Merriam-Webster

Spanish-English
Dictionary

Merriam-Webster's Spanish-English Dictionary

MERRIAM-WEBSTER, INCORPORATED
Springfield, Massachusetts, U.S.A.

A GENUINE MERRIAM-WEBSTER

The name *Webster* alone is no guarantee of excellence. It is used by a number of publishers and may serve mainly to mislead an unwary buyer.

Merriam-Webster™ is the name you should look for when you consider the purchase of dictionaries or other fine reference books. It carries the reputation of a company that has been publishing since 1831 and is your assurance of quality and authority.

Merriam-Webster's Spanish-English Dictionary, principal copyright 1998

MADE IN THE UNITED STATES OF AMERICA

3rd printing OPM Dallas, PA 11/2023

Contents   Índice

Preface

MERRIAM-WEBSTER'S SPANISH-ENGLISH DICTIONARY is a completely new dictionary designed to meet the needs of English and Spanish speakers in a time of ever-expanding communication among the countries of the Western Hemisphere. It is intended for language learners, teachers, office workers, tourists, business travelers—anyone who needs to communicate effectively in the Spanish and English languages as they are spoken and written in the Americas. This new dictionary provides accurate and up-to-date coverage of current vocabulary in both languages, as well as abundant examples of words used in context to illustrate idiomatic usage. The selection of Spanish words and idioms was based on evidence drawn from a wide variety of modern Latin-American sources and interpreted by trained Merriam-Webster bilingual lexicographers. The English entries were chosen by Merriam-Webster editors from the most recent Merriam-Webster dictionaries, and they represent the current basic vocabulary of American English.

All of this material is presented in a format which is based firmly upon and, in many important ways, is similar to the traditional styling found in the Merriam-Webster monolingual dictionaries. The reader who is familiar with Merriam-Webster dictionaries will immediately recognize this style, with its emphasis on convenience and ease of use, clarity and conciseness of the information presented, precise discrimination of senses, and frequent inclusion of example phrases showing words in actual use. Other features include pronunciations (in the International Phonetic Alphabet) for all English words, full coverage of irregular verbs in both languages, a section on basic Spanish grammar, tables of the most common Spanish and English abbreviations, and a detailed Explanatory Notes section which answers any questions the reader might have concerning the use of this book.

Merriam-Webster's Spanish-English Dictionary represents the combined efforts of many members of the Merriam-Webster Editorial Department, along with advice and assistance from consultants outside the company. The primary defining work was done by Charlene M. Chateauneuf, Seán O'Mannion-Espejo, Karen L. Wilkinson, and Jocelyn Woods; early contributions to the text were also submitted by Cèsar Alegre, Hilton Alers, Marién Díaz, Anne Gatschet, and María D. Guijarro, with Victoria E. Neufeldt, Ph.D., and James L. Rader providing helpful suggestions regarding style. Proofreading was done by Susan L. Brady, Daniel B. Brandon, Charlene M. Chateauneuf, Deanna Stathis Chiasson, Seán O'Mannion-Espejo, James L. Rader, Donna L. Rickerby, Adrienne M. Scholz, Amy West, Karen L. Wilkinson, and Linda Picard Wood. Brian M. Sietsema, Ph.D., provided the pronunciations. Cross-reference services were provided by Donna L. Rickerby.

Karen L. Levister assisted in inputting revisions. Carol Fugiel contributed many hours of clerical assistance and other valuable support. The editorial work relating to typesetting and production was begun by Jennifer Goss Duby and continued by Susan L. Brady, who also offered helpful suggestions regarding format. Madeline L. Novak provided guidance on typographic matters. John M. Morse was responsible for the conception of this book as well as for numerous ideas and continued support along the way.

Eileen M. Haraty
Editor
2003

This new revision of *Merriam-Webster's Spanish-English Dictionary* adds more than 350 new words and meanings from areas such as science, medicine, technology, and popular culture, and provides updates to nearly 130 existing vocabulary entries. It builds on the substantial work already completed in previous updates, which added more than 4,600 new vocabulary terms, updated more than 6,000 existing entries, and incorporated significantly expanded coverage of more than 700 of the entries for the most essential English and Spanish vocabulary. Included in this expanded coverage were many additional meanings, thousands of new examples showing how the words are typically used in context, and more than 2,000 common idioms and phrasal verbs in which these essential words often appear.

Many members of the Merriam-Webster editorial staff contributed to this update. Defining and cross-reference work were done by Sarah S. Carragher. Proofreading was done by Paul S. Wood and editor Carragher, with outside assistance from Mark A. Stevens and Tasha Martino Bigelow. Joshua S. Guenter, Ph.D., provided the pronunciations. Data file management was performed by Anne E. McDonald, who also entered the revisions. Editor Wood oversaw the book's typesetting and final production. Madeline L. Novak and Emily A. Vezina assisted in planning the update, and also provided guidance and support throughout the course of the project.

Karen L. Wilkinson
Editor
2021

Prefacio

El Diccionario Español-Inglés Merriam-Webster es un diccionario completamente nuevo, diseñado con el fin de satisfacer las necesidades de lenguaje de angloparlantes e hispanoparlantes en una era de continuo crecimiento en la comunicación entre los países del hemisferio occidental. El diccionario está destinado a los estudiantes de estos idiomas, así como a los maestros, oficinistas, turistas, viajeros de negocios, o a cualquier persona que necesite expresarse claramente y eficazmente en los idiomas inglés o español tal como se hablan y se escriben en las Américas. Este diccionario provee una cobertura exacta y actualizada del vocabulario corriente en ambos idiomas, así como abundantes ejemplos de palabras empleadas en contexto para ilustrar su uso idiomático. La selección de vocablos y modismos en español se efectuó a base de una vasta gama de fuentes latinoamericanas modernas y fue interpretada por especialistas en lexicografía bilingüe de Merriam-Webster. Las voces inglesas fueron extraídas de los más recientes diccionarios Merriam-Webster por editores de Merriam-Webster, y representan el vocabulario básico actual del inglés americano.

El material se ha organizado en un formato basado en el estilo tradicional característico de los diccionarios monolingües Merriam-Webster. El lector ya familiarizado con los diccionarios Merriam-Webster reconocerá de inmediato este estilo, con su énfasis en la conveniencia y la facilidad de uso, en la claridad y la concisión de la información presentada, en el preciso discernimiento de los sentidos de cada vocablo, y en la frecuente inclusión de frases ejemplares que ilustran el uso de una palabra. Aparecen también pronunciaciones (compuestas en el Alfabeto Fonético Internacional) para todas las voces inglesas, así como una cobertura plena de verbos irregulares en ambos idiomas, una sección de gramática inglesa básica, tablas de abreviaturas comunes, y una sección de Notas explicativas que contesta en detalle cualquier pregunta que pueda tener el lector tocante al uso de este libro.

El *Diccionario Español-Inglés Merriam-Webster* es el fruto del esfuerzo combinado de muchos miembros del departamento editorial de Merriam-Webster, junto con el asesoramiento y la asistencia de consultores exteriores. La obra de definición primaria fue llevada a cabo por Charlene M. Chateauneuf, Seán O'Mannion-Espejo, Karen L. Wilkinson, y Jocelyn Woods; contribuciones textuales preliminares fueron aportadas por Cèsar Alegre, Hilton Alers, Marién Díaz, Anne Gatschet, y María D. Guijarro, y valiosas sugerencias con respecto al estilo del diccionario fueron hechas por Victoria E. Neufeldt, Ph.D., y James L. Rader. La corrección de pruebas fue realizada por Susan L. Brady, Daniel B. Brandon, Charlene M. Chateauneuf, Deanna Stathis Chiasson, Seán O'Mannion-Espejo, James L. Rader, Donna L. Rickerby, Adrienne M. Scholz, Amy West, Karen L. Wilkinson, y Linda Picard Wood.

Las pronunciaciones fueron proporcionadas por Brian M. Sietsema, Ph.D. Los servicios de remisión textual fueron provistos por Donna L. Rickerby. Karen L. Levister ayudó con la entrada de revisiones. Carol Fugiel contribuyó muchas horas de labor de oficina y otros valiosos apoyos. La labor editorial de composición y producción fue comenzada por Jennifer Goss Duby y fue continuada por Susan L. Brady, la cual también ofreció sugerencias importantes con respecto al formato. Madeline L. Novak proveyó orientación en asuntos tipográficos. John M. Morse fue responsable de la concepción de este libro, y contribuyó numerosas ideas y apoyo continuo durante su elaboración.

Eileen M. Haraty
Editor
2003

Esta nueva versión corregida del *Diccionario Español-Inglés Merriam-Webster* añade más de 350 vocablos y significados nuevos de áreas tales como la ciencia, la medicina, la tecnología, y la cultura popular, y proporciona actualizaciones de casi 130 entradas ya existentes. Continúa el considerable trabajo ya realizado en versiones anteriores, en las cuales se añadieron más de 4600 vocablos, se actualizaron más de 6000 entradas, y se incorporaron cobertura considerablemente ampliada en más de 700 de las entradas que corresponden al vocabulario más esencial del inglés y el español. Esta ampliación abarcaba muchos significados adicionales, miles de ejemplos que muestran el uso típico de las palabras en contexto, y más de dos mil de los modismos y verbos preposicionales en los cuales estas palabras tan esenciales suelen aparecer.

Muchos miembros del departamento editorial de Merriam-Webster contribuyeron a la actualización de este libro. La obra de definición primaria y de verificación de remisiones fue realizada por Sarah S. Carragher. La corrección de pruebas fue hecha por Paul S. Wood y la redactora Carragher, con la ayuda externa de Mark A. Stevens y Tasha Martino Bigelow. Las pronunciaciones fueron provistas por Joshua S. Guenter, Ph.D. La administración de archivos de datos fue ejecutada por Anne E. McDonald, quien también tecleó las revisiones. El redactor Wood supervisó la composición del libro. Madeline L. Novak y Emily A. Vezina ayudaron con la planificación del proyecto de actualización, y también proporcionaron orientación y apoyo general en el curso del proyecto.

Karen L. Wilkinson
Editora
2021

Explanatory Notes

Entries

1. Headwords

A boldface letter, word, or phrase appearing at the left edge of a column of type is a headword or main entry word. The headword may consist of letters set solid, of letters joined by a hyphen, or of letters separated by a space:

> **cafetalero**[1], **-ra** *adj* ...
> **lip–read** ... *vi* ...
> **computer science** *n* ...

The headword, together with the material that follows it on the same line and succeeding indented lines, constitutes a dictionary entry.

2. Order of Entries

Alphabetical order throughout the dictionary follows the order of the English alphabet, with one exception: the Spanish letter *ñ* follows the letter *n* and comes before the letter *o*. The headwords are ordered alphabetically letter by letter without regard to intervening spaces or hyphens; for example, *shake-up* follows *shaker*.

Homographs (words with the same spelling) having different parts of speech are usually given separate dictionary entries. These entries have superscript numerals after the headword:

> **hail**[1] ... *vt* ...
> **hail**[2] *n* ...
> **hail**[3] *interj* ...
> **madrileño**[1], **-ña** *adj* ...
> **madrileño**[2], **-ña** *n* ...

Headwords in a numbered sequence are listed in this order: verb, adverb, adjective, noun, conjunction, preposition, pronoun, interjection, article.

Homographs having the same part of speech are normally included at the same dictionary entry even if they have different origins. On the English-to-Spanish side, however, separate entries are made if the homographs have different inflected forms or if they have different pronunciations. On the Spanish-to-English side, separate entries are made if the homographs differ in gender.

3. Guide Words

A pair of guide words is printed at the top of each page, indicating the first and last main entries that appear on that page:

balanca · bañar

4. Variants

When a headword is followed by the word *or* and another spelling, the two spellings are variants. Both are standard, and you may choose to use either one:

> **jailer** *or* **jailor** . . . *n* . . .
> **quizá** *or* **quizás** *adv* . . .

Occasionally, a variant spelling is used only for a particular sense of a word. In these cases, the variant spelling is listed after the sense number of the sense to which it pertains:

> **electric** . . . *adj* **1** *or* **electrical** . . .

Sometimes the headword is used interchangeably with a longer phrase containing the headword. For the purposes of this dictionary, such phrases are considered variants of the headword:

> **bunk²** *n* **1** *or* **bunk bed** . . .
> **angina** *nf* **1** *or* **angina de pecho** . . .

Variant wordings of boldface phrases may also be shown:

> **madera** *nf* . . . **2** **madera dura** *or*
> **madera noble** . . .
> **atención¹** *nf* . . . **2 poner atención** *or*
> **prestar atención** . . .
> **gasto** *nm* . . . **3 gastos fijos/generales/indirectos** . . .

5. Run-On Entries

A main entry may be followed by one or more derivatives or by a homograph with a different functional label. These are run-on entries. Each is introduced by a boldface dash and each has a functional label. They are not defined, however, since their equivalents can be readily derived by adding the corresponding foreign-language suffix to the terms used to define the main entry word or, in the case of homographs, simply substituting the appropriate part of speech:

> **illegal** . . . *adj* : ilegal — **illegally** *adv*
> [the Spanish adverb is *ilegalmente*]
> **transferir** . . . *vt* TRASLADAR : to
> transfer — **transferible** *adj*
> [the English adjective is *transferable*]
> **Bosnian** . . . *n* : bosnio *m*, -nia *f* —
> **Bosnian** *adj*
> [the Spanish adjective is *bosnio, -nia*]

On the Spanish-to-English side of the dictionary, reflexive verbs are sometimes run on undefined:

> **enrollar** *vt* : to roll up, to coil —
> **enrollarse** *vr*

The absence of a definition means that *enrollarse* has the simple reflexive meaning "to become rolled up or coiled," "to roll itself up."

6. Boldface phrases

A main entry may be followed by one or more phrases in dark, boldface type that contain the main entry word or an inflected form of it. Each boldface phrase is defined at its own numbered sense:

> **álamo** *nm* 1 : poplar 2 **álamo tem-blón** : aspen
>
> **hold¹** . . . *v* . . . — *vi* . . . 3 **to hold forth** : . . . 4 **to hold off** WAIT : . . .

If the boldface phrase consists only of the entry word and a single preposition, the entry word is represented by a boldface swung dash ~ :

> **pegar** . . . *vt* . . . — *vi* . . . 3 ~ **con** : . . .

The same boldface phrase may appear at two or more senses if it has more than one distinct meaning:

> **wear¹** . . . *v* . . . *vt* . . . 8 **to wear out** : gastar . . . 9 **to wear out** EXHAUST : agotar, fatigar . . .
>
> **estar** . . . *v aux* . . . *vi* . . . 16 ~ **por** : to be in favor of 17 ~ **por** : to be about to . . .

A slash / is used between words in a boldface phrase when either of the words separated by the slash can be used in that part of the phrase:

> **casa** *nf* . . . 11 **echar/tirar/botar la casa por la ventana** . . .
>
> **same²** *pron* . . . 4 **all/just the same** . . .

Words separated by slashes in boldface phrases do not always have the same meaning.

When a boldface phrase contains a slash, a corresponding slash may or may not be included in the definition that follows the phrase:

> **agua** *nf* . . . 4 **agua dulce/salada** : fresh/salt water . . .
>
> **go¹** . . . *v* . . . *vi* . . . 59 **to go down well/badly** : caer bien/mal, tener una buena/mala acogida . . .
>
> **pedir** . . . *vt* . . . 3 **pedir disculpas/perdón** : to apologize . . .
>
> **break¹** . . . *v* . . . *vt* . . . — *vi* . . . 17 **to break free/loose** : soltarse . . .

When no corresponding slash is included in the definition, all wordings shown for the boldface phrase have the same meaning.

If a word in a boldface phrase is followed by "(etc.)", other words similar to the one that precedes the "(etc.)" may be used in that place in the phrase:

> **part²** *n* . . . 6 **for my/his (etc.) part** : por mi/su (etc.) parte . . .

> **hablar** . . . — **hablarse** *vr* . . . **2 se**
> **habla inglés (etc.) :** English (etc.)
> spoken

A corresponding "(etc.)" is included in the definition unless a verbal illustration is shown instead of a definition, or the definition is worded in a way that makes the inclusion of "(etc.)" unnecessary:

> **ser**[1] . . . *vi* . . . **17 sea cual/quien**
> **(etc.) sea** <sean cuales sean las circunstancias : whatever the circumstances might be> . . .

> **hell** . . . *n* . . . **8 like hell I did/will**
> **(etc.)!** *fam* : ¡y un cuerno! . . .

If the use of the entry word is commonly restricted to one particular phrase, then only the phrase will be defined:

> **ward**[1] . . . *vt* **to ward off :** desviar,
> protegerse contra

Pronunciation

1. Pronunciation of English Entry Words

The text between a pair of brackets [ ] following the entry word of an English-to-Spanish entry indicates the pronunciation. The symbols used are explained in the Pronunciation Symbols chart on page 85a.

When more than one pronunciation is shown for a word, different educated speakers of English pronounce that word in different ways. The pronunciation shown second may be just as common as the one shown first. All pronunciations shown are common and acceptable:

> **tomato** [təˈmeɪt̬o, -ˈmɑ-] . . .

When less than a full pronunciation is shown for a compound word, the rest of the pronunciation can be found at the separate entry for that individual part of the compound:

> **gamma ray** [ˈgæmə] . . .
> **ray** [ˈreɪ] . . .
> **smoke**[1] [ˈsmoːk] . . .
> **smoke detector** [dɪˈtɛktər] . . .

In general, no pronunciation is given for open compounds consisting of two or more English words that are main entries at their own alphabetical place:

> **water lily** *n* : nenúfar *m*

Only the first headword in a series of numbered homographs is given a pronunciation if their pronunciations are the same:

> **dab**[1] [ˈdæb] *vt* . . .
> **dab**[2] *n* . . .

No pronunciation is shown for principal parts of verbs that are formed regularly by adding a suffix or for other derivative words formed by common suffixes.

2. Pronunciation of Spanish Entry Words

Spanish pronunciation is highly regular, so no pronunciations are given in most Spanish-to-English entries. Exceptions have been made for certain words (such as foreign borrowings) whose Spanish pronunciations are not evident from their spellings:

> **pizza** [ˈpitsa, ˈpisa] . . .
> **footing** [ˈfuˌtɪŋ] . . .

Functional Labels

An italic label indicating a part of speech or some other functional classification follows the pronunciation or, if no pronunciation is given, the headword. The eight traditional parts of speech—adjective, adverb, conjunction, interjection, noun, preposition, pronoun, and verb—are indicated as follows:

> **daily²** *adj* . . .
> **vagamente** *adv* . . .
> **and** . . . *conj* . . .
> **huy** *interj* . . .
> **jackal** . . . *n* . . .
> **para** *prep* . . .
> **neither³** *pron* . . .
> **leer** . . . *v* . . .

Verbs that are intransitive are labeled *vi,* and verbs that are transitive are labeled *vt*:

> **deliberar** *vi* : to deliberate . . .
> **necessitate** . . . *vt* **-tated; -tating**
> : necesitar, requerir

Verbs that are both transitive and intransitive are labeled *v* if all listed senses are both transitive and intransitive. If some senses are only transitive or only intransitive, the entry is subdivided into transitive and intransitive sections, each with its own *vt* or *vi* label, respectively:

> **scrawl¹** . . . *v* : garabatear
> **crack¹** . . . *vt* . . . — *vi* . . .
> **esperar** *vt* . . . — *vi* . . .

If a subdivided verb entry includes irregular verb inflections, it is labeled *v* immediately before the inflections, with the labels *vt* and *vi* serving to introduce the transitive and intransitive subdivisions:

> **satisfy** . . . *v* **-fied; -fying** *vt* . . . —
> *vi* . . .

Spanish reflexive verbs are labeled *vr*:

> **jactarse** *vr* . . .
>
> **abandonar** *vt* . . . — **abando-**
> **narse** . . . *vr* . . .

Two other labels are used to indicate functional classifications of verbs: *v aux* (auxiliary verb) and *v impers* (impersonal verb).

> **may** . . . *v aux, past* **might** . . .
>
> **hacer** . . . *vt* . . . — *vi* . . . — *v impers*
> **1** *(referring to weather)* <hace frío
> : it's cold> . . .

Entries for prefixes are labeled *pref*:

> **ciber-** *pref* . . .
>
> **e-** *pref* . . .

Entries for suffixes are labeled *suf*:

> **-less** . . . *suf* . . .
>
> **-ísimo, -ma** *suf* . . .

Entries for English-language and Spanish-language trademarks are labeled *trademark* and *marca registrada*, respectively:

> **Q–tips** . . . *trademark* — se usa para
> hisopos
>
> **Kleenex** . . . *marca registrada, m* —
> used for a paper tissue

Entries for English-language service marks (words or names that organizations use to identify their services) are labeled *service mark*:

> **Realtor** . . . *service mark* . . .

Gender Labels

In Spanish-to-English noun entries and trademark entries, the gender of the headword is indicated by an italic *m* (masculine), *f* (feminine), or *mf* (masculine or feminine). In noun entries, the gender label immediately follows the functional label:

> **magnesio** *nm* . . .
>
> **galaxia** *nf* . . .
>
> **turista** *nmf* . . .

In trademark entries, the gender label follows the functional label and is preceded by a comma and a space:

> **Ping–Pong** *marca registrada, m* . . .

If both the masculine and feminine forms are shown for a noun referring to a person, the label is simply *n:*

> **director, -tora** *n* . . .

Spanish noun equivalents of English headwords are also labeled for gender:

> **amnesia** ... *n* : amnesia *f*
> **earache** ... *n* : dolor *m* de oído(s)
> **gamekeeper** ... *n* : guardabosque *mf*

Inflected Forms

1. Nouns

The plurals of nouns are shown in this dictionary when they are irregular, if the root word changes in spelling or accentuation when a plural suffix is added, when an English noun ends in a consonant plus -*o* or in -*ey*, when an English noun ends in -*oo*, when an English noun is a compound that pluralizes the first element instead of the last, when a noun has variant plurals, or whenever the dictionary user might have reasonable doubts regarding the spelling of a plural:

> **tooth** ... *n, pl* **teeth** ...
> **garrafón** *nm, pl* **-fones** ...
> **potato** ... *n, pl* **-toes** ...
> **abbey** ... *n, pl* **-beys** ...
> **cuckoo**[2] *n, pl* **-oos** ...
> **brother–in–law** ... *n, pl* **brothers– in–law** ...
> **fish**[2] *n, pl* **fish** *or* **fishes** ...
> **hábitat** *nm, pl* **-tats** ...
> **tahúr** *nm, pl* **tahúres** ...

Cutback (partial) inflected forms are shown for most nouns on the English-to-Spanish side, regardless of the number of syllables in the word. On the Spanish-to-English side, cutback inflections are given for nouns that have three or more syllables; plurals for shorter words are written out in full:

> **shampoo**[2] *n, pl* **-poos** ...
> **calamity** ... *n, pl* **-ties** ...
> **mouse** ... *n, pl* **mice** ...
> **sartén** *nmf, pl* **sartenes** ...
> **hámster** ... *nm, pl* **hámsters** ...
> **federación** *nf, pl* **-ciones** ...

If only one gender form has a plural which is irregular, that plural form will be given with the appropriate label:

> **campeón, -peona** *n, mpl* **-peones**
> : champion

The plurals of nouns are usually not shown when the base word is unchanged by the addition of the regular plural suffix or when the noun is unlikely to occur in the plural:

> **apple** ... *n* : manzana *f*
> **inglés**[3] *nm* : English (language)

Nouns that are always plural in form and occur in plural constructions are labeled *npl* for English nouns, *nmpl* for Spanish masculine nouns, *nfpl* for Spanish feminine nouns, or *nmfpl* for Spanish nouns that can be masculine or feminine:

> **knickers** . . . *npl* . . .
> **enseres** *nmpl* . . .
> **mancuernas** *nfpl* . . .
> **panties** . . . *nmfpl* . . .

Entry words that are unchanged in the plural are labeled *ns & pl* for English nouns, *nms & pl* for Spanish masculine nouns, *nfs & pl* for Spanish feminine nouns, or *nmfs & pl* for Spanish nouns that can be masculine or feminine:

> **deer** . . . *ns & pl* . . .
> **lavaplatos** *nms & pl* . . .
> **tesis** *nfs & pl* . . .
> **rompehuelgas** *nmfs & pl* . . .

2. Verbs

ENGLISH VERBS

The principal parts of verbs are shown in English-to-Spanish entries when they are irregular, if the spelling of the root word changes when the verb suffix is added, when the verb ends in *-ey*, when there are variant inflected forms, or whenever the dictionary user might have reasonable doubts about the spelling of an inflected form:

> **break**[1] . . . *v* **broke** . . . ; **broken** . . . ;
> **breaking** . . .
> **drag**[1] . . . *v* **dragged; dragging** . . .
> **monkey**[1] . . . *vi* **-keyed; -keying** . . .
> **label**[1] . . . *vt* **-beled** *or* **-belled; -bèling**
> *or* **-belling** . . .
> **imagine** . . . *vt* **-ined; -ining** . . .

Cutback inflected forms are usually shown when the verb has two or more syllables:

> **multiply** . . . *v* **-plied; -plying** . . .
> **bevel**[1] . . . *v* **-eled** *or* **-elled; -eling** *or*
> **-elling** . . .
> **forgo** *or* **forego** . . . *vt* **-went; -gone;**
> **-going** . . .
> **commit** . . . *vt* **-mitted; -mitting** . . .

The principal parts of an English verb are not shown if the base word does not change when *-s, -ed,* and *-ing* are added:

> **delay**[1] . . . *vt*
> **pitch**[1] . . . *vt*

SPANISH VERBS

Entries for irregular Spanish verbs are cross-referenced by number to the model conjugations appearing in the Conjugation of Spanish Verbs section on pages 72a–78a:

> **abnegarse** {49} *vr* ...
>
> **volver** {89} *vi* ...

Entries for Spanish verbs with regular conjugations are not cross-referenced; however, model conjugations for regular Spanish verbs are included on pages 68a–69a in the Conjugation of Spanish Verbs section.

3. Adverbs and Adjectives

The comparative and superlative forms of English adjective and adverb main entries are shown if the spelling of the root word changes when the suffix is added, if the inflection is irregular, or if there are variant inflected forms:

> **wet²** *adj* wetter; wettest ...
>
> **good²** *adj* better ... ; best ...
>
> **evil¹** ... *adj* eviler *or* eviller; evilest
> *or* evillest ...

For adjectives and adverbs that have more than one syllable, only the shortened form -*est* is usually shown for the superlative:

> **early¹** ... *adv* earlier; -est ...
>
> **gaudy** ... *adj* gaudier; -est ...
>
> **secure²** *adj* securer; -est ...

At a few entries only the superlative form is shown because there is no evidence that the comparative form is used:

> **mere** ... *adj, superlative* merest ...

The comparative and superlative forms of adjectives and adverbs are usually not shown if the base word does not change when the suffix is added:

> **quiet³** *adj* 1 ...

Usage

1. Usage Labels

Two types of usage labels are used in this dictionary—regional and stylistic. Spanish words that are limited in use to a specific area or areas of Latin America, or to Spain, are given labels indicating the countries in which they are most commonly used:

> **guarachear** *vi Cuba, PRi fam* ...
>
> **bucket** ... *n* : ... cubeta *f Mex*

The following regional labels are used in this dictionary: *Arg* (Argentina), *Bol* (Bolivia), *CA* (Central America), *Car* (Caribbean), *Chile* (Chile), *Col* (Colombia), *CoRi* (Costa Rica), *Cuba* (Cuba), *DomRep* (Dominican Republic), *Ecua* (Ecuador), *Sal* (El Salvador), *Guat* (Guatemala), *Hond* (Honduras), *Mex* (Mexico), *Nic* (Nicaragua), *Pan* (Panama), *Par* (Paraguay), *Peru* (Peru), *PRi* (Puerto Rico), *Spain* (Spain), *Uru* (Uruguay), *Ven* (Venezuela).

Since this dictionary focuses on the Spanish spoken in Latin America, only the most common regionalisms from Spain have been included.

A number of words are given a *fam* (familiar) label, indicating that these words are suitable for informal contexts but would not normally be used in formal writing or speaking. The labels *disparaging*, *vulgar*, and *offensive* are used for words or senses that are intended to hurt or shock or that are likely to give offense; such words are entered and defined in this dictionary only if they are very commonly used. The labels are intended to warn the reader that the word or sense in question may be inappropriate in polite conversation.

2. Usage Notes

Usage notes that give information about meaning or grammar may appear in parentheses before the definition:

> **not** ... *adv* **1** (*used to form a negative*) : no ...
>
> **within²** *prep* ... **2** (*in expressions of distance*) : ... **3** (*in expressions of time*) : ...
>
> **e²** *conj* (*used instead of* y *before words beginning with* i- *or* hi-) : ...
>
> **poder¹** ... *v aux* ... **2** (*expressing possibility*) : ... **3** (*expressing permission*) : ...

Orientation about meaning is also sometimes given in parentheses within the definition:

> **calibrate** ... *vt* ... : calibrar (armas), graduar (termómetros)
>
> **palco** *nm* : box (in a theater or stadium)

Occasionally a usage note is used in place of a definition. This is usually done when the entry word has no simple equivalent in the other language. This type of usage note is accompanied by examples of common use:

> **shall** ... *v aux* ... **1** (*used formally to express a command*) <you shall do as I say : harás lo que te digo> ...

3. Illustrations of Usage

Definitions are sometimes followed by verbal illustrations that show a typical use of the word in context or a common idiomatic usage. These verbal illustrations include a translation and are enclosed in angle brackets:

> **lejos** *adv* **1** : far away, distant <a lo lejos : in the distance, far off> ...
>
> **make**[1] ... *v* ... *vt* ... **15** ... : hacer (dinero, amigos) <to make a living : ganarse la vida> ...

A slash / is used between words in a verbal illustration when either of the words separated by the slash can occur in that position in the phrase:

> **tener** ... *vt* ... **2** : to have (available) <tener dinero/tiempo para : to have money/time for> ...
>
> **money** ... *n* ... **1** : dinero *m*, plata *f* <to make/lose money : ganar/perder dinero> ...

Words separated by slashes in verbal illustrations do not always have the same meaning.

When a word in a verbal illustration is followed by "(etc.)," other words similar to the one before the "(etc.)" can occur in that position in the phrase:

> **dar** ... *vt* ... **16** CAUSAR : to cause <darle miedo/sed (etc.) a alguien : to make someone frightened/thirsty (etc.)> ...
>
> **turn**[2] *n* ... **3** INTERSECTION : bocacalle *f* <we took a wrong turn : nos equivocamos de calle/salida (etc.), ...> ...

Occasionally verbal illustrations are used in place of a definition. This is usually done when a boldface phrase has no single-phrase equivalent in the other language, or when its use is more easily understood in context:

> **saber**[1] ... *vt* ... **6 qué sé yo** <diamantes, perlas, y qué sé yo : diamonds, pearls, and whatnot> <y qué sé yo dónde : and who knows where (else)> ...
>
> **all**[1] ... *adv* ... **8 ~ over** *fam* <to be all over someone for something : criticar duramente a alguien por algo> ...

Definitions

A definition in this dictionary consists of one or more translations for a single sense of a main entry word, a run-on entry word, or a boldface phrase. A boldface colon is used to introduce a definition:

> **fable** ... *n* : fábula *f*
>
> **sonrojar** ... — **sonrojarse** *vr* : to blush

> **aback** . . . *adv* . . . **2 to be taken**
> **aback :** quedarse desconcertado

If more than one translation word or phrase is included in the same definition, the translations are usually separated by commas:

> **as of** *prep* : desde, a partir de

When commas are used within a definition for other reasons, the translations are separated by semicolons instead of commas:

> **love**[2] *n* . . . **3** BELOVED : amor *m;*
> amado *m,* -da *f;* enamorado *m,* -da
> *f* . . .

A slash / is used between words in a translation phrase when either of the words separated by the slash can be used in that position in the phrase:

> **bajar** *vt* . . . **2 :** to bring/take/carry
> down, to get/lift down . . .

Words separated by slashes in translations do not always have the same meaning.

Sense Division

When a word has more than one sense, each sense begins with a boldface numeral:

> **laguna** *nf* **1 :** lagoon **2 :** gap

Whenever some information (such as a synonym, a boldface word or phrase, a usage note, a cross-reference, or a label) follows a sense number, it applies only to that specific sense:

> **abanico** *nm* . . . **2** GAMA : . . .
> **tonic**[2] *n* . . . **2** *or* **tonic water :** . . .
> **grillo** *nm* . . . **2 grillos** *nmpl* : . . .
> **fairy** . . . *n, pl* **fairies** . . . **2 fairy tale**
> **:** . . .
> **myself** . . . *pron* **1** (*used reflexively*)
> **:** . . .
> **pike** . . . *n* . . . **3** → turnpike
> **atado**[2] *nm* . . . **2** *Arg* : . . .

Cross-References

An arrow in an entry means that information about the word you have looked up is available at the separate entry for the word that appears after the arrow. If the word you have looked up is an inflected form, the cross-reference after the arrow will point you to the base form of the word:

> **fue, etc.** → **ir, ser**
> **mice** → **mouse**

In other cases, the cross-reference will point you to the entry for a word that has the same meaning as the word you have looked up:

> scapula . . . → shoulder blade
>
> amuck . . . → amok

Synonyms

A synonym in small capital letters is often provided before the boldface colon that precedes a definition:

> seleccionar *vt* ELEGIR : . . .
>
> turn[1] *vt* . . . — *vi* . . . 1 ROTATE, SPIN
> : . . .
>
> carta *nf* . . . 2 NAIPE : . . .

These synonyms are all main entries or boldface phrases elsewhere in the dictionary. They serve as a helpful guide to the meaning of the entry or sense and also give you an additional term that might be substituted in a similar context.

Notas explicativas

Entradas

1. Lemas

Toda letra, palabra o frase en negrita que aparece al margen izquierdo de una columna de texto de la que forma parte es un lema, o entrada principal. La composición del lema puede constar de letras continuas, de letras unidas por un guión, o bien de letras separadas por un espacio:

> **cafetalero**[1], **-ra** *adj* . . .
> **lip—read** . . . *vi* . . .
> **computer science** *n* . . .

El lema, junto con el texto que lo sigue tanto en la misma línea como en las líneas sangradas subsiguientes, constituye una entrada del diccionario.

2. Orden de los lemas

El orden alfabético del diccionario concuerda con el orden alfabético latino universal, en el que la letra *ñ* aparece después de la *n* y antes de la *o*, y la *ch* y la *ll* no se consideran letras independientes. Los lemas se suceden alfabéticamente, letra por letra, sin tener en cuenta guiones o espacios intermediarios; por ejemplo, *shake-up* aparece después de *shaker*.

Los homógrafos (palabras que se escriben igual) que pertenecen a distintas categorías gramaticales por lo general aparecen en entradas individuales. Estas entradas tienen un número volado:

> **hail**[1] . . . *vt* . . .
> **hail**[2] *n* . . .
> **hail**[3] *interj* . . .
> **madrileño**[1], **-ña** *adj* . . .
> **madrileño**[2], **-ña** *n* . . .

Las entradas que siguen una secuencia numerada se listan en el siguiente orden: verbo, adverbio, adjetivo, sustantivo, conjunción, preposición, pronombre, interjección, y por último, artículo.

Los homógrafos que se clasifican bajo una misma categoría gramatical son normalmente incluidos dentro de la misma entrada del diccionario, sin tener en cuenta diferencias de origen semántico. Sin embargo, en la sección Inglés-Español se les asigna a cada uno de estos homógrafos una entrada individual si entre ellos existe alguna diferencia ya sea en la inflexión o en la pronunciación. En la sección Español-Inglés, se les asigna una entrada individual si existe una diferencia de género.

3. Palabras guía

En el margen superior de cada página aparecen dos palabras guía, que indican la primera y última entrada de la página correspondiente:

balanca · bañar

4. Variantes

Cuando un lema aparece seguido de la palabra *or* y otra ortografía, las dos ortografías se consideran como variantes. Ambas ortografías son estándares, y cualquiera de las dos puede usarse:

> **jailer** *or* **jailor** . . . *n* . . .
>
> **quizá** *or* **quizás** *adv* . . .

Hay ocasiones en las que una variante ortográfica se emplea
únicamente para una de las acepciones de una palabra. En tales
casos, la variante ortográfica aparece después del número de la
acepción a la cual corresponde:

> **electric** . . . *adj* **1** *or* **electrical** . . .

En otros casos, el lema puede usarse intercambiablemente con
una frase de la que forma parte. Para los fines de este diccionario,
tales frases se consideran como variantes del lema:

> **bunk**² *n* **1** *or* **bunk bed** . . .
>
> **angina** *nf* **1** *or* **angina de pecho** . . .

Las frases en negrita también pueden, a su vez, presentar
variantes:

> **madera** *nf* . . . **3 madera dura** *or*
> **madera noble** . . .
>
> **atención**¹ *nf* . . . **2 poner atención** *or*
> **prestar atención** . . .
>
> **gasto** *nm* . . . **3 gastos fijos/genera-
> les/indirectos** . . .

5. Entradas secundarias

Una entrada principal puede ser seguida de uno o más derivados
del lema, o de un homógrafo de distinta categoría gramatical. Éstas
son entradas secundarias. Cada una de estas entradas aparece después de un guión en negrita, y cada una posee su propio calificativo.
Tales entradas aparecen sin definición, ya que sus equivalentes en
el idioma extranjero pueden derivarse fácilmente al combinar la
definición del lema con el sufijo correspondiente, o como sucede
con los homógrafos, al sustituir la categoría gramatical por otra.
Véase por ejemplo:

> **illegal** . . . *adj* : ilegal — **illegally** *adv*
> [el adverbio español es *ilegalmente*]
>
> **transferir** . . . *vt* TRASLADAR : to
> transfer — **transferible** *adj*
> [el adjetivo inglés es *transferable*]
>
> **Bosnian** . . . *n* : bosnio *m*, -nia *f* —
> **Bosnian** *adj*
> [el adjetivo español es *bosnio, -nia*]

En la sección Español-Inglés, los verbos pronominales aparecen
en ocasiones como entradas secundarias, sin definición:

> **enrollar** *vt* : to roll up, to coil —
> **enrollarse** *vr*

La ausencia de la definición en este caso comunica al lector que el verbo *enrollarse* tiene una función expresamente reflexiva. Esto elimina la necesidad de agregar una definición que resultaría superflua como "to become rolled up or coiled," o "to roll itself up."

6. Frases en negrita

Un lema puede aparecer acompañado de una o varias frases en negrita que contienen ya sea el lema, o una inflexión de éste. Cada una de estas frases se presenta como una de las acepciones numeradas del lema:

> **álamo** *nm* **1** : poplar **2 álamo temblón** : aspen
>
> **hold**[1] . . . *v* . . . — *vi* . . . **3 to hold forth** : . . . **4 to hold off** WAIT : . . .

Cuando la frase en negrita consta únicamente de una combinación del lema con una preposición, el lema se representa entonces por medio de una tilde en negrita ~ :

> **pegar** . . . *vt* . . . — *vi* . . . **3 ~ con** : . . .

Si la frase en cuestión tiene más de un sentido, entonces puede aparecer en dos o más acepciones del mismo lema:

> **wear**[1] . . . *v* . . . *vt* . . . **8 to wear out** : gastar . . . **9 to wear out** EXHAUST : agotar, fatigar . . .
>
> **estar** . . . *v aux* . . . *vi* . . . **16 ~ por** : to be in favor of **17 ~ por** : to be about to . . .

Se utiliza una barra inclinada / entre las palabras de una frase en negrita para indicar que cualquiera de las palabras así separadas puede usarse en esa posición dentro de la frase:

> **casa** *nf* . . . **11 echar/tirar/botar la casa por la ventana** : . . .
>
> **same**[2] *pron* . . . . **4 all/just the same** . . .

Las palabras separadas por barras no siempre tienen el mismo significado.

Cuando una frase en negrita contiene una barra, la definición que sigue puede o no contener una barra correspondiente:

> **agua** *nf* . . . **4 agua dulce/salada** : fresh/salt water . . .
>
> **go**[1] . . . *v* . . . *vi* . . . **59 to go down well/badly** : caer bien/mal, tener una buena/mala acogida . . .
>
> **pedir** . . . *vt* . . . **3 pedir disculpas/perdón** : to apologize . . .
>
> **break**[1] . . . *v* . . . *vt* . . . — *vi* . . . **17 to break free/loose** : soltarse . . .

Si la definición no incluye una barra correspondiente, esto indica que todas las versiones de la frase en negrita tienen el mismo significado.

Cuando una de las palabras de una frase en negrita aparece
seguida de "(etc.)", esto indica que hay otras palabras parecidas a
la que precede al "(etc.)" que pueden usarse en esa posición dentro
de la frase:

> **part²** *n* . . . **6 for my/his (etc.) part**
> : por mi/su (etc.) parte . . .
>
> **hablar** . . . — **hablarse** *vr* . . . **2 se
> habla inglés (etc.) :** English (etc.)
> spoken

Un "(etc.)" correspondiente se incluye en la definición que sigue
a no ser que ésta o se sustituya por un ejemplo de uso o esté cons-
truída de tal manera que el "(etc.)" no haga falta:

> **ser¹** . . . *vi* . . . **17 sea cual/quien
> (etc.) sea** <sean cuales sean las cir-
> cunstancias : whatever the circum-
> stances might be> . . .
>
> **hell** . . . *n* . . . **8 like hell I did/will
> (etc.)!** *fam* : ¡y un cuerno! . . .

Si el uso común de una palabra es generalmente limitado a una frase
determinada, la frase es presentada como la única acepción del lema:

> **ward¹** . . . *vt* **to ward off :** desviar,
> protegerse contra

Pronunciación

1. Pronunciación de los lemas ingleses

El texto que aparece entre corchetes [ ] inmediatamente después
de un lema en la sección Inglés-Español indica la pronunciación del
lema. Para una explicación de los símbolos empleados, véase la tabla
titulada Símbolos de pronunciación que aparece en la página 85a.

Cuando se incluyen dos o más pronunciaciones que corresponden a la misma palabra, esto indica que diferentes hablantes edu-
cados del idioma pronuncian esta palabra de distintas maneras. La
segunda variante puede ser tan común como la primera. Todas las
pronunciaciones incluidas son comunes y aceptables:

> **tomato** [tə'meɪt̬o, -'mɑ-] . . .

Cuando un término compuesto aparece con sólo una pronunciación parcial, el resto de la pronunciación puede obtenerse bajo la
entrada que corresponde a la parte del término cuya pronunciación se ha omitido:

> **gamma ray** ['gæmə] . . .
>
> **ray** ['reɪ] . . .
>
> **smoke¹** ['smoːk] . . .
>
> **smoke detector** [dɪ'tɛktər] . . .

En general, no se indica la pronunciación de términos compues-
tos cuando éstos están formados de dos o más palabras inglesas
que aparecen en el diccionario como lemas:

> **water lily** *n* : nenúfar *m*

Solamente la primera entrada en una serie de homógrafos nume-
rados incluye la pronunciación si ésta es la misma para todos los
otros homógrafos:

> **dab¹** [ˈdæb] *vt* . . .
> **dab²** *n* . . .

No se indica la pronunciación de las partes principales de los
verbos formados regularmente por añadir un sufijo, ni por otros
derivados formados por sufijos comunes.

2. Pronunciación de los lemas españoles

Dada la alta regularidad de la pronunciación del español, no se
indica la pronunciación de la mayor parte de las entradas que aparecen en la sección Español-Inglés. Sin embargo, se han hecho
excepciones para ciertas palabras (tales como aquéllas que se han
adaptado de otras lenguas) cuya pronunciación en español no
puede derivarse naturalmente de su ortografía:

> **pizza** [ˈpitsa, ˈpisa] . . .
> **footing** [ˈfuˌtɪŋ] . . .

Calificativos funcionales

Un calificativo en itálicas que indica la categoría gramatical u
otra clasificación funcional del lema aparece inmediatamente después de la pronunciación, o si la pronunciación se ha omitido,
después del lema. Las ocho categorías gramaticales tradiciona-
les—el adjetivo, el adverbio, la conjunción, la interjección, el sustantivo, la preposición, el pronombre, y el verbo—se indican como
sigue:

> **daily²** *adj* . . .
> **vagamente** *adv* . . .
> **and** . . . *conj* . . .
> **huy** *interj* . . .
> **jackal** . . . *n* . . .
> **para** *prep* . . .
> **neither³** *pron* . . .
> **leer** . . . *v* . . .

Los verbos intransitivos se identifican con el calificativo *vi,* y los
transitivos, *vt*:

> **deliberar** *vi* : to deliberate . . .
> **necessitate** . . . *vt* **-tated; -tating**
>   : necesitar, requerir

Los verbos que son a la vez transitivos e intransitivos llevan el
calificativo *v* si todas las acepciones que aparecen en la entrada son
tanto transitivas como intransitivas; si algunas son o únicamente
transitivas o únicamente intransitivas, la entrada se subdivide en

dos secciones, y cada una de éstas es introducida con el calificativo *vt* o *vi*, respectivamente:

> **scrawl**[1] . . . *v* : garabatear
> **crack**[1] . . . *vt* . . . — *vi* . . .
> **esperar** *vt* . . . — *vi* . . .

Si una entrada así subdividida incluye inflexiones irregulares, el calificativo *v* aparece inmediatamente delante de las inflexiones, y las acepciones transitivas e intransitivas son introducidas con los calificativos *vt* y *vi*, respectivamente:

> **satisfy** . . . *v* **-fied; -fying** *vt* . . . —
>   *vi* . . .

Los verbos pronominales españoles se identifican con el calificativo *vr*:

> **jactarse** *vr* . . .
> **abandonar** *vt* . . . — **abando-**
>   **narse** . . . *vr* . . .

Por último, dos otros calificativos se emplean para indicar la clasificación funcional de los verbos: *v aux* (auxiliary verb) y *v impers* (impersonal verb).

> **may** . . . *v aux, past* **might** . . .
> **hacer** . . . *vt* . . . — *vi* . . . — *v impers*
>   **1** *(referring to weather)* <hace frío
>   : it's cold> . . .

Los prefijos se identifican con el calificativo *pref*:

> **ciber-** *pref* . . .
> **e-** *pref* . . .

Los sufijos se identifican con el calificativo *suf*:

> **-less** . . . *suf* . . .
> **-ísimo, -ma** *suf* . . .

Los lemas ingleses y españoles que son marcas registradas se indican con los calificativos *trademark* y *marca registrada*, respectivamente:

> **Q–tips** . . . *trademark* — se usa para
>   hisopos
> **Kleenex** . . . *marca registrada, m* —
>   used for a paper tissue

Los lemas ingleses que son marcas de servicio (palabras o nombres utilizados por una organización para identificar sus servicios) se indican con el calificativo *service mark*:

> **Realtor** . . . *service mark* . . .

Calificativos de género

En toda entrada de la sección Español-Inglés cuyo lema es un sustantivo o una marca registrada, el género del lema se indica con los calificativos *m* (masculino), *f* (femenino), o *mf* (masculino o femenino). Si el lema es un sustantivo, el calificativo de género aparece inmediatamente después del calificativo funcional:

> **magnesio** *nm* . . .
> **galaxia** *nf* . . .
> **turista** *nmf* . . .

Si el lema es una marca registrada, el calificativo de género aparece después del calificativo funcional y va precedido por una coma y un espacio:

> **Ping–Pong** *marca registrada, m* . . .

Si se dan las formas tanto masculina como femenina de un sustantivo que denota a una persona, se aplica el calificativo *n*:

> **director, -tora** *n* . . .

Todo sustantivo español que aparece como definición de un lema inglés es acompañado de un calificativo de género:

> **amnesia** . . . *n* : amnesia *f*
> **earache** . . . *n* : dolor *m* de oído(s)
> **gamekeeper** . . . *n* : guardabosque
>   *mf*

Inflexiones

1. Sustantivos

En este diccionario se indica el plural de un sustantivo en los siguientes casos: cuando el plural es irregular, cuando la acentuación o la ortografía del vocablo raíz cambia al añadir el sufijo del plural, cuando un sustantivo inglés termina en una consonante seguida de *-o* o de *-ey*, cuando un sustantivo inglés termina en *-oo*, cuando un sustantivo inglés es un término compuesto del cual el elemento a pluralizar es el primero y no el último, cuando un sustantivo tiene variantes en el plural, o cuando podría suscitarse una duda razonable en cuanto a la ortografía del plural:

> **tooth** . . . *n, pl* **teeth** . . .
> **garrafón** *nm, pl* **-fones** . . .
> **potato** . . . *n, pl* **-toes** . . .
> **abbey** . . . *n, pl* **-beys** . . .
> **cuckoo**[2] *n, pl* **-oos** . . .
> **brother–in–law** . . . *n, pl* **brothers–**
>   **in–law** . . .
> **fish**[2] *n, pl* **fish** *or* **fishes** . . .
> **hábitat** *nm, pl* **-tats** . . .
> **tahúr** *nm, pl* **tahúres** . . .

En la sección Inglés-Español, la forma plural de la mayor parte de los sustantivos se indica por medio de una inflexión reducida, sin tener en cuenta el número de sílabas que el lema contenga. En la sección Español-Inglés, se dan inflexiones reducidas sólo para aquellos sustantivos que contengan tres o más sílabas, mientras que las formas plurales de sustantivos más breves se presentan enteras:

> **shampoo²** *n, pl* **-poos** ...
> **calamity** ... *n, pl* **-ties** ...
> **mouse** ... *n, pl* **mice** ...
> **sartén** *nmf, pl* **sartenes** ...
> **hámster** ... *nm, pl* **hámsters** ...
> **federación** *nf, pl* **-ciones** ...

Si se produce un plural irregular en sólo uno de los géneros, la forma plural se da con el calificativo correspondiente:

> **campeón, -peona** *n, mpl* **-peones**
>   : champion

La forma plural de un sustantivo generalmente no aparece si el vocablo raíz permanece inalterado por la adición del sufijo plural regular, o cuando no es probable que el sustantivo se use en el plural:

> **apple** ... *n* : manzana *f*
> **inglés³** *nm* : English (language)

Aquellos sustantivos que siempre son plurales en forma y que ocurren en construcciones plurales son clasificados *npl* si son sustantivos ingleses, *nmpl* si son sustantivos masculinos españoles, *nfpl* si son sustantivos femeninos españoles, o *nmfpl* si son sustantivos españoles que pueden ser o masculino o femenino:

> **knickers** ... *npl* ...
> **enseres** *nmpl* ...
> **mancuernas** *nfpl* ...
> **panties** ... *nmfpl* ...

Toda entrada que permanece inalterada en el plural es clasificada *ns & pl* si es un sustantivo inglés, *nms & pl* si es un sustantivo masculino español, *nfs & pl* si es un sustantivo femenino español, y *nmfs & pl* si es un sustantivo español que puede ser o masculino o femenino:

> **deer** ... *ns & pl* ...
> **lavaplatos** *nms & pl* ...
> **tesis** *nfs & pl* ...
> **rompehuelgas** *nmfs & pl* ...

2. Verbos

VERBOS INGLESES

En la sección Inglés-Español, las partes principales de los verbos se indican en los siguientes casos: cuando el verbo es irregular, cuando la ortografía del vocablo raíz cambia al añadir un sufijo verbal, cuando el verbo termina en *-ey*, cuando una inflexión tiene variantes, o cuando puede suscitarse una duda razonable en cuanto a la ortografía de una inflexión:

> **break¹** . . . *v* **broke** . . . ; **broken** . . . ;
>   **breaking** . . .
>
> **drag¹** . . . *v* **dragged; dragging** . . .
>
> **monkey¹** . . . *vi* **-keyed; -keying** . . .
>
> **label¹** . . . *vt* **-beled** *or* **-belled; -beling**
>   *or* **-belling** . . .
>
> **imagine** . . . *vt* **-ined; -ining** . . .

Si el verbo consta de dos o más sílabas, se da generalmente una forma reducida de la inflexión:

> **multiply** . . . *v* **-plied; -plying** . . .
>
> **bevel¹** . . . *v* **-eled** *or* **-elled; -eling** *or*
>   **-elling** . . .
>
> **forgo** *or* **forego** . . . *vt* **-went; -gone;**
>   **-going** . . .
>
> **commit** . . . *vt* **-mitted; -mitting** . . .

Las partes principales de un verbo inglés no aparecen cuando el vocablo raíz no cambia al añadir *-s, -ed,* y *-ing*:

> **delay¹** . . . *vt*
>
> **pitch¹** . . . *vt*

VERBOS ESPAÑOLES

En cada entrada correspondiente a un verbo irregular español aparece un número entre llaves que remite al lector a los modelos de conjugación que aparecen en las páginas 72a a 78a de la sección titulada Conjugation of Spanish Verbs:

> **abnegarse** {49} *vr* . . .
>
> **volver** {89} *vi* . . .

Aunque estas remisiones no aparecen en las entradas que corresponden a los verbos regulares españoles, los modelos de conjugación de estas formas pueden consultarse en la susodicha sección, que comienza en la página 68a.

3. Adverbios y adjetivos

ADVERBIOS Y ADJETIVOS INGLESES

Los lemas de adjetivos y adverbios ingleses incluyen las formas comparativas y superlativas cuando la ortografía del vocablo raíz cambia al añadir un sufijo, cuando la inflexión es de forma irregular, o cuando existen variantes de la inflexión:

> **wet²** *adj* **wetter; wettest** . . .
>
> **good²** *adj* **better** . . . ; **best** . . .
>
> **evil¹** . . . *adj* **eviler** *or* **eviller; evilest**
>   *or* **evillest** . . .

Las formas superlativas de adjetivos y adverbios ingleses de más de una sola sílaba son representadas generalmente por la forma reducida *-est*:

> **early**[1] ... *adv* **earlier; -est** ...
>
> **gaudy** ... *adj* **gaudier; -est** ...
>
> **secure**[2] *adj* **securer; -est** ...

En algunas entradas aparece únicamente la forma superlativa porque no existe evidencia del uso de la forma comparativa:

> **mere** ... *adj, superlative* **merest** ...

Las formas comparativas y superlativas de los adjetivos y adverbios generalmente no se muestran si el vocablo raíz no cambia al añadir el sufijo:

> **quiet**[3] *adj* **1** ...

Uso

1. Calificativos de uso

En este diccionario se emplean dos tipos de calificativo de uso: regional y estilístico. Las palabras españolas cuyo uso se limita a ciertas regiones de Latinoamérica o a España reciben calificativos que indican los países en que suelen usarse con más frecuencia:

> **guarachear** *vi Cuba, PRi fam* ...
>
> **bucket** ... *n* : ... cubeta *f Mex*

Los siguientes calificativos regionales se han empleado en la redacción de este libro: *Arg* (Argentina), *Bol* (Bolivia), *CA* (Centroamérica), *Car* (el Caribe), *Chile* (Chile), *Col* (Colombia), *CoRi* (Costa Rica), *Cuba* (Cuba), *DomRep* (República Dominicana), *Ecua* (Ecuador), *Sal* (El Salvador), *Guat* (Guatemala), *Hond* (Honduras), *Mex* (México), *Nic* (Nicaragua), *Pan* (Panamá), *Par* (Paraguay), *Peru* (Perú), *PRi* (Puerto Rico), *Spain* (España), *Uru* (Uruguay), *Ven* (Venezuela).

Dado el foco primordialmente latinoamericano de este diccionario, la mayoría de los regionalismos que contiene provienen de América Latina. Sin embargo, se han incluido también algunos regionalismos comunes de España.

Varios vocablos reciben un calificativo de *fam* (familiar), lo cual indica que el uso de tales palabras es apropiado solamente en contextos informales. Los calificativos *disparaging* (despreciativo), *vulgar* (vulgar o soez), y *offensive* (ofensivo) se emplean para palabras o acepciones que se usan con la intención de lastimar o escandalizar, o que tienen una alta probabilidad de ofender. Tales voces aparecen definidas en este diccionario solamente si su uso es muy común. El propósito de estos calificativos es, pues, de servir de advertencia al lector.

2. Notas de uso

En algunos casos, una acepción puede venir precedida de una nota entre paréntesis que proporciona al lector información semántica o gramatical:

> **not** ... *adv* **1** (*used to form a negative*)
> : no ...
>
> **within**[2] *prep* ... **2** (*in expressions of distance*) : ... **3** (*in expressions of time*) : ...
>
> **e**[2] *conj* (*used instead of* **y** *before words beginning with* i- *or* hi-) : ...
>
> **poder**[1] ... *v aux* ... **2** (*expressing possibility*) : ... **3** (*expressing permission*) : ...

Este tipo de orientación semántica puede aparecer también entre paréntesis como parte de la definición:

> **calibrate** ... *vt* ... : calibrar (armas), graduar (termómetros)
>
> **palco** *nm* : box (in a theater or stadium)

En algunas ocasiones, una nota de uso aparece en lugar de una definición. Esto ocurre generalmente cuando el lema carece de un equivalente sencillo en el otro idioma. Estas notas de uso aparecen acompañadas de ejemplos que ilustran el uso común del lema:

> **shall** ... *v aux* ... **1** (*used formally to express a command*) <you shall do as I say : harás lo que te digo> ...

3. Ejemplos de uso

Varias definiciones vienen acompañadas de ejemplos de uso. Estos ejemplos sirven para ilustrar un empleo típico del lema en un contexto dado, o un uso idiomático común de la palabra. Los ejemplos de uso incluyen una traducción, y aparecen entre paréntesis angulares:

> **lejos** *adv* **1** : far away, distant <a lo lejos : in the distance, far off> ...
>
> **make**[1] ... *v* ... *vt* ... **15** ... : hacer (dinero, amigos) <to make a living : ganarse la vida> ...

Se utiliza una barra inclinada / entre las palabras de un ejemplo de uso para indicar que cualquiera de las palabras así separadas puede usarse en esa posición dentro de la frase:

> **tener** ... *vt* ... **2** : to have (available) <tener dinero/tiempo para : to have money/time for> ...
>
> **money** ... *n* ... **1** : dinero *m*, plata *f* <to make/lose money : ganar/perder dinero> ...

Las palabras separadas por barras no siempre tienen el mismo significado.

Cuando una de las palabras de un ejemplo de uso aparece seguida de "(etc.)", esto indica que hay otras palabras parecidas a la que precede al "(etc.)" que pueden usarse en esa posición dentro de la frase:

dar . . . *vt* . . . **16** CAUSAR : to cause <darle miedo/sed (etc.) a alguien : to make someone frightened/thirsty (etc.)> . . .

turn² *n* . . . **3** INTERSECTION : boca-calle *f* <we took a wrong turn : nos equivocamos de calle/salida (etc.), . . .> . . .

En algunas ocasiones, un ejemplo de uso aparece en lugar de una definición. Esto ocurre generalmente cuando una frase en negrita carece de un equivalente en el otro idioma de una sola frase, o cuando su uso se entiende mejor en contexto:

saber¹ . . . *vt* . . . **6 qué sé yo** <dia-mantes, perlas, y qué sé yo : dia-monds, pearls, and whatnot> <y qué sé yo dónde : and who knows where (else)> . . .

all¹ . . . *adv* . . . **8** ~ **over** *fam* <to be all over someone for something : cri-ticar duramente a alguien por algo> . . .

Definiciones

En este diccionario, una definición consta de una o más traduc-ciones que corresponden a una sola acepción de un lema, una entrada secundaria, o una frase en negrita. Se introduce una acep-ción o definición por medio de dos puntos en negrita:

fable . . . *n* : fábula *f*

sonrojar . . . — **sonrojarse** *vr* : to blush

aback . . . *adv* . . . **2 to be taken aback** : quedarse desconcertado

Si se incluye más de una traducción dentro de la misma definición, las traducciones generalmente se separan por comas:

as of *prep* : desde, a partir de

Cuando las comas aparecen en una definición por otras razones, las traducciones se separan por un punto y coma en lugar de una coma:

love² *n* . . . **3** BELOVED : amor *m;* amado *m,* -da *f;* enamorado *m,* -da *f* . . .

Se utiliza una barra inclinada / entre las palabras de una traduc-ción para indicar que cualquiera de las palabras así separadas puede usarse en esa posición dentro de la frase:

bajar *vt* . . . **2** : to bring/take/carry down, to get/lift down . . .

Las palabras separadas por barras no siempre tienen el mismo sig-nificado.

División de las acepciones

Cuando una entrada principal tiene varias acepciones, éstas se indican con un número arábigo, compuesto también en negrita:

laguna *nf* **1** : lagoon **2** : gap

Cuando alguna información (como un sinónimo, una palabra o frase en negrita, una nota de uso, una remisión, o un calificativo) aparece después de un número de acepción, ésta se aplica específicamente a dicha acepción:

> **abanico** *nm* ... **2** GAMA : ...
>
> **tonic²** *n* ... **2** *or* **tonic water** : ...
>
> **grillo** *nm* ... **2 grillos** *nmpl* : ...
>
> **fairy** ... *n, pl* **fairies** ... **2 fairy tale**
> : ...
>
> **myself** ... *pron* **1** (*used reflexively*)
> : ...
>
> **pike** ... *n* ... **3** → **turnpike**
>
> **atado²** *nm* ... **2** *Arg* : ...

Remisiones

Una flecha indica que información correspondiente al lema que precede a la flecha puede encontrarse en la entrada que corresponde a la palabra que la sigue. Si el lema es una inflexión, la remisión que viene después de la flecha dirige al lector a la forma raíz de la palabra:

> **fue, etc.** → **ir, ser**
>
> **mice** → **mouse**

En otros casos, la remisión señala otro lema que tiene el mismo significado que la palabra buscada:

> **scapula** ... → **shoulder blade**
>
> **amuck** ... → **amok**

Sinónimos

Frecuentemente se provee un sinónimo compuesto en mayúsculas pequeñas antes de los dos puntos en negrita que preceden a una definición:

> **seleccionar** *vt* ELEGIR : ...
>
> **turn¹** *vt* ... — *vi* ... **1** ROTATE, SPIN
> : ...
>
> **carta** *nf* ... **2** NAIPE : ...

Toda palabra empleada como sinónimo tiene su propia entrada en el diccionario, ya sea como lema o como frase en negrita. El propósito de estos sinónimos es de orientar al lector y ayudarlo a elegir la acepción correcta, así como de proveer un término que podría usarse alternativamente en el mismo contexto.

Spanish Grammar

Accentuation

Spanish word stress is generally determined according to the following rules:

- Words ending in a vowel, or in *-n* or *-s*, are stressed on the next-to-last syllable (*za<u>pa</u>to*, *<u>lla</u>man*).

- Words ending in a consonant other than *-n* or *-s* are stressed on the last syllable (*per<u>diz</u>*, *curiosi<u>dad</u>*).

Exceptions to these rules have a written accent mark over the stressed vowel (*<u>fá</u>cil*, *habla<u>rá</u>*, *<u>úl</u>timo*).

There are also a few words which take accent marks in order to distinguish them from homonyms (*si, sí; que, qué; el, él;* etc.).*

Adverbs ending in *-mente* have two stressed syllables since they retain both the stress of the root word and of the *-mente* suffix (*<u>len</u>ta<u>men</u>te*, *di<u>fí</u>cil<u>men</u>te*). Many compounds also have two stressed syllables (*<u>lim</u>piapara<u>bri</u>sas*).

Punctuation and Capitalization

Questions and exclamations in Spanish are preceded by an inverted question mark ¿ and an inverted exclamation mark ¡, respectively:

¿Cuándo llamó Ana?
Y tú, ¿qué piensas?

¡No hagas eso!
Pero, ¡qué lástima!

In Spanish, unlike English, the following words are not capitalized:

- Names of days, months, and languages (*jueves, octubre, español*).

- Spanish adjectives or nouns derived from proper nouns (*los nicaragüenses, una teoría marxista*).

---

*The Real Academia Española (Royal Spanish Academy) now recommends always omitting the accent marks from the adverb *solo*, which was previously written as *sólo* to distinguish it from the adjective *solo*; and from all demonstrative pronouns (see Demonstrative Pronouns on page 51a for more information about the latter). Nevertheless, the accented variants of these words are still commonly encountered as of this writing.

Articles

1. Definite Article

Spanish has five forms of the definite article: *el* (masculine singular), *la* (feminine singular), *los* (masculine plural), *las* (feminine plural), and *lo* (neuter). The first four agree in gender and number with the nouns they limit (*el carro*, the car; *las tijeras*, the scissors), although the form *el* is used with feminine singular nouns beginning with a stressed *a-* or *ha-* (*el águila, el hambre*).

The neuter article *lo* is used with the masculine singular form of an adjective to express an abstract concept (*lo mejor de este método*, the best thing about this method; *lo meticuloso de su trabajo*, the meticulousness of her work; *lo mismo para mí*, the same for me).

Whenever the masculine article *el* immediately follows the words *de* or *a*, it combines with them to form the contractions *del* and *al*, respectively (*viene del campo*, *vi al hermano de Roberto*).

The use of *el, la, los,* and *las* in Spanish corresponds largely to the use of *the* in English; some exceptions are noted below.

The definite article is used:

- When referring to something as a class (*los gatos son ágiles*, cats are agile; *me gusta el café*, I like coffee).

- In references to meals and in most expressions of time (*¿comiste el almuerzo?*, did you eat lunch?; *vino el año pasado*, he came last year; *son las dos*, it's two o'clock; *prefiero el verano*, I prefer summer; *la reunión es el lunes*, the meeting is on Monday; but: *hoy es lunes*, today is Monday).

- Before titles (except *don, doña, san, santo, santa, fray*, and *sor*) in third-person references to people (*la señora Rivera llamó*, Mrs. Rivera called; but: *hola, señora Rivera*, hello, Mrs. Rivera).

- In references to body parts and personal possessions (*me duele la cabeza*, my head hurts; *dejó el sombrero*, he left his hat).

- To mean "the one" or "the ones" when the subject is already understood (*la de plástico*, the plastic one; *los que vi ayer*, the ones I saw yesterday).

The definite article is omitted:

- Before a noun in apposition, if the noun is not modified (*Caracas, capital de Venezuela;* but: *Pico Bolívar, la montaña más alta de Venezuela*).

- Before a number in a royal title (*Carlos Quinto*, Charles the Fifth).

2. Indefinite Article

The forms of the indefinite article in Spanish are *un* (masculine singular), *una* (feminine singular), *unos* (masculine plural), and *unas* (feminine plural). They agree in number and gender with the nouns they limit (*una mesa*, a table; *unos platos*, some plates), although the form *un* is used with feminine singular nouns beginning with a stressed *a-* or *ha-* (*un ala, un hacha*).

The use of *un, una, unos,* and *unas* in Spanish corresponds largely to the use of *a, an,* and *some* in English, with some exceptions:

- Indefinite articles are generally omitted before nouns identifying someone or something as a member of a class or category (*Paco es profesor/católico,* Paco is a professor/Catholic; *se llama páncreas,* it's called a pancreas).

- They are also often omitted in instances where quantity is understood from context (*vine sin chaqueta,* I came without a jacket; *no tengo carro,* I don't have a car).

Nouns

1. Gender

Nouns in Spanish are either masculine or feminine. A noun's gender can often be determined according to the following guidelines:

- Nouns ending in *-aje, -o,* or *-or* are usually masculine (*el traje, el libro, el sabor*), with some exceptions (*la mano, la foto, la labor,* etc.).

- Nouns ending in *-a, -dad, -ión, -tud,* or *-umbre* are usually feminine (*la alfombra, la capacidad, la excepción, la juventud, la certidumbre*). Exceptions include: *el día, el mapa,* and many learned borrowings ending in *-ma* (*el idioma, el tema*).

Most nouns referring to people or animals agree in gender with the subject (*el hombre, la mujer; el hermano, la hermana; el perro, la perra*). However, some nouns referring to people, including those ending in *-ista*, use the same form for both sexes (*el artista, la artista; el modelo, la modelo;* etc.).

A few names of animals exist in only one gender form (*la jirafa, el sapo,* etc.). In these instances, the adjectives *macho* and *hembra* are sometimes used to distinguish males and females (*una jirafa macho,* a male giraffe).

2. Pluralization

Plurals of Spanish nouns are formed as follows:

- Nouns ending in an unstressed vowel or an accented *-é* are pluralized by adding *-s* (*la vaca, las vacas; el café, los cafés*).

- Nouns ending in a consonant other than -s, or in a stressed vowel other than -é, are generally pluralized by adding -es (el papel, los papeles; el rubí, los rubíes). Exceptions include papá (papás) and mamá (mamás).

- Nouns with an unstressed final syllable ending in -s usually have a zero plural (la crisis, las crisis; el jueves, los jueves). Other nouns ending in -s add -es to form the plural (el mes, los meses; el país, los países).

- Nouns ending in -z are pluralized by changing the -z to -c and adding -es (el lápiz, los lápices; la vez, las veces).

- Many compound nouns have a zero plural (el paraguas, los paraguas; el aguafiestas, los aguafiestas).

- The plurals of cualquiera and quienquiera are cualesquiera and quienesquiera, respectively.

Adjectives

1. Gender and Number

Most adjectives agree in gender and number with the nouns they modify (un chico alto, una chica alta, unos chicos altos, unas chicas altas). Some adjectives, including those ending in -e and -ista (fuerte, altruista) and comparative adjectives ending in -or (mayor, mejor), vary only for number.

Adjectives whose masculine singular forms end in -o generally change the -o to -a to form the feminine (pequeño → pequeña). Masculine adjectives ending in -án, -ón, or -dor, and masculine adjectives of nationality which end in a consonant, usually add -a to form the feminine (holgazán → holgazana; llorón → llorona; trabajador → trabajadora; irlandés → irlandesa).

Adjectives are pluralized in much the same manner as nouns:

- The plurals of adjectives ending in an unstressed vowel or an accented -é are formed by adding an -s (un postre rico, unos postres ricos; una camisa café, unas camisas cafés).

- Adjectives ending in a consonant, or in a stressed vowel other than -é, are generally pluralized by adding -es (un niño cortés, unos niños corteses; una persona iraní, unas personas iraníes).

- Adjectives ending in -z are pluralized by changing the -z to -c and adding -es (una respuesta sagaz, unas respuestas sagaces).

2. Shortening

- The following masculine singular adjectives drop their final -o when they occur before a masculine singular noun: bueno (buen), malo (mal), uno (un), alguno (algún), ninguno (ningún), primero (primer), tercero (tercer).

- *Grande* shortens to *gran* before any singular noun.
- *Ciento* shortens to *cien* before any noun.
- *Cualquiera* shortens to *cualquier* before any noun.
- The title *Santo* shortens to *San* before all masculine names except those beginning with *To-* or *Do-* (*San Juan, Santo Tomás*).

3. Position

Descriptive adjectives generally follow the nouns they modify (*una cosa útil, un actor famoso*). However, adjectives that express an inherent quality often precede the noun (*la blanca nieve*).

Some adjectives change meaning depending on whether they occur before or after the noun: *un pobre niño*, a poor (pitiable) child; *un niño pobre*, a poor (not rich) child; *un gran hombre*, a great man; *un hombre grande*, a big man; *el único libro*, the only book; *el libro único*, the unique book; etc.

4. Comparative and Superlative Forms

The comparative of Spanish adjectives is generally rendered as *más . . . que* (more . . . than) or *menos . . . que* (less . . . than): *soy más alta que él*, I'm taller than he (is), I'm taller than him *fam*; *son menos inteligentes que tú*, they're less intelligent than you.

The superlative of Spanish adjectives usually follows the formula *definite article + (noun +) más/menos + adjective*: *ella es la estudiante más trabajadora*, she is the hardest-working student; *él es el menos conocido*, he's the least known.

A few Spanish adjectives have irregular comparative and superlative forms:

Adjective	Comparative/Superlative
bueno (good)	**mejor** (better, best)
malo (bad)	**peor** (worse, worst)
grande[1] (big, great), **viejo** (old)	**mayor** (greater, older; greatest, oldest)
pequeño[1] (little), **joven** (young)	**menor** (lesser, younger; least, youngest)
mucho (much), **muchos** (many)	**más** (more, most)
poco (little), **pocos** (few)	**menos** (less, least)

[1] These words have regular comparative and superlative forms when used in reference to physical size: *él es más grande que yo; nuestra casa es la más pequeña*.

ABSOLUTE SUPERLATIVE

The absolute superlative is formed by placing *muy* before the adjective, or by adding the suffix *-ísimo* (*ella es muy simpática* or *ella es simpatiquísima*, she is very nice). The absolute superlative using *-ísimo* is formed according to the following rules:

- Adjectives ending in a consonant other than *-z* simply add the *-ísimo* ending (*fácil → facilísimo*).

- Adjectives ending in *-z* change this consonant to *-c* and add *-ísimo* (*feliz → felicísimo*).

- Adjectives ending in a vowel or diphthong drop the vowel or diphthong and add *-ísimo* (*claro → clarísimo; amplio → amplísimo*).

- Adjectives ending in *-co* or *-go* change these endings to *-qu* and *-gu*, respectively, and add *-ísimo* (*rico → riquísimo; largo → larguísimo*).

- Adjectives ending in *-ble* change this ending to *-bil* and add *-ísimo* (*notable → notabilísimo*).

- Adjectives containing the stressed diphthong *ie* or *ue* will sometimes change these to *e* and *o*, respectively (*ferviente → fervientísimo* or *ferventísimo; bueno → buenísimo* or *bonísimo*).

Adverbs

Adverbs can be formed by adding the adverbial suffix *-mente* to virtually any adjective (*fácil → fácilmente*). If the adjective varies for gender, the feminine form is used as the basis for forming the adverb (*rápido → rápidamente*).

Pronouns

1. Personal Pronouns

The personal pronouns in Spanish are:

Person	Singular		Plural	
FIRST	yo	I	nosotros, -tras	we
SECOND	tú	you (familiar)	vosotros[2], -tras[2]	you, all of you
	vos[1]	you		
	usted	you (formal)	ustedes[3]	you, all of you
THIRD	él	he	ellos, ellas	they
	ella	she		
	ello	it (neuter)		

[1] Familiar form used in addition to *tú* in South and Central America.

[2] Familiar form used in Spain.

[3] Formal form used in Spain; familiar and formal form used in Latin America.

FAMILIAR VS. FORMAL

The second-person personal pronouns exist in both familiar and formal forms. The familiar forms are generally used when addressing relatives, friends, and children, although usage varies considerably from region to region; the formal forms are used in other contexts to show courtesy, respect, or emotional distance.

In Spain and in the Caribbean, *tú* is used exclusively as the familiar singular "you." In South and Central America, however, *vos* either competes with *tú* to varying degrees or replaces it entirely. (For a more detailed explanation of *vos* and its corresponding verb forms, refer to the Conjugation of Spanish Verbs section.)

The plural familiar form *vosotros, -tras* is used only in Spain, where *ustedes* is reserved for formal contexts. In Latin America, *vosotros, -tras* is not used, and *ustedes* serves as the all-purpose plural "you."

It should be noted that while *usted* and *ustedes* are regarded as second-person pronouns, they take the third-person form of the verb.

USAGE

In Spanish, personal pronouns are generally omitted (*voy al cine*, I'm going to the movies; *¿llamaron?*, did they call?), although they are sometimes used for purposes of emphasis or clarity (*se lo diré yo*, I will tell them; *vino ella, pero él se quedó*, she came, but he stayed behind). The forms *usted* and *ustedes* are usually included out of courtesy (*¿cómo está usted?*, how are you?).

Personal pronouns are not generally used in reference to inanimate objects or living creatures other than humans; in these instances, the pronoun is most often omitted (*¿es nuevo? no, es viejo*, is it new? no, it's old).

The neuter third-person pronoun *ello* is reserved for indefinite subjects (such as abstract concepts): *todo ello implica* . . . , all of this implies . . . ; *por si ello fuera poco* . . . , as if that weren't enough . . . . It most commonly appears in formal writing and speech. In less formal contexts, *ello* is often either omitted or replaced with *esto, eso,* or *aquello.*

2. Prepositional Pronouns

Prepositional pronouns are used as the objects of prepositions (*¿es para mí?*, is it for me?; *se lo dio a ellos*, he gave it to them).

The prepositional pronouns in Spanish are:

Singular		Plural	
mí	me	**nosotros, -tras**	us
ti	you	**vosotros[1], -tras[1]**	you
usted	you (formal)	**ustedes**	you
él	him	**ellos, ellas**	them
ella	her		
ello	it (neuter)		
sí	yourself, himself, herself, itself, oneself	**sí**	yourselves, themselves

[1] Used primarily in Spain.

When the preposition *con* is followed by *mí, ti,* or *sí,* both words are replaced by *conmigo, contigo,* and *consigo,* respectively (*¿vienes conmigo?*, are you coming with me?; *habló contigo,* he spoke with you; *no lo trajo consigo,* she didn't bring it with her).

3. Object Pronouns

DIRECT OBJECT PRONOUNS

Direct object pronouns indicate the person or thing that receives the action of a verb. The direct object pronouns in Spanish are:

Singular		Plural	
me	me	**nos**	us
te	you	**os[1]**	you
le[2]	you, him	**les[2]**	you[3], them
lo	you (formal), him, it	**los**	you[3], them
la	you (formal), her, it	**las**	you[3], them

[1] Used only in Spain.
[2] Used mainly in Spain.
[3] See explanation below.

Agreement

The third-person forms agree in both gender and number with the nouns they replace or the people they refer to (*pintó las paredes,* she painted the walls → *las pintó,* she painted them; *visitaron al señor Juárez,* they visited Mr. Juárez → *lo visitaron,* they visited him). The remaining forms vary only for number.

Position

Direct object pronouns are normally affixed to the end of an affirmative command, a simple infinitive, or a present participle (*¡hazlo!,* do it!; *es difícil hacerlo,* it's difficult to do it; *haciéndolo, aprenderás,* you'll learn by doing it). With constructions involving an auxiliary verb and an infinitive or present participle, the pronoun may occur either immediately before the construction or suffixed to it (*lo voy a hacer* or *voy a hacerlo,* I'm going to do it; *estoy haciéndolo* or *lo estoy haciendo,* I'm doing it). In all other cases, the pronoun immediately precedes the conjugated verb (*no lo haré,* I won't do it).

Regional Variation

The second-person ("you") familiar plural form *os* is restricted to Spain. In most parts of Latin America, *los* and *las* are used as both the familiar and formal second-person plural forms.

In Spain and in a few areas of Latin America, *le* and *les* are used in place of *lo* and *los,* respectively, when referring to or addressing people (*le vieron,* they saw him; *les vistió,* she dressed them; *encantado de conocerle,* pleased to meet you).

INDIRECT OBJECT PRONOUNS

Indirect object pronouns represent the secondary goal of the action of a verb (*me dio el regalo,* he gave me the gift; *les dije que no,* I told them no). The indirect object pronouns in Spanish are:

Singular		Plural	
me	(to, for, from) me	**nos**	(to, for, from) us
te	(to, for, from) you	**os**[1]	(to, for, from) you
le	(to, for, from) you, him, her, it	**les**	(to, for, from) you, them
se[2]		**se**[2]	

[1] Used only in Spain.
[2] See explanation below.

Position

Indirect object pronouns follow the same rules as direct object pronouns with regard to their position in relation to verbs. When they occur with direct object pronouns, the indirect object pronoun always precedes (*nos lo dio,* she gave it to us; *estoy trayéndotela,* I'm bringing it to you).

Use of *Se*

When the indirect object pronouns *le* or *les* occur before any direct object pronoun beginning with an *l-,* the indirect object pronouns *le* and *les* convert to *se* (*les mandé la carta,* I sent them the letter → *se la mandé,* I sent it to them; *vamos a comprarle los aretes,* let's buy her the earrings → *vamos a comprárselos,* let's buy them for her).

4. Reflexive Pronouns

Reflexive pronouns are used to refer back to the subject of the verb (*me hice daño,* I hurt myself; *se vistieron,* they got dressed, they dressed themselves; *nos lo compramos,* we bought it for ourselves).

The reflexive pronouns in Spanish are:

Singular		Plural	
me	myself	**nos**	ourselves
te	yourself	**os**[1]	yourselves
se	yourself, himself, herself, itself	**se**	yourselves, themselves

[1] Used only in Spain.

Reflexive pronouns are also used:

- When the verb describes an action performed to one's own body, clothing, etc. (*me quité los zapatos,* I took off my shoes; *se arregló el pelo,* he fixed his hair).

- In the plural, to indicate reciprocal action (*se hablan con frecuencia,* they speak with each other frequently).

- In the third-person singular and plural, as an indefinite subject reference (*se dice que es verdad,* they say it's true; *nunca se sabe,* one never knows; *se escribieron miles de páginas,* thousands of pages were written).

It should be noted that many verbs which take reflexive pronouns in Spanish have intransitive equivalents in English (*ducharse,* to shower; *quejarse,* to complain; etc.).

5. Relative Pronouns

Relative pronouns introduce subordinate clauses acting as nouns or modifiers (*el libro que escribió* . . . , the book that he wrote . . . ; *las chicas a quienes conociste* . . . , the girls whom you met . . .). In Spanish, the relative pronouns are:

que (that, which, who, whom)

quien, quienes (who, whom, that, whoever, whomever)

el cual, la cual, los cuales, las cuales (which, who)

el que, la que, los que, las que (which, who, whoever)

lo cual (which)

lo que (what, which, whatever)

cuanto, cuanta, cuantos, cuantas (all those that, all that, whatever, whoever, as much as, as many as)

Relative pronouns are not omitted in Spanish as they often are in English: *el carro que vi ayer*, the car (that) I saw yesterday. When relative pronouns are used with prepositions, the preposition precedes the clause (*la película sobre la cual le hablé*, the film I spoke to you about).

The relative pronoun *que* can be used in reference to both people and things. Unlike other relative pronouns, *que* does not take the personal *a** when used as a direct object referring to a person (*el hombre que llamé*, the man that I called; but: *el hombre a quien llamé*, the man whom I called).

Quien is used only in reference to people. It varies in number with the explicit or implied antecedent (*las mujeres con quienes charlamos . . .* , the women we chatted with; *quien lo hizo pagará*, whoever did it will pay).

El cual and *el que* vary for both number and gender, and are therefore often used in situations where *que* or *quien(es)* might create ambiguity: *nos contó algunas cosas sobre los libros, las cuales eran interesantes,* he told us some things about the books which (the things) were interesting.

Lo cual and *lo que* are used to refer back to a whole clause, or to something indefinite (*dijo que iría, lo cual me alegró*, he said he would go, which made me happy; *pide lo que quieras*, ask for whatever you want).

Cuanto varies for both number and gender with the implied antecedent: *conté a cuantas (personas) pude*, I counted as many (people) as I could. If an indefinite mass quantity is referred to, the masculine singular form is used (*anoté cuanto decía*, I jotted down whatever he said).

---

*The personal *a* is generally used: 1) before direct objects (except direct object pronouns or reflexive pronouns) that refer to people or to something that is personified: *cuida a los niños*, he takes care of the children; *amar a la patria*, to love one's country; and 2) before indirect objects (except indirect object pronouns or reflexive pronouns): *permiten a los pasajeros usar sus teléfonos*, they allow passengers to use their phones; *a mí no me importa*, it doesn't matter to me.

Possessives

1. Possessive Adjectives

UNSTRESSED FORMS

Singular		Plural	
mi(s)	my	nuestro(s), nuestra(s)	our
tu(s)	your	vuestro(s)[1], vuestra(s)[1]	your
su(s)	your, his, her, its	su(s)	your, their

[1] Used only in Spain.

STRESSED FORMS

Singular		Plural	
mío(s), mía(s)	my, mine, of mine	nuestro(s), nuestra(s)	our, ours, of ours
tuyo(s), tuya(s)	your, yours, of yours	vuestro(s)[1], vuestra(s)[1]	your, yours, of yours
suyo(s), suya(s)	your, yours, of yours; his, of his; her, hers, of hers; its, of its	suyo(s), suya(s)	your, yours, of yours; their, theirs, of theirs

[1] Used only in Spain.

The unstressed forms of possessive adjectives precede the nouns they modify (*mis zapatos,* my shoes; *nuestra escuela,* our school).

The stressed forms occur after the noun and are often used for purposes of emphasis (*el carro tuyo,* your car; *la pluma es mía,* the pen is mine; *unos amigos nuestros,* some friends of ours).

All possessive adjectives agree with the noun in number. The stressed forms, as well as the unstressed forms *nuestro* and *vuestro,* also vary for gender.

2. Possessive Pronouns

The possessive pronouns have the same forms as the stressed possessive adjectives (see table above). They are always preceded by the definite article, and they agree in number and gender with the nouns they replace (*las llaves mías,* my keys → *las mías,* mine; *los guantes nuestros,* our gloves → *los nuestros,* ours).

Demonstratives

1. Demonstrative Adjectives

The demonstrative adjectives in Spanish are:

Singular		Plural	
este, esta	this	**estos, estas**	these
ese, esa	that	**esos, esas**	those
aquel, aquella	that	**aquellos, aquellas**	those

Demonstrative adjectives agree in gender and number with the nouns they modify (*esta chica, aquellos árboles*). They normally precede the noun, but may occasionally occur after for purposes of emphasis or to express contempt: *en la época aquella de cambio*, in that era of change; *el perro ese ha ladrado toda la noche*, that (awful, annoying, etc.) dog barked all night long.

The forms *aquel, aquella, aquellos*, and *aquellas* are generally used in reference to people and things that are relatively distant from the speaker in space or time: *ese libro*, that book (a few feet away); *aquel libro*, that book (way over there).

2. Demonstrative Pronouns

The demonstrative pronouns in Spanish are orthographically identical to the demonstrative adjectives. Formerly, Spanish rules of orthography required that the demonstrative pronouns include an accent mark over the stressed vowel (*éste, ése, aquél*, etc.) to distinguish them from the corresponding demonstrative adjectives. However, the Real Academia Española (Royal Spanish Academy) now recommends the omission of the accent mark from these pronouns. This supersedes a previous recommendation calling for the inclusion of the accent mark only when needed to resolve cases of ambiguity. Nevertheless, both the accented and unaccented variants are in common use as of this writing, and are reflected in this dictionary.

In addition, there are three neuter forms—*esto, eso*, and *aquello*—which are used when referring to abstract ideas or unidentified things (*¿te dijo eso?*, he said that to you?; *¿qué es esto?*, what is this?; *tráeme todo aquello*, bring me all that stuff).

Except for the neuter forms, demonstrative pronouns agree in gender and number with the nouns they replace (*esta silla*, this chair → *esta/ésta*, this one; *aquellos vasos*, those glasses → *aquellos/aquéllos*, those ones).

Gramática inglesa

El adjetivo

El adjetivo inglés es invariable en cuanto a número o género, y suele preceder al sustantivo que modifica:

the *tall* woman
(la mujer *alta*)

the *tall* women
(las mujeres *altas*)

a *happy* child
(un niño *contento*)

happy children
(niños *contentos*)

1. Adjetivos positivos, comparativos, y superlativos

Las formas comparativas y superlativas del adjetivo inglés se pueden construir de tres maneras. Cuando el adjetivo positivo consta de una sola sílaba, la construcción más común es de añadir los sufijos -*er* o -*est* al vocablo raíz; si el adjetivo positivo consta de más de dos sílabas, suele entonces combinarse con los adverbios *more, most, less* o *least;* al adjetivo positivo de dos sílabas puede aplicarse cualquiera de las dos fórmulas; y por último, existen los adjetivos irregulares cuyas formas comparativas y superlativas son únicas:

Positivo	Comparativo	Superlativo
clean (limpio)	**cleaner** (más limpio)	**cleanest** (el más limpio)
narrow (angosto)	**narrower** (más angosto)	**narrowest** (el más angosto)
meaningful (significativo)	**more meaningful** (más significativo)	**most meaningful** (el más significativo)
less meaningful (menos significativo)	**least meaningful** (el menos significativo)	
good (bueno)	**better** (mejor)	**best** (el mejor)
bad (malo)	**worse** (peor)	**worst** (el peor)

2. Adjetivos demostrativos

Los adjetivos demostrativos *this* y *that* corresponden a los adjetivos españoles *este* y *ese*, respectivamente, y sirven esencialmente la misma función. Debe notarse que este tipo de adjetivo es el único que tiene forma plural:

Singular		Plural	
this	este, esta	**these**	estos, estas
that	ese, esa	**those**	esos, esas

3. Adjetivos descriptivos

Un adjetivo descriptivo describe o indica una cualidad, clase o condición (*a fascinating conversation,* una conversación fascinante; *a positive attitude,* una actitud positiva; *a fast computer,* una computadora rápida).

4. Adjetivos indefinidos

Un adjetivo indefinido se usa para designar personas o cosas no identificadas (*some children,* unos niños *o* algunos niños; *other hotels,* otros hoteles).

5. Adjetivos interrogativos

El adjetivo interrogativo se usa para formular preguntas:

Whose office is this?
(¿*De quién* es esta oficina?)

Which book do you want?
(¿*Cuál* libro quieres?)

6. El sustantivo empleado como adjetivo

Un sustantivo puede usarse para modificar otro sustantivo. De esta manera el sustantivo funciona igual que un adjetivo (*the Vietnam War,* la Guerra de Vietnam; *word processing,* procesamiento de textos).

7. Adjetivos posesivos

Llámase adjetivo posesivo a la forma posesiva del pronombre personal. A continuación se listan los adjetivos posesivos ingleses y algunos ejemplos de su uso:

Singular	Plural
my	our
your	your
his/her/its	their

Where's *my* watch?
(¿Dónde está *mi* reloj?)

Your cab's here.
(Ha llegado *su/tu* taxi.)

It was *her* idea.
(Fue *su* idea.)

They read *his* book.
(Leyeron *su* libro.)

the box and *its* contents
(la caja y *su* contenido)

We paid for *their* ticket.
(Pagamos por *su* boleto.)

Your tables are ready.
(*Sus* mesas están listas.)

8. Adjetivos predicativos

Un adjetivo predicativo modifica el sujeto de un verbo copulativo (como *be, become, feel, taste, smell,* o *seem*):

She is *happy* with the outcome.
(Está *contenta* con el resultado.)

The milk tastes *sour*.
(La leche sabe *agria*.)

The student seems *puzzled*.
(El estudiante parece estar *desconcertado*.)

9. Adjetivos propios

Un adjetivo propio es derivado de un nombre propio y suele escribirse con mayúscula:

Victorian furniture
(muebles *victorianos*)

a *Puerto Rican* product
(un producto *puertorriqueño*)

10. Adjetivos relativos

Un adjetivo relativo (tal como *which, that, who, whom, whose, where*) se emplea para introducir una cláusula adjetival o sustantiva:

toward late April, by *which* time the report should be finished
(para fines de abril, fecha para *la cual* deberá estar listo el reporte)

a person *whose* identity is unknown
(una persona *cuya* identidad se desconoce)

El adverbio

La mayor parte de los adverbios ingleses se forman a partir de un adjetivo al que se le agrega el sufijo *-ly*:

mad*ly*
(loca*mente*)

wonderful*ly*
(maravillosa*mente*)

Para formar un adverbio de un adjetivo que termina en *-y*, suele cambiarse primero esta terminación a una *-i*, y luego se añade el sufijo *-ly*:

happ*ily*
(feliz*mente*)

daint*ily*
(delicada*mente*)

La forma adverbial que corresponde a varios adjetivos que terminan en *-ic* recibe el sufijo *-ally*:

basic*ally*
(básica*mente*)

numeric*ally*
(numérica*mente*)

Si un adjetivo termina en *-ly*, el adverbio que le corresponde suele escribirse de la misma manera:

she called her mother *daily*
(llamaba a su madre *todos los días*)

the show started *early*
(la función empezó *temprano*)

Por último, hay adverbios que no terminan en *-ly*, por ejemplo:

again (otra vez)
now (ahora)

too (demasiado)
too (también)

1. Adverbios positivos, comparativos, y superlativos

Al igual que el adjetivo, la mayoría de los adverbios ingleses poseen tres grados de comparación: positivo, comparativo, y superlativo. Como regla general, a un adverbio monosilábico se le añade el sufijo *-er* cuando es comparativo, y *-est* cuando es superlativo. Si el adverbio consta de tres o más sílabas, las formas comparativas y superlativas se forman al combinarlo con los adverbios *more/most* o *less/least*. Las formas comparativas y superlativas de un adverbio de dos sílabas pueden obtenerse empleando uno u otro de los dos métodos:

Positivo	Comparativo	Superlativo
fast	fast*er*	fast*est*
easy	easi*er*	easi*est*
madly	more mad*ly*	most mad*ly*
happily	more happi*ly*	most happi*ly*

Finalmente, hay algunos adverbios, tales como *quite* y *very*, que no poseen comparativo.

2. Adverbios de énfasis

Adverbios tales como *just* y *only* suelen usarse para poner el énfasis en otras palabras. El énfasis producido puede cambiar según la posición del adverbio en la oración:

He *just* nodded to me as he passed.
(*Sólo* me saludó con la cabeza al pasar.)

He nodded to me *just* as he passed.
(Me saludó con la cabeza *justamente* cuando me pasó.)

3. Adverbios relativos

Los adverbios relativos (tales como *when*, *where*, y *why*) se utilizan principalmente para introducir preguntas:

When will he return?
(¿*Cuándo* volverá?)

Where have the children gone?
(¿*A dónde* fueron los niños?)

Why did you do it?
(¿*Por qué* lo hiciste?)

El artículo

1. El artículo definido

En inglés existe solamente una forma del artículo definido, *the*. Este artículo es invariable en cuanto a género o número:

The boys were expelled.
(*Los* chicos fueron expulsados.)

The First Lady dined with *the* ambassador.
(*La* Primera Dama cenó con *el* embajador.)

2. El artículo indefinido

El artículo indefinido *a* se usa con cualquier sustantivo o abreviatura que comience ya sea con una consonante, o con un *sonido* consonántico:

a door	*a* hat
a B.A. degree	*a* one-way street
a union	*a* U.S. Senator

El artículo *a* se emplea también antes de un sustantivo cuya primera sílaba comienza con *h-*, y esta sílaba o no es acentuada, o tiene solamente una acentuación moderada (*a historian, a heroic attempt, a hilarious performance*). Sin embargo, en el inglés hablado, suele más usarse el artículo *an* en estos casos (*an historian, an heroic attempt, an hilarious performance*). Ambas formas son perfectamente aceptables.

El artículo indefinido *an* se usa con cualquier sustantivo o abreviatura que comience con un *sonido* vocal, sin tener en cuenta si la primera letra del sustantivo es vocal o consonante (*an icicle, an nth degree, an honor, an FBI investigation*).

La conjunción

Existen tres tipos principales de conjunciones: la conjunción coordinante, la correlativa, y la subordinante.

1. Conjunciones coordinantes

Las conjunciones coordinantes, tales como *and, because, but, or, nor, since, so*, y *yet*, se emplean para unir elementos gramaticales de igual valor. Estos elementos pueden ser palabras, frases, cláusulas subordinadas, cláusulas principales, u oraciones completas. Las conjunciones coordinantes se emplean para unir elementos similares, para excluir o contrastar, para indicar una alternativa, para indicar una razón, o para precisar un resultado:

unión de elementos similares:
She ordered pencils, pens, *and* erasers.

exclusión o contraste:
He is a brilliant *but* arrogant man.
They offered a promising plan, *but* it had not yet been tested.

alternativa:
She can wait here *or* go on ahead.

razón:
The report is useless, *since* its information is no longer current.

resultado:
His diction is excellent, *so* every word is clear.

2. Conjunciones correlativas

Las conjunciones correlativas se usan en pares, y sirven para unir alternativas y elementos de igual valor gramatical:

Either you go *or* you stay.
(*O* te vas *o* te quedas.)

He had *neither* looks *nor* wit.
(No tenía *ni* atractivo físico *ni* inteligencia.)

3. Conjunciones subordinantes

Las conjunciones subordinantes se usan para unir una cláusula subordinada a una cláusula principal. Estas conjunciones pueden emplearse para expresar la causa, la condición o concesión, el modo, el propósito o resultado, el tiempo, el lugar o la circunstancia, así como las condiciones o posibilidades alternativas:

causa:
Because she learns quickly, she is doing well in her new job.

condición o concesión:
Don't call *unless* you are coming.

modo:
We'll do it *however* you tell us to.

propósito o resultado:
He distributes the mail early *so that* they can read it.

tiempo:
She kept meetings to a minimum *when* she was president.

El sustantivo

A diferencia del sustantivo español, el sustantivo inglés generalmente carece de género. En algunos sustantivos, el género femenino se identifica por la presencia del sufijo *-ess* (*empress, hostess*); existen también aquellos sustantivos que sólo se aplican a miembros de uno u otro sexo, por ejemplo: *husband, wife; father, mother; brother, sister;* así como nombres de ciertos animales: *bull, cow; buck, doe;* etc. Sin embargo, la mayoría de los sustantivos ingleses son neutros. Cuando es preciso atribuirle un género a un sustantivo neutro, suele combinarse éste con palabras como *male, female, man, woman,* etc., por ejemplo:

a *male* parrot
(un loro *macho*)

women writers
(escritoras)

1. Usos básicos

Los sustantivos ingleses suelen usarse como sujetos, objetos directos, objetos de una preposición, objetos indirectos, objetos retenidos, nominativos predicativos, complementos objetivos, construcciones apositivas, y en trato directo:

sujeto:
The *office* was quiet.

objeto directo:
He locked the *office*.

objeto de una preposición:
The file is in the *office*.

objeto indirecto:
He gave his *client* the papers.

objeto retenido:
His client was given the *papers*.

nominativo predicativo:
Mrs. Adams is the managing *partner*.

complemento objetivo:
They made Mrs. Adams managing *partner*.

construcción apositiva:
Mrs. Adams, the managing *partner*, wrote that memo.

trato directo:
Mrs. Adams, may I present Mr. Bonkowski.

2. El sustantivo empleado como adjetivo

Los sustantivos desempeñan una función adjetival cuando preceden a otros sustantivos:

olive oil
(aceite *de oliva*)

business management
(administración *de empresas*)

emergency room
(sala *de emergencias*)

3. La formación del plural

La mayoría de los sustantivos ingleses se pluralizan añadiendo -*s* al final del singular (*book, books; cat, cats; dog, dogs; tree, trees*).

Cuando el sustantivo singular termina en -*s*, -*x*, -*z*, -*ch*, o -*sh*, su forma plural se obtiene añadiendo -*es* al final (*cross, crosses; fox, foxes; witch, witches; wish, wishes; fez, fezes*).

Si el sustantivo singular termina en -*y* precedida de una consonante, la -*y* es convertida en -*i* y se le añade la terminación -*es* (*fairy*, *fairies*; *pony*, *ponies*; *guppy*, *guppies*).

No todos los sustantivos ingleses obedecen estas normas. Hay algunos sustantivos (generalmente nombres de animales) que no siempre cambian en el plural (*fish*, *fish* o *fishes*; *caribou*, *caribou* o *caribous*). Por último, hay algunos sustantivos que poseen una forma plural única (*foot*, *feet*; *mouse*, *mice*; *knife*, *knives*).

4. El posesivo

La forma posesiva del sustantivo singular generalmente se obtiene al añadir un apóstrofe seguido de una -*s* al final:

Jackie's passport
(el pasaporte *de Jackie*)

this hat is *Billy's*
(este sombrero es *de Billy*)

Cuando el sustantivo termina en -*s*, suele añadirse únicamente el apóstrofe, como sigue:

the *neighbors'* dog
(el perro *de los vecinos*)

Mr. Collins' briefcase
(el portafolios *del Sr. Collins*)

La preposición

La preposición inglesa se combina generalmente con un sustantivo, un pronombre, o el equivalente de un sustantivo (como una frase o cláusula) para formar una frase con función adjetival, adverbial, o sustantiva. Suele distinguirse dos tipos de preposiciones: la preposición simple, es decir, aquélla que consta de una sola palabra (p. ej., *against, from, near, of, on, out,* o *without*), y la compuesta, que consta de más de un elemento (como *according to, by means of,* o *in spite of*).

1. Usos básicos

La preposición se emplea generalmente para unir un sustantivo, un pronombre, o el equivalente de un sustantivo al resto de la oración. Una frase preposicional suele emplearse como adverbio o adjetivo:

She expected resistance *on his part*.
He sat down *beside her*.

2. La conjunción vs. la preposición

Las palabras inglesas *after, before, but, for*,* y *since* pueden funcionar como preposiciones así como conjunciones. El papel que

---

*La conjunción *for* se emplea principalmente en el lenguaje formal y literario.

desempeñan estas palabras suele determinarse según su posición dentro de la oración. Las conjunciones generalmente sirven para unir dos elementos de igual valor gramatical, mientras que las preposiciones suelen preceder a un sustantivo, un pronombre, o una frase sustantiva:

conjunción:
I was a bit concerned *but* not panicky. (*but* vincula dos adjetivos)

preposición:
I was left with nothing *but* hope. (*but* precede a un sustantivo)

conjunción:
The device conserves fuel, *for* it is battery-powered. (*for* vincula dos cláusulas)

preposición:
The device conserves fuel *for* residual heating. (*for* precede a una frase sustantiva)

3. Posición

Una preposición puede aparecer antes de un sustantivo o un pronombre (*below the desk, beside them*), después de un adjetivo (*antagonistic to, insufficient in, symbolic of*), o después de un elemento verbal con el cual combina para formar una frase con función verbal (*take for, take over, come across*).

A diferencia de la preposición española, la preposición inglesa puede aparecer al final de una oración, lo cual sucede frecuentemente en el uso común, especialmente si la preposición forma parte de una frase con función verbal:

After Rourke left, Joyce took *over*.
What does this all add up *to*?

El pronombre

Los pronombres pueden poseer las características siguientes: caso (nominativo, posesivo, u objetivo); número (singular o plural); persona (primera, segunda, o tercera), y género (masculino, femenino, o neutro). Los pronombres ingleses se clasifican en siete categorías principales, de las cuales cada una juega un papel específico.

1. Pronombres demostrativos

Las palabras *this, that, these* y *those* se consideran como pronombres cuando funcionan como sustantivos. (Se les clasifica como adjetivos demostrativos cuando modifican un sustantivo.) El pronombre demostrativo indica a una persona o cosa para distinguirla de otras:

These are the best designs we've seen to date.
Those are strong words.

El pronombre demostrativo también se usa para distinguir a una persona o cosa cercana de otra que se encuentre a mayor distancia (*this is my desk; that is yours*).

2. Pronombres indefinidos

El pronombre indefinido se emplea para designar a una persona o cosa cuya identidad se desconoce o no se puede establecer de inmediato. Estos pronombres se usan generalmente como referencias en la tercera persona, y no se distinguen en cuanto a género. A continuación se listan ejemplos de pronombres indefinidos:

all	either	none
another	everybody	no one
any	everyone	one
anybody	everything	other
anyone	few	several
anything	many	some
both	much	somebody
each	neither	someone
each one	nobody	something

Los pronombres indefinidos deben concordar en cuanto a número con los verbos que les corresponden. Los siguientes pronombres son singulares y deben usarse con un verbo conjugado en singular: *another, anything, each, each one, everything, much, nobody, no one, one, other, someone, something.*

Much is being done.
No one wants to go.

Los pronombres indefinidos *both, few, many, several* entre otros son plurales, y por lo tanto deben emplearse con verbos conjugados en plural:

Many were called; *few were* chosen.

Algunos pronombres, tales como *all, any, none,* y *some,* pueden presentar un problema ya que pueden usarse tanto con verbos singulares como plurales. Como regla general, los pronombres que se usan con sustantivos no numerables emplean verbos singulares, mientras que aquéllos que se usan con sustantivos numerables suelen tomar un verbo plural:

con sustantivo no numerable:
All of the property *is* affected.
None of the soup *was* spilled.
Some of the money *was* spent.

con sustantivo numerable:
All of my shoes *are* black.
None of the clerks *were* available.
Some of your friends *were* there.

3. Pronombres interrogativos

Los pronombres interrogativos *what, which, who, whom,* y *whose,* así como las combinaciones de estos con el sufijo *-ever* (*whatever, whichever,* etc.) se usan para introducir una pregunta:

Who is she?
He asked me *who* she was.

Whoever can that be?
We wondered *whoever* that could be.

4. Pronombres personales

El pronombre personal refleja la persona, el número, y el género del ser u objeto que representa. La mayoría de los pronombres personales toman una forma distinta para cada uno de estos tres casos:

Persona	Nominativo	Posesivo	Objetivo
PRIMERA			
SINGULAR:	I	my, mine	me
PLURAL:	we	our, ours	us
SEGUNDA			
SINGULAR:	you	your, yours	you
PLURAL:	you	your, yours	you
TERCERA			
SINGULAR:	he	his, his	him
	she	her, hers	her
	it	its, its	it
PLURAL:	they	their, theirs	them

Nótese que los pronombres personales en el caso posesivo no llevan apóstrofe, y no deben confundirse con los homófonos *you're, they're, there's, it's.*

5. Pronombres recíprocos

Los pronombres recíprocos *each other* y *one another* se emplean para indicar una acción o relación mutua:

They do not quarrel with *one another*.
(No se pelean (el uno con el otro).)

Lou and Andy saw *each other* at the party.
(Lou y Andy se vieron en la fiesta.)

Un pronombre recíproco puede usarse también en el caso posesivo:

They always borrowed *one another's* money.
(Siempre se prestaban dinero.)

The two companies depend on *each other's* success.
(Cada una de las dos compañías depende del éxito de la otra.)

6. Pronombres reflexivos

Los pronombres reflexivos se forman al combinar los pronombres personales *him, her, it, my, our, them* y *your* con *-self* o *-selves*. El pronombre reflexivo se usa generalmente para expresar una acción reflexiva, o bien para recalcar el sujeto de una oración, cláusula, o frase:

She dressed *herself*.
He asked *himself* if it was worth it.
I *myself* am not concerned.

7. Pronombres relativos

Los pronombres relativos son *that, what, which, who, whom,* y *whose,* así como las combinaciones de éstos con la terminación *-ever*. Estos pronombres se emplean para introducir oraciones subordinadas con función sustantiva o adjetival.

El pronombre relativo *who* se usa para referirse a personas y, en ciertas ocasiones, algunos animales. *Which* suele usarse para referirse a animales o cosas, y *that* puede usarse para personas, animales, o cosas:

a man *who* sought success
a woman *whom* we trust
Kentucky Firebolt, *who* won yesterday's horse race
a movie *which* was a big hit
a dog *which* kept barking
a boy *that* behaves well
a movie *that* was a big hit
a dog *that* kept barking

En ciertas ocasiones el pronombre relativo puede omitirse:

The man (*whom*) I was talking to is the senator.

El verbo

El verbo inglés posee típicamente las siguientes características: inflexión (p. ej., *help, helps, helping, helped*), persona (primera, segunda, o tercera), número (singular o plural), tiempo (presente, pasado, futuro), aspecto (categorías temporales distintas a los tiempos simples de presente, pasado y futuro), voz (activa o pasiva), y modo (indicativo, subjuntivo e imperativo).

1. La inflexión

Los verbos regulares ingleses tienen cuatro inflexiones diferentes, las cuales se producen al añadir los sufijos -*s* o -*es*, -*ed*, e -*ing*. La mayoría de los verbos irregulares poseen cuatro o cinco inflexiones (p. ej., *see, sees, seeing, saw, seen*); y el verbo *be* tiene ocho (*be, is, am, are, being, was, were, been*).

Los verbos que terminan en una -*e* muda conservan por lo general la -*e* al añadírsele un sufijo que comienza con una consonante (como -*s*), pero esta -*e* desaparece si el sufijo comienza con una vocal (como sucede con -*ed* o -*ing*):

arrange; arranges; arranged; arranging
hope; hopes; hoped; hoping

Sin embargo, algunos de estos verbos conservan la -*e* final para no ser confundidos con otras palabras de ortografía igual, por ejemplo:

dye; dyes; dyed; dyeing
(vs. *dying*, del verbo *die*)
singe; singes; singed; singeing
(vs. *singing*, del verbo *sing*)

Si un verbo consta de una sílaba y termina en una sola consonante a la cual precede una sola vocal, la consonante final se repite al añadir el sufijo -*ed* o -*ing*:

brag; brags; bragged; bragging
grip; grips; gripped; gripping

Cuando un verbo posee esta misma terminación, pero consta de dos o más sílabas, y la última de éstas es acentuada, se repite también al añadir el sufijo -*ed* o -*ing*:

commit; commits; committed; committing
occur; occurs; occurred; occurring

Los verbos que terminan en -*y*, precedida de una consonante, suelen cambiar esta -*y* en -*i* en toda inflexión excepto cuando el sufijo correspondiente es -*ing:*

carry; carries; carried; carrying
study; studies; studied; studying

Cuando un verbo termina en -*c*, se le añade una -*k* en inflexiones cuyos sufijos comienzan con -*e* o -*i*:

mimic; mimics; mimicked; mimicking
traffic; traffics; trafficked; trafficking

2. El tiempo y el aspecto

Los verbos ingleses exhiben generalmente su presente simple o pasado simple en una sola palabra, por ejemplo:

I *do*, I *did*
we *write*, we *wrote*

El tiempo futuro suele expresarse al combinar el verbo auxiliar *shall* o *will* con la forma presente simple o presente progresiva del verbo:

I *shall do* it.
(Lo *haré*.)

We *will come* tomorrow.
(*Vendremos* mañana.)

He *will be arriving* later.
(*Llegará* más tarde.)

Llámase aspecto de un verbo a aquellos tiempos que difieren del presente simple, pasado simple, o futuro simple. A continuación se presentan cuatro de estos tiempos o aspectos: el progresivo, el presente perfecto, el pasado perfecto, y el futuro perfecto.

El tiempo progresivo expresa una acción en progreso:

He *is reading* the paper.
(*Está leyendo* el periódico.)

I *was working* when she called.
(*Estaba trabajando* cuando llamó.)

El presente perfecto se emplea para expresar una acción que ha comenzado en el pasado y que continúa en el presente, o también para expresar una acción que haya tenido lugar en un momento indefinido del pasado:

She *has written* a book.
(*Ha escrito* un libro.)

El pasado perfecto expresa una acción que fue llevada a cabo antes de otra acción o evento en el pasado:

She *had written* many books previously.
(*Había escrito* muchos libros anteriormente.)

El futuro perfecto indica una acción que será llevada a cabo antes de una acción o evento en el futuro:

We *will have finished* the project by then.
(A esas alturas *habremos terminado* el proyecto.)

3. La voz

La voz (activa o pasiva) indica si el sujeto de la oración es el que desempeña la acción del verbo o si es el objeto de esta acción:

Voz activa:
He *respected* his colleagues.
(*Respetaba* a sus colegas.)

Voz pasiva:
He *was respected* by his colleagues.
(*Era respetado* por sus colegas.)

4. El modo

En inglés existen tres modos: indicativo, imperativo, y subjuntivo.

El modo indicativo se emplea ya sea para indicar un hecho, o para hacer una pregunta:

He *is* here.
(*Está* aquí.)

Is he here?
(*¿Está* aquí?)

El modo imperativo se usa para expresar una orden o una petición:

Come here.
(*Ven* aquí.)

Please *come* here.
(*Ven* aquí, por favor.)

El modo subjuntivo expresa una condición contraria a los hechos. El modo subjuntivo en inglés ha caído en desuso, pero suele aparecer en cláusulas introducidas por *if*, y después del verbo *wish*:

I wish he *were* here.
(Quisiera que *estuviera* él aquí.)

If she *were* there, she could have answered that.
(Si *estuviera* ella allá, podría haberlo contestado.)

5. Verbos transitivos e intransitivos

Como en español, el verbo inglés puede ser transitivo o intransitivo. El verbo transitivo es el que puede llevar un complemento directo:

She *sold* her car.
(*Vendió* su coche.)

El verbo intransitivo no lleva un complemento directo:

He *talked* all day.
(*Habló* todo el día.)

Conjugation of Spanish Verbs

Simple Tenses

Tense	Regular Verbs Ending in -AR hablar	
PRESENT INDICATIVE	hablo	hablamos
	hablas	habláis
	habla	hablan
PRESENT SUBJUNCTIVE	hable	hablemos
	hables	habléis
	hable	hablen
PRETERIT INDICATIVE	hablé	hablamos
	hablaste	hablasteis
	habló	hablaron
IMPERFECT INDICATIVE	hablaba	hablábamos
	hablabas	hablabais
	hablaba	hablaban
IMPERFECT SUBJUNCTIVE	hablara	habláramos
	hablaras	hablarais
	hablara	hablaran
	or	
	hablase	hablásemos
	hablases	hablaseis
	hablase	hablasen
FUTURE INDICATIVE	hablaré	hablaremos
	hablarás	hablaréis
	hablará	hablarán
FUTURE SUBJUNCTIVE	hablare	habláremos
	hablares	hablareis
	hablare	hablaren
CONDITIONAL	hablaría	hablaríamos
	hablarías	hablaríais
	hablaría	hablarían
IMPERATIVE		hablemos
	habla	hablad
	hable	hablen
PRESENT PARTICIPLE (GERUND)	hablando	
PAST PARTICIPLE	hablado	

Regular Verbs Ending in -ER		Regular Verbs Ending in -IR	
comer		vivir	
como	comemos	vivo	vivimos
comes	coméis	vives	vivís
come	comen	vive	viven
coma	comamos	viva	vivamos
comas	comáis	vivas	viváis
coma	coman	viva	vivan
comí	comimos	viví	vivimos
comiste	comisteis	viviste	vivisteis
comió	comieron	vivió	vivieron
comía	comíamos	vivía	vivíamos
comías	comíais	vivías	vivíais
comía	comían	vivía	vivían
comiera	comiéramos	viviera	viviéramos
comieras	comierais	vivieras	vivierais
comiera	comieran	viviera	vivieran
or		*or*	
comiese	comiésemos	viviese	viviésemos
comieses	comieseis	vivieses	vivieseis
comiese	comiesen	viviese	viviesen
comeré	comeremos	viviré	viviremos
comerás	comeréis	vivirás	viviréis
comerá	comerán	vivirá	vivirán
comiere	comiéremos	viviere	viviéremos
comieres	comiereis	vivieres	viviereis
comiere	comieren	viviere	vivieren
comería	comeríamos	viviría	viviríamos
comerías	comeríais	vivirías	viviríais
comería	comerían	viviría	vivirían
	comamos		vivamos
come	comed	vive	vivid
coma	coman	viva	vivan
comiendo		viviendo	
comido		vivido	

Compound Tenses

1. Perfect Tenses

The perfect tenses are formed with *haber* and the past participle:

PRESENT PERFECT

he hablado, etc. (*indicative*)
haya hablado, etc. (*subjunctive*)

PAST PERFECT

había hablado, etc. (*indicative*)
hubiera hablado, etc. (*subjunctive*)
or
hubiese hablado, etc. (*subjunctive*)

PRETERIT PERFECT

hube hablado, etc. (*indicative*)

FUTURE PERFECT

habré hablado, etc. (*indicative*)

CONDITIONAL PERFECT

habría hablado, etc. (*indicative*)

2. Progressive Tenses

The progressive tenses are formed with *estar* and the present participle:

PRESENT PROGRESSIVE

estoy llamando, etc. (*indicative*)
esté llamando, etc. (*subjunctive*)

IMPERFECT PROGRESSIVE

estaba llamando, etc. (*indicative*)
estuviera llamando, etc. (*subjunctive*)
or
estuviese llamando, etc. (*subjunctive*)

PRETERIT PROGRESSIVE

estuve llamando, etc. (*indicative*)

FUTURE PROGRESSIVE

estaré llamando, etc. (*indicative*)

CONDITIONAL PROGRESSIVE

estaría llamando, etc. (*indicative*)

PRESENT PERFECT PROGRESSIVE

> he estado llamando, etc. (*indicative*)
> haya estado llamando, etc. (*subjunctive*)

PAST PERFECT PROGRESSIVE

> había estado llamando, etc. (*indicative*)
> hubiera estado llamando, etc. (*subjunctive*)
> *or*
> hubiese estado llamando, etc. (*subjunctive*)

Use of *Vos*

In parts of South and Central America, *vos* often replaces or competes with *tú* as the second-person familiar personal pronoun. It is particularly well established in the Río de la Plata region and much of Central America.

The pronoun *vos* often takes a distinct set of verb forms, usually in the present tense and the imperative. These vary widely from region to region; examples of the most common forms are shown below:

INFINITIVE FORM	hablar	comer	vivir
PRESENT INDICATIVE	vos hablás	vos comés	vos vivís
PRESENT SUBJUNCTIVE	vos hablés	vos comás	vos vivás
IMPERATIVE	hablá	comé	viví

In some areas, *vos* may take the *tú* or *vosotros* forms of the verb, while in others (such as Uruguay), *tú* is combined with the *vos* verb forms.

Irregular Verbs

The *imperfect subjunctive,* the *future subjunctive,* the *conditional,* and most forms of the *imperative* are not included in the model conjugations list, but can be derived as follows:

The *imperfect subjunctive* and the *future subjunctive* are formed from the third-person plural form of the preterit tense by removing the last syllable (*-ron*) and adding the appropriate suffix:

PRETERIT INDICATIVE, THIRD-PERSON PLURAL (querer)	quisieron
IMPERFECT SUBJUNCTIVE (querer)	quisiera, quisieras, etc.
	or
	quisiese, quisieses, etc.
FUTURE SUBJUNCTIVE (querer)	quisiere, quisieres, etc.

The conditional uses the same stem as the future indicative:

FUTURE INDICATIVE (poner)   pondré, pondrás, etc.
CONDITIONAL (poner)   pondría, pondrías, etc.

The third-person singular, first-person plural, and third-person plural forms of the *imperative* are the same as the corresponding forms of the present subjunctive.

The second-person plural (*vosotros*) form of the *imperative* is formed by removing the final *-r* of the infinitive form and adding a *-d* (ex.: *oír → oíd*).

Model Conjugations of Irregular Verbs

The model conjugations below include the following simple tenses: the *present indicative* (IND), the *present subjunctive* (SUBJ), the *preterit indicative* (PRET), the *imperfect indicative* (IMPF), the *future indicative* (FUT), the second-person singular form of the *imperative* (IMPER), the *present participle* or *gerund* (PRP), and the *past participle* (PP). Each set of conjugations is preceded by the corresponding infinitive form of the verb, shown in bold type. Only tenses containing irregularities are listed, and the irregular verb forms within each tense are displayed in bold type.

Each irregular verb entry in the Spanish-English section of this dictionary is cross-referred by number to one of the following model conjugations. These cross-reference numbers are shown in curly braces { } immediately following the entry's functional label.

1 **abolir** *(defective verb)* : IND abolimos, abolís *(other forms not used)*; SUBJ *(not used)*; IMPER *(only second-person plural is used)*

2 **abrir** : PP abierto

3 **actuar** : IND actúo, **actúas, actúa,** actuamos, actuáis, **actúan;** SUBJ **actúe, actúes, actúe,** actuemos, actuéis, **actúen;** IMPER **actúa**

4 **adquirir** : IND adquiero, adquieres, adquiere, adquirimos, adquirís, adquieren; SUBJ adquiera, adquieras, adquiera, adquiramos, adquiráis, adquieran; IMPER adquiere

5 **airar** : IND aíro, aíras, aíra, airamos, airáis, aíran; SUBJ aíre, aíres, aíre, airemos, airéis, aíren; IMPER aíra

6 **andar** : PRET anduve, anduviste, anduvo, anduvimos, anduvisteis, anduvieron

7 **asir** : IND asgo, ases, ase, asimos, asís, asen; SUBJ asga, asgas, asga, asgamos, asgáis, asgan

8 **aunar** : IND aúno, aúnas, aúna, aunamos, aunáis, aúnan; SUBJ aúne, aúnes, aúne, aunemos, aunéis, aúnen; IMPER aúna

9 **avergonzar** : *IND* **avergüenzo, avergüenzas, avergüenza,** avergonzamos, avergonzáis, **avergüenzan;** *SUBJ* **avergüence, avergüences, avergüence, avergoncemos, avergoncéis, avergüencen;** *PRET* **avergoncé;** *IMPER* **avergüenza**

10 **averiguar** : *SUBJ* **averigüe, averigües, averigüe, averigüemos, averigüéis, averigüen;** *PRET* **averigüé,** averiguaste, averiguó, averiguamos, averiguasteis, averiguaron

11 **bendecir** : *IND* **bendigo, bendices, bendice,** bendecimos, bendecís, **bendicen;** *SUBJ* **bendiga, bendigas, bendiga, bendigamos, bendigáis, bendigan;** *PRET* **bendije, bendijiste, bendijo, bendijimos, bendijisteis, bendijeron;** *IMPER* **bendice**

12 **caber** : *IND* **quepo,** cabes, cabe, cabemos, cabéis, caben; *SUBJ* **quepa, quepas, quepa, quepamos, quepáis, quepan;** *PRET* **cupe, cupiste, cupo, cupimos, cupisteis, cupieron;** *FUT* **cabré, cabrás, cabrá, cabremos, cabréis, cabrán**

13 **caer** : *IND* **caigo,** caes, cae, caemos, caéis, caen; *SUBJ* **caiga, caigas, caiga, caigamos, caigáis, caigan;** *PRET* **caí, caíste, cayó, caímos, caísteis, cayeron;** *PRP* **cayendo;** *PP* **caído**

14 **cocer** : *IND* **cuezo, cueces, cuece,** cocemos, cocéis, **cuecen;** *SUBJ* **cueza, cuezas, cueza, cozamos, cozáis, cuezan;** *IMPER* **cuece**

15 **coger** : *IND* **cojo,** coges, coge, cogemos, cogéis, cogen; *SUBJ* **coja, cojas, coja, cojamos, cojáis, cojan**

16 **colgar** : *IND* **cuelgo, cuelgas, cuelga,** colgamos, colgáis, **cuelgan;** *SUBJ* **cuelgue, cuelgues, cuelgue, colguemos, colguéis, cuelguen;** *PRET* **colgué,** colgaste, colgó, colgamos, colgasteis, colgaron; *IMPER* **cuelga**

17 **concernir** *(defective verb; used only in the third-person singular and plural of the present indicative, present subjunctive, and imperfect subjunctive) see* **25 discernir**

18 **conocer** : *IND* **conozco,** conoces, conoce, conocemos, conocéis, conocen; *SUBJ* **conozca, conozcas, conozca, conozcamos, conozcáis, conozcan**

19 **contar** : *IND* **cuento, cuentas, cuenta,** contamos, contáis, **cuentan;** *SUBJ* **cuente, cuentes, cuente,** contemos, contéis, **cuenten;** *IMPER* **cuenta**

20 **creer** : *PRET* **creí, creíste, creyó, creímos, creísteis, creyeron;** *PRP* **creyendo;** *PP* **creído**

21 **cruzar** : *SUBJ* **cruce, cruces, cruce, crucemos, crucéis, crucen;** *PRET* **crucé,** cruzaste, cruzó, cruzamos, cruzasteis, cruzaron

22 **dar** : *IND* **doy,** das, da, damos, **dais,** dan; *SUBJ* **dé,** des, **dé,** demos, **deis,** den; *PRET* **di,** diste, **dio, dimos, disteis, dieron**

23 **decir** : *IND* **digo, dices, dice,** decimos, decís, **dicen;** *SUBJ* **diga, digas, diga, digamos, digáis, digan;** *PRET* **dije, dijiste, dijo, dijimos, dijisteis, dijeron;** *FUT* **diré, dirás, dirá, diremos, diréis, dirán;** *IMPER* **di;** *PRP* **diciendo;** *PP* **dicho**

24 **delinquir** : *IND* **delinco,** delinques, delinque, delinquimos, delin-
quís, delinquen; *SUBJ* **delinca, delincas, delinca, delincamos,
delincáis, delincan**

25 **discernir** : *IND* **discierno, disciernes, discierne,** discernimos, dis-
cernís, **disciernen;** *SUBJ* **discierna, disciernas, discierna,** dis-
cernamos, discernáis, **disciernan;** *IMPER* **discierne**

26 **distinguir** : *IND* **distingo,** distingues, distingue, distinguimos, dis-
tinguís, distinguen; *SUBJ* **distinga, distingas, distinga, distinga-
mos, distingáis, distingan**

27 **dormir** : *IND* **duermo, duermes, duerme,** dormimos, dormís,
duermen; *SUBJ* **duerma, duermas, duerma, durmamos,
durmáis, duerman;** *PRET* dormí, dormiste, **durmió,** dormimos,
dormisteis, **durmieron;** *IMPER* **duerme;** *PRP* **durmiendo**

28 **elegir** : *IND* **elijo,** eliges, elige, elegimos, elegís, **eligen;** *SUBJ* **elija,
elijas, elija, elijamos, elijáis, elijan;** *PRET* elegí, elegiste, **eligió,**
elegimos, elegisteis, **eligieron;** *IMPER* **elige;** *PRP* **eligiendo**

29 **empezar** : *IND* **empiezo, empiezas, empieza,** empezamos,
empezáis, **empiezan;** *SUBJ* **empiece, empieces, empiece, empecemos, empecéis, empiecen;** *PRET* **empecé,** empezaste, empezó,
empezamos, empezasteis, empezaron; *IMPER* **empieza**

30 **enraizar** : *IND* **enraízo, enraízas, enraíza,** enraizamos, enraizáis,
enraízan; *SUBJ* **enraíce, enraíces, enraíce, enraicemos, enrai-
céis, enraícen;** *PRET* **enraicé,** enraizaste, enraizó, enraizamos,
enraizasteis, enraizaron; *IMPER* **enraíza**

31 **erguir** : *IND* **irgo** *or* **yergo, irgues** *or* **yergues, irgue** *or* **yergue,**
erguimos, erguís, **irguen** *or* **yerguen;** *SUBJ* **irga** *or* **yerga, irgas**
or **yergas, irga** *or* **yerga, irgamos, irgáis, irgan** *or* **yergan;**
PRET erguí, erguiste, **irguió,** erguimos, erguisteis, **irguieron;**
IMPER **irgue** *or* **yergue;** *PRP* **irguiendo**

32 **errar** : *IND* **yerro, yerras, yerra,** erramos, erráis, **yerran;** *SUBJ*
yerre, yerres, yerre, erremos, erréis, **yerren;** *IMPER* **yerra**

33 **escribir** : *PP* **escrito**

34 **estar** : *IND* **estoy, estás, está,** estamos, estáis, **están;** *SUBJ* **esté,
estés, esté,** estemos, estéis, **estén;** *PRET* **estuve, estuviste,
estuvo, estuvimos, estuvisteis, estuvieron;** *IMPER* **está**

35 **exigir** : *IND* **exijo,** exiges, exige, exigimos, exigís, exigen; *SUBJ*
exija, exijas, exija, exijamos, exijáis, exijan

36 **forzar** : *IND* **fuerzo, fuerzas, fuerza,** forzamos, forzáis, **fuerzan;**
SUBJ **fuerce, fuerces, fuerce, forcemos, forcéis, fuercen;** *PRET*
forcé, forzaste, forzó, forzamos, forzasteis, forzaron; *IMPER*
fuerza

37 **freír** : *IND* **frío, fríes, fríe, freímos,** freís, **fríen;** *SUBJ* **fría, frías,
fría, friamos, friáis, frían;** *PRET* freí, **freíste,** frió, **freímos,
freísteis, frieron;** *IMPER* **fríe;** *PRP* **friendo;** *PP* **frito**

38 **gruñir** : *PRET* gruñí, gruñiste, **gruñó,** gruñimos, gruñisteis,
gruñeron; *PRP* **gruñendo**

39 **haber** : *IND* **he, has, ha, hemos,** habéis, **han;** *SUBJ* **haya, hayas, haya, hayamos,** hayáis, **hayan;** *PRET* **hube, hubiste, hubo, hubimos, hubisteis, hubieron;** *FUT* **habré, habrás, habrá, habremos, habréis, habrán;** *IMPER* **he**

40 **hacer** : *IND* **hago,** haces, hace, hacemos, hacéis, hacen; *SUBJ* **haga, hagas, haga, hagamos, hagáis, hagan;** *PRET* **hice, hiciste, hizo, hicimos, hicisteis, hicieron;** *FUT* **haré, harás, hará, haremos, haréis, harán;** *IMPER* **haz;** *PP* **hecho**

41 **huir** : *IND* **huyo, huyes, huye,** huimos, huís, **huyen;** *SUBJ* **huya, huyas, huya, huyamos,** huyáis, **huyan;** *PRET* huí, huiste, **huyó,** huimos, huisteis, **huyeron;** *IMPER* **huye;** *PRP* **huyendo**

42 **imprimir** : *PP* **impreso**

43 **ir** : *IND* **voy, vas, va, vamos, vais, van;** *SUBJ* **vaya, vayas, vaya, vayamos,** vayáis, **vayan;** *PRET* **fui, fuiste, fue, fuimos, fuisteis, fueron;** *IMPF* **iba, ibas, iba, íbamos, ibais, iban;** *IMPER* **ve;** *PRP* **yendo;** *PP* **ido**

44 **jugar** : *IND* **juego, juegas, juega,** jugamos, jugáis, **juegan;** *SUBJ* **juegue, juegues, juegue, juguemos, juguéis, jueguen;** *PRET* **jugué,** jugaste, jugó, jugamos, jugasteis, jugaron; *IMPER* **juega**

45 **lucir** : *IND* **luzco,** luces, luce, lucimos, lucís, lucen; *SUBJ* **luzca, luzcas, luzca, luzcamos, luzcáis, luzcan**

46 **morir** : *IND* **muero, mueres, muere,** morimos, morís, **mueren;** *SUBJ* **muera, mueras, muera, muramos, muráis, mueran;** *PRET* morí, moriste, **murió,** morimos, moristeis, **murieron;** *IMPER* **muere;** *PRP* **muriendo;** *PP* **muerto**

47 **mover** : *IND* **muevo, mueves, mueve,** movemos, movéis, **mueven;** *SUBJ* **mueva, muevas, mueva,** movamos, mováis, **muevan;** *IMPER* **mueve**

48 **nacer** : *IND* **nazco,** naces, nace, nacemos, nacéis, nacen; *SUBJ* **nazca, nazcas, nazca, nazcamos, nazcáis, nazcan**

49 **negar** : *IND* **niego, niegas, niega,** negamos, negáis, **niegan;** *SUBJ* **niegue, niegues, niegue, neguemos, neguéis, nieguen;** *PRET* **negué,** negaste, negó, negamos, negasteis, negaron; *IMPER* **niega**

50 **oír** : *IND* **oigo, oyes, oye, oímos,** oís, **oyen;** *SUBJ* **oiga, oigas, oiga, oigamos, oigáis, oigan;** *PRET* oí, **oíste, oyó, oímos, oísteis, oyeron;** *IMPER* **oye;** *PRP* **oyendo;** *PP* **oído**

51 **oler** : *IND* **huelo, hueles, huele,** olemos, oléis, **huelen;** *SUBJ* **huela, huelas, huela,** olamos, oláis, **huelan;** *IMPER* **huele**

52 **pagar** : *SUBJ* **pague, pagues, pague, paguemos, paguéis, paguen;** *PRET* **pagué,** pagaste, pagó, pagamos, pagasteis, pagaron

53 **parecer** : *IND* **parezco,** pareces, parece, parecemos, parecéis, parecen; *SUBJ* **parezca, parezcas, parezca, parezcamos, parezcáis, parezcan**

54 **pedir** : *IND* **pido, pides, pide,** pedimos, pedís, **piden;** *SUBJ* **pida, pidas, pida, pidamos, pidáis, pidan;** *PRET* pedí, pediste, **pidió,** pedimos, pedisteis, **pidieron;** *IMPER* **pide;** *PRP* **pidiendo**

55 **pensar** : *IND* **pienso, piensas, piensa,** pensamos, pensáis, **piensan;** *SUBJ* **piense, pienses, piense,** pensemos, penséis, **piensen;** *IMPER* **piensa**

56 **perder** : *IND* **pierdo, pierdes, pierde,** perdemos, perdéis, **pierden;** *SUBJ* **pierda, pierdas, pierda,** perdamos, perdáis, **pierdan;** *IMPER* **pierde**

57 **placer** : *IND* **plazco,** places, place, placemos, placéis, placen; *SUBJ* **plazca, plazcas, plazca, plazcamos, plazcáis, plazcan;** *PRET* plací, placiste, plació *or* **plugo,** placimos, placisteis, placieron *or* **pluguieron**

58 **poder** : *IND* **puedo, puedes, puede,** podemos, podéis, **pueden;** *SUBJ* **pueda, puedas, pueda,** podamos, podáis, **puedan;** *PRET* pude, pudiste, pudo, pudimos, pudisteis, pudieron; *FUT* podré, podrás, podrá, podremos, podréis, podrán; *IMPER* **puede;** *PRP* **pudiendo**

59 **podrir** *or* **pudrir** : *PP* podrido *(all other forms based on* pudrir*)*

60 **poner** : *IND* **pongo,** pones, pone, ponemos, ponéis, ponen; *SUBJ* **ponga, pongas, ponga, pongamos, pongáis, pongan;** *PRET* puse, pusiste, puso, pusimos, pusisteis, pusieron; *FUT* pondré, pondrás, pondrá, pondremos, pondréis, pondrán; *IMPER* **pon;** *PP* **puesto**

61 **producir** : *IND* **produzco,** produces, produce, producimos, producís, producen; *SUBJ* **produzca, produzcas, produzca, produzcamos, produzcáis, produzcan;** *PRET* **produje, produjiste, produjo, produjimos, produjisteis, produjeron**

62 **prohibir** : *IND* **prohíbo, prohíbes, prohíbe,** prohibimos, prohibís, **prohíben;** *SUBJ* **prohíba, prohíbas, prohíba,** prohibamos, prohibáis, *IMPER* **prohíbe**

63 **proveer** : *PRET* proveí, **proveíste,** proveyó, **proveímos, proveísteis,** proveyeron; *PRP* proveyendo; *PP* provisto

64 **querer** : *IND* **quiero, quieres, quiere,** queremos, queréis, **quieren;** *SUBJ* **quiera, quieras, quiera,** queramos, queráis, **quieran;** *PRET* quise, quisiste, quiso, quisimos, quisisteis, quisieron; *FUT* querré, querrás, querrá, querremos, querréis, querrán; *IMPER* **quiere**

65 **raer** : *IND* rao *or* **raigo** *or* **rayo,** raes, rae, raemos, raéis, raen; *SUBJ* **raiga** *or* **raya, raigas** *or* **rayas, raiga** *or* **raya, raigamos** *or* **rayamos, raigáis** *or* **rayáis, raigan** *or* **rayan;** *PRET* raí, raíste, rayó, raímos, raísteis, rayeron; *PRP* rayendo; *PP* raído

66 **reír** : *IND* **río, ríes, ríe, reímos,** reís, **ríen;** *SUBJ* **ría, rías, ría, riamos, riáis, rían;** *PRET* reí, reíste, rió, reímos, reísteis, rieron; *IMPER* **ríe;** *PRP* **riendo;** *PP* **reído**

67 **reñir** : *IND* **riño, riñes, riñe,** reñimos, reñís, **riñen;** *SUBJ* **riña, riñas, riña, riñamos, riñáis, riñan;** *PRET* reñí, reñiste, **riñó,** reñimos, reñisteis, **riñeron;** *IMPER* **riñe;** *PRP* **riñendo**

68 **reunir** : *IND* **reúno, reúnes, reúne,** reunimos, reunís, **reúnen;** *SUBJ* **reúna, reúnas, reúna,** reunamos, reunáis, **reúnan;** *IMPER* **reúne**

69 **roer** : *IND* roo *or* **roigo** *or* **royo,** roes, roe, roemos, roéis, roen; *SUBJ* roa *or* **roiga** *or* **roya,** roas *or* **roigas** *or* **royas,** roa *or* **roiga** *or* **roya,** roamos *or* **roigamos** *or* **royamos,** roáis *or* **roigáis** *or* **royáis,** roan *or* **roigan** *or* **royan;** *PRET* roí, **roíste, royó, roímos, roísteis, royeron;** *PRP* **royendo;** *PP* **roído**

70 **romper** : *PP* **roto**

71 **saber** : *IND* **sé,** sabes, sabe, sabemos, sabéis, saben; *SUBJ* **sepa, sepas, sepa, sepamos, sepáis, sepan;** *PRET* **supe, supiste, supo, supimos, supisteis, supieron;** *FUT* **sabré, sabrás, sabrá, sabremos, sabréis, sabrán**

72 **sacar** : *SUBJ* **saque, saques, saque, saquemos, saquéis, saquen;** *PRET* **saqué,** sacaste, sacó, sacamos, sacasteis, sacaron

73 **salir** : *IND* **salgo,** sales, sale, salimos, salís, salen; *SUBJ* **salga, salgas, salga, salgamos, salgáis, salgan;** *FUT* **saldré, saldrás, saldrá, saldremos, saldréis, saldrán;** *IMPER* **sal**

74 **satisfacer** : *IND* **satisfago,** satisfaces, satisface, satisfacemos, satisfacéis, satisfacen; *SUBJ* **satisfaga, satisfagas, satisfaga, satisfagamos, satisfagáis, satisfagan;** *PRET* **satisfice, satisficiste, satisfizo, satisficimos, satisficisteis, satisficieron;** *FUT* **satisfaré, satisfarás, satisfará, satisfaremos, satisfaréis, satisfarán;** *IMPER* **satisfaz** *or* satisface; *PP* **satisfecho**

75 **seguir** : *IND* **sigo, sigues, sigue,** seguimos, seguís, **siguen;** *SUBJ* **siga, sigas, siga, sigamos, sigáis, sigan;** *PRET* seguí, seguiste, **siguió,** seguimos, seguisteis, **siguieron;** *IMPER* **sigue;** *PRP* **siguiendo**

76 **sentir** : *IND* **siento, sientes, siente,** sentimos, sentís, **sienten;** *SUBJ* **sienta, sientas, sienta, sintamos, sintáis, sientan;** *PRET* sentí, sentiste, **sintió,** sentimos, sentisteis, **sintieron;** *IMPER* **siente;** *PRP* **sintiendo**

77 **ser** : *IND* **soy, eres, es, somos, sois, son;** *SUBJ* **sea, seas, sea, seamos, seáis, sean;** *PRET* **fui, fuiste, fue, fuimos, fuisteis, fueron;** *IMPF* **era, eras, era, éramos, erais, eran;** *IMPER* **sé;** *PRP* **siendo;** *PP* **sido**

78 **soler** (*defective verb; used only in the present, preterit, and imperfect indicative, and the present and imperfect subjunctive*) see **47 mover**

79 **tañer** : *PRET* tañí, tañiste, **tañó,** tañimos, tañisteis, **tañeron;** *PRP* **tañendo**

80 **tener** : *IND* **tengo, tienes, tiene,** tenemos, tenéis, **tienen;** *SUBJ* **tenga, tengas, tenga, tengamos, tengáis, tengan;** *PRET* **tuve, tuviste, tuvo, tuvimos, tuvisteis, tuvieron;** *FUT* **tendré, tendrás, tendrá, tendremos, tendréis, tendrán;** *IMPER* **ten**

81 **traer** : *IND* **traigo**, traes, trae, traemos, traéis, traen; *SUBJ* **traiga, traigas, traiga, traigamos, traigáis, traigan**; *PRET* **traje, trajiste, trajo, trajimos, trajisteis, trajeron**; *PRP* **trayendo**; *PP* **traído**

82 **trocar** : *IND* **trueco, truecas, trueca**, trocamos, trocáis, **truecan**; *SUBJ* **trueque, trueques, trueque, troquemos, troquéis, truequen**; *PRET* **troqué**, trocaste, trocó, trocamos, trocasteis, trocaron; *IMPER* **trueca**

83 **uncir** : *IND* **unzo**, unces, unce, uncimos, uncís, uncen; *SUBJ* **unza, unzas, unza, unzamos, unzáis, unzan**

84 **valer** : *IND* **valgo**, vales, vale, valemos, valéis, valen; *SUBJ* **valga, valgas, valga, valgamos, valgáis, valgan**; *FUT* **valdré, valdrás, valdrá, valdremos, valdréis, valdrán**

85 **variar** : *IND* **varío, varías, varía**, variamos, variáis, **varían**; *SUBJ* **varíe, varíes, varíe**, variemos, variéis, **varíen**; *IMPER* **varía**

86 **vencer** : *IND* **venzo**, vences, vence, vencemos, vencéis, vencen; *SUBJ* **venza, venzas, venza, venzamos, venzáis, venzan**

87 **venir** : *IND* **vengo, vienes, viene**, venimos, venís, **vienen**; *SUBJ* **venga, vengas, venga, vengamos, vengáis, vengan**; *PRET* **vine, viniste, vino, vinimos, vinisteis, vinieron**; *FUT* **vendré, vendrás, vendrá, vendremos, vendréis, vendrán**; *IMPER* **ven**; *PRP* **viniendo**

88 **ver** : *IND* veo, **ves, ve, vemos, veis, ven**; *PRET* **vi**, viste, vio, vimos, visteis, vieron; *IMPER* **ve**; *PRP* **viendo**; *PP* **visto**

89 **volver** : *IND* **vuelvo, vuelves, vuelve**, volvemos, volvéis, **vuelven**; *SUBJ* **vuelva, vuelvas, vuelva**, volvamos, volváis, **vuelvan**; *IMPER* **vuelve**; *PP* **vuelto**

90 **yacer** : *IND* **yazco** *or* **yazgo** *or* **yago**, yaces, yace, yacemos, yacéis, yacen; *SUBJ* **yazca** *or* **yazga** *or* **yaga, yazcas** *or* **yazgas** *or* **yagas, yazca** *or* **yazga** *or* **yaga, yazcamos** *or* **yazgamos** *or* **yagamos, yazcáis** *or* **yazgáis** *or* **yagáis, yazcan** *or* **yazgan** *or* **yagan**; *IMPER* **yace** *or* **yaz**

Verbos irregulares en inglés

INFINITIVO	PRETÉRITO	PARTICIPIO PASADO
arise	arose	arisen
awake	awoke	awoken *o* awaked
be	was, were	been
bear	bore	borne
beat	beat	beaten *o* beat
become	became	become
befall	befell	befallen
begin	began	begun
behold	beheld	beheld
bend	bent	bent
beseech	beseeched *o* besought	beseeched *o* besought
beset	beset	beset
bet	bet	bet
bid	bade *o* bid	bidden *o* bid
bind	bound	bound
bite	bit	bitten
bleed	bled	bled
blow	blew	blown
break	broke	broken
breed	bred	bred
bring	brought	brought
build	built	built
burn	burned *o* burnt	burned *o* burnt
burst	burst	burst
buy	bought	bought
can	could	—
cast	cast	cast
catch	caught	caught
choose	chose	chosen
cling	clung	clung
come	came	come
cost	cost	cost
creep	crept	crept
cut	cut	cut
deal	dealt	dealt
dig	dug	dug
dive	dived *o* dove	dived
do	did	done
draw	drew	drawn
dream	dreamed *o* dreamt	dreamed *o* dreamt
drink	drank	drunk *o* drank
drive	drove	driven
dwell	dwelled *o* dwelt	dwelled *o* dwelt
eat	ate	eaten
fall	fell	fallen
feed	fed	fed
feel	felt	felt
fight	fought	fought
find	found	found
flee	fled	fled
fling	flung	flung
fly	flew	flown
forbid	forbade	forbidden

INFINITIVO	PRETÉRITO	PARTICIPIO PASADO
forecast	forecast	forecast
forego	forewent	foregone
foresee	foresaw	foreseen
foretell	foretold	foretold
forget	forgot	forgotten *o* forgot
forgive	forgave	forgiven
forsake	forsook	forsaken
freeze	froze	frozen
get	got	got *o* gotten
give	gave	given
go	went	gone
grind	ground	ground
grow	grew	grown
hang	hung	hung
have	had	had
hear	heard	heard
hide	hid	hidden *o* hid
hit	hit	hit
hold	held	held
hurt	hurt	hurt
keep	kept	kept
kneel	knelt *o* kneeled	knelt *o* kneeled
know	knew	known
lay	laid	laid
lead	led	led
leap	leaped *o* leapt	leaped *o* leapt
leave	left	left
lend	lent	lent
let	let	let
lie	lay	lain
light	lit *o* lighted	lit *o* lighted
lose	lost	lost
make	made	made
may	might	—
mean	meant	meant
meet	met	met
mow	mowed	mowed *o* mown
overcome	overcame	overcome
pay	paid	paid
put	put	put
quit	quit	quit
read	read	read
rend	rent	rent
rid	rid	rid
ride	rode	ridden
ring	rang	rung
rise	rose	risen
run	ran	run
saw	sawed	sawed *o* sawn
say	said	said
see	saw	seen
seek	sought	sought

INFINITIVO	PRETÉRITO	PARTICIPIO PASADO
sell	sold	sold
send	sent	sent
set	set	set
sew	sewed	sewn *o* sewed
shake	shook	shaken
shall	should	—
shear	sheared	sheared *o* shorn
shed	shed	shed
shine	shone *o* shined	shone *o* shined
shoot	shot	shot
show	showed	shown *o* showed
shrink	shrank *o* shrunk	shrunk *o* shrunken
shut	shut	shut
sing	sang *o* sung	sung
sink	sank *o* sunk	sunk
sit	sat	sat
slay	slew	slain
sleep	slept	slept
slide	slid	slid
sling	slung	slung
smell	smelled *o* smelt	smelled *o* smelt
sow	sowed	sown *o* sowed
speak	spoke	spoken
speed	sped *o* speeded	sped *o* speeded
spend	spent	spent
spin	spun	spun
spit	spit *o* spat	spit *o* spat
split	split	split
spread	spread	spread
spring	sprang *o* sprung	sprung
stand	stood	stood
steal	stole	stolen
stick	stuck	stuck
sting	stung	stung
stink	stank *o* stunk	stunk
stride	strode	stridden
strike	struck	struck
swear	swore	sworn
sweep	swept	swept
swell	swelled	swelled *o* swollen
swim	swam	swum
swing	swung	swung
take	took	taken
teach	taught	taught
tear	tore	torn
tell	told	told
think	thought	thought
throw	threw	thrown
thrust	thrust	thrust
tread	trod	trodden *o* trod
undergo	underwent	undergone
understand	understood	understood

INFINITIVO	PRETÉRITO	PARTICIPIO PASADO
undo	undid	undone
wake	woke	woken *o* waked
waylay	waylaid	waylaid
wear	wore	worn
weave	wove *o* weaved	woven *o* weaved
weep	wept	wept
will	would	—
win	won	won
wind	wound	wound
withdraw	withdrew	withdrawn
withhold	withheld	withheld
withstand	withstood	withstood
wring	wrung	wrung
write	wrote	written

Abbreviations in This Work (Abreviaturas empleadas en este libro)

Abbreviation (Abreviatura)	English Expansion (Expansión en inglés)	Spanish Meaning (Significado en español)
adj	adjective	adjetivo
adv	adverb	adverbio
Arg	Argentina	Argentina
Bol	Bolivia	Bolivia
Brit	British	británico
CA	Central America	Centroamérica
Car	Caribbean region	Región del Caribe
Col	Colombia	Colombia
conj	conjunction	conjunción
CoRi	Costa Rica	Costa Rica
DomRep	Dominican Republic	República Dominicana
Ecua	Ecuador	Ecuador
esp	especially	especialmente
f	feminine	femenino
fam	familiar or colloquial	familiar o coloquial
fpl	feminine plural	femenino plural
Guat	Guatemala	Guatemala
Hond	Honduras	Honduras
interj	interjection	interjección
m	masculine	masculino
Mex	Mexico	México
mf	masculine or feminine	masculino o femenino
mfpl	masculine or feminine plural	plural masculino o femenino
mpl	masculine plural	plural masculino
n	noun	sustantivo
nf	feminine noun	sustantivo femenino
nfpl	feminine plural noun	sustantivo plural femenino
nfs & pl	invariable singular or plural feminine noun	sustantivo femenino, invariable en cuanto a número
Nic	Nicaragua	Nicaragua
nm	masculine noun	sustantivo masculino
nmf	masculine or feminine noun	sustantivo masculino o femenino
nmfpl	plural noun invariable for gender	sustantivo plural, invariable en cuanto a género
nmfs & pl	noun invariable for both gender and number	sustantivo invariable en cuanto a género y número
nmpl	masculine plural noun	sustantivo plural masculino

Abbreviation (Abreviatura)	English Expansion (Expansión en inglés)	Spanish Meaning (Significado en español)
nms & pl	invariable singular or plural masculine noun	sustantivo masculino, invariable en cuanto a número
npl	plural noun	sustantivo plural
ns & pl	noun invariable for plural	sustantivo invariable en cuanto a número
Pan	Panama	Panamá
Par	Paraguay	Paraguay
pl	plural	plural
pp	past participle	participio pasado
pref	prefix	prefijo
prep	preposition	preposición
PRi	Puerto Rico	Puerto Rico
pron	pronoun	pronombre
s	singular	singular
Sal	El Salvador	El Salvador
suf	suffix	sufijo
Uru	Uruguay	Uruguay
usu	usually	generalmente
v	verb	verbo
v aux	auxiliary verb	verbo auxiliar
Ven	Venezuela	Venezuela
vi	intransitive verb	verbo intransitivo
v impers	impersonal verb	verbo impersonal
vr	reflexive verb	verbo pronominal
vt	transitive verb	verbo transitivo

Pronunciation Symbols
(Símbolos de pronunciación)

VOWELS (VOCALES)

æ	ask, bat, glad	ask, bat, glad
ɑ	cot, bomb	cot, bomb
a	*New England* aunt, *British* ask, glass, *Spanish* casa	*Nueva Inglaterra* aunt, *inglés británico* ask, glass, *español* casa
e	*Spanish* peso, jefe	*español* peso, jefe
ɛ	egg, bet, fed	egg, bet, fed
ə	about, javelin, Alabama	about, javelin, Alabama
ə	indicates a syllabic pronunciation of the consonant as in bottle, prism	denota una pronunciación silábica del consonante, como en bottle, prism
i	very, any, thirty, *Spanish* piña	very, any, thirty, *español* piña
i:	eat, bead, bee	eat, bead, bee
ɪ	id, bid, pit	id, bid, pit
o	Ohio, yellower, potato, *Spanish* óvalo	Ohio, yellower, potato, *español* óvalo
o:	oats, own, zone, blow	oats, own, zone, blow
ɔ	awl, maul, caught, paw	awl, maul, caught, paw
ʊ	should, could	should, could
u	*Spanish* uva, culpa	*español* uva, culpa
u:	boot, few, coo	boot, few, coo
ʌ	under, putt, bud	under, putt, bud
eɪ	eight, wade, bay	eight, wade, bay
aɪ	ice, bite, tie	ice, bite, tie
aʊ	out, gown, plow	out, gown, plow
ɔɪ	oyster, coil, boy	oyster, coil, boy
ər	further, stir	further, stir
ø	*French* deux, *German* Höhle	*francés* deux, *alemán* Höhle
~	(tilde as in ɔ̃) *French* bon	(tilde como en ɔ̃) *francés* bon
:	indicates that the preceding vowel is long	indica que la vocal precedente es larga

CONSONANTS (CONSONANTES)

b	baby, labor, cab	baby, labor, cab
d	day, ready, kid	day, ready, kid
dʒ	just, badger, fudge	just, badger, fudge
ð	then, either, bathe	then, either, bathe
f	foe, tough, buff	foe, tough, buff
g	go, bigger, bag	go, bigger, bag
h	hot, aha	hot, aha
j	yes, vineyard	yes, vineyard
k	cat, keep, lacquer, flock	cat, keep, lacquer, flock
l	law, hollow, boil	law, hollow, boil
m	mat, hemp, hammer, rim	mat, hemp, hammer, rim
n	new, tent, tenor, run	new, tent, tenor, run
ŋ	rung, hang, swinger	rung, hang, swinger
p	pay, lapse, top	pay, lapse, top
r	rope, burn, tar	rope, burn, tar
s	sad, mist, kiss	sad, mist, kiss
ʃ	shoe, mission, slush	shoe, mission, slush

t	toe, button, mat	toe, button, mat
t̬	indicates a voiced alveolar flap [ɾ], as in later, catty, battle	indica un flap alveolar sonoro [ɾ], como en later, catty, battle
ʧ	choose, batch	choose, batch
θ	thin, ether, bath	thin, ether, bath
v	vat, never, cave	vat, never, cave
w	wet, software	wet, software
x	*German* Bach, *Scots* loch, *Spanish* gente, jefe	*alemán* Bach, *escocés* loch, *español* gente, jefe
z	zoo, easy, buzz	zoo, easy, buzz
ʒ	jaborandi, azure, beige	jaborandi, azure, beige
h, k, *p, t*	indicate sounds which are present in the pronunciation of some speakers of English but absent in that of others	denotan sonidos presentes en la forma de pronunciar de algunos angloparlantes pero ausentes en el habla de otros angloparlantes

STRESS MARKS (MARCAS DE ACENTUACIÓN)

ˈ	[high stress] **pen**manship	[acento alto] **pen**manship
ˌ	[low stress] penman**ship**	[acento bajo] penman**ship**

Spelling-to-Sound Correspondences in Spanish

For example words for the phonetic symbols below, see Pronunciation Symbols on page 85a.

VOWELS

a   [a]

e   [e] in open syllables (syllables ending with a vowel); [ɛ] in closed syllables (syllables ending with a consonant)

i   [i]; before another vowel in the same syllable pronounced as [j] ([ʒ] or [ʃ] in Argentina and Uruguay; [ʤ] when at the beginning of a word in the Caribbean)

o   [o] in open syllables (syllables ending with a vowel); [ɔ] in closed syllables (syllables ending with a consonant)

u   [u]; before another vowel in the same syllable pronounced as [w]

y   [i]; before another vowel in the same syllable pronounced as [j] ([ʒ] or [ʃ] in Argentina and Uruguay; [ʤ] when at the beginning of a word in the Caribbean)

CONSONANTS

b   [b] at the beginning of a word or after *m* or *n*; [β] elsewhere

c   [s] before *i* or *e* in Latin America and parts of southern Spain; [θ] in northern Spain; [k] elsewhere

ch [ʧ]; frequently [ʃ] in Chile and Panama; sometimes [ts] in Chile

d   [d] at the beginning of a word or after *n* or *l*; [ð] elsewhere, frequently silent between vowels

f   [f]; [Φ] in Honduras (no English equivalent for this sound; like [f] but made with both lips)

g   [x] before *i* or *e* ([h] in the Caribbean and Central America); [g] at the beginning of a word or after *n* and not before *i* or *e*; [ɣ] elsewhere, frequently silent between vowels

gu [gw] at the beginning of a word before *a, o*; [ɣw] elsewhere before *a, o*; frequently just [w] between vowels; [g] at the beginning of a word before *i, e*; [ɣ] elsewhere before *i, e*; frequently silent between vowels

gü [gw] at the beginning of a word, [ɣw] elsewhere; frequently just [w] between vowels

h   silent

j   [x] ([h] in the Caribbean and Central America)

k   [k]

l   [l]

ll [j]; [ʒ] or [ʃ] in Argentina and Uruguay; [ʤ] when at the beginning of a word in the Caribbean; [lʲ] in Bolivia, Paraguay, Peru, and parts of northern Spain (no English equivalent; like "lli" in *million*)

m   [m]

n   [n]; frequently [ŋ] at the end of a word when next word begins with a vowel

ñ   [n]

p   [p]

qu [k]

r   [r] (no English equivalent; a trilled sound) at the beginning of words; [t]/[ɾ] elsewhere

rr [r] (no English equivalent; a trilled sound)

s   [s]; frequently [z] before *b, d, g, m, n, l, r*; at the end of a word [h] or silent in many parts of Latin America and some parts of Spain

t   [t]

v   [b] at the beginning of a word or after *m* or *n*; [β] elsewhere

x   [ks] or [gz] between vowels; [s] before consonants

z   [s] in Latin America and parts of southern Spain, [θ] in northern Spain; at the end of a word [h] or silent in many parts of Latin America and some parts of Spain

Diccionario
Español-Inglés

Spanish-English
Dictionary

A

a¹ *nf* : first letter of the Spanish alphabet

a² *prep* **1** (*indicating direction*) : to ⟨vamos a México : we're going to Mexico⟩ ⟨fui a casa : I went home⟩ ⟨gira a la derecha : turn right⟩ **2** (*indicating location*) : at ⟨llegué al hotel : I arrived at the hotel⟩ ⟨al fondo del pasillo : at the end of the hall⟩ ⟨a mi lado : beside me⟩ ⟨vivo a cinco minutos de aquí : I live five minutes from here⟩ **3** (*used before direct objects referring to persons*) ⟨¿llamaste a tu papá? : did you call your dad?⟩ **4** (*used before indirect objects*) ⟨como a usted le guste : as you wish⟩ ⟨le echó un vistazo a la página : she glanced over the page⟩ **5** : in the manner of ⟨papas a la francesa : french fries⟩ ⟨una boda a lo Hollywood : a Hollywood-style wedding⟩ **6** : on, by means of ⟨a pie : on foot⟩ ⟨a mano : by hand⟩ **7** : per, each ⟨tres pastillas al día : three pills per day⟩ **8** (*indicating rate or measure*) ⟨lo venden a 50 pesos el kilo : they sell it for 50 pesos a kilo⟩ ⟨a una velocidad de . . . : at a speed of . . .⟩ **9** (*indicating comparison*) : to ⟨prefiero el vino a la cerveza : I prefer wine to beer⟩ ⟨un margen de dos a uno : a two-to-one margin⟩ **10** (*indicating time*) : at, on ⟨a las dos : at two o'clock⟩ ⟨al principio : at first⟩ ⟨al salir : on/upon leaving⟩ ⟨al día siguiente : on the following day⟩ **11** (*with infinitive*) ⟨enséñales a leer : teach them to read⟩ ⟨problemas a resolver : problems to be solved⟩

a- *pref* : a-

ábaco *nm* : abacus

abad *nm* : abbot

abadesa *nf* : abbess

abadía *nf* : abbey

abajo *adv* **1** : down ⟨póngalo más abajo : put it lower (down)⟩ ⟨arriba y abajo : up and down⟩ ⟨cuesta/río abajo : downhill/downstream⟩ **2** : downstairs ⟨los vecinos de abajo : the downstairs neighbors⟩ **3** : under, beneath ⟨el abajo firmante : the undersigned⟩ **4** : down with ⟨¡abajo la violencia! : down with violence!⟩ **5 ~ de** : under, beneath **6 de ~** : bottom ⟨el cajón de abajo : the bottom drawer⟩ **7 hacia ~** *or* **para ~** : downwards

abalanzarse {21} *vr* : to hurl oneself, to rush

abalorio *nm* : glass bead

abanderado, -da *n* : standard-bearer

abandonado, -da *adj* **1** : abandoned, deserted **2** : neglected **3** : slovenly, unkempt

abandonar *vt* **1** DEJAR : to abandon, to leave **2** : to give up, to quit ⟨abandonaron la búsqueda : they gave up the search⟩ — **abandonarse** *vr* **1** : to neglect oneself **2 ~ a** : to succumb to, to give oneself over to

abandono *nm* **1** : abandonment **2** : neglect **3** : withdrawal ⟨ganar por abandono : to win by default⟩

abanicar {72} *vt* : to fan — **abanicarse** *vr*

abanico *nm* **1** : fan **2** GAMA : range, gamut

abaratamiento *nm* : price reduction

abaratar *vt* : to lower the price of — **abaratarse** *vr* : to go down in price

abarcar {72} *vt* **1** : to cover, to include, to embrace **2** : to undertake **3** : to monopolize

abaritonado, -da *adj* : baritone

abarrotado, -da *adj* : packed, crammed

abarrotar *vt* : to fill up, to pack

abarrotería *nf CA, Mex* : grocery store

abarrotero, -ra *n Col, Mex* : grocer

abarrotes *nmpl* **1** : groceries, supplies **2 tienda de abarrotes** : general store, grocery store

abastecedor, -dora *n* : supplier

abastecer {53} *vt* : to supply, to stock — **abastecerse** *vr* : to stock up

abastecimiento → **abasto**

abasto *nm* : supply, supplying ⟨no da abasto : there isn't enough for all⟩

abatible *adj* **1** : reclining (of a chair) **2** : folding

abatido, -da *adj* : dejected, depressed

abatimiento *nm* **1** : drop, reduction **2** : dejection, depression

abatir *vt* **1** DERRIBAR : to demolish, to knock down **2** : to shoot down **3** DEPRIMIR : to depress, to bring low — **abatirse** *vr* **1** DEPRIMIRSE : to get depressed **2 ~ sobre** : to swoop down on

abdicación *nf, pl* **-ciones** : abdication

abdicar {72} *vt* : to relinquish, to abdicate

abdomen *nm, pl* **-dómenes** : abdomen

abdominal *adj* : abdominal

abecé *nm* : ABC's *pl*

abecedario *nm* ALFABETO : alphabet

abedul *nm* : birch (tree)

abeja *nf* : bee

abejorro *nm* : bumblebee

aberración *nf, pl* **-ciones** : aberration

aberrante *adj* : aberrant, perverse

abertura *nf* **1** : aperture, opening **2** AGUJERO : hole **3** : slit (in a skirt, etc.) **4** GRIETA : crack

abeto *nm* : fir (tree)

abierto¹ *pp* → **abrir**

abierto², -ta *adj* **1** : open ⟨una puerta/boca/caja abierta : an open door/mouth/box⟩ ⟨heridas abiertas : open wounds⟩ ⟨con los brazos abiertos : with open arms⟩ **2** : open (for business, traffic, etc.) **3** DESABROCHADO : open, undone **4** : unlocked, open **5** : on, running (of a faucet) **6** : open, overt ⟨guerra abierta : open warfare⟩ **7** FRANCO : open, frank **8** RECEPTIVO : open, receptive — **abiertamente** *adv*

abigarrado, -da *adj* : multicolored, variegated

abigeato *nm* : rustling (of livestock)

abismal *adj* : abysmal, vast
abismo *nm* : abyss, chasm ⟨al borde del abismo : on the brink of ruin⟩
abjurar *vi* ∼ **de** : to abjure — **abjuración** *nf*
ablandamiento *nm* : softening, moderation
ablandar *vt* **1** SUAVIZAR : to soften **2** CALMAR : to soothe, to appease — *vi* : to moderate, to get milder — **ablandarse** *vr* **1** : to become soft, to soften **2** CEDER : to yield, to relent
-able *suf* : -able
ablución *nf, pl* **-ciones** : ablution
abnegación *nf, pl* **-ciones** : self-denial
abnegado, -da *adj* : self-sacrificing, selfless
abnegarse {49} *vr* : to deny oneself
abobado, -da *adj* **1** : silly, stupid **2** : bewildered
abocado, -da *adj* ∼ **a** **1** : headed for **2** : committed to
abocarse {72} *vr* **1** DIRIGIRSE : to head, to direct oneself **2** DEDICARSE : to dedicate oneself
abochornar *vt* AVERGONZAR : to embarrass, to shame — **abochornarse** *vr*
abofetear *vt* : to slap
abogacía *nf* : law, legal profession
abogado, -da *n* : lawyer, attorney
abogar {52} *vi* ∼ **por** : to plead for, to defend, to advocate
abolengo *nm* LINAJE : lineage, ancestry
abolición *nf, pl* **-ciones** : abolition
abolir {1} *vt* DEROGAR : to abolish, to repeal
abolladura *nf* : dent
abollar *vt* : to dent
abombar *vt* : to warp, to cause to bulge — **abombarse** *vr* : to decompose, to go bad
abominable *adj* ABORRECIBLE : abominable
abominación *nf, pl* **-ciones** : abomination
abominar *vt* ABORRECER : to abominate, to abhor
abonado, -da *n* : subscriber
abonar *vt* **1** : to pay **2** FERTILIZAR : to fertilize — **abonarse** *vr* : to subscribe
abono *nm* **1** : payment, installment **2** FERTILIZANTE : fertilizer **3** : season ticket
abordaje *nm* : boarding
abordar *vt* **1** : to address, to broach **2** : to accost, to waylay **3** : to come on board
aborigen¹ *adj, pl* **-rígenes** : aboriginal, native
aborigen² *nmf, pl* **-rígenes** : aborigine, indigenous inhabitant
aborrecer {53} *vt* ABOMINAR, ODIAR : to abhor, to detest, to hate
aborrecible *adj* ABOMINABLE, ODIOSO : abominable, detestable
aborrecimiento *nm* : abhorrence, loathing
abortar *vi* : to have an abortion — *vt* **1** : to abort **2** : to quash, to suppress
abortivo, -va *adj* : abortive
aborto *nm* **1** : abortion **2** : miscarriage

abotonar *vt* : to button — **abotonarse** *vr* : to button up
abovedado, -da *adj* : vaulted
abrasador, -dora *adj* : burning, scorching
abrasar *vt* QUEMAR : to burn, to sear, to scorch
abrasivo¹, -va *adj* : abrasive
abrasivo² *nm* : abrasive
abrazadera *nf* : clamp, brace
abrazar {21} *vt* : to hug, to embrace — **abrazarse** *vr*
abrazo *nm* : hug, embrace
abrebotellas *nms & pl* : bottle opener
abrecartas *nms & pl* : letter opener
abrelatas *nms & pl* : can opener
abrevadero *nm* BEBEDERO : watering trough
abreviación *nf, pl* **-ciones** : abbreviation
abreviar *vt* **1** : to abbreviate **2** : to shorten, to cut short
abreviatura → **abreviación**
abridor *nm* : bottle opener, can opener
abrigadero *nm* : shelter, windbreak
abrigado, -da *adj* **1** : sheltered **2** : warm, wrapped up (with clothing)
abrigar {52} *vt* **1** : to shelter, to protect **2** : to keep warm, to dress warmly **3** : to cherish, to harbor ⟨abrigar esperanzas : to cherish hopes⟩ — **abrigarse** *vr* : to dress warmly
abrigo *nm* **1** : coat, overcoat **2** : shelter, refuge
abril *nm* : April ⟨el dos de abril : (on) April second⟩
abrillantador *nm* : polish
abrillantar *vt* : to polish, to shine
abrir {2} *vt* **1** : to open (a door, an umbrella, etc.) **2** : to open, to clear ⟨abrir paso a : to make way for⟩ **3** : to open (a business, an account) **4** : to unlock (a lock, a house), to undo (clothing) **5** : to turn on (a tap or faucet) **6** INICIAR : to open, to start — *vi* : to open, to open up ⟨abren a las nueve : they open at nine⟩ — **abrirse** *vr* **1** : to open, to open up **2** : to clear (of the skies)
abrochar *vt* : to button, to fasten — **abrocharse** *vr* : to fasten, to hook up
abrogación *nf, pl* **-ciones** : annulment, repeal
abrogar {52} *vt* : to abrogate, to annul, to repeal
abrojo *nm* : bur (of a plant)
abrumador, -dora *adj* : crushing, overwhelming
abrumar *vt* **1** AGOBIAR : to overwhelm **2** OPRIMIR : to oppress, to burden
abrupto, -ta *adj* **1** : abrupt **2** ESCARPADO : steep — **abruptamente** *adv*
absceso *nm* : abscess
absolución *nf, pl* **-ciones** **1** : absolution **2** : acquittal
absolutismo *nm* : absolutism
absoluto, -ta *adj* **1** : absolute, unconditional **2** **en** ∼ : (not) at all ⟨no me gustó en absoluto : I did not like it at all⟩ — **absolutamente** *adv*
absolver {89} *vt* **1** : to absolve **2** : to acquit
absorbencia *nf* : absorbency

absorbente *adj* **1** : absorbent **2** : absorbing, engrossing

absorber *vt* **1** : to absorb, to soak up **2** : to occupy, to take up, to engross

absorción *nf, pl* **-ciones** : absorption

absorto, -ta *adj* : absorbed, engrossed

abstemio¹, -mia *adj* : abstemious, teetotal

abstemio², -mia *n* : teetotaler

abstención *nf, pl* **-ciones** : abstention — **abstencionismo** *nm*

abstenerse {80} *vr* : to abstain, to refrain

abstinencia *nf* : abstinence

abstracción *nf, pl* **-ciones** : abstraction

abstracto, -ta *adj* : abstract

abstraer {81} *vt* : to abstract — **abstraerse** *vr* : to lose oneself in thought

abstraído, -da *adj* : preoccupied, withdrawn

abstruso, -sa *adj* : abstruse

abstuvo, etc. → **abstenerse**

absuelto *pp* → **absolver**

absurdo¹, -da *adj* DISPARATADO, RIDÍCULO : absurd, ridiculous — **absurdamente** *adv*

absurdo² *nm* : absurdity

abuchear *vt* : to boo, to jeer

abucheo *nm* : booing, jeering

abuela *nf* **1** : grandmother **2** : old woman **3** ¡tu abuela! *fam* : no way!, forget about it!

abuelita *nf fam* : grandma *fam*

abuelito *nm fam* : grandpa *fam*

abuelo *nm* **1** : grandfather **2** : old man **3** **abuelos** *nmpl* : grandparents, ancestors

abulia *nf* : apathy, lethargy

abúlico, -ca *adj* : lethargic, apathetic

abultado, -da *adj* : bulging, bulky

abultar *vi* : to bulge — *vt* : to enlarge, to expand

abundancia *nf* : abundance

abundante *adj* : abundant, plentiful — **abundantemente** *adv*

abundar *vi* **1** : to abound, to be plentiful **2** ~ **en** : to be in agreement with

aburrido, -da *adj* **1** : bored, tired, fed up **2** TEDIOSO : boring, tedious

aburrimiento *nm* : boredom, weariness

aburrir *vt* : to bore, to tire — **aburrirse** *vr* : to get bored

abusado, -da *adj Mex fam* : sharp, on the ball

abusador, -dora *n* : abuser

abusar *vi* **1** : to go too far, to do something to excess **2** ~ **de** : to abuse (as drugs) **3** ~ **de** : to take unfair advantage of

abusivo, -va *adj* **1** : abusive **2** : outrageous, excessive

abuso *nm* **1** : abuse **2** : injustice, outrage

abyecto, -ta *adj* : despicable, contemptible

acá *adv* **1** AQUÍ : here, over here ⟨ven acá! : come here!⟩ ⟨de acá para allá : back and forth⟩ **2** (*in expressions of time*) ⟨de 2010 (para) acá : from 2010 to now, since 2010⟩

acabado¹, -da *adj* **1** : finished, done, completed **2** : old, worn-out

acabado² *nm* : finish ⟨un acabado brillante : a glossy finish⟩

acabar *vi* **1** TERMINAR : to finish, to end ⟨ya acabo : I'm almost done⟩ **2** ~ **de** : to have just ⟨acabo de ver a tu hermano : I just saw your brother⟩ **3** ~ **con** : to put an end to, to stamp out **4** **acabar por hacer algo** *or* **acabar haciendo algo** : to end up doing something — *vt* TERMINAR : to finish — **acabarse** *vr* TERMINARSE : to come to an end, to run out ⟨se me acabó el dinero : I ran out of money⟩ ⟨¡se acabó! : that's it!⟩

acabose *or* **acabóse** *nm fam* COLMO : extreme, limit ⟨¡esto es el acabóse! : this is the limit!⟩

acacia *nf* : acacia

academia *nf* : academy

académico¹, -ca *adj* : academic, scholastic — **académicamente** *adv*

académico², -ca *n* : academic, academician

acaecer {53} *vt* (*3rd person only*) : to happen, to take place

acalambrarse *vr* : to cramp up, to get a cramp

acallar *vt* : to quiet, to silence

acalorado, -da *adj* : emotional, heated

acaloramiento *nm* **1** : heat **2** : ardor, passion

acalorar *vt* : to heat up, to inflame — **acalorarse** *vr* : to get upset, to get worked up

acampada *nf* : camp, camping ⟨ir de acampada : to go camping⟩

acampar *vi* : to camp

acanalar *vt* **1** : to groove, to furrow **2** : to corrugate

acantilado *nm* : cliff

acanto *nm* : acanthus

acantonar *vt* : to station, to quarter

acaparador, -dora *adj* : greedy, selfish

acaparar *vt* **1** : to stockpile, to hoard **2** : to monopolize

acápite *nm* : paragraph

acaramelado, -da *adj* **1** : caramel-coated **2** : caramel-colored **3** : sugary **4** : very affectionate (of a couple)

acariciar *vt* : to caress, to stroke, to pet

ácaro *nm* : mite

acarrear *vt* **1** : to haul, to carry **2** : to bring, to give rise to ⟨los problemas que acarrea : the problems that come along with it⟩

acarreo *nm* : transport, haulage

acartonarse *vr* **1** : to stiffen **2** : to become wizened

acaso *adv* **1** : perhaps, by any chance **2** **por si acaso** : just in case

acatamiento *nm* : compliance, observance

acatar *vt* : to comply with, to respect

acatarrarse *vr* : to catch a cold

acaudalado, -da *adj* RICO : wealthy, rich

acaudillar *vt* : to lead, to command

acceder *vi* ~ **a** **1** : to accede to, to agree to **2** : to assume (a position) **3** : to gain access to

accesar *vt* : to access (on a computer)

accesibilidad *nf* : accessibility

accesible *adj* ASEQUIBLE : accessible, attainable

acceso *nm* **1** : access **2** : admittance, entrance

accesorio[1], **-ria** *adj* **1** : accessory **2** : incidental

accesorio[2] *nm* **1** : accessory **2** : prop (in the theater)

accidentado[1], **-da** *adj* **1** : eventful, turbulent **2** : rough, uneven **3** : injured

accidentado[2], **-da** *n* : accident victim

accidental *adj* : accidental, unintentional — **accidentalmente** *adv*

accidentarse *vr* : to have an accident

accidente *nm* **1** : accident **2** : unevenness **3 accidente geográfico** : geographical feature

acción *nf, pl* **acciones 1** : action **2** ACTO : act, deed **3** : share, stock

accionamiento *nm* : activation

accionar *vt* : to put into motion, to activate — *vi* : to gesticulate

accionario, -ria *adj* : stock ⟨mercado accionario : stock market⟩

accionista *nmf* : stockholder, shareholder

acebo *nm* : holly

acechar *vt* **1** : to watch, to spy on **2** : to stalk, to lie in wait for

acecho *nm* **al acecho** : lying in wait

acedera *nf* : sorrel (herb)

aceitar *vt* : to oil

aceite *nm* **1** : oil **2 aceite de ricino** : castor oil **3 aceite de oliva** : olive oil

aceitera *nf* **1** : cruet (for oil) **2** : oilcan **3** *Mex* : oil refinery

aceitoso, -sa *adj* : oily

aceituna *nf* OLIVA : olive

aceituno *nm* OLIVO : olive tree

aceleración *nf, pl* **-ciones** : acceleration, speeding up

acelerado, -da *adj* : accelerated, speedy

acelerador *nm* : accelerator

aceleramiento *nm* → **aceleración**

acelerar *vt* **1** : to accelerate, to speed up **2** AGILIZAR : to expedite — *vi* : to accelerate (of an automobile) — **acelerarse** *vr* : to hasten, to hurry up

acelga *nf* : chard, Swiss chard

acendrar *vt* : to purify, to refine

acento *nm* **1** : accent **2** : stress, emphasis

acentuado, -da *adj* : marked, pronounced

acentuar {3} *vt* **1** : to accent **2** : to emphasize, to stress — **acentuarse** *vr* : to become more pronounced

acepción *nf, pl* **-ciones** SIGNIFICADO : sense, meaning

aceptabilidad *nf* : acceptability

aceptable *adj* : acceptable

aceptación *nf, pl* **-ciones 1** : acceptance **2** APROBACIÓN : approval

aceptar *vt* **1** : to accept **2** : to approve

acequia *nf* **1** : irrigation ditch **2** *Mex* : sewer

acera *nf* : sidewalk

acerado, -da *adj* **1** : made of steel **2** : steely, tough

acerbo, -ba *adj* **1** : harsh, cutting ⟨comentarios acerbos : cutting remarks⟩ **2** : bitter — **acerbamente** *adv*

acerca *prep* ~ **de** : about, concerning

acercamiento *nm* : rapprochement, reconciliation

acercar {72} *vt* APROXIMAR, ARRIMAR : to bring near, to bring closer — **acercarse** *vr* APROXIMARSE, ARRIMARSE : to approach, to draw near

acería *nf* : steel mill

acerico *nm* : pincushion

acero *nm* : steel ⟨acero inoxidable : stainless steel⟩

acérrimo, -ma *adj* **1** : staunch, steadfast **2** : bitter ⟨un acérrimo enemigo : a bitter enemy⟩

acertado, -da *adj* CORRECTO : accurate, correct, on target — **acertadamente** *adv*

acertante[1] *adj* : winning

acertante[2] *nmf* : winner

acertar {55} *vt* : to guess correctly — *vi* **1** ATINAR : to be correct, to be on target **2** ~ **a** : to manage to

acertijo *nm* ADIVINANZA : riddle

acervo *nm* **1** : pile, heap **2** : wealth, heritage ⟨el acervo artístico del instituto : the artistic treasures of the institute⟩

acetato *nm* : acetate

acetileno *nm* : acetylene

acetona *nf* **1** : acetone **2** : nail-polish remover

achacar {72} *vt* : to attribute, to impute ⟨te achaca todos sus problemas : he blames all his problems on you⟩

achacoso, -sa *adj* : frail, sickly

achaparrado, -da *adj* : stunted, scrubby ⟨árboles achaparrados : scrubby trees⟩

achaque *nm* : ailment

achaques *nmpl* : aches and pains

achatar *vt* : to flatten

achicar {72} *vt* **1** REDUCIR : to make smaller, to reduce **2** : to intimidate **3** : to bail out (water) — **achicarse** *vr* : to become intimidated

achicharrar *vt* : to scorch, to burn to a crisp

achicoria *nf* : chicory

achiote *or* **achote** *nm* : annatto

achispado, -da *adj fam* : tipsy

achuchón *nm, pl* **-chones 1** : push, shove **2** *fam* : squeeze, hug **3** *fam* : mild illness

aciago, -ga *adj* : fateful, unlucky

acicalar *vt* **1** PULIR : to polish **2** : to dress up, to adorn — **acicalarse** *vr* : to get dressed up

acicate *nm* **1** : spur **2** INCENTIVO : incentive, stimulus

acidez *nf, pl* **-deces 1** : acidity **2** : sourness **3 acidez estomacal** : heartburn

ácido[1], **-da** *adj* AGRIO : acid, sour

ácido[2] *nm* **1** : acid **2 ácido clorhídrico** : hydrochloric acid **3 ácido nítrico** : nitric acid **4 ácido sulfúrico** : sulfuric acid

acierto *nm* **1** : correct answer, right choice **2** : accuracy, skill

acimut *nm* : azimuth

acitronar *vt Mex* : to fry until crisp

aclamación *nf, pl* **-ciones** : acclaim, acclamation

aclamar *vt* : to acclaim, to cheer, to applaud

aclaración *nf, pl* **-ciones** CLARIFICACIÓN : clarification, explanation

aclarar *vt* **1** CLARIFICAR : to clarify, to explain, to resolve **2** : to lighten **3 aclarar la voz** : to clear one's throat — *vi* **1** : to get light, to dawn **2** : to clear up — **aclararse** *vr* : to become clear

aclaratorio, -ria *adj* : explanatory

aclimatar *vt* : to acclimatize — **aclimatarse** *vr* ~ **a** : to get used to — **aclimatación** *nf*

acné *nm* : acne

acobardar *vt* INTIMIDAR : to frighten, to intimidate — **acobardarse** *vr* **1** : to get frightened, to chicken out **2** : to cower

acodarse *vr* ~ **en** : to lean (one's elbows) on

acogedor, -dora *adj* : cozy, warm, friendly

acoger {15} *vt* **1** REFUGIAR : to take in, to shelter **2** : to receive, to welcome — **acogerse** *vr* **1** REFUGIARSE : to take refuge **2** ~ **a** : to resort to, to avail oneself of

acogida *nf* **1** AMPARO, REFUGIO : refuge, protection **2** RECIBIMIENTO : reception, welcome

acolchar *vt* **1** : to pad (a wall, etc.) **2** : to quilt

acólito *nm* **1** MONAGUILLO : altar boy **2** : follower, helper, acolyte

acomedido, -da *adj* : helpful, obliging

acometer *vt* **1** ATACAR : to attack, to assail **2** EMPRENDER : to undertake, to begin — *vi* ~ **contra** : to rush against

acometida *nf* ATAQUE : attack, assault

acomodado, -da *adj* **1** : suitable, appropriate **2** : well-to-do, prosperous

acomodador, -dora *n* : usher, usherette *f*

acomodar *vt* **1** : to accommodate, to make room for **2** : to adjust, to adapt — **acomodarse** *vr* **1** : to settle in **2** ~ **a** : to adapt to

acomodaticio, -cia *adj* : accommodating, obliging

acomodo *nm* **1** : job, position **2** : arrangement, placement **3** : accommodation, lodging

acompañamiento *nm* : accompaniment

acompañante *nmf* **1** COMPAÑERO : companion **2** : accompanist

acompañar *vt* : to accompany, to go with

acompasado, -da *adj* : rhythmic, regular, measured

acompasar *vt* : to synchronize

acomplejado, -da *adj* : full of complexes, neurotic

acomplejar *vt* : to give a complex, to make neurotic

acondicionado, -da *adj* **1** : equipped **2 bien acondicionado** : in good shape, in a fit state

acondicionador *nm* **1** : conditioner **2 acondicionador de aire** : air conditioner

acondicionar *vt* **1** : to condition **2** : to fit out, to furnish

acongojado, -da *adj* : distressed, upset

acongojarse *vr* : to grieve, to become distressed

aconsejable *adj* : advisable

aconsejar *vt* : to advise, to counsel

acontecer {53} *vt* (*3rd person only*) : to occur, to happen

acontecimiento *nm* SUCESO : event

acopiar *vt* : to gather, to collect, to stockpile

acopio *nm* : collection, stock

acoplamiento *nm* : connection, coupling

acoplar *vt* : to couple, to connect — **acoplarse** *vr* : to fit together

acoquinar *vt* : to intimidate

acorazado¹, -da *adj* BLINDADO : armored

acorazado² *nm* : battleship

acordado, -da *adj* : agreed upon

acordar {19} *vt* **1** : to agree on **2** OTORGAR : to award, to bestow — **acordarse** *vr* RECORDAR : to remember, to recall

acorde¹ *adj* **1** : in agreement, in accordance **2** ~ **con** : in keeping with

acorde² *nm* : chord

acordeón *nm, pl* **-deones** : accordion — **acordeonista** *nmf*

acordonar *vt* **1** : to cordon off **2** : to lace up **3** : to mill (coins)

acorralar *vt* ARRINCONAR : to corner, to hem in, to corral

acortar *vt* : to shorten, to cut short — **acortarse** *vr* **1** : to become shorter **2** : to end early

acosar *vt* PERSEGUIR : to pursue, to hound, to harass

acoso *nm* ASEDIO : harassment ⟨acoso sexual : sexual harassment⟩

acostar {19} *vt* **1** : to lay (something) down **2** : to put to bed — **acostarse** *vr* **1** : to lie down **2** : to go to bed

acostumbrado, -da *adj* **1** HABITUADO : accustomed **2** HABITUAL : usual, customary

acostumbrar *vt* : to accustom — *vi* : to be accustomed, to be in the habit — **acostumbrarse** *vr*

acotación *nf, pl* **-ciones** **1** : marginal note **2** : stage direction

acotado, -da *adj* : enclosed

acotamiento *nm* Mex : shoulder (of a road)

acotar *vt* **1** ANOTAR : to note, to annotate **2** DELIMITAR : to mark off (land), to demarcate

acre¹ *adj* **1** : acrid, pungent **2** MORDAZ : caustic, biting

acre² *nm* : acre

acrecentamiento *nm* : growth, increase

acrecentar {55} *vt* AUMENTAR : to increase, to augment

acreditación *nf, pl* **-ciones** : accreditation

acreditado, -da *adj* **1** : accredited, authorized **2** : reputable

acreditar *vt* **1** : to accredit, to authorize **2** : to credit **3** : to prove, to verify — **acreditarse** *vr* : to gain a reputation

acreedor¹, -dora *adj* : deserving, worthy

acreedor², -dora *n* : creditor

acribillar *vt* **1** : to riddle, to pepper (with bullets, etc.) **2** : to hound, to harass

acrílico *nm* : acrylic

acrimonia *nf* **1** : pungency **2** : acrimony

acrimonioso, -sa *adj* : acrimonious

acriollarse *vr* : to adopt local customs, to go native

acristalamiento *nm Spain* : glazing, windows *pl*

acritud *nf* **1** : pungency, bitterness **2** : intensity, sharpness **3** : harshness, asperity

acrobacia *nf* : acrobatics

acróbata *nmf* : acrobat

acrobático, -ca *adj* : acrobatic

acrónimo *nm* : acronym

acta *nf* **1** : document, certificate ⟨acta de nacimiento/defunción : birth/death certificate⟩ **2 actas** *nfpl* : minutes (of a meeting)

actitud *nf* **1** : attitude **2** : posture, position

activación *nf, pl* **-ciones 1** : activation, stimulation **2** ACELERACIÓN : acceleration, speeding up

activar *vt* **1** : to activate **2** : to stimulate, to energize **3** : to speed up

actividad *nf* : activity

activista *nmf* : activist — **activismo** *nm*

activo¹, -va *adj* : active — **activamente** *adv*

activo² *nm* : assets *pl* ⟨activo y pasivo : assets and liabilities⟩

acto *nm* **1** ACCIÓN : act, deed **2** : act (in a play) **3 el acto sexual** : sexual intercourse **4 en el acto** : right away, on the spot **5 acto seguido** : immediately after

actor *nm* ARTISTA : actor

actriz *nf, pl* **actrices** ARTISTA : actress

actuación *nf, pl* **-ciones 1** : performance **2 actuaciones** *nfpl* DILIGENCIAS : proceedings

actual *adj* PRESENTE : present, current

actualidad *nf* **1** : present time ⟨en la actualidad : at present⟩ **2 actualidades** *nfpl* : current affairs

actualización *nf, pl* **-ciones** : updating, modernization

actualizar {21} *vt* : to modernize, to bring up to date

actualmente *adv* : at present, nowadays

actuar {3} *vi* : to act, to perform

actuarial *adj* : actuarial

actuario, -ria *n* : actuary

acuarela *nf* : watercolor

acuario *nm* : aquarium

Acuario¹ *nm* : Aquarius (sign or constellation)

Acuario² *nmf* : Aquarius (person)

acuartelar *vt* : to quarter (troops)

acuático, -ca *adj* : aquatic, water

acuchillar *vt* APUÑALAR : to knife, to stab

acuciante *adj* : pressing, urgent

acucioso, -sa → **acuciante**

acudir *vi* **1** : to go, to come (someplace for a specific purpose) ⟨acudió a la puerta : he went to the door⟩ ⟨acudimos en su ayuda : we came to her aid⟩ **2** : to be present, to show up ⟨acudí a la cita : I showed up for the appointment⟩ **3** ~ **a** : to turn to, to have recourse to ⟨hay que acudir al médico : you must consult the doctor⟩

acueducto *nm* : aqueduct

acuerdo *nm* **1** : agreement **2 estar de acuerdo** : to agree **3 de acuerdo con** : in accordance with **4 de** ~ : OK, all right

acullá *adv* : yonder, over there

acumulación *nf, pl* **-ciones** : accumulation

acumulador *nm* : storage battery

acumular *vt* : to accumulate, to amass — **acumularse** *vr* : to build up, to pile up

acumulativo, -va *adj* : cumulative — **acumulativamente** *adv*

acunar *vt* : to rock, to cradle

acuñar *vt* : to coin, to mint

acuoso, -sa *adj* : aqueous, watery

acupuntura *nf* : acupuncture

acurrucarse {72} *vr* : to cuddle, to nestle, to curl up

acusación *nf, pl* **-ciones 1** : accusation, charge **2 la acusación** : the prosecution

acusado¹, -da *adj* : prominent, marked

acusado², -da *n* : defendant ⟨el acusado : the defendant, the accused⟩

acusador, -dora *n* **1** : accuser **2** FISCAL : prosecutor

acusar *vt* **1** : to accuse, to charge **2** : to reveal, to betray ⟨sus ojos acusaban la desconfianza : his eyes revealed distrust⟩ — **acusarse** *vr* : to confess

acusativo *nm* : objective (in grammar)

acusatorio, -ria *adj* : accusatory

acuse *nm* **acuse de recibo** : acknowledgment of receipt

acústica *nf* : acoustics

acústico, -ca *adj* : acoustic

adagio *nm* REFRÁN : adage, proverb

adalid *nm* : leader, champion

adaptable *adj* : adaptable — **adaptabilidad** *nf*

adaptación *nf, pl* **-ciones** : adaptation, adjustment

adaptado, -da *adj* : suited, adapted

adaptador *nm* : adapter (in electricity)

adaptar *vt* **1** MODIFICAR : to adapt **2** : to adjust, to fit — **adaptarse** *vr* : to adapt oneself, to conform

adecentar *vt* : to tidy up

adecuación *nf, pl* **-ciones** ADAPTACIÓN : adaptation

adecuadamente *adv* : adequately

adecuado, -da *adj* **1** IDÓNEO : suitable, appropriate **2** : adequate

adecuar {8} *vt* : to adapt, to make suitable — **adecuarse** *vr* ~ **a** : to be appropriate for, to fit in with

adefesio *nm* : eyesore, monstrosity

adelantado, -da *adj* **1** : advanced, ahead **2** : fast (of a clock or watch) **3 por** ~ : in advance

adelantamiento *nm* **1** : advancement **2** : speeding up

adelantar *vt* **1** : to advance, to move forward ⟨adelantar el reloj : to set one's watch/clock ahead⟩ ⟨adelantar una fecha : to move up a date⟩ **2** : to pass, to overtake **3** : to reveal (information) in advance **4** : to advance, to lend (money) — **adelantarse** *vr* **1** : to go ahead ⟨se adelantó para recibirlos : she went ahead to meet them⟩ **2** : to run fast (of a watch or clock) **3** : to get ahead ⟨alguien se me adelantó : someone beat me to it⟩ ⟨no nos adelantemos : let's not get ahead of ourselves⟩ **4 adelantarse a su tiempo** : to be ahead of one's time

adelante *adv* **1** : forward, ahead, in front ⟨dar un paso adelante : to take a step forward⟩ ⟨seguimos adelante con el proyecto : we went ahead with the project⟩ **2 de ahora/ahí en adelante** : from now/then on **3 hacia/para ∼** : forward, toward the front **4 más adelante** : further on, later on **5 ¡adelante!** : come in!

adelanto *nm* **1** : advance, progress **2** : advance payment **3** : earliness ⟨llevamos una hora de adelanto : we're running an hour ahead of time⟩

adelfa *nf* : oleander

adelgazar {21} *vt* : to thin, to reduce — *vi* : to lose weight

ademán *nm, pl* **-manes 1** GESTO : gesture **2 ademanes** *nmpl* : manners

además *adv* **1** : besides, furthermore **2 ∼ de** : in addition to, as well as

adenoides *nfpl* : adenoids

adentrarse *vr* **∼ en** : to go into, to penetrate

adentro *adv* **1** : in, inside ⟨fuimos adentro : we went inside⟩ ⟨estoy aquí adentro : I'm in here⟩ **2 mar adentro** : out to sea **3 tierra adentro** : inland

adentros *nmpl* **decirse para sus adentros** : to say to oneself ⟨me dije para mis adentros que nunca regresaría : I told myself that I'd never go back⟩

adepto¹, -ta *adj* : supportive ⟨ser adepto a : to be a follower of⟩

adepto², -ta *n* PARTIDARIO : follower, supporter

aderezar {21} *vt* **1** SAZONAR : to season, to dress (salad) **2** : to embellish, to adorn

aderezo *nm* **1** : dressing, seasoning **2** : adornment, embellishment

adeudar *vt* **1** : to debit **2** DEBER : to owe

adeudo *nm* **1** DÉBITO : debit **2** *Mex* : debt, indebtedness

adherencia *nf* **1** : adherence (to a rule, etc.) **2** : adhesion

adherente *adj* : adhesive, sticky

adherir {76} *vt* : to stick to — **adherirse** *vr* : to adhere, to stick

adhesión *nf, pl* **-siones 1** : adhesion **2** : attachment, commitment (to a cause, etc.)

adhesivo¹, -va *adj* : adhesive

adhesivo² *nm* : adhesive

adicción *nf, pl* **-ciones** : addiction

adición *nf, pl* **-ciones** : addition

adicional *adj* : additional — **adicionalmente** *adv*

adicionar *vt* : to add

adictivo, -va *adj* : addictive

adicto¹, -ta *adj* **1** : addicted **2** : devoted, dedicated

adicto², -ta *n* **1** : addict **2** PARTIDARIO : supporter, advocate

adiestrador, -dora *n* : trainer

adiestramiento *nm* : training

adiestrar *vt* : to train

adinerado, -da *adj* : moneyed, wealthy

adiós *nm, pl* **adioses 1** DESPEDIDA : farewell, good-bye **2 ¡adiós!** : good-bye!

aditamento *nm* : attachment, accessory

aditivo *nm* : additive

adivinación *nf, pl* **-ciones 1** : guess **2** : divination, prediction

adivinanza *nf* ACERTIJO : riddle

adivinar *vt* **1** : to guess **2** : to foretell, to predict

adivino, -na *n* : fortune-teller

adjetivo¹, -va *adj* : adjectival

adjetivo² *nm* : adjective

adjudicación *nf, pl* **-ciones 1** : adjudication **2** : allocation, awarding, granting

adjudicar {72} *vt* **1** : to judge, to adjudicate **2** : to assign, to allocate ⟨adjudicar la culpa : to assign the blame⟩ **3** : to award, to grant

adjuntar *vt* : to enclose, to attach

adjunto¹, -ta *adj* : enclosed, attached

adjunto², -ta *n* : deputy, assistant

adjunto³ *nm* **1** : adjunct **2** : attachment (in an e-mail)

administración *nf, pl* **-ciones 1** : administration, management **2 administración de empresas** : business administration

administrador, -dora *n* : administrator, manager

administrar *vt* : to administer, to manage, to run

administrativo, -va *adj* : administrative — **administrativamente** *adv*

admirable *adj* : admirable, impressive — **admirablemente** *adv*

admiración *nf, pl* **-ciones** : admiration

admirador, -dora *n* : admirer

admirar *vt* **1** : to admire **2** : to amaze, to astonish — **admirarse** *vr* : to be amazed

admirativo, -va *adj* : admiring

admisible *adj* : admissible, allowable

admisión *nf, pl* **-siones** : admission, admittance

admitir *vt* **1** : to admit, to let in **2** : to acknowledge, to concede **3** : to allow, to make room for ⟨la ley no admite cambios : the law doesn't allow for changes⟩

admonición *nf, pl* **-ciones** : admonition, warning

admonitorio, -ria *adj* : admonishing

ADN *nm* (*ácido desoxirribonucleico*) : DNA

adobar *vt* : to marinate

adobe *nm* : adobe

adobo *nm* **1** : marinade, seasoning **2** *Mex* : spicy marinade used for cooking pork

adoctrinamiento *nm* : indoctrination

adoctrinar *vt* : to indoctrinate

adolecer {53} *vi* PADECER : to suffer ⟨adolece de timidez : he suffers from shyness⟩

adolescencia *nf* : adolescence

adolescente¹ *adj* : adolescent, teenage

adolescente² *nmf* : adolescent, teenager

adonde *conj* : where ⟨el lugar adonde vamos es bello : the place where we're going is beautiful⟩

adónde *adv* : where ⟨¿adónde vamos? : where are we going?⟩

adondequiera *adv* : wherever, anywhere ⟨adondequiera que vayas : anywhere you go⟩

adopción *nf, pl* **-ciones** : adoption

adoptar *vt* **1** : to adopt (a measure), to take (a decision) **2** : to adopt (children)

adoptivo, -va *adj* **1** : adopted (children, country) **2** : adoptive (parents)

adoquín *nm, pl* **-quines** : paving stone, cobblestone

-ador, -adora *suf* : -er ⟨trabajador, trabajadora : worker⟩

adorable *adj* : adorable, lovable

adoración *nf, pl* **-ciones** : adoration, worship

adorador¹, -dora *adj* : adoring, worshipping

adorador², -dora *n* : worshipper

adorar *vt* : to adore, to worship

adormecer {53} *vt* **1** : to make sleepy, to lull to sleep **2** : to numb — **adormecerse** *vr* **1** : to doze off **2** : to go numb

adormecimiento *nm* **1** SUEÑO : drowsiness, sleepiness **2** INSENSIBILIDAD : numbness

adormilarse *vr* : to doze, to drowse

adornar *vt* DECORAR : to decorate, to adorn

adorno *nm* : ornament, decoration

adosado, -da *adj* : attached (of a structure) ⟨casa adosada : duplex, row house⟩

adosar *vt* **1** : to place against, to affix **2** : to enclose, to attach (to a letter)

adquirido, -da *adj* **1** : acquired **2 mal adquirido** : ill-gotten

adquirir {4} *vt* **1** : to acquire, to gain **2** COMPRAR : to purchase

adquisición *nf, pl* **-ciones** **1** : acquisition **2** COMPRA : purchase

adquisitivo, -va *adj* **poder adquisitivo** : purchasing power

adrede *adv* : intentionally, on purpose

adrenalina *nf* : adrenaline

adscribir {33} *vt* : to assign, to appoint — **adscribirse** *vr* ~ **a** : to become a member of

adscripción *nf, pl* **-ciones** : assignment, appointment

adscrito *pp* → **adscribir**

aduana *nf* : customs, customs office

aduanero¹, -ra *adj* : customs

aduanero², -ra *n* : customs officer

aducir {61} *vt* : to adduce, to offer as proof

adueñarse *vr* ~ **de** : to take possession of, to take over

adulación *nf, pl* **-ciones** : adulation, flattery

adulador¹, -dora *adj* : flattering

adulador², -dora *n* : flatterer, toady

adular *vt* LISONJEAR : to flatter

adulteración *nf, pl* **-ciones** : adulteration

adulterar *vt* : to adulterate

adulterio *nm* : adultery

adúltero¹, -ra *adj* : adulterous

adúltero², -ra *n* : adulterer

adultez *nf* : adulthood

adulto, -ta *adj & n* : adult

adusto, -ta *adj* : harsh, severe

advenedizo, -za *n* **1** : upstart, parvenu **2** : newcomer

advenimiento *nm* : advent

adverbio *nm* : adverb — **adverbial** *adj*

adversario¹, -ria *adj* : opposing, contrary

adversario², -ria *n* OPOSITOR : adversary, opponent

adversidad *nf* : adversity

adverso, -sa *adj* DESFAVORABLE : adverse, unfavorable — **adversamente** *adv*

advertencia *nf* AVISO : warning

advertir {76} *vt* **1** AVISAR : to warn **2** : to notice, to tell ⟨no advertí que estuviera enojada : I couldn't tell she was angry⟩

Adviento *nm* : Advent

adyacente *adj* : adjacent

aéreo, -rea *adj* **1** : aerial, air **2 correo aéreo** : airmail

aeróbic *nm* : aerobics

aeróbico, -ca *adj* : aerobic

aerobio, -bia *adj* : aerobic

aerodeslizador *nm* : hovercraft

aerodinámica *nf* : aerodynamics

aerodinámico, -ca *adj* : aerodynamic, streamlined

aeródromo *nm* : airfield

aeroespacial *adj* : aerospace

aerogenerador *nm* : wind-powered generator

aerolínea *nf* : airline

aeromozo, -za *n* : flight attendant, steward *m*, stewardess *f*

aeronáutica *nf* : aeronautics

aeronáutico, -ca *adj* : aeronautical

aeronave *nf* : aircraft

aeropostal *adj* : airmail

aeropuerto *nm* : airport

aerosol *nm* : aerosol, aerosol spray

aeróstata *nmf* : balloonist

aerotransportado, -da *adj* : airborne

aerotransportar *vt* : to airlift

afabilidad *nf* : affability

afable *adj* : affable — **afablemente** *adv*

afamado, -da *adj* : well-known, famous

afán *nm, pl* **afanes** **1** ANHELO : eagerness, desire **2** EMPEÑO : effort, determination

afanador, -dora *n Mex* : cleaning person, cleaner

afanarse *vr* : to toil, to strive

afanosamente *adv* : zealously, industriously, busily

afanoso, -sa *adj* **1** : eager, industrious **2** : arduous, hard

afear *vt* : to make ugly, to disfigure

afección *nf, pl* **-ciones** **1** : fondness, affection **2** : illness, complaint

afectación *nf, pl* **-ciones** : affectation

afectado, -da *adj* **1** : affected, mannered **2** : influenced **3** : afflicted **4** : feigned

afectar *vt* **1** : to affect **2** : to upset **3** : to feign, to pretend

afectísimo, -ma *adj* **suyo afectísimo** : yours truly

afectivo, -va *adj* : emotional

afecto¹, -ta *adj* **1** : affected, afflicted **2** : fond, affectionate

afecto² *nm* CARIÑO : affection

afectuoso, -sa *adj* CARIÑOSO : affectionate — **afectuosamente** *adv*

afeitadora *nf* : shaver, electric razor

afeitar *vt* RASURAR : to shave — **afeitarse** *vr*

afelpado, -da *adj* : plush

afeminado, -da *adj* : effeminate

aferrado, -da *adj* : obstinate, stubborn

aferrarse {55} *vr* : to cling, to hold on

affidávit *nm, pl* **-dávits** : affidavit

afgano, -na *adj & n* : Afghan

AFI *nm* (*Alfabeto Fonético Internacional*) : IPA

afianzar {21} *vt* **1** : to secure, to strengthen **2** : to guarantee, to vouch for — **afianzarse** *vr* ESTABLECERSE : to establish oneself — **afianzamiento** *nm*

afiche *nm* : poster

afición *nf, pl* **-ciones 1** : enthusiasm, penchant, fondness ⟨afición al deporte : love of sports⟩ **2** PASATIEMPO : hobby

aficionado¹, -da *adj* ENTUSIASTA : enthusiastic, keen

aficionado², -da *n* **1** ENTUSIASTA : enthusiast, fan **2** : amateur

aficionar *vt* : to interest ⟨aficionar a alguien a algo : to get someone interested in something⟩ — **aficionarse** *vr*

áfido *nm* : aphid

afiebrado, -da *adj* : feverish

afilado, -da *adj* **1** : sharp **2** : long, pointed ⟨una nariz afilada : a sharp nose⟩

afilador *nm* : sharpener

afilalápices *nms & pl* : pencil sharpener

afilar *vt* : to sharpen

afiliación *nf, pl* **-ciones** : affiliation

afiliado¹, -da *adj* : affiliated

afiliado², -da *n* : member

afiliarse *vr* ~ **a** : to become a member of, to join

afín *adj, pl* **afines 1** PARECIDO : related, similar ⟨la biología y disciplinas afines : biology and related disciplines⟩ **2** PRÓXIMO : adjacent, nearby

afinación *nf, pl* **-ciones 1** : tune-up **2** : tuning (of an instrument)

afinador, -dora *n* : tuner (of musical instruments)

afinar *vt* **1** : to perfect, to refine **2** : to tune (an instrument) — *vi* : to sing or play in tune

afincarse {72} *vr* : to establish oneself, to settle in

afinidad *nf* : affinity, similarity

afirmación *nf, pl* **-ciones 1** : statement **2** : affirmation

afirmar *vt* **1** : to state, to affirm **2** REFORZAR : to make firm, to strengthen

afirmativo, -va *adj* : affirmative — **afirmativamente** *adj*

aflicción *nf, pl* **-ciones** DESCONSUELO, PESAR : grief, sorrow

afligido, -da *adj* : grief-stricken, sorrowful

afligir {35} *vt* **1** : to distress, to upset **2** : to afflict — **afligirse** *vr* : to grieve

aflojar *vt* **1** : to loosen, to slacken **2** *fam* : to pay up, to fork over — *vi* : to slacken, to ease up — **aflojarse** *vr* : to become loose, to slacken

aflorar *vi* **1** : to come to the surface, to emerge

afluencia *nf* **1** : flow, influx **2** : abundance, plenty

afluente *nm* : tributary

afluir {41} *vi* **1** : to flock ⟨la gente afluía a la frontera : people were flocking to the border⟩ **2** : to flow

afónico, -ca *adj* **quedarse afónico** : to lose one's voice, to get laryngitis

aforismo *nm* : aphorism

aforo *nm* **1** : appraisal, assessment **2** : maximum capacity (of a theater, highway, etc.)

afortunado, -da *adj* : fortunate, lucky — **afortunadamente** *adv*

afrecho *nm* : bran, mash

afrenta *nf* : affront, insult

afrentar *vt* : to affront, to dishonor, to insult

africano, -na *adj & n* : African

afroamericano, -na *adj & n* : Afro-American

afrodisiaco *or* **afrodisíaco** *nm* : aphrodisiac

afrontamiento *nm* : confrontation

afrontar *vt* : to confront, to face up to

afrutado, -da *adj* : fruity

aftershave [ˈaftərˌʃeif] *nm* : aftershave

afuera *adv* **1** (*indicating direction*) : out, outside ⟨¡afuera! : get out!⟩ **2** (*indicating location*) FUERA : out, outside ⟨estoy aquí afuera : I'm out here, I'm outside⟩ **3 afuera de** : out of, outside

afueras *nfpl* ALEDAÑOS : outskirts

agachadiza *nf* : snipe (bird)

agachar *vt* : to lower (a part of the body) ⟨agachar la cabeza : to bow one's head⟩ — **agacharse** *vr* : to crouch, to stoop, to bend down

agalla *nf* **1** BRANQUIA : gill **2 tener agallas** *fam* : to have guts, to have courage

agarradera *nf* ASA, ASIDERO : handle, grip

agarrado, -da *adj fam* : cheap, stingy

agarrar *vt* **1** : to grab, to grasp **2** : to catch, to take — *vi* **agarrar y** *fam* : to do (something) abruptly ⟨el día siguiente agarró y se fue : the next day he up and left⟩ — **agarrarse** *vr* **1** : to hold on, to cling **2** *fam* : to get into a fight ⟨se agarraron a golpes : they came to blows⟩

agarre *nm* : grip, grasp

agarrotarse *vr* **1** : to stiffen up **2** : to seize up

agasajar *vt* : to fête, to wine and dine

agasajo *nm* : lavish attention

ágata *nf* : agate

agazaparse *vr* **1** AGACHARSE : to crouch **2** : to hide

agencia *nf* : agency, office

agenciar *vt* : to obtain, to procure — **agenciarse** *vr* : to manage, to get by

agenda *nf* **1** : agenda **2** : appointment book

agénero *adj* : agender ⟨las personas agénero : agender people⟩

agente *nmf* **1** : agent **2 agente de viajes**
: travel agent **3 agente de bolsa** : stockbroker **4 agente de tráfico** : traffic officer

agigantado, -da *adj* GIGANTESCO : gigantic

agigantar *vt* **1** : to increase greatly, to
enlarge **2** : to exaggerate

ágil *adj* **1** : agile, nimble **2** : sharp, lively
(of a response, etc.) — **ágilmente** *adv*

agilidad *nf* : agility, nimbleness

agilizar {21} *vt* ACELERAR : to expedite, to
speed up

agitación *nf, pl* **-ciones 1** : agitation **2**
NERVIOSISMO : nervousness

agitado, -da *adj* **1** : agitated, excited **2**
: choppy, rough, turbulent

agitador, -dora *n* PROVOCADOR : agitator

agitar *vt* **1** : to agitate, to shake **2** : to
wave, to flap **3** : to stir up — **agitarse** *vr*
1 : to toss about, to flap around **2** : to get
upset

aglomeración *nf, pl* **-ciones 1** : conglomeration, mass **2** GENTÍO : crowd

aglomerar *vt* : to cluster, to amass —
aglomerarse *vr* : to crowd together

aglutinar *vt* : to bring together, to bind

agnóstico, -ca *adj & n* : agnostic

agobiado, -da *adj* : weary, worn-out,
weighted down

agobiante *adj* **1** : exhausting, overwhelming **2** : stifling, oppressive

agobiar *vt* **1** OPRIMIR : to oppress, to
burden **2** ABRUMAR : to overwhelm **3**
: to wear out, to exhaust

agobio *nm Spain fam* : burden, pressure

agolparse *vr* : to crowd together

agonía *nf* : agony, death throes

agonizante *adj* : dying

agonizar {21} *vi* **1** : to be dying **2** : to be
in agony **3** : to dim, to fade

agorero, -ra *adj* : ominous

agostar *vt* **1** : to parch **2** : to wither —
agostarse *vr*

agosto *nm* **1** : August ⟨el cinco de
agosto : (on) August fifth⟩ **2 hacer uno
su agosto** : to make a fortune, to make
a killing

agotado, -da *adj* **1** : exhausted, used up
2 : sold out **3** FATIGADO : worn-out,
tired

agotador, -dora *adj* : exhausting

agotamiento *nm* FATIGA : exhaustion

agotar *vt* **1** : to exhaust, to use up **2** : to
weary, to wear out — **agotarse** *vr*

agraciado[1], -da *adj* **1** : attractive **2** : fortunate

agraciado[2], -da *n* : winner

agradable *adj* **1** GRATO, PLACENTERO
: pleasant, agreeable **2 ser agradable a
la vista** : to be easy on the eye(s) —
agradablemente *adv*

agradar *vi* : to be pleasing ⟨nos agradó
mucho el resultado : we were very
pleased with the result⟩

agradecer {53} *vt* **1** : to be grateful for **2**
: to thank

agradecido, -da *adj* : grateful, thankful

agradecimiento *nm* : gratitude, thankfulness

agrado *nm* **1** GUSTO : taste, liking ⟨no es
de su agrado : it's not to his liking⟩ **2**
: graciousness, helpfulness **3 con** ∼
: with pleasure, willingly ⟨lo haré con
agrado : I will be happy to do it⟩

agrandar *vt* **1** : to exaggerate **2** : to enlarge — **agrandarse** *vr*

agrario, -ria *adj* : agrarian, agricultural

agravación *nf, pl* **-ciones** : aggravation,
worsening

agravante *adj* : aggravating

agravar *vt* **1** : to increase (weight), to
make heavier **2** EMPEORAR : to aggravate, to worsen — **agravarse** *vr*

agraviar *vt* INJURIAR, OFENDER : to offend, to insult

agravio *nm* INJURIA : affront, offense, insult

agredir {1} *vt* : to assail, to attack

agregado[1], -da *n* **1** : attaché **2** : assistant professor

agregado[2] *nm* **1** : aggregate **2** AÑADI-
DURA : addition, something added

agregar {52} *vt* **1** AÑADIR : to add, to attach **2** : to appoint — **agregarse** *vr* : to
join

agresión *nf, pl* **-siones 1** : aggression **2**
ATAQUE : attack

agresividad *nf* : aggressiveness, aggression

agresivo, -va *adj* : aggressive — **agresi-
vamente** *adv*

agresor[1], -sora *adj* : hostile, attacking

agresor[2], -sora *n* **1** : aggressor **2** : assailant, attacker

agreste *adj* **1** CAMPESTRE : rural **2**
: wild, untamed

agriar *vt* **1** : to sour, to make sour **2** : to
embitter — **agriarse** *vr* : to turn sour

agrícola *adj* : agricultural

agricultor, -tora *n* : farmer, grower

agricultura *nf* : agriculture, farming

agridulce *adj* **1** : bittersweet **2** : sweet-
and-sour

agrietar *vt* : to crack — **agrietarse** *vr* **1**
: to crack **2** : to become chapped

agrimensor, -sora *n* : surveyor

agrimensura *nf* : surveying

agrio, agria *adj* **1** ÁCIDO : sour **2** : caustic, acrimonious

agriparse *vr* : to catch the flu

agroindustria *nf* : agribusiness

agropecuario, -ria *adj* : pertaining to livestock and agriculture

agrupación *nf, pl* **-ciones** GRUPO : group,
association

agrupamiento *nm* : grouping, concentration

agrupar *vt* : to group together

agua *nf* **1** : water **2 agua bendita** : holy
water **3 agua corriente** : running water
4 agua dulce/salada : fresh/salt water
5 agua mineral : mineral water **6 agua
oxigenada** : hydrogen peroxide **7 agua
potable** : drinking water **8 aguas** *nfpl*
: waters ⟨en aguas internacionales : in
international waters⟩ **9 aguas negras/
residuales** : sewage **10 como agua
para chocolate** *Mex fam* : furious **11
echar aguas** *Mex fam* : to keep an eye

out, to be on the lookout **12 ¡aguas!**
Mex fam : look out!

aguacate *nm* : avocado

aguacero *nm* : shower, downpour

aguado, -da *adj* **1** DILUIDO : diluted **2**
CA, Col, Mex fam : soft, flabby **3** *Mex,
Peru fam* : dull, boring

aguafiestas *nmfs & pl* : killjoy, stick-in-
the-mud, spoilsport

aguafuerte *nm* : etching

aguamarina *nf* **1** : aquamarine **2** color
aguamarina : aqua

aguanieve *nf* : sleet ⟨caer aguanieve : to
be sleeting⟩

aguantar *vt* **1** SOPORTAR : to bear, to tolerate **2** : to hold ⟨aguántame la puerta
: hold the door for me⟩ **3** : to take, to
withstand (weight, etc.) **4** DURAR : to
last **5 aguantar las ganas (de hacer
algo)** : to resist the urge (to do something) — *vi* **1** : to tolerate ⟨no aguanto
más : I can't take it anymore⟩ **2** : to
hold out, to last **3** : to hold (under pressure, etc.) — **aguantarse** *vr* **1** : to resign oneself **2** : to restrain oneself

aguante *nm* **1** TOLERANCIA : tolerance,
patience **2** RESISTENCIA : endurance,
strength

aguar {10} *vt* **1** : to water down, to dilute
2 aguar la fiesta *fam* : to spoil the party

aguardar *vt* ESPERAR : to wait for, to
await — *vi* : to be in store

aguardiente *nm* : clear brandy

aguarrás *nm* : turpentine

agudeza *nf* **1** : keenness, sharpness **2**
: sharpness (of a sound) **3** : witticism

agudizar {21} *vt* : to intensify, to heighten

agudo, -da *adj* **1** : sharp (of a point, etc.)
2 : acute (of an angle), sharp (of an increase) **3** : acute (of an illness), severe
(of a crisis) ⟨un dolor agudo : a sharp
pain⟩ **4** ESTRIDENTE : shrill **5** : sharp
(of eyes or ears) **6** PERSPICAZ : clever,
shrewd **7** : acute (of an accent) — **agudamente** *adv*

agüero *nm* AUGURIO, PRESAGIO : augury,
omen

aguijón *nm, pl* **-jones** **1** : stinger (of a
bee, etc.) **2** : goad

aguijonear *vt* : to goad

águila *nf* **1** : eagle **2 águila o sol** *Mex*
: heads or tails

aguileño, -ña *adj* : aquiline

aguilera *nf* : aerie, eagle's nest

aguilón *nm, pl* **-lones** : gable

aguinaldo *nm* **1** : Christmas bonus, year-
end bonus **2** *PRi, Ven* : Christmas carol

agüitarse *vr* *Mex fam* : to have the blues,
to feel discouraged

aguja *nf* **1** : needle **2** : steeple, spire

agujerear *vt* : to make a hole in, to pierce

agujero *nm* **1** : hole **2 agujero negro**
: black hole (in astronomy)

agujeta *nf* **1** *Mex* : shoelace **2 agujetas**
nfpl : muscular soreness or stiffness

agusanado, -da *adj* : wormy

aguzar {21} *vt* **1** : to sharpen ⟨aguzar el
ingenio : to sharpen one's wits⟩ **2 aguzar el oído** : to prick up one's ears

ah *interj* : oh!

ahí *adv* **1** : there ⟨ahí está : there it is⟩
⟨pasé por ahí : I went by/through there⟩
⟨ahí está el problema : therein lies the
problem⟩ **2** : then ⟨desde ahí : since
then⟩ **3 por ~** : (around) there ⟨lo he
visto por ahí : I've seen him around
there⟩ ⟨debe estar por ahí : it must be
there somewhere⟩ ⟨en 1950 o por ahí
: in 1950 or thereabouts⟩ **4 de ahí**
: hence **5 de ahí que** : with the result
that, so that

ahijado, -da *n* : godchild, godson *m*, goddaughter *f*

ahijar {5} *vt* : to adopt (a child)

ahínco *nm* : eagerness, zeal

ahogar {52} *vt* **1** : to drown **2** : to
smother **3** : to choke back, to stifle —
ahogarse *vr*

ahogo *nm* : breathlessness, suffocation

ahondar *vt* : to deepen — *vi* : to elaborate,
to go into detail

ahora *adv* **1** : now ⟨ahora voy : I'm coming now⟩ **2** : just (now) ⟨como te decía
ahora . . . : as I was just telling you
(now) . . .⟩ **3 ahora bien** : however **4
ahora mismo** : right now **5 hasta ~**
: so far **6 por ~** : for the time being

ahorcar {72} *vt* : to hang, to kill by hanging — **ahorcarse** *vr*

ahorita *adv fam* : right now, right away

ahorquillado, -da *adj* : forked

ahorrador, -dora *adj* : thrifty

ahorrante *nmf Chile, CoRi, DomRep, Hon*
AHORRISTA : investor (in savings)

ahorrar *vt* **1** : to save (money) **2** : to
spare, to conserve — *vi* : to save up —
ahorrarse *vr* : to spare oneself

ahorrativo, -va *adj* : thrifty, frugal

ahorrista *nmf Arg, Uru, Ven* AHORRANTE
: investor (in savings)

ahorro *nm* : saving ⟨cuenta de ahorro(s)
: savings account⟩

ahuecar {72} *vt* **1** : to hollow out **2** : to
cup (one's hands) **3** : to plump up, to
fluff up

ahuizote *nm Mex fam* : annoying person,
pain in the neck

ahumado, -da *adj* : smoked

ahumar {8} *vt* : to smoke, to cure

ahuyentar *vt* **1** : to scare away, to chase
away **2** : to banish, to dispel ⟨ahuyentar
las dudas : to dispel doubts⟩

airado, -da *adj* FURIOSO : angry, irate

airar {5} *vt* : to make angry, to anger

airbag [ˈerbag] *nm, pl* **airbags** *or* **airbag**
: airbag

aire *nm* **1** : air ⟨aire frío : cold air⟩ ⟨un
aire caliente : a hot breeze⟩ **2** : air ⟨un
aire de autoridad : an air of authority⟩
3 aire acondicionado : air-conditioning
4 al aire libre : in the open air **5 darse
aires** : to give oneself airs **6 en el aire**
: on the air, broadcasting **7 en el aire**
: up in the air, unresolved

airear *vt* : to air, to air out — **airearse** *vr*
: to get some fresh air

airoso, -sa *adj* **1** : elegant, graceful **2
salir airoso** : to come out winning

aislado, -da *adj* : isolated, alone

aislador *nm* : insulator (part)

aislamiento *nm* **1** : isolation **2** : insulation

aislante *nm* : insulator, nonconductor

aislar {5} *vt* **1** : to isolate **2** : to insulate

ajado, -da *adj* **1** : worn, shabby **2** : wrinkled, crumpled

ajar *vt* : to wear out, to spoil

ajardinar *vt* : to landscape

ajedrecista *nmf* : chess player

ajedrez *nm*, *pl* **-dreces 1** : chess **2** : chess set

ajeno; -na *adj* **1** : alien **2** : of another, of others ⟨propiedad ajena : somebody else's property⟩ **3** ~ **a** : foreign to **4** ~ **de** : devoid of, free from

ajetreado, -da *adj* : hectic, busy

ajetrearse *vr* : to bustle about, to rush around

ajetreo *nm* : hustle and bustle, fuss

ají *nm*, *pl* **ajíes** : chili pepper

ajillo *nm* **al ajillo** : in a garlic sauce

ajo *nm* : garlic

ajonjolí *nm*, *pl* **-líes** : sesame

ajuar *nm* : trousseau

ajustable *adj* : adjustable

ajustado, -da *adj* **1** CEÑIDO : tight, tight-fitting **2** : close, tight ⟨una ajustada victoria : a close victory⟩

ajustar *vt* **1** : to adjust (wages, settings, etc.) **2** ADECUAR : to adapt **3** : to tighten (a bolt, etc.) **4** : to fit (a part) **5** : to take in (clothing) **6** : to fix, to set (a price) **7** SALDAR : to settle — *vi* : to fit — **ajustarse** *vr* : to fit, to conform

ajuste *nm* **1** : adjustment **2** : tightening

ajusticiar *vt* EJECUTAR : to execute, to put to death

al *prep contraction of* A *and* EL → **a²**

ala *nf* **1** : wing **2** : brim (of a hat) **3** : end (in football) ⟨ala cerrada : tight end⟩

Alá *nm* : Allah

alabanza *nf* ELOGIO : praise

alabar *vt* : to praise — **alabarse** *vr* : to boast

alabastro *nm* : alabaster

alabear *vt* : to warp — **alabearse** *vr*

alabeo *nm* : warp, warping

alacena *nf* : cupboard, larder

alacrán *nm*, *pl* **-cranes** ESCORPIÓN : scorpion

ala delta *nf* **1** : hang glider **2** → **aladeltismo**

aladeltismo *nm* : hang gliding

alado, -da *adj* : winged

alambique *nm* : still (to distill alcohol)

alambrada *nf* : wire fence

alambre *nm* **1** : wire **2 alambre de púas** : barbed wire

alameda *nf* **1** : poplar grove **2** : tree-lined avenue

álamo *nm* **1** : poplar **2 álamo temblón** : aspen

alar *nm* : eaves *pl*

alarde *nm* **1** : show, display **2 hacer alarde de** : to make show of, to boast about

alardear *vi* PRESUMIR : to boast, to brag

alargado, -da *adj* : elongated, slender

alargador *nm* : extension cord

alargamiento *nm* : lengthening, extension, elongation

alargar {52} *vt* **1** : to extend, to lengthen **2** PROLONGAR : to prolong — **alargarse** *vr*

alargue *nm* **1** *Arg* → **alargador 2** *Arg, Chile, Uru* : overtime (in sports)

alarido *nm* : howl, shriek

alarma *nf* : alarm

alarmante *adj* : alarming — **alarmantemente** *adv*

alarmar *vt* : to alarm

alazán *nm*, *pl* **-zanes** : sorrel (color or animal)

alba *nf* AMANECER : dawn, daybreak

albacea *nmf* TESTAMENTARIO : executor, executrix *f*

albahaca *nf* : basil

albanés, -nesa *adj & n*, *mpl* **-neses** : Albanian

albañil *nmf* : bricklayer, mason

albañilería *nf* : bricklaying, masonry

albaricoque *nm* : apricot

albatros *nm* : albatross

albedrío *nm* : will ⟨libre albedrío : free will⟩

alberca *nf* **1** : reservoir, tank **2** *Mex* : swimming pool

albergar {52} *vt* ALOJAR : to house, to lodge, to shelter

albergue *nm* **1** : shelter, refuge **2** : hostel

albino, -na *adj & n* : albino — **albinismo** *nm*

albóndiga *nf* : meatball

albor *nm* **1** : dawning, beginning **2** BLANCURA : whiteness

alborada *nf* : dawn

alborear *v impers* : to dawn

alborotado, -da *adj* **1** : excited, agitated **2** : rowdy, unruly

alborotador¹, -dora *adj* **1** : noisy, boisterous **2** : rowdy, unruly

alborotador², -dora *n* : agitator, troublemaker, rioter

alborotar *vt* **1** : to excite, to agitate **2** : to incite, to stir up — **alborotarse** *vr* **1** : to get excited **2** : to riot

alboroto *nm* **1** : disturbance, ruckus **2** MOTÍN : riot

alborozado, -da *adj* : jubilant

alborozar {21} *vt* : to gladden, to cheer

alborozo *nm* : joy, elation

álbum *nm* : album ⟨álbum de fotos : photo album⟩ ⟨álbum de recortes : scrapbook⟩

albúmina *nf* : albumin

albur *nm* **1** : chance, risk **2** *Mex* : pun

alca *nf* : auk

alcachofa *nf* : artichoke

alcahuete, -ta *n* CHISMOSO : gossip

alcaide *nm* : warden (in a prison)

alcalde, -desa *n* : mayor

alcaldía *nf* **1** : mayor's office (job) **2** AYUNTAMIENTO : city hall

álcali *nm* : alkali

alcalino, -na *adj* : alkaline — **alcalinidad** *nf*

alcance *nm* **1** : reach **2** : range, scope

alcancía *nf* **1** : piggy bank, money box **2** : collection box (for alms, etc.)

alcanfor *nm* : camphor
alcantarilla *nf* CLOACA : sewer, drain
alcantarillado *nm* : sewer system
alcanzar {21} *vt* 1 : to reach 2 : to catch up with 3 LOGRAR : to achieve, to attain — *vi* 1 DAR : to suffice, to be enough 2 ～ a : to manage to
alcaparra *nf* : caper
alcapurria *nf* PRi : stuffed fritter made with taro and green banana
alcaravea *nf* : caraway
alcayata *nf* : hook
alcázar *nm* : fortress, castle
alce¹, etc. → alzar
alce² *nm* : moose, European elk
alcista *adj* : upward (of a trend), bullish (of markets)
alcoba *nf* : bedroom
alcohol *nm* : alcohol
alcoholemia *nf* prueba de alcoholemia : sobriety test
alcohólico, -ca *adj & n* : alcoholic
alcoholismo *nm* : alcoholism
alcoholizarse {21} *vr* : to become an alcoholic
alcornoque *nm* 1 : cork oak 2 *fam* PRINCIPIANTE : idiot, fool
alcurnia *nf* : ancestry, lineage
aldaba *nf* : door knocker
aldea *nf* : village
aldeano¹, -na *adj* : village, rustic
aldeano², -na *n* : villager
aleación *nf, pl* **-ciones** : alloy
alear *vt* : to alloy
aleatorio, -ria *adj* : random, fortuitous — **aleatoriamente** *adv*
alebrestar *vt* : to excite, to make nervous — **alebrestarse** *vr*
aleccionar *vt* : to lecture, to teach
aledaño, -ña *adj* : bordering, neighboring
aledaños *nmpl* AFUERAS : outskirts, surrounding area
alegación *nf, pl* **-ciones** 1 *CA, Car* : allegation 2 : statement (in law)
alegar {52} *vt* : to assert, to allege — *vi* DISCUTIR : to argue
alegato *nm* 1 : allegation, claim 2 *Mex* : argument, summation (in law) 3 : argument, dispute
alegoría *nf* : allegory
alegórico, -ca *adj* : allegorical
alegrar *vt* : to make happy, to cheer up ⟨me alegra mucho que . . .⟩ : I'm very happy that . . .⟩ — **alegrarse** *vr* : to be glad, to be happy ⟨me alegro de (ver) que . . .⟩ : I'm glad (to see) that . . .⟩ ⟨me alegro por ti : I'm happy for you⟩
alegre *adj* 1 : glad, cheerful 2 : colorful, bright 3 *fam* : tipsy
alegremente *adv* : happily, cheerfully
alegría *nf* : joy, cheer, happiness
alejado, -da *adj* : remote
alejamiento *nm* 1 : removal, separation 2 : estrangement
alejar *vt* 1 : to remove, to move away 2 : to estrange, to alienate — **alejarse** *vr* 1 : to move away, to stray 2 : to drift apart
alelado, -da *adj* 1 : bewildered, stupefied 2 : foolish, stupid

aleluya *interj* : hallelujah!, alleluia!
alemán¹, -mana *adj & n, mpl* **-manes** : German
alemán² *nm* : German (language)
alentador, -dora *adj* : encouraging
alentar {55} *vt* : to encourage, to inspire — *vi* : to breathe
alerce *nm* : larch
alérgeno *nm* : allergen
alergia *nf* : allergy
alérgico, -ca *adj* : allergic
alero *nm* 1 : eaves *pl* 2 : forward (in basketball)
alerón *nm, pl* **-rones** : aileron
alerta¹ *adv* : on the alert
alerta² *adj & nf* : alert
alertar *vt* : to alert
aleta *nf* 1 : fin 2 : flipper 3 : small wing
aletargado, -da *adj* : lethargic, sluggish, torpid
aletargarse {52} *vr* : to feel drowsy, to become lethargic
aletear *vi* : to flutter, to flap one's wings
aleteo *nm* : flapping, flutter
alevín *nm, pl* **-vines** 1 : fry, young fish 2 PRINCIPIANTE : beginner
alevosía *nf* 1 : treachery 2 : premeditation
alevoso, -sa *adj* : treacherous
alfabético, -ca *adj* : alphabetical — **alfabéticamente** *adv*
alfabetismo *nm* : literacy
alfabetizado, -da *adj* : literate
alfabetizar {21} *vt* : to alphabetize — **alfabetización** *nf*
alfabeto *nm* : alphabet
alfalfa *nf* : alfalfa
alfanje *nm* : cutlass
alfarería *nf* : pottery
alfarero, -ra *n* : potter
alféizar *nm* : sill, windowsill
alfeñique *nm fam* : wimp, weakling
alférez *nmf, pl* **-reces** 1 : second lieutenant 2 : ensign
alfil *nm* : bishop (in chess)
alfiler *nm* 1 : pin 2 BROCHE : brooch
alfiletero *nm* : pincushion
alfombra *nf* : carpet, rug
alfombrado *nm* : carpeting
alfombrar *vt* : to carpet
alfombrilla *nf* 1 : small rug, mat 2 alfombrilla de/para ratón : mouse pad
alforfón *nm, pl* **-fones** : buckwheat
alforja *nf* : saddlebag
alforza *nf* : pleat, tuck
alga *nf* 1 : aquatic plant, alga 2 : seaweed
algarabía *nf* 1 : gibberish, babble 2 : hubbub, uproar
álgebra *nf* : algebra
algebraico, -ca *adj* : algebraic
álgido, -da *adj* 1 : critical, decisive 2 : icy cold
algo¹ *adv* : somewhat, rather ⟨estaba algo nervioso : he was a little nervous⟩
algo² *pron* 1 : something, anything ⟨¿pasa algo? : is something wrong?⟩ ⟨¿dijo algo más? : did he say anything else?⟩ ⟨por algo lo escogió : she chose him for a reason⟩ ⟨algo para/de comer

: something to eat⟩ **2 ~ de** : some, a little ⟨tengo algo de dinero : I've got some money⟩ **3 (o) algo así** : (or) something like that

algodón *nm, pl* **-dones** : cotton

algodoncillo *nm* : milkweed

algodón de azúcar *nm* : cotton candy

algodonero¹, -ra *adj* : cotton

algodonero², -ra *n* : cotton farmer

algoritmo *nm* : algorithm

alguacil *nm* : constable

alguien *pron* **1** : somebody, someone ⟨alguien gritó : someone shouted⟩ ⟨hablaba con alguien : he was talking to somebody⟩ **2** : anybody, anyone ⟨¿hay alguien en casa? : is there anybody home?⟩

alguno¹, -na *adj* (**algún** before masculine singular nouns) **1** : some, any ⟨en algunos casos : in some cases⟩ ⟨algún día : someday, one day⟩ ⟨algunas semanas después : a few weeks later⟩ ⟨¿alguna pregunta? : any questions?⟩ **2** (*in negative constructions*) : not any, not at all ⟨no tengo noticia alguna : I have no news at all⟩ **3 algún que otro, alguna que otra** : the odd, the occasional

alguno², -na *pron* **1** : one, any ⟨alguno de los libros/niños : one of the books/children⟩ ⟨alguno se ofendió : someone got offended⟩ ⟨¿falta alguno? : are there any missing?⟩ **2 algunos, -nas** : some, a few, any ⟨algunos de los libros/niños : some of the books/children⟩ ⟨algunos dicen que . . . : some (people) say that . . .⟩ ⟨hay algunos que te gusten? : are there any that you like?⟩

alhaja *nf* : jewel, gem

alhajar *vt* : to adorn with jewels

alhajero *nm* : jewelry box

alharaca *nf* : fuss

alhelí *nm, pl* **alhelíes** : wallflower

aliado¹, -da *adj* : allied

aliado², -da *n* : ally

alianza *nf* : alliance

aliar {85} *vt* : to ally — **aliarse** *vr* : to form an alliance, to ally oneself

alias *adv & nm* : alias

alicaído, -da *adj* : depressed, discouraged

alicates *nmpl* PINZAS : pliers

aliciente *nm* **1** INCENTIVO : incentive **2** ATRACCIÓN : attraction

alienación *nf, pl* **-ciones** : alienation, derangement

alienar *vt* ENAJENAR : to alienate

aliento *nm* **1** : breath **2** : courage, strength **3 dar aliento a** : to encourage

aligerar *vt* **1** : to lighten **2** ACELERAR : to hasten, to quicken

alijo *nm* : cache, consignment (of contraband)

alimaña *nf* : pest, vermin

alimentación *nf, pl* **-ciones** **1** NUTRICIÓN : nutrition, nourishment **2** : feed ⟨mecanismo de alimentación : feed (mechanism)⟩

alimentar *vt* **1** NUTRIR : to feed, to nourish **2** MANTENER : to support (a family) **3** FOMENTAR : to nurture, to foster — **alimentarse** *vr* **~ con** : to live on

alimentario, -ria → **alimenticio**

alimenticio, -cia *adj* **1** : nutritional, food, dietary **2** : nutritious, nourishing

alimento *nm* : food, nourishment

alineación *nf, pl* **-ciones** **1** : alignment **2** : lineup (in sports)

alineamiento *nm* : alignment

alinear *vt* **1** : to align **2** : to line up — **alinearse** *vr* **1** : to fall in, to line up **2 ~ con** : to align oneself with

aliñar *vt* **1** : to dress (salad) **2** CONDIMENTAR : to season

aliño *nm* : seasoning, dressing

alipús *nm, pl* **-puses** *Mex fam* : booze, drink

alisar *vt* : to smooth

aliscafo or **alíscafo** *nm* : hydrofoil

alistamiento *nm* : enlistment, recruitment

alistar *vt* **1** : to recruit **2** : to make ready — **alistarse** *vr* : to join up, to enlist

aliteración *nf, pl* **-ciones** : alliteration

aliviar *vt* MITIGAR : to relieve, to alleviate, to soothe — **aliviarse** *vr* : to recover, to get better

alivio *nm* : relief

aljaba *nf* : quiver (for arrows)

aljibe *nm* : cistern, well

allá *adv* **1** : there, over there ⟨allá arriba : up there⟩ ⟨allá en Cuba : over (there) in Cuba⟩ **2 ~ por** : back in ⟨allá por los años 80 : back in the 80's⟩ **3 allá tú** : that's up to you **4 ¡allá voy!** : here I come!, here I go! **5 más allá** : farther away **6 más allá de** : beyond

allanamiento *nm* **1** : (police) raid **2 allanamiento de morada** : breaking and entering

allanar *vt* **1** : to raid, to search **2** : to resolve, to solve **3** : to smooth, to level off/out — **allanarse** *vr* : to even out, to level off/out

allegado¹, -da *adj* : close, intimate

allegado², -da *n* : close friend, relation ⟨parientes y allegados : friends and relations⟩

allegar {52} *vt* : to gather, to collect

allende¹ *adv* : beyond, on the other side

allende² *prep* : beyond ⟨allende las montañas : beyond the mountains⟩

allí *adv* : there, over there ⟨todos están allí : everyone's there⟩ ⟨allí mismo : right there⟩ ⟨hasta allí : up to that point⟩

alma *nf* **1** : soul **2** : person, human being **3 no tener alma** : to be pitiless **4 tener el alma en un hilo** : to have one's heart in one's mouth

almacén *nm, pl* **-cenes** **1** BODEGA : warehouse, storehouse **2** TIENDA : shop, store **3 gran almacén** *Spain* : department store

almacenaje → **almacenamiento**

almacenamiento *nm* : storage ⟨almacenamiento de datos : data storage⟩

almacenar *vt* : to store, to put in storage

almacenero, -ra *n* : shopkeeper

almacenista *nm* MAYORISTA : wholesaler

almádena *nf* : sledgehammer

almanaque *nm* : almanac

almeja *nf* : clam

almendra *nf* **1** : almond **2** : kernel
almendro *nm* : almond tree
almiar *nm* : haystack
almíbar *nm* : syrup
almidón *nm, pl* **-dones** : starch
almidonar *vt* : to starch
alminar *nm* MINARETE : minaret
almirantazgo *nm* : admiralty
almirante *nm* : admiral
almizcle *nm* : musk
almohada *nf* : pillow
almohadilla *nf* **1** : small pillow, cushion **2** : bag, base (in baseball) **3 almohadilla de/para ratón** : mouse pad
almohadón *nm, pl* **-dones** : bolster, cushion
almohazar {21} *vt* : to curry (a horse)
almoneda *nf* SUBASTA : auction
almorranas *nfpl* HEMORROIDES : hemorrhoids, piles
almorzar {36} *vi* : to have lunch — *vt* : to have for lunch
almuerzo *nm* : lunch
alocado, -da *adj* **1** : crazy **2** : wild, reckless **3** : silly, scatterbrained
alocución *nf, pl* **-ciones** : speech, address
áloe *or* **aloe** *nm* : aloe
alojamiento *nm* : lodging, accommodations *pl*
alojar *vt* ALBERGAR : to house, to lodge — **alojarse** *vr* : to lodge, to room
alondra *nf* : lark, skylark
alpaca *nf* : alpaca
alpargata *nf Arg, Spain, Uru, Ven* : espadrille
alpinismo *nm* : mountain climbing, mountaineering
alpinista *nmf* : mountain climber
alpino, -na *adj* : Alpine, alpine
alpiste *nm* : birdseed
alquilar *vt* ARRENDAR : to rent, to lease
alquiler *nm* ARRENDAMIENTO : rent, rental
alquimia *nf* : alchemy
alquimista *nmf* : alchemist
alquitrán *nm, pl* **-tranes** BREA : tar
alquitranar *vt* : to tar, to cover with tar
alrededor *adv* **1** : around ⟨lo que sucede alrededor : the things happening around us/you (etc.)⟩ **2** ~ **de** : around ⟨la Tierra gira alrededor del sol : the Earth revolves around the sun⟩ **3** ~ **de** : about, around ⟨alrededor de quince personas : about fifteen people⟩ ⟨alrededor de diciembre : around December⟩ **4 a mi/tu (etc.) alrededor** : around me/you (etc.)
alrededores *nmpl* ALEDAÑOS : surroundings, outskirts
alta *nf* **1** : admission, entry, enrollment **2 dar de alta** : to release, to discharge (a patient)
altanería *nf* ALTIVEZ, ARROGANCIA : arrogance, haughtiness
altanero, -ra *adj* ALTIVO, ARROGANTE : arrogant, haughty — **altaneramente** *adv*
altar *nm* : altar
altavoz *nm, pl* **-voces** ALTOPARLANTE : loudspeaker

alteración *nf, pl* **-ciones** **1** MODIFICACIÓN : alteration, modification **2** PERTURBACIÓN : disturbance, disruption
alterado, -da *adj* : upset
alterar *vt* **1** MODIFICAR : to alter, to modify **2** PERTURBAR : to disturb, to disrupt — **alterarse** *vr* : to get upset, to get worked up
altercado *nm* DISCUSIÓN, DISPUTA : altercation, argument, dispute
altercar {72} *vi* : to argue
alternador *nm* : alternator
alternancia *nf* : alternation, rotation
alternar *vi* **1** : to alternate **2** : to mix, to socialize — *vt* : to alternate — **alternarse** *vr* : to take turns
alternativa *nf* OPCIÓN : alternative, option
alternativo, -va *adj* **1** : alternating **2** : alternative — **alternativamente** *adv*
alterno, -na *adj* : alternate ⟨corriente alterna : alternating current⟩
alteza *nf* **1** : loftiness, lofty height **2 Alteza** : Highness
altibajos *nmpl* **1** : unevenness (of terrain) **2** : ups and downs
altiplanicie *nf* → **altiplano**
altiplano *nm* : high plateau, upland
altisonante *adj* **1** : pompous, affected (of language) **2** *Mex* : rude, obscene (of language)
altitud *nf* : altitude
altivez *nf, pl* **-veces** ALTANERÍA, ARROGANCIA : arrogance, haughtiness
altivo, -va *adj* ALTANERO, ARROGANTE : arrogant, haughty
alto¹ *adv* **1** : high **2** : loud, loudly — **altamente** *adv*
alto², -ta *adj* **1** : tall, high ⟨un hombre/edificio alto : a tall man/building⟩ ⟨altas montañas : high mountains⟩ **2** : high ⟨altas temperaturas : high temperatures⟩ ⟨de alta calidad : of high quality⟩ **3** : high ⟨la alta sociedad : high society⟩ ⟨un alto funcionario : a high-ranking official⟩ **4** : upper ⟨el Alto Nilo : the Upper Nile⟩ **5** : loud ⟨en voz alta : aloud, out loud⟩ **6 en alta mar** : on the high seas **7 en alto** : in the air ⟨con la cabeza en alto : with her head held high⟩ **8 en lo alto de** : high up on/in **9 por todo lo alto** : in high style
alto³ *nm* **1** ALTURA : height, elevation ⟨tiene un metro de alto : it's one meter tall/high⟩ **2** : stop, halt **3 altos** *nmpl* : upper floors
alto⁴ *interj* : halt!, stop!
alto el fuego *nm, pl* **altos el fuego** : ceasefire
altoparlante *nm* ALTAVOZ : loudspeaker
altozano *nm* : hillock
altruismo *nm* : altruism
altruista *adj* : altruistic
altura *nf* **1** : height ⟨una altura de dos metros : a height of two meters⟩ ⟨a la altura del pecho : at chest height⟩ ⟨no estuvo a la altura de las expectativas : it didn't meet our expectations⟩ **2** : altitude **3** : loftiness, nobleness **4 a la altura de** : (up) by, (up) near ⟨en la avenida San Antonio a la

altura de la calle Tres : on San Antonio Avenue up by Third Street⟩ **5 a estas alturas** : at this point, at this stage

alubia *nf* : kidney bean

alucinación *nf, pl* **-ciones** : hallucination

alucinante *adj* : hallucinatory

alucinar *vi* : to hallucinate

alucinógeno¹, -na *adj* : hallucinogenic

alucinógeno² *nm* : hallucinogen

alud *nm* AVALANCHA : avalanche, landslide

aludido, -da *n* **1** : person in question ⟨el aludido : the aforesaid⟩ **2 darse por aludido** : to take it personally

aludir *vi* : to allude, to refer

alumbrado *nm* ILUMINACIÓN : lighting

alumbramiento *nm* **1** : lighting **2** : childbirth

alumbrar *vt* **1** ILUMINAR : to light, to illuminate **2** : to give birth to

alumbre *nm* : alum

aluminio *nm* : aluminum

alumnado *nm* : student body

alumno, -na *n* : pupil, student ⟨ex-alumno, ex-alumna : alumnus, alumna⟩ ⟨ex-alumnos, ex-alumnas : alumni, alumnae⟩

alusión *nf, pl* **-siones** : allusion, reference

alusivo, -va *adj* ~ **a** : in reference to, regarding

aluvión *nm, pl* **-viones** : flood, barrage

alza *nf* SUBIDA : rise ⟨precios en alza : rising prices⟩

alzacuello *nm* : clerical collar

alzamiento *nm* LEVANTAMIENTO : uprising, insurrection

alzar {21} *vt* **1** ELEVAR, LEVANTAR : to lift, to raise **2** : to erect — **alzarse** *vr* LEVANTARSE : to rise up ⟨alzarse en armas : to rise up in arms⟩

Alzheimer [al'seimer] *nm* : Alzheimer's, Alzheimer's disease

ama *nf* → **amo**

amabilidad *nf* : kindness

amable *adj* : kind, nice — **amablemente** *adv*

amado¹, -da *adj* : beloved, darling

amado², -da *n* : sweetheart, loved one

amaestrar *vt* : to train (animals)

amafiarse *vr Mex fam* : to conspire, to be in cahoots *fam*

amagar {52} *vt* **1** : to show signs of (an illness, etc.) **2** : to threaten — *vi* **1** : to be imminent, to threaten **2** : to feint, to dissemble

amago *nm* **1** AMENAZA : threat **2** : sign, hint

amainar *vi* : to abate, to ease up, to die down

amalgama *nf* : amalgam

amalgamar *vt* : to amalgamate, to unite

amamantar *v* : to breast-feed, to nurse, to suckle

amanecer¹ {53} *v impers* **1** : to dawn **2** : to begin to show, to appear **3** : to wake up (in the morning)

amanecer² *nm* ALBA : dawn, daybreak

amanerado, -da *adj* : affected, mannered

amansar *vt* **1** : to tame **2** : to soothe, to calm down — **amansarse** *vr*

amante¹ *adj* : loving, fond

amante² *nmf* : lover

amañar *vt* : to rig, to fix, to tamper with — **amañarse** *vr* **amañárselas** : to manage

amaño *nm* **1** : skill, dexterity **2** : trick, ruse

amapola *nf* : poppy

amar *vt* : to love — **amarse** *vr*

amargado, -da *adj* : embittered, bitter

amargar {52} *vt* : to make bitter, to embitter — *vi* : to taste bitter

amargo¹, -ga *adj* : bitter — **amargamente** *adv*

amargo² *nm* : bitterness, tartness

amargura *nf* **1** : bitterness **2** : grief, sorrow

amarilis *nf* : amaryllis

amarillear *vi* : to yellow, to turn yellow

amarillento, -ta *adj* : yellowish

amarillismo *nm* : sensationalism

amarillo¹, -lla *adj* : yellow

amarillo² *nm* : yellow

amarra *nf* **1** : mooring, mooring line **2 soltar las amarras de** : to loosen one's grip on

amarrar *vt* **1** : to moor (a boat) **2** ATAR : to fasten, to tie up, to tie down

amartillar *vt* : to cock (a gun)

amasar *vt* **1** : to amass **2** : to knead **3** : to mix, to prepare

amasijo *nm* : jumble, hodgepodge

amasio, -sia *n* : lover

amateur *adj & nmf* : amateur — **amateurismo** *nm*

amatista *nf* : amethyst

amazona *nf* **1** : Amazon (in mythology) **2** : horsewoman

amazónico, -ca *adj* : amazonian

ambages *nmpl* **sin** ~ : without hesitation, straight to the point

ámbar *nm* **1** : amber **2 ámbar gris** : ambergris

ambición *nf, pl* **-ciones** : ambition

ambicionar *vt* : to aspire to, to seek

ambicioso, -sa *adj* : ambitious — **ambiciosamente** *adv*

ambidextro, -tra *adj* : ambidextrous

ambientación *nf, pl* **-ciones** : setting, atmosphere

ambiental *adj* : environmental — **ambientalmente** *adv*

ambientalista *nmf* : environmentalist

ambientar *vt* : to give atmosphere to, to set (in literature and drama) — **ambientarse** *vr* : to adjust, to get one's bearings

ambiente *nm* **1** : atmosphere **2** : environment **3** : surroundings *pl*

ambigüedad *nf* : ambiguity

ambiguo, -gua *adj* : ambiguous

ámbito *nm* : domain, field, area

ambivalencia *nf* : ambivalence

ambivalente *adj* : ambivalent

ambos, -bas *adj & pron* : both

ambulancia *nf* : ambulance

ambulante *adj* **1** : traveling, itinerant **2 vendedor ambulante** : street vendor

ambulatorio¹, -ria *adj* : outpatient

ambulatorio² *nm Spain, Ven* : clinic

ameba *nf* : amoeba — **amébico** *adj*

amedrentar *vt* : to frighten, to intimidate — **amedrentarse** *vr*

amén *nm, pl* **amenes** 1 : amen 2 ~ **de** : in addition to, besides 3 **en un decir amén** : in an instant

amenaza *nf* : threat ⟨amenazas de muerte/ bomba : death/bomb threats⟩

amenazador, -dora *adj* : threatening, menacing

amenazante → **amenazador**

amenazar {21} *vt* : to threaten ⟨me amenazó con demandarme : she threatened to sue me⟩ ⟨fue amenazado de muerte : he received death threats⟩ — *vi* : to threaten ⟨amenazan con sanciones : they're threatening sanctions⟩

amenguar {10} *vt* 1 : to diminish 2 : to belittle, to dishonor

amenidad *nf* : pleasantness, amenity

amenizar {21} *vt* 1 : to make pleasant 2 : to brighten up, to add life to

ameno, -na *adj* : agreeable, pleasant

americano, -na *adj & n* : American

amerindio, -dia *adj & n* → **nativo americano**

ameritar *vt* MERECER : to deserve

ametralladora *nf* : machine gun

amianto *nm* : asbestos

amiba → **ameba**

amienemigo, -ga *n fam* : frenemy

amigable *adj* : friendly, amicable — **amigablemente** *adv*

amígdala *nf* : tonsil

amigdalitis *nf* : tonsillitis

amigo¹, -ga *adj* 1 : friendly, close ⟨es muy amigo mío : he's a very good friend of mine⟩ 2 **hacerse (muy) amigo (de)** : to become (good) friends (with) 3 **ser (muy) amigo de algo** : to be (very) fond of something

amigo², -ga *n* 1 : friend ⟨un buen/íntimo amigo : a good/close friend⟩ ⟨es una amiga suya : she's a friend of his⟩ 2 **hacer amigos** : to make friends

amigote *nm* : crony, pal

amilanar *vt* 1 : to frighten 2 : to daunt, to discourage — **amilanarse** *vr* : to lose heart

aminoácido *nm* : amino acid

aminorar *vt* : to reduce, to lessen — *vi* : to diminish

amistad *nf* : friendship

amistoso, -sa *adj* : friendly — **amistosamente** *adv*

amnesia *nf* : amnesia

amnésico, -ca *adj & n* : amnesiac

amnistía *nf* : amnesty

amnistiar {85} *vt* : to grant amnesty to

amo, ama *n* 1 : master *m*, mistress *f* 2 : owner, keeper (of an animal) 3 **ama de casa** : housewife 4 **ama de llaves** : housekeeper

amodorrado, -da *adj* : drowsy

amolar {19} *vt* 1 : to grind, to sharpen 2 : to pester, to annoy

amoldable *adj* : adaptable

amoldar *vt* 1 : to mold 2 : to adapt, to adjust — **amoldarse** *vr*

amonestación *nf, pl* **-ciones** 1 APERCIBIMIENTO : admonition, warning 2 **amonestaciones** *nfpl* : banns

amonestar *vt* APERCIBIR : to admonish, to warn

amoníaco *or* **amoniaco** *nm* : ammonia

amontonamiento *nm* : accumulation, piling up

amontonar *vt* 1 APILAR : to pile up, to heap up 2 : to collect, to gather 3 : to hoard — **amontonarse** *vr*

amor *nm* 1 : love ⟨un poema de amor : a love poem⟩ ⟨su amor por/a la música : his love of music⟩ 2 : loved one, beloved ⟨sí, mi amor : yes, my love⟩ 3 **amor propio** : self-esteem 4 **hacer el amor** : to make love 5 **por amor al arte** : for the love of it 6 **¡por el amor de Dios!** : for God's sake!

amoral *adj* : amoral

amoratado, -da *adj* : black-and-blue, bruised, livid

amordazar {21} *vt* 1 : to gag, to muzzle 2 : to silence

amorfo, -fa *adj* : shapeless, amorphous

amorío *nm* : love affair, fling

amoroso, -sa *adj* 1 : loving, affectionate 2 : amorous ⟨una mirada amorosa : an amorous glance⟩ 3 : charming, cute — **amorosamente** *adv*

amortiguación *nf* : cushioning, absorption

amortiguador *nm* : shock absorber

amortiguar {10} *vt* : to soften (an impact)

amortizar {21} *vt* : to amortize, to pay off — **amortización** *nf*

amotinado¹, -da *adj* : rebellious, insurgent, mutinous

amotinado², -da *n* : rebel, insurgent, mutineer

amotinamiento *nm* : uprising, rebellion

amotinar *vt* : to incite (to riot), to agitate — **amotinarse** *vr* : to riot, to rebel 2 : to mutiny

amparar *vt* : to safeguard, to protect — **ampararse** *vr* 1 ~ **de** : to take shelter from 2 ~ **en** : to have recourse to

amparo *nm* ACOGIDA, REFUGIO : protection, refuge

amperímetro *nm* : ammeter

amperio *nm* : ampere

ampliación *nf, pl* **-ciones** : expansion, extension

ampliar {85} *vt* 1 : to expand, to extend 2 : to widen 3 : to enlarge (photographs) 4 : to elaborate on, to develop (ideas)

amplificador *nm* : amplifier

amplificar {72} *vt* : to amplify — **amplificación** *nf*

amplio, -plia *adj* 1 : broad, wide (of a street, etc.), spacious (of a room, etc.) ⟨una amplia gama de : a broad range of⟩ ⟨en el sentido más amplio : in the broadest sense⟩ 2 : full, comprehensive 3 : loose, full (of clothes) — **ampliamente** *adj*

amplitud *nf* 1 : breadth, extent 2 : space, spacious quality

ampolla *nf* 1 : blister 2 : vial

ampollar *vt* : to blister — **ampollarse** *vr*

ampolleta *nf* 1 : small vial 2 : hourglass 3 *Chile* : light bulb

ampulosidad *nf* : pomposity, bombast

ampuloso, -sa *adj* GRANDILOCUENTE : pompous, bombastic — **ampulosamente** *adv*

amputar *vt* : to amputate — **amputación** *nf*

amueblar *vt* : to furnish

amuleto *nm* TALISMÁN : amulet, charm

amurallar *vt* : to wall in, to fortify

anacardo *nm* : cashew nut

anaconda *nf* : anaconda

anacrónico, -ca *adj* : anachronistic

anacronismo *nm* : anachronism

ánade *nmf* **1** : duck **2 ánade real** : mallard

anagrama *nm* : anagram

anal *adj* : anal

anales *nmpl* : annals

analfabetismo *nm* : illiteracy

analfabeto, -ta *adj & n* : illiterate

analgésico¹, -ca *adj* : analgesic

analgésico² *nm* : painkiller, analgesic

análisis *nm* : analysis

analista *nmf* : analyst

analítico, -ca *adj* : analytical, analytic — **analíticamente** *adv*

analizar {21} *vt* : to analyze

analogía *nf* : analogy

analógico, -ca *adj* **1** : analogical **2** : analog ⟨computadora analógica : analog computer⟩

análogo, -ga *adj* : analogous, similar

ananá *or* **ananás** *nm, pl* **-nás** : pineapple

anaquel *nm* REPISA : shelf

anaranjado¹, -da *adj* NARANJA : orange-colored

anaranjado² *nm* NARANJA : orange (color)

anarquía *nf* : anarchy

anárquico, -ca *adj* : anarchic

anarquismo *nm* : anarchism

anarquista *adj & nmf* : anarchist

anatema *nf* : anathema

anatomía *nf* : anatomy — **anatomista** *nmf*

anatómico, -ca *adj* : anatomical — **anatómicamente** *adv*

ancas *nfpl* **1** : haunches, hindquarters **2 ancas de rana** : frogs' legs

ancestral *adj* **1** : ancient, traditional **2** : ancestral

ancestro *nm* ASCENDIENTE : ancestor, forefather *m*

ancho¹, -cha *adj* **1** : wide, broad ⟨calles anchas : wide streets⟩ **2** : full, loose-fitting **3 a lo ancho** : across (the width of) **4 a sus anchas** : at home, comfortable

ancho² *nm* **1** : width, breadth ⟨tiene dos metros de ancho : it's two meters wide⟩ **2 ancho de banda** : bandwidth

anchoa *nf* : anchovy

anchura *nf* : width, breadth

ancianidad *nf* SENECTUD : old age

anciano¹, -na *adj* : aged, old, elderly

anciano², -na *n* : elderly person

ancla *nf* : anchor

ancladero → **anclaje**

anclaje *nm* : anchorage

anclar *v* FONDEAR : to anchor

andadas *nfpl* **1** : tracks **2 volver a las andadas** : to go back to one's old ways, to backslide

andador¹ *nm* **1** : walker, baby walker **2** *Mex* : walkway

andador², -dora *n* : walker, one who walks

andadura *nf* : course, journey ⟨su agotadora andadura al campeonato : his exhausting journey to the championship⟩

ándale → **andar**

andaluz, -luza *adj & n, mpl* **-luces** : Andalusian

andamiaje *nm* **1** : scaffolding **2** ESTRUCTURA : structure, framework

andamio *nm* : scaffold

andanada *nf* **1** : volley, broadside **2 soltarle una andanada a alguien** : to reprimand someone

andanzas *nfpl* : adventures

andar¹ {6} *vi* **1** CAMINAR : to walk **2** IR : to go, to travel **3** FUNCIONAR : to run, to function ⟨el auto anda bien : the car runs well⟩ **4** : to ride ⟨andar en bicicleta : to ride a bike⟩ ⟨andar a caballo : to ride on horseback⟩ **5** : to be ⟨su madre no anda bien : his mother isn't well⟩ ⟨lo andaban buscando : they were looking for him⟩ **6 ¡anda!** *or Mex* **¡ándale!** : come on!, go on! **7** ~ **con** SALIR CON : to go out with, to date **8** ~ **con** : to associate with **9** ~ **con/sin** ⟨andaba sin camisa : he had no shirt on⟩ ⟨siempre anda con su guitarra : she always has her guitar with her⟩ **10 andar detrás de** : to be after **11** ~ **en** : to be involved with **12** ~ **en** REVOLVER : to rummage through **13** ~ **por** : to be about ⟨anda por los 25 años : she's about 25 years old⟩ — *vi* : to walk, to travel — **andarse** *vr* : to leave, to go

andar² *nm* : walk, gait

andas *nfpl* : stand (for a coffin), bier

andén *nm, pl* **andenes** **1** : (train) platform **2** *CA, Col* : sidewalk

andino, -na *adj* : Andean

andorrano, -na *adj & n* : Andorran

andrajos *nmpl* : rags, tatters

andrajoso, -sa *adj* : ragged, tattered

andrógino, -na *adj* : androgynous

andurriales *nmpl* : remote place

anea *nf* : cattail

anduvo, etc. → **andar**

anécdota *nf* : anecdote

anecdótico, -ca *adj* : anecdotal

anegar {52} *vt* **1** INUNDAR : to flood **2** AHOGAR : to drown **3** : to overwhelm — **anegarse** *vr* : to be flooded

anejo *nm* → **anexo²**

anemia *nf* : anemia

anémico, -ca *adj* : anemic

anémona *nf* : anemone

anestesia *nf* : anesthesia

anestesiar *vt* : to anesthetize

anestésico¹, -ca *adj* : anesthetic

anestésico² *nm* : anesthetic

anestesista *nmf* : anesthetist

aneurisma *nmf* : aneurysm

anexar *vt* : to annex, to attach

anexión *nf, pl* **-xiones** : annexation

anexo¹, -xa *adj* : attached, joined, annexed

anexo² *nm* **1** : annex **2** : supplement (to a book), appendix

anfetamina *nf* : amphetamine

anfibio¹, -bia *adj* : amphibious

anfibio² *nm* : amphibian

anfiteatro *nm* **1** : amphitheater **2** : lecture hall

anfitrión, -triona *n, mpl* **-triones** : host, hostess *f*

ánfora *nf* **1** : urn, jar (with two handles) **2** *Mex, Peru* : ballot box

ángel *nm* **1** : angel **2 ángel de la guarda** : guardian angel **3 ángel exterminador** : Angel of Death

angelical *adj* : angelic, angelical

angélico, -ca *adj* → angelical

angina *nf* **1** *or* **angina de pecho** : angina **2** *Mex* : tonsil

anglicano, -na *adj & n* : Anglican

angloparlante¹ *adj* : English-speaking

angloparlante² *nmf* : English speaker

anglosajón, -jona *adj & n, mpl* **-jones** : Anglo-Saxon

angoleño, -ña *adj & n* : Angolan

angora *nf* : angora

angostar *vt* : to narrow — **angostarse** *vr*

angosto, -ta *adj* : narrow

angostura *nf* : narrowness

anguila *nf* : eel

angular *adj* : angular — **angularidad** *nf*

ángulo *nm* **1** : angle **2** : corner **3 ángulo muerto** : blind spot

anguloso, -sa *adj* : angular, sharp ⟨una cara angulosa : an angular face⟩ — **angulosidad** *nf*

angustia *nf* **1** CONGOJA : anguish, distress **2** : anxiety, worry

angustiar *vt* **1** : to anguish, to distress **2** : to worry — **angustiarse** *vr*

angustioso, -sa *adj* **1** : anguished, distressed **2** : distressing, worrisome

anhelante *adj* : yearning, longing

anhelar *vt* : to yearn for, to crave

anhelo *nm* : longing, yearning

anidar *vi* **1** : to nest **2** : to make one's home, to dwell — *vt* : to shelter

anilla *nf* : ring

anillo *nm* SORTIJA : ring

ánima *n* ALMA : soul

animación *nf, pl* **-ciones** **1** : animation **2** VIVEZA : liveliness

animado, -da *adj* **1** : animated, lively **2** : cheerful — **animadamente** *adv*

animador, -dora *n* **1** : (television) host **2** : cheerleader

animadversión *nf, pl* **-siones** ANIMOSIDAD : animosity, antagonism

animal¹ *adj* **1** : animal **2** ESTÚPIDO : stupid, idiotic **3** : rough, brutish

animal² *nm* : animal

animal³ *nmf* **1** IDIOTA : idiot, fool **2** : brute, beastly person

animar *vt* **1** ALENTAR : to encourage, to inspire **2** : to animate, to enliven **3** : to brighten up, to cheer up — **animarse** *vr*

anímico, -ca *adj* : mental ⟨estado anímico : state of mind⟩

ánimo *nm* **1** ALMA : spirit, soul **2** : mood, spirits *pl* **3** : encouragement **4** PROPÓSITO : intention, purpose ⟨sociedad sin ánimo de lucro : nonprofit organization⟩ **5** : energy, vitality

animosidad *nf* ANIMADVERSIÓN : animosity, ill will

animoso, -sa *adj* : brave, spirited — **animosamente** *adv*

añiñado, -da *adj* : childlike

aniquilación *nf* → **aniquilamiento**

aniquilamiento *nm* : annihilation, extermination

aniquilar *vt* **1** : to annihilate, to wipe out **2** : to overwhelm, to bring to one's knees — **aniquilarse** *vr*

anís *nm* **1** : anise **2 semilla de anís** : aniseed

aniversario *nm* : anniversary

ano *nm* : anus

anoche *adv* : last night

anochecer¹ {53} *v impers* : to get dark

anochecer² *nm* : dusk, nightfall

anodino, -na *adj* : insipid, dull

ánodo *nm* : anode

anomalía *nf* : anomaly

anómalo, -la *adj* : anomalous

anonadado, -da *adj* : dumbfounded, speechless

anonadar *vt* : to dumbfound, to stun

anonimato *nm* : anonymity

anónimo, -ma *adj* : anonymous — **anónimamente** *adv*

anorak [ano'rak] *nm, pl* **-raks** : anorak

anorexia *nf* : anorexia

anoréxico, -ca *adj* : anorexic

anormal *adj* : abnormal — **anormalmente** *adv*

anormalidad *nf* : abnormality

anotación *nf, pl* **-ciones** **1** : annotation, note **2** : scoring (in sports) ⟨lograron una anotación : they managed to score a goal⟩

anotador, -dora *n* : scorer (in sports) ⟨el máximo anotador : the top scorer, the top-scoring player⟩

anotar *vt* **1** : to annotate **2** APUNTAR, ESCRIBIR : to write down, to jot down **3** : to score (in sports) — *vi* : to score

anquilosado, -da *adj* **1** : stiff (of a joint) **2** : stagnated, stale

anquilosamiento *nm* **1** : stiffness (of joints) **2** : stagnation, paralysis

anquilosarse *vr* **1** : to stagnate **2** : to become stiff or paralyzed

anquilostoma *nm* : hookworm

ánsar *nm* : goose

ansarino *nm* : gosling

ansia *nf* **1** INQUIETUD : anxiety, uneasiness **2** ANGUSTIA : anguish, distress **3** ANHELO : longing, yearning

ansiar {85} *vt* : to long for, to yearn for

ansiedad *nf* : anxiety

ansioso, -sa *adj* **1** : anxious, worried **2** : eager — **ansiosamente** *adv*

antagónico, -ca *adj* : conflicting, opposing

antagonismo *nm* : antagonism

antagonista¹ *adj* : antagonistic

antagonista² *nmf* : antagonist, opponent

antagonizar {21} *vt* : to antagonize

antaño *adv* : yesteryear, long ago

antártico, -ca *adj* **1** : antarctic **2 círculo antártico** : antarctic circle

ante¹ *nm* **1** : elk, moose **2** : suede

ante² *prep* **1** : before, in front of **2** : considering, in view of **3 ante todo** : first and foremost, above all

anteanoche adv : the night before last
anteayer adv : the day before yesterday
antebrazo nm : forearm
antecedente[1] adj : previous, prior
antecedente[2] nm 1 : precedent 2 **antecedentes** nmpl : record, background
anteceder v : to precede
antecesor, -sora n 1 ANTEPASADO : ancestor 2 PREDECESOR : predecessor
antedicho, -cha adj : aforesaid, above
antelación nf, pl -ciones 1 : advance notice 2 con ~ : in advance, beforehand
antemano adv de ~ : in advance ⟨se lo agradezco de antemano : I thank you in advance⟩
antena nf : antenna ⟨antena parabólica : satellite dish⟩
antenoche → anteanoche
anteojera nf 1 : glasses case 2 **anteojeras** nfpl : blinders
anteojos nmpl GAFAS : glasses, eyeglasses
antepasado[1], **-da** adj : before last ⟨el domingo antepasado : the Sunday before last⟩
antepasado[2], **-da** n ANTECESOR : ancestor
antepecho nm 1 : guardrail 2 : ledge, sill
antepenúltimo, -ma adj : third from last
anteponer {60} vt 1 : to place before ⟨anteponer al interés de la nación el interés de la comunidad : to place the interests of the community before national interest⟩ 2 : to prefer
anteproyecto nm 1 : draft, proposal 2 **anteproyecto de ley** : bill
antera nf : anther
anterior adj 1 : previous 2 : earlier ⟨tiempos anteriores : earlier times⟩ 3 : anterior, forward, front
anterioridad nf 1 : priority 2 con ~ : beforehand, in advance
anteriormente adv : previously, beforehand
antes adv 1 : before ⟨no se me ocurrió antes : it didn't occur to me before⟩ ⟨es igual que antes : it's the same as before⟩ ⟨una hora antes : an hour earlier⟩ ⟨antes eran más baratos : they used to be cheaper⟩ 2 : rather, sooner ⟨antes prefiero morir : I'd rather die⟩ 3 ~ de : before, previous to ⟨antes de hoy : before today⟩ ⟨antes de salir : before leaving⟩ ⟨antes de un mes : within a month⟩ 4 **antes que** : before ⟨antes que llegue Luis : before Luis arrives⟩ 5 **cuanto antes** or **lo antes posible** : as soon as possible 6 **antes bien** : on the contrary
antesala nf 1 : lobby, waiting room 2 : prelude, prologue
anti- pref : anti-, against, opposing
antiaborto, -ta adj : antiabortion
antiácido nm : antacid
antiadherente adj : nonstick
antiaéreo, -rea adj : antiaircraft
antiamericano, -na adj : anti-American
antibalas adj : bulletproof
antibiótico[1], **-ca** adj : antibiotic
antibiótico[2] nm : antibiotic
anticipación nf, pl -ciones 1 : expectation, anticipation 2 con ~ : in advance

anticipado, -da adj 1 : advance, early 2 por ~ : in advance
anticipar vt 1 : to anticipate, to forestall, to deal with in advance 2 : to pay in advance — **anticiparse** vr 1 : to be early 2 ADELANTARSE : to get ahead
anticipo nm 1 : advance (payment) 2 : foretaste, preview
anticlimático, -ca adj : anticlimactic
anticlímax nm : anticlimax
anticomunismo nm : anticommunism
anticomunista adj & nmf : anticommunist
anticoncepción nf, pl -ciones : birth control, contraception
anticonceptivo nm : contraceptive — **anticonceptivo, -va** adj
anticongelante nm : antifreeze
anticonstitucional adj : not constitutional
anticuado, -da adj : antiquated, outdated
anticuario[1], **-ria** adj : antique, antiquarian
anticuario[2], **-ria** n : antiquarian, antiquary
anticuario[3] nm : antique shop
anticuerpo nm : antibody
antidemocrático, -ca adj : antidemocratic
antidepresivo nm : antidepressant
antidisturbios[1] adj : riot ⟨policía antidisturbios : riot police⟩
antidisturbios[2] nmpl : riot police
antídoto nm : antidote
antidrogas adj : antidrug
antier → anteayer
antiestético, -ca adj : unsightly, unattractive
antifascista adj & nmf : antifascist
antifaz nm, pl -faces : mask
antifeminista adj & nmf : antifeminist
antífona nf : anthem
antígeno nm : antigen
antigualla nf 1 : antique 2 : relic, old thing
antiguamente adv 1 : formerly, once 2 : long ago
antigüedad nf 1 : antiquity 2 : seniority 3 : age ⟨con siglos de antigüedad : centuries-old⟩ 4 **antigüedades** nfpl : antiques
antiguo, -gua adj 1 : ancient, old 2 : former 3 : old-fashioned ⟨a la antigua : in the old-fashioned way⟩ 4 **Antiguo Testamento** : Old Testament
antihigiénico, -ca adj INSALUBRE : unhygienic, unsanitary
antihistamínico nm : antihistamine
antiimperialismo nm : anti-imperialism
antiimperialista adj & nmf : anti-imperialist
antiinflacionario, -ria adj : anti-inflationary
antiinflamatorio, -ria adj : anti-inflammatory
antillano[1], **-na** adj CARIBEÑO : Caribbean, West Indian
antillano[2], **-na** n : West Indian
antílope nm : antelope
antimonio nm : antimony
antimonopolista adj : antitrust

antinatural *adj* : unnatural, perverse

antipatía *nf* : aversion, dislike

antipático, -ca *adj* : obnoxious, unpleasant

antipatriótico, -ca *adj* : unpatriotic

antirrábico, -ca *adj* : rabies ⟨vacuna antirrábica : rabies vaccine⟩

antirreglamentario, -ria *adj* **1** : unlawful, illegal **2** : foul (in sports)

antirrevolucionario, -ria *adj & n* : antirevolutionary

antirrobo, -ba *adj* : antitheft

antisemita *adj* : anti-Semitic

antisemitismo *nm* : anti-Semitism

antiséptico¹, -ca *adj* : antiseptic

antiséptico² *nm* : antiseptic

antisocial *adj* : antisocial

antitabaco *adj* : antismoking

antiterrorista *adj* : antiterrorist

antítesis *nf* : antithesis

antitoxina *nf* : antitoxin

antitranspirante *nm* : antiperspirant

antiviral *adj* : antiviral

antivirus *nm, pl* **antivirus** : antivirus software

antojadizo, -za *adj* CAPRICHOSO : capricious

antojarse *vr* **1** APETECER : to be appealing, to be desirable ⟨se me antoja un helado : I feel like having ice cream⟩ **2** : to seem, to appear ⟨los árboles se antojaban fantasmas : the trees seemed like ghosts⟩

antojitos *nmpl Mex* : traditional Mexican snack foods

antojo *nm* **1** CAPRICHO : whim **2** : craving

antología *nf* **1** : anthology **2** de ~ *fam* : fantastic, incredible

antónimo *nm* : antonym

antonomasia *nf* por ~ : par excellence

antorcha *nf* : torch

antracita *nf* : anthracite

antro *nm* **1** : cave, den **2** : dive, seedy nightclub

antropofagia *nf* CANIBALISMO : cannibalism

antropófago¹, -ga *adj* : cannibalistic

antropófago², -ga *n* CANÍBAL : cannibal

antropoide *adj & nmf* : anthropoid

antropología *nf* : anthropology

antropológico, -ca *adj* : anthropological

antropólogo, -ga *n* : anthropologist

anual *adj* : annual, yearly — **anualmente** *adv*

anualidad *nf* : annuity

anuario *nm* : yearbook, annual

anudar *vt* : to knot, to tie in a knot — **anudarse** *vr*

anuencia *nf* : consent

anulación *nf, pl* **-ciones** : annulment, cancellation

anular *vt* : to annul, to cancel

anunciador, -dora *n* → **anunciante**

anunciante *nmf* : advertiser

anunciar *vt* **1** : to announce **2** : to advertise

anuncio *nm* **1** : announcement **2** : advertisement, commercial

anzuelo *nm* **1** : fishhook **2 morder el anzuelo** : to take the bait

añadido *nm* : addition

añadidura *nf* **1** : additive, addition **2** por ~ : in addition, furthermore

añadir *vt* **1** AGREGAR : to add **2** AUMENTAR : to increase

añejar *vt* : to age, to ripen

añejo, -ja *adj* **1** : aged, vintage **2** : ancient, musty, stale

añicos *nmpl* : smithereens, bits ⟨hacer(se) añicos : to shatter⟩

añil *nm* **1** : indigo **2** : bluing

año *nm* **1** : year ⟨el año pasado : last year⟩ ⟨en el año 1990 : in (the year) 1990⟩ ⟨en los años '70 : in the '70's⟩ ⟨tiene diez años : she is ten years old⟩ ⟨cumple hoy 80 años : he turns 80 today⟩ ⟨los menores de 18 años : those under the age of 18⟩ **2** : grade ⟨cuarto año : fourth grade⟩ **3 año bisiesto** : leap year **4 año luz** : light-year **5 Año Nuevo** : New Year

añoranza *nf* : longing, yearning

añorar *vt* **1** DESEAR : to long for **2** : to grieve for, to miss — *vi* : to mourn, to grieve

añoso, -sa *adj* : aged, old

añublo *nm* : blight

aorta *nf* : aorta

apa *interj Mex fam* : wow!

apabullante *adj* : overwhelming, crushing

apabullar *vt* : to overwhelm

apacentar {55} *vt* : to pasture, to put to pasture

apache *adj & nmf* : Apache

apachurrado, -da *adj fam* : depressed, down

apachurrar *vt* : to crush, to squash

apacible *adj* : gentle, mild, calm — **apaciblemente** *adv*

apaciguador, -dora *adj* : calming

apaciguamiento *nm* : appeasement

apaciguar {10} *vt* APLACAR : to appease, to pacify — **apaciguarse** *vr* : to calm down

apadrinar *vt* **1** : to be a godparent to **2** : to sponsor, to support

apagado, -da *adj* **1** : off, out ⟨la luz está apagada : the light is off⟩ **2** : dull, subdued

apagador *nm Mex* : switch

apagar {52} *vt* **1** : to turn off, to shut off **2** : to put out, to extinguish — **apagarse** *vr* **1** : to go out (of a light, flame, etc.) **2** DISMINUIR : to wane, to die down

apagón *nm, pl* **-gones** : blackout (of power), power failure

apalabrar *vt* : to arrange with (someone), to arrange for (something)

apalancamiento *nm* : leverage

apalancar {72} *vt* **1** : to jack up **2** : to pry open

apalear *vt* : to beat up, to thrash

apanar *Col, Ecua, Peru* → **empanar**

apantallar *vt Mex* : to dazzle, to impress

apañar *vt* **1** : to seize, to grasp **2** : to repair, to mend — **apañarse** *vr* : to manage, to get along

apaño *nm fam* **1** : patch **2** HABILIDAD : skill, knack

apapachar *vt Mex fam* : to cuddle, to caress — **apapacharse** *vr*

apapacho *nm Mex fam* : cuddle, caress

aparador *nm* **1** : sideboard, cupboard **2** ESCAPARATE, VITRINA : shop window

aparato *nm* **1** : machine, appliance, apparatus ⟨aparato auditivo : hearing aid⟩ ⟨aparato de televisión : television set⟩ : system ⟨aparato digestivo : digestive system⟩ **3** : display, ostentation ⟨sin aparato : without ceremony⟩ **4 aparatos** *nmpl* : braces (for the teeth) **5** : ride (in an amusement park)

aparatoso, -sa *adj* **1** : ostentatious : spectacular

aparcamiento *nm Spain* **1** : parking **2** : parking lot

aparcar {72} *v Spain* : to park

aparcero, -ra *n* : sharecropper

aparear *vt* **1** : to mate (animals) **2** : to match up — **aparearse** *vr* : to mate

aparecer {53} *vi* **1** : to appear **2** PRESENTARSE : to show up **3** : to turn up, to be found — **aparecerse** *vr* : to appear

aparejado, -da *adj* **1 ir aparejado con** : to go hand in hand with **2 llevar aparejado** : to entail

aparejar *vt* **1** PREPARAR : to prepare, to make ready **2** : to harness (a horse) **3** : to fit out (a ship)

aparejo *nm* **1** : equipment, gear **2** : harness, saddle **3** : rig, rigging (of a ship)

aparentar *vt* **1** : to seem, to appear ⟨no aparentas tu edad : you don't look your age⟩ **2** FINGIR : to feign, to pretend

aparente *adj* **1** : apparent **2** : showy, striking — **aparentemente** *adv*

aparición *nf, pl* **-ciones 1** : appearance **2** PUBLICACIÓN : publication, release **3** FANTASMA : apparition, vision

apariencia *nf* **1** ASPECTO : appearance, look **2 en ~** : seemingly, apparently

apartado *nm* **1** : section, paragraph **2 apartado postal** : P.O. Box

apartamento *nm* DEPARTAMENTO : apartment

apartar *vt* **1** ALEJAR : to move away, to put at a distance **2** : to put aside, to set aside, to separate — **apartarse** *vr* **1** : to step aside, to move away **2** DESVIARSE : to stray

aparte[1] *adv* **1** : apart, aside ⟨modestia aparte : if I say so myself⟩ **2** : separately **3 ~ de** : apart from, besides

aparte[2] *adj* : separate, special

aparte[3] *nm* : aside (in theater)

apartheid *nm* : apartheid

apasionado, -da *adj* : passionate, enthusiastic — **apasionadamente** *adv*

apasionante *adj* : fascinating, exciting

apasionar *vt* **1** : to enthuse, to excite — **apasionarse** *vr*

apatía *nf* : apathy

apático, -ca *adj* : apathetic.

apátrida *adj* **1** : without nationality **2** *Ven* : unpatriotic

apearse *vr* **1** DESMONTAR : to dismount **2** : to get out of or off (a vehicle)

apechugar {52} *vi fam* : to put up with the situation ⟨apechugar con : to put up with, to deal with⟩

apedrear *vt* : to stone, to throw stones at

apegado, -da *adj* : attached, close, devoted ⟨es muy apegado a su familia : he is very devoted to his family⟩

apegarse {52} *vr ~ a* : to become attached to, to grow fond of

apego *nm* AFICIÓN : attachment, fondness, inclination

apelación *nf, pl* **-ciones** : appeal (in court)

apelar *vi* **1** : to appeal **2 ~ a** : to resort to

apelativo *nm* APELLIDO : last name, surname

apellidarse *vr* : to have for a last name ⟨¿cómo se apellida? : what is your last name?⟩

apellido *nm* : last name, surname

apelotonar *vt* : to roll into a ball, to bundle up

apenar *vt* : to sadden — **apenarse** *vr* **1** : to be saddened **2** : to become embarrassed

apenas[1] *adv* : hardly, scarcely

apenas[2] *conj* : as soon as

apéndice *nm* **1** : appendix **2** : appendage

apendicectomía *nf* : appendectomy

apendicitis *nf* : appendicitis

apercibimiento *nm* **1** : preparation **2** AMONESTACIÓN : warning

apercibir *vt* **1** DISPONER : to prepare, to make ready **2** AMONESTAR : to warn **3** OBSERVAR : to observe, to perceive — **apercibirse** *vr* **1** : to get ready **2 ~ de** : to notice

aperitivo *nm* **1** : appetizer **2** : aperitif

apero *nm* : tool, implement

apersonarse *vr* **1** : to appear, to show up **2 ~ de** *Col* : to take charge of, to oversee

apertura *nf* **1** : opening, aperture **2** : commencement, beginning **3** : openness

apesadumbrar *vt* : to distress, to sadden — **apesadumbrarse** *vr* : to be weighed down

apestar *vt* **1** : to infect with the plague **2** : to corrupt — *vi* : to stink

apestoso, -sa *adj* : stinking, foul

apetecer {53} *vt* **1** : to crave, to long for ⟨apeteció la fama : he longed for fame⟩ **2** : to appeal to ⟨me apetece un bistec : I feel like having a steak⟩ ⟨¿cuándo te apetece ir? : when do you want to go?⟩ — *vi* : to be appealing

apetecible *adj* : appetizing, appealing

apetito *nm* : appetite

apetitoso, -sa *adj* : appetizing

apiadarse *vr ~ de* : to take pity on

apiario *nm* : apiary

ápice *nm* **1** : apex, summit **2** PIZCA : bit, smidgen

apicultor, -tora *n* : beekeeper

apicultura *nf* : beekeeping

apilar *vt* AMONTONAR : to heap up, to pile up — **apilarse** *vr*

apiñado, -da *adj* : jammed, crowded

apiñar *vt* : to pack, to cram — **apiñarse** *vr* : to crowd together, to huddle

apio *nm* : celery

apisonadora *nf* : steamroller
apisonar *vt* : to pack down, to tamp
aplacamiento *nm* : appeasement
aplacar {72} *vt* APACIGUAR : to appease, to placate — **aplacarse** *vr* : to calm down
aplanadora *nf* : steamroller
aplanar *vt* : to flatten, to level
aplastante *adj* : crushing, overwhelming
aplastar *vt* : to crush, to squash
aplaudir *v* : to applaud
aplauso *nm* 1 : applause, clapping 2 : praise, acclaim
aplazamiento *nm* : postponement
aplazar {21} *vt* : to postpone, to defer
aplicable *adj* : applicable — **aplicabilidad** *nf*
aplicación *nf, pl* **-ciones** 1 : application 2 : diligence, dedication
aplicado, -da *adj* : diligent, industrious
aplicador *nm* : applicator
aplicar {72} *vt* : to apply — **aplicarse** *vr* : to apply oneself
aplique *or* **apliqué** *nm* : appliqué
aplomar *vt* : to plumb, to make vertical
aplomo *nm* : aplomb, composure
apocado, -da *adj* : timid
apocalipsis *nms & pl* : apocalypse ⟨el Libro del Apocalipsis : the Book of Revelation⟩
apocalíptico, -ca *adj* : apocalyptic
apocamiento *nm* : timidity
apocarse {72} *vr* 1 : to shy away, to be intimidated 2 : to humble oneself, to sell oneself short
apócrifo, -fa *adj* : apocryphal
apodar *vt* : to nickname, to call — **apodarse** *vr*
apoderado, -da *n* : proxy, agent
apoderar *vt* : to authorize, to empower — **apoderarse** *vr* ~ **de** : to seize, to take over
apodo *nm* SOBRENOMBRE : nickname
apogeo *nm* : acme, peak, zenith
apolillado, -da *adj* 1 : moth-eaten, worm-eaten 2 : old-fashioned
apolítico, -ca *adj* : apolitical
apología *nf* : defense, apology
apoplejía *nf* : apoplexy, stroke
apoplético, -ca *adj* : apoplectic
aporrear *vt* : to bang on, to beat, to bludgeon
aportación *nf, pl* **-ciones** : contribution
aportar *vt* CONTRIBUIR : to contribute, to provide
aporte *nm* → **aportación**
aposento *nm* : chamber, room ⟨los aposentos reales : the royal chambers⟩
apósito *nm* : dressing (for a wound)
apostador, -dora *n* : bettor, better
apostar {19} *v* : to bet, to wager ⟨apuesto que no viene : I bet he's not coming⟩
apostasía *nf* : apostasy
apóstata *nmf* : apostate
apostilla *nf* : note
apostillar *vt* : to annotate
apóstol *nm* : apostle
apostólico, -ca *adj* : apostolic
apóstrofe *nmf* → **apóstrofo**
apóstrofo *nm* : apostrophe

apostura *nf* : elegance, gracefulness
apoteósico, -ca *adj* : tremendous
apoyabrazos *nms & pl* : armrest
apoyacabezas *nms & pl* : headrest
apoyapiés *nms & pl* : footrest
apoyar *vt* 1 : to support, to back 2 : to lean, to rest — **apoyarse** *vr* 1 ~ **en** : to lean on 2 ~ **en** : to be based on, to rest on
apoyo *nm* : support, backing
app ['ap] *nf, pl* **apps** : app, application
apreciable *adj* : appreciable, substantial, considerable
apreciación *nf, pl* **-ciones** 1 : appreciation 2 : appraisal, evaluation
apreciar *vt* 1 ESTIMAR : to appreciate, to value 2 EVALUAR : to appraise, to assess — **apreciarse** *vr* : to appreciate, to increase in value
apreciativo, -va *adj* : appreciative
aprecio *nm* 1 ESTIMO : esteem, appreciation 2 EVALUACIÓN : appraisal, assessment
aprehender *vt* 1 : to apprehend, to capture 2 : to conceive of, to grasp
aprehensión *nf, pl* **-siones** : apprehension, capture, arrest
apremiante *adj* : pressing, urgent
apremiar *vt* INSTAR : to pressure, to urge — *vi* URGIR : to be urgent ⟨el tiempo apremia : time is of the essence⟩
apremio *nm* : pressure, urgency
aprender *v* : to learn — **aprenderse** *vr*
aprendiz, -diza *n, mpl* **-dices** : apprentice, trainee
aprendizaje *nm* 1 : apprenticeship 2 : learning
aprensión *nf, pl* **-siones** : apprehension, dread
aprensivo, -va *adj* : apprehensive, worried
apresamiento *nm* : seizure, capture
apresar *vt* : to capture, to seize
aprestar *vt* : to make ready, to prepare — **aprestarse** *vr* : to get ready
apresuradamente *adv* 1 : hurriedly 2 : hastily, too fast
apresurado, -da *adj* : hurried, in a rush
apresuramiento *nm* : hurry, haste
apresurar *vt* : to quicken, to speed up — **apresurarse** *vr* : to hurry up, to make haste
apretado, -da *adj* 1 : tight 2 *fam* : cheap — **apretadamente** *adv*
apretar {55} *vt* 1 : to press, to push (a button) 2 : to tighten 3 : to squeeze, to clasp ⟨apretar el gatillo : to pull the trigger⟩ 4 : to press together ⟨apretar los dientes : to grit one's teeth⟩ — *vi* 1 : to press, to push 2 : to fit tightly, to be too tight ⟨los zapatos me aprietan : my shoes are too tight⟩ — **apretarse** *vr*
apretón *nm, pl* **-tones** 1 : squeeze 2 **apretón de manos** : handshake
apretujado, -da *adj* : cramped, squeezed together
apretujar *vt* : to squash, to squeeze — **apretujarse** *vr*
aprieto *nm* APURO : predicament, difficulty ⟨estar en un aprieto : to be in a fix⟩

aprisa *adv* : quickly, hurriedly

aprisionar *vt* **1** : to imprison **2** : to trap, to box in

aprobación *nf, pl* **-ciones** : approval, endorsement

aprobar {19} *vt* **1** : to approve of **2** : to pass (a law) **3** : to pass (an exam) **4** : to pass (a student) — *vi* : to pass (in school)

aprobatorio, -ria *adj* : approving

aprontar *vt Chile, Uru* : to prepare, to ready — **aprontarse** *vr* : to get ready

apropiación *nf, pl* **-ciones** : appropriation

apropiado, -da *adj* : appropriate, proper, suitable — **apropiadamente** *adv*

apropiarse *vr* ~ **de** : to take possession of, to appropriate

aprovechable *adj* : usable

aprovechado¹, -da *adj* **1** : diligent, hardworking **2** : pushy, opportunistic

aprovechado², -da *n* : pushy person, opportunist

aprovechamiento *nm* : use, exploitation

aprovechar *vt* : to take advantage of (an opportunity, etc.), to make good use of (time, etc.) — *vi* : to make the most of it — **aprovecharse** *vr* ~ **de** : to take advantage of, to exploit

aprovisionamiento *nm* : provisions *pl*, supplies *pl*

aprovisionar *vt* : to provide, to supply (with provisions)

aproximación *nf, pl* **-ciones** **1** : approximation, estimate **2** : rapprochement

aproximado, -da *adj* : approximate, estimated — **aproximadamente** *adv*

aproximar *vt ACERCAR, ARRIMAR* : to approximate, to bring closer — **aproximarse** *vr ACERCARSE, ARRIMARSE* : to approach, to move closer

aptitud *nf* : aptitude, capability

apto, -ta *adj* **1** : suitable, suited, fit **2** *HÁBIL* : capable, competent

apuesta *nf* : bet, wager

apuesto, -ta *adj* : elegant, good-looking

apuntador, -dora *n* : prompter

apuntalar *vt* : to prop up, to shore up

apuntar *vt* **1** : to point (a finger, etc.) **2** : to point at **3** *ANOTAR* : to write down **4** *INSCRIBIR* : to sign up **5** : to point out (a fact, etc.) **6** : to prompt (in the theater) — *vi* **1** : to aim ⟨apuntó al blanco con el revólver : she aimed the gun at the target⟩ **2** ~ **a/hacia** : to point to/toward — **apuntarse** *vr* **1** : to sign up, to enroll **2** : to score

apunte *nm* : note

apuñalar *vt* : to stab

apuradamente *adv* **1** : with difficulty **2** : hurriedly, hastily

apurado, -da *adj* **1** *APRESURADO* : rushed, pressured **2** : poor, needy **3** : difficult, awkward **4** : embarrassed

apurar *vt* **1** *APRESURAR* : to hurry, to rush **2** : to use up, to exhaust **3** : to trouble — **apurarse** *vr* **1** *APRESURARSE* : to hurry up **2** *PREOCUPARSE* : to worry

apuro *nm* **1** : predicament, jam ⟨en apuros : in a bind⟩ ⟨me sacó del apuro : he

got me out of a jam⟩ **2** : rush, hurry ⟨tengo apuro : I'm in a hurry⟩ ⟨con/sin apuro : in a hurried/leisurely way⟩ **3** : embarrassment

aquejado, -da *adj* ~ **de** : suffering from

aquejar *vt* : to afflict

aquel¹, aquella *adj, mpl* **aquellos** : that, those

aquel², aquella *or* **aquél, aquélla** *pron, mpl* **aquellos** *or* **aquéllos** **1** : that (one), those (ones) ⟨aquel/aquél fue un año récord : that was a record year⟩ ⟨aquellos/ aquéllos que la conocieron : those who knew her⟩ **2** : the former (of two) **3** **todo aquel/aquél que** : anyone who

aquello *pron* (*neuter*) : that, that matter, that business ⟨aquello fue algo serio : that was something serious⟩

aquí *adv* **1** : here ⟨aquí está : here it is⟩ ⟨ven aquí : come here⟩ ⟨aquí adentro : in here⟩ ⟨aquí mismo : right here⟩ ⟨como dicen (por) aquí . . . : as they say (around) here . . .⟩ ⟨de aquí para allá : back and forth⟩ **2** : now ⟨de aquí en adelante : from now on⟩

aquiescente *adj* : acquiescent

aquiescencia *nf* : acquiescence, approval

aquietar *vt* : to allay, to calm — **aquietarse** *vr* : to calm down

aquilatar *vt* **1** : to assay **2** : to assess, to size up

ara *nf* **1** : altar **2 en aras de** : in the interests of, for the sake of

árabe¹ *adj & nmf* : Arab, Arabian

árabe² *nm* : Arabic (language)

arabesco *nm* : arabesque — **arabesco, -ca** *adj*

arábigo, -ga *adj* **1** : Arabic, Arabian **2 número arábigo** : Arabic numeral

arable *adj* : arable

arado *nm* : plow

aragonés¹, -nesa *adj, mpl* **-neses** : of or from Aragón

aragonés², -nesa *n, mpl* **-neses** : person from Aragón

arancel *nm* : tariff, duty

arancelario, -ria *adj* : tariff, duty ⟨barreras arancelarias : tariff barriers⟩

arándano *nm* : blueberry

arandela *nf* : washer (for a faucet, etc.)

araña *nf* **1** : spider **2** : chandelier

arañar *v* : to scratch, to claw

arañazo *nm* : scratch

arar *v* : to plow

arbitraje *nm* **1** : arbitration **2** : refereeing (in sports)

arbitrar *v* **1** : to arbitrate **2** : to referee, to umpire

arbitrariedad *nf* **1** : arbitrariness **2** *INJUSTICIA* : injustice, wrong

arbitrario, -ria *adj* **1** : arbitrary **2** : unfair, unjust — **arbitrariamente** *adv*

arbitrio *nm* **1** *ALBEDRÍO* : will **2** *JUICIO* : judgment

árbitro, -tra *n* **1** : arbitrator, arbiter **2** : referee, umpire

árbol *nm* **1** : tree **2 árbol genealógico** : family tree

arbolado¹, -da *adj* : wooded

arbolado² *nm* : woodland

arboleda *nf* : grove, wood
arbóreo, -rea *adj* : arboreal
arbusto *nm* : shrub, bush, hedge
arca *nf* **1** : ark **2** : coffer, chest
arcada *nf* **1** : arcade, series of arches **2** **arcadas** *nfpl* : retching ⟨hacer arcadas : to retch⟩
arcaico, -ca *adj* : archaic
arcángel *nm* : archangel
arcano, -na *adj* : arcane
arce *nm* : maple tree
arcén *nm*, *pl* **arcenes** : hard shoulder, berm
archiconocido, -da *adj* : well-known, famous
archidiócesis *nfs & pl →* **arquidiócesis**
archipiélago *nm* : archipelago
archivador *nm* : filing cabinet
archivar *vt* **1** : to file **2** : to archive
archivero, -ra *n* : archivist
archivista *nmf* : archivist
archivo *nm* **1** : file **2** : archive, archives *pl*
arcilla *nf* : clay
arco *nm* **1** : arch, archway **2** : bow (in archery) **3** : arc **4** : wicket (in croquet) **5** PORTERÍA : goal, goalposts *pl* **6** **arco iris** : rainbow
arcón *nm*, *pl* **-cones** : large chest
arder *vi* **1** : to burn ⟨el bosque está ardiendo : the forest is in flames⟩ ⟨arder de ira : to burn with anger, to be seething⟩ **2** : to smart, to sting, to burn ⟨le ardía el estómago : he had heartburn⟩
ardid *nm* : scheme, ruse
ardiente *adj* **1** : burning **2** : ardent, passionate — **ardientemente** *adv*
ardilla *nf* **1** : squirrel **2** *or* **ardilla listada** : chipmunk
ardor *nm* **1** : heat **2** : passion, ardor
ardoroso, -sa *adj* : heated, impassioned
arduo, -dua *adj* : arduous, grueling — **arduamente** *adv*
área *nf* : area
arena *nf* **1** : sand ⟨arena movediza : quicksand⟩ **2** : arena
arenal *nm* : sandy area
arenga *nf* : harangue, lecture
arengar {52} *vt* : to harangue, to lecture
arenilla *nf* **1** : fine sand **2** **arenillas** *nfpl* : kidney stones
arenisca *nf* : sandstone
arenoso, -sa *adj* : sandy, gritty
arenque *nm* : herring
arepa *nf* : cornmeal bread
arete *nm* : earring
argamasa *nf* : mortar (cement)
argelino, -na *adj & n* : Algerian
argentino, -na *adj & n* : Argentinian, Argentine
argolla *nf* : hoop, ring
argón *nm* : argon
argot *nm* : slang
argucia *nf* : sophistry, subtlety
argüir {41} *vi* : to argue — *vt* **1** ARGUMENTAR : to contend, to argue **2** INFERIR : to deduce **3** PROBAR : to prove
argumentación *nf*, *pl* **-ciones** : line of reasoning, argument
argumentar *vt* : to argue, to contend

argumento *nm* **1** : argument, reasoning **2** : plot, story line
aria *nf* : aria
aridez *nf*, *pl* **-deces** : aridity, dryness
árido, -da *adj* : arid, dry
Aries¹ *nm* : Aries (sign or constellation)
Aries² *nmf* : Aries (person)
ariete *nm* : battering ram
arisco, -ca *adj* : surly, sullen, unsociable
arista *nf* **1** : ridge, edge **2** : beard (of a plant) **3** **aristas** *nfpl* : rough edges, complications, problems
aristocracia *nf* : aristocracy
aristócrata *nmf* : aristocrat
aristocrático, -ca *adj* : aristocratic
aritmética *nf* : arithmetic
aritmético, -ca *adj* : arithmetic, arithmetical — **aritméticamente** *adv*
arlequín *nm*, *pl* **-quines** : harlequin
arma *nf* **1** : weapon ⟨arma nuclear : nuclear weapon⟩ ⟨arma química/biológica : chemical/biological weapon⟩ ⟨arma de destrucción masiva : weapon of mass destruction⟩ **2** **armas** *nfpl* : armed forces **3** **arma blanca** : sharp object (used as a weapon) **4** **arma de fuego** : firearm
armada *nf* : navy, fleet
armadillo *nm* : armadillo
armado, -da *adj* **1** : armed **2** : assembled, put together **3** *PRi* : obstinate, stubborn
armador, -dora *n* : owner of a ship
armadura *nf* **1** : armor **2** ARMAZÓN : skeleton, framework
armamento *nm* : armament, arms *pl*, weaponry
armar *vt* **1** : to assemble, to put together **2** : to create, to cause ⟨armar un escándalo : to cause a scene⟩ **3** : to arm (soldiers, etc.) — **armarse** *vr* ~ **de** : to arm oneself with ⟨armarse de valor : to steel oneself⟩
armario *nm* **1** CLÓSET, ROPERO : closet **2** ALACENA : cupboard
armatoste *nm fam* : monstrosity, contraption
armazón *nmf*, *pl* **-zones** **1** ESQUELETO : framework, skeleton ⟨armazón de acero : steel framework⟩ **2** : frames *pl* (of eyeglasses)
armenio, -nia *adj & n* : Armenian
armería *nf* **1** : armory **2** : arms museum **3** : gunsmith's shop **4** : gunsmith's craft
armero, -ra *n* : gunsmith
armiño *nm* : ermine
armisticio *nm* : armistice
armonía *nf* : harmony
armónica *nf* : harmonica
armónico, -ca *adj* **1** : harmonic **2** : harmonious — **armónicamente** *adv*
armonioso, -sa *adj* : harmonious — **armoniosamente** *adv*
armonizar {21} *vt* **1** : to harmonize **2** : to reconcile — *vi* : to harmonize, to blend together
arnés *nm*, *pl* **arneses** : harness
aro *nm* **1** : hoop **2** : napkin ring **3** *Arg, Chile, Uru* : earring
aroma *nm* : aroma, scent
aromático, -ca *adj* : aromatic

arpa *nf* : harp

arpillera *nf* : burlap

arpista *nmf* : harpist

arpón *nm, pl* **arpones** : harpoon — **arponear** *vt*

arquear *vt* : to arch, to bend ⟨arquear las cejas : to raise one's eyebrows⟩ — **arquearse** *vr* : to bend, to bow

arqueología *nf* : archaeology

arqueológico, -ca *adj* : archaeological

arqueólogo, -ga *n* : archaeologist

arquero, -ra *n* **1** : archer **2** PORTERO : goalkeeper, goalie

arquetípico, -ca *adj* : archetypal

arquetipo *nm* : archetype

arquidiócesis *nfs & pl* : archdiocese

arquitecto, -ta *n* : architect

arquitectónico, -ca *adj* : architectural — **aquitectónicamente** *adv*

arquitectura *nf* : architecture

arrabal *nm* **1** : slum **2 arrabales** *nmpl* : outskirts, outlying area

arracada *nf* : hoop earring

arracimarse *vr* : to cluster together

arraigado, -da *adj* : deep-seated, ingrained

arraigar {52} *vi* : to take root, to become established — **arraigarse** *vr*

arraigo *nm* : roots *pl* ⟨con mucho arraigo : deep-rooted⟩

arrancar {72} *vt* **1** : to pull out (hair), to tear out (a page), to pull up (a weed), to pull off (a piece) **2** : to pick (a flower) **3** : to draw (applause, tears) **4** : to start (a car, etc.), to boot (a computer) **5** ARREBATAR : to snatch — *vi* **1** : to start, to boot (a computer) **2** : to get going — **arrancarse** *vr* : to pull out, to pull off

arrancón *nm, pl* **-cones** *Mex* **1** : sudden loud start (of a car) **2 carrera de arrancones** : drag race

arranque *nm* **1** : starter (of a car) **2** ARREBATO : outburst, fit **3 punto de arranque** : beginning, starting point

arrasar *vt* **1** : to level, to smooth **2** : to devastate, to destroy **3** : to fill to the brim

arrastrar *vt* **1** : to drag, to tow **2** : to draw, to attract — *vi* : to hang down, to trail — **arrastrarse** *vr* **1** : to crawl **2** : to grovel

arrastre *nm* **1** : dragging **2** : pull, attraction **3 red de arrastre** : dragnet, trawling net

arrayán *nm, pl* **-yanes** MIRTO : myrtle

arrear *vt* : to urge on, to drive — *vi* : to hurry along

arrebatado, -da *adj* **1** PRECIPITADO : impetuous, hotheaded, rash **2** : flushed, blushing

arrebatador, -dora *adj* : breathtaking, impressive

arrebatar *vt* **1** : to snatch, to seize **2** CAUTIVAR : to captivate — **arrebatarse** *vr* : to get carried away (with anger, etc.)

arrebato *nm* ARRANQUE : fit, outburst

arreciar *vi* : to intensify, to worsen

arrecife *nm* : reef

arreglado, -da *adj* **1** : fixed, repaired **2** : settled, sorted out **3** : neat, tidy **4** : smart, dressed-up

arreglar *vt* **1** COMPONER : to repair, to fix **2** : to tidy, to straighten ⟨arregla tu cuarto : pick up your room⟩ ⟨deja que te arregle : let me fix your clothes/hair⟩ **3** : to arrange (flowers, etc.) **4** : to solve (a problem), to work out (plans) ⟨quiero arreglar este asunto : I want to settle this matter⟩ — **arreglarse** *vr* **1** : to get ready, to get dressed (up) **2** : to fix, to do ⟨arreglarse el pelo : to fix/do one's hair⟩ **3** : to have/get done ⟨arreglarse el pelo : to have/get one's hair done⟩ **4** **arreglárselas** *fam* : to get by, to manage

arreglo *nm* **1** : repair **2** : arrangement **3** : agreement, understanding

arrellanarse *vr* : to settle (in a chair)

arremangarse {52} *vr* : to roll up one's sleeves

arremeter *vi* EMBESTIR : to attack, to charge

arremetida *nf* EMBESTIDA : attack, onslaught

arremolinarse *vr* **1** : to crowd around, to mill about **2** : to swirl (about)

arrendador, -dora *n* **1** : landlord, landlady *f* **2** : tenant, lessee

arrendajo *nm* : jay

arrendamiento *nm* **1** ALQUILER : rental, leasing **2 contrato de arrendamiento** : lease

arrendar {55} *vt* ALQUILAR : to rent, to lease

arrendatario, -ria *n* : tenant, lessee, renter

arreos *nmpl* GUARNICIONES : tack, harness, trappings

arrepentido, -da *adj* : repentant, remorseful

arrepentimiento *nm* : regret, remorse, repentance

arrepentirse {76} *vr* **1** : to regret, to be sorry **2** : to repent

arrestar *vt* DETENER : to arrest, to detain

arresto *nm* **1** DETENCIÓN : arrest **2 arrestos** *nmpl* : boldness, daring

arriar {85} *vt* **1** : to lower (a flag, etc.) **2** : to slacken (a rope, etc.)

arriate *nm Mex, Spain* : bed (for plants), border

arriba *adv* **1** : up, upwards ⟨póngalo más arriba : put it higher (up)⟩ ⟨arriba y abajo : up and down⟩ ⟨¡manos arriba! : (put your) hands up!⟩ ⟨cuesta/río arriba : uphill/upstream⟩ **2** : above, overhead ⟨desde arriba : from above⟩ ⟨el arriba mencionado : the above-mentioned⟩ **3** : upstairs ⟨los vecinos de arriba : the upstairs neighbors⟩ **4** : up with ⟨¡arriba la democracia! : up with democracy!⟩ **5 ~ de** : above, on top of **6 ~ de** : more than ⟨arriba de cien : more than a hundred⟩ **7 de ~** : top, upper ⟨el cajón de arriba : the top drawer⟩ **8 de arriba abajo** : from top to bottom, from head to foot **9 hacia/para ~** : upwards

arribar *vi* **1** : to arrive **2** : to dock, to put into port

arribista *nmf* : parvenu, upstart

arribo *nm* : arrival

arriendo *nm* ARRENDAMIENTO : rent, rental

arriero, -ra n : mule driver

arriesgado, -da adj 1 : risky 2 : bold, daring

arriesgar {52} vt : to risk, to venture — **arriesgarse** vr : to take a chance

arrimado, -da n Mex fam : sponger, freeloader

arrimar vt ACERCAR, APROXIMAR : to bring closer, to draw near — **arrimarse** vr ACERCARSE, APROXIMARSE : to approach, to get close

arrinconar vt 1 ACORRALAR : to corner, to box in 2 : to push aside, to abandon

arroba nf 1 (used for the symbol @) : at sign ⟨arroba merriam-webster punto com : at merriam-webster dot com⟩ 2 : former unit of measurement

arrobamiento nm : rapture, ecstasy

arrobar vt : to enrapture, to enchant — **arrobarse** vr

arrocero¹, -ra adj : rice

arrocero², -ra n : rice grower

arrodillarse vr : to kneel (down)

arrogancia nf ALTANERÍA, ALTIVEZ : arrogance, haughtiness

arrogante adj ALTANERO, ALTIVO : arrogant, haughty

arrogarse {52} vr : to usurp, to arrogate

arrojado, -da adj : daring, fearless

arrojar vt 1 : to hurl, to cast, to throw 2 : to give off, to spew out 3 : to yield, to produce 4 fam : to vomit — **arrojarse** vr PRECIPITARSE : to throw oneself, to leap

arrojo nm : boldness, fearlessness

arrollador, -dora adj : sweeping, overwhelming

arrollar vt 1 : to sweep away, to carry away 2 : to crush, to overwhelm 3 : to run over (with a vehicle)

arropar vt : to clothe, to cover (up) — **arroparse** vr

arrostrar vt : to confront, to face (up to)

arroyo nm 1 RIACHUELO : brook, creek, stream 2 : gutter

arroz nm, pl **arroces** : rice

arrozal nm : rice field, rice paddy

arruga nf : wrinkle, fold, crease

arrugado, -da adj : wrinkled, creased, lined

arrugar {52} vt : to wrinkle, to crease, to pucker — **arrugarse** vr

arruinar vt : to ruin, to wreck — **arruinarse** vr 1 : to be ruined 2 : to fall into ruin, to go bankrupt

arrullar vt : to lull to sleep — vi : to coo

arrullo nm 1 : lullaby 2 : coo (of a dove)

arrumaco nm fam : kissing, cuddling

arrumbar vt 1 : to lay aside, to put away 2 : to floor, to leave speechless

arsenal nm : arsenal

arsénico nm : arsenic

arte nmf (usually m in singular, f in plural) 1 : art ⟨artes y oficios : arts and crafts⟩ ⟨bellas artes : fine arts⟩ ⟨obra de arte : work of art⟩ 2 HABILIDAD : art, skill ⟨el arte de hacer amigos : the art of making friends⟩ ⟨tener arte para : to be skilled at⟩ 3 **artes** nfpl : cunning, guile

artefacto nm 1 : artifact 2 DISPOSITIVO : device

artemisa nf : sagebrush

arteria nf : artery — **arterial** adj

arteriosclerosis nf : arteriosclerosis, hardening of the arteries

artero, -ra adj : wily, crafty

artesanal adj : pertaining to crafts or craftsmanship, handmade

artesanía nf 1 : craftsmanship 2 : handicrafts pl

artesano, -na n : artisan, craftsman

ártico, -ca adj : arctic

articulación nf, pl **-ciones** 1 : articulation, pronunciation 2 COYUNTURA : joint

articular vt 1 : to articulate, to utter 2 : to connect with a joint 3 : to coordinate, to orchestrate

articulista nmf : columnist

artículo nm 1 : article, thing 2 : item, feature, report 3 **artículo de comercio** : commodity 4 **artículos de primera necesidad** : essentials 5 **artículos de tocador** : toiletries

artífice nmf 1 ARTESANO : artisan 2 : mastermind, architect

artificial adj 1 : artificial, man-made 2 : feigned, false — **artificialmente** adv

artificio nm 1 HABILIDAD : skill 2 APARATO : device, appliance 3 ARDID : artifice, ruse

artificioso, -sa adj 1 : skillful 2 : cunning, deceptive

artillería nf : artillery

artillero, -ra n : gunner

artilugio nm : gadget, contraption

artimaña nf : ruse, trick

artista nmf 1 : artist 2 ACTOR, ACTRIZ : actor, actress f

artístico, -ca adj : artistic — **artísticamente** adv

artrítico, -ca adj : arthritic

artritis nfs & pl : arthritis

artrópodo nm : arthropod

arveja nf GUISANTE : pea

arzobispado nm : archbishopric

arzobispo nm : archbishop

as nm : ace

asa nf AGARRADERA, ASIDERO : handle, grip

asado¹, -da adj : roasted, grilled, broiled

asado² nm 1 : roast 2 : barbecued meat 3 : barbecue, cookout

asador nm : spit, rotisserie

asaduras nfpl : entrails, offal

asalariado¹, -da adj : wage-earning, salaried

asalariado², -da n : wage earner

asaltante nmf 1 : mugger, robber 2 : assailant

asaltar vt 1 : to assault 2 : to mug, to rob 3 **asaltar al poder** : to seize power

asalto nm 1 : assault 2 : mugging, robbery 3 : round (in boxing) 4 **asalto al poder** : coup d'état

asamblea nf : assembly, meeting

asambleísta nmf : assemblyman m, assemblywoman f

asar vt : to roast, to grill — **asarse** vr fam : to roast, to be dying from heat

asbesto nm : asbestos

ascendencia *nf* 1 : ancestry, descent 2 ~ **sobre** : influence over

ascendente *adj* : ascending, upward ⟨un curso ascendente : an upward trend⟩

ascender {56} *vi* 1 : to ascend, to rise up 2 : to be promoted ⟨ascendió a gerente : she was promoted to manager⟩ 3 ~ **a** : to amount to, to reach ⟨las deudas ascienden a 20 millones de pesos : the debt amounts to 20 million pesos⟩ — *vt* : to promote

ascendiente *nmf* ANCESTRO : ancestor

ascendiente² *nm* INFLUENCIA : influence, ascendancy

ascensión *nf, pl* -**siones** 1 : ascent, rise 2 **Fiesta de la Ascensión** : Ascension Day

ascenso *nm* 1 : ascent, rise 2 : promotion

ascensor *nm* ELEVADOR : elevator

asceta *nmf* : ascetic

ascético, -ca *adj* : ascetic

ascetismo *nm* : asceticism

asco *nm* 1 : disgust ⟨¡qué asco! : that's disgusting!, how revolting!⟩ 2 **darle asco a alguien** : to disgust someone 3 **estar hecho un asco** : to be filthy 4 **hacerle ascos a algo** : to turn up one's nose at something

ascua *nf* 1 BRASA : ember 2 **estar en ascuas** *fam* : to be on edge

aseado, -da *adj* : clean, neat

asear *vt* 1 : to wash, to clean 2 : to tidy up — **asearse** *vr*

asechanza *nf* : snare, trap

asechar *vt* : to set a trap for

asediar *vt* 1 SITIAR : to besiege 2 ACOSAR : to harass

asedio *nm* 1 : siege 2 ACOSO : harassment

asegurador¹, -dora *adj* 1 : insuring, assuring 2 : pertaining to insurance

asegurador², -dora *n* : insurer, underwriter

aseguradora *nf* : insurance company

asegurar *vt* 1 : to assure 2 : to secure 3 : to insure — **asegurarse** *vr* 1 CERCIORARSE : to make sure 2 : to take out insurance, to insure oneself

asemejar *vt* 1 : to make similar ⟨ese bigote te asemeja a tu abuelo : that mustache makes you look like your grandfather⟩ 2 *Mex* : to be similar to, to resemble — **asemejarse** *vr* ~ **a** : to look like, to resemble

asentaderas *nfpl fam* : bottom, buttocks *pl*

asentado, -da *adj* : settled, established

asentamiento *nm* : settlement

asentar {55} *vt* 1 : to lay down, to set down, to place 2 : to settle, to establish 3 *Mex* : to state, to affirm — **asentarse** *vr* 1 : to settle 2 ESTABLECERSE : to settle down, to establish oneself

asentimiento *nm* : assent, consent

asentir {76} *vi* : to consent, to agree

aseo *nm* : cleanliness

aséptico, -ca *adj* : aseptic

asequible *adj* ACCESIBLE : accessible, attainable

aserción *nf, pl* -**ciones** → **aserto**

aserradero *nm* : sawmill

aserrar {55} *vt* : to saw

aserrín *nm, pl* -**rrines** : sawdust

aserto *nm* : assertion, affirmation

asesinar *vt* 1 : to murder 2 : to assassinate

asesinato *nm* 1 : murder 2 : assassination

asesino¹, -na *adj* : murderous, homicidal

asesino², -na *n* 1 : murderer, killer 2 : assassin

asesor, -sora *n* : advisor, consultant

asesoramiento *nm* : advice, counsel

asesorar *vt* : to advise, to counsel — **asesorarse** *vr* ~ **de** : to consult

asesoría *nf* 1 : consulting, advising 2 : consultant's office

asestar {55} *vt* 1 : to aim, to point (a weapon) 2 : to deliver, to deal (a blow)

aseveración *nf, pl* -**ciones** : assertion, statement

aseverar *vt* : to assert, to state

asexual *adj* : asexual — **asexualmente** *adv*

asfaltado¹, -da *adj* : paved (with asphalt)

asfaltado² *nm* PAVIMENTO : pavement, asphalt

asfaltar *vt* : to pave, to blacktop

asfalto *nm* : asphalt

asfixia *nf* : asphyxia, asphyxiation, suffocation

asfixiante *adj* 1 : asphyxiating 2 AGOBIANTE : oppressive

asfixiar *vt* : to asphyxiate, to suffocate, to smother — **asfixiarse** *vr*

asga, etc. → **asir**

así¹ *adv* 1 : like this, like that, so ⟨así se hace : that's how it's done⟩ ⟨no puede seguir así : it can't go on like this⟩ ⟨así sea : so be it⟩ ⟨y así sucesivamente : and so on⟩ 2 **así así** : so-so, fair 3 ~ **como** : as well as 4 **así como así** *or* **así nomás** : just like that 5 ~ **de** : so, about so ⟨una caja así de grande : a box about so big⟩ 6 **así mismo** → **asimismo** 7 **así que** : so, therefore 8 **así y todo** : even so

así² *adj* : such, such a, like that ⟨un talento así : a talent like that⟩ ⟨algo así : something like that⟩ ⟨así es la vida : that's life⟩ ⟨si es así . . . : if that's the case . . .⟩

así³ *conj* AUNQUE : even if, even though ⟨no irá, así le paguen : he won't go, even if they pay him⟩

asiático¹, -ca *adj* : Asian

asiático², -ca *n* : Asian

asidero *nm* 1 AGARRADERA, ASA : grip, handle 2 AGARRE : grip, hold

asiduamente *adv* : regularly, frequently

asiduidad *nf* **con** ~ : regularly, frequently

asiduo, -dua *adj* 1 : assiduous 2 : frequent, regular

asiento *nm* 1 : seat, chair ⟨asiento trasero : back seat⟩ 2 : location, site

asignación *nf, pl* -**ciones** 1 : allocation 2 : appointment, designation 3 : allowance, pay 4 *PRi* : homework, assignment

asignar *vt* **1** : to assign, to allocate **2** : to appoint

asignatura *nf* MATERIA : subject, course

asilado, -da *n* : exile, refugee

asilo *nm* : asylum, refuge, shelter

asimetría *nf* : asymmetry

asimétrico, -ca *adj* : asymmetrical, asymmetric

asimilación *nf, pl* **-ciones** : assimilation

asimilar *vt* : to assimilate — **asimilarse** *vr* ~ **a** : to be similar to, to resemble

asimismo *adv* **1** IGUALMENTE : similarly, likewise **2** TAMBIÉN : as well, also

asir {7} *vt* : to seize, to grasp — **asirse** *vr* ~ **a** : to cling to

asistencia *nf* **1** : attendance **2** : assistance **3** : assist (in sports) **4** **asistencia médica** *or Spain* **asistencia sanitaria** : health care, medical care

asistente¹ *adj* : attending, in attendance

asistente² *nmf* **1** : assistant **2 los asistentes** : those present, those in attendance

asistido, -da *adj* : assisted

asistir *vi* : to attend, to be present ⟨asistir a clase : to attend class⟩ — *vt* : to aid, to assist

asma *nf* : asthma

asmático, -ca *adj* : asthmatic

asno *nm* BURRO : ass, donkey

asociación *nf, pl* **-ciones** **1** : association, relationship **2** : society, group, association

asociado¹, -da *adj* : associate, associated

asociado², -da *n* : associate, partner

asociar *vt* **1** : to associate, to connect **2** : to pool (resources) **3** : to take into partnership — **asociarse** *vr* **1** : to become partners **2** ~ **a** : to join, to become a member of

asolar {19} *vt* : to devastate, to destroy

asoleado, -da *adj* : sunny

asolear *vt* : to put in the sun — **asolearse** *vr* : to sunbathe

asomar *vt* : to show, to stick out — *vi* : to appear, to become visible — **asomarse** *vr* **1** : to show, to appear **2** : to lean out, to look out ⟨se asomó por la ventana : he leaned out the window⟩

asombrar *vt* MARAVILLAR : to amaze, to astonish — **asombrarse** *vr* : to marvel, to be amazed

asombro *nm* : amazement, astonishment

asombroso, -sa *adj* : amazing, astonishing — **asombrosamente** *adv*

asomo *nm* **1** : hint, trace **2 ni por asomo** : by no means

aspa *nf* : blade (of a fan or propeller)

aspaviento *nm* : exaggerated movement, fuss, flounce

aspecto *nm* **1** : aspect **2** APARIENCIA : appearance, look

aspereza *nf* RUDEZA : roughness, coarseness

áspero, -ra *adj* : rough, coarse, abrasive — **ásperamente** *adv*

aspersión *nf, pl* **-siones** : sprinkling

aspersor *nm* : sprinkler

aspiración *nf, pl* **-ciones** **1** : inhalation, breathing in **2** ANHELO : aspiration, desire

aspiradora *nf* : vacuum cleaner

aspirante *nmf* : applicant, candidate

aspirar *vi* ~ **a** : to aspire to — *vt* : to inhale, to breathe in

aspirina *nf* : aspirin

asqueante *adj* : sickening, disgusting

asquear *vt* : to sicken, to disgust

asquerosidad *nf* : filth, foulness

asqueroso, -sa *adj* : disgusting, sickening, repulsive — **asquerosamente** *adv*

asta *nf* **1** : flagpole ⟨a media asta : at half-mast⟩ **2** : horn, antler **3** : shaft (of a weapon)

ástaco *nm* : crayfish

astado, -da *adj* : horned

aster *nm* : aster

asterisco *nm* : asterisk

asteroide *nm* : asteroid

astigmatismo *nm* : astigmatism

astil *nm* : shaft (of an arrow or feather)

astilla *nf* **1** : splinter, chip **2 de tal palo, tal astilla** : like father, like son

astillar *vt* : to splinter — **astillarse** *vr*

astillero *nm* : dry dock, shipyard

astral *adj* : astral

astringente *adj & nm* : astringent — **astringencia** *nf*

astro *nm* **1** : heavenly body **2** : star

astrología *nf* : astrology

astrológico, -ca *adj* : astrological

astrólogo, -ga *n* : astrologer

astronauta *nmf* : astronaut

astronáutica *nf* : astronautics

astronáutico, -ca *adj* : astronautic, astronautical

astronave *nf* : spaceship

astronomía *nf* : astronomy

astronómico, -ca *adj* : astronomical — **astronómicamente** *adv*

astrónomo, -ma *n* : astronomer

astroso, -sa *adj* DESALIÑADO : slovenly, untidy

astucia *nf* **1** : astuteness, shrewdness **2** : cunning, guile

astuto, -ta *adj* **1** : astute, shrewd **2** : crafty, tricky — **astutamente** *adv*

asueto *nm* : time off, break

asumir *vt* **1** : to assume, to take on ⟨asumir el cargo : to take office⟩ **2** SUPONER : to assume, to suppose

asunción *nf, pl* **-ciones** : assumption

asunto *nm* **1** CUESTIÓN, TEMA : affair, matter, subject **2 asuntos** *nmpl* : affairs, business

asustadizo, -za *adj* : nervous, jumpy, skittish

asustado, -da *adj* : frightened, afraid

asustar *vt* ESPANTAR : to scare, to frighten — **asustarse** *vr*

atacante *nmf* : assailant, attacker

atacar {72} *v* : to attack

atado¹, -da *adj* : shy, inhibited

atado² *nm* **1** : bundle, bunch **2** *Arg* : pack (of cigarettes)

atadura *nf* LIGADURA : tie, bond

atajada *nf* : save (in sports)

atajar *vt* **1** IMPEDIR : to block, to stop **2** INTERRUMPIR : to interrupt, to cut off **3** CONTENER : to hold back, to restrain — *vi* ~ **por** : to take a shortcut through

atajo *nm* : shortcut
atalaya *nf* **1** : watchtower **2** : vantage point
atañer {79} *vt* ~ **a** (*3rd person only*) : to concern, to have to do with ⟨eso no me atañe : that does not concern me⟩
ataque *nm* **1** : attack, assault **2** : fit ⟨ataque de risa : fit of laughter⟩ **3 ataque de nervios** : nervous breakdown **4 ataque de pánico/ansiedad** : panic/anxiety attack **5 ataque cardíaco** or **ataque al corazón** : heart attack
atar *vt* AMARRAR : to tie, to tie up, to tie down — **atarse** *vr*
atarantado, -da *adj fam* **1** : restless **2** : dazed, stunned
atarantar *vt fam* : to daze, to stun
atarazana *nf* : shipyard
atardecer[1] {53} *v impers* : to get dark
atardecer[2] *nm* : late afternoon, dusk
atareado, -da *adj* : busy, overworked
atascar {72} *vt* **1** ATORAR : to block, to clog, to stop up **2** : to hinder — **atascarse** *vr* **1** : to become obstructed **2** : to get bogged down **3** PARARSE : to stall
atasco *nm* **1** : blockage **2** EMBOTELLAMIENTO : traffic jam
ataúd *nm* : coffin, casket
ataviar {85} *vt* : to dress, to clothe — **ataviarse** *vr* : to dress up
atavío *nm* ATUENDO : dress, attire
ateísmo *nm* : atheism
atemorizar {21} *vt* : to frighten, to intimidate — **atemorizarse** *vr*
atemperar *vt* : to temper, to moderate
atención[1] *nf, pl* **-ciones 1** : attention **2 poner atención** or **prestar atención** : to pay attention **3 llamar la atención** : to attract attention **4 en atención a** : in view of
atención[2] *interj* **1** : attention! **2** : watch out!
atender {56} *vt* **1** : to help, to wait on **2** : to look after, to take care of **3** : to heed, to listen to — *vi* : to pay attention
atenerse {80} *vr* : to abide ⟨tendrás que atenerte a las reglas : you will have to abide by the rules⟩
atentado *nm* : attack, assault
atentamente *adv* **1** : attentively, carefully **2** (*used in correspondence*) : sincerely, sincerely yours
atentar {55} *vi* ~ **contra** : to make an attempt on, to threaten ⟨atentaron contra su vida : they made an attempt on his life⟩
atento, -ta *adj* **1** : attentive, mindful **2** CORTÉS : courteous
atenuación *nf, pl* **-ciones 1** : lessening **2** : understatement
atenuante[1] *adj* : extenuating, mitigating
atenuante[2] *nmf* : extenuating circumstance, excuse
atenuar {3} *vt* **1** MITIGAR : to extenuate, to mitigate **2** : to dim (light), to tone down (colors) **3** : to minimize, to lessen
ateo[1], **atea** *adj* : atheistic
ateo[2], **atea** *n* : atheist
aterciopelado, -da *adj* : velvety, downy
aterido, -da *adj* : freezing, frozen

aterrador, -dora *adj* : terrifying
aterrar {55} *vt* : to terrify, to frighten
aterrizaje *nm* : landing (of a plane)
aterrizar {21} *vt* : to land, to touch down
aterrorizar {21} *vt* **1** : to terrify **2** : to terrorize — **aterrorizarse** *vr* : to be terrified
atesorar *vt* : to hoard, to amass
atestado, -da *adj* : crowded, packed
atestar {55} *vt* **1** ATIBORRAR : to crowd, to pack **2** : to witness, to testify to — *vi* : to testify
atestiguar {10} *vt* : to testify to, to bear witness to — *vi* DECLARAR : to testify
atiborrar *vt* : to pack, to crowd — **atiborrarse** *vr* : to stuff oneself
ático *nm* **1** : penthouse **2** BUHARDILLA, DESVÁN : attic
atigrado, -da *adj* : tabby (of cats), striped (of fur)
atildado, -da *adj* : smart, neat, dapper
atildar *vt* **1** : to put a tilde over **2** : to clean up, to smarten up — **atildarse** *vr* : to get spruced up
atinar *vi* ACERTAR : to be accurate, to be on target
atingencia *nf* : bearing, relevance
atípico, -ca *adj* : atypical
atiplado, -da *adj* : shrill, high-pitched
atirantar *vt* : to make taut, to tighten
atisbar *vt* **1** : to spy on, to watch **2** : to catch a glimpse of, to make out
atisbo *nm* : glimpse, sign, hint
atizador *nm* : poker (for a fire)
atizar {21} *vt* **1** : to poke, to stir, to stoke (a fire) **2** : to stir up, to rouse **3** *fam* : to give, to land (a blow)
atlántico, -ca *adj* : Atlantic
atlas *nm* : atlas
atleta *nmf* : athlete
atlético, -ca *adj* : athletic
atletismo *nm* : athletics
atmósfera *nf* : atmosphere
atmosférico, -ca *adj* : atmospheric
atole *nm Mex* **1** : thick hot beverage prepared with cornmeal **2 darle atole con el dedo a alguien** : to string someone along
atolladero *nm* : predicament, fix
atollarse *vr* : to get stuck, to get bogged down
atolón *nm, pl* **-lones** : atoll
atolondrado, -da *adj* **1** ATURDIDO : bewildered, dazed **2** DESPISTADO : scatterbrained, absentminded
atómico, -ca *adj* : atomic
atomizador *nm* : atomizer
atomizar {21} *vt* FRAGMENTAR : to fragment, to break into bits
átomo *nm* : atom
atónito, -ta *adj* : astonished, amazed
atontar *vt* **1** : to stupefy **2** : to bewilder, to confuse
atorar *vt* ATASCAR : to block, to clog — **atorarse** *vr* **1** ATASCARSE : to get stuck **2** ATRAGANTARSE : to choke
atormentador, -dora *n* : tormentor
atormentar *vt* : to torment, to torture — **atormentarse** *vr* : to torment oneself, to agonize
atornillar *vt* : to screw (in, on, down)

atorrante *nmf Arg* : bum, loafer
atosigar {52} *vt* : to harass, to annoy
atracadero *nm* : dock, pier
atracador, -dora *n* : robber, mugger
atracar {72} *vt* : to dock, to land — *vi* : to hold up, to rob, to mug — **atracarse** *vr fam* ~ **de** : to gorge oneself with
atracción *nf, pl* **-ciones** : attraction
atraco *nm* : holdup, robbery
atracón *nm, pl* **-cones** *fam* **darse un atracón (de)** : to pig out (on)
atractivo¹, -va *adj* : attractive — **atractivamente** *adv*
atractivo² *nm* : attraction, appeal, charm
atraer {81} *vt* : to attract — **atraerse** *vr* 1 : to attract (each other) 2 **GANARSE** : to gain, to win
atragantarse *vr* : to choke (on food)
atrancar {72} *vt* : to block, to bar — **atrancarse** *vr*
atrapada *nf* : catch
atrapar *vt* : to trap, to capture
atrás *adv* 1 **DETRÁS** : back, behind ⟨la parte de atrás : the back/rear part⟩ ⟨dar un paso atrás : to take a step back⟩ 2 **ANTES** : ago ⟨mucho tiempo atrás : long ago⟩ 3 ~ **de** : in back of, behind 4 **desde** ~ : from behind, from the rear 5 **hacia/para** ~ : backwards, toward the rear 6 **dejar atrás** : to leave (the past, etc.) behind 7 **quedarse atrás** : to fall behind, to get left behind
atrasado, -da *adj* 1 : late, overdue 2 : backward 3 : old-fashioned 4 : slow (of a clock or watch)
atrasar *vt* : to delay, to put off — *vi* : to lose time — **atrasarse** *vr* : to fall behind
atraso *nm* 1 **RETRASO** : lateness, delay ⟨llegó con 20 minutos de atraso : he was 20 minutes late⟩ 2 : backwardness 3 **atrasos** *nmpl* : arrears
atravesar {55} *vt* 1 **CRUZAR** : to cross, to go across 2 : to pierce 3 : to lay across 4 : to go through (a situation or crisis) — **atravesarse** *vr* 1 : to be in the way ⟨se me atravesó : it blocked my path⟩ 2 : to interfere, to meddle
atrayente *adj* : attractive
atreverse *vr* 1 : to dare 2 : to be insolent
atrevido, -da *adj* 1 : bold, daring 2 : insolent
atrevimiento *nm* 1 : daring, boldness 2 : insolence
atribución *nf, pl* **-ciones** : attribution
atribuible *adj* **IMPUTABLE** : attributable, ascribable
atribuir {41} *vt* 1 : to attribute, to ascribe 2 : to grant, to confer — **atribuirse** *vr* : to take credit for
atribular *vt* : to afflict, to trouble — **atribularse** *vr*
atributo *nm* : attribute
atril *nm* : lectern, stand
atrincherar *vt* : to entrench — **atrincherarse** *vr* 1 : to dig in, to entrench oneself 2 ~ **en** : to hide behind
atrio *nm* 1 : atrium 2 : portico
atrocidad *nf* : atrocity
atrofia *nf* : atrophy

atrofiar *v* : to atrophy
atronador, -dora *adj* : thunderous, deafening
atropellado, -da *adj* 1 : rash, hasty 2 : brusque, abrupt — **atropelladamente** *adv*
atropellamiento → **atropello**
atropellar *vt* 1 : to knock down, to run over 2 : to violate, to abuse — **atropellarse** *vr* : to rush through (a task), to trip over one's words
atropello *nm* : abuse, violation, outrage
atroz *adj, pl* **atroces** : atrocious, appalling — **atrozmente** *adv*
atuendo *nm* **ATAVÍO** : attire, costume
atufar *vt* : to vex, to irritate — **atufarse** *vr* 1 : to get angry 2 : to smell bad, to stink
atún *nm, pl* **atunes** : tuna fish, tuna
aturdimiento *nm* : bewilderment, confusion
aturdir *vt* 1 : to stun, to shock 2 : to bewilder, to confuse, to stupefy — **aturdido, -da** *adj*
atuvo, etc. → **atenerse**
audacia *nf* **OSADÍA** : boldness, audacity
audaz *adj, pl* **audaces** : bold, audacious, daring — **audazmente** *adv*
audible *adj* : audible
audición *nf, pl* **-ciones** 1 : hearing 2 : audition
audiencia *nf* : audience
audífono *nm* 1 : hearing aid 2 **audífonos** *nmpl* : headphones, earphones
audio *nm* : audio
audiolibro *nm* : audiobook
audiovisual *adj* : audiovisual
auditar *vt* : to audit
auditivo, -va *adj* : auditory, hearing, aural ⟨aparato auditivo : hearing aid⟩
auditor, -tora *n* : auditor
auditoría *nf* : audit
auditorio *nm* 1 : auditorium 2 : audience
auge *nm* 1 : peak, height 2 : boom, upturn
augur *nm* : augur
augurar *vt* : to predict, to foretell
augurio *nm* **AGÜERO, PRESAGIO** : augury, omen
augusto, -ta *adj* : august
aula *nf* : classroom
aullar {8} *vt* : to howl, to wail
aullido *nm* : howl, wail
aumentar *vt* **ACRECENTAR** : to increase, to raise — *vi* : to rise, to increase, to grow
aumento *nm* **INCREMENTO** : increase, rise
aun *adv* 1 : even ⟨ni aun en coche llegaría a tiempo : I wouldn't arrive on time even if I drove⟩ 2 **aun así** : even so 3 **aun más** : even more
aún *adv* **TODAVÍA** : still, yet ⟨aún falta mucho por hacer : there's still a lot left to do⟩ ⟨aún no lo sabe : she doesn't know yet⟩
aunar {8} *vt* : to join, to combine — **aunarse** *vr* : to unite
aunque *conj* 1 : though, although, even if, even though 2 **aunque sea** : at least
aura *nf* 1 : aura 2 : turkey buzzard

áureo, -rea adj : golden
aureola nf **1** : halo **2** : aura (of power, fame, etc.)
aurícula nf : auricle
auricular nm **1** : telephone receiver **2 auriculares** nmpl : headphones, earphones **3 auriculares de tapón** : earbuds
aurora nf **1** : dawn **2 aurora boreal** : aurora borealis
ausencia nf : absence
ausentarse vr **1** : to leave, to go away **2 ~ de** : to stay away from
ausente[1] adj : absent, missing
ausente[2] nmf **1** : absentee **2** : missing person
auspiciar vt **1** PATROCINAR : to sponsor **2** FOMENTAR : to foster, to promote
auspicios nmpl : sponsorship, auspices
austeridad nf : austerity
austero, -ra adj : austere
austral[1] adj : southern
austral[2] nm : former monetary unit of Argentina
australiano, -na adj & n : Australian
austriaco or **austríaco, -ca** adj & n : Austrian
autenticar {72} vt : to authenticate — **autenticación** nf
autenticidad nf : authenticity
auténtico, -ca adj : authentic — **auténticamente** adv
autentificar {72} vt : to authenticate — **autentificación** nf
autismo nm : autism
autista adj : autistic
auto nm : auto, car
auto- pref : self-
autoabastecerse {18} vr : to be self-sufficient
autoayuda nf : self-help
autobiografía nf : autobiography
autobiográfico, -ca adj : autobiographical
autobomba nf Arg, Spain, Uru : fire truck
auto bomba nm Chile : car bomb
autobús nm, pl **-buses** : bus
autocar Spain → **autobús**
autocine nm : drive-in
autocompasión nf : self-pity
autocontrol nm : self-control
autocorrector nm : autocorrect
autocracia nf : autocracy
autócrata nmf : autocrat
autocrático, -ca adj : autocratic
autóctono, -na adj : indigenous, native ⟨arte autóctono : indigenous art⟩
autodefensa nf : self-defense
autodenominarse vr : to call oneself
autodestrucción nf : self-destruction — **autodestructivo, -va** adj
autodeterminación nf : self-determination
autodidacta[1] adj : self-taught
autodidacta[2] nmf : self-taught person
autodidacto[1], **-ta** adj → **autodidacta**[1]
autodidacto[2], **-ta** n → **autodidacta**[2]
autodisciplina nf : self-discipline
autoedición nf : desktop publishing
autoescuela nf Spain : driving school
autoestima nf : self-esteem

autofoto nf : selfie
autogobierno nm : self-government
autografiar vt : to autograph
autógrafo nm : autograph
autoinfligido, -da adj : self-inflicted
automación → **automatización**
autómata nm : automaton
automático, -ca adj : automatic — **automáticamente** adv
automatización nf : automation
automatizar {21} vt : to automate
**aut
mercado** nm Ven : supermarket
automotor, -tora adj **1** : self-propelled **2** : automotive, car
automotriz[1] adj, pl **-trices** : automotive, car
automotriz[2] nf, pl **-trices** : automaker
automóvil nm : automobile
automovilista nmf : motorist
automovilístico, -ca adj : automobile, car ⟨accidente automovilístico : automobile accident⟩
autonombrado, -da adj : self-appointed
autonomía nf : autonomy
autonómico, -ca adj : autonomous
autónomo, -ma adj : autonomous — **autónomamente** adv
autopista nf : expressway, highway
autoproclamado, -da adj : self-proclaimed, self-appointed
autopropulsado, -da adj : self-propelled
autopsia nf : autopsy
autor, -tora n **1** : author **2** : perpetrator
autoría nf : authorship
autoridad nf : authority
autoritario, -ria adj : authoritarian
autorización nf, pl **-ciones** : authorization
autorizado, -da adj **1** : authorized **2** : authoritative
autorizar {21} vt : to authorize, to approve
autorretrato nm : self-portrait
autoservicio nm **1** : self-service restaurant **2** SUPERMERCADO : supermarket
autostop nm **1** : hitchhiking **2 hacer autostop** : to hitchhike
autostopista nmf : hitchhiker
autosuficiencia nf : self-sufficiency — **autosuficiente** adj
autovía nf : divided highway
auxiliar[1] vt : to aid, to assist
auxiliar[2] adj : assistant, auxiliary
auxiliar[3] nmf **1** : assistant, helper **2 auxiliar de vuelo** : flight attendant
auxilio nm **1** : aid, assistance **2 primeros auxilios** : first aid
aval nm : guarantee, endorsement
avalancha nf ALUD : avalanche
avalar vt : to guarantee, to endorse
avaluar {3} vt : to evaluate, to appraise
avalúo nm : appraisal, evaluation
avance nm ADELANTO : advance
avanzado, -da adj **1** : advanced **2** : progressive
avanzar {21} vi : to advance, to move forward, to make progress — vt **1** : to advance, to move forward **2** : to advance, to put forward
avaricia nf CODICIA : greed, avarice
avaricioso, -sa adj : avaricious, greedy

avaro¹, -ra *adj* : miserly, greedy
avaro², -ra *n* : miser
avasallador, -dora *adj* : overwhelming
avasallamiento *nm* : domination
avasallar *vt* : to overpower, to subjugate
avatar *nm* **1** : avatar **2 avatares** *nmpl* : vagaries, vicissitudes
ave *nf* **1** : bird **2 aves de corral** : poultry **3 ave rapaz** *or* **ave de presa** : bird of prey
avecinarse *vr* : to approach, to come near
avecindarse *vr* : to settle, to take up residence
avellana *nf* : hazelnut, filbert
avellano *nm* : hazel
avena *nf* **1** : oat, oats *pl* **2** : oatmeal
avenencia *nf* : agreement, pact
avenida *nf* : avenue
avenir {87} *vt* : to reconcile, to harmonize — **avenirse** *vr* **1** : to agree, to come to terms **2** : to get along
aventajado, -da *adj* : outstanding
aventajar *vt* **1** : to be ahead of, to lead **2** : to surpass, to outdo
aventar {55} *vt* **1** : to fan **2** : to winnow **3** *Col, Mex* : to throw, to toss — **aventarse** *vr* *Col, Mex* : to hurl oneself **2** *Mex fam* : to dare, to take a chance
aventón *nm*, *pl* **-tones** *Col, Mex fam* : ride, lift
aventura *nf* **1** : adventure **2** RIESGO : venture, risk **3** : love affair
aventurado, -da *adj* : hazardous, risky
aventurar *vt* : to venture, to risk — **aventurarse** *vr* : to take a risk
aventurero¹, -ra *adj* : adventurous
aventurero², -ra *n* : adventurer
avergonzado, -da *adj* **1** : ashamed **2** : embarrassed
avergonzar {9} *vt* APENAR : to shame, to embarrass — **avergonzarse** *vr* APENARSE : to be ashamed, to be embarrassed
avería *nf* **1** : damage **2** : breakdown, malfunction
averiado, -da *adj* **1** : damaged, faulty **2** : broken down
averiar {85} *vt* : to damage — **averiarse** *vr* : to break down
averiguación *nf*, *pl* **-ciones** : investigation, inquiry
averiguar {10} *vt* **1** : to find out, to ascertain **2** : to investigate
aversión *nf*, *pl* **-siones** : aversion, dislike
avestruz *nm*, *pl* **-truces** : ostrich
avezado, -da *adj* : seasoned, experienced
aviación *nf*, *pl* **-ciones** : aviation
aviador, -dora *n* : aviator, flyer
aviar {85} *vt* **1** : to prepare, to make ready **2** : to tidy up **3** : to equip, to supply
avícola *adj* : poultry
avicultor, -tora *n* : poultry farmer
avicultura *nf* : poultry farming
avidez *nf*, *pl* **-deces** : eagerness
ávido, -da *adj* : eager, avid — **ávidamente** *adv*
avieso, -sa *adj* **1** : twisted, distorted **2** : wicked, depraved
avinagrado, -da *adj* : vinegary, sour
avío *nm* **1** : preparation, provision **2** : loan (for agriculture or mining) **3** **avíos** *nmpl* : gear, equipment

avión *nm*, *pl* **aviones** : airplane
avionazo *nm Mex* : plane crash
avioneta *nf* : light airplane
avisar *vt* **1** : to notify, to inform **2** : to advise, to warn
aviso *nm* **1** : notice **2** : advertisement, ad **3** ADVERTENCIA : warning **4 estar sobre aviso** : to be on the alert
avispa *nf* : wasp
avispado, -da *adj fam* : clever, sharp
avispero *nm* : wasps' nest
avispón *nm*, *pl* **-pones** : hornet
avistamiento *nm* : sighting
avistar *vt* : to sight, to catch sight of
avituallar *vt* : to supply with food, to provision
avivar *vt* **1** : to enliven, to brighten **2** : to strengthen, to intensify
avizorar *vt* **1** ACECHAR : to spy on, to watch **2** : to observe, to perceive ⟨se avizoran dificultades : difficulties are expected⟩
axila *nf* : armpit
axioma *nm* : axiom
axiomático, -ca *adj* : axiomatic
ay *interj* **1** : oh! **2** : ouch!, ow!
ayer¹ *adv* : yesterday ⟨ayer por/en la mañana : yesterday morning⟩ ⟨antes de ayer : the day before yesterday⟩
ayer² *nm* ANTAÑO : yesteryear, days gone by
ayote *nm CA, Mex* : squash, pumpkin
ayuda *nf* **1** : help, assistance **2 ayuda de cámara** : valet
ayudante *nmf* : helper, assistant
ayudar *vt* : to help, to assist ⟨ayúdame a levantar esta caja : help me lift this box⟩ ⟨¿en qué puedo ayudarle? : how can I help you?⟩ ⟨¿te ayudo con tus cosas? : can I help you with your things?⟩ — **ayudarse** *vr* ~ **de** : to make use of
ayunar *vi* : to fast
ayunas *nfpl* **en ~** : fasting ⟨este medicamento ha de tomarse en ayunas : this medication should be taken on an empty stomach⟩
ayuno *nm* : fast
ayuntamiento *nm* **1** : town hall, city hall **2** : town or city council
azabache *nm* : jet ⟨negro azabache : jet black⟩
azada *nf* : hoe
azafata *nf* **1** : stewardess *f* **2** : hostess *f* (on a TV show)
azafrán *nm*, *pl* **-franes** **1** : saffron **2** : crocus
azahar *nm* : orange blossom
azalea *nf* : azalea
azar *nm* **1** : chance ⟨juegos de azar : games of chance⟩ **2** : accident, misfortune **3 al azar** : at random, randomly
azaroso, -sa *adj* **1** : perilous, hazardous **2** : turbulent, eventful
azimut *nm* : azimuth
azogue *nm* : mercury
azorado, -da *adj* **1** : embarrassed, flustered **2** : amazed, stunned
azorar *vt* **1** : to alarm, to startle **2** : to fluster, to embarrass — **azorarse** *vr* : to get embarrassed

azotar *vt* **1** : to whip, to flog **2** : to lash, to batter **3** : to devastate, to afflict

azote *nm* **1** LÁTIGO : whip, lash **2** *fam* : spanking, licking **3** : calamity, scourge

azotea *nf* : flat roof, terraced roof

azteca *adj & nmf* : Aztec

azúcar *nmf* : sugar — **azucarar** *vt*

azucarado, -da *adj* : sweetened, sugary

azucarera *nf* : sugar bowl

azucarero, -ra *adj* : sugar ⟨industria azucarera : sugar industry⟩

azucena *nf* : white lily

azuela *nf* : adze

azufre *nm* : sulfur — **azufroso, -sa** *adj*

azul *adj & nm* : blue

azulado, -da *adj* : bluish

azulejo *nm* : ceramic tile, floor tile

azuloso, -sa *adj* : bluish

azulete *nm* : bluing

azur¹ *adj* CELESTE : azure

azur² *n* CELESTE : azure, sky blue

azuzar {21} *vt* : to incite, to egg on

B

b *nf* : second letter of the Spanish alphabet

baba *nf* **1** : spittle, saliva **2** : dribble, drool (of a baby) **3** : slime, ooze

babear *vi* **1** : to drool, to slobber **2** : to ooze

babero *nm* : bib

babor *nm* : port, port side ⟨a babor : to port⟩

babosa *nf* : slug (mollusk)

babosada *nf CA, Mex* : silly act or remark

baboso, -sa *adj* **1** : drooling, slobbering **2** : slimy **3** *CA, Mex fam* : silly, dumb

babucha *nf* : slipper

babuino *nm* : baboon

baca *nf* : luggage/roof rack

bacalao *nm* : cod (fish)

bacán¹ *adj, pl* **bacanes** *fam* **1** *Arg, Uru* : posh, classy, rich **2** *Chile, Ecua, Peru* : cool, neat, great

bacán² *n, pl* **bacanes** *Arg, Col, Uru* : rich person

bacano, -na *adj Col fam* : cool, great

bache *nm* **1** : pothole **2** : air pocket **3** : bad period, rough time, slump

bachiller *nmf* : high school graduate

bachillerato *nm* : high school diploma

bacinica *nf* : chamber pot, potty (for children)

bacon *nm Spain* : bacon

bacteria *nf* : bacterium

bacteriano, -na *adj* : bacterial

báculo *nm* : staff, stick

badajo *nm* : clapper (of a bell)

badén *nm, pl* **badenes** **1** VADO : ford **2** : dip, ditch (in a road) **3** : speed bump

bádminton *nm* : badminton

bafle *or* **baffle** *nm* : speaker, loudspeaker

bagaje *nm* **1** → **equipaje** **2** : background, knowledge ⟨bagaje cultural : cultural heritage⟩

bagre *nm* : catfish

baguette *nf* : baguette

bah *interj* (*expressing disapproval*) : huh!

bahía *nf* : bay

bailar *vt* : to dance — *vi* **1** : to dance **2** : to spin **3** : to be loose, to be too big

bailarín¹, -rina *adj, mpl* **-rines** **1** : dancing **2** : fond of dancing

bailarín², -rina *n, mpl* **-rines** **1** : dancer **2** : ballet dancer, ballerina *f* ⟨prima bailarina : prima ballerina⟩

baile *nm* **1** : dance **2** : dance party, ball **3** **llevarse al baile a** *Mex fam* : to take advantage of

baja *nf* **1** DESCENSO : fall, drop **2** : slump, recession **3** : loss, casualty **4** **dar de baja** : to discharge, to dismiss **5** **darse de baja** : to withdraw, to drop out, to resign

bajada *nf* **1** : descent **2** : dip, slope **3** : decrease, drop **4** **bajada de bandera** *Arg, Spain* : minimum fare

bajar *vt* **1** : to lower (a blind, zipper, etc.), to let down (a hem) **2** : to bring/take/carry down, to get/lift down **3** REDUCIR : to lower (prices, a fever, one's voice, etc.) **4** INCLINAR : to lower (the eyes, etc.), to bow (the head) **5** : to go/come down (stairs) **6** DESCARGAR : to download **7** **bajar de categoría** : to downgrade — *vi* **1** DISMINUIR : to drop, to fall, to go down **2** : to come/go down ⟨bajar por la escalera : to come/go down the stairs⟩ **3** : to ebb (of tides) — **bajarse** *vr* ~ **de** : to get off (a train, etc.), to get out of (a car)

bajeza *nf* **1** : low or despicable act **2** : baseness

bajío *nm* **1** : lowland **2** : shoal, sandbank, shallows

bajista *nmf* : bass player, bassist

bajo¹ *adv* **1** : low **2** : softly, quietly

bajo², -ja *adj* **1** : low **2** : short (of stature) **3** : soft, faint, low ⟨en voz baja : in a low voice⟩ **4** : low, deep (in tone) **5** : lower ⟨el bajo Amazonas : the lower Amazon⟩ ⟨la planta baja : the ground/first floor⟩ **6** : lowered ⟨con la mirada baja : with lowered eyes⟩ **7** : base, vile **8 los bajos fondos** : the underworld

bajo³ *nm* **1** : bass, double bass **2** : bass, bass guitar **3** : first floor, ground floor **4** : hemline

bajo⁴ *prep* : under, beneath, below

bajón *nm, pl* **bajones** : sharp drop, slump

bajorrelieve *nm* : bas-relief

bala *nf* **1** : bullet ⟨a prueba de balas : bulletproof⟩ **2** : bale **3 lanzamiento de bala** : shot put

balacear → **balear**

balacera *nf* → **baleo**

balada *nf* : ballad

balance *nm* **1** : balance **2** : balance sheet **3** : outcome, result **4 hacer balance de** : to take stock of

balancear *vt* **1** : to balance **2** : to swing (one's arms, etc.) **3** : to rock (a boat) — **balancearse** *vr* OSCILAR : to swing, to sway, to rock

balanceo *nm* : swaying, rocking, swinging

balancín *nm, pl* **-cines 1** : rocking chair **2** SUBIBAJA : seesaw

balandra *nf* : sloop

balanza *nf* : scales *pl*, balance ⟨balanza comercial : balance of trade⟩ ⟨balanza de pagos : balance of payments⟩

balar *vi* : to bleat

balaustrada *nf* : balustrade

balazo *nm* **1** TIRO : shot, gunshot **2** : bullet wound

balboa *nf* : balboa (monetary unit of Panama)

balbucear *vi* **1** : to mutter, to stammer **2** : to babble

balbuceo *nm* **1** : mumbling, stammering **2** : babbling

balbucir → **balbucear**

balcánico, -ca *adj* : Balkan

balcón *nm, pl* **balcones** : balcony

balde *nm* **1** CUBO : bucket, pail **2 en ∼** : in vain, to no avail

baldío¹, -día *adj* **1** : fallow **2** : useless, vain

baldío² *nm* **1** : wasteland **2** *Mex* : vacant lot

baldosa *nf* LOSETA : floor tile, paving tile/stone, paving block

balear *vt* : to shoot, to shoot at

baleo *nm* : shooting, shoot-out

balero *nm* **1** *Mex* : ball bearing **2** *Mex, PRi* : cup-and-ball toy

balido *nm* : bleat

balín *nm, pl* **balines** : pellet

balística *nf* : ballistics

balístico, -ca *adj* : ballistic

baliza *nf* **1** : buoy **2** : beacon (for aircraft)

ballena *nf* : whale

ballenero¹, -ra *adj* : whaling

ballenero², -ra *n* : whaler

ballenero³ *nm* : whaleboat, whaler

ballesta *nf* **1** : crossbow **2** : spring (of an automobile)

ballet [ba'le] *nm* : ballet

balneario *nm* : spa, bathing resort

balompié *nm* FUTBOL : soccer

balón *nm, pl* **balones 1** : ball **2** TANQUE : tank

baloncelista *PRi* → **basquetbolista**

baloncesto *nm* BASQUETBOL : basketball

balonmano *nm* : handball

balsa *nf* **1** : raft **2** : balsa **3** : pond, pool

balsámico, -ca *adj* : soothing

bálsamo *nm* : balsam, balm

balsero, -ra *n* : boat person, refugee

báltico, -ca *adj* : Baltic

baluarte *nm* : bulwark, bastion

bambalina *nf* **tras/entre bambalinas** : behind the scenes

bambolear *vi* **1** : to sway, to swing **2** : to wobble — **bambolearse** *vr*

bamboleo *nm* **1** : swaying, swinging **2** : wobbling

bambú *nm, pl* **bambúes** *or* **bambús** : bamboo

banal *adj* : banal — **banalidad** *nf*

banana *nf* : banana

bananero¹, -ra *adj* : banana

bananero² *nm* : banana tree

banano *nm* **1** : banana tree **2** *CA, Col* : banana

banca *nf* **1** : banking, banks **2** : bank (in games) **3** BANCO : bench **4** BANQUILLO : bench (in sports)

bancada *nf* **1** : group, faction **2** : workbench

bancal *nm* **1** : terrace (in agriculture) **2** : plot (of land)

bancario, -ria *adj* : bank, banking

bancarrota *nf* QUIEBRA : bankruptcy ⟨en bancarrota : bankrupt⟩

banco *nm* **1** : bank ⟨banco central : central bank⟩ ⟨banco de datos : data bank⟩ ⟨banco de sangre : blood bank⟩ **2** BARRA : bank, bar ⟨banco de arena : sandbank⟩ **3** BANCA : stool, bench **4** : pew **5** : school (of fish)

banda *nf* **1** : band, strip **2** : band (on arm), sash **3** *Mex* : belt ⟨banda transportadora : conveyor belt⟩ **4** : (frequency) band **5** : band (of musicians) **6** : gang (of persons), flock (of birds) **7** : side (of a ship) **8** : touchline (in soccer) **9 banda ancha** : broadband **10 banda de rodadura** : tread (of a tire) **11 banda sonora** *or* **banda de sonido** : sound track

bandada *nf* : flock (of birds), school (of fish)

bandazo *nm* **dar bandazos** : to move from side to side

bandearse *vr* : to look after oneself, to cope

bandeja *nf* **1** : tray, platter **2 bandeja de entrada** : in-box **3 bandeja de salida** : out-box

bandera *nf* : flag, banner

banderazo *nm* : starting signal (in sports)

banderilla *nf* : dart (in bullfighting)

banderín *nm, pl* **-rines** : pennant, small flag

bandido, -da *n* BANDOLERO : bandit, outlaw

bando *nm* **1** FACCIÓN : faction, side **2** EDICTO : proclamation

bandolero, -ra *n* BANDIDO : bandit, outlaw

banjo *nm* : banjo

banquero, -ra *n* : banker

banqueta *nf* **1** : footstool, stool, bench **2** *Mex* : sidewalk

banquete *nm* : banquet ⟨banquete de bodas : wedding reception⟩

banquetear *v* : to feast

banquillo *nm* **1** BANCA : bench (in sports) **2** : dock, defendant's seat

banquina *nf* *Arg, Uru* : shoulder (of a road)

bañadera *Arg, Uru* → **bañera**

bañador *nm* *Spain* : swimsuit, bathing suit

bañar *vt* **1** : to bathe, to wash **2** : to immerse, to dip **3** : to coat, to cover

⟨bañado en lágrimas : bathed in tears⟩
— **bañarse** *vr* **1** : to take a bath, to bathe **2** : to go swimming
bañera *nf* **1** TINA : bathtub **2 bañera de hidromasaje** : hot tub, whirlpool, Jacuzzi *trademark*
bañero, -ra *n Arg, Uru* : lifeguard
bañista *nmf* : bather
baño *nm* **1** : bath ⟨darse un baño : to take a bath⟩ ⟨baño de espuma/burbujas : bubble bath⟩ **2** : swim, dip **3** : bathroom ⟨baños públicos : public restrooms⟩ **4** BAÑERA : bathtub **5** GLASEADO : icing, frosting **6 baño de sangre** : bloodbath
baptista → **bautista**
baqueta *nf* **1** : ramrod **2 baquetas** *nfpl* : drumsticks
bar *nm* : bar
baraja *nf* : deck of cards
barajar *vt* **1** : to shuffle (cards) **2** : to consider
baranda *nf* → **barandal 1**
barandal *nm* **1** : rail, railing **2** : banister, handrail
barandilla *nf Spain* → **barandal**
barata *nf* **1** *Mex* : sale, bargain **2** *Chile* : cockroach
baratija *nf* **1** : bauble, trinket
baratillo *nm* : rummage sale, flea market
barato[1] *adv* : cheap, cheaply ⟨te lo vendo barato : I'll sell it to you cheap⟩
barato[2]**, -ta** *adj* : cheap, inexpensive
barba *nf* **1** : beard, stubble **2** : chin
barbacoa *nf* **1** PARRILLA : barbecue **2** : barbecued meat
bárbaramente *adv* : barbarously
barbaridad *nf* **1** : barbarity, atrocity **2** BURRADA : stupid act or remark **3** MONTÓN : ton, load **4 ¡qué barbaridad!** : that's outrageous!
barbarie *nf* : savagery
bárbaro[1] *adv* **pasarlo bárbaro** *fam* : to have a great time
bárbaro[2]**, -ra** *adj* **1** : barbarian (in history) **2** CRUEL : cruel **3** GROSERO : rude, crass **4** *fam* : great, fantastic
bárbaro[3]**, -ra** *n* : barbarian
barbecho *nm* : fallow land ⟨dejar en barbecho : to leave fallow⟩
barbería *nf* : barbershop
barbero *nm* : barber
barbilla *nf* MENTÓN : chin
barbitúrico *nm* : barbiturate
barbudo[1]**, -da** *adj* : bearded
barbudo[2] *nm* : bearded man
barca *nf* : boat
barcaza *nf* : barge
barcia *nf* : chaff
barco *nm* **1** BARCA : boat ⟨viajar en barco : to travel by boat/ship⟩ ⟨barco de guerra/vapor/vela : warship/steamship/sailboat⟩ ⟨barco pesquero : fishing boat⟩ **2** BUQUE, NAVE : ship
barda *nf Mex* **1** MURO : wall **2** CERCO : fence
bardo *nm* : bard
baremo *nm* : scale
barítono *nm* : baritone
barman *nm* : bartender

barniz *nm, pl* **barnices** : varnish
barnizar {21} *vt* : to varnish
barómetro *nm* : barometer — **barométrico, -ca** *adj*
barón *nm, pl* **barones** : baron
baronesa *nf* : baroness
barquero, -ra *n* : boatman *m*, boatwoman *f*
barquillo *nm* **1** : wafer **2** CONO : ice-cream cone
barra *nf* **1** : bar (of metal), rod (for curtains) **2** : bar (of soap, etc.), block (of ice) **3** MOSTRADOR : bar, counter **4** : gang (of friends) **5** : slash (in punctuation) ⟨barra oblicua : forward slash⟩ ⟨barra invertida/inversa : backslash⟩ **6** BANCO : bar, bank ⟨barra de arena : sandbar⟩ **7 barra de herramientas** : toolbar **8 barra de labios** : lipstick
barra de pan *Mex, Spain* : baguette
barraca *nf* **1** CHOZA : shack **2** PUESTO, CASETA : booth, stall
barracuda *nf* : barracuda
barranca *nf* **1** : hillside, slope **2** → **barranco**
barranco *nm* : ravine, gorge
barredora *nf* : street sweeper (machine)
barrena *nf* **1** TALADRO : drill, auger, gimlet **2** : tailspin
barrenar *vt* : to drill
barrendero, -ra *n* : sweeper, street cleaner
barrer *vt* **1** : to sweep **2** : to sweep away **3** : to crush, to defeat — *vi* **1** : to sweep **2** : to make a clean sweep **3** ~ **con** : to sweep away **4** ~ **con** : to wipe out (an enemy), to crush (a sports opponent) — **barrerse** *vr* : to slide (in sports)
barrera *nf* OBSTÁCULO : barrier, obstacle ⟨barrera de sonido : sound barrier⟩ ⟨barrera comercial : trade barrier⟩
barreta *nf Arg, Mex* : crowbar
barriada *nf* **1** : district, quarter **2** : shantytown, slums *pl*
barrica *nf* BARRIL, TONEL : barrel, cask, keg
barricada *nf* : barricade
barrida *nf* **1** : sweep **2** : slide (in sports) **3** : clean sweep (in a competition)
barrido *nm* : sweeping
barriga *nf* : belly
barrigón, -gona *adj, mpl* **-gones** *fam* : potbellied
barril *nm* **1** BARRICA : barrel, keg **2 cerveza de barril** : draft beer
barrio *nm* **1** : neighborhood, district **2 barrios bajos** : slums *pl* **3 barrio de invasión** *Col* → **invasión 4 barrio de chabolas** *Spain* : shantytown, slums *pl*
barrizal *nm* : quagmire
barro *nm* **1** LODO : mud **2** ARCILLA : clay ⟨vajilla de barro : earthenware dishes⟩ **3** ESPINILLA, GRANO : pimple, blackhead
barroco, -ca *adj* : baroque — **barroco** *nm*
barroso, -sa *adj* ENLODADO : muddy
barrote *nm* : bar (on a window)
bártulos *nmpl* : things, belongings ⟨liar los bártulos : to pack one's things⟩
barullo *nm* **1** BULLA : racket, ruckus **2** CONFUSIÓN : mess, confusion
basa *nf* : base, pedestal

basalto *nm* : basalt
basar *vt* FUNDAR : to base — **basarse** *vr*
FUNDARSE **1** ~ **en** : to be based on **2**
~ **en** : to base one's position on
báscula *nf* BALANZA : balance, scales *pl*
base *nf* **1** : base, bottom **2** : base (in
baseball) **3** FUNDAMENTO : basis, foundation ⟨sentar las bases de : to lay the
foundation for⟩ **4** : base ⟨base naval/
aérea : naval/air base⟩ **5** REGLAS : rules
pl **6** *or* **base de maquillaje** : foundation
(makeup) **7 a base de** : based on, by
means of **8 base de datos** : database **9**
en base a : based on, on the basis of
básico, -ca *adj* FUNDAMENTAL : basic —
básicamente *adv*
basílica *nf* : basilica
basket *or* **básquet** → **basquetbol**
basquetbol *or* **básquetbol** *nm* BALON-
CESTO : basketball
basquetbolista *nmf* : basketball player
basset *nm* : basset hound
bastante[1] *adv* **1** : enough, sufficiently
⟨he trabajado bastante : I have worked
enough⟩ ⟨lo bastante alto (como) para
alcanzar : tall enough to reach⟩ **2**
: fairly, rather, quite ⟨llegaron bastante
temprano : they arrived quite early⟩ ⟨me
gustó bastante : I liked it a lot⟩
bastante[2] *adj* **1** : enough, sufficient ⟨¿hay
bastantes sillas? : are there enough
chairs?⟩ **2** : plenty of, a lot of ⟨había bastante gente : there were a lot of people⟩
bastante[3] *pron* : enough ⟨hemos visto
bastante : we have seen enough⟩ ⟨no hay
bastantes : there aren't enough⟩
bastar *vi* : to be enough, to suffice ⟨con
uno basta (y sobra) : one is (more than)
enough⟩ ⟨¡basta (ya)! : that's enough!⟩
— **bastarse** *vr* : to be able to manage on
one's own
bastardilla *nf* CURSIVA : italic type, italics *pl*
bastardo[1], **-da** *adj* **1** ILEGÍTIMO : bastard
2 VIL : base
bastardo[2], **-da** *n* : bastard *usu offensive*
bastidor *nm* **1** : framework, frame **2**
: wing (in theater) ⟨entre bastidores
: backstage, behind the scenes⟩
bastión *nf*, *pl* **bastiones** BALUARTE : bastion, bulwark
basto[1], **-ta** *adj* : coarse, rough
basto[2] *nm* : club (in the Spanish deck of
cards)
bastón *nm*, *pl* **bastones** **1** : cane, walking stick **2** : baton **3** *or* **bastón de esquí** : ski pole **4 bastón de mando**
: staff (of authority)
basura *nf* : garbage, trash ⟨tirar/echar/
botar algo a la basura : to throw something in the garbage⟩ ⟨sacar la basura
: to take out the garbage⟩
basural → **basurero 2**
basurero[1], **-ra** *n* : garbage collector
basurero[2] *nm*. **1** *Mex* : garbage can **2**
VERTEDERO, BASURAL : garbage dump
bata *nf* **1** : bathrobe, housecoat **2**
: smock, coveralls, lab coat
batacazo *nm* **1** : wallop **2 dar el/un batacazo** *Arg, Uru* : to pull off an unexpected win

batalla *nf* **1** : battle ⟨batalla campal
: pitched battle⟩ **2** : fight, struggle **3 de**
~ : ordinary, everyday
batallar *vi* LIDIAR, LUCHAR : to battle, to
fight
batallón *nm*, *pl* **-llones** : battalion
batata *nf* : yam, sweet potato
batazo *nm* HIT : hit (in baseball)
bate *nm* : baseball bat
batea *nf* **1** : tray, pan **2** : punt (boat)
bateador, -dora *n* : batter, hitter
batear *vi* : to bat — *vt* : to hit
bateo *nm* : batting (in baseball)
batería *nf* **1** PILA : battery **2** : drum kit,
drums *pl* **3 batería de cocina** : kitchen
utensils *pl*
baterista *nmf* : drummer
batida *nf* REDADA, ALLANAMIENTO : raid
batido *nm* LICUADO : milk shake
batidor *nm* : eggbeater, whisk, mixer
batidora *nf* : (electric) mixer
batir *vt* **1** GOLPEAR : to beat, to hit **2**
VENCER : to defeat **3** : to whisk, to beat
(eggs), to whip (cream), to cream (butter
and sugar) **4** : to flap, to beat (wings) **5**
RASTREAR : to comb, to search **6** : to
break (a record) **7 batir palmas** : to
clap — **batirse** *vr* : to fight
batuta *nf* **1** : baton **2 llevar la batuta**
: to be in charge
baúl *nm* **1** : trunk, chest **2** (*in various
countries*) : trunk (of a car)
bautismal *adj* : baptismal
bautismo *nm* : baptism, christening
bautista *adj & nmf* : Baptist
bautizar {21} *vt* : to baptize, to christen
bautizo → **bautismo**
bávaro, -ra *adj & n* : Bavarian
baya *nf* : berry
bayeta *nf* : cleaning cloth
bayoneta *nf* : bayonet
baza *nf* : trick (in card games)
bazar *nm* : bazaar
bazo *nm* : spleen
bazofia *nf* **1** : table scraps *pl* **2** : slop,
swill **3** : rubbish
bazuca *nf* : bazooka
be *or* **be larga** *or* **be grande** *nf* : (letter) b
beagle *nm* : beagle
beatífico, -ca *adj* : beatific
beato, -ta *adj* **1** : blessed **2** : devout **3**
: overly devout
bebe, -ba *n Arg, Uru* : baby
bebé *nm* : baby
bebedero *nm* **1** ABREVADERO : watering
trough **2** *Mex* : drinking fountain
bebedor, -dora *n* : (heavy) drinker
beber *v* TOMAR : to drink
bebida *nf* : drink, beverage
bebido, -da *adj* BORRACHO : drunk
beca *nf* : grant, scholarship
becado, -da *n* : grant recipient, scholarship holder
becar {72} *vt* : to award a grant or scholarship to
becario, -ria → **becado**
becerro, -rra *n* : calf
bedel *nmf* : janitor
begonia *nf* : begonia
beige *adj & nm* : beige

beisbol or **béisbol** nm : baseball
beisbolista nmf : baseball player
beldad nf BELLEZA, HERMOSURA : beauty
belén nf, pl **belenes** NACIMIENTO : Nativity scene
belga adj & nmf : Belgian
belicista[1] adj : militaristic
belicista[2] nmf : warmonger
bélico, -ca adj GUERRERO : war, fighting, military ⟨conflicto bélico : armed conflict⟩
belicoso, -sa adj 1 : warlike, martial 2 : aggressive, belligerent
beligerancia nf : belligerence
beligerante adj & nmf : belligerent
bellaco[1], **-ca** adj : sly, cunning
bellaco[2], **-ca** n : rogue, scoundrel
belleza nf BELDAD, HERMOSURA : beauty
bello, -lla adj 1 HERMOSO : beautiful 2 **bellas artes** : fine arts — **bellamente** adv
bellota nf : acorn
bemol nm : flat (in music) — **bemol** adj
bencina nf Chile GASOLINA : gas, gasoline
bencinera nf Chile : gas station
bendecir {11} vt 1 : to bless 2 **bendecir la mesa** : to say grace
bendición nf, pl **-ciones** : benediction, blessing
bendiga, bendijo etc. → **bendecir**
bendito[1], **-ta** adj 1 : blessed, holy 2 : fortunate
bendito[2], **-ta** n : simple person
benefactor[1], **-tora** adj : charitable
benefactor[2], **-tora** n : benefactor, benefactress f
beneficencia nf : charity
beneficiar vt : to benefit — **beneficiarse** vr : to benefit ⟨beneficiarse con/de : to benefit from⟩
beneficiario, -ria n 1 : beneficiary 2 : payee (of a check)
beneficio nm 1 GANANCIA : profit 2 : benefit 3 **en/a beneficio de** : in aid of, to benefit 4 **en beneficio de alguien** : in someone's interest
beneficioso, -sa adj : beneficial
benéfico, -ca adj : charitable
benemérito, -ta adj : meritorious, worthy
beneplácito nm : approval, consent
benevolencia nf BONDAD : benevolence, kindness
benevolente → **benévolo**
benévolo, -la adj BONDADOSO : benevolent, kind, good
bengala nf **luz de bengala** 1 : flare (signal) 2 : sparkler
benigno, -na adj : benign, mild
benjamín, -mina n, mpl **-mines** : youngest child
beodo, -da adj & n : drunk
berberecho nm : cockle
berenjena nf : eggplant
bergantín nm, pl **-tines** : brig (ship)
berlinés[1], **-nesa** adj : of or from Berlin
berlinés[2], **-nesa** n : person from Berlin
berma nf Chile, Col, Ecua, Peru : shoulder (of a road)
bermudas nfpl : Bermuda shorts
berrear vi 1 : to bellow, to low 2 : to bawl, to howl

berrido nm 1 : bellowing 2 : howl, scream
berrinche nm fam : tantrum ⟨hacer (un) berrinche : to throw a tantrum⟩
berro nm : watercress
besar vt : to kiss — **besarse** vr : to kiss (each other)
beso nm : kiss ⟨tirarle un beso a alguien : to blow someone a kiss⟩
bestia[1] adj 1 : ignorant, stupid 2 : boorish, rude
bestia[2] nf 1 : beast — 2 BRUTO : brute
bestia[3] nmf 1 IGNORANTE : ignoramus 2 : brute
bestial adj 1 : bestial, beastly 2 fam : huge, enormous ⟨hace un frío bestial : it's freezing cold⟩ 3 fam : great, fantastic
bestialidad nf 1 BRUTALIDAD : brutality 2 DISPARATE : stupid act or remark 3 MONTÓN : load, ton
best-seller [bes'seler] nm, pl **-sellers** : best seller
beta nf : beta (software)
besuquear vt fam : to cover with kisses — **besuquearse** vr fam : to neck, to smooch
betabel nm Mex : beet
betún nm, pl **betunes** 1 : shoe polish 2 Mex : icing
bi- pref : bi-
bianual adj : biannual
biberón nm, pl **-rones** : baby's bottle ⟨le dio el biberón al bebé : she gave the baby his bottle⟩
biblia nf 1 : bible 2 **la Biblia** : the Bible
bíblico, -ca adj : biblical
bibliografía nf : bibliography — **bibliográfico, -ca** adj
bibliógrafo, -fa n : bibliographer
biblioteca nf 1 : library 2 ESTANTERÍA : bookcase, bookshelves
bibliotecario, -ria n : librarian
bicameral adj : bicameral
bicarbonato nm 1 : bicarbonate 2 **bicarbonato de soda** : sodium bicarbonate, baking soda
bicentenario nm : bicentennial
bíceps nms & pl : biceps
bicho nm 1 : small animal 2 INSECTO : bug 3 **bicho raro** : weirdo
bici nf fam : bike
bicicleta nf 1 : bicycle ⟨ir en bicicleta : to cycle, to bicycle⟩ ⟨andar/montar en bicicleta : to ride a bicycle⟩ 2 **bicicleta de montaña** mountain bike
bicolor adj : two-tone
bidé or **bidet** nm : bidet
bidireccional adj : two-way
bidón nm, pl **bidones** : large can, (oil) drum
bien[1] adv 1 : well ⟨¿dormiste bien? : did you sleep well?⟩ ⟨todo va bien : everything's going well⟩ 2 : well, right, properly ⟨nos trata bien : she treats us well⟩ ⟨funcionar bien : to work right⟩ 3 : well, skillfully ⟨canta bien : she sings well⟩ ⟨¡bien dicho! : well said!⟩ 4 : well, thoroughly ⟨piénsalo bien : think it over carefully⟩ ⟨bien documentado : well-

documented⟩ **5** : very, quite ⟨era bien divertido : it was very enjoyable⟩ **6** : easily ⟨bien podría decirse que . . . : it could very well be said that . . .⟩ **7 bien que** : willingly, readily ⟨no ayuda pero bien que critica : he doesn't help but he's quick to criticize⟩ **8 más bien** : rather **9 no bien** : as soon as **10 si bien** : although

bien² *adj* **1** : well, OK, all right ⟨¿te sientes bien? : are you feeling all right?⟩ ⟨estoy bien, gracias : I'm fine, thanks⟩ **2** : good, nice, pleasant ⟨las flores huelen bien : the flowers smell very nice⟩ ⟨se está bien aquí : it's very pleasant here⟩ **3** : fine, OK, all right ⟨me parece bien : it seems fine to me⟩ ⟨está bien, no te preocupes : it's OK—don't worry about it⟩ **4** : right, correct, proper ⟨esta frase no está bien : this sentence isn't right⟩ ⟨no está bien que te hable así : it's not right for him to speak to you like that⟩

bien³ *nm* **1** : good ⟨el bien y el mal : good and evil⟩ **2** : good, sake ⟨por tu (propio) bien : for your (own) good⟩ **3 bienes** *nmpl* : property, goods, possessions ⟨bienes de consumo : consumer goods⟩ ⟨bienes muebles : personal property⟩ ⟨bienes raíces/inmuebles : real estate⟩

bien⁴ *conj* (o) bien . . . (o) bien . . . : either . . . or . . .

bien⁵ *interj* **1** BUENO : well, so ⟨bien, empecemos : well, let's get started⟩ ⟨bien, como iba diciendo . . . : so as I was saying . . .⟩ **2 ¡(muy) bien!** : (very) good!, well done! **3 ¡qué bien!** : great!

bienal *adj & nf* : biennial — **bienalmente** *adv*

bienaventurado, -da *adj* **1** : blessed **2** : fortunate, happy

bienestar *nm* **1** : welfare, well-being **2** CONFORT : comfort

bienintencionado, -da *adj* : well-meaning

bienvenida *nf* **1** : welcome **2 dar la bienvenida a** : to welcome

bienvenido, -da *adj* : welcome

bies *nm* : bias (in sewing)

bife *nm Arg, Chile, Uru* : steak

bífido, -da *adj* : forked

bifocales *nmpl* : bifocals — **bifocal** *adj*

bifurcación *nf, pl* **-ciones** : fork (in a river or road)

bifurcarse {72} *vr* : to fork

bigamia *nf* : bigamy

bígamo, -ma *n* : bigamist

bigote *nm* **1** : mustache **2** : whisker (of an animal)

bigotón, -tona *adj, mpl* **-tones** CA, Mex : having a big mustache

bikini *nm* : bikini

bilateral *adj* : bilateral — **bilateralmente** *adv*

biliar *adj* : bile ⟨cálculo biliar : gallstone⟩

bilingüe *adj* : bilingual

bilis *nf* : bile

billar *nm* : pool, billiards

billete *nm* **1** : bill ⟨un billete de cinco dólares : a five-dollar bill⟩ ⟨billete de banco : banknote⟩ **2** *Spain* → **boleto**

billetera *nf* : billfold, wallet

billetero, -ra *n CA, Car* : lottery ticket vendor

billón *nm, pl* **billones 1** : billion (Great Britain) **2** : trillion (U.S.A.)

bimensual *adj* : bimonthly, semimonthly

bimestral *adj* : bimonthly ⟨una revista bimestral : a bimonthly magazine, a magazine that's published every two months⟩ — **bimestralmente** *adv*

bimestre *nm* : two-month period

bimotor *adj* : twin-engine

binacional *adj* : binational

binario, -ria *adj* : binary

bingo *nm* : bingo

binocular *adj* : binocular

binoculares *nmpl* : binoculars

bio- *pref* : bio-

biodegradable *adj* : biodegradable

biodiversidad *nf* : biodiversity

biografía *nf* : biography

biográfico, -ca *adj* : biographical

biógrafo, -fa *n* : biographer

biología *nf* : biology

biológico, -ca *adj* : biological, biologic — **biológicamente** *adv*

biólogo, -ga *n* : biologist

biombo *nm* MAMPARA : folding screen, room divider

biopsia *nf* : biopsy

bioquímica *nf* : biochemistry

bioquímico¹, -ca *adj* : biochemical

bioquímico², -ca *n* : biochemist

biosfera *or* **biósfera** *nf* : biosphere

biotecnología *nf* : biotechnology — **biotecnológico, -ca** *adj*

bip *nm* PITIDO : beep

bipartidismo *nm* : two-party system

bipartidista *adj* : bipartisan

bípedo *nm* : biped

biquini → **bikini**

birlar *vt fam* : to swipe, to pinch

birmano, -na *adj & n* : Burmese

birrete *nm* **1** : mortarboard **2** : biretta

bis¹ *adv* **1** : twice, again (in music) **2** : a, A ⟨artículo 47 bis : Article 47A⟩ ⟨calle 15, número 70 bis : 15th Street, number 70A⟩

bis² *nm* : encore

bis- *pref* : great ⟨bisnieto : great-grandson⟩

bisabuelo, -la *n* : great-grandfather *m*, great-grandmother *f*, great-grandparent

bisagra *nf* : hinge

bisecar {72} *vt* : bisect

bisel *nm* : bevel

biselar *vt* : to bevel

bisexual *adj* : bisexual — **bisexualidad** *nf*

bisiesto *adj* año bisiesto : leap year

bisnieto, -ta *n* : great-grandson *m*, great-granddaughter *f*, great-grandchild

bisonte *nm* : bison, buffalo

bisoñé *nm* : hairpiece, toupee

bisoño¹, -ña *adj* : inexperienced

bisoño², -ña *n* : rookie

bistec *nm* : steak, beefsteak

bisturí *nm, pl* **-ríes** ESCALPELO : scalpel

bisutería *nf* : costume jewelry

bit *nm* : bit (unit of information)

bitácora *nf* 1 : ship's log 2 BLOG : blog
bitcoin [bit'koin] *nm, pl* **bitcoins** : Bitcoin
bizco, -ca *adj* : cross-eyed
bizcocho *nm* 1 : sponge cake 2 : biscuit
blanca *nf* : half note (in music)
blanco¹, -ca *adj* 1 : white 2 **en blanco** : blank (of a paper, etc.) 3 **pasar la noche en blanco** : to have a sleepless night
blanco², -ca *n* : white person
blanco³ *nm* 1 : white (color) 2 : white (of the eye) 3 : target, bull's-eye ⟨dar en el blanco : to hit the target, to hit the nail on the head⟩
blancura *nf* : whiteness
blancuzco, -ca *adj* 1 : whitish, off-white 2 PÁLIDO : pale
blandir {1} *vt* : to wave, to brandish
blando, -da *adj* 1 SUAVE : soft (of a bed, etc.), tender (of meat) 2 : weak (in character) 3 : lenient
blandura *nf* 1 : softness, tenderness 2 : leniency
blanqueador *nm* : bleach, whitener
blanquear *vt* 1 : to bleach (clothes), to whitewash (a wall) 2 : to shut out (in sports) 3 : to launder (money) — *vi* : to turn white
blanqueo *nm* 1 : bleaching, whitewashing 2 : money laundering
blanquillo *nm CA, Mex* : egg
blasfemar *vi* : to blaspheme
blasfemia *nf* : blasphemy
blasfemo, -ma *adj* : blasphemous
blazer *nm* : blazer
bledo *nm* (no) **me importa un bledo** *fam* : I don't give a damn
blindado, -da *adj* ACORAZADO : armored
blindaje *nm* 1 : armor, armor plating 2 : shield (for cables, machinery, etc.)
bloc *nm, pl* **blocs** : notepad, pad (of paper)
blof *nm Col, Mex* : bluff
blofear *vi Col, Mex* : to bluff
blog ['blox] *nm, pl* **blogs** BITÁCORA : blog
blondo, -da *adj* : blond, flaxen
bloque *nm* 1 : block (of wood, etc.) 2 GRUPO : bloc ⟨el bloque comunista : the Communist bloc⟩ 3 **en bloque** : en masse
bloquear *vt* 1 OBSTRUIR : to block (a road, etc.) 2 : to blockade (a port) 3 : to jam (a mechanism) 4 : to freeze (an account) — **bloquearse** *vr* : to jam, to stick, to lock
bloqueo *nm* 1 : blocking 2 : blockade (of a port, etc.)
blues ['blus] *nm* : blues (music)
blusa *nf* : blouse
blusón *nm, pl* **blusones** : loose shirt, smock
boa *nf* : boa
boato *nm* : ostentation, show
bobada *nf* 1 : stupid remark or action 2 **decir bobadas** : to talk nonsense
bobalicón, -cona *adj, mpl* **-cones** *fam* : silly, stupid
bobina *nf* 1 : roll, spool (of thread), bobbin (in sewing machine) 2 : (electrical) coil

bobo¹, -ba *adj* : silly, stupid
bobo², -ba *n* : fool
bobsleigh ['bobsle] *nm* : bobsled
boca *nf* 1 : mouth 2 : entrance 3 : mouth (of a jar, etc.), muzzle (of a gun) 4 **boca arriba** : face up 5 **boca abajo** : face down 6 **boca del estómago** : pit of the stomach 7 **boca de riego/incendios** : hydrant 8 **correr de boca en boca** : to spread by word of mouth 9 **el boca a boca** : mouth-to-mouth (resuscitation) ⟨hacerle el boca a boca a alguien : to give someone mouth-to-mouth⟩ 10 **en boca de todos** : on everyone's lips 11 **por boca de** : according to
bocacalle *nf* : entrance to a street ⟨gire a la última bocacalle : turn onto the last side street⟩
bocadillo *nm Spain* : sandwich
bocado *nm* 1 : bite, mouthful ⟨no probó bocado : he didn't have a bite to eat⟩ 2 FRENO : bit (of a bridle)
bocajarro *nm* **a ~** : point-blank
bocallave *nf* : keyhole
bocanada *nf* 1 : mouthful (of smoke, etc.) 2 : gust (of air)
boceto *nm* : sketch, outline
bochinche *nm fam* : ruckus, uproar
bochorno *nm* 1 VERGÜENZA : embarrassment 2 : hot and humid weather 3 : hot flash
bochornoso, -sa *adj* 1 EMBARAZOSO : embarrassing 2 : hot and muggy
bocina *nf* 1 : horn, trumpet 2 : automobile horn 3 : mouthpiece (of a telephone) 4 *Mex* : loudspeaker
bocinazo *nm* : honk (of a horn)
bocio *nm* : goiter
bocón, -cona *n, mpl* **bocones** *fam* : blabbermouth, loudmouth
boda *nf* : wedding ⟨bodas de oro/plata : golden/silver anniversary⟩
bodega *nf* 1 : wine cellar 2 : wine shop 3 : wine bar 4 : winery, wine producer 5 SÓTANO : cellar 6 : (ship's) hold 7 *Chile, Col, Mex* : storeroom, warehouse 8 *(in various countries)* : grocery store
bodegón *nm, pl* **-gones** : still life
bofetada *nf* CACHETADA : slap on the face
bofetear *vt* CACHETEAR : to slap
bofetón *nm, pl* **-tones** → **bofetada**
boga *nf* : fashion, vogue ⟨estar en boga : to be in style⟩
bogey ['bogi] *nm* : bogey (in golf)
bogotano¹, -na *adj* : of or from Bogotá
bogotano², -na *n* : person from Bogotá
bohemio, -mia *adj & n* : bohemian, Bohemian
bohío *nm (in various countries)* : hut
boicot *nm, pl* **boicots** : boycott
boicotear *vt* : to boycott
bóiler *nm Mex* : water heater
boina *nf* : beret
bol *nm* : bowl
bola *nf* 1 : ball ⟨bola de nieve : snowball⟩ ⟨bola de billar : billiard ball⟩ 2 CANICA : marble 3 : scoop (of ice cream) 4 *fam* : lie, fib 5 *Mex fam* : bunch ⟨una bola de rateros/mentiras : a bunch of thieves/lies⟩ 6 *Mex* : up-

roar, tumult **7 hacerse bolas con** *Mex*
: to muddle up (facts), to make a mess of
bolchevique *adj & nmf* : Bolshevik
bolear *vt Mex* : to polish (shoes)
bolera *nf* : bowling alley
bolero[1] *nm* : bolero
bolero[2], **-ra** *n Mex* : shoeshine boy/man
m, shoeshine girl/woman *f*
boleta *nf* **1** : receipt, ticket, slip **2**
: (traffic/parking) ticket **3** *Arg, Mex*
FACTURA : bill **4** *or* **boleta electoral**
: ballot **5 boleta de calificaciones** *Mex*
: report card
boletaje *nm Mex* : tickets *pl*
boletería *nf* TAQUILLA : box office, ticket
office
boletín *nm, pl* **-tines 1** : bulletin **2**
: journal, review **3 boletín informativo**
: news bulletin **4 boletín de prensa**
: press release
boleto *nm* **1** : ticket, fare ⟨bolcto de ida/
de ida y vuelta : one-way/round-trip
ticket⟩ **2** : ticket (for a lottery, etc.)
boli *nm Spain* → **bolígrafo**
boliche *nm* **1** BOLOS : bowling **2** BO-
LERA : bowling alley **3** *Arg, Uru* : bar,
nightclub **4** *Arg, Chile, Uru* : small store
bólido *nm* **1** : race car **2** METEORO
: meteor
bolígrafo *nm* : ballpoint pen
bolillo *nm* **1** : bobbin **2** *Mex* : roll, bun
bolita *nf* CANICA : marble
bolívar *nm* : bolivar (monetary unit of
Venezuela)
boliviano[1], **-na** *adj & n* : Bolivian
boliviano[2] *nm* : boliviano (monetary unit
of Bolivia)
bollo *nm* **1** : bun, sweet roll **2** *Arg, Uru*
: ball
bolo *nm* : bowling pin
bolos *nmpl* BOLICHE : bowling
bolsa *nf* **1** : bag, sack ⟨bolsa de basura/
plástico : garbage/plastic bag⟩ **2** *Mex*
: pocketbook, purse **3** *Mex* : pocket **4**
: pouch (of a marsupial) **5** : pocket (of
minerals, etc.) **6** *or* **Bolsa** *or* **bolsa de
valores** : stock market, stock exchange
7 bolsa de agua caliente : hot-water
bottle **8 bolsa de aire** : airbag **9 bolsa
de trabajo** : job bank
bolsear *vt Mex* : to pick (someone's)
pocket
bolsillo *nm* **1** : pocket **2 dinero de bolsillo** : pocket change
bolsita *nf* : small bag ⟨bolsita de té : tea
bag⟩
bolso *nm* : pocketbook, handbag
bomba *nf* **1** : bomb ⟨bomba atómica
: atomic/atom bomb⟩ ⟨bomba de
tiempo, bomba de relojería *Spain* : time
bomb⟩ **2** : bubble **3** : pump ⟨bomba de
agua : water pump⟩ **4** *or* **bomba destapacaños** : plunger (for toilets, etc.) **5**
(in various countries) : gas station **6**
BOMBAZO : bombshell, shocker **7 pasarlo bomba** : to have a great time
bombacha *nf Arg, Uru* **1** : panties **2** →
bombachos
bombachos *nmpl* : baggy pants, bloomers

bombardear *vt* **1** : to bomb **2** : to bombard
bombardeo *nm* **1** : bombing, shelling **2**
: bombardment
bombardero *nm* : bomber (airplane)
bombástico, **-ca** *adj* : bombastic
bombazo *nm* **1** : bombshell, shocker **2**
Mex : (bomb) explosion
bombear *vt* : to pump
bombero, **-ra** *n* : firefighter, fireman *m*
bombilla *nf* **1** : lightbulb **2** : tube, straw
(for maté)
bombillo *nm CA, Col, Ven* : lightbulb
bombita *Arg, Uru* → **bombilla**
bombo *nm* **1** : bass drum **2** *fam* : fanfare, hype ⟨con bombos y platillos : with
great fanfare⟩
bombón *nm, pl* **bombones 1** : bonbon,
chocolate **2** *Mex* : marshmallow
bombona *nf Ecua, Spain, Ven* : tank (container)
bonachón[1], **-chona** *adj, mpl* **-chones** *fam*
: good-natured, kindhearted
bonachón[2], **-chona** *n, mpl* **-chones** *fam*
BUENAZO : kindhearted person
bonaerense[1] *adj* : of or from Buenos Aires
bonaerense[2] *nmf* : person from Buenos
Aires
bonanza *nf* **1** PROSPERIDAD : prosperity
2 : calm weather **3** : rich ore deposit,
bonanza
bondad *nf* BENEVOLENCIA : goodness,
kindness ⟨tener la bondad de hacer algo
: to be kind enough to do something⟩
bondadoso, **-sa** *adj* BENÉVOLO : kind,
kindly, good — **bondadosamente** *adv*
bonete *nm* : cap, mortarboard
bongo *or* **bongó** *nm, pl* **bongos** *or* **bon-
góes** : bongo
boniato *nm* : sweet potato
bonificación *nf, pl* **-ciones 1** : discount
2 : bonus, extra
bonito[1] *adv* : nicely, well
bonito[2], **-ta** *adj* LINDO : pretty, lovely
bonito[3] *nm* : bonito (tuna)
bono *nm* **1** : bond ⟨bono bancario
: bank bond⟩ **2** : voucher
boqueada *nf* : gasp ⟨dar la última boqueada : to give one's last gasp⟩
boquear *vi* **1** : to gasp **2** : to be dying
boquerón *nm, pl* **-rones** : anchovy
boquete *nm* : hole, opening
boquiabierto, **-ta** *adj* : open-mouthed,
speechless, agape
boquilla *nf* **1** : mouthpiece (of a musical
instrument), stem (of a pipe) **2** : cigarette holder **3** : nozzle
borbotar *or* **borbotear** *vi* : to bubble
borboteo *nm* : bubbling
borbotón *nm, pl* **-tones 1 hervir a bor-
botones** : to boil rapidly **2 salir a bor-
botones** : to gush out
borda *nf* : gunwale ⟨echar/tirar algo por la
borda : to throw something overboard⟩
bordado *nm* : embroidery
bordar *v* : to embroider
borde *nm* **1** : edge (of a table, etc.), rim
(of a glass, etc.) **2** : side (of a road, etc.)
3 al borde de : on the verge of

bordear *vt* **1** : to border (a city, etc.), to line (a street) **2** : to skirt, to follow (a coastline, etc.) **3** : to border on ⟨bordea la genialidad : it borders on genius⟩

bordillo *nm* : curb

bordo *nm* a ∼ : aboard, on board

bordón *nm, pl* **-dones 1** : bass string (of a guitar, etc.), snare (of a drum) **2** BASTÓN : staff

boreal *adj* : northern

borgoña *nf* : burgundy

boricua *adj & nmf fam* : Puerto Rican

borinqueño, -ña → boricua

borla *nf* **1** : pom-pom, tassel **2** : powder puff

borrachera *nf* : drunkenness ⟨(se) agarró una borrachera : he got drunk⟩

borrachín, -china *n, mpl* **-chines** *fam* : lush, drunk

borracho¹, -cha *adj* EBRIO : drunk

borracho², -cha *n* : drunk, drunkard

borrador *nm* **1** : rough copy, first draft ⟨en borrador : in the rough⟩ **2** BOSQUEJO : sketch **3** : (blackboard) eraser

borrar *vt* **1** : to erase (on paper), to delete (on a computer) **2** : to wipe, to erase (a disk, etc.) **3** : to erase, to wipe off (a blackboard) **4** : to erase, to blot out (a memory) — **borrarse** *vr* **1** : to fade, to fade away **2** : to resign, to drop out **3** *Mex fam* : to split, to leave ⟨me borro : I'm out of here⟩

borrasca *nf* **1** : area of low pressure **2** TORMENTA : squall, storm

borrascoso, -sa *adj* : blustery, stormy

borrego, -ga *n* : lamb, sheep

borrico → burro

borrón *nm, pl* **borrones** : smudge, blot ⟨hacer borrón y cuenta nueva : to start with a clean slate⟩

borronear *vt* : to smudge, to blot

borroso, -sa *adj* : blurry, fuzzy

boscoso, -sa *adj* : wooded

bosnio, -nia *adj & n* : Bosnian

bosque *nm* : woods, forest ⟨bosque tropical : rain forest⟩

bosquecillo *nm* : grove, copse, thicket

bosquejar *vt* ESBOZAR : to outline, to sketch

bosquejo *nm* **1** TRAZADO : outline, sketch **2** : draft

bostezar {21} *vi* : to yawn

bostezo *nm* : yawn

bot [ᵇbot] *nm, pl* **bots** : bot

bota *nf* **1** : boot **2** : wineskin (small) **3** botas vaqueras *Mex* : cowboy boots

botadero *nm* : garbage dump

botana *nf Mex* : snack, appetizer

botánica *nf* : botany

botánico¹, -ca *adj* : botanical

botánico², -ca *n* : botanist

botar *vt* **1** ARROJAR : to throw, to fling, to hurl **2** TIRAR : to throw out, to throw away **3** ECHAR : to throw (someone) out **4** : to bounce **5** : to launch (a ship) — *vi* **1** SALTAR : to jump **2** *Spain* REBOTAR : to bounce

bote *nm* **1** : small boat ⟨bote de remos : rowboat⟩ ⟨bote salvavidas : lifeboat⟩ **2** : can, jar **3** : jump, bounce ⟨dar botes : to bounce⟩ **4** *Mex fam* : jail **5 bote de basura** *CA, Mex* : garbage can, trash can

botella *nf* : bottle

botica *nf* FARMACIA : drugstore, pharmacy

boticario, -ria *n* FARMACÉUTICO : pharmacist, druggist

botín *nm, pl* **botines 1** : baby's bootee **2** : ankle boot **3** : booty, plunder

botiquín *nm, pl* **-quines 1** : medicine cabinet **2** : first aid kit

botón *nm, pl* **botones 1** : button **2** : bud **3** INSIGNIA : badge

botones *nmfs & pl* : bellhop

botulismo *nm* : botulism

boulevard [ˌbuleᵇvar] → **bulevar**

bouquet [buᵇke] *nm, pl* **-quets 1** RAMO : bouquet **2** : bouquet, aroma

bourbon *nm* : bourbon

boutique [buᵗtik] *nf* : boutique

bóveda *nf* **1** : vault, dome **2** CRIPTA : crypt

bovino, -na *adj* : bovine

box *nm, pl* **boxes 1** : pit (in auto racing) **2** *CA, Mex* : boxing

boxeador, -dora *n* : boxer

boxear *vi* : to box

boxeo *nm* : boxing

boxers *nmpl* : boxer shorts

boya *nf* : buoy

boyante *adj* : buoyant

bozal *nm* **1** : muzzle **2** : halter (for a horse)

bracear *vi* **1** : to wave one's arms **2** : to make strokes (in swimming)

bracero, -ra *n* : migrant worker, day laborer

bragas *nfpl Spain* : panties

braguero *nm* : truss (in medicine)

bragueta *nf* : fly, pants zipper

braille *adj & nm* : braille

bramante *nm* : twine, string

bramar *vi* **1** RUGIR : to roar, to bellow **2** : to howl (of the wind)

bramido *nm* : bellowing, roar

brandy *nm* : brandy

branquia *nf* AGALLA : gill

brasa *nf* ASCUA : ember ⟨a la brasa : grilled⟩

brasero *nm* : brazier

brasier *or* **brassiere** *nm Col, Mex* : brassiere, bra

brasileño, -ña *adj & n* : Brazilian

brasilero, -ra → brasileño

bravata *nf* **1** JACTANCIA : boast **2** AMENAZA : threat

bravío, -vía *adj* : wild, fierce

bravo, -va *adj* **1** FEROZ : ferocious, fierce **2** : angry **3** : rough (of the sea) **4 ¡bravo!** : bravo!, well done!

bravucón, -cona *n, mpl* **-cones** : bully

bravuconadas *nfpl* : bravado

bravura *nf* **1** FEROCIDAD : fierceness, ferocity **2** VALENTÍA : bravery

braza *nf* **1** *or* **estilo braza** *Spain* : breaststroke ⟨nadar a braza : to swim the breaststroke⟩ **2** : fathom (unit of length)

brazada *nf* : stroke (in swimming)

brazalete *nm* **1** PULSERA : bracelet, bangle **2** BANDA : armband

brazo *nm* **1** : arm ⟨tomar del brazo : to take by the arm⟩ ⟨con los brazos cruzados : with one's arms crossed⟩ ⟨llevar en brazos : to carry in one's arms⟩ **2** : arm (of an object), limb (of a tree) **3** : branch (of a river), inlet (of the sea) **brazo derecho** : right-hand man **5 brazos** *nmpl* : hands, laborers

brea *nf* ALQUITRÁN : tar, pitch

brebaje *nm* : potion, brew

brecha *nf* **1** : gap, breach, opening **2** : breach (of defenses) **3** DIFERENCIA : gap, difference **4** TAJO : gash

brega *nf* **1** LUCHA : struggle **2** : hard work

bregar {52} *vi* **1** LUCHAR : to struggle **2** : to toil **3 ~ con** : to deal with

breve *adj* **1** CORTO : brief, short **2 en ~** : shortly, in short — **brevemente** *adv*

brevedad *nf* **1** : brevity, shortness **2 con la mayor brevedad** *or* **a la brevedad posible** : as soon as possible

brezo *nm* : heather

bribón, -bona *n, mpl* **bribones** : rascal, scamp

bricolaje *or* **bricolage** *nm* : do-it-yourself, DIY

brida *nf* : bridle

bridge ['brɪʤ, 'brɪʒ, 'brɪtʃ] *nm* : bridge (game)

brigada *nf* **1** : brigade **2** : team, squad

brigadier *nm* : brigadier

brillante[1] *adj* **1** : bright (of color, light, etc.) **2** LUSTROSO : shiny, glossy **3** RELUCIENTE : sparkling **4** GENIAL : brilliant — **brillantemente** *adv*

brillante[2] *nm* DIAMANTE : diamond

brillantez *nf* : brilliance, brightness

brillar *vi* : to shine, to sparkle

brillo *nm* **1** : brilliance **2** : luster, shine, gloss ⟨sacarle/darle brillo a : to polish⟩ **3** ESPLENDOR : splendor

brilloso, -sa *adj* LUSTROSO : lustrous, shiny

brincar {72} *vi* **1** SALTAR : to jump (up and down) ⟨brincar de alegría : to jump for joy⟩ **2** : to hop (of a rabbit, etc.), to gambol

brinco *nm* **1** SALTO : jump, leap, skip **2 dar un brinco** : to jump

brindar *vi* : to drink a toast ⟨brindar por : to toast, to drink to⟩ — *vt* : to offer, to provide — **brindarse** *vr* **brindarse a hacer algo** : to volunteer to do something

brindis *nm* : toast, drink ⟨hacer un brindis : to drink a toast⟩

brinque, etc. → **brincar**

brío *nm* **1** : force, determination **2** : spirit, verve

brioso, -sa *adj* : spirited

brisa *nf* : breeze

británico[1], **-ca** *adj* : British

británico[2], **-ca** *n* **1** : British person **2 los británicos** : the British

brizna *nf* **1** : strand **2** : blade (of grass)

broca *nf* : drill bit

brocado *nm* : brocade

brocha *nf* : paintbrush

broche *nm* **1** ALFILER : brooch **2** : fastener, clasp, clip **3** *Mex* : barrette, hair

clip **4** *Arg* GRAPA : staple **5 broche de oro** : finishing touch

brocheta *nf* : skewer

brócoli *nm* : broccoli

broma *nf* **1** : joke, prank ⟨le hizo una broma : she played a joke on him⟩ **2 en ~** : in jest, jokingly

bromear *vi* : to joke

bromista[1] *adj* : joking, playful

bromista[2] *nmf* : joker, prankster

bromo *nm* : bromine

bronca *nf* **1** *fam* : fight, quarrel, fuss ⟨armar una bronca : to kick up a fuss⟩ **2** *fam* : anger ⟨dar bronca : to piss off⟩ ⟨estar con bronca : to be pissed off⟩ ⟨tener bronca con : to have a beef with⟩ **3** *fam* : scolding ⟨echarle (la) bronca a alguien : to tell someone off⟩

bronce *nm* : bronze

bronceado[1], **-da** *adj* **1** : tanned, suntanned **2** : bronze

bronceado[2] *nm* **1** : suntan, tan **2** : bronzing

bronceador *nm* : suntan lotion

broncear *vt* : to tan — **broncearse** *vr* : to get a suntan

bronco, -ca *adj* **1** : harsh, rough **2** : untamed, wild

bronquial *adj* : bronchial

bronquio *nm* : bronchial tube

bronquitis *nf* : bronchitis

broqueta *nf* : skewer

brotar *vi* **1** : to bud, to sprout **2** : to spring up, to stream, to gush forth **3** : to appear (of a rash, etc.)

brote *nm* **1** : outbreak **2** : sprout, bud, shoot

broza *nf* **1** : brushwood **2** MALEZA : scrub, undergrowth

bruces → **de bruces**

brujería *nf* HECHICERÍA : witchcraft, sorcery

brujo[1], **-ja** *adj* : bewitching

brujo[2], **-ja** *n* : witch *f*, sorcerer

brújula *nf* : compass

bruma *nf* : haze, mist

brumoso, -sa *adj* : hazy, misty

bruñir {38} *vt* : to burnish, to polish (metals)

brusco, -ca *adj* **1** SÚBITO : sudden, abrupt **2** : curt, brusque — **bruscamente** *adv*

brusquedad *nf* **1** : abruptness, suddenness **2** : brusqueness

brutal *adj* **1** : brutal **2** *fam* : incredible, terrific — **brutalmente** *adv*

brutalidad *nf* : brutality

brutalizar {21} *vt* : to brutalize, to maltreat

bruto[1], **-ta** *adj* **1** : gross ⟨peso bruto : gross weight⟩ ⟨ingresos brutos : gross income⟩ **2** : raw, unrefined ⟨petróleo (en) bruto : crude oil⟩ ⟨diamantes en bruto : uncut diamonds⟩ **3** ESTÚPIDO : brutish, stupid

bruto[2], **-ta** *n* **1** : brute **2** : dunce, blockhead

bubónico, -ca *adj* : bubonic ⟨peste bubónica : bubonic plague⟩

bucal *adj* : oral

bucanero *nm* : buccaneer
buceador, -dora *n* : diver, scuba diver
bucear *vi* **1** : to dive, to swim underwater **2** : to explore, to delve
buceo *nm* : diving; scuba diving
buche *nm* **1** : crop (of a bird) **2** *fam* : belly **3 hacer buches** : to rinse one's mouth
bucle *nm* **1** : curl, ringlet **2** : loop
bucólico, -ca *adj* : bucolic
budín *nm*, *pl* **budines** : pudding
budismo *nm* : Buddhism
budista *adj & nmf* : Buddhist
buen *adj* → **bueno**[1]
buenamente *adv* **1** : easily **2** : willingly
buenaventura *nf* **1** : good luck **2** : fortune, future ⟨le dijo la buenaventura : she told his fortune⟩
buenazo, -za *n fam* BONACHÓN : kindhearted person
bueno[1], **-na** *adj* (**buen** *before masculine singular nouns*) **1** : good ⟨una buena idea : a good idea⟩ ⟨en buenas condiciones : in good condition⟩ **2** : good, kind ⟨un buen hombre : a good man⟩ ⟨ser bueno con alguien : to be good to someone⟩ **3** : good, proper ⟨buenos modales : good manners⟩ ⟨es bueno ayudar a la gente : it's good to help people⟩ **4** : good, pleasant ⟨buen tiempo : good weather⟩ **5** : good, tasty ⟨esta sopa está buena : this soup is good⟩ **6** FRESCO : fresh **7** : good, healthy ⟨una buena alimentación : a good diet⟩ ⟨es bueno para el corazón : it's good for your heart⟩ **8** *fam* : sexy, hot *fam* ⟨está bueno : he's a hunk⟩ **9** : good, competent ⟨un buen abogado : a good lawyer⟩ ⟨hiciste un buen trabajo : you did a good job⟩ ⟨ser bueno para/en algo : to be good at something⟩ **10** : considerable, goodly ⟨una buena cantidad : a goodly amount, a lot⟩ **11 buenos días** : hello, good day **12 buenas tardes** : good afternoon **13 buenas noches** : good evening, good night **14 de buenas a primeras** : suddenly **15 ¡qué bueno!** : great! **16 un buen día** : one day
bueno[2] *interj* **1** : OK!, all right! **2** *Mex* : hello! (on the telephone)
bueno[3], **-na** *n* **1** : good guy (in a story, etc.) **2 el bueno de, la buena de** : good old ⟨el bueno de Carlos : good old Carlos⟩
buey *nm* : ox, steer
búfalo *nm* **1** : buffalo **2 búfalo de agua** : water buffalo
bufanda *nf* : scarf
bufar *vi* : to snort
bufet *or* **bufé** *nm* : buffet (meal)
bufete *nm* : law firm, law office
bufido *nm* : snort
bufo, -fa *adj* : comic
bufón, -fona *n*, *mpl* **bufones 1** : jester **2** : clown, buffoon
bufonada *nf* : antic ⟨hacer bufonadas : to clown around⟩
buhardilla *nf* **1** ÁTICO, DESVÁN : attic **2** : dormer window
búho *nm* **1** : owl **2** *fam* : hermit, recluse
buhonero, -ra *n* MERCACHIFLE : peddler

buitre *nm* : vulture
bujía *nf* : spark plug
bula *nf* : papal bull
bulbo *nm* : bulb
bulboso, -sa *adj* : bulbous
bulevar *nm* : boulevard
búlgaro, -ra *adj & n* : Bulgarian
bulla *nf* BARULLO : racket, rowdiness
bulldog [bul'dog] *nm*, *pl* **bulldogs** : bulldog
bulldozer [bul'doser] *nm*, *pl* **-zers** : bulldozer
bullicio *nm* **1** : ruckus, uproar **2** : hustle and bustle
bullicioso, -sa *adj* : noisy, busy, turbulent
bullir {38} *vi* **1** HERVIR : to boil **2** MOVERSE : to stir, to bustle about
bullying ['bulin] *nm* : bullying
bulto *nm* **1** : package, bundle **2** : piece of luggage, bag **3** : size, bulk, volume **4** : form, shape ⟨pude distinguir unos bultos : I could make out some shapes⟩ **5** : lump (on the body), swelling, bulge
bumerán *nm*, *pl* **-ranes** : boomerang
búnker *nm*, *pl* **búnkers** : bunker
búnquer → **búnker**
buñuelo *nm* : doughnut, fried pastry
buque *nm* BARCO : ship, vessel ⟨buque de guerra : warship⟩
burbuja *nf* : bubble
burbujeante *adj* : bubbly
burbujear *vi* **1** : to bubble **2** : to fizz
burdel *nm* : brothel
burdo, -da *adj* **1** : coarse, rough **2** : crude, clumsy ⟨una burda mentira : an obvious lie⟩ — **burdamente** *adj*
burgués, -guesa *adj & n*, *mpl* **burgueses** : bourgeois
burguesía *nf* : bourgeoisie, middle class
burla *nf* **1** : mockery, ridicule **2** : joke, trick **3 hacer burla de** : to make fun of, to mock
burlar *vt* **1** ENGAÑAR : to trick, to deceive **2** ELUDIR : to evade — **burlarse** *vr* ~ **de** : to make fun of
burlesco, -ca *adj* : burlesque, comic
burlón[1], **-lona** *adj*, *mpl* **burlones** : joking, mocking
burlón[2], **-lona** *n*, *mpl* **burlones** : joker
burocracia *nf* : bureaucracy
burócrata *nmf* : bureaucrat
burocrático, -ca *adj* : bureaucratic
burrada *nf fam* : stupid act or remark, nonsense
burrito *nm* : burrito
burro[1], **-rra** *adj fam* : dumb, stupid
burro[2], **-rra** *n* **1** ASNO : donkey, ass **2** *fam* : idiot, dunce
burro[3] *nm* **1** : sawhorse **2** *Mex* : ironing board **3** *Mex* : stepladder
bursátil *adj* : stock-market
bus *nm* : bus
busca[1] *nf* : search ⟨en busca de : in search of⟩
busca[2] *nm Spain* → **buscapersonas**
buscador[1] *nm* : search engine
buscador[2], **-dora** *n* : hunter (for treasure, etc.), prospector
buscapersonas *nms & pl* : beeper, pager
buscapleitos *nmfs & pl* : troublemaker

buscar {72} *vt* **1** : to look for (a person, an object, etc.), to seek (revenge, etc.) **2** : to fetch, to get ⟨ve a buscar ayuda : go (and) get help⟩ **3** : to look for (trouble, etc.) **4** : to look up (in a book, etc.), to search (on the Web) **5 ir a buscar** RE-COGER : to pick up (at a place) — *vi* : to look, to search ⟨buscó en los bolsillos : he searched through his pockets⟩ — **buscarse** *vr* : to ask for, to look for ⟨te la estás buscando : you're asking for it/trouble⟩

buscavidas *nmfs & pl* : go-getter

busero, -ra *n CA* : bus driver

buseta *nf Col, CoRi, Ecua, Ven* : minibus

busque, etc. → buscar

búsqueda *nf* : search ⟨en búsqueda de : in search of⟩ ⟨la búsqueda de la verdad : the search for the truth⟩

busto *nm* : bust

butaca *nf* **1** SILLÓN : armchair, easy chair **2** : seat (in a theatre) **3** *Mex* : pupil's desk

buzo¹, -za *adj Mex fam* : smart, astute ⟨¡ponte buzo! : get with it!, get on the ball!⟩

buzo² *nm* **1** : diver **2** *Arg, Col* : sweatshirt, hoodie **3** *Uru* : sweater **4** *Chile, Peru* : tracksuit

buzón *nm, pl* **buzones** : mailbox ⟨buzón de voz : voice mail⟩

byte *nm* : byte

C

c *nf* : third letter of the Spanish alphabet

cabal *adj* **1** : exact, correct **2** : complete **3** : upright, honest

cabales *nmpl* **no estar en sus cabales** : not to be in one's right mind

cabalgar {52} *vi* : to ride (on horseback)

cabalgata *nf* : cavalcade, procession

cabalidad *nf* **a ~** : thoroughly, conscientiously

caballa *nf* : mackerel

caballar *adj* EQUINO : horse, equine

caballeresco, -ca *adj* : gallant, chivalrous

caballería *nf* **1** : cavalry **2** : horse, mount **3** : knighthood, chivalry

caballeriza *nf* : stable

caballero¹ → caballeroso

caballero² *nm* **1** : gentleman **2** : knight ⟨caballero andante : knight errant⟩

caballerosidad *nf* : chivalry, gallantry

caballeroso, -sa *adj* : gentlemanly, chivalrous

caballete *nm* **1** : ridge **2** : easel **3** : trestle (for a table, etc.) **4** : bridge (of the nose) **5** : sawhorse

caballista *nmf* : horseman *m*, horsewoman *f*

caballito *nm* **1** : rocking horse **2 caballito de mar** : sea horse **3 caballitos** *nmpl* : merry-go-round

caballo *nm* **1** : horse **2** : knight (in chess) **3 caballo de fuerza** *or* **caballo de vapor** : horsepower

cabalmente *adv* : fully, exactly

cabaña *nf* : cabin, hut

cabaret [kaba'ɾe] *nm, pl* **-rets** : nightclub, cabaret

cabecear *vt* : to head (in soccer) — *vi* **1** : to nod one's head **2** : to lurch, to pitch

cabeceo *nm* : pitch (of a boat, etc.)

cabecera *nf* **1** : headboard **2** : head ⟨cabecera de la mesa : head of the table⟩ **3** : heading, headline **4** : headwaters *pl* **5 médico de cabecera** : family doctor **6 cabecera municipal** *CA, Mex* : downtown area

cabecilla *nmf* : ringleader

cabellera *nf* : head of hair, mane

cabello *nm* : hair

cabelludo, -da *adj* **1** : hairy **2 cuero cabelludo** : scalp

caber {12} *vi* **1** : to fit, to go ⟨¿cabremos todos? : will we all fit?⟩ **2** : to be possible ⟨no cabe duda alguna : there's no doubt about it⟩ ⟨cabe la posibilidad que llegue mañana : it's possible he'll come tomorrow⟩

cabestrillo *nm* : sling ⟨llevo el brazo en cabestrillo : my arm is in a sling⟩

cabestro *nm* : halter (for an animal)

cabeza *nf* **1** : head ⟨de pies a cabeza : from head to toe⟩ ⟨negar/asentir con la cabeza : to shake/nod one's head⟩ ⟨levantar/bajar/volver la cabeza : to raise/lower/turn one's head⟩ **2** : head, mind ⟨pasar por la cabeza : to cross one's mind⟩ **3** PELO : hair **4** : head, leader **5** : head, front, top **6** : head ⟨por cabeza : each, a head⟩ ⟨500 cabezas de ganado : 500 head of cattle⟩ **7** : head (of cabbage, etc.) **8** : head (measurement) **9 de ~** : headfirst **10 dolor de cabeza** : headache

cabezada *nf* **1** : head butt **2** : nod ⟨echar una cabezada : to take a nap, to doze off⟩ **3 → cabeceo**

cabezal *nm* : bolster

cabeza rapada *nmf* : skinhead

cabezazo *nm* : head butt

cabezón, -zona *adj, mpl* **-zones** *fam* **1** : having a big head **2** : pigheaded, stubborn

cabida *nf* **1** : room, space, capacity **2 dar cabida a** : to accommodate, to hold

cabildear *vi* : to lobby

cabildeo *nm* : lobbying

cabildero, -ra *n* : lobbyist

cabildo *nm* AYUNTAMIENTO **1** : town or city hall **2** : town or city council

cabina *nf* **1** : cabin **2** : booth **3** : cab (of a truck), cockpit (of an airplane)

cabizbajo, -ja *adj* : dejected, downcast

cable *nm* **1** : cable ⟨cables de arranque, cables pasacorriente : jumper cables⟩ **2** : cable, cable television **3 cable tensor** : guy, guy line

cableado *nm* : wiring
cabo *nm* **1** : end ⟨al cabo de dos semanas : at the end of two weeks⟩ **2** : stub, end piece **3** : corporal **4** : cape, headland ⟨el Cabo Cañaveral : Cape Canaveral⟩ **5 al fin y al cabo** : after all, in the end **6 llevar a cabo** : to carry out, to do
cabrá, etc. → **caber**
cabra *nf* : goat
cabrío, -ría *adj* : goat
cabriola *nf* **1** : skip, jump **2 hacer cabriolas** : to prance
cabriolar *vi* : to prance
cabrito *nm* : kid, baby goat
cabro, cabra *n* : kid, youth
cabrón, cabrona *n, mpl* **cabrones** *Spain, Mex offensive* : bastard *m offensive*, bitch *f fam + offensive*
cabús *nm, pl* **cabuses** *Mex* : caboose
caca *nf fam* : poop ⟨hacer caca : to poop⟩ ⟨hacerse caca : to poop one's pants/diaper (etc.)⟩
cacahuate *nm Mex* : peanut
cacahuete *nm Spain* : peanut
cacalote *nm Mex* : crow
cacao *nm* **1** : cacao, cocoa bean **2** : hot chocolate, cocoa (drink)
cacarear *vi* : to crow, to cackle, to cluck — *vt fam* : to boast about, to crow about
cacareo *nm* **1** : clucking (of a hen), crowing (of a rooster) **2** : boasting
cacatúa *nf* : cockatoo
cace, etc. → **cazar**
cacería *nf* **1** CAZA : hunt, hunting **2** : hunting party
cacerola *nf* : pan, saucepan
cacha *nf* : butt (of a gun)
cachalote *nm* : sperm whale
cachar *vt fam* : to catch
cacharro *nm* **1** *fam* : thing, piece of junk **2** *fam* : jalopy **3 cacharros** *nmpl* : pots and pans
cache *nm* : cache, cache memory
caché *nm* : cachet
cachear *vt* : to search, to frisk
cachemir *nm* : cashmere
cachemira *nf* → **cachemir**
cacheo *nm* : frisking, body search
cachetada *nf* BOFETADA : slap on the face
cachete *nm* : cheek
cachetear *vt* BOFETEAR : to slap
cachiporra *nf* : bludgeon, club, blackjack
cachirul *nm Mex fam* : cheating ⟨hacer cachirul : to cheat⟩
cachivache *nm fam* : thing, piece of junk ⟨cachivaches : stuff, junk⟩
cacho *nm fam* : piece, bit
cachondo, -da *adj Mex & Spain fam* : horny, lustful
cachorro, -rra *n* **1** : cub **2** PERRITO : puppy
cachucha *nf Mex* : cap, baseball cap
cacique *nm* **1** : chief (of a tribe) **2** : boss (in politics)
caco *nm fam* : thief
cacofonía *nf* : cacophony
cacto *nm* : cactus
cactus → **cacto**
cada *adj* **1** : each, every ⟨cuestan diez pesos cada una : they cost ten pesos each⟩ ⟨cada vez : each/every time⟩ **2** : every ⟨cada dos semanas : every two weeks, every other week⟩ ⟨cada cinco metros : every five meters⟩ **3** : every ⟨cuatro de cada cinco : four out of (every) five⟩ **4** : such, some ⟨sales con cada historia : you come up with such crazy stories⟩ **5 cada vez más** : more and more, increasingly **6 cada vez menos** : less and less
cadalso *nm* : scaffold, gallows
cadáver *nm* : corpse, cadaver
cadavérico, -ca *adj* **1** : cadaverous **2** : cadaveric (in medicine)
caddie *or* **caddy** *nmf, pl* **caddies** : caddy
cadena *nf* **1** : chain **2** : network, channel **3 cadena de montaje** : assembly line **4 cadena perpetua** : life sentence
cadencia *nf* : cadence, rhythm
cadencioso, -sa *adj* : rhythmic, rhythmical
cadera *nf* : hip
cadete *nmf* : cadet
cadmio *nm* : cadmium
caducar {72} *vi* : to expire
caducidad *nf* : expiration
caduco, -ca *adj* **1** : outdated, obsolete **2** : deciduous
caer {13} *vi* **1** : to fall ⟨cayó al suelo : he fell on the floor/ground⟩ ⟨lo dejó caer : she dropped it⟩ **2** : to drop away, to slope **3** : to fall (of night) **4** : to collapse, to fall **5** : to hang (down) **6** : to realize, to understand ⟨caer (en) que . . . : to realize that . . .⟩ **7 — en** : to fall into (a trap, etc.) ⟨caer en el error de : to make the mistake of⟩ ⟨caer en manos de : to fall into the hands of⟩ ⟨caer en la tentación : to give in to temptation⟩ **8 caer en desgracia** : to fall out of favor **9 caer enfermo** : to fall ill **10 caerle bien/mal a alguien** *fam* : to sit well/poorly with someone ⟨me caes bien : I like you⟩ — **caerse** *vr* : to fall (down) ⟨se cayó de rodillas : she fell to her knees⟩
café¹ *adj* : brown ⟨ojos cafés : brown eyes⟩
café² *nm* **1** : coffee **2** : café
cafeína *nf* : caffeine
cafetal *nm* : coffee plantation
cafetalero¹, -ra *adj* : coffee ⟨cosecha cafetalera : coffee harvest⟩
cafetalero², -ra *n* : coffee grower
cafetera *nf* : coffeepot, coffeemaker
cafetería *nf* **1** : coffee shop, café **2** : lunchroom, cafeteria
cafetero¹, -ra *adj* : coffee-producing
cafetero², -ra *n* : coffee grower
caficultura *Mex* → **caficultura**
caficultor, -tora *n* : coffee grower
caficultura *nf* : coffee industry
caguama *nf* **1** : large Caribbean turtle **2** *Mex* : large bottle of beer
caída *nf* **1** BAJA, DESCENSO : fall, drop **2** : collapse, downfall
caído, -da *adj* **1** : fallen **2** : drooping, sagging
caiga, etc. → **caer**
caimán *nm, pl* **caimanes** : alligator

caimito *nm* : star apple
caja *nf* **1** : box, case **2** *or* **caja registradora** : cash register, checkout **3** : bed (of a truck) **4** *fam* : coffin **5 caja de cambios** : gearbox **6 caja fuerte** *or* **caja de caudales** : safe **7 caja de seguridad** : safe-deposit box **8 caja negra** : black box **9 caja torácica** : rib cage
cajero, -ra *n* **1** : cashier **2** : teller **3 cajero automático** : automated teller machine, ATM
cajeta *nf Mex* : sweet caramel-flavored spread
cajetilla *nf* : pack (of cigarettes)
cajón *nm, pl* **cajones 1** : drawer, till **2** : crate, case **3** ATAÚD : coffin, casket **4 cajón de arena** : sandbox **5 cajón de estacionamiento** *Mex* : parking space
cajuela *nf Mex* : trunk (of a car)
cal *nf* : lime
cala *nf* : cove, inlet
calabacín *nm, pl* **-cines** : zucchini
calabacita *nf Mex* : zucchini
calabaza *nf* **1** : pumpkin, squash **2** : gourd **3 dar calabazas a** : to give the brush-off to, to jilt
calabozo *nm* **1** : prison **2** : jail cell
calado¹, -da *adj* : drenched
calado² *nm* : draft (of a ship)
calamar *nm* **1** : squid **2 calamares** *nmpl* : calamari
calambre *nm* **1** ESPASMO : cramp **2** : electric shock, jolt
calamidad *nf* DESASTRE : calamity, disaster
calamina *nf* : calamine
calamitoso, -sa *adj* : calamitous, disastrous
calaña *nf* : ilk, kind, sort ⟨una persona de mala calaña : a bad sort⟩
calar *vt* **1** : to soak through **2** : to pierce, to penetrate — *vi* : to catch on — **calarse** *vr* : to get drenched
calavera¹ *nf* **1** : skull **2** *Mex* : taillight
calavera² *nm* : rake, rogue
calcar {72} *vt* **1** : to trace **2** : to copy, to imitate
calce, etc. → **calzar**
calceta *nf* : knee-high stocking
calcetería *nf* : hosiery
calcetín *nm, pl* **-tines** : sock
calcinar *vt* : to char, to burn
calcio *nm* : calcium
calco *nm* **1** : transfer, tracing **2** : copy, image
calcomanía *nf* : decal, transfer
calculador, -dora *adj* : calculating
calculadora *nf* : calculator
calcular *vt* **1** : to calculate, to estimate **2** : to plan, to scheme
cálculo *nm* **1** : calculation, estimation **2** : calculus **3** : plan, scheme **4 cálculo biliar** : gallstone **5 hoja de cálculo** : spreadsheet
caldear *vt* : to heat, to warm — **caldearse** *vr* **1** : to heat up **2** : to become heated, to get tense
caldera *nf* **1** : cauldron **2** : boiler
caldero *nm* : cauldron
caldo *nm* **1** : broth, stock **2 caldo de cultivo** : culture medium, breeding ground

caldoso, -sa *adj* : watery
calefacción *nf, pl* **-ciones** : heating, heat
calefactor *nm* : heater
caleidoscopio → **calidoscopio**
calendario *nm* **1** : calendar **2** : timetable, schedule
caléndula *nf* : marigold
calentador *nm* : heater
calentamiento *nm* **1** : heating, warming ⟨calentamiento global : global warming⟩ **2** : warm-up (in sports)
calentar {55} *vt* **1** : to heat, to warm **2** *fam* : to annoy, to anger **3** *fam* : to excite, to turn on — **calentarse** *vr* **1** : to get warm, to heat up **2** : to warm up (in sports) **3** *fam* : to become sexually aroused **4** *fam* : to get mad
calentura *nf* **1** FIEBRE : temperature, fever **2** : cold sore
calesa *nf* : buggy
calibrador *nm* : gauge, calipers *pl*
calibrar *vt* : to calibrate — **calibración** *nf*
calibre *nm* **1** : caliber, gauge **2** : importance, excellence **3** : kind, sort ⟨un problema de grueso calibre : a serious problem⟩
calicó *nm* : calico (cloth)
calidad *nf* **1** : quality, grade **2** : position, status **3 en calidad de** : as, in the capacity of
cálido, -da *adj* **1** : hot ⟨un clima cálido : a hot climate⟩ **2** : warm ⟨una cálida bienvenida : a warm welcome⟩
calidoscopio *nm* : kaleidoscope
caliente *adj* **1** : hot, warm ⟨mantenerse caliente : to stay warm⟩ **2** : heated, fiery ⟨una disputa caliente : a heated argument⟩ **3** *fam* : sexually excited, horny
califa *nm* : caliph
calificación *nf, pl* **-ciones 1** NOTA : grade (for a course) **2** : rating, score **3** CLASIFICACIÓN : qualification, qualifying ⟨ronda de calificación : qualifying round⟩
calificar {72} *vt* **1** : to grade **2** : to describe, to rate ⟨la calificaron de buena alumna : they described her as a good student⟩ **3** : to qualify, to modify (in grammar)
calificativo¹, -va *adj* : qualifying
calificativo² *nm* : qualifier, epithet
caligrafía *nf* **1** LETRA : handwriting **2** : calligraphy
calipso *nm* : calypso
calistenia *nf* : calisthenics
cáliz *nm, pl* **cálices 1** : chalice, goblet **2** : calyx
caliza *nf* : limestone
calizo, -za *adj* : chalky, limy
callado, -da *adj* : quiet, silent — **calladamente** *adv*
callampa *nf Chile* **1** : mushroom **2 callampas** *pl* : slums, shantytown
callar *vi* **1** : to keep quiet, to be silent — *vt* **1** : to silence, to hush ⟨¡calla a los niños! : keep the children quiet!⟩ **2** : to keep secret — **callarse** *vr* **1** : to remain silent ⟨¡cállate! : be quiet!, shut up!⟩
calle *nf* : street, road ⟨calle de sentido único : one-way street⟩ ⟨calle sin salida

: dead-end street ⟨salir a la calle : to go out/outside⟩ ⟨salir a la(s) calle(s) : to take to the streets⟩ ⟨la echó a la calle : he kicked her out⟩

callejear *vi* : to wander about the streets, to hang out

callejero, -ra *adj* : street ⟨perro callejero : stray dog⟩

callejón *nm, pl* **-jones** 1 : alley 2 **callejón sin salida** : dead-end street

callejuela *nf* 1 : alley 2 : narrow street, side street

callo *nm* 1 : callus, corn 2 **callos** *nmpl* : tripe

calloso, -sa *adj* : callous

calma *nf* : calm, quiet

calmante[1] *adj* : calming, soothing

calmante[2] *nm* : tranquilizer, sedative

calmar *vt* 1 : to calm, to soothe — **calmarse** *vi* 1 : to calm down 2 : to ease (of pain, etc.)

calmo, -ma *adj* : calm, tranquil

calmoso, -sa *adj* 1 : calm, quiet 2 LENTO : slow

caló *nm* : Gypsy slang

calor *nm* 1 : heat ⟨hace calor : it's hot outside⟩ ⟨tener calor : to feel hot⟩ ⟨entrar en calor : to warm up, to get warm⟩ 2 : warmth, affection 3 : ardor, passion

caloría *nf* : calorie

calórico, -ca *adj* : caloric

calorífico, -ca *adj* : caloric

calque, etc. → calcar

calumnia *nf* : slander, libel — **calumnioso, -sa** *adj*

calumniar *vt* : to slander, to libel

caluroso, -sa *adj* 1 : hot 2 : warm, enthusiastic — **calurosamente** *adv*

calva *nf* : bald spot, bald head

calvario *nm* : ordeal, misery ⟨vivir un calvario : to go through hell⟩

calvicie *nf* : baldness

calvo[1]**, -va** *adj* : bald

calvo[2]**, -va** *n* : bald person

calza *nf* : block, wedge

calzada *nf* : roadway, avenue

calzado *nm* : footwear

calzador *nm* : shoehorn

calzar {21} *vt* 1 : to wear (shoes) ⟨¿de cuál calza? : what is your shoe size?⟩ ⟨calzar tenis : to wear sneakers⟩ 2 : to provide with shoes

calzoncillos *nmpl* : underpants, briefs

calzones *nmpl* : underpants, panties

cama *nf* 1 : bed 2 **cama elástica** : trampoline

camada *nf* : litter, brood

camafeo *nm* : cameo

camaleón *nm, pl* **-leones** : chameleon

cámara *nf* 1 : camera 2 : chamber, room 3 : house (in government) 4 : inner tube

camarada *nmf* 1 : comrade, companion 2 : colleague

camaradería *nf* : camaraderie

camarero, -ra *n* 1 MESERO : waiter, waitress *f* 2 BARMAN : bartender 3 : bellhop *m*, chambermaid *f* (in a hotel) 4 : steward *m*, stewardess *f* (on a ship, etc.)

camarilla *nf* : political clique

camarín *nm, pl* **-rines** 1 *Chile, Peru, Uru* : locker room 2 *Arg, Uru* : dressing room

camarógrafo, -fa *n* : cameraman *m*, camerawoman *f*

camarón *nm, pl* **-rones** 1 : shrimp 2 : prawn

camarote *nm* : cabin, stateroom

camastro *nm* : small hard bed, pallet

cambalache *nm fam* : swap

cambiable *adj* : changeable

cambiante *adj* 1 : changing 2 VARIABLE : changeable, variable

cambiar *vt* 1 : to change ⟨le cambió la vida : it changed her life⟩ ⟨cambiaron el menú : they changed the menu⟩ ⟨cambiar algo de lugar : to move something⟩ 2 : to exchange, to trade ⟨lo cambió por otro : she exchanged it for another⟩ 3 : to change (money) ⟨cambiar pesos a euros : to change pesos into euros⟩ 4 : to change, to replace ⟨cambió la llanta/contraseña : he changed the tire/password⟩ ⟨le cambié el pañal : I changed her diaper⟩ — *vi* 1 : to change ⟨el tiempo cambió : the weather changed⟩ ⟨cambiar de color : to change color⟩ ⟨cambiar de tema : to change the subject⟩ ⟨cambiar de opinión/idea : to change one's mind⟩ 2 **cambiar de velocidad** : to shift gears — **cambiarse** *vr* 1 : to change ⟨se ha cambiado mucho : she's changed a lot⟩ 2 *or* **cambiarse de ropa** : to change (clothes) 3 MUDARSE : to move (to a new address)

cambio *nm* 1 : change, alteration ⟨cambio climático : climate change⟩ ⟨cambio de horario : schedule change⟩ ⟨cambio de domicilio : change of address⟩ 2 : exchange (of goods, etc.) 3 : change (money) 4 : currency exchange 5 : gear ⟨palanca de cambio : gearshift⟩ ⟨caja de cambios : gearbox⟩ 6 **a cambio (de)** : in exchange (for) 7 **en ~** : instead 8 **en ~** : however, on the other hand

cambista *nmf* : exchange broker, money changer

camboyano, -na *adj & n* : Cambodian

cambur *nm Ven* : banana

camello *nm* 1 : camel 2 *fam* TRAFICANTE : drug dealer, pusher

camellón *nm, pl* **-llones** *Mex* : traffic island

camerino *nm* : dressing room

camilla *nf* : stretcher

camillero, -ra *n* : orderly (in a hospital)

caminante *nmf* : wayfarer, walker

caminar *vi* 1 ANDAR : to walk ⟨prefiero ir caminando : I prefer to walk⟩ 2 : to move, to progress 3 FUNCIONAR : to work, to run — *vt* : to walk, to cover (a distance)

caminata *nf* : hike, long walk

camino *nm* 1 : path, road 2 : journey ⟨ponerse en camino : to set off⟩ 3 : way ⟨a medio camino : halfway there⟩

camión *nm, pl* **camiones** 1 : truck 2 *Mex* : bus

camionero, -ra *n* 1 : truck driver 2 *Mex* : bus driver

camioneta *nf* : light truck, van

camisa *nf* **1** : shirt **2 camisa de fuerza** : straitjacket

camiseta *nf* **1** : T-shirt **2** : undershirt

camisón *nm, pl* **-sones** : nightshirt, nightgown

camomila *nf* MANZANILLA : chamomile

camorra *nf fam* : fight, trouble ⟨buscar camorra : to pick a fight⟩

camote *nm* **1** : root vegetable similar to the sweet potato **2 hacerse camote** *Mex fam* : to get mixed up

campal *adj* : pitched, fierce (of a battle)

campamento *nm* : camp

campana *nf* : bell

campanada *nf* : stroke (of a clock), peal (of bells)

campanario *nm* : bell tower, belfry

campanazo *nm* **1** → **campanada 2 campanazo inicial** : starting bell

campanilla *nf* **1** : bluebell **2** : uvula **3 campanilla blanca** : snowdrop

campante *adj* : nonchalant, smug ⟨seguir tan campante : to go on as if nothing had happened⟩

campaña *nf* **1** CAMPO : countryside, country **2** : campaign **3 tienda de campaña** : tent

campañol *nm* : vole

campechana *nf Mex* : puff pastry

campechano, -na *adj* : friendly and down-to-earth

campeón, -peona *n, mpl* **-peones** : champion

campeonato *nm* : championship

cámper *nm* : camper (vehicle)

campera *nf* CHAQUETA : jacket

campero, -ra *adj* : country, rural

campesino, -na *n* : peasant, farm laborer

campestre *adj* : rural, rustic

camping *nm* **1** : camping **2** : campsite

campiña *nf* CAMPO : countryside, country

campista *nmf* : camper

campo *nm* **1** CAMPAÑA : countryside, country **2** : field (of crops, ice, etc.) **3** : field (in sports), course (in golf) **4** : field, area ⟨su campo de responsabilidad : her area of responsibility⟩ ⟨el campo tecnológico : the field of technology⟩ **5** : camp ⟨campo de refugiados : refugee camp⟩ ⟨campo de concentración : concentration camp⟩ **6 campo de aviación** : airfield **7 campo de batalla** : battlefield **8 campo magnético** : magnetic field **9 estudio de campo** : field study

camposanto *nm* : graveyard, cemetery

campus *nms & pl* : campus

camuflaje *nm* : camouflage

camuflajear *vt* : to camouflage

camuflar → **camuflajear**

can *nm* : hound, dog

cana *nf* **1** : gray hair ⟨le salen canas : he's going gray⟩ **2 echar una cana al aire** : to let one's hair down

canadiense *adj & nmf* : Canadian

canal¹ *nm* **1** : canal **2** : channel **3** : feed (on social media)

canal² *nmf* : gutter, groove

canalé *nm* : rib, ribbing (in fabric)

canaleta *nf* : gutter

canalete *nm* : paddle

canalizar {21} *vt* : to channel

canalla¹ *adj fam* : low, rotten

canalla² *nmf fam* : bastard, swine

canapé *nm* **1** : canapé **2** SOFÁ : couch, sofa

canario¹, -ria *adj* : of or from the Canary Islands

canario², -ria *n* : Canary Islander

canario³ *nm* : canary

canasta *nf* : basket

canasto *nm* {21} : (large) basket

cancel *nm* **1** : sliding door **2** : partition

cancelación *nf, pl* **-ciones 1** : cancellation **2** : payment in full

cancelar *vt* **1** : to cancel **2** : to pay off, to settle

cáncer *nm* : cancer

Cáncer¹ *nm* : Cancer (sign or constellation)

Cáncer² *nmf* : Cancer (person)

cancerígeno¹, -na *adj* : carcinogenic

cancerígeno² *nm* : carcinogen

canceroso, -sa *adj* : cancerous

cancha *nf* : court, field (for sports) ⟨cancha de golf : golf course⟩

canciller *nm* : chancellor

cancillería *nf* : ministry of foreign affairs

canción *nf, pl* **canciones 1** : song **2 canción de cuna** : lullaby

cancionero¹ *nm* : songbook

cancionero², -ra *n Mex* : singer

candado *nm* : padlock

candela *nf* **1** : flame, fire **2** : candle

candelabro *nm* : candelabra

candelero *nm* **1** : candlestick **2 estar en el candelero** : to be in the spotlight

candente *adj* : red-hot, white-hot

candidato, -ta *n* : candidate, applicant

candidatura *nf* : candidacy

candidez *nf* **1** : simplicity **2** INGENUIDAD : naïveté, ingenuousness

cándido, -da *adj* **1** : simple, unassuming **2** INGENUO : naive, ingenuous

candil *nm* : oil lamp

candilejas *nfpl* : footlights

candor *nm* : naïveté, innocence

caneca *nf Col* **1** : garbage can **2** PAPELERA : wastebasket **3** BIDÓN : drum

canela *nf* : cinnamon

canelones *nmpl* : cannelloni

cangrejo *nm* JAIBA : crab

canguro¹ *nm* : kangaroo

canguro² *nmf Spain fam* : baby-sitter

caníbal¹ *adj* : cannibalistic

caníbal² *nmf* ANTROPÓFAGO : cannibal

canibalismo *nm* ANTROPOFAGIA : cannibalism

canica *nf* : marble ⟨jugar a las canicas : to play marbles⟩

caniche *nm* : poodle

canijo, -ja *adj* **1** *fam* : puny, weak **2** *Mex fam* DIFÍCIL : tough, hard

canilla *nf* **1** : shin **2** *Arg, Uru* : faucet

canillita *nmf Arg* : newspaper vendor

canino¹, -na *adj* : canine

canino² *nm* **1** COLMILLO : canine (tooth) **2** : dog, canine

canje *nm* : exchange, trade

canjeable *adj* : exchangeable
canjear *vt* : to exchange, to trade
cannabis *nm* : cannabis
cano, -na *adj* : gray ⟨un hombre de pelo cano : a gray-haired man⟩
canoa *nf* : canoe
canon *nm, pl* **cánones** : canon
canónico, -ca *adj* : canonical
canónigo *nm* : canon (of a church)
canonizar {21} *vt* : to canonize — **canonización** *nf*
canoso, -sa → **cano**
cansado, -da *adj* **1** : tired ⟨estar cansado : to be tired⟩ **2** : tiresome ⟨ser cansado : to be tiring⟩
cansancio *nm* : tiredness
cansar *vt* : to tire — *vi* : to be tiresome — **cansarse** *vr* **1** : to tire oneself out **2** : to get bored
cansino, -na *adj* : slow, weary, lethargic
cantaleta *nf fam* : nagging ⟨la misma cantaleta : the same old story⟩
cantalupo *nm* : cantaloupe
cantante[1] *adj* : singing
cantante[2] *nmf* : singer
cantar[1] *vi* **1** : to sing **2** CACAREAR : to crow ⟨CHIRRIAR : to chirp (of insects) — *vt* **1** : to sing **2** : to call out, to recite ⟨cantar victoria : to claim victory⟩
cantar[2] *nm* : song, ballad
cántaro *nm* **1** : pitcher, jug **2 llover a cántaros** *fam* : to rain cats and dogs
cantata *nf* : cantata
cantautor, -tora *n* : singer-songwriter
cantera *nf* : quarry
cantero *nm* **1** MAMPOSTERO : mason, stonemason **2** ARRIATE : bed (for plants)
cántico *nm* : chant
cantidad[1] *adv fam* : a lot ⟨me gustó cantidad : I liked it a lot⟩ ⟨ese carro me costó cantidad : that car cost me plenty⟩
cantidad[2] *nf* **1** : quantity **2** : sum, amount (of money) **3** *fam* : a lot, a great many ⟨había cantidad de gente : there were tons of people⟩
cantillos *nmpl* : jacks *pl*
cantimplora *nf* : canteen, water bottle
cantina *nf* **1** : tavern, bar **2** : canteen, mess, dining quarters *pl*
cantinero, -ra *n* : bartender
canto *nm* **1** : singing **2** : chant ⟨canto gregoriano : Gregorian chant⟩ **3** : song (of a bird) **4** : edge, end ⟨de canto : on end, sideways⟩ **5 canto rodado** : boulder
cantón *nm, pl* **cantones** **1** : canton **2** *Mex fam* : place, home
cantonés[1], **-nesa** *adj & n, mpl* **-neses** : Cantonese
cantonés[2] *nm, pl* **-neses** : Cantonese (language)
cantor[1], **-tora** *adj* **1** : singing **2 pájaro cantor** : songbird
cantor[2], **-tora** *n* **1** : singer **2** : cantor
canturrear *v* : to sing softly
caña *nf* **1** : cane ⟨caña de azúcar : sugarcane⟩ **2** : reed **3 caña de pescar** : fishing rod **4 caña del timón** : tiller (of a boat)

cañada *nf* : ravine, gully
cáñamo *nm* : hemp
cañaveral *nm* : sugarcane field
cañería *nf* TUBERÍA : pipes *pl*, piping
cañero[1], **-ra** *adj* : sugar cane
cañero[2], **-ra** *n* **1** : sugar cane grower **2** : sugar cane worker
caño *nm* **1** : pipe **2** : spout **3** : channel (for navigation)
cañón *nm, pl* **cañones** **1** : cannon **2** : barrel (of a gun) **3** : canyon
cañonazo *nm* : firing (of a cannon) ⟨saludo de 21 cañonazos : 21-gun salute⟩
cañonear *vt* : to shell, to bombard
cañonero *nm* : gunboat
caoba *nf* : mahogany
caos *nm* : chaos
caótico, -ca *adj* : chaotic
capa *nf* **1** : cape, cloak **2** : coating **3** : layer, stratum **4** : (social) class, stratum
capacidad *nf* **1** : capacity **2** : capability, ability
capacitación *nf, pl* **-ciones** : training
capacitar *vt* : to train, to qualify
capar *vt* : to castrate
caparazón *nm, pl* **-zones** : shell
capataz[1] *nmf, pl* **-taces** : foreman *m*, forewoman *f*
capataz[2], **-taza** *n* → **capataz**[1]
capaz *adj, pl* **capaces** **1** : capable, able ⟨capaz de trabajar : able to work⟩ ⟨es capaz de cualquier cosa : he's capable of anything⟩ **2** COMPETENTE : competent, capable **3** : spacious ⟨capaz para : with room for⟩
capcioso, -sa *adj* : cunning, deceptive ⟨pregunta capciosa : trick question⟩
capea *nf* : amateur bullfight
capear *vt* **1** : to make a pass with the cape (in bullfighting) **2** : to weather (a storm, crisis, etc.)
capellán *nm, pl* **-llanes** : chaplain
capilar[1] *adj* **1** : capillary **2** : hair
capilar[2] *nm* : capillary
capilla *nf* : chapel
capirotada *nf Mex* : traditional bread pudding
capirotazo *nm* : flip, flick
capital[1] *adj* **1** : capital **2** : chief, principal
capital[2] *nm* : capital ⟨capital de riesgo : venture capital⟩
capital[3] *nf* : capital, capital city
capitalino[1], **-na** *adj* : of or from a capital city
capitalino[2], **-na** *n* : inhabitant of a capital city
capitalismo *nm* : capitalism
capitalista *adj & nmf* : capitalist
capitalizar {21} *vt* : to capitalize — **capitalización** *nf*
capitán, -tana *n, mpl* **-tanes** **1** : captain **2 capitán de corbeta** : lieutenant commander
capitanear *vt* : to captain, to command
capitel *nm* : capital (of a column)
capitolio *nm* : capitol
capitulación *nf, pl* **-ciones** : capitulation
capitular *vi* : to capitulate, to surrender

capítulo *nm* **1** : chapter, section **2** : matter, subject

capo, capa *n* : boss

capó *nm* : hood (of a car)

capón, pl capones *adj* : capon

caporal *nm* **1** : chief, leader **2** : foreman (on a ranch)

capot → **capó**

capota *nf* : top (of a convertible)

capote *nm* **1** : cloak, overcoat **2** : bullfighter's cape **3** *Mex* : hood (of a car)

capricho *nm* : whim, caprice

caprichoso, -sa *adj* : capricious, fickle

Capricornio[1] *nm* : Capricorn (sign or constellation)

Capricornio[2] *nmf* : Capricorn (person)

cápsula *nf* : capsule

captar *vt* **1** : to catch, to grasp **2** : to gain, to attract **3** : to harness, to collect (waters)

captor, -tora *n* : captor

captura *nf* : capture, seizure

capturar *vt* : to capture, to seize

capucha *nf* : hood, cowl

capuchino *nm* : cappuccino

capullo *nm* **1** : cocoon **2** : bud (of a flower)

caqui *adj & nm* : khaki

cara *nf* **1** : face **2** : look, appearance ⟨¡qué buena cara tiene ese pastel! : that cake looks delicious!⟩ **3** *fam* : nerve, gall **4 (de) cara a** : facing **5 de cara a** : in view of, in the light of

carabina *nf* : carbine

carabinero, -ra *n* : police officer

caracol *nm* **1** : snail **2** CONCHA : conch, seashell **3** : ringlet

caracola *nf* : conch

carácter *nm, pl* **caracteres 1** ÍNDOLE : character, kind, nature **2** TEMPERAMENTO : character, temperament **3** : character (in writing)

característica *nf* RASGO : trait, feature, characteristic

característico, -ca *adj* : characteristic — **característicamente** *adv*

caracterizar {21} *vt* : to characterize — **caracterización** *nf*

caradura *adj* DESCARADO : cheeky, impudent

caramba *interj* **1** (*expressing annoyance or anger*) : darn!, heck! **2** (*expressing surprise*) : wow!, good Lord!

carámbano *nm* : icicle

carambola *nf* **1** : carom **2** : ruse, trick ⟨por carambola : by a lucky chance⟩

caramelo *nm* **1** : caramel **2** DULCE : candy

caramillo *nm* **1** : pipe, small flute **2** : heap, pile

caraqueño[1]**, -ña** *adj* : of or from Caracas

caraqueño[2]**, -ña** *n* : person from Caracas

carátula *nf* **1** : title page **2** : cover, dust jacket **3** CARETA : mask **4** *Mex* : face, dial (of a clock or watch)

caravana *nf* **1** : caravan **2** : convoy **3** REMOLQUE : trailer

caray → **caramba**

carbohidrato *nm* : carbohydrate

carbón *nm, pl* **carbones 1** : coal **2** : charcoal

carbonatado, -da *adj* : carbonated

carboncillo *nm* : charcoal

carbonera *nf* : coal cellar, coal bunker (on a ship)

carbonero, -ra *adj* : coal

carbonizar {21} *vt* : to char — **carbonizarse** *vr*

carbono *nm* : carbon

carburador *nm* : carburetor

carburante *nm* : fuel

carca *nmf fam* : old fogy

carcacha *nf fam* : jalopy, wreck

carcaj *nm* : quiver (for arrows)

carcajada *nf* : loud laugh, guffaw ⟨reírse a carcajadas : to roar with laughter⟩

carcajearse *vr* : to roar with laughter, to be in stitches

cárcel *nf* PRISIÓN : jail, prison

carcelario, -ria *adj* : prison

carcelero, -ra *n* : jailer

carcinogénico, -ca *adj* → **cancerígeno**

carcinógeno *nm* → **cancerígeno**

carcinoma *nm* : carcinoma

carcomer *vt* : to eat away at, to consume

carcomido, -da *adj* **1** : worm-eaten **2** : decayed, rotten

cardar *vt* : to card, to comb

cardenal *nm* **1** : cardinal (in religion) **2** : bruise

cardíaco *or* **cardiaco, -ca** *adj* : cardiac, heart

cárdigan *nm, pl* **-gans** : cardigan

cardinal *adj* : cardinal

cardiología *nf* : cardiology

cardiólogo, -ga *n* : cardiologist

cardiovascular *adj* : cardiovascular

cardo *nm* : thistle

cardumen *nm* : school of fish

carecer {53} *vi* **~ de** : to lack ⟨el cheque carecía de fondos : the check had insufficient funds⟩

carencia *nf* **1** FALTA : lack **2** ESCASEZ : shortage **3** DEFICIENCIA : deficiency

carente *adj* **~ de** : lacking (in)

careo *nm* : confrontation, face-off

carero, -ra *adj fam* : pricey

carestía *nf* **1** : rise in cost ⟨la carestía de la vida : the high cost of living⟩ **2** : dearth, scarcity

careta *nf* MÁSCARA : mask

carey *nm* **1** : sea turtle **2** : tortoiseshell

carga *nf* **1** : loading **2** : freight, load, cargo **3** : burden, responsibility **4** : charge ⟨carga eléctrica : electrical charge⟩ **5** : attack, charge

cargada *nf Arg, Uru* : joke

cargado, -da *adj* **1** : loaded **2** : bogged down, weighted down **3** : close, stuffy **4** : full, fraught ⟨cargado de tensión/errores : fraught with tension/errors⟩ **5** FUERTE : strong ⟨café cargado : strong coffee⟩ **6 cargado de hombros** : round-shouldered

cargador[1]**, -dora** *n* : longshoreman *m*, longshorewoman *f*

cargador[2] *nm* **1** : magazine (for a firearm) **2** : charger (for batteries)

cargamento *nm* : cargo, load

cargar {52} *vt* **1** : to carry **2** : to load, to fill **3** : to charge **4** : to burden ⟨car-

gado de deudas : burdened with debts⟩
5 SUBIR : to upload — *vi* **1** : to load **2**
: to rest (in architecture) **3** ~ **con** : to
shoulder, to take on (a responsibility,
etc.) **4** ~ **sobre** : to fall upon
cargo *nm* **1** : burden, load **2** : charge ⟨estar a cargo de : to be in charge of⟩ ⟨correr
a cargo de : to be paid by⟩ ⟨hacerse cargo
de : to take charge of, to take care of⟩
⟨tener a su cargo : to be in charge of⟩ **3**
: charge, cost **4** : position, office
cargue[1], etc. → **cargar**
cargue[2] *nm* Col : loading
carguero[1], **-ra** *adj* : freight, cargo ⟨tren
carguero : freight train⟩
carguero[2] *nm* : freighter, cargo ship
cariarse *vr* : to decay (of teeth)
caribe *adj* : Caribbean ⟨el mar Caribe
: the Caribbean Sea⟩
caribeño, -ña *adj* : Caribbean
caribú *nm, pl* **caribúes** : caribou
caricatura *nf* **1** : caricature **2** : cartoon
caricaturista *nmf* : caricaturist, cartoonist
caricaturizar {21} *vt* : to caricature
caricia *nf* **1** : caress **2 hacer caricias**
: to pet, to stroke
caridad *nf* : charity
caries *nfs & pl* : cavity (in a tooth)
cariño[1] *nm* AFECTO : affection, love
cariño[2], **-ña** *n* : darling, sweetheart
cariñoso, -sa *adj* AFECTUOSO : affectionate, loving — **cariñosamente** *adv*
carioca[1] *adj* : of or from Rio de Janeiro
carioca[2] *nmf* : person from Rio de Janeiro
carisma *nf* : charisma
carismático, -ca *adj* : charismatic
carita *adj* Mex fam : cute (said of a man)
⟨se cree muy carita : he thinks he's gorgeous⟩
carita sonriente *nf* : smiley face (emoticon or drawing)
caritativo, -va *adj* : charitable
cariz *nm, pl* **carices** : appearance, aspect
carmesí *adj & nm* : crimson
carmín *nm, pl* **carmines** **1** : carmine **2**
: lipstick
carnada *nf* CEBO : bait
carnal *adj* **1** : carnal **2 primo carnal**
: first cousin
carnaval *nm* : carnival
carne *nf* **1** : meat ⟨carne molida : ground
beef⟩ **2** : flesh ⟨carne de gallina : goose
bumps⟩
carné → **carnet**
carnero *nm* **1** : ram, sheep **2** : mutton
carnet *nm* **1** : identification card, ID **2**
: membership card **3 carnet de conducir** Spain : driver's license
carnicería *nf* **1** : butcher shop **2** MATANZA : slaughter, carnage
carnicero, -ra *n* : butcher
carnitas *nfpl* Mex : small chunks of
cooked pork
carnívoro[1], **-ra** *adj* : carnivorous
carnívoro[2] *nm* : carnivore
carnoso, -sa *adj* : fleshy, meaty
caro[1] *adv* : a lot ⟨costar/pagar caro : to
cost/pay a lot⟩ ⟨vender caro : to sell

high, to sell at a high price⟩ ⟨un error
que me costó caro : a mistake that cost
me dearly⟩
caro[2], **-ra** *adj* **1** : expensive, dear ⟨es
muy/demasiado caro : it's very/too expensive⟩ **2** QUERIDO : dear, beloved
carpa *nf* **1** : carp **2** : big top (of a circus)
3 : tent
carpeta *nf* : folder, binder, portfolio (of
drawings, etc.)
carpetazo *nm* **dar carpetazo a** : to shelve,
to defer
carpintería *nf* **1** : carpentry **2** : carpenter's workshop
carpintero, -ra *n* : carpenter
carraspear *vi* : to clear one's throat
carraspera *nf* : hoarseness ⟨tener carraspera : to have a frog in one's throat⟩
carrera *nf* **1** : run, running ⟨a la carrera
: at full speed⟩ ⟨de carrera : hastily⟩ **2**
: race ⟨carrera de caballos : horse race⟩
3 : course of study ⟨estudiar la carrera
de medicina : to study medicine⟩ **4** : career, profession **5** : run (in baseball)
carreta *nf* : cart, wagon
carrete *nm* **1** : spool (for thread), bobbin
(in sewing machine), reel (for film, etc.)
⟨carrete de pesca : fishing reel⟩ **2** : roll
of film **3** : (electrical) coil
carretear *vi* : to taxi
carretel → **carrete**
carretera *nf* : highway, road ⟨carretera de
peaje : turnpike⟩
carretero, -ra *adj* : highway ⟨el sistema
carretero : the highway system⟩
carretilla *nf* **1** : wheelbarrow **2 carretilla elevadora** : forklift
carril *nm* **1** : lane ⟨carretera de doble
carril : two-lane highway⟩ **2** : rail (on a
railroad track)
carrillo *nm* : cheek, jowl
carrito *nm* : cart ⟨carrito de compras, carrito de la compra Mexico, Spain : shopping cart⟩
carrizo *nm* JUNCO : reed
carro *nm* **1** COCHE : car **2** : cart **3**
Chile, Mex : coach (of a train) **4 carro
alegórico** : float (in a parade) **5 carro
bomba** : car bomb **6 carro de compras**
or **carro de la compra** Spain : shopping
cart
carrocería *nf* : bodywork, body (of a vehicle)
carroña *nf* : carrion
carroñero, -ra *n* : scavenger (animal)
carroza *nf* **1** : carriage **2** : float (in a
parade)
carruaje *nm* : carriage
carrusel *nm* **1** : merry-go-round **2** : carousel ⟨carrusel de equipaje : luggage
carousel⟩
carta *nf* **1** : letter ⟨carta de amor : love
letter⟩ ⟨carta de renuncia : letter of resignation⟩ **2** NAIPE : playing card **3**
: charter, constitution **4** MENÚ : menu
5 : map, chart **6 tomar cartas en** : to
intervene in
carta blanca *nf* : carte blanche
carta bomba *nf* : letter bomb

cartearse *vr* : to write to one another, to correspond

cartel *nm* : sign, poster

cártel *or* **cartel** *nm* : cartel

cartelera *nf* **1** : billboard **2** : marquee

cartera *nf* **1** BILLETERA : wallet, billfold **2** BOLSO : pocketbook, purse **3** : portfolio ⟨cartera de acciones : stock portfolio⟩

carterista *nmf* : pickpocket

cartero, -ra *n* : letter carrier, mailman *m*

cartílago *nm* : cartilage

cartilla *nf* **1** : primer, reader **2** : booklet ⟨cartilla de ahorros : bankbook⟩

cartografía *nf* : cartography

cartógrafo, -fa *n* : cartographer

cartón *nm*, *pl* **cartones** **1** : cardboard ⟨cartón madera : fiberboard⟩ **2** : carton

cartucho *nm* : cartridge

cartulina *nf* : poster board, cardboard

casa *nf* **1** : house ⟨una casa de dos pisos : a two-story house⟩ ⟨la casa blanca : the White House⟩ **2** HOGAR : home ⟨en casa : at home⟩ ⟨ir a casa : to go home⟩ **3** : home (in sports) ⟨equipo de casa : home team⟩ ⟨partido en casa : home game⟩ ⟨partido fuera de casa : away game⟩ **4** : household, family **5** : company, firm **6** casa de cambio : currency exchange **7** casa de empeños : pawnshop **8** casa de (altos) estudios : institute of (higher) learning, college, university **9** casa de salud : clinic **10** casa matriz : headquarters **11** echar/tirar/botar la casa por la ventana : to spare no expense

casaca *nf* : jacket

casado[1], -da *adj* : married

casado[2], -da *n* : married person

casamentero, -ra *n* : matchmaker

casamiento *nm* **1** : marriage **2** BODA : wedding

casar *vt* : to marry ⟨el cura que nos casó : the priest who married us⟩ — *vi* : to go together, to match up — **casarse** *vr* **1** : to get married **2** ∼ **con** : to marry

casateniente *nmf* *Mex* : landlord, landlady *f*

cascabel[1] *nm* : small bell

cascabel[2] *nf* : rattlesnake

cascada *nf* CATARATA, SALTO : waterfall, cascade

cascajo *nm* **1** : pebble, rock fragment **2** *fam* : piece of junk

cascanueces *nms & pl* : nutcracker

cascar {72} *vt* : to crack (a shell) — **cascarse** *vr* : to crack, to chip

cáscara *nf* **1** : skin, peel, rind, husk **2** : shell (of a nut or egg)

cascarón *nm*, *pl* **-rones** **1** : eggshell **2** *Mex* : shell filled with confetti

cascarrabias *nmfs & pl fam* : grouch, crab

casco *nm* **1** : helmet **2** : hull **3** : hoof **4** : fragment, shard **5** : center (of a town) **6** *Mex* : empty bottle **7** cascos *nmpl* : headphones

caserío *nm* **1** : country house **2** : hamlet

casero[1], -ra *adj* **1** : domestic, household **2** : homemade

casero[2], -ra *n* DUEÑO : landlord *m*, landlady *f*

caseta *nf* **1** : booth, stand, stall ⟨caseta de peaje, caseta de cobro *CA*, *Mex* : tollbooth⟩ **2** : doghouse **3** : dugout (in sports)

casete → **cassette**

casi *adv* **1** : almost, nearly ⟨casi un año : almost a year⟩ ⟨casi me desmayo : I almost fainted⟩ **2** (*in negative phrases*) : hardly ⟨casi nunca : hardly ever⟩ ⟨no hace casi nada : he hardly does anything⟩

casilla *nf* **1** : booth **2** : pigeonhole **3** : box (on a form) **4** casilla de correos *Arg* : P.O. box

casillero *nm* **1** : pigeonhole **2** : set of pigeonholes

casino *nm* **1** : casino **2** : (social) club

caso *nm* **1** : case ⟨en caso de : in case of⟩ ⟨en este/ese caso : in this/that case⟩ ⟨en todo/cualquier caso : in any case⟩ ⟨en el mejor/peor de los casos : at best/worst⟩ ⟨el caso es que . . . : the fact/thing is (that) . . .⟩ **2** : case (in law or medicine) **3** hacer caso : to pay attention ⟨hacer caso de algo : to pay attention to something, to notice something⟩ ⟨hacerle caso a alguien : to pay attention to someone, to listen to someone⟩ **4** hacer caso omiso de : to ignore, to take no notice of **5** no hay caso : it's useless, there's no point **6** no venir al caso : to be beside the point

caspa *nf* : dandruff

casque, etc. → **cascar**

casquete *nm* **1** : skullcap **2** casquete glaciar : ice cap **3** casquete polar : polar ice cap **4** casquete corto *Mex* : crew cut

casquillo *nm* : case, casing (of a bullet)

cassette *nmf* : cassette

casta *nf* **1** : caste **2** : lineage, stock ⟨de casta : thoroughbred, purebred⟩ **3** sacar la casta *Mex* : to come out ahead

castaña *nf* : chestnut

castañetear *vi* : to chatter (of teeth)

castañeteo *nm* : chatter, chattering (of teeth)

castaño[1], -ña *adj* : chestnut, brown

castaño[2] *nm* **1** : chestnut tree **2** : chestnut, brown

castañuela *nf* : castanet

castellano[1], -na *adj & n* : Castilian

castellano[2] *nm* ESPAÑOL : Spanish, Castilian (language)

castidad *nf* : chastity

castigar {52} *vt* : to punish

castigo *nm* : punishment

castillo *nm* **1** : castle **2** castillo de proa : forecastle **3** castillo de arena : sand castle

castizo, -za *adj* **1** AUTÉNTICO : authentic, genuine, pure **2** TRADICIONAL : traditional

casto, -ta *adj* : chaste, pure — **castamente** *adv*

castor *nm* : beaver

castración *nf, pl* **-ciones** : castration

castrar *vt* **1** : to castrate, to spay, to neuter **2** DEBILITAR : to weaken, to debilitate

castrense *adj* : military

casual *adj* **1** : chance ⟨no es casual : it's no accident⟩ **2** *Mex* : casual (of clothing)

casualidad *nf* **1** : chance **2** **por** ∼ *or* **de** ∼ : by chance, by any chance

casualmente *adv* : accidentally, by chance

casucha *or* **casuca** *nf* : shanty, hovel

cataclismo *nm* : cataclysm

catacumbas *nfpl* : catacombs

catador, -dora *n* : wine taster

catalán[1], -lana *adj & n, mpl* **-lanes** : Catalan

catalán[2] *nm* : Catalan (language)

catalizador *nm* **1** : catalyst **2** : catalytic converter

catalogar {52} *vt* : to catalog, to classify

catálogo *nm* : catalog

catamarán *nm, pl* **-ranes** : catamaran

cataplasma *nf* : poultice

catapulta *nf* : catapult

catapultar *vt* : to catapult

catar *vt* **1** : to taste, to sample **2** : to look at, to examine

catarata *nf* **1** CASCADA, SALTO : waterfall **2** : cataract

catarro *nm* RESFRIADO : cold, catarrh

catarsis *nf* : catharsis — **catártico, -ca** *adj*

catastro *nm* : property registry

catástrofe *nf* DESASTRE : catastrophe, disaster

catastrófico, -ca *adj* DESASTROSO : catastrophic, disastrous

catcher *nmf* : catcher (in baseball)

catecismo *nm* : catechism

cátedra *nf* **1** : (tenured) professorship **2** : department chair (at a university) **3** : subject, class **4 libertad de cátedra** : academic freedom

catedral *nf* : cathedral

catedrático, -ca *n* **1** PROFESOR : (tenured) professor **2** : department chair (at a university)

categoría *nf* **1** CLASE : category **2** RANGO : rank, standing **3 categoría gramatical** : part of speech **4 de** ∼ : first-rate, outstanding

categórico, -ca *adj* : categorical, unequivocal — **categóricamente** *adv*

categorizar {21} *vt* : categorize

cateo *CA, Mex* → **cacheo**

catering *or* **cátering** *nm* : catering, food service

catéter *nm* : catheter

cátodo *nm* : cathode

catolicismo *nm* : Catholicism

católico, -ca *adj & n* : Catholic

catorce *adj & nm* : fourteen — **catorce** *pron*

catorceavo[1], -va *adj* : fourteenth

catorceavo[2] *nm* : fourteenth

catre *nm* : cot

catsup *nm* : ketchup

caucásico, -ca *adj & n* : Caucasian

cauce *nm* **1** LECHO : riverbed **2** : means *pl*, channel

caucho *nm* **1** GOMA : rubber **2** : rubber tree **3** *Ven* : tire

caución *nf, pl* **cauciones** FIANZA : bail, security

caudal *nm* **1** : volume of water **2** RIQUEZA : capital, wealth **3** ABUNDANCIA : abundance

caudaloso, -sa *adj* **1** : large, mighty (of a river) **2** RICO : rich, wealthy

caudillo *nm* : leader, commander

causa *nf* **1** MOTIVO : cause, reason, motive ⟨a causa de : because of⟩ **2** IDEAL : cause ⟨morir por una causa : to die for a cause⟩ **3** : lawsuit

causal[1] *adj* : causal — **causalidad** *nf*

causal[2] *nm* : cause, grounds *pl*

causante[1] *adj* ∼ **de** : causing, responsible for

causante[2] *nmf Mex* : taxpayer

causar *vt* **1** : to cause **2** : to provoke, to arouse ⟨eso me causa gracia : I find that funny⟩

cáustico, -ca *adj* : caustic

cautela *nf* : caution, prudence

cautelar *adj* : precautionary, preventive

cauteloso, -sa *adj* : cautious, prudent — **cautelosamente** *adv*

cauterizar {21} *vt* : to cauterize

cautivador, -dora *adj* : captivating

cautivar *vt* : to captivate, to charm

cautiverio *nm* : captivity

cautivo, -va *adj & n* : captive

cauto, -ta *adj* : cautious, careful

cava *nm* : a Spanish sparkling wine

cavar *vt* : to dig — *vi* ∼ **en** : to delve into, to probe

caverna *nf* : cavern, cave

cavernícola *nmf* : caveman *m*, cavewoman *f*

cavernoso, -sa *adj* **1** : cavernous **2** : deep, resounding

caviar *nm* : caviar

cavidad *nf* : cavity

cavilar *vi* : to ponder, to deliberate

cayado *nm* : crook, staff

cayena *nf* : cayenne pepper

cayo *nm* ISLOTE : key, islet

cayó, etc. → **caer**

caza[1] *nf* **1** CACERÍA : hunt, hunting **2** : game

caza[2] *nm* : fighter plane

cazador, -dora *n* **1** : hunter **2 cazador furtivo** : poacher

cazadora *nf* : jacket, bomber jacket

cazar {21} *vt* **1** : to hunt **2** : to catch, to bag **3** *fam* : to land (a job, a spouse) — *vi* : to go hunting

cazatalentos *nmfs & pl* : talent scout

cazo *nm* **1** : saucepan, pot **2** CUCHARÓN : ladle

cazuela *nf* **1** : pan, saucepan **2** : casserole

cazurro, -rra *adj* : sullen, surly

CD *nm* : CD, compact disk

CD–ROM [sede'rom] *nm* : CD-ROM

ce *nf* : (letter) c

cebada *nf* : barley

cebar *vt* **1** : to bait **2** : to feed, to fatten **3** : to prime (a pump, etc.) — **cebarse** *vr* ~ **en** : to take it out on

cebo *nm* **1** CARNADA : bait **2** : feed **3** : primer (for firearms)

cebolla *nf* : onion

cebolleta *nf* : scallion, green onion

cebollino *nm* **1** : chive **2** : scallion

cebra *nf* : zebra

cebú *nm, pl* **cebús** *or* **cebúes** : zebu (cattle)

cecear [θeθe'ar] *vi* **1** : to lisp **2** : to pronounce the Spanish letter *s* as /θ/

ceceo [θe'θeo] *nm* **1** : lisp **2** : pronunciation of the Spanish letter *s* as /θ/

cecina *nf* : dried beef, beef jerky

cedazo *nm* : sieve

ceder *vi* **1** : to yield, to give way **2** : to diminish, to abate **3** : to give in, to relent — *vt* : to cede, to hand over

cedro *nm* : cedar

cédula *nf* : document, certificate

cegador, -dora *adj* : blinding

cegar {49} *vt* **1** : to blind **2** : to block, to stop up — *vi* : to be blinded, to go blind

ceguera *nf* : blindness

ceiba *nf* : silk-cotton tree

ceja *nf* **1** : eyebrow ⟨fruncir las cejas : to knit one's brows⟩ **2** : flange, rim

cejar *vi* : to give in, to back down

celada *nf* : trap, ambush

celador, -dora *n* GUARDIA : guard, warden

celda *nf* : cell (of a jail)

celebración *nf, pl* **-ciones** : celebration

celebrado, -da *adj* → **célebre**

celebrante *nmf* OFICIANTE : celebrant

celebrar *vt* **1** : to celebrate **2** : to hold (a meeting) **3** : to say (Mass) **4** : to welcome, to be happy about — *vi* : to be glad — **celebrarse** *vr* **1** : to be celebrated, to fall **2** : to be held, to take place

célebre *adj* : celebrated, famous

celebridad *nf* **1** : celebrity **2** FAMA : fame, celebrity

celeridad *nf* : swiftness

celeste[1] *adj* **1** : celestial **2** : sky blue, azure

celeste[2] *nm* : sky blue

celestial *adj* : heavenly, celestial

celibato *nm* : celibacy

célibe *adj & nmf* : celibate

cello ['tʃelo] → **chelo**

celo *nm* **1** : zeal, fervor **2** : heat (of females), rut (of males) **3** **celos** *nmpl* : jealousy ⟨tenerle celos a alguien : to be jealous of someone⟩

celofán *nm, pl* **-fanes** : cellophane

celosía *nf* : lattice window ⟨lattice, trellis

celoso, -sa *adj* **1** : jealous **2** : zealous — **celosamente** *adv*

celta[1] *adj* : Celtic

celta[2] *nmf* : Celt

célula *nf* : cell ⟨célula madre : stem cell⟩

celular[1] *adj* : cellular

celular[2] *nm* : cell phone

celulitis *nf* : cellulite

celuloide *nm* **1** : celluloid **2** : film, cinema

celulosa *nf* : cellulose

cementar *vt* : to cement

cementerio *nm* : cemetery

cemento *nm* : cement

cena *nf* : supper, dinner

cenador *nm* : arbor, gazebo

cenagal *nm* : bog, quagmire

cenagoso, -sa *adj* : swampy

cenar *vi* : to have dinner, to have supper — *vt* : to have for dinner or supper ⟨cenamos tamales : we had tamales for supper⟩

cencerro *nm* : cowbell

cenicero *nm* : ashtray

ceniciento, -ta *adj* : ashen

cenit *nm* : zenith, peak

ceniza *nf* **1** : ash **2 cenizas** *nfpl* : ashes (of a deceased person)

cenizo *nm* : jinx

cenote *nm Mex* : natural deposit of spring water

censar *vt* : to take a census of

censo *nm* : census

censor, -sora *n* : censor, critic

censura *nf* **1** : censorship **2** : censure, criticism

censurable *adj* : reprehensible, blameworthy

censurar *vt* **1** : to censor **2** : to censure, to criticize

centauro *nm* : centaur

centavo *nm* **1** : cent (in English-speaking countries) **2** : centavo (unit of currency in various Latin-American countries)

centella *nf* **1** : lightning flash **2** : spark

centellear *vi* **1** : to twinkle **2** : to gleam, to sparkle

centelleo *nm* : twinkling, sparkle

centena *nf* : hundred ⟨una centena de personas : a hundred people⟩

centenar *nm* **1** : hundred **2 a centenares** : by the hundreds

centenario[1]**, -ria** *adj & n* : hundred-year-old

centenario[2] *nm* : centennial

centeno *nm* : rye

centésima *nf* : hundredth

centésimo[1]**, -ma** *adj* : hundredth

centésimo[2] *nm* **1** : hundredth **2** : centesimo (Panamanian and Uruguayan unit of currency)

centi- *pref* : centi-

centígrado *adj* : centigrade, Celsius

centigramo *nm* : centigram

centímetro *nm* : centimeter

céntimo *nm* **1** : centimo (unit of currency in various Spanish- and Portuguese-speaking countries) **2** : cent (subdivision of the euro) **2** : centime (unit of currency in various French- and Portuguese-speaking countries)

centinela *nmf* : sentinel, sentry

centrado, -da *adj* **1** EQUILIBRADO : stable **2** : centered **3** ~ **en** : focused on

central[1] *adj* **1** : central **2** PRINCIPAL : main, principal

central[2] *nf* **1** : main office, headquarters **2** : power plant, power station **3 central camionera** *Mex* : bus terminal

centralista *adj & nmf* : centralist

centralita *nf* : switchboard
centralizar {21} *vt* : to centralize — **centralización** *nf*
centrar *vt* **1** : to center **2** : to focus — **centrarse** *vr* ~ **en** : to focus on, to concentrate on
céntrico, -ca *adj* : central
centrifugar {52} *vt* : to spin (clothing)
centrista *adj & nmf* : centrist
centro[1] *nmf* : center (in sports)
centro[2] *nm* **1** MEDIO : center ⟨centro de atención/gravedad : center of attention/gravity⟩ **2** : downtown **3 centro comercial** : shopping plaza **4 centro de mesa** : centerpiece **5 centro de votación** : polling place
centroamericano, -na *adj & n* : Central American
centrocampista *nmf* : midfielder
ceñido, -da *adj* AJUSTADO : tight, tight-fitting
ceñir {67} *vt* **1** : to encircle, to surround **2** : to hug, to cling to ⟨me ciñe demasiado : it's too tight on me⟩ — **ceñirse** *vr* ~ **a** : to restrict oneself to, to stick to
ceño *nm* **1** : frown, scowl **2 fruncir el ceño** : to frown, to knit one's brows
cepa *nf* **1** : stump (of a tree) **2** : stock (of a vine) **3** LINAJE : ancestry, stock
cepillar *vt* **1** : to brush **2** : to plane (wood) — **cepillarse** *vr*
cepillo *nm* **1** : brush ⟨cepillo de dientes : toothbrush⟩ **2** : plane (for woodworking)
cepo *nm* : trap (for animals)
cera *nf* **1** : wax ⟨cera de abejas : beeswax⟩ **2** : polish
cerámica *nf* **1** : ceramics *pl* **2** : pottery
cerámico, -ca *adj* : ceramic
ceramista *nmf* ALFARERO : potter
cerca[1] *adv* **1** : nearby, close by ⟨vive cerca : he lives nearby⟩ **2** : close, near ⟨cerca de aquí : near here⟩ ⟨su cumpleaños está cerca : her birthday is almost here⟩ **3** ~ **de** : nearly, almost, close to ⟨cerca de 100 personas : nearly 100 people⟩ **4 de** ~ : close up ⟨seguir de cerca : to follow closely⟩
cerca[2] *nf* **1** : fence **2** : (stone) wall
cercado *nm* : enclosure
cercanía *nf* **1** PROXIMIDAD : proximity, closeness **2 cercanías** *nfpl* : outskirts, suburbs
cercano, -na *adj* : near, close
cercar {72} *vt* **1** : to fence in, to enclose **2** : to surround
cercenar *vt* **1** : to cut off, to amputate, to sever **2** : to diminish, to curtail
cerceta *nf* : teal (duck)
cerciorarse *vr* ASEGURARSE ~ **de** : to make sure of, to verify
cerco *nm* **1** : siege **2** : cordon, circle **3** : fence
cerda *nf* **1** : bristle **2** : sow
cerdo *nm* **1** : pig, hog **2 carne de cerdo** : pork
cereal *nm* : cereal — **cereal** *adj*
cerebelo *nm* : cerebellum
cerebral *adj* : cerebral
cerebro *nm* : brain

ceremonia *nf* : ceremony ⟨sin ceremonias : informal/informally, without ceremony⟩ — **ceremonial** *adj*
ceremonioso, -sa *adj* : ceremonious
cereza *nf* : cherry
cerezo *nm* : cherry tree
cerilla *nf* **1** : match **2** : earwax
cerillo *nm* (*in various countries*) : match
cerner {56} *vt* : to sift — **cernerse** *vr* **1** : to hover **2** ~ **sobre** : to loom over, to threaten
cernidor *nm* : sieve
cernir → **cerner**
cero *nm* : zero
ceroso, -sa *adj* : waxy
cerque, etc. → **cercar**
cerquillo *nm* : bangs *pl*
cerquita *adv fam* : very close, very near
cerrado, -da *adj* **1** : closed, shut **2** : thick, broad (of an accent) **3** : cloudy, overcast **4** : quiet, reserved **5** : dense, stupid
cerradura *nf* : lock
cerrajería *nf* : locksmith's shop
cerrajero, -ra *n* : locksmith
cerrar {55} *vt* **1** : to close, to shut (a door, a book, etc.) ⟨cerrar los ojos : to close one's eyes⟩ ⟨cerrar algo (con llave) : to lock something⟩ **2** : to turn off (a faucet, etc.) **3** : to close, to put the top on (a jar, etc.) **4** : to fasten, to button up (buttons), to zip up (a zipper) **5** CONCLUIR : to bring to an end, to close ⟨cerrar (la) sesión : to log off/out⟩ **6** : to close (a business, an account) **7** : to close, to close off (a street, etc.) — *vi* **1** : to close up, to lock up **2** : to close down — **cerrarse** *vr* **1** : to close **2** : to fasten, to button up, to zip up **3** : to conclude, to end
cerrazón *nf*, *pl* **-zones** : obstinacy, stubbornness
cerro *nm* COLINA, LOMA : hill
cerrojo *nm* PESTILLO : bolt, latch
certamen *nm*, *pl* **-támenes** : competition, contest
certero, -ra *adj* : accurate, precise — **certeramente** *adv*
certeza *nf* : certainty
certidumbre *nf* : certainty
certificable *adj* : certifiable
certificación *nf*, *pl* **-ciones** : certification
certificado[1], **-da** *adj* **1** : certified **2** : registered (of mail)
certificado[2] *nm* **1** : certificate ⟨certificado de matrimonio/difunción/nacimiento : marriage/death/birth certificate⟩ ⟨certificado de regalo : gift certificate⟩ **2** : registered letter
certificar {72} *vt* **1** : to certify **2** : to register (mail)
cerumen *nm* : earwax
cervato *nm* : fawn
cervecera *nf* : brewery
cervecero, -ra *n* : brewer
cervecería *nf* **1** : brewery **2** : beer hall, bar
cerveza *nf* : beer ⟨cerveza de barril : draft beer⟩
cervical *adj* : cervical

cerviz *nf, pl* **cervices** : nape of the neck
cesación *nf, pl* **-ciones** : cessation, suspension
cesante *adj* : laid off, unemployed
cesantia *nf* : unemployment
cesar *vi* : to cease, to stop — *vt* : to dismiss, to lay off
cesárea *nf* : cesarean
cesáreo, -rea *adj* : cesarean
cese *nm* **1** : cessation, stop ⟨cese del fuego : cease-fire⟩ **2** : dismissal
cesio *nm* : cesium
cesión *nf, pl* **cesiones** : transfer, assignment (of property, etc.)
césped *nm* : lawn, grass
cesta *nf* **1** : basket **2** : jai alai racket
cesto *nm* **1** : hamper **2** : basket (in basketball) **3 cesto de (la) basura** : wastebasket
cetro *nm* : scepter
ch *nf* : fourth letter of the Spanish alphabet — not usually considered a separate letter in alphabetization
chabacano¹, -na *adj* : tacky, tasteless
chabacano² *nm Mex* : apricot
chabola *nf Spain* : shack, shanty **2 barrio de chabolas** → **barrio**
chacal *nm* : jackal
cháchara *nf fam* **1** : small talk, chatter **2 chácharas** *nfpl* : trinkets, junk
chacharear *vi fam* : to chatter, to gab
chacra *nf Arg, Chile, Peru* : small farm
chal *nm* MANTÓN : shawl
chalado¹, -da *adj fam* : crazy, nuts
chalado², -da *n* : nut, crazy person
chalán *nm, pl* **chalanes** *Mex* : barge
chalé → **chalet**
chaleco *nm* : vest
chalet *nm Spain* : house
chalupa *nf* **1** : small boat **2** *Mex* : small stuffed tortilla
chamaco, -ca *n Mex fam* : kid, boy *m*, girl *f*
chamarra *nf* **1** : sheepskin jacket **2** : poncho, blanket
chamba *nf Mex, Peru fam* : job, work
chambear *vi Mex, Peru fam* : to work
chamo, -ma *n Ven fam* **1** : kid, boy *m*, girl *f* **2** : buddy, pal
champaña *or* **champán** *nm* : champagne
champiñón *nm, pl* **-ñones** : mushroom
champú *nm, pl* **-pus** *or* **-púes** : shampoo
champurrado *nm Mex* : hot chocolate thickened with cornstarch
chamuco *nm Mex fam* : devil
chamuscar {72} *vt* : to singe, to scorch — **chamuscarse** *vr*
chamusquina *nf* : scorch
chance *nm* OPORTUNIDAD : chance, opportunity
chancho¹, -cha *adj fam* : dirty, filthy, gross
chancho², -cha *n* **1** : pig, hog **2** *fam* : slob
chanchullero, -ra *adj fam* : shady, crooked
chanchullo *nm fam* : shady deal, scam
chancla *nf* **1** : thong sandal, slipper **2** : old shoe
chancleta → **chancla**

chanclo *nm* **1** : clog **2 chanclos** *nmpl* : overshoes, galoshes, rubbers
chándal *nm, pl* **chándals** *Spain* : sweatsuit, tracksuit
changarro *nm Mex* : small shop, stall
chango, -ga *n Mex* : monkey
chantaje *nm* : blackmail
chantajear *vt* : to blackmail
chantajista *nmf* : blackmailer
chanza *nf* **1** : joke, jest **2** *Mex fam* : chance, opportunity
chao *interj fam* : bye!
chapa *nf* **1** *Arg, Uru* : license plate **2** : sheet, panel, veneer **3** : lock **4** : badge **5** TAPÓN : cap, bottle cap
chapado, -da *adj* **1** : plated **2 chapado a la antigua** : old-fashioned
chapar *vt* **1** : to add a veneer to **2** : to plate (metals)
chaparro¹, -rra *adj* : short and squat, stocky
chaparro², -rra *n* : short, stocky person
chaparrón *nm, pl* **-rrones** **1** : downpour **2** : great quantity, torrent
chápeado, -da *adj Col, Mex* : flushed
chaperón, -rona *n, mpl* **-rones** : chaperon, chaperone
chapín, chapina *adj & n CA* : Guatemalan
chapopote *nm Mex* : tar, blacktop
chapotear *vi* : to splash about
chapucero¹, -ra *adj* **1** : crude, shoddy **2** *Mex fam* : dishonest
chapucero², -ra *n* **1** : sloppy worker, bungler **2** *Mex fam* : cheat, swindler
chapulín *nm, pl* **-lines** *CA, Mex* : grasshopper, locust
chapurrear *or* **chapurrar** *vt* **chapurrear el inglés/español (etc.)** : to speak broken English/Spanish (etc.)
chapuza *nf* **1** : botched job **2** *Mex fam* : fraud, trick ⟨hacer chapuzas : to cheat⟩
chapuzón *nm, pl* **-zones** : dip, swim ⟨darse un chapuzón : to go for a quick dip⟩
chaqueta *nf* : jacket
chara *nf* : jay
charada *nf* : charades (game)
charango *nm* : traditional Andean stringed instrument
charca *nf* : pond, pool
charco *nm* : puddle, pool
charcutería *nf* : delicatessen
charla *nf* : chat, talk
charlar *vi* : to chat, to talk
charlatán¹, -tana *adj* : talkative, chatty
charlatán², -tana *n, mpl* **-tanes** **1** : chatterbox **2** FARSANTE : charlatan, phony
charol *nm* **1** : lacquer, varnish **2** : patent leather **3** : tray
charola *nf Bol, Mex, Peru* : tray
charqui *nm Chile, Peru* : dried beef, beef jerky
charreada *nf Mex* : rodeo
charretera *nf* : epaulet
charro¹, -rra *adj* **1** : gaudy, tacky **2** *Mex* : pertaining to charros
charro², -rra *n Mex* : charro (Mexican cowboy or cowgirl)
charrúa *adj & nmf* : Uruguayan

chárter *adj* : charter
chascarrillo *nm fam* : joke, funny story
chasco *nm* **1** BROMA : trick, joke **2** DE-
CEPCIÓN : disappointment
chasis *or* **chasis** *nm* : chassis
chasquear *vt* **1** : to snap (the fingers), to
click (the tongue) **2** : to snap (a whip)
chasquido *nm* **1** : snap (of fingers), click
(of the tongue) **2** : snap, crack
chat *nm, pl* **chats** : chat room
chatarra *nf* : scrap metal
chato, -ta *adj* **1** : pug-nosed **2** : flat
chauvinismo *nm* : chauvinism
chauvinista[1] *adj* : chauvinistic
chauvinista[2] *nmf* : chauvinist
chaval, -vala *n fam* : kid, boy *m*, girl *f*
chavalo, -vala *Mex, Nic* → **chaval**
chavo[1], **-va** *adj Mex fam* : young
chavo[2], **-va** *n Mex fam* : kid, boy *m*, girl *f*
chavo[3] *nm fam* : cent, buck ⟨no tengo un
chavo : I'm broke⟩
che[1] *nf* : (letter) ch
che[2] *interj Arg, Uru* ⟨che, ¡mirá! : hey,
look!⟩ ⟨che, ¡qué mal! : wow, how awful!⟩ ⟨en serio, che : hey, I'm being seri-
ous⟩
checar {72} *vt Mex* : to check, to verify
checo[1], **-ca** *adj & n* : Czech
checo[2] *nm* : Czech (language)
checoslovaco, -ca *adj & n* : Czechoslovakian
cheddar *nm* : cheddar
chef *nm* : chef
chelín *nm, pl* **chelines** : shilling
chelo *nm* : cello, violoncello
cheque[1], etc. → **checar**
cheque[2] *nm* **1** : check **2 cheque de viajero** : traveler's check
chequear *vt* **1** : to check, to verify **2** : to
check in (baggage)
chequeo *nm* **1** INSPECCIÓN : check, inspection **2** : checkup, examination
chequera *nf* : checkbook
chévere *adj fam* : great, fantastic
chic *adj & nm* : chic
chica → **chico**
chicano, -na *adj & n* : Chicano *m*, Chicana *f*
chicha *nf* : fermented alcoholic beverage
made from corn
chícharo *nm* : pea
chicharra *nf* **1** CIGARRA : cicada **2**
: buzzer
chicharrón *nm, pl* **-rrones** **1** : pork rind
2 darle chicharrón a algo/alguien *Mex
fam* : to get rid of something/someone
chiche *nm Arg, Uru* JUGUETE : toy
chichón *nm, pl* **chichones** : bump, swelling
chicle *nm* : chewing gum
chicloso *nm Mex* : taffy
chico[1], **-ca** *adj* **1** : little, small **2** : young
chico[2], **-ca** *n* **1** : child, boy *m*, girl *f* **2**
: young man *m*, young woman *f*
chicote *nm* LÁTIGO : whip, lash
chido, -da *adj Mex fam* : cool, great
chiffon → **chifón**
chiflado[1], **-da** *adj fam* : nuts, crazy
chiflado[2], **-da** *n fam* : crazy person, lunatic

chiflar *vi* : to whistle. — *vt* : to whistle at,
to boo — **chiflarse** *vr fam* ~ **por** : to be
crazy about
chiflido *nm* : whistle, whistling
chiflón *nm, pl* **chiflones** : draft (of air)
chifón *nm, pl* **chifones** : chiffon
chii[1] *adj* CHIITA : Shiite
chii[2] *nmf* CHIITA : Shia, Shiite
chiismo *or* **chiísmo** *nm* : Shia
chiita[1] *or* **chiíta** *adj* → **chii**[1]
chiita[2] *or* **chiíta** *nmf* → **chii**[2]
chilango[1], **-ga** *adj Mex fam* : of or from
Mexico City
chilango[2], **-ga** *n Mex fam* : person from
Mexico City
chilaquiles *nmpl Mex* : shredded tortillas
in sauce
chile *nm* : chili pepper
chileno, -na *adj & n* : Chilean
chillar *vi* **1** : to squeal, to screech **2** : to
scream, to yell **3** : to be gaudy, to clash
chillido *nm* **1** : scream, shout **2** : squeal,
screech, cry (of an animal)
chillo *nm PRi* : red snapper
chillón, -llona *adj, mpl* **chillones** **1**
: piercing, shrill **2** : loud, gaudy
chilpayate *nmf Mex fam* : child, little kid
chimbo[1], **-ba** *adj* **1** : fake, false ⟨un
cheque chimbo : a bad check⟩ **2** *Ven*
: crummy, lousy
chimbo[2] *nm Hond* : tank (container)
chimenea *nf* **1** : chimney **2** : fireplace
chimichurri *nm Arg* : traditional hot
sauce
chimpancé *nm* : chimpanzee
china *nf* **1** : pebble, small stone **2** *PRi*
: orange
chinchar *vt Spain fam* : to annoy, to pester — **chincharse** *vr Spain fam* : to put
up with something
chinche[1] *nf* **1** : bedbug **2** *Ven* : ladybug
3 : thumbtack
chinche[2] *nmf fam* : nuisance, pain in the
neck
chinchilla *nf* : chinchilla
chino[1], **-na** *adj* **1** : Chinese **2** *Mex*
: curly, kinky
chino[2], **-na** *n* : Chinese person
chino[3] *nm* : Chinese (language)
chintz [ˈtʃints] *or* **chinz** *nm* : chintz
chip *nm, pl* **chips** : chip ⟨chip de memoria : memory chip⟩
chipote *nm Mex fam* : bump (on the
head)
chipotle *nm Mex* : chipotle
chiquear *vt Mex* : to spoil, to indulge
chiquero *nm* POCILGA : pigpen, pigsty
chiquillada *nf* : childish prank
chiquillo[1], **-lla** *adj* : very young, little
chiquillo[2], **-lla** *n* : kid, youngster
chiquito[1], **-ta** *adj* : tiny
chiquito[2], **-ta** *n* : little one, baby
chiribita *nf* **1** : spark **2 chiribitas** *nfpl*
: spots before the eyes
chiribitil *nm* **1** DESVÁN : attic, garret **2**
: cubbyhole
chirigota *nf* : joke
chirimía *nf* : traditional reed pipe
chiripa *nf* **1** : fluke **2 de ~** : by sheer
luck

chirivía *nf* : parsnip

chirona *nf fam* : jail

chirriar {85} *vi* **1** : to squeak, to creak **2** : to screech — **chirriante** *adj*

chirrido *nm* **1** : squeak, squeaking **2** : screech, screeching

chirrión *nm, pl* **chirriones** *Mex* : whip, lash

chis *or* **chist** *interj* **1** : sh! **2** : hey!

chisme *nm* **1** : gossip, tale **2** *Spain fam* : gadget, thingamajig

chismear *vi* : to gossip

chismorrear → **chismear**

chismoso[1], **-sa** *adj* : gossipy, gossiping

chismoso[2], **-sa** *n* **1** : gossiper, gossip **2** *Mex fam* : tattletale

chispa[1] *adj* **1** *Mex fam* : lively, vivacious ⟨un perrito chispa : a frisky puppy⟩ **2** *Spain fam* : tipsy

chispa[2] *nf* **1** : spark **2 echar chispas** : to be furious

chispeante *adj* : sparkling, scintillating

chispear *vi* **1** : to give off sparks **2** : to sparkle

chisporrotear *vi* : to crackle, to sizzle

chistar *vi* **sin chistar** : without a word (of complaint)

chiste *nm* **1** : joke, funny story **2 tener chiste** : to be funny **3 tener su chiste** *Mex* : to be tricky

chistera *nf Spain* : top hat

chistoso[1], **-sa** *adj* **1** : funny, humorous **2** : witty

chistoso[2], **-sa** *n* : wit, joker

chiva *nf* **1** *Col, Ecua, Pan* : rural bus **2 chivas** *nfpl Mex fam* : stuff, odds and ends

chivato, -ta *n Cuba, Spain* **1** : informant, snitch **2** : tattletale

chivo[1], **-va** *n* **1** : kid, young goat **2 chivo expiatorio** : scapegoat

chivo[2] *nm* **1** : billy goat **2** : fit of anger

chocante *adj* **1** : shocking **2** : unpleasant, rude

chocar {72} *vi* **1** : to crash, to collide **2** : to clash, to conflict **3** : to be shocking ⟨le chocó : he was shocked⟩ **4** *Mex, Ven fam* : to be unpleasant or obnoxious ⟨me choca tu jefe : I can't stand your boss⟩ — *vt* **1** : to shake (hands) **2** : to clink glasses

chochear *vi* **1** : to be senile **2** ~ **por** : to dote on, to be soft on

chochín *nm, pl* **-chines** : wren

chocho, -cha *adj* **1** : senile **2** : doting

choclo *nm* **1** : ear of corn, corncob **2** : corn **3 meter el choclo** *Mex fam* : to make a mistake

chocolate *nm* **1** : chocolate ⟨chocolate con leche : milk chocolate⟩ ⟨chocolate oscuro/amargo/negro : dark chocolate⟩ ⟨chocolate blanco : white chocolate⟩ **2** : hot chocolate, cocoa

chocolatín *nm, pl* **-tines** → **chocolatina**

chocolatina *nf* : chocolate bar

chofer *or* **chófer** *nm* **1** : chauffeur **2** : driver

choke *nm* : choke (of an automobile)

chole *interj Mex fam* ¡ya chole! : enough!, cut it out!

cholo, -la *adj & n* : mestizo

cholla *nf fam* : head

chollo *nm Spain fam* : bargain

chongo *nm* **1** *Mex* : bun (chignon) **2 chongos** *nmpl Mex* : dessert made with fried bread

choque[1], etc. → **chocar**

choque[2] *nm* **1** : crash, collision **2** : clash, conflict **3** : shock

chorizo *nm* : chorizo, pork sausage

choro *nm* **1 MEJILLÓN** : mussel **2** : crook, criminal

chorrear *vi* **1** : to drip **2** : to pour out, to gush out

chorrito *nm* : squirt, splash

chorro *nm* **1** : flow, stream, jet **2** *Mex fam* : heap, ton

choteado, -da *adj Mex fam* : worn-out, stale ⟨esa canción está bien choteada : that song's been played to death⟩

chotear *vt* : to make fun of

choteo *nm* : joking around, kidding

chovinismo, chovinista → **chauvinismo, chauvinista**

chow–chow [ˈtʃautʃau] *nmf* : chow

choza *nf* : hut, shack

christmas *or* **crismas** *nm Spain* : Christmas card

chubasco *nm* : downpour, storm

chuchería *nf* : knickknack, trinket

chucho, -cha *n fam* **1** *CA, Mex, Spain* : mongrel, mutt **2 chuchos de frío** *Arg, Uru* : shivers

chueco, -ca *adj* **1** : crooked, bent **2** *Chile, Mex fam* : dishonest, shady

chulada *nf Mex, Spain fam* : cute or pretty thing ⟨qué chulada de vestido! : what a lovely dress!⟩

chulear *vt Mex fam* : to compliment

chuleta *nf* : cutlet, chop

chulla *nmf* : person from Quito, Ecuador

chulo[1], **-la** *adj* **1** *fam* : cute, pretty **2** *Spain fam* : cocky, arrogant

chulo[2] *nm Spain* : pimp

chupada *nf* **1** : suck, sucking **2** : puff, drag (on a cigarette)

chupado, -da *adj fam* **1** : gaunt, skinny **2** : plastered, drunk

chupaflor *nm* **COLIBRÍ** : hummingbird

chupamirto *nm Mex* : hummingbird

chupar *vt* **1** : to suck **2** : to absorb **3** : to puff on **4** *fam* : to drink, to guzzle — *vi* : to suckle — **chuparse** *vr* **1** : to waste away **2** *fam* : to put up with **3** ¡chúpate esa! *fam* : take that!

chupete *nm* **1** : pacifier **2** *Chile, Peru* : lollipop

chupetear *vt* : to suck (at)

chupón *nm, pl* **chupones 1** : sucker (of a plant) **2** : baby bottle, pacifier

churrasco *nm* **1** : steak **2** : barbecued meat

churro *nm* **1** : fried dough **2** *fam* : attractive person

chusco, -ca *adj* : funny, amusing

chusma *nf* **GENTUZA** : riffraff, rabble

chutar *vi* : to shoot (in soccer)

chute *nm* : shot (in soccer)

chutney [ˈtʃatni] *nm* : chutney

CI *or* **coeficiente intelectual** *nm* : IQ, intelligence quotient

cianotipo *nm* : blueprint
cianuro *nm* : cyanide
ciber- *pref* : cyber-
ciberacoso *nm* : cyberbullying
cibercafé *nm* : Internet café
cibernético, -ca *adj* : cybernetic, cyber-
cicatriz *nf, pl* **-trices** : scar
cicatrizar {21} *vi* : to form a scar, to heal
cicatrizarse *vr* → **cicatrizar**
cíclico, -ca *adj* : cyclical
ciclismo *nm* : bicycling
ciclista *nmf* : bicyclist
ciclo *nm* : cycle
ciclomotor *nm* : moped
ciclón *nm, pl* **ciclones** : cyclone
cicuta *nf* : hemlock
ciega, ciegue etc. → **cegar**
ciego[1], -ga *adj* **1** INVIDENTE : blind **2 a
ciegas** : blindly **3 quedarse ciego** : to
go blind — **ciegamente** *adv*
ciego[2], -ga *n* INVIDENTE : blind person
cielo *nm* **1** : sky **2** : heaven **3** : ceiling
ciempiés *nms & pl* : centipede
cien[1] *adj* **1** : a hundred ⟨las
primeras cien páginas : the first hundred
pages⟩ **2 cien por cien** *or* **cien por
ciento** : a hundred percent, through and
through, wholeheartedly — **cien** *pron*
cien[2] *nm* : one hundred
ciénaga *nf* : swamp, bog
ciencia *nf* **1** : science **2** : learning,
knowledge **3 a ciencia cierta** : for a
fact, for certain
cieno *nm* : mire, mud, silt
científico[1], -ca *adj* : scientific — **científi-
camente** *adv*
científico[2], -ca *n* : scientist
ciento[1] *adj* (*used in compound numbers*)
: one hundred ⟨ciento uno : one hundred and one⟩
ciento[2] *nm* **1** : hundred ⟨cientos de per-
sonas/años : hundreds of people/years⟩
2 por ~ : percent
cierne, etc. → **cerner**
cierra, etc. → **cerrar**
cierre *nm* **1** : closing, closure **2** : fastener, clasp, zipper
cierto, -ta *adj* **1** : true, certain, definite
⟨lo cierto es que . . . : the fact is that . . .⟩
2 : certain, one ⟨cierto día de verano
: one summer day⟩ ⟨bajo ciertas circunstancias : under certain circumstances⟩
3 por ~ : in fact, as a matter of fact —
ciertamente *adv*
ciervo, -va *n* : deer, stag *m*, hind *f*
cifra *nf* **1** : figure, number **2** : quantity,
amount **3** CLAVE : code, cipher
cifrar *vt* **1** : to write in code **2** : to place,
to pin ⟨cifró su esperanza en la lotería
: he pinned his hopes on the lottery⟩ **3**
: to encrypt (a file, etc.) — **cifrarse** *vr*
: to amount ⟨cifrarse en : to amount to⟩
cigarra *nf* CHICHARRA : cicada
cigarrera *nf* : cigarette case
cigarrillo *nm* **1** : cigarette **2 cigarrillo
electrónico** : electronic cigarette, e-cigarette
cigarro *nm* **1** : cigarette **2** PURO : cigar
cigoto *nm* : zygote
cigüeña *nf* : stork

cilantro *nm* : cilantro, coriander
cilindrada *nf* : cubic capacity (of an engine)
cilíndrico, -ca *adj* : cylindrical
cilindro *nm* : cylinder
cima *nf* CUMBRE : peak, summit, top
cimarrón, -rrona *adj, mpl* **-rrones** : untamed, wild
címbalo *nm* : cymbal
cimbrar *vt* : to shake, to rock — **cim-
brarse** *vr* : to sway, to swing
cimentar {55} *vt* **1** : to lay the foundation
of, to establish **2** : to strengthen, to cement
cimientos *nmpl* : base, foundation(s)
cinc *nm* : zinc
cincel *nm* : chisel
cincelar *vt* **1** : to chisel **2** : to engrave
cincha *nf* : cinch, girth
cinchar *vt* : to cinch (a horse)
cinco[1] *adj & nm* : five ⟨mi hija tiene cinco
años : my daughter is five (years old)⟩
⟨el cinco de junio : (on) the fifth of June,
(on) June fifth⟩
cinco[2] *pron* : five ⟨seremos cinco : there
will be five of us⟩ ⟨son las cinco y media
: it's five-thirty⟩
cincuenta *adj & nm* : fifty — **cincuenta**
pron
cincuentavo[1], -va *adj* : fiftieth
cincuentavo[2] *nm* : fiftieth (fraction)
cine *nm* **1** : cinema, movies *pl* **2** : movie
theater
cineasta *nmf* : filmmaker
cinéfilo, -la *n* : cinephile, movie buff
cinematografía *nf* : cinematography
cinematográfico, -ca *adj* : movie, film,
cinematic ⟨la industria cinematográfica
: the film industry⟩
cínico[1], -ca *adj* **1** : cynical **2** : shameless, brazen — **cínicamente** *adv*
cínico[2], -ca *n* : cynic
cinismo *nm* : cynicism
cinta *nf* **1** : ribbon **2** : tape ⟨cinta
métrica : tape measure⟩ **3** : strap, belt
⟨cinta transportadora : conveyor belt⟩
cinto *nm* : strap, belt
cintura *nf* **1** : waist, waistline **2 meter
en cintura** *fam* : to bring into line, to
discipline
cinturilla *nf* : waistband
cinturón *nm, pl* **-rones** **1** : belt **2 cinturón de seguridad** : seat belt **3 cinturón de miseria** : shantytown, slums *pl*
ciñe, etc. → **ceñir**
ciprés *nm, pl* **cipreses** : cypress
circo *nm* : circus
circuitería *nf* : circuitry
circuito *nm* : circuit
circulación *nf, pl* **-ciones** **1** : circulation
2 : movement **3** : traffic
circular[1] *vi* **1** : to circulate **2** : to move
along **3** : to drive
circular[2] *adj* : circular
circular[3] *nf* : circular, flier
circulatorio, -ria *adj* : circulatory
círculo *nm* : circle **2** : club, group
circuncidar *vt* : to circumcise
circuncisión *nf, pl* **-siones** : circumcision
circundar *vt* : to surround — **circun-
dante** *adj*

circunferencia *nf* : circumference
circunflejo, -ja *adj* **acento circunflejo** : circumflex
circunlocución *nf, pl* **-ciones** : circumlocution
circunloquio *nm* → **circunlocución**
circunnavegar {52} *vt* : to circumnavigate — **circunnavegación** *nf*
circunscribir {33} *vt* : to circumscribe, to constrict, to limit — **circunscribirse** *vr*
circunscripción *nf, pl* **-ciones** **1** : limitation, restriction **2** : constituency
circunscrito *pp* → **circunscribir**
circunspecto, -ta *adj* : circumspect, prudent
circunstancia *nf* : circumstance
circunstancial *adj* : circumstantial, incidental
circunstante *nmf* **1** : onlooker, bystander **2 los circunstantes** : those present
circunvalación *nf, pl* **-ciones** : surrounding, encircling ⟨carretera de circunvalación : bypass, beltway⟩
circunvecino, -na *adj* : surrounding, neighboring
cirio *nm* : large candle
cirrosis *nf* : cirrhosis
ciruela *nf* **1** : plum **2 ciruela pasa** : prune
cirugía *nf* : surgery ⟨cirugía cardíaca : heart surgery⟩ ⟨cirugía plástica/estética : plastic/cosmetic surgery⟩
cirujano, -na *n* : surgeon
cisgénero *adj* : cisgender, cis ⟨las personas cisgénero : cisgender people⟩
cisma *nm* : schism, rift
cisne *nm* : swan
cisterna *nf* : cistern, tank
cita *nf* **1** : quote, quotation **2** : appointment, date
citable *adj* : quotable
citación *nf, pl* **-ciones** EMPLAZAMIENTO : summons, subpoena
citadino¹, -na *adj* : of the city, urban
citadino², -na *n* : city dweller
citado, -da *adj* : said, aforementioned
citar *vt* **1** : to quote, to cite **2** : to make an appointment with **3** : to summon (to court), to subpoena — **citarse** *vr* ~ **con** : to arrange to meet (someone)
citatorio *nm* : subpoena
-cito *suf* → **-ito**
cítrico *nm* : citrus
ciudad *nf* **1** : city, town **2 ciudad deportiva** : sports complex **3 ciudad natal** : native city/town **4 ciudad perdida** *Mex* : shantytown **5 ciudad universitaria** : college or university campus
ciudadanía *nf* **1** : citizenship **2** : citizenry, citizens *pl*
ciudadano¹, -na *adj* : civic, city
ciudadano², -na *n* **1** NACIONAL : citizen **2** HABITANTE : resident, city dweller
ciudadela *nf* : citadel, fortress
cívico, -ca *adj* **1** : civic **2** : civic-minded
civil¹ *adj* **1** : civil **2** : civilian **3 de ~** : in plain/civilian clothes ⟨un policía de civil : a plainclothes policeman⟩
civil² *nmf* : civilian

civilidad *nf* : civility, courtesy
civilización *nf, pl* **-ciones** : civilization
civilizado, -da *adj* : civilized
civilizar {21} *vt* : to civilize
civismo *nm* : community spirit, civics
cizaña *nf* **sembrar cizaña** : to sow discord
clamar *vi* : to clamor, to raise a protest — *vt* : to cry out for
clamor *nm* : clamor, outcry
clamoroso, -sa *adj* : clamorous, resounding, thunderous
clan *nm* : clan
clandestinidad *nf* : secrecy ⟨en la clandestinidad : underground⟩
clandestino, -na *adj* : clandestine, secret — **clandestinamente** *adv*
clara *nf* : egg white
claraboya *nf* : skylight
claramente *adv* : clearly
clarear *v impers* **1** : to clear, to clear up **2** : to get light, to dawn — *vi* : to go gray, to turn white
claridad *nf* **1** NITIDEZ : clarity **2** : brightness, light
clarificación *nf, pl* **-ciones** ACLARACIÓN : clarification, explanation
clarificar {72} *vt* ACLARAR : to clarify, to explain
clarín *nm, pl* **clarines** : bugle
clarinete *nm* : clarinet
clarividencia *nf* **1** : clairvoyance **2** : perspicacity, discernment
clarividente¹ *adj* **1** : clairvoyant **2** : perspicacious, discerning
clarividente² *nmf* : clairvoyant
claro¹ *adv* **1** : clearly ⟨habla más claro : speak more clearly⟩ **2** : of course, surely ⟨¡claro!, ¡claro que sí! : absolutely!, of course!⟩ ⟨claro que entendió : of course she understood⟩
claro², -ra *adj* **1** : bright, clear **2** : pale, fair, light **3** : clear, evident
claro³ *nm* **1** : clearing **2 claro de luna** : moonlight
clase *nf* **1** : class **2** ÍNDOLE, TIPO : sort, kind, type **3 clase alta/baja** : upper/lower class
clasicismo *nm* : classicism
clásico¹, -ca *adj* **1** : classic **2** : classical
clásico² *nm* : classic
clasificación *nf, pl* **-ciones** **1** : classification, sorting out **2** : rating **3** CALIFICACIÓN : qualification (in competitions)
clasificado, -da *adj* : classified ⟨aviso clasificado : classified ad⟩
clasificar {72} *vt* **1** : to classify, to sort out **2** : to rate, to rank — *vi* CALIFICAR : to qualify (in competitions) — **clasificarse** *vr*
clasificatorio, -ria *adj* : qualifying
claudicación *nf, pl* **-ciones** : surrender, abandonment of one's principles
claudicar {72} *vi* : to back down, to abandon one's principles
claustro *nm* : cloister
claustrofobia *nf* : claustrophobia
claustrofóbico, -ca *adj* : claustrophobic
cláusula *nf* : clause
clausura *nf* **1** : closure, closing **2** : closing ceremony **3** : cloister

clausurar *vt* **1** : to close, to bring to a close **2** : to close down

clavada *nf* : slam dunk (in basketball)

clavadista *nmf* : diver

clavado¹, -da *adj* **1** : nailed, fixed, stuck **2** *fam* : punctual, on the dot **3** *fam* : identical ⟨es clavado a su padre : he's the image of his father⟩

clavado² *nm* : dive

clavar *vt* **1** : to nail, to hammer **2** HINCAR : to plunge, to stick **3** : to fix (one's eyes) on — **clavarse** *vr* : to stick oneself (with a sharp object)

clave¹ *adj* : key, essential

clave² *nf* **1** CIFRA : code **2** : key ⟨la clave del misterio : the key to the mystery⟩ **3** : clef ⟨clave de sol/fa : treble/bass clef⟩

clavel *nm* : carnation

clavelito *nm* : pink (flower)

clavicémbalo *nm* : harpsichord

clavícula *nf* : collarbone

clavija *nf* **1** : plug **2** : peg, pin

clavo *nm* **1** : nail ⟨clavo grande : spike⟩ **2** : clove **3 dar en el clavo** : to hit the nail on the head

claxon *nm, pl* **cláxones** : horn (of an automobile)

clemencia *nf* : clemency, mercy

clemente *adj* : merciful

cleptomanía *nf* : kleptomania

cleptómano, -na *n* : kleptomaniac

clerecía *nf* : ministry, ministers *pl*

clerical *adj* : clerical

clérigo, -ga *n* : cleric, member of the clergy

clero *nm* : clergy

clic *or* **click** *nm, pl* **clics** *or* **clicks** : click ⟨haz clic aquí : click here⟩ ⟨doble clic : double click⟩ ⟨hacer clic derecho/izquierdo : to right/left-click⟩

cliché *nm* **1** : cliché **2** : stencil **3** : negative (of a photograph)

cliente, -ta *n* : customer, client

clientela *nf* : clientele, customers *pl*

clima *nm* **1** : climate **2** AMBIENTE : atmosphere, ambience

climático, -ca *adj* : climatic

climatización *nf, pl* **-ciones** : air-conditioning

climatizar {21} *vt* : to air-condition — **climatizado, -da** *adj*

clímax *nm* : climax

clinch *nm* : clinch (in boxing)

clínica *nf* : clinic

clínico, -ca *adj* : clinical — **clínicamente** *adv*

clip *nm, pl* **clips** **1** : clip **2** : paper clip

clíper *nm* : clipper

clítoris *nms & pl* : clitoris

cloaca *nf* ALCANTARILLA : sewer

clocar {82} *vi* : to cluck

cloche *nm* CA, Car, Col, Ven : clutch (of an automobile)

clon *nm* : clone

clonar *vt* : to clone

cloqué, etc. → **clocar**

cloquear *vi* : to cluck

cloqueo *nm* : cluck, clucking

clorar *vt* : to chlorinate — **cloración** *nf*

clorhídrico, -ca *adj* **ácido clorhídrico →** **ácido²**

cloro *nm* : chlorine

clorofila *nf* : chlorophyll

cloroformo *nm* : chloroform

cloruro *nm* : chloride

clóset *nm, pl* **clósets** **1** : closet **2** : cupboard

club *nm* : club

clueca, clueque etc. → **clocar**

clutch ['klatʃ] *nm* : clutch

coa *nf Mex* : hoe

coacción *nf, pl* **-ciones** : coercion, duress

coaccionar *vt* : to coerce

coactivo, -va *adj* : coercive

coagular *v* : to clot, to coagulate — **coagulación** *nf*

coágulo *nm* : clot

coalición *nf, pl* **-ciones** : coalition

coartada *nf* : alibi

coartar *vt* : to restrict, to limit

coba *nf fam* **1** : flattery ⟨darle coba a alguien : to suck up to someone⟩ **2** *Ven* MENTIRA : lie

cobalto *nm* : cobalt

cobarde¹ *adj* : cowardly

cobarde² *nmf* : coward

cobardía *nf* : cowardice

cobaya *nf* : guinea pig

cobertizo *nm* : shed, shelter

cobertor *nm* COLCHA : bedspread, quilt

cobertura *nf* **1** : coverage **2** : cover, collateral

cobija *nf* FRAZADA, MANTA : blanket

cobijar *vt* : to shelter — **cobijarse** *vr* : to take shelter

cobijo *nm* : shelter

cobra *nf* : cobra

cobrador, -dora *n* **1** : collector **2** : conductor (of a bus or train)

cobrar *vt* **1** : to charge **2** : to collect, to draw, to earn **3** : to acquire, to gain **4** : to recover, to retrieve **5** : to cash (a check) **6** : to claim, to take (a life) **7** : to shoot (game), to bag — *vi* **1** : to be paid **2 llamar por cobrar** *Mex* : to call collect

cobre *nm* : copper

cobrizo, -za *adj* : coppery

cobro *nm* : collection (of money), cashing (of a check)

coca *nf* **1** : coca **2** *fam* : coke, cocaine

Coca *nf* (*Coca-Cola*, marca registrada) : Coke™, Coca-Cola™

cocaína *nf* : cocaine

cocal *nm* : coca plantation

cocción *nf, pl* **cocciones** : cooking

cocear *vi* : to kick (of an animal)

cocer {14} *vt* **1** COCINAR : to cook **2** HERVIR : to boil

cochambre *nmf fam* : filth, grime

cochambroso, -sa *adj* : filthy, grimy

coche *nm* **1** : car, automobile **2** : coach, carriage **3 coche bomba** : car bomb **4 coche cama** : sleeping car **5 coche fúnebre** : hearse

cochecito *nm* : baby carriage, stroller

cochera *nf* GARAJE : garage, carport

cochinada *nf fam* **1** : filthy language **2** : disgusting behavior **3** : dirty trick

cochinillo *nm* : suckling pig, piglet
cochino¹, -na *adj* **1** : dirty, filthy, disgusting **2** *fam* : rotten, lousy
cochino², -na *n* : pig, hog
cocido¹, -da *adj* **1** : boiled, cooked **2 bien cocido** : well-done
cocido² *nm* ESTOFADO, GUISADO : stew
cociente *nm* : quotient
cocimiento *nm* : cooking, baking
cocina *nf* **1** : kitchen **2** : stove **3** : cuisine, cooking
cocinar *v* : to cook
cocinero, -ra *n* : cook, chef
cocineta *nf* *Mex* : kitchenette
coco *nm* **1** : coconut **2** *fam* : head **3** *fam* : bogeyman
cocoa *nf* : cocoa, hot chocolate
cocodrilo *nm* : crocodile
cocotero *nm* : coconut palm
coctel *or* **cóctel** *nm* **1** : cocktail **2** : cocktail party
coctelera *nf* : cocktail shaker
codazo *nm* **1 darle un codazo a alguien** : to elbow someone, to nudge someone **2 abrirse paso a codazos** : to elbow one's way through
codear *vt* : to elbow, to jog, to nudge — **codearse** *vr* : to rub elbows, to hobnob
codeína *nf* : codeine
códice *nm* : codex, manuscript
codicia *nf* AVARICIA : avarice
codiciar *vt* : to covet
codicioso, -sa *adj* : avaricious, covetous
codificar {72} *vt* **1** : to codify **2** : to code, to encode
código *nm* **1** : code **2 código de barras** : bar code **3 código postal** : zip code **4 código morse** : Morse code
codo¹, -da *adj* *Mex* : cheap, stingy
codo², -da *n* *Mex* : tightwad, cheapskate
codo³ *nm* : elbow
codorniz *nf, pl* **-nices** : quail
coeficiente *nm* **1** : coefficient **2 coeficiente intelectual** : IQ, intelligence quotient
coexistir *vi* : to coexist — **coexistencia** *nf*
cofradía *nf* **1** : (religious) brotherhood **2** GREMIO : guild
cofre *nm* **1** BAÚL : trunk, chest **2** *Mex* CAPOTE : hood (of a car)
coger {15} *vt* **1** : to seize, to take hold of **2** : to catch **3** : to pick up **4** : to gather, to pick **5** : to gore — **cogerse** *vr* AGARRARSE : to hold on
cogida *nf* : gathering, harvest **2** : goring
cognición *nf, pl* **-ciones** : cognition
cognitivo, -va *adj* : cognitive
cogollo *nm* **1** : heart (of a vegetable) **2** : bud, bulb **3** : core, crux ⟨el cogollo de la cuestión : the heart of the matter⟩
cogote *nm* : scruff, nape
cohabitar *vi* : to cohabit — **cohabitación** *nf*
cohechar *vt* SOBORNAR : to bribe
cohecho *nm* SOBORNO : bribe, bribery
coherencia *nf* : coherence — **coherente** *adj*
cohesión *nf, pl* **-siones** : cohesion

cohesivo, -va *adj* : cohesive
cohete *nm* : rocket
cohibición *nf, pl* **-ciones** **1** : (legal) restraint **2** INHIBICIÓN : inhibition
cohibido, -da *adj* : inhibited, shy
cohibir {62} *vt* : to inhibit, to make self-conscious — **cohibirse** *vr* : to feel shy or embarrassed
cohorte *nf* : cohort
coima *nf* *Arg, Chile, Peru* : bribe
coimear *vi* *Arg, Chile, Peru* : to bribe
coincidencia *nf* **1** CASUALIDAD : coincidence **2** ACUERDO : agreement
coincidente *adj* **1** : coincident **2** ACORDE : coinciding
coincidir *vi* **1** : to coincide **2** : to agree
coito *nm* : sexual intercourse, coitus
coja, etc. → **coger**
cojear *vi* **1** : to limp **2** : to wobble, to rock **3 cojear del mismo pie** : to be two of a kind
cojera *nf* : limp
cojín *nm, pl* **cojines** : cushion, throw pillow
cojinete *nm* **1** : bearing, bushing **2 cojinete de bola** : ball bearing
cojo¹, -ja *adj* **1** : limping, lame **2** : wobbly **3** : weak, ineffectual
cojo², -ja *n* : lame person
cojones *nmpl usu vulgar* **1** : balls *pl, usu vulgar*; testicles *pl* **2** : balls *pl, usu vulgar*; guts *pl*; courage
col *nf* **1** REPOLLO : cabbage **2 col de Bruselas** : Brussels sprout **3 col rizada** : kale
cola *nf* **1** RABO : tail ⟨cola de caballo : ponytail⟩ **2** FILA : line (of people) ⟨hacer cola : to wait in line⟩ **3** : cola, drink **4** : train (of a dress) **5** : tails *pl* (of a tuxedo) **6** PEGAMENTO : glue **7** *fam* : buttocks *pl*, rear end
colaboracionista *nmf* : collaborator, traitor
colaborador, -dora *n* **1** : contributor (to a periodical) **2** : collaborator
colaborar *vi* : to collaborate — **colaboración** *nf*
colación *nf, pl* **-ciones** **1** : light meal **2** : conferring (of a degree) **3 traer a colación** : to bring up, to broach
colada *nf* *Spain* : laundry, wash, washing
coladera *nf* *Mex* : drain
colador *nm* **1** : colander, strainer **2** *PRi* : small coffeepot
colapsar *vt* **1** : to collapse **2** : to paralyze, to bring to a standstill — *vi* : to collapse
colapso *nm* **1** : collapse **2** : standstill
colar {19} *vt* **1** : to strain, to filter — **colarse** *vr* **1** : to sneak in **2** : to cut in line **3** : to slip up, to make a mistake
colateral¹ *adj* : collateral — **colateralmente** *adv*
colateral² *nm* : collateral
colcha *nf* COBERTOR : bedspread, quilt
colchón *nm, pl* **colchones** **1** : mattress **2** : cushion, padding, buffer
colchoneta *nf* : mat (for gymnastic sports)
colear *vi* **1** : to wag its tail **2 vivito y coleando** *fam* : alive and kicking

colección *nf, pl* **-ciones** : collection
coleccionable *adj* : collectible
coleccionar *vt* : to collect, to keep a collection of
coleccionista *nmf* : collector
colecta *nf* : collection (of donations)
colectar *vt* : to collect
colectivero, -ra *n* **1** *Arg* : bus driver **2** *Chile* : taxi driver
colectividad *nf* : community, group
colectivo¹, -va *adj* : collective — **colectivamente** *adv*
colectivo² *nm* **1** : collective **2** (*in various countries*) : city bus **3** *Chile* : fixed-route taxi
colector¹, -tora *n* : collector ⟨colector de impuestos : tax collector⟩
colector² *nm* **1** : sewer **2** : manifold (of an engine)
colega *nmf* **1** : colleague **2** HOMÓLOGO : counterpart **3** *fam* : buddy
colegiado, -da *n* **1** ÁRBITRO : referee **2** : member (of a professional association)
colegial¹, -giala *adj* **1** : school **2** *Mex fam* : green, inexperienced
colegial², -giala *n* : schoolboy *m*, schoolgirl *f*
colegiatura *nf Mex* : tuition
colegio *nm* **1** : school **2** : college ⟨colegio electoral : electoral college⟩ **3** : professional association
colegir {28} *vt* **1** JUNTAR : to collect, to gather **2** INFERIR : to infer, to deduce
cólera¹ *nm* : cholera
cólera² *nf* FURIA, IRA : anger, rage
colérico, -ca *adj* **1** FURIOSO : angry **2** IRRITABLE : irritable
colesterol *nm* : cholesterol
coleta *nf* **1** : ponytail **2** : pigtail
coletazo *nm* : lash, flick (of a tail)
colgado, -da *adj* **1** : hanging, hanged **2** : pending **3** dejar colgado a : to disappoint, to let down
colgante¹ *adj* : hanging, dangling
colgante² *nm* : pendant, charm (on a bracelet)
colgar {16} *vt* **1** : to hang (up), to put up **2** AHORCAR : to hang (someone) **3** : to hang up (a telephone) **4** *fam* : to fail (an exam) — **colgarse** *vr* **1** : to hang, to be suspended **2** AHORCARSE : to hang oneself **3** : to hang up a telephone
colibrí *nm* CHUPAFLOR : hummingbird
cólico *nm* : colic
coliflor *nf* : cauliflower
colilla *nf* : butt (of a cigarette)
colín *nm, pl* **colines** *Spain* : breadstick
colina *nf* CERRO, LOMA : hill
colindante *adj* CONTIGUO : adjacent, neighboring
colindar *vi* : to adjoin, to be adjacent
colirio *nm* : eyedrops *pl*
coliseo *nm* : coliseum
colisión *nf, pl* **-siones** : collision
colisionar *vi* : to collide
collage *nm* : collage
collar *nm* **1** : collar (for an animal) **2** : necklace
collie [ˈkoli] *nmf* : collie
colmado, -da *adj* : heaping

colmar *vt* **1** : to fill to the brim **2** : to fulfill, to satisfy **3** : to heap, to shower ⟨me colmaron de regalos : they showered me with gifts⟩
colmena *nf* : beehive
colmenar *nm* APIARIO : apiary
colmillo *nm* **1** CANINO : canine (tooth), fang **2** : tusk
colmilludo, -da *adj Mex, PRi* : astute, shrewd, crafty
colmo *nm* : height, extreme, limit ⟨el colmo de la locura : the height of folly⟩ ⟨¡eso es el colmo! : that's the last straw!⟩ ⟨para colmo : to top it all off⟩
colocación *nf, pl* **-ciones** **1** : placement, placing **2** : position, job **3** : investment
colocar {72} *vt* **1** PONER : to place, to put **2** : to find a job for **3** : to invest — **colocarse** *vr* **1** SITUARSE : to position oneself **2** : to get a job
colofonia *nf* : rosin
colombiano, -na *adj & n* : Colombian
colon *nm* : (intestinal) colon
colón *nm, pl* **colones** : colón (Costa Rican and Salvadoran unit of currency)
colonia *nf* **1** : colony **2** : cologne **3** *Mex* : residential area, neighborhood
colonial *adj* : colonial
colonización *nf, pl* **-ciones** : colonization
colonizador¹, -dora *adj* : colonizing
colonizador², -dora *n* : colonist
colonizar {21} *vt* : to colonize, to settle
colono, -na *n* **1** : settler, colonist **2** : tenant farmer
coloquial *adj* : colloquial
coloquio *nm* **1** : discussion, talk **2** : conference, symposium
color *nm* **1** : color **2** : paint, dye **3** colores *nmpl* : colored pencils
coloración *nf, pl* **-ciones** : coloring, coloration
colorado¹, -da *adj* **1** ROJO : red **2** ponerse colorado : to blush **3** chiste colorado *Mex* : off-color joke
colorado² *nm* ROJO : red
colorante *nm* : coloring ⟨colorante de alimentos : food coloring⟩
colorear *vt* : to color — *vi* **1** : to redden **2** : to ripen
colorete *nm* : blush, rouge
colorido *nm* : color, coloring
colorín *nm, pl* **-rines** **1** : bright color **2** : goldfinch
colosal *adj* : colossal
coloso *nm* : colossus
coludir *vi* : to conspire
columna *nf* **1** : column **2** columna vertebral : spine, backbone
columnata *nf* : colonnade
columnista *nmf* : columnist
columpiar *vt* : to push (on a swing) — **columpiarse** *vr* : to swing
columpio *nm* : swing
colusión *nf, pl* **-siones** : collusion
colza *nf* : rape (plant)
coma¹ *nm* : coma ⟨entrar en coma : to go into a coma⟩
coma² *nf* **1** : comma **2** coma decimal : decimal point

comadre *nf* **1** : godmother of one's child **2** : mother of one's godchild **3** *fam* : neighbor, female friend **4** *fam* : gossip
comadrear *vi fam* : to gossip
comadreja *nf* : weasel
comadrona *nf* : midwife
comal *nm CA, Mex* : tortilla griddle
comanche *nmf* : Comanche
comandancia *nf* **1** : command headquarters **2** : command
comandante *nmf* **1** : commander, commanding officer **2** : major
comandar *vt* : to command, to lead
comando *nm* **1** : commando **2** : command (for computers)
comarca *nf REGIÓN* : region
comarcal *adj REGIONAL* : regional, local
comatoso, -sa *adj* : comatose
comba *nf* **1** : bend, sag **2** *Spain* : jump rope
combar *vt* : to bend, to curve — **combarse** *vr* **1** : to bend, to buckle **2** : to warp, to bulge, to sag
combate *nm* **1** : combat **2** : fight, boxing match
combatiente *nmf* : combatant, fighter
combatir *vt* : to combat, to fight against — *vi* : to fight
combatividad *nf* : fighting spirit
combativo, -va *adj* : combative, spirited
combi *nf Arg, Mex, Peru* : minibus
combinación *nf, pl* -**ciones** **1** : combination **2** : connection (in travel)
combinado, -da **1** *COCTEL* : cocktail **2** *EQUIPO* : team
combinar *vt* **1** *UNIR* : to combine, to mix together **2** : to match, to put together — **combinarse** *vr* : to get together, to conspire
combo *nm* **1** : (musical) band **2** *Chile, Peru* : sledgehammer **3** *Chile, Peru* : punch
combustible¹ *adj* : combustible
combustible² *nm* : fuel
combustión *nf, pl* -**tiones** : combustion
comedero *nm* : trough, feeder
comedia *nf* : comedy
comediante *nmf* **1** : actor, actress *f FARSANTE* : fraud
comedido, -da *adj MESURADO* : moderate, restrained
comediógrafo, -fa *n* : playwright
comedor *nm* : dining room
comején *nm, pl* -**jenes** : termite
comelón¹, -lona *adj, mpl* -**lones** *fam* : gluttonous
comelón², -lona *n, pl* -**lones** *fam* : big eater, glutton
comensal *nmf* : dinner guest
comentador, -dora *n* → comentarista
comentar *vt* **1** : to comment on, to discuss **2** : to mention, to remark
comentario *nm* **1** : comment, remark ⟨sin comentarios : no comment⟩ **2** : commentary
comentarista *nmf* : commentator
comenzar {29} *v EMPEZAR* : to begin, to start ⟨comenzó a trabajar : he started to work⟩ ⟨comenzó diciendo que . . . , comenzó por decir que . . . : she started by saying that . . .⟩

comer¹ *vt* **1** : to eat **2** : to consume, to eat up, to eat into — *vi* **1** : to eat **2** *CENAR* : to have a meal **3 dar de comer** : to feed — **comerse** *vr* : to eat up
comer² *nm* : eating, dining
comercial *adj & nm* : commercial — **comercialmente** *adv*
comercializar {21} *vt* **1** : to commercialize **2** : to market — **comercialización** *nf*
comerciante *nmf* : merchant, dealer
comerciar *vi* : to do business, to trade
comercio *nm* **1** : commerce, trade **2** *NEGOCIO* : business, place of business **3 comercio electrónico** : e-commerce
comestible¹ *adj* : edible
comestible² *nm* **1** : foodstuff, food **2 comestibles** *nmpl VÍVERES* : groceries, food
cometa¹ *nm* : comet
cometa² *nf* : kite
cometer *vt* **1** : to commit **2 cometer un error** : to make a mistake
cometido *nm* : assignment, task
comezón *nf, pl* -**zones** *PICAZÓN* : itchiness, itching
comible *adj fam* : eatable, edible
cómic *or* **cómic** *nm* : comic strip, comic book
comicidad *nf HUMOR* : humor, wit
comicios *nmpl* : elections, voting
cómico¹, -ca *adj* : comic, comical
cómico², -ca *n HUMORISTA* : comic, comedian, comedienne *f*
comida *nf* **1** : food **2** : meal **3** *CENA* : dinner **3** *Mex, Spain ALMUERZO* : lunch **5 comida basura** *or* **comida chatarra** : junk food **6 comida rápida** : fast food
comidilla *nf* : talk, gossip
comienzo *nm* **1** : start, beginning **2 al comienzo** : at first **3 dar comienzo** : to begin
comillas *nfpl* : quotation marks ⟨entre comillas : in quotes⟩
comilón, -lona → comelón, -lona
comilona *nf fam* : feast
comino *nm* **1** : cumin **2 me vale un comino** *fam* : not to matter to someone ⟨no me importa un comino : I couldn't care less⟩
comisaría *nf* : police station
comisario, -ria *n* : commissioner
comisión *nf, pl* -**siones** **1** : commission, committing **2** : committee, commission **3** : percentage, commission ⟨comisión sobre las ventas : sales commission⟩ ⟨trabajar a comisión : to work on commission⟩
comisionado¹, -da *adj* : commissioned, entrusted
comisionado², -da *n* → comisario
comisionar *vt* : to commission
comisura *nf* **comisura de los labios** : corner of the mouth
comité *nm* : committee
comitiva *nf* : retinue, entourage
como¹ *adv* **1** : around, about ⟨cuesta como 500 pesos : it costs around 500 pesos⟩ **2** : kind of, like ⟨tengo como mareos : I'm kind of dizzy⟩

como² *conj* **1** : how, as ⟨hazlo como dijiste que lo harías : do it the way you said you would⟩ **2** : since, given that ⟨como estaba lloviendo, no salí : since it was raining, I didn't go out⟩ **3** : if ⟨como lo vuelva a hacer lo arrestarán : if he does that again he'll be arrested⟩ **4 como quiera** : in any way

como³ *prep* **1** : like, as ⟨ligero como una pluma : light as a feather⟩ **2 así como** : as well as

cómo *adv* : how ⟨¿cómo estás? : how are you?⟩ ⟨¿a cómo están las peras? : how much are the pears?⟩ ⟨¿cómo? : excuse me?, what was that?⟩ ⟨no sé cómo lo hace : I don't know how she does it⟩ ⟨¿cómo es eso? : how come?⟩ ⟨¡cómo que no hay dinero? : what do you mean there's no money?⟩ ⟨¿se puede? ¡cómo no! : may I? of course!⟩ ⟨¡cómo cambian los tiempos! : how times change!⟩

cómoda *nf* : bureau, chest of drawers

comodidad *nf* **1** : comfort **2** : convenience

comodín *nm, pl* **-dines** **1** : joker, wild card **2** : wildcard (symbol) **3** : all-purpose word or thing **4** : pretext, excuse

cómodo, -da *adj* **1** COMFORTABLE : comfortable **2** : convenient — **cómodamente** *adv*

comodoro *nm* : commodore

comoquiera *adv* **1** : in any way **2 comoquiera que** : in whatever way, however ⟨comoquiera que sea eso : however that may be⟩

compa *nm fam* : buddy, pal

compactar *vt* : to compact, to compress

compact disc [¹kompak¹dis, -¹disk] *nm, pl* **compact discs** [¹kompak¹dis, -¹disks] : compact disc, CD

compacto, -ta *adj* : compact

compadecer {53} *vt* : to sympathize with, to feel sorry for — **compadecerse** *vr* **1** ~ **de** : to take pity on **2** ~ **con** : to fit, to accord (with)

compadre *nm* **1** : godfather of one's child **2** : father of one's godchild **3** *fam* : buddy, pal

compaginar *vt* **1** COORDINAR : to combine, to coordinate **2** : to collate

compañerismo *nm* : camaraderie

compañero, -ra *n* : companion, mate, partner ⟨compañero de clase : classmate⟩ ⟨compañero de trabajo : coworker⟩

compañía *nf* **1** : company ⟨en compañía de su madre : accompanied by his mother⟩ ⟨me hacía compañía : she was keeping me company⟩ ⟨andar en/con malas compañías : to keep bad company⟩ **2** EMPRESA, FIRMA : company, firm **3** : company (in theater) **4** : company (in the military)

comparable *adj* : comparable

comparación *nf, pl* **-ciones** : comparison

comparado, -da *adj* : comparative ⟨literatura comparada : comparative literature⟩

comparar *vt* : to compare

comparativo¹, -va *adj* : comparative, relative — **comparativamente** *adv*

comparativo² *nm* : comparative degree or form

comparecencia *nf* **1** : appearance (in court) **2 orden de comparecencia** : subpoena, summons

comparecer {53} *vi* : to appear (in court)

comparsa *nmf* : extra (in a film, etc.)

compartimiento *or* **compartimento** *nm* : compartment

compartir *vt* : to share

compás *nm, pl* **-pases** **1** : beat, rhythm, time **2** : compass

compasión *nf, pl* **-siones** : compassion, pity

compasivo, -va *adj* : compassionate

compatibilidad *nf* : compatibility

compatible *adj* : compatible

compatriota *nmf* PAISANO : compatriot, fellow countryman

compeler *vt* : to compel

compendiar *vt* **1** : to summarize, to condense

compendio *nm* : summary

compenetración *nf, pl* **-ciones** : rapport, mutual understanding

compenetrarse *vr* **1** : to understand each other **2** ~ **con** : to identify oneself with

compensación *nf, pl* **-ciones** : compensation

compensar *vt* : to compensate for, to make up for — *vi* : to be worth one's while

compensatorio, -ria *adj* : compensatory

competencia *nf* **1** : competition, rivalry **2** : competence

competente *adj* : competent, able — **competentemente** *adv*

competición *nf, pl* **-ciones** : competition

competidor¹, -dora *adj* RIVAL : competing, rival

competidor², -dora *n* RIVAL : competitor, rival

competir {54} *vi* : to compete

competitividad *nf* : competitiveness

competitivo, -va *adj* : competitive — **competitivamente** *adv*

compilar *vt* : to compile — **compilación** *nf*

compinche *nmf fam* **1** : buddy, pal **2** : partner in crime, accomplice

complacencia *nf* : pleasure, satisfaction

complacer {57} *vt* : to please — **complacerse** *vr* ~ **en** : to take pleasure in

complaciente *adj* : obliging, eager to please

complejidad *nf* : complexity

complejo¹, -ja *adj* : complex

complejo² *nm* : complex

complementar *vt* : to complement, to supplement — **complementarse** *vr*

complementario, -ria *adj* : complementary

complemento *nm* **1** : complement, supplement **2** : supplementary pay, allowance

completamente *adv* : completely, totally

completar *vt* TERMINAR : to complete, to finish

completo, -ta *adj* **1** : complete, full, whole ⟨las obras completas : the complete works⟩ ⟨su nombre completo : his full name⟩ **2** : complete, absolute ⟨por completo : completely⟩ **3** DETALLADO : full, detailed **4** VERSÁTIL : well-rounded, versatile

complexión *nf, pl* **-xiones** : (physical) constitution

complicación *nf, pl* **-ciones** : complication

complicado, -da *adj* : complicated

complicar {72} *vt* **1** : to complicate **2** : to involve — **complicarse** *vr*

cómplice *nmf* : accomplice

complicidad *nf* : complicity

complot *nm, pl* **complots** CONFABULACIÓN, CONSPIRACIÓN : conspiracy, plot

componenda *nf* : shady deal, scam

componente *adj & nm* : component, constituent

componer {60} *vt* **1** ARREGLAR : to fix, to repair **2** CONSTITUIR : to make up, to compose **3** : to compose, to write **4** : to set (a bone) — **componerse** *vr* **1** : to improve, to get better **2** ~ **de** : to consist of

comportamiento *nm* CONDUCTA : behavior, conduct

comportarse *vr* : to behave, to conduct oneself

composición *nf, pl* **-ciones** **1** OBRA : composition, work **2** : makeup, arrangement

compositor, -tora *n* : composer, songwriter

compostura *nf* **1** : composure **2** : mending, repair

compota *nf* : compote

compra *nf* **1** : purchase **2** ir de compras : to go shopping **3** orden de compra : purchase order

comprador, -dora *n* : buyer, shopper

comprar *vt* : to buy, to purchase

compraventa *nf* : buying and selling

comprender *vt* **1** ENTENDER : to comprehend, to understand **2** ABARCAR : to cover, to include — *vi* : to understand ⟨¡ya comprendo! : now I understand!⟩

comprensible *adj* : understandable — **comprensiblemente** *adv*

comprensión *nf, pl* **-siones** **1** : comprehension, understanding **2** : understanding, sympathy

comprensivo, -va *adj* : understanding

compresa *nf* **1** : compress **2 or compresa higiénica** : sanitary napkin

compresión *nf, pl* **-siones** : compression

compresor *nm* : compressor

comprimido *nm* PÍLDORA, TABLETA : pill, tablet

comprimir *vt* : to compress

comprobable *adj* : provable

comprobación *nf, pl* **-ciones** : verification, confirmation

comprobante *nm* **1** : proof ⟨comprobante de identidad : proof of identity⟩ **2** : voucher, receipt ⟨comprobante de ventas : sales slip⟩

comprobar {19} *vt* **1** : to verify, to check **2** : to prove

comprometedor, -dora *adj* : compromising

comprometer *vt* **1** : to compromise **2** : to jeopardize **3** : to commit, to put under obligation — **comprometerse** *vr* **1** : to commit oneself **2** ~ **con** : to get engaged to

comprometido, -da *adj* **1** : compromising, awkward **2** : committed, obliged **3** : engaged (to be married)

compromiso *nm* **1** : obligation, commitment **2** : engagement ⟨anillo de compromiso : engagement ring⟩ **3** : agreement **4** : awkward situation, fix

compuerta *nf* : floodgate

compuesto¹ *pp* → **componer**

compuesto², -ta *adj* **1** : fixed, repaired **2** : compound, composite **3** : decked out, spruced up **4** ~ **de** : made up of, consisting of

compuesto³ *nm* : compound

compulsión *nf, pl* **-siones** : compulsion

compulsivo, -va *adj* **1** : compelling, urgent **2** : compulsive — **compulsivamente** *adv*

compungido, -da *adj* : contrite, remorseful

compungirse {35} *vr* : to feel remorse

compuso, etc. → **componer**

computable *adj* : countable ⟨años computables : years accrued⟩ ⟨ingresos computables : qualifying income⟩

computación *nf, pl* **-ciones** : computing, computers *pl*

computador *nm* → **computadora**

computadora *nf* **1** : computer **2 computadora portátil** : laptop computer

computar *vt* : to compute, to calculate

computarizar {21} *vt* : to computerize

cómputo *nm* : computation, calculation

comulgar {52} *vi* : to receive Communion

común *adj, pl* **comunes** **1** : common **2 común y corriente** : ordinary, regular **3 por lo común** : generally, as a rule

comuna *nf* : commune

comunal *adj* : communal

comunicación *nf, pl* **-ciones** **1** : communication **2** : access, link **3** : message, report

comunicado *nm* **1** : communiqué **2 comunicado de prensa** : press release

comunicador, -dora *n* : commentator, analyst

comunicar {72} *vt* **1** : to communicate, to convey **2** : to notify — **comunicarse** *vr* ~ **con** **1** : to contact, to get in touch with **2** : to be connected to

comunicativo, -va *adj* : communicative, talkative

comunidad *nf* : community

comunión *nf, pl* **-niones** **1** : communion, sharing **2** : Communion

comunismo *nm* : communism, Communism

comunista *adj & nmf* : communist

comunitario, -ria *adj* : community, communal

comúnmente *adv* : commonly

con *prep* **1** : with ⟨vengo con mi padre : I'm going with my father⟩ ⟨¿con quién hablas? : who are you speaking to?⟩ **2** : in spite of ⟨con todo : in spite of it all⟩

3 : to, towards ⟨ser amable con : to be kind to⟩ 4 : by ⟨con llegar temprano : by arriving early⟩ 5 con (tal) que : as/ so long as

conato *nm* : attempt, effort ⟨conato de robo : attempted robbery⟩

cóncavo, -va *adj* : concave

concebible *adj* : conceivable

concebir {54} *vt* 1 : to conceive 2 : to conceive of, to imagine — *vi* : to conceive, to become pregnant

conceder *vt* 1 : to grant, to bestow 2 : to concede, to admit

concejal, -jala *n* : councilman *m*, councilwoman *f*; alderman *mf*

concejo *nm* : council ⟨concejo municipal : town council⟩

concentración *nf, pl* **-ciones** : concentration

concentrado *nm* : concentrate

concentrar *vt* : to concentrate — **concentrarse** *vr*

concéntrico, -ca *adj* : concentric

concepción *nf, pl* **-ciones** : conception

concepto *nm* NOCIÓN : concept, idea, opinion

conceptual *adj* : conceptual — **conceptualmente** *adv*

conceptualizar {21} *vt* : conceptualize — **conceptualización** *nf*

conceptuar {3} *vt* : to regard, to judge

concernir {17} *vi* : to be of concern

concertar {55} *vt* 1 : to arrange, to set up 2 : to agree on, to settle 3 : to harmonize — *vi* : to be in harmony

concesión *nf, pl* **-siones** 1 : concession 2 : awarding, granting

concesionario, -ria *n* : franchisee

concha *nf* : conch, seashell

concho *nm DomRep* : fixed-route taxi

conciencia *nf* 1 : conscience 2 : consciousness, awareness

concienciar → **concientizar**

concientización *nf, pl* **-ciones** : awareness, awareness-raising

concientizar {21} *vt* : to make aware — **concientizarse** *vr* ~ **de** : to realize, to become aware of

concienzudo, -da *adj* : conscientious

concierto *nm* 1 : concert 2 : agreement 3 : concerto

conciliador¹, -dora *adj* : conciliatory

conciliador², -dora *n* : arbitrator, peacemaker

conciliar *vt* : to reconcile — **conciliación** *nf*

conciliatorio, -ria *adj* → **conciliador¹**

concilio *nm* : (church) council

conciso, -sa *adj* : concise — **concisamente** *adv* — **concisión** *nf*

concitar *vt* : to arouse

conciudadano, -na *n* : fellow citizen

cónclave *nm* : conclave, private meeting

concluir {41} *vt* 1 TERMINAR : to conclude, to finish 2 DEDUCIR : to deduce, to conclude — *vi* : to end, to conclude

conclusión *nf, pl* **-siones** : conclusion

concluyente *adj* : conclusive

concomitante *adj* : accompanying, attendant

concordancia *nf* : agreement, accordance

concordar {19} *vi* : to agree, to coincide — *vt* : to reconcile

concordia *nf* : concord, harmony

concretar *vt* 1 : to pinpoint, to specify 2 : to fulfill, to realize — **concretarse** *vr* : to become real, to take shape

concretizar → **concretar**

concreto¹, -ta *adj* 1 : concrete, actual 2 : definite, specific ⟨en concreto : specifically⟩ — **concretamente** *adv*

concreto² *nm* HORMIGÓN : concrete

concurrencia *nf* 1 : audience, turnout 2 : concurrence

concurrente *adj* : concurrent — **concurrentemente** *adv*

concurrido, -da *adj* : busy, crowded

concurrir *vi* 1 : to converge, to come together 2 : to concur, to agree 3 : to take part, to participate 4 : to attend, to be present ⟨concurrir a una reunión : to attend a meeting⟩ 5 ~ **a** : to contribute to

concursante *nmf* : contestant, competitor

concursar *vt* : to compete in — *vi* : to compete, to participate

concurso *nm* 1 : contest, competition 2 : concurrence, coincidence 3 : crowd, gathering 4 : cooperation, assistance

condado *nm* 1 : county 2 : earldom

conde, -desa *n* : count *m*, earl *m*, countess *f*

condecoración *nf, pl* **-ciones** : decoration, medal

condecorar *vt* : to decorate, to award (a medal)

condena *nf* 1 : condemnation 2 SENTENCIA : sentence

condenable *adj* : reprehensible

condenación *nf, pl* **-ciones** 1 : condemnation 2 : damnation

condenado¹, -da *adj* 1 : fated, doomed 2 : convicted, sentenced 3 *fam* : darn, damned

condenado², -da *n* : convict

condenar *vt* 1 : to condemn 2 : to sentence 3 : to board up, to wall up — **condenarse** *vr* : to be damned

condenatorio, -ria *adj* : condemning ⟨sentencia condenatoria : conviction⟩

condensación *nf, pl* **-ciones** : condensation

condensar *vt* : to condense

condesa *nf* → **conde**

condescendencia *nf* : condescension

condescender {56} *vi* 1 : to condescend 2 : to agree, to acquiesce

condescendiente *adj* 1 : condescending 2 : accommodating, obliging

condición *nf, pl* **-ciones** 1 : condition, state ⟨en buenas/malas condiciones : in good/bad condition⟩ ⟨no está en condiciones de trabajar : she's in no shape to work⟩ 2 : capacity, position ⟨estar en condiciones de : to be in a position to⟩ 3 : condition, stipulation ⟨a condición de que, con la condición de que : on the condition that⟩ 4 **condiciones** *nfpl* : conditions, circumstances ⟨condicio-

nes de vida : living conditions⟩ ⟨en igualdad de condiciones : on equal footing⟩
condicional *adj* : conditional — **condi-
cionalmente** *adv*
condicionamiento *nm* : conditioning
condicionar *vt* **1** : to condition, to determine **2** ~ **a** : to be contingent on, to
depend on
condimentar *vt* SAZONAR : to season, to
spice
condimento *nm* : condiment, seasoning,
spice
condolencia *nf* : condolence, sympathy
condolerse {47} *vr* : to sympathize
condominio *nm* : condominium, condo
condón *nm, pl* **condones** : condom
cóndor *nm* : condor
conducción *nf, pl* **-ciones** **1** : conduction (of electricity, etc.) **2** DIRECCIÓN
: management, direction
conducir {61} *vt* **1** DIRIGIR, GUIAR : to
direct, to lead **2** MANEJAR : to drive (a
vehicle) — *vi* **1** : to drive a vehicle **2** ~
a : to lead to — **conducirse** *vr* POR-
TARSE : to behave, to conduct oneself
conducta *nf* COMPORTAMIENTO : conduct, behavior
conductividad *nf* : conductivity
conducto *nm* : conduit, channel, duct
conductor[1], **-tora** *adj* : conducting, leading
conductor[2], **-tora** *n* : driver
conductor[3] *nm* : conductor (of electricity, etc.)
conectar *vt* : to connect — *vi* ~ **con** : to
link up with, to communicate with
conectivo, -va *adj* : connective — **conec-
tividad** *nf*
conector *nm* : connector
conejera *nf* : rabbit hutch
conejillo *nm* **conejillo de Indias** : guinea
pig
conejo, -ja *n* : rabbit
conexión *nf, pl* **-xiones** : connection
confabulación *nf, pl* **-ciones** COMPLOT,
CONSPIRACIÓN : plot, conspiracy
confabularse *vr* : to plot, to conspire
confección *nf, pl* **-ciones** **1** : preparation **2** : tailoring, dressmaking
confeccionar *vt* : to make, to produce, to
prepare
confederación *nf, pl* **-ciones** : confederation
confederarse *vr* : to confederate, to form
a confederation
conferencia *nf* **1** REUNIÓN : conference,
meeting **2** : lecture
conferenciante *nmf* : lecturer
conferencista → **conferenciante**
conferir {76} *vt* : to confer, to bestow
confesar {55} *v* **1** : to confess — **confesarse** *vr* : to go to confession
confesión *nf, pl* **-siones** **1** : confession
2 : creed, denomination
confesionario *nm* : confessional
confesor *nm* : confessor
confeti *nm* : confetti
confiable *adj* : trustworthy, reliable
confiado, -da *adj* **1** : confident, self-confident **2** : trusting — **confiadamente**
adv

confianza *nf* **1** : trust ⟨de poca confianza
: untrustworthy⟩ **2** : confidence, self-
confidence
confianzudo, -da *adj* : forward, presumptuous
confiar {85} *vt* **1** : to confide **2** : to entrust — *vi* ~ **en** : to trust, to have faith/
confidence in — **confiarse** *vr* **1** : to be
overconfident **2** ~ **a** : to confide in
confidencia *nf* : confidence, secret
confidencial *adj* : confidential — **confi-
dencialmente** *adv*
confidencialidad *nf* : confidentiality
confidente *nmf* **1** : confidant, confidante
f **2** : informer
configuración *nf, pl* **-ciones** : configuration, shape
configurar *vt* **1** : to shape, to form **2** : to
configure (a computer, etc.)
confín *nm, pl* **confines** : boundary, limit
confinamiento *nm* : confinement
confinar *vt* **1** : to confine, to limit **2** : to
exile — *vi* ~ **con** : to border on
confirmación *nf, pl* **-ciones** : confirmation
confirmar *vt* : to confirm, to substantiate
confiscación *nf, pl* **-ciones** : confiscation
confiscar {72} *vt* DECOMISAR : to confiscate, to seize
confitado, -da *adj* : candied
confite *nm* : sugar-coated candy
confitería *nf* **1** DULCERÍA : candy store,
confectionery **2** : tearoom, café
confitero, -ra *n* : confectioner
confitura *nf* : preserves, jam
conflagración *nf, pl* **-ciones** **1** : conflagration, fire **2** : war
conflictivo, -va *adj* **1** : troubled **2** : controversial
conflicto *nm* : conflict
confluencia *nf* : junction, confluence
confluir {41} *vi* **1** : to converge, to join **2**
: to gather, to assemble
conformación *nf, pl* **-ciones** : makeup,
composition
conformar *vt* **1** : to form, to create **2**
: to constitute, to make up — **conformarse** *vr* **1** RESIGNARSE : to resign oneself **2** : to comply, to conform **3** ~
con : to be content with
conforme[1] *adj* **1** : content, satisfied **2** ~
a : in accordance with
conforme[2] *conj* : as ⟨irá mejorando conforme avance el día : it will improve as
the day goes on⟩
conformidad *nf* **1** : agreement, consent
2 : resignation
confort *nm* : comfort
confortable *adj* CÓMODO : comfortable
confortar *vt* CONSOLAR : to comfort, to
console
confraternidad *nf* : brotherhood, fraternity
confraternizar {21} *vi* : to fraternize —
confraternización *nf*
confrontación *nf, pl* **-ciones** : confrontation
confrontar *vt* **1** ENCARAR : to confront
2 : to compare **3** : to bring face-to-face
— *vi* : to border — **confrontarse** *vr* ~
con : to face up to

confundir *vt* : to confuse, to mix up — **confundirse** *vr* : to make a mistake, to be confused ⟨confundirse de número : to get the wrong number⟩

confusión *nf, pl* **-siones** : confusion

confuso, -sa *adj* **1** DESORDENADO : confused, confusing ⟨ideas confusas : confused ideas⟩ ⟨una situación confusa : a confused/confusing situation⟩ ⟨unas voces confusas : a confusion of voices⟩ **2** ATURDIDO, TURBADO : confused, flustered, embarrassed **3** VAGO : hazy, indistinct

congelación *nf, pl* **-ciones 1** : freezing **2** : frostbite (on skin), exposure

congelado, -da *adj* HELADO : frozen

congelador *nm* HELADORA : freezer

congelamiento *nm* → **congelación**

congelar *vt* : to freeze — **congelarse** *vr*

congeniar *vi* : to get along (with someone)

congénito, -ta *adj* : congenital

congestión *nf, pl* **-tiones** : congestion

congestionado, -da *adj* : congested

congestionamiento *nm* → **congestión**

congestionarse *vr* **1** : to become flushed **2** : to become congested

conglomerado¹, -da *adj* : conglomerate, mixed

conglomerado² *nm* : conglomerate, conglomeration

congoja *nf* ANGUSTIA : anguish, grief

congoleño, -ña *adj & n* : Congolese

congraciarse *vr* : to ingratiate oneself

congratular *vt* FELICITAR : to congratulate

congregación *nf, pl* **-ciones** : congregation, gathering

congregar {52} *vt* : to bring together — **congregarse** *vr* : to congregate, to assemble

congresista *nmf* : congressman *m*, congresswoman *f*

congreso *nm* : congress, conference

congruencia *nf* **1** : congruence **2** COHERENCIA : coherence — **congruente** *adj*

cónico, -ca *adj* : conical, conic

conífera *nf* : conifer

conífero, -ra *adj* : coniferous

conjetura *nf* : conjecture, guess

conjeturar *vt* : to guess, to conjecture

conjugación *nf, pl* **-ciones** : conjugation

conjugar {52} *vt* **1** : to conjugate **2** : to combine

conjunción *nf, pl* **-ciones** : conjunction

conjuntivitis *nf* : conjunctivitis

conjuntivo, -va *adj* : connective ⟨tejido conjuntivo : connective tissue⟩

conjunto¹, -ta *adj* : joint — **conjuntamente** *adv*

conjunto² *nm* **1** : collection, group **2** : ensemble, outfit **3** : ensemble, musical group **4** : whole, entirety ⟨en conjunto : as a whole, altogether⟩

conjurar *vt* **1** : to exorcise **2** : to avert, to ward off — *vi* CONSPIRAR : to conspire, to plot

conjuro *nm* **1** : exorcism **2** : spell

conllevar *vt* **1** : to bear, to suffer **2** IMPLICAR : to entail, to involve

conmemorar *vt* : to commemorate — **conmemoración** *nf*

conmemorativo, -va *adj* : commemorative, memorial

conmigo *pron* : with me ⟨habló conmigo : he talked with me⟩

conminar *vt* AMENAZAR : to threaten, to warn

conmiseración *nf, pl* **-ciones** : pity, commiseration

conmoción *nf, pl* **-ciones 1** : shock, upheaval **2** *or* **conmoción cerebral** : concussion

conmocionar *vt* : to shake, to shock

conmovedor, -dora *adj* EMOCIONANTE : moving, touching

conmover {47} *vt* **1** EMOCIONAR : to move, to touch **2** : to shake up — **conmoverse** *vr*

conmutador *nm* **1** : switch **2** : switchboard

conmutar *vt* **1** : to commute (a sentence) **2** : to switch, to exchange

connivencia *nf* : connivance

connotación *nf, pl* **-ciones** : connotation

connotar *vt* : to connote, to imply

cono *nm* : cone

conocedor¹, -dora *adj* : knowledgeable

conocedor², -dora *n* : connoisseur, expert

conocer {18} *vt* **1** : to know, to be acquainted with ⟨¿lo conoces? : do you know him?⟩ **2** : to meet ⟨ya la conocí : I've already met her⟩ **3** : to know, to be familiar with (a topic, etc.) **4** : to get to know, to experience ⟨me gustaría conocer otros países : I'd like to visit other countries⟩ ⟨conocer de primera mano : to experience firsthand⟩ **5** RECONOCER : to recognize ⟨no te conocí : I didn't recognize you⟩ **6 dar a conocer** : to disclose, to announce **7 darse a conocer** : to make oneself known — **conocerse** *vr* **1** : to know each other **2** : to meet **3** : to know oneself

conocible *adj* : knowable

conocido¹, -da *adj* **1** : familiar **2** : well-known, famous

conocido², -da *n* : acquaintance

conocimiento *nm* **1** : knowledge **2** SENTIDO : consciousness

conque *conj* : so, so then, and so ⟨¡ah, conque esas tenemos! : oh, so that's what's going on!⟩

conquista *nf* : conquest

conquistador¹, -dora *adj* : conquering

conquistador², -dora *n* : conqueror

conquistar *vt* : to conquer

consabido, -da *adj* : usual, typical

consagración *nf, pl* **-ciones** : consecration

consagrar *vt* **1** : to consecrate **2** DEDICAR : to dedicate, to devote

consciencia → **conciencia**

consciente *adj* : conscious, aware — **conscientemente** *adv*

conscripción *nf, pl* **-ciones** : conscription, draft

conscripto, -ta *n* : conscript, inductee

consecución *nf, pl* **-ciones** : attainment

consecuencia *nf* **1** : consequence, result ⟨a consecuencia de : as a result of⟩ **2** en ~ : accordingly
consecuente *adj* : consistent — **consecuentemente** *adv*
consecutivo, -va *adj* : consecutive, successive — **consecutivamente** *adv*
conseguir {75} *vt* **1** : to get, to obtain **2** : to achieve, to attain (a goal, etc.) **3** : to manage to ⟨consiguió acabar : she managed to finish⟩ ⟨conseguí que lo aceptara : I got him to accept it⟩
consejero, -ra *n* : adviser, counselor
consejo *nm* **1** : piece of advice ⟨me dio algunos consejos : she gave me some advice⟩ ⟨por consejo de : on the advice of⟩ **2** : council ⟨consejo de guerra : court-martial⟩
consenso *nm* : consensus
consensuar *vt* : to reach a consensus on
consentido, -da *adj* : spoiled, pampered
consentimiento *nm* : consent, permission
consentir {76} *vt* **1** PERMITIR : to consent to, to allow **2** MIMAR : to pamper, to spoil — *vi* ~ en : to agree to, to approve of
conserje *nmf* : custodian, janitor, caretaker
conserva *nf* **1** : preserve(s), jam **2** conservas *nfpl* : canned goods
conservación *nf, pl* **-ciones** : conservation, preservation
conservacionista *nmf* : conservationist
conservador¹, -dora *adj & n* : conservative
conservador² *nm* : preservative
conservadurismo *nm* : conservatism
conservante *nm* : preservative
conservar *vt* **1** : to preserve **2** GUARDAR : to keep, to conserve
conservatorio *nm* : conservatory
considerable *adj* : considerable — **considerablemente** *adv*
consideración *nf, pl* **-ciones** **1** : consideration **2** : respect **3** de ~ : considerable, important
considerado, -da *adj* **1** : considerate, thoughtful **2** : respected
considerar *vt* **1** : to consider, to think about ⟨considerar la posibilidad : to consider the possibility⟩ ⟨considerando su edad : considering his age⟩ **2** : to consider, to regard as ⟨lo considera necesario : she considers it necessary⟩ **3** : to treat with consideration — **considerarse** *vr* : to consider oneself
consigna *nf* **1** ESLOGAN : slogan **2** : assignment, orders *pl* **3** : luggage storage
consignación *nf, pl* **-ciones** **1** : consignment **2** ASIGNACIÓN : allocation
consignar *vt* **1** : to consign **2** : to record, to write down **3** : to assign, to allocate
consigo *pron* : with her, with him, with you, with oneself ⟨se llevó las llaves consigo : she took the keys with her⟩
consiguiente *adj* **1** : resulting, consequent **2** por ~ : consequently, as a result
consistencia *nf* : consistency

consistente *adj* **1** : firm, strong, sound **2** : consistent — **consistentemente** *adv*
consistir *vi* **1** ~ en : to consist of **2** ~ en : to lie in, to consist in
consola *nf* : console
consolación *nf, pl* **-ciones** : consolation ⟨premio de consolación : consolation prize⟩
consolar {19} *vt* CONFORTAR : to console, to comfort
consolidar *vt* : to consolidate — **consolidación** *nf*
consomé *nm* CALDO : consommé, clear soup
consonancia *nf* **1** : harmony **2** en consonancia con : in accordance with
consonante¹ *adj* : consonant, harmonious
consonante² *nf* : consonant
consorcio *nm* : consortium
consorte *nmf* : consort, spouse
conspicuo, -cua *adj* : eminent, famous
conspiración *nf, pl* **-ciones** COMPLOT, CONFABULACIÓN : conspiracy, plot
conspirador, -dora *n* : conspirator
conspirar *vi* CONJURAR : to conspire, to plot
constancia *nf* **1** PRUEBA : proof, certainty **2** : record, evidence ⟨que quede constancia : for the record⟩ **3** : perseverance, constancy
constante¹ *adj* : constant — **constantemente** *adv*
constante² *nf* : constant
constar *vi* **1** : to be evident, to be on record ⟨que conste : believe me, have no doubt⟩ **2** ~ de : to consist of
constatación *nf, pl* **-ciones** : confirmation, proof
constatar *vt* **1** : to verify **2** : to state
constelación *nf, pl* **-ciones** : constellation
consternación *nf, pl* **-ciones** : consternation, dismay
consternar *vt* : to dismay, to appall
constipación *nf, pl* **-ciones** : constipation
constipado¹, -da *adj* estar constipado : to have a cold
constipado² *nm* RESFRIADO : cold
constiparse *vr* : to catch a cold
constitución *nf, pl* **-ciones** : constitution — **constitucional** *adj* — **constitucionalmente** *adv*
constitucionalidad *nf* : constitutionality
constituir {41} *vt* **1** FORMAR : to constitute, to make up, to form **2** FUNDAR : to establish, to set up — **constituirse** *vr* ~ en : to set oneself up as, to become
constitutivo, -va *adj* : constituent, component
constituyente *adj & nmf* : constituent
constreñir {67} *vt* **1** FORZAR, OBLIGAR : to constrain, to oblige **2** LIMITAR : to restrict, to limit
construcción *nf, pl* **-ciones** : construction, building
constructivo, -va *adj* : constructive — **constructivamente** *adv*
constructor, -tora *n* : builder
constructora *nf* : construction company

construir {41} *vt* : to build, to construct

consuelo *nm* : consolation, comfort

consuetudinario, -ria *adj* **1** : customary, habitual **2 derecho consuetudinario** : common law

cónsul *nmf* : consul — **consular** *adj*

consulado *nm* : consulate

consulta *nf* **1** : consultation **2** : inquiry

consultar *vt* : to consult

consultivo, -va *adj* : advisory

consultor¹, -tora *adj* : consulting ⟨firma consultora : consulting firm⟩

consultor², -tora *n* : consultant

consultoría *nf* : consultancy

consultorio *nm* **1** : office (of a doctor or dentist) **2** → **consultoría**

consumación *nf, pl* **-ciones** : consummation

consumado, -da *adj* : consummate, perfect

consumar *vt* **1** : to consummate, to complete **2** : to commit, to carry out

consumible *adj* : consumable

consumición *nf, pl* **-ciones 1** : consumption **2** : drink (in a restaurant)

consumido, -da *adj* : thin, emaciated

consumidor, -dora *n* : consumer

consumir *vt* : to consume — **consumirse** *vr* : to waste away

consumismo *nm* : consumerism

consumo *nm* : consumption (of food, fuel, etc.)

contabilidad *nf* **1** : accounting, bookkeeping **2** : accountancy

contabilizar {21} *vt* : to enter, to record (in accounting)

contable¹ *adj* : countable

contable² *nmf Spain* : accountant, bookkeeper

contactar *vt* : to contact — *vi* ∼ **con** : to get in touch with, to contact

contacto *nm* : contact

contado¹, -da *adj* **1** : counted ⟨tenía los días contados : his days were numbered⟩ **2** : rare, scarce ⟨en contadas ocasiones : on rare occasions⟩

contado² *nm* **al contado** : cash ⟨pagar al contado : to pay in cash⟩

contador¹, -dora *n* : accountant

contador² *nm* : meter ⟨contador de agua : water meter⟩ ⟨contador Geiger : Geiger counter⟩

contaduría *nf* **1** : accounting office **2** CONTABILIDAD : accountancy

contagiar *vt* **1** : to infect **2** : to transmit (a disease) — **contagiarse** *vr* **1** : to be contagious **2** : to become infected

contagio *nm* : contagion, infection

contagioso, -sa *adj* : contagious, catching

contaminación *nf, pl* **-ciones** : contamination, pollution

contaminante *nm* : pollutant, contaminant

contaminar *vt* : to contaminate, to pollute

contante *adj* **dinero contante y sonante** → **dinero**

contar {19} *vt* **1** : to count ⟨contar el dinero : to count the money⟩ **2** : to tell ⟨cuéntame un cuento : tell me a story⟩ ⟨me lo contó todo : she told me everything⟩ **3** : to include, to count — *vi* **1** : to count (up) ⟨contar de diez en diez : to count by tens⟩ **2** : to count, to matter ⟨eso no cuenta : that doesn't count⟩ **3** ∼ **con** : to count on, to rely on **4** ∼ **con** : to expect, to count on ⟨no contaba con que . . . : I didn't count on the fact that . . .⟩ **5** ∼ **con** : to have (support, resources, etc.) — **contarse** *vr* ∼ **entre** : to be numbered among

contemplación *nf, pl* **-ciones** : contemplation — **contemplativo, -va** *adj*

contemplar *vt* **1** : to contemplate, to ponder **2** : to gaze at, to look at

contemporáneo, -nea *adj & n* : contemporary

contención *nf, pl* **-ciones** : containment, holding

contencioso, -sa *adj* : contentious

contender {56} *vi* **1** : to contend, to compete **2** : to fight

contendiente *nmf* : contender

contenedor *nm* **1** : container, receptacle **2** : Dumpster™

contener {80} *vt* **1** : to contain, to hold **2** ATAJAR : to restrain, to hold back — **contenerse** *vr* : to restrain oneself

contenido¹, -da *adj* : restrained, reserved

contenido² *nm* : contents *pl*, content

contentar *vt* : to please, to make happy — **contentarse** *vr* : to be satisfied, to be pleased

contento¹, -ta *adj* : contented, glad, happy

contento² *nm* : joy, happiness

conteo *nm* : count

contestación *nf, pl* **-ciones 1** : answer, reply **2** : protest

contestador *nm* **or contestador automático** : answering machine

contestadora *nf* → **contestador**

contestar *vt* RESPONDER : to answer — *vi* **1** RESPONDER : to answer, to reply **2** : to talk back, to be disrespectful

contexto *nm* : context

contienda *nf* **1** : dispute, conflict **2** : contest, competition

contigo *pron* : with you ⟨voy contigo : I'm going with you⟩

contiguo, -gua *adj* COLINDANTE : contiguous, adjacent

continente *nm* : continent — **continental** *adj*

contingencia *nf* : contingency, eventuality

contingente *adj & nm* : contingent

continuación *nf, pl* **-ciones 1** : continuation **2 a** ∼ : next ⟨más detalles a continuación : more details below⟩ **3 a continuación de** : after, following

continuar {3} *v* : to continue ⟨continuó trabajando : she continued working, she continued to work⟩ ⟨continuar (con) algo : to continue (with) something⟩

continuidad *nf* : continuity

continuo, -nua *adj* : continuous, steady, constant — **continuamente** *adv*

contonearse *vr* : to sway one's hips

contoneo *nm* : swaying, wiggling (of the hips)

contorno *nm* **1** : outline **2 contornos** *nmpl* : outskirts

contorsión *nf, pl* **-siones** : contortion

contra[1] *nf* **1** *fam* : difficulty, snag **2 llevar la contra a** : to oppose, to contradict

contra[2] *nm* : con ⟨los pros y los contras : the pros and cons⟩

contra[3] *prep* **1** : against ⟨se apoyó contra la pared : he leaned against the wall⟩ ⟨luchar contra : to fight against⟩ **2 en contra** : against ⟨las razones en contra : the reasons against it⟩ ⟨protestas en contra del gobierno : anti-government protests⟩

contra- *pref* : counter- ⟨contraataque : counterattack⟩

contraalmirante *nm* : rear admiral

contraatacar {72} *v* : to counterattack — **contraataque** *nm*

contrabajo *nm* : double bass

contrabalancear *vt* : to counterbalance — **contrabalanza** *nf*

contrabandear *v* : to smuggle

contrabandista *nmf* : smuggler, black market dealer

contrabando *nm* **1** : smuggling **2** : contraband

contracción *nf, pl* **-ciones** : contraction

contracepción *nf, pl* **-ciones** : contraception

contraceptivo *nm* ANTICONCEPTIVO : contraceptive

contrachapado *nm* : plywood

contracorriente *nf* **1** : crosscurrent **2 ir a contracorriente** : to go against the tide

contractual *adj* : contractual

contradecir {11} *vt* DESMENTIR : to contradict — **contradecirse** *vr* DESDECIRSE : to contradict oneself

contradicción *nf, pl* **-ciones** : contradiction

contradictorio, -ria *adj* : contradictory

contraer {81} *vt* **1** : to contract (a disease) **2** : to establish by contract ⟨contraer matrimonio : to get married⟩ **3** : to tighten, to contract — **contraerse** *vr* : to contract, to tighten up

contrafuerte *nm* : buttress

contragolpe *nm* **1** : counterattack **2** : backlash

contrahuella *nf* : riser (of a stair)

contralor, -lora *n* : comptroller

contraloría *nf* : office of the comptroller

contralto *nmf* : contralto

contraluz *nm, pl* **-luces a contraluz** : against the light

contramandar *vt* : to countermand

contramano *nm* **a ~** : the wrong way (on a street)

contramedida *nf* : countermeasure

contraparte *nf* **1** : counterpart **2 en ~** : on the other hand

contrapartida *nf* : compensation

contrapelo *nm* **a ~** : in the wrong direction, against the grain

contrapesar *vt* : to counterbalance

contrapeso *nm* : counterbalance

contraponer {60} *vt* **1** : to counter, to oppose **2** : to contrast, to compare

contraportada *nf* : back cover, back page

contraposición *nf, pl* **-ciones** : comparison

contraproducente *adj* : counterproductive

contrapunto *nm* : counterpoint

contrariar {85} *vt* **1** : to contradict, to oppose **2** : to vex, to annoy

contrariedad *nf* **1** : setback, obstacle **2** : vexation, annoyance

contrario, -ria *adj* **1** : contrary, opposite ⟨al contrario : on the contrary⟩ **2** : conflicting, opposed

contrarreloj *adj* **1** : timed **2 a ~** : against the clock

contrarrestar *vt* : to counteract

contrarrevolución *nf, pl* **-ciones** : counterrevolution — **contrarrevolucionario, -ria** *adj & n*

contrasentido *nm* : contradiction

contraseña *nf* : password

contrastante *adj* : contrasting

contrastar *vt* **1** : to resist **2** : to check, to confirm — *vi* : to contrast

contraste *nm* : contrast

contratar *vt* **1** : to contract for **2** : to hire, to engage

contratiempo *nm* **1** PERCANCE : mishap, accident **2** DIFICULTAD : setback, difficulty

contratista *nmf* : contractor

contrato *nm* : contract

contravenir {87} *vt* : to contravene, to infringe

contraventana *nf* : shutter

contravía *nf* *Col* **ir en contravía** : to drive the wrong way (down a street)

contribución *nf, pl* **-ciones** : contribution

contribuidor, -dora *n* : contributor

contribuir {41} *vt* APORTAR : to contribute **2** : to pay (in taxes) — *vi* **1** : contribute, to help out **2** : to pay taxes

contribuyente[1] *adj* : contributing

contribuyente[2] *nmf* : taxpayer

contrición *nf, pl* **-ciones** : contrition

contrincante *nmf* : rival, opponent

contrito, -ta *adj* : contrite, repentant

control *nm* **1** : control ⟨control remoto : remote control⟩ ⟨control de natalidad : birth control⟩ **2** : inspection, check **3** : checkpoint, roadblock

controlable *adj* : controllable

controlador, -dora *n* : controller ⟨controlador aéreo : air traffic controller⟩

controlar *vt* **1** : to control **2** : to monitor, to check

controversia *nf* : controversy

controversial → **controvertido**

controvertido, -da *adj* : controversial

controvertir {76} *vt* : to dispute, to argue about — *vi* : to argue, to debate

contubernio *nm* : conspiracy

contundencia *nf* **1** : forcefulness, weight **2** : severity

contundente *adj* **1** : blunt ⟨un objeto contundente : a blunt instrument⟩ **2** : forceful, convincing — **contundentemente** *adv*

contusión *nf, pl* **-siones** : bruise, contusion

contusionar *vt* MAGULLAR : to bruise

contuvo, etc. → **contener**

conurbano *nm Arg* : suburbs *pl*

convalecencia *nf* : convalescence

convalecer {53} *vi* : to convalesce, to recover

convaleciente *adj & nmf* : convalescent

convalidar *vt* : to recognize, to validate

convección *nf, pl* **-ciones** : convection

convencer {86} *vt* : to convince, to persuade — **convencerse** *vr*

convencimiento *nm* : belief, conviction

convención *nf, pl* **-ciones** 1 : convention, conference 2 : pact, agreement 3 : convention, custom

convencional *adj* : conventional — **convencionalmente** *adv*

conveniencia *nf* 1 : convenience 2 : fitness, suitability, advisability

conveniente *adj* 1 : convenient 2 : suitable, advisable

convenio *nm* PACTO : agreement, pact

convenir {87} *vi* 1 : to be suitable, to be advisable 2 : to agree

conventillo *nm Arg, Uru* : tenement

convento *nm* 1 : convent 2 : monastery

convergencia *nf* : convergence

convergente *adj* : convergent, converging

converger {15} *or* **convergir** {35} *vi* 1 : to converge 2 ~ **en** : to concur on

conversación *nf, pl* **-ciones** : conversation

conversador, -dora *n* : conversationalist, talker

conversar *vi* : to converse, to talk

conversatorio *nm CA, Carib, Mex* : talk, discussion

conversión *nf, pl* **-siones** : conversion

converso, -sa *n* : convert

convertible *adj & nm* : convertible

convertidor *nm* : converter ⟨convertidor catalítico : catalytic converter⟩

convertir {76} *vt* 1 : to convert (someone) 2 : to convert (money, etc.) 3 ~ **en** : to turn (someone or something) into (something) — **convertirse** *vr* 1 : to convert 2 ~ **en** : to turn into, to become

convexo, -xa *adj* : convex

convicción *nf, pl* **-ciones** : conviction

convicto¹, -ta *adj* : convicted

convicto², -ta *n* : convict, prisoner

convidado, -da *n* : guest

convidar *vt* 1 INVITAR : to invite 2 : to offer

convincente *adj* : convincing — **convincentemente** *adv*

convivir *vi* 1 : to coexist 2 : to live together

convocar {72} *vt* : to convoke, to call together

convocatoria *nf* : summons, call

convoy *nm* : convoy

convulsión *nf, pl* **-siones** 1 : convulsion 2 : agitation, upheaval

convulsionar *vt* : to shake, to convulse — **convulsionarse** *vr*

convulsivo, -va *adj* : convulsive

conyugal *adj* : conjugal

cónyuge *nmf* : spouse, partner

coñac *nm* : cognac, brandy

cooperación *nf, pl* **-ciones** : cooperation

cooperador, -dora *adj* : cooperative

cooperar *vi* : to cooperate

cooperativa *nf* : cooperative, co-op

cooperativo, -va *adj* : cooperative

cooptar *vt* : to co-opt

coordenada *nf* : coordinate

coordinación *nf, pl* **-ciones** : coordination

coordinador, -dora *n* : coordinator

coordinar *vt* COMPAGINAR : to coordinate, to combine

copa *nf* 1 : wineglass, goblet 2 : drink ⟨irse de copas : to go out drinking⟩ 3 : cup, trophy 4 : top, crown (of a tree) 5 **copas** *nfpl* : cups (suit in the Spanish deck of cards)

copar *vt* 1 : to take ⟨ya está copado el puesto : the job is already taken⟩ 2 : to fill, to crowd

copartícipe *nmf* : joint partner

copero, -ra *adj* : cup ⟨partido copero : cup game⟩

copete *nm* 1 : tuft (of hair) 2 **estar hasta el copete** : to be completely fed up

copia *nf* 1 : copy 2 : imitation, replica 3 **copia oculta** : blind carbon copy

copiadora *nf* : photocopier

copiar *vt* : to copy

copiloto *nmf* : copilot

copión, -piona *n, pl* **copiones** : copycat

copioso, -sa *adj* : copious, abundant

copla *nf* 1 : popular song or ballad 2 : stanza

copo *nm* 1 : snowflake 2 **copos de avena** : rolled oats 3 **copos de maíz** : cornflakes

coprotagonista *nmf* : co-star

cópula *nf* : copulation

copular *vi* : to copulate

coque *nm* : coke (fuel)

coqueta *nf* : dressing table

coquetear *vi* : to flirt

coqueteo *nm* : flirting

coqueto¹, -ta *adj* : flirtatious

coqueto², -ta *n* : flirt

coraje *nm* 1 VALOR : valor, courage 2 IRA : anger ⟨darle coraje a alguien : to make someone angry⟩

corajudo, -da *adj* : brave

coral¹ *adj* : choral

coral² *nm* 1 : coral 2 : chorale

coral³ *nf* : choir

Corán *nm* **el Corán** : the Koran

coraza *nf* 1 : armor, armor plating 2 : shell (of an animal)

corazón *nm, pl* **-zones** 1 : heart ⟨de todo corazón : wholeheartedly⟩ ⟨de buen corazón : kindhearted⟩ 2 : core 3 : darling, sweetheart

corazonada *nf* : hunch, impulse

corbata *nf* : tie, necktie

corcel *nm* : steed, charger

corchete *nm* 1 : hook and eye, clasp 2 : square bracket

corcho *nm* : cork

corcholata *nf Mex* : cap, bottle top

corcovear *vi* : to buck

cordel *nm* : cord, string
cordero *nm* : lamb
cordial[1] *adj* : cordial, affable — **cordialmente** *adv*
cordial[2] *nm* : cordial (liqueur)
cordialidad *nf* : cordiality, warmth
cordillera *nf* : mountain range
córdoba *nf* : córdoba (Nicaraguan unit of currency)
cordón *nm, pl* **cordones** 1 : cord ⟨cordón umbilical : umbilical cord⟩ 2 : cordon
cordoncillo *nm* : piping (of clothing, etc.)
cordura *nf* 1 : sanity 2 : prudence, good judgment
coreano[1], **-na** *adj & n* : Korean
coreano[2] *nm* : Korean (language)
corear *vt* : to chant, to chorus
coreografía *nf* : choreography
coreografiar {85} *vt* : to choreograph
coreográfico, -ca *adj* : choreographic
coreógrafo, -fa *n* : choreographer
corista *nmf* 1 : chorister 2 : chorus girl *f*
cormorán *nm, pl* **-ranes** : cormorant
cornada *nf* : goring, butt (with the horns)
córnea *nf* : cornea
cornear *vt* : to gore
cornejo *nm* : dogwood (tree)
córner *nm* : corner kick
corneta *nf* : bugle, horn, cornet
cornisa *nf* : cornice
cornucopia *nf* : cornucopia
cornudo, -da *adj* : horned
coro *nm* 1 : choir 2 : chorus
corola *nf* : corolla
corolario *nm* : corollary
corona *nf* 1 : crown 2 : wreath, garland 3 : corona (in astronomy)
coronación *nf, pl* **-ciones** : coronation
coronar *vt* 1 : to crown 2 : to reach the top of, to culminate
coronario, -ria *adj* : coronary
coronel, -nela *n* : colonel
coronilla *nf* 1 : crown (of the head) 2 **estar hasta la coronilla** : to be completely fed up
corpiño *nm* 1 : bodice 2 *Arg* : brassiere, bra
corporación *nf, pl* **-ciones** : corporation
corporal *adj* : corporal, bodily
corporativo, -va *adj* : corporate
corpóreo, -rea *adj* : corporeal, physical
corpulencia *nf* : stoutness, sturdiness
corpulento, -ta *adj* : robust, stout, sturdy
corpúsculo *nm* : corpuscle
corral *nm* 1 : farmyard 2 : corral, pen, stockyard 3 *or* **corralito** : playpen
correa *nf* 1 : strap, belt 2 TRAÍLLA : leash
correcaminos *nms & pl* : roadrunner
corrección *nf, pl* **-ciones** 1 : correction 2 : correctness, propriety 3 : rebuke, reprimand 4 **corrección de pruebas** : proofreading 5 **corrección ortográfica** : spell-check
correccional *nm* REFORMATORIO : reform school
correctivo, -va *adj* : corrective ⟨lentes correctivos : corrective lenses⟩

correcto, -ta *adj* 1 : correct, right 2 : courteous, polite — **correctamente** *adv*
corrector, -tora *n* : proofreader
corrector automático *nm* : autocorrect
corrector ortográfico *nm* : spellchecker
corredizo, -za *adj* : sliding ⟨puerta corrediza : sliding door⟩ ⟨nudo corredizo : slipknot⟩
corredor[1], **-dora** *n* 1 : runner, racer 2 : agent, broker ⟨corredor de bolsa : stockbroker⟩
corredor[2] *nm* PASILLO : corridor, hallway
correduría *nf → corretaje*
corregir {28} *vt* 1 : to correct, to edit (text), to grade (exams) 2 : to reprimand 3 **corregir pruebas** : to proofread — **corregirse** *vr* : to reform, to mend one's ways
correlación *nf, pl* **-ciones** : correlation
correo *nm* 1 : mail 2 : post office 3 **correo aéreo** : airmail 4 **correo electrónico** : e-mail, email
correoso, -sa *adj* : leathery, rough
correr *vi* 1 : to run ⟨corrió a/hacia la puerta : he ran to/towards the door⟩ ⟨salí corriendo : I took off running⟩ 2 : to race (in sports) 3 : to rush ⟨corre, que se acaban! : hurry, they're almost gone/done!⟩ 4 : to flow, to run 5 **a todo correr** : at top speed, in a hurry — *vt* 1 : to run, to race in 2 : to move, to slide, to roll, to draw (curtains) 3 ~ **con** : to be responsible for ⟨correr con los gastos : to foot the bill⟩ 4 **correr peligro** : to be in danger 5 **correr un riesgo** : to run a risk — **correrse** *vr* 1 : to move along 2 : to run, to spill over
correspondencia *nf* 1 : correspondence, mail 2 : equivalence 3 : connection, interchange
corresponder *vi* 1 : to correspond ⟨corresponder a/con : to correspond to/with, to match, to fit⟩ 2 : to belong ⟨el título que le corresponde : the title that is rightfully hers⟩ 3 : to be the responsibility of ⟨no le corresponde intervenir : it's not his place to intervene⟩ 4 : to be appropriate, to be fitting ⟨como corresponde : as is appropriate⟩ 5 : to reciprocate — **corresponderse** *vr* : to write to each other
correspondiente *adj* : corresponding, respective
corresponsal *nmf* : correspondent
corretaje *nm* : brokerage
corretear *vi* 1 VAGAR : to loiter, to wander about 2 : to run around, to scamper about — *vt* : to pursue, to chase
correteo *nm* : running around
corrida *nf* 1 : run, dash 2 : bullfight
corrido[1], **-da** *adj* 1 : straight, continuous 2 : worldly, experienced
corrido[2] *nm* : Mexican narrative folk song
corriente[1] *adj* 1 : common, everyday 2 : current, present 3 *Mex* : cheap, trashy 4 **perro corriente** *Mex* : mutt
corriente[2] *nf* 1 : current ⟨corriente alterna : alternating current⟩ ⟨corriente

continua : direct current⟩ **2** : draft **3**
TENDENCIA : tendency, trend
corrillo *nm* : small group, clique
corro *nm* : ring, circle (of people)
corroboración *nf, pl* **-ciones** : corroboration
corroborar *vt* : to corroborate
corroer {69} *vt* **1** : to corrode **2** : to
erode, to wear away
corromper *vt* **1** : to corrupt **2** : to rot —
corromperse *vr*
corrompido, -da *adj* CORRUPTO : corrupt, rotten
corrosión *nf, pl* **-siones** : corrosion
corrosivo, -va *adj* : corrosive
corrugar {52} *vt* : to corrugate — **corrugación** *nf*
corrupción *nf, pl* **-ciones** **1** : decay
: corruption
corruptela *nf* : corruption, abuse of
power
corruptible *adj* : corruptible
corrupto, -ta *adj* CORROMPIDO : corrupt
corsé *nm* : corset
cortacésped *nm Spain* : lawn mower
cortada *nf* : cut, gash
cortador, -dora *n* : cutter
cortadora *nf* : cutter, slicer
cortadura *nf* : cut, slash
cortafuegos *nms & pl* **1** : firebreak **2**
: firewall (program)
cortante *adj* : cutting, sharp
cortar *vt* **1** : to cut ⟨lo cortó en dos : he
cut it in half⟩ ⟨cortar en pedazos : to cut
into pieces⟩ ⟨cortar en rebanadas/trozos
(etc.) : to slice⟩ ⟨cortar leña : to chop
wood⟩ ⟨cortar el pasto : to mow the
lawn, to cut the grass⟩ **2** CERCENAR : to
cut off, to sever **3** TALAR : to cut down,
to chop down **4** RECORTAR : to cut out,
to clip (coupons, etc.) **5** EDITAR : to
cut, to edit **6** INTERRUMPIR : to cut off,
to interrupt **7** BLOQUEAR, CERRAR : to
block (off), to close (off) **8** : to curdle
(milk) — *vi* **1** : to cut **2** : to break up
⟨cortar con alguien : to break up with
someone⟩ **3** : to hang up (the telephone) — **cortarse** *vr* **1** : to cut oneself
⟨cortarse el pelo : to cut one's hair⟩ **2**
: to be cut off **3** : to sour, to separate (of
milk)
cortaúñas *nms & pl* : nail clippers
corte¹ *nm* **1** : cut, cutting ⟨corte de pelo
: haircut⟩ **2** : cut of clothes) **3** : cutoff, interruption ⟨corte comercial/publicitario : commercial break⟩ ⟨corte de
luz, corte de energía eléctrica : power
failure⟩
corte² *nf* **1** : court ⟨corte suprema : supreme court⟩ **2 hacer la corte a** : to
court, to woo
cortejar *vt* GALANTEAR : to court, to woo
cortejo *nm* **1** GALANTEO : courtship **2**
: retinue, entourage
cortés *adj* : courteous, polite — **cortésmente** *adv*
cortesano¹, -na *adj* : courtly
cortesano², -na *n* : courtier
cortesía *nf* **1** : courtesy, politeness **2 de
~** : complimentary, free

corteza *nf* **1** : bark **2** : crust **3** : peel,
rind **4** : cortex ⟨corteza cerebral : cerebral cortex⟩
cortijo *nm* : farmhouse
cortina *nf* : curtain
cortisona *nf* : cortisone
corto¹, -ta *adj* **1** : short (in length or duration) **2** : scarce **3** : timid, shy **4**
corto de vista : nearsighted
corto² *nm* → **cortometraje**
cortocircuito *nm* : short circuit
cortometraje *nm* : short (film)
corvejón *nm, pl* **-jones** JARRETE : hock
corvo, -va *adj* : curved, bent
cosa *nf* **1** : thing, object **2** : matter, affair **3 otra cosa** : anything else, something else
cosecha *nf* : harvest, crop
cosechador, -dora *n* : harvester, reaper
cosechadora *nf* : harvester (machine)
cosechar *vt* **1** : to harvest, to reap **2** : to
win, to earn, to garner — *vi* : to harvest
coser *vt* **1** : to sew **2** : to stitch up — *vi*
: to sew
cosmético¹, -ca *adj* : cosmetic
cosmético² *nm* : cosmetic
cósmico, -ca *adj* : cosmic
cosmonauta *nmf* : cosmonaut
cosmopolita *adj & nmf* : cosmopolitan
cosmos *nm* : cosmos
cosquillas *nfpl* **1** : tickling **2 hacer cosquillas** : to tickle
cosquilleo *nm* : tickling sensation, tingle
cosquilloso, -sa *adj* : ticklish
costa *nf* **1** : coast, shore **2** : cost ⟨a toda
costa : at all costs⟩ ⟨a costa de : at the
expense of⟩
costado *nm* **1** : side **2 al costado**
: alongside
costal *nm* **1** : sack **2 ser harina de otro
costal** → **harina**
costanera *nf* : boardwalk, waterfront
path
costar {19} *v* : to cost ⟨¿cuánto cuesta?
: how much does it cost?⟩
costarricense *adj & nmf* : Costa Rican
costarriqueño, -ña → **costarricense**
coste → **costo**
costear *vt* : to pay for, to finance
costero, -ra *adj* : coastal, coast
costilla *nf* **1** : rib **2** : chop, cutlet **3** *fam*
: better half, wife
costo *nm* **1** : cost, price **2 costo de
vida** : cost of living
costoso, -sa *adj* : costly, expensive
costra *nf* **1** : crust **2** POSTILLA : scab
costumbre *nf* **1** : custom **2** HÁBITO
: habit
costura *nf* **1** : seam **2** : sewing, dressmaking **3 alta costura** : haute couture
costurera *nf* : seamstress
costurero *nm* : sewing box
cota *nf* **1** : altitude **2** : level ⟨su máxima
cota : its maximum level⟩
cotejar *vt* : to compare, to collate
cotejo *nm* **1** : comparison **2** : match,
game
cotidiano, -na *adj* : daily, everyday ⟨la
vida cotidiana : daily life⟩
cotilla *nmf Spain fam* : gossip, gossiper

cotización *nf, pl* **-ciones 1** : market price **2** : quote, estimate
cotizado, -da *adj* : in demand, sought after
cotizar {21} *vt* : to quote, to value — **cotizarse** *vr* : to be worth
coto *nm* **1** : enclosure, reserve **2 poner coto a** : to put a stop to
cotonete *nf Mex* : (cotton) swab
cotorra *nf* **1** : small parrot **2** *fam* : chatterbox
cotorrear *vi fam* : to chatter, to gab, to blab
cotorreo *nm fam* : chatter, prattle
cowboy [kaoˈboi] *nm, pl* **-boys** [kaoˈbois] : cowboy
coyote *nm* **1** : coyote **2** *Mex fam* : smuggler (of illegal immigrants)
coyuntura *nf* **1** ARTICULACIÓN : joint **2** : occasion, moment
coz *nf, pl* **coces** : kick (of an animal)
CPU [sepeˈu] *nmf* : CPU
crac *nm, pl* **cracs** : crash (of the stock market)
crack *nm* : crack (cocaine)
cozamos, etc. → **cocer**
craneal *adj* : cranial
craneano, -na *adj* : cranial
cráneo *nm* : cranium, skull — **craneano, -na** *adj*
cráter *nm* : crater
crayón *nm, pl* **-yones** : crayon
creación *nf, pl* **-ciones** : creation
creador¹, -dora *adj* : creative, creating
creador², -dora *n* : creator
crear *vt* **1** : to create, to cause **2** : to originate
creatividad *nf* : creativity
creativo, -va *adj* : creative — **creativamente** *adv*
creces *nfpl* **con creces** ⟨cumple con creces las expectativas : it more than meets expectations⟩ ⟨superar con creces : to greatly exceed⟩ ⟨pagar con creces : to pay dearly (for)⟩
crecer {53} *vi* **1** : to grow **2** : to increase, to grow (in number, etc.)
crecida *nf* : flooding, floodwater
crecido, -da *adj* **1** : grown, grown-up **2** : large (of numbers)
creciente *adj* **1** : growing, increasing **2 luna creciente** : waxing moon
crecimiento *nm* **1** : growth **2** : increase
credencial *adj* **cartas credenciales** : credentials
credenciales *nfpl* : documents, documentation, credentials ⟨credenciales de acceso/usuario : login/user credentials⟩
credibilidad *nf* : credibility
crediticio, -cia *adj* : credit
crédito *nm* : credit
credo *nm* : creed, credo
credulidad *nf* : credulity
crédulo, -la *adj* : credulous, gullible
creencia *nf* : belief
creer {20} *v* **1** : to believe ⟨creer en : to believe in⟩ **2** : to think, to suppose ⟨creo que sí : I think so⟩ ⟨no creo que no : I don't think so⟩ ⟨no creo que sea necesario : I don't think it's necessary⟩ **3 ¡ya**

lo creo! : of course!, indeed! — **creerse** *vr* **1** : to believe, to think **2** : to regard oneself as ⟨se cree muy guapo : he thinks he's so handsome⟩
creíble *adj* : believable, credible
creído, -da *adj* **1** *fam* : conceited **2** : confident, sure
crema *nf* **1** : cream ⟨crema batida : whipped cream⟩ **2 la crema y nata** : the pick of the crop
cremación *nf, pl* **-ciones** : cremation
cremallera *nf* : zipper
cremar *vt* : to cremate
crematorio *nm* : crematorium
cremoso, -sa *adj* : creamy
crepa *nf Mex* : crepe (pancake)
crepe *or* **crep** *nmf* : crepe (pancake)
crepé *nm* **1** → **crespón 2 papel crepé** : crepe paper
crepúsculo *nm* : twilight
crescendo *nm* : crescendo
crespo, -pa *adj* : curly, frizzy
crespón *nm, pl* **crespones** : crepe (fabric)
cresta *nf* **1** : crest **2** : comb (of a rooster)
creta *nf* : chalk (mineral)
cretino, -na *n* **1** : cretin *often offensive* **2** : idiot, moron, cretin
creyente¹ *adj* : faithful ⟨personas creyentes : believers⟩
creyente² *nmf* : believer
creyó, etc. → **creer**
crezca, etc. → **crecer**
cría *nf* **1** : breeding, rearing **2** : young **3** : litter
criadero *nm* : hatchery
criado¹, -da *adj* **1** : raised, brought up **2 bien criado** : well-bred
criado², -da *n* : servant, maid *f*
criador, -dora *n* : breeder
crianza *nf* : upbringing, rearing
criar {85} *vt* **1** : to breed **2** : to bring up, to raise — **criarse** *vr* : to grow up
criatura *nf* **1** : baby, child **2** : creature
criba *nf* : sieve, screen
cribar *vt* : to sift
cric *nm, pl* **crics** : jack
cricket *nm* : cricket (sport)
crimen *nm, pl* **crímenes** : crime
criminal *adj & nmf* : criminal
criminalidad *nf* : crime ⟨alta criminalidad : high crime rates⟩
crin *nf* **1** : mane **2** : horsehair
crío, cría *n Spain* : kid
criollo¹, -lla *adj* **1** : Creole **2** : native, national ⟨comida criolla : native cuisine⟩
criollo², -lla *n* : Creole
criollo³ *nm* : Creole (language)
cripta *nf* : crypt
críptico, -ca *adj* **1** : cryptic, coded **2** : enigmatic, cryptic
criptodivisa → **criptomoneda**
criptomoneda *nf* : cryptocurrency
criptón *nm* : krypton
críquet *nm* : cricket (game)
crisálida *nf* : chrysalis, pupa
crisantemo *nm* : chrysanthemum
crisis *nf* **1** : crisis **2 crisis nerviosa** : nervous breakdown

crisma *nf fam* : head ⟨romperle la crisma a alguien : to knock someone's block off⟩

crismas → **christmas**

crisol *nm* **1** : crucible **2** : melting pot

crispar *vt* **1** : to cause to contract **2** : to irritate, to set on edge ⟨eso me crispa : that gets on my nerves⟩ — **crisparse** *vr* : to tense up

cristal *nm* **1** VIDRIO : glass, piece of glass **2** : crystal

cristalería *nf* **1** : glassware shop **2** : glassware, crystal

cristalino¹, -na *adj* : crystalline, clear

cristalino² *nm* : lens (of the eye)

cristalizar {21} *vi* : to crystallize — **cristalización** *nf*

cristiandad *nf* : Christendom

cristianismo *nm* : Christianity

cristiano, -na *adj & n* : Christian

Cristo *nm* : Christ

criterio *nm* **1** : criterion **2** : judgment, sense

crítica *nf* **1** : criticism **2** : review, critique

criticar {72} *vt* : to criticize

crítico¹, -ca *adj* : critical — **críticamente** *adv*

crítico², -ca *n* : critic

criticón¹, -cona, *mpl* **-cones** *fam* : hypercritical

criticón², -cona *n,* *mpl* **-cones** *fam* : faultfinder, critic

croar *vi* : to croak

croata *adj & nmf* : Croatian

crocante *adj* : crunchy

croché *or* **crochet** *nm* : crochet

croissant [krwaˈsan, -ˈzan] *nm, pl* **croissants** [krwaˈsans, -ˈzans] : croissant

crol *nm* : crawl (in swimming)

cromático, -ca *adj* : chromatic

cromo *nm* **1** : chromium, chrome **2** : picture card, sports card

cromosoma *nm* : chromosome

crónica *nf* **1** : news report **2** : chronicle, history

crónico, -ca *adj* : chronic

cronista *nmf* **1** : reporter, newscaster **2** HISTORIADOR : chronicler, historian

cronograma *nm* : schedule, timetable

cronología *nf* : chronology

cronológico, -ca *adj* : chronological — **cronológicamente** *adv*

cronometrador, -dora *n* : timekeeper

cronometrar *vt* : to time, to clock

cronómetro *nm* : chronometer

croquet *nm* : croquet

croqueta *nf* : croquette

croquis *nm* : rough sketch

cruasán *nm, pl* **cruasanes** → **croissant**

cruce¹, etc. → **cruzar**

cruce² *nm* **1** : crossing, cross **2** : crossroads, intersection ⟨cruce peatonal : crosswalk⟩

crucero *nm* **1** : cruise **2** : cruiser, warship **3** *Mex* : intersection

crucial *adj* : crucial — **crucialmente** *adv*

crucificar {72} *vt* : to crucify

crucifijo *nm* : crucifix

crucifixión *nf, pl* **-fixiones** : crucifixion

crucigrama *nm* : crossword puzzle

cruda *nf Mex fam* : hangover

crudeza *nf* : harshness

crudo¹, -da *adj* **1** : raw **2** : crude, harsh

crudo² *nm* : crude oil

cruel *adj* : cruel — **cruelmente** *adv*

crueldad *nf* : cruelty ⟨la crueldad del tirano : the tyrant's cruelty⟩ ⟨las crueldades de la guerra : the cruelties of war⟩

cruento, -ta *adj* : bloody

crujido *nm* **1** : rustling **2** : creaking **3** : crackling (of a fire) **4** : crunching

crujiente *adj* : crunchy, crisp

crujir *vi* **1** : to rustle **2** : to creak, to crack **3** : to crunch

crup *nm* : croup

crustáceo *nm* : crustacean

crutón *nm, pl* **crutones** : crouton

cruz *nf, pl* **cruces** : cross

cruza *nf* : cross (hybrid)

cruzada *nf* : crusade

cruzado¹, -da *adj* : crossed

cruzado² *nm* **1** : crusader **2** : Brazilian unit of currency

cruzar {21} *vt* **1** : to cross ⟨cruzar la calle : to cross the street⟩ ⟨cruzar las piernas : to cross one's legs⟩ **2** : to exchange (words, greetings) **3** : to cross, to interbreed — *vi* : to cross — **cruzarse** *vr* **1** : to intersect **2** : to meet, to pass each other **3 cruzarse de brazos** : to cross one's arms

cuaderno *nm* LIBRETA : notebook

cuadra *nf* **1** : city block **2** : stable

cuadrado¹, -da *adj* : square

cuadrado² *nm* : square ⟨elevar al cuadrado : to square (a number)⟩

cuadragésimo¹, -ma *adj* : fortieth, forty- (in a series)

cuadragésimo², -ma *n* : fortieth, forty- (in a series)

cuadrante *nm* **1** : quadrant **2** : dial

cuadrar *vi* **1** : to conform, to agree — *vt* : to square — **cuadrarse** *vr* : to stand at attention

cuadriculado *nm* : grid (on a map, etc.)

cuadrilátero *nm* **1** : quadrilateral **2** : ring (in sports)

cuadrilla *nf* : gang, team, group

cuadro *nm* **1** : square ⟨una blusa a cuadros : a checkered blouse⟩ **2** : painting, picture **3** : baseball diamond, infield **4** : panel, board, cadre

cuádruple *adj* : quadruple

cuadruplicar {72} *vt* : to quadruple — **cuadruplicarse** *vr*

cuajada *nf* : curd

cuajar *vi* **1** : to curdle **2** COAGULAR : to clot, to coagulate **3** : to set, to jell **4** : to be accepted ⟨su idea no cuajó : his idea didn't catch on⟩ — *vt* **1** : to curdle **2** ~ **de** : to fill with

cual¹ *prep* : like, as

cual² *pron* **1 el cual, la cual, los cuales, las cuales** : who, whom, which ⟨la razón por la cual lo dije : the reason I said it⟩ **2 lo cual** : which ⟨se rió, lo cual me dio rabia : he laughed, which made me mad⟩ **3 cada cual** : everyone, everybody

cuál¹ *adj* : which, what ⟨¿cuáles libros? : which books?⟩

cuál² *pron* **1** (*in questions*) : which (one), what (one) ⟨¿cuál es el mejor? : which one is the best?⟩ ⟨¿cuál es tu apellido? : what is your last name?⟩ **2 cuál más, cuál menos** : some more, some less

cualidad *nf* : quality, trait

cualificado, -da *adj Spain* : qualified, trained

cualitativo, -va *adj* : qualitative — **cualitativamente** *adv*

cualquier *adj* → **cualquiera¹**

cualquiera¹ *cualquier* before nouns *adj*, *pl* **cualesquiera 1** : any, whichever ⟨cualquier persona : any person⟩ **2** : everyday, ordinary ⟨un hombre cualquiera : an ordinary man⟩

cualquiera² *pron*, *pl* **cualesquiera 1** : anyone, anybody, whoever **2** : whatever, whichever

cuán *adv* : how ⟨¡cuán feliz era! : how happy I was!⟩

cuando¹ *conj* **1** : when ⟨cuando llegó : when he arrived⟩ **2** : since, if ⟨cuando lo dices : if you say so⟩ **3 cuando más/menos** : at the most/least **4 de vez en cuando** : from time to time

cuando² *prep* : during, at the time of ⟨cuando la guerra : during the war⟩

cuándo *adv & conj* **1** : when ⟨¿cuándo llegará? : when will she arrive?⟩ ⟨no sabemos cuándo será : we don't know when it will be⟩ **2 ¿de cuándo acá?** : since when?, how come?

cuantía *nf* **1** : quantity, extent **2** : significance, import

cuántico, -ca *adj* : quantum ⟨teoría cuántica : quantum theory⟩

cuantificar {72} *vt* : to quantify

cuantioso, -sa *adj* **1** : abundant, considerable **2** : heavy, grave ⟨cuantiosos daños : heavy damage⟩

cuantitativo, -va *adj* : quantitative — **cuantitativamente** *adv*

cuanto¹ *adv* **1** : as much as ⟨come cuanto puedas : eat as much as you can⟩ **2 cuanto antes** : as soon as possible **3 en ∼** : as soon as **4 en cuanto a** : as for, as regards

cuanto², -ta *adj* : as many, whatever ⟨llévate cuantas flores quieras : take as many flowers as you wish⟩

cuanto³, -ta *pron* **1** : as much as, all that, everything ⟨tengo cuanto deseo : I have all that I want⟩ **2 unos cuantos, unas cuantas** : a few

cuánto¹ *adv* : how much, how many ⟨¿a cuánto están las peras? : how much are the pears?⟩ ⟨no sé cuánto desean : I don't know how much they want⟩

cuánto², -ta *adj* : how much, how many ⟨¿cuántos niños tiene? : how many children do you have?⟩

cuánto³, -ta *pron* : how much, how many ⟨¿cuántos quieren participar? : how many want to take part?⟩ ⟨¿cuánto cuesta? : how much does it cost?⟩

cuáquero, -ra *adj & n* : Quaker

cuarenta *adj & nm* : forty — **cuarenta** *pron*

cuarentavo¹, -va *adj* : fortieth

cuarentavo² *adj & nm* : fortieth (fraction)

cuarentena *nf* **1** : group of forty **2** : quarantine

Cuaresma *nf* : Lent

cuarta *nf* : fourth (gear)

cuartear *vt* **1** : to quarter **2** : to divide up — **cuartearse** *vr* AGRIETARSE : to crack, to split

cuartel *nm* **1** : barracks, headquarters **2** : mercy ⟨una guerra sin cuartel : a merciless war⟩

cuartelazo *nm* : coup d'état

cuarteto *nm* : quartet

cuartilla *nf* : sheet (of paper)

cuarto¹, -ta *adj & n* : fourth ⟨la cuarta (persona) : the fourth (person)⟩ ⟨llegó la cuarta : she came in fourth (place)⟩ ⟨una/la cuarta parte de : a quarter of, a fourth of⟩

cuarto² *nm* **1** : quarter, fourth ⟨un cuarto de : a quarter of, a fourth of⟩ ⟨cuarto de galón : quart⟩ **2** HABITACIÓN : room

cuarto oscuro *nm* : darkroom

cuarzo *nm* : quartz

cuasi- *pref* : quasi-

cuate, -ta *n Mex* **1** : twin **2** *fam* : buddy, pal

cuatrero, -ra *n* : rustler

cuatrillizo, -za *n* : quadruplet

cuatro¹ *adj & nm* : four ⟨tiene cuatro años : she's four years old⟩ ⟨el cuatro de agosto : (on) the fourth of August, (on) August fourth⟩

cuatro² *pron* : four ⟨son cuatro : there are four of them⟩ ⟨son las cuatro y cuarto : it's four fifteen, it's (a) quarter after four⟩

cuatrocientos, -tas *adj & nm* : four hundred — **cuatrocientos** *pron*

cuba *nf* BARRIL : cask, barrel

cubano, -na *adj & n* : Cuban

cubertería *nf* : flatware, silverware

cubeta *nf* **1** : keg, cask **2** : bulb (of a thermometer) **3** *Mex* : bucket, pail

cúbico, -ca *adj* : cubic, cubed

cubículo *nm* : cubicle

cubierta *nf* **1** : covering **2** FORRO : cover, jacket (of a book) **3** : deck

cubierto *pp* → **cubrir**

cubierto² *nm* **1** : cover, shelter ⟨bajo cubierto : under cover⟩ **2** : table setting **3** : utensil, piece of silverware

cubil *nm* : den, lair

cúbito *nm* : ulna

cubo *nm* **1** : cube **2** *Spain* BALDE : pail, bucket, can ⟨cubo de basura : garbage can⟩ **3** : hub (of a wheel)

cubrecama *nm* COLCHA : bedspread

cubrir {2} *vt* **1** : to cover ⟨cubierto de algo : covered in/with something⟩ **2** : to cover (costs, etc.) — **cubrirse** *vr*

cucaracha *nf* : cockroach, roach

cuchara *nf* : spoon

cucharada *nf* : spoonful

cucharadita *nf* : teaspoon, teaspoonful

cucharilla *or* **cucharita** *nf* : teaspoon

cucharón *nm*, *pl* **-rones** : ladle

cuchichear *vi* : to whisper

cuchicheo *nm* : whisper

cuchilla nf **1** : kitchen knife, cleaver **2** : blade ⟨cuchilla de afeitar : razor blade, (safety) razor⟩ **3** : crest, ridge

cuchillada nf : stab, knife wound

cuchillo nm : knife

cuclillas nfpl en ~ : squatting, crouching

cuclillo nm : cuckoo

cuco¹, -ca adj fam : pretty, cute

cuco² nm **1** : cuckoo **2** Arg, Chile, Peru, Uru fam COCO : bogeyman

cucurucho nm : ice-cream cone

cuece, cueza etc. → **cocer**

cuela, etc. → **colar**

cuelga, cuelgue etc. → **colgar**

cuello nm **1** : neck **2** : collar, neck (of a shirt) ⟨cuello en V : V-neck⟩ **3** cuello del útero : cervix

cuenca nf **1** : river basin **2** : eye socket

cuenco nm : bowl, basin

cuenta¹, etc. → **contar**

cuenta² nf **1** : calculation, count **2** : account ⟨cuenta corriente : checking account⟩ ⟨cuenta de ahorro(s) : savings account⟩ ⟨cuenta de correo(s) electrónico(s), cuenta de email : e-mail account⟩ **3** : responsibility, liability ⟨corre por cuenta del gobierno : the government is footing the bill⟩ ⟨trabajar por cuenta propia : to be self-employed⟩ **4** : check, bill **5 a fin de cuentas** : in the end **6 darse cuenta** : to realize **7 en buenas cuentas** Chile : in short **8 por cuenta de** : on account of, because of **9 rendir cuentas** : to be held accountable **10 tener en cuenta** : to bear in mind **11 tomar en cuenta** : to take into account

cuentagotas nfs & pl **1** : dropper **2 con ~** : little by little

cuentakilómetros nm **1** : odometer **2** VELOCÍMETRO : speedometer

cuentista nmf **1** : short story writer **2** fam : liar, fibber

cuento nm **1** : story, tale **2 cuento chino** : tall tale **3 cuento de hadas** : fairy tale **4 sin ~** : countless

cuerda nf **1** : cord, rope, string **2 cuerdas vocales** : vocal cords **3 darle cuerda a algo** : to wind something up

cuerdo, -da adj : sane, sensible

cuerno nm **1** : horn, antler **2** : cusp (of the moon) **3** : horn (musical instrument)

cuero nm **1** : leather, hide **2 cuero cabelludo** : scalp

cuerpo nm **1** : body **2** : corps ⟨cuerpo policial : police force⟩

cuervo nm : crow, raven

cuesta¹, etc. → **costar**

cuesta² nf **1** : slope ⟨cuesta arriba : uphill⟩ **2 a cuestas** : on one's back

cuestión nf, pl **-tiones** ASUNTO, TEMA : matter, affair

cuestionable adj : questionable, dubious

cuestionamiento nm **1** : question, doubt ⟨hacer cuestionamientos a/sobre : to raise questions about⟩ **2** : questioning

cuestionar vt : to question

cuestionario nm **1** : questionnaire **2** : quiz

cueva nf : cave

cuidado nm **1** : care ⟨cuidado personal : self-care⟩ **2** : worry, concern **3 tener cuidado** : to be careful **4 ¡cuidado!** : watch out!, be careful!

cuidador, -dora n : caretaker

cuidadoso, -sa adj : careful, attentive — **cuidadosamente** adv

cuidar vt **1** : to take care of, to look after **2** : to pay attention to — vi **1 ~ de** : to look after **2 cuidar de que** : to make sure that — **cuidarse** vr : to take care of oneself

culata nf : butt (of a gun)

culatazo nf : kick, recoil

culebra nf SERPIENTE : snake

culebrón nm, pl **-brones** : soap, soap opera

culinario, -ria adj : culinary

culminante adj punto culminante : peak, high point, climax

culminar vi : to culminate — **culminación** nf

culo nm **1** fam : backside, behind **2** : bottom (of a glass)

culpa nf **1** : fault, blame ⟨echarle la culpa a alguien : to blame someone⟩ **2** : sin

culpabilidad nf : guilt

culpable¹ adj : guilty

culpable² nmf : culprit, guilty party

culpar vt : to blame

culposo, -sa adj : culpable, negligent

cultivable adj : arable

cultivado, -da adj **1** : cultivated, farmed **2** : cultured

cultivador, -dora n : grower

cultivar vt **1** : to cultivate **2** : to foster

cultivo nm **1** : cultivation, farming **2** : crop

culto¹, -ta adj : cultured, educated

culto² nm **1** : worship **2** : cult

cultura nf : culture

cultural adj : cultural — **culturalmente** adv

culturismo nm : bodybuilding

cumbre nf CIMA : top, peak, summit

cumpleañero, -ra n **1** : birthday boy m, birthday girl f

cumpleaños nms & pl : birthday

cumplido¹, -da adj **1** : complete, full **2** : courteous, correct

cumplido² nm : compliment, courtesy ⟨por cumplido : out of courtesy⟩ ⟨andarse con cumplidos : to stand on ceremony⟩

cumplidor, -dora adj : reliable

cumplimentar vt **1** : to congratulate **2** : to carry out, to perform

cumplimiento nm **1** : completion, fulfillment **2** : performance

cumplir vt **1** : to accomplish, to carry out **2** : to comply with, to fulfill **3** : to attain, to reach ⟨su hermana cumple (los) 20 (años) el viernes : her sister will be 20 on Friday⟩ — vi **1** : to expire, to fall due **2** : to fulfill one's obligations ⟨cumplir con su deber : to do one's duty⟩ ⟨cumplir con su palabra : to keep one's word⟩ — **cumplirse** vr **1** : to come true, to be fulfilled ⟨se cumplieron

sus sueños : her dreams came true⟩ 2
: to run out, to expire
cúmulo *nm* 1 MONTÓN : heap, pile 2
: cumulus
cuna *nf* 1 : cradle 2 : birthplace, origin
cundir *vi* 1 : to spread, to propagate (of
panic, etc.) 2 : to progress, to make
headway
cuneta *nf* : ditch (in a road), gutter
cuña *nf* : wedge
cuñado, -da *n* : brother-in-law *m*, sister-
in-law *f*
cuño *nm* : die (for stamping)
cuota *nf* 1 : fee, dues 2 : quota, share 3
: installment, payment
cupé *nm* : coupe
cupo[1]**, etc.** → **caber**
cupo[2] *nm* 1 : quota, share 2 : capacity,
room
cupón *nm, pl* **cupones** 1 : coupon,
voucher 2 **cupón federal** : food stamp
cúpula *nf* : dome, cupola
cura[1] *nm* : priest
cura[2] *nf* 1 CURACIÓN, TRATAMIENTO
: cure, treatment 2 : dressing, bandage
curación *nf, pl* **-ciones** CURA, TRATA-
MIENTO : cure, treatment
curador, -dora *n* 1 : healer 2 CONSER-
VADOR : curator
curandero, -ra *nm* 1 : witch doctor 2
: quack, charlatan
curar *vt* 1 : to cure, to heal 2 : to treat,
to dress 3 CURTIR : to tan 4 : to cure
(meat) — *vi* : to get well, to recover —
curarse *vr*
curativo, -va *adj* : healing
curiosear *vi* 1 : to snoop, to pry 2 : to
browse — *vt* : to look over, to check
curiosidad *nf* 1 : curiosity 2 : curio
curioso, -sa *adj* 1 : curious, inquisitive
2 : strange, unusual, odd — **curiosamente** *adv*
curita *nf* (*Curitas*, marca registrada)
: bandage, Band-Aid™

currículo → **currículum**
currículum *nm, pl* **-lums** 1 : résumé, curriculum vitae 2 : curriculum, course of
study
curruca *nf* : warbler
curry [¹kurri] *nm, pl* **-rries** 1 : curry powder 2 : curry (dish)
cursar *vt* 1 : to attend (school), to take (a
course) 2 : to dispatch, to pass on
cursi *adj fam* : affected, pretentious
cursilería *nf* 1 : vulgarity, poor taste 2
: pretentiousness
cursillo *nm* : short course
cursiva *nf* BASTARDILLA : italic type, italics *pl*
cursivo, -va *adj* : italic
curso *nm* 1 : course, direction 2
: school year 3 : course, subject (in
school)
cursor *nm* : cursor
curtido, -da *adj* : weather-beaten, leathery (of skin)
curtidor, -dora *n* : tanner
curtiduría *nf* : tannery
curtir *vt* 1 : to tan 2 : to harden, to
weather — **curtirse** *vr*
curul *nf* ESCAÑO : seat (in a legislative
body)
curva *nf* : curve, bend
curvar *vt* : to bend
curvatura *nf* : curvature
curvilíneo, -nea *adj* : shapely
curvo, -va *adj* : curved, bent
cúspide *nf* : zenith, apex, peak
custodia *nf* : custody
custodiar *vt* : to guard, to look after
custodio, -dia *n* : keeper, guardian
cutáneo, -nea *adj* : skin, cutaneous
cúter *nm* : cutter (boat)
cutícula *nf* : cuticle
cutis *nms & pl* : skin, complexion
cuyo, -ya *adj* 1 : whose, of whom, of
which 2 **en cuyo caso** : in which case

D

d *nf* : fifth letter of the Spanish alphabet
dactilar *adj* **huellas dactilares** : finger-
prints
dádiva *nf* : gift, handout
dadivoso, -sa *adj* : generous
dado, -da *adj* 1 : given 2 **dado que**
: given that, since
dados *nmpl* : dice
daga *nf* : dagger
dalia *nf* : dahlia
dálmata *nm* : dalmatian
daltónico, -ca *adj* : color-blind
daltonismo *nm* : color blindness
dama *nf* 1 : lady 2 **damas** *nfpl* : checkers
damasco *nm* : damask
damisela *nf* : damsel
damnificado, -da *n* : victim (of a disaster)
dance, etc. → **danzar**
dandi *nm* : dandy

danés[1]**, -nesa** *adj* : Danish
danés[2]**, -nesa** *n, mpl* **daneses** : Dane,
Danish person
danza *nf* : dance, dancing ⟨danza
folklórica : folk dance⟩
danzante, -ta *n* BAILARÍN : dancer
danzar {21} *v* BAILAR : to dance
dañar *vt* 1 : to damage, to spoil 2 : to
harm, to hurt — **dañarse** *vr*
dañino, -na *adj* : harmful
daño *nm* 1 : damage 2 : harm, injury
⟨daños colaterales : collateral damages⟩
3 **hacer daño a** : to harm, to damage 4
hacerse daño : to hurt oneself ⟨me he
hecho daño en la mano : I've hurt my
hand⟩ 5 **daños y perjuicios** : damages
dar {22} *vt* 1 : to give (a gift, a donation,
etc.) 2 ENTREGAR : to give, to hand
(over) 3 PROPORCIONAR : to give (sup-

plies, support, etc.⟩ ⟨dale una oportunidad : give him a chance⟩ **4** CONCEDER : to give (time, permission, etc.) **5** ADMINISTRAR : to give (medicine, etc.) **6** EXPRESAR : to give, to express ⟨dales recuerdos de mi parte : give them my regards⟩ ⟨darle las gracias a : to thank⟩ ⟨dar su palabra : to give one's word⟩ **7** MOSTRAR : to give (an indication, etc.) **8** OFRECER : to give (a reason, etc.) **9** : to give (an impression, etc.) **10** GOLPEAR : to hit ⟨me dio en la cara : it hit me in the face⟩ **11** : to strike ⟨el reloj dio las doce : the clock struck twelve⟩ **12** PRODUCIR : to yield, to produce **13** : to give (a performance, a party, etc.), to show (a film, etc.) **14** : to do (an action) ⟨dar un grito : to give a shout⟩ ⟨dar un paseo : to go for a walk⟩ ⟨me dio un beso : she gave me a kiss⟩ **15** VENDER : to give, to sell **16** CAUSAR : to cause ⟨darle miedo/sed (etc.) a alguien : to make someone frightened/thirsty (etc.)⟩ ⟨me da risa : it makes me laugh, it's funny⟩ ⟨le da problemas/esperanza : it gives her trouble/hope⟩ **17** APLICAR : to apply ⟨dale una mano de pintura : give it a coat of paint⟩ ⟨dar un impulso a : to give a boost to⟩ **18** CONFERIR : to give, to impart (a quality) **19 dar como/por** : to regard as, to consider ⟨dar por hecho : to take for granted⟩ ⟨dar a alguien por muerto : to give someone up for dead⟩ — *vi* **1** : to provide (enough) ⟨no me da para dos pasajes : I don't have enough for two fares⟩ ⟨no me da tiempo : I don't have time⟩ ⟨esto no da para más : this can't go on⟩ ⟨a todo lo que da : at full speed/power (etc.)⟩ **2** : to hand something over ⟨dame : give it to me⟩ **3** : to deal (in cards) **4** : to hit ⟨dar en el blanco : to hit the target⟩ **5** : to give a result ⟨dio positivo al virus : he tested positive for the virus⟩ **6 dale que dale** *or Spain* **dale que te pego** ⟨están dale que dale con el teléfono : they're constantly on the phone⟩ ⟨y ella dale que te pego con sus problemas : and she was going on and on about her problems⟩ **7 darle a** : to press (a button, etc.), to turn (a dial, etc.) **8 ~ a/sobre** : to overlook, to look out on **9 ~ con** : to run into **10 ~ con** : to hit upon (an idea) **11 dar de sí** : to give, to stretch (of clothing, etc.) — **darse** *vr* **1** : to consider oneself ⟨se dio por vencido : he gave in⟩ **2** : to occur, to arise **3** : to grow, to come up **4 ~ con/contra** : to hit oneself against, to bump into **5 dárselas de** : to boast about ⟨se las da de muy listo : he thinks he's very smart⟩ **6 dársele bien algo a uno** : to be good at something ⟨se le dan muy bien las matemáticas : she's very good at math⟩
dardo *nm* : dart
dársena *nf* : dock
data *nf* **1** : byline **2 de larga data** : long-standing
datar *vt* : to date — *vi* **~ de** : to date from, to date back to

dátil *nm* : date (fruit)
dato *nm* **1** : fact, piece of information **2 datos** *nmpl* : data, information
dé → **dar**
de¹ *nf* : (letter) d
de² *prep* **1** (*indicating connection or belonging*) : of ⟨la casa de Pepe : Pepe's house⟩ ⟨el cuatro de abril : the fourth of April, April fourth⟩ ⟨la reina de Inglaterra : the Queen of England⟩ ⟨el mejor de todos : the best of all⟩ **2** (*indicating a quality or condition*) : of ⟨un asunto de gran importancia : a matter of great importance⟩ ⟨un niño de tres años : a three-year-old boy⟩ ⟨estoy de vacaciones : I'm on vacation⟩ **3** (*indicating content, material, or quantity*) : of ⟨un vaso de agua : a glass of water⟩ ⟨una casa de ladrillo : a brick house, a house made of brick⟩ ⟨una gran cantidad de lluvia : a large amount of rain⟩ **4** (*indicating a source or starting point*) : from ⟨es de Managua : she's from Managua⟩ ⟨salió del edificio : he left the building⟩ **5** (*with time*) : in, at ⟨a las tres de la mañana : at three in the morning⟩ ⟨salen de noche : they go out at night⟩ **6** (*with numbers*) : than ⟨más de tres : more than three⟩ **7** (*indicating a particular example*) : of ⟨el mes de junio : the month of June⟩ **8** (*indicating a cause*) ⟨morirse de hambre : to be dying of/from starvation⟩ ⟨gritar de alegría : to shout with/for joy⟩ **9** : about ⟨libros de historia : history books, books about history⟩ **10** (*indicating purpose*) : for ⟨ropa de deporte : sportswear, athletic clothes⟩ ⟨máquina de coser : sewing machine⟩ **11** : as ⟨ella trabaja de camionera : she works as a truck driver⟩ **12** : if ⟨de haberlo sabido : if I had known⟩ ⟨de continuar esta situación : if this situation continues⟩
deambular *vi* : to wander, to roam
deán *nm, pl* **deanes** : dean (of clergy)
debacle *nf* : debacle
debajo *adv* **1** : underneath, below, on the bottom **2 ~ de** : under, underneath **3 por ~** : below, beneath
debate *nm* : debate
debatir *vt* : to debate, to discuss — **debatirse** *vr* : to struggle
debe *nm* : debit column, debit
deber¹ *vt* : to owe — *v aux* **1** : must, have to ⟨debo ir : I must go⟩ ⟨no debes hacerlo : you mustn't do it⟩ **2** : should, ought to ⟨deberías buscar trabajo : you should look for work⟩ ⟨debería darte vergüenza : you ought to be ashamed of yourself⟩ **3** (*expressing probability*) : must ⟨debe ser muy tarde : it must be very late⟩ — **deberse** *vr* **1 ~ a** : to be due to **2 ~ a** : to have a responsibility towards
deber² *nm* **1** OBLIGACIÓN : duty, obligation **2 deberes** *nmpl Spain* : homework
debidamente *adv* : properly, duly
debido, -da *adj* **1** : right, proper, due **2 ~ a** : due to, owing to
débil *adj* : weak, feeble — **débilmente** *adv*

debilidad *nf* : weakness, debility, feebleness

debilitamiento *nm* : weakening

debilitar *vt* : to debilitate, to weaken — **debilitarse** *vr*

debilucho¹, -cha *adj* : weak, frail

debilucho², -cha *n* : weakling

debitar *vt* : to debit

débito *nm* **1** DEUDA : debt **2** : debit

de bruces *adv* : facedown, face-first ⟨caer de bruces : to fall flat on one's face⟩

debut [de'but] *nm, pl* **debuts** : debut

debutante¹ *nmf* : beginner, newcomer

debutante² *nf* : debutante *f*

debutar *vi* : to debut, to make a debut

década *nf* DECENIO : decade

decadencia *nf* **1** : decadence **2** : decline

decadente *adj* **1** : decadent **2** : declining

decaer {13} *vi* **1** : to decline, to decay, to deteriorate **2** FLAQUEAR : to weaken, to flag

decaído, -da *adj fam* : depressed, sad

decaiga, etc. → **decaer**

decano, -na *n* **1** : dean **2** : senior member

decapitar *vt* : to decapitate, to behead

decayó, etc. → **decaer**

decena *nf* : group of ten

decencia *nf* : decency

decenio *nm* DÉCADA : decade

decente *adj* : decent — **decentemente** *adv*

decepción *nf, pl* **-ciones** : disappointment, letdown

decepcionante *adj* : disappointing

decepcionar *vt* : to disappoint, to let down — **decepcionarse** *vr*

deceso *nm* DEFUNCIÓN : death, passing

dechado *nm* **1** : sampler (of embroidery) **2** : model, paragon

decibelio *or* **decibel** *nm* : decibel

decidido, -da *adj* : decisive, determined, resolute — **decididamente** *adv*

decidir *vt* **1** : to decide ⟨decidí ir : I decided to go⟩ ⟨no he decidido nada : I haven't made a decision⟩ **2** : to make (someone) decide, to persuade (someone) — *vi* : to decide ⟨decidir sobre : to make a decision about⟩ — **decidirse** *vr* : to make up one's mind ⟨decidirse por : to decide on, to choose⟩

décima *nf* : tenth (fraction)

decimal *adj* : decimal

décimo¹, -ma *adj & n* : tenth ⟨la décima (persona) : the tenth (person)⟩ ⟨una/la décima parte de : a tenth of, one tenth of⟩ ⟨en décimo lugar : in tenth place⟩

décimo² *nm Spain* → **décima**

decimoctavo¹, -va *adj* : eighteenth

decimoctavo², -va *n* : eighteenth (in a series)

decimocuarto¹, -ta *adj* : fourteenth

decimocuarto², -ta *n* : fourteenth (in a series)

decimonoveno¹, -na *or* **decimonono, -na** *adj* : nineteenth

decimonoveno², -na *or* **decimonono, -na** *n* : nineteenth (in a series)

decimoquinto¹, -ta *adj* : fifteenth

decimoquinto², -ta *n* : fifteenth (in a series)

decimoséptimo¹, -ma *adj* : seventeenth

decimoséptimo², -ma *n* : seventeenth (in a series)

decimosexto¹, -ta *adj* : sixteenth

decimosexto², -ta *n* : sixteenth (in a series)

decimotercero¹, -ra *adj* : thirteenth

decimotercero², -ra *n* : thirteenth (in a series)

decir¹ {23} *vt* **1** : to say ⟨dice que no irá : she says she won't go⟩ **2** : to tell ⟨dime lo que estás pensando : tell me what you're thinking⟩ ⟨ya te lo decía yo : I told you so⟩ **3** : to tell, to say ⟨haz lo que te digo : do as I say, do what I tell you⟩ ⟨te dije que callaras : I told you to be quiet⟩ **4** : to speak, to talk ⟨no digas tonterías : don't talk nonsense⟩ **5** : to call ⟨me dicen Rosy : they call me Rosy⟩ **6 como quien dice** : so to speak **7 es decir** : that is to say **8 dicho y hecho** : no sooner said than done **9 (o) mejor dicho** : (or) rather **10 ¡no me digas!** : you're kidding!, you don't say! **11 por así decirlo** : so to speak **12 querer decir** : to mean ⟨¿qué quiere decir? : what do you mean?⟩ — **decirse** *vr* **1** : to say to oneself **2** : to be said ⟨¿cómo se dice "lápiz" en francés? : how do you say "pencil" in French?⟩

decir² *nm* DICHO : saying, expression

decisión *nf, pl* **-siones** **1** : decision, choice ⟨tomar una decisión : to make a decision⟩ **2** : decisiveness

decisivo, -va *adj* : decisive, conclusive — **decisivamente** *adv*

declamar *vi* : to declaim — *vt* : to recite

declaración *nf, pl* **-ciones** **1** : declaration, statement ⟨hacer una declaración : to issue a statement⟩ **2** TESTIMONIO : deposition, testimony ⟨prestar declaración : to give evidence, to testify⟩ **3 declaración de derechos** : bill of rights **4 declaración jurada** : affidavit **5 declaración de la renta** : income tax return

declarado, -da *adj* : professed, open — **declaradamente** *adv*

declarar *vt* : to declare, to state ⟨declarar culpable : to find guilty⟩ ⟨declarar inocente : to find not guilty⟩ — *vi* ATESTIGUAR : to testify — **declararse** *vr* **1** : to declare oneself (to be) ⟨declararse en huelga : to go on strike⟩ ⟨declararse en bancarrota : to declare bankruptcy⟩ **2** : to confess one's love **3** : to plead (in court) ⟨declararse culpable : to plead guilty⟩ ⟨declararse inocente : to plead not guilty⟩ **4** : to testify **5** : to break out (of a fire, etc.)

declinar *vt* : to decline, to turn down — *vi* **1** : to draw to a close **2** : to diminish, to decline

declive *nm* **1** DECADENCIA : decline **2** : slope, incline

decodificador *nm* : decoder

decolar *vi Chile, Col, Ecua* : to take off (of an airplane)

decolorar vt : to bleach — **decolorarse** vr : to fade

decomisar vt CONFISCAR : to seize, to confiscate

decomiso nm : seizure, confiscation

decoración nf, pl -ciones 1 : decoration 2 : decor 3 : stage set, scenery

decorado nm : stage set, scenery

decorador, -dora n : decorator

decorar vt ADORNAR : to decorate, to adorn

decorativo, -va adj : decorative, ornamental

decoro nm : decorum, propriety

decoroso, -sa adj : decent, proper, respectable

decrecer {53} vi : to decrease, to wane, to diminish — **decreciente** adj

decrecimiento nm : decrease, decline

decrépito, -ta adj : decrepit

decretar vt : to decree, to order

decreto nm : decree

decúbito nm : horizontal position ⟨en decúbito prono/supino : prone/supine⟩

dedal nm : thimble

dedalera nf DIGITAL : foxglove

dedicación nf, pl -ciones : dedication, devotion

dedicar {72} vt : to dedicate, to devote — **dedicarse** vr ~ **a** : to devote oneself to, to engage in

dedicatoria nf : dedication (of a book, song, etc.)

dedillo nm **conocer algo al dedillo** : to know something backward and forward

dedo nm 1 : finger ⟨dedo meñique : little finger⟩ ⟨no mover un dedo : not to lift a finger⟩ ⟨hacer dedo, ir a dedo : to hitchhike⟩ ⟨poner el dedo en la llaga : to hit a nerve⟩ 2 **dedo del pie** : toe

deducción nf, pl -ciones : deduction

deducible adj : deductible

deducir {61} vt 1 INFERIR : to deduce 2 DESCONTAR : to deduct

defecar {72} vi : to defecate — **defecación** nf

defecto nm 1 : defect, flaw, shortcoming 2 **en su defecto** : lacking that, in the absence of that

defectuoso, -sa adj : defective, faulty

defender {56} vt : to defend, to protect — **defenderse** vr 1 : to defend oneself 2 : to get by, to know the basics ⟨su inglés no es perfecto pero se defiende : his English isn't perfect but he gets by⟩

defendible adj : tenable

defensa[1] nf 1 : defense ⟨salió en nuestra defensa : he came to our defense⟩ ⟨actuar en defensa propia : to act in self-defense⟩ ⟨clase de defensa personal : self-defense class⟩ 2 : defense (in sports)

defensa[2] nmf : defender, back (in sports)

defensiva nf : defensive

defensivo, -va adj : defensive — **defensivamente** adv

defensor[1], **-sora** adj : defending, defense

defensor[2], **-sora** n 1 : defender, advocate 2 : defense counsel

defeño, -ña n : person from the Federal District (Mexico City)

deferencia nf : deference

deferir {76} vi **deferir a** : to defer to

deficiencia nf : deficiency, flaw

deficiente adj : deficient

déficit nm, pl -cits 1 : deficit 2 : shortage, lack

deficitario, -ria adj : with a deficit (of a country, etc.), negative (of a balance) ⟨una empresa deficitaria : a business that is losing money⟩

definición nf, pl -ciones : definition

definido, -da adj : definite, well-defined

definir vt 1 : to define 2 : to determine

definitivamente adv 1 : finally 2 : permanently, for good 3 : definitely, absolutely

definitivo, -va adj 1 : definitive, conclusive 2 **en definitiva** : all in all, on the whole 3 **en definitiva** Mex : permanently, for good

deflación nf, pl -ciones : deflation

deforestación nf, pl -ciones : deforestation

deformación nf, pl -ciones 1 : deformation 2 : distortion

deformar vt 1 : to deform, to disfigure 2 : to distort — **deformarse** vr

deforme adj : deformed, misshapen

deformidad nf : deformity

defraudación nf, pl -ciones : fraud

defraudar vt 1 ESTAFAR : to defraud, to cheat 2 : to disappoint

defunción nf, pl -ciones DECESO : death, passing

degeneración nf, pl -ciones 1 : degeneration 2 DEPRAVACIÓN : depravity

degenerado, -da adj DEPRAVADO : degenerate

degenerar vi : to degenerate

degenerativo, -va adj : degenerative

degollar {19} vt 1 : to slit the throat of, to slaughter 2 DECAPITAR : to behead 3 : to ruin, to destroy

degradación nf, pl -ciones 1 : degradation 2 : demotion

degradante adj : degrading

degradar vt 1 : to degrade, to debase 2 : to demote

degustación nf, pl -ciones : tasting, sampling

degustador, -dora n : taster

degustar vt : to taste

dehesa nf : meadow

deidad nf : deity

deificar {72} vt : to idolize, to deify

dejadez nf : neglect, slovenliness

dejado, -da adj 1 : slovenly 2 : careless, lazy

dejar vt 1 : to leave ⟨dejé la cartera en casa : I left my purse at home⟩ ⟨déjalo allí : leave it there⟩ ⟨déjalo conmigo : leave it with me⟩ 2 : to drop (someone) off 3 : to leave (a tip, a package, etc.) 4 LEGAR : to leave, to bequeath 5 ABANDONAR : to leave (a spouse, a job, etc.), to give up (an activity) 6 : to leave alone, to let be 7 : to drop (a subject) ⟨déjalo, no importa : forget it—it's not important〉 **8** POSPONER : to leave, to put off **9** : to leave 〈dejé las luces encendidas : I left the lights on〉〈no me dejes esperando : don't leave me waiting〉 **10** GUARDAR : to leave, to set aside **11** : to leave (a mark, etc.) **12** PERMITIR : to let, to allow 〈déjalo hablar : let him speak〉〈deja que se enfríe : let it cool〉 — *vi* **1** ~ **de** : to stop, to quit 〈dejar de fumar : to quit smoking〉 **2 no dejar de** : to be sure to 〈no dejes de llamar : be sure to call〉 — **dejarse** *vr* **1** : to let oneself be 〈se deja insultar : he lets himself be insulted〉 **2** : to forget, to leave 〈me dejé las llaves en el carro : I left the keys in the car〉 **3** : to neglect oneself, to let oneself go **4** : to grow 〈me estoy dejando el pelo largo : I'm growing my hair long〉

dejo *nm* **1** : aftertaste **2** : touch, hint **3** : (regional) accent

del *contraction of* DE *and* EL → **de**

delación *nf, pl* **-ciones** : denunciation, betrayal

delantal *nm* **1** : apron **2** : pinafore

delante *adv* **1** ENFRENTE : ahead, in front **2** ~ **de** : before, in front of

delantera *nf* **1** : front, front part, front row 〈tomar la delantera : to take the lead〉 **2** : forward line (in sports)

delantero¹, -ra *adj* **1** : front, forward **2 tracción delantera** : front-wheel drive

delantero², -ra *n* : forward (in sports)

delatar *vt* **1** : to betray, to reveal **2** : to denounce, to inform against

delator, -tora *adj* : incriminating

delegación *nf, pl* **-ciones** : delegation

delegado, -da *n* : delegate, representative

delegar {52} *vt* : to delegate

deleitar *vt* : to delight, to please — **deleitarse** *vr*

deleite *nm* : delight, pleasure

deletrear *vi* : to spell 〈¿como se deletrea? : how do you spell it?〉

deleznable *adj* **1** : brittle, crumbly **2** : slippery **3** : weak, fragile 〈una excusa deleznable : a weak excuse〉

delfín *nm, pl* **delfines** : dolphin

delgadez *nf* : thinness

delgado, -da *adj* **1** FLACO : thin, skinny **2** ESBELTO : slender, slim **3** DELICADO : delicate, fine **4** AGUDO : sharp, clever

deliberado, -da *adj* : deliberate, intentional — **deliberadamente** *adv*

deliberar *vi* : to deliberate — **deliberación** *nf*

delicadamente *adv* : delicately

delicadeza *nf* **1** : delicacy, fineness **2** : gentleness, softness **3** : tact, discretion, consideration

delicado, -da *adj* **1** : delicate, fine **2** : sensitive, frail **3** : delicate, tricky **4** : fussy **5** : tactful, considerate

delicia *nf* : delight

delicioso, -sa *adj* **1** RICO : delicious **2** : delightful

delictivo, -va *adj* : criminal

delictuoso, -sa → **delictivo**

delimitación *nf, pl* **-ciones** **1** : demarcation **2** : defining, specifying

delimitar *vt* **1** : to demarcate **2** : to define, to specify

delincuencia *nf* : delinquency, crime

delincuente¹ *adj* : delinquent

delincuente² *nmf* CRIMINAL : delinquent, criminal

delineador *nm* : eyeliner

delinear *vt* **1** : to delineate, to outline **2** : to draft, to draw up

delinquir {24} *vi* : to break the law

delirante *adj* : delirious

delirar *vi* **1** DESVARIAR : to be delirious **2** : to rave, to talk nonsense

delirio *nm* **1** : delirium **2** FRENESÍ : mania, frenzy 〈¡fue el delirio! : it was wild!〉 **3 delirios** *pl* DISPARATES : nonsense, ravings *pl* 〈delirios de grandeza : delusions of grandeur〉

delito *nm* : crime, offense

delta *nm* : delta

demacrado, -da *adj* : emaciated, gaunt

demagogo, -ga *n* : demagogue

demanda *nf* **1** : demand 〈la oferta y la demanda : supply and demand〉〈tener mucha demanda : to be in great demand〉 **2** : petition, request **3** : lawsuit

demandado, -da *n* : defendant

demandante *nmf* : plaintiff

demandar *vt* **1** : to demand **2** REQUERIR : to call for, to require **3** : to sue, to file a lawsuit against

demarcar {72} *vt* : to demarcate — **demarcación** *nf*

demás¹ *adj* : remaining 〈las demás tareas : the rest of the chores〉

demás² *pron* **1 lo (la, los, las) demás** : the rest, everyone else, everything else 〈Pepe, Rosa, y los demás : Pepe, Rosa, and everybody else〉 **2 estar por demás** : to be of no use, to be pointless 〈no estaría por demás : it couldn't hurt, it's worth a try〉 **3 por demás** : extremely **4 por lo demás** : otherwise **5 y demás** : and so on, et cetera

demasía *nf* **en** ~ : excessively, in excess

demasiado¹ *adv* **1** : too 〈vas demasiado aprisa : you're going too fast〉 **2** : too much 〈comí demasiado : I ate too much〉

demasiado², -da *adj* : too much, too many, excessive

demencia *nf* **1** : dementia **2** LOCURA : madness, insanity

demencial *adj fam* : crazy, insane

demente¹ *adj* : insane, mad

demente² *nmf* : insane person

demeritar *vt* **1** : to detract from **2** : to discredit

demérito *nm* **1** : fault **2** : discredit, disrepute

demo *nf* **1** : demo, demo product/version (etc.) **2** : demo, demo tape

democracia *nf* : democracy

demócrata¹ *adj* : democratic

demócrata² *nmf* : democrat

democrático, -ca *adj* : democratic — **democráticamente** *adv*

democratizar {21} *vt* : to democratize, to make democratic — **democratización** *nf*

demografía *nf* **1** : demography **2** : demographics *pl*

demográfico, -ca *adj* : demographic

demoledor, -dora *adj* : devastating

demoler {47} *vt* DERRIBAR, DERRUMBAR : to demolish, to destroy

demolición *nf, pl* **-ciones** : demolition

demoníaco, -ca *adj* : demonic, demoniac

demonio *nm* **1** DIABLO : devil, demon **2** ¿qué demonios . . . ? : what on earth . . . ?, what the hell . . . ?

demora *nf* : delay

demorar *vt* **1** RETRASAR : to delay **2** TARDAR : to take, to last ⟨la reparación demorará varios días : the repair will take several days⟩ — *vi* : to delay, to linger ⟨no demores : don't delay, don't take too long⟩ — **demorarse** *vr* **1** : to be slow, to take a long time **2** : to take too long

demostración *nf, pl* **-ciones** : demonstration

demostrar {19} *vt* **1** PROBAR : to demonstrate, to prove **2** MANIFESTAR : to show **3** : to demonstrate (a procedure, etc.)

demostrativo, -va *adj* : demonstrative

demudar *vt* : to change, to alter — **demudarse** *vr* : to change one's expression

denegación *nf, pl* **-ciones** : denial, refusal

denegar {49} *vt* : to deny, to turn down

dengue *nm* : dengue

denigrante *adj* : degrading, humiliating

denigrar *vt* **1** DIFAMAR : to denigrate, to disparage **2** : to degrade, to humiliate

denominación *nf, pl* **-ciones** **1** : name, designation **2** : denomination (of money)

denominador *nm* : denominator

denominar *vt* : to designate, to name, to call

denostar {19} *vt* : to revile

denotar *vt* : to denote, to show

densidad *nf* : density, thickness

denso, -sa *adj* : dense, thick — **densamente** *adv*

dentado, -da *adj* SERRADO : serrated, jagged

dentadura *nf* **1** : teeth *pl* **2** dentadura postiza : dentures *pl*

dental *adj* : dental

dentellada *nf* **1** : bite **2** : tooth mark

dentera *nf* **1** : envy, jealousy **2** dar dentera : to set one's teeth on edge

dentífrico *nm* : toothpaste

dentista *nmf* : dentist

dentro *adv* **1** ADENTRO : in, inside ⟨por dentro : on the inside⟩ ⟨estoy aquí dentro : I'm in here⟩ **2** ~ de : within, inside, in ⟨dentro de la tienda : inside the store⟩ ⟨dentro de los límites de : within the limits of⟩ **3** ~ de : in, within (a time period) ⟨dentro de poco : soon, shortly⟩ **4** dentro de todo : all in all, all things considered **5** por ~ : inwardly, inside

denuncia *nf* **1** : denunciation, condemnation **2** : police report

denunciante *nmf* : accuser (of a crime)

denunciar *vt* **1** : to denounce, to condemn **2** : to report (to the authorities)

deparar *vt* : to have in store for, to provide with ⟨no sabemos lo que nos depara el destino : we don't know what fate has in store for us⟩

departamental *adj* **1** : departmental **2** tienda departamental *Mex* : department store

departamento *nm* **1** : department **2** APARTAMENTO : apartment

departir *vi* : to converse

dependencia *nf* **1** : dependence, dependency ⟨dependencia del alcohol : dependence on alcohol⟩ **2** : agency, branch office

depender *vi* **1** : to depend **2** ~ de : to depend on **3** ~ de : to be subordinate to

dependiente[1] *adj* : dependent

dependiente[2], **-ta** *n* : clerk, salesperson

depilar *vt* : to wax, to shave

deplorable *adj* : deplorable

deplorar *vt* **1** : to deplore **2** LAMENTAR : to regret

deponer {60} *vt* **1** : to depose, to overthrow **2** : to abandon (an attitude or stance) **3** deponer las armas : to lay down one's arms — *vi* **1** TESTIFICAR : to testify, to make a statement **2** EVACUAR : to defecate

deportación *nf, pl* **-ciones** : deportation

deportar *vt* : to deport

deporte *nm* **1** : sport, sports *pl* ⟨hacer deporte : to engage in sports⟩ ⟨practicar un deporte : to do a sport⟩ ⟨por deporte : for the fun of it, for sport⟩ **2** deporte extremo : extreme sport **3** deporte de invierno/equipo : winter/team sport

deportista[1] *adj* **1** : fond of sports **2** : sporty

deportista[2] *nmf* **1** : sports fan **2** : athlete, sportsman *m*, sportswoman *f*

deportividad *nf Spain* : sportsmanship

deportivo, -va *adj* **1** : sports, sporting ⟨artículos deportivos : sporting goods⟩ **2** : sporty

deposición *nf, pl* **-ciones** **1** : statement, testimony **2** : removal from office

depositar *vt* **1** : to deposit, to place **2** : to store — **depositarse** *vr* : to settle

depósito *nm* **1** : deposit ⟨hacer un depósito : to make a deposit⟩ **2** : warehouse, storehouse ⟨depósito de armas : arms depot⟩ **3** : tank ⟨depósito de gasolina : gas tank⟩

depravación *nf, pl* **-ciones** : depravity

depravado, -da *adj* DEGENERADO : depraved, degenerate

depravar *vt* : to deprave, to corrupt

depreciación *nf, pl* **-ciones** : depreciation

depreciar *vt* : to depreciate, to reduce the value of — **depreciarse** *vr* : to lose value

depredador[1], **-dora** *adj* : predatory

depredador[2] *nm* **1** : predator **2** SAQUEADOR : plunderer

depresión *nf, pl* **-siones** **1** : depression **2** : hollow, recess **3** : drop, fall **4** : slump, recession

depresivo nm : depressant
deprimente adj : depressing
deprimir vt 1 : to depress 2 : to lower —
— **deprimirse** vr ABATIRSE : to get depressed
deprisa adv : fast
depuesto pp → **deponer**
depuración nf, pl **-ciones** 1 PURIFICACIÓN : purification 2 PURGA : purge 3 : refinement, polish
depurar vt 1 PURIFICAR : to purify 2 PURGAR : to purge
depuso, etc. → **deponer**
derby nm, pl **derbies** or **derbys** 1 : derby (in horse racing) 2 : derby (hat) 3 Spain : local game
derecha nf 1 : right 2 : right hand, right side 3 : right wing, right (in politics)
derechazo nm 1 : pass with the cape on the right hand (in bullfighting) 2 : right (in boxing) 3 : forehand (in tennis)
derechista[1] adj : rightist, right-wing
derechista[2] nmf : right-winger, rightist
derecho[1] adv 1 : straight ⟨todo derecho : straight ahead⟩ 2 : upright, directly ⟨ir derecho al tema : to get straight to the point⟩
derecho[2], **-cha** adj 1 : right 2 : right-hand ⟨el margen derecho : the right-hand margin⟩ 3 RECTO : straight, upright, erect ⟨siéntate derecho : sit up straight⟩
derecho[3] nm 1 : right ⟨derechos humanos : human rights⟩ ⟨el derecho al voto : the right to vote⟩ ⟨derecho de nacimiento : birthright⟩ ⟨tener derecho a : to have a right to⟩ ⟨hacer valer sus derechos : to exercise one's rights⟩ ⟨estás en tu derecho : you're within your rights⟩ ⟨no hay derecho : it's not fair⟩ 2 : law ⟨derecho civil : civil law⟩ ⟨derecho de familia : family law⟩ ⟨un estudiante de derecho : a law student⟩ 3 : right side (of cloth or clothing) ⟨ponlo del derecho : turn it right side up/out⟩
de refilón adv 1 : sidelong, obliquely 2 : briefly
deriva nf 1 : drift 2 **a la deriva** : adrift
derivación nf, pl **-ciones** 1 : derivation 2 RAMIFICACIÓN : ramification, consequence
derivar vi 1 : to drift 2 ~ **de** : to come from, to derive from 3 ~ **en** : to result in — vt : to steer, to direct ⟨derivó la discusión hacia la política : he steered the discussion over to politics⟩ — **derivarse** vr : to be derived from, to arise from
dermatología nf : dermatology
dermatólogo, -ga n : dermatologist
derogación nf, pl **-ciones** : abolition, repeal
derogar {52} vt ABOLIR : to abolish, to repeal
derramamiento nm 1 : spilling, overflowing 2 **derramamiento de sangre** : bloodshed
derramar vt 1 : to spill 2 : to shed (tears, blood) — **derramarse** vr 1 : to spill over 2 : to scatter

derrame nm 1 : spilling, shedding 2 : leakage, overflow 3 : discharge, hemorrhage ⟨derrame cerebral : stroke⟩
derrapar vi : to skid
derrape nm : skid
derredor nm **al derredor** or **en derredor** : around, round about
derrengado, -da adj 1 : bent, twisted 2 : exhausted
derretir {54} vt : to melt, to thaw — **derretirse** vr 1 : to melt, to thaw 2 ~ **por** fam : to be crazy about
derribar vt 1 DEMOLER, DERRUMBAR : to demolish, to knock down 2 : to shoot down, to bring down (an airplane) 3 DERROCAR : to overthrow
derribo nm 1 : demolition, razing 2 : shooting down 3 : overthrow
derrocamiento nm : overthrow
derrocar {72} vt DERRIBAR : to overthrow, to topple
derrochador[1], **-dora** adj : extravagant, wasteful
derrochador[2], **-dora** n : spendthrift
derrochar vt : to waste, to squander
derroche nm : extravagance, waste
derrota nf 1 : defeat, rout 2 : course (at sea)
derrotar vt : to defeat
derrotero nm RUTA : course
derrotista adj & nmf : defeatist
derruir {41} vt : to demolish, to tear down
derrumbamiento nm : collapse
derrumbar vt 1 DEMOLER, DERRIBAR : to demolish, to knock down 2 DESPEÑAR : to cast down, to topple — **derrumbarse** vr DESPLOMARSE : to collapse, to break down
derrumbe nm 1 DESPLOME : collapse, fall ⟨el derrumbe del comunismo : the fall of Communism⟩ 2 : landslide
des- pref : de-, dis-, un-
desabastecimiento nm : shortage, scarcity
desabasto nm Mex : shortage, scarcity
desabotonar vt : to unbutton, to undo — **desabotonarse** vr : to come undone
desabrido, -da adj : tasteless, bland
desabrigar {52} vt 1 : to undress 2 : to uncover 3 : to deprive of shelter
desabrochar vt : to unbutton, to undo — **desabrocharse** vr : to come undone
desacato nm 1 : disrespect 2 : contempt (of court)
desacelerar vi : to decelerate, to slow down
desacertado, -da adj 1 : mistaken 2 : unwise
desacertar {55} vi ERRAR : to err, to be mistaken
desacierto nm ERROR : error, mistake
desaconsejable adj : inadvisable
desaconsejado, -da adj : ill-advised, unwise
desaconsejar vt : to advise against
desacostumbrado, -da adj : unaccustomed, unusual
desacreditar vt DESPRESTIGIAR : to discredit, to disgrace
desactivar vt : to deactivate, to defuse

desacuerdo *nm* : disagreement

desafiante *adj* : defiant

desafiar {85} *vt* RETAR : to defy, to challenge

desafilado, -da *adj* : blunt

desafilar *vt* : to dull, to blunt

desafinado, -da *adj* : out-of-tune, off-key

desafinarse *vr* : to go out of tune

desafío *nm* **1** RETO : challenge **2** RESISTENCIA : defiance

desaforado, -da *adj* : wild, unrestrained

desafortunado, -da *adj* : unfortunate, unlucky — **desafortunadamente** *adv*

desafuero *nm* ABUSO : injustice, outrage

desagradable *adj* : unpleasant, disagreeable — **desagradablemente** *adv*

desagradar *vi* : to be unpleasant, to be disagreeable

desagradecido, -da *adj* : ungrateful

desagrado *nm* **1** : displeasure **2 con ~** : reluctantly

desagravio *nm* **1** : apology **2** : amends, reparation

desagregarse {52} *vr* : to break up, to disintegrate

desaguar {10} *vi* : to drain, to empty

desagüe *nm* **1** : drain **2** : drainage

desaguisado *nm* : mess

desahogado, -da *adj* **1** : well-off, comfortable **2** : spacious, roomy

desahogar {52} *vt* **1** : to relieve, to ease **2** : to give vent to — **desahogarse** *vr* **1** : to recover, to feel better **2** : to unburden oneself, to let off steam

desahogo *nm* **1** : relief, outlet **2 con ~** : comfortably

desahuciar *vt* **1** : to deprive of hope **2** : to evict — **desahuciarse** *vr* : to lose all hope

desahucio *nm* : eviction

desairar {5} *vt* : to snub, to rebuff

desaire *nm* : rebuff, snub, slight

desajustar *vt* **1** : to disarrange, to put out of order **2** : to upset (plans)

desajuste *nm* **1** : maladjustment **2** : imbalance **3** : upset, disruption

desalentador, -dora *adj* : discouraging, disheartening

desalentar {55} *vt* DESANIMAR : to discourage, to dishearten — **desalentarse** *vr*

desaliento *nm* : discouragement

desaliñado, -da *adj* : sloppy, untidy (of a person's appearance) — **desaliñadamente** *adv*

desaliño *nm* : sloppiness, untidiness (of a person's appearance)

desalmado, -da *adj* : heartless, callous

desalojar *vt* **1** : to remove, to clear **2** EVACUAR : to evacuate, to vacate **3** : to evict

desalojo *nm* **1** : removal, expulsion **2** : evacuation **3** : eviction

desamarrar *vt* : to cast off **2** : to untie

desamor *nm* **1** FRIALDAD : indifference **2** ENEMISTAD : dislike, enmity

desamparado, -da *adj* DESVALIDO : helpless, destitute

desamparar *vt* : to abandon, to forsake

desamparo *nm* **1** : abandonment, neglect **2** : helplessness

desamueblado, -da *adj* : unfurnished

desandar {6} *vt* : to go back, to return to the starting point

desangelado, -da *adj* : dull, lifeless

desangrar *vt* : to bleed, to bleed dry — **desangrarse** *vr* **1** : to be bleeding **2** : to bleed to death

desanimar *vt* DESALENTAR : to discourage, to dishearten — **desanimarse** *vr*

desánimo *nm* DESALIENTO : discouragement, dejection

desapacible *adj* : unpleasant, disagreeable

desaparecer {53} *vt* : to cause to disappear — *vi* : to disappear, to vanish

desaparecido¹, -da *adj* **1** : late, deceased **2** : missing

desaparecido², -da *n* : missing person

desaparición *nf, pl* **-ciones** : disappearance

desapasionado, -da *adj* : dispassionate, impartial — **desapasionadamente** *adv*

desapego *nm* : coolness, indifference

desapercibido, -da *adj* **1** : unnoticed **2** DESPREVENIDO : unprepared, off guard

desaprobación *nf, pl* **-ciones** : disapproval

desaprobar {19} *vt* REPROBAR : to disapprove of

desaprovechar *vt* MALGASTAR : to waste, to misuse — *vi* : to lose ground, to slip back

desarmador *nm Mex* : screwdriver

desarmar *vt* **1** : to disarm **2** DESMONTAR : to disassemble, to take apart

desarme *nm* : disarmament

desarraigado, -da *adj* : rootless

desarraigar {52} *vt* : to uproot, to root out

desarregladamente *adv* : untidily, messily

desarreglado, -da *adj* : untidy, disorganized

desarreglar *vt* **1** : to mess up **2** : to upset, to disrupt

desarreglo *nm* **1** : untidiness **2** : disorder, confusion

desarrollar *vt* **1** : to develop **2** : to carry out (an action, etc.) **3** : to explain (a theory, etc.) — **desarrollarse** *vr* **1** : to develop **2** : to take place, to unfold

desarrollo *nm* : development ⟨países en vías de desarrollo : developing countries⟩

desarticulación *nf, pl* **-ciones** **1** : dislocation **2** : breaking up, dismantling

desarticular *vt* **1** DISLOCAR : to dislocate **2** : to break up, to dismantle

desasosiego *nm* : sense of unease

desastre *nm* CATÁSTROFE : disaster

desastroso, -sa *adj* : disastrous, catastrophic — **desastrosamente** *adv*

desatar *vt* **1** : to undo, to untie **2** : to unleash **3** : to trigger, to precipitate — **desatarse** *vr* **1** : to come undone **2** : to break out, to erupt

desatascador *nm* : plunger (for toilets, etc.)

desatascar {72} *vt* : to unblock, to clear

desatención *nf, pl* **-ciones** **1** : absentmindedness, distraction **2** : discourtesy

desatender {56} *vt* **1** : to disregard **2** : to neglect **3** : to leave unattended

desatento, -ta *adj* **1** DISTRAÍDO : absent-minded **2** GROSERO : discourteous, rude

desatinado, -da *adj* : foolish, silly

desatino *nm* : folly, mistake

desatorador *nm* **1** : plunger (for toilets, etc.) **2** : drain cleaner (liquid)

desatornillar → **destornillar**

desautorizar {21} *vt* : to deprive of authority, to discredit

desavenencia *nf* DISCORDANCIA : disagreement, dispute

desayunar *vi* : to have breakfast — *vt* : to have for breakfast

desayuno *nm* : breakfast

desazón *nf, pl* **-zones** INQUIETUD : uneasiness, anxiety

desbalance *nm* : imbalance

desbancar {72} *vt* : to displace, to oust

desbandada *nf* : scattering, dispersal

desbarajuste *nm* DESORDEN : disarray, disorder, mess

desbaratar *vt* **1** ARRUINAR : to destroy, to ruin **2** DESCOMPONER : to break, to break down — **desbaratarse** *vr* : to fall apart

desbloquear *vt* **1** : to open up, to clear, to break through **2** : to free, to release

desbocado, -da *adj* : unbridled, rampant

desbocarse {72} *vr* : to run away, to bolt

desbordamiento *nm* : overflowing

desbordante *adj* : overflowing, bursting ⟨desbordante de energía : bursting with energy⟩

desbordar *vt* **1** : to overflow, to spill over **2** : to surpass, to exceed — **desbordarse** *vr*

descabellado, -da *adj* : outlandish, ridiculous

descafeinado, -da *adj* : decaffeinated

descalabrar *vt* : to hit on the head — **descalabrarse** *vr*

descalabro *nm* : setback, misfortune, loss

descalificación *nf, pl* **-ciones** **1** : disqualification **2** : disparaging remark

descalificar {72} *vt* **1** : to disqualify **2** DESACREDITAR : to discredit — **descalificarse** *vr*

descalzarse {21} *vr* : take off one's shoes

descalzo, -za *adj* : barefoot

descampado *nm* : open area

descansado, -da *adj* **1** : rested, refreshed **2** : restful, peaceful

descansar *vi* : to rest, to relax ⟨¡descansen! : at ease!⟩ — *vt* : to rest ⟨descansar la vista : to rest one's eyes⟩

descansillo *nm Spain* DESCANSO : landing (of a staircase)

descanso *nm* **1** : rest, relaxation **2** : break **3** : landing (of a staircase) **4** : intermission (in a show), halftime (in sports)

descapotable *adj & nm* : convertible

descarado, -da *adj* : brazen, impudent — **descaradamente** *adv*

descarga *nf* **1** : discharge **2** : unloading

descargable *adj* : downloadable

descargar {52} *vt* **1** : to discharge **2** : to unload **3** : to release, to free **4** : to take out, to vent (anger, etc.) **5** : to download (a file, etc.) — **descargarse** *vr* **1** : to unburden oneself **2** : to quit **3** : to lose power

descargo *nm* **1** : unloading **2** : defense ⟨testigo de descargo : witness for the defense⟩

descarnado, -da *adj* : scrawny, gaunt

descaro *nm* : audacity, nerve

descarriado, -da *adj* : lost, gone astray

descarriarse *vr* : to go astray

descarrilar *vi* : to derail — **descarrilarse** *vr* — **descarrilamiento** *nm*

descartar *vt* : to rule out, to reject — **descartarse** *vr* : to discard

descascarar *vt* : to peel, to shell, to husk — **descascararse** *vr* : to peel off, to chip

descendencia *nf* **1** : descendants *pl* **2** LINAJE : descent, lineage

descendente *adj* : downward, descending

descender {56} *vi* **1** : to descend, to go down **2** BAJAR : to lower, to take down, to let down — *vi* **1** : to descend, to come down **2** : to drop, to fall **3** ∼ **de** : to be a descendant of

descendiente *adj & nm* : descendant

descenso *nm* **1** : descent **2** BAJA, CAÍDA : drop, fall

descentralizar {21} *vt* : to decentralize — **descentralizarse** *vr* — **descentralización** *nf*

descifrar *vt* : to decipher, to decode — **descifrable** *adj*

desclasificar {72} *vt* : to declassify

descodificador → **decodificador**

descodificar {72} *vt* : to decode

descolgar {16} *vt* **1** : to take down, to let down **2** : to pick up, to answer (the telephone)

descollar {19} *vi* SOBRESALIR : to stand out, to be outstanding, to excel

descolorido, -da *adj* : discolored, faded

descomponer {60} *vt* **1** : to rot, to decompose **2** DESBARATAR : to break, to break down **3** : to damage **4** : to mess up — **descomponerse** *vr* **1** : to break down **2** : to decompose

descomposición *nf, pl* **-ciones** **1** : breakdown, decomposition **2** : decay

descompuesto[1] *pp* → **descomponer**

descompuesto[2], **-ta** *adj* **1** : broken down, out of order **2** : rotten, decomposed

descomunal *adj* **1** ENORME : enormous, huge **2** EXTRAORDINARIO : extraordinary

desconcentrar *vt* DISTRAER : to distract

desconcertante *adj* : disconcerting

desconcertar {55} *vt* : to disconcert — **desconcertarse** *vr*

desconchar *vt* : to chip — **desconcharse** *vr* : to chip off, to peel

desconcierto *nm* : uncertainty, confusion

desconectar *vt* **1** : to disconnect, to switch off **2** : to unplug

desconfiado, -da adj : distrustful, suspicious

desconfianza nf RECELO : distrust, suspicion

desconfiar {85} vi ~ **de** : to distrust, to be suspicious of

descongelar vt **1** : to thaw **2** : to defrost (a refrigerator, etc.) **3** : to unfreeze (assets) — **descongelarse** vr

descongestionante adj & nm : decongestant

descongestionar vt : to clear, to unclog ⟨descongestionar el tráfico : to reduce traffic congestion⟩

desconocer {18} vt **1** IGNORAR : to be unaware of **2** : to fail to recognize

desconocido¹, -da adj : unknown, unfamiliar

desconocido², -da n EXTRAÑO : stranger

desconocimiento nm : ignorance

desconsiderado, -da : inconsiderate, thoughtless — **desconsideradamente** adj

desconsolado, -da adj : disconsolate, heartbroken, despondent

desconsuelo nm AFLICCIÓN : grief, distress, despair

descontaminar vt : to decontaminate — **descontaminación** nf

descontar {19} vt **1** : to discount, to deduct **2** EXCEPTUAR : to except, to exclude

descontento¹, -ta adj : discontented, dissatisfied

descontento² nm : discontent, dissatisfaction

descontinuar {3} vt : to discontinue (a product, etc.)

descontrol nm : lack of control, disorder, chaos

descontrolarse vr : to get out of control, to be out of hand

desconvocar {72} vt : to cancel

descorazonado, -da adj : disheartened, discouraged

descorchar vt : to uncork

descorrer vt : to draw back

descortés adj, pl **-teses** : discourteous, rude

descortesía nf : discourtesy, rudeness

descrédito nm DESPRESTIGIO : discredit

descremado, -da adj : nonfat, skim

describir {33} vt : to describe

descripción nf, pl **-ciones** : description

descriptivo, -va adj : descriptive

descrito pp → **describir**

descuartizar {21} vt **1** : to cut up, to quarter **2** : to tear to pieces

descubierto¹ pp → **descubrir**

descubierto², -ta adj **1** : exposed, revealed **2 al descubierto** : out in the open

descubridor, -dora n : discoverer, explorer

descubrimiento nm : discovery

descubrir {2} vt **1** HALLAR : to discover, to find out **2** REVELAR : to uncover, to reveal **3** DEVELAR : to unveil **4** DELATAR : to give away — **descubrirse** vr

descuento nm REBAJA : discount

descuidado, -da adj **1** : neglectful, careless **2** : neglected, unkempt

descuidar vt : to neglect, to overlook — vi : to be careless — **descuidarse** vr **1** : to be careless, to drop one's guard **2** : to let oneself go

descuido nm **1** : carelessness, negligence **2** : slip, oversight

desde prep **1** : from ⟨desde arriba : from above⟩ ⟨desde la cabeza hasta los pies : from head to foot/toe⟩ **2** : since, from ⟨desde el lunes : since Monday⟩ ⟨desde el principio : right from the start⟩ ⟨desde la mañana hasta la noche : from morning to/until night⟩ **3 desde ahora** : from now on **4 desde entonces** : since then **5 desde hace** : for, since (a time) ⟨ha estado nevando desde hace dos días : it's been snowing for two days⟩ **6 desde luego** : of course **7 desde que** : since, ever since **8 desde ya** : right now, immediately

desdecir {11} vi **1** ~ **de** : to be unworthy of **2** ~ **de** : to clash with — **desdecirse** vr **1** CONTRADECIRSE : to contradict oneself **2** RETRACTARSE : to go back on one's word

desdén nm, pl **desdenes** DESPRECIO : disdain, scorn

desdentado, -da adj : toothless

desdeñar vt DESPRECIAR : to disdain, to scorn, to despise

desdeñoso, -sa adj : disdainful, scornful — **desdeñosamente** adv

desdibujar vt : to blur — **desdibujarse** vr

desdicha nf **1** : misery **2** : misfortune

desdichado¹, -da adj **1** : unfortunate **2** : miserable, unhappy

desdichado², -da n : wretch

desdicho pp → **desdecir**

desdiga, desdijo etc. → **desdecir**

desdoblar vt DESPLEGAR : to unfold

deseable adj : desirable

desear vt **1** : to wish ⟨te deseo buena suerte : I wish you good luck⟩ **2** QUERER : to want, to desire ⟨dejar mucho que desear : to leave much to be desired⟩

desecar {72} vt : to dry (flowers, etc.)

desechable adj : disposable

desechar vt **1** : to discard, to throw away **2** RECHAZAR : to reject

desecho nm **1** : reject **2 desechos** nmpl RESIDUOS : rubbish, waste

desembarazarse {21} vr ~ **de** : to get rid of

desembarcar {72} vi : to disembark — vt : to unload

desembarco nm **1** : landing, arrival **2** : unloading

desembarque → **desembarco**

desembocadura nf **1** : mouth (of a river) **2** : opening, end (of a street)

desembocar {72} vi ~ **en** or ~ **a 1** : to flow into, to join **2** : to lead to, to result in

desembolsar vt PAGAR : to disburse, to pay out

desembolso nm PAGO : disbursement, payment

desempacar {72} *v* : to unpack
desempatar *vi* : to break a tie
desempate *nm* : tiebreaker, play-off
desempeñar *vt* **1** : to play (a role) **2** : to fulfill, to carry out **3** : to redeem (from a pawnshop) — **desempeñarse** *vr* : to function, to act
desempeño *nm* **1** : fulfillment, carrying out **2** : performance
desempleado¹, -da *adj* : unemployed
desempleado², -da *n* : unemployed person
desempleo *nm* : unemployment
desempolvar *vt* **1** : to dust off **2** : to resurrect, to revive
desencadenar *vt* **1** : to unchain **2** : to trigger, to unleash — **desencadenarse** *vr*
desencajar *vt* **1** : to dislocate (a bone) **2** : to pop out of place, to disengage — **desencajarse** *vr*
desencantar *vt* : to disenchant, to disillusion — **desencantarse** *vr*
desencanto *nm* : disenchantment, disillusionment
desenchufar *vt* : to disconnect, to unplug
desenfadado, -da *adj* **1** : uninhibited, carefree **2** : confident, self-assured
desenfado *nm* **1** DESENVOLTURA : self-assurance, confidence **2** : naturalness, ease
desenfocado, -da *adj* : unfocused, blurry
desenfrenadamente *adv* : wildly, with abandon
desenfrenado, -da *adj* : unbridled, unrestrained
desenfreno *nm* : abandon, lack of restraint
desenfundar *vt* : to draw (a gun)
desenganchar *vt* : to unhitch, to uncouple
desengañar *vt* : to disillusion, to disenchant — **desengañarse** *vr*
desengaño *nm* : disenchantment, disillusionment
desenlace *nm* : ending, outcome
desenmarañar *vt* : to disentangle, to unravel
desenmascarar *vt* : to unmask, to expose
desenredar *vt* **1** : to untangle, to disentangle **2** : to straighten out, to sort out
desenrollar *vt* : to unroll, to unwind
desenroscar *vt* **1** : to unscrew **2** : to unroll — **desenroscarse** *vr*
desentenderse {56} *vr* **1** ~ **de** : to want nothing to do with, to be uninterested in **2** ~ **de** : to pretend ignorance of
desenterrar {55} *vt* **1** EXHUMAR : to exhume **2** : to unearth, to dig up
desentonar *vi* **1** : to clash, to conflict **2** : to be out of tune, to sing off-key
desentrañar *vt* : to get to the bottom of, to unravel
desenvainar *vt* : to draw, to unsheathe (a sword)
desenvoltura *nf* **1** DESENFADO : confidence, self-assurance **2** ELOCUENCIA : eloquence, fluency
desenvolver {89} *vt* : to unwrap, to open — **desenvolverse** *vr* **1** : to unfold, to develop **2** : to manage, to cope
desenvuelto¹ *pp* → **desenvolver**

desenvuelto², -ta *adj* : confident, relaxed, self-assured
deseo *nm* : wish, desire
deseoso, -sa *adj* : eager, anxious
desequilibrado, -da *adj* **1** : off-balance **2** : insane
desequilibrar *vt* : to unbalance, to throw off balance — **desequilibrarse** *vr*
desequilibrio *nm* : imbalance
deserción *nf, pl* **-ciones** : desertion, defection
desertar *vi* **1** : to desert, to defect **2** ~ **de** : to abandon, to neglect
desértico, -ca *adj* **1** : desert **2** : uninhabited
desertor, -tora *n* : deserter, defector
desesperación *nf, pl* **-ciones** : desperation, despair
desesperado, -da *adj* : desperate, despairing, hopeless — **desesperadamente** *adv*
desesperante *adj* **1** : exasperating **2** : agonizing, excruciating
desesperanza *nf* : despair, hopelessness
desesperar *vt* : to exasperate — *vi* : to despair, to lose hope — **desesperarse** *vr* : to become exasperated
desestabilizar {21} *vt* : to make unstable
desestimar *vt* **1** : to reject, to disallow **2** : to have a low opinion of
desfachatez *nf, pl* **-teces** : audacity, nerve, cheek
desfalcador, -dora *n* : embezzler
desfalcar {72} *vt* : to embezzle
desfalco *nm* : embezzlement
desfallecer {53} *vi* **1** : to weaken **2** : to faint
desfallecimiento *nm* **1** : weakness **2** : fainting
desfasado, -da *adj* **1** : out of sync **2** : out of step, behind the times
desfase *nm* : gap, lag ⟨desfase (de) horario : jet lag⟩
desfavorable *adj* : unfavorable, adverse — **desfavorablemente** *adv*
desfavorecido, -da *adj* : underprivileged
desfigurar *vt* **1** : to disfigure, to mar **2** : to distort, to misrepresent
desfiladero *nm* : narrow gorge, defile
desfilar *vi* : to parade, to march
desfile *nm* : parade, procession
desfogar {52} *vt* **1** : to vent **2** *Mex* : to unclog, to unblock — **desfogarse** *vr* : to vent one's feelings, to let off steam
desgajar *vt* **1** : to tear off **2** : to break apart — **desgajarse** *vr* : to come apart
desgana *nf* **1** INAPETENCIA : lack of appetite **2** APATÍA : apathy, unwillingness, reluctance
desgano *nm* → **desgana**
desgarbado, -da *adj* : ungainly
desgarrador, -dora *adj* : heartbreaking
desgarradura *nf* : tear, rip
desgarrar *vt* **1** : to tear, to rip **2** : to break (one's heart) — **desgarrarse** *vr*
desgarre → **desgarro**
desgarro *nm* : tear
desgarrón *nm, pl* **-rrones** : rip, tear
desgastar *vt* **1** : to use up **2** : to wear away, to wear down

desgaste *nm* : deterioration, wear and tear

desglosar *vt* : to break down, to itemize

desglose *nm* : breakdown, itemization

desgobierno *nm* : anarchy, disorder

desgracia *nf* 1 : misfortune 2 : disgrace 3 **por** ~ : unfortunately

desgraciadamente *adv* : unfortunately

desgraciado¹, -da *adj* 1 : unfortunate, unlucky 2 : vile, wretched

desgraciado², -da *n* : unfortunate person, wretch

desgranar *vt* : to shuck, to shell

desgravar *vt* : to deduct (from taxes), to exempt — **desgravación** *n*

desguazar {21} *vt Spain* : to scrap

deshabitado, -da *adj* : unoccupied, uninhabited

deshacer {40} *vt* 1 : to destroy, to ruin 2 DESATAR : to undo, to untie 3 : to break apart, to crumble 4 : to dissolve, to melt 5 : to break, to cancel — **deshacerse** *vr* 1 : to fall apart, to come undone 2 ~ **de** : to get rid of

deshecho¹ *pp* → **deshacer**

deshecho², -cha *adj* 1 : destroyed, ruined 2 : devastated, shattered 3 : undone, untied

deshelar {55} *vt* 1 : to thaw 2 : to deice (a plane), to defrost — **deshelarse** *vr* 1 : to thaw 2 : to defrost

desherbar *vt* : to weed

desheredado, -da *adj* MARGINADO : dispossessed, destitute

desheredar *vt* : to disinherit

deshicieron, etc. → **deshacer**

deshidratar *vt* : to dehydrate — **deshidratación** *nf*

deshielo *nm* : thaw, thawing

deshierbar → **desherbar**

deshilachar *vt* : to fray — **deshilacharse** *vr*

deshizo → **deshacer**

deshojar *vt* 1 : to remove petals from 2 : to remove pages from

deshollinador, -dora *n* : chimney sweep

deshonestidad *nf* : dishonesty

deshonesto, -ta *adj* : dishonest

deshonor *nm* : dishonor, disgrace

deshonra *nf* : dishonor, disgrace

deshonrar *vt* : to dishonor, to disgrace

deshonroso, -sa *adj* : dishonorable, disgraceful

deshora *nf* **a deshoras** : at odd times

deshuesadero *nm Mex* : dump

deshuesar *vt* 1 : to pit (a fruit, etc.) 2 : to bone

desidia *nf* 1 APATÍA : apathy, indolence 2 NEGLIGENCIA : negligence, sloppiness

desierto¹, -ta *adj* : deserted, uninhabited

desierto² *nm* : desert

designación *nf, pl* **-ciones** NOMBRAMIENTO : appointment, naming (to an office, etc.)

designar *vt* NOMBRAR : to designate, to appoint, to name

designio *nm* : plan

desigual *adj* 1 : unequal 2 DISPAREJO : uneven 3 : variable, changeable — **desigualmente** *adv*

desigualdad *nf* 1 : inequality 2 : unevenness

desilusión *nf, pl* **-siones** DESENCANTO, DESENGAÑO : disillusionment, disenchantment

desilusionar *vt* DESENCANTAR, DESENGAÑAR : to disillusion, to disenchant — **desilusionarse** *vr*

desinfectante *adj & nm* : disinfectant

desinfectar *vt* : to disinfect — **desinfección** *nf*

desinflar *vt* : to deflate — **desinflarse** *vr*

desinformar *vt* : to misinform

desinhibido, -da *adj* : uninhibited, unrestrained

desintegración *nf, pl* **-ciones** : disintegration

desintegrar *vt* : to disintegrate, to break up — **desintegrarse** *vr*

desinterés *nm* 1 : lack of interest, indifference 2 : unselfishness

desinteresado, -da *adj* GENEROSO : unselfish

desintoxicación *nf, pl* **-ciones** : detoxification, detox *fam*

desintoxicar {72} *vt* : to detoxify, to detox *fam* — **desintoxicarse** *vr*

desistir *vi* 1 : to desist, to stop 2 ~ **de** : to give up, to relinquish

deslave *nm Mex* : landslide

desleal *adj* INFIEL : disloyal — **deslealmente** *adv*

deslealtad *nf* : disloyalty

desligar {52} *vt* 1 : to separate, to undo 2 : to free (from an obligation) — **desligarse** *vr* ~ **de** : to extricate oneself from

deslindar *vt* 1 : to mark the limits of, to demarcate 2 : to define, to clarify

deslinde *nm* : demarcation

desliz *nm, pl* **deslices** : error, mistake, slip ⟨desliz de la lengua : slip of the tongue⟩

deslizador *nm* 1 : speedboat 2 *Mex* : hang glider

deslizamiento *nm* : slip, slide ⟨deslizamiento de tierras : landslide⟩

deslizar {21} *vt* 1 : to slide, to slip 2 : to slip in — **deslizarse** *vr* 1 : to slide, to glide 2 : to slip away

deslomarse *vr* : to wear oneself out, to work oneself to death

deslucido, -da *adj* 1 : lackluster, dull 2 : faded, dingy, tarnished

deslucir {45} *vt* 1 : to spoil 2 : to fade, to dull, to tarnish 3 : to discredit

deslumbrar *vt* : to dazzle — **deslumbrante** *adj*

deslustrado, -da *adj* : dull, lusterless

deslustrar *vt* : to tarnish, to dull

deslustre *nm* : tarnish

desmadrarse *vr* : to get out of hand

desmadre *nm fam* : chaos

desmán *nm, pl* **desmanes** 1 : outrage, abuse 2 : misfortune

desmandarse *vr* : to behave badly, to get out of hand

desmantelar *vt* DESMONTAR : to dismantle

desmañado, -da *adj* : clumsy, awkward

desmarcarse {72} *vr* : to distance oneself
desmayado, -da *adj* 1 : fainting, weak 2 : dull, pale
desmayar *vi* : to lose heart, to falter — **desmayarse** *vr* DESVANECERSE : to faint, to swoon
desmayo *nm* 1 : faint, fainting 2 **sufrir un desmayo** : to faint
desmedido, -da *adj* DESMESURADO : excessive, undue
desmejorar *vt* : to weaken, to make worse — *vi* : to decline (in health), to get worse
desmembrar {55} *vt* 1 : to dismember 2 : to break up
desmemoriado, -da *adj* : absentminded, forgetful
desmentido *nm* : denial
desmentir {76} *vt* 1 NEGAR : to deny, to refute 2 CONTRADECIR : to contradict
desmenuzar {21} *vt* 1 : to break down, to scrutinize 2 : to crumble, to shred — **desmenuzarse** *vr*
desmerecer {53} *vt* : to be unworthy of — *vi* 1 : to decline in value 2 ~ **de** : to compare unfavorably with
desmesurado, -da *adj* DESMEDIDO : excessive, inordinate — **desmesuradamente** *adv*
desmigajar *vt* : to crumble — **desmigajarse** *vr*
desmilitarizar {21} *vt* : to demilitarize
desmitificar {72} *vt* : to demystify, to dispel the myths surrounding
desmontable *adj* : removable
desmontar *vt* 1 : to clear, to level off 2 DESMANTELAR : to dismantle, to take apart — *vi* : to dismount
desmonte *nm* : clearing, leveling
desmoralizador, -dora *adj* : demoralizing
desmoralizante → **desmoralizador**
desmoralizar {21} *vt* DESALENTAR : to demoralize, to discourage
desmoronamiento *nm* : crumbling, falling apart
desmoronar *vt* : to wear away, to erode — **desmoronarse** *vr* : to crumble, to deteriorate, to fall apart
desmovilizar {21} *vt* : to demobilize — **desmovilización** *nf*
desnatado, -da *Spain* → **descremado**
desnaturalizar {21} *vt* 1 : to denature 2 : to distort, to alter
desnivel *nm* 1 : disparity, difference 2 : unevenness (of a surface)
desnivelado, -da *adj* 1 : uneven 2 : unbalanced
desnivelar *vt* 1 : to make uneven 2 : to tip (the balance)
desnucar {72} *vt* : to break the neck of — **desnucarse** *vr* : to break one's neck
desnudar *vt* 1 : to undress 2 : to strip, to lay bare — **desnudarse** *vr* : to undress, to strip off one's clothing
desnudez *nf, pl* **-deces** : nudity, nakedness
desnudo¹, -da *adj* : nude, naked, bare
desnudo² *nm* : nude
desnutrición *nf, pl* **-ciones** MALNUTRICIÓN : malnutrition
desnutrido, -da *adj* MALNUTRIDO : malnourished, undernourished

desobedecer {53} *v* : to disobey
desobediencia *nf* : disobedience — **desobediente** *adj*
desocupación *nf, pl* **-ciones** : unemployment
desocupado, -da *adj* 1 : vacant, empty 2 : free, unoccupied 3 : unemployed
desocupar *vt* 1 : to empty 2 : to vacate, to move out of — **desocuparse** *vr* : to leave, to quit (a job)
desodorante *adj & nm* : deodorant
desolación *nf, pl* **-ciones** : desolation
desolado, -da *adj* 1 : desolate 2 : devastated, distressed
desolador, -dora *adj* 1 : devastating 2 : bleak, desolate
desolar {19} *vt* : to devastate
desollar *vt* : to skin, to flay
desorbitado, -da *adj* 1 : excessive, exorbitant 2 **con los ojos desorbitados** : with eyes popping out of one's head
desorden *nm, pl* **desórdenes** 1 DESBARAJUSTE : disorder, mess 2 : disorder, disturbance, upset
desordenadamente *adv* : messily, in a disorderly way
desordenado, -da *adj* 1 : untidy, messy 2 : disorderly, unruly
desordenar *vt* : to mess up — **desordenarse** *vr* : to get messed up
desorganización *nf, pl* **-ciones** : disorganization
desorganizar {21} *vt* : to disrupt, to disorganize
desorientar *vt* : to disorient, to mislead, to confuse — **desorientarse** *vr* : to become disoriented, to lose one's way
desovar *vi* : to spawn
despachar *vt* 1 : to complete, to conclude 2 : to deal with, to take care of, to handle 3 : to dispatch, to send off 4 *fam* : to finish off, to kill 5 : to serve — *vi* : to serve — **despacharse** *vr fam* : to gulp down, to polish off
despacho *nm* 1 : dispatch, shipment 2 OFICINA : office, study
despacio *adv* LENTAMENTE, LENTO : slowly, slow ⟨¡despacio! : take it easy!, easy does it!⟩
despampanante *adj fam* : breathtaking, stunning
desparasitar *vt* : to worm (an animal), to rid of fleas/ticks/lice (etc.)
desparpajo *nm fam* 1 : self-confidence, nerve 2 *CA* : confusion, muddle
desparramar *vt* 1 : to spill, to splatter 2 : to spread, to scatter
despatarrarse *vr* : to sprawl (out)
despavorido, -da *adj* : terrified, horrified
despecho *nm* 1 : spite 2 **a despecho de** : despite, in spite of
despectivo, -va *adj* 1 : contemptuous, disparaging 2 : derogatory, pejorative — **despectivamente** *adv*
despedazar {21} *vt* : to cut to pieces, to tear apart
despedida *nf* 1 : farewell, good-bye 2 **despedida de soltera** : bridal shower
despedir {54} *vt* 1 : to see off, to show out 2 : to dismiss, to fire 3 EMITIR : to

give off, to emit ⟨despedir un olor : to give off an odor⟩ — **despedirse** vr : to take one's leave, to say good-bye

despegado, -da adj **1** : separated, detached **2** : cold, distant

despegar {52} vt : to remove, to detach — vi : to take off, to lift off, to blast off

despegue nm : takeoff, liftoff

despeinar vt **despeinar a alguien** : to mess up someone's hair — **despeinarse** vr ⟨me despeiné : I messed up my hair, my hair got messed up⟩

despejado, -da adj **1** : clear, fair **2** : alert **3** : uncluttered, unobstructed

despejar vt **1** : to clear, to free **2** : to clarify — vi **1** : to clear up **2** : to punt (in sports)

despeje nm **1** : clearing **2** : punt (in sports)

despellejar vt : to skin (an animal)

despelote nm : mess, disaster

despenalizar {21} vt : to legalize — **despenalización** nf

despensa nf **1** : pantry, larder **2** PROVISIONES : provisions pl, supplies pl

despeñadero nm : cliff, precipice

despeñar vt : to hurl down

desperdiciar vt **1** DESAPROVECHAR, MALGASTAR : to waste **2** : to miss, to miss out on

desperdicio nm **1** : waste **2 desperdicios** nmpl RESIDUOS : refuse, scraps, rubbish

desperdigar {52} vt DISPERSAR : to disperse, to scatter

desperezarse {21} vr : to stretch

desperfecto nm **1** DEFECTO : flaw, defect **2** : damage

despertador nm : alarm clock

despertar {55} vi : to awaken, to wake up — vt **1** : to arouse, to wake **2** EVOCAR : to elicit, to evoke — **despertarse** vr : to wake (oneself) up

despiadado, -da adj CRUEL : cruel, merciless, pitiless — **despiadadamente** adv

despido nm : dismissal, layoff

despierto, -ta adj **1** : awake, alert **2** LISTO : clever, sharp ⟨con la mente despierta : with a sharp mind⟩

despilfarrador[1], -dora adj : extravagant, wasteful

despilfarrador[2], -dora n : spendthrift, prodigal

despilfarrar vt MALGASTAR : to squander, to waste

despilfarro nm : extravagance, wastefulness

despintar vt : to strip the paint from — **despintarse** vr : to fade, to wash off, to peel off

despistado[1], -da adj **1** DISTRAÍDO : absentminded, forgetful, scatterbrained **2** CONFUSO : confused, bewildered

despistado[2], -da n : absentminded person

despistar vt : to throw off the track, to confuse — **despistarse** vr

despiste nm **1** : absentmindedness **2** : mistake, slip

desplantador nm : garden trowel

desplante nm : insolence, rudeness

desplazamiento nm **1** : movement, displacement **2** : journey

desplazar {21} vt **1** : to replace, to displace **2** TRASLADAR : to move, to shift **3** : to scroll (in computing) — **desplazarse** vr

desplegar {49} vt **1** : to display, to show, to manifest **2** DESDOBLAR : to unfold, to unfurl **3** : to spread (out) **4** : to deploy

despliegue nm **1** : display **2** : deployment

desplomarse vr **1** : to plummet, to fall **2** DERRUMBARSE : to collapse, to break down

desplome nm **1** : fall, drop **2** : collapse

desplumar vt **1** : to pluck (a chicken, etc.)

despoblación nf, pl **-ciones** : large population decrease

despoblado[1], -da adj : uninhabited, deserted

despoblado[2] nm : open country, deserted area

despoblar {19} vt : to reduce the population of ⟨un lugar despoblado : a deserted place⟩

despojar vt **1** : to strip, to clear **2** : to divest, to deprive — **despojarse** vr **1** ~ **de** : to remove (clothing) **2** ~ **de** : to relinquish, to renounce

despojos nmpl **1** : remains, scraps **2** : plunder, spoils

desportillar vt : to chip — **desportillarse** vr

desposar vt : to marry — **desposarse** vr

desposeer {20} vt : to dispossess

déspota nmf : despot, tyrant

despotismo nm : despotism — **despótico, -ca** adj

despotricar {72} vi : to rant and rave, to complain excessively

despreciable adj **1** : despicable, contemptible **2** : negligible ⟨nada despreciable : not inconsiderable, significant⟩

despreciar vt DESDEÑAR, MENOSPRECIAR : to despise, to scorn, to disdain

despreciativo, -va adj : scornful, disdainful

desprecio nm DESDÉN, MENOSPRECIO : disdain, contempt, scorn

desprender vt **1** SOLTAR : to detach, to loosen, to unfasten **2** EMITIR : to emit, to give off — **desprenderse** vr **1** : to come off, to come undone **2** : to be inferred, to follow **3** ~ **de** : to part with, to get rid of

desprendido, -da adj : generous, unselfish, disinterested

desprendimiento nm **1** : detachment **2** GENEROSIDAD : generosity **3 desprendimiento de tierras** : landslide

despreocupación nf, pl **-ciones** : indifference, lack of concern

despreocupadamente adv : in a carefree, easygoing, or unconcerned way

despreocupado, -da adj : carefree, easygoing, unconcerned

desprestigiar vt DESACREDITAR : to discredit, to disgrace — **desprestigiarse** vr : to lose prestige

desprestigio *nm* DESCRÉDITO : discredit, disrepute

desprevenido, -da *adj* DESAPERCIBIDO : unprepared, off guard, unsuspecting

desprolijo, -ja *adj* : untidy, messy

desproporción *nf, pl* **-ciones** : disproportion, disparity

desproporcionado, -da *adj* : out of proportion

despropósito *nm* : piece of nonsense, absurdity

desprotegido, -da *adj* : unprotected, vulnerable

desprovisto, -ta *adj* ∼ **de** : devoid of, lacking in

después *adv* **1** : afterward, later ⟨mucho después : much later⟩ ⟨me lo dijo después : she told me about it afterward⟩ **2** : then, next ⟨primero uno y después el otro : first one and then the other⟩ ⟨¿que hago después? : what do I do next?⟩ **3** ∼ **de** : after, next after ⟨después de comer : after eating⟩ ⟨después del semáforo : after the stoplight⟩ **4 después (de) que** : after ⟨después que lo acabé : after I finished it⟩ **5 después de todo** : after all **6 poco después** : shortly after, soon thereafter

despuntar, -da *adj* : blunt, dull

despuntar *vt* : to blunt — *vi* **1** : to dawn **2** : to sprout **3** : to excel, to stand out

desquiciado, -da *adj* : crazy

desquiciar *vt* **1** : to unhinge (a door) **2** : to drive crazy — **desquiciarse** *vr* : to go crazy

desquitarse *vr* **1** : to get even, to retaliate **2** ∼ **con** : to take it out on

desquite *nm* : revenge

desregulación *nf, pl* **-ciones** : deregulation

desregular *vt* : to deregulate

desregularización *nf, pl* **-ciones** → **desregulación**

destacadamente *adv* : outstandingly, prominently

destacado, -da *adj* **1** : outstanding, prominent **2** : stationed, posted

destacamento *nm* : detachment (of troops)

destacar {72} *vt* **1** ENFATIZAR, SUBRAYAR : to emphasize, to highlight, to stress ⟨cabe destacar . . . : it's worth mentioning . . .⟩ **2** REALZAR : to highlight, to bring out **3** : to station, to post — *vi* : to stand out — **destacarse** *vr* : to stand out

destajo *nm* **1** : piecework **2 a** ∼ : by the item, by the job

destapacaños *nm Mex* : plunger (for toilets, etc.)

destapador *nm* : bottle opener

destapar *vt* **1** : to open, to take the top off **2** DESCUBRIR : to reveal, to uncover **3** : to unblock, to unclog

destape *nm* : uncovering, revealing

destartalado, -da *adj* : dilapidated, tumbledown

destellar *vi* **1** : to sparkle, to flash, to glint **2** : to twinkle

destello *nm* **1** : flash, sparkle, twinkle **2** : glimmer, hint

destemplado, -da *adj* **1** : out of tune **2** : irritable, out of sorts **3** : unpleasant (of weather)

desteñir {67} *vi* : to run, to fade — **desteñirse** *vr* : to fade

desterrado¹, -da *adj* : banished, exiled

desterrado², -da *n* : exile

desterrar {55} *vt* **1** EXILIAR : to banish, to exile **2** ERRADICAR : to eradicate, to do away with

destetar *vt* : to wean

destiempo *adv* **a** ∼ : at the wrong time

destierro *nm* EXILIO : exile

destilación *nf, pl* **-ciones** : distillation

destilador, -dora *n* : distiller

destilar *vt* **1** : to exude **2** : to distill

destilería *nf* : distillery

destinación *nf, pl* **-ciones** DESTINO : destination

destinado, -da *adj* : destined, bound

destinar *vt* **1** : to appoint, to assign **2** ASIGNAR : to earmark, to allot

destinatario, -ria *n* **1** : addressee **2** : payee

destino *nm* **1** : destiny, fate **2** DESTINACIÓN : destination **3** : use **4** : assignment, post

destitución *nf, pl* **-ciones** : dismissal, removal from office

destituir {41} *vt* : to dismiss, to remove from office

destornillador *nm* : screwdriver

destornillar *vt* : to unscrew

destrabar *vt* **1** : to untie, to undo, to ease up **2** : to separate

destreza *nf* HABILIDAD : dexterity, skill

destronar *vt* : to depose, to dethrone

destrozado, -da *adj* **1** : ruined, destroyed **2** : devastated, brokenhearted

destrozar {21} *vt* **1** : to smash, to shatter **2** : to destroy, to wreck — **destrozarse** *vr*

destrozo *nm* **1** DAÑO : damage **2** : havoc, destruction

destrucción *nf, pl* **-ciones** : destruction

destructivo, -va *adj* : destructive

destructor¹, -tora *adj* : destructive

destructor² *nm* : destroyer (ship)

destruir {41} *vt* : to destroy — **destruirse** *vr*

desubicado, -da *adj* **1** : out of place **2** : confused, disoriented

desunión *nf, pl* **-niones** : lack of unity

desunir *vt* : to split, to divide

desusado, -da *adj* **1** INSÓLITO : unusual **2** OBSOLETO : obsolete, disused, antiquated

desuso *nm* : disuse, obsolescence ⟨caer en desuso : to fall into disuse⟩

desvaído, -da *adj* **1** : pale, washed-out **2** : vague, blurred

desvalido, -da *adj* DESAMPARADO : destitute, helpless

desvalijar *vt* **1** : to ransack **2** : to rob

desvalorización *nf, pl* **-ciones** **1** DEVALUACIÓN : devaluation **2** : depreciation

desvalorizar {21} *vt* : to devalue

desván *nm, pl* **desvanes** ÁTICO, BUHARDILLA : attic

desvanecer {53} *vt* **1** DISIPAR : to make disappear, to dispel **2** : to fade, to blur

— **desvanecerse** *vr* **1** : to vanish, to disappear **2** : to fade **3** DESMAYARSE : to faint, to swoon

desvanecimiento *nm* **1** : disappearance **2** DESMAYO : faint **3** : fading

desvariar {85} *vi* **1** DELIRAR : to be delirious **2** : to rave, to talk nonsense

desvarío *nm* **1** DELIRIO : delirium **2** **desvaríos** *nmpl* : ravings *pl*

desvelado, -da *adj* : sleepless

desvelar *vt* **1** : to keep awake **2** REVELAR : to reveal, to disclose — **desvelarse** *vr* **1** : to stay awake **2** : to do one's utmost

desvelo *nm* **1** : insomnia **2** **desvelos** *nmpl* : efforts, pains

desvencijado, -da *adj* : dilapidated, rickety

desventaja *nf* : disadvantage, drawback

desventajoso, -sa *adj* : disadvantageous, unfavorable

desventura *nf* INFORTUNIO : misfortune

desventurado, -da *adj* : unfortunate, ill-fated

desvergonzado, -da *adj* : shameless, impudent

desvergüenza *nf* : audacity, impudence

desvestir {54} *vt* : to undress — **desvestirse** *vr* : to get undressed

desviación *nf*, *pl* -**ciones** **1** : deviation, departure **2** : detour, diversion

desviar {85} *vt* **1** : to change the course of, to divert **2** : to turn away, to deflect — **desviarse** *vr* **1** : to branch off **2** APARTARSE : to stray

desvinculación *nf*, *pl* -**ciones** : dissociation

desvincular *vt* ~ **de** : to separate from, to dissociate from — **desvincularse** *vr*

desvío *nm* **1** : diversion, detour **2** : deviation

desvirtuar {3} *vt* **1** : to impair, to spoil **2** : to detract from **3** : to distort, to misrepresent

desvivirse *vr* : to be devoted to

detalladamente *adv* : in detail, at great length

detallar *vt* : to detail

detalle *nm* **1** : detail ⟨entrar en detalles : to go into detail⟩ **2** **al detalle** : retail **3** : thoughtful gesture ⟨tener un detalle con alguien : to do something nice for someone⟩

detallista[1] *adj* **1** : meticulous **2** : retail

detallista[2] *nmf* **1** : perfectionist **2** : retailer

detección *nf*, *pl* -**ciones** : detection

detectar *vt* : to detect — **detectable** *adj*

detective *nmf* : detective ⟨detective privado/privada : private detective⟩

detector *nm* : detector ⟨detector de mentiras : lie detector⟩

detención *nf*, *pl* -**ciones** **1** ARRESTO : detention, arrest **2** : stop, halt **3** : delay, holdup

detener {80} *vt* **1** ARRESTAR : to arrest, to detain **2** PARAR : to stop, to halt **3** : to keep, to hold back — **detenerse** *vr* **1** : to stop **2** : to delay, to linger

detenidamente *adv* : thoroughly, at length

detenimiento *nm* **con** ~ : carefully, in detail

detentar *vt* : to hold, to retain

detergente *nm* : detergent

deteriorado, -da *adj* : damaged, worn

deteriorar *vt* ESTROPEAR : to damage, to spoil — **deteriorarse** *vr* **1** : to get damaged, to wear out **2** : to deteriorate, to worsen

deterioro *nm* **1** : deterioration, wear **2** : worsening, decline

determinación *nf*, *pl* -**ciones** **1** : determination, resolve **2** **tomar una determinación** : to make a decision

determinado, -da *adj* **1** : certain, particular **2** : determined, resolute

determinante[1] *adj* : determining, deciding

determinante[2] *nm* : determinant

determinar *vt* **1** : to determine **2** : to cause, to bring about — **determinarse** *vr* : to make up one's mind, to decide

detestar *vt* : to detest — **detestable** *adj*

detonación *nf*, *pl* -**ciones** : detonation

detonador *nm* : detonator

detonante[1] *adj* : detonating, explosive

detonante[2] *nm* **1** → **detonador** **2** : catalyst, cause

detonar *vi* : to detonate, to explode

detractor, -tora *n* : detractor, critic

detrás *adv* **1** : behind ⟨caminábamos detrás : we walked along behind⟩ **2** ~ **de** : in back of, behind **3 por** ~ : from behind, in/at the back

detrimento *nm* : detriment ⟨en detrimento de : to the detriment of⟩

detuvo, etc. → **detener**

deuda *nf* **1** DÉBITO : debt **2** **en deuda con** : indebted to

deudo, -da *n* : relative

deudor[1], -**dora** *adj* : indebted

deudor[2], -**dora** *n* : debtor

devaluación *nf*, *pl* -**ciones** DESVALORIZACIÓN : devaluation

devaluar {3} *vt* : to devalue — **devaluarse** *vr* : to depreciate

devanarse *vr* **devanarse los sesos** : to rack one's brains

devaneo *nm* **1** : flirtation, fling **2** : idle pursuit

devastador, -dora *adj* : devastating

devastar *vt* : to devastate — **devastación** *nf*

develar *vt* **1** REVELAR : to reveal, to uncover **2** : to unveil

devenir {87} *vi* **1** : to come about **2** ~ **en** : to become, to turn into

devoción *nf*, *pl* -**ciones** : devotion

devolución *nf*, *pl* -**ciones** REEMBOLSO : return, refund

devolver {89} *vt* **1** : to return, to give back **2** REEMBOLSAR : to refund, to pay back **3** : to vomit, to bring up — *vi* : to vomit, to throw up — **devolverse** *vr* : to return, to come back, to go back

devorar *vt* **1** : to devour **2** : to consume

devoto[1], -**ta** *adj* : devout — **devotamente** *adv*

devoto[2], -**ta** *n* : devotee, admirer

di → **dar, decir**
día *nm* **1** : day ⟨buenos días : hello, good morning⟩ ⟨todos los días : every day⟩ ⟨todo el día : all day⟩ ⟨un día sí y otro no : every other day⟩ ⟨ocho horas al día : eight hours a day⟩ ⟨día hábil : work-day, business day⟩ ⟨día festivo/feriado : public holiday⟩ ⟨día de pago : payday⟩ ⟨¿qué día es hoy? : what day is today?⟩ ⟨el día 21 de abril : the 21st of April, April 21st⟩ ⟨el día anterior : the previous day, the day before⟩ **2** : daytime, daylight ⟨de día : by day, in the daytime⟩ ⟨en pleno día : in broad daylight⟩ ⟨día y noche : day and night⟩ **3 al día** : up-to-date ⟨ponerse al día con : to get up to date with, to catch up on⟩ ⟨poner al día : to bring up to date, to update⟩ **4 en su día** : in due time **5 hoy (en) día** : nowadays, these days
diabetes *nf* : diabetes
diabético, -ca *adj & n* : diabetic
diablillo *nm* : little devil, imp
diablo *nm* **1** DEMONIO : devil **2 ¿qué diablos . . . ?** : what on earth . . . ?, what the hell . . . ?
diablura *nf* **1** : prank **2 diabluras** *nfpl* : mischief
diabólico, -ca *adj* : diabolical, diabolic, devilish
diaconisa *nf* : deaconess
diácono *nm* : deacon
diacrítico, -ca *adj* : diacritic, diacritical
diadema *nf* : diadem, crown
diáfano, -na *adj* **1** CLARO : clear **2** TRASLÚCIDO : sheer (of fabric), translucent **3** : bright (of a light, room, etc.)
diafragma *nm* : diaphragm
diagnosticar {72} *vt* : to diagnose
diagnóstico[1], -ca *adj* : diagnostic
diagnóstico[2] *nm* : diagnosis
diagonal[1] *adj* : diagonal — **diagonalmente** *adv*
diagonal[2] *nf* **1** : diagonal **2** : slash (punctuation mark)
diagrama *nm* **1** : diagram **2 diagrama de flujo** ORGANIGRAMA : flow chart
dial *nm* : dial (on a radio, etc.)
dialecto *nm* : dialect
dialogar {52} *vi* : to have a talk, to converse
diálogo *nm* : dialogue
diamante *nm* : diamond
diámetro *nm* : diameter
diana *nf* **1** : target, bull's-eye **2 or toque de diana** : reveille
diapasón *nm, pl* **-sones** : tuning fork
diapositiva *nf* : slide, transparency
diariamente *adv* : daily, every day
diario[1] *adv Mex* : every day, daily
diario[2], -ria *adj* **1** : daily, everyday ⟨la vida diaria : everyday life⟩ ⟨ocho horas diarias : eight hours a day⟩ **2 a diario** : every day, daily
diario[3] *nm* **1** : diary **2** PERIÓDICO : newspaper **3 de ~** : everyday
diarrea *nf* : diarrhea
diatriba *nf* : diatribe, tirade
dibujante *nmf* **1** : draftsman *m*, draftswoman *f* **2** CARICATURISTA : cartoonist

dibujar *vt* **1** : to draw, to sketch **2** : to portray, to depict
dibujo *nm* **1** : drawing ⟨dibujo lineal : line drawing⟩ ⟨dibujo a lápiz : pencil drawing⟩ ⟨dibujo a pulso, dibujo a mano alzada : freehand sketch⟩ **2** : design, pattern **3 dibujos animados** : (animated) cartoons
dicción *nf, pl* **-ciones** : diction
diccionario *nm* : dictionary
dícese → **decir**
dicha *nf* **1** SUERTE : good luck **2** FELICIDAD : happiness, joy
dicho[1] *pp* → **decir**
dicho[2], -cha *adj* : said, aforementioned ⟨las personas dichas : the aforementioned people⟩
dicho[3] *nm* DECIR : saying, proverb
dichoso, -sa *adj* **1** : blessed **2** FELIZ : happy **3** AFORTUNADO : fortunate, lucky
diciembre *nm* : December ⟨el primero de diciembre : (on) December first⟩
diciendo → **decir**
dictado *nm* : dictation
dictador, -dora *n* : dictator
dictadura *nf* : dictatorship
dictamen *nm, pl* **dictámenes** **1** : report **2** : judgment, opinion
dictaminar *vt* : to report — *vi* : to give an opinion, to pass judgment
dictar *vt* **1** : to dictate **2** : to pronounce (a judgment) **3** : to give, to deliver (a lecture, etc.)
dictatorial *adj* : dictatorial
didáctico, -ca *adj* : didactic
diecinueve *adj & nm* : nineteen — **diecinueve** *pron*
diecinueveavo[1], -va *adj* : nineteenth
diecinueveavo[2] *nm* : nineteenth (fraction)
dieciocho *adj & nm* : eighteen — **dieciocho** *pron*
dieciochoavo[1], -va *or* **dieciochavo, -va** *adj* : eighteenth
dieciochoavo[2] *or* **dieciochavo** *nm* : eighteenth (fraction)
dieciséis *adj & nm* : sixteen — **dieciséis** *pron*
dieciseisavo[1], -va *adj* : sixteenth
dieciseisavo[2] *nm* : sixteenth (fraction)
diecisiete *adj & nm* : seventeen — **diecisiete** *pron*
diecisieteavo[1], -va *adj* : seventeenth
diecisieteavo[2] *nm* : seventeenth (in a series)
diente *nm* **1** : tooth ⟨diente canino : eyetooth, canine tooth⟩ ⟨cepillarse los dientes : to brush one's teeth⟩ ⟨le están saliendo los dientes : he's teething⟩ **2** : tusk, fang **3** : prong, tine **4** : clove (of garlic) **5 diente de león** : dandelion **6 entre dientes** : under one's breath, quietly ⟨hablar entre dientes : to mutter, to mumble⟩
dieron, etc. → **dar**
diesel [ˈdisɛl] *nm* : diesel
diestra *nf* : right hand
diestro[1], -tra *adj* **1** : right **2** : skillful, accomplished

diestro² *nm* : bullfighter, matador
dieta *nf* : diet
dietético, -ca *adj* : dietary, diet
dietista *nmf* : dietitian
diez¹ *nm, pl* **dieces** : ten ⟨el diez de julio : (on) the tenth of July, (on) July tenth⟩ ⟨un as y dos dieces : an ace and two tens⟩
diez² *adj* : ten ⟨tiene diez años : he's ten (years old)⟩
diez³ *pron* : ten ⟨somos diez : there are ten of us⟩ ⟨son las diez : it's ten o'clock⟩
difamación *nf, pl* **-ciones** : defamation, slander
difamar *vt* : to defame, to slander
difamatorio, -ria *adj* : slanderous, defamatory, libelous
diferencia *nf* **1** : difference ⟨partir la diferencia : to split the difference⟩ **2 a diferencia de** : unlike, in contrast to **3 con ∼** : by far
diferenciación *nf, pl* **-ciones** : differentiation
diferencial *adj & nm* : differential
diferenciar *vt* : to differentiate between, to distinguish — **diferenciarse** *vr* : to differ
diferendo *nm* : dispute, conflict
diferente *adj* DISTINTO : different ⟨diferente a/de : different from⟩ — **diferentemente** *adv*
diferido *adj* **en ∼** ⟨un programa en diferido : a prerecorded program⟩ ⟨transmitir en diferido : to broadcast later⟩
diferir {76} *vt* DILATAR, POSPONER : to postpone, to put off — *vi* : to differ
difícil *adj* : difficult, hard ⟨difícil de describir : hard to describe⟩ ⟨una persona difícil : a difficult person⟩ ⟨lo veo difícil : I think it's unlikely⟩
difícilmente *adv* **1** : with difficulty **2** : hardly
dificultad *nf* : difficulty
dificultar *vt* : to make difficult, to obstruct
dificultoso, -sa *adj* : difficult, hard
difteria *nf* : diphtheria
difuminar *vt* : to blur
difundir *vt* **1** : to diffuse, to spread out **2** : to broadcast, to spread
difunto, -ta *adj & n* FALLECIDO : deceased
difusión *nf, pl* **-siones** **1** : spreading **2** : diffusion (of heat, etc.) **3** : broadcast, broadcasting ⟨los medios de difusión : the media⟩
difuso, -sa *adj* : diffuse, widespread
diga, etc. → **decir**
digerir {76} *vt* : to digest — **digerible** *adj*
digestión *nf, pl* **-tiones** : digestion
digestivo, -va *adj* : digestive
digital¹ *adj* : digital — **digitalmente** *adv*
digital² *nf* DEDALERA : foxglove
digitalizar {21} *vt* : to digitalize
digitaria *nf* : crabgrass
dígito *nm* : digit
dignarse *vr* : to deign, to condescend ⟨no se dignó contestar : he didn't deign to answer⟩
dignatario, -ria *n* : dignitary

dignidad *nf* **1** : dignity **2** : dignitary
dignificar {72} *vt* : to dignify
digno, -na *adj* **1** HONORABLE : honorable **2** : worthy ⟨digno de : worthy of⟩ **3** : decent (of a salary, etc.) — **dignamente** *adv*
digresión *nf, pl* **-ciones** : digression
dije *nm* : charm (on a bracelet)
dijo, etc. → **decir**
dilación *nf, pl* **-ciones** : delay
dilapidar *vt* : to waste, to squander
dilatar *vt* **1** : to dilate, to widen, to expand **2** DIFERIR, POSPONER : to put off, to postpone — **dilatarse** *vr* **1** : to expand (of gases, metals, etc.) **2** *Mex* : to take long, to be long
dilatorio, -ria *adj* : delaying
dilema *nm* : dilemma
diletante *nmf* : dilettante
diligencia *nf* **1** : diligence, care **2** : promptness, speed **3** : action, step **4** : task, errand **5** : stagecoach **6 diligencias** *nfpl* : judicial procedures, formalities
diligente *adj* : diligent — **diligentemente** *adv*
dilucidar *vt* : to elucidate, to clarify
dilución *nf, pl* **-ciones** : dilution
diluir {41} *vt* : to dilute
diluviar *v impers* : to pour (with rain), to pour down
diluvio *nm* **1** : flood **2** : downpour
dimensión *nf, pl* **-siones** : dimension — **dimensional** *adj*
dimensionar *vt* : to measure, to gauge
diminutivo¹, -va *adj* : diminutive
diminutivo² *nm* : diminutive
diminuto, -ta *adj* : minute, tiny
dimisión *nf, pl* **-siones** : resignation
dimitir *vi* : to resign, to step down
dimos → **dar**
dinámica *nf* : dynamics
dinámico, -ca *adj* : dynamic — **dinámicamente** *adv*
dinamismo *nm* : energy, vigor
dinamita *nf* : dynamite
dinamitar *vt* : to dynamite
dínamo *or* **dinamo** *nm* : dynamo
dinastía *nf* : dynasty
dineral *nm* : fortune, large sum of money
dinero *nm* **1** : money ⟨hacer/ganar/recaudar dinero : to make/earn/raise money⟩ **2 dinero de bolsillo** : pocket money **3 dinero contante y sonante** : cold cash, hard cash **4 dinero en efectivo** : cash
dinosaurio *nm* : dinosaur
dintel *nm* : lintel
dio, etc. → **dar**
diócesis *nfs & pl* : diocese
dios, diosa *n* : god, goddess *f*
Dios *nm* : God ⟨gracias a Dios : thank God⟩ ⟨si Dios quiere : God willing⟩ ⟨¡por Dios! : for God's sake!⟩ ⟨¡Dios mío! : good God!⟩ ⟨¡vaya con Dios : for heaven's sake!⟩ ⟨¡Dios me libre! : God/heaven forbid!⟩ ⟨que Dios te bendiga : God bless you⟩ ⟨como Dios manda : proper, properly⟩
dióxido de carbono *nm* : carbon dioxide
diploma *nm* : diploma
diplomacia *nf* : diplomacy

diplomado[1], **-da** *adj* : qualified, trained
diplomado[2] *nm Mex* : seminar
diplomático[1], **-ca** *adj* : diplomatic — **diplomáticamente** *adv*
diplomático[2], **-ca** *n* : diplomat
diptongo *nm* : diphthong
diputación *nf, pl* **-ciones** : deputation, delegation
diputado, -da *n* : delegate, representative
dique *nm* : dike
dirá, etc. → **decir**
dirección *nf, pl* **-ciones 1** : address ⟨dirección particular/electrónica : home/e-mail address⟩ **2** : direction ⟨en dirección a : towards⟩ ⟨en dirección contraria : the opposite direction, the other way⟩ **3** : management, leadership **4** : steering (of an automobile) ⟨dirección asistida : power steering⟩
direccional[1] *adj* : directional
direccional[2] *nf* : directional, turn signal
directa *nf* : high gear
directamente *adv* : straight, directly
directiva *nf* **1** ORDEN : directive **2** DIRECTORIO, JUNTA : board of directors
directivo[1], **-va** *adj* : executive, managerial
directivo[2], **-va** *n* : executive, director
directo, -ta *adj* **1** : direct, straight, immediate **2 en ~** : live (in broadcasting)
director, -tora *n* **1** : director, manager, head **2** : conductor (of an orchestra)
directorial → **directivo**[1]
directorio *nm* **1** : directory **2** DIRECTIVA, JUNTA : board of directors
directriz *nf, pl* **-trices** : guideline
dirigencia *nf* : leaders *pl*, leadership
dirigente[1] *adj* : directing, leading
dirigente[2] *nmf* : director, leader
dirigible *nm* : dirigible, blimp
dirigir {35} *vt* **1** : to run, to manage (a business, etc.), to lead (a group, etc.) **2** : to conduct (music), to direct (a film) **3** : to address (a letter, comment, etc.) **4** : to aim, to point ⟨dirigir la mirada a/hacia : to look at/towards⟩ ⟨dirigir la atención hacia : to turn one's attention to⟩ — **dirigirse** *vr* **~ a 1** : to go towards **2** : to speak to, to address
dirimir *vt* **1** : to resolve, to settle **2** : to annul, to dissolve (a marriage)
discapacidad *nf* MINUSVALÍA : disability, handicap *sometimes offensive*
discapacitado[1], **-da** *adj* : disabled, handicapped *sometimes offensive*
discapacitado[2], **-da** *n* : disabled person, handicapped person *sometimes offensive*
discar {72} *v* : to dial
discernimiento *nm* : discernment
discernir {25} *v* : to discern, to distinguish
disciplina *nf* : discipline
disciplinar *vt* : to discipline — **disciplinario, -ria** *adj*
discípulo, -la *n* : disciple, follower
disc jockey [ˌdiskˈjokeɪ, -ˈdʒo-] *nmf* : disc jockey
disco *nm* **1** : record ⟨parecer un disco rayado : to sound like a broken record⟩ **2** : disc, disk ⟨disco compacto : compact disc⟩ ⟨disco volador : Frisbee *trademark*⟩ **3** : discus

disco duro *nm* **1** : hard disk **2** *or* **unidad de disco duro** : hard drive
discografía *nf* : list of records (by a musician)
díscolo, -la *adj* : unruly, disobedient
disconforme *adj* : in disagreement
discontinuidad *nf* : discontinuity
discontinuo, -nua *adj* : discontinuous
discordancia *nf* DESAVENENCIA : conflict, disagreement
discordante *adj* **1** : discordant **2** : conflicting
discordia *nf* : discord
discoteca *nf* **1** : disco, discotheque **2** *CA, Mex* : record store
discreción *nf, pl* **-ciones** : discretion
discrecional *adj* : discretionary
discrepancia *nf* : discrepancy
discrepar *vi* **1** : to disagree **2** : to differ
discreto, -ta *adj* : discreet — **discretamente** *adv*
discriminación *nf, pl* **-ciones** : discrimination
discriminar *vt* **1** : to discriminate against **2** : to distinguish, to differentiate
discriminatorio, -ria *adj* : discriminatory
disculpa *nf* **1** : apology **2** : excuse
disculpable *adj* : excusable
disculpar *vt* : to excuse, to pardon — **disculparse** *vr* : to apologize
discurrir *vi* **1** : to flow **2** : to pass, to go by **3** : to ponder, to reflect
discurso *nm* **1** ORACIÓN : speech, address **2** : discourse, treatise
discusión *nf, pl* **-siones 1** : discussion **2** ALTERCADO, DISPUTA : argument
discutible *adj* : arguable, debatable
discutidor, -dora *adj* : argumentative
discutir *vt* **1** : to discuss **2** : to dispute — *vi* ALTERCAR : to argue, to quarrel
disecar {72} *vt* **1** : to dissect **2** : to stuff (for preservation)
disección *nf, pl* **-ciones** : dissection
diseminación *nf, pl* **-ciones** : dissemination, spreading
diseminar *vt* : to disseminate, to spread
disensión *nf, pl* **-siones** : dissension, disagreement
disenso *nm* : dissent, disagreement
disentería *nf* : dysentery
disentimiento → **disenso**
disentir {76} *vi* **1** : to dissent, to disagree
diseñador, -dora *n* : designer
diseñar *vt* **1** : to design, to plan **2** : to lay out, to outline
diseño *nm* : design
disertación *nf, pl* **-ciones 1** : lecture, talk **2** : dissertation
disertar *vi* : to lecture, to give a talk
disfraz *nm, pl* **disfraces 1** : disguise **2** : costume **3** : front, pretense
disfrazar {21} *vt* **1** : to disguise **2** : to mask, to conceal — **disfrazarse** *vr* : to wear a costume, to be in disguise
disfrutar *vt* : to enjoy — *vi* : to enjoy oneself, to have a good time
disfrute *nm* : enjoyment
disfunción *nf, pl* **-ciones** : dysfunction — **disfuncional** *adj*

disgregar {52} vt : to break up, to disintegrate — **disgregarse** vr

disgustar vt : to upset, to displease, to make angry ⟨darle un disgusto a alguien : to upset someone⟩ ⟨llevarse un disgusto : to be upset⟩ — **disgustarse** vr

disgusto nm 1 : annoyance, displeasure 2 : argument, quarrel 3 : trouble, misfortune

disidencia nf : dissent

disidente adj & nmf : dissident

disímbolo, -la adj Mex : dissimilar

disímil adj : dissimilar

disimuladamente adv : furtively, slyly

disimulado, -da adj 1 : concealed, disguised 2 : furtive, sly

disimular vt : to dissemble, to pretend — vt : to conceal, to hide

disimulo nm 1 : dissembling, pretense 2 : slyness, furtiveness 3 : tolerance

disipar vt 1 : to dissipate, to dispel 2 : to squander — **disiparse** vr

diskette [di'sket] nm : floppy disk, diskette

dislexia nf : dyslexia — **disléxico, -ca** adj

dislocar {72} vt : to dislocate — **dislocación** nf

disminución nf, pl -ciones : decrease, drop, fall

disminuir {41} vt REDUCIR : to reduce, to decrease, to lower — vi 1 : to lower 2 : to drop, to fall

disociar vt : to dissociate, to separate — **disociación** nf

disolución nf, pl -ciones 1 : dissolution, dissolving 2 : breaking up 3 : dissipation

disoluto, -ta adj : dissolute, dissipated

disolvente nm : solvent

disolver {89} vt 1 : to dissolve 2 : to break up — **disolverse** vr

disonancia nf : dissonance — **disonante** adj

dispar adj 1 : different, disparate 2 DIVERSO : diverse 3 DESIGUAL : inconsistent

disparado, -da adj salir disparado fam : to take off in a hurry, to rush away

disparar vi 1 : to shoot, to fire 2 Mex fam : to pay — vt 1 : to shoot 2 Mex fam : to treat to, to buy — **dispararse** vr : to shoot up, to skyrocket

disparatado, -da adj ABSURDO, RIDÍCULO : absurd, ridiculous, crazy

disparate nm : silliness, stupidity ⟨decir disparates : to talk nonsense⟩

disparejo, -ja adj DESIGUAL : uneven

disparidad nf : disparity

disparo nm TIRO : shot

dispendio nm : wastefulness, extravagance

dispendioso, -sa adj : wasteful, extravagant

dispensa nf : dispensation

dispensador nm : dispenser

dispensar vt 1 : to dispense, to give, to grant 2 EXCUSAR : to excuse, to forgive 3 EXIMIR : to exempt

dispensario nm 1 : dispensary, clinic 2 Mex : dispenser

dispersar vt DESPERDIGAR : to disperse, to scatter

dispersión nf, pl -siones : dispersion

disperso, -sa adj : dispersed, scattered

displicencia nf : indifference, coldness, disdain

displicente adj : indifferent, cold, disdainful

disponer {60} vt 1 : to arrange, to lay out 2 : to stipulate, to order 3 : to prepare — vi ~ de : to have at one's disposal — **disponerse** vr ~ a : to prepare to, to be about to

disponibilidad nf : availability

disponible adj : available

disposición nf, pl -ciones 1 : disposition 2 : aptitude, talent 3 : order, arrangement 4 : willingness, readiness 5 última disposición : last will and testament

dispositivo nm 1 APARATO, MECANISMO : device, mechanism 2 : force, detachment

dispositivo intrauterino nm : intrauterine device, IUD

dispuesto¹ pp → disponer

dispuesto², -ta adj PREPARADO : ready, prepared, disposed

dispuso, etc. → disponer

disputa nf ALTERCADO, DISCUSIÓN : dispute, argument

disputar vi : to argue, to contend, to vie — vt : to dispute, to question — **disputarse** vr : to compete for

disquera nf : record label, recording company

disquete → diskette

disquisición nf, pl -ciones 1 : formal discourse 2 disquisiciones nfpl : digressions

distancia nf 1 : distance ⟨la distancia entre la Tierra y el Sol : the distance between the Earth and the Sun⟩ ⟨está a dos cuadras de distancia : it's two blocks away⟩ 2 : (emotional) distance ⟨guardar/mantener las distancias : to keep one's distance⟩ 3 a ~ : from/at a distance ⟨mando a distancia : remote control⟩

distanciamiento nm 1 : distancing 2 : rift, estrangement

distanciar vt 1 : to space out 2 : to draw apart — **distanciarse** vr : to grow apart, to become estranged

distante adj 1 : distant, far-off 2 : aloof

distar vi ~ de : to be far from ⟨dista de ser perfecto : he is far from perfect⟩

diste → dar

distender {56} vt : to distend, to stretch

distendido, -da adj : relaxed

distensión nf, pl -siones : easing of relations

distinción nf, pl -ciones : distinction

distinguible adj : distinguishable

distinguido, -da adj : distinguished, refined

distinguir {26} vt 1 : to distinguish 2 : to honor 3 : to characterize — **distinguirse** vr

distintivo, -va adj : distinctive — **distintivamente** adv

distinto, -ta *adj* 1 DIFERENTE : different ⟨distinto de/a : different from/than⟩ 2 CLARO : distinct, clear, evident 3 distintos, -tas *pl* : various
distorsión *nf, pl* -siones : distortion
distorsionar *vt* : to distort
distracción *nf, pl* -ciones 1 : distraction, amusement 2 : forgetfulness 3 : oversight
distraer {81} *vt* 1 : to distract 2 ENTRETENER : to entertain, to amuse — distraerse *vr* 1 : to get distracted 2 : to amuse oneself
distraídamente *adv* : absentmindedly
distraído¹ *pp* → distraer
distraído², -da *adj* 1 : distracted, preoccupied 2 DESPISTADO : absentminded
distribución *nf, pl* -ciones : distribution
distribuidor, -dora *n* : distributor
distribuir {41} *vt* : to distribute
distributivo, -va *adj* : distributive
distrital *adj* : district, of the district
distrito *nm* : district
distrofia *nf* : dystrophy ⟨distrofia muscular : muscular dystrophy⟩
disturbio *nm* : disturbance
disuadir *vt* : to dissuade, to discourage
disuasión *nf, pl* -siones : deterrence
disuasivo, -va *adj* : deterrent, discouraging
disuasorio, -ria *adj* : discouraging
disuelto *pp* → disolver
disyuntiva *nf* : dilemma
DIU ['diu] *nm* (*dispositivo intrauterino*) : IUD, intrauterine device
diurno, -na *adj* : day, daytime
diva *nf* → divo
divagar {52} *vi* : to digress
diván *nm, pl* divanes : divan
divergencia *nf* : divergence, difference
divergente *adj* : divergent, differing
divergir {35} *vi* 1 : to diverge 2 : to differ, to disagree
diversidad *nf* : diversity, variety
diversificación *nf, pl* -ciones : diversification
diversificar {72} *vt* : to diversify
diversión *nf, pl* -siones ENTRETENIMIENTO : fun, amusement, diversion
diverso, -sa *adj* : diverse, various ⟨opiniones diversas : diverse opinions⟩ ⟨de diverso(s) tipo(s) : of various kinds⟩
divertido, -da *adj* 1 : amusing, funny 2 : entertaining, enjoyable
divertir {76} *vt* ENTRETENER : to amuse, to entertain — divertirse *vr* : to have fun, to have a good time
dividendo *nm* : dividend
dividir *vt* 1 : to divide, to split 2 : to distribute, to share out — dividirse *vr*
divinidad *nf* : divinity
divino, -na *adj* : divine
divisa *nf* 1 : currency 2 LEMA : motto 3 : emblem, insignia
divisar *vt* : to discern, to make out
divisible *adj* : divisible
división *nf, pl* -siones : division
divisivo, -va *adj* : divisive
divisor *nm* : denominator
divisorio, -ria *adj* : dividing

divo, -va *n* 1 : prima donna 2 : celebrity, star
divorciado¹, -da *adj* 1 : divorced 2 : split, divided
divorciado², -da *n* : divorcé *m*, divorcée *f*
divorciar *vt* : to divorce — divorciarse *vr* : to get a divorce
divorcio *nm* : divorce
divulgación *nf, pl* -ciones 1 : spreading, dissemination 2 : popularizing
divulgar {52} *vt* 1 : to spread, to circulate 2 REVELAR : to divulge, to reveal 3 : to popularize — divulgarse *vr*
dizque *adv* : supposedly, apparently
do *nm* 1 : C ⟨do sostenido/bemol : C sharp/flat⟩ 2 : do (in singing)
dobladillo *nm* : hem
doblado, -da *adj* 1 : folded 2 : dubbed
doblaje *nm* : dubbing
doblar *vt* 1 : to double 2 PLEGAR : to fold, to bend 3 : to turn ⟨doblar la esquina : to turn the corner⟩ 4 : to dub — *vi* 1 : to turn 2 : to toll, to ring — doblarse *vr* 1 : to fold up, to double over 2 : to give in, to yield
doble¹ *adj* : double ⟨doble el número de : double the number of⟩ ⟨doble sentido : double meaning⟩ — doblemente *adv*
doble² *nm* 1 : double 2 : toll (of a bell), knell
doble³ *nmf* : stand-in, double
doblegar {52} *vt* 1 : to fold, to crease 2 : to force to yield — doblegarse *vr* : to yield, to bow
doble uve *nf Spain* → ve doble
doble ve → ve doble
doblez¹ *nm, pl* dobleces : fold, crease
doblez² *nmf* : duplicity, deceitfulness
doce *adj & nm* : twelve — doce *pron*
doceavo¹, -va *adj* : twelfth
doceavo² *nm* : twelfth (fraction)
docena *nf* 1 : dozen 2 docena de fraile : baker's dozen
docencia *nf* : teaching
docente¹ *adj* : educational, teaching
docente² *n* : teacher, lecturer
dócil *adj* : docile — dócilmente *adv*
docilidad *nf* : meekness
docto, -ta *adj* : learned, erudite
doctor, -tora *n* : doctor ⟨doctor en pedagogía : doctor of education⟩
doctorado *nm* : doctorate
doctorarse *vr* : to earn one's doctorate
doctrina *nf* : doctrine — doctrinal *adj*
documentación *nf, pl* -ciones : documentation
documental *adj & nm* : documentary
documentar *vt* : to document
documento *nm* : document
dogma *nm* : dogma
dogmático, -ca *adj* : dogmatic
dogmatismo *nm* : dogmatism
doguillo *nm* : pug (dog)
dólar *nm* : dollar
dolencia *nf* : ailment, malaise
doler {47} *vi* 1 : to hurt, to ache ⟨me duele la cabeza : my head hurts⟩ ⟨no duele nada : it doesn't hurt at all⟩ 2 : to grieve — dolerse *vr* 1 : to be distressed 2 : to complain

doliente *nmf* : mourner, bereaved

dolor *nm* **1** : pain, ache ⟨dolor de cabeza/muelas/espalda : headache/toothache/backache⟩ **2** PENA, TRISTEZA : grief, sorrow

dolorido, -da *adj* **1** : sore, aching : hurt, upset

doloroso, -sa *adj* **1** : painful **2** : distressing — **dolorosamente** *adv*

doloso, -sa *adj* : fraudulent — **dolosamente** *adv*

domador, -dora *n* : tamer

domar *vt* : to tame, to break in

domesticado, -da *adj* : domesticated, tame

domésticamente *adv* : domestically

domesticar {72} *vt* : to domesticate, to tame

doméstico, -ca *adj* : domestic, household

domiciliado, -da *adj* : residing

domiciliario, -ria *adj* **1** : home **2 arresto domiciliario** : house arrest

domiciliarse *vr* RESIDIR : to reside

domicilio *nm* : home, residence ⟨cambio de domicilio : change of address⟩

dominación *nf*, *pl* **-ciones** : domination

dominante *adj* **1** : dominant **2** : domineering

dominar *vt* **1** : to dominate **2** : to master, to be proficient at **3** : to overlook, to offer a view of — *vi* : to predominate, to prevail — **dominarse** *vr* : to control oneself

domingo *nm* : Sunday ⟨el domingo : on Sunday⟩ ⟨Domingo de Pascua/Resurrección : Easter Sunday⟩

dominical *adj* : Sunday ⟨periódico dominical : Sunday newspaper⟩

dominicano, -na *adj* & *n* : Dominican

dominico, -ca *adj* & *n* : Dominican (in religion)

dominio *nm* **1** : dominion, power ⟨dominio de/sobre sí mismo : self-control⟩ **2** : mastery **3** : domain, field

dominó *nm*, *pl* **-nós** **1** : domino (tile) **2** : dominoes *pl* (game)

domo *nm* : dome

don¹ *nm* **1** : gift, present **2** : talent, gift ⟨don de gente(s)/mando : people/leadership skills⟩ ⟨tener el don de la palabra : to have a way with words⟩

don² *nm* **1** : title of courtesy preceding a man's first name **2 don nadie** : nobody, insignificant person

dona *nf Mex* : doughnut, donut

donación *nf*, *pl* **-ciones** : donation

donador, -dora *n* : donor

donaire *nm* **1** GARBO : grace, poise **2** : witticism

donante *nf* → **donador**

donar *vt* : to donate

donativo *nm* : donation

doncella *nf* : maiden, damsel

donde¹ *conj* : where ⟨el pueblo donde vivo : the town where I live⟩ ⟨el lugar de donde viene : the place that/where he comes from⟩ ⟨regresamos por donde venimos : we went back the way we came⟩

donde² *prep* : over by ⟨lo encontré donde la silla : I found it over by the chair⟩

dónde *adv* : where ⟨¿dónde está su casa? : where is your house?⟩ ⟨¿de dónde eres? : where are you from?⟩ ⟨no sé por dónde empezar : I don't know where to begin⟩

dondequiera *adv* **1** : anywhere, no matter where **2 dondequiera que** : wherever, everywhere

donqueo *nm* : slam dunk

doña *nf* : title of courtesy preceding a woman's first name

dopado, -da *adj* : drugged

dopar *vt* : to drug, to dope — **doparse** *vr*

doping *nm* : doping (in sports)

doquier *adv* por ∼ : everywhere, all over

dorado¹, -da *adj* : gold, golden

dorado², -da *nm* : gilt

dorar *vt* **1** : to gild **2** : to brown (food)

dormido, -da *adj* **1** : asleep **2** : numb ⟨tiene el pie dormido : her foot's numb, her foot's gone to sleep⟩

dormilón, -lona *n*, *mpl* **-lones** : late riser

dormir {27} *vi* : to sleep — *vt* **1** : to put to sleep/bed **2** : to put to sleep (from boredom, etc.) **3** ANESTESIAR : to put to sleep, to anesthetize **4 dormir la siesta** : to have a nap — **dormirse** *vr* : to fall asleep

dormitar *vi* : to snooze, to doze

dormitorio *nm* **1** : bedroom **2** : dormitory

dorsal¹ *adj* : dorsal

dorsal² *nm* : number (worn in sports)

dorso *nm* **1** : back ⟨el dorso de la mano : the back of the hand⟩ **2** *or* **estilo dorso** *Mex* : backstroke

dos¹ *adj* & *nm* : two ⟨ella tiene dos años : she's two (years old)⟩ ⟨el dos de junio : (on) the second of June, (on) June second⟩

dos² *pron* : two ⟨somos dos : there are two of us⟩ ⟨ya somos dos : that makes two of us⟩ ⟨son las dos de la tarde : it's two o'clock in the afternoon⟩

doscientos¹, -tas *adj* & *pron* : two hundred

doscientos² *nms* & *pl* : two hundred (in a series)

dosel *nm* : canopy

dosificación *nf*, *pl* **-ciones** : dosage

dosificar {72} *vt* **1** : to dose **2** : to use sparingly

dosis *nfs* & *pl* **1** : dose **2** : amount, quantity

dossier *nm* : dossier

dotación *nf*, *pl* **-ciones** **1** : endowment, funding **2** : staff, personnel

dotado, -da *adj* **1** : gifted **2** ∼ **de** : endowed with, equipped with

dotar *vt* **1** : to provide, to equip **2** : to endow

dote *nf* **1** : dowry **2 dotes** *nfpl* : talent, gift

doy → **dar**

draga *nf* : dredge

dragado *nm* : dredging

dragar {52} *vt* : to dredge

dragón *nm*, *pl* **dragones** **1** : dragon **2** : snapdragon

drague, etc. → **dragar**

drama *nm* : drama
dramático, -ca *adj* : dramatic — **dramáticamente** *adv*
dramatizar {21} *vt* : to dramatize — **dramatización** *nf*
dramaturgo, -ga *n* : dramatist, playwright
drástico, -ca *adj* : drastic — **drásticamente** *adv*
drenaje *nm* : drainage
drenar *vt* : to drain
drene *nm Mex* : drain
driblar *vi* : to dribble (in basketball)
drible *nm* : dribble (in basketball)
droga *nf* : drug
drogadicción *nf, pl* **-ciones** : drug addiction
drogadicto, -ta *n* : drug addict
drogar {52} *vt* : to drug — **drogarse** *vr* : to take drugs
drogodependiente *nmf* : drug addict
drogue, etc. → drogar
droguería *nf* FARMACIA : drugstore
dromedario *nm* : dromedary
dual *adj* : dual
dualidad *nf* : duality
dualismo *nm* : dualism
ducha *nf* : shower ⟨darse una ducha : to take a shower⟩
ducharse *vr* : to take a shower
ducho, -cha *adj* : experienced, skilled, expert
ducto *nm* 1 : duct, shaft 2 : pipeline
duda *nf* 1 : doubt ⟨no cabe duda : there's no doubt about it⟩ ⟨no tengo ninguna duda que . . . : I have no doubt that . . .⟩ ⟨si tienes alguna duda . . . : if you have any questions . . .⟩ ⟨poner algo en duda : to call something into question⟩ ⟨salir de dudas : to set one's mind at ease⟩ ⟨sin sombra de duda : beyond the shadow of a doubt⟩ 2 sin ～ : undoubtedly, without a doubt, no doubt
dudar *vt* : to doubt ⟨lo dudo mucho : I doubt that very much⟩ — *vi* ～ **en** : to hesitate to ⟨no dudes en pedirme ayuda : don't hesitate to ask me for help⟩
dudoso, -sa *adj* 1 : doubtful 2 : dubious, questionable — **dudosamente** *adv*
duela *nf Mex* : floorboard
duele, etc. → doler
duelo *nm* 1 : duel 2 LUTO : mourning

duende *nm* 1 : elf, goblin 2 ENCANTO : magic, charm ⟨una bailarina que tiene duende : a dancer with a certain magic⟩
dueño, -ña *n* 1 : owner, proprietor 2 : landlord, landlady *f*
duerme, etc. → dormir
dueto *nm* : duet
dulce[1] *adv* : sweetly, softly
dulce[2] *adj* 1 : sweet 2 : mild, gentle, mellow — **dulcemente** *adv*
dulce[3] *nm* : candy, sweet
dulcería *nf* : candy store
dulcificar {72} *vt* : to sweeten
dulzura *nf* 1 : sweetness 2 : gentleness, mellowness
duna *nf* : dune
dúo *nm* : duo, duet
duodécimo[1], **-ma** *adj* : twelfth
duodécimo[2], **-ma** *nm* : twelfth (in a series)
dúplex *nms & pl* : duplex apartment
duplicación *nf, pl* **-ciones** : duplication, copying
duplicado *nm* : duplicate, copy
duplicar {72} *vt* 1 : to double 2 : to duplicate, to copy
duplicidad *nf* : duplicity
duque *nm* : duke
duquesa *nf* : duchess
durabilidad *nf* : durability
durable → duradero
duración *nf, pl* **-ciones** : duration, length
duradero, -ra *adj* : durable, lasting
duramente *adv* 1 : harshly, severely 2 : hard
durante *prep* : during ⟨durante todo el día : all day long⟩ ⟨trabajó durante tres horas : he worked for three hours⟩
durar *v* : to last
durazno *nm* 1 : peach 2 : peach tree
dureza *nf* 1 : hardness, toughness 2 : severity, harshness
durmiente[1] *adj* : sleeping
durmiente[2] *nmf* : sleeper
durmió, etc. → dormir
duro[1] *adv* : hard ⟨trabajé tan duro : I worked so hard⟩
duro[2], **-ra** *adj* 1 FIRME : hard (of a surface, etc.), tough (of meat) 2 DIFÍCIL : hard, tough 3 : harsh, severe ⟨no seas tan duro con él : don't be so hard on him⟩
DVD *nm* : DVD

E

e[1] *nf* : sixth letter of the Spanish alphabet
e[2] *conj* (*used instead of* y *before words beginning with* i- *or* hi-) : and
ebanista *nmf* : cabinetmaker
ébano *nm* : ebony
e-book ['ibuk] *nm, pl* **e-books** : e-book, electronic book
ebriedad *nf* EMBRIAGUEZ : inebriation, drunkenness
ebrio, -bria *adj* EMBRIAGADO : inebriated, drunk
ebullición *nf, pl* **-ciones** : boiling

eccema → eczema
eccéntrico → excéntrico
echar *vt* 1 LANZAR : to throw, to toss (a coin), to cast (an anchor, a net) ⟨lo echó a la basura : she threw it away⟩ ⟨echar la cabeza hacia atrás : to throw one's head back⟩ 2 : to throw out (of a place), to expel (from school) ⟨me echaron de la casa : they threw me out of the house⟩ 3 DESPEDIR : to fire, to dismiss 4 EMITIR : to emit, to give off 5 BROTAR : to sprout 6 : to put in, to add 7 : to take,

to have (a look) **8** : to mail **9** : to pour **10** : to give (a blessing, etc.), to put (a curse) on **11** : to turn (a key), to slide (a bolt) ⟨echarle (la) llave (a la puerta) : to lock the door⟩ **12 echar abajo** : to demolish **13 echar a perder** : to spoil, to ruin **14 echar de menos** : to miss ⟨echan de menos a su madre : they miss their mother⟩ — *vi* **1** : to start off **2** ~ **a** : to begin to ⟨se echó a llorar : he began to cry⟩ — **echarse** *vr* **1** : to throw oneself ⟨se echó en sus brazos : she threw herself into his arms⟩ **2** : to lie down **3** : to put on **4** ~ **a** : to begin to **5 echarse a perder** : to go bad, to spoil **6 echárselas de** : to pose as

ecléctico, -ca *adj* : eclectic

eclesiástico¹, -ca *adj* : ecclesiastical, ecclesiastic

eclesiástico² *nm* CLÉRIGO : cleric, clergyman

eclipsar *vt* **1** : to eclipse **2** : to outshine, to surpass

eclipse *nm* : eclipse

eco *nm* **1** : echo **2 hacerse eco de** : to echo, to repeat

eco- *pref* : eco-

ecografía *nf* : ultrasound scanning

ecología *nf* : ecology

ecológico, -ca *adj* : ecological — **ecológicamente** *adv*

ecologismo *nm* : environmentalism

ecologista *nmf* : ecologist, environmentalist

ecólogo, -ga *n* : ecologist

economía *nf* **1** : economy **2** : economics

económicamente *adv* : financially

económico, -ca *adj* : economic, economical

economista *nmf* : economist

economizar {21} *vt* : to save, to economize on — *vi* : to save money, to be frugal

ecosistema *nm* : ecosystem

ecoturismo *nm* : ecotourism — **ecoturístico, -ca** *adj*

ecuación *nf, pl* **-ciones** : equation

ecuador *nm* : equator

ecuánime *adj* **1** : even-tempered **2** : impartial

ecuanimidad *nf* **1** : equanimity **2** : impartiality

ecuatorial *adj* : equatorial

ecuatoriano, -na *adj & n* : Ecuadorian

ecuestre *adj* : equestrian

ecuménico, -ca *adj* : ecumenical

eczema *nm* : eczema

edad *nf* **1** : age ⟨¿qué edad tiene? : how old is she?⟩ ⟨tiene 20 años de edad : she is 20 years old⟩ ⟨ser mayor de edad : to be of age⟩ ⟨ser menor de edad : to be a minor, to be underage⟩ ⟨una persona de edad : an elderly person⟩ ⟨desde temprana edad : from an early age⟩ **2** : age, epoch, era ⟨la edad media : the Middle Ages⟩ ⟨la edad de oro/bronce : the Golden/Bronze Age⟩

edamame *nm* : edamame

edecán *nm, pl* **-canes** : aide, assistant

edema *nm* : edema

Edén *nm, pl* **Edenes** : Eden, paradise

edición *nf, pl* **-ciones** **1** : edition **2** : publication, publishing

edicto *nm* : edict, proclamation

edificación *nf, pl* **-ciones** **1** : edification **2** : construction, building

edificar {72} *vt* **1** : to edify **2** CONSTRUIR : to build, to construct

edificio *nm* : building, edifice

edil, edila *n* : councillor, councilman *m*, councilwoman *f*

editar *vt* **1** : to edit **2** PUBLICAR : to publish

editor¹, -tora *adj* : publishing ⟨casa editora : publishing house⟩

editor², -tora *n* **1** : editor **2** : publisher

editor³ *nm* : editor (software)

editora *nf* : publisher, publishing company

editorial¹ *adj* **1** : publishing **2** : editorial

editorial² *nm* : editorial

editorial³ *nf* : publishing house

edredón *nm, pl* **-dones** COBERTOR, COLCHA : comforter, eiderdown, quilt

educación *nf, pl* **-ciones** **1** ENSEÑANZA : education ⟨educación primaria/secundaria/superior : primary/secondary/higher education⟩ **2** : manners *pl* ⟨es de mala educación : it's bad manners⟩ — **educacional** *adj*

educado, -da *adj* : polite, well-mannered

educador, -dora *n* : educator

educando, -da *n* ALUMNO, PUPILO : pupil, student

educar {72} *vt* **1** : to educate **2** CRIAR : to bring up, to raise **3** : to train — **educarse** *vr* : to be educated

educativo, -va *adj* : educational

efe *nf* : (letter) f

efectista *adj* : dramatic, sensational

efectivamente *adv* : really, actually

efectividad *nf* : effectiveness

efectivo¹, -va *adj* **1** : effective **2** : real, actual **3** : permanent, regular (of employment)

efectivo² *nm* : cash

efecto *nm* **1** : effect ⟨tener efecto : to take effect⟩ ⟨surtir efecto, producir un efecto : to have an effect⟩ ⟨bajo los efectos del alcohol : under the influence of alcohol⟩ **2 en** ~ : actually, in fact **3 efecto dominó** : domino effect **4 efecto secundario** : side effect **5 efectos** *nmpl* : goods, property ⟨efectos personales : personal effects⟩ **6 efectos** *nmpl* : effects ⟨efectos especiales : special effects⟩ ⟨efectos de sonido : sound effects⟩

efeméride *nf* : major event

efectuar {3} *vt* : to carry out, to bring about

efervescencia *nf* : effervescence — **efervescente** *adj*

eficacia *nf* **1** : effectiveness, efficacy **2** : efficiency

eficaz *adj, pl* **-caces** **1** : effective **2** EFICIENTE : efficient — **eficazmente** *adv*

eficiencia *nf* : efficiency

eficiente *adj* EFICAZ : efficient — **eficientemente** *adv*

eficientizar {21} *vt Mex* : to streamline, to make more efficient
efigie *nf* : effigy
efímera *nf* : mayfly
efímero, -ra *adj* : ephemeral
efluentes *nmpl* : effluent(s), (liquid) waste
efusión *nf*, *pl* **-siones 1** : warmth, effusiveness **2 con ~** : effusively
efusivo, -va *adj* : effusive — **efusivamente** *adv*
egipcio, -cia *adj & n* : Egyptian
eglefino *nm* : haddock
ego *nm* : ego
egocéntrico, -ca *adj* : egocentric, self-centered
egoísmo *nm* : selfishness, egoism
egoísta[1] *adj* : selfish, egoistic
egoísta[2] *nmf* : egoist, selfish person
egotismo *nm* : egotism, conceit
egotista[1] *adj* : egotistic, egotistical, conceited
egotista[2] *nmf* : egotist, conceited person
egresado, -da *n* : graduate
egresar *vi* : to graduate
egreso *nm* **1** : graduation **2 ingresos y egresos** : income and expenditure
eh *interj* **1** : hey! **2** : eh?, huh?
eje *nm* **1** : axle **2** : axis
ejecución *nf*, *pl* **-ciones** : execution
ejecutante *nmf* : performer
ejecutar *vt* **1** : to execute, to put to death **2** : to carry out, to perform
ejecutivo, -va *adj & n* : executive
ejecutor, -tora *n* : executor
ejem *interj* : ahem!
ejemplar[1] *adj* : exemplary, model
ejemplar[2] *nm* **1** : copy (of a book, magazine, etc.) **2** : specimen, example
ejemplificar {72} *vt* : to exemplify, to illustrate
ejemplo *nm* **1** : example **2 por ~** : for example **3 dar ejemplo** : to set an example
ejercer {86} *vi* **~ de** : to practice as, to work as — *vt* **1** : to practice **2** : exercise (a right) **3** : to exert
ejercicio *nm* **1** : exercise **2** : practice
ejercitar *vt* **1** : to exercise **2** ADIESTRAR : to drill, to train
ejército *nm* : army
ejidal *adj Mex* : cooperative
ejidatario, -ria *n Mex* : member of a cooperative
ejido *nm* **1** : common land **2** *Mex* : cooperative
ejote *nm Mex* : green bean
el[1] *pron (referring to masculine nouns)* **1** : the one ⟨me gusta el verde : I like the green one⟩ ⟨el de la camisa roja : the one with the red shirt⟩ ⟨mi papá y el tuyo : my dad and yours⟩ ⟨el partido de ayer y el de hoy : yesterday's game and today's⟩ **2 el que** : the one that/who, whoever, he who ⟨el que vino ayer : the one who came yesterday⟩ ⟨el que compré : the one (that) I bought⟩ ⟨el que gane : whoever wins⟩ ⟨el que trabaja duro estará contento : he who works hard will be happy⟩

el[2], **la** *art*, *pl* **los, las** : the ⟨los niños están en la casa : the boys/children are in the house⟩ ⟨me duele el pie : my foot hurts⟩ ⟨¿te gusta el té? : do you like tea?⟩ ⟨los gatos son inteligentes : cats are intelligent⟩ ⟨el lago Titicaca : Lake Titicaca⟩ ⟨llamó el señor Núñez : Mr. Núñez called⟩ ⟨viene el lunes : he's coming on Monday⟩ ⟨son las dos : it's two o'clock⟩ ⟨el cinco por ciento : five percent⟩ ⟨un dólar la docena : a dollar a dozen⟩
él *pron* : he, him ⟨él es mi amigo : he's my friend⟩ ⟨un amigo de él : a friend of his⟩ ⟨a él no le interesa : it doesn't interest him⟩ ⟨hablaremos con él : we will speak with him⟩
elaboración *nf*, *pl* **-ciones 1** PRODUCCIÓN : production, making **2** : preparation, devising
elaborado, -da *adj* : elaborate
elaborar *vt* **1** : to make, to produce **2** : to devise, to draw up
elasticidad *nf* : elasticity
elástico[1], **-ca** *adj* **1** FLEXIBLE : flexible **2** : elastic
elástico[2] *nm* **1** : elastic (material) **2** : rubber band
elastizado, -da *adj* : elastic
ele *nf* : (letter) l
elección *nf*, *pl* **-ciones 1** SELECCIÓN : choice, selection **2** : election
electivo, -va *adj* : elective
electo, -ta *adj* : elect ⟨el presidente electo : the president-elect⟩
elector, -tora *n* : voter
electorado *nm* : electorate
electoral *adj* : electoral, election
electricidad *nf* : electricity
electricista *nmf* : electrician
eléctrico, -ca *adj* : electric, electrical
electrificar {72} *vt* : to electrify — **electrificación** *nf*
electrizar {21} *vt* : to electrify, to thrill — **electrizante** *adj*
electrocardiógrafo *nm* : electrocardiograph
electrocardiograma *nm* : electrocardiogram
electrocutar *vt* : to electrocute — **electrocución** *nf*
electrodo *nm* : electrode
electrodoméstico *nm* : electric appliance
electroimán *nm*, *pl* **-manes** : electromagnet
electrólisis *nfs & pl* : electrolysis
electrólito *nm* : electrolyte
electromagnético, -ca *adj* : electromagnetic
electromagnetismo *nm* : electromagnetism
electrón *nm*, *pl* **-trones** : electron
electrónica *nf* : electronics
electrónico, -ca *adj* : electronic, electronics — **electrónicamente** *adv*
elefante, -ta *n* : elephant
elegancia *nf* : elegance
elegante *adj* : elegant, smart — **elegantemente** *adv*
elegía *nf* : elegy
elegíaco, -ca *adj* : elegiac

elegible *adj* : eligible — **elegibilidad** *nf*

elegido, -da *adj* **1** : chosen, selected **2** : elected

elegir {28} *vt* **1** ESCOGER, SELECCIONAR : to choose, to select **2** : to elect

elemental *adj* **1** : elementary, basic **2** : fundamental, essential

elemento *nm* : element

elenco *nm* : cast (of actors)

elevación *nf, pl* **-ciones** : elevation, height

elevado, -da *adj* **1** : elevated, lofty **2** : high

elevador *nm* ASCENSOR : elevator

elevar *vt* **1** ALZAR : to raise, to lift **2** AUMENTAR : to raise, to increase **3** : to elevate (in a hierarchy), to promote **4** : to present, to submit — **elevarse** *vr* : to rise

elfo *nm* : elf

eliminación *nf, pl* **-ciones** : elimination, removal

eliminar *vt* **1** : to eliminate, to remove **2** : to do in, to kill

eliminatoria *nf* : qualifying round (in a competition)

eliminatorio, -ria *adj* : qualifying

elipse *nf* : ellipse

elipsis *nf* : ellipsis

elíptico, -ca *adj* : elliptical, elliptic

elite *or* **élite** *nf* : elite

elitista *adj & nmf* : elitist

elixir *or* **elíxir** *nm* : elixir

ella *pron* : she, her ⟨ella es mi amiga : she is my friend⟩ ⟨un amigo de ella : a friend of hers⟩ ⟨a ella no le interesa : it doesn't interest her⟩ ⟨nos fuimos con ella : we left with her⟩

ello *pron* : it ⟨es por ello que me voy : that's why I'm going⟩

ellos, ellas *pron pl* **1** : they, them ⟨ellas son mis hermanas : they're my sisters⟩ ⟨un amigo de ellos : a friend of theirs⟩ ⟨a ellos no les interesa : it doesn't interest them⟩ ⟨fuimos con ellos : we went with them⟩ **2 de ellos, de ellas** : theirs

elocución *nf, pl* **-ciones** : elocution

elocuencia *nf* : eloquence

elocuente *adj* : eloquent — **elocuentemente** *adv*

elogiar *vt* ENCOMIAR : to praise

elogio *nm* : praise

elote *nm* **1** *Mex* : corn, maize **2** *CA, Mex* : corncob

elucidación *nf, pl* **-ciones** ESCLARECIMIENTO : elucidation

elucidar *vt* ESCLARECER : to elucidate

eludir *vt* EVADIR : to evade, to avoid, to elude

em- → **en-**

email ['imeil] *nm, pl* **emails** : e-mail ⟨enviar algo por email : to e-mail something⟩

emanación *nf, pl* **-ciones** : emanation

emanar *vi* ~ **de** : to emanate from — *vt* : to exude

emancipar *vt* : to emancipate — **emancipación** *nf*

embadurnar *vt* EMBARRAR : to smear, to daub

embajada *nf* : embassy

embajador, -dora *n* : ambassador

embalaje *nm* : packing, packaging

embalar *vt* EMPAQUETAR : to pack

embaldosar *vt* : to tile, to pave with tiles

embalsamar *vt* : to embalm

embalse *nm* : dam, reservoir

embarazada¹ *adj* ENCINTA, PREÑADA : pregnant, expecting

embarazada² *nf* : pregnant woman

embarazar {21} *vt* **1** : to obstruct, to hamper **2** PREÑAR : to make pregnant

embarazo *nm* **1** : pregnancy **2** IMPEDIMENTO : obstacle, obstruction **3** VERGÜENZA : embarrassment

embarazoso, -sa *adj* : embarrassing, awkward

embarcación *nf, pl* **-ciones** : boat, craft

embarcadero *nm* : wharf, pier, jetty

embarcar {72} *vi* : to embark, to board — *vt* : to load

embarco *nm* : embarkation

embargar {52} *vt* **1** : to seize, to impound **2** : to overwhelm

embargo *nm* **1** : seizure **2** : embargo **3** **sin** ~ : however, nevertheless

embarque *nm* **1** : embarkation **2** : shipment

embarrancar {72} *vi* **1** : to run aground **2** : to get bogged down

embarrar *vt* **1** : to cover with mud **2** EMBADURNAR : to smear

embaucador, -dora *n* : swindler, deceiver

embaucar {72} *vt* : to trick, to swindle

embeber *vt* : to absorb, to soak up — *vi* : to shrink

embelesado, -da *adj* : spellbound

embelesar *vt* : to enchant, to captivate

embellecer {53} *vt* : to embellish, to beautify

embellecimiento *nm* : beautification, embellishment

embestida *nf* **1** : charge (of a bull) **2** ARREMETIDA : attack, onslaught

embestir {54} *vt* : to hit, to run into, to charge at — *vi* ARREMETER : to charge, to attack

emblanquecer {53} *vt* BLANQUEAR : to bleach, to whiten — **emblanquecerse** *vr* : to turn white

emblema *nm* : emblem

emblemático, -ca *adj* : emblematic

embobado, -da *adj* **1** : captivated, spellbound **2** : dazed

embolar *vt* *Col* : to polish (shoes)

embolia *nf* : embolism

émbolo *nm* : piston

embolsarse *vr* **1** : to pocket (money) **2** : to collect (payment)

embonar *vi* *Mex* ENCAJAR : to fit

emborracharse *vr* EMBRIAGARSE : to get drunk

emborronar *vt* **1** : to blot, to smudge **2** GARABATEAR : to scribble

emboscada *nf* : ambush

emboscar {72} *vt* : to ambush — **emboscarse** *vr* : to lie in ambush

embotar *vt* **1** : to dull, to blunt **2** : to weaken, to enervate

embotellamiento *nm* ATASCO : traffic jam

embotellar *vt* ENVASAR : to bottle — **embotellado, -da** *adj*

embragar {52} *vi* : to engage the clutch

embrague *nm* : clutch

embriagado, -da *adj* : inebriated, drunk

embriagador, -dora *adj* : intoxicating

embriagar {52} *vt* : to intoxicate, to make drunk — **embriagarse** *vr* EMBORRACHARSE : to get drunk

embriaguez *nf* EBRIEDAD : drunkenness, inebriation

embridar *vt* : to bridle (a horse)

embrión *nm, pl* **embriones** : embryo

embrionario, -ria *adj* : embryonic

embrollo *nm* ENREDO : confusion, mess, tangle

embrujado *adj* 1 : bewitched 2 : haunted (of a house, etc.)

embrujar *vt* HECHIZAR : to bewitch

embrujo *nm* : spell, curse

embrutecer {18} *vt* 1 : to make dull 2 ATONTAR : to stupefy

embudo *nm* : funnel

embuste *nm* 1 MENTIRA : lie, fib *fam* 2 ENGAÑO : trick, hoax

embustero¹, -ra *adj* : lying, deceitful

embustero², -ra *n* : liar, cheat

embutido *nm* 1 : sausage 2 : inlaid work

embutir *vt* 1 : to cram, to stuff, to jam 2 : to inlay

eme *nf* : (letter) m

emergencia *nf* 1 : emergency 2 : emergence

emergente *adj* 1 : emergent 2 : consequent, resultant

emerger {15} *vi* : to emerge, to surface

emigración *nf, pl* **-ciones** 1 : emigration 2 : migration

emigrante *adj & nmf* : emigrant

emigrar *vi* 1 : to emigrate 2 : to migrate

eminencia *nf* : eminence

eminente *adj* : eminent, distinguished

eminentemente *adv* : basically, essentially

emisario¹, -ria *n* : emissary

emisario² *nm* : outlet (of a body of water)

emisión *nf, pl* **-siones** 1 : emission 2 : broadcast 3 : issue ⟨emisión de acciones : stock issue⟩

emisor *nm* TRANSMISOR : television or radio transmitter

emisora *nf* : radio station

emitir *vt* 1 : to emit, to give off 2 : to broadcast 3 : to issue 4 : to cast (a vote)

emoción *nf, pl* **-ciones** : emotion — **emocional** *adj* — **emocionalmente** *adv*

emocionado, -da *adj* 1 : moved, affected by emotion 2 ENTUSIASMADO : excited

emocionante *adj* 1 CONMOVEDOR : moving, touching 2 EXCITANTE : exciting, thrilling

emocionar *vt* 1 CONMOVER : to move, to touch 2 : to excite, to thrill — **emocionarse** *vr*

emoji [e'moji] *nm, pl* **emojis** *or* **emoji** : emoji

emoticón *or* **emoticono** *nm, pl* **-cones** *or* **-conos** : emoticon

emotivo, -va *adj* : emotional, moving

empacador, -dora *n* : packer

empacar {72} *vt* 1 EMPAQUETAR : to pack 2 : to bale — *vi* : to pack — **empacarse** *vr* 1 : to balk, to refuse to budge 2 *Col, Mex fam* : to eat ravenously, to devour

empachar *vt* 1 ESTORBAR : to obstruct 2 : to give indigestion to 3 DISFRAZAR : to disguise, to mask — **empacharse** *vr* 1 INDIGESTARSE : to get indigestion 2 AVERGONZARSE : to be embarrassed

empacho *nm* 1 INDIGESTIÓN : indigestion 2 VERGÜENZA : embarrassment 3 **no tener empacho en** : to have no qualms about

empadronarse *vr* : to register to vote

empalagar {52} *vt* 1 : to seem cloying to ⟨me empalaga : I find it cloying⟩ 2 FASTIDIAR : to annoy, to bother

empalagoso, -sa *adj* MELOSO : cloying

empalar *vt* : to impale

empalizada *nf* : palisade (fence)

empalmar *vt* 1 : to splice, to link 2 : to combine — *vi* : to meet, to converge

empalme *nm* 1 CONEXIÓN : connection, link 2 : junction

empanada *nf* : pie, turnover

empanadilla *nf* : meat or seafood pie

empanar *vt* : to bread

empantanar *vt* 1 INUNDAR : to swamp, to bog down 2 ESTANCAR : to bog down, to delay — **empantanarse** *vr*

empañar *vt* 1 : to steam up 2 : to tarnish, to sully

empapado, -da *adj* : soggy, sodden

empapar *vt* MOJAR : to soak, to drench — **empaparse** *vr* 1 : to get soaking wet 2 ~ **de** : to absorb, to be imbued with

empapelar *vt* : to wallpaper

empaque *nm fam* 1 : presence, bearing 2 : pomposity 3 DESCARO : impudence, nerve

empaquetar *vt* EMBALAR : to pack, to package — **empaquetarse** *vr fam* : to dress up

emparedado *nm* : sandwich

emparedar *vt* : to wall in, to confine

emparejar *vt* 1 : to pair, to match up 2 : to make even, to even out — *vi* : to catch up — **emparejarse** *vr* 1 : to pair up 2 : to become even, to even out

emparentado, -da *adj* : related

emparentar {55} *vi* : to become related by marriage

emparrillado *nm Mex* : gridiron (in football)

empastar *vt* 1 : to fill (a tooth) 2 : to bind (a book)

empaste *nm* : filling (of a tooth)

empatar *vt* : to tie, to connect.— *vi* : to result in a draw, to be tied — **empatarse** *vr Ven* : to hook up, to link together

empate *nm* : draw, tie

empatía *nf* : empathy

empecinado, -da *adj* TERCO : stubborn

empecinarse *vr* OBSTINARSE : to be stubborn, to persist

empedernido, -da *adj* INCORREGIBLE : hardened, inveterate

empedrado *nm* : paving, pavement
empedrar {55} *vt* : to pave (with stones)
empeine *nm* : instep
empellón *nm, pl* **-llones** : shove, push
empelotado, -da *adj* 1 *Mex fam* : madly in love 2 *fam* : stark naked
empeñado, -da *adj* : determined, committed
empeñar *vt* 1 : to pawn 2 : to pledge, to give (one's word) — **empeñarse** *vr* 1 : to insist stubbornly 2 : to make an effort
empeño *nm* 1 : pledge, commitment 2 : insistence 3 ESFUERZO : effort, determination ⟨poner mucho empeño : to put in a lot of effort⟩ ⟨trabajar con empeño : to work hard⟩ 4 : pawning ⟨casa de empeños : pawnshop⟩
empeoramiento *nm* : worsening, deterioration
empeorar *vi* : to deteriorate, to get worse — *vt* : to make worse
empequeñecer {53} *vi* : to diminish, to become smaller — *vt* : to minimize, to make smaller
emperador *nm* : emperor
emperatriz *nf, pl* **-trices** : empress
empero *conj* : however, nevertheless
empezar {29} *v* COMENZAR : to start, to begin ⟨empezar a hacer algo : to start to do something, to start doing something⟩ ⟨empezar por algo/alguien : to start with something/someone⟩ ⟨empezar por hacer algo : to start by doing something⟩ ⟨empezó diciendo que . . . : she started out by saying that . . .⟩ ⟨para empezar : to begin with⟩
empinado, -da *adj* : steep
empinar *vt* ELEVAR : to lift, to raise — **empinarse** *vr* : to stand on tiptoe
empírico, -ca *adj* : empirical — **empíricamente** *adv*
emplasto *nm* : poultice, dressing
emplazamiento *nm* 1 : location, site 2 CITACIÓN : summons, subpoena
emplazar {21} *vt* 1 CONVOCAR : to convene, to summon 2 : to subpoena 3 UBICAR : to place, to position
empleado, -da *n* : employee
empleador, -dora *n* PATRÓN : employer
emplear *vt* 1 : to employ 2 USAR : to use — **emplearse** *vr* 1 : to get a job 2 : to occupy oneself
empleo *nm* 1 OCUPACIÓN : employment, occupation, job 2 : use, usage
emplomadura *nm Arg, Uru* : filling (in a tooth)
emplumar *vt* : to feather
empobrecer {53} *vt* : to impoverish — *vi* : to become poor — **empobrecerse** *vr*
empobrecimiento *nm* : impoverishment
empollar *vi* : to brood eggs — *vt* : to incubate
empolvar *vt* 1 : to cover with dust 2 : to powder — **empolvarse** *vr* 1 : to gather dust 2 : to powder one's face
emporio *nm* 1 : center, capital, empire ⟨un emporio cultural : a cultural center⟩ ⟨un emporio financiero : a financial empire⟩ 2 : department store

empotrado, -da *adj* : built-in ⟨armarios empotrados : built-in cabinets⟩
empotrar *vt* : to build into, to embed
emprendedor, -dora *adj* : enterprising
emprender *vt* : to undertake, to begin
empresa *nf* 1 COMPAÑÍA, FIRMA : company, corporation, firm 2 : undertaking, venture
empresariado *nm* 1 : business world 2 : management, managers *pl*
empresarial *adj* : business, managerial, corporate
empresario, -ria *n* 1 : manager 2 : businessman *m*, businesswoman *f* 3 : impresario
empréstito *nm* : loan
empujar *vi* : to push, to shove — *vt* 1 : to push 2 PRESIONAR : to spur on, to press
empuje *nm* : impetus, drive
empujón *nm, pl* **-jones** : push, shove
empuñadura *nf* MANGO : hilt, handle
empuñar *vt* 1 ASIR : to grasp 2 **empuñar las armas** : to take up arms
emú *nm, pl* **emú** *or* **emús** *or* **emúes** : emu
emular *vt* IMITAR : to emulate — **emulación** *nf*
emulsión *nf, pl* **-siones** : emulsion
emulsionante *nm* : emulsifier
emulsionar *vt* : to emulsify
en *prep* 1 : in (a box, building, city, etc.) ⟨en el aire : in the air⟩ ⟨en el bolsillo : in one's pocket⟩ 2 : on (a surface, etc.) ⟨está en la mesa : it's on the table⟩ ⟨en la costa : on the coast⟩ ⟨en la planta baja : on the ground floor⟩ ⟨en la calle Sur : on South Street⟩ 3 : at (a place or event) ⟨en casa : at home⟩ ⟨en el trabajo : at work⟩ ⟨en la reunión : at the meeting⟩ ⟨todos en la mesa : everyone at the table⟩ ⟨en el 30 de la calle Sur : at 30 South Street⟩ 4 : in, on, as part of ⟨en la película : in the movie⟩ ⟨en el equipo : on the team⟩ 5 : on (television, etc.) 6 : by (plane, train, etc.) 7 : in, within (a day, week, etc.) 8 : in, during (a period) 9 : on, at ⟨en esa ocasión : on that occasion⟩ ⟨en ese momento : at that moment⟩ 10 : in (a form) ⟨en francés/metros/pedazos : in French/meters/pieces⟩ 11 (*with numbers*) ⟨se ubica en el 26% : it's at 26%⟩ ⟨aumentó en un 90% : it increased by 90%⟩ ⟨se cifran en millones : they amount to millions⟩ 12 : in, made of (a material) 13 : in (a state, manner, circumstance) ⟨en peligro : in danger⟩ ⟨en broma : in jest⟩ ⟨en ese caso : in that case⟩ 14 : on (a subject) ⟨un experto en animales : an animal expert⟩ 15 : in (a field or profession) 16 (*with an infinitive verb*) ⟨el primero en ganar el título : the first to win the title⟩
en- *or* **em-** *pref* : en-, em- ⟨enredar : entangle⟩ ⟨empatía : empathy⟩
enagua *nf* : petticoat, slip
enajenación *nf, pl* **-ciones** 1 : transfer (of property) 2 : alienation 3 : absent-mindedness
enajenado, -da *adj* : out of one's mind
enajenar *vt* 1 : to transfer (property) 2 : to alienate 3 : to enrapture — **enaje-**

narse *vr* **1** : to become estranged **2** : to go mad

enaltecer {53} *vt* : to praise, to extol

enamorado[1], -da *adj* : in love

enamorado[2], -da *n* : lover, sweetheart

enamoramiento *nm* : infatuation, crush

enamorar *vt* **1** : to enamor, to win the love of — enamorarse *vr* : to fall in love

enamorizado, -da *adj* : amorous, passionate

enano[1], -na *adj* : tiny, minute

enano[2], -na *n* **1** *sometimes offensive* : little person, dwarf *sometimes offensive*, midget *sometimes offensive* **2** : dwarf (in stories) **3** *often disparaging* : shorty, shrimp *usu disparaging*

enarbolar *vt* **1** : to hoist, to raise **2** : to brandish

enardecer {53} *vt* **1** : to arouse (anger, passions) **2** : to stir up, to excite — enardecerse *vr*

encabezado *nm Mex* : headline

encabezamiento *nm* **1** : heading **2** : salutation, opening

encabezar {21} *vt* **1** : to head, to lead **2** : to put a heading on

encabritarse *vr* **1** : to rear up **2** *fam* : to get angry

encadenar *vt* **1** : to chain **2** : to connect, to link **3** INMOVILIZAR : to immobilize

encajar *vi* : to fit, to fit together, to fit in — *vt* **1** : to insert, to stick **2** : to take, to cope with (encajó el golpe : he withstood the blow)

encaje *nm* **1** : lace **2** : financial reserve

encajonar *vt* **1** : to box, to crate **2** : to cram in

encalar *vt* : to whitewash

encallar *vi* **1** : to run aground **2** : to get stuck

encallecido, -da *adj* : callused

encamar *vt* : to confine to a bed

encaminado, -da *adj* **1** : on the right track ~ a : aimed at, designed to

encaminar *vt* **1** : to direct, to channel **2** : to head in the right direction — encaminarse *vr* ~ a : to head for, to aim at

encandilar *vt* : to dazzle

encanecer {53} *vi* : to gray, to go gray

encantado, -da *adj* **1** : charmed, bewitched **2** : delighted **3** : haunted

encantador[1], -dora *adj* : charming, delightful

encantador[2], -dora *n* : magician

encantamiento *nm* : enchantment, spell

encantar *vt* **1** : to enchant, to bewitch **2** : to charm, to delight (me encanta esta canción : I love this song)

encanto *nm* **1** : charm, fascination **2** HECHIZO : spell **3** : delightful person or thing

encañonar *vt* : to point (a gun) at, to hold up

encapotado, -da *adj* : cloudy, overcast

encaprichado, -da *adj* : infatuated

encaprichamiento *nm* : infatuation

encapuchado, -da *adj* : hooded

encarado, -da *adj* estar mal encarado *fam* : to be ugly-looking, to look mean

encaramar *vt* : to raise, to lift up — encaramarse *vr* : to perch

encarar *vt* CONFRONTAR : to face, to confront

encarcelación *nf, pl* -ciones → encarcelamiento

encarcelamiento *nm* : incarceration, imprisonment

encarcelar *vt* : to incarcerate, to imprison

encarecer {53} *vt* **1** : to increase, to raise (price, value) **2** : to beseech, to entreat — encarecerse *vr* : to become more expensive

encarecidamente *adv* : insistently, urgently

encarecimiento *nm* : increase, rise (in price)

encargado[1], -da *adj* : in charge

encargado[2], -da *n* : manager, person in charge

encargar {52} *vt* **1** : to put in charge of **2** : to recommend, to advise **3** : to order, to request — encargarse *vr* ~ de : to take charge of

encargo *nm* **1** : errand **2** : job assignment **3** : order (hecho de encargo : custom-made, made to order)

encariñarse *vr* ~ con : to become fond of, to grow attached to

encarnación *nf, pl* -ciones : incarnation, embodiment

encarnado[1], -da *adj* **1** : incarnate **2** : flesh-colored **3** : red **4** : ingrown

encarnado[2] *nm* : red

encarnar *vt* : to incarnate, to embody — encarnarse *vr* encarnarse una uña : to have an ingrown nail

encarnizado, -da *adj* **1** : bloodshot, inflamed **2** : fierce, bloody

encarnizar {21} *vt* : to enrage, to infuriate — encarnizarse *vr* : to be brutal, to attack viciously

encarrilar *vt* : to guide, to put on the right track

encasillar *vt* CLASIFICAR : to classify, to pigeonhole, to categorize

encausar *vt* : to prosecute, to charge

encauzar {21} *vt* : to channel, to guide — encauzarse *vr*

encebollado, -da *adj* : cooked with onions

encefalitis *nms & pl* : encephalitis

enceguecedor, -dora *n* : blinding

encendedor *nm* : lighter

encender {56} *vi* : to light — *vt* **1** : to light, to set fire to **2** PRENDER : to switch on **3** : to start (a motor) **4** : to arouse, to kindle — encenderse *vr* **1** : to get excited **2** : to blush

encendido[1], -da *adj* **1** : burning **2** : flushed **3** : fiery, passionate

encendido[2] *nm* : ignition

encerado *nm* **1** : waxing, polishing **2** : blackboard

encerar *vt* : to wax, to polish

encerrar {55} *vt* **1** : to lock (up), to shut away/up (la encerraron en una celda : they locked her in a cell) (está encerrado en su cuarto : he's shut up in his room) **2** : to contain, to include **3** : to involve, to entail

encerrona *nf* **1** TRAMPA : trap, setup **2** **prepararle una encerrona a alguien** : to set a trap for someone, to set someone up

encestar *vi* : to make a basket (in basketball)

enchapado *nm* : plating, coating (of metal)

encharcamiento *nm* : flood, flooding

encharcar {72} *vt* : to flood — **encharcarse** *vr* **1** : to flood, to get flooded **2** : to pool

enchilada *nf* : enchilada

enchilar *vt Mex* : to season with chili

enchuecar {72} *vt Chile, Mex fam* : to make crooked, to twist

enchufar *vt* **1** : to plug in **2** : to connect, to fit together

enchufe *nm* **1** : connection **2** : plug, socket

encía *nf* : gum (tissue)

-encia *suf* : -ence ⟨independencia : independence⟩

enciclopedia *nf* : encyclopedia — **enciclopédico, -ca** *adj*

encierro *nm* **1** : confinement **2** : enclosure

encima *adv* **1** : on, on top (of) ⟨se me cayó encima : it fell on (top of) me⟩ ⟨con queso (por) encima : with cheese on top⟩ ⟨no llevo dinero encima : I don't have any money on me⟩ **2** ADEMÁS : as well, besides ⟨y encima : and on top of that⟩ **3** ~ **de** : on, on top of, over, above ⟨encima de la mesa : on (top of) the table⟩ ⟨encima de las nubes : above the clouds⟩ ⟨viven encima de la librería : they live above the bookstore⟩ ⟨miró por encima del hombro : he looked over his shoulder⟩ **4** **por** ~ : superficially **5** **por encima de** : above, beyond ⟨por encima de la ley : above the law⟩ ⟨por encima de la media : above average⟩ ⟨por encima de todo : above all⟩ ⟨vive por encima de sus posibilidades : she lives above her means⟩ **6** **echarse encima** : to take upon oneself **7** **estar encima de** *fam* : to nag, to criticize **8** **quitarse de encima** : to get rid of

encina *nf* : evergreen oak

encinta *adj* EMBARAZADA, PREÑADA : pregnant, expecting

enclaustrado, -da *adj* : cloistered, shut away

enclavado, -da *adj* : buried

enclenque *adj* : weak, sickly

encoger {15} *vt* **1** : to shrink, to make smaller **2** : to intimidate — *vi* : to shrink, to contract — **encogerse** *vr* **1** : to shrink **2** : to be intimidated, to cower, to cringe **3 encogerse de hombros** : to shrug (one's shoulders)

encogido, -da *adj* **1** : shriveled, shrunken **2** TÍMIDO : shy, inhibited

encogimiento *nm* **1** : shrinking, shrinkage **2** : shrug **3** TIMIDEZ : shyness

encolerizar {21} *vt* ENFURECER : to enrage, to infuriate — **encolerizarse** *vr*

encomendar {55} *vt* CONFIAR : to entrust, to commend — **encomendarse** *vr*

encomiable *adj* : commendable, praiseworthy

encomiar *vt* ELOGIAR : to praise, to pay tribute to

encomienda *nf* **1** : charge, mission **2** : royal land grant **3** : parcel

encomio *nm* : praise, eulogy

enconar *vt* **1** : to irritate, to anger **2** : to inflame — **enconarse** *vr* **1** : to become heated **2** : to fester

encono *nm* **1** RENCOR : animosity, rancor **2** : inflammation, infection

encontrado, -da *adj* : contrary, opposing

encontrar {19} *vt* **1** HALLAR : to find ⟨encontré el libro : I found the book⟩ ⟨encontraron al culpable : they found the culprit⟩ **2** : to encounter, to meet **3** : to find ⟨lo encuentro muy interesante : I find it very interesting⟩ — **encontrarse** *vr* **1** : to clash, to conflict **2** : to be, to feel ⟨su padre se encuentra mejor : her father is (feeling/doing) better⟩ **3** ~ **con** : to meet, to bump into

encorvar *vt* : to bend, to curve — **encorvarse** *vr* : to hunch over, to stoop

encrespar *vt* **1** : to curl, to ruffle, to ripple **2** : to annoy, to irritate — **encresparse** *vr* **1** : to curl one's hair **2** : to become choppy **3** : to get annoyed

encriptar *vt* : to encrypt

encrucijada *nf* : crossroads

encuadernación *nf, pl* **-ciones** : binding (of books)

encuadernar *vt* EMPASTAR : to bind (a book) — **encuadernador, -dora** *n*

encuadrar *vt* **1** ENMARCAR : to frame **2** ENCAJAR : to fit, to insert **3** COMPRENDER : to contain, to include

encubierto *pp* → **encubrir**

encubrimiento *nm* : cover-up

encubrir {2} *vt* : to cover up, to conceal

encuentro *nm* **1** : meeting, encounter **2** : conference, congress

encuerado, -da *adj fam* : naked

encuerar *vt fam* : to undress

encuesta *nf* **1** INVESTIGACIÓN, PESQUISA : inquiry, investigation **2** SONDEO : survey

encuestador, -dora *n* : pollster

encuestar *vt* : to poll, to take a survey of

encumbrado, -da *adj* **1** : lofty, high **2** : eminent, distinguished

encumbrar *vt* **1** : to exalt, to elevate **2** : to extol — **encumbrarse** *vr* : to reach the top

encurtir *vt* ESCABECHAR : to pickle

ende *adv* **por** ~ : therefore, consequently

endeble *adj* : feeble, weak

endemoniado, -da *adj* : fiendish, diabolical

enderezar {21} *vt* **1** : to straighten (out) **2** : to stand on end, to put upright — **enderezarse** *vr* **1** : to straighten up, to sit/stand (up) straight **2** ARREGLARSE : to straighten out, to improve

endeudado, -da *adj* : in debt, indebted

endeudamiento *nm* : indebtedness, debt

endeudarse *vr* **1** : to go into debt **2** : to feel obliged

endiablado, -da *adj* **1** : devilish, diabolical **2** : complicated, difficult

endibia or **endivia** nf : endive
endilgar {52} vt fam : to spring, to foist ⟨me endilgó la responsabilidad : he saddled me with the responsibility⟩
endocrino, -na adj : endocrine
endogamia nf : inbreeding
endosar vt : to endorse
endoso nm : endorsement
endulzante nm : sweetener
endulzar {21} vt **1** : to sweeten **2** : to soften, to mellow — **endulzarse** vr
endurecer {53} vt : to harden, to toughen — **endurecerse** vr
ene nf : (letter) n
enebro nm : juniper
eneldo nm : dill
enema nm : enema
enemigo, -ga adj & n : enemy
enemistad nf : enmity, hostility
enemistar vt : to make enemies of — **enemistarse** vr ~ **con** : to fall out with
energético, -ca adj **1** : energy ⟨consumo energético : energy consumption⟩ **2** : lively, spirited
energía nf : energy
enérgico, -ca adj **1** : energetic, vigorous **2** : forceful, emphatic — **enérgicamente** adv
energúmeno, -na n fam : lunatic, crazy person
enero nm : January ⟨el primero de enero : (on) January first⟩
enervar vt **1** : to enervate **2** fam : to annoy, to get on one's nerves — **enervante** adj
enésimo, -ma adj : umpteenth, nth
enfadado, -da adj : angry, annoyed
enfadar vt : to annoy, to make angry — **enfadarse** vr : to get angry, to get annoyed
enfado nm : anger, annoyance
enfardar vt : to bale
énfasis nms & pl : emphasis
enfático, -ca adj : emphatic — **enfáticamente** adv
enfatizar {21} vt DESTACAR, SUBRAYAR : to emphasize
enfermar vt : to make sick — vi : to fall ill, to get sick — **enfermarse** vr
enfermedad nf **1** INDISPOSICIÓN : illness, sickness ⟨por enfermedad : due to illness⟩ **2** : illness, disease ⟨contraer una enfermedad : to catch/contract an illness⟩ ⟨enfermedad infecciosa : infectious disease⟩ ⟨enfermedad mental : mental illness⟩ ⟨enfermedad de Alzheimer : Alzheimer's disease⟩
enfermería nf : infirmary
enfermero, -ra n : nurse
enfermizo, -za adj : sickly
enfermo[1], **-ma** adj : sick, ill
enfermo[2], **-ma** n **1** : sick person, invalid **2** PACIENTE : patient
enfilar vt **1** : to take, to go along ⟨enfiló la carretera de Montevideo : she went up the road to Montevideo⟩ **2** : to line up, to put in a row **3** : to string, to thread **4** : to aim, to direct — vi : to make one's way
enflaquecer {53} vi : to lose weight, to become thin — vt : to emaciate

enfocar {72} vt **1** : to focus (on) **2** : to consider, to look at
enfoque nm : focus
enfrascarse {72} vr ~ **en** : to immerse oneself in, to get caught up in
enfrentamiento nm : clash, confrontation
enfrentar vt : to confront, to face — **enfrentarse** vr **1** ~ **con** : to clash with **2** ~ **a** : to face up to
enfrente adv **1** DELANTE : in front **2** : opposite
enfriamiento nm **1** CATARRO : chill, cold **2** : cooling off, damper
enfriar {85} vt **1** : to chill, to cool **2** : to cool down, to dampen — vi : to get cold — **enfriarse** vr : to get chilled, to catch a cold
enfundar vt : to sheathe, to encase
enfurecer {53} vt ENCOLERIZAR : to infuriate — **enfurecerse** vr : to fly into a rage
enfurecido, -da adj : furious, raging
enfurruñarse vr fam : to sulk
engalanar vt : to decorate, to deck out — **engalanarse** vr : to dress up
enganchar vt **1** : to hook, to snag **2** : to attach, to hitch up — **engancharse** vr **1** : to get snagged, to get hooked **2** : to enlist
enganche nm **1** : hook **2** : coupling, hitch **3** Mex : down payment
engañar vt **1** EMBAUCAR : to trick, to deceive, to mislead **2** : to cheat on, to be unfaithful to — **engañarse** vr **1** : to be mistaken **2** : to deceive oneself
engaño nm **1** : deception, trick **2** : fake, feint (in sports)
engañoso, -sa adj **1** : deceitful **2** : misleading, deceptive
engarzar {21} vt **1** : to set (a gem) **2** ENSARTAR : to string **3** HILAR : to string together — **engarzarse** vr ~ **en** : to get involved in, to get caught up in
engatusar vt : to coax, to cajole
engendrar vt **1** : to beget, to father **2** : to give rise to, to engender
engendro nm **1** : fetus **2** MONSTRUO : monstrosity, freak
engentarse vr Mex : to become confused and overwhelmed
englobar vt : to include, to embrace
engomado nm Mex : sticker
engomar vt : to glue, to coat with glue
engordar vt : to fatten, to fatten up — vi : to gain weight
engorroso, -sa adj : bothersome
engranaje nm : gears pl, cogs pl
engranar vt : to mesh, to engage — vi : to mesh gears
engrandecer {53} vt **1** : to enlarge **2** : to exaggerate **3** : to exalt
engrandecimiento nm **1** : enlargement **2** : exaggeration **3** : exaltation
engrane nm Mex : cogwheel
engrapadora nf : stapler
engrapar vt : to staple
engrasar vt : to grease, to lubricate
engrase nm : greasing, lubrication
engreído, -da adj PRESUMIDO, VANIDOSO : vain, conceited, stuck-up

engreimiento *nm* ARROGANCIA : arrogance, conceit

engreir {66} *vt* ENVANECER : to make vain — **engreírse** *vr* : to become conceited

engrosar {19} *vt* : to enlarge, to increase, to swell — *vi* ENGORDAR : to gain weight

engrudo *nm* : paste

engullir {38} *vt* : to gulp down, to gobble up — **engullirse** *vr*

enharinar *vt* : to flour

enhebrar *vt* ENSARTAR : to string, to thread

enhilar *vt* : to thread (a needle, etc.)

enhorabuena *nf* FELICIDADES : congratulations *pl*

enigma *nm* : enigma, mystery

enigmático, -ca *adj* : enigmatic — **enigmáticamente** *adv*

enjabonar *vt* : to soap up, to lather — **enjabonarse** *vr*

enjaezar {21} *vt* : to harness

enjalbegar {52} *vt* : to whitewash

enjambrar *vi* : to swarm

enjambre *nm* 1 : swarm 2 MUCHEDUMBRE : crowd, mob

enjaular *vt* 1 : to cage 2 *fam* : to jail, to lock up

enjuagar {52} *vt* : to rinse — **enjuagarse** *vr* : to rinse out

enjuague *nm* 1 : rinse 2 **enjuague bucal** : mouthwash

enjugar {52} *vt* : to wipe away (tears)

enjuiciar *vt* 1 : to indict, to prosecute 2 JUZGAR : to try

enlace *nm* 1 : bond, link, connection 2 : liaison 3 HIPERENLACE : link

enlatar *vt* ENVASAR : to can — **enlatado, -da** *adj*

enlazar {21} *v* : to join, to link, to fit together

enlistar *vt* : to list — **enlistarse** *vr* : to enlist

enlodado, -da *adj* LODOSO : muddy

enlodar *vt* 1 : to cover with mud 2 : to stain, to sully — **enlodarse** *vr*

enlodazar → enlodar

enloquecedor, -dora *adj* : maddening

enloquecer {53} *vt* : to drive crazy — **enloquecerse** *vr* : to go crazy

enlutarse *vr* : to go into mourning

enmarañar *vt* 1 : to tangle 2 : to complicate 3 : to confuse, to mix up — **enmarañarse** *vr*

enmarcar {72} *vt* 1 ENCUADRAR : to frame 2 : to provide the setting for

enmascarar *vt* : to mask, to disguise — **enmascarado, -da** *adj*

enmasillar *vt* : to putty, to caulk

enmendar {55} *vt* 1 : to amend 2 CORREGIR : to emend, to correct 3 COMPENSAR : to compensate for — **enmendarse** *vr* : to mend one's ways

enmienda *nf* 1 : amendment 2 : correction, emendation

enmohecerse {53} *vr* 1 : to become moldy 2 OXIDARSE : to rust, to become rusty

enmudecer {53} *vt* : to mute, to silence — *vi* : to fall silent

ennegrecer {53} *vt* : to blacken, to darken — **ennegrecerse** *vr*

ennoblecer {53} *vt* 1 : to ennoble 2 : to embellish

enojadizo, -za *adj* IRRITABLE : irritable, cranky

enojado, -da *adj* 1 : annoyed 2 : angry, mad

enojar *vt* 1 : to anger 2 : to annoy, to upset — **enojarse** *vr*

enojo *nm* 1 CÓLERA : anger 2 : annoyance

enojón, -jona *adj, pl* **-jones** *Chile, Mex fam* : irritable, cranky

enojoso, -sa *adj* FASTIDIOSO, MOLESTOSO : annoying, irritating

enorgullecer {53} *vt* : to make proud — **enorgullecerse** *vr* : to pride oneself

enorme *adj* INMENSO : enormous, huge — **enormemente** *adv*

enormidad *nf* 1 : enormity, seriousness 2 : immensity, hugeness

enraizado, -da *adj* : deep-seated, deeply rooted

enraizar {30} *vi* : to take root

enramada *nf* : arbor, bower

enramar *vt* : to cover with branches

enrarecer {53} *vt* : to rarefy — **enrarecerse** *vr*

enredadera *nf* : climbing plant, vine

enredar *vt* 1 : to tangle up, to entangle 2 : to confuse, to complicate 3 : to involve, to implicate — **enredarse** *vr*

enredo *nm* 1 EMBROLLO : muddle, confusion 2 MARAÑA : tangle

enrejado *nm* 1 : railing 2 : grating, grille 3 : trellis, lattice

enrevesado, -da *adj* : complicated, involved

enriquecer {53} *vt* : to enrich — **enriquecerse** *vr* : to get rich

enriquecido, -da *adj* : enriched

enriquecimiento *nm* : enrichment

enrojecer {53} *vt* : to make red, to redden — **enrojecerse** *vr* : to blush

enrolar *vt* RECLUTAR : to recruit — **enrolarse** *vr* INSCRIBIRSE : to enlist, to sign up

enrollado, -da *adj* 1 : rolled up, coiled 2 **estar enrollado con** *Spain* : to be involved with (romantically)

enrollar *vt* : to roll up, to coil — **enrollarse** *vr*

enronquecerse {53} *vr* : to become hoarse

enroscar {72} *vt* TORCER : to twist — **enroscarse** *vr* : to coil, to twine

ensacar {72} *vt* : to bag (up)

ensalada *nf* : salad

ensaladera *nf* : salad bowl

ensalmo *nm* : incantation, spell

ensalzar {21} *vt* 1 : to praise, to extol 2 EXALTAR : to exalt

ensamblaje *nm* : assembly

ensamblar *vt* 1 : to assemble 2 : to join, to fit together

ensanchar *vt* 1 : to widen 2 : to expand, to extend — **ensancharse** *vr*

ensanche *nm* 1 : widening 2 : expansion, development

ensangrentado, -da *adj* : bloody, blood-stained

ensangrentar {55} *vt* : to cover or stain with blood

ensañarse *vr* : to act cruelly, to be merciless

ensartar *vt* **1** ENHEBRAR : to string, to thread **2** : to skewer, to pierce

ensayar *vi* : to rehearse — *vt* **1** : to try out, to test **2** : to assay

ensayista *nmf* : essayist

ensayo *nm* **1** : essay **2** : trial, test **3** : rehearsal **4** : assay (of metals)

enseguida *adv* INMEDIATAMENTE : right away, immediately, at once

ensenada *nf* : cove, inlet

enseña *nf* INSIGNIA : emblem, insignia **2** : standard, banner

enseñanza *nf* **1** EDUCACIÓN : education **2** : teaching

enseñar *vt* **1** : to teach **2** MOSTRAR : to show, to display — **enseñarse** *vr* ~ **a** : to learn to, to get used to

enseres *nmpl* : equipment, furnishings *pl* ⟨enseres domésticos : household goods⟩

ensillar *vt* : to saddle (up)

ensimismado, -da *adj* : absorbed, engrossed

ensimismarse *vr* : to lose oneself in thought

ensombrecer {53} *vt* : to cast a shadow over, to darken — **ensombrecerse** *vr*

ensoñación *nf, pl* **-ciones** : fantasy

ensopar *vt* **1** : to drench **2** : to dunk, to dip

ensordecedor, -dora *adj* : deafening, thunderous

ensordecer {53} *vt* : to deafen — *vi* : to go deaf

ensuciar *vt* : to soil, to dirty — **ensuciarse** *vr*

ensueño *nm* **1** : daydream, reverie **2** FANTASÍA : illusion, fantasy

entablar *vt* **1** : to cover with boards **2** : to initiate, to enter into, to start

entallar *vt* AJUSTAR : to tailor, to fit, to take in — *vi* QUEDAR : to fit

entarimado *nm* : flooring, floorboards *pl*

ente *nm* **1** : being, entity **2** : body, organization ⟨ente rector : ruling body⟩ **3** *fam* : eccentric, crackpot

entenado, -da *n Mex* : stepchild, stepson *m*, stepdaughter *f*

entender¹ {56} *vt* **1** COMPRENDER : to understand ⟨no entiendo por qué : I don't understand why⟩ ⟨me has entendido mal : you've misunderstood me⟩ ⟨mis padres no me entienden : my parents don't understand me⟩ ⟨dar a entender : to imply⟩ **2** : to think, to believe ⟨él no lo entiende así : he doesn't see it that way⟩ **3** : to know, to get ⟨si me entiendes : if you know what I mean⟩ **4** : to infer ⟨dar algo a entender : to imply something⟩ — *vi* **1** : to understand ⟨¡ya entiendo! : now I understand!⟩ **2** ~ **de** : to know about **3** ~ **en** : to be in charge of — **entenderse** *vr* **1** : to be understood **2** : to get along well **3** ~ **con** : to deal with

entender² *nm* **a mi entender** : in my opinion

entendible *adj* : understandable

entendido¹, -da *adj* **1** : skilled, expert, knowledgeable **2 tener entendido** : to understand, to be under the impression ⟨teníamos entendido que vendrías : we were under the impression you would come⟩ **3 darse por entendido** : to go without saying

entendido² *nm* : expert, authority, connoisseur

entendimiento *nm* **1** : intellect, mind **2** : understanding, agreement

enterado, -da *adj* : aware, well-informed ⟨estar enterado de : to be privy to⟩ ⟨darse por enterado : to get the message⟩

enteramente *adv* : entirely, completely

enterar *vt* INFORMAR : to inform — **enterarse** *vr* INFORMARSE : to find out, to learn

entereza *nf* **1** INTEGRIDAD : integrity **2** FORTALEZA : fortitude **3** FIRMEZA : resolve

enternecedor, -dora *adj* CONMOVEDOR : touching, moving

enternecer {53} *vt* CONMOVER : to move, to touch

entero¹, -ra *adj* **1** : entire, whole **2** : complete, absolute **3** : intact — **enteramente** *adv*

entero² *nm* **1** : integer, whole number **2** : point (in finance)

enterramiento *nm* : burial

enterrar {55} *vt* : to bury

entibiar *vt* : to cool (down) — **entibiarse** *vr* : to become lukewarm

entidad *nf* **1** ENTE : entity **2** : body, organization **3** : firm, company **4** : importance, significance

entierro *nm* **1** : burial **2** : funeral

entintar *vt* : to ink

entoldado *nm* : awning

entomología *nf* : entomology

entomólogo, -ga *n* : entomologist

entonación *nf, pl* **-ciones** : intonation

entonar *vi* : to be in tune — *vt* **1** : to intone **2** : to tone up

entonces *adv* **1** : then **2 desde** ~ : since then **3 en aquel entonces** : in those days

entornado, -da *adj* ENTREABIERTO : half-closed, ajar

entornar *vt* ENTREABRIR : to leave ajar

entorno *nm* : surroundings *pl*, environment

entorpecer {53} *vt* **1** : to hinder, to obstruct **2** : to dull — **entorpecerse** *vr* : to dull the senses

entrada *nf* **1** : entrance, entry ⟨prohibida la entrada : do not enter⟩ **2** : entrance ⟨entrada principal : main entrance⟩ **3** : ticket, admission ⟨entrada gratuita/libre : free admission⟩ **4** : beginning, onset ⟨de entrada : from the start⟩ **5** : entrée **6** : cue (in music) **7 entradas** *nfpl* : income ⟨entradas y salidas : income and expenditures⟩ **8 tener entradas** : to have a receding hairline

entrado, -da *adj* **entrado en años** : elderly

entramado *nm* : framework

entrampar *vt* **1** ATRAPAR : to entrap, to ensnare **2** ENGAÑAR : to deceive, to trick

entrante *adj* **1** : next, upcoming ⟨el año entrante : next year⟩ **2** : incoming, new ⟨el presidente entrante : the president elect⟩

entraña *nf* **1** MEOLLO : core, heart, crux **2 entrañas** *nfpl* VÍSCERAS : entrails

entrañable *adj* : close, intimate

entrañar *vt* : to entail, to involve

entrar *vi* **1** : to enter, to go in, to come in ⟨entré a la casa : I went in the house⟩ ⟨entrar por : to come/go in (through)⟩ ⟨¿puedo entrar? : can I come in?⟩ ⟨la llave no entra : the key won't go in⟩ **2** : to fit ⟨este vestido no me entra : this dress doesn't fit me⟩ **3** : to begin ⟨entro a trabajar a las ocho : I start work at eight⟩ **4** : to affect ⟨me entra el hambre : I'm getting hungry⟩ **5 ~ en** : to enter (a phase, etc.) **6 ~ en** : to be included/considered in **7 ~ en** : to go into, to discuss (details, etc.) **8 ~ en** : to enter into (negotiations, battle, etc.), to come into (contact, conflict, etc.), to go into (effect) **9 ~ en** : to enter (college), to join (an organization), to go into (a profession) — *vt* **1** : to bring in, to introduce **2** : to access

entre *prep* **1** : between ⟨entre las dos ciudades/fechas : between the two cities/dates⟩ ⟨lo dividimos entre los dos : we divided it between the two of us⟩ ⟨la diferencia entre los dos : the difference between the two⟩ ⟨entre todos lo logramos : between all of us we managed it⟩ ⟨entre tú y yo : between you and me⟩ **2** : among ⟨entre las hojas : among the leaves⟩ ⟨entre amigos : among friends⟩ ⟨lo dividimos entre los cuatro : we divided it among the four of us⟩ ⟨conversaban entre sí : they talked among themselves⟩

entreabierto¹ *pp* → **entreabrir**

entreabierto², -ta *adj* ENTORNADO : half-open, ajar

entreabrir {2} *vt* ENTORNAR : to leave ajar

entreacto *nm* : intermission, interval

entrecano, -na *adj* : grayish, graying

entrecejo *nm* **fruncir el entrecejo** : to knit one's brows

entrecomillar *vt* : to place in quotation marks

entrecortadamente *adv* **1** : breathlessly **2** : falteringly

entrecortado, -da *adj* **1** : labored, difficult ⟨respiración entrecortada : shortness of breath⟩ **2** : faltering, hesitant ⟨con la voz entrecortada : with a catch in his voice⟩

entrecortarse *vr* : to falter (of the voice or breath)

entrecruzar {21} *vt* ENTRELAZAR : to interweave, to intertwine — **entrecruzarse** *vr*

entredicho *nm* **1** DUDA : doubt, question **2** : prohibition

entrega *nf* **1** : delivery **2** : handing over, surrender **3** : installment ⟨entrega inicial : down payment⟩

entregar {52} *vt* **1** : to deliver **2** DAR : to give, to present **3** : to hand in, to hand over — **entregarse** *vr* **1** : to surrender, to give in **2** : to devote oneself

entrelazar {21} *vt* ENTRECRUZAR : to interweave, to intertwine

entremedias *adv* **1** : in between, halfway **2** : in the meantime

entremés *nm, pl* **-meses 1** APERITIVO : appetizer, hors d'oeuvre **2** : interlude, short play

entremeterse → **entrometerse**

entremetido *nm* → **entrometido**

entremezclar *vt* : to intermingle

entrenador, -dora *n* : trainer, coach

entrenamiento *nm* : training, drill, practice

entrenar *vt* : to train, to drill, to practice — **entrenarse** *vr* : to train, to spar (in boxing)

entrepierna *nf* **1** : inner thigh **2** : crotch **3** : inseam

entrepiso *nm* : mezzanine

entretanto¹ *adv* : meanwhile

entretanto² *nm* **en el entretanto** : in the meantime

entretejer *vt* : to interweave

entretela *nf* : facing (of a garment)

entretelones *nmpl* : inside details

entretención *nf, pl* **-ciones** ENTRETENIMIENTO : entertainment

entretener {80} *vt* **1** DIVERTIR : to entertain, to amuse **2** DISTRAER : to distract **3** DEMORAR : to delay, to hold up — **entretenerse** *vr* **1** : to amuse oneself **2** : to dally

entretenido, -da *adj* DIVERTIDO : entertaining, amusing

entretenimiento *nm* **1** : entertainment, pastime **2** DIVERSIÓN : fun, amusement

entretiempo *nm* **1** → **medio tiempo 2** : period between seasons

entrever {88} *vt* **1** : to catch a glimpse of **2** : to make out, to see indistinctly

entreverar *vt* : to mix, to intermingle

entrevero *nm* : confusion, disorder

entrevista *nf* : interview

entrevistador, -dora *n* : interviewer

entrevistar *vt* : to interview — **entrevistarse** *vr* REUNIRSE **~ con** : to meet with

entristecer {53} *vt* : to sadden

entrometerse *vr* : to interfere, to meddle

entrometido, -da *n* : meddler, busybody

entroncar {72} *vt* RELACIONAR : to establish a relationship between, to connect — *vi* **1** : to be related **2** : to link up, to be connected

entronque *nm* **1** : kinship **2** VÍNCULO : link, connection

entuerto *nm* : wrong, injustice

entumecer {53} *vt* : to make numb, to be numb — **entumecerse** *vr* : to go numb, to fall asleep

entumecido, -da *adj* **1** : numb **2** : stiff (of muscles, joints, etc.)

entumecimiento *nm* : numbness

enturbiar *vt* **1** : to cloud **2** : to confuse — **enturbiarse** *vr*
entusiasmar *vt* : to excite, to fill with enthusiasm — **entusiasmarse** *vr* : to get excited
entusiasmo *nm* : enthusiasm
entusiasta[1] *adj* : enthusiastic
entusiasta[2] *nmf* AFICIONADO : enthusiast
enumerar *vt* : to enumerate — **enumeración** *nf*
enunciación *nf, pl* **-ciones** : enunciation, statement
enunciado *nm* : statement
enunciar *vt* : to enunciate, to state
envainar *vt* : to sheathe
envalentonar *vt* : to make bold, to encourage — **envalentonarse** *vr*
envanecer {53} *vt* ENGREÍR : to make vain — **envanecerse** *vr*
envasar *vt* **1** EMBOTELLAR : to bottle **2** ENLATAR : to can **3** : to pack in a container
envase *nm* **1** : packaging, packing **2** : container **3** LATA : can **4** : empty bottle
envejecer {53} *vt* : to age, to make look old — *vi* : to age, to grow old
envejecido, -da *adj* : aged, old-looking
envejecimiento *nm* : aging
envenenamiento *nm* : poisoning
envenenar *vt* **1** : to poison **2** : to embitter
envergadura *nf* **1** : span, breadth, spread **2** : importance, scope
envés *nm, pl* **enveses** : reverse, opposite side
enviado, -da *n* : envoy, correspondent
enviar {85} *vt* **1** : to send **2** : to ship
envidia *nf* : envy, jealousy
envidiar *vt* : to envy — **envidiable** *adj*
envidioso, -sa *adj* : envious, jealous
envilecer {53} *vt* : to degrade, to debase
envío *nm* **1** : shipment **2** : remittance
enviudar *vi* : to be widowed, to become a widower
envoltorio *nm* **1** : bundle, package **2** : wrapping, wrapper
envoltura *nf* : wrapper, wrapping
envolver {89} *vt* **1** : to wrap **2** : to envelop, to surround **3** : to entangle, to involve — **envolverse** *vr* **1** : to become involved **2** : to wrap oneself (up)
envuelto *pp* → **envolver**
enyerbar *vt Mex* : to bewitch
enyesar *vt* **1** : to plaster **2** ESCAYOLAR : to put (a broken limb) in a cast
enzima *nf* : enzyme
eón *nm, pl* **eones** : aeon
eperlano *nm* : smelt (fish)
epicentro *nm* : epicenter
épico, -ca *adj* : epic
epicúreo[1]**, -rea** *adj* : epicurean
epicúreo[2]**, -rea** *n* : epicure
epidemia *nf* : epidemic
epidémico, -ca *adj* : epidemic
epidemiología *nf* : epidemiology — **epidemiológico, -ca** *adj*
epifanía *nf* : feast of the Epiphany (January 6th)
epigrama *nm* : epigram
epilepsia *nf* : epilepsy

epiléptico, -ca *adj & n* : epileptic
epílogo *nm* : epilogue
episcopal *adj* : episcopal
episcopaliano, -na *adj & n* : Episcopalian
episódico, -ca *adj* : episodic
episodio *nm* : episode
epístola *nf* : epistle
epitafio *nm* : epitaph
epíteto *nm* : epithet, name
epítome *nm* : summary, abstract
época *nf* **1** EDAD, ERA, PERÍODO : epoch, age, period **2** : time of year, season **3** de ~ : vintage, antique
epopeya *nf* : epic poem
equidad *nf* JUSTICIA : equity, justice, fairness
equilátero, -ra *adj* : equilateral
equilibrado, -da *adj* : well-balanced
equilibrar *vt* : to balance — **equilibrarse** *vr*
equilibrio *nm* **1** : balance, equilibrium ⟨perder el equilibrio : to lose one's balance⟩ ⟨equilibrio político : balance of power⟩ **2** : poise, aplomb
equilibrista *nmf* ACRÓBATA : acrobat, tightrope walker
equino, -na *adj* : equine
equinoccio *nm* : equinox
equipaje *nm* BAGAJE : baggage, luggage
equipamiento *nm* : equipping, equipment
equipar *vt* : to equip — **equiparse** *vr*
equiparable *adj* : comparable
equiparar *vt* **1** ~ a/con : to put on the same level as/with **2** COMPARAR : to compare
equipo *nm* **1** : team, crew **2** : gear, equipment
equis *nf* : (letter) x
equitación *nf, pl* **-ciones** : horseback riding, horsemanship
equitativo, -va *adj* JUSTO : equitable, fair, just — **equitativamente** *adv*
equivalencia *nf* : equivalence
equivalente *adj & nm* : equivalent
equivaler {84} *vi* : to be equivalent
equivocación *nf, pl* **-ciones** ERROR : error, mistake
equivocado, -da *adj* : mistaken, wrong — **equivocadamente** *adv*
equivocar {72} *vt* **1** : to confuse (someone), to make (someone) mess up **2** : to choose badly — **equivocarse** *vr* : to make a mistake, to be wrong ⟨se equivocó de casa : he got the wrong house⟩
equívoco[1]**, -ca** *adj* AMBIGUO : ambiguous, equivocal
equívoco[2] *nm* : misunderstanding
era[1]**, etc.** → **ser**
era[2] *nf* EDAD, ÉPOCA : era, age
erario *nm* : public treasury
ere *nf* : (letter) r
erección *nf, pl* **-ciones** : erection, raising
erecto, -ta *adj* : erect
eremita *nmf* ERMITAÑO : hermit
ergonomía *nf* : ergonomics
erguido, -da *adj* : erect, upright
erguir {31} *vt* : to raise, to lift up — **erguirse** *vr* : to straighten up
erigir {35} *vt* : to build, to erect — **erigirse** *vr* ~ en : to set oneself up as

erizado, -da *adj* : bristly

erizar {21} *vt* 1 : to make (hair, etc.) stand on end ⟨me eriza la piel : it gives me goose bumps⟩ 2 : to irritate, to grate on (someone) — **erizarse** *vr* : to stand on end

erizo *nm* 1 : hedgehog 2 **erizo de mar** : sea urchin

ermitaño[1], -ña *n* EREMITA : hermit, recluse

ermitaño[2] *nm* : hermit crab

erogación *nf, pl* -ciones : expenditure

erogar {52} *vt* 1 : to pay out 2 : to distribute

erosión *nf, pl* -siones : erosion

erosionar *vt* : to erode

erótico, -ca *adj* : erotic

erotismo *nm* : eroticism

erradicar {72} *vt* : to eradicate — **erradicación** *nf*

errado, -da *adj* : wrong, mistaken

errante *adj* VAGABUNDO : errant, wandering

errar {32} *vt* FALLAR : to miss — *vi* 1 DESACERTAR : to be wrong, to be mistaken 2 VAGAR : to wander

errata *nf* : misprint, error

errático, -ca *adj* : erratic — **erráticamente** *adv*

erre *nf* : (letter) r (especially when trilled)

erróneo, -nea *adj* EQUIVOCADO : erroneous, wrong — **erróneamente** *adv*

error *nm* EQUIVOCACIÓN : error, mistake ⟨cometer un error : to make a mistake⟩ ⟨estar en un error : to be mistaken⟩ ⟨por error : by mistake⟩ ⟨error de cálculo : miscalculation⟩ ⟨error de imprenta : misprint⟩ ⟨error de hecho : factual error⟩

eructar *vi* : to belch, to burp

eructo *nm* : belch, burp

erudición *nf, pl* -ciones : erudition, learning

erudito[1], -ta *adj* LETRADO : erudite, learned

erudito[2], -ta *n* : scholar

erupción *nf, pl* -ciones 1 : eruption 2 SARPULLIDO : rash

eruptivo, -va *adj* : eruptive

es → ser

esbelto, -ta *adj* DELGADO : slender, slim

esbirro *nm* : henchman

esbozar {21} *vt* BOSQUEJAR : to sketch, to outline

esbozo *nm* 1 : sketch 2 : rough draft

escabechar *vt* 1 ENCURTIR : to pickle 2 *fam* : to kill, to rub out

escabeche *nm* : brine (for pickling)

escabel *nm* : footstool

escabroso, -sa *adj* 1 : rugged, rough 2 : difficult, tough 3 : risqué

escabullirse {38} *vr* : to slip away, to escape

escafandra *nf* : (protective) suit

escala *nf* 1 : scale ⟨en escala de 1 a 10 : on a scale of 1 to 10⟩ ⟨a escala : to scale⟩ ⟨a escala mundial : on a worldwide scale⟩ ⟨producción a gran escala : large-scale production⟩ 2 : scale (in music) 3 ESCALERA : ladder 4 : stopover, layover ⟨hacer escala : to lay over⟩

escalada *nf* : ascent, climb

escalador, -dora *n* ALPINISTA : mountain climber

escalafón *nm, pl* -fones 1 : list of personnel 2 : salary scale, rank

escalar *vt* : to climb, to scale — *vi* 1 : to go climbing 2 : to escalate

escaldar *vt* : to scald

escalera *nf* 1 : ladder ⟨escalera de tijera : stepladder⟩ 2 : stairs *pl*, staircase 3 **escalera mecánica** : escalator

escalfar *vt* : to poach (eggs)

escalinata *nf* : flight of stairs

escalofriante *adj* : horrifying, bloodcurdling

escalofrío *nm* : shiver, chill, shudder

escalón *nm, pl* -lones 1 : echelon 2 : step, rung

escalonado, -da *adj* GRADUAL : gradual, staggered

escalonar *vt* 1 : to terrace 2 : to stagger, to alternate

escalpelo *nm* BISTURÍ : scalpel

escama *nf* 1 : scale (of fish or reptiles) 2 : flake (of skin)

escamar *vt* 1 : to scale (fish) 2 : to make suspicious

escamocha *nf Mex* : fruit salad

escamoso, -sa *adj* : scaly

escamotear *vt* 1 : to palm, to conceal 2 *fam* : to lift, to swipe 3 : to hide, to cover up

escampar *v impers* : to stop raining

escandalizar {21} *vt* : to shock, to scandalize — *vi* : to make a fuss — **escandalizarse** *vr* : to be shocked

escándalo *nm* 1 : scandal 2 : scene, commotion

escandaloso, -sa *adj* 1 : shocking, scandalous 2 RUIDOSO : noisy, rowdy 3 : flagrant, outrageous — **escandalosamente** *adv*

escandinavo, -va *adj & n* : Scandinavian

escandir *vt* : to scan (poetry)

escanear *vt* : to scan (documents)

escáner *nm* 1 : scan 2 : scanner

escaño *nm* 1 : seat (in a legislative body) 2 BANCO : bench

escapada *nf* HUIDA : flight, escape

escapar *vi* HUIR : to escape, to flee, to run away — **escaparse** *vr* : to escape notice, to leak out

escaparate *nm* 1 : shop window 2 : showcase

escapatoria *nf* 1 : loophole, excuse, pretext ⟨no tener escapatoria : to have no way out⟩ 2 ESCAPADA : escape, flight

escape *nm* 1 FUGA : escape 2 : exhaust (from a vehicle)

escapismo *nm* : escapism — **escapista** *adj*

escápula *nf* OMÓPLATO : scapula, shoulder blade

escarabajo *nm* : beetle

escaramuza *nf* 1 : skirmish 2 : scrimmage

escaramuzar {21} *vi* : to skirmish

escarapela *nf* : rosette (ornament)

escarbar *vt* 1 : to dig, to scratch up 2 : to poke, to pick 3 ~ **en** : to investigate, to pry into

escarcha *nf* 1 : frost 2 *Mex, PRi* : glitter

escarchar *vt* 1 : to frost, to sugar 2 : to candy (fruit)

escardar *vt* 1 : to weed, to hoe 2 : to weed out

escarlata *adj & nf* : scarlet

escarlatina *nf* : scarlet fever

escarmentar {55} *vt* : to punish, to teach a lesson to — *vi* : to learn one's lesson

escarmiento *nm* 1 : lesson, warning 2 CASTIGO : punishment

escarnio *nm* : ridicule, mockery

escarola *nf* : escarole

escarpa *nf* : escarpment, steep slope

escarpado, -da *adj* : steep, sheer

escasamente *adv* : scarcely, barely

escasear *vi* : to be scarce, to run short

escasez *nf, pl* **-seces** : shortage, scarcity

escaso, -sa *adj* 1 : scarce, scant 2 ~ **de** : short of

escatimar *vt* : to skimp on, to be sparing with ⟨no escatimar esfuerzos : to spare no effort⟩

escayola *nf Spain* 1 : plaster (for casts) 2 : cast (in medicine)

escayolar *vt Spain* : to put (a broken limb) in a cast

escena *nf* 1 : scene 2 : stage

escenario *nm* 1 ESCENA : stage 2 : setting, scene ⟨el escenario del crimen : the scene of the crime⟩

escénico, -ca *adj* 1 : scenic 2 : stage

escenificar {72} *vt* : to stage, to dramatize

escenografía *nf* : set design

escepticismo *nm* : skepticism

escéptico[1], -ca *adj* : skeptical

escéptico[2], -ca *n* : skeptic

escindirse *vr* 1 : to split 2 : to break away

escisión *nf, pl* **-siones** : split, division

esclarecer {53} *vt* 1 ELUCIDAR : to elucidate, to clarify 2 ILUMINAR : to illuminate, to light up

esclarecimiento *nm* ELUCIDACIÓN : elucidation, clarification

esclavitud *nf* : slavery

esclavización *nf, pl* **-ciones** : enslavement

esclavizar {21} *vt* : to enslave

esclavo, -va *n* : slave

esclerosis *nf* esclerosis múltiple : multiple sclerosis

esclusa *nf* : floodgate, lock (of a canal)

escoba *nf* : broom

escobilla *nf* : small broom, brush, whisk broom

escocer {14} *vi* ARDER : to smart, to sting — **escocerse** *vr* : to be sore

escocés[1], -cesa *adj, mpl* **-ceses** 1 : Scottish 2 : tartan, plaid

escocés[2], -cesa *n, mpl* **-ceses** : Scottish person, Scot

escocés[3] *nm* 1 : Scottish, Scots (language) 2 *pl* **-ceses** : Scotch (whiskey)

escofina *nf* : file, rasp

escoger {15} *vt* ELEGIR, SELECCIONAR : to choose, to select

escogido, -da *adj* : choice, select

escolar[1] *adj* : school

escolar[2] *nmf* : student, pupil

escolaridad *nf* : schooling ⟨escolaridad obligatoria : compulsory education⟩

escolarización *nf, pl* **-ciones** : education, schooling

escolarizar {21} *vt* : to educate

escollo *nm* 1 : reef 2 OBSTÁCULO : obstacle

escolta *nmf* : escort

escoltar *vt* : to escort, to accompany

escombro *nm* 1 : debris, rubbish 2 **escombros** *nmpl* : ruins, rubble

esconder *vt* OCULTAR : to hide, to conceal

escondidas *nfpl* 1 : hide-and-seek 2 **a** ~ : secretly, in secret

escondite *nm* 1 ESCONDRIJO : hiding place 2 ESCONDIDAS : hide-and-seek

escondrijo *nm* ESCONDITE : hiding place

escopeta *nf* : shotgun

escoplo *nm* : chisel

escorar *vi* : to list, to heel (of a boat)

escorbuto *nm* : scurvy

escoria *nf* 1 : slag, dross 2 HEZ : dregs *pl*, scum ⟨la escoria de la sociedad : the dregs of society⟩

Escorpio[1] *or* **Escorpión** *nm* : Scorpio (sign or constellation)

Escorpio[2] *or* **Escorpión** *nmf* : Scorpio (person)

escorpión *nm, pl* **-piones** ALACRÁN : scorpion

escotado, -da *adj* : low-cut (of clothing)

escote *nm* 1 : (low) neckline ⟨escote en V : V-neck⟩ 2 **pagar a escote** : to go dutch

escotilla *nf* : hatch, hatchway

escozor *nm* : smarting, stinging

escriba *nm* : scribe

escribanía *nf CoRi, Arg, Uru* : office of a notary public

escribano, -na *n* 1 : court clerk 2 NOTARIO : notary public

escribir {33} *v* 1 : to write ⟨escribir una novela/palabra : to write a novel/word⟩ ⟨escribir a lápiz : to write in pencil⟩ ⟨escribir a mano : to write by hand⟩ ⟨escribir a máquina : to type⟩ 2 : to spell ⟨¿cómo se escribe? : how do you spell it?⟩ — **escribirse** *vr* CARTEARSE : to write to one another, to correspond

escrito[1] *pp* → escribir

escrito[2], -ta *adj* : written

escrito[3] *nm* 1 : written document 2 **escritos** *nmpl* : writings, works

escritor, -tora *n* : writer

escritorio *nm* : desk

escritorzuelo, -la *n* : hack (writer)

escritura *nf* 1 : writing, handwriting 2 : deed 3 **las Escrituras** : the Scriptures

escroto *nm* : scrotum

escrúpulo *nm* : scruple

escrupuloso, -sa *adj* 1 : scrupulous 2 METICULOSO : exact, meticulous — **escrupulosamente** *adv*

escrutador, -dora *adj* : penetrating, searching

escrutar *vt* ESCUDRIÑAR : to scrutinize, to examine closely

escrutinio *nm* : scrutiny

escuadra *nf* **1** : square (instrument) **2** : fleet, squadron

escuadrilla *nf* : squadron, formation, flight

escuadrón *nm, pl* **-drones** : squadron

escuálido, -da *adj* **1** : skinny, scrawny **2** INMUNDO : filthy, squalid

escuchar *vt* **1** : to listen to **2** : to hear — *vi* : to listen — **escucharse** *vr*

escudar *vt* : to shield — **escudarse** *vr ~* **en** : to hide behind

escudería *nf* : team (in car racing)

escudero *nm* : squire

escudo *nm* **1** : shield **2 escudo de armas** : coat of arms

escudriñar *vt* **1** ESCRUTAR : to scrutinize **2** : to inquire into, to investigate

escuela *nf* **1** : school ⟨escuela privada/pública : private/public school⟩ ⟨escuela nocturna : night school⟩ ⟨escuela de verano : summer school⟩ **2** DEPARTAMENTO : school, department

escueto, -ta *adj* **1** : plain, simple **2** : succinct, concise — **escuetamente** *adv*

escuincle, -cla *n Mex fam* : child, kid

esculcar {72} *vt* : to search

esculpir *vt* **1** : to sculpt **2** : to carve, to engrave — *vi* : to sculpt

escultor, -tora *n* : sculptor

escultórico, -ca *adj* : sculptural

escultura *nf* : sculpture

escultural *adj* : statuesque

escupir *v* : to spit

escupitajo *nm* : spit, gob of spit

escurridizo, -za *adj* : slippery, elusive

escurridor *nm* **1** : dish rack **2** : colander

escurrir *vt* **1** : to wring out **2** : to drain — *vi* **1** : to drain **2** : to drip, to drip-dry — **escurrirse** *vr* : to slip away

ese¹, esa *adj, mpl* **esos** : that, those ⟨ese mismo día : that very day⟩ ⟨esos niños : those children⟩ ⟨sale con la chica esa : he's dating that girl⟩

ese² *nf* : (letter) s

ese³, esa *or* **ése, ésa** *pron, mpl* **esos** *or* **ésos** : that (one), those (ones) *pl* ⟨ese/ése es el mío : that one is mine⟩ ⟨esa/ésa no fue la primera vez : that wasn't the first time⟩ ⟨ese/ése no es el hombre : that's not the man⟩

esencia *nf* : essence

esencial *adj* : essential — **esencialmente** *adv*

esfera *nf* **1** : sphere (object or shape) **2** : sphere ⟨esfera de influencia : sphere of influence⟩ ⟨en las altas esferas : in the highest circles⟩ **3** : face, dial (of a clock)

esférico¹, -ca *adj* : spherical

esférico² *nm* : ball (in sports)

esfinge *nf* : sphinx

esforzado, -da *adj* **1** : energetic, vigorous **2** VALIENTE : courageous, brave

esforzar {36} *vt* : to strain — **esforzarse** *vr* : to make an effort

esfuerzo *nm* **1** : effort **2** ÁNIMO, VIGOR : spirit, vigor **3 sin ~** : effortlessly

esfumar *vt* : to tone down, to soften — **esfumarse** *vr* **1** : to fade away, to vanish **2** *fam* : to take off, to leave

esgrima *nf* : fencing (sport)

esgrimir *vt* **1** : to brandish, to wield **2** : to use, to resort to — *vi* : to fence

esgrimista *nmf* : fencer

esguince *nm* : sprain, strain (of a muscle)

eslabón *nm, pl* **-bones** : link

eslavo¹, -va *adj* : Slavic

eslavo², -va *n* : Slav

eslogan *nm, pl* **-lóganes** : slogan

eslora *nf* : length

eslovaco, -ca *adj & n* : Slovakian, Slovak

esloveno, -na *adj & nm* : Slovene, Slovenian

esmaltar *vt* : to enamel

esmalte *nm* **1** : enamel **2 esmalte de uñas** : nail polish

esmerado, -da *adj* : careful, painstaking

esmeralda *nf* : emerald

esmerarse *vr* : to take great pains, to do one's utmost

esmeril *nm* : emery

esmero *nm* : meticulousness, great care

esmoquin *nm, pl* **-quins** **1** : tuxedo (suit) **2** : tuxedo jacket, dinner jacket

esnob¹ *adj, pl* **esnobs** : snobbish

esnob² *nmf, pl* **esnobs** : snob

esnobismo *nm* : snobbery, snobbishness

esnórquel *nm* : snorkel

eso *pron (neuter)* **1** : that ⟨eso no me gusta : I don't like that⟩ **2 ¡eso es!** : that's it!, that's right! **3 a eso de** : around ⟨a eso de las tres : around three o'clock⟩ **4 en ~** : at that point, just then **5 por ~** : for that reason ⟨por eso me voy : that's why I'm leaving⟩

esófago *nm* : esophagus

esos → ese

ésos → ése

esotérico, -ca *adj* : esoteric — **esotéricamente** *adv*

espabilado, -da *adj* : bright, smart

espabilarse *vr* **1** : to awaken **2** : to get a move on **3** : to get smart, to wise up

espacial *adj* **1** : space **2** : spatial

espaciar *vt* DISTANCIAR : to space out, to spread out

espacio *nm* **1** : space, room ⟨hay mucho espacio : there is plenty of space⟩ ⟨ocupa demasiado espacio : it takes up too much space⟩ ⟨espacios abiertos : open spaces⟩ **2** : space (in printing) ⟨a doble espacio : double-spaced⟩ **3** : period, length (of time) ⟨por espacio de : over a period of⟩ **4** : time slot (in television, etc.) **5** : program ⟨espacio televisivo : television program⟩ **6 espacio exterior** : outer space

espacioso, -sa *adj* : spacious, roomy

espada¹ *nf* **1** : sword **2 espadas** *nfpl* : swords (in the Spanish deck of cards)

espada² *nm* MATADOR, TORERO : bullfighter, matador

espadaña *nf* **1** : belfry **2** : cattail

espagueti *nm or* **espaguetis** *nmpl* : spaghetti

espalda *nf* **1** : back **2 espaldas** *nfpl* : shoulders, back **3** *or* **estilo espalda** : backstroke **4 por la espalda** : from behind

espaldarazo *nm* **1** : recognition, support **2** : slap on the back

espantajo *nm* : scarecrow

espantapájaros *nms & pl* : scarecrow

espantar *vt* ASUSTAR : to scare, to frighten — **espantarse** *vr*

espanto *nm* : fright, fear, horror

espantoso, -sa *adj* **1** : frightening, terrifying **2** : frightful, dreadful — **espantosamente** *adv*

español¹, -ñola *adj* : Spanish

español², -ñola *n* : Spaniard

español³ *nm* CASTELLANO : Spanish (language)

esparadrapo *nm* : adhesive bandage, Band-Aid™

esparcimiento *nm* **1** DIVERSIÓN, RECREO : entertainment, recreation **2** DESCANSO : relaxation **3** DISEMINACIÓN : dissemination, spreading

esparcir {83} *vt* DISPERSAR : to scatter, to spread — **esparcirse** *vr* **1** : to spread out **2** DESCANSARSE : to take it easy **3** DIVERTIRSE : to amuse oneself

espárrago *nm* : asparagus

espartano, -na *adj* : severe, austere

espasmo *nm* : spasm

espasmódico, -ca *adj* : spasmodic — **espasmódicamente** *adv*

espástico, -ca *adj* : spastic

espátula *nf* : spatula

especia *nf* : spice

especial *adj & nm* : special

especialidad *nf* : specialty

especialista *nmf* : specialist, expert

especialización *nf, pl* **-ciones** : specialization

especializarse {21} *vr* : to specialize

especialmente *adv* : especially, particularly

especie *nf* **1** : species **2** CLASE, TIPO : type, kind, sort

especificación *nf, pl* **-ciones** : specification

especificar {72} *vt* : to specify

específico, -ca *adj* : specific — **específicamente** *adv*

espécimen *nm, pl* **especímenes** : specimen

espectacular *adj* : spectacular — **espectacularmente** *adv*

espectáculo *nm* **1** : spectacle, sight **2** : show, performance

espectador, -dora *n* : spectator, onlooker

espectro *nm* **1** : ghost, specter **2** : spectrum

especulación *nf, pl* **-ciones** : speculation

especulador, -dora *n* : speculator

especular *vi* : to speculate

especulativo, -va *adj* : speculative

espejismo *nm* **1** : mirage **2** : illusion

espejo *nm* : mirror

espejuelos *nmpl* ANTEOJOS : spectacles, glasses

espeluznante *adj* : hair-raising, terrifying

espera *nf* : wait

esperado, -da *adj* : anticipated

esperanza *nf* : hope, expectation ⟨dar esperanzas : to give hope⟩ ⟨perder la esperanza : to lose hope⟩ ⟨esperanza de vida : life expectancy⟩

esperanzado, -da *adj* : hopeful

esperanzador, -dora *adj* : encouraging, promising

esperanzar {21} *vt* : to give hope to

esperar *vt* **1** AGUARDAR : to wait for ⟨espero a un amigo : I'm waiting for a friend⟩ ⟨esperé una hora : I waited for an hour⟩ **2** : to expect ⟨no esperaba visitas : I wasn't expecting visitors⟩ ⟨como era de esperar : as was to be expected⟩ ⟨cuando uno menos lo espera : when you least expect it⟩ **3** : to hope ⟨espero poder trabajar : I hope to be able to work⟩ ⟨espero que sí/no : I hope so/not⟩ ⟨espero que llame : I hope he calls⟩ — *vi* : to wait ⟨espere un momento, por favor : just a moment, please⟩ ⟨hay que esperar a que llueva : we have to wait for it to rain⟩ — **esperarse** *vr* **1** : to expect, to be hoped ⟨como podría esperarse : as would be expected⟩ **2** : to hold on, to hang on ⟨espérate un momento : hold on a minute⟩

esperma *nmf* : sperm

esperpéntico, -ca *adj* GROTESCO : grotesque

esperpento *nm fam* MAMARRACHO : sight, fright ⟨voy hecha un esperpento : I really look a sight⟩

espesante *nm* : thickener

espesar *vt* : to thicken — **espesarse** *vr*

espeso, -sa *adj* : thick, heavy, dense

espesor *nm* : thickness, density

espesura *nf* **1** : thickness **2** : thicket

espetar *vt* **1** : to blurt out **2** : to skewer

espía *nmf* : spy

espiar {85} *vt* : to spy on, to observe — *vi* : to spy

espiga *nf* **1** : ear (of wheat) **2** : spike (of flowers)

espigado, -da *adj* : willowy, slender

espigar {52} *vt* : to glean, to gather — **espigarse** *vr* : to grow quickly, to shoot up

espigón *nm, pl* **-gones** : breakwater

espina *nf* **1** : thorn **2** : spine ⟨espina dorsal : spinal column⟩ **3** : fish bone **4** **darle mala espina a alguien** : to make someone uneasy

espinaca *nf* **1** : spinach (plant) **2** **espinacas** *nfpl* : spinach (food)

espinal *adj* : spinal

espinazo *nm* : backbone

espinilla *nf* **1** BARRO, GRANO : pimple **2** : shin

espino *nm* : hawthorn

espinoso, -sa *adj* **1** : thorny, prickly **2** : bony (of fish) **3** : knotty, difficult

espionaje *nm* : espionage

espiración *nf, pl* **-ciones** : exhalation

espiral *adj & nf* : spiral

espirar *vt* EXHALAR : to breathe out, to give off — *vi* : to exhale

espiritismo *nm* : spiritualism

espiritista *nmf* : spiritualist

espíritu *nm* **1** : spirit **2** ÁNIMO : state of mind, spirits *pl* **3** **el Espíritu Santo** : the Holy Ghost

espiritual *adj* : spiritual — **espiritualmente** *adv*

espiritualidad *nf* : spirituality

espita *nf* : spigot, tap

esplendidez *nf, pl* **-deces** ESPLENDOR : magnificence, splendor

espléndido, -da *adj* **1** : splendid, magnificent **2** : generous, lavish — **espléndidamente** *adv*

esplendor *nm* ESPLENDIDEZ : splendor

esplendoroso, -sa *adj* MAGNÍFICO : magnificent, grand

espliego *nm* LAVANDA : lavender

espolear *vt* : to spur on

espoleta *nf* **1** DETONADOR : detonator, fuse **2** : wishbone

espolón *nm, pl* **-lones** : spur (of poultry), fetlock (of a horse)

espolvorear *vt* : to sprinkle, to dust

esponja *nf.* **1** : sponge **2 tirar la esponja** : to throw in the towel

esponjado, -da *adj* : spongy

esponjoso, -sa *adj* **1** : spongy **2** : soft, fluffy

esponsales *nmpl* : betrothal, engagement

espontaneidad *nf* : spontaneity

espontáneo, -nea *adj* : spontaneous — **espontáneamente** *adv*

espora *nf* : spore

esporádico, -ca *adj* : sporadic — **esporádicamente** *adv*

esposar *vt* : to handcuff

esposas *nfpl* : handcuffs

esposo, -sa *n* : spouse, wife *f,* husband *m*

espray *nm, pl* **esprays** : spray

esprint *nm* : sprint

esprintar *vi* : to sprint

esprínter *nmf* : sprinter

espuela *nf* : spur

espuma *nf* **1** : foam 〈espuma de afeitar : shaving cream〉 〈espuma de baño : bubble bath (soap)〉 〈baño de espuma : bubble bath〉 〈crecer/subir como la espuma : to mushroom, to skyrocket〉 **2** : lather **3** : froth, head (on beer)

espumadera *nf* : slotted spoon

espumar *vi* : to foam, to froth — *vt* : to skim off

espumoso, -sa *adj* : foamy, frothy

espurio, -ria *adj* : spurious

esqueje *nm* : cutting (from a plant)

esquela *nf* **1** : note **2** : notice, announcement

esquelético, -ca *adj* : emaciated, skeletal

esqueleto *nm* **1** : skeleton **2** ARMAZÓN : framework

esquema *nm* BOSQUEJO : outline, sketch, plan

esquemático, -ca *adj* : schematic

esquí *nm, pl* **esquíes 1** : ski **2 esquí acuático** : water ski, waterskiing

esquiador, -dora *n* : skier

esquiar {85} *vi* : to ski

esquilar *vt* TRASQUILAR : to shear

esquimal *adj & nmf* : Eskimo *now sometimes offensive*

esquina *nf* : corner

esquinazo *nm* **1** : corner **2 dar esquinazo a** *fam* : to stand up, to give the slip to

esquirla *nf* : splinter (of bone, glass, etc.)

esquirol *nm* ROMPEHUELGAS : strikebreaker, scab

esquisto *nm* : shale

esquivar *vt* **1** EVADIR : to dodge, to evade **2** EVITAR : to avoid

esquivo, -va *adj* **1** HURAÑO : aloof, unsociable **2** : shy **3** : elusive, evasive

esquizofrenia *nf* : schizophrenia

esquizofrénico, -ca *adj & n* : schizophrenic

esta *adj → este[1]*

ésta → éste

estabilidad *nf* : stability

estabilizar {21} *vt* : to stabilize — **estabilizarse** *vr* — **estabilización** *nf* — **estabilizador** *nm*

estable *adj* : stable, steady

establecer {53} *vt* **1** FUNDAR, INSTITUIR : to establish, to found (a city, etc.), to set up (a system, etc.) **2** : to establish (a law, etc.), to set (a standard, etc.) **3** : to establish (relations, etc.) **4** DEMOSTRAR : to establish, to show, to prove — **establecerse** *vr* **1** INSTALARSE : to settle, to establish oneself **2** : to establish, to show, to prove

establecimiento *nm* **1** : establishing **2** : establishment, institution, office

establo *nm* : stable

estaca *nf* : stake, picket, post

estacada *nf* **1** : picket fence **2** : stockade

estacar {72} *vt* **1** : to stake out **2** : to fasten down with stakes — **estacarse** *vr* : to remain rigid

estación *nf. pl* **-ciones 1** : station 〈estación de servicio : service station, gas station〉 **2** : season

estacional *adj* : seasonal

estacionamiento *nm* **1** : parking **2** : parking lot

estacionar *vt* **1** : to place, to station **2** : to park — **estacionarse** *vr* **1** : to park **2** : to remain stationary

estacionario, -ria *adj* **1** : stationary **2** : stable

estada *nf → estadía*

estadía *nf* ESTANCIA : stay, sojourn

estadio *nm* **1** : stadium **2** : phase, stage

estadista *nmf* : statesman

estadística *nf* **1** : statistic, figure **2** : statistics

estadístico[1], -ca *adj* : statistical — **estadísticamente** *adv*

estadístico[2], -ca *n* : statistician

estado *nm* **1** : state, condition 〈estar en buen/mal estado : to be in good/bad condition〉 **2** : state (nation or region) 〈los Estados Unidos : the United States〉 **3** : state, government **4** : status 〈estado civil : marital status〉 **5 estado de ánimo** : state of mind **6 estado de cuenta** : account statement **7 estado de emergencia** : state of emergency **8 estado de la nación** : state of the nation **9 estado de salud** : (state of) health, condition **10 estar en estado** : to be expecting, to be pregnant

estadounidense *adj & nmf* AMERICANO, NORTEAMERICANO : American

estafa *nf* : swindle, fraud

estafador, -dora *n* : cheat, swindler

estafar *vt* DEFRAUDAR : to swindle, to defraud

estafeta *nf* 1 : baton (in a relay race) 2 : post office

estalactita *nf* : stalactite

estalagmita *nf* : stalagmite

estallar *vi* 1 REVENTAR : to burst, to explode, to erupt 2 : to break out

estallido *nm* 1 EXPLOSIÓN : explosion 2 : report (of a gun) 3 : outbreak, outburst

estambre *nm* 1 : worsted (fabric) 2 : stamen

estamento *nm* : stratum, class

estampa *nf* 1 ILUSTRACIÓN, IMAGEN : printed image, illustration 2 ASPECTO : appearance, demeanor

estampado¹, -da *adj* : patterned, printed

estampado² *nm* : print, pattern

estampar *vt* : to stamp, to print, to engrave

estampida *nf* : stampede

estampido *nm* ESTALLIDO : bang

estampilla *nf* 1 : rubber stamp 2 SELLO, TIMBRE : postage stamp

estancado, -da *adj* : stagnant

estancamiento *nm* : stagnation

estancar {72} *vt* 1 : to dam up, to hold back 2 : to bring to a halt, to deadlock — **estancarse** *vr* 1 : to stagnate 2 : to be brought to a standstill, to be deadlocked

estancia *nf* 1 ESTADÍA : stay, sojourn 2 : ranch, farm

estanciero, -ra *n* : rancher, farmer

estanco, -ca *adj* : watertight

estándar *adj & nm* : standard

estandarización *nf, pl* **-ciones** : standardization

estandarizar {21} *vt* : to standardize

estandarte *nm* : standard, banner

estanque *nm* 1 : pool, pond 2 : tank, reservoir

estanquillo *nm Mex* : general store

estante *nm* REPISA : shelf

estantería *nf* : shelves *pl*, bookcase

estaño *nm* : tin

estaquilla *nf* 1 : peg 2 ESPIGA : spike

estar {34} *v aux* 1 : to be ⟨estoy aprendiendo inglés : I'm learning English⟩ ⟨está terminado : it's finished⟩ — *vi* 1 (*indicating a state or condition*) : to be ⟨está lleno : it's full⟩ ⟨está claro que . . . : it's clear that . . .⟩ ⟨¿ya estás mejor? : are you feeling better now?⟩ ⟨estoy casado : I'm married⟩ ⟨está sin trabajo : she's out of work, she has no job⟩ ⟨está muy alto : he's so tall, he's gotten very tall⟩ 2 (*indicating location*) : to be ⟨están en la mesa : they're on the table⟩ ⟨estamos en la página 2 : we're on page 2⟩ ⟨ahí está el problema : therein lies the problem⟩ 3 : to be at home ⟨¿está Julia? : is Julia in?⟩ 4 : to be, to remain ⟨estaré aquí 5 días : I'll be here for 5 days⟩ 5 : to be ready, to be done ⟨estará para las diez

: it will be ready by ten o'clock⟩ 6 : to agree ⟨¿estamos? : are we in agreement?⟩ ⟨estoy contigo : I'm with you⟩ 7 ¿cómo estás? : how are you? 8 ¡está bien! : all right!, that's fine! 9 ~ a : to cost 10 ~ a : to be ⟨¿a qué día estamos? : what day is today?, what's today's date?⟩ ⟨está a 15 kilómetros del centro : it's 15 kilometers from the downtown⟩ 11 ~ con : to have ⟨está con fiebre : she has a fever⟩ 12 ~ de : to be ⟨estoy de vacaciones : I'm on vacation⟩ ⟨está de director hoy : he's acting as director today⟩ 13 estar bien/mal : to be well/sick 14 ~ para : to be in the mood for 15 ~ para : to be for (a purpose) ⟨para eso está : that's what it's here for⟩ 16 ~ por : to be in favor of 17 ~ por : to be about to ⟨está por cerrar : it's on the verge of closing⟩ 18 estar de más : to be unnecessary 19 estar que (*indicating a state or condition*) ⟨está que echa chispas : he's hopping mad⟩ — **estarse** *vr* QUEDARSE : to stay, to remain ⟨estáte quieto! : be still!⟩

estarcir {83} *vt* : to stencil

estárter *nm* : choke (of a motor)

estatal *adj* : state, national

estática *nf* : static

estático, -ca *adj* : static

estatizar {21} *vt* : to nationalize — **estatización** *nf*

estatua *nf* : statue

estatuilla *nf* : statuette, figurine

estatura *nf* : height, stature ⟨de mediana estatura : of medium height⟩

estatus *nm* : status, prestige

estatutario, -ria *adj* : statutory

estatuto *nm* : statute

este¹, esta *adj, mpl* **estos** : this, these ⟨este año : this year⟩ ⟨estas señoras : these ladies⟩ ⟨es un sinvergüenza el tipo este : this guy is a crook⟩

este² *adj* : eastern, east

este³ *nm* 1 ORIENTE : east 2 : east wind 3 el Este : the East, the Orient

este⁴, esta *or* **éste, ésta** *pron, mpl* **estos** *or* **éstos** 1 : this (one), these (ones) *pl* ⟨este/éste es el mío : this one is mine⟩ ⟨esta/ésta no es la primera vez : this isn't the first time⟩ ⟨un día de estos/éstos : one of these days⟩ 2 : the latter ⟨se lo dijo a su hijo, y este/éste me llamó : he told his son, who called me⟩

estela *nf* 1 : wake (of a ship) 2 RASTRO : trail (of dust, smoke, etc.)

estelar *adj* : stellar

estelarizar {21} *vt Mex* : to star in, to be the star of

esténcil *nm* : stencil

estepa *nf* : steppe

estera *nf* : mat

estéreo *adj & nm* : stereo

estereofónico, -ca *adj* : stereophonic

estereotipado, -da *adj* : stereotyped

estereotipar *vt* : to stereotype

estereotipo *nm* : stereotype

estéril *adj* 1 : sterile 2 : infertile, sterile, barren 3 : futile, vain

esterilidad *nf* 1 : sterility 2 : infertility

esterilizar {21} *vt* **1** : to sterilize, to disinfect **2** : to sterilize (a person), to spay (an animal) — **esterilización** *nf*

esterlina *adj* : sterling

esternón *nm, pl* **-nones** : sternum

estero *nm* : estuary

esteroide *nm* : steroid

estertor *nm* : death rattle

estética *nf* : aesthetics

esteticista *nmf* : beautician

estético, -ca *adj* : aesthetic — **estéticamente** *adv*

estetoscopio *nm* : stethoscope

estibador, -dora *n* : longshoreman, stevedore

estiércol *nm* : dung, manure

estigma *nm* : stigma

estigmatizar {21} *vt* : to stigmatize, to brand

estilarse *vr* : to be in fashion

estilete *nm* : stiletto

estilista *nmf* : stylist

estilizar {21} *vt* : to stylize

estilo *nm* **1** : style ⟨estilo de vida : lifestyle⟩ **2** : fashion, manner **3** : stylus

estilográfica *nf* : fountain pen

estima *nf* ESTIMACIÓN : esteem, regard

estimable *adj* **1** : considerable **2** : estimable, esteemed

estimación *nf, pl* **-ciones** **1** ESTIMA : esteem, regard **2** : estimate

estimado, -da *adj* : esteemed, dear ⟨Estimado señor Ortiz : Dear Mr. Ortiz⟩

estimar *vt* **1** APRECIAR : to esteem, to respect **2** EVALUAR : to estimate, to appraise **3** OPINAR : to consider, to deem

estimulación *nf, pl* **-ciones** **1** : stimulation **2** estimulación hidráulica *Arg, Col* : fracking

estimulante¹ *adj* : stimulating

estimulante² *nm* : stimulant

estimular *vt* **1** : to stimulate **2** : to encourage

estímulo *nm* **1** : stimulus **2** INCENTIVO : incentive, encouragement

estío *nm* : summertime

estipendio *nm* **1** : salary **2** : stipend, remuneration

estipular *vt* : to stipulate — **estipulación** *nf*

estirado, -da *adj* **1** : stretched, extended **2** PRESUMIDO : stuck-up, conceited

estiramiento *nm* **1** : stretching **2** estiramiento facial : face-lift

estirar *vt* : to stretch (out), to extend — **estirarse** *vr*

estirón *nm, pl* **-rones** **1** : pull, tug **2** dar un estirón : to grow quickly, to shoot up

estirpe *nf* LINAJE : lineage, stock

estival *adj* VERANIEGO : summer

esto *pron* (*neuter*) **1** : this ⟨¿qué es esto? : what is this?⟩ **2 en ~** : at this point **3 por ~** : for this reason

estocada *nf* **1** : final thrust (in bullfighting) **2** : thrust, lunge (in fencing)

estofa *nf* CLASE : class, quality ⟨de baja estofa : low-class, poor-quality⟩

estofado *nm* COCIDO, GUISADO : stew

estofar *vt* GUISAR : to stew

estoicismo *nm* : stoicism

estoico¹, -ca *adj* : stoic, stoical

estoico², -ca *n* : stoic

estola *nf* : stole

estolón *nm, pl* **-lones** : runner (of a plant)

estomacal *adj* GÁSTRICO : stomach, gastric

estómago *nm* : stomach

estoniano, -na *adj & n* : Estonian

estonio, -nia *adj & n* : Estonian

estopa *nf* **1** : tow (yarn or cloth) **2** : burlap

estopilla *nf* : cheesecloth

estoque *nm* : rapier, sword

estorbar *vt* OBSTRUIR : to obstruct, to hinder — *vi* : to get in the way

estorbo *nm* **1** : obstacle, hindrance **2** : nuisance

estornino *nm* : starling

estornudar *vi* : to sneeze

estornudo *nm* : sneeze

estos *adj* → **este¹**

éstos → **éste**

estoy → **estar**

estrabismo *nm* : squint

estrado *nm* **1** : dais, platform **2** : bench (of a judge) **3** : witness stand **4 estrados** *nmpl* : courts of law

estrafalario, -ria *adj* ESTRAMBÓTICO, EXCÉNTRICO : eccentric, bizarre

estragar {52} *vt* DEVASTAR : to ruin, to devastate

estragón *nm* : tarragon

estragos *nmpl* **1** : ravages, destruction, devastation ⟨los estragos de la guerra : the ravages of war⟩ **2 hacer estragos en** *or* **causar estragos entre** : to play havoc with

estrambótico, -ca *adj* ESTRAFALARIO, EXCÉNTRICO : eccentric, bizarre

estrangulador, -dora *n* : strangler

estrangulamiento *nm* : strangling, strangulation

estrangular *vt* AHOGAR : to strangle — **estrangulación** *nf*

estratagema *nf* ARTIMAÑA : stratagem, ruse

estratega *nmf* : strategist

estrategia *nf* : strategy

estratégico, -ca *adj* : strategic, tactical — **estratégicamente** *adv*

estratificado, -da *adj* : stratified

estrato *nm* : stratum, layer

estratosfera *nf* : stratosphere

estratosférico, -ca *adj* **1** : stratospheric **2** : astronomical, exorbitant

estrechamiento *nm* **1** : narrowing **2** : narrow point **3** : tightening, strengthening (of relations)

estrechar *vt* **1** : to narrow **2** : to tighten, to strengthen (a bond) **3** : to hug, to embrace **4 estrechar la mano de** : to shake hands with — **estrecharse** *vr*

estrechez *nf, pl* **-checes** **1** : tightness, narrowness **2 estrecheces** *nfpl* : financial problems

estrecho¹, -cha *adj* **1** : tight, narrow **2** ÍNTIMO : close — **estrechamente** *adv*

estrecho² *nm* : strait, narrows

estrella *nf* **1** ASTRO : star ⟨estrella fugaz : shooting star⟩ **2** : destiny ⟨tener buena estrella : to be born lucky⟩ 3 : movie star 4 estrella de mar : starfish

estrellado, -da adj 1 : starry 2 : starshaped 3 huevos estrellados : fried eggs

estrellamiento nm : crash, collision

estrellar vt : to smash, to crash — estrellarse vr : to crash, to collide

estrellato nm : stardom

estremecedor, -dora adj : horrifying

estremecer {53} vt : to cause to shake — vi : to tremble, to shake — estremecerse vr : to shudder, to shiver (with emotion)

estremecimiento nm : trembling, shaking, shivering

estrenar vt 1 : to use for the first time 2 : to premiere, to open — estrenarse vr : to make one's debut

estreno nm DEBUT : debut, premiere

estreñido, -da adj : constipated

estreñimiento nm : constipation

estreñir {67} vt : to constipate, to make constipated — vi : to cause constipation — estreñirse vr : to get constipated

estrépito nm ESTRUENDO : clamor, din

estrepitoso, -sa adj : clamorous, noisy — estrepitosamente adv

estrés nm, pl estreses : stress

estresante adj : stressful

estresar vt : to stress, to stress out — estresado, -da adj

estría nf : fluting, groove

estribación nf, pl -ciones 1 : spur, ridge 2 estribaciones nfpl : foothills

estribar vi FUNDARSE ~ en : to be due to, to stem from

estribillo nm : refrain, chorus

estribo nm 1 : stirrup 2 : abutment, buttress 3 perder los estribos : to lose one's temper

estribor nm : starboard

estricto, -ta adj SEVERO : strict, severe — estrictamente adv

estridente adj : strident, shrill, loud — estridentemente adv

estrofa nf : stanza, verse

estrógeno nm : estrogen

estropajo nm : scouring pad

estropear vt 1 ARRUINAR : to ruin, to spoil 2 : to break, to damage — estropearse vr 1 : to spoil, to go bad 2 : to break down — estropeado, -da adj

estropicio nm DAÑO : damage, breakage

estructura nf : structure, framework

estructuración nf, pl -ciones : structuring, structure

estructural adj : structural — estructuralmente adv

estructurar vt : to structure, to organize

estruendo nm ESTRÉPITO : racket, din, roar

estruendoso, -sa adj : resounding, thunderous

estrujar vt APRETAR : to press, to squeeze

estuario nm : estuary

estuche nm : kit, case

estuco nm : stucco

estudiado, -da adj : affected, mannered

estudiantado nm : student body, students pl

estudiante nmf : student

estudiantil adj : student ⟨la vida estudiantil : student life⟩

estudiar v : to study

estudio nm 1 : study ⟨estar en estudio : to be under consideration⟩ ⟨un estudio sobre la salud nacional : a study of the nation's health⟩ 2 : studio (room or office) 3 : studio (for filming, etc.) 4 : studio (apartment) 5 estudios nmpl : studies, education ⟨estudios primarios/secundarios/superiores : primary/secondary/higher education⟩ ⟨tener estudios en/de algo : to have studied something⟩

estudioso, -sa adj : studious

estufa nf 1 : stove, heater 2 Col, Mex : cooking stove, range

estupefacción nf, pl -ciones : astonishment

estupefaciente[1] adj : narcotic

estupefaciente[2] nm DROGA, NARCÓTICO : drug, narcotic

estupefacto, -ta adj : astonished, stunned

estupendo, -da adj MARAVILLOSO : stupendous, marvelous — estupendamente adv

estupidez nf, pl -deces 1 : stupidity 2 : nonsense

estúpido[1], -da adj : stupid — estúpidamente adv

estúpido[2], -da n IDIOTA : idiot, fool

estupor nm 1 : stupor 2 : amazement

esturión nm, pl -riones : sturgeon

estuvo, etc. → estar

esvástica nf : swastika

etanol nm : ethanol

etapa nf FASE : stage, phase

etcétera[1] : et cetera, and so on

etcétera[2] nmf : et cetera

éter nm : ether

etéreo, -rea adj : ethereal, heavenly

eternidad nf : eternity

eternizar {21} vt PERPETUAR : to make eternal, to perpetuate — eternizarse vr fam : to take forever

eterno, -na adj : eternal, endless — eternamente adv

ética nf : ethics

ético, -ca adj : ethical — éticamente adv

etílico, -ca adj 1 : alcohol, alcoholic ⟨intoxicación etílica : alcohol poisoning⟩ 2 : inebriated, drunken

etimología nf : etymology

etimológico, -ca adj : etymological

etíope adj & nmf : Ethiopian

etiqueta nf 1 : etiquette 2 : tag, label 3 : hashtag (on social media) 4 de ~ : formal, dressy

etiquetar vt : to label

etnia nf : ethnic group

étnico, -ca adj : ethnic

eucalipto nm : eucalyptus

Eucaristía nf : Eucharist, communion

eufemismo nm : euphemism

eufemístico, -ca adj : euphemistic

euforia nf : euphoria, joyousness

eufórico, -ca adj : euphoric, exuberant, joyous — eufóricamente adv

eunuco nm : eunuch

euro nm : euro
europeo, -pea adj & n : European
euskera nm : Basque (language)
eutanasia nf : euthanasia
evacuación nf, pl -ciones : evacuation
evacuar vt 1 : to evacuate, to vacate 2 : to carry out — vi : to have a bowel movement, to move one's bowels
evadir vt ELUDIR : to evade, to avoid — **evadirse** vr : to escape, to slip away
evaluación nf, pl -ciones : assessment, evaluation
evaluador, -dora n : assessor
evaluar {3} vt : to evaluate, to assess, to appraise
evangélico, -ca adj : evangelical — **evangélicamente** adv
evangelio nm : gospel
evangelismo nm : evangelism
evangelista nm : evangelist
evangelizador, -dora n : evangelist, missionary
evaporación nf, pl -ciones : evaporation
evaporar vt : to evaporate — **evaporarse** vr ESFUMARSE : to disappear, to vanish
evasión nf, pl -siones 1 : escape, flight 2 : evasion, dodge
evasiva nf : excuse, pretext
evasivo, -va adj : evasive
evento nm : event
eventual adj 1 : possible 2 : temporary ⟨trabajadores eventuales : temporary workers⟩ — **eventualmente** adv
eventualidad nf : possibility, eventuality
evidencia nf 1 : evidence, proof 2 **poner en evidencia** : to demonstrate, to make clear
evidenciar vt : to demonstrate, to show — **evidenciarse** vr : to be evident
evidente adj : evident, obvious, clear — **evidentemente** adv
eviscerar vt : to eviscerate
evitable adj : avoidable, preventable
evitar vt 1 : to avoid 2 PREVENIR : to prevent 3 ELUDIR : to escape, to elude
evocación nf, pl -ciones : evocation
evocador, -dora adj : evocative
evocar {72} vt 1 : to evoke 2 RECORDAR : to recall
evolución nf, pl -ciones 1 : evolution 2 : development, progress
evolucionar vi 1 : to evolve 2 : to change, to develop
evolutivo, -va adj : evolutionary
ex nmf : ex
ex- or **ex** pref : ex-, former ⟨exmarido, ex marido : ex-husband⟩
exabrupto nm : pointed remark
exacerbar vt 1 : to exacerbate, to aggravate 2 : to irritate, to exasperate
exactamente adv : exactly
exactitud nf PRECISIÓN : accuracy, precision, exactitude
exacto, -ta adj PRECISO : accurate, precise, exact
exageración nf, pl -ciones : exaggeration
exagerado, -da adj 1 : exaggerated 2 : excessive — **exageradamente** adv
exagerar v : to exaggerate

exaltación nf, pl -ciones 1 : exaltation 2 : excitement, agitation
exaltado[1], -da adj : excitable, hotheaded
exaltado[2], -da n : hothead
exaltar vt 1 ENSALZAR : to exalt, to extol 2 : to excite, to agitate — **exaltarse** vr ACALORARSE : to get overexcited
ex-alumno → alumno
examen nm, pl exámenes 1 : examination, test ⟨examen final/oral : final/written exam⟩ ⟨examen de manejo/conducir : driving test⟩ ⟨hacer/dar un examen : to take a test⟩ 2 : consideration, investigation ⟨someter algo a examen : to examine something⟩
examinar vt 1 : to examine 2 INSPECCIONAR : to inspect — **examinarse** vr : to take an exam
exánime adj 1 : lifeless 2 : exhausted
exasperante adj : exasperating
exasperar vt IRRITAR : to exasperate, to irritate — **exasperación** nf
excavación nf, pl -ciones : excavation
excavadora nf : excavator
excavar v : to excavate, to dig
excedente[1] adj 1 : excessive 2 : excess, surplus
excedente[2] nm : surplus, excess
exceder vt : to exceed, to surpass — **excederse** vr : to go too far
excelencia nf 1 : excellence 2 : excellency ⟨Su Excelencia : His Excellency⟩
excelente adj : excellent — **excelentemente** adv
excelso, -sa adj : lofty, sublime
excentricidad nf : eccentricity
excéntrico, -ca adj & n : eccentric
excepción nf, pl -ciones : exception ⟨a/con excepción de : with the exception of⟩
excepcional adj EXTRAORDINARIO : exceptional, extraordinary, rare — **excepcionalmente** adv
excepto prep SALVO : except
exceptuar {3} vt EXCLUIR : to except, to exclude
excesivo, -va adj : excessive — **excesivamente** adv
exceso nm 1 : excess 2 excesos nmpl : excesses, abuses 3 **exceso de velocidad** : speeding
excitabilidad nf : excitability
excitación nf, pl -ciones : excitement
excitante adj : exciting
excitar vt : to excite, to arouse — **excitarse** vr
exclamación nf, pl -ciones : exclamation
exclamar v : to exclaim
excluir {41} vt EXCEPTUAR : to exclude, to leave out
exclusión nf, pl -siones : exclusion
exclusividad nf 1 : exclusiveness 2 : exclusive rights pl
exclusivo, -va adj : exclusive — **exclusivamente** adv
excombatiente nmf : war veteran
excomulgar {52} vt : to excommunicate
excomunión nf, pl -niones : excommunication
excreción nf, pl -ciones : excretion

excremento *nm* : excrement
excretar *vt* : to excrete
exculpar *vt* : to exonerate, to exculpate —
 exculpación *nf*
excursión *nf, pl* **-siones** : excursion, outing
excursionista *nmf* **1** : sightseer, tourist
 2 : hiker
excusa *nf* **1** PRETEXTO : excuse ⟨poner
 excusas : to make excuses⟩ **2** DISCULPA
 : apology
excusado *nm Mex* : toilet
excusar *vt* **1** : to excuse **2** : to exempt
 — **excusarse** *vr* : to apologize, to send
 one's regrets
execrable *adj* : detestable, abominable
exención *nf, pl* **-ciones** : exemption
exento, -ta *adj* **1** : exempt, free **2**
 exento de impuestos : tax-exempt
exequias *nfpl* FUNERALES : funeral rites
exesposa *or* **ex esposa** *nf* : ex-wife
exhalación *nf, pl* **-ciones** **1** : exhalation
 2 : shooting star ⟨salió como una exhalación : he took off like a shot⟩
exhalar *vt* ESPIRAR : to exhale, to give off
exhaustivo, -va *adj* : exhaustive — **ex-
 haustivamente** *adv*
exhausto, -ta *adj* AGOTADO : exhausted,
 worn-out
exhibición *nf, pl* **-ciones** **1** : exhibition,
 show **2** : showing
exhibir *vt* : to exhibit, to show, to display
 — **exhibirse** *vr*
exhortación *nf, pl* **-ciones** : exhortation
exhortar *vt* : to exhort
exhumar *vt* DESENTERRAR : to exhume
 — **exhumación** *nf*
exigencia *nf* : demand, requirement
exigente *adj* : demanding, exacting
exigir {35} *vt* **1** : to demand, to require **2**
 : to exact, to levy
exiguo, -gua *adj* : meager
exiliado¹, -da *adj* : exiled, in exile
exiliado², -da *n* : exile
exiliar *vt* DESTERRAR : to exile, to banish
 — **exiliarse** *vr* : to go into exile
exilio *nm* DESTIERRO : exile
eximio, -mia *adj* : distinguished, eminent
eximir *vt* EXONERAR : to exempt
existencia *nf* **1** : existence **2** **existencias** *nfpl* MERCANCÍA : goods, stock
existente *adj* **1** : existing, in existence **2**
 : in stock
existir *vi* : to exist
exitazo *nm* : big/huge success, big/huge
 hit, smash
éxito *nm* **1** TRIUNFO : success, hit **2** tener **éxito** : to be successful
exitoso, -sa *adj* : successful — **exitosa-
 mente** *adv*
exmarido *or* **ex marido** *nm* : ex-husband
éxodo *nm* : exodus
exoneración *nf, pl* **-ciones** EXENCIÓN
 : exoneration, exemption
exonerar *vt* **1** EXIMIR : to exempt, to exonerate **2** DESPEDIR : to dismiss
exorbitante *adj* : exorbitant
exorcismo *nm* : exorcism — **exorcista**
 nmf
exorcizar {21} *vt* : to exorcise

exótico, -ca *adj* : exotic
expandir *vt* EXPANSIONAR : to expand —
 expandirse *vr* : to spread
expansión *nf, pl* **-siones** **1** : expansion,
 spread **2** DIVERSIÓN : recreation, relaxation
expansionar *vt* EXPANDIR : to expand —
 expansionarse *vr* **1** : to expand **2** DI-
 VERTIRSE : to amuse oneself, to relax
expansivo, -va *adj* : expansive
expatriado, -da *adj & n* : expatriate
expatriar {85} *vt* : to expatriate, to exile
 — **expatriarse** *vr* **1** EMIGRAR : to emigrate **2** : to go into exile
expectación *nf, pl* **-ciones** : expectation,
 anticipation
expectante *adj* : expectant
expectativa *nf* **1** : expectation, hope ⟨es-
 tar a la expectativa de : to await, to wait
 for⟩ ⟨expectativa(s) de la vida : life expec-
 tancy⟩ **2** **expectativas** *nfpl* : prospects
expedición *nf, pl* **-ciones** : expedition
expediente *nm* **1** : expedient, means **2**
 ARCHIVO : file, dossier, record
expedir {54} *vt* **1** EMITIR : to issue **2**
 DESPACHAR : to dispatch, to send
expedito, -ta *adj* **1** : free, clear **2**
 : quick, easy
expeler *vt* : to expel, to eject
expendedor, -dora *n* : dealer, seller
expendio *nm* TIENDA : store, shop
expensas *nfpl* **1** : expenses, costs **2 a
 expensas de** : at the expense of
experiencia *nf* **1** : experience **2** EXPERI-
 MENTO : experiment
experimentación *nf, pl* **-ciones** : experimentation
experimentado, -da *adj* : experienced
experimental *adj* : experimental
experimentar *vi* : to experiment — *vt* **1**
 : to experiment with, to test out **2** : to
 experience
experimento *nm* EXPERIENCIA : experiment
experto, -ta *adj & n* : expert
expiación *nf, pl* **-ciones** : expiation,
 atonement
expiar {85} *vt* : to expiate, to atone for
expiración *nf, pl* **-ciones** VENCIMIENTO
 : expiration
expirar *vi* **1** FALLECER, MORIR : to pass
 away, to die **2** : to expire
explanada *nf* **1** TERRAZA : terrace **2** PA-
 TIO : courtyard, patio **3** : seaside walk,
 boardwalk
explayar *vt* : to extend — **explayarse** *vr*
 : to expound, to speak at length
explicable *adj* : explicable, explainable
explicación *nf, pl* **-ciones** : explanation
explicar {72} *vt* : to explain — **explicarse**
 vr **1** : to understand **2** : to explain oneself
explicativo, -va *adj* : explanatory
explicitar *vt* : to state explicitly, to specify
explícito, -ta *adj* : explicit — **explícita-
 mente** *adv*
exploración *nf, pl* **-ciones** : exploration
explorador, -dora *n* : explorer, scout
explorar *vt* : to explore — **exploratorio,
 -ria** *adj*

explosión *nf, pl* **-siones 1** ESTALLIDO : explosion **2** : outburst ⟨una explosión de ira : an outburst of anger⟩

explosionar *vi* : to explode

explosivo, -va *adj* : explosive

explotación *nf, pl* **-ciones 1** : exploitation **2** : operation, running

explotar *vt* **1** : to exploit **2** : to operate, to run — *vi* ESTALLAR, REVENTAR : to explode — **explotable** *adj*

exponencial *adj* : exponential — **exponencialmente** *adv*

exponente *nm* : exponent

exponer {60} *vt* **1** : to exhibit, to show, to display **2** : to explain, to present, to set forth **3** : to expose, to risk — *vi* : to exhibit

exportación *nf, pl* **-ciones 1** : exportation **2 exportaciones** *nfpl* : exports

exportador, -dora *n* : exporter

exportar *vt* : to export — **exportable** *adj*

exposición *nf, pl* **-ciones 1** EXHIBICIÓN : exposition, exhibition **2** : exposure **3** : presentation, statement

expósito, -ta *n* : foundling

expositor, -tora *n* **1** : exhibitor **2** : exponent

exprés¹ *adj* : express

exprés² *nms & pl* **1** : express, express train **2** : espresso

expresamente *adv* : expressly, on purpose

expresar *vt* : to express — **expresarse** *vr*

expresión *nf, pl* **-siones** : expression

expresivo, -va *adj* **1** : expressive **2** CARIÑOSO : affectionate — **expresivamente** *adv*

expreso¹, -sa *adj* **1** : express, specific **2** : express ⟨correo expreso : express mail⟩

expreso² *nm* **1** : express train, express **2** : express mail

express → exprés

exprimidor *nm* : juicer

exprimir *vt* **1** : to squeeze **2** : to exploit

expropiar *vt* : to expropriate, to commandeer — **expropiación** *nf*

expuesto¹ *pp → exponer*

expuesto², -ta *adj* **1** : exposed **2** : hazardous, risky

expulsar *vt* : to expel, to eject — **expulsarse** *vr*

expulsión *nf, pl* **-siones** : expulsion

expurgar {52} *vt* : to expurgate

expuso, etc. → exponer

exquisitez *nf, pl* **-teces 1** : exquisiteness, refinement **2** : delicacy, special dish

exquisito, -ta *adj* **1** : exquisite **2** : delicious

extasiarse {85} *vr* : to be in ecstasy, to be enraptured

éxtasis *nms & pl* **1** : ecstasy, rapture **2** : Ecstasy (drug)

extático, -ca *adj* : ecstatic

extemporáneo, -nea *adj* **1** : unseasonable **2** : untimely

extender {56} *vt* **1** : to spread out, to stretch out **2** : to broaden, to expand ⟨extender la influencia : to broaden one's influence⟩ **3** : to draw up (a document), to write out (a check) — **extenderse** *vr* **1** : to spread **2** : to last

extendido, -da *adj* **1** : outstretched **2** : widespread **3** : extended ⟨garantía extendida : extended warranty⟩

extensamente *adv* : extensively, at length

extensible *adj* : extendable

extensión *nf, pl* **-siones 1** : extension, stretching **2** : expanse, spread **3** : extent, range **4** : length, duration **5** : extension cord

extensivamente *adv* : widely, broadly

extensivo, -va *adj* **1** : extensive **2 hacer extensivo** : to extend

extenso, -sa *adj* **1** : extensive, detailed **2** : spacious, vast

extenuar {3} *vt* : to exhaust, to tire out — **extenuarse** *vr* — **extenuante** *adj*

exterior¹ *adj* **1** : exterior, external **2** : foreign ⟨asuntos exteriores : foreign affairs⟩

exterior² *nm* **1** : outside **2** : abroad

exteriorizar {21} *vt* : to express, to reveal

exteriormente *adv* : outwardly

exterminador¹, -dora *adj → ángel*

exterminador², -dora *n* **exterminador - dora de plagas** : exterminator

exterminar *vt* : to exterminate — **exterminación** *nf*

exterminio *nm* : extermination

externalización *nf, pl* **-ciones** : outsourcing

externalizar {21} *vt* : to outsource

externar *vt Mex* : to express, to display

externo, -na *adj* : external, outward

extinción *nf, pl* **-ciones** : extinction

extinguidor *nm* : fire extinguisher

extinguir {26} *vt* **1** APAGAR : to extinguish, to put out **2** : to wipe out — **extinguirse** *vr* **1** APAGARSE : to go out, to fade out **2** : to die out, to become extinct

extinto, -ta *adj* : extinct

extintor *nm* : extinguisher

extirpación *n, pl* **-ciones** : removal (of a tumor, etc.)

extirpar *vt* : to eradicate, to remove, to excise — **extirparse** *vr*

extorsión *nf, pl* **-siones 1** : extortion **2** : harm, trouble

extorsionar *vt* : to extort

extra¹ *adv* : extra

extra² *adj* **1** : additional, extra **2** : superior, top-quality

extra³ *nmf* : extra (in movies)

extra⁴ *nm* : extra expense ⟨paga extra : bonus⟩

**extra- ** *pref* : extra-

extracción *nf, pl* **-ciones** : extraction

extracto *nm* **1** : extract ⟨extracto de vainilla : vanilla extract⟩ **2** : abstract, summary

extractor *nm* : extractor

extracurricular *adj* : extracurricular

extradición *nf, pl* **-ciones** : extradition

extraditar *vt* : to extradite

extraer {81} *vt* : to extract

extraído *pp → extraer*

extrajudicial *adj* : out-of-court

extrajudicialmente *adv* : out of court

extralimitarse *vr* : to go too far, to overstep one's bounds

extramatrimonial *adj* : extramarital
extranjero¹, -ra *adj* : foreign
extranjero², -ra *n* : foreigner
extranjero³ *nm* : foreign countries *pl* ⟨viajó al extranjero : he traveled abroad⟩ ⟨trabajan en el extranjero : they work overseas⟩
extrañamente *adv* : strangely, oddly
extrañamiento *nm* ASOMBRO : amazement, surprise, wonder
extrañar *vt* : to miss (someone) — **extrañarse** *vr* : to be surprised
extrañeza *nf* **1** : strangeness, oddness **2** : surprise
extraño¹, -ña *adj* **1** RARO : strange, odd **2** EXTRANJERO : foreign
extraño², -ña *n* DESCONOCIDO : stranger
extraoficial *adj* OFICIOSO : unofficial — **extraoficialmente** *adv*
extraordinario, -ria *adj* EXCEPCIONAL : extraordinary — **extraordinariamente** *adv*
extrapolar *vt* : to extrapolate — **extrapolación** *nf*
extrarradio *nm* : outskirts *pl*
extrasensorial *adj* : extrasensory ⟨percepción extrasensorial : extrasensory perception⟩
extraterrestre *adj* & *nmf* : extraterrestrial, alien
extravagancia *nf* **1** : extravagance, flamboyance **2** : outrageous or outlandish thing
extravagante *adj* **1** : extravagant, flamboyant **2** : outrageous, outlandish
extraviado, -da *adj* : lost, stray
extraviar {85} *vt* **1** : to mislead, to lead astray **2** : to misplace, to lose — **extraviarse** *vr* : to get lost, to go astray
extravío *nm* **1** PÉRDIDA : loss **2** : misconduct

extremado, -da *adj* : extreme — **extremadamente** *adv*
extremar *vt* : to carry to extremes — **extremarse** *vr* : to do one's utmost
extremidad *nf* **1** : extremity, tip, edge **2 extremidades** *nfpl* : extremities
extremista *adj* & *nmf* : extremist
extremo¹, -ma *adj* **1** : extreme, great ⟨frío extremo : extreme cold⟩ ⟨extrema pobreza : extreme poverty⟩ **2** : extreme, severe ⟨condiciones extremas : extreme conditions⟩ **3** EXTREMISTA : extreme ⟨opiniones extremas : extreme views⟩ **4** : extreme ⟨deportes extremos : extreme sports⟩ **5 en caso extremo** : as a last resort
extremo² *nm* **1** : extreme ⟨de un extremo a otro : from one extreme to the other⟩ **2** : end ⟨al otro extremo de la calle : the other end of the street⟩ ⟨el extremo sur : the southern end/tip⟩ **3 al extremo de** : to the point of **4 en ~** : in the extreme
extrovertido¹, -da *adj* : extroverted, outgoing
extrovertido², -da *n* : extrovert
extrudir *vt* : to extrude
exuberancia *nf* **1** : exuberance **2** : luxuriance, lushness
exuberante *adj* : exuberant, luxuriant — **exuberantemente** *adv*
exudar *vt* : to exude
exultación *nf, pl* **-ciones** : exultation, elation
exultante *adj* : exultant, elated — **exultantemente** *adv*
exultar *vi* : to exult, to rejoice
eyacular *vi* : to ejaculate — **eyaculación** *nf*
eyección *nf, pl* **-ciones** : ejection, expulsion
eyectar *vt* : to eject, to expel — **eyectarse** *vr*

F

f *nf* : seventh letter of the Spanish alphabet
fa *nm* **1** : F ⟨fa sostenido/bemol : F sharp/flat⟩ **2** : fa (in singing)
fábrica *nf* FACTORÍA : factory
fabricación *nf, pl* **-ciones** : manufacture
fabricante *nmf* : manufacturer
fabricar {72} *vt* MANUFACTURAR : to manufacture, to make
fabril *adj* INDUSTRIAL : industrial, manufacturing
fábula *nf* **1** : fable **2** : fabrication, fib *fam*
fabuloso, -sa *adj* **1** : fabulous, fantastic **2** : mythical, fabled
facción *nf, pl* **facciones 1** : faction **2 facciones** *nfpl* RASGOS : features
faceta *nf* : facet
facha *nf* : appearance, look ⟨estar hecho una facha : to look a sight⟩
fachada *nf* : facade
facial *adj* : facial

fácil *adj* **1** : easy **2** : likely, probable ⟨es fácil que no pase : it probably won't happen⟩
facilidad *nf* **1** : facility, ease ⟨con facilidad : with ease, easily⟩ ⟨tener facilidad para : to have a gift for⟩ **2 facilidades** *nfpl* : facilities, services ⟨facilidades de pago : payment plans⟩ **3 facilidades** *nfpl* : opportunities ⟨tenían todas las facilidades : they had every opportunity⟩
facilitar *vt* **1** : to make easier, to facilitate **2** : to provide, to supply — **facilitador, -dora** *n*
fácilmente *adv* : easily, readily
facsímil *nm* **1** : facsimile, copy **2** : fax
factibilidad *nf* : feasibility
factible *adj* : feasible, practicable
factor¹, -tora *n* **1** : agent, factor **2** : baggage clerk
factor² *nm* ELEMENTO : factor, element
factoría *nf* FÁBRICA : factory
factura *nf* **1** : making, manufacturing **2** : bill, invoice

facturación *nf, pl* **-ciones 1** : invoicing, billing **2** : check-in

facturar *vt* **1** : to bill, to invoice **2** : to register, to check in

facultad *nf* **1** : faculty, ability ⟨facultades mentales : mental faculties⟩ **2** : authority, power **3** : school (of a university) ⟨facultad de derecho : law school⟩

facultar *vt* : to authorize, to empower

facultativo, -va *adj* **1** OPTATIVO : voluntary, optional **2** : medical ⟨informe facultativo : medical report⟩

faena *nf* : task, job, work ⟨faenas domésticas : housework⟩

faenar *vi* **1** : to work, to labor **2** PESCAR : to fish

fagot *nm* : bassoon

Fahrenheit *adj* : Fahrenheit

faisán *nm, pl* **faisanes** : pheasant

faja *nf* **1** : sash, belt **2** : girdle **3** : strip (of land)

fajar *vt* **1** : to wrap (a sash or girdle) around **2** : to hit, to thrash — **fajarse** *vr* **1** : to put on a sash or girdle **2** : to come to blows

fajín *nm, pl* **-jines** : sash, belt

fajo *nm* : bundle, sheaf ⟨un fajo de billetes : a wad of cash⟩

falacia *nf* : fallacy

falaz, -laza *adj, mpl* **falaces** FALSO : fallacious, false

falda *nf* **1** : skirt ⟨falda escocesa : kilt⟩ ⟨falda de tubo : pencil skirt⟩ **2** REGAZO : lap (of the body) **3** VERTIENTE : side, slope

faldón *nm, pl* **-dones 1** : tail (of a shirt, etc.) **2** : full skirt **3** : christening gown

falible *adj* : fallible

fálico, -ca *adj* : phallic

falla *nf* **1** : flaw, defect **2** : (geological) fault **3** : fault, failing

fallar *vi* FRACASAR : to fail, to go wrong **2** : to rule (in a court of law) — *vt* **1** ERRAR : to miss (a target) **2** : to pronounce judgment on

fallecer {53} *vi* MORIR : to pass away, to die

fallecido, -da *adj & n* DIFUNTO : deceased

fallecimiento *nm* : demise, death

fallido, -da *adj* : failed, unsuccessful

fallo *nm* **1** SENTENCIA : sentence, judgment, verdict **2** : error, fault

falo *nm* : phallus, penis

falsamente *adv* : falsely

falsear *vt* **1** : to falsify, to fake **2** : to distort — *vi* **1** CEDER : to give way **2** : to be out of tune

falsedad *nf* **1** : falseness, hypocrisy **2** MENTIRA : falsehood, lie

falsete *nm* : falsetto

falsificación *nf, pl* **-ciones 1** : counterfeit, forgery **2** : falsification

falsificador, -dora *n* : counterfeiter, forger

falsificar {72} *vt* **1** : to counterfeit, to forge **2** : to falsify

falso, -sa *adj* **1** FALAZ : false, untrue **2** : counterfeit, forged

falta *nf* **1** CARENCIA : lack ⟨falta de dinero/interés : lack of money/interest⟩ **2** DEFECTO : defect, fault, error ⟨falta de ortografía : spelling mistake⟩ ⟨falta de educación : bad manners⟩ **3** AUSENCIA : absence **4** : offense, misdemeanor **5** : foul (in basketball), fault (in tennis) **6** **a falta de** : in the absence of **7** **hacer falta** : to be lacking, to be needed ⟨nos hace falta un líder : we need a leader⟩ ⟨no hace falta : it's not necessary⟩ ⟨me hace mucha falta mi familia : I really miss my family⟩ **8** **por falta de** : for lack of **9** **sin ~** : without fail

faltar *vi* **1** : to be lacking, to be needed ⟨me falta tiempo : I don't have time⟩ ⟨le falta imaginación : he lacks imagination⟩ ⟨le falta sal : it needs salt⟩ ⟨falta algo : something's missing⟩ ⟨al libro le falta una página : the book is missing a page⟩ ⟨nos faltan sillas : we need more chairs⟩ **2** : to be absent, to be missing ⟨faltan Juan y María : Juan and María aren't here⟩ ⟨faltar al trabajo/colegio : to miss work/school⟩ **3** QUEDAR : to remain, to be left ⟨falta un mes para la boda : there's a month to go until the wedding, the wedding is a month away⟩ ⟨falta mucho por hacer : there is still a lot to be done⟩ ⟨¿te falta mucho? : are you almost ready/done?⟩ **4** **faltar a su promesa/palabra** : not to keep one's promise/word **5** **¡no faltaba más!** : don't mention it!, you're welcome!

faltante *nm* : shortage

falto, -ta *adj* **~ de** : lacking (in), short of

fama *nf* **1** : fame **2** REPUTACIÓN : reputation **3** **de mala fama** : disreputable

famélico, -ca *adj* HAMBRIENTO : starving, famished

familia *nf* **1** : family ⟨ser como de la familia : to be like one of the family⟩ ⟨sentir como en familia : to feel at home⟩ ⟨le viene de familia : he inherited it, it runs in the family⟩ **2** **en ~** : in private **3** **familia nuclear** : nuclear family **4** **familia política** : in-laws

familiar¹ *adj* **1** CONOCIDO : familiar **2** : familial, family **3** INFORMAL : informal

familiar² *nmf* PARIENTE : relation, relative

familiaridad *nf* **1** : familiarity **2** : informality

familiarizar {21} *vt* : to familiarize — **familiarizarse** *vr*

famoso¹, -sa *adj* CÉLEBRE : famous

famoso², -sa *n* : celebrity

fan *nmf, pl* **fans** AFICIONADO : fan

fanal *nm* **1** : beacon, signal light **2** *Mex* : headlight

fanático, -ca *adj & n* : fanatic

fanatismo *nm* : fanaticism

fandango *nm* : fandango

fanfarria *nf* **1** : (musical) fanfare **2** : pomp, ceremony

fanfarrón¹, -rrona *adj, mpl* **-rrones** *fam* : bragging, boastful

fanfarrón², -rrona *n, mpl* **-rrones** *fam* : braggart

fanfarronada *nf* : boast, bluster

fanfarronear *vi* : to brag, to boast

fango *nm* LODO : mud, mire
fangoso, -sa *adj* LODOSO : muddy
fantasear *vi* : to fantasize, to daydream
fantasía *nf* **1** : fantasy **2** : imagination
fantasioso, -sa *adj* : fanciful
fantasma *nm* : ghost, phantom
fantasmagórico, -ca *adj* : ghostly, eerie
fantasmal *adj* : ghostly
fantástico, -ca *adj* **1** : fantastic, imaginary, unreal **2** *fam* : great, fantastic
FAQ [ˈfak] *nm, pl* **FAQs** : FAQ
farándula *nf* : show business, theater
faraón *nm, pl* **faraones** : pharaoh
fardo *nm* **1** : bale **2** : bundle
farfullar *v* : to jabber
faringe *nf* : pharynx
fariña *nf* : coarse manioc flour
farmacéutico¹, -ca *adj* : pharmaceutical
farmacéutico², -ca *n* : pharmacist
farmacia *nf* : drugstore, pharmacy
fármaco *nm* : medicine, drug
farmacología *nf* : pharmacology
faro *nm* **1** : lighthouse **2** : headlight
farol *nm* **1** : streetlight **2** : lantern, lamp **3** *fam* : bluff **4** *Mex* : headlight
farola *nf* **1** : lamppost **2** : streetlight
farra *nf* : spree, revelry
fárrago *nm* REVOLTIJO : hodgepodge, jumble
farsa *nf* **1** : farce **2** : fake, sham
farsante *nmf* CHARLATÁN : charlatan, fraud, phony
fascículo *nm* : part (of a publication)
fascinación *nf, pl* **-ciones** : fascination
fascinante *adj* : fascinating
fascinar *vt* **1** : to fascinate **2** : to charm, to captivate
fascismo *nm* : fascism
fascista *adj & nmf* : fascist
fase *nf* : phase, stage
fastidiar *vt* **1** MOLESTAR : to annoy, to bother, to hassle **2** ABURRIR : to bore — *vi* : to be annoying or bothersome — **fastidiarse** *vr* : to put up with something
fastidio *nm* **1** MOLESTIA : annoyance, nuisance, hassle **2** ABURRIMIENTO : boredom
fastidioso, -sa *adj* **1** MOLESTO : annoying, bothersome **2** ABURRIDO : boring — **fastidiosamente** *adv*
fastuoso, -sa *adj* : lavish, luxurious
fatal *adj* **1** MORTAL : fatal **2** *fam* : awful, terrible **3** : fateful, unavoidable
fatalidad *nf* **1** : fatality **2** DESGRACIA : misfortune, bad luck
fatalismo *nm* : fatalism
fatalista¹ *adj* : fatalistic
fatalista² *nmf* : fatalist
fatalmente *adv* **1** : unavoidably **2** : unfortunately
fatídico, -ca *adj* : fateful, momentous
fatiga *nf* CANSANCIO : fatigue
fatigado, -da *adj* AGOTADO : weary, tired
fatigar {52} *vt* CANSAR : to fatigue, to tire — **fatigarse** *vr* : to wear oneself out
fatigoso, -sa *adj* : fatiguing, tiring
fatuo, -tua *adj* **1** : fatuous **2** PRESUMIDO : vain
fauces *nfpl* : jaws *pl*, maw
faul *nm, pl* **fauls** : foul, foul ball

fauna *nf* : fauna
fausto *nm* : splendor, magnificence
favor *nm* **1** : favor ⟨¿me haces un favor? : will you do me a favor?⟩ ⟨quiero pedirte un favor : I want to ask you (for) a favor⟩ **2** a/en favor de : in favor of **3** en favor de : in support of, in the interests of ⟨trabajar en favor de una causa : to work for a cause⟩ **4** por ~ : please
favorable *adj* : favorable — **favorablemente** *adv*
favorecedor, -dora *adj* : becoming, flattering
favorecer {53} *vt* **1** : to favor **2** : to look well on, to suit
favorecido, -da *adj* **1** : flattering **2** : fortunate
favoritismo *nm* : favoritism
favorito, -ta *adj & n* : favorite
fax *nm* : fax, facsimile
fayuca *nf Mex* **1** : contraband **2** : black market
faz *nf* **1** : face, countenance ⟨la faz de la tierra : the face of the earth⟩ **2** : side (of coins, fabric, etc.)
fe *nf* **1** : faith **2** : assurance, testimony ⟨dar fe de : to bear witness to⟩ **3** : intention, will ⟨de buena fe : bona fide, in good faith⟩
fealdad *nf* : ugliness
febrero *nm* : February ⟨el primero de febrero : (on) February first⟩
febril *adj* : feverish — **febrilmente** *adv*
fecal *adj* : fecal
fecha *nf* **1** : date ⟨hasta la fecha : to date⟩ ⟨a partir de esta fecha : from today⟩ ⟨adelantar/atrasar la fecha : to move up/back the date⟩ **2** fecha de caducidad/vencimiento : expiration date **3** fecha límite : deadline
fechar *vt* : to date, to put a date on
fechoría *nf* : misdeed
fécula *nf* : starch (food)
fecundar *vt* : to fertilize (an egg) — **fecundación** *nf*
fecundidad *nf* **1** : fecundity, fertility **2** : productivity
fecundo, -da *adj* FÉRTIL : fertile, fecund
federación *nf, pl* **-ciones** : federation
federal *adj* : federal
federalismo *nm* : federalism — **federalista** *adj & nmf*
federar *vt* : to federate
fehaciente *adj* : reliable, irrefutable — **fehacientemente** *adv*
felicidad *nf* **1** : happiness **2** ¡felicidades! : best wishes!, congratulations!, happy birthday!
felicitación *nf, pl* **-ciones** **1** : congratulation ⟨¡felicitaciones! : congratulations!⟩ **2** : greeting card
felicitar *vt* CONGRATULAR : to congratulate — **felicitarse** *vr* ~ de : to be glad about
feligrés, -gresa *n, mpl* **-greses** : parishioner
feligresía *nf* : parish
felino, -na *adj & n* : feline
feliz *adj, pl* **felices** **1** : happy **2** Feliz Navidad : Merry Christmas

felizmente adv 1 : happily 2 : fortunately, luckily
felonía nf 1 : felony
felpa nf 1 : terry cloth 2 : plush
felpudo nm : doormat
femenil adj : women's, girls' ⟨futbol femenil : women's soccer⟩
femenino, -na adj 1 : feminine 2 : women's ⟨derechos femeninos : women's rights⟩ 3 : female
fémina nf : woman
femineidad or **feminidad** nf : femininity
feminismo nm : feminism
feminista adj & nmf : feminist
femoral adj : femoral
fémur nm : femur, thighbone
fenecer {53} vi 1 : to die, to pass away 2 : to come to an end, to cease
fénix nm : phoenix
fenomenal adj 1 : phenomenal 2 fam : fantastic, terrific — **fenomenalmente** adv
fenómeno nm 1 : phenomenon 2 : prodigy, genius
feo[1] adv : badly, bad
feo[2], **fea** adj 1 : ugly 2 : unpleasant, nasty ⟨un olor feo : a nasty smell⟩ ⟨me dijo cosas feas : he said awful things to me⟩ ⟨la cosa se pone fea : things are getting ugly⟩
féretro nm ATAÚD : coffin, casket
feria nf 1 : fair, market 2 : festival, holiday 3 Mex : change (money)
feriado, -da adj día feriado : public holiday
ferial nm : fairground
fermentar v : to ferment — **fermentación** nf
fermento nm : ferment
ferocidad nf : ferocity, fierceness
feroz adj, pl **feroces** FIERO : ferocious, fierce — **ferozmente** adv
férreo, -rrea adj 1 : iron 2 : strong, steely ⟨una voluntad férrea : an iron will⟩ 3 : strict, severe 4 vía férrea : railroad track
ferretería nf 1 : hardware store 2 : hardware 3 : foundry, ironworks
ferrocarril nm : railroad, railway
ferrocarrilero → **ferroviario**
ferroviario, -ria adj : rail, railroad
ferry nm, pl **ferrys** : ferry
fértil adj FECUNDO : fertile, fruitful
fertilidad nf : fertility
fertilizante[1] adj : fertilizing ⟨droga fertilizante : fertility drug⟩
fertilizante[2] nm ABONO : fertilizer
fertilizar vt ABONAR : to fertilize — **fertilización** nf
ferviente adj FERVOROSO : fervent — **fervientemente** adv
fervor nm : fervor, zeal
fervoroso, -sa adj FERVIENTE : fervent, zealous
festejar vt 1 CELEBRAR : to celebrate 2 AGASAJAR : to entertain, to wine and dine 3 Mex fam : to thrash, to beat
festejo nm : celebration, festivity
festín nm, pl **festines** : banquet, feast
festinar vt : to hasten, to hurry up

festival nm : festival
festividad nf 1 : festivity 2 : (religious) feast, holiday
festivo, -va adj 1 : festive 2 día festivo : holiday — **festivamente** adv
festón nm, pl **-tones** : scallop (decoration)
fetal adj : fetal
fetiche nm : fetish
fétido, -da adj : fetid, foul
feto nm : fetus
feudal adj : feudal — **feudalismo** nm
fiabilidad nf : reliability, trustworthiness
fiable adj : trustworthy, reliable
fiado, -da adj : on credit
fiador, -dora n : bondsman, guarantor
fiambrería nf : delicatessen
fiambres nmpl : cold cuts
fianza nf 1 CAUCIÓN : bail, bond 2 : surety, deposit
fiar {85} vt 1 : to sell on credit 2 : to guarantee — **fiarse** vr ~ **de** : to place trust in
fiasco nm FRACASO : fiasco, failure
fibra nf 1 : fiber 2 fibra de vidrio : fiberglass
fibroso, -sa adj : fibrous
ficción nf, pl **ficciones** 1 : fiction 2 : fabrication, lie
ficha nf 1 : index card 2 : file, record 3 : token 4 : domino, checker, counter, poker chip
fichaje nm : signing (in sports)
fichar vt 1 : to open a file on 2 : to sign up — vi : to punch in, to punch out
fichero nm 1 : card file 2 : filing cabinet
ficticio, -cia adj : fictitious
fidedigno, -na adj FIABLE : reliable, trustworthy
fideicomisario, -ria n : trustee
fideicomiso nm : trust ⟨guardar en fideicomiso : to hold in trust⟩
fidelidad nf : fidelity, faithfulness
fideo nm : noodle
fiduciario[1], **-ria** adj : fiduciary
fiduciario[2], **-ria** n : trustee
fiebre nf 1 CALENTURA : fever, temperature ⟨fiebre amarilla : yellow fever⟩ 2 : fever, excitement
fiel[1] adj 1 : faithful, loyal 2 : accurate — **fielmente** adv
fiel[2] nm 1 : pointer (of a scale) 2 los **fieles** : the faithful
fieltro nm : felt
fiera nf 1 : wild animal, beast 2 : fiend, demon ⟨una fiera para el trabajo : a demon for work⟩
fiereza nf : fierceness, ferocity
fiero, -ra adj FEROZ : fierce, ferocious
fierro nm HIERRO : iron
fiesta nf 1 : party, fiesta ⟨fiesta de cumpleaños : birthday party⟩ ⟨no estoy para fiestas : I am in no mood to celebrate⟩ ⟨aguarle la fiesta a alguien : to rain on someone's parade⟩ 2 : holiday, feast day (in religion) ⟨hoy es (día de) fiesta : today is a holiday⟩
figura nf 1 : figure ⟨figura retórica : figure of speech⟩ ⟨figuras políticas : political figures⟩ 2 : shape, form 3 : figure, body shape

figuración *nf, pl* **-ciones** : imagining
figurado, -da *adj* : figurative — **figuradamente** *adv*
figurar *vi* **1** : to figure, to be included ⟨Rivera figura entre los más grandes pintores de México : Rivera is among Mexico's greatest painters⟩ **2** : to be prominent, to stand out — *vt* : to represent ⟨esta línea figura el horizonte : this line represents the horizon⟩ — **figurarse** *vr* : to imagine, to think ⟨figúrate el lío en que se metió! : imagine the mess she got into!⟩
fijación *nf, pl* **-ciones** **1** : fixation, obsession **2** : fixing, establishing **3** : fastening, securing
fijador *nm* : hair spray
fijamente *adv* : fixedly
fijar *vt* **1** : to fasten, to affix **2** ESTABLECER : to establish, to set up ⟨fijar su residencia : to take up residence⟩ **3** CONCRETAR : to set, to fix ⟨fijar la fecha : to set the date⟩ ⟨fijar la atención en : to focus one's attention on⟩ ⟨fijar la mirada en : to fix one's gaze on⟩ — **fijarse** *vr* **1** : to settle, to become fixed **2** : to notice ⟨fijarse en algo : to notice something, to pay attention to something⟩ ⟨me he fijado que . . . : I noticed that . . .⟩
fijeza *nf* **1** : firmness (of convictions) **2** : persistence, constancy ⟨mirar con fijeza a : to stare at⟩
fijo, -ja *adj* **1** : fixed, firm, steady **2** PERMANENTE : permanent
fila *nf* **1** HILERA : line, file ⟨ponerse en fila : to get in line⟩ ⟨en fila india : (in) single file⟩ **2** : rank, row **3 filas** *nfpl* : ranks ⟨cerrar filas : to close ranks⟩
filamento *nm* : filament
filantropía *nf* : philanthropy
filantrópico, -ca *adj* : philanthropic
filántropo, -pa *n* : philanthropist
filarmónica *nf* : philharmonic
filatelia *nf* : philately, stamp collecting
fildeador, -dora *n* : fielder
filete *nm* **1** : fillet **2** SOLOMILLO : sirloin **3** : thread (of a screw)
filiación *nf, pl* **-ciones** **1** : affiliation, connection **2** : particulars *pl*, (police) description
filial[1] *adj* : filial
filial[2] *nf* : affiliate, subsidiary
filigrana *nf* **1** : filigree **2** : watermark (on paper)
filipino, -na *adj & n* : Filipino
filmación *nf, pl* **-ciones** : filming, shooting
filmar *vt* : to film, to shoot
filme *or* **film** *nm* PELÍCULA : film, movie
filmoteca *nf* : film library
filo *nm* **1** : cutting edge, blade **2** : edge ⟨al filo del escritorio : at the edge of the desk⟩ ⟨al filo de la medianoche : at the stroke of midnight⟩
filón *nm, pl* **filones** **1** : seam, vein (of minerals) **2** *fam* : successful business, gold mine
filoso, -sa *adj* : sharp
filosofar *vi* : to philosophize
filosofía *nf* : philosophy

filosófico, -ca *adj* : philosophic, philosophical — **filosóficamente** *adv*
filósofo, -fa *n* : philosopher
filtración *nf, pl* **-ciones** : seeping, leaking
filtrar *v* : to filter — **filtrarse** *vr* : to seep through, to leak
filtro *nm* : filter
fin *nm* **1** : end ⟨dar/poner fin a : to end, to put an end to⟩ ⟨llegar a su fin : to come to an end⟩ **2** : purpose, aim, objective **3 a fin de cuentas** : in the end **4 a fin de que** : in order to **5 a fines de mes/año (etc.)** : at the end of the month/year (etc.) **6 al fin y al cabo** : after all **7 con el fin de** *or* **a fin de** : with the purpose of **8 con este fin** : to this end, with this purpose **9 en ~** : in short **10 fin de semana** : weekend **11 por ~** : finally, at last
finado, -da *adj & n* DIFUNTO : deceased
final[1] *adj* : final, ultimate — **finalmente** *adv*
final[2] *nm* **1** CONCLUSIÓN : end ⟨al final : at the end⟩ **2 a finales de mes/año (etc.)** : at the end of the month/year (etc.)
final[3] *nf* : final, play-off
finalidad *nf* **1** : purpose, aim **2** : finality
finalista *nmf* : finalist
finalización *nf, pl* **-ciones** : completion, end
finalizar {21} *v* : to finish, to end
financiación *nf, pl* **-ciones** : financing, funding
financiamiento *nm* → **financiación**
financiar *vt* : to finance, to fund
financiero[1], **-ra** *adj* : financial
financiero[2], **-ra** *n* : financier
financista *nmf* : financier
finanzas *nfpl* : finances, finance ⟨altas finanzas : high finance⟩
finca *nf* **1** : farm, ranch **2** : country house
fineza *nf* FINURA, REFINAMIENTO : refinement
fingido, -da *adj* : false, feigned
fingimiento *nm* : pretense
fingir {35} *v* : to feign, to pretend
finiquitar *vt* **1** : to settle (an account) **2** : to conclude, to bring to an end
finiquito *nm* : settlement (of an account)
finito, -ta *adj* : finite
finja, etc. → **fingir**
finlandés, -desa *adj & n* : Finnish
fino[1], **-na** *adj* **1** : fine, excellent **2** : delicate, slender **3** REFINADO : refined **4** : sharp, acute ⟨olfato fino : keen sense of smell⟩ **5** : subtle
fino[2] *nm* : dry sherry
finta *nf* : feint
fintar *or* **fintear** *vi* : to feint
finura *nf* **1** : fineness, high quality **2** FINEZA, REFINAMIENTO : refinement
fiordo *nm* : fjord
firma *nf* **1** : signature **2** : signing **3** EMPRESA : firm, company
firmamento *nm* : firmament, sky
firmante *nmf* : signer, signatory
firmar *v* : to sign
firme *adj* **1** : firm, resolute **2** : steady, stable

firmemente *adv* : firmly
firmeza *nf* **1** : firmness, stability **2** : strength, resolve
fiscal[1] *adj* : fiscal — **fiscalmente** *adv*
fiscal[2] *nmf* : district attorney, prosecutor
fiscalizar {21} *vt* **1** : to audit, to inspect **2** : to oversee **3** : to criticize
fisco *nm* : Treasury (en EEUU), Exchequer (en Gran Bretaña)
fisgar {52} *vt* HUSMEAR : to pry into, to snoop on
fisgón, -gona *n, mpl* **fisgones** : snoop, busybody
fisgonear *vi* : to snoop, to pry
fisgue, etc. → **fisgar**
física *nf* : physics
físico[1], **-ca** *adj* : physical — **físicamente** *adv*
físico[2], **-ca** *n* : physicist
físico[3] *nm* : physique, figure
fisiología *nf* : physiology
fisiológico, -ca *adj* : physiological, physiologic
fisiólogo, -ga *n* : physiologist
fisión *nf, pl* **fisiones** : fission — **fisionable** *adj*
fisionomía → **fisonomía**
fisioterapeuta *nmf* : physical therapist
fisioterapia *nf* : physical therapy
fisonomía *nf* : physiognomy, features *pl*
fistol *nm Mex* : tie clip
fisura *nf* : fissure, crevasse
flaccidez *nf* : limpness
fláccido, -da *or* **flácido, -da** *adj* : flaccid, flabby
flaco, -ca *adj* **1** DELGADO : thin, skinny **2** : feeble, weak ⟨una flaca excusa : a feeble excuse⟩
flagelo *nm* **1** : scourge, whip **2** : calamity
flagrante *adj* : flagrant, glaring, blatant — **flagrantemente** *adv*
flama *nf* LLAMA : flame
flamable *adj Mex* : flammable
flamante *adj* **1** : bright, brilliant **2** : brand-new
flamear *vi* **1** LLAMEAR : to flame, to blaze **2** ONDEAR : to flap, to flutter
flamenco[1], **-ca** *adj* **1** : flamenco **2** : Flemish
flamenco[2], **-ca** *n* : Fleming, Flemish person
flamenco[3] *nm* **1** : Flemish (language) **2** : flamingo **3** : flamenco (music or dance)
flan *nm* : flan
flanco *nm* : flank, side
flanquear *vt* : to flank
flaquear *vi* DECAER : to flag, to weaken
flaqueza *nf* **1** DEBILIDAD : frailty, feebleness **2** : thinness **3** : weakness, failing
flash *nm* : flash (in photography)
flashback *nm, pl* **flashbacks** : flashback
flatulento, -ta *adj* : flatulent — **flatulencia** *nf*
flauta *nf* **1** : flute **2 flauta dulce** : recorder
flautín *nm, pl* **flautines** : piccolo
flautista *nmf* : flute player, flutist
flecha *nf* : arrow

flechazo *nm* : love at first sight
fleco *nm* **1** : bangs *pl* **2** : fringe
flema *nf* : phlegm
flemático, -ca *adj* : phlegmatic, stolid, impassive
flequillo *nm* : bangs *pl*
fletar *vt* **1** : to charter, to hire **2** : to load (freight)
flete *nm* **1** : charter fee **2** : shipping cost **3** : freight, cargo
fletero *nm* : shipper, carrier
flexibilidad *nf* : flexibility
flexibilizar {21} *vt* : to make more flexible
flexible[1] *adj* : flexible
flexible[2] *nm* **1** : flexible electrical cord **2** : soft hat
flexión *nf, pl* **flexiones** **1** : push-up **2** : squat
flexionar *vt* : to bend (a limb, etc.)
flirtear *vi* : to flirt
flojear *vi* **1** DEBILITARSE : to weaken, to flag **2** : to idle, to loaf around
flojedad *nf* : weakness
flojera *nf fam* **1** : lethargy, feeling of weakness **2** : laziness
flojo, -ja *adj* **1** SUELTO : loose, slack **2** : weak, poor ⟨está flojo en las ciencias : he's weak in science⟩ **3** PEREZOSO : lazy
flor *nf* **1** : flower **2 a flor de piel** : easily noticed or affected ⟨con los nervios a flor de piel : with one's nerves on edge⟩ ⟨canta con las emociones a flor de piel : her singing is full of emotion⟩ **3 en ~** : in bloom **4 flor de Pascua** : poinsettia
flora *nf* : flora
floración *nf, pl* **-ciones** : flowering ⟨en plena floración : in full bloom⟩
floral *adj* : floral
floreado, -da *adj* : flowered, flowery
florear *vi* FLORECER : to flower, to bloom — *vt* **1** : to adorn with flowers **2** *Mex* : to flatter, to compliment
florecer {53} *vi* **1** : to bloom, to blossom **2** : to flourish, to thrive
floreciente *adj* **1** : flowering **2** PRÓSPERO : flourishing, thriving
florecimiento *nm* : flowering
floreo *nm* : flourish
florería *nf* : flower shop, florist's
florero[1], **-ra** *n* : florist
florero[2] *nm* JARRÓN : vase
florete *nm* : foil (in fencing)
florido, -da *adj* **1** : full of flowers **2** : florid, flowery ⟨escritos floridos : flowery prose⟩
florista *nmf* : florist
floristería → **florería**
floritura *nf* : frill, embellishment
flota *nf* : fleet
flotabilidad *nf* : buoyancy
flotación *nf, pl* **-ciones** : flotation
flotador *nm* **1** : float **2** : life preserver
flotante *adj* : floating, buoyant
flotar *vi* : to float
flote *nm* **a ~** : afloat
flotilla *nf* : flotilla, fleet
fluctuar {3} *vi* **1** : to fluctuate **2** VACILAR : to vacillate — **fluctuación** *nf* — **fluctuante** *adj*

fluidez *nf* 1 : fluency 2 : fluidity
fluido¹, -da *adj* 1 : flowing 2 : fluent 3 : fluid
fluido² *nm* : fluid
fluir {41} *vi* : to flow
flujo *nm* 1 : flow ⟨el flujo y reflujo : the ebb and flow⟩ 2 : discharge
flúor *nm* : fluorine
fluorescencia *nf* : fluorescence — **fluorescente** *adj*
fluorescente *nm* : fluorescent light — **fluorescente** *adj*
fluoruro *nm* : fluoride
fluye, etc. → **fluir**
fobia *nf* : phobia
foca *nf* : seal (animal)
focal *adj* : focal
foco *nm* 1 : focus 2 : center, pocket 3 : lightbulb 4 : spotlight 5 : headlight
fofo, -fa *adj* 1 ESPONJOSO : soft, spongy 2 : flabby
fogata *nf* : campfire, bonfire
fogón *nm, pl* **fogones** 1 : bonfire, campfire 2 : burner, stove 3 : fireplace
fogonazo *nm* : flash, explosion
fogoso, -sa *adj* ARDIENTE : ardent
foguear *vt* : to inure, to accustom
fogueo *nm* **de ~** ⟨un cartucho de fogueo : a blank, a dummy round⟩
foja *nf* : sheet (of paper)
folículo *nm* : follicle
folio *nm* : folio, leaf
folk ['fok, 'folk] *nm* : folk (music) — **folk** *adj*
folklore *nm* : folklore
folklórico, -ca *adj* : folk, traditional
follaje *nm* : foliage
folleto *nm* : pamphlet, leaflet, circular
follón *nm, pl* **follones** *Spain* 1 : commotion, fuss 2 : mess
fomentar *vt* 1 : to foment, to stir up 2 PROMOVER : to promote, to foster
fomento *nm* : promotion, encouragement
fonda *nf* 1 POSADA : inn 2 : small restaurant
fondeado, -da *adj fam* : rich, in the money
fondear *vt* 1 : to sound 2 : to sound out, to examine 3 *Mex* : to fund, to finance — *vi* ANCLAR : to anchor — **fondearse** *vr fam* : to get rich
fondeo *nm* 1 : anchoring 2 *Mex* : funding, financing
fondillos *mpl* : seat, bottom (of clothing)
fondista *nmf* : long-distance runner
fondo *nm* 1 : bottom ⟨el fondo del océano/barril : the bottom of the ocean/barrel⟩ ⟨llegar al fondo de algo : to get to the bottom of something⟩ 2 : rear, back, end ⟨al fondo de la casa : at the back of the house⟩ 3 PROFUNDIDAD : depth 4 : background ⟨al fondo : in the background⟩ ⟨música de fondo : background music⟩ 5 CONTENIDO : content 6 *Mex* : slip, petticoat 7 : fund ⟨fondo de inversiones/pensiones : investment/pension fund⟩ ⟨fondo común : joint fund⟩ 8 **fondos** *nmpl* : funds, resources ⟨cheque sin fondos : bounced check⟩ ⟨recaudar fondos : to

raise funds⟩ ⟨fondos públicos : public funds⟩ ⟨fondos de campaña : campaign funds⟩ 9 **a ~** : thoroughly, in depth 10 **de ~** : fundamental 11 **de ~** : long-distance (in sports) 12 **en ~** : abreast 13 **en el fondo** : deep down, at heart 14 **tocar fondo** : to touch bottom (in the sea, etc.), to hit rock bottom
fondue *nf* : fondue
fonema *nm* : phoneme
fonética *nf* : phonetics
fonético, -ca *adj* : phonetic
fontanería *nf* PLOMERÍA : plumbing
fontanero, -ra *n* PLOMERO : plumber
footing ['fu,tɪŋ] *nm* : jogging ⟨hacer footing : to jog⟩
forajido, -da *n* : bandit, fugitive, outlaw
foráneo, -nea *adj* : foreign, strange
forastero, -ra *n* : stranger, outsider
forcejear *vi* : to struggle
forcejeo *nm* : struggle
fórceps *nms & pl* : forceps *pl*
forense¹ *adj* : forensic, legal
forense² *nmf* : forensic scientist
forestal *adj* : forest
forja *nf* FRAGUA : forge
forjar *vt* 1 : to forge 2 : to shape, to create ⟨forjar un compromiso : to hammer out a compromise⟩ 3 : to invent, to concoct
forma *nf* 1 : form, shape ⟨tomar forma : to take shape⟩ ⟨dar forma a : to form, to give shape to⟩ ⟨en forma de corazón : in the shape of a heart⟩ 2 MANERA, MODO : manner, way ⟨su forma de vida : their way of life⟩ ⟨formas de pago : payment methods⟩ 3 : fitness ⟨estar en forma : to be fit, to be in shape⟩ ⟨estar en baja forma : to be out of shape⟩ 4 **formas** *nfpl* : appearances, conventions ⟨guardar las formas : to keep up appearances⟩ 5 **de cualquier forma** or **de todas formas** : anyway, in any case 6 **de forma que** : so that
formación *nf, pl* **-ciones** 1 : formation 2 : training ⟨formación profesional : vocational training⟩
formal *adj* 1 : formal 2 : serious, dignified 3 : dependable, reliable
formaldehído *nm* : formaldehyde
formalidad *nf* 1 : formality 2 : seriousness, dignity 3 : reliability
formalizar {21} *vt* : to formalize, to make official
formalmente *adv* : formally
formar *vt* 1 : to form, to make 2 CONSTITUIR : to make up, to constitute 3 : to train, to educate — **formarse** *vr* 1 DESARROLLARSE : to develop, to take shape 2 EDUCARSE : to be educated
formatear *vt* : to format
formativo, -va *adj* : formative
formato *nm* : format
formidable *adj* 1 : formidable, tremendous 2 *fam* : fantastic, terrific
formón *nm, pl* **formones** : chisel
fórmula *nf* : formula
formulación *nf, pl* **-ciones** : formulation
formular *vt* 1 : to formulate, to draw up 2 : to make, to lodge (a protest or complaint)

formulario *nm* : form ⟨rellenar un formulario : to fill out a form⟩
fornicar {72} *vi* : to fornicate — **fornicación** *nf*
fornido, -da *adj* : well-built, burly, hefty
foro *nm* **1** : forum **2** : public assembly, open discussion
forraje *nm* **1** : fodder **2** : foraging **3** *fam* : hodgepodge
forrajear *vi* : to forage
forrar *vt* **1** : to line (a garment) **2** : to cover (a book)
forro *nm* **1** : lining **2** CUBIERTA : book cover
forsitia *nf* : forsythia
fortalecer {53} *vt* : to strengthen, to fortify — **fortalecerse** *vr*
fortalecimiento *nm* **1** : strengthening, fortifying **2** : fortifications
fortaleza *nf* **1** : fortress **2** FUERZA : strength **3** : resolution, fortitude
fortificación *nf, pl* **-ciones** : fortification
fortificar {72} *vt* **1** : to fortify **2** : to strengthen
fortín *nm, pl* **fortines** : small fort
fortuito, -ta *adj* : fortuitous
fortuna *nf* **1** SUERTE : fortune, luck **2** RIQUEZA : wealth, fortune
forúnculo *nm* : boil
forzado, -da *adj* : forced (of a smile, etc.)
forzar {36} *vt* **1** OBLIGAR : to force, to compel **2** : to force open **3** : to strain ⟨forzar los ojos : to strain one's eyes⟩
forzosamente *adv* **1** : forcibly, by force **2** : necessarily, inevitably ⟨forzosamente tendrán que pagar : they'll have no choice but to pay⟩
forzoso, -sa *adj* **1** : forced, compulsory **2** : necessary, inevitable
fosa *nf* **1** : ditch, pit ⟨fosa séptica : septic tank⟩ **2** TUMBA : grave **3** : cavity ⟨fosas nasales : nasal cavities, nostrils⟩
fosfato *nm* : phosphate
fosforescencia *nf* : phosphorescence — **fosforescente** *adj*
fósforo *nm* **1** CERILLA : match **2** : phosphorus
fósil[1] *adj* : fossilized, fossil
fósil[2] *nm* : fossil
fosilizar {21} *vt* : to fossilize — **fosilizarse** *vr*
foso *nm* **1** FOSA, ZANJA : ditch **2** : pit (of a theater) **3** : moat
foto *nf* : photo, picture
fotocopia *nf* : photocopy — **fotocopiar** *vt*
fotocopiadora *nf* COPIADORA : photocopier
fotoeléctrico, -ca *adj* : photoelectric
fotogénico, -ca *adj* : photogenic
fotografía *nf* **1** : photograph **2** : photography
fotografiar {85} *vt* : to photograph
fotográfico, -ca *adj* : photographic — **fotográficamente** *adv*
fotógrafo, -fa *n* : photographer
fotosíntesis *nf* : photosynthesis
foul *nm, pl* **fouls** : foul (in sports)
frac *nm, pl* **fracs** : tailcoat, tails *pl*
fracasado[1], **-da** *adj* : unsuccessful, failed
fracasado[2], **-da** *n* : failure

fracasar *vi* **1** FALLAR : to fail **2** : to fall through
fracaso *nm* FIASCO : failure
fracción *nf, pl* **fracciones** **1** : fraction **2** : part, fragment **3** : faction, splinter group
fraccionamiento *nm* **1** : division, breaking up **2** *Mex* : residential area, housing development
fraccionar *vt* : to divide, to break up
fraccionario, -ria *adj* : fractional
fracking [ˈfrakɪŋ] *nm* : fracking
fractura *nf* **1** : fracture **2** **fractura hidráulica** : fracking
fracturación hidráulica *nf* : fracking
fracturar *vt* : to fracture — **fracturarse** *vr*
fragancia *nf* : fragrance, scent
fragante *adj* : fragrant
fragata *nf* : frigate
frágil *adj* **1** : fragile **2** : frail, delicate
fragilidad *nf* **1** : fragility **2** : frailty, delicacy
fragmentar *vt* : to fragment — **fragmentación** *nf*
fragmentario, -ria *adj* : fragmentary, sketchy
fragmento *nm* **1** : fragment, shard **2** : bit, snippet **3** : excerpt, passage
fragor *nm* : clamor, din, roar
fragua *nf* FORJA : forge
fraguar {10} *vt* **1** : to forge **2** : to conceive, to concoct, to hatch — *vi* : to set, to solidify
fraile *nm* : friar, monk
frambuesa *nf* : raspberry
francamente *adv* **1** : frankly, candidly **2** REALMENTE : really ⟨es francamente admirable : it's really impressive⟩
francés[1], **-cesa** *adj, mpl* **franceses** : French
francés[2], **-cesa** *n, mpl* **franceses** : French person, Frenchman *m*, Frenchwoman *f*
francés[3] *nm* : French (language)
franciscano, -na *adj & n* : Franciscan
francmasón, -sona *n, mpl* **-sones** : Freemason — **francmasonería** *nf*
franco[1], **-ca** *adj* **1** CÁNDIDO : frank, candid **2** PATENTE : clear, obvious **3** : free ⟨franco a bordo : free on board⟩
franco[2] *nm* : franc
francotirador, -dora *n* : sniper
franela *nf* : flannel
franja *nf* **1** : stripe, band **2** : border, fringe
franquear *vt* **1** : to clear **2** ATRAVESAR : to cross, to go through **3** : to pay the postage on
franqueo *nm* : postage
franqueza *nf* : frankness
franquicia *nf* **1** EXENCIÓN : exemption **2** : franchise
frasco *nm* : small bottle, flask, vial
frase *nf* **1** : phrase **2** ORACIÓN : sentence
frasear *vt* : to phrase
fraternal *adj* : fraternal, brotherly
fraternidad *nf* **1** : brotherhood **2** : fraternity
fraternizar {21} *vi* : to fraternize — **fraternización** *nf*

fraterno, -na *adj* : fraternal, brotherly

fraude *nm* : fraud

fraudulento, -ta *adj* : fraudulent — **fraudulentamente** *adv*

fray *nm* : brother (title of a friar) ⟨Fray Bartolomé : Brother Bartholomew⟩

frazada *nf* COBIJA, MANTA : blanket

frecuencia *nf* : frequency

frecuentar *vt* : to frequent, to haunt

frecuente *adj* : frequent — **frecuentemente** *adv*

freelance[1] [fri'lans] *adj, pl* **freelance** : freelance

freelance[2] *nmf* : freelancer

fregadero *nm* : kitchen sink

fregado[1], **-da** *adj fam* : annoying, bothersome

fregado[2] *nm* **1** : scrubbing, scouring **2** *fam* : mess, muddle

fregar {49} *vt* **1** : to scrub, to scour, to wash ⟨fregar los trastes : to do the dishes⟩ ⟨fregar el suelo : to scrub the floor⟩ **2** *fam* : to annoy — *vi* **1** : to wash the dishes **2** : to clean, to scrub **3** *fam* : to be annoying

fregona *nf Spain* : mop

freidera *nf Mex* : frying pan

freír {37} *vt* : to fry — **freírse** *vr*

fréjol *Ecua* → **frijol**

frenado *nm* : braking (of a vehicle)

frenar *vt* **1** : to brake **2** DETENER : to curb, to check — *vi* : to apply the brakes — **frenarse** *vr* : to restrain oneself

frenazo *nm* : sudden stop (in a vehicle) ⟨dar un frenazo : to brake hard⟩

frenesí *nm, pl* **-síes** : frenzy

frenético, -ca *adj* : frantic, frenzied — **frenéticamente** *adv*

freno *nm* **1** : brake ⟨freno de mano : handbrake, emergency brake⟩ **2** : bit (of a bridle) **3** : check, restraint **4 frenos** *nmpl Mex* : braces (for teeth)

frente[1] *nm* **1** : front ⟨en frente : in front, opposite⟩ **2** : facade **3** : front line, front **4** : front (in politics) **5** : front (in meteorology) ⟨frente frío : cold front⟩ **6 de ~** : head-on ⟨chocar de frente a/con : to run head-on into⟩ **7 de frente a** : facing **8 ~ a** : opposite, in front of **9 ~ a** : in the face of (a crisis, etc.), against (an opponent, etc.) **10 estar al ~ de** : to be at the head of, to lead **11 hacer frente a** : to face up to

frente[2] *nf* **1** : forehead, brow **2 frente a frente** : face to face

fresa *nf* **1** : strawberry **2** : drill (in dentistry)

fresco[1], **-ca** *adj* **1** : fresh **2** : cool **3** *fam* : insolent, nervy

fresco[2] *nm* **1** : coolness **2** : fresh air ⟨al fresco : in the open air, outdoors⟩ **3** : fresco **4** → **refresco**

frescor *nm* : cool air ⟨el frescor de la noche : the cool of the evening⟩

frescura *nf* **1** : freshness **2** : coolness **3** : calmness **4** DESCARO : nerve, audacity

fresno *nm* : ash (tree)

frialdad *nf* **1** : coldness **2** INDIFERENCIA : coldness, indifference

fríamente *adv* : coldly, indifferently

fricción *nf, pl* **fricciones** **1** : friction **2** : rubbing, massage **3** : discord, disagreement ⟨fricción entre los hermanos : friction between the brothers⟩

friccionar *vt* **1** FROTAR : to rub **2** : to massage

friega[1], **friegue, etc.** → **fregar**

friega[2] *nf* **1** FRICCIÓN : massage **2** : annoyance, bother

frigidez *nf* : (sexual) frigidity

frigorífico *nm Spain* : refrigerator

frijol *nm* : bean ⟨frijoles refritos : refried beans⟩

frío[1], **fría** *adj* **1** : cold **2** INDIFERENTE : cool, indifferent ⟨me deja frío : it leaves me cold⟩ **3** ESTUPEFACTO, PASMADO : shocked, stunned

frío[2] *nm* **1** : cold ⟨hace mucho frío esta noche : it's very cold tonight⟩ **2** INDIFERENCIA : coldness, indifference **3 tener frío** : to feel cold ⟨tengo frío : I'm cold⟩ **4 tomar frío** RESFRIARSE : to catch a cold

friolento, -ta *adj* : sensitive to cold

friolera *nf* (*used ironically or humorously*) : trifling amount ⟨una friolera de mil dólares : a mere thousand dollars⟩

friolero, -ra → **friolento**

friso *nm* : frieze

fritar *vt* : to fry

frito[1] *pp* → **freír**

frito[2], **-ta** *adj* **1** : fried **2** *fam* : worn-out, fed up ⟨tener frito a alguien : to get on someone's nerves⟩ **3** *fam* : fast asleep ⟨se quedó frito en el sofá : she fell asleep on the couch⟩ **4** *Arg, Chile, Peru, Uru fam* : done for, in trouble

fritura *nf* **1** : frying **2** : fried food

frivolidad *nf* : frivolity

frívolo, -la *adj* : frivolous — **frívolamente** *adv*

fronda *nf* **1** : frond **2 frondas** *nfpl* : foliage

frondoso, -sa *adj* : leafy, luxuriant

frontal *adj* : frontal, head-on ⟨un choque frontal : a head-on collision⟩

frontalmente *adv* : head-on

frontera *nf* : border, frontier

fronterizo, -za *adj* : border, on the border ⟨estados fronterizos : neighboring states⟩

frontón *nm, pl* **frontones** **1** : jai alai **2** : jai alai court

frotar *vt* **1** : to rub **2** : to strike (a match) — **frotarse** *vr* : to rub (together)

frote *nm* : rubbing, rub

fructífero, -ra *adj* : fruitful, productive

fructificar {72} *vi* **1** : to bear or produce fruit **2** : to be productive

fructuoso, -sa *adj* : fruitful

frugal *adj* : frugal, thrifty — **frugalmente** *adv*

frugalidad *adj* : frugality

fruncido *nm* : gathering (of fabric)

fruncir {83} *vt* **1** : to gather (fabric) **2 fruncir el ceño** : to knit one's brow, to frown **3 fruncir la boca** : to pucker up, to purse one's lips

frunza, etc. → **fruncir**

frustración *nf, pl* **-ciones** : frustration

frustrado, -da *adj* **1** : frustrated **2** : failed, unsuccessful

frustrante *adj* : frustrating

frustrar *vt* : to frustrate, to thwart — **frustrarse** *vr* FRACASAR : to fail, to come to nothing ⟨se frustraron sus esperanzas : his hopes were dashed⟩

fruta *nf* : fruit

frutal[1] *adj* : fruit, fruit-bearing

frutal[2] *nm* : fruit tree

frutería *nf* : fruit store

frutero[1], **-ra** *n* : fruit seller

frutero[2] *nm* : fruit bowl

frutilla *nf* : South American strawberry

fruto *nm* **1** : fruit ⟨los frutos de la tierra : the fruits of the earth⟩ **2** : fruit, result ⟨los frutos de su trabajo : the fruits of his labor⟩

fucsia *adj & nm* : fuchsia

fue, etc. → **ir, ser**

fuego *nm* **1** : fire ⟨prender fuego a algo : to set something on fire⟩ ⟨jugar con fuego : to play with fire⟩ ⟨abrir fuego contra : to open fire on⟩ **2** : light ⟨¿tienes fuego? : have you got a light?⟩ **3** : flame, burner (on a stove) ⟨a fuego lento : on low heat⟩ **4** : ardor, passion **5** : skin eruption, cold sore **6 fuegos artificiales** : fireworks

fuelle *nm* : bellows

fuente *nf* **1** MANANTIAL : spring **2** : fountain **3** ORIGEN : source ⟨fuentes informativas : sources of information⟩ ⟨fuente de alimentación/energía : food/ energy source⟩ **4** : platter, serving dish **5 fuente de noticias** : news feed **6 fuente de soda** : soda fountain

fuera *adv* **1** AFUERA : outside, out ⟨por fuera : on the outside⟩ ⟨hacia fuera : out, outside, outwards⟩ **2** : abroad, away **3** ~ **de** : out of, outside of, beyond ⟨fuera del alcance : out of reach⟩ ⟨fuera de peligro : out of danger⟩ **4** ~ **de** : besides, in addition to ⟨fuera de eso : aside from that⟩ **5 fuera de lugar** : out of place, amiss

fuerce, fuerza etc. → **forzar**

fuero *nm* **1** JURISDICCIÓN : jurisdiction **2** : privilege, exemption **3 fuero interno** : conscience, heart of hearts

fuerte[1] *adv* **1** : strongly, tightly, hard **2** : loudly **3** : abundantly

fuerte[2] *adj* **1** : strong ⟨brazos fuertes : strong arms⟩ **2** RESISTENTE : strong, sturdy **3** : intense (of pain, etc.), strong (of a drug, odor, etc.) **4** : powerful, strong (of wind), heavy (of rain) ⟨un fuerte golpe : a hard blow⟩ **5** : sharp, marked ⟨un fuerte incremento : a sharp increase⟩ **6** : loud ⟨hablar más fuerte : to speak up⟩ **7** : extreme, excessive **8 hacerse fuerte** : to pull oneself together — **fuertemente** *adv*

fuerte[3] *nm* **1** : fort, stronghold **2** : forte, strong point

fuerza *nf* **1** : strength ⟨tener fuerzas para : to have the strength to⟩ ⟨cobrar fuerza : to gather strength⟩ ⟨recuperar fuerzas : to get one's strength back⟩ ⟨con todas sus fuerzas : with all your might⟩ **2** VIO-

LENCIA : force ⟨fuerza bruta : brute force⟩ **3** : force, strength, power ⟨la fuerza del impacto : the force of the impact⟩ **4** : force, power ⟨fuerza de costumbre : force of habit⟩ ⟨fuerza de voluntad : willpower⟩ ⟨la fuerza de la razón : the power of reason⟩ **5** : (natural) force ⟨la fuerza de la gravedad : the force of gravity⟩ **6** : force ⟨fuerzas armadas/militares : armed/military forces⟩ ⟨fuerzas de seguridad : security forces⟩ ⟨fuerza pública, fuerzas del orden : police⟩ ⟨fuerza de trabajo : workforce⟩ **7 a fuerza de** : by, by dint of **8 a/por la fuerza** : by force, forcibly **9 con** ~ : hard, firmly, tightly **10 por** ~ : necessarily, unavoidably

fuerza centrífuga *nf* : centrifugal force

fuete *nm* : riding crop

fuga *nf* **1** HUIDA : flight, escape **2** : fugue **3** : leak ⟨fuga de gas : gas leak⟩

fugarse {52} *vr* **1** : to escape **2** HUIR : to flee, to run away **3** : to elope

fugaz *adj, pl* **fugaces** : brief, fleeting

fugitivo, -va *adj & n* : fugitive

fulana *nf disparaging* : hooker, slut *disparaging + offensive*

fulano, -na *n* : so-and-so, what's-his-name, what's-her-name ⟨fulano, mengano, y zutano : Tom, Dick, and Harry⟩ ⟨señora fulana de tal : Mrs. so-and-so⟩

fulcro *nm* : fulcrum

fulgor *nm* : brilliance, splendor

fulminante *adj* : devastating, terrible ⟨una mirada fulminante : a withering look⟩

fulminar *vt* : to strike down ⟨fulminar a alguien con la mirada : to look daggers at someone⟩

fumador, -dora *n* : smoker

fumar *v* : to smoke

fumble *nm* : fumble (in football)

fumblear *vt* : to fumble (in football)

fumigar {52} *vt* : to fumigate — **fumigación** *nf* — **fumigador, -dora** *n*

función *nf, pl* **funciones 1** : function **2** : duty ⟨el presidente en funciones : the acting president⟩ **3** : performance, show **4 en función de** : according to

funcional *adj* : functional — **funcionalmente** *adv*

funcionamiento *nm* **1** : functioning **2 en** ~ : in operation

funcionar *vi* **1** : to function **2** : to run, to work

funcionario, -ria *n* : civil servant, official

funda *nf* **1** : case, cover, sheath **2** : pillowcase

fundación *nf, pl* **-ciones** : foundation, establishment

fundado, -da *adj* : well-founded, justified

fundador, -dora *n* : founder

fundamental *adj* BÁSICO : fundamental, basic — **fundamentalmente** *adv*

fundamentalismo *nm* : fundamentalism — **fundamentalista** *nmf*

fundamentar *vt* **1** : to lay the foundations for **2** : to support, to back up **3** : to base, to found

fundamento *nm* : basis, foundation, groundwork

fundar *vt* **1** ESTABLECER, INSTITUIR : to found, to establish **2** BASAR : to base — **fundarse** *vr* ~ **en** : to be based on, to stem from

fundición *nf, pl* **-ciones 1** : founding, smelting **2** : foundry

fundir *vt* **1** : to melt down, to smelt **2** : to fuse, to merge **3** : to burn out (a lightbulb) — **fundirse** *vr* **1** : to fuse together, to blend, to merge **2** : to melt, to thaw **3** : to fade (in television or movies)

fúnebre *adj* **1** : funeral, funereal **2** LÚGUBRE : gloomy, mournful

funeral[1] *adj* : funeral

funeral[2] *nm* **1** : funeral **2 funerales** *nmpl* EXEQUIAS : funeral rites

funeraria *nf* **1** : funeral home, funeral parlor **2 director de funeraria** : funeral director, undertaker

funerario, -ria *adj* : funeral

funesto, -ta *adj* : terrible, disastrous ⟨consecuencias funestas : disastrous consequences⟩

fungicida *nm* : fungicide

fungir {35} *vi* : to act, to function ⟨fungir de asesor : to act as a consultant⟩

funicular *nm* : cable car (on a mountain)

funja, etc. → **fungir**

furgón *nm, pl* **furgones 1** : van, truck **2** : freight car, boxcar **3 furgón de cola** : caboose

furgoneta *nf* : van

furia *nf* **1** CÓLERA, IRA : fury, rage **2** : violence, fury ⟨la furia de la tormenta : the fury of the storm⟩

furibundo, -da *adj* : furious

furiosamente *adv* : furiously, frantically

furioso, -sa *adj* **1** AIRADO : furious, irate **2** : intense, violent

furor *nm* **1** : fury, rage **2** : violence (of the elements) **3** : passion, frenzy **4** : enthusiasm ⟨hacer furor : to be all the rage⟩

furtivo, -va *adj* : furtive — **furtivamente** *adv*

fuselaje *nm* : fuselage

fusible *nm* : (electrical) fuse

fusil *nm* : rifle

fusilar *vt* **1** : to shoot, to execute (by firing squad) **2** *fam* : to plagiarize, to pirate

fusilería *nf* **1** : rifles *pl*, rifle fire **2 descarga de fusilería** : fusillade

fusión *nf, pl* **fusiones 1** : fusion **2** : union, merger

fusionar *vt* **1** : to fuse **2** : to merge, to amalgamate — **fusionarse** *vr*

fusta *nf* : riding crop

fuste *nm* **1** : shaft **2 de fuste** : important, significant

fustigar {52} *vt* **1** AZOTAR : to whip, to lash **2** : to upbraid, to berate

futbol *or* **fútbol** *nm* **1** : soccer **2 futbol americano** : football

futbolista *nmf* : soccer player

fútbol sala *nm* : indoor soccer

futesa *nf* **1** : small thing, trifle **2 futesas** *nfpl* : small talk

fútil *adj* : trifling, trivial

futón *nm, pl* **-tones** : futon

futurista *adj* : futuristic

futuro[1]**, -ra** *adj* : future

futuro[2] *nm* PORVENIR : future

G

g *nf* : eighth letter of the Spanish alphabet

gabán *nm, pl* **gabanes** : topcoat, overcoat

gabardina *nf* **1** : gabardine **2** : trench coat, raincoat

gabarra *nf* : barge

gabinete *nm* **1** : cabinet (in government) **2** : study, office (in the home) **3** : (professional) office

gablete *nm* : gable

gabonés, -nesa *adj & n, mpl* **-neses** : Gabonese

gacela *nf* : gazelle

gaceta *nf* : gazette, newspaper

gachas *nfpl* : porridge

gacho, -cha *adj* **1** : drooping, turned downward **2** *Mex fam* : nasty, awful **3 ir a gachas** *fam* : to go on all fours

gaélico[1]**, -ca** *adj* : Gaelic

gaélico[2] *nm* : Gaelic (language)

gafas *nfpl* ANTEOJOS : eyeglasses, glasses

gafe *nm Spain fam* : jinx, bad luck

gaita *nf* : bagpipes *pl*

gajes *nmpl* **gajes del oficio** : occupational hazards

gajo *nm* **1** : broken branch (of a tree) **2** : cluster, bunch (of fruit) **3** : segment (of citrus fruit)

gala *nf* **1** : gala ⟨vestido de gala : formal dress⟩ ⟨tener algo a gala : to be proud of something⟩ **2 galas** *nfpl* : finery, attire

galáctico, -ca *adj* : galactic

galán *nm, pl* **galanes 1** : ladies' man, gallant **2** : leading man, hero **3** : boyfriend, suitor

galano, -na *adj* **1** : elegant **2** *Mex* : mottled

galante *adj* : gallant, attentive — **galantemente** *adv*

galantear *vt* **1** CORTEJAR : to court, to woo **2** : to flirt with

galanteo *nm* **1** CORTEJO : courtship **2** : flirtation, flirting

galantería *nf* **1** : gallantry, attentiveness **2** : compliment

galápago *nm* : aquatic turtle

galardón *nm, pl* **-dones** : award, prize

galardonado, -da *adj* : prizewinning

galardonar *vt* : to give an award to

galaxia *nf* : galaxy

galeno *nm fam* : physician, doctor

galeón *nm, pl* **galeones** : galleon

galera *nf* : galley

galería *nf* **1** : gallery, balcony (in a theater) ⟨galería comercial : shopping mall⟩ **2** : corridor, passage

galerón *nm, pl* **-rones** *Mex* : large hall
galés[1], **-lesa** *adj* : Welsh
galés[2], **-lesa** *n, mpl* **galeses** 1 : Welshman *m*, Welshwoman *f* 2 **los galeses** : the Welsh
galés[3] *nm* : Welsh (language)
galgo *nm* : greyhound
galimatías *nms & pl* : gibberish, nonsense
galio *nm* : gallium
gallardete *nm* : pennant, streamer
gallardía *nf* 1 VALENTÍA : bravery 2 APOSTURA : elegance, gracefulness
gallardo, -da *adj* 1 VALIENTE : brave 2 APUESTO : elegant, graceful
gallear *vi* : to show off, to strut around
gallego[1], **-ga** *adj* 1 : Galician 2 *fam* : Spanish
gallego[2], **-ga** *n* 1 : Galician 2 *fam* : Spaniard
galleta *nf* 1 : cookie 2 : cracker
gallina *nf* 1 : hen 2 **gallina de Guinea** : guinea fowl
gallinazo *nm* : vulture, buzzard
gallinero *nm* : chicken coop
gallito, -ta *adj fam* : cocky, belligerent
gallo *nm* 1 : rooster, cock 2 *fam* : squeak or crack in the voice 3 *Mex* : serenade 4 **gallo de pelea** : gamecock
galochas *nfpl* : galoshes
galón *nm, pl* **galones** 1 : gallon 2 : stripe (military insignia)
galopada *nf* : gallop
galopante *adj* : galloping ⟨inflación galopante : galloping inflation⟩
galopar *vi* : to gallop
galope *nm* : gallop
galpón *nm, pl* **galpones** : shed, storehouse
galvanizar {21} *vt* : to galvanize — **galvanización** *nf*
gama *nf* 1 : range, spectrum, gamut 2 → gamo
gamba *nf Arg, Spain, Uru* : large shrimp, prawn
gamberrada *nf Spain* 1 : act of vandalism 2 : crude thing (to say or do)
gamberro, -rra *n Spain* : hooligan, troublemaker
gambiano, -na *adj & n* : Gambian
gambito *nm* : gambit (in chess)
gamo, -ma *n* : fallow deer
gamuza *nf* 1 : suede 2 : chamois
gana *nf* 1 : desire, inclination 2 **con ∼s** : enthusiastically, heartily ⟨trabajar con ganas : to work enthusiastically⟩ ⟨llover con ganas : to be pouring rain⟩ 3 **darle ganas a alguien de hacer algo** : to make someone feel like doing something 4 **de buena gana** : willingly, readily, gladly 5 **de mala gana** : reluctantly, halfheartedly 6 **tener ganas de hacer algo** : to feel like doing something ⟨tengo ganas de bailar : I feel like dancing⟩ 7 **morirse de ganas de hacer algo** : to be dying to do something 8 **ponerle ganas a algo** : to put effort into something 9 **quedarse con las ganas (de hacer algo)** : to end up not doing something

ganadería *nf* 1 : cattle raising 2 : cattle ranch 3 GANADO : cattle *pl*, livestock
ganadero[1], **-ra** *adj* : cattle, ranching
ganadero[2], **-ra** *n* : rancher
ganado *nm* 1 : cattle *pl*, livestock 2 **ganado ovino** : sheep *pl* 3 **ganado porcino** : swine *pl*
ganador[1], **-dora** *adj* : winning
ganador[2], **-dora** *n* : winner
ganancia *nf* 1 : profit 2 **ganancias** *nfpl* : winnings, gains
ganancioso, -sa *adj* : profitable
ganar *vt* 1 : to win 2 : to gain ⟨ganar tiempo : to buy time⟩ 3 : to earn ⟨ganar dinero : to make money⟩ 4 : to acquire, to obtain — *vi* 1 : to win 2 : to profit ⟨salir ganando : to come out ahead⟩ — **ganarse** *vr* 1 : to gain, to win ⟨ganarse a alguien : to win someone over⟩ 2 : to earn ⟨ganarse la vida : to make a living⟩ 3 : to deserve
ganchillo *nm* : crochet hook
gancho *nm* 1 : hook 2 : clothes hanger 3 : hairpin, bobby pin 4 *Col* : safety pin
gandul[1] *nm CA, Car, Col* : pigeon pea
gandul[2], **-dula** *n fam* : idler, lazybones
gandulear *vi* : to idle, to loaf, to lounge about
ganga *nf* : bargain
ganglio *nm* 1 : ganglion 2 : gland
gangrena *nf* : gangrene — **gangrenoso, -sa** *adj*
gángster *nmf, pl* **gángsters** : gangster
gansada *nf* : silly thing, nonsense
ganso, -sa *n* 1 : goose, gander *m* 2 : idiot, fool
gañido *nm* : yelp (of a dog)
gañir {38} *vi* : to yelp
garabatear *v* : to scribble, to scrawl, to doodle
garabato *nm* 1 : doodle 2 **garabatos** *nmpl* : scribble, scrawl
garaje *nm* : garage
garante *nmf* : guarantor
garantía *nf* 1 : guarantee, warranty 2 : security ⟨garantía de trabajo : job security⟩
garantizar {21} *vt* : to guarantee
garapiña *nf* : pineapple drink
garapiñar *vt* : to candy
garbanzo *nm* : chickpea
garbo *nm* 1 DONAIRE : grace, poise 2 : jauntiness
garboso, -sa *adj* 1 : graceful 2 : elegant, stylish
garceta *nf* : egret
gardenia *nf* : gardenia
garfio *nm* : hook, gaff
gargajo *nm fam* : phlegm
garganta *nf* 1 : throat 2 : neck (of a person or a bottle) 3 : ravine, narrow pass
gargantilla *nf* : choker, necklace
gárgara *nf* 1 : gargle, gargling 2 **hacer gárgaras** : to gargle
gargarizar *vi* : to gargle
gárgola *nf* : gargoyle
garita *nf* 1 : cabin, hut 2 : sentry box, lookout post
garito *nm* : gambling hall

garoso, -sa *adj Col, Ven* : gluttonous, greedy
garra *nf* 1 : claw 2 : hand, paw 3 **garras** *nfpl* : claws, clutches ⟨caer en las garras de alguien : to fall into someone's clutches⟩
garrafa *nf* : decanter, carafe
garrafal *adj* : terrible, monstrous
garrafón *nm, pl* **-fones** : large decanter, large bottle
garrapata *nf* : tick
garrobo *nm CA* : large lizard, iguana
garrocha *nf* 1 PICA : lance, pike 2 : pole ⟨salto con/de garrocha : pole vault⟩
garrotazo *nm* : blow (with a club)
garrote *nm* 1 : club, stick 2 *Mex* : brake
garúa *nf* : drizzle
garuar {3} *v impers* LLOVIZNAR : to drizzle
garza *nf* : heron
garzón, -zona *n, mpl* **-zones** *Chile* : waiter *m*, waitress *f*
gas *nm* : gas, vapor, fumes *pl* ⟨gas lacrimógeno : tear gas⟩
gasa *nf* : gauze
gasear *vt* 1 : to gas 2 : to aerate (a liquid)
gaseosa *nf* REFRESCO : soda, soft drink
gaseoso, -sa *adj* 1 : gaseous 2 : carbonated, fizzy
gasfitería *nf Chile, Peru* : plumbing
gasfitero, -ra *n Chile, Peru* : plumber
gasoducto *nm* : gas pipeline
gasoil *nm* : diesel oil, fuel oil
gasóleo → gasoil
gasolina *nf* : gasoline, gas
gasolinera *nf* : gas station, service station
gastado, -da *adj* 1 : spent 2 : worn, worn-out
gastador¹, -dora *adj* : extravagant, spendthrift
gastador², -dora *n* : spendthrift
gastar *vt* 1 : to spend 2 CONSUMIR : to consume, to use up 3 : to squander, to waste 4 : to wear ⟨gasta un bigote : he sports a mustache⟩ — **gastarse** *vr* 1 : to spend, to expend 2 : to run down, to wear out
gasto *nm* 1 : expense, expenditure 2 DETERIORO : wear 3 **gastos fijos/generales/indirectos** : overhead 4 **cubrir gastos** : to cover costs, to break even 5 **gastos de seguro** : insurance costs 6 **gastos de la casa** : household expenses 7 **gastos de viaje** : travel expenses 8 **gastos de envío** : shipping and handling 9 **gasto público** : public spending
gástrico, -ca *adj* : gastric
gastronomía *nf* : gastronomy
gastronómico, -ca *adj* : gastronomic
gastrónomo, -ma *n* : gourmet
gatas *adv* andar a gatas : to crawl, to go on all fours
gatear *vi* 1 : to crawl 2 : to climb, to clamber (up)
gatillero *nm Mex* : gunman
gatillo *nm* : trigger
gatito, -ta *n* : kitten
gato¹, -ta *n* 1 : cat ⟨gato manchado : calico cat⟩ ⟨gato montés : wildcat⟩ 2

(aquí) hay gato encerrado : there's something fishy going on (here) 3 **dar gato por liebre a alguien** : to swindle someone 4 **llevarse el gato al agua** : to pull it off, to manage it
gato² *nm* : jack (for an automobile)
gauchada *nf Arg, Uru* : favor, kindness
gaucho *nm* : gaucho
gaveta *nf* 1 CAJÓN : drawer 2 : till
gavilán *nm, pl* **-lanes** : sparrow hawk
gavilla *nf* 1 : gang, band 2 : sheaf
gaviota *nf* : gull, seagull
gay [ˈge, ˈgai] *adj* : gay (homosexual)
gaza *nf* : loop
gazapo *nm* 1 : young rabbit 2 : misprint, error
gazmoñería *nf* MOJIGATERÍA : prudery, primness
gazmoño¹, -ña *adj* : prudish, prim
gazmoño², -ña *n* MOJIGATO : prude, prig
gaznate *nm* : throat, gullet
gazpacho *nm* : gazpacho
ge *nf* : (letter) g
géiser *or* **géyser** *nm* : geyser
gel *nm* : gel
gelatina *nf* : gelatin
gélido, -da *adj* : icy, freezing cold
gelificarse *vr* : to jell
gema *nf* : gem
gemelo¹, -la *adj & n* MELLIZO : twin
gemelo² *nm* 1 : cuff link 2 **gemelos** *nmpl* BINOCULARES : binoculars
gemido *nm* : moan, groan, wail
Géminis¹ *nm* : Gemini (sign or constellation)
Géminis² *nmf* : Gemini (person)
gemir {54} *vi* : to moan, to groan, to wail
gen *or* **gene** *nm* : gene
gendarme *nmf* POLICÍA : police officer, policeman *m*, policewoman *f*
gendarmería *nf* : police
genealogía *nf* : genealogy
genealógico, -ca *adj* : genealogical
generación *nf, pl* **-ciones** 1 : generation ⟨tercera generación : third generation⟩ 2 : generating, creating 3 : class ⟨la generación del '97 : the class of '97⟩
generacional *adj* : generation, generational
generador *nm* : generator
general¹ *adj* 1 : general 2 **en ~** *or* **por lo general** : in general, generally
general² *nmf* 1 : general 2 **general de división** : major general
generalidad *nf* 1 : generality, generalization 2 : majority
generalización *nf, pl* **-ciones** 1 : generalization 2 : escalation, spread
generalizado, -da *adj* : generalized, widespread
generalizar {21} *vi* : to generalize — *vt* : to spread, to spread out — **generalizarse** *vr* : to become widespread
generalmente *adv* : usually, generally
generar *vt* : to generate — **generarse** *vr*
genérico, -ca *adj* : generic
género *nm* 1 : genre, class, kind ⟨el género humano : the human race, mankind⟩ 2 : gender (in grammar) 3 : gender (of a person) ⟨identidad de género

: gender identity⟩ **4 géneros** *nmpl*
: goods, commodities **5 de género neutro** : gender-neutral
generosidad *nf* : generosity
generoso, -sa *adj* **1** : generous, unselfish
2 : ample — **generosamente** *adv*
genética *nf* : genetics
genético, -ca *adj* : genetic — **genéticamente** *adv*
genetista *nmf* : geneticist
genial *adj* **1** AGRADABLE : genial, pleasant **2** : brilliant ⟨una obra genial : a
work of genius⟩ **3** *fam* FORMIDABLE
: fantastic, terrific
genialidad *nf* **1** : genius **2** : stroke of
genius **3** : eccentricity
genio *nm* **1** : genius **2** : temper, disposition ⟨de mal genio : bad-tempered⟩ **3**
: genie
genital *adj* : genital
genitales *nmpl* : genitals
genocidio *nm* : genocide
gente *nf* **1** : people **2** : relatives *pl*, folks
pl **3 gente menuda** *fam* : children, kids
pl **4 ser buena gente** : to be nice, to be
kind
gentil[1] *adj* **1** AMABLE : kind **2** : gentile
gentil[2] *nmf* : gentile
gentileza *nf* **1** AMABILIDAD : kindness **2**
CORTESÍA : courtesy
gentilicio, -cia *adj* **1** : national, tribal **2**
: family
gentilmente *adv* : kindly
gentío *nm* MUCHEDUMBRE, MULTITUD
: crowd, mob
gentuza *nf* CHUSMA : riffraff, rabble
genuflexión *nf*, *pl* **-xiones** **1** : genuflection **2 hacer una genuflexión** : to genuflect
genuino, -na *adj* : genuine — **genuina-
mente** *adv*
geografía *nf* : geography
geográfico, -ca *adj* : geographic, geographical — **geográficamente** *adv*
geógrafo, -fa *n* : geographer
geología *nf* : geology
geológico, -ca *adj* : geologic, geological
— **geológicamente** *adv*
geólogo, -ga *n* : geologist
geometría *nf* : geometry
geométrico, -ca *adj* : geometric, geometrical — **geométricamente** *adv*
geopolítico, -ca *adj* : geopolitical
georgiano, -na *adj & n* : Georgian
geranio *nm* : geranium
gerbo *nm* : gerbil
gerencia *nf* : management, administration
gerencial *adj* : managerial
gerente *nmf* : manager, director
geriatría *nf* : geriatrics
geriátrico, -ca *adj* : geriatric
germanio *nm* : germanium
germano, -na *adj* : Germanic, German
germen *nm*, *pl* **gérmenes** : germ
germicida *nf* : germicide
germinación *nf*, *pl* **-ciones** : germination
germinar *vi* : to germinate, to sprout
gerundio *nm* : gerund
gesta *nf* : deed, exploit

gestación *nf*, *pl* **-ciones** : gestation
gesticular *vi* : to gesticulate — **gesticula-
ción** *nf*
gestión *nf*, *pl* **gestiones** **1** TRÁMITE
: procedure, step **2** ADMINISTRACIÓN
: management **3 gestiones** *nfpl* : negotiations **4 gestión de datos** : data management
gestionar *vt* **1** : to negotiate, to work towards **2** ADMINISTRAR : to manage, to
handle
gesto *nm* **1** ADEMÁN : gesture **2** : facial
expression **3** MUECA : grimace
gestor[1], **-tora** *adj* : facilitating, negotiat-
ing, managing
gestor[2], **-tora** *n* : facilitator, manager
géyser → géiser
ghanés, -nesa *adj & n*, *mpl* **ghaneses**
: Ghanaian
ghetto → gueto
giba *nf* **1** : hump (of an animal) **2** : person with a hump, hunchback *offensive*,
humpback *offensive*
gibón *nm*, *pl* **gibones** : gibbon
giboso[1], **-sa** *adj* : hunchbacked, humpbacked
giboso[2], **-sa** *n* : person with a hump,
hunchback *offensive*, humpback *offensive*
giga[1] *nf* : jig
giga[2] *nmf fam* : gig, gigabyte
gigabyte *nm* : gigabyte
gigante[1] *adj* : giant, gigantic
gigante[2], **-ta** *n* : giant
gigantesco, -ca *adj* : gigantic, huge
gime, etc. → gemir
gimnasia *nf* : gymnastics
gimnasio *nm* : gymnasium, gym
gimnasta *nmf* : gymnast
gimnástico, -ca *adj* : gymnastic
gimotear *vi* LLORIQUEAR : to whine, to
whimper
gimoteo *nm* : whimpering
ginebra *nf* : gin
ginecología *nf* : gynecology
ginecológico, -ca *adj* : gynecologic, gynecological
ginecólogo, -ga *n* : gynecologist
ginseng *nm* : ginseng
gira *nf* : tour
giralda *nf* : weather vane
girar *vi* **1** : to turn around, to revolve **2**
: to swing around, to swivel — *vt* **1** : to
turn, to twist, to rotate **2** : to draft
(checks) **3** : to transfer (funds)
girasol *nm* MIRASOL : sunflower
giratorio, -ria *adj* : revolving
giro *nm* **1** VUELTA : turn, rotation **2**
: change of direction ⟨giro de 180 grados, giro en U : U-turn, about-face⟩ **3
giro bancario** : bank draft **4 giro postal** : money order
giroscopio *or* **giróscopo** *nm* : gyroscope
gis *nm Mex* : chalk
gitano, -na *adj & n* : Gypsy *sometimes offensive*
glacial *adj* : glacial, icy — **glacialmente**
adv
glaciar *nm* : glacier
gladiador *nm* : gladiator

gladiolo or **gladíolo** nm : gladiolus

glamping ['glampiŋ] nm fam : glamping

glándula nf : gland — **glandular** adj

glaseado nm : glaze, icing

glasear vt : to glaze

glaucoma nm : glaucoma

glena nf : socket

glicerina nf : glycerin

glicinia nf : wisteria

global adj 1 : global, worldwide 2 : full, comprehensive 3 : total, overall

globalizar {21} vt 1 ABARCAR : to include, to encompass 2 : to extend worldwide — **globalización** nf

globalmente adv : globally, as a whole

globo nm 1 : globe, sphere 2 : balloon 3 **globo ocular** : eyeball

glóbulo nm 1 : globule 2 : blood cell, corpuscle

gloria nf 1 : glory 2 : fame, renown 3 : delight, enjoyment 4 : star, legend ⟨las glorias del cine : the great names in motion pictures⟩

glorieta nf 1 : rotary, traffic circle 2 : bower, arbor 3 : gazebo

glorificar {72} vt ALABAR : to glorify — **glorificación** nf

glorioso, -sa adj : glorious — **gloriosamente** adv

glosa nf 1 : gloss 2 : annotation, commentary

glosar vt 1 : to gloss 2 : to annotate, to comment on (a text)

glosario nm : glossary

glotón¹, -tona adj, mpl **glotones** : gluttonous

glotón², -tona n, mpl **glotones** : glutton

glotón³ nm, pl **glotones** : wolverine

glotonería nf GULA : gluttony

glucosa nf : glucose

glutinoso, -sa adj : glutinous

gnomo ['nomo] nm : gnome

gobernación nf, pl **-ciones** : governing, government

gobernador, -dora n : governor

gobernante¹ adj : ruling, governing

gobernante² nmf : ruler, leader, governor

gobernar {55} vt 1 : to govern, to rule 2 : to steer, to sail (a ship) — vi 1 : to govern 2 : to steer

gobierno nm : government

goce¹, etc. → gozar

goce² nm 1 PLACER : enjoyment, pleasure 2 : use, possession

gol nm : goal (in soccer)

goleada nf : rout, defeat (in sports)

goleador, -dora n : scorer (of goals) ⟨el máximo goleador del equipo : the team's top scorer⟩

golear vt : to rout, to score many goals against (in soccer)

goleta nf : schooner

golf nm : golf

golfista nmf : golfer

golfo nm : gulf, bay

golondrina nf 1 : swallow (bird) 2 **golondrina de mar** : tern

golosina nf : sweet, snack

goloso, -sa adj : fond of sweets ⟨ser goloso : to have a sweet tooth⟩

golpazo nm : heavy blow, bang, thump

golpe nm 1 : blow ⟨caerle/cogerle a golpes a alguien : to give someone a beating⟩ ⟨darse un golpe en la cabeza : to hit one's head⟩ 2 : knock 3 : job, heist ⟨dar el golpe : to do the job⟩ 4 **de ~** : suddenly 5 **de un golpe** : all at once, in one fell swoop 6 **golpe de estado** : coup, coup d'etat 7 **golpe de gracia** : coup de grâce 8 **golpe de suerte** : stroke of luck 9 **golpe de viento** : gust of wind 10 **no dar/pegar (ni) golpe** : not to lift a finger, not to do a bit of work

golpeado, -da adj 1 : beaten, hit 2 : bruised (of fruit) 3 : dented

golpear vt 1 : to beat (up), to hit 2 : to slam, to bang, to strike — vi 1 : to knock (at a door) 2 : to beat ⟨la lluvia golpeaba contra el tejado : the rain beat against the roof⟩ — **golpearse** vr

golpetear v 1 : to knock, to rattle, to tap

golpeteo nm : banging, knocking, tapping

golpista¹ adj 1 : coup, coup-related ⟨intentona golpista : attempted coup, coup attempt⟩ 2 : pro-coup

golpista² mf 1 : coup supporter 2 : military insurgent

golpiza nf : beating, pummeling

goma nf 1 : gum ⟨goma de mascar : chewing gum⟩ ⟨goma de pegar : glue⟩ 2 CAUCHO : rubber ⟨goma espuma : foam rubber⟩ 3 PEGAMENTO : glue 4 : rubber band 5 Arg : tire 6 or **goma de borrar** : eraser 6 CA fam : hangover

gomina nf : hair gel

gomita nf : rubber band

gomoso, -sa adj : gummy, sticky

góndola nf : gondola

gong nm : gong

gonorrea nf : gonorrhea

googlear [gugle'ar] vt (Google, marca registrada) : to google

gorda nf Mex : thick corn tortilla

gordinflón¹, -flona adj, mpl **-flones** fam : chubby, pudgy

gordinflón², -flona n, mpl **-flones** fam : chubby person

gordo¹, -da adj 1 : fat 2 : thick 3 : fatty, greasy, oily 4 : unpleasant ⟨me cae gorda tu tía : I can't stand your aunt⟩

gordo², -da n : fat person

gordo³ nm 1 GRASA : fat 2 : jackpot

gordura nf : fatness, flab

gorgojo nm : weevil

gorgorito nm : trill

gorgotear vi : to gurgle, to bubble

gorgoteo nm : gurgle

gorila nm 1 : gorilla 2 Spain fam : bouncer

gorjear vi 1 : to chirp, to tweet, to warble 2 : to gurgle

gorjeo nm 1 : chirping, warbling 2 : gurgling

gorra nf 1 : bonnet 2 : cap 3 **de ~** fam : for free, at someone else's expense ⟨vivir de gorra : to sponge, to freeload⟩

gorrear vt fam : to bum, to scrounge — vi fam : to freeload gorrero, -ra *n fam* : freeloader, sponger

gorrión *nm, pl* gorriones : sparrow

gorro *nm* 1 : cap ⟨gorro de ducha : shower cap⟩ 2 estar hasta el gorro : to be fed up

gorrón, -rrona *n, mpl* gorrones *fam* : freeloader, scrounger

gorronear *vt fam* : to bum, to scrounge — *vi fam* : to freeload

gota *nf* 1 : drop ⟨una gota de sudor : a bead of sweat⟩ ⟨como dos gotas de agua : like two peas in a pod⟩ ⟨sudar la gota gorda : to sweat buckets, to work very hard⟩ 2 : gout

gotear *vi* 1 : to drip 2 : to leak — *v impers* LLOVIZNAR : to drizzle

goteo *nm* : drip, dripping

gotera *nf* 1 : leak 2 : stain (from dripping water)

gotero *nm* : (medicine) dropper

gótico, -ca *adj* : Gothic

gourmet *nmf* : gourmet

gozar {21} *vi* 1 : to enjoy oneself, to have a good time 2 ~ de : to enjoy, to have, to possess ⟨gozar de buena salud : to enjoy good health⟩ 3 ~ con : to take delight in

gozne *nm* BISAGRA : hinge

gozo *nm* 1 : joy 2 PLACER : enjoyment, pleasure

gozoso, -sa *adj* : joyful

GPS [hepe'ese] *nm, pl* GPS : GPS

grabación *nf, pl* -ciones : recording

grabado *nm* 1 : engraving 2 grabado al aguafuerte : etching

grabador, -dora *n* 1 : engraver 2 → grabadora

grabadora *nf* : recorder, tape recorder ⟨grabadora de DVD : DVD recorder⟩

grabar *vt* 1 : to engrave 2 : to record, to tape — *vi* grabar al aguafuerte : to etch — grabarse *vr* grabársele a alguien en la memoria : to become engraved on someone's mind

gracia *nf* 1 : grace ⟨lo hizo con gracia : she did it gracefully⟩ ⟨una casa con mucha gracia : a very stylish/elegant house⟩ 2 : favor, kindness ⟨por la gracia de Dios : by the grace of God⟩ 3 : humor, wit ⟨su comentario no me hizo gracia : I wasn't amused by his remark⟩ ⟨tener gracia : to be funny⟩ 4 : grace, respite ⟨una semana de gracia : a week's grace⟩ ⟨período de gracia : grace period⟩ 5 gracias *nfpl* : thanks ⟨¡gracias! : thank you!⟩ ⟨dar gracias : to give thanks⟩

grácil *adj* 1 : graceful 2 : delicate, slender, fine

gracilidad *nm* : gracefulness

gracioso, -sa *adj* 1 CHISTOSO : funny, amusing 2 : cute, attractive

grada *nf* 1 : harrow 2 PELDAÑO : step, stair 3 gradas *nfpl* : bleachers, grandstand

gradación *nf, pl* -ciones : gradation, scale

gradar *vt* : to harrow, to hoe

gradería *nf* : tiers *pl*, stands *pl*, rows *pl* (in a theater)

gradiente *nf* : gradient, slope

grado *nm* 1 : degree (in meteorology and mathematics) ⟨grado centígrado : degree centigrade⟩ 2 : extent, level, degree ⟨en grado sumo : greatly, to the highest degree⟩ 3 RANGO : rank 4 : year, class (in education) 5 de buen grado : willingly, readily

graduable *adj* : adjustable

graduación *nf, pl* -ciones 1 : graduation (from a school) 2 GRADO : rank 3 : alcohol content, proof

graduado¹, -da *adj* 1 : graduated 2 lentes graduados : prescription lenses

graduado², -da *n* : graduate

gradual *adj* : gradual — gradualmente *adv*

graduar {3} *v* 1 : to regulate, to adjust 2 CALIBRAR : to calibrate, to gauge — graduarse *vr* : to graduate (from a school)

graffiti *or* grafiti *nmpl* : graffiti *pl*

gráfica *nf* → gráfico²

gráfico¹, -ca *adj* : graphic — gráficamente *adv*

gráfico² *nm* 1 : graph, chart 2 : graphic (for a computer, etc.) 3 gráfico de barras : bar graph

grafismo *nm* : graphics *pl*

grafito *nm* : graphite

gragea *nf* 1 : coated pill or tablet 2 grageas *nfpl* : sprinkles, jimmies

grajo *nm* : rook (bird)

grama *nf* : grass

gramática *nf* : grammar

gramatical *adj* : grammatical — gramaticalmente *adv*

gramilla *f* : crabgrass

gramo *nm* : gram

gran → grande

grana *nf* : scarlet, deep red

granada *nf* 1 : pomegranate 2 : grenade ⟨granada de mano : hand grenade⟩

granaderos *nmpl Mex* : riot squad

granadino, -na *adj & n* : Grenadian

granado, -da *adj* 1 DISTINGUIDO : distinguished 2 : choice, select

granate *nm* 1 : garnet 2 : deep red, maroon

grande *adj* (gran *before singular nouns*) 1 : large, big ⟨un libro grande : a big book⟩ ⟨un grupo grande : a large group⟩ ⟨grandes cantidades : large quantities⟩ ⟨grandes corporaciones : big corporations⟩ ⟨esta camisa me queda grande : this shirt's (too) big on me⟩ 2 ALTO : tall ⟨qué grande estás! : look how much you've grown!⟩ 3 NOTABLE : great ⟨un gran autor : a great writer⟩ 4 (*indicating significance*) : big ⟨un gran error : a big mistake⟩ ⟨su gran oportunidad : his big chance⟩ 5 (*indicating degree*) : great, big ⟨con gran placer : with great pleasure⟩ ⟨un gran éxito : a big/great success⟩ ⟨a gran velocidad : at great speed⟩ ⟨grandes amigos : great friends⟩ ⟨un gran admirador : a great/big admirer, a big fan⟩ 6 : old, grown-up, big ⟨hijos grandes : grown children⟩ ⟨ya eres (una niña/un niño) grande

: you're a big girl/boy now〉 **7 a lo
grande** : in style
grandeza *nf* 1 MAGNITUD : greatness,
size 2 : nobility 3 : generosity, graciousness 4 : grandeur, magnificence
grandilocuencia *nf* : bombast
grandilocuente *adj* : bombastic
grandiosidad *nf* : grandeur
grandioso, -sa *adj* 1 MAGNÍFICO : grand,
magnificent 2 : grandiose
granel *adv* 1 a ∼ : galore, in great quan-
tities 2 a ∼ : in bulk 〈vender a granel
: to sell in bulk〉
granero *nm* : barn, granary
granito *nm* : granite
granizada *nf* : hailstorm
granizado *nm* : drink made with crushed
ice
granizar {21} *v impers* : to hail
granizo *nm* : hail
granja *nf* : farm
granjear *vt* : to earn, to win — **granjearse**
vr : to gain, to earn
granjero, -ra *n* : farmer
grano *nm* 1 PARTÍCULA : grain, particle
〈un grano de arena : a grain of sand〉
2 : grain (of rice, etc.), bean (of coffee),
seed 3 : grain (of wood or rock) 4 BA-
RRO, ESPINILLA : pimple 5 **apartar el
grano de la paja** *fam* : to separate the
wheat from the chaff 6 **ir al grano** : to
get to the point
granoso, -sa *adj* : grainy
granuja *nmf* PILLUELO : rascal, urchin
granular *adj* : granular, grainy
granularse *vr* : to break out in spots
granuloso, -sa → granular
granza *nf* : chaff
grapa *nf* 1 : staple 2 : clamp
grapadora *nf* ENGRAPADORA : stapler
grapar *vt* ENGRAPAR : to staple
grasa *nf* 1 : grease 2 : fat 3 *Mex* : shoe
polish
grasiento, -ta *adj* : greasy, oily
graso, -sa *adj* 1 : fatty 2 : greasy, oily
grasoso, -sa *adj* GRASIENTO : greasy, oily
gratificación *nf, pl* -ciones 1 SATISFAC-
CIÓN : gratification 2 : bonus 3 RE-
COMPENSA : recompense, reward
gratificante *adj* : satisfying, gratifying
gratificar {72} *vt* 1 SATISFACER : to satisfy, to gratify 2 RECOMPENSAR : to reward 3 : to give a bonus to
gratinado, -da *adj* : au gratin
gratis[1] *adv* GRATUITAMENTE : free, for
free, gratis
gratis[2] *adj* GRATUITO : free, gratis
gratitud *nf* : gratitude
grato, -ta *adj* AGRADABLE, PLACENTERO
: pleasant, agreeable — **gratamente** *adv*
gratuitamente *adv* 1 : gratuitously 2
GRATIS : free, for free, gratis
gratuito, -ta *adj* 1 : gratuitous, unwarranted 2 GRATIS : free, gratis
grava *nf* : gravel
gravamen *nm, pl* -vámenes 1 : burden,
obligation 2 : (property) tax
gravar *vt* 1 : to burden, to encumber 2
: to levy (a tax)

grave *adj* 1 : grave, important 2 : serious, somber 3 : serious (of an illness)
gravedad *nf* 1 : gravity 〈centro de gravedad : center of gravity〉 2 : seriousness,
severity, gravity
gravemente *adv* : gravely, seriously
gravilla *nf* : (fine) gravel
gravitación *nf, pl* -ciones : gravitation
gravitacional *adj* : gravitational
gravitar *vi* 1 : to gravitate 2 ∼ **sobre**
: to rest on 3 ∼ **sobre** : to loom over
gravoso, -sa *adj* 1 ONEROSO : burdensome, onerous 2 : costly
graznar *vi* : to caw, to honk, to quack, to
squawk
graznido *nm* : cawing, honking, quack-
ing, squawking
gregario, -ria *adj* : gregarious
gremial *adj* SINDICAL : union, labor
gremialista *nmf* : union supporter
gremio *nm* SINDICATO : union, guild
greña *nf* 1 : mat, tangle 2 **greñas** *nfpl*
MELENAS : shaggy hair, mop
greñudo, -da *n* HIPPIE, MELENUDO : hippie
gresca *nf fam* : fight, ruckus
grey *nf* : congregation, flock
griego[1], **-ga** *adj & n* : Greek
griego[2] *nm* : Greek (language)
grieta *nf* : crack, crevice
grifo *nm* 1 : faucet 〈agua del grifo : tap
water〉 2 *Peru* : gas station
grillete *nm* : shackle
grillo *nm* 1 : cricket 2 **grillos** *nmpl* : fetters, shackles
grima *nf* 1 : disgust, uneasiness 2 **darle
grima a alguien** : to get on someone's
nerves
gringo, -ga *adj & n often disparaging* YAN-
QUI : Yankee, gringo *often disparaging*
gripa *nf Col, Mex* : flu
gripe *nf* : flu
gris *adj* 1 : gray 2 : overcast, cloudy
grisáceo, -cea *adj* : grayish
grisín *nm, pl* grisines *Arg, Uru* : breadstick
gritar *v* : to shout, to scream, to cry
gritería *nf* : shouting, clamor
grito *nm* 1 : shout, scream, cry 〈a grito
pelado : at the top of one's voice〉 2 **ser
el último grito** : to be the latest fashion
groenlandés, -desa *adj & n* : Greenlander
grogui *adj fam* : dazed, groggy
grosella *nf* 1 : currant 2 **grosella espinosa** : gooseberry
grosería *nf* 1 : insult, coarse language 2
: rudeness, discourtesy
grosero[1], **-ra** *adj* 1 : rude, fresh 2
: coarse, vulgar — **groseramente** *adv*
grosero[2], **-ra** *n* : rude person
grosor *nm* : thickness
grosso *adj* **a grosso modo** : roughly,
broadly, approximately
grotesco, -ca *adj* : grotesque, hideous
grúa *nf* 1 : crane (machine) 2 : tow truck
gruesa *nf* : gross
grueso[1], **-sa** *adj* 1 : thick, bulky 2
: heavy, big 3 : stout
grueso[2] *nm* 1 : thickness 2 : main body,
mass 3 **en** ∼ : in bulk

grulla *nf* : crane (bird)

grumo *nm* : lump, glob

gruñido *nm* : growl, grunt

gruñir {38} *vi* **1** : to growl, to grunt **2** : to grumble

gruñón¹, -ñona *adj, mpl* **gruñones** *fam* : grumpy, crabby

gruñón², -ñona *n, mpl* **gruñones** *fam* : grumpy person, nag

grupa *nf* : rump, hindquarters *pl*

grupo *nm* : group

gruta *nf* : grotto, cave

guacal *nm Col, Mex, Ven* : crate

guacamayo *nm* : macaw

guacamole *or* **guacamol** *nm* : guacamole

guacamote *nm Mex* : manioc, cassava

guachimán *nm, pl* **-manes** *fam* : watchman

guachinango → huachinango

guacho, -cha *adj* **1** *Arg, Col, Chile, Peru* : orphaned **2** *Chile, Peru* : odd (of a shoe, glove, etc.)

guadaña *nf* : scythe

guagua *nf* **1** *Arg, Col, Chile, Peru* : baby **2** *Cuba, PRi* : bus

guaira *nf* **1** *CA* : traditional flute **2** *Peru* : smelting furnace

guajiro, -ra *n Cuba* : peasant

guajolote *nm Mex* : turkey

guanábana *nf* : soursop (fruit)

guanaco *nm* : guanaco (South American mammal)

guandú *nm, pl* **guandú** *or* **guandúes** *CA, Car, Col* : pigeon pea

guango, -ga *adj Mex* **1** : loose-fitting, baggy **2** : slack, loose

guano *nm* : guano

guante *nm* **1** : glove ⟨guante de boxeo : boxing glove⟩ **2 arrojarle el guante (a alguien)** : to throw down the gauntlet (to someone)

guantelete *nm* : gauntlet

guantera *nf* : glove compartment

guapo, -pa *adj* **1** : handsome, good-looking, attractive **2** : elegant, smart **3** *fam* : bold, dashing

guarache → huarache

guarachear *vi Cuba, PRi fam* : to go on a spree, to go out on the town

guarangada *nf Arg, Uru fam* : rude or insulting remark

guaraní¹ *nmf, pl* **-níes** : Guarani (person) — **guaraní** *adj*

guaraní² *nm* **1** : Guarani (language of Paraguay) **2** : guarani (Paraguayan unit of currency)

guarda *nmf* **1** GUARDIÁN : security guard **2** : keeper, custodian

guardabarros *nms & pl* : fender, mudguard

guardabosque *nmf* : forest ranger, gamekeeper

guardacostas¹ *nmfs & pl* : member of the coast guard

guardacostas² *nms & pl* : coast guard vessel

guardaespaldas *nmfs & pl* : bodyguard

guardafangos *nms & pl* : fender

guardameta *nmf* ARQUERO, PORTERO : goalkeeper, goalie

guardapelo *nm* : locket

guardapolvo *nm* **1** : dustcover **2** : duster, housecoat

guardar *vt* **1** : to guard **2** : to maintain, to preserve **3** CONSERVAR : to put away **4** RESERVAR : to save **5** : to keep (a secret or promise) — **guardarse** *vr* **1** ~ **de** : to refrain from **2** ~ **de** : to guard against, to be careful not to

guardarropa *nm* **1** : coat check **2** ARMARIO : closet, wardrobe

guardavallas *nmf* : goalkeeper

guardería *nf* : nursery, day-care center

guardia¹ *nf* **1** : guard, defense **2** : guard duty, watch **3 en** ~ : on guard

guardia² *nmf* **1** : sentry, guard **2** : police officer, policeman *m*, policewoman *f*

guardiamarina *nmf* : midshipman

guardián, -diana *n, mpl* **guardianes** **1** GUARDA : security guard, watchman **2** : guardian, keeper **3 perro guardián** : watchdog

guarecer {53} *vt* : to shelter, to protect — **guarecerse** *vr* : to take shelter

guarida *nf* **1** : den, lair **2** : hideout

guarismo *nm* : figure, numeral

guarnecer {53} *vt* **1** : to adorn **2** : to garnish **3** : to garrison

guarnición *nf, pl* **-ciones** **1** : garnish **2** : garrison **3** : decoration, trimming, setting (of a jewel)

guaro *nm CA* : liquor distilled from sugarcane

guarrada *nf Spain fam* **1** : filthy mess **2** : dirty trick **3 decir guarradas** : to say filthy/disgusting things, to be vulgar

guarro¹, -ra *adj Spain fam* : dirty, filthy

guarro², -ra *n Spain fam* : filthy, disgusting, or vulgar person

guarura *nm Mex fam* : bodyguard

guasa *nf fam* **1** : joking, fooling around **2 de** ~ : in jest, as a joke

guasón¹, -sona *adj, mpl* **guasones** *fam* : funny, witty

guasón², -sona *n, mpl* **guasones** *fam* : joker, clown

guatemalteco, -ca *adj & n* : Guatemalan

guau *interj* : wow!

guay *adj Spain fam* : cool, neat, great

guayaba *nf* : guava (fruit)

guayín *nm, pl* **guayines** *Mex* : station wagon

gubernamental *adj* : governmental

gubernativo, -va → **gubernamental**

gubernatura *nf Mex* : governing body

guepardo *nm* : cheetah

güero, -ra *adj Mex* : blond, fair

guerra *nf* **1** : war ⟨declarar la guerra : to declare war⟩ ⟨estar en guerra : to be at war⟩ ⟨guerra sin cuartel : all-out war⟩ ⟨guerra civil/nuclear : civil/nuclear war⟩ ⟨hacer la guerra : to wage war⟩ **2** : warfare ⟨guerra de guerrillas : guerrilla warfare⟩ ⟨guerra biológica : biological warfare⟩ **3** LUCHA : conflict, struggle ⟨guerra a muerte : fight to the death⟩ **4 dar guerra** *fam* : to be annoying, to cause trouble

guerrear *vi* : to wage war

guerrero¹, -ra *adj* **1** : war, fighting **2** : warlike

guerrero², -ra *n* : warrior

guerrilla *nf* : guerrilla warfare
guerrillero, -ra *adj & n* : guerrilla
gueto *nm* : ghetto
guía[1] *nf* **1** : directory, guidebook **2** ORIENTACIÓN : guidance, direction ⟨la conciencia me sirve como guía : conscience is my guide⟩
guía[2] *nmf* : guide, leader ⟨guía de turismo : tour guide⟩
guiar {85} *vt* **1** : to guide, to lead **2** CONDUCIR : to manage — **guiarse** *vr* : to be guided by, to go by
guija *nf* : pebble
guijarro *nm* : pebble
guillotina *nf* : guillotine — **guillotinar** *vt*
guinda[1] *adj & nm Mex* : maroon (color)
guinda[2] *nf* : morello (cherry)
guindilla *nf* : chili
guineo *nm Car* : banana
guinga *nf* : gingham
guiñada → **guiño**
guiñar *vi* : to wink
guiño *nm* : wink
guiñol *nm* : puppet theater
guión *nm, pl* **guiones 1** : script, screenplay **2** : hyphen, dash **3** ESTANDARTE : standard, banner
guionista *nmf* : scriptwriter
guirnalda *nf* : garland
guisa *nf* **1** : manner, fashion **2 a guisa de** : like, by way of **3 de tal guisa** : in such a way
guisado ESTOFADO *nm* : stew
guisante *nm* : pea
guisar *vt* **1** ESTOFAR : to stew **2** *Spain* : to cook
guiso *nm* **1** : stew **2** : casserole
güisqui → **whisky**
guita *nf* : string, twine

guitarra *nf* : guitar
guitarrista *nmf* : guitarist
gula *nf* GLOTONERÍA : gluttony, greed
guppy *nm* : guppy
gusano *nm* **1** LOMBRIZ : worm, earthworm ⟨gusano de seda : silkworm⟩ **2** : caterpillar, maggot, grub
gustar *vt* **1** : to taste **2** : to like ⟨¿gustan pasar? : would you like to come in?⟩ — *vi* **1** : to be pleasing ⟨me gustan los dulces : I like sweets⟩ ⟨a María le gusta Carlos : Maria is attracted to Carlos⟩ ⟨no me gusta que me griten : I don't like to be yelled at⟩ **2 ~ de** : to like, to enjoy ⟨no gusta de chismes : she doesn't like gossip⟩ **3 como guste** : as you wish, as you like
gustativo, -va *adj* : taste ⟨papilas gustativas : taste buds⟩
gusto *nm* **1** : flavor, taste ⟨tiene gusto a chocolate : it tastes like chocolate⟩ **2** : taste, style ⟨de buen/mal gusto : in good/bad taste⟩ ⟨no es de mi gusto : it's not to my taste⟩ **3** : pleasure, liking ⟨tener el gusto de : to have the pleasure of⟩ ⟨con mucho gusto : gladly, with pleasure⟩ ⟨dar gusto : to be a pleasure⟩ ⟨darse el gusto de : to treat oneself to⟩ **4** : whim, fancy ⟨a gusto : at will⟩ **5 a ~** : comfortable, at ease **6 al gusto** : to taste, as one likes **7 mucho gusto** : pleased to meet you **8 por ~** : for pleasure
gustosamente *adv* : gladly
gustoso, -sa *adj* **1** : willing, glad ⟨nuestra empresa participará gustosa : our company will be pleased to participate⟩ **2** : zesty, tasty
gutural *adj* : guttural

H

h *nf* : ninth letter of the Spanish alphabet
ha → **haber**
haba *nf* : broad bean
habanero[1]**, -ra** *adj* : of or from Havana
habanero[2]**, -ra** *n* : native or resident of Havana
habano, -na *n* **1** → **habanero 2** : cigar from Havana
haber[1] {39} *v aux* **1** : have, has ⟨no ha llegado el envío : the shipment hasn't arrived⟩ ⟨de haberlo sabido : if I had known⟩ ⟨debería haberlo pensado : I should have thought of it⟩ **2 ~ de** : must ⟨ha de ser tarde : it must be late⟩ — *v impers* (**hay** *in the present indicative*) **1** : there is, there are ⟨hay dos mensajes : there are two messages⟩ ⟨¿hay postre? : do you have any dessert?⟩ ⟨hubo muchos errores : there were a lot of errors⟩ ⟨ha habido varios casos : there have been various cases⟩ **2 hay que** : it is necessary ⟨hay que trabajar más rápido : you/we (etc.) have to work faster⟩ ⟨habrá que hacerlo : it will have

to be done⟩ ⟨hubo que esperar : we had to wait⟩ **3 no hay de qué** : you're welcome, don't mention it **4 ¿qué hay?** *fam* : what's up?, how are things? **5 ¿qué hay de nuevo?** *fam* : what's new?
haber[2] *nm* **1** : assets *pl* **2** : credit, credit side **3 haberes** *nmpl* : salary, income, remuneration
habichuela *nf* **1** : bean, kidney bean **2** : green bean
hábil *adj* **1** : able, skillful **2** : work, working ⟨días hábiles : workdays, business days⟩
habilidad *nf* CAPACIDAD : ability, skill
habilidoso, -sa *adj* : skillful, clever
habilitación *nf, pl* **-ciones 1** : authorization **2** : furnishing, equipping
habilitar *vt* **1** : to enable, to authorize, to empower (someone) **2** : to equip, to furnish
hábilmente *adv* : skillfully, expertly
habiloso, -sa *adj Chile fam* : bright, smart, clever
habitable *adj* : habitable, inhabitable

habitación *nf, pl* **-ciones 1** CUARTO : room **2** DORMITORIO : bedroom **3** : habitation, occupancy

habitante *nmf* : inhabitant, resident

habitar *vt* : to inhabit — *vi* : to reside, to dwell

hábitat *nm, pl* **-tats** : habitat

hábito *nm* **1** : habit, custom **2** : habit (of a monk or nun)

habitual *adj* : habitual, customary — **habitualmente** *adv*

habituar {3} *vt* : to accustom, to habituate — **habituarse** *vr* ~ **a** : to get used to, to grow accustomed to

habla *nf* **1** : speech ⟨dejar a alguien sin habla : to leave someone speechless⟩ ⟨quedarse sin habla : to be left speechless⟩ **2** : language, dialect **3** **de** ~ : speaking ⟨de habla inglesa : English-speaking⟩

hablado, -da *adj* **1** : spoken **2 mal hablado** : foulmouthed

hablador[1]**, -dora** *adj* : talkative

hablador[2]**, -dora** *n* : chatterbox

habladuría *nf* **1** : rumor **2 habladurías** *nfpl* : gossip, scandal

hablante *nmf* : speaker

hablar *vi* **1** : to speak, to talk ⟨hablar en broma : to be joking⟩ ⟨hablar más alto : to speak up, to speak/talk louder⟩ ⟨hablar más bajo : to lower one's voice, to speak/talk more quietly⟩ **2** ~ **con** : to talk to, to speak to/with **3** ~ **de** : to mention, to talk about ⟨hablar bien/mal de : to speak well/ill of⟩ **4 dar que hablar** : to make people talk ⟨va a dar que hablar : people will start talking/gossiping about him⟩ **5 ¡ni hablar!** : no way! — *vt* **1** : to speak (a language) **2** : to talk about, to discuss ⟨háblalo con tu jefe : discuss it with your boss⟩ — **hablarse** *vr* **1** : to speak to each other, to be on speaking terms **2 se habla inglés** (etc.) : English (etc.) spoken

habrá, etc. → **haber**

hacedor, -dora *n* : creator, maker, doer

hacendado, -da *n* : landowner

hacendoso, -sa *adj* : hardworking, industrious

hacer {40} *vt* **1** CREAR, CONSTRUIR : to make (a cake, a list, a law, etc.), to build (a building), to write (a book, a check) ⟨hacer planes : to make plans⟩ ⟨hacer una película : to make a movie⟩ ⟨hacer un fuego : to make/build a fire⟩ ⟨lo hizo de madera : he made it out of wood⟩ **2** : to do (a task, an activity, etc.), to make (a gesture, a trip, an agreement, etc.), to pay (a visit) ⟨hacer mandados : to do/run errands⟩ ⟨hacer los deberes : to do one's homework⟩ ⟨¿me haces un favor? : will you do me a favor?⟩ **3** : to make, to cause, to produce ⟨hacer ruido : to make noise⟩ **4** EXPRESAR : to voice (an objection, etc.), to ask (a question) **5** : to make, to force, to oblige ⟨los hice esperar : I made them wait⟩ ⟨hizo que todos se callaran : he made everyone be quiet⟩ **6** : to make, to cause, to provoke ⟨me hizo reír/llorar : it made me laugh/cry⟩ ⟨¿te hice daño? : did I hurt you?⟩ **7** : to make, to cause to (be) ⟨la hizo famosa : it made her famous⟩ ⟨te hará (un) hombre : it will make a man out of you⟩ ⟨lo hizo funcionar : she made it work⟩ ⟨hace que el color parezca más oscuro : it makes the color seem darker⟩ **8** : to make (a bed), to pack (a suitcase) **9** PREPARAR : to make, to fix (a meal, etc.) **10** ADQUIRIR : to make (money, friends, etc.) — *vi* **1** : to act ⟨haces bien : you're doing the right thing⟩ **2** : to serve as, to function as **3** ~ **de** : to play, to perform as ⟨hizo de Ofelia en "Hamlet" : she played Ophelia in "Hamlet"⟩ **4 hacer como que/si** : to act as if **5 hacer por** : to try to ⟨hicieron por entendernos : they tried to understand us⟩ **6 hacer y deshacer** : to do as one pleases — *v impers* **1** (*referring to weather*) ⟨hace frío : it's cold⟩ ⟨hacía mucho viento : it was very windy⟩ **2** (*referring to time*) ⟨eso pasó hace mucho tiempo : that happened a long time ago⟩ ⟨vivo aquí desde hace dos años, hace dos años que vivo aquí : I've lived here for two years⟩ ⟨hacía años que no sabía nada de él : I hadn't heard from him in years⟩ **3 hacer falta** : to be necessary, to be needed **4 no le hace** : it doesn't matter, it makes no difference — **hacerse** *vr* **1** : to become **2** : to pretend, to act, to play ⟨hacerse el tonto : to play dumb⟩ **3** : to seem ⟨el examen se me hizo difícil : the exam seemed difficult to me⟩ **4** : to get, to grow ⟨se hace tarde : it's getting/growing late⟩

hacha *nf* : hatchet, ax

hachazo *nm* : blow, chop (with an ax)

hache *nf* : (letter) h

hachís *nm* : hashish

hacia *prep* **1** : toward, towards ⟨hacia abajo : downward⟩ ⟨hacia adelante : forward⟩ **2** : near, around, about ⟨hacia las seis : about six o'clock⟩

hacienda *nf* **1** : estate, ranch, farm **2** : property **3** : livestock **4 la Hacienda** : department of revenue, tax office

hacinamiento *nm* : overcrowding

hacinar *vt* **1** : to pile up, to stack **2** : to crowd, to cram — **hacinarse** *vr* **1** : to crowd together

hackear *vt fam* : to hack, to hack into (a system, etc.)

hacker *nmf, pl* **hackers** *fam* : hacker

hada *nf* : fairy

hado *nm* : destiny, fate

haga, etc. → **hacer**

haitiano, -na *adj & n* : Haitian

hala *interj Spain* **1** (*expressing encouragement or disbelief*) : come on! **2** (*expressing surprise*) : wow! **3** (*expressing protest*) : hey!

halagador[1]**, -dora** *adj* : flattering

halagador[2]**, -dora** *n* : flatterer

halagar {52} *vt* : to flatter, to compliment

halago *nm* : flattery, praise

halagüeño, -ña *adj* **1** : flattering **2** : encouraging, promising

halar *vt CA, Car* → **jalar**

halcón *nm, pl* **halcones** : hawk, falcon
halibut *nm, pl* **-buts** : halibut
hálito *nm* **1** : breath **2** : gentle breeze
hallar *vt* **1** ENCONTRAR : to find **2** DESCUBRIR : to discover, to find out — **hallarse** *vr* **1** : to be situated, to find oneself **2** : to feel ⟨no se halla bien : he doesn't feel comfortable, he feels out of place⟩
hallazgo *nm* **1** : discovery **2** : find ⟨es un verdadero hallazgo! : it's a real find!⟩
halo *nm* **1** : halo **2** : aura
halterofilia *nf* : weight lifting
hamaca *nf* : hammock
hambre *nf* **1** : hunger **2** : starvation **3** **tener hambre** : to be hungry **4** **dar hambre** : to make hungry
hambriento, -ta *adj* : hungry, starving
hambruna *nf* : famine
hamburguesa *nf* **1** : hamburger, burger **2** : patty, burger ⟨una hamburguesa de pavo : a turkey patty/burger⟩
hampa *nf* : criminal underworld
hampón, -pona *n, mpl* **hampones** : criminal, thug
hámster ['xamster] *nm, pl* **hámsters** : hamster
han → haber
handicap *or* **hándicap** ['handi,kap] *nm, pl* **-caps** : handicap (in sports)
hangar *nm* : hangar
Hanukkah → Janucá
hará, etc. → hacer
haragán¹, -gana *adj, mpl* **-ganes** : lazy, idle
haragán², -gana *n, mpl* **-ganes** HOLGAZÁN : slacker, good-for-nothing
haraganear *vi* : to be lazy, to waste one's time
haraganería *nf* : laziness
harapiento, -ta *adj* : ragged, tattered
harapos *nmpl* ANDRAJOS : rags, tatters
hardware ['hard,wer] *nm* : computer hardware
harén *nm, pl* **harenes** : harem
harina *nf* **1** : flour **2** **harina de maíz** : cornmeal **3** **ser harina de otro costal** : to be a horse of a different color
hartar *vt* **1** : to glut, to satiate **2** FASTIDIAR : to tire, to irritate, to annoy — **hartarse** *vr* **1** : to be weary, to get fed up **2** ~ **de** : to gorge oneself on
harto¹ *adv* : most, extremely, very
harto², -ta *adj* **1** : full, satiated **2** : fed up **3** MUCHO : a lot of, much ⟨tiene harto dinero : he lots of money⟩
hartura *nf* **1** : surfeit **2** : abundance, plenty
has → haber
hashtag ['ha∫tag] *nm, pl* **hashtags** : hashtag
hasta¹ *adv* : even
hasta² *prep* **1** : until, up until ⟨hasta ahora/entonces : until now/then⟩ ⟨until Friday : hasta el viernes⟩ ⟨¡hasta luego! : see you later!⟩ **2** : as far as ⟨nos fuimos hasta Managua : we went all the way to Managua⟩ **3** : to, up/down to ⟨hasta cierto punto : up to a certain point⟩ ⟨tengo el pelo hasta la cintura

: my hair is down to my waist⟩ **4** **hasta que** : until ⟨hasta que lleguen : until they arrive⟩
hastiar {85} *vt* **1** : to make weary, to bore **2** : to disgust, to sicken — **hastiarse** *vr* ~ **de** : to get tired of
hastío *nm* **1** TEDIO : tedium **2** REPUGNANCIA : disgust
hatchback *nm* : hatchback (car)
hatillo *nm* : bundle (of clothes)
hato *nm* **1** : flock, herd **2** : bundle (of possessions)
hawaiano, -na *adj & n* : Hawaiian
hay → haber¹
haya¹, etc. → haber
haya² *nf* : beech (tree and wood)
hayuco *nm* : beechnut
haz¹ → hacer
haz² *nm, pl* **haces** **1** FARDO : bundle **2** : beam (of light)
haz³ *nf, pl* **haces** **1** : face **2** **haz de la tierra** : surface of the earth
hazaña *nf* PROEZA : feat, exploit
hazmerreír *nm fam* : laughingstock
he¹ {39} → haber
he² *v impers* **he aquí** : here is, here are, behold
hebilla *nf* : buckle, clasp
hebra *nf* : strand, thread
hebreo¹, -brea *adj & n* : Hebrew
hebreo² *nm* : Hebrew (language)
hecatombe *nf* **1** MATANZA : massacre **2** : disaster
heces → hez
hechicería *nf* **1** BRUJERÍA : sorcery, witchcraft **2** : curse, spell
hechicero¹, -ra *adj* : bewitching, enchanting
hechicero², -ra *n* : sorcerer, sorceress *f*
hechizar {21} *vt* **1** EMBRUJAR : to bewitch **2** CAUTIVAR : to charm
hechizo *nm* **1** SORTILEGIO : spell, enchantment **2** ENCANTO : charm, fascination
hecho¹ *pp* → hacer
hecho², -cha *adj* **1** : made, done ⟨hecho a mano : handmade⟩ **2** : complete, finished ⟨hecho y derecho : full-fledged⟩
hecho³ *nm* **1** : fact **2** : event ⟨hechos históricos : historic events⟩ **3** : act, action **4** **de** ~ : in fact, in reality
hechura *nf* **1** : style **2** : craftsmanship, workmanship **3** : product, creation
hectárea *nf* : hectare
heder {56} *vi* : to stink, to reek
hediondez *nf, pl* **-deces** : stink, stench
hediondo, -da *adj* MALOLIENTE : foul-smelling, stinking
hedor *nm* : stench, stink
hegemonía *nf* **1** : dominance **2** : hegemony (in politics)
helada *nf* : frost (in meteorology)
heladería *nf* : ice-cream parlor, ice-cream stand
helado¹, -da *adj* **1** GÉLIDO : icy, freezing cold **2** CONGELADO : frozen
helado² *nm* : ice cream
heladora *nf* CONGELADOR : freezer
helar {55} *v* CONGELAR : to freeze — *v impers* : to produce frost ⟨anoche heló : there was frost last night⟩ — **helarse** *vr*

helecho *nm* : fern, bracken
hélice *nf* **1** : spiral, helix **2** : propeller
helicóptero *nm* : helicopter
helio *nm* : helium
helipuerto *nm* : heliport
hematoma *nm* **1** : hematoma **2** MORE-
TÓN : bruise
hembra *adj & nf* : female
hemisférico, -ca *adj* : hemispheric, hemispherical
hemisferio *nm* : hemisphere
hemofilia *nf* : hemophilia
hemofílico, -ca *adj & n* : hemophiliac
hemoglobina *nf* : hemoglobin
hemorragia *nf* **1** : hemorrhage **2 hemorragia nasal** : nosebleed
hemorroides *nfpl* ALMORRANAS : hemorrhoids, piles
hemos → **haber**
henchido, -da *adj* : swollen, bloated
henchir {54} *vt* **1** : to stuff, to fill **2** : to
swell, to swell up — **henchirse** *vr* **1** : to
stuff oneself **2** LLENARSE : to fill up, to
be full
hender {56} *vt* : to cleave, to split
hendidura *nf* : crack, crevice, fissure
heno *nm* : hay
hepatitis *nf* : hepatitis
heráldica *nf* : heraldry
heráldico, -ca *adj* : heraldic
heraldo *nm* : herald
herbario, -ria *adj* : herbal
herbicida *nm* : herbicide, weed killer
herbívoro[1], -ra *adj* : herbivorous
herbívoro[2] *nm* : herbivore
hercio *nm* : hertz
hercúleo, -lea *adj* : herculean
heredar *vt* : to inherit
heredero, -ra *n* : heir, heiress *f*
hereditario, -ria *adj* : hereditary
hereje *nmf* : heretic
herejía *nf* : heresy
herencia *nf* **1** : inheritance **2** : heritage
3 : heredity
herético, -ca *adj* : heretical
herida *nf* : injury, wound
herido[1], -da *adj* **1** : injured, wounded **2**
: hurt, offended
herido[2], -da *n* : injured person, casualty
herir {76} *vt* **1** : to injure, to wound **2**
: to hurt, to offend
hermafrodita *nmf* : hermaphrodite
hermanar *vt* **1** : to unite, to bring together **2** : to match up, to twin (cities)
hermanastro, -tra *n* **1** : half brother *m*,
half sister *f* **2** : stepbrother *m*, stepsister
f
hermandad *nf* **1** FRATERNIDAD : brotherhood ⟨hermandad de mujeres : sisterhood, sorority⟩ **2** : association
hermano, -na *n* : sibling, brother *m*, sister
f ⟨hermano mayor/menor : big/little
brother⟩ ⟨hermana gemela : twin sister⟩
hermético, -ca *adj* : hermetic, watertight
— **herméticamente** *adv*
hermoso, -sa *adj* BELLO : beautiful,
lovely — **hermosamente** *adv*
hermosura *nf* BELLEZA : beauty, loveliness
hernia *nf* : hernia

herniarse *vr* : to get a hernia, to rupture
oneself
héroe *nm* : hero
heroicidad *nf* : heroism, heroic deed
heroico, -ca *adj* : heroic — **heroica-
mente** *adv*
heroína *nf* **1** : heroine **2** : heroin
heroinómano, -na *n* : heroin addict
heroísmo *nm* : heroism
herpes *nms & pl* **1** : herpes **2** : shingles
herradura *nf* : horseshoe
herraje *nm* : ironwork
herramienta *nf* : tool
herrar {55} *vt* : to shoe (a horse)
herrería *nf* : blacksmith's shop
herrero, -ra *n* : blacksmith
herrumbre *nf* ORÍN : rust
herrumbroso, -sa *adj* OXIDADO : rusty
hertzio → **hercio**
hervidero *nm* **1** : mass, swarm **2** : hotbed (of crime, etc.)
hervidor *nm* : kettle
hervir {76} *vi* **1** BULLIR : to boil, to bubble **2** ~ **de** : to teem with, to be swarm-
ing with — *vt* : to boil
hervor *nm* **1** : boiling **2** : fervor, ardor
heterogéneo, -nea *adj* : heterogeneous
heterosexual *adj & nmf* : heterosexual
heterosexualidad *nf* : heterosexuality
hexágono *nm* : hexagon — **hexagonal**
adj
hez *nf, pl* **heces 1** ESCORIA : scum, dregs
pl **2** : sediment, lees *pl* **3 heces** *nfpl*
: feces, excrement
hiato *nm* : hiatus
hibernar *vi* : to hibernate — **hibernación**
nf
híbrido[1], -da *adj* : hybrid
híbrido[2] *nm* : hybrid
hicieron, etc. → **hacer**
hidalgo, -ga *n* : nobleman *m*, noblewoman *f*
hidrante *nm* CA, Col : hydrant
hidratar *vt* : to moisturize — **hidratante**
adj
hidrato de carbono *nm* : carbohydrate
hidráulico, -ca *adj* : hydraulic
hidroala *nm* : hydrofoil
hidroavión *nm, pl* **-viones** : seaplane
hidrocarburo *nm* : hydrocarbon
hidroeléctrico, -ca *adj* : hydroelectric
hidrofobia *nf* RABIA : hydrophobia, rabies
hidrófugo, -ga *adj* : water-repellent
hidrógeno *nm* : hydrogen
hidromasaje *nm* **bañera de hidromasaje**
→ **bañera**
hidroplano *nm* : hydroplane
hiede, etc. → **heder**
hiedra *nf* **1** : ivy **2 hiedra venenosa**
: poison ivy
hiel *nf* **1** BILIS : bile **2** : bitterness
hiela, etc. → **helar**
hielo *nm* **1** : ice **2** : coldness, reserve
⟨romper el hielo : to break the ice⟩
hiena *nf* : hyena
hiende, etc. → **hender**
hierba *nf* **1** : herb **2** : grass **3 mala
hierba** : weed
hierbabuena *nf* : mint, spearmint
hiere, etc. → **herir**

hierra, etc. → herrar
hierro *nm* **1** : iron ⟨hierro fundido : cast iron⟩ **2** : branding iron
hierve, etc. → hervir
hígado *nm* : liver
higiene *nf* : hygiene
higiénico, -ca *adj* : hygienic — **higiénicamente** *adv*
higienista *nmf* : hygienist
higo *nm* **1** : fig **2 higo chumbo** : prickly pear (fruit)
higrómetro *nm* : hygrometer
higuera *nf* : fig tree
hijab → hiyab
hijastro, -tra *n* : stepson *m*, stepdaughter *f*
hijo, -ja *n* : son *m*, daughter *f* ⟨hijo adoptivo : adopted son⟩ ⟨soy hija única : I'm an only child⟩ ⟨tiene dos hijos/hijas : she has two sons/daughters⟩ ⟨nuestros hijos : our children⟩
hijo de puta *nm sometimes offensive* : son of a bitch *sometimes offensive*, bastard *offensive*
hijole *interj Mex* : wow!, good grief!
hilacha *nf* **1** : ravel, loose thread **2 mostrar la hilacha** : to show one's true colors
hilado *nm* **1** : spinning **2** HILO : yarn, thread
hilar *vt* **1** : to spin (thread) **2** : to consider, to string together (ideas) — *vi* **1** : to spin ⟨hilar delgado : to split hairs⟩
hilarante *adj* **1** : humorous, hilarious **2 gas hilarante** : laughing gas
hilaridad *nf* : hilarity
hilera *nf* FILA : file, row, line
hilo *nm* **1** : thread ⟨colgar de un hilo : to hang by a thread⟩ ⟨hilo dental : dental floss⟩ **2** LINO : linen **3** : (electric) wire ⟨conexión sin hilos : wireless connection⟩ **4** : theme, thread (of a discourse) **5** : trickle (of water, etc.)
hilvanar *vt* **1** : to baste, to tack **2** : to piece together
himnario *nm* : hymnal
himno *nm* **1** : hymn **2 himno nacional** : national anthem
hincapié *nm* **hacer hincapié en** : to emphasize, to stress
hincar {72} *vt* CLAVAR : to stick, to plunge — **hincarse** *vr* **hincarse de rodillas** : to kneel down, to fall to one's knees
hincha *nmf fam* : fan, supporter
hinchado, -da *adj* **1** : swollen, inflated **2** : pompous, overblown
hinchar *vt* INFLAR : to inflate **2** : to exaggerate — **hincharse** *vr* **1** : to swell up **2** : to become conceited, to swell with pride
hinchazón *nf, pl* **-zones** : swelling
hinche, etc. → henchir
hindi *nm* : Hindi
hindú *adj & nmf* : Hindu
hinduismo *nm* : Hinduism
hiniesta *nf* : broom (plant)
hinojo *nm* **1** : fennel **2 de hinojos** : on bended knee
hinque, etc. → hincar
hipar *vi* : to hiccup
hiperactividad *nf* : hyperactivity

hiperactivo, -va *adj* : hyperactive, overactive
hipérbole *nf* : hyperbole
hiperbólico, -ca *adj* : hyperbolic, exaggerated
hipercrítico, -ca *adj* : hypercritical
hiperenlace *nm* : hyperlink
hipermercado *nm* : large supermarket, hypermarket
hipermétrope *adj* : farsighted
hipermetropía *nf* : farsightedness
hipersensibilidad *nf* : hypersensitivity
hipertensión *nf, pl* **-siones** : hypertension, high blood pressure
hip-hop [ˌxipˈxop] *nm* : hip-hop (music)
hípico, -ca *adj* : equestrian ⟨concurso hípico : horse show⟩
hipil → huipil
hipnosis *nfs & pl* : hypnosis
hipnótico, -ca *adj* : hypnotic
hipnotismo *nm* : hypnotism
hipnotizador¹, -dora *adj* **1** : hypnotic **2** : spellbinding, mesmerizing
hipnotizador², -dora *n* : hypnotist
hipnotizar {21} *vt* : to hypnotize
hipo *nm* : hiccup, hiccups *pl*
hipocampo *nm* : sea horse
hipocondría *nf* : hypochondria
hipocondríaco, -ca *adj & n* : hypochondriac
hipocresía *nf* : hypocrisy
hipócrita¹ *adj* : hypocritical — **hipócritamente** *adv*
hipócrita² *nmf* : hypocrite
hipodérmico, -ca *adj* **aguja hipodérmica** : hypodermic needle
hipódromo *nm* : racetrack
hipopótamo *nm* : hippopotamus
hipoteca *nf* : mortgage
hipotecar {72} *vt* **1** : to mortgage **2** : to compromise, to jeopardize
hipotecario, -ria *adj* : mortgage
hipotensión *nf, pl* **-siones** : low blood pressure
hipotenusa *nf* : hypotenuse
hipotermia *nf* : hypothermia
hipótesis *nfs & pl* : hypothesis
hipotético, -ca *adj* : hypothetical — **hipotéticamente** *adv*
hippie *or* **hippy** [ˈhipi] *nmf, pl* **hippies** [-pis] : hippie
hiriente *adj* : hurtful, offensive
hirió, etc. → herir
hirsuto, -ta *adj* **1** : hairy **2** : bristly, wiry
hirviente *adj* : boiling
hirvió, etc. → hervir
hisopo *nm* : cotton swab
hispánico, -ca *adj & n* : Hispanic
hispano¹, -na *adj* : Hispanic ⟨de habla hispana : Spanish-speaking⟩
hispano², -na *n* : Hispanic (person)
hispanoamericano¹, -na *adj* LATINOAMERICANO : Latin-American
hispanoamericano², -na *n* LATINOAMERICANO : Latin American
hispanohablante¹ *adj* : Spanish-speaking
hispanohablante² *nmf* : Spanish speaker
histerectomía *nf* : hysterectomy
histeria *nf* **1** : hysteria **2** : hysterics

histérico, -ca *adj* : hysterical — **histéricamente** *adv*

histerismo *nm* **1** : hysteria **2** : hysterics

historia *nf* **1** : history ⟨historia universal : world history⟩ ⟨pasará a la historia como un gran jugador de béisbol : he'll go down in history as a great baseball player⟩ **2** NARRACIÓN, RELATO : story **3 dejarse de ~s** : to say something directly, to stop beating around the bush **4 hacer ~** : to make history

historiador, -dora *n* : historian

historial *nm* **1** : record, document **2** CURRÍCULUM : résumé, curriculum vitae

histórico, -ca *adj* **1** : historical **2** : historic, important — **históricamente** *adv*

historieta *nf* : comic strip

histrionismo *nm* : histrionics, acting

hit [ˈhit] *nm, pl* **hits** **1** ÉXITO : hit, popular song **2** : hit (in baseball)

hito *nm* : milestone, landmark

hiyab *nm, pl* **hiyabs** : hijab

hizo → hacer

hobby [ˈhɔbi] *nm, pl* **hobbies** [-bis] : hobby

hocico *nm* : snout, muzzle

hockey [ˈhɔke, -ki] *nm* : hockey ⟨hockey sobre césped : field hockey⟩

hogar *nm* **1** : home ⟨labores del hogar : housework⟩ ⟨hogar, dulce hogar : home sweet home⟩ **2** : hearth, fireplace

hogareño, -ña *adj* **1** : domestic, homey **2 ser muy hogareño** : to be a homebody

hogaza *nf* : large loaf (of bread)

hoguera *nf* **1** FOGATA : bonfire, campfire **2 morir en la hoguera** : to burn at the stake

hoja *nf* **1** : leaf, petal, blade (of grass) **2** : sheet (of paper), page (of a book) ⟨hoja de cálculo : spreadsheet⟩ **3** FORMULARIO : form ⟨hoja de pedido : order form⟩ **4** : blade (of a knife) ⟨hoja de afeitar : razor blade⟩

hojalata *nf* : tinplate

hojaldre *nm* : puff pastry

hojarasca *nf* : fallen leaves *pl*

hojear *vt* : to leaf through (a book or magazine)

hojuela *nf* **1** : leaflet, young leaf **2** : flake

hola *interj* : hello!, hi!

holandés¹, -desa *adj, mpl* **-deses** : Dutch

holandés², -desa *n, mpl* **-deses** : Dutch person ⟨los holandeses : the Dutch⟩

holandés³ *nm* : Dutch (language)

holgadamente *adv* : comfortably, easily ⟨vivir holgadamente : to be well-off⟩

holgado, -da *adj* **1** : loose, baggy **2** : at ease, comfortable

holganza *nf* : leisure, idleness

holgar {16} *vi* : to be unnecessary ⟨huelga decir que . . . : it goes without saying that . . .⟩

holgazán¹, -zana *adj, mpl* **-zanes** : lazy

holgazán², -zana *n, mpl* **-zanes** HARAGÁN : slacker, idler

holgazanear *vi* HARAGANEAR : to laze around, to loaf

holgazanería *nf* PEREZA : idleness, laziness

holgura *nf* **1** : looseness **2** COMODIDAD : comfort, ease

holístico, -ca *adj* : holistic

hollar {19} *vt* : to tread on, to trample

hollín *nm, pl* **hollines** TIZNE : soot

holocausto *nm* : holocaust

holograma *nm* : hologram

hombre¹ *nm* **1** : man ⟨el hombre : man, mankind⟩ ⟨la escuela hizo de él un hombre : the school made a man out of him⟩ **2 hombre de confianza** : right-hand man **3 hombre de estado** : statesman **4 hombre de negocios** : businessman **5 hombre lobo** : werewolf **6 el hombre de la calle** : the man in/on the street, the average person

hombre² *interj fam* **1** : well, hey **2** : of course!, you bet! **3** : come on!

hombrera *nf* **1** : shoulder pad **2** : epaulet

hombría *nf* : manliness

hombro *nm* **1** : shoulder ⟨encogerse de hombros : to shrug one's shoulders⟩ ⟨hombro con hombro : shoulder to shoulder⟩ ⟨llevé mi hija en hombros : I carried my daughter on my shoulders⟩ **2 arrimar el hombro** : to lend a hand, to pull one's weight

hombruno, -na *adj* : mannish

homenaje *nm* : homage, tribute ⟨rendir homenaje a : to pay tribute to⟩

homenajeado, -da *n* : guest of honor

homenajear *vt* : to pay homage to, to honor

homeopatía *nf* : homeopathy — **homeopático, -ca** *adj*

homicida¹ *adj* : homicidal, murderous

homicida² *nmf* ASESINO : murderer

homicidio *nm* ASESINATO : homicide, murder

homilía *nf* : homily, sermon

homófono *nm* : homophone

homogeneidad *nf* : homogeneity

homogeneizar {21} *vt* : to homogenize

homogéneo, -nea *adj* : homogeneous — **homogéneamente** *adv*

homógrafo *nm* : homograph

homologación *nf, pl* **-ciones** **1** : sanctioning, approval **2** : parity

homologar {52} *vt* **1** : to sanction **2** : to bring into line

homólogo¹, -ga *adj* : homologous, equivalent

homólogo², -ga *n* : counterpart

homónimo¹, -ma *n* TOCAYO : namesake

homónimo² *nm* : homonym

homosexual *adj & nmf* : homosexual

homosexualidad *nf* : homosexuality

honda *nf* : sling

hondo¹ *adv* : deeply

hondo², -da *adj* PROFUNDO : deep ⟨en lo más hondo de : in the depths of⟩ — **hondamente** *adv*

hondonada *nf* **1** : hollow, depression **2** : ravine, gorge

hondura *nf* : depth

hondureño, -ña *adj & n* : Honduran

honestidad *nf* 1 : decency, modesty 2 : honesty

honesto, -ta *adj* 1 : decent, virtuous 2 : honest, honorable — **honestamente** *adv*

hongo *nm* 1 : fungus 2 : mushroom

honor *nm* 1 : honor ⟨en honor a la verdad : to be quite honest⟩ 2 **honores** *nmpl* : honors ⟨hacer los honores : to do the honors⟩

honorable *adj* HONROSO : honorable — **honorablemente** *adv*

honorario, -ria *adj* : honorary

honorarios *nmpl* : payment, fees (for professional services)

honorífico, -ca *adj* : honorary ⟨mención honorífica : honorable mention⟩

honra *nf* 1 : dignity, self-respect ⟨tener a mucha honra : to take great pride in⟩ 2 : good name, reputation

honradamente *adv* : honestly, decently

honradez *nf, pl* **-deces** : honesty, integrity, probity

honrado, -da *adj* 1 HONESTO : honest, upright 2 : honored

honrar *vt* 1 : to honor 2 : to be a credit to ⟨su generosidad lo honra : his generosity does him credit⟩

honroso, -sa *adj* 1 HONORABLE : honorable — **honrosamente** *adv*

hora *nf* 1 : hour ⟨media hora : half an hour⟩ ⟨se pasa horas viendo televisión : he spends hours watching television⟩ 2 : time ⟨¿qué hora es? : what time is it?⟩ ⟨llegar a la hora : to arrive on time⟩ ⟨a la hora en punto : on the dot⟩ ⟨a la hora de comer : at mealtime⟩ ⟨a la última hora : at the last minute⟩ ⟨a primera hora : first thing⟩ ⟨antes de la hora : early, ahead of time⟩ ⟨es hora de irnos a casa : it's time to go home⟩ ⟨ya es hora de tomarlo en serio : it's about time we took it seriously⟩ 3 CITA : appointment ⟨pedir/dar/tener hora : to make/ give/have an appointment⟩ 4 **hora de cierre** : closing time 5 **hora local** : local time 6 **horas de oficina/trabajo** : office/work hours 7 **hora pico** : rush hour 8 **horas extras** : overtime 9 **las altas horas** : the wee hours 10 **trabajar por horas** : to work by the hour

horadar *vt* : to drill a hole in

horario *nm* : schedule, timetable, hours *pl* ⟨horario de visita : visiting hours⟩

horca *nf* 1 : gallows *pl* 2 : pitchfork

horcajadas *nfpl a* ~ : astride, astraddle

horchata *nf* : cold sweet drink usually made with a kind of tuber

horcón *nm, pl* **horcones** : wooden post, prop

horda *nf* : horde

horizontal *adj* : horizontal — **horizontalmente** *adv*

horizonte *nm* : horizon, skyline

horma *nf* 1 : shoe tree 2 : shoemaker's last

hormiga *nf* : ant

hormigón *nm, pl* **-gones** CONCRETO : concrete

hormigonera *nf* : cement mixer

hormigueo *nm* 1 : tingling, pins and needles *pl* 2 : uneasiness

hormiguero *nm* 1 : anthill 2 : swarm (of people)

hormona *nf* : hormone — **hormonal** *adj*

hornacina *nf* : niche, recess

hornada *nf* : batch

hornear *vt* : to bake

hornilla *nf* : burner (of a stove)

hornillo *nm* : portable stove

horno *nm* 1 : oven ⟨horno de microondas : microwave oven⟩ 2 : kiln

horóscopo *nm* : horoscope

horqueta *nf* 1 : fork (in a river or road) 2 : crotch (in a tree) 3 : small pitchfork

horquilla *nf* 1 : hairpin, bobby pin 2 : pitchfork

horrendo, -da *adj* : horrendous, horrible

horrible *adj* : horrible, dreadful — **horriblemente** *adv*

horripilante *adj* : horrifying, hair-raising

horripilar *vt* : to horrify, to terrify

horror *nm* : horror, dread

horrorizado, -da *adj* : terrified

horrorizar {21} *vt* : to horrify, to terrify — **horrorizarse** *vr*

horroroso, -sa *adj* 1 : horrifying, terrifying 2 : dreadful, bad

hortaliza *nf* 1 : vegetable 2 **hortalizas** *nfpl* : garden produce

hortera *adj Spain fam* : tacky, gaudy

hortícola *adj* : horticultural

horticultura *nf* : horticulture

hosco, -ca *adj* : sullen, gloomy — **hoscamente** *adv*

hospedaje *nm* : lodging, accommodations *pl*

hospedar *vt* : to provide with lodging, to put up — **hospedarse** *vr* : to stay, to lodge

hospicio *nm* : orphanage

hospital *nm* : hospital

hospitalario, -ria *adj* : hospitable

hospitalidad *nf* : hospitality

hospitalización *nf, pl* **-ciones** : hospitalization

hospitalizar {21} *vt* : to hospitalize — **hospitalizarse** *vr*

hostal *nm* : cheap hotel

hostelería *nf* : the hotel industry

hostería *nf* POSADA : inn

hostia *nf* : host, Eucharist

hostigamiento *nm* : harassment

hostigar {52} *vt* ACOSAR, ASEDIAR : to harass, to pester

hostil *adj* : hostile

hostilidad *nf* 1 : hostility, antagonism 2 **hostilidades** *nfpl* : (military) hostilities

hostilizar {21} *vt* : to harass

hotel *nm* : hotel

hotelero[1], -ra *adj* : hotel ⟨la industria hotelera : the hotel business⟩

hotelero[2], -ra *n* : hotel manager, hotelier

hoy *adv* 1 : today ⟨hoy mismo : right now, this very day⟩ 2 : now, nowadays ⟨de hoy en adelante : from now on⟩

hoyo *nm* AGUJERO : hole

hoyuelo *nm* : dimple

hoz *nf, pl* **hoces** : sickle

hozar {21} *vi* : to root (of a pig)

huachinango *nm Mex* : red snapper
huarache *nm* : sandal
hubo, etc. → haber
hueco[1], **-ca** *adj* 1 : hollow, empty 2 : soft, spongy 3 : hollow, resonant 4 : proud, conceited 5 : superficial
hueco[2] *nm* 1 : hole, hollow, cavity 2 : gap, space 3 : recess, alcove
huele, etc. → oler
huelga *nf* 1 PARO : strike 2 hacer huelga : to strike, to go on strike
huelguista *nmf* : striker
huella[1], **etc.** → hollar
huella[2] *nf* 1 : footprint ⟨seguir las huellas de alguien : to follow in someone's footsteps⟩ 2 : mark, impact ⟨dejar huella : to leave one's mark⟩ ⟨sin dejar huella : without a trace⟩ 3 huella digital *or* huella dactilar : fingerprint
huérfano[1], **-na** *adj* 1 : orphan, orphaned 2 : defenseless 3 ~ de : lacking, devoid of
huérfano[2], **-na** *n* : orphan
huerta *nf* 1 : large vegetable garden, truck farm 2 : orchard 3 : irrigated land
huerto *nm* 1 : vegetable garden 2 : orchard
hueso *nm* 1 : bone 2 : pit, stone (of a fruit)
huésped[1], **-peda** *n* INVITADO : guest
huésped[2] *nm* : host ⟨organismo huésped : host organism⟩
huestes *nfpl* 1 : followers 2 : troops, army
huesudo, -da *adj* : bony
hueva *nf* : roe, spawn
huevo *nm* 1 : egg ⟨huevos revueltos : scrambled eggs⟩ ⟨huevo de Pascua : Easter egg⟩ 2 huevos *nmpl usu vulgar* : balls *pl, usu vulgar*; testicles *pl*
huida *nf* : flight, escape
huidizo, -za *adj* 1 ESCURRIDIZO : elusive, slippery 2 : shy, evasive
huipil *nm CA, Mex* : traditional sleeveless blouse or dress
huir {41} *vi* 1 ESCAPAR : to escape, to flee 2 ~ de : to avoid
huiro *nm Chile, Peru* : seaweed
huizache *nm* : acacia
hule *nm* 1 : oilcloth, oilskin 2 *Mex* : rubber 3 hule espuma *Mex* : foam rubber
hulera *nf Mex* : slingshot
humanidad *nf* 1 : humanity, mankind 2 : humanity, compassion 3 humanidades *nfpl* : humanities *pl*
humanismo *nm* : humanism
humanista *nmf* : humanist
humanístico, -ca *adj* : humanistic
humanitario, -ria *adj & n* : humanitarian
humanizar {21} *vt* : to humanize
humano[1], **-na** *adj* 1 : human 2 BENÉVOLO : humane, benevolent — **humanamente** *adv*
humano[2] *nm* : human being, human
humareda *nf* : cloud of smoke
humeante *adj* 1 : smoky 2 : smoking, steaming

humear *vi* 1 : to smoke 2 : to steam
humectante[1] *adj* : moisturizing
humectante[2] *nm* : moisturizer
humedad *nf* 1 : humidity 2 : dampness, moistness
humedecer {53} *vt* 1 : to humidify 2 : to moisten, to dampen
húmedo, -da *adj* 1 : humid 2 : moist, damp
humidificador *nm* : humidifier
humidificar {72} *vt* : to humidify
humildad *nf* 1 : humility 2 : lowliness
humilde *adj* 1 : humble 2 : lowly ⟨gente humilde : poor people⟩
humildemente *adv* : meekly, humbly
humillación *nf, pl* **-ciones** : humiliation
humillante *adj* : humiliating
humillar *vt* : to humiliate — **humillarse** *vr* : to humble oneself ⟨humillarse a hacer algo : to stoop to doing something⟩
humo *nm* 1 : smoke, steam, fumes 2 humos *nmpl* : airs *pl*, conceit
humor *nm* 1 : humor 2 : mood, temper ⟨está de buen humor : she's in a good mood⟩
humorada *nf* 1 BROMA : joke, witticism 2 : whim, caprice
humorismo *nm* : humor, wit
humorista *nmf* : humorist, comedian, comedienne *f*
humorístico, -ca *adj* : humorous — **humorísticamente** *adv*
humoso, -sa *adj* : smoky, steamy
humus *nm* : humus
hundido, -da *adj* 1 : sunken 2 : depressed
hundimiento *nm* 1 : sinking 2 : collapse, ruin
hundir *vt* 1 : to sink 2 : to destroy, to ruin — **hundirse** *vr* 1 : to sink down 2 : to cave in 3 : to break down, to go to pieces
húngaro[1], **-ra** *adj & n* : Hungarian
húngaro[2] *nm* : Hungarian (language)
húngaro *nm, pl* **-canes** : hurricane
huraño, -ña *adj* 1 : unsociable, aloof 2 : timid, skittish (of an animal)
hurgar {52} *vt* : to poke, to jab, to rake (a fire) — *vi* ~ en : to rummage in, to poke through
hurgue, etc. → hurgar
hurón *nm, pl* **hurones** : ferret
huronear *vi* : to pry, to snoop
hurra *interj* : hurrah!, hooray!
hurtadillas *nfpl* a ~ : stealthily, on the sly
hurtar *vt* ROBAR : to steal
hurto *nm* 1 : theft, robbery 2 : stolen property, loot
husmear *vt* 1 : to follow the scent of, to track 2 : to sniff out, to pry into — *vi* 1 : to pry, to snoop 2 : to sniff around (of an animal)
huso *nm* 1 : spindle 2 huso horario : time zone
huy *interj* : ow!, ouch!
huye, etc. → huir

I

I *nf* : tenth letter of the Spanish alphabet

i- → **in-**

iba, etc. → **ir**

ibérico, -ca *adj* : Iberian

ibero, -ra *or* **íbero, -ra** : Iberian

iberoamericano, -na *adj* HISPANOAMERI-CANO, LATINOAMERICANO : Latin-American

-ible *suf* : -ible

ice, etc. → **izar**

iceberg *nm, pl* **icebergs** : iceberg

icono *nm* : icon

iconoclasia *nf* : iconoclasm

iconoclasta *nmf* : iconoclast

ictericia *nf* : jaundice

ictérico, -ca *adj* : jaundiced

id *nm* : id

ida *nf* **1** : going, departure **2 ida y vuelta** : round trip **3 idas y venidas** : comings and goings

idea *nf* **1** : idea, notion ⟨una buena/mala idea : a good/bad idea⟩ ⟨tengo una idea : I have an idea⟩ ⟨no tengo (ni) idea : I have no idea⟩ ⟨me hago una idea de cómo es : I'm getting an/some idea of what he's like⟩ **2** : opinion, belief ⟨siempre puedes cambiar de idea : you can always change your mind⟩ ⟨¿de dónde sacaste esa idea? : where did you get that idea?⟩ **3** PROPÓSITO : intention, idea ⟨la idea era llegar temprano : the idea was to arrive early⟩

ideal *adj & nm* : ideal — **idealmente** *adv*

idealismo *nm* : idealism

idealista¹ *adj* : idealistic

idealista² *nmf* : idealist

idealizar {21} *vt* : to idealize — **idealización** *nf*

idear *vt* : to devise, to think up

ideario *nm* : ideology

idem *nm* : the same, ditto

idéntico, -ca *adj* : identical, alike — **idénticamente** *adv*

identidad *nf* : identity

identificable *adj* : identifiable

identificación *nf, pl* **-ciones 1** : identification, identifying **2** : identification document, ID

identificar {72} *vt* : to identify — **identificarse** *vr* **1** : to identify oneself **2** ~ **con** : to identify with

ideología *nf* : ideology — **ideológicamente** *adv*

ideológico, -ca *adj* : ideological

ideólogo, -ga *n* : ideologue

idílico, -ca *adj* : idyllic

idilio *nm* **1** : idyll **2** AMORÍO : love affair, romance

idioma *nm* **1** : language ⟨el idioma inglés : the English language⟩

idiomático, -ca *adj* : idiomatic — **idiomáticamente** *adv*

idiosincrasia *nf* : idiosyncrasy

idiosincrásico, -ca *adj* : idiosyncratic

idiota¹ *adj* : idiotic, stupid, foolish

idiota² *nmf* **1** : idiot, foolish person **2** *dated, now offensive* : idiot (in medicine) *dated, now offensive*

idiotez *nf, pl* **-teces 1** : idiocy (in medicine) *dated, now offensive* **2** : idiotic act or remark ⟨¡no digas idioteces! : don't talk nonsense!⟩

ido¹, ida *adj* : crazy, nutty

ido² *pp* → **ir**

idólatra¹ *adj* : idolatrous

idólatra² *nmf* : idolater

idolatrar *vt* : to idolize

idolatría *nf* : idolatry

ídolo *nm* : idol

idoneidad *nf* : suitability

idóneo, -nea *adj* ADECUADO : suitable, fitting

iglesia *nf* : church

iglú *nm, pl* **iglús** *or* **iglúes** : igloo

ignición *nf, pl* **-ciones** : ignition

ignífugo, -ga *adj* : fireproof

ignominia *nf* : ignominy, disgrace

ignominioso, -sa *adj* : ignominious, shameful

ignorancia *nf* : ignorance

ignorante¹ *adj* : ignorant — **ignorantemente** *adv*

ignorante² *nmf* : ignorant person, ignoramus

ignorar *vt* **1** : to ignore **2** DESCONOCER : to be unaware of ⟨lo ignoramos por absoluto : we have no idea⟩

ignoto, -ta *adj* : unknown

i griega *nf* : (letter) i

igual¹ *adv* **1** : in the same way ⟨las cosas siguen igual : things are the same as ever⟩ **2** : perhaps ⟨igual llueve : it might rain, it may rain⟩ **3** : anyway ⟨iba a venir igual : I was going to come anyway⟩ **4 al igual que** : as well as **5 igual que** : (just) like, the same as ⟨juega básquetbol, igual que su prima : she plays basketball, just like her cousin⟩ ⟨pienso igual que tú : I agree with you, I think the same thing⟩ **6 por** ~ : equally

igual² *adj* **1** : equal ⟨ser igual a : to be equal to⟩ **2** IDÉNTICO : the same, alike ⟨son iguales : they're the same⟩ ⟨ser igual a : to be the same as⟩ ⟨me es/da igual : it makes no difference to me⟩ **3** : even, smooth **4** SEMEJANTE : similar **5** CONSTANTE : constant

igual³ *nmf* : equal, peer ⟨sin igual : without equal, unequaled⟩

igualado, -da *adj* **1** : even (of a score) **2** : level **3** *Mex* : disrespectful

igualar *vt* **1** : to equalize **2** NIVELAR : to level, to flatten, to straighten **3** : to tie ⟨igualar el marcador : to even the score⟩ — **igualarse** *vr* ~ **a/con** : to equal, to be equal to, to be a match for

igualdad *nf* **1** : equality **2** UNIFORMIDAD : evenness, uniformity

igualitario, -ria *adj* : egalitarian

igualmente *adv* **1** : equally **2** ASIMISMO : likewise

iguana *nf* : iguana

ijada *nf* : flank, loin, side

ijar *nm* → **ijada**

ilegal[1] *adj* : illegal, unlawful — **ilegalmente** *adv*
ilegal[2] *nmf CA, Mex* : illegal alien
ilegalidad *nf* : illegality
ilegibilidad *nf* : illegibility
ilegible *adj* : illegible — **ilegiblemente** *adv*
ilegitimidad *nf* : illegitimacy
ilegítimo, -ma *adj* : illegitimate, unlawful
ileso, -sa *adj* : uninjured, unharmed
ilícito, -ta *adj* : illicit — **ilícitamente** *adv*
ilimitado, -da *adj* : unlimited
ilógico, -ca *adj* : illogical — **ilógicamente** *adv*
iluminación *nf, pl* **-ciones** 1 : illumination 2 ALUMBRADO : lighting
iluminado, -da *adj* : illuminated, lighted
iluminar *vt* 1 : to illuminate, to light (up) 2 : to enlighten
ilusión *nf, pl* **-siones** 1 : illusion, delusion 2 ESPERANZA : hope ⟨hacerse ilusiones : to get one's hopes up⟩ 3 *Spain* : happiness, excitement, enthusiasm ⟨¡me hace mucha ilusión que te haya gustado! : I'm so glad you liked it!⟩ ⟨no me hace ilusión ir : I'm not looking forward to going⟩ 4 **ilusión óptica** : optical illusion
ilusionado, -da *adj* ESPERANZADO : hopeful, eager
ilusionar *vt* : to build up hope, to excite — **ilusionarse** *vr* : to get one's hopes up
iluso[1], **-sa** *adj* : naive, gullible
iluso[2], **-sa** *n* SOÑADOR : dreamer, visionary
ilusorio, -ria *adj* ENGAÑOSO : illusory, misleading
ilustración *nf, pl* **-ciones** 1 : illustration 2 : erudition ⟨la Ilustración : the Enlightenment⟩
ilustrado, -da *adj* 1 : illustrated 2 DOCTO : learned, erudite
ilustrador, -dora *n* : illustrator
ilustrar *vt* 1 : to illustrate 2 ACLARAR, CLARIFICAR : to explain
ilustrativo, -va *adj* : illustrative
ilustre *adj* : illustrious, eminent
im- → in-
imagen *nf, pl* **imágenes** : image, picture
imaginable *adj* : imaginable, conceivable
imaginación *nf, pl* **-ciones** : imagination
imaginar *vt* : to imagine — **imaginarse** *vr* 1 : to suppose, to imagine 2 : to picture
imaginario, -ria *adj* : imaginary
imaginativo, -va *adj* : imaginative — **imaginativamente** *adv*
imaginería *nf* 1 : imagery 2 : image making (in religion)
imán *nm, pl* **imanes** : magnet
imantar *vt* : to magnetize
imbatible *adj* : unbeatable
imbécil[1] *adj* : stupid, idiotic
imbécil[2] *nmf* 1 *dated, now offensive* : imbecile (in medicine) *dated, now offensive* 2 *fam* : idiot, dope
imbecilidad *nf* 1 : imbecility (in medicine) *dated, now offensive* 2 IDIOTEZ : stupid thing to say or do
imborrable *adj* : indelible
imbuir {41} *vt* : to imbue — **imbuirse** *vr*

imitación *nf, pl* **-ciones** 1 : imitation 2 : mimicry, impersonation
imitador[1], **-dora** *adj* : imitative
imitador[2], **-dora** *n* 1 : imitator 2 : mimic
imitar *vt* 1 : to imitate, to copy 2 : to mimic, to impersonate
imitativo, -va *adj* → **imitador**[1]
impaciencia *nf* : impatience
impacientar *vt* : to make impatient, to exasperate — **impacientarse** *vr*
impaciente *adj* : impatient — **impacientemente** *adv*
impactado, -da *adj* : shocked, stunned
impactante *adj* 1 : shocking 2 : impressive, powerful
impactar *vt* 1 GOLPEAR : to hit 2 IMPRESIONAR : to impact, to affect — **impactarse** *vr*
impacto *nm* 1 : impact, effect 2 : shock, collision
impagable *adj* 1 : unpayable 2 : priceless
impago[1] *adj* : outstanding, unpaid
impago[2] *nm* : nonpayment
impala *nm* : impala
impalpable *adj* INTANGIBLE : impalpable, intangible
impar[1] *adj* : odd ⟨números impares : odd numbers⟩
impar[2] : odd number
imparable *adj* : unstoppable
imparcial *adj* : impartial — **imparcialmente** *adv*
imparcialidad *nf* : impartiality
impartir *vt* : to impart, to give
impasible *adj* : impassive, unmoved — **impasiblemente** *adv*
impasse *nm* : impasse
impavidez *nf* : fearlessness
impávido, -da *adj* : undaunted
impecable *adj* INTACHABLE : impeccable, faultless — **impecablemente** *adv*
impedido[1], **-da** *adj* : disabled, crippled
impedido[2], **-da** *n* : disabled person, handicapped person *sometimes offensive*
impedimento *nm* 1 : impediment, obstacle 2 : disability
impedir {54} *vt* 1 : to prevent, to block 2 : to impede, to hinder
impeler *vt* 1 : to drive, to propel 2 : to impel
impenetrable *adj* : impenetrable — **impenetrabilidad** *nf*
impenitente *adj* : unrepentant
impensable *adj* : unthinkable
impensado, -da *adj* : unforeseen, unexpected
imperante *adj* : prevailing
imperar *vi* 1 : to reign, to rule 2 PREDOMINAR : to prevail
imperativo[1], **-va** *adj* 1 : imperative 2 : authoritative, commanding
imperativo[2] *nm* : imperative
imperceptible *adj* : imperceptible — **imperceptiblemente** *adv*
imperdible *nm Spain* : safety pin
imperdonable *adj* : unforgivable
imperecedero, -ra *adj* 1 : imperishable 2 INMORTAL : immortal, everlasting

imperfección *nf, pl* **-ciones** 1 : imperfection 2 DEFECTO : defect, flaw
imperfecto[1], **-ta** *adj* : imperfect, flawed
imperfecto[2] *nm* : imperfect tense
imperial *adj* : imperial
imperialismo *nm* : imperialism
imperialista *adj & nmf* : imperialist
impericia *nf* : lack of skill, incompetence
imperio *nm* 1 : empire 2 : authority, rule ⟨el imperio de la ley : the rule of law⟩
imperioso, -sa *adj* 1 : imperious 2 : pressing, urgent — **imperiosamente** *adv*
impermeabilizante *nm* : water repellent, waterproofing
impermeabilizar {21} *vt* : to waterproof
impermeable[1] *adj* 1 : impervious 2 : impermeable, waterproof
impermeable[2] *nm* : raincoat
impersonal *adj* : impersonal — **impersonalmente** *adv*
impersonar *vt Mex* : to impersonate
impertinencia *nf* INSOLENCIA : impertinence, insolence
impertinente *adj* 1 INSOLENTE : impertinent, insolent 2 INOPORTUNO : inappropriate, uncalled-for 3 IRRELEVANTE : irrelevant
impertinentemente *adv* : impertinently
imperturbable *adj* : imperturbable, impassive, stolid
ímpetu *nm* 1 : impetus, momentum 2 : vigor, energy 3 : force, violence
impetuoso, -sa *adj* : impetuous, impulsive — **impetuosamente** *adv*
impiedad *nf* : impiety
impío, -pía *adj* : impious, ungodly
implacable *adj* : implacable, relentless — **implacablemente** *adv*
implantación *nf, pl* **-ciones** 1 : implantation 2 ESTABLECIMIENTO : establishment, introduction
implantado, -da *adj* : well-established
implantar *vt* 1 : to implant 2 ESTABLECER : to establish, to introduce — **implantarse** *vr*
implante *nm* : implant
implementar *vt* : to implement — **implementarse** *vr* — **implementación** *nf*
implemento *nm* : implement, tool
implicación *nf, pl* **-ciones** : implication
implicancia *nf* : implication
implicar {72} *vt* 1 ENREDAR, ENVOLVER : to involve, to implicate 2 : to imply
implícito, -ta *adj* : implied, implicit — **implícitamente** *adv*
implorar *vt* : to implore
implosión *nf, pl* **-siones** : implosion — **implosivo, -va** *adj*
implosionar *vi* : to implode
imponderable *adj & nm* : imponderable
imponente *adj* : imposing, impressive
imponer {60} *vt* 1 : to impose 2 : to confer 3 : to introduce, to establish, to set (a fashion) — *vi* : to be impressive, to command respect — **imponerse** *vr* 1 : to take on (a duty) 2 : to assert oneself 3 : to prevail
imponible *adj* : taxable

impopular *adj* : unpopular — **impopularidad** *nf*
importación *nf, pl* **-ciones** 1 : importation 2 **importaciones** *nfpl* : imports
importado, -da *adj* : imported
importador[1], **-dora** *adj* : importing
importador[2], **-dora** *n* : importer
importancia *nf* : importance
importante *adj* : important, significant — **importantemente** *adv*
importar *vi* 1 : to matter, to be important ⟨no importa : it doesn't matter, it's not important⟩ ⟨lo que importa es el resultado : what matters is the result⟩ ⟨no le importa lo que piensen : she doesn't care what they think⟩ ⟨¿qué importa que no les guste? : who cares if they don't like it?⟩ ⟨(no) me importa un bledo/comino : I don't give a damn, I couldn't care less⟩ ⟨no te importo : you don't care about me⟩ 2 : to bother ⟨no le importa hacerlo : he doesn't mind doing it⟩ ⟨si no te importa : if you don't mind, if it's OK with you⟩ — *vt* 1 : to import (goods, etc.) 2 : to import (in computing)
importe *nm* 1 : price, cost 2 : sum, amount
importunar *vt* : to bother, to inconvenience — *vi* : to be inconvenient
importuno, -na *adj* 1 : inopportune, inconvenient 2 : bothersome, annoying
imposibilidad *nf* : impossibility
imposibilitado, -da *adj* 1 : disabled, crippled 2 **verse imposibilitado** : to be unable (to do something)
imposibilitar *vt* 1 : to make impossible 2 : to disable, to incapacitate — **imposibilitarse** *vr* : to become disabled
imposible *adj* : impossible — **imposiblemente** *adv*
imposición *nf, pl* **-ciones** 1 : imposition 2 EXIGENCIA : demand, requirement 3 : tax 4 : deposit
impositivo, -va *adj* : tax ⟨tasa impositiva : tax rate⟩
impostor, -tora *n* : impostor
impostura *nf* 1 : fraud 2 CALUMNIA : slander
impotencia *nf* 1 : impotence, helplessness, powerlessness 2 : impotence (in medicine)
impotente *adj* 1 : helpless, powerless 2 : impotent
impracticable *adj* : impracticable
imprecisión *nf, pl* **-siones** 1 : imprecision, vagueness 2 : inaccuracy
impreciso, -sa *adj* 1 : imprecise, vague 2 : inaccurate
impredecible *adj* : unpredictable
impregnar *vt* : to impregnate
imprenta *nf* 1 : printing 2 : printing shop, press 3 **letra(s) de imprenta** → **letra**
imprescindible *adj* : essential, indispensable
impresión *nf, pl* **-siones** 1 : print, printing 2 : impression, feeling ⟨causar una buena/mala impresión : to make a good/bad impression⟩
impresionable *adj* : impressionable

impresionante *adj* : impressive, incredible, amazing, shocking (of video, etc.), horrific (of an accident, etc.) — **impresionantemente** *adv*
impresionar *vt* **1** : to impress, to strike **2** : to affect, to move **3** : to shock **4** : to expose (film) to light — *vi* : to make an impression — **impresionarse** *vr* : to be affected, to be moved
impresionismo *nm* : impressionism
impresionista¹ *adj* : impressionist
impresionista² *nmf* : impressionist
impreso¹ *pp* → **imprimir**
impreso², **-sa** *adj* : printed
impreso³ *nm* **1** PUBLICACIÓN : printed matter, publication **2** FORMULARIO : form
impresor, **-sora** *n* : printer
impresora *nf* **1** : (computer) printer **2 impresora de inyección de tinta** : inkjet printer **3 impresora láser** : laser printer
imprevisible *adj* : unforeseeable, unpredictable
imprevisión *nf, pl* **-siones** : lack of foresight, thoughtlessness
imprevisto¹, **-ta** *adj* : unexpected, unforeseen
imprevisto² *nm* : unexpected occurrence, contingency
imprimir {42} *vt* **1** : to print **2** : to imprint, to stamp, to impress
improbabilidad *nf* : improbability
improbable *adj* : improbable, unlikely
improcedente *adj* **1** : inadmissible **2** : inappropriate, improper
improductivo, **-va** *adj* : unproductive
impronta *nf* : mark, stamp ⟨dejar su impronta : to leave one's mark⟩
improperio *nm* : affront, insult
impropiedad *nf* : impropriety
impropio, **-pia** *adj* **1** : improper, incorrect **2** INADECUADO : unsuitable, inappropriate
improvisación *nf, pl* **-ciones** : improvisation, ad-lib
improvisado, **-da** *adj* : improvised, ad-lib
improvisar *v* : to improvise, to ad-lib
improviso *adj* de ~ : all of a sudden, unexpectedly
imprudencia *nf* **1** : mistake, indiscretion **2** : carelessness, recklessness
imprudente *adj* **1** : imprudent, unwise, indiscreet **2** : careless, reckless — **imprudentemente** *adv*
impúdico, **-ca** *adj* : shameless, indecent
impuesto¹ *pp* → **imponer**
impuesto² *nm* : tax
impugnar *vt* : to challenge, to contest
impulsar *vt* **1** : to propel, to drive **2** : to boost, to promote
impulsividad *nf* : impulsiveness
impulsivo, **-va** *adj* : impulsive — **impulsivamente** *adv*
impulso *nm* **1** : drive, thrust **2** : impulse, urge
impulsor, **-sora** *n* : force, impetus ⟨el principal impulsor de la iniciativa : the main/driving force behind the initiative⟩
impune *adj* : unpunished
impunemente *adv* : with impunity

impunidad *nf* : impunity
impuntualidad *nf* : lack of punctuality
impureza *nf* : impurity
impuro, **-ra** *adj* : impure
impuso, etc. → **imponer**
imputable *adj* ATRIBUIBLE : attributable
imputación *nf, pl* **-ciones** **1** : attribution **2** : accusation
imputar *vt* ATRIBUIR : to impute, to attribute
in- or **im-** or **i-** or **ir-** *pref* : in-, im-, il-, un- ⟨inexacto : inexact⟩ ⟨imperfecto : imperfect⟩ ⟨ilegal : illegal⟩ ⟨inaceptable : unacceptable⟩
inacabable *adj* : endless
inacabado, **-da** *adj* INCONCLUSO : unfinished
inaccesibilidad *nf* : inaccessibility
inaccesible *adj* **1** : inaccessible **2** : unattainable
inacción *nf, pl* **-ciones** : inactivity, inaction
inaceptable *adj* : unacceptable
inactividad *nf* : inactivity, idleness
inactivo, **-va** *adj* : inactive, idle
inadaptado¹, **-da** *adj* : maladjusted
inadaptado², **-da** *n* : misfit
inadecuación *nf, pl* **-ciones** : inadequacy
inadecuado, **-da** *adj* **1** : inadequate **2** IMPROPIO : inappropriate — **inadecuadamente** *adv*
inadmisible *adj* **1** : inadmissible **2** : unacceptable
inadvertencia *nf* : oversight
inadvertidamente *adv* : inadvertently
inadvertido, **-da** *adj* **1** : unnoticed ⟨pasar inadvertido : to go unnoticed⟩ **2** DESPISTADO, DISTRAÍDO : inattentive, distracted
inagotable *adj* : inexhaustible
inaguantable *adj* INSOPORTABLE : insufferable, unbearable
inalámbrico, **-ca** *adj* : wireless, cordless ⟨acceso inalámbrico a Internet : wireless Internet access⟩ ⟨un teléfono inalámbrico : a cordless phone⟩
inalcanzable *adj* : unreachable, unattainable
inalienable *adj* : inalienable
inalterable *adj* **1** : unalterable, unchangeable **2** : impassive **3** : colorfast
inamovible *adj* : immovable, fixed
inanición *nf, pl* **-ciones** : starvation
inanimado, **-da** *adj* : inanimate
inapelable *adj* : unappealable
inapetencia *nf* : lack of appetite
inaplicable *adj* : inapplicable
inapreciable *adj* **1** : imperceptible, negligible **2** : invaluable
inapropiado, **-da** *adj* : inappropriate, unsuitable — **inapropiadamente** *adv*
inarticulado, **-da** *adj* : inarticulate, unintelligible — **inarticuladamente** *adv*
inasequible *adj* : unattainable, inaccessible
inasistencia *nf* AUSENCIA : absence
inatacable *adj* : unassailable, indisputable
inaudible *adj* : inaudible
inaudito, **-ta** *adj* : unheard-of, unprecedented

inauguración *nf, pl* **-ciones** 1 : inauguration, opening 2 : inauguration, beginning

inaugural *adj* : inaugural, opening

inaugurar *vt* 1 : to inaugurate 2 : to open

inauténtico, -ca *adj* : counterfeit, inauthentic

inca *adj & nmf* : Inca

incaico, -ca *adj* : Inca, Incan

incalculable *adj* : incalculable

incalificable *adj* : indescribable

incandescencia *nf* : incandescence — **incandescente** *adj*

incansable *adj* INFATIGABLE : tireless — **incansablemente** *adv*

incapacidad *nf* 1 : inability, incapacity 2 : disability, handicap *sometimes offensive* 3 : incompetence 4 *Col, CoRi* : sick leave

incapacitado, -da *adj* 1 : disqualified 2 : disabled, handicapped

incapacitar *vt* 1 : to incapacitate, to disable 2 : to disqualify

incapaz *adj, pl* **-paces** 1 : incapable, unable 2 : incompetent, inept

incautación *nf, pl* **-ciones** : seizure, confiscation

incautar *vt* CONFISCAR : to confiscate, to seize — **incautarse** *vr*

incauto, -ta *adj* : unwary, unsuspecting

incendiar *vt* : to set fire to, to burn (down) — **incendiarse** *vr* : to catch fire, to burn down

incendiario¹, -ria *adj* : incendiary, inflammatory

incendiario², -ria *n* : arsonist

incendio *nm* 1 : fire 2 **incendio provocado** : arson

incensario *nm* : censer

incentivar *vt* : to encourage, to stimulate

incentivo *nm* : incentive

incertidumbre *nf* : uncertainty, suspense

incesante *adj* : incessant — **incesantemente** *adv*

incesto *nm* : incest

incestuoso, -sa *adj* : incestuous

incidencia *nf* 1 : incident 2 : effect, impact 3 **por ～** : by chance, accidentally

incidental *adj* : incidental

incidentalmente *adv* : by chance

incidente *nm* : incident, occurrence

incidir *vi* 1 ～ **en** : to fall into, to enter into ⟨incidimos en el mismo error : we fell into the same mistake⟩ 2 ～ **en** : to affect, to influence, to have a bearing on

incienso *nm* : incense

incierto, -ta *adj* 1 : uncertain 2 : untrue 3 : unsteady, insecure

incinerador *nm* : incinerator

incinerar *vt* 1 : to incinerate 2 : to cremate

incipiente *adj* : incipient

incisión *nf, pl* **-siones** : incision

incisivo¹, -va *adj* : incisive

incisivo² *nm* : incisor

inciso *nm* 1 : digression, aside 2 : paragraph, subsection

incitación *nf, pl* **-ciones** : incitement

incitador¹, -dora *n* : instigator, agitator

incitador², -dora *adj* : provocative

incitante *adj* : provocative

incitar *vt* : to incite, to rouse

incivilizado, -da *adj* : uncivilized

inclemencia *nf* : inclemency, severity

inclemente *adj* : inclement

inclinación *nf, pl* **-ciones** 1 PROPENSIÓN : inclination, tendency 2 : incline, slope 3 : bow ⟨inclinación de cabeza : nod⟩

inclinado, -da *adj* 1 : sloping, tilted 2 : inclined, apt

inclinar *vt* : to tilt, to lean, to incline ⟨inclinar la cabeza : to bow one's head⟩ — **inclinarse** *vr* 1 : to lean, to lean over 2 : to bow 3 ～ **a** : to be inclined to

incluir {41} *vt* : to include

inclusión *nf, pl* **-siones** : inclusion

inclusive *adv* : inclusive ⟨niños de entre dos y cinco años inclusive : children ages two through five inclusive⟩ ⟨hasta el sábado inclusive : up to and including Saturday, through Saturday⟩

inclusivo, -va *adj* : inclusive, open

incluso *adv* AUN : even, in fact ⟨es importante e incluso crucial : it is important and even crucial⟩

incógnita *nf* 1 : unknown quantity (in mathematics) 2 : mystery

incógnito, -ta *adj* 1 : unknown 2 **de incógnito** : incognito

incoherencia *nf* : incoherence

incoherente *adj* : incoherent — **incoherentemente** *adv*

incoloro, -ra *adj* : colorless

incombustible *adj* : fireproof

incomible *adj* : inedible

incomodar *vt* 1 : to make uncomfortable 2 : to inconvenience — **incomodarse** *vr* : to put oneself out, to take the trouble

incomodidad *nf* 1 : discomfort, awkwardness 2 MOLESTIA : inconvenience, bother

incómodo, -da *adj* 1 : uncomfortable, awkward 2 INCONVENIENTE : inconvenient — **incómodamente** *adv*

incomparable *adj* : incomparable

incompatibilidad *nf* : incompatibility

incompatible *adj* : incompatible

incompetencia *nf* : incompetence

incompetente *adj & nmf* : incompetent

incompleto, -ta *adj* : incomplete

incomprendido, -da *adj* : misunderstood

incomprensible *adj* : incomprehensible

incomprensión *nf, pl* **-siones** : lack of understanding, incomprehension

incomunicación *nf, pl* **-ciones** : lack of communication

incomunicado, -da *adj* 1 : cut off, isolated 2 : in solitary confinement

inconcebible *adj* : inconceivable, unthinkable — **inconcebiblemente** *adv*

inconcluso, -sa *adj* INACABADO : unfinished

incondicional *adj* : unconditional — **incondicionalmente** *adv*

inconexo, -xa *adj* 1 : unrelated, unconnected 2 : disjointed

inconfesable *adj* : unspeakable, shameful

inconforme *adj & nmf* : nonconformist

inconformidad *nf* : nonconformity

inconformista *adj & nmf* : nonconformist
inconfundible *adj* : unmistakable, obvious — **inconfundiblemente** *adv*
incongruencia *nf* : incongruity
incongruente *adj* : incongruous
inconmensurable *adj* : vast, immeasurable
inconquistable *adj* : unyielding
inconsciencia *nf* **1** : unconsciousness, lack of awareness **2** : irresponsibility
inconsciente[1] *adj* **1** : unconscious, unaware **2** : reckless, needless — **inconscientemente** *adv*
inconsciente[2] *nm* **el inconsciente** : the unconscious
inconsecuente *adj* : inconsistent — **inconsecuencia** *nf*
inconsiderado, -da *adj* : inconsiderate, thoughtless
inconsistencia *nf* : inconsistency
inconsistente *adj* **1** : weak, flimsy **2** : inconsistent, weak (of an argument)
inconsolable *adj* : inconsolable — **inconsolablemente** *adv*
inconstancia *nf* : fickleness
inconstante *adj* : fickle, changeable
inconstitucional *adj* : unconstitutional — **inconstitucionalidad** *nf*
incontable *adj* INNUMERABLE : countless, innumerable
incontenible *adj* : uncontrollable, unstoppable
incontestable *adj* INCUESTIONABLE, INDISCUTIBLE : irrefutable, indisputable
incontinencia *nf* : incontinence — **incontinente** *adj*
incontrolable *adj* : uncontrollable
incontrolado, -da *adj* : uncontrolled, out of control
incontrovertible *adj* : indisputable
inconveniencia *nf* **1** : inconvenience, trouble **2** : inappropriateness **3** : tactless remark
inconveniente[1] *adj* **1** INCÓMODO : inconvenient **2** INAPROPIADO : improper, unsuitable
inconveniente[2] *nm* **1** : obstacle, problem, snag **2** : objection ⟨no tengo inconveniente en hacerlo : I don't mind doing it⟩ **3** : disadvantage, drawback ⟨las ventajas e inconvenientes : the advantages and disadvantages⟩
incordiar *vt Spain* : to annoy, to pester
incorporación *nf, pl* **-ciones** : incorporation
incorporado *adj* : built-in
incorporar *vt* **1** : to incorporate **2** : to add, to include — **incorporarse** *vr* **1** : to sit up **2** ~ **a** : to join
incorpóreo, -rea *adj* : incorporeal, bodiless
incorrección *n, pl* **-ciones** : impropriety, improper word or action
incorrecto, -ta *adj* **1** : incorrect **2** : impolite, rude — **incorrectamente** *adv*
incorregible *adj* : incorrigible — **incorregibilidad** *nf*
incorruptible *adj* : incorruptible
incredulidad *nf* : incredulity, skepticism
incrédulo[1], **-la** *adj* : incredulous, skeptical

incrédulo[2], **-la** *n* : skeptic
increíble *adj* : incredible, unbelievable — **increíblemente** *adv*
incrementar *vt* : to increase — **incrementarse** *vr*
incremento *nm* AUMENTO : increase
increpar *vt* : to·tell off *fam*, to yell at, to rebuke
incriminar *vt* : to incriminate — **incriminación** *nf*
incriminatorio, -ria *adj* : incriminating, incriminatory
incruento, -ta *adj* : bloodless
incrustación *nf, pl* **-ciones** : inlay
incrustar *vt* **1** : to embed **2** : to inlay — **incrustarse** *vr* : to become embedded
incubación *nf, pl* **-ciones** : incubation
incubadora *nf* : incubator
incubar *v* : to incubate
incuestionable *adj* INCONTESTABLE, INDISCUTIBLE : unquestionable, indisputable — **incuestionablemente** *adv*
inculcar {72} *vt* : to inculcate, to instill
inculpado, -da *n* : defendant ⟨el inculpado : the defendant, the accused⟩
inculpar *vt* ACUSAR : to accuse, to charge
inculto, -ta *adj* **1** : uncultured, ignorant **2** : uncultivated, fallow
incultura *adj* : ignorance, lack of culture
incumbencia *nf* : obligation, responsibility
incumbir *vi (3rd person only)* ~ **a** : to be incumbent upon, to be of concern to ⟨a mí no me incumbe : it's not my concern⟩
incumplido, -da *adj* : irresponsible, unreliable
incumplimiento *nm* **1** : failure to fulfill (conditions, obligations, etc.) ⟨incumplimiento de la ley : failure to comply with the law⟩ ⟨incumplimiento de pago : failure to make payment, default⟩ **2 incumplimiento de contrato** : breach of contract **3 incumplimiento de deberes** : neglect of duty
incumplir *vt* : to fail to carry out, to break (a promise, a contract)
incurable *adj* : incurable
incurrir *vi* **1** ~ **en** : to incur ⟨incurrir en gastos : to incur expenses⟩ **2** ~ **en** : to fall into, to commit ⟨incurrió en un error : he made a mistake⟩
incursión *nf, pl* **-siones** : incursion, raid
incursionar *vi* **1** : to raid **2** ~ **en** : to go into, to enter ⟨el actor incursionó en el baile : the actor worked in dance for a while⟩
indagación *nf, pl* **-ciones** : investigation, inquiry
indagar {52} *vt* : to inquire into, to investigate
indagatoria *nf* **1** : statement, deposition **2** : investigation, inquiry, inquest
indebido, -da *adj* : improper, undue — **indebidamente** *adv*
indecencia *nf* : indecency, obscenity
indecente *adj* : indecent, obscene
indecible *adj* : indescribable, inexpressible
indecisión *nf, pl* **-siones** : indecision
indeciso, -sa *adj* **1** IRRESOLUTO : indecisive **2** : undecided

indeclinable *adj* : unavoidable

indecoro *nm* : impropriety, indecorousness

indecoroso, -sa *adj* : indecorous, unseemly

indefectible *adj* : unfailing, sure

indefendible *adj* : indefensible

indefensión *nf* : defenselessness

indefenso, -sa *adj* : defenseless, helpless

indefinible *adj* : indefinable

indefinido, -da *adj* **1** : undefined, vague **2** INDETERMINADO : indefinite — **indefinidamente** *adv*

indeleble *adj* : indelible — **indeleblemente** *adv*

indelicado, -da *adj* : indelicate, tactless

indemne *adj* : unharmed, unhurt

indemnidad *nf* : indemnity

indemnización *nf, pl* **-ciones 1** : indemnity **2 indemnización por despido** : severance pay

indemnizar {21} *vt* : to indemnify, to compensate

independencia *nf* : independence

independiente *adj* : independent — **independientemente** *adv*

independista[1] *adj* : pro-independence

independista[2] *nmf* : independence supporter

independizar {21} *vt* : to make independent — **independizarse** *vr*

indescifrable *adj* : indecipherable

indescriptible *adj* : indescribable — **indescriptiblemente** *adv*

indeseable *adj & nmf* : undesirable

indestructible *adj* : indestructible

indeterminado, -da *adj* **1** INDEFINIDO : indefinite **2** : indeterminate

indexar *vt* INDICIAR : to index (wages, prices, etc.)

indicación *nf, pl* **-ciones 1** : sign, signal **2** : direction, instruction **3** : suggestion, hint

indicado, -da *adj* **1** APROPIADO : appropriate, suitable **2** : specified, indicated ⟨al día indicado : on the specified day⟩

indicador *nm* **1** : gauge, dial, meter **2** : indicator ⟨indicadores económicos : economic indicators⟩

indicar {72} *vt* **1** SEÑALAR : to indicate **2** ENSEÑAR, MOSTRAR : to show

indicativo[1], **-va** *adj* : indicative

indicativo[2] *nm* : indicative (mood)

índice *nm* **1** : index **2** : contents *pl*, table of contents **3** : index finger, forefinger **4** INDICIO : indication

indiciar *vt* : to index (prices, wages, etc.)

indicio *nm* **1** : indication, sign **2 indicios** *nmpl* : evidence

indiferencia *nf* : indifference

indiferente *adj* **1** : indifferent, unconcerned **2 ser indiferente** : to be of no concern ⟨me es indiferente : it doesn't matter to me⟩

indiferentemente *adv* : indifferently

indígena[1] *adj* : indigenous, native

indígena[2] *nmf* : native

indigencia *nf* MISERIA : poverty, destitution

indigente *adj & nmf* : indigent

indigestarse *vr* **1** EMPACHARSE : to have indigestion **2** *fam* : to nauseate, to disgust ⟨ese tipo se me indigesta : that guy makes me sick⟩

indigestión *nf, pl* **-tiones** EMPACHO : indigestion

indigesto, -ta *adj* : indigestible, difficult to digest

indignación *nf, pl* **-ciones** : indignation

indignado, -da *adj* : indignant

indignante *adj* : outrageous, infuriating

indignar *vt* : to outrage, to infuriate — **indignarse** *vr*

indignidad *nf* : indignity

indigno, -na *adj* **1** : unworthy **2** : contemptible, despicable

índigo *nm* : indigo

indio, -dia *adj & n* **1** *sometimes offensive* : Indian *often offensive*, Native American **2** : Indian (from India)

indio–americano, india–americana → **nativo americano**

indirecta *nf* **1** : hint, innuendo **2 echar indirectas** *or* **lanzar indirectas** : to drop a hint, to insinuate

indirecto, -ta *adj* : indirect — **indirectamente** *adv*

indisciplina *nf* : lack of discipline, unruliness

indisciplinado, -da *adj* : undisciplined, unruly

indiscreción *nf, pl* **-ciones 1** IMPRUDENCIA : indiscretion **2** : tactless remark

indiscreto, -ta *adj* IMPRUDENTE : indiscreet, imprudent — **indiscretamente** *adv*

indiscriminado, -da *adj* : indiscriminate — **indiscriminadamente** *adv*

indiscutible *adj* **1** INCONTESTABLE, INCUESTIONABLE : indisputable, unquestionable **2** : undisputed ⟨el campeón indiscutible : the undisputed champion⟩ — **indiscutiblemente** *adv*

indiscutido, -da *adj* : undisputed

indispensable *adj* : indispensable — **indispensablemente** *adv*

indisponer {60} *vt* **1** : to spoil, to upset **2** : to make ill — **indisponerse** *vr* **1** : to become ill **2** ∼ **con** : to fall out with

indisposición *nf, pl* **-ciones** : illness

indispuesto, -ta *adj* : unwell, indisposed

indistinguible *adj* : indistinguishable

indistintamente *adv* **1** : indistinctly **2** : indiscriminately

indistinto, -ta *adj* : indistinct, vague, faint

individual[1] *adj* : individual — **individualmente** *adv*

individual[2] *nm* **1** : place mat **2 individuales** *nmpl* : singles (in sports)

individualidad *nf* : individuality

individualismo *nm* : individualism

individualista[1] *adj* : individualistic

individualista[2] *nmf* : individualist

individualizar {21} *vt* : to individualize

individuo *nm* : individual, person

indivisible *adj* : indivisible — **indivisibilidad** *nf*

indocumentado, -da *n* : illegal immigrant

índole *nf* **1** : nature, character **2** CLASE, TIPO : sort, kind

indolencia *nf* : indolence, laziness
indolente *adj* : indolent, lazy
indoloro, -ra *adj* : painless
indomable *adj* 1 : indomitable 2 : unruly, unmanageable
indómito, -ta *adj* 1 : indomitable 2 : untamed
indonesio, -sia *adj & n* : Indonesian
inducción *nf, pl* **-ciones** : induction
inducir {61} *vt* 1 : to induce, to cause 2 : to infer, to deduce
inductivo, -va *adj* : inductive
indudable *adj* : unquestionable, beyond doubt
indudablemente *adv* : undoubtedly, unquestionably
indulgencia *nf* 1 : indulgence, leniency 2 : indulgence (in religion)
indulgente *adj* : indulgent, lenient
indultar *vt* : to pardon, to reprieve
indulto *nm* : pardon, reprieve
indumentaria *nf* : clothing, attire
industria *nf* : industry
industrial[1] *adj* : industrial
industrial[2] *nmf* : industrialist, manufacturer
industrialización *nf, pl* **-ciones** : industrialization
industrializar {21} *vt* : to industrialize
industrioso, -sa *adj* : industrious
inédito, -ta *adj* 1 : unpublished 2 : unprecedented
inefable *adj* : ineffable
ineficacia *nf* 1 : inefficiency 2 : lack of effectiveness
ineficaz *adj, pl* **-caces** 1 : inefficient 2 : ineffective — **ineficazmente** *adv*
ineficiencia *nf* : inefficiency
ineficiente *adj* : inefficient — **ineficientemente** *adv*
inelegancia *nf* : inelegance — **inelegante** *adj*
inelegible *adj* : ineligible — **inelegibilidad** *nf*
ineludible *adj* : inescapable, unavoidable — **ineludiblemente** *adv*
ineptitud *nf* : ineptitude, incompetence
inepto[1]**, -ta** *adj* : inept, incompetent
inepto[2]**, -ta** *n* : incompetent
inequidad *nf* : inequity
inequitativo, -va *adj* : inequitable
inequívoco, -ca *adj* : unequivocal, unmistakable — **inequívocamente** *adv*
inercia *nf* 1 : inertia 2 : apathy 3 **por ~** : out of habit
inerme *adj* : unarmed, defenseless
inerte *adj* : inert
inescrupuloso, -sa *adj* : unscrupulous
inescrutable *adj* : inscrutable
inesperado, -da *adj* : unexpected — **inesperadamente** *adv*
inestabilidad *nf* : instability, unsteadiness
inestable *adj* 1 : unstable, unsteady 2 : changeable (of weather)
inestimable *adj* : inestimable, invaluable
inevitabilidad *nf* : inevitability
inevitable *adj* : inevitable, unavoidable — **inevitablemente** *adv*
inexactitud *nf* : inaccuracy
inexacto, -ta *adj* : inexact, inaccurate

inexcusable *adj* 1 : inexcusable, unforgivable 2 : unavoidable
inexistencia *nf* : lack, nonexistence
inexistente *adj* : nonexistent
inexorable *adj* : inexorable — **inexorablemente** *adv*
inexperiencia *nf* : inexperience
inexperto, -ta *adj* : inexperienced, unskilled
inexplicable *adj* : inexplicable — **inexplicablemente** *adv*
inexplorado, -da *adj* : unexplored
inexpresable *adj* : inexpressible
inexpresivo, -va *adj* : expressionless
inexpugnable *adj* : impregnable
inextricable *adj* : inextricable — **inextricablemente** *adv*
infalibilidad *nf* : infallibility
infalible *adj* : infallible — **infaliblemente** *adv*
infame *adj* 1 : infamous 2 : loathsome, vile ⟨tiempo infame : terrible weather⟩
infamia *nf* : infamy, disgrace
infancia *nf* 1 **NIÑEZ** : infancy, childhood 2 : children *pl* 3 : beginnings *pl*
infante[1]**, -ta** *n* : prince *m*, princess *f*
infante[2] *nm* : infantry soldier
infantería *nf* 1 : infantry 2 **infantería de marina** : marines *pl*
infantil *adj* 1 : childish, infantile 2 : child's, children's
infarto *nm* 1 : heart attack 2 **infarto cerebral** : stroke
infatigable *adj* : indefatigable, tireless — **infatigablemente** *adv*
infección *nf, pl* **-ciones** : infection
infeccioso, -sa *adj* : infectious
infectar *vt* : to infect — **infectarse** *vr*
infecto, -ta *adj* 1 : infected 2 : repulsive, sickening
infecundidad *nf* : infertility
infecundo, -da *adj* : infertile, barren
infelicidad *nf* : unhappiness
infeliz[1] *adj, pl* **-lices** 1 : unhappy 2 : hapless, unfortunate, wretched
infeliz[2] *nmf, pl* **-lices** : wretch
inferencia *nf* : inference
inferior[1] *adj* : inferior, lower
inferior[2] *nmf* : inferior, underling
inferioridad *nf* : inferiority
inferir {76} *vt* 1 **DEDUCIR** : to infer, to deduce 2 : to cause (harm or injury), to inflict
infernal *adj* : infernal, hellish
infertilidad *nf* : infertility
infestación *n, pl* **-ciones** : infestation
infestar *vt* 1 : to infest ⟨infestar de : to infest with⟩ 2 : to overrun, to invade
infición *nf, pl* **-ciones** *Mex* : pollution
infidelidad *nf* : unfaithfulness, infidelity
infiel[1] *adj* : unfaithful, disloyal
infiel[2] *nmf* : infidel, heathen *often offensive*
infierno *nm* 1 : hell 2 : bedlam, madness 3 : hellhole, hellish place 4 **el quinto infierno** : the middle of nowhere
infiltrado, -da *n* : infiltrator
infiltrar *vt* : to infiltrate — **infiltrarse** *vr* — **infiltración** *nf*
ínfimo, -ma *adj* 1 : minuscule, negligible 2 : lousy, very poor

infinidad *nf* 1 : infinity 2 SINFÍN : great number, huge quantity ⟨una infinidad de veces : countless times⟩
infinitesimal *adj* : infinitesimal
infinitivo *nm* : infinitive
infinito¹ *adv* : infinitely, vastly
infinito², -ta *adj* 1 : infinite 2 : limitless, endless — **infinitamente** *adv*
infinito³ *nm* : infinity
inflable *adj* : inflatable
inflación *nf, pl* **-ciones** : inflation
inflacionario, -ria *adj* : inflationary
inflacionista → **inflacionario**
inflamable *adj* : flammable
inflamación *nf, pl* **-ciones** 1 : inflammation 2 : ignition, combustion
inflamar *vt* 1 : to inflame 2 : to ignite
inflamatorio, -ria *adj* : inflammatory
inflar *vt* 1 HINCHAR : to inflate 2 EXAGERAR : to exaggerate — **inflarse** *vr* 1 : to swell 2 : to become conceited
inflexibilidad *nf* : inflexibility
inflexible *adj* : inflexible, unyielding
inflexión *nf, pl* **-xiones** : inflection
infligir {35} *vt* : to inflict
influencia *nf* 1 INFLUJO : influence 2 **influencias** *nfpl* : contacts *pl*, influence ⟨tráfico de influencias : influence peddling⟩
influenciable *adj* : easily influenced, suggestible
influenciar *vt* : to influence
influenza *nf* : influenza
influir {41} *vt* : to influence — *vi* ∼ **en** *or* ∼ **sobre** : to have an influence on, to affect
influjo *nm* INFLUENCIA : influence
influyente *adj* : influential
infografía *nf* : computer graphics *pl*
información *nf, pl* **-ciones** 1 : information ⟨centro/oficina de información : information center/office⟩ 2 : information, directory assistance 3 INFORME : report, inquiry 4 NOTICIAS : news
informado, -da *adj* : informed ⟨bien informado : well-informed⟩
informador, -dora *n* : informer, informant
informal *adj* 1 : unreliable (of persons) 2 : informal, casual 3 : informal, unofficial (in economics) — **informalmente** *adv*
informalidad *nf* : informality
informante *nmf* : informant
informar *vt* ENTERAR : to inform — *vi* : to report — **informarse** *vr* ENTERARSE : to get information, to find out
informática *nf* : computer science, computing
informático¹, -ca *adj* : computer ⟨sistema informático : computer system⟩
informático², -ca *n* : computer specialist
informativo¹, -va *adj* : informative, informational
informativo² *nm* : news program, news
informatización *nf, pl* **-ciones** : computerization
informatizar {21} *vt* : to computerize
informe¹ *adj* AMORFO : shapeless, formless

informe² *nm* 1 : report 2 : reference (for employment) 3 **informes** *nmpl* : information, data
infortunado, -da *adj* : unfortunate, unlucky
infortunio *nm* 1 DESGRACIA : misfortune 2 CONTRATIEMPO : mishap
infracción *nf, pl* **-ciones** : violation, offense, infraction
infractor, -tora *n* : offender
infraestructura *nf* : infrastructure
in fraganti *adv* : red-handed
infrahumano, -na *adj* : subhuman
infranqueable *adj* 1 : impassable 2 : insurmountable
infrarrojo, -ja *adj* : infrared
infrecuente *adj* : infrequent
infringir {35} *vt* : to infringe, to breach
infructuoso, -sa *adj* : fruitless — **infructuosamente** *adv*
ínfulas *nfpl* 1 : conceit 2 **darse ínfulas** : to put on airs
infundado, -da *adj* : unfounded, baseless
infundio *nm* : false story, lie, tall tale ⟨todo eso son infundios : that's a pack of lies⟩
infundir *vt* 1 : to instill (fear, confidence), to arouse (enthusiasm) 2 **infundir ánimo a** : to encourage
infusión *nf, pl* **-siones** : infusion, tea
ingeniar *vt* : to devise, to think up — **ingeniarse** *vr* : to manage, to find a way
ingeniería *nf* : engineering
ingeniero, -ra *n* : engineer
ingenio *nm* 1 : ingenuity 2 CHISPA : wit, wits 3 : device, apparatus 4 **ingenio azucarero** : sugar refinery
ingenioso, -sa *adj* 1 : ingenious 2 : clever, witty — **ingeniosamente** *adv*
ingente *adj* : huge, enormous
ingenuidad *nf* : naïveté, ingenuousness
ingenuo¹, -nua *adj* CÁNDIDO : naive — **ingenuamente** *adv*
ingenuo², -nua *n* : naive person
ingerencia → **injerencia**
ingerir {76} *vt* : to ingest, to consume
ingesta *nf* : consumption, ingestion
ingestión *nf, pl* **-tiones** : ingestion
ingle *nf* : groin
inglés¹, -glesa *adj, mpl* **ingleses** : English
inglés², -glesa *n, mpl* **ingleses** : Englishman *m*, Englishwoman *f*
inglés³ *nm* : English (language)
inglete *nm* : miter joint
ingobernable *adj* : ungovernable, lawless
ingratitud *nf* : ingratitude
ingrato¹, -ta *adj* 1 : ungrateful 2 : thankless, difficult
ingrato², -ta *n* : ingrate
ingrávido, -da *adj* : weightless
ingrediente *nm* : ingredient
ingresar *vt* 1 : to admit ⟨ingresaron a Luis al hospital : Luis was admitted into the hospital⟩ 2 : to deposit — *vi* 1 : to enter, to go in 2 ∼ **en** : to join, to enroll in
ingreso *nm* 1 : entrance, entry 2 : admission 3 : deposit 4 **ingresos** *nmpl* : income, earnings
íngrimo, -ma *adj* : all alone, all by oneself

inhábil *adj* : clumsy
inhabilidad *nf* **1** : lack of skill **2** : lack of suitability
inhabilitar *vt* **1** : to disqualify, to bar **2** : to disable
inhabitable *adj* : uninhabitable
inhabitado, -da → **deshabitado**
inhabituado, -da *adj* ∼ **a** : unaccustomed to
inhalador *nm* : inhaler
inhalante *nm* : inhalant
inhalar *vt* : to inhale — **inhalación** *nf*
inherente *adj* : inherent
inhibición *nf, pl* **-ciones** COHIBICIÓN : inhibition
inhibir *vt* : to inhibit — **inhibirse** *vr*
inhóspito, -ta *adj* : inhospitable
inhumación *nf, pl* **-ciones** : interment, burial
inhumanidad *nf* : inhumanity
inhumano, -na *adj* : inhuman, cruel, inhumane
inhumar *vt* : to inter, to bury
iniciación *nf, pl* **-ciones** **1** : initiation **2** : introduction
iniciado, -da *n* : initiate
iniciador¹, -dora *adj* : initiatory
iniciador², -dora *n* : originator
inicial¹ *adj* : initial, original — **inicialmente** *adv*
inicial² *nf* : initial (letter)
iniciar *vt* **1** COMENZAR : to initiate, to begin ⟨iniciar (la) sesión : to log in/on⟩ **2** : to initiate (someone) — **iniciarse** *vr*
iniciativa *nf* : initiative
inicio *nm* COMIENZO : beginning
inicuo, -cua *adj* : iniquitous, wicked
inigualable *adj* : incomparable (of a person, view, etc.), unrivaled (of popularity, etc.), unbeatable (of prices, etc.)
inigualado, -da *adj* : unequaled
inimaginable *adj* : unimaginable
inimitable *adj* : inimitable
ininteligible *adj* : unintelligible
ininterrumpido, -da *adj* : uninterrupted, continuous — **ininterrumpidamente** *adv*
iniquidad *nf* : iniquity, wickedness
injerencia *nf* : interference
injerirse {76} *vr* ENTROMETERSE, INMISCUIRSE : to meddle, to interfere
injertar *vt* : to graft
injerto *nm* : graft ⟨injerto de piel : skin graft⟩
injuria *nf* AGRAVIO : affront, insult
injuriar *vt* INSULTAR : to insult, to revile
injurioso, -sa *adj* : insulting, abusive
injusticia *nf* : injustice, unfairness
injustificable *adj* : unjustifiable
injustificadamente *adv* : unjustifiably, unfairly
injustificado, -da *adj* : unjustified, unwarranted
injusto, -ta *adj* : unfair, unjust — **injustamente** *adv*
inmaculado, -da *adj* : immaculate, spotless
inmadurez *nf, pl* **-reces** : immaturity
inmaduro, -ra *adj* **1** : immature **2** : unripe

inmediaciones *nfpl* : environs, surrounding area
inmediatamente *adv* ENSEGUIDA : immediately
inmediatez *nf, pl* **-teces** : immediacy
inmediato, -ta *adj* **1** : immediate **2** CONTIGUO : adjoining **3** de ∼ : immediately, right away **4** ∼ a : next to, close to
inmejorable *adj* : excellent, unbeatable
inmemorial *adj* : immemorial ⟨tiempos inmemoriales : time immemorial⟩
inmensidad *nf* : immensity, vastness
inmenso, -sa *adj* ENORME : immense, huge, vast — **inmensamente** *adv*
inmensurable *adj* : boundless, immeasurable
inmerecido, -da *adj* : undeserved — **inmerecidamente** *adv*
inmersión *nf, pl* **-siones** : immersion
inmerso, -sa *adj* **1** : immersed **2** : involved, absorbed
inmigración *nf, pl* **-ciones** : immigration
inmigrado, -da *adj & n* : immigrant
inmigrante *adj & nmf* : immigrant
inmigrar *vi* : to immigrate
inminencia *nf* : imminence
inminente *adj* : imminent — **inminentemente** *adv*
inmiscuirse {41} *vr* ENTROMETERSE, INJERIRSE : to meddle, to interfere
inmobiliaria *nf* **1** : real estate agency **2** : developer
inmobiliario, -ria *adj* : real estate, property
inmoderación *n, pl* **-ciones** : intemperance, lack of moderation
inmoderado, -da *adj* : immoderate, excessive — **inmoderamente** *adv*
inmodestia *nf* : immodesty — **inmodesto, -ta** *adj*
inmoral *adj* : immoral
inmoralidad *nf* : immorality
inmortal *adj & nmf* : immortal
inmortalidad *nf* : immortality
inmortalizar {21} *vt* : to immortalize
inmotivado, -da *adj* **1** : unmotivated **2** : groundless
inmovible *adj* : immovable, fixed
inmóvil *adj* **1** : still, motionless **2** : steadfast
inmovilidad *nf* : immobility
inmovilizar {21} *vt* : to immobilize — **inmovilización** *nf*
inmueble *nm* : building, property
inmundicia *nf* : dirt, filth, trash
inmundo, -da *adj* : dirty, filthy, nasty
inmune *adj* : immune
inmunidad *nf* : immunity
inmunizar {21} *vt* : to immunize — **inmunización** *nf*
inmunología *nf* : immunology
inmunológico, -ca *adj* : immune ⟨sistema inmunológico : immune system⟩
inmutable *adj* : immutable, unchangeable
inmutar *vt* : to upset — **inmutarse** *vr* : to get upset, to look upset ⟨ni se inmutó : he didn't even bat an eyelash⟩
innato, -ta *adj* : innate, inborn
innecesario, -ria *adj* : unnecessary — **innecesariamente** *adv*

innegable *adj* : undeniable

innoble *adj* : ignoble — **innoblemente** *adv*

innovación *nf, pl* **-ciones** : innovation

innovador[1], **-dora** *adj* : innovative

innovador[2], **-dora** *n* : innovator

innovar *vt* : to introduce — *vi* : to innovate

innumerable *adj* INCONTABLE : innumerable, countless

inobjetable *adj* : indisputable, unobjectionable

inocencia *nf* : innocence

inocentada *nf* : practical joke

inocente[1] *adj* 1 : innocent 2 INGENUO : naive — **inocentemente** *adv*

inocente[2] *nmf* : innocent person

inocentón[1], **-tona** *adj, mpl* **-tones -tones** : naive, gullible

inocentón[2], **-tona** *n, mpl* **-tones** : simpleton, dupe

inocuidad *nf* : harmlessness

inocular *vt* : to inoculate, to vaccinate — **inoculación** *nf*

inocuo, -cua *adj* : innocuous, harmless

inodoro[1], **-ra** *adj* : odorless

inodoro[2] *nm* : toilet

inofensivo, -va *adj* : inoffensive, harmless

inolvidable *adj* : unforgettable

inoperable *adj* : inoperable

inoperante *adj* : ineffective, inoperative

inopinado, -da *adj* : unexpected — **inopinadamente** *adv*

inoportuno, -na *adj* : untimely, inopportune, inappropriate

inorgánico, -ca *adj* : inorganic

inoxidable *adj* 1 : rustproof 2 **acero inoxidable** : stainless steel

inquebrantable *adj* : unshakable, unwavering

inquietamente *adv* 1 : anxiously, uneasily 2 : restlessly

inquietante *adj* : disturbing, worrisome

inquietar *vt* PREOCUPAR : to disturb, to upset, to worry — **inquietarse** *vr*

inquieto, -ta *adj* 1 : anxious, uneasy, worried 2 : restless

inquietud *nf* 1 : anxiety, uneasiness, worry 2 AGITACIÓN : restlessness

inquilinato *nm* : tenancy

inquilino, -na *n* : tenant, occupant

inquina *nf* 1 : aversion, dislike 2 : ill will ⟨tener inquina a alguien : to have a grudge against someone⟩

inquirir {4} *vi* : to make inquiries — *vt* : to investigate

inquisición *nf, pl* **-ciones** : investigation, inquiry

inquisidor[1], **-dora** *adj* : inquisitive

inquisidor[2] *nm* : inquisitor

inquisitivo, -va *adj* : inquisitive, curious — **inquisitivamente** *adv*

insaciable *adj* : insatiable

insalubre *adj* 1 : unhealthy 2 ANTIHIGIÉNICO : unsanitary

insalvable *adj* : insurmountable

insano, -na *adj* 1 LOCO : insane, mad 2 INSALUBRE : unhealthy

insatisfacción *nf, pl* **-ciones** : dissatisfaction

insatisfactorio *nm* : unsatisfactory

insatisfecho, -cha *adj* 1 : dissatisfied 2 : unsatisfied

inscribir {33} *vt* 1 MATRICULAR : to enroll, to register 2 GRABAR : to engrave — **inscribirse** *vr* : to register, to sign up

inscripción *nf, pl* **-ciones** 1 MATRÍCULA : enrollment, registration 2 : inscription

inscrito *pp* → **inscribir**

insecticida[1] *adj* : insecticidal

insecticida[2] *nm* : insecticide

insecto *nm* : insect

inseguridad *nf* 1 : insecurity 2 : lack of safety 3 : uncertainty

inseguro, -ra *adj* 1 : insecure 2 : unsafe 3 : uncertain — **inseguramente** *adv*

inseminar *vt* : to inseminate — **inseminación** *nf*

insensatez *nf, pl* **-teces** : foolishness, stupidity

insensato[1], **-ta** *adj* : foolish, senseless — **insensatamente** *adv*

insensato[2], **-ta** *n* : fool

insensibilidad *nf* : insensitivity

insensible *adj* : insensitive, unfeeling — **insensiblemente** *adv*

inseparable *adj* : inseparable — **inseparablemente** *adv*

inserción *nf, pl* **-ciones** : insertion

insertar *vt* : to insert

inservible *adj* INÚTIL : useless, unusable

insidia *nf* 1 : snare, trap 2 : malice

insidioso, -sa *adj* : insidious

insigne *adj* : noted, famous

insignia *nf* ENSEÑA : insignia, emblem, badge

insignificancia *nf* 1 : insignificance 2 NIMIEDAD : trifle, triviality

insignificante *adj* : insignificant

insincero, -ra *adj* : insincere — **insinceramente** *adv* — **insinceridad** *nf*

insinuación *nf, pl* **-ciones** : insinuation, hint

insinuante *adj* : suggestive

insinuar {3} *vt* : to insinuate, to hint at — **insinuarse** *vr* 1 ~ **a** : to make advances to 2 ~ **en** : to worm one's way into

insípido, -da *adj* : insipid, bland

insistencia *nf* : insistence

insistente *adj* : insistent — **insistentemente** *adv*

insistir *v* : to insist

insociable *adj* : unsociable

insolación *nf, pl* **-ciones** : sunstroke

insolencia *nf* IMPERTINENCIA : insolence

insolente *adj* IMPERTINENTE : insolent — **insolentemente** *adv*

insólito, -ta *adj* : rare, unusual

insoluble *adj* : insoluble — **insolubilidad** *nf*

insolvencia *nf* : insolvency, bankruptcy

insolvente *adj* : insolvent, bankrupt

insomne *adj & nmf* : insomniac

insomnio *nm* : insomnia

insonorizado, -da *adj* : soundproof

insoportable *adj* INAGUANTABLE : unbearable, intolerable

insoslayable *adj* : unavoidable, inescapable

insospechado, -da *adj* : unexpected, unforeseen

insostenible *adj* **1** : not sustainable (of a rate, etc.) **2** : untenable

inspección *nf, pl* **-ciones** : inspection

inspeccionar *vt* : to inspect

inspector, -tora *n* : inspector

inspiración *nf, pl* **-ciones** **1** : inspiration **2** INHALACIÓN : inhalation

inspirador, -dora *adj* : inspiring

inspirar *vt* : to inspire — *vi* INHALAR : to inhale — **inspirarse** *vr*

instalación *nf, pl* **-ciones** : installation

instalar *vt* **1** : to install (a device, etc.) **2** : to install, to induct — **instalarse** *vr* ESTABLECERSE : to settle, to establish oneself

instancia *nf* **1** : petition, request **2 en última instancia** : as a last resort

instantánea *nf* : snapshot

instantáneo, -nea *adj* **1** : instantaneous **2** : instant ⟨café instantáneo : instant coffee⟩ — **instantáneamente** *adv*

instante *nm* **1** : instant, moment **2 al instante** : immediately **3 a cada instante** : frequently, all the time **4 por instantes** : constantly, incessantly

instar *vt* APREMIAR : to urge, to press — *vi* URGIR : to be urgent or pressing ⟨insta que vayamos pronto : it is imperative that we leave soon⟩

instauración *nf, pl* **-ciones** : establishment

instaurar *vt* : to establish

instigador, -dora *n* : instigator

instigar {52} *vt* : to instigate, to incite

instintivo, -va *adj* : instinctive — **instintivamente** *adv*

instinto *nm* : instinct

institución *nf, pl* **-ciones** : institution

institucional *adj* : institutional — **institucionalmente** *adv*

institucionalizar {21} *vt* : to institutionalize

instituir {41} *vt* ESTABLECER, FUNDAR : to institute, to establish, to found

instituto *nm* : institute

institutriz *nf, pl* **-trices** : governess *f*

instrucción *nf, pl* **-ciones** **1** EDUCACIÓN : education, training **2 instrucciones** *nfpl* : instructions, directions

instructivo, -va *adj* : instructive, educational

instructor, -tora *n* : instructor

instruir {41} *vt* **1** ADIESTRAR : to instruct, to train **2** ENSEÑAR : to educate, to teach

instrumentación *nf, pl* **-ciones** : orchestration

instrumental¹ *adj* : instrumental

instrumental² *nm* : instruments *pl*

instrumentar *vt* : to orchestrate

instrumentista *nmf* : instrumentalist

instrumento *nm* **1** : (musical) instrument **2** : instrument (tool or device) **3** : instrument, means *pl*

insubordinado, -da *adj* : insubordinate — **insubordinación** *nf*

insubordinarse *vr* : to rebel

insuficiencia *nf* **1** : insufficiency, inadequacy **2 insuficiencia cardíaca** : heart failure

insuficiente¹ *adj* **1** : insufficient, inadequate **2** : poor, unsatisfactory — **insuficientemente** *adv*

insuficiente² *nm* : F, failing grade

insufrible *adj* : insufferable

insular *adj* : insular

insularidad *nf* : insularity

insulina *nf* : insulin

insulso, -sa *adj* **1** INSÍPIDO : insipid, bland **2** : dull

insultante *adj* : insulting

insultar *vt* : to insult

insulto *nm* : insult

insumos *nmpl* : supplies ⟨insumos agrícolas : agricultural supplies⟩

insuperable *adj* **1** : insurmountable **2** : unbeatable

insurgente *adj & nmf* : insurgent — **insurgencia** *nf*

insurrección *nf, pl* **-ciones** : insurrection, uprising

insustancial *adj* : insubstantial, flimsy

insustituible *adj* : irreplaceable

intachable *adj* : irreproachable, faultless

intacto, -ta *adj* : intact

intangible *adj* IMPALPABLE : intangible, impalpable

integración *nf, pl* **-ciones** : integration

integral *adj* **1** : integral, essential **2 pan integral** : whole grain bread

integrante¹ *adj* : integrating, integral

integrante² *nmf* : member

integrar *vt* : to make up, to compose — **integrarse** *vr* : to integrate, to fit in

integridad *nf* **1** RECTITUD : integrity, honesty **2** : integrity, soundness ⟨integridad física : personal safety⟩

integrismo *nm* : fundamentalism

integrista *adj & nmf* : fundamentalist

íntegro, -gra *adj* **1** : honest, upright **2** ENTERO : whole, complete **3** : unabridged

intelecto *nm* : intellect

intelectual *adj & nmf* : intellectual — **intelectualmente** *adv*

intelectualidad *nf* : intelligentsia

inteligencia *nf* : intelligence

inteligente *adj* : intelligent — **inteligentemente** *adv*

inteligible *adj* : intelligible — **inteligibilidad** *nf*

intemperancia *adj* : intemperance, excess

intemperie *nf* **1** : bad weather, elements *pl* **2 a la intemperie** : in the open air, outside

intempestivo, -va *adj* : inopportune, untimely — **intempestivamente** *adv*

intención *nf, pl* **-ciones** **1** : intention, plan ⟨tenías buenas intenciones : you had good intentions, your intentions were good⟩ ⟨tener la intención de hacer algo : to intend to do something⟩ ⟨con/sin intención : intentionally/unintentionally⟩ ⟨con la mejor intención : with the best (of) intentions⟩ **2 segunda intención** : ulterior motive

intencionadamente → **intencionalmente**

intencionado, -da → **intencional**
intencional *adj* : intentional
intencionalmente *adv* : intentionally
intendencia *nf* **1** : management, administration **2** *Arg, Par, Uru* : city council, town council **3** *Chile* : governorship
intendente *nmf* **1** : quartermaster **2** *Arg, Par, Uru* : mayor **3** *Chile* : governor
intensidad *nf* : intensity
intensificación *nf, pl* **-ciones** : intensification
intensificador *nm* : intensifier (in linguistics)
intensificar {72} *vt* : to intensify — **intensificarse** *vr*
intensivo, -va *adj* : intensive — **intensivamente** *adv*
intenso, -sa *adj* : intense — **intensamente** *adv*
intentar *vt* : to attempt, to try
intento *nm* **1** PROPÓSITO : intent, intention **2** TENTATIVA : attempt, try
intentona *nf* : attempt ⟨intentona golpista : attempted coup⟩
inter- *pref* : inter-
interacción *nf, pl* **-ciones** : interaction
interactivo, -va *adj* : interactive
interactuar {3} *vi* : to interact
intercalar *vt* : to intersperse, to insert
intercambiable *adj* : interchangeable
intercambiar *vt* CANJEAR : to exchange, to trade
intercambio *nm* CANJE : exchange, trade
interceder *vi* : to intercede
intercepción → **interceptación**
interceptación *nf, pl* **-ciones** : interception
interceptar *vt* **1** : to intercept, to block **2 interceptar las líneas** : to wiretap
intercesión *nf, pl* **-siones** : intercession
interconectar *vt* : to connect, to interconnect
interconfesional *adj* : interdenominational
intercontinental *adj* : intercontinental
interdepartamental *adj* : interdepartmental
interdependencia *nf* : interdependence — **interdependiente** *adj*
interdicción *nf, pl* **-ciones** : prohibition
interdisciplinario, -ria *adj* : interdisciplinary
interés *nm, pl* **-reses 1** : interest ⟨su interés por la ciencia : her interest in science⟩ ⟨tiene interés en aprender español : he is interested in learning Spanish⟩ ⟨perder interés : to lose interest⟩ **2** BENEFICIO : interest ⟨por su propio interés : for one's own benefit⟩ ⟨por puro interés : purely out of self-interest⟩ ⟨el interés público : the public interest⟩ ⟨conflicto de intereses : conflict of interest⟩ **3** : interest, interest rate **4 intereses** *nmpl* : interest, stake ⟨tener intereses en : to have an interest in⟩
interesado¹, -da *adj* **1** : interested **2** : selfish, self-seeking
interesado², -da *n* **1** : interested party ⟨los interesados deberán rellenar una solicitud : anyone who is interested should

fill out an application⟩ **2** : self-centered person
interesante *adj* : interesting
interesar *vt* : to interest — *vi* : to be of interest, to be interesting — **interesarse** *vr*
interestatal *adj* : interstate ⟨autopista interestatal : interstate highway⟩
interestelar *adj* : interstellar
interfase → **interfaz**
interfaz *nf, pl* **-faces** : interface
interferencia *nf* : interference, static
interferir {76} *vi* : to interfere, to meddle — *vt* : to interfere with, to obstruct
interfón *nm, pl* **-fones** *Mex* : intercom
interfono *nm* *Spain* : intercom
intergaláctico, -ca *adj* : intergalactic
intergubernamental *adj* : intergovernmental
interín¹ *or* **ínterin** *adv* : meanwhile
interín² *or* **ínterin** *nm, pl* **-rines** : meantime, interim ⟨en el interín : in the meantime⟩
interinamente *adv* : temporarily
interinato *nm* : temporary position
interino¹, -na *adj* : acting, temporary, interim
interino², -na *n* : substitute, temp
interior¹ *adj* **1** : interior, inside, inner ⟨parte interior : inside⟩ ⟨bolsillo interior : inside pocket⟩ ⟨patio interior : inner courtyard⟩ **2** : inner ⟨voz interior : inner voice⟩ **3** : domestic, internal
interior² *nm* **1** : interior, inside **2** : inland region
interiormente *adv* : inwardly
interjección *nf, pl* **-ciones** : interjection
interlocutor, -tora *n* : speaker
interludio *nm* : interlude
intermediario, -ria *adj & n* : intermediary, go-between
intermedio¹, -dia *adj* : intermediate
intermedio² *nm* **1** : intermission **2 por intermedio de** : by means of
interminable *adj* : interminable, endless — **interminablemente** *adv*
intermisión *nf, pl* **-siones** : intermission, pause
intermitente¹ *adj* **1** : intermittent **2** : flashing, blinking (of a light) — **intermitentemente** *adv*
intermitente² *nm* : blinker, turn signal
internacional *adj* : international — **internacionalmente** *adv*
internacionalizar {21} *vt* : to internationalize — **internacionalización** *nf*
internado *nm* : boarding school
internamiento *nm* **1** : internment, confinement **2** : admission
internar *vt* : to admit (to a hospital, etc.), to commit (to an institution) — **internarse** *vr* **1** : to penetrate, to advance into **2 ~ en** : to go into, to enter **3 ~ en** : to be admitted to
internauta *nmf* : Internet user
Internet *or* **internet** *nmf* : Internet
internista *nmf* : internist
interno¹, -na *adj* : internal ⟨la política interna : domestic policy⟩ — **internamente** *adv*

interno², **-na** n 1 : intern 2 : inmate
interpelación nf, pl **-ciones** : appeal, plea
interpelar vt : to question (formally)
interpersonal adj : interpersonal
interpolar vt : to insert, to interpolate
interponer {60} vt : to interpose — **interponerse** vr : to intervene
interpretación nf, pl **-ciones** : interpretation
interpretar vt 1 : to interpret 2 : to play, to perform
interpretativo, **-va** adj : interpretive
intérprete nmf 1 TRADUCTOR : interpreter 2 : performer
interpuesto pp → **interponer**
interracial adj : interracial
interrelación nf, pl **-ciones** : interrelationship
interrelacionar vi : to interrelate
interrogación nf, pl **-ciones** 1 : interrogation, questioning 2 or **signo de interrogación** : question mark
interrogador, **-dora** n : interrogator, questioner
interrogante¹ adj : questioning
interrogante² nm : question mark
interrogante³ nmf : question
interrogar {52} vt : to interrogate, to question
interrogativo, **-va** adj : interrogative
interrogatorio nm : interrogation, questioning
interrumpir v : to interrupt
interrupción nf, pl **-ciones** : interruption
interruptor nm 1 : (electrical) switch 2 : circuit breaker
intersecarse {72} vr Spain → **intersectarse**
intersección nf, pl **-ciones** : intersection
intersectarse vr : to intersect
intersticio nm : interstice — **intersticial** adj
interuniversitario, **-ria** adj : intercollegiate
interurbano, **-na** adj 1 : intercity 2 : long-distance ⟨llamadas interurbanas : long-distance calls⟩
intervalo nm : interval
intervención nf, pl **-ciones** 1 : intervention 2 : audit 3 : intercepting (of mail, etc.), tapping (of phones) 4 **intervención quirúrgica** : operation
intervenir {87} vi 1 : to take part 2 INTERCEDER : to intervene, to intercede — vt 1 : to control, to supervise 2 : to audit 3 : to operate on 4 : to tap, to wire-tap (a phone)
interventor, **-tora** n 1 : inspector 2 : auditor, comptroller
intestado, **-da** adj : intestate
intestinal adj : intestinal
intestino¹, **-na** adj : internal, internecine
intestino² nm : intestine
intimar vi ∼ **con** : to become friendly with — vt : to require, to call on
intimidación nf, pl **-ciones** : intimidation
intimidad nf 1 : intimacy 2 : privacy, private life
intimidante adj : intimidating
intimidar vt ACOBARDAR : to intimidate

intimidatorio, **-ria** adj : intimidating
íntimo, **-ma** adj 1 : intimate, close 2 PRIVADO : private — **íntimamente** adv
intitular : to entitle, to title
intocable adj : untouchable
intolerable adj : intolerable, unbearable
intolerancia nf : intolerance
intolerante¹ adj : intolerant
intolerante² nmf : intolerant person, bigot
intoxicación nf, pl **-ciones** : poisoning
intoxicante nm : poison
intoxicar {72} vt : to poison
intranquilidad nf PREOCUPACIÓN : worry, anxiety
intranquilizar {21} vt : to upset, to make uneasy — **intranquilizarse** vr : to get worried, to be anxious
intranquilo, **-la** adj PREOCUPADO : uneasy, worried
intransferible adj : nontransferable
intransigencia nf : intransigence
intransigente adj : intransigent, unyielding
intransitable adj : impassable
intransitivo, **-va** adj : intransitive
intrascendente adj : unimportant, insignificant
intratable adj 1 : intractable 2 : awkward 3 : unsociable
intravenoso, **-sa** adj : intravenous
intrepidez nf : fearlessness
intrépido, **-da** adj : intrepid, fearless
intriga nf : intrigue
intrigante nmf : schemer
intrigar {52} v : to intrigue — **intrigante** adj
intrincado, **-da** adj : intricate, involved
intrínseco, **-ca** adj : intrinsic — **intrínsecamente** adv
introducción nf, pl **-ciones** : introduction
introducir {61} vt 1 : to introduce 2 : to bring in 3 : to insert 4 : to input, to enter — **introducirse** vr : to penetrate, to get into
introductorio, **-ria** adj : introductory
intromisión nf, pl **-siones** : interference, meddling
introspección nf, pl **-ciones** : introspection
introspectivo, **-va** adj : introspective
introvertido¹, **-da** adj : introverted
introvertido², **-da** n : introvert
intrusión nf, pl **-siones** : intrusion
intruso¹, **-sa** adj : intrusive
intruso², **-sa** n : intruder
intuición nf, pl **-ciones** : intuition
intuir {41} vt : to intuit, to sense
intuitivo, **-va** adj : intuitive — **intuitivamente** adv
inundación nf, pl **-ciones** : flood, inundation
inundar vt : to flood, to inundate — **inundarse** vr
inusitado, **-da** adj : unusual, uncommon — **inusitadamente** adv
inusual adj : unusual, uncommon — **inusualmente** adv
inútil¹ adj INSERVIBLE : useless — **inútilmente** adv
inútil² nmf : good-for-nothing

inutilidad *nf* : uselessness
inutilizar {21} *vt* **1** : to make useless **2** INCAPACITAR : to disable, to put out of commission
invadir *vt* : to invade
invalidar *vt* : to nullify, to invalidate
invalidez *nf, pl* **-deces 1** : invalidity **2** : disability
inválido, -da *adj & n* : invalid
invalorable *adj* : invaluable
invaluable *adj* : invaluable
invariable *adj* : invariable — **invariablemente** *adv*
invasión *nf, pl* **-siones 1** : invasion **2** *or* **barrio de invasión** *Col* : shantytown, slums *pl*
invasivo, -va *adj* : invasive
invasor¹, -sora *adj* : invading
invasor², -sora *n* : invader
invectiva *nf* : invective, abuse
invencibilidad *nf* : invincibility
invencible *adj* **1** : invincible **2** : insurmountable
invención *nf, pl* **-ciones 1** INVENTO : invention **2** MENTIRA : fabrication, lie
inventar *vt* **1** : to invent **2** : to fabricate, to make up — **inventarse** *vr* : to fabricate, to make up
inventariar {85} *vt* : to inventory
inventario *nm* : inventory
inventiva *nf* : ingenuity, inventiveness
inventivo, -va *adj* : inventive
invento *nm* INVENCIÓN : invention
inventor, -tora *n* : inventor
invernadero *nm* : greenhouse, hothouse
invernal *adj* : winter, wintry
invernar {55} *vi* **1** : to spend the winter **2** HIBERNAR : to hibernate
inverosímil *adj* : unlikely, far-fetched
inverosimilitud *nf* : implausibility, improbability
inversión *nf, pl* **-siones 1** : inversion **2** : investment
inversionista *nmf* : investor
inverso¹, -sa *adj* **1** : inverse, inverted **2** CONTRARIO : opposite **3 a la inversa** : the other way around, vice versa **4 en orden inverso** : in reverse order — **inversamente** *adv*
inverso² *n* : inverse
inversor, -sora *n* : investor
invertebrado¹, -da *adj* : invertebrate
invertebrado² *nm* : invertebrate
invertir {76} *vt* **1** : to invert, to reverse **2** : to invest — *vi* : to make an investment — **invertirse** *vr* : to be reversed
investidura *nf* : investiture, inauguration
investigación *nf, pl* **-ciones 1** ENCUESTA, INDAGACIÓN : investigation, inquiry **2** : research ⟨investigación y desarrollo : research and development⟩
investigador¹, -dora *adj* : investigative
investigador², -dora *n* **1** : investigator ⟨investigador privado, investigadora privada : private investigator⟩ **2** : researcher
investigar {52} *vt* **1** INDAGAR : to investigate **2** : to research — *vi* ~ **sobre** : to do research into
investigativo, -va *adj* : investigative

investir {54} *vt* **1** : to empower **2** : to swear in, to inaugurate
inveterado, -da *adj* : inveterate, deep-seated
inviable *adj* : not viable, not feasible
invicto, -ta *adj* : undefeated
invidente¹ *adj* CIEGO : blind, sightless
invidente² *nmf* CIEGO : blind person
invierno *nm* : winter, wintertime
inviolable *adj* : inviolable — **inviolabilidad** *nf*
inviolado, -da *adj* : inviolate, pure
invisibilidad *nf* : invisibility
invisible *adj* : invisible — **invisiblemente** *adv*
invitación *nf, pl* **-ciones** : invitation
invitado, -da *n* : guest
invitar *vt* : to invite — *vi* : to pay for ⟨invita la casa : it's on the house⟩ ⟨invito yo : it's on me, it's my treat⟩
invocación *nf, pl* **-ciones** : invocation
invocar {72} *vt* : to invoke, to call on
involucramiento *nm* : involvement
involucrar *vt* : to implicate, to involve — **involucrarse** *vr* : to get involved
involuntario, -ria *adj* : involuntary — **involuntariamente** *adv*
invulnerable *adj* : invulnerable
inyección *nf, pl* **-ciones** : injection, shot
inyectado, -da *adj* **ojos inyectados** : bloodshot eyes
inyectar *vt* : to inject — **inyectarse** *vr*
ion *nm* : ion
iónico, -ca *adj* : ionic
ionizar {21} *vt* : to ionize — **ionización** *nf*
ionosfera *nf* : ionosphere
ir {43} *vi* **1** : to go ⟨ir a pie : to go on foot, to walk⟩ ⟨ir a caballo : to ride horseback⟩ ⟨ir a casa : to go home⟩ ⟨ir por mar : to go by sea⟩ ⟨iba para el aeropuerto : he was headed for the airport⟩ ⟨fui a ver una película : I went to see a movie⟩ ⟨el ir y venir de la gente : the comings and goings (of the people)⟩ ⟨vamos : let's go⟩ ⟨¡voy! : I'm coming!⟩ **2** : to lead, to extend, to stretch ⟨el camino va de Cali a Bogotá : the road goes from Cali to Bogotá⟩ **3** FUNCIONAR : to work, to function ⟨esta computadora ya no va : this computer doesn't work anymore⟩ **4** : to get on, to get along ⟨¿cómo te va? : how are you?, how's it going?⟩ ⟨el negocio no va bien : the business isn't doing well⟩ ⟨ir a mejor/peor : to get better/worse⟩ ⟨ir de mal en peor : to go from bad to worse⟩ **5** : to suit ⟨ese vestido te va bien : that dress really suits you⟩ ⟨el cambio te irá bien : the change will do you good⟩ **6** ~ **a** ASISTIR : to go to, to attend **7** ~ **con/en/de** : to wear ⟨voy a ir con/en falda : I'm going to wear a skirt⟩ ⟨iba de azul : she was wearing blue⟩ **8** ~ **con** (*with a noun*) : to be ⟨ir con prisa : to be in a hurry⟩ ⟨ir con cuidado : to be cautious⟩ **9** ~ **con** : to go with, to complement **10** ~ **para** : to be studying to be ⟨va para médico : she's studying to be a doctor⟩ **11** ~ **para** : to be going on, to be close to (an age) **12** ~ **por** : to be aimed at ⟨también va por

ti : that goes for you, too⟩ **13** ~ **por** : to follow, to go along ⟨fueron por la costa : they followed the shoreline⟩ **14** ~ **por** : to be up to (a point or stage) ⟨voy por la última página : I'm on the last page⟩ **15** ~ **por** : to go (and) get, to fetch **16 dejarse ir** : to let oneself go **17 ir a parar** : to end up **18** ¡qué val *fam* : hardly! **19** ¡vamos! : come on! **20 vamos a ver** : let's see — *v aux* **1** (*indicating manner*) ⟨ir caminando : to walk, to go on foot⟩ ⟨¡voy corriendo! : I'll be right there!⟩ **2** (*indicating a process*) ⟨va mejorando : he's getting better⟩ ⟨lo iremos haciendo poco a poco : we'll do it little by little⟩ **3** ~ **a** : to be going to ⟨voy a hacerlo : I'm going to do it⟩ ⟨el avión va a despegar : the plane is about to take off⟩ — **irse** *vr* **1** : to leave, to go ⟨¡vámonos! : let's go!⟩ ⟨todo el mundo se fue : everyone left⟩ **2 ESCAPARSE** : to leak **3 GASTARSE** : to be used up, to be gone

ira *nf* **CÓLERA, FURIA** : wrath, anger
iracundo, -da *adj* **1** : irate, angry ⟨estar iracundo : to be angry⟩ **2** : irascible ⟨ser iracundo : to be irascible⟩
iraní *adj & nmf* : Iranian
iraquí *adj & nmf* : Iraqi
irascible *adj* : irascible, irritable — **irascibilidad** *nf*
irga, irgue *etc.* → **erguir**
iridio *nm* : iridium
iridiscencia *nf* : iridescence — **iridiscente** *adj*
iris *nms & pl* **1** : iris **2 arco iris** : rainbow
irlandés¹, -desa *adj, mpl* **-deses -deses** : Irish
irlandés², -desa *n, pl* **-deses** : Irish person, Irishman *m*, Irishwoman *f*
irlandés³ *nm* : Irish (language)
ironía *nf* : irony
irónico, -ca *adj* : ironic, ironical — **irónicamente** *adv*
ironizar {21} *vi* : to speak ironically — *vt* : to say ironically
irracional *adj* : irrational — **irracionalmente** *adv*
irracionalidad *nf* : irrationality
irradiación *nf, pl* **-ciones** : irradiation
irradiar *vt* : to radiate, to irradiate
irrazonable *adj* : unreasonable
irreal *adj* : unreal
irrebatible *adj* : unanswerable, irrefutable
irreconciliable *adj* : irreconcilable
irreconocible *adj* : unrecognizable
irrecuperable *adj* : irrecoverable, irretrievable
irredimible *adj* : irredeemable
irreductible *adj* : unyielding
irreemplazable *adj* : irreplaceable
irreflexión *nf, pl* **-xiones** : thoughtlessness
irreflexivo, -va *adj* : rash, unthinking — **irreflexivamente** *adv*
irrefrenable *adj* : uncontrollable, unstoppable ⟨un impulso irrefrenable : an irresistible urge⟩
irrefutable *adj* : irrefutable

irregular *adj* : irregular — **irregularmente** *adv*
irregularidad *nf* : irregularity
irrelevante *adj* : irrelevant — **irrelevancia** *nf*
irreligioso, -sa *adj* : irreligious
irremediable *adj* : incurable — **irremediablemente** *adv*
irreparable *adj* : irreparable
irrepetible *adj* : unrepeatable, unique
irreprimible *adj* : irrepressible
irreprochable *adj* : irreproachable
irresistible *adj* : irresistible — **irresistiblemente** *adv*
irresolución *nf, pl* **-ciones** : indecision, hesitation
irresoluto, -ta *adj* **INDECISO** : undecided
irrespetar *vt* **CA, Carib** : to disrespect, to be disrespectful to
irrespeto *nm* : disrespect
irrespetuoso, -sa *adj* : disrespectful — **irrespetuosamente** *adv*
irrespirable *adj* : unbreathable
irresponsabilidad *nf* : irresponsibility
irresponsable *adj* : irresponsible — **irresponsablemente** *adv*
irrestricto, -ta *adj* : unrestricted, unconditional
irreverencia *nf* : disrespect
irreverente *adj* : irreverent, disrespectful
irreversible *adj* : irreversible
irrevocable *adj* : irrevocable — **irrevocablemente** *adv*
irrigar {52} *vt* : to irrigate — **irrigación** *nf*
irrisible *adj* : laughable
irrisión *nf, pl* **-siones** : derision, ridicule
irrisorio, -ria *adj* **RISIBLE** : ridiculous, ludicrous
irritabilidad *nf* : irritability
irritable *adj* : irritable
irritación *nf, pl* **-ciones** : irritation
irritante *adj* : irritating
irritar *vt* : to irritate
irrompible *adj* : unbreakable
irrumpir *vi* ~ **en** : to burst into
irrupción *nf, pl* **-ciones** **1** : emergence **2** : invasion
-ísimo, -ma *suf* : very, extremely
isla *nf* : island
Islam *nm* : Islam
islámico, -ca *adj* : Islamic, Muslim
islamismo *nm* **1** : Islam **2** : Islamism — **islamista** *adj & nmf*
islandés¹, -desa *adj, mpl* **-deses** : Icelandic
islandés², -desa *n, pl* **-deses** : Icelander
islandés³ *nm* : Icelandic (language)
isleño¹, -ña *adj* : island
isleño², -ña *n* : islander
islote *nm* : islet
isometría *nfs & pl* : isometrics
isométrico, -ca *adj* : isometric
isósceles *adj* : isosceles ⟨triángulo isósceles : isosceles triangle⟩
isótopo *nm* : isotope
israelí *adj & nmf* : Israeli
istmo *nm* : isthmus
itacate *nm* **Mex** : pack, provisions *pl*
italiano¹, -na *adj & n* : Italian
italiano² *nm* : Italian (language)

ítem *nm* : item

itinerante *adj* AMBULANTE : traveling, itinerant

itinerario *nm* : itinerary, route

-ito *or* **-cito** *suf* **1** : little ⟨un pedacito : a little piece⟩ ⟨su hermanita : his little/baby sister⟩ ⟨sólo un ratito : just a little while⟩ **2** (*used to show affection*) ⟨mi abuelito : my grandpa⟩ ⟨¡pobrecita! : poor thing!⟩ ⟨dame un besito : give me a kiss⟩ ⟨¿quieres un cafecito? : do you want a nice cup of coffee?⟩ **3** (*used for emphasis*) ⟨bien calentito : nice and hot⟩ ⟨al verlo se quedó calladita : when she saw him she went quiet⟩

izar {21} *vt* : to hoist, to raise ⟨izar la bandera : to raise the flag⟩

izquierda *nf* : left

izquierdista *adj & nmf* : leftist

izquierdo, -da *adj* : left

J

j *nf* : tenth letter of the Spanish alphabet

ja *interj* **1** : ha! **2 ja, ja** : ha-ha!

jaba *nf* **1** *Car* : bag, sack **2** *Mex, CA* : crate, box

jabalí *nm, pl* **-líes** : wild boar

jabalina *nf* : javelin

jabón *nm, pl* **jabones** : soap

jabonar *vt* ENJABONAR : to soap up, to lather — **jabonarse** *vr*

jabonera *nf* : soap dish

jabonoso, -sa *adj* : soapy

jaca *nf* **1** : pony **2** YEGUA : mare

jacal *nm Mex* : shack, hut

jacinto *nm* : hyacinth

jactancia *nf* **1** : boastfulness **2** : boasting, bragging

jactancioso[1], -sa *adj* : boastful

jactancioso[2], -sa *n* : boaster, braggart

jactarse *vr* : to boast, to brag ⟨jactarse de algo : to brag about something⟩

Jacuzzi [ja'kuzi, -'kusi] *marca registrada, m* — used for a whirlpool bath

jade *nm* : jade

jadear *vi* : to pant, to gasp, to puff — **jadeante** *adj*

jadeo *nm* : panting, gasping, puffing

jaez *nm, pl* **jaeces 1** : harness **2** : kind, sort, ilk **3 jaeces** *nmpl* : trappings

jaguar *nm* : jaguar

jai alai *nm* : jai alai

jaiba *nf* CANGREJO : crab

jalapeño *nm Mex* : jalapeño pepper

jalar *vt* **1** : to pull, to tug **2** *fam* : to attract, to draw in ⟨las ideas nuevas lo jalan : new ideas appeal to him⟩ — *vi* **1** : to pull, to pull together ⟨jalar de algo : to pull on something⟩ **2** *fam* : to hurry up, to get going **3** *Mex fam* : to be in working order ⟨esta máquina no jala : this machine doesn't work⟩

jalbegue *nm* : whitewash

jalea *nf* : jelly

jalear *vt* : to encourage, to urge on

jaleo *nm* **1** *fam* : uproar, ruckus, racket **2** *fam* : confusion, mess, hassle **3** : cheering and clapping (for a dance)

jalón *nm, pl* **jalones 1** : milestone, landmark **2** TIRÓN : pull, tug

jalonar *vt* : to mark, to stake out

jalonear *vt Mex, Peru fam* : to tug at — *vi* **1** *fam* : to pull, to tug **2** *CA fam* : to haggle

jamaicano, -na → **jamaiquino**

jamaiquino, -na *adj & n* : Jamaican

jamás *adv* **1** NUNCA : never ⟨jamás vi tal cosa : I've never seen such a thing⟩ ⟨no lo olvidaré jamás : I'll never forget it⟩ **2 nunca jamás** *or* **jamás de los jamases** : never ever **3 para siempre jamás** : for ever and ever

jamba *nf* : jamb

jamelgo *nm* : nag (horse)

jamón *nm, pl* **jamones 1** : ham **2 jamón serrano** : cured Spanish ham

Janucá *or* **Januká** *nmf* : Hanukkah

japonés[1], -nesa *adj & n, mpl* **-neses** : Japanese ⟨los japoneses : the Japanese (people)⟩

japonés[2] *nm, pl* **-neses** : Japanese (language)

jaque *nm* **1** : check (in chess) ⟨jaque mate : checkmate⟩ ⟨dar jaque mate a : to checkmate⟩ **2 tener en jaque** : to intimidate, to bully

jaquear *vi* : to check (in chess)

jaqueca *nf* : headache, migraine

jarabe *nm* **1** : syrup ⟨jarabe para la tos : cough syrup⟩ **2** : Mexican folk dance

jarana *nf* **1** *fam* : revelry, partying, spree **2** *fam* : joking, fooling around **3** : small guitar

jaranear *vi fam* : to go on a spree, to party

jarcia *nf* **1** : rigging **2** : fishing tackle

jardín *nm, pl* **jardines 1** : garden **2** : yard (of a house) **3 jardín de niños** *CA, Mex or* **jardín infantil** *Chile or* **jardín de infancia** *Spain* : kindergarten **4 jardín izquierdo/central/derecho** : left/center/right field **5 los jardines** : the outfield

jardinera *nf* **1** : planter **2** : plant stand

jardinería *nf* : gardening

jardinero, -ra *n* **1** : gardener **2** : outfielder (in baseball)

jarra *nf* **1** : pitcher, jug **2** : stein, mug **3 de jarras** *or* **en jarras** : akimbo

jarrete *nm* **1** : back of the knee **2** CORVEJÓN : hock

jarro *nm* **1** : pitcher, jug **2** : mug

jarrón *nm, pl* **jarrones** FLORERO : vase

jaspe *nm* : jasper

jaspeado, -da *adj* **1** VETEADO : streaked, veined **2** : speckled, mottled

jaula *nf* : cage

jauría *nf* : pack of hounds

javanés, -nesa *adj & n* : Javanese

jazmín *nm, pl* **jazmines** : jasmine

jazz [ˈjas, ˈdʒas] *nm* : jazz

je *interj* → **ja**

jeans [ˈjins, ˈdʒins] *nmpl* : jeans

jeep [ˈjip, ˈdʒip] *nm, pl* **jeeps** : jeep (military vehicle)

Jeep *marca registrada, m* — used for a small truck

jefatura *nf* **1** : leadership **2** : headquarters ⟨jefatura de policía : police headquarters⟩

jefe, -fa *n* **1** : chief, head, leader ⟨jefe de bomberos/policía : fire/police chief⟩ ⟨jefe del departamento : department head⟩ ⟨jefe de oficina : office manager⟩ ⟨jefe de Estado/gobierno : head of state/government⟩ ⟨jefe de redacción : editor in chief⟩ **2** : boss

Jehová *nm* : Jehovah

jején *nm, pl* **jejenes** : gnat, small mosquito

jengibre *nm* : ginger

jeque *nm* : sheikh, sheik

jerarca *nmf* : leader, chief

jerarquía *nf* **1** : hierarchy **2** RANGO : rank

jerárquico, -ca *adj* : hierarchical

jerbo *nm* : gerbil

jerez *nm, pl* **jereces** : sherry

jerga *nf* **1** : jargon, slang **2** : coarse cloth

jerigonza *nf* GALIMATÍAS : mumbo jumbo, gibberish

jeringa *nf* : syringe

jeringar {52} *vt* **1** : to inject **2** *fam* JOROBAR : to annoy, to pester — *vi fam* JOROBAR : to be annoying, to be a nuisance

jeringuear → **jeringar**

jeringuilla → **jeringa**

jeroglífico *nm* : hieroglyphic

jersey *nm, pl* **jerseys** **1** : jersey (fabric) **2** *Spain* : sweater

Jesucristo *nm* : Jesus Christ

jesuita *adj & nm* : Jesuit

Jesús *nm* **1** : Jesus **2** ¡Jesús! : goodness!, good heavens! **3** ¡Jesús! : bless you! (said to someone who has sneezed)

jet *nm* : jet (airplane)

jeta *nf* **1** : snout **2** *fam* : face, mug

jíbaro, -ra *adj* **1** : Jívaro **2** : rustic, rural

jibia *nf* : cuttlefish

jícama *nf* : jicama

jícara *nf Mex* : calabash

jicotea *nf CA, Car, Mex* : turtle

jihad *nmf* → **yihad**

jilguero *nm* : European goldfinch

jinete *nmf* : horseman, horsewoman *f*, rider

jinetear *vt* **1** : to ride, to perform (on horseback) **2** DOMAR : to break in (a horse) — *vi* CABALGAR : to ride horseback

jingoísmo [ˌjiŋɡoˈizmo, ˌdʒiŋ-] *nm* : jingoism

jingoísta *adj* : jingoist, jingoistic

jiote *nm Mex* : rash

jira *nf* : outing, picnic

jirafa *nf* **1** : giraffe **2** : boom microphone

jirón *nm, pl* **jirones** **1** : shred, rag ⟨hecho jirones : in tatters⟩ **2** *Peru* : street

jitomate *nm Mex* : tomato

jockey [ˈjɔki, ˈdʒɔ-] *nmf, pl* **jockeys** [-kis] : jockey

jocosidad *nf* : humor, jocularity

jocoso, -sa *adj* : playful, jocular — **jocosamente** *adv*

jofaina *nf* : washbowl

jogging [ˈjɔɡin, ˈdʒɔ-] *nm* **1** : jogging **2** *Arg* : sweatpants **3** *Arg* : sweatsuit, tracksuit

jolgorio *nm* : merrymaking, fun

jonrón *nm, pl* **jonrones** : home run

jordano, -na *adj & n* : Jordanian

jornada *nf* **1** : expedition, day's journey **2** jornada laboral *or* jornada de trabajo : workday **3** jornadas *nfpl* : conference, congress

jornal *nm* **1** : day's pay **2 a ~** : by the day

jornalero, -ra *n* : day laborer

joroba *nf* **1** GIBA : hump **2** *fam* : nuisance, pain in the neck

jorobado¹, -da *adj* GIBOSO : hunchbacked, humpbacked

jorobado², -da *n* GIBOSO : person with a hump, hunchback *offensive*, humpback *offensive*

jorobar *vt fam* JERINGAR : to bother, to annoy — *vi fam* JERINGAR : to be annoying, to be a nuisance

jorongo *nm Mex* : full-length poncho

jota *nf* **1** : jot, bit ⟨no entiendo ni jota : I don't understand a word of it⟩ ⟨no se ve ni jota : you can't see a thing⟩ **2** : jack (in playing cards) **3** : (letter) j

joven¹ *adj, pl* **jóvenes** **1** : young **2** : youthful

joven² *nmf, pl* **jóvenes** : young man *m*, young woman *f*, young person

jovial *adj* : jovial, cheerful — **jovialmente** *adv*

jovialidad *nf* : joviality, cheerfulness

joya *nf* **1** : jewel, piece of jewelry **2** : treasure, gem ⟨la nueva empleada es una joya : the new employee is a real gem⟩

joyería *nf* **1** : jewelry store **2** : jewelry **3** joyería de fantasía : costume jewelry

joyero, -ra *n* **1** : jeweler **2** : jewelry box

joystick [ˈjoistik] *nm, pl* **joysticks** : joystick

juanete *nm* : bunion

jubilación *nf, pl* **-ciones** **1** : retirement ⟨jubilación anticipada : early retirement⟩ **2** PENSIÓN : pension

jubilado¹, -da *adj* : retired, in retirement

jubilado², -da *nmf* : retired person, retiree

jubilar *vt* **1** : to retire, to pension off **2** *fam* : to get rid of, to discard — **jubilarse** *vr* : to retire

jubileo *nm* : jubilee

júbilo *nm* : jubilation, joy

jubiloso, -sa *adj* : jubilant, joyous

judaico, -ca *adj* : Judaic, Jewish

judaísmo *nm* : Judaism

judía *nf* **1** : bean **2** *or* judía verde : green bean, string bean

judicatura *nf* **1** : judiciary, judges *pl* **2** : office of judge

judicial *adj* : judicial — **judicialmente**
adv

judío¹, -día *adj* : Jewish

judío², -día *n* : Jewish person, Jew

judo [ˈjuðo, ˈdʒu-] *nm* : judo

juega, juegue etc. → **jugar**

juego *nm* **1** : play, playing ⟨poner/entrar
en juego : to bring/come into play⟩
⟨juego limpio/sucio : fair/foul play⟩ **2**
: game, sport ⟨juego de cartas : card
game⟩ ⟨juego de mesa : board game⟩
⟨juego de azar : game of chance⟩
⟨Juegos Olímpicos : Olympic Games⟩ **3**
: gaming, gambling ⟨el juego ilegal : illegal gambling⟩ ⟨estar en juego : to be at
stake⟩ **4** : ride (at an amusement park)
5 : set ⟨un juego de herramientas/platos
: a set of tools/dishes⟩ **6** SOLTURA
: play, slack **7 fuera de juego** : offside
8 hacer juego : to go together, to match
9 hacerle el juego a : to play along with
10 juego de manos : trick, sleight of
hand **11 juego de palabras** : play on
words, pun

juerga *nf* : partying, binge ⟨irse de juerga
: to go on a spree⟩

juerguista *nmf* : reveler, carouser

jueves *nms & pl* : Thursday ⟨el jueves
: (on) Thursday⟩ ⟨los jueves : (on)
Thursdays⟩ ⟨cada (dos) jueves : every
(other) Thursday⟩ ⟨el jueves pasado
: last Thursday⟩ ⟨el próximo jueves
: next Thursday⟩

juez¹ *nmf, pl* **jueces 1** : judge **2** ÁRBI-
TRO : umpire, referee **3 juez de paz**
: justice of the peace

juez², jueza *n* → **juez¹**

jugada *nf* **1** : play, move **2** : trick ⟨hacer
una mala jugada : to play a dirty trick⟩

jugador, -dora *n* **1** : player **2** : gambler

jugar {44} *vi* **1** : to play ⟨jugar al fútbol
: to play soccer⟩ ⟨jugar a la lotería : to
play the lottery⟩ ⟨jugar a las muñecas
: to play with dolls⟩ ⟨jugar limpio/sucio
: to play fair/dirty⟩ **2** APOSTAR : to
gamble, to bet ⟨jugar a la Bolsa : to play
the stock market⟩ **3** : to joke, to kid **4**
jugar con alguien : to toy with someone
— *vt* **1** : to play ⟨jugar un papel : to
play a role⟩ ⟨jugar una carta : to play a
card⟩ **2** : to bet ⟨jugarlo todo a : to bet
everything on⟩ — **jugarse** *vr* **1** : to risk,
to gamble away ⟨jugarse la vida : to risk
one's life⟩ **2 jugarse el todo por el todo**
: to risk everything

jugarreta *nf fam* : prank, dirty trick

juglar *nm* : minstrel

jugo *nm* **1** : juice ⟨jugo de naranja : orange juice⟩ **2** : substance, essence
⟨sacarle el jugo a algo : to get the most
out of something⟩

jugosidad *nf* : juiciness

jugoso, -sa *adj* **1** : juicy **2** : lucrative,
profitable

juguete *nm* **1** : toy **2 de ~** : toy ⟨un
camión de juguete : a toy truck⟩

juguetear *vi* **1** : to play, to cavort, to
frolic **2** : to toy, to fiddle

juguetería *nf* : toy store

juguetón, -tona *adj, mpl* **-tones** : playful
— **juguetonamente** *adv*

juicio *nm* **1** : good judgment, reason,
sense ⟨perder el juicio : to lose one's
mind⟩ ⟨en su sano juicio : in one's right
mind⟩ **2** : opinion ⟨a mi juicio : in my
opinion⟩ **3** : trial ⟨llevar/ir a juicio : to
take/go to court⟩ ⟨un juicio civil/crimi-
nal : a civil/criminal trial⟩

juicioso, -sa *adj* : judicious, wise — **jui-
ciosamente** *adv*

julio *nm* : July ⟨el primero de julio : (on)
July first⟩

jumper [ˈdʒumper] *nm, pl* **jumpers**
[ˈdʒumpers] : jumper, pinafore

juncia *nf* : sedge

junco *nm* **1** : reed, rush **2** : junk (boat)

jungla *nf* : jungle

junio *nm* : June ⟨el primero de junio
: (on) June first⟩

junquillo *nm* : jonquil

junta *nf* **1** : board, committee ⟨junta directiva : board of directors⟩ **2** REUNIÓN
: meeting, session **3** : junta **4** : regional
government (in Spain) **5** : joint, gasket

juntamente *adv* **1** : jointly, together
⟨juntamente con : together with⟩ **2** : at
the same time

juntar *vt* **1** UNIR : to unite, to combine,
to put together **2** REUNIR : to collect, to
gather together, to assemble **3** : to close
partially ⟨juntar la puerta : to leave the
door ajar⟩ — **juntarse** *vr* **1** : to join together **2** : to move closer together **3**
: to get together ⟨nos juntamos a conversar : we got together to chat⟩ ⟨volvió a
juntarse con el grupo : he got back together with the group⟩

junto, -ta *adj* **1** UNIDO : joined, united **2**
: close, adjacent ⟨colgaron los dos retra-
tos juntos : they hung the two paintings
side by side⟩ **3** (*used adverbially*) : together ⟨llegamos juntos : we arrived to-
gether⟩ ⟨sabe más que todos juntos : she
knows more than all of us put together⟩
4 ~ a : next to, alongside of **5 ~ con**
: together with, along with

juntura *nf* : joint, coupling

Júpiter *nm* : Jupiter

jura *nf* : oath, pledge ⟨jura de bandera
: pledge of allegiance⟩

jurado¹ *nm* : jury (in a trial), panel of
judges (in a contest)

jurado², -da *nmf* **1** : juror **2** : judge (in a
contest)

juramentación *nf, pl* **-ciones** : swearing
in

juramentar *vt* : to swear in

juramento *nm* **1** : oath ⟨prestar juramento : to swear, to take an oath⟩ ⟨to-
marle juramento a : to swear in (an official), to place (a witness) under oath⟩ **2**
: swearword, oath

jurar *vt* **1** : to swear ⟨jurar lealtad : to
swear loyalty⟩ ⟨jurar bandera : to pledge
allegiance to the flag⟩ ⟨no lo sabía, ¡te lo
juro! : I swear I didn't know!⟩ **2** : to
take an oath ⟨el alcalde juró su cargo
: the mayor took the oath of office⟩ **3**

tenérsela jurada a alguien : to have it in for someone — *vi* : to curse, to swear
jurídico, -ca *adj* : legal
jurisdicción *nf, pl* **-ciones** : jurisdiction — **jurisdiccional** *adj*
jurisprudencia *nf* : jurisprudence, law
jurista *nmf* : jurist
justa *nf* **1** : joust **2** TORNEO : tournament, competition
justamente *adv* **1** PRECISAMENTE : precisely, exactly **2** : justly, fairly
justar *vi* : to joust
justicia *nf* **1** : justice, fairness ⟨hacerle justicia a : to do justice to⟩ ⟨ser de justicia : to be only fair⟩ ⟨en justicia : in all fairness⟩ ⟨pedir justicia : to demand justice⟩ **2 la justicia** : the law ⟨tomarse la justicia por su mano : to take the law into one's own hands⟩
justiciero, -ra *adj* : righteous, avenging
justificable *adj* : justifiable
justificación *nf, pl* **-ciones** : justification
justificante *nm* **1** : justification **2** : proof, voucher
justificar {72} *vt* **1** : to justify **2** : to excuse, to vindicate — **justificarse** *vr*

justo[1] *adv* **1** : justly **2** : right, exactly ⟨justo en ese momento : right at that moment⟩ ⟨justo en el centro : right in the center/middle⟩ ⟨justo a tiempo : just in time⟩ **3** : tightly
justo[2], **-ta** *adj* **1** : just, fair **2** : right, exact ⟨la cantidad justa : the exact amount⟩ ⟨lo justo para vivir : just enough to live on⟩ **3** : tight ⟨estos zapatos me quedan muy justos : these shoes are too tight⟩
justo[3], **-ta** *n* : just person ⟨los justos : the just⟩
juvenil *adj* **1** : juvenile (of crimes, etc.), youth ⟨una organización juvenil : a youth organization⟩ **2** : young, youthful (in appearance, etc.) **3** ADOLESCENTE : teenage **4** : junior (in sports)
juventud *nf* **1** : youth **2** : young people
juzgado *nm* TRIBUNAL : court, tribunal
juzgar {52} *vt* **1** : to try, to judge (a case in court) **2** : to pass judgment on **3** CONSIDERAR : to consider, to deem ⟨a juzgar por los resultados : judging by the results⟩
juzgue, etc. → juzgar

K

k *nf* : twelfth letter of the Spanish alphabet
ka *nf* : (letter) k
káiser *nm* : kaiser
kaki → caqui
kaleidoscopio → caleidoscopio
kamikaze *adj & nm* : kamikaze
kan *nm* : khan
karaoke *nm* : karaoke
karate *or* **kárate** *nm* : karate
kayac *or* **kayak** *nm, pl* **kayacs** *or* **kayaks** : kayak
kebab [ke'bab] *nm, pl* **kebabs** [ke'babs] : kebab
keniano, -na *adj & n* : Kenyan
kermesse *or* **kermés** [kɛr'mɛs] *nf, pl* **kermesses** *or* **kermeses** [-'mɛsɛs] : charity fair, bazaar
kerosene *or* **kerosén** *or* **keroseno** *nm* : kerosene, paraffin
ketchup ['ketʃap, -tʃup] *nm* : ketchup, catsup
kibutz *or* **kibbutz** *nms & pl* : kibbutz
kilo *nm* **1** : kilo, kilogram **2** *fam* : large amount
kilobyte [ˌkilo'bait] *nm* : kilobyte
kilociclo *nm* : kilocycle
kilogramo *nm* : kilogram

kilohertzio *nm* : kilohertz
kilometraje *nm* : distance in kilometers, mileage
kilométrico, -ca *adj fam* : endless, very long
kilómetro *nm* : kilometer
kilovatio *nm* : kilowatt
kimono *nm* : kimono
kinder ['kɪndɛr,] → **kindergarten**
kindergarten [ˌkɪndɛr'garten] *nm, pl* **kindergartens** [-tɛns] **1** : kindergarten **2** : nursery school
kinesiología *nf* : physical therapy
kinesiólogo, -ga *n* : physical therapist
kiosco, kiosko → quiosco
kiosquero, -ra → quiosquero
kit *nm, pl* **kits** : kit
kiwi ['kiwi] *nm* **1** : kiwi (bird) **2** : kiwifruit
klaxon → claxon
Kleenex ['klines, -neks] *marca registrada, m* — used for a paper tissue
knockout [nɔ'kaut] → **nocaut**
koala *nm* : koala bear
kriptón *nm* : krypton
kurdo[1], **-da** *adj* : Kurdish
kurdo[2], **-da** *n* : Kurd
kuwaití [kuˌwai'ti] *adj & nmf* : Kuwaiti

L

l *nf* : thirteenth letter of the Spanish alphabet

la¹ *nm* **1** : A ⟨la sostenido/bemol : A sharp/flat⟩ **2** : la (in singing)

la² *pron* (*referring to feminine nouns*) **1** : her, it ⟨llámala hoy : call her today⟩ ⟨sacó la botella y la abrió : he took out the bottle and opened it⟩ **2** (*formal*) : you ⟨no la vi a usted, Señora Díaz : I didn't see you, Mrs. Díaz⟩ **3** : the one ⟨me gusta la roja : I like the red one⟩ ⟨la de la camisa azul : the one with the blue shirt⟩ ⟨mi mamá y la tuya : my mom and yours⟩ ⟨la clase de ayer y la de hoy : yesterday's class and today's⟩ **4 la que** : the one that/who, whoever, she who ⟨la que vino ayer : the one who came yesterday⟩ ⟨la que compré : the one (that) I bought⟩ ⟨la que gane : whoever wins⟩

la³ *art* → **el²**

laberíntico, -ca *adj* : labyrinthine

laberinto *nm* : labyrinth, maze

labia *nf fam* : gift of gab ⟨tu amigo tiene labia : your friend has a way with words⟩

labial *adj* : labial, lip ⟨lápiz labial : lipstick⟩

labio *nm* : lip

labor *nf* : work, labor

laborable *adj* **1** : arable **2** : work, working ⟨día laborable : workday, business day⟩

laboral *adj* : work, labor ⟨costos laborales : labor costs⟩

laborar *vi* : to work

laboratorio *nm* : laboratory, lab

laboriosamente *adv* **1** : laboriously **2** : industriously, diligently

laboriosidad *nf* : industriousness, diligence

laborioso, -sa *adj* **1** : laborious, hard **2** : industrious, hardworking

labrado¹, -da *adj* **1** : cultivated, tilled **2** : carved, wrought

labrado² *nm* : cultivated field

labrador, -dora *n* : farmer

labranza *nf* : farming

labrar *vt* **1** : to carve, to work (metal) **2** : to cultivate, to till **3** : to cause, to bring about

labriego, -ga *n* : farm worker

laburar *vi Arg, Uru* TRABAJAR : to work

laburo *nm Arg, Uru* TRABAJO : work, job

laca *nf* **1** : lacquer, shellac **2** : hair spray **3 laca de uñas** : nail polish

lace, etc. → **lazar**

lacear *vt* : to lasso

laceración *nf, pl* **-ciones** : laceration

lacerante *adj* : hurtful, wounding

lacerar *vt* **1** : to lacerate, to cut **2** : to hurt, to wound (one's feelings)

lacio, -cia *adj* **1** : limp, lank **2 pelo lacio** : straight hair

lacónico, -ca *adj* : laconic — **lacónicamente** *adv*

lacra *nf* **1** : scar, mark (on the skin) **2** : stigma, blemish

lacrar *vt* : to seal (with wax)

lacrimógeno, -na *adj* : gas lacrimógeno : tear gas

lacrimoso, -sa *adj* : tearful, moving

lacrosse *nm* : lacrosse

lactancia *nf* : breast-feeding

lactante *nmf* : nursing infant, suckling

lactar *v* : to breast-feed

lácteo¹, -tea *adj* **1** : dairy **2 Vía Láctea** : Milky Way

lácteo² *nm* : dairy product ⟨evito los lácteos : I avoid dairy⟩

ladeado, -da *adj* : crooked, tilted, lopsided

ladear *vt* : to tilt, to tip — **ladearse** *vr* : to bend (over)

ladera *nf* : slope, hillside

ladino¹, -na *adj* **1** : cunning, shrewd **2** *CA, Mex* : mestizo

ladino², -na *n* **1** : trickster **2** *CA, Mex* : Spanish-speaking person of indigenous descent **3** *CA, Mex* : mestizo

lado *nm* **1** : side ⟨el lado izquierdo/derecho : the left/right side⟩ ⟨el otro lado : the other side⟩ ⟨el lado de arriba/abajo : the top/bottom⟩ **2** PARTE : place ⟨miró por todos lados : he looked everywhere⟩ **3** : side (in an argument, etc.) ⟨se puso de mi lado : she took my side⟩ **4 al ~** ⟨los que viven al lado : the people who live next door⟩ ⟨tenemos una tienda al lado : there's a store beside/near us⟩ **5 al lado de** : next to, beside ⟨al lado de la calle : on/at the side of the road⟩ ⟨a mi lado : beside me⟩ **6 de al lado** ⟨los de al lado : the next-door neighbors⟩ ⟨el asiento de al lado : the seat next to mine/yours (etc.)⟩ **7 de ~** : tilted, sideways ⟨está de lado : it's lying on its side⟩ **8 de un lado a otro** : to and fro, back and forth **9 dejar a un lado** : to set aside **10 hacerse a un lado** : to step aside **11 lado a lado** : side by side **12 por un lado . . . , por otro lado . . .** : on the one hand . . . , on the other hand . . .

ladrar *vi* : to bark

ladrido *nm* : bark (of a dog), barking

ladrillo *nm* **1** : brick **2** AZULEJO : tile

ladrón, -drona *n, mpl* **ladrones** : robber, thief, burglar

lagartija *nf* : small lizard

lagarto *nm* **1** : lizard **2 lagarto de Indias** : alligator

lago *nm* : lake

lágrima *nf* : tear, teardrop

lagrimal *nm* : corner of the eye

lagrimear *vi* **1** : to water (of eyes) **2** : to weep easily

laguna *nf* **1** : lagoon **2** : gap

laicado *nm* : laity

laico¹, -ca *adj* : lay, secular

laico², -ca *n* : layman *m*, laywoman *f*

laja *nf* : slab

lama¹ *nf* : slime, ooze

lama² *nm* : lama

lamber *vt* : to lick

lamentable *adj* **1** : unfortunate, lamentable **2** : pitiful, sad
lamentablemente *adv* : unfortunately, regrettably
lamentación *nf, pl* **-ciones** : lamentation, groaning, moaning
lamentar *vt* **1** : to lament **2** : to regret ⟨lo lamento : I'm sorry⟩ — **lamentarse** *vr* : to grumble, to complain
lamento *nm* : lament, groan, cry
lamer *vt* **1** : to lick **2** : to lap against
lamida *nf* : lick
lámina *nf* **1** PLANCHA : sheet, plate **2** : plate, illustration
laminado¹, -da *adj* : laminated
laminado² *nm* : laminate
laminar *vt* : to laminate — **laminación** *nf*
lámpara *nf* : lamp
lampiño, -ña *adj* : hairless
lamprea *nf* : lamprey
lana *nf* **1** : wool ⟨lana de acero : steel wool⟩ **2** *Mex fam* : money, dough
lance¹, etc. → **lanzar**
lance² *nm* **1** INCIDENTE : event, incident **2** RIÑA : quarrel **3** : throw, cast (of a net, etc.) **4** : move, play (in a game), throw (of dice)
lancear *vt* : to spear
lancha *nf* **1** : small boat, launch **2** lancha motora : motorboat, speedboat
langosta *nf* **1** : lobster **2** : locust
langostino *nm* : prawn, crayfish
languidecer {53} *vi* : to languish
languidez *nf, pl* **-deces** : languor, listlessness
lánguido, -da *adj* : languid, listless — **lánguidamente** *adv*
lanolina *nf* : lanolin
lanudo, -da *adj* : woolly
lanza *nf* : spear, lance
lanzadera *nf* **1** : shuttle (for weaving) **2** lanzadera espacial : space shuttle
lanzado, -da *adj* **1** : impulsive, brazen **2** : forward, determined ⟨ir lanzado : to hurtle along⟩
lanzador, -dora *n* : thrower, pitcher
lanzallamas *nms & pl* : flamethrower
lanzamiento *nm* **1** : throw **2** : pitch (in baseball) **3** : launching, launch
lanzar {21} *vt* **1** : to throw, to hurl **2** : to pitch **3** : to launch — **lanzarse** *vr* **1** : to throw oneself (at, into) **2** ∼ a : to embark upon, to undertake
laosiano, -na *adj & n* : Laotian
lapa *nf* : limpet
lapicera *nf Arg, Uru* : pen
lapicero *nm* **1** : mechanical pencil **2** *CA, Peru* : ballpoint pen
lápida *nf* : marker, tombstone
lapidar *vt* APEDREAR : to stone
lápiz *nm, pl* **lápices** **1** : pencil **2** lápiz labial *or* lápiz de labios : lipstick
lapón, -pona *adj & n, mpl* **lapones** : Lapp
lapso *nm* : lapse, space (of time)
lapsus *nms & pl* : error, slip
laptop *nm, pl* **laptops** : laptop
laquear *vt* : to lacquer, to varnish, to shellac
larga *nf* **1** a la larga : in the long run **2** darle largas a : to put off, to stall

largamente *adv* **1** : at length, extensively **2** : easily, comfortably **3** : generously
largar {52} *vt* **1** SOLTAR : to let loose, to release **2** AFLOJAR : to loosen, to slacken **3** *fam* : to give, to hand over **4** *fam* : to hurl, to let fly (insults, etc.) — **largarse** *vr fam* : to scram, to beat it
largo¹, -ga *adj* **1** : long **2** a lo largo : lengthwise **3** a lo largo de : along **4** a lo largo y ancho de : the length and breadth of, all over
largo² *nm* : length ⟨tres metros de largo : three meters long⟩
largometraje *nm* : feature film
largue, etc. → **largar**
largueza *nf* : generosity, largesse
larguirucho, -cha *adj fam* : lanky
largura *nf* : length
laringe *nf* : larynx
laringitis *nfs & pl* : laryngitis
larva *nf* : larva — **larval** *adj*
las → **el², los¹**
lasaña *nf* : lasagna
lasca *nf* : chip, chipping
lascivia *nf* : lasciviousness, lewdness
lascivo, -va *adj* : lascivious, lewd — **lascivamente** *adv*
láser *nm* : laser
lasitud *nf* : weariness
laso, -sa *adj* : languid, weary
lástima *nf* **1** : compassion, pity **2** PENA : shame, pity ⟨¡qué lástima! : what a shame!⟩ ⟨es una lástima que . . . : it's a shame that . . .⟩ ⟨tener/sentir lástima de : to feel sorry for⟩
lastimadura *nf* : injury, wound
lastimar *vt* **1** DAÑAR, HERIR : to hurt, to injure **2** AGRAVIAR : to offend — **lastimarse** *vr* : to hurt oneself
lastimero, -ra *adj* : pitiful, wretched
lastimoso, -sa *adj* **1** : shameful **2** : pitiful, terrible
lastrar *vt* **1** : to ballast **2** : to burden, to encumber
lastre *nm* **1** : burden **2** : ballast
lata *nf* **1** : tin **2** : tin can **3** *fam* : pest, bother, nuisance **4** dar lata *fam* : to bother, to annoy
latente *adj* : latent
lateral¹ *adj* **1** : lateral, side **2** : indirect — **lateralmente** *adv*
lateral² *nm* : end piece, side
látex *nms & pl* : latex
latido *nm* : beat, throb ⟨latido del corazón : heartbeat⟩
latifundio *nm* : large estate
latigazo *nm* : lash (with a whip)
látigo *nm* AZOTE : whip
latín *nm* : Latin (language)
latino¹, -na *adj* **1** : Latin **2** *fam* : Latin-American
latino², -na *n fam* : Latin American
latinoamericano¹, -na *adj* HISPANOAMERICANO : Latin American
latinoamericano², -na *n* : Latin American
latir *vi* **1** : to beat, to throb **2** latirle a uno *Mex fam* : to have a hunch ⟨me late que no va a venir : I have a feeling he's not going to come⟩
latitud *nf* **1** : latitude **2** : breadth

lato, -ta *adj* **1** : extended, lengthy **2** : broad (in meaning)

latón *nm, pl* **latones** : brass

latoso¹, -sa *adj fam* : annoying, bothersome

latoso², -sa *n fam* : pest, nuisance

latrocinio *nm* : larceny

laúd *nm* : lute

laudable *adj* : laudable, praiseworthy

laudo *nm* : findings, decision

laureado, -da *adj & n* : laureate

laurear *vt* : to award, to honor

laurel *nm* **1** : laurel, bay (in cooking) ⟨hoja de laurel : bay leaf⟩ **2 dormirse en sus laureles** : to rest on one's laurels

lava *nf* : lava

lavable *adj* : washable

lavabo *nm* **1** LAVAMANOS : sink, washbowl **2** : lavatory, toilet

lavadero *nm* : laundry room

lavado *nm* **1** : laundry, wash **2** : laundering ⟨lavado de dinero : money laundering⟩

lavadora *nf* : washing machine

lavamanos *nms & pl* LAVABO : sink, washbowl

lavanda *nf* ESPLIEGO : lavender

lavandería *nf* : laundry (service)

lavandero, -ra *n* : launderer, laundress *f*

lavaplatos *nms & pl* **1** : dishwasher **2** *Chile, Col, Mex* : kitchen sink

lavar *vt* **1** : to wash, to clean **2** : to launder (money) **3 lavar en seco** : to dryclean — **lavarse** *vr* **1** : to wash oneself **2 lavarse las manos de** : to wash one's hands of

lavarropas *nms & pl Arg, Uru* : washing machine

lavativa *nf* : enema

lavatorio *nm* : lavatory, washroom

lavavajillas *nms & pl* : dishwasher

laxante *adj & nm* : laxative

laxitud *nf* : laxity, slackness

laxo, -xa *adj* : lax, slack

lazada *nf* : bow, loop

lazar {21} *vt* : to rope, to lasso

lazo *nm* **1** VÍNCULO : link, bond **2** : bow, ribbon **3** : lasso, lariat

LCD *nm* : LCD, liquid crystal display

le *pron* **1** : to her, to him, to it ⟨¿qué le dijiste? : what did you tell him?⟩ **2** : from her, from him, from it ⟨el ladrón le robó la cartera : the thief stole his wallet⟩ **3** : for her, for him, for it ⟨cómprale flores a tu mamá : buy your mom some flowers⟩ **4** *(formal)* : to you, for you ⟨le traje un regalo : I brought you a gift⟩

leal *adj* : loyal, faithful — **lealmente** *adv*

lealtad *nf* : loyalty, allegiance

lebrel *nm* : hound

lección *nf, pl* **lecciones** : lesson

lechada *nf* **1** : whitewash **2** : grout

lechal *adj* : suckling ⟨cordero lechal : suckling lamb⟩

leche *nf* **1** : milk ⟨leche en polvo : powdered milk⟩ **2** : milk (of a plant) **3 leche de magnesia** : milk of magnesia

lechera *nf* **1** : milk jug **2** : dairymaid *f*

lechería *nf* : dairy store

lechero¹, -ra *adj* : dairy

lechero², -ra *n* : milkman *m*, milk dealer

lecho *nm* **1** : bed ⟨un lecho de rosas : a bed of roses⟩ ⟨lecho de muerte : deathbed⟩ **2** : riverbed **3** : layer, stratum (in geology)

lechón, -chona *n, mpl* **lechones** : suckling pig

lechoso, -sa *adj* : milky

lechuga *nf* : lettuce

lechuza *nf* BÚHO : owl, barn owl

lectivo, -va *adj* : school ⟨año lectivo : school year⟩

lector¹, -tora *adj* : reading ⟨nivel lector : reading level⟩

lector², -tora *n* : reader

lector³ *nm* **1** : scanner, reader **2 lector electrónico** *or* **lector de libros electrónicos** : e-reader

lectura *nf* **1** : reading **2** : reading matter

LED *or* **led** *nm* : LED

leer {20} *v* : to read ⟨leer los labios : to lip-read, to read lips⟩ ⟨leer entre las líneas : to read between the lines⟩

legación *nf, pl* **-ciones** : legation

legado *nm* **1** : legacy, bequest **2** : legate, emissary

legajo *nm* : dossier, file

legal *adj* : legal, lawful — **legalmente** *adv*

legalidad *nf* : legality

legalista *adj* : legalistic

legalizar {21} *vt* : to legalize — **legalización** *nf*

legañas *nfpl* : sleep (in the eyes)

legar {52} *vt* **1** : to bequeath, to hand down **2** DELEGAR : to delegate

legendario, -ria *adj* : legendary

legible *adj* : legible — **legibilidad** *nf*

legión *nf, pl* **legiones** : legion

legionario, -ria *n* : legionnaire

legislación *nf, pl* **-ciones** **1** : legislation (act) **2** : laws *pl*, legislation

legislador¹, -dora *adj* : legislative

legislador², -dora *n* : legislator

legislar *vi* : to legislate

legislativo, -va *adj* : legislative

legislatura *nf* **1** : legislature **2** : term of office

legitimar *vt* **1** : to legitimize **2** : to authenticate — **legitimación** *nf*

legitimidad *nf* : legitimacy

legítimo, -ma *adj* **1** : legitimate **2** : genuine, authentic — **legítimamente** *adv*

lego¹, -ga *adj* **1** : secular, lay **2** : uninformed, ignorant

lego², -ga *n* : layperson, layman *m*, laywoman *f*

legua *nf* **1** : league **2 notarse a leguas** : to be very obvious ⟨se notaba a leguas : you could tell from a mile away⟩

legue, etc. → **legar**

legumbre *nf* **1** HORTALIZA : vegetable **2** : legume

leíble *adj* : readable

leída *nf* : reading, read ⟨de una leída : in one reading, at one go⟩

leído¹ *pp* → **leer**

leído², -da *adj* : well-read

lejanía *nf* : remoteness, distance

lejano, -na *adj* : remote, distant, far away

lejía *nf* 1 : lye 2 : bleach
lejos *adv* 1 : far away, distant ⟨a lo lejos : in the distance, far off⟩ ⟨desde lejos : from a distance⟩ 2 : long ago, a long way off ⟨está lejos de los 50 años : he's a long way from 50 years old⟩ 3 de ~ : by far ⟨esta decisión fue de lejos la más fácil : this decision was by far the easiest⟩ 4 ~ de : far from ⟨lejos de ser reprobado, recibió una nota de B : far from failing, he got a B⟩ 5 ir demasiado lejos : to go too far
lelo, -la *adj* : silly, stupid
lema *nm* : motto, slogan
lemming *nm* : lemming
lempira *nf* : lempira (Honduran unit of currency)
lencería *nf* : lingerie
lengua *nf* 1 : tongue ⟨se me traba la lengua : I have trouble speaking, I get tongue-tied⟩ 2 IDIOMA : language ⟨lengua materna : mother tongue⟩ ⟨lengua nativa : native language⟩ ⟨lengua muerta : dead language⟩ 3 : tongue (of flame) 4 : spit (of land) 5 irse de la lengua : to let something slip, to blab 6 morderse la lengua : to bite one's tongue 7 sacarle la lengua a alguien : to stick one's tongue out at someone
lenguado *nm* : sole, flounder
lenguaje *nm* 1 : language, speech 2 lenguaje gestual *or* lenguaje de gestos : sign language 3 lenguaje de programación : programming language
lengüeta *nf* 1 : tongue (of a shoe), tab, flap 2 : reed (of a musical instrument) 3 : barb, point
lengüetada *nf* beber a lengüetadas : to lap (up)
lenidad *nf* : leniency
lenitivo, -va *adj* : soothing
lente *nmf* 1 : lens ⟨lentes de contacto : contact lenses⟩ 2 lentes *nmpl* ANTEOJOS : eyeglasses ⟨lentes de sol : sunglasses⟩
lenteja *nf* : lentil
lentejuela *nf* : sequin, spangle
lentilla *nf* *Spain* : contact lens
lentitud *nf* : slowness
lento[1] *adv* DESPACIO : slowly
lento[2], -ta *adj* 1 : slow 2 : slow-witted, dull — **lentamente** *adv*
leña *nf* : wood, firewood
leñador, -dora *n* : lumberjack, woodcutter
leñera *nf* : woodshed
leño *nm* : log
leñoso, -sa *adj* : woody
Leo[1] *nm* : Leo (sign or constellation)
Leo[2] *nm* : Leo (person)
león, -ona *n, mpl* **leones** 1 : lion, lioness *f* 2 (*in various countries*) : puma, cougar
leonado, -da *adj* : tawny
leonino, -na *adj* 1 : lion-like 2 : one-sided, unfair
leopardo *nm* : leopard
leotardo *nm* MALLA : leotard, tights *pl*
leperada *nf Mex* : obscenity
lépero, -ra *adj Mex* : vulgar, coarse
lepra *nf* : leprosy

leproso[1], -sa *adj* : leprous
leproso[2], -sa *n* : leper
lerdo, -da *adj* 1 : clumsy 2 : dull, oafish, slow-witted
les *pron* 1 : to them ⟨dales una propina : give them a tip⟩ 2 : from them ⟨se les privó de su herencia : they were deprived of their inheritance⟩ 3 : for them ⟨les hice sus tareas : I did their homework for them⟩ 4 : to you *pl*, for you *pl* ⟨les compré un regalo : I bought you all a present⟩
lesbiana *nf* : lesbian — **lesbiano, -na** *adj*
lesbianismo *nm* : lesbianism
lesera *nf Chile fam* : stupid thing
lesión *nf, pl* **lesiones** HERIDA : lesion, wound, injury ⟨una lesión grave : a serious injury⟩
lesionado, -da *adj* HERIDO : injured, wounded
lesionar *vt* : to injure, to wound — **lesionarse** *vr* : to hurt oneself
lesivo, -va *adj* : harmful, damaging
letal *adj* MORTÍFERO : deadly, lethal — **letalmente** *adv*
letanía *nf* 1 : litany 2 *fam* : spiel, song and dance
letárgico, -ca *adj* : lethargic
letargo *nm* : lethargy, torpor
letón[1], -tona *adj & n, mpl* **letones** : Latvian
letón[2] *nm* : Latvian (language)
letra *nf* 1 : letter ⟨letra mayúscula/minúscula : capital/lowercase letter⟩ ⟨letra en negrilla/negrita : boldface, bold type⟩ ⟨letra cursiva : italics, italic type⟩ ⟨leer la letra pequeña/chica : to read the small print⟩ ⟨aprender las primeras letras : to learn how to read and write⟩ 2 CALIGRAFÍA : handwriting, lettering 3 : lyrics *pl* 4 al pie de la letra : word for word, by the book 5 letra(s) de molde *or* letra(s) de imprenta : print ⟨escribió su nombre en/con letra(s) de molde/imprenta : she printed her name⟩ 6 letras *nfpl* : arts (in education)
letrado[1], -da *adj* ERUDITO : learned, erudite
letrado[2], -da *n* : attorney, lawyer
letrero *nm* RÓTULO : sign, notice
letrina *nf* : latrine
letrista *nmf* : lyricist, songwriter
leucemia *nf* : leukemia
leva *nf* : cam
levadura *nf* 1 : yeast, leavening 2 levadura en polvo : baking powder
levantado, -da *adj* : awake, up
levantamiento *nm* 1 ALZAMIENTO : uprising 2 : raising, lifting ⟨levantamiento de pesas : weight lifting⟩
levantar *vt* 1 ALZAR : to lift, to raise ⟨levanté la tapa : I lifted the lid⟩ ⟨levantar pesas : to lift weights⟩ ⟨levantar las manos : to raise one's hand⟩ ⟨levantar la mirada/vista : to look up⟩ ⟨levantar la voz : to raise one's voice⟩ 2 : to put up, to erect (a building, etc.) 3 : to give a boost to ⟨me levantó el ánimo : it lifted my spirits⟩ ⟨un plan para levantar al país : a plan to get the country back on its

feet⟩ **4** : to lift (an embargo, etc.), to call off (a strike, etc.), to adjourn (a meeting, etc.) **5** : to give rise to, to arouse ⟨levantar sospechas : to arouse suspicion⟩ ⟨levantar una polémica : to spark controversy⟩ **6 levantar cabeza** : to get back on one's feet, to recover — **levantarse** vr **1** : to rise, to stand up **2** : to get out of bed, to get up ⟨se levanta a las seis : he gets up at six⟩
levante nm **1** : east (direction) **2** : east wind
levar vt levar anclas : to weigh anchor
leve adj **1** : light, slight **2** : trivial, unimportant — **levemente** adv
levedad nf : lightness
levemente adv LIGERAMENTE : lightly, softly
leviatán nm, pl **-tanes** : leviathan
levitar vi : to levitate
léxico¹, -ca adj : lexical
léxico² nm : lexicon, glossary
lexicografía nf : lexicography
lexicográfico, -ca adj : lexicographical, lexicographic
lexicógrafo, -fa n : lexicographer
ley nf **1** : law ⟨aprobar/derogar una ley : to pass/repeal a law⟩ ⟨violar la ley : to break the law⟩ ⟨fuera de la ley : outside the law⟩ ⟨proyecto de ley : bill (of law)⟩ ⟨la ley de gravedad : the law of gravity⟩ ⟨es ley de vida : it's a fact of life⟩ ⟨con todas las de la ley : proper, properly⟩ **2** : purity (of metals) ⟨oro de ley : pure gold⟩
leyenda nf **1** : legend **2** : caption, inscription
leyó, etc. → **leer**
liar {85} vt **1** ATAR : to bind, to tie (up) **2** : to roll (a cigarette) **3** : to confuse — **liarse** vr : to get mixed up
libanés, -nesa adj & n, mpl **-neses** : Lebanese
libar vt **1** : to suck (nectar) **2** : to sip, to swig (liquor, etc.)
libelo nm **1** : libel, lampoon **2** : petition (in court)
libélula nf : dragonfly
liberación nf, pl **-ciones** : liberation, deliverance ⟨liberación de la mujer : women's liberation⟩
liberado, -da adj **1** : liberated ⟨una mujer liberada : a liberated woman⟩ **2** : freed, delivered
liberal adj & nmf : liberal
liberalidad nf : generosity, liberality
liberalismo nm : liberalism
liberalizar {21} vt : to liberalize — **liberalización** nf
liberar vt : to liberate, to free — **liberarse** vr : to get free of
liberiano, -na adj & n : Liberian
libertad nf **1** : freedom, liberty ⟨tomarse la libertad de : to take the liberty of⟩ ⟨poner a alguien en libertad : to set someone free⟩ ⟨libertad de expresión : freedom of speech⟩ **2 libertad bajo fianza** : bail **3 libertad condicional** : parole, probation
libertador¹, -dora adj : liberating

libertador², -dora n : liberator
libertar vt LIBRAR : to set free
libertario, -ria adj & n : libertarian
libertinaje nm : licentiousness, dissipation
libertino¹, -na adj : licentious, dissolute
libertino², -na n : libertine
libidinoso, -sa adj : lustful, lewd
libido nf : libido
libio, -bia adj & n : Libyan
libra nf **1** : pound **2 libra esterlina** : pound sterling
Libra¹ nm : Libra (sign or constellation)
Libra² nmf : Libra (person)
libramiento nm **1** : liberating, freeing **2** LIBRANZA : order of payment **3** Mex : beltway
libranza nf : order of payment
librar vt **1** LIBERTAR : to free (from punishment, etc.), to save (from death, etc.) ⟨líbranos del mal : deliver us from evil⟩ ⟨librar de culpas : to absolve of guilt⟩ **2** : to wage ⟨librar batalla : to do battle⟩ **3** : to issue ⟨librar una orden : to issue an order⟩ — **librarse** vr ~ **de** : to free oneself from, to get out of ⟨se libró de pagar una multa : he got out of paying a fine⟩ ⟨librarse de morir : to escape death⟩
libre¹ adj **1** : free ⟨un país libre : a free country⟩ ⟨libre de : free from, exempt from⟩ ⟨libre albedrío : free will⟩ ⟨ratos libres : free/spare time⟩ **2** DESOCUPADO : vacant **3 día libre** : day off
libre² nm Mex : taxi
librea nf : livery
libremente adv : freely
librería nf : bookstore
librero¹, -ra n : bookseller
librero² nm Mex : bookcase
libresco, -ca adj : bookish
libreta nf CUADERNO : notebook
libretista nmf **1** : librettist **2** : scriptwriter
libreto nm : libretto, script
libro nm **1** : book ⟨libro de texto/cocina : textbook/cookbook⟩ ⟨libro de consulta : reference book⟩ ⟨libro en rústica, libro de tapa/pasta blanda : paperback⟩ ⟨libro de tapa/pasta dura : hardcover⟩ ⟨libro de instrucciones : instruction manual⟩ **2 libros** nmpl : books (in bookkeeping), accounts ⟨llevar los libros : to keep the books⟩
liceal nmf Uru : high school student
liceano, -na n Chile → **liceal**
liceísta nmf CoRi, Ven → **liceal**
licencia nf **1** : permission **2** : leave, leave of absence **3** : permit, license ⟨licencia de conducir : driver's license⟩
licenciado, -da n **1** : university graduate **2** ABOGADO : lawyer
licenciar vt **1** : to license, to permit, to allow **2** : to discharge **3** : to grant a university degree to — **licenciarse** vr : to graduate
licenciatura nf **1** : college degree **2** : course of study (at a college or university)
licencioso, -sa adj : licentious, lewd
liceo nm (in various countries) : secondary school, high school

licitación *nf, pl* **-ciones** : bid, bidding
licitar *vt* : to bid on
lícito, -ta *adj* **1** : lawful, licit **2** JUSTO : just, fair
licor *nm* **1** : liquor **2** : liqueur
licorera *nf* : decanter
licuado *nm* BATIDO : milk shake
licuadora *nf* : blender
licuar {3} *vt* : to liquefy — **licuarse** *vr*
lid *nf* **1** : fight, combat **2** : argument, dispute **3 lides** *nfpl* : matters, affairs **4 en buena lid** : fair and square
líder[1] *adj* : leading, foremost
líder[2] *nmf* : leader
liderar *vt* DIRIGIR : to lead, to head
liderato *nm* : leadership, leading
liderazgo → liderato
lidia *nf* **1** : bullfighting **2** : bullfight
lidiar *vt* : to fight — *vi* BATALLAR, LUCHAR : to struggle, to battle, to wrestle
liebre *nf* : hare
liendre *nf* : nit
lienzo *nm* **1** : linen **2** : canvas, painting **3** : stretch of wall or fencing
liga *nf* **1** ASOCIACIÓN : league **2** GOMITA : rubber band **3** : garter
ligado, -da *adj* : linked, connected
ligadura *nf* **1** ATADURA : tie, bond **2** : ligature
ligamento *nm* : ligament
ligar {52} *vt* : to bind, to tie (up)
ligeramente *adv* **1** : slightly **2** LEVEMENTE : lightly, gently **3** : casually, lightly
ligereza *nf* **1** : lightness **2** : flippancy **3** : agility
ligero, -ra *adj* **1** : light, lightweight **2** : slight, minor **3** : agile, quick **4** : light-hearted, superficial
light [ˈlait] *adj* : light, low-calorie
ligue, etc. → ligar
liguero, -ra *adj* : league
lija *nf or* **papel de lija** : sandpaper
lijar *vt* : to sand
lila[1] *adj* : lilac, light purple
lila[2] *nf* : lilac
lima *nf* **1** : lime (fruit) **2** : file ⟨lima de uñas : nail file⟩
limar *vt* **1** : to file **2** : to polish, to put the final touch on **3** : to smooth over ⟨limar asperezas : to iron out differences⟩
limbo *nm* **1** : limbo **2** : limb (in botany and astronomy)
limeño[1], **-ña** *adj* : of or from Lima, Peru
limeño[2], **-ña** *n* : person from Lima, Peru
limero *nm* : lime tree
limitación *nf, pl* **-ciones** **1** : limitation **2** : limit, restriction ⟨sin limitación : unlimited⟩
limitado, -da *adj* **1** RESTRINGIDO : limited **2** : dull, slow-witted
limitar *vt* RESTRINGIR : to limit, to restrict — *vi* ~ **con** : to border on — **limitarse** *vr* ~ **a** : to limit oneself to
límite *nm* **1** : boundary, border **2** : limit ⟨el límite de mi paciencia : the limit of my patience⟩ ⟨límite de velocidad : speed limit⟩ **3 fecha límite** : deadline
limítrofe *adj* LINDANTE, LINDERO : bordering, adjoining

limo *nm* : slime, mud
limón *nm, pl* **limones** **1** : lemon **2** : lemon tree **3 limón verde** *Mex* : lime
limonada *nf* : lemonade
limonero *nm* : lemon tree
limosna *nf* : alms, charity
limosnear *vi* : to beg (for alms)
limosnero, -ra *n* MENDIGO : beggar
limoso, -sa *adj* : slimy
limpiabotas *nmfs & pl* : shoeshine boy/man *m*, shoeshine girl/woman *f*
limpiacristales *nms & pl Spain* **1** : glass cleaner (fluid) **2** : window washer (person)
limpiador[1], **-dora** *adj* : cleaning
limpiador[2], **-dora** *n* : cleaning person, cleaner
limpiamente *adv* : cleanly, honestly, fairly
limpiaparabrisas *nms & pl* : windshield wiper
limpiar *vt* **1** : to clean, to cleanse **2** : to clean up, to remove defects **3** *fam* : to clean out (in a game) **4** *fam* : to swipe, to pinch — *vi* : to clean — **limpiarse** *vr*
limpiavidrios *nmfs & pl* **1** *Mex* : windshield wiper **2** : glass cleaner (fluid) **3** : window washer (person)
límpido, -da *adj* : limpid
limpieza *nf* **1** : cleanliness, tidiness **2** : cleaning **3** HONRADEZ : integrity, honesty **4** DESTREZA : skill, dexterity
limpio[1] *adv* : fairly
limpio[2], **-pia** *adj* **1** : clean, neat **2** : honest ⟨un juego limpio : a fair game⟩ **3** : free ⟨limpio de impurezas : pure, free from impurities⟩ **4** : clear, net ⟨ganancia limpia : clear profit⟩
limusina *nf* : limousine
linaje *nm* ABOLENGO : lineage, ancestry
lince *nm* : lynx
linchamiento *nm* : lynching
linchar *vt* : to lynch
lindante *adj* LIMÍTROFE, LINDERO : bordering, adjoining
lindar *vi* ~ **con** : to border, to skirt **2** ~ **con** BORDEAR : to border on, to verge on
linde *nmf* : boundary, limit
lindero[1], **-ra** *adj* LIMÍTROFE, LINDANTE : bordering, adjoining
lindero[2] *nm* : boundary, limit
lindeza *nf* **1** : prettiness **2** : clever remark **3 lindezas** *nfpl* (*used ironically*) : insults
lindo[1] *adv* **1** : beautifully, wonderfully ⟨canta lindo tu mujer : your wife sings beautifully⟩ **2 de lo lindo** : a lot, a great deal ⟨los zancudos nos picaban de lo lindo : the mosquitoes were biting away at us⟩
lindo[2], **-da** *adj* **1** BONITO : pretty, lovely **2** MONO : cute
línea *nf* **1** : line ⟨línea divisoria : dividing line⟩ ⟨línea de banda : sideline⟩ ⟨línea de meta : finish line⟩ ⟨línea de puntos : dotted line⟩ ⟨líneas enemigas : enemy lines⟩ ⟨línea de producción : production line⟩ ⟨leer entre líneas : to read between the lines⟩ **2** : line, course, position ⟨en

líneas generales : in general terms, along general lines ⟨línea de conducta : course of action⟩ ⟨línea de investigación : line of inquiry⟩ ⟨la línea del partido : the party line⟩ 3 : line, range ⟨línea de productos : product line⟩ 4 : line, side ⟨línea de sucesión : line of succession⟩ ⟨un primo suyo por línea materna : a cousin on his mother's side⟩ 5 : line, service ⟨línea aérea : airline⟩ ⟨línea telefónica : telephone line⟩ ⟨en línea : online⟩ ⟨fuera de línea : off-line⟩ 6 : figure ⟨guardar la línea : to watch one's figure⟩

línea de crédito *nf* : line of credit

lineal *adj* : linear

lineamientos *nmpl* : guidelines

linfa *nf* : lymph

linfático, -ca *adj* : lymphatic

lingote *nm* : ingot

lingüista *nmf* : linguist

lingüística *nf* : linguistics

lingüístico, -ca *adj* : linguistic

linimento *nm* : liniment

lino *nm* 1 : linen 2 : flax

linóleo *nm* : linoleum

linterna *nf* 1 : lantern 2 : flashlight

lío *nm fam* 1 : confusion, mess 2 : hassle, trouble, jam ⟨meterse en un lío : to get into a jam⟩ 3 : affair, liaison

liofilizar {21} *vt* : to freeze-dry

lioso, -sa *adj fam* : confusing, muddled

liquen *nm* : lichen

liquidación *nf, pl* **-ciones** 1 : liquidation 2 : clearance sale 3 : settlement, payment

liquidar *vt* 1 : to liquefy 2 : to liquidate 3 : to settle, to pay off 4 *fam* : to rub out, to kill

liquidez *nf, pl* **-deces** : liquidity

líquido¹, -da *adj* 1 : liquid, fluid 2 : net ⟨ingresos líquidos : net income⟩

líquido² *nm* 1 : liquid, fluid ⟨líquido de frenos : brake fluid⟩ 2 : ready cash, liquid assets

lira *nf* : lyre

lírica *nf* : lyric poetry

lírico, -ca *adj* : lyric, lyrical

lirio *nm* 1 : iris 2 **lirio de los valles** MUGUETE : lily of the valley

lirón *nm, pl* **lirones** : dormouse

lisiado¹, -da *adj* : disabled, crippled

lisiado², -da *n offensive* : disabled person, cripple *offensive*

lisiar *vt* : to cripple, to disable — **lisiarse** *vr*

liso, -sa *adj* 1 : smooth 2 : flat 3 : straight ⟨pelo liso : straight hair⟩ 4 : plain, unadorned ⟨liso y llano : plain and simple⟩

lisonja *nf* : flattery

lisonjear *vt* ADULAR : to flatter

lista *nf* 1 : list ⟨es la primera/última de la lista : she's first/last on the list⟩ 2 : roster, roll ⟨pasar lista : to take attendance⟩ 3 : stripe, strip 4 : menu

listado¹, -da *adj* : striped

listado² *nm* : listing

listar *vt* : to list

listeza *nf* : smartness, alertness

listo, -ta *adj* 1 DISPUESTO, PREPARADO : ready ⟨¿estás listo? : are you ready?⟩ 2 : clever, smart ⟨pasarse de listo : to be too clever⟩

listón *nm, pl* **listones** 1 : ribbon 2 : strip (of wood), lath 3 : high bar (in sports)

lisura *nf* : smoothness

litera *nf* : bunk bed, berth

literal *adj* : literal — **literalmente** *adv*

literario, -ria *adj* : literary

literato, -ta *n* : writer, author

literatura *nf* : literature

litigante *adj & nmf* : litigant

litigar {52} *vi* : to litigate, to be in litigation

litigio *nm* 1 : litigation, lawsuit 2 **en ~** : in dispute

litio *nm* : lithium

litografía *nf* 1 : lithography 2 : lithograph

litógrafo, -fa *n* : lithographer

litoral¹ *adj* : coastal

litoral² *nm* : shore, seaboard

litosfera *nf* : lithosphere

litro *nm* : liter

lituano¹, -na *adj & n* : Lithuanian

lituano² *nm* : Lithuanian (language)

liturgia *nf* : liturgy

litúrgico, -ca *adj* : liturgical — **litúrgicamente** *adv*

liviandad *nf* LIGEREZA : lightness

liviano, -na *adj* 1 : light, slight 2 INCONSTANTE : fickle

lividez *nf* PALIDEZ : pallor

lívido, -da *adj* 1 AMORATADO : livid 2 PÁLIDO : pallid, extremely pale

living *nm* : living room

ll *nf* : fourteenth letter of the Spanish alphabet not usually considered a separate letter in alphabetization

llaga *nf* : sore, wound

llama *nf* 1 : flame 2 : llama

llamada *nf* : call ⟨llamada a larga distancia : long-distance call⟩ ⟨llamada al orden : call to order⟩

llamado¹, -da *adj* : named, called ⟨una mujer llamada Rosa : a woman called Rosa⟩

llamado² → **llamamiento**

llamador *nm* : door knocker

llamamiento *nm* : call, appeal

llamar *vt* 1 : to name, to call ⟨la llamamos Paulita : we call her Paulita⟩ ⟨lo llamaban loco : they called him crazy⟩ ⟨así lo llamamos en Cuba : that's what we call it in Cuba⟩ 2 : to call, to summon ⟨llamar un taxi : to call a taxi⟩ ⟨me llamó desde abajo : she called up to me (from downstairs)⟩ ⟨fue llamado a declarar : he was called to testify⟩ 3 : to call (up), to phone ⟨me llama todos los días : she calls me every day⟩ — *vi* : to knock (on a door), to ring a doorbell ⟨llaman a la puerta : there's someone at the door⟩ — **llamarse** *vr* : to be called, to be named ⟨¿cómo te llamas? : what's your name?⟩ ⟨me llamo Ana : my name is Ana⟩

llamarada *nf* 1 : flare-up, sudden blaze 2 : flushing (of the face)

llamativo, -va *adj* : flashy, showy, striking

llameante *adj* : flaming, blazing

llamear *vi* : to flame, to blaze

llana *nf* **1** : trowel **2** → **llano²**

llanamente *adv* : simply, plainly ⟨es, simple y llanamente, un desastre : it's a disaster, plain and simple⟩

llaneza *nf* : simplicity, naturalness

llano¹, -na *adj* **1** : even, flat **2** : frank, open **3** LISO : plain, simple

llano² *nm* : plain

llanta *nf* **1** NEUMÁTICO : tire **2** : rim

llantén *nm, pl* **llantenes** : plantain (weed)

llanto *nm* : crying, weeping

llanura *nf* : plain, prairie

llave *nf* **1** : key ⟨bajo llave : under lock and key⟩ ⟨llave maestra : master key⟩ ⟨cerrar (algo) con llave : to lock (something)⟩ **2** : faucet **3** : valve (in plumbing) **4** INTERRUPTOR : switch **5** : (curly) brace, curly bracket (punctuation mark) **6** : wrench ⟨llave inglesa : monkey wrench⟩

llavero *nm* : key chain, key ring

llegada *nf* : arrival

llegar {52} *vi* **1** : to arrive ⟨llegar temprano/tarde : to arrive early/late⟩ ⟨llegué a Lisboa : I arrived in Lisbon⟩ ⟨llegué al hotel : I arrived at the hotel⟩ ⟨llegó hasta la frontera : he got as far as the border⟩ ⟨cuando llegue el momento : when the time comes⟩ ⟨va a llegar lejos : she's going to go far⟩ **2** : to be enough ⟨no nos llega el sueldo para todo : we can't afford it all on our salary⟩ **3** ∼ **a/hasta** : to reach ⟨llega hasta el techo : it goes (all the way) up to the ceiling⟩ ⟨llegué hasta la página 85 : I got up to page 85, I got as far as page 85⟩ ⟨podría llegar a los 35 grados : it could get up to 35 degrees⟩ **4** ∼ **a** : to reach (an agreement, etc.) **5** ∼ **a** : to manage to ⟨llegó a terminar la novela : she managed to finish the novel⟩ **6 llegar a ser** : to become ⟨llegó a ser presidente : he became President⟩

llegue, etc. → **llegar**

llenar *vt* **1** : to fill, to fill up, to fill in **2** : to meet, to fulfill ⟨los regalos no llenaron sus expectativas : the gifts did not meet her expectations⟩ — **llenarse** *vr* : to fill up, to become full

llenito, -ta *adj fam* REGORDETE : chubby, plump

lleno¹, -na *adj* **1** : full, filled **2 de** ∼ : completely, fully **3 estar lleno de sí mismo** : to be full of oneself

lleno² *nm* **1** *fam* : plenty, abundance **2** : full house

llevadero, -ra *adj* : bearable

llevar *vt* **1** : to carry, to take (away) ⟨le llevé las maletas : I carried her bags⟩ ⟨siempre lo lleva consigo : he always has it with him⟩ ⟨me gusta, me lo llevo : I like it—I'll take it⟩ **2** : to wear ⟨llevaba un vestido azul : she wore a blue dress⟩ ⟨llevar el pelo corto/largo : to wear one's hair short/long⟩ **3** : to take ⟨llevamos a Pedro al cine : we took Pedro to the movies⟩ ⟨la llevaron al hospital : they took her to the hospital⟩ **4** : to lead ⟨nos llevó por un pasillo : he led us down a hallway⟩ ⟨me lleva a pensar que . . . : it leads me to believe that . . .⟩ **5** : to lead ⟨llevar una vida sana : to lead a healthy life⟩ **6** : to run, to be in charge of ⟨lleva la biblioteca : she runs the library⟩ **7** : to keep ⟨llevar el ritmo : to keep time⟩ ⟨llevar un diario : to keep a diary⟩ **8** : to take, to require ⟨le llevó horas hacerlo : it took him hours to do it⟩ **9** : to have . . . more than ⟨nos llevan cinco puntos : they're five points ahead of us⟩ ⟨te llevo tres años : I'm three years older than you⟩ **10 llevar a cabo** : to carry out **11 llevar adelante** : to carry on with, to keep going with — *vi* : to lead ⟨un problema lleva al otro : one problem leads to another⟩ — *v aux* : to have ⟨llevo mucho tiempo buscándolo : I've been looking for it for a long time⟩ ⟨lleva leído medio libro : he's halfway through the book⟩ — **llevarse** *vr* **1** : to take away, to carry off/away ⟨una ola se lo llevó : a wave carried him away⟩ ⟨se llevó el primer premio : she took/won first prize⟩ **2** : to get along ⟨siempre nos llevábamos bien : we always got along well⟩

llorar *vi* : to cry, to weep — *vt* : to mourn, to bewail

lloriquear *vi* : to whimper, to whine

lloriqueo *nm* : whimpering, whining

lloro *nm* : crying

llorón, -rona *n, mpl* **llorones** : crybaby, whiner

lloroso, -sa *adj* : tearful, sad

llovedizo, -za *adj* : rain ⟨agua llovediza : rainwater⟩

llover {47} *v impers* : to rain ⟨está lloviendo : it's raining⟩ ⟨llover a cántaros : to rain cats and dogs⟩ — *vi* : to rain down, to shower ⟨le llovieron regalos : he was showered with gifts⟩

llovizna *nf* : drizzle, sprinkle

lloviznar *v impers* : to drizzle, to sprinkle

llueve, etc. → **llover**

lluvia *nf* **1** : rain, rainfall **2** : barrage, shower **3 lluvia ácida** : acid rain

lluvioso, -sa *adj* : rainy

lo¹ *pron* (referring to masculine nouns) **1** : him, it ⟨lo vi ayer : I saw him yesterday⟩ ⟨lo entiendo : I understand it⟩ ⟨no lo creo : I don't believe so⟩ **2** (formal) : you ⟨disculpe, señor, no lo oí : excuse me, sir, I didn't hear you⟩ **3 lo que** : what, that which ⟨eso es lo que más le gusta : that's what he likes the most⟩

lo² *art* **1** : the ⟨lo mejor : the best, the best thing⟩ **2** : how ⟨sé lo bueno que eres : I know how good you are⟩ ⟨lo más rápido posible : as quickly as possible⟩

loa *nf* : praise

loable *adj* : laudable, praiseworthy — **loablemente** *adv*

loar *vt* : to praise, to laud

lobato, -ta *n* : wolf cub

lobby *nm* : lobby, pressure group

lobo, -ba *n* : wolf

lobotomía *nf* : lobotomy

lóbrego, -ga *adj* SOMBRÍO : gloomy, dark

lobulado, -da *adj* : lobed

lóbulo *nm* : lobe ⟨lóbulo de la oreja : earlobe⟩

locación *nf, pl* **-ciones** 1 : location (for filming) 2 *Mex* : place

local¹ *adj* : local — **localmente** *adv*

local² *nm* : premises *pl*

localidad *nf* : town, locality

localización *nf, pl* **-ciones** 1 : locating, localization 2 : location

localizar {21} *vt* 1 UBICAR : to locate, to find 2 : to localize — **localizarse** *vr* UBICARSE : to be located ⟨se localiza en el séptimo piso : it is located on the seventh floor⟩

locamente *adv* 1 : madly 2 : wildly, recklessly

locatario, -ria *n* : tenant

loción *nf, pl* **lociones** : lotion

lócker *nm, pl* **lóckers** : locker

loco¹, -ca *adj* 1 DEMENTE : crazy, insane, mad 2 **a lo loco** : wildly, recklessly 3 **volverse loco** : to go mad

loco², -ca *n* 1 : crazy person, lunatic 2 **hacerse el loco** : to act the fool

locomoción *nf, pl* **-ciones** : locomotion

locomotor, -tora *adj* : locomotive

locomotora *nf* 1 : locomotive 2 : driving force

locuaz *adj, pl* **locuaces** : loquacious, talkative

locución *nf, pl* **-ciones** : locution, phrase ⟨locución adverbial : adverbial phrase⟩

locura *nf* 1 : insanity, madness 2 : crazy thing, folly

locutor, -tora *n* : announcer

lodazal *nm* : bog, quagmire

lodo *nm* BARRO : mud, mire

lodoso, -sa *adj* : muddy

logaritmo *nm* : logarithm

logia *nf* : lodge ⟨logia masónica : Masonic lodge⟩

lógica *nf* : logic

lógico, -ca *adj* : logical — **lógicamente** *adv*

login [ˈlogin] *nm* 1 : login, logon (act of logging in) 2 : login (user credentials)

logística *nf* : logistics *pl*

logístico, -ca *adj* : logistic

logo → **logotipo**

logotipo *nm* : logo

logrado, -da *adj* : successful, skillfully done ⟨un efecto muy logrado : a very convincing effect⟩

lograr *vt* 1 : to get, to obtain 2 : to achieve, to attain — **lograrse** *vr* : to be successful

logro *nm* : achievement, attainment

loma *nf* : hill, hillock

lombriz *nf, pl* **lombrices** : worm ⟨lombriz de tierra : earthworm, night crawler⟩ ⟨lombriz solitaria : tapeworm⟩ ⟨tener lombrices : to have worms⟩

lomo *nm* 1 : back (of an animal) 2 : loin ⟨lomo de cerdo : pork loin⟩ 3 : spine (of a book) 4 : blunt edge (of a knife)

lona *nf* : canvas

loncha *nf* LONJA, REBANADA : slice

lonche *nm* 1 *Mex* ALMUERZO : lunch 2 *Mex* : submarine sandwich 3 *Peru* MERIENDA : afternoon snack, tea

lonchería *nf Mex* : snack bar

londinense¹ *adj* : of or from London

londinense² *nmf* : Londoner

longaniza *nf* : spicy pork sausage

longevidad *nf* : longevity

longevo, -va *adj* : long-lived

longitud *nf* 1 LARGO : length ⟨longitud de onda : wavelength⟩ 2 : longitude

longitudinal *adj* : longitudinal — **longitudinalmente** *adv*

lonja *nf* LONCHA, REBANADA : slice

lontananza *nf* : background ⟨en lontananza : in the distance, far away⟩

lord *nm, pl* **lores** (*title in England*) : lord

loro *nm* : parrot

los¹, las *pron* 1 : them ⟨no los conozco muy bien : I don't know them very well⟩ ⟨hice galletas y se las di a los nuevos vecinos : I made cookies and gave them to the new neighbors⟩ 2 : you ⟨voy a llevarlos a los dos : I am going to take both of you⟩ 3 : the ones ⟨me gustan las rojas : I like the red ones⟩ ⟨los de las camisas azules : the ones in the blue shirts⟩ ⟨mis padres y los tuyos : my parents and yours⟩ ⟨las reuniones de ayer y las de hoy : yesterday's meetings and today's⟩ 4 **los que, las que** : those, who, the ones ⟨los que van a cantar deben venir temprano : those who are singing must come early⟩ 5 (*used with* **haber**) ⟨los hay en varios colores : they come in various colors⟩

los² *art* → **el²**

losa *nf* : flagstone, paving stone

loseta *nf* BALDOSA : floor tile

lote *nm* 1 : part, share 2 : batch, lot 3 : plot of land, lot

lotería *nf* : lottery

loto *nm* : lotus

loza *nf* 1 : crockery, earthenware 2 : china

lozanía *nf* 1 : healthiness, robustness 2 : luxuriance, lushness

lozano, -na *adj* 1 : robust, healthy-looking ⟨un rostro lozano : a smooth, fresh face⟩ 2 : lush, luxuriant

LSD *nm* : LSD

lubina *nf* : sea bass

lubricante¹ *adj* : lubricating

lubricante² *nm* : lubricant

lubricar {72} *vt* : to lubricate, to oil — **lubricación** *nf*

lucero *nm* : bright star ⟨lucero del alba : morning star⟩

lucha *nf* 1 : struggle, fight 2 : wrestling

luchador, -dora *n* 1 : fighter 2 : wrestler

luchar *vi* 1 : to fight, to struggle 2 : to wrestle

luchón, -chona *adj, mpl* **luchones** *Mex* : industrious, hardworking

lucidez *nf, pl* **-deces** : lucidity, clarity

lucido, -da *adj* MAGNÍFICO : magnificent, splendid

lúcido, -da *adj* : lucid

luciente *adj* : bright, shining

luciérnaga *nf* : firefly, glowworm
lucimiento *nm* 1 : brilliance, splendor, sparkle 2 : triumph, success ⟨salir con lucimiento : to succeed with flying colors⟩
lucio *nm* : pike (fish)
lucir {45} *vi* 1 : to shine 2 : to look good, to stand out 3 : to seem, to appear ⟨ahora luce contento : he looks happy now⟩ — *vt* 1 : to wear, to sport 2 : to flaunt, to show off — **lucirse** *vr* 1 : to distinguish oneself, to excel 2 : to show off
lucrarse *vr* : to make a profit
lucrativo, -va *adj* : lucrative, profitable — **lucrativamente** *adv*
lucro *nm* GANANCIA : profit, gain
luctuoso, -sa *adj* : mournful, tragic
lúdico, -ca *adj* : play, playful
luego[1] *adv* 1 DESPUÉS : then, afterwards 2 : later (on) 3 desde ∼ : of course 4 ¡hasta luego! : see you later! 5 luego que : as soon as 6 luego luego *Mex fam* : right away, immediately
luego[2] *conj* : therefore ⟨pienso, luego existo : I think, therefore I am⟩
lugar *nm* 1 : place, position ⟨lugar de nacimiento/trabajo : birthplace/workplace⟩ ⟨en algún lugar : somewhere⟩ ⟨en otro lugar : somewhere else⟩ ⟨cambiar algo de lugar : to move something⟩ ⟨poner las cosas en su lugar : to put things away, to straighten up⟩ ⟨te guardo el lugar : I'll save your spot⟩ ⟨yo en tu lugar : if I were in your place, if I were you⟩ ⟨se llevó el primer lugar : she took first place⟩ 2 ESPACIO : space, room ⟨no hay lugar para todos : there isn't room for everyone⟩ 3 dar lugar a : to give rise to, to lead to ⟨puede dar lugar a complicaciones : it can lead to complications⟩ 4 en lugar de : instead of, on behalf of 5 en primer lugar : in the first place, firstly 6 en último lugar : last, lastly 7 lugar común : cliché, platitude 8 sin lugar a dudas : without a doubt, undoubtedly 9 tener lugar : to take place
lugareño[1], **-ña** *adj* : village, rural
lugareño[2], **-ña** *nf* : villager
lugarteniente *nmf* : lieutenant, deputy
lúgubre *adj* : gloomy, lugubrious
lujo *nm* 1 : luxury 2 de ∼ : deluxe
lujoso, -sa *adj* : luxurious
lujuria *nf* : lust, lechery
lujurioso, -sa *adj* : lustful, lecherous
lumbago *nm* : lumbago
lumbar *adj* : lumbar

lumbre *nf* 1 FUEGO : fire 2 : brilliance, splendor 3 poner en la lumbre : to put on the stove, to warm up
lumbrera *nf* 1 : skylight 2 : vent, port 3 : brilliant person, luminary
luminaria *nf* 1 : altar lamp 2 LUMBRERA : luminary, celebrity
luminiscencia *nf* : luminescence — **luminiscente** *adj*
luminosidad *nf* : luminosity, brightness
luminoso, -sa *adj* : shining, luminous
luna *nf* 1 : moon 2 luna de miel : honeymoon
lunar[1] *adj* : lunar
lunar[2] *nm* 1 : mole, beauty spot 2 : defect, blemish 3 : polka dot
lunático, -ca *adj* & *n* : lunatic
lunes *nms* & *pl* : Monday ⟨el lunes : (on) Monday⟩ ⟨los lunes : (on) Mondays⟩ ⟨cada (dos) lunes : every (other) Monday⟩ ⟨el lunes pasado : last Monday⟩ ⟨el lunes por la noche : on Monday night⟩ ⟨el próximo lunes : next Monday⟩
luneta *nf* 1 : lens (of eyeglasses) 2 : windshield (of an automobile) 3 : crescent
lupa *nf* : magnifying glass
lúpulo *nm* : hops (plant)
lustrabotas → **limpiabotas**
lustrar *vt* : to shine, to polish
lustre *nm* 1 BRILLO : luster, shine 2 : glory, distinction
lustro *nm* : five-year period
lustroso, -sa *adj* BRILLOSO : lustrous, shiny
luto *nm* : mourning ⟨estar de luto : to be in mourning⟩
luxación *nf, pl* **-ciones** : dislocation
luz *nf, pl* **luces** 1 : light ⟨luz del sol : sunlight⟩ ⟨luz eléctrica/artificial : electric/artificial light⟩ ⟨iluminado con una luz tenue : dimly lit⟩ ⟨a plena luz del día : in full/broad daylight⟩ 2 *fam* : power, electricity ⟨se fue la luz : the power/electricity went out⟩ ⟨cortar la luz : to cut off the power⟩ ⟨pagar la luz : to pay the electricity bill⟩ 3 : light, lamp ⟨apagar la luz : to turn off the light⟩ ⟨encender/prender la luz : to turn on the light⟩ ⟨luz de bengala : flare⟩ ⟨luz neón/LED : neon/LED light⟩ 4 : span, spread (between supports) 5 a la luz de : in light of 6 a todas luces : by any measure 7 dar a luz : to give birth 8 sacar a la luz : to make known, to bring to light 9 salir a la luz : to become known, to come to light 10 traje de luces : matador's costume
luzca, etc. → **lucir**

M

m *nf* : fifteenth letter of the Spanish alphabet

macabro, -bra *adj* : macabre

macadán *nm, pl* **-danes** : macadam

macana *nf* **1** : club, cudgel **2** *fam* : nonsense, silliness **3** *fam* : lie, fib *fam*

macanear *vi Arg, Chile, Uru fam* : to talk nonsense — *vt Mex, PRi fam* : to beat

macanudo, -da *adj fam* : great, fantastic

macarrón *nm, pl* **-rrones 1** : macaroon **2 macarrones** *nmpl* : macaroni

macerar *vt* : to soak (food)

maceta *nf* **1** : flowerpot **2** : mallet **3** *Mex fam* : head

macetero *nm* **1** : plant stand **2 TIESTO** : flowerpot, planter

machacar {72} *vt* **1** : to crush, to grind **2** : to beat, to pound — *vi* : to insist, to go on (about)

machacón, -cona *adj, mpl* **-cones** : insistent, tiresome

machete *nm* : machete

machetear *vt* : to hack with a machete — *vi fam* : to plod, to work tirelessly

machismo *nm* **1** : machismo **2** : male chauvinism

machista *nm* : male chauvinist

macho¹ *adj* **1** : male **2** : macho, virile, tough

macho² *nm* **1** : male **2** : he-man

machote *nm* **1** *fam* : tough guy, he-man **2** *CA, Mex* : rough draft, model **3** *Mex* : blank form

machucar {72} *vt* **1** : to pound, to beat, to crush **2** : to bruise

machucón *nm, pl* **-cones 1 MORETÓN** : bruise **2** : smashing, pounding

macilento, -ta *adj* : gaunt, wan

macis *nm* : mace (spice)

macizo, -za *adj* **1** : solid ⟨oro macizo : solid gold⟩ **2** : strong, strapping **3** : massive

mácula *nf* : blemish, stain

macuto *nm Spain* : backpack

madeja *nf* **1** : skein, hank **2** : tangle (of hair)

madera *nf* **1** : wood ⟨de madera : made of wood, wooden⟩ ⟨tener madera de algo : to have the makings of something⟩ **2** : lumber, timber **3 madera dura** *or* **madera noble** : hardwood

maderero, -ra *adj* : timber, lumber

madero *nm* : piece of lumber, plank

madrastra *nf* : stepmother

madrazo *nm Mex fam* : punch, blow ⟨se agarraron a madrazos : they beat each other up⟩

madre *nf* **1** : mother ⟨madre biológica/adoptiva : biological/adoptive mother⟩ ⟨madre de alquiler : surrogate mother⟩ ⟨madre soltera : single/unwed mother⟩ **2 madre política** : mother-in-law **3 la Madre Patria** : the mother country (said of Spain)

madrear *vt Mex fam* : to beat up

madreperla *nf* NÁCAR : mother-of-pearl

madreselva *nf* : honeysuckle

madriguera *nf* : burrow, den, lair

madrileño¹, -ña *adj* : of or from Madrid

madrileño², -ña *n* : person from Madrid

madrina *nf* **1** : godmother **2** : mother of the groom, matron of honor **3** : sponsor

madrugada *nf* **1** : early morning, wee hours **2 ALBA** : dawn, daybreak

madrugador, -dora *n* : early riser

madrugar {52} *vi* **1** : to get up early **2** : to get a head start

madurar *v* **1** : to ripen **2** : to mature

madurez *nf, pl* **-reces 1** : maturity **2** : ripeness

maduro, -ra *adj* **1** : mature **2** : ripe

maestría *nf* **1** : mastery, skill **2** : master's degree

maestro¹, -tra *adj* **1** : masterly, skilled **2** : chief, main **3** : trained ⟨un elefante maestro : a trained elephant⟩

maestro², -tra *n* **1** : teacher (in elementary and middle school) ⟨no hay mejor maestro que la necesidad : necessity is the mother of invention⟩ **2** : expert, master ⟨maestro de cocina : chef⟩ ⟨maestro de ceremonias : master of ceremonies⟩ **3** : maestro

Mafia *nf* : Mafia

mafioso, -sa *n* : mafioso, gangster

magdalena *nf* : bun, muffin

magenta *adj & n* : magenta

magia *nf* : magic

mágico, -ca *adj* : magic, magical — **mágicamente** *adv*

magisterio *nm* **1** : teaching **2** : teachers *pl*, teaching profession

magistrado, -da *n* : magistrate, judge

magistral *adj* : masterful, skillful

magistralmente *adv* : masterfully, brilliantly

magistratura *nf* : office of judge/magistrate

magma *nm* : magma

magnanimidad *nf* : magnanimity

magnánimo, -ma *adj* GENEROSO : magnanimous — **magnánimamente** *adv*

magnate *nmf* : magnate, tycoon

magnesio *nm* : magnesium

magnético, -ca *adj* : magnetic

magnetismo *nm* : magnetism

magnetizar {21} *vt* : to magnetize

magnetofónico, -ca *adj* **cinta magnetofónica** : magnetic tape

magnificar {72} *vt* **1** : to magnify **2 EXAGERAR** : to exaggerate **3 ENSALZAR** : to exalt, to extol, to praise highly

magnificencia *nf* : magnificence, splendor

magnífico, -ca *adj* ESPLENDOROSO : magnificent, splendid — **magníficamente** *adv*

magnitud *nf* : magnitude

magnolia *nf* : magnolia (flower)

magnolio *nm* : magnolia (tree)

mago, -ga *n* **1** : magician **2** : wizard (in folk tales, etc.) **3 los Reyes Magos** : the Magi

magro, -gra *adj* 1 : lean (of meat) 2 : meager

maguey *nm* : maguey

magulladura *nf* MORETÓN : bruise

magullar *vt* : to bruise — **magullarse** *vr*

mahometano¹, -na *adj* ISLÁMICO : Islamic, Muslim

mahometano², -na *n* : Muslim

mahonesa → **mayonesa**

maicena *nf* : cornstarch

mainframe ['mein,freim] *nm* : mainframe

maíz *nm* : corn, maize

maizal *nm* : cornfield

maja *nf* : pestle

majadería *nf* 1 TONTERÍA : stupidity, foolishness 2 *Mex* LEPERADA : insult, obscenity

majadero¹, -ra *adj* 1 : foolish, silly 2 *Mex* LÉPERO : crude, vulgar

majadero², -ra *n* 1 TONTO : fool 2 *Mex* : rude person, boor

majar *vt* : to crush, to mash

majestad *nf* : majesty ⟨Su Majestad : Your Majesty⟩

majestuosamente *adv* : majestically

majestuosidad *nf* : majesty, grandeur

majestuoso, -sa *adj* : majestic, stately

majo, -ja *adj Spain* 1 : nice, likeable 2 GUAPO : attractive, good-looking

mal¹ *adv* 1 : badly, poorly ⟨baila muy mal : he dances very badly⟩ ⟨hablar mal de alguien : to speak ill of someone⟩ ⟨hice mal en decirlo : I was wrong to say it⟩ ⟨comió algo que le hizo mal : he ate something that didn't agree with him⟩ ⟨algo anda mal : something's wrong⟩ ⟨todo le salió mal : everything went wrong for her⟩ ⟨el primer día no me fue mal : my first day wasn't bad⟩ 2 : wrong, incorrectly ⟨me entendió mal : she misunderstood me⟩ ⟨no lo tomes a mal : don't take it the wrong way⟩ ⟨esta palabra está mal escrita : this word is spelled wrong⟩ ⟨si mal no recuerdo : if I remember correctly⟩ 3 : hardly, with difficulty ⟨te oigo mal : I can hardly hear you⟩ ⟨mal se pueden comparar : you can hardly compare them⟩ ⟨mal puedo esperar : I can hardly wait⟩ 4 **de mal en peor** : from bad to worse 5 **menos mal** : it's a good thing, it's just as well ⟨menos mal que reaccioné a tiempo : it's a good thing I reacted in time⟩ ⟨menos mal que no viniste : it's just as well you didn't come⟩

mal² *adj* → **malo**

mal³ *nm* 1 : evil, wrong ⟨un mal necesario : a necessary evil⟩ 2 DAÑO : harm, damage ⟨las acusaciones le hicieron mucho mal : the accusations did him a lot of harm⟩ 3 DESGRACIA : misfortune 4 ENFERMEDAD : illness, sickness 5 **mal de ojo** : evil eye

malabar *adj* **juegos malabares** : juggling

malabares *nmpl* : juggling ⟨hacer malabares : to juggle⟩

malabarismos → **malabares**

malabarista *nmf* : juggler

malaconsejado, -da *adj* : ill-advised

malacostumbrado, -da *adj* CONSENTIDO : spoiled, pampered

malacostumbrar *vt* : to spoil

malagradecido, -da *adj* INGRATO : ungrateful

malaisio → **malasio**

malanga *nf* TARO : taro

malaria *nf* PALUDISMO : malaria

malasio, -sia *adj & n* : Malaysian

malauiano, -na *adj & n* : Malawian

malaventura *nf* : misadventure, misfortune

malaventurado, -da *adj* MALHADADO : ill-fated, unfortunate

malayo, -ya *adj & n* : Malay, Malayan

malbaratar *vt* 1 MALGASTAR : to squander 2 : to undersell

malcriado¹, -da *adj* 1 : ill-bred, ill-mannered 2 : spoiled, pampered

malcriado², -da *n* : spoiled brat

malcriar *vt* : to spoil, to raise badly

maldad *nf* 1 : evil, wickedness 2 : evil deed

maldecir {11} *vt* : to curse, to damn — *vi* 1 : to curse, to swear 2 ~ **de** : to speak ill of, to slander, to defame

maldición *nf, pl* **-ciones** : curse

maldiga, maldijo etc. → **maldecir**

maldito, -ta *adj* 1 : cursed, damned ⟨¡maldita sea! : damn it all!⟩ 2 : wicked

maldoso, -sa *adj Mex* : mischievous

maleable *adj* : malleable

maleante *nmf* : crook, thug

malecón *nm, pl* **-cones** : jetty, breakwater

maleducado, -da *adj* : ill-mannered, rude

maleficio *nm* : curse, hex

maléfico, -ca *adj* : evil, harmful

malentender {56} *vt* : to misunderstand

malentendido *nm* : misunderstanding

malestar *nm* 1 : discomfort 2 IRRITACIÓN : annoyance 3 INQUIETUD : uneasiness, unrest

maleta *nf* : suitcase, bag ⟨haz tus maletas : pack your bags⟩

maletera *nf Peru* → **maletero²**

maletero¹, -ra *n* : porter

maletero² *nm* : trunk (of an automobile)

maletín *nm, pl* **-tines** 1 PORTAFOLIO : briefcase 2 : overnight bag, satchel

malevolencia *nf* : malevolence, wickedness

malévolo, -la *adj* : malevolent, wicked

maleza *nf* 1 : thicket, underbrush 2 : weeds *pl*

malformación *nf, pl* **-ciones** : malformation

malgache *adj & nmf* : Madagascan

malgastar *vt* : to squander (resources), to waste (time, effort)

mal habido, -da *adj* : ill-gotten, dirty

malhablado, -da *adj* : foulmouthed

malhadado, -da *adj* MALAVENTURADO : ill-fated

malhechor, -chora *n* : criminal, delinquent, wrongdoer

malherir {76} *vt* : to injure seriously

malhumor *nm* : bad mood

malhumorado, -da *adj* : bad-tempered, cross

malicia *nf* **1** : wickedness, malice **2** : mischief, naughtiness **3** : cunning, craftiness

malicioso, -sa *adj* **1** : malicious **2** PÍCARO : mischievous

malignidad *nf* **1** : malignancy **2** MALDAD : evil

maligno, -na *adj* **1** : malignant ⟨un tumor maligno : a malignant tumor⟩ **2** : evil, harmful, malign

malinchismo *nm Mex* : preference for foreign goods or people — **malinchista** *adj*

malintencionado, -da *adj* : malicious, spiteful

malinterpretar *vt* : to misinterpret

mall ['mol] *nm, pl* **malls** : (shopping) mall

malla *nf* **1** : mesh **2** LEOTARDO : leotard, tights *pl* **3 malla de baño** *Arg, Uru* : swimsuit, bathing suit

mallorquín, -quina *adj & n* : Majorcan

malnutrición *nf, pl* **-ciones** DESNUTRICIÓN : malnutrition

malnutrido, -da *adj* DESNUTRIDO : malnourished, undernourished

malo¹, -la *adj* (**mal** *before masculine singular nouns*) **1** : bad ⟨mala suerte : bad luck⟩ ⟨malas noticias : bad news⟩ ⟨es mala idea : it's a bad idea⟩ ⟨mal aliento : bad breath⟩ ⟨un mal sabor : a bad taste⟩ ⟨un mal actor : a bad actor⟩ ⟨tener un mal día : to have a bad day⟩ ⟨una situación muy mala : a very bad situation⟩ ⟨recibió muy malas críticas : it got very bad reviews⟩ ⟨ese sombrero te queda mal : that hat doesn't look good on you⟩ ⟨llegaste en mal momento : you arrived at a bad time⟩ **2** : bad, poor ⟨en malas condiciones : in bad condition⟩ ⟨es de mala calidad : it's poor quality⟩ **3** : bad, wicked, naughty ⟨una mala persona : a bad person⟩ ⟨malas intenciones : bad intentions⟩ ⟨fuiste muy malo : you were very bad⟩ **4** : bad, improper ⟨ser de mala educación : to be bad manners⟩ ⟨malas palabras : bad words⟩ **5** : bad, harmful ⟨malo para la salud : bad for one's health⟩ **6** (*using the form* **mal**) : sick, ill, unwell ⟨estar/ponerse mal : to be/fall ill⟩ ⟨me siento/encuentro mal : I feel sick⟩ ⟨ando mal del estómago : my stomach is upset⟩ ⟨estar mal del corazón : to have heart trouble⟩ **7** : bad, spoiled (of food) **8 estar de malas** : to be in a bad mood

malo², -la *n* : villain, bad guy (in novels, movies, etc.)

malogrado, -da *adj* : failed, unsuccessful

malograr *vt* **1** : to spoil, to ruin **2** : to waste (an opportunity, time) — **malograrse** *vr* **1** FRACASAR : to fail **2** : to die young

malogro *nm* **1** : untimely death **2** FRACASO : failure

maloliente *adj* HEDIONDO : foul-smelling, smelly

malparado, -da *adj* **salir malparado** *or* **quedar malparado** : to come out of (something) badly, to end up in a bad state

malpensado, -da *adj* : distrustful, suspicious

malquerencia *nf* AVERSIÓN : ill will, dislike

malquerer {64} *vt* : to dislike

malquiso, etc. → **malquerer**

malsano, -na *adj* : unhealthy

malsonante *adj* : rude, offensive ⟨palabras malsonantes : foul language⟩

malta *nf* : malt

malteada *nf* : malted milk ⟨malteada de chocolate : chocolate malt⟩

maltratar *vt* **1** : to mistreat, to abuse **2** : to damage, to spoil

maltrato *nm* : mistreatment, abuse

maltrecho, -cha *adj* : battered, damaged

malucho, -cha *adj fam* : sick, under the weather

malva *adj & nm* : mauve

malvado¹, -da *adj* : evil, wicked

malvado², -da *n* : evildoer, wicked person

malvavisco *nm* : marshmallow

malvender *vt* : to sell at a loss

malversación *nf, pl* **-ciones** : misappropriation (of funds), embezzlement

malversador, -dora *n* : embezzler

malversar *vt* : to embezzle

malvivir *vi* : to live badly, to just scrape by

malware ['malwer] *nm* : malware

mamá *nf fam* : mom, mama

mamadera *nf* : baby bottle

mamar *vi* **1** : to suckle **2 darle de mamar a** : to breast-feed — *vt* **1** : to suckle, to nurse **2** : to learn from childhood, to grow up with — **mamarse** *vr fam* : to get drunk

mamario, -ria *adj* : mammary

mamarracho *nm fam* **1** ESPERPENTO : mess, sight **2** : laughingstock, fool **3** : rubbish, junk

mambo *nm* : mambo

mameluco *nm* : overalls *pl*

mami *nf fam* : mommy

mamífero¹, -ra *adj* : mammalian

mamífero² *nm* : mammal

mamila *nf* **1** : nipple **2** *Mex* : baby bottle, pacifier

mamografía *nf* : mammogram

mamola *nf* : pat, chuck under the chin

mamotreto *nm fam* **1** : huge book, tome **2** ARMATOSTE : hulk, monstrosity

mampara *nf* BIOMBO : screen, room divider

mamparo *nm* : bulkhead

mampostería *nf* : masonry, stonemasonry

mampostero *nm* : mason, stonemason

mamut *nm, pl* **mamuts** : mammoth

maná *nm* : manna

manada *nf* **1** : flock, herd, pack **2** *fam* : horde, mob ⟨llegaron en manada : they came in droves⟩

manager *or* **mánager** *nmf, pl* **-gers** : manager

manantial *nm* **1** FUENTE : spring **2** : source

manar *vi* **1** : to flow **2** : to abound

manaza *nf* MANO : hand, mitt

manazas *nmfs & pl* : clumsy person, klutz, oaf

manatí *nm, pl* **-tíes** : manatee

mancha *nf* **1** : stain, spot, mark ⟨mancha de sangre : bloodstain⟩ **2** : blemish, blot ⟨una mancha en su reputación : a blemish on his reputation⟩ **3** : patch

manchado, -da *adj* : stained

manchar *vt* **1** ENSUCIAR : to stain, to soil **2** DESHONRAR : to sully, to tarnish — **mancharse** *vr* : to get dirty

mancillar *vt* : to sully, to besmirch

manco, -ca *adj* : one-armed, with one arm/hand

mancomunar *vt* **1** : to combine, to pool — **mancomunarse** *vr* : to unite, to join together

mancomunidad *nf* **1** : commonwealth **2** : association, confederation

mancuernas *nfpl* : cuff links

mancuernillas *nf Mex* : cuff links

mandadero, -ra *n* : errand boy *m*, errand girl *f*, messenger

mandado *nm* **1** : order, command **2** : errand ⟨hacer los mandados : to run errands, to go shopping⟩

mandamás *nmf, pl* **-mases** *fam* : boss, bigwig, honcho

mandamiento *nm* **1** : commandment **2** : command, order, warrant ⟨mandamiento judicial : warrant, court order⟩

mandar *vt* **1** ORDENAR : to command, to order ⟨los mandó (a) callar, los mandó (a) que callaran : she ordered them to be quiet⟩ ⟨mandó (a) construir un monumento : he had a monument built⟩ **2** ENVIAR : to send ⟨te manda saludos : he sends you his regards⟩ ⟨la mandaron a Buenos Aires : they sent her to Buenos Aires⟩ **3** ECHAR : to hurl, to throw **4** ¿mande? *Mex* : yes?, pardon? **5 mandar algo a arreglar** : to have something fixed **6 mandar (a) decir** : to send word, to send a message **7 mandar (a) llamar** : to send for, to summon — *vi* : to be the boss, to be in charge — **mandarse** *vr Mex* : to take liberties, to take advantage

mandarín *nm* : Mandarin

mandarina *nf* : mandarin orange, tangerine

mandatario, -ria *n* **1** : leader (in politics) ⟨primer mandatario : head of state⟩ **2** : agent (in law)

mandato *nm* **1** : term of office **2** : mandate

mandíbula *nf* **1** : jaw **2** : mandible

mandil *nm* **1** DELANTAL : apron **2** : horse blanket

mandilón *nm, pl* **-lones** *fam* : wimp, coward

mandioca *nf* **1** : manioc, cassava **2** : tapioca

mando *nm* **1** : command, leadership **2** : control (for a device) ⟨mando a distancia : remote control⟩ **3 al mando de** : in charge of **4 al mando de** : under the command of

mandolina *nf* : mandolin

mandón, -dona *adj, mpl* **mandones** : bossy, domineering

mandonear *vt fam* MANGONEAR : to boss around

manecilla *nf* : hand (of a clock), pointer

manejable *adj* **1** : manageable **2** : docile, easily led

manejar *vt* **1** CONDUCIR : to drive (a car) **2** OPERAR : to handle, to operate **3** : to manage **4** : to manipulate (a person) — *vi* : to drive — **manejarse** *vr* **1** COMPORTARSE : to behave **2** : to get along, to manage

manejo *nm* **1** : handling, operation **2** : management

manera *nf* **1** MODO : way, manner, fashion ⟨cada uno lo hace a su manera : everyone does it their own way⟩ ⟨a mi manera de ver : the way I see it⟩ ⟨de esta/esa manera : in this/that way⟩ ⟨de una manera u otra : one way or another⟩ ⟨de manera inmediata : immediately⟩ ⟨de mala manera : badly, rudely⟩ **2 a manera de** : by way of **3 de alguna manera** : somehow, in some way **4 de cualquier manera** *or* **de todas maneras** : anyway, anyhow ⟨de todas maneras tenía que hacerlo : I had to do it anyway⟩ **5 de manera que** : so, in order that **6 de ninguna manera** : by no means, absolutely not **7 de otra manera** : differently, in another way ⟨para decirlo de otra manera : in other words⟩ ⟨de otra manera no hubiera sobrevivido : otherwise he wouldn't have survived⟩ **8 manera de ser** : personality, demeanor **9 no hay manera** : there's no way, it's not possible ⟨no hay manera de saberlo : there's no way to know⟩ **10 maneras** *nfpl* : manners

manga *nf* **1** : sleeve ⟨en mangas de camisa : in shirt sleeves⟩ ⟨sin mangas : without sleeves, sleeveless⟩ **2** MANGUERA : hose

manganeso *nm* : manganese

manglar *nm* : mangrove swamp

mangle *nm* : mangrove

mango *nm* **1** : hilt, handle **2** : mango

mangonear *vt fam* : to boss around, to bully — *vi* **1** : to be bossy **2** : to loaf, to fool around

mangosta *nf* : mongoose

manguera *nf* : hose

manguito *nm* **1** : muff **2** : sleeve (of a pipe, etc.), hose (of a car)

maní *nm, pl* **maníes** : peanut

manía *nf* **1** OBSESIÓN : mania, obsession **2** : craze, fad **3** : odd habit, peculiarity **4** : dislike, aversion

maníaco¹, -ca *or* **maniaco, -ca** *adj* **1** : manic **2** *fam* CRAZED : maniacal

maníaco², -ca *or* **maniaco, -ca** *n* : maniac

maniatar *vt* : to tie the hands of

maniático¹, -ca *adj* **1** MANÍACO : maniacal **2** : obsessive **3** : fussy, finicky

maniático², -ca *n* **1** MANÍACO : maniac, lunatic **2** : obsessive person, fanatic **3** : eccentric, crank

manicomio *nm fam* **1** : insane asylum, madhouse *now often offensive* **2** (*used figuratively*) : madhouse

manicura *nf* : manicure

manicuro, -ra *n* : manicurist

manido, -da *adj* : hackneyed, stale, trite

manifestación *nf, pl* **-ciones** 1 : manifestation, sign 2 : demonstration, rally
manifestante *nmf* : demonstrator
manifestar {55} *vt* 1 : to demonstrate, to show 2 : to declare — **manifestarse** *vr* 1 : to be or become evident 2 : to state one's position ⟨se han manifestado a favor del acuerdo : they have declared their support for the agreement⟩ 3 : to demonstrate, to rally
manifiesto¹, -ta *adj* : manifest, evident, clear — **manifiestamente** *adv*
manifiesto² *nm* : manifesto
manija *nf* MANGO : handle
manilla → **manecilla**
manillar *nm* : handlebars *pl*
maniobra *nf* : maneuver, stratagem
maniobrar *v* : to maneuver
manipulación *nf, pl* **-ciones** : manipulation
manipulador¹, -dora *adj* : manipulating, manipulative
manipulador², -dora *n* : manipulator
manipular *vt* 1 : to manipulate 2 MANEJAR : to handle
maniquí¹ *nmf, pl* **-quíes** : mannequin, model
maniquí² *nm, pl* **-quíes** : mannequin, dummy
manirroto¹, -ta *adj* : extravagant
manirroto², -ta *n* : spendthrift
manitas *nmfs & pl Spain* : handyman *m*, handywoman *f*
manito, -ta → **mano²**
manivela *nf* : crank
manjar *nm* : delicacy, special dish
mano¹ *nf* 1 : hand ⟨lávate las manos : wash your hands⟩ ⟨agárralo con las dos manos : hold it with both hands⟩ ⟨tenía algo en la mano : she had something in her hand⟩ ⟨con mis propias manos : with my own two hands⟩ 2 : coat (of paint or varnish) 3 : hand (in games) 4 **a ~** : by hand ⟨a la ~ *or* a la mano : handy, at hand, nearby ⟨tenía los libros a (la) mano : I kept the books handy⟩ 6 **bajo ~** : secretly, on the sly 7 **caer en manos de** : to fall into the hands of 8 **con las manos en la masa** : red-handed 9 **darle la mano a alguien** : to shake someone's hand 10 **darse la mano** : to shake hands 11 **de la mano** : by the hand, hand in hand ⟨me tomó de la mano : he took me by the hand⟩ ⟨la política y la economía van de la mano : politics and economics go hand in hand⟩ 12 **de mano en mano** : from one person to the next ⟨pasar de mano en mano : to be passed along/around⟩ 13 **de primera mano** : firsthand, at firsthand ⟨conocer de primera mano : to experience firsthand⟩ 14 **de segunda mano** : secondhand, used ⟨ropa de segunda mano : secondhand clothing⟩ 15 **echar una mano** : to lend a hand 16 **mano a mano** : one-on-one 17 **mano de obra** : labor, manpower 18 **mano de mortero** : pestle 19 **mano negra** *Mex fam* : shady dealings *pl* 20 ¡**manos arriba**! *or* ¡**arriba las manos**! : stick 'em up!, (put your) hands up! 21 **tener (buena) mano para** : to be good at
mano², -na *n fam* : buddy, pal ⟨joye, mano! : hey man!⟩
manojo *nm* PUÑADO : handful, bunch ⟨ser un manojo de nervios : to be a bag/bundle of nerves⟩
manómetro *nm* : pressure gauge
manopla *nf* 1 : mitten, mitt 2 : brass knuckles *pl*
manosear *vt* 1 : to handle or touch excessively 2 ACARICIAR : to fondle, to caress
manoseo *nm* 1 : touching, handling 2 : groping, fondling
manotazo *nm* : slap, smack, swipe
manotear *vi* : to wave one's hands, to gesticulate
mansalva *adv* **a ~** : at close range
mansarda *nf* BUHARDILLA : attic
mansedumbre *nf* : gentleness, meekness
mansión *nf, pl* **-siones** : mansion
manso, -sa *adj* 1 : gentle, meek 2 : tame — **mansamente** *adv*
manta *nf* 1 COBIJA, FRAZADA : blanket 2 : poncho 3 *Mex* : coarse cotton fabric
manteca *nf* 1 GRASA : lard, fat 2 : butter
mantecado *nm* 1 PRi HELADO : ice cream 2 (*in various countries*) : unflavored ice cream 3 *Spain* : shortbread (made with lard)
mantecoso, -sa *adj* : buttery
mantel *nm* 1 : tablecloth 2 : altar cloth
mantelería *nf* : table linen
mantener {80} *vt* 1 SUSTENTAR : to support, to feed ⟨mantener uno su familia : to support one's family⟩ 2 CONSERVAR : to keep, to preserve ⟨mantener la calma : to keep one's calm⟩ ⟨mantener la paz : to keep the peace⟩ 3 CONTINUAR : to keep up, to sustain ⟨mantener una correspondencia : to keep up a correspondence⟩ 4 AFIRMAR : to maintain, to affirm — **mantenerse** *vr* 1 : to support oneself, to subsist 2 **mantenerse firme** : to hold one's ground
mantenimiento *nm* 1 : maintenance, upkeep 2 : sustenance, food 3 : preservation
mantequera *nf* 1 : churn 2 : butter dish
mantequería *nf* 1 : creamery, dairy 2 : grocery store
mantequilla *nf* : butter
mantilla *nf* : scarf (worn over the head and shoulders)
mantis *nf* **mantis religiosa** : praying mantis
manto *nm* 1 : cloak 2 : mantle (in geology)
mantón *nm, pl* **-tones** CHAL : shawl
mantuvo, etc. → **mantener**
manual¹ *adj* 1 : manual ⟨trabajo manual : manual labor⟩ 2 : handy, manageable — **manualmente** *adv*
manual² *nm* : manual, handbook
manualidades *nfpl* : handicrafts (in schools)
manubrio *nm* 1 : handle, crank 2 : handlebars *pl*

manufactura *nf* 1 FABRICACIÓN : manufacture 2 : manufactured item, product 3 FÁBRICA : factory
manufacturar *vt* FABRICAR : to manufacture
manufacturero[1], -ra *adj* : manufacturing
manufacturero[2], -ra *n* FABRICANTE : manufacturer
manuscrito[1], -ta *adj* : handwritten
manuscrito[2] *nm* : manuscript
manutención *nf, pl* **-ciones** : maintenance, support
manzana *nf* 1 : apple 2 CUADRA : block (enclosed by streets or buildings) 3 *or* **manzana de Adán** : Adam's apple
manzanal *nm* 1 : apple orchard 2 MANZANO : apple tree
manzanar *nm* : apple orchard
manzanilla *nf* 1 : chamomile 2 : chamomile tea
manzano *nm* : apple tree
maña *nf* 1 : dexterity, skill 2 : cunning, guile 3 **mañas** *or* **malas mañas** *nfpl* : bad habits, vices
mañana *nf* 1 : morning ⟨a las cuatro de la mañana : at four in the morning⟩ ⟨por la mañana : in the morning⟩ 2 : tomorrow
mañanero, -ra *adj* MATUTINO : morning ⟨rocío mañanero : morning dew⟩
mañanitas *nfpl Mex* : birthday serenade
mañoso, -sa *adj* 1 HÁBIL : skillful 2 ASTUTO : cunning, crafty 3 : fussy, finicky
mapa *nm* CARTA : map
mapache *nm* : raccoon
mapamundi *nm* : map of the world
maqueta *nf* : model
maquila *nf* 1 : production, manufacture (for export) 2 → **maquiladora**
maquiladora *nf* : foreign-owned factory
maquillador, -dora *n* : makeup artist
maquillaje *nm* : makeup
maquillarse *vr* : to put on makeup, to make oneself up
máquina *nf* 1 : machine ⟨máquina de afeitar : electric razor⟩ ⟨máquina de coser : sewing machine⟩ ⟨máquina de escribir : typewriter⟩ ⟨máquina tragamonedas : slot machine⟩ ⟨máquina del tiempo : time machine⟩ ⟨máquina de votación : voting machine⟩ ⟨máquina expendedora : vending machine⟩ ⟨hecho a máquina : machine-made⟩ ⟨escribir a máquina : to type⟩ 2 LOCOMOTORA : engine, locomotive 3 : machine (in politics) 4 *or* **máquina de fotos** CÁMARA : camera 5 **a toda máquina** : at full speed
maquinación *nf, pl* **-ciones** : machination, scheme, plot
maquinal *adj* : mechanical, automatic — **maquinalmente** *adv*
maquinar *vt* : to plot, to scheme
maquinaria *nf* 1 : machinery 2 : mechanism, works *pl*
maquinilla *nf* 1 : small machine or device 2 *CA, Car* : typewriter
maquinista *nmf* 1 : machinist 2 : railroad engineer
mar *nmf* 1 : sea ⟨un mar agitado : a rough sea⟩ ⟨hacerse a la mar : to set sail⟩ 2 **alta mar** : high seas

maraca *nf* : maraca
maraña *nf* 1 : thicket 2 ENREDO : tangle, mess
marasmo *nm* : paralysis, stagnation
maratón *nm, pl* **-tones** : marathon
maravilla *nf* 1 : wonder, marvel ⟨a las mil maravillas : wonderfully, marvelously⟩ ⟨hacer maravillas : to work wonders⟩ 2 : marigold
maravillar *vt* ASOMBRAR : to astonish, to amaze — **maravillarse** *vr* : to be amazed, to marvel
maravilloso, -sa *adj* ESTUPENDO : wonderful, marvelous — **maravillosamente** *adv*
marbete *nm* 1 ETIQUETA : label, tag 2 *PRi* : registration sticker (of a car)
marca *nf* 1 : mark ⟨marca de nacimiento : birthmark⟩ 2 : brand, make ⟨artículos de marca : brand-name items⟩ 3 : trademark ⟨marca registrada : registered trademark⟩ 4 : record (in sports) ⟨batir la marca : to beat the record⟩
marcado, -da *adj* : marked ⟨un marcado contraste : a marked contrast⟩ — **marcadamente** *adv*
marcador *nm* 1 TANTEADOR : scoreboard 2 : marker, felt-tip pen 3 **marcador de libros** : bookmark
marcaje *nm* 1 : scoring (in sports) 2 : guarding (in sports)
marcapasos *nms & pl* : pacemaker
marcar {72} *vt* 1 : to mark 2 : to brand (livestock) 3 : to indicate, to show 4 RESALTAR : to emphasize 5 : to dial (a telephone) 6 : to guard (an opponent) 7 ANOTAR : to score (a goal, a point) — *vi* 1 ANOTAR : to score 2 : to dial
marcha *nf* 1 : march ⟨cerrar la marcha : to bring up the rear⟩ 2 : hike, walk ⟨ir de marcha : to go hiking⟩ 3 : pace, speed ⟨a toda marcha : at top speed⟩ 4 : gear (of an automobile) ⟨marcha atrás : reverse, reverse gear⟩ ⟨dar marcha atrás : to go into reverse⟩ 5 : departure 6 : march (in music) ⟨marcha fúnebre/nupcial : funeral/wedding march⟩ 7 : course ⟨la marcha de los acontecimientos : the course of events⟩ 8 **dar marcha atrás (en algo)** : to backtrack (on something) 9 **en ~** : in motion, in gear, under way ⟨poner en marcha : to activate, to start, to set in motion⟩ ⟨ponerse en marcha : to set off⟩
marchar *vi* 1 IR : to go, to travel 2 ANDAR : to walk 3 FUNCIONAR : to work, to go 4 : to march — **marcharse** *vr* : to leave
marchitar *vi* : to make wither, to wilt — **marchitarse** *vr* 1 : to wither, to shrivel up, to wilt 2 : to languish, to fade away
marchito, -ta *adj* : withered, faded
marcial *adj* : martial, military
marciano, -na *adj & n* : Martian
marco *nm* 1 : frame, framework 2 : goalposts *pl* 3 AMBIENTE : setting, atmosphere 4 : mark (unit of currency)
marea *nf* 1 : tide 2 **marea negra** : oil slick

mareado, -da *adj* **1** : dizzy, light-headed **2** : queasy, nauseous **3** : seasick, airsick, carsick

marear *vt* **1** : to make sick ⟨los gases me marearon : the fumes made me sick⟩ **2** : to bother, to annoy — **marearse** *vr* **1** : to get sick, to become nauseated **2** : to feel dizzy **3** : to get tipsy

marejada *nf* **1** : surge, swell (of the sea) **2** : undercurrent, ferment, unrest

maremoto *nm* : tidal wave

mareo *nm* **1** : dizzy spell **2** : nausea **3** : seasickness, motion sickness **4** : annoyance, vexation

marfil *nm* : ivory

margarina *nf* : margarine

margarita *nf* **1** : daisy **2** : margarita (cocktail)

margen[1] *nf, pl* **márgenes** : bank (of a river), side (of a street)

margen[2] *nm, pl* **márgenes** **1** : edge, border ⟨dejar al margen : to exclude⟩ **2** : margin ⟨margen de ganancia : profit margin⟩ ⟨margen de error : margin of error⟩

marginación *nf, pl* **-ciones** : marginalization, exclusion

marginado[1], **-da** *adj* **1** DESHEREDADO : outcast, alienated, dispossessed **2 clases marginadas** : underclass

marginado[2], **-da** *n* : outcast, misfit

marginal *adj* : marginal, fringe

marginar *vt* : to ostracize, to exclude

mariachi *nm* **1** : mariachi band **2** : mariachi musician **3** : mariachi music

maridaje *nm* : marriage, union

maridar *vt* UNIR : to marry, to unite

marido *nm* ESPOSO : husband

marihuana *or* **mariguana** *or* **marijuana** *nf* : marihuana

marimacho *nmf fam* **1** : mannish woman **2** : tomboy

marimba *nf* : marimba

marina *nf* **1** : coast, coastal area **2** : navy, fleet ⟨marina mercante : merchant marine⟩

marinada *nf* : marinade

marinar *vt* : to marinate

marinero[1], **-ra** *adj* **1** : seaworthy **2** : sea, marine

marinero[2] *nm* : sailor

marino[1], **-na** *adj* : marine, sea

marino[2] *nm* : sailor, seaman

marioneta *nf* TÍTERE : puppet, marionette

mariposa *nf* **1** : butterfly **2 mariposa nocturna** : moth

mariquita[1] *nf* : ladybug

mariquita[2] *nm fam + disparaging* : sissy *fam + disparaging*, wimp

mariscal *nm* **1** : marshal **2 mariscal de campo** : field marshal (in the military), quarterback (in football)

marisco *nm* **1** : shellfish **2 mariscos** *nmpl* : seafood

marisma *nf* : marsh, salt marsh

marital *adj* : marital, married ⟨la vida marital : married life⟩

marítimo, -ma *adj* : maritime, shipping ⟨la industria marítima : the shipping industry⟩

marketing [ˈmarketin] *nm* : marketing

marmita *nf* : (cooking) pot

mármol *nm* : marble

marmóreo, -rea *adj* : marble

marmota *nf* **1** : marmot **2 marmota de América** : woodchuck, groundhog

maroma *nf* **1** : rope **2** : acrobatic stunt **3** *Mex* : somersault

marque, etc. → **marcar**

marqués, -quesa *n, pl* **marqueses** : marquis *m*, marquess *m*, marquise *f*, marchioness *f*

marquesina *nf* **1** : marquee, canopy **2** : shelter (at a bus stop, etc.)

marqueta *nf Mex* : block (of chocolate), lump (of sugar or salt)

marranada *nf* **1** : disgusting thing **2** : dirty trick

marrano[1], **-na** *adj* : filthy, disgusting

marrano[2], **-na** *n* **1** CERDO : pig, hog **2** *fam* : dirty pig, slob

marrar *vt* : to miss (a target) — *vi* : to fail, to go wrong

marras *adv* **1** : long ago **2 de ∼** : said, aforementioned ⟨el individuo de marras : the individual in question⟩

marrasquino *nm* : maraschino

marrón *adj & nm, pl* **marrones** CASTAÑO : brown

marroquí *adj & nmf, pl* **-quíes** : Moroccan

marsopa *nf* : porpoise

marsupial *nm* : marsupial

marta *nf* **1** : marten **2 marta cebellina** : sable (animal)

Marte *nm* : Mars

martes *nms & pl* **1** : Tuesday ⟨el martes : (on) Tuesday⟩ ⟨los martes : (on) Tuesdays⟩ ⟨cada (dos) martes : every (other) Tuesday⟩ ⟨el martes pasado : last Tuesday⟩ ⟨el próximo martes : next Tuesday⟩ **2 martes de Carnaval** : Mardi Gras

martillar *or* **martillear** *v* : to hammer

martillazo *nm* : blow with a hammer

martillo *nm* **1** : hammer **2 martillo neumático** : jackhammer

martín pescador *nm, pl* **martines pescadores** : kingfisher

martinete *nm* **1** : heron **2** : pile driver

mártir *nmf* : martyr

martirio *nm* **1** : martyrdom **2** : ordeal, torment

martirizar {21} *vt* **1** : to martyr **2** ATORMENTAR : to torment

marxismo *nm* : Marxism

marxista *adj & nmf* : Marxist

marzo *nm* : March ⟨el nueve de marzo : (on) the ninth of March, (on) March ninth⟩

mas *conj* PERO : but

más[1] *adv* **1** : more ⟨¿hay algo más grande? : is there anything bigger?⟩ ⟨unos días más tarde : a few days later⟩ ⟨es más complicado de lo que parece : it's more complicated than it seems⟩ ⟨no puedo esperar más : I can't wait any longer⟩ ⟨éste me gusta más que ése : I like this one better than that one⟩ ⟨ahora más que nunca : now more than ever⟩ **2** : most ⟨Luis es el más alto (del grupo) : Luis is the tallest (in the group)⟩ ⟨el que más me gusta : the one I like the most/best⟩ ⟨estudia lo más posible : he studies as much as possible⟩ **3** : rather ⟨más querría andar : I would rather walk⟩ **4 a ~** : besides, in addition **5 más allá** : further, farther ⟨la tienda está más allá : the shop is farther down⟩ **6 más allá de** : beyond, past ⟨está más allá de la iglesia : it's beyond/past the church⟩ ⟨ir más allá de los límites : to go beyond the limits⟩ **7 ~ de** : more than (a number or amount) ⟨más de cien personas : more than a hundred people⟩ ⟨más de una hora : more than an hour⟩ **8 qué ... más ...** : what ..., what a ... ⟨qué día más bonito! : what a beautiful day!⟩

más² *adj* **1** : more ⟨dáme dos kilos más : give me two more kilos⟩ **2** : most ⟨la que ganó más dinero : the one who earned the most money⟩ **3** : else ⟨¿quién más quiere vino? : who else wants wine?⟩ ⟨nadie más : nobody else⟩

más³ *n* : plus sign

más⁴ *prep* : plus ⟨tres más dos es igual a cinco : three plus two equals five⟩

más⁵ *pron* **1** : more ⟨¿tienes más? : do you have more?⟩ **2 a lo más** : at most **3 de ~** : extra, excess **4 ~ bien** : rather **5 más o menos** : more or less, approximately **6 por más que** : no matter how much ⟨por más que corras no llegarás a tiempo : no matter how fast you run you won't arrive on time⟩

masa *nf* **1** : mass, volume ⟨masa atómica : atomic mass⟩ ⟨producción en masa : mass production⟩ **2** : dough, batter **3 masas** *nfpl* : people, masses ⟨las masas populares : the common people⟩ **4 masa harina** *Mex* : corn flour (for tortillas, etc.) **5 en masa** : en masse

masacrar *vt* : to massacre

masacre *nf* : massacre

masaje *nm* : massage

masajear *vt* : to massage

masajista *nmf* : masseur *m*, masseuse *f*

mascar {72} *v* MASTICAR : to chew

máscara *nf* **1** CARETA : mask **2** : appearance, pretense **3 máscara antigás** : gas mask

mascarada *nf* : masquerade

mascarilla *nf* **1** : mask (in medicine) ⟨mascarilla de oxígeno : oxygen mask⟩ **2** : facial mask (treatment)

mascota *nf* **1** : mascot **2** : pet

masculinidad *nf* : masculinity

masculino, -na *adj* **1** : masculine, male **2** : manly **3** : masculine (in grammar)

mascullar *v* : to mumble, to mutter

masificación *nf, pl* **-ciones** **1** : mass adoption, propagation **2** *Spain* : overcrowding

masificado, -da *adj* : overcrowded

masilla *nf* : putty

masivamente *adv* : en masse

masivo, -va *adj* : mass ⟨comunicación masiva : mass communication⟩

masón *nm, pl* **masones** FRANCMASÓN : Mason, Freemason

masonería *nf* FRANCMASONERÍA : Masonry, Freemasonry

masónico, -ca *adj* : Masonic

masoquismo *nm* : masochism

masoquista¹ *adj* : masochistic

masoquista² *nmf* : masochist

masque, etc. → mascar

Máster *nm* : Master's degree

masticar {72} *v* MASCAR : to chew, to masticate

mástil *nm* **1** : mast **2** ASTA : flagpole **3** : neck (of a stringed instrument)

mastín *nm, pl* **mastines** : mastiff

mástique *nm* : putty, filler

mastodonte *nm* : mastodon

masturbación *nf, pl* **-ciones** : masturbation

masturbarse *vr* : to masturbate

mata *nf* **1** ARBUSTO : bush, shrub **2** : plant ⟨mata de tomate : tomato plant⟩ **3** : sprig, tuft **4 mata de pelo** : mop of hair

matadero *nm* : slaughterhouse, abattoir

matado, -da *adj Mex* : strenuous, exhausting

matador *nm* TORERO : matador, bullfighter

matamoscas *nms & pl* : flyswatter

matanza *nf* MASACRE : slaughter, butchering

matar *vt* **1** : to kill **2** : to slaughter, to butcher **3** APAGAR : to extinguish, to put out (fire, light) **4** : to tone down (colors) **5** : to pass, to waste (time) **6** : to trump (in card games) — *vi* : to kill — **matarse** *vr* **1** : to be killed **2** SUICIDARSE : to commit suicide **3** *fam* : to exhaust oneself ⟨se mató tratando de terminarlo : he knocked himself out trying to finish it⟩

matasanos *nms & pl fam* : quack

matasellar *vt* : to cancel (a stamp), to postmark

matasellos *nms & pl* : postmark

matatena *nf Mex* : jacks

mate¹ *adj* : matte, dull

mate² *nm* **1** : maté **2** : slam dunk (in basketball) **3 jaque mate** : checkmate ⟨darle mate a *or* darle jaque mate a : to checkmate⟩

matemática → matemáticas

matemáticas *nfpl* : mathematics, math

matemático¹, -ca *adj* : mathematical — **matemáticamente** *adv*

matemático², -ca *n* : mathematician

materia *nf* **1** : matter ⟨materia gris : gray matter⟩ **2** : material ⟨materia prima : raw material⟩ **3** : (academic) subject **4 en materia de** : on the subject of, concerning

material¹ *adj* **1** : material, physical, real **2 daños materiales** : property damage

material² *nm* **1** : material ⟨material de construcción : building material⟩ **2** EQUIPO : equipment, gear **3 material gráfico** : illustrations *pl*, artwork

materialismo *nm* : materialism

materialista¹ *adj* : materialistic

materialista² *nmf* **1** : materialist **2** *Mex* : truck driver

materializar {21} *vt* : to bring to fruition, to realize — **materializarse** *vr* : to materialize, to come into being

materialmente *adv* **1** : physically ⟨materialmente imposible : physically impossible⟩ **2** : really, absolutely

maternal *adj* : maternal, motherly

maternidad *nf* **1** : maternity, motherhood **2** : maternity hospital, maternity ward

materno, -na *adj* : maternal

matinal *adj* MATUTINO : morning ⟨la pálida luz matinal : the pale morning light⟩

matinée *or* **matiné** *nf* : matinee

matiz *nm, pl* **matices** **1** : hue, shade **2** : nuance

matización *nf, pl* **-ciones** **1** : tinting, toning, shading **2** : clarification (of a statement)

matizar {21} *vt* **1** : to tinge, to tint (colors) **2** : to vary, to modulate (sounds) **3** : to qualify (statements)

matón *nm, pl* **matones** : thug, bully

matorral *nm* **1** : thicket **2** : scrub

matraca *nf* **1** : rattle, noisemaker **2 dar la matraca a** : to pester, to nag

matriarca *nf* : matriarch

matriarcado *nm* : matriarchy

matrícula *nf* **1** : list, roll, register **2** INSCRIPCIÓN : registration, enrollment **3** : registration number (of a vehicle) **4 placa de matrícula** : license plate, tag

matriculación *nf, pl* **-ciones** : matriculation, registration

matricular *vt* INSCRIBIR : to enroll, to register (a person) **2** : to register (a vehicle) — **matricularse** *vr* : to matriculate

matrimonial *adj* : marital, matrimonial ⟨la vida matrimonial : married life⟩

matrimonio *nm* **1** : marriage, matrimony ⟨matrimonio civil/religioso : civil/religious wedding⟩ ⟨nació fuera del matrimonio : he was born out(side) of wedlock⟩ **2** : married couple

matriz *nf, pl* **matrices** **1** : uterus, womb **2** : original, master copy **3** : main office, headquarters **4** : stub (of a check) **5** : matrix ⟨matriz de puntos : dot matrix⟩

matrona *nf* : matron

matronal *adj* : matronly

matutino¹, -na *adj* : morning ⟨la edición matutina : the morning edition⟩

matutino² *nm* : morning paper

maullar {8} *vi* : to meow

maullido *nm* : meow

mauritano, -na *adj & n* : Mauritanian

mausoleo *nm* : mausoleum

maxilar *nm* : jaw, jawbone

máxima *nf* : maxim

máxime *adv* ESPECIALMENTE : especially, principally

maximizar {21} *vt* : to maximize

máximo¹, -ma *adj* : maximum, greatest, highest

máximo² *nm* **1** : maximum **2 al máximo** : to the utmost **3 como ~** : at the most, at the latest

maya¹ *adj & nmf* : Mayan

maya² *nmf* : Maya, Mayan

mayo *nm* : May ⟨el primero de mayo : (on) the first of May, (on) May first⟩

mayonesa *nf* : mayonnaise

mayor¹ *adj* **1** *comparative of* GRANDE : bigger, larger, greater, elder, older **2** *superlative of* GRANDE : biggest, largest, greatest, eldest, oldest **3** : grown-up, mature ⟨hacerse mayor : to grow up⟩ **4** : main, major **5** : elderly **6** : major ⟨una sonata en re mayor : a sonata in D major⟩ **7 mayor de edad** : of (legal) age **8 al por mayor** *or* **por ~** : wholesale

mayor² *nmf* **1** : major (in the military) **2** : adult, grown-up ⟨tus mayores : your elders⟩ ⟨las personas mayores : the elderly⟩

mayoral *nm* CAPATAZ : foreman, overseer

mayordomo *nm* : butler

mayoreo *nm* : wholesale

mayoría *nf* **1** : majority ⟨la mayoría de : most of, the majority of⟩ ⟨estar en mayoría : to be in the majority⟩ ⟨mayoría de edad : adulthood, age of majority⟩ **2 en su mayoría** : on the whole

mayorista¹ *adj* ALMACENISTA : wholesale

mayorista² *nmf* : wholesaler

mayoritariamente *adv* : primarily, chiefly

mayoritario, -ria *adj & n* : majority ⟨un consenso mayoritario : a majority consensus⟩

mayormente *adv* : primarily, chiefly

mayúscula *nf* : capital letter

mayúsculo, -la *adj* **1** : capital, uppercase **2** : huge, terrible ⟨un problema mayúsculo : a huge problem⟩

maza *nf* **1** : mace (weapon) **2** : drumstick **3** *fam* : bore, pest

mazacote *nm* **1** : concrete **2** : lumpy mess (of food) **3** : eyesore, crude work of art

mazapán *nm, pl* **-panes** : marzipan

mazmorra *nf* CALABOZO : dungeon

mazo *nm* **1** : mallet **2** : pestle **3** MANOJO : handful, bunch

mazorca *nf* **1** CHOCLO : cob, ear of corn **2 pelar la mazorca** *Mex fam* : to smile from ear to ear

me *pron* **1** : me ⟨me vieron : they saw me⟩ **2** : to me, for me, from me ⟨dame el libro : give me the book⟩ ⟨me lo compró : he bought it for me⟩ ⟨me robaron la cartera : they stole my pocketbook⟩ **3** : myself, to myself, for myself, from myself ⟨me preparé una buena comida : I cooked myself a good dinner⟩ ⟨me equivoqué : I made a mistake⟩

meada *nf usu vulgar* : piss *usu vulgar* ⟨echar una meada : to take a piss⟩

meados *nmpl usu vulgar* ORINA : piss *usu vulgar*

mear *vi usu vulgar* : to piss *usu vulgar*, to take a piss *usu vulgar*

mecánica *nf* : mechanics

mecánico¹, -ca *adj* : mechanical — **mecánicamente** *adv*

mecánico², -ca *n* **1** : mechanic **2** : technician ⟨mecánico dental : dental technician⟩

mecanismo *nm* : mechanism
mecanización *nf, pl* **-ciones** : mechanization
mecanizar {21} *vt* : to mechanize
mecanografía *nf* : typing
mecanografiar {85} *vt* : to type
mecanógrafo, -fa *n* : typist
mecate *nm CA, Mex, Ven* : rope, twine, cord
mecedor *nm* : glider (seat)
mecedora *nf* : rocking chair
mecenas *nmfs & pl* : patron (of the arts), sponsor
mecenazgo *nm* PATROCINIO : sponsorship, patronage
mecer {86} *vt* **1** : to rock **2** COLUMPIAR : to push (on a swing) — **mecerse** *vr* : to rock, to swing, to sway
mecha *nf* **1** : fuse **2** : wick **3 mechas** *nfpl* : highlights (in hair)
mechero *nm* **1** : burner **2** *Spain* : lighter
mechón *nm, pl* **mechones** : lock (of hair)
medalla *nf* : medal, medallion
medallista *nmf* : medalist
medallón *nm, pl* **-llones** **1** : medallion **2** : locket
media *nf* **1** CALCETÍN : sock **2** : average, mean **3 medias** *nfpl* : stockings, hose, tights **4 a medias** : by halves, half and half, halfway ⟨ir a medias : to go halves⟩ ⟨verdad a medias : half-truth⟩
mediación *nf, pl* **-ciones** : mediation
mediado, -da *adj* **1** : half full, half empty, half over **2** : halfway through ⟨mediada la tarea : halfway through the job⟩
mediador, -dora *n* : mediator
mediados *nmpl* **a mediados de** : halfway through, in the middle of ⟨a mediados del mes : towards the middle of the month, mid-month⟩
medialuna *nf* **1** : crescent **2** : croissant, crescent roll
medianamente *adv* : fairly, moderately
medianero, -ra *adj* **1** : dividing **2** : mediating
medianía *nf* **1** : middle position **2** : mediocre person, mediocrity
mediano, -na *adj* **1** : medium, average ⟨la mediana edad : middle age⟩ **2** : mediocre
medianoche *nf* : midnight
mediante *prep* : through, by means of ⟨Dios mediante : God willing⟩
mediar *vi* **1** : to mediate ⟨mediar en algo : to mediate something⟩ ⟨mediar por : to intercede on behalf of⟩ ⟨mediar con/ante : to intercede with⟩ **2** : to be in the middle, to be halfway through **3** : to elapse, to pass ⟨mediaron cinco años entre el inicio de la guerra y el armisticio : five years passed between the start of the war and the armistice⟩ **4** : to be a consideration ⟨media el hecho de que cuesta mucho : one must take into account that it is costly⟩ **5** : to come up, to happen ⟨medió algo urgente : something pressing came up⟩
mediatizar {21} *vt* : to influence, to interfere with

medicación *nf, pl* **-ciones** : medication, treatment
medicamento *nm* : medication, medicine, drug
medicar {72} *vt* : to medicate — **medicarse** *vr* : to take medicine
medicatura *nf Ven* : first aid clinic
medicina *nf* : medicine
medicinal *adj* **1** : medicinal **2** : medicated
medicinar *vt* : to give medication to, to dose
medición *nf, pl* **-ciones** : measuring, measurement
médico¹, -ca *adj* : medical ⟨una receta médica : a doctor's prescription⟩
médico², -ca *n* DOCTOR : doctor, physician
medida *nf* **1** : measurement, measure ⟨hecho a medida : custom-made⟩ ⟨tomar las medidas de algo : to measure something⟩ ⟨tomarle las medidas a alguien : to measure someone⟩ **2** : measure, step ⟨tomar medidas : to take steps⟩ ⟨medidas cautelares : precautionary measures⟩ ⟨medidas de seguridad : security measures⟩ **3** : moderation, prudence ⟨sin medida : immoderately⟩ **4** : extent, degree ⟨en cierta/gran medida : to a certain/great extent⟩ ⟨en la medida de lo posible : as far as possible, to the extent possible⟩ **5 a medida que** : as ⟨a medida que aumenta : as it increases⟩
medidor *nm* : meter, gauge
medieval *adj* : medieval — **medievalista** *nmf*
medievo → **medioevo**
medio¹ *adv* **1** : half ⟨está medio dormida : she's half asleep⟩ **2** : rather, kind of ⟨está medio aburrida esta fiesta : this party is rather boring⟩
medio², -dia *adj* **1** : half ⟨una media hora : half an hour⟩ ⟨medio hermano : half brother⟩ ⟨estar a media luz : to be dimly lit⟩ ⟨son las tres y media : it's half past three, it's three-thirty⟩ **2** : midway, halfway ⟨a medio camino : halfway there⟩ ⟨a media tarde : (in the) mid-afternoon⟩ **3** : middle ⟨la clase media : the middle class⟩ **4** : average ⟨la temperatura media : the average temperature⟩
medio³ *nm* **1** CENTRO : middle, center ⟨en medio de : in the middle of, amid⟩ ⟨estar en medio : to be in the way⟩ ⟨ponerse en medio : to get in the way⟩ **2** AMBIENTE : milieu, environment **3** : medium, spirituality **4** : means *pl*, way ⟨por medio de : by means of⟩ ⟨los medios de comunicación : the media⟩ ⟨medios sociales : social media⟩ **5 medios** *nmpl* : means, resources
medioambiental *adj* : environmental
medio ambiente *nm* : environment
mediocampista *nmf* : midfielder
mediocre *adj* : mediocre, average
mediocridad *nf* : mediocrity
mediodía *nm* : noon, midday
medioevo *nm* : Middle Ages

medio tiempo *nm* : halftime
medir {54} *vt* **1** : to measure **2** : to weigh, to consider ⟨medir los riesgos : to weigh the risks⟩ — *vi* : to measure
medirse *vr* : to be moderate, to exercise restraint
meditabundo, -da *adj* PENSATIVO : pensive, thoughtful
meditación *nf*, *pl* **-ciones** : meditation, thought
meditar *vi* : to meditate, to think ⟨meditar sobre la vida : to contemplate life⟩ — *vt* **1** : to think over, to consider **2** : to plan, to work out
meditativo, -va *adj* : pensive
mediterráneo, -nea *adj* : Mediterranean
médium *nmf*, *pl* **médiums** : medium (person)
medrar *vi* **1** PROSPERAR : to prosper, to thrive **2** AUMENTAR : to increase, to grow
medro *nm* PROSPERIDAD : prosperity, growth
medroso, -sa *adj* : fainthearted, fearful
médula *nf* **1** : marrow, pith **2 médula espinal** : spinal cord
medular *adj* : fundamental, core ⟨el punto medular : the crux of the matter⟩
medusa *nf* : jellyfish
megabyte *nm* : megabyte
megáfono *nm* : megaphone
megahercio *nm* : megahertz
megahertzio *nm* : megahertz
megatón *nm*, *pl* **-tones** : megaton
megavatio *nm* : megawatt
mejicano → mexicano
mejilla *nf* : cheek
mejillón *nm*, *pl* **-llones** : mussel
mejor[1] *adv* **1** : better ⟨Carla cocina mejor que Ana : Carla cooks better than Ann⟩ **2** : best ⟨ella es la que lo hace mejor : she's the one who does it best⟩ **3** : rather ⟨mejor morir que rendirme : I'd rather die than give up⟩ **4** : it's better that . . . ⟨mejor te vas : you'd better go⟩ **5 a lo mejor** : maybe, perhaps
mejor[2] *adj* **1** *comparative of* BUENO : better ⟨a falta de algo mejor : for lack of something better⟩ **2** *comparative of* BIEN : better ⟨está mucho mejor : he's much better⟩ **3** *superlative of* BUENO : best, the better ⟨mi mejor amigo : my best friend⟩ **4** *superlative of* BIEN : best, the better ⟨duermo mejor en un clima seco : I sleep best in a dry climate⟩ **5** PREFERIBLE : preferable, better **6 lo mejor** : the best thing, the best part
mejor[3] *nmf* (*with definite article*) : the better (one), the best (one)
mejora *nf* : improvement
mejoramiento *nm* : improvement
mejorana *nf* : marjoram
mejorar *vt* : to improve, to make better — *vi* : to improve, to get better — **mejorarse** *vr*
mejoría *nf* : improvement, betterment
mejunje *nm* : concoction, brew
melancolía *nf* : melancholy, sadness
melancólico, -ca *adj* : melancholy, sad
melanoma *nm* : melanoma

melaza *nf* : molasses
melena *nf* **1** : mane **2** : long hair **3 melenas** *nfpl* GREÑAS : shaggy hair, mop
melenudo, -da *adj fam* : long-haired
melindroso[1], **-sa** *adj* **1** : affected **2** : fussy, finicky
melindroso[2], **-sa** *n* : finicky person, fussbudget
melisa *nf* : lemon balm
mella *nf* **1** : dent, nick **2 hacer mella en** : to have an effect on, to make an impression on
mellado, -da *adj* **1** : chipped, dented **2** : gap-toothed
mellar *vt* : to dent, to nick
mellizo, -za *adj & n* GEMELO : twin
melocotón *nm*, *pl* **-tones** : peach
melodía *nf* : melody, tune
melódico, -ca *adj* : melodic
melodioso, -sa *adj* : melodious
melodrama *nm* : melodrama
melodramático, -ca *adj* : melodramatic
melón *nm*, *pl* **melones** : melon, cantaloupe
meloso, -sa *adj* **1** : sweet **2** EMPALAGOSO : cloying, saccharine
membrana *nf* **1** : membrane **2 membrana interdigital** : web, webbing (of a bird's foot) — **membranoso, -sa** *adj*
membresía *nf* : membership, members *pl*
membrete *nm* : letterhead, heading ⟨papel con membrete : official stationery, letterhead⟩
membrillo *nm* : quince
membrudo, -da *adj* FORNIDO : muscular, well-built
memez *nf*, *pl* **memeces** : stupid thing
memo, -ma *adj* : silly, stupid
memorabilia *nf* : memorabilia
memorable *adj* : memorable
memorándum *or* **memorando** *nm*, *pl* **-dums** *or* **-dos** **1** : memorandum, memo **2** : memo book, appointment book
memoria *nf* **1** : memory ⟨de memoria : by heart⟩ ⟨hacer memoria : to try to remember⟩ ⟨traer a la memoria : to call to mind⟩ **2** RECUERDO : remembrance, memory ⟨su memoria perdurará para siempre : his memory will live forever⟩ **3** : report ⟨memoria anual : annual report⟩ **4** : memory (in computing) **5 memorias** *nfpl* : memoirs *pl* **6 memoria de acceso aleatorio** : random-access memory, RAM **7 memoria flash** : flash memory
memorizar {21} *vt* : to memorize — **memorización** *nf*
mena *nf* : ore
menaje *nm* : household goods *pl*, furnishings *pl*
mención *nf*, *pl* **-ciones** : mention
mencionar *vt* : to mention, to refer to
mendaz *adj*, *pl* **mendaces** : false, untruthful, dishonest
mendicidad *nf* : begging
mendigar {52} *vi* : to beg — *vt* : to beg for
mendigo, -ga *n* LIMOSNERO : beggar
mendrugo *nm* : crust (of bread)
menear *vt* **1** : to shake (one's head) **2** : to sway, to wiggle (one's hips) **3** : to

wag (a tail) **4** : to stir (a liquid) —
menearse *vr* **1** : to wiggle one's hips **2**
: to fidget
meneo *nm* **1** : movement **2** : shake, toss
3 : swaying, wagging, wiggling **4** : stir,
stirring
menester *nm* **1** : activity, occupation,
duties *pl* **2 ser menester** : to be necessary ⟨es menester que vengas : you must
come⟩
menestra *nf* **1** *Ecua* : legume stew **2**
Peru : legume **3** *Spain* : mixed cooked
vegetables
mengano, -na → **fulano**
mengua *nf* **1** : decrease, decline **2**
: lack, want **3** : discredit, dishonor
menguar *vt* : to diminish, to lessen — *vi*
1 : to decline, to decrease **2** : to wane —
menguante *adj*
meningitis *nf* : meningitis
menisco *nm* : cartilage
menjurje → **mejunje**
menopausia *nf* : menopause
menopáusico, -ca *nf* : menopausal
menor[1] *adj* **1** *comparative of* PEQUEÑO
: smaller, lesser, younger ⟨es menor que
su hermana : he's younger than his sis-
ter⟩ ⟨en menor medida : to a lesser ex-
tent/degree⟩ **2** *superlative of* PEQUEÑO
: smallest, least, youngest **3** : minor ⟨un
problema menor : a minor problem⟩ **4**
: minor (in music) ⟨en tono de mi menor
: in the key of E minor⟩ **5 al por menor**
: retail **6 ser menor de edad** : to be a
minor, to be underage
menor[2] *nmf* : minor, juvenile
menos[1] *adv* **1** : less ⟨llueve menos en
agosto : it rains less in August⟩ ⟨éste me
gusta menos que ése : I like this one less
than that one⟩ ⟨soy menos alta que mis
hermanas : I'm not as tall as my sisters⟩
⟨es menos difícil de lo que parece : it's
less difficult than it looks⟩ **2** : least ⟨el
coche menos caro : the least expensive
car⟩ ⟨en el momento menos pensado
: when you least expect it⟩ ⟨es lo menos
que puedo hacer : it's the least I can do⟩
⟨trabaja lo menos posible : he works as
little as possible⟩ ⟨los que menos ganan
: those who earn the least⟩ ⟨lo que menos necesitamos es otra crisis : the last
thing we need is another crisis⟩ **3 ~ de**
: less than, fewer than ⟨tienen menos de
50 empleados : they have fewer than 50
employees⟩ ⟨en menos de un minuto : in
less than a minute⟩
menos[2] *adj* **1** : less, fewer ⟨tengo más
trabajo y menos tiempo : I have more
work and less time⟩ ⟨hay menos sillas
que personas : there are fewer chairs
than people⟩ **2** : least, fewest ⟨la clase
que tiene menos estudiantes : the class
that has the fewest students⟩
menos[3] *prep* **1** SALVO, EXCEPTO : except
2 : minus ⟨quince menos cuatro son
once : fifteen minus four is eleven⟩
menos[4] *pron* **1** : less, fewer ⟨no deberías
aceptar menos : you shouldn't accept
less⟩ **2 al menos** *or* **por lo menos** : at

least **3 a menos que** : unless **4 lo de
menos** : the least important thing
menoscabar *vt* **1** : to lessen, to diminish
2 : to disgrace, to discredit **3** PERJUDI-
CAR : to harm, to damage
menoscabo *nm* **1** : lessening, diminishing **2** : disgrace, discredit **3** : harm,
damage
menospreciar *vt* **1** DESPRECIAR : to
scorn, to look down on **2** : to underestimate, to undervalue
menosprecio *nm* DESPRECIO : contempt,
scorn
mensaje *nm* **1** : message **2 mensaje
instantáneo** : instant message
mensajear *v fam* : to message, to text
mensajería *nf* **1** : messaging **2 mensajería instantánea** : instant messaging
mensajero, -ra *n* : messenger
menso, -sa *adj Mex fam* : foolish, stupid
menstrual *adj* : menstrual
menstruar {3} *vi* : to menstruate —
menstruación *nf*
mensual *adj* : monthly
mensualidad *nf* **1** : monthly payment,
installment **2** : monthly salary
mensualmente *adv* : every month,
monthly
mensurable *adj* : measurable
menta *nf* **1** : mint, peppermint **2 menta
verde** : spearmint
mentado, -da *adj* **1** : aforementioned **2**
FAMOSO : renowned, famous
mental *adj* : mental, intellectual — **mentalmente** *adv*
mentalidad *nf* : mentality
mentalizar {21} *vt* : to prepare mentally
— **mentalizarse** *vr*
mentar {55} *vt* **1** : to mention, to name **2
mentar la madre a** *fam* : to insult, to
swear at
mente *nf* : mind ⟨tener en mente : to have
in mind⟩
-mente *suf* : -ly ⟨frecuentemente : fre-
quently⟩
mentecato[1], **-ta** *adj* : foolish, simple
mentecato[2], **-ta** *n* : fool, idiot
mentir {76} *vi* : to lie
mentira *nf* : lie
mentirijillas *nfpl fam* **de ~** : as a joke, in
fun
mentiroso[1], **-sa** *adj* EMBUSTERO : lying,
untruthful
mentiroso[2], **-sa** *n* EMBUSTERO : liar
mentís *nm, pl* **mentises** : denial, repudiation ⟨dar el mentís a : to deny, to refute⟩
mentol *nm* : menthol — **mentolado, -da**
adj
mentón *nm, pl* **mentones** BARBILLA
: chin
mentor *nm* : mentor, counselor
menú *nm, pl* **menús** : menu
menudear *vi* : to occur frequently — *vt*
: to do repeatedly
menudencia *nf* **1** : trifle **2 menudencias** *nfpl* : giblets
menudeo *nm* : retail, retailing
menudillos *nmpl* : giblets
menudo[1], **-da** *adj* **1** : minute, small **2 a
~ FRECUENTEMENTE** : often, frequently

menudo² *nm* **1** *Mex* : tripe stew **2 menudos** *nmpl* : giblets

meñique *nm or* **dedo meñique** : little finger, pinkie

meollo *nm* **1** MÉDULA : marrow **2** SESO : brains *pl* **3** ENTRAÑA : essence, core ⟨el meollo del asunto : the heart of the matter⟩

mequetrefe *nm fam* : good-for-nothing

meramente *adv* : merely, purely

mercachifle *nm* : peddler, hawker

mercadeo *nm* : marketing

mercader *nmf* : merchant

mercadería *nf* : merchandise, goods *pl*

mercadillo *nm Spain* : flea market

mercado *nm* **1** : market **2 mercado de pulgas** (*in various countries*) : flea market **3 mercado de trabajo/valores** : labor market **4 mercado de valores** *or* **mercado bursátil** : stock market

mercadotecnia *nf* : marketing

mercancía *nf* : merchandise, goods *pl*

mercante *nmf* : merchant, dealer

mercantil *adj* COMERCIAL : commercial, mercantile

merced *nf* **1** : favor **2 ~ a** : thanks to, due to **3 a merced de** : at the mercy of

mercenario, -ria *adj & n* : mercenary

mercería *nf* : notions store

Mercosur *nm* : economic community consisting of Argentina, Brazil, Paraguay, and Uruguay

mercurio *nm* : mercury

Mercurio *nm* : Mercury (planet)

merecedor, -dora *adj* : deserving, worthy

merecer {53} *vt* : to deserve, to merit — *vi* : to be worthy

merecidamente *adv* : rightfully, deservedly

merecido *nm* : something merited, due ⟨recibieron su merecido : they got their just deserts⟩

merecimiento *nm* : merit, worth

merendar {55} *vi* : to have an afternoon snack — *vt* : to have as an afternoon snack

merendero *nm* **1** : lunchroom, snack bar **2** : picnic area

merengue *nm* **1** : meringue **2** : merengue (music or dance)

meridiano¹, -na *adj* **1** : midday **2** : crystal clear

meridiano² *nm* : meridian

meridional *adj* SUREÑO : southern

merienda *nf* : afternoon snack, tea

mérito *nm* : merit

meritorio¹, -ria *adj* : deserving, meritorious

meritorio², -ria *n* : intern, trainee

merluza *nf* : hake

merma *nf* **1** : decrease, cut **2** : waste, loss

mermar *vi* : to decrease, to diminish — *vt* : to reduce, to cut down

mermelada *nf* : marmalade, jam

mero¹, -ra *adv Mex fam* **1** : nearly, almost ⟨ya mero me caí : I almost fell⟩ **2** : just, exactly ⟨aquí mero : right here⟩

mero², -ra *adj* **1** : mere, simple **2** *Mex fam* (*used as an intensifier*) : very ⟨en el

mero centro : in the very center of town⟩

mero³ *nm* : grouper

merodeador, -dora *n* **1** : marauder **2** : prowler

merodear *vi* **1** : to maraud, to pillage **2** : to prowl around, to skulk

mes *nm* : month

mesa *nf* **1** : table ⟨mesa de cocina : kitchen table⟩ ⟨mesa de noche : nightstand, night table⟩ **2** : committee, board ⟨mesa directiva : executive board⟩

mesada *nf* : allowance, pocket money

mesarse *vr* : to pull at ⟨mesarse los cabellos : to tear one's hair⟩

mesero, -ra *n* CAMARERO : waiter, waitress *f*

meseta *nf* : plateau

Mesías *nm* : Messiah

mesita *or Spain* **mesilla** *nf* **1** : small table **2** *or* **mesita/mesilla de noche** : nightstand, night table

mesón *nm, pl* **mesones** : inn

mesonero, -ra *nm* : innkeeper

mesteño, -ña *adj* **caballo mesteño** : wild horse, mustang

mestizo¹, -za *adj* **1** : of mixed ancestry, mestizo **2** HÍBRIDO : hybrid

mestizo², -za *n* : person of mixed ancestry, mestizo

mesura *nf* **1** MODERACIÓN : moderation, discretion **2** CORTESÍA : courtesy **3** GRAVEDAD : seriousness, dignity

mesurado, -da *adj* COMEDIDO : moderate, restrained

mesurar *vt* : to moderate, to restrain, to temper — **mesurarse** *vr* : to restrain oneself

meta *nf* : goal, objective

metabólico, -ca *adj* : metabolic

metabolismo *nm* : metabolism

metabolizar {21} *vt* : to metabolize

metafísica *nf* : metaphysics

metafísico, -ca *adj* : metaphysical

metáfora *nf* : metaphor

metafórico, -ca *adj* : metaphoric, metaphorical

metal *nm* **1** : metal **2** *or* **metales** *nmpl* : brass, brass section (in an orchestra)

metálico, -ca *adj* : metallic, metal

metalistería *nf* : metalworking

metalizado, -da *adj* : metallic

metalurgia *nf* : metallurgy

metalúrgico¹, -ca *adj* : metallurgical

metalúrgico², -ca *n* : metalworker

metamorfosis *nfs & pl* : metamorphosis

metano *nm* : methane

metedura *nf* **metedura de pata** : blunder, faux pas

meteórico, -ca *adj* : meteoric

meteorito *nm* : meteorite

meteoro *nm* : meteor

meteorología *nf* : meteorology

meteorológico, -ca *adj* : meteorologic, meteorological

meteorólogo, -ga *n* : meteorologist

meter *vt* **1** : to put ⟨lo metió en un cajón : he put it in a drawer⟩ ⟨metieron su dinero en el banco : they put their money in the bank⟩ ⟨se le metió en la

cabeza que . . . : he got it in his head
that . . .⟩ **2** : to shut (in a place) ⟨la
metieron en la cárcel : they put her in
jail⟩ ⟨estuve todo el día metida en la casa
: I was stuck in the house all day⟩ **3** : to
fit, to squeeze ⟨puedes meter dos líneas
más en esa página : you can fit two more
lines on that page⟩ **4** : to place (in a job)
⟨lo metieron de dependiente : they got
him a job as a store clerk⟩ **5** : to involve
⟨lo metió en un buen lío : she got him in
an awful mess⟩ **6** : to make, to cause
⟨meten demasiado ruido : they make too
much noise⟩ ⟨un cuento que mete
miedo : a scary story⟩ **7** : to spread (a
rumor) **8** : to strike (a blow) **9** : to
score (a goal or point) **10** : to take up,
to take in (clothing) **11 a todo meter**
: at top speed — **meterse** *vr* **1** : to get
(in), to enter ⟨se metió en la cama : she
got in bed⟩ ⟨el ladrón se metió por la
ventana : the thief got in through the
window⟩ ⟨¿dónde te has metido?
: where are you hiding?, where have you
gotten to?⟩ **2** : to put, to stick ⟨no te lo
metas en la boca : don't put it in your
mouth⟩ ⟨se metió la mano en el bolsillo
: he stuck his hand in his pocket⟩ **3** *fam*
: to meddle ⟨no te metas en lo que no te
importa : mind your own business⟩ **4**
~ **con** *fam* : to pick a fight with, to provoke ⟨no te metas conmigo : don't mess
with me⟩ **5** ~ **a/de** : to become ⟨se
metió a monja : she became a nun⟩
metiche[1] *adj Mex fam* : nosy
metiche[2] *nmf Mex fam* : busybody
meticulosidad *nf* : thoroughness, meticulousness
meticuloso, -sa *adj* : meticulous, thorough — **meticulosamente** *adv*
metida *nf* **metida de pata** *fam* : blunder,
gaffe, blooper
metódico, -ca *adj* : methodical — **metó-
dicamente** *adv*
metodista *adj & nmf* : Methodist
método *nm* : method
metodología *nf* : methodology
metomentodo *nmf fam* : busybody
metraje *nm* : length (of a film) ⟨de largo
metraje : feature-length⟩
metralla *nf* : shrapnel
metralleta *nf* : submachine gun
métrico, -ca *adj* **1** : metric **2 cinta métrica** : tape measure
metro *nm* **1** : meter **2** : subway
metrónomo *nm* : metronome
metrópoli *nf or* **metrópolis** *nfs & pl* : metropolis
metropolitano, -na *adj* : metropolitan
mexicanismo *nm* : Mexican word or expression
mexicano, -na *adj & n* : Mexican
mexicoamericano, -na *adj & n* : Mexi-
can-American
mexiquense[1] *adj Mex* : of or from Mexico City
mexiquense[2] *nmf Mex* : person from
Mexico City
meza, etc. → **mecer**

mezcla *nf* **1** : mixing **2** : mixture, blend
3 : mortar (masonry material)
mezclar *vt* **1** : to mix, to blend **2** : to mix
up, to muddle **3** INVOLUCRAR : to in-
volve — **mezclarse** *vr* **1** : to get mixed
up (in) **2** : to mix, to mingle (socially)
mezclilla *nf Chile, Mex* : denim ⟨panta-
lones de mezclilla : jeans⟩
mezcolanza *nf* : jumble, hodgepodge
mezquindad *nf* **1** : meanness, stinginess
2 : petty deed, mean action
mezquino[1]**, -na** *adj* **1** : mean, petty **2**
: stingy **3** : paltry
mezquino[2] *nm Mex* : wart
mezquita *nf* : mosque
mi[1] *adj* : my
mi[2] *nm* **1** : E ⟨mi sostenido/bemol : E
sharp/flat⟩ **2** : mi (in singing)
mí *pron* **1** : me ⟨es para mí : it's for me⟩
⟨a mí no me importa : it doesn't matter
to me⟩ **2 mí mismo, mí misma** : myself
miasma *nm* : miasma
miau *nm* : meow
mica *nf* : mica
mico *nm* : monkey, long-tailed monkey
micro *nm* **1** *Chile, Arg* : minibus **2** : microphone
micro- *pref* : micro-
microbio *nm* : microbe, germ
microbiología *nf* : microbiology
microbús *nm, pl* **-buses** : minibus
microchip *nm, pl* **microchips** : microchip
microcomputadora *nf* : microcomputer
microcosmos *nms & pl* : microcosm
microfilm *nm, pl* **-films** : microfilm
micrófono *nm* : microphone
micrómetro *nm* : micrometer
microonda *nf* : microwave
microondas *nms & pl* : microwave, microwave oven
microordenador *nm Spain* : microcomputer
microorganismo *nm* : microorganism
microprocesador *nm* : microprocessor
microscópico, -ca *adj* : microscopic
microscopio *nm* : microscope
mide, etc. → **medir**
miedo *nm* **1** TEMOR : fear ⟨le tiene
miedo al perro : he's scared of the dog⟩
⟨tenían miedo de hablar : they were
afraid to speak⟩ ⟨morirse de miedo : to
be scared to death⟩ ⟨temblar de miedo
: to tremble with fear⟩ ⟨miedo escénico
: stage fright⟩ **2 dar miedo** : to frighten
miedoso, -sa *adj* TEMEROSO : fearful
miel *nf* : honey
miembro *nm* **1** : member **2** EXTREMI-
DAD : limb, extremity
mienta, etc. → **mentar**
miente, etc. → **mentir**
-miento *suf* : -ment ⟨entretenimiento : en-
tertainment⟩
mientras[1] *adv* **1** *or* **mientras tanto**
: meanwhile, in the meantime **2 mientras más** : the more ⟨mientras más
como, más quiero : the more I eat, the
more I want⟩
mientras[2] *conj* **1** : while, as ⟨roncaba
mientras dormía : he snored while he
was sleeping⟩ **2** : as long as ⟨luchará

mientras pueda : he will fight as long as he is able⟩ **3 mientras que** : while, whereas ⟨él es alto mientras que ella es muy baja : he is tall, whereas she is very short⟩

miércoles *nms & pl* **1** : Wednesday ⟨el miércoles : (on) Wednesday⟩ ⟨los miércoles : (on) Wednesdays⟩ ⟨cada (dos) miércoles : every (other) Wednesday⟩ ⟨el miércoles pasado : last Wednesday⟩ ⟨el próximo miércoles : next Wednesday⟩ ⟨el miércoles por la noche : Wednesday night⟩ **2 Miércoles de Ceniza** : Ash Wednesday

miga *nf* **1** : crumb **2 hacer buenas (malas) migas con** : to get along well (poorly) with

migaja *nf* **1** : crumb **2 migajas** *nfpl* SOBRAS : leftovers, scraps

migra *nf Mex fam* **la migra** : the immigration police

migración *nf, pl* **-ciones** : migration

migrante *nmf* : migrant

migraña *nf* : migraine

migrar *vi* : to migrate

migratorio, -ria *adj* : migratory

mijo *nm* : millet

mil[1] *adj & pron* : thousand

mil[2] *nm* : one thousand, a thousand

milagro *nm* : miracle ⟨de milagro : miraculously⟩

milagroso, -sa *adj* : miraculous, marvelous — **milagrosamente** *adv*

milenario[1], **-ria** *adj* : millennial

milenario[2], **-ria** *n* : millennial (person born in the 1980s or 1990s)

milenial → **milenario**[2]

milenio *nm* : millennium

milésima *nf* → **milésimo**[2]

milésimo[1], **-ma** *adj* : thousandth

milésimo[2] *nm* : thousandth

mili *nf Spain fam* : military service

milicia *nf* **1** : militia **2** : military service

miligramo *nm* : milligram

mililitro *nm* : milliliter

milímetro *nm* : millimeter

militancia *nf* : militancy

militante[1] *adj* : militant

militante[2] *nmf* : militant, activist

militar[1] *vi* **1** : to serve (in the military) **2** : to be active (in politics)

militar[2] *adj* : military

militar[3] *nmf* SOLDADO : soldier

militarismo *nm* : militarism

militarista *adj* : militaristic

militarizar {21} *vt* : to militarize

milla *nf* : mile

millar *nm* : thousand

millón *nm, pl* **millones** : million

millonario, -ria *n* : millionaire

millonésima *nf* → **millonésimo**[2]

millonésimo[1], **-ma** *adj* : millionth

millonésimo[2] *nm* **1** : millionth (in a series) **2** : millionth (fraction)

mil millones *nms & pl* : billion

milmillonésimo[1], **-ma** *adj* : billionth

milmillonésimo[2] *nm* **1** : billionth (in a series) **2** : billionth (fraction)

milpa *nf CA, Mex* : cornfield

milpiés *nms & pl* : millipede

mimar *vt* CONSENTIR : to pamper, to spoil

mimbre *nm* : wicker

mimeógrafo *nm* : mimeograph

mímica *nf* **1** : mime, sign language **2** IMITACIÓN : mimicry

mimo *nm* **1** : pampering, indulgence ⟨hacerle mimos a alguien : to pamper someone⟩ **2** : mime

mimoso, -sa *adj* **1** : fussy, finicky **2** : affectionate, clinging

mina *nf* **1** : mine **2** : lead (for pencils)

minar *vt* **1** : to mine **2** DEBILITAR : to undermine

minarete *nm* ALMINAR : minaret

mineral *adj & nm* : mineral

mineralogía *nf* : mineralogy

minería *nf* : mining

minero[1], **-ra** *adj* : mining

minero[2], **-ra** *n* : miner, mine worker

mini- *pref* : mini-

miniatura *nf* : miniature

minicomputadora *nf* : minicomputer

minifalda *nf* : miniskirt

minifundio *nm* : small farm

minimizar {21} *vt* : to minimize

mínimo[1], **-ma** *adj* **1** : minimum ⟨salario mínimo : minimum wage⟩ **2** : least, smallest ⟨es lo mínimo que puede hacer : it's the least he can do⟩ **3** : very small, minute ⟨no tengo la más mínima idea : I haven't the slightest idea⟩

mínimo[2] *nm* **1** : minimum, least amount **2** : modicum, small amount **3 como ∼** : at least

minino, -na *n fam* : kitty, pussy

miniserie *nf* : miniseries

ministerial *adj* : ministerial

ministerio *nm* : ministry, department

ministro, -tra *n* : minister, secretary ⟨primer ministro, primera ministra : prime minister⟩ ⟨Ministro de Defensa : Secretary of Defense⟩

minivan [ˌminiˈban, -ˈvan] *nf, pl* **-vanes** : minivan

minoría *nf* : minority

minorista[1] *adj* : retail

minorista[2] *nmf* : retailer

minoritario, -ria *adj* : minority

mintió, etc. → **mentir**

minucia *nf* **1** : (minor) detail **2** INSIGNIFICANCIA : trifle, triviality **3 con minucia** : in detail

minuciosamente *adv* **1** : minutely **2** : in great detail **3** : thoroughly, meticulously

minucioso, -sa *adj* **1** : minute **2** DETALLADO : detailed **3** : thorough, meticulous

minué *nm* : minuet

minúsculo, -la *adj* DIMINUTO : tiny, miniscule

minusvalía *nf* : disability, handicap *sometimes offensive*

minusválido[1], **-da** *adj* : handicapped, disabled

minusválido[2], **-da** *n* : handicapped person

minuta *nf* **1** BORRADOR : rough draft **2** : bill, fee

minutero *nm* : minute hand

minuto *nm* : minute

mío¹, mía *adj* **1** : my, of mine ⟨Dios mío! : my God!, good heavens!⟩ ⟨una amiga mía : a friend of mine⟩ **2** : mine ⟨es mío : it's mine⟩

mío², mía *pron* (*with definite article*) : mine, my own ⟨tus zapatos son iguales a los míos : your shoes are just like mine⟩

miope *adj* : nearsighted, myopic

miopía *nf* : myopia, nearsightedness

mira *nf* **1** : sight (of a firearm or instrument) **2** : aim, objective ⟨con miras a : with the intention of, with a view to⟩ ⟨de amplias miras : broad-minded⟩ ⟨poner la mira en : to aim at, to aspire to⟩

mirada *nf* **1** : look, glance, gaze ⟨apartar la mirada : to look away⟩ ⟨dirigir/lanzar la mirada a : to glance at⟩ ⟨hay miradas que matan : if looks could kill⟩ **2** EXPRESIÓN : look, expression ⟨una mirada de sorpresa : a look of surprise⟩

mirado, -da *adj* **1** : cautious, careful **2** : considerate **3 bien mirado** : well thought of **4 mal mirado** : disliked, disapproved of

mirador *nm* : balcony, lookout, vantage point

miramiento *nm* **1** CONSIDERACIÓN : consideration, respect **2 sin miramientos** : without due consideration, carelessly

mirar *vt* **1** : to look at ⟨miró el reloj : she looked at her watch⟩ ⟨mirar fijamente : to stare at⟩ ⟨mirar algo (muy) por encima : to glance something over⟩ ⟨la miré en los ojos : I looked her straight in the eye⟩ **2** OBSERVAR : to watch ⟨mirar televisión : to watch television⟩ **3** REFLEXIONAR : to consider, to think over ⟨míralo desde su punto de vista : look at it from her point of view⟩ **4** (*used for emphasis*) ⟨¡mira que eres lista! : you're so clever!⟩ ⟨mire que no soy experto, pero . . . : I'm no expert, but . . .⟩ ⟨¡mira qué gracia! : how funny!⟩ — *vi* **1** : to look ⟨miraba por la ventana : I was looking out the window⟩ ⟨mira bien y lo verás : look carefully and you'll see it⟩ ⟨¡mira! ahí está : look! there he is⟩ ⟨mira, a mí no me importa : look, it doesn't matter to me⟩ **2** : to face, to overlook **3 ~ por** : to look after, to look out for — **mirarse** *vr* **1** : to look at oneself **2** : to look at each other

mirasol *nm* GIRASOL : sunflower

miríada *nf* : myriad

mirlo *nm* : blackbird

mirón, rona *n, mpl* **-rones** **1** : gawker, onlooker **2** : voyeur

mirra *nf* : myrrh

mirto *nm* ARRAYÁN : myrtle

misa *nf* : Mass

misantropía *nf* : misanthropy

misantrópico, -ca *adj* : misanthropic

misántropo, -pa *n* : misanthrope

miscelánea *nf* : miscellany

misceláneo, -nea *adj* : miscellaneous

miserable *adj* **1** LASTIMOSO : miserable, ˙wretched **2** : paltry, meager **3** MEZ-

QUINO : stingy, miserly **4** : despicable, vile

miserablemente *adv* **1** : miserably, wretchedly **2** : shamefully, disgracefully

miseria *nf* **1** POBREZA : poverty **2** : misery, suffering **3** : pittance, meager amount

misericordia *nf* COMPASIÓN : mercy, compassion

misericordioso, -sa *adj* : merciful

mísero, -ra *adj* **1** : wretched, miserable **2** : stingy **3** : paltry, meager

misil *nm* : missile

misión *nf, pl* **misiones** : mission

misionero, -ra *adj & n* : missionary

misiva *nf* : missive, letter

mismísimo, -ma *adj* (*used as an intensifier*) : very, selfsame ⟨el mismísimo día : that very same day⟩

mismo¹ *adv* (*used as an intensifier*) : right, exactly ⟨hazlo ahora mismo : do it right now⟩ ⟨te llamará hoy mismo : he'll definitely call you today⟩

mismo², -ma *adj* **1** : same ⟨la misma historia de siempre : the same old story⟩ ⟨ya no es el mismo de antes : he's not the same as he was before⟩ **2** (*used as an intensifier*) : very ⟨en ese mismo momento : at that very moment⟩ **3** : oneself ⟨lo hizo ella misma : she made it herself⟩ **4 por lo mismo** : for that reason

misoginia *nf* : misogyny

misógino *nm* : misogynist

miss *nf* : miss ⟨Miss Universo : Miss Universe⟩

misterio *nm* : mystery

misterioso, -sa *adj* : mysterious — **misteriosamente** *adv*

misticismo *nm* : mysticism

místico¹, -ca *adj* : mystic, mystical

místico², -ca *n* : mystic

mitad *nf* **1** : half ⟨mitad y mitad : half and half⟩ **2** MEDIO : middle ⟨a mitad de : halfway through⟩ ⟨por la mitad : in half⟩

mítico, -ca *adj* : mythical, mythic

mitigar {52} *vt* ALIVIAR : to mitigate, to alleviate — **mitigación** *nf*

mitin *nm, pl* **mítines** : (political) meeting, rally

mito *nm* LEYENDA : myth, legend

mitología *nf* : mythology

mitológico, -ca *adj* : mythological

mitosis *nfs & pl* : mitosis

mitra *nf* : miter (bishop's hat)

mixto, -ta *adj* **1** : mixed, joint **2** : coeducational

mixtura *nf* : mixture, blend

mnemónico, -ca *adj* : mnemonic

mobbing [ˈmobiŋ] *nm Spain* : workplace bullying

mobiliario *nm* : furniture

mocasín *nm, pl* **-sines** : moccasin

mocedad *nf* **1** JUVENTUD : youth **2** : youthful prank

mochila *nf* MORRAL : backpack, knapsack

moción *nf, pl* **-ciones** **1** MOVIMIENTO : motion, movement **2** : motion (to a court or assembly)

moco nm **1** : mucus **2** fam : snot ⟨limpiarse los mocos : to wipe one's (runny) nose⟩

mocoso, -sa n disparaging : kid, brat disparaging

moda nf **1** : fashion, style **2 a la moda** or **de ∼** : in style, fashionable **3 moda pasajera** : fad

modales nmpl : manners

modalidad nf **1** CLASE : kind, type **2** MANERA : way, manner

modelaje nm (in various countries) : modeling

modelar vt : to model, to mold — **modelarse** vr : to model oneself after, to emulate

modelo¹ adj : model ⟨una casa modelo : a model home⟩

modelo² nm : model, example, pattern

modelo³ nmf : model, mannequin

módem or **modem** ['moðem] nm : modem

moderación nf, pl **-ciones** MESURA : moderation

moderado, -da adj & n : moderate — **moderadamente** adv

moderador, -dora n : moderator, chair

moderar vt **1** TEMPERAR : to temper, to moderate **2** : to curb, to reduce ⟨moderar gastos : to curb spending⟩ **3** PRESIDIR : to chair (a meeting) — **moderarse** vr **1** : to restrain oneself **2** : to diminish, to calm down

modernidad nf **1** : modernity **2** : modern age

modernismo nm : modernism

modernista¹ adj : modernist

modernista² nmf : modernist

modernizar {21} vt : to modernize — **modernización** nf

moderno, -na adj : modern, up-to-date

modestia nf : modesty

modesto, -ta adj : modest — **modestamente** adv

módico, -ca adj : modest, reasonable

modificación nf, pl **-ciones** : alteration

modificador¹, -dora adj : modifying, moderating

modificador² → **modificante**

modificante nm : modifier

modificar {72} vt ALTERAR : to modify, to alter, to adapt

modismo nm : idiom

modista nmf **1** : dressmaker **2** : fashion designer

modisto nm : fashion designer

modo nm **1** MANERA : way, manner, mode ⟨de un modo u otro : one way or another⟩ ⟨a mi modo de ver : to my way of thinking⟩ ⟨modo de vida : way of life⟩ **2** : mood (in grammar) **3** : mode (in music) **4 a modo de** : by way of, in the manner of, like ⟨a modo de ejemplo : by way of example⟩ **5 de este/ese modo** : in this/that way **6 de cualquier modo** : in any case, anyway **7 de modo que** : so, in such a way that **8 de ningún modo** : (in) no way **9 de todos modos** : in any case, anyway **10 en cierto modo** : in a way, to a certain extent

modorra nf : drowsiness, lethargy

modular¹ v : to modulate — **modulación** nf

modular² adj : modular

módulo nm : module, unit

mofa nf **1** : mockery, ridicule **2 hacer mofa de** : to make fun of, to ridicule

mofarse vr ∼ **de** : to scoff at, to make fun of

mofeta nf ZORRILLO : skunk

mofle nm CA, Mex : muffler (of a car)

moflete nm fam : fat cheek

mofletudo, -da adj fam : chubby-cheeked, chubby

mohín nm, pl **mohines** : grimace, face

mohino, -na adj : gloomy, melancholy

moho nm **1** : mold, mildew **2** : rust

mohoso, -sa adj **1** : moldy **2** : rusty

moisés nm, pl **moiseses** : bassinet, cradle

mojado¹, -da adj : wet

mojado², -da n Mex fam : illegal immigrant

mojar vt **1** : to wet, to moisten **2** : to dunk — **mojarse** vr : to get wet

mojigatería nf **1** : hypocrisy **2** GAZMOÑERÍA : primness, prudery

mojigato¹, -ta adj : prudish, prim — **mojigatamente** adv

mojigato², -ta n : prude, prig

mojón nm, pl **mojones** : boundary stone, marker

molar nm MUELA : molar

molcajete nm Mex : mortar

molde nm **1** : mold, form **2 letra(s) de molde** → **letra**

moldear vt **1** FORMAR : to mold, to shape **2** : to cast

moldura nf : molding

mole¹ nm Mex **1** : spicy sauce made with chilies and usually chocolate **2** : meat served with mole sauce

mole² nf : mass, bulk

molécula nf : molecule — **molecular** adj

moler {47} vt **1** : to grind, to crush **2** CANSAR : to exhaust, to wear out

molestar vt **1** FASTIDIAR : to annoy, to bother ⟨no me molesta : it doesn't bother me, I don't mind⟩ **2** : to disturb, to disrupt — vi : to be a nuisance — **molestarse** vr **1** : to get annoyed, to be offended **2** ∼ **en** : to take the trouble to

molestia nf **1** FASTIDIO : annoyance, bother, nuisance **2** : trouble ⟨se tomó la molestia de investigar : she took the trouble to investigate⟩ **3** MALESTAR : discomfort

molesto, -ta adj **1** ENOJADO : bothered, annoyed **2** FASTIDIOSO : bothersome, annoying

molestoso, -sa adj : bothersome, annoying

molido, -da adj **1** MACHACADO : ground, crushed **2 estar molido** : to be exhausted

molienda nf : milling, grinding

molinero, -ra n : miller

molinillo nm : grinder, mill ⟨molinillo de café : coffee grinder⟩

molino *nm* 1 : mill 2 **molino de viento** : windmill

molla *nf* : soft fleshy part, flesh (of fruit), lean part (of meat)

molleja *nf* : gizzard

molusco *nm* : mollusk

momentáneamente *adv* : momentarily

momentáneo, -nea *adj* 1 : momentary 2 TEMPORARIO : temporary

momento *nm* 1 : moment, instant ⟨espera un momentito : wait just a moment⟩ 2 : time, period of time ⟨momentos difíciles : hard times⟩ 3 : time, moment (in time) ⟨en este momento : right now, at the moment⟩ ⟨llegar en mal momento : to come at a bad time⟩ ⟨momento decisivo : turning point, critical time⟩ 4 : present, moment ⟨los atletas del momento : the athletes of the moment, today's popular athletes⟩ 5 : momentum 6 **a cada momento** : constantly 7 **al momento** : right away, at once 8 **de ∼** : at the moment, for the moment 9 **de un momento a otro** : any time now 10 **en algún momento** : at some point, sometime 11 **en cualquier momento** : at any time 12 **en ningún momento** : never, at no time 13 **en todo momento** : at all times 14 **en un primer momento** : at first, initially 15 **por el momento** : for the time being 16 **por ∼s** : at times

momia *nf* : mummy

monada *nf* 1 : attractive person 2 : cute or pretty thing

monaguillo *nm* ACÓLITO : altar boy

monarca *nmf* : monarch

monarquía *nf* : monarchy

monárquico, -ca *n* : monarchist

monasterio *nm* : monastery

monástico, -ca *adj* : monastic

monda *nf* 1 : peel 2 **ser la monda** *Spain fam* : to be hilarious

mondadientes *nms & pl* PALILLO : toothpick

mondar *vt* : to peel

mondongo *nm* ENTRAÑAS : innards *pl*, insides *pl*, guts *pl*

moneda *nf* 1 : coin 2 : money, currency

monedero *nm* : change purse

monetario, -ria *adj* : monetary, financial

mongol, -gola *adj & n* : Mongol, Mongolian

monigote *nm* 1 : rag doll 2 : paper doll

monitor¹, -tora *n* : instructor (in sports)

monitor² *nm* : monitor ⟨monitor de televisión : television monitor⟩

monitorear *vt* : to monitor

monja *nf* : nun

monje *nm* : monk

mono¹, -na *adj fam* : lovely, pretty, cute, darling

mono², -na *n* : monkey

monóculo *nm* : monocle

monogamia *nf* : monogamy

monógamo, -ma *adj* : monogamous

monografía *nf* : monograph

monograma *nm* : monogram

monolingüe *adj* : monolingual

monolítico, -ca *adj* : monolithic

monolito *nm* : monolith

monólogo *nm* : monologue

monomanía *nf* : obsession

monopatín *nm, pl* **-tines** 1 : scooter 2 : skateboard

monopatinaje *nm* : skateboarding

monopolio *nm* : monopoly

monopolizar {21} *vt* : to monopolize — **monopolización** *nf*

monosilábico, -ca *adj* : monosyllabic

monosílabo *nm* : monosyllable

monoteísmo *nm* : monotheism

monoteísta¹ *adj* : monotheistic

monoteísta² *nmf* : monotheist

monotonía *nf* 1 : monotony 2 : monotone

monótono, -na *adj* : monotonous — **monótonamente** *adv*

monóxido *nm* **monóxido de carbono** : carbon monoxide

monovolumen *nm, pl* **-lúmenes** *Spain* : minivan

monseñor *nm* : monsignor

monserga *nf* : gibberish, drivel

monstruo *nm* : monster

monstruosidad *nf* : monstrosity

monstruoso, -sa *adj* : monstrous — **monstruosamente** *adv*

monta *nf* 1 : sum, total 2 : importance, value ⟨de poca monta : unimportant, insignificant⟩

montacargas *nms & pl* : freight elevator

montaje *nm* 1 : assembling, assembly 2 : montage

montante *nm* : transom, fanlight

montaña *nf* 1 MONTE : mountain 2 **montaña rusa** : roller coaster

montañero, -ra *n* : mountaineer, mountain climber

montañismo *nm* : mountaineering, (mountain) climbing

montañoso, -sa *adj* : mountainous

montar *vt* 1 : to mount, to get on 2 : to ride (a horse, a bicycle, etc.) 3 ESTABLECER : to set up, to establish 4 ARMAR : to assemble, to put together, to set up 5 : to set, to mount (gems, etc.) 6 : to edit (a film) 7 : to stage, to put on (a show) 8 : to cock (a gun) 9 : to mount (of a male animal) — *vi* 1 : to get on (a bus, etc), to get in (a car, a truck), to mount (a horse) 2 **montar en bicicleta** : to ride a bicycle 3 **montar a caballo** CABALGAR : to ride horseback —

montarse *vr* : to get in, to get on, to mount ⟨se montó en el avión : she got on the plane⟩ ⟨volvió a montarse : he got back on again⟩

monte *nm* 1 MONTAÑA : mountain, mount 2 : woodland ⟨monte bajo : underbrush⟩ 3 : outskirts (of a town), surrounding country 4 **monte de piedad** : pawnshop

montés *adj, pl* **monteses** : wild (of animals or plants)

montículo *nm* 1 : mound, heap 2 : hillock, knoll

monto *nm* : amount, total

montón *nm, pl* **-tones** 1 : heap, pile 2 *fam* : ton, load ⟨un montón de preguntas

: a ton of questions⟩ ⟨montones de gente
: loads of people⟩
montonero, -ra *n* : guerrilla
montura *nf* **1** : mount (horse) **2** : saddle, tack **3** : setting, mounting (of jewelry) **4** : frame (of glasses)
monumental *adj fam* **1** : tremendous, terrific **2** : massive, huge
monumento *nm* : monument
monzón *nm, pl* **monzones** : monsoon
moño *nm* **1** : bun (chignon) **2** LAZO : bow, knot ⟨corbata de moño : bow tie⟩
moquear *vi* : to snivel
moqueta *nf Spain* : wall-to-wall carpet
moquette *nf Arg, Uru* : wall-to-wall carpet
moquillo *nm* : distemper
mora *nf* **1** : blackberry **2** : mulberry
morada *nf* RESIDENCIA : dwelling, abode
morado¹, -da *adj* : purple
morado² *nm* : purple
morador, -dora *n* : dweller, inhabitant
moral¹ *adj* : moral — **moralmente** *adv*
moral² *nf* **1** MORALIDAD : ethics, morality, morals *pl* **2** ÁNIMO : morale, spirits *pl*
moraleja *nf* : moral (of a story)
moralidad *nf* : morality
moralista¹ *adj* : moralistic
moralista² *nmf* : moralist
morar *vi* : to dwell, to reside
moratón *nm, pl* **-tones** : bruise
moratoria *nf* : moratorium
mórbido, -da *adj* : morbid
morbo *nm* : morbid fascination
morboso, -sa *adj* : morbid — **morbosidad** *nf*
morcilla *nf* : blood sausage, blood pudding
mordacidad *nf* : bite, sharpness
mordaz *adj* : caustic, scathing
mordaza *nf* **1** : gag **2** : clamp
mordedura *nf* : bite (of an animal)
morder {47} *v* : to bite — **morderse** *vr* : to bite ⟨morderse la lengua/las uñas : to bite one's tongue/nails⟩
mordida *nf* **1** : bite **2** *CA, Mex* : bribe, payoff
mordisco *nm* : bite, nibble
mordisquear *vt* : to nibble (on), to bite
morena *nf* **1** : moraine **2** : moray (eel)
moreno¹, -na *adj* **1** : brunette **2** : dark, dark-skinned
moreno², -na *n* **1** : brunette **2** : dark-skinned person
morera *nf* : mulberry
moretón *nm, pl* **-tones** : bruise
morfina *nf* : morphine
morfología *nf* : morphology
morgue *nf* : morgue
moribundo¹, -da *adj* : dying, moribund
moribundo², -da *n* : dying person
morillo *nm* : andiron
morir {46} *vi* **1** FALLECER : to die ⟨murió de cáncer : he died of cancer⟩ **2** APAGARSE : to die out, to go out — **morirse** *vr* **1** : to die **2** ~ **de** (*expressing an extreme state*) ⟨¡me muero de frío/hambre! : I'm freezing/starving!⟩ ⟨cuando lo vi casi me muero de vergüenza : when I saw it I nearly died of embarrassment⟩

⟨morirse de risa : to die laughing⟩ **3** ~ **por** : to be dying for (something), to be dying to (do something) ⟨se muere por jugar : she's dying to play⟩ ⟨se muere por ti : he's crazy about you⟩
mormón, -mona *adj & n, pl* **mormones** : Mormon
moro¹, -ra *adj* : Moorish
moro², -ra *n* **1** : Moor **2** : Muslim
morocho¹, -cha *adj* : dark-haired
morocho², -cha *n* : dark-haired person
morosidad *nf* **1** : delinquency (in payment) **2** : slowness
moroso, -sa *adj* **1** : delinquent, in arrears ⟨cuentas morosas : delinquent accounts⟩ **2** : slow, sluggish
morral *nm* MOCHILA : backpack, knapsack
morralla *nf* **1** : small fish **2** : trash, riffraff **3** *Mex* : small change
morriña *nf* : homesickness
morro *nm* HOCICO : snout
morsa *nf* : walrus
morse *nm* : Morse code
mortadela *nf* : mortadella
mortaja *nf* SUDARIO : shroud
mortal¹ *adj* **1** : mortal **2** FATAL : fatal, deadly — **mortalmente** *adv*
mortal² *nmf* : mortal
mortalidad *nf* : mortality
mortandad *nf* **1** : loss of life, death toll **2** : carnage, slaughter
mortero *nm* : mortar (bowl, cannon, or building material)
mortífero, -ra *adj* LETAL : deadly, fatal
mortificación *nf, pl* **-ciones** **1** : mortification **2** TORMENTO : anguish, torment
mortificar {72} *vt* **1** : to mortify **2** TORTURAR : to trouble, to torment — **mortificarse** *vr* : to be mortified, to feel embarrassed
mosaico *nm* : mosaic
mosca *nf* **1** : fly **2** **mosca común** : housefly
moscada *adj* **nuez moscada** : nutmeg
mosquearse *vr* **1** : to become suspicious **2** : to take offense
mosquete *nm* : musket
mosquetero *nm* : musketeer
mosquitero *nm* : mosquito net
mosquito *nm* ZANCUDO : mosquito
mostachón *nm, pl* **-chones** : macaroon
mostaza *nf* : mustard
mosto *nm* : must (from a grape)
mostrador *nm* : counter (in a store)
mostrar {19} *vt* **1** : to show **2** EXHIBIR : to exhibit, to display — **mostrarse** *vr* : to show oneself, to appear
mota *nf* **1** : fleck, speck **2** : defect, blemish
mote *nm* SOBRENOMBRE : nickname
moteado, -da *adj* : dotted, spotted, dappled
motel *nm* : motel
motín *nm, pl* **motines** **1** : riot **2** : rebellion, mutiny
motivación *nf, pl* **-ciones** : motivation — **motivacional** *adj*
motivar *vt* **1** CAUSAR : to cause **2** IMPULSAR : to motivate

motivo *nm* **1** MÓVIL : motive ⟨el motivo del crimen : the motive for the crime⟩ **2** CAUSA : cause, reason ⟨da motivos para el optimismo : it's cause for optimism⟩ **3** TEMA : theme, motif

moto *nf* : motorcycle, motorbike

motocicleta *nf* : motorcycle

motociclismo *nm* : motorcycling

motociclista *nmf* : motorcyclist

motoneta *nf* : scooter

motor¹, -ra *adj* MOTRIZ : motor

motor² *nm* **1** : motor, engine **2** : driving force, cause

motora *nf* : motorboat

motorismo *nm* : motorcycle riding, motorcycling

motorista *nmf* : motorist

motorizado, -da *adj* : motorized

motriz *adj, pl* **matrices** : driving

motu proprio *adv* **de motu proprio** [de¹-motu¹proprio] : voluntarily, of one's own accord

mousse [ˈmus] *nmf* : mousse

movedizo, -za **1** : movable **2** : moving **3** : restless

mover {47} *vt* **1** TRASLADAR : to move, to shift **2** AGITAR : to shake, to move ⟨mover la cabeza (diciendo que sí) : to nod⟩ ⟨mover la cabeza (diciendo que no) : to shake one's head⟩ **3** ACCIONAR : to power, to drive **4** ~ **a** : to cause to (do something) ⟨me movió a pensar : it made me think⟩ ⟨lo movió a escribir : it inspired him to write⟩ — **moverse** *vr* **1** : to move **2** : to hurry, to get a move on **3** : to get moving, to make an effort

movible *adj* : movable

movida *nf* : move (in a game)

móvil¹ *adj* : mobile

móvil² *nm* **1** MOTIVO : motive **2** : mobile

movilidad *nf* : mobility

movilizar {21} *vt* : to mobilize — **movilización** *nf*

movimiento *nm* : movement, motion ⟨movimiento del cuerpo : bodily movement⟩ ⟨movimiento sindicalista : labor movement⟩

mozo¹, -za *adj* : young, youthful

mozo², -za *n* **1** JOVEN : young man *m*, young woman *f*, youth **2** : helper, servant *Arg, Chile, Col, Peru* : waiter *m*, waitress *f*

MP3 *nm, pl* **MP3** : MP3

mucamo, -ma *n* : servant, maid *f*

muchacha *nf* : maid

muchacho, -cha *n* **1** : kid, boy *m*, girl *f* **2** JOVEN : young man *m*, young woman *f*

muchedumbre *nf* MULTITUD : crowd, multitude

mucho¹ *adv* **1** : (very) much, a lot ⟨mucho más fácil/rápido/grande : much easier/faster/bigger⟩ ⟨mucho más tarde : much later⟩ ⟨te quiero mucho : I love you very much⟩ ⟨lo siento mucho : I'm very sorry⟩ ⟨le gusta mucho : he likes it a lot⟩ ⟨¿viajas mucho? : do you travel a lot?⟩ ⟨no habla mucho : she doesn't talk (very) much⟩

mucho², -cha *adj* **1** : a lot of, many, much ⟨mucha gente : a lot of people, many people⟩ ⟨mucho dinero : a lot of money⟩ ¡muchas gracias! : thank you very much!⟩ ⟨no tengo mucha hambre : I'm not very hungry⟩ ⟨hace mucho tiempo que no lo veo : I haven't seen him in ages⟩ **2 muchas veces** : often

mucho³, -cha *pron* **1** : a lot, many, much ⟨hay mucho que hacer : there is a lot to do⟩ ⟨muchos no vinieron : many didn't come⟩ **2 mucho** : long, a long time ⟨tardó mucho en venir : he was a long time getting here⟩ ⟨¿te falta mucho? : will you be much longer?⟩ ⟨hace mucho que no te veo : it's been a long time since I've seen you⟩ **3 cuando/como** ~ : at most **4 con** ~ : by far **5 ni mucho menos** : not at all, far from it **6 por mucho que** : no matter how much, (as) much as ⟨por mucho que quiera no puedo : as much as I would like to, I can't⟩

mucílago *nm* : mucilage

mucosidad *nf* : mucus

mucoso, -sa *adj* : mucous, slimy

muda *nf* **1** : change ⟨muda de ropa : change of clothes⟩ **2** : molt, molting

mudanza *nf* **1** CAMBIO : change **2** TRASLADO : move, moving

mudar *v* **1** CAMBIAR : to change **2** : to molt, to shed — **mudarse** *vr* **1** TRASLADARSE : to move (one's residence) **2** : to change (clothes)

mudo¹, -da *adj* **1** SILENCIOSO : silent ⟨el cine mudo : silent films⟩ **2** : mute, dumb *now often offensive*

mudo², -da *n* : mute *sometimes offensive*

mueble *nm* **1** : piece of furniture **2 muebles** *nmpl* : furniture, furnishings

mueblería *nf* : furniture store

mueca *nf* : grimace, face

muela *nf* **1** : tooth, molar ⟨dolor de muelas : toothache⟩ ⟨muela de juicio : wisdom tooth⟩ **2** : millstone **3** : whetstone

muele, etc. → **moler**

muelle¹ *adj* : soft, comfortable, easy

muelle² *nm* **1** : wharf, dock **2** RESORTE : spring

muérdago *nm* : mistletoe

muerde, etc. → **morder**

muere, etc. → **morir**

muerte *nf* : death ⟨amenaza de muerte : death threat⟩ ⟨dar un susto de muerte : to scare half to death⟩ ⟨morir de muerte natural : to die of natural causes⟩

muerto¹ *pp* → **morir**

muerto², -ta *adj* **1** : dead ⟨caer muerto : to die, to drop dead⟩ **2** : lifeless, flat, dull **3** ~ **de** : dying of ⟨estoy muerto de hambre : I'm dying of hunger⟩ ⟨muerto de miedo : scared to death⟩

muerto³, -ta *nm* DIFUNTO : dead person, deceased

muesca *nf* : nick, notch

muestra¹, etc. → **mostrar**

muestra² *nf* **1** : sample **2** SEÑAL : sign, show ⟨una muestra de respeto : a show of respect⟩ **3** EXPOSICIÓN : exhibition, exposition **4** : pattern, model

muestreo *nm* : sample

mueve, etc. → **mover**
mugido *nm* : moo, lowing, bellow
mugir {35} *vi* : to moo, to low, to bellow
mugre *nf* SUCIEDAD : grime, filth
mugriento, -ta *adj* : filthy
muguete *nm* : lily of the valley
muja, etc. → **mugir**
mujer *nf* **1** : woman **2** ESPOSA : wife
mújol *nm* : mullet (fish)
mulato, -ta *adj & n* : mulatto *now sometimes offensive*
muleta *nf* : crutch
muletilla *nf* : favorite word or phrase
mullido, -da *adj* **1** : soft, fluffy **2**
: spongy, springy
mulo, -la *n* : mule
multa *nf* : fine
multar *vt* : to fine
multi- *pref* : multi-
multicine *nm* : multiplex
multicolor *adj* : multicolored
multicultural *adj* : multicultural
multidisciplinario, -ria *adj* : multidisciplinary
multifacético, -ca *adj* : multifaceted
multifamiliar *adj* : multifamily
multilateral *adj* : multilateral
multimedia *nf* : multimedia
multimillonario, -ria *n* : multimillionaire
multinacional *adj* : multinational
múltiple *adj* : multiple
multiplicación *nf, pl* **-ciones** : multiplication
multiplicar {72} *v* **1** : to multiply **2** : to increase — **multiplicarse** *vr* **1** : to multiply, to reproduce **2** : to increase, to multiply ⟨multiplicarse por cinco : to increase fivefold⟩
multiplicidad *nf* : multiplicity
múltiplo *nm* : multiple
multipropiedad *nf* : time share
multitarea *nf* : multitasking
multitud *nf* MUCHEDUMBRE : crowd, multitude
multitudinario, -ria *adj* : well-attended ⟨manifestaciones multitudinarias : mass protests⟩ ⟨un concierto multitudinario : a concert with a huge turnout⟩
multiuso, -sa *adj* : multipurpose
multivitamínico, -ca *adj* : multivitamin
mundano, -na *adj* : worldly, earthly
mundial *adj* : world, worldwide
mundialmente *adv* : worldwide, all over the world
mundo *nm* **1** : world ⟨alrededor del mundo : around the world⟩ ⟨el mundo entero : the whole world⟩ ⟨el mundo actual : today's world⟩ ⟨el Tercer Mundo : the Third World⟩ ⟨el mundo de la moda : the world of fashion⟩ **2** VIDA : world, life ⟨su mundo se derrumbó : his world fell apart⟩ **3** PLANETA : world, planet **4 del mundo** : in the world ⟨el mejor del mundo : the best in the world⟩ ⟨por nada del mundo : not for anything in the world⟩ ⟨tener todo el tiempo del mundo : to have all the time

in the world⟩ **5 el otro mundo** : the afterlife, the hereafter ⟨no es nada del otro mundo : it's nothing special⟩ **6 en su mundo** *fam* : in one's own world, in a world of one's own **7 por/en/de todo el mundo** : the (whole) world over **8 todo el mundo** : everyone, everybody
municiones *nfpl* : ammunition, munitions
municipal *adj* : municipal
municipio *nm* **1** : municipality **2** AYUNTAMIENTO : town council
muñeca *nf* **1** : doll ⟨muñeca de trapo : rag doll⟩ **2** MANIQUÍ : mannequin **3** : wrist
muñeco *nm* **1** : doll, boy doll **2** MARIONETA : puppet
muñequera *nf* : wristband
muñón *nm, pl* **muñones** : stump (of an arm or leg)
mural *adj & nm* : mural
muralla *nf* : rampart, wall
murciélago *nm* : bat (animal)
murga *nf* : band of street musicians
murió, etc. → **morir**
murmullo *nm* **1** : murmur, murmuring **2** : rustling, rustle ⟨el murmullo de las hojas : the rustling of the leaves⟩
murmuraciones *nfpl* : gossip
murmurar *vt* **1** : to murmur, to mutter **2** : to whisper (gossip) — *vi* **1** : to murmur **2** CHISMEAR : to gossip
muro *nm* : wall
musa *nf* : muse
musaraña *nf* : shrew
muscular *adj* : muscular
musculatura *nf* : muscles *pl*, musculature
músculo *nm* : muscle
musculoso, -sa *adj* : muscular, brawny
muselina *nf* : muslin
museo *nm* : museum
musgo *nm* : moss
musgoso, -sa *adj* : mossy
música *nf* : music
musical *adj* : musical — **musicalmente** *adv*
músico¹, -ca *adj* : musical
músico², -ca *n* : musician
musitar *vt* : to mumble, to murmur
muslo *nm* : thigh
mustio, -tia *adj* : withered (of a plant)
musulmán, -mana *adj & n, mpl* **-manes** : Muslim
mutación *nf, pl* **-ciones** : mutation
mutante *adj & nm* : mutant
mutar *v* : to mutate
mutilar *vt* : to mutilate — **mutilación** *nf*
mutis *nm* **1** : exit (in theater) **2** : silence
mutismo *nm* : silence
mutual *adj* : mutual
mutuo, -tua *adj* : mutual, reciprocal — **mutuamente** *adv*
muy *adv* **1** : very, quite ⟨es muy inteligente : she's very intelligent⟩ ⟨muy bien : very well, fine⟩ ⟨eso es muy americano : that's typically American⟩ ⟨muy poca comida : very little food⟩ **2** : too ⟨es muy grande para él : it's too big for him⟩

N

n *nf* : sixteenth letter of the Spanish alphabet

nabo *nm* : turnip

nácar *nm* MADREPERLA : mother-of-pearl

nacarado, -da *adj* : pearly

nacer {48} *vi* **1** : to be born ⟨nací en Guatemala : I was born in Guatemala⟩ ⟨no nació ayer : he wasn't born yesterday⟩ **2** : to hatch **3** : to bud, to sprout **4** : to rise, to originate **5 nacer para algo** : to be born to be something **6 volver a nacer** : to have a lucky escape

nacido¹, -da *adj* **1** : born **2 recién nacido** : newborn

nacido², -da *n* **1 los nacidos** : those born (at a particular time) **2 recién nacido** : newborn baby

naciente *adj* **1** : newfound, growing **2** : rising ⟨el sol naciente : the rising sun⟩

nacimiento *nm* **1** : birth **2** : source (of a river) **3** : beginning, origin **4** BELÉN : Nativity scene, créche

nación *nf, pl* **naciones** : nation, country, people (of a country)

nacional¹ *adj* : national

nacional² *nmf* CIUDADANO : national, citizen

nacionalidad *nf* : nationality

nacionalismo *nm* : nationalism

nacionalista¹ *adj* : nationalist, nationalistic

nacionalista² *nmf* : nationalist

nacionalización *nf, pl* **-ciones 1** : nationalization **2** : naturalization

nacionalizar {21} *vt* **1** : to nationalize **2** : to naturalize (as a citizen) — **nacionalizarse** *vr*

naco, -ca *adj Mex* : trashy, vulgar, common

nada¹ *adv* : not at all, not in the least ⟨no estamos nada cansados : we are not at all tired⟩ ⟨no me importa nada : it doesn't matter at all to me⟩

nada² *nf* **1** : nothingness **2** : smidgen, bit ⟨una nada le disgusta : the slightest thing upsets him⟩

nada³ *pron* **1** : nothing ⟨no estoy haciendo nada : I'm not doing anything⟩ ⟨es mejor que nada : it's better than nothing⟩ ⟨empecé sin nada : I started out with nothing⟩ ⟨no tengo nada que decir : I have nothing to say⟩ ⟨no tiene nada de extraño : there's nothing strange about it⟩ ⟨esta pluma no sirve para nada : this pen is useless⟩ ⟨no me interesa para nada : it doesn't interest me at all⟩ ⟨no es nada comparado con . . . : it's nothing compared to . . .⟩ ⟨no hay nada como la comida casera : there's nothing like home cooking⟩ **2 antes que nada** : first of all (in order), above all (in importance) **3 casi nada** : next to nothing **4 de ～** : you're welcome **5 dentro de nada** : very soon, in no time **6 nada de eso** : nothing of the kind, nothing like that **7 nada más** : nothing else, nothing

more **8 nada más** : as soon as, no sooner . . . than ⟨nada más comenzar el partido, marcó : as soon as the game started, he scored; no sooner did the game start than he scored⟩ **9 pues nada** *fam* : anyway

nadador, -dora *n* : swimmer

nadar *vi* **1** : to swim **2 ～ en** : to be swimming in, to be rolling in — *vt* : to swim

nadería *nf* : small thing, trifle

nadie *pron* : nobody, no one ⟨no vi a nadie : I didn't see anyone⟩

nadir *nm* : nadir

nado *nm* **1** *Mex* : swimming **2 a ～** : swimming ⟨cruzó el río a nado : he swam across the river⟩

nafta *nf* **1** : naphtha **2** (*in various countries*) : gasoline

naftalina *nf* : mothballs *pl*

náhuatl¹ *adj & nmf, pl* **nahuas** : Nahuatl

náhuatl² *nm* : Nahuatl (language)

nailon → nilón

naipe *nm* : playing card

nalga *nf* **1** : buttock **2 nalgas** *nfpl* : buttocks, bottom

nalgada *nf* : smack on the bottom, spanking

namibio, -bia *adj & n* : Namibian

nana *nf* **1** : lullaby **2** *fam* : grandma **3** *CA, Col, Mex, Ven* : nanny

nanay *interj fam* : no way!, not likely!

nanotecnología *nf* : nanotechnology

naranja¹ *adj & nm* : orange (color)

naranja² *nf* : orange (fruit)

naranjada *nf* : orangeade

naranjal *nm* : orange grove

naranjo *nm* : orange tree

narcisismo *nm* : narcissism

narcisista¹ *adj* : narcissistic

narcisista² *nmf* : narcissist

narciso *nm* : narcissus, daffodil

narco *nmf fam* → **narcotraficante**

narcótico¹, -ca *adj* : narcotic

narcótico² *nm* : narcotic

narcotizar {21} *vt* : to drug, to dope

narcotraficante *nmf* : drug trafficker

narcotráfico *nm* : drug trafficking

narigón, -gona *adj, mpl* **-gones** : big-nosed

narigudo → narigón

nariz *nf, pl* **narices 1** : nose ⟨sonar(se) la nariz : to blow one's nose⟩ **2** : sense of smell

narración *nf, pl* **-ciones** : narration, account

narrador, -dora *n* : narrator

narrar *vt* : to narrate, to tell

narrativa *nf* : narrative, story

narrativo, -va *adj* : narrative

nasa *nf* : creel

nasal *adj* : nasal

nata *nf* **1** *Spain* : cream ⟨nata montada : whipped cream⟩ **2** : skin (on boiled milk)

natación *nf, pl* **-ciones** : swimming

natal *adj* : native, natal

natalicio *nm* : birthday ⟨el natalicio de George Washington : George Washington's birthday⟩
natalidad *nf* : birthrate
natillas *nfpl* : custard
natividad *nf* : birth, nativity
nativo, -va *adj & n* : native
nativo americano, nativa americana *adj & n* : Native American
nato, -ta *adj* : born, natural
natural¹ *adj* **1** : natural **2** : normal ⟨como es natural : naturally, as expected⟩ **3** ~ **de** : native of, from **4 de tamaño natural** : life-size
natural² *nm* **1** CARÁCTER : disposition, temperament **2** : native ⟨un natural de Venezuela : a native of Venezuela⟩
naturaleza *nf* **1** : nature ⟨la madre naturaleza : mother nature⟩ **2** ÍNDOLE : nature, disposition, constitution ⟨la naturaleza humana : human nature⟩ **3 naturaleza muerta** : still life
naturalidad *nf* : simplicity, naturalness
naturalismo *nm* : naturalism
naturalista¹ *adj* : naturalistic
naturalista² *nmf* : naturalist
naturalización *nf, pl* **-ciones** : naturalization
naturalizar {21} *vt* : to naturalize — **naturalizarse** *vr* NACIONALIZARSE : to become naturalized
naturalmente *adv* **1** : naturally, inherently **2** : of course
naufragar {52} *vi* **1** : to be shipwrecked **2** FRACASAR : to fail, to collapse
naufragio *nm* **1** : shipwreck **2** FRACASO : failure, collapse
náufrago¹, -ga *adj* : shipwrecked, castaway
náufrago², -ga *n* : shipwrecked person, castaway
náusea *nf* **1** : nausea **2 dar náuseas** : to nauseate, to disgust **3 náuseas matutinas** : morning sickness
nauseabundo, -da *adj* : nauseating, sickening
náutica *nf* : navigation
náutico, -ca *adj* : nautical
nautilo *nm* : nautilus
navaja *nf* **1** : pocketknife, penknife ⟨navaja de muelle : switchblade⟩ **2 navaja de afeitar** : straight razor
navajazo *nm* : knife wound
navajo, -ja *adj & n* : Navajo
naval *adj* : naval
nave *nf* **1** : ship ⟨nave capitana : flagship⟩ ⟨nave espacial : spaceship⟩ **2** : nave ⟨nave lateral : aisle⟩ **3 quemar uno sus naves** : to burn one's bridges
navegabilidad *nf* : navigability
navegable *adj* : navigable
navegación *nf, pl* **-ciones** : navigation
navegador *nm* : browser ⟨navegador web : web browser⟩
navegante¹ *adj* : sailing, seafaring
navegante² *nmf* : navigator
navegar {52} *v* : to navigate, to sail
Navidad *nf* : Christmas ⟨Feliz Navidad : Merry Christmas⟩
navideño, -ña *adj* : Christmas

naviero, -ra *adj* : shipping
navío *nm* : (large) ship
nazca, etc. → **nacer**
nazi *adj & nmf* : Nazi
nazismo *nm* : Nazism
neandertal *or* **neanderthal** *nm* **1** Neandertal *or* Neanderthal *or* hombre de Neandertal/Neanderthal : Neanderthal (man) **2 fam** : Neanderthal
nébeda *nf* : catnip
neblina *nf* : light fog, mist
neblinoso, -sa *adj* : misty, foggy
nebulosa *nf* : nebula
nebulosidad *nf* : mistiness, haziness
nebuloso, -sa *adj* **1** : hazy, misty **2** : nebulous, vague
necedad *nf* : stupidity, foolishness ⟨decir necedades : to talk nonsense⟩
necesariamente *adv* : necessarily
necesario, -ria *adj* **1** : necessary **2 si es necesario** : if need be **3 hacerse necesario** : to be required
neceser *nm* : toilet kit, vanity case
necesidad *nf* **1** : need, necessity ⟨por necesidad : out of necessity⟩ ⟨en caso de necesidad : if necessary, if need be⟩ **2** : poverty, want **3 necesidades** *nfpl* : hardships **4 hacer sus necesidades** : to relieve oneself
necesitado, -da *adj* : needy
necesitar *vt* **1** : to need **2** : to necessitate, to require — *vi* ~ **de** : to have need of
necio¹, -cia *adj* **1** : foolish, silly, dumb **2 fam** : naughty **3** *Mex* : stubborn
necio², -cia *n* **1** ESTÚPIDO : fool, idiot **2** *Mex* : stubborn person
necrología *nf* : obituary
necrópolis *nfs & pl* : cemetery
néctar *nm* : nectar
nectarina *nf* : nectarine
neerlandés¹, -desa *adj, mpl* **-deses** HOLANDÉS : Dutch
neerlandés², -desa *n, mpl* **-deses** HOLANDÉS : Dutch person
nefando, -da *adj* : unspeakable, heinous
nefario, -ria *adj* : nefarious
nefasto, -ta *adj* **1** : ill-fated, unlucky **2** : disastrous, terrible
negación *nf, pl* **-ciones** **1** : negation, denial **2** : negative (in grammar)
negado, -da *adj* : useless
negar {49} *vt* **1** : to deny **2** REHUSAR : to refuse **3** : to disown — **negarse** *vr* **1** : to refuse **2** : to deny oneself
negativa *nf* **1** : denial **2** : refusal
negativo¹, -va *adj* : negative — **negativamente** *adv*
negativo² *nm* : negative (of a photograph)
negligé *nm* : negligee
negligencia *nf* : negligence
negligente *adj* : neglectful, negligent — **negligentemente** *adv*
negociable *adj* : negotiable
negociación *nf, pl* **-ciones** **1** : negotiation **2 negociación colectiva** : collective bargaining
negociador, -dora *n* : negotiator
negociante *nmf* : businessman *m*, businesswoman *f*

negociar vt : to negotiate — vi : to deal, to do business

negocio nm 1 : business, place of business ⟨el mundo de los negocios : the business world⟩ 2 : deal, transaction 3 **negocios** nmpl : commerce, trade, business

negra nf : quarter note

negrero, -ra n 1 : slave trader 2 fam : slave driver, brutal boss

negrita or **negrilla** nf : boldface (type)

negro¹, -gra adj 1 : black, dark 2 BRONCEADO : suntanned 3 : gloomy, awful, desperate ⟨la cosa se está poniendo negra : things are looking bad⟩ 4 **mercado negro** : black market

negro², -gra n 1 : dark-skinned person, black person 2 fam : darling, dear

negro³ nm : black (color)

negrura nf : blackness

negruzco, -ca adj : blackish

nene, -na n : baby, small child

nenúfar nm : water lily

neocelandés → neozelandés

neófito, -ta n : neophyte, novice

neologismo nm : neologism

neón nm, pl **neones** : neon

neoyorquino¹, -na adj : of or from New York

neoyorquino², -na n : New Yorker

neozelandés¹, -desa adj, mpl **-deses** : of or from New Zealand

neozelandés², -desa n, mpl **-deses** : New Zealander

nepalés, -lesa adj & n, mpl **-leses** : Nepali

nepotismo nm : nepotism

Neptuno nm : Neptune

nervio nm 1 : nerve 2 : tendon, sinew, gristle (in meat) 3 : energy, drive 4 : rib (of a vault) 5 **nervios** nmpl : nerves ⟨estar mal de los nervios : to be a bag/bundle of nerves⟩ ⟨tener los nervios de punta : to be on edge, to have one's nerves on edge⟩ ⟨crisparle los nervios a alguien : to get on someone's nerves⟩ ⟨ataque de nervios : nervous breakdown⟩ ⟨una guerra de nervios : a war of nerves⟩ ⟨nervios de acero : nerves of steel⟩

nerviosamente adv : nervously

nerviosidad → nerviosismo

nerviosismo nf : nervousness, anxiety

nervioso, -sa adj 1 : nervous, nerve ⟨sistema nervioso : nervous system⟩ 2 : high-strung, restless, anxious ⟨ponerse nervioso : to get nervous⟩ 3 : vigorous, energetic

nervudo, -da adj : sinewy, wiry

neta nf Mex fam : truth ⟨la neta es que me cae mal : the truth is, I don't like her⟩

netamente adv : clearly, obviously

neto, -ta adj 1 : net ⟨peso neto : net weight⟩ 2 : clear, distinct

neumático¹, -ca adj : pneumatic

neumático² nm LLANTA : tire

neumonía nf PULMONÍA : pneumonia

neural adj : neural

neuralgia nf : neuralgia

neuritis nf : neuritis

neurología nf : neurology

neurológico, -ca adj : neurological, neurologic

neurólogo, -ga n : neurologist

neurosis nfs & pl : neurosis

neurótico, -ca adj & n : neurotic

neutral adj : neutral

neutralidad nf : neutrality

neutralizar {21} vt : to neutralize — **neutralización** nf

neutro, -tra adj 1 : neutral 2 : neuter

neutrón nm, pl **neutrones** : neutron

nevada nf : snowfall

nevado, -da adj 1 : snowcapped 2 : snow-white

nevar {55} v impers : to snow

nevasca nf : snowstorm, blizzard

nevera nf REFRIGERADOR : refrigerator

nevería nf Mex : ice cream parlor

nevisca nf : light snowfall, flurry

nevoso, -sa adj : snowy

nexo nm VÍNCULO : link, connection, nexus

ni conj 1 : neither, nor ⟨no es (ni) bueno ni malo : it's neither good nor bad⟩ ⟨ni hoy ni mañana : neither today nor tomorrow⟩ ⟨ni confirma ni niega las acusaciones : he neither confirms nor denies the allegations⟩ ⟨zonas sin agua ni electricidad : areas without water or power, areas with no water or power⟩ ⟨no pagó ni un centavo : he didn't pay a single cent⟩ ⟨él no lo cree, ni yo tampoco : he doesn't believe it, and neither do I⟩ ⟨no le beneficia a ella ni a nadie : it doesn't benefit her or anyone else⟩ 2 **ni que** : not even if, not as if ⟨ni que me pagaran : not even if they paid me⟩ ⟨ni que fuera (yo) su madre : it's not as if I were his mother⟩ 3 **ni siquiera** : not even ⟨ni siquiera nos llamaron : they didn't even call us⟩

nicaragüense adj & nmf : Nicaraguan

nicho nm : niche

nicotina nf : nicotine

nidada nf : brood (of chicks)

nido nm 1 : nest 2 : hiding place, den

niebla nf : fog, mist

niega, niegue etc. → negar

nieto, -ta n 1 : grandson m, granddaughter f 2 **nietos** nmpl : grandchildren

nieva, etc. → nevar

nieve nf 1 : snow 2 Cuba, Mex, PRi : sherbet

nigeriano, -na adj & n : Nigerian

nigua nf : sand flea, chigger

nihilismo nm : nihilism

nilón or **nilon** nm, pl **nilones** : nylon

nimbo nm : halo

nimiedad nf INSIGNIFICANCIA : trifle, triviality

nimio, -mia adj INSIGNIFICANTE : insignificant, trivial

ninfa nf : nymph

ningunear vt Mex fam : to disrespect

ninguno¹, -na (**ningún** before masculine singular nouns) adj, mpl **ningunos** : no, none ⟨no es ninguna tonta : she's no fool⟩ ⟨no dieron ninguna razón : they gave no reason, they didn't give a reason⟩ ⟨no debe hacerse en ningún mo-

mento : that should never be done⟩ ⟨no
tenemos ninguna idea : we have no idea⟩
ninguno², -na *pron* **1** : neither, none
⟨ninguno de los dos ha vuelto aún : neither one has returned yet⟩ ⟨ninguno de
ellos : none of them⟩ **2** : no one, no
other ⟨te quiero más que a ninguna : I
love you more than any other⟩ ⟨ninguno
me dice nada : nobody tells me any-
thing⟩
niña *nf* **1** PUPILA : pupil (of the eye) **2 la
niña de los ojos** : the apple of one's eye
niñada *nf* **1** : childishness **2** : trifle, silly
thing
niñería → niñada
niñero, -ra *n* : baby-sitter, nanny
niñez *nf, pl* **niñeces** INFANCIA : childhood
niño, -ña *n* : child, boy *m*, girl *f* ⟨los niños
: the children⟩ ⟨esperar un niño : to be
pregnant, to be expecting a baby⟩
nipón, -pona *adj & n, mpl* **nipones** JA-
PONÉS : Japanese
níquel *nm* : nickel
nitidez *nf, pl* **-deces** CLARIDAD : clarity,
vividness, sharpness
nítido, -da *adj* CLARO : clear, vivid, sharp
nitrato *nm* : nitrate
nítrico, -ca *adj* **ácido nítrico** → ácido²
nitrógeno *nm* : nitrogen
nitroglicerina *nf* : nitroglycerin
nivel *nm* **1** : level, height ⟨nivel del mar
: sea level⟩ ⟨al nivel de : level with⟩ ⟨al
nivel del suelo : at floor level⟩ **2** : level,
standard ⟨nivel de vida : standard of liv-
ing⟩ ⟨al mismo nivel que : on a level/par
with⟩ ⟨de alto nivel : high-level⟩
nivelador, -dora *n* : leveler
nivelar *vt* **1** : to level (off/out), to even (out)
— nivelarse *vr*
nixtamal *nm Mex* : corn cooked with lime
(used for tortillas)
no¹ *adv* **1** (*indicating a negative response*)
: no ⟨¿quieres más? no, gracias : do you
want more? no, thanks⟩ ⟨¿la conoces?
no : do you know her? no⟩ ⟨no? : no, not
⟨no sé : I don't know⟩ ⟨no tengo ni idea
: I have no idea⟩ ⟨no hagas eso! : don't
do that!⟩ ⟨no le gusta : she doesn't like
it⟩ ⟨no es fácil : it's not easy⟩ ⟨creo que
no : I don't think so⟩ ⟨no puedo ver
nada : I can't see a thing, I can't see any-
thing⟩ ⟨no hay nadie : there's no one
there⟩ ⟨es interesante, ¿no? : it's interesting, isn't it?⟩ ⟨se casó! ¡no! : he got
married! no way!⟩ **3** : non- ⟨no fumador : non-smoker⟩ **4 ¡cómo no!** : of
course! **5 no bien** : as soon as, no
sooner
no² *nm, pl* **noes** : no
noble¹ *adj* : noble **— noblemente** *adv*
noble² *nmf* : nobleman *m*, noblewoman *f*
nobleza *nf* **1** : nobility **2** HONRADEZ
: honesty, integrity
nocaut *nm* : knockout, KO
noche *nf* **1** : night, nighttime, evening
⟨esta noche : tonight⟩ ⟨la noche anterior
: the night before⟩ ⟨la noche del lunes
: (on) Monday night⟩ ⟨todas las noches
: every night⟩ ⟨a altas horas de la noche

: late at night⟩ ⟨en medio/mitad de la
noche : in the middle of the night⟩ ⟨las
diez de la noche : ten (o'clock) at night⟩
⟨al caer la noche : at nightfall⟩ ⟨pasar la
noche : to spend the night⟩ **2 buenas
noches** : good evening, good night **3 de
noche** *or* **en/por/a la noche** : at night
⟨salir de noche : to go out at night⟩ ⟨era
de noche : it was nighttime⟩ ⟨mañana
en/por/a la noche : tomorrow night⟩ **4
de la noche a la mañana** : overnight,
suddenly **5 hacerse de noche** : to get
dark
Nochebuena *nf* : Christmas Eve
nochecita *nf* : dusk
Nochevieja *nf* : New Year's Eve
noción *nf, pl* **nociones** **1** CONCEPTO
: notion, concept **2 nociones** *nfpl*
: smattering, rudiments *pl*
nocivo, -va *adj* DAÑINO : harmful, noxious
noctámbulo, -la *n* **1** : sleepwalker **2**
: night owl
nocturno¹, -na *adj* : night, nocturnal
nocturno² *nm* : nocturne
nodriza *nf* : wet nurse
nódulo *nm* : nodule
nogal *nm* **1** : walnut tree **2** *Mex* : pecan
tree **3 nogal americano** : hickory
nómada¹ *adj* : nomadic
nómada² *nmf* : nomad
nomás *adv* : only, just ⟨lo hice nomás
porque sí : I did it just because⟩ ⟨nomás
de recordarlo me enojo : I get angry just
remembering it⟩ ⟨nomás faltan dos semanas para Navidad : there are only two
weeks left till Christmas⟩
nombradía *nf* RENOMBRE : fame, renown
nombrado, -da *adj* : famous, well-known
nombramiento *nm* : appointment, nomination
nombrar *vt* **1** : to appoint **2** : to mention, to name
nombre *nm* **1** : name ⟨nombre y apellido
: first and last name, full name⟩ ⟨nom-
bre de pila : first name⟩ ⟨nombre de
soltera : maiden name⟩ ⟨nombre de usuario : user name⟩ ⟨nombre artístico
: stage name⟩ ⟨nombre de pluma : pen
name⟩ ⟨nombre comercial : trade name⟩
⟨en nombre de : on behalf of⟩ ⟨sin nombre : nameless⟩ ⟨sólo de nombre : in
name only⟩ ⟨lo cambiaron de nombre
: they changed its name⟩ ⟨no lo conozco
de nombre : I don't know him by name⟩
⟨lo que están haciendo no tiene nombre
: what they're doing is an outrage⟩ **2**
: noun ⟨nombre propio : proper noun⟩
3 : fame, renown ⟨hacerse un nombre
: to make a name for oneself⟩
nomenclatura *nf* : nomenclature
nomeolvides *nmfs & pl* : forget-me-not
nómina *nf* : payroll
nominación *nf, pl* **-ciones** : nomination
nominal *adj* : nominal **— nominalmente**
adv
nominar *vt* : to nominate
nominativo¹, -va *adj* : nominative
nominativo² *nm* : nominative (case)
nomo *nm* : gnome

non[1] *adj* IMPAR : odd, not even

non[2] *nm* : odd number

nonagésimo[1], **-ma** *adj* : ninetieth, ninety-

nonagésimo[2], **-ma** *n* : ninetieth, ninety- (in a series)

nono, -na *adj* : ninth — **nono** *nm*

nopal *nm* : prickly pear

nopalitos *nmpl Mex* : pickled prickly pear leaves

noquear *vt* : to knock out, to KO

norcoreano, -na *adj & n* : North Korean

nordeste[1] *or* **noreste** *adj* 1 : northeastern 2 : northeasterly

nordeste[2] *or* **noreste** *nm* : northeast

nórdico, -ca *adj & n* 1 ESCANDINAVO : Scandinavian 2 : Norse

noreste → **nordeste**

noria *nf* 1 : waterwheel 2 : Ferris wheel

norirlandés[1], **-desa** *adj, mpl* **-deses** : Northern Irish

norirlandés[2], **-desa** *n, mpl* **-deses** : person from Northern Ireland

norma *nf* 1 : rule, regulation 2 : norm, standard

normal *adj* 1 : normal, usual 2 : standard 3 **escuela normal** : teacher-training college

normalidad *nf* : normality, normalcy

normalización *nf, pl* **-ciones** *nf* 1 REGULARIZACIÓN : normalization 2 ESTANDARIZACIÓN : standardization

normalizar {21} *vt* 1 REGULARIZAR : to normalize 2 ESTANDARIZAR : to standardize — **normalizarse** *vr* : to return to normal

normalmente *adv* GENERALMENTE : ordinarily, generally

noroeste[1] *adj* 1 : northwestern 2 : northwesterly

noroeste[2] *nm* : northwest

norte[1] *adj* : north, northern

norte[2] *nm* 1 : north 2 : north wind 3 META : aim, objective

norteamericano, -na *adj & n* 1 : North American 2 AMERICANO, ESTADOUNIDENSE : American, native or inhabitant of the United States

norteño[1], **-ña** *adj* : northern

norteño[2], **-ña** *n* : Northerner

noruego[1], **-ga** *adj & n* : Norwegian

noruego[2] *nm* : Norwegian (language)

nos *pron pl* 1 : us ⟨nos enviaron a la frontera : they sent us to the border⟩ 2 : ourselves ⟨nos divertimos muchísimo : we enjoyed ourselves a great deal⟩ 3 : each other, one another ⟨nos vimos desde lejos : we saw each other from far away⟩ 4 : to us, for us, from us ⟨nos lo dio : he gave it to us⟩ ⟨nos lo compraron : they bought it from us⟩

nosotros, -tras *pron pl* 1 : we ⟨nosotros llegamos ayer : we arrived yesterday⟩ 2 : us ⟨ven con nosotros : come with us⟩ ⟨a nosotros no nos afecta : it doesn't affect us⟩ ⟨ninguna de nosotras : neither of us⟩ ⟨el de nosotros es mejor : ours is better⟩ 3 **nosotros mismos** : ourselves ⟨lo arreglamos nosotros mismos : we fixed it ourselves⟩

nostalgia *nf* 1 : nostalgia, longing 2 : homesickness

nostálgico, -ca *adj* 1 : nostalgic 2 : homesick

nota *nf* 1 : note, message ⟨tomar notas : to take notes⟩ 2 : announcement ⟨nota de prensa : press release⟩ 3 : grade, mark (in school) 4 : characteristic, feature, touch 5 : note (in music) 6 : bill, check (in a restaurant)

notable *adj* 1 : notable, noteworthy 2 : outstanding

notablemente *adv* 1 : notably, markedly 2 : outstandingly

notación *nf, pl* **-ciones** : notation

notar *vt* 1 : to notice ⟨hacer notar algo : to point out something⟩ 2 : to tell ⟨la diferencia se nota inmediatamente : you can tell the difference right away⟩ — **notarse** *vr* 1 : to be evident, to show 2 : to feel, to seem

notaría *nf* : notary's office

notario, -ria *n* : notary, notary public

notebook *nf* : notebook (computer)

noticia *nf* 1 : news item, piece of news ⟨noticia bomba : shocking news, bombshell⟩ 2 **noticias** *nfpl* : news

noticiero *or* **noticiario** *nm* : news, news program, newscast

noticioso, -sa *adj* : news ⟨agencia noticiosa : news agency⟩

notificación *nf, pl* **-ciones** : notification

notificar {72} *vt* : to notify, to inform

notoriedad *nf* 1 : knowledge 2 : fame, notoriety

notorio, -ria *adj* 1 OBVIO : obvious, evident 2 CONOCIDO : well-known

novato[1], **-ta** *adj* : inexperienced, new

novato[2], **-ta** *n* : beginner, novice

novecientos[1], **-tas** *adj & pron* : nine hundred

novecientos[2] *nms & pl* : nine hundred

novedad *nf* 1 : newness, novelty 2 : innovation 3 : news, development 4 **sin ~** : the same as before 5 **sin ~** : without incident, safely

novedoso, -sa *adj* : original, novel

novel *adj* NOVATO : inexperienced, new

novela *nf* 1 : novel 2 : soap opera

novelar *vt* : to make a novel out of

novelesco, -ca *adj* 1 : fictional 2 : fantastic, fabulous

novelista *nmf* : novelist

novena *nf* : novena

noveno, -na *adj & n* : ninth ⟨el noveno piso : the ninth floor⟩ ⟨la novena (persona) : the ninth (person)⟩ ⟨un noveno de . . . : one ninth of . . .⟩

noventa *adj & nm* : ninety — **noventa** *pron*

noventavo[1], **-va** *adj* : ninetieth

noventavo[2] *nm* : ninetieth (fraction)

noviar *vi* : to date, to go out ⟨noviar con : to go out with⟩

noviazgo *nm* 1 : courtship, relationship 2 : engagement, betrothal

novicio, -cia *n* 1 : novice (in religion) 2 PRINCIPIANTE : novice, beginner

noviembre *nm* : November ⟨el primero de noviembre : (on) November first⟩

novilla *nf* : heifer
novillada *nf* : bullfight featuring young bulls
novillero, -ra *n* : apprentice bullfighter
novillo *nm* : young bull
novio, -via *n* **1** : boyfriend *m*, girlfriend *f* **2** PROMETIDO : fiancé *m*, fiancée *f* **3** : bridegroom *m*, bride *f*
novocaína *nf* : novocaine
nubarrón *nm*, *pl* **-rrones** : storm cloud
nube *nf* **1** : cloud ⟨andar en las nubes : to have one's head in the clouds⟩ ⟨por las nubes : sky-high⟩ **2** : cloud (of dust), swarm (of insects, etc.) **3** : cloud ⟨computación en la nube : cloud computing⟩
nublado¹, -da *adj* **1** NUBOSO : cloudy, overcast **2** : clouded, dim
nublado² *nm* **1** : storm cloud **2** AMENAZA : menace, threat
nublar *vt* **1** : to cloud **2** OSCURECER : to obscure — **nublarse** *vr* : to get cloudy
nubosidad *nf* : cloudiness
nuboso, -sa *adj* NUBLADO : cloudy
nuca *nf* : nape, back of the neck
nuclear *adj* : nuclear
núcleo *nm* **1** : nucleus **2** : center, heart, core
nudillo *nm* : knuckle
nudismo *nm* : nudism
nudista *adj & nmf* : nudist
nudo *nm* **1** : knot ⟨nudo de rizo : square knot⟩ ⟨nudo corredizo : slipknot⟩ ⟨un nudo en la garganta : a lump in one's throat⟩ **2** : node **3** : junction, hub ⟨nudo de comunicaciones : communication center⟩ **4** : crux, heart (of a problem, etc.)
nudoso, -sa *adj* : knotty, gnarled
nuera *nf* : daughter-in-law
nuestro¹, -tra *adj* : our
nuestro², -tra *pron* ⟨with definite article⟩ : ours, our own ⟨el nuestro es más grande : ours is bigger⟩ ⟨es de los nuestros : it's one of ours⟩
nuevamente *adv* : again, anew
nuevas *nfpl* : tidings *pl*
nueve¹ *adj & nm* : nine ⟨tengo nueve años : I am nine years old⟩ ⟨el nueve de noviembre : (on) the ninth of November, (on) November ninth⟩
nueve² *pron* : nine ⟨somos nueve : there are nine of us⟩ ⟨son las nueve : it's nine o'clock⟩
nuevecito, -ta *adj* : brand-new
nuevo, -va *adj* **1** : new ⟨una casa nueva : a new house⟩ ⟨¿qué hay de nuevo? : what's new?⟩ **2 de ~** : again, once more **3 Nuevo Testamento** : New Testament
nuez *nf*, *pl* **nueces 1** : nut **2** : walnut **3** *Mex* : pecan **4 nuez de Adán** : Adam's apple **5 nuez de Brasil** : Brazil nut **6 nuez moscada** : nutmeg

nulidad *nf* **1** : nullity **2** : incompetent person ⟨¡es una nulidad! : he's hopeless!⟩
nulo, -la *adj* **1** : null, null and void **2** INEPTO : useless, inept ⟨es nula para la cocina : she's hopeless at cooking⟩
numen *nm* : poetic muse, inspiration
numerable *adj* : countable
numeración *nf*, *pl* **-ciones 1** : numbering **2** : numbers *pl*, numerals *pl* ⟨numeración romana : Roman numerals⟩
numerador *nm* : numerator
numeral *adj* : numeral
numerar *vt* : to number
numerario, -ria *adj* : long-standing, permanent ⟨profesor numerario : tenured professor⟩
numérico, -ca *adj* : numerical — **numéricamente** *adv*
número *nm* **1** : number ⟨número impar : odd number⟩ ⟨número primo : prime number⟩ ⟨número ordinal : ordinal number⟩ ⟨número arábigo : Arabic numeral⟩ ⟨número quebrado : fraction⟩ **2** : issue (of a publication) **3** : size ⟨¿qué número calza? : what's his shoe size?⟩ **4** : lottery ticket **5** : act, routine, number **6 sin ~** : countless
numeroso, -sa *adj* : numerous
numismática *nf* : numismatics
nunca *adv* **1** : never, ever ⟨nunca es tarde : it's never too late⟩ ⟨no trabaja casi nunca : he hardly ever works⟩ **2 nunca más** : never again **3 nunca jamás** : never ever
nuncio *nm* : harbinger, herald
nupcial *adj* : nuptial, wedding
nupcias *nfpl* : nuptials *pl*, wedding
nutria *nf* **1** : otter **2** : nutria
nutrición *nf*, *pl* **-ciones** : nutrition, nourishment
nutricionista *nmf* : nutritionist
nutrido, -da *adj* **1** : nourished ⟨mal nutrido : undernourished, malnourished⟩ **2** : considerable, abundant ⟨de nutrido : full of, abounding in⟩
nutriente *nm* : nutrient
nutrimento *nm* : nutriment
nutrir *vt* **1** ALIMENTAR : to feed, to nourish **2** : to foster, to provide
nutritivo, -va *adj* : nourishing, nutritious
nylon → **nilón**
ñ *nf* : seventeenth letter of the Spanish alphabet
ñame *nm* : yam
ñandú *nm*, *pl* **ñandú** *or* **ñandúes** : rhea
ñapa *nf* : extra amount ⟨de ñapa : for good measure⟩
ñato, -ta *adj* : snub-nosed
ñoñear *vi fam* : to whine
ñoñería *nf* : inanity
ñoño, -ña *adj fam* : whiny, fussy ⟨no seas tan ñoño : don't be such a wimp⟩
ñu *nm* : gnu

O

o¹ *nf* : eighteenth letter of the Spanish alphabet

o² *conj* (**u** *before words beginning with* o- *or* ho-) **1** : or ⟨¿vienes con nosotros o te quedas? : are you coming with us or staying?⟩ **2** : either ⟨o vienes con nosotros o te quedas : either you come with us or you stay⟩ **3 o sea** : that is to say, in other words

oasis *nms & pl* : oasis

obcecado, -da *adj* **1** : blinded ⟨obcecado por la ira : blinded by rage⟩ **2** : stubborn, obstinate

obcecar {72} *vt* : to blind (by emotions) — **obcecarse** *vr* : to become stubborn

obedecer {53} *vt* : to obey ⟨obedecer órdenes : to obey orders⟩ ⟨obedece a tus padres : obey your parents⟩ — *vi* **1** : to obey **2 ~ a** : to respond to **3 ~ a** : to be due to, to result from

obediencia *nf* : obedience

obediente *adj* : obedient — **obedientemente** *adv*

obelisco *nm* : obelisk

obertura *nf* : overture

obesidad *nf* : obesity

obeso, -sa *adj* : obese

óbice *nm* : obstacle, impediment

obispado *nm* DIÓCESIS : bishopric, diocese

obispo *nm* : bishop

obituario *nm* : obituary

objeción *nf*, *pl* **-ciones** : objection ⟨ponerle objeciones a algo : to object to something⟩

objetar *v* : to object ⟨no tengo nada que objetar : I have no objections⟩

objetividad *nf* : objectivity

objetivo¹, -va *adj* : objective — **objetivamente** *adv*

objetivo² *nm* **1** META : objective, goal, target **2** : lens

objeto *nm* **1** COSA : object, thing ⟨objetos de valor : valuables⟩ **2** OBJETIVO : objective, purpose ⟨con objeto de : in order to, with the aim of⟩ **3 objeto volador no identificado** : unidentified flying object

objetor, -tora *n* : objector ⟨objetor de conciencia : conscientious objector⟩

oblea *nf* **1** : wafer **2 hecho una oblea** *fam* : skinny as a rail

oblicuo, -cua *adj* : oblique — **oblicuamente** *adv*

obligación *nf*, *pl* **-ciones 1** DEBER : obligation, duty **2** : bond

obligado, -da *adj* **1** : obliged **2** : obligatory, compulsory **3** : customary

obligar {52} *vt* : to force, to require, to oblige — **obligarse** *vr* : to commit oneself, to undertake (to do something)

obligatorio, -ria *adj* : mandatory, required, compulsory

obliterar *vt* : to obliterate, to destroy — **obliteración** *nf*

oblongo, -ga *adj* : oblong

obnubilación *nf*, *pl* **-ciones** : bewilderment, confusion

obnubilar *vt* : to daze, to bewilder

oboe¹ *nm* : oboe

oboe² *nmf* : oboist

obra *nf* **1** : work ⟨obra de arte : work of art⟩ ⟨obra de teatro : play⟩ ⟨obra de consulta : reference work⟩ **2** : deed ⟨una buena obra : a good deed⟩ **3** : construction work ⟨en obra(s) : under construction⟩ ⟨obras viales : roadwork⟩ **4** : construction site, building site **5 obra maestra** : masterpiece **6 obras públicas** : public works **7 poner en obra** : to put into effect **8 por obra de** : thanks to, because of

obrar *vt* : to work, to produce ⟨obrar milagros : to work miracles⟩ — *vi* **1** : to act, to behave ⟨obrar con cautela : to act with caution⟩ **2 obrar en poder de** : to be in possession of

obrero¹, -ra *adj* : working ⟨la clase obrera : the working class⟩

obrero², -ra *n* : worker, laborer

obscenidad *nf* : obscenity

obsceno, -na *adj* : obscene

obscurecer, obscuridad, obscuro → **oscurecer, oscuridad, oscuro**

obsequiar *vt* REGALAR : to give, to present ⟨lo obsequiaron con una placa : they presented him with a plaque⟩

obsequio *nm* REGALO : gift, present

obsequiosidad *nf* : attentiveness, deference

obsequioso, -sa *adj* : obliging, attentive

observable *adj* : observable

observación *nf*, *pl* **-ciones 1** : observation, watching ⟨bajo/en observación : under observation⟩ **2** : remark, comment

observador¹, -dora *adj* : observant

observador², -dora *n* : observer, watcher

observancia *nf* : observance

observante *adj* : observant ⟨los judíos observantes : observant Jews⟩

observar *vt* **1** : to observe, to watch ⟨estábamos observando a los niños : we were watching the children⟩ **2** NOTAR : to notice **3** ACATAR : to obey, to abide by **4** COMENTAR : to remark, to comment

observatorio *nm* : observatory

obsesión *nf*, *pl* **-siones** : obsession

obsesionar *vt* : to obsess, to preoccupy excessively — **obsesionarse** *vr*

obsesivo, -va *adj* : obsessive

obseso, -sa *adj* : obsessed

obsolescencia *nf* DESUSO : obsolescence — **obsolescente** *adj*

obsoleto, -ta *adj* DESUSADO : obsolete

obstaculizar {21} *vt* IMPEDIR : to obstruct, to hinder

obstáculo *nm* IMPEDIMENTO : obstacle

obstante¹ *conj* **no obstante** : nevertheless, however

obstante² *prep* **no obstante** : in spite of, despite ⟨mantuvo su inocencia no obstante la evidencia : he maintained his innocence in spite of the evidence⟩

obstar *v impers* ∼ **a** *or* ∼ **para** : to hinder, to prevent ⟨eso no obsta para que me vaya : that doesn't prevent me from leaving⟩

obstetra *nmf* TOCÓLOGO : obstetrician

obstetricia *nf* : obstetrics

obstétrico, -ca *adj* : obstetric, obstetrical

obstinación *nf, pl* **-ciones** 1 TERQUEDAD : obstinacy, stubbornness 2 : perseverance, tenacity

obstinado, -da *adj* 1 TERCO : obstinate, stubborn 2 : persistent — **obstinadamente** *adv*

obstinarse *vr* EMPECINARSE : to be obstinate, to be stubborn

obstrucción *nf, pl* **-ciones** : obstruction, blockage

obstruccionismo *nm* : filibustering (en política)

obstruccionista *adj* : filibustering (en política)

obstructor, -tora *adj* : obstructive

obstruir {41} *vt* BLOQUEAR : to obstruct, to block, to clog — **obstruirse** *vr*

obtención *nf, pl* **-ciones** : obtaining, procurement

obtener {80} *vt* : to obtain, to secure, to get — **obtenible** *adj*

obturador *nm* : shutter (of a camera)

obturar *vt* : to block

obtuso, -sa *adj* : obtuse

obtuvo, etc. → obtener

obús *nm, pl* **obuses** 1 : mortar (weapon) 2 : mortar shell

obviar *vt* : to get around (a difficulty), to avoid

obvio, -via *adj* : obvious — **obviamente** *adv*

oca *nf* : goose

ocasión *nf, pl* **-siones** 1 : occasion, time ⟨en alguna ocasión : occasionally, sometimes⟩ 2 : opportunity, chance 3 : bargain 4 de ∼ : secondhand 5 aviso de ocasión *Mex* : classified ad

ocasional *adj* 1 : occasional 2 : chance, fortuitous

ocasionalmente *adv* 1 : occasionally 2 : by chance

ocasionar *vt* CAUSAR : to cause, to occasion

ocaso *nm* 1 ANOCHECER : sunset, sundown 2 DECADENCIA : decline, fall

occidental *adj* : western

occidente *nm* 1 OESTE, PONIENTE : west 2 el Occidente : the West

oceánico, -ca *adj* : oceanic

océano *nm* : ocean

oceanografía *nf* : oceanography — **oceanográfico, -ca** *adj*

ocelote *nm* : ocelot

ochenta *adj & nm* : eighty — **ochenta** *pron*

ochentavo¹, -va *adj* : eightieth

ochentavo² *nm* : eightieth (fraction)

ocho¹ *adj & nm* : eight ⟨tiene ocho años : he's eight (years old)⟩ ⟨el ocho de mayo : (on) the eighth of May, (on) May eighth⟩

ocho² *pron* : eight ⟨somos ocho : there are eight of us⟩ ⟨son las ocho : it's eight o'clock⟩

ochocientos¹, -tas *adj & pron* : eight hundred

ochocientos² *nms & pl* : eight hundred

ocio *nm* 1 : free time, leisure 2 : idleness

ociosamente *adv* : idly

ociosidad *nf* : idleness, inactivity

ocioso, -sa *adj* 1 INACTIVO : idle, inactive 2 INÚTIL : pointless, useless

ocre *nm* : ocher

octágono *nm* : octagon — **octagonal** *adj*

octava *nf* : octave

octavilla *nf* : pamphlet

octavo, -va *adj & n* : eighth ⟨el octavo grado : the eighth grade⟩ ⟨la octava (persona) : the eighth (person)⟩ ⟨un octavo de . . . : one eighth of . . .⟩

octeto *nm* : byte

octogésimo¹, -ma *adj* : eightieth, eighty-

octogésimo², -ma *n* : eightieth, eighty- (in a series)

octubre *nm* : October ⟨el primero de octubre : (on) October first⟩

ocular *adj* 1 : ocular, eye ⟨músculos oculares : eye muscles⟩ 2 **testigo ocular** : eyewitness

oculista *nmf* : oculist, ophthalmologist

ocultación *nf, pl* **-ciones** : concealment

ocultar *vt* ESCONDER : to conceal, to hide — **ocultarse** *vr*

oculto, -ta *adj* 1 ESCONDIDO : hidden, concealed 2 : occult

ocupación *nf, pl* **-ciones** 1 : occupation, activity 2 : occupancy 3 EMPLEO : employment, job

ocupacional *adj* : occupational, job-related

ocupado, -da *adj* 1 : busy 2 : taken ⟨este asiento está ocupado : this seat is taken⟩ 3 : occupied ⟨territorios ocupados : occupied territories⟩ 4 **señal de ocupado** : busy signal

ocupante *nmf* : occupant

ocupar *vt* 1 : to occupy, to take possession of 2 : to hold (a position) 3 : to employ, to keep busy 4 : to fill (space, time) 5 : to inhabit (a dwelling) 6 : to bother, to concern — **ocuparse** *vr* ∼ **de** 1 : to be concerned with 2 : to take care of

ocurrencia *nf* 1 : occurrence, event 2 : witticism 3 : bright idea

ocurrente *adj* 1 : witty 2 : clever, sharp

ocurrir *vi* : to occur, to happen — **ocurrirse** *vr* ∼ **a** : to occur to, to strike ⟨se me ocurrió una mejor idea : a better idea occurred to me⟩

oda *nf* : ode

odiar *vt* ABOMINAR, ABORRECER : to hate

odio *nm* : hate, hatred

odioso, -sa *adj* ABOMINABLE, ABORRECIBLE : hateful, detestable

odisea *nf* : odyssey

odómetro *nm* : odometer

odontología *nf* : dentistry, dental surgery

odontólogo, -ga *n* : dentist, dental surgeon

odre nm : wineskin
oeste¹ adj **1** : west, western ⟨la región oeste : the western region⟩ **2** : westerly
oeste² nm **1** : west, West **2** : west wind
ofender vt AGRAVIAR : to offend, to insult — vi : to offend, to be insulting — **ofenderse** vr : to take offense
ofensa nf : offense, insult
ofensiva nf : offensive ⟨pasar a la ofensiva : to go on the offensive⟩
ofensivo, -va adj : offensive, insulting — **ofensivamente** adv
ofensor, -sora n : offender
oferente nmf **1** : supplier **2** FUENTE : source ⟨un oferente no identificado : an unidentified source⟩
oferta nf **1** : offer **2** : sale, bargain ⟨las camisas están en oferta : the shirts are on sale⟩ **3 oferta y demanda** : supply and demand
ofertar vt OFRECER : to offer
oficial¹ adj : official — **oficialmente** adv
oficial² nmf **1** : officer, police officer, commissioned officer (in the military) **2** : skilled worker
oficializar {21} vt : to make official
oficiante nmf : celebrant
oficiar vi **1** : to inform officially **2** : to officiate at, to celebrate (Mass) — vi ~ **de** : to act as
oficina nf : office
oficinista nmf : office worker
oficio nm **1** : trade, profession ⟨es electricista de oficio : he's an electrician by trade⟩ **2** : function, role **3** : official communication **4** : experience ⟨tener oficio : to be experienced⟩ **5** : religious ceremony
oficioso, -sa adj **1** EXTRAOFICIAL : unofficial **2** : officious — **oficiosamente** adv
ofimática nf : office automation, office computing
ofrecer {53} vt **1** : to offer **2** : to provide, to give **3** : to present (an appearance, etc.) — **ofrecerse** vr **1** : to offer oneself, to volunteer **2** : to open up to, to present itself
ofrecimiento nm : offer, offering
ofrenda nf : offering
oftalmología nf : ophthalmology
oftalmólogo, -ga n : ophthalmologist
ofuscación nf, pl **-ciones** : blindness, confusion
ofuscar {72} vt **1** : to blind, to dazzle **2** CONFUNDIR : to bewilder, to confuse — **ofuscarse** vr ~ **con** : to be blinded by
ogro nm : ogre
oh interj : oh ⟨¡oh, no! : oh no!⟩ ⟨oh, ¡qué raro! : oh, how odd!⟩
ohm nm, pl **ohms** : ohm
ohmio → ohm
oídas nfpl **de** ~ : by hearsay
oído nm **1** : ear ⟨oído interno : inner ear⟩ **2** : hearing ⟨duro de oído : hard of hearing⟩ **3 tocar de oído** : to play by ear
oiga, etc. → oír
oír {50} vi : to hear — vt **1** : to hear **2** ESCUCHAR : to listen to **3** : to pay atten-

tion to, to heed **4 ¡oye!** or **¡oiga!** : listen!, excuse me!, look here!
ojal nm : buttonhole
ojalá interj **1** : I hope so!, if only!, God willing! **2** : I hope, I wish, hopefully ⟨¡ojalá que le vaya bien! : I hope things go well for her!⟩ ⟨¡ojalá no llueva! : hopefully it won't rain!⟩
ojeada nf : glimpse, glance ⟨echar una ojeada : to have a quick look⟩
ojear vt : to eye, to have a look at
ojeras nfpl : bags/circles under one's eyes
ojeriza nf fam : grudge
ojeroso, -sa adj : with bags/circles under one's eyes
ojete nm : eyelet
ojiva nf : warhead
ojo nm **1** : eye ⟨un hombre con/de ojos verdes : a man with green eyes⟩ ⟨ojos negros : dark eyes⟩ ⟨la miré a los ojos : I looked her in the eye⟩ ⟨lo vi con mis propios ojos : I saw it with my own two eyes⟩ ⟨apareció ante nuestros ojos : it appeared before our very eyes⟩ ⟨con los ojos abiertos : with one's eyes open⟩ **2** : judgment, sharpness ⟨tener buen ojo para : to be a good judge of, to have a good eye for⟩ **3** : hole (in cheese), eye (in a needle), center (of a storm) ⟨ojo de cerradura : keyhole⟩ **4** : span (of a bridge) **5 a ojos vistas** : obviously, visibly **6 andar con ojo** : to be careful **7 costar un ojo de la cara** : to cost an arm and a leg **8 en un abrir y cerrar de ojos** : in the blink of an eye **9 ojo de agua** Mex : spring, source **10 ¡ojo!** : look out!, pay attention! **11 tener ojos de águila** : to have eyes like a hawk
okupa nf fam : squatter
ola nf **1** : wave **2 ola de calor** : heat wave
oleada nf : swell, wave ⟨una oleada de protestas : a wave of protests⟩
oleaje nm : waves pl, surf
óleo nm **1** : oil **2** : oil painting
oleoducto nm : oil pipeline
oleoso, -sa adj : oily
oler {51} vt **1** : to smell **2** INQUIRIR : to pry into, to investigate **3** AVERIGUAR : to smell out, to uncover — vi **1** : to smell ⟨huele mal : it smells bad⟩ ⟨todo esto huele mal : there's something fishy about all of this⟩ **2** ~ **a** : to smell like, to smell of ⟨huele a pino : it smells like pine⟩ — **olerse** vr : to have a hunch, to suspect
olfatear vt **1** : to sniff **2** : to sense, to sniff out
olfativo, -va adj : olfactory
olfato nm **1** : sense of smell **2** : nose, instinct
oligarquía nf : oligarchy
olimpiada or **olimpíada** nf **1** : Olympiad **2** or **olympiadas** nfpl : Olympics pl
olímpico, -ca adj : Olympic
olisquear vt : to sniff at
oliva nf ACEITUNA : olive ⟨aceite de oliva : olive oil⟩
olivar nm : olive grove
olivo nm : olive tree

olla *nf* **1** : pot ⟨olla de presión : pressure cooker⟩ ⟨olla de cocción lenta, olla de cocimiento lento : slow cooker⟩ **2 olla podrida** : Spanish stew **3 olla vaporera → vaporera**

olmeca *adj & nmf* : Olmec
olmo *nm* : elm
olor *nm* : smell, odor
oloroso, -sa *adj* : scented, fragrant
olote *nm* *Mex* : cob, corncob
olvidadizo, -za *adj* : forgetful, absent-minded
olvidar *vt* **1** : to forget, to forget about ⟨olvida lo que pasó : forget about what happened⟩ **2** : to leave behind ⟨olvidé mi chequera en la casa : I left my checkbook at home⟩ — **olvidarse** *vr* : to forget ⟨se me olvidó mi cuaderno : I forgot my notebook⟩ ⟨se le olvidó llamarme : he forgot to call me⟩
olvido *nm* **1** : forgetfulness **2** : oblivion **3** DESCUIDO : oversight
omaní *adj & nmf* : Omani
ombligo *nm* : navel, belly button
ombudsman *nmfs & pl* : ombudsman
omelette *nmf* : omelet
ominoso, -sa *adj* : ominous — **ominosamente** *adv*
omisión *nf, pl* **-siones** : omission, neglect
omiso, -sa *adj* **1** NEGLIGENTE : neglectful **2 hacer caso omiso de → caso**
omitir *vt* **1** : to omit, to leave out **2** : to fail to ⟨omitió dar su nombre : he failed to give his name⟩
ómnibus *n, pl* **-bus** *or* **-buses** : bus, coach
omnipotencia *nf* : omnipotence
omnipotente *adj* TODOPODEROSO : omnipotent, almighty
omnipresencia *nf* : omnipresence
omnipresente *adj* : ubiquitous, omnipresent
omnisciente *adj* : omniscient — **omnisciencia** *nf*
omnívoro, -ra *adj* : omnivorous
omóplato *or* **omoplato** *nm* : shoulder blade
once¹ *adj & nm* : eleven ⟨tiene once años : she's eleven (years old)⟩ ⟨el once de noviembre : (on) the eleventh of November, (on) November eleventh⟩
once² *pron* : eleven ⟨son las once : it's eleven o'clock⟩ ⟨somos once : there are eleven of us⟩
onceavo¹, -va *adj* : eleventh
onceavo² *nm* : eleventh (fraction)
onda *nf* **1** : wave, ripple, undulation ⟨onda sonora : sound wave⟩ **2** : wave (in hair) **3** : scallop (on clothing) **4** *fam* : wavelength, understanding ⟨agarrar la onda : to get the point⟩ ⟨en la onda : on the ball, with it⟩ **5 ¿qué onda?** *fam* : what's happening?, what's up?
ondear *vi* : to ripple, to undulate, to flutter
ondulación *nf, pl* **-ciones** : undulation
ondulado, -da *adj* **1** : wavy ⟨pelo ondulado : wavy hair⟩ **2** : undulating
ondulante *adj* : undulating
ondular *vt* : to wave (hair) — *vi* : to undulate, to ripple

oneroso, -sa *adj* GRAVOSO : onerous, burdensome
ónix *nm* : onyx
online [on'lain] *adj & adv* : online
onza *nf* : ounce
opacar {72} *vt* **1** : to make opaque or dull **2** : to outshine, to overshadow
opacidad *nf* **1** : opacity **2** : dullness
opaco, -ca *adj* **1** : opaque **2** : dull
ópalo *nm* : opal
opción *nf, pl* **opciones 1** ALTERNATIVA : option, choice **2** : right, chance ⟨tener opción a : to be eligible for⟩
opcional *adj* : optional — **opcionalmente** *adv*
ópera *nf* : opera
operación *nf, pl* **-ciones 1** : operation **2** : transaction, deal
operacional *adj* : operational
operador, -dora *n* **1** : operator **2** : projectionist, camera operator
operante *adj* : operating, working
operar *vt* **1** : to produce, to bring about **2** INTERVENIR : to operate on ⟨me operaron : I had an operation, I had surgery⟩ ⟨me operaron de la rodilla : I had surgery on my knee, I had knee surgery⟩ ⟨la operaron de cáncer : she had cancer surgery⟩ ⟨fue operado de un tumor : he had surgery to remove a tumor⟩ **3** *Mex* : to operate, to run (a machine) — *vi* **1** : to operate, to function **2** : to deal, to do business — **operarse** *vr* **1** : to come about, to take place **2** : to have an operation, to have surgery
operario, -ria *n* : laborer, worker
operático, -ca → operístico
operativo¹, -va *adj* **1** : operating ⟨capacidad operativa : operating capacity⟩ **2** : operative
operativo² *nm* : operation ⟨operativo militar : military operation⟩
opereta *nf* : operetta
operístico, -ca *adj* : operatic
opiato *nm* : opiate
opinable *adj* : arguable
opinar *vi* **1** : to think, to have an opinion **2** : to express an opinion **3 opinar bien de** : to think highly of — *vt* : to think ⟨opinamos lo mismo : we're of the same opinion, we're in agreement⟩
opinión *nf, pl* **-niones** : opinion, belief
opio *nm* : opium
oponente *nmf* : opponent
oponer {60} *vt* **1** CONTRAPONER : to oppose, to place against **2 oponer resistencia** : to resist, to put up a fight — **oponerse** *vr* **~ a** : to object to, to be against
oporto *nm* : port (wine)
oportunamente *adv* **1** : at the right time, opportunely **2** : appropriately
oportunidad *nf* : opportunity, chance
oportunismo *nm* : opportunism
oportunista¹ *adj* : opportunistic
oportunista² *nmf* : opportunist
oportuno, -na *adj* **1** : opportune, timely **2** : suitable, appropriate
oposición *nf, pl* **-ciones** : opposition
opositor, -tora *n* ADVERSARIO : opponent

oposum *nm* ZARIGÜEYA : opossum
opresión *nf*, *pl* **-siones** 1 : oppression 2 **opresión de pecho** : tightness in the chest
opresivo, -va *adj* : oppressive
opresor¹, -sora *adj* : oppressive
opresor², -sora *n* : oppressor
oprimir *vt* 1 : to oppress 2 : to press, to squeeze ⟨oprima el botón : push the button⟩
oprobio *nm* : opprobrium, shame
optar *vi* 1 — **por** : to opt for, to choose 2 — **a** : to aspire to, to apply for ⟨dos candidatos optan a la presidencia : two candidates are running for president⟩
optativo, -va *adj* FACULTATIVO : optional
óptica *nf* 1 : optics 2 : optician's shop 3 : viewpoint
óptico¹, -ca *adj* : optical, optic
óptico², -ca *n* : optician
optimismo *nm* : optimism
optimista¹ *adj* : optimistic
optimista² *nmf* : optimist
óptimo, -ma *adj* : optimum, optimal
optometría *nf* : optometry — **optometrista** *nmf*
opuesto¹ *pp* → **oponer**
opuesto² *adj* 1 : opposite, contrary 2 : opposed
opulencia *nf* : opulence — **opulento, -ta** *adj*
opus *nm* : opus
opuso, etc. → **oponer**
ora *conj* : now ⟨los matices eran variados, ora verdes, ora ocres : the hues were varied, now green, now ocher⟩
oración *nf*, *pl* **-ciones** 1 DISCURSO : oration, speech 2 PLEGARIA : prayer 3 FRASE : sentence, clause
oráculo *nm* : oracle
orador, -dora *n* : speaker, orator
oral *adj* : oral — **oralmente** *adv*
órale *interj Mex fam* 1 : sure!, OK! ⟨¿los dos por cinco pesos? ¡órale! : both for five pesos? you've got a deal!⟩ 2 : come on! ⟨¡órale, vámonos! : come on, let's go!⟩
orangután *nm*, *pl* **-tanes** : orangutan
orar *vi* REZAR : to pray
oratoria *nf* : oratory
oratorio *nm* 1 CAPILLA : oratory, chapel 2 : oratorio
orbe *nm* 1 : orb, sphere 2 GLOBO : globe, world
órbita *nf* 1 : orbit 2 : eye socket 3 ÁMBITO : sphere, field
orbital *adj* : orbital
orbitar *v* : to orbit
orca *nf* : orca, killer whale
orden¹ *nm*, *pl* **órdenes** 1 : order ⟨todo está en orden : everything's in order⟩ ⟨por orden cronológico : in chronological order⟩ 2 **orden del día** : agenda (at a meeting) 3 **orden público** : law and order
orden² *nf*, *pl* **órdenes** 1 : order ⟨una orden religiosa : a religious order⟩ ⟨una orden de tacos : an order of tacos⟩ 2 **orden de compra** : purchase order 3 **estar a la orden del día** : to be the order of the day, to be prevalent

ordenación *nf*, *pl* **-ciones** 1 : ordination 2 : ordering, organizing
ordenadamente *adv* : in an orderly fashion, neatly
ordenado, -da *adj* : orderly, neat
ordenador *nm Spain* : computer
ordenamiento *nm* 1 : ordering, organizing 2 : code (of laws)
ordenanza¹ *nf* REGLAMENTO : ordinance, regulation
ordenanza² *nm* : orderly (in the armed forces)
ordenar *vt* 1 MANDAR : to order, to command 2 ARREGLAR : to put in order, to arrange 3 : to ordain (a priest) — **ordenarse** *vr* : to be ordained
ordeñar *vt* : to milk
ordeño *nm* : milking
ordinal *nm* : ordinal (number)
ordinariamente *adv* 1 : usually 2 : coarsely
ordinariez *nf* : coarseness, vulgarity
ordinario, -ria *adj* 1 : ordinary 2 : coarse, common, vulgar 3 de ~ : usually
orear *vt* : to air
orégano *nm* : oregano
oreja *nf* : ear
orfanato *nm* : orphanage
orfanatorio *nm Mex* : orphanage
orfandad *nf* : state of being an orphan
orfebre *nmf* : goldsmith, silversmith
orfebrería *nf* : articles of gold or silver
orfelinato *nm* : orphanage
orgánico, -ca *adj* : organic — **orgánicamente** *adv*
organigrama *nm* : organization chart, flow chart
organismo *nm* 1 : organism 2 : agency, organization
organista *nmf* : organist
organización *nf*, *pl* **-ciones** : organization
organizador¹, -dora *adj* : organizing
organizador², -dora *n* : organizer ⟨organizador de bodas : wedding planner⟩
organizar {21} *vt* : to organize, to arrange — **organizarse** *vr* : to get organized
organizativo, -va *adj* : organizational
órgano *nm* : organ
orgasmo *nm* : orgasm
orgía *nf* : orgy
orgullo *nm* : pride
orgulloso, -sa *adj* : proud — **orgullosamente** *adv*
orientación *nf*, *pl* **-ciones** 1 : orientation 2 DIRECCIÓN : direction, course 3 GUÍA : guidance, direction
oriental¹ *adj* 1 : eastern 2 *now sometimes offensive when used of people* : oriental *now usu offensive when used of people* 3 *Arg, Uru* : Uruguayan
oriental² *nmf* 1 : Easterner 2 *dated now sometimes offensive when used of people* : Oriental *dated, now usu offensive* 3 *Arg, Uru* : Uruguayan
orientar *vt* 1 : to orient, to position 2 : to guide, to direct — **orientarse** *vr* 1 : to orient oneself, to get one's bearings 2 ~ **hacia** : to turn towards, to lean towards
oriente *nm* 1 : east, East 2 **el Oriente** : the Orient

orífice *nmf* : goldsmith

orificio *nm* : orifice, opening

origen *nm, pl* **orígenes** 1 : origin 2 : lineage, birth 3 **dar origen a** : to give rise to 4 **en su origen** : originally

original *adj & nm* : original — **originalmente** *adv*

originalidad *nf* : originality

originar *vt* : to originate, to give rise to — **originarse** *vr* : to originate, to begin

originario, -ria *adj* ~ **de** : native of

originariamente *adv* : originally

orilla *nf* 1 **BORDE** : border, edge 2 : bank (of a river) 3 : shore

orillar *vt* 1 : to skirt, to go around 2 : to trim, to edge (cloth) 3 : to settle, to wind up 4 *Mex* : to pull over (a vehicle)

orín *nm* 1 **HERRUMBRE** : rust 2 **orines** *nmpl* : urine

orina *nf* : urine

orinación *nf* : urination

orinal *nm* : urinal (vessel)

orinar *vi* : to urinate — **orinarse** *vr* : to wet oneself

oriol *nm* **OROPÉNDOLA** : oriole

oriundo, -da *adj* ~ **de** : native of

orla *nf* : border, edging

orlar *vt* : to edge, to trim

ornamentación *nf, pl* **-ciones** : ornamentation

ornamental *adj* : ornamental

ornamentar *vt* **ADORNAR** : to ornament, to adorn

ornamento *nm* : ornament, adornment

ornar *vt* : to adorn, to decorate

ornitología *nf* : ornithology

ornitólogo, -ga *n* : ornithologist

ornitorrinco *nm* : platypus

oro *nm* 1 : gold 2 **oros** *nmpl* : gold coins (in the Spanish deck of cards)

orondo, -da *adj* 1 : rounded, potbellied (of a container) 2 *fam* : smug, self-satisfied

oropel *nm* : glitz, glitter, tinsel

oropéndola *nf* : oriole

orquesta *nf* : orchestra ⟨orquesta sinfónica : symphony (orchestra)⟩ — **orquestal** *adj*

orquestar *vt* : to orchestrate — **orquestación** *nf*

orquídea *nf* : orchid

ortiga *nf* : nettle

ortodoncia *nf* : orthodontics

ortodoncista *nmf* : orthodontist

ortodoxia *nf* : orthodoxy

ortodoxo, -xa *adj* : orthodox

ortografía *nf* : orthography, spelling

ortográfico, -ca *adj* : orthographic, spelling

ortopedia *nf* : orthopedics

ortopédico, -ca *adj* : orthopedic

ortopedista *nmf* : orthopedist

oruga *nf* 1 : caterpillar 2 : track (of a tank, etc.)

orzuelo *nm* : sty, stye (in the eye)

os *pron pl objective form of* **VOSOTROS** 1 *Spain* : you, to you ⟨os veo pronto : I'll see you soon⟩ 2 : yourselves, to yourselves 3 : each other, to each other

osa *nf* → **oso**

osadía *nf* 1 **VALOR** : boldness, daring 2 **AUDACIA** : audacity, nerve

osado, -da *adj* 1 : bold, daring 2 : audacious, impudent — **osadamente** *adv*

osamenta *nf* : skeletal remains *pl*, bones *pl*

osar *vi* : to dare

oscilación *nf, pl* **-ciones** 1 : oscillation 2 : fluctuation 3 : vacillation, wavering

oscilar *vi* 1 **BALANCEARSE** : to swing, to sway, to oscillate 2 **FLUCTUAR** : to fluctuate 3 : to vacillate, to waver

oscuramente *adv* : obscurely

oscurecer {53} *vt* 1 : to darken 2 : to obscure, to confuse, to cloud 3 **al oscurecer** : at dusk, at nightfall — *v impers* : to grow dark, to get dark — **oscurecerse** *vr* : to darken, to dim

oscuridad *nf* 1 : darkness 2 : obscurity

oscuro, -ra *adj* 1 : dark 2 : obscure 3 **a oscuras** : in the dark, in darkness

óseo, ósea *adj* : skeletal, bony

ósmosis *or* **osmosis** *nf* : osmosis

oso, osa *n* 1 : bear 2 **Osa Mayor** : Big Dipper 3 **Osa Menor** : Little Dipper 4 **oso blanco** : polar bear 5 **oso hormiguero** : anteater 6 **oso de peluche** : teddy bear

ostensible *adj* : ostensible, apparent — **ostensiblemente** *adv*

ostentación *nf, pl* **-ciones** : ostentation, display

ostentar *vt* 1 : to display, to flaunt 2 **POSEER** : to have, to hold ⟨ostenta el récord mundial : he holds the world record⟩

ostentoso, -sa *adj* : ostentatious, showy — **ostentosamente** *adv*

osteópata *nmf* : osteopath

osteopatía *n* : osteopathy

osteoporosis *nf* : osteoporosis

ostión *nm, pl* **ostiones** 1 *Mex* : oyster 2 *Chile* : scallop

ostra *nf* : oyster

ostracismo *nm* : ostracism

otear *vt* : to scan, to survey, to look over

otero *nm* : knoll, hillock

otitis *nf* : otitis, inflammation of the ear

otomana *nf* : ottoman (furniture)

otomano, -na *adj & n* : Ottoman

otoñal *adj* : autumn, autumnal

otoño *nm* : autumn, fall

otorgamiento *nm* : granting, awarding

otorgar {52} *vt* 1 : to grant, to award 2 : to draw up, to frame (a legal document)

otorrino, -na *n* : ear, nose, and throat doctor

otro¹, otra *adj* 1 : other 2 : another ⟨en otro juego, ellos ganaron : in another game, they won⟩ 3 **otra vez** : again 4 **de otra manera** : otherwise 5 **otra parte** : elsewhere 6 **en otro tiempo** : once, formerly

otro², otra *pron* 1 : another one ⟨dame otro : give me another⟩ ⟨otra! : encore!⟩ 2 : other one ⟨el uno o el otro : one or the other⟩ 3 **los otros, las otras** : the others, the rest ⟨me dio una y se quedó con las otras : he gave me one and kept the rest⟩

ovación *nf, pl* **-ciones** : ovation
ovacionar *vt* : to cheer, to applaud
oval → **ovalado**
ovalado, -da *adj* : oval
óvalo *nm* : oval
ovárico, -ca *adj* : ovarian
ovario *nm* : ovary
oveja *nf* **1** : sheep, ewe **2 oveja negra** : black sheep
overol *nm* : overalls *pl*
ovillar *vt* : to roll into a ball
ovillo *nm* **1** : ball (of yarn) **2** : tangle
ovni *or* **OVNI** *nm* (*objeto volador no identificado*) : UFO
ovoide *adj* : ovoid, ovoidal
ovulación *nf, pl* **-ciones** : ovulation
ovular *vi* : to ovulate

óvulo *nm* : ovum
oxidación *nf, pl* **-ciones** **1** : oxidation **2** : rusting
oxidado, -da *adj* : rusty
oxidar *vt* **1** : to cause to rust **2** : to oxidize — **oxidarse** *vr* : to rust, to become rusty
óxido *nm* **1** HERRUMBRE, ORÍN : rust **2** : oxide
oxigenar *vt* **1** : to oxygenate **2** : to bleach (hair)
oxígeno *nm* : oxygen
oxiuro *nm* : pinworm
oye, etc. → **oír**
oyente *nmf* **1** : listener **2** : auditor, auditing student
ozono *nm* : ozone

P

p *nf* : nineteenth letter of the Spanish alphabet
pabellón *nm, pl* **-llones** **1** : pavilion (at a fair, etc.) **2** GLORIETA : gazebo, pavilion **3** : building (of a hospital, etc.) **4** : flag (of a vessel)
pabilo *nm* MECHA : wick
paca *nf* FARDO : bale
pacana *nf* : pecan
pacer {48} *v* : to graze, to pasture
paces → **paz**
pachanga *nf fam* : party, bash
paciencia *nf* : patience ⟨tener paciencia : to be patient⟩ ⟨perder la paciencia : to lose (one's) patience⟩
paciente *adj & nmf* : patient — **pacientemente** *adv*
pacíficamente *adv* : peacefully, peaceably
pacificar {72} *vt* : to pacify, to calm — **pacificarse** *vr* : to calm down, to abate — **pacificación** *nf*
pacífico, -ca *adj* : peaceful, pacific
pacifismo *nm* : pacifism
pacifista *adj & nmf* : pacifist
pacotilla *nf* de ⟨~⟩ : shoddy, trashy
pactar *vt* : to agree on (terms, etc.) — *vi* : to come to an agreement
pacto *nm* CONVENIO : pact, agreement
paddock ['padok] *nm* : paddock
padecer {53} *vt* : to suffer (hardship, etc.), to suffer from (an illness) — *vi* **1** ADOLECER : to suffer **2** ~ **de** : to suffer from
padecimiento *nm* **1** : suffering **2** : ailment, condition
padrastro *nm* **1** : stepfather **2** : hangnail
padre¹ *adj Mex fam* : fantastic, great
padre² *nm* **1** : father **2** : Father (title of a priest) **3 padres** *nmpl* : parents
padrenuestro *nm* : Lord's Prayer
padrino *nm* **1** : godfather **2** : father of the bride **3** : sponsor, patron **4 padrinos** *nmpl* : godparents

padrón *nm, pl* **padrones** : register, roll ⟨padrón municipal : city register⟩ ⟨padrón electoral : electoral/voter roll⟩
paella *nf* : paella
paga *nf* **1** : payment **2** : pay, wages *pl* **3** : allowance (given to a child)
pagadero, -ra *adj* : payable
pagado, -da *adj* **1** : paid **2 pagado de sí mismo** : self-satisfied, smug
pagador, -dora *n* : payer
paganismo *nm* : paganism
pagano, -na *adj & n* : pagan
pagar {52} *vt* **1** : to pay (a bill), to pay for (a purchase), to pay off (a debt) **2** : to pay for (a crime, etc.) **3** : to repay (a favor) — *vi* : to pay
pagaré *nm* VALE : promissory note, IOU
página *nf* **1** : page ⟨la página seis : page six⟩ **2 página de inicio** : home page **3 página web** : web page
pago *nm* **1** : payment **2 en pago de** : in return for **3 pago al contado** : cash payment **4 pago anticipado** : advance payment **5 pago inicial** : down payment
pagoda *nf* : pagoda
pague, etc. → **pagar**
paila *nf* **1** : large shallow dish or pan **2** *Hond* : cargo area (of a vehicle)
país *nm* **1** NACIÓN : country, nation **2** REGIÓN : region, territory
paisaje *nm* : scenery, landscape
paisajismo *nm* : landscaping
paisajista *nmf* : landscaper
paisano, -na *n* **1** COMPATRIOTA : compatriot, fellow countryman **2 de** ~ : in plain/civilian clothes ⟨un policía de paisano : a plainclothes policeman⟩
paja *nf* **1** : straw **2** *fam* : trash, tripe
pajar *nm* : hayloft, haystack
pajarera *nf* : aviary
pajarita *nf Spain* : bow tie
pájaro *nm* **1** : bird ⟨pájaro cantor : songbird⟩ ⟨pájaro bobo : penguin⟩ ⟨pájaro carpintero : woodpecker⟩

paje *nm* : page (person)
pajita *or* **pajilla** *nf* : (drinking) straw
pajote *nm* : straw, mulch
pakistaní *adj & nmf, pl* **-níes** : Pakistani
pala *nf* **1** : shovel, spade **2** : blade (of an oar or a rotor) **3** : paddle, racket **4** : spatula (for serving food)
palabra *nf* **1** VOCABLO : word ⟨en otras palabras : in other words⟩ ⟨no dijo ni una palabra : she didn't say a word⟩ **2** PROMESA : word, promise ⟨un hombre de palabra : a man of his word⟩ ⟨cumplió (con) su palabra : she kept her word⟩ ⟨le di mi palabra : I gave him my word⟩ **3** HABLA : speech ⟨acuerdo de palabra : verbal agreement⟩ **4** : right to speak ⟨tener/tomar la palabra : to have/take the floor⟩ ⟨pidió la palabra : he asked to speak⟩
palabrería *nf* : empty talk
palabrota *nf* : swearword ⟨decir palabrotas : to swear⟩
palacio *nm* **1** : palace, mansion **2** palacio de justicia : courthouse **3** palacio municipal : city hall
paladar *nm* **1** : palate **2** GUSTO : taste
paladear *vt* SABOREAR : to savor
paladín *nm, pl* **-dines** : champion, defender
palanca *nf* **1** : lever, crowbar **2** *fam* : leverage, influence **3** palanca de cambios/velocidad : gearshift **4** palanca de mando JOYSTICK : joystick
palangana *nf* : washbowl
palanqueta *nf* : jimmy, small crowbar
palapa *nf Mex* : shelter (thatched with palms)
palco *nm* : box (in a theater or stadium)
palear *vt* **1** : to shovel **2** : to paddle
palenque *nm* **1** ESTACADA : stockade, palisade **2** : arena, ring
paleontología *nf* : paleontology
paleontólogo, -ga *n* : paleontologist
palestino, -na *adj & n* : Palestinian
palestra *nf* : arena ⟨salir a la palestra : to join the fray⟩
paleta *nf* **1** : palette {53} **2** : trowel **3** : spatula **4** : blade, vane **5** : paddle **6** *CA, Mex* : lollipop, Popsicle
paletilla *nf* : shoulder blade
paliacate *nm Mex* : bandanna, scarf
paliar *vt* MITIGAR : to alleviate
paliativo¹, -va *adj* : palliative ⟨cuidados paliativos : palliative care⟩ ⟨centro de cuidados paliativos : hospice⟩
paliativo² *nm* : palliative
palidecer {53} *vi* : to turn pale
palidez *nf, pl* **-deces** : paleness, pallor
pálido, -da *adj* : pale ⟨se puso pálida : she turned pale⟩
palillo *nm* **1** *or* palillo de dientes MONDADIENTES : toothpick **2** *or* palillo de tambor : drumstick **3** palillos *nmpl* : chopsticks
paliza *nf* **1** : beating, pummeling ⟨darle una paliza a : to beat, to thrash⟩ **2** DERROTA : rout, defeat
palma *nf* **1** : palm (of the hand) **2** : palm (tree or leaf) **3** batir/dar palmas : to clap, to applaud **4** llevarse la palma *fam* : to take the cake

palmada *nf* **1** : pat ⟨le dio unas palmadas en el hombro : she patted him on the shoulder⟩ **2** BOFETADA, CACHETADA : slap **3** : clap ⟨dar palmadas : to clap⟩
palmarés *nm* : record (of achievements)
palmario, -ria *adj* MANIFIESTO : clear, manifest
palmeado, -da *adj* : webbed
palmear *vt* : to slap on the back — *vi* : to clap, to applaud
palmera *nf* : palm tree
palmito *nm* : heart of palm
palmo *nm* **1** : span, small amount **2** palmo a palmo : bit by bit, inch by inch **3** palmo a palmo : thoroughly **4** dejar con un palmo de narices : to disappoint
palmotear *vi* : to applaud
palmoteo *nm* : clapping, applause
palo *nm* **1** : stick, pole, post **2** : shaft, handle ⟨palo de escoba : broomstick⟩ **3** : mast, spar **4** *or* palo de golf : golf club **5** : wood **6** : blow (with a stick) **7** : suit (of cards) **8 de tal palo, tal astilla** : he/she (etc.) is a chip off the old block
paloma *nf* **1** : pigeon, dove **2 paloma de la paz** : dove of peace **3 paloma mensajera** : carrier pigeon
palomilla *nf* : moth
palomitas *nfpl* : popcorn
palpable *adj* : palpable, tangible
palpar *vt* : to feel, to touch — **palparse** *vr* ⟨se palpó la cabeza : he felt/touched his head⟩
palpitación *nf, pl* **-ciones** : palpitation
palpitar *vi* : to palpitate, to throb — **palpitante** *adj*
pálpito *nm* : feeling, hunch
palta *nf Arg, Chile, Peru, Uru* : avocado
paludismo *nm* MALARIA : malaria
palurdo, -da *n* : boor, yokel, bumpkin
pampa *nf* : pampas *pl*
pampeano, -na *adj* : pampas
pampero → pampeano
pan *nm* **1** : bread ⟨una rebanada de pan : a slice of bread⟩ ⟨pan rallado : (grated) bread crumbs⟩ **2** : loaf of bread **3** : cake, bar ⟨pan de jabón : bar of soap⟩ **4 pan árabe** *Arg, Ven, Uru* : pita, pita bread **5 pan blanco** : white bread **6 pan de molde** : sandwich bread (baked in a loaf pan) **7 pan dulce** *CA, Mex* : traditional pastry **8 pan integral** : whole wheat bread **9 pan tostado** : toast **10 ser pan comido** *fam* : to be a piece of cake, to be a cinch
pan- *pref* : pan- ⟨panacea : panacea⟩
pana¹ *nf* : corduroy
pana² *nmf PRi, Ven* : buddy, friend
panacea *nf* : panacea
panadería *nf* : bakery, bread shop
panadero, -ra *n* : baker
panal *nm* : honeycomb
panameño, -ña *adj & n* : Panamanian
pancarta *nf* : placard, sign, banner
panceta *nf* : bacon
pancho *nm Arg, Uru* : hot dog
pancita *nf Mex* : tripe
páncreas *nms & pl* : pancreas
panda *nmf* : panda
pandeado, -da *adj* : warped

pandearse *vr* 1 : to warp 2 : to bulge, to sag

pandemonio *or* **pandemónium** *nm* : pandemonium

pandereta *nf* : tambourine

pandero *nm* : tambourine

pandilla *nf* 1 : group, clique 2 : gang

panecillo *Spain* → **panecito**

panecito *nm* : roll, bun

panegírico *nm* : eulogy

panel *nm* 1 : panel ⟨paneles de madera : wood panels⟩ ⟨panel solar : solar panel⟩ 2 TABLERO : board — **panelista** *nmf*

panela *nf Col, Ecua* : unrefined sugar

panera *nf* : bread box (for storage), bread basket (for serving)

panfleto *nm* : pamphlet

pánico *nm* : panic ⟨tener(le) pánico a algo : to be terrified of something⟩ ⟨pánico escénico : stage fright⟩

panificadora *nf* : bakery

panini *nm, pl* **panini** *or* **paninis** : panini

panorama *nm* 1 VISTA : panorama, view 2 : scene, situation ⟨el panorama nacional : the national scene⟩ 3 PERSPECTIVA : outlook

panorámico, -ca *adj* : panoramic

panqueque *nm* : pancake

pansexual *adj* : pansexual ⟨las personas pansexuales : pansexual people⟩

pantaletas *nfpl* : panties

pantalla *nf* 1 : screen, monitor 2 : lampshade 3 : fan 4 **pantalla táctil** : touchscreen

pantalón *nm, pl* **-lones** 1 : pants *pl*, trousers *pl* 2 **pantalones cortos** : shorts 3 **pantalones vaqueros/tejanos** : jeans 4 **pantalones de mezclilla** *Chile, Mex* : jeans 5 **pantalones de montar** : jodhpurs

pantano *nm* 1 : swamp, marsh, bayou 2 : reservoir 3 : obstacle, difficulty

pantanoso, -sa *adj* 1 : marshy, swampy 2 : difficult, thorny

panteón *nm, pl* **-teones** 1 CEMENTERIO : cemetery 2 : pantheon, mausoleum

pantera *nf* : panther

panties *or* **pantys** *or* **pantis** *nmfpl* 1 CA, Car : panties *pl* 2 Spain : panty hose

pantimedias *nfpl Mex* : panty hose

pantomima *nf* : pantomime

pantorrilla *nf* : calf (of the leg)

pants *nms & pl Mex* 1 : sweatpants *pl* : sweatsuit, tracksuit

pantufla *nf* ZAPATILLA : slipper

panty *or* **panti** *nmf, pl* **-tys** *or* **-ties** *or* **-tis** → **panties**

panza *nf* BARRIGA : belly, paunch

panzón, -zona *adj, mpl* **panzones** : pot-bellied

pañal *nm* 1 : diaper ⟨pañal desechable : disposable diaper⟩ 2 **estar en pañales** : to be in its infancy (of things), to be a beginner (of people)

pañería *nf* 1 : cloth, material 2 : fabric store

pañito *nm* : doily

paño *nm* 1 : cloth ⟨en paños menores : in one's underwear⟩ 2 : rag, dust cloth

3 *or* **paño de cocina** : dishcloth 4 **paño higiénico** : sanitary napkin

pañoleta *nf* 1 : head scarf 2 : kerchief, scarf (for the neck) 3 CHAL : shawl

pañuelo *nm* 1 : handkerchief 2 : head scarf 3 : scarf (for the neck)

papa[1] *nm* 1 : pope ⟨el Papa : the Pope⟩

papa[2] *nf* 1 : potato 2 **papa dulce** : sweet potato 3 **papas fritas** : potato chips, french fries 4 **papas a la francesa** *Mex* : french fries

papá *nm fam* 1 : dad *fam*, pop *fam* 2 **papás** *nmpl* : parents, folks *fam*

papada *nf* 1 : double chin, jowl 2 : dewlap

papagayo *nm* LORO : parrot

papal *adj* : papal

papalote *nm CA, Car, Mex* : kite

Papanicolau *nm* : Pap smear

Papá Noel *nm* : Santa Claus

papaya *nf* : papaya

papel *nm* 1 : paper, piece of paper 2 : role, part ⟨hizo el papel de Romeo : he played the part of Romeo⟩ ⟨jugar un papel importante en algo : to play an important role in something⟩ 3 **papel (de) aluminio** : tinfoil, aluminum foil 4 **papel de carta** : writing paper 5 **papel de empapelar** *or* **papel pintado** : wallpaper 6 **papel de envolver** : wrapping paper 7 **papel de fumar** : cigarette paper 8 **papel de lija** : sandpaper 9 **papel de periódico** : newspaper, newsprint 10 **papel de seda** : tissue paper 11 **papel film** : plastic wrap 12 **papel higiénico** : toilet paper, bathroom tissue 13 **papel maché** : papier-mâché 14 **papel moneda** : paper money

papeleo *nm* : paperwork, red tape

papelera *nf* 1 : wastebasket (indoors), trash can (on street) 2 : paper mill

papelería *nf* : stationery store

papelero, -ra *adj* : paper

papeleta *nf* 1 : ballot 2 : ticket, slip

paperas *nfpl* : mumps

papi *nm fam* : daddy, papa

papila gustativa *nf* : taste bud

papilla *nf* 1 : pap (for sick people), baby food 2 **hacer papilla** : to beat to a pulp

papiro *nm* : papyrus

paprika *nf* : paprika

paquete *nm* 1 BULTO : package, parcel ⟨paquete bomba : mail bomb⟩ 2 : package (of cookies, etc.), pack (of cigarettes) 3 : package, bundle ⟨paquete turístico : tour package⟩ ⟨paquete de software : software bundle⟩

paquistaní *adj & nmf* : Pakistani

par[1] *adj* : even (in number)

par[2] *nm* 1 : pair, couple ⟨un par de zapatos : a pair of shoes⟩ 2 : equal, peer ⟨sin par : matchless, peerless⟩ 3 : par (in golf) 4 : rafter 5 **de par en par** : wide open

par[3] *nf* 1 : par ⟨por encima de la par : above par⟩ 2 **a la par que** : at the same time as, as well as ⟨interesante a la par que instructivo : both interesting and informative⟩

para *prep* 1 (*indicating a recipient*) : for ⟨un regalo para ti : a present for you⟩ 2 (*indicating a purpose or goal*) : for ⟨la comida es para la fiesta : the food is for the party⟩ ⟨¿para qué? : what for?⟩ **3** (*indicating comparison*) : for ⟨alta para su edad : tall for her age⟩ ⟨es bueno para lo que cuesta : it's good for what it costs⟩ **4** : for (a time) ⟨una cita para el lunes : an appointment for Monday⟩ **5** : to (a time) ⟨faltan cinco para las ocho : it's five (minutes) to eight⟩ **6** : around, by (a time) ⟨para mañana estarán listos : they'll be ready by tomorrow⟩ **7** : to, towards ⟨para adelante/atrás : forwards/backwards⟩ ⟨para la derecha/izquierda : to the right/left⟩ ⟨van para el río : they're heading towards the river⟩ **8** (*used before an infinitive*) : to, in order to ⟨lo hace para molestarte : he does it to annoy you⟩ ⟨para no ser visto : in order not to be seen⟩ **9** (*used before an infinitive*) : to ⟨estoy listo para salir : I'm ready to leave⟩ ⟨demasiado joven para entender : too young to understand⟩ ⟨lo compré para devolverlo el mismo día : I bought it only to return it the same day⟩ **10 para que** : so, so that, in order that ⟨te lo digo para que sepas : I'm telling you so you'll know⟩

parabién *nm, pl* **-bienes** : congratulations *pl*

parábola *nf* **1** : parable **2** : parabola

parabrisas *nms & pl* : windshield

paracaídas *nms & pl* : parachute ⟨saltar/lanzarse en paracaídas : to parachute⟩

paracaidista *nmf* **1** : parachutist **2** : paratrooper

parachoques *nms & pl* : bumper

parada *nf* **1** : stop ⟨parada de autobús : bus stop⟩ **2** : stop (action) **3** : catch, save, parry (in sports) **4** DESFILE : parade

paradero *nm* **1** : whereabouts **2** : bus stop

paradigma *nm* : paradigm

paradisíaco, -ca *or* **paradisiaco, -ca** *adj* : heavenly

parado¹, -da *adj* **1** : motionless, idle, stopped **2** : standing (up) ⟨estar parado : to stand, to be standing⟩ **3** : confused, bewildered **4 bien/mal parado** : in good/bad shape ⟨salió bien parado : it turned out well for him⟩

parado², -da *n Spain* : unemployed person

paradoja *nf* : paradox

paradójico, -ca *adj* : paradoxical

parador *nm* **1** : roadside inn **2** : state-run hotel (in Spain) **3 parador en corto** *Car, Mex, Ven* : shortstop

parafernalia *nf* : paraphernalia

parafina *nf* **1** : paraffin **2** *Chile* : kerosene

parafrasear *vt* : to paraphrase

paráfrasis *nfs & pl* : paraphrase

paragolpes *nms & pl Arg, Par, Uru* : bumper

paraguas *nms & pl* : umbrella

paraguayo, -ya *adj & n* : Paraguayan

paraíso *nm* **1** : paradise, heaven **2 paraíso fiscal** : tax shelter

paraje *nm* : spot, place

paralelismo *nm* : parallel, similarity

paralelo¹, -la *adj* : parallel

paralelo² *nm* : parallel

paralelogramo *nm* : parallelogram

parálisis *nfs & pl* **1** : paralysis **2** : standstill **3 parálisis cerebral** : cerebral palsy

paralizar {21} *vt* **1** : to paralyze **2** : to paralyze, to bring to a standstill — **paralizarse** *vr*

paramédico, -ca *n* : paramedic

parámetro *nm* : parameter

páramo *nm* : barren plateau, moor

parangón *nm, pl* **-gones 1** : comparison **2 sin ~** : incomparable

paraninfo *nm* : auditorium, assembly hall

paranoia *nf* : paranoia

paranoico, -ca *adj & n* : paranoid

paranormal *adj* : paranormal

parapente *nm* : paragliding

parapetarse *vr* : to take cover

parapeto *nm* : parapet, rampart

parapléjico, -ca *adj & n* : paraplegic

parar *vt* **1** DETENER : to stop **2** : to stand, to prop ⟨parar la oreja : to perk up one's ears⟩ **3** : to stop, to block (a blow, etc.) — *vi* **1** CESAR : to stop ⟨habla sin parar : she talks nonstop⟩ ⟨no paraba de llorar : he wouldn't stop crying⟩ **2** : to stay, to put up **3** : to go on strike **4 ir a parar** : to end up, to wind up ⟨ir a parar a manos de alguien : to fall into someone's hands⟩ ⟨va a parar al hospital : he's going to end up in the hospital⟩ — **pararse** *vr* **1** : to stop ⟨pararse en seco : to stop dead⟩ **2** ATASCARSE : to stall (out) **3** : to stand up, to get up

pararrayos *nms & pl* : lightning rod

parasitario, -ria *adj* : parasitic

parásito *nm* : parasite

parasol *nm* SOMBRILLA : parasol

parcela *nf* : parcel, tract of land

parcelar *vt* : to parcel (land)

parchar *vt* : to patch, to patch up

parche *nm* : patch

parcial¹ *adj* **1** : partial ⟨un éxito parcial : a partial success⟩ **2** TENDENCIOSO : partial, biased — **parcialmente** *adv*

parcial² *nm* : exam (covering a portion of a semester's or trimester's material)

parcialidad *nf* : partiality, bias

parco, -ca *adj* **1** : sparing, frugal **2** : moderate, temperate **3** LACÓNICO : laconic, concise

pardo, -da *adj* : brownish grey

pardusco → **pardo**

parecer¹ {53} *vi* **1** : to seem, to look, to appear to be ⟨parece fácil : it looks easy⟩ ⟨parece que van a ganar : it looks like they're going to win⟩ ⟨así parece : so it seems⟩ ⟨pareces una princesa : you look like a princess⟩ **2** (*expressing an opinion*) ⟨¿qué te parece? : what do you think?⟩ ⟨me parece que sí : I think so⟩ ⟨me parece bien : that seems fine to me⟩ **3** : to like, to be in agreement ⟨si te parece : if you like, if it's all right with you⟩ — **parecerse** *vr* ~ **a** : to resemble

parecer² *nm* **1** OPINIÓN : opinion ⟨en mi parecer : in my opinion⟩ ⟨es del parecer

que . . . : he's of the opinion that . . .⟩ 2
ASPECTO : appearance ⟨al parecer : ap-
parently⟩
parecido¹, -da adj 1 : similar, alike 2
bien parecido : good-looking
parecido² nm : resemblance, similarity
⟨tener un parecido con : to bear a resemblance to⟩
pared nf 1 : wall ⟨las paredes oyen : the
walls have ears⟩ 2 : face (of a mountain)
paredón nm, pl -dones 1 : rock face 2
: wall (for executions by firing squad)
pareja nf 1 : couple, pair ⟨por parejas
: in pairs⟩ ⟨vivir en pareja : to live to-
gether⟩ ⟨pareja de hecho : unmarried
couple living together⟩ 2 : partner,
mate ⟨tu pareja ideal : your ideal mate⟩
3 : mate (to a glove, etc.)
parejo, -ja adj 1 : even, smooth, level 2
: equal, similar 3 al parejo de : on a par
with
parentela nf : relations pl, kinfolk
parentesco nm : relationship, kinship
paréntesis nms & pl 1 : parenthesis ⟨en-
tre paréntesis : in parentheses⟩ 2 : digression 3 entre ~ : by the way
parentético, -ca adj : parenthetic, parenthetical
pargo nm : red snapper
paria nmf : pariah, outcast
paridad nf : parity, equality
pariente nmf : relative, relation
parir vi : to give birth — vt : to give birth
to, to bear
paritario, -ria adj : equal, of peers/equals
parka nf : parka
parking nm : parking lot
parkour [par'kor] nm : parkour
parlamentario¹, -ria adj : parliamentary
parlamentario², -ria n : member of parliament
parlamento nm 1 : parliament 2 : negotiations pl, talks pl
parlanchín¹, -china adj, mpl -chines
: chatty, talkative
parlanchín², -china n, mpl -chines : chatterbox
parlante nm ALTOPARLANTE : loudspeaker
parlotear vi fam : to gab, to chat, to prattle
parloteo nm fam : prattle, chatter
paro nm 1 HUELGA : strike 2 : stoppage, stopping 3 Spain : unemployment
4 Spain : unemployment benefits 5
paro cardíaco/cardiaco : cardiac arrest
6 paro forzoso : layoff
parodia nf : parody
parodiar vt : to parody
paroxismo nm 1 : fit, paroxysm 2
: peak, height ⟨llevar al paroxismo : to
carry to the extreme⟩
parpadear vi 1 : to blink 2 : to flicker
parpadeo nm 1 : blink, blinking 2
: flickering
párpado nm : eyelid
parque nm 1 : park 2 CORRAL : playpen
(for children) 3 parque de diversio-

nes/atracciones : amusement park 4
parque infantil : playground 5 parque
natural : nature preserve 6 parque nacional : national park 7 parque
temático : theme park
parqueadero nm Col : parking lot
parquear vt : to park — **parquearse** vr
parqueo nm : parking
parquet or **parqué** nm : parquet
parquímetro nm : parking meter
parra nf : vine, grapevine
párrafo nm : paragraph
parranda nf fam : party, spree ⟨irse de
parranda : to party, to go partying⟩
parrilla nf 1 : broiler, grill ⟨a la parrilla
: broiled, grilled⟩ 3 : grill (restaurant)
4 : grate 5 BACA : luggage rack, roof
rack
parrillada nf 1 BARBACOA : barbecue 2
: grill (restaurant)
párroco nm : parish priest
parroquia nf 1 : parish 2 : parish church
3 : customers pl, clientele
parroquial adj : parochial
parroquiano, -na nm 1 : parishioner 2
: customer, patron
parsimonia nf 1 : calm 2 : thrift
parsimonioso, -sa adj 1 : calm, unhurried 2 : parsimonious, thrifty
parte¹ nm : report, dispatch ⟨parte meteorológico : weather report⟩
parte² nf 1 : part (of a whole) ⟨la mayor
parte de : the majority of⟩ ⟨una quinta
parte de : one fifth of⟩ 2 : place, part
⟨en alguna/cualquier parte : some-
where/anywhere⟩ ⟨en ninguna parte
: nowhere, not anywhere⟩ ⟨por todas
partes : everywhere⟩ ⟨ir a otra parte : to
go somewhere else⟩ 3 : party (in negotiations, etc.) 4 de parte de : on behalf
of ⟨de mi parte : on my behalf, for me⟩
5 ¿de parte de quién? : may I ask who's
calling? 6 en gran parte : largely, in
large part 7 en ~ : partly, in part 8 la
mayor parte de : most of, the majority
of 9 por otra parte : on the other hand
10 por parte de : on the part of ⟨por mi
parte : on my part, as far as I'm con-
cerned⟩ 11 tomar parte : to take part
partero, -ra n : midwife
partición nf, pl -ciones : division, sharing
participación nf, pl -ciones 1 : participation 2 : share, interest 3 : announcement, notice
participante nmf 1 : participant 2
: competitor, entrant
participar vi 1 : to participate, to take
part ⟨participar en algo : to participate
in something⟩ 2 ~ en : to have a share
in — vt : to announce, to notify
partícipe nmf : participant
participio nm : participle
partícula nf : particle
particular¹ adj 1 : particular, specific ⟨en
particular : in particular⟩ 2 : private
⟨clases particulares : private lessons⟩
⟨una casa particular : a private home⟩
3 : special, unique ⟨¿qué tiene de particular? : what's so special about it?⟩ 4
de ~ Arg, Uru : in plain/civilian clothes

⟨un policía de particular : a plainclothes policeman⟩

particular² *nm* **1** : matter, detail **2** : individual

particularidad *nf* : characteristic, peculiarity

particularizar {21} *vt* **1** : to distinguish, to characterize **2** : to specify

particularmente *adv* **1** : particularly, especially **2** : personally

partida *nf* **1** : departure **2** : item, entry **3** : certificate ⟨partida de nacimiento : birth certificate⟩ **4** : game, match, hand **5** : party, group

partidario, -ria *n* : follower, supporter ⟨soy partidario de . . . : I'm in favor of . . . , I support . . .⟩

partido *nm* **1** : (political) party **2** : game, match ⟨partido de futbol : soccer game⟩ ⟨partido amistoso : non-league game, non-championship game⟩ **3** APOYO : support, following **4** PROVECHO : profit, advantage ⟨sacar partido de : to profit from⟩ **5 un buen partido** : a good catch (for marriage)

partir *vt* **1** : to cut, to split **2** : to break, to crack **3** : to share (out), to divide — *vi* **1** : to leave, to depart **2 ~ de** : to start from **3 a partir de** : as of, from ⟨a partir de hoy : as of today⟩ — **partirse** *vr* **1** : to smash, to split open **2** : to become chapped

partisano, -na *adj & n* : partisan

partitura *nf* : (musical) score

parto *nm* **1** : childbirth, delivery, labor ⟨estar de parto : to be in labor⟩ **2** : product, creation, brainchild

parvulario *nm* **1** : nursery school **2** : kindergarten

párvulo, -la *n* : toddler, preschooler

pasa *nf* **1** : raisin **2 pasa de Corinto** : currant

pasable *adj* : passable, tolerable — **pasablemente** *adv*

pasada *nf* **1** : passage, passing **2** : pass, wipe, coat (of paint) **3 de ~** : in passing **4 mala pasada** : dirty trick

pasadizo *nm* : passageway, corridor

pasado¹, -da *adj* **1** : past ⟨el año pasado : last year⟩ ⟨pasado mañana : the day after tomorrow⟩ ⟨pasadas las siete : after seven o'clock⟩ **2** : overripe (of fruit), slightly spoiled **3** : well done (of meat), overcooked **4** : past tense (in grammar) **5** *or* **pasado de moda** : old-fashioned, out-of-date

pasado² *nm* : past

pasador *nm* **1** : bolt, latch **2** : barrette **3** *Mex* : bobby pin **4** : quarterback (in American football)

pasaje *nm* **1** : ticket (for travel) **2** TARIFA : fare **3** : passageway **4** : passengers *pl* **5** : passage (from a book, etc.)

pasajero¹, -ra *adj* : passing, fleeting

pasajero², -ra *n* : passenger

pasamanos *nms & pl* : banister (of a staircase), handrail

pasamontañas *nms & pl* : balaclava, ski mask

pasante *nmf* : assistant

pasapalos *nmpl* *Ven* : snacks, hors d'oeuvres

pasaporte *nm* : passport

pasar *vi* **1** : to pass, to go ⟨la gente que pasa : the people who are passing (by), the people who pass by⟩ ⟨nos dejaron pasar : they let us (go) through⟩ ⟨pasamos por el centro : we went through the downtown⟩ ⟨nunca paso por esa calle : I never go down that street⟩ ⟨pasé por delante de la escuela : I went by/past the school⟩ **2** : to pass (of time) **3** : to pass, to pass down ⟨el trono pasó a su hijo : the throne passed to his son⟩ **4** : to go (on), to move (on) ⟨pasaron a la final : they moved on to the finals⟩ ⟨pasar a ser : to go on to become⟩ ⟨pasar de . . . a . . . : to go from . . . to . . .⟩ **5** : to drop by/in, to stop by ⟨pasamos por su casa : we dropped by his house⟩ **6** : to come in, to enter ⟨¿se puede pasar? : may we come in?⟩ **7** CABER : to go through, to fit **8** : to happen ⟨¿qué pasa? : what's happening?, what's going on?⟩ ⟨lo que pasa es que . . . : what's happening is that . . . , the thing is that . . .⟩ ⟨¿qué le pasa? : what's the matter with him?⟩ ⟨pase lo que pase : come what may⟩ **9** : to manage, to get by ⟨pasar sin algo : to manage without something⟩ **10** : to be acceptable, to pass ⟨puede pasar : it will do⟩ **11** : to pass (in an exam, etc.) **12** TERMINAR : to be over, to end **13 ~ de** : to exceed, to go beyond **14 ~ por** : to pass as/for ⟨podría pasar por tu hermana : she could pass as/for your sister⟩ **15 ~ por** : to go through, to experience (difficulties, etc.) — *vt* **1** : to pass, to give ⟨¿me pasas la sal? : would you pass me the salt?⟩ **2** PEGAR : to give (an illness) **3** : to pass (a test) **4** : to cross (a bridge, river, etc.), to go through (a barrier) **5** : to spend (time) ⟨pasamos una semana en Acapulco : we spent a week in Acapulco⟩ **6** TOLERAR : to tolerate **7** SUFRIR : to go through, to suffer **8** : to show (a movie, etc.) **9** ADELANTAR, SUPERAR : to overtake, to pass, to surpass **10** : to pass (something over something) ⟨le pasó un trapo : he wiped it with a cloth⟩ ⟨pasar la aspiradora (por algo) : to vacuum (something)⟩ **11 ~ con** : to put (a caller) through to ⟨pásame con el jefe : put me through to the boss⟩ **12 pasar de largo** : to go right past (without stopping) **13 pasarlo/pasarla bien** : to have a good time **14 pasarlo/pasarla mal** : to have a bad time, to have a hard time **15 ~ por** : to put through ⟨pasa la sopa por un colador : put the soup through a strainer⟩ **16 pasar por alto** : to overlook, to omit — **pasarse** *vr* **1** : to pass, to go away ⟨se me pasó el mareo : the/my nausea has passed⟩ **2** : to stop by **3** : to slip one's mind, to slip by ⟨la fecha se me pasó : the date slipped by me⟩ **4** : to go too far ⟨se pasa de listo : he's too clever for his own good⟩ ⟨no te pases con la sal

: go easy with/on the salt⟩ **5** : to go bad, to spoil

pasarela *nf* **1** : gangplank **2** : footbridge **3** : runway, catwalk

pasatiempo *nm* : pastime, hobby

Pascua *nf* **1** : Easter ⟨Domingo de Pascua : Easter Sunday⟩ **2** : Passover **3** : Christmas **4 Pascuas** *nfpl* : Christmas season

pase *nm* **1** PERMISO : pass, permit **2** : pass (in sports) **3 pase de abordar** *Mex* : boarding pass

paseante *nmf* : walker (person)

pasear *vi* : to take a walk, to go for a ride — *vt* **1** : to take for a walk **2** : to parade around, to show off — **pasearse** *vr* : to walk around, to go for a ride

paseo *nm* **1** : walk, stroll ⟨dar un paseo : to go for a walk⟩ **2** : ride **3** EXCURSIÓN : outing, trip **4** : avenue, walk **5** *or* **paseo marítimo** : boardwalk

pasiflora *nf* PASIONARIA : passionflower

pasillo *nm* CORREDOR : hallway, corridor, aisle

pasión *nf, pl* **pasiones** : passion

pasional *adj* : passionate ⟨crimen pasional : crime of passion⟩

pasionaria → **pasiflora**

pasivo¹, -va *adj* : passive — **pasivamente** *adv*

pasivo² *nm* **1** : liability ⟨activos y pasivos : assets and liabilities⟩ **2** : debit side (of an account)

pasmado, -da *adj* : stunned, flabbergasted

pasmar *vt* : to amaze, to stun — **pasmarse** *vr*

pasmo *nm* **1** : shock, astonishment **2** : wonder, marvel

pasmoso, -sa *adj* : incredible, amazing — **pasmosamente** *adv*

paso¹, -sa *adj* : dried ⟨ciruela pasa : prune⟩

paso² *nm* **1** : passage, passing ⟨de paso : in passing, on the way⟩ ⟨estar de paso : to be passing through⟩ ⟨el paso del tiempo : the passage of time⟩ **2** : way, path ⟨abrir/dejar paso a : to make way for⟩ ⟨ceda el paso : yield⟩ ⟨prohibido el paso : do not enter, no entry⟩ **3** : crossing ⟨paso de peatones : crosswalk⟩ ⟨paso elevado : overpass⟩ ⟨paso subterráneo : underpass, tunnel⟩ ⟨paso a desnivel : underpass, overpass⟩ ⟨paso a nivel : railroad crossing⟩ **4** : pass (through mountains) ⟨salir del paso : to get out of a jam⟩ **5** : step ⟨dar un paso para adelante/atrás : to take a step forward/back⟩ ⟨estar a un paso de : to be within spitting distance of⟩ ⟨oír pasos : to hear footsteps⟩ **6** : step (in a process) ⟨paso a paso : step by step⟩ ⟨un paso positivo : a step in the right direction⟩ **7** : pace, gait ⟨a buen paso : quickly, at a good rate⟩ ⟨a este paso : at this rate⟩

pasta *nf* **1** : paste ⟨pasta de dientes *or* pasta dental : toothpaste⟩ **2** : pasta **3** : pastry dough **4 libro en pasta dura** : hardcover book **5 tener pasta de** : to have the makings of

pastar *vi* : to graze — *vt* : to put to pasture

pastel¹ *adj* : pastel

pastel² *nm* **1** : cake ⟨pastel de cumpleaños : birthday cake⟩ **2** : pie, turnover **3** : pastel

pastelería *nf* **1** : bakery, pastry shop **2** : baking, pastry making

pasteurización *nf, pl* **-ciones** : pasteurization

pasteurizar {21} *vt* : to pasteurize

pastilla *nf* **1** COMPRIMIDO, PÍLDORA : pill, tablet **2** : lozenge ⟨pastilla para la tos : cough drop⟩ **3** : cake (of soap), bar (of chocolate)

pastizal *nm* : pasture, grazing land

pasto *nm* **1** : pasture **2** HIERBA : grass, lawn

pastor, -tora *n* **1** : shepherd, shepherdess *f* **2** : minister, pastor **3 pastor alemán** : German shepherd

pastoral *adj & nf* : pastoral

pastorear *vt* : to shepherd, to tend

pastorela *nf Mex* : traditional Christmas play

pastoso, -sa *adj* **1** : pasty, doughy **2** : smooth, mellow (of sounds)

pata¹ *nf* **1** : paw, leg (of an animal) **2** *fam* : foot, leg (of a person) **3** : foot, leg (of furniture) **4 mala pata** *fam* : bad luck **5 meter la pata** *fam* : to put one's foot in it, to make a faux pas **6 patas de gallo** : crow's-feet **7 patas (para) arriba** : upside-down

pata² *nm Peru* : pal, buddy

patada *nf* **1** PUNTAPIÉ : kick ⟨le dio una patada : she kicked him⟩ **2** : stamp (of the foot)

patalear *vi* **1** : to kick **2** : to stamp one's feet

pataleta *nf fam* : tantrum

patán¹ *adj, pl* **patanes** : boorish, crude

patán² *nm, pl* **patanes** : boor, lout

patata *nf Spain* **1** : potato **2 patatas fritas** : potato chips, french fries

paté *nm* : pâté

pateador, -dora *n* : kicker (in sports)

patear *vt* : to kick — *vi* : to stamp one's foot

patentar *vt* : to patent

patente¹ *adj* EVIDENTE : obvious, patent — **patentemente** *adv*

patente² *nf* **1** : patent **2** *Arg, Chile, Uru* : license plate

paternal *adj* : fatherly, paternal

paternidad *nf* **1** : fatherhood, paternity **2** : parenthood **3** : authorship

paterno, -na *adj* : paternal ⟨abuela paterna : paternal grandmother⟩

patético, -ca *adj* : pathetic, moving

patetismo *nm* : pathos

patíbulo *nm* : gallows, scaffold

patilla *nf* **1** : arm (of glasses) **2** *Col* : watermelon **3 patillas** *nfpl* : sideburns

patín *nm, pl* **patines** : skate ⟨patín de ruedas : roller skate⟩ ⟨patín en línea : in-line skate⟩

pátina *nf* : patina

patinador, -dora *n* : skater

patinaje *nm* : skating ⟨patinaje artístico : figure skating⟩

patinar *vi* **1** : to skate **2** : to skid, to slip **3** *fam* : to slip up, to blunder

patinazo *nm* **1** : skid **2** *fam* : blunder, slipup

patineta *nf* **1** : scooter **2** : skateboard

patinete *nm* : scooter

patio *nm* **1** : courtyard, patio **2 patio de recreo** : playground

patito, -ta *n* : duckling

patizambo, -ba *adj* : knock-kneed

pato, -ta *n* **1** : duck **2 pato real** : mallard **3 pagar el pato** *fam* : to take the blame

patología *nf* : pathology

patológico, -ca *adj* : pathological

patólogo, -ga *n* : pathologist

patoso, -sa *adj Spain* : clumsy

patovica *nf Arg, Uru fam* : bouncer

patraña *nf* : tall tale, humbug, nonsense

patria *nf* : native land

patriarca *nm* : patriarch — **patriarcal** *adj*

patriarcado *nm* : patriarchy

patrimonio *nm* : patrimony, legacy

patrio, -tria *adj* **1** : native, home ⟨suelo patrio : native soil⟩ **2** : paternal

patriota[1] *adj* : patriotic

patriota[2] *nmf* : patriot

patriotería *nf* : jingoism, chauvinism

patriotero[1], **-ra** *adj* : jingoistic, chauvinistic

patriotero[2], **-ra** *n* : jingoist, chauvinist

patriótico, -ca *adj* : patriotic

patriotismo *nm* : patriotism

patrocinador, -dora *n* : sponsor, patron

patrocinar *vt* : to sponsor

patrocinio *nm* : sponsorship, patronage

patrón[1], **-trona** *n, mpl* **patrones** **1** JEFE : boss **2** CAPITÁN : skipper **3** *Spain* CASERO : landlord *m*, landlady *f* **4** : patron saint

patrón[2] *nm, pl* **patrones** **1** : standard **2** : pattern (in sewing)

patronal *adj* **1** : management, employers' ⟨sindicato patronal : employers' association⟩ **2** : pertaining to a patron saint ⟨fiesta patronal : patron saint's day⟩

patronato *nm* **1** : board, council **2** : foundation, trust

patrono, -na *n* **1** : employer **2** : patron saint

patrulla *nf* **1** : patrol **2** : police car, cruiser

patrullar *v* : to patrol

patrullero *nm* **1** : police car **2** : patrol boat **3** : patrol plane

paulatino, -na *adj* : gradual

paupérrimo, -ma *adj* : destitute, poverty-stricken

pausa *nf* : pause, break ⟨hacer una pausa : to pause, to break⟩ ⟨pausa comercial/publicitaria : commercial break⟩

pausado[1] *adv* : slowly, deliberately ⟨habla más pausado : speak more slowly⟩

pausado[2], **-da** *adj* : slow, deliberate — **pausadamente** *adv*

pauta *nf* **1** : rule, guideline **2** : lines *pl* (on paper)

pava *nf Arg, Bol, Chile* : kettle

pavimentar *vt* : pave

pavimento *nm* : pavement

pavo, -va *n* **1** : turkey **2 pavo real** : peacock **3 comer pavo** : to be a wallflower

pavón *nm, pl* **pavones** : peacock

pavonearse *vr* **1** : to strut, to swagger **2 pavonearse de** : to brag about

pavoneo *nm* : strut, swagger

pavor *nm* TERROR : dread, terror

pavoroso, -sa *adj* ATERRADOR : dreadful, terrifying

paya *nf Chile* → **payada**

payada *nf Arg, Uru* : song with improvised lyrics

payasada *nf* **1** : antic ⟨hacer payasadas : to clown around⟩ **2** TONTERÍA : foolish thing **3** FARSA : joke, farce

payasear *vi* : to clown around

payaso, -sa *n* **1** : clown **2** : clown, funny person

paz *nf, pl* **paces** **1** : peace **2 descanse en paz** : rest in peace **3 dejar en paz** : to leave alone **4 hacer las paces** : to make up, to reconcile

pazca, etc. → **pacer**

PC [pe'se, pi'si] *nmf* : PC, personal computer

PDA [pede'a, pidi'e] *nm* : PDA

pe *nf* : (letter) p

peaje *nm* : toll

peatón *nm, pl* **-tones** : pedestrian

peatonal *adj* : pedestrian

peca *nf* : freckle

pecado *nm* : sin

pecador[1], **-dora** *adj* : sinful, sinning

pecador[2], **-dora** *n* : sinner

pecaminoso, -sa *adj* : sinful

pecar {72} *vi* **1** : to sin **2 ~ de** ⟨pecan de optimistas/optimismo : they're too optimistic⟩

pécari *or* **pecarí** *nm* : peccary

pececillo *nm* : small fish

pecera *nf* : fishbowl, fish tank

pecho *nm* **1** : chest **2** SENO : breast, bosom **3** : heart, courage **4 dar el pecho** : to breast-feed **5** *or* **estilo (de) pecho** : breaststroke **6 tomarse algo a pecho** : to take something to heart

pechuga *nf* : breast (of fowl)

pecoso, -sa *adj* : freckled

pectoral *adj* : pectoral

peculado *nm* : embezzlement

peculiar *adj* **1** CARACTERÍSTICO : particular, characteristic **2** RARO : peculiar, uncommon

peculiaridad *nf* : peculiarity

pecuniario, -ria *adj* : pecuniary

pedagogía *nf* : pedagogy

pedagógico, -ca *adj* : pedagogic, pedagogical

pedagogo, -ga *n* : educator

pedal *nm* : pedal ⟨pedal del acelerador : accelerator pedal⟩

pedalear *vi* : to pedal

pedante[1] *adj* : pedantic

pedante[2] *nmf* : pedant

pedantería *nf* : pedantry

pedazo *nm* TROZO : piece, bit, chunk ⟨caerse a pedazos : to fall to pieces⟩

* ⟨hacer pedazos : to tear into shreds, to smash to pieces⟩
pedernal nm : flint
pedestal nm : pedestal
pedestre adj : commonplace, pedestrian
pediatra nmf : pediatrician
pediatría nf : pediatrics
pediátrico, -ca adj : pediatric
pedido nm 1 : order (of merchandise) ⟨hacer un pedido : to place an order⟩ 2 : request
pedigrí nm, pl **-gríes** : pedigree
pedir {54} vt 1 : to ask for, to request ⟨le pedí un préstamo a Claudia : I asked Claudia for a loan⟩ ⟨le pedí que nos llamara : I asked her to call us⟩ ⟨me pidieron ayuda/permiso : they asked me for help/permission⟩ ⟨pide 200 dólares por la bici : he's asking 200 dollars for the bike⟩ 2 : to order (food, merchandise) 3 **pedir disculpas/perdón** : to apologize — vi 1 : to order 2 : to beg
pedo nm fam : fart often vulgar
pedrada nf 1 : blow (with a rock or stone) ⟨la ventana se quebró de una pedrada : the window was broken by a rock⟩ 2 fam : cutting remark, dig
pedregal nm : rocky ground
pedregoso, -sa adj : rocky, stony
pedrera nf CANTERA : quarry
pedrería nf : precious stones pl, gems pl
pega nf Chile : work
pegadizo, -za adj : catchy
pegado, -da adj 1 : glued, stuck, stuck together 2 ∼ a : right next to
pegajoso, -sa adj 1 : sticky, gluey 2 : catchy ⟨una tonada pegajosa : a catchy tune⟩ 3 : clingy (of a person)
pegamento nm : adhesive, glue
pegar {52} vt 1 : to stick, to glue, to paste 2 : to attach, to sew on 3 : to infect with, to give ⟨me pegó el resfriado : he gave me his cold⟩ 4 : to give (a slap, a kick, etc.), to deal (a blow) ⟨le pegó un tiro/puñetazo : she shot/punched him⟩ ⟨me pegó un susto : he startled me⟩ 5 : to give (a shout, a jump, etc.) ⟨pegó un alarido : she let out a scream⟩ 6 : to put against, to put near 7 : to paste (into a computer document) — vi 1 ADHERIRSE : to stick, to adhere 2 : to hit ⟨pegar en algo : to hit (against) something⟩ ⟨pegarle a alguien : to hit someone⟩ 3 ∼ con : to match, to go with — **pegarse** vr 1 : to hit oneself ⟨me pegué en el codo : I hit my elbow⟩ 2 : to hit each other 3 : to stick, to take hold 4 : to be contagious
pegote nm 1 : sticky mess 2 Mex : sticker, adhesive label
pegue, etc. → pegar
peinado nm : hairstyle, hairdo
peinador, -dora n : hairdresser
peinar vt 1 : to comb (hair) 2 : to style, to do (hair) 3 RASTREAR : to comb, to search — **peinarse** vr : to comb one's hair 2 : to get one's hair done
peine nm : comb
peineta nf : ornamental comb
peladez nf, pl **-deces** Mex fam : obscenity, bad language

pelado, -da adj 1 : bald, hairless 2 : peeled 3 : bare, barren 4 : broke, penniless 5 Mex fam : coarse, crude
pelador nm : peeler
pelagra nf : pellagra
pelaje nm : coat (of an animal), fur
pelapapas nms & pl : (potato) peeler
pelar vt 1 : to peel, to shell 2 : to skin 3 : to pluck 4 : to remove hair from 5 fam : to clean out (of money) — **pelarse** vr 1 : to peel 2 fam : to get a haircut 3 Mex fam : to split, to leave
peldaño nm 1 : step, stair 2 : rung
pelea nf 1 LUCHA : fight 2 : quarrel
pelear vi 1 LUCHAR : to fight 2 DISPUTAR : to quarrel — **pelearse** vr
pelele nm : puppet
peleón, -ona adj, mpl **-ones** Spain : quarrelsome, argumentative
peleonero, -ra adj Mex : quarrelsome
peletería nf 1 : fur shop 2 : fur trade
peletero, -ra n : furrier
peliagudo, -da adj : tricky, difficult, ticklish
pelícano nm : pelican
película nf 1 : movie, film ⟨dar/poner una película : to show a movie⟩ ⟨película de acción/suspenso/terror : action/suspense/horror movie⟩ ⟨película de vaqueros : Western⟩ 2 : (photographic) film 3 : thin covering, layer
peligrar vi : to be in danger
peligro nm 1 : danger, peril ⟨estar en peligro : to be in danger⟩ ⟨estar fuera de peligro : to be out of danger⟩ ⟨poner en peligro : to put in danger, to endanger⟩ ⟨peligro de incendio : fire hazard⟩ 2 : risk ⟨correr (el) peligro de : to run the risk of⟩
peligroso, -sa adj : dangerous, hazardous
pelirrojo¹, -ja adj : red-haired, redheaded
pelirrojo², -ja n : redhead
pellejo nm 1 : hide, skin 2 **salvar el pellejo** : to save one's neck
pellizcar {72} vt 1 : to pinch 2 : to nibble on
pellizco nm : pinch ⟨me dio un pellizco : she gave me a pinch⟩ ⟨un pellizco de : a pinch of⟩
pelmazo¹, -za adj fam : boring
pelmazo², -za n fam : bore
pelo nm 1 : hair 2 : fur 3 : pile, nap 4 **a pelo** : bareback 5 **con pelos y señales** : in great detail 6 **no tener pelos en la lengua** : not to mince words, to be blunt 7 **ponerle los pelos de punta a alguien** : to make someone's hair stand on end 8 **por un pelo** : just barely 9 **tomarle el pelo a alguien** : to tease someone, to pull someone's leg
pelón¹, -lona adj, mpl **pelones** 1 : bald 2 fam : broke 3 Mex fam : tough, difficult
pelón², -lona n, mpl **pelones** : bald person
pelota nf 1 : ball 2 fam : head 3 **en pelotas** fam : naked 4 **jugar a la pelota** : to play ball 5 **pasar la pelota** fam : to pass the buck 6 **pelota vasca** : jai alai
pelotera nf 1 : fight 2 : ruckus, row

pelotón *nm, pl* **-tones** : squad, detachment

peltre *nm* : pewter

peluca *nf* : wig

peluche *nm* : plush (fabric) ⟨oso de peluche : teddy bear⟩

peludo, -da *adj* : hairy, shaggy, bushy

peluquería *nf* **1** : hairdresser's, barbershop **2** : hairdressing

peluquero, -ra *n* : barber, hairdresser

peluquín *nm, pl* **-quines** TUPÉ : hairpiece, toupee

pelusa *nf* **1** : down **2** : lint (on clothes)

pélvico, -ca *adj* : pelvic

pelvis *nfs & pl* : pelvis

pena *nf* **1** SENTENCIA : sentence, penalty ⟨pena de muerte, pena capital : death penalty⟩ **2** AFLICCIÓN : sorrow, grief ⟨me da pena : it makes me sad⟩ ⟨morir de pena : to die of a broken heart⟩ ⟨¡qué pena! : what a shame!, how sad!⟩ **3** VERGÜENZA : shame, embarrassment **4 penas** *nfpl* : problems, troubles ⟨olvidar tus penas : to forget your troubles⟩ **5 penas** *nfpl* : difficulty, trouble ⟨a duras penas : with great difficulty⟩ **6 valer la pena** : to be worthwhile

penacho *nm* **1** : crest, tuft **2** : plume (of feathers)

penal¹ *adj* : criminal, penal

penal² *nm* CÁRCEL : prison, penitentiary

penalidad *nf* **1** : hardship **2** : penalty, punishment

penalizar {21} *vt* : to penalize

penalty *nm* : penalty (in sports)

penar *vt* : to punish, to penalize — *vi* : to suffer, to grieve

pendenciero, -ra *adj* : argumentative, quarrelsome

pender *vi* **1** : to hang **2** : to be pending

pendiente¹ *adj* **1** : pending ⟨asuntos pendientes : unfinished business⟩ ⟨cuentas pendientes : outstanding bills⟩ **2 estar pendiente de** : to pay a lot of attention to **3 estar pendiente de** : to be awaiting

pendiente² *nm Spain* : earring

pendiente³ *nm* : slope, incline

pendón *nm, pl* **pendones** : banner

péndulo *nm* : pendulum

pene *nm* : penis

penetración *nf, pl* **-ciones** **1** : penetration **2** : insight

penetrante *adj* **1** : penetrating ⟨una mirada/mente penetrante : a penetrating look/mind⟩ **2** : bitter (of cold or wind), pungent (of smells) **3** ESTRIDENTE : piercing, shrill

penetrar *vi* **1** : to penetrate, to sink in **2** ~ **por** *or* ~ **en** : to pierce, to go in, to enter into ⟨el frío penetra por la ventana : the cold comes right in through the window⟩ — *vt* **1** : to penetrate, to permeate **2** : to pierce ⟨el dolor penetró su corazón : sorrow pierced her heart⟩ **3** : to fathom, to understand

penicilina *nf* : penicillin

península *nf* : peninsula — **peninsular** *adj*

penique *nm* : penny

penitencia *nf* : penance, penitence

penitenciaría *nf* : penitentiary

penitente *adj & nmf* : penitent

penol *nm* : yardarm

penosamente *adv* : with difficulty

penoso, -sa *adj* **1** : painful, distressing **2** : difficult, arduous **3** : shy, bashful

pensado, -da *adj* **1 bien pensado** : well thought-out **2 en el momento menos pensado** : when least expected **3 poco pensado** : badly thought-out **4 mal pensado** : evil-minded

pensador, -dora *n* : thinker

pensamiento *nm* **1** : thought **2** : thinking **3** : pansy

pensar {55} *vi* **1** : to think ⟨pensar bien/mal de alguien : to think well/poorly of someone⟩ **2** ~ **en** : to think about ⟨pensaba en otra cosa : I was thinking about something else⟩ **3 dar que pensar** : to provide food for thought — *vt* **1** : to think ⟨pienso que es necesario : I think it's necessary⟩ ⟨¿qué piensas de su nueva canción? : what do you think about her new song?⟩ **2** : to think about ⟨está pensando comprar una casa : she's thinking about buying a house⟩ **3** : to intend, to plan on ⟨¿qué piensas hacer? : what do you plan to do?⟩ ⟨no pienso casarme : I don't intend to get married⟩ — **pensarse** *vr* : to think over

pensativo, -va *adj* : pensive, thoughtful

pensión *nf, pl* **pensiones** **1** JUBILACIÓN : pension **2** : boarding house **3 pensión alimenticia** : alimony

pensionado, -da *n* → **pensionista**

pensionista *nmf* **1** JUBILADO : pensioner, retiree **2** : boarder, lodger

pentágono *nm* : pentagon — **pentagonal** *adj*

pentagrama *nm* : staff (in music)

penthouse ['pent,haus] *nm* : penthouse

penúltimo, -ma *adj* : next to last, penultimate

penumbra *nf* : partial darkness, shadow

penuria *nf* **1** ESCASEZ : shortage, scarcity **2** : poverty

peña *nf* : rock, crag

peñasco *nm* : crag, large rock

peñascoso, -sa *adj* : craggy

peñón → **peñasco**

peón *nm, pl* **peones** **1** : laborer, peon **2** : pawn (in chess)

peonía *nf* : peony

peor¹ *adv* **1** *comparative of* MAL : worse ⟨se llevan peor que antes : they get along worse than before⟩ **2** *superlative of* MAL : worst ⟨me fue peor que a nadie : I did the worst of all⟩ ⟨el secreto peor guardado : the worst-kept secret⟩ **3 cada vez peor** : worse and worse **4 de mal en peor** : from bad to worse

peor² *adj* **1** *comparative of* MALO : worse ⟨es peor que el original : it's worse than the original⟩ **2** *superlative of* MALO : worst ⟨la peor parte : the worst part⟩ ⟨el peor de todos : the worst of all⟩

pepa *nf* : seed, pit (of a fruit)

pepenador, -dora *n CA, Mex* : scavenger

pepenar *vt CA, Mex* : to scavenge, to scrounge

pepinillo *nm* : pickle, gherkin
pepino *nm* : cucumber
pepita *nf* **1** : seed, pip **2** : nugget **3** *Mex* : dried pumpkin seed
peque, etc. → **pecar**
pequeñez *nf, pl* **-ñeces 1** : smallness **2** : trifle, triviality **3 pequeñez de espíritu** : pettiness
pequeño¹, -ña *adj* **1** : small, little ⟨un libro pequeño : a small book⟩ **2** : young, little ⟨su hermana pequeña : his little sister⟩ **3** CORTO : short **4** LIGERO : slight
pequeño², -ña *n* : child, little one
pera *nf* **1** : pear **2** *Arg, Chile, Uru* BARBILLA, MENTÓN : chin **3** *Arg, Chile, Uru* : goatee **4** : rubber bulb (for suction, etc.) **5 pedirle peras al olmo** : to ask the impossible
peral *nm* : pear tree
peraltar *vt* : to bank (a road)
peralte *nm* : bank (of a road)
perca *nf* : perch (fish)
percal *nm* : percale
percance *nm* : mishap, misfortune
per cápita *adv & adj* : per capita
percatarse *vr* ~ **de** : to notice, to become aware of
percebe *nm* : barnacle
percepción *nf, pl* **-ciones 1** : perception **2** : idea, notion **3** COBRO : receipt (of payment), collection
perceptible *adj* : perceptible, noticeable — **perceptiblemente** *adv*
percha *nf* **1** : perch **2** : coat hanger **3** : coatrack, coat hook
perchero *nm* : coatrack
percibir *vt* **1** : to perceive, to notice, to sense **2** : to earn, to draw (a salary)
percudido, -da *adj* : grimy
percudir *vt* : to make grimy — **percudirse** *vr*
percusión *nf, pl* **-siones** : percussion
percusor *or* **percutor** *nm* : hammer (of a firearm)
perdedor¹, -dora *adj* : losing
perdedor², -dora *n* : loser
perder {56} *vt* **1** : to lose ⟨perdió las llaves : he lost his keys⟩ ⟨perder dinero/peso : to lose money/weight⟩ ⟨perder la paciencia/confianza : to lose patience/confidence⟩ ⟨perder la vida : to lose one's life⟩ **2** : to lose (a game, contest, etc.) **3** : to miss (a train, an event, etc.) ⟨perdimos la oportunidad : we missed the opportunity⟩ **4** : to waste (time) — *vi* : to lose — **perderse** *vr* **1** EXTRAVIARSE : to get lost **2** : to miss **3** DESAPARECER : to disappear
perdición *nf, pl* **-ciones** : ruin
pérdida *nf* **1** : loss ⟨pérdidas económicas : economic losses⟩ **2** : waste (of time, money, etc.) **3** : leak (of liquid, gas, etc.)
perdidamente *adv* : hopelessly
perdido, -da *adj* **1** : lost ⟨objetos perdidos : lost and found⟩ ⟨una bala perdida : a stray bullet⟩ **2** : inveterate, incorrigible ⟨es un caso perdido : he's a hopeless case⟩ ⟨dar algo por perdido : to give

something up as a lost cause⟩ **3 de** ~ *Mex fam* : at least **4 estar perdido** : to be in trouble, to be done for
perdigón *nm, pl* **-gones** : shot, pellet
perdiz *nf, pl* **perdices** : partridge
perdón¹ *nm, pl* **perdones** : forgiveness, pardon ⟨me pidió perdón : she apologized to me⟩
perdón² *interj* : excuse me!, sorry!
perdonable *adj* : forgivable
perdonar *vt* **1** DISCULPAR : to forgive, to pardon ⟨¿me perdonas? : do you forgive me?⟩ ⟨perdona que te interrumpa : pardon me for interrupting⟩ **2** : to excuse from (a task, etc.), to write off (a debt) ⟨perdonarle la vida a alguien : to spare someone's life⟩ — *vi* : to excuse, to pardon ⟨perdona, pero . . . : excuse/pardon me, but . . .⟩
perdurable *adj* : lasting
perdurar *vi* : to last, to endure, to survive
perecedero, -ra *adj* : perishable
perecer {53} *vi* : to perish, to die
peregrinación *nf, pl* **-ciones** : pilgrimage
peregrinaje *nm* → **peregrinación**
peregrino¹, -na *adj* **1** : unusual, odd **2** MIGRATORIO : migratory
peregrino², -na *n* : pilgrim
perejil *nm* : parsley
perenne *adj* : perennial ⟨árbol de hoja perenne : evergreen tree⟩
perentorio, -ria *adj* **1** : peremptory **2** URGENTE : urgent **3** FIJO : fixed, set
pereza *nf* FLOJERA, HOLGAZANERÍA : laziness, idleness
perezoso¹, -sa *adj* FLOJO, HOLGAZÁN : lazy
perezoso² *nm* : sloth (animal)
perfección *nf, pl* **-ciones** : perfection ⟨a la perfección : perfectly⟩
perfeccionamiento *nm* : perfecting, refinement
perfeccionar *vt* **1** : to perfect **2** : to improve, to refine
perfeccionismo *nm* : perfectionism
perfeccionista *nmf* : perfectionist
perfecto, -ta *adj* : perfect — **perfectamente** *adv*
perfidia *nf* : treachery
pérfido, -da *adj* : perfidious
perfil *nm* **1** : profile ⟨de perfil : from the side, in profile⟩ **2** CONTORNO : profile, outline **3 perfiles** *nmpl* RASGOS : features, characteristics
perfilar *vt* : to outline, to define — **perfilarse** *vr* **1** : to be outlined, to be silhouetted **2** : to take shape
perforación *nf, pl* **-ciones 1** : perforation **2** : drilling
perforadora *nf* **1** : hole punch (for paper) **2** : drill (in mining, etc.)
perforar *vt* **1** : to perforate, to pierce **2** : to drill, to bore
perfumar *vt* : to perfume, to scent — **perfumarse** *vr* : to put on perfume
perfume *nm* : perfume, scent
perfumería *nf* **1** : perfume shop **2** : perfumes *pl* **3** : perfume industry
pergamino *nm* : parchment
pérgola *nf* : arbor

pericia *nf* : skill, expertise
pericial *adj* : expert ⟨testigo pericial : expert witness⟩
perico *nm* COTORRA : small parrot
periferia *nf* : periphery, outskirts
periférico¹, -ca *adj* : outlying, peripheral
periférico² *nm* **1** *CA, Mex* : beltway **2** : peripheral
perilla *nf* **1** : goatee **2** : pommel (on a saddle) **3** *Col, Mex* : knob, handle **4 perilla de la oreja** : earlobe **5 de perillas** *fam* : handy, just right
perímetro *nm* : perimeter
periódico¹, -ca *adj* : periodic — **periódicamente** *adv*
periódico² *nm* DIARIO : newspaper
periodismo *nm* : journalism
periodista *nmf* : journalist
periodístico, -ca *adj* : journalistic, news
período *or* **periodo** *nm* : period
peripecia *nf* VICISITUD : vicissitude, reversal ⟨las peripecias de su carrera : the ups and downs of her career⟩ ⟨contar las peripecias de : to tell the adventures of⟩
periquera *nf Mex* : high chair (for a baby)
periquito *nm* : parakeet
periscopio *nm* : periscope
perito, -ta *adj & n* : expert
perjudicar {72} *vt* : to harm, to be detrimental to ⟨perjudicar la salud : to be bad for your health⟩
perjudicial *adj* : harmful, detrimental ⟨ser perjudicial para : to be harmful to⟩
perjuicio *nm* **1** : harm, damage ⟨causar perjuicio a : to cause damage to⟩ **2 en perjuicio de** : to the detriment of **3 sin perjuicio de** : without detriment to, without affecting
perjurar *vi* : to perjure oneself
perjurio *nm* : perjury
perla *nf* **1** : pearl **2 de perlas** *fam* : wonderfully ⟨me viene de perlas : it suits me just fine⟩
permanecer {53} *vi* **1** QUEDARSE : to remain, to stay **2** SEGUIR : to remain, to continue to be
permanencia *nf* **1** : permanence, continuance **2** ESTANCIA : stay
permanente¹ *adj* : permanent **2** : constant — **permanentemente** *adv*
permanente² *nf* : perm, permanent (wave) ⟨hacerse la permanente : to get a perm⟩
permeabilidad *nf* : permeability
permeable *adj* : permeable
permisible *adj* : permissible, allowable
permisividad *nf* : permissiveness
permisivo, -va *adv* : permissive
permiso *nm* **1** : permission ⟨dar permiso : to give permission⟩ **2** : permit, license ⟨permiso de conducir : driver's license⟩ ⟨permiso de residencia : green card⟩ ⟨permiso de trabajo : work permit⟩ **3** : leave, furlough **4 con ∼** : excuse me, pardon me **5 de ∼** : on leave
permitir *vt* : to permit, to allow ⟨no me permitió pasar : he wouldn't let me through⟩ ⟨¿me permite? : may I?⟩ **2** POSIBILITAR : to enable, to allow — **permitirse** *vr* : to allow oneself ⟨permitirse

el lujo de : to allow oneself the luxury of⟩
permuta *nf* : exchange
permutación *nf, pl* **-ciones** : permutation
permutar *vt* INTERCAMBIAR : to exchange
pernera *nf* : leg (of pants, etc.)
pernicioso, -sa *adj* : pernicious, destructive
pernil *nm* **1** : haunch (of an animal) **2** : leg (of meat), ham **3** : trouser leg
perno *nm* : bolt, pin
pernoctar *vi* : to stay overnight, to spend the night
pero¹ *nm* **1** : fault, defect ⟨ponerle peros a : to find fault with⟩ **2** : objection
pero² *conj* **1** : but ⟨lo siento, pero no puedo : I'm sorry, but I can't⟩ ⟨*used for emphasis*⟩ ⟨¿pero que le ve? : what on earth does she see in him?⟩ ⟨es muy, pero muy caro : it's extremely expensive⟩
perogrullada *nf* : truism, platitude, cliché
peroné *nm* : fibula
perorar *vi* : to deliver a speech
perorata *nf* : oration, long-winded speech
peróxido *nm* : peroxide
perpendicular *adj & nf* : perpendicular
perpetrar *vt* : to perpetrate
perpetuar {3} *vt* ETERNIZAR : to perpetuate
perpetuidad *nf* : perpetuity
perpetuo, -tua *adj* : perpetual — **perpetuamente** *adv*
perplejidad *nf* : perplexity
perplejo, -ja *adj* : perplexed, puzzled
perrada *nf fam* : dirty trick
perrera *nf* : kennel, dog pound
perrero, -ra *n* : dogcatcher
perrito, -ta *n* CACHORRO : puppy, small dog
perro, -rra *n* **1** : dog, bitch *f* **2 perro callejero** : stray dog **3 perro caliente** : hot dog **4 perro cobrador** : retriever **5 perro faldero** : lapdog **6 perro guardián** : guard dog **7 perro guía/lazarillo** : guide dog **8 perro pastor** : sheepdog **9 perro policía** : police dog **10 perro rastreador** : tracking dog **11 perro salchicha** : dachshund
persa¹ *adj & nmf* : Persian
persa² *nm* : Persian (language)
per se *adv* : per se
persecución *nf, pl* **-ciones** **1** : pursuit, chase **2** : persecution
perseguible *adj* : chargeable
perseguidor, -dora *n* **1** : pursuer **2** : persecutor
perseguir {75} *vt* **1** : to pursue, to chase **2** : to persecute **3** : to pester, to annoy
perseverancia *nf* : perseverance
perseverante *adj* : persistent
perseverar *vi* : to persevere
persiana *nf* : blind, venetian blind
persignarse *vr* SANTIGUARSE : to cross oneself, to make the sign of the cross
persistir *vi* **1** : to persist **2 ∼ en** : to persist in — **persistencia** *nf* — **persistente** *adj*
persona *nf* **1** : person ⟨miles de personas : thousands of people⟩ **2 en ∼** : in person **3 por ∼** : per person

personaje *nm* **1** : character (in drama or literature) **2** : personage, celebrity

personal[1] *adj* : personal — **personalmente** *adv*

personal[2] *nm* : personnel, staff

personalidad *nf* **1** : personality **2** PERSONAJE : personage, celebrity

personalizar {21} *vt* : to personalize — *vi* : to name names

personero, -ra *n* **1** : representative **2** : spokesperson, spokesman *m*, spokeswoman *f*

personificar {72} *vi* : to personify — **personificación** *nf*

perspectiva *nf* **1** : perspective **2** VISTA : view **3** : prospect, outlook ⟨tener buenas perspectivas : to have good prospects⟩ ⟨en perspectiva : in the offing, in prospect⟩ **4** : perspective, point of view ⟨mirándolo en perspectiva : looking back (at it), (looking at it) in retrospect/hindsight⟩

perspicacia *nf* : shrewdness, perspicacity, insight

perspicaz *adj, pl* **-caces** : shrewd, perspicacious

persuadir *vt* : to persuade ⟨lo persuadí de/para que viniera : I persuaded him to come⟩ — **persuadirse** *vr* : to become convinced

persuasión *nf, pl* **-siones** : persuasion

persuasivo, -va *adj* : persuasive

pertenecer {53} *vi* : to belong ⟨pertenecer a : to belong to⟩

perteneciente *adj* ~ **a** : belonging to

pertenencia *nf* **1** : membership **2** : ownership **3 pertenencias** *nfpl* : belongings, possessions

pértiga *nf* GARROCHA : pole ⟨salto con/de pértiga : pole vault⟩

pertinaz *adj, pl* **-naces** **1** OBSTINADO : obstinate **2** PERSISTENTE : persistent

pertinencia *nf* : pertinence, relevance

pertinente *adj* **1** : pertinent, relevant **2** : appropriate

pertrechos *nmpl* : equipment, gear

perturbación *nf, pl* **-ciones** : disturbance, disruption

perturbador, -dora *adj* **1** INQUIETANTE : disturbing, troubling **2** : disruptive

perturbar *vt* **1** : to disturb, to trouble **2** : to disrupt

peruano, -na *adj & n* : Peruvian

perversidad *nf* : perversity, depravity

perversión *nf, pl* **-siones** : perversion

perverso, -sa *adj* : wicked, depraved

pervertido[1], **-da** *adj* DEPRAVADO : perverted, depraved

pervertido[2], **-da** *n* : pervert

pervertir {76} *vt* : to pervert, to corrupt

pesa *nf* **1** : weight **2 levantamiento de pesas** : weight lifting

pesadamente *adv* **1** : heavily **2** : slowly, clumsily

pesadez *nf, pl* **-deces** **1** : heaviness **2** ABURRIMIENTO : tediousness **3** PLOMO : drag, bore

pesadilla *nf* : nightmare

pesado[1], **-da** *adj* **1** : heavy **2** LENTO : slow **3** MOLESTO : irritating, annoying

4 ABURRIDO : tedious, boring **5** DIFÍCIL : tough, difficult

pesado[2], **-da** *n fam* : bore, pest

pesadumbre *nf* AFLICCIÓN : grief, sorrow, sadness

pésame *nm* : condolences *pl* ⟨darle el pésame a alguien : to give someone one's condolences⟩ ⟨mi más sentido pésame : my heartfelt condolences⟩

pesar[1] *vt* **1** : to weigh ⟨pesa dos kilos : it weighs two kilos⟩ **2** EXAMINAR : to consider, to think over — *vi* **1** : to weigh ⟨¿cuánto pesa? : how much does it weigh?⟩ **2** : to be heavy **3** : to weigh heavily, to be a burden ⟨la responsabilidad le pesa : the responsibility is a burden on him⟩ **4** INFLUIR : to carry weight, to have bearing **5** (*with personal pronouns*) : to grieve, to sadden ⟨me pesa mucho no haber ido : I really regret not having gone⟩ **6 pese a** : in spite of, despite **7 pese a que** : in spite of the fact that

pesar[2] *nm* **1** AFLICCIÓN, PENA : sorrow, grief **2** REMORDIMIENTO : remorse **3 a pesar de** : in spite of, despite ⟨a pesar de todo : in spite of it all⟩ **4 a pesar de que** : in spite of the fact that

pesaroso, -sa *adj* **1** : sad, mournful **2** ARREPENTIDO : sorry, regretful

pesca *nf* **1** : fishing ⟨ir de pesca : to go fishing⟩ **2** : catch

pescadería *nf* : fish market

pescado *nm* : fish (as food)

pescador, -dora *n* : fisherman *m*, fisherwoman *f*

pescar {72} *vt* **1** : to fish for **2** : to catch **3** *fam* : to get a hold of, to land — *vi* : to fish, to go fishing

pescuezo *nm* : neck

pesebre *nm* **1** : manger **2** : Nativity scene

pesebrera *nf Col* : stable

pesera *nf* → **pesero**

pesero *nm Mex* : minibus

peseta *nf* : peseta (Spanish unit of currency)

pesimismo *nm* : pessimism

pesimista[1] *adj* : pessimistic

pesimista[2] *nmf* : pessimist

pésimo, -ma *adj* : dreadful, abominable

peso *nm* **1** : weight, heaviness ⟨perder/ganar peso : to lose/gain weight⟩ ⟨peso bruto/neto : gross/net weight⟩ **2** : burden, responsibility **3** : weight (in sports) ⟨peso pesado : heavyweight⟩ **4** BÁSCULA : scale **5** : peso (currency)

pesque, etc. → **pescar**

pesquería *nf* : fishery

pesquero[1], **-ra** *adj* : fishing ⟨pueblo pesquero : fishing village⟩

pesquero[2] *nm* : fishing boat

pesquisa *nf* INVESTIGACIÓN : inquiry, investigation

pestaña *nf* **1** : eyelash **2** : flange, rim **3** : tab (in a browser, etc.)

pestañear *vi* : to blink

pestañeo *nm* : blink

peste *nf* **1** : plague, pestilence **2** : stench, stink **3** : nuisance, pest

pesticida *nm* : pesticide
pestilencia *nf* 1 : stench, foul odor 2 : pestilence
pestillo *nm* CERROJO : bolt, latch
petaca *nf* 1 *Mex* : suitcase 2 **petacas** *nfpl Mex fam* : bottom, behind
pétalo *nm* : petal
petardear *vi* : to backfire
petardeo *nm* : backfiring
petardo *nm* : firecracker
petate *nm Hond, Mex* : mat
petición *nf, pl* **-ciones** : petition, request ⟨a petición de : at the request of⟩
peticionar *vt* : to petition
peticionario, -ria *n* : petitioner
petirrojo *nm* : robin
petiso, -sa *or* **petizo, -za** *n* : shorty
peto *nm* : bib (of clothing)
pétreo, -trea *adj* : stone, stony
petrificar {72} *vt* : to petrify
petróleo *nm* : oil, petroleum
petrolero¹, -ra *adj* : oil ⟨industria petrolera : oil industry⟩
petrolero² *nm* : oil tanker
petrolífero, -ra *adj* → petrolero¹
petulancia *nf* INSOLENCIA : insolence, petulance
petulante *adj* INSOLENTE : insolent, petulant — **petulantemente** *adv*
petunia *nf* : petunia
peyorativo, -va *adj* : pejorative
pez¹ *nm, pl* **peces** 1 : fish 2 **pez de colores** : goldfish 3 **pez espada** : swordfish 4 **pez gordo** : big shot
pez² *nf, pl* **peces** : pitch, tar
pezón *nm, pl* **pezones** : nipple
pezuña *nf* : hoof ⟨pezuña hendida : cloven hoof⟩
pH [ˈpeˈatʃe, ˈpiˈetʃ] *nm* : pH
phishing [ˈfiʃiŋ] *nm* : phishing
phylum [ˈfilum] *nm* : phylum
pi *nf* : pi
piadoso, -sa *adj* 1 : compassionate, merciful 2 DEVOTO : pious, devout — **piadosamente** *adv*
pianista *nmf* : pianist, piano player
piano *nm* : piano ⟨piano de cola : grand piano⟩
piar {85} *vi* : to chirp, to cheep, to tweet
pibe, -ba *n Arg, Uru fam* : kid, child
pica *nf* 1 : pike, lance 2 : goad (in bullfighting) 3 : spade (in playing cards)
picada *nf* 1 : bite, sting (of an insect) 2 : sharp descent
picadero *nm* 1 : exercise ring (for horses) 2 : riding school
picadillo *nm* 1 : minced meat, hash 2 **hacer picadillo a** : to beat to a pulp
picado, -da *adj* 1 : perforated 2 : ground (of meat), chopped 3 : decayed (of teeth) 4 : choppy, rough 5 *fam* : annoyed, miffed
picador *nm* : picador
picadura *nf* 1 : sting, bite 2 : prick, puncture 3 : decay, cavity
picaflor *nm* 1 COLIBRÍ : hummingbird 2 : womanizer
picana *nf* : goad, prod
picante¹ *adj* 1 : hot, spicy 2 : sharp, cutting 3 : racy, risqué

picante² *nm* 1 : spiciness 2 : hot spices *pl*, hot sauce
picaporte *nm* 1 : latch 2 : door handle 3 ALDABA : door knocker
picar {72} *vt* 1 : to sting (of bees, etc.), to bite (of fleas, etc.) 2 : to peck at (of birds) 3 COMER : to nibble on 4 : to prick (of a needle, etc.), to punch (a ticket) 5 : to break, to chip (stone, etc.) 6 : to grind, to chop 7 : to goad, to incite 8 : to pique, to provoke — *vi* 1 : to itch ⟨esta camisa me pica : this shirt is itchy⟩ 2 : to sting 3 : to be spicy, to be hot 4 : to nibble 5 : to take the bait 6 ~ **en** : to dabble in 7 **picar muy alto** : to aim too high — **picarse** *vr* 1 : to get a cavity, to decay 2 : to go bad (of food) 3 : to get annoyed, to take offense 4 : to become choppy (of the sea)
picardía *nf* 1 : cunning, craftiness 2 : prank, dirty trick
picaresco, -ca *adj* 1 : picaresque 2 : mischievous, naughty
pícaro¹, -ra *adj* 1 : mischievous 2 : cunning, sly 3 : off-color, risqué
pícaro², -ra *n* 1 : rogue, scoundrel 2 : rascal
picazón *nf, pl* **-zones** COMEZÓN : itch
picea *nf* : spruce (tree)
pichel *nm* : pitcher, jug
pichón, -chona *n, mpl* **pichones** 1 : young pigeon, squab 2 *Mex fam* : novice, greenhorn
picnic *nm* : picnic
pico *nm* 1 : peak 2 : point 3 : corner 4 : beak, bill 5 *fam* : mouth 6 : pick, pickax 7 **y pico** : and a little, and a bit ⟨las siete y pico : a little after seven⟩ ⟨dos metros y pico : a bit over two meters⟩
picor *nm* : itch, irritation
picoso, -sa *adj Mex* : very hot, spicy
picota *nf* 1 : pillory, stock 2 **poner a alguien en la picota** : to put someone on the spot
picotada *nf* → picotazo
picotazo *nm* : peck (of a bird)
picotear *vt* : to peck — *vi* : to nibble, to pick
pictórico, -ca *adj* : pictorial
picudo, -da *adj* 1 : pointy, sharp 2 ~ **para** *Mex fam* : clever at, good at
pide, etc. → pedir
pie *nm* 1 : foot 2 : base, bottom, stem, foot ⟨pie de la cama : foot of the bed⟩ ⟨pie de una lámpara : base of a lamp⟩ ⟨pie de la escalera : bottom of the stairs⟩ ⟨pie de una copa : stem of a glass⟩ ⟨pie de la página : foot of the page⟩ ⟨pie de foto : caption⟩ 3 : foot (in measurement) ⟨pie cuadrado : square foot⟩ 4 : cue (in theater) 5 **a** ~ : on foot 6 **de** ~ : on one's feet, standing ⟨estar de pie : to be standing⟩ ⟨ponerse de pie : to stand up⟩ 7 **en** ~ : standing ⟨mantenerse en pie : to remain standing⟩ ⟨seguir en pie : to remain valid, to stand⟩ 8 **al pie de la letra** : word for word 9 **con buen pie** : well ⟨comenzar con buen pie : to start on the right foot, to get off to a

good start⟩ **10 con pies de plomo** : very cautiously **11 dar pie a** : to give cause for, to give rise to **12 de a pie** : average, ordinary **13 de pies a cabeza** : from head to toe **14 en pie de guerra** : ready for war **15 en pie de igualdad** : on equal footing **16 hacer pie** : to touch bottom (in water) **17 no tener ni pies ni cabeza** : to make no sense

piedad *nf* **1** COMPASIÓN : mercy, pity **2** DEVOCIÓN : piety, devotion

piedra *nf* **1** : stone **2** : flint (of a lighter) **3** : hailstone **4 piedra angular** : cornerstone **5 piedra arenisca** : sandstone **6 piedra caliza** : limestone **7 piedra de afilar** : whetstone, grindstone **8 piedra de molino** : millstone **9 piedra de pómez** : pumice stone **10 piedra de toque** : touchstone **11 piedra imán** : lodestone **12 piedra preciosa** : precious stone

piel *nf* **1** : skin **2** CUERO : leather, hide ⟨piel de venado : deerskin⟩ **3** : fur, pelt **4** CÁSCARA : peel, skin **5 piel de gallina** : goose bumps *pl* ⟨me pone la piel de gallina : it gives me goose bumps⟩

piélago *nm* **el piélago** : the deep, the ocean

piensa, etc. → **pensar**

pienso *nm* : feed, fodder

pierde, etc. → **perder**

pierna *nf* : leg ⟨cruzar las piernas : to cross one's legs⟩

pieza *nf* **1** ELEMENTO : piece, part, component ⟨vestido de dos piezas : two-piece dress⟩ ⟨pieza de recambio/repuesto : spare part⟩ ⟨pieza clave : key element⟩ **2** : piece (in chess) **3** OBRA : piece, work ⟨pieza de teatro : play⟩ **4** : room, bedroom

pífano *nm* : fife

pifia *nf fam* : goof, blunder

pifiar *vt fam* : to mess up, to bungle

pigargo *nm* : osprey

pigmentación *nf, pl* **-ciones** : pigmentation

pigmento *nm* : pigment

pigmeo, -mea *adj & n* : pygmy, Pygmy

pijama *nm* : pajamas *pl*

pila *nf* **1** BATERÍA : battery ⟨pila de linterna : flashlight battery⟩ **2** MONTÓN : pile, heap **3** : sink, basin, font ⟨pila bautismal : baptismal font⟩ ⟨pila para pájaros : birdbath⟩

pilar *nm* **1** : pillar, column **2** : support, mainstay

píldora *nf* PASTILLA : pill ⟨tomar la píldora (anticonceptiva) : to be on the pill⟩

pileta *nf Arg, Uru* **1** FREGADERO, LAVABO : sink **2** PISCINA : swimming pool

pillaje *nm* : pillage, plunder

pillar *vt* **1** *fam* : to catch ⟨¡cuidado! ¡nos pillarán! : watch out! they'll catch us!⟩ **2** *fam* : to grasp, to catch on ⟨¿no lo pillas? : don't you get it?⟩ — **pillarse** *vr* : to catch (one's finger, etc.)

pillo¹, -lla *adj* : cunning, crafty

pillo², -lla *n* **1** : rascal, brat **2** : rogue, scoundrel

pilluelo, -la *n* : urchin

pilón *nm, pl* **pilones 1** PILA : basin **2** : pillar, tower (for cables), pylon (of a bridge) **3** *Mex* : extra, free gift

pilotar *vt* : to pilot (a plane), to steer (a ship), to drive (an automobile)

pilote *nm* : pile (stake)

pilotear → **pilotar**

piloto¹ *nm* **1** : pilot light **2** *Arg* : raincoat **3 piloto automático** : autopilot, automatic pilot

piloto² *nmf* : pilot (of a plane or ship), driver (of an automobile)

piltrafa *nf* **1** : poor quality meat **2** : wretch **3 piltrafas** *nfpl* : food scraps

pimentero *nm* : pepper shaker

pimentón *nm, pl* **-tones 1** : paprika **2** : cayenne pepper

pimienta *nf* **1** : pepper (condiment) ⟨pimienta blanca/negra : white/black pepper⟩ **2 pimienta de Jamaica** : allspice

pimiento *nm* : pepper (fruit) ⟨pimiento verde : green pepper⟩ ⟨pimiento morrón : pimiento, pimento⟩

pináculo *nm* **1** : pinnacle (of a building) **2** : peak, acme

pinar *nm* : pine forest

pinball [pin'bol] *nm* : pinball

pincel *nm* **1** : paintbrush **2** : makeup brush

pincelada *nf* **1** : brushstroke **2 últimas pinceladas** : final touches

pinchar *vt* **1** : to puncture (a tire, balloon, etc.) **2** : to prick, to stick, to jab **3** PROVOCAR : to goad, to tease, to needle **4** : to give an injection **5** : to click on (a link, etc.) ⟨pinche aquí : click here⟩ **6** *fam* : to tap, to wiretap (a phone) — *vi* **1** : to be prickly **2** : to get a flat tire **3** *fam* : to get beaten, to lose out — **pincharse** *vr* **1** INYECTARSE : to shoot up **2** : to go flat (of a tire)

pinchazo *nm* **1** : prick, jab **2** : puncture, flat tire

pinche¹ *adj Mex* MALDITO : damned

pinche² *nmf* : kitchen assistant

pincho *nm* **1** : thorn, spine (of a plant) **2** *Spain* : bar snack

Ping–Pong *marca registrada, m* — used for table tennis

pingüe *adj* **1** : rich, huge (of profits) **2** : lucrative

pingüino *nm* : penguin

pininos *or* **pinitos** *nmpl* : first steps ⟨hacer pininos : to take one's first steps, to toddle⟩

pino *nm* : pine, pine tree

pinta *nf* **1** : dot, spot **2** : pint **3** *fam* : aspect, appearance ⟨las peras tienen buena pinta : the pears look good⟩ ⟨tener pinta de : to look like⟩ **4 pintas** *nfpl Mex* : graffiti

pintadas *nfpl* : graffiti

pintado, -da *adj* : spotted

pintalabios *nms & pl* : lipstick

pintar *vt* **1** : to paint **2** : to draw, to mark **3** : to describe, to depict — *vi* **1** : to paint, to draw **2** : to look ⟨no pinta bien : it doesn't look good⟩ **3** *fam* : to count ⟨aquí no pinta nada : he has no say here⟩ — **pintarse** *vr* **1** MAQUI-

LLARSE : to put on makeup 2
pintárselas solo *fam* : to manage by
oneself, to know it all
pintarrajear *vt* : to daub (with paint)
pinto, -ta *adj* : speckled, spotted
pintor, -tora *n* 1 : painter (artist) 2 *or*
pintor de brocha gorda : painter (of
buildings, etc.)
pintoresco, -ca *adj* : picturesque, quaint
pintura *nf* 1 : paint 2 : painting ⟨pintura
al óleo : oil painting⟩ ⟨pintura a la acuarela : watercolor painting⟩
pinza *nf* - 1 : clothespin 2 HORQUILLA
: bobby pin 3 : claw, pincer (of a crab,
etc.) 4 : pleat, dart (in clothing) 5 pinzas *nfpl* : tweezers 6 pinzas *nfpl* ALICA-
TES : pliers, pincers 7 pinzas *nfpl*
: tongs (for food)
pinzón *nm*, *pl* pinzones : finch
piña *nf* 1 : pineapple 2 : pine cone
piñata *nf* : piñata
piñón *nm*, *pl* piñones 1 : pine nut 2
: pinion (of a machine), sprocket (of a
bicycle)
pío¹, pía *adj* 1 DEVOTO : pious, devout 2
: pied, dappled
pío² *nm* 1 : peep, tweet, cheep 2 **no decir ni pío** : not to say a word
piocha *nf* 1 : pickax 2 *Mex* : goatee
piojo *nm* : louse
piojoso, -sa *adj* 1 : lousy 2 : filthy
piola¹ *adj fam* 1 *Arg* : cool *fam*, good 2
pasar piola *Chile, Peru* : to go unnoticed
piola² *nf* : cord
pionero¹, -ra *adj* : pioneering
pionero², -ra *n* : pioneer
pipa *nf* 1 : pipe (for smoking) 2 *Cuba,
Mex* : tanker truck 3 *Spain* : seed
pipí *nm fam* : pee *fam* ⟨hacer pipí : to
take a pee⟩
pipián *nm*, *pl* pipianes *Mex* : a spicy
sauce or stew
pipiolo, -la *n fam* 1 : greenhorn, novice
2 : kid, youngster
pique¹, etc. → picar
pique² *nm* 1 : pique, resentment 2 : rivalry, competition 3 **a pique de** : about
to, on the verge of 4 **irse a pique** : to
sink, to founder
piqueta *nf* : pickax
piquete *nm* 1 : picketers *pl*, picket line
2 : squad, detachment 3 *Mex* : prick,
jab 4 *Mex* : insect bite
piquetear *vt* 1 : to picket 2 *Mex* : to
prick, to jab
pira *nf* : pyre
piragua *nf* : canoe
piragüismo *nm* : canoeing
piragüista *nmf* : canoeist, canoer
pirámide *nf* : pyramid
piraña *nf* : piranha
pirata¹ *adj* 1 : bootleg, pirated 2 : pirate
⟨un barco pirata : a pirate ship⟩
pirata² *nmf* 1 : pirate 2 : pirate, bootlegger 3 **pirata aéreo** : hijacker 4 **pirata
informático** : hacker
piratear *vt* 1 : to hijack, to commandeer
2 : to bootleg, to pirate
piratería *nf* : piracy, bootlegging
piromanía *nf* : pyromania

pirómano, -na *n* : pyromaniac
piropo *nm* : flirtatious compliment
pirotecnia *nf* : fireworks *pl*, pyrotechnics
pl
pirotécnico, -ca *adj* : fireworks, pyrotechnic
pírrico, -ca *adj* : Pyrrhic
pirueta *nf* : pirouette
piruli *nm* : cone-shaped lollipop
pis → pipí
pisada *nf* 1 : footstep 2 HUELLA : footprint
pisapapeles *nms & pl* : paperweight
pisar *vt* 1 : to step on/in ⟨no pises las
flores : don't step on the flowers⟩ 2 : to
set foot in (a place) 3 : to walk all over,
to mistreat — *vi* : to step, to walk, to
tread
piscina *nf* 1 : swimming pool 2 : fish
pond
Piscis¹ *nm* : Pisces (sign or constellation)
Piscis² *nmf* : Pisces (person)
piso *nm* 1 PLANTA : floor, story 2 SUELO
: floor 3 PAVIMENTO : surface (of a road)
4 CAPA : layer 5 *Spain* : apartment
pisotear *vt* 1 : to stamp on, to trample 2
PISAR : to walk all over 3 : to flout, to
disregard
pisotón *nm*, *pl* -tones : stamp, step ⟨su-
frieron empujones y pisotones : they
were pushed and stepped on⟩
pista *nf* 1 RASTRO : trail, track ⟨siguen la
pista de los sospechosos : they're on the
trail of the suspects⟩ 2 : clue 3 CA-
MINO : road, trail 4 : track, racetrack
5 *Chile* : lane (of a road) 6 : ring, arena,
rink ⟨pista de patinaje/hielo : skating/ice
rink⟩ 7 : track (of a recording) 8 **pista
de aterrizaje** : runway, airstrip 9 **pista
de baile** : dance floor 10 **pista de tenis**
Spain : tennis court
pistacho *nm* : pistachio
pistilo *nm* : pistil
pistola *nf* 1 : pistol, handgun 2 : spray
gun
pistolera *nf* : holster
pistolero *nm* : gunman
pistón *nm*, *pl* pistones 1 : piston 2
: key, valve (of an instrument)
pita *nf* 1 : twine 2 : pita (bread)
pitar *vi* 1 : to blow a whistle 2 : to whistle, to boo 3 : to beep, to honk, to toot
— *vt* 1 : to whistle at, to boo 2 : to call,
to signal (a foul)
pitido *nm* 1 : whistle, whistling 2 : beep,
honk, toot
pitillo *nm* : cigarette
pito *nm* 1 SILBATO : whistle 2 CLAXON,
BOCINA : horn 3 **no me importa un pito**
fam : I don't give a damn
pitón *nm*, *pl* pitones 1 : python 2
: point of a bull's horn
pitonisa *nf* : fortune-teller
pituitario, -ria *adj* : pituitary
pívot *nmf*, *pl* pivots : center (in basketball)
pivote *nm* : pivot
piyama *nmf* : pajamas *pl*
pizarra *nf* 1 : slate 2 : blackboard 3
: scoreboard

pizarrón *nm, pl* **-rrones** : blackboard, chalkboard

pizca *nf* **1** : pinch ⟨una pizca de canela : a pinch of cinnamon⟩ **2** : speck, trace ⟨ni pizca : not a bit⟩ **3** *Mex* : harvest

pizcar {72} *vt Mex* : to harvest

pizque, etc. → **pizcar**

pizza [ˈpitsa, ˈpisa] *nf* : pizza

pizzería *nf* : pizzeria, pizza parlor

placa *nf* **1** : sheet, plate **2** : plaque **3** : plate (in photography) **4** : badge, insignia **5 placa de circuito(s)** : circuit board **6 placa de matrícula** : license plate, tag **7 placa dental** : plaque, tartar

placard [plaˈkar] *nm, pl* **-cards** *Arg, Uru* : built-in closet

placebo *nm* : placebo

placenta *nf* : placenta

placentero, -ra *adj* AGRADABLE, GRATO : pleasant, agreeable — **placenteramente** *adv*

placer¹ {57} *vi* GUSTAR : to be pleasing ⟨hazlo como te plazca : do it however you please⟩

placer² *nm* **1** : pleasure, enjoyment ⟨ha sido un placer : it has been a pleasure⟩ **2 a** ~ : as much as one wants

plácido, -da *adj* TRANQUILO : placid, calm

plaga *nf* **1** : plague, infestation (of insects, etc.), blight (of crops, etc.) **2** CALAMIDAD : disaster, scourge

plagado, -da *adj* ~ **de** : filled with, covered with

plagar {52} *vt* : to plague

plagiar *vt* **1** : to plagiarize **2** SECUESTRAR : to kidnap, to abduct

plagiario, -ria *n* **1** : plagiarist **2** SECUESTRADOR : kidnapper, abductor

plagio *nm* **1** : plagiarism **2** SECUESTRO : kidnapping, abduction

plague, etc. → **plagar**

plan *nm* **1** : plan, strategy, program ⟨plan de inversiones : investment plan⟩ ⟨plan de estudios : curriculum⟩ **2** PLANO : plan, diagram **3** : attitude, intent, purpose ⟨ponte en plan serio : be serious⟩ ⟨estamos en plan de divertirnos : we're looking to have some fun⟩

plana *nf* **1** : page ⟨noticias en primera plana : front-page news⟩ **2 plana mayor** : staff (in the military)

plancha *nf* **1** : iron, ironing **2** : grill, griddle ⟨a la plancha : grilled⟩ **3** : sheet, plate ⟨plancha para hornear : baking sheet⟩ **4** *fam* : blunder, blooper

planchada *nf* : ironing, pressing

planchado *nm* → **planchada**

planchar *v* : to iron

planchazo *nm fam* : goof, blunder

plancton *nm* : plankton

planeación *nf, pl* **-ciones** *Col, Hon, Mex* → **planeamiento**

planeador *nm* : glider (aircraft)

planeamiento *nm* : plan, planning

planear *vt* : to plan — *vi* : to glide (in the air)

planeo *nm* : gliding, soaring

planeta *nm* : planet

planetario¹, -ria *adj* **1** : planetary **2** : global, worldwide

planetario² *nm* : planetarium

planicie *nf* : plain

planificación *nf, pl* **-ciones** : planning ⟨planificación familiar : family planning⟩

planificador, -dora *n* : planner

planificar {72} *vt* : to plan

planilla *nf* **1** LISTA : list **2** NÓMINA : payroll **3** TABLA : chart, table **4** *Mex* : slate, ticket (of candidates) **5 planilla de cálculo** *Arg, Chile* : spreadsheet

plano¹, -na *adj* : flat, level, plane

plano² *nm* **1** PLAN : map, plan **2** : plane (surface) **3** NIVEL : level ⟨en un plano personal : on a personal level⟩ **4** : shot (in photography) ⟨primer plano : close-up⟩ **5 de** ~ : flatly, outright, directly ⟨se negó de plano : he flatly refused⟩

planta *nf* **1** : plant ⟨planta de interior : houseplant⟩ **2** FÁBRICA : plant, factory **3** PISO : floor, story ⟨planta baja : ground floor, first floor⟩ **4** : staff, employees *pl* **5** : sole (of the foot)

plantación *nf, pl* **-ciones** **1** : plantation **2** : planting

plantado, -da *adj* **1** : planted **2 dejar plantado** *fam* : to stand up (a date), to dump (a lover)

plantar *vt* **1** : to plant, to sow ⟨plantar de flores : to plant with flowers⟩ **2** : to put in, to place **3** *fam* : to plant, to land ⟨plantar un beso : to plant a kiss⟩ **4** *fam* : to leave, to jilt — **plantarse** *vr* **1** : to stand firm **2** *fam* : to arrive, to show up **3** *fam* : to balk

planteamiento *nm* **1** : approach, position ⟨el planteamiento feminista : the feminist viewpoint⟩ **2** : explanation, exposition **3** : proposal, suggestion, plan

plantear *vt* **1** : to set forth (an argument, etc.), to bring up (a topic, possibility, etc.), to suggest (an idea, etc.) ⟨no lo plantearía así : I wouldn't describe/explain it like that⟩ **2** : to establish, to set up **3** : to create, to pose (a problem) — **plantearse** *vr* **1** : to think about **2** : to arise

plantel *nm* **1** : educational institution **2** : staff, team

planteo → **planteamiento**

plantilla *nf* **1** : insole **2** : pattern, template, stencil **3** *Mex, Spain* : staff, roster of employees

plantío *nm* : field (planted with a crop)

plantón *nm, pl* **plantones** **1** : seedling **2** : long wait ⟨darle (un) plantón a alguien : to stand someone up⟩

plañidero¹, -ra *adj* : mournful

plañidero², -ra *nf* : hired mourner

plañir {38} *v* : to mourn, to lament

plasma *nm* : plasma

plasmar *vt* : to express, to give form to — **plasmarse** *vr*

plasta *nf* : soft mass, lump

plástica *nf* : modeling, sculpture

plasticidad *nf* : plasticity

plástico¹, -ca *adj* : plastic

plástico² *nm* : plastic

plastificar {72} *vt* : to laminate

plata *nf* **1** : silver (metal) **2** : silver, silverware **3** : money

plataforma *nf* **1** ESTRADO, TARIMA : platform, dais **2** : platform (in politics) **3** : springboard, stepping stone **4 plataforma continental** : continental shelf **5 plataforma de lanzamiento** : launchpad **6 plataforma petrolífera** : oil rig (at sea)

platal *nm* : large sum of money, fortune

platanal *or* **platanar** *nm* : banana plantation

platanero¹, -ra *adj* : banana, banana-producing

platanero², -ra *n* : banana grower

plátano *nm* **1** : banana (plant, fruit) **2** : plantain (plant, fruit) **3** : plane tree **plátano macho** *Mex* : plantain

platea *nf* : orchestra seats *pl* (in a theater)

plateado, -da *adj* **1** : silver, silvery **2** : silver-plated

platería *nf* **1** : silver, silverware **2** : silver shop

plática *nf* **1** : talk, lecture **2** : chat, conversation

platicar {72} *vi* : to talk, to chat — *vt Mex* : to tell, to say

platija *nf* : flatfish, flounder

platillo *nm* **1** : saucer ⟨platillo volador : flying saucer⟩ **2** : cymbal **3** : pan (of a scale) **4** *Mex* : dish ⟨platillos típicos : local dishes⟩

platino *nm* : platinum

plato *nm* **1** : plate, dish ⟨lavar los platos : to do the dishes⟩ **2** : serving, helping **3** : course (of a meal) ⟨primer/segundo plato : first/second course⟩ ⟨plato fuerte/principal : main course⟩ **4** : dish ⟨plato típico : typical dish⟩ ⟨plato dulce/salado : sweet/savory dish⟩ **5** : home plate (in baseball) **6 plato hondo** : soup bowl **7 plato llano** : dinner plate

plató *nm* : set (in the movies)

platónico, -ca *adj* : platonic

playa *nf* **1** : beach, seashore **2 playa de estacionamiento** : parking lot

playera *nf* **1** : canvas sneaker **2** *CA, Mex* : T-shirt

playboy [pleiˈboi] *nm, pl* **playboys** : playboy

plaza *nf* **1** : square, plaza **2** : marketplace **3** : space, seat (in a vehicle) **4** EMPLEO, PUESTO : post, position **5** : place, spot (on a team, etc.) **6 plaza fuerte** : stronghold, fortified city **7 plaza de toros** : bullring

plazca, etc. → placer

plazo *nm* **1** : period, term ⟨un plazo de cinco días : a period of five days⟩ ⟨préstamos a corto/largo plazo : short-term/long-term loans⟩ ⟨el plazo se cumplió : the deadline has passed⟩ **2** ABONO : installment ⟨pagar a plazos : to pay in installments⟩

plazoleta *nf* : small square

plazuela → plazoleta

pleamar *nf* : high tide

plebe *nf* : common people, masses *pl*

plebeyo¹, -ya *adj* : plebeian

plebeyo², -ya *n* : plebeian, commoner

plegable *adj* : folding, collapsible

plegadizo → plegable

plegar {49} *vt* DOBLAR : to fold, to bend — **plegarse** *vr* : to give in, to yield

plegaria *nf* ORACIÓN : prayer

pleito *nm* **1** : lawsuit **2** : fight, argument, dispute

plenamente *adv* COMPLETAMENTE : fully, completely

plenario, -ria *adj* : full

plenilunio *nm* : full moon

plenitud *nf* : fullness, abundance

pleno, -na *adj* (*often used as an intensifier*) COMPLETO : full, complete ⟨en pleno uso de sus facultades : in full command of his faculties⟩ ⟨en plena noche : in the middle of the night⟩ ⟨a plena luz (del día) : in broad daylight⟩ ⟨en pleno corazón de la ciudad : right in the heart of the city⟩ ⟨en plena cara : right in the face⟩

plétora *nf* : plethora

pleuresía *nf* : pleurisy

plexiglás *nm* (*Plexiglas, trademark*) *Spain* : plexiglass

pliega, pliegue etc. → plegar

pliego *nm* **1** HOJA : sheet of paper **2** : sealed document

pliegue *nm* **1** DOBLEZ : crease, fold **2** : pleat

plisar *vt* : to pleat

plomada *nf* **1** : plumb line **2** : weight, sinker

plomería *nf* FONTANERÍA : plumbing

plomero, -ra *n* FONTANERO : plumber

plomizo, -za *adj* : leaden

plomo *nm* **1** : lead ⟨sin plomo : unleaded⟩ **2** : plumb line **3** : weight, sinker **4** *Spain* FUSIBLE : fuse **5** *fam* : bore, drag **6 a ~** : plumb, straight

plugo, etc. → placer

pluma *nf* **1** : feather, quill (for writing) **2** : pen **3** LLAVE : faucet **4 pluma fuente** : fountain pen

plumaje *nm* : plumage

plumero *nm* : feather duster

plumilla *nf* : nib

plumón *nm, pl* **plumones** **1** : down **2** : marker, felt-tip pen

plumoso, -sa *adj* : feathery, downy

plural *adj & nm* : plural

pluralidad *nf* : plurality

pluralizar {21} *vt* **1** : to pluralize **2** : to expand, to multiply

pluriempleado, -da *adj* : holding more than one job

pluriempleo *nm* : moonlighting

plus *nm* : bonus

pluscuamperfecto *nm* : pluperfect — **pluscuamperfecto, -ta** *adj*

plusvalía *nf* : appreciation, capital gain

Plutón *nm* : Pluto

plutocracia *nf* : plutocracy

plutonio *nm* : plutonium

población *nf, pl* **-ciones** **1** : population ⟨población activa : working population⟩ **2** : city, town, village **3 población callampa** *Chile* : shantytown, slums *pl*

poblado¹, -da *adj* **1** : inhabited, populated **2** : full, thick ⟨cejas pobladas : bushy eyebrows⟩

poblado² *nm* : village, settlement

poblador, -dora *n* : settler

poblar {19} *vt* **1** : to populate, to inhabit **2** : to settle, to colonize **3 ~ de** : to stock with, to plant with — **poblarse** *vr* : to fill up, to become crowded

pobre[1] *adj* **1** : poor, impoverished **2** : poor, unfortunate ⟨¡pobre de mí! : poor me!⟩ **3** : poor, bad (in quality) ⟨pobres resultados : poor results⟩ **4** : poor, deficient ⟨una dieta pobre : a poor diet⟩

pobre[2] *nmf* : poor person ⟨los pobres : the poor⟩ ⟨¡pobre! : poor thing!⟩

pobremente *adv* : poorly

pobreza *nf* : poverty

pocilga *nf* CHIQUERO : pigsty, pigpen

pocillo *nm* : small coffee cup, demitasse

poción *or* **pócima** *nf, pl* **pociones** *or* **pócimas** : potion

poco[1] *adv* **1** : little, not much ⟨poco probable : not very likely⟩ ⟨come poco : he doesn't eat much⟩ **2** : a short time, a while ⟨tardaremos poco : we won't be very long⟩ **3** *poco antes* : shortly before **4** *poco después* : shortly after

poco[2], **-ca** *adj* **1** : little, not much, (a) few ⟨tengo poco dinero : I don't have much money⟩ ⟨en no pocas ocasiones : on more than a few occasions⟩ ⟨unos pocos meses : a few months⟩ ⟨muy poca gente : very few people⟩ **2** *pocas veces* : rarely

poco[3], **-ca** *pron* **1** : little, few ⟨le falta poco para terminar : he's almost finished⟩ ⟨uno de los pocos que quedan : one of the remaining few⟩ **2** *un poco* : a little, a bit ⟨un poco de vino : a little wine⟩ ⟨un poco extraño : a bit strange⟩ **3** *a ~ Mex (used to express disbelief)* ⟨¿a poco no se te hizo difícil? : you mean you didn't find it difficult?⟩ **4** *de a poco* : little by little **5** *dentro de poco* : shortly, in a little while **6** *hace poco* : not long ago **7** *poco a poco* : little by little **8** *por ~* : nearly, almost

podar *vt* : to prune, to trim

podcast [pod'kast] *nm, pl* **podcasts** : podcast

poder[1] {58} *v aux* **1** : to be able to, can ⟨no puede hablar : he can't speak⟩ ⟨no pude acabarlo : I couldn't finish it⟩ **2** *(expressing possibility)* : might, may ⟨puede llover : it may rain at any moment⟩ ⟨¿cómo puede ser? : how can that be?⟩ ⟨se podría/podía haber evitado : it could have been avoided⟩ **3** *(expressing permission)* : can, may ⟨¿puedo ir a la fiesta? : can I go to the party?⟩ ⟨¿se puede? : may I come in?⟩ **4** *(expressing a request)* : can ⟨¿me puedes ayudar? : can you help me?⟩ ⟨¿me lo podrías explicar? : could/would you explain it to me?⟩ **5** *(expressing annoyance)* : can ⟨¿no puedes estarte quieto? : can't you sit still?⟩ ⟨¡podrías/podías haberme llamado! : you could have called me!⟩ **6** *(expressing moral obligation)* : can ⟨no puedo juzgarlo : I can't judge him⟩ — *vi* **1** : to beat, to defeat ⟨cree que le puede a cualquiera : he thinks he can beat anyone⟩ **2** : to be possible ⟨¿crees que vendrán? — puede (que sí) : do you think they'll come? — maybe⟩ **3** *~ con* : to

cope with, to manage ⟨¡no puedo con estos niños! : I can't handle these children!⟩ **4** *a/hasta más no poder* ⟨es competitivo a más no poder : he's as competitive as they come⟩ ⟨comimos hasta más no poder : we ate until we couldn't eat another bite⟩ **5** *no poder más* : to have had enough ⟨no puede más : she can't take anymore⟩ **6** *no poder menos que* : not to be able to help (doing something) ⟨no pudo menos que asombrarse : she couldn't help but be amazed⟩

poder[2] *nm* **1** : power, control ⟨tener poder sobre alguien : to have power over someone⟩ **2** : power, influence ⟨el poder del amor : the power of love⟩ **3** : power, ability ⟨poderes mágicos : magical powers⟩ ⟨poder adquisitivo : purchasing power⟩ **4** : power, control (of a country, etc.) ⟨llegar al poder : to come to power⟩ ⟨estar en el poder : to be in power⟩ **5** : power, authority ⟨el poder de veto : veto power⟩ ⟨tener el poder para : to have the authority to⟩ **6** : branch (of government) ⟨el poder legislativo : the legislature⟩ ⟨los poderes públicos : the authorities⟩ **7** : power, force ⟨poder militar : military might⟩ **8** : possession ⟨estar en el poder de : to be in the hands of⟩ **9** : power of attorney

poderío *nm* **1** : power **2** : wealth, influence

poderosamente *adv* : powerfully

poderoso, -sa *adj* **1** : powerful **2** : wealthy, influential **3** : effective

podiatría *nf* : podiatry

podio *nm* : podium

pódium → **podio**

podología *nf* : podiatry, chiropody

podólogo, -ga *n* : podiatrist, chiropodist

podrá, etc. → **poder**

podredumbre *nf* **1** : decay, rottenness **2** : corruption

podrido, -da *adj* **1** : rotten, decayed **2** : corrupt **3** *Arg, Chile, Uru* HARTO : fed up

podrir → **pudrir**

poema *nm* : poem

poesía *nf* **1** : poetry **2** POEMA : poem

poeta *nmf* : poet

poético, -ca *adj* : poetic, poetical

poetisa *nf* : poetess *f*, poet

pogrom *nm* : pogrom

póker *or* **poker** *nm* : poker (card game)

polaco[1], **-ca** *adj* : Polish

polaco[2], **-ca** *n* : Pole, Polish person

polaco[3] *nm* : Polish (language)

polar *adj* : polar

polarizar {21} *vt* : to polarize — **polarizarse** *vr* — **polarización** *nf*

Polaroid *marca registrada, f* — used for a camera that produces developed photos or for the photos produced in this way

polea *nf* : pulley

polémica *nf* CONTROVERSIA : controversy, polemics

polémico, -ca *adj* CONTROVERTIDO : controversial, polemical

polemizar {21} *vi* : to argue, to debate

polemonio *nm* : phlox

polen *nm, pl* **pólenes** : pollen
polera *nf Chile* : T-shirt
polerón *nm, pl* **-rones** *Chile* : sweatshirt
policía[1] *nf* : police
policía[2] *nmf* : police officer, policeman *m*, policewoman *f*
policíaco, -ca *or* **policiaco, -ca** *adj* : police ⟨novela policíaca : detective story⟩
policial *adj* : police
polideportivo *nm* : sports center
poliéster *nm* : polyester
polifacético, -ca *adj* : versatile, multifaceted
poligamia *nf* : polygamy
polígamo[1]**, -ma** *adj* : polygamous
polígamo[2]**, -ma** *n* : polygamist
poligonal *adj* : polygonal
polígono *nm* **1** : polygon **2** *Spain* : zone
poliinsaturado, -da *adj* : polyunsaturated
polilla *nf* : moth
polímero *nm* : polymer
polinesio, -sia *adj & n* : Polynesian
polinizar {21} *vt* : to pollinate — **polinización** *nf*
polio *nf* : polio
poliomielitis *nf* : poliomyelitis, polio
polisón *nm, pl* **-sones** : bustle (on clothing)
politeísmo *nm* : polytheism — **politeísta** *adj & nmf*
política *nf* **1** : politics **2** : policy ⟨política interior/exterior : domestic/foreign policy⟩
políticamente *adv* : politically
político[1]**, -ca** *adj* **1** : political **2** : tactful, politic **3** : by marriage ⟨padre político : father-in-law⟩
político[2]**, -ca** *n* : politician
póliza *nf* : policy ⟨póliza de seguros : insurance policy⟩
polizón *nm, pl* **-zones** : stowaway ⟨viajar de polizón : to stow away⟩
polka *nf* : polka
polla *nf* **1** APUESTA : bet **2** *Chile* LOTERÍA : lottery
pollera *nf* **1** : chicken coop **2** : skirt
pollero, -ra *n* **1** : poultry farmer **2** : poultry farm **3** *Mex fam* COYOTE : smuggler of illegal immigrants
pollito, -ta *n* : chick, young bird, fledgling
pollo, -lla *n* **1** : chicken **2** POLLITO : chick **3** JOVEN : young man *m*, young lady *f*
polluelo *nm* → **pollito**
polo *nm* **1** : pole ⟨el Polo Norte : the North Pole⟩ ⟨polo negativo : negative pole⟩ **2** : polo (sport) **3** : polo shirt **4** : focal point, center **5** **polo opuesto** : exact opposite
pololo, -la *n Chile fam* : boyfriend *m*, girlfriend *f*
poltrona *nf* : armchair, easy chair
polución *nf, pl* **-ciones** CONTAMINACIÓN : pollution
polvareda *nf* **1** : cloud of dust **2** : uproar, fuss
polvera *nf* : compact (for face powder)
polvo *nm* **1** : dust ⟨quitar/limpiar el polvo : to dust⟩ **2** : powder ⟨polvo(s) de hornear : baking powder⟩ **3** **polvos**

nmpl : face powder **4** **en ~** : powdered, ground **5** **estar hecho polvo** *fam* : to be worn out **6** **hacer polvo** *fam* : to crush, to shatter
pólvora *nf* **1** : gunpowder **2** : fireworks *pl*
polvoriento, -ta *adj* : dusty, powdery
polvorín *nm, pl* **-rines** : magazine, ammunition dump
pomada *nf* : ointment, cream
pomelo *nm* : grapefruit
pómez *nf or* **piedra pómez** : pumice
pomo *nm* **1** : pommel (on a sword) **2** : knob, handle **3** : perfume bottle
pompa *nf* **1** : bubble **2** : pomp, splendor **3** **pompas fúnebres** : funeral
pompón *nm, pl* **pompones** BORLA : pompom
pomposidad *nf* **1** : pomp, splendor **2** : pomposity, ostentation
pomposo, -sa *adj* : pompous — **pomposamente** *adv*
pómulo *nm* : cheekbone
pon → **poner**
ponchadura *nf Mex* : puncture, flat (tire)
ponchar *vt* **1** *Car, CA, Col, Ven* : to strike out (in baseball) **2** *Mex* : to puncture — **poncharse** *vr* **1** *Car, CA, Col, Ven* : to strike out (in baseball) **2** *Mex* : to blow out (of a tire)
ponche *nm* **1** : punch (drink) **2** **ponche de huevo** : eggnog
poncho *nm* : poncho
ponderación *nf, pl* **-ciones** **1** : consideration, deliberation **2** : high praise
ponderar *vt* **1** : to weigh, to consider **2** : to speak highly of
pondrá, etc. → **poner**
ponedora *nf* : layer (bird)
ponencia *nf* **1** DISCURSO : paper, presentation, address **2** INFORME : report
ponente *nmf* : speaker, presenter
poner {60} *vt* **1** COLOCAR : to put, to place ⟨pon el libro en la mesa : put the book on the table⟩ **2** AGREGAR, AÑADIR : to put in, to add (an ingredient, etc.) **3** : to put on (clothes) ⟨le puse el suéter : I put her sweater on (her)⟩ **4** CONTRIBUIR : to contribute **5** ESCRIBIR : to put in writing ⟨no le puso su nombre : he didn't put his name on it⟩ **6** : to give (a task, etc.), to impose (a fine) **7** : to prepare, to arrange ⟨poner la mesa : to set the table⟩ **8** : to name ⟨le pusimos Ana : we called her Ana⟩ **9** ESTABLECER : to set up, to establish ⟨puso un restaurante : he opened up a restaurant⟩ **10** INSTALAR : to install, to put in **11** (*with an adjective or adverb*) : to make ⟨me pone nervioso : it makes me nervous⟩ ⟨siempre lo pones de mal humor : you always put him in a bad mood⟩ **12** : to turn on, to switch on **13** : to set (an alarm, etc.) ⟨pon la música más alta/fuerte : turn up the music⟩ **14** SUPONER : to suppose ⟨pongamos que no viene : supposing he doesn't come⟩ **15** : to give (an example) **16** : to raise (objections), to create (problems) etc.) **17** : to lay (eggs) **18** **~ a** : to start (some-

one doing something) ⟨lo puse a trabajar : I put him to work⟩ **19 ~ de** : to place as ⟨la pusieron de directora : they made her director⟩ **20 ~ en** : to put in (a state or condition) ⟨poner en duda : to call into question⟩ ⟨lo puso en peligro : he put him in danger⟩ — *vi* **1** : to contribute **2** : to lay eggs — **ponerse** *vr* **1** : to move (into a position) ⟨ponerse de pie : to stand up⟩ **2** : to put on, to wear **3** : to become, to turn ⟨se puso colorado : he turned red⟩ **4** : to start ⟨me puse a llorar : I started to cry⟩ **5** : to set (of the sun or moon)

poni *or* **poney** *nm* : pony

ponga, etc. → poner

poniente *nm* **1** OCCIDENTE : west **2** : west wind

ponqué *nm Col, Ven* : cake

pontificar {72} *vi* : to pontificate

pontífice *nm* : pontiff, pope

pontón *nm, pl* **pontones** : pontoon

ponzoña *nf* VENENO : poison — **ponzoñoso, -sa** *adj*

pop ['pop] *adj & nm* : pop (music)

popa *nf* **1** : stern **2 a ~** : astern, abaft, aft

popelín *nm, pl* **-lines** : poplin

popelina *nf* : poplin

popó *nm fam* **1** : poop **2 hacer popó** : to poop, to go poop

popote *nm Mex* : straw, drinking straw

populachero, -ra *adj* : common, popular, vulgar

populacho *nm* : rabble, masses *pl*

popular *adj* **1** : popular **2** : traditional **3** : colloquial — **popularmente** *adv*

popularidad *nf* : popularity

popularizar {21} *vt* : to popularize — **popularizarse** *vr*

populista *adj & nmf* : populist — **populismo** *nm*

populoso, -sa *adj* : populous

popurrí *nm* : potpourri

por *prep* **1** : for, during ⟨se quedaron allí por la semana : they stayed there for the week⟩ ⟨por el momento : for now, at the moment⟩ **2** : around, during ⟨por noviembre empieza a nevar : around November it starts to snow⟩ ⟨por la mañana : in the morning⟩ ⟨por la noche : at night⟩ **3** : around (a place) ⟨debe estar por allí : it must be over there⟩ ⟨por todas partes : everywhere⟩ **4** : by, through, along ⟨por la puerta : through the door⟩ ⟨pasamos por el centro : we went through the downtown⟩ ⟨pasé por tu casa : I stopped by your house⟩ ⟨por la costa : along the coast⟩ ⟨caminando por la calle : walking down the street⟩ **5** : for, for the sake of ⟨lo hizo por su madre : he did it for his mother⟩ ⟨¡por Dios! : for heaven's sake!⟩ **6** : because of, on account of ⟨llegué tarde por el tráfico : I arrived late because of the traffic⟩ ⟨dejar por imposible : to give up as impossible⟩ ⟨perdón por la demora : sorry for the delay⟩ **7** : per ⟨60 millas por hora : 60 miles per hour⟩ ⟨por docena : by the dozen⟩ **8** : for, in ex-

change for, instead of ⟨su hermana habló por él : his sister spoke on his behalf⟩ ⟨lo vendió por cien dólares : he sold it for a hundred dollars⟩ **9** : by means of ⟨hablar por teléfono : to talk on the phone⟩ ⟨por escrito : in writing⟩ ⟨por avión : by plane⟩ **10** : as for ⟨por mí : as far as I'm concerned⟩ **11** : times ⟨tres por dos son seis : three times two is six⟩ **12** SEGÚN : from, according to ⟨por lo que dices : judging from what you're telling me⟩ **13** : as, for ⟨por ejemplo : for example⟩ **14** : by ⟨hecho por mi abuela : made by my grandmother⟩ ⟨por correo : by mail⟩ **15** : for, in order to ⟨lucha por ganar su respeto : he struggles to win her respect⟩ **16 estar por** : to be about to **17 por ciento** : percent **18 por favor** : please **19 por lo tanto** : therefore, consequently **20 ¿por qué?** : why? **21 por que →** porque **22 por . . . que** : no matter how ⟨por mucho que intente : no matter how hard I try⟩ **23 por si** *or* **por si acaso** : just in case

porcelana *nf* : china, porcelain

porcentaje *nm* : percentage

porche *nm* : porch

porción *nf, pl* **porciones 1** : portion **2** PARTE : part, share **3** RACIÓN : serving, helping

pordiosear *vi* MENDIGAR : beg

pordiosero, -ra *n* MENDIGO : beggar

porfiado, -da *adj* OBSTINADO, TERCO : obstinate, stubborn — **porfiadamente** *adv*

porfiar {85} *vi* **1** : to insist, to persist

pormenor *nm* DETALLE : detail

pormenorizar {21} *vi* : to go into detail — *vt* : to tell in detail

pornografía *nf* : pornography

pornográfico, -ca *adj* : pornographic

poro *nm* : pore

poroso, -sa *adj* : porous — **porosidad** *nf*

poroto *nm Arg, Chile, Uru* : bean

porque *conj* **1** : because **2** *or* **por que** : in order that

porqué *nm* : reason, cause ⟨no explicó el porqué : he didn't explain the reason⟩

porquería *nf* **1** SUCIEDAD : dirt, filth **2** : nastiness, vulgarity **3** : worthless thing, trifle **4** : junk food

porra *nf* **1** : nightstick, club **2** *Mex* : fans *pl* **3** *Mex* : cheer, yell ⟨los aficionados le echaban porras : the fans cheered him on⟩ **4 mandar a alguien a la porra** : to tell someone to go to hell

porrazo *nm* **1** : blow, whack **2 de golpe y porrazo** : suddenly

porrista *nmf* **1** : cheerleader **2** : fan, supporter

porro *nm fam* : joint *fam*, marijuana cigarette

portaaviones *nms & pl* : aircraft carrier

portada *nf* **1** : title page **2** : cover **3** : facade, front

portador, -dora *n* : carrier, bearer ⟨cheque al portador : check payable to bearer⟩

portaequipajes *nms & pl* **1** : luggage rack, roof rack **2** : trunk (of a car)

portafolio *or* **portafolios** *nm, pl* **-lios** 1 MALETÍN : briefcase 2 : portfolio (of investments)

portal *nm* 1 : portal, doorway 2 VESTÍBULO : vestibule, hall 3 : portal (on the web)

portar *vt* 1 : to carry, to bear 2 : to wear — **portarse** *vr* CONDUCIRSE : to behave ⟨pórtate bien : behave yourself⟩ ⟨se portó mal con ella : he treated her badly⟩

portátil[1] *adj* : portable

portátil[2] *nmf* : laptop computer

portaviandas *nms & pl* : lunch box

portaviones *nm* → **portaaviones**

portavoz *nmf, pl* **-voces** : spokesperson, spokesman *m*, spokeswoman *f*

portazo *nm* : slam ⟨dar un portazo : to slam the door⟩

porte *nm* 1 ASPECTO : bearing, demeanor 2 TRANSPORTE : transport, carrying ⟨porte pagado : postage paid⟩ 3 : size ⟨de gran porte : large-sized⟩

portento *nm* MARAVILLA : marvel, wonder

portentoso, -sa *adj* MARAVILLOSO : marvelous, wonderful

porteño, -ña *adj* : of or from Buenos Aires

portería *nf* 1 ARCO : goal, goalposts *pl* 2 : superintendent's office

portero, -ra *n* 1 ARQUERO : goalkeeper, goalie 2 : doorman *m* (at a hotel, etc.), bouncer (at a nightclub, etc.) 3 : janitor, superintendent

pórtico *nm* : portico

portilla *nf* : porthole

portón *nm, pl* **portones** 1 : main door 2 : gate

portorriqueño, -ña → **puertorriqueño**

portugués[1], **-guesa** *adj & n, mpl* **-gueses** : Portuguese

portugués[2] *nm* : Portuguese (language)

porvenir *nm* FUTURO : future

pos *adv* **en pos de** : in pursuit of

pos- *or* **post-** *pref* : post-

posada *nf* 1 : inn 2 *Mex* : Advent celebration

posaderas *nfpl* : bottom, backside

posadero, -ra *n* : innkeeper

posar *vi* : to pose — *vt* : to place, to lay — **posarse** *vr* 1 : to land, to light, to perch 2 : to settle, to rest

posavasos *nms & pl* : coaster (for drinks)

posdata → **postdata**

pose *nf* : pose

poseedor, -dora *n* : possessor, holder

poseer {20} *vt* : to possess, to hold, to have

poseído, -da *adj* : possessed

posesión *nf, pl* **-siones** : possession

posesionarse *vr* **~ de** : to take possession of, to take over

posesivo[1], **-va** *adj* : possessive

posesivo[2] *nm* : possessive case

posfechar *vt* : to postdate

posguerra *nf* : postwar period

posibilidad *nf* 1 : possibility ⟨existe la posibilidad de que . . . : the possibility exists that . . .⟩ 2 **posibilidades** *nfpl* : means, income

posibilitar *vt* : to make possible, to permit

posible *adj* 1 : possible ⟨es posible que . . . : it's possible that . . .⟩ 2 **a/de ser posible** : if possible 3 **dentro de lo posible** *or* **en lo posible** : as far as possible 4 **hacer todo lo posible** : to do everything possible 5 **lo mejor/antes (etc.) posible** : as well/soon (etc.) as possible 6 **si es posible** : if possible — **posiblemente** *adv*

posición *nf, pl* **-ciones** 1 : position, place ⟨en posición vertical : in an upright position⟩ 2 : status, standing 3 : attitude, stance

posicionar *vt* 1 : to position, to place 2 : to establish — **posicionarse** *vr*

positivo[1], **-va** *adj* : positive — **positivamente** *adv*

positivo[2] *nm* : print (in photography)

posmoderno, -na *adj* : postmodern

poso *nm* 1 : sediment, dregs *pl* 2 : grounds *pl* (of coffee)

posoperatorio, -ria *adj* : postoperative

posparto *adj* : postnatal ⟨depresión posparto : postpartum depression⟩

posponer {60} *vt* 1 : to postpone 2 : to put behind, to subordinate

pospuso, etc. → **posponer**

post *nm, pl* **post** *or* **posts** : post (on social media)

posta *nf* 1 : relay race 2 : post, station 3 *Chile* : emergency medical center

postal[1] *adj* : postal

postal[2] *nf* : postcard

postdata *nf* : postscript

poste *nm* 1 : post, pole ⟨poste de teléfonos : telephone pole⟩ 2 : goalpost (in sports)

postear *vt fam* : to post (on social media)

posteo *nm* → **post**

póster *or* **poster** *nm, pl* **pósters** *or* **posters** : poster, placard

postergación *nf, pl* **-ciones** : postponement, deferring

postergar {52} *vt* 1 : to delay, to postpone 2 : to pass over (an employee)

posteridad *nf* : posterity

posterior *adj* 1 ULTERIOR : later, subsequent 2 TRASERO : back, rear

posterioridad *nf* **con ~** : subsequently, later

posteriormente *adv* : subsequently

postgrado *nm* : graduate course

postgraduado, -da *n* : graduate student, postgraduate

postguerra → **posguerra**

postigo *nm* 1 CONTRAVENTANA : shutter 2 : small door, wicket gate

postilla *nf* : scab

Post–it *marca registrada, m* — used for a slip of paper with a sticky edge

postizo, -za *adj* : artificial, false ⟨dentadura postiza : dentures⟩

postnatal *adj* : postnatal

postor, -tora *n* : bidder ⟨mejor postor : highest bidder⟩

postración *nf, pl* **-ciones** 1 : prostration 2 ABATIMIENTO : depression

postrado, -da *adj* 1 : prostrate 2 **postrado en cama** : bedridden

potranco, -ca n → **potro**[1]

postrar *vt* DEBILITAR : to debilitate, to weaken — **postrarse** *vr* : to prostrate oneself

postre[1] *nm* : dessert ⟨de postre comimos helado : we had ice cream for dessert⟩

postre[2] *nf* **a la postre** : in the end

postrero, -ra *adj* (*postrer before masculine singular nouns*) ÚLTIMO : last

postulación *nf, pl* **-ciones** 1 : collection 2 : nomination (of a candidate)

postulado *nm* : postulate, assumption

postulante, -ta *n* : candidate, applicant

postular *vt* 1 : to postulate 2 : to nominate 3 : to propose — **postularse** *vr* : to run, to be a candidate

póstumo, -ma *adj* : posthumous — **póstumamente** *adv*

postura *nf* 1 : posture, position (of the body) 2 ACTITUD, POSICIÓN : position, stance

potable *adj* : drinkable, potable ⟨agua potable : (safe) drinking water⟩

potaje *nm* : thick vegetable soup

potasa *nf* : potash

potasio *nm* : potassium

pote *nm* 1 OLLA : pot 2 : jar, container

potencia *nf* 1 : power ⟨potencias extranjeras : foreign powers⟩ ⟨elevado a la tercera potencia : raised to the third power⟩ 2 : capacity, potency 3 **en ~** : in the making ⟨un líder en potencia : a leader in the making⟩

potencial *adj & nm* : potential

potenciar *vt* : to promote, to foster

potenciómetro *nm* : dimmer, dimmer switch

potentado, -da *n* 1 SOBERANO : sovereign, ruler 2 MAGNATE : tycoon, magnate

potente *adj* 1 : powerful, strong 2 : potent, virile

potestad *nf* 1 AUTORIDAD : authority, jurisdiction 2 **patria potestad** : custody, guardianship

potrero *nm* 1 : field, pasture 2 : cattle ranch

potro[1]**, -tra** *n* : colt *m*, filly *f*

potro[2] *nm* 1 : rack (for torture) 2 : horse (in gymnastics)

pozo *nm* 1 : well ⟨pozo de petróleo, pozo petrolero : oil well⟩ 2 : deep pool (in a river) 3 : mine shaft 4 *Arg, Par, Uru* : pothole 5 **pozo séptico** : cesspool

pozole *nm Mex* : spicy stew made with pork and hominy

práctica *nf* 1 : practice, experience 2 : practice ⟨la práctica de la medicina : the practice of medicine⟩ 3 : practice ⟨en la práctica : in practice⟩ ⟨poner en práctica : to put into practice⟩ 4 **prácticas** *nfpl* : practice, training

practicable *adj* : practicable, feasible

prácticamente *adv* : practically

practicante[1] *adj* : practicing ⟨católicos practicantes : practicing Catholics⟩

practicante[2] *nmf* : practitioner

practicar {72} *vt* 1 : to practice 2 : to perform, to carry out 3 : to exercise (a

profession), to play (a sport) — *vi* : to practice

práctico, -ca *adj* : practical ⟨a efectos prácticos : for all practical purposes⟩

pradera *nf* : grassland, prairie

prado *nm* 1 CAMPO : field, meadow 2 : park

pragmático, -ca *adj* : pragmatic — **pragmáticamente** *adv*

pragmatismo *nm* : pragmatism

pre- *pref* : pre-

preadolescente *nmf* : preteen

preámbulo *nm* 1 INTRODUCCIÓN : preamble, introduction 2 RODEO : evasion ⟨gastar preámbulos : to beat around the bush⟩

prebélico, -ca *adj* : antebellum

prebenda *nf* : privilege

precalentar {55} *vt* : to preheat

precariedad *nf* : precariousness

precario, -ria *adj* : precarious — **precariamente** *adv*

precaución *nf, pl* **-ciones** 1 : precaution ⟨medidas de precaución : precautionary measures⟩ 2 PRUDENCIA : caution, care ⟨con precaución : cautiously⟩

precautorio, -ria *adj* : precautionary

precaver *vt* PREVENIR : to prevent, to guard against — **precaverse** *vr* PREVENIRSE : to take precautions, to be on guard

precavido, -da *adj* CAUTELOSO : cautious, prudent

precedencia *nf* : precedence, priority

precedente[1] *adj* : preceding, previous

precedente[2] *nm* : precedent

preceder *v* : to precede

precepto *nm* : rule, precept

preciado, -da *adj* : esteemed, prized, valuable

preciarse *vr* 1 JACTARSE : to boast, to brag 2 **~ de** : to pride oneself on

precintar *vt* 1 : to seal 2 : to shut down (a business), to seal off (an area)

precinto *nm* : seal

precio *nm* 1 : price ⟨¿qué precio tiene? : how much is it?⟩ ⟨no tener precio : to be priceless⟩ 2 : cost, sacrifice ⟨a cualquier precio : at any cost⟩ 3 **precio de salida** : starting price 4 **precio de venta** : retail price

preciosidad *nf* : beautiful thing ⟨este vestido es una preciosidad : this dress is lovely⟩

precioso, -sa *adj* 1 HERMOSO : beautiful, exquisite 2 VALIOSO : precious, valuable

precipicio *nm* 1 : precipice 2 RUINA : ruin

precipitación *nf, pl* **-ciones** 1 PRISA : haste, hurry, rush 2 : precipitation, rain, snow

precipitado, -da *adj* 1 : hasty, sudden 2 : rash — **precipitadamente** *adv*

precipitar *vt* 1 APRESURAR : to hasten, to speed up 2 ARROJAR : to hurl, to throw — **precipitarse** *vr* 1 APRESURARSE : to rush 2 : to act rashly ⟨tal vez me precipito : perhaps I'm being too hasty⟩ 3 ARROJARSE : to throw oneself

precisamente *adv* JUSTAMENTE : precisely, exactly
precisar *vt* **1** : to specify, to determine exactly **2** NECESITAR : to need, to require — *vi* : to be necessary
precisión *nf, pl* **-siones 1** EXACTITUD : precision, accuracy **2** CLARIDAD : clarity (of style, etc.) **3** NECESIDAD : necessity ⟨tener precisión de : to have need of⟩
preciso, -sa *adj* **1** EXACTO : precise **2** : very, exact ⟨en ese preciso instante : at that very instant⟩ **3** NECESARIO : necessary ⟨es preciso que . . . : it is necessary that . . .⟩
precocidad *nf* : precocity
precocinar *vt* : to precook
preconcebido, -da *adj* : preconceived
precondición *nf, pl* **-ciones** : precondition
preconizar {21} *vt* **1** : to recommend, to advocate **2** : to extol
precoz *adj, pl* **precoces 1** : precocious **2** : early, premature — **precozmente** *adv*
precursor, -sora *n* : forerunner, precursor
predecesor, -sora *n* ANTECESOR : predecessor
predecir {11} *vt* : to foretell, to predict
predestinado, -da *adj* : predestined, fated
predestinar *vt* : to predestine — **predestinación** *nf*
predeterminar *vt* : to predetermine
prédica *nf* SERMÓN : sermon
predicado *nm* : predicate
predicador, -dora *n* : preacher
predicar {72} *v* : to preach
predicción *nf, pl* **-ciones 1** : prediction **2** PRONÓSTICO : forecast ⟨predicción del tiempo : weather forecast⟩
prediga, predijo etc. → predecir
predilección *nf, pl* **-ciones** : predilection, preference
predilecto, -ta *adj* : favorite
predio *nm* : property, piece of land
predisponer {60} *vt* **1** : to predispose, to incline **2** : to prejudice, to bias
predisposición *nf, pl* **-ciones 1** : predisposition, tendency **2** : prejudice, bias
predispuesto, -ta *adj* ~ **a** : prone to
predominante *adj* : predominant — **predominantemente** *adv*
predominar *vi* PREVALECER : to predominate, to prevail
predominio *nm* : predominance, prevalence
preeminente *adj* : preeminent — **preeminencia** *nf*
preescolar *adj & nm* : preschool
preestreno *nm* : preview
prefabricado, -da *adj* : prefabricated
prefacio *nm* : preface
prefecto *nm* : prefect
preferencia *nf* **1** : preference **2** PRIORIDAD : priority **3** : right-of-way (of traffic) **4 de** ~ : preferably
preferencial *adj* : preferential
preferente *adj* : preferential, special ⟨trato preferente : special treatment⟩

preferentemente *adv* : preferably
preferible *adj* : preferable ⟨es preferible que . . . : it's better that . . .⟩ ⟨ser preferible a : to be preferable to⟩
preferido, -da *adj & n* : favorite
preferir {76} *vt* : to prefer ⟨prefiero ir : I'd rather go⟩ ⟨prefiero que no vayas : I'd rather (that) you didn't go⟩ ⟨prefiero éste a ése : I prefer this one to/over that one⟩
prefigurar *vt* : foreshadow, prefigure
prefijo *nm* **1** : prefix (in linguistics) **2** *Spain* : area code
pregonar *vt* **1** : to proclaim, to announce **2** : to hawk (merchandise) **3** : to extol **4** : to reveal, to disclose
pregrabado, -da *adj* : prerecorded
pregunta *nf* **1** : question **2 hacer una pregunta** : to ask a question
preguntar *vt* : to ask, to question — *vi* : to ask, to inquire ⟨preguntar por : to ask about⟩ — **preguntarse** *vr* : to wonder
preguntón, -tona *adj, mpl* **-tones** : inquisitive
prehistórico, -ca *adj* : prehistoric
prejuiciado, -da *adj* : prejudiced
prejuicio *nm* : prejudice ⟨tener prejuicios contra : to be prejudiced against⟩
prejuzgar {52} *vt* : to prejudge
prelado *nm* : prelate
preliminar *adj & nm* : preliminary
preludio *nm* : prelude
prematrimonial *adj* : premarital
prematuro, -ra *adj* : premature
premeditación *nf, pl* **-ciones** : premeditation
premeditar *vt* : to premeditate, to plan
premenstrual *adj* : premenstrual
premiado¹, -da *adj* : winning, prizewinning
premiado², -da *n* : prizewinner
premiar *vt* **1** : to award a prize to **2** : to reward
premier *nmf* : premier, prime minister
premio *nm* **1** : prize ⟨premio gordo : grand prize, jackpot⟩ ⟨dar/ganar un premio : to give/win a prize⟩ **2** : reward **3** : premium
premisa *nf* : premise, basis
premolar *nm* : bicuspid (tooth)
premonición *nf, pl* **-ciones** : premonition
premura *nf* : haste, urgency
prenatal *adj* : prenatal
prenda *nf* **1** : piece of clothing **2** : security, pledge **3** : forfeit (in a game)
prendar *vt* **1** : to charm, to captivate **2** : to pawn, to pledge — **prendarse** *vr* ~ **de** : to fall in love with
prendedor *nm* : brooch, pin
prender *vt* **1** SUJETAR : to pin, to fasten **2** APRESAR : to catch, to apprehend **3** : to light (a cigarette, a match) **4** : to turn on ⟨prende la luz : turn on the light⟩ **5 prender fuego a** : to set fire to — *vi* **1** : to take root **2** : to catch fire **3** : to catch on — **prenderse** *vr* : to catch fire
prensa *nf* **1** : printing press **2** : press ⟨conferencia de prensa : press conference⟩ ⟨la prensa : the press, the newspapers⟩

prensar *vt* : to press
prensil *adj* : prehensile
preñado, -da *adj* **1** : pregnant **2** ~ **de** : filled with
preñar *vt* INEMBARAZAR : to make pregnant
preñez *nf, pl* **preñeces** : pregnancy
preocupación *nf, pl* **-ciones** INQUIETUD : worry, concern
preocupado, -da *adj* : worried ⟨preocupado por : worried about⟩
preocupante *adj* : worrisome
preocupar *vt* INQUIETAR : to worry, to concern ⟨eso me preocupa : that worries me⟩ — **preocuparse** *vr* **1** APURARSE : to worry, to be concerned ⟨preocuparse por : to worry about⟩ **2** ~ **de** : to take care of (something) ⟨preocuparse de que . . . : to make sure that . . .⟩
preparación *nf, pl* **-ciones** **1** : preparation, readiness **2** : education, training **3** : (medicinal) preparation
preparado¹, -da *adj* **1** : ready, prepared **2** : trained
preparado² *nm* : preparation, mixture
preparar *vt* **1** : to prepare ⟨preparé el almuerzo : I made lunch, I got lunch ready⟩ ⟨preparar un examen : to prepare for an exam⟩ **2** : to teach, to train, to coach — **prepararse** *vr* **1** : to get ready, to prepare ⟨prepararse para algo : to get ready for something⟩ ⟨se prepara para salir : she's getting ready to leave⟩
preparativos *nmpl* : preparations
preparatoria *nf Mex* : high school
preparatorio, -ria *adj* : preparatory
preponderante *adj* : preponderant, predominant — **preponderancia** *nf* — **preponderantemente** *adv*
preposición *nf, pl* **-ciones** : preposition — **preposicional** *adj*
prepotente *adj* : arrogant, domineering, overbearing — **prepotencia** *nf*
prerrogativa *nf* : prerogative, privilege
presa *nf* **1** : capture, seizure ⟨hacer presa de : to seize⟩ **2** : catch, prey ⟨presa de : prey to, seized with⟩ **3** : claw, fang **4** DIQUE : dam **5** : morsel, piece (of food)
presagiar *vt* : to presage, to portend
presagio *nm* : omen, portent
presbiterio *nm* : sanctuary (of a church)
prescindible *adj* : expendable, dispensable
prescindir *vi* ~ **de 1** : to do without, to dispense with **2** DESATENDER : to ignore, to disregard **3** OMITIR : to omit, to skip
prescribir {33} *vt* : to prescribe
prescripción *nf, pl* **-ciones** : prescription
prescrito *pp* → **prescribir**
presencia *nf* **1** : presence ⟨en presencia de : in the presence of⟩ **2** ASPECTO : appearance
presenciar *vt* **1** : to witness **2** : to be present at, to attend
presentable *adj* : presentable
presentación *nf, pl* **-ciones** **1** : presentation **2** : introduction **3** : appearance
presentador, -dora *n* : host (of a show), anchor (of a newscast)

presentar *vt* **1** MOSTRAR : to present, to show **2** : to have, to show (a symptom) **3** : to offer, to give (an excuse, etc.) **4** : to submit (a document), to file (a complaint) **5** : to launch (a product) **6** : to introduce (a person) **7** : to host (a show), to anchor (a newscast) — **presentarse** *vr* **1** : to show up, to appear ⟨preséntese en la oficina central : report to the central office⟩ **2** SURGIR : to arise, to come up **3** : to introduce oneself **4** ~ **a** : to enter (a competition), to run in (an election)
presente¹ *adj* **1** : present, in attendance **2** : present, current ⟨del presente mes/año : of the current month/year⟩ **3 tener presente** : to keep in mind
presente² *nf* **por la presente** : hereby (in a letter)
presente³ *nm* : present (time, tense)
presente⁴ *nmf* : one present ⟨entre los presentes se encontraban . . . : those present included . . .⟩
presentimiento *nm* : premonition, hunch, feeling
presentir {76} *vt* : to sense, to intuit ⟨presentía lo que iba a pasar : he sensed what was going to happen⟩
preservación *nf, pl* **-ciones** : preservation
preservar *vt* **1** : to preserve **2** : to protect
preservativo *nm* CONDÓN : condom
presidencia *nf* **1** : presidency **2** : chairmanship
presidencial *adj* : presidential
presidente¹ *nmf* → **presidente²**
presidente², -ta *n* **1** : president **2** : chair, chairperson (of a group or event) **3** : presiding judge
presidiario, -ria *n* : convict, prisoner
presidio *nm* : prison, penitentiary
presidir *vt* **1** MODERAR : to preside over, to chair **2** : to dominate, to rule over
presilla *nf* : eye, loop, fastener
presión *nf, pl* **presiones** **1** : pressure **2 presión arterial** : blood pressure
presionar *vt* **1** : to pressure **2** : to press, to push — *vi* : to put on the pressure
preso¹, -sa *adj* **1** : imprisoned ⟨estar preso : to be imprisoned⟩ **2 llevarse/tomar preso a** : to imprison, to take prisoner
preso², -sa *n* : prisoner
prestación *nf, pl* **-ciones** **1** : providing, provision **2** : benefit ⟨prestaciones sociales : welfare, government assistance⟩ **3** : feature
prestado, -da *adj* **1** : borrowed, on loan **2 pedir prestado** : to borrow, to ask to borrow **3 tomar prestado** : to borrow
prestamista *nmf* : moneylender, pawnbroker
préstamo *nm* **1** : loan **2** : lending, borrowing **3** BARBARISMO : loanword, borrowing
prestar *vt* **1** : to lend ⟨¿me prestas el paraguas? : can I borrow your umbrella?⟩ **2** : to render (a service), to give (aid) **3 prestar atención** : to pay atten-

tion **4 prestar declaración** : to testify
5 prestar juramento : to take an oath —
prestarse vr ~ **a/para** 1 : to lend oneself to ⟨se presta a confusiones : it lends itself to confusion⟩ 2 : to agree to 3 : to participate in
prestatario, -ria n : borrower
presteza nf : promptness, speed
prestidigitación nf, pl **-ciones** : sleight of hand
prestidigitador, -dora n : conjurer, magician
prestigio nm : prestige — **prestigioso, -sa** adj
presto¹ adv : promptly, at once
presto², -ta adj 1 : quick, prompt 2 DISPUESTO, PREPARADO : ready
presumido, -da adj VANIDOSO : conceited, vain
presumir vt SUPONER : to presume, to suppose — vi 1 ALARDEAR : to boast, to show off 2 ~ **de** : to consider oneself ⟨presume de inteligente : he thinks he's intelligent⟩
presunción nf, pl **-ciones** 1 SUPOSICIÓN : presumption, supposition 2 VANIDAD : conceit, vanity
presunto, -ta adj : presumed, supposed, alleged — **presuntamente** adv
presuntuoso, -sa adj : conceited
presuponer {60} vt : to presuppose
presupuestal adj : budget, budgetary
presupuestar vi : to budget — vt : to budget for
presupuestario, -ria adj : budget, budgetary
presupuesto nm 1 : budget, estimate 2 : assumption, supposition
presurizar {21} vt : to pressurize
presuroso, -sa adj : hasty, quick
pretencioso, -sa adj : pretentious — **pretenciosamente** adv
pretender vt 1 INTENTAR : to attempt, to try ⟨pretendo estudiar : I'm trying to study⟩ 2 AFIRMAR : to claim ⟨pretende ser pobre : he claims he's poor⟩ 3 : to seek, to aspire to ⟨¿qué pretendes tú? : what are you after?⟩ 4 CORTEJAR : to court 5 **pretender que** : to expect ⟨¿pretendes que lo crea? : do you expect me to believe you?⟩
pretendido, -da adj 1 SUPUESTO : supposed, so-called 2 FALSO : feigned, false
pretendiente¹ nmf 1 : candidate, applicant 2 : pretender, claimant (to a throne, etc.)
pretendiente² nm : suitor
pretensión nf, pl **-siones** 1 : intention, hope, plan 2 : claim (to a throne, etc.) 3 : pretension ⟨sin pretensiones : unpretentious⟩
pretérito nm : preterit, past (tense)
pretextar vt : to claim, to feign
pretexto nm EXCUSA : pretext, excuse
pretil nm : parapet, railing
prevalecer {53} vi : to prevail, to triumph
prevaleciente adj : prevailing, prevalent
prevalerse {84} vr ~ **de** : to avail oneself of, to take advantage of
prevención nf, pl **-ciones** 1 : prevention 2 : preparation, readiness 3 : precautionary measure 4 : prejudice, bias

prevenido, -da adj 1 PREPARADO : prepared, ready 2 ADVERTIDO : forewarned 3 CAUTELOSO : cautious
prevenir {87} vt 1 : to prevent 2 : to warn — **prevenirse** vr ~ **contra** or ~ **de** : to take precautions against
preventivo, -va adj : preventive, precautionary
prever {88} vt 1 ANTICIPAR : to foresee, to anticipate 2 PLANEAR : to plan
previo¹, -via adj 1 : previous, prior 2 PRELIMINAR : preliminary
previo², -via prep : after, upon ⟨previo pago : after paying, upon payment⟩
previsible adj : foreseeable
previsión nf, pl **-siones** 1 : foresight 2 : prediction, forecast 3 : precaution 4 **previsión social** : welfare
previsor, -sora adj : farsighted, prudent
prieto, -ta adj 1 : dark 2 Car, Mex : dark-skinned 3 : tight, compressed
prima nf 1 : premium 2 : bonus 3 → **primo**
primacía nf 1 : precedence, priority 2 : superiority, supremacy
primado nm : primate (bishop)
primario, -ria adj : primary
primate nm : primate
primavera nf 1 : spring (season) 2 PRÍMULA : primrose
primaveral adj : spring
primera nf 1 : first (gear) 2 : first class
primeramente adv : firstly, first of all
primero¹ adv 1 : first 2 : rather, sooner
primero², -ra adj (**primer** before masculine singular nouns) 1 : first ⟨el primer paso : the first step⟩ 2 : top, leading ⟨de primera clase : first-class⟩ 3 : main, basic ⟨nuestro primer objetivo : our main objective⟩ ⟨lo primero es no alarmarse : the most important thing is not to panic⟩ 4 **de primera** : first-rate
primero³, -ra n : first ⟨el primero de enero : (on) the first of January, (on) January first⟩ ⟨el primero en llegar : the first to arrive⟩ ⟨la primera de tres fases : the first of three stages⟩
primicia nf 1 : first fruits 2 : scoop, exclusive
primigenio, -nia adj : original, primary
primitivo, -va adj 1 : primitive 2 ORIGINAL : original
primo¹ adj 1 : prime (of a number) 2 : raw ⟨materia prima : raw material⟩
primo², -ma n 1 : cousin ⟨primo hermano : first cousin⟩ 2 Spain : sucker
primogénito, -ta adj & n : firstborn
primor nm 1 : skill, care 2 : beauty, elegance
primordial adj 1 : primordial 2 : basic, fundamental
primoroso, -sa adj 1 : exquisite, fine, delicate 2 : skillful
prímula nf : primrose
princesa nf : princess
principado nm : principality
principal¹ adj 1 : main, principal 2 : foremost, leading
principal² nm : capital, principal
principalmente adv : mainly, chiefly

príncipe *nm* : prince
principesco, -ca *adj* : princely
principiante[1] *adj* : beginning
principiante[2] *nmf* : beginner, novice
principiar *vt* EMPEZAR : to begin
principio *nm* 1 COMIENZO : beginning ⟨empieza por el principio : start at the beginning⟩ 2 : principle (theory, law) 3 : principle (moral belief) 4 al principio : at first 5 a principios de : at the beginning of ⟨a principios de agosto : at the beginning of August⟩ 6 en ~ : in principle 7 en un principio : at first 8 por ~ : on principle
pringar {52} *vt* 1 : to dip (in grease) 2 : to soil, to spatter (with grease) — pringarse *vr*
pringoso, -sa *adj* : greasy
pringue[1], etc. → pringar
pringue[2] *nmf* : grease, drippings *pl*
prior, priora *n* : prior *m*, prioress *f*
priorato *nm* : priory
prioridad *nf* : priority, precedence
prisa *nf* 1 : hurry, rush 2 a ~ *or* de ~ : quickly, fast 3 a toda prisa : as fast as possible 4 correr prisa : to be urgent 5 darse prisa : to hurry 6 tener prisa : to be in a hurry
prisión *nf, pl* prisiones 1 CÁRCEL : prison, jail 2 ENCARCELAMIENTO : imprisonment
prisionero, -ra *n* : prisoner
prisma *nm* : prism
prismáticos *nmpl* : binoculars
prístino, -na *adj* : pristine
privacidad *nf* : privacy
privación *nf, pl* -ciones 1 : deprivation ⟨privación de libertad : deprivation of liberty⟩ 2 : privation, want
privado, -da *adj* : private ⟨en privado : in private⟩ — privadamente *adv*
privar *vt* 1 DESPOJAR : to deprive ⟨privar a alguien de algo : to deprive someone of something⟩ 2 : to stun, to knock out — privarse *vr* : to deprive oneself
privativo, -va *adj* : exclusive, particular
privatizar {21} *vt* : to privatize
privilegiado, -da *adj* 1 : privileged 2 EXCEPCIONAL : exceptional
privilegiar *vt* : to grant a privilege to, to favor
privilegio *nm* : privilege
pro[1] *nm* 1 : pro, advantage ⟨los pros y contras : the pros and cons⟩ 2 en pro de : for, in favor of
pro[2] *prep* : for, in favor of ⟨grupos pro derechos humanos : groups supporting human rights⟩
pro- *pref* : pro-
proa *nf* : bow, prow
probabilidad *nf* : probability ⟨con toda probabilidad : in all likelihood⟩
probable *adj* : probable, likely ⟨es probable que pierdan : it's likely that they'll lose⟩
probablemente *adv* : probably
probador[1] *nm* : fitting room, dressing room
probador[2], -dora *n* : tester
probar {19} *vt* 1 : to demonstrate, to prove 2 : to test, to try out 3 : to try on

(clothing) 4 : to taste, to sample — *vi* : to try ⟨probar a hacer algo : to try doing something⟩ — probarse *vr* : to try on (clothing)
probeta *nf* : test tube
probidad *nf* : probity
problema *nm* : problem ⟨resolver un problema : to solve a problem⟩
problemática *nf* : set of problems ⟨la problemática que debemos enfrentar : the problems we must face⟩
probóscide *nf* : proboscis
problemático, -ca *adj* : problematic
procaz *adj, pl* procaces 1 : insolent, impudent 2 : indecent
procedencia *nf* : origin, source
procedente *adj* 1 : proper, fitting 2 ~ de : coming from
proceder *vi* 1 AVANZAR : to proceed 2 : to act, to behave 3 : to be appropriate, to be fitting 4 ~ a : to proceed to 5 ~ de : to originate from, to come from
procedimiento *nm* 1 : procedure, process 2 : proceedings *pl* (in law)
prócer *nmf* : eminent person, leader
procesado, -da *n* : accused, defendant
procesador *nm* : processor ⟨procesador de textos : word processor⟩
procesamiento *nm* : processing ⟨procesamiento de datos : data processing⟩
procesar *vt* 1 : to prosecute, to try 2 : to process
procesión *nf, pl* -siones : procession
proceso *nm* 1 : process 2 : trial, proceedings *pl* 3 → procesamiento
proclama *nf* : proclamation
proclamación *nf, pl* -ciones : proclamation
proclamar *vt* : to proclaim — proclamarse *vr*
proclive *adj* ~ a : inclined to, prone to
proclividad *nf* : proclivity, inclination
procrear *vi* : to procreate — procreación *nf*
procurador, -dora *n* ABOGADO : attorney
procurar *vt* 1 INTENTAR : to try, to endeavor ⟨procura llegar temprano : try to arrive early⟩ ⟨procura que no se enteren : make sure they don't find out⟩ 2 CONSEGUIR : to obtain, to procure
prodigar {52} *vt* : to lavish, to be generous with
prodigio *nm* : wonder, marvel
prodigioso, -sa *adj* : prodigious, marvelous
pródigo[1], -ga *adj* 1 : generous, lavish 2 : wasteful, prodigal
pródigo[2], -ga *n* : spendthrift, prodigal
producción *nf, pl* -ciones 1 : production (action or quantity) 2 : production (in cinema, etc.) 3 producción en serie : mass production
producir {61} *vt* 1 : to produce, to make, to manufacture 2 : to cause, to bring about 3 : to bear (interest) — producirse *vr* : to take place, to occur
productividad *nf* : productivity
productivo, -va *adj* 1 : productive 2 LUCRATIVO : profitable
producto *nm* : product ⟨producto alimenticio : foodstuff⟩ ⟨producto interno

bruto : gross domestic product⟩ 2 : proceeds *pl*, yield

productor¹, -tora *adj* : producing

productor², -tora *n* : producer

productora *nf* : production company

proeza *nf* HAZAÑA : feat, exploit

profanar *vt* : to profane, to desecrate — **profanación** *nf*

profano¹, -na *adj* **1** : profane **2** : worldly, secular, lay

profano², -na *n* **1** : layman *mf*, layperson *mf* **2** LAICO : layman *m*, laywoman *f*, layperson *mf* (in religion)

profecía *nf* : prophecy

proferir {76} *vt* **1** : to utter **2** : to hurl (insults)

profesar *vt* **1** : to profess, to declare **2** : to practice, to exercise

profesión *nf*, *pl* **-siones** : profession, occupation

profesional *adj & nmf* : professional — **profesionalmente** *adv*

profesionalismo *nm* : professionalism

profesionalizar {21} *vt* : to make (more) professional

profesionista *nmf Mex* : professional

profesor, -sora *n* **1** : teacher (of older children) **2** : professor (in a university) **3** : instructor, tutor

profesorado *nm* **1** : faculty **2** : teaching profession

profeta *nm* : prophet

profético, -ca *adj* : prophetic

profetizar {21} *vt* : to prophesy

prófugo, -ga *adj & n* : fugitive

profundidad *nf* **1** : depth, profundity **2** en ∼ : in depth, thoroughly

profundizar {21} *vt* **1** : to deepen **2** : to study in depth — *vi* ∼ **en** : to go deeply into, to study in depth

profundo, -da *adj* **1** HONDO : deep ⟨poco profundo : shallow⟩ **2** : profound — **profundamente** *adv*

profusión *nf*, *pl* **-siones** : abundance, profusion

profuso, -sa *adj* : profuse, abundant, extensive

progenie *nf* : progeny, offspring

progenitor, -tora *n* **1** : father *m*, mother *f* ⟨sus progenitores : his parents⟩ **2** ANTEPASADO : ancestor, progenitor

progesterona *nf* : progesterone

prognóstico *nm* : prognosis

programa *nm* **1** : program (on television, etc.) **2** : program (pamphlet) **3** : plan, schedule **4** : program (on a computer) **5** *or* **programa de estudios** : curriculum, syllabus

programable *adj* : programmable

programación *nf*, *pl* **-ciones** **1** : programming (on television) **2** : programming (of computers) **3** : planning (of an event)

programador, -dora *n* : programmer

programar *vt* **1** : to schedule (times, shows, etc.), to plan (an event) **2** : to program (a computer, etc.)

progresar *vi* : to progress, to make progress

progresista *adj & nmf* : progressive

progresivo, -va *adj* : progressive, gradual — **progresivamente** *adv*

progreso *nm* : progress ⟨hacer progresos : to make progress⟩

prohibición *nf*, *pl* **-ciones** : ban, prohibition

prohibir {62} *vt* **1** : to prohibit, to ban, to forbid ⟨prohibido fumar : no smoking⟩ ⟨prohibido el paso : do not enter⟩ ⟨me prohibió ir : she forbade me to go⟩ ⟨se prohíbe el uso de pesticidas : the use of pesticides is banned/prohibited⟩

prohibitivo, -va *adj* : prohibitive

prohijar {5} *vt* ADOPTAR : to adopt

prójimo *nm* : neighbor, fellow man

prole *nf* : offspring, progeny

proletariado *nm* : proletariat, working class

proletario, -ria *adj & n* : proletarian

proliferar *vi* : to proliferate — **proliferación** *nf*

prolífico, -ca *adj* : prolific

prolijo, -ja *adj* : wordy, long-winded

prólogo *nm* : prologue, preface, foreword

prolongación *nf*, *pl* **-ciones** : extension, lengthening

prolongar {52} *vt* **1** : to prolong (a life, a war, etc.), to extend (a visit, etc.) **2** : to extend, to lengthen (in size) — **prolongarse** *vr* CONTINUAR : to last, to continue

promediar *vt* **1** : to average **2** : to divide in half — *vi* : to be half over

promedio *nm* **1** : average ⟨como promedio : on average⟩ **2** : middle, midpoint

promesa *nf* : promise ⟨cumplir (con) una promesa : to keep a promise⟩

prometedor, -dora *adj* : promising, hopeful

prometer *vt* : to promise ⟨¿me lo prometes? : (do you) promise?⟩ — *vi* : to show promise — **prometerse** *vr* COMPROMETERSE : to get engaged

prometido¹, -da *adj* : engaged

prometido², -da *n* NOVIO : fiancé *m*, fiancée *f*

prominente *adj* : prominent — **prominencia** *nf* — **prominentemente** *adv*

promiscuo, -cua *adj* : promiscuous — **promiscuidad** *nf*

promisorio, -ria *adj* **1** : promising **2** : promissory

promoción *nf*, *pl* **-ciones** **1** : promotion **2** : class, year **3** : play-off (in soccer)

promocionar *vt* : to promote — **promocional** *adj*

promontorio *nm* : promontory, headland

promotor, -tora *n* **1** : promoter **2** INSTIGADOR : instigator **3** : developer (of real estate)

promover {47} *vt* **1** FOMENTAR : to promote, to encourage **2** : to promote (in rank, etc.) **3** PROVOCAR : to provoke, to cause

promulgación *nf*, *pl* **-ciones** **1** : enactment **2** : proclamation, enactment

promulgar {52} *vt* **1** : to promulgate, to proclaim **2** : to enact (a law or decree)

prono, -na *adj* : prone

pronombre *nm* : pronoun

pronosticar {72} vt : to predict, to forecast

pronóstico nm 1 PREDICCIÓN : forecast, prediction ⟨pronóstico del tiempo : weather forecast⟩ 2 : prognosis

prontitud nf 1 PRESTEZA : promptness, speed 2 con ~ : promptly, quickly

pronto¹ adv 1 : quickly, promptly 2 : soon 3 de ~ : suddenly 4 ¡hasta pronto! : see you soon! 5 lo más pronto posible : as soon as possible 6 por de pronto : for now 7 tan pronto como : as soon as

pronto², -ta adj 1 RÁPIDO : quick, speedy, prompt 2 PREPARADO : ready

pronunciación nf, pl -ciones : pronunciation

pronunciado, -da adj 1 : pronounced, sharp, steep 2 : marked, noticeable

pronunciamiento nm 1 : pronouncement 2 : military uprising

pronunciar vt 1 : to pronounce, to say 2 : to give, to deliver (a speech) 3 pronunciar un fallo : to pronounce sentence — pronunciarse vr : to declare oneself (for or against), to make a statement

propagación nf, pl -ciones : propagation, spreading

propaganda nf 1 : propaganda 2 PUBLICIDAD : advertising (activity or materials)

propagar {52} vt 1 : to propagate 2 : to spread, to disseminate — propagarse vr

propalar vt 1 : to divulge 2 : to spread

propano nm : propane

propasarse vr 1 : to go too far, to overstep one's bounds 2 ~ con : to make sexual advances towards

propensión nf, pl -siones INCLINACIÓN : inclination, propensity

propenso, -sa adj ~ a : prone to, susceptible to

propiamente adv 1 : properly, correctly 2 : exactly, precisely ⟨propiamente dicho : strictly speaking⟩

propiciar vt 1 : to propitiate 2 : to favor, to foster

propicio, -cia adj : favorable, propitious

propiedad nf 1 : property ⟨propiedad privada : private property⟩ ⟨ser propiedad de : to be the property of⟩ 2 : ownership 3 CUALIDAD : property, quality 4 : suitability, appropriateness ⟨con propiedad : appropriately, properly⟩

propietario¹, -ria adj : proprietary

propietario², -ria n DUEÑO : proprietor (of a business), owner

propina nf : tip, gratuity ⟨le di una buena propina : I tipped him well⟩

propinar vt : to give, to strike ⟨propinar una paliza : to give a beating⟩

propio, -pia adj 1 : own ⟨su propia casa : his own house⟩ ⟨tienen recursos propios : they have their own resources⟩ 2 APROPIADO : appropriate, suitable 3 CARACTERÍSTICO : characteristic, typical ⟨es propio de la región : it's typical of the region⟩ 4 MISMO : oneself ⟨el propio director : the director himself⟩

proponer {60} vt 1 : to propose, to suggest 2 : to nominate — proponerse vr : to intend, to plan, to set out ⟨lo que se propone lo cumple : he does what he sets out to do⟩

proporción nf, pl -ciones 1 : proportion ⟨en proporción a : in proportion to⟩ 2 : ratio (in mathematics) 3 proporciones nfpl : proportions, size ⟨de grandes proporciones : very large⟩

proporcionado, -da adj 1 : proportionate 2 : proportioned ⟨bien proporcionado : well-proportioned⟩ — proporcionadamente adv

proporcional adj : proportional — proporcionalmente adv

proporcionar vt 1 : to provide, to give ⟨les proporcionó la información : she provided them with the information⟩ 2 : to proportion, to adapt

proposición nf, pl -ciones : proposal, proposition

propósito nm 1 INTENCIÓN : purpose, intention 2 a ~ : by the way 3 a ~ : on purpose, intentionally 4 a propósito de : on the subject of

propuesta nf PROPOSICIÓN : proposal

propulsar vt 1 IMPULSAR : to propel, to drive 2 PROMOVER : to promote, to encourage

propulsión nf, pl -siones : propulsion ⟨propulsión a chorro : jet propulsion⟩

propulsor¹ nm : propellant

propulsor², -sora n : promoter, proponent

propulsor³, -sora adj : propellant

propuso, etc. → proponer

prórroga nf 1 : extension, deferment 2 : overtime (in sports)

prorrogar {52} vt 1 : to extend (a deadline) 2 : to postpone

prorrumpir vi : to burst forth, to break out ⟨prorrumpí en lágrimas : I burst into tears⟩

prosa nf : prose

prosaico, -ca adj : prosaic, mundane

proscribir {33} v 1 PROHIBIR : to prohibit, to ban, to proscribe 2 DESTERRAR : to banish, to exile

proscripción nf, pl -ciones 1 PROHIBICIÓN : ban 2 DESTIERRO : banishment

proscrito¹ pp → proscribir

proscrito², -ta n 1 DESTERRADO : exile 2 : outlaw

prosecución nf, pl -ciones 1 : continuation 2 : pursuit

proseguir {75} vt 1 CONTINUAR : to continue 2 : to pursue (studies, goals) — vi : to continue, to go on

prospección nf, pl -ciones : prospecting, exploration

prospectar vi : to prospect

prospecto nm 1 : leaflet, brochure 2 : prospectus (for investors, etc.)

prospector, -tora n : prospector

prosperar vi : to prosper, to thrive

prosperidad nf : prosperity

próspero, -ra adj : prosperous, flourishing

próstata nf : prostate

prostíbulo *nm* : brothel
prostitución *nf, pl* **-ciones** : prostitution
prostituir {41} *vt* : to prostitute — **prostituirse** *vr* : to prostitute oneself
prostituto, -ta *n* : prostitute
protagonista *nmf* **1** : protagonist, main character **2** : star (in a film, etc.) **3** : leader, central figure
protagonizar {21} *vt* **1** : to star in **2** : to cause (an accident, etc.), to carry out (an attack, a campaign, etc.)
protección *nf, pl* **-ciones** : protection
protector¹, -tora *adj* : protective ⟨chaleco protector : chest protector⟩
protector², -tora *n* **1** : protector, guardian **2** : patron
protector³ *nm* : protector, guard ⟨protector de pantallas : screen saver⟩
protectorado *nm* : protectorate
proteger {15} *vt* : to protect, to defend ⟨proteger de/contra algo : to protect against something⟩ — **protegerse** *vr*
protegido, -da *n* : protégé
proteína *nf* : protein
prótesis *nfs & pl* : prosthesis
protesta *nf* **1** : protest **2** *Mex* : promise, oath
protestante *adj & nmf* : Protestant
protestantismo *nm* : Protestantism
protestar *vi* **1** : to protest, to object **2** ~ **por** : to complain about — *vt* : to protest, to object to
protocolo *nm* : protocol
protón *nm, pl* **protones** : proton
protoplasma *nm* : protoplasm
prototipo *nm* : prototype
protuberancia *nf* : protuberance — **protuberante** *adj*
provecho *nm* **1** : benefit, advantage ⟨sacar provecho de : to benefit from⟩ **2** ¡buen provecho! : bon appétit!
provechoso, -sa *adj* BENEFICIOSO : beneficial, profitable, useful — **provechosamente** *adv*
proveedor, -dora *n* : provider, supplier
proveedor de servicios de Internet *or* **PSI** *nm* : Internet service provider, ISP
proveer {63} *vt* : to provide, to supply ⟨proveer a alguien de algo : to provide someone with something⟩ — **proveerse** *vr* ~ **de** : to obtain, to supply oneself with
provenir {87} *vi* ~ **de** : to come from
provenzal¹ *adj* : Provençal
provenzal² *nmf* : Provençal
provenzal³ *nm* : Provençal (language)
proverbio *nm* REFRÁN : proverb — **proverbial** *adj*
providencia *nf* **1** : providence, foresight **2** : Providence, God **3 providencias** *nfpl* : steps, measures
providencial *adj* : providential
provincia *nf* : province — **provincial** *adj*
provinciano, -na *adj* : provincial, unsophisticated
provisión *nf, pl* **-siones** **1** : provision, providing **2 provisiones** *nfpl* : provisions, supplies
provisional *adj* : provisional, temporary

provisionalmente *adv* : provisionally, tentatively
provisorio, -ria *adj* : provisional, temporary
provisto *pp* → **proveer**
provocación *nf, pl* **-ciones** : provocation
provocador¹, -dora *adj* : provocative, provoking
provocador², -dora *n* AGITADOR : agitator
provocar {72} *vt* **1** CAUSAR : to provoke, to cause **2** IRRITAR : to provoke, to pique **3** : to arouse (sexually) **4** *Col, Peru, Ven fam* APETECER : to appeal to ⟨¿qué te provoca comer? : what would you like to eat?⟩
provocativo, -va *adj* : provocative
proxeneta *nmf* : pimp *m*
próximamente *adv* : shortly, soon
proximidad *nf* **1** : nearness, proximity **2 proximidades** *nfpl* : vicinity
próximo, -ma *adj* **1** : near, close ⟨la Navidad está próxima : Christmas is almost here⟩ ⟨las próximas elecciones : the coming election⟩ ⟨en un futuro próximo : in the near future⟩ ⟨próximo a la ciudad : near the city⟩ **2** SIGUIENTE : next, following ⟨la próxima semana : the following week, next week⟩ — **próximo, -ma** *pron*
proyección *nf, pl* **-ciones** **1** : projection **2** : showing, screening (of a film) **3** : range, influence, diffusion
proyeccionista *nmf* : projectionist
proyectar *vt* **1** : to plan **2** LANZAR : to throw, to hurl **3** : to project, to cast (light or shadow) **4** : to show, to screen (a film)
proyectil *nm* : projectile, missile
proyecto *nm* **1** : plan, project **2 proyecto de ley** : bill
proyector *nm* **1** : projector **2** : spotlight
prudencia *nf* : prudence, care, discretion
prudencial *adj* : prudent, sensible, cautious ⟨a una distancia prudencial : at a safe distance⟩
prudente *adj* : prudent, sensible, cautious
prueba¹, etc. → **probar**
prueba² *nf* **1** : proof, (piece of) evidence ⟨como prueba de : as proof of⟩ ⟨pruebas científicas : scientific evidence⟩ **2** : trial, test ⟨prueba del embarazo : pregnancy test⟩ ⟨vamos a hacer la prueba : let's try it⟩ **3** : proof (in printing or photography) **4** : event, qualifying round (in sports) **5 a** ~ : on a trial basis **6 a prueba de agua** : waterproof **7 prueba de fuego** : acid test **8 poner a prueba** : to put to the test
prurito *nm* **1** : itching **2** : desire, urge
PSI → **proveedor de servicios de Internet**
psicoanálisis *nm* : psychoanalysis — **psicoanalista** *nmf*
psicoanalítico, -ca *adj* : psychoanalytic
psicoanalizar {21} *vt* : to psychoanalyze
psicodélico, -ca *adj* : psychedelic
psicología *nf* : psychology
psicológico, -ca *adj* : psychological — **psicológicamente** *adv*

psicólogo, -ga n : psychologist
psicópata nmf : psychopath
psicopático, -ca adj : psychopathic
psicosis nfs & pl : psychosis
psicosomático, -ca adj : psychosomatic
psicoterapeuta nmf : psychotherapist
psicoterapia nf : psychotherapy
psicótico, -ca adj & n : psychotic
psique nf : psyche
psiquiatra nmf : psychiatrist
psiquiatría nf : psychiatry
psiquiátrico¹, -ca adj : psychiatric
psiquiátrico² nm : mental hospital
psíquico, -ca adj : psychic
psiquis nfs & pl : psyche
psoriasis nf : psoriasis
púa nf 1 : barb ⟨alambre de púas : barbed wire⟩ 2 : tooth (of a comb) 3 : quill, spine (of an animal) 4 : thorn, spine (of a plant) 5 : pick (for a guitar, etc.)
pub ['pub, 'pab] nm, pl **pubs** : bar, nightclub
pubertad nf : puberty
pubiano → **púbico**
púbico, -ca adj : pubic
publicación nf, pl **-ciones** : publication
publicar {72} vt 1 : to publish 2 DIVULGAR : to divulge, to disclose
publicidad nf 1 : publicity 2 : advertising
publicista nmf : publicist
publicitar vt 1 : to publicize 2 : to advertise
publicitario, -ria adj : advertising, publicity ⟨agencia publicitaria : advertising agency⟩
público¹, -ca adj : public ⟨hacer público : to make public⟩ — **públicamente** adv
público² nm 1 : public ⟨en público : in public⟩ 2 : audience, spectators pl
puchero nm 1 : pot 2 : stew 3 : pout ⟨hacer pucheros : to pout⟩
pucho nm 1 : waste, residue 2 : cigarette 3 : cigarette butt 4 **a puchos** : little by little, bit by bit
púdico, -ca adj : chaste, modest
pudiente adj 1 : powerful 2 : rich, wealthy
pudín nm, pl **pudines** BUDÍN : pudding
pudo, etc. → **poder**
pudor nm : modesty, reserve
pudoroso, -sa adj : modest, reserved, shy
pudrir {59} vt 1 : to rot 2 fam : to annoy, to upset — **pudrirse** vr 1 : to rot 2 : to languish
puebla, etc. → **poblar**
pueblerino, -na adj : provincial
pueblo nm 1 NACIÓN : people 2 : common people 3 ALDEA, POBLADO : town, village 4 **pueblo joven** Peru : shantytown, slums pl
puede, etc. → **poder**
puente nm 1 : bridge 2 : bridge (in dentistry) 3 **puente aéreo** : airlift (military), air shuttle (commercial) 4 **puente levadizo** : drawbridge
puerco¹, -ca adj : dirty, filthy
puerco², -ca n 1 CERDO, MARRANO : pig, hog 2 : pig, dirty or greedy person 3 **puerco espín** : porcupine

puericultura nf : infant care, childcare
pueril adj : childish, puerile
puerro nm : leek
puerta nf 1 : door (of a house, etc.), entrance (of a hotel, etc.), gate (in a fence, etc.) ⟨llamar a la puerta : to knock at/on the door⟩ ⟨puerta principal : front door, main entrance⟩ ⟨puerta trasera : back door⟩ 2 **a las puertas de** : on the verge of 3 **a puerta cerrada** : behind closed doors 4 **puerta de embarque** : gate (in an airport)
puerto nm 1 : port, harbor ⟨puerto pesquero : fishing port⟩ ⟨puerto marítimo : seaport⟩ 2 : mountain pass 3 : port (in a computer)
puertorriqueño, -ña adj & n : Puerto Rican
pues conj 1 : since, because, for ⟨lo hicieron, pues consideraron que era necesario : they did it because they considered it necessary⟩ 2 (used interjectionally) : well, then ⟨pues claro que sí! : well, of course!⟩ ⟨¡pues no voy! : well then, I'm not going!⟩
puesta nf 1 : setting ⟨puesta de/del sol : sunset⟩ 2 : laying (of eggs) 3 **puesta al día** : updating 4 **puesta a punto** : tune-up 5 **puesta en escena** : production (in theater) 6 **puesta en marcha** : start, starting up
puestero, -ra n : seller, vendor
puesto¹ pp → **poner**
puesto², -ta adj 1 : dressed ⟨bien puesto : well-dressed⟩ 2 : set (of a table)
puesto³ nm 1 LUGAR, SITIO : place, position 2 : place (in a ranking) 3 : kiosk, stand, stall 4 : post, station ⟨puesto de policía : police station⟩ ⟨puesto de socorro : first-aid post⟩ 5 or **puesto de trabajo** : position, job 6 **puesto que** : since, given that
púgil → **pugilista**
pugilato nm BOXEO : boxing
pugilista nmf BOXEADOR : boxer (athlete)
pugna nf 1 CONFLICTO, LUCHA : conflict, struggle 2 **en ~** : at odds, in conflict
pugnar vi ~ **por** : to strive to (do something), to strive for (something)
pugnaz adj : pugnacious
pujante adj : mighty, powerful
pujanza nf : strength, vigor ⟨pujanza económica : economic strength⟩
pujar vi 1 : to push, to strain 2 ~ **por** : to struggle to (do something), to struggle for (something)
pulcritud nf 1 : neatness, tidiness 2 ESMERO : meticulousness
pulcro, -cra adj 1 : clean, neat 2 : exquisite, delicate, refined
pulga nf 1 : flea 2 **tener malas pulgas** : to be bad-tempered
pulgada nf : inch
pulgar nm 1 : thumb 2 : big toe
pulir vt 1 : to polish, to shine 2 REFINAR : to refine, to perfect
pulla nf 1 : cutting remark, dig, gibe 2 : obscenity
pulmón nm, pl **pulmones** : lung

pulmonar adj : pulmonary
pulmonía nf NEUMONÍA : pneumonia
pulóver nm, pl **-veres** : pullover, sweater
pulpa nf : pulp, flesh
pulpería nf : small grocery store
púlpito nm : pulpit
pulpo nm : octopus
pulque nm : Mexican alcoholic drink made from maguey sap
pulsación nf, pl **-ciones** 1 : beat, pulsation, throb 2 : keystroke
pulsar vt 1 APRETAR : to press, to push 2 : to strike (a key), to pluck (a string) 3 : to assess — vi : to beat, to throb
pulsera nf : bracelet
pulso nm 1 : pulse ⟨tomarle el pulso a alguien : to take someone's pulse⟩ ⟨tomarle el pulso a la opinión : to sound out opinion⟩ 2 : steady hand ⟨dibujo a pulso : freehand sketch⟩ ⟨a pulso : through effort, through hard work⟩
pulular vi ABUNDAR : to abound, to swarm ⟨en el río pululan los peces : the river is teeming with fish⟩
pulverizador nm 1 : atomizer, spray 2 : spray gun
pulverizar {21} vt 1 : to pulverize, to crush 2 : to spray
pum interj : bang!
puma nf : cougar, puma
puna nf 1 : Andean plateau 2 : altitude sickness
punción nf, pl **punciones** : puncture
punible adj : punishable
punitivo, -va adj : punitive
punce, etc. → punzar
punk[1] adj : punk
punk[2] nm : punk, punk rock
punk[3] nmf : punk, punk rocker
punta nf 1 : tip, end ⟨punta del dedo : fingertip⟩ ⟨en la punta de la lengua : at the tip of one's tongue⟩ ⟨en la otra punta del país : on the other side of the country⟩ ⟨cortar las puntas : to trim (hair)⟩ 2 : point (of a weapon, pencil, etc.) ⟨punta de lanza : spearhead⟩ ⟨acabar en punta : to be pointed⟩ ⟨sacar punta a : to sharpen⟩ 3 : point, headland 4 : bunch, lot ⟨una punta de ladrones : a bunch of thieves⟩ 5 a punta de : by, by dint of 6 de ∼ : on end
puntada nf 1 : stitch (in sewing) 2 PUNZADA : sharp pain, stitch, twinge 3 Mex : witticism, quip
puntal nm : prop, support
puntapié nm PATADA : kick ⟨darle un puntapié a alguien : to kick someone⟩
puntazo nm CORNADA : wound (from a goring)
puntear vt 1 : to pluck (a guitar) 2 : to lead (in sports)
puntería nf : aim, marksmanship
puntero nm 1 : pointer 2 : leader
puntiagudo, -da adj : sharp, pointed
puntilla nf 1 : lace edging 2 : dagger (in bullfighting) 3 de puntillas : on tiptoe
puntilloso, -sa adj : punctilious
punto nm 1 : dot, spot 2 : period (in punctuation) 3 : point, item, question 4 : spot, place 5 : point, moment, stage

6 : point, extent 7 : point (in a score) 8 : stitch 9 en ∼ : on the dot, sharp ⟨a las dos en punto : at two o'clock sharp⟩ 10 al punto : at once 11 a punto de : about to, on the verge of ⟨estaba a punto de salir : I was about to leave⟩ ⟨a punto del colapso : on the verge of collapse⟩ 12 a punto fijo : exactly, certainly 13 dos puntos : colon 14 en su punto : just right 15 hasta cierto punto : up to a point 16 punto decimal : decimal point 17 punto de partida : starting point 18 punto de vista : point of view 19 punto final : period (in punctuation) ⟨poner punto final a algo : to end something⟩ 20 punto fuerte/débil : strong/weak point 21 punto muerto : neutral (in an automobile), deadlock (in talks, etc.) 22 puntos cardinales : points of the compass 23 puntos suspensivos : ellipsis (in punctuation) 24 punto y aparte : (period and) new paragraph 25 punto y coma : semicolon 26 y punto : period ⟨es el mejor que hay y punto : it's the best there is, period⟩
puntocom nm, pl **puntocom** : dot-com
puntuación nf, pl **-ciones** 1 : punctuation 2 : scoring (action), score, grade
puntual adj 1 : prompt, punctual 2 : exact, accurate — **puntualmente** adv
puntualidad nf : promptness, punctuality
puntualizar {21} vt 1 : to specify, to state 2 : to point out
puntuar {3} vt : to punctuate — vi : to score points
punzada nf : sharp pain, twinge, stitch
punzante adj 1 : sharp 2 CÁUSTICO : biting, caustic
punzar {21} vt : to pierce, to puncture
punzón nm, pl **punzones** 1 : awl 2 : hole punch
puñado nm 1 : handful 2 a puñados : lots of, by the handful
puñal nm DAGA : dagger
puñalada nf : stab, stab wound
puñetazo nm : punch (with the fist) ⟨le dio un puñetazo en la cara : she punched him in the face⟩
puño nm 1 : fist 2 : handful, fistful 3 : cuff (of a shirt) 4 : handle, hilt 5 de su puño y letra : in one's own handwriting
pupa nf CRISÁLIDA : pupa, chrysalis
pupila nf : pupil (of the eye)
pupilente nm Mex : contact lens
pupilo, -la n 1 : pupil, student 2 : ward, charge
pupitre nm : writing desk
puramente adv : purely
puré nm : puree ⟨puré de papas : mashed potatoes⟩
pureza nf : purity
purga nf 1 : laxative 2 : purge
purgante adj & nm : laxative, purgative
purgar {52} vt 1 : to purge, to cleanse 2 : to liquidate (in politics) 3 : to give a laxative to — **purgarse** vr 1 : to take a laxative 2 ∼ de : to purge oneself of
purgatorio nm : purgatory
purgue, etc. → purgar
purificador nm : purifier

purificar {72} *vt* : to purify — **purificación** *nf*

puritano¹, -na *adj* : puritanical, puritan

puritano², -na *n* 1 : Puritan 2 : puritan

puro¹ *adv* : sheer, much ⟨de puro terco : out of sheer stubbornness⟩

puro², -ra *adj* 1 : pure ⟨aire puro : fresh air⟩ 2 : plain, simple, sheer ⟨por pura curiosidad : from sheer curiosity⟩ 3 : only, just ⟨emplean puras mujeres : they only employ women⟩ 4 **pura sangre** : Thoroughbred horse

puro³ *nm* : cigar

púrpura *nf* : purple

purpúreo, -rea *adj* : purple

purpurina *nf* : glitter (for decoration)

pus *nm* : pus

pusilánime *adj* COBARDE : cowardly

puso, etc. → **poner**

pústula *nf* : pustule, pimple

puta *nf offensive* : whore, prostitute

putrefacción *nf, pl* **-ciones** : putrefying, rotting

putrefacto, -ta *adj* 1 PODRIDO : putrid, rotten 2 : decayed

pútrido, -da *adj* : putrid, rotten

puya *nf* 1 : point (of a lance) 2 **lanzar una puya** : to gibe, to taunt

Q

q *nf* : twentieth letter of the Spanish alphabet

que¹ *conj* 1 : that ⟨dice que está listo : he says (that) he's ready⟩ ⟨espero que lo haga : I hope (that) she does it⟩ ⟨es posible que vuelva a pasar : it's possible (that) it will happen again⟩ ⟨estaba tan cansado que casi se durmió : he was so tired (that) he almost fell asleep⟩ ⟨me di cuenta de que era ella : I realized (that) it was her⟩ 2 : than ⟨ella es más alta que él : she is taller than he is⟩ ⟨más que nada : more than anything⟩ 3 (*expressing permission or desire*) ⟨¡que entre! : send him in!⟩ ⟨¡que te vaya bien! : I wish you well!⟩ 4 (*used in repeating a statement or question*) ⟨¡que no lo toques! : I told you not to touch it!⟩ ⟨que sí quieres más : I asked if you wanted more⟩ ⟨¿cómo que no lo sabes? : what do you mean you don't know?⟩ 5 (*indicating a reason or cause*) ⟨¡cuidado, que te caes! : be careful, you're about to fall!⟩ ⟨no provoques al perro, que te va a morder : don't provoke the dog or (else) he'll bite⟩ 6 (*indicating a continuing or repeated action*) ⟨estaba todo el día corre que (te) corre : I was running around nonstop all day⟩ 7 **es que** : the thing is that, I'm afraid that ⟨es que no tengo ganas de ir : the thing is that I don't want to go⟩ 8 **yo que tú** : if I were you

que² *pron* 1 : who, that ⟨la niña que viene : the girl who is coming⟩ ⟨todos los chicos que están aquí : all (of) the boys who are here⟩ ⟨el hombre que llamó ayer : he's the man who called yesterday⟩ ⟨no conozco a nadie que lo crea : I don't know anyone who believes it⟩ 2 : whom, that ⟨los alumnos que enseñé : the students that I taught⟩ ⟨la persona con que habló : the person with whom he spoke⟩ ⟨el hombre al que pertenece : the man to whom it belongs⟩ 3 : that, which ⟨el carro que me gusta : the car that I like⟩ ⟨el asunto al que hizo referencia : the matter to which she referred⟩ ⟨el delito del que fue acusado : the crime of which he was accused⟩ 4 **el (la, lo, las, los) que** → **el¹, la¹, lo¹, los¹**

qué¹ *adv* : how, what ⟨¡qué bonito! : how pretty!⟩

qué² *adj* : what, which ⟨¿qué hora es? : what time is it?⟩

qué³ *pron* : what ⟨¿qué quieres? : what do you want?⟩ ⟨¿y qué? : so what?⟩ ⟨¿qué es eso? : what is that?⟩ ⟨¿sabes qué? : you know what?⟩ ⟨qué de . . . : what a lot of . . .⟩

quebracho *nm* : quebracho (tree)

quebrada *nf* DESFILADERO : ravine, gorge

quebradero *nm* **quebradero de cabeza** : headache, problem

quebradizo, -za *adj* FRÁGIL : breakable, delicate, fragile

quebrado¹, -da *adj* 1 : bankrupt 2 : rough, uneven 3 ROTO : broken

quebrado² *nm* : fraction

quebrantamiento *nm* 1 : breaking 2 : deterioration, weakening

quebrantar *vt* 1 : to break, to split, to crack 2 : to weaken 3 : to violate (a law or contract)

quebranto *nm* 1 : break, breaking 2 AFLICCIÓN : affliction, grief 3 PÉRDIDA : loss

quebrar {55} *vt* 1 ROMPER : to break 2 DOBLAR : to bend, to twist — *vi* 1 : to go bankrupt 2 : to fall out, to break up — **quebrarse** *vr*

queda *nf* : curfew

quedar *vi* 1 PERMANECER : to remain, to stay ⟨queda abierto hasta el 31 : it will remain open until the 31st⟩ 2 : to be, to end up being ⟨quedamos contentos con las mejoras : we were pleased with the improvements⟩ ⟨el partido quedó empatado : the game ended in a tie⟩ ⟨el pastel quedó muy rico : the cake came out really well, the cake was delicious⟩ ⟨queda claro que . . . : it's clear that . . .⟩ 3 : to be situated ⟨queda muy lejos : it's very far, it's too far away⟩ 4 : to be left ⟨quedan sólo dos alternativas : there are only two options left⟩ ⟨no me queda mucho dinero : I don't have much money left⟩ ⟨queda mucho por hacer : there's still a lot left to do⟩ 5 : to fit, to suit ⟨estos zapatos no me quedan : these shoes don't fit⟩ ⟨me queda grande : it's big on me⟩ ⟨ese color te queda bien : that color looks good on you⟩ 6 : to agree to meet ⟨¿a qué hora quedamos? : what time are we meeting?⟩ ⟨quedé con un amigo para cenar : I arranged to have dinner with a friend⟩ 7 quedar bien/mal con alguien : to make a good/bad impression on someone 8 ～ en : to agree, to arrange ⟨¿en qué quedamos? : what's the plan?, what are we doing?⟩ — quedarse vr 1 : to stay ⟨se quedó en casa : she stayed at home⟩ 2 : to keep on ⟨se quedó esperando : he kept on waiting⟩ 3 quedarse atrás : to stay behind, to get left behind ⟨no quedarse atrás : to be no slouch⟩ 4 ～ con : to remain ⟨me quedé con hambre después de comer : I was still hungry after I ate⟩

quedo¹ adv : softly, quietly

quedo², -da adj : quiet, still

queer [ˈker] adj & nmf, pl **queer** or **queers** : queer sometimes disparaging + offensive

quehacer nm 1 : work 2 **quehaceres** nmpl : chores

queja nf : complaint

quejarse vr 1 : to complain 2 : to groan, to moan

quejica¹ adj fam : whiny

quejica² nmf fam : whiny person

quejido nm 1 : groan, moan 2 : whine, whimper

quejoso, -sa adj : complaining, whining

quema nf 1 FUEGO : fire 2 : burning

quemado, -da adj 1 : burned, burnt 2 : annoyed 3 : burned out 4 : sunburned

quemador nm : burner

quemadura nf : burn

quemar vt 1 : to burn (wood, letters, etc.), to burn down (a building) 2 : to burn (calories, etc.) 3 : to burn, to overcook 4 : to burn (skin, clothes, etc.) ⟨te ha quemado el sol : you have a sunburn⟩ 5 DERROCHAR : to squander 6 : to burn (a DVD, etc.) 7 : to burn out (an engine), to blow (a fuse) — vi 1 : to burn ⟨en el trópico el sol quema mucho : the sun is very strong in the tropics⟩ 2 : to be burning hot — **quemarse** vr 1 : to burn, to burn down 2 : to burn oneself ⟨me quemé la mano : I burned my hand⟩ 3 : to get sunburned 4 : to burn out, to blow

quemarropa nf a ～ : point-blank

quemazón nf, pl **-zones** 1 : burning 2 : intense heat 3 : itch 4 : cutting remark

quena nf : Peruvian reed flute

quepa, etc. → caber

querella nf 1 : complaint 2 : lawsuit

querellante nmf : plaintiff

querellarse vr ～ **contra** : to bring suit against, to sue

querer¹ {64} vt 1 DESEAR : to want, to desire ⟨quiere ser profesor : he wants to

be a teacher⟩ ⟨¿cuánto quieres por esta computadora? : how much do you want for this computer?⟩ ⟨¿qué quieres que haga? : what do you want me to do?⟩ ⟨quiero que ella me ayude : I want her to help me⟩ ⟨quisiera cancelar la cuenta : I'd like to cancel the account⟩ ⟨quisiera que no fuera así : I wish it weren't so⟩ ⟨léelo cuando quieras : read it whenever you like⟩ ⟨no quería decírselo : he didn't want to tell her⟩ ⟨no quiso dar detalles : she wouldn't give any details⟩ 2 : to love, to like, to be fond of ⟨te quiero : I love you⟩ ⟨te quiere bien : he's very fond of you⟩ 3 (indicating a request) ⟨¿quieres pasarme la leche? : please pass the milk⟩ ⟨¿quieres decirme qué pasa? : do you mind telling me what's going on?⟩ 4 querer decir : to mean ⟨¿qué quieres decir con eso? : what do you mean by that?⟩ ⟨eso no es lo que quiero decir : that's not what I meant to say⟩ 5 sin ～ : unintentionally — vi : like, want ⟨si quieres : if you like⟩ ⟨¡no quiero! : I don't want to!⟩

querer² nm : love, affection

querido, -da adj : dear, beloved

querido², -da n : dear, sweetheart

queroseno nm : kerosene

querrá, etc. → querer

querúbico, -ca adj : cherubic

querubín nm, pl **-bines** : cherub

quesadilla nf : quesadilla

quesería nf : cheese shop

queso nm : cheese

quetzal nm 1 : quetzal (bird) 2 : quetzal (monetary unit of Guatemala)

quiche nf : quiche

quicio nm 1 estar fuera de quicio : to be beside oneself 2 sacar de quicio : to exasperate, to drive crazy

quid nm : crux, gist ⟨el quid de la cuestión : the crux of the matter⟩

quiebra¹, etc. → quebrar

quiebra² nf 1 : break, crack 2 BANCARROTA : failure, bankruptcy

quien pron, pl **quienes** 1 : who, whom ⟨no sé quien ganará : I don't know who will win⟩ ⟨las personas con quienes trabajo : the people with whom I work⟩ ⟨su amigo, a quien conoció en México : his friend, whom he met in Mexico⟩ 2 : whoever, whomever ⟨quien quiere salir que salga : whoever wants to can leave⟩ 3 : anyone, some people ⟨hay quienes no están de acuerdo : some people don't agree⟩ ⟨no hay quien lo aguante : there's no one who would tolerate it⟩

quién pron, pl **quiénes** 1 : who, whom ⟨¿quién sabe? : who knows?⟩ ⟨¿con quién hablo? : with whom am I speaking?⟩ 2 de ～ : whose ⟨¿de quién es este libro? : whose book is this?⟩

quienquiera pron, pl **quienesquiera** : whoever, whomever

quiere, etc. → querer

quieto, -ta adj 1 : calm, quiet 2 INMÓVIL : still

quietud nf 1 : calm, tranquility 2 INMOVILIDAD : stillness

quijada *nf* : jaw, jawbone
quijotesco, -ca *adj* : quixotic
quilate *nm* : karat
quilla *nf* : keel
quimera *nf* : chimera, illusion
quimérico, -ca *adj* : fanciful
química *nf* : chemistry
químico¹, -ca *adj* : chemical
químico², -ca *n* : chemist
quimioterapia *nf* : chemotherapy
quimono *nm* : kimono
quincalla *nf* : trinkets *pl*
quince *adj & nm* : fifteen — **quince** *pron*
quinceañero, -ra *n* : fifteen-year-old, teenager
quinceavo¹, -va *adj* : fifteenth
quinceavo² *nm* : fifteenth (fraction)
quincena *nf* : two week period, fortnight
quincenal *adj* : bimonthly, semimonthly
quincuagésimo¹, -ma *adj* : fiftieth, fifty-
quincuagésimo², -ma *n* : fiftieth, fifty-
  (in a series)
quingombó *nm* : okra
quiniela *nf* : sports lottery
quinientos¹, -tas *adj & pron* : five hundred
quinientos² *nms & pl* : five hundred
quinina *nf* : quinine
quino *nm* : cinchona
quinqué *nm* : oil lamp
quinquenal *adj* : five-year ⟨un plan quinquenal : a five-year plan⟩
quinta *nf* : country house, villa
quintaesencia *nf* : quintessence — **quintaesencial** *adj*
quintal *nm* : hundredweight
quinteto *nm* : quintet
quintillizo, -za *n* : quintuplet
quinto, -ta *adj & n* : fifth ⟨el quinto grado : the fifth grade⟩ ⟨la quinta (persona) : the fifth (person)⟩ ⟨llegó el quinto : he came in fifth (place)⟩ ⟨un quinto de : a fifth of⟩
quintuplo, -la *adj* : quintuple, five-fold
quiosco *nm* **1** : kiosk **2** : newsstand **3** **quiosco de música** : bandstand
quiosquero, -ra *n* : kiosk vendor

quirófano *nm* : operating room
quiromancia *nf* : palmistry
quiropráctica *nf* : chiropractic
quiropráctico, -ca *n* : chiropractor
quirúrgico, -ca \ *adj* : surgical — **quirúrgicamente** *adv*
quiso, etc. → querer
quisquilloso¹, -sa *adj* : fastidious, fussy
quisquilloso², -sa *n* : fussy person, fuss-budget
quiste *nm* : cyst
quitaesmalte *nm* : nail polish remover
quitamanchas *nms & pl* : stain remover
quitanieves *nms & pl* : snowplow
quitar *vt* **1** : to remove, to take away/off/out ⟨quita la olla del fuego : take the pot off the heat/burner⟩ ⟨quitarle el polvo a algo : to dust something⟩ ⟨quítalo de en medio : get it out of the way⟩ ⟨¡quítame las manos (de encima)! : get your hands off me!⟩ **2** : to take, to take away ⟨le quitó las llaves : she took away his keys⟩ ⟨trataron de quitarle el dinero : they tried to take her money⟩ ⟨le quitaron la vida : they took his life, they killed him⟩ ⟨no me quita el sueño : I'm not losing any sleep over it⟩ **3** : to take off (clothes) ⟨le quitó los zapatos al paciente : she took the patient's shoes off⟩ **4** : to get rid of, to relieve ⟨quitar el dolor : to relieve the pain⟩ ⟨nadie le va a quitar esa idea de la cabeza : nobody's going to change his mind⟩ **5** : to take up (time) — **quitarse** *vr* **1** : to withdraw, to leave, to go away ⟨se me quitaron las ganas de salir : I don't feel like going out anymore⟩ **2** : to take off (one's clothes) **3** ~ **de** : to give up (a habit) **4 quitarse de encima** : to get rid of ⟨me he quitado un peso de encima : that's a load off my mind⟩
quitasol *nm* : parasol
quiteño¹, -ña *adj* : of or from Quito
quiteño², -ña *n* : person from Quito
quizá *or* **quizás** *adv* : maybe, perhaps
quórum *nm, pl* **quórums** : quorum

R

r *nf* : twenty-first letter of the Spanish alphabet
rábano *nm* **1** : radish **2 rábano picante** : horseradish
rabí *nmf, pl* **rabíes** : rabbi
rabia *nf* **1** HIDROFOBIA : rabies, hydrophobia **2** : rage, anger
rabiar *vi* **1** : to rage, to be furious **2** : to be in great pain **3 a ~** *fam* : like crazy, like mad
rabieta *nf* BERRINCHE : tantrum
rabillo *nm* : corner (of the eye)
rabino, -na *n* : rabbi
rabioso, -sa *adj* **1** : enraged, furious **2** : rabid
rabo *nm* **1** COLA : tail **2 el rabo del ojo** : the corner of one's eye

rácano, -na *adj fam* : stingy
racha *nf* **1** : gust of wind **2** : run, series, string ⟨racha perdedora : losing streak⟩
racheado, -da *adj* : gusty, windy
racial *adj* : racial
racimo *nm* : bunch, cluster ⟨un racimo de uvas : a bunch of grapes⟩
raciocinio *nm* : reason, reasoning
ración *nf, pl* **raciones** **1** : share, ration **2** PORCIÓN : portion, helping
racional *adj* : rational, reasonable — **racionalmente** *adv*
racionalidad *nf* : rationality
racionalización *nf, pl* **-ciones** : rationalization
racionalizar {21} *vt* **1** : to rationalize **2** : to streamline

racionamiento *nm* : rationing
racionar *vt* : to ration
racismo *nm* : racism
racista *adj & nmf* : racist
radar *nm* : radar
radiación *nf, pl* **-ciones** : radiation, irradiation
radiactividad *nf* : radioactivity
radiactivo, -va *adj* : radioactive
radiador *nm* : radiator
radial *adj* **1** : radial **2** : radio, broadcasting ⟨emisora radial : radio transmitter⟩
radiante *adj* : radiant — **radiantemente** *adv*
radiar *vt* **1** : to radiate **2** : to irradiate **3** : to broadcast (on the radio)
radical¹ *adj* : radical, extreme — **radicalmente** *adv*
radical² *nmf* : radical
radicalismo *nm* : radicalism
radicar {72} *vi* **1** : to be found, to lie **2** ARRAIGAR : to take root — **radicarse** *vr* : to settle, to establish oneself
radio¹ *nm* **1** : radius **2** : radium
radio² *nmf* : radio
radioactividad *nf* : radioactivity
radioactivo, -va *adj* : radioactive
radioaficionado, -da *n* : ham radio operator
radiodifusión *nf, pl* **-siones** : radio broadcasting
radiodifusora *nf* : radio station
radioemisora *nf* : radio station
radiofaro *nm* : radio beacon
radiofónico, -ca *adj* : radio ⟨estación radiofónica pública : public radio station⟩
radiofrecuencia *nf* : radio frequency
radiografía *nf* : X ray (photograph)
radiografiar {85} *vt* : to x-ray
radiología *nf* : radiology
radiólogo, -ga *n* : radiologist
radionovela *nf* : radio soap opera
radioterapia *nf* : radiation therapy
radioyente *nmf* : radio listener
radón *nm* : radon
raer {65} *vt* RASPAR : to scrape, to scrape off
ráfaga *nf* **1** : gust (of wind) **2** : flash, burst ⟨una ráfaga de luz : a flash of light⟩
rafting *nm* : rafting
ragtime *nm* : ragtime
raid *nm* CA, *Mex fam* : lift, ride
raído, -da *adj* : worn, shabby
raiga, etc. → **raer**
raíz *nf, pl* **raíces** **1** : root **2** : origin, source **3 a raíz de** : following, as a result of **4 echar raíces** : to take root
raja *nf* **1** : crack, slit **2** : slice, wedge
rajá *nm* : raja
rajadura *nf* : crack, split
rajar *vt* HENDER : to crack, to split — *vi* **1** *fam* : to chatter **2** *fam* : to boast, to brag — **rajarse** *vr* **1** : to crack, to split open **2** *fam* : to back out
rajatabla *adv* **a ~** : strictly, to the letter
ralea *nf* : kind, sort, ilk ⟨son de la misma ralea : they're two of a kind⟩
ralentí *nm* **dejar al ralentí** : to leave (a motor) idling

rallado, -da *adj* **1** : grated **2 pan rallado** : bread crumbs *pl*
rallador *nm* : grater
rallar *vt* : to grate
ralo, -la *adj* : sparse, thin
RAM *nf* : RAM, random-access memory
rama *nf* : branch
Ramadán *nm, pl* **-danes** : Ramadan
ramaje *nm* : branches *pl*
ramal *nm* **1** : spur (of a railroad line) **2** : halter, strap
rambla *nf* **1** : avenue, boulevard **2** *Arg, Uru* : seaside walk, boardwalk
ramera *nf* : harlot, prostitute
ramificación *nf, pl* **-ciones** : ramification
ramificarse {72} *vr* : to branch out, to divide into branches
ramillete *nm* **1** RAMO : bouquet **2** : select group, cluster
ramo *nm* **1** : branch **2** RAMILLETE : bouquet **3** : division (of science or industry) **4 Domingo de Ramos** : Palm Sunday
rampa *nf* : ramp, incline
rana *nf* **1** : frog **2 rana toro** : bullfrog
ranchera *nf Mex* : traditional folk song
ranchería *nf* : settlement
ranchero, -ra *n* : rancher, farmer
rancho *nm* **1** : ranch, farm **2** : hut **3** : settlement, camp **4** : food, mess (for soldiers, etc.)
rancio, -cia *adj* **1** : aged, mellow (of wine) **2** : ancient, old **3** : rancid
rango *nm* **1** : rank, status **2** : high social standing **3** : pomp, splendor
ransomware ['ransomwer] *nm* : ransomware
ranúnculo *nm* : buttercup
ranura *nf* : groove, slot
rap *nm* : rap (music)
rapar *vt* **1** : to crop **2** : to shave
rapaz¹ *adj, pl* **rapaces** : rapacious, predatory
rapaz², -paza *n, mpl* **rapaces** : youngster, child
rape *nm* : close haircut
rapé *nm* : snuff
rapero, -ra *n* : rapper, rap artist
rapidez *nf* : rapidity, speed
rápido¹ *adv* : quickly, fast ⟨¡manejas tan rápido! : you drive so fast!⟩
rápido², -da *adj* : rapid, quick — **rápidamente** *adv*
rápido³ *nm* **1** : express train **2 rápidos** *nmpl* : rapids
rapiña *nf* **1** : plunder, pillage **2 ave de rapiña** : bird of prey
raposa *nf* : vixen (fox)
rapsodia *nf* : rhapsody
raptar *vt* SECUESTRAR : to abduct, to kidnap
rapto *nm* **1** SECUESTRO : kidnapping, abduction **2** ARREBATO : fit, outburst
raptor, -tora *n* SECUESTRADOR : kidnapper
raquero, -ra *n* : beachcomber
raqueta *nf* **1** : racket (in sports) **2** : snowshoe
raquítico, -ca *adj* **1** : scrawny, weak **2** : measly, skimpy

raquitismo nm : rickets

raramente adv : seldom, rarely

rareza nf 1 : rarity 2 : peculiarity, oddity

raro, -ra adj 1 EXTRAÑO : odd, strange, peculiar 2 : unusual, rare 3 : exceptional 4 **rara vez** : seldom, rarely

ras nm **a ras de** : level with

rasar vt 1 : to skim, to graze 2 : to level

rascacielos nms & pl : skyscraper

rascar {72} vt 1 : to scratch 2 : to scrape — **rascarse** vr : to scratch an itch

rasgadura nf : tear, rip

rasgar {52} vt : to rip, to tear — **rasgarse** vr

rasgo nm 1 : stroke (of a pen) ⟨a grandes rasgos : in broad outlines⟩ 2 CARACTERÍSTICA : trait, characteristic 3 : gesture, deed 4 **rasgos** nmpl FACCIONES : features

rasgón nm, pl **rasgones** : rip, tear

rasgue, etc. → rasgar

rasguear vt : to strum

rasguñar vt 1 : to scratch 2 : to sketch, to outline

rasguño nm 1 : scratch 2 : sketch

raso¹, -sa adj 1 : level, flat 2 **soldado raso** : private (in the army) ⟨los soldados rasos : the ranks⟩

raso² nm : satin

raspadura nf 1 : scratching, scraping 2 **raspaduras** nfpl : scrapings

raspar vt 1 : to scrape 2 : to file down, to smooth — vi : to be rough

rasposo, -sa adj : rough, scratchy

rasque, etc. → rascar

rastra nf 1 : harrow 2 **a rastras** : by dragging, unwillingly

rastrear vt 1 : to track, to trace 2 : to comb, to search 3 : to trawl

rastrero, -ra adj 1 : creeping, crawling 2 : vile, despicable

rastrillar vt : to rake, to harrow

rastrillo nm 1 : rake 2 Mex : razor

rastro nm 1 PISTA : trail, track 2 VESTIGIO : trace, sign

rastrojo nm : stubble (of plants)

rasuradora nf Mex, CA : electric razor, shaver

rasurar vt AFEITAR : to shave — **rasurarse** vr

rata¹ nm fam : pickpocket, thief

rata² nf 1 : rat 2 Col, Pan, Peru : rate, percentage

rata almizclera nf : muskrat

ratear vt : to pilfer, to steal

ratero, -ra n : petty thief

ratificación nf, pl **-ciones** : ratification

ratificar {72} vt 1 : to ratify 2 : to confirm

rato nm 1 : while 2 **pasar el rato** : to pass the time 3 **a cada rato** : all the time, constantly ⟨les sacaba dinero a cada rato : he was always taking money from them⟩ 4 **al poco rato** : later, shortly after 5 **pasar un mal rato** : to have a bad/hard/tough time

ratón¹, -tona n, mpl **ratones** 1 : mouse 2 **ratón de biblioteca** fam : bookworm

ratón² nm, pl **ratones** 1 : (computer) mouse 2 CoRi : biceps

ratonera nf : mousetrap

raudal nm 1 : torrent 2 **a raudales** : in abundance

raviolis or **ravioles** nmpl : ravioli

raya¹, etc. → raer

raya² nf 1 : line ⟨pasarse de la raya : to go over the line, to go too far⟩ 2 : stripe 3 : skate, ray 4 : part (in the hair) ⟨hacerse la raya : to part one's hair⟩ 5 : crease (in clothing)

rayado, -da adj : striped, lined

rayar vt 1 ARAÑAR : to scratch 2 : to scrawl on, to mark up ⟨rayaron las paredes : they covered the walls with graffiti⟩ — vi 1 : to scratch 2 AMANECER : to dawn, to break ⟨al rayar el alba : at break of day⟩ 3 ~ con : to be adjacent to, to be next to 4 ~ en : to border on, to verge on ⟨su respuesta raya en lo ridículo : his answer borders on the ridiculous⟩ — **rayarse** vr

rayo nm 1 : ray, beam ⟨rayo láser : laser beam⟩ ⟨rayo gamma : gamma ray⟩ ⟨rayo de sol : sunbeam⟩ 2 RELÁMPAGO : lightning bolt 3 **rayo X** : X-ray

rayón nm, pl **rayones** : rayon

rayuela nf : hopscotch

raza nf 1 : race ⟨raza humana : human race⟩ 2 : breed, strain 3 **de ~** : thoroughbred (of a horse), purebred, pedigreed

razón nf, pl **razones** 1 MOTIVO : reason, motive ⟨en razón de : by reason of, because of⟩ ⟨tuvo sus razones : she had her reasons⟩ ⟨razón de más para hacerlo : all the more reason to do it⟩ 2 : reasoning, sense ⟨perder la razón : to lose one's mind⟩ 3 **con ~** : with good reason ⟨se quejaron, y con razón : they complained, and with good reason⟩ ⟨con razón no tiene novia : no wonder he doesn't have a girlfriend⟩ 4 **con razón o sin ella** : rightly or wrongly 5 **tener razón** : to be right ⟨en algo tiene razón : he's right about one thing⟩ 6 **darle la razón a alguien** : to say/admit that someone is right

razonable adj : reasonable — **razonablemente** adv

razonado, -da adj : itemized, detailed

razonamiento nm : reasoning

razonar v : to reason, to think

re nm 1 : D ⟨re sostenido/bemol : D sharp/flat⟩ 2 : re (in singing)

re- pref : re-

reabastecimiento nm : replenishment

reabierto pp → **reabrir**

reabrir {2} vt : to reopen — **reabrirse** vr

reacción nf, pl **-ciones** 1 : reaction 2 **motor a reacción** : jet engine

reaccionar vi : to react, to respond

reaccionario, -ria adj & n : reactionary

reacio, -cia adj : resistant, opposed

reacondicionar vt : to recondition

reactivación nf, pl **-ciones** : reactivation, revival

reactivar vt : reactivate, revive

reactor nm 1 : reactor ⟨reactor nuclear : nuclear reactor⟩ 2 : jet engine 3 : jet airplane, jet

reafirmar *vt* : to reaffirm, to assert, to strengthen

reagruparse *vr* : to regroup

reajustar *vt* : to readjust, to adjust

reajuste *nm* : readjustment ⟨reajuste de precios : price increase⟩

real[1] *adj* **1** : real, true **2** : royal

real[2] *nm* : real (monetary unit of Brazil)

realce *nm* **1** : embossing, relief **2 dar realce** : to highlight, to bring out

realeza *nf* : royalty

realidad *nf* **1** : reality **2 en ∼** : in truth, actually **3 realidad aumentada** : augmented reality

realinear *vt* : to realign — **realineamiento** *nm*

realismo *nm* **1** : realism **2** : royalism

realista[1] *adj* **1** : realistic **2** : realist **3** : royalist

realista[2] *nmf* **1** : realist **2** : royalist

realizable *adj* : feasible, attainable, workable

realización *nf, pl* **-ciones** : execution, realization

realizador, -dora *n* : (television or movie) producer

realizar {21} *vt* **1** : to carry out, to execute **2** : to produce, to direct (a film or play) **3** : to fulfill, to achieve **4** : to realize (a profit) — **realizarse** *vr* **1** : to come true **2** : to fulfill oneself

realmente *adv* : really, in reality

realzar {21} *vt* **1** : to heighten, to raise **2** : to highlight, to enhance

reanimación *nf, pl* **-ciones** : revival, resuscitation

reanimar *vt* **1** : to revive, to restore **2** : to resuscitate — **reanimarse** *vr* : to come around, to recover

reanudación *nf, pl* **-ciones** : resumption, renewal

reanudar *vt* : to resume, to renew — **reanudarse** *vr* : to resume, to continue

reaparecer {53} *vi* **1** : to reappear **2** : to make a comeback

reaparición *nf, pl* **-ciones** : reappearance

reapertura *nf* : reopening

reata *nf* **1** : rope **2** *Mex* : lasso, lariat **3 de ∼** : single file

reavivar *vt* : to revive, to reawaken

rebaja *nf* **1** : reduction **2** DESCUENTO : discount **3 rebajas** *nfpl* : sale

rebajar *vt* **1** : to reduce, to lower ⟨a precios rebajados : at reduced prices, on sale⟩ **2** : to lessen, to diminish **3** : to humiliate — **rebajarse** *vr* **1** : to humble oneself **2 rebajarse a** : to stoop to

rebanada *nf* : slice

rebanadora *nf* : slicer

rebañar *vt* : to mop up, to sop up

rebaño *nm* **1** : flock **2** : herd

rebasar *vt* **1** : to surpass, to exceed **2** *Mex* : to pass, to overtake

rebatiña *nf* : scramble, fight (over something)

rebatir *vt* REFUTAR : to refute

rebato *nm* **1** : surprise attack **2 tocar a rebato** : to sound the alarm

rebeca *nf Spain* : cardigan

rebelarse *vr* : to rebel

rebelde[1] *adj* : rebellious, unruly

rebelde[2] *nmf* **1** : rebel **2** : defaulter

rebeldía *nf* **1** : rebelliousness **2 en ∼** : in default

rebelión *nf, pl* **-liones** : rebellion

reblandecer {18} *vt* : to soften

rebobinar *vt* : to rewind

reborde *nm* : border, flange, rim

rebosante *adj* : brimming, overflowing ⟨rebosante de salud : brimming with health⟩

rebosar *vi* **1** : to overflow **2 ∼ de** : to abound in, to be bursting with — *vt* : to radiate

rebotar *vi* **1** : to bounce **2** : to ricochet, to rebound

rebote *nm* **1** : bounce **2** : rebound, ricochet

rebozar {21} *vt* : to coat in batter

rebozo *nm* **1** : shawl, wrap **2 sin ∼** : frankly, openly

rebullir {38} *v* : to move, to stir — **rebullirse** *vr*

rebuscado, -da *adj* : affected, pretentious

rebuscar {72} *vi* : to search thoroughly

rebuznar *vi* : to bray

rebuzno *nm* : bray, braying

recabar *vt* **1** : to gather, to obtain, to collect **2 recabar fondos** : to raise money

recado *nm* **1** : message ⟨mandar recado : to send word⟩ **2** *Spain* : errand

recaer {13} *vi* **1** : to relapse **2 ∼ en** *or* **∼ sobre** : to fall on, to fall to

recaída *nf* : relapse

recaiga, etc. → recaer

recalar *vi* : to arrive

recalcar {72} *vt* : to emphasize, to stress

recalcitrante *adj* : recalcitrant

recalentar {55} *vt* **1** : to reheat, to warm up **2** : to overheat

recámara *nf* **1** *Col, Mex, Pan* : bedroom **2** : chamber (of a firearm)

recamarera *nf Mex* : chambermaid

recambio *nm* **1** : spare part **2** : refill (for a pen, etc.)

recapacitar *vi* **1** : to reconsider **2 ∼ en** : to reflect on, to weigh

recapitular *v* : to recapitulate — **recapitulación** *nf*

recargable *adj* : rechargeable

recargado, -da *adj* : overly elaborate or ornate

recargar {52} *vt* **1** : to recharge (a battery), to reload (a gun) **2** : to reload (a web page, etc.) **3** : to overload — **recargarse** *vr Mex* **∼ contra** : to lean against

recargo *nm* : surcharge

recatado, -da *adj* MODESTO : modest, demure

recato *nm* PUDOR : modesty

recaudación *nf, pl* **-ciones** **1** : collection **2** : earnings *pl*, takings *pl*

recaudador, -dora *n* **recaudador de impuestos** : tax collector

recaudar *vt* : to collect

recaudo *nm* : safe place ⟨a (buen) recaudo : in safe keeping⟩

recayó, etc. → recaer

rece, etc. → rezar

recelar *vt* **∼ de** : to distrust, to be suspicious of ⟨recelábamos de ella : we didn't trust her, we were suspicious of her⟩

recelo *nm* : distrust, suspicion
receloso, -sa *adj* : distrustful, suspicious
recepción *nf, pl* **-ciones** : reception
recepcionista *nmf* : receptionist
receptáculo *nm* : receptacle
receptividad *nf* : receptiveness
receptivo, -va *adj* : receptive
receptor¹, -tora *n* : receiving
receptor², -tora *n* **1** : recipient **2** : catcher (in baseball), receiver (in football)
receptor³ *nm* : receiver ⟨receptor de televisión : television set⟩
recesión *nf, pl* **-siones** : recession
recesivo, -va *adj* : recessive
receso *nm* : recess, adjournment
receta *nf* **1** : recipe **2** : prescription
recetar *vt* : to prescribe (medications)
rechazar {21} *vt* **1** : to reject **2** : to turn down, to refuse
rechazo *nm* : rejection, refusal
rechifla *nf* : booing, jeering
rechinar *vi* **1** : to squeak **2** : to grind, to gnash ⟨hacer rechinar los dientes : to grind one's teeth⟩
rechistar *vi* : to complain, to answer back ⟨trabajó sin rechistar : he worked without complaint⟩
rechoncho, -cha *adj fam* : chubby, squat
rechupete *adj fam de* ~ : delicious, scrumptious
recibidor *nm* : vestibule, entrance hall
recibimiento *nm* : reception, welcome
recibir *vt* **1** : to receive, to get **2** : to receive, to greet (visitors) — *vi* : to receive visitors — **recibirse** *vr* **1** : to graduate **2** ~ **de** : to qualify as
recibo *nm* : receipt
reciclable *adj* : recyclable
reciclado → **reciclaje**
reciclaje *nm* **1** : recycling **2** : retraining
reciclar *vt* **1** : to recycle **2** : to retrain
recién *adv* **1** : newly, recently ⟨recién nacido : newborn⟩ ⟨recién casados : newlyweds⟩ ⟨recién llegado : newcomer⟩ **2** : just, only just ⟨recién ahora me acordé : I just now remembered⟩
reciente *adj* : recent — **recientemente** *adv*
recinto *nm* **1** : enclosure **2** : site, premises *pl*
recio¹ *adv* **1** : strongly, hard **2** : loudly, loud
recio², -cia *adj* **1** : severe, harsh **2** : tough, strong
recipiente¹ *nm* : container, receptacle
recipiente² *nmf* : recipient
reciprocar {72} *vi* : to reciprocate
reciprocidad *nf* : reciprocity
recíproco, -ca *adj* : reciprocal, mutual — **recíprocamente** *adv*
recitación *nf, pl* **-ciones** : recitation, recital
recital *nm* : recital
recitar *vt* : to recite
reclamación *nf, pl* **-ciones** **1** : claim, demand **2** QUEJA : complaint
reclamar *vt* **1** EXIGIR : to demand, to require **2** : to claim — *vi* : to complain

reclamo *nm* **1** : bird call, lure **2** : lure, decoy **3** : inducement, attraction **4** : advertisement **5** : complaint
reclinable *adj* : reclining
reclinar *vt* : to rest, to lean — **reclinarse** *vr* : to recline, to lean back
recluir {41} *vt* : to confine, to lock up — **recluirse** *vr* : to shut oneself up, to withdraw
reclusión *nf, pl* **-siones** : imprisonment
recluso, -sa *n* **1** : inmate, prisoner **2** SOLITARIO : recluse
recluta *nmf* : recruit, draftee
reclutamiento *nm* : recruitment, recruiting
reclutar *vt* ENROLAR : to recruit, to enlist
recobrar *vt* : to recover, to regain — **recobrarse** *vr* : to recover, to recuperate
recocer {14} *vt* : to overcook, to cook over
recodo *nm* : bend
recogedor *nm* : dustpan
recogepelotas *nmfs & pl* : ball boy *m*, ball girl *f*
recoger {15} *vt* **1** : to collect, to gather **2** : to get, to pick up, to retrieve **3** : to clean up, to tidy (up)
recogido, -da *adj* : quiet, secluded
recogimiento *nm* **1** : collecting, gathering **2** : withdrawal **3** : absorption, concentration
recolección *nf, pl* **-ciones** **1** : collection ⟨recolección de basura : trash pickup⟩ **2** : harvest
recolectar *vt* **1** : to gather, to collect **2** : to harvest, to pick
recomendable *adj* : advisable, recommended
recomendación *nf, pl* **-ciones** : recommendation
recomendar {55} *vt* **1** : to recommend **2** ACONSEJAR : to advise
recompensa *nf* : reward, recompense
recompensar *vt* **1** PREMIAR : to reward **2** : to compensate
reconciliación *nf, pl* **-ciones** : reconciliation
reconciliar *vt* : to reconcile — **reconciliarse** *vr*
recóndito, -ta *adj* **1** : remote, isolated **2** : hidden **3 en lo más recóndito de** : in the depths of
reconfortar *vt* : to comfort — **reconfortante** *adj*
reconocer {18} *vt* **1** : to recognize **2** : to admit **3** : to examine
reconocible *adj* : recognizable
reconocido, -da *adj* **1** : recognized, accepted **2** : grateful
reconocimiento *nm* **1** : acknowledgment, recognition, avowal **2** : (medical) examination **3** : reconnaissance
reconquista *nf* : reconquest
reconquistar *vt* **1** : to reconquer, to recapture **2** RECUPERAR : to regain, to recover
reconsiderar *vt* : to reconsider — **reconsideración** *nf*
reconstrucción *nf, pl* **-ciones** : reconstruction

reconstructivo, -va *adj* : reconstructive
reconstruir {41} *vt* : to rebuild, to reconstruct
reconversión *nf, pl* **-siones** : restructuring
reconvertir {76} *vt* **1** : to restructure **2** : to retrain
recopilación *nf, pl* **-ciones** **1** : summary **2** : collection, compilation
recopilar *vt* : to compile, to collect
récord *or* **record** ['rekɔr] *nm, pl* **récords** *or* **records** [-kɔrs] : record ⟨record mundial : world record⟩ — **récord** *or* **record** *adj*
recordar {19} *vt* **1** : to recall, to remember **2** : to remind — *vi* **1** ACORDARSE : to remember ⟨si mal no recuerdo : if I recall/remember correctly⟩ **2** DESPERTAR : to wake up
recordatorio¹, -ria *adj* : commemorative
recordatorio² *nm* : reminder
recorrer *vt* **1** : to travel through, to tour **2** : to cover (a distance) **3** : to go over, to look over
recorrido *nm* **1** : journey, trip **2** : path, route, course **3** : round (in golf)
recortar *vt* **1** : to cut, to reduce **2** : to cut out **3** : to trim, to cut off **4** : to outline — **recortarse** *vr* : to stand out ⟨los árboles se recortaban en el horizonte : the trees were silhouetted against the horizon⟩
recorte *nm* **1** : cut, reduction **2** : clipping ⟨recortes de periódicos : newspaper clippings⟩
recostar {19} *vt* : to lean, to rest — **recostarse** *vr* : to lie down, recline
recoveco *nm* **1** VUELTA : bend, turn **2** : nook, corner **3** **recovecos** *nmpl* : intricacies, ins and outs
recreación *nf, pl* **-ciones** **1** : re-creation **2** DIVERSIÓN : recreation, entertainment
recrear *vt* **1** : to re-create **2** : to entertain, to amuse — **recrearse** *vr* : to enjoy oneself
recreativo, -va *adj* : recreational
recreo *nm* **1** DIVERSIÓN : entertainment, amusement **2** : recess, break
recriminación *nf, pl* **-ciones** : reproach, recrimination
recriminar *vt* : to reproach — **recriminarse** *vr*
recrudecer {53} *v* : to intensify, to worsen — **recrudecerse** *vr*
recta *nf* : straight line
rectal *adj* : rectal
rectangular *adj* : rectangular
rectángulo *nm* : rectangle
rectificación *nf, pl* **-ciones** : rectification, correction
rectificar {72} *vt* **1** : to rectify, to correct **2** : to straighten (out)
rectitud *nf* : honesty, rectitude
recto¹ *adv* : straight
recto², -ta *adj* **1** : straight **2** : upright, honorable **3** : sound
recto³ *nm* : rectum
rector¹, -tora *adj* : governing, managing
rector², -tora *n* : rector
rectoría *nf* : rectory

recuadro *nm* : box (containing text, etc.)
recubierto *pp* → **recubrir**
recubrir {2} *vt* : to cover, to coat
recuento *nm* : recount, count ⟨un recuento de los votos : a recount of the votes⟩
recuerdo *nm* **1** : memory **2** : souvenir, memento **3** **recuerdos** *nmpl* : regards
recular *vi* **1** : to back up **2** REPLEGARSE : to retreat, to fall back **3** RETRACTARSE : to back down
recuperación *nf, pl* **-ciones** **1** : recovery, recuperation **2** **recuperación de datos** : data retrieval
recuperar *vt* **1** : to recover, to get back, to retrieve **2** : to recuperate **3** : to make up for ⟨recuperar el tiempo perdido : to make up for lost time⟩ — **recuperarse** *vr* ~ **de** : to recover from, to get over
recurrente *adj* : recurrent, recurring
recurrir *vi* **1** ~ **a** : to turn to, to appeal to **2** ~ **a** : to resort to **3** : to appeal (in law)
recurso *nm* **1** : recourse ⟨el último recurso : the last resort⟩ **2** : appeal (in law) **3** **recursos** *nmpl* : resources, means ⟨recursos naturales : natural resources⟩
red *nf* **1** : net, mesh **2** : network, system, chain ⟨redes sociales : social media⟩ **3** : trap, snare **4** **la red/Red** : the Internet, the Web **5** **red barredera** : dragnet
redacción *nf, pl* **-ciones** **1** : writing, composition **2** : editing
redactar *vt* **1** : to write, to draft **2** : to edit
redactor, -tora *n* : editor
redada *nf* **1** : raid **2** : catch, haul
redecorar *v* : to redecorate
redefinir *vt* : to redefine — **redefinición** *nf*
redención *nf, pl* **-ciones** : redemption
redentor¹, -tora *adj* : redeeming
redentor², -tora *n* : redeemer
redescubierto *pp* → **redescubrir**
redescubrir {2} *vt* : to rediscover
redicho, -cha *adj fam* : affected, pretentious
redil *nm* **1** : sheepfold **2** **volver al redil** : to return to the fold
redimir *vt* : to redeem, to deliver (from sin)
rediseñar *vt* : to redesign
redistribuir {41} *vt* : to redistribute — **redistribución** *nf*
rédito *nm* : return, yield
redituar {3} *vt* : to produce, to yield
redoblar *vt* : to redouble, to strengthen — **redoblado, -da** *adj*
redoble *nm* : drum roll
redomado, -da *adj* **1** : sly, crafty **2** : utter, out-and-out
redonda *nf* **1** : region, surrounding area **2** **a la redonda** ALREDEDOR : around ⟨de diez millas a la redonda : for ten miles around⟩ **3** : whole note
redondear *vt* : to round off, to round out
redondel *nm* **1** : ring, circle **2** : bullring, arena

redondez *nf* : roundness
redondo, -da *adj* **1** : round ⟨mesa redonda : round table⟩ **2** : great, perfect ⟨un negocio redondo : an excellent deal⟩ **3** : straightforward, flat ⟨un rechazo redondo : a flat refusal⟩ **4** *Mex* : round-trip **5 en ∼** : around
reducción *nf, pl* **-ciones** : reduction, decrease
reducido, -da *adj* **1** : reduced, limited **2** : small
reducir {61} *vt* **1** DISMINUIR : to reduce, to decrease, to cut **2** : to subdue **3** : to boil down — **reducirse** *vr* ∼ **a** : to come down to, to be nothing more than
redundancia *nf* : redundancy
redundante *adj* : redundant
reedición *nf, pl* **-ciones** : reprint
reeditar *vt* : to reprint
reelegir {28} *vt* : to reelect — **reelección** *nf*
reembolsable *adj* : refundable
reembolsar *vt* **1** : to refund, to reimburse **2** : to repay
reembolso *nm* : refund, reimbursement
reemplazable *adj* : replaceable
reemplazar {21} *vt* : to replace, to substitute
reemplazo *nm* : replacement, substitution
reencarnación *nf, pl* **-ciones** : reincarnation
reencuentro *nm* : reunion
reestablecer {53} *vt* : to reestablish
reestructurar *vt* : to restructure
reexaminar *vt* : to reexamine
refacción *nf, pl* **-ciones** **1** *Mex* : spare part, replacement part **2** : repair, renovation
refaccionar *vt* : to repair, to renovate
refaccionaria *nf Mex* : repair shop
referencia *nf* **1** : reference **2 hacer referencia a** : to refer to
referendo → referéndum
referéndum *nm, pl* **-dums** : referendum
referente *adj* ∼ **a** : concerning
réferi *or* **referi** ['referi] *nmf* : referee
referir {76} *vt* **1** : to relate, to tell **2** : to refer ⟨nos refirió al diccionario : she referred us to the dictionary⟩ — **referirse** *vr* ∼ **a** **1** : to refer to **2** : to be concerned, to be in reference to ⟨en lo que se refiere a la educación : as far as education is concerned⟩
refilón → de refilón
refinado¹, -da *adj* : refined
refinado² *nm* : refining
refinamiento *nm* **1** : refining **2** FINURA : refinement
refinanciar *vt* : to refinance
refinar *vt* : to refine
refinería *nf* : refinery
reflectante *adj* : reflective, reflecting
reflector¹, -tora *adj* : reflecting
reflector² *nm* **1** : spotlight, searchlight **2** : reflector
reflejar *vt* : to reflect — **reflejarse** *vr* : to be reflected ⟨la decepción se refleja en su rostro : the disappointment shows on her face⟩

reflejo *nm* **1** : reflection **2** : reflex **3 reflejos** *nmpl* : highlights, streaks (in hair)
reflexión *nf, pl* **-xiones** : reflection, thought
reflexionar *vi* : to reflect, to think
reflexivo, -va *adj* **1** : reflective, thoughtful **2** : reflexive
reflujo *nm* **1** : ebb, ebb tide **2 el flujo y reflujo** : the ebb and flow
reforma *nf* **1** : reform **2** : alteration, renovation
reformador, -dora *n* : reformer
reformar *vt* **1** : to reform **2** : to change, to alter **3** : to renovate, to repair — **reformarse** *vr* : to mend one's ways
reformatorio *nm* : reform school
reforzar {36} *vt* **1** : to reinforce, to strengthen **2** : to encourage, to support
refracción *nf, pl* **-ciones** : refraction
refractar *vt* : to refract — **refractarse** *vr*
refrán *nm, pl* **refranes** ADAGIO : proverb, saying
refregar {49} *vt* : to scrub
refrenar *vt* **1** : to rein in (a horse) **2** : to restrain, to check — **refrenarse** *vr* : to restrain oneself
refrendar *vt* **1** : to countersign, to endorse **2** : to stamp (a passport)
refrescante *adj* : refreshing
refrescar {72} *vt* **1** : to refresh, to cool **2** : to brush up (on) **3 refrescar la memoria** : to refresh one's memory — *vi* : to turn cooler
refresco *nm* : refreshment, soft drink ⟨refresco de cola : cola⟩
refriega *nf* : skirmish, scuffle
refrigeración *nf, pl* **-ciones** **1** : refrigeration **2** : air-conditioning
refrigerador *nmf* NEVERA : refrigerator
refrigeradora *nf Col, Peru* : refrigerator
refrigerante *nm* : coolant
refrigerar *vt* **1** : to refrigerate **2** : to air-condition
refrigerio *nm* : snack, refreshments *pl*
refrito¹, -ta *adj* : refried
refrito² *nm* : fried dish
refuerzo *nm* : reinforcement, support
refugiado, -da *n* : refugee
refugiar *vt* : to shelter — **refugiarse** *vr* ACOGERSE : to take refuge
refugio *nm* : refuge, shelter
refulgencia *nf* : brilliance, splendor
refulgir {35} *vi* : to shine brightly
refundir *vt* **1** : to recast (metals) **2** : to revise, to rewrite
refunfuñar *vi* : to grumble, to groan
refutar *vt* : to refute — **refutación** *nf*
regadera *nf* **1** : watering can **2** : shower head, shower **3** : sprinkler
regaderazo *nm Mex* : shower
regadío *nm* **tierra de** ∼ : irrigated land
regalado, -da *adj* **1** : dirt cheap **2** : comfortable, easy
regalar *vt* **1** OBSEQUIAR : to present (as a gift), to give away **2** : to regale, to entertain **3** : to flatter, to make a fuss over — **regalarse** *vr* : to pamper oneself
regalía *nf* : royalty, payment
regaliz *nm, pl* **-lices** : licorice

regalo *nm* **1** OBSEQUIO : gift, present **2** : pleasure, comfort **3** : treat

regalón, -lona *adj, mpl* **-lones** *Chile fam* : spoiled (of a person)

regañadientes *mpl* **a ~** : reluctantly, unwillingly

regañar *vt* : to scold, to give a talking to — *vi* **1** QUEJARSE : to grumble, to complain **2** REÑIR : to quarrel, to argue

regañina *nf fam* : scolding

regaño *nm fam* : scolding

regañón, -ñona *adj, mpl* **-ñones** *fam* : grumpy, irritable

regar {49} *vt* **1** : to irrigate **2** : to water **3** : to wash, to hose down **4** : to spill, to scatter

regata *nf* : regatta, yacht race

regate *nm* : dodge, feint

regatear *vt* **1** : to haggle over **2** ESCATIMAR : to skimp on, to be sparing with — *vi* : to bargain, to haggle

regateo *nm* : bargaining, haggling

regatón *nm, pl* **-tones** : cap, tip

regazo *nm* : lap (of a person)

regencia *nf* : regency

regenerar *vt* : to regenerate — **regenerarse** *vr* — **regeneración** *nf*

regentar *vt* : to run, to manage

regente *nmf* : regent

reggae ['rege, 'rigi] *nm* : reggae

regidor, -dora *n* : town councillor

régimen *nm, pl* **regímenes 1** : regime **2** : diet **3** : regimen, rules *pl* ⟨régimen de vida : lifestyle⟩

regimiento *nm* : regiment

regio, -gia *adj* **1** : great, magnificent **2** : regal, royal

región *nf, pl* **regiones** : region, area

regional *adj* : regional — **regionalmente** *adv*

regir {28} *vt* **1** : to rule **2** : to manage, to run **3** : to control, to govern ⟨las costumbres que rigen la conducta : the customs which govern behavior⟩ — *vi* : to apply, to be in force ⟨las leyes rigen en los tres países : the laws apply in all three countries⟩ — **regirse** *vr* **~ por** : to go by, to be guided by

registrador[1], -dora *adj* **caja registradora** : cash register

registrador[2], -dora *n* : registrar, recorder

registrar *vt* **1** : to register, to record **2** GRABAR : to record, to tape **3** : to search, to examine — **registrarse** *vr* **1** INSCRIBIRSE : to register **2** OCURRIR : to happen, to occur

registro *nm* **1** : register **2** : registration **3** : registry, record office **4** : range (of a voice or musical instrument) **5** : search

regla *nf* **1** NORMA : rule, regulation **2** : ruler ⟨regla de cálculo : slide rule⟩ **3** MENSTRUACIÓN : period, menstruation

reglamentación *nf, pl* **-ciones 1** : regulation **2** : rules *pl*

reglamentar *vt* : to regulate, to set rules for

reglamentario, -ria *adj* : regulation, official ⟨equipo reglamentario : standard equipment⟩

reglamento *nm* : regulations *pl*, rules *pl* ⟨reglamento de tráfico : traffic regulations⟩

regocijar *vt* : to gladden, to delight — **regocijarse** *vr* : to rejoice

regocijo *nm* : delight, rejoicing

regodearse *vr* : to delight, to gloat ⟨regodearse en/con : to delight in, to gloat about/over⟩

regordete, -ta *adj fam* LLENITO : chubby

regresar *vt* DEVOLVER : to give back — *vi* : to return, to come back, to go back

regresión *nf, pl* **-siones** : regression, return

regresivo, -va *adj* : regressive

regreso *nm* **1** : return **2 estar de regreso** : to be back, to be home

reguero *nm* **1** : irrigation ditch **2** : trail, trace **3 propagarse como reguero de pólvora** : to spread like wildfire

regulable *adj* : adjustable

regulación *nf, pl* **-ciones** : regulation, control

regulador[1], -dora *adj* : regulating, regulatory

regulador[2] *nm* **1** : regulator, governor **2 regulador de tiro** : damper (in a chimney)

regular[1] *vt* : to regulate, to control

regular[2] *adj* **1** : regular **2** : fair, OK, soso **3** : medium, average **4 por lo regular** : in general, generally

regularidad *nf* : regularity

regularización *nf, pl* **-ciones** NORMALIZACIÓN : normalization

regularizar {21} *vt* NORMALIZAR : to normalize, to make regular

regularmente *adv* : regularly

regurgitar *vi* : to regurgitate

regusto *nm* : aftertaste

rehabilitar *vt* **1** : to rehabilitate **2** : to reinstate **3** : renovate, to restore — **rehabilitación** *nf*

rehacer {40} *vt* **1** : to redo **2** : to remake, to repair, to renew — **rehacerse** *vr* **1** : to recover **2 ~ de** : to get over

rehecho *pp* → **rehacer**

rehén *nm, pl* **rehenes** : hostage

rehicieron, etc. → **rehacer**

rehizo → **rehacer**

rehuir {41} *vt* : to avoid, to shun

rehusar {8} *v* : to refuse

reimprimir *vt* : to reprint

reina *nf* : queen

reinado *nm* : reign

reinante *adj* **1** : reigning **2** : prevailing, current

reinar *vi* **1** : to reign **2** : to prevail

reincidencia *nf* : recidivism

reincidente *adj & nmf* : recidivist

reincidir *vi* : to backslide, to relapse

reincorporar *vt* : to reinstate — **reincorporarse** *vr* **~ a** : to return to, to rejoin

reiniciar *vt* **1** : to resume, to restart **2** : to reboot (a computer)

reino *nm* : kingdom, realm ⟨reino animal : animal kingdom⟩

reinstalar *vt* **1** : to reinstall **2** : to reinstate

reintegración *nf, pl* **-ciones 1** : reinstatement, reintegration **2** : refund, reimbursement

reintegrar *vt* **1** : to reintegrate, reinstate **2** : to refund, to reimburse — **reintegrarse** *vr* ~ **a** : to return to, to rejoin

reintegro *nm* : refund, reimbursement

reintroducir {61} *vt* : to reintroduce

reír {66} *vi* : to laugh — *vt* : to laugh at — **reírse** *vr*

reiteración *nf, pl* **-ciones** : reiteration, repetition

reiterado, -da *adj* : repeated ⟨lo explicó en reiteradas ocasiones : he explained it repeatedly⟩ — **reiteradamente** *adv*

reiterar *vt* : to reiterate, to repeat

reiterativo, -va *adj* : repetitive, repetitious

reivindicación *nf, pl* **-ciones** **1** : demand, claim **2** : vindication

reivindicar {72} *vt* **1** : to vindicate **2** : to demand, to claim **3** : to restore

reja *nf* **1** : grille, grating ⟨entre rejas : behind bars⟩ **2** : plowshare

rejego, -ga *adj Mex fam* : stubborn

rejilla *nf* : grille, grate, screen

rejuvenecer {53} *vt* : to rejuvenate — *vi* : to be rejuvenated — **rejuvenecerse** *vr*

rejuvenecimiento *nm* : rejuvenation

relación *nf, pl* **-ciones** **1** : relation, connection, relevance **2** : relationship **3** RELATO : account **4** LISTA : list **5** : ratio (in mathematics) **6 con relación a** *or* **en relación con** : in relation to, concerning **7 relaciones públicas** : public relations, PR

relacionar *vt* : to relate, to connect — **relacionarse** *vr* ~ **con** : to be connected to, to be linked with

relajación *nf, pl* **-ciones** : relaxation

relajado, -da *adj* **1** : relaxed, loose **2** : dissolute, depraved

relajante *adj* : relaxing

relajar *vt* : to relax, to slacken — *vi* : to be relaxing — **relajarse** *vr*

relajo *nm* **1** : commotion, ruckus **2** : joke, laugh ⟨lo hizo de relajo : he did it for a laugh⟩

relamerse *vr* : to smack one's lips, to lick one's chops

relámpago *nm* : flash of lightning

relampaguear *vi* : to flash

relanzar {21} *vt* : to relaunch

relatar *vt* : to relate, to tell

relatividad *nf* : relativity

relativismo *nm* : relativism

relativo, -va *adj* **1** : relative **2 en lo relativo a** : with regard to, concerning — **relativamente** *adv*

relato *nm* **1** : story, tale **2** : account

relax [re'las] *nm* : relaxation

releer {20} *vt* : to reread

relegar {52} *vt* **1** : to relegate **2 relegar al olvido** : to consign to oblivion

relevante *adj* : outstanding, important

relevar *vt* **1** : to relieve, to take over from **2** ~ **de** : to exempt from — **relevarse** *vr* : to take turns

relevo *nm* **1** : relief, replacement **2** : relay ⟨carrera de relevos : relay race⟩

relicario *nm* **1** : shrine, container (for relics) **2** : locket

relieve *nm* **1** : relief, projection ⟨mapa en relieve : relief map⟩ ⟨letras en relieve : embossed letters⟩ **2** : prominence, importance **3 poner en relieve** : to highlight, to emphasize

religión *nf, pl* **-giones** : religion

religiosamente *adv* : religiously, faithfully

religioso[1], -sa *adj* : religious

religioso[2], -sa *n* : monk *m*, nun *f*

relinchar *vi* : to neigh, to whinny

relincho *nm* : neigh, whinny

reliquia *nf* **1** : relic **2 reliquia de familia** : family heirloom

rellano *nm* : landing (of a stairway)

rellenar *vt* **1** : to refill **2** : to stuff, to fill **3** : to fill out

relleno[1], -na *adj* : stuffed, filled

relleno[2] *nm* : stuffing, filling

reloj *nm* **1** : clock **2** : watch **3 reloj de arena** : hourglass **4 reloj de pulsera** : wristwatch **5 como un reloj** : like clockwork

relojería *nf* **1** : watchmaker's shop **2** : watchmaking, clockmaking

relojero, -ra *n* : watchmaker, clockmaker

reluciente *adj* : brilliant, shining

relucir {45} *vi* **1** : to glitter, to shine **2** **salir a relucir** : to come to the surface **3** **sacar a relucir** : to bring up, to mention

relumbrante *adj* : dazzling

relumbrar *vi* : to shine brightly

relumbrón *nm, pl* **-brones** **1** : flash, glare **2 de ~** : flashy, showy

remachar *vt* **1** : to rivet **2** : to clinch (a nail) **3** : to stress, to drive home — *vi* : to smash, to spike (a ball)

remache *nm* **1** : rivet **2** : smash, spike (in sports)

remanente *nm* **1** : remainder, balance **2** : surplus

remangar {52} *vt* : to roll up — **remangarse** *vr* : to roll up one's sleeves

remanso *nm* : pool

remar *vi* **1** : to row, to paddle **2** : to struggle, to toil

remarcar {72} *vt* : to emphasize, to stress

rematado, -da *adj* : utter, complete

rematador, -dora *n* : auctioneer

rematar *vt* **1** : to finish off **2** : to auction — *vi* **1** : to shoot **2** : to end

remate *nm* **1** : shot (in sports) ⟨sacar un remate : to take a shot⟩ **2** : auction **3** : end, conclusion **4 como ~** : to top it off **5 de ~** : completely, utterly

remecer {86} *vt* : to sway, to swing

remedar *vt* **1** IMITAR : to imitate, to copy **2** : to mimic, to ape

remediar *vt* **1** : to remedy, to repair **2** : to help out, to assist **3** EVITAR : to prevent, to avoid

remedio *nm* **1** : remedy, cure **2** : solution **3** : option ⟨no me quedó más remedio : I had no other choice⟩ ⟨no hay remedio : it can't be helped⟩ **4 poner remedio a** : to put a stop to **5 sin ~** : unavoidable, inevitable

remedo *nm* : imitation

rememorar *vt* : to recall ⟨rememorar los viejos tiempos : to reminisce⟩

remendar {55} *vt* **1** : to mend, to patch, to darn **2** : to correct

remera *nf Arg, Uru* : T-shirt
remero, -ra *n* : rower
remesa *nf* 1 : remittance 2 : shipment
remezón *nm, pl* **-zones** : mild earthquake, tremor
remiendo *nm* 1 : patch 2 : correction
remilgado, -da *adj* 1 : prim, prudish 2 : affected
remilgo *nm* : primness, affectation
reminiscencia *nf* : reminiscence
remisión *nf, pl* **-siones** 1 ENVÍO : sending, delivery 2 : remission 3 : reference, cross-reference
remiso, -sa *adj* 1 : lax, remiss 2 : reluctant
remite *nm* : return address
remitente¹ *nm* : return address
remitente² *nmf* : sender (of a letter, etc.)
remitir *vt* 1 : to send, to remit 2 ~ a : to refer to, to direct to ⟨nos remitió al diccionario : he referred us to the dictionary⟩ — *vi* : to subside, to let up — **remitirse** *vr* ~ a : to refer to
remo *nm* 1 : paddle, oar 2 : rowing (sport)
remoción *nf, pl* **-ciones** 1 : removal 2 : dismissal
remodelación *nf, pl* **-ciones** 1 : remodeling 2 : reorganization, restructuring
remodelar *vt* 1 : to remodel 2 : to restructure
remojar *vt* 1 : to soak, to steep 2 : to dip, to dunk 3 : to celebrate with a drink
remojo *nm* 1 : soaking, steeping 2 **poner en remojo** : to soak, to leave soaking
remolacha *nf* : beet
remolcador *nm* : tugboat
remolcar {72} *vt* : to tow, to haul
remolino *nm* 1 : whirlwind 2 : eddy, whirlpool 3 : crowd, throng 4 : cowlick
remolón, -lona *adj, mpl* **-lones** : lazy
remolque *nm* 1 : towing, tow 2 : trailer 3 **a** ~ : in tow
remontar *vt* 1 : to overcome 2 SUBIR : to go up — **remontarse** *vr* 1 : to soar 2 ~ a : to date from, to go back to
rémora *nf* : obstacle, hindrance
remorder {47} *vt* INQUIETAR : to trouble, to distress
remordimiento *nm* : remorse
remotamente *adv* : remotely, vaguely
remoto, -ta *adj* 1 : remote, unlikely ⟨hay una posibilidad remota : there is a slim possibility⟩ 2 : distant, far-off
remover {47} *vt* 1 : to stir 2 : to move around, to turn over 3 : to stir up 4 : to remove 5 : to dismiss
removible *adj* : removable
remozamiento *nm* : renovation
remozar {21} *vt* 1 : to renew, to brighten up 2 : to redo, to renovate
remuneración *nf, pl* **-ciones** : remuneration, pay
remunerar *vt* : to pay, to remunerate
renacer {48} *vi* : to be reborn, to revive
renacimiento *nm* 1 : rebirth, revival 2 **el Renacimiento** : the Renaissance
renacuajo *nm* : tadpole, pollywog

renal *adj* : renal, kidney
rencilla *nf* : quarrel
renco, -ca *adj* : lame
rencor *nm* 1 : rancor, enmity, hostility 2 **guardar rencor** : to hold a grudge ⟨guardarle rencor a alguien por algo : to resent someone for something, to hold a grudge against someone for something⟩
rencoroso, -sa *adj* : resentful, bitter, rancorous
rendición *nf, pl* **-ciones** 1 : surrender, submission 2 : yield, return
rendido, -da *adj* 1 : submissive 2 : worn-out, exhausted 3 : devoted
rendija *nf* GRIETA : crack, split
rendimiento *nm* 1 : performance 2 : yield, efficiency
rendir {54} *vt* 1 : to render, to give ⟨rendir las gracias : to give thanks⟩ ⟨rendir homenaje a : to pay homage to⟩ 2 : to yield 3 CANSAR : to exhaust — *vi* 1 CUNDIR : to progress, to make headway 2 : to last, to go a long way — **rendirse** *vr* : to surrender, to give up
renegado, -da *n* : renegade
renegar {49} *vi* 1 ~ **de** : to renounce, to disown, to give up 2 ~ **de** : to complain about — *vt* 1 : to deny vigorously 2 : to abhor, to hate
renglón *nm, pl* **renglones** 1 : line (of writing) 2 : merchandise, line (of products)
rengo, -ga *adj* : lame
renguear *vi* : to limp
reno *nm* : reindeer
renombrado, -da *adj* : renowned, famous
renombre *nm* NOMBRADÍA : renown, fame
renovable *adj* : renewable
renovación *nf, pl* **-ciones** 1 : renewal ⟨renovación de un contrato : renewal of a contract⟩ 2 : change, renovation
renovar {19} *vt* 1 : to renew, to restore 2 : to renovate
renquear *vi* : to limp, to hobble
renquera *nf* COJERA : limp, lameness
renta *nf* 1 : income 2 : rent 3 **impuesto sobre la renta** : income tax
rentable *adj* : profitable — **rentabilidad** *nf*
rentar *vt* 1 : to produce, to yield 2 ALQUILAR : to rent
renuencia *nf* : reluctance, unwillingness
renuente *adj* : reluctant, unwilling
renuncia *nf* 1 : resignation 2 : renunciation 3 : waiver
renunciar *vi* : to resign 2 ~ **a** : to renounce, to relinquish ⟨renunció al título : he relinquished the title⟩
reñido, -da *adj* 1 : tough, hard-fought 2 : at odds, on bad terms
reñir {67} *vi* 1 : to argue 2 ~ **con** : to fall out with, to go up against — *vt* : to scold, to reprimand
reo, rea *n* 1 : accused, defendant 2 : offender, culprit
reojo *nm* **de** ~ : out of the corner of one's eye ⟨una mirada de reojo : a sidelong glance⟩
reorganizar {21} *vt* : to reorganize — **reorganización** *nf*

repantigarse {52} *vr* : to slouch, to loll about

reparación *nf, pl* **-ciones 1** : reparation, amends **2** : repair

reparador, -dora *adj* : refreshing

reparar *vt* **1** : to repair, to fix, to mend **2** : to make amends for **3** : to correct **4** : to restore, to refresh — *vi* **1** ~ **en** : to observe, to take notice of **2** ~ **en** : to consider, to think about ⟨sin reparar en las consecuencias : without thinking about the consequences⟩ ⟨no repararon en gastos : they spared no expense, money was no object⟩

reparo *nm* **1** : repair, restoration **2** : reservation, qualm ⟨no tuvieron reparos en decírmelo : they didn't hesitate to tell me⟩ **3 poner reparos a** : to find fault with, to object to

repartición *nf, pl* **-ciones 1** : distribution **2** : department, division

repartidor¹, -dora *adj* : delivery ⟨camión repartidor : delivery truck⟩

repartidor², -dora *n* : delivery person, distributor

repartimiento *nm* → repartición

repartir *vt* **1** : to allocate **2** DISTRIBUIR : to distribute, to hand out **3** : to spread

reparto *nm* **1** : allocation **2** : distribution **3** : cast (of characters)

repasador *nm Arg, Uru* : dish towel

repasar *vt* **1** : to pass by again **2** : to review, to go over **3** : to mend

repaso *nm* **1** : review **2** : mending **3** : checkup, overhaul

repatriar {85} *vt* : to repatriate — **repatriación** *nf*

repavimentar *vt* : to resurface

repelente¹ *adj* : repellent, repulsive

repelente² *nm* : repellent ⟨repelente de insectos : insect repellent⟩

repeler *vt* **1** : to repel, to resist, to repulse **2** : to reject **3** : to disgust ⟨el sabor me repele : I find the taste repulsive⟩

repensar {55} *v* : to rethink, to reconsider

repente *nm* **1** : sudden movement, start ⟨de repente : suddenly⟩ **2** : fit, outburst ⟨un repente de ira : a fit of anger⟩

repentino, -na *adj* : sudden — **repentinamente** *adv*

repercusión *nf, pl* **-siones** : repercussion

repercutir *vi* **1** : to reverberate, to echo **2** ~ **en** : to have effects on, to have repercussions on

repertorio *nm* : repertoire

repetición *nf, pl* **-ciones 1** : repetition **2** : rerun, repeat

repetidamente *adv* : repeatedly

repetido, -da *adj* **1** : repeated, numerous **2 repetidas veces** : time and again

repetir {54} *vt* **1** : to repeat **2** : to have a second helping of — *vi* **1** : to repeat a year (in school) **2** : to have a second helping **3** : to give indigestion — **repetirse** *vr* **1** : to repeat oneself **2** : to recur

repetitivo, -va *adj* : repetitive, repetitious

repicar {72} *vt* : to ring — *vi* : to ring out, to peal

repique *nm* : ringing, pealing

repiqueteo *nm* **1** : ringing, pealing **2** : drumming

repisa *nf* : shelf, ledge ⟨repisa de chimenea : mantelpiece⟩ ⟨repisa de ventana : windowsill⟩

replantear *vt* : to redefine, to restate — **replantearse** *vr* : to reconsider

replegar {49} *vt* : to fold — **replegarse** *vr* RETIRARSE : to retreat, to withdraw

repleto, -ta *adj* **1** : replete, full **2** ~ **de** : packed with, crammed with

réplica *nf* **1** : reply **2** : replica, reproduction **3** : aftershock

replicación *nf, pl* **-ciones** : replication

replicar {72} *vi* **1** : to reply, to retort **2** : to argue, to answer back

repliegue *nm* **1** : fold **2** : retreat, withdrawal

repollo *nm* COL : cabbage

reponer {60} *vt* **1** : to replace, to put back **2** : to reinstate **3** : to reply — **reponerse** *vr* : to recover

reportaje *nm* : article, story, report

reportar *vt* **1** : to check, to restrain **2** : to bring, to carry, to yield ⟨me reportó numerosos beneficios : it brought me many benefits⟩ **3** : to report — **reportarse** *vr* **1** CONTENERSE : to control oneself **2** PRESENTARSE : to report, to show up

reporte *nm* : report

reportear *vt* : to report on, to cover

reportero, -ra *n* **1** : reporter **2 reportero gráfico** : photojournalist

reposado, -da *adj* : calm

reposapiés *nm, pl* **reposapiés** : footrest

reposar *vi* **1** : to rest, to repose **2** : to stand, to settle ⟨deje reposar la masa media hora : let the dough stand for half an hour⟩ **3** : to lie, to be buried — **reposarse** *vr* : to settle

reposición *nf, pl* **-ciones 1** : replacement **2** : reinstatement **3** : revival

repositorio *nm* : repository

reposo *nm* : repose, rest

repostar *vi* **1** : to stock up **2** : to refuel

repostear *vt* : to repost (on social media)

repostería *nf* **1** : confectioner's shop **2** : pastry-making

repostero, -ra *n* : confectioner

repreguntar *vt* : to cross-examine

repreguntas *nfpl* : cross-examination

reprender *vt* : to reprimand, to scold

reprensible *adj* : reprehensible

represa *nf* : dam

represalia *nf* **1** : reprisal, retaliation **2 tomar represalias** : to retaliate

represar *vt* : to dam

representación *nf, pl* **-ciones 1** : representation **2** : performance **3 en representación de** : on behalf of

representante *nmf* **1** : representative **2** : performer

representar *vt* **1** : to represent, to act for **2** : to perform **3** : to look, to appear as **4** : to symbolize, to stand for **5** : to signify, to mean — **representarse** *vr* : to imagine, to picture

representativo, -va *adj* : representative

represión *nf, pl* **-siones** : repression
represivo, -va *adj* : repressive
reprimenda *nf* : reprimand
reprimir *vt* **1** : to repress **2** : to suppress, to stifle
reprobable *adj* : reprehensible, culpable
reprobación *nf, pl* **-ciones** : disapproval
reprobar {19} *vt* **1** DESAPROBAR : to condemn, to disapprove of **2** : to fail (a course)
reprobatorio, -ria *adj* : disapproving, admonishing
reprochable *adj* : reprehensible
reprochar *vt* : to reproach — **reprocharse** *vr*
reproche *nm* : reproach
reproducción *nf, pl* **-ciones** : reproduction
reproducir {61} *vt* : to reproduce — **reproducirse** *vr* **1** : to breed, to reproduce **2** : to recur
reproductor¹, -tora *adj* : reproductive
reproductor² *nm* : player ⟨reproductor de DVD : DVD player⟩
reptar *vi* : to crawl, to slither
reptil¹ *adj* : reptilian
reptil² *nm* : reptile
república *nf* : republic
republicano, -na *adj & n* : republican — **republicanismo** *nm*
repudiar *vt* : to repudiate — **repudiación** *nf*
repudio *nm* : repudiation
repuesto¹ *pp* → **reponer**
repuesto² *nm* **1** : spare part **2 de ~** : spare ⟨rueda de repuesto : spare wheel⟩
repugnancia *nf* : repugnance
repugnante *adj* : repulsive, repugnant, revolting
repugnar *vt* : to cause repugnance, to disgust — **repugnarse** *vr*
repujar *vt* : to emboss
repulsa *nf* **1** : rejection **2** : condemnation
repulsivo, -va *adj* : repulsive
repuntar *vt Arg, Chile* : to round up (cattle) — *vi* : to begin to appear — **repuntarse** *vr* : to fall out, to quarrel
repuso, etc. → **reponer**
reputación *nf, pl* **-ciones** : reputation
reputar *vt* : to consider, to deem
requerir {76} *vt* **1** : to require, to call for **2** : to summon, to send for
requesón *nm, pl* **-sones** : curd cheese, cottage cheese
réquiem *nm* : requiem
requisa *nf* **1** : requisition **2** : seizure **3** : inspection
requisar *vt* **1** : to requisition **2** : to seize **3** INSPECCIONAR : to inspect
requisito *nm* **1** : requirement **2 requisito previo** : prerequisite
res *nf* **1** : beast, animal **2** *CA, Mex* : beef **3 reses** *nfpl* : cattle ⟨60 reses : 60 head of cattle⟩
resabio *nm* **1** VICIO : bad habit, vice **2** DEJO : aftertaste
resaca *nf* **1** : undertow **2** : hangover
resaltar *vi* **1** SOBRESALIR : to stand out **2 hacer resaltar** : to bring out, to highlight — *vt* : to stress, to emphasize

resarcimiento *nm* **1** : compensation **2** : reimbursement
resarcir {83} *vt* : to compensate, to indemnify — **resarcirse** *vr* **~ de** : to make up for
resbalada *nf* : slip
resbaladizo, -za *adj* **1** RESBALOSO : slippery **2** : tricky, ticklish, delicate
resbalar *vi* **1** : to slip, to slide **2** : to slip up, to make a mistake **3** : to skid — **resbalarse** *vr*
resbalón *nm, pl* **-lones** : slip
resbaloso, -sa *adj* : slippery
rescatar *vt* **1** : to rescue, to save **2** : to recover, to get back
rescate *nm* **1** : rescue **2** : recovery **3** : ransom
rescindir *vt* : to rescind, to annul, to cancel
rescisión *nf, pl* **-siones** : annulment, cancellation
rescoldo *nm* : embers *pl*
resecar {72} *vt* : to make dry, to dry up — **resecarse** *vr* : to dry up
reseco, -ca *adj* : dry
resentido, -da *adj* : resentful
resentimiento *nm* : resentment
resentirse {76} *vr* **1** : to suffer, to be weakened **2** OFENDERSE : to be/get upset ⟨se resintió porque la insultaron : she got upset when they insulted her, she resented being insulted⟩ **3 ~ de** : to feel the effects of — **resentir** *vt* **1** : to feel (effects, etc.) **2** : to resent
reseña *nf* **1** : report, summary, review **2** : description
reseñar *vt* **1** : to review **2** DESCRIBIR : to describe
reserva *nf* **1** : reservation **2** : reserve **3** : confidence, privacy ⟨con la mayor reserva : in strictest confidence⟩ **4 de ~** : spare, in reserve **5 reservas** *nfpl* : reservations, doubts
reservación *nf, pl* **-ciones** : reservation
reservado, -da *adj* **1** : reserved, reticent **2** : confidential
reservar *vt* : to reserve — **reservarse** *vr* **1** : to save oneself **2** : to conceal, to keep to oneself
reservorio *nm* : reservoir, reserve
resfriado *nm* CATARRO : cold
resfriar {85} *vt* : to cool — **resfriarse** *vr* **1** : to cool off **2** : to catch a cold
resfrío *nm* : cold
resguardar *vt* : to safeguard, to protect — **resguardarse** *vr*
resguardo *nm* **1** : safeguard, protection **2** : receipt, voucher **3** : border guard, coast guard
residencia *nf* **1** : residence **2** : boarding house
residencial *adj* : residential
residente *adj & nmf* : resident
residir *vi* **1** VIVIR : to reside, to dwell **2 ~ en** : to lie in, to consist of
residual *adj* : residual
residuo *nm* **1** : residue **2** : remainder **3 residuos** *nmpl* : waste ⟨residuos nucleares : nuclear waste⟩
resignación *nf, pl* **-ciones** : resignation

resignar vt : to resign — **resignarse** vr ∼ **a** : to resign oneself to

resina nf 1 : resin 2 **resina epoxídica** : epoxy

resistencia nf 1 : resistance 2 AGUANTE : endurance, strength, stamina 3 : heating element

resistente adj 1 : resistant 2 : strong, tough

resistir vt 1 TOLERAR : to stand, to bear, to tolerate 2 : to withstand, to resist 3 : to resist (temptation, etc.) — vi : to resist ⟨resistió hasta el último minuto : he held out until the last minute⟩ — **resistirse** vr ∼ **a** : to be resistant to, to be reluctant ⟨se resiste a aceptarlo : she's reluctant to accept it⟩

resma nf : ream

resollar {19} vi : to breathe heavily, to wheeze

resolución nf, pl -ciones 1 : resolution, settlement 2 : decision 3 : determination, resolve

resolver {89} vt 1 : to resolve, to settle 2 : to decide — **resolverse** vr : to make up one's mind

resonancia nf 1 : resonance 2 : impact, repercussions pl

resonante adj 1 : resonant 2 : tremendous, resounding ⟨un éxito resonante : a resounding success⟩

resonar {19} vi : to resound, to ring

resoplar vi 1 : to puff, to pant 2 : to snort

resoplo nm 1 : puffing, panting 2 : snort

resorte nm 1 MUELLE : spring 2 : elasticity 3 : influence, means pl ⟨tocar resortes : to pull strings⟩

resortera nf Mex : slingshot

respaldar vt : to back, to support, to endorse — **respaldarse** vr : to lean back

respaldo nm 1 : back (of an object) 2 : support, backing

respectar vt : to concern, to relate to ⟨por lo que a mí respecta : as far as I'm concerned⟩

respectivo, -va adj : respective — **respectivamente** adv

respecto nm 1 ∼ **a** : in regard to, concerning 2 **al respecto** : on this matter, in this respect

respetable adj : respectable — **respetabilidad** nf

respetar vt : to respect

respeto nm 1 : respect, consideration 2 **respetos** nmpl : respects ⟨presentar sus respetos : to pay one's respects⟩

respetuosidad nf : respectfulness

respetuoso, -sa adj : respectful — **respetuosamente** adv

respingado, -da adj : snub-nosed

respingo nm : start, jump

respiración nf, pl -ciones 1 : respiration, breathing 2 **respiración boca a boca** : mouth-to-mouth resuscitation

respiradero nm : vent, ventilation shaft

respirador nm : respirator

respirar v : to breathe

respiratorio, -ria adj : respiratory

respiro nm 1 : breath 2 : respite, break

resplandecer {53} vi 1 : to shine 2 : to stand out

resplandeciente adj 1 : resplendent, shining 2 : radiant

resplandor nm 1 : brightness, brilliance, radiance 2 : flash

responder vt : to answer — vi 1 : to answer, to reply, to respond 2 ∼ **a** : to respond to ⟨responder al tratamiento : to respond to treatment⟩ 3 ∼ **de** : to answer for, to vouch for (something) 4 ∼ **por** : to vouch for (someone)

respondón, -dona adj, mpl -dones fam : sassy, fresh, impertinent

responsabilidad nf : responsibility ⟨tener la responsabilidad de : to be responsible for⟩ ⟨exigen responsabilidades a la compañía : the company is being held responsible/accountable⟩

responsabilizarse {21} vr : to accept responsibility ⟨responsabilizarse de : to accept responsibility for⟩

responsable[1] adj : responsible — **responsablemente** adv

responsable[2] nmf : person responsible ⟨los responsables del proyecto : those in charge of the project⟩ ⟨los responsables del desastre : those responsible for the disaster⟩

respuesta nf : answer, response

resquebrajar vt : to split, to crack — **resquebrajarse** vr

resquemor nm : resentment, bitterness

resquicio nm 1 : crack 2 : opportunity, chance 3 : trace ⟨sin un resquicio de remordimiento : without a trace of remorse⟩ 4 **resquicio legal** : loophole

resta nf SUSTRACCIÓN : subtraction

restablecer {53} vt : to reestablish, to restore — **restablecerse** vr : to recover

restablecimiento nm 1 : reestablishment, restoration 2 : recovery

restallar vi : to crack, to crackle, to click

restallido nm : crack, crackle

restante adj 1 : remaining 2 **lo restante, los restantes** : the rest

restañar vt : to stanch

restar vt 1 : to deduct, to subtract ⟨restar un punto : to deduct a point⟩ 2 : to minimize, to play down — vi : to remain, to be left

restauración nf, pl -ciones 1 : restoration 2 : catering, food service

restaurante nm : restaurant

restaurar vt : to restore

restitución nf, pl -ciones : restitution, return

restituir {41} vt : to return, to restore, to reinstate

resto nm 1 : rest, remainder 2 **restos** nmpl : remains ⟨restos de comida : leftovers⟩ ⟨restos arqueológicos : archeological ruins⟩ 3 **restos mortales** : mortal remains

restorán nm, pl -ranes : restaurant

restregadura nf : scrub, scrubbing

restregar {49} vt 1 : to rub 2 : to scrub — **restregarse** vr

restricción *nf, pl* **-ciones** : restriction, limitation

restrictivo, -va *adj* : restrictive

restringido, -da *adj* LIMITADO : limited, restricted

restringir {35} *vt* LIMITAR : to restrict, to limit

restructuración *nf, pl* **-ciones** : restructuring

restructurar *vt* : to restructure

resucitación *nf, pl* **-ciones** : resuscitation ⟨resucitación cardiopulmonar : CPR, cardiopulmonary resuscitation⟩

resucitar *vt* **1** : to resuscitate, to revive, to resurrect **2** : to revitalize

resuello *nm* **1** : puffing, heavy breathing, wheezing **2** : break, breather

resueltamente *adv* : resolutely

resuelto¹ *pp* → **resolver**

resuelto², -ta *adj* : determined, resolved, resolute

resulta *nf* **1** : consequence, result **2 a resultas de** *or* **de resultas de** : as a result of

resultado *nm* : result, outcome

resultante *adj & nf* : resultant

resultar *vi* **1** : to work, to work out ⟨mi idea no resultó : my idea didn't work out⟩ **2** : to be, to turn out to be, to end up being ⟨resultó bien simpático : he turned out to be very nice⟩ ⟨resultó cancelado : it was canceled, it ended up being canceled⟩ ⟨resulta más sencillo/barato : it's simpler/cheaper, it ends up being simpler/cheaper⟩ ⟨me resulta muy interesante : I find it very interesting⟩ ⟨resultó (ser) una falsa alarma : it turned out to be a false alarm⟩ ⟨resulta que ya lo había hecho : it turns out she'd already done it⟩ ⟨resultó con heridas graves : he sustained serious injuries⟩ **3** **~ en** : to lead to, to result in **4** **~ de** : to be the result of

resumen *nm, pl* **-súmenes 1** : summary, summation **2 en ~** : in summary, in short

resumidero *nm* : drain

resumir *v* : to summarize, to sum up

resurgimiento *nm* : resurgence

resurgir {35} *vi* : to reappear, to revive

resurrección *nf, pl* **-ciones** : resurrection **2** *or* **Domingo de Resurrección** : Easter, Easter Sunday

retablo *nm* : tableau

retador, -dora *n* : challenger (in sports)

retaguardia *nf* : rear guard

retahíla *nf* : string, series ⟨una retahíla de insultos : a volley of insults⟩

retaliación *nf, pl* **-ciones** : retaliation

retama *nf* : broom (plant)

retar *vt* DESAFIAR : to challenge, to defy

retardar *vt* **1** RETRASAR : to delay, to retard **2** : to postpone

retazo *nm* **1** : remnant, scrap **2** : fragment, piece ⟨retazos de su obra : bits and pieces from his writings⟩

retén *nm, pl* **retenes 1** : squad, patrol ⟨de retén : on call, on duty⟩ **2** CONTROL : checkpoint, roadblock **3** *Ven* : reform school

retención *nf, pl* **-ciones 1** : retention **2** : deduction, withholding

retener {80} *vt* **1** : to retain, to keep **2** : to withhold **3** : to detain

retentivo, -va *adj* : retentive

reticencia *nf* **1** : reluctance, reticence **2** : insinuation

reticente *adj* **1** : reluctant, reticent **2** : insinuating, misleading

retina *nf* : retina

retintín *nm, pl* **-tines 1** : jingle, jangle **2 con ~** : sarcastically

retirada *nf* **1** : retreat ⟨batirse en retirada : to withdraw, to beat a retreat⟩ **2** : withdrawal (of funds) **3** : retirement **4** : refuge, haven

retirado, -da *adj* **1** : remote, distant, far off **2** : secluded, quiet

retirar *vt* **1** : to remove, to take away, to recall **2** : to withdraw, to take out — **retirarse** *vr* **1** REPLEGARSE : to retreat, to withdraw **2** JUBILARSE : to retire

retiro *nm* **1** JUBILACIÓN : retirement **2** : withdrawal, retreat **3** : seclusion

reto *nm* DESAFÍO : challenge, dare

retocar {72} *vt* : to touch up

retomar *vt* : to pick up, to resume

retoñar *vi* : to sprout

retoño *nm* : sprout, shoot

retoque *nm* : touch-up, finishing touch

retorcer {14} *vt* **1** : to twist **2** : to wring — **retorcerse** *vr* **1** : to get twisted, to get tangled up **2** : to squirm, to writhe, to wiggle about

retorcido, -da *adj* **1** : twisted **2** : complicated

retorcijón *nm, pl* **-jones** : cramp, sharp pain

retórica *nf* : rhetoric

retórico, -ca *adj* : rhetorical — **retóricamente** *adv*

retornar *v* : to return

retorno *nm* : return

retozar {21} *vi* : to frolic, to romp

retozo *nm* : frolicking

retozón, -zona *adj, mpl* **-zones** : playful

retracción *nf, pl* **-ciones** : retraction, withdrawal

retractable *adj* : retractable

retractación *nf, pl* **-ciones** : retraction (of a statement, etc.)

retractarse *vr* **1** : to withdraw, to back down **2 ~ de** : to take back, to retract

retraer {81} *vt* **1** : to bring back **2** : to dissuade — **retraerse** *vr* **1** RETIRARSE : to withdraw, to retire **2** REFUGIARSE : to take refuge

retraído, -da *adj* : withdrawn, retiring, shy

retraimiento *nm* **1** : shyness, timidity **2** : withdrawal

retransmisión *nf, pl* **-siones** *Spain* : broadcast

retransmitir *vt* *Spain* : to broadcast

retrasado¹, -da *adj* *dated, now usu offensive* : retarded, now usu offensive, mentally slow **2** : behind, in arrears **3** : backward (of a country) **4** : slow (of a watch)

retrasado², -da *n or* **retrasado mental** *dated, now offensive* : retarded person *dated, now usu offensive*; moron *dated, now offensive*

retrasar *vt* **1** DEMORAR, RETARDAR : to delay, to hold up **2** : to put off, to postpone **3** : to turn back (a clock) — **retrasarse** *vr* **1** : to be late **2** : to fall behind **3** : to lose time (of a clock)

retraso *nm* **1** ATRASO : delay, lateness **2** **retraso mental** *dated, now sometimes offensive* : mental retardation *dated, now sometimes offensive*

retratar *vt* **1** : to portray, to depict **2** : to photograph **3** : to paint a portrait of

retrato *nm* **1** : depiction, portrayal **2** : portrait, photograph

retrete *nm* : restroom, toilet

retribución *nf, pl* **-ciones** **1** : pay, payment **2** : reward

retribuir {41} *vt* **1** : to pay **2** : to reward

retroactivo, -va *adj* : retroactive — **retroactivamente** *adv*

retroalimentación *nf, pl* **-ciones** : feedback

retroceder *vi* **1** : to move back, to turn back **2** : to back off, to back down **3** : to recoil (of a firearm)

retroceso *nm* **1** : backward movement **2** : backing down **3** : setback, relapse **4** : recoil

retrógrado, -da *adj* **1** : reactionary **2** : retrograde

retropropulsión *nf* : jet propulsion

retroproyector *nm* : overhead projector

retrospectiva *nf* : retrospective, hindsight

retrospectivamente *adv* : in retrospect

retrospectivo, -va *adj* **1** : retrospective **2** **mirada retrospectiva** : backward glance

retrovisor *nm* : rearview mirror

retruécano *nm* : pun, play on words

retuitear *vt* : to retweet

retumbar *vi* **1** : to boom, to thunder **2** : to resound, to reverberate

retumbo *nm* : booming, thundering, roll

retuvo, etc. → **retener**

reubicar {72} *vt* : to relocate — **reubicación** *nf*

reuma *or* **reúma** *nmf* → **reumatismo**

reumático, -ca *adj* : rheumatic

reumatismo *nm* : rheumatism

reunión *nf, pl* **-niones** **1** : meeting **2** : gathering, reunion

reunir {68} *vt* **1** : to unite, to join, to bring together **2** : to have, to possess ⟨reunieron los requisitos necesarios : they fulfilled the necessary requirements⟩ **3** : to gather, to collect, to raise (funds) — **reunirse** *vr* : to meet

reutilizable *adj* : reusable

reutilizar {21} *vt* : to recycle, to reuse

revalidar *vt* **1** : to confirm, to ratify **2** : to defend (a title)

revalorizar {21} *vt* : to reevaluate, to reassess

revaluar {3} *vt* : to reevaluate — **revaluación** *n*

revancha *nf* **1** DESQUITE : revenge **2** : rematch

revelación *nf, pl* **-ciones** : revelation

revelado *nm* : developing (of film)

revelador¹, -dora *adj* : revealing

revelador² *nm* : developer

revelar *vt* **1** : to reveal, to disclose **2** : to develop (film)

revendedor, -dora *n* **1** : scalper **2** DETALLISTA : retailer

revender *vt* **1** : to resell **2** : to scalp

reventa *nf* **1** : resale **2** : scalping

reventar {55} *vi* **1** ESTALLAR, EXPLOTAR : to burst, to blow up **2** ~ **de** : to be bursting with — *vt* **1** : to burst **2** *fam* : to annoy, to rile — **reventarse** *vr* : to burst

reventón *nm, pl* **-tones** **1** : burst, bursting **2** : blowout, flat tire **3** *Mex fam* : bash, party

reverberar *vi* : to reverberate — **reverberación** *nf*

reverdecer {53} *vi* **1** : to grow green again **2** : to revive

reverencia *nf* **1** : reverence **2** : bow, curtsy

reverenciar *vt* : to revere, to venerate

reverendo¹, -da *adj* **1** : reverend **2** *fam* : total, absolute ⟨es un reverendo imbécil : he is a complete idiot⟩

reverendo², -da *n* : reverend

reverente *adj* : reverent

reversa *nf Col, Mex* : reverse (gear)

reversible *adj* : reversible

reversión *nf, pl* **-siones** : reversion

reverso *nm* **1** : back, other side **2** **el reverso de la medalla** : the complete opposite

revertir {76} *vi* **1** : to revert, to go back **2** ~ **en** : to result in, to end up as — *vt* : to reverse (a decision, etc.)

revés *nm, pl* **reveses** **1** : back, wrong side **2** : setback, reversal **3** : backhand (in sports) **4** **al revés** : the other way around, upside down, inside out **5** **al revés de** : contrary to

revestimiento *nm* : covering, facing (of a building)

revestir {54} *vt* **1** : to coat, to cover, to surface **2** : to conceal, to disguise **3** : to take on, to assume ⟨la reunión revistió gravedad : the meeting took on a serious note⟩

revisar *vt* **1** : to examine, to inspect, to check **2** : to check over, to overhaul (machinery) **3** : to revise

revisión *nf, pl* **-siones** **1** : revision **2** : inspection, check ⟨revisión de cuentas : (financial) audit⟩ ⟨revisión médica : checkup⟩

revisor, -sora *n* **1** : inspector **2** : conductor (on a train)

revista *nf* **1** : magazine, journal **2** : revue **3** **pasar revista** : to review, to inspect

revistar *vt* : to review, to inspect

revistero *nm* : magazine rack

revitalizar {21} *vt* : to revitalize — **revitalización** *nf*

revivir *vi* : to revive, to come alive again — *vt* : to relive

revocación *nf, pl* **-ciones** **1** : revocation, repeal **2** : reversal

revocar {72} *vt* **1** : to revoke, to repeal **2** : to plaster (a wall)

revolcar {82} *vt* : to knock over, to knock down — **revolcarse** *vr* : to roll around, to wallow

revolcón *nm*, *pl* **-cones** *fam* : tumble, fall

revolotear *vi* : to flutter around, to flit

revoloteo *nm* : fluttering, flitting

revoltijo *or* **revoltillo** *nm* **1** FÁRRAGO : mess, jumble **2** *Mex* : traditional seafood dish

revoltoso, -sa *adj* : unruly, rebellious

revolución *nf*, *pl* **-ciones** : revolution

revolucionar *vt* : to revolutionize

revolucionario, -ria *adj & n* : revolutionary

revolver {89} *vt* **1** : to move about, to mix, to shake, to stir **2** : to upset (one's stomach) **3** : to mess up, to rummage through ⟨revolver la casa : to turn the house upside down⟩ — **revolverse** *vr* **1** : to toss and turn **2** VOLVERSE : to turn around

revólver *nm* : revolver

revoque *nm* : plaster

revuelo *nm* **1** : fluttering **2** : commotion, stir

revuelta *nf* : uprising, revolt

revuelto[1] *pp* → **revolver**

revuelto[2], **-ta** *adj* **1** : choppy, rough ⟨mar revuelto : rough sea⟩ **2** : untidy **3 huevos revueltos** : scrambled eggs

rey *nm* : king

reyerta *nf* : brawl, fight

rezagado, -da *n* : straggler, latecomer

rezagar {52} *vt* **1** : to leave behind **2** : to postpone — **rezagarse** *vr* : to fall behind, to lag

rezar {21} *vi* **1** : to pray **2** : to say ⟨como reza el refrán : as the saying goes⟩ **3** ∼ **con** : to concern, to have to do with — *vt* : to say, to recite ⟨rezar un Ave María : to say a Hail Mary⟩

rezo *nm* : prayer, praying

rezongar {52} *vi* : to gripe, to grumble

rezumar *v* : to ooze, to leak

ría, etc. → **reír**

riachuelo *nm* ARROYO : brook, stream

riada *nf* : flood

ribera *nf* : bank, shore

ribete *nm* **1** : border, trim **2** : frill, adornment **3 ribetes** *nmpl* : hint, touch ⟨tiene sus ribetes de genio : there's a touch of genius in him⟩

ribetear *vt* : to border, to edge, to trim

ricachón[1], **-chona** *adj*, *mpl* **-chones** *fam* : rich, wealthy

ricachón[2], **-chona** *n*, *mpl* **-chones** *fam* : rich person

ricamente *adv* : richly, splendidly

rice, etc. → **rizar**

rickshaw [ˈrikʃo] *nm* : rickshaw

rico[1], **-ca** *adj* **1** : rich, wealthy **2** : fertile **3** : luxurious, valuable **4** : delicious **5** : adorable, lovely **6** : great, wonderful

rico[2], **-ca** *n* : rich person

ridiculez *nf*, *pl* **-leces** : absurdity

ridiculizar {21} *vt* : to ridicule

ridículo[1], **-la** *adj* ABSURDO, DISPARATADO : ridiculous, ludicrous — **ridículamente** *adv*

ridículo[2], **-la** *n* **1 hacer el ridículo** : to make a fool of oneself **2 poner en ridículo** : to ridicule

ríe, etc. → **reír**

riega, riegue etc. → **regar**

riego *nm* : irrigation

riel *nm* : rail, track

rienda *nf* **1** : rein **2 dar rienda suelta a** : to give free rein to **3 llevar las riendas** : to be in charge **4 tomar las riendas** : to take control

riesgo *nm* : risk

riesgoso, -sa *adj* : risky

rifa *nf* : raffle

rifar *vt* : to raffle — *vi* : to quarrel, to fight

rifle *nm* : rifle

rige, rija etc. → **regir**

rigidez *nf*, *pl* **-deces** **1** : rigidity, stiffness ⟨rigidez cadavérica : rigor mortis⟩ **2** : inflexibility

rígido, -da *adj* **1** : rigid, stiff **2** : strict — **rígidamente** *adv*

rigor *nm* **1** : rigor, harshness **2** : precision, meticulousness **3 de** ∼ : usual ⟨la respuesta de rigor : the standard reply⟩ **4 de** ∼ : essential, obligatory **5 en** ∼ : strictly speaking, in reality

riguroso, -sa *adj* : rigorous — **rigurosamente** *adv*

rima *nf* **1** : rhyme **2 rimas** *nfpl* : verse, poetry

rimar *vi* : to rhyme

rimbombante *adj* **1** : grandiose, showy **2** : bombastic, pompous

rímel *or* **rimel** *or* **rimmel** *nm* : mascara

rin *nm* *Col*, *Mex* : wheel, rim (of a tire)

rincón *nm*, *pl* **rincones** : corner, nook

rinde, etc. → **rendir**

ring [ˈrin] *nm*, *pl* **rings** : (boxing) ring

ringtone [ˈrinˌton] *nm* : ringtone

rinoceronte *nm* : rhinoceros

riña *nf* **1** : fight, brawl **2** : dispute, quarrel

riñe, etc. → **reñir**

riñón *nm*, *pl* **riñones** : kidney

río[1] → **reír**

río[2] *nm* **1** : river **2** : torrent, stream ⟨un río de lágrimas : a flood of tears⟩

ripio *nm* **1** : debris, rubble **2** : gravel

riqueza *nf* **1** : wealth, riches *pl* **2** : richness **3 riquezas naturales** : natural resources

risa *nf* **1** : laughter, laugh **2 dar risa** : to make laugh ⟨me dio mucha risa : I found it very funny⟩ **3** *fam* **morirse de la risa** : to die laughing, to crack up

risco *nm* : crag, cliff

risible *adj* IRRISORIO : ludicrous, laughable

risita *nf* : giggle, titter, snicker

risotada *nf* : guffaw

ristra *nf* : string, series *pl*

risueño, -ña *adj* **1** : cheerful, pleasant **2** : promising

rítmico, -ca *adj* : rhythmical, rhythmic — **rítmicamente** *adv*

ritmo *nm* **1** : rhythm **2** : pace, tempo ⟨trabajó a ritmo lento : she worked at a slow pace⟩

rito *nm* : rite, ritual

ritual *adj & nm* : ritual — **ritualmente** *adv*

rival *adj & nmf* COMPETIDOR : rival

rivalidad *nf* : rivalry, competition

rivalizar {21} *vi* ~ **con** : to rival, to compete with

rizado, -da *adj* **1** : curly **2** : ridged **3** : rippled, undulating

rizar {21} *vt* **1** : to curl **2** : to ripple, to ruffle (a surface) **3** : to crumple, to fold — **rizarse** *vr* **1** : to frizz **2** : to ripple

rizo *nm* **1** : curl **2** : loop (in aviation)

robalo *or* **róbalo** *nm* : sea bass

robar *vt* **1** : to steal **2** : to rob, to burglarize **3** SECUESTRAR : to abduct, to kidnap **4** : to captivate — *vi* ~ **en** : to break into

roble *nm* : oak

robo *nm* : robbery, theft ⟨robo de identidad : identity theft⟩

robot *nm, pl* **robots** : robot — **robótico, -ca** *adj*

robótica *nf* : robotics

robustecer {53} *vt* : to grow stronger, to strengthen

robustez *nf* : sturdiness, robustness

robusto, -ta *adj* : robust, sturdy

roca *nf* : rock, boulder

roce[1], etc. → **rozar**

roce[2] *nm* **1** : rubbing, chafing **2** : brush, graze, touch **3** : close contact, familiarity **4** : friction, disagreement

rociador *nm* : sprinkler

rociar {85} *vt* : to spray, to sprinkle

rocío *nm* **1** : dew **2** : shower, light rain

rock *or* **rock and roll** *nm* : rock, rock and roll

rocola *nf* : jukebox

rocoso, -sa *adj* : rocky

rodada *nf* : track (of a tire), rut

rodado, -da *adj* **1** : wheeled **2** : dappled (of a horse)

rodadura *nf* : rolling, taxiing

rodaja *nf* : round, slice

rodaje *nm* **1** : filming, shooting **2** : breaking in (of a vehicle)

rodamiento *nm* **1** : bearing ⟨rodamiento de bolas : ball bearings⟩ **2** : rolling

rodante *adj* : rolling

rodar {19} *vi* **1** : to roll, to roll down, to roll along ⟨rodé por la escalera : I tumbled down the stairs⟩ ⟨todo rodaba bien : everything was going along well⟩ **2** GIRAR : to turn, to go around **3** : to move about, to travel ⟨andábamos rodando por todas partes : we drifted along from place to place⟩ — *vt* **1** : to film, to shoot **2** : to break in (a new vehicle)

rodear *vt* **1** : to surround ⟨rodeado de montañas : surrounded by mountains⟩ **2** : to round up (cattle) — *vi* **1** : to go around **2** : to beat around the bush — **rodearse** *vr* ~ **de** : to surround oneself with

rodeo *nm* **1** : rodeo, roundup **2** DESVÍO : detour **3** : evasion ⟨andar con rodeos : to beat around the bush⟩ ⟨sin rodeos : without reservations⟩

rodilla *nf* : knee

rodillera *nf* : knee pad

rodillo *nm* **1** : roller **2** : rolling pin

rododendro *nm* : rhododendron

roedor[1], **-dora** *adj* : gnawing

roedor[2] *nm* : rodent

roer {69} *vt* **1** : to gnaw **2** : to eat away at, to torment

rogar {16} *vt* **1** : to beg, to request — *vi* **1** : to beg, to plead **2** : to pray

roiga, etc. → **roer**

rojez *nf* : redness

rojizo, -za *adj* : reddish

rojo[1], **-ja** *adj* **1** : red **2 ponerse rojo** : to blush

rojo[2] *nm* : red

rol *nm* **1** : role **2** : list, roll

rollizo, -za *adj* : chubby, plump

rollo *nm* **1** : roll, coil ⟨un rollo de cinta : a roll of tape⟩ ⟨en rollo : rolled up⟩ **2** *fam* : roll of fat **3** *fam* : boring speech, lecture

ROM *nf, pl* **ROM** *or* **ROMs** : ROM

romance *nm* **1** : Romance language **2** : ballad **3** : romance **4 en buen romance** : simply stated, simply put

romano, -na *adj & n* : Roman

romanticismo *nm* : romanticism

romántico, -ca *adj* : romantic — **romántico, -ca** *n* — **románticamente** *adv*

rombo *nm* : rhombus

romería *nf* **1** : pilgrimage, procession **2** : crowd, gathering

romero[1], **-ra** *n* PEREGRINO : pilgrim

romero[2] *nm* : rosemary

romo, -ma *adj* : blunt, dull

rompecabezas *nms & pl* : puzzle, riddle

rompecorazones *nmfs & pl* : heartbreaker

rompehielos *nms & pl* : icebreaker (ship)

rompehuelgas *nmfs & pl* ESQUIROL : strikebreaker, scab

rompenueces *nms & pl* : nutcracker

rompeolas *ns & pl* : breakwater, jetty

romper {70} *vt* **1** : to break (a glass, a bone, etc.) **2** : to rip, to tear (cloth, paper) **3** : to break off (relations), to break (a contract) **4** : to break through/down (a door, etc.) **5** GASTAR : to wear out **6** : to break ⟨romper el hielo/silencio : to break the ice/silence⟩ — *vi* **1** : to break ⟨al romper del día : at the break of day⟩ **2** ~ **a** : to begin to, to burst out with ⟨romper a llorar : to burst into tears⟩ **3** ~ **con** : to break with (tradition, etc.), to break away from **4** ~ **con alguien** : to break up with someone — **romperse** *vr*

rompope *nm CA, Mex* : drink similar to eggnog

ron *nm* : rum

roncar {72} *vi* **1** : to snore **2** : to roar

roncha *nf* : rash

ronco, -ca *adj* **1** : hoarse **2** : husky (of the voice) — **roncamente** *adv*

ronda *nf* **1** : beat, patrol **2** : round (of drinks, of negotiations, of a game)

rondar *vt* **1** : to patrol **2** : to hang around ⟨siempre está rondando la calle : he's always hanging around the street⟩ **3** : to be approximately ⟨debe rondar los cincuenta : he must be about 50⟩ — *vi* **1** : to be on patrol **2** : to prowl around, to roam about

ronque, etc. → **roncar**

ronquera *nf* : hoarseness
ronquido *nm* 1 : snore 2 : roar
ronronear *vi* : to purr
ronroneo *nm* : purr, purring
ronzal *nm* : halter (for an animal)
ronzar {21} *v* : to munch, to crunch
roña *nf* 1 : mange 2 : dirt, filth 3 *fam* : stinginess
roñoso, -sa *adj* 1 : mangy 2 : dirty 3 *fam* : stingy
ropa *nf* 1 : clothes *pl*, clothing ⟨ropa sucia : dirty clothes, (dirty) laundry⟩ ⟨ropa de abrigo : warm clothes⟩ ⟨cambiarse de ropa : to change one's clothes, to get changed⟩ 2 **ropa interior** : underwear
ropaje *nm* : apparel, garments *pl*, regalia
ropero *nm* ARMARIO, CLÓSET : wardrobe, closet
rosa[1] *adj* : rose-colored, pink
rosa[2] *nm* : rose, pink (color)
rosa[3] *nf* : rose (flower)
rosáceo, -cea *adj* : pinkish
rosado[1], **-da** *adj* 1 : pink 2 **vino rosado** : rosé
rosado[2] *nm* : pink (color)
rosal *nm* : rosebush
rosario *nm* 1 : rosary 2 : series ⟨un rosario de islas : a string of islands⟩
rosbif *nm* : roast beef
rosca *nf* 1 : thread (of a screw) ⟨una tapa a rosca : a screw top⟩ 2 : ring, coil
roscón *nm, pl* **roscones** : ring-shaped cake
roseta *nf* : rosette
rosetón *nm, pl* **-tones** : rose window
rosquilla *nf* : ring-shaped pastry, doughnut
rostro *nm* : face, countenance
rotación *nf, pl* **-ciones** : rotation
rotar *vt* : to rotate, to turn — *vi* : to turn, to spin
rotativo[1], **-va** *adj* : rotary
rotativo[2] *nm* : newspaper
rotatorio, -ria *adj* → **rotativo**[1]
roto[1] *pp* → **romper**
roto[2], **-ta** *adj* 1 : broken 2 : ripped, torn
rotonda *nf* 1 : traffic circle, rotary 2 : rotunda
rotor *nm* : rotor
rotoso, -sa *adj Arg, Uru, Peru* : ragged, scruffy
rótula *nf* : kneecap
rotulador *nm Spain* 1 : felt-tip pen 2 : highlighter
rotular *vt* 1 : to head, to entitle 2 : to label
rótulo *nm* 1 : heading, title 2 : label, sign
rotundo, -da *adj* 1 REDONDO : round 2 : categorical, absolute ⟨un éxito rotundo : a resounding success⟩ — **rotundamente** *adv*
rotura *nf* : break, tear, fracture
rough ['ruf, 'raf] *nm* **el rough** : the rough (in golf)
router *nm, pl* **routers** : router (in computing)
roya[1] *nf* : plant rust
roya[2], etc. → **roer**
rozado, -da *adj* GASTADO : worn

rozadura *nf* 1 : scratch, abrasion 2 : rubbed spot, sore
rozamiento *nf* : rubbing, friction
rozar {21} *vt* 1 : to chafe, to rub against 2 : to border on, to touch on 3 : to graze, to touch lightly — **rozarse** *vr* ∼ **con** *fam* : to rub shoulders with
ruandés, -desa *adj & n* : Rwandan
rubéola *nf* : German measles, rubella
rubí *nm, pl* **rubíes** : ruby
rubicundo, -da *adj* : ruddy ⟨una cara rubicunda : a ruddy face⟩
rubio, -bia *adj & n* : blond
rublo *nm* : ruble
rubor *nm* 1 : flush, blush 2 : blush, rouge
ruborizarse {21} *vr* : to blush
rúbrica *nf* : title, heading
rubricar {72} *vt* 1 : sign with a flourish ⟨firmado y rubricado : signed and sealed⟩ 2 : to endorse, to sanction
rubro *nm* 1 : heading, title 2 : line, area (in business)
rucio, rucia *adj* : gray
rudeza *nf* ASPEREZA : roughness, coarseness
rudimentario, -ria *adj* : rudimentary — **rudimentariamente** *adv*
rudimento *nm* : rudiment, basics *pl*
rudo, -da *adj* 1 : rough, harsh 2 : coarse, unpolished — **rudamente** *adv*
rueda[1], etc. → **rodar**
rueda[2] *nf* 1 : wheel 2 RODAJA : round slice 3 : circle, ring 4 **rueda de andar** : treadmill 5 **rueda de prensa** : press conference 6 **ir sobre ruedas** : to go smoothly
ruedita *nf* : caster (on furniture)
ruedo *nm* 1 : bullring, arena 2 : rotation, turn 3 : hem
ruega, ruegue etc. → **rogar**
ruego *nm* : request, appeal, plea
rufián *nf, pl* **rufianes** : villain, scoundrel, ruffian
rugby *nm* : rugby
rugido *nm* : roar
rugir {35} *vi* : to roar
rugoso, -sa *adj* 1 : rough, bumpy 2 : wrinkled
ruibarbo *nm* : rhubarb
ruido *nm* : noise, sound
ruidoso, -sa *adj* : loud, noisy — **ruidosamente** *adv*
ruin *adj* 1 : base, despicable 2 : mean, stingy
ruina *nf* 1 : ruin, destruction ⟨llevar a alguien a la ruina : to ruin someone, to bring someone to ruin⟩ ⟨estar en la ruina : to be ruined⟩ 2 : ruin, downfall ⟨la avaricia será su ruina : greed will be his ruin⟩ 3 : collapse (of a building, etc.) ⟨amenazar ruina : to threaten to collapse⟩ 4 **ruinas** *nfpl* : ruins, remains ⟨ruinas romanas : Roman ruins⟩ ⟨estar/quedar en ruinas : to be/lie in ruins⟩
ruinoso, -sa *adj* 1 : run-down, dilapidated 2 : ruinous, disastrous
ruiseñor *nm* : nightingale
ruja, etc. → **rugir**
rulero *nm Arg, Peru, Uru* : curler, roller

ruleta nf : roulette
ruletero, -ra n Mex fam : taxi driver
rulo nm : curler, roller
ruma nf Chile, Peru, Ven : pile, heap
rumano, -na n : Romanian, Rumanian
rumba nf : rumba
rumbo nm **1** : direction, course ⟨con rumbo a : bound for, heading for⟩ ⟨perder el rumbo : to go off course, to lose one's bearings⟩ ⟨sin rumbo : aimless, aimlessly⟩ **2** : ostentation, pomp **3** : lavishness, generosity
rumiante adj & nm : ruminant
rumiar vt : to ponder, to mull over — vi **1** : to chew the cud **2** : to ruminate, to ponder
rummy nm : rummy (card game)
rumor nm **1** : rumor **2** : murmur
rumorearse or **rumorarse** vr : to be rumored ⟨se rumorea que se va : rumor

has it that she's leaving⟩ — **rumoreado, -da** adj
rumoroso, -sa adj : murmuring, babbling ⟨un arroyo rumoroso : a babbling brook⟩
rupestre adj : cave ⟨pinturas rupestres : cave paintings⟩
rupia nf : rupee
ruptura nf **1** : break **2** : breaking, breach (of a contract) **3** : breaking off, breakup
rural adj : rural
ruso¹, -sa adj & n : Russian
ruso² nm : Russian (language)
rústico¹, -ca adj : rural, rustic
rústico², -ca n : rustic, country dweller
ruta nf : route
rutina nf : routine, habit
rutinario, -ria adj : routine, ordinary ⟨visita rutinaria : routine visit⟩ — **rutinariamente** adv

S

s nf : twenty-second letter of the Spanish alphabet
sábado nm **1** : Saturday ⟨el sábado : (on) Saturday⟩ ⟨los sábados : (on) Saturdays⟩ ⟨cada (dos) sábados : every (other) Saturday⟩ ⟨el sábado pasado : last Saturday⟩ ⟨el próximo sábado : next Saturday⟩ **2** : Sabbath
sábalo nm : shad
sabana nf : savanna
sábana nf : sheet, bedsheet
sabandija nf BICHO : bug, small reptile, pesky creature
sabático, -ca adj : sabbatical
sabedor, -dora adj : aware, informed
sabelotodo nmf fam : know-it-all
saber¹ {71} vt **1** : to know ⟨no lo sé : I don't know⟩ ⟨no sé qué decirte : I don't know what to tell you⟩ ⟨no sabes lo que te espera : you don't know what you're in for⟩ ⟨saber la respuesta : to know the answer⟩ ⟨sabe mucho de política : he knows a lot about politics⟩ ⟨¿sabes dónde está? : do you know where it is?⟩ ⟨creo que no, pero ¿qué sé yo? : I don't think so, but what do I know?⟩ ⟨quién sabe qué va a pasar : who knows what will happen⟩ **2** : to know how to, to be able to ⟨sabe tocar el violín : she can play the violin⟩ **3** : to learn, to find out ⟨lo supe ayer : I found out yesterday⟩ ⟨no sé nada de ellos : I haven't heard from them⟩ **4 a** ～ : to wit, namely **5 que yo sepa** : as far as I know **6 qué sé yo** ⟨diamantes, perlas, y qué sé yo : diamonds, pearls, and whatnot⟩ ⟨y qué sé yo dónde : and who knows where (else)⟩ — vi **1** : to know, to suppose ⟨¿quién sabe? : who knows?⟩ ⟨nunca se sabe : you never know, one never knows⟩ **2** : to be informed ⟨supimos del desastre : we heard about the disaster⟩ **3** : to taste ⟨esto no sabe bien : this doesn't

taste right⟩ **4** ～ **a** : to taste like ⟨sabe a naranja : it tastes like orange⟩ — **saberse** vr : to know ⟨ese chiste no me lo sé : I don't know that joke⟩
saber² nm : knowledge, learning
sabiamente adv : wisely
sabido, -da adj : well-known
sabiduría nf **1** : wisdom **2** : learning, knowledge
sabiendas adv **1 a** ～ : knowingly **2 a sabiendas de que** : knowing full well that
sabihondo, -da n fam : know-it-all
sabio¹, -bia adj **1** PRUDENTE : wise, sensible **2** DOCTO : learned
sabio², -bia n **1** : wise person **2** : learned person
sable nm : saber, cutlass
sablear vt **1** : to bum, to scrounge, to sponge **2** : to scrounge off, to sponge off
sabor nm **1** : flavor, taste **2 sin** ～ : flavorless
saborear vt **1** : to taste, to savor **2** : to enjoy, to relish
saborizante nm : flavor, flavoring
sabotaje nm : sabotage
saboteador, -dora n : saboteur
sabotear vt : to sabotage
sabrá, etc. → saber
sabroso, -sa adj **1** RICO : delicious, tasty **2** AGRADABLE : pleasant, nice, lovely
sabueso nm **1** : bloodhound **2** fam : detective, sleuth
sacacorchos nms & pl : corkscrew
sacapuntas nms & pl : pencil sharpener
sacar {72} vt **1** : to pull out, to take out ⟨saca el pollo del congelador : take the chicken out of the freezer⟩ ⟨me sacaron de la cama : they dragged me out of bed⟩ ⟨sacó un as : he drew an ace⟩ ⟨sacar la basura : to take out the garbage⟩ ⟨¡sácalo de la casa! : get it out of the

house!⟩ **2** : to get, to obtain ⟨saqué un 100 en el examen : I got 100 on the exam⟩ ⟨sacó cuatro puntos de ventaja : she got a four-point lead⟩ **3** : to get out, to extract ⟨le saqué la información : I got the information from him⟩ ⟨sacar sangre : to draw blood⟩ ⟨me sacó de un apuro : she got me out of a jam⟩ ⟨sacar provecho de : to benefit from⟩ **4** : to take (someone) out ⟨lo saqué a comer : I took him out to eat⟩ ⟨la sacó a bailar : he asked her to dance⟩ **5** : to stick out ⟨sacar la lengua : to stick out one's tongue⟩ **6** : to bring out, to introduce ⟨sacar un libro : to publish a book⟩ ⟨sacaron una moda nueva : they introduced a new style⟩ ⟨sacar algo a la venta : to release something for sale⟩ ⟨sacar a relucir un tema : to bring up a topic⟩ **7** : to take (a photo, a shot) **8** : to make (copies) **9** RETIRAR : to withdraw (money) **10** : to draw, to reach (a conclusion) **11** CALCULAR : to work out, to tally up **12 sacar adelante** AVANZAR : to get started, to move forward **13 sacar adelante** MANTENER : to support, to keep afloat **14 sacar de encima** — *vi* **1** : to kick off (in soccer or football) **2** : to serve (in sports)

sacarina *nf* : saccharin

sacarosa *nf* : sucrose

sacerdocio *nm* : priesthood

sacerdotal *adj* : priestly

sacerdote, -tisa *n* : priest *m*, priestess *f*

saciar *vt* **1** HARTAR : to sate, to satiate **2** SATISFACER : to satisfy

saciedad *nf* **1** : fullness ⟨comer hasta la saciedad : to eat one's fill⟩ **2 hacer algo hasta la saciedad** : to do something ad nauseam

saco *nm* **1** : bag, sack **2** : sac **3** : jacket, sport coat

sacramento *nm* : sacrament — **sacramental** *adj*

sacrificar {72} *vt* **1** : to sacrifice **2** : to euthanize, to put down — **sacrificarse** *vr* : to sacrifice oneself, to make sacrifices

sacrificio *nm* : sacrifice

sacrilegio *nm* : sacrilege

sacrílego, -ga *adj* : sacrilegious

sacristán *nm, pl* **-tanes** : sexton

sacristía *nf* : vestry

sacro, -cra *adj* SAGRADO : sacred ⟨arte sacro : sacred art⟩

sacrosanto, -ta *adj* : sacrosanct

sacudida *nf* **1** : shaking **2** : jerk, jolt, shock **3** : shake-up, upheaval

sacudir *vt* **1** : to shake, to beat **2** : to jerk, to jolt **3** : to dust off **4** CONMOVER : to shake up, to shock — **sacudirse** *vr* : to shake off

sacudón *nm, pl* **-dones** : intense jolt or shake-up

sádico¹, -ca *adj* : sadistic

sádico², -ca *n* : sadist

sadismo *nm* : sadism

safari *nm* : safari

saga *nf* : saga

sagacidad *nf* : shrewdness

sagaz *adj, pl* **sagaces** PERSPICAZ : shrewd, discerning, sagacious

sagazmente *adv* : shrewdly

Sagitario¹ *nm* : Sagittarius (sign or constellation)

Sagitario² *nmf* : Sagittarius (person)

sagrado, -da *adj* : sacred, holy

sainete *nm* : comedy sketch, one-act farce ⟨este proceso es un sainete : these proceedings are a farce⟩

sajar *vt* : to lance, to cut open

sal¹ → **salir**

sal² *nf* **1** : salt **2** *CA, Mex* : misfortune, bad luck

sala *nf* **1** : living room **2** : room, hall ⟨sala de conferencias : lecture hall⟩ ⟨sala de urgencias : emergency room⟩ ⟨sala de baile : ballroom⟩

salado, -da *adj* **1** : salty **2 agua salada** : salt water

salamandra *nf* : salamander

salami *nm* : salami

salar *vt* **1** : to salt **2** : to spoil, to ruin **3** *CoRi, Mex* : to jinx, to bring bad luck

salarial *adj* : salary, salary-related

salario *nm* **1** : salary **2 salario mínimo** : minimum wage

salaz *adj, pl* **salaces** : salacious, lecherous

salchicha *nf* **1** : sausage **2** : frankfurter, wiener

salchichón *nf, pl* **-chones** : a type of deli meat

salchichonería *nf Mex* **1** : delicatessen **2** : cold cuts *pl*

saldar *vt* : to settle, to pay off ⟨saldar una cuenta : to settle an account⟩

saldo *nm* **1** : settlement, payment **2** : balance ⟨saldo de cuenta : account balance⟩ **3** : remainder, leftover merchandise

saldrá, etc. → **salir**

salero *nm* **1** : salt shaker **2** : wit, charm

salga, etc. → **salir**

salida *nf* **1** : exit ⟨salida de emergencia/incendios : emergency/fire exit⟩ ⟨una calle sin salida : a dead-end street⟩ **2** : leaving, departure **3** SOLUCIÓN : way out, solution **4** : start (of a race) **5** OCURRENCIA : wisecrack, joke **6 salida del sol** : sunrise

salido *adj* : protuding

saliente¹ *adj* **1** : departing, outgoing **2** : projecting **3** DESTACADO : salient, prominent

saliente² *nm* **1** : projection, protrusion **2 ventana en saliente** : bay window

salinidad *nf* : salinity, saltiness

salino, -na *adj* : saline ⟨solución salina : saline solution⟩

salir {73} *vi* **1** : to go out, to come out, to get out ⟨salió del edificio : she came/went out of the building⟩ ⟨salí a la calle : I went outside⟩ ⟨salimos todas las noches : we go out every night⟩ ⟨salimos a desayunar : we went out for breakfast⟩ ⟨me ayudó a salir del apuro : he helped me out of a jam⟩ ⟨salieron ilesos : they escaped unharmed⟩ ⟨por la tarde salió el sol : in the afternoon the sun came out⟩

2 PARTIR : to leave, to depart ⟨salí de casa a las seis : I left home at six (o'clock)⟩ ⟨salió del hospital : she's out of the hospital⟩ ⟨salieron para Bogotá : they left for Bogotá⟩ ⟨salió a buscarla : he went to go pick her up⟩ ⟨¿a qué hora sale el vuelo? : what time does the flight leave?⟩ ⟨salió corriendo : she took off running⟩ **3** APARECER : to appear ⟨salió en todos los diarios : it came out in all the papers⟩ ⟨le están saliendo los dientes : she's teething⟩ ⟨me salen canas : I'm going gray, I'm getting gray hairs⟩ ⟨le salen granos : she breaks out, she gets pimples⟩ ⟨le salió un sarpullido : he broke out in a rash⟩ **4** : to come out, to become available ⟨su libro acaba de salir : her book just came out⟩ ⟨salir a la venta : to be released (for sale)⟩ **5** : to rise (of the sun) **6** : to come up (of a topic), to come out (of news) ⟨salir a relucir : to come out, to come to light⟩ **7** : to project, to stick out **8** : to cost, to come to ⟨sale muy caro : it's very expensive⟩ **9** RESULTAR : to turn out, to prove ⟨salir bien/mal : to turn out well/badly⟩ **10** : to come up, to occur ⟨salga lo que salga : whatever happens⟩ ⟨salió una oportunidad : an opportunity came up⟩ **11** ~ **a** : to take after, to look like, to resemble **12 salir adelante** : to overcome difficulties, to advance ⟨salir adelante en la vida : to get ahead in life⟩ ⟨es difícil, pero saldremos adelante : it's difficult, but we'll get through it⟩ ⟨sin ello el país/proyecto no saldrá adelante : without it the country/project won't move forward⟩ **13** ~ **con** : to go out with, to date — **salirse** *vr* **1** : to escape, to get out, to leak out **2** : to come loose, to come off **3 salirse con la suya** : to get one's own way

saliva *nf* : saliva

salival *adj* : salivary ⟨glándula salival : salivary gland⟩

salivar *vi* : to salivate

salmo *nm* : psalm

salmodia *nf* : chant

salmodiar *v* : to chant

salmón[1] *adj* : salmon-colored

salmón[2] *nm*, *pl* **salmones** : salmon

salmuera *nf* : brine

salobre *adj* : brackish, briny

salón *nm*, *pl* **salones** **1** : hall, large room ⟨salón de clase : classroom⟩ ⟨salón de baile : ballroom⟩ **2** : salon ⟨salón de belleza : beauty salon⟩ **3** : parlor, sitting room

salpicadera *nf Mex* : fender

salpicadero *nm Spain* : dashboard

salpicadura *nf* : spatter, splash

salpicar {72} *vt* **1** : to spatter, to splash **2** : to sprinkle, to scatter about

salpimentar {55} *vt* **1** : to season (with salt and pepper) **2** : to spice up

salpullido → **sarpullido**

salsa *nf* **1** : sauce ⟨salsa picante : hot sauce⟩ ⟨salsa inglesa : Worcestershire sauce⟩ ⟨salsa tártara : tartar sauce⟩ **2** : gravy **3** : salsa (music) **4 salsa mexicana** : salsa (sauce)

salsero, -ra *n* : salsa musician

saltador, -dora *n* : jumper

saltamontes *nms & pl* : grasshopper

saltar *vi* **1** BRINCAR : to jump, to leap ⟨saltó de la silla : he jumped out of his chair⟩ ⟨el gato saltó sobre el ratón : the cat pounced on the mouse⟩ ⟨saltó a la fama : she rose to fame⟩ **2** REBOTAR : to bounce **3** : to come off, to pop out ⟨el corcho saltó de la botella : the cork popped out of the bottle⟩ **4** : to shatter, to break **5** : to explode, to blow up **6** : to jump, to increase ⟨saltó de 500.000 a un millón : it jumped from 500,000 to a million⟩ **7 saltar a la vista** : to be glaringly obvious **8 saltar de alegría** : to jump for joy — *vt* **1** : to jump, to jump over ⟨saltó la reja : he jumped over the railing⟩ **2** : to skip, to miss — **saltarse** *vr* **1** OMITIR : to skip, to omit ⟨me salté ese capítulo : I skipped that chapter⟩ **2** : to come off, to fall off

saltarín, -rina *adj, mpl* **-rines** : leaping, hopping ⟨frijol saltarín : jumping bean⟩

salteado, -da *adj* **1** : sautéed **2** : jumbled up ⟨los episodios se transmitieron salteados : the episodes were broadcast in random order⟩

salteador *nm* : highwayman

saltear *vt* **1** SOFREÍR : to sauté **2** : to skip around, to skip over

saltimbanqui *nmf* : acrobat

salto *nm* **1** BRINCO : jump, leap, skip — *vt* : jump, dive (in sports) ⟨salto de longitud, salto (en) largo : long jump⟩ **3** : gap, omission **4 dar saltos** : to jump up and down **5** *or* **salto de agua** CATARATA : waterfall

saltón, -tona *adj, mpl* **saltones** : bulging, protruding

salubre *adj* : healthful, salubrious

salubridad *nf* : healthiness, health

salud *nf* **1** : health ⟨buena salud : good health⟩ **2 ¡salud!** : bless you! (when someone sneezes) **3 ¡salud!** : cheers!, to your health!

saludable *adj* **1** SALUBRE : healthful **2** SANO : healthy, well

saludar *vt* **1** : to greet, to say hello to **2** : to salute — **saludarse** *vr*

saludo *nm* **1** : greeting, regards *pl* **2** : salute

salutación *nf, pl* **-ciones** : salutation

salva *nf* **1** : salvo, volley **2 salva de aplausos** : round of applause

salvación *nf, pl* **-ciones** **1** : salvation **2** RESCATE : rescue

salvado *nm* : bran

salvador, -dora *n* **1** : savior, rescuer **2 el Salvador** : the Savior

salvadoreño, -ña *adj & n* : Salvadoran, El Salvadoran

salvaguardar *vt* : to safeguard

salvaguardia *or* **salvaguarda** *nf* : safeguard, defense

salvajada *nf* ATROCIDAD : atrocity, act of savagery

salvaje[1] *adj* **1** : wild ⟨animales salvajes : wild animals⟩ **2** : savage, cruel **3** : primitive, uncivilized

salvaje² *nmf* : savage
salvajismo *nm* : savagery
salvamanteles *nms & pl* : trivet
salvamento *nm* **1** : rescuing, lifesaving **2** : salvation **3** : refuge
salvapantallas *nms & pl* : screen saver
salvar *vt* **1** : to save, to rescue **2** : to cover (a distance) **3** : to get around (an obstacle), to overcome (a difficulty) **4** : to cross, to jump across **5 salvando** : except for, excluding — **salvarse** *vr* **1** : to survive, to escape **2** : to save one's soul
salvavidas¹ *nms & pl* **1** : life preserver **2 bote salvavidas** : lifeboat
salvavidas² *nmf* : lifeguard
salvedad *nf* **1** EXCEPCIÓN : exception **2** : proviso, stipulation
salvia *nf* : sage (plant)
salvo¹, -va *adj* **1** : unharmed, sound ⟨sano y salvo : safe and sound⟩ **2 a ~** : safe from danger
salvo² *prep* **1** EXCEPTO : except (for), save ⟨todos asistirán salvo Jaime : all will attend except for Jaime⟩ **2 salvo que** : unless ⟨salvo que llueva : unless it rains⟩
salvoconducto *nm* : safe-conduct
samba *nf* : samba
San *adj* → **santo¹**
sanar *vt* : to heal, to cure — *vi* : to get well, to recover
sanatorio *nm* **1** : sanatorium **2** : clinic, private hospital
sanción *nf, pl* **sanciones** : sanction
sancionar *vt* **1** : to penalize, to impose a sanction on **2** : to sanction, to approve
sancochar *vt* : to parboil
sandalia *nf* : sandal
sándalo *nm* : sandalwood
sandez *nf, pl* **sandeces** ESTUPIDEZ : nonsense, silly thing to say
sandía *nf* : watermelon
sandwich ['sandwitʃ, 'saŋgwitʃ] *nm, pl* **sandwiches** [-dwitʃes, -gwi-] EMPAREDADO : sandwich
saneamiento *nm* **1** : cleaning up, sanitation **2** : reorganizing, streamlining
sanear *vt* **1** : to clean up, to sanitize **2** : to reorganize, to streamline
sangrante *adj* **1** : bleeding **2** : flagrant, blatant
sangrar *vi* : to bleed — *vt* : to indent (a paragraph, etc.)
sangre *nf* **1** : blood **2 a sangre fría** : in cold blood **3 a sangre y fuego** : by violent force **4 pura sangre** : thoroughbred
sangría *nf* **1** : bleeding (in medicine) **2** : sangria (wine punch) **3** : drain, draining ⟨una sangría fiscal : a financial drain⟩ **4** : indentation, indenting
sangriento, -ta *adj* **1** : bloody **2** : cruel
sanguijuela *nf* **1** : leech, bloodsucker **2** : sponger, leech
sanguinario, -ria *adj* : bloodthirsty
sanguíneo, -nea *adj* **1** : blood ⟨vaso sanguíneo : blood vessel⟩ **2** : sanguine, ruddy
sanidad *nf* **1** : health **2** : public health, sanitation

sanitario¹, -ria *adj* **1** : sanitary **2** : health ⟨centro sanitario : health center⟩
sanitario², -ria *n* : sanitation worker
sanitario³ *nm* Col, Mex, Ven : toilet ⟨los sanitarios : the toilets, the restroom⟩
sano, -na *adj* **1** SALUDABLE : healthy **2** : wholesome **3** : whole, intact
santiaguino, -na *adj* : of or from Santiago, Chile
santiamén *nm* **en un santiamén** : in no time at all
santidad *nf* : holiness, sanctity
santificar {72} *vt* : to sanctify, to consecrate, to hallow
santiguarse {10} *vr* PERSIGNARSE : to cross oneself
santo¹, -ta *adj* **1** : holy, saintly ⟨el Santo Padre : the Holy Father⟩ ⟨una vida santa : a saintly life⟩ **2 Santo, Santa** (*San before names of masculine saints except those beginning with D or T*) : Saint ⟨Santa Clara : Saint Claire⟩ ⟨Santo Tomás : Saint Thomas⟩ ⟨San Francisco : Saint Francis⟩
santo², -ta *n* : saint
santo³ *nm* **1** : saint's day **2** CUMPLEAÑOS : birthday
santuario *nm* : sanctuary
santurrón, -rrona *adj, mpl* **-rrones** : overly pious, sanctimonious — **santurronamente** *adv*
saña *nf* **1** : fury, rage **2** : viciousness ⟨con saña : viciously⟩
sapo *nm* : toad
saque¹, etc. → **sacar**
saque² *nm* **1** : kickoff (in soccer or football) **2** : serve, service (in sports)
saqueador, -dora *n* DEPREDADOR : plunderer, looter
saquear *vt* : to sack, to plunder, to loot
saqueo *nm* : sacking, plunder, looting
sarampión *nm* : measles *pl*
sarape *nm* CA, Mex : blanket (worn as a poncho)
sarcasmo *nm* : sarcasm
sarcástico, -ca *adj* : sarcastic
sarcófago *nm* : sarcophagus
sardina *nf* : sardine
sardónico, -ca *adj* : sardonic
sarga *nf* : serge
sargento *nmf* : sergeant
sari *nm* : sari
sarna *nf* : mange
sarnoso, -sa *adj* : mangy
sarpullido *nm* ERUPCIÓN : rash
sarro *nm* **1** : deposit, coating **2** : tartar, plaque
sarta *nf* **1** : string, series (of insults, etc.) **2** : string (of pearls, etc.)
sartén *nmf, pl* **sartenes** **1** : frying pan **2 tener la sartén por el mango** : to call the shots, to be in control
sasafrás *nm* : sassafras
sastre, -tra *n* : tailor
sastrería *nf* **1** : tailoring **2** : tailor's shop
Satanás *or* **Satán** *nm* : Satan, the devil
satánico, -ca *adj* : satanic
satélite *nm* : satellite
satín *or* **satén** *nm, pl* **satines** *or* **satenes** : satin

satinado, -da *adj* : satin, glossy
sátira *nf* : satire
satírico, -ca *adj* : satirical, satiric
satirizar {21} *vt* : to satirize
sátiro *nm* : satyr
satisfacción *nf, pl* **-ciones** : satisfaction
satisfacer {74} *vt* **1** : to satisfy **2** : to fulfill, to meet **3** : to pay, to settle — **satisfacerse** *vr* **1** : to be satisfied **2** : to take revenge
satisfactorio, -ria *adj* : satisfactory — **satisfactoriamente** *adv*
satisfecho, -cha *adj* : satisfied, content, pleased
saturación *nf, pl* **-ciones** : saturation
saturar *vt* **1** : to saturate, to fill up **2** : to satiate, to surfeit
saturnismo *nm* : lead poisoning
Saturno *nm* : Saturn
sauce *nm* : willow
saúco *nm* : elder (tree)
saudí *or* **saudita** *adj & nmf* : Saudi, Saudi Arabian
sauna *nmf* : sauna
savia *nf* : sap
saxo¹ *nm fam* : sax *fam*, saxophone
saxo² *nmf fam* : sax player *fam*, saxophone player
saxofón *nm, pl* **-fones** : saxophone — **saxofonista** *nmf*
sazón¹ *nf, pl* **sazones** **1** : flavor, seasoning **2** : ripeness, maturity ⟨en sazón : in season, ripe⟩ **3 a la sazón** : at that time, then
sazón² *nmf, pl* **sazones** *Mex* : flavor, seasoning
sazonar *vt* CONDIMENTAR : to season, to spice
scanner [es'kaner] → **escáner**
scout [es'kaut] *nmf, pl* **scouts** : scout
se *pron* **1** : to him, to her, to you, to them ⟨se los daré a ella : I'll give them to her⟩ **2** : each other, one another ⟨se abrazaron : they hugged each other⟩ **3** : himself, herself, itself, oneself, yourselves, themselves ⟨se afeitó antes de salir : he shaved before leaving⟩ **4** (*used in passive constructions*) ⟨se dice que es hermosa : they say she's beautiful⟩ ⟨se habla inglés : English spoken⟩
sé → **saber, ser**
sea, etc. → **ser**
sebo *nm* **1** : grease, fat **2** : tallow **3** : suet
secado *nm* : drying
secador *nm* : hair dryer
secadora *nf* **1** : dryer, clothes dryer **2** *Mex* : hair dryer
secamente *adv* : curtly, brusquely
secante *nm* : blotting paper, blotter
secar {72} *v* : to dry — **secarse** *vr* **1** : to get dry **2** : to dry up
sección *nf, pl* **secciones** **1** : section ⟨sección transversal : cross section⟩ **2** : department, division
seccionar *vt* : to section, to divide
seco, -ca *adj* **1** : dry **2** DISECADO : dried ⟨fruta seca : dried fruit⟩ **3** : thin, lean **4** : curt, brusque **5** : sharp ⟨un golpe seco : a sharp blow⟩ **6** : dry, alcohol-

free **7 a secas** : simply, just ⟨se llama Chico, a secas : he's just called Chico⟩ **8 en ~** : abruptly, suddenly ⟨frenar en seco : to make a sudden stop⟩
secoya *nf* : sequoia, redwood
secreción *nf, pl* **-ciones** : secretion
secretar *vt* : to secrete
secretaría *nf* **1** : secretariat, administrative department **2** *Mex* : ministry, cabinet office
secretariado *nm* **1** : secretariat **2** : secretarial profession
secretario, -ria *n* : secretary — **secretarial** *adj*
secreto¹, -ta *adj* : secret — **secretamente** *adv*
secreto² *nm* **1** : secret **2** : secrecy
secta *nf* : sect
sectario, -ria *adj & n* : sectarian
sector *nm* : sector
secuaz *nmf, pl* **secuaces** : follower, henchman, underling
secuela *nf* : consequence, sequel ⟨las secuelas de la guerra : the aftermath of the war⟩
secuencia *nf* : sequence
secuestrador, -dora *n* **1** : kidnapper, abductor **2** : hijacker
secuestrar *vt* **1** RAPTAR : to kidnap, to abduct **2** : to hijack, to commandeer **3** CONFISCAR : to confiscate, to seize
secuestro *nm* **1** RAPTO : kidnapping, abduction **2** : hijacking **3** : seizure, confiscation
secular *adj* : secular — **secularismo** *nm* — **secularización** *nf*
secundar *vt* : to support, to second
secundaria *nf* **1** : secondary education, high school **2** *Mex* : junior high school, middle school
secundario, -ria *adj* : secondary
secuoya *nf* : sequoia
sed *nf* **1** : thirst ⟨tener sed : to be thirsty⟩ **2 tener sed de** : to hunger for, to thirst for
seda *nf* : silk
sedación *nf, pl* **-ciones** : sedation
sedal *nm* : fishing line
sedán *nm, pl* **sedanes** : sedan
sedante *adj & nm* CALMANTE : sedative
sedar *vt* : to sedate
sede *nf* **1** : seat, headquarters **2** : venue, site **3 la Santa Sede** : the Holy See
sedentario, -ria *adj* : sedentary
sedición *nf, pl* **-ciones** : sedition — **sedicioso, -sa** *adj*
sediento, -ta *adj* : thirsty, thirsting
sedimento *nm* : sediment — **sedimentario, -ria** *adj* — **sedimentación** *nf*
sedoso, -sa *adj* : silky, silken
seducción *nf, pl* **-ciones** : seduction
seducir {61} *vt* **1** : to seduce **2** : to captivate, to charm
seductivo, -va *adj* : seductive
seductor¹, -tora *adj* **1** SEDUCTIVO : seductive **2** ENCANTADOR : charming, alluring
seductor², -tora *n* : seducer
segador¹, *nm* : daddy longlegs
segador², -dora *n* : harvester

segar {49} *vt* **1** : to reap, to harvest, to cut **2** : to sever abruptly ⟨una vida segada por la enfermedad : a life cut short by illness⟩

seglar[1] *adj* LAICO : lay, secular

seglar[2] *nm* LAICO : layperson, layman *m*, laywoman *f*

segmentado, -da *adj* : segmented

segmento *nm* : segment

segregación *nf, pl* **-ciones** : segregation

segregar {52} *vt* **1** : to segregate **2** SE-CRETAR : to secrete

seguida *nf* **en** ~ : right away, immediately ⟨vuelvo en seguida : I'll be right back⟩

seguidamente *adv* **1** : next, immediately after **2** : without a break, continuously

seguido[1] *adv* **1** RECTO : straight, straight ahead **2** : often, frequently

seguido[2], **-da** *adj* **1** CONSECUTIVO : consecutive, successive ⟨tres días seguidos : three days in a row⟩ **2** : straight, unbroken **3** ~ **por** *or* ~ **de** : followed by

seguidor, -dora *n* : follower, supporter

seguimiento *nm* **1** : following, pursuit **2** : continuation ⟨darle seguimiento a : to follow up (on)⟩ **3** : tracking, monitoring

seguir {75} *vt* **1** : to follow ⟨el policía los siguió : the policeman followed them⟩ ⟨me siguieron con la mirada : they followed me with their eyes⟩ ⟨seguiré tu consejo : I'll follow your advice⟩ ⟨seguir el ejemplo de : to follow the example of⟩ ⟨me cuesta seguirle el ritmo : I have trouble keeping up with her⟩ ⟨seguir el procedimiento : to follow procedure⟩ ⟨en los meses que siguieron a una tragedia : in the months that followed the tragedy⟩ **2** : to go along, to keep on ⟨seguimos toda la carretera panamericana : we continued along the PanAmerican Highway⟩ ⟨siguió hablando : he kept on talking⟩ ⟨sigue aumentando : it continues to increase⟩ ⟨lo sigue creyendo : he still believes it⟩ ⟨seguir el curso : to stay on course⟩ **3** : to take (a course, a treatment) — *vi* **1** : to go on, to keep going ⟨sigue adelante : keep going, carry on⟩ ⟨sigue derecho : keep going straight⟩ **2** : to remain, to continue to be ⟨¿todavía sigues aquí? : you're still here?⟩ ⟨sigue con vida : she's still alive⟩ ⟨todo sigue igual : everything's still the same⟩ ⟨seguimos a la espera de noticias : we're still awaiting news⟩ **3** : to follow, to come after ⟨la frase que sigue : the following sentence⟩ ⟨¿qué sigue después? : what comes next?⟩

según[1] *adv* : it depends ⟨según y como : it all depends on⟩

según[2] *conj* **1** COMO, CONFORME : as, just as ⟨según lo dejé : just as I left it⟩ ⟨hace anotaciones según va leyendo : she makes notes as she reads⟩ **2** : depending on how ⟨según se vea : depending on how one sees it⟩

según[3] *prep* **1** : according to ⟨según los rumores : according to the rumors⟩ **2** : depending on ⟨según los resultados : depending on the results⟩

segundero *nm* : second hand (on a clock)

segundo[1], **-da** *adj* : second ⟨el segundo lugar : second place⟩ ⟨el segundo piso : the second floor⟩ ⟨llegó la segunda : she came in second⟩

segundo[2], **-da** *n* **1** : second (in a series) **2** : second (person), second in command

segundo[3] *nm* : second ⟨sesenta segundos : sixty seconds⟩

seguramente *adv* **1** : for sure, surely **2** : probably

seguridad *nf* **1** : safety (against accidents, etc.), security (against attacks, etc.) ⟨seguridad ciudadana : public safety⟩ ⟨seguridad nacional : national security⟩ ⟨de alta/máxima seguridad : high/maximum security⟩ ⟨medidas de seguridad : safety/security measures⟩ **2** : (financial) security ⟨seguridad social : Social Security⟩ **3** CERTEZA : certainty, assurance ⟨con toda seguridad : with complete certainty⟩ **4** : confidence, self-confidence

seguro[1] *adv* : certainly, definitely ⟨va a llover, seguro : it's going to rain for sure⟩ ⟨¡seguro que sí! : of course!⟩

seguro[2], **-ra** *adj* **1** : safe, secure **2** : sure, certain ⟨estoy segura que es él : I'm sure that's him⟩ **3** : reliable, trustworthy **4** : self-assured

seguro[3] *nm* **1** : insurance ⟨seguro de vida : life insurance⟩ **2** : fastener, clasp **3** *Mex* : safety pin

seis[1] *adj & nm* : six ⟨tiene seis años : she's six (years old)⟩ ⟨el seis de agosto : (on) the sixth of August, (on) August sixth⟩

seis[2] *pron* : six ⟨somos seis : there are six of us⟩ ⟨son las seis : it's six o'clock⟩

seiscientos[1], **-tas** *adj & pron* : six hundred

seiscientos[2] *nms & pl* : six hundred

seísmo *nm Spain* : earthquake

selección *nf, pl* **-ciones** **1** ELECCIÓN : selection, choice **2 selección natural** : natural selection

seleccionador, -dora *n* : manager (in sports)

seleccionar *vt* ELEGIR : to select, to choose

selectividad *nf Spain* : entrance examination

selectivo, -va *adj* : selective — **selectivamente** *adv*

selecto, -ta *adj* **1** : choice, select **2** EX-CLUSIVO : exclusive

selenio *nm* : selenium

selfie *or* **selfi** [ˈselfi] *nm* : selfie

self-service [selfˈserbis] *nm* : self-service restaurant

sellar *vt* **1** : to seal **2** : to stamp

sello *nm* **1** : seal **2** ESTAMPILLA, TIMBRE : postage stamp **3** : hallmark, characteristic

selva *nf* **1** BOSQUE : woods *pl*, forest ⟨selva húmeda : rain forest⟩ **2** JUNGLA : jungle

selvático, -ca *adj* **1** : forest, jungle ⟨sendero selvático : jungle path⟩ **2** : wild

semáforo *nm* **1** : traffic light **2** : stop signal

semana *nf* : week

semanal *adj* : weekly — **semanalmente** *adv*

semanario *nm* : weekly (publication)

semántica *nf* : semantics

semántico, -ca *adj* : semantic

semblante *nm* 1 : countenance, face 2 : appearance, look

semblanza *nf* : biographical sketch, profile

sembrado *nm* : cultivated field

sembrar {55} *vt* 1 : to plant, to sow 2 : to scatter, to strew ⟨sembrar el pánico : to spread panic⟩

semejante[1] *adj* 1 PARECIDO : similar, alike 2 TAL : such ⟨nunca he visto cosa semejante : I have never seen such a thing⟩

semejante[2] *nm* PRÓJIMO : fellowman

semejanza *nf* PARECIDO : similarity, resemblance

semejar *vi* : to resemble, to look like — **semejarse** *vr* : to be similar, to look alike

semen *nm* : semen

semental *nm* : stud (animal) ⟨caballo semental : stallion⟩

semestral *adj* : biannual, semiannual

semestre *nm* : semester

semi- *pref* : semi-

semibreve *nf* : whole note

semicírculo *nm* : semicircle, half circle

semiconductor *nm* : semiconductor

semidiós *nm*, *pl* **-dioses** : demigod *m*

semifinal *nf* : semifinal

semilla *nf* : seed

semillero *nm* 1 : bed (for plants), seed tray 2 : hotbed, breeding ground

seminario *nm* 1 : seminary 2 : seminar, graduate course

semiprecioso, -sa *adj* : semiprecious

semita *nmf* : Semite — **semítico, -ca** *adj*

sémola *nf* : semolina

sempiterno, -na *adj* ETERNO : eternal, everlasting

senado *nm* : senate

senador, -dora *n* : senator

sencillamente *adv* : simply, plainly

sencillez *nf* : simplicity

sencillo[1], **-lla** *adj* 1 : simple, easy 2 : plain, unaffected 3 : single

sencillo[2] *nm* 1 : single (recording) 2 : small change (coins) 3 : one-way ticket

senda *nf* CAMINO, SENDERO : path, way

senderismo *nm* : hiking

sendero *nm* CAMINO, SENDA : path, way

sendos, -das *adj pl* : each, both ⟨llevaban sendos vestidos nuevos : they were each wearing a new dress⟩

senectud *nf* ANCIANIDAD : old age

senegalés, -lesa *adj & n*, *mpl* **-leses** : Senegalese

senil *adj* : senile — **senilidad** *nf*

seno *nm* 1 : breast, bosom ⟨los senos : the breasts⟩ ⟨el seno de la familia : the bosom of the family⟩ 2 : sinus 3 **seno materno** : womb

sensación *nf*, *pl* **-ciones** 1 IMPRESIÓN : feeling ⟨tener la sensación : to have a feeling⟩ 2 : sensation ⟨causar sensación : to cause a sensation⟩

sensacional *adj* : sensational

sensacionalismo *nm* : sensationalism — **sensacionalista** *adj*

sensatez *nf* 1 : good sense 2 **con ~** : sensibly

sensato, -ta *adj* : sensible, sound — **sensatamente** *adv*

sensibilidad *nf* 1 : sensitivity, sensibility 2 SENSACIÓN : feeling

sensibilizar {21} *vt* : to sensitize

sensible *adj* 1 : sensitive 2 APRECIABLE : considerable, significant 3 : sentient, capable of feeling

sensiblemente *adv* : considerably, significantly

sensiblería *nf* : sentimentality, mush

sensiblero, -ra *adj* : mawkish, sentimental, mushy

sensitivo, -va *adj* 1 : sense ⟨órganos sensitivos : sense organs⟩ 2 : sentient, capable of feeling

sensor *nm* : sensor

sensorial *adj* : sensory

sensual *adj* : sensual, sensuous — **sensualmente** *adv*

sensualidad *nf* : sensuality

sentado, -da *adj* 1 : sitting, seated 2 : established, settled ⟨dar por sentado : to take for granted⟩ ⟨dejar sentado : to make clear⟩ 3 : sensible, steady, judicious

sentar {55} *vt* 1 : to seat, to sit 2 : to establish, to set — *vi* 1 : to suit ⟨ese color te sienta : that color suits you⟩ 2 : to agree with (of food or drink) ⟨las cebollas no me sientan : onions don't agree with me⟩ 3 : to please ⟨le sentó mal el paseo : she didn't enjoy the trip⟩ — **sentarse** *vr* : to sit, to sit down ⟨siéntese, por favor : please have a seat⟩

sentencia *nf* 1 : sentence, judgment 2 : maxim, saying

sentenciar *vt* : to sentence

sentido[1], **-da** *adj* 1 : heartfelt, sincere ⟨mi más sentido pésame : my sincerest condolences⟩ 2 : touchy, sensitive 3 : offended, hurt

sentido[2] *nm* 1 : sense ⟨sentido común : common sense⟩ ⟨los cinco sentidos : the five senses⟩ ⟨sin sentido : senseless⟩ 2 CONOCIMIENTO : consciousness 3 SIGNIFICADO : meaning, sense ⟨doble sentido : double entendre⟩ 4 : direction ⟨calle de sentido único : one-way street⟩

sentimental *adj* 1 : sentimental 2 : love, romantic ⟨vida sentimental : love life⟩

sentimentalismo *nm* : sentimentality

sentimiento *nm* 1 : feeling, emotion 2 PESAR : regret, sorrow

sentir {76} *vt* 1 : to feel, to experience ⟨no siento nada de dolor : I don't feel any pain⟩ ⟨sentía sed : he was feeling thirsty⟩ ⟨sentir amor : to feel love⟩ 2 PERCIBIR : to perceive, to sense ⟨sentir un ruido : to hear a noise⟩ 3 LAMENTAR : to regret, to feel sorry for ⟨lo siento mucho : I'm very sorry⟩ — *vi* 1 : to have feeling, to feel 2 **sin ~** : without noticing, inadvertently — **sentirse** *vr* 1 : to feel ⟨¿te sientes mejor? : are you feeling better?⟩ **2** *Chile, Mex* : to take offense

seña *nf* **1** : sign, signal ⟨hablar por señas : to talk in sign language⟩ **2 dar señas de** : to show signs of

señal *nf* **1** : signal ⟨señales de radio/televisión : radio/television signals⟩ **2** : sign ⟨señal de tráfico/tránsito : traffic sign⟩ **3** : signal (with the hand, etc.) ⟨señales de humo : smoke signals⟩ **4** INDICIO : sign, indication ⟨señales de vida : signs of life⟩ ⟨señal de alarma/alerta : warning sign⟩ ⟨no hay señales de violencia : there are no signs of violence⟩ ⟨como señal de protesta : as a sign of protest⟩ ⟨en señal de : as a token of⟩ ⟨sin dejar señal : without leaving a trace⟩ ⟨una buena señal : a good sign⟩ **5** MARCA : mark

señalado, -da *adj* : distinguished, notable

señalador *nm* : marker ⟨señalador de libros : bookmark⟩

señalar *vt* **1** INDICAR : to indicate, to show **2** : to mark **3** : to point out, to stress **4** : to fix, to set — **señalarse** *vr* : to distinguish oneself

señalización *nf, pl* **-ciones 1** : signs *pl*, signage **2** : installing of signs

señalizar {21} *vt* **1** : to mark (with signs or guides) ⟨la ruta está claramente señalizada : the route is clearly marked⟩ **2** : to put up signs on/in

señor, -ñora *n* **1** : gentleman *m*, man *m*, lady *f*, woman *f*, wife *f* ⟨señoras y señores : ladies and gentlemen⟩ ⟨un señor de setenta años : a 70-year-old man⟩ ⟨la señora de la casa : the lady of the house⟩ ⟨mi señora : my wife⟩ **2** : Mr. *m*, Mrs. *f* ⟨buenos días, señor López : good morning, Mr. López⟩ ⟨¿conoces a la señora Ortega? : do you know Mrs. Ortega?⟩ **3** : Sir *m*, Madam *f* ⟨Estimados señores : Dear Sirs⟩ **4** : Mr. *m*, Madam *f* ⟨Señora presidenta: . . . : Madam President: . . .⟩ ⟨Señor presidente: . . . : Mr. President: . . .⟩ ⟨habló con el señor embajador : she spoke with the ambassador⟩ **5** : lord *m*, lady *f* ⟨el Señor : the Lord⟩

señoría *nf* **1** : lordship **2 Su Señoría** : Your Honor

señorial *adj* : stately, regal

señorío *nm* **1** : manor, estate **2** : dominion, power **3** : elegance, class

señorita *nf* **1** : young lady, young woman **2** : Miss

señuelo *nm* **1** : decoy **2** : bait

sepa, etc. → **saber**

separación *nf, pl* **-ciones 1** : separation, division **2** : gap, space

separadamente *adv* : separately, apart

separado¹, -da *adj* **1** : separated **2** : separate ⟨vidas separadas : separate lives⟩ **3 por ~** : separately

separado², -da *n* : person who is separated ⟨separados y divorciados : separated and divorced people⟩

separador *nm* : divider

separar *vt* **1** : to separate, to divide **2** : to split up, to pull apart **3** : to put aside, to set aside — **separarse** *vr* **1** : to

separate, to split up ⟨sus padres se separaron : his parents separated⟩ ⟨separarse de alguien : to separate from someone⟩ **2** : to split up (of a group, etc.)

separo *nm Mex* : cell (in a jail or prison)

sepelio *nm* : interment, burial

sepia¹ *adj & nm* : sepia

sepia² *nf* : cuttlefish

septentrional *adj* : northern

septiembre *nm* : September ⟨el cinco de septiembre : (on) the fifth of September⟩

séptico, -ca *adj* : septic

séptimo, -ma *adj & n* : seventh ⟨el séptimo piso : the seventh floor⟩ ⟨llegó la séptima : she came in seventh (place)⟩ ⟨un séptimo de : a seventh of⟩

septuagésimo¹, -ma *adj* : seventieth

septuagésimo² *nm* : seventieth

sepulcral *adj* **1** : deathly **2** : dismal, gloomy

sepulcro *nm* TUMBA : tomb, sepulchre

sepultar *vt* ENTERRAR : to bury

sepultura *nf* **1** : burial **2** TUMBA : grave, tomb

seque, etc. → **secar**

sequedad *nf* **1** : dryness **2** : brusqueness, curtness

sequía *nf* : drought

séquito *nm* : retinue, entourage

ser¹ {77} *vi* **1** (*expressing identity*) : to be ⟨él es mi hermano : he is my brother⟩ ⟨¿quién es? : who is it?⟩ ⟨soy yo : it's me⟩ **2** (*expressing a quality*) : to be ⟨Camila es linda : Camila is pretty⟩ ⟨no seas tonto : don't be silly⟩ ⟨éste es el mejor : this one is the best⟩ ⟨es mío : it's mine⟩ ⟨es para ti : it's for you⟩ ⟨es para abrir latas : it's for opening cans⟩ ⟨son de Juan : they're Juan's⟩ ⟨somos de Managua : we're from Managua⟩ ⟨no creo que sea necesario : I don't think it's necessary⟩ ⟨quiero que seas feliz : I want you to be happy⟩ **3** (*indicating group, category, etc.*) : to be ⟨soy abogada : I'm a lawyer⟩ ⟨es un mamífero : it's a mammal⟩ **4** : to be, to exist, to live ⟨ser, o no ser : to be or not to be⟩ **5** : to be, to take place, to occur ⟨el concierto es el domingo : the concert is on Sunday⟩ ⟨la reunión fue en la escuela : the meeting was at the school⟩ **6** (*expressing time, date, season*) ⟨son las diez : it's ten o'clock⟩ ⟨hoy es el 9 : today's the 9th⟩ **7** : to be (a price), to cost, to come to ⟨¿cuánto es? : how much is it?⟩ **8** : to be, to equal ⟨dos más dos son cuatro : two plus two is four⟩ **9** (*with the future tense*) ⟨¿será posible? : can it be possible?⟩ ⟨serán las ocho : it must be eight o'clock⟩ **10 a no ser que** : unless **11 como sea** *or* **sea como sea** : one way or another, somehow ⟨hay que terminarlo como sea; hay que terminarlo, sea como sea : one way or another, we have to finish it⟩ **12 cuando sea** : anytime, whenever **13 donde sea** : anywhere, wherever **14 es que** : the thing is that ⟨es que no lo conozco : it's just that I don't know him⟩ **15 o sea** : in other words **16 ¡sea!** : agreed!, all right! **17 sea**

cual/quien (etc.) **sea** ⟨sean cuales sean las circunstancias : whatever the circumstances might be⟩ ⟨sea quien sea, no lo van a permitir : no matter who he is, they're not going to allow it⟩ **18 sea . . . sea** : either . . . or — *v aux* (*used in passive constructions*) : to be ⟨la cuenta ha sido pagada : the bill has been paid⟩ ⟨él fue asesinado : he was murdered⟩

ser² *nm* : being ⟨ser humano : human being⟩

seráfico, -ca *adj* : angelic

serbio¹, -bia *adj & n* : Serb, Serbian

serbio² *nm* : Serbian (language)

serbocroata¹ *adj* : Serbo-Croatian

serbocroata² *nm* : Serbo-Croatian (language)

serenar *vt* : to calm, to soothe — **serenarse** *vr* CALMARSE : to calm down

serenata *nf* : serenade

serenidad *nf* : serenity, calmness

sereno¹, -na *adj* **1** SOSEGADO : serene, calm, composed **2** : fair, clear (of weather) **3** : calm, still (of the sea) — **serenamente** *adv*

sereno² *nm* : night watchman

seriado, -da *adj* : serial

serial *nm* : serial (on radio or television)

seriamente *adv* : seriously

serie *nf* **1** : series **2** SERIAL : serial **3 fabricación en serie** : mass production **4 fuera de serie** : extraordinary, amazing

seriedad *nf* **1** : seriousness, earnestness **2** : gravity, importance

serio, -ria *adj* **1** : serious, earnest **2** : reliable, responsible **3** : important **4 en ~** : seriously, in earnest — **seriamente** *adv*

sermón *nm, pl* **sermones 1** : sermon **2** *fam* : harangue, lecture

sermonear *vt fam* : to harangue, to lecture

seropositivo *adj* **1** : positive (in blood testing) ⟨es seropositivo : he's positive, he tested positive⟩ **2** : HIV positive

serpentear *vi* : to twist, to wind — **serpenteante** *adj*

serpentina *nf* : paper streamer

serpiente *nf* : serpent, snake

serrado, -da *adj* DENTADO : serrated

serranía *nf* : mountainous area

serrano, -na *adj* : from the mountains

serrar {55} *vt* : to saw

serrín *nm, pl* **serrines** : sawdust

serruchar *vt* : to saw up

serrucho *nm* : saw, handsaw

servicentro *nm Peru* : gas station

servicial *adj* : obliging, helpful

servicio *nm* **1** : service ⟨servicio postal : postal service⟩ ⟨servicios sociales : social services⟩ ⟨servicio público : public service⟩ **2** SAQUE : serve (in sports) **3** : help, servants *pl* **4 servicios** *nmpl* : restrooms **5 fuera de servicio** : out of service

servidor, -dora *n* **1** : servant **2 su seguro servidor** : yours truly (in correspondence)

servidumbre *nf* **1** : servitude **2** : help, servants *pl*

servil *adj* **1** : servile, subservient **2** : menial

servilismo *nm* : servility

servilleta *nf* : napkin

servir {54} *vi* **1** : to work, to be useful ⟨esta máquina no sirve para nada : this machine is completely useless⟩ ⟨esa excusa no sirve : that excuse doesn't work⟩ ⟨su talento no le sirvió de mucho : his talent didn't do him much good⟩ ⟨deshazte de lo que no te sirve : get rid of what you don't need⟩ ⟨¿para qué sirve? : what's it for?⟩ **2** : to serve ⟨¿en qué puedo servirle? : how may I help you?⟩ **3** : to serve (in sports) **4** : to serve (in the military, etc.) **5 ~ de** : to serve as ⟨servir de ejemplo : to serve as an example⟩ — *vt* **1** : to serve ⟨¿en qué puedo servirlo? : how may I help you?⟩ ⟨¿te sirvo más café? : would you like more coffee?⟩ **2** SURTIR : to fill (an order) — **servirse** *vr* **1** : to help oneself **2** : to be kind enough ⟨sírvase enviarnos un catálogo : please send us a catalog⟩

sésamo *nm* AJONJOLÍ : sesame, sesame seeds *pl*

sesear *vi* : to pronounce the Spanish letter *c* before *i* or *e* or the Spanish letter *z* as /s/

sesenta *adj & nm* : sixty — **sesenta** *pron*

sesentavo¹, -va *adj* : sixtieth

sesentavo² *n* : sixtieth (fraction)

seseo *nm* : pronunciation of the Spanish letter *c* before *i* or *e* or the Spanish letter *z* as /s/

sesgado, -da *adj* **1** : inclined, tilted **2** : slanted, biased

sesgar {52} *vt* **1** : to cut on the bias **2** : to tilt **3** : to bias, to slant

sesgo *nm* : bias

sesgue, etc. → **sesgar**

sesión *nf, pl* **sesiones 1** : session (of a legislature, etc.), meeting **2** : showing, performance ⟨sesión de tarde : afternoon showing⟩

sesionar *vi* REUNIRSE : to meet, to be in session

seso *nm* **1** : brains, intelligence **2 sesos** *nmpl* : brains (as food)

sesudo, -da *adj* **1** : prudent, sensible **2** : brainy

set *nm, pl* **sets** : set (in tennis)

seta *nf* : mushroom

setecientos¹, -tas *adj & pron* : seven hundred

setecientos² *nms & pl* : seven hundred

setenta *adj & nm* : seventy — **setenta** *pron*

setentavo¹, -va *adj* : seventieth

setentavo² *nm* : seventieth

setiembre → **septiembre**

seto *nm* **1** : fence, enclosure **2 seto vivo** : hedge

setter *nm, pl* **setter** *or* **setters** : setter (dog)

seudónimo *nm* : pseudonym

severidad *nf* **1** : harshness, severity **2** : strictness

severo, -ra *adj* **1** : harsh, severe **2** ESTRICTO : strict — **severamente** *adv*

sexagésimo[1], **-ma** *adj* : sixtieth, sixty-
sexagésimo[2], **-ma** *n* : sixtieth, sixty- (in a
series)
sexismo *nm* : sexism — **sexista** *adj &
nmf*
sexo *nm* : sex
sextante *nm* : sextant
sexteto *nm* : sextet
sexto, -ta *adj & n* : sixth ⟨el sexto lugar
: sixth place⟩ ⟨llegó la sexta : she came in
sixth (place)⟩ ⟨un sexto de : a sixth of⟩
sexual *adj* : sexual, sex ⟨educación sexual
: sex education⟩ — **sexualmente** *adv*
sexualidad *nf* : sexuality
sexy *adj, pl* **sexy** *or* **sexys** : sexy
sheriff *nmf, pl* **sheriffs** : sheriff
shock [ˈʃɔk, ˈtʃɔk] *nm* : shock ⟨estado de
shock : state of shock⟩
short *nm, pl* **shorts** : shorts *pl*
show *nm, pl* **shows** : show
si[1] *nm* 1 : B ⟨si sostenido/bemol : B
sharp/flat⟩ 2 : ti (in singing)
si[2] *conj* 1 : if ⟨lo haré si me pagan : I'll do
it if they pay me⟩ ⟨si lo supiera te lo diría
: if I knew it I would tell you⟩ 2
: whether, if ⟨no importa si funciona o
no : it doesn't matter whether it works
(or not)⟩ 3 (*expressing desire, protest, or
surprise*) ⟨si supiera la verdad : if only I
knew the truth⟩ ⟨¡si no quiero! : but I
don't want to!⟩ 4 **si bien** : although ⟨si
bien se ha progresado : although progress has been made⟩ 5 **si no** : otherwise, or else ⟨si no, no voy : otherwise I
won't go⟩
sí[1] *adv* 1 : yes ⟨sí, gracias : yes, please⟩
⟨creo que sí : I think so⟩ 2 **sí que** : indeed, absolutely ⟨esta vez sí que ganaré
: this time I'm sure to win⟩ 3 **porque sí**
fam : because, just because ⟨lo hizo
porque sí : she did it just because⟩
sí[2] *nm, pl* **síes** : yes ⟨dar el sí : to say yes,
to express consent⟩
sí[3] *pron* 1 : oneself, yourself, yourselves
pl, itself, himself, herself, themselves *pl*
⟨puede decidir por sí mismo : he can decide for himself⟩ ⟨los hechos hablan por
sí solos : the facts speak for themselves⟩
⟨se culpa a sí misma : she blames her-
self⟩ ⟨dio lo mejor de sí : he gave it his
all⟩ 2 **de por sí** *or* **en sí** : by itself, in
itself, per se 3 **fuera de sí** : beside one-
self/yourself (etc.) 4 **para sí** (mism@)
: to oneself/yourself (etc.), for oneself/
yourself (etc.) ⟨¿qué quiere decir?—dijo
para sí : "what does it mean?" she said to
herself⟩ ⟨lo hicieron para sí mismos
: they did it for themselves⟩ 5 **entre ~**
: among themselves
siamés, -mesa *adj & n, mpl* **siameses**
: Siamese
sicario, -ria *n* : hired killer, hit man
siciliano, -na *adj & n* : Sicilian
sico- → **psico-**
sicómoro *or* **sicómoro** *nm* : sycamore
SIDA *or* **sida** *nm* (síndrome de inmunodeficiencia adquirida) : AIDS
siderurgia *nf* : iron and steel industry
siderúrgico, -ca *adj* : steel, iron ⟨la industria siderúrgica : the steel industry⟩

sidra *nf* : hard cider
siega[1], **siegue, etc.** → **segar**
siega[2] *nf* 1 : harvesting 2 : harvest time
3 : harvested crop
siembra[1], **etc.** → **sembrar**
siembra[2] *nf* 1 : sowing 2 : sowing season 3 SEMBRADO : cultivated field
siempre *adv* 1 : always ⟨siempre tienes
hambre : you're always hungry⟩ 2 : still
⟨¿siempre te vas? : are you still going?⟩
3 *Mex* : after all ⟨siempre no fui : I didn't
go after all⟩ 4 **siempre que** : whenever,
every time ⟨siempre que pasa : every
time he walks by⟩ 5 **para ~** : forever,
for good 6 **siempre y cuando** : provided that
sien *nf* : temple (on the forehead)
sienta, etc. → **sentar**
siente, etc. → **sentir**
sierpe *nf* : serpent, snake
sierra[1], **etc.** → **serrar**
sierra[2] *nf* 1 : saw ⟨sierra de vaivén : jig-
saw⟩ 2 CORDILLERA : mountain range
3 : mountains *pl* ⟨viven en la sierra
: they live in the mountains⟩
siervo, -va *n* 1 : slave 2 : serf
siesta *nf* : nap, siesta
siete[1] *adj & nm* : seven ⟨tiene siete años
: she's seven (years old)⟩ ⟨la página siete
: page seven⟩ ⟨el siete de junio : (on) the
seventh of June, (on) June seventh⟩
siete[2] *pron* : seven ⟨somos siete : there
are seven of us⟩ ⟨son las siete : it's seven
o'clock⟩
sífilis *nf* : syphilis
sifón *nm, pl* **sifones** : siphon
siga, sigue etc. → **seguir**
sigilo *nm* : secrecy, stealth
sigiloso, -sa *adj* FURTIVO : furtive,
stealthy — **sigilosamente** *adv*
sigla *nf* : acronym, abbreviation
siglo *nm* 1 : century 2 : age ⟨el Siglo de
Oro : the Golden Age⟩ ⟨hace siglos que
no te veo : I haven't seen you in ages⟩ 3
: world, secular life
signar *vt* : to sign (a treaty or agreement)
signatario, -ria *n* : signatory
significación *nf, pl* **-ciones** 1 : significance, importance 2 : meaning
significado *nm* 1 : sense, meaning 2
: significance
significante *adj* : significant
significar {72} *vt* 1 : to mean, to signify
2 : to express, to make known — **signifi-
carse** *vr* 1 : to draw attention, to become known 2 : to take a stance
significativo, -va *adj* 1 : significant, important 2 : meaningful — **significativa-
mente** *adv*
signo *nm* 1 : sign ⟨signo de igual : equal
sign⟩ ⟨un signo de alegría : a sign of hap-
piness⟩ 2 : (punctuation) mark ⟨signo
de interrogación : question mark⟩ ⟨si-
gno de admiración : exclamation point⟩
⟨signo de intercalación : caret⟩
siguiente *adj* : next, following
sílaba *nf* : syllable
silábico, -ca *adj* : syllabic
silbar *v* : to whistle
silbato *nm* PITO : whistle

silbido *nm* : whistle, whistling
silenciador *nm* **1** : muffler (of an automobile) **2** : silencer
silenciar *vt* **1** : to silence **2** : to muffle
silencio *nm* **1** : silence, quiet ⟨¡silencio! : be quiet!⟩ **2** : rest (in music)
silencioso, -sa *adj* : silent, quiet — **silenciosamente** *adv*
sílice *nf* : silica
silicio *nm* : silicon
silla *nf* **1** : chair **2 silla alta** : high chair (for a baby) **3 silla de ruedas** : wheelchair
sillín *nm*, *pl* **sillines** : saddle
sillón *nm*, *pl* **sillones** : armchair, easy chair
silo *nm* : silo
silueta *nf* **1** : silhouette **2** : figure, shape
silvestre *adj* : wild ⟨flor silvestre : wildflower⟩
silvicultor, -tora *n* : forester
silvicultura *nf* : forestry
sima *nf* ABISMO : chasm, abyss
simbólico, -ca *adj* : symbolic — **simbólicamente** *adj*
simbolismo *nm* : symbolism
simbolizar {21} *vt* : to symbolize
símbolo *nm* : symbol
simetría *nf* : symmetry
simétrico, -ca *adj* : symmetrical, symmetric
simiente *nf* : seed
símil *nm* **1** : simile **2** : analogy, comparison
similar *adj* SEMEJANTE : similar, alike
similitud *nf* : similarity, resemblance
simio *nm* : ape
simpatía *nf* **1** : liking, affection ⟨tomarle simpatía a : to take a liking to⟩ **2** : warmth, friendliness **3** : support, solidarity
simpático, -ca *adj* : nice, friendly, likeable
simpatizante *nf* : sympathizer, supporter
simpatizar {21} *vi* **1** : to get along, to hit it off ⟨simpaticé mucho con él : I really liked him⟩ **2** ~ **con** : to sympathize with, to support
simple[1] *adj* **1** SENCILLO : plain, simple, easy **2** : pure, mere ⟨por simple vanidad : out of pure vanity⟩ **3** : simpleminded, foolish
simple[2] *n* : fool, simpleton
simplemente *adv* : simply, merely, just
simpleza *nf* **1** : foolishness **2** NECEDAD : nonsense
simplicidad *nf* : simplicity
simplificar {72} *vt* : to simplify — **simplificación** *nf*
simplista *adj* : simplistic
simposio *or* **simposium** *nm* : symposium
simulación *nf*, *pl* **-ciones** : simulation
simulacro *nm* : imitation, sham ⟨simulacro de juicio : mock trial⟩
simular *vt* **1** : to simulate **2** : to feign, to pretend
simultáneo, -nea *adj* : simultaneous — **simultáneamente** *adv*
sin *prep* **1** : without ⟨sin querer : unintentionally⟩ ⟨sin refinar : unrefined⟩ ⟨café sin leche : coffee without milk⟩ ⟨un vuelo sin escalas : a nonstop flight⟩ **2 sin que** : without ⟨lo hicimos sin que él se diera cuenta : we did it without him noticing⟩
sinagoga *nf* : synagogue
sinceridad *nf* : sincerity
sincero, -ra *adj* : sincere, honest, true — **sinceramente** *adv*
síncopa *nf* : syncopation
sincopar *vt* : to syncopate
sincronizar {21} *vt* : to synchronize — **sincronización** *nf*
sindical *adj* GREMIAL : union, labor ⟨representante sindical : union representative⟩
sindicalismo *nm* : unionism — **sindicalista** *nmf*
sindicalizar {21} *vt* : to unionize — **sindicalizarse** *vr* **1** : to form a union **2** : to join a union
sindicar → **sindicalizar**
sindicato *nm* GREMIO : union, guild
síndrome *nm* : syndrome ⟨síndrome de Down : Down's syndrome⟩ ⟨síndrome tóxico : poisoning⟩
síndrome premenstrual *nm* : premenstrual syndrome, PMS
sinfín *nm* : endless number ⟨un sinfín de problemas : no end of problems⟩
sinfonía *nf* : symphony
sinfónica *nf* : symphony orchestra
sinfónico, -ca *adj* : symphonic, symphony
singular[1] *adj* **1** : singular, unique **2** PARTICULAR : peculiar, odd **3** : singular (in grammar) — **singularmente** *adv*
singular[2] *nm* : singular
singularidad *nf* **1** : uniqueness **2** : strangeness, peculiarity
singularizar {21} *vt* : to make unique or distinct — **singularizarse** *vr* : to stand out, to distinguish oneself
siniestrado, -da *adj* : damaged, wrecked ⟨zona siniestrada : disaster zone⟩
siniestro[1], **-tra** *adj* **1** IZQUIERDO : left, left-hand **2** MALVADO : sinister, evil
siniestro[2] *nm* : accident, disaster
sinnúmero → **sinfín**
sino *conj* **1** : but, rather ⟨no será hoy, sino mañana : it won't be today, but tomorrow⟩ **2** EXCEPTO : but, except ⟨no hace sino despertar suspicacias : it does nothing but arouse suspicion⟩
sinónimo[1], **-ma** *adj* : synonymous
sinónimo[2] *nm* : synonym
sinopsis *nfs* & *pl* RESUMEN : synopsis, summary
sinrazón *nf*, *pl* **-zones** : wrong, injustice
sinsabores *nmpl* : woes, troubles
sinsonte *nm* : mockingbird
sintáctico, -ca *adj* : syntactic
sintaxis *nfs* & *pl* : syntax
síntesis *nfs* & *pl* **1** : synthesis, fusion **2** SINOPSIS : synopsis, summary
sintético, -ca *adj* : synthetic — **sintéticamente** *adv*
sintetizador *nm* : synthesizer
sintetizar {21} *vt* **1** : to synthesize **2** RESUMIR : to summarize
sintió, etc. → **sentir**

síntoma *nm* : symptom
sintomático, -ca *adj* : symptomatic
sintonía *nf* **1** : tuning in (of a radio) **2 en sintonía con** : in tune with, attuned to
sintonizador *nm* : tuner, knob for tuning (of a radio, etc.)
sintonizar {21} *vt* : to tune (in) to — *vi* **1** : to tune in **2** ~ **con** : to be in tune with, to empathize with
sinuoso, -sa *adj* **1** : winding, sinuous **2** : devious
sinvergüenza[1] *adj* **1** DESCARADO : shameless, brazen, impudent **2** TRAVIESO : naughty
sinvergüenza[2] *nmf* **1** : rogue, scoundrel **2** : brat, rascal
sionista *adj & nmf* : Zionist — **sionismo** *nm*
siqui- → **psiqui-**
siquiera *adv* **1** : at least ⟨dame siquiera un poquito : at least give me a little bit⟩ **2** (*in negative constructions*) : not even ⟨ni siquiera nos saludaron : they didn't even say hello to us⟩
sir *nm* : sir (in titles)
sirena *nf* **1** : mermaid **2** : siren ⟨sirena de niebla : foghorn⟩
sirio, -ria *adj & n* : Syrian
sirope *nm* : syrup
sirve, etc. → **servir**
sirviente, -ta *n* : servant, maid *f*
sisear *vi* : to hiss
siseo *nm* : hiss
sísmico, -ca *adj* : seismic
sismo *nm* **1** TERREMOTO : earthquake **2** TEMBLOR : tremor
sismógrafo *nm* : seismograph
sistema *nm* **1** : system ⟨sistema nervioso : nervous system⟩ ⟨el sistema métrico : the metric system⟩ ⟨sistema solar : solar system⟩ ⟨entrar al sistema : to log in⟩ ⟨salir del sistema : to log out⟩ **2** : method ⟨trabajar con sistema : to work methodically⟩
sistemático, -ca *adj* : systematic — **sistemáticamente** *adv*
sistematizar {21} *vt* : to systematize
sistémico, -ca *adj* : systemic
sitiar *vt* ASEDIAR : to besiege
sitio *nm* **1** LUGAR : place, site ⟨vámonos a otro sitio : let's go somewhere else⟩ **2** ESPACIO : room, space ⟨hacer sitio a : to make room for⟩ **3** : siege ⟨estado de sitio : state of siege⟩ **4** *Mex* : taxi stand **5** *or* **sitio web** : site, web site
situación *nf, pl* **-ciones** : situation
situado, -da *adj* : situated, placed
situar {3} *vt* UBICAR : to place, to locate — **situarse** *vr* **1** : to be placed, to be located **2** : to make a place for oneself, to do well
skateboard [es'keitbor] *nm, pl* **skateboards** : skateboard
skateboarding [es'keitbordin] *nm* : skateboarding
sketch *nm* : sketch, skit
slider [esli'der] *nm, pl* **sliders** : slider (in baseball)
slip *nm* : briefs *pl*, underpants *pl*

smartphone ['smartfon] *nm* : smartphone
smog *nm* : smog
smoking → **esmoquin**
SMS ['ese'eme'ese, 'es'em'es] *nm, pl* **SMS** : text message
snob → **esnob**
snorkel → **esnórquel**
snowboard *nm, pl* **snowboards** **1** : snowboard **2** : snowboarding
so *prep* : under ⟨so pena de : under penalty of⟩
sobaco *nm* : armpit
sobado, -da *adj* **1** : worn, shabby **2** : well-worn, hackneyed
sobar *vt* **1** : to finger, to handle **2** : to knead **3** : to rub, to massage **4** *fam* : to beat, to pummel
soberanía *nf* : sovereignty
soberano, -na *adj & n* : sovereign
soberbia *nf* **1** ORGULLO : pride, arrogance **2** MAGNIFICENCIA : magnificence
soberbio, -bia *adj* **1** : proud, arrogant **2** : grand, magnificent
sobornar *vt* : to bribe
soborno *nm* **1** : bribery **2** : bribe
sobra *nf* **1** : excess, surplus **2 de** ~ : extra, to spare **3 sobras** *nfpl* : leftovers, scraps
sobrado, -da *adj* : abundant, excessive, more than enough
sobrante[1] *adj* : remaining, superfluous
sobrante[2] *nm* : remainder, surplus
sobrar *vi* : to be in excess, to be superfluous ⟨más vale que sobre a que falte : it's better to have too much than not enough⟩
sobre[1] *nm* **1** : envelope **2** : packet ⟨un sobre de sazón : a packet of seasoning⟩
sobre[2] *prep* **1** : on, on top of ⟨sobre la mesa : on the table⟩ ⟨apilados uno sobre otro : piled one on top of another⟩ **2** : over, above ⟨hay montañas sobre la ciudad : there are mountains above the city⟩ ⟨se inclinó sobre mí : she leaned over me⟩ ⟨temperaturas sobre los 30 grados : temperatures above 30 degrees⟩ **3** : about ⟨¿tiene libros sobre Bolivia? : do you have books on Bolivia?⟩ **4 sobre todo** : especially, above all
sobrealimentar *vt* : to overfeed
sobrecalentar {55} *vt* : to overheat — **sobrecalentarse** *vr*
sobrecama *nmf* : bedspread
sobrecarga *nf* **1** : excess weight **2** : overload
sobrecargar {52} *vt* : to overload, to overburden, to weigh down
sobrecargo *nm* : purser
sobrecogedor, -dora *adj* : shocking
sobrecoger {15} *vt* **1** : to surprise, to startle **2** : to scare — **sobrecogerse** *vr*
sobrecubierta *nf* : dust jacket
sobredosis *nfs & pl* : overdose
sobreentender {56} *vt* : to infer, to understand
sobreestimar *vt* : to overestimate, to overrate
sobreexcitado, -da *adj* : overexcited
sobreexponer {60} *vt* : to overexpose

sobregirar vt : to overdraw
sobregiro nm : overdraft
sobrehumano, -na adj : superhuman
sobrellevar vt : to endure, to bear
sobremanera adv : exceedingly
sobremesa nf : after-dinner conversation
sobrenatural adj : supernatural
sobrenombre nm APODO : nickname
sobrentender → **sobreentender**
sobrepasar vt : to exceed, to surpass —
  sobrepasarse vr PASARSE : to go too far
sobrepeso nm 1 : excess weight 2
  : overweight, obesity
sobrepoblación, sobrepoblado → **superpoblación, superpoblado**
sobreponer {60} vt 1 SUPERPONER : to
  superimpose 2 ANTEPONER : to put
  first, to give priority to — **sobrepo-
  nerse** vr 1 : to pull oneself together 2
  ~ **a** : to overcome
sobreprecio nm : surcharge
sobreprotector, -tora adj : overprotective
sobresaliente[1] adj 1 : protruding, projecting 2 : outstanding, noteworthy 3
  : significant, salient
sobresaliente[2] nmf : understudy
sobresalir {73} vi 1 : to protrude, to jut
  out, to project 2 : to stand out, to excel
sobresaltar vt : to startle, to frighten —
  sobresaltarse vr
sobresalto nm : start, fright
sobresueldo nm : bonus, additional pay
sobretasa nf : surcharge ⟨sobretasa a la
  gasolina : gas tax⟩
sobretodo nm : overcoat
sobrevalorar or **sobrevaluar** {3} vt : to
  overrate
sobrevender vt : to oversell
sobrevenir {87} vi ACAECER : to take
  place, to come about ⟨podrían sobrevenir complicaciones : complications
  could occur⟩
sobrevivencia → **supervivencia**
sobreviviente → **superviviente**
sobrevivir vi : to survive — vt : to outlive,
  to outlast
sobrevolar {19} vt : to fly over, to overfly
sobriedad nf : sobriety, moderation
sobrino, -na n : nephew m, niece f
sobrio, -bria adj : sober — **sobriamente**
  adv
socarrón, -rrona adj, mpl **-rrones** 1 : sly,
  cunning 2 : sarcastic
socavar vt : to undermine
socavón nm, pl **-vones** : pothole
sociabilidad nf : sociability
sociable adj : sociable
social adj : social — **socialmente** adv
socialista adj & nmf : socialist — **socialismo** nm
socializar {21} vt 1 : to nationalize 2
  : to socialize — vi : to socialize
sociedad nf 1 : society ⟨sociedad
  democrática : democratic society⟩ ⟨una
  sociedad secreta : a secret society⟩ 2
  : company, enterprise 3 **sociedad anónima** : incorporated company
socio, -cia n 1 : member 2 : partner
socioeconómico, -ca adj : socioeconomic

sociología nf : sociology
sociológico, -ca adj : sociological — **so-
  ciológicamente** adv
sociólogo, -ga n : sociologist
socorrer vt : to assist, to come to the aid of
socorrido, -da adj ÚTIL : handy, practical
socorrismo nm : lifesaving
socorrista nmf 1 : rescue worker 2
  : lifeguard
socorro nm AUXILIO 1 : aid, help
  ⟨equipo de socorro : rescue team⟩ 2
  ¡socorro! : help!
soda nf 1 : soda, soda water 2 CA, Car
  REFRESCO : soda, soda pop
sodio nf : sodium
soez adj, pl **soeces** GROSERO : rude, vulgar — **soezmente** adv
sofá nm : couch, sofa
sofistería nf : sophistry — **sofista** nmf
sofisticación nf, pl **-ciones** : sophistication
sofisticado, -da adj : sophisticated
sofocante adj : suffocating, stifling
sofocar {72} vt 1 AHOGAR : to suffocate,
  to smother 2 EXTINGUIR : to extinguish, to put out (a fire) 3 APLASTAR
  : to crush, to put down ⟨sofocar una rebelión : to crush a rebellion⟩ — **sofocarse** vr 1 : to suffocate 2 fam : to get
  upset, to get mad
sofoco nm : hot flash
sofreír {66} vt : to sauté
sofrito[1], -ta adj : sautéed
sofrito[2] nm : seasoning sauce
softbol nm : softball
software nm : software
soga nf : rope
soja → **soya**
sojuzgar vt : to subdue, to conquer, to
  subjugate
sol[1] nm 1 : G ⟨sol sostenido/bemol : G
  sharp/flat⟩ 2 : so, sol (in singing)
sol[2] nm 1 : sun ⟨a pleno sol : in the sun⟩
  ⟨tomar el sol : to sunbathe⟩ 2 : sol (Peruvian unit of currency)
solamente adv SÓLO : only, just
solapa nf 1 : lapel (of a jacket) 2 : flap
  (of an envelope)
solapado, -da adj : secret, underhanded
solapar vt : to cover up, to keep secret —
  solaparse vr : to overlap
solar[1] {19} vt : to floor, to tile
solar[2] adj : solar, sun
solar[3] nm 1 TERRENO : lot, piece of land,
  site 2 Cuba, Peru : tenement building
solariego, -ga adj : ancestral
solaz nm, pl **solaces** 1 CONSUELO : solace, comfort 2 DESCANSO : relaxation,
  recreation
solazarse {21} vr : to relax, to enjoy oneself
soldado nm 1 : soldier 2 **soldado raso**
  : private, enlisted man
soldador[1], **-dora** n : welder
soldador[2] nm : soldering iron
soldadura nf 1 : welding 2 : soldering,
  solder
soldar {19} vt 1 : to weld 2 : to solder
soleado, -da adj : sunny
soledad nf : loneliness, solitude

solemne *adj* : solemn — **solemnemente** *adv*
solemnidad *nf* : solemnity
soler {78} *vi* : to be in the habit of, to tend to ⟨solía tomar café por la tarde : she usually drank coffee in the afternoon⟩ ⟨eso suele ocurrir : that frequently happens⟩
solera *nf* 1 : prop, support 2 : tradition
solfeo *nm* : sol-fa
solicitante *nmf* : applicant
solicitar *vt* 1 : to request, to solicit 2 : to apply for ⟨solicitar empleo : to apply for employment⟩
solícito, -ta *adj* : solicitous, attentive, obliging
solicitud *nf* 1 : solicitude, concern 2 : request 3 : application
solidaridad *nf* : solidarity
solidario, -ria *adj* : supportive, united in support ⟨se declararon solidarios con la nueva ley : they declared their support for the new law⟩ ⟨espíritu solidario : spirit of solidarity⟩
solidarizar {21} *vi* : to be in solidarity ⟨solidarizamos con la huelga : we support the strike⟩
solidez *nf* 1 : solidity, firmness 2 : soundness (of an argument, etc.)
solidificar {72} *vt* : to solidify, to make solid — **solidificarse** *vr* — **solidificación** *nf*
sólido¹, -da *adj* 1 : solid, firm 2 : sturdy, well-made 3 : sound, well-founded — **sólidamente** *adv*
**sólido² *nm* : solid
soliloquio *nm* : soliloquy
solista *nmf* : soloist
solitaria *nf* TENIA : tapeworm
solitario¹, -ria *adj* 1 : lonely 2 : lone, solitary 3 DESIERTO : deserted, lonely ⟨una calle solitaria : a deserted street⟩
solitario², -ria *n* : recluse, loner
solitario³ *nm* : solitaire
sollozar {21} *vi* : to sob
sollozo *nm* : sob
solo¹, -la *adj* 1 : alone, by oneself ⟨me dejaron solo : they left me on my own⟩ ⟨lo hizo ella sola : she did it all by herself⟩ 2 : lonely 3 ÚNICO : only, sole, unique ⟨hay un solo problema : there's only one problem⟩ 4 **a solas** : alone
**solo² *nm* : solo
solo³ *or* **sólo** *adv* SOLAMENTE : just, only
solomillo *nm* : sirloin, loin
solsticio *nm* : solstice
soltar {19} *vt* 1 : to let go of, to drop ⟨¡suéltame el brazo! : let go of my arm!⟩ ⟨soltó las riendas : he dropped the reins⟩ 2 : to release, to set free 3 : to pay out (a rope, etc.) 4 AFLOJAR : to loosen, to slacken 5 : to undo, to untie (a knot, etc.) 6 : to give, to let out (a shout, etc.) 7 : to come out with (a swearword, etc.) — **soltarse** *vr* 1 : to get loose, to break free 2 : to come undone
soltería *nf* : state of being single
soltero¹, -ra *adj* : single, unmarried
soltero², -ra *n* 1 : bachelor *m*, single man *m*, single woman *f* 2 **apellido de soltera** : maiden name

soltura *nf* 1 : looseness, slackness 2 : fluency (of language) 3 : agility, ease of movement
soluble *adj* : soluble — **solubilidad** *nf*
solución *nf*, *pl* **-ciones** 1 : solution (in a liquid) 2 : answer, solution
solucionar *vt* RESOLVER : to solve, to resolve — **solucionarse** *vr*
solvencia *nf* 1 : solvency 2 : settling, payment (of debts) 3 : reliability ⟨solvencia moral : trustworthiness⟩
solvente¹ *adj* 1 : solvent 2 : reliable, trustworthy
**solvente² *nm* : solvent
sombra *nf* 1 : shadow 2 : shade 3 **sombras** *nfpl* : darkness, shadows *pl* 4 **sin sombra de duda** : without a shadow of a doubt 5 **sombra de ojos** : eye shadow
sombreado, -da *adj* 1 : shady 2 : shaded, darkened
sombrear *vt* : to shade
sombrerero, -ra *n* : milliner, hatter
sombrero *nm* 1 : hat 2 **sin ~** : bareheaded 3 **sombrero hongo** : derby
sombrilla *nf* : parasol, umbrella
sombrío, -bría *adj* LÓBREGO : dark, somber, gloomy — **sombríamente** *adv*
somero, -ra *adj* : superficial, cursory, shallow
someter *vt* 1 : to subjugate, to conquer 2 : to subordinate 3 : to subject (to treatment or testing) 4 : to submit, to present ⟨lo someterán a votación : they will put it to a vote⟩ ⟨someter a la justicia : to bring to justice⟩ — **someterse** *vr* 1 : to submit, to yield 2 : to undergo
sometimiento *nm* 1 : submission, subjection 2 : presentation
somier *nm*, *pl* **somieres** *or* **somiers** : box spring
somnífero¹, -ra *adj* : soporific
**somnífero² *nm* : sleeping pill
somnolencia *nf* : drowsiness, sleepiness
somnoliento, -ta *adj* : drowsy, sleepy
somorgujo *or* **somormujo** *nm* : loon, grebe
somos → **ser¹**
son¹ → **ser**
son² *nm* 1 : sound ⟨al son de la trompeta : at the sound of the trumpet⟩ 2 : news, rumor 3 **en son de : as, in the manner of, by way of ⟨en son de broma : as a joke⟩ ⟨en son de paz : in peace⟩
sonado, -da *adj* : celebrated, famous, much-discussed
sonaja *nf* : rattle
sonajero *nm* : rattle (toy)
sonambulismo *nm* : sleepwalking
sonámbulo, -la *n* : sleepwalker
sonante *adj* **dinero contante y sonante** → **dinero**
sonar¹ {19} *vi* 1 : to sound ⟨suena bien : it sounds good⟩ ⟨sonaba contenta : she sounded happy⟩ 2 : to sound, to ring (of bells, a phone, etc.), to go off (of an alarm), to ring out (of shots), to play (of music) 3 : to be pronounced (of a letter) 4 : to look or sound familiar ⟨me suena ese nombre : that name rings a bell⟩ 5 : to fly (of rumors), to be talked

about ⟨suena para reemplazar a Díaz : there is talk that he might replace Díaz⟩ 6 ~ a : to sound like — *vt* 1 : to ring 2 : to blow (a trumpet, a nose) — **sonarse** *vr* : to blow one's nose

sonar[2] *nm* : sonar

sonata *nf* : sonata

sonda *nf* 1 : sounding line 2 : probe 3 CATÉTER : catheter

sondar *vt* 1 : to sound, to probe (in medicine, drilling, etc.) 2 : to probe, to explore (outer space)

sondear *vt* 1 : to sound 2 : to probe 3 : to sound out, to test (opinions, markets)

sondeo *nm* 1 : sounding, probing 2 : drilling 3 ENCUESTA : survey, poll

soneto *nm* : sonnet

sónico, -ca *adj* : sonic

sonido *nm* : sound

sonoridad *nf* : resonance

sonoro, -ra *adj* 1 : resonant, sonorous, voiced (in linguistics) 2 : resounding, loud 3 **banda sonora** : soundtrack

sonreír {66} *vi* : to smile

sonriente *adj* : smiling

sonrisa *nf* : smile

sonrojar *vt* : to cause to blush — **sonrojarse** *vr* : to blush

sonrojo *nm* RUBOR : blush

sonrosado, -da *adj* : rosy, pink

sonsacar {72} *vt* : to wheedle, to extract

sonsonete *nm* 1 : tapping 2 : drone 3 : mocking tone

soñador[1], **-dora** *adj* : dreamy

soñador[2], **-dora** *n* : dreamer

soñar {19} *v* 1 : to dream 2 ~ **con** : to dream about 3 **soñar despierto** : to daydream

soñoliento, -ta *adj* : sleepy, drowsy

sopa *nf* 1 : soup 2 **estar hecho una sopa** : to be soaked to the bone

sopapa *nm Arg* : plunger (for toilets, etc.)

sopapo *nm fam* : slap

sopera *nf* : soup tureen

sopesar *vt* : to weigh, to evaluate

soplar *vi* : to blow — *vt* : to blow on, to blow out, to blow off

soplete *nm* : blowtorch

soplido *nm* : puff

soplo *nm* : puff, gust

soplón, -plona *n, mpl* **soplones** *fam* : tattletale, sneak

soponcio *nm fam* 1 : fainting spell ⟨sufrió un soponcio : he fainted⟩ 2 : shock, fit ⟨cuando se enteró le dio un/el soponcio : when he found out, he was horrified⟩

sopor *nm* SOMNOLENCIA : drowsiness, sleepiness

soporífero, -ra *adj* : soporific

soportable *adj* : bearable, tolerable

soportar *vt* 1 SOSTENER : to support, to hold up 2 RESISTIR : to withstand, to resist 3 AGUANTAR : to bear, to tolerate

soporte *nm* : base, stand, support

soprano *nmf* : soprano

sor *nf* : Sister (religious title)

sorber *vt* 1 : to sip, to suck in 2 : to absorb, to soak up

sorbete *nm* : sherbet

sorbo *nm* 1 : sip, gulp, swallow 2 **beber a sorbos** : to sip

sordera *nf* : deafness

sórdido, -da *adj* : sordid, dirty, squalid

sordina *nf* : mute (for a musical instrument)

sordo, -da *adj* 1 : deaf 2 : muted, muffled

sordomudo, -da *n offensive* : deaf-mute *often offensive*

sorgo *nm* : sorghum

soriasis *nfs & pl* : psoriasis

sorna *nf* : sarcasm, mocking tone

soroche *nm Peru* : altitude sickness

sorprendente *adj* : surprising — **sorprendentemente** *adv*

sorprender *vt* : to surprise — **sorprenderse** *vr*

sorpresa *nf* : surprise

sorpresivo, -va *adj* 1 : surprising, surprise 2 IMPREVISTO : sudden, unexpected

sortear *vt* 1 RIFAR : to raffle, to draw lots for 2 : to dodge, to avoid

sorteo *nm* : drawing, raffle

sortija *nf* 1 ANILLO : ring 2 : curl, ringlet

sortilegio *nm* 1 HECHIZO : spell, charm 2 HECHICERÍA : sorcery

SOS *nm* : SOS

sosegado, -da *adj* SERENO : calm, tranquil, serene

sosegar {49} *vt* : to calm, to pacify — **sosegarse** *vr*

sosiego *nm* : tranquillity, serenity, calm

soslayar *vt* ESQUIVAR : to dodge, to evade

soslayo *nm* **de** ~ : obliquely, sideways ⟨mirar de soslayo : to look askance⟩

soso, -sa *adj* 1 INSÍPIDO : bland, flavorless 2 ABURRIDO : dull, boring

sospecha *nf* : suspicion

sospechar *vt* : to suspect — *vi* : to be suspicious

sospechosamente *adv* : suspiciously

sospechoso[1], **-sa** *adj* : suspicious, suspect

sospechoso[2], **-sa** *n* : suspect

sostén *nm, pl* **sostenes** 1 APOYO : support 2 : sustenance 3 : brassiere, bra

sostener {80} *vt* 1 : to support, to hold up 2 : to hold ⟨sostenme la puerta : hold the door for me⟩ ⟨sostener una conversación : to hold a conversation⟩ 3 : to sustain, to maintain — **sostenerse** *vr* 1 : to stand, to hold oneself up 2 : to continue, to remain

sostenible *adj* : sustainable, tenable — **sostenibilidad** *nf*

sostenido[1], **-da** *adj* 1 : sustained, prolonged 2 : sharp (in music)

sostenido[2] *nm* : sharp (in music)

sostuvo, etc. → **sostener**

sota *nf* : jack (in the Spanish deck of cards)

sotana *nf* : cassock

sótano *nm* : basement

sotavento *nm* : lee ⟨a sotavento : leeward⟩

soterrar {55} *vt* 1 : to bury 2 : to conceal, to hide away

soto *nm* : grove, copse
souvenir *nm, pl* **-nirs** RECUERDO : souvenir, memento
soviético, -ca *adj* : Soviet
soy → **ser**
soya *nf* : soy, soybean
spaghetti → **espagueti**
spam *nm, pl* **spams** : spam (e-mail)
spaniel *nm, pl* **spaniels** : spaniel
SPM → **síndrome premenstrual**
sport [ɛˈspor] *adj* : sport, casual
sprint [ɛˈsprin, -ˈsprint] *nm* : sprint — **sprinter** *nmf*
squash [ɛˈskwaʃ, -ˈskwatʃ] *nm* : squash (sport)
Sr. *nm* : Mr.
Sra. *nf* : Mrs., Ms.
Srta. *or* **Srita.** *nf* : Miss, Ms.
staccato *adj* : staccato
stand *nm, pl* **stands** : stand, kiosk
standard → **estándar**
statu quo *nm* : status quo
stop [ɛsˈtop] *nm* : stop sign
streaming [ˈstrimiŋ] *nm* : streaming (of audio, video, etc.) ⟨un streaming en vivo : a livestream⟩
stress → **estrés**
su *adj* **1** : his, her, its, their, one's ⟨su libro : her book⟩ ⟨sus consecuencias : its consequences⟩ **2** (*formal*) : your ⟨tómese su medicina, señor : take your medicine, sir⟩
suave *adj* **1** BLANDO : soft **2** LISO : smooth **3** : gentle, mild **4** *Mex fam* : great, fantastic
suavemente *adv* : smoothly, gently, softly
suavidad *nf* : softness, smoothness, mellowness
suavizante *nm* : softener, fabric softener
suavizar {21} *vt* **1** : to soften, to smooth out **2** : to tone down — **suavizarse** *vr*
sub- *pref* : sub-
subacuático, -ca *adj* : underwater
subalterno[1], -na *adj* **1** SUBORDINADO : subordinate **2** SECUNDARIO : secondary
subalterno[2], -na *n* SUBORDINADO : subordinate
subarrendar {55} *vt* : to sublet
subasta *nf* : auction
subastador, -dora *n* : auctioneer
subastar *vt* : to auction, to auction off
subcampeón, -peona *n, mpl* **-peones** : runner-up
subcomisión *nf, pl* **-siones** : subcommittee
subcomité *nm* : subcommittee
subconsciente *adj & nm* : subconscious — **subconscientemente** *adv*
subcontratar *vt* : to subcontract
subcontratista *nmf* : subcontractor
subcultura *nf* : subculture
subdesarrollado, -da *adj* : underdeveloped
subdesarrollo *nm* : underdevelopment
subdirector, -tora *n* : assistant manager
súbdito, -ta *n* : subject (of a monarch)
subdividir *vt* : to subdivide
subdivisión *nf, pl* **-siones** : subdivision
subestimar *vt* : to underestimate, to undervalue

subexponer {60} *vt* : to underexpose
subexposición *nf, pl* **-ciones** : underexposure
subgrupo *nm* : subgroup
subibaja *nm* : seesaw
subida *nf* **1** : ascent, climb **2** : rise, increase **3** : slope, hill ⟨ir de subida : to go uphill⟩
subido, -da *adj* **1** : intense, strong ⟨amarillo subido : bright yellow⟩ **2 subido de tono** : risqué
subir *vt* **1** : to bring/take/carry up, to lift up **2** : to climb, to go/come up (stairs, etc.) **3** : to raise (a blind, etc.), to pull up (a zipper, etc.), to take up (a hem) **4** AUMENTAR : to raise (prices, etc.) ⟨subir el volumen : to turn up the volume⟩ **5** CARGAR : to upload — *vi* **1** : to go/come up **2** AUMENTAR : to rise, to increase **3** : to be promoted **4 ~ a** : to get on, to mount ⟨subir a un tren : to get on a train⟩ — **subirse** *vr* **1** : to climb (up) **2** : to pull up (clothing) **3 subirse a la cabeza** : to go to one's head
súbito, -ta *adj* **1** REPENTINO : sudden **2 de ~** : all of a sudden, suddenly — **súbitamente** *adv*
subjetivo, -va *adj* : subjective — **subjetivamente** *adv* — **subjetividad** *nf*
subjuntivo[1], -va *adj* : subjunctive
subjuntivo[2] *nm* : subjunctive
sublevación *nf, pl* **-ciones** ALZAMIENTO : uprising, rebellion
sublevar *vt* : to incite to rebellion — **sublevarse** *vr* : to rebel, to rise up
sublimar *vt* : to sublimate — **sublimación** *nf*
sublime *adj* : sublime
submarinismo *nm* : scuba diving
submarinista *nmf* : scuba diver
submarino[1], -na *adj* : submarine, undersea
submarino[2] *nm* : submarine
subnormal[1] *adj* **1** *usu offensive* : mentally handicapped *sometimes offensive* **2** : idiotic
subnormal[2] *nmf* **1** *usu offensive* : mentally handicapped person **2** : moron, idiot
suboficial *nmf* : noncommissioned officer, petty officer
subordinado, -da *adj & n* : subordinate
subordinar *vt* : to subordinate — **subordinarse** *vr* — **subordinación** *nf*
subproducto *nm* : by-product
subrayar *vt* **1** : to underline, to underscore **2** ENFATIZAR : to highlight, to emphasize
subrepticio, -cia *adj* : surreptitious — **subrepticiamente** *adv*
subsanar *vt* **1** RECTIFICAR : to rectify, to correct **2** : to overlook, to excuse **3** : to make up for
subscribir → **suscribir**
subsecretario, -ria *n* : undersecretary
subsecuente *adj* : subsequent — **subsecuentemente** *adv*
subsidiar *vt* : to subsidize
subsidiaria *nf* : subsidiary
subsidio *nm* : subsidy

subsiguiente *adj* : subsequent
subsistencia *nf* 1 : subsistence 2 : sustenance
subsistir *vi* 1 : to subsist, to live 2 : to endure, to survive
substancia → **sustancia**
subte *nm Arg, Uru* : subway
subteniente *nmf* : second lieutenant
subterfugio *nm* : subterfuge
subterráneo[1], **-nea** *adj* : underground, subterranean
subterráneo[2] *nm* 1 : underground passage, tunnel 2 *Arg, Uru* : subway
subtitular *vt* : to subtitle
subtítulo *nm* : subtitle, subheading
subtotal *nm* : subtotal
suburbano, -na *adj* : suburban
suburbio *nm* 1 : suburb 2 : slum (outside a city)
subvención *nf, pl* **-ciones** : subsidy, grant
subvencionar *vt* : to subsidize
subversivo, -va *adj & n* : subversive — **subversión** *nf*
subvertir {76} *vt* : to subvert
subyacente *adj* : underlying
subyacer *vi* — **en/a** *vi* : to underlie
subyugar {52} *vt* : to subjugate — **subyugación** *nf*
succión *nf, pl* **succiones** : suction
succionar *vt* : to suck up, to draw in
sucedáneo *nm* : substitute ⟨sucedáneo de azúcar : sugar substitute⟩
suceder *vi* 1 OCURRIR : to happen, to occur ⟨¿qué sucede? : what's going on?⟩ ⟨suceda lo que suceda : come what may⟩ 2 ~ **a** : to follow, to succeed ⟨a la primavera sucede el verano : summer follows spring⟩ — *vt* : to succeed ⟨suceder a alguien : to succeed someone⟩
sucesión *nf, pl* **-siones** 1 : succession 2 : sequence, series 3 : issue, heirs *pl* 4 : estate, inheritance
sucesivamente *adv* : successively, consecutively ⟨y así sucesivamente : and so on⟩
sucesivo, -va *adj* : successive ⟨en los días sucesivos : in the days that followed⟩
suceso *nm* 1 : event, happening, occurrence 2 : incident, crime
sucesor, -sora *n* : successor
suciedad *nf* 1 : dirtiness, filthiness 2 MUGRE : dirt, filth
sucinto, -ta *adj* CONCISO : succinct, concise — **sucintamente** *adv*
sucio, -cia *adj* : dirty, filthy
sucre *nm* : Ecuadoran unit of currency
suculento, -ta *adj* : succulent
sucumbir *vi* : to succumb
sucursal *nf* : branch (of a business)
sudadera *nf* 1 : sweatshirt 2 : sweatsuit, tracksuit
sudado, -da → **sudoroso**
sudafricano, -na *adj & n* : South African
sudamericano, -na *adj & n* : South American
sudanés, -nesa *adj & n, mpl* **-neses** : Sudanese
sudar *vi* TRANSPIRAR : to sweat, to perspire
sudario *nm* : shroud

sudeste → **sureste**
sudoeste → **suroeste**
sudor *nm* TRANSPIRACIÓN : sweat, perspiration
sudoroso, -sa *adj* : sweaty
sueco[1], **-ca** *adj* : Swedish
sueco[2], **-ca** *n* : Swede
sueco[3] *nm* : Swedish (language)
suegro, -gra *n* 1 : father-in-law *m*, mother-in-law *f* 2 **suegros** *nmpl* : in-laws
suela *nf* : sole (of a shoe)
suelda, etc. → **soldar**
sueldo *nm* : salary, wage
suele, etc. → **soler**
suelo *nm* 1 : ground ⟨caerse al suelo : to fall down, to hit the ground⟩ 2 : floor, flooring 3 TIERRA : soil, land
suelta, etc. → **soltar**
suelto[1], **-ta** *adj* 1 : loose, free, unattached ⟨dinero suelto : loose change⟩ ⟨una camisa suelta : a loose shirt⟩ ⟨cabos sueltos : loose ends⟩ ⟨el perro estaba suelto : the dog was loose⟩ ⟨un papelito suelto : a scrap of paper⟩ ⟨con el pelo suelto : with one's hair down⟩ 2 : individual, separate, odd ⟨¿las venden sueltas? : do they sell them individually?⟩ 3 : fluent, fluid
suelto[2] *nm* : loose change
suena, etc. → **sonar**
sueña, etc. → **soñar**
sueño *nm* 1 : dream 2 : sleep ⟨perder el sueño : to lose sleep⟩ 3 : sleepiness ⟨tener sueño : to be sleepy⟩
suero *nm* 1 : serum 2 : whey 3 **suero de mantequilla/manteca** : buttermilk
suerte *nf* 1 FORTUNA : luck, fortune ⟨tener suerte : to be lucky⟩ ⟨estar de suerte : to be in luck⟩ ⟨le deseo suerte : I wish him luck⟩ ⟨¡buena suerte! : good luck!⟩ ⟨por suerte : luckily⟩ ⟨con suerte : with any luck⟩ ⟨traer mala suerte : to be/bring bad luck⟩ ⟨fue una suerte que . . . : it's a lucky thing that . . .⟩ 2 DESTINO : fate, destiny, lot ⟨tentar a la suerte : to tempt fate⟩ ⟨la dejaron a su suerte : they left her to her fate⟩ ⟨correr la misma suerte : to meet the same fate⟩ 3 CLASE, GÉNERO : sort, kind ⟨toda suerte de cosas : all kinds of things⟩
suertudo[1], **-da** *adj fam* : lucky
suertudo[2], **-da** *n fam* : lucky person
suéter *nm* : sweater
suficiencia *nf* 1 : adequacy 2 : competence, fitness 3 : self-satisfaction
suficiente *adj* 1 BASTANTE : enough, sufficient ⟨tener suficiente : to have enough⟩ 2 : suitable, fit 3 : smug, complacent
suficientemente *adv* : sufficiently, enough
sufijo *nm* : suffix
suflé *nm* : soufflé
sufragar {52} *vt* 1 AYUDAR : to help out, to support 2 : to defray (costs) — *vi* : to vote
sufragio *nm* : suffrage, vote
sufrido, -da *adj* 1 : long-suffering, patient 2 : sturdy, serviceable (of clothing)

sufrimiento *nm* : suffering
sufrir *vt* **1** : to suffer ⟨sufrir una pérdida : to suffer a loss⟩ **2** : to tolerate, to put up with ⟨ella no lo puede sufrir : she can't stand him⟩ — *vi* : to suffer
sugerencia *nf* : suggestion
sugerente *adj* **1** : suggestive (of words, etc.), revealing (of clothes) **2** : intriguing, provocative
sugerir {76} *vt* **1** PROPONER, RECOMENDAR : to suggest, to recommend, to propose **2** : to suggest, to bring to mind
sugestión *nf*, *pl* **-tiones** : suggestion, prompting ⟨poder de sugestión : power of suggestion⟩
sugestionable *adj* : suggestible, impressionable
sugestionar *vt* : to influence, to sway — **sugestionarse** *vr* ~ **con** : to talk oneself into, to become convinced of
sugestivo, -va *adj* **1** : suggestive **2** : interesting, stimulating
suicida[1] *adj* : suicidal
suicida[2] *nmf* : suicide victim, suicide
suicidarse *vr* : to commit suicide
suicidio *nm* : suicide
suite *nf* : suite
suizo, -za *adj & n* : Swiss
sujeción *nf*, *pl* **-ciones** **1** : holding, fastening **2** : subjection
sujetador *nm* **1** : fastener **2** : holder ⟨sujetador de tazas : cup holder⟩
sujetalibros *nms & pl* : bookend
sujetapapeles *nms & pl* CLIP : paper clip
sujetar *vt* **1** : to hold on to, to steady, to hold down **2** FIJAR : to fasten, to attach **3** DOMINAR : to subdue, to conquer — **sujetarse** *vr* **1** : to hold on, to hang on **2** ~ **a** : to abide by
sujeto[1], **-ta** *adj* **1** : secure, fastened **2** ~ **a** : subject to
sujeto[2] *nm* **1** INDIVIDUO : individual, character **2** : subject (in grammar)
sulfúrico, -ca *adj* ácido sulfúrico → ácido[2]
sulfuro *nm* : sulfur
sultán *nm*, *pl* **sultanes** : sultan
suma *nf* **1** CANTIDAD : sum, quantity **2** : addition
sumamente *adv* : extremely, exceedingly
sumar *vt* **1** : to add, to add up **2** : to add up to, to total — *vi* : to add up — **sumarse** *vr* ~ **a** : to join
sumariamente *adv* : summarily
sumario[1], **-ria** *adj* SUCINTO : succinct, summary
sumario[2] *nm* : summary
sumergible *adj* : waterproof
sumergir {35} *vt* : to submerge, to immerse, to plunge — **sumergirse** *vr*
sumersión *nf*, *pl* **-siones** : submerging, immersion
sumidero *nm* : drain, sewer
suministrar *vt* : to supply, to provide
suministro *nm* : supply, provision
sumir *vt* SUMERGIR : to plunge, to immerse, to sink — **sumirse** *vr*
sumisión *nf*, *pl* **-siones** **1** : submission **2** : submissiveness

sumiso, -sa *adj* : submissive, acquiescent, docile
sumo, -ma *adj* **1** : extreme, great, high ⟨la suma autoridad : the highest authority⟩ **2 a lo sumo** : at the most
sunita *nmf* : Sunni
suntuoso, -sa *adj* : sumptuous, lavish — **suntuosamente** *adv*
supeditar *vt* SUBORDINAR : to subordinate — **supeditación** *nf*
super[1] *or* **súper** *adj fam* : super, great
super[2] *nm* SUPERMERCADO : market, supermarket
super- *pref* : super-
superabundancia *nf* : overabundance — **superabundante** *adj*
superación *nf*, *pl* **-ciones** : surpassing, overcoming
superar *vt* **1** : to surpass, to exceed **2** : to overcome, to surmount — **superarse** *vr* : to improve oneself
superávit *nm*, *pl* **-vit** *or* **-vits** : surplus
supercheria *nf* : trickery, fraud
supercomputadora *nf* : supercomputer
superdotado, -da *n* : a very talented person
superestrella *nf* : superstar
superestructura *nf* : superstructure
superficial *adj* : superficial — **superficialmente** *adv*
superficialidad *nf* : superficiality
superficie *nf* **1** : surface **2** : area ⟨la superficie de un triángulo : the area of a triangle⟩
superfluo, -flua *adj* : superfluous — **superfluidad** *nf*
superintendente *nmf* : supervisor, superintendent
superior[1] *adj* **1** : superior **2** : upper ⟨nivel superior : upper level⟩ **3** : higher ⟨educación superior : higher education⟩ **4** ~ **a** : above, higher than, in excess of
superior[2] *nm* : superior
superioridad *nf* : superiority
superlativo[1], **-va** *adj* : superlative
superlativo[2] *nm* : superlative
supermercado *nm* : supermarket
superpoblación *nf*, *pl* **-ciones** : overpopulation
superpoblado, -da *adj* : overpopulated
superponer {60} *vt* : to superimpose
superpotencia *nf* : superpower
superproducción → **sobreproducción**
supersónico, -ca *adj* : supersonic
superstición *nf*, *pl* **-ciones** : superstition
supersticioso, -sa *adj* : superstitious
supervisar *vt* : to supervise, to oversee
supervisión *nf*, *pl* **-siones** : supervision
supervisor, -sora *n* : supervisor, overseer
supervivencia *nf* : survival
superviviente *nmf* : survivor
supino, -na *adj* : supine
suplantación *nf*, *pl* **-ciones** : supplanting, replacement ⟨suplantación de identidad : identity theft⟩
suplantar *vt* : to supplant, to replace
suplemental → **suplementario**
suplementario, -ria *adj* : supplementary, additional, extra

suplemento *nm* : supplement

suplencia *nf* : substitution, replacement

suplente *adj & nmf* : substitute ⟨equipo suplente : replacement team⟩

supletorio, -ria *adj* : extra, additional ⟨teléfono supletorio : extension phone⟩ ⟨cama supletoria : spare bed⟩

súplica *nf* : plea, entreaty

suplicar {72} *vt* IMPLORAR, ROGAR : to entreat, to implore, to supplicate

suplicio *nm* TORMENTO : ordeal, torture

suplir *vt* **1** COMPENSAR : to make up for, to compensate for **2** REEMPLAZAR : to replace, to substitute

supo, etc. → saber

suponer {60} *vt* **1** PRESUMIR : to suppose, to assume ⟨supongo que sí : I guess so, I suppose so⟩ ⟨se supone que van a llegar mañana : they're supposed to arrive tomorrow⟩ **2** : to imply, to suggest **3** : to involve, to entail ⟨el éxito supone mucho trabajo : success involves a lot of work⟩

suposición *nf, pl* **-ciones** PRESUNCIÓN : supposition, assumption

supositorio *nm* : suppository

supremacía *nf* : supremacy

supremo, -ma *adj* : supreme

supresión *nf, pl* **-siones 1** : suppression, elimination **2** : deletion

suprimir *vt* **1** : to suppress, to eliminate **2** : to delete

supuestamente *adv* : supposedly, allegedly

supuesto, -ta *adj* **1** : supposed, alleged ⟨los supuestos expertos : the supposed experts⟩ ⟨un nombre supuesto : an assumed name⟩ **2 por ~** : of course, absolutely

supurar *vi* : to ooze, to discharge

supuso, etc. → suponer

sur¹ *adj* : southern, southerly, south

sur² *nm* **1** : south, South **2** : south wind

surafricano, -na → sudafricano

suramericano, -na → sudamericano

surcar {72} *vt* **1** : to plow (through) **2** : to groove, to score, to furrow

surco *nm* : groove, furrow, rut

sureño¹, -ña *adj* : southern, Southern

sureño², -ña *n* : Southerner

sureste¹ *adj* **1** : southeast, southeastern **2** : southeasterly

sureste² *nm* : southeast, Southeast

surf *nm* : surfing

surfear *vi* : to surf

surfing → surf

surfista *nmf* : surfer

surgimiento *nm* : rise, emergence

surgir {35} *vi* : to rise, to arise, to emerge

suroeste¹ *adj* **1** : southwest, southwestern **2** : southwesterly

suroeste² *nm* : southwest, Southwest

surrealismo *nm* : surrealism

surrealista¹ *adj* : surreal, surrealistic

surrealista² *nmf* : surrealist

surtido¹, -da *adj* **1** : assorted, varied **2** : stocked, provisioned

surtido² *nm* : assortment, selection

surtidor *nm* **1** : jet, spout **2** *Arg, Chile, Spain* : gas pump

surtir *vt* **1** : to supply, to provide ⟨surtir un pedido : to fill an order⟩ **2 surtir efecto** : to have an effect — *vi* : to spout, to spurt up — **surtirse** *vr* : to stock up

susceptible *adj* : susceptible, sensitive — **susceptibilidad** *nf*

suscitar *vt* : to provoke, to give rise to

suscribir {33} *vt* **1** : to sign (a formal document) **2** : to endorse, to sanction — **suscribirse** *vr* ~ **a** : to subscribe to

suscripción *nf, pl* **-ciones 1** : subscription **2** : endorsement, sanction **3** : signing

suscriptor, -tora *n* : subscriber

susodicho, -cha *adj* : aforementioned, aforesaid

suspender *vt* **1** COLGAR : to suspend, to hang **2** : to suspend, to discontinue **3** : to suspend, to dismiss

suspense *nm Spain* → **suspenso**

suspensión *nf, pl* **-siones** : suspension

suspenso *nm* : suspense

suspensores *nmpl Chile* : suspenders

suspicacia *nf* : suspicion, mistrust

suspicaz *adj, pl* **-caces** DESCONFIADO : suspicious, wary

suspirar *vi* : to sigh

suspiro *nm* : sigh

surque, etc. → surcar

suscrito *pp* → **suscribir**

sustancia *nf* **1** : substance **2 sin ~** : shallow, lacking substance

sustancial *adj* **1** : substantial **2** ESENCIAL, FUNDAMENTAL : essential, fundamental — **sustancialmente** *adv*

sustancioso, -sa *adj* **1** NUTRITIVO : hearty, nutritious **2** : substantial, solid

sustantivo *nm* : noun

sustentación *nf, pl* **-ciones** SOSTÉN : support

sustentar *vt* **1** : to support, to hold up **2** : to sustain, to nourish **3** : to maintain, to hold (an opinion) — **sustentarse** *vr* : to support oneself

sustento *nm* **1** : means of support, livelihood **2** : sustenance, food

sustitución *nf, pl* **-ciones** : replacement, substitution

sustituir {41} *vt* **1** : to replace, to substitute for **2** : to stand in for

sustituto, -ta *n* : substitute, stand-in

susto *nm* : fright, scare

sustracción *nf, pl* **-ciones 1** RESTA : subtraction **2** : theft

sustraer {81} *vt* **1** : to remove, to take away **2** RESTAR : to subtract **3** : to steal — **sustraerse** *vr* ~ **a** : to avoid, to evade

susurrar *vi* **1** : to whisper **2** : to murmur **3** : to rustle (leaves, etc.) — *vt* : to whisper

susurro *nm* **1** : whisper **2** : murmur **3** : rustle, rustling

sutil *adj* **1** : delicate, thin, fine **2** : subtle — **sutilmente** *adv*

sutileza *nf* **1** : delicacy **2** : subtlety

sutura *nf* : suture, stitch

SUV [esu'bi, esju-] *nm, pl* **SUV** *or* **SUVs** [esu'bis, esju-] : SUV

suyo¹, -ya *adj* **1** : his, her, its, theirs ⟨los libros suyos : his books⟩ ⟨un amigo suyo : a friend of hers⟩ ⟨esta casa es suya : this house is theirs⟩ **2** (*formal*) : yours ⟨¿este abrigo es suyo, señor? : is this your coat, sir?⟩

suyo², -ya *pron* **1** : his, hers, theirs ⟨mi guitarra y la suya : my guitar and hers⟩ ⟨ellos trajeron las suyas : they brought theirs, they brought their own⟩ **2** (*formal*) : yours ⟨usted olvidó la suya : you forgot yours⟩

switch *nm* : switch

T

t *nf* : twenty-third letter of the Spanish alphabet

taba *nf* : anklebone

tabacalero¹, -ra *adj* : tobacco ⟨industria tabacalera : tobacco industry⟩

tabacalero², -ra *n* : tobacco grower

tabaco *nm* : tobacco

tábano *nm* : horsefly

tabaquería *nf* : tobacco shop

tabaquismo *nm* **tabaquismo pasivo** : passive smoking

taberna *nf* : tavern, bar

tabernáculo *nm* : tabernacle

tabernero, -ra *n* **1** : bar owner **2** : bartender

tabicar {72} *vt* : to wall up

tabique *nm* : thin wall, partition

tabla *nf* **1** : table, list ⟨tabla de multiplicar : multiplication table⟩ **2** : board, plank, slab ⟨tabla de planchar : ironing board⟩ **3** : plot, strip (of land) **4** : box pleat **5 tablas** *nfpl* : stage, boards *pl*

tablado *nm* **1** : floor **2** : platform, scaffold **3** : stage

tablao *nm* : flamenco bar

tablero *nm* **1** : bulletin board **2** : board (in games) ⟨tablero de ajedrez : chessboard⟩ ⟨tablero de damas : checkerboard⟩ ⟨tablero de circuitos : circuit board⟩ **3** PIZARRA : blackboard **4** : switchboard **5 tablero de instrumentos** : dashboard, instrument panel

tablet → tableta

tableta *nf* **1** COMPRIMIDO, PÍLDORA : tablet, pill **2** : bar (of chocolate) **3** : tablet (computer)

tabletear *vi* : to rattle, to clack

tableteo *nm* : clack, rattling

tablilla *nf* **1** : small board or tablet **2** : bulletin board **3** : splint

tabloide *nm* : tabloid

tablón *nm, pl* **tablones 1** : plank, beam **2 tablón de anuncios** : bulletin board

tabú¹ *adj* : taboo

tabú² *nm, pl* **tabúes** *or* **tabús** : taboo

tabulador *nm* **1** : tabulator **2** : tab, tab key

tabular¹ *vt* : to tabulate

tabular² *adj* : tabular

taburete *nm* : footstool, stool

tacañería *nf* : stinginess

tacaño¹, -ña *adj* MEZQUINO : stingy, miserly

tacaño², -ña *n* : miser, tightwad

tacha *nf* **1** : flaw, blemish, defect **2 poner tacha a** : to find fault with **3 sin ∼** : flawless

tachadura *nf* : erasure, correction

tachar *vt* **1** : to cross out, to delete **2 ∼ de** : to accuse of, to label as ⟨lo tacharon de mentiroso : they accused him of being a liar⟩

tacho *nm Arg, Chile, Ecua, Peru, Uru* **1** : wastebasket **2 ∼ de (la) basura** : garbage can

tachón *nm, pl* **tachones** : stud, hobnail

tachonar *vt* : to stud

tachuela *nf* : tack, hobnail, stud

tácito, -ta *adj* : tacit, implicit — **tácitamente** *adv*

taciturno, -na *adj* **1** : taciturn **2** : sullen, gloomy

tacle *nm* : tackle

tacleada *nf* : tackle (in football)

taclear *vt* : to tackle (in football)

taco *nm* **1** : wad, stopper, plug **2** : pad (of paper) **3** : cleat **4** : heel (of a shoe) **5** : cue (in billiards) **6** : light snack, bite **7** : taco

tacón *nm, pl* **tacones** : heel (of a shoe) ⟨de tacón alto : high-heeled⟩

taconazo *nm* **1** PATADA : (heel) kick **2** : stamp, heel tap ⟨dar un taconazo : to click one's heels⟩

táctica *nf* : tactic, tactics *pl*

táctico, -ca *adj* : tactical

táctil *adj* : tactile

tacto *nm* **1** : touch, touching, feel **2** DELICADEZA : tact

tafeta *nf Arg, Mex, Uru* : taffeta

tafetán *nm, pl* **-tanes** : taffeta

tahúr *nm, pl* **tahúres** : gambler

tailandés¹, -desa *adj & n, pl* **-deses** : Thai

tailandés² *nm* : Thai (language)

taimado, -da *adj* **1** : crafty, sly **2** *Chile* : sullen, sulky

tajada *nf* **1** : slice **2 sacar tajada** *fam* : to get one's share

tajante *adj* **1** : cutting, sharp **2** : decisive, categorical

tajantemente *adj* : emphatically, categorically

tajar *vt* : to cut, to slice

tajear *vt* **1** : to cut **2** : to hack, to slash

tajo *nm* **1** : cut, slash, gash **2** ESCARPA : steep cliff

tal¹ *adj* **1** : so, in such a way **2 tal como** : just as ⟨tal como lo hice : just the way I did it⟩ **3 con tal que** : provided that, as long as **4 ¿qué tal?** : how are you?, how's it going?

tal² *adj* **1** : such, such a ⟨a tal grado : to such a degree⟩ ⟨de tal manera que : such that, in such a way that⟩ ⟨yo no dije tal cosa! : I said no such thing!〉 **2** (*indicating an unspecified person or thing*) 〈en tal día, a tal hora : on such and such a day at such and such a time〉 〈un tal Pérez : a Mr. Pérez, some guy named Pérez〉 **3 tal vez** : maybe, perhaps

tal³ *pron* **1** : such a one, someone **2** : such a thing, something **3 tal para cual** : two of a kind

tala *nf* : felling (of trees)

taladradora *nf* : jackhammer

taladrar *vt* : to drill

taladro *nm* : drill, auger 〈taladro eléctrico : power drill〉

talante *nm* **1** HUMOR : mood, disposition **2** VOLUNTAD : will, willingness

talar *vt* **1** : to cut down, to fell **2** DEVASTAR : to devastate, to destroy

talco *nm* **1** : talc **2** : talcum powder

talego *nm* : sack

talento *nm* : talent, ability

talentoso, -sa *adj* : talented, gifted

talismán *nm, pl* **-manes** AMULETO : talisman, charm

talla *nf* **1** ESTATURA : height **2** : size (in clothing) **3** : stature, status **4** : sculpture, carving

tallar *vt* **1** : to sculpt, to carve **2** : to measure (someone's height) **3** : to deal (cards)

tallarín *nf, pl* **-rines** : noodle

talle *nm* **1** : size **2** : waist, waistline **3** : figure, shape

taller *nm* **1** : shop, workshop **2** : studio (of an artist)

tallo *nm* : stalk, stem 〈tallo de maíz : cornstalk〉

talón *nm, pl* **talones 1** : heel (of the foot) **2** : stub (of a check) **3 talón de Aquiles** : Achilles' heel

talonario *nm* : checkbook

taltuza *nf* : gopher

talud *nm* : slope, incline

tamal *nm* : tamale

tamaño¹, -ña *adj* : such a big 〈¿crees tamaña mentira? : do you believe such a lie?〉

tamaño² *nm* **1** : size **2 de tamaño natural** : life-size

tamarindo *nm* : tamarind

tambaleante *adj* **1** : wobbly, unsteady, teetering **2** : staggering, swaying, tottering

tambalear *vi* → **tambalearse**

tambalearse *vr* **1** : to teeter, to stagger, to sway, to totter

tambaleo *nm* : staggering, lurching, swaying

también *adv* : too, as well, also

tambor *nm* : drum

tamborilear *vi* : to drum, to tap

tamborileo *nm* : tapping, drumming

tamiz *nm* : sieve

tamizar {21} *vt* : to sift

tampoco *adv* : neither, not either 〈ni yo tampoco : me neither〉

tampón *nm, pl* **tampones 1** : ink pad **2** : tampon

tam—tam *nm* : tom-tom

tan¹ *adv* **1** : so, so very 〈no es tan difícil : it is not that difficult〉 **2** : as 〈tan

pronto como : as soon as〉 **3 tan siquiera** : at least, at the least **4 tan sólo** : only, merely

tan² *pron* **tan es así** : so much so

tanda *nf* **1** : turn, shift **2** : batch, lot, series

tándem *nm* **1** : tandem (bicycle) **2** : duo, pair

tangente *adj & nf* : tangent — **tangencial** *adj*

tangerina *nf* : tangerine

tangible *adj* : tangible

tango *nm* : tango

tanino *nm* : tannin

tanque *nm* **1** : tank 〈buque tanque : tanker (ship)〉 **2** : tank (vehicle)

tanteador *nm* MARCADOR : scoreboard

tantear *vt* **1** : to feel, to grope **2** : to size up, to weigh — *vi* **1** : to keep score **2** : to feel one's way

tanteo *nm* **1** : estimate, rough calculation **2** : testing, sizing up **3** : scoring

tanto¹ *adv* **1** : so much 〈te quiero tanto : I love you so much〉 〈ha cambiado tanto que no lo reconocí : he has changed so much that I didn't recognize him〉 〈tanto mejor : so much the better〉 **2** : so long 〈¿por qué te tardaste tanto? : why did you take so long?〉 **3 tanto como** : as much as 〈trabajo tanto como ella : I work as much as she does〉 〈¿te gustó tanto como a mí? : did you like it as much as I did?〉

tanto², -ta *adj* **1** : so much, so many, such 〈no hagas tantas preguntas : don't ask so many questions〉 〈tiene tanto encanto : he has such charm, he's so charming〉 **2** : as much, as many 〈come tantos dulces como yo : she eats as many sweets as I do〉 **3** : odd, however many 〈cuarenta y tantos años : forty-odd years〉

tanto³ *nm* **1** : certain amount **2** : goal, point (in sports) **3 al tanto** : abreast, in the picture **4 un tanto** : somewhat, rather 〈un tanto cansado : rather tired〉

tanto⁴, -ta *pron* **1** : so much, so many 〈tiene tanto que hacer : she has so much to do〉 〈no me des tantos : don't give me so many!〉 **2 en ~** : while **3 entre ~** : meanwhile **4 otro tanto** : again as much, again as many 〈tiene un metro de ancho y otro tanto de altura : it's a meter wide and a meter high〉 〈otro tanto podría decirse de . . . : the same can be said of . . .〉 **5 por lo tanto** : therefore **6 tanto es así** : so much so

tañer {79} *vt* **1** : to ring (a bell) **2** : to play (a musical instrument)

tañido *nm* **1** CAMPANADA : ring, peal, toll **2** : sound (of an instrument)

tapa *nf* **1** : cover, top, lid **2** *Spain* : bar snack

tapacubos *nms & pl* : hubcap

tapadera *nf* **1** : cover, lid **2** : front, cover (for an organization or person)

tapar *vt* **1** CUBRIR : to cover, to cover up **2** OBSTRUIR : to block, to obstruct — **taparse** *vr*

taparrabos *nms & pl* : loincloth

tapete *nm* **1** : small rug, mat **2** : table cover **3 poner sobre el tapete** : to bring up for discussion

tapia *nf* : (adobe) wall, garden wall

tapiar *vt* **1** : to wall in **2** : to enclose, to block off

tapicería *nf* **1** : upholstery **2** TAPIZ : tapestry

tapicero, -ra *n* : upholsterer

tapioca *nf* : tapioca

tapir *nm* : tapir

tapiz *nm, pl* **tapices** : tapestry

tapizado *nm* : upholstery

tapizar {21} *vt* **1** : to upholster **2** : to cover, to carpet

tapón *nm, pl* **tapones** **1** : cork **2** : bottle cap **3** : plug, stopper **4** *fam* : traffic jam **5** *Arg* : fuse.

taponar *vt* **1** : to block, to stop up

tapujo *nm* **1** : deceit, pretension **2 sin tapujos** : openly, frankly

taquigrafía *nf* : stenography, shorthand

taquigráfico, -ca *adj* : stenographic

taquígrafo, -fa *n* : stenographer

taquilla *nf* **1** : box office, ticket office **2** : earnings *pl*, take

taquillero, -ra *adj* : box-office, popular ⟨un éxito taquillero : a box-office success⟩

tara *nf* : defect

tarántula *nf* : tarantula

tararear *vt* : to hum

tardanza *nf* : lateness, delay

tardar *vi* **1** : to take time, to delay ⟨tardaron en responder : they took a while to respond⟩ ⟨no tardes : don't take too long⟩ **2 a más tardar** : at the latest — *vt* DEMORAR : to take (time) ⟨tarda una hora : it takes an hour⟩ ⟨tardar mucho : to take a long time⟩ ⟨tardar el doble : to take twice as long⟩ — **tardarse** *vr*

tarde[1] *adv* **1** : late **2 tarde o temprano** : sooner or later

tarde[2] *nf* **1** : afternoon, evening **2 ¡buenas tardes!** : good afternoon!, good evening! **3 en la tarde** *or* **por la tarde** : in the afternoon, in the evening

tardío, -día *adj* : late, tardy

tardo, -da *adj* : slow

tarea *nf* **1** : task, job **2** : homework

tarifa *nf* **1** : rate ⟨tarifas postales : postal rates⟩ **2** : fare (for transportation) **3** : price list **4** ARANCEL : duty

tarima *nf* PLATAFORMA : dais, platform, stage

tarjeta *nf* : card ⟨tarjeta de crédito/débito : credit/debit card⟩ ⟨tarjeta postal : postcard⟩ ⟨tarjeta (de) regalo : gift card⟩ ⟨tarjeta de felicitación : greeting card⟩ ⟨tarjeta navideña, tarjeta de Navidad : Christmas card⟩ ⟨tarjeta de video/memoria : video/memory card⟩ ⟨tarjeta de visita : business card, calling card⟩

taro *nm* : taro

tarrina *nf* : tub

tarro *nm* **1** : jar, pot **2** *Arg, Chile, CoRi, Uru* : can, tin

tarta *nf* **1** : tart **2** *Spain* : cake

tartaleta *nf* : tart

tartamudear *vi* : to stammer, to stutter

tartamudeo *nm* : stutter, stammer

tartamudo[1]**, -da** *adj* : stuttering, stammering

tartamudo[2]**, -da** *n* : person who stutters or stammers

tartán *nm, pl* **tartanes** : tartan, plaid

tártaro *nm* : tartar

tartera *nf* *Spain* : lunch box

tasa *nf* **1** : rate ⟨tasa de desempleo : unemployment rate⟩ **2** : tax, fee **3** : appraisal, valuation

tasación *nf, pl* **-ciones** : appraisal, assessment

tasador, -dora *n* : assessor, appraiser

tasajo *nm* : dried beef, beef jerky

tasar *vt* **1** VALORAR : to appraise, to value **2** : to set the price of **3** : to ration, to limit

tasca *nf* : cheap bar, dive

tatarabuela *nf* : great-great-grandmother

tatarabuelo *nm* : great-great-grandfather

tatuaje *nm* : tattoo, tattooing

tatuar {3} *vt* : to tattoo

taurino, -na *adj* : bull, bullfighting

Tauro[1] *nm* : Taurus (sign or constellation)

Tauro[2] *nmf* : Taurus (person)

tauromaquia *nf* : (art of) bullfighting

taxi *nm, pl* **taxis** : taxi, taxicab

taxidermia *nf* : taxidermy

taxidermista *nmf* : taxidermist

taxista *nmf* : taxi driver

taza *nf* **1** : cup **2** : cupful **3** : (toilet) bowl **4** : basin (of a fountain)

tazón *nm, pl* **tazones** **1** : bowl **2** : large cup, mug

te[1] *nf* : (letter) t

te[2] *pron* **1** : you ⟨te quiero : I love you⟩ **2** : for you, to you, from you ⟨me gustaría dártelo : I would like to give it to you⟩ **3** : yourself, for yourself, to yourself, from yourself ⟨¡cálmate! : calm yourself!⟩ ⟨¿te guardaste uno? : did you keep one for yourself?⟩ **4** : thee

té *nm* **1** : tea **2** : tea party

tea *nf* : torch

teatral *adj* : theatrical — **teatralmente** *adv*

teatro *nm* **1** : theater **2 hacer teatro** : to put on an act, to exaggerate

teca *nf* : teak

techado *nm* **1** : roof **2 bajo techado** : under cover, indoors

techar *vt* : to roof, to shingle

techo *nm* **1** TEJADO : roof **2** : ceiling **3** : upper limit, ceiling

techumbre *nf* : roofing

tecla *nf* **1** : key (of a musical instrument or a machine) ⟨la tecla Tab : the tab key⟩ **2 dar en la tecla** : to hit the nail on the head

teclado *nm* **1** : keyboard — **2 teclado numérico** : (number) keypad

teclear *vt* : to type in, to enter

técnica *nf* **1** : technique, skill **2** : technology

técnico[1]**, -ca** *adj* : technical — **técnicamente** *adv*

técnico[2]**, -ca** *n* : technician, expert, engineer.

tecnología *nf* : technology

tecnológico, -ca *adj* : technological — **tecnológicamente** *adv*
tecolote *nm Mex* : owl
tedio *nm* : tedium, boredom
tedioso, -sa *adj* : tedious, boring — **tediosamente** *adv*
tee ['ti] *nm* : tee (in golf)
teja *nf* : tile
tejado *nm* TECHO : roof
tejanos *nmpl* : jeans
tejar *vt* : to tile
tejedor, -dora *n* : weaver
tejemaneje *nm* **1** : intrigue, machination **2** : fuss, commotion
tejer *vt* **1** : to knit, to crochet **2** : to weave **3** FABRICAR : to concoct, to make up, to fabricate
tejido *nm* **1** TELA : fabric, cloth **2** : weave, texture **3** : tissue ⟨tejido muscular : muscle tissue⟩
tejo *nm* **1** : yew **2** : hopscotch (children's game)
tejón *nm, pl* **tejones** : badger
tela *nf* **1** : fabric, cloth, material **2 tela de araña** : spiderweb **3 poner en tela de juicio** : to call into question, to doubt
telar *nm* : loom
telaraña *nf* : spiderweb, cobweb
tele *nf fam* : TV, television
telecomunicación *nf, pl* **-ciones** : telecommunication
teleconferencia *nf* : teleconference
telediario *nm Spain* : news, news program
teledifusión *nf, pl* **-siones** : television broadcasting
teledirigido, -da *adj* : remote-controlled
teleférico *nm* : cable car
telefonazo *nm fam* : (telephone) call
telefonear *v* : to telephone, to call
telefónico, -ca *adj* : phone, telephone ⟨llamada telefónica : phone call⟩
telefonista *nmf* : telephone operator
teléfono *nm* **1** : telephone ⟨contestar el teléfono : to answer the phone⟩ ⟨número de teléfono : phone number⟩ ⟨teléfono celular : cell phone, mobile phone⟩ **2 llamar por teléfono** : to telephone, to make a phone call **3 teléfono inteligente** : smartphone
telegrafiar {85} *v* : to telegraph
telégrafo *nm* : telegraph
telegrama *nm* : telegram
telemárketing *nm* : telemarketing
telenovela *nf* : soap opera
telepatía *nf* : telepathy
telepático, -ca *adj* : telepathic — **telepáticamente** *adv*
telerrealidad *nf* : reality TV, reality television
telescópico, -ca *adj* : telescopic
telescopio *nm* : telescope
telesilla *nf* : ski lift
telespectador, -dora *n* : (television) viewer
telesquí *nm, pl* **-squís** : ski lift
televidente *nmf* : (television) viewer
televisar *v* : to televise
televisión *nf, pl* **-siones** : television, TV ⟨televisión de alta definición : high definition television⟩ ⟨hay un programa de ciencia en la televisión : there's a science program on TV⟩

televisivo, -va *adj* : television ⟨serie televisiva : television series⟩
televisor *nm* : television set
telón *nm, pl* **telones** **1** : curtain (in theater) **2 telón de fondo** : backdrop, background
tema *nm* **1** ASUNTO : theme, topic, subject **2** MOTIVO : motif, central theme
temario *nm* **1** : set of topics (for study) **2** : agenda
temática *nf* : subject matter
temático, -ca *adj* : thematic
temblar {55} *vi* **1** : to tremble, to shake, to shiver ⟨le temblaban las rodillas : his knees were shaking⟩ **2** : to shudder, to be afraid ⟨tiemblo con sólo pensarlo : I shudder to think of it⟩
temblor *nm* **1** : shaking, trembling **2** : tremor, earthquake
temblorosamente *adv* : shakily
tembloroso, -sa *adj* : tremulous, trembling, shaking ⟨con la voz temblorosa : with a shaky voice⟩
temer *vt* : to fear, to dread ⟨temíamos lo peor : we feared the worst⟩ — *vi* : to be afraid ⟨temer por alguien/algo : to fear for someone/something⟩ — **temerse** *vr*
temerario, -ria *adj* : reckless, rash — **temerariamente** *adv*
temeridad *nf* **1** : temerity, recklessness, rashness **2** : rash act
temeroso, -sa *adj* MIEDOSO : fearful, frightened
temible *adj* : fearsome, dreadful
temor *nm* MIEDO : fear, dread
témpano *nm* : ice floe
temperamento *nm* : temperament — **temperamental** *adj*
temperancia *nf* : temperance
temperar *vt* MODERAR : to temper, to moderate — *vi* : to have a change of air
temperatura *nf* : temperature
tempestad *nf* **1** : storm, tempest **2 tempestad de arena** : sandstorm
tempestuoso, -sa *adj* : tempestuous, stormy
templado, -da *adj* **1** : temperate, mild **2** : moderate, restrained **3** : warm, lukewarm **4** VALIENTE : courageous, bold
templanza *nf* **1** : temperance, moderation **2** : mildness (of weather)
templar *vt* **1** : to temper (steel) **2** : to restrain, to moderate **3** : to tune (a musical instrument) **4** : to warm up, to cool down — **templarse** *vr* **1** : to be moderate **2** : to warm up, to cool down
temple *nm* **1** : temper (of steel, etc.) **2** HUMOR : mood ⟨de buen temple : in a good mood⟩ **3** : tuning **4** VALOR : courage
templo *nm* **1** : temple **2** : church, chapel
tempo *nm* : tempo (in music)
temporada *nf* **1** : season, time ⟨temporada de béisbol : baseball season⟩ **2** : period, spell ⟨por temporadas : on and off⟩
temporal[1] *adj* **1** : temporal **2** : temporary

temporal² *nm* **1** : storm **2 capear el temporal** : to weather the storm
temporalmente *adv* : temporarily
temporario, -ria *adj* : temporary — **temporariamente** *adv*
temporero¹, -ra *adj* : temporary, seasonal
temporero², -ra *n* : temporary or seasonal worker
temporizador *nm* : timer
tempranero, -ra *adj* : early
temprano¹ *adv* : early ⟨lo más temprano posible : as soon as possible⟩ ⟨por la mañana temprano : early in the morning⟩
temprano², -na *adj* : early ⟨la parte temprana del siglo : the early part of the century⟩
ten → tener
tenacidad *nf* : tenacity, perseverance
tenacillas *nfpl* **1** : tongs **2** : curling iron (for hair)
tenaz *adj, pl* **tenaces 1** : tenacious, persistent **2** : strong, tough
tenaza *nf, or* **tenazas** *nfpl* **1** : pliers, pincers **2** : tongs **3** : claw (of a crustacean)
tenazmente *adv* : tenaciously
tendedero *nm* : clothesline
tendencia *nf* **1 PROPENSIÓN** : tendency, inclination **2** : trend
tendencioso, -sa *adj* : biased
tendente → tendiente
tender {56} *vt* **1 EXTENDER** : to spread out, to lay out **2 EXTENDER** : to extend, to hold out (one's hand) **3** : to hang out (clothes) **4** : to run (cables, etc.) **5** : to set (a trap) **6** : to set (a table), to make (a bed) — *vi* ~ **a** : to tend to, to have a tendency towards — **tenderse** *vr* : to stretch out, to lie down
tenderete *nm* : (market) stall
tendero, -ra *n* : shopkeeper, storekeeper
tendido *nm* **1** : laying (of cables, etc.) **2** : seats *pl*, section (at a bullfight)
tendiente *adj* : aimed at, designed to
tendón *nm, pl* **tendones** : tendon
tendrá, etc. → tener
tenebrosidad *nf* : darkness, gloom
tenebroso, -sa *adj* **1 OSCURO** : gloomy, dark **2 SINIESTRO** : sinister
tenedor¹, -dora *n* **1** : holder **2 tenedor de libros, tenedora de libros** : bookkeeper
tenedor² *nm* : table fork
teneduría *nf* **teneduría de libros** : bookkeeping
tenencia *nf* **1** : possession, holding **2** : tenancy **3** : tenure
tener {80} *vt* **1** : to have ⟨tiene un coche azul : he has a blue car⟩ ⟨¿lo tienes contigo? : do you have it with you?⟩ ⟨tienen tres hijos : they have three children⟩ ⟨tiene ojos verdes : she has green eyes⟩ ⟨tiene mucha experiencia : she has a lot of experience⟩ ⟨¿tiene hora? : do you have the time?, can you tell me what time it is?⟩ **2** : to have (available) ⟨tener dinero/tiempo para : to have money/time for⟩ ⟨no tuve más remedio : I had no choice⟩ **3** : to have (plans, etc.) ⟨tengo mucho que hacer : I have a lot to do⟩ ⟨hoy tiene clase : he has class today⟩ **4** : to have, to cause (consequences, etc.)

5 (*indicating age*) ⟨tiene veinte años : he's twenty years old⟩ **6** (*indicating dimensions*) ⟨tiene un metro de largo : it's one meter long⟩ **7** (*expressing thoughts, feelings, or sensations*) ⟨tengo frío/hambre/miedo : I'm cold/hungry/scared⟩ ⟨no tengo ni idea : I have no idea⟩ ⟨tengo confianza en ti : I have confidence in you⟩ ⟨eso nos tiene contentos : that makes us happy⟩ **8** : to have (an illness or injury) **9** : to have, to experience (problems, etc.) ⟨tuve un buen día : I had a good day⟩ **10** : to have, to receive (news, etc.) **11** : to have, to show (a quality) ⟨tienes razón : you're right⟩ ⟨eso no tiene sentido : that doesn't make sense⟩ ⟨no tiene nada de malo/raro : there's nothing bad/strange about it⟩ **12** : to have, to include ⟨el libro tiene 500 páginas : the book has 500 pages⟩ **13** : to use, to exercise ⟨tener cuidado : to be careful⟩ **14** (*indicating condition*) ⟨tenía la camisa manchada : his shirt was stained⟩ **15** (*indicating position*) ⟨tenía las manos en los bolsillos : she had her hands in her pockets⟩ **16** : to hold ⟨ten esto : hold this⟩ **17** : to have, to give birth to **18** ~ **por** : to think, to consider ⟨me tienes por loco : you think I'm crazy⟩ — *v aux* **1 tener que** : to have to ⟨tengo que salir : I have to leave⟩ ⟨tiene que estar aquí : it has to be here, it must be here⟩ **2** (*with past participle*) ⟨tenía pensado escribirte : I've been thinking of writing to you⟩ **3** (*in expressions of time*) ⟨tengo diez años haciendo esto : I have been doing this for ten years⟩ ⟨tiene años de estar aquí : it's been here for years⟩ — **tenerse** *vr* **1** : to stand up **2** ~ **por** : to consider oneself ⟨me tengo por afortunado : I consider myself lucky⟩
tenería *nf* **CURTIDURÍA** : tannery
tenga, etc. → tener
tenia *nf* **SOLITARIA** : tapeworm
teniente *nmf* **1** : lieutenant **2 teniente coronel** : lieutenant colonel
tenis *nms & pl* **1** : tennis **2 tenis** *nmpl* : sneakers *pl*
tenista *nmf* : tennis player
tenor *nm* **1** : tenor **2** : tone, sense
tensar *vt* **1** : to tense, to make taut **2** : to draw (a bow) — **tensarse** *vr* : to become tense
tensión *nf, pl* **tensiones 1** : tension, tautness **2** : stress, strain **3 tensión arterial** : blood pressure **4** : voltage, tension ⟨de alta tensión : high-tension⟩
tenso, -sa *adj* : tense — **tensamente** *adv*
tentación *nf, pl* **-ciones** : temptation ⟨caer en la tentación : to give in to temptation⟩ ⟨caer en la tentación de : to be tempted into⟩ ⟨resistir la tentación de : to resist the temptation to⟩
tentáculo *nm* : tentacle, feeler
tentador¹, -dora *adj* : tempting
tentador², -dora *n* : tempter, temptress *f*
tentar {55} *vt* **1 TOCAR** : to feel, to touch **2 PROBAR** : to test, to try **3 ATRAER** : to tempt, to entice

tentativa *nf* : attempt, try

tentempié *nm fam* : snack, bite

tenue *adj* 1 : tenuous 2 : faint, weak, dim 3 : light, fine 4 : thin, slender

teñir {67} *vt* 1 : to dye 2 : to stain

teología *nf* : theology

teológico, -ca *adj* : theological

teólogo, -ga *n* : theologian

teorema *nm* : theorem

teoría *nf* : theory

teórico[1], -ca *adj* : theoretical — teóricamente *adv*

teórico[2], -ca *n* : theorist

teorizar {21} *vi* : to theorize

tepe *nm* : sod, turf

teponaztle *nm Mex* : traditional drum

tequila *nm* : tequila

terapeuta *nmf* : therapist

terapéutica *nf* : therapeutics

terapéutico, -ca *adj* : therapeutic

terapia *nf* 1 : therapy 2 terapia intensiva : intensive care

tercer → tercero

tercermundista *adj* : third-world

tercero[1], -ra *adj* (*tercer before masculine singular nouns*) 1 : third ⟨el tercer piso/grado : the third floor/grade⟩ ⟨una/la tercera parte de : a third of, one third of⟩ 2 el Tercer Mundo : the Third World

tercero[2], -ra *n* : third (in a series)

terceto *nm* 1 : triplet (in literature) 2 : trio (in music)

terciar *vt* 1 : to place diagonally 2 : to divide into three parts — *vi* 1 : to mediate 2 ~ en : to take part in

terciario, -ria *adj* : tertiary

tercio[1], -cia → tercero

tercio[2] *nm* : third ⟨dos tercios : two thirds⟩

terciopelo *nm* : velvet

terco, -ca *adj* OBSTINADO : obstinate, stubborn

tergiversación *nf, pl* -ciones : distortion

tergiversar *vt* : to distort, to twist

termal *adj* : thermal, hot

termas *nfpl* : hot springs

térmico, -ca *adj* : thermal, heat ⟨energía térmica : thermal energy⟩

terminación *nf, pl* -ciones : termination, conclusion

terminal[1] *adj* : terminal — terminalmente *adv*

terminal[2] *nm* (*in some regions f*) : (electric or electronic) terminal

terminal[3] *nf* (*in some regions m*) : terminal, station

terminante *adj* : final, definitive, categorical — terminantemente *adv*

terminar *vt* 1 CONCLUIR : to end, to conclude 2 ACABAR : to complete, to finish off — *vi* 1 : to finish 2 : to stop, to end — terminarse *vr* 1 : to run out 2 : to come to an end

término *nm* 1 CONCLUSIÓN : end, conclusion 2 : term, expression 3 : period, term of office 4 : place, position ⟨en primer término : first of all⟩ 5 término medio : happy medium 6 por término medio : on average 7 términos *nmpl*

: terms, specifications ⟨los términos del acuerdo : the terms of the agreement⟩

terminología *nf* : terminology

termita *nf* : termite

termo *nm* : thermos

termodinámica *nf* : thermodynamics

termómetro *nm* : thermometer

termostato *nm* : thermostat

ternera *nf* : veal

ternero, -ra *n* : calf

terno *nm* 1 : set of three 2 : three-piece suit

ternura *nf* : tenderness

terquedad *nf* OBSTINACIÓN : obstinacy, stubbornness

terracota *nf* : terra-cotta

terraplén *nm, pl* -plenes : terrace, embankment

terráqueo, -quea *adj* 1 : earth 2 globo terráqueo : the earth, globe (of the earth)

terrateniente *nmf* : landowner

terraza *nf* 1 : terrace, veranda 2 : balcony (in a theater) 3 : terrace (in agriculture)

terremoto *nm* : earthquake

terrenal *adj* : worldly, earthly

terreno *nm* 1 : terrain 2 SUELO : earth, ground 3 : plot, tract of land 4 perder terreno : to lose ground 5 preparar el terreno : to pave the way

terrestre *adj* : terrestrial

terrible *adj* : terrible, horrible — terriblemente *adv*

terrier *nmf* : terrier

territorial *adj* : territorial

territorio *nm* : territory

terrón *nm, pl* terrones 1 : clod (of earth) 2 terrón de azúcar : lump of sugar

terror *nm* : terror

terrorífico, -ca *adj* : horrific, terrifying

terrorismo *nm* : terrorism

terrorista *adj & nmf* : terrorist

terroso, -sa *adj* : earthy ⟨colores terrosos : earthy colors⟩

terruño *nm* : native land, homeland

terso, -sa *adj* 1 : smooth 2 : glossy, shiny 3 : polished, flowing (of a style)

tersura *nf* 1 : smoothness 2 : shine

tertulia *nf* : gathering, group ⟨tertulia literaria : literary circle⟩

tesauro *nm* : thesaurus

tesis *nfs & pl* : thesis

tesón *nm* : persistence, tenacity

tesonero, -ra *adj* : persistent, tenacious

tesorería *nf* : treasurer's office

tesorero, -ra *n* : treasurer

tesoro *nm* 1 : treasure 2 : thesaurus 3 : treasury

test *nm* : test

testaferro *nm* : figurehead

testamentario, -ria *n* ALBACEA : executor

testamento *nm* : testament, will

testar *vi* : to draw up a will

testarudo, -da *adj* : stubborn, pigheaded

testículo *nm* : testicle

testificar {72} *v* : to testify

testigo *nmf* 1 : witness 2 testigo presencial : eyewitness

testimonial *adj* 1 : testimonial 2 : token

testimoniar *vi* : to testify

testimonio *nm* : testimony, statement
teta *nf* : teat
tétano *or* **tétanos** *nm* : tetanus, lockjaw
tetera *nf* **1** : teapot **2** : teakettle
tetilla *nf* **1** : teat **2** : nipple
tetina *nf* : nipple (on a bottle)
tétrico, -ca *adj* : somber, gloomy
textear *v fam* : to text
textil *adj & nm* : textile
texto *nm* : text
textual *adj* : literal, exact — **textualmente** *adv*
textura *nf* : texture
tez *nf, pl* **teces** : complexion, coloring
thumbnail ['tomneil] *nm, pl* **thumbnails** : thumbnail (in computing)
ti *pron* **1** : you ⟨es para ti : it's for you⟩ **2 ti mismo, ti misma** : yourself **3** : thee
tía → tío
tiamina *nf* : thiamine
tianguis *nm Mex* : open-air market
tibetano¹, -na *adj & n* : Tibetan
tibetano² *nm* : Tibetan (language)
tibia *nf* : tibia
tibieza *nf* **1** : warmth, mildness **2** : lack of enthusiasm, coolness, indifference
tibio, -bia *adj* **1** : lukewarm, tepid **2** : cool, unenthusiastic
tiburón *nm, pl* **-rones 1** : shark **2** : raider (in finance)
tic *nm* **1** : click, tick **2 tic nervioso** : tic
tico, -ca *adj & n fam* : Costa Rican
tictac *nm* **1** : ticking, tick-tock **2 hacer tictac** : to tick
tiembla, etc. → temblar
tiempo *nm* **1** : time ⟨justo a tiempo : just in time⟩ ⟨ahorrar/matar/perder tiempo : to save/kill/waste time⟩ ⟨ganar tiempo : to buy time⟩ ⟨tiempo libre : spare time⟩ ⟨al poco tiempo : soon after⟩ ⟨al tiempo que : (while) at the same time⟩ ⟨con tiempo : in good time, in advance⟩ ⟨con el tiempo : in/with/over time⟩ ⟨no tengo tiempo, no me da tiempo : I don't have time⟩ ⟨hace tiempo que vive aquí : she has lived here for a while⟩ ⟨desde hace mucho tiempo : for quite a while⟩ **2** : period of time ⟨un tiempo de : a period of⟩ ⟨esperamos un tiempo : we waited a while⟩ ⟨cada cierto tiempo : every so often⟩ ⟨en los tiempos que corren : nowadays⟩ **3** : season, moment ⟨antes de tiempo : prematurely⟩ ⟨fuera de tiempo : at the wrong time⟩ **4** : weather ⟨hace buen tiempo : the weather is fine, it's nice outside⟩ **5** : tempo (in music) **6** : half (in sports) **7** : tense (in grammar) **8** : half (in sports) ⟨medio tiempo : halftime⟩ **9 medio tiempo** *or* **tiempo parcial** ⟨un empleo de medio tiempo, un empleo a tiempo parcial : a part-time job⟩ ⟨trabajar medio tiempo, trabajar a tiempo parcial : to work part-time⟩ **10 tiempo compartido** : timeshare **11 tiempo completo** : full-time ⟨un empleo de tiempo completo : a full-time job⟩ ⟨trabajar a/de tiempo completo : to work full-time⟩
tienda *nf* **1** : store, shop **2** *or* **tienda de campaña** : tent

tiende, etc. → tender
tiene, etc. → tener
tienta¹, etc. → tentar
tienta² *nf* **andar a tientas** : to feel one's way, to grope around
tiernamente *adv* : tenderly
tierno, -na *adj* **1** : affectionate, tender **2** : tender, young
tierra *nf* **1** : land ⟨vender tierra : to sell land⟩ **2** SUELO : ground, earth ⟨camino de tierra : dirt road⟩ ⟨tomar tierra : to land⟩ ⟨caer a tierra : to fall to earth⟩ **3** : country, homeland, soil **4 tierra adentro** : inland **5 tierra firme** : dry/solid ground **6 tierra natal** : native land **7 tierras altas** : highlands **8 tierras bajas** : lowlands **9 la Tierra** : the Earth
tieso, -sa *adj* **1** : stiff, rigid **2** : upright, erect
tiesto *nm* MACETA : flowerpot
tiesura *nf* : stiffness, rigidity
tifoidea *nf* : typhoid
tifoideo, -dea *adj* : typhoid ⟨fiebre tifoidea : typhoid fever⟩
tifón *nm, pl* **tifones** : typhoon
tifus *nm* : typhus
tigre, -gresa *n* **1** : tiger, tigress *f* **2** : jaguar
tijera *nf* **1** *or* **tijeras** *nfpl* : scissors **2 de ~** : folding ⟨escalera de tijera : stepladder⟩
tijereta *nf* : earwig
tijeretada *nf or* **tijeretazo** *nm* : cut, snip
tila *nf* : lime blossom tea
tildar *vt* **~ de** : to brand as, to call ⟨lo tildaron de traidor : they branded him as a traitor⟩
tilde *nf* **1** : accent mark **2** : tilde (accent over ñ)
tilín *nm, pl* **tilines** : tinkle
tilo *nm* : linden (tree)
timador, -dora *n* : swindler
timar *vt* : to swindle, to cheat
timbal *nm* **1** : kettledrum **2 timbales** *nmpl* : timpani
timbre *nm* **1** : bell ⟨tocar el timbre : to ring the doorbell⟩ **2** : tone, timbre **3** SELLO : seal, stamp **4** *CA, Mex* : postage stamp
timidez *nf* : timidity, shyness
tímido, -da *adj* : timid, shy — **tímidamente** *adv*
timo *nm fam* : swindle, trick, hoax
timón *nm, pl* **timones** : rudder ⟨estar al timón : to beat the helm⟩
timonel *nm* : coxswain
timorato, -ta *adj* **1** : timorous **2** : sanctimonious
tímpano *nm* **1** : eardrum **2 tímpanos** *nmpl* : timpani, kettledrums
tina *nf* **1** BAÑERA : tub, bathtub **2** : vat
tinaco *nm Mex* : water tank
tinaja *nf* : large clay pot/jar
tinieblas *nfpl* **1** OSCURIDAD : darkness **2** : ignorance
tino *nm* **1** : good judgment, sense **2** : tact, sensitivity, insight
tinta *nf* : ink
tinte *nm* **1** : dye, coloring **2** : overtone ⟨tintes raciales : racial overtones⟩

tintero *nm* **1** : inkwell **2 quedarse en el tintero** : to remain unsaid

tintinear *vt* : to jingle, to clink, to tinkle

tintineo *nm* : clink, jingle, tinkle

tinto, -ta *adj* **1** : dyed, stained ⟨tinto en sangre : bloodstained⟩ **2** : red (of wine)

tintorería *nf* : dry cleaner (service)

tintura *nf* **1** : dye, tint **2** : tincture ⟨tintura de yodo : tincture of iodine⟩

tiña *nf* : ringworm

tiñe, etc. → **teñir**

tío, tía *n* **1** : uncle *m*, aunt *f*

tiovivo *nm* : merry-go-round

tipear *vt* (*in various countries*) : to type

tipi *nm* : tepee

típico, -ca *adj* : typical — **típicamente** *adv*

tipificar {72} *vt* **1** : to classify, to categorize **2** : to typify

tiple *nm* : soprano

tipo[1] *nm* **1** CLASE : type, kind, sort **2** : figure, build, appearance **3** : rate ⟨tipo de interés : interest rate⟩ **4** : (printing) type, typeface **5** : style, model ⟨un vestido tipo 60's : a 60's-style dress⟩

tipo[2], -pa *n fam* : guy *m*, gal *f*, character

tipografía *nf* : typography, printing

tipográfico, -ca *adj* : typographic, typographical

tipógrafo, -fa *n* : printer, typographer

tique *or* **tiquet** *nm* **1** : ticket **2** : receipt

tira *nf* **1** : strip, strap **2 tira cómica** : comic, comic strip

tirabuzón *nf, pl* **-zones** : corkscrew

tirachinas *nms & pl* : slingshot

tirada *nf* **1** : throw **2** : distance, stretch **3** IMPRESIÓN : printing, issue

tiradero *nm Mex* **1** : dump **2** : mess, clutter

tirado, -da *adj Spain fam* **1** : dirt cheap **2** : very easy

tirador[1] *nm* : handle, knob

tirador[2], -dora *n* : marksman *m*, markswoman *f*

tiragomas *nms & pl* : slingshot

tiranía *nf* : tyranny

tiránico, -ca *adj* : tyrannical

tiranizar {21} *vt* : to tyrannize

tirano[1], -na *adj* : tyrannical, despotic

tirano[2], -na *n* : tyrant

tirante[1] *adj* **1** : tense, strained **2** : taut

tirante[2] *nm* **1** : shoulder strap **2 tirantes** *nmpl* : suspenders

tirantez *nf* **1** : tautness **2** : tension, friction, strain

tirar *vt* **1** : to throw, to hurl, to toss ⟨tírame la pelota : throw/toss me the ball⟩ **2** BOTAR : to throw away/out (garbage), to waste (money, etc.) **3** DERRIBAR : to knock down **4** : to shoot, to fire, to launch (a rocket), to drop (a bomb) **5** : to shoot (in sports) **6** *Car, Spain* : to take (a photo) **7** : to print, to run off **8** *Arg, Chile, Uru* : to pull — *vi* **1** : to pull, to draw **2** : to shoot ⟨tirar a matar : to shoot to kill⟩ **3** : to shoot (in sports) **4** : to attract **5** : to get by, to manage ⟨va tirando : he's getting along, he's managing⟩ **6 ~ a** : to tend towards, to be rather ⟨tira a picante : it's a

bit spicy⟩ — **tirarse** *vr* **1** : to throw oneself **2** *fam* : to spend (time)

tiritar *vi* : to shiver, to tremble

tiro *nm* **1** BALAZO, DISPARO : shot, gunshot ⟨pegarle un tiro a alguien : to shoot someone⟩ ⟨matar a alguien a tiros : to shoot someone dead⟩ ⟨errar el tiro : to miss the mark⟩ **2** : shot, kick (in sports) ⟨tiro libre : free shot/throw/kick⟩ ⟨tiro penal : penalty shot/kick⟩ **3** : flue **4** : team (of horses, etc.) **5 a ~** : within range ⟨ponerse a tiro : to come within range⟩ ⟨estar a tiro : to be within range, to be within reach⟩ **6 al tiro** : right away **7 tiro de gracia** : coup de grâce, death blow

tiroideo, -dea *adj* : thyroid

tiroides *nmf* : thyroid, thyroid gland — **tiroides** *adj*

tirolés, -lesa *adj* : Tyrolean

tirón *nm, pl* **tirones** **1** : pull, tug, yank **2 de un tirón** : all at once, in one go **3 tirón de orejas** : slap on the wrist, minor punishment

tiroteo *nm* **1** : shooting **2** : gunfight, shoot-out

tirria *nf* **tener tirria a** *fam* : to have a grudge against

titánico, -ca *adj* : titanic, huge

titanio *nm* : titanium

títere *nm* : puppet

tití *nm, pl* **tití** *or* **titíes** *or* **titís** : marmoset

titilar *vi* : to twinkle, to flicker

titileo *nm* : twinkle, flickering

titiritero, -ra *n* **1** : puppeteer **2** : acrobat

tito, tita *n fam* : uncle *m*, auntie *f*

titubear *vi* **1** : to hesitate **2** : to stutter, to stammer — **titubeante** *adj*

titubeo *nm* **1** : hesitation **2** : stammering

titulado, -da *adj* **1** : titled, entitled **2** : qualified

titular[1] *vt* : to title, to entitle — **titularse** *vr* **1** : to be called, to be entitled **2** : to receive a degree

titular[2] *adj* : titular, official

titular[3] *nm* : headline

titular[4] *nmf* **1** : owner, holder **2** : officeholder, incumbent

titularidad *nf* **1** : ownership, title **2** : position, office (with a title) **3** : starting position (in sports)

título *nm* **1** : title **2** : degree, qualification **3** : security, bond **4 a título de** : by way of, in the capacity of

tiza *nf* : chalk

tiznar *vt* : to blacken (with soot, etc.)

tizne *nm* HOLLÍN : soot

tiznón *nm, pl* **tiznones** : stain, smudge

tlapalería *nf Mex* : hardware store

TNT *nm* (*trinitrotolueno*) : TNT

toalla *nf* **1** : towel **2 tirar la toalla** : to throw in the towel

toallita *nf* : washcloth

tobillo *nm* : ankle

tobogán *nm, pl* **-ganes** **1** : toboggan, sled **2** : slide, chute

tocadiscos *nms & pl* : record player

tocado[1], -da *adj* **1** : bad, bruised (of fruit) **2** *fam* : touched, not all there

tocado[2] *nm* : headdress
tocador[1] *nm* **1** : dressing table, vanity table **2 artículos de tocador** : toiletries
tocador[2], **-dora** *n* : player (of music)
tocante *adj* ~ **a** : with regard to, regarding
tocar {72} *vt* **1** : to touch, to feel, to handle **2** : to touch on, to refer to **3** : to concern, to affect **4** : to play (a musical instrument) **5** : to ring (a bell) **6 tocar fondo** : to hit/reach rock bottom — *vi* **1** : to knock ⟨tocar a la puerta : to knock on the door⟩ **2** : to sound, to ring ⟨tocó el timbre : the doorbell rang⟩ **3** : to fall to, to be up to, to be one's turn ⟨¿a quién le toca manejar? : whose turn is it to drive?⟩ ⟨a él le toca decidir : it's up to him to decide⟩ ⟨nos toca el 50 por ciento : we get 50 percent⟩ **4** : to come by chance ⟨les tocó la lotería : they won the lottery⟩ ⟨nos toca vivir en tiempos difíciles : it's our fate to live in difficult times⟩ **5** ~ **en** : to touch on, to border on ⟨eso toca en lo ridículo : that's almost ludicrous⟩ — **tocarse** *vr* **1** : to touch ⟨se tocó la frente : he touched his forehead⟩ **2** : to touch (each other)
tocayo, -ya *n* : namesake
tocineta *nf Col, Ven* : bacon
tocino *nm* **1** : bacon **2** : salt pork
tocología *nf* OBSTETRICIA : obstetrics
tocólogo, -ga *n* OBSTETRA : obstetrician
tocón *nm, pl* **tocones** CEPA : stump (of a tree)
todavía *adv* **1** AÚN : still, yet ⟨todavía puedes verlo : you can still see it⟩ **2** : even ⟨todavía más rápido : even faster⟩ **3 todavía no** : not yet
todo[1], **-da** *adj* **1** : all, whole, entire ⟨toda la comunidad : the whole community⟩ ⟨toda la noche : all night, the whole night⟩ ⟨todo tipo de : all kinds of⟩ ⟨con toda sinceridad : with all sincerity⟩ **2** : every, each, any ⟨a todo nivel : at every level⟩ ⟨todos los días : every day⟩ ⟨toda persona menor de 18 años : anyone under the age of 18⟩ **3** : maximum ⟨a toda velocidad : at top speed⟩ **4 todo el mundo** : everyone, everybody
todo[2] *nm* : whole
todo[3], **-da** *pron* **1** : everything, all, every bit ⟨lo sabe todo : he knows it all⟩ ⟨tienen de todo : they have some of everything⟩ ⟨hizo todo lo que pudo : she did everything she could⟩ ⟨no los encontré todos : I didn't find all of them⟩ ⟨es todo un soldado : he's a soldier through and through⟩ ⟨fue todo un éxito : it was quite a success⟩ **2 todos, -das** *pl* : everybody, everyone, all ⟨todos estamos de acuerdo : everybody agrees, we all agree⟩ ⟨¿estamos todos? : are we all here?⟩ ⟨es mejor para todos : it's better for everyone⟩ ⟨agradeció a todos : he thanked everyone⟩ ⟨es la más famosa de todos : she's the most famous of them all⟩ **3 ante** ~ : above all, first and foremost **4 con todo (y eso)** : even so, nevertheless **5 del todo** : completely **6 sobre** ~ : above all

todopoderoso, -sa *adj* OMNIPOTENTE : almighty
todoterreno *nm* : all-terrain vehicle
toga *nf* **1** : toga **2** : gown, robe (for magistrates, etc.)
toldo *nm* : awning, canopy
tolerable *adj* : tolerable — **tolerablemente** *adv*
tolerancia *nf* : tolerance, toleration
tolerante *adj* : tolerant — **tolerantemente** *adv*
tolerar *vt* : to tolerate
tolete *nm* : oarlock
tolva *nf* : hopper (container)
toma *nf* **1** : taking, seizure, capture **2** DOSIS : dose **3** : take, shot **4 toma de corriente** : wall socket, outlet **5 toma y daca** : give-and-take
tomado *adj* : drunk
tomar *vt* **1** : to take ⟨tomé el libro : I took the book⟩ ⟨tomar un taxi : to take a taxi⟩ ⟨tomar una foto : to take a photo⟩ ⟨toma dos años : it takes two years⟩ ⟨tomaron medidas drásticas : they took drastic measures⟩ **2** : to make (a decision) **3** BEBER : to drink **4** CONSUMIR : to have (food), to take (medicine) **5** CAPTURAR : to capture, to seize **6** : to take, to interpret ⟨no lo tomes a mal : don't take it the wrong way⟩ **7** ~ **por** : to take for, to mistake for **8 tomar el sol** : to sunbathe **9 tomar prestado** : to borrow **10 tomar tierra** : to land — *vi* **1** : to take something ⟨toma, te lo presto : here, I'll lend it to you⟩ **2** : to drink (alcohol) — **tomarse** *vr* **1** : to take ⟨tomarse la molestia de : to take the trouble to⟩ **2** : to drink, to eat, to have
tomate *nm* : tomato
tomillo *nm* : thyme
tomo *nm* : volume, tome
ton *nm* **sin ton ni son** : without rhyme or reason
tonada *nf* **1** : tune, song **2** : accent
tonalidad *nf* : tones *pl*, color scheme
tonel *nm* BARRICA : barrel, cask
tonelada *nf* : ton
tonelaje *nm* : tonnage
tónica *nf* **1** : tonic (water) **2** : tonic (in music) **3** : trend, tone ⟨dar la tónica : to set the tone⟩
tónico[1], **-ca** *adj* : tonic
tónico[2] *nm* : tonic ⟨tónico capilar : hair tonic⟩
tonificar {72} *vt* : to tone, to tone up
tono *nm* **1** : tone ⟨tono muscular : muscle tone⟩ **2** : shade (of colors) **3** : key (in music) **4 tono de llamada** : ringtone
tontamente *adv* : foolishly, stupidly
tontear *vi* **1** : to fool around, to play the fool **2** : to flirt
tontería *nf* **1** : foolishness **2** : stupid remark or action **3 decir tonterías** : to talk nonsense
tonto[1], **-ta** *adj* **1** : dumb, stupid **2** : silly **3 a tontas y a locas** : without thinking, haphazardly
tonto[2], **-ta** *n* : fool, idiot
topacio *nm* : topaz

toparse *vr* ~ **con** : to bump into, to run into, to come across ⟨me topé con algunas dificultades : I ran into some problems⟩

tope *nm* **1** : limit, end ⟨hasta el tope : to the limit, to the brim⟩ **2** : stop, check, buffer ⟨tope de puerta : doorstop⟩ **3** : bump, collision **4** *Mex* : speed bump

tópico[1], **-ca** *adj* **1** : topical, external **2** : trite, commonplace

tópico[2] *nm* **1** : topic, subject **2** : cliché, trite expression

topo *nm* **1** : mole (animal) **2** *fam* : clumsy person

topografía *nf* : topography

topográfico, -ca *adj* : topographic, topographical

toque[1], etc. → **tocar**

toque[2] *nm* **1** : touch ⟨el último toque : the finishing touch⟩ ⟨un toque de color : a touch of color⟩ **2** : ringing, peal, chime **3** *Mex* : shock, jolt **4 toque de queda** : curfew **5 toque de diana** : reveille

toquetear *vt* : to touch, to handle, to finger

toquilla *nf* : shawl

tórax *nm* : thorax

torbellino *nm* : whirlwind

torcedura *nf* **1** : twisting, buckling **2** : sprain

torcer {14} *vt* **1** : to bend, to twist **2** : to sprain **3** : to turn (a corner) **4** : to wring, to wring out **5** : to distort — *vi* : to turn — **torcerse** *vr*

torcido, -da *adj* **1** : twisted, crooked **2** : devious

tordo *nm* ZORZAL : thrush

torear *vt* **1** : to fight (bulls) **2** : to dodge, to sidestep

toreo *nm* : bullfighting

torero, -ra *n* MATADOR : bullfighter, matador

tormenta *nf* **1** : storm ⟨tormenta de nieve : snowstorm⟩ **2** : turmoil, frenzy

tormento *nm* **1** : torment, anguish **2** : torture

tormentoso, -sa *adj* : stormy, turbulent — **tormentosamente** *adv*

tornado *nm* : tornado

tornamesa *nmf* : turntable

tornar *vt* **1** : to return, to give back **2** : to make, to render — *vi* : to go back — **tornarse** *vr* : to become, to turn into

tornasol *nm* **1** : reflected light **2** : sunflower **3** : litmus

tornear *vt* : to turn (in carpentry)

torneo *nm* : tournament

tornillo *nm* **1** : screw **2 tornillo de banco** : vise

torniquete *nm* **1** : tourniquet **2** : turnstile

torno *nm* **1** : lathe **2** : winch **3 torno de banco** : vise **4 en torno a** : around, about ⟨en torno a este asunto : about this issue⟩ ⟨en torno suyo : around him⟩

toro *nm* : bull

toronja *nf* : grapefruit

toronjil *nm* : balm, lemon balm

torpe *adj* **1** DESMAÑADO : clumsy, awkward **2** : stupid, dull — **torpemente** *adv*

torpedear *vt* : to torpedo

torpedero, -ra *n* : shortstop

torpedo *nm* : torpedo

torpeza *nf* **1** : clumsiness, awkwardness **2** : stupidity **3** : blunder

torre *nf* **1** : tower ⟨torre de perforación : oil rig⟩ **2** : turret **3** : rook, castle (in chess)

torreja *nf* : French toast

torrencial *adj* : torrential — **torrencialmente** *adv*

torrente *nm* **1** : torrent **2 torrente sanguíneo** : bloodstream

torreón *nm*, *pl* **-rreones** : tower (of a castle)

torreta *nf* : turret (of a tank, ship, etc.)

tórrido, -da *adj* : torrid

torrija *nf* *Spain* → **torreja**

torso *nm* : torso, trunk

torta *nf* **1** (*in various countries*) : cake **2** : pie, tart **3** *Mex* : sandwich

tortazo *nm* *fam* : blow, wallop

tortícolis *nf* : stiff neck

tortilla *nf* **1** : tortilla **2** *or* **tortilla de huevo** : omelet

tórtola *nf* : turtledove

tortuga *nf* **1** : turtle, tortoise **2 tortuga de agua dulce** : terrapin **3 tortuga boba** : loggerhead

tortuoso, -sa *adj* : tortuous, winding

tortura *nf* : torture

torturador, -dora *n* : torturer

torturar *vt* : to torture, to torment

torvo, -va *adj* : grim, stern, baleful

torzamos, etc. → **torcer**

tos *nf* **1** : cough **2 tos ferina** : whooping cough

tosco, -ca *adj* : rough, coarse

toser *vi* : to cough

tosquedad *nf* : coarseness, roughness

tostada *nf* **1** : piece of toast **2** *Mex* : fried tortilla

tostador *nm* **1** : toaster **2** : roaster (for coffee)

tostadora *nf* **1** : toaster **2** : roaster (for coffee)

tostar {19} *vt* **1** : to toast **2** : to roast (coffee) **3** : to tan — **tostarse** *vr* : to get a tan

tostón *nm*, *pl* **tostones** *Car* : fried plantain chip

total[1] *adv* : in the end, so ⟨total, que no fui : in short, I didn't go⟩

total[2] *adj* & *nm* : total — **totalmente** *adv*

totalidad *nf* : totality, whole

totalitario, -ria *adj* & *n* : totalitarian

totalitarismo *nm* : totalitarianism

totalizar {21} *vt* : to total, to add up to

tótem *nm*, *pl* **tótems** : totem

totopo *nm* *CA*, *Mex* : tortilla chip

totuma *nf* : calabash

touchdown *nm* : touchdown (in football)

tour ['tur] *nm*, *pl* **tours** : tour, excursion

toxicidad *nf* : toxicity

tóxico[1], **-ca** *adj* : toxic, poisonous

tóxico[2] *nm* : poison

toxicomanía *nf* : drug addiction

toxicómano, -na *n* : drug addict

toxina *nf* : toxin

tozudez *nf* : stubbornness, obstinacy

tozudo, -da *adj* : stubborn, obstinate — **tozudamente** *adv*

traba *nf* **1** : tie, bond **2** : obstacle, hindrance

trabajador¹, -dora *adj* : hardworking

trabajador², -dora *n* : worker

trabajar *vi* **1** : to work ⟨trabaja mucho : he works hard⟩ ⟨trabajo de secretaria : I work as a secretary⟩ **2** : to strive ⟨trabajan por mejores oportunidades : they're striving for better opportunities⟩ **3** : to act, to perform ⟨trabajar en una película : to be in a movie⟩ — *vt* **1** : to work (metal) **2** : to knead **3** : to till **4** : to work on ⟨tienes que trabajar el español : you need to work on your Spanish⟩

trabajo *nm* **1** : work, job **2** LABOR : labor, work ⟨tengo mucho trabajo : I have a lot of work to do⟩ ⟨¡buen trabajo! : good job!, good work!⟩ **3** TAREA : task **4** ESFUERZO : effort **5** : piece of writing, essay, paper **6 costar trabajo** : to be difficult **7 tomarse el trabajo** : to take the trouble **8 trabajo en equipo** : teamwork **9 trabajos** *nmpl* : hardships, difficulties

trabajoso, -sa *adj* LABORIOSO : laborious — **trabajosamente** *adv*

trabalenguas *nms & pl* : tongue twister

trabar *vt* **1** : to join, to connect **2** : to impede, to hold back **3** : to strike up (a conversation), to form (a friendship) **4** : to thicken (sauces) — **trabarse** *vr* **1** : to jam **2** : to become entangled **3** : to be tongue-tied, to stammer

trabucar {72} *vt* : to confuse, to mix up

trabuco *nm* : blunderbuss

tracalero, -ra *adj Mex* : dishonest, tricky

tracción *nf* : traction

trace, etc. → trazar

tracto *nm* : tract

tractor *nm* : tractor

tradición *nf*, *pl* **-ciones** : tradition

tradicional *adj* : traditional — **tradicionalmente** *adv*

traducción *nf*, *pl* **-ciones** : translation

traducible *adj* : translatable

traducir {61} *vt* **1** : to translate **2** : to convey, to express — **traducirse** *vr* ∼ **en** : to result in

traductor, -tora *n* : translator

traer {81} *vt* **1** : to bring ⟨trae una ensalada : bring a salad⟩ **2** CAUSAR : to cause, to bring about ⟨el problema puede traer graves consecuencias : the problem could have serious consequences⟩ **3** : to carry, to have ⟨todos los periódicos traían las mismas noticias : all of the newspapers carried the same news⟩ **4** LLEVAR : to wear — **traerse** *vr* **1** : to bring along **2 traérselas** : to be difficult

traficante *nmf* : dealer, trafficker

traficar {72} *vi* **1** : to trade, to deal **2** ∼ **con** : to traffic in

tráfico *nm* **1** : trade **2** : traffic

tragaluz *nf*, *pl* **-luces** : skylight, fanlight

tragamonedas *nmfs & pl* : slot machine

tragaperras *nmfs & pl Spain →* **tragamonedas**

tragar {52} *v* : to swallow — **tragarse** *vr*

tragedia *nf* : tragedy

trágico, -ca *adj* : tragic — **trágicamente** *adv*

trago *nm* **1** : swallow, swig **2** : drink, liquor **3 trago amargo** : hard time

trague, etc. → tragar

traición *nf*, *pl* **traiciones 1** : treason **2** : betrayal, treachery

traicionar *vt* : to betray

traicionero, -ra → traidor

traidor¹, -dora *adj* : traitorous, treacherous

traidor², -dora *n* : traitor

traiga, etc. → traer

tráiler ['trailer] *or* **trailer** ['trailer, 'treiler] *nm* : trailer

trailla *nf* **1** : leash **2** : harrow

traje *nm* **1** : suit **2** : dress **3** : costume **4 traje de baño** : swimsuit, bathing suit **5 traje de luces** : matador's outfit **6 traje de neopreno/buzo** : wet suit

trajín *nm*, *pl* **trajines 1** : transport **2** *fam* : hustle and bustle

trajinar *vt* : to transport, to carry — *vi* : to rush around

trajo, etc. → traer

trama *nf* **1** : plot **2** : weave, weft (fabric)

tramar *vt* **1** : to plot, to plan **2** : to weave

tramitación *nf*, *pl* **-ciones** : processing

tramitar *vt* : to transact, to negotiate, to handle

trámite *nm* : procedure, step

tramo *nm* **1** : stretch, section **2** : flight (of stairs)

trampa *nf* **1** : trap ⟨trampa mortal : death trap⟩ **2 hacer trampas** : to cheat

trampear *vt* : to cheat

trampero, -ra *n* : trapper

trampilla *nf* : trapdoor

trampolín *nm*, *pl* **-lines 1** : diving board **2** : trampoline **3** : springboard ⟨un trampolín al éxito : a springboard to success⟩ **4** : ski jump

tramposo¹, -sa *adj* : crooked, cheating

tramposo², -sa *n* : cheat, swindler

tranca *nf* **1** : stick, club **2** : bar, crossbar

trancar {72} *vt* : to bar (a door or window)

trancazo *nm* GOLPE : blow, hit

trance *nm* **1** : critical juncture, tough time **2** : trance **3 en trance de** : in the process of ⟨en trance de extinción : on the verge of extinction⟩

tranco *nm* **1** : stride **2** UMBRAL : threshold

tranque, etc. → trancar

tranquilidad *nf* : tranquility, peace

tranquilizador, -dora *adj* **1** : soothing **2** : reassuring

tranquilizante¹ *adj* **1** : reassuring **2** : tranquilizing

tranquilizante² *nm* : tranquilizer

tranquilizar {21} *vt* CALMAR : to calm down, to soothe ⟨tranquilizar la conciencia : to ease the conscience⟩ — **tranquilizarse** *vr*

tranquilo, -la *adj* CALMO : calm, tranquil ⟨una vida tranquila : a quiet life⟩ — **tranquilamente** *adv*

trans ['trans] *adj* **1** TRANSGÉNERO : trans, transgender **2** TRANSEXUAL : trans, transsexual

transacción *nf, pl* **-ciones** : transaction

transar *vi* TRANSIGIR : to give way, to compromise — *vt* : to buy and sell

transatlántico[1], **-ca** *adj* : transatlantic

transatlántico[2] *nm* : ocean liner

transbordador *nm* **1** : ferry **2 transbordador espacial** : space shuttle

transbordar *v* : to transfer

transbordo *nm* : transfer

transcendencia → trascendencia

transcender → trascender

transcribir {33} *vt* : to transcribe

transcrito *pp* → transcribir

transcripción *nf, pl* **-ciones** : transcription

transcurrir *vi* : to elapse, to pass

transcurso *nm* : course, progression ⟨en el transcurso de cien años : over the course of a hundred years⟩

transeúnte *nmf* **1** : passerby **2** : transient

transexual *adj & nmf* : transsexual

transferencia *nf* : transfer, transference

transferir {76} *vt* TRASLADAR : to transfer — **transferible** *adj*

transfigurar *vt* : to transfigure, to transform — **transfiguración** *nf*

transformación *nf, pl* **-ciones** : transformation, conversion

transformador *nm* : transformer

transformar *vt* **1** CONVERTIR : to convert **2** : to transform, to change, to alter — **transformarse** *vr*

tránsfuga *nmf* : defector, turncoat

transfusión *nf, pl* **-siones** : transfusion

transgénero *adj* : transgender ⟨las personas transgénero : transgender people⟩

transgénico[1], **-ca** *adj* : genetically modified

transgénico[2] *nm* : genetically modified plant or animal

transgredir {1} *vt* : to transgress — **transgresión** *nf* — **transgresor, -sora** *n*

transición *nf, pl* **-ciones** : transition ⟨período de transición : transition period⟩

transido, -da *adj* : overcome, beset ⟨transido de dolor : racked with pain⟩

transigir {35} *vi* **1** : to give in, to compromise **2** ~ **con** : to tolerate, to put up with

transistor *nm* : transistor

transitable *adj* : passable

transitar *vi* : to go, to pass, to travel ⟨transitar por la ciudad : to travel through the city⟩

transitivo, -va *adj* : transitive

tránsito *nm* **1** TRÁFICO : traffic ⟨hora de máximo tránsito : rush hour⟩ **2** : transit, passage, movement **3** : death, passing

transitorio, -ria *adj* **1** : transitory **2** : provisional, temporary — **transitoriamente** *adv*

translúcido, -da *adj* : translucent

translucir → traslucir

transmisible *adj* : transmissible

transmisión *nf, pl* **-siones** **1** : transmission, broadcast **2** : transfer **3** : transmission (of an automobile)

transmisor *nm* : transmitter

transmitir *vt* **1** : to transmit, to broadcast **2** : to pass on, to transfer — *vi* : to transmit, to broadcast

transparencia *nf* : transparency

transparentar *vt* : to reveal, to betray — **transparentarse** *vr* **1** : to be transparent **2** : to show through

transparente[1] *adj* : transparent — **transparentemente** *adv*

transparente[2] *nm* : shade, blind

transpiración *nf, pl* **-ciones** SUDOR : perspiration, sweat

transpirado, -da *adj* : sweaty

transpirar *vi* **1** SUDAR : to perspire, to sweat **2** : to transpire

transplantar, transplante → trasplantar, trasplante

transponer {60} *vt* **1** : to transpose, to move about **2** TRASPLANTAR : to transplant — **transponerse** *vr* **1** OCULTARSE : to hide **2** PONERSE : to set, to go down (of the sun or moon) **3** DORMITAR : to doze off

transportación *nf, pl* **-ciones** : transportation

transportador *nm* **1** : protractor **2** : conveyor

transportar *vt* **1** : to transport, to carry **2** : to transmit **3** : to transpose (music) — **transportarse** *vr* : to get carried away

transporte *nm* : transport, transportation ⟨transporte público : public transit, mass transit⟩

transportista *nmf* : hauler, carrier, trucker

transpuso, etc. → transponer

transversal *adj* : transverse, cross ⟨corte transversal : cross section⟩

transversalmente *adv* : obliquely

transverso, -sa *adj* : transverse

tranvía *nm* : streetcar, trolley

trapeador *nm* : mop

trapear *vt* : to mop

trapecio *nm* **1** : trapezoid **2** : trapeze

trapecista *nmf* : trapeze artist

trapezoide *nm* : trapezoid

trapo *nm* **1** : cloth, rag ⟨trapo de polvo : dust cloth⟩ **2 soltar el trapo** : to burst into tears **3 trapos** *nmpl fam* : clothes

tráquea *nf* : trachea, windpipe

traquetear *vi* : to clatter, to jolt

traqueteo *nm* **1** : jolting **2** : clattering, clatter

tras *prep* **1** : after ⟨día tras día : day after day⟩ ⟨uno tras otro : one after another⟩ **2** : behind ⟨tras la puerta : behind the door⟩

trasbordar, trasbordo → transbordar, transbordo

trascendencia *nf* **1** : importance, significance **2** : transcendence

trascendental *adj* **1** : transcendental **2** : important, momentous

trascendente *adj* **1** : important, significant **2** : transcendent

trascender {56} *vi* **1** : to leak out, to become known **2** : to spread, to have a

wide effect 3 ~ a : to smell of ⟨la casa
trascendía a flores : the house smelled of
flowers⟩ 4 ~ de : to transcend, to go
beyond — vt : to transcend
trasero[1], **-ra** adj POSTERIOR : rear, back
trasero[2] nm : buttocks
trasfondo nm 1 : background, backdrop
2 : undertone, undercurrent
trasformación → transformación
trasgo nm : goblin, imp
trasgredir → transgredir
trashumante adj : seasonally migratory
trasiego nm 1 : coming and going 2
: transfer
trasladar vt 1 TRANSFERIR : to transfer,
to move 2 POSPONER : to postpone 3
TRADUCIR : to translate 4 COPIAR : to
copy, to transcribe — **trasladarse** vr
MUDARSE : to move, to relocate
traslado nm 1 : transfer, move 2 : copy
traslapar vt : to overlap — **traslaparse** vr
traslapo nm : overlap
traslúcido, -da → translúcido
traslucir {45} vi : to reveal, to show —
traslucirse vr : to show through
trasluz nm, pl **-luces al trasluz** : against
the light
trasmano nm **a ~** : out of the way, out of
reach
**trasmisión, trasmitir → transmisión,
transmitir**
trasnochar vi : to stay up all night
traspapelar vt : to misplace, to mislay (papers, etc.)
**trasparencia, trasparente → transparen-
cia, transparente**
traspasar vt 1 PERFORAR : to pierce, to
go through 2 : to go beyond ⟨traspasar
los límites : to overstep the limits⟩ 3
ATRAVESAR : to cross, to go across 4
: to sell, to transfer
traspaso nm : transfer, sale
traspié nm 1 : stumble 2 : blunder
traspiración → transpiración
trasplantar vt : to transplant
trasplante nm : transplant
trasponer → transponer
trasportar → transportar
trasquilar vt ESQUILAR : to shear
trastada nf fam : dirty trick
traste nm 1 : fret (on a guitar) 2 CA,
Mex, PRi : kitchen utensil ⟨lavar los trastes : to do the dishes⟩ 3 **dar al traste
con** : to ruin, to destroy 4 **irse al traste**
: to fall through
trastero nm : junk room
trastienda nf : back room
trastornar vt : to disturb, to upset, to disrupt — **trastornarse** vr
trastorno nm 1 : disorder ⟨trastorno
mental : mental disorder⟩ 2 : disturbance, upset
trastos nmpl 1 : implements, utensils 2
fam : pieces of junk, stuff
trasunto nm : image, likeness
tratable adj 1 : friendly, sociable 2
: treatable
tratado nm 1 : treatise 2 : treaty
tratamiento nm : treatment
tratante nmf : dealer, trader

tratar vi 1 ~ **con** : to deal with, to have
contact with ⟨no trato mucho con los
clientes : I don't have much contact with
customers⟩ 2 ~ **de** : to try to ⟨estoy
tratando de comer : I am trying to eat⟩
3 ~ **de/sobre** : to be about, to concern
⟨el libro trata de las plantas : the book is
about plants⟩ 4 ~ **en** : to deal in ⟨trata
en herramientas : he deals in tools⟩ — vt
1 : to treat ⟨tratan bien a sus empleados
: they treat their employees well⟩ 2 : to
treat (a patient, a condition) 3 : to handle ⟨trató el tema con delicadeza : he
handled the subject tactfully⟩ 4 : to
treat (wood, etc.) — **tratarse** vr 1 : to
socialize with 2 ~ **de** : to be about, to
concern
trato nm 1 : deal, agreement 2 : relationship, dealings pl 3 : treatment
⟨malos tratos : ill-treatment⟩
trauma nm : trauma
traumático, -ca adj : traumatic —
traumáticamente adv
traumatismo nm : injury ⟨traumatismo
cervical : whiplash⟩
través nm 1 **a través de** : across, through
2 **al través** : crosswise, across 3 **de través** : sideways
travesaño nm 1 : crossbar 2 : transom
(of a window), crosspiece
travesía nf : voyage, crossing (of the sea)
travesti or **travestí** adj & nmf, pl **-tis** or
-tíes : transvestite
travesura nf 1 : prank, mischievous act
2 **travesuras** nfpl : mischief
travieso, -sa adj : mischievous, naughty
— **traviesamente** adv
trayecto nm 1 : journey 2 : route 3
: trajectory, path
trayectoria nf 1 : course, path, trajectory
2 : history (of a company, etc.), career
(of a person)
trayendo → traer
traza nf 1 DISEÑO : design, plan 2 : appearance
trazado nm 1 BOSQUEJO : outline, sketch
2 PLAN : plan, layout
trazar {21} vt 1 : to trace 2 : to draw up,
to devise 3 : to outline, to sketch
trazo nm 1 : stroke, line 2 : sketch, outline
trébol nm 1 : clover, shamrock 2 : club
(playing card)
trece adj & nm : thirteen — **trece** pron
treceavo[1], **-va** adj : thirteenth
treceavo[2] nm : thirteenth (fraction)
trecho nm 1 : stretch, period ⟨de trecho en
trecho : at intervals⟩ 2 : distance, space
tregua nf 1 : truce 2 : lull, respite 3 **sin
~** : relentless, unrelenting
treinta adj & nm : thirty — **treinta** pron
treintavo[1], **-va** adj : thirtieth
treintavo[2] nm : thirtieth (fraction)
tremendamente adv : tremendously
tremendo, -da adj 1 : tremendous, enormous 2 : terrible, dreadful 3 fam
: great, super
trementina nf AGUARRÁS : turpentine
trémulo, -la adj 1 : trembling, shaky 2
: flickering

tren *nm* **1** : train **2** : set, assembly ⟨tren de aterrizaje : landing gear⟩ ⟨tren motriz : drive train⟩ **3** : speed, pace ⟨a todo tren : at top speed⟩

trenca *nf Spain* : duffle coat

trence, etc. → trenzar

trenza *nf* : braid, pigtail

trenzar {21} *vt* : to braid — **trenzarse** *vr* : to get involved

trepador, -dora *adj* : climbing ⟨rosal trepador : rambling rose⟩

trepadora *nf* **1** : climbing plant, climber **2** : nuthatch

trepar *vi* **1** : to climb ⟨trepar a un árbol : to climb up a tree⟩ **2** : to creep, to spread (of a plant)

trepidación *nf, pl* **-ciones** : vibration

trepidante *adj* **1** : vibrating **2** : fast, frantic

trepidar *vi* **1** : to shake, to vibrate **2** : to hesitate, to waver

tres[1] *adj & nm* : three ⟨tiene tres años : she's three years old⟩ ⟨el tres de mayo : (on) the third of May, (on) May third⟩ ⟨el siglo tres : the third century⟩

tres[2] *pron* : three ⟨somos tres : there are three of us⟩ ⟨son las tres : it's three (o'clock)⟩

trescientos[1], **-tas** *adj & pron* : three hundred

trescientos[2] *nms & pl* : three hundred

tresillo *nm* **1** : three-piece suit **2** *Spain* : three-piece furniture set **3** *Spain* : three-seat sofa

treta *nf* : trick, ruse

tri- *pref* : tri-

tríada *nf* : triad

triángulo *nm* : triangle — **triangular** *adj*

tribal *adj* : tribal

tribu *nf* : tribe

tribulación *nf, pl* **-ciones** : tribulation

tribuna *nf* **1** : dais, platform **2** : stands *pl*, bleachers *pl*, grandstand

tribunal *nm* : court, tribunal

tributar *vt* : to pay, to render — *vi* : to pay taxes

tributario[1], **-ria** *adj* : tax ⟨evasión tributaria : tax evasion⟩

tributario[2] *nm* : tributary

tributo *nm* **1** : tax **2** : tribute

triciclo *nm* : tricycle

tricolor *adj* : tricolor

tricotar *vt Spain* : to knit

tridente *nm* : trident

tridimensional *adj* : three-dimensional, 3-D

trienal *adj* : triennial

trifulca *nf fam* : row, ruckus

trigal *nm* : wheat field

trigésimo[1], **-ma** *adj* : thirtieth, thirty-

trigésimo[2], **-ma** *n* : thirtieth, thirty- (in a series)

trigo *nm* **1** : wheat **2 trigo sarraceno** : buckwheat

trigonometría *nf* : trigonometry

trigueño, -ña *adj* **1** : light brown (of hair) **2** *MORENO* : dark, olive-skinned

trillado, -da *adj* : trite, hackneyed

trilladora *nf* : thresher, threshing machine

trillar *vt* : to thresh

trillizo, -za *n* : triplet

trilogía *nf* : trilogy

trimestral *adj* : quarterly — **trimestralmente** *adv*

trimestre *nm* : trimester

trinar *vi* **1** : to thrill **2** : to warble

trinchar *vt* : to carve, to cut up

trinchera *nf* **1** : trench, ditch **2** : trench coat

trineo *nm* : sled, sleigh

trinidad *nf* **la Trinidad** : the Trinity

trino *nm* : trill, warble

trinquete *nm* : ratchet

trío *nm* : trio

tripa *nf* **1** *INTESTINO* : gut, intestine **2 tripas** *nfpl fam* : belly, tummy, insides *pl* ⟨dolerle a uno las tripas : to have a stomach ache⟩

tripartito, -ta *adj* : tripartite

triple *adj & nm* : triple

triplicado *nm* : triplicate

triplicar {72} *vt* : to triple, to treble

trípode *nm* : tripod

tripulación *nf, pl* **-ciones** : crew

tripulante *nmf* : crew member

tripular *vt* : to man

triquiñuela *nf* : trick

tris *nm* **estar en un tris de** : to be within an inch of, to be very close to

triste *adj* **1** : sad, gloomy ⟨ponerse triste : to become sad⟩ **2** : desolate, dismal ⟨una perspectiva triste : a dismal outlook⟩ **3** : sorry, sorry-looking ⟨la triste verdad : the sorry truth⟩

tristemente *adv* : sadly

tristeza *nf* *DOLOR* : sadness, grief

tristón, -tona *adj, mpl* **-tones** : melancholy, downhearted

tritón *nm, pl* **tritones** : newt

triturador *nm* → **trituradora**

trituradora *nf* **1** : grinder **2 trituradora de papel** : paper shredder **3 trituradora de basura** : garbage disposal

triturar *vt* : to crush, to grind

triunfador[1], **-dora** *adj* : triumphal, triumphant

triunfador[2], **-dora** *n* : winner

triunfal *adj* : triumphal, triumphant — **triunfalmente** *adv*

triunfante *adj* : triumphant, victorious

triunfar *vi* : to triumph, to win

triunfo *nm* **1** : triumph, victory **2** *ÉXITO* : success **3** : trump (in card games)

triunvirato *nm* : triumvirate

trivial *adj* **1** : trivial **2** : trite, commonplace

trivialidad *nf* : triviality

triza *nf* **1** : shred, bit **2 hacer trizas** : to tear into shreds, to smash to pieces

trocar {82} *vt* **1** *CAMBIAR* : to exchange, to trade **2** *CAMBIAR* : to change, to alter, to transform **3** *CONFUNDIR* : to confuse, to mix up

trocear *vt* : to carve, to cut up

trocha *nf* : path, trail

troce, etc. → trozar

trofeo *nm* : trophy

tromba *nf* **1** : whirlwind **2 tromba de agua** : downpour, cloudburst

trombón *nm, pl* **trombones 1** : trombone **2** : trombonist — **trombonista** *nmf*

trombosis *nf* : thrombosis
trompa *nf* **1** : trunk (of an elephant), proboscis (of an insect) **2** : horn ⟨trompa de caza : hunting horn⟩ **3** : tube, duct (in the body)
trompada *nf fam* **1** : punch, blow **2** : bump, collision (of persons)
trompazo *nm fam* : bang, bump, smack
trompear *vt fam* : to punch
trompeta *nf* : trumpet
trompetista *nmf* : trumpet player, trumpeter
trompicón *nm, pl* **-cones 1** : stumble, lurch **2 a trompicones** : in fits and starts
trompo *nm* : spinning top
trona *nf Spain* : high chair (for a baby)
tronada *nf* : thunderstorm
tronado, -da *adj fam* : nuts, crazy
tronar {19} *vi* **1** : to thunder, to roar **2** : to be furious, to rage **3** *CA, Mex fam* : to shoot — *v impers* : to thunder ⟨está tronando : it's thundering⟩
tronchar *vt* **1** : to snap, to break off **2** : to cut off (relations)
tronco *nm* **1** : trunk (of a tree) **2** : log **3** : torso
trono *nm* **1** : throne **2** *fam* : toilet
tropa *nf* **1** : troop, soldiers *pl* **2** : crowd, mob **3** : herd (of livestock)
tropel *nm* : mob, swarm
tropezar {29} *vi* **1** : to trip, to stumble **2** : to slip up, to blunder **3 ~ con** : to run into, to bump into **4 ~ con** : to come up against (a problem) — **tropezarse** *vr* **~ con** : to run into, to bump into
tropezón *nm, pl* **-zones 1** : stumble **2** : mistake, slip
tropical *adj* : tropical
trópico *nm* **1** : tropic ⟨trópico de Cáncer : tropic of Cancer⟩ **2 el trópico** : the tropics
tropiezo *nm* **1** CONTRATIEMPO : snag, setback **2** EQUIVOCACIÓN : mistake, slip
troqué, etc. → **trocar**
troquel *nm* : die (for stamping)
trotamundos *nmf* : globe-trotter
trotar *vi* **1** : to trot **2** : to jog **3** *fam* : to rush about
trote *nm* **1** : trot **2** *fam* : rush, bustle **3 de ~** : durable, for everyday use
troupe *nf* : troupe
trovador, -dora *n* : troubadour
trozar {21} *vt* : to cut up, to dice
trozo *nm* **1** PEDAZO : piece, bit, chunk **2** : passage, extract
trucha *nf* : trout
truco *nm* **1** : trick **2** : knack
truculento, -ta *adj* : horrifying, gruesome
trueca, trueque etc. → **trocar**
truena, etc. → **tronar**
trueno *nm* : thunder
trueque *nm* : barter, exchange
trufa *nf* : truffle
truhán, truhana *n, pl* **truhanes** : rogue, scoundrel
truncar {72} *vt* **1** : to truncate, to cut short **2** : to thwart, to frustrate ⟨truncó sus esperanzas : she shattered their hopes⟩

trunco, -ca *adj* **1** : truncated **2** : unfinished, incomplete
trunque, etc. → **truncar**
trust *nm* : trust (business group)
tu *adj* **1** : your ⟨tu vestido : your dress⟩ ⟨toma tus vitaminas : take your vitamins⟩ **2** : thy
tú *pron* **1** : you ⟨tú eres mi hijo : you are my son⟩ **2** : thou
tuba *nf* : tuba
tubérculo *nm* : tuber
tuberculosis *nf* : tuberculosis
tuberculoso, -sa *adj* : tuberculous, tubercular
tubería *nf* : pipes *pl*, tubing
tuberoso, -sa *adj* : tuberous
tubo *nm* **1** : tube ⟨tubo de ensayo : test tube⟩ **2** : pipe ⟨tubo de desagüe : drainpipe⟩ **3 tubo digestivo** : alimentary canal
tubular *adj* : tubular
tuerca *nf* : nut ⟨tuercas y tornillos : nuts and bolts⟩
tuerce, etc. → **torcer**
tuerto, -ta *adj* : one-eyed, blind in one eye
tuerza, etc. → **torcer**
tuesta, etc. → **tostar**
tuétano *nm* : marrow
tufo *nm* **1** : fume, vapor **2** *fam* : stench, stink
tugurio *nm* : hovel
tuit *nm, pl* **tuits** : tweet (on the social network Twitter)
tuitear *v* : to tweet (on the social network Twitter)
tul *nm* : tulle
tulipán *nm, pl* **-panes** : tulip
tullido[1], -da *adj* : disabled, crippled
tullido[2], -da *n* : disabled person
tumba *nf* **1** SEPULCRO : tomb **2** FOSA : grave **3** : felling of trees
tumbar *vt* **1** : to knock down **2** : to fell, to cut down — *vi* : to fall down — **tumbarse** *vr* ACOSTARSE : to lie down
tumbo *nm* **1** : tumble, fall **2 dar tumbos** : to jolt, to bump around
tumbona *nf Spain* : deck chair
tumor *nm* : tumor
túmulo *nm* : burial mound
tumulto *nm* **1** ALBOROTO : commotion, tumult **2** MOTÍN : riot **3** MULTITUD : crowd
tumultuoso, -sa *adj* : tumultuous
tuna *nf* : prickly pear (fruit)
tunante, -ta *n* : crook, scoundrel
tundra *nf* : tundra
tunecino, -na *adj & n* : Tunisian
túnel *nm* : tunnel
tungsteno *nm* : tungsten
túnica *nf* : tunic
tupé *nm* PELUQUÍN : toupee
tupido, -da *adj* **1** DENSO : dense, thick **2** OBSTRUIDO : obstructed, blocked up
turba *nf* **1** : peat **2** : mob, throng
turbación *nf, pl* **-ciones 1** : disturbance **2** : alarm, concern **3** : confusion
turbante *nm* : turban
turbar *vt* **1** : to disturb, to disrupt **2** : to worry, to upset **3** : to confuse
turbina *nf* : turbine

turbio, -bia *adj* **1** : cloudy, murky, turbid **2** : dim, blurred **3** : shady, crooked
turbulencia *nf* : turbulence
turbulento, -ta *adj* : turbulent
turco¹, -ca *adj* : Turkish
turco², -ca *n* : Turk
turco³ *nm* : Turkish (language)
turgente *adj* : turgid, swollen
turismo *nm* : tourism, tourist industry
turista *nmf* : tourist, vacationer
turístico, -ca *adj* : tourist, travel
turnar *vi* : to take turns, to alternate
turno *nm* **1** : turn ⟨ya te tocará tu turno : you'll get your turn⟩ **2** : shift, duty ⟨turno de noche : night shift⟩ **3 por turno** : alternately
turón *nm, pl* **turones** : polecat
turquesa *nf* : turquoise
turrón *nm, pl* **turrones** : nougat

tusa *nf* : corn husk
tutear *vt* : to address as *tú*
tutela *nf* **1** : guardianship **2** : tutelage, protection
tuteo *nm* : addressing as *tú*
tutor, -tora *n* **1** : tutor **2** : guardian
tutoría *nf* : guardianship
tutorial *nm* : tutorial
tuvo, etc. → **tener**
tuyo¹, -ya *adj* : yours, of yours ⟨un amigo tuyo : a friend of yours⟩ ⟨¿es tuya esta casa? : is this house yours?⟩
tuyo², -ya *pron* **1** : yours ⟨ése es el tuyo : that one is yours⟩ ⟨trae la tuya : bring your own⟩ **2 los tuyos** : your relations, your friends ⟨¿vendrán los tuyos? : are your folks coming?⟩
tweed [ˈtwið] *nm* : tweed
tweet [ˈtwit] *nm* : tuit
twittear → **tuitear**

U

u¹ *nf* : twenty-fourth letter of the Spanish alphabet
u² *conj* (*used instead of* **o** *before words beginning with o- or ho-*) : or
uapití *nm, pl* **-tíes** *or* **-tís** *or* **-tí** : American elk, wapiti
ubicación *nf, pl* **-ciones** : location, position
ubicar {72} *vt* **1** SITUAR : to place, to put, to position **2** LOCALIZAR : to locate, to find — **ubicarse** *vr* **1** LOCALIZARSE : to be placed, to be located **2** SITUARSE : to position oneself
ubicuo, -cua *adj* : ubiquitous
ubre *nf* : udder
UCP [useˈpe] (*unidad central de procesamiento*) → **CPU**
ucraniano¹, -na *adj & n* : Ukrainian
ucraniano² *nm* : Ukrainian (language)
Ud., Uds. → **usted**
uf *interj* : phew!
ufanarse *vr* ~ **de** : to boast about
ufano, -na *adj* **1** ORGULLOSO : proud **2** : self-satisfied, smug
ugandés, -desa *adj & n, mpl* **-deses** : Ugandan
ukelele *nm* : ukulele
úlcera *nf* : ulcer — **ulceroso, -sa** *adj*
ulcerar *vt* : to ulcerate — **ulcerarse** *vr*
ulterior *adj* : later, subsequent — **ulteriormente** *adv*
últimamente *adv* : lately, recently
ultimar *vt* **1** : to complete, to finish, to finalize **2** MATAR : to kill
ultimátum *nm, pl* **-tums** : ultimatum
último¹, -ma *adj* **1** : last, final ⟨la última galleta : the last cookie⟩ ⟨en último caso : as a last resort⟩ ⟨estar en último lugar : to be in last place⟩ **2** : last, latest, most recent ⟨su último viaje a España : her last trip to Spain⟩ ⟨en los últimos años : in recent years⟩ ⟨las últimas noticias : the latest news⟩ ⟨a última hora : at the

last moment⟩ **3** : last, farthest ⟨el último piso : the top floor⟩ **4 por** ~ : finally
último², -ma *n* : last one
ultra- *pref* : ultra-
ultrajar *vt* : to offend, to outrage, to insult
ultraje *nm* : outrage, insult
ultramar *nm de* ~ *or en* ~ : overseas, abroad
ultranza *nf* **1 a** ~ : to the extreme ⟨defender a ultranza : to defend fiercely⟩ **2 a** ~ : extreme, out-and-out ⟨perfeccionismo a ultranza : rabid perfectionism⟩
ultrarrojo, -ja *adj* : infrared
ultrasecreto, -ta *adj* : top secret
ultrasónico, -ca *adj* : ultrasonic
ultrasonido *nm* : ultrasound
ultravioleta *adj* : ultraviolet
ulular *vi* **1** : to hoot **2** : to howl, to wail
ululato *nm* : hoot (of an owl), wail (of a person)
umbilical *adj* : umbilical ⟨cordón umbilical : umbilical cord⟩
umbral *nm* : threshold, doorstep
un¹ *adj* → **uno¹**
un², una *art, mpl* **unos** **1** : a, an ⟨un año : a year⟩ ⟨una persona : a person⟩ **2 unos** *or* **unas** *pl* : some, a few ⟨hace unas semanas : a few weeks ago⟩ **3 unos** *or* **unas** *pl* : about, approximately ⟨unos veinte años antes : about twenty years before⟩
unánime *adj* : unanimous — **unánimemente** *adv*
unanimidad *nf* **1** : unanimity **2 por** ~ : unanimously
uncir {83} *vt* : to yoke
undécimo¹, -ma *adj* : eleventh
undécimo², -ma *n* : eleventh (in a series)
ungir {35} *vt* : to anoint
ungüento *nm* : ointment, salve
ungulado, -da *adj* : hoofed
únicamente *adv* : only, solely

único¹, -ca *adj* **1** : only, sole ⟨lo único que necesito : the only thing I need⟩ ⟨es hijo único : he's an only child⟩ **2** : unique, extraordinary

único², -ca *n* : only one ⟨los únicos que vinieron : the only ones who showed up⟩

unicornio *nm* : unicorn

unidad *nf* **1** : unity **2** : unit (of army, currency, etc.) **3** : drive, unit ⟨unidad (de memoria) flash : flash drive⟩

unido, -da *adj* **1** : joined, united **2** : close (of friends, etc.)

unificar {72} *vt* : to unify — **unificación** *nf*

uniformado, -da *adj* : uniformed

uniformar *vt* : to standardize, to make uniform

uniforme¹ *adj* : uniform — **uniformemente** *adv*

uniforme² *nm* : uniform

uniformidad *nf* : uniformity

unilateral *adj* : unilateral — **unilateralmente** *adv*

unión *nf*, *pl* **uniones** **1** : union (partnership) ⟨Unión Europea : European Union⟩ **2** : union, joining **3** JUNTURA : joint, coupling

unir *vt* **1** JUNTAR : to unite, to join **2** CONECTAR : to link, to connect **3** COMBINAR : to blend — **unirse** *vr* **1** : to join together **2** : to combine, to mix together **3** ~ **a** : to join (a group, etc.)

unísono *nm* : unison ⟨al unísono : in unison⟩

unitario, -ria *adj* : unitary, unit ⟨precio unitario : unit price⟩

universal *adj* : universal — **universalidad** *nf* — **universalmente** *adv*

universidad *nf* : university

universitario¹, -ria *adj* : university, college

universitario², -ria *n* : university student, college student

universo *nm* : universe

unja, etc. → **ungir**

uno¹, una *adj* (*un* before masculine singular nouns) : one ⟨una cosa más : one more thing⟩ ⟨tiene treinta y un años : he's thirty-one years old⟩ ⟨el tomo uno : volume one⟩

uno² *nm* : one, number one

uno³, una *pron* **1** : one (number) ⟨uno por uno : one by one⟩ ⟨es la una : it's one o'clock⟩ **2** : one (person or thing) ⟨una es mejor que las otras : one (of them) is better than the others⟩ ⟨hacerlo uno mismo : to do it oneself⟩ ⟨uno no puede vivir así : you/one can't live like that⟩ **3** *unos, unas* *pl* : some (ones), some people **4 uno y otro** : both **5 unos y otros** : all of them **6 el uno al otro** : one another, each other ⟨se enseñaron los unos a los otros : they taught each other⟩

untar *vt* **1** : to anoint **2** : to smear, to grease **3** : to bribe

unza, etc. → **uncir**

uña *nf* **1** : fingernail, toenail **2** : claw, hoof, stinger

UPC [upe'se] (*unidad de procesamiento central*) → CPU

uranio *nm* : uranium

Urano *nm* : Uranus

urbanismo *nm* : city planning

urbanización *nf, pl* **-ciones** : housing development, residential area

urbanizar {21} *vt* : to develop (an area) — **urbanizado, -da** *adj* — **urbanizadora** *nf*

urbano, -na *adj* **1** : urban **2** CORTÉS : urbane, polite

urbe *nf* : large city, metropolis

urdimbre *nf* : warp (in a loom)

urdir *vt* : to engineer, to devise

uretra *nf* : urethra

urgencia *nf* **1** : urgency ⟨con urgencia : urgently⟩ **2** EMERGENCIA : emergency ⟨sala de urgencias : emergency room⟩ ⟨fue intervenido de urgencia : he had emergency surgery⟩

urgente *adj* **1** : urgent **2** : express (mail) — **urgentemente** *adv*

urgido, -da *adj* **estar urgido de** : to be in urgent need of

urgir {35} *v impers* : to be urgent, to be pressing ⟨me urge localizarlo : I urgently need to find him⟩ ⟨el tiempo urge : time is running out⟩

urinario, -ria *adj* : urinary

urja, etc. → **urgir**

urna *nf* **1** : urn **2** : ballot box ⟨acudir a las urnas : to go to the polls⟩

urogallo *nm* : grouse (bird)

urraca *nf* **1** : magpie **2 urraca de América** : blue jay

urticaria *nf* : hives

uruguayo, -ya *adj & n* : Uruguayan

usado, -da *adj* **1** : used, secondhand **2** : worn, worn-out

usanza *nf* : custom, usage

usar *vt* **1** : to use, to make use of ⟨lo usó de martillo : he used it as a hammer⟩ **2** CONSUMIR : to consume, to use (up) **3** LLEVAR : to wear **4 de usar y tirar** : disposable — **usarse** *vr* **1** : to be used **2** : to be in fashion

usina *nf* : power plant

uso *nm* **1** : use ⟨hacer uso de : to make use of⟩ ⟨objetos de uso personal : personal items⟩ **2** : wear ⟨uso y desgaste : wear and tear⟩ **3** COSTUMBRE : custom **4 al uso** : typical, standard ⟨una casa al uso : a typical house⟩

usted *pron* **1** (*formal form of address in most countries; often written as* **Ud.** *or* **Vd.**) : you ⟨usted la conoce : you know her⟩ ⟨¿a usted le gusta el café? : do you like coffee?⟩ ⟨con/para usted : with/for you⟩ **2 ustedes** *pl* (*often written as* **Uds.** *or* **Vds.**) : you, all of you ⟨muchos de ustedes : many of you⟩

usual *adj* : usual, common, normal ⟨poco usual : not very common⟩ — **usualmente** *adv*

usuario, -ria *n* : user

usura *nf* : usury

usurpador, -dora *n* : usurper

usurpar *vt* : to usurp — **usurpación** *nf*

utensilio *nm* : utensil, tool

uterino, -na *adj* : uterine

útero *nm* : uterus, womb
útil *adj* : useful, handy, helpful
utilería *nf* : props *pl*
útiles *nmpl* : implements, tools
utilidad *nf* **1** : utility, usefulness **2 utilidades** *nfpl* : profits
utilitario, -ria *adj* : utilitarian
utilizable *adj* : usable, fit for use
utilización *nf, pl* **-ciones** : utilization, use

utilizar {21} *vt* : to use, to utilize
útilmente *adv* : usefully
utopía *nf* : utopia
utópico, -ca *adj* : utopian
uva *nf* : grape
uve *nf Spain* → **ve²**
uve doble *nf Spain* → **ve doble**
úvula *nf* : uvula
uy *interj* **1** : oh! **2** : ow!

V

v *nf* : twenty-fifth letter of the Spanish alphabet
va → **ir**
vaca *nf* : cow
vacación *nf, pl* **-ciones** **1** : vacation ⟨dos semanas de vacaciones : two weeks of vacation⟩ **2 estar de vacaciones** : to be on vacation **3 irse de vacaciones** : to go on vacation
vacacionar *vi Mex* : to vacation
vacacionista *nmf CA, Mex* : vacationer
vacante¹ *adj* : vacant, empty
vacante² *nf* : vacancy (for a job)
vaciar {85} *vt* **1** : to empty, to empty out, to drain **2** AHUECAR : to hollow out : to cast (in a mold) — *vi* ~ **en** : to flow into, to empty into
vacilación *nf, pl* **-ciones** : hesitation, vacillation
vacilante *adj* **1** : hesitant, unsure **2** : shaky, unsteady **3** : flickering
vacilar *vi* **1** : to hesitate, to vacillate, to waver **2** : to be unsteady, to wobble **3** : to flicker **4** *fam* : to joke, to fool around
vacío¹, -cía *adj* **1** : vacant **2** : empty **3** : meaningless
vacío² *nm* **1** : emptiness, void **2** : space, gap **3** : vacuum **4 hacerle el vacío a alguien** : to ostracize someone, to give someone the cold shoulder
vacuidad *nf* : vacuousness
vacuna *nf* : vaccine
vacunación *nf, pl* **-ciones** INOCULACIÓN : vaccination, inoculation
vacunar *vt* INOCULAR : to vaccinate, to inoculate
vacuno¹, -na *adj* : bovine ⟨ganado vacuno : cattle⟩
vacuno² *nm* : bovine
vacuo, -cua *adj* : empty, shallow, inane
vadear *vt* : to ford, to wade across
vado *nm* : ford
vagabundear *vi* : to wander, to roam about
vagabundo¹, -da *adj* **1** ERRANTE : wandering **2** : stray
vagabundo², -da *n* : vagrant, bum, vagabond
vagamente *adv* : vaguely
vagancia *nf* **1** : vagrancy **2** PEREZA : laziness, idleness
vagar {52} *vi* ERRAR : to roam, to wander
vagina *nf* : vagina — **vaginal** *adj*

vago¹, -ga *adj* **1** : vague **2** PEREZOSO : lazy, idle
vago², -ga *n* **1** : idler, loafer **2** VAGABUNDO : vagrant, bum
vagón *nm, pl* **vagones** : car (of a train)
vagoneta *nf* : station wagon
vague, etc. → **vagar**
vaguedad *nf* : vagueness
vahído *nm* : dizzy spell
vaho *nm* **1** : breath **2** : vapor, steam (on glass, etc.)
vaina *nf* **1** : sheath, scabbard **2** : pod (of a pea or bean) **3** *fam* MOLESTIA : nuisance, bother **4** *fam* COSA : thing
vainilla *nf* : vanilla
vaivén *nm, pl* **vaivenes** **1** : swinging, swaying, rocking **2** : change, fluctuation ⟨los vaivenes de la vida : life's ups and downs⟩
vajilla *nf* : dishes *pl*, set of dishes
valdrá, etc. → **valer**
vale *nm* **1** : voucher **2** PAGARÉ : promissory note, IOU
valedero, -ra *adj* : valid
valentía *nf* : courage, valor
valer {84} *vt* **1** : to be worth ⟨valen una fortuna : they're worth a fortune⟩ ⟨no vale protestar : there's no point in protesting⟩ ⟨valer la pena : to be worth the trouble⟩ **2** : to cost ⟨¿cuánto vale? : how much does it cost?⟩ **3** : to earn, to gain ⟨le valió una reprimenda : it earned him a reprimand⟩ **4** : to protect, to aid ⟨¡válgame Dios! : God help me!⟩ **5** : to be equal to — *vi* **1** : to have value ⟨sus consejos no valen para nada : his advice is worthless⟩ **2** : to be valid, to count ⟨¡eso no vale! : that doesn't count!⟩ **3 hacerse valer** : to assert oneself **4 más vale** : it's better ⟨más vale que te vayas : you'd better go⟩ — **valerse** *vr* **1** ~ **de** : to take advantage of **2 valerse solo** *or* **valerse por sí mismo** ⟨ : to look after oneself **3** *Mex* : to be fair ⟨no se vale : it's not fair⟩
valeroso, -sa *adj* : brave, valiant
valet [ˈbalet, -ˈle] *nm* : jack (in playing cards)
valga, etc. → **valer**
valía *nf* : value, worth
validar *vt* : to validate — **validación** *nf*
validez *nf* : validity
válido, -da *adj* : valid
valiente *adj* **1** : brave, valiant **2** (*used ironically*) : fine, great ⟨¡valiente amiga!⟩

: what a fine friend!⟩ — **valientemente**
adv
valija nf : suitcase, valise
valioso, -sa adj PRECIOSO : valuable, precious
Valium marca registrada, m — used for a drug that reduces anxiety and stress
valla nf **1** : fence, barricade **2** : hurdle (in sports) **3** : obstacle, hindrance
vallar vt : to fence, to put a fence around
valle nm : valley, vale
valor nm **1** : value, worth, importance **2** CORAJE : courage, valor **3 valores** nmpl : values, principles **4 valores** nmpl : securities, bonds **5 sin ~** : worthless
valoración nf, pl **-ciones 1** EVALUACIÓN : valuation, appraisal, assessment **2** APRECIACIÓN : appreciation
valorar vt **1** EVALUAR : to evaluate, to appraise, to assess **2** APRECIAR : to value, to appreciate
valorizarse {21} vr : to appreciate, to increase in value — **valorización** nf
vals nm : waltz
valuación nf, pl **-ciones** : valuation, appraisal
valuar {3} vt : to value, to appraise, to assess
válvula nf **1** : valve **2 válvula reguladora** : throttle
vamos → **ir**
vampiro nm : vampire
van → **ir**
vanagloriarse vr : to boast, to brag
vandalismo : vandalism
vándalo nm : vandal — **vandalismo** nm
vanguardia nf **1** : vanguard **2** : avant-garde **3 a la vanguardia** : at the forefront
vanguardista[1] adj : avant-garde
vanguardista[2] nmf : avant-gardist
vanidad nf : vanity
vanidoso, -sa adj PRESUMIDO : vain, conceited
vano, -na adj **1** INÚTIL : vain, useless **2** : vain, worthless ⟨vanas promesas : empty promises⟩ **3 en ~** : in vain, of no avail — **vanamente** adv
vapear v : to vape
vapor nm **1** : vapor, steam **2** : steamer, steamship **3 al vapor** : steamed
vaporeador nm : e-cigarette
vaporera nf : steamer (for cooking)
vaporizador nm **1** : vaporizer **2** : e-cigarette
vaporizar {21} vt : to vaporize — **vaporizarse** vr — **vaporización** nf
vaporoso, -sa adj : sheer, airy
vapulear vt : to beat, to thrash
vaquero[1], **-ra** adj : cowboy ⟨pantalón vaquero : jeans⟩
vaquero[2], **-ra** n : cowboy m, cowgirl f
vaqueros nmpl JEANS : jeans
vaquilla nf : heifer
vara nf **1** : pole, stick, rod **2** : staff (of office) **3** : lance, pike (in bullfighting) **4** : yardstick **5 vara de oro** : goldenrod
varado, -da adj **1** : beached, aground **2** : stranded
varar vt : to beach (a ship), to strand — vi : to run aground

variable adj & nf : variable — **variabilidad** nf
variación nf, pl **-ciones** : variation
variado, -da adj : varied, diverse
variante adj & nf : variant
varianza nf : variance
variar {85} vt **1** : to change, to alter **2** : to diversify — vi **1** : to vary, to change **2 variar de opinión** : to change one's mind
varicela nf : chicken pox
várices or **varices** nfpl : varicose veins
varicoso, -sa adj : varicose
variedad nf DIVERSIDAD : variety, diversity
varilla nf **1** : rod, bar **2** : spoke (of a wheel) **3** : rib (of an umbrella)
vario, -ria adj **1** : varied, diverse **2** : variegated, motley **3** : changeable **4 varios, varias** pl : various, several
variopinto, -ta adj : diverse, assorted, motley
varita nf : wand ⟨varita mágica : magic wand⟩
varón nm, pl **varones 1** HOMBRE : man, male **2** NIÑO : boy
varonil adj **1** : masculine, manly **2** : mannish
vas → **ir**
vasallo, -lla n : vassal — **vasallaje** nm
vasco[1], **-ca** adj & n : Basque
vasco[2] nm : Basque (language)
vascular adj : vascular
vaselina nf : petroleum jelly
vasija nf : container, vessel
vaso nm **1** : glass, tumbler **2** : glassful **3** : vessel ⟨vaso sanguíneo : blood vessel⟩ **4 ahogarse en un vaso de agua** : to make a mountain out of a molehill **5 una tormenta en un vaso de agua** : a tempest in a teapot
vástago nm **1** : offspring, descendant **2** : shoot (of a plant)
vastedad nf : vastness, immensity
vasto, -ta adj : vast, immense
vataje nm : wattage
váter nm **1** : toilet **2** : bathroom
vaticinar vt : to predict, to foretell
vaticinio nm : prediction, prophecy
vatio nm : watt
vaya, etc. → **ir**
Vd., Vds. → **usted**
ve[1], **etc.** → **ir**, **ver**
ve[2] or **ve corta** or **ve pequeña** or **ve chica** nf : (letter) v
vea, etc. → **ver**
vecinal adj : local
vecindad nf **1** : neighborhood, vicinity **2 casa de vecindad** : tenement
vecindario nm **1** : neighborhood, area **2** : residents pl
vecino[1], **-na** adj : neighboring
vecino[2], **-na** n **1** : neighbor **2** : resident, inhabitant
veda nf **1** PROHIBICIÓN : prohibition **2** : closed season (for hunting or fishing)
vedar vt **1** : to prohibit, to ban **2** IMPEDIR : to impede, to prevent
ve doble or **doble ve** nf : (letter) w
vegetación nf, pl **-ciones 1** : vegetation **2 vegetaciones** nfpl : adenoids

vegetal *adj & nm* : vegetable, plant
vegetar *vi* : to vegetate
vegetariano, -na *adj & n* : vegetarian — **vegetarianismo** *nm*
vegetativo, -va *adj* : vegetative
vehemente *adj* : vehement — **vehemencia** *nf* — **vehementemente** *adv*
vehículo *nm* : vehicle ⟨vehículo deportivo utilitario : sport-utility vehicle⟩ — **vehicular** *adj*
veía, etc. → **ver**
veinte *adj & nm* : twenty — **veinte** *pron*
veinteavo¹, -va *adj* : twentieth
veinteavo² *nm* : twentieth (fraction)
veintena *nf* : group of twenty, score ⟨una veintena de participantes : about twenty participants⟩
vejación *nf, pl* **-ciones** : ill-treatment, humiliation
vejete *nm* : old fellow, codger
vejez *nf* : old age
vejiga *nf* **1** : bladder **2** AMPOLLA : blister
vela *nf* **1** : watch, vigil, wake **2** : candle **3** : sail **4** : sailing **5 pasar la noche en vela** : to be up all night
velada *nf* : evening party
velado, -da *adj* **1** : veiled, hidden **2** : blurred **3** : muffled
velador¹, -dora *n* : guard, night watchman
velador² *nm* **1** : candlestick **2** : night table
velar *vt* **1** : to hold a wake over **2** : to watch over, to sit up with **3** : to blur, to expose (a photo) **4** : to veil, to conceal — *vi* **1** : to stay awake **2** ~ **por** : to watch over, to look after
velatorio *nm* VELORIO : wake (for the dead)
velcro *marca registrada, m* — used for a type of nylon fastener
veleidad *nf* **1** : fickleness **2** : whim, caprice
veleidoso, -sa : fickle, capricious
velero *nm* **1** : sailing ship **2** : sailboat
veleta *nf* : weather vane
vello *nm* **1** : body hair **2** : down, fuzz
vellón *nm, pl* **vellones** **1** : fleece, sheepskin **2** PRi : nickel (coin)
vellosidad *nf* : fuzziness, hairiness
velloso, -sa *adj* : downy, fuzzy, hairy
velludo, -da *adj* : hairy
velo *nm* : veil
velocidad *nf* **1** : speed, velocity ⟨límite de velocidad : speed limit⟩ ⟨exceso de velocidad : speeding⟩ ⟨a gran velocidad : at high speed⟩ ⟨de alta velocidad : high-speed⟩ **2** MARCHA : gear (of an automobile)
velocímetro *nm* : speedometer
velocista *nmf* : sprinter
velorio *nm* VELATORIO : wake (for the dead)
velour *nm* : velour, velours
veloz *adj, pl* **veloces** : fast, quick, swift — **velozmente** *adv*
ven → **venir**
vena *nf* **1** : vein ⟨vena yugular : jugular vein⟩ **2** : vein, seam, lode **3** : grain (of wood) **4** : style ⟨en vena lírica : in a

lyrical vein⟩ **5** : strain, touch ⟨una vena de humor : a touch of humor⟩ **6** : mood
venado *nm* **1** : deer **2** : venison
venal *adj* : venal
vencedor, -dora *n* : winner, victor
vencejo *nm* : swift (bird)
vencer {86} *vt* **1** DERROTAR : to vanquish, to defeat **2** SUPERAR : to overcome, to surmount — *vi* **1** GANAR : to win, to triumph **2** CADUCAR : to expire ⟨el plazo vence el jueves : the deadline is Thursday⟩ **3** : to be due, to mature — **vencerse** *vr* **1** DOMINARSE : to control oneself **2** : to break, to collapse
vencido, -da *adj* **1** : defeated **2** : expired **3** : due, payable **4 darse por vencido** : to give up
vencimiento *nm* **1** : defeat **2** : expiration **3** : maturity (of a loan)
venda *nf* : bandage
vendaje *nm* : bandage, dressing
vendar *vt* **1** : to bandage **2 vendar los ojos** : to blindfold
vendaval *nm* : gale, strong wind
vendedor, -dora *n* : salesperson, salesman *m*, saleswoman *f*
vender *vt* **1** : to sell **2** : to sell out, to betray — **venderse** *vr* **1** : to be sold ⟨se vende : for sale⟩ **2** : to sell out
vendetta *nf* : vendetta
vendible *adj* : salable, marketable
vendimia *nf* : grape harvest
vendrá, etc. → **venir**
veneno *nm* **1** : poison **2** : venom
venenoso, -sa *adj* : poisonous, venomous
venerable *adj* : venerable
veneración *nf, pl* **-ciones** : veneration, reverence
venerar *vt* : to venerate, to revere
venéreo, -rea *adj* : venereal ⟨enfermedad venérea : venereal disease⟩
venero *nm* **1** VENA : seam, lode, vein **2** MANANTIAL : spring **3** FUENTE : origin, source
venezolano, -na *adj & n* : Venezuelan
venga, etc. → **venir**
venganza *nf* : vengeance, revenge
vengar {52} *vt* : to avenge — **vengarse** *vr* : to get even, to revenge oneself
vengativo, -va *adj* : vindictive, vengeful
vengue, etc. → **vengar**
venia *nf* **1** PERMISO : permission, leave **2** PERDÓN : pardon **3** : bow (of the head)
venial *adj* : venial
venida *nf* **1** LLEGADA : arrival, coming **2** REGRESO : return **3 idas y venidas** : comings and goings
venidero, -ra *adj* : coming, future
venir {87} *vi* **1** : to come ⟨lo vi venir : I saw him coming⟩ ⟨vino a verte : she came to see you⟩ ⟨vino a/de la oficina : he came to/from the office⟩ ⟨¡no me vengas con cuentos! : I don't want to hear your excuses!⟩ ⟨¡venga! : come on!⟩ **2** : to arrive ⟨vinieron en coche : they came by car⟩ **3** : to come, to originate ⟨sus zapatos vienen de Italia : her shoes are from Italy⟩ **4** : to come, to be available ⟨viene envuelto en plástico : it

comes wrapped in plastic⟩ **5** : to come back, to return ⟨no vengas tarde : don't come back late⟩ **6** : to affect, to overcome ⟨me vino un vahído : a dizzy spell came over me⟩ **7** : to fit ⟨te viene un poco grande : it's a little big for you⟩ **8** (*with the present participle*) : to have been ⟨viene entrenando diariamente : he's been training daily⟩ **9** ~ **a** (*with the infinitive*) : to end up, to turn out ⟨viene a ser lo mismo : it comes out the same⟩ **10 que viene** : coming, next ⟨el año que viene : next year⟩ **11 venir bien** : to be suitable, to be just right — **venirse** *vr* **1** : to come, to arrive ⟨¿te vienes conmigo? : are you coming with me?⟩ **2** : to come back **3 venirse abajo** : to fall apart, to collapse

venta *nf* **1** : sale **2 venta al por menor** *or* **venta al detalle** : retail **3 venta al por mayor** : wholesale **4 venta por correo** : mail order

ventaja *nf* **1** : advantage **2** : lead, head start ⟨llevar (la) ventaja : to be in the lead⟩ **3 ventajas** *nfpl* : perks, extras

ventajoso, -sa *adj* **1** : advantageous **2** : profitable — **ventajosamente** *adv*

ventana *nf* **1** : window (of a building) **2** : window (on a computer) **3 ventana de la nariz** : nostril

ventanal *nm* : large window

ventanilla *nf* **1** : window (of a vehicle or airplane) **2** : ticket window, box office

ventero, -ra *n* : innkeeper

ventilación *nf, pl* **-ciones** : ventilation

ventilador *nm* **1** : ventilator **2** : fan

ventilar *vt* **1** : to ventilate, to air out **2** : to air, to discuss **3** : to make public, to reveal — **ventilarse** *vr* : to get some air

ventisca *nf* : snowstorm, blizzard

ventisquero *nm* : snowdrift

ventolera *nf* : gust of wind

ventosa *nf* : sucker

ventosear *vi* : to break wind

ventosidad *nf* : wind, flatulence

ventoso, -sa *adj* : windy

ventrículo *nm* : ventricle

ventrílocuo, -cua *n* : ventriloquist

ventriloquia *nf* : ventriloquism

ventura *nf* **1** : fortune, luck, chance **2** : happiness **3 a la ventura** : at random, as it comes

venturoso, -sa *adj* **1** AFORTUNADO : fortunate, lucky **2** : successful

Venus *nm* : Venus

venza, etc. → **vencer**

ver¹ {88} *vt* **1** : to see ⟨no veo nada : I can't see anything⟩ ⟨lo vi con mis propios ojos : I saw it with my own eyes⟩ ⟨vimos una película : we saw a movie⟩ **2** ENTENDER : to understand, to see ⟨ya lo veo : now I get it⟩ ⟨no veo por qué : I don't see why⟩ ⟨¿ves lo que quiero decir? : do you see what I mean?⟩ **3** EXAMINAR : to examine, to look into ⟨lo veré : I'll take a look at it⟩ **4** JUZGAR : to see, to judge ⟨otra forma de verlo : another way of looking at it⟩ ⟨lo veo bien : I think it's good/fine⟩ **5** VISITAR : to see, to meet, to visit ⟨vino a verte

: she came to see you⟩ **6** AVERIGUAR : to see, to find out ⟨vino a ver cómo estabas : she came to see how you were⟩ — *vi* **1** : to see **2** ENTERARSE : to learn, to find out **3** ENTENDER : to understand ⟨ya veo : (so) I see⟩ ⟨a mi modo de ver : to my way of thinking, the way I see it⟩ **4 (vamos) a ver** : let's see — **verse** *vr* **1** HALLARSE : to find oneself **2** PARECER : to look, to appear **3** ENCONTRARSE : to see each other, to meet

ver² *nm* **1** : looks *pl*, appearance **2** : opinion ⟨a mi ver : in my view⟩

vera *nf* : side ⟨a la vera del camino : alongside the road⟩

veracidad *nf* : truthfulness, veracity

veranda *nf* : veranda

veraneante *nmf* : summer vacationer

veranear *vi* : to spend the summer

veraneo *nm* : summer vacation

veraniego, -ga *adj* **1** ESTIVAL : summer ⟨el sol veraniego : the summer sun⟩ **2** : summery

verano *nm* : summer

veras *nfpl* **de** ~ : really, truly

veraz *adj, pl* **veraces** : truthful

verbal *adj* : verbal — **verbalmente** *adv*

verbalizar {21} *vt* : to verbalize, to express

verbena *nf* FIESTA : festival, fair

verbigracia *adv* : for example

verbo *nm* : verb

verbosidad *nf* : wordiness

verboso, -sa *adj* : verbose, wordy

verdad *nf* **1** : truth ⟨es verdad : it's true⟩ ⟨a decir verdad : to tell the truth⟩ **2 de** ~ : really, truly **3 de** ~ : real ⟨un amigo de verdad : a true friend⟩ **4 ¿verdad?** : right?, isn't that so?

verdaderamente *adv* : really, truly

verdadero, -dera *adj* **1** REAL, VERÍDICO : true, real **2** AUTÉNTICO : genuine

verde¹ *adj* **1** : green (in color) **2** : green, unripe **3** : inexperienced, green **4** : dirty, risqué

verde² *nm* : green

verdeante *adj* : verdant

verdín *nm, pl* **verdines** : slime, scum

verdor *nm* : greenness

verdoso, -sa *adj* : greenish

verdugo *nm* **1** : executioner, hangman **2** : tyrant

verdugón *nm, pl* **-gones** : welt (on the body)

verdulería *nf* : greengrocer's store

verdulero, -ra *n* : greengrocer

verdura *nf* : vegetable(s), green(s)

vereda *nf* **1** SENDA : path, trail **2** : sidewalk, pavement

veredicto *nm* : verdict

verga *nf* : spar, yard (of a ship)

vergonzoso, -sa *adj* **1** : disgraceful, shameful **2** : bashful, shy — **vergonzosamente** *adv*

vergüenza *nf* **1** : embarrassment ⟨me hiciste pasar vergüenza : you embarrassed me⟩ ⟨me da vergüenza : I'm embarrassed (about it)⟩ ⟨¡qué vergüenza! : how embarrassing!⟩ **2** : disgrace, shame ⟨ser una vergüenza para : to be a disgrace to⟩ **3** : bashfulness, shyness

vericueto nm : rough terrain
verídico, -ca adj **1** REAL, VERDADERO : true, real **2** VERAZ : truthful
verificación nf, pl **-ciones 1** : verification **2** : testing, checking
verificador, -dora n : inspector, tester
verificar {72} vt **1** : to verify, to confirm **2** : to test, to check **3** : to carry out, to conduct — **verificarse** vr **1** : to take place, to occur **2** : to come true
verja nf **1** : rails pl (of a fence) **2** : grating, grille **3** : gate
vermut nm, pl **vermuts** : vermouth
vernáculo, -la adj : vernacular
vernal adj : vernal, spring
verosímil adj **1** : probable, likely **2** : credible, realistic
verosimilitud nf **1** : probability, plausibility **2** : realism
verraco nm : boar
verruga nf : wart
versado, -da adj ~ **en** : versed in, knowledgeable about
versar vi ~ **sobre** : to deal with, to be about
versátil adj **1** : versatile **2** : fickle
versatilidad nf **1** : versatility **2** : fickleness
versículo nm : verse (in the Bible)
versión nf, pl **versiones 1** : version **2** : translation
verso nm : verse
versus prep : versus, against
vértebra nf : vertebra — **vertebral** adj
vertebrado¹, -da adj : vertebrate
vertebrado² nm : vertebrate
vertedero nm **1** : garbage dump **2** DESAGÜE : drain, outlet
verter {56} vt **1** : to pour (liquid), to dump (waste) **2** DERRAMAR : to spill, to shed **3** VACIAR : to empty out **4** EXPRESAR : to express, to voice **5** TRADUCIR : to translate, to render — vi : to flow
vertical adj & nf : vertical — **verticalmente** adv
vértice nm : vertex, apex
vertido nm : spilling, spill
vertiente nf **1** : slope **2** : aspect, side, element
vertiginoso, -sa adj : dizzying — **vertiginosamente** adv
vértigo nm : vertigo, dizziness
vesícula nf **1** : vesicle **2 vesícula biliar** : gallbladder
vespertino, -na adj : evening
vestíbulo nm : vestibule, hall, lobby, foyer
vestido nm **1** : dress, costume, clothes pl **2** : dress (garment)
vestidor nm : dressing room
vestiduras nfpl **1** : clothing, raiment, regalia **2** : vestments (of a priest)
vestigio nm : vestige, sign, trace
vestimenta nf ROPA : clothing, clothes pl
vestir {54} vt **1** : to dress, to clothe **2** LLEVAR : to wear ⟨vestir de blanco : to wear white⟩ **3** ADORNAR : to decorate, to dress up — vi **1** : to dress ⟨vestir bien : to dress well⟩ **2** : to look good, to suit

the occasion — **vestirse** vr **1** : to get dressed **2** ~ **con** : to wear, to dress in **3** ~ **de** : to dress up as ⟨se vistieron de soldados : they dressed up as soldiers⟩ **4** ~ **de** : to wear, to dress in
vestuario nm **1** : wardrobe **2** : dressing room, locker room
veta nf **1** : grain (in wood) **2** : vein, seam, lode **3** : trace, streak ⟨una veta de terco : a stubborn streak⟩
veteado, -da adj : streaked, veined
veteranía nf **1** EXPERIENCIA : experience **2** ANTIGÜEDAD : seniority
veterano, -na adj & n : veteran
veterinaria nf : veterinary medicine
veterinario¹, -ria adj : veterinary
veterinario², -ria n : veterinarian
veto nm : veto
vetusto, -ta adj ANTIGUO : ancient, very old
vez nf, pl **veces** : time, occasion ⟨a la vez : at the same time⟩ ⟨a veces : at times, occasionally⟩ ⟨algunas veces : sometimes⟩ ⟨cada vez : each/every time⟩ ⟨cada vez más : more and more⟩ ⟨cada vez menos : less and less⟩ ⟨de vez en cuando : from time to time⟩ **2** (with numbers) : time ⟨una vez : once⟩ ⟨dos veces : twice⟩ ⟨de una vez : all at once⟩ ⟨de una vez para siempre : once and for all⟩ ⟨una y otra vez : time after time, again and again⟩ **3** : turn ⟨a su vez : in turn⟩ ⟨en vez de : instead of⟩ ⟨hacer las veces de : to act as, to stand in for⟩ **4**
alguna vez : sometime (in the future), on occasion (in the past) ⟨¿has viajado alguna vez? : have you ever traveled?⟩
vía¹ nf **1** RUTA, CAMINO : road, route, way ⟨vía pública : public thoroughfare⟩ ⟨Vía Láctea : Milky Way⟩ **2** MEDIO : means, way ⟨por la vía diplomática : through diplomatic channels⟩ ⟨por vía aérea : by air, airmail⟩ ⟨por vía oral : orally⟩ **3** : track, line (of a railroad) **4** : tract ⟨vía urinaria : urinary tract⟩ **5**
en vías de : in the process of ⟨en vías de solución : on the road to a solution⟩ ⟨países en vías de desarrollo : developing countries⟩ ⟨animales en vías de extinción : endangered animals⟩
vía² prep : via
viable adj : viable, feasible — **viabilidad** nf
viaducto nm : viaduct
viajante mf : traveling salesman, traveling saleswoman
viajar vi : to travel, to journey
viaje nm : trip, journey ⟨ir de viaje : to go on a trip⟩ ⟨estar de viaje : to be away⟩ ⟨¡buen viaje! : have a good trip!⟩ ⟨viaje de ida : one-way trip⟩ ⟨viaje de ida y vuelta/regreso : round trip⟩ ⟨viaje de regreso/vuelta : return trip⟩ ⟨viaje de negocios : business trip⟩ ⟨viaje en tren : train trip⟩
viajero¹, -ra adj : traveling
viajero², -ra n **1** : traveler **2** PASAJERO : passenger
vial adj : road, traffic

viático *nm* : travel allowance, travel expenses *pl*

víbora *nf* : viper

vibración *nf, pl* **-ciones** : vibration

vibrador *nm* : vibrator

vibrante *adj* **1** : vibrant **2** : vibrating

vibrar *vi* : to vibrate

vicario, -ria *n* : vicar

vice- *pref* : vice-

vicealmirante *nmf* : vice admiral

vicepresidente, -ta *n* : vice president — **vicepresidencia** *nf*

viceversa *adv* : vice versa, conversely

viciado, -da *adj* : stuffy, close

viciar *vt* **1** : to corrupt **2** : to invalidate **3** FALSEAR : to distort **4** : to pollute, to adulterate

vicio *nm* **1** : vice, depravity **2** : bad habit **3** : defect, blemish

vicioso, -sa *adj* : depraved, corrupt

vicisitud *nf* : vicissitude

víctima *nf* : victim

victimario, -ria *n* ASESINO : killer, murderer

victimizar {21} *vt Arg, Mex* : to victimize

victoria *nf* : victory — **victorioso, -sa** *adj* — **victoriosamente** *adv*

victoriano, -na *adj* : Victorian

vid *nf* : vine, grapevine

vida *nf* **1** : life ⟨con vida : alive⟩ ⟨sin vida : lifeless, dead⟩ ⟨perder/quitarse la vida : to lose/take one's life⟩ **2** : life ⟨la vida cotidiana : everyday life⟩ ⟨vida nocturna : nightlife⟩ ⟨estilo de vida : lifestyle, way of life⟩ ⟨así es la vida : that's life⟩ **3** : life, lifetime ⟨nunca en mi/la vida : never in my life⟩ ⟨de por vida : for life⟩ **4** : life ⟨vida animal/vegetal : animal/plant life⟩ **5** BIOGRAFÍA : life, biography **6** : living, livelihood ⟨ganarse la vida : to earn one's living⟩ **7** VIVEZA : life, liveliness **8 media vida** : half-life

vidente *nmf* **1** : psychic, clairvoyant **2** : sighted person

video *or* **vídeo** *nm* : video

videocinta *nf* : videotape

videocasete *or* **videocassette** *nm* : videocassette

videocasetera *or* **videocassettera** *nf* : videocassette recorder, video recorder, VCR

videocámara *nf* : video camera

videoclip *nm, pl* **-clips** : video

videoclub *nm* : video store

videoconferencia *nf* : videoconference

videograbar *vt Mex* : to videotape

videojuego *nm* : video game

videojugador, -dora *n* : gamer

videollamada *nf* : video call

vidriado *nm* : glaze

vidriar *vt* : to glaze (pottery, tile, etc.)

vidriera *nf* **1** : stained-glass window **2** : glass door or window **3** : store window

vidriero, -ra *n* : glazier

vidrio *nm* **1** : glass, piece of glass **2** : windowpane

vidrioso, -sa *adj* **1** : brittle, fragile **2** : slippery **3** : glassy, glazed (of eyes) **4** : touchy, delicate

vieira *nf* **1** : scallop **2** : scallop shell

viejo¹, -ja *adj* **1** ANCIANO : old, elderly **2** ANTIGUO : former, long-standing ⟨viejas tradiciones : old traditions⟩ ⟨viejos amigos : old friends⟩ **3** GASTADO : old, worn, worn-out **4 hacerse viejo** : to get old

viejo², -ja *n* ANCIANO : old man *m*, old woman *f*

viene, etc. → **venir**

viento *nm* **1** : wind **2 hacer viento** : to be windy **3 contra viento y marea** : against all odds **4 viento en popa** : splendidly, successfully

vientre *nm* **1** : abdomen, belly **2** : womb **3** : bowels *pl*

viernes *nms & pl* : Friday ⟨el viernes : (on) Friday⟩ ⟨los viernes : (on) Fridays⟩ ⟨cada (dos) viernes : every (other) Friday⟩ ⟨el viernes pasado : last Friday⟩ ⟨el próximo viernes : next Friday⟩

vierte, etc. → **verter**

vietnamita¹ *adj & nmf* : Vietnamese

vietnamita² *nm* : Vietnamese (language)

viga *nf* **1** : beam, rafter, girder **2 viga voladiza** : cantilever

vigencia *nf* **1** : validity **2** : force, effect ⟨entrar en vigencia : to go into effect⟩

vigente *adj* : valid, in force

vigésimo¹, -ma *adj* : twentieth, twenty- ⟨la vigésima segunda edición : the twenty-second edition⟩

vigésimo², -ma *n* : twentieth, twenty- (in a series)

vigía *nmf* : lookout

vigilancia *nf* **1** : vigilance, watchfulness ⟨bajo vigilancia : under surveillance⟩

vigilante¹ *adj* : vigilant, watchful

vigilante² *nmf* : watchman, guard

vigilar *vt* **1** CUIDAR : to look after, to keep an eye on **2** GUARDAR : to watch over, to guard — *vi* **1** : to be watchful **2** : to keep watch

vigilia *nf* **1** VELA : wakefulness **2** : night work **3** : vigil (in religion)

vigor *nm* **1** : vigor, energy, strength **2** VIGENCIA : force, effect ⟨entrar en vigor : to take effect⟩

vigorizante *adj* : invigorating

vigorizar {21} *vt* : to strengthen, to invigorate

vigoroso, -sa *adj* : vigorous — **vigorosamente** *adv*

VIH *nm* (virus de inmunodeficiencia humana) : HIV

vikingo, -ga *adj & n* : Viking

vil *adj* : vile, despicable, base

vileza *nf* **1** : vileness **2** : despicable action, villainy

vilipendiar *vt* : to vilify, to revile

villa *nf* **1** : town, village **2** : villa **3 villa miseria** *or* **villa de emergencia** *Arg* : shantytown, slums *pl*

villancico *nm* : carol, Christmas carol

villano, -na *n* **1** : villain **2** : peasant

vilmente *adv* : basely

vilo *nm* **1 en ~** : in the air **2 en ~** : uncertain, in suspense

vinagre *nm* : vinegar

vinagrera *nf* : cruet (for vinegar)

vinagreta *nf* : vinaigrette

vinatería *nf* : wine shop
vinculación *nf, pl* **-ciones** 1 : linking 2 RELACIÓN : bond, link, connection
vincular *vt* CONECTAR, RELACIONAR : to tie, to link, to connect
vínculo *nm* 1 LAZO : tie, link, bond 2 HIPERENLACE : link
vindicación *nf, pl* **-ciones** : vindication
vindicar *vt* 1 : to vindicate 2 : to avenge
vinilo *nm* : vinyl
vino¹, etc. → **venir**
vino² *nm* : wine
viña *nf* : vineyard
viñedo *nm* : vineyard
viñeta *nf* : cartoon
vio, etc. → **ver**
viola *nf* : viola
violación *nf, pl* **-ciones** 1 : violation, offense 2 : rape
violador¹, -dora *n* : violator, offender
violador² *nm* : rapist
violar *vt* 1 : to rape 2 : to violate (a law or right) 3 PROFANAR : to desecrate
violencia *nf* : violence
violentamente *adv* : by force, violently
violentar *vt* 1 FORZAR : to break open, to force 2 : to distort (words or ideas) — **violentarse** *vr* : to force oneself
violento, -ta *adj* 1 : violent 2 EMBARAZOSO, INCÓMODO : awkward, embarrassing
violeta¹ *adj & nm* : violet (color)
violeta² *nf* : violet (flower)
violín *nm, pl* **-lines** : violin
violinista *nmf* : violinist
violonchelista *nmf* : cellist
violonchelo *nm* : cello, violoncello
VIP *nmf, pl* **VIPs** : VIP
viraje *nm* 1 : turn, swerve 2 : change
viral *adj* : viral
virar *vi* : to tack, to turn, to veer
virgen¹ *adj* : virgin ⟨lana virgen : virgin wool⟩
virgen² *nmf, pl* **vírgenes** : virgin ⟨la Santísima Virgen : the Blessed Virgin⟩
virginal *adj* : virginal, chaste
virginidad *nf* : virginity
Virgo¹ *nm* : Virgo (sign or constellation)
Virgo² *nmf* : Virgo (person)
vírico, -ca *adj Spain* : viral
viril *adj* : virile — **virilidad** *nf*
virrey, -rreina *n* : viceroy *m*
virtual *adj* : virtual — **virtualmente** *adv*
virtud *nf* 1 : virtue 2 **en virtud de** : by virtue of
virtuosismo *nm* : virtuosity
virtuoso¹, -sa *adj* : virtuous
virtuoso², -sa *n* : virtuoso
viruela *nf* 1 : smallpox 2 : pockmark
virulencia *nf* : virulence
virulento, -ta *adj* : virulent
virus *nm* : virus
viruta *nf* : shaving
visa *nf* : visa
visado *nm Spain* : visa
visceral *adj* : visceral
vísceras *nfpl* : viscera, entrails
viscosidad *nf* : viscosity
viscoso, -sa *adj* : viscous
visera *nf* : visor

visibilidad *nf* : visibility
visible *adj* : visible — **visiblemente** *adv*
visillo *nm* : sheer curtain, lace curtain
visión *nf, pl* **visiones** 1 : vision, eyesight 2 : view, perspective 3 : vision, illusion ⟨ver visiones : to be seeing things⟩
visionario, -ria *adj & n* : visionary
visita *nf* 1 : visit, call ⟨hacer una visita : to pay a visit⟩ ⟨ir de visita : to go visiting⟩ 2 : visitor ⟨tener visita(s) : to have company⟩
visitador, -dora *n* : visitor, frequent caller
visitante¹ *adj* : visiting
visitante² *nmf* : visitor
visitar *vt* : to visit
vislumbrar *vt* 1 : to discern, to make out 2 : to begin to see, to have an inkling of
vislumbre *nf* : glimmer, gleam
viso *nm* 1 APARIENCIA : appearance ⟨tener visos de : to seem, to show signs of⟩ 2 DESTELLO : glint, gleam 3 : sheen, iridescence
visón *nm, pl* **visones** : mink
visor *nm* 1 : viewfinder (of a camera), sight (of a gun) 2 : scout (in sports)
víspera *nf* 1 : eve, day before 2 **vísperas** *nfpl* : vespers
vista *nf* 1 VISIÓN : vision, eyesight ⟨perder la vista : to lose one's eyesight⟩ 2 MIRADA : look, gaze, glance ⟨bajó la vista : he looked down⟩ ⟨fijar la vista en : to fix one's gaze on⟩ 3 PANORAMA : view, vista, panorama 4 : hearing (in court) 5 **a la vista** : in sight, in view 6 **a primera vista** : at first sight 7 **con vistas a** : with a view to 8 **en vista de** : in view of 9 **hacer la vista gorda** : to turn a blind eye 10 **¡hasta la vista!** : so long!, see you! 11 **perder de vista** : to lose sight of 12 **punto de vista** : point of view 13 **saltar a la vista** : to be obvious, to stand out
vistazo *nm* : glance, look
viste, etc. → **ver¹, vestir**
visto¹ *pp* → **ver**
visto², -ta *adj* 1 : obvious, clear 2 : in view of, considering 3 **estar bien visto** : to be approved of 4 **estar mal visto** : to be frowned upon 5 **por lo visto** : apparently 6 **nunca visto** : unheard-of 7 **visto que** : since, given that
visto³ *nm* **visto bueno** : approval
vistoso, -sa *adj* : colorful, bright
visual *adj* : visual — **visualmente** *adv*
visualizador *nm* : display (of a device)
visualizar {21} *vt* 1 : to visualize 2 : to display (on a screen)
vital *adj* 1 : vital 2 : lively, dynamic
vitalicio, -cia *adj* : life, lifetime
vitalidad *nf* : vitality
vitamina *nf* : vitamin
vitamínico, -ca *adj* : vitamin ⟨complejos vitamínicos : vitamin compounds⟩
viticultor, -ra *n* : wine producer
viticultura *nf* : wine producing
vítor *nm* : cheer
vitorear *vt* : to cheer
vitral *nm* : stained-glass window
vítreo, -rea *adj* : glass, glassy

vitrina *nf* **1** : showcase, display case **2** : store window

vitriolo *nm* : vitriol

vituperar *vt* : to condemn, to lambaste

viudez *nf* : state of being widowed ⟨su primer año de viudez : his first year as a widower⟩

viudo, -da *n* : widower *m*, widow *f*

viva *nm* : cheer

vivacidad *nf* VIVEZA : vivacity, liveliness

vivamente *adv* **1** : in a lively manner **2** : vividly **3** : strongly, acutely ⟨lo recomendamos vivamente : we strongly recommend it⟩

vivar *vi* : to cheer

vivaracho, -cha *adj* **1** : lively, vivacious **2** : bright, sparkling

vivaz *adj, pl* **vivaces 1** : lively, vivacious **2** : clever, sharp **3** : perennial

vivencia *nf* : experience

víveres *nmpl* : provisions, supplies, food

vivero *nm* **1** : nursery (for plants) **2** : hatchery, fish farm

viveza *nf* **1** VIVACIDAD : liveliness **2** BRILLO : vividness, brightness **3** ASTUCIA : cleverness, sharpness

vívidamente *adv* : vividly

vívido, -da *adj* : vivid, lively

vividor, -dora *n* : sponger, parasite

vivienda *nf* **1** : housing **2** MORADA : dwelling, home

viviente *adj* : living

vivificar {72} *vt* : to revitalize, to give life to

vivir *vi* **1** : to live, to be alive ⟨¡viva la democracia! : long live democracy!⟩ **2** SUBSISTIR : to subsist, to make a living **3** RESIDIR : to reside **4** : to spend one's life ⟨vive para trabajar : she lives to work⟩ **5** ~ **de** : to live on — *vt* **1** : to live ⟨vivir su vida : to live one's life⟩ **2** EXPERIMENTAR : to go through, to experience

vivir² *nm* **1** : life, lifestyle **2 de mal vivir** : disreputable

vivisección *nf, pl* **-ciones** : vivisection

vivo, -va *adj* **1** : alive **2** INTENSO : vivid, bright, intense **3** ANIMADO : lively, vivacious **4** ASTUTO : sharp, clever **5 en ~** : live ⟨transmisión en vivo : live broadcast⟩ **6 al rojo vivo** : red-hot

vocablo *nm* PALABRA : word

vocabulario *nm* : vocabulary

vocación *nf, pl* **-ciones** : vocation

vocacional *adj* : vocational

vocal¹ *adj* : vocal

vocal² *nmf* : member (of a committee, board, etc.)

vocal³ *nf* : vowel

vocalista *nmf* CANTANTE : singer, vocalist

vocalizar {21} *vi* : to vocalize

vocear *vi* : to shout

vocerío *nm* : clamor, shouting

vocero, -ra *n* PORTAVOZ : spokesperson, spokesman *m*, spokeswoman *f*

vociferante *adj* : vociferous

vociferar *vi* GRITAR : to shout, to yell

vodevil *nm* : vaudeville

vodka *nm* : vodka

voladizo¹, -za *adj* : projecting

voladizo² *nm* : projection

volador, -dora *adj* : flying

volando *adv* : quickly, in a hurry

volante¹ *adj* : flying

volante² *nm* **1** : steering wheel **2** FOLLETO : flier, circular **4** : shuttlecock **4** : flywheel **5** : balance wheel (of a watch) **6** : ruffle, flounce

volantín *nm, pl* **-tines** : kite

volar {19} *vi* **1** : to fly **2** CORRER : to go quickly, to rush ⟨el tiempo vuela : time flies⟩ ⟨pasar volando : to fly past⟩ **3** DESAPARECER : to disappear ⟨el dinero ya voló : the money's already gone⟩ — *vt* **1** : to blow up, to demolish **2** : to irritate

volátil *adj* : volatile — **volatilidad** *nf*

volcán *nm, pl* **volcanes** : volcano

volcánico, -ca *adj* : volcanic

volcar {82} *vt* **1** : to upset, to knock over, to turn over **2** : to empty out **3** : to make dizzy **4** : to cause a change of mind in **5** : to irritate — *vi* **1** : to overturn, to tip over **2** : to capsize — **volcarse** *vr* **1** : to overturn **2** : to do one's utmost

volea *nf* : volley (in sports)

volear *vi* : to volley (in sports)

voleibol *nm* : volleyball

voleo *nm* **al voleo** : haphazardly, at random

volframio *nm* : wolfram, tungsten

volibol *Car, Hond, Mex* → **voleibol**

volición *nf, pl* **-ciones** : volition

volqué, etc. → **volcar**

voltaje *nm* : voltage ⟨de alto voltaje : high-voltage⟩

voltear *vt* **1** : to turn over, to turn upside down **2** : to reverse, to turn inside out **3** : to turn ⟨voltear la cara : to turn one's head⟩ **4** : to knock down — *vi* **1** : to roll over, to do somersaults **2** : to turn ⟨volteó a la izquierda : he turned left⟩ — **voltearse** *vr* **1** : to turn around **2** : to change one's allegiance

voltereta *nf* : somersault, tumble

voltio *nm* : volt

volubilidad *nf* : fickleness

voluble *adj* : fickle, changeable

volumen *nm, pl* **-lúmenes 1** TOMO : volume, book **2** : capacity, size, bulk **3** CANTIDAD : amount ⟨el volumen de ventas : the volume of sales⟩ **4** : volume, loudness

voluminoso, -sa *adj* : voluminous, massive, bulky

voluntad *nf* **1** : will, volition ⟨por propia voluntad : of one's own free will⟩ **2** DESEO : desire, wish **3** INTENCIÓN : intention **4 a voluntad** : at will **5 buena voluntad** : good will **6 mala voluntad** : ill will **7 fuerza de voluntad** : willpower

voluntariado *nm* : volunteer service ⟨programa de voluntariado : volunteer program⟩

voluntario¹, -ria *adj* : voluntary — **voluntariamente** *adv*

voluntario², -ria *n* : volunteer

voluntarioso, -sa *adj* **1** : stubborn **2** : willing, eager

voluptuosidad *nf* : voluptuousness

voluptuoso, -sa adj : voluptuous — **voluptuosamente** adv

voluta nf : spiral, column (of smoke)

volver {89} vi 1 : to return, to come/go back ⟨volver a casa : to return home⟩ ⟨volver de vacaciones : to get back from vacation⟩ ⟨no vuelvas por aquí : don't come back here⟩ ⟨volver atrás : to turn back⟩ 2 ~ a : to return to ⟨volver al tema : to get back to the subject⟩ ⟨volver a la normalidad : to get back to normal⟩ 3 ~ a : to do again ⟨volvieron a llamar : they called again⟩ ⟨volver a pasar/ ocurrir/suceder : to happen again⟩ 4 **volver en sí** : to come to, to regain consciousness — vt 1 : to turn, to turn over, to turn inside out 2 : to return, to repay, to restore 3 : to cause, to make ⟨la volvía loca : it was driving her crazy⟩ — **volverse** vr 1 : to become ⟨se volvió deprimido : he became depressed⟩ 2 : to turn around

vomitar vi : to vomit — vt 1 : to vomit 2 : to spew out (lava, etc.)

vómito nm 1 : vomiting 2 : vomit

voracidad nf : voracity

vorágine nf : whirlpool, maelstrom

voraz adj, pl **voraces** : voracious — **vorazmente** adv

vórtice nm 1 : whirlpool, vortex 2 TORBELLINO : whirlwind

vos pron (in some regions of Latin America) : you ⟨para vos : for you⟩ ⟨¿vos sos José? : are you José?⟩

vosear vt : to address as **vos**

vosotros, -tras pron pl Spain 1 : you, yourselves 2 : ye

votación nf, pl **-ciones** : vote, voting ⟨someter a votación : to put to a vote, to vote on⟩

votante nmf : voter

votar vi : to vote ⟨votar por : to vote for⟩ ⟨votar a favor de : to vote in favor of⟩ ⟨votar en contra de : to vote against⟩ — vt : to vote for

voto nm 1 : vote 2 : vow (in religion) 3 **votos** nmpl : good wishes

voy → **ir**

voz nf, pl **voces** 1 : voice ⟨alzar la voz : to raise one's voice⟩ 2 : opinion, say 3 GRITO : shout, yell 4 : sound 5 VOCABLO : word, term 6 : rumor 7 **a voces** : loudly, in a loud voice 8 **a voz en cuello** : at the top of one's lungs 9 **dar voces** : to shout 10 **en voz alta** : aloud, in a loud voice 11 **en voz baja** : softly, in a low voice

vudú nm : voodoo

vuelco nm 1 : upset, overturning ⟨dar un vuelco : to overturn⟩ ⟨me dio un vuelco el corazón : my heart skipped a beat⟩ 2 : drastic change, reversal ⟨dar un vuelco inesperado : to take an unexpected turn⟩

vuela, etc. → **volar**

vuelca, vuelque etc. → **volcar**

vuelo nm 1 : flight, flying ⟨alzar el vuelo : to take flight⟩ ⟨remontar el vuelo : to climb, to fly up⟩ 2 : flight (of an aircraft) ⟨un vuelo directo : a direct flight⟩ 3 : flare, fullness (of clothing) 4 **al vuelo** : on the wing

vuelta nf 1 GIRO : turn ⟨se dio la vuelta : he turned around⟩ ⟨vuelta en U : U-turn, about-face⟩ 2 REVOLUCIÓN : circle, revolution ⟨dio la vuelta al mundo : she went around the world⟩ ⟨las ruedas daban vueltas : the wheels were spinning⟩ 3 : flip, turn ⟨le dio la vuelta : she flipped it over⟩ 4 : bend, curve ⟨a la vuelta de la esquina : around the corner⟩ 5 REGRESO : return ⟨de ida y vuelta : round-trip⟩ ⟨a vuelta de correo : by return mail⟩ 6 : round, lap (in sports or games) 7 PASEO : walk, drive, ride ⟨dio una vuelta : he went for a walk⟩ 8 DORSO, REVÉS : back, other side ⟨a la vuelta : on the back⟩ 9 : cuff (of pants) 10 **darle vueltas a algo** : to think something over 11 **darle vuelta a la página** : to move on, to begin a new phase 12 **dar una vuelta de campana** : to roll over (completely) 13 **estar de vuelta** : to be back

vuelto pp → **volver**

vuelve, etc. → **volver**

vuestro[1], -tra adj Spain : your, of yours ⟨vuestros coches : your cars⟩ ⟨una amiga vuestra : a friend of yours⟩

vuestro[2], -tra pron Spain (with definite article) : yours ⟨la vuestra es más grande : yours is bigger⟩ ⟨esos son los vuestros : those are yours⟩

vulgar adj 1 : common 2 : vulgar

vulgaridad nf : vulgarity

vulgarmente adv : vulgarly, popularly

vulgo nm **el vulgo** : the masses, common people

vulnerable adj : vulnerable — **vulnerabilidad** nf

vulnerar vt 1 : to injure, to damage (one's reputation or honor) 2 : to violate, to break (a law or contract)

W

w *nf* : twenty-sixth letter of the Spanish alphabet
wafle *nm* : waffle
waflera *nf* : waffle iron
wapiti *nm*, *pl* **-ties** *or* **-tis** *or* **-ti** : wapiti, elk
wáter → **váter**
web *nmf* : web, World Wide Web
webcam *nf*, *pl* **webcams** : webcam

webmaster *nmf*, *pl* **-ters** : Webmaster
western *nm*, *pl* **westerns** : western
whisky *nm*, *pl* **whiskys** *or* **whiskies** : whiskey
wicca *nf* : Wicca
wiccano, -na *adj & n* : Wiccan
wigwam *nm* : wigwam
windsurf ['winsurf] *nm* : windsurfing

X

x *nf* : twenty-seventh letter of the Spanish alphabet
xenofobia *nf* : xenophobia
xenófobo[1], -ba *adj* : xenophobic
xenófobo[2], -ba *n* : xenophobe

xenón *nm* : xenon
xerografiar *vt* : to photocopy, to xerox
Xerox *marca registrada, f* — used for a photocopier
xilófono *nm* : xylophone

Y

y[1] *nf* : twenty-eighth letter of the Spanish alphabet
y[2] *conj* (**e** *before words beginning with i- or hi-*) **1** : and ⟨mi hermano y yo : my brother and I⟩ ⟨más y más : more and more⟩ ⟨¿y los demás? : and (what about) the others?⟩ **2** (*used in numbers*) ⟨cincuenta y cinco : fifty-five⟩ **3** *fam* : well ⟨y por supuesto : well, of course⟩ **4** ¿**y qué?** : so what?
ya[1] *adv* **1** : already ⟨ya terminó : she's finished already⟩ ⟨ya en los años sesenta : as early as the 1960's⟩ **2** : now, right now ⟨¡hazlo ya! : do it now!⟩ ⟨ya mismo : right away⟩ ⟨desde ya : as of now, immediately⟩ **3** : later, soon ⟨ya iremos : we'll go later on⟩ **4** : no longer, anymore ⟨ya no fuma : he no longer smokes⟩ **5** : yes, right ⟨ya, pero . . . : yes, I know, but . . .⟩ **6** (*used for emphasis*) ⟨¡ya lo sé! : I know!⟩ ⟨ya lo creo : of course⟩ **7 ya no** : not only ⟨no ya lloran sino gritan : they're not only crying but screaming⟩ **8 ya que** : now that, since ⟨ya que sabe la verdad : now that she knows the truth⟩
ya[2] *conj* **ya . . . ya** : whether . . . or, first . . . then ⟨ya le gusta, ya no : first he likes it, then he doesn't⟩
yac *nm* : yak
yacer {90} *vi* : to lie ⟨en esta tumba yacen sus abuelos : his grandparents lie in this grave⟩
yacimiento *nm* : bed, deposit ⟨yacimiento petrolífero : oil field⟩
yaga, etc. → **yacer**
yang *nm* : yang ⟨el yin y el yang : (the) yin and yang⟩
yanqui *adj & nmf* : Yankee
yarda *nf* : yard

yate *nm* : yacht
yayo, yaya *n fam* : grandpa *m*, grandma *f*
yaz, yazca yazga etc. → **yacer**
yedra *nf* : ivy
yegua *nf* : mare
yelmo *nm* : helmet
yema *nf* **1** : bud, shoot **2** : yolk (of an egg) **3 yema del dedo** : fingertip
yen *nm* : yen (currency)
yendo → **ir**
yerba *nf* **1** *or* **yerba mate** : maté **2** → **hierba**
yerga, yergue etc. → **erguir**
yermo[1], -ma *adj* : barren, deserted
yermo[2] *nm* : wasteland
yerno *nm* : son-in-law
yerra, etc. → **errar**
yerro *nm* : blunder, mistake
yesca *nf* : tinder
yeso *nm* **1** : plaster (material) **2** : cast (for a limb) **3** : gypsum
yiddish [ˈjidiʃ] *or* **yidis** [ˈjidis] *adj & nm* : Yiddish
yihad [jiˈad] *nmf*, *pl* **yihads** : jihad — **yihadista** *nmf*
yin *nm* : yin ⟨el yin y el yang : (the) yin and yang⟩
yo[1] *nm* : ego, self
yo[2] *pron* **1** : I ⟨yo la vi : I saw her⟩ ⟨¿quién lo hizo? yo : who did it? I did⟩ **2** : me ⟨todos menos yo : everyone except me⟩ ⟨tan bajo como yo : as short as me⟩ **3 soy yo** : it's me
yodo *nm* : iodine
yoga *nm* : yoga
yogurt *or* **yogur** *nm* : yogurt
Yom Kippur *n* : Yom Kippur
yoyo *or* **yoyó** *nm* : yo-yo
yuca *nf* **1** : yucca (plant) **2** : cassava, manioc

yucateco¹, -ca *adj* : of or from the Yucatán

yucateco², -ca *n* : person from the Yucatán

yudo → **judo**

yugo *nm* : yoke

yugoslavo, -va *adj & n* : Yugoslavian

yugular *adj* : jugular ⟨vena yugular : jugular vein⟩

yungas *nfpl Bol, Chile, Peru* : warm tropical valleys

yunque *nm* : anvil

yunta *nf* : yoke, team (of oxen)

yuppy *nmf, pl* **yuppies** : yuppie

yute *nm* : jute

yuxtaponer {60} *vt* : to juxtapose — **yuxtaposición** *nf*

yuyo *nm* (*in various countries*) **1** : weed **2** : herb

Z

z *nf* : twenty-ninth letter of the Spanish alphabet

zacate *nm CA, Mex* **1** : grass, fodder **2** : hay

zafacón *nm, pl* **-cones** *Car* : wastebasket

zafar *vt* : to loosen, to untie — **zafarse** *vr* **1** : to loosen up, to come undone **2** : to get free of

zafio, -fia *adj* : coarse, crude

zafiro *nm* : sapphire

zaga *nf* **1** : defense (in sports) **2 a la zaga** *or* **en ~** : behind, in the rear

zagual *nm* : paddle (of a canoe)

zaguán *nm, pl* **zaguanes** : front hall, vestibule

zaherir {76} *vt* **1** : to criticize sharply **2** : to wound, to mortify

zahones *nmpl* : chaps

zaino, -na *adj* : chestnut (color)

zalamería *nf* : flattery, sweet talk

zalamero¹, -ra *adj* : flattering, fawning

zalamero², -ra *n* : flatterer

zambullida *nf* : dive, plunge

zambullir {38} *vt* : to dip, to submerge — **zambullirse** *vr* : to dive, to plunge

zamparse *vr* : to gobble, to wolf down (food)

zanahoria *nf* : carrot

zancada *nf* : stride, step

zancadilla *nf* **1** : trip, stumble **2** *fam* : trick, ruse

zanco *nm* : stilt

zancuda *nf* : wading bird

zancudo *nm* MOSQUITO : mosquito

zángano *nm* : drone, male bee

zanja *nf* : ditch, trench

zanjar *vt* ACLARAR : to settle, to clear up, to resolve

zapallo *nm Arg, Chile, Peru, Uru* : pumpkin

zapapico *nm* : pickax

zapata *nf* : brake shoe

zapatear *vi* : to stamp one's feet

zapatería *nf* **1** : shoemaker's, shoe factory **2** : shoe store

zapatero¹, -ra *adj* : dry, tough, poorly cooked

zapatero², -ra *n* : shoemaker, cobbler

zapatilla *nf* **1** PANTUFLA : slipper **2** *Mex* : women's shoe **3** *or* **zapatilla de deporte** : sneaker

zapato *nm* : shoe

zapping [ˈsapin, ˈθapin] *nm* : channel surfing

zar, zarina *n* : czar *m*, czarina *f*

zarandear *vt* **1** : to sift, to sieve **2** : to shake, to jostle, to jiggle

zarapito *nm* : curlew

zarcillo *nm* **1** : earring **2** : tendril (of a plant)

zarigüeya *nf* : opossum

zarpa *nf* : paw

zarpar *vi* : to set sail, to raise anchor

zarpazo *nm* : swipe (with a paw)

zarza *nf* : bramble, blackberry bush

zarzamora *nf* **1** : blackberry **2** : bramble, blackberry bush

zarzaparrilla *nf* : sarsaparilla

zarzuela *nf* : Spanish operetta

zas *interj* : bam!, wham!

zepelín *nm, pl* **-lines** : zeppelin

zeta *nf* : (letter) z

zigoto *nm* : zygote

zigzag *nm, pl* **zigzags** *or* **zigzagues** : zigzag

zigzaguear *vi* : to zigzag

zimbabuense *adj & nmf* : Zimbabwean

zinc *nm* : zinc

zinnia *nf* : zinnia

zíper *nm CA, Mex* : zipper

zócalo *nm Mex* : main square

zodíaco *or* **zodiaco** *nm* : zodiac — **zodiacal** *adj*

zombi *or* **zombie** *nmf* : zombie

zona *nf* : zone, district, area ⟨zona comercial : business district⟩ ⟨zonas rurales/urbanas : rural/urban areas⟩ ⟨zona de conflicto : conflict zone⟩

zonzo¹, -za *adj* : stupid, silly

zonzo², -za *n* : idiot, nitwit

zoo *nm* : zoo

zoología *nf* : zoology

zoológico¹, -ca *adj* : zoological

zoológico² *nm* : zoo

zoólogo, -ga *n* : zoologist

zoom *nm* : zoom lens

zopilote *nm CA, Mex* : buzzard

zoquete *nmf fam* : oaf, blockhead

zorrillo *nm* MOFETA : skunk

zorro¹, -rra *adj* : sly, crafty

zorro², -rra *n* **1** : fox, vixen **2** : sly crafty person

zorzal *nm* : thrush

zozobra *nf* : anxiety, worry

zozobrar *vi* : to capsize

zueco *nm* : clog (shoe)

zulú *adj & nmf, pl* **zulúes** *or* **zulús** *or* **zulú** : Zulu

zulú² *nm* : Zulu (language)
zumaque *nm* : sumac
zumbar *vi* : to buzz, to hum ⟨le zumba-
ban los oídos : her ears were ringing⟩ —
vt fam **1** : to hit, to thrash **2** : to make
fun of
zumbido *nm* : buzzing, humming

zumo *nf* JUGO : juice
zurcir {83} *vt* : to darn, to mend
zurdo¹, -da *adj* : left-handed
zurdo², -da *n* : left-handed person
zurrón *nm, pl* **zurrones** : leather bag
zurza, etc. → zurcir
zutano, -na → fulano

English-Spanish Dictionary

Diccionario Inglés-Español

A

a¹ [ˈeɪ] *n, pl* **a's** *or* **as** [ˈeɪz] **1** : primera letra del alfabeto inglés **2 A** : la *m* ⟨A sharp/flat : la sostenido/bemol⟩

a² [ə, ˈeɪ] (**an** [ən, ˈæn] *before vowel or silent h*) *art* **1** : un *m*, una *f* ⟨a house : una casa⟩ ⟨a little more : un poco más⟩ ⟨half an hour : media hora⟩ ⟨what a surprise! : ¡qué sorpresa!⟩ ⟨she's a lawyer : es abogada⟩ ⟨it's a Rembrandt : es un Rembrandt⟩ ⟨a Mr. Jones called : llamó un tal señor Jones⟩ **2** PER : por, a la, al ⟨30 kilometers an hour : 30 kilómetros por hora⟩ ⟨twice a month : dos veces al mes⟩

a- [ə] *pref* : a-

aardvark [ˈɑrdˌvɑrk] *n* : oso *m* hormiguero

aback [əˈbæk] *adv* **1** : por sorpresa **2 to be taken aback** : quedarse desconcertado

abacus [ˈæbəkəs] *n, pl* **abaci** [ˈæbəˌsaɪ, -ˌkiː] *or* **abacuses** : ábaco *m*

abaft [əˈbæft] *adv* : a popa

abandon¹ [əˈbændən] *vt* **1** DESERT, FORSAKE : abandonar, desamparar (a alguien), desertar de (algo) **2** GIVE UP, SUSPEND : renunciar a, suspender ⟨he abandoned the search : suspendió la búsqueda⟩ **3** EVACUATE, LEAVE : abandonar, evacuar, dejar ⟨to abandon ship : abandonar el buque⟩ **4 to abandon oneself** : entregarse, abandonarse

abandon² *n* : desenfreno *m* ⟨with wild abandon : desenfrenadamente⟩

abandoned [əˈbændənd] *adj* **1** DESERTED : abandonado **2** UNRESTRAINED : desenfrenado, desinhibido

abandonment [əˈbændənmənt] *n* : abandono *m*, desamparo *m*

abase [əˈbeɪs] *vt* **abased; abasing** : degradar, humillar, rebajar

abash [əˈbæʃ] *vt* : avergonzar, abochornar

abashed [əˈbæʃt] *adj* : avergonzado

abate [əˈbeɪt] *vi* **abated; abating** : amainar, menguar, disminuir

abattoir [ˈæbəˌtwɑr] *n* : matadero *m*

abbess [ˈæbɪs, -ˌbɛs, -bəs] *n* : abadesa *f*

abbey [ˈæbi] *n, pl* **-beys** : abadía *f*

abbot [ˈæbət] *n* : abad *m*

abbreviate [əˈbriːviˌeɪt] *vt* **-ated; -ating** : abreviar

abbreviation [ə,briːviˈeɪʃən] *n* : abreviación *f*, abreviatura *f*

ABC's [ˌeɪˌbiːˈsiːz] *npl* : abecé *m*

abdicate [ˈæbdɪˌkeɪt] *v* **-cated; -cating** : abdicar

abdication [ˌæbdɪˈkeɪʃən] *n* : abdicación *f*

abdomen [ˈæbdəmən, æbˈdoːmən] *n* : abdomen *m*, vientre *m*

abdominal [æbˈdɑmənəl] *adj* : abdominal — **abdominally** *adv*

abduct [æbˈdʌkt] *vt* : raptar, secuestrar

abduction [æbˈdʌkʃən] *n* : rapto *m*, secuestro *m*

abductor [æbˈdʌktər] *n* : raptor *m*, -tora *f*; secuestrador *m*, -dora *f*

abed [əˈbɛd] *adv & adj* : en cama

aberrant [æˈbɛrənt, ˈæbərənt] *adj* **1** ABNORMAL : anormal, aberrante **2** ATYPICAL : anómalo, atípico

aberration [ˌæbəˈreɪʃən] *n* **1** : aberración *f* **2** DERANGEMENT : perturbación *f* mental

abet [əˈbɛt] *vt* **abetted; abetting** ASSIST : ayudar ⟨to aid and abet : ser cómplice de⟩

abeyance [əˈbeɪənts] *n* : desuso *m*, suspensión *f*

abhor [əbˈhɔr, æb-] *vt* **-horred; -horring** : abominar, aborrecer

abhorrence [əbˈhɔrənts, æb-] *n* : aborrecimiento *m*, odio *m*

abhorrent [əbˈhɔrənt, æb-] *adj* : abominable, aborrecible, odioso

abide [əˈbaɪd] *v* **abode** [əˈboːd] *or* **abided; abiding** *vt* STAND : soportar, tolerar ⟨I can't abide them : no los puedo ver⟩ — *vi* **1** ENDURE : quedar, permanecer **2** DWELL : morar, residir **3 to abide by** : atenerse a

ability [əˈbɪləti] *n, pl* **-ties 1** CAPABILITY : aptitud *f*, capacidad *f*, facultad *f* **2** COMPETENCE : competencia *f* **3** TALENT : talento *m*, don *m*, habilidad *f*

abject [ˈæbˌdʒɛkt, æbˈ-] *adj* **1** WRETCHED : miserable, desdichado **2** HOPELESS : abatido, desesperado **3** SERVILE : servil ⟨abject flattery : halagos serviles⟩ — **abjectly** *adv*

abjure [əbˈdʒʊr] *vt* **-jured; -juring** : abjurar de

ablaze [əˈbleɪz] *adj* **1** BURNING : ardiendo, en llamas **2** RADIANT : resplandeciente, radiante

able [ˈeɪbəl] *adj* **abler; ablest 1** CAPABLE : capaz, hábil **2** COMPETENT : competente

-able *suf* : -able

ablution [əˈbluːʃən] *n* : ablución *f* ⟨to perform one's ablutions : lavarse⟩

ably [ˈeɪbəli] *adv* : hábilmente, eficientemente

abnormal [æbˈnɔrməl] *adj* : anormal — **abnormally** *adv*

abnormality [ˌæbnərˈmæləti, -nɔr-] *n, pl* **-ties** : anormalidad *f*

aboard¹ [əˈbɔrd] *adv* : a bordo

aboard² *prep* : a bordo de

abode¹ → **abide**

abode² [əˈboːd] *n* : morada *f*, residencia *f*, vivienda *f*

abolish [əˈbɑlɪʃ] *vt* : abolir, suprimir

abolition [ˌæbəˈlɪʃən] *n* : abolición *f*, supresión *f*

abominable [əˈbɑmənəbəl] *adj* DETESTABLE : abominable, aborrecible, espantoso

abominate [əˈbɑməˌneɪt] *vt* **-nated; -nating** : abominar, aborrecer

abomination [ə,bɑməˈneɪʃən] *n* : abominación *f*

aboriginal [ˌæbəˈrɪdʒənəl] *adj* : aborigen, indígena

aborigine [ˌæbəˈrɪdʒəni] *n* NATIVE : aborigen *mf*, indígena *mf*

abort [əˈbɔrt] *vt* 1 : abortar (en medicina) 2 CALL OFF : suspender, abandonar — *vi* : abortar, hacerse un aborto

abortion [əˈbɔrʃən] *n* : aborto *m*

abortive [əˈbɔrtɪv] *adj* UNSUCCESSFUL : fracasado, frustrado, malogrado

abound [əˈbaʊnd] *vi* **to abound in** : abundar en, estar lleno de

about¹ [əˈbaʊt] *adv* 1 APPROXIMATELY : aproximadamente, casi, más o menos ⟨about a hundred dollars : unos cien dólares⟩ 2 AROUND : por todas partes, alrededor ⟨the children are running about : los niños están corriendo por todas partes⟩ 3 **to be about to** : estar a punto de 4 **to be out and about** → out³ 5 **to be up and about** → up³

about² *prep* 1 AROUND : alrededor de (un lugar, una persona, etc.) 2 CONCERNING : de, acerca de, sobre ⟨she always talks about politics : siempre habla de política⟩ ⟨she's worried about him : está preocupada por él⟩ ⟨you need to do something about it : tienes que hacer algo⟩ 3 (*indicating a quality*) ⟨there's something weird about it : hay algo raro (en el asunto)⟩ ⟨there's something about her : tiene algo, tiene un no sé qué⟩ 4 (*indicating manner*) ⟨be quick about it : date prisa, apúrate⟩ 5 **to be (all) about** : tratarse de (dícese de un asunto), ser muy partidario de (dícese de una persona)

about–face [əˈbaʊtˈfeɪs] *n* 1 : media vuelta *f* 2 : cambio *m* total (de opinión, etc.), giro *m* de 180 grados

above¹ [əˈbʌv] *adv* 1 OVERHEAD : por encima, arriba ⟨the floor above : el piso de arriba⟩ ⟨I looked at the sky above : alcé la vista hacia el cielo⟩ 2 : más arriba (as stated above : como se indica más arriba) 3 OVER, MORE : más ⟨groups of six and above : grupos de seis o más⟩ ⟨children age 10 and above : niños a partir de los 10 años⟩ 4 : sobre cero (dícese de temperaturas) 5 **from above** : de arriba, desde arriba ⟨looking down from above : mirando desde arriba⟩ ⟨orders from above : órdenes de arriba⟩

above² *adj* 1 : anterior, antedicho ⟨for the above reasons : por las razones antedichas⟩ 2 **the above** : lo anterior

above³ *prep* 1 OVER : encima de, arriba de, sobre 2 : superior a, por encima de ⟨he's above those things : él está por encima de esas cosas⟩ 3 : más de, superior a ⟨he earns above $50,000 : gana más de $50,000⟩ ⟨a number above 10 : un número superior a 10⟩ 4 **above all** : sobre todo

aboveboard¹ [əˈbʌvˈbord, -ˌbord] *adv or* **open and aboveboard** : sin tapujos

aboveboard² *adj* : legítimo, sincero

aboveground *adj* : sobre el nivel del suelo

abrade [əˈbreɪd] *vt* **abraded; abrading** 1 ERODE : erosionar, corroer 2 SCRAPE : raspar

abrasion [əˈbreɪʒən] *n* 1 SCRAPE, SCRATCH : raspadura *f*, rasguño *m* 2 EROSION : erosión *f*

abrasive¹ [əˈbreɪsɪv] *adj* 1 ROUGH : abrasivo, áspero 2 BRUSQUE, IRRITATING : brusco, irritante

abrasive² *n* : abrasivo *m*

abreast [əˈbrest] *adv* 1 : en fondo, al lado ⟨to march three abreast : marchar de tres en fondo⟩ 2 **to keep abreast** : mantenerse al día

abridge [əˈbrɪdʒ] *vt* **abridged; abridging** : compendiar, resumir

abridgment *or* **abridgement** [əˈbrɪdʒmənt] *n* : compendio *m*, resumen *m*

abroad [əˈbrɔd] *adv* 1 ABOUT, WIDELY : por todas partes, en todas direcciones ⟨the news spread abroad : la noticia corrió por todas partes⟩ 2 OVERSEAS : en el extranjero, en el exterior

abrogate [ˈæbrəˌgeɪt] *vt* **-gated; -gating** : abrogar

abrupt [əˈbrʌpt] *adj* 1 SUDDEN : abrupto, repentino, súbito 2 BRUSQUE, CURT : brusco, cortante — **abruptly** *adv*

abruptness [əˈbrʌptnəs] *n* 1 SUDDENNESS : lo repentino 2 BRUSQUENESS : brusquedad *f*

abscess [ˈæbˌses] *n* : absceso *m*

abscond [æbˈskɑnd] *vi* : huir, fugarse

absence [ˈæbsənts] *n* 1 : ausencia *f* (de una persona) 2 LACK : falta *f*, carencia *f*

absent¹ [æbˈsent] *vt* **to absent oneself** : ausentarse

absent² [ˈæbsənt] *adj* : ausente

absentee [ˌæbsənˈtiː] *n* : ausente *mf*

absentminded [ˌæbsəntˈmaɪndəd] *adj* : distraído, despistado

absentmindedly [ˌæbsəntˈmaɪndədli] *adv* : distraídamente

absentmindedness [ˌæbsəntˈmaɪndədnəs] *n* : distracción *f*, despiste *m*

absolute [ˈæbsəˌluːt, ˌæbsəˈluːt] *adj* 1 COMPLETE, PERFECT : completo, pleno, perfecto 2 UNCONDITIONAL : absoluto, incondicional 3 DEFINITE : categórico, definitivo

absolutely [ˈæbsəˌluːtli, ˌæbsəˈluːtli] *adv* 1 COMPLETELY : completamente, absolutamente 2 CERTAINLY : desde luego ⟨do you agree? absolutely! : ¿estás de acuerdo? ¡desde luego!⟩

absolution [ˌæbsəˈluːʃən] *n* : absolución *f*

absolutism [ˈæbsəˌluːˌtɪzəm] *n* : absolutismo *m*

absolve [əbˈzɑlv, æb-, -ˈsɑlv] *vt* **solved; -solving** : absolver, perdonar

absorb [əbˈzɔrb, æb-, -ˈsɔrb] *vt* 1 : absorber, embeber (un líquido), amortiguar (un golpe, la luz) 2 ENGROSS : absorber 3 ASSIMILATE : asimilar

absorbed [əbˈzɔrbd, æb-, -ˈsɔrbd] *adj* ENGROSSED : absorto, ensimismado

absorbency [əbˈzɔrbəntsi, æb-, -ˈsɔr-] *n* : absorbencia *f*

absorbent [əbˈzɔrbənt, æb-, -ˈsɔr-] *adj* : absorbente

absorbing [əbˈzɔrbɪŋ, æb-, -ˈsɔr-] *adj* : absorbente, fascinante

absorption [əb'zɔrpʃən, æb-, -'sɔrp-] n 1
: absorción f 2 CONCENTRATION : concentración f

abstain [əb'steɪn, æb-] vi : abstenerse

abstainer [əb'steɪnər, æb-] n : abstemio
m, -mia f

abstemious [æb'stiːmiəs] adj : abstemio,
sobrio — **abstemiously** adv

abstention [əb'stɛntʃən, æb-] n : abstención f

abstinence ['æbstənənts] n : abstinencia f

abstract[1] [æb'strækt, 'æb,-] vt 1 EXTRACT
: abstraer, extraer 2 SUMMARIZE : compendiar, resumir

abstract[2] adj : abstracto — **abstractly**
[æb'stræktli, 'æb,-] adv

abstract[3] ['æb,strækt] n : resumen m,
compendio m, sumario m

abstraction [æb'strækʃən] n 1 : abstracción f, idea f abstracta 2 ABSENTMIND-
EDNESS : distracción f

abstruse [əb'struːs, æb-] adj : abstruso,
recóndito — **abstrusely** adv

absurd [əb'sɔrd, -'zɔrd] adj : absurdo,
ridículo, disparatado — **absurdly** adv

absurdity [əb'sɔrdəti, -'zɔr-] n, pl **-ties** 1
: absurdo m 2 NONSENSE : disparate m,
despropósito m

abundance [ə'bʌndənts] n : abundancia f

abundant [ə'bʌndənt] adj : abundante,
cuantioso, copioso

abundantly [ə'bʌndəntli] adv : abundantemente, en abundancia

abuse[1] [ə'bjuːz] vt **abused; abusing** 1
MISUSE : abusar de 2 MISTREAT
: maltratar 3 REVILE : insultar, injuriar,
denostar

abuse[2] [ə'bjuːs] n 1 MISUSE : abuso m 2
MISTREATMENT : abuso m, maltrato
m 3 INSULTS : insultos mpl, impro-
perios mpl ⟨a string of abuse : una serie
de improperios⟩

abuser [ə'bjuːzər] n : abusador m, -dora f

abusive [ə'bjuːsɪv] adj 1 ABUSING : abusivo 2 INSULTING : ofensivo, injurioso,
insultante — **abusively** adv

abut [ə'bʌt] v **abutted; abutting** vt : bordear — vi to abut on : colindar con

abutment [ə'bʌtmənt] n BUTTRESS : contrafuerte m, estribo m

abysmal [ə'bɪzməl] adj TERRIBLE : atroz,
desastroso

abysmally [ə'bɪzməli] adv : desastrosamente, terriblemente

abyss [ə'bɪs, 'æbɪs] n : abismo m, sima f

acacia [ə'keɪʃə] n : acacia f

academic[1] [ˌækə'dɛmɪk] adj 1
: académico 2 THEORETICAL : teórico
— **academically** [-mɪkli] adv

academic[2] n : académico m, -ca f

academician [ˌækədə'mɪʃən] n → academic

academy [ə'kædəmi] n, pl **-mies** : academia f

acanthus [ə'kænθəs] n : acanto m

accede [æk'siːd] vi **-ceded; -ceding** 1
AGREE : acceder, consentir 2 ASCEND
: subir, acceder ⟨he acceded to the
throne : subió al trono⟩

accelerate [ɪk'sɛləˌreɪt, æk-] v **-ated;
-ating** vt : acelerar, apresurar — vi
: acelerar (dícese de un carro)

acceleration [ɪkˌsɛlə'reɪʃən, æk-] n : aceleración f

accelerator [ɪk'sɛləˌreɪtər, æk-] n : acelerador m

accent[1] ['æk,sɛnt, æk'sɛnt] vt : acentuar

accent[2] ['æk,sɛnt, -sənt] n 1 : acento
m 2 EMPHASIS, STRESS : énfasis m, acento m

accentuate [ɪk'sɛntʃuˌeɪt, æk-] vt **-ated;
-ating** : acentuar, poner énfasis en

accept [ɪk'sɛpt, æk-] vt 1 : aceptar 2 AC-
KNOWLEDGE : admitir, reconocer

acceptability [ɪkˌsɛptə'bɪləti, æk-] n
: aceptabilidad f

acceptable [ɪk'sɛptəbəl, æk-] adj : aceptable, admisible — **acceptably** [-bli] adv

acceptance [ɪk'sɛptənts, æk-] n : aceptación f, aprobación f

access[1] ['æk,sɛs] vt : obtener acceso a, entrar a

access[2] n : acceso m

accessibility [ɪkˌsɛsə'bɪləti] n, pl **-ties**
: accesibilidad f

accessible [ɪk'sɛsəbəl, æk-] adj : accesible, asequible

accession [ɪk'sɛʃən, æk-] n 1 : ascenso f,
subida f (al trono, etc.) 2 ACQUISITION
: adquisición f

accessory[1] [ɪk'sɛsəri, æk-] adj : auxiliar

accessory[2] n, pl **-ries** 1 : accesorio m,
complemento m 2 ACCOMPLICE : cóm-
plice mf

accident ['æksədənt] n 1 MISHAP : accidente m 2 CHANCE : casualidad f

accidental [ˌæksə'dɛntəl] adj : accidental,
casual, imprevisto, fortuito

accidentally [ˌæksə'dɛntəli, -'dɛntli] adv 1
BY CHANCE : por casualidad 2 UNIN-
TENTIONALLY : sin querer, involuntaria-
mente

acclaim[1] [ə'kleɪm] vt : aclamar, elogiar

acclaim[2] n : aclamación f, elogio m

acclamation [ˌæklə'meɪʃən] n : aclamación
f

acclimate ['æklə,meɪt, ə'klaɪmət] → **acclimatize**

acclimatize [ə'klaɪmə,taɪz] v **-tized; -tiz-
ing** vt 1 : aclimatar 2 to acclimatize
oneself : aclimatarse

accolade ['ækə,leɪd, -,lɑd] n 1 PRAISE
: elogio m 2 AWARD : galardón m

accommodate [ə'kamə,deɪt] vt **-dated;
-dating** 1 ADAPT : acomodar, adaptar 2
SATISFY : tener en cuenta, satisfacer 3
HOLD : dar cabida a, tener cabida para

accommodating [ə'kamə,deɪtɪŋ] adj
: complaciente, acomodaticio

accommodation [ə,kamə'deɪʃən] n 1
: adaptación f, adecuación f 2 accommodations npl LODGING : alojamiento
m, hospedaje m

accompaniment [ə'kʌmpənəmənt, -'kʌm-]
n : acompañamiento m

accompanist [ə'kʌmpənɪst, -'kʌm-] n
: acompañante mf

accompany [ə'kʌmpəni, -'kʌm-] vt **-nied;
-nying** : acompañar

accomplice [ə'kɑmpləs, -'kʌm-] n : cómplice mf

accomplish [ə'kɑmplɪʃ, -'kʌm-] vt : efectuar, realizar, lograr, llevar a cabo

accomplished [ə'kɑmplɪʃt, -'kʌm-] adj : consumado, logrado

accomplishment [ə'kɑmplɪʃmənt, -'kʌm-] n 1 ACHIEVEMENT : logro m, éxito m 2 SKILL : destreza f, habilidad f

accord¹ [ə'kɔrd] vt GRANT : conceder, otorgar — vi to accord with : concordar con, conformarse con

accord² n 1 AGREEMENT : acuerdo m, convenio m 2 VOLITION : voluntad f ⟨of one's own accord : voluntariamente, de motu proprio⟩

accordance [ə'kɔrdənts] n 1 ACCORD : acuerdo m, conformidad f 2 in accordance with : conforme a, según, de acuerdo con

accordingly [ə'kɔrdɪŋli] adv 1 CORRESPONDINGLY : en consecuencia 2 CONSEQUENTLY : por consiguiente, por lo tanto

according to [ə'kɔrdɪŋ] prep : según, de acuerdo con, conforme a

accordion [ə'kɔrdiən] n : acordeón m

accordionist [ə'kɔrdiənɪst] n : acordeonista mf

accost [ə'kɔst] vt : abordar, dirigirse a

account¹ [ə'kaʊnt] vt : considerar, estimar ⟨he accounts himself lucky : se considera afortunado⟩ — vi to account for : dar cuenta de, explicar

account² n 1 : cuenta f ⟨bank/checking account : cuenta bancaria/corriente⟩ ⟨savings account : cuenta de ahorro(s)⟩ ⟨e-mail account : cuenta de email, cuenta de correo(s) electrónico(s)⟩ 2 EXPLANATION : versión f, explicación f 3 REPORT : relato m, relación f 4 IMPORTANCE : importancia f ⟨to be of no account : no tener importancia⟩ 5 accounts npl : contabilidad f 6 by all accounts : a decir de todos 7 by one's own account ⟨by her own account : según ella misma⟩ 8 on account of BECAUSE OF : a causa de, debido a, por 9 on no account : de ninguna manera 10 on someone's account : por alguien 11 to take into account : tener en cuenta

accountability [ə,kaʊntə'bɪləti] n : responsabilidad f

accountable [ə'kaʊntəbəl] adj : responsable

accountancy [ə'kaʊntəntsi] n : contabilidad f

accountant [ə'kaʊntənt] n : contador m, -dora f; contable mf Spain

accounting [ə'kaʊntɪŋ] n : contabilidad f

accoutrements or accouterments [ə'ku:trəmənts, -'ku:tər-] npl 1 EQUIPMENT : equipo m, avíos mpl 2 ACCESSORIES : accesorios mpl 3 TRAPPINGS : símbolos mpl ⟨the accoutrements of power : los símbolos del poder⟩

accredit [ə'krɛdət] vt : acreditar, autorizar

accreditation [ə,krɛdə'teɪʃən] n : acreditación f, homologación f

accrual [ə'kru:əl] n : incremento m, acumulación f

accrue [ə'kru:] vi -crued; -cruing : acumularse, aumentar

accumulate [ə'kju:mjə,leɪt] v -lated; -lating — vt : acumular, amontonar — vi : acumularse, amontonarse

accumulation [ə,kju:mjə'leɪʃən] n : acumulación f, amontonamiento m

accuracy ['ækjərəsi] n : exactitud f, precisión f

accurate ['ækjərət] adj : exacto, correcto, fiel, preciso — accurately adv

accusation [,ækjə'zeɪʃən] n : acusación f

accusatory [ə'kju:zə,tori] adj : acusatorio

accuse [ə'kju:z] vt -cused; -cusing : acusar, delatar, denunciar

accused [ə'kju:zd] ns & pl DEFENDANT : acusado m, -da f

accuser [ə'kju:zər] n : acusador m, -dora f

accustom [ə'kʌstəm] vt : acostumbrar, habituar

ace ['eɪs] n : as m

acerbic [ə'sərbɪk, æ-] adj : acerbo, mordaz

acetate ['æsə,teɪt] n : acetato m

acetone ['æsə,to:n] n : acetona f

acetylene [ə'sɛtələn, -,li:n] n : acetileno m

ache¹ ['eɪk] vi ached; aching 1 : doler 2 to ache for : anhelar, ansiar

ache² n : dolor m

achieve [ə'tʃi:v] vt achieved; achieving : lograr, alcanzar, conseguir, realizar

achievement [ə'tʃi:vmənt] n : logro m, éxito m, realización f

Achilles' heel [ə'kɪliz-] n : talón m de Aquiles

acid¹ ['æsəd] adj 1 SOUR : ácido, agrio 2 CAUSTIC, SHARP : acerbo, mordaz — acidly adv

acid² n : ácido m

acidic [ə'sɪdɪk, æ-] adj : ácido

acidity [ə'sɪdəti, æ-] n, pl -ties : acidez f

acid rain n : lluvia f ácida

acid test n : prueba f de fuego

acknowledge [ɪk'nɑlɪdʒ, æk-] vt -edged; -edging 1 ADMIT : reconocer, admitir 2 RECOGNIZE : reconocer 3 to acknowledge receipt of : acusar recibo de

acknowledgment [ɪk'nɑlɪdʒmənt, æk-] n 1 RECOGNITION : reconocimiento m 2 THANKS : agradecimiento m

acme ['ækmi] n : colmo m, apogeo m, cúspide f

acne ['ækni] n : acné m

acolyte ['ækə,laɪt] n : acólito m

acorn ['eɪ,kɔrn, -kərn] n : bellota f

acoustic [ə'ku:stɪk] or acoustical [-stɪkəl] adj : acústico — acoustically adv

acoustics [ə'ku:stɪks] ns & pl : acústica f

acquaint [ə'kweɪnt] vt 1 INFORM : enterar, informar 2 FAMILIARIZE : familiarizar 3 to be acquainted with : conocer a (una persona), estar al tanto de (un hecho)

acquaintance [ə'kweɪntənts] n 1 KNOWLEDGE : conocimiento m 2 : co-

nocido m, -da f ⟨friends and acquaintances : amigos y conocidos⟩
acquiesce [ˌækwiˈɛs] vi -esced; -escing : consentir, conformarse
acquiescence [ˌækwiˈɛsənts] n : consentimiento m, aquiescencia f
acquiescent [ˌækwiˈɛsənt] adj : acquiescente
acquire [əˈkwaɪr] vt -quired; -quiring : adquirir, obtener
acquisition [ˌækwəˈzɪʃən] n : adquisición f
acquisitive [əˈkwɪzətɪv] adj : adquisitivo, codicioso
acquit [əˈkwɪt] vt -quitted; -quitting 1 : absolver, exculpar 2 **to acquit oneself** : comportarse, defenderse
acquittal [əˈkwɪtəl] n : absolución f, exculpación f
acre [ˈeɪkər] n : acre m
acreage [ˈeɪkərɪdʒ] n : superficie f en acres
acrid [ˈækrəd] adj 1 BITTER : acre 2 CAUSTIC : acre, mordaz — **acridly** adv
acrimonious [ˌækrəˈmoːniəs] adj : áspero, cáustico, sarcástico
acrimony [ˈækrəˌmoːni] n, pl -nies : acrimonia f
acrobat [ˈækrəˌbæt] n : acróbata mf, saltimbanqui mf
acrobatic [ˌækrəˈbætɪk] adj : acrobático
acrobatics [ˌækrəˈbætɪks] ns & pl : acrobacia f
acronym [ˈækrəˌnɪm] n : acrónimo m
across[1] [əˈkrɔs] adv 1 CROSSWISE : al través 2 : a través, del otro lado ⟨he's already across : ya está del otro lado⟩ 3 : de ancho ⟨40 feet across : 40 pies de ancho⟩
across[2] prep 1 : al otro lado de ⟨across the street : al otro lado de la calle⟩ 2 : a través de ⟨a log across the road : un tronco a través del camino⟩
across–the–board adj : general, para todos
acrylic [əˈkrɪlɪk] n : acrílico m
act[1] [ˈækt] vi 1 : actuar ⟨he acted alone : actuó solo⟩ ⟨she acted courageously : actuó con coraje⟩ ⟨to act in one's own interests : actuar uno en su propio interés⟩ 2 : tomar medidas ⟨he acted to save the business : tomó medidas para salvar el negocio⟩ 3 BEHAVE : comportarse ⟨to act like children : actuar como niños⟩ 4 PERFORM : actuar, interpretar 5 : fingir, simular ⟨he acted as if dumb : hacerse el tonto⟩ ⟨he acted as if nothing had happened : actuó como si no hubiera pasado nada⟩ 6 FUNCTION : actuar, servir, funcionar 7 **to act as** : servir de, hacer de 8 **to act on** : seguir (un consejo, etc.), actuar respecto a 9 **to act on** AFFECT : actuar sobre 10 **to act out** MISBEHAVE : portarse mal (para hacerse notar) 11 **to act out** PERFORM : representar 12 **to act up** MISBEHAVE : portarse mal 13 **to act up** MALFUNCTION : funcionar mal 14 **to act up** WORSEN : agravarse
act[2] n 1 DEED : acto m, hecho m, acción f 2 DECREE : ley f, decreto m 3 : acto m

(en una obra de teatro), número m (en un espectáculo) 4 PRETENSE : fingimiento m
acting[1] [ˈæktɪŋ] adj INTERIM : interino, en funciones
acting[2] n : interpretación f, actuación f
action [ˈækʃən] n 1 DEED : acción f, acto m, hecho m ⟨to take action : tomar medidas⟩ 2 BEHAVIOR : actuación f, comportamiento m 3 LAWSUIT : demanda f 4 MOVEMENT : movimiento m 5 COMBAT : combate m 6 PLOT : acción f, trama f 7 MECHANISM : mecanismo m 8 **in** ∼ : en acción 9 **to go into action** : entrar en acción
activate [ˈæktəˌveɪt] vt -vated; -vating : activar
activation [ˌæktəˈveɪʃən] n : activación f
active [ˈæktɪv] adj 1 MOVING : activo, en movimiento 2 LIVELY : vigoroso, enérgico 3 : en actividad ⟨an active volcano : un volcán en actividad⟩ 4 OPERATIVE : vigente
actively [ˈæktɪvli] adv : activamente, enérgicamente
activist [ˈæktɪvɪst] n : activista mf — **activism** [-ˌvɪzəm] n — **activist** adj
activity [ækˈtɪvəti] n, pl -ties 1 MOVEMENT : actividad f, movimiento m 2 VIGOR : vigor m, energía f 3 OCCUPATION : actividad f, ocupación f
actor [ˈæktər] n : actor m, artista mf
actress [ˈæktrəs] n : actriz f
actual [ˈækt͡ʃuəl] adj : real, verdadero
actuality [ˌækt͡ʃuˈæləti] n, pl -ties : realidad f
actually [ˈækt͡ʃuəli, -ʃəli] adv : realmente, en realidad
actuary [ˈækt͡ʃuˌɛri] n, pl -aries : actuario m, -ria f de seguros — **actuarial** [ˌækt͡ʃuˈɛriəl] adj
acumen [əˈkjuːmən] n : perspicacia f
acupuncture [ˈækjuˌpʌŋkt͡ʃər] n : acupuntura f
acute [əˈkjuːt] adj acuter; acutest 1 SHARP : agudo 2 PERCEPTIVE : perspicaz, sagaz 3 KEEN : fino, muy desarrollado, agudo ⟨an acute sense of smell : un fino olfato⟩ 4 SEVERE : grave 5 **acute angle** : ángulo m agudo
acutely [əˈkjuːtli] adv : intensamente ⟨to be acutely aware : estar perfectamente consciente⟩
acuteness [əˈkjuːtnəs] n : agudeza f
ad [ˈæd] → **advertisement**
adage [ˈædɪdʒ] n : adagio m, refrán m, dicho m
adamant [ˈædəmənt, -ˌmænt] adj : firme, categórico, inflexible — **adamantly** adv
Adam's apple [ˈædəmz] n : nuez f de Adán
adapt [əˈdæpt] vt : adaptar, ajustar — vi : adaptarse
adaptability [əˌdæptəˈbɪləti] n : adaptabilidad f, flexibilidad f
adaptable [əˈdæptəbəl] adj : adaptable, amoldable
adaptation [ˌæˌdæpˈteɪʃən, -dəp-] n 1 : adaptación f, modificación f 2 VERSION : versión f

adapter [ə'dæptər] *n* : adaptador *m*
add ['æd] *vt* 1 : añadir, agregar ⟨add the flour : añadir la harina⟩ 2 : agregar, añadir ⟨to add a comment : añadir una observación⟩ 3 : sumar (números) 4 INCLUDE : incluir 5 **to add up** : sumar ⟨add up the costs : suma los gastos⟩ — *vi* 1 : sumar 2 **to add to** INCREASE : aumentar ⟨to add to the confusion : para aumentar la confusión⟩ 3 **to add up** SQUARE : cuadrar 4 **to add up to** : sumar en total
adder ['ædər] *n* : víbora *f*
addict¹ [ə'dıkt] *vt* : causar adicción en
addict² ['ædıkt] *n* 1 : adicto *m*, -ta *f* 2 **drug addict** : drogadicto *m*, -ta *f*; toxicómano *m*, -na *f*
addicted [ə'dıktəd] *adj* : adicto
addiction [ə'dıkʃən] *n* 1 : adicción *f*, dependencia *f* 2 **drug addiction** : drogadicción *f*
addictive [ə'dıktıv] *adj* : adictivo
addition [ə'dıʃən] *n* 1 : adición *f*, añadidura *f* 2 **in ~** : además, también
additional [ə'dıʃənəl] *adj* : extra, adicional, de más
additionally [ə'dıʃənəli] *adv* : además, adicionalmente
additive ['ædətıv] *n* : aditivo *m*
addle ['ædəl] *vt* **-dled; -dling** : confundir, enturbiar
address¹ [ə'drɛs] *vt* 1 : dirigirse a, pronunciar un discurso ante ⟨to address a jury : dirigirse a un jurado⟩ 2 : dirigir, ponerle la dirección a ⟨to address a letter : dirigir una carta⟩
address² [ə'drɛs, 'æˌdrɛs] *n* 1 SPEECH : discurso *m*, alocución *f* 2 : dirección *f* (de una residencia, etc.)
addressee [ˌæˌdrɛ'siː, ə-] *n* : destinatario *m*, -ria *f*
adduce [ə-'duːs, 'djuːs] *vt* **-duced; -ducing** : aducir
adenoids ['ædˌnɔıd, -dənˌɔıd] *npl* : adenoides *fpl*
adept [ə'dɛpt] *adj* : experto, hábil — **adeptly** *adv*
adequacy ['ædıkwəsi] *n*, *pl* **-cies** : lo adecuado, lo suficiente
adequate ['ædıkwət] *adj* 1 SUFFICIENT : adecuado, suficiente 2 ACCEPTABLE, PASSABLE : adecuado, aceptable
adequately ['ædıkwətli] *adv* : suficientemente, apropiadamente
adhere [æd'hır, əd-] *vi* **-hered; -hering** 1 STICK : pegarse, adherirse 2 **to adhere to** : adherirse a (una política, etc.), cumplir con (una promesa)
adherence [æd'hırənts, əd-] *n* : adhesión *f*, adherencia *f*, observancia *f* (de una ley, etc.)
adherent¹ [æd'hırənt, əd-] *adj* : adherente, adhesivo, pegajoso
adherent² *n* : adepto *m*, -ta *f*; partidario *m*, -ria *f*
adhesion [æd'hiːʒən, əd-] *n* : adhesión *f*, adherencia *f*
adhesive¹ [æd'hiːsıv, əd-, -zıv] *adj* : adhesivo
adhesive² *n* : adhesivo *m*, pegamento *m*

adjacent [ə'dʒeısənt] *adj* : adyacente, colindante, contiguo
adjective ['ædʒıktıv] *n* : adjetivo *m* — **adjectival** [ˌædʒık'taıvəl] *adj*
adjoin [ə'dʒɔın] *vt* : lindar con, colindar con
adjoining [ə'dʒɔınıŋ] *adj* : contiguo, colindante
adjourn [ə'dʒərn] *vt* : levantar, suspender ⟨the meeting is adjourned : se levanta la sesión⟩ — *vi* : aplazarse
adjournment [ə'dʒərnmənt] *n* : suspensión *f*, aplazamiento *m*
adjudicate [ə'dʒuːdıˌkeıt] *vt* **-cated; -cating** : juzgar, arbitrar
adjudication [əˌdʒuːdı'keıʃən] *n* 1 JUDGING : arbitrio *m* (judicial) 2 JUDGMENT : fallo *m*
adjunct ['æˌdʒʌŋkt] *n* : adjunto *m*, complemento *m*
adjust [ə'dʒʌst] *vt* : ajustar, arreglar, regular — *vi* **to adjust to** : adaptarse a
adjustable [ə'dʒʌstəbəl] *adj* : ajustable, regulable, graduable
adjustment [ə'dʒʌstmənt] *n* : ajuste *m*, modificación *f*
ad-lib¹ ['æd'lıb] *v* **-libbed; -libbing** : improvisar
ad-lib² *adj* : improvisado
administer [æd'mınəstər, əd-] *vt* : administrar
administration [ædˌmınə'streıʃən, əd-] *n* 1 MANAGING : administración *f*, dirección *f* 2 GOVERNMENT, MANAGEMENT : administración *f*, gobierno *m*
administrative [æd'mınəˌstreıtıv, əd-] *adj* : administrativo — **administratively** *adv*
administrator [æd'mınəˌstreıtər, əd-] *n* : administrador *m*, -dora *f*
admirable ['ædmərəbəl] *adj* : admirable, loable — **admirably** *adv*
admiral ['ædmərəl] *n* : almirante *mf*
admiralty ['ædmərəlti] *n* : almirantazgo *m*
admiration [ˌædmə'reıʃən] *n* : admiración *f*
admire [æd'maır] *vt* **-mired; -miring** : admirar
admirer [æd'maırər] *n* : admirador *m*, -dora *f*
admiring [æd'maırıŋ] *adj* : admirativo, de admiración
admiringly [æd'maırıŋli] *adv* : con admiración
admissible [æd'mısəbəl] *adj* : admisible, aceptable
admission [æd'mıʃən] *n* 1 ADMITTANCE : entrada *f*, admisión *f* 2 ACKNOWLEDGMENT : reconocimiento *m*, admisión *f*
admit [æd'mıt, əd-] *vt* **-mitted; -mitting** 1 : admitir, dejar entrar ⟨the museum admits children : el museo deja entrar a los niños⟩ 2 ACKNOWLEDGE : reconocer, admitir
admittance [æd'mıtənts, əd-] *n* : admisión *f*, entrada *f*, acceso *m*
admittedly [æd'mıtədli, əd-] *adv* : la verdad es que, lo cierto es que ⟨admittedly we went too fast : la verdad es que fuimos demasiado de prisa⟩
admonish [æd'manıʃ, əd-] *vt* : amonestar, reprender

admonition [ˌædməˈnɪʃən] n : admonición f

ad nauseam [ædˈnɔziəm] adv : hasta la saciedad

ado [əˈduː] n **1** FUSS : ruido m, alboroto m **2** TROUBLE : dificultad f, lío m **3 without further ado** : sin más preámbulos

adobe [əˈdoːbi] n : adobe m

adolescence [ˌædəlˈɛsənts] n : adolescencia f

adolescent¹ [ˌædəlˈɛsənt] adj : adolescente, de adolescencia

adolescent² n : adolescente mf

adopt [əˈdɑpt] vt : adoptar

adopted [əˈdɑptəd] adj : adoptivo

adoption [əˈdɑpʃən] n : adopción f

adoptive [əˈdɑptɪv] adj : adoptivo

adorable [əˈdorəbəl] adj : adorable, encantador

adorably [əˈdorəbli] adv : de manera adorable

adoration [ˌædəˈreɪʃən] n : adoración f

adore [əˈdor] vt **adored; adoring 1** WORSHIP : adorar **2** LOVE : querer, adorar **3** LIKE : encantarle (algo a uno), gustarle mucho (algo a uno) ⟨I adore your new dress : me encanta tu vestido nuevo⟩

adorn [əˈdorn] vt : adornar, ornar, engalanar

adornment [əˈdornmənt] n : adorno m, decoración f

adrenaline [əˈdrɛnələn] n : adrenalina f

adrift [əˈdrɪft] adj & adv : a la deriva

adroit [əˈdrɔɪt] adj : diestro, hábil — **adroitly** adv

adroitness [əˈdrɔɪtnəs] n : destreza f, habilidad f

adulation [ˌædʒəleɪʃən] n : adulación f

adult¹ [əˈdʌlt, ˈæˌdʌlt] adj : adulto

adult² n : adulto m, -ta f

adulterate [əˈdʌltəˌreɪt] vt **-ated; -ating** : adulterar — **adulteration** [əˌdʌltəˈreɪʃən] n

adulterer [əˈdʌltərər] n : adúltero m, -ra f

adulterous [əˈdʌltərəs] adj : adúltero

adultery [əˈdʌltəri] n, pl **-teries** : adulterio m

adulthood [əˈdʌltˌhʊd] n : adultez f, edad f adulta

advance¹ [ædˈvænts, əd-] v **-vanced; -vancing** vt **1** : avanzar, adelantar ⟨to advance troops : avanzar las tropas⟩ **2** PROMOTE : ascender, promover **3** PROPOSE : proponer, presentar **4** : adelantar, anticipar ⟨they advanced me next month's salary : me adelantaron el sueldo del próximo mes⟩ — vi **1** PROCEED : avanzar, adelantarse **2** PROGRESS : progresar

advance² adj : anticipado ⟨advance notice : previo aviso⟩

advance³ n **1** PROGRESSION : avance m **2** PROGRESS : adelanto m, mejora f, progreso m **3** RISE : aumento m, alza f **4** LOAN : anticipo m, préstamo m **5 in ~** : por adelantado

advanced [ædˈvæntst, əd-] adj **1** DEVELOPED : avanzado, desarrollado **2** PRECOCIOUS : adelantado, precoz **3** HIGHER : superior

advancement [ædˈvæntsmənt, əd-] n **1** FURTHERANCE : fomento m, adelantamiento m, progreso m **2** PROMOTION : ascenso m

advantage [ədˈvæntɪʤ, æd-] n **1** SUPERIORITY : ventaja f, superioridad f ⟨to have the/an advantage : tener ventaja⟩ **2** GAIN : provecho m, partido m **3 to take advantage of** : aprovecharse de

advantageous [ˌædˌvænˈteɪʤəs, -vən-] adj : ventajoso, provechoso — **advantageously** adv

advent [ˈædˌvɛnt] n **1 Advent** : Adviento m **2** ARRIVAL : advenimiento m, venida f

adventure [ædˈvɛntʃər, əd-] n : aventura f

adventurer [ædˈvɛntʃərər, əd-] n : aventurero m, -ra f

adventurous [ædˈvɛntʃərəs, əd-] adj **1** : intrépido, aventurero ⟨an adventurous traveler : un viajero intrépido⟩ **2** RISKY : arriesgado, aventurado

adverb [ˈædˌvərb] n : adverbio m — **adverbial** [ædˈvərbiəl] adj

adversary [ˈædvərˌseri] n, pl **-saries** : adversario m, -ria f

adverse [ædˈvərs, ˈædˌ] adj **1** OPPOSING : opuesto, contrario **2** UNFAVORABLE : adverso, desfavorable — **adversely** adv

adversity [ædˈvərsəti, əd-] n, pl **-ties** : adversidad f

advertise [ˈædvərˌtaɪz] v **-tised; -tising** vt : anunciar, hacerle publicidad a — vi : hacer publicidad, hacer propaganda

advertisement [ˈædvərˌtaɪzmənt;, ˌædˈvərtəzmənt] n : anuncio m, aviso m

advertiser [ˈædvərˌtaɪzər] n : anunciante mf

advertising [ˈædvərˌtaɪzɪŋ] n : publicidad f, propaganda f

advice [ædˈvaɪs] n : consejo m, recomendación f ⟨take my advice : sigue mis consejos⟩

advisability [ædˌvaɪzəˈbɪləti, əd-] n : conveniencia f

advisable [ædˈvaɪzəbəl, əd-] adj : aconsejable, recomendable, conveniente

advise [ædˈvaɪz, əd-] v **-vised; -vising** vt **1** COUNSEL : aconsejar, asesorar ⟨I advise that you wait : le aconsejo que espere⟩ ⟨I advise you to wait : le aconsejo esperar⟩ ⟨she advised us against buying it : nos aconsejó que no lo compráramos⟩ **2** RECOMMEND : recomendar ⟨I advise that you wait, I advise waiting : les aconsejo que esperen⟩ ⟨he advised caution : aconsejó actuar con cautela⟩ **3** INFORM : informar, notificar ⟨they advised him of his rights : le informaron de sus derechos⟩ — vi : dar consejo ⟨to advise against : desaconsejar⟩

adviser or **advisor** [ædˈvaɪzər, əd-] n : consejero m, -ra f; asesor m, -sora f

advisory [ædˈvaɪzəri, əd-] adj **1** : consultivo **2 in an advisory capacity** : como asesor

advocacy [ˈædvəkəsi] n : promoción f, apoyo m

advocate¹ [ˈædvəˌkeɪt] vt **-cated; -cating** : recomendar, abogar por, ser partidario de

advocate² ['ædvə,kət] *n* : defensor *m*, -sora *f*; partidario *m*, -ria *f*

adze ['ædz] *n* : azuela *f*

aeon ['i:ən, 'i:,ɑn] *n* : eón *m*, siglo *m*, eternidad *f*

aerate ['ær,eɪt] *vt* **-ated; -ating** : gasear (un líquido), oxigenar (la sangre)

aerial¹ ['æriəl] *adj* : aéreo

aerial² *n* : antena *f*

aerie ['æri, 'ɪri, 'eɪəri] *n* : aguilera *f*

aerobic [,ær'o:bɪk] *adj* : aerobio, aeróbico ⟨aerobic exercises : ejercicios aeróbicos⟩

aerobics [,ær'o:bɪks] *ns & pl* : aeróbic *m*

aerodynamic [,æro:daɪ'næmɪk] *adj* : aerodinámico — **aerodynamically** [-mɪkli] *adv*

aerodynamics [,æro:daɪ'næmɪks] *n* : aerodinámica *f*

aeronautical [,ærə'nɔtɪkəl] *adj* : aeronáutico

aeronautics [,ærə'nɔtɪks] *n* : aeronáutica *f*

aerosol ['ærə,sɔl] *n* : aerosol *m*

aerospace¹ ['æro:,speɪs] *adj* : aeroespacial

aerospace² *n* : espacio *m*

aesthetic [ɛs'θɛtɪk] *adj* : estético — **aesthetically** [-ɪkli] *adv*

aesthetics [ɛs'θɛtɪks] *n* : estética *f*

afar [ə'fɑr] *adv* : lejos, a lo lejos

affability [,æfə'bɪləti] *n* : afabilidad *f*

affable ['æfəbəl] *adj* : afable — **affably** *adv*

affair [ə'fær] *n* **1** MATTER : asunto *m*, cuestión *f*, caso *m* **2** EVENT : ocasión *f*, acontecimiento *m* **3** LIAISON : amorío *m*, aventura *f* **4 business affairs** : negocios *mpl* **5 current affairs** : actualidades *fpl*

affect [ə'fɛkt, æ-] *vt* **1** INFLUENCE, TOUCH : afectar, tocar **2** FEIGN : fingir

affectation [,æ,fɛk'teɪʃən] *n* : afectación *f*

affected [ə'fɛktəd, æ-] *adj* **1** FEIGNED : afectado, fingido **2** MOVED : conmovido

affecting [ə'fɛktɪŋ, æ-] *adj* : conmovedor

affection [ə'fɛkʃən] *n* : afecto *m*, cariño *m*

affectionate [ə'fɛkʃənət] *adj* : afectuoso, cariñoso — **affectionately** *adv*

affidavit [,æfə'deɪvət, 'æfə,-] *n* : declaración *f* jurada, affidávit *m*

affiliate¹ [ə'fɪli,eɪt] *v* **-ated; -ating** *vt* **to be affiliated with** : estar afiliado a

affiliate² [ə'fɪliət] *n* : afiliado *m*, -da *f* (persona), filial *f* (organización)

affiliation [ə,fɪli'eɪʃən] *n* : afiliación *f*, filiación *f*

affinity [ə'fɪnəti] *n, pl* **-ties** : afinidad *f*

affirm [ə'fərm] *vt* : afirmar, aseverar, declarar

affirmation [,æfər'meɪʃən] *n* : afirmación *f*, aserto *m*, declaración *f*

affirmative¹ [ə'fərmətɪv] *adj* : afirmativo ⟨affirmative action : acción afirmativa⟩

affirmative² *n* **1** : afirmativa *f* **2 to answer in the affirmative** : responder afirmativamente, dar una respuesta afirmativa

affix [ə'fɪks] *vt* : fijar, poner, pegar

afflict [ə'flɪkt] *vt* **1** : afligir, aquejar **2 to be afflicted with** : padecer de, sufrir de

affliction [ə'flɪkʃən] *n* **1** TRIBULATION : tribulación *f* **2** AILMENT : enfermedad *f*, padecimiento *m*

affluence ['æ,flu:ənts;, æ'flu:-, ə-] *n* : afluencia *f*, abundancia *f*, prosperidad *f*

affluent ['æ,flu:ənt;, æ'flu:-, ə-] *adj* : próspero, adinerado

afford [ə'ford] *vt* **1** : tener los recursos para, permitirse el lujo de ⟨I can afford it : puedo permitírmelo, tengo con que comprarlo⟩ **2** PROVIDE : ofrecer, proporcionar, dar

affordable [ə'fordəbəl] *adj* : asequible (dícese de precios)

affront¹ [ə'frʌnt] *vt* : afrentar, insultar, ofender

affront² *n* : afrenta *f*, insulto *m*, ofensa *f*

Afghan ['æf,gæn, -gən] *n* : afgano *m*, -na *f* — **Afghan** *adj*

afield [ə'fi:ld] *adv* **farther afield** : más lejos

afire [ə'faɪr] *adj* : ardiendo, en llamas

aflame [ə'fleɪm] *adj* : llameante, en llamas

afloat [ə'flo:t] *adv & adj* : a flote

afoot [ə'fʊt] *adj* **1** WALKING : a pie, andando **2** UNDER WAY : en marcha ⟨something suspicious is afoot : algo sospechoso se está tramando⟩

aforementioned [ə'for'mentʃənd] *adj* : antedicho, susodicho

aforesaid [ə'for,sɛd] *adj* : antes mencionado, antedicho

afraid [ə'freɪd] *adj* **1 to be afraid** : tener miedo ⟨she's afraid of the dark : le tiene miedo a la oscuridad⟩ ⟨I was afraid to look down : me daba miedo mirar para abajo⟩ **2 to be afraid that** : temerse que ⟨I'm afraid not : me temo que no⟩

afresh [ə'frɛʃ] *adv* **1** : de nuevo, otra vez **2 to start afresh** : volver a empezar

African ['æfrɪkən] *n* : africano *m*, -na *f* — **African** *adj*

African–American¹ [,æfrɪkənə'mɛrɪkən] *adj* : afroamericano

African–American² *n* : afroamericano *m*, -na *f*

Afro–American¹ [,æfro:ə'mɛrɪkən] *adj* → **African–American¹**

Afro–American² *n* → **African–American²**

aft ['æft] *adv* : a popa

after¹ ['æftər] *adv* **1** AFTERWARD : después **2** BEHIND : detrás, atrás

after² *adj* : posterior, siguiente ⟨in after years : en los años posteriores⟩

after³ *conj* : después de, después de que ⟨after we ate : después de que comimos, después de comer⟩

after⁴ *prep* **1** FOLLOWING : después de, tras ⟨after Saturday/lunch : después del sábado/almuerzo⟩ ⟨after a year : después de un año⟩ ⟨day after day : día tras día⟩ ⟨the day after tomorrow : pasado mañana⟩ ⟨it's ten (minutes) after six : son las seis y diez⟩ ⟨I shouted after him : le grité (mientras se alejaba)⟩ ⟨I'm not cleaning up after you : no voy a limpiar lo que tú ensucias⟩ **2** BEHIND : tras, detrás de ⟨she ran after the dog : corrió tras el perro⟩ **3** CONCERNING : por ⟨they asked after you : preguntaron por ti⟩ **4** CONSIDERING : después de 5 PURSUING : tras ⟨to be after someone : andar tras alguien⟩ 6 : al estilo de ⟨to be named after : llevar el nombre de⟩ ⟨to take after : parecerse a⟩ 7 after all : después de todo

aftereffect ['æftərɪ,fɛkt] n : efecto m secundario

afterlife ['æftər,laɪf] n : vida f venidera, vida f después de la muerte

aftermath ['æftər,mæθ] n : consecuencias fpl, resultados mpl

afternoon [,æftər'nu:n] n : tarde f

aftershave ['æftər,ʃeɪv] n : aftershave m, loción f para después de afeitarse

aftershock ['æftər,ʃak] n : réplica f (de un terremoto)

aftertaste ['æftər,teɪst] n : resabio m, regusto m

afterthought ['æftər,θɔt] n : ocurrencia f tardía, idea f tardía

afterward ['æftərwərd] or **afterwards** [-wərdz] adv : después, luego ⟨soon afterward : poco después⟩

again [ə'gɛn, -'gɪn] adv 1 ANEW, OVER : de nuevo, otra vez ⟨all over again : otra vez desde el principio⟩ ⟨never again : nunca más⟩ ⟨again and again : una y otra vez⟩ 2 BESIDES : además 3 then again : por otra parte ⟨I may stay, then again I may not : puede ser que me quede, por otra parte, puede que no⟩

against [ə'gɛnst, -'gɪnst] prep 1 TOUCHING : contra ⟨against the wall : contra la pared⟩ 2 OPPOSING : contra, en contra de ⟨I voted against the proposal : voté en contra de la propuesta⟩ ⟨he acted against my advice : no siguió mi consejo⟩ ⟨against her wishes/will : en contra de su voluntad⟩

agape [ə'geɪp] adj : boquiabierto

agate ['ægət] n : ágata f

age¹ ['eɪdʒ] vi **aged; aging** : envejecer, madurar

age² n 1 : edad f ⟨ten years of age : diez años de edad⟩ ⟨at the age of 35 : a los 35 años, a la edad de 35⟩ ⟨at your age : a tu edad⟩ ⟨people of all ages : personas de todas las edades⟩ ⟨those under age 18 : los menores de 18 años⟩ ⟨from an early age : desde pequeño⟩ ⟨to be of age : ser mayor de edad⟩ ⟨to come of age : cumplir la mayoría de edad⟩ ⟨he came of age as a writer : alcanzó su madurez como escritor⟩ ⟨to act one's age : actuar con madurez⟩ 2 PERIOD : era f, siglo m, época f 3 old age : vejez f 4 ages npl : siglos mpl, eternidad f ⟨it's been ages since I've seen her : hace mucho tiempo que no la veo⟩

aged adj 1 ['eɪdʒəd, 'eɪdʒd] OLD : anciano, viejo, vetusto 2 ['eɪdʒd] (indicating a specified age) ⟨a girl aged 10 : una niña de 10 años de edad⟩

ageless ['eɪdʒləs] adj 1 YOUTHFUL : eternamente joven 2 TIMELESS : eterno, perenne

agency ['eɪdʒəntsi] n, pl **-cies** 1 : agencia f, oficina f ⟨travel agency : agencia de viajes⟩ 2 through the agency of : a través de, por medio de

agenda [ə'dʒɛndə] n : agenda f, orden m del día

agender [eɪ'dʒɛndər] adj : agénero ⟨agender people : las personas agénero⟩

agent ['eɪdʒənt] n 1 MEANS : agente m, medio m, instrumento m 2 REPRESENTATIVE : agente mf, representante mf

aggravate ['ægrə,veɪt] vt **-vated; -vating** 1 WORSEN : agravar, empeorar 2 ANNOY : irritar, exasperar

aggravation [,ægrə'veɪʃən] n 1 WORSENING : empeoramiento m 2 ANNOYANCE : molestia f, irritación f, exasperación f

aggregate¹ ['ægrɪ,geɪt] vt **-gated; -gating** : juntar, sumar

aggregate² ['ægrɪgət] adj : total, global, conjunto

aggregate³ ['ægrɪgət] n 1 CONGLOMERATE : agregado m, conglomerado m 2 WHOLE : total m, conjunto m

aggression [ə'grɛʃən] n 1 ATTACK : agresión f 2 AGGRESSIVENESS : agresividad f

aggressive [ə'grɛsɪv] adj : agresivo — **aggressively** adv

aggressiveness [ə'grɛsɪvnəs] n : agresividad f

aggressor [ə'grɛsər] n : agresor m, -sora f

aggrieved [ə'gri:vd] adj : ofendido, herido

aghast [ə'gæst] adj : espantado, aterrado, horrorizado

agile ['ædʒəl] adj : ágil

agility [ə'dʒɪləti] n, pl **-ties** : agilidad f

aging¹ ['eɪdʒɪŋ] adj 1 : envejecido 2 : anticuado

aging² ['eɪdʒɪŋ] n : envejecimiento m

agitate ['ædʒə,teɪt] v **-tated; -tating** vt 1 SHAKE : agitar 2 UPSET : inquietar, perturbar — vi to agitate against : hacer campaña en contra de

agitated ['ædʒə,teɪtəd] adj : agitado, inquieto

agitation [,ædʒə'teɪʃən] n : agitación f, inquietud f

agitator ['ædʒə,teɪtər] n : agitador m, -dora f

agnostic [æg'nɑstɪk] n : agnóstico m, -ca f

ago [ə'go:] adv : hace ⟨two years ago : hace dos años⟩ ⟨long ago : hace tiempo, hace mucho tiempo⟩

agog [ə'gɑg] adj : ansioso, curioso

agonize ['ægə,naɪz] vi **-nized; -nizing** 1 : atormentarse, angustiarse 2 to agonize over : preocuparse mucho por

agonizing ['ægə,naɪzɪŋ] adj : angustioso, terrible — **agonizingly** [-zɪŋli] adv

agony ['ægəni] n, pl **-nies** 1 PAIN : dolor m 2 ANGUISH : angustia f

agrarian [ə'grɛriən] adj : agrario

agree [ə'gri:] v **-greed; agreeing** vt 1 : estar de acuerdo ⟨we all agree that . . . : todos estamos de acuerdo que . . .⟩ 2 ADMIT, CONCEDE : reconocer, admitir 3 : acceder a, consentir en ⟨she agreed to come : accedió a venir⟩ ⟨she agreed that she could come : consintió en que viniera⟩ ⟨she agreed to be interviewed : concedió una entrevista⟩ — vi 1 CON-

CUR : estar de acuerdo ⟨to agree with someone/something : estar de acuerdo con alguien/algo⟩ ⟨we agree on/about . . . : estamos de acuerdo en . . .⟩ ⟨we can't agree on a date : no nos ponemos de acuerdo en la fecha⟩ **2** TALLY, SQUARE : concordar **3** : concordar (en gramática) **4 to agree on** : ponerse de acuerdo en **5 to agree to** : acceder a ⟨he agreed to the plan : accedió al plan⟩ **6 to agree with** SUIT : sentarle bien (a alguien)

agreeable [ə'griːəbəl] *adj* **1** PLEASANT : agradable, simpático **2** WILLING : dispuesto **3** ACCEPTABLE : aceptable ⟨is it agreeable to you? : ¿te parece bien?⟩

agreeableness [ə'griːəbəlnəs] *n* **1** PLEASANTNESS : simpatía *f* **2** WILLINGNESS : disposición *f*, buena voluntad *f* **3** ACCEPTABILITY : aceptabilidad *f*

agreeably [ə'griːəbli] *adv* : agradablemente

agreement [ə'griːmənt] *n* **1** : acuerdo *m*, conformidad *f* ⟨in agreement with : de acuerdo con⟩ **2** CONTRACT, PACT : acuerdo *m*, pacto *m*, convenio *m* **3** CONCORD, HARMONY : concordia *f*

agribusiness ['ægrɪˌbɪznəs, -nəz] *n* : agroindustria *f*

agricultural [ˌægrɪ'kʌltʃərəl] *n* : agrícola *f*

agriculture ['ægrɪˌkʌltʃər] *n* : agricultura *f*

aground [ə'graʊnd] *adj* : encallado, varado

ahead [ə'hed] *adv* **1** : al frente, delante, adelante ⟨he walked ahead : caminó delante⟩ ⟨to go straight ahead : ir todo recto⟩ **2** BEFOREHAND : por adelantado, con antelación **3** LEADING : a la delantera **4 to get ahead** : adelantar, progresar **5 to look/think ahead** : mirar hacia el futuro

ahead of *prep* **1** : al frente de, delante de, antes de **2 to get ahead of** : adelantarse a

ahem [ə'hem] *interj* : ¡ejem!

ahoy [ə'hɔɪ] *interj* ship ahoy! : ¡barco a la vista!

aid[1] ['eɪd] *vt* : ayudar, auxiliar

aid[2] *n* **1** HELP : ayuda *f*, asistencia *f* **2** ASSISTANT : asistente *mf*

aide ['eɪd] *n* : ayudante *mf*

AIDS ['eɪdz] *n* : SIDA *m*, sida *m*

ail ['eɪl] *vt* : molestar, afligir — *vi* : sufrir, estar enfermo

aileron ['eɪləˌrɑn] *n* : alerón *m*

ailment ['eɪlmənt] *n* : enfermedad *f*, dolencia *f*, achaque *m*

aim[1] ['eɪm] *vt* **1** POINT : apuntar (un arma, una cámara, etc.) **2** DIRECT : dirigir ⟨he aimed the stone at the window : arrojó la piedra hacia la ventana⟩ ⟨a well-aimed blow : un golpe certero⟩ **3** INTEND : proponerse, querer ⟨he aims to do it tonight : se propone hacerlo esta noche⟩ ⟨we aim to please : nuestro objetivo es complacer⟩ **4 to be aimed at** ⟨his criticism wasn't aimed at her : sus críticas no iban dirigidas a ella⟩ ⟨it's aimed at reducing costs : tiene como objetivo la reducción de gastos⟩ — *vi* **1**

POINT : apuntar ⟨she aimed at the target : le apuntó al blanco⟩ **2** ASPIRE : aspirar ⟨to aim high/low : aspirar a mucho/poco⟩ **3 to aim at/for** ⟨it aims at reducing costs : tiene como objetivo la reducción de gastos⟩ ⟨to aim for a goal : proponerse como meta⟩

aim[2] *n* **1** MARKSMANSHIP : puntería *f* **2** GOAL : propósito *m*, objetivo *m*, fin *m*

aimless ['eɪmləs] *adj* : sin rumbo, sin objeto

aimlessly ['eɪmləsli] *adv* : sin rumbo, sin objeto

ain't ['eɪnt] *fam contraction of* AM NOT *or* ARE NOT *or* IS NOT *or* HAVE NOT *or* HAD NOT → **be, have**

air[1] ['ær] *vt* **1** *or* **to air out** : airear, ventilar ⟨to air out a mattress : airear un colchón⟩ **2** EXPRESS : airear, manifestar, comunicar **3** BROADCAST : transmitir, emitir

air[2] *n* **1** : aire *m* ⟨in the open air : al aire libre⟩ ⟨to vanish into thin air : desaparecerse⟩ **2** MELODY : aire *m* **3** APPEARANCE : aire *m*, aspecto *m* **4** → **air-conditioning** **5 airs** *npl* : aires *mpl*, afectación *f* **6 by ~** : por avión (dícese de una carta), en avión (dícese de una persona) **7 to be on the air** : estar en el aire, estar emitiendo **8 to be up in the air** : estar en el aire, no estar resuelto

airbag ['ærˌbæg] *n* : bolsa *f* de aire, airbag *m*

airbase ['ærˌbeɪs] *n* : base *f* aérea

airborne ['ærˌbɔrn] *adj* **1** : aerotransportado ⟨airborne troops : tropas aerotransportadas⟩ **2** FLYING : volando, en el aire

air-condition [ˌærkən'dɪʃən] *vt* : climatizar, condicionar con el aire

air-conditioned [-ʃənd] *adj* : climatizado, con aire acondicionado

air conditioner [ˌærkən'dɪʃənər] *n* : acondicionador *m* de aire

air-conditioning [ˌærkən'dɪʃənɪŋ] *n* : aire *m* acondicionado

aircraft ['ærˌkræft] *ns & pl* **1** : avión *m*, aeronave *f* **2 aircraft carrier** : portaaviones *m*

airfield ['ærˌfiːld] *n* : aeródromo *m*, campo *m* de aviación

air force *n* : fuerza *f* aérea

airlift ['ærˌlɪft] *n* : puente *m* aéreo, transporte *m* aéreo

airline ['ærˌlaɪn] *n* : aerolínea *f*, línea *f* aérea

airliner ['ærˌlaɪnər] *n* : avión *m* de pasajeros

airmail[1] ['ærˌmeɪl] *vt* : enviar por vía aérea

airmail[2] *n* : correo *m* aéreo

airman ['ærmən] *n*, *pl* **-men** [-mən, -ˌmen] **1** AVIATOR : aviador *m*, -dora *f* **2** : soldado *m* de la fuerza aérea

airplane ['ærˌpleɪn] *n* : avión *m*

airport ['ærˌpɔrt] *n* : aeropuerto *m*

airship ['ærˌʃɪp] *n* : dirigible *m*, zepelín *m*

airsick ['ærˌsɪk] *adj* : mareado (al viajar en avión)

airstrip ['ærˌstrɪp] *n* : pista *f* de aterrizaje

airtight ['ær'taɪt] *adj* : hermético, herméticamente cerrado

air vent → **vent²**

airwaves ['ær,weɪvz] *npl* : radio *m*, televisión *f*

airy ['æri] *adj* **airier** [-iər]; **-est** **1** DELICATE, LIGHT : delicado, ligero **2** BREEZY : aireado, bien ventilado

aisle ['aɪl] *n* : pasillo *m*, nave *f* lateral (de una iglesia)

ajar [ə'dʒɑr] *adj* : entreabierto, entornado

akimbo [ə'kɪmbo] *adj & adv* : en jarras

akin [ə'kɪn] *adj* **1** RELATED : emparentado **2** SIMILAR : semejante, parecido

alabaster ['ælə,bæstər] *n* : alabastro *m*

alacrity [ə'lækrəṭi] *n* : presteza *f*, prontitud *f*

alarm¹ [ə'lɑrm] *vt* **1** WARN : alarmar, alertar **2** FRIGHTEN : asustar

alarm² *n* **1** WARNING : alarma *f*, alerta *f* **2** APPREHENSION, FEAR : aprensión *f*, inquietud *f*, temor *m* **3** alarm clock : despertador *m*

alarming [ə'lɑrmɪŋ] *adj* : alarmante

alas [ə'læs] *interj* : ¡ay!

Albanian [æl'beɪniən] *n* : albanés *m*, -nesa *f* — **Albanian** *adj*

albatross ['ælbə,trɔs] *n, pl* **-tross** or **-trosses** : albatros *m*

albeit [ɔl'bi:ət, æl-] *conj* : aunque

albino [æl'baɪno] *n, pl* **-nos** : albino *m*, -na *f*

album ['ælbəm] *n* : álbum *m* ⟨photo album : álbum de fotos⟩

albumen [æl'bju:mən] *n* **1** : clara *f* de huevo **2** → **albumin**

albumin [æl'bju:mən] *n* : albúmina *f*

alchemist ['ælkəmɪst] *n* : alquimista *mf*

alchemy ['ælkəmi] *n, pl* **-mies** : alquimia *f*

alcohol ['ælkə,hɔl] *n* **1** ETHANOL : alcohol *m*, etanol *m* **2** LIQUOR : alcohol *m*, bebidas *fpl* alcohólicas

alcohol–free *adj* : sin alcohol

alcoholic¹ ['ælkə'hɔlɪk] *adj* : alcohólico

alcoholic² *n* : alcohólico *m*, -ca *f*

alcoholism ['ælkəhə,lɪzəm] *n* : alcoholismo *m*

alcove ['æl,ko:v] *n* : nicho *m*, hueco *m*

alderman ['ɔldərmən] *n, pl* **-men** [-mən, -,mɛn] : concejal *mf*

ale ['eɪl] *n* : cerveza *f*

alert¹ [ə'lərt] *vt* : alertar, poner sobre aviso

alert² *adj* **1** WATCHFUL : alerta, vigilante **2** QUICK : listo, vivo

alert³ *n* : alerta *f*, alarma *f*

alertly [ə'lərtli] *adv* : con listeza

alertness [ə'lərtnəs] *n* **1** WATCHFULNESS : vigilancia *f* **2** ASTUTENESS : listeza *f*, viveza *f*

alfalfa [æl'fælfə] *n* : alfalfa *f*

alga ['ælgə] *n, pl* **-gae** ['æl,dʒi:] : alga *f*

algebra ['ældʒəbrə] *n* : álgebra *m*

algebraic [,ældʒə'breɪk] *adj* : algebraico — **algebraically** [-ikli] *adv*

Algerian [æl'dʒɪriən] *n* : argelino *m*, -na *f* — **Algerian** *adj*

algorithm ['ælgə,rɪðəm] *n* : algoritmo *m*

alias¹ ['eɪliəs] *adv* : alias

alias² *n* : alias *m*

alibi ['ælə,baɪ] *vi* : ofrecer una coartada

alibi² *n* **1** : coartada *f* **2** EXCUSE : pretexto *m*, excusa *f*

alien¹ ['eɪliən] *adj* **1** STRANGE : ajeno, extraño **2** FOREIGN : extranjero, foráneo **3** EXTRATERRESTRIAL : extraterrestre

alien² *n* **1** FOREIGNER : extranjero *m*, -ra *f*; forastero *m*, -ra *f* **2** EXTRATERRESTRIAL : extraterrestre *mf*

alienate ['eɪliə,neɪt] *vt* **-ated; -ating** **1** ESTRANGE : alienar, enajenar **2** to alienate oneself : alejarse, distanciarse

alienation [,eɪliə'neɪʃən] *n* : alienación *f*, enajenación *f*

alight [ə'laɪt] *vi* **1** DISMOUNT : bajarse, apearse **2** LAND : posarse, aterrizar

align [ə'laɪn] *vt* : alinear

alignment [ə'laɪnmənt] *n* : alineación *f*, alineamiento *m*

alike¹ [ə'laɪk] *adv* : igual, del mismo modo

alike² *adj* : igual, semejante, parecido

alimentary [,ælə'mɛntəri] *adj* **1** : alimenticio **2** alimentary canal : tubo *m* digestivo

alimony ['ælə,mo:ni] *n, pl* **-nies** : pensión *f* alimenticia

alive [ə'laɪv] *adj* **1** LIVING : vivo, viviente ⟨alive and kicking : vivito y coleando⟩ **2** LIVELY : animado, activo **3** ACTIVE : vigente, en uso **4** AWARE : consciente ⟨alive to the danger : consciente del peligro⟩

alkali ['ælkə,laɪ] *n, pl* **-lies** [-,laɪz] or **-lis** [-,laɪz] : álcali *m*

alkaline ['ælkələn, -,laɪn] *adj* : alcalino

all¹ ['ɔl] *adv* **1** COMPLETELY : todo, completamente ⟨all wet : todo mojado⟩ ⟨all alone : completamente solo⟩ ⟨all too often : con demasiada frecuencia⟩ ⟨it's all yours : es todo para ti⟩ ⟨I'm all for it : estoy totalmente a su favor⟩ ⟨she forgot all about it : lo olvidó por completo⟩ **2** : igual ⟨the score is 14 all : es 14 iguales, están empatados a 14⟩ **3** all around : para todos **4** all but ALMOST : casi **5** ~ of ONLY : sólo, solamente **6** ~ of AT LEAST : por lo menos **7** ~ over EVERYWHERE : por todas partes **8** ~ over *fam* ⟨to be all over someone for something : criticar duramente a alguien por algo⟩ **9** ~ over : aglomerados alrededor de ⟨to be all over each other : estar muy acaramelados⟩ **10** all that : tan ⟨it hasn't changed all that much : no ha cambiado tanto/demasiado⟩ ⟨it's not all that bad : no es para tanto⟩ **11** all the better : tanto mejor **12** all the more : aún más, todavía más

all² *adj* : todo ⟨all the children : todos los niños⟩ ⟨in all likelihood : con toda probabilidad, con la mayor probabilidad⟩ ⟨all night : toda la noche⟩ ⟨people of all kinds : gente de todo tipo⟩

all³ *pron* **1** : todo ⟨they ate it all : lo comieron todo⟩ ⟨that's all : eso es todo⟩ ⟨enough for all : suficiente para todos⟩ ⟨the best of all : el mejor de todos⟩ ⟨some of the girls, but not all : algunas de las muchachas, pero no todas⟩ ⟨all I know is that . . . : lo único que sé es que . . . , todo lo que sé es que . . .⟩ ⟨for all I know : que yo sepa⟩ **2 all in all** : en general **3 all told** *or* **in all** : en total **4 and all** : y todo eso **5 at all** (*in questions*) ⟨did you find out anything at all? : ¿supiste algo?⟩ **6 (not) at all** (*in negative constructions*) : en absoluto, para nada ⟨he did nothing at all, he didn't do anything at all : no hizo nada en absoluto⟩ ⟨I don't like it at all : no me gusta para nada⟩ **7 to give it one's all** : dar todo de sí **8 when all is said and done** : a fin de cuentas

Allah [ˈɑlə, ɑˈlɑ] *n* : Alá *m*

all–around [ˌɔlɔˈraʊnd] *adj* : completo, amplio

allay [əˈleɪ] *vt* **1** ALLEVIATE : aliviar, mitigar **2** CALM : aquietar, calmar

allegation [ˌælɪˈɡeɪʃən] *n* : alegato *m*, acusación *f*

allege [əˈlɛdʒ] *vt* **-leged; -leging 1** : alegar, afirmar **2 to be alleged** : decirse, pretenderse ⟨she is alleged to be wealthy : se dice que es adinerada⟩

alleged [əˈlɛdʒd, əˈlɛdʒəd] *adj* : presunto, supuesto

allegedly [əˈlɛdʒədli] *adv* : supuestamente, según se alega

allegiance [əˈliːdʒənts] *n* : lealtad *f*, fidelidad *f* ⟨to pledge allegiance to : jurar lealtad a⟩

allegorical [ˌæləˈɡɔrɪkəl] *adj* : alegórico

allegory [ˈæləˌɡori] *n*, *pl* **-ries** : alegoría *f*

alleluia [ˌɑləˈluːjə, ˌæ-] → **hallelujah**

allergen [ˈælərdʒən] *n* : alérgeno *m*

allergic [əˈlərdʒɪk] *adj* : alérgico

allergy [ˈælərdʒi] *n*, *pl* **-gies** : alergia *f*

alleviate [əˈliːviˌeɪt] *vt* **-ated; -ating** : aliviar, mitigar, paliar

alleviation [əˌliːviˈeɪʃən] *n* : alivio *m*

alley [ˈæli] *n*, *pl* **-leys 1** : callejón *m* **2 bowling alley** : bolera *f*

alliance [əˈlaɪənts] *n* : alianza *f*, coalición *f*

alligator [ˈæləˌɡeɪtər] *n* : caimán *m*

all–important [ˌɔlɪmˈpɔrtənt] *adj* : crucial, de fundamental importancia

alliteration [əˌlɪtəˈreɪʃən] *n* : aliteración *f*

all–night [ˈɔlˈnaɪt] *adj* **1** : que dura toda la noche (dícese de una fiesta, etc.) **2** : que está abierto toda la noche (dícese de un restaurante, etc.)

all–nighter [ˈɔlˈnaɪtər] *n fam* **to pull an all–nighter** : trasnochar (estudiando, etc.)

allocate [ˈæləˌkeɪt] *vt* **-cated; -cating** : asignar, adjudicar

allocation [ˌæləˈkeɪʃən] *n* : asignación *f*, reparto *m*, distribución *f*

allot [əˈlɑt] *vt* **-lotted; -lotting** : repartir, distribuir, asignar

allotment [əˈlɑtmənt] *n* : reparto *m*, asignación *f*, distribución *f*

all–out [ˈɔlˈaʊt] *adj* : total, con todo ⟨all-out war : guerra sin cuartel⟩

allow [əˈlaʊ] *vt* **1** PERMIT : permitir, dejar ⟨she allowed him to leave : le permitió irse, le permitió que se fuera⟩ ⟨we won't allow that to happen : no permitiremos que eso pase⟩ ⟨it allows you to create web pages : permite crear páginas web⟩ ⟨no dogs allowed : no se admiten perros⟩ **2** ALLOT : conceder, dar (tiempo, etc.) **3** ADMIT, CONCEDE : admitir, conceder **4** : admitir (pruebas) — *vi* **to allow for** : tener en cuenta

allowable [əˈlaʊəbəl] *adj* **1** PERMISSIBLE : permisible, lícito **2** : deducible ⟨allowable expenditure : gasto deducible⟩

allowance [əˈlaʊənts] *n* **1** : complemento *m* (para gastos, etc.), mesada *f* (para niños) **2 to make allowance(s)** : tener en cuenta, disculpar

alloy [ˈælˌlɔɪ] *n* : aleación *f*

all–purpose [ˈɔlˈpərpəs] *adj* : multiuso ⟨all-purpose flour : harina común⟩

all right[1] *adv* **1** YES : sí, por supuesto **2** WELL : bien ⟨I did all right : me fue bien⟩ **3** DEFINITELY : bien, ciertamente, sin duda ⟨he's sick all right : está bien enfermo⟩

all right[2] *adj* **1** OK : bien ⟨are you all right? : ¿estás bien?⟩ **2** SATISFACTORY : bien, bueno ⟨your work is all right : tu trabajo es bueno⟩

all–round [ˈɔlˈraʊnd] → **all-around**

allspice [ˈɔlspaɪs] *n* : pimienta *f* de Jamaica

all–terrain vehicle [ˈɔltəˈreɪn-] *n* : todoterreno *m*, vehículo *m* todoterreno

all–time [ˈɔlˌtaɪm] *adj* : de todos los tiempos, histórico ⟨my all-time favorite : mi favorito de todos los tiempos⟩ ⟨an all-time record/high/low : un récord/máximo/mínimo histórico⟩

allude [əˈluːd] *vi* **-luded; -luding** : aludir, referirse

allure[1] [əˈlʊr] *vt* **-lured; -luring** : cautivar, atraer

allure[2] *n* : atractivo *m*, encanto *m*

allusion [əˈluːʒən] *n* : alusión *f*

ally[1] [əˈlaɪ, ˈæˌlaɪ] *vi* **-lied; -lying** : aliarse

ally[2] [ˈæˌlaɪ, əˈlaɪ] *n* : aliado *m*, -da *f*

almanac [ˈɔlməˌnæk, ˈæl-] *n* : almanaque *m*

almighty [ɔlˈmaɪti] *adj* : omnipotente, todopoderoso

almond [ˈɑmənd, ˈɑl-, ˈæ-, ˈæl-] *n* : almendra *f*

almost [ˈɔlˌmoːst, ɔlˈmoːst] *adv* : casi, prácticamente

aims [ˈɑmz, ˈɑlmz, ˈælmz] *ns & pl* : limosna *f*, caridad *f*

aloe [ˈæloː] *n* : áloe *m*

aloft [əˈlɔft] *adv* : en alto, en el aire

alone[1] [əˈloːn] *adv* : sólo, solamente, únicamente

alone[2] *adj* : solo ⟨they're alone in the house : están solos en la casa⟩

along[1] [əˈlɔŋ] *adv* **1** FORWARD : adelante ⟨farther along : más adelante⟩ ⟨move along! : ¡circulen, por favor!⟩ **2 to bring along** : traer **3 ∼ with** : con, junto con **4 all along** : desde el principio

along[2] *prep* **1** : por, a lo largo de ⟨along the coast : a lo largo de la costa⟩ **2** : en, en el curso de, por ⟨along the way : en el curso del viaje⟩

alongside[1] [əˌlɔŋˈsaɪd] *adv* : al costado, al lado

alongside[2] *or* **alongside of** *prep* : junto a, al lado de

aloof [ə'lu:f] *adj* : distante, reservado

aloofness [ə'lu:fnəs] *n* : reserva *f*, actitud *f* distante

aloud [ə'laʊd] *adv* : en voz alta

alpaca [æl'pækə] *n* : alpaca *f*

alphabet ['ælfə,bɛt] *n* : alfabeto *m*

alphabetical [,ælfə'bɛtɪkəl] *or* **alphabetic** [-'bɛtɪk] *adj* : alfabético — **alphabetically** [-tɪkli] *adv*

alphabetize ['ælfəbə,taɪz] *vt* **-ized; -izing** : alfabetizar, poner en orden alfabético

alpine ['æl,paɪn] *adj* : alpino

already [ɔl'rɛdi] *adv* : ya

also ['ɔl,so:] *adv* : también, además

altar ['ɔltər] *n* : altar *m*

alter ['ɔltər] *vt* : alterar, cambiar, modificar

alteration [,ɔltə'reɪʃən] *n* : alteración *f*, cambio *m*, modificación *f*

altercation [,ɔltər'keɪʃən] *n* : altercado *m*, disputa *f*

alternate¹ ['ɔltər,neɪt] *v* **-nated; -nating** : alternar

alternate² ['ɔltərnət] *adj* **1** : alterno ⟨alternate cycles of inflation and depression : ciclos alternos de inflación y depresión⟩ **2** : uno sí y otro no ⟨he cooks on alternate days : cocina un día sí y otro no⟩

alternate³ ['ɔltərnət] *n* : suplente *mf*; sustituto *m*, -ta *f*

alternately ['ɔltərnətli] *adv* : alternativamente, por turno

alternating current ['ɔltər,neɪtɪŋ] *n* : corriente *f* alterna

alternation [,ɔltər'neɪʃən] *n* : alternancia *f*, rotación *f*

alternative¹ [ɔl'tərnətɪv] *adj* : alternativo

alternative² *n* : alternativa *f*

alternatively [ɔl'tərnətɪvli] *adv* (*indicating another option*) ⟨(or,) alternatively, you could come here : (o,) si prefieres, podrías venir aquí⟩

alternator ['ɔltər,neɪtər] *n* : alternador *m*

although [ɔl'ðo:] *conj* : aunque, a pesar de que

altitude ['æltə,tu:d, -,tju:d] *n* : altitud *f*, altura *f*

alto ['æl,to:] *n, pl* **-tos** : alto *mf*, contralto *mf*

altogether [,ɔltə'gɛðər] *adv* **1** COMPLETELY : completamente, totalmente, del todo **2** ON THE WHOLE : en suma, en general

altruism ['æltru,ɪzəm] *n* : altruismo *m*

altruistic [,æltru'ɪstɪk] *adj* : altruista — **altruistically** [-tɪkli] *adv*

alum ['æləm] *n* : alumbre *m*

aluminum [ə'lu:mənəm] *n* : aluminio *m*

alumna [ə'lʌmnə] *n, pl* **-nae** [-,ni:] : exalumna *f*

alumnus [ə'lʌmnəs] *n, pl* **-ni** [-,naɪ] : exalumno *m*

always ['ɔlwiz, -,weiz] *adv* **1** INVARIABLY : siempre, invariablemente **2** FOREVER : para siempre

Alzheimer's ['ɑlts,haɪmərz] *or* **Alzheimer's disease** *n* : (enfermedad *f* de) Alzheimer *m*

am → be

amalgam [ə'mælgəm] *n* : amalgama *f*

amalgamate [ə'mælgə,meɪt] *vt* **-ated; -ating** : amalgamar, unir, fusionar

amalgamation [ə,mælgə'meɪʃən] *n* : fusión *f*, unión *f*

amaryllis [,æmə'rɪləs] *n* : amarilis *f*

amass [ə'mæs] *vt* : amasar, acumular

amateur ['æmət̬ər, -tər, -,tur, -,tjur] *n* **1** : amateur *mf* **2** BEGINNER : principiante *mf*; aficionado *m*, -da *f*

amateurish ['æmə,tʃərɪʃ, -,tər-, -,tur-, -,tjur-] *adj* : amateur, inexperto

amaze [ə'meɪz] *vt* **amazed; amazing** : asombrar, maravillar, pasmar

amazement [ə'meɪzmənt] *n* : asombro *m*, sorpresa *f*

amazing [ə'meɪzɪŋ] *adj* : asombroso, sorprendente — **amazingly** [-zɪŋli] *adv*

Amazon ['æmə,zɑn] *n* : amazona *f* (en mitología)

Amazonian [,æmə'zo:niən] *adj* : amazónico

ambassador [æm'bæsədər] *n* : embajador *m*, -dora *f*

amber ['æmbər] *n* : ámbar *m*

ambergris ['æmbər,grɪs, -,gri:s] *n* : ámbar *m* gris

ambidextrous [,æmbɪ'dɛkstrəs] *adj* : ambidiextro — **ambidextrously** *adv*

ambience *or* **ambiance** ['æmbiən̬s, 'ambi,ɑn̬s] *n* : ambiente *m*, atmósfera *f*

ambiguity [,æmbə'gju:ət̬i] *n, pl* **-ties** : ambigüedad *f*

ambiguous [æm'bɪgjuəs] *adj* : ambiguo

ambition [æm'bɪʃən] *n* : ambición *f*

ambitious [æm'bɪʃəs] *adj* : ambicioso — **ambitiously** *adv*

ambivalence [æm'bɪvələn̬s] *n* : ambivalencia *f*

ambivalent [æm'bɪvələnt] *adj* : ambivalente

amble¹ ['æmbəl] *vi* **-bled; -bling** : ir tranquilamente, pasearse despreocupadamente

amble² *n* : paseo *m* tranquilo

ambulance ['æmbjələn̬s] *n* : ambulancia *f*

ambush¹ ['æm,bʊʃ] *vt* : emboscar

ambush² *n* : emboscada *f*, celada *f*

ameliorate [ə'mi:ljə,reɪt] *v* **-rated; -rating** IMPROVE : mejorar

amelioration [ə,mi:ljə'reɪʃən] *n* : mejora *f*

amen ['eɪ'mɛn, 'ɑ-] *interj* : amén

amenable [ə'mi:nəbəl, -'mɛ-] *adj* RESPONSIVE : susceptible, receptivo, sensible

amend [ə'mɛnd] *vt* **1** IMPROVE : mejorar, enmendar **2** CORRECT : enmendar, corregir

amendment [ə'mɛndmənt] *n* : enmienda *f*

amends [ə'mɛndz] *ns & pl* : compensación *f*, reparación *f*, desagravio *m*

amenity [ə'mɛnət̬i, -'mi:-] *n, pl* **-ties 1** PLEASANTNESS : lo agradable, amenidad *f* **2 amenities** *npl* : servicios *mpl*, comodidades *fpl*

American [ə'mɛrɪkən] *n* : americano *m*, -na *f* — **American** *adj*

American Indian *n sometimes offensive* → Native American

amethyst ['æməθəst] *n* : amatista *f*

amiability [,eimiə'bɪlət̬i] *n* : amabilidad *f*, afabilidad *f*

amiable ['eɪmiːəbəl] *adj* : amable, afable
— amiably [-bli] *adv*

amicable ['æmɪkəbəl] *adj* : amigable, amistoso, cordial — amicably [-bli] *adv*

amid [ə'mɪd] *or* amidst [ə'mɪdst] *prep* : en medio de, entre

amino acid [ə'miːno] *n* : aminoácido *m*

amiss[1] [ə'mɪs] *adv* : mal, fuera de lugar ⟨to take amiss : tomar a mal, llevar a mal⟩

amiss[2] *adj* 1 WRONG : malo, inoportuno 2 there's something amiss : pasa algo, algo anda mal

ammeter ['æˌmiːtər] *n* : amperímetro *m*

ammonia [ə'moːnjə] *n* : amoníaco *m*

ammunition [ˌæmjə'nɪʃən] *n* 1 : municiones *fpl* 2 ARGUMENTS : argumentos *mpl*

amnesia [æm'niːʒə] *n* : amnesia *f*

amnesiac [æm'niːʒiˌæk] *n* : amnésico *m*, -ca *f* — amnesiac *adj*

amnesty ['æmnəsti] *n, pl* -ties : amnistía *f*

amoeba [ə'miːbə] *n, pl* -bas *or* -bae [-ˌbiː] : ameba *f* — amoebic [ə'miːbɪk] *adj*

amok [ə'mʌk, -'mɑk] *adv* to run amok : correr a ciegas, enloquecerse, desbocarse (dícese de la economía, etc.)

among [ə'mʌŋ] *or* amongst [ə'mʌŋkst] *prep* : entre

amoral [eɪ'mɔrəl] *adj* : amoral

amorous ['æmərəs] *adj* 1 PASSIONATE : apasionado 2 ENAMORED : enamorado 3 LOVING : amoroso, cariñoso

amorously ['æmərəsli] *adv* : con cariño

amorphous [ə'mɔrfəs] *adj* : amorfo, informe

amortize ['æmərˌtaɪz, ə'mɔr-] *vt* -tized; -tizing : amortizar

amount[1] [ə'maʊnt] *vi* to amount to 1 : equivaler a, significar ⟨that amounts to treason : eso equivale a la traición⟩ 2 : ascender (a) ⟨my debts amount to $2000 : mis deudas ascienden a $2000⟩

amount[2] *n* : cantidad *f*, suma *f*

ampere ['æmˌpɪr] *n* : amperio *m*

ampersand ['æmpərˌsænd] *n* : el signo & : ampersand *m*

amphetamine [æm'fɛtəˌmiːn] *n* : anfetamina *f*

amphibian [æm'fɪbiən] *n* : anfibio *m*

amphibious [æm'fɪbiəs] *adj* : anfibio

amphitheater ['æmfəˌθiːətər] *n* : anfiteatro *m*

ample ['æmpəl] *adj* ampler; amplest 1 LARGE, SPACIOUS : amplio, extenso, grande 2 ABUNDANT : abundante, generoso

amplifier ['æmpləˌfaɪər] *n* : amplificador *m*

amplify ['æmpləˌfaɪ] *vt* -fied; -fying : amplificar

amply ['æmpli] *adv* : ampliamente, abundantemente, suficientemente

amputate ['æmpjəˌteɪt] *vt* -tated; -tating : amputar

amputation [ˌæmpjə'teɪʃən] *n* : amputación *f*

amuck [ə'mʌk] → amok

amulet ['æmjələt] *n* : amuleto *m*, talismán *m*

amuse [ə'mjuːz] *vt* amused; amusing 1 ENTERTAIN : entretener, distraer 2

: hacer reír, divertir ⟨the joke amused us : la broma nos hizo reír⟩

amusement [ə'mjuːzmənt] *n* 1 ENTERTAINMENT : diversión *f*, entretenimiento *m*, pasatiempo *m* 2 LAUGHTER : risa *f*

amusement park *n* : parque *m* de diversiones

an *art* → a[2]

anachronism [ə'nækrəˌnɪzəm] *n* : anacronismo *m*

anachronistic [əˌnækrə'nɪstɪk] *adj* : anacrónico

anaconda [ˌænə'kɑndə] *n* : anaconda *f*

anagram ['ænəˌgræm] *n* : anagrama *m*

anal ['eɪnəl] *adj* : anal

analgesic [ˌænəl'dʒiːzɪk, -sɪk] *n* : analgésico *m*

analog ['ænəˌlɔg] *adj* : analógico

analogical [ˌænə'lɑdʒɪkəl] *adj* : analógico — analogically [-kli] *adv*

analogous [ə'næləgəs] *adj* : análogo

analogy [ə'nælədʒi] *n, pl* -gies : analogía *f*

analysis [ə'næləsəs] *n, pl* -yses [-ˌsiːz] 1 : análisis *m* 2 PSYCHOANALYSIS : psicoanálisis *m*

analyst ['ænələst] *n* 1 : analista *mf* 2 PSYCHOANALYST : psicoanalista *mf*

analytic [ˌænə'lɪtɪk] *or* analytical [-tɪkəl] *adj* : analítico — analytically [-tɪkli] *adv*

analyze ['ænəˌlaɪz] *vt* -lyzed; -lyzing : analizar

anarchic [æ'nɑrkɪk] *adj* : anárquico — anarchically [-kɪkli] *adv*

anarchism ['ænərˌkɪzəm, -nɑr-] *n* : anarquismo *m*

anarchist ['ænərkɪst, -nɑr-] *n* : anarquista *mf*

anarchy ['ænərki, -nɑr-] *n* : anarquía *f*

anathema [ə'næθəmə] *n* : anatema *m*

anatomic [ˌænə'tɑmɪk] *or* anatomical [-mɪkəl] *adj* : anatómico — anatomically [-mɪkli] *adv*

anatomy [ə'nætəmi] *n, pl* -mies : anatomía *f*

ancestor ['ænˌsɛstər] *n* : antepasado *m*, -da *f*; antecesor *m*, -sora *f*

ancestral [æn'sɛstrəl] *adj* : ancestral, de los antepasados

ancestry ['ænˌsɛstri] *n* 1 DESCENT : ascendencia *f*, linaje *m*, abolengo *m* 2 ANCESTORS : antepasados *mpl*, -das *fpl*

anchor[1] ['æŋkər] *vt* 1 MOOR : anclar, fondear 2 FASTEN : sujetar, asegurar, fijar

anchor[2] *n* 1 : ancla *f* 2 → anchorman 3 → anchorwoman

anchorage ['æŋkərɪdʒ] *n* : anclaje *m*

anchorman ['æŋkərˌmæn] *n, pl* -men [-mən, -ˌmɛn] : presentador *m* (de televisión)

anchorwoman ['æŋkərˌwʊmən] *n, pl* -women [-ˌwɪmən] : presentadora *f* (de televisión)

anchovy ['ænˌtʃoːvi, æn'tʃoː-] *n, pl* -vies *or* -vy : anchoa *f*, boquerón *m*

ancient ['eɪntʃənt] *adj* 1 : antiguo ⟨ancient history : historia antigua⟩ 2 OLD : viejo

ancients ['eɪntʃənts] *npl* : los antiguos *mpl*

and ['ænd] *conj* 1 : y (e *before words beginning with* i- *or* hi-) ⟨books and papers

: libros y papeles⟩ ⟨six and a half : seis y medio⟩ ⟨a hundred and ten : ciento diez⟩ ⟨2 and 2 equals 4 : 2 más 2 es igual a 4⟩ ⟨at (the corner of) First and Main : en la esquina de First y Main⟩ **2** : con ⟨ham and eggs : huevos con jamón⟩ **3** IN ORDER TO : a, de ⟨go and see : ve a ver⟩ ⟨try and finish it : trata de terminarlo⟩ **4** (*indicating continuation*) ⟨she cried and cried : no dejaba de llorar⟩ **5** (*used for emphasis*) ⟨hundreds and hundreds of people : cientos de personas⟩ ⟨more and more difficult : cada vez más difícil⟩

Andalusian [ˌændə'luːʒən] *n* : andaluz *m*, -luza *f* — **Andalusian** *adj*

Andean ['ændiən] *adj* : andino

andiron ['ænˌdaɪərn] *n* : morillo *m*

Andorran [æn'dɔrən] *n* : andorrano *m*, -na *f* — **Andorran** *adj*

androgynous [æn'drɑdʒənəs] *adj* : andrógino

anecdotal [ˌænɪk'doːtəl] *adj* : anecdótico

anecdote ['ænɪkˌdoːt] *n* : anécdota *f*

anemia [ə'niːmiə] *n* : anemia *f*

anemic [ə'niːmɪk] *adj* : anémico

anemone [ə'nɛməni] *n* : anémona *f*

anesthesia [ˌænəs'θiːʒə] *n* : anestesia *f*

anesthetic¹ [ˌænəs'θɛtɪk] *adj* : anestésico

anesthetic² *n* : anestésico *m*

anesthetist [ə'nɛsθətɪst] *n* : anestesista *mf*

anesthetize [ə'nɛsθəˌtaɪz] *vt* **-tize;** **-tized** : anestesiar

aneurysm ['ænjəˌrɪzəm] *n* : aneurisma *m*

anew [ə'nuː:, -'njuː] *adv* : de nuevo, otra vez, nuevamente

angel ['eɪndʒəl] *n* : ángel *m* ⟨the Angel of Death : el ángel exterminador⟩

angelic [æn'dʒɛlɪk] *or* **angelical** [-lɪkəl] *adj* : angélico, angelical — **angelically** [-lɪkli] *adv*

anger¹ ['æŋgər] *vt* : enojar, enfadar

anger² *n* : enojo *m*, enfado *m*, ira *f*, cólera *f*, rabia *f*

angina [æn'dʒaɪnə] *n* : angina *f*

angle¹ ['æŋgəl] *v* **angled;** **angling** *vt* DIRECT, SLANT : orientar, dirigir — *vi* FISH : pescar (con caña)

angle² *n* **1** : ángulo *m* **2** POINT OF VIEW : perspectiva *f*, punto *m* de vista

angler ['æŋglər] *n* : pescador *m*, -dora *f*

Anglican ['æŋglɪkən] *n* : anglicano *m*, -na *f* — **Anglican** *adj*

angling ['æŋglɪŋ] *n* : pesca *f* con caña

Anglo–Saxon¹ [ˌæŋglo'sæksən] *adj* : anglosajón

Anglo–Saxon² *n* : anglosajón *m*, -jona *f*

Angolan [æn'goːlən, æn-] *n* : angoleño *m*, -ña *f* — **Angolan** *adj*

angora [æn'gorə, æn-] *n* : angora *f*

angrily ['æŋgrəli] *adv* : furiosamente, con ira

angry ['æŋgri] *adj* **angrier;** **-est** : enojado, enfadado, furioso

anguish ['æŋgwɪʃ] *n* : angustia *f*, congoja *f*

anguished ['æŋgwɪʃt] *adj* : angustiado, acongojado

angular ['æŋgjələr] *adj* : angular (dícese de las formas), anguloso (dícese de las caras)

animal ['ænəməl] *n* **1** : animal *m* **2** BRUTE : bruto *m*, -ta *f*

animate¹ ['ænəˌmeɪt] *vt* **-mated;** **-mating** : animar

animate² ['ænəmət] *adj* : animado

animated ['ænəˌmeɪtəd] *adj* **1** LIVELY : animado, vivo, vivaz **2 animated cartoon** : dibujos *mpl* animados

animation [ˌænə'meɪʃən] *n* : animación *f*

animosity [ˌænə'mɑsəti] *n*, *pl* **-ties** : animosidad *f*, animadversión *f*

anise ['ænəs] *n* : anís *m*

aniseed ['ænəsˌsiːd] *n* : anís *m*, semilla *f* de anís

ankle ['æŋkəl] *n* : tobillo *m*

anklebone ['æŋkəlˌboːn] *n* : taba *f*

annals ['ænəlz] *npl* : anales *mpl*, crónica *f*

annatto [ə'nɑto] *n* : achiote *m*

anneal [ə'niːl] *vt* **1** TEMPER : templar **2** STRENGTHEN : fortalecer

annex¹ [ə'nɛks, 'æˌnɛks] *vt* : anexar

annex² ['æˌnɛks, -nɪks] *n* : anexo *m*, anejo *m*

annexation [ˌæˌnɛk'seɪʃən] *n* : anexión *f*

annihilate [ə'naɪəˌleɪt] *vt* **-lated;** **-lating** : aniquilar

annihilation [əˌnaɪə'leɪʃən] *n* : aniquilación *f*, aniquilamiento *m*

anniversary [ˌænə'vərsəri] *n*, *pl* **-ries** : aniversario *m*

annotate ['ænəˌteɪt] *vt* **-tated;** **-tating** : anotar

annotation [ˌænə'teɪʃən] *n* : anotación *f*

announce [ə'naʊn*t*s] *vt* **-nounced;** **-nouncing** : anunciar

announcement [ə'naʊn*t*smənt] *n* : anuncio *m*

announcer [ə'naʊn*t*sər] *n* : anunciador *m*, -dora *f*; comentarista *mf*; locutor *m*, -tora *f*

annoy [ə'nɔɪ] *vt* : molestar, fastidiar, irritar

annoyance [ə'nɔɪən*t*s] *n* **1** IRRITATION : irritación *f*, fastidio *m* **2** NUISANCE : molestia *f*, fastidio *m*

annoying [ə'nɔɪɪŋ] *adj* : molesto, fastidioso, engorroso — **annoyingly** [-ɪŋli] *adv*

annual¹ ['ænjəl] *adj* : anual — **annually** *adv*

annual² *n* **1** : planta *f* anual **2** YEARBOOK : anuario *m*

annuity [ə'nuːəti] *n*, *pl* **-ties** : anualidad *f*

annul [ə'nʌl] *vt* **-nulled;** **-nulling** : anular, invalidar

annulment [ə'nʌlmənt] *n* : anulación *f*

anode ['æˌnoːd] *n* : ánodo *m*

anoint [ə'nɔɪnt] *vt* : ungir

anomalous [ə'nɑmələs] *adj* : anómalo

anomaly [ə'nɑməli] *n*, *pl* **-lies** : anomalía *f*

anonymity [ˌænə'nɪmət̪i] *n* : anonimato *m*

anonymous [ə'nɑnəməs] *adj* : anónimo — **anonymously** *adv*

anorak ['ænəˌræk] *n* : anorak *m*

anorexia [ˌænə'rɛksiə] *n* : anorexia *f*

anorexic [ˌænə'rɛksɪk] *adj* : anoréxico

another¹ [ə'nʌðər] *adj* **1** : otro ⟨another drink : otra copa⟩ ⟨another two days : dos días más, otros dos días⟩ ⟨yet another example : otro ejemplo más⟩ ⟨it was just another day : fue un día como cualquier otro⟩ **2** : otro ⟨at another time : en otro momento, en otra ocasión⟩ ⟨that's another matter : eso es otra cuestión⟩ **3** (*indicating similarity*) : otro ⟨another Great Depression : otra Gran Depresión⟩

another² *pron* : otro ⟨one after another : uno tras otro, una tras otra⟩ ⟨at one time or another : en algún momento⟩ ⟨for one reason or another : por alguna razón⟩ ⟨one way or another : de una u otra forma/manera⟩

answer¹ [ˈænʦsər] *vt* **1** : contestar (a) ⟨to answer the telephone : contestar el teléfono⟩ ⟨to answer a question : contestar (a) una pregunta⟩ ⟨he didn't answer me : no me contestó⟩ **2** FULFILL : satisfacer **3** : responder a (acusaciones, etc.) — *vi* **1** : contestar, responder **2** to answer back TALK BACK : contestar (con impertinencia) **3** to answer for someone : contestar por alguien **4** to answer for something : responder de algo, pagar por algo ⟨she'll answer for that mistake : pagará por ese error⟩ **5** to answer to : responder a

answer² *n* **1** REPLY : respuesta *f*, contestación *f* ⟨a straight answer : una respuesta clara⟩ ⟨there's no answer : no contestan (el teléfono)⟩ ⟨I never got an answer : nunca me dieron respuesta⟩ ⟨in answer to your question : en respuesta a su pregunta⟩ **2** : respuesta *f*, solución *f* (en un examen, etc.) **3** SOLUTION : solución *f* ⟨there's no easy answer : no tiene una solución fácil⟩

answerable [ˈænʦsərəbəl] *adj* : responsable

answering machine *n* : contestador *m* (automático)

ant [ˈænt] *n* : hormiga *f*

antacid [æntˈæsəd, ˈæn,tæ-] *n* : antiácido *m*

antagonism [ænˈtægəˌnɪzəm] *n* : antagonismo *m*, hostilidad *f*

antagonist [ænˈtægənɪst] *n* : antagonista *mf*

antagonistic [ænˌtægəˈnɪstɪk] *adj* : antagonista, hostil

antagonize [ænˈtægəˌnaɪz] *vt* -nized; -nizing : antagonizar

antarctic [æntˈɑrktɪk, -ˈɑrtɪk] *adj* : antártico

antarctic circle *n* : círculo *m* antártico

anteater [ˈæntˌiːtər] *n* : oso *m* hormiguero

antebellum [ˌæntiˈbɛləm] *adj* : prebélico

antecedent¹ [ˌæntəˈsiːdənt] *adj* : antecedente, precedente

antecedent² *n* : antecedente *mf*; precursor *m*, -sora *f*

antelope [ˈæntəlˌoːp] *n, pl* -lope *or* -lopes : antílope *m*

antenatal [ˌæntiˈneɪtəl] → **prenatal**

antenna [ænˈtɛnə] *n, pl* -nae [-ˌniː, -ˌnaɪ] *or* -nas : antena *f*

anterior [ænˈtɪriər] *adj* : anterior

anthem [ˈænθəm] *n* : himno *m* ⟨national anthem : himno nacional⟩

anther [ˈænθər] *n* : antera *f*

anthill [ˈæntˌhɪl] *n* : hormiguero *m*

anthology [ænˈθɑlədʒi] *n, pl* -gies : antología *f*

anthracite [ˈænθrəˌsaɪt] *n* : antracita *f*

anthropoid¹ [ˈænθrəˌpɔɪd] *adj* : antropoide

anthropoid² *n* : antropoide *mf*

anthropological [ˌænθrəpəˈlɑdʒɪkəl] *adj* : antropológico

anthropologist [ˌænθrəˈpɑlədʒɪst] *n* : antropólogo *m*, -ga *f*

anthropology [ˌænθrəˈpɑlədʒi] *n* : antropología *f*

anti- [ˌænti, ˌæntaɪ] *pref* : anti-

antiabortion [ˌæntiəˈbɔrʃən, ˌæntaɪ-] *adj* : antiaborto

antiaircraft [ˌæntiˈærˌkræft, ˌæntaɪ-] *adj* : antiaéreo

anti-American [ˌæntiəˈmɛrɪkən, ˌæntaɪ-] *adj* : antiamericano

antibiotic¹ [ˌæntibaɪˈɑtɪk, ˌæntaɪ-, -bi-] *adj* : antibiótico

antibiotic² *n* : antibiótico *m*

antibody [ˈæntiˌbɑdi] *n, pl* -bodies : anticuerpo *m*

antic¹ [ˈæntɪk] *adj* : extravagante, juguetón

antic² *n* : payasada *f*, travesura *f*

anticipate [ænˈtɪsəˌpeɪt] *vt* -pated; -pating **1** FORESEE : anticipar, prever **2** EXPECT : esperar, contar con

anticipation [ænˌtɪsəˈpeɪʃən] *n* **1** FORESIGHT : previsión *f* **2** EXPECTATION : anticipación *f*, expectación *f*, esperanza *f*

anticipatory [ænˈtɪsəpəˌtori] *adj* : en anticipación, en previsión

anticlimactic [ˌæntiklaɪˈmæktɪk] *adj* : anticlimático, decepcionante

anticlimax [ˌæntiˈklaɪˌmæks] *n* : anticlímax *m*

anticommunism [ˌæntiˈkɑmjəˌnɪzəm, ˌæntaɪ-] *n* : anticomunismo *m*

anticommunist [ˌæntiˈkɑmjənɪst, ˌæntaɪ-] *adj* : anticomunista

anticommunist² *n* : anticomunista *mf*

antidemocratic [ˌæntiˌdɛməˈkrætɪk, ˌæntaɪ-] *adj* : antidemocrático

antidepressant [ˌæntidɪˈprɛsənt] *n* : antidepresivo *m* — **antidepressant** *adj*

antidote [ˈænti,doːt] *n* : antídoto *m*

antidrug [ˌæntiˈdrʌg, ˌæntaɪ-;, ˈæntiˌdrʌg, ˈæntaɪ-] *adj* : antidrogas

antifascist [ˌæntiˈfæʃɪst, ˌæntaɪ-] *adj* : antifascista

antifeminist [ˌæntiˈfɛmənɪst, ˌæntaɪ-] *adj* : antifeminista

antifreeze [ˈæntiˌfriːz] *n* : anticongelante *m*

antigen [ˈæntɪdʒən, -ˌdʒɛn] *n* : antígeno *m*

antihistamine [ˌæntiˈhɪstəˌmiːn, -mən] *n* : antihistamínico *m*

anti-imperialism [ˌæntiɪmˈpɪriəˌlɪzəm, ˌæntaɪ-] *n* : antiimperialismo *m*

anti-imperialist [ˌæntiɪmˈpɪriəlɪst, ˌæntaɪ-] *adj* : antiimperialista

anti-inflammatory [ˌæntiɪmˈflæmətori] *adj* : antiinflamatorio

anti-inflationary [ˌæntiɪmˈfleɪʃəˌnɛri, ˌæntaɪ-] *adj* : antiinflacionario

antimony [ˈæntəˌmoːni] *n* : antimonio *m*

antipathy [ænˈtɪpəθi] *n, pl* -thies : antipatía *f*, aversión *f*

antiperspirant [‚ænti'pərspərənt, ‚æntaɪ-] *n* : antitranspirante *m*

antiquarian[1] [‚æntə'kweriən] *adj* : antiguo, anticuario ⟨an antiquarian book : un libro antiguo⟩

antiquarian[2] *n* : anticuario *m*, -ria *f*

antiquary ['æntə‚kweri] *n* → **antiquarian**[2]

antiquated ['æntə‚kweɪtəd] *adj* : anticuado, pasado de moda

antique[1] [æn'ti:k] *adj* **1** OLD : antiguo, de época ⟨an antique mirror : un espejo antiguo⟩ **2** OLD-FASHIONED : anticuado, pasado de moda

antique[2] *n* : antigüedad *f*

antiquity [æn'tɪkwəţi] *n, pl* **-ties** : antigüedad

antirevolutionary [‚ænti‚revə'lu:ʃə‚neri, ‚æntaɪ-] *adj* : antirrevolucionario

anti–Semitic [‚æntisə'mɪţɪk, ‚æntaɪ-] *adj* : antisemita

anti–Semitism [‚ænti'semə‚tɪzəm, ‚æntaɪ-] *n* : antisemitismo *m*

antiseptic[1] [‚ænti'septɪk] *adj* : antiséptico — **antiseptically** [-tɪkli] *adv*

antiseptic[2] *n* : antiséptico *m*

antismoking [‚ænti'smo:kɪŋ, ‚æntaɪ-] *adj* : antitabaco

antisocial [‚ænti'so:ʃəl, ‚æntaɪ-] *adj* **1** : antisocial **2** UNSOCIABLE : poco sociable

antiterrorist [‚ænti'terərɪst, ‚æntaɪ-] *adj* : antiterrorista

antitheft [‚ænti'θeft, ‚æntaɪ-] *adj* : antirrobo

antithesis [æn'tɪθəsɪs] *n, pl* **-eses** [-‚si:z] : antítesis *f*

antitoxin [‚ænti'tɑksən, ‚æntaɪ-] *n* : antitoxina *f*

antitrust [‚ænti'trʌst, ‚æntaɪ-] *adj* : antimonopolista

antiviral [‚ænti'vaɪrəl, ‚æntaɪ-] *adj* : antiviral

antivirus [‚ænti'vaɪrəs, ‚æntaɪ-] *adj* → **antiviral**

antivirus software *n* : antivirus *m*

antler ['æntlər] *n* : asta *f*, cuerno *m*

antonym ['æntə‚nɪm] *n* : antónimo *m*

anus ['eɪnəs] *n* : ano *m*

anvil ['ænvəl, -vɪl] *n* : yunque *m*

anxiety [æŋk'zaɪəţi] *n, pl* **-eties** **1** UNEASINESS : inquietud *f*, preocupación *f*, ansiedad *f* **2** APPREHENSION : ansiedad *f*, angustia *f*

anxious ['æŋkʃəs] *adj* **1** WORRIED : inquieto, preocupado, ansioso **2** WORRISOME : preocupante, inquietante **3** EAGER : ansioso, deseoso

anxiously ['æŋkʃəsli] *adv* : con inquietud, con ansiedad

any[1] ['eni] *adv* **1** : algo ⟨is it any better? : ¿está (algo) mejor?⟩ ⟨I can't stand it any more : no lo soporto más⟩ ⟨do you want any more? : ¿quiere más?⟩ **2** : para nada ⟨it is not any good : no sirve para nada⟩

any[2] *adj* **1** : alguno ⟨is there any doubt? : ¿hay alguna duda?⟩ ⟨call me if you have any questions : llámeme si tiene alguna pregunta⟩ **2** : cualquier ⟨I can

answer any question : puedo responder a cualquier pregunta⟩ **3** : todo ⟨in any case : en todo caso⟩ **4** : ningún ⟨he would not accept it under any circumstances : no lo aceptaría bajo ninguna circunstancia⟩

any[3] *pron* **1** : alguno ⟨are there any left? : ¿queda alguno?⟩ ⟨did you see any of the girls? : ¿viste a alguna de las chicas?⟩ **2** : ninguno ⟨I don't want any : no quiero ninguno⟩ ⟨I couldn't attend any of the meetings : no pude asistir a ninguna de las reuniones⟩

anybody ['eni‚bʌdi, -‚bɑ-] *pron* → **anyone**

anyhow ['eni‚haʊ] *adv* **1** HAPHAZARDLY : de cualquier manera **2** IN ANY CASE : de todos modos, en todo caso

anymore [‚eni'mor] *adv* **1** : ya, ya más ⟨he doesn't dance anymore : ya no baila más⟩ **2** : todavía ⟨do they sing anymore? : ¿cantan todavía?⟩

anyone ['eni‚wʌn] *pron* **1** : alguien ⟨is anyone here? : ¿hay alguien aquí?⟩ ⟨if anyone wants to come : si alguno quiere venir⟩ **2** : cualquiera ⟨anyone can play : cualquiera puede jugar⟩ **3** : nadie ⟨I don't want anyone here : no quiero a nadie aquí⟩

anyplace ['eni‚pleɪs] → **anywhere**

anything ['eni‚θɪŋ] *pron* **1** : algo, alguna cosa ⟨do you want anything (else)? : ¿quieres algo (más)?, ¿quieres alguna cosa (más)?⟩ **2** : nada ⟨hardly anything : casi nada⟩ **3** : cualquier cosa ⟨I eat anything : como de todo⟩ **4** ~ **but** : no . . . ni mucho menos ⟨he was anything but pleased : no estaba contento, ni mucho menos⟩ **5 anything goes** : todo vale **6** ~ **like** ⟨it wasn't anything like what I expected : no fue en absoluto lo que esperaba⟩ ⟨we don't have anything like enough : no tenemos suficiente, ni mucho menos⟩

anytime ['eni‚taɪm] *adv* : en cualquier momento, a cualquier hora, cuando sea

anyway ['eni‚weɪ] *or* **anyways** [-‚weɪz] → **anyhow**

anywhere ['eni‚ʍwer] *adv* **1** : en algún sitio, en alguna parte ⟨do you see it anywhere? : ¿lo ves en alguna parte?⟩ **2** : en ningún sitio, por ninguna parte ⟨I can't find it anywhere : no puedo encontrarlo por ninguna parte⟩ **3** : en cualquier parte, dondequiera, donde sea ⟨put it anywhere : ponlo dondequiera⟩

aorta [eɪ'ortə] *n, pl* **-tas** *or* **-tae** [-ți, -‚taɪ] : aorta *f*

Apache [ə'pætʃi] *n, pl* **Apache** *or* **Apaches** : apache *mf*

apart [ə'pɑrt] *adv* **1** SEPARATELY : aparte, separadamente **2** ASIDE : aparte, a un lado **3 to fall apart** : deshacerse, hacerse pedazos **4 to take apart** : desmontar, desmantelar

apartheid [ə'pɑr‚teɪt, -‚taɪt] *n* : apartheid *m*

apartment [ə'pɑrtmənt] *n* : apartamento *m*, departamento *m*, piso *m* *Spain*

apartment building *n* : bloque *m* de apartamentos/departamentos, bloque *m* de pisos *Spain*

apathetic [ˌæpəˈθεtɪk] *adj* : apático, indiferente — **apathetically** [-ˌtɪkli] *adv*

apathy [ˈæpəθi] *n* : apatía *f*, indiferencia *f*

ape[1] [ˈeɪp] *vt* **aped; aping** : imitar, remedar

ape[2] *n* : simio *m*; mono *m*, -na *f*

aperitif [əˌpɛrəˈtiːf] *n* : aperitivo *m*

aperture [ˈæpərtʃər, -ˌtʃʊr] *n* : abertura *f*, rendija *f*, apertura *f* (en fotografía)

apex [ˈeɪˌpɛks] *n, pl* **apexes** *or* **apices** [ˈeɪpəˌsiːz, ˈæ-] : ápice *m*, cúspide *f*, cima *f*

aphid [ˈeɪfɪd, ˈæ-] *n* : áfido *m*

aphorism [ˈæfəˌrɪzəm] *n* : aforismo *m*

aphrodisiac [ˌæfrəˈdiːziˌæk, -ˈdɪ-] *n* : afrodisíaco *m*

apiary [ˈeɪpiˌɛri] *n, pl* **-aries** : apiario *m*, colmenar *m*

apiece [əˈpiːs] *adv* : cada uno

aplenty [əˈplɛnti] *adj* : en abundancia

aplomb [əˈplɑm, -ˈplʌm] *n* : aplomo *m*

apocalypse [əˈpɑkəˌlɪps] *n* : apocalipsis *m*

apocalyptic [əˌpɑkəˈlɪptɪk] *adj* : apocalíptico

apocrypha [əˈpɑkrəfə] *n* : textos *mpl* apócrifos

apocryphal [əˈpɑkrəfəl] *adj* : apócrifo

apolitical [ˌeɪpəˈlɪtɪkəl] *adj* : apolítico

apologetic [əˌpɑləˈdʒɛtɪk] *adj* : lleno de disculpas

apologetically [əˌpɑləˈdʒɛtɪkli] *adv* : disculpándose, con aire de disculpas

apologize [əˈpɑləˌdʒaɪz] *vi* **-gized; -gizing** : disculparse, pedir perdón

apology [əˈpɑlədʒi] *n, pl* **-gies** : disculpa *f*, excusa *f*

apoplectic [ˌæpəˈplɛktɪk] *adj* : apoplético

apoplexy [ˈæpəˌplɛksi] *n* : apoplejía *f*

apostasy [əˈpɑstəsi] *n, pl* **-sies** : apostasía *f*

apostate [əˈpɑsˌteɪt] *n* : apóstata *mf*

apostle [əˈpɑsəl] *n* : apóstol *m*

apostolic [ˌæpəˈstɑlɪk] *adj* : apostólico

apostrophe [əˈpɑstrəˌfiː] *n* : apóstrofo *m* (ortográfico)

apothecary [əˈpɑθəˌkɛri] *n, pl* **-caries** : boticario *m*, -ria *f*

app [ˈæp] *n* : app *f*, aplicación *f*

appall [əˈpɔl] *vt* : consternar, horrorizar

appalling [əˈpɔlɪŋ] *adj* : atroz, horroroso

apparatus [ˌæpəˈrætəs, -ˈreɪ-] *n, pl* **-tuses** *or* **-tus** : aparato *m*, equipo *m*

apparel [əˈpærəl] *n* : atavío *m*, ropa *f*

apparent [əˈpærənt] *adj* **1** VISIBLE : visible **2** OBVIOUS : claro, evidente, manifiesto **3** SEEMING : aparente, ostensible

apparently [əˈpærəntli] *adv* : aparentemente, al parecer

apparition [ˌæpəˈrɪʃən] *n* : aparición *f*, visión *f*

appeal[1] [əˈpiːl] *vt* : apelar ⟨to appeal a decision : apelar contra una decisión⟩ — *vi* **1 to appeal for** : pedir, solicitar **2 to appeal to** : atraer a ⟨that doesn't appeal to me : eso no me atrae⟩

appeal[2] *n* **1** : apelación *f* (en derecho) **2** PLEA : ruego *m*, súplica *f* **3** ATTRACTION : atracción *f*, atractivo *m*, interés *m*

appear [əˈpɪr] *vi* **1** : aparecer, aparecerse, presentarse ⟨he suddenly appeared

: apareció de repente⟩ **2** COME OUT : aparecer, salir, publicarse **3** : comparecer (ante el tribunal), actuar (en el teatro) **4** SEEM : parecer

appearance [əˈpɪrənts] *n* **1** APPEARING : aparición *f*, presentación *f*, comparecencia *f* (ante un tribunal), publicación *f* (de un libro) **2** LOOK : apariencia *f*, aspecto *m* **3 by all appearances** : según parece **4 to keep up appearances** : guardar las apariencias **5 to make an appearance** : hacer acto de presencia

appease [əˈpiːz] *vt* **-peased; -peasing 1** CALM, PACIFY : aplacar, apaciguar, sosegar **2** SATISFY : satisfacer, mitigar

appeasement [əˈpiːzmənt] *n* : aplacamiento *m*, apaciguamiento *m*

append [əˈpɛnd] *vt* : agregar, añadir, adjuntar

appendage [əˈpɛndɪdʒ] *n* **1** ADDITION : apéndice *m*, añadidura *f* **2** LIMB : miembro *m*, extremidad *f*

appendectomy [ˌæpənˈdɛktəmi] *n, pl* **-mies** : apendicectomía *f*

appendicitis [əˌpɛndəˈsaɪtəs] *n* : apendicitis *f*

appendix [əˈpɛndɪks] *n, pl* **-dixes** *or* **-dices** [-dəˌsiːz] : apéndice *m*

appetite [ˈæpəˌtaɪt] *n* **1** CRAVING : apetito *m*, deseo *m*, ganas *fpl* **2** PREFERENCE : gusto *m*, preferencia *f* ⟨the cultural appetites of today : los gustos culturales de hoy⟩

appetizer [ˈæpəˌtaɪzər] *n* : aperitivo *m*, entremés *m*, botana *f* Mex, tapa *f* Spain

appetizing [ˈæpəˌtaɪzɪŋ] *adj* : apetecible, apetitoso — **appetizingly** [-ˌzɪŋli] *adv*

applaud [əˈplɔd] *v* : aplaudir

applause [əˈplɔz] *n* : aplauso *m*

apple [ˈæpəl] *n* : manzana *f*

apple tree *n* : manzano *m*

appliance [əˈplaɪənts] *n* **1** : aparato *m* **2 household appliance** : electrodoméstico *m*, aparato *m* electrodoméstico

applicability [ˌæplɪkəˈbɪləti, əˌplɪkə-] *n* : aplicabilidad *f*

applicable [ˈæplɪkəbəl, əˈplɪkə-] *adj* : aplicable, pertinente

applicant [ˈæplɪkənt] *n* : solicitante *mf*, aspirante *mf*, postulante *mf*; candidato *m*, -ta *f*

application [ˌæpləˈkeɪʃən] *n* **1** USE : aplicación *f*, empleo *m*, uso *m* **2** DILIGENCE : aplicación *f*, diligencia *f*, dedicación *f* **3** REQUEST : solicitud *f*, petición *f*, demanda *f* **4** PROGRAM : aplicación *f*, app *f*

applicator [ˈæpləˌkeɪtər] *n* : aplicador *m*

appliqué[1] [ˌæpləˈkeɪ] *vt* : decorar con apliques

appliqué[2] *n* : aplique *m*

apply [əˈplaɪ] *v* **-plied; -plying** *vt* **1** : aplicar (una sustancia, los frenos, el conocimiento) **2 to apply oneself** : dedicarse, aplicarse — *vi* **1** : aplicarse, referirse ⟨the rules apply to everyone : las reglas se aplican a todos⟩ **2 to apply for** : solicitar, pedir

appoint [əˈpɔɪnt] *vt* **1** NAME : nombrar, designar **2** FIX, SET : fijar, señalar, desig-

nar ⟨to appoint a date : fijar una fecha⟩
3 EQUIP : equipar ⟨a well-appointed office
: una oficina bien equipada⟩
appointee [ə‚pɔɪnˈtiː, ‚æ-] n : persona f
designada
appointment [əˈpɔɪntmənt] n 1 APPOIN-
TING : nombramiento m, designación
f 2 ENGAGEMENT : cita f, hora f ⟨to
have/make an appointment : tener/con-
certar una cita⟩ 3 POST : puesto m
apportion [əˈporʃən] vt : distribuir, repartir
apportionment [əˈporʃənmənt] n : distribución f, repartición f, reparto m
apposite [ˈæpəzət] adj : apropiado, oportuno, pertinente — **appositely** adv
appraisal [əˈpreɪzəl] n : evaluación f, valoración f, tasación f, apreciación f
appraise [əˈpreɪz] vt -praised; -praising
: evaluar, valorar, tasar, apreciar
appraiser [əˈpreɪzər] n : tasador m, -dora
f
appreciable [əˈpriːʃəbəl, -ˈprɪʃiə-] adj
: apreciable, sensible, considerable —
appreciably [-bli] adv
appreciate [əˈpriːʃiˌeɪt, -ˈprɪ-] v -ated;
-ating vt 1 VALUE : apreciar, valorar 2
: agradecer ⟨we appreciate his frankness
: agradecemos su franqueza⟩ 3 UN-
DERSTAND : darse cuenta de, entender
— vi : apreciarse, valorizarse
appreciation [ə‚priːʃiˈeɪʃən, -‚prɪ-] n 1
GRATITUDE : agradecimiento m, reconocimiento m 2 VALUING : apreciación f,
valoración f, estimación f ⟨art appreciation : apreciación artística⟩ 3 UNDERS-
TANDING : comprensión f, entendimiento m
appreciative [əˈpriːʃətɪv, -ˈprɪ-, əˈpriːʃiˌeɪt-]
adj 1 : apreciativo ⟨an appreciative audience : un público apreciativo⟩ 2 GRA-
TEFUL : agradecido 3 ADMIRING : de
admiración
apprehend [‚æprɪˈhend] vt 1 ARREST
: aprehender, detener, arrestar 2
DREAD : temer 3 COMPREHEND : comprender, entender
apprehension [‚æprɪˈhentʃən] n 1
ARREST : arresto m, detención f, aprehensión f 2 ANXIETY : aprensión f, ansiedad
f, temor m 3 UNDERSTANDING : comprensión f, percepción f
apprehensive [‚æprɪˈhensɪv] adj : aprensivo, inquieto — **apprehensively** adv
apprentice[1] [əˈprentɪs] vt -ticed; -ticing
: colocar de aprendiz
apprentice[2] n : aprendiz m, -diza f
apprenticeship [əˈprentɪsˌʃɪp] n : aprendizaje f
apprise [əˈpraɪz] vt -prised; -prising : informar, avisar
approach[1] [əˈproːtʃ] vt 1 NEAR : acercarse a 2 APPROXIMATE : aproximarse a
3 : abordar, dirigirse a ⟨I approached my
boss with the proposal : me dirigí a mi
jefe con la propuesta⟩ 4 TACKLE : abordar, enfocar, considerar — vi : acercarse,
aproximarse
approach[2] n 1 NEARING : acercamiento
m, aproximación f 2 POSITION : en-

foque m, planteamiento m 3 OFFER
: propuesta f, oferta f 4 ACCESS : acceso
m, vía f de acceso
approachable [əˈproːtʃəbəl] adj : accesible, asequible
approbation [‚æprəˈbeɪʃən] n : aprobación f
appropriate[1] [əˈproːpriˌeɪt] vt -ated; -ating
1 SEIZE : apropiarse de 2 ALLOCATE
: destinar, asignar
appropriate[2] [əˈproːpriət] adj : apropiado,
adecuado, idóneo — **appropriately** adv
appropriateness [əˈproːpriətnəs] n : idoneidad f, propiedad f
appropriation [ə‚proːpriˈeɪʃən] n 1 SEI-
ZURE : apropiación f 2 ALLOCATION
: asignación f
approval [əˈpruːvəl] n 1 : aprobación f,
visto m bueno 2 **on approval** : a prueba
approve [əˈpruːv] vt -proved; -proving 1
: aprobar, sancionar, darle el visto bueno
a 2 **to approve of** : consentir en, aprobar ⟨he doesn't approve of smoking
: está en contra del tabaco⟩
approximate[1] [əˈprɑksəˌmeɪt] vt -mated;
-mating : aproximarse a, acercarse a
approximate[2] [əˈprɑksəmət] adj : aproximado
approximately [əˈprɑksəmətli] adv : aproximadamente, más o menos
approximation [ə‚prɑksəˈmeɪʃən] n
: aproximación f
appurtenance [əˈpərtənənts] n : accesorio
m
apricot [ˈæprəˌkɑt, ˈeɪ-] n : albaricoque m,
chabacano m Mex
April [ˈeɪprəl] n : abril m ⟨they arrived on
the 23rd of April, they arrived on April
the 23rd : llegaron el 23 de abril⟩
apron [ˈeɪprən] n : delantal m, mandil m
apropos[1] [‚æprəˈpoː, ˈæprəˌpoː] adv : a
propósito
apropos[2] adj : pertinente, oportuno,
acertado
apropos of prep : a propósito de
apt [ˈæpt] adj 1 FITTING : apto, apropiado, acertado, oportuno 2 LIABLE
: propenso, inclinado 3 CLEVER, QUICK
: listo, despierto
aptitude [ˈæptəˌtuːd, -ˌtjuːd] n 1 : aptitud
f, capacidad f ⟨aptitude test : prueba de
aptitud⟩ 2 TALENT : talento m, facilidad f
aptly [ˈæptli] adv : acertadamente
aqua [ˈækwə, ˈɑ-] n : color m aguamarina
aquamarine [‚ɑkwəməˈriːn, ‚æ-] n 1 : aguamarina f 2 → aqua
aquarium [əˈkwæriəm] n, pl -iums or -ia
[-iə] : acuario m
Aquarius [əˈkwæriəs] n 1 : Acuario m
(signo o constelación) 2 : Acuario mf
(persona)
aquatic [əˈkwɑtɪk, -ˈkwæ-] adj : acuático
aqueduct [ˈækwəˌdʌkt] n : acueducto m
aqueous [ˈeɪkwiəs, ˈæ-] adj : acuoso
aquiline [ˈækwəˌlaɪn, -lən] adj : aguileño
Arab[1] [ˈærəb] adj : árabe
Arab[2] n : árabe mf
arabesque [‚ærəˈbesk] n : arabesco m
Arabian[1] [əˈreɪbiən] adj : árabe

Arabian² *n* → Arab²
Arabic¹ ['ærəbɪk] *adj* : árabe
Arabic² *n* : árabe *m* (idioma)
arable ['ærəbəl] *adj* : arable, cultivable
arbiter ['arbətər] *n* : árbitro *m*, -tra *f*
arbitrariness ['arbə,trɛrinəs] *n* : arbitrariedad *f*
arbitrary ['arbə,trɛri] *adj* : arbitrario — arbitrarily [,arbə'trɛrəli] *adv*
arbitrate ['arbə,treɪt] *v* -trated; -trating : arbitrar
arbitration [,arbə'treɪʃən] *n* : arbitraje *m*
arbitrator ['arbə,treɪtər] *n* : árbitro *m*, -tra *f*
arbor ['arbər] *n* : cenador *m*, pérgola *f*
arboreal [ar'boriəl] *adj* : arbóreo
arc¹ ['ark] *vi* arced; arcing : formar un arco
arc² *n* : arco *m*
arcade [ar'keɪd] *n* 1 ARCHES : arcada *f* 2 MALL : galería *f* comercial
arcane [ar'keɪn] *adj* : arcano, secreto, misterioso
arch¹ ['artʃ] *vt* : arquear — *vi* : formar un arco, arquearse
arch² *adj* 1 CHIEF : principal 2 MISCHIEVOUS : malicioso, pícaro
arch³ *n* : arco *m*
archaeological [,arkiə'ladʒɪkəl] *or* archeological *adj* : arqueológico
archaeologist [,arki'alədʒɪst] *or* archeologist *n* : arqueólogo *m*, -ga *f*
archaeology *or* archeology [,arki'alədʒi] *n* : arqueología *f*
archaic [ar'keɪɪk] *adj* : arcaico — archaically [-ɪkli] *adv*
archangel ['ark,eɪndʒəl] *n* : arcángel *m*
archbishop [artʃ'bɪʃəp] *n* : arzobispo *m*
archbishopric [artʃ'bɪʃəprɪk] *n* : arzobispado *m*
archdiocese [artʃ'daɪəsəs, -,si:z, -,si:s] *n* : arquidiócesis *f*, archidiócesis *f*
archer ['artʃər] *n* : arquero *m*, -ra *f*
archery ['artʃəri] *n* : tiro *m* al arco
archetypal [,arkɪ'taɪpəl] *adj* : arquetípico
archetype ['arkɪ,taɪp] *n* : arquetipo *m*
archipelago [,arkə'pɛlə,go:, ,artʃə-] *n*, *pl* -goes *or* -gos [-go:z] : archipiélago *m*
architect ['arkə,tɛkt] *n* : arquitecto *m*, -ta *f*
architectural [,arkə'tɛktʃərəl] *adj* : arquitectónico — architecturally *adv*
architecture ['arkə,tɛktʃər] *n* : arquitectura *f*
archive¹ ['ar,kaɪv] *vt* archived; archiving : archivar
archive² *n or* archives ['ar,kaɪvz] *npl* : archivo *m*
archivist ['arkəvɪst, -,kaɪ-] *n* : archivero *m*, -ra *f*; archivista *mf*
archway ['artʃ,weɪ] *n* : arco *m*, pasadizo *m* abovedado
arctic ['arktɪk, 'artʃ-] *adj* 1 : ártico ⟨arctic regions : zonas árticas⟩ 2 FRIGID : glacial
arctic circle *n* : círculo *m* ártico
ardent ['ardənt] *adj* 1 PASSIONATE : ardiente, fogoso, apasionado 2 FERVENT : ferviente, fervoroso — ardently *adv*
ardor ['ardər] *n* : ardor *m*, pasión *f*, fervor *m*

arduous ['ardʒuəs] *adj* : arduo, duro, riguroso — arduously *adv*
arduousness ['ardʒuəsnəs] *n* : dureza *f*, rigor *m*
are → be
area ['æriə] *n* 1 SURFACE : área *f*, superficie *f* 2 REGION : área *f*, región *f*, zona *f* 3 FIELD : área *f*, terreno *m*, campo *m* (de conocimiento)
area code *n* : código *m* de la zona, prefijo *m* *Spain*
arena [ə'ri:nə] *n* 1 : arena *f*, estadio *m* ⟨sports arena : estadio deportivo⟩ 2 : arena *f*, ruedo *m* ⟨the political arena : el ruedo político⟩
aren't ['arənt] *contraction of* ARE NOT → be
Argentine ['ardʒən,taɪn, -,ti:n] *or* Argentinean *or* Argentinian [,ardʒən'tɪniən] *n* : argentino *m*, -na *f* — Argentine *or* Argentinean *or* Argentinian *adj*
argon ['ar,gan] *n* : argón *m*
argot ['argət, -,go:] *n* : argot *m*
arguable ['argjuəbəl] *adj* : discutible — arguably [-bli] *adv*
argue ['ar,gju:] *v* -gued; -guing *vi* 1 REASON : argumentar, argüir, razonar ⟨to argue for something : abogar por algo, argumentar a favor de algo⟩ ⟨to argue against something : argumentar en contra de algo⟩ 2 DISPUTE : discutir, pelear(se), alegar ⟨to argue about something : discutir por algo, pelear(se) por algo⟩ — *vt* 1 SUGGEST : sugerir 2 MAINTAIN : alegar, argüir, sostener 3 DISCUSS : discutir, debatir
argument ['argjəmənt] *n* 1 REASONING : argumento *m*, razonamiento *m* 2 DISCUSSION : discusión *f*, debate *m* 3 QUARREL : pelea *f*, riña *f*, disputa *f*
argumentative [,argjə'mɛntətɪv] *adj* : discutidor
argyle ['ar,gaɪl] *n* : diseño *m* de rombos
aria ['ariə] *n* : aria *f*
arid ['ærəd] *adj* : árido
aridity [ə'rɪdəti, æ-] *n* : aridez *f*
Aries ['ɛri:z, -i,i:z] *n* 1 : Aries *m* (signo o constelación) 2 : Aries *mf* (persona)
arise [ə'raɪz] *vi* arose [ə'ro:z]; arisen [ə'rɪzən]; arising 1 ASCEND : ascender, subir, elevarse 2 ORIGINATE : originarse, surgir, presentarse 3 GET UP : levantarse
aristocracy [,ærə'stakrəsi] *n*, *pl* -cies : aristocracia *f*
aristocrat [ə'rɪstə,kræt] *n* : aristócrata *mf*
aristocratic [ə,rɪstə'krætɪk] *adj* : aristocrático, noble
arithmetic¹ [,ærɪθ'mɛtɪk] *or* arithmetical [-ʧkəl] *adj* : aritmético
arithmetic² [ə'rɪθmə,tɪk] *n* : aritmética *f*
ark ['ark] *n* : arca *f*
arm¹ ['arm] *vt* : armar — *vi* : armarse
arm² *n* 1 : brazo *m* (del cuerpo, de un sillón, de una máquina), manga *f* (de una prenda) ⟨he took her (by the) arm : la tomó del brazo⟩ 2 BRANCH : rama *f*, sección *f* 3 WEAPON : arma *f* ⟨to take up arms : tomar las armas⟩ 4 ~ in ~ : del brazo 5 → coat of arms

armada [ɑrˈmɑdə, -ˈmeɪ-] n : armada f, flota f

armadillo [ˌɑrməˈdɪlo] n, pl **-los** : armadillo m

armament [ˈɑrməmənt] n : armamento m

armband [ˈɑrmˌbænd] n : brazalete m

armchair [ˈɑrmˌtʃɛr] n : butaca f, sillón m

armed [ˈɑrmd] adj 1 : armado ⟨armed robbery : robo a mano armada⟩ 2 **armed forces** : fuerzas fpl armadas 3 (used in combination) : de brazos ⟨long-armed : de brazos largos⟩ ⟨one-armed : manco⟩

Armenian [ɑrˈmiːniən] n : armenio m, -nia f — **Armenian** adj

armistice [ˈɑrməstɪs] n : armisticio m

armor [ˈɑrmər] n : armadura f, coraza f

armored [ˈɑrmərd] adj : blindado, acorazado

armory [ˈɑrməri] n, pl **-mories** : arsenal m (almacén), armería f (museo), fábrica f de armas

armpit [ˈɑrmˌpɪt] n : axila f, sobaco m

armrest [ˈɑrmˌrɛst] n : apoyabrazos m

army [ˈɑrmi] n, pl **-mies** 1 : ejército m (militar) 2 MULTITUDE : legión f, multitud f, ejército m

aroma [əˈroːmə] n : aroma f

aromatic [ˌærəˈmætɪk] adj : aromático

around¹ [əˈraʊnd] adv 1 : en un círculo ⟨to go around (and around) : dar vueltas⟩ ⟨to turn around : darse la vuelta, voltearse⟩ ⟨the road goes around the lake : la carretera bordea el lago⟩ 2 : de circunferencia ⟨a tree three feet around : un árbol de tres pies de circunferencia⟩ 3 : alrededor ⟨for miles around : por millas a la redonda⟩ ⟨all around : por todos lados, todo alrededor⟩ ⟨he looked around : miró a su alrededor⟩ ⟨they crowded around to watch : se aglomeraron para observar⟩ 4 : por ahí ⟨they're around somewhere : deben estar por ahí⟩ ⟨there was no one around : no había nadie⟩ ⟨is your mother around? : ¿está tu madre?⟩ ⟨I'll see you around! : ¡nos vemos!⟩ 5 : por/en muchas partes ⟨to wander around : deambular⟩ ⟨scattered around : esparcidos⟩ 6 APPROXIMATELY : más o menos, aproximadamente ⟨around 5 o'clock : a eso de las 5⟩ ⟨it's around 50 dollars : cuesta unos 50 dólares⟩ 7 **the wrong way around** : al revés

around² prep 1 SURROUNDING : alrededor de, en torno a 2 THROUGH : por, en ⟨he traveled around Mexico : viajó por México⟩ ⟨around the house : en casa⟩ 3 : a la vuelta de ⟨around the corner : a la vuelta de la esquina⟩ 4 NEAR : alrededor de, cerca de

arousal [əˈraʊzəl] n : excitación f

arouse [əˈraʊz] vt **aroused; arousing** 1 AWAKE : despertar 2 EXCITE : despertar, suscitar, excitar

arraign [əˈreɪn] vt : hacer comparecer (ante un tribunal)

arraignment [əˈreɪnmənt] n : orden m de comparecencia, acusación f

arrange [əˈreɪndʒ] vt **-ranged; -ranging** 1 ORDER : arreglar, poner en orden, dis-

poner 2 SETTLE : arreglar, fijar, concertar 3 ADAPT : arreglar, adaptar

arrangement [əˈreɪndʒmənt] n 1 ORDER : arreglo m, orden m 2 ARRANGING : disposición f ⟨floral arrangement : arreglo floral⟩ 3 AGREEMENT : arreglo m, acuerdo m, convenio m 4 **arrangements** npl : preparativos mpl, planes mpl

array¹ [əˈreɪ] vt 1 ORDER : poner en orden, presentar, formar 2 GARB : vestir, ataviar, engalanar

array² n 1 ORDER : orden m, formación f 2 ATTIRE : atavío m, galas mpl 3 RANGE, SELECTION : selección f, serie f, gama f ⟨an array of problems : una serie de problemas⟩

arrears [əˈrɪrz] npl : atrasos mpl ⟨to be in arrears : estar atrasado en los pagos⟩

arrest¹ [əˈrɛst] vt 1 APPREHEND : arrestar, detener 2 CHECK, STOP : detener, parar

arrest² n 1 APPREHENSION : arresto m, detención f ⟨under arrest : detenido⟩ 2 STOPPING : paro m

arrival [əˈraɪvəl] n : llegada f, venida f, arribo m

arrive [əˈraɪv] vi **-rived; -riving** 1 COME : llegar, arribar 2 SUCCEED : triunfar, tener éxito

arrogance [ˈærəgənts] n : arrogancia f, soberbia f, altanería f, altivez f

arrogant [ˈærəgənt] adj : arrogante, soberbio, altanero, altivo — **arrogantly** adv

arrogate [ˈærəˌgeɪt] vt **-gated; -gating** **to arrogate to oneself** : arrogarse

arrow [ˈæro] n : flecha f

arrowhead [ˈæroˌhɛd] n : punta f de flecha

arroyo [əˈroɪo] n : arroyo m

arsenal [ˈɑrsənəl] n : arsenal m

arsenic [ˈɑrsənɪk] n : arsénico m

arson [ˈɑrsən] n : incendio m premeditado

arsonist [ˈɑrsənɪst] n : incendiario m, -ria f; pirómano m, -na f

art [ˈɑrt] n 1 : arte m 2 SKILL : destreza f, habilidad f, maña f 3 **arts** npl : letras fpl (en la educación) 4 **arts and crafts** : artes y oficios 5 **fine arts** : bellas artes fpl

arterial [ɑrˈtɪriəl] adj : arterial

arteriosclerosis [ɑrˌtɪrioskləˈroːsɪs] n : arteriosclerosis f

artery [ˈɑrtəri] n, pl **-teries** 1 : arteria f 2 THOROUGHFARE : carretera f principal, arteria f

artful [ˈɑrtfəl] adj 1 INGENIOUS : ingenioso, diestro 2 CRAFTY : astuto, taimado, ladino, artero — **artfully** adv

art gallery → gallery

arthritic [ɑrˈθrɪtɪk] adj : artrítico

arthritis [ɑrˈθraɪtəs] n, pl **-tides** [ɑrˈθrɪtəˌdiːz] : artritis f

arthropod [ˈɑrθrəˌpɑd] n : artrópodo m

artichoke [ˈɑrtəˌtʃoːk] n : alcachofa f

article [ˈɑrtɪkəl] n 1 ITEM : artículo m, objeto m 2 ESSAY : artículo m 3 CLAUSE : artículo m, cláusula f 4 : artículo m ⟨definite article : artículo determinado⟩

articulate[1] [ɑr'tɪkjə,leɪt] *vt* **-lated; -lating**
1 UTTER : articular, enunciar, expresar
2 CONNECT : articular (en anatomía)

articulate[2] [ɑr'tɪkjələt] *adj* **to be articulate** : poder articular palabras, expresarse bien

articulately [ɑr'tɪkjələtli] *adv* : elocuentemente, con fluidez

articulateness [ɑr'tɪkjələtnəs] *n* : elocuencia *f*, fluidez *f*

articulation [ɑr,tɪkjə'leɪʃən] *n* **1** JOINT : articulación *f* **2** UTTERANCE : articulación *f*, declaración *f* **3** ENUNCIATION : articulación *f*, pronunciación *f*

artifact ['ɑrtə,fækt] *n* : artefacto *m*

artifice ['ɑrtəfəs] *n* : artificio *m*

artificial [,ɑrtə'fɪʃəl] *adj* **1** SYNTHETIC : artificial, sintético **2** FEIGNED : artificial, falso, afectado

artificially [,ɑrtə'fɪʃəli] *adv* : artificialmente, con afectación

artillery [ɑr'tɪləri] *n, pl* **-leries** : artillería *f*

artisan ['ɑrtəzən, -sən] *n* : artesano *m*, -na *f*

artist ['ɑrtɪst] *n* : artista *mf*

artistic [ɑr'tɪstɪk] *adj* : artístico — **artistically** [-tɪkli] *adv*

artistry ['ɑrtəstri] *n* : maestría *f*, arte *m*

artless ['ɑrtləs] *adj* : sencillo, natural, ingenuo, cándido — **artlessly** *adv*

artlessness ['ɑrtləsnəs] *n* : ingenuidad *f*, candidez *f*

artwork ['ɑrt,wərk] *n* **1** : obra *f* de arte **2** WORKS : arte *f*, obra *f* **3** ILLUSTRATIONS : material *m* gráfico

arty ['ɑrti] *or* **artsy** ['ɑrtsi] *adj* **artier; -est** : pretenciosamente artístico

as[1] ['æz] *adv* **1** : tan, tanto ⟨this one's not as difficult : éste no es tan difícil⟩ ⟨he has a lot of time, but I don't have as much : él tiene mucho tiempo, pero yo no tengo tanto⟩ ⟨he was angry, but she was just as angry : él estaba enojado, pero ella estaba tan enojada como él⟩ **2** SUCH AS : como ⟨some trees, such as oak and pine : algunos árboles, como el roble y el pino⟩

as[2] *conj* **1** LIKE : como, igual que ⟨(as) white as snow : blanca como la nieve⟩ ⟨she's as smart/guilty as he is : ella es tan inteligente/culpable como él⟩ ⟨she's Italian, as am I : es italiana, igual que yo⟩ ⟨she believes it, as do I : ella lo cree, y yo también⟩ ⟨twice as big as : el doble de grande que⟩ ⟨as soon as possible : lo más pronto posible⟩ **2** : como ⟨do (it) as I do : haz como yo⟩ ⟨knowing them as I do : conociéndolo como lo conozco⟩ ⟨as it happens . . . : da la casualidad de que . . .⟩ ⟨as is often/usually the case : como suele ocurrir⟩ ⟨as was to be expected : como era de esperar⟩ **3** WHEN, WHILE : cuando, mientras, a la vez que ⟨I saw it as I was leaving : lo vi cuando salía⟩ **4** BECAUSE : porque ⟨as I was tired, I stayed home : porque estaba cansada, me quedé en casa⟩ **5** THOUGH : aunque, por más que ⟨strange as it may appear : por extraño que parezca⟩ ⟨much as it pains me to say so : aunque me da pena decirlo⟩ ⟨try as he might

: por más que trataba⟩ **6** as for CONCERNING : en cuanto a **7** as if : como si ⟨it looks as if : parece que⟩ ⟨as if I weren't there : como si yo no estuviera ahí⟩ **8** as is : tal (y) como está ⟨it's being sold as is : se vende tal como está⟩ **9** as it is : tal (y) como está ⟨leave it as it is : déjalo tal como está⟩ **10** as it is ALREADY : ya ⟨we have too much to do as it is : ya tenemos demasiado que hacer⟩ **11** as of : a partir de **12** as to CONCERNING : en cuanto a ⟨I'm at a loss as to how to explain it : no sé como explicarlo⟩ **13** so as IN ORDER TO : para

as[3] *prep* **1** : de ⟨I met her as a child : la conocí de pequeña⟩ ⟨he works as a secretary : trabaja de secretario⟩ **2** LIKE : como ⟨behave as a man : compórtate como un hombre⟩ ⟨I'm telling you this as a friend : te lo digo como amigo⟩

as[4] *pron* : que ⟨in the same building as my brother : en el mismo edificio que mi hermano⟩

asbestos [æz'bɛstəs, æs-] *n* : asbesto *m*, amianto *m*

ascend [ə'sɛnd] *vi* : ascender, subir — *vt* : subir, subir a, escalar

ascendancy [ə'sɛndənsi] *n* : ascendiente *m*, predominio *m*

ascendant[1] [ə'sɛndənt] *adj* **1** RISING : ascendente **2** DOMINANT : superior, dominante

ascendant[2] *n* to be in the ascendant : estar en alza, ir ganando predominio

ascension [ə'sɛnʧən] *n* : ascensión *f*

ascent [ə'sɛnt] *n* **1** RISE : ascensión *f*, subida *f*, ascenso *m* **2** SLOPE : cuesta *f*, pendiente *f*

ascertain [,æsər'teɪn] *vt* : determinar, establecer, averiguar

ascetic[1] [ə'sɛtɪk] *adj* : ascético

ascetic[2] *n* : asceta *mf*

asceticism [ə'sɛtə,sɪzəm] *n* : ascetismo *m*

ascribable [ə'skraɪbəbəl] *adj* : atribuible, imputable

ascribe [ə'skraɪb] *vt* **-cribed; -cribing** : atribuir, imputar

aseptic [eɪ'sɛptɪk] *adj* : aséptico

asexual [,eɪ'sɛkʃʊəl] *adj* : asexual

as for *prep* CONCERNING : en cuanto a, respecto a, para

ash ['æʃ] *n* **1** : ceniza *f* ⟨to reduce to ashes : reducir a cenizas⟩ **2** : fresno *m* (árbol)

ashamed [ə'ʃeɪmd] *adj* : avergonzado, abochornado, apenado — **ashamedly** [ə'ʃeɪmədli] *adv*

ashen ['æʃən] *adj* : lívido, ceniciento, pálido

ashore [ə'ʃor] *adv* **1** : en tierra **2 to go ashore** : desembarcar

ashtray ['æʃ,treɪ] *n* : cenicero *m*

Ash Wednesday *n* : Miércoles *m* de Ceniza

Asian[1] ['eɪʒən, -ʃən] *adj* : asiático

Asian[2] *n* : asiático *m*, -ca *f*

aside [ə'saɪd] *adv* **1** : a un lado ⟨to step aside : hacerse a un lado⟩ **2** : de lado, aparte ⟨jesting aside : bromas aparte⟩ **3 to set aside** : guardar, apartar, reservar

aside from prep **1** BESIDES : además de **2** EXCEPT : aparte de, menos

as if conj : como si

asinine ['æsən,aɪn] adj : necio, estúpido

ask ['æsk] vt **1** : preguntar ⟨to ask a question : hacer una pregunta⟩ ⟨ask him if he's coming : pregúntale si viene⟩, **2** REQUEST : pedir, solicitar ⟨to ask someone (for) a favor, to ask a favor of someone : pedirle un favor a alguien⟩ **3** INVITE : invitar ⟨she asked us to the party : nos invitó a la fiesta⟩ ⟨we asked them over for dinner : los invitamos a cenar⟩ ⟨he asked her out : la invitó a salir⟩ — vi **1** INQUIRE : preguntar ⟨I asked about/after her children : pregunté por sus niños⟩ **2** REQUEST : pedir ⟨we asked for help : pedimos ayuda⟩ ⟨if you need help, ask : si necesitas ayuda, pídela⟩ **3 to ask for it/trouble** : buscársela

askance [ə'skæns] adv **1** SIDELONG : de reojo, de soslayo **2** SUSPICIOUSLY : con recelo, con desconfianza

askew [ə'skju:] adj : torcido, ladeado

asleep [ə'sli:p] adj **1** : dormido, durmiendo **2 to fall asleep** : quedarse dormido

as of prep : desde, a partir de

asparagus [ə'spærəgəs] n : espárrago m

aspect ['æ,spɛkt] n : aspecto m

aspen ['æspən] n : álamo m temblón

asperity [æ'spɛrəṭi, ə-] n, pl **-ties** : aspereza f

aspersion [ə'spərʒən] n : difamación f, calumnia f

asphalt ['æs,fɔlt] n : asfalto m

asphyxia [æ'sfɪksiə, ə-] n : asfixia f

asphyxiate [æ'sfɪksi,eɪt] v **-ated; -ating** vt : asfixiar — vi : asfixiarse

asphyxiation [æ,sfɪksi'eɪʃən] n : asfixia f

aspirant ['æspərənt, ə'spaɪrənt] n : aspirante mf, pretendiente mf

aspiration [,æspə'reɪʃən] n **1** DESIRE : aspiración f, anhelo m, ambición f **2** BREATHING : aspiración f

aspire [ə'spaɪr] vi **-pired; -piring** : aspirar

aspirin ['æsprən, 'æspə-] n, pl **aspirin** or **aspirins** : aspirina f

ass ['æs] n **1** : asno m **2** IDIOT : imbécil mf, idiota mf

assail [ə'seɪl] vt : atacar, asaltar

assailant [ə'seɪlənt] n : asaltante mf, atacante mf

assassin [ə'sæsən] n : asesino m, -na f

assassinate [ə'sæsən,eɪt] vt **-nated; -nating** : asesinar

assassination [ə,sæsən'eɪʃən] n : asesinato m

assault¹ [ə'sɔlt] vt : atacar, asaltar, agredir

assault² n : ataque m, asalto m, agresión f

assay¹ [æ'seɪ, 'æ,seɪ] vt : ensayar

assay² ['æ,seɪ, æ'seɪ] n : ensayo m

assemble [ə'sɛmbəl] v **-bled; -bling** vt **1** GATHER : reunir, recoger, juntar **2** CONSTRUCT : ensamblar, montar, construir — vi : reunirse, congregarse

assembly [ə'sɛmbli] n, pl **-blies** **1** MEETING : reunión f **2** CONSTRUCTING : ensamblaje m, montaje m

assembly line n : cadena f de montaje

assemblyman [ə'sɛmblimən] n, pl **-men** [-mən, -,mɛn] : asambleísta m

assemblywoman [ə'sɛmbli,wʊmən] n, pl **-women** [-,wɪmən] : asambleísta f

assent¹ [ə'sɛnt] vi : asentir, consentir

assent² n : asentimiento m, aprobación f

assert [ə'sərt] vt **1** AFFIRM : afirmar, aseverar, mantener **2 to assert oneself** : imponerse, hacerse valer

assertion [ə'sərʃən] n : afirmación f, aseveración f, aserto m

assertive [ə'sərṭɪv] adj : firme, enérgico

assertiveness [ə'sərṭɪvnəs] n : seguridad f en sí mismo

assess [ə'sɛs] vt **1** IMPOSE : gravar (un impuesto), imponer **2** EVALUATE : evaluar, valorar, aquilatar

assessment [ə'sɛsmənt] n : evaluación f, valoración f

assessor [ə'sɛsər] n : evaluador m, -dora f; tasador m, -dora f

asset ['æ,sɛt] n **1** : ventaja f, recurso m **2 assets** npl : bienes mpl, activo m ⟨assets and liabilities : activo y pasivo⟩

assiduous [ə'sɪdʒʊəs] adj : diligente, aplicado, asiduo — **assiduously** adv

assign [ə'saɪn] vt **1** APPOINT : designar, nombrar **2** ALLOT : asignar, señalar **3** ATTRIBUTE : atribuir, dar, conceder

assignment [ə'saɪnmənt] n **1** TASK : función f, tarea f, misión f **2** HOMEWORK : tarea f, asignación f PRi, deberes mpl Spain **3** APPOINTMENT : nombramiento m **4** ALLOCATION : asignación f

assimilate [ə'sɪmə,leɪt] v **-lated; -lating** vt : asimilar — vi : adaptarse, integrarse

assimilation [ə,sɪmə'leɪʃən] n : asimilación f

assist¹ [ə'sɪst] vt : asistir, ayudar

assist² n : asistencia f, contribución f

assistance [ə'sɪstənts] n : asistencia f, ayuda f, auxilio m

assistant [ə'sɪstənt] n : ayudante mf, asistente mf

associate¹ [ə'so:ʃi,eɪt, -si-] v **-ated; -ating** vt **1** CONNECT, RELATE : asociar, relacionar **2 to be associated with** : estar relacionado con, estar vinculado a — vi **to associate with** : relacionarse con, frecuentar

associate² [ə'so:ʃiət, -siət] n : asociado m, -da f; colega mf; socio m, -cia f

association [ə,so:ʃi'eɪʃən, -si-] n **1** ORGANIZATION : asociación f, sociedad f **2** RELATIONSHIP : asociación f, relación f

as soon as conj : en cuanto, tan pronto como

assorted [ə'sɔrṭəd] adj : surtido

assortment [ə'sɔrtmənt] n : surtido m, variedad f, colección f

assuage [ə'sweɪdʒ] vt **-suaged; -suaging** **1** EASE : aliviar, mitigar **2** CALM : calmar, aplacar **3** SATISFY : saciar, satisfacer

assume [ə'su:m] vt **-sumed; -suming** **1** SUPPOSE : suponer, asumir **2** UNDERTAKE : asumir, encargarse de **3** TAKE ON : adquirir, adoptar, tomar ⟨to assume importance : tomar importancia⟩ **4** FEIGN : adoptar, afectar, simular

assumed [ə'suːmd] *adj* : fingido, falso ⟨an assumed air of confidence : un aire de falsa confianza⟩ ⟨an assumed name : un nombre falso/ficticio/supuesto, un seudónimo⟩

assumption [ə'sʌmpʃən] *n* : asunción *f*, presunción *f*

assurance [ə'ʃurənts] *n* **1** CERTAINTY : certidumbre *f*, certeza *f* **2** CONFIDENCE : confianza *f*, aplomo *m*, seguridad *f*

assure [ə'ʃur] *vt* **-sured; -suring** : asegurar, garantizar ⟨I assure you that I'll do it : te aseguro que lo haré⟩

assured [ə'ʃurd] *adj* **1** CERTAIN : seguro, asegurado **2** CONFIDENT : confiado, seguro de sí mismo

aster ['æstər] *n* : aster *m*

asterisk ['æstə,rɪsk] *n* : asterisco *m*

astern [ə'stərn] *adv* **1** BEHIND : detrás, a popa **2** BACKWARDS : hacia atrás

asteroid ['æstə,rɔɪd] *n* : asteroide *m*

asthma ['æzmə] *n* : asma *m*

asthmatic [æz'mætɪk] *adj* : asmático

as though → as if

astigmatism [ə'stɪgmə,tɪzəm] *n* : astigmatismo *m*

as to *prep* **1** ABOUT : sobre, acerca de **2** → according to

astonish [ə'stanɪʃ] *vt* : asombrar, sorprender, pasmar

astonishing [ə'stanɪʃɪŋ] *adj* : asombroso, sorprendente, increíble — **astonishingly** *adv*

astonishment [ə'stanɪʃmənt] *n* : asombro *m*, estupefacción *f*, sorpresa *f*

astound [ə'staund] *vt* : asombrar, pasmar, dejar estupefacto

astounding [ə'staundɪŋ] *adj* : asombroso, pasmoso — **astoundingly** *adv*

astraddle [ə'strædəl] *adv* : a horcajadas

astral ['æstrəl] *adj* : astral

astray [ə'streɪ] *adv & adj* : perdido, extraviado, descarriado

astride [ə'straɪd] *adv* : a horcajadas

astringency [ə'strɪndʒəntsi] *n* : astringencia *f*

astringent¹ [ə'strɪndʒənt] *adj* : astringente

astringent² *n* : astringente *m*

astrologer [ə'stralədʒər] *n* : astrólogo *m*, -ga *f*

astrological [,æstrə'lɑdʒɪkəl] *adj* : astrológico

astrology [ə'stralədʒi] *n* : astrología *f*

astronaut ['æstrə,nɔt] *n* : astronauta *mf*

astronautic [,æstrə'nɔtɪk] *or* **astronautical** [-tɪkəl] *adj* : astronáutico

astronautics [,æstrə'nɔtɪks] *ns & pl* : astronáutica *f*

astronomer [ə'stranəmər] *n* : astrónomo *m*, -ma *f*

astronomical [,æstrə'nɑmɪkəl] *adj* **1** : astronómico **2** ENORMOUS : astronómico, enorme, gigantesco

astronomy [ə'stranəmi] *n, pl* **-mies** : astronomía *f*

astute [ə'stuːt, -'stjuːt] *adj* : astuto, sagaz, perspicaz — **astutely** *adv*

astuteness [ə'stuːtnəs, -'stjuːt-] *n* : astucia *f*, sagacidad *f*, perspicacia *f*

asunder [ə'sʌndər] *adv* : en dos, en pedazos ⟨to tear asunder : hacer pedazos⟩

as well as¹ *conj* : tanto como

as well as² *prep* BESIDES : además de, aparte de

as yet *adv* : aún, todavía

asylum [ə'saɪləm] *n* **1** REFUGE : refugio *m*, santuario *m*, asilo *m* **2** **insane asylum** : manicomio *m*

asymmetrical [,eɪsə'mɛtrɪkəl] *or* **asymmetric** [-'mɛtrɪk] *adj* : asimétrico

asymmetry [,eɪ'sɪmətri] *n* : asimetría *f*

at ['æt] *prep* **1** (*indicating location*) : en, a ⟨at the top : en lo alto⟩ ⟨at the fondo⟩ ⟨at Ann's house : en casa de Ana⟩ ⟨is she at home? : ¿está en casa?⟩ ⟨he was sitting at the table : estaba sentado a la mesa⟩ ⟨someone is knocking at the door : llaman a la puerta⟩ **2** (*indicating the recipient of an action, motion, or feeling*) ⟨she shouted at me : me gritó⟩ ⟨don't look at me! : ¡a mí no me mires!⟩ ⟨he's laughing at you : está riéndose de ti⟩ ⟨to be angry at someone : estar enojado con alguien⟩ **3** (*indicating a reaction or cause*) ⟨he laughed at the joke : se rió con el chiste⟩ ⟨to be surprised at something : sorprenderse por algo⟩ ⟨at the invitation of : por invitación de⟩ **4** (*indicating an activity or state*) ⟨children who are at play : niños que están jugando⟩ ⟨you're good at this : eres bueno para esto⟩ ⟨he's at peace now : ahora descansa en paz⟩ ⟨at peace/war : en paz/guerra⟩ ⟨to be at risk : peligrar⟩ **5** (*used for the symbol @*) : arroba ⟨at merriam-webster dot com : arroba merriam-webster punto com⟩ **6** (*indicating a rate or measure*) : a ⟨at 80 miles an hour : a 80 millas por hora⟩ ⟨they sell at a dollar each : se venden a un dólar cada uno⟩ **7** (*indicating an age or time*) : a ⟨at ten o'clock : a las diez⟩ ⟨at age 65 : a los 65 años (de edad)⟩ ⟨at last : por fin⟩ **8 at it** ⟨while we're at it : ya que estamos (en ello)⟩ ⟨they're at it again! : ¡ya empezaron otra vez!⟩

at all *adv* : en absoluto, para nada

ate → eat

atheism ['eɪθi,ɪzəm] *n* : ateísmo *m*

atheist ['eɪθiɪst] *n* : ateo *m*, atea *f*

atheistic [,eɪθi'ɪstɪk] *adj* : ateo

athlete ['æθ,liːt] *n* : atleta *mf*

athletic [æθ'lɛtɪk] *adj* : atlético

athletics [æθ'lɛtɪks] *ns & pl* : atletismo *m*

Atlantic [ət'læntɪk, æt-] *adj* : atlántico

atlas ['ætləs] *n* : atlas *m*

ATM [,eɪ,tiː'ɛm] *n* : cajero *m* automático

atmosphere ['ætmə,sfɪr] *n* **1** AIR : atmósfera *f*, aire *m* **2** AMBIENCE : ambiente *m*, atmósfera *f*, clima *m*

atmospheric [,ætmə'sfɪrɪk, -'sfɛr-] *adj* : atmosférico — **atmospherically** [-ɪkli] *adv*

atoll ['æ,tɔl, 'eɪ-, -,tɑl] *n* : atolón *m*

atom ['ætəm] *n* **1** : átomo *m* **2** SPECK : ápice *m*, pizca *f*

atomic [ə'tamɪk] *adj* : atómico

atomic bomb *n* : bomba *f* atómica

atomizer ['ætə,maɪzər] *n* : atomizador *m*, pulverizador *m*

atone [ə'to:n] *vt* atoned; atoning to atone for : expiar

atonement [ə'to:nmənt] *n* : expiación *f*, desagravio *m*

atop[1] [ə'tɑp] *adj* : encima

atop[2] *prep* : encima de, sobre

atrium ['eɪtriəm] *n, pl* **atria** [-triə] *or* **atriums** 1 : atrio *m* 2 : aurícula *f* (del corazón)

atrocious [ə'tro:ʃəs] *adj* : atroz — **atrociously** *adv*

atrocity [ə'trɑsəti] *n, pl* **-ties** : atrocidad *f*

atrophy[1] ['ætrəfi] *vt* **-phied; -phying** : atrofiar

atrophy[2] *n, pl* **-phies** : atrofia *f*

at sign *n* (*used for the symbol @*) : arroba *f*

attach [ə'tætʃ] *vt* 1 FASTEN : sujetar, atar, amarrar, pegar 2 JOIN : juntar, adjuntar 3 ATTRIBUTE : dar, atribuir ⟨I attached little importance to it : le di poca importancia⟩ 4 SEIZE : embargar 5 to become attached to someone : encariñarse con alguien

attaché [ˌætɑ'ʃeɪ, ˌæ,tæ-, ˌə,tæ-] *n* : agregado *m*, -da *f*

attaché case *n* : maletín *m*

attachment [ə'tætʃmənt] *n* 1 ACCESSORY : accesorio *m* 2 CONNECTION : conexión *f*, acoplamiento *m* 3 FONDNESS : apego *m*, cariño *m*, afición *f* 4 : adjunto *m* (en un email)

attack[1] [ə'tæk] *vt* 1 ASSAULT : atacar, asaltar, agredir 2 TACKLE : acometer, combatir, enfrentarse con

attack[2] *n* 1 : ataque *m* ⟨an attack on/against : un ataque a/contra⟩ ⟨to launch an attack : lanzar un ataque⟩ 2 : ataque *m* ⟨heart attack : ataque cardíaco, infarto⟩ ⟨panic/anxiety attack : ataque de pánico/ansiedad⟩

attacker [ə'tækər] *n* : asaltante *mf*

attain [ə'teɪn] *vt* 1 ACHIEVE : lograr, conseguir, alcanzar, realizar 2 REACH : alcanzar, llegar a

attainable [ə'teɪnəbəl] *adj* : realizable, asequible

attainment [ə'teɪnmənt] *n* : logro *m*, consecución *f*, realización *f*

attempt[1] [ə'tempt] *vt* : intentar, tratar de

attempt[2] *n* : intento *m*, tentativa *f*

attend [ə'tend] *vt* 1 : asistir a ⟨to attend a meeting : asistir a una reunión⟩ 2 : atender, ocuparse de, cuidar ⟨to attend a patient : atender a un paciente⟩ 3 HEED : atender a, hacer caso de 4 ACCOMPANY : acompañar

attendance [ə'tendənts] *n* 1 ATTENDING : asistencia *f* 2 TURNOUT : concurrencia *f*

attendant[1] [ə'tendənt] *adj* : concomitante, inherente

attendant[2] *n* : asistente *mf*, acompañante *mf*, guarda *mf*

attention [ə'tentʃən] *n* 1 : atención *f* ⟨I brought the problem to his attention : le informé del problema⟩ ⟨it has come to our attention that . . . : se nos ha informado que . . .⟩ ⟨to attract someone's attention : atraer la atención de alguien⟩ 2 to pay attention : prestar atención, hacer caso ⟨to pay attention to someone/something : prestarle atención a algo/alguien⟩ ⟨don't pay any attention to him : no le hagas caso⟩ ⟨she didn't pay attention to the rumors : no hizo caso de los rumores⟩ 3 to stand at attention : estar firme

attentive [ə'tentɪv] *adj* : atento — **attentively** *adv*

attentiveness [ə'tentɪvnəs] *n* 1 THOUGHTFULNESS : cortesía *f*, consideración *f* 2 CONCENTRATION : atención *f*, concentración *f*

attest [ə'test] *vt* : atestiguar, dar fe de

attestation [ˌæ,ts'teɪʃən] *n* : testimonio *m*

attic ['ætɪk] *n* : ático *m*, desván *m*, buhardilla *f*

attire[1] [ə'taɪr] *vt* **-tired; -tiring** : ataviar

attire[2] *n* : atuendo *m*, atavío *m*

attitude ['ætə,tu:d, -,tju:d] *n* 1 FEELING : actitud *f* 2 POSTURE : postura *f*

attorney [ə'tərni] *n, pl* **-neys** : abogado *m*, -da *f*

attract [ə'trækt] *vt* 1 : atraer 2 to attract attention : llamar la atención

attraction [ə'trækʃən] *n* : atracción *f*, atractivo *m*

attractive [ə'træktɪv] *adj* : atractivo, atrayente

attractively [ə'træktɪvli] *adv* : de manera atractiva, de buen gusto, hermosamente

attractiveness [ə'træktɪvnəs] *n* : atractivo *m*

attributable [ə'trɪbjutəbəl] *adj* : atribuible, imputable

attribute[1] [ə'trɪ,bju:t] *vt* **-tributed; -tributing** : atribuir

attribute[2] ['ætrə,bju:t] *n* : atributo *m*, cualidad *f*

attribution [ˌætrə'bju:ʃən] *n* : atribución *f*

attrition [ə'trɪʃən] *n* : desgaste *m* ⟨war of attrition : guerra de desgaste⟩

attune [ə'tu:n, -'tju:n] *vt* **-tuned; -tuning** 1 ADAPT : adaptar, adecuar 2 to be attuned to : estar en armonía con

ATV [ˌeɪ,ti:'vi:] → all-terrain vehicle

atypical [ˌeɪ'tɪpɪkəl] *adj* : atípico

aubergine ['o:bər,ʒi:n] → eggplant

auburn ['ɔbərn] *adj* : castaño rojizo

auction[1] ['ɔkʃən] *vt* : subastar, rematar

auction[2] *n* : subasta *f*, remate *m*

auctioneer [ˌɔkʃə'nɪr] *n* : subastador *m*, -dora *f*; rematador *m*, -dora *f*

audacious [ɔ'deɪʃəs] *adj* : audaz, atrevido

audacity [ɔ'dæsəti] *n, pl* **-ties** : audacia *f*, atrevimiento *m*, descaro *m*

audible ['ɔdəbəl] *adj* : audible — **audibly** [-bli] *adv*

audience ['ɔdiənts] *n* 1 INTERVIEW : audiencia *f* 2 PUBLIC : audiencia *f*, público *m*, auditorio *m*, espectadores *mpl*

audio[1] ['ɔdi,o:] *adj* : de sonido, de audio

audio[2] *n* : audio *m*

audiobook ['ɔdi,o:'bʊk] *n* : audiolibro *m*

audiovisual [ˌɔdio'vɪʒʊəl] *adj* : audiovisual

audit[1] ['ɔdət] *vt* 1 : auditar (finanzas) 2 : asistir como oyente a (una clase o un curso)

audit² n : auditoría f
audition¹ [ɔ'dɪʃən] vi : hacer una audición
audition² n : audición f
auditor ['ɔdətər] n 1 : auditor m, -tora f (de finanzas) 2 STUDENT : oyente mf
auditorium [,ɔdə'toriəm] n, pl -riums or -ria [-riə] : auditorio m, sala f
auditory ['ɔdə,tori] adj : auditivo
auger ['ɔgər] n : taladro m, barrena f
augment [ɔg'ment] vt : aumentar, incrementar
augmentation [,ɔgmən'teɪʃən] n : aumento m, incremento m
augmented reality n : realidad f aumentada
au gratin [o:'grɑtən, -'græ-] adj : gratinado
augur¹ ['ɔgər] vt : augurar, presagiar — vi **to augur well** : ser de buen agüero
augur² n : augur m
augury ['ɔgjuri, -gər-] n, pl -ries : augurio m, presagio m, agüero m
august [ɔ'gʌst] adj : augusto
August ['ɔgəst] n : agosto m ⟨they arrived on the 20th of August, they arrived on August 20th : llegaron el 20 de agosto⟩
auk ['ɔk] n : alca f
aunt ['ænt, 'ɑnt] n : tía f
auntie ['ænti, 'ɑnti] n : tita f
aura ['ɔrə] n : aura f
aural ['ɔrəl] adj : auditivo
auricle ['ɔrɪkəl] n : aurícula f
aurora borealis [ə'rorə,bori'æləs] n : aurora f boreal
auspices ['ɔspəsəz, -,si:z] npl : auspicios mpl
auspicious [ɔ'spɪʃəs] adj : prometedor, propicio, de buen augurio
austere [ɔ'stɪr] adj : austero, severo, adusto — **austerely** adv
austerity [ɔ'sterəti] n, pl -ties : austeridad f
Australian [ɔ'streɪljən] n : australiano m, -na f — **Australian** adj
Austrian ['ɔstriən] n : austriaco m, -ca f — **Austrian** adj
authentic [ə'θentɪk, ɔ-] adj : auténtico, genuino — **authentically** [-tɪkli] adv
authenticate [ə'θentɪ,keɪt, ɔ-] vt -cated; -cating : autenticar, autentificar
authenticity [,ɔθen'tɪsəti] n : autenticidad f
author ['ɔθər] n 1 WRITER : escritor m, -tora f; autor m, -tora f 2 CREATOR : autor m, -tora f; creador m, -dora f; artífice mf
authoritarian [ə,θorə'teriən, ə-] adj : autoritario
authoritative [ə'θorə,teɪtɪv, ɔ-] adj 1 RELIABLE : fidedigno, autorizado 2 DICTATORIAL : autoritario, dictatorial, imperioso
authoritatively [ə'θorə,teɪtɪvli, ɔ-] adv 1 RELIABLY : con autoridad 2 DICTATORIALLY : de manera autoritaria
authority [ə'θorəti, ɔ-] n, pl -ties 1 EXPERT : autoridad f 2 POWER : autoridad f 3 AUTHORIZATION : autorización f 4 **the authorities** : las autoridades 5 **on good authority** : de buena fuente ⟨he

has it on good authority that . . . : sabe de buena fuente que . . .⟩
authorization [,ɔθərə'zeɪʃən] n : autorización f
authorize ['ɔθə,raɪz] vt -rized; -rizing : autorizar, facultar
authorship ['ɔθər,ʃɪp] n : autoría f
autism ['ɔ,tɪzəm] n : autismo m
autistic [ɔ'tɪstɪk] adj : autista
auto ['ɔto] → **automobile**
auto- ['ɔto] pref 1 SELF- : auto- 2 : automático
autobiographical [,ɔto,baɪə'græfɪkəl] adj : autobiográfico
autobiography [,ɔtobaɪ'ɑgrəfi] n, pl -phies : autobiografía f
autocorrect ['ɔ,to:kə'rekt] n : autocorrector m, corrector m automático
autocracy [ɔ'tɑkrəsi] n, pl -cies : autocracia f
autocrat ['ɔtə,kræt] n : autócrata mf
autocratic [,ɔtə'krætɪk] adj : autocrático — **autocratically** [-tɪkli] adv
autograph¹ ['ɔtə,græf] vt : autografiar
autograph² n : autógrafo m
automaker ['ɔto:meɪkər] n : fabricante mf de autos, automotriz f
automate ['ɔtə,meɪt] vt -mated; -mating : automatizar
automatic [,ɔtə'mætɪk] adj : automático — **automatically** [-tɪkli] adv
automatic pilot → **autopilot**
automation [,ɔtə'meɪʃə n] n : automatización f
automaton [ɔ'tɑmə,tɑn] n, pl -atons or -ata [-tə, -,tɑ] : autómata m
automobile [,ɔtəmo'bi:l, -'mo:,bi:l] n : automóvil m, auto m, carro m, coche m
automotive [,ɔtə'mo:tɪv] adj : automotor
autonomous [ɔ'tɑnəməs] adj : autónomo — **autonomously** adv
autonomy [ɔ'tɑnəmi] n, pl -mies : autonomía f
autopilot ['ɔto:,paɪlət] n : piloto m automático
autopsy ['ɔ,tɑpsi, -təp-] n, pl -sies : autopsia f
autumn ['ɔtəm] n : otoño m
autumnal [ɔ'tʌmnəl] adj : otoñal
auxiliary¹ [ɔg'zɪljəri, -'zɪləri] adj : auxiliar
auxiliary² n, pl -ries : auxiliar mf, ayudante mf
avail¹ [ə'veɪl] vt **to avail oneself** : aprovecharse, valerse
avail² n 1 : provecho m, utilidad f 2 **to no avail** : en vano 3 **to be of no avail** : no servir de nada, ser inútil
availability [ə,veɪlə'bɪləti] n, pl -ties : disponibilidad f
available [ə'veɪləbəl] adj : disponible
avalanche ['ævə,læntʃ] n : avalancha f, alud m
avant–garde¹ [,ɑ,vɑnt'gɑrd] adj : vanguardista
avant–garde² n : vanguardia f — **avant–gardist** [,ɑ,vɑnt'gɑrdɪst] n
avarice ['ævərəs] n : avaricia f, codicia f
avaricious [,ævə'rɪʃəs] adj : avaricioso, codicioso
avatar ['ævə,tɑr] n : avatar m

avenge [əˈvɛndʒ] *vt* **avenged; avenging** , : vengar

avenue [ˈævəˌnuː, -ˌnjuː] *n* **1** : avenida *f* **2** MEANS : vía *f*, camino *m*

average¹ [ˈævrɪdʒ, ˈævə-] *vt* **-aged; -aging** **1** : hacer un promedio de ⟨he averages 8 hours a day : hace un promedio de 8 horas diarias⟩ **2** : calcular el promedio de, promediar (en matemáticas)

average² *adj* **1** MEAN : medio ⟨the average temperature : la temperatura media⟩ **2** ORDINARY : común, ordinario ⟨the average man : el hombre común⟩

average³ *n* : promedio *m*

averse [əˈvərs] *adj* : reacio, opuesto

aversion [əˈvərʒən] *n* : aversión *f*

avert [əˈvərt] *vt* **1** : apartar, desviar ⟨he averted his eyes from the scene : apartó los ojos de la escena⟩ **2** AVOID, PREVENT : evitar, prevenir

aviary [ˈeɪviˌɛri] *n, pl* **-aries** : pajarera *f*

aviation [ˌeɪviˈeɪʃən] *n* : aviación *f*

aviator [ˈeɪviˌeɪtər] *n* : aviador *m*, -dora *f*

avid [ˈævɪd] *adj* **1** GREEDY : ávido, codicioso **2** ENTHUSIASTIC : ávido, entusiasta, ferviente — **avidly** *adv*

avocado [ˌævəˈkɑdo, ˌɑvə-] *n, pl* **-dos** : aguacate *m*, palta *f*

avocation [ˌævəˈkeɪʃən] *n* : pasatiempo *m*, afición *f*

avoid [əˈvɔɪd] *vt* **1** SHUN : evitar, eludir **2** FORGO : evitar, abstenerse de ⟨I always avoided gossip : siempre evitaba los chismes⟩ **3** EVADE : evitar ⟨if I can avoid it : si puedo evitarlo⟩

avoidable [əˈvɔɪdəbəl] *adj* : evitable

avoidance [əˈvɔɪdənts] *n* : el evitar

avoirdupois [ˌævərdəˈpɔɪz] *n* : sistema *m* inglés de pesos y medidas

avow [əˈvau] *vt* : reconocer, confesar

avowal [əˈvauəl] *n* : reconocimiento *m*, confesión *f*

await [əˈweɪt] *vt* : esperar

awake¹ [əˈweɪk] *v* **awoke** [əˈwoːk]; **awoken** [əˈwoːkən] *or* **awaked; awaking** : despertar

awake² *adj* : despierto

awaken [əˈweɪkən] → **awake¹**

award¹ [əˈwɔrd] *vt* : otorgar, conceder, conferir

award² *n* **1** PRIZE : premio *m*, galardón *m* **2** MEDAL : condecoración *f*

aware [əˈwær] *adj* : consciente ⟨to be aware of : darse cuenta de, estar consciente de⟩

awareness [əˈwærnəs] *n* : conciencia *f*, conocimiento *m*

awash [əˈwɔʃ] *adj* : inundado

away¹ [əˈweɪ] *adv* **1** : de aquí, de allí ⟨it's 10 miles away (from here) : queda/está a 10 millas (de aquí)⟩ ⟨she's away from the office : está fuera de la oficina⟩ ⟨far away from home : lejos de casa⟩ ⟨go

away! : ¡fuera de aquí!, ¡vete!⟩ ⟨he walked away : se alejó (caminando)⟩ ⟨she looked away : desvió la mirada⟩ ⟨stay away from the dog : no te acerques al perro⟩ **2** : en un lugar seguro ⟨she tucked it away in a drawer : lo guardó en un cajón⟩ ⟨the files are locked away : los archivos están guardados bajo llave⟩ **3** (*indicating a gradual diminishing*) ⟨to fade away : desvanecerse, apagarse⟩ ⟨to waste away (from illness) : consumirse (por enfermedad)⟩ **4** NONSTOP, STEADILY : sin parar, a un ritmo constante ⟨she was typing away at the computer : estaba tecleando en la computadora⟩ **5** : fuera de casa (en deportes) ⟨they played at home and away : jugaron en casa y fuera de casa⟩

away² *adj* **1** ABSENT : ausente ⟨away for the week : ausente por la semana⟩ **2** **away game** : partido *m* fuera de casa

awe¹ [ˈɔ] *vt* **awed; awing** : abrumar, asombrar, impresionar

awe² *n* : asombro *m*

awesome [ˈɔsəm] *adj* **1** IMPOSING : imponente, formidable **2** AMAZING : asombroso

awestruck [ˈɔˌstrʌk] *adj* : asombrado

awful [ˈɔfəl] *adj* **1** AWESOME : asombroso **2** DREADFUL : horrible, terrible, atroz **3** ENORMOUS : enorme, tremendo ⟨an awful lot of people : muchísima gente, la mar de gente⟩

awfully [ˈɔfəli] *adv* **1** EXTREMELY : terriblemente, extremadamente **2** BADLY : muy mal, espantosamente

awhile [əˈhwaɪl] *adv* : un rato, algún tiempo

awkward [ˈɔkwərd] *adj* **1** CLUMSY : torpe, desmañado **2** EMBARRASSING : embarazoso, delicado ⟨an awkward position : una situación embarazosa⟩ — **awkwardly** *adv*

awkwardness [ˈɔkwərdnəs] *n* **1** CLUMSINESS : torpeza *f* **2** INCONVENIENCE : incomodidad *f*

awl [ˈɔl] *n* : punzón *m*

awning [ˈɔnɪŋ] *n* : toldo *m*

awry [əˈraɪ] *adj* **1** ASKEW : torcido **2 to go awry** : salir mal, fracasar

ax *or* **axe** [ˈæks] *n* : hacha *m*

axiom [ˈæksiəm] *n* : axioma *m*

axiomatic [ˌæksiəˈmætɪk] *adj* : axiomático

axis [ˈæksɪs] *n, pl* **axes** [-ˌsiːz] : eje *m*

axle [ˈæksəl] *n* : eje *m*

aye¹ [ˈaɪ] *adv* : sí

aye² *n* : sí *m*

azalea [əˈzeɪljə] *n* : azalea *f*

azimuth [ˈæzəməθ] *n* : azimut *m*, acimut *m*

Aztec [ˈæzˌtɛk] *n* : azteca *mf*

azure¹ [ˈæʒər] *adj* : azur, celeste

azure² *n* : azur *m*

B

b ['bi:] *n, pl* **b's** *or* **bs** ['bi:z] **1** : segunda letra del alfabeto inglés **2 B** : si *m* ⟨B sharp/flat : si sostenido/bemol⟩

babble[1] ['bæbəl] *vi* **-bled; -bling 1** PRATTLE : balbucear **2** CHATTER : parlotear *fam* **3** MURMUR : murmurar

babble[2] *n* : balbuceo *m* (de bebé), parloteo *m* (de adultos), murmullo *m* (de voces, de un arroyo)

babe ['beɪb] *n* → **baby**[3]

baboon [bæ'bu:n] *n* : babuino *m*

baby[1] ['beɪbi] *vt* **-bied; -bying** : mimar, consentir

baby[2] *adj* **1** : de niño ⟨a baby carriage : un cochecito⟩ ⟨baby talk : habla infantil⟩ **2** TINY : pequeño, minúsculo

baby[3] *n, pl* **-bies** : bebé *m*; niño *m*, -ña *f*; bebe *m*, -ba *f Arg, Uru*

babyhood ['beɪbi,hʊd] *n* : niñez *f*, primera infancia *f*

babyish ['beɪbiʃ] *adj* : infantil, pueril

baby–sit ['beɪbi,sɪt] *vi* **-sat** [-,sæt]; **-sitting** : cuidar niños, hacer de canguro *Spain*

baby–sitter ['beɪbi,sɪtər] *n* : niñero *m*, -ra *f*; canguro *mf Spain*

baccalaureate [,bætʃələriət] *n* : licenciatura *f*

bachelor ['bætʃələr] *n* **1** : soltero *m* **2** : licenciado *m*, -da *f* ⟨bachelor of arts degree : licenciatura en filosofía y letras⟩

back[1] ['bæk] *vt* **1** *or* **to back up** SUPPORT : apoyar, respaldar **2** *or* **to back up** REVERSE : dar marcha atrás a, dar reversa a *Col, Mex* ⟨un vehículo⟩ **3** : estar detrás de, formar el fondo de ⟨trees back the garden : detrás del jardín hay unos árboles⟩ **4** : apostar por (un caballo, etc.) **5** *or* **to back up** : acompañar (en música) **6 to back up** : hacer una copia de seguridad de (archivos, etc.) **7 to back up** BLOCK : atascar — *vi* **1** *or* **to back away/up** : echarse atrás **2** *or* **to back up** : dar marcha atrás, dar reversa *Col, Mex* (en un vehículo) **3 to back off** : dejar a alguien en paz **4 to back off/down** : volverse atrás, echarse para atrás **5 to back off/out** RENEGE : volverse atrás, echarse para atrás, rajarse *fam* **6 to back up** : hacer copias de seguridad

back[2] *adv* **1** : atrás, hacia atrás, detrás ⟨to move back : moverse atrás⟩ ⟨to step back : dar un paso atrás⟩ ⟨to lean back : reclinarse⟩ ⟨it's two miles back : queda dos millas atrás⟩ ⟨back and forth : de acá para allá⟩ **2** AGO : atrás, antes, ya ⟨some years back : unos años atrás, ya unos años⟩ ⟨10 months back : hace diez meses⟩ **3** : de vuelta, de regreso ⟨we're back : estamos de vuelta⟩ ⟨I'll be back soon : vuelvo enseguida⟩ ⟨she ran back : volvió corriendo⟩ ⟨he never went back : nunca regresó⟩ ⟨I forgot to put it back : me olvidé de devolverlo a su lugar⟩ **4** : como respuesta, en cambio ⟨to call back : llamar de nuevo⟩ ⟨he smiled back

at me : me devolvió la sonrisa⟩ ⟨she gave the money back : devolvió el dinero⟩

back[3] *adj* **1** REAR : de atrás, posterior, trasero **2** OVERDUE : atrasado **3 back pay** : atrasos *mpl*

back[4] *n* **1** : espalda *f* (de un ser humano), lomo *m* (de un animal) **2** : respaldo *m* (de una silla), espalda *f* (de ropa) **3** REVERSE : reverso *m*, dorso *m*, revés *m* ⟨the back of an envelope : el reverso de un sobre⟩ **4** REAR : fondo *m*, parte *f* de atrás **5** : defensa *mf* (en deportes) **6 back to back** : espalda con espalda **7 back to back** CONSECUTIVE : seguido **8 back to front** BACKWARD : al revés **9 behind someone's back** : a espaldas de alguien ⟨behind my back : a mis espaldas⟩ **10 in** ∼ : en la parte de atrás, al fondo **11 in back of** : detrás de **12 out** ∼ : detrás de la casa (etc.) **13 to turn one's back on someone** : volverle la espalda a alguien

backache ['bæk,eɪk] *n* : dolor *m* de espalda

backbite ['bæk,baɪt] *v* **-bit** [-,bɪt], **-bitten** [-,bɪtən]; **-biting** *vt* : calumniar, hablar mal de — *vi* : murmurar

backbone ['bæk,bo:n] *n* **1** : columna *f* vertebral **2** FIRMNESS : firmeza *f*, carácter *m*

backdrop ['bæk,drɑp] *n* : telón *m* de fondo

backer ['bækər] *n* **1** SUPPORTER : partidario *m*, -ria *f* **2** SPONSOR : patrocinador *m*, -dora *f*

backfire[1] ['bæk,faɪr] *vi* **-fired; -firing 1** : petardear (dícese de un automóvil) **2** FAIL : fallar, salir el tiro por la culata

backfire[2] *n* : petardeo *m*, explosión *f*

background ['bæk,graʊnd] *n* **1** : fondo *m* (de un cuadro, etc.) ⟨background color : color de fondo⟩ ⟨background noise/music : ruido/música de fondo⟩ **2** : segundo plano *m* ⟨a shy person who stays in the background : una persona tímida que permanece en (un) segundo plano⟩ ⟨the program runs in the background : el programa se ejecuta en segundo plano⟩ **3** *or* **background information** : antecedentes *mpl* (de una situación) **4** : historial *m*, antecedentes *mpl* (de una persona) ⟨family background : historial familiar⟩ ⟨professional background : experiencia profesional⟩ ⟨background check : verificación de antecedentes⟩

backhand[1] ['bæk,hænd] *adv* : de revés, con el revés

backhand[2] *n* : revés *m*

backhanded ['bæk,hændəd] *adj* **1** : dado con el revés, de revés **2** INDIRECT : indirecto, ambiguo

backing ['bækɪŋ] *n* **1** SUPPORT : apoyo *m*, respaldo *m* **2** REINFORCEMENT : refuerzo *m* **3** SUPPORTERS : partidarios *mpl*, -rias *fpl*

backlash ['bæk,læʃ] *n* : reacción *f* violenta

backlog ['bæk,lɔg] n : atraso m, trabajo m acumulado
backpack¹ ['bæk,pæk] vi : viajar con mochila
backpack² n : mochila f
backrest ['bæk,rɛst] n : respaldo m
backside ['bæk,saɪd] n : trasero m
backslash ['bæk,slæʃ] n : barra f invertida, barra f inversa
backslide ['bæk,slaɪd] vi -slid [-,slɪd]; -slid or -slidden [-,slɪdən]; -sliding : recaer, reincidir
backstage [,bæk'steɪʤ, 'bæk,-] adv & adj : entre bastidores
backstroke ['bæk,stro:k] n : estilo m espalda, estilo m dorso Mex
backtrack ['bæk,træk] vi : dar marcha atrás, volverse atrás
backup ['bæk,ʌp] n 1 SUPPORT : respaldo m, apoyo m 2 : copia f de seguridad (de un archivo, etc.)
backward¹ ['bækwərd] or **backwards** [-wərdz] adv 1 : hacia atrás 2 : de espaldas ⟨he fell backwards : se cayó de espaldas⟩ 3 : al revés ⟨you're doing it backwards : lo estás haciendo al revés⟩ 4 to bend over backwards : hacer todo lo posible
backward² adj 1 : hacia atrás ⟨a backward glance : una mirada hacia atrás⟩ 2 RETARDED : retrasado 3 SHY : tímido 4 UNDERDEVELOPED : atrasado
backwardness ['bækwərdnəs] n : atraso m (dícese de una región), retraso m (dícese de una persona)
backwoods [,bæk'wʊdz] npl : monte m, región f alejada
backyard [,bæk'jard] n : jardín m trasero
bacon ['beɪkən] n : tocino m, tocineta f Col, Ven, bacon m Spain
bacterial [bæk'tɪriəl] adj : bacteriano
bacterium [bæk'tɪriəm] n, pl -ria [-iə] : bacteria f
bad¹ ['bæd] adv → badly
bad² adj 1 POOR : malo ⟨a bad example : un mal ejemplo⟩ ⟨a bad idea : una mala idea⟩ ⟨in bad shape : en malas condiciones⟩ 2 UNPLEASANT, UNFAVORABLE : malo ⟨bad news : malas noticias⟩ ⟨bad luck : mala suerte⟩ ⟨bad reviews : mala crítica⟩ ⟨a bad dream : una pesadilla⟩ ⟨it smells/tastes bad : huele/sabe mal⟩ 3 UNSUITABLE : malo ⟨bad lighting : mala iluminación⟩ ⟨you've come at a bad time : llegas en mal momento⟩ 4 INCORRECT, FAULTY : malo ⟨bad spelling : mala ortografía⟩ ⟨a bad check : un cheque sin fondos⟩ 5 ROTTEN : podrido ⟨to go bad : echarse a perder⟩ 6 UNHEALTHY, SERIOUS : malo, grave ⟨to have bad eyesight : tener mala vista⟩ ⟨a bad injury : una herida grave⟩ ⟨he's in bad health, his health is bad : está mal de salud⟩ 7 HARMFUL : malo, perjudicial 8 CORRUPT, EVIL : malo, corrupto ⟨the bad guys : los malos⟩ 9 NAUGHTY : malo, travieso 10 from bad to worse : de mal en peor 11 to be bad about

something : ser malo para algo 12 to be in a bad way : estar mal 13 too bad! : ¡qué lástima!
bad³ n 1 : lo malo ⟨the good and the bad : lo bueno y lo malo⟩
bade → **bid**
badge ['bæʤ] n : insignia f, botón m, chapa f
badger¹ ['bæʤər] vt : fastidiar, acosar, importunar
badger² n : tejón m
badly ['bædli] adv 1 : mal 2 URGENTLY : mucho, con urgencia 3 SEVERELY : gravemente
badminton ['bæd,mɪntən, -,mɪt-] n : bádminton m
badness ['bædnəs] n : maldad f
bad–tempered ['bæd'tempərd] adj : malhumorado
baffle ['bæfəl] vi -fled; -fling 1 PERPLEX : desconcertar, confundir 2 FRUSTRATE : frustrar
bafflement ['bæfəlmənt] n : desconcierto m, confusión f
bag¹ ['bæg] v **bagged; bagging** vi SAG : formar bolsas — vt 1 : ensacar, poner en una bolsa 2 : cobrar (en la caza), cazar
bag² n 1 : bolsa f, saco m 2 HANDBAG : cartera f, bolso m, bolsa f Mex 3 SUITCASE : maleta f, valija f 4 to have bags under one's eyes : tener ojeras
bagel ['beɪgəl] n : rosquilla f de pan
baggage ['bægɪʤ] n : equipaje m
baggie ['bægi] n : bolsita f de plástico
baggy ['bægi] adj **baggier; -est** : holgado, ancho
bagpipe ['bæg,paɪp] n or **bagpipes** ['bæg,paɪps] npl : gaita f
baguette [bæ'gɛt] n : baguette f, barra f de pan Mex, Spain
bail¹ ['beɪl] vt 1 : achicar (agua de un bote) 2 to bail out : poner en libertad (de una cárcel) bajo fianza 3 to bail out EXTRICATE : sacar de apuros — vi 1 or to bail out fam : largarse fam, rajarse fam ⟨when things got difficult, she bailed (out on us) : cuando las cosas se pusieron difíciles, nos dejó colgados⟩ 2 to bail out : tirarse en paracaídas (de un avión)
bail² n : fianza f, caución f
bailiff ['beɪləf] n : alguacil mf
bailiwick ['beɪli,wɪk] n : dominio m
bailout ['beɪl,aʊt] n : rescate m (financiero)
bait¹ ['beɪt] vt 1 : cebar (un anzuelo o cepo) 2 HARASS : acosar
bait² n : cebo m, carnada f
bake¹ ['beɪk] vt **baked; baking** : hornear, hacer al horno
bake² n : fiesta con platos hechos al horno
baker ['beɪkər] n : panadero m, -ra f
baker's dozen n : docena f de fraile
bakery ['beɪkəri] n, pl -ries : panadería f
bakeshop ['beɪk,ʃɑp] n : pastelería f, panadería f

baking powder n : levadura f en polvo
baking soda → **sodium bicarbonate**
balaclava [ˌbæləˈklɑvə, -ˈklæ-] n : pasamontañas m
balance¹ [ˈbælənts] v **-anced; -ancing** vt 1 : hacer el balance de (una cuenta) ⟨to balance the books : cuadrar las cuentas⟩ 2 EQUALIZE : balancear, equilibrar 3 HARMONIZE : armonizar — vi : balancearse
balance² n 1 SCALES : balanza f, báscula f 2 COUNTERBALANCE : contrapeso m 3 EQUILIBRIUM : equilibrio m ⟨to keep/lose one's balance : mantener/perder el equilibrio⟩ 4 REMAINDER : balance m, resto m 5 **balance of trade** : balanza comercial 6 **balance of payments** : balanza de pagos 7 **to be/hang in the balance** : estar en el aire
balanced [ˈbælənst] adj : equilibrado, balanceado
balboa [bælˈboːə] n : balboa f (unidad monetaria)
balcony [ˈbælkəni] n, pl **-nies** 1 : balcón m, terraza f (de un edificio) 2 : galería f (de un teatro)
bald [ˈbɔld] adj 1 : calvo, pelado, pelón 2 PLAIN : simple, puro ⟨the bald truth : la pura verdad⟩
balding [ˈbɔldɪŋ] adj : quedándose calvo
baldly [ˈbɔldli] adv : sin reparos, sin rodeos, francamente
baldness [ˈbɔldnəs] n : calvicie f
bale¹ [ˈbeɪl] vt **baled; baling** : empacar, hacer balas de
bale² n : bala f, fardo m, paca f
baleful [ˈbeɪlfəl] adj 1 DEADLY : mortífero 2 SINISTER : siniestro, funesto, torvo ⟨a baleful glance : una mirada torva⟩
balk¹ [ˈbɔk] vt : obstaculizar, impedir — vi 1 : plantarse fam (dícese de un caballo, etc.) 2 **to balk at** : resistirse a, mostrarse reacio a
balk² n : obstáculo m
Balkan [ˈbɔlkən] adj : balcánico
balky [ˈbɔki] adj **balkier; -est** : reacio, obstinado, terco
ball¹ [ˈbɔl] vt : apelotonar, ovillar
ball² n 1 : pelota f, bola f, balón m, bollo m Arg, Uru ⟨ball of yarn : ovillo de lana⟩ 2 DANCE : baile m (de etiqueta) 3 : bola f, bola f mala (en béisbol) 4 : parte f anterior de la planta (de un pie) 5 **balls** npl usu vulgar : cojones mpl, usu vulgar; huevos mpl, usu vulgar; testículos mpl 6 **balls** npl GUTS : cojones mpl, usu vulgar; agallas fpl fam 7 **on the ball** : espabilado, alerta 8 **the ball is in your/his (etc.) court** ⟨the ball is in your court : ahora te corresponde a ti⟩ 9 **to drop the ball** : cometer un gran error 10 **to get/set/start the ball rolling** : poner las cosas en marcha 11 **to keep the ball rolling** : mantener el impulso 12 **to play ball** : jugar al béisbol/baloncesto (etc.) 13 **to play ball** COOPERATE : cooperar
ballad [ˈbæləd] n : romance m, balada f
balladeer [ˌbæləˈdɪr] n : cantante mf de baladas

ballast¹ [ˈbæləst] vt : lastrar
ballast² n : lastre m
ball bearing n : cojinete m de bola
ballerina [ˌbæləˈriːnə] n : bailarina f ⟨prima ballerina : primera bailarina⟩
ballet [bæˈleɪ, ˈbæˌleɪ] n : ballet m
ballet dancer n : bailarín m, -rina f
ball game n : partido m de beisbol
ballistic [bəˈlɪstɪk] adj : balístico
ballistics [bəˈlɪstɪks] ns & pl : balística f
balloon¹ [bəˈluːn] vi 1 : viajar en globo 2 SWELL : hincharse, inflarse
balloon² n : globo m
balloonist [bəˈluːnɪst] n : aerostata mf
ballot¹ [ˈbælət] vi : votar
ballot² n 1 : papeleta f (de voto), boleta f electoral 2 BALLOTING : votación f 3 VOTE : voto m
ballot box n : urna f
ballpoint pen [ˈbɔlˌpɔɪnt] n : bolígrafo m
ballroom [ˈbɔlˌruːm, -ˌrʊm] n : sala f de baile
ballyhoo [ˈbæliˌhuː] n : propaganda f, publicidad f, bombo m fam
balm [ˈbɑm, ˈbɑlm] n : bálsamo m, ungüento m
balmy [ˈbɑmi, ˈbɑl-] adj **balmier; -est** 1 MILD : templado, agradable 2 SOOTHING : balsámico 3 CRAZY : chiflado fam, chalado fam
baloney [bəˈloːni] n NONSENSE : tonterías fpl, estupideces fpl
balsa [ˈbɔlsə] n : balsa f
balsam [ˈbɔlsəm] n or **balsam fir** : abeto m balsámico
Baltic [ˈbɔltɪk] adj : báltico
balustrade [ˈbæləˌstreɪd] n : balaustrada f
bam¹ [ˈbæm] n BANG : explosión f, estallido m, estampido m
bam² interj : ¡zas!
bamboo [bæmˈbuː] n : bambú m
bamboozle [bæmˈbuːzəl] vt **-zled; -zling** : engañar, embaucar
ban¹ [ˈbæn] vt **banned; banning** : prohibir, proscribir
ban² n : prohibición f, proscripción f
banal [bəˈnɑl, bəˈnæl, ˈbeɪnəl] adj : banal, trivial
banality [bəˈnæləti] n, pl **-ties** : banalidad f, trivialidad f
banana [bəˈnænə] n : banano m, plátano m, banana f, cambur m Ven, guineo m Car
band¹ [ˈbænd] vt 1 BIND : fajar, atar 2 **to band together** : unirse, juntarse
band² n 1 STRIP : banda f, cinta f (de un sombrero, etc.) 2 STRIPE : franja f 3 : banda f (de radiofrecuencia) 4 RING : anillo m 5 GROUP : banda f, grupo m, conjunto m ⟨jazz band : conjunto de jazz⟩
bandage¹ [ˈbændɪdʒ] vt **-daged; -daging** : vendar
bandage² n : vendaje m, venda f
Band-Aid [ˈbændˌeɪd] trademark se usa para una venda adhesiva
bandanna or **bandana** [bænˈdænə] n : pañuelo m (de colores)
bandit [ˈbændət] n : bandido m, -da f; bandolero m, -ra f

bandstand ['bænd,stænd] n : quiosco m de música

bandwagon ['bænd,wægən] n 1 : carroza f de músicos 2 **to jump on the bandwagon** : subirse al carro, seguir la moda

bandwidth ['bænd,wɪdθ] n : ancho m de banda

bandy ['bændi] vt **-died; -dying** 1 EXCHANGE : intercambiar 2 **to bandy about** : circular, propagar

bane ['beɪn] n 1 POISON : veneno m 2 RUIN : ruina f, pesadilla f

baneful ['beɪnfəl] adj : nefasto, funesto

bang[1] ['bæŋ] vt 1 STRIKE : golpear, darse ⟨he banged his elbow against the door : se dio con el codo en la puerta⟩ 2 SLAM : cerrar (la puerta) con/de un portazo 3 **to bang up** : rayar o abollar (algo), dejar (a alguien) con moretones — vi 1 SLAM : cerrarse de un golpe 2 **to bang on** : aporrear, golpear ⟨she was banging on the table : aporreaba la mesa⟩

bang[2] adv : directamente, exactamente

bang[3] n 1 BLOW : golpe m, porrazo m, trancazo m 2 EXPLOSION : explosión f, estallido m, estampido m 3 SLAM : portazo m 4 **bangs** npl : flequillo m, fleco m

bang[4] interj : ¡pum!

bangle ['bæŋgəl] n : brazalete m, pulsera f

banish ['bænɪʃ] vt 1 EXILE : desterrar, exiliar 2 EXPEL : expulsar

banishment ['bænɪʃmənt] n 1 EXILE : destierro m, exilio m 2 EXPULSION : expulsión f

banister ['bænəstər] n HANDRAIL : pasamanos m, barandilla f, barandal m

banjo ['bæn,dʒo:] n, pl **-jos** : banjo m

bank[1] ['bæŋk] vt 1 TILT : peraltar (una carretera), ladear (un avión) 2 HEAP : amontonar 3 : cubrir (un fuego) 4 : depositar (dinero en un banco) — vi 1 : ladearse (dícese de un avión) 2 : tener una cuenta (en un banco) 3 **to bank on** : contar con

bank[2] n 1 MASS : montón m, montículo m, masa f 2 : orilla f, ribera f (de un río) 3 : peralte m (de una carretera) 4 : banco m ⟨World Bank : Banco Mundial⟩ ⟨blood bank : banco de sangre⟩ 5 : banca f (en juegos)

bankbook ['bæŋk,bʊk] n : libreta f bancaria, libreta f de ahorros

banker ['bæŋkər] n : banquero m, -ra f

banking ['bæŋkɪŋ] n : banca f

banknote n : billete m de banco

bankrupt[1] ['bæŋ,krʌpt] vt : hacer quebrar, llevar a la quiebra, arruinar

bankrupt[2] adj 1 : en bancarrota, en quiebra 2 ~ **of** LACKING : carente de, falto de

bankrupt[3] n : fallido m, -da f; quebrado m, -da f

bankruptcy ['bæŋ,krʌptsi] n, pl **-cies** : ruina f, quiebra f, bancarrota f

bank statement → statement

bank teller → teller

banner[1] ['bænər] adj : excelente

banner[2] n : estandarte m, bandera f

banns ['bænz] npl : amonestaciones fpl

banquet[1] ['bæŋkwət] vi : celebrar un banquete

banquet[2] n : banquete m

banter[1] ['bæntər] vi : bromear, hacer bromas

banter[2] n : bromas fpl

baptism ['bæp,tɪzəm] n : bautismo m

baptismal [bæp'tɪzməl] adj : bautismal

baptismal font → font

Baptist ['bæptɪst] n : bautista mf, baptista mf — **Baptist** adj

baptize [bæp'taɪz, 'bæp,taɪz] vt **-tized; -tizing** : bautizar

bar[1] ['bar] vt **barred; barring** 1 OBSTRUCT : obstruir, bloquear 2 EXCLUDE : excluir 3 PROHIBIT : prohibir 4 SECURE : atrancar, asegurar ⟨bar the door! : ¡atranca la puerta!⟩

bar[2] n 1 : barra f, barrote m (de una ventana), tranca f (de una puerta) ⟨behind bars : entre rejas⟩ 2 BARRIER : barrera f, obstáculo m 3 LAW : abogacía f 4 STRIPE : franja f 5 COUNTER : mostrador m, barra f 6 TAVERN : bar m, taberna f 7 MEASURE : compás m (en música)

bar[3] prep 1 : excepto, con excepción de 2 **bar none** : sin excepción

barb ['barb] n 1 POINT : púa f, lengüeta f 2 GIBE : pulla f

barbarian[1] [bar'bæriən] adj 1 : bárbaro 2 CRUDE : tosco, bruto

barbarian[2] n : bárbaro m, -ra f

barbaric [bar'bærɪk] adj 1 PRIMITIVE : primitivo 2 CRUEL : brutal, cruel

barbarity [bar'bærəṭi] n, pl **-ties** : barbaridad f

barbarous ['barbərəs] adj 1 UNCIVILIZED : bárbaro 2 MERCILESS : despiadado, cruel

barbarously ['barbərəsli] adv : bárbaramente

barbecue[1] ['barbɪ,kju:] vt **-cued; -cuing** : asar a la parrilla

barbecue[2] n : barbacoa f, parrillada f

barbed ['barbd] adj 1 : con púas ⟨barbed wire : alambre de púas⟩ 2 BITING : mordaz

barber ['barbər] n : barbero m, -ra f

barbershop ['barbər,ʃap] n : peluquería f, barbería f

barbiturate [bar'bɪtʃərət] n : barbitúrico m

bar code n : código m de barras

bard ['bard] n : bardo m

bare[1] ['bær] vt **bared; baring** : desnudar

bare[2] adj 1 NAKED : desnudo 2 EXPOSED : descubierto, sin protección 3 EMPTY : desprovisto, vacío 4 MINIMUM : mero, mínimo ⟨the bare necessities : las necesidades mínimas⟩ 5 PLAIN : puro, sencillo

bareback ['bær,bæk] or **barebacked** [-,bækt] adv & adj : a pelo

barefaced ['bær,feɪst] adj : descarado

barefoot ['bær,fʊt] or **barefooted** [-,fʊṭəd] adv & adj : descalzo

bareheaded ['bær'hɛdəd] *adv & adj* : sin sombrero, con la cabeza descubierta

barely ['bærli] *adv* : apenas, por poco

bareness ['bærnəs] *n* : desnudez *f*

barf¹ ['barf] *v fam* → **vomit¹**

barf² *n fam* → **vomit¹**

bargain¹ ['bargən] *vi* HAGGLE : regatear, negociar — *vt* BARTER : trocar, cambiar

bargain² *n* **1** AGREEMENT : acuerdo *m*, convenio *m* ⟨to strike a bargain : cerrar un trato⟩ ⟨in/into the bargain : además, encima⟩ **2** : ganga *f* ⟨bargain price : precio de ganga⟩

bargaining *n* : regateo *m*, negociación *f*

barge¹ ['bardʒ] *vi* **barged; barging 1** : mover con torpeza **2 to barge in** : entrometerse, interrumpir

barge² *n* : barcaza *f*, gabarra *f*

bar graph *n* : gráfico *m* de barras

baritone ['bærə,to:n] *n* : barítono *m*

bark¹ ['bark] *vi* : ladrar — *vt or* **to bark out** : gritar ⟨to bark out an order : dar una orden a gritos⟩

bark² *n* **1** : ladrido *m* (de un perro) **2** : corteza *f* (de un árbol) **3** *or* **barque** : tipo de embarcación con velas de proa y popa

barley ['barli] *n* : cebada *f*

barmaid ['bar,meɪd] *n* : camarera *f*

barman ['bar,mən] *n, pl* **-men** [-mən, -,mɛn] → **bartender**

barn ['barn] *n* : granero *m* (para cosechas), establo *m* (para ganado)

barnacle ['barnɪkəl] *n* : percebe *m*

barnyard ['barn,jard] *n* : corral *m*

barometer [bə'ramətər] *n* : barómetro *m*

barometric [,bærə'mɛtrɪk] *adj* : barométrico

baron ['bærən] *n* **1** : barón *m* **2** TYCOON : magnate *mf*

baroness ['bærənɪs, -nəs, -,nɛs] *n* : baronesa *f*

baronial [bə'ro:niəl] *adj* **1** : de barón **2** STATELY : señorial, majestuoso

baroque [bə'ro:k, -'rak] *adj* : barroco

barracks ['bærəks] *ns & pl* : cuartel *m*

barracuda [,bærə'ku:də] *n, pl* **-da** *or* **-das** : barracuda *f*

barrage ['bəraʒ, -'radʒ] *n* **1** : descarga *f* (de artillería) **2** DELUGE : aluvión *m* ⟨a barrage of questions : un aluvión de preguntas⟩

barred ['bard] *adj* : excluido, prohibido

barrel¹ ['bærəl] *v* **-reled** *or* **-relled; -reling** *or* **-relling** *vi* : ir disparado

barrel² *n* **1** : barril *m*, tonel *m* **2** : cañón *m* (de un arma de fuego), cilindro *m* (de una cerradura)

barren ['bærən] *adj* **1** STERILE : estéril (dícese de las plantas o la mujer), árido (dícese del suelo) **2** DESERTED : yermo, desierto

barrette [bɑ'rɛt, bə-] *n* : pasador *m*, broche *m* para el cabello

barricade¹ ['bærə,keɪd, ,bærə'-] *vt* **-caded; -cading** : cerrar con barricadas

barricade² *n* : barricada *f*

barrier ['bæriər] *n* **1** : barrera *f* **2** OBSTACLE : obstáculo *m*, impedimento *m*

barring ['barɪŋ] *prep* : excepto, salvo, a excepción de

barrio ['bario, 'bær-] *n* : barrio *m*

barroom ['bar,ru:m, -,rʊm] *n* : bar *m*

barrow ['bær,o:] → **wheelbarrow**

bartender ['bar,tɛndər] *n* : camarero *m*, -ra *f*; barman *m*

barter¹ ['bartər] *vt* : cambiar, trocar

barter² *n* : trueque *m*, permuta *f*

basalt [bə'sɔlt, 'beɪ-] *n* : basalto *m*

base¹ ['beɪs] *vt* **based; basing** : basar, fundamentar, establecer

base² *adj* **baser; basest 1** : de baja ley (dícese de un metal) **2** CONTEMPTIBLE : vil, despreciable

base³ *n, pl* **bases** **1** : base *f* **2** : pie *m* (de una montaña, una estatua, etc.)

baseball ['beɪs,bɔl] *n* : beisbol *m*, béisbol *m*

baseball cap *n* : gorra *f* de visera, gorra *f* de beisbol

baseless ['beɪsləs] *adj* : infundado

basely ['beɪsli] *adv* : vilmente

basement ['beɪsmənt] *n* : sótano *m*

baseness ['beɪsnəs] *n* : vileza *f*, bajeza *f*

bash¹ ['bæʃ] *vt* : golpear violentamente

bash² *n* **1** BLOW : golpe *m*, porrazo *m*, madrazo *m* Mex fam **2** PARTY : fiesta *f*, juerga *f* fam

bashful ['bæʃfəl] *adj* : tímido, vergonzoso, penoso

bashfulness ['bæʃfəlnəs] *n* : timidez *f*

basic¹ ['beɪsɪk] *adj* **1** FUNDAMENTAL : básico, fundamental **2** RUDIMENTARY : básico, elemental **3** : básico (en química)

basic² *n* : fundamento *m*, rudimento *m*

basically ['beɪsɪkli] *adv* : fundamentalmente

basil ['beɪzəl, 'bæzəl] *n* : albahaca *f*

basilica [bə'sɪlɪkə] *n* : basílica *f*

basin ['beɪsən] *n* **1** WASHBOWL : palangana *f*, lavamanos *m*, lavabo *m* **2** : cuenca *f* (de un río)

basis ['beɪsɪs] *n, pl* **bases** [-,si:z] **1** BASE : base *f*, pilar *m* **2** FOUNDATION : fundamento *m*, base *f* **3 on a weekly basis** : semanalmente

bask ['bæsk] *vi* : disfrutar, deleitarse ⟨to bask in the sun : disfrutar del sol⟩

basket ['bæskət] *n* : cesta *f*, cesto *m*, canasta *f*

basketball ['bæskət,bɔl] *n* : baloncesto *m*, basquetbol *m*, basket *m*

Basque ['bæsk, 'bask] *n* : Basque *mf* — **Basque** *adj*

bas–relief [,bari'li:f] *n* : bajorrelieve *m*

bass¹ ['beɪs] *adj* : de bajo (dícese de una voz, etc.) ⟨bass clef : clave de fa⟩ ⟨bass string : bordón⟩

bass² ['bæs] *n, pl* **bass** *or* **basses** : róbalo *m* (pesca)

bass³ ['beɪs] *n* **1** : bajo *m* (tono, voz, cantante) **2** → **bass guitar 3** → **double bass**

bass drum *n* : bombo *m*

basset hound ['bæsət,haʊnd] *n* : basset *m*

bass guitar *n* : bajo *m* (guitarra)

bassinet [,bæsə'nɛt] *n* : moisés *m*, cuna *f*

bassist ['beɪsɪst] *n* : bajista *mf*

bassoon [bə'su:n, bæ-] *n* : fagot *m*
bass viol ['beɪs'vaɪəl, -ˌɔːl] → **double bass**
bastard[1] ['bæstərd] *adj* : bastardo
bastard[2] *n* **1** *usu offensive* : bastardo *m*, -da *f* **2** *offensive* : hijo *m* de puta *sometimes offensive*; cabrón *m Mex, Spain offensive* **3** *sometimes offensive* : tipo *m* ⟨the poor bastard : el pobre diablo⟩ ⟨what a lucky bastard! : ¡qué suertudo!⟩
bastardize ['bæstərˌdaɪz] *vt* **-ized; -izing** DEBASE : degradar, envilecer
baste ['beɪst] *vt* **basted; basting 1** STITCH : hilvanar **2** : bañar (con su jugo durante la cocción)
bastion ['bæstʃən] *n* : bastión *m*, baluarte *m*
bat[1] ['bæt] *vt* **batted; batting 1** HIT : batear **2 without batting an eye** : sin pestañear
bat[2] *n* **1** : murciélago *m* (animal) **2** : bate *m* ⟨baseball bat : bate de beisbol⟩
batch ['bætʃ] *n* : hornada *f*, tanda *f*, grupo *m*, cantidad *f*
bate ['beɪt] *vt* **bated; bating 1** : aminorar, reducir **2 with bated breath** : con ansiedad, aguantando la respiración
bath ['bæθ, 'baθ] *n, pl* **baths** ['bæðz, 'bæθs, 'baðz, 'baθs] **1** BATHING : baño *m* ⟨to take a bath : bañarse⟩ **2** : baño *m* (en fotografía, etc.) **3** BATHROOM : baño *m*, cuarto *m* de baño **4** SPA : balneario *m* **5** LOSS : pérdida *f*
bathe ['beɪð] *v* **bathed; bathing** *vt* **1** WASH : bañar, lavar **2** SOAK : poner en remojo **3** FLOOD : inundar ⟨to bathe with light : inundar de luz⟩ — *vi* : bañarse, ducharse
bather ['beɪðər] *n* : bañista *mf*
bathing suit → **swimsuit**
bathrobe ['bæθˌroːb] *n* : bata *f* (de baño)
bathroom ['bæθˌruːm, -ˌrʊm] *n* : baño *m*, cuarto *m* de baño
bathroom tissue → **toilet paper**
bathtub ['bæθˌtʌb] *n* : bañera *f*, tina *f* (de baño)
baton [bə'tɑn] *n* : batuta *f*, bastón *m*
battalion [bə'tæljən] *n* : batallón *m*
batten ['bætən] *vt* **to batten down the hatches** : cerrar las escotillas
batter[1] ['bætər] *vt* **1** BEAT : aporrear, golpear **2** MISTREAT : maltratar
batter[2] *n* **1** : masa *f* para rebozar **2** HITTER : bateador *m*, -dora *f*
battered ['bætərd] *adj* **1** ABUSED : maltratado **2** DAMAGED : maltrecho **3** INJURED : apaleado, aporreado
battering ram *n* : ariete *m*
battery ['bætəri] *n, pl* **-teries 1** : lesiones *fpl* ⟨assault and battery : agresión con lesiones⟩ **2** ARTILLERY : batería *f* **3** : batería *f*, pila *f* (de electricidad) **4** SERIES : serie *f*
batting ['bætɪŋ] *n* **1** *or* **cotton batting** : algodón en láminas **2** : bateo *m* (en beisbol)
battle[1] ['bætəl] *vi* **-tled; -tling** : luchar, pelear
battle[2] *n* : batalla *f*, lucha *f*, pelea *f*

battle-ax ['bætəlˌæks] *n* : hacha *f* de guerra
battlefield ['bætəlˌfiːld] *n* : campo *m* de batalla
battleship ['bætəlˌʃɪp] *n* : acorazado *m*
batty ['bæti] *adj* **battier; -est** : chiflado *fam*, chalado *fam*
bauble ['bɔbəl] *n* : chuchería *f*, baratija *f*
Bavarian [bə'veriən] *n* : bávaro *m*, -ra *f* — **Bavarian** *adj*
bawdiness ['bɔdinəs] *n* : picardía *f*
bawdy ['bɔdi] *adj* **bawdier; -est** : subido de tono, verde, colorado *Mex*
bawl[1] ['bɔl] *vi* : llorar a gritos
bawl[2] *n* : grito *m*, alarido *m*
bawl out *vt* SCOLD : regañar
bay[1] ['beɪ] *vi* HOWL : aullar
bay[2] *adj* : castaño, zaino (dícese de los caballos)
bay[3] *n* **1** : bahía *f* ⟨Bay of Campeche : Bahía de Campeche⟩ **2** *or* **bay horse** : caballo *m* castaño **3** LAUREL : laurel *m* (en cocina) ⟨bay leaf : hoja de laurel⟩ **4** HOWL : aullido *m* **5** : saliente *m* ⟨bay window : ventana en saliente⟩ **6** COMPARTMENT : área *f*, compartimento *m* **7** at ⟨sim⟩ : acorralado
bayonet[1] [ˌbeɪə'nɛt, 'beɪəˌnɛt] *vt* **-neted; -neting** : herir *o* matar) con bayoneta
bayonet[2] *n* : bayoneta *f*
bayou ['baɪˌuː, -ˌoː] *n* : pantano *m*
bazaar [bə'zɑr] *n* **1** : bazar *m* **2** SALE : venta *f* benéfica
bazooka [bə'zuːkə] *n* : bazuca *f*
BB ['biːbi] *n* : balín *m*
bcc [ˌbiːsiː'siː] *vt* **bcc'd; bcc'ing** : enviarle una copia oculta a (alguien), enviar una copia oculta de (un mensaje)
be ['biː] *v* **was** ['wɑz, 'wʌz]; **were** ['wər]; **been** ['bɪn]; **being; am** ['æm]; **is** ['ɪz]; **are** ['ɑr] *vi* **1** (*expressing identity or category*) : ser ⟨José is a doctor : José es doctor⟩ ⟨I'm Ann's sister : soy la hermana de Ann⟩ ⟨who is it? it's me : ¿quién es? soy yo⟩ ⟨apes are mammals : los simios son mamíferos⟩ ⟨if I were you : yo en tu lugar, yo que tú⟩ **2** (*expressing a quality*) : ser ⟨the dress is red : el vestido es rojo⟩ ⟨she's very intelligent : ella es muy inteligente⟩ ⟨she's 10 years old : tiene 10 años⟩ ⟨you're so silly! : ¡qué tonto eres!⟩ ⟨I want you to be happy : quiero que seas feliz⟩ **3** (*expressing origin or possession*) : ser ⟨she's from Managua : es de Managua⟩ ⟨it's mine : es mío⟩ **4** (*expressing location*) : estar, quedar ⟨he's not at home : no está en casa⟩ ⟨the cups are on the table : las tazas están en la mesa⟩ ⟨it's ten miles away : está/queda diez millas de aquí⟩ **5** EXIST : ser, existir ⟨to be or not to be : ser, o no ser⟩ ⟨I think, therefore I am : pienso, luego existo⟩ **6** COME, GO : estar, ir, venir ⟨have you been to Paris? : ¿has estado en París?, ¿has ido a París?⟩ ⟨she's been and gone : llegó y se fue⟩ **7** (*expressing a state of being*) : estar, tener ⟨how are you? : ¿cómo estás?⟩ ⟨I'm cold/hungry : tengo frío/hambre⟩ ⟨they're sick : están enfermos⟩ ⟨she's angry : está enojada⟩ ⟨to be

frank : para serte franco⟩ **8** COST : ser, costar ⟨it's $5 : cuesta $5⟩ **9** EQUAL : ser (igual a) ⟨two plus two is four : dos más dos son cuatro⟩ **10** OCCUR : ser ⟨the concert is (on) Sunday : el concierto es el domingo⟩ — *v impers* **1** (*indicating time*) : ser ⟨it's eight o'clock : son las ocho⟩ ⟨it's Friday : hoy es viernes⟩ **2** (*indicating a condition*) : hacer, estar ⟨it's sunny : hace sol⟩ ⟨it's very dark in here : está muy oscuro aquí dentro⟩ **3** (*used with* there) : haber ⟨there's a book on the table : hay un libro en la mesa⟩ ⟨there was an accident : hubo un accidente⟩ ⟨there's someone at the door : llaman a la puerta⟩ — *v aux* **1** (*expressing progression*) : estar ⟨I'm working : estoy trabajando⟩ ⟨what were you saying? : ¿qué estabas diciendo?⟩ ⟨it's snowing : está nevando⟩ ⟨we've been waiting : hemos estado esperando⟩ **2** (*expressing future action*) ⟨I'm seeing him tonight : voy a verlo esta noche⟩ ⟨are you coming tomorrow? : ¿vienes mañana?⟩ ⟨she was never/not to see him again : nunca volvería a verlo⟩ ⟨the best is yet to come : lo mejor está por venir⟩ **3** (*used in passive constructions*) : ser ⟨it was finished yesterday : fue acabado ayer, se acabó ayer⟩ **4** (*expressing possibility*) : poderse ⟨can she be trusted? : ¿se puede confiar en ella?⟩ ⟨it was nowhere to be found : no se pudo encontrar por ninguna parte⟩ ⟨you're not to blame : no tienes la culpa⟩ **5** (*expressing obligation*) : deber ⟨you are to stay here : debes quedarte aquí⟩ ⟨he was to come yesterday : se esperaba que viniese ayer⟩ **6 to be oneself** : ser uno mismo ⟨be yourself : sé tú mismo⟩

beach¹ [ˈbiːtʃ] *vt* : hacer varar, hacer encallar

beach² *n* : playa *f*

beachcomber [ˈbiːtʃˌkoːmər] *n* : raquero *m*, -ra *f*

beachhead [ˈbiːtʃˌhɛd] *n* : cabeza *f* de playa

beacon [ˈbiːkən] *n* : faro *m*

bead¹ [ˈbiːd] *vi* : formarse en gotas

bead² *n* **1** : cuenta *f* **2** DROP : gota *f* **3 beads** *npl* NECKLACE : collar *m*

beady [ˈbiːdi] *adj* **beadier; -est 1** : de forma de cuenta **2 beady eyes** : ojos *mpl* pequeños y brillantes

beagle [ˈbiːgəl] *n* : beagle *m*

beak [ˈbiːk] *n* : pico *m*

beaker [ˈbiːkər] *n* **1** CUP : taza *f* alta **2** : vaso *m* de precipitados (en un laboratorio)

beam¹ [ˈbiːm] *vi* **1** SHINE : brillar **2** SMILE : sonreír radiantemente — *vt* BROADCAST : transmitir, emitir

beam² *n* **1** : viga *f*, barra *f* **2** RAY : rayo *m*, haz *m* de luz **3** : haz *m* de radiofaro (para guiar pilotos, etc.)

bean [ˈbiːn] *n* **1** : habichuela *f*, frijol *m* **2 broad bean** : haba *f* **3 string bean** : judía *f*

bear¹ [ˈbær] *v* **bore** [ˈbor]; **borne** [ˈbɔrn]; **bearing** *vt* **1** CARRY : llevar, portar **2** : dar a luz a (un niño) **3** PRODUCE : dar

(frutas, cosechas) **4** ENDURE, SUPPORT : soportar, resistir, aguantar **5** SHOW : llevar, tener ⟨to bear a resemblance to : tener una similitud con (algo), tener un parecido con (alguien)⟩ **6 to bear out** : corroborar — *vi* **1** TURN : doblar, dar la vuelta, girar ⟨bear right : doble a la derecha⟩ **2 to bear up** : resistir **3 to bear with** : tener paciencia con

bear² *n, pl* **bears** *or* **bear** : oso *m*, osa *f*

bearable [ˈbærəbəl] *adj* : soportable

beard [ˈbɪrd] *n* **1** : barba *f* **2** : arista *f* (de plantas)

bearded [ˈbɪrdəd] *adj* : barbudo, de barba

bearer [ˈbærər] *n* : portador *m*, -dora *f*

bearing [ˈbærɪŋ] *n* **1** CONDUCT, MANNERS : comportamiento *m*, modales *mpl* **2** SUPPORT : soporte *f* **3** SIGNIFICANCE : relación *f*, importancia *f* ⟨to have no bearing on : no tener nada que ver con⟩ **4** : cojinete *m*, rodamiento *m* (de una máquina) **5** COURSE, DIRECTION : dirección *f*, rumbo *m* ⟨to get one's bearings : orientarse⟩

beast [ˈbiːst] *n* **1** : bestia *f*, fiera *f* ⟨beast of burden : animal de carga⟩ **2** BRUTE : bruto *m*, -ta *f*; bestia *mf*

beastly [ˈbiːstli] *adj* : detestable, repugnante

beat¹ [ˈbiːt] *v* **beat; beaten** [ˈbiːtən] *or* **beat; beating** *vt* **1** STRIKE : golpear, pegar, darle una paliza (a alguien) **2** DEFEAT : vencer, derrotar (a un rival, etc.), batir (un récord) **3** : superar, ser mejor que ⟨nothing beats a nice, hot bath : no hay nada mejor que un baño caliente⟩ **4** AVOID : anticiparse a, evitar ⟨to beat the crowd : evitar el gentío⟩ **5** STIR, WHIP : batir **6** : batir (alas) **7 beat it!** *fam* : ¡lárgate! **8 it beats me** : no sé **9 to beat down** : echar abajo (una puerta) **10 to beat out** DEFEAT : vencer, derrotar **11 to beat up** : darle una paliza (a alguien) **12 to beat up on** : darle frecuentes palizas (a alguien) — *vi* **1** : batir **2** THROB : palpitar, latir **3 to beat down** : pegar fuerte, caer a plomo (dícese del sol)

beat² *adj* EXHAUSTED : derrengado, muy cansado ⟨I'm beat! : ¡estoy molido!⟩

beat³ *n* **1** : golpe *m*, redoble *m* (de un tambor), latido *m* (del corazón) **2** RHYTHM : ritmo *m*, tiempo *m*

beater [ˈbiːtər] *n* **1** : batidor *m*, -dora *f* **2** EGGBEATER : batidor *m*

beatific [ˌbiːəˈtɪfɪk] *adj* : beatífico

beating [ˈbiːtɪŋ] *n* **1** : paliza *f* **2** DEFEAT : derrota *f*

beau [ˈboː] *n, pl* **beaux** *or* **beaus** : pretendiente *m*, galán *m*

beautician [bjuˈtɪʃən] *n* : esteticista *mf*

beautification [ˌbjuːtəfəˈkeɪʃən] *n* : embellecimiento *m*

beautiful [ˈbjuːtɪfəl] *adj* : hermoso, bello, lindo, precioso

beautifully [ˈbjuːtɪfəli] *adv* **1** ATTRACTIVELY : maravillosamente, excelentemente **2** EXCELLENTLY : maravillosamente, excelentemente

beautify [ˈbjuːtəˌfaɪ] *vt* **-fied; -fying** : embellecer

beauty ['bjuːṭi] *n, pl* **-ties** : belleza *f*, hermosura *f*, beldad *f*

beauty shop *or* **beauty parlor** *or* **beauty salon** *n* : salón *m* de belleza

beauty spot *n* : lunar *m*

beaver ['biːvər] *n* : castor *m*

because [bɪ'kʌz, -'kɔz] *conj* : porque

because of *prep* : por, a causa de, debido a

beck ['bɛk] *n* **to be at the beck and call of** : estar a la entera disposición de, estar sometido a la voluntad de

beckon ['bɛkən] *vi* **to beckon to someone** : hacerle señas a alguien

become [bɪ'kʌm] *v* **-came** [-'keɪm]; **-come; -coming** *vi* : hacerse, volverse, ponerse ⟨he became famous : se hizo famoso⟩ ⟨to become sad : ponerse triste⟩ ⟨to become accustomed to : acostumbrarse a⟩ — *vt* **1** BEFIT : ser apropiado para **2** SUIT : favorecer, quedarle bien a (alguien) ⟨that dress becomes you : ese vestido te favorece⟩

becoming [bɪ'kʌmɪŋ] *adj* **1** SUITABLE : apropiado **2** FLATTERING : favorecedor

bed¹ ['bɛd] *v* **bedded; bedding** *vt* : acostar — *vi* : acostarse

bed² *n* **1** : cama *f*, lecho *m* ⟨to make the bed : hacer la cama⟩ ⟨to go to bed : acostarse⟩ ⟨to be time for bed : ser hora de acostarse⟩ **2** : cauce *m* (de un río), fondo *m* (del mar) **3** : arriate *m* (para plantas) **4** LAYER, STRATUM : capa *f*, estrato *m* **5** : caja *f* (de una camioneta)

bed and breakfast *n* : pensión *f* con desayuno

bedbug ['bɛd,bʌg] *n* : chinche *f*

bedclothes ['bɛd,kloːðz, -,kloːz] *npl* : ropa *f* de cama, sábanas *fpl*

bedding ['bɛdɪŋ] *n* **1** → **bedclothes 2** : cama *f* (para animales)

bedeck [bɪ'dɛk] *vt* : adornar, engalanar

bedevil [bɪ'dɛvəl] *vt* **-iled** *or* **-illed; -iling** *or* **-illing** : acosar, plagar

bedlam ['bɛdləm] *n* : locura *f*, caos *m*, alboroto *m*

bedraggled [bɪ'drægəld] *adj* : desaliñado, despeinado

bedridden ['bɛd,rɪdən] *adj* : postrado en cama

bedrock ['bɛd,rɑk] *n* : lecho *m* de roca

bedroom ['bɛd,ruːm, -,rʊm] *n* : dormitorio *m*, habitación *f*, pieza *f*, recámara *f* *Col, Mex, Pan*

bedsheet → **sheet**

bedside table ['bɛd,saɪd-] *n* : mesita *f* de noche

bedspread ['bɛd,sprɛd] *n* : cubrecama *m*, colcha *f*, cobertor *m*

bedtime ['bɛd,taɪm] *n* : hora *f* de acostarse

bee ['biː] *n* **1** : abeja *f* (insecto) **2** GATHERING : círculo *m*, reunión *f*

beech ['biːtʃ] *n, pl* **beeches** *or* **beech** : haya *f*

beechnut ['biːtʃ,nʌt] *n* : hayuco *m*

beef¹ ['biːf] *vt* **to beef up** : fortalecer, reforzar — *vi* COMPLAIN : quejarse

beef² *n, pl* **beefs** ['biːfs] *or* **beeves** ['biːvz] : carne *f* de vaca, carne *f* de res *CA, Mex*

beefsteak ['biːf,steɪk] *n* : filete *m*, bistec *m*

beehive ['biː,haɪv] *n* : colmena *f*

beekeeper ['biː,kiːpər] *n* : apicultor *m*, -tora *f*

beekeeping ['biː,kiːpɪŋ] *n* : apicultura *f*

beeline ['biː,laɪn] *n* **to make a beeline for** : ir derecho a, ir directo hacia

been → **be**

beep¹ ['biːp] *v* : pitar

beep² *n* : pitido *m*

beeper ['biːpər] *n* : buscapersonas *m*, busca *m Spain*

beer ['bɪr] *n* : cerveza *f*

beeswax ['biːz,wæks] *n* : cera *f* de abejas

beet ['biːt] *n* : remolacha *f*, betabel *m Mex*

beetle ['biːṭəl] *n* : escarabajo *m*

befall [bɪ'fɔl] *v* **-fell** [-'fɛl]; **-fallen** [-'fɔlən] *vt* : sucederle a, acontecerle a — *vi* : acontecer

befit [bɪ'fɪt] *vt* **-fitted; -fitting** : convenir a, ser apropiado para

before¹ [bɪ'for] *adv* **1** : antes ⟨before and after : antes y después⟩ **2** : anterior ⟨the month before : el mes anterior⟩

before² *conj* : antes que ⟨he would die before surrendering : moriría antes de rendirse⟩

before³ *prep* **1** : antes de ⟨before eating : antes de comer⟩ **2** : delante de, ante ⟨I stood before the house : estaba parada delante de la casa⟩ ⟨before the judge : ante el juez⟩

beforehand [bɪ'for,hænd] *adv* : antes, por adelantado, de antemano, con anticipación

befriend [bɪ'frɛnd] *vt* : hacerse amigo de

befuddle [bɪ'fʌdəl] *n* **-dled; -dling** : aturdir, ofuscar, confundir

beg ['bɛg] *v* **begged; begging** *vt* **1** : mendigar, pedir (dinero, etc.) **2** : pedir, suplicar ⟨I begged him to go : le supliqué que fuera⟩ — *vi* **1** : mendigar, pedir limosna **2 to beg for** : suplicar ⟨she begged for mercy : imploró clemencia⟩

beget [bɪ'gɛt] *vt* **-got** [-'gɑt]; **-gotten** [-'gɑtən] *or* **-got; -getting** : engendrar

beggar ['bɛgər] *n* : mendigo *m*, -ga *f*; pordiosero *m*, -ra *f*

begin [bɪ'gɪn] *v* **-gan** [-'gæn]; **-gun** [-'gʌn]; **-ginning** *vt* : empezar, comenzar, iniciar ⟨she began to work, she began working : empezó a trabajar⟩ — *vi* **1** START : empezar, comenzar, iniciarse **2** ORIGINATE : nacer, originarse **3 to begin with** : en primer lugar, para empezar

beginner [bɪ'gɪnər] *n* : principiante *mf*

beginning [bɪ'gɪnɪŋ] *n* : principio *m*, comienzo *m* ⟨at the beginning of the week : a principios de la semana⟩

begone [bɪ'gɔn] *interj* : ¡fuera de aquí!

begonia [bɪ'goːnjə] *n* : begonia *f*

begrudge [bɪ'grʌdʒ] *vt* **-grudged; -grudging 1** : dar/hacer (etc.) de mala gana ⟨he did the work, but he begrudged every minute of it : hizo el trabajo, pero de muy mala gana⟩ ⟨I don't begrudge the money I spent : no me molesta el dinero que gasté⟩ **2** (*indicating disapproval*)

⟨he begrudges (her) her success : a él le molesta que ella tenga éxito⟩

beguile [bɪ'gaɪl] *vt* **-guiled; -guiling** 1 DECEIVE : engañar 2 AMUSE : divertir, entretener

behalf [bɪ'hæf, -'haf] *n* 1 : favor *m*, beneficio *m*, parte *f* 2 **on behalf of** or **in behalf of** : de parte de, en nombre de

behave [bɪ'heɪv] *vi* **-haved; -having** : comportarse, portarse

behavior [bɪ'heɪvjər] *n* : comportamiento *m*, conducta *f*

behead [bɪ'hɛd] *vt* : decapitar

behest [bɪ'hɛst] *n* 1 : mandato *m*, orden *f* 2 **at the behest of** : a instancia de

behind¹ [bɪ'haɪnd] *adv* : atrás, detrás ⟨to fall behind : quedarse atrás⟩

behind² *prep* 1 : atrás de, detrás de, tras ⟨behind the house : detrás de la casa⟩ ⟨one behind another : uno tras otro⟩ 2 : atrasado con, después de ⟨behind schedule : atrasado con el trabajo⟩ ⟨I arrived behind the others : llegué después de los otros⟩ 3 SUPPORTING : en apoyo de, detrás ⟨we're behind you all the way! : ¡tienes todo nuestro apoyo!⟩

behind³ [bɪ'haɪnd, 'bi:,haɪnd] *n* : trasero *m*

behold [bɪ'ho:ld] *vt* **-held; -holding** : contemplar

beholder [bɪ'ho:ldər] *n* : observador *m*, -dora *f*

behoove [bɪ'hu:v] *vt* **-hooved; -hooving** : convenirle a, corresponderle a ⟨it behooves us to help him : nos conviene ayudarlo⟩

beige¹ ['beɪʒ] *adj* : beige

beige² *n* : beige *m*

being ['bi:ɪŋ] *n* 1 EXISTENCE : ser *m*, existencia *f* 2 CREATURE : ser *m*, ente *m*

belabor [bɪ'leɪbər] *vt* **to belabor the point** : extenderse sobre el tema

belated [bɪ'leɪtəd] *adj* : tardío, retrasado

belch¹ ['bɛltʃ] *vi* 1 BURP : eructar 2 EXPEL : expulsar, arrojar

belch² *n* : eructo *m*

beleaguer [bɪ'li:gər] *vt* 1 BESIEGE : asediar, sitiar 2 HARASS : fastidiar, molestar

belfry ['bɛlfri] *n, pl* **-fries** : campanario *m*

Belgian ['bɛldʒən] *n* : belga *mf* — **Belgian** *adj*

belie [bɪ'laɪ] *vt* **-lied; -lying** 1 MISREPRESENT : falsear, ocultar 2 CONTRADICT : contradecir, desmentir

belief [bɪ'li:f] *n* 1 TRUST : confianza *f* 2 CONVICTION : creencia *f*, convicción *f* 3 FAITH : fe *f*

believable [bə'li:vəbəl] *adj* : verosímil, creíble

believe [bə'li:v] *v* **-lieved; -lieving** *vt* : creer ⟨I don't believe it! : ¡no puedo creerlo!⟩ ⟨believe it or not : aunque no lo creas, lo creas o no⟩ ⟨I can't believe my eyes : si no lo veo, no lo creo⟩ ⟨you'd better believe it! : ¡ya lo creo!, ¡por supuesto!⟩ — *vi* : creer

believer [bə'li:vər] *n* 1 : creyente *mf* 2 : partidario *m*, -ria *f*; entusiasta *mf* ⟨she's a great believer in vitamins : ella es una gran partidaria de las vitaminas⟩

belittle [bɪ'lɪṭəl] *vt* **-littled; -littling** 1 DISPARAGE : menospreciar, denigrar, rebajar 2 MINIMIZE : minimizar, quitar importancia a

bell¹ ['bɛl] *vt* : ponerle un cascabel a

bell² *n* : campana *f*, cencerro *m* (para una vaca o cabra), cascabel *m* (para un gato), timbre *m* (de teléfono, de la puerta)

belle ['bɛl] *n* : belleza *f*, beldad *f*

bellhop ['bɛl,hɑp] *n* : botones *m*

bellicose ['bɛlɪ,ko:s] *adj* : belicoso *m*

belligerence [bə'lɪdʒərənts] *n* : agresividad *f*, beligerancia *f*

belligerent¹ [bə'lɪdʒərənt] *adj* : agresivo, beligerante

belligerent² *n* : beligerante *mf*

bellow¹ ['bɛ,lo:] *vi* : bramar, mugir — *vt* : gritar

bellow² *n* : bramido *m*, grito *m*

bellows ['bɛ,lo:z] *ns & pl* : fuelle *m*

bellwether ['bɛl,wɛðər] *n* : líder *mf*

belly¹ ['bɛli] *vi* **-lied; -lying** SWELL : hincharse, inflarse

belly² *n, pl* **-lies** : abdomen *m*, vientre *m*, barriga *f*, panza *f*

bellyache¹ ['bɛli,eɪk] *vi fam* → **grouse**¹

bellyache² → **stomachache**

belly button *n* : ombligo *m*

belong [bɪ'lɔŋ] *vi* 1 : pertenecer (a), ser propiedad (de) ⟨it belongs to her : pertenece a ella, es suyo, es de ella⟩ 2 : ser parte (de), ser miembro (de) ⟨he belongs to the club : es miembro del club⟩ 3 : deber estar, ir ⟨your coat belongs in the closet : tu abrigo va en el ropero⟩

belongings [bɪ'lɔŋɪŋz] *npl* : pertenencias *fpl*, efectos *mpl* personales

beloved¹ [bɪ'lʌvd, -'lʌvd] *adj* : querido, amado

beloved² *n* : amado *m*, -da *f*; enamorado *m*, -da *f*; amor *m*

below¹ [bɪ'lo:] *adv* 1 : abajo ⟨the floor below : el piso de abajo⟩ ⟨the pilot looked at the ground below : el piloto miraba el suelo allá abajo⟩ ⟨from below : desde abajo⟩ 2 : más abajo ⟨as stated below : como se indica más abajo⟩ 3 UNDER, LOWER : más bajo ⟨children age 10 and below : niños menores de los 11 años⟩ 4 : abajo (en un navío) 5 : bajo cero (dícese de temperaturas)

below² *prep* 1 : abajo de, debajo de ⟨below the window : debajo de la ventana⟩ 2 : por debajo de, bajo ⟨below average : por debajo del promedio⟩ ⟨5 degrees below zero : 5 grados bajo cero⟩

belt¹ ['bɛlt] *vt* 1 : ceñir con un cinturón, ponerle un cinturón a 2 THRASH : darle una paliza a, darle un trancazo a

belt² *n* 1 : cinturón *m*, cinto *m* (para el talle) 2 BAND, STRAP : cinta *f*, correa *f*, banda *f Mex* 3 AREA : franja *f*, zona *f*

beltway ['bɛlt,weɪ] *n* : carretera *f* de circunvalación; periférico *m CA, Mex*; libramiento *m Mex*

bemoan [bɪ'mo:n] *vt* : lamentarse de

bemuse [bɪ'mju:z] *vt* **-mused; -musing** 1 BEWILDER : confundir, desconcertar 2 ENGROSS : absorber

bench ['bɛntʃ] n **1** SEAT : banco m, escaño m, banca f **2** : estrado m (de un juez) **3** COURT : tribunal m **4** : banca f (en deportes)

bend¹ ['bɛnd] v **bent** ['bɛnt]; **bending** vt : torcer, doblar, curvar, flexionar — vi **1** : torcerse, agacharse ⟨to bend over : inclinarse⟩ **2** TURN : torcer, hacer una curva **3 on bended knee** : de rodillas, de hinojos

bend² n **1** TURN : vuelta f, recodo m **2** CURVE : curva f, ángulo m, codo m

beneath¹ [bɪ'ni:θ] adv : bajo, abajo, debajo

beneath² prep : bajo de, abajo de, por debajo de

benediction [ˌbɛnə'dɪkʃən] n : bendición f

benefactor ['bɛnəˌfæktər] n : benefactor m, -tora f

benefactress ['bɛnəˌfæktrɪs] n : benefactora f

beneficial [ˌbɛnə'fɪʃəl] adj : beneficioso, provechoso — **beneficially** adv

beneficiary [ˌbɛnə'fɪʃiˌɛri, -'fɪʃəri] n, pl **-ries** : beneficiario m, -ria f

benefit¹ ['bɛnəfɪt] vt : beneficiar — vi : beneficiarse

benefit² n **1** ADVANTAGE : beneficio m, ventaja f, provecho m **2** AID : asistencia f, beneficio m **3** : función f benéfica (para recaudar fondos)

benevolence [bə'nɛvələnts] n : bondad f, benevolencia f

benevolent [bə'nɛvələnt] adj : benévolo, bondadoso — **benevolently** adv

benign [bɪ'naɪn] adj **1** GENTLE, KIND : benévolo, amable **2** FAVORABLE : propicio, favorable **3** MILD : benigno ⟨a benign tumor : un tumor benigno⟩

bent¹ ['bɛnt] n : aptitud f, inclinación f

benumb [bɪ'nʌm] vt : entumecer

bequeath [bɪ'kwi:θ, -'kwi:ð] vt : legar, dejar en testamento

bequest [bɪ'kwɛst] n : legado m

berate [bɪ'reɪt] vt **-rated; -rating** : reprender, regañar

bereaved¹ [bɪ'ri:vd] adj : que está de luto, afligido (por la muerte de alguien)

bereaved² n **the bereaved** : los deudos del difunto (o de la difunta)

bereavement [bɪ'ri:vmənt] n **1** SORROW : dolor m, pesar m **2** LOSS : pérdida f

bereft [bɪ'rɛft] adj : privado, desprovisto

beret [bə'reɪ] n : boina f

berm ['bərm] n : arcén m

Bermuda shorts [bər'mju:də-] npl : bermudas fpl

berry ['bɛri] n, pl **-ries** : baya f

berserk [bər'sərk, -'zərk] adj **1** : enloquecido **2 to go beserk** : volverse loco

berth¹ ['bərθ] vi : atracar

berth² n **1** DOCK : atracadero m **2** ACCOMMODATION : litera f, camarote m **3** POSITION : trabajo m, puesto m

beseech [bɪ'si:tʃ] vt **-seeched** or **-sought** [-'sɔt]; **-seeching** : suplicar, implorar, rogar

beset [bɪ'sɛt] vt **-set; -setting 1** HARASS : acosar **2** SURROUND : rodear

beside [bɪ'saɪd] prep : al lado de, junto a ⟨the car beside mine : el coche al lado

del mío⟩ ⟨that's beside the point : eso no tiene nada que ver, eso no viene al caso⟩

besides¹ [bɪ'saɪdz] adv **1** ALSO : además, también, aparte **2** MOREOVER : además, por otra parte

besides² prep **1** : además de, aparte de ⟨six others besides you : seis otros además de ti⟩ **2** EXCEPT : excepto, fuera de, aparte de

besiege [bɪ'si:dʒ] vt **-sieged; -sieging** : asediar, sitiar, cercar

besmirch [bɪ'smərtʃ] vt : ensuciar, mancillar

besotted [bɪ'sɑtəd] adj : enamorado

best¹ ['bɛst] vt : superar, ganar a

best² adv (superlative of WELL) : mejor ⟨as best I can : lo mejor que pueda⟩

best³ adj (superlative of GOOD) : mejor ⟨my best friend : mi mejor amigo⟩

best⁴ n **1 the best** : lo mejor, el mejor, la mejor, los mejores, las mejores **2 at ~** : a lo más **3 to do one's best** : hacer todo lo posible **4 to make the best of** ⟨I'll just have to make the best of it : tendré que arreglármelas como pueda⟩

best-case adj **a/the best-case scenario** : el mejor de los casos

bestial ['bɛstʃəl, 'bi:s-] adj **1** : bestial **2** BRUTISH : brutal, salvaje

bestie ['bɛsti] n fam : mejor amigo m, mejor amiga f

best man n : padrino m

bestow [bɪ'sto:] vt : conferir, otorgar, conceder

bestowal [bɪ'sto:əl] n : concesión f, otorgamiento m

best seller n : best-seller m

bet¹ ['bɛt] v **bet; betting** vt : apostar — vi **1 to bet on** : apostarle a **2 you bet!** : ¡ya lo creo!, ¡por supuesto!

bet² n : apuesta f

beta ['beɪtə] n : beta f (software)

betoken [bɪ'to:kən] vt : denotar, ser indicio de

betray [bɪ'treɪ] vt **1** : traicionar ⟨to betray one's country : traicionar uno a su patria⟩ **2** DIVULGE, REVEAL : delatar, revelar ⟨to betray a secret : revelar un secreto⟩

betrayal [bɪ'treɪəl] n : traición f, delación f, revelación f ⟨betrayal of trust : abuso de confianza⟩

betrothal [bɪ'tro:ðəl, -'trɔ-] n : esponsales mpl, compromiso m

betrothed [bɪ'tro:ðd, -'trɔθt] n FIANCÉ : prometido m, -da f

better¹ ['bɛtər] vt **1** IMPROVE : mejorar **2** SURPASS : superar

better² adv (comparative of WELL) **1** : mejor **2** MORE : más ⟨better than 50 miles : más de 50 millas⟩

better³ adj (comparative of GOOD) **1** : mejor ⟨the weather is better today : hace mejor tiempo hoy⟩ ⟨I was sick, but now I'm better : estuve enfermo, pero ahora estoy mejor⟩ **2** : mayor ⟨the better part of a month : la mayor parte de un mes⟩

better⁴ n **1** : el mejor, la mejor ⟨the better of the two : el mejor de los dos⟩ **2 to**

get the better of : vencer a, quedar por encima de, superar

betterment [ˈbɛt̬ərmənt] n : mejoramiento m, mejora f

better off adj (comparative of WELL OFF) **1** : mejor ⟨to be better off : salir ganando, venirle mejor a uno⟩ **2** WEALTHIER : más adinerado

betting [ˈbɛt̬ɪŋ] n : apuestas fpl

bettor or **better** [ˈbɛt̬ər] n : apostador m, -dora f

between[1] [brˈtwiːn] adv **1** : en medio, por lo medio **2 in ~** : intermedio

between[2] prep : entre ⟨between the chair and the wall : entre la silla y la pared⟩ ⟨between now and then : de aquí a entonces⟩ ⟨between nine and ten o'clock : entre las nueve y las diez⟩ ⟨between five and ten people : entre cinco y diez personas⟩ ⟨between you and me : entre nosotros⟩ ⟨they divided it between them : se lo dividieron entre ellos/sí⟩ ⟨the difference between the two brands : la diferencia entre las dos marcas⟩ ⟨to choose between two options : escoger entre dos opciones⟩

bevel[1] [ˈbɛvəl] v **-eled** or **-elled; -eling** or **-elling** vt : biselar — vi INCLINE : inclinarse

bevel[2] n : bisel m

beverage [ˈbɛvrɪdʒ, ˈbɛvə-] n : bebida f

bevy [ˈbɛvi] n, pl **bevies** : grupo m (de personas), bandada f (de pájaros)

bewail [brˈweɪl] vt : lamentarse de, llorar

beware [brˈwær] vi **to beware of** : tener cuidado con ⟨beware of the dog! : ¡cuidado con el perro!⟩ — vt : guardarse de, cuidarse de

bewilder [brˈwɪldər] vt : desconcertar, dejar perplejo

bewilderment [brˈwɪldərmənt] n : desconcierto m, perplejidad f

bewitch [brˈwɪtʃ] vt **1** : hechizar, embrujar **2** CHARM : cautivar, encantar

bewitchment [brˈwɪtʃmənt] n : hechizo m

beyond[1] [biˈjɑnd] adv **1** FARTHER, LATER : más allá, más lejos (en el espacio), más adelante (en el tiempo) **2** MORE : más ⟨$50 and beyond : $50 o más⟩

beyond[2] n **the beyond** : el más allá, lo desconocido

beyond[3] prep **1** : más allá de ⟨beyond the frontier : más allá de la frontera⟩ **2** : fuera de ⟨beyond one's reach : fuera de su alcance⟩ **3** BESIDES : además de

BFF [ˌbiːˌɛfˈɛf] n (Best Friends Forever) : amigo m íntimo, amiga f íntima

bi- pref : bi-

biannual [ˌbaɪˈænjʊəl] adj : bianual — **biannually** adv

bias[1] [ˈbaɪəs] vt **-ased** or **-assed; -asing** or **-assing 1** : predisponer, sesgar, influir en, afectar **2 to be biased against** : tener prejuicio contra

bias[2] n **1** : sesgo m, bies m (en la costura) **2** PREJUDICE : prejuicio m **3** TENDENCY : inclinación f, tendencia f

biased [ˈbaɪəst] adj : tendencioso, parcial

bib [ˈbɪb] n **1** : peto m **2** : babero m (para niños)

Bible [ˈbaɪbəl] n : Biblia f

biblical [ˈbɪblɪkəl] adj : bíblico

bibliographer [ˌbɪbliˈɑgrəfər] n : bibliógrafo m, -fa f

bibliography [ˌbɪbliˈɑgrəfi] n, pl **-phies** : bibliografía f — **bibliographic** [ˌbɪbliəˈgræfɪk] adj

bicameral [ˌbaɪˈkæmərəl] adj : bicameral

bicarbonate [ˌbaɪˈkɑrbənət, -ˌneɪt] n : bicarbonato m

bicentennial [ˌbaɪsɛnˈtɛniəl] n : bicentenario m

biceps [ˈbaɪˌsɛps] ns & pl : bíceps m

bicker[1] [ˈbɪkər] vi : pelear, discutir, reñir

bicker[2] n : pelea f, riña f, discusión f

bicuspid [baɪˈkʌspɪd] n : premolar m

bicycle[1] [ˈbaɪsɪkəl, -ˌsɪ-] n **-cled; -cling** : ir en bicicleta

bicycle[2] n : bicicleta f

bicycling [ˈbaɪsɪkəlɪŋ] n : ciclismo m

bicyclist [ˈbaɪsɪkəlɪst] n : ciclista m/f

bid[1] [ˈbɪd] vt **bade** [ˈbæd, ˈbeɪd] or **bid; bidden** [ˈbɪdən] or **bid; bidding 1** ORDER : pedir, mandar **2** INVITE : invitar **3** SAY : dar, decir ⟨to bid good evening : dar las buenas noches⟩ ⟨to bid farewell to : decir adiós a⟩ **4** : ofrecer (en una subasta), declarar (en juegos de cartas)

bid[2] n **1** OFFER : oferta f (en una subasta), declaración f (en juegos de cartas) **2** INVITATION : invitación f **3** ATTEMPT : intento m, tentativa f

bidder [ˈbɪdər] n : postor m, -tora f

bide [ˈbaɪd] v **bode** [ˈboːd] or **bided; biding** vi : esperar, aguardar ⟨to bide one's time : esperar el momento oportuno⟩ — vi DWELL : morar, vivir

bidet [biˈdeɪ] n : bidé m, bidet m

biennial [baɪˈɛniəl] adj : bienal — **biennially** adv

bier [ˈbɪr] n **1** STAND : andas fpl **2** COFFIN : ataúd m, féretro m

bifocals [ˈbaɪˌfoːkəlz] npl : lentes mpl bifocales, bifocales mpl — **bifocal** [ˈbaɪˌfoːkəl] adj

big [ˈbɪg] adj **bigger; biggest 1** LARGE : grande ⟨a big guy : un tipo grande⟩ ⟨a great big house : una casa grandísima⟩ ⟨a big group : un grupo grande/numeroso⟩ ⟨big words : palabras difíciles⟩ **2** (indicating degree) ⟨to be a big eater : ser un comelón⟩ ⟨to be a big believer in something : ser un gran partidario de algo⟩ **3** IMPORTANT, MAJOR : importante, grande ⟨a big decision : una gran decisión⟩ **4** POPULAR : popular, famoso, conocido ⟨the next big thing : el próximo exitazo⟩ **5** KIND : generoso ⟨it was very big of him : fue muy generoso de su parte⟩ **6 to be big on** : ser entusiasta de

bigamist [ˈbɪgəmɪst] n : bígamo m, -ma f

bigamous [ˈbɪgəməs] adj : bígamo

bigamy [ˈbɪgəmi] n : bigamia f

Big Dipper → dipper

big-headed [ˈbɪgˈhɛdəd] adj fam : creído

bighorn [ˈbɪgˌhɔrn] n, pl **-horn** or **-horns** or **bighorn sheep** : oveja f salvaje de las montañas

bight ['baɪt] *n* : bahía *f*, ensenada *f*, golfo *m*

bigot ['bɪgət] *n* : intolerante *mf*

bigoted ['bɪgətəd] *adj* : intolerante, prejuiciado, fanático

bigotry ['bɪgətri] *n, pl* **-tries** : intolerancia *f*

big picture *n* **to look at the big picture** : ver las cosas desde una perspectiva global

big shot *n* : pez *m* gordo *fam*, mandamás *mf*

big toe *n* : dedo *m* gordo (del pie)

bigwig ['bɪg,wɪg] → **big shot**

bike ['baɪk] *n* **1** : bicicleta *f*, bici *f fam* **2** : motocicleta *f*, moto *f*

bike lane *or* **bicycle lane** *n* : carril *m* para bicicletas

bikini [bə'ki:ni] *n* : bikini *m*

bilateral [baɪ'læʧərəl] *adj* : bilateral — **bilaterally** *adv*

bile ['baɪl] *n* **1** : bilis *f* **2** IRRITABILITY : mal genio *m*

bilingual [baɪ'lɪŋgwəl] *adj* : bilingüe

bilk ['bɪlk] *vt* : burlar, estafar, defraudar

bill¹ ['bɪl] *vt* : pasarle la cuenta a — *vi* : acariciar ⟨to bill and coo : acariciarse⟩

bill² *n* **1** LAW : proyecto *m* de ley, ley *f* **2** INVOICE : cuenta *f*, factura *f* **3** POSTER : cartel *m* **4** PROGRAM : programa *m* (del teatro) **5** : billete *m* ⟨a five-dollar bill : un billete de cinco dólares⟩ **6** BEAK : pico *m*

billboard ['bɪl,bɔrd] *n* : cartelera *f*

billet¹ ['bɪlət] *vt* : acuartelar, alojar

billet² *n* : alojamiento *m*

billfold ['bɪl,fo:ld] *n* : billetera *f*, cartera *f*

billiard ['bɪljərd] *adj* : de billar ⟨billiard ball : bola de billar⟩

billiards ['bɪljərdz] *n* : billar *m*

billion ['bɪljən] *n, pl* **billions** *or* **billion** : mil millones *mpl*

billionth ['bɪljənθ] *n* : milmillonésimo *m* — **billionth** *adj*

billow¹ ['bɪlo] *vi* : hincharse, inflarse

billow² *n* **1** WAVE : ola *f* **2** CLOUD : nube *f* ⟨a billow of smoke : un nube de humo⟩

billowy ['bɪlowi] *adj* : ondulante

billy goat ['bɪli,go:t] *n* : macho *m* cabrío

bimonthly [baɪ'mʌnθli] *adj* **1** SEMI-MONTHLY : bimensual, quincenal **2** : bimestral

bin ['bɪn] *n* : cubo *m*, cajón *m*

binary ['baɪnəri, -,nɛri] *adj* : binario *m*

binational [,baɪ'næʃənəl] *adj* : binacional

bind ['baɪnd] *vt* **bound** ['baʊnd]; **binding** **1** TIE : atar, amarrar **2** OBLIGATE : obligar **3** UNITE : aglutinar, ligar, unir **4** BANDAGE : vendar **5** : encuadernar (un libro)

binder ['baɪndər] *n* **1** FOLDER : carpeta *f* **2** : encuadernador *m*, -dora *f* (de libros)

binding ['baɪndɪŋ] *n* **1** : encuadernación *f* (de libros) **2** COVER : cubierta *f*, forro *m*

binge ['bɪnʤ] *n* : juerga *f*, parranda *f fam*

bingo ['bɪŋ,go:] *n, pl* **-gos** : bingo *m*

binocular [baɪ'nɑkjələr, bə-] *adj* : binocular

binoculars [bə'nɑkjələrz, baɪ-] *npl* : binoculares *mpl*

bio- *pref* : bio- ⟨biochemistry : bioquímica⟩

biochemical¹ [,baɪo'kɛmɪkəl] *adj* : bioquímico

biochemical² *n* : bioquímico *m*

biochemist [,baɪo'kɛmɪst] *n* : bioquímico *m*, -ca *f*

biochemistry [,baɪo'kɛmɪstri] *n* : bioquímica *f*

biodegradable [,baɪodɪ'greɪdəbəl] *adj* : biodegradable

biodiversity [,baɪodə'vərsəti, -daɪ-] *n, pl* **-ties** : biodiversidad *f*

biographer [baɪ'ɑgrəfər] *n* : biógrafo *m*, -fa *f*

biographical [,baɪə'græfɪkəl] *adj* : biográfico

biography [baɪ'ɑgrəfi, bi:-] *n, pl* **-phies** : biografía *f*

biologic [,baɪə'lɑʤɪk] *or* **biological** [-ʤɪkəl] *adj* : biológico

biological weapon *n* : arma *f* biológica

biologist [baɪ'ɑləʤɪst] *n* : biólogo *m*, -ga *f*

biology [baɪ'ɑləʤi] *n* : biología *f*

biopsy ['baɪˌɑpsi] *n, pl* **-sies** : biopsia *f*

biosphere ['baɪəˌsfɪr] *n* : biosfera *f*, biósfera *f*

biotechnology [,baɪotɛk'nɑləʤi] *n* : biotecnología *f* — **biotechnological** [,baɪoˌtɛknə'lɑʤɪkəl] *adj*

bipartisan [baɪ'pɑrʧəzən, -sən] *adj* : bipartidista, de dos partidas

biped ['baɪˌpɛd] *n* : bípedo *m*

birch ['bərʧ] *n* : abedul *m*

bird ['bərd] *n* : pájaro *m* (pequeño), ave *f* (grande)

birdbath ['bərd,bæθ, -,baθ] *n* : pila *f* para pájaros

bird dog *n* : perro *m*, -rra *f* de caza

bird of prey *n* : ave *f* rapaz, ave *f* de presa

birdseed ['bərd,si:d] *n* : alpiste *m*

bird's-eye ['bərdz,aɪ] *adj* **1** : visto desde arriba ⟨bird's-eye view : vista aérea⟩ **2** CURSORY : rápido, somero

birdwatching ['bərd,wɑʧɪŋ] *n* : observación *f* de aves

biretta [bə'rɛʧə] *n* : birrete *m*

birth ['bərθ] *n* **1** : nacimiento *m*, parto *m* **2** ORIGIN : origen *m*, nacimiento *m*

birth certificate *n* : partida *f* de nacimiento, acta *f* de nacimiento, certificado *m* de nacimiento

birth control *n* : control *m* de natalidad

birthday ['bərθ,deɪ] *n* : cumpleaños *m*, aniversario *m* ⟨birthday boy/girl : cumpleañero/cumpleañera⟩

birthmark ['bərθ,mɑrk] *n* : mancha *f* de nacimiento

birthplace ['bərθ,pleɪs] *n* : lugar *m* de nacimiento

birthrate ['bərθ,reɪt] *n* : índice *m* de natalidad

birthright ['bərθ,raɪt] *n* : derecho *m* de nacimiento

biscuit ['bɪskət] *n* : bizcocho *m*

bisect ['baɪ,sɛkt, ,baɪ'-] *vt* : bisecar

bisexual [,baɪ'sɛkʃʊəl] *adj* : bisexual — **bisexuality** [,baɪˌsɛkʃʊ'æləti] *n*

bishop ['bɪʃəp] *n* 1 : obispo *m* 2 : alfil *m* (en ajedrez)

bishopric ['bɪʃəprɪk] *n* : obispado *m*

bison ['baɪzən, -sən] *ns & pl* : bisonte *m*

bistro ['bi:stro, 'bɪs-] *n, pl* **-tros** : bar *m*, restaurante *m* pequeño

bit[1] *n* 1.FRAGMENT, PIECE : pedazo *m*, trozo *m* ⟨he smashed it to bits : lo hizo pedazos⟩ 2 : freno *m*, bocado *m* (de una brida) 3 : broca *f* (de un taladro) 4 : bit *m* (de información) 5 : rato *m*, momento *m* ⟨stay a bit (longer) : quédate un ratito⟩ 6 SKETCH : sketch *m* (en teatro, etc.) 7 **a bit** SOMEWHAT : un poco 8 **a bit of** : un poco de 9 **bit by bit** : poco a poco 10 **every bit as . . . as** : tan . . . como 11 **quite a bit** : bastante

bitch[1] ['bɪtʃ] *vi* COMPLAIN : quejarse, reclamar

bitch[2] *n* 1 : perra *f* 2 *fam offensive* : bruja *f*; cabrona *f* *Spain, Mex offensive* 3 *fam* : cosa *f* difícil ⟨the exam was a bitch : el examen fue dificilísimo⟩ ⟨life's a bitch : la vida es dura⟩

Bitcoin ['bɪt,kɔɪn] *n* : bitcoin *m*

bite[1] ['baɪt] *v* **bit** ['bɪt]; **bitten** ['bɪtən]; **biting** *vt* 1 : morder 2 STING : picar 3 PUNCTURE : punzar, pinchar 4 GRIP : agarrar 5 **to bite one's tongue** : morderse la lengua 6 **to bite someone's head off** : explotar, perder los estribos (sin provocación) 7 **to bite the bullet** : hacer de tripas corazón 8 **to bite the dust** : morder el polvo (dícese de una persona), pasar a mejor vida (dícese de una cosa) — *vi* 1 : morder ⟨that dog bites : ese perro muerde⟩ 2 STING : picar (dícese de un insecto), cortar (dícese del viento) 3 : picar ⟨the fish are biting now : ya están picando los peces⟩ 4 GRAB : agarrarse

bite[2] *n* 1 BITING : mordisco *m*, dentellada *f* 2 SNACK : bocado *m* ⟨a bite to eat : algo de comer⟩ 3 : picadura *f* (de un insecto), mordedura *f* (de un animal) 4 SHARPNESS : mordacidad *f*, penetración *f*

biting ['baɪtɪŋ] *adj* 1 PENETRATING : cortante, penetrante 2 CAUSTIC : mordaz, sarcástico

bit part *n* : papel *m* secundario

bitter ['bɪtər] *adj* 1 ACRID : amargo, acre 2 PENETRATING : cortante, penetrante ⟨bitter cold : frío glacial⟩ 3 HARSH : duro, amargo ⟨to the bitter end : hasta el final⟩ 4 INTENSE, RELENTLESS : intenso, extremo, implacable ⟨bitter hatred : odio implacable⟩

bitterly ['bɪtərli] *adv* : amargamente

bitterness ['bɪtərnəs] *n* : amargura *f*

bittersweet ['bɪtər,swi:t] *adj* : agridulce

bizarre [bə'zɑr] *adj* : extraño, singular, estrafalario, estrambótico — **bizarrely** *adv*

blab ['blæb] *vi* **blabbed**; **blabbing** : parlotear fam, cotorrear fam

blabbermouth ['blæbər,maʊθ] *n fam* : bocón *m*, -cona *f fam*

black[1] ['blæk] *vt* : ennegrecer

black[2] *adj* 1 : negro (color, raza) 2 SOILED : sucio 3 DARK : oscuro, negro 4 WICKED : malvado, perverso, malo 5 GLOOMY : negro, sombrío, deprimente

black[3] *n* 1 : negro *m* (color) 2 : negro *m*, -gra *f* (persona)

black–and–blue [,blækən'blu:] *adj* : amoratado

blackball ['blæk,bɔl] *vt* 1 OSTRACIZE : hacerle el vacío a, aislar 2 BOYCOTT : boicotear

blackberry ['blæk,bɛri] *n, pl* **-ries** : mora *f*

blackbird ['blæk,bərd] *n* : mirlo *m*

blackboard ['blæk,bord] *n* : pizarra *f*, pizarrón *m*

black box *n* : caja *f* negra

blacken ['blækən] *vt* 1 BLACK : ennegrecer 2 DEFAME : deshonrar, difamar, manchar

black eye *n* : ojo *m* morado

blackhead ['blæk,hɛd] *n* : espinilla *f*, punto *m* negro

black hole *n* : agujero *m* negro

blackish ['blækɪʃ] *adj* : negruzco

blackjack ['blæk,dʒæk] *n* 1 : cachiporra *f* (arma) 2 : veintiuna *f* (juego de cartas)

blacklist[1] ['blæk,lɪst] *vt* : poner en la lista negra

blacklist[2] *n* : lista *f* negra

blackmail[1] ['blæk,meɪl] *vt* : chantajear, hacer chantaje a

blackmail[2] *n* : chantaje *m*

blackmailer ['blæk,meɪlər] *n* : chantajista *mf*

blackness ['blæknəs] *n* : negrura *f*

blackout ['blæk,aʊt] *n* 1 : apagón *m* (de poder eléctrico) 2 FAINT : desmayo *m*, desvanecimiento *m*

black out *vt* : dejar sin luz — *vi* FAINT : perder el conocimiento, desmayarse

black sheep *n* : oveja *f* negra

blacksmith ['blæk,smɪθ] *n* : herrero *m*

blacktop ['blæk,tɑp] *n* : asfalto *m*

bladder ['blædər] *n* : vejiga *f*

blade ['bleɪd] *n* : hoja *f* (de un cuchillo), cuchilla *f* (de un patín), pala *f* (de un remo o una hélice), brizna *f* (de hierba)

blamable ['bleɪməbəl] *adj* : culpable

blame[1] ['bleɪm] *vt* **blamed**; **blaming** : culpar, echar la culpa a

blame[2] *n* : culpa *f*

blameless ['bleɪmləs] *adj* : intachable, sin culpa, inocente — **blamelessly** *adv*

blameworthiness ['bleɪm,wərðinəs] *n* : culpa *f*, culpabilidad *f*

blameworthy ['bleɪm,wərði] *adj* : culpable, reprochable, censurable

blanch ['blæntʃ] *vt* WHITEN : blanquear — *vi* PALE : palidecer

bland ['blænd] *adj* : soso, insulso, desabrido ⟨a bland smile : una sonrisa insulsa⟩ ⟨a bland diet : una dieta fácil de digerir⟩

blandishments ['blændɪʃmənts] *npl* : lisonjas *fpl*, halagos *mpl*

blandly ['blændli] *adv* : de manera insulsa

blandness ['blændnəs] *n* : lo insulso, lo desabrido

blank[1] ['blæŋk] *vt* OBLITERATE : borrar

blank[2] *adj* 1 DAZED : perplejo, desconcertado 2 EXPRESSIONLESS : sin expresión, inexpresivo **3** : en blanco (dícese de un papel), liso (dícese de una pared) **4** EMPTY : vacío, en blanco ⟨a blank stare : una mirada vacía⟩ ⟨his mind went blank : se quedó en blanco⟩

blank³ n **1** SPACE : espacio m en blanco **2** FORM : formulario m **3** CARTRIDGE : cartucho m de fogueo **4** or **blank key** : llave f ciega

blank check n **1** : cheque m en blanco **2** CARTE BLANCHE : carta f blanca

blanket¹ ['blæŋkət] vt : cubrir

blanket² adj : global

blanket³ n : manta f, cobija f, frazada f

blankly ['blæŋkli] adv : sin comprender

blankness ['blæŋknəs] n **1** PERPLEXITY : desconcierto m, perplejidad f **2** EMPTINESS : vacío m, vacuidad f

blare¹ ['blær] vi **blared; blaring** : resonar

blare² n : estruendo m

blarney ['blɑrni] n : labia f fam

blasé [blɑ'zeɪ] adj : displicente, indiferente

blaspheme [blæs'fiːm, 'blæs‚-] vi **-phemed; -pheming** : blasfemar

blasphemer [blæs'fiːmər, 'blæs‚-] n : blasfemo m, -ma f

blasphemous ['blæsfəməs] adj : blasfemo

blasphemy ['blæsfəmi] n, pl **-mies** : blasfemia f

blast¹ ['blæst] vt **1** BLOW UP : volar, hacer volar **2** ATTACK : atacar, arremeter contra

blast² n **1** GUST : ráfaga f **2** EXPLOSION : explosión f

blast–off ['blæst‚ɔf] n : despegue m

blast off vi : despegar

blatant ['bleɪtənt] adj : descarado — **blatantly** ['bleɪtəntli] adv

blaze¹ ['bleɪz] v **blazed; blazing** vi SHINE : arder, brillar, resplandecer — vt MARK : marcar, señalar ⟨to blaze a trail : abrir un camino⟩

blaze² n **1** FIRE : fuego m **2** BRIGHTNESS : resplandor m, brillantez f **3** OUTBURST : arranque m ⟨a blaze of anger : un arranque de cólera⟩ **4** DISPLAY : alarde m, llamarada f ⟨a blaze of color : un derroche de color⟩

blazer ['bleɪzər] n : chaqueta f deportiva, blazer m

bleach¹ ['bliːtʃ] vt : blanquear, decolorar

bleach² n : lejía f, blanqueador m

bleachers ['bliːtʃərz] ns & pl : gradas fpl, tribuna f descubierta

bleak ['bliːk] adj **1** DESOLATE : inhóspito, sombrío, desolado **2** DEPRESSING : deprimente, triste, sombrío

bleakly ['bliːkli] adv : sombríamente

bleakness ['bliːknəs] n : lo inhóspito, lo sombrío

blear ['blɪr] adj : empañado, nublado

bleary ['blɪri] adj **1** : adormilado, fatigado **2** **bleary–eyed** : con los ojos nublados

bleat¹ ['bliːt] vi : balar

bleat² n : balido m

bleed ['bliːd] v **bled** ['blɛd]; **bleeding** vi **1** : sangrar **2** GRIEVE : sufrir, afligirse **3** EXUDE : exudar (dícese de una planta),

correrse (dícese de los colores) — vt **1** : sangrar (a una persona), purgar (frenos) **2 to bleed someone dry** : sacarle todo el dinero a alguien

blemish¹ ['blɛmɪʃ] vt : manchar, marcar

blemish² n : imperfección f, mancha f, marca f

blend¹ ['blɛnd] vt **1** MIX : mezclar **2** COMBINE : combinar, aunar

blend² n : mezcla f, combinación f

blender ['blɛndər] n : licuadora f

bless ['blɛs] vt **blessed** ['blɛst]; **blessing 1** : bendecir ⟨God bless you! : ¡que Dios te bendiga!⟩ ⟨you did the dishes? bless you! : ¿lavaste los trastes? ¡mil gracias!⟩ ⟨he's a little forgetful, bless his heart : es un poco olvidadizo, el pobre⟩ **2 bless you!** (said to someone who has sneezed) : ¡salud! **3 to bless with** : dotar de **4 to bless oneself** : santiguarse

blessed ['blɛsəd] or **blest** ['blɛst] adj : bienaventurado, bendito, dichoso

blessedly ['blɛsədli] adv : felizmente, alegremente, afortunadamente

blessing ['blɛsɪŋ] n **1** : bendición f **2** APPROVAL : aprobación f, consentimiento m

blew → blow

blight¹ ['blaɪt] vt : arruinar, infestar

blight² n **1** : añublo m **2** PLAGUE : peste f, plaga f **3** DECAY : deterioro m, ruina f

blimp ['blɪmp] n : dirigible m

blind¹ ['blaɪnd] vt **1** : cegar, dejar ciego **2** DAZZLE : deslumbrar

blind² adj **1** SIGHTLESS : ciego ⟨to go blind : quedarse ciego⟩ **2** INSENSITIVE : ciego, insensible, sin razón **3** CLOSED : sin salida ⟨blind alley : callejón sin salida⟩

blind³ n **1** : persiana f (para una ventana) **2** COVER : escondite m, escondrijo m

blind carbon copy n : copia f oculta

blind date n : cita f a ciegas

blinders ['blaɪndərz] npl : anteojeras fpl

blindfold¹ ['blaɪnd‚foːld] vt : vendar los ojos

blindfold² n : venda f (para los ojos)

blinding ['blaɪndɪŋ] adj : enceguecedor, cegador ⟨with blinding speed : con una rapidez inusitada⟩

blindly ['blaɪndli] adv : a ciegas, ciegamente

blindness ['blaɪndnəs] n : ceguera f

blind spot n **1** : ángulo m muerto (de un vehículo) **2** WEAKNESS : punto m débil

blink¹ ['blɪŋk] vi **1** WINK : pestañear, parpadear **2** : brillar intermitentemente

blink² n : pestañeo m, parpadeo m

blinker ['blɪŋkər] n : intermitente m, direccional f

bliss ['blɪs] n **1** HAPPINESS : dicha f, felicidad f absoluta **2** PARADISE : paraíso m

blissful ['blɪsfəl] adj : dichoso, feliz — **blissfully** adv

blister¹ ['blɪstər] vi : ampollarse

blister² n : ampolla f (en la piel o una superficie), burbuja f (en una superficie)

blithe ['blaɪθ, 'blaɪð] adj **blither; blithest 1** CAREFREE : despreocu-

pado **2** CHEERFUL : alegre, risueño —
blithely adv
blitz[1] [ˈblɪts] vt **1** BOMBARD : bombardear **2** : atacar con rapidez
blitz[2] n **1** : bombardeo m aéreo **2** CAM-
PAIGN : ataque m, acometida f
blizzard [ˈblɪzərd] n : tormenta f de nieve,
ventisca f
bloat [ˈbloːt] vi : hincharse, inflarse
blob [ˈblɑb] n : gota f, mancha f, borrón m
bloc [ˈblɑk] n : bloque m
block[1] [ˈblɑk] vt **1** OBSTRUCT : bloquear
(una calle, una arteria, etc.) ⟨you're
blocking my light : me estás tapando la
luz⟩ **2** or **to block up** CLOG : obstruir,
atascar, atorar (una tubería, etc.) **3** IM-
PEDE : bloquear, impedir **4** : bloquear
(en deportes) **5 to block in** : cerrarle el
paso a (un vehículo) **6 to block off** BAR-
RICADE : cortar (una calle) **7 to block
out** : tapar (el sol, etc.) **8 to block out**
FORGET, IGNORE : borrar de la mente
block[2] n **1** PIECE : bloque m ⟨building
blocks : cubos de construcción⟩ ⟨auc-
tion block : plataforma de subastas⟩
⟨starting block : taco de salida⟩ **2** OBS-
TRUCTION : obstrucción f, bloqueo m
⟨mental block : bloqueo mental⟩ **3**
: cuadra f, manzana f (de edificios) ⟨to
go around the block : dar la vuelta a la
cuadra⟩ **4** BUILDING : edificio m (de
apartamentos, oficinas, etc.) **5** SERIES,
GROUP : serie f, grupo m ⟨a block of
tickets : una serie de entradas⟩ **6 block
and tackle** : aparejo m de poleas
blockade[1] [blɑˈkeɪd] vt **-aded; -ading**
: bloquear
blockade[2] n : bloqueo m
blockage [ˈblɑkɪʤ] n : bloqueo m, obstrucción f
blockbuster [ˈblɑkˌbʌstər] n : gran éxito
m (de taquilla)
blockhead [ˈblɑkˌhɛd] n : bruto m, -ta f;
estúpido m, -da f
block letters npl : letras fpl de molde/im-
prenta (mayúsculas)
blog [ˈblɔg, ˈblɑg] n : blog m, bitácora f
blond[1] or **blonde** [ˈblɑnd] adj : rubio,
güero Mex, claro (dícese de la madera)
blond[2] or **blonde** n : rubio m, -bia f; güero
m, -ra f Mex
blood [ˈblʌd] n **1** : sangre f ⟨to draw blood
: sacar sangre⟩ **2** LIFEBLOOD : vida f,
alma f **3** LINEAGE : linaje m, sangre f
⟨blood relatives : parientes consanguí-
neos⟩ **4 in cold blood** : a sangre fría
blood bank n : banco m de sangre
bloodbath [ˈblʌdˌbæθ, -ˌbɑθ] n : masacre
f, baño m de sangre
bloodcurdling [ˈblʌdˌkərdlɪŋ] adj : espeluznante, aterrador
blood donor n : donador m, -dora f de
sangre; donante mf de sangre
blooded [ˈblʌdəd] adj : de sangre ⟨cold-
blooded animal : animal de sangre fría⟩
blood group n : grupo m sanguíneo
bloodhound [ˈblʌdˌhaʊnd] n : sabueso m
bloodless [ˈblʌdləs] adj **1** : incruento,
sin derramamiento de sangre **2** LIFE-
LESS : desanimado, insípido, sin vida

bloodmobile [ˈblʌdmoˌbiːl] n : unidad f
móvil para donantes de sangre
blood pressure n : tensión f, presión f (arterial)
bloodshed [ˈblʌdˌʃɛd] n : derramamiento
m de sangre
bloodshot [ˈblʌdˌʃɑt] adj : inyectado de
sangre
bloodstain [ˈblʌdˌsteɪn] n : mancha f de
sangre
bloodstained [ˈblʌdˌsteɪnd] adj : manchado de sangre
bloodstream [ˈblʌdˌstriːm] n : torrente m
sanguíneo, corriente f sanguínea
bloodsucker [ˈblʌdˌsʌkər] n : sanguijuela f
blood test n : análisis m de sangre
bloodthirsty [ˈblʌdˌθərsti] adj : sanguinario
blood transfusion n : transfusión f de
sangre
blood vessel n : vaso m sanguíneo
bloody [ˈblʌdi] adj **bloodier; -est** : ensangrentado, sangriento
bloom[1] [ˈbluːm] vi **1** FLOWER : florecer **2** MATURE : madurar
bloom[2] n **1** FLOWER : flor f ⟨to be in
bloom : estar en flor⟩ **2** FLOWERING
: floración f ⟨in full bloom : en plena flo-
ración⟩ **3** : rubor m (de la tez) ⟨in the
bloom of youth : en plena juventud, en
la flor de la vida⟩
bloomers [ˈbluːmərz] npl : bombachos
mpl
blooper [ˈbluːpər] n : metedura f de pata
fam
blossom[1] [ˈblɑsəm] vi : florecer, dar flor
blossom[2] n : flor f
blot[1] [ˈblɑt] vt **blotted; blotting 1** SPOT
: emborronar, borronear **2** DRY : secar
blot[2] n **1** STAIN : mancha f, borrón m **2**
BLEMISH : mancha f, tacha f
blotch[1] [ˈblɑtʃ] vt : emborronar, borronear
blotch[2] n : mancha f, borrón m
blotchy [ˈblɑtʃi] adj **blotchier; -est** : lleno
de manchas
blotter [ˈblɑtər] n : hoja f de papel secante, secante m
blouse [ˈblaʊs, ˈblaʊz] n : blusa f
blow[1] [ˈbloː] v **blew** [ˈbluː]; **blown** [ˈbloːn];
blowing vi **1** : soplar (dícese del
viento) **2** : agitarse (etc.) con el viento
⟨to blow open/shut : abrirse/cerrarse⟩
⟨to blow off/away : volar⟩ **3** SOUND
: sonar (dícese de un silbato, etc.) **4 to
blow off** fam : dejar plantado a (alguien)
fam, no ir a (una cita, etc.) **5 to blow
out** : fundirse (dícese de un fusible eléctrico), reventarse (dícese de una
llanta) **6 to blow over** : pasar, dispersarse (dícese de una tormenta) **7 to
blow over** : pasar, calmarse, caer en el
olvido (dícese de una situación) — vt **1**
: soplar, echar ⟨to blow smoke : echar
humo⟩ **2** SOUND : tocar, sonar **3**
SHAPE : soplar, dar forma a (vidrio,
etc.) **4** BUNGLE : echar a perder **5 to
blow one's nose** : sonarse la nariz
blow[2] n **1** PUFF : soplo m, soplido m **2**
GALE : vendaval f **3** HIT, STROKE : golpe

m 4 CALAMITY : golpe *m*, desastre *m* 5
to come to blows : llegar a las manos
blow–dry [ˈbloˑˌdraɪ] *n, pl* **-dries** : secado
m (de pelo)
blower [ˈbloˑər] *n* FAN : ventilador *m*
blowout [ˈbloˑˌaʊt] *n* : reventón *m*
blowtorch [ˈbloˑˌtɔrtʃ] *n* : soplete *m*
blow up *vi* EXPLODE : estallar, hacer explosión — *vt* BLAST : volar, hacer volar
blubber[1] [ˈblʌbər] *vi* : lloriquear
blubber[2] *n* : esperma *f* de ballena
bludgeon [ˈblʌdʒən] *vt* : aporrear
blue[1] [ˈbluː] *adj* **bluer; bluest** 1 : azul *m*
2 MELANCHOLY : melancólico, triste
blue[2] *n* : azul *m*
bluebell [ˈbluːˌbɛl] *n* : campanilla *f*
blueberry [ˈbluːˌbɛri] *n, pl* **-ries** : arándano *m*
bluebird [ˈbluːˌbərd] *n* : azulejo *m*
blue cheese *n* : queso *m* azul
blue–collar [ˈbluːˈkɑlər] *adj* : obrero
blueprint [ˈbluːˌprɪnt] *n* 1 : plano *m*, proyecto *m*, cianotipo *m* 2 PLAN : anteproyecto *m*, programa *m*
blues [ˈbluːz] *npl* 1 DEPRESSION : depresión *f*, melancolía *f* 2 : blues *m* ⟨to sing the blues : cantar blues⟩
bluff[1] [ˈblʌf] *vi* : hacer un farol, blofear *Col, Mex*
bluff[2] *adj* 1 STEEP : escarpado 2 FRANK : campechano, franco, directo
bluff[3] *n* 1 : farol *m*; blof *m Col, Mex* 2 CLIFF : acantilado *m*, risco *m*
bluing or **blueing** [ˈbluːɪŋ] *n* : añil *m*, azulete *m*
bluish [ˈbluːɪʃ] *adj* : azulado
blunder[1] [ˈblʌndər] *vi* 1 STUMBLE : tropezar, dar traspiés 2 ERR : cometer un error, tropezar, meter la pata *fam*
blunder[2] *n* : error *m*, fallo *m* garrafal, metedura *f* de pata *fam*
blunderbuss [ˈblʌndərˌbʌs] *n* : trabuco *m*
blunt[1] [ˈblʌnt] *vt* 1 : despuntar (un lápiz, etc.), desafilar (un cuchillo, etc.) 2 : embotar (la mente, etc.), suavizar (críticas)
blunt[2] *adj* 1 DULL : desafilado, despuntado 2 DIRECT : directo, franco, categórico
bluntly [ˈblʌntli] *adv* : sin rodeos, francamente, bruscamente
bluntness [ˈblʌntnəs] *n* 1 DULLNESS : falta *f* de filo 2 FRANKNESS : franqueza *f*
blur[1] [ˈblər] *vt* **blurred; blurring** : desdibujar, hacer borroso
blur[2] *n* 1 SMEAR : mancha *f*, borrón *m* 2 : aspecto *m* borroso ⟨everything was just a blur : todo se volvió borroso⟩
blurb [ˈblərb] *n* : propaganda *f*, nota *f* publicitaria
blurred [ˈblərd] *adj* : borroso
blurry [ˈbləri] *adj* : borroso
blurt [ˈblərt] *vt* : espetar, decir impulsivamente
blush[1] [ˈblʌʃ] *vi* : ruborizarse, sonrojarse, hacerse colorado
blush[2] *n* : rubor *m*, sonrojo *m*
bluster[1] [ˈblʌstər] *vi* 1 BLOW : soplar con fuerza 2 BOAST : fanfarronear, echar bravatas

bluster[2] *n* : fanfarronada *f*, bravatas *fpl*
blustery [ˈblʌstəri] *adj* : borrascoso, tempestuoso
boa [ˈboˑə] *n* : boa *f*
boar [ˈbor] *n* : cerdo *m* macho, verraco *m*
board[1] [ˈbord] *vt* 1 : embarcarse en, subir a bordo de (una nave o un avión), subir a (un tren o carro) 2 LODGE : hospedar, dar hospedaje con comidas a 3 **to board up** : cerrar con tablas
board[2] *n* 1 PLANK : tabla *f*, tablón *m* 2 : tablero *m* ⟨chessboard : tablero de ajedrez⟩ 3 → cardboard 4 → bulletin board 5 → blackboard 6 → surfboard 7 MEALS : comida *f* ⟨board and lodging : comida y alojamiento⟩ 8 COMMITTEE, COUNCIL : junta *f*, consejo *m* 9 **across the board** : en general, para todos 10 **on** ~ → aboard 11 **on** ~ ⟨to get someone on board : conseguir el apoyo de alguien⟩ ⟨to be on board : apoyar algo, apoyar a alguien⟩
boarder [ˈbordər] *n* LODGER : huésped *m*, -peda *f*
board game *n* : juego *m* de mesa
boardinghouse [ˈbordɪŋˌhaʊs] *n* : casa *f* de huéspedes
boarding school *n* : internado *m*
boardroom [ˈbordˌruːm, -ˌrʊm] *n* : sala *f* de juntas
boardwalk [ˈbordˌwɔk] *n* : paseo *m* marítimo
boast[1] [ˈboːst] *vi* : alardear, presumir, jactarse
boast[2] *n* : jactancia *f*, alarde *m*
boaster [ˈboːstər] *n* : presumido *m*, -da *f*; fanfarrón *m*, -rrona *f fam*
boastful [ˈboːstfəl] *adj* : jactancioso, fanfarrón *fam*
boastfully [ˈboːstfəli] *adv* : de manera jactanciosa
boastfulness [ˈboːstfəlnəs] *n* : jactancia *f*
boat[1] [ˈboːt] *vt* : transportar en barco, poner a bordo
boat[2] *n* : barco *m*, embarcación *f*, bote *m*, barca *f*
boatman [ˈboːtmən] *n, pl* **-men** [-mən, -ˌmɛn] : barquero *m*
boat person *n* : balsero *m*, -ra *f*
boatwoman [ˈboːtˌwʊmən] *n, pl* **-women** [-ˌwɪmən] : barquera *f*
bob[1] [ˈbɑb] *v* **bobbed; bobbing** *vi* 1 : balancearse, mecerse ⟨to bob up and down : subir y bajar⟩ 2 *or* **to bob up** APPEAR : presentarse, surgir — *vt* 1 : inclinar (la cabeza o el cuerpo) 2 CUT : cortar, recortar ⟨she bobbed her hair : se cortó el pelo⟩
bob[2] *n* 1 : inclinación *f* (de la cabeza, del cuerpo), sacudida *f* 2 FLOAT : flotador *m*, corcho *m* (de pesca) 3 : pelo *m* corto
bobbin [ˈbɑbən] *n* : bobina *f*, carrete *m* (de una máquina de coser)
bobby pin [ˈbɑbiˌpɪn] *n* : horquilla *f*
bobcat [ˈbɑbˌkæt] *n* : lince *m* rojo
bobolink [ˈbɑbəˌlɪŋk] *n* : tordo *m* arrocero
bobsled [ˈbɑbˌslɛd] *n* : bobsleigh *m*
bobwhite [ˈbɑbˈʰwaɪt] *n* : codorniz *m* (del Nuevo Mundo)

bode¹ ['boːd] *v* **boded; boding** *vt* : presagiar, augurar — *vi* **to bode well** : ser de buen agüero

bode² → **bide**

bodice ['badəs] *n* : corpiño *m*

bodied ['badid] *adj* : de cuerpo ⟨lean-bodied : de cuerpo delgado⟩ ⟨able-bodied : no discapacitado⟩

bodiless ['badiləs, 'badələs] *adj* : incorpóreo

bodily¹ ['badəli] *adv* : en peso ⟨to lift someone bodily : levantar a alguien en peso⟩

bodily² *adj* : corporal, del cuerpo ⟨bodily harm : daños corporales⟩

body ['badi] *n, pl* **bodies** **1** : cuerpo *m*, organismo *m* **2** CORPSE : cadáver *m* **3** PERSON : persona *f*, ser *m* humano **4** : nave *f* (de una iglesia), carrocería *f* (de un automóvil), fuselaje *m* (de un avión), casco *m* (de una nave) **5** COLLECTION, MASS : conjunto *m*, grupo *m*, masa *f* ⟨in a body : todos juntos, en masa⟩ **6** ORGANIZATION : organismo *m*, organización *f*

bodybuilding ['badi,bɪldɪŋ] *n* : culturismo *m*

bodyguard ['badi,gard] *n* : guardaespaldas *mf*

bodywork ['badi,wərk] *n* : carrocería *f*

bog¹ ['bag, 'bɔg] *v* **bogged; bogging** *vt* **1** **to bog down** SWAMP : empantanar, inundar ⟨to get bogged down : quedar empantanado⟩ **2** STALL : estancar, paralizar — *vi* **to bog down 1** STICK : embarrancar, empantanarse **2** STALL : estancarse, empantanarse

bog² *n* : lodazal *m*, ciénaga *f*, cenagal *m*

bogey ['bugi, 'boː-] *n* **1** : bogey *m* (en golf) **2** → **bugaboo**

bogeyman ['bugi,mæn, 'boː-] *n, pl* **-men** [-mən] : coco *m fam*; cuco *m Arg, Chile, Peru, Uru fam* ⟨the bogeyman will get you! : ¡viene el coco!⟩ ⟨he's the bogeyman of conservatives : es el coco de los conservativos⟩

boggle ['bagəl] *vi* **-gled; -gling** : quedarse atónito, quedarse pasmado ⟨the mind boggles! : ¡es increíble!⟩

boggy ['bagi, 'bɔ-] *adj* **boggier; -est** : cenagoso

bogus ['boːgəs] *adj* : falso, fingido, falaz

bohemian [boː'hiːmiən] *n* : bohemio *m*, -mia *f* — **bohemian** *adj*

boil¹ ['bɔɪl] *vi* **1** : hervir **2 to boil down to** : reducirse a **3 to make one's blood boil** : hervirle la sangre a uno — *vt* **1** : hervir, hacer hervir ⟨to boil water : hervir agua⟩ **2** : cocer, hervir ⟨to boil potatoes : cocer papas⟩ **3 to boil something down** : reducir algo a

boil² *n* **1** BOILING : hervor *m* **2** : forúnculo *m* (en medicina)

boiler ['bɔɪlər] *n* : caldera *f*

boiling ['bɔɪlɪŋ] *adj* **1** : hirviendo **2** HOT : caliente ⟨I'm boiling : me muero de calor⟩

boiling point *n* : punto *m* de ebullición

boisterous ['bɔɪstərəs] *adj* : bullicioso, escandaloso — **boisterously** *adv*

bold¹ ['boːld] *adj* **1** COURAGEOUS : valiente **2** INSOLENT : insolente, descarado **3** DARING : atrevido, audaz — **boldly** *adv*

bold² → **boldface**

boldface ['boːld,feɪs] *or* **boldface type** *n* : negrita *f*

boldness ['boːldnəs] *n* **1** COURAGE : valor *m*, coraje *m* **2** INSOLENCE : atrevimiento *m*, insolencia *f*, descaro *m* **3** DARING : audacia *f*

bolero [bə'lero] *n, pl* **-ros** : bolero *m*

bolivar [bə'liː,var, 'baləvər] *n* : bolívar *m* (unidad monetaria)

Bolivian [bə'lɪvian] *n* : boliviano *m*, -na *f* — **Bolivian** *adj*

boliviano [bə,lɪvi'ano] *n* : boliviano *m* (unidad monetaria)

boll ['boːl] *n* : cápsula *f* (del algodón)

boll weevil *n* : gorgojo *m* del algodón

bologna [bə'loːni] *n* : salchicha *f* ahumada

Bolshevik ['boːlʃə,vɪk, 'bəl-] *n* : bolchevique *nmf* — **Bolshevik** *adj*

bolster¹ ['boːlstər] *vt* **-stered; -stering** : reforzar, reafirmar ⟨to bolster morale : levantar la moral⟩

bolster² *n* : cabezal *m*, almohadón *m*

bolt¹ ['boːlt] *vt* **1** : atornillar, sujetar con pernos ⟨bolted to the floor : sujetado con pernos al suelo⟩ **2** : cerrar con pestillo, echar el cerrojo a ⟨to bolt the door : echar el cerrojo a la puerta⟩ **3 to bolt down** : engullir ⟨she bolted down her dinner : engulló su comida⟩ — *vi* : echar a correr, salir corriendo ⟨he bolted from the room : salió corriendo de la sala⟩

bolt² *n* **1** LATCH : pestillo *m*, cerrojo *m* **2** : tornillo *m*, perno *m* ⟨nuts and bolts : tuercas y tornillos⟩ **3** : rollo *m* ⟨a bolt of cloth : un rollo de tela⟩ **4** lightning bolt : relámpago *m*, rayo *m*

bomb¹ ['bam] *vt* : bombardear

bomb² *n* **1** : bomba *f* **2** FAILURE : desastre *m*

bombard [bam'bard, bəm-] *vt* : bombardear

bombardment [bam'bardmənt] *n* : bombardeo *m*

bombast ['bam,bæst] *n* : grandilocuencia *f*, ampulosidad *f*

bombastic [bam'bæstɪk] *adj* : grandilocuente, ampuloso, bombástico

bomber ['bamər] *n* : bombardero *m*

bombing ['bamɪŋ] *n* : bombardeo *m*

bombproof ['bam,pruːf] *adj* : a prueba de bombas

bombshell ['bam,ʃɛl] *n* : bomba *f* ⟨a political bombshell : una bomba política⟩

bona fide ['boːnə,faɪd, 'baː-, ,boːnə'faɪd] *adj* **1** : de buena fe ⟨a bona fide offer : una oferta de buena fe⟩ **2** GENUINE : genuino, auténtico

bonanza [bə'nænzə] *n* : bonanza *f*

bon appétit ['bounæpə'tiː] *interj* : ¡buen provecho!

bonbon ['ban,ban] *n* : bombón *m*

bond¹ ['band] *vt* **1** INSURE : dar fianza a, asegurar **2** STICK : adherir, pegar — *vi* : adherirse, pegarse

bond² *n* **1** LINK, TIE : vínculo *m*, lazo *m* **2** BAIL : fianza *f*, caución *f* **3** : bono *m* ⟨stocks and bonds : acciones y bonos⟩ **4 bonds** *npl* FETTERS : cadenas *fpl*

bondage ['bɑndɪdʒ] *n* : esclavitud *f*

bondholder ['bɑnd,hoːldər] *n* : tenedor *m*, -dora *f* de bonos

bondsman ['bɑndzmən] *n, pl* **-men** [-mən, -,mn] **1** SLAVE : esclavo *m* **2** SURETY : fiador *m*, -dora *f*

bone¹ ['boːn] *vt* **boned**; **boning 1** : deshuesar **2 to bone up on** *fam* : estudiar

bone² *n* **1** : hueso *m* **2 to feel it in one's bones** : tener un presentimiento **3 to have a bone to pick with someone** : tener que arreglar cuentas con alguien **4 to the bone** : muchísimo ⟨it chilled me to the bone : se me helό la sangre⟩ **5 to throw someone a bone** : hacerle una pequeña concesión a alguien

boneless ['boːnləs] *adj* : sin huesos, sin espinas

boner ['boːnər] *n* : metedura *f* de pata, metida *f* de pata

bonfire ['bɑn,faɪr] *n* : hoguera *f*, fogata *f*, fogόn *m*

bongo ['bɑngo, 'bɔn-] *n* : bongό *m*, bongo *m*

bonito [bə'niːto] *n, pl* **-tos** *or* **-to** : bonito *m*

bonnet ['bɑnət] *n* : sombrero *m* (de mujer), gorra *f* (de niño)

bonus ['boːnəs] *n* **1** : prima *f*, bonificaciόn *f* (pagado al empleado) **2** ADVANTAGE, BENEFIT : beneficio *m*, provecho *m*

bony ['boːni] *adj* **bonier; -est** : huesudo

boo¹ ['buː] *vt* : abuchear

boo² *n, pl* **boos** : abucheo *m*

booby ['buːbi] *n, pl* **-bies** FOOL : bobo *m*, -ba *f*; tonto *m*, -ta *f*

boogeyman ['bʊgi,mæn] *n, pl* **-men** [-mən, -,mɛn] → **bogeyman**

book¹ ['bʊk] *vt* : reservar ⟨to book a flight : reservar un vuelo⟩ — *vi* : hacer una reservaciόn

book² *n* **1** : libro *m* **2 the Book** : la Biblia **3 by the book** : segύn las reglas

bookcase ['bʊk,keɪs] *n* : estantería *f*, librero *m* Mex, biblioteca *f*

bookend ['bʊk,ɛnd] *n* : sujetalibros *m*

bookie ['bʊki] → **bookmaker**

bookish ['bʊkɪʃ] *adj* : libresco

bookkeeper ['bʊk,kiːpər] *n* : tenedor *m*, -dora *f* de libros; contable *mf* Spain

bookkeeping ['bʊk,kiːpɪŋ] *n* : contabilidad *f*, teneduría *f* de libros

booklet ['bʊklət] *n* : folleto *m*

bookmaker ['bʊk,meɪkər] *n* : corredor *m*, -dora *f* de apuestas

bookmark¹ ['bʊk,mɑrk] *n* **1** : señalador *m* de libros, marcador *m* de libros **2** : marcador *m* (de Internet)

bookmark² *vt* : marcar (una página web)

bookseller ['bʊk,sɛlər] *n* : librero *m*, -ra *f*

bookshelf ['bʊk,ʃɛlf] *n, pl* **-shelves** : estante *m* **2 bookshelves** *npl* : estantería *f*

bookstore ['bʊk,stor] *n* : librería *f*

bookworm ['bʊk,wərm] *n* : ratόn *m* de biblioteca *fam*

boom¹ ['buːm] *vi* **1** THUNDER : tronar, resonar **2** FLOURISH, PROSPER : estar en auge, prosperar

boom² *n* **1** BOOMING : bramido *m*, estruendo *m* **2** FLOURISHING : auge *m* ⟨population boom : auge de poblaciόn⟩

boomerang ['buːmə,ræŋ] *n* : bumerán *m*

boon¹ ['buːn] *adj* **boon companion** : amigo *m*, -ga *f* del alma

boon² *n* : ayuda *f*, beneficio *m*, adelanto *m*

boondocks ['buːn,dɑks] *npl* : área *f* rural remota, regiόn *f* alejada

boor ['bʊr] *n* : grosero *m*, -ra *f*

boorish ['bʊrɪʃ] *adj* : grosero

boost¹ ['buːst] *vt* **1** LIFT : levantar, alzar **2** INCREASE : aumentar, incrementar **3** PROMOTE : promover, fomentar, hacer publicidad por

boost² *n* **1** THRUST : impulso *m*, empujόn *m* **2** ENCOURAGEMENT : estímulo *m*, aliento *m* **3** INCREASE : aumento *m*, incremento *m*

booster ['buːstər] *n* **1** SUPPORTER : partidario *m*, -ria *f* **2 booster rocket** : cohete *m* propulsor **3 booster shot** : vacuna *f* de refuerzo

boot¹ ['buːt] *vt* KICK : dar una patada a, patear

boot² *n* **1** : bota *f*, botín *m* **2** KICK : puntapié *m*, patada *f*

bootee *or* **bootie** ['buːti] *n* : botita *f*, botín *m*

booth ['buːθ] *n, pl* **booths** ['buːðz, 'buːθs] : cabina *f* (de teléfono, de votar), caseta *f* (de informaciόn), barraca *f* (a una feria)

bootleg¹ ['buːt,lɛg] *adj* : pirata ⟨bootleg software : software pirata⟩

bootleg² *vt* : piratear (un video, etc.)

bootlegger ['buːt,lɛgər] *n* : contrabandista *mf* del alcohol

bootlegging ['buːt,lɛgɪŋ] *n* : piratería *f*

booty ['buːti] *n, pl* **-ties** : botín *m*

booze ['buːz] *n fam* : alcohol *m*

border¹ ['bɔrdər] *vt* **1** EDGE : ribetear, bordear **2** BOUND : limitar con, lindar con — *vi* : rayar, lindar ⟨that borders on absurdity : eso raya en lo absurdo⟩

border² *n* **1** EDGE : borde *m*, orilla *f* **2** TRIM : ribete *m* **3** FRONTIER : frontera *f*

borderline¹ ['bɔrdər,laɪn] *adj* : dudoso

borderline² *n* : límite *m*

bore¹ ['bɔr] *vt* **bored; boring 1** PIERCE : taladrar, perforar ⟨to bore metals : taladrar metales⟩ **2** OPEN : hacer, abrir ⟨to bore a tunnel : abrir un túnel⟩ **3** WEARY : aburrir

bore² → **bear**¹

bore³ *n* **1** : pesado *m*, -da *f* (persona aburrida) **2** TEDIOUSNESS : pesadez *f*, lo aburrido **3** DIAMETER : calibre *m*

bored ['bɔrd] *adj* : aburrido ⟨to be bored stiff, to be bored to tears/death : aburrirse como una ostra⟩

boredom ['bɔrdəm] *n* : aburrimiento *m*

boring ['bɔrɪŋ] *adj* : aburrido, pesado

born ['bɔrn] *adj* **1** : nacido *m* : nato ⟨she's a born singer : es una cantante nata⟩ ⟨he's a born leader : naciό para mandar⟩

borne *pp* → bear¹

borough ['bərə] *n* : distrito *m* municipal

borrow ['baro] *vt* 1 : pedir prestado, tomar prestado 2 APPROPRIATE : apropiarse de, adoptar

borrower ['barəwər] *n* : prestatario *m*, -ria *f*

borrowing ['barəwiŋ] *n* : préstamo *m* (en lingüística)

Bosnian ['bazniən, 'baz-] *n* : bosnio *m*, -nia *f* — **Bosnian** *adj*

bosom¹ ['buzəm, 'bu:-] *adj* : íntimo

bosom² *n* 1 CHEST : pecho *m* 2 BREAST : pecho *m*, seno *m* 3 CLOSENESS : seno *m* ⟨in the bosom of her family : en el seno de su familia⟩

bosomed ['buzəmd, 'bu:-] *adj* : con busto ⟨big-bosomed : con mucho busto⟩

boss¹ ['bɔs] *vt* 1 SUPERVISE : dirigir, supervisar 2 to boss around : mandonear *fam*, mangonear *fam*

boss² *n* : jefe *m*, -fa *f*; patrón *m*, -trona *f*

bossy ['bɔsi] *adj* bossier; -est : mandón *fam*, autoritario, dominante

bot ['bat] *n* : bot *m*

botanist ['batənɪst] *n* : botánico *m*, -ca *f*

botany ['batəni] *n* : botánica *f* — **botanical** [bə'tænɪkəl] *adj*

botch¹ ['bat͡ʃ] *vt* : hacer una chapuza de, estropear

botch² *n* : chapuza *f*

both¹ ['boθ] *adj* : ambos, ambas; los dos, las dos ⟨both classes : ambas clases, las dos clases⟩

both² *conj* : tanto como ⟨both Ann and her mother are tall : tanto Ana como su madre son altas⟩

both³ *pron* : ambos ambas; los dos, las dos ⟨both of the women laughed : ambas mujeres rieron, las dos mujeres rieron⟩ ⟨we both went : fuimos los dos⟩ ⟨he knows both of my sisters : conoce a mis dos hermanas⟩

bother¹ ['baðər] *vt* 1 IRK : preocupar ⟨nothing's bothering me : nada me preocupa⟩ ⟨what's bothering him? : ¿qué le pasa?⟩ 2 PESTER : molestar, fastidiar — *vi* to bother to : molestarse en, tomar la molestia de

bother² *n* 1 TROUBLE : molestia *f*, problemas *mpl* 2 ANNOYANCE : molestia *f*, fastidio *m*

bothersome ['baðərsəm] *adj* : molesto, fastidioso

bottle¹ ['batəl] *vt* bottled; bottling : embotellar, envasar

bottle² *n* : botella *f*, frasco *m*

bottleneck ['batəl,nɛk] *n* 1 : cuello *m* de botella (en un camino) 2 : embotellamiento *m*, atasco *m* (de tráfico) 3 OBSTACLE : obstáculo *m*

bottle opener *n* : abrebotellas *m*

bottom¹ ['batəm] *adj* : más bajo, inferior, de abajo

bottom² *n* 1 : fondo *m* (de una caja, de una taza, del mar), pie *m* (de una escalera, una página, una montaña), asiento *m* (de una silla), parte *f* de abajo (de una pila) 2 CAUSE : origen *m*, causa *f* ⟨to get to the bottom of : llegar al fondo de⟩ 3 BUTTOCKS : trasero *m*, nalgas *fpl*

bottomless ['batəmləs] *adj* : sin fondo, sin límites

bottom line *n* 1 : balance *m* final (en contabilidad) 2 the bottom line : lo esencial, lo más importante 3 the bottom line : el resultado final

botulism ['bat͡ʃə,lɪzəm] *n* : botulismo *m*

boudoir [bə'dwar, bʊ-; 'bu:,-, 'bʊ-] *n* : tocador *m*

bough ['baʊ] *n* : rama *f*

bought → buy¹

bouillon ['bu:jan;, 'bʊl,jan, -jən] *n* : caldo *m*

boulder ['boldər] *n* : canto *m* rodado, roca *f* grande

boulevard ['bʊlə,vard, 'bu:-] *n* : bulevar *m*, boulevard *m*

bounce¹ ['baʊnts] *v* bounced; bouncing *vt* 1 : hacer rebotar 2 to bounce a check : emitir un cheque sin fondos — *vi* 1 : rebotar 2 : ser devuelto (dícese de un cheque)

bounce² *n* : rebote *m*

bouncer ['baʊntsər] *n* : portero *m*; patovica *m Arg, Uru fam*; gorila *m Spain fam*

bouncy ['baʊntsi] *adj* bouncier; -est 1 LIVELY : vivo, exuberante, animado 2 RESILIENT : elástico, flexible 3 : que rebota (dícese de una pelota)

bound¹ ['baʊnd] *vt* : delimitar, rodear — *vi* LEAP : saltar, dar brincos

bound² *adj* 1 OBLIGED : obligado 2 : encuadernado, empastado ⟨a book bound in leather : un libro encuadernado en cuero⟩ 3 DETERMINED : decidido, empeñado 4 to be bound to : ser seguro que, tener que, no caber duda que ⟨it was bound to happen : tenía que suceder⟩ 5 bound for : con rumbo a ⟨bound for Chicago : con rumbo a Chicago⟩ ⟨to be homeward bound : ir camino a casa⟩

bound³ *n* 1 LIMIT : límite *m* 2 LEAP : salto *m*, brinco *m*

boundary ['baʊndri, -dəri] *n, pl* -aries : límite *m*, línea *f* divisoria, linde *mf*

boundless ['baʊndləs] *adj* : sin límites, infinito

bounteous ['baʊntiəs] *adj* 1 GENEROUS : generoso 2 ABUNDANT : copioso, abundante — **bounteously** *adv*

bountiful ['baʊntɪfəl] *adj* 1 GENEROUS, LIBERAL : pródigo, generoso 2 ABUNDANT : copioso, abundante

bounty ['baʊnti] *n, pl* -ties 1 GENEROSITY : generosidad *f* 2 REWARD : recompensa *f*

bouquet [bo'keɪ, bu:-] *n* 1 : ramo *m*, ramillete *m* 2 FRAGRANCE : bouquet *m*, aroma *m*

bourbon ['bərbən, 'bʊr-] *n* : bourbon *m*, whisky *m* americano

bourgeois¹ ['bʊrʒ,wa, bʊrʒ'wa] *adj* : burgués

bourgeois² *n* : burgués *m*, -guesa *f*

bourgeoisie [,bʊrʒ,wa'zi] *n* : burguesía *f*

bout ['baʊt] *n* 1 : encuentro *m*, combate *m* (en deportes) 2 ATTACK : ataque *m* (de una enfermedad) 3 PERIOD, SPELL : período *m* (de actividad)

boutique [bu:'ti:k] *n* : boutique *f*

bovine¹ ['bo:₁vaɪn, -₁vi:n] *adj* : bovino, vacuno

bovine² *n* : bovino *m*

bow¹ ['baʊ] *vi* **1** : hacer una reverencia, inclinarse **2** SUBMIT : ceder, resignarse, someterse — *vt* **1** LOWER : inclinar, bajar **2** BEND : doblar

bow² ['baʊ] *n* **1** BOWING : reverencia *f*, inclinación *f* **2** : proa *f* (de un barco)

bow³ ['bo:] *vi* CURVE : arquearse, doblarse

bow⁴ ['bo:] *n* **1** ARCH, CURVE : arco *m*, curva *f* **2** : arco *m* (arma o vara para tocar varios instrumentos de música) **3** : lazo *m*, moño *m* ⟨to tie a bow : hacer un moño⟩

bowel ['baʊəl] *n* **1** INTESTINE : intestino *m* ⟨to move one's bowels, to have a bowel movement : evacuar (el vientre)⟩ **2 the bowels** : las entrañas ⟨in the bowels of the earth : en las entrañas de la tierra⟩

bower ['baʊər] *n* : enramada *f*

bowl¹ ['bo:l] *vi* : jugar a los bolos

bowl² *n* : tazón *m*, cuenco *m*, bol *m* ⟨salad bowl : ensaladera⟩

bowler ['bo:lər] *n* : jugador *m*, -dora *f* de bolos

bowling ['bo:lɪŋ] *n* : bolos *mpl*

bowling alley *n* : bolera *f*, boliche *m*

bowling pin *n* : bolo *m*

bow tie *n* : corbata *f* de moño, pajarita *f* *Spain*

box¹ ['baks] *vt* **1** PACK : empaquetar, embalar, encajonar **2** SLAP : bofetear, cachetear — *vi* : boxear

box² *n* **1** CONTAINER : caja *f*, cajón *m* **2** COMPARTMENT : compartimento *m*, palco *m* (en el teatro) **3** SLAP : bofetada *f*, cachetada *f*

boxcar ['baks₁kar] *n* : vagón *m* de carga, furgón *m*

boxer ['baksər] *n* **1** : boxeador *m*, -dora *f* **2 boxers** *pl* → **boxer shorts**

boxer shorts *n* : boxers *mpl*, calzoncillos *mpl*, calzones *mpl*

boxing ['baksɪŋ] *n* : boxeo *m*

box–office ['baks'ɔfəs] *adj* : taquillero

box office *n* : taquilla *f*, boletería *f*

box spring *n* : somier *m*

boy ['bɔɪ] *n* **1** : chico *m*, muchacho *m* **2** *or* **little boy** : niño *m*, chico *m* **3** SON : hijo *m*

boycott¹ ['bɔɪ₁kat] *vt* : boicotear

boycott² *n* : boicot *m*

boyfriend ['bɔɪ₁frɛnd] *n* **1** FRIEND : amigo *m* **2** SWEETHEART : novio *m*

boyhood ['bɔɪ₁hʊd] *n* : niñez *f*

boyish ['bɔɪʃ] *adj* : de niño, juvenil

bra ['bra] → **brassiere**

brace¹ ['breɪs] *v* **braced; bracing** *vt* **1** PROP UP, SUPPORT : apuntalar, apoyar, sostener **2** INVIGORATE : vigorizar **3** REINFORCE : reforzar — *vi* **to brace oneself** PREPARE : prepararse

brace² *n* **1** CLAMP, REINFORCEMENT : abrazadera *f*, refuerzo *m* **2** → **curly brace 3 braces** *npl* : aparatos *mpl* (de ortodoncia), frenos *mpl* *Mex*

bracelet ['breɪslət] *n* : brazalete *m*, pulsera *f*

bracken ['brækən] *n* : helecho *m*

bracket¹ ['brækət] *vt* **1** SUPPORT : asegurar, apuntalar **2** : poner entre corchetes **3** CATEGORIZE, GROUP : catalogar, agrupar

bracket² *n* **1** SUPPORT : soporte *m* **2** : corchete *m* (marca de puntuación) **3** CATEGORY, CLASS : clase *f*, categoría *f*

brackish ['brækɪʃ] *adj* : salobre

brad ['bræd] *n* : clavo *n*ɪ con cabeza pequeña, clavito *m*

brag¹ ['bræg] *vi* **bragged; bragging** : alardear, fanfarronear, jactarse

brag² *n* : alarde *m*, jactancia *f*, fanfarronada *f*

braggart ['brægərt] *n* : fanfarrón *m*, -rrona *f fam*; jactancioso *m*, -sa *f*

braid¹ ['breɪd] *vt* : trenzar

braid² *n* : trenza *f*

braille ['breɪl] *n* : braille *m*

brain¹ ['breɪn] *vt* : romper la crisma a, aplastar el cráneo a

brain² *n* **1** : cerebro *m* **2 brains** *npl* INTELLECT : inteligencia *f*, sesos *mpl*

brainchild ['breɪn₁tʃaɪld] *n* IDEA : creación *f*, invento *m*

brainless ['breɪnləs] *adj* : estúpido, tonto

brainstorm ['breɪn₁stɔrm] *n* : idea *f* brillante, idea *f* genial

brainy ['breɪni] *adj* **brainier; -est** : inteligente, listo

braise ['breɪz] *vt* **braised; braising** : cocer a fuego lento, estofar

brake¹ ['breɪk] *v* **braked; braking** : frenar

brake² *n* : freno *m*

bramble ['bræmbəl] *n* : zarza *f*, zarzamora *f*

bran ['bræn] *n* : salvado *m*

branch¹ ['bræntʃ] *vi* **1** : echar ramas (dícese de una planta) **2** *or* **to branch off** DIVERGE : ramificarse, separarse **3 to branch out** : diversificarse

branch² *n* **1** : rama *f* (de una planta) **2** EXTENSION : ramal *m* (de un camino, un ferrocarril, un río), brazo *m* (de un río), rama *f* (de una familia o un campo de estudio), sucursal *f* (de una empresa), agencia *f* (del gobierno)

brand¹ ['brænd] *vt* **1** : marcar (ganado) **2** LABEL : tachar, tildar ⟨they branded him as a liar : lo tacharon de mentiroso⟩

brand² *n* **1** : marca *f* (de ganado) **2** STIGMA : estigma *m* **3** MAKE : marca *f*

brandish ['brændɪʃ] *vt* : blandir

brand–name ['brænd'neɪm] *adj* : de marca

brand name *n* : marca *f*

brand–new ['brænd'nu:, -'nju:] *adj* : nuevo, flamante

brandy ['brændi] *n*, *pl* **-dies** : brandy *m*

brash ['bræʃ] *adj* **1** IMPULSIVE : impulsivo, impetuoso **2** BRAZEN : excesivamente desenvuelto, descarado

brass ['bræs] *n* **1** : latón *m* **2** GALL, NERVE : descaro *m*, cara *f fam* **3** OFFICERS : mandamases *mpl fam* **4** : metal *m*, metales *mpl* (de una orquesta)

brass band *n* : banda *f* de metales

brassiere [brə'zɪr, bra-] *n* : sostén *m*, brasier *m Col, Mex*

brassy ['bræsi] *adj* **brassier; -est** : dorado

brat [brat] *n disparaging* : mocoso *m*, -sa *f disparaging*; niño *m* mimado, niña *f* mimada

bravado [brə'vado] *n, pl* **-does** *or* **-dos** : bravuconadas *fpl*, bravatas *fpl*

brave¹ ['breɪv] *vt* **braved; braving** : afrontar, hacer frente a

brave² *adj* **braver; bravest** : valiente, valeroso — **bravely** *adv*

brave³ *n* : guerrero *m* (nativo americano)

bravery ['breɪvəri] *n* : valor *m*, valentía *f*

bravo ['brɑ,vo:] *n, pl* **-vos** : bravo *m*

brawl¹ ['brɔl] *vi* : pelearse, pegarse

brawl² *n* : pelea *f*, reyerta *f*

brawn ['brɔn] *n* : fuerza *f* muscular

brawny ['brɔni] *adj* **brawnier; -est** : musculoso

bray¹ ['breɪ] *vi* : rebuznar

bray² *n* : rebuzno *m*

brazen ['breɪzən] *adj* **1** : de latón **2** BOLD : descarado, directo

brazenly ['breɪzənli] *adv* : descaradamente, insolentemente

brazenness ['breɪzənnəs] *n* : descaro *m*, atrevimiento *m*

brazier ['breɪʒər] *n* : brasero *m*

Brazilian [brə'zɪljən] *n* : brasileño *m*, -ña *f* — **Brazilian** *adj*

Brazil nut [brə'zɪl,nʌt] *n* : nuez *f* de Brasil

breach¹ ['britʃ] *vt* **1** PENETRATE : abrir una brecha en, penetrar **2** VIOLATE : infringir, violar

breach² *n* **1** VIOLATION : infracción *f*, violación *f* ⟨breach of trust : abuso de confianza⟩ ⟨breach of contract : incumplimiento de contrato⟩ **2** GAP, OPENING : brecha *f*

bread¹ ['brɛd] *vt* : empanar

bread² *n* : pan *m*

bread box *n* : panera *f*

breadstick ['brɛd,stɪk] *n* : palito *m* de pan; grisín *m Arg, Uru*; colín *m Spain*

breadth ['brɛtθ] *n* : ancho *m*, anchura *f*

breadwinner ['brɛd,wɪnər] *n* : sostén *m* de la familia

break¹ ['breɪk] *v* **broke** ['bro:k]; **broken** ['bro:kən]; **breaking** *vt* **1** : romper, quebrar (cristales, un hueso, etc.) ⟨to break something in two : partir algo en dos⟩ **2** : descomponer, romper (un aparato, etc.) **3** *or* **to break up** DIVIDE, SPLIT : dividir, separar **4** : abrir (la piel), salir a (la superficie) **5** : romper (el suelo) **6** VIOLATE : infringir, violar (la ley, etc.), romper (un contrato), faltar a (una promesa) ⟨to break the speed limit : exceder el límite de velocidad⟩ **7** SURPASS : batir (un récord), superar **8** CRUSH, RUIN : arruinar, deshacer, destrozar ⟨to break someone's spirit : quebrantar el espíritu de alguien⟩ **9** *or* **to break in** TAME : domar **10** : dar, comunicar ⟨to break the news to someone : darle la noticia a alguien⟩ **11** INTERRUPT, END : interrumpir, cortar (un circuito), romper (el silencio), hacer perder (la concentración), perder (una mala costumbre), superar (un punto muerto) **12**
or **to break up** DISRUPT : romper (la monotonía, etc.) **13** SLOW : amortiguar (una caída) ⟨without breaking one's stride : sin cambiar el paso⟩ **14** SOLVE : esclarecer (un caso), descifrar (un código) **15** : cambiar ⟨to break a twenty : cambiar un billete de veinte dólares⟩ **16** **to break down** KNOCK DOWN : derribar, romper **17** **to break down** DIVIDE : desglosar (gastos, etc.), dividir **18** **to break in** : ablandar (zapatos) **19** **to break in** TRAIN : capacitar (a un nuevo empleado, etc.) **20** **to break off** : partir, romper, separar (un pedazo) **21** **to break open** : forzar (una puerta, etc.) **22** **to break someone of something** : quitarle a alguien la costumbre de hacer algo **23** **to break up** STOP : poner fin a, disolver (una manifestación, etc.), detener (una pelea) **24** **to break up** : hacer pedazos (algo), deshacer (grumos, etc.) — *vi* **1** : romperse, quebrarse ⟨my computer broke : se me rompió la computadora⟩ **2** DISSIPATE : disiparse **3** DIVIDE, SPLIT : dividirse **4** : desatarse (dícese de una tormenta), romper (dícese del día) **5** : romper (dícese de olas) **6** CHANGE : cambiar (dícese de la voz), acabarse (dícese del calor, etc.) **7** FALTER : entrecortarse (dícese de la voz) **8** : no poder resistir ⟨he broke under the strain : no pudo con el estrés⟩ **9** DECREASE : bajar ⟨my fever broke : me bajó la fiebre⟩ **10** PAUSE : parar, hacer una pausa **11** : divulgarse, revelarse ⟨the news broke : la noticia se divulgó⟩ **12** **to break away** : separarse **13** **to break down** SEPARATE : descomponerse **14** **to break down** MALFUNCTION : averiarse, descomponerse, estropearse **15** **to break down** : perder el control ⟨she broke down in tears : rompió a llorar⟩ **16** **to break even** : alcanzar su punto de equilibrio (financiero) **17** **to break free/loose** : soltarse **18** **to break in** : entrar (por la fuerza) **19** **to break into** : entrar a (una casa, etc.) para robar **20** **to break off** DETACH : romperse, desprenderse **21** **to break off** END : romper (relaciones, etc.) ⟨she broke off in the middle of a sentence : se detuvo en la mitad de una frase⟩ **22** **to break out** ERUPT : desencadenarse **23** **to break out in** : salirle a uno (un sarpullido, etc.) **24** **to break out of** : escaparse de **25** **to break through** : penetrar **26** **to break up** FRAGMENT : hacerse pedazos **27** **to break up** DISPERSE : disolverse **28** **to break up** : separarse ⟨they broke up : se separaron⟩ ⟨she broke up with him : rompió con él⟩

break² *n* **1** : ruptura *f*, rotura *f*, fractura *f* (de un hueso), claro *m* (entre las nubes), cambio *m* (del tiempo) **2** CHANCE : oportunidad *f* ⟨a lucky break : un golpe de suerte⟩ **3** REST : descanso *m* ⟨to take a break : tomar(se) un descanso⟩ **4** : corte *m*, pausa *f* ⟨commercial break : corte comercial/publicitaria, pausa publicitaria/comercial⟩

breakable ['breɪkəbəl] *adj* : quebradizo, frágil

breakage ['breɪkɪʤ] *n* **1** BREAKING : rotura *f* **2** DAMAGE : destrozos *mpl*, daños *mpl*

breakdown ['breɪk,daʊn] *n* **1** : avería *f* (de máquinas), interrupción *f* (de comunicaciones), fracaso *m* (de negociaciones) **2** ANALYSIS : análisis *m*, desglose *m* **3** *or* **nervous breakdown** : crisis *f* nerviosa

break down *vi* **1** : estropearse, descomponerse ⟨the machine broke down : la máquina se descompuso⟩ **2** FAIL : fracasar **3** CRY : echarse a llorar — *vt* **1** DESTROY : derribar, echar abajo **2** OVERCOME : vencer (la resistencia), disipar (sospechas) **3** ANALYZE : analizar, descomponer

breaker ['breɪkər] *n* **1** WAVE : ola *f* grande **2** : interruptor *m* automático (de electricidad)

breakfast¹ ['brɛkfəst] *vi* : desayunar

breakfast² *n* : desayuno *m*

break–in ['breɪk,ɪn] *n* : robo *m*

breakneck ['breɪk,nɛk] *adj* **at breakneck speed** : a una velocidad vertiginosa

break out *vi* **1** : salirse ⟨she broke out in spots : le salieron granos⟩ **2** ERUPT : estallar (dícese de una guerra, la violencia, etc.) **3** ESCAPE : fugarse, escaparse

breakthrough ['breɪk,θruː] *n* : avance *m* (importante)

breakup ['breɪk,əp] *n* **1** DIVISION : desintegración *f* **2** : ruptura *f*

break up *vt* **1** DIVIDE : dividir **2** : disolver (una muchedumbre, una pelea, etc.) — *vi* **1** BREAK : romperse **2** SEPARATE : deshacerse, separarse ⟨I broke up with him : terminé con él⟩

breakwater ['breɪk,wɔtər, -,wɑ-] *n* : rompeolas *m*, malecón *m*, espigón *m*

breast ['brɛst] *n* **1** : pecho *m*, seno *m* (de una mujer) **2** CHEST : pecho *m*

breastbone ['brɛst,boːn] *n* : esternón *m*

breast–feed ['brɛst,fiːd] *vt* **-fed** [-,fɛd]; **-feeding** : amamantar, darle de mamar (a un niño)

breaststroke ['brɛst,stroːk] *adj* : estilo *m* (de) pecho, estilo *m* braza *Spain*

breath ['brɛθ] *n* **1** BREATHING : aliento *m* ⟨to hold one's breath : aguantar la respiración⟩ ⟨she was short of breath : le faltaba el aire⟩ **2** BREEZE : soplo *m* ⟨a breath of fresh air : un soplo de aire fresco⟩ **3** **under one's breath** : entre dientes, en voz baja

breathe ['briːð] *v* **breathed; breathing** *vi* **1** : respirar **2** LIVE : vivir, respirar **3** **to breathe in** : aspirar **4** **to breathe out** : espirar — *vt* **1** : respirar, aspirar ⟨to breathe fresh air : respirar el aire fresco⟩ ⟨to breathe a sigh of relief : suspirar aliviado⟩ **2** UTTER : decir ⟨I won't breathe a word of this : no diré nada de esto⟩ **3** **to breathe in** : aspirar (aire, etc.) **4** **to breathe out** : espirar (aire, etc.)

breather ['briːðər] *n* : respiro *m*, resuello *m*

breathing ['briːðɪŋ] *n* : respiración *f*

breathless ['brɛθləs] *adj* : sin aliento, jadeante

breathlessly ['brɛθləsli] *adv* : entrecortadamente, jadeando

breathlessness ['brɛθləsnəs] *n* : dificultad *f* al respirar

breathtaking ['brɛθ,teɪkɪŋ] *adj* IMPRESSIVE : impresionante, imponente

breeches ['brɪtʃəz, 'briː-] *npl* : pantalones *mpl*, calzones *mpl*, bombachos *mpl*

breed¹ ['briːd] *v* **bred** ['brɛd]; **breeding** *vt* **1** : criar (animales) **2** ENGENDER : engendrar, producir ⟨familiarity breeds contempt : la confianza hace perder el respeto⟩ **3** RAISE, REAR : criar, educar — *vi* REPRODUCE : reproducirse

breed² *n* **1** : variedad *f* (de plantas), raza *f* (de animales) **2** CLASS : clase *f*, tipo *m*

breeder ['briːdər] *n* : criador *m*, -dora *f* (de animales); cultivador *m*, -dora *f* (de plantas)

breeze¹ ['briːz] *vi* **breezed; breezing** : pasar con ligereza ⟨to breeze in : entrar como si nada⟩

breeze² *n* : brisa *f*, soplo *m* (de aire)

breezy ['briːzi] *adj* **breezier; -est 1** AIRY, WINDY : aireado, ventoso **2** LIVELY : animado, alegre **3** NONCHALANT : despreocupado

brethren → **brother**

brevity ['brɛvəti] *n, pl* **-ties** : brevedad *f*, concisión *f*

brew¹ ['bruː] *vt* **1** : fabricar, elaborar (cerveza) **2** FOMENT : tramar, maquinar, fomentar — *vi* **1** : fabricar cerveza **2** : amenazar ⟨a storm is brewing : una tormenta amenaza⟩

brew² *n* **1** BEER : cerveza *f* **2** POTION : brebaje *m*

brewer ['bruːər] *n* : cervecero *m*, -ra *f*

brewery ['bruːəri, 'bruri] *n, pl* **-eries** : cervecería *f*

briar ['braɪər] → **brier**

bribe¹ ['braɪb] *vt* **bribed; bribing** : sobornar, cohechar, coimear *Arg, Chile, Peru*

bribe² *n* : soborno *m*, cohecho *m*, coima *f Arg, Chile, Peru*, mordida *f CA, Mex*

bribery ['braɪbəri] *n, pl* **-eries** : soborno *m*, cohecho *m*, coima *f*, mordida *f CA, Mex*

bric-a-brac ['brɪkə,bræk] *npl* : baratijas *fpl*, chucherías *fpl*

brick¹ ['brɪk] *vt* **to brick up** : tabicar, tapiar

brick² *n* : ladrillo *m*

bricklayer ['brɪk,leɪər] *n* : albañil *mf*

bricklaying ['brɪk,leɪɪŋ] *n* : albañilería *f*

bridal ['braɪdəl] *adj* : nupcial, de novia

bride ['braɪd] *n* : novia *f*

bridegroom ['braɪd,gruːm] *n* : novio *m*

bridesmaid ['braɪd,meɪd] *n* : dama *f* de honor

bridge¹ ['brɪʤ] *vt* **bridged; bridging 1** : tender un puente sobre **2** **to bridge the gap** : salvar las diferencias

bridge² *n* **1** : puente *m* **2** : caballete *m* (de la nariz) **3** : puente *m* de mando (de un barco) **4** : puente *m* (dental) **5** : bridge *m* (juego de naipes)

bridle¹ ['braɪdəl] v **-dled; -dling** vt 1
: embridar (un caballo) 2 RESTRAIN
: refrenar, dominar, contener — vi **to
bridle at** : molestarse por, picarse por
bridle² n : brida f
brief¹ ['briːf] vt : dar órdenes a, instruir
brief² adj : breve, sucinto, conciso
brief³ n 1 : resumen m, sumario m 2
briefs npl : calzoncillos mpl
briefcase ['briːfˌkeɪs] n : portafolio m,
maletín m
briefing ['briːfɪŋ] n : reunión f informativa
briefly ['briːfli] adv : brevemente, por
poco tiempo
brier ['braɪər] n 1 BRAMBLE : zarza f, rosal m silvestre 2 HEATH : brezo m veteado
brig ['brɪg] n 1 : bergantín m (barco) 2
: calabozo m (en un barco)
brigade [brɪˈgeɪd] n : brigada f
brigadier [ˌbrɪgəˈdɪr] n : brigadier m
brigadier general [ˌbrɪgəˈdɪr] n : general
m de brigada
brigand ['brɪgənd] n : bandolero m, -ra f;
forajido m, -da f
bright ['braɪt] adj 1 : brillante (dícese del
sol, de los ojos), vivo (dícese de un color),
claro, fuerte 2 CHEERFUL : alegre, animado ⟨bright and early : muy tem-
prano⟩ 3 INTELLIGENT : listo, inteligente ⟨a bright idea : una idea luminosa⟩
brighten ['braɪtən] vt 1 ILLUMINATE : iluminar 2 ENLIVEN : alegrar, animar —
vi 1 : hacerse más brillante 2 **to
brighten up** : animarse, alegrarse, mejorar
brightly ['braɪtli] adv : vivamente, intensamente, alegremente
brightness ['braɪtnəs] n 1 LUMINOSITY
: luminosidad f, brillantez f, resplandor
m, brillo m 2 CHEERFULNESS : alegría
f, ánimo m
brilliance ['brɪljənts] n 1 BRIGHTNESS
: resplandor m, fulgor m, brillo m, brillantez f 2 INTELLIGENCE : inteligencia
f, brillantez f
brilliancy ['brɪljəntsi] → **brilliance**
brilliant ['brɪljənt] adj : brillante
brilliantly ['brɪljəntli] adv : brillantemente, con brillantez
brim¹ ['brɪm] vi **brimmed; brimming** 1 or
to brim over : desbordarse, rebosar 2
to brim with tears : llenarse de lágrimas
brim² n 1 : ala f (de un sombrero) 2
: borde m (de una taza o un vaso)
brimful ['brɪmˈfʊl] adj : lleno hasta el
borde, repleto, rebosante
brimless ['brɪmləs] adj : sin ala
brimstone ['brɪmˌstoːn] n : azufre m
brindled ['brɪndəld] adj : manchado,
pinto
brine ['braɪn] n 1 : salmuera f, escabeche
m (para encurtir) 2 OCEAN : océano m,
mar m
bring ['brɪŋ] vt **brought** ['brɔt]; **bringing** 1 : traer, llevar ⟨bring me some
coffee : tráigame un taza⟩ 2 ATTRACT
: traer, atraer 3 : traer (problemas),
conseguir (la paz), dar (alegría), obtener
(ganancias) ⟨it brought him fame : lo

lanzó a la fama⟩ ⟨it brought a smile to
her face : la hizo sonreír⟩ 4 : llevar (a
un estado) ⟨bring it to a boil : dejarlo
hervir⟩ 5 YIELD : rendir, alcanzar ⟨to
bring a good price : alcanzar un precio
alto⟩ 6 : aportar (experiencia, etc.) 7
: presentar (cargos, etc.) 8 : llevar (a un
tema) 9 **to bring about** : ocasionar,
provocar 10 **to bring around** CON-
VINCE : convencer 11 **to bring back**
RETURN : devolver 12 **to bring back**
REINSTATE, REINTRODUCE : restablecer,
reintroducir 13 **to bring back** : traer
(de otro lugar) 14 **to bring back** : recordar, traer (recuerdos) 15 **to bring
down** LOWER : hacer bajar 16 **to bring
down** OVERTHROW : derrocar 17 **to
bring down** : derribar (a balazos,
etc.) 18 **to bring forth** PRODUCE : producir 19 **to bring in** : invitar a (expertos), atraer (clientes) 20 **to bring in**
: ganar (dinero), obtener (ganancias) 21
to bring on : provocar ⟨you brought this
on yourself : te la buscaste⟩ 22 **to bring
oneself to** : animarse a (hacer algo) 23
to bring out : sacar, publicar (un libro,
etc.) 24 **to bring out** EMPHASIZE : hacer
resaltar 25 **to bring to** REVIVE : resucitar 26 **to bring up** REAR : criar 27 **to
bring up** MENTION : sacar, mencionar
brininess ['braɪnɪnəs] n : salinidad f
brink ['brɪŋk] n : borde m
briny ['braɪni] adj **brinier; -est** : salobre
brisk ['brɪsk] adj 1 LIVELY : rápido,
enérgico, brioso 2 INVIGORATING
: fresco, estimulante
brisket ['brɪskət] n : falda f
briskly ['brɪskli] adv : rápidamente, enérgicamente, con brío
briskness ['brɪsknəs] n : brío m, rapidez f
bristle¹ ['brɪsəl] vi **-tled; -tling** 1 : erizarse, ponerse de punta 2 : enfurecerse,
enojarse ⟨she bristled at the suggestion
: se enfureció ante tal sugerencia⟩ 3
: estar plagado, estar repleto ⟨a city bris-
tling with tourists : una ciudad repleta
de turistas⟩
bristle² n : cerda f (de un animal), pelo m
(de una planta)
bristly ['brɪsəli] adj **bristlier; -est** : áspero
y erizado
British¹ ['brɪtɪʃ] adj : británico
British² n **the British** (used with a plural
verb) : los británicos
brittle ['brɪtəl] adj **brittler; brittlest**
: frágil, quebradizo
brittleness ['brɪtəlnəs] n : fragilidad f
broach ['broːtʃ] vt BRING UP : mencionar,
abordar, sacar
broad ['brɔd] adj 1 WIDE : ancho 2 SPA-
CIOUS : amplio, extenso 3 FULL : pleno
⟨in broad daylight : en pleno día⟩ 4 OB-
VIOUS : claro, evidente 5 TOLERANT
: tolerante, liberal 6 GENERAL : general 7 ESSENTIAL : principal, esencial
⟨the broad outline : los rasgos esencia-
les⟩
broadband¹ ['brɔdˌbænd] adj : de banda
ancha
broadband² n : banda f ancha

broad bean *n* : haba *f*

broadcast¹ ['brɔd,kæst] *vt* **-cast; -casting** **1** SCATTER : esparcir, diseminar **2** CIRCULATE, SPREAD : divulgar, difundir, propagar **3** TRANSMIT : transmitir, emitir

broadcast² *n* **1** TRANSMISSION : transmisión *f*, emisión *f* **2** PROGRAM : programa *m*, emisión *f*

broadcaster ['brɔd,kæstər] *n* : presentador *m*, -dora *f*; locutor *m*, -tora *f*

broadcloth ['brɔd,klɔθ] *n* : paño *m* fino

broaden ['brɔdən] *vt* : ampliar, ensanchar — *vi* : ampliarse, ensancharse

broadloom ['brɔd,lu:m] *adj* : tejido en telar ancho

broadly ['brɔdli] *adv* **1** GENERALLY : en general, aproximadamente **2** WIDELY : extensivamente

broad–minded ['brɔd'maɪndəd] *adj* : tolerante, de amplias miras

broad–mindedness ['brɔd'maɪndədnəs] *n* : tolerancia *f*

broadside ['brɔd,saɪd] *n* **1** VOLLEY : andanada *f* **2** ATTACK : ataque *m*, invectiva *f*, andanada *f*

brocade [bro'keɪd] *n* : brocado *m*

broccoli ['brɑkəli] *n* : brócoli *m*

brochure [bro'ʃʊr] *n* : folleto *m*

brogue ['bro:g] *n* : acento *m* irlandés

broil¹ ['brɔɪl] *vt* : asar a la parrilla

broil² *n* : asado *m*

broiler ['brɔɪlər] *n* **1** GRILL : parrilla *f* **2** : pollo *m* para asar

broke¹ ['bro:k] → **break¹**

broke² *adj* : pelado, arruinado ⟨to go broke : arruinarse, quebrar⟩

broken ['bro:kən] *adj* **1** DAMAGED, SHATTERED : roto, quebrado, fracturado **2** IRREGULAR, UNEVEN : accidentado, irregular, recortado **3** VIOLATED : roto, quebrantado **4** INTERRUPTED : interrumpido, discontinuo **5** CRUSHED : abatido, quebrantado ⟨a broken man : un hombre destrozado⟩ **6** IMPERFECT : mal ⟨to speak broken English : hablar el inglés con dificultad⟩

brokenhearted [,bro:kən'hɑrtəd] *adj* : descorazonado, desconsolado

broker¹ ['bro:kər] *vt* : hacer corretaje de

broker² *n* **1** : agente *mf*; corredor *m*, -dora *f* **2** → **stockbroker**

brokerage ['bro:kərɪdʒ] *n* : corretaje *m*, agencia *f* de corredores

bromine ['bro:,mi:n] *n* : bromo *m*

bronchial ['brɑŋkiəl] *adj* : bronquial

bronchitis [brɑn'kaɪtəs, brɑŋ-] *n* : bronquitis *f*

bronze¹ ['brɑnz] *vt* **bronzed; bronzing** : broncear

bronze² *n* : bronce *m*

brooch ['bro:tʃ, 'bru:tʃ] *n* : broche *m*, prendedor *m*

brood¹ ['bru:d] *vt* **1** INCUBATE : empollar, incubar **2** PONDER : sopesar, considerar — *vi* **1** INCUBATE : empollar **2** REFLECT : rumiar, reflexionar **3** WORRY : ponerse melancólico, inquietarse

brood² *adj* : de cría

brood³ *n* : nidada *f* (de pájaros), camada *f* (de mamíferos)

brooder ['bru:dər] *n* **1** THINKER : pensador *m*, -dora *f* **2** INCUBATOR : incubadora *f*

brook¹ ['brʊk] *vt* TOLERATE : tolerar, admitir

brook² *n* : arroyo *m*

broom ['bru:m, 'brʊm] *n* **1** : retama *f*, hiniesta *f* **2** : escoba *f* (para barrer)

broomstick ['bru:m,stɪk, 'brʊm-] *n* : palo *m* de escoba

broth ['brɔθ] *n, pl* **broths** ['brɔθs, 'brɔðz] : caldo *m*

brothel ['brɑθəl, 'brɔ-] *n* : burdel *m*

brother ['brʌðər] *n, pl* **brothers** *also* **brethren** ['brɛðrən, -ðərn] **1** : hermano *m* **2** KINSMAN : pariente *m*, familiar *m*

brotherhood ['brʌðər,hʊd] *n* **1** FELLOWSHIP : fraternidad *f* **2** ASSOCIATION : hermandad *f*

brother–in–law ['brʌðərɪn,lɔ] *n, pl* **brothers–in–law** : cuñado *m*

brotherly ['brʌðərli] *adj* : fraternal

brought → **bring**

brow ['braʊ] *n* **1** EYEBROW : ceja *f* **2** FOREHEAD : frente *f* **3** : cima *f* ⟨the brow of a hill : la cima de una colina⟩

browbeat ['braʊ,bi:t] *vt* **-beat; -beaten** [-,bi:tən] *or* **-beat; -beating** : intimidar

brown¹ ['braʊn] *vt* **1** : dorar (en cocina) **2** TAN : broncear — *vi* **1** : dorarse (en cocina) **2** TAN : broncearse

brown² *adj* : marrón, café, castaño (dícese del pelo), moreno (dícese de la piel)

brown³ *n* : marrón *m*, café *m*

brown bread *n* **1** : pan *m* integral **2** : pan *m* negro (dulce)

brownie ['braʊni] *n* : bizcocho *m* de chocolate y nueces

brownish ['braʊnɪʃ] *adj* : pardo

brown rice *n* : arroz *m* integral

browse ['braʊz] *v* **browsed; browsing** *vt* **1** LOOK : mirar **2** : explorar (la Internet) — *vi* **1** GRAZE : pacer **2** LOOK : mirar, echar un vistazo **3** : navegar (en/por Internet)

browser ['braʊzər] *or* **Web browser** *n* : navegador *m* (web)

bruin ['bru:ɪn] *n* BEAR : oso *m*

bruise¹ ['bru:z] *vt* **bruised; bruising** **1** : contusionar, machucar, magullar (a una persona) **2** DAMAGE : magullar, dañar (frutas) **3** CRUSH : majar **4** HURT : herir (los sentimientos)

bruise² *n* : moretón *m*, cardenal *m*, magulladura *f* (dícese de frutas)

brunch ['brʌntʃ] *n* : combinación *f* de desayuno y almuerzo

brunet¹ *or* **brunette** [bru:'nɛt] *adj* : moreno

brunet² *or* **brunette** *n* : moreno *m*, -na *f*

brunt ['brʌnt] *n* **to bear the brunt of** : llevar el peso de, aguantar el mayor impacto de

brush¹ ['brʌʃ] *vt* **1** : cepillar ⟨I brushed my teeth : me cepillé los dientes⟩ **2** SWEEP : quitar, sacudir ⟨he brushed the dirt off his pants : se sacudió el polvo de los pantalones⟩ **3** PAINT, APPLY : pintar **4** GRAZE : rozar **5 to brush off** DISREGARD : hacer caso omiso de (algo), no hacerle caso (a alguien) — *vi* **to brush up (on)** : repasar, refrescar, dar un repaso a

brush² *n* **1** *or* **brushwood** ['brʌʃ,wʊd] : broza *f* **2** SCRUB, UNDERBRUSH : maleza *f* **3** : cepillo *m*, pincel *m* (de artista), brocha *f* (de pintor) **4** TOUCH : roce *m* **5** SKIRMISH : escaramuza *f*

brush-off ['brʌʃ,ɔf] *n* **to give the brush-off to** : dar calabazas a

brushstroke ['brʌʃ,stro:k] *n* : pincelada *f*

brusque ['brʌsk] *adj* : brusco — **brusquely** *adv*

brusqueness ['brʌsknəs] *n* : brusquedad *f*

brussels sprout ['brʌsəlz,spraʊt] *n* : col *f* de Bruselas

brutal ['bru:təl] *adj* : brutal, cruel, salvaje — **brutally** *adv*

brutality [bru:'tæləṭi] *n, pl* **-ties** : brutalidad *f*

brutalize ['bru:ṭəl,aɪz] *vt* **-ized; -izing** : brutalizar, maltratar

brute¹ ['bru:t] *adj* : bruto ⟨brute force : fuerza bruta⟩

brute² *n* **1** BEAST : bestia *f*, animal *m* **2** : bruto *m*, -ta *f*; bestia *mf* (persona)

brutish ['bru:ṭɪʃ] *adj* **1** : de animal **2** CRUEL : brutal, salvaje **3** STUPID : bruto, estúpido

bubble¹ ['bʌbəl] *vi* **-bled; -bling** : burbujear ⟨to bubble over with joy : rebosar de alegría⟩

bubble² *n* : burbuja *f*

bubble bath *n* **1** : baño *m* de espuma/burbujas **2** : espuma *f* de baño (jabón)

bubble gum *n* : chicle *m* (de) globo, chicle *m* (de) bomba

bubbly ['bʌbli] *adj* **bubblier; -est 1** BUBBLING : burbujeante **2** LIVELY : vivaz, lleno de vida

bubonic plague [bu:'bɑnɪk-, 'bju:-] *n* : peste *f* bubónica

buccaneer [,bʌkə'nɪr] *n* : bucanero *m*

buck¹ ['bʌk] *vi* **1** : corcovear (dícese de un caballo o un burro) **2** JOLT : dar sacudidas **3 to buck against** : resistirse a, rebelarse contra **4 to buck up** : animarse, levantar el ánimo — *vt* OPPOSE : oponerse a, ir en contra de

buck² *n, pl* **buck** *or* **bucks 1** : animal *m* macho, ciervo *m* (macho) **2** DOLLAR : dólar *m* **3 to pass the buck** *fam* : pasar la pelota *fam*

bucket ['bʌkət] *n* : balde *m*, cubo *m*, cubeta *f Mex*

bucketful ['bʌkət,fʊl] *n* : balde *m* lleno

buckle¹ ['bʌkəl] *v* **-led; -ling** *vt* **1** FASTEN : abrochar **2** BEND, TWIST : combar, torcer — *vi* **1** BEND, TWIST : combarse, torcerse, doblarse (dícese de las rodillas) **2 to buckle down** : ponerse a trabajar con esmero **3 to buckle up** : abrocharse

buckle² *n* **1** : hebilla *f* **2** TWISTING : torcedura *f*

buckshot ['bʌk,ʃɑt] *n* : perdigón *m*

buckskin ['bʌk,skɪn] *n* : gamuza *f*

buck tooth *n* : diente *m* saliente, diente *m* salido

bucktoothed ['bʌk,tu:θt] *adj* : de dientes salientes, de dientes salidos

buckwheat ['bʌk,ʰwi:t] *n* : alforfón *m*, trigo *m* sarraceno

bucolic [bju:'kɑlɪk] *adj* : bucólico

bud¹ ['bʌd] *v* **budded; budding** *vt* GRAFT : injertar — *vi* : brotar, hacer brotes

bud² *n* : brote *m*, yema *f*, capullo *m* (de una flor)

Buddhism ['bu:,dɪzəm, 'bʊ-] *n* : budismo *m*

Buddhist ['bu:dɪst, 'bʊ-] *n* : budista *mf* — **Buddhist** *adj*

budding ['bʌdɪŋ] *adj* : en ciernes

buddy ['bʌdi] *n, pl* **-dies** *fam* : amigo *m*, -ga *f*; compinche *mf fam*; cuate *m*, -ta *f Mex fam*

budge ['bʌdʒ] *vi* **budged; budging 1** MOVE : moverse, desplazarse **2** YIELD : ceder

budget¹ ['bʌdʒət] *vt* : presupuestar (gastos), asignar (dinero) — *vi* : presupuestar, planear el presupuesto

budget² *n* : presupuesto

budgetary ['bʌdʒə,teri] *adj* : presupuestario

buff¹ ['bʌf] *vt* POLISH : pulir, sacar brillo a, lustrar

buff² *adj* : beige, amarillento

buff³ *n* **1** : beige *m*, amarillento *m* **2** ENTHUSIAST : aficionado *m*, -da *f*; entusiasta *mf*

buffalo ['bʌfə,lo:] *n, pl* **-lo** *or* **-loes 1** : búfalo *m* **2** BISON : bisonte *m*

buffer ['bʌfər] *n* **1** BARRIER : barrera *f* ⟨buffer state : estado tapón⟩ **2** SHOCK ABSORBER : amortiguador *m*

buffet¹ ['bʌfət] *vt* : golpear, zarandear, sacudir

buffet² *n* BLOW : golpe *m*

buffet³ [,bʌ'feɪ, ,bə-] *n* **1** : bufete *m*, bufé *m* (comida) **2** SIDEBOARD : aparador *m*

buffoon [,bʌ'fu:n] *n* : bufón *m*, -fona *f*; payaso *m*, -sa *f*

bug¹ ['bʌg] *vt* **bugged; bugging 1** PESTER : fastidiar, molestar **2** : ocultar micrófonos en

bug² *n* **1** INSECT : bicho *m*, insecto *m* **2** DEFECT : defecto *m*, falla *f*, problema *m* **3** GERM : microbio *m*, virus *m* **4** MICROPHONE : micrófono *m*

bugaboo ['bʌgə,bu:] : pesadilla *f*, terror *m*, coco *m*

bugbear ['bʌg,bær] *n* : problema *m*, obstáculo *f*

buggy ['bʌgi] *n, pl* **-gies 1** : calesa *f* (tirada por caballos) **2** : cochecito *m* (para niños)

bugle ['bju:gəl] *n* : clarín *m*, corneta *f*

bugler ['bju:gələr] *n* : corneta *mf*

build¹ ['bɪld] *v* **built** ['bɪlt]; **building** *vt* **1** CONSTRUCT : construir, edificar, ensamblar, levantar **2** DEVELOP : desarrollar, elaborar, forjar **3** INCREASE : incrementar, aumentar — *vi* **1 to build on** : ampliar (conocimientos, etc.) **2 to build up** : aumentar, intensificar

build² *n* PHYSIQUE : físico *m*, complexión *f*

builder ['bɪldər] *n* : constructor *m*, -tora *f*; contratista *mf*

building ['bɪldɪŋ] *n* **1** EDIFICE : edificio *m* **2** CONSTRUCTION : construcción *f*

buildup [ˈbɪldˌʌp] *n* : acumulación *f*
built-in [ˈbɪltˈɪn] *adj* **1** : empotrado ⟨built-in cabinets : armarios empotrados⟩ **2** INHERENT : incorporado, intrínseco
built-up [ˈbɪltˌʌp] *adj* : urbanizado
bulb [ˈbʌlb] *n* **1** : bulbo *m* (de una planta), cabeza *f* (de ajo), cubeta *f* (de un termómetro) **2** LIGHTBULB : bombilla *f*, foco *m*, bombillo *m* CA, Col, Ven
bulbous [ˈbʌlbəs] *adj* : bulboso
Bulgarian [bʌlˈgæriən, bʊl-] *n* **1** : búlgaro *m*, -ra *f* **2** : búlgaro *m* (idioma) — **Bulgarian** *adj*
bulge¹ [ˈbʌldʒ] *vi* **bulged; bulging** : abultar, sobresalir
bulge² *n* : bulto *m*, protuberancia *f*
bulk¹ [ˈbʌlk] *vi* : hinchar — *vi* EXPAND, SWELL : ampliarse, hincharse
bulk² *n* **1** SIZE, VOLUME : volumen *m*, tamaño *m* **2** FIBER : fibra *f* **3** MASS : mole *f* **4 the bulk of** : la mayor parte de **5 in ~** : en grandes cantidades
bulkhead [ˈbʌlkˌhɛd] *n* : mamparo *m*
bulky [ˈbʌlki] *adj* **bulkier; -est** : voluminoso, grande
bull¹ [ˈbʊl] *adj* : macho
bull² *n* **1** : toro *m*, macho *m* (de ciertas especies) **2** : bula *f* (papal) **3** DECREE : decreto *m*, edicto *m*
bulldog [ˈbʊlˌdɔg] *n* : bulldog *m*
bulldoze [ˈbʊlˌdoːz] *vt* **-dozed; -dozing** **1** LEVEL : nivelar (el terreno), derribar (un edificio) **2** FORCE : forzar ⟨he bulldozed his way through : se abrió paso a codazos⟩
bulldozer [ˈbʊlˌdoːzər] *n* : bulldozer *m*
bullet [ˈbʊlət] *n* : bala *f*
bulletin [ˈbʊlətən, -lətən] *n* **1 or news bulletin** : boletín *m* informativo, boletín *m* de noticias **2** NEWSLETTER : boletín *m*
bulletin board *n* : tablón *m* de anuncios
bulletproof [ˈbʊlətˌpruːf] *adj* : antibalas, a prueba de balas
bullfight [ˈbʊlˌfaɪt] *n* : corrida *f* (de toros)
bullfighter [ˈbʊlˌfaɪtər] *n* : torero *m*, -ra *f*; matador *m*
bullfighting [ˈbʊlˌfaɪtɪŋ] *n* : lidia *f*, toreo *m*
bullfrog [ˈbʊlˌfrɔg] *n* : rana *f* toro
bullheaded [ˈbʊlˈhɛdəd] *adj* : testarudo
bullion [ˈbʊljən] *n* : oro *m* en lingotes, plata *f* en lingotes
bullish [ˈbʊlɪʃ] *adj* : alcista
bullock [ˈbʊlək] *n* **1** STEER : buey *m*, toro *m* castrado **2** : toro *m* joven, novillo *m*
bullring [ˈbʊlˌrɪŋ] *n* : plaza *f* de toros, redondel *m*, ruedo *m*
bull's-eye [ˈbʊlzˌaɪ] *n, pl* **bull's-eyes** : diana *f*, blanco *m*
bully¹ [ˈbʊli] *vt* **-lied; -lying** : intimidar, amedrentar, mangonear
bully² *n, pl* **-lies** : matón *m*; bravucón *m*, -cona *f*
bullying [ˈbʊliɪŋ] *n* : bullying *m*, acoso *m* ⟨school bullying : bullying/acoso escolar⟩
bulrush [ˈbʊlˌrʌʃ] *n* : especie *f* de junco
bulwark [ˈbʊlˌwərk, -ˌwɔrk:, ˈbʌlˌwərk] *n* : baluarte *m*, bastión *f*
bum¹ [ˈbʌm] *v* **bummed; bumming** *vi* to **bum around** : vagabundear, vagar — *vt* : gorronear *fam*, sablear *fam*

bum² *adj* : inútil, malo ⟨a bum rap : una acusación falsa⟩
bum³ *n* **1** LOAFER : vago *m*, -ga *f* **2** HOBO, TRAMP : vagabundo *m*, -da *f*
bumblebee [ˈbʌmbəlˌbiː] *n* : abejorro *m*
bump¹ [ˈbʌmp] *vt* : chocar contra, golpear contra, dar ⟨to bump one's head : darse (un golpe) en la cabeza⟩ — *vi* to **bump into** MEET : encontrarse con, tropezar con
bump² *n* **1** BULGE : bulto *m*, protuberancia *f* **2** IMPACT : golpe *m*, choque *m* **3** JOLT : sacudida *f*
bumper¹ [ˈbʌmpər] *adj* : extraordinario, récord ⟨a bumper crop : una cosecha abundante⟩
bumper² *n* : parachoques *mpl*
bumpkin [ˈbʌmpkən] *n* : palurdo *m*, -da *f*
bumpy [ˈbʌmpi] *adj* **bumpier; -est** : desigual, lleno de baches (dícese de un camino), agitado (dícese de un vuelo en avión)
bun [ˈbʌn] *n* **1** : bollo *m* (dulce) **2** ROLL : panecito *m* **3** CHIGNON : moño *m*, chongo *m* Mex
bunch¹ [ˈbʌntʃ] *vt* : agrupar, amontonar — *vi* to **bunch up** : amontonarse, agruparse, fruncirse (dícese de una tela)
bunch² *n* : grupo *m*, montón *m*, ramo *m* (de flores)
bundle¹ [ˈbʌndəl] *vt* **-dled; -dling** : liar, atar
bundle² *n* **1** : fardo *m*, atado *m*, bulto *m*, haz *m* (de palos) **2** PARCEL : paquete *m* **3** LOAD : montón *m* ⟨a bundle of money : un montón de dinero⟩
bungalow [ˈbʌŋgəˌloː] *n* : tipo de casa de un solo piso
bungle¹ [ˈbʌŋgəl] *vt* to **bungle** : echar a perder, malograr
bungle² *n* : chapuza *f*, desatino *m*
bungler [ˈbʌŋgələr] *n* : chapucero *m*, -ra *f*; inepto *m*, -ta *f*
bunion [ˈbʌnjən] *n* : juanete *m*
bunk¹ [ˈbʌŋk] *vi* : dormir (en una litera)
bunk² *n* **1 or bunk bed** : litera *f* **2** NONSENSE : tonterías *fpl*, bobadas *fpl*
bunker [ˈbʌŋkər] *n* **1** : carbonera *f* (en un barco) **2** SHELTER : búnker *m*
bunny [ˈbʌni] *n, pl* **-nies** : conejo *m*, -ja *f*
buoy¹ [ˈbuːi, ˈbɔɪ] *vt* to **buoy up 1** : mantener a flote **2** CHEER, HEARTEN : animar, levantar el ánimo a
buoy² *n* : boya *f*
buoyancy [ˈbɔɪəntsi, ˈbuːjən-] *n* **1** : flotabilidad *f* **2** OPTIMISM : confianza *f*, optimismo *m*
buoyant [ˈbɔɪənt, ˈbuːjənt] *adj* : boyante, flotante
bur *or* **burr** [ˈbər] *n* : abrojo *m* (de una planta)
burden¹ [ˈbərdən] *vt* : cargar, oprimir
burden² *n* : carga *f*, peso *m*
burdensome [ˈbərdənsəm] *adj* : oneroso
bureau [ˈbjʊroː] *n* **1** CHEST OF DRAWERS : cómoda *f* **2** DEPARTMENT : departamento *m* (del gobierno) **3** AGENCY : agencia *f* ⟨travel bureau : agencia de viajes⟩
bureaucracy [bjʊˈrɑkrəsi] *n, pl* **-cies** : burocracia *f*

bureaucrat ['bjʊrə,kræt] *n* : burócrata *mf*
bureaucratic [,bjʊrə'krætɪk] *adj* : buro-crático
burgeon ['bərdʒən] *vi* : florecer, retoñar, crecer
burger ['bərgər] *n* 1 → hamburger 2 PATTY : hamburguesa *f* ⟨a turkey burger : una hamburguesa de pavo⟩
burglar ['bərglər] *n* : ladrón *m*, -drona *f*
burglar alarm : alarma *f* antirrobo
burglarize ['bərglə,raɪz] *vt* -ized; -izing : robar
burglary ['bərgləri] *n*, *pl* -glaries : robo *m*
burgle ['bərgəl] *vt* -gled; -gling : robar
burgundy ['bərgəndi] *n*, *pl* -dies : bor-goña *m*, vino *m* de Borgoña
burial ['bɛriəl] *n* : entierro *m*, sepelio *m*
burlap ['bər,læp] *n* : arpillera *f*
burlesque¹ [bər'lɛsk] *vt* -lesqued; -lesqu-ing : parodiar
burlesque² *n* 1 PARODY : parodia *f* 2 REVUE : revista *f* (musical)
burly ['bərli] *adj* **burlier; -est** : fornido, corpulento, musculoso
Burmese [,bər'miːz, -'miːs] *n* : birmano *m*, -na *f* — **Burmese** *adj*
burn¹ ['bərn] *v* **burned** ['bərnd, 'bərnt] *or* **burnt** ['bərnt]; **burning** *vt* 1 : quemar (leña, etc.) ⟨to burn a candle : encender una vela⟩ 2 : quemar (piel, ropa, etc.) ⟨I burned my hand : me quemé la mano⟩ ⟨to burn a hole in something : quemar algo (haciendo un agujero)⟩ 3 STING : hacer escocer 4 OVERCOOK : que-mar 5 CONSUME : usar, gastar ⟨a gas-burning engine : un motor que funciona con gas⟩ ⟨to burn (up) calories : quemar calorías⟩ 6 CHEAT : estafar, timar 7 RECORD, WRITE : quemar (un DVD, etc.) 8 *or* **to burn down** : quemar, in-cendiar (un edificio) 9 **to burn out** : quemar (un motor, etc.) 10 **to burn up** : quemar, incendiar ⟨the fire burned up homes and forests : el incendio arrasó con casas y bosques⟩ — *vi* 1 : arder (dícese de un fuego o un edificio), que-marse ⟨I smell something burning : huele a quemado⟩ ⟨the house burned to the ground : la casa fue arrasada por el incendio⟩ 2 : estar prendido, estar encendido ⟨we left the lights burning : dejamos las luces encendidas⟩ 3 STING : arder 4 : quemarse (dícese de la comida) 5 *or* **to burn up** : tener fiebre ⟨you're burning (up)! : ¡estás hir-viendo!⟩ 6 : arder (dícese de las meji-llas, etc.) 7 **to burn down** : incendiarse, quemarse 8 **to burn off** : disiparse (dícese de la niebla, etc.) 9 **to burn out** : consumirse, apagarse 10 **to burn out** : quemarse (dícese de un motor, etc.) 11 **to burn out** : quemarse, agotarse (dícese de una persona) 12 **to burn to death** : morir quemado 13 **to burn up** : desin-tegrarse (dícese de un asteroide, etc.) 14 **to burn with** : arder de ⟨he was burning with jealousy : ardía de celos⟩
burn² *n* : quemadura *f*
burned out *or* **burnt out** *adj* 1 : con el interior destruido (dícese de un edifi-

cio) 2 : quemado, agotado (dícese de una persona)
burner ['bərnər] *n* : quemador *m*
burnish ['bərnɪʃ] *vt* : bruñir
burp¹ ['bərp] *vi* : eructar — *vt* : hacer eructar
burp² *n* : eructo *m*
burrito [bə'riːto] *n*, *pl* **-tos** : burrito *m*
burro ['bʊro, 'bʌr-] *n*, *pl* **-os** : burro *m*
burrow¹ ['bəro] *vi* 1 : cavar, hacer una madriguera ⟨to burrow into : hurgar en⟩ — *vt* : cavar, excavar
burrow² *n* : madriguera *f*, coneja *f* (de un conejo)
bursar ['bərsər] *n* : administrador *m*, -dora *f*
burst¹ ['bərst] *v* **burst; bursting** *vi* 1 : reventarse (dícese de una llanta o un globo), estallar (dícese de obuses o fuegos artificiales), romperse (dícese de un dique) 2 **to burst in** : irrumpir en 3 **to burst into (something)** *or* **to burst out in (something)** : empezar a (hacer algo), echar a (hacer algo) ⟨to burst into tears : echarse a llorar⟩ — *vt* : reventar
burst² *n* 1 EXPLOSION : estallido *m*, ex-plosión *f*, reventón *m* (de una llanta) 2 OUTBURST : arranque *m* (de actividad, de velocidad), arrebato *m* (de ira), salva *f* (de aplausos)
bury ['bɛri] *vt* **buried; burying** 1 INTER : enterrar, sepultar 2 HIDE : esconder, ocultar 3 **to bury oneself in** : enfras-carse en
bus¹ ['bʌs] *v* **bused** *or* **bussed** ['bʌst]; **busing** *or* **bussing** ['bʌsɪŋ] *vt* : transpor-tar en autobús — *vi* : viajar en autobús
bus² *n* : autobús *m*, bus *m*, camión *m* Mex, colectivo *m* Arg, Bol, Peru
busboy ['bʌs,bɔɪ] *n* : ayudante *mf* de ca-marero
bus driver *n* : chofer *mf* (de autobús); conductor *m*, -tora *f* (de autobús); busero *m*, -ra *f* CA; camionero *m*, -ra *f* Mex; colectivero *m*, -ra *f* Arg
bush ['bʊʃ] *n* 1 SHRUB : arbusto *m*, mata *f* 2 THICKET : maleza *f*, matorral *m*
bushel ['bʊʃəl] *n* : medida de áridos igual a 35.24 litros
bushing ['bʊʃɪŋ] *n* : cojinete *m*
bushy ['bʊʃi] *adj* **bushier; -est** : espeso, poblado ⟨bushy eyebrows : cejas pobla-das⟩
busily ['bɪzəli] *adv* : afanosamente, dili-gentemente
business ['bɪznəs, -nəz] *n* 1 OCCUPA-TION : ocupación *f*, oficio *m* 2 DUTY, MISSION : misión *f*, deber *m*, responsabi-lidad *f* 3 ESTABLISHMENT, FIRM : em-presa *f*, firma *f*, negocio *m*, comercio *m* 4 COMMERCE : negocios *mpl*, comer-cio *m* ⟨to go out of business : cerrar⟩ ⟨to open for business : abrir al público⟩ ⟨business hours : horas de atención al público⟩ ⟨business meeting/trip : re-unión/viaje de negocios⟩ 5 AFFAIR, MATTER : asunto *m*, cuestión *f*, cosa *f* ⟨it's none of your business : no es asunto tuyo⟩ ⟨to have no business doing some-thing : no tener derecho a hacer algo⟩

business class n : clase f ejecutiva, clase f preferente Spain

business day n : día m hábil, día m laborable

businesslike ['bɪznəs,laɪk, -nəz-] n : profesional

businessman ['bɪznəs,mæn, -nəz-] n, pl **-men** [-mən, -,mɛn] : empresario m, hombre m de negocios

businesswoman ['bɪznəs,wʊmən, -nəz-] n, pl **-women** [-,wɪmən] : empresaria f, mujer f de negocios

bus shelter n : marquesina f

bus station n : estación f de autobús, terminal f de autobús

bus stop n : parada f de autobús

bust¹ ['bʌst] vt **1** BREAK, SMASH : romper, estropear, destrozar **2** TAME : domar, amansar (un caballo) — vi : romperse, estropearse

bust² n **1** : busto m (en la escultura) **2** BREASTS : pecho m, senos mpl, busto m

bustle¹ ['bʌsəl] vi **-tled; -tling** to bustle about : ir y venir, trajinar, ajetrearse

bustle² n **1** or hustle and bustle : bullicio m, ajetreo m **2** : polisón m (en la ropa femenina)

busy¹ ['bɪzi] vt busied; busying to busy oneself with : ocuparse con, ponerse a, entretenerse con

busy² adj busier; -est **1** OCCUPIED : ocupado, atareado ⟨he's busy working : está ocupado en su trabajo⟩ ⟨the telephone was busy : el teléfono estaba ocupado⟩ **2** BUSTLING : concurrido, animado ⟨a busy street : una calle concurrida, una calle con mucho tránsito⟩

busybody ['bɪzi,badi] n, pl **-bodies** : entrometido m, -da f; metiche mf fam; metomentodo mf

busy signal n : tono m de ocupado, señal f de comunicando Spain

but¹ ['bʌt] conj **1** NEVERTHELESS : pero, no obstante, sin embargo ⟨I called her but she didn't answer : la llamé pero no contestó⟩ **2** EXCEPT : pero ⟨I'd do it, but I don't have time : lo haría pero no me da tiempo⟩ ⟨I had no choice but to leave : no tuve más remedio que irme⟩ ⟨they do nothing but argue : no hacen más que discutir⟩ **3** (used for emphasis) : pero ⟨but it's not fair! : ¡pero no es justo!⟩ **4** THAT : que ⟨there's no doubt but he is lazy : no cabe duda que es perezoso⟩ **5** WITHOUT : sin que **6** YET : pero ⟨he was poor but proud : era pobre pero orgulloso⟩ **7** but then HOWEVER : pero

but² prep **1** EXCEPT : excepto, menos ⟨everyone but Charles : todos menos Charles⟩ ⟨no one but you would think that : sólo a ti te ocurriría eso⟩ ⟨we've had nothing but rain : no hace más que llover⟩ ⟨the last but one : el penúltimo⟩ **2** but for : si no fuera por

butcher¹ ['bʊtʃər] vt **1** SLAUGHTER : matar (animales) **2** KILL : matar, asesinar, masacrar **3** BOTCH : estropear, hacer una chapuza

butcher² n **1** : carnicero m, -ra f **2** KILLER : asesino m, -na f **3** BUNGLER : chapucero m, -ra f

butcher shop n : carnicería f

butler ['bʌtlər] n : mayordomo m

butt¹ ['bʌt] vt **1** : embestir (con los cuernos), darle un cabezazo a **2** ABUT : colindar con, bordear — vi to butt in **1** INTERRUPT : interrumpir **2** MEDDLE : entrometerse, meterse

butt² n **1** BUTTING : embestida f (de cuernos), cabezazo m **2** TARGET : blanco m ⟨the butt of their jokes : el blanco de sus bromas⟩ **3** BOTTOM, END : extremo m, culata f (de un rifle), colilla f (de un cigarrillo)

butte ['bju:t] n : colina f empinada y aislada

butter¹ ['bʌtər] vt **1** : untar con mantequilla **2** to butter up : halagar

butter² n : mantequilla f

buttercup ['bʌtər,kʌp] n : ranúnculo m

butterfat ['bʌtər,fæt] n : grasa f de la leche

butterfly ['bʌtər,flaɪ] n, pl **-flies** : mariposa f

buttermilk ['bʌtər,mɪlk] n : suero m de mantequilla/manteca

butternut ['bʌtər,nʌt] n : nogal m ceniciento (árbol)

butterscotch ['bʌtər,skatʃ] n : caramelo m duro hecho con mantequilla

buttery ['bʌtəri] adj : mantecoso

buttock ['bʌtək, -,tak] n : nalga f

button¹ ['bʌtən] vt : abrochar, abotonar — vi : abrocharse, abotonarse

button² n : botón m

buttonhole¹ ['bʌtən,ho:l] vt **-holed; -holing** : acorralar

buttonhole² n : ojal m

buttress¹ ['bʌtrəs] vt : apoyar, reforzar

buttress² n **1** : contrafuerte m (en la arquitectura) **2** SUPPORT : apoyo m, sostén m

buxom ['bʌksəm] adj : con mucho busto, con mucho pecho

buy¹ ['baɪ] v bought ['bɔt]; buying vt **1** : comprar **2** BELIEVE : tragarse **3** BRIBE : comprar **4** to buy into : comprar acciones de **5** to buy into BELIEVE : tragarse **6** to buy off BRIBE : comprar **7** to buy out : comprar la parte de **8** to buy time : ganar tiempo **9** to buy up : comprar (en grandes cantidades) — vi : comprar

buy² n BARGAIN : compra f, ganga f

buyer ['baɪər] n : comprador m, -dora f

buzz¹ ['bʌz] vi : zumbar (dícese de un insecto), sonar (dícese de un teléfono o un despertador)

buzz² n **1** : zumbido m (de insectos) **2** : murmullo m, rumor m (de voces)

buzzard ['bʌzərd] n VULTURE : buitre m, zopilote m CA, Mex

buzzer ['bʌzər] n : timbre m, chicharra f

buzzword ['bʌz,wərd] n : palabra f de moda

by¹ ['baɪ] adv **1** NEAR : cerca ⟨he lives close by : vive muy cerca⟩ **2** PAST : pasando ⟨the train went by : pasó el tren⟩ ⟨they rushed by : pasaron corriendo⟩

⟨as time goes by : con el paso del tiempo⟩ **3 by and by** : poco después, dentro de poco **4 by and large** : en general **5 to put by** : reservar, poner a un lado, apartar **6 to stop by** : pasar por casa, hacer una visita

by² *prep* **1** NEAR : cerca de, al lado de, junto a ⟨she was standing by the window : estaba parada al lado de la ventana⟩ **2** PAST : por, por delante de ⟨they walked by him : pasaron por delante de él⟩ **3** VIA : por ⟨she left by the back door : salió por la puerta trasera⟩ **4** (*indicating manner*) : hecho a mano ⟨he took her by the hand : la tomó de la mano⟩ ⟨you learn by making mistakes : uno aprende equivocándose⟩ ⟨I know her by sight/name : la conozco de vista/nombre⟩ ⟨she read by candlelight : leía a la luz de una vela⟩ ⟨to travel by train : viajar en tren⟩ ⟨to pay by credit card : pagar con tarjeta de crédito⟩ **5** (*indicating cause or agent*) : por ⟨built by the Romans : construido por los romanos⟩ ⟨a book by Borges : un libro de Borges⟩ ⟨I was surprised by the result : el resultado me sorprendió⟩ **6** AT : por ⟨stop/come by my house tonight : pásate por casa esta noche⟩ **7** DURING : de, durante ⟨by night : de noche⟩ **8** (*in expressions of time*) : para ⟨we'll be there by ten : estaremos allí para las diez⟩ ⟨by then : para entonces⟩ **9** : por ⟨I swear by all that's sacred : te lo juro por todo lo sagrado⟩ ⟨he said he'd do it, and by God, he did it! : dijo que lo haría y, efectivamente, lo hizo⟩ **10** : con ⟨what do you mean by that? : ¿qué quieres decir con eso?⟩ **11** (*with numbers, rates, and amounts*) : por ⟨to pay by the hour : pagar por hora⟩ ⟨it was reduced by 10 percent : se redujo (en) un 10 por ciento⟩ ⟨by a narrow margin : por un estrecho margen⟩ ⟨10 feet by 20 feet : 10 pies por 20 pies⟩ ⟨divide 100 by 10 : dividir 100 por/entre 10⟩ **12** : según ⟨by my watch, it's ten o'clock : según mi reloj, son las diez⟩ ⟨that's fine by me : por mí no hay problema⟩ ⟨to play by the rules : respetar las reglas⟩ **13** : a ⟨little by little : poco a poco⟩ **14** : por ⟨one by one : uno por uno⟩ ⟨two by two : de dos en dos⟩ **15 by oneself** : solo

by and by *adv* : dentro de poco
bye ['baɪ] *interj fam* : ¡adiós!, ¡chao!, ¡hasta luego!
bygone¹ ['baɪ,ɡɔn] *adj* : pasado
bygone² *n* **let bygones be bygones** : lo pasado, pasado está
bylaw *or* **byelaw** ['baɪ,lɔ] *n* : norma *f*, reglamento *m*
byline ['baɪ,laɪn] *n* : data *f*
bypass¹ ['baɪ,pæs] *vt* : evitar
bypass² *n* **1** BELTWAY : carretera *f* de circunvalación **2** DETOUR : desvío *m*
by-product ['baɪ,prɑdəkt] *n* : subproducto *m*, producto *m* derivado
bystander ['baɪ,stændər] *n* : espectador *m*, -dora *f*
byte ['baɪt] *n* : byte *m*
byway ['baɪ,weɪ] *n* : camino *m* (apartado), carretera *f* secundaria
byword ['baɪ,word] *n* **1** PROVERB : proverbio *m*, refrán *m* **2 to be a byword for** : ser sinónimo de

C

c ['si:] *n, pl* **c's** *or* **cs** **1** : tercera letra del alfabeto inglés — **2** : do *m* ⟨C sharp/flat : do sostenido/bemol⟩
cab ['kæb] *n* **1** TAXI : taxi *m* **2** : cabina *f* (de un camión o una locomotora) **3** CARRIAGE : coche *m* de caballos
cabal [kə'bɑl, -'bæl] *n* **1** INTRIGUE, PLOT : conspiración *f*, complot *m*, intriga *f* **2** : grupo *m* de conspiradores
cabaret [,kæbə'reɪ] *n* : cabaret *m*
cabbage ['kæbɪdʒ] *n* : col *f*, repollo *m*
cabbie *or* **cabby** ['kæbi] *n* : taxista *mf*
cabin ['kæbən] *n* **1** HUT : cabaña *f*, choza *f*, barraca *f* **2** STATEROOM : camarote *m* **3** : cabina *f* (de un automóvil o avión)
cabinet ['kæbnət] *n* **1** CUPBOARD : armario *m* **2** : gabinete *m*, consejo *m* de ministros **3 medicine cabinet** : botiquín *m*
cabinetmaker ['kæbnət,meɪkər] *n* : ebanista *mf*
cable¹ ['keɪbəl] *vt* **-bled; -bling** : enviar un cable, telegrafiar
cable² *n* **1** : cable *m* (para colgar o sostener algo) **2** : cable *m* eléctrico **3** → **cable television**

cable car *n* **1** → **streetcar** **2** : funicular *m* (en una montaña), teleférico *m*
cable television *n* : cable *m*, televisión *f* por cable
caboose [kə'bu:s] *n* : furgón *m* de cola, cabús *m Mex*
cabstand ['kæb,stænd] *n* : parada *f* de taxis
cacao [kə'kaʊ, -'keɪo] *n, pl* **cacaos** : cacao *m*
cache¹ ['kæʃ] *vt* **cached; caching** : esconder, guardar en un escondrijo
cache² *n* **1** : escondite *m*, escondrijo *m* ⟨cache of weapons : escondite de armas⟩ **2** : cache ⟨cache memory : memoria cache⟩
cachet [kæ'feɪ] *n* : caché *m*, prestigio *m*
cackle¹ ['kækəl] *vi* **-led; -ling** **1** CLUCK : cacarear **2** : reírse o carcajearse estridentemente ⟨he was cackling with delight : estaba carcajeándose de gusto⟩
cackle² *n* **1** : cacareo *m* (de una polla) **2** LAUGH : risa *f* estridente
cacophony [kæ'kɑfəni, -'kɔ-] *n, pl* **-nies** : cafofonía *f*

cactus [ˈkæktəs] *n, pl* **cacti** [-ˌtaɪ] *or* **-tuses** : cacto *m*, cactus *m*

cadaver [kəˈdævər] *n* : cadáver *m*

cadaveric [kəˈdævərɪk] *adj* : cadavérico (en medicina)

cadaverous [kəˈdævərəs] *adj* : cadavérico

caddie¹ *or* **caddy** [ˈkædi] *vi* **caddied; caddying** : trabajar de caddie, hacer de caddie

caddie² *or* **caddy** *n, pl* **-dies** : caddie *mf*

caddy [ˈkædi] *n, pl* **-dies** : cajita *f* para té

cadence [ˈkeɪdənts] *n* : cadencia *f*, ritmo *m*

cadenced [ˈkeɪdənʧt] *adj* : cadencioso, rítmico

cadet [kəˈdɛt] *n* : cadete *mf*

cadmium [ˈkædmiəm] *n* : cadmio *m*

cadre [ˈkæˌdreɪ, ˈkɑ-, -ˌdriː] *n* : cuadro *m* (de expertos)

café [kæˈfeɪ, kə-] *n* : café *m*, cafetería *f*

cafeteria [ˌkæfəˈtɪriə] *n* : cafetería *f*, restaurante *m* de autoservicio

caffeinated [ˈkæfəˌneɪtəd] *adj* : con cafeína

caffeine [kæˈfiːn] *n* : cafeína *f*

cage¹ [ˈkeɪdʒ] *vt* **caged; caging** : enjaular

cage² *n* : jaula *f*

cagey [ˈkeɪdʒi] *adj* **cagier; -est** 1 CAUTIOUS : cauteloso, reservado 2 SHREWD : astuto, vivo — **cagily** [-dʒəli] *adv*

cahoots [kəˈhuːts] *n* **to be in cahoots** *fam* : estar confabulado

caisson [ˈkeɪˌsɑn, -sən] *n* 1 : cajón *m* de municiones 2 : cajón *m* hidráulico

cajole [kəˈdʒoːl] *vt* **-joled; -joling** : engatusar

cake¹ [ˈkeɪk] *v* **caked; caking** *vt* : cubrir ⟨caked with mud : cubierto de barro⟩ — *vi* : endurecerse

cake² *n* 1 : torta *f*, bizcocho *m*, pastel *m* 2 : pastilla *f* (de jabón) 3 **to take the cake** : llevarse la palma, ser el colmo

calabash [ˈkæləˌbæʃ] *n* : calabaza *f*

calamari [ˌkɑləˈmɑri] *ns & pl* : calamares *mpl*

calamine [ˈkæləˌmaɪn] *n* : calamina *f* ⟨calamine lotion : loción de calamina⟩

calamitous [kəˈlæmətəs] *adj* : desastroso, catastrófico, calamitoso — **calamitously** *adv*

calamity [kəˈlæməti] *n, pl* **-ties** : desastre *m*, desgracia *f*, calamidad *f*

calcium [ˈkælsiəm] *n* : calcio *m*

calculate [ˈkælkjəˌleɪt] *v* **-lated; -lating** *vt* 1 COMPUTE : calcular, computar 2 ESTIMATE : calcular, creer 3 INTEND : planear, tener la intención de ⟨I calculated on spending $100 : planeaba gastar $100⟩ — *vi* : calcular, hacer cálculos

calculated [ˈkælkjəˌleɪtəd] *adj* 1 ESTIMATED : calculado 2 DELIBERATE : intencional, premeditado, deliberado

calculating [ˈkælkjəˌleɪtɪŋ] *adj* SHREWD : calculador, astuto

calculation [ˌkælkjəˈleɪʃən] *n* : cálculo *m*

calculator [ˈkælkjəˌleɪtər] *n* : calculadora *f*

calculus [ˈkælkjələs] *n, pl* **-li** [-ˌlaɪ] 1 : cálculo *m* ⟨differential calculus : cálculo diferencial⟩ 2 TARTAR : sarro *m* (dental)

caldron [ˈkɔldrən] → **cauldron**

calendar [ˈkæləndər] *n* 1 : calendario *m* 2 SCHEDULE : calendario *m*, programa *m*, agenda *f*

calf [ˈkæf, ˈkaf] *n, pl* **calves** [ˈkævz, ˈkavz] 1 : becerro *m*, -rra *f*; ternero *m*, -ra *f* (de vacunos) 2 : cría *f* (de otros mamíferos) 3 : pantorrilla *f* (de la pierna)

calfskin [ˈkæfˌskɪn] *n* : piel *f* de becerro

caliber *or* **calibre** [ˈkæləbər] *n* 1 : calibre *m* ⟨a .38 caliber gun : una pistola de calibre .38⟩ 2 ABILITY : calibre *m*, valor *m*, capacidad *f*

calibrate [ˈkæləˌbreɪt] *vt* **-brated; -brating** : calibrar (armas), graduar (termómetros)

calibration [ˌkæləˈbreɪʃən] *n* : calibrado *m*, calibración *f*

calico [ˈkælɪˌkoː] *n, pl* **-coes** *or* **-cos** 1 : calicó *m*, percal *m* (estampado) 2 *or* **calico cat** : gato *m* manchado

calipers [ˈkæləpərz] *npl* : calibrador *m*

caliph *or* **calif** [ˈkeɪləf, ˈkæ-] *n* : califa *m*

calisthenics [ˌkæləsˈθɛnɪks] *ns & pl* : calistenia *f*

calk [ˈkɔk] → **caulk**

call¹ [ˈkɔl] *vi* 1 CRY, SHOUT : llamar, gritar ⟨she called to me from upstairs : me llamó desde arriba⟩ 2 VISIT : hacer (una) visita, visitar 3 SING : cantar (dícese de las aves) 4 **to call back** : volver a llamar (por teléfono) 5 **to call for** : exigir, requerir, necesitar ⟨it calls for patience : requiere mucha paciencia⟩ 6 **to call for** SUMMON : llamar 7 **to call for** DEMAND : pedir 8 **to call in** : llamar ⟨to call in sick : reportarse enfermo⟩ 9 **to call on** VISIT : visitar 10 **to call on** IMPLORE : intimar, apelar — *vt* 1 SUMMON : llamar ⟨un perro, un taxi, a una persona, etc.⟩ ⟨he called her name : la llamó⟩ ⟨I was called away : tuve que ausentarme⟩ 2 *or* **to call up** TELEPHONE : llamar (por teléfono), telefonear ⟨she called me (up) at work : me llamó al trabajo⟩ ⟨he called 911 : llamó al 911⟩ 3 NAME : llamar ⟨what do you call this? : ¿cómo se llama esto?⟩ ⟨call me Kathy : llámeme Kathy⟩ ⟨to call someone names : insultar a alguien⟩ 4 ANNOUNCE, READ : anunciar, leer ⟨to call...roll : pasar lista⟩ 5 CONSIDER : considerar ⟨call me crazy, but . . . : quizá esté loco, pero . . .⟩ ⟨give me a dollar and we'll call it even : dame un dólar y estamos en paz⟩ ⟨let's call it a day : basta por hoy⟩ 6 PREDICT : pronosticar 7 : convocar (elecciones, etc.) 8 CANCEL : cancelar (un partido) 9 : cobrar (un penal, etc.) 10 **to call down** REPRIMAND : reprender, reñir 11 **to call in a favor** : cobrar un favor 12 **to call in an order** : llamar para hacer un pedido 13 **to call into question/doubt** : poner en duda 14 **to call off** CANCEL : cancelar 15 **to call off** : llamar (un perro) 16 **to call someone on something** *fam* ⟨he's rude, but no one calls him on it : es maleducado, pero nadie le dice nada⟩ **17 to call up** DRAFT : llamar a filas

call² n **1** SHOUT : grito m, llamada f **2** : grito m (de un animal), reclamo m (de un pájaro) **3** SUMMONS : llamada f ⟨call to action : llamada a la acción⟩ **4** DEMAND : llamado m, petición f **5** VISIT : visita f ⟨to pay a call on someone : hacerle una visita a alguien⟩ **6** DECISION : decisión f (en deportes) **7** ANNOUNCEMENT : llamada f, aviso m (para pasajeros, etc.) **8** : llamada f (telephone/phone call : llamada (telefónica) ⟩ ⟨video call : videollamada⟩ ⟨to return someone's call : devolverle la llamada a alguien⟩ **9 to be on call** : estar de guardia

call center n : centro m de atención (telefónica), centro m de llamadas

caller [ˈkɔlər] n **1** VISITOR : visita f **2** : persona f que llama (por teléfono)

calligraphy [kəˈlɪgrəfi] n, pl **-phies** : caligrafía f

calling [ˈkɔlɪŋ] n : vocación f, profesión f

calliope [kəˈlaɪəˌpiː, ˈkæliˌoːp] n : órgano m de vapor

callous [ˈkæləs] adj **1** CALLUSED : calloso, encallecido **2** UNFEELING : insensible, desalmado, cruel

callously [ˈkæləsli] adv : cruelmente, insensiblemente

callousness [ˈkæləsnəs] n : insensibilidad f, crueldad f

callow [ˈkæloː] adj : inexperto, inmaduro

callus [ˈkæləs] n : callo m

callused [ˈkæləst] adj : encallecido, calloso

calm¹ [ˈkam, ˈkalm] vt : tranquilizar, calmar, sosegar — vi or **to calm down** : tranquilizarse, calmarse ⟨calm down! : ¡tranquilízate!⟩

calm² adj **1** TRANQUIL : calmo, tranquilo, sereno, ecuánime **2** STILL : en calma (dícese del mar), sin viento (dícese del aire)

calm³ n : tranquilidad f, calma f

calmly [ˈkamli, ˈkalm-] adv : con calma, tranquilamente

calmness [ˈkamnəs, ˈkalm-] n : calma f, tranquilidad f

caloric [kəˈlɔrɪk] adj : calórico (dícese de los alimentos), calorífico (dícese de la energía)

calorie [ˈkæləri] n : caloría f

calumniate [kəˈlʌmniˌeɪt] vt **-ated; -ating** : calumniar, difamar

calumny [ˈkæləmni] n, pl **-nies** : calumnia f, difamación f

calve [ˈkæv, ˈkav] vi **calved; calving** : parir (dícese de los mamíferos)

calves → **calf**

calypso [kəˈlɪpˌsoː] n, pl **-sos** : calipso m

calyx [ˈkeɪlɪks, ˈkæ-] n, pl **-lyxes** or **-lyces** [-ləˌsiːz] : cáliz m

cam [ˈkæm] n : leva f

camaraderie [ˌkamˈradəri, ˌkæm-:, ˌkamˈra-] n : compañerismo m, camaradería f

Cambodian [kæmˈboːdiən] n : camboyano m, -na f — **Cambodian** adj

camcorder [ˈkæmˌkɔrdər] n : videocámara f

came → **come**

camel [ˈkæməl] n : camello m

cameo [ˈkæmiˌoː] n, pl **-eos 1** : camafeo m **2** or **cameo performance** : actuación f especial

camera [ˈkæmrə, ˈkæmərə] n : cámara f, máquina f fotográfica

cameraman [ˈkæmrəˌmæn, ˈkæmərə-] n, pl **-men** [-mən, -ˌmɛn] : cámara m

camerawoman [ˈkæmrəˌwʊmən, ˈkæmərə-] n, pl **-women** [ˌwɪmən] : cámara f

camouflage¹ [ˈkæməˌflɑʒ, -ˌflɑdʒ] vt **-flaged; -flaging** : camuflajear, camuflar

camouflage² n : camuflaje m

camp¹ [ˈkæmp] vi : acampar, ir de camping

camp² n **1** : campamento m **2** FACTION : campo m, bando m ⟨in the same camp : del mismo bando⟩ **3 to pitch camp** : acampar, poner el campamento **4 to break camp** : levantar el campamento

campaign¹ [kæmˈpeɪn] vi : hacer (una) campaña

campaign² n : campaña f

campaigner [kæmˈpeɪnər] n : defensor m, -sora f ⟨civil rights campaigners : defensores de los derechos civiles⟩

campanile [ˌkæmpəˈniːˌliː, -ˈniːl] n, pl **-niles** or **-nili** [-ˈniːˌliː] : campanario m

camp bed n : cama f plegable

camper [ˈkæmpər] n **1** : campista mf (persona) **2** : cámper m (vehículo)

campfire [ˈkæmpˌfaɪr] n : fogata f, hoguera f, fogón m

campground [ˈkæmpˌgraʊnd] n : campamento m, camping m

camphor [ˈkæmpfər] n : alcanfor m

camping [ˈkæmpɪŋ] n : camping m

campsite [ˈkæmpˌsaɪt] n : campamento m, camping m

campus [ˈkæmpəs] n : campus m, recinto m universitario

can¹ [ˈkæn] v aux, past **could** [ˈkʊd] present s & pl **can** **1** (referring to ability) : poder ⟨I can't hear you : no te oigo⟩ ⟨I can do it myself : puedo hacerlo yo mismo⟩ ⟨I can't decide : no me decido⟩ ⟨it can withstand high temperatures : puede soportar altas temperaturas⟩ **2** (referring to knowledge) : saber ⟨he can already read and write : ya sabe leer y escribir⟩ **3** MAY : poder ⟨can I sit down? : ¿puedo sentarme?⟩ **4** (expressing possibility) : poder ⟨can/could you help me? : ¿podría ayudarme?⟩ ⟨sorry, I can't : lo siento pero no puedo⟩ ⟨I'll do what I can : haré lo que pueda⟩ ⟨she can't come : no puede venir⟩ ⟨he can be annoying : a veces es pesado⟩ ⟨it can get crowded : a veces se llena de gente⟩ ⟨it can't be! : ¡no puede ser!⟩ ⟨you can't be serious! : ¡no lo dirás en serio!⟩ ⟨where can they be? : ¿dónde estarán?⟩ ⟨we were as happy as can be : estábamos contentísimos⟩ **5** (used to suggest or demand) : poder ⟨why can't you be more romantic? : ¿por qué no puedes ser más romántico?⟩ ⟨you can always ask for help : siempre puedes pedir ayuda⟩ ⟨you

can't leave so soon! : ¡no te vayas tan pronto!⟩ 6 **no can do** *fam* : no puedo
can² ['kæn] *vt* **canned; canning** 1 : enlatar, envasar ⟨to can tomatoes : enlatar tomates⟩ 2 DISMISS, FIRE : despedir, echar
can³ *n* : lata *f*, envase *m*, cubo *m* ⟨a can of beer : una lata de cerveza⟩ ⟨garbage can : cubo de basura⟩
Canadian [kə'neɪdiən] *n* : canadiense *mf* — **Canadian** *adj*
canal [kə'næl] *n* 1 : canal *m*, tubo *m* ⟨alimentary canal : tubo digestivo⟩ 2 : canal *m* ⟨Panama Canal : Canal de Panamá⟩
canapé ['kænəpi, -ˌpeɪ] *n* : canapé *m*
canary [kə'neri] *n, pl* **-naries** : canario *m*
cancel ['kænsəl] *vt* **-celed** *or* **-celled; -celing** *or* **-celling** 1 : cancelar 2 **to cancel out** : anular
cancellation [ˌkænsə'leɪʃən] *n* : cancelación *f*
cancer ['kænsər] *n* : cáncer *m*
Cancer *n* 1 : Cáncer *m* (signo o constelación) 2 : Cáncer *mf* (persona)
cancerous ['kænsərəs] *adj* : canceroso
candelabrum [ˌkændə'lɑbrəm, -'læ-] *or* **candelabra** [-brə] *n, pl* **-bra** *or* **-bras** : candelabro *m*
candid ['kændɪd] *adj* 1 FRANK : franco, sincero, abierto 2 : natural, espontáneo (en la fotografía)
candidacy ['kændədəsi] *n, pl* **-cies** : candidatura *f*
candidate ['kændəˌdeɪt, -dət] *n* : candidato *m*, -ta *f*
candidly ['kændɪdli] *adv* : con franqueza
candied ['kændid] *adj* : confitado
candle ['kændəl] *n* : vela *f*, candela *f*, cirio *m* (ceremonial)
candlelight ['kændəlˌlaɪt] *n* **by ~** : a la luz de una vela
candlestick ['kændəlˌstɪk] *n* : candelero *m*
candor ['kændər] *n* : franqueza *f*
candy ['kændi] *n, pl* **-dies** : dulce *m*, caramelo *m*
cane¹ ['keɪn] *vt* **caned; caning** 1 : tapizar (muebles) con mimbre 2 FLOG : azotar con una vara
cane² *n* 1 : bastón *m* (para andar), vara *f* (para castigar) 2 REED : caña *f*, mimbre *m* (para muebles)
canine¹ ['keɪˌnaɪn] *adj* : canino
canine² *n* 1 DOG : canino *m*; perro *m*, -rra *f* 2 *or* **canine tooth** : colmillo *m*, diente *m* canino
canister ['kænəstər] *n* : lata *f*, bote *m*
canker ['kæŋkər] *n* : úlcera *f* bucal
cannabis ['kænəbɪs] *n* : cannabis *m*
cannelloni [ˌkænə'loːni] *n* : canelones *mpl*
cannery ['kænəri] *n, pl* **-ries** : fábrica *f* de conservas
cannibal ['kænəbəl] *n* : caníbal *mf*; antropófago *m*, -ga *f*
cannibalism ['kænəbəˌlɪzəm] *n* : canibalismo *m*, antropofagia *f*
cannibalistic [ˌkænəbə'lɪstɪk] *adj* : antropófago, caníbal
cannily ['kænəli] *adv* : astutamente, sagazmente

cannon ['kænən] *n, pl* **-nons** *or* **-non** : cañón *m*
cannot (**can not**) ['kænˌɑt, kə'nɑt] → **can¹**
canny ['kæni] *adj* **-nier; -est** SHREWD : astuto, sagaz
canoe¹ [kə'nuː] *vi* **-noed; -noeing** : ir en canoa
canoe² *n* : canoa *f*, piragua *f*
canoeing [kə'nuːɪŋ] *n* : piragüismo *m*
canoeist [kə'nuːɪst] *or* **canoer** [kə'nuːər] *n* : piragüista *mf*
canon ['kænən] *n* 1 : canon *m* ⟨canon law : derecho canónico⟩ 2 WORKS : canon *m* ⟨the canon of American literature : el canon de la literatura americana⟩ 3 : canónigo *m* (de una catedral) 4 STANDARD : canon *m*, norma *f*
canonical [kə'nɑnɪkəl] *adj* : canónico
canonize ['kænəˌnaɪz] *vt* **-ized; -izing** : canonizar
can opener *n* : abrelatas *m*
canopy ['kænəpi] *n, pl* **-pies** : dosel *m*, toldo *m*
cant¹ ['kænt] *vt* TILT : ladear, inclinar — *vi* 1 SLANT : ladearse, inclinarse, escorar (dícese de un barco) 2 : hablar insinceramente
cant² *n* 1 SLANT : plano *m* inclinado 2 JARGON : jerga *f* 3 : palabras *fpl* insinceras
can't ['kænt, 'kɑnt] *contraction of* CAN NOT → **can¹**
cantaloupe ['kæntəlˌoːp] *n* : melón *m*, cantalupo *m*
cantankerous [kæn'tæŋkərəs] *adj* : irritable, irascible — **cantankerously** *adv*
cantankerousness [kæn'tæŋkərəsnəs] *n* : irritabilidad *f*, irascibilidad *f*
cantata [kən'tɑtə] *n* : cantata *f*
canteen [kæn'tiːn] *n* 1 FLASK : cantimplora *f* 2 CAFETERIA : cantina *f*, comedor *m* 3 : club *m* para actividades sociales y recreativas
canter¹ ['kæntər] *vi* : ir a medio galope
canter² *n* : medio galope *m*
cantilever ['kæntəˌliːvər, -ˌlevər] *n* 1 : viga *f* voladiza 2 **cantilever bridge** : puente *m* voladizo
canto ['kænˌtoː] *n, pl* **-tos** : canto *m*
canton ['kæntən, -ˌtɑn] *n* : cantón *m*
Cantonese [ˌkæntən'iːz, -'iːs] *n* 1 : cantonés *m*, -nesa *f* 2 : cantonés *m* (idioma) — **Cantonese** *adj*
cantor ['kæntər] *n* : solista *mf*
canvas ['kænvəs] *n* 1 : lona *f* 2 SAILS : velas *fpl* (de un barco) 3 : lienzo *m*, tela *f* (de pintar) 4 PAINTING : pintura *f*, óleo *m*, cuadro *m*
canvass¹ ['kænvəs] *vt* 1 SOLICIT : solicitar votos o pedidos de, hacer campaña entre 2 SOUND OUT : sondear (opiniones, etc.)
canvass² *n* SURVEY : sondeo *m*, encuesta *f*
canyon ['kænjən] *n* : cañón *m*
cap¹ ['kæp] *vt* **capped; capping** 1 COVER : tapar (un recipiente), enfundar (un diente), cubrir (una montaña) 2 CLIMAX : coronar, ser el punto culminante de ⟨to cap it all off : para colmo⟩ 3 LIMIT : limitar, poner un tope a

cap² *n* **1** : gorra *f*, gorro *m*, cachucha *f* *Mex* ⟨baseball cap : gorra de béisbol⟩ **2** COVER, TOP : tapa *f*, tapón *m* (de botellas), corchota *f* *Mex* **3** LIMIT : tope *m*, límite *m*

capability [ˌkeɪpəˈbɪləti] *n, pl* **-ties** : capacidad *f*, habilidad *f*, competencia *f*

capable [ˈkeɪpəbəl] *adj* : competente, capaz, hábil — **capably** [-bli] *adv*

capacious [kəˈpeɪʃəs] *adj* : amplio, espacioso, de gran capacidad

capacity² [kəˈpæsəti] *n, pl* **-ties 1** ROOM, SPACE : capacidad *f*, cabida *f*, espacio *m* **2** CAPABILITY : habilidad *f*, competencia *f* **3** FUNCTION, ROLE : calidad *f*, función *f* ⟨in his capacity as ambassador : en su calidad de embajador⟩

cape¹ [ˈkeɪp] *n* **1** : capa *f* **2** : cabo *m* ⟨Cape Horn : el Cabo de Hornos⟩

caper¹ [ˈkeɪpər] *vi* : dar saltos, correr y brincar

caper² *n* **1** : alcaparra *f* ⟨olives and capers : aceitunas y alcaparras⟩ **2** ANTIC, PRANK : broma *f*, travesura *f* **3** LEAP : brinco *m*, salto *m*

capful [ˈkæpˌfʊl] *n* : tapa *f*, tapita *f*

capillary¹ [ˈkæpəˌlɛri] *adj* : capilar

capillary² *n, pl* **-ries** : capilar *m*

capital¹ [ˈkæpətəl] *adj* **1** : capital ⟨capital punishment : pena capital⟩ **2** : mayúsculo (dícese de las letras) **3** : de capital ⟨capital assets : activo fijo⟩ ⟨capital gain : ganancia de capital, plusvalía⟩ **4** EXCELLENT : excelente, estupendo

capital² *n* **1** *or* **capital city** : capital *f*, sede *f* del gobierno **2** WEALTH : capital *m* **3** *or* **capital letter** : mayúscula *f* **4** : capitel *m* (de una columna)

capitalism [ˈkæpətəlˌɪzəm] *n* : capitalismo *m*

capitalist¹ [ˈkæpətəlɪst] *or* **capitalistic** [ˌkæpətəlˈɪstɪk] *adj* : capitalista

capitalist² *n* : capitalista *mf*

capitalization [ˌkæpətələˈzeɪʃən] *n* : capitalización *f*

capitalize [ˈkæpətəlˌaɪz] *v* **-ized; -izing** *vt* **1** FINANCE : capitalizar, financiar **2** : escribir con mayúscula — *vi* **to capitalize on** : sacar partido de, aprovechar

capitol [ˈkæpətəl] *n* : capitolio *m*

capitulate [kəˈpɪtʃəˌleɪt] *vi* **-lated; -lating** : capitular

capitulation [kəˌpɪtʃəˈleɪʃən] *n* : capitulación *f*

capon [ˈkeɪˌpɑn, -pən] *n* : capón *m*

cappuccino [ˌkæpəˈtʃiːnoː] *n* : capuchino *m* (café)

caprice [kəˈpriːs] *n* : capricho *m*, antojo *m*

capricious [kəˈprɪʃəs, -ˈpriː-] *adj* : caprichoso — **capriciously** *adv*

Capricorn [ˈkæprɪˌkɔrn] *n* **1** : Capricornio *m* (signo o constelación) **2** : Capricornio *mf* (persona)

capsize [ˈkæpˌsaɪz, kæpˈsaɪz] *v* **-sized; -sizing** *vi* : volcar, volcarse — *vt* : hacer volcar

capsule [ˈkæpsəl, -ˌsuːl] *n* **1** : cápsula *f* (en la farmacéutica y botánica) **2** **space capsule** : cápsula *f* espacial

captain¹ [ˈkæptən] *vt* : capitanear

captain² *n* **1** : capitán *m*, -tana *f* **2** HEADWAITER : jefe *m*, -fa *f* de comedor **3 captain of industry** : magnate *mf*

caption¹ [ˈkæpʃən] *vt* : ponerle una leyenda a (una ilustración), titular (un artículo), subtitular (una película)

caption² *n* **1** HEADING : titular *m*, encabezamiento *m* **2** : leyenda *f* (al pie de una ilustración) **3** SUBTITLE : subtítulo *m*

captivate [ˈkæptəˌveɪt] *vt* **-vated; -vating** CHARM : cautivar, hechizar, encantar

captivating [ˈkæptəˌveɪtɪŋ] *adj* : cautivador, hechicero, encantador

captive¹ [ˈkæptɪv] *adj* : cautivo

captive² *n* : cautivo *m*, -va *f*

captivity [kæpˈtɪvəti] *n* : cautiverio *m*

captor [ˈkæptər] *n* : captor *m*, -tora *f*

capture¹ [ˈkæptʃər] *vt* **-tured; -turing 1** SEIZE : capturar, apresar **2** CATCH : captar ⟨to capture one's interest : captar el interés de uno⟩

capture² *n* : captura *f*, apresamiento *m*

car [ˈkɑr] *n* **1** AUTOMOBILE : automóvil *m*, carro *m*, coche *m* **2** : vagón *m*, coche *m* (de un tren) **3** : cabina *f* (de un ascensor)

carafe [kəˈræf, -ˈrɑf] *n* : garrafa *f*

caramel [ˈkɑrməl;, ˈkærəməl, -ˌmɛl] *n* **1** : caramelo *m*, azúcar *f* quemada **2** *or* **caramel candy** : caramelo *m*, dulce *m* de leche

carat [ˈkærət] *n* : quilate *m*

caravan [ˈkærəˌvæn] *n* : caravana *f*

caraway [ˈkærəˌweɪ] *n* : alcaravea *f*

carb [ˈkɑrb] *n fam* → **carbohydrate**

carbine [ˈkɑrˌbaɪn, -ˌbiːn] *n* : carabina *f*

carbohydrate [ˌkɑrboˈhaɪˌdreɪt, -drət] *n* : carbohidrato *m*, hidrato *m* de carbono

car bomb *n* : carro *m* bomba, coche *m* bomba, auto *m* bomba *Chile*

carbon [ˈkɑrbən] *n* **1** : carbono *m* **2** → **carbon paper 3** → **carbon copy**

carbonated [ˈkɑrbəˌneɪtəd] *adj* : carbonatado (dícese del agua), gaseoso (dícese de las bebidas)

carbon copy *n* **1** : copia *f* al carbón **2** DUPLICATE : duplicado *m*, copia *f* exacta

carbon dioxide [-daɪˈɑkˌsaɪd] *n* : dióxido *m* de carbono

carbon footprint *n* : huella *f* de carbono

carbon monoxide [-məˈnɑkˌsaɪd] *n* : monóxido *m* de carbono

carbon paper *n* : papel *m* carbón

carburetor [ˈkɑrbəˌreɪtər, -bjə-] *n* : carburador *m*

carcass [ˈkɑrkəs] *n* : cuerpo *m* (de un animal muerto)

carcinogen [kɑrˈsɪnədʒən, ˈkɑrsənəˌdʒɛn] *n* : carcinógeno *m*, cancerígeno *m*

carcinogenic [ˌkɑrsənoˈdʒɛnɪk] *adj* : carcinogénico

carcinoma [ˌkɑrsəˈnoːmə] *n* : carcinoma *m*

card¹ [ˈkɑrd] *vt* : cardar (fibras)

card² *n* **1** : carta *f*, naipe *m* ⟨to play cards : jugar a las cartas⟩ ⟨a deck of cards

: una baraja⟩ **2** : tarjeta *f* ⟨birthday card : tarjeta de cumpleaños⟩ ⟨business card : tarjeta (de visita)⟩ **3** : tarjeta *f* (bancaria) ⟨credit/debit card : tarjeta de crédito/débito⟩ **4** : tarjeta *f* (de memoria, etc.) **5 to be in the cards** : estar escrito ⟨it just wasn't in the cards : estaba escrito que no iba a pasar⟩

cardboard ['kɑrd,bord] *n* : cartón *m*, cartulina *f*

cardiac ['kɑrdi,æk] *adj* : cardíaco, cardiaco

cardigan ['kɑrdɪgən] *n* : cárdigan *m*, chaqueta *f* de punto

cardinal¹ ['kɑrdənəl] *adj* FUNDAMENTAL : cardinal, fundamental

cardinal² *n* : cardenal *m*

cardinal number *n* : número *m* cardinal

cardinal point *n* : punto *m* cardinal

cardiologist [,kɑrdi'ɑlədʒɪst] *n* : cardiólogo *m*, -ga *f*

cardiology [,kɑrdi'ɑlədʒi] *n* : cardiología *f*

cardiopulmonary resuscitation [,kɑrdio'pʊlmənɛri-, -'pʌl-] *n* → CPR

cardiovascular [,kɑrdio'væskjələr] *adj* : cardiovascular

care¹ ['kær] *v* **cared; caring** *vi* **1** : importarle a uno ⟨they don't care : no les importa⟩ ⟨I could/couldn't care less : (no) me importa un bledo/comino⟩ ⟨see if I care! : ¡me tiene sin cuidado!⟩ ⟨who cares? : ¿y qué?, ¿qué importa?⟩ **2** LOVE : querer ⟨show her that you care (about her) : demuéstrale que la quieres⟩ **3** : preocuparse, inquietarse ⟨she cares about the poor : se preocupa por los pobres⟩ **4 to care for** TEND : cuidar (de), atender, encargarse de **5 to care for** LOVE : querer, sentir cariño por **6 to care for** LIKE : gustarle (algo a uno) ⟨I don't care for your attitude : tu actitud no me agrada⟩ — *vt* **1** WISH : desear, querer ⟨if you care to go : si deseas ir⟩ **2** : importarle a uno ⟨I don't care what happens to her : a mí no me importa lo que le pase⟩ ⟨for all I care, he can quit right now : por mí, puede renunciarse ahora mismo⟩ ⟨what does she care? : ¿a ella qué le importa?⟩

care² *n* **1** ANXIETY : inquietud *f*, preocupación *f* ⟨to be without a care in the world : no tener ninguna preocupación⟩ **2** CAREFULNESS : cuidado *m*, atención *f* ⟨handle with care : manejar con cuidado⟩ **3** : cargo *m*, cuidado *m* ⟨medical care : asistencia médica⟩ ⟨hair care : el cuidado del cabello/pelo⟩ ⟨the children are in my care : los niños están a mi cuidado/cargo⟩ **4 care of** : a casa de (en una carta) **5 take care!** : ¡cuídate! **6 to take care** : tener cuidado **7 to take care of** CARE FOR : cuidar (de), atender **8 to take care of** DEAL WITH : encargarse de

careen [kə'ri:n] *vi* **1** SWAY : oscilar, balancearse **2** CAREER : ir a toda velocidad

career¹ [kə'rɪr] *vi* : ir a toda velocidad

career² *n* VOCATION : vocación *f*, profesión *f*, carrera *f*

carefree ['kær,fri:, ,kær'-] *adj* : despreocupado

careful ['kærfəl] *adj* **1** CAUTIOUS : cuidadoso, cauteloso ⟨be careful : ten cuidado⟩ ⟨you can't be too careful : toda prudencia es poca⟩ **2** PAINSTAKING : cuidadoso, esmerado, meticuloso ⟨after careful consideration : después de considerarlo detenidamente⟩

carefully ['kærfəli] *adv* : con cuidado, cuidadosamente

carefulness ['kærfəlnəs] *n* **1** CAUTION : cuidado *m*, cautela *f* **2** METICULOUSNESS : esmero *m*, meticulosidad *f*

caregiver ['kær,gɪvər] *n* : persona *f* que cuida a niños o enfermos

careless ['kærləs] *adj* : descuidado, negligente — **carelessly** *adv*

carelessness ['kærləsnəs] *n* : descuido *m*, negligencia *f*

caress¹ [kə'res] *vt* : acariciar

caress² *n* : caricia *f*

caret ['kærət] *n* : signo *m* de intercalación

caretaker ['kɛr,teɪkər] *n* : conserje *mf*; velador *m*, -dora *f*

cargo ['kɑr,go:] *n, pl* **-goes** or **-gos** : cargamento *m*, carga *f*

Caribbean [,kærə'bi:ən, kə'rɪbiən] *adj* : caribeño ⟨the Caribbean Sea : el mar Caribe⟩

caribou ['kærə,bu:] *n, pl* **-bou** or **-bous** : caribú *m*

caricature¹ ['kærɪkə,tʃur] *vt* **-tured; -turing** : caricaturizar

caricature² *n* : caricatura *f*

caricaturist ['kærɪkə,tʃurɪst] *n* : caricaturista *mf*

caries ['kær,i:z] *ns & pl* : caries *f*

caring ['kærɪŋ] *n* **1** AFFECTIONATE : cariñoso, solícito **2** KIND : bondadoso

carjacking ['kɑr,dʒækɪŋ] *n* : robo *m* de un vehículo (por asalto)

carmine ['kɑrmən, -,maɪn] *n* : carmín *m*

carnage ['kɑrnɪdʒ] *n* : matanza *f*, carnicería *f*

carnal ['kɑrnəl] *adj* : carnal

carnation [kɑr'neɪʃən] *n* : clavel *m*

carnival ['kɑrnəvəl] *n* : carnaval *m*, feria *f*

carnivore ['kɑrnə,vor] *n* : carnívoro *m*

carnivorous [kɑr'nɪvərəs] *adj* : carnívoro

carol¹ ['kærəl] *vi* **-oled** or **-olled; -oling** or **-olling** : cantar villancicos

carol² *n* : villancico *m*

caroler or **caroller** ['kærələr] *n* : persona *f* que canta villancicos

carom¹ ['kærəm] *vi* **1** REBOUND : rebotar ⟨the bullet caromed off the wall : la bala rebotó contra el muro⟩ **2** : hacer carambola (en billar)

carom² *n* : carambola *f*

carouse [kə'rauz] *vi* **-roused; -rousing** : irse de parranda, irse de juerga

carousel or **carrousel** [,kærə'sɛl, 'kærə,-] *n* : carrusel *m*, tiovivo *m*

carouser [kə'rauzər] *n* : juerguista *mf*

carp¹ ['kɑrp] *vi* **1** COMPLAIN : quejarse **2 to carp at** : criticar

carp² *n, pl* **carp** or **carps** : carpa *f*

carpenter ['kɑrpəntər] *n* : carpintero *m*, -ra *f*

carpentry ['kɑrpəntri] *n* : carpintería *f*

carpet¹ ['kɑrpət] *vt* : alfombrar

carpet[2] *n* : alfombra *f*

carpeting [ˈkɑrpətɪŋ] *n* : alfombrado *m*

carport [ˈkɑr.pɔrt] *n* : cochera *f*, garaje *m* abierto

carriage [ˈkæriʤ] *n* **1** TRANSPORT : transporte *m* **2** POSTURE : porte *m*, postura *f* **3** *or* **horse-drawn carriage** : carruaje *m*, coche *m* **4** *or* **baby carriage** : cochecito *m*

carrier [ˈkæriər] *n* **1** : transportista *mf*, empresa *f* de transportes **2** : portador *m*, -dora *f* (de una enfermedad) **3** aircraft carrier : portaaviones *m*

carrier pigeon : paloma *f* mensajera

carrion [ˈkæriən] *n* : carroña *f*

carrot [ˈkærət] *n* : zanahoria *f*

carry [ˈkæri] *v* **-ried; -rying** *vt* **1** : llevar, cargar, transportar (cargamento) ⟨to carry a bag : cargar una bolsa⟩ ⟨to carry money : llevar dinero encima, traer dinero consigo⟩ **2** : llevar (sangre, agua, etc.) **3** HAVE : tener (una garantía, etc.), llevar (una advertencia) **4** BEAR : soportar, aguantar, resistir (peso) **5** STOCK : vender, tener en abasto **6** ENTAIL : llevar, implicar, acarrear **7** WIN, PASS : ganar (una elección o competición), aprobar (una moción) **8** : estar embarazada (de un hijo) **9** : portar, ser portador de (un virus, etc.) **10** : llevar (en matemáticas) **11 to be/get carried away** : pasarse, excederse ⟨to be/get carried away by something : dejarse llevar por algo⟩ **12 to carry a tune** : cantar bien **13 to carry off** ACHIEVE : conseguir, lograr **14 to carry off** TAKE : llevarse **15 to carry on** CONTINUE : seguir con, continuar con **16 to carry on** CONDUCT : realizar, ejercer, mantener ⟨to carry on research : realizar investigaciones⟩ ⟨to carry on a correspondence : mantener una correspondencia⟩ **17 to carry oneself** : portarse, comportarse ⟨he carried himself honorably : se comportó dignamente⟩ **18 to carry out** COMPLETE : llevar a cabo, realizar, efectuar **19 to carry out** FULFILL : cumplir (una orden, etc.) **20 to carry through** SUSTAIN : sustentar, sostener — *vi* **1** : oírse, proyectarse ⟨her voice carries well : su voz se puede oír desde lejos⟩ **2 to carry on** CONTINUE : seguir, continuar **3 to carry on** : portarse de manera escandalosa o inapropiada ⟨it's embarrassing how he carries on : su manera de comportarse da vergüenza⟩

carryall [ˈkæri.ɔl] *n* : bolsa *f* de viaje

carsick [ˈkɑr.sɪk] *adj* : mareado (de ir en coche)

cart[1] [ˈkɑrt] *vt* : acarrear, llevar

cart[2] *n* : carreta *f*, carro *m*

carte blanche [ˈkɑrt'blɑnch] *n* : carta *f* blanca

cartel [kɑrˈtɛl] *n* : cártel *m*

cartilage [ˈkɑrtəlɪʤ] *n* : cartílago *m*

cartographer [kɑrˈtɑgrəfər] *n* : cartógrafo *m*, -fa *f*

cartography [kɑrˈtɑgrəfi] *n* : cartografía *f*

carton [ˈkɑrtən] *n* : caja *f* de cartón

cartoon [kɑrˈtuːn] *n* **1** : chiste *m* (gráfico), caricatura *f* ⟨a political cartoon : un chiste político⟩ **2** COMIC STRIP : tira *f* cómica, historieta *f* **3** : dibujo *m* animado ⟨to watch cartoons : mirar dibujos animados⟩

cartoonist [kɑrˈtuːnɪst] *n* : caricaturista *mf*, dibujante *mf* (de chistes)

cartridge [ˈkɑrtrɪʤ] *n* : cartucho *m*

cartwheel [ˈkɑrtˌʍiːl] *n* : voltereta *f* lateral

carve [ˈkɑrv] *vt* **carved; carving** **1** : tallar (madera), esculpir (piedra), grabar ⟨he carved his name in the bark : grabó su nombre en la corteza⟩ **2** SLICE : cortar, trinchar (carne) **3 to carve out** : hacerse, conquistar

carving [ˈkɑrvɪŋ] *n* : talla *f*, escultura *f* (de madera, piedra, etc.)

cascade[1] [kæsˈkeɪd] *vi* **-caded; -cading** : caer en cascada

cascade[2] *n* : cascada *f*, salto *m* de agua

case[1] [ˈkeɪs] *vt* **cased; casing** **1** BOX, PACK : embalar, encajonar **2** INSPECT : observar, inspeccionar (antes de cometer un delito)

case[2] *n* **1** : caso *m* ⟨an unusual case : un caso insólito⟩ ⟨a case of the flu : un caso de gripe⟩ ⟨a murder case : un caso de asesinato⟩ **2** BOX : caja *f* **3** CONTAINER : funda *f*, estuche *m* **4** SUITCASE : maleta *f*, valija *f* **5** ARGUMENT : argumento *m* ⟨to make a case for : presentar argumentos a favor de⟩ **6** : caso *m* (en gramática) **7 in any case** : en todos modos, en cualquier caso **8 in ~** : como precaución ⟨just in case : por si acaso⟩ **9 in case of** : en caso de **10 in that case** : en ese caso

casement [ˈkeɪsmənt] *n* : ventana *f* con bisagras

cash[1] [ˈkæʃ] *vt* : convertir en efectivo, cobrar, cambiar (un cheque) — *vi* **to cash in on** : sacar partido de

cash[2] *n* : efectivo *m*, dinero *m* en efectivo ⟨cash on delivery : entrega contra reembolso⟩ ⟨hard/cold cash : dinero contante y sonante⟩

cashew [ˈkæ.ʃuː, kəˈʃuː] *n* : anacardo *m*

cashier[1] [kæˈʃɪr] *vt* : destituir, despedir

cashier[2] *n* : cajero *m*, -ra *f*

cashmere [ˈkæʒ.mɪr, ˈkæʃ-] *n* : cachemir *m*

cash register *n* : caja *f* registradora

casing [ˈkeɪsɪŋ] *n* **1** : caja *f*, cubierta *f* **2** : casquillo *m* (de una bala, etc.) **3** FRAME : marco *m* (de una puerta o ventana)

casino [kəˈsiːˌnoː] *n*, *pl* **-nos** : casino *m*

cask [ˈkæsk] *n* : tonel *m*, barrica *f*, barril *m*

casket [ˈkæskət] *n* COFFIN : ataúd *m*, féretro *m*

cassava [kəˈsɑvə] *n* : mandioca *f*, yuca *f*

casserole [ˈkæsə.roːl] *n* **1** : cazuela *f* **2** : guiso *m*, guisado *m* ⟨tuna casserole : guiso de atún⟩

cassette [kəˈsɛt, kæ-] *n* : cassette *mf*

cassock [ˈkæsək] *n* : sotana *f*

cast[1] [ˈkæst] *vt* **cast; casting** **1** THROW : tirar, echar, arrojar ⟨the die is cast : la suerte está echada⟩ **2** DIRECT : echar ⟨he cast a glance at the door : echó una mirada a la puerta⟩ **3** : depositar (un voto) **4** : asignar ⟨to cast a role : asignar un papel⟩ ⟨to cast someone as : asignarle a alguien el papel de⟩ **5** MOLD : moldear, fundir, vaciar **6** : proyectar (luz, etc.) ⟨to cast a shadow : proyectar una sombra⟩ ⟨to cast a shadow/pall on : ensombrecer⟩ **7 to be cast away** : quedarse varado (en un lugar remoto tras naufragar) **8 to cast adrift** : dejar a la deriva **9 to cast aside** : desechar (las preocupaciones, etc.) **10 to cast a spell on** : hechizar **11 to cast off** GET RID OF : deshacerse de **12 to cast out** EXPEL : expulsar — *vi* **1 to cast about/around for** : tratar de encontrar **2 to cast off** : desamarrar, soltar (las amarras) **3 to cast off** : cerrar (puntos) **4 to cast on** : montar puntos

cast² *n* **1** THROW : lance *m*, lanzamiento *m* **2** APPEARANCE : aspecto *m*, forma *f* **3** : elenco *m*, reparto *m* (de una obra de teatro) **4** MOLD : molde *m* **5** : yeso *m*, escayola *f* Spain (en medicina)

castanet [ˌkæstəˈnɛt] *n* : castañuela *f*

castaway¹ [ˈkæstəˌweɪ] *adj* : náufrago

castaway² *n* : náufrago *m*, -ga *f*

caste [ˈkæst] *n* : casta *f*

caster [ˈkæstər] *n* : ruedita *f* (de un mueble)

castigate [ˈkæstəˌgeɪt] *vt* **-gated; -gating** : castigar severamente, censurar, reprobar

Castilian [kæˈstɪljən] *n* **1** : castellano *m*, -na *f* **2** : castellano *m* (idioma) — **Castilian** *adj*

cast iron *n* : hierro *m* fundido

castle [ˈkæsəl] *n* **1** : castillo *m* **2** : torre *f* (en ajedrez)

cast-off [ˈkæstˌɔf] *adj* : desechado

castoff [ˈkæstˌɔf] *n* : desecho *m*

castor oil [ˈkæstər-] *n* : aceite *m* de ricino

castrate [ˈkæsˌtreɪt] *vt* **-trated; -trating** : castrar

castration [kæˈstreɪʃən] *n* : castración *f*

casual [ˈkæʒuəl] *adj* **1** FORTUITOUS : casual, fortuito **2** INDIFFERENT : indiferente, despreocupado **3** INFORMAL : informal **4** IRREGULAR, OCCASIONAL : eventual, ocasional — **casually** [ˈkæʒʰuəli, ˈkæʒʒli] *adv*

casualness [ˈkæʒuəlnəs] *n* **1** INDIFFERENCE : indiferencia *f*, despreocupación *f* **2** INFORMALITY : informalidad *f*

casualty [ˈkæʒuəlti, ˈkæʒəl-] *n, pl* **-ties 1** ACCIDENT : accidente *m* serio, desastre *m* **2** VICTIM : víctima *f*; baja *f*; herido *m*, -da *f*

cat [ˈkæt] *n* : gato *m*, -ta *f*

cataclysm [ˈkætəˌklɪzəm] *n* : cataclismo *m*

cataclysmal [ˌkætəˈklɪzməl] *or* **cataclysmic** [ˌkætəˈklɪzmɪk] *adj* : catastrófico

catacombs [ˈkætəˌkoːmz] *npl* : catacumbas *fpl*

Catalan [ˈkætələn, -ˌlæn] *n* **1** : catalán *m*, catalana *f* **2** : catalán *m* (idioma) — **Catalan** *adj*

catalog¹ *or* **catalogue** [ˈkætəˌlɔg] *vt* **-loged** *or* **-logued; -loging** *or* **-loguing** : catalogar

catalog² *n* : catálogo *m*

catalyst [ˈkætələst] *n* : catalizador *m*

catalytic converter [ˌkætəˈlɪtɪk-] *n* : catalizador *m*, convertidor *m* catalítico

catamaran [ˌkætəməˈræn, ˈkætəməˌræn] *n* : catamarán *m*

catapult¹ [ˈkætəˌpʌlt, -ˌpʊlt] *vt* : catapultar

catapult² *n* : catapulta *f*

cataract [ˈkætəˌrækt] *n* : catarata *f*

catarrh [kəˈtɑr] *n* : catarro *m*

catastrophe [kəˈtæstrəˌfiː] *n* : catástrofe *f*

catastrophic [ˌkætəˈstrɑfɪk] *adj* : catastrófico — **catastrophically** [-fɪkli] *adv*

catcall [ˈkætˌkɔl] *n* : rechifla *f*, abucheo *m*

catch [ˈkætʃ, ˈkɛtʃ] *v* **caught** [ˈkɔt]; **catching** *vt* **1** GRASP : agarrar, coger Spain **2** CAPTURE, TRAP : capturar, agarrar, atrapar, coger Spain **3** SURPRISE, INTERRUPT : agarrar, pillar Spain, coger Spain ⟨they caught him red-handed : lo pillaron con las manos en la masa⟩ ⟨to catch by surprise : tomar por sorpresa⟩ ⟨we got caught in the rain : nos agarró la lluvia⟩ ⟨you've caught me at a bad time : llegas en mal momento⟩ ⟨I caught her just as she was leaving : llegué justo cuando ella salía⟩ **4** ENTANGLE : enganchar, enredar ⟨to get caught up in something : quedarse enredado en algo⟩ **5** MAKE : alcanzar (un tren, etc.) ⟨to catch a train : tomar un tren, etc.⟩ **7** : contagiarse de ⟨to catch a cold : contagiarse de un resfriado, resfriarse⟩ **8** ATTRACT : llamar (la atención), captar (el interés) **9** UNDERSTAND : captar ⟨if you catch my drift : si me entiendes⟩ **10** PERCEIVE : percibir ⟨to catch a glimpse of : alcanzar a ver⟩ **11** NOTICE, DETECT : darse cuenta de, detectar **12** : ver (una película), ir a (un concierto, etc.) — *vi* **1** GRASP : agarrar **2** HOOK : engancharse **3** IGNITE : prender, agarrar **4 to catch on** : hacerse popular **5 to catch on** LEARN : agarrarle la onda **6 to catch on** UNDERSTAND : entender, darse cuenta **7 to catch up** : ponerse al día ⟨to catch up on the news : ponerse al día con las noticias⟩ **8 to catch up to/with** : alcanzar

catch² *n* **1** CATCHING : captura *f*, atrapada *f*, parada *f* (de una pelota) **2** : redada *f* (de pescado), presa *f* (de caza) ⟨he's a good catch : es un buen partido⟩ **3** LATCH : pestillo *m*, pasador *m* **4** DIFFICULTY, TRICK : problema *m*, trampa *f*, truco *m*

catcher [ˈkætʃər, ˈkɛ-] *n* : catcher *mf*; receptor *m*, -tora *f* (en béisbol)

catching [ˈkætʃɪŋ, ˈkɛ-] *adj* : contagioso

catchphrase [ˈkætʃˌfreɪz, ˈkɛtʃ-] *n* : eslogan *m*, lema *m*

catchup [ˈkætʃəp, ˈkɛ-] → **ketchup**

catchword [ˈkætʃˌwərd, ˈkɛtʃ-] *n* : eslogan *m*, lema *m*

catchy [ˈkætʃi, ˈkɛ-] *adj* **catchier; -est** : pegajoso ⟨a catchy song : una canción pegajosa⟩

catechism ['kætə,kɪzəm] n : catecismo m

categorical [,kætə'gɔrɪkəl] adj : categórico, absoluto, rotundo — categorically [-kli] adv

categorize ['kætɪgə,raɪz] vt -rized; -rizing : clasificar, catalogar

category ['kætə,gori] n, pl -ries : categoría f, género m, clase f

cater ['keɪtər] vi 1 : proveer servicio de alimentos (para fiestas, bodas, etc.) 2 to cater to : atender a ⟨to cater to all tastes : atender a todos los gustos⟩ — vt : proveer servicio de alimentos para

catercorner¹ ['kætɚ,kɔrnɚ, 'kætə-, 'kɪti-] or cater-cornered [-,kɔrnɚrd] adv : diagonalmente, en diagonal

catercorner² or cater-cornered adj : diagonal

caterer ['keɪtərɚr] n : proveedor m, -dora f de comida

catering ['keɪtərɪŋ] n : servicio m de alimentos, catering m

caterpillar ['kætɚr,pɪlɚr] n : oruga f

catfish ['kæt,fɪʃ] n : bagre m

catgut ['kæt,gʌt] n : cuerda f de tripa

catharsis [kə'θɑrsɪs] n, pl catharses [-,siːz] : catarsis f

cathartic¹ [kə'θɑrtɪk] adj : catártico

cathartic² n : purgante m

cathedral [kə'θiːdrəl] n : catedral f

catheter ['kæθətər] n : catéter m, sonda f

cathode ['kæ,θoːd] n : cátodo m

catholic ['kæθəlɪk] adj 1 BROAD, UNIVERSAL : liberal, universal 2 Catholic : católico

Catholic n : católico m, -ca f

Catholicism [kə'θɑlə,sɪzəm] n : catolicismo m

catlike ['kæt,laɪk] adj : felino

catnap¹ ['kæt,næp] vi -napped; -napping : tomarse una siestecita

catnap² n : siesta f breve, siestecita f

catnip ['kæt,nɪp] n : nébeda f

catsup ['kɛtʃəp, 'kætsəp] → ketchup

cattail ['kæt,teɪl] n : espadaña f, anea f

cattiness ['kætinəs] n : malicia f

cattle ['kætəl] npl : ganado m, reses fpl

cattleman ['kætəlmən, -,mæn] n, pl -men [-mən, -,mɛn] : ganadero m

catty ['kæti] adj cattier; -est : malicioso, malintencionado

catwalk ['kæt,wɔk] n : pasarela f

Caucasian¹ [kɔ'keɪʒən] adj : caucásico

Caucasian² n : caucásico m, -ca f

caucus ['kɔkəs] n : junta f de políticos

caught → catch

cauldron ['kɔldrən] n : caldera f

cauliflower ['kɑlɪ,flaʊər, 'kɔ-] n : coliflor f

caulk¹ ['kɔk] vt : enmasillar (una grieta)

caulk² n : masilla f

causal ['kɔzəl] adj : causal — causality [kɔ'zæləti] n

cause¹ ['kɔz] vt caused; causing : causar, provocar, ocasionar

cause² n 1 ORIGIN : causa f, origen m 2 REASON : causa f, razón f, motivo m 3 LAWSUIT : litigio m, pleito m 4 MOVEMENT : causa f, movimiento m

causeless ['kɔzləs] adj : sin causa

causeway ['kɔz,weɪ] n : camino m elevado

caustic ['kɔstɪk] adj 1 CORROSIVE : cáustico, corrosivo 2 BITING : mordaz, sarcástico

cauterize ['kɔtə,raɪz] vt -ized; -izing : cauterizar

caution¹ ['kɔʃən] vt : advertir

caution² n 1 WARNING : advertencia f, aviso m 2 CARE, PRUDENCE : precaución f, cuidado m, cautela f

cautionary ['kɔʃə,nɛri] adj : admonitorio ⟨cautionary tale : cuento moral⟩

cautious ['kɔʃəs] adj : cauteloso, cuidadoso, precavido

cautiously ['kɔʃəsli] adv : cautelosamente, con precaución

cautiousness ['kɔʃəsnəs] n : cautela f, precaución f

cavalcade [,kævəl'keɪd, 'kævəl,-] n 1 : cabalgata f 2 SERIES : serie f

cavalier¹ [,kævə'lɪr] adj : altivo, desdeñoso — cavalierly adv

cavalier² n : caballero m

cavalry ['kævəlri] n, pl -ries : caballería f

cave¹ ['keɪv] vi caved; caving or to cave in : derrumbarse

cave² n : cueva f

caveman ['keɪv,mæn] n, pl -men [-mən, -,mɛn] : cavernícola m

cavern ['kævɚrn] n : caverna f

cavernous ['kævɚrnəs] adj : cavernoso — cavernously adv

cavewoman ['keɪv,wʊmən] n, pl -women [-,wɪmən] : cavernícola f

caviar or caviare ['kævi,ɑr, 'kɑ-] n : caviar m

cavity ['kævəti] n, pl -ties 1 HOLE : cavidad f, hueco m 2 CARIES : caries f

cavort [kə'vɔrt] vi : brincar, hacer cabriolas

caw¹ ['kɔ] vi : graznar

caw² n : graznido m

cayenne pepper [,kaɪ'ɛn, ,keɪ-] n : pimienta f cayena, pimentón m

cc [,si:'si:] vt cc'd; cc'ing : enviarle una copia a (alguien), enviar una copia de (un email, etc.)

CD [,si:'di:] n : CD m, disco m compacto

CD–ROM [,si:,di:'rɑm] n : CD-ROM m

cease ['si:s] v ceased; ceasing vt : dejar de ⟨they ceased bickering : dejaron de discutir⟩ — vi : cesar, pasarse

cease–fire ['si:s'faɪr] n : alto m el fuego, cese m del fuego

ceaseless ['si:sləs] adj : incesante, continuo

cedar ['si:dər] n : cedro m

cede ['si:d] vt ceded; ceding : ceder, conceder

ceiling ['si:lɪŋ] n 1 : techo m, cielo m raso 2 LIMIT : límite m, tope m

celebrant ['sɛləbrənt] n : celebrante mf, oficiante mf

celebrate ['sɛlə,breɪt] v -brated; -brating vt 1 : celebrar, oficiar ⟨to celebrate Mass : celebrar la misa⟩ 2 : celebrar, festejar ⟨we're celebrating our anniversary : estamos celebrando nuestro aniversario⟩ 3 EXTOL : alabar, ensalzar, exaltar — vi : estar de fiesta, divertirse

celebrated [ˈsɛləˌbreɪtəd] *adj* : célebre, famoso, renombrado
celebration [ˌsɛləˈbreɪʃən] *n* : celebración *f*, festejos *mpl*
celebrity [səˈlɛbrəti] *n, pl* **-ties 1** RENOWN : fama *f*, renombre *m*, celebridad *f* **2** PERSONALITY : celebridad *f*, personaje *m*
celery [ˈsɛləri] *n, pl* **-eries** : apio *m*
celestial [səˈlɛstʃəl, -ˈlstiəl] *adj* **1** : celeste **2** HEAVENLY : celestial, paradisiaco
celibacy [ˈsɛləbəsi] *n* : celibato *m*
celibate¹ [ˈsɛləbət] *adj* : célibe
celibate² *n* : célibe *mf*
cell [ˈsɛl] *n* **1** : célula *f* (de un organismo) **2** : celda *f* (en una cárcel, etc.) **3** : elemento *m* (de una pila)
cellar [ˈsɛlər] *n* **1** BASEMENT : sótano *m* **2** : bodega *f* (de vinos)
cellist [ˈtʃɛlɪst] *n* : violonchelista *mf*
cello [ˈtʃɛˌloː] *n, pl* **-los** : chelo *m*, violonchelo *m*
cellophane [ˈsɛləˌfeɪn] *n* : celofán *m*
cell phone *n* : teléfono *m* celular
cellular [ˈsɛljələr] *adj* : celular
cellulite [ˈsɛljəˌlaɪt] *n* : celulitis *f*
celluloid [ˈsɛljəˌlɔɪd] *n* : celuloide *m*
cellulose [ˈsɛljəˌloːs] *n* : celulosa *f*
Celsius [ˈsɛlsiəs] *adj* : centígrado ⟨100 degrees Celsius : 100 grados centígrados⟩
Celt [ˈkɛlt, ˈsɛlt] *n* : celta *mf*
Celtic¹ [ˈkɛltɪk, ˈsɛl-] *adj* : celta
Celtic² *n* : celta *m*
cement¹ [sɪˈmɛnt] *vi* : unir o cubrir algo con cemento, cementar
cement² *n* **1** : cemento *m* **2** GLUE : pegamento *m*
cement mixer *n* : hormigonera *f*
cemetery [ˈsɛməˌteri] *n, pl* **-teries** : cementerio *m*, panteón *m*
censer [ˈsɛnsər] *n* : incensario *m*
censor¹ [ˈsɛnsər] *vt* : censurar
censor² *n* : censor *m*, -sora *f*
censorious [sɛnˈsoriəs] *adj* : de censura, crítico
censorship [ˈsɛnsərˌʃɪp] *n* : censura *f*
censure¹ [ˈsɛntʃər] *vt* **-sured; -suring** : censurar, criticar, reprobar — **censurable** [-tʃərəbəl] *adj*
censure² *n* : censura *f*, reproche *m* oficial
census [ˈsɛnsəs] *n* : censo *m*
cent [ˈsɛnt] *n* **1** : centavo *m* **2** : céntimo *m* (fracción del euro)
centaur [ˈsɛnˌtɔr] *n* : centauro *m*
centavo [sɛnˈtavo] *n* : centavo *m* (unidad monetaria)
centennial¹ [sɛnˈtɛniəl] *adj* : del centenario
centennial² *n* : centenario *m*
center¹ [ˈsɛntər] *vt* **1** : centrar **2** CONCENTRATE : concentrar, fijar, enfocar — *vi* : centrarse, enfocarse
center² *n* **1** : centro *m* ⟨center of gravity : centro de gravedad⟩ **2** : centro *mf* (en futbol americano), pívot *mf* (en basquetbol)
centerpiece [ˈsɛntərˌpiːs] *n* : centro *m* de mesa
centesimo [sɛnˈtɛsəˌmo] *n* : centésimo *m* (unidad monetaria)

centi- [ˈsɛntə] *pref* : centi-
centigrade [ˈsɛntəˌgreɪd, ˈsan-] *adj* : centígrado
centigram [ˈsɛntəˌgræm, ˈsan-] *n* : centigramo *m*
centime [ˈsanˌtiːm] *n* : céntimo *m* (unidad monetaria en varios países de habla francesa y portuguesa)
centimeter [ˈsɛntəˌmiːtər, ˈsan-] *n* : centímetro *m*
centimo [ˈsɛntəmo] *n* : céntimo *m* (unidad monetaria en varios países de habla española y portuguesa)
centipede [ˈsɛntəˌpiːd] *n* : ciempiés *m*
central [ˈsɛntrəl] *adj* **1** : céntrico, central ⟨in a central location : en un lugar céntrico⟩ **2** MAIN, PRINCIPAL : central, fundamental, principal
Central American¹ *adj* : centroamericano
Central American² *n* : centroamericano *m*, -na *f*
centralist [ˈsɛntrəlɪst] *n* : centralista *mf* — **centralist** *adj*
centralization [ˌsɛntrələˈzeɪʃən] *n* : centralización *f*
centralize [ˈsɛntrəˌlaɪz] *vt* **-ized; -izing** : centralizar
centrally [ˈsɛntrəli] *adv* **1 centrally heated** : con calefacción central **2 centrally located** : céntrico, en un lugar céntrico
centre [ˈsɛntər] → **center**
centrifugal force [sɛnˈtrɪfjəgəl-, -ˈtrɪfɪ-] *n* : fuerza *f* centrífuga
centrist [ˈsɛntrɪst] *n* : centrista *mf* — **centrist** *adj*
century [ˈsɛntʃəri] *n, pl* **-ries** : siglo *m*
CEO [ˌsiːˌiːˈoː] *n* (chief executive officer) : director *m*, -tora *f* general (de una compañía)
ceramic¹ [səˈræmɪk] *adj* : de cerámica
ceramic² *n* **1** : objeto *m* de cerámica, cerámica *f* **2 ceramics** *npl* : cerámica *f*
cereal¹ [ˈsiriəl] *adj* : cereal
cereal² *n* : cereal *m*
cerebellum [ˌsɛrəˈbɛləm] *n, pl* **-bellums** *or* **-bella** [-ˈbɛlə] : cerebelo *m*
cerebral [səˈriːbrəl, ˈsɛrə-] *adj* : cerebral
cerebral palsy *n* : parálisis *f* cerebral
cerebrum [səˈriːbrəm, ˈsɛrə-] *n, pl* **-brums** *or* **-bra** [-brə] : cerebro *m*
ceremonial¹ [ˌsɛrəˈmoːniəl] *adj* : ceremonial
ceremonial² *n* : ceremonial *m*
ceremonious [ˌsɛrəˈmoːniəs] *adj* **1** FORMAL : ceremonioso, formal **2** CEREMONIAL : ceremonial
ceremony [ˈsɛrəˌmoːni] *n, pl* **-nies** : ceremonia *f* ⟨without ceremony : sin ceremonias⟩ ⟨not to stand on ceremony : dejarse de ceremonias⟩
cerise [səˈriːs] *n* : rojo *m* cereza
certain¹ [ˈsərtən] *adj* **1** DEFINITE : cierto, determinado ⟨a certain percentage : un porcentaje determinado⟩ **2** TRUE : cierto, con certeza ⟨I don't know for certain : no sé exactamente⟩ **3** : cierto, alguno ⟨it has a certain charm : tiene cierta gracia⟩ **4** INEVITABLE : seguro, inevitable **5** ASSURED : seguro, asegu-

rado ⟨she's certain to do well : seguro
que le irá bien⟩
certain² *pron* SOME : ciertos, algunos
⟨certain of my friends : algunos de mis
amigos⟩
certainly [ˈsərtənli] *adv* **1** DEFINITELY
: ciertamente, seguramente **2** OF
COURSE : por supuesto
certainty [ˈsərtənti] *n, pl* **-ties** : certeza *f*,
certidumbre *f*, seguridad *f*
certifiable [ˌsərtəˈfaɪəbəl] *adj* : certificable
certificate [sərˈtɪfɪkət] *n* : certificado *m*,
acta *f* ⟨birth certificate : partida/acta/
certificado de nacimiento⟩
certification [ˌsərtəfəˈkeɪʃən] *n* : certificación *f*
certified [ˈsərtəˌfaɪd] *adj* **1** ACCREDITED
: acreditado, certificado, diplomado, titulado **2** VERIFIED : certificado **3** *fam*
REAL : verdadero, auténtico
certify [ˈsərtəˌfaɪ] *vt* **-fied; -fying** **1** VER-
IFY : certificar, verificar, confirmar,
constatar **2** ENDORSE : endosar, aprobar oficialmente **3** ACCREDIT, LICENSE
: acreditar, autorizar
certitude [ˈsərtəˌtuːd, -ˌtjuːd] *n* : certeza *f*,
certidumbre *f*
cervical [ˈsərvɪkəl] *adj* **1** : cervical (dícese
del cuello) **2** : del cuello del útero
cervix [ˈsərvɪks] *n, pl* **-vices** [-vəˌsiːz] *or*
-vixes : cuello *m* del útero
cesarean¹ [sɪˈzæriən] *adj* : cesáreo
cesarean² *or* **cesarean section** *n*
: cesárea *f*
cesium [ˈsiːziəm] *n* : cesio *m*
cessation [sɛˈseɪʃən] *n* : cesación *f*, cese
m
cesspool [ˈsɛsˌpuːl] *n* : pozo *m* séptico
chafe [ˈtʃeɪf] *v* **chafed; chafing** *vi* : enojarse, irritarse — *vt* : rozar
chaff [ˈtʃæf] *n* **1** : barcia *f*, granzas *fpl* **2**
to separate the wheat from the chaff
: separar el grano de la paja
chagrin¹ [ʃəˈgrɪn] *vt* : desilusionar, avergonzar
chagrin² *n* : desilusión *f*, disgusto *m*
chain¹ [ˈtʃeɪn] *vt* : encadenar
chain² *n* **1** : cadena *f* ⟨steel chain : cadena de acero⟩ ⟨restaurant chain : ca-
dena de restaurantes⟩ **2** SERIES : serie *f*
⟨chain of events : serie de eventos⟩ **3**
chains *npl* FETTERS : grillos *mpl*
chain–smoke [ˈtʃeɪnˈsmoːk] *n* : fumar un
cigarrillo tras otro
chair¹ [ˈtʃɛr] *vt* : presidir, moderar
chair² *n* **1** : silla *f* **2** CHAIRMANSHIP
: presidencia *f* **3** *or* **chairman, chairwoman, chairperson** **4** *or* **department
chair** : catedrático *m*, -ca *f* (de una universidad)
chairlift [ˈtʃɛrˌlɪft] *n* : telesilla *mf*
chairman [ˈtʃɛrmən] *n, pl* **-men** [-mən,
-ˌmɛn] : presidente *m*
chairmanship [ˈtʃɛrmənˌʃɪp] *n* : presidencia *f*
chairperson [ˈtʃɛrˌpərsən] *n* : presidente
mf, presidenta *f*
chairwoman [ˈtʃɛrˌwʊmən] *n, pl* **-women**
[-ˌwɪmən] : presidenta *f*

chalet [ʃæˈleɪ] *n* : chalet *m*, chalé *m*
chalice [ˈtʃælɪs] *n* : cáliz *m*
chalk¹ [ˈtʃɔk] *vt* : escribir con tiza
chalk² *n* **1** LIMESTONE : creta *f*, caliza
f **2** : tiza *f*, gis *m Mex* (para escribir)
chalkboard [ˈtʃɔkˌbord] → **blackboard**
chalk up *vt* **1** ASCRIBE : atribuir, adscribir **2** SCORE : apuntarse, anotarse (una
victoria, etc.)
chalky [ˈtʃɔki] *adj* **chalkier; -est** **1** PALE
: pálido **2** POWDERY : polvoriento
challenge¹ [ˈtʃælɪndʒ] *vt* **-lenged; -leng-
ing** **1** DISPUTE : disputar, cuestionar,
poner en duda **2** DARE : desafiar, retar **3** STIMULATE : estimular, incentivar
challenge² *n* : reto *m*, desafío *m*
challenger [ˈtʃælɪndʒər] *n* : retador *m*,
-dora *f*; contendiente *mf*
challenging [ˈtʃælɪndʒɪŋ] *adj* **1** DEMAND-
ING : exigente **2** DEFIANT : desafiante,
de desafío **3** STIMULATING : estimulante, provocador
chamber [ˈtʃeɪmbər] *n* **1** ROOM : cámara
f, sala *f* ⟨the senate chamber : la cámara
del senado⟩ **2** : recámara *f* (de un arma
de fuego), cámara *f* (de combustión) **3**
: cámara *f* ⟨chamber of commerce
: cámara de comercio⟩ **4 chambers** *npl*
or **judge's chambers** : despacho *m* del
juez
chambermaid [ˈtʃeɪmbərˌmeɪd] *n* : camarera *f*
chamber music *n* : música *f* de cámara
chamber pot *n* : bacinica *f*
chameleon [kəˈmiːljən, -liən] *n* : camaleón *m*
chamois [ˈʃæmi] *n, pl* **chamois** [-mi, -miz]
: gamuza *f*
chamomile [ˈkæməˌmaɪl, -ˌmiːl] *n* **1**
: manzanilla *f*, camomila *f* **2 chamomile tea** : manzanilla *f*
champ¹ [ˈtʃæmp, ˈtʃɑmp] *vi* **1** : masticar
ruidosamente **2 to champ at the bit**
: impacientarse, comerle a uno la impaciencia
champ² [ˈtʃæmp] *n* : campeón *m*, -peona *f*
champagne [ʃæmˈpeɪn] *n* : champaña *m*,
champán *m*
champion¹ [ˈtʃæmpiən] *vt* : defender,
luchar por (una causa)
champion² *n* **1** ADVOCATE, DEFENDER
: paladín *m*; campeón *m*, -peona *f*; defensor *m*, -sora *f* **2** WINNER : campeón *m*,
-peona *f* ⟨world champion : campeón
mundial⟩
championship [ˈtʃæmpiənˌʃɪp] *n* : campeonato *m*
chance¹ [ˈtʃænts] *v* **chanced; chancing**
vi **1** HAPPEN : ocurrir por casualidad **2
to chance upon** : encontrar por casualidad — *vt* RISK : arriesgarse a (hacer
algo) ⟨we can't chance it : no podemos
arriesgarnos⟩
chance² *adj* : fortuito, casual ⟨a chance
encounter : un encuentro casual⟩
chance³ *n* **1** FATE, LUCK : azar *m*, suerte
f, fortuna *f* **2** OPPORTUNITY : oportunidad *f*, ocasión *f* **3** PROBABILITY : probabilidad *f*, posibilidad *f* **4** RISK : riesgo

m **5** : boleto *m* (de una rifa o lotería) **6 by chance** : por casualidad

chancellor [ˈtʃænʦələr] *n* **1** : canciller *m* **2** : rector *m*, -tora *f* (de una universidad)

chancy [ˈtʃænʦi] *adj* **chancier; -est** : riesgoso, arriesgado

chandelier [ˌʃændəˈlɪr] *n* : araña *f* de luces

change¹ [ˈtʃeɪndʒ] *v* **changed; changing** *vt* **1** ALTER : cambiar ⟨to change one's mind : cambiar de idea/opinión⟩ ⟨to change direction : cambiar de dirección⟩ **2** EXCHANGE, REPLACE : cambiar (pilas, etc.), cambiar de ⟨he changed the subject : cambió de tema⟩ ⟨to change jobs : cambiar de trabajo⟩ ⟨to change places : cambiar de sitio⟩ **3** : cambiar (dinero) ⟨can you change a twenty? : ¿me puedes cambiar un billete de veinte dólares?⟩ ⟨to change dollars into yen : cambiar dólares a yen⟩ **4** : cambiar ⟨I changed the baby, I changed the baby's diaper : le cambié el pañal al bebé⟩ ⟨to change the bed/sheets : cambiar las sábanas⟩ ⟨to change one's clothes : cambiarse (de ropa)⟩ **5 to change hands** : cambiar de manos/dueño — *vi* **1** : cambiar ⟨you haven't changed : no has cambiado⟩ **2** : cambiarse (de ropa) **3 to change over to** : cambiar a (otro sistema, etc.)

change² *n* **1** ALTERATION : cambio *m* ⟨a change for the better/worse : un cambio para mejor/peor⟩ ⟨for a change : para variar⟩ ⟨to make changes to : hacerle cambios a⟩ **2** REPLACEMENT, EXCHANGE : cambio *m* ⟨an oil change : un cambio de aceite⟩ ⟨a change of address : un cambio de dirección⟩ ⟨a change of scenery : un cambio de aire(s)⟩ ⟨a change of clothes : una muda de ropa⟩ **3** : cambio *m*, vuelto *m* ⟨two dollars change : dos dólares de vuelto⟩ ⟨do you have change for a twenty? : ¿tienes cambio de veinte dólares?⟩ **4** COINS : cambio *m*, monedas *fpl* ⟨loose change : dinero suelto⟩

changeable [ˈtʃeɪndʒəbəl] *adj* : cambiante, variable

changeless [ˈtʃeɪndʒləs] *adj* : invariable, constante

changeover [ˈtʃeɪndʒˌoːvər] *n* : cambio *m*

changing [ˈtʃeɪndʒɪŋ] *adj* : cambiante, variable

changing room *n* FITTING ROOM : probador *m*

changing table *n* : cambiador *m*

channel¹ [ˈtʃænəl] *vt* **-neled** *or* **-nelled; -neling** *or* **-nelling** : encauzar, canalizar

channel² *n* **1** RIVERBED : cauce *m* **2** STRAIT : canal *m*, estrecho *m* ⟨English Channel : Canal de la Mancha⟩ **3** COURSE, MEANS : vía *f*, conducto *m* ⟨the usual channels : las vías normales⟩ **4** : canal *m* (de televisión)

channel surfing *n* : zapping *m*

chant¹ [ˈtʃænt] *v* : salmodiar, cantar

chant² *n* **1** : salmodia *f* **2 Gregorian chant** : canto *m* gregoriano

Chanukah [ˈxɑnəkə, ˈhɑ–] → **Hanukkah**

chaos [ˈkeɪˌɑs] *n* : caos *m*

chaotic [keɪˈɑtɪk] *adj* : caótico — **chaotically** [-tɪkli] *adv*

chap *n* FELLOW : tipo *m*, hombre *m*

chapel [ˈtʃæpəl] *n* : capilla *f*

chaperon¹ *or* **chaperone** [ˈʃæpəˌroːn] *vt* **-oned; -oning** : ir de chaperón, acompañar

chaperon² *or* **chaperone** *n* : chaperón *m*, -rona *f*; acompañante *mf*

chaplain [ˈtʃæplɪn] *n* : capellán *m*

chapped [ˈtʃæpt] *adj* : agrietado ⟨chapped lips : labios agrietados⟩

chapter [ˈtʃæptər] *n* **1** : capítulo *m* (de un libro) **2** BRANCH : sección *f*, división *f* (de una organización)

char [ˈtʃɑr] *v* **charred; charring** *vt* **1** BURN : carbonizar **2** SCORCH : chamuscar — *vi* **1** : carbonizarse **2** : chamuscarse

character [ˈkærɪktər] *n* **1** LETTER, SYMBOL : carácter *m* ⟨Chinese characters : caracteres chinos⟩ **2** DISPOSITION : carácter *m*, personalidad *f* ⟨of good character : de buena reputación⟩ ⟨to build character : forjar el carácter⟩ **3** REPUTATION : carácter *m*, reputación *f* ⟨character attacks : ataques personales⟩ **4** NATURE, QUALITIES : carácter *m* ⟨the national character : el carácter nacional⟩ ⟨the character of the wine : el carácter del vino⟩ ⟨the room has no character : la habitación no tiene carácter⟩ **5** : tipo *m*, personaje *m* peculiar ⟨he's quite a character! : ¡él es algo serio!⟩ **6** : personaje *m* (ficticio) **7 to be in character** : ser típico de alguien **8 to be out of character** : no ser típico de alguien

characteristic¹ [ˌkærɪktəˈrɪstɪk] *adj* : característico, típico — **characteristically** [-tɪkli] *adv*

characteristic² *n* : característica *f*

characterization [ˌkærɪktərəˈzeɪʃən] *n* : caracterización *f*

characterize [ˈkærɪktəˌraɪz] *vt* **-ized; -izing** : caracterizar

charades [ʃəˈreɪdz] *ns & pl* : charada *f*

charcoal [ˈtʃɑrˌkoːl] *n* : carbón *m*

chard [ˈtʃɑrd] → **Swiss chard**

charge¹ [ˈtʃɑrdʒ] *v* **charged; charging** *vt* **1** : cargar ⟨to charge the batteries : cargar las pilas⟩ **2** ENTRUST : encomendar, encargar **3** COMMAND : ordenar, mandar **4** ACCUSE : acusar ⟨charged with robbery : acusado de robo⟩ **5** : cargar a una cuenta, comprar a crédito — *vi* **1** : cargar (contra el enemigo) ⟨charge! : ¡a la carga!⟩ **2** : cobrar ⟨they charge too much : cobran demasiado⟩

charge² *n* **1** : carga *f* (eléctrica) **2** : carga *f* (de dinamita, etc.) **3** BURDEN : carga *f*, peso *m* **4** RESPONSIBILITY : cargo *m*, responsabilidad *f* ⟨to take charge of : hacerse cargo de⟩ ⟨to be in charge : ser el responsable⟩ ⟨to be in charge of : tener a su cargo⟩ **5** : persona *f* al cuidado de alguien ⟨her young charges : los niños que están a su cargo⟩ **6** ACCUSATION : cargo *m*, acusación f ⟨to press charges : presentar cargos⟩ **7** COST : costo m, cargo m, precio m ⟨free of charge : gratis⟩ ⟨they gave it to us free of charge : nos lo regalaron gratuitamente⟩ **8** ATTACK : carga f, ataque m **9** to get a charge out of EN-JOY : disfrutar de, deleitarse con

chargeable [ˈtʃɑrdʒəbəl] adj **1** : perseguible (dícese de un delito) **2** ~ to : a cargo de (una cuenta)

charge card → credit card

charger [ˈtʃɑrdʒər] n : corcel m, caballo m (de guerra)

chariot [ˈtʃæriət] n : carro m (de guerra)

charisma [kəˈrɪzmə] n : carisma m

charismatic [ˌkærəzˈmætɪk] adj : carismático

charitable [ˈtʃærətəbəl] adj **1** GENEROUS : caritativo ⟨a charitable organization : una organización benéfica⟩ **2** KIND, UNDERSTANDING : generoso, benévolo, comprensivo — **charitably** [-bli] adv

charitableness [ˈtʃærətəbəlnəs] n : caridad f

charity [ˈtʃærəti] n, pl **-ties 1** GENEROS-ITY : caridad f **2** ALMS : caridad f, limosna f **3** : organización f benéfica, obra f de beneficencia

charlatan [ˈʃɑrlətən] n : charlatán m, -tana f; farsante mf

charley horse [ˈtʃɑrliˌhɔrs] n : calambre m

charm¹ [ˈtʃɑrm] vt : encantar, cautivar, fascinar

charm² n **1** AMULET : amuleto m, talismán m **2** ATTRACTION : encanto m, atractivo m ⟨it has a certain charm : tiene cierto atractivo⟩ **3** : dije m, colgante m ⟨charm bracelet : pulsera de dijes⟩

charmer [ˈtʃɑrmər] n : persona f encantadora

charming [ˈtʃɑrmɪŋ] adj : encantador, fascinante

chart¹ [ˈtʃɑrt] vt **1** : trazar un mapa de, hacer un gráfico de **2** PLAN : trazar, planear ⟨to chart a course : trazar un derrotero⟩

chart² n **1** MAP : carta f, mapa m **2** DIA-GRAM : gráfico m, cuadro m, tabla f

charter¹ [ˈtʃɑrtər] vt **1** : establecer los estatutos de (una organización) **2** RENT : alquilar, fletar

charter² adj : chárter ⟨a charter flight : un vuelo chárter⟩

charter³ n **1** STATUTES : estatutos mpl **2** CONSTITUTION : carta f, constitución f

chartreuse [ʃɑrˈtruːz, -ˈtruːs] n : color m verde-amarillo intenso

chary [ˈtʃæri] adj **charier; -est 1** WARY : cauteloso, precavido **2** SPARING : parco

chase¹ [ˈtʃeɪs] vt **chased; chasing 1** PURSUE : perseguir, ir a la caza de **2** DRIVE : ahuyentar, echar ⟨he chased the dog from the garden : ahuyentó al perro del jardín⟩ **3** : grabar (metales)

chase² n **1** PURSUIT : persecución f, caza f **2** the chase HUNTING : caza f

chaser [ˈtʃeɪsər] n **1** PURSUER : perse-

guidor m, -dora f **2** : bebida f que se toma después de un trago de licor

chasm [ˈkæzəm] n : abismo m, sima f

chassis [ˈtʃæsi, ˈʃæsi] n, pl **chassis** [-siz] : chasis m, armazón m

chaste [ˈtʃeɪst] adj **chaster; -est 1** : casto **2** MODEST : modesto, puro **3** AUSTERE : austero, sobrio

chastely [ˈtʃeɪstli] adv : castamente

chasten [ˈtʃeɪsən] vt : castigar, sancionar

chasteness [ˈtʃeɪstnəs] n **1** MODESTY : modestia f, castidad f **2** AUSTERITY : sobriedad f, austeridad f

chastise [ˈtʃæs.taɪz, tʃæsˈ-] vt **-tised; -tis-ing 1** REPRIMAND : reprender, corregir, reprobar **2** PUNISH : castigar

chastisement [ˈtʃæs.taɪzmənt, tʃæsˈtaɪz-, ˈtʃæstəz-] n : castigo m, corrección f

chastity [ˈtʃæstəti] n : castidad f, decencia f, modestia f

chat¹ [ˈtʃæt] vi **chatted; chatting** : charlar, platicar

chat² n : charla f, plática f

château [ʃæˈtoː] n, pl **-teaus** [-ˈtoːz] or **-teaux** [-ˈtoː, -ˈtoːz] : mansión f campestre

chat room n : chat m, sala f de chat

chattel [ˈtʃætəl] n : bienes fpl muebles, enseres mpl

chatter¹ [ˈtʃætər] vi **1** : castañetear (dícese de los dientes) **2** GAB : parlotear fam, cotorrear fam

chatter² n **1** CHATTERING : castañeteo m (de dientes) **2** GABBING : parloteo m fam, cotorreo m fam, cháchara f fam

chatterbox [ˈtʃætərˌbɑks] n : parlanchín m, -china f; charlatán m, -tana f; hablador m, -dora f

chatty [ˈtʃæti] adj **chattier; -est 1** TALKA-TIVE : parlanchín, charlatán **2** CONVER-SATIONAL : familiar, conversador ⟨a chatty letter : una carta llena de noticias⟩

chauffeur¹ [ˈʃoːfər, ʃoːˈfər] vi : trabajar de chofer privado — vt : hacer de chofer para

chauffeur² n : chofer m privado

chauvinism [ˈʃoːvəˌnɪzəm] n : chauvinismo m, patriotería f

chauvinist [ˈʃoːvənɪst] n : chauvinista mf; patriotero m, -ra f

chauvinistic [ˌʃoːvəˈnɪstɪk] adj : chauvinista, patriotero

cheap¹ [ˈtʃiːp] adv : barato ⟨to sell cheap : vender barato⟩

cheap² adj **1** INEXPENSIVE : barato, económico **2** SHODDY : barato, mal hecho **3** STINGY : tacaño, agarrado fam, codo Mex

cheapen [ˈtʃiːpən] vt : degradar, rebajar

cheaply [ˈtʃiːpli] adv : barato, a precio bajo

cheapness [ˈtʃiːpnəs] n **1** : precio m bajo **2** STINGINESS : tacañería f

cheapskate [ˈtʃiːpˌskeɪt] n : tacaño m, -ña f; codo m, -da f Mex

cheat¹ [ˈtʃiːt] vt **1** : defraudar, estafar, engañar **2** to cheat on : engañar (a un/una amante) — vi : hacer trampa

cheat² n **1** CHEATING : engaño m, fraude m, trampa f **2** → **cheater**

cheater [ˈtʃiːt̬ər] n : estafador m, -dora f; tramposo m, -sa f

check¹ [ˈtʃɛk] vt 1 VERIFY : verificar, comprobar (la ortografía, etc.) 2 IN-SPECT : revisar, chequear, inspeccionar 3 CONSULT : consultar, chequear ⟨let me check the files : déjame chequear los archivos⟩ 4 HALT : frenar, parar, detener 5 RESTRAIN : refrenar, contener, reprimir 6 MARK : marcar, señalar 7 or to check in : chequear, facturar (maletas, equipaje) 8 CHECKER : marcar con cuadros 9 to check off : marcar (algo en una lista) 10 to check out INVESTIGATE : investigar 11 to check out fam LOOK AT : mirar 12 to check out SIGN OUT : sacar (libros) 13 to check out RING UP : cobrar (en una tienda) — vi 1 VERIFY : comprobar, verificar 2 to check back with fam : volver a contactar ⟨I'll check back with you later : te llamaré/hablaré (etc.) más tarde⟩ 3 to check in : registrarse (en un hotel) 4 to check into INVESTIGATE : investigar 5 to check off on APPROVE : aprobar 6 to check on : ir a ver, visitar, llamar ⟨she checks on the patients regularly : visita a los pacientes regularmente⟩ 7 to check out : pagar e irse (de un hotel) 8 to check out SQUARE : cuadrar 9 to check up on : vigilar, controlar 10 to check with : consultar

check² n 1 HALT : detención f súbita, parada f 2 RESTRAINT : control m, freno m 3 INSPECTION : verificación f, comprobación f, inspección f, chequeo m ⟨she gave the list a quick check : le echó una ojeada a la lista⟩ ⟨security/background check : verificación de identidad/antecedentes⟩ ⟨system check : comprobación del sistema⟩ ⟨sound check : prueba de sonido⟩ 4 : cheque m ⟨to pay by check : pagar con cheque⟩ 5 VOUCHER : resguardo m, comprobante m 6 BILL : cuenta f (en un restaurante) 7 : jaque m (en ajedrez) 8 or check mark : marca f 9 or check pattern : dibujo m a/de cuadros

checkbook [ˈtʃɛkˌbʊk] n : chequera f

checked adj : a/de cuadros

checker¹ [ˈtʃɛkər] vt : marcar con cuadros

checker² n 1 : pieza f (en el juego de damas) 2 : verificador m, -dora f 3 CASHIER : cajero m, -ra f

checkerboard [ˈtʃɛkərˌbord] n : tablero m de damas

checkered adj 1 → checked 2 TROU-BLED : accidentado

checkers [ˈtʃɛkərz] n : damas fpl

check-in [ˈtʃɛkˌɪn] n 1 : facturación f 2 or check-in desk/counter : mostrador m de facturación

checking account n : cuenta f corriente

checklist [ˈtʃɛkˌlɪst] n : lista f de control

checkmate [ˈtʃɛkˌmeɪt] vt -mated; -mating 1 : dar jaque mate a (en ajedrez) 2 THWART : frustrar, arruinar

checkmate² n : jaque mate m

checkout [ˈtʃɛkˌaʊt] n or checkout counter : caja f

checkpoint [ˈtʃɛkˌpɔɪnt] n : puesto m de control

checkroom [ˈtʃɛkˌruːm, -ˌrʊm] n : guardarropa m

checkup [ˈtʃɛkˌʌp] n : examen m médico, chequeo m

cheddar [ˈtʃɛdər] n : queso m Cheddar

cheek [ˈtʃiːk] n 1 : mejilla f, cachete m 2 IMPUDENCE : insolencia f, descaro m

cheekbone [ˈtʃiːkˌboːn] n : pómulo m

cheeked [ˈtʃiːkt] adj (used in combination) : de mejillas ⟨rosy-cheeked : de mejillas sonrosadas⟩

cheeky [ˈtʃiːki] adj cheekier; -est : descarado, insolente, atrevido

cheep¹ [ˈtʃiːp] vi : piar

cheep² n : pío m

cheer¹ [ˈtʃɪr] vt 1 ENCOURAGE : alentar, animar 2 GLADDEN : alegrar, levantar el ánimo a 3 ACCLAIM : aclamar, vitorear, echar porras a

cheer² n 1 CHEERFULNESS : alegría f, buen humor m, jovialidad f 2 APPLAUSE : aclamación f, ovación f, aplausos mpl ⟨three cheers for the chief! : ¡viva el jefe!⟩ 3 cheers! : ¡salud!

cheerful [ˈtʃɪrfəl] adj : alegre, de buen humor

cheerfully [ˈtʃɪrfəli] adv : alegremente, jovialmente

cheerfulness [ˈtʃɪrfəlnəs] n : buen humor m, alegría f

cheerily [ˈtʃɪrəli] adv : alegremente

cheeriness [ˈtʃɪrinəs] n : buen humor m, alegría f

cheerleader [ˈtʃɪrˌliːdər] n : porrista mf

cheerless [ˈtʃɪrləs] adj BLEAK : triste, sombrío

cheery [ˈtʃɪri] adj cheerier; -est : alegre, de buen humor

cheese [ˈtʃiːz] n : queso m

cheeseburger [ˈtʃiːzˌbərgər] n : hamburguesa f con queso

cheesecake [ˈtʃiːzˌkeɪk] n : tarta f de queso

cheesecloth [ˈtʃiːzˌklɔθ] n : estopilla f

cheesy [ˈtʃiːzi] adj cheesier; -est 1 : a queso 2 : que contiene queso 3 CHEAP : barato, de mala calidad

cheetah [ˈtʃiːt̬ə] n : guepardo m

chef [ˈʃɛf] n : chef m

chemical¹ [ˈkɛmɪkəl] adj : químico — **chemically** [-mɪkli] adv

chemical² n : sustancia f química

chemical weapon n : arma f química

chemise [ʃəˈmiːz] n 1 : camiseta f, prenda f interior de una pieza 2 : vestido m holgado

chemist [ˈkɛmɪst] n : químico m, -ca f

chemistry [ˈkɛmɪstri] n, pl -tries : química f

chemotherapy [ˌkiːmoˈθɛrəpi, ˌkɛmo-] n, pl -pies : quimioterapia f

cherish [ˈtʃɛrɪʃ] vt 1 VALUE : apreciar, valorar 2 HARBOR : abrigar, albergar

cherry [ˈtʃɛri] n, pl -ries 1 : cereza f (fruta) 2 : cerezo m (árbol)

cherub [ˈtʃɛrəb] n 1 pl -ubim [ˈtʃɛrəˌbɪm, ˈtʃɛrjə-] ANGEL : ángel m, querubín m 2 *pl* **-ubs** : niño *m* regordete, niña *f* regordeta

cherubic [tʃəˈruːbɪk] *adj* : querúbico, angelical

chess [ˈtʃɛs] *n* : ajedrez *m*

chessboard [ˈtʃɛsˌbord] *n* : tablero *m* de ajedrez

chessman [ˈtʃɛsmən, -ˌmæn] *n, pl* **-men** [-mən, -ˌmɛn] : pieza *f* de ajedrez

chest [ˈtʃɛst] *n* **1** : cofre *m*, baúl *m* **2** : pecho *m* ⟨chest pains : dolores de pecho⟩

chestnut [ˈtʃɛstˌnʌt] *n* **1** : castaña *f* (fruto) **2** : castaño *m* (árbol)

chest of drawers *n* : cómoda *f*

chevron [ˈʃɛvrən] *n* : galón *m* (de un oficial militar)

chew¹ [ˈtʃuː] *vt* **1** : masticar, mascar **2 to chew out** SCOLD : regañar **3 to chew the fat** CHAT : charlar, platicar **4 to chew up** : destrozar a mordiscos **5 to chew up** DESTROY : destrozar — *vi* **to chew on/over** THINK OVER : pensar

chew² *n* : algo que se masca (como tabaco)

chewing gum *n* : goma *f* de mascar, chicle *m*

chewy [ˈtʃuːi] *adj* **chewier; -est 1** : fibroso (dícese de las carnes o los vegetales) **2** : pegajoso, chicloso (dícese de los dulces)

chic¹ [ˈʃiːk] *adj* : chic, elegante, de moda

chic² *n* : chic *m*, elegancia *f*

Chicana [tʃɪˈkɑnə] *n* : chicana *f*

Chicano [tʃɪˈkɑno] *n* : chicano *m*, -na *f* — **Chicano** *adj*

chick [ˈtʃɪk] *n* **1** : pollito *m*, -ta *f*; polluelo *m* **2** *fam, sometimes offensive* : chica *f*; mujer *f*

chicken¹ [ˈtʃɪkən] *adj* : miedoso, cobarde

chicken² *n* **1** FOWL : pollo *m* **2** COWARD : cobarde *mf*

chickenhearted [ˈtʃɪkənˌhɑrtəd] *adj* : miedoso, cobarde

chicken out *vi fam* : acobardarse, rajarse

chicken pox *n* : varicela *f*

chickpea [ˈtʃɪkˌpiː] *n* : garbanzo *m*

chicle [ˈtʃɪkəl] *n* : chicle *m* (resina)

chicory [ˈtʃɪkəri] *n, pl* **-ries 1** : endibia *f* (para ensaladas) **2** : achicoria *f* (aditivo de café)

chide [ˈtʃaɪd] *vt* **chid** [ˈtʃɪd] *or* **chided; chid** *or* **chidden** [ˈtʃɪdən] *or* **chided; chiding** [ˈtʃaɪdɪŋ] : regañar, reprender

chief¹ [ˈtʃiːf] *adj* : principal, capital ⟨chief negotiator : negociador en jefe⟩ — **chiefly** *adv*

chief² *n* : jefe *m*, -fa *f* ⟨fire/police chief : jefe de bomberos/policía⟩

chief executive officer *n* → CEO

chieftain [ˈtʃiːftən] *n* : jefe *m*, -fa *f* (de una tribu)

chiffon [ʃɪˈfɑn, ˈʃɪ-] *n* : chifón *m*

chigger [ˈtʃɪgər] *n* : nigua *f*

chignon [ˈʃiːnˌjɑn, -ˌjɑn] *n* : moño *m*, chongo *m Mex*

child [ˈtʃaɪld] *n, pl* **children** [ˈtʃɪldrən] **1** BABY, YOUNGSTER : niño *m*, -ña *f*; criatura *f* **2 children** *npl* OFFSPRING : hijo *m*, -ja *f*; progenie *f*

childbearing¹ [ˈtʃaɪlbɛrɪŋ] *adj* : relativo al parto ⟨of childbearing age : en edad fértil⟩

childbearing² → **childbirth**

childbirth [ˈtʃaɪldˌbərθ] *n* : parto *m*

childcare [ˈtʃaɪldˌkær] *n* : cuidado *m* de los niños, puericultura *f*

childhood [ˈtʃaɪldˌhʊd] *n* : infancia *f*, niñez *f*

childish [ˈtʃaɪldɪʃ] *adj* : infantil, inmaduro — **childishly** *adv*

childishness [ˈtʃaɪldɪʃnəs] *n* : inmadurez *f*

childless [ˈtʃaɪldləs] *adj* : sin hijos

childlike [ˈtʃaɪldˌlaɪk] *adj* : infantil, inocente ⟨a childlike imagination : una imaginación infantil⟩

childproof [ˈtʃaɪldˌpruːf] *adj* : a prueba de niños

Chilean [ˈtʃɪliən, tʃɪˈleɪən] *n* : chileno *m*, -na *f* — **Chilean** *adj*

chili *or* **chile** *or* **chilli** [ˈtʃɪli] *n, pl* **chilies** *or* **chiles** *or* **chillies 1** *or* **chili pepper** : chile *m*, ají *m* **2** : chile *m* con carne

chill¹ [ˈtʃɪl] *v* : enfriar

chill² *adj* : frío, gélido ⟨a chill wind : un viento frío⟩

chill³ *n* **1** CHILLINESS : fresco *m*, frío *m* **2** SHIVER : escalofrío *m* **3** DAMPER : enfriamiento *m*, frío *m* ⟨to cast a chill over : enfriar⟩

chilliness [ˈtʃɪlinəs] *n* : frío *m*, fresco *m*

chilly [ˈtʃɪli] *adj* **chillier; -est** : frío ⟨it's chilly tonight : hace frío esta noche⟩

chime¹ [ˈtʃaɪm] *v* **chimed; chiming** *vt* : hacer sonar (una campana) — *vi* : sonar una campana, dar campanadas

chime² *n* **1** BELLS : juego *m* de campanitas sintonizadas, carillón *m* **2** PEAL : tañido *m*, campanada *f*

chime in *vi* : meterse en una conversación

chimera *or* **chimaera** [kaɪˈmɪrə, kə-] *n* : quimera *f*

chimney [ˈtʃɪmni] *n, pl* **-neys** : chimenea *f*

chimney sweep *n* : deshollinador *m*, -dora *f*

chimp [ˈtʃɪmp, ˈʃɪmp] → **chimpanzee**

chimpanzee [ˌtʃɪmˌpænˈziː, ˌʃɪm-; tʃɪmˈpænzi, ʃɪm-] *n* : chimpancé *m*

chin [ˈtʃɪn] *n* : barbilla *f*, mentón *m*, barba *f*, pera *f Arg, Chile, Uru*

china [ˈtʃaɪnə] *n* **1** PORCELAIN : porcelana *f*, loza *f* **2** CROCKERY, TABLEWARE : loza *f*, vajilla *f*

chinchilla [tʃɪnˈtʃɪlə] *n* : chinchilla *f*

Chinese¹ [ˈtʃaɪˈniːz, -ˈniːs] *adj* : chino

Chinese² *n* **1** : chino *m* (idioma) **2 the Chinese** (*used with a plural verb*) : los chinos

chink [ˈtʃɪŋk] *n* : grieta *f*, abertura *f*

chintz [ˈtʃɪnts] *n* : chintz *m*, chinz *m*

chip¹ [ˈtʃɪp] *v* **chipped; chipping** *vt* : desportillar, desconchar, astillar (madera) — *vi* : desportillarse, desconcharse, descascararse (dícese de la pintura, etc.)

chip² *n* **1** : astilla *f* (de madera o vidrio), lasca *f* (de piedra) ⟨he's a chip off the old block : de tal palo, tal astilla⟩ **2** : bocado *m* pequeño (en rodajas o rebanadas) ⟨tortilla chips : totopos, tortillitas

tostadas⟩ **3** : ficha *f* (de póker, etc.) **4**
NICK : mella *f* **5** : chip *m* ⟨memory chip
: chip de memoria⟩
chip in *v* CONTRIBUTE : contribuir
chipmunk [ˈtʃɪpˌmʌŋk] *n* : ardilla *f* listada
chipotle [tʃəˈpoːtleɪ, tʃi-] *n* : chipotle *m*
chipper [ˈtʃɪpər] *adj* : alegre y vivaz
chiropodist [kəˈrɑpədɪst, ʃə-] *n* : podólogo
m, -ga *f*
chiropody [kəˈrɑpədi, ʃə-] *n* : podología *f*
chiropractic [ˈkaɪrəˌpræktɪk] *n* : quiropráctica *f*
chiropractor [ˈkaɪrəˌpræktər] *n* : quiropráctico *m*, -ca *f*
chirp[1] [ˈtʃərp] *vi* : gorjear (dícese de los
pájaros), chirriar (dícese de los grillos)
chirp[2] *n* : gorjeo *m* (de un pájaro), chirrido *m* (de un grillo)
chisel[1] [ˈtʃɪzəl] *vt* **-eled** *or* **-elled; -eling** *or*
-elling **1** : cincelar, tallar, labrar **2**
CHEAT : estafar, defraudar
chisel[2] *n* : cincel *m* (para piedras y metales), escoplo *m* (para madera), formón *f*
chiseler [ˈtʃɪzələr] *n* SWINDLER : estafador *m*, -dora *f*; fraude *mf*
chit [ˈtʃɪt] *n* : resguardo *m*, recibo *m*
chitchat [ˈtʃɪtˌtʃæt] *n* : cotorreo *m*, charla
f
chivalric [ʃəˈvælrɪk] → **chivalrous**
chivalrous [ˈʃɪvəlrəs] *adj* **1** KNIGHTLY
: caballeresco, relativo a la caballería **2**
GENTLEMANLY : caballeroso, honesto,
cortés
chivalrousness [ˈʃɪvəlrəsnəs] *n* : caballerosidad *f*, cortesía *f*
chivalry [ˈʃɪvəlri] *n, pl* **-ries 1**
KNIGHTHOOD : caballería *f* **2** CHIVAL-
ROUSNESS : caballerosidad *f*, nobleza *f*,
cortesía *f*
chive [ˈtʃaɪv] *n* : cebollino *m*
chloride [ˈklorˌaɪd] *n* : cloruro *m*
chlorinate [ˈklorəˌneɪt] *vt* **-nated; -nating**
: clorar
chlorination [ˌklorəˈneɪʃən] *n* : cloración *f*
chlorine [ˈklorˌiːn] *n* : cloro *m*
chloroform [ˈklorəˌfɔrm] *n* : cloroformo
m
chlorophyll [ˈklorəˌfɪl] *n* : clorofila *f*
chock-full [ˈtʃɑkˈful, ˈtʃʌk-] *adj* : colmado, repleto
chocolate [ˈtʃɑkələt, ˈtʃɔk-] *n* **1** : chocolate *m* **2** BONBON : bombón *m* **3**
: color *m* chocolate, marrón *m*
choice[1] [ˈtʃɔɪs] *adj* **choicer; choicest** : selecto, escogido, de primera calidad
choice[2] *n* **1** CHOOSING : elección *f*, selección *f* **2** OPTION : elección *f*, opción *f* ⟨I
have no choice : no tengo alternativa⟩ **3**
PREFERENCE : preferencia *f*, elección
f **4** VARIETY : variedad *f*, selección *f* ⟨a
wide choice : un gran surtido⟩
choir [ˈkwaɪr] *n* : coro *m*
choirboy [ˈkwaɪrˌbɔɪ] *n* : niño *m* de coro
choke[1] [ˈtʃoːk] *v* **choked; choking** *vt* **1**
ASPHYXIATE, STRANGLE : sofocar, asfix-
iar, ahogar, estrangular **2** BLOCK
: tapar, obstruir — *vi* **1** SUFFOCATE
: asfixiarse, sofocarse, ahogarse ⟨to
choke on food : atragantarse con
comida⟩ **2** CLOG : taparse, obstruirse

choke[2] *n* **1** CHOKING : estrangulación
f **2** : choke *m*, estárter *m* (de un motor)
choker [ˈtʃoːkər] *n* : gargantilla *f*
cholera [ˈkɑlərə] *n* : cólera *m*
cholesterol [kəˈlɛstəˌrɔl] *n* : colesterol *m*
choose [ˈtʃuːz] *v* **chose** [ˈtʃoːz]; **chosen**
[ˈtʃoːzən]; **choosing** *vt* **1** SELECT : escoger, elegir ⟨choose only one : escoja sólo
uno⟩ **2** DECIDE : decidir ⟨he chose to
leave : decidió irse⟩ **3** PREFER : preferir
⟨which one do you choose? : ¿cuál prefiere?⟩ — *vi* : escoger ⟨much to choose
from : mucho de donde escoger⟩
choosy *or* **choosey** [ˈtʃuːzi] *adj* **choos-
ier; -est** : exigente, remilgado
chop[1] [ˈtʃɑp] *vt* **chopped; chopping 1**
MINCE : picar, cortar, moler (carne) **2**
to chop down : cortar, talar (un árbol)
chop[2] *n* **1** CUT : hachazo *m* (con una hacha), tajo *m* (con una cuchilla) **2** BLOW
: golpe *m* (penetrante) ⟨karate chop
: golpe de karate⟩ **3** : chuleta *f* ⟨pork
chops : chuletas de cerdo⟩
chopper [ˈtʃɑpər] → **helicopter**
choppy [ˈtʃɑpi] *adj* **choppier; -est 1**
: agitado, picado (dícese del mar) **2** DIS-
CONNECTED : incoherente, inconexo
chops [ˈtʃɑps] *npl* **1** : quijada *f*, mandíbula *f*, boca *f* (de una persona) **2 to**
lick one's chops : relamerse
chopsticks [ˈtʃɑpˌstɪks] *npl* : palillos *mpl*
choral [ˈkorəl] *adj* : coral
chorale [kəˈræl, -ˈrɑl] *n* **1** : coral *f* (composición musical vocal) **2** CHOIR, CHO-
RUS : coral *f*, coro *m*
chord [ˈkɔrd] *n* **1** : acorde *m* (en
música) **2** : cuerda *f* (en anatomía o
geometría)
chore [ˈtʃor] *n* **1** TASK : tarea *f* rutinaria **2** BOTHER, NUISANCE : lata *f*
fam, fastidio *m* **3** **chores** *npl* WORK
: quehaceres *mpl*, faenas *fpl*
choreograph [ˈkoriəˌgræf] *vt* : coreografiar
choreographer [ˌkoriˈɑgrəfər] *n* : coreógrafo *m*, -fa *f*
choreographic [ˌkoriəˈgræfɪk] *adj*
: coreográfico
choreography [ˌkoriˈɑgrəfi] *n, pl* **-phies**
: coreografía *f*
chorister [ˈkorəstər] *n* : corista *mf*
chorizo [tʃəˈriːzo, -so] *n* : chorizo *m*
chortle[1] [ˈtʃɔrtəl] *vi* **-tled; -tling** : reírse
(con satisfacción o júbilo)
chortle[2] *n* : risa *f* (de satisfacción o júbilo)
chorus[1] [ˈkorəs] *vt* : corear
chorus[2] *n* **1** : coro *m* (grupo o composición musical) **2** REFRAIN : coro *m*,
estribillo *m*
chose → **choose**
chosen [ˈtʃoːzən] *adj* : elegido, selecto
chow [ˈtʃaʊ] *n* **1** FOOD : comida *f* **2**
: chow-chow *mf* (perro)
chowder [ˈtʃaʊdər] *n* : sopa *f* de pescado
Christ [ˈkraɪst] *n* **1** : Cristo *m* **2 for**
Christ's sake : ¡por Dios!
christen [ˈkrɪsən] *vt* **1** BAPTIZE : bautizar **2** NAME : bautizar con el nombre de
Christendom [ˈkrɪsəndəm] *n* : cristiandad
f

christening [ˈkrɪsənɪŋ] n : bautismo m, bautizo m
Christian¹ [ˈkrɪstʃən] adj : cristiano
Christian² n : cristiano m, -na f
Christianity [ˌkrɪstʃiˈænəti, ˌkrɪsˈtʃæ-] n : cristianismo m
Christian name n : nombre m de pila
Christmas [ˈkrɪsməs] n : Navidad f ⟨Christmas season : las Navidades⟩
Christmas carol n → carol²
Christmas eve n : Nochebuena f
chromatic [kroˈmætɪk] adj : cromático ⟨chromatic scale : escala cromática⟩
chrome [ˈkroːm] n : cromo m (metal)
chromium [ˈkroːmiəm] n : cromo m (elemento)
chromosome [ˈkroːməˌsoːm, -ˌzoːm] n : cromosoma m
chronic [ˈkrɑnɪk] adj : crónico — **chronically** [-nɪkli] adv
chronicle¹ [ˈkrɑnɪkəl] vt -cled; -cling : escribir (una crónica o historia)
chronicle² n : crónica f, historia f
chronicler [ˈkrɑnɪklər] n : historiador m, -dora f; cronista mf
chronological [ˌkrɑnəlˈɑdʒɪkəl] adj : cronológico — **chronologically** [-kli] adv
chronology [krəˈnɑlədʒi] n, pl -gies : cronología f
chronometer [krəˈnɑmətər] n : cronómetro m
chrysalis [ˈkrɪsələs] n, pl **chrysalides** [krɪˈsæləˌdiz] or **chrysalises** : crisálida f
chrysanthemum [krɪˈsænθəməm] n : crisantemo m
chubbiness [ˈtʃʌbinəs] n : gordura f
chubby [ˈtʃʌbi] adj **chubbier; -est** : gordito, regordete, rechoncho
chuck¹ [ˈtʃʌk] vt 1 TOSS : tirar, lanzar, aventar Col, Mex 2 to chuck under the chin : hacer la mamola
chuck² n 1 PAT : mamola f, palmada f 2 TOSS : lanzamiento m 3 or **chuck steak** : corte m de carne de res
chuckle¹ [ˈtʃʌkəl] vi -led; -ling : reírse entre dientes
chuckle² n : risita f, risa f ahogada
chug [ˈtʃʌɡ] vi **chugged; chugging** : resoplar, traquetear
chum¹ [ˈtʃʌm] vi **chummed; chumming** : ser camaradas, ser cuates Mex fam
chum² n : amigo m, -ga f; camarada mf; compinche mf fam
chummy [ˈtʃʌmi] adj **chummier; -est** : amistoso ⟨they're very chummy : son muy amigos⟩
chump [ˈtʃʌmp] n : tonto m, -ta f; idiota mf
chunk [ˈtʃʌŋk] n 1 PIECE : cacho m, pedazo m, trozo m 2 : cantidad f grande ⟨a chunk of money : mucho dinero⟩
chunky [ˈtʃʌŋki] adj **chunkier; -est** 1 STOCKY : fornido, robusto 2 : que contiene pedazos
church [ˈtʃərtʃ] n 1 : iglesia f ⟨to go to church : ir a la iglesia⟩ 2 CHRISTIANS : iglesia f, conjunto m de fieles cristianos 3 DENOMINATION : confesión f, secta f 4 CONGREGATION : feligreses mpl, fieles mpl

churchgoer [ˈtʃərtʃˌgoːər] n : practicante mf
churchyard [ˈtʃərtʃˌjɑrd] n : cementerio m (junto a una iglesia)
churn¹ [ˈtʃərn] vt 1 : batir (crema), hacer (mantequilla) 2 : agitar con fuerza, revolver 3 to churn out : producir en masa — vi : agitarse, arremolinarse
churn² n : mantequera f
chute [ˈʃuːt] n : conducto m inclinado, vertedero m (para basuras)
chutney [ˈtʃʌtni] n, pl -neys : chutney m
chutzpah [ˈhʊtspə, ˈxʊt-, -ˌspɑ] n : descaro m, frescura f, cara f fam
cicada [səˈkeɪdə, -ˈkɑ-] n : cigarra f, chicharra f
cider [ˈsaɪdər] n 1 : jugo m (de manzana, etc.) 2 hard cider : sidra f
cigar [sɪˈɡɑr] n : puro m, cigarro m
cigarette [ˌsɪɡəˈrɛt, ˈsɪɡəˌrɛt] n : cigarrillo m, cigarro m
cilantro [sɪˈlɑntro, -ˈlæn-] n : cilantro m
cinch¹ [ˈsɪntʃ] vt 1 : cinchar (un caballo) 2 ASSURE : asegurar
cinch² n 1 : cincha f (para caballos) 2 : algo fácil o seguro ⟨it's a cinch : es bien fácil, es pan comido⟩
cinchona [sɪŋˈkoːnə] n : quino m
cinder [ˈsɪndər] n 1 EMBER : brasa f, ascua f 2 cinders npl ASHES : cenizas fpl
cinema [ˈsɪnəmə] n : cine m
cinematic [ˌsɪnəˈmætɪk] adj : cinematográfico
cinematography [ˌsɪnəməˈtɑɡrəfi] n : cinematografía f
cinephile [ˈsɪnəˌfaɪl] n : cinéfilo m, -fila f
cinnamon [ˈsɪnəmən] n : canela f
cipher [ˈsaɪfər] n 1 ZERO : cero m 2 CODE : cifra f, clave f
circa [ˈsərkə] prep : alrededor de, hacia ⟨circa 1800 : hacia el año 1800⟩
circle¹ [ˈsərkəl] v -cled; -cling vt 1 : encerrar en un círculo, poner un círculo alrededor de 2 : girar alrededor de, dar vueltas a ⟨we circled the building twice : le dimos vueltas al edificio dos veces⟩ — vi : dar vueltas
circle² n 1 : círculo m 2 CYCLE : ciclo m ⟨to come full circle : volver al punto de partida⟩ 3 GROUP : círculo m, grupo m (social) 4 to have (dark) circles under one's eyes : tener ojeras
circuit [ˈsərkət] n 1 BOUNDARY : circuito m, perímetro m (de una zona o un territorio) 2 TOUR : circuito m, recorrido m, tour m 3 : circuito m (eléctrico) ⟨a short circuit : un cortocircuito⟩
circuitous [ˌsərˈkjuːətəs] adj : sinuoso, tortuoso
circuitry [ˈsərkətri] n, pl -ries : sistema m de circuitos
circular¹ [ˈsərkjələr] adj ROUND : circular, redondo
circular² n : circular f
circulate [ˈsərkjəˌleɪt] v -lated; -lating vi : circular — vt 1 : circular (noticias, etc.) 2 DISSEMINATE : hacer circular, divulgar
circulation [ˌsərkjəˈleɪʃən] n : circulación f

circulatory ['sərkjələ,tori] *adj* : circulatorio

circumcise ['sərkəm,saɪz] *vt* -cised; -cising : circuncidar

circumcision [,sərkəm'sɪʒən, 'sərkəm,-] *n* : circuncisión *f*

circumference [sər'kʌmpfrən/s] *n* : circunferencia *f*

circumflex ['sərkəm,flɛks] *n* : acento *m* circunflejo

circumlocution [,sərkəmlo'kju:ʃən] *n* : circunlocución *f*

circumnavigate [,sərkəm'nævə,geɪt] *vt* -gated; -gating : circunnavegar

circumscribe ['sərkəm,skraɪb] *vt* -scribed; -scribing 1 : circunscribir, trazar una figura alrededor de 2 LIMIT : circunscribir, limitar

circumspect ['sərkəm,spɛkt] *adj* : circunspecto, prudente, cauto

circumstance ['sərkəm,stæn/s] *n* 1 EVENT : circunstancia *f*, acontecimiento *m* 2 circumstances *npl* SITUATION : circunstancias *fpl*, situación *f* ⟨under the circumstances : dadas las circunstancias⟩ ⟨under no circumstances : de ninguna manera, bajo ningún concepto⟩ 3 circumstances *npl* : situación *f* económica

circumstantial [,sərkəm'stæntʃəl] *adj* : circunstancial

circumvent [,sərkəm'vɛnt] *vt* : evadir, burlar (una ley o regla), sortear (una responsabilidad o dificultad)

circumvention [,sərkəm'vɛntʃən] *n* : evasión *f*

circus ['sərkəs] *n* : circo *m*

cirrhosis [sə'ro:sɪs] *n*, *pl* -rhoses [-'ro:,si:z] : cirrosis *f*

cis ['sɪs] → cisgender

cisgender [(,)sɪs'dʒɛndər] *adj* : cisgénero ⟨cisgender people : las personas cisgénero⟩

cistern ['sɪstərn] *n* : cisterna *f*, aljibe *m*

citadel ['sɪtədəl, -,dɛl] *n* FORTRESS : ciudadela *f*, fortaleza *f*

citation [saɪ'teɪʃən] *n* 1 SUMMONS : emplazamiento *m*, citación *f*, convocatoria *f* (judicial) 2 QUOTATION : cita *f* 3 COMMENDATION : elogio *m*, mención *f* (de honor)

cite ['saɪt] *vt* cited; citing 1 ARRAIGN, SUBPOENA : emplazar, citar, hacer comparecer (ante un tribunal) 2 QUOTE : citar 3 COMMEND : elogiar, honrar (oficialmente)

citizen ['sɪtəzən] *n* : ciudadano *m*, -na *f*

citizenry ['sɪtəzənri] *n*, *pl* -ries : ciudadanía *f*, conjunto *m* de ciudadanos

citizenship ['sɪtəzən,ʃɪp] *n* : ciudadanía *f* ⟨Nicaraguan citizenship : ciudadanía nicaragüense⟩

citrus ['sɪtrəs] *n*, *pl* -rus *or* -ruses : cítrico *m*

city ['sɪti] *n*, *pl* cities : ciudad *f*

civic ['sɪvɪk] *adj* : cívico

civic-minded ['sɪvɪk'maɪndəd] *adj* : cívico

civics ['sɪvɪks] *ns & pl* : civismo *m*

civil ['sɪvəl] *adj* 1 : civil ⟨civil law : derecho civil⟩ 2 POLITE : civil, cortés

civilian [sə'vɪljən] *n* : civil *mf* ⟨soldiers and civilians : soldados y civiles⟩

civility [sə'vɪləti] *n*, *pl* -ties : cortesía *f*, educación *f*

civilization [,sɪvələ'zeɪʃən] *n* : civilización *f*

civilize ['sɪvə,laɪz] *vt* -lized; -lizing : civilizar — civilized *adj*

civil liberties *npl* : derechos *mpl* civiles

civilly ['sɪvəli] *adv* : cortésmente

civil rights *npl* : derechos *mpl* civiles

civil servant *n* : funcionario *m*, -ria *f*

civil service *n* : administración *f* pública

civil war *n* : guerra *f* civil

clack¹ ['klæk] *vi* : tabletear

clack² *n* : tableteo *m*

clad ['klæd] *adj* 1 CLOTHED : vestido 2 COVERED : cubierto

claim¹ ['kleɪm] *vt* 1 DEMAND : reclamar, reivindicar ⟨she claimed her rights : reclamó sus derechos⟩ 2 MAINTAIN : afirmar, sostener ⟨they claim it's theirs : sostienen que es suyo⟩

claim² *n* 1 DEMAND : demanda *f*, reclamación *f* 2 DECLARATION : declaración *f*, afirmación *f* 3 to stake a claim : reclamar, reivindicar

claimant ['kleɪmənt] *n* : demandante *mf* (ante un juez), pretendiente *mf* (al trono, etc.)

clairvoyance [klær'vɔɪənts] *n* : clarividencia *f*

clairvoyant¹ [klær'vɔɪənt] *adj* : clarividente

clairvoyant² *n* : clarividente *mf*

clam ['klæm] *n* : almeja *f*

clamber ['klæmbər] *vi* : treparse o subirse torpemente

clammy ['klæmi] *adj* clammier; -est : húmedo y algo frío

clamor¹ ['klæmər] *vi* : gritar, clamar

clamor² *n* : clamor *m*

clamorous ['klæmərəs] *adj* : clamoroso, ruidoso, estrepitoso

clamp¹ ['klæmp] *vt* : sujetar con abrazaderas

clamp² *n* : abrazadera *f*

clam up *vi fam* : callarse, negarse a hablar

clan ['klæn] *n* : clan *m*

clandestine [klæn'dɛstɪn] *adj* : clandestino, secreto

clang¹ ['klæŋ] *vi* : hacer resonar (dícese de un objeto metálico)

clang² *n* : ruido *m* metálico fuerte

clangor ['klæŋər, -,gər] *n* : estruendo *m* metálico

clank¹ ['klæŋk] *vi* : producir un ruido metálico seco

clank² *n* : ruido *m* metálico seco

clap¹ ['klæp] *v* clapped; clapping *vt* 1 SLAP, STRIKE : golpear ruidosamente, dar una palmada ⟨to clap one's hands : batir palmas, dar palmadas⟩ 2 APPLAUD : aplaudir — *vi* APPLAUD : aplaudir

clap² *n* 1 SLAP : palmada *f*, golpecito *m* 2 NOISE : ruido *m* seco ⟨a clap of thunder : un trueno⟩

clapboard ['klæbərd, 'klæp,bord] *n* : tabla *f* de madera (para revestir muros)

clapper ['klæpər] *n* : badajo *m* (de una campana)

clapping ['klæpɪŋ] *n* : aplausos *mpl*

clarification [ˌklærəfə'keɪʃən] *n* : clarificación *f*

clarify ['klærəˌfaɪ] *vt* **-fied; -fying 1** EXPLAIN : aclarar **2** : clarificar (un líquido)

clarinet [ˌklærə'nɛt] *n* : clarinete *m*

clarion ['klæriən] *adj* : claro y sonoro

clarity ['klærəti] *n* : claridad *f*, nitidez *f*

clash¹ ['klæʃ] *vi* **1** : sonar, chocarse ⟨the cymbals clashed : los platillos sonaron⟩ **2** : chocar, enfrentarse ⟨the students clashed with the police : los estudiantes se enfrentaron con la policía⟩ **3** CONFLICT : estar en conflicto, oponerse **4** : desentonar (dícese de los colores), coincidir (dícese de los datos)

clash² *n* **1** : ruido *m* (producido por un choque) **2** CONFLICT, CONFRONTATION : enfrentamiento *m*, conflicto *m*, choque *m*

clasp¹ ['klæsp] *vt* **1** FASTEN : sujetar, abrochar **2** EMBRACE, GRASP : agarrar, sujetar, abrazar

clasp² *n* **1** FASTENING : broche *m*, cierre *m* **2** EMBRACE, SQUEEZE : apretón *m*, abrazo *m*

class¹ ['klæs] *vt* : clasificar, catalogar

class² *n* **1** KIND, TYPE : clase *f*, tipo *m*, especie *f* **2** : clase *f*, rango *m* social ⟨the working class : la clase obrera⟩ **3** LESSON : clase *f*, curso *m* ⟨English class : clase de inglés⟩ ⟨to take a class : tomar/hacer un curso⟩ **4** : clase *f* ⟨she told the whole class : se lo dijo a toda la clase⟩ ⟨the class of '97 : la promoción del 97⟩ **5** STYLE : clase *f*, estilo *m* **6** : clase *f* (en un vuelo) ⟨business class : clase ejecutiva⟩

classic¹ ['klæsɪk] *adj* : clásico

classic² *n* : clásico *m*, obra *f* clásica

classical ['klæsɪkəl] *adj* : clásico — **classically** [-kli] *adv*

classicism ['klæsəˌsɪzəm] *n* : clasicismo *m*

classification [ˌklæsəfə'keɪʃən] *n* : clasificación *f*

classified ['klæsəˌfaɪd] *adj* **1** : clasificado ⟨classified ads : avisos clasificados⟩ **2** RESTRICTED : confidencial, secreto ⟨classified documents : documentos secretos⟩

classify ['klæsəˌfaɪ] *vt* **-fied; -fying** : clasificar, catalogar

classless ['klæsləs] *adj* : sin clases

classmate ['klæsˌmeɪt] *n* : compañero *m*, -ra *f* de clase

classroom ['klæsˌruːm] *n* : aula *f*, salón *m* de clase

classy ['klæsi] *adj* **classier; -est** : con clase

clatter¹ ['klætər] *vi* : traquetear, hacer ruido

clatter² *n* : traqueteo *m*, ruido *m*, estrépito *m*

clause ['klɔz] *n* : cláusula *f*

claustrophobia [ˌklɔstrə'foːbiə] *n* : claustrofobia *f*

claustrophobic [ˌklɔstrə'foːbɪk] *adj* : claustrofóbico

clavicle ['klævɪkəl] *n* : clavícula *f*

claw¹ ['klɔ] *v* : arañar

claw² *n* : garra *f*, uña *f* (de un gato), pinza *f* (de un crustáceo)

clay ['kleɪ] *n* : arcilla *f*, barro *m*

clean¹ ['kliːn] *vt* **1** *or* to clean up : limpiar ⟨to clean oneself up : lavarse⟩ **2** : limpiar (pescado, etc.) **3** to clean one's plate : comérselo todo **4** to clean out : limpiar y ordenar (un lugar) **5** to clean out : dejar pelado, limpiar, robarle todo — *vi* **1** *or* to clean up : limpiar ⟨to clean up after dinner : lavar los platos/trastes⟩ ⟨I'm not cleaning up after you : no voy a limpiar lo que tú ensucias⟩ **2** to clean up : hacerse su agosto, enriquecerse

clean² *adv* : limpio, limpiamente ⟨to play clean : jugar limpio⟩

clean³ *adj* **1** : limpio **2** UNADULTERATED : puro ⟨clean water : agua pura⟩ **3** IRREPROACHABLE : intachable, sin mancha ⟨to have a clean record : no tener antecedentes penales⟩ **4** GREEN : limpio ⟨clean energy : energía limpia⟩ **5** CLEAR, SHARP : claro, nítido ⟨clean lines : líneas sencillas/puras⟩ **6** DECENT : decente **7** COMPLETE : completo, absoluto ⟨a clean break with the past : un corte radical con el pasado⟩

cleaner ['kliːnər] *n* **1** : limpiador *m*, -dora *f* **2** : producto *m* de limpieza ⟨glass/window cleaner : limpiavidrios⟩ **3** DRY CLEANER : tintorería *f* ⟨the cleaner/cleaner's/cleaners : la tintorería⟩

cleaning ['kliːnɪŋ] *n* : limpieza *f*

cleanliness ['klɛnlinəs] *n* : limpieza *f*, aseo *m*

cleanly¹ ['kliːnli] *adv* : limpiamente, con limpieza

cleanly² ['klɛnli] *adj* **cleanlier; -est** : limpio, pulcro

cleanness ['kliːnnəs] *n* : limpieza *f*

cleanse ['klɛnz] *vt* **cleansed; cleansing** : limpiar, purificar

cleanser ['klɛnzər] *n* : limpiador *m*, purificador *m*

clean sweep *n* : barrida *f* (en una competencia)

clear¹ ['klɪr] *vt* **1** CLARIFY : aclarar, clarificar (un líquido) **2** : despejar (una superficie), desatascar (un tubo), desmontar (una selva) ⟨to clear the table : levantar la mesa⟩ ⟨to clear a path : abrir un camino⟩ ⟨to clear a space por : hacer lugar para⟩ ⟨to clear one's throat : carraspear, aclararse la voz⟩ **3** EMPTY, EVACUATE : vaciar, evacuar **4** EXONERATE : absolver, limpiar el nombre de **5** EARN : ganar, sacar (una ganancia de) **6** : pasar sin tocar ⟨he cleared the hurdle : saltó por encima de la valla⟩ **7** AUTHORIZE : autorizar **8** to clear away : poner en su sitio **9** to clear off : quitar de ⟨let me clear (the papers) off the table : déjame quitar los papeles de la mesa⟩ **10** to clear out : ordenar **11** to clear up RESOLVE : aclarar, resolver, esclarecer

— *vi* **1** DISPERSE : irse, despejarse, disiparse **2** : ser compensado (dícese de un cheque) **3 to clear up** : despejar (dícese del tiempo), mejorarse (dícese de una enfermedad)

clear² *adv* : claro, claramente

clear³ *adj* **1** BRIGHT : claro, lúcido **2** FAIR : claro, despejado **3** TRANSPARENT : transparente, translúcido **4** EVIDENT, UNMISTAKABLE : claro, evidente, obvio ⟨a clear explanation : una explicación clara⟩ ⟨is that clear?, do I make myself clear? : ¿está claro?⟩ ⟨I want to be clear : (quiero) que quede claro⟩ **5** SHARP : claro, nítido **6** CERTAIN : seguro ⟨to be clear on something : entender algo⟩ **7** ALERT : despejado, lúcido ⟨to have a clear head : estar despejado⟩ **8** : despejado (dícese de las vías, etc.) ⟨keep the area clear of clutter : mantener la zona libre de objetos⟩

clear⁴ *n* **1 in the clear** : inocente, libre de toda sospecha **2 in the clear** SAFE : fuera de peligro

clearance ['klɪrənts] *n* **1** CLEARING : despeje *m* **2** SPACE : espacio *m* (libre), margen *m* **3** AUTHORIZATION : autorización *f*, despacho *m* (de la aduana)

clear-cut ['klɪr'kʌt] *adj* : bien definido

clearing ['klɪrɪŋ] *n* : claro *m* (de un bosque)

clearly ['klɪrli] *adv* **1** DISTINCTLY : claramente, directamente **2** OBVIOUSLY : obviamente, evidentemente

cleat ['kli:t] *n* **1** : taco *m* **2 cleats** *npl* : zapatos *mpl* deportivos (con tacos)

cleavage ['kli:vɪdʒ] *n* **1** CLEFT : hendidura *f*, raja *f* **2** : escote *m* (del busto)

cleave¹ ['kli:v] *vi* cleaved ['kli:vd] *or* clove ['klo:v]; cleaving ADHERE : adherirse, unirse

cleave² *vt* cleaved; cleaving SPLIT : hender, dividir, partir

cleaver ['kli:vər] *n* : cuchilla *f* de carnicero

clef ['klɛf] *n* : clave *f*

cleft ['klɛft] *n* : hendidura *f*, raja *f*, grieta *f*

clemency ['klɛməntsi] *n* : clemencia *f*

clement ['klɛmənt] *adj* **1** MERCIFUL : clemente, piadoso **2** MILD : clemente, apacible

clench ['klɛntʃ] *vt* **1** CLUTCH : agarrar **2** TIGHTEN : apretar (el puño, los dientes)

clergy ['klərdʒi] *n*, *pl* -gies : clero *m*

clergyman ['klərdʒimən] *n*, *pl* -men [-mən, -ˌmɛn] : clérigo *m*

cleric ['klɛrɪk] *n* : clérigo *m*, -ga *f*

clerical ['klɛrɪkəl] *adj* **1** : clerical ⟨a clerical collar : un alzacuello⟩ **2** : de oficina ⟨clerical staff : personal de oficina⟩

clerk¹ ['klərk, *Brit* 'klɑrk] *vi* : trabajar de oficinista, trabajar de dependiente

clerk² *n* **1** : funcionario *m*, -ria *f* (de una oficina gubernamental) **2** : oficinista *mf*, empleado *m*, -da *f* de oficina **3** SALESPERSON : dependiente *m*, -ta *f*

clever ['klɛvər] *adj* **1** SKILLFUL : ingenioso, hábil **2** SMART : listo, inteligente, astuto

cleverly ['klɛvərli] *adv* **1** SKILLFULLY

: ingeniosamente, hábilmente **2** INTELLIGENTLY : inteligentemente

cleverness ['klɛvərnəs] *n* **1** SKILL : ingenio *m*, habilidad *f* **2** INTELLIGENCE : inteligencia *f*

clew ['klu:] → **clue**

cliché [kli:'ʃeɪ] *n* : cliché *m*, tópico *m*

click¹ ['klɪk] *vt* **1** : chasquear (los dedos, etc.) ⟨to click one's heels : dar un taconazo⟩ **2** : hacer clic/click en (un botón, etc.) — *vi* **1** : hacer clic/click **2** SNAP : chasquear **3** SUCCEED : tener éxito **4** GET ALONG : congeniar, llevarse bien

click² *n* **1** : chasquido *m* (de los dedos, etc.) **2** : clic *m*, click *m* (de un botón, etc.)

client ['klaɪənt] *n* : cliente *m*, -ta *f*

clientele [ˌklaɪən'tɛl, ˌkli:-] *n* : clientela *f*

cliff ['klɪf] *n* : acantilado *m*, precipicio *m*, risco *m*

climate ['klaɪmət] *n* : clima *m*

climatic [klaɪ'mætɪk, klə-] *adj* : climático

climax¹ ['klaɪˌmæks] *vi* : llegar al punto culminante, culminar — *vt* : ser el punto culminante de

climax² *n* : clímax *m*, punto *m* culminante

climb¹ ['klaɪm] *vt* : escalar, trepar a, subir a ⟨to climb a mountain : escalar una montaña⟩ — *vi* **1** RISE : subir, ascender ⟨prices are climbing : los precios están subiendo⟩ **2** : subirse, treparse ⟨to climb up a tree : treparse a un árbol⟩

climb² *n* : ascenso *m*, subida *f*

climber ['klaɪmər] *n* **1** : escalador *m*, -dora *f* ⟨a mountain climber : un alpinista⟩ **2** : trepadora *f* (planta)

climbing ['klaɪmɪŋ] *n* MOUNTAINEERING : montañismo *m*, alpinismo *m*

clinch¹ ['klɪntʃ] *vt* **1** FASTEN, SECURE : remachar (un clavo), afianzar, abrochar **2** SETTLE : decidir, cerrar ⟨to clinch the title : ganar el título⟩

clinch² *n* : abrazo *m*, clinch *m* (en el boxeo)

clincher ['klɪntʃər] *n* : argumento *m* decisivo

cling ['klɪŋ] *vi* clung ['klʌŋ]; clinging **1** STICK : adherirse, pegarse **2** : aferrarse, agarrarse ⟨he clung to the railing : se aferró a la barandilla⟩

clingy ['klɪŋi] *adj* clingier; -est **1** : ajustado, ceñido (dícese de la ropa) **2** : pegajoso (dícese de una persona)

clinic ['klɪnɪk] *n* : clínica *f*

clinical ['klɪnɪkəl] *adj* : clínico — **clinically** [-kli] *adv*

clink¹ ['klɪŋk] *vi* : tintinear

clink² *n* : tintineo *m*

clip¹ ['klɪp] *vt* clipped; clipping **1** CUT : cortar, recortar **2** HIT : golpear, dar un puñetazo a **3** FASTEN : sujetar (con un clip)

clip² *n* **1** → **clippers 2** BLOW : golpe *m*, puñetazo *m* **3** PACE : paso *m* rápido **4** FASTENER : clip *m* ⟨a paper clip : un sujetapapeles⟩

clipper ['klɪpər] *n* **1** : clíper *m* (buque de vela) **2 clippers** *npl* : tijeras *fpl* ⟨nail clippers : cortaúñas⟩

clipping [ˈklɪpɪŋ] n 1 : recorte m (de un periódico) 2 BIT : pedazo m, trozo m (de uña, etc.), recorte m (de pasto, etc.)

clique [ˈkliːk, ˈklɪk] n : grupo m exclusivo, camarilla f (de políticos)

clitoris [ˈklɪt̬ərəs, klɪˈtɔrəs] n, pl **clitorides** [-ˈtɔrəˌdiːz] : clítoris m

cloak¹ [ˈkloːk] vt : encubrir, envolver (en un manto de)

cloak² n : capa f, capote m, manto m ⟨under the cloak of darkness : al amparo de la oscuridad⟩

cloakroom [ˈkloːkˌruːm, -ˌrʊm] n : guardarropa m

clobber [ˈklɑbər] vt : dar una paliza a

clock¹ [ˈklɑk] vt 1 : cronometrar 2 to **clock in/out** : fichar (al entrar/salir)

clock² n 1 : reloj m (de pared), cronómetro m (en deportes o competencias) 2 **around the clock** : las veinticuatro horas

clockmaker [ˈklɑkˌmeɪkər] n : relojero m, -ra f

clockmaking [ˈklɑkˌmeɪkɪŋ] n : relojería f

clockwise [ˈklɑkˌwaɪz] adv & adj : en la dirección de las manecillas del reloj

clockwork [ˈklɑkˌwərk] n : mecanismo m de relojería

clod [ˈklɑd] n 1 : terrón m 2 OAF : zoquete mf

clog¹ [ˈklɑg] v **clogged**; **clogging** vt 1 HINDER : estorbar, impedir 2 BLOCK : atascar, tapar — vi : atascarse, taparse

clog² n 1 OBSTACLE : traba f, impedimento m, estorbo m 2 : zueco m (zapato)

cloister [ˈklɔɪstər] n : claustro m

clone¹ [ˈkloːn] vt : clonar

clone² n 1 : clon m (de un organismo) 2 COPY : copia f, reproducción f

close¹ [ˈkloːz] v **closed**; **closing** vt 1 : cerrar (una puerta, un libro, un archivo, etc.) ⟨to close one's eyes : cerrar los ojos⟩ 2 or to **close up** : cerrar (una empresa, etc.) ⟨they close the store at five o'clock : cierran la tienda a las cinco⟩ 3 or to **close down** : cerrar (una empresa, etc.) ⟨they had to close the restaurant : tuvieron que cerrar el restaurante⟩ 4 or to **close off** : cerrar (una calle) 5 or to **close out** : cerrar (una cuenta) 6 or to **close out** END : concluir, terminar 7 : hacer, cerrar (un trato) 8 REDUCE : cerrar, reducir (una distancia) 9 to **close up** : cerrar (una casa, etc.) — vi 1 : cerrarse, cerrar ⟨the door closed behind her : la puerta se cerró tras ella⟩ ⟨they close on Sundays : cierran los domingos⟩ 2 TERMINATE : concluirse, terminar 3 to **close at** (a **price**) : cotizar (a un precio) al cierre 4 to **close down** : cerrar (dícese de una empresa, etc.) 5 to **close in** APPROACH : acercarse, aproximarse 6 to **close on** : cerrar (un trato), cerrar la compra/venta (de una casa)

close² [ˈkloːs] adv : cerca, de cerca

close³ [ˈkloːs] adj **closer**; **closest** 1 NEAR : cercano, próximo ⟨stay close to me : no te separes de mi lado⟩ ⟨don't get too close to the fire : no te acerques al fuego⟩ ⟨we must be getting close by now : ya estaremos muy cerca⟩ ⟨Christmas is getting close : se acerca la Navidad⟩ ⟨at close range/quarters : de cerca⟩ ⟨to live in close quarters : vivir muy apretados⟩ 2 SIMILAR : parecido, similar ⟨they're close in age : tienen casi la misma edad⟩ ⟨close in size : de tamaño parecido⟩ ⟨to bear a close resemblance to : tener un gran parecido con/a⟩ 3 (indicating approximation) ⟨did I guess right? — no, but you're close : ¿acerté? — no, pero casi⟩ ⟨not even close : ni por asomo⟩ ⟨close, but no cigar : casi, pero no⟩ 4 (indicating that something nearly did or didn't happen) ⟨that was close!, that was a close one/call/shave! : ¡nos salvamos por los pelos!⟩ ⟨we won, but it was close : ganamos por los pelos⟩ 5 STRICT : estricto, detallado ⟨keep a close eye/watch on him : vigílalo bien⟩ ⟨to pay close attention : prestar mucha atención a⟩ 6 STUFFY : de aire viciado o sofocante (dícese de un lugar) 7 TIGHT : apretado, entallado, ceñido ⟨it's a close fit : es muy apretado⟩ 8 : cercano ⟨close relatives : parientes cercanos⟩ 9 INTIMATE : íntimo ⟨close friends : amigos íntimos⟩ ⟨those close to the president : los allegados del presidente⟩ 10 ACCURATE : fiel, exacto 11 : reñido ⟨a close election : una elección muy reñida⟩ ⟨she came in a close second : quedó en segundo lugar por una diferencia mínima⟩ 12 to be **close to** : estar a punto de, estar al borde de ⟨he was close to crying/tears : estaba a punto de llorar, estaba a punto de las lágrimas⟩ ⟨to be close to death : estar al borde de la muerte⟩

close⁴ [ˈkloːz] n : fin m, final m, conclusión f

close–knit [ˈkloːsˈnɪt] adj : unido, íntimo

closely [ˈkloːsli] adv : cerca, de cerca

closeness [ˈkloːsnəs] n 1 NEARNESS : cercanía f, proximidad f 2 INTIMACY : intimidad f

closet¹ [ˈklɑzət] vt to be **closeted with** : estar encerrado con

closet² n : armario m, guardarropa f, clóset m

close–up [ˈkloːsˌʌp] n : primer plano m

closure [ˈkloːʒər] n 1 CLOSING, END : cierre m, clausura f, fin m 2 FASTENER : cierre m

clot¹ [ˈklɑt] v **clotted**; **clotting** vt : coagular, cuajar — vi : cuajarse, coagularse

clot² n : coágulo m

cloth [ˈklɔθ] n, pl **cloths** [ˈklɔðz, ˈklɔθs] 1 FABRIC : tela f 2 RAG : trapo m 3 TABLECLOTH : mantel m

clothe [ˈkloːð] vt **clothed** or **clad** [ˈklæd]; **clothing** DRESS : vestir, arropar, ataviar

clothes [ˈkloːz, ˈkloːðz] npl 1 CLOTHING : ropa f 2 BEDCLOTHES : ropa f de cama

clothesline [ˈkloːzˌlaɪn] n : tendedero m

clothespin [ˈkloːzˌpɪn] n : pinza f (para la ropa)

clothing [ˈkloːðɪŋ] n : ropa f, indumentaria f

cloud¹ [ˈklaʊd] vt : nublar, oscurecer — vi **to cloud over** : nublarse

cloud² n 1 : nube f ⟨to have one's head in the clouds : andar en las nubes⟩ 2 : nube f (de polvo, etc.) 3 : nube f ⟨cloud computing : computación en la nube⟩

cloudburst [ˈklaʊdˌbərst] n : chaparrón m, aguacero m

cloudiness [ˈklaʊdinəs] n : nubosidad f

cloudless [ˈklaʊdləs] adj : despejado, claro

cloudy [ˈklaʊdi] adj **cloudier; -est** : nublado, nuboso

clout¹ [ˈklaʊt] vt : bofetear, dar un tortazo a

clout² n 1 BLOW : golpe m, tortazo m fam 2 INFLUENCE : influencia f, palanca f fam

clove¹ [ˈkloːv] n 1 : diente m (de ajo) 2 : clavo m (especia)

clove² → cleave

cloven hoof [ˈkloːvən] n : pezuña f hendida

clover [ˈkloːvər] n : trébol m

cloverleaf [ˈkloːvərˌliːf] n, pl **-leafs** or **-leaves** [-ˌliːvz] : intersección f en trébol

clown¹ [ˈklaʊn] vi : payasear, bromear ⟨stop clowning around : déjate de payasadas⟩

clown² n : payaso m, -sa f

clownish [ˈklaʊnɪʃ] adj 1 : de payaso 2 BOORISH : grosero — **clownishly** adv

cloying [ˈklɔɪɪŋ] adj : empalagoso, meloso

club¹ [ˈklʌb] vt **clubbed; clubbing** : aporrear, dar garrotazos a

club² n 1 CUDGEL : garrote m, porra f : palo m ⟨golf club : palo de golf⟩ 3 : trébol m, basto m (en la baraja española) 4 ASSOCIATION : club m

clubfoot [ˈklʌbˌfʊt] n, pl **-feet** : pie m deforme

clubhouse [ˈklʌbˌhaʊs] n : sede f de un club

cluck¹ [ˈklʌk] vi : cloquear, cacarear

cluck² n : cloqueo m, cacareo m

clue¹ [ˈkluː] vt **clued; clueing** or **cluing** or **to clue in** : dar una pista a, informar

clue² n : pista f, indicio m

clump¹ [ˈklʌmp] vi 1 : caminar con pisadas fuertes 2 LUMP : agruparse, aglutinarse — vt : amontonar

clump² n 1 : grupo m (de arbustos o árboles), terrón m (de tierra) 2 : pisada f fuerte

clumsily [ˈklʌmzəli] adv : torpemente, sin gracia

clumsiness [ˈklʌmzinəs] n : torpeza f

clumsy [ˈklʌmzi] adj **clumsier; -est** 1 AWKWARD : torpe, desmañado 2 TACTLESS : carente de tacto, poco delicado

clung → cling

clunky [ˈklʌŋki] adj : torpe, poco elegante

cluster¹ [ˈklʌstər] vt : agrupar, juntar — vi : agruparse, apiñarse, arracimarse

cluster² n : grupo m, conjunto m, racimo m (de uvas)

clutch¹ [ˈklʌtʃ] vt : agarrar, asir — vi **to clutch at** : tratar de agarrar

clutch² n 1 GRASP, GRIP : agarre m, apretón m 2 : embrague m, clutch m

(de una máquina) 3 **clutches** npl : garras fpl ⟨he fell into their clutches : cayó en sus garras⟩

clutter¹ [ˈklʌtər] vt : atiborrar o atestar de cosas, llenar desordenadamente

clutter² n : desorden m, revoltijo m

coach¹ [ˈkoːtʃ] vt : entrenar (atletas, artistas), preparar (alumnos)

coach² n 1 CARRIAGE : coche m, carruaje m, carroza f 2 : vagón m de pasajeros (de un tren) 3 BUS : autobús m, ómnibus m 4 : pasaje m aéreo de segunda clase 5 TRAINER : entrenador m, -dora f

coagulate [koˈæɡjəˌleɪt] v **-lated; -lating** vt : coagular, cuajar — vi : coagularse, cuajarse

coal [ˈkoːl] n 1 EMBER : ascua f, brasa f 2 : carbón m ⟨a coal mine : una mina de carbón⟩

coalesce [ˌkoːəˈlɛs] vi **-alesced; -alescing** : unirse

coalition [ˌkoːəˈlɪʃən] n : coalición f

coarse [ˈkors] adj **coarser; coarsest** 1 : grueso (dícese de la arena o la sal), basto (dícese de las telas), áspero (dícese de la piel) 2 CRUDE, ROUGH : basto, tosco, ordinario 3 VULGAR : grosero — **coarsely** adv

coarsen [ˈkorsən] vt : hacer áspero o basto — vi : volverse áspero o basto

coarseness [ˈkorsnəs] n : aspereza f, tosquedad f

coast¹ [ˈkoːst] vi : deslizarse, rodar sin impulso

coast² n : costa f, litoral m

coastal [ˈkoːstəl] adj : costero

coaster [ˈkoːstər] n : posavasos m

coast guard n : guardia f costera, guardacostas mpl

coastline [ˈkoːstˌlaɪn] n : costa f

coat¹ [ˈkoːt] vt : cubrir, revestir, bañar (en un líquido)

coat² n 1 : abrigo m ⟨a sport coat : una chaqueta, un saco⟩ 2 : pelaje m (de animales) 3 LAYER : capa f, mano f (de pintura)

coat check n : guardarropa m

coat hanger n : percha f, gancho m

coating [ˈkoːtɪŋ] n : capa f

coat of arms n : escudo m de armas

coatrack [ˈkoːtˌræk] n : percha f, perchero m

coax [ˈkoːks] vt : engatusar, persuadir

cob [ˈkab] → corncob

cobalt [ˈkoːˌbɔlt] n : cobalto m

cobble [ˈkabəl] vt **cobbled; cobbling** 1 : fabricar o remendar (zapatos) 2 **to cobble together** : improvisar, hacer apresuradamente

cobbler [ˈkablər] n 1 SHOEMAKER : zapatero m, -ra f 2 **fruit cobbler** : tarta f de fruta

cobblestone [ˈkabəlˌstoːn] n : adoquín m

cobra [ˈkoːbrə] n : cobra f

cobweb [ˈkabˌwɛb] n : telaraña f

coca [ˈkoːkə] n : coca f

cocaine [koˈkeɪn, ˈkoːˌkeɪn] n : cocaína f

cock¹ [ˈkak] vt 1 : ladear ⟨to cock one's head : ladear la cabeza⟩ 2 : montar, amartillar (un arma de fuego)

cock² *n* **1** ROOSTER : gallo *m* **2** FAUCET : grifo *m*, llave *f* **3** : martillo *m* (de un arma de fuego)

cockatoo [ˈkɑkəˌtuː] *n, pl* **-toos** : cacatúa *f*

cockeyed [ˈkɑkˌaɪd] *adj* **1** ASKEW : ladeado, torcido, chueco **2** ABSURD : disparatado, absurdo

cockfight [ˈkɑkˌfaɪt] *n* : pelea *f* de gallos

cockiness [ˈkɑkinəs] *n* : arrogancia *f*

cockle [ˈkɑkəl] *n* : berberecho *m*

cockpit [ˈkɑkˌpɪt] *n* : cabina *f*

cockroach [ˈkɑkˌroːtʃ] *n* : cucaracha *f*

cocktail [ˈkɑkˌteɪl] *n* **1** : coctel *m*, cóctel *m* **2** APPETIZER : aperitivo *m*

cocky [ˈkɑki] *adj* **cockier; -est** : creído, engreído

cocoa [ˈkoːˌkoː] *n* **1** CACAO : cacao *m* **2** : cocoa *f*, chocolate *m* (bebida)

coconut [ˈkoːkəˌnʌt] *n* : coco *m*

cocoon [kəˈkuːn] *n* : capullo *m*

cod [ˈkɑd] *n, pl* **cod** : bacalao *m*

coddle [ˈkɑdəl] *vt* **-dled; -dling** : mimar, consentir

code¹ [ˈkoːd] *vt* **coded; coding 1** ENCODE : cifrar (mensajes, etc.) **2** ENCODE : codificar (datos, etc.) **3** MARK : codificar

code² *n* **1** : código *m* ⟨civil code : código civil⟩ **2** : código *m*, clave *f* ⟨secret code : clave secreta⟩

codeine [ˈkoːˌdiːn] *n* : codeína *f*

codex [ˈkoːˌdeks] *n, pl* **-dexes** [-ˌdeksəz] *or* **-dices** [-dəˌsiːz] : códice *m*

codger [ˈkɑdʒər] *n* : viejo *m*, vejete *m*

codify [ˈkɑdəˌfaɪ, ˈkoː-] *vt* **-fied; -fying** : codificar

coeducational [ˌkoːˌɛdʒəˈkeɪʃənəl] *adj* : mixto

coefficient [ˌkoːəˈfɪʃənt] *n* : coeficiente *m*

coerce [koˈərs] *vt* **-erced; -ercing** : coaccionar, forzar, obligar

coercion [koˈərʒən, -ʃən] *n* : coacción *f*

coercive [koˈərsɪv] *adj* : coactivo

coexist [ˌkoːɪgˈzɪst] *vi* : coexistir

coexistence [ˌkoːɪgˈzɪstəns] *n* : coexistencia *f*

coffee [ˈkɔfi] *n* : café *m*

coffeemaker [ˈkɔfiˌmeɪkər] *n* : cafetera *f*

coffeepot [ˈkɔfiˌpɑt] *n* : cafetera *f*

coffee table *n* : mesa *f* de centro

coffer [ˈkɔfər] *n* : cofre *m*

coffin [ˈkɔfən] *n* : ataúd *m*, féretro *m*

cog [ˈkɑg] *n* : diente *m* (de una rueda dentada)

cogent [ˈkoːdʒənt] *adj* : convincente, persuasivo

cogitate [ˈkɑdʒəˌteɪt] *vi* **-tated; -tating** : reflexionar, meditar, discurrir

cogitation [ˌkɑdʒəˈteɪʃən] *n* : reflexión *f*, meditación *f*

cognac [ˈkoːnˌjæk] *n* : coñac *m*

cognate [ˈkɑgˌneɪt] *adj* : relacionado, afín

cognition [kɑgˈnɪʃən] *n* : cognición *f*

cognitive [ˈkɑgnətɪv] *adj* : cognitivo

cogwheel [ˈkɑgˌʰwiːl] *n* : rueda *f* dentada

cohabit [ˌkoːˈhæbət] *vi* : cohabitar — **cohabitation** [ˌkoːˌhæbəˈteɪʃən] *n*

cohere [koˈhɪr] *vi* **-hered; -hering 1** ADHERE : adherirse, pegarse **2** : ser coherente o congruente

coherence [koˈhɪrənts] *n* : coherencia *f*, congruencia *f*

coherent [koˈhɪrənt] *adj* : coherente, congruente — **coherently** *adv*

cohesion [koˈhiːʒən] *n* : cohesión *f*

cohesive [koːˈhiːsɪv, -zɪv] *adj* : cohesivo

cohort [ˈkoːˌhɔrt] *n* **1** : cohorte *f* (de soldados) **2** COMPANION : compañero *m*, -ra *f*; colega *mf*

coiffure [kwɑˈfjʊr] *n* : peinado *m*

coil¹ [ˈkɔɪl] *vt* : enrollar — *vi* : enrollarse, enroscarse

coil² *n* **1** : rollo *m* (de cuerda, etc.), espiral *f* (de humo) **2** : bobina *f* (eléctrica)

coin¹ [ˈkɔɪn] *vt* **1** MINT : acuñar (moneda) **2** INVENT : acuñar, crear, inventar ⟨to coin a phrase : como se suele decir⟩

coin² *n* : moneda *f*

coincide [ˌkoːɪnˈsaɪd, ˈkoːɪnˌsaɪd] *vi* **-cided; -ciding** : coincidir

coincidence [koˈɪntsədənts] *n* : coincidencia *f*, casualidad *f* ⟨what a coincidence! : ¡qué casualidad!⟩

coincident [koˈɪntsədənt] *adj* : coincidente, concurrente

coincidental [koˌɪntsəˈdentəl] *adj* : casual, accidental, fortuito

coitus [ˈkoːətəs] *n* : coito *m*

coke [ˈkoːk] *n* : coque *m*

Coke [ˈkoːk] *trademark* se usa para un refresco de cola

cola [ˈkoːlə] *n* : refresco *m* de cola

colander [ˈkɑləndər, ˈkʌ-] *n* : colador *m*

cold¹ [ˈkoːld] *adj* : frío ⟨it's cold out : hace frío⟩ ⟨a cold reception : una fría recepción⟩ ⟨in cold blood : a sangre fría⟩

cold² *n* **1** : frío *m* ⟨to feel the cold : sentir frío⟩ **2** : resfriado *m*, catarro *m* ⟨to catch a cold : resfriarse⟩

cold–blooded [ˈkoːldˈblʌdəd] *adj* **1** CRUEL : cruel, despiadado **2** : de sangre fría (dícese de los reptiles, etc.)

cold cuts *npl* : fiambres *mpl*

coldly [ˈkoːldli] *adv* : fríamente, con frialdad

coldness [ˈkoːldnəs] *n* : frialdad *f* (de una persona o una actitud), frío *m* (de la temperatura)

cold sore *n* : fuego *m*, calentura *f*

coleslaw [ˈkoːlˌslɔ] *n* : ensalada *f* de col

colic [ˈkɑlɪk] *n* : cólico *m*

coliseum [ˌkɑləˈsiːəm] *n* : coliseo *m*, arena *f*

collaborate [kəˈlæbəˌreɪt] *vi* **-rated; -rating** : colaborar

collaboration [kəˌlæbəˈreɪʃə n] *n* : colaboración *f*

collaborator [kəˈlæbəˌreɪtər] *n* **1** COLLEAGUE : colaborador *m*, -dora *f* **2** TRAITOR : colaboracionista *mf*

collage [kəˈlɑʒ] *n* : collage *m*

collapse¹ [kəˈlæps] *vi* **-lapsed; -lapsing 1** : derrumbarse, desplomarse, hundirse ⟨the building collapsed : el edificio se derrumbó⟩ **2** FALL : desplomarse, caerse ⟨he collapsed on the bed : se desplomó en la cama⟩ ⟨to collapse with laughter : morirse de risa⟩ **3** FAIL : fracasar, quebrar, arruinarse **4** FOLD : plegarse

collapse² n **1** FALL : derrumbe m, desplome m **2** BREAKDOWN, FAILURE : fracaso m, colapso m (físico), quiebra f (económica)
collapsible [kə'læpsəbəl] adj : plegable
collar¹ ['kɑlər] vt : agarrar, atrapar
collar² n **1** : cuello m **2** : collar m (para un animal)
collarbone ['kɑlər,bo:n] n : clavícula f
collate [kə'leɪt;, 'kɑ,leɪt, 'ko:-] vt -lated; -lating **1** COMPARE : cotejar, comparar · **2** : ordenar, recopilar (páginas)
collateral¹ [kə'læt̬ərəl] adj : colateral
collateral² n : garantía f, fianza f, prenda f
colleague ['kɑ,li:g] n : colega mf; compañero m, -ra f
collect¹ [kə'lɛkt] vt **1** GATHER : recopilar, reunir, recoger ⟨she collected her thoughts : puso en orden sus ideas⟩ **2** : coleccionar, juntar ⟨to collect stamps : coleccionar timbres⟩ **3** : cobrar (una deuda), recaudar (un impuesto) **4** PICK UP : recoger, ir a buscar **5** DRAW : cobrar, percibir (un sueldo, etc.) — vi **1** ACCUMULATE : acumularse, juntarse **2** CONGREGATE : congregarse, reunirse
collect² adv & adj : por cobrar, a cobro revertido
collectible or **collectable** [kə'lɛkt̬əbəl] adj : coleccionable
collection [kə'lɛkʃən] n **1** COLLECTING : colecta f (de contribuciones), cobro m (de deudas), recaudación f (de impuestos) **2** GROUP : colección f (de objetos), grupo m (de personas)
collective¹ [kə'lɛkt̬ɪv] adj : colectivo — **collectively** adv
collective² n : colectivo m
collector [kə'lɛkt̬ər] n **1** : coleccionista mf (de objetos) **2** : cobrador m, -dora f (de deudas)
college ['kɑlɪʤ] n **1** : universidad f **2** : colegio m (de electores o profesionales)
collegiate [kə'li:ʤət] adj : universitario
collide [kə'laɪd] vi -lided; -liding : chocar, colisionar, estrellarse
collie ['kɑli] n : collie m
collision [kə'lɪʒən] n : choque m, colisión f
colloquial [kə'lo:kwiəl] adj : coloquial
colloquialism [kə'lo:kwiə,lɪzəm] n : expresión f coloquial
collusion [kə'lu:ʒən] n : colusión f
cologne [kə'lo:n] n : colonia f
Colombian [kə'lʌmbiən] n : colombiano m, -na f — **Colombian** adj
colon¹ ['ko:lən] n, pl **colons** or **cola** [-lə] : colon m (de los intestinos)
colon² n, pl **colons** : dos puntos mpl (signo ortográfico)
colón [kə'lo:n] n, pl -**lones** [-'lo:,neɪs] : colón m (unidad monetaria)
colonel ['kərnəl] n : coronel m
colonial¹ [kə'lo:niəl] adj : colonial
colonial² n : colono m, -na f
colonist ['kɑlənɪst] n : colono m, -na f; colonizador m, -dora f
colonization [,kɑlənə'zeɪʃən] n : colonización f
colonize ['kɑlə,naɪz] vt -nized; -nizing **1**

: establecer una colonia en **2** SETTLE : colonizar
colonnade [,kɑlə'neɪd] n : columnata f
colony ['kɑləni] n, pl -**nies** : colonia f
color¹ ['kʌlər] vt **1** : colorear, pintar **2** INFLUENCE : influir en, influenciar — vi BLUSH : sonrojarse, ruborizarse
color² n **1** : color m ⟨primary colors : colores primarios⟩ **2** INTEREST, LIVENESS : color m, colorido m ⟨local color : color local⟩
coloration [kʌlə'reɪʃən] n : coloración f
color-blind ['kʌlər,blaɪnd] adj : daltónico
color blindness n : daltonismo m
colored ['kʌlərd] adj **1** : de color **2** dated, now offensive : de color dated, now offensive; negro (dícese de las personas)
colorfast ['kʌlər,fæst] adj : que no se destiñe
colorful ['kʌlərfəl] adj **1** : lleno de colorido, de colores vivos **2** PICTURESQUE, STRIKING : pintoresco, llamativo
coloring ['kʌlərɪŋ] n **1** : color m, colorido m **2** food coloring : colorante m
colorless ['kʌlərləs] adj **1** : incoloro, sin color **2** DULL : soso, aburrido
color scheme n : combinación f de colores, tonalidad f
colossal [kə'lɑsəl] adj : colosal
colossus [kə'lɑsəs] n, pl -**si** [-,saɪ] : coloso m
colt ['ko:lt] n : potro m, potranco m
column ['kɑləm] n : columna f
columnist ['kɑləmnɪst, -ləmɪst] n : columnista m
coma ['ko:mə] n : coma m, estado m de coma
Comanche [kə'mæntʃi] n : comanche mf — **Comanche** adj
comatose ['ko:mə,to:s, 'kɑ-] adj : comatoso, en estado de coma
comb¹ ['ko:m] vt **1** : peinar (el pelo) **2** SEARCH : peinar, rastrear, registrar a fondo
comb² n **1** : peine m **2** : cresta f (de un gallo)
combat¹ [kəm'bæt, 'kʌm,bæt] vt -bated or -batted; -bating or -batting : combatir, luchar contra
combat² ['kʌm,bæt] n : combate m, lucha f
combatant [kəm'bæt̬ənt] n : combatiente mf
combative [kəm'bæt̬ɪv] adj : combativo
combination [,kɑmbə'neɪʃən] n : combinación f
combine¹ [kəm'baɪn] v -bined; -bining vt : combinar, aunar — vi : combinarse, mezclarse
combine² ['kɑm,baɪn] n **1** ALLIANCE : alianza f comercial o política **2** HARVESTER : cosechadora f
combustible [kəm'bʌstəbəl] adj : inflamable, combustible
combustion [kəm'bʌstʃən] n : combustión f
come ['kʌm] vi **came** ['keɪm]; **come**; **coming** **1** APPROACH : venir, aproximarse ⟨here he comes : acá viene⟩ **2** ARRIVE : venir, llegar ⟨she came yesterday

: vino ayer⟩ ⟨did the mail come? : ¿llegó el correo?⟩ **3** : venir (a un lugar, una reunión, etc.) ⟨come with me : ven conmigo⟩ ⟨are you coming to the wedding? : ¿vienes a la boda?⟩ ⟨come (and) visit us! : ¡ven a visitarnos!⟩ ⟨I'm coming! : ¡voy!⟩ **4** HAPPEN : ocurrir, pasar ⟨to come at a bad time : llegar en mal momento⟩ **5** : venir ⟨it comes in three colors : viene en tres colores⟩ **6** : estar, ir (en una serie) ⟨B comes after A : la B va después de la A⟩ **7 come again?** : ¿cómo? **8 come on!** (used to encourage or urge) : ¡vamos! **9 come on!** (expressing surprise, disbelief, etc.) : ¡anda! **10 to come to think of it** : ahora que lo pienso **11 come what may** : pase lo que pase **12 if it comes to that** : si es necesario **13 to be coming up** : acercarse (dícese de una fecha, etc.) ⟨her birthday is coming up : falta poco para su cumpleaños⟩ **14 to come about** HAPPEN : ocurrir, pasar **15 to come across** FIND : tropezarse con, dar con **16 to come across as** : dar la impresión de ser, parecer ser **17 to come along** APPEAR, ARRIVE : aparecer, llegar **18 to come along** : venir con alguien ⟨would you like to come along? : ¿quieres venir conmigo?⟩ **19 to come along** PROGRESS : ir ⟨how's the project coming along? : ¿qué tal va el proyecto?⟩ **20 to come apart** : deshacerse **21 to come around** : convencerse al final **22 to come around** : venir, pasar ⟨why don't you come around to my place tonight? : ¿por qué no pasas por casa esta noche?⟩ **23 to come back** RETURN : volver ⟨come back here! : ¡vuelve acá!⟩ ⟨that style's coming back : ese estilo está volviendo⟩ **24 to come back** RETORT : replicar, contestar **25 to come between** : interponerse entre **26 to come by** STOP BY : pasar por casa **27 to come by** GET, OBTAIN : conseguir **28 to come clean** : confesar, desahogar la conciencia **29 to come down** : caer (dícese de la lluvia, etc.), bajar (dícese de los precios, etc.) **30 to come down hard on** : ser duro con **31 to come down to** : reducirse a **32 to come down with** : caer enfermo de **33 to come forward** : presentarse **34 to come from** : venir de (un lugar, etc.) **35 to come in** ENTER : entrar, pasar **36 to come in** : llegar **37 to come in** : desempeñar una función ⟨that's where you come in : ahí es donde entras tú⟩ ⟨to come in handy : venir bien, ser útil⟩ **38 to come into** ACQUIRE : adquirir ⟨to come into a fortune : heredar una fortuna⟩ **39 to come of** : resultar de **40 to come off** DETACH : soltarse, desprenderse **41 to come off** SUCCEED : tener éxito, ser un éxito **42 to come off as** : dar la impresión de ser, parecer ser **43 to come off well/poorly** : irle bien/mal a uno ⟨he came off poorly in the debate : le fue mal en el debate⟩ **44 to come on** TURN ON : encenderse **45 to come on** BEGIN : empezar **46 to come on to someone** : insinuársele a alguien **47 to come out** : salir, aparecer, publicarse **48 to come out** : declararse ⟨to come out in favor of : declararse a favor de⟩ **49 to come out and say** : decir sin rodeos **50 to come out and say** : declararse homosexual **51 to come over** STOP BY : pasar por casa **52 to come over** someone : sobrevenirle (una emoción) a alguien ⟨I don't know what came over her : no sé qué le pasó⟩ **53 to come through** : pasar por, sobrevivir a **54 to come through** SHOW : ser evidente **55 to come through** : recibirse (dícese de una señal, etc.), llegar **56 to come through** : recobrar el conocimiento, volver en sí **57 to come to** : llegar a (un lugar) **58 to come to** : llegar a, ascender a (una cantidad) **59 to come to** REACH : llegar a, alcanzar (un acuerdo, etc.) ⟨to come to an end : llegar a su fin⟩ ⟨to come to a boil : empezar a hervir⟩ **60 to come to** : ocurrírsele (a alguien) ⟨the answer came to me : la respuesta me vino, se me ocurrió la respuesta⟩ **61 to come to be/believe (etc.)** : llegar a ser/creer (etc.) **62 to come to pass** HAPPEN : acontecer **63 to come to terms** : llegar a un acuerdo **64 to come under** ⟨to come under attack/criticism : ser atacado/criticado⟩ ⟨to come under the control of : quedar bajo el control de⟩ **65 to come under** : ir bajo (una categoría, etc.) **66 to come undone** : desatarse, desabrocharse **67 to come up** ARISE : surgir **68 to come up** RISE, APPEAR : salir **69 to come up** : resultar, salir, quedar ⟨the shot came up short : el tiro se quedó corto⟩ ⟨to come up heads/tails : salir cara/cruz⟩ **70 to come up against** : enfrentarse a, tropezar con **71 to come up to someone** : acercarse a alguien **72 to come up with** : encontrar (una solución), idear (un plan), conseguir (dinero) ⟨we couldn't come up with a better idea : no se nos ocurrió nada mejor⟩ **73 to have it coming** : tenerlo merecido **74 what's coming to someone** ⟨one day he'll get what's coming to him : algún día recibirá su merecido⟩ **75 when it comes to** : en cuanto a, cuando se trata de ⟨when it comes to chess, he's the best : cuando se trata de ajedrez, él es el mejor⟩

comeback [ˈkʌm͵bæk] n **1** RETORT : réplica f, respuesta f **2** RETURN : retorno m, regreso m ⟨the champion announced his comeback : el campeón anunció su regreso⟩

comedian [kəˈmiːdiən] n : cómico m, -ca f; humorista mf

comedienne [kə͵miːdiˈɛn] n : cómica f, humorista f

comedy [ˈkɑmədi] n, pl **-dies** : comedia f

comely [ˈkʌmli] adj **comelier; -est** : bello, bonito

comet [ˈkɑmət] n : cometa m

comfort[1] [ˈkʌmp͵fərt] vt **1** CHEER : confortar, alentar **2** CONSOLE : consolar

comfort² *n* **1** CONSOLATION : consuelo *m* **2** WELL-BEING : confort *m*, bienestar *m* **3** CONVENIENCE : comodidad *f* ⟨the comforts of home : las comodidades del hogar⟩

comfortable [ˈkʌmpfərtəbəl, ˈkʌmpftə-] *adj* : cómodo, confortable — **comfortably** [ˈkʌmpfərtəbli, ˈkʌmpftə-] *adv*

comforter [ˈkʌmpfərtər] *n* QUILT : edredón *m*, cobertor *m*

comic¹ [ˈkɑmɪk] *adj* : cómico, humorístico

comic² *n* **1** COMEDIAN : cómico *m*, -ca *f*; humorista *mf* **2** *or* **comic book** : historieta *f*, cómic *m*

comical [ˈkɑmɪkəl] *adj* : cómico, gracioso, chistoso

comic strip *n* : tira *f* cómica, historieta *f*

coming¹ [ˈkʌmɪŋ] *adj* : siguiente, próximo, que viene

coming² *n* **1** ARRIVAL : llegada *f* **2 comings and goings** : idas y venidas *fpl*

comma [ˈkɑmə] *n* : coma *f*

command¹ [kəˈmænd] *vt* **1** ORDER : ordenar, mandar **2** CONTROL, DIRECT : comandar, tener el mando de — *vi* **1** : dar órdenes **2** GOVERN : estar al mando *m*, gobernar

command² *n* **1** CONTROL, LEADERSHIP : mando *m*, control *m*, dirección *f* **2** ORDER : orden *f*, mandato *m* **3** MASTERY : maestría *f*, destreza *f*, dominio *m* **4** : tropa *f* asignada a un comandante

commandant [ˈkɑmənˌdɑnt, -ˌdænt] *n* : comandante *mf*

commandeer [ˌkɑmənˈdɪr] *vt* : piratear, secuestrar (un vehículo, etc.)

commander [kəˈmændər] *n* : comandante *mf*

commanding [kəˈmændɪŋ] *adj* AUTHORITATIVE : autoritario, imperativo, imperioso

commandment [kəˈmændmənt] *n* : mandamiento *m*, orden *f* ⟨the Ten Commandments : los diez mandamientos⟩

commando [kəˈmændoː] *n* : comando *m*

commemorate [kəˈmɛməˌreɪt] *vt* **-rated; -rating** : conmemorar

commemoration [kəˌmɛməˈreɪʃən] *n* : conmemoración *f*

commemorative [kəˈmɛmrətɪv, -ˈmɛməˌreɪtɪv] *adj* : conmemorativo

commence [kəˈmɛnts] *v* **-menced; -mencing** *vt* : iniciar, comenzar — *vi* : iniciarse, comenzar

commencement [kəˈmɛntsmənt] *n* **1** BEGINNING : inicio *m*, comienzo *m* **2** : ceremonia *f* de graduación

commend [kəˈmɛnd] *vt* **1** ENTRUST : encomendar **2** RECOMMEND : recomendar **3** PRAISE : elogiar, alabar

commendable [kəˈmɛndəbəl] *adj* : loable, meritorio, encomiable

commendation [ˌkɑmənˈdeɪʃən, -ˌmɛn-] *n* : elogio *m*, encomio *m*

commensurate [kəˈmɛntsərət, -ˈmɛntʃʊrət] *adj* : proporcionado ⟨commensurate with : en proporción a⟩

comment¹ [ˈkɑˌmɛnt] *vi* **1** : hacer comentarios **2 to comment on** : comentar,

hacer observaciones sobre — **commenter** *n*

comment² *n* : comentario *m*, observación *f*

commentary [ˈkɑmənˌteri] *n, pl* **-taries** : comentario *m*, crónica *f* (deportiva)

commentator [ˈkɑmənˌteɪtər] *n* **1** HOST, ANCHOR : comentarista *mf*, cronista *mf* (de deportes) **2** : comentarista *mf* ⟨political commentators : comentaristas políticos⟩

commerce [ˈkɑmərs] *n* : comercio *m*

commercial¹ [kəˈmərʃəl] *adj* : comercial — **commercially** *adv*

commercial² *n* : comercial *m*

commercialize [kəˈmərʃəˌlaɪz] *vt* **-ized; -izing** : comercializar

commiserate [kəˈmɪzəˌreɪt] *vi* **-ated; -ating** : compadecerse, consolarse

commiseration [kəˌmɪzəˈreɪʃən] *n* : conmiseración *f*

commission¹ [kəˈmɪʃən] *vt* **1** : nombrar (un oficial) **2** : comisionar, encargar ⟨to commission a painting : encargar una pintura⟩

commission² *n* **1** : nombramiento *m* (al grado de oficial) **2** COMMITTEE : comisión *f*, comité *m* **3** COMMITTING : comisión *f*, realización *f* (de un acto) **4** PERCENTAGE : comisión *f* ⟨sales commissions : comisiones de venta⟩

commissioned officer *n* : oficial *mf*

commissioner [kəˈmɪʃənər] *n* **1** : comisionado *m*, -da *f*; miembro *m* de una comisión **2** : comisario *m*, -ria *f* (de policía, etc.)

commit [kəˈmɪt] *vt* **-mitted; -mitting** **1** ENTRUST : encomendar, confiar **2** CONFINE : internar (en un hospital), encarcelar (en una prisión) **3** PERPETRATE : cometer ⟨to commit a crime : cometer un crimen⟩ **4 to commit oneself** : comprometerse

commitment [kəˈmɪtmənt] *n* **1** RESPONSIBILITY : compromiso *m*, responsabilidad *f* **2** DEDICATION : dedicación *f*, devoción *f* ⟨commitment to the cause : devoción a la causa⟩

committee [kəˈmɪti] *n* : comité *m*

commodious [kəˈmoːdiəs] *adj* SPACIOUS : amplio, espacioso

commodity [kəˈmɑdəti] *n, pl* **-ties** : artículo *m* de comercio, mercancía *f*, mercadería *f*

commodore [ˈkɑməˌdor] *n* : comodoro *m*

common¹ [ˈkɑmən] *adj* **1** PUBLIC : común, público ⟨the common good : el bien común⟩ **2** SHARED : común ⟨a common interest : un interés común⟩ **3** GENERAL : común, general ⟨it's common knowledge : todo el mundo lo sabe⟩ **4** ORDINARY : ordinario, común y corriente ⟨the common man : el hombre medio, el hombre de la calle⟩

common² *n* **1** : tierra *f* comunal **2 in ~** : en común

common cold *n* : resfriado *m* común

common denominator *n* : denominador *m* común

commoner [ˈkɑmənər] *n* : plebeyo *m*, -ya *f*

common law *n* : derecho *m* consuetudinario

commonly ['kɑmənli] *adv* **1** FREQUENTLY : comúnmente, frecuentemente **2** USUALLY : normalmente

common noun *n* : nombre *m* común

commonplace¹ ['kɑmən,pleɪs] *adj* : común, ordinario

commonplace² *n* : cliché *m*, tópico *m*

common sense *n* : sentido *m* común

commonwealth ['kɑmən,wɛlθ] *n* : entidad *f* política ⟨the British Commonwealth : la Mancomunidad Británica⟩

commotion [kə'moːʃən] *n* **1** RUCKUS : alboroto *m*, jaleo *m*, escándalo *m* **2** STIR, UPSET : revuelo *m*, conmoción *f*

communal [kə'mjuːnəl] *adj* : comunal

commune¹ [kə'mjuːn] *vi* **-muned; -muning** : estar en comunión

commune² ['kɑ,mjuːn, kə'mjuːn] *n* : comuna *f*

communicable [kə'mjuːnɪkəbəl] *adj* CONTAGIOUS : transmisible, contagioso

communicate [kə'mjuːnə,keɪt] *v* **-cated; -cating** *vt* **1** CONVEY : comunicar, expresar, hacer saber **2** TRANSMIT : transmitir (una enfermedad), contagiar — *vi* : comunicarse, expresarse

communication [kə,mjuːnə'keɪʃən] *n* : comunicación *f*

communicative [kə'mjuːnɪ,keɪtɪv, -kətɪv] *adj* : comunicativo

communion [kə'mjuːnjən] *n* **1** SHARING : comunión *f* **2** **Communion** : comunión *f*, eucaristía *f*

communiqué [kə'mjuːnə,keɪ, -,mjuːnə-'keɪ] *n* : comunicado *m*

communism *or* **Communism** ['kɑmjə-,nɪzəm] *n* : comunismo *m*

communist¹ *or* **Communist** ['kɑmjə,nɪst] *adj* : comunista ⟨the Communist Party : el Partido Comunista⟩

communist² *or* **Communist** *n* : comunista *mf*

communistic *or* **Communistic** [,kɑmjə-'nɪstɪk] *adj* : comunista

community¹ [kə'mjuːnəti] *n*, *pl* **-ties** : comunidad *f*

community² *adj* : comunitario

commute [kə'mjuːt] *v* **-muted; -muting** *vt* REDUCE : conmutar, reducir (una sentencia) — *vi* : viajar de la residencia al trabajo

commuter [kə'mjuːtər] *n* : persona *f* que viaja diariamente al trabajo

compact¹ [kəm'pækt, 'kɑm,pækt] *vt* : compactar, consolidar, comprimir

compact² [kəm'pækt, 'kɑm,pækt] *adj* **1** DENSE, SOLID : compacto, macizo, denso **2** CONCISE : breve, conciso

compact³ ['kɑm,pækt] *n* **1** AGREEMENT : acuerdo *m*, pacto *m* **2** : polvera *f*, estuche *m* de maquillaje **3** *or* **compact car** : auto *m* compacto

compact disc ['kɑm,pækt'dɪsk] *n* : disco *m* compacto, compact disc *m*

compactly [kəm'pæktli, 'kɑm,pækt-] *adv* **1** DENSELY : densamente **2** CONCISELY : concisamente, brevemente

companion [kəm'pænjən] *n* **1** COMRADE : compañero *m*, -ra *f*; acompañante *mf* **2** MATE : pareja *f* (de un zapato, etc.)

companionable [kəm'pænjənəbəl] *adj* : sociable, amigable

companionship [kəm'pænjən,ʃɪp] *n* : compañerismo *m*, camaradería *f*

company ['kʌmpəni] *n*, *pl* **-nies** **1** FIRM : compañía *f*, empresa *f* **2** GROUP : compañía *f* (de actores o soldados) **3** GUESTS : visita *f* ⟨we have company : tenemos visita⟩ **4** COMPANIONSHIP : compañía *f* ⟨to keep someone company : hacerle compañía a alguien⟩ ⟨I enjoy her company : me gusta estar con ella⟩ **5 to be in good company** : no ser el único

comparable ['kɑmpərəbəl] *adj* : comparable, parecido

comparative¹ [kəm'pærətɪv] *adj* RELATIVE : comparativo, relativo — **comparatively** *adv*

comparative² *n* : comparativo *m*

compare¹ [kəm'pær] *v* **-pared; -paring** *vt* : comparar — *vi* **to compare with** : poder comparar con, tener comparación con

compare² *n* : comparación *f* ⟨beyond compare : sin igual, sin par⟩

comparison [kəm'pærəsən] *n* : comparación *f*

compartment [kəm'pɑrtmənt] *n* : compartimento *m*, compartimiento *m*

compass ['kʌmpəs, 'kɑm-] *n* **1** RANGE, SCOPE : alcance *m*, extensión *f*, límites *mpl* **2** : compás *m* (para trazar circunferencias) **3** : compás *m*, brújula *f* ⟨the points of the compass : los puntos cardinales⟩

compassion [kəm'pæʃən] *n* : compasión *f*, piedad *f*, misericordia *f*

compassionate [kəm'pæʃənət] *adj* : compasivo

compatibility [kəm,pætə'bɪləti] *n* : compatibilidad *f*

compatible [kəm'pætəbəl] *adj* : compatible, afín

compatriot [kəm'peɪtriət, -'pæ-] *n* : compatriota *mf*; paisano *m*, -na *f*

compel [kəm'pɛl] *vt* **-pelled; -pelling** : obligar, compeler

compelling [kəm'pɛlɪŋ] *adj* **1** FORCEFUL : fuerte **2** ENGAGING : absorbente **3** PERSUASIVE : persuasivo, convincente

compendium [kəm'pɛndiəm] *n*, *pl* **-diums** *or* **-dia** [-diə] : compendio *m*

compensate ['kɑmpən,seɪt] *v* **-sated; -sating** *vi* **to compensate for** : compensar — *vt* : indemnizar, compensar

compensation [,kɑmpən'seɪʃən] *n* : compensación *f*, indemnización *f*

compensatory [kəm'pɛntsə,tori] *adj* : compensatorio

compete [kəm'piːt] *vi* **-peted; -peting** : competir, contender, rivalizar

competence ['kɑmpətənts] *n* : competencia *f*, aptitud *f*

competency ['kɑmpətəntsi] → **competence**

competent ['kɑmpətənt] *adj* : competente, capaz

competition [ˌkampəˈtɪʃən] *n* : competencia *f*, concurso *m*

competitive [kəmˈpɛtətɪv] *adj* : competitivo

competitively [kəmˈpɛtətɪvli] *adv* : competitivamente ⟨competitively priced : a precios competitivos⟩

competitiveness [kəmˈpɛtətɪvnəs] *n* : competitividad *f*

competitor [kəmˈpɛtətər] *n* : competidor *m*, -dora *f*

compilation [ˌkampəˈleɪʃən] *n* : recopilación *f*, compilación *f*

compile [kəmˈpaɪl] *vt* **-piled; -piling** : compilar, recopilar

complacency [kəmˈpleɪsənsi] *n* : satisfacción *f* consigo mismo, suficiencia *f*

complacent [kəmˈpleɪsənt] *adj* : satisfecho de sí mismo, suficiente

complain [kəmˈpleɪn] *vi* **1** GRIPE : quejarse, regañar, rezongar **2** PROTEST : reclamar, protestar

complaint [kəmˈpleɪnt] *n* **1** GRIPE : queja *f* **2** AILMENT : afección *f*, dolencia *f* **3** ACCUSATION : reclamo *m*, acusación *f*

complement¹ [ˈkampləˌmɛnt] *vt* : complementar

complement² [ˈkampləmənt] *n* : complemento *m*

complementary [ˌkampləˈmɛntəri] *adj* : complementario

complete¹ [kəmˈpliːt] *vt* **-pleted; -pleting 1** : completar, hacer entero ⟨this piece completes the collection : esta pieza completa la colección⟩ **2** FINISH : completar, acabar, terminar ⟨she completed her studies : completó sus estudios⟩

complete² *adj* **completer; -est 1** WHOLE : completo, entero, íntegro **2** FINISHED : terminado, acabado **3** TOTAL : completo, total, absoluto

completely [kəmˈpliːtli] *adv* : completamente, totalmente

completion [kəmˈpliːʃən] *n* : finalización *f*, cumplimiento *m*

complex¹ [kamˈplɛks, kəm-;, ˈkamˌplɛks] *adj* : complejo, complicado

complex² [ˈkamˌplɛks] *n* : complejo *m*

complexion [kəmˈplɛkʃən] *n* : cutis *m*, tez *f* ⟨of dark complexion : de tez morena⟩

complexity [kəmˈplɛksəti, kam-] *n, pl* **-ties** : complejidad *f*

compliance [kəmˈplaɪənts] *n* : conformidad *f* ⟨in compliance with the law : conforme a la ley⟩

compliant [kəmˈplaɪənt] *adj* : dócil, sumiso

complicate [ˈkampləˌkeɪt] *vt* **-cated; -cating** : complicar

complicated [ˈkampləˌkeɪtəd] *adj* : complicado

complication [ˌkampləˈkeɪʃən] *n* : complicación *f*

complicity [kəmˈplɪsəti] *n, pl* **-ties** : complicidad *f*

compliment¹ [ˈkampləˌmɛnt] *vt* : halagar, florear *Mex*

compliment² [ˈkampləmənt] *n* **1** : halago *m*, cumplido *m* **2 compliments** *npl* : saludos *mpl* ⟨give them my compliments : déles saludos de mi parte⟩

complimentary [ˌkampləˈmɛntəri] *adj* **1** FLATTERING : halagador, halagüeño **2** FREE : de cortesía, gratis

comply [kəmˈplaɪ] *vi* **-plied; -plying** : cumplir, acceder, obedecer

component¹ [kəmˈpoːnənt, ˈkam-ˌpoː-] *adj* : componente

component² *n* : componente *m*, elemento *m*, pieza *f*

compose [kəmˈpoːz] *vt* **-posed; -posing 1** : componer, crear ⟨to compose a melody : componer una melodía⟩ **2** CALM : calmar, serenar ⟨to compose oneself : serenarse⟩ **3** CONSTITUTE : constar, componer ⟨to be composed of : constar de⟩ **4** : componer (un texto a imprimirse)

composed [kəmˈpoːzd] *adj* : tranquilo

composer [kəmˈpoːzər] *n* : compositor *m*, -tora *f*

composite¹ [kamˈpazət, kəm-;, ˈkampəzət] *adj* : compuesto (de varias partes)

composite² *n* : compuesto *m*, mezcla *f*

composition [ˌkampəˈzɪʃən] *n* **1** MAKEUP : composición *f* **2** ESSAY : ensayo *m*, trabajo *m*

compost [ˈkamˌpoːst] *n* : abono *m* vegetal

composure [kəmˈpoːʒər] *n* : compostura *f*, serenidad *f*

compote [ˈkamˌpoːt] *n* : compota *f*

compound¹ [kamˈpaʊnd, kəm-;, ˈkamˌpaʊnd] *vt* **1** COMBINE, COMPOSE : combinar, componer **2** AUGMENT : agravar, aumentar ⟨to compound a problem : agravar un problema⟩

compound² [ˈkamˌpaʊnd;, kamˈpaʊnd, kəm-] *adj* : compuesto ⟨compound interest : interés compuesto⟩

compound³ [ˈkamˌpaʊnd] *n* **1** MIXTURE : compuesto *m*, mezcla *f* **2** ENCLOSURE : recinto *m* (de residencias, etc.)

comprehend [ˌkamprɪˈhɛnd] *vt* **1** UNDERSTAND : comprender, entender **2** INCLUDE : comprender, incluir, abarcar

comprehensible [ˌkamprɪˈhɛntsəbəl] *adj* : comprensible

comprehension [ˌkamprɪˈhɛntʃən] *n* : comprensión *f*

comprehensive [ˌkamprɪˈhɛntsɪv] *adj* **1** INCLUSIVE : inclusivo, exhaustivo **2** BROAD : extenso, amplio

compress¹ [kəmˈprɛs] *vt* : comprimir

compress² [ˈkamˌprɛs] *n* : compresa *f*

compression [kəmˈprɛʃən] *n* : compresión *f*

compressor [kəmˈprɛsər] *n* : compresor *m*

comprise [kəmˈpraɪz] *vt* **-prised; -prising 1** INCLUDE : comprender, incluir **2** : componerse de, constar de ⟨the installation comprises several buildings : la instalación está compuesta de varios edificios⟩

compromise¹ [ˈkamprəˌmaɪz] *v* **-mised; -mising** *vi* : transigir, avenirse — *vt* JEOPARDIZE : comprometer, poner en peligro compromise² n : acuerdo m mutuo, compromiso m

comptroller [kən'troːlər, 'kɑmp-,troː-] n : contralor m, -lora f; interventor m, -tora f

compulsion [kəm'pʌlʃən] n 1 COERCION : coacción f 2 URGE : compulsión f, impulso m

compulsive [kəm'pʌlsɪv] adj : compulsivo

compulsory [kəm'pʌlsəri] adj : obligatorio

compunction [kəm'pʌŋkʃən] n 1 QUALM : reparo m, escrúpulo m 2 REMORSE : remordimiento m

computation [,kɑmpju'teɪʃən] n : cálculo m, cómputo m

compute [kəm'pjuːt] vt -puted; -puting : computar, calcular

computer [kəm'pjuːtər] n : computadora f, computador m, ordenador m Spain

computerization [kəm,pjuːtərə'zeɪʃən] n : informatización f

computerize [kəm'pjuːtə,raɪz] vt -ized; -izing : computarizar, informatizar

computer programmer → programmer

computer programming → programming

computer science n : informática f

computing [kəm'pjuːtɪŋ] n : informática f

comrade ['kʌm,ræd] n : camarada mf; compañero m, -ra f

con¹ ['kɑn] vt conned; conning SWINDLE : estafar, timar

con² adv : contra

con³ n : contra m ⟨the pros and cons : los pros y los contras⟩

concave [kɑn'keɪv, 'kɑn,keɪv] adj : cóncavo

conceal [kən'siːl] vt : esconder, ocultar, disimular

concealment [kən'siːlmənt] n : ocultación f

concede [kən'siːd] vt -ceded; -ceding 1 ALLOW, GRANT : conceder 2 ADMIT : conceder, reconocer ⟨to concede defeat : reconocer la derrota⟩

conceit [kən'siːt] n : engreimiento m, presunción f

conceited [kən'siːtəd] adj : presumido, engreído, presuntuoso

conceivable [kən'siːvəbəl] adj : concebible, imaginable

conceivably [kən'siːvəbli] adv : posiblemente, de manera concebible

conceive [kən'siːv] v -ceived; -ceiving vi : concebir, embarazarse — vt IMAGINE : concebir, imaginar

concentrate¹ ['kɑntsən,treɪt] v -trated; -trating vt : concentrar — vi : concentrarse

concentrate² n : concentrado m

concentration [,kɑntsən'treɪʃən] n : concentración f

concentration camp n : campo m de concentración

concentric [kən'sɛntrɪk] adj : concéntrico

concept ['kɑn,sɛpt] n : concepto m, idea f

conception [kən'sɛpʃən] n 1 : concepción f (de un bebé) 2 IDEA : concepto m, idea f

conceptual [kən'sɛptʃəwəl] adj : conceptual — conceptually adv

conceptualize [kən'sɛptʃəwə,laɪz] vt -ized; -izing : conceptualizar, formarse un concepto de — conceptualization [kən'sɛptʃəwələ'zeɪʃən] n

concern¹ [kən'sərn] vt 1 : tratarse de, tener que ver con ⟨the novel concerns a sailor : la novela se trata de un marinero⟩ 2 INVOLVE : concernir, incumbir a, afectar ⟨that does not concern me : eso no me incumbe⟩

concern² n 1 AFFAIR : asunto m 2 WORRY : inquietud f, preocupación f 3 BUSINESS : negocio m

concerned [kən'sərnd] adj 1 ANXIOUS : preocupado, ansioso 2 INTERESTED, INVOLVED : interesado, afectado

concerning [kən'sərnɪŋ] prep REGARDING : con respecto a, acerca de, sobre

concert ['kɑn,sərt] n 1 AGREEMENT : concierto m, acuerdo m 2 : concierto m (musical)

concerted [kən'sərtəd] adj 1 : concertado, coordinado ⟨to make a concerted effort : coordinar los esfuerzos⟩

concerto [kən'tʃɛrtoː] n, pl -ti [-ti, -,tiː] or -tos : concierto m ⟨violin concerto : concierto para violín⟩

concession [kən'sɛʃən] n : concesión f

conch ['kɑŋk, 'kɑntʃ] n, pl conchs ['kɑŋks] or conches ['kɑntʃəz] : caracol m (animal), caracola f (concha)

conciliatory [kən'sɪliə,tori] adj : conciliador, conciliatorio

concise [kən'saɪs] adj : conciso, breve — concisely adv

conclave ['kɑn,kleɪv] n : cónclave m

conclude [kən'kluːd] v -cluded; -cluding vt 1 END : concluir, finalizar ⟨to conclude a meeting : concluir una reunión⟩ 2 DECIDE : concluir, llegar a la conclusión de — vi END : concluir, terminar

conclusion [kən'kluːʒən] n 1 INFERENCE : conclusión f 2 END : fin m, final m

conclusive [kən'kluːsɪv] adj : concluyente, decisivo — conclusively adv

concoct [kən'kɑkt, kɑn-] vt 1 PREPARE : preparar, confeccionar 2 DEVISE : inventar, tramar

concoction [kən'kɑkʃən] n : invención f, mejunje m, brebaje m

concord ['kɑn,kɔrd, 'kɑŋ-] n 1 HARMONY : concordia f, armonía f 2 AGREEMENT : acuerdo m

concordance [kən'kɔrdənts] n : concordancia f

concourse ['kɑn,kors] n : explanada f, salón m (para pasajeros)

concrete¹ [kɑn'kriːt, 'kɑn,kriːt] adj 1 REAL : concreto ⟨concrete objects : objetos concretos⟩ 2 SPECIFIC : determinado, específico 3 : de concreto, de hormigón ⟨concrete walls : paredes de concreto⟩

concrete² ['kɑn,kri:t, kɑn'kri:t] *n* : concreto *m*, hormigón *m*

concur [kən'kər] *vi* **concurred; concurring 1** COINCIDE : concurrir, coincidir **2** AGREE : concurrir, estar de acuerdo

concurrence [kən'kərənts] *n* **1** AGREEMENT : coincidencia *f* **2** COINCIDENCE : concurrencia *f*, concurso *m*, coincidencia *f*

concurrent [kən'kərənt] *adj* : concurrente, simultáneo

concussion [kən'kʌʃən] *n* : conmoción *f* cerebral

condemn [kən'dem] *vt* **1** CENSURE : condenar, reprobar, censurar **2** : declarar insalubre (alimentos), declarar ruinoso (un edificio) **3** SENTENCE : condenar ⟨condemned to death : condenado a muerte⟩

condemnation [,kɑn,dem'neɪʃən] *n* : condena *f*, reprobación *f*

condensation [,kɑn,den'seɪʃən, -dən-] *n* : condensación *f*

condense [kən'dents] *v* **-densed; -densing** *vt* **1** ABRIDGE : condensar, resumir **2** : condensar (vapor, etc.) — *vi* : condensarse

condescend [,kɑndɪ'send] *vi* **1** DEIGN : condescender, dignarse **2 to condescend to someone** : tratar a alguien con condescendencia

condescending [,kɑndɪ'sendɪŋ] *adj* : condescendiente

condescension [,kɑndɪ'sentʃən] *n* : condescendencia *f*

condiment [ˈkɑndəmənt] *n* : condimento *m*

condition¹ [kən'dɪʃən] *vt* **1** DETERMINE : condicionar, determinar **2** : acondicionar (el pelo o el aire), poner en forma (el cuerpo)

condition² *n* **1** STIPULATION : condición *f*, estipulación *f* ⟨on the condition that : a condición de que⟩ **2** STATE : condición *f*, estado *m* ⟨in good/poor condition : en buenas/malas condiciones⟩ ⟨he's in good condition : está en buena forma⟩ ⟨he's out of condition : no está en forma⟩ **3 conditions** *npl* : condiciones *fpl*, situación *f* ⟨working conditions : condiciones del trabajo⟩

conditional [kən'dɪʃənəl] *adj* : condicional — **conditionally** *adv*

conditioner [kən'dɪʃənər] *n* : acondicionador *m*

condo [ˈkɑndo:] → **condominium**

condolence [kən'do:lənts] *n* **1** SYMPATHY : condolencia *f* **2 condolences** *npl* : pésame *m*

condom [ˈkɑndəm] *n* : condón *m*

condominium [,kɑndə'mɪniəm] *n*, *pl* **-ums** : condominio *m*

condone [kən'do:n] *vt* **-doned; -doning** : aprobar, perdonar, tolerar

condor [ˈkɑndər, -,dɔr] *n* : cóndor *m*

conducive [kən'du:sɪv, -'dju:-] *adj* : propicio, favorable

conduct¹ [kən'dʌkt] *vt* **1** GUIDE : guiar, conducir ⟨to conduct a tour : guiar una visita⟩ **2** DIRECT : conducir, dirigir ⟨to

conduct an orchestra : dirigir una orquesta⟩ **3** CARRY OUT : realizar, llevar a cabo ⟨to conduct an investigation : llevar a cabo una investigación⟩ **4** TRANSMIT : conducir, transmitir (calor, electricidad, etc.) **5 to conduct oneself** BEHAVE : conducirse, comportarse

conduct² [ˈkɑn,dʌkt] *n* **1** MANAGEMENT : conducción *f*, dirección *f*, manejo *m* ⟨the conduct of foreign affairs : la conducción de asuntos exteriores⟩ **2** BEHAVIOR : conducta *f*, comportamiento *m*

conduction [kən'dʌkʃən] *n* : conducción *f*

conductivity [,kɑn,dʌk'tɪvəţi] *n*, *pl* **-ties** : conductividad *f*

conductor [kən'dʌktər] *n* **1** : conductor *m*, -tora *f*; revisor *m*, -sora *f* (en un tren); cobrador *m*, -dora *f* (en un bus); director *m*, -tora *f* (de una orquesta) **2** : conductor *m* (de electricidad, etc.)

conduit [ˈkɑn,du:ət, -,dju:-] *n* : conducto *m*, canal *m*, vía *f*

cone [ˈko:n] *n* **1** : piña *f* (fruto de las coníferas) **2** : cono *m* (en geometría) **3 ice–cream cone** : cono *m*, barquillo *m*, cucurucho *m*

confection [kən'fekʃən] *n* : dulce *m*

confectioner [kən'fekʃənər] *n* : confitero *m*, -ra *f*

confectionery [kən'fekʃə,neri] *n*, *pl* **-eries 1** : dulces *mpl*, golosinas *fpl* **2** or **confectionery shop** : confitería *f* (tienda)

confederacy [kən'fedərəsi] *n*, *pl* **-cies** : confederación *f*

confederate¹ [kən'fedə,reɪt] *v* **-ated; -ating** *vt* : unir, confederar — *vi* : confederarse, aliarse

confederate² [kən'fedərət] *adj* : confederado

confederate³ *n* : cómplice *mf*; aliado *m*, -da *f*

confederation [kən,fedə'reɪʃən] *n* : confederación *f*, alianza *f*

confer [kən'fər] *v* **-ferred; -ferring** *vt* : conferir, otorgar — *vi* **to confer with** : consultar

conference [ˈkɑnfrənts, -fərənts] *n* : conferencia *f* ⟨press conference : conferencia de prensa⟩

confess [kən'fes] *vt* : confesar — *vi* **1** : confesar ⟨the prisoner confessed : el detenido confesó⟩ **2** : confesarse (en religión)

confession [kən'feʃən] *n* : confesión *f*

confessional [kən'feʃənəl] *n* : confesionario *m*

confessor [kən'fesər] *n* : confesor *m*

confetti [kən'feţi] *n* : confeti *m*

confidant [ˈkɑnfə,dɑnt, -,dænt] *n* : confidente *mf*

confidante [ˈkɑnfə,dɑnt, -,dænt] *n* : confidente *f*

confide [kən'faɪd] *v* **-fided; -fiding** : confiar

confidence [ˈkɑnfədənts] *n* **1** TRUST : confianza *f* **2** SELF-ASSURANCE : confianza *f* en sí mismo, seguridad *f* en sí mismo **3** SECRET : confidencia *f*, secreto *m*

confident ['kɑnfədənt] adj 1 SURE : seguro 2 SELF-ASSURED : confiado, seguro de sí mismo

confidential [ˌkɑnfə'dentʃəl] adj : confidencial — **confidentially** [ˌkɑnfə'dentʃəli] adv

confidentiality [ˌkɑnfəˌdentʃi'æləti] n : confidencialidad f

confidently ['kɑnfədəntli] adv : con seguridad, con confianza

configuration [kənˌfɪgjə'reɪʃən] n : configuración f

configure [kən'fɪgjər] vt : configurar (un sistema, etc.)

confine [kən'faɪn] vt **-fined; -fining** 1 LIMIT : confinar, restringir, limitar 2 IMPRISON : recluir, encarcelar, encerrar

confined [kən'faɪnd] adj SMALL : limitado ⟨confined spaces : espacios limitados⟩

confinement [kən'faɪnmənt] n : confinamiento m, reclusión f, encierro m

confines ['kɑnˌfaɪnz] npl : límites mpl, confines mpl

confirm [kən'fərm] vt 1 RATIFY : ratificar 2 VERIFY : confirmar, verificar 3 : confirmar (en religión)

confirmation [ˌkɑnfər'meɪʃən] n : confirmación f

confiscate ['kɑnfəˌskeɪt] vt **-cated; -cating** : confiscar, incautar, decomisar

confiscation [ˌkɑnfə'skeɪʃən] n : confiscación f, incautación f, decomiso m

conflagration [ˌkɑnflə'greɪʃən] n : conflagración f

conflict¹ [kən'flɪkt] vi : estar en conflicto, oponerse

conflict² ['kɑnˌflɪkt] n : conflicto m ⟨to be in conflict : estar en desacuerdo⟩

confluence [kən'fluːənts, kən'fluːənts] n : confluencia f

conform [kən'fərm] vi 1 ACCORD, COMPLY : ajustarse, adaptarse, conformarse ⟨it conforms with our standards : se ajusta a nuestras normas⟩ 2 CORRESPOND : corresponder, encajar ⟨to conform to the truth : corresponder a la verdad⟩

conformity [kən'fərməti] n, pl **-ties** : conformidad f

confound [kən'faʊnd, kɑn-] vt : confundir, desconcertar

confront [kən'frʌnt] vt : afrontar, enfrentarse a, encarar

confrontation [ˌkɑnfrən'teɪʃən] n : enfrentamiento m, confrontación f

confuse [kən'fjuːz] vt **-fused; -fusing** 1 PUZZLE : confundir, enturbiar 2 COMPLICATE : confundir, enredar, complicar ⟨to confuse the issue : complicar las cosas⟩

confused [kən'fjuːzd] adj 1 : confundido (dícese de una persona) 2 : confuso (dícese de una explicación, etc.)

confusing [kən'fjuːzɪŋ] adj : complicado, que confunde

confusion [kən'fjuːʒən] n 1 PERPLEXITY : confusión f 2 MESS, TURMOIL : confusión f, embrollo m, lío m fam

congeal [kən'dʒiːl] vi 1 FREEZE : congelarse 2 COAGULATE, CURDLE : coagularse, cuajarse

congenial [kən'dʒiːniəl] adj : agradable, simpático

congenital [kən'dʒenətəl] adj : congénito

congest [kən'dʒest] vt 1 : congestionar (en la medicina) 2 CROWD : abarrotar, atestar, congestionar (el tráfico) — vi : congestionarse

congested [kən'dʒestəd] adj : congestionado

congestion [kən'dʒestʃən] n : congestión f

conglomerate¹ [kən'glɑmərət] adj : conglomerado

conglomerate² [kən'glɑmərət] n : conglomerado m

conglomeration [kənˌglɑmə'reɪʃən] n : conglomerado m, acumulación f

Congolese [ˌkɑŋgə'liːz, -'liːs] n : congoleño m, -ña f — **Congolese** adj

congratulate [kən'grædʒəˌleɪt, -'grætʃə-] vt **-lated; -lating** : felicitar

congratulation [kənˌgrædʒə'leɪʃən, -ˌgrætʃə-] n : felicitación f ⟨congratulations! : ¡felicidades!, ¡enhorabuena!⟩

congregate ['kɑŋgrɪˌgeɪt] v **-gated; -gating** vt : congregar, reunir — vi : congregarse, reunirse

congregation [ˌkɑŋgrɪ'geɪʃən] n 1 GATHERING : congregación f, fieles mpl (a un servicio religioso) 2 PARISHIONERS : feligreses mpl

congress ['kɑŋgrəs] n : congreso m

congressional [kən'greʃənəl, kɑn-] adj : del congreso

congressman ['kɑŋgrəsmən] n, pl **-men** [-mən, -ˌmen] : congresista m, diputado m

congresswoman ['kɑŋgrəsˌwʊmən] n, pl **-women** [-ˌwɪmən] : congresista f, diputada f

congruence [kən'gruːənts, 'kɑŋgruːənts] n : congruencia f

congruent [kən'gruːənt, 'kɑŋgruːənt] adj : congruente

conic ['kɑnɪk] → **conical**

conical ['kɑnɪkəl] adj : cónico

conifer ['kɑnəfər, 'koː-] n : conífera f

coniferous [koː'nɪfərəs, kə-] adj : conífero

conjecture¹ [kən'dʒektʃər] v **-tured; -turing** : conjeturar

conjecture² n : conjetura f, presunción f

conjugal ['kɑndʒɪgəl, kən'dʒuː-] adj : conyugal

conjugate ['kɑndʒəˌgeɪt] vt **-gated; -gating** : conjugar

conjugation [ˌkɑndʒə'geɪʃən] n : conjugación f

conjunction [kən'dʒʌŋkʃən] n : conjunción f ⟨in conjunction with : en combinación con⟩

conjunctivitis [kənˌdʒʌŋkti'vaɪtəs] n : conjuntivitis f

conjure ['kɑndʒər, 'kʌn-] v **-jured; -juring** vt 1 ENTREAT : rogar, suplicar 2 to **conjure up** : hacer aparecer (apariciones), evocar (memorias, etc.) — vi : practicar la magia

conjurer or **conjuror** ['kɑndʒərər, 'kʌn-] n : mago m, -ga f; prestidigitador m, -dora f

con man n : timador m

connect [kə'nɛkt] *vt* **1** JOIN, LINK : conectar (cables, etc.), comunicar (habitaciones) **2** RELATE : relacionar, asociar (ideas) ⟨evidence that connects him with the crime : evidencias que lo vinculan con el crimen⟩ — *vi* **1** : conectar, comunicarse ⟨to connect to the Internet : conectar a la Internet⟩ **2 to connect with someone** : sintonizar con alguien

connection [kə'nɛkʃən] *n* : conexión *f*, enlace *m* ⟨professional connections : relaciones profesionales⟩

connective [kə'nɛktɪv] *adj* : conectivo, conjuntivo ⟨connective tissue : tejido conjuntivo⟩ — **connectivity** *n*

connector [kə'nɛktər] *n* : conector *m*

connivance [kə'naɪvənts] *n* : connivencia *f*, complicidad *f*

connive [kə'naɪv] *vi* **-nived; -niving** CONSPIRE, PLOT : actuar en connivencia, confabularse, conspirar

connoisseur [ˌkɑnə'sər, -'sur] *n* : conocedor *m*, -dora *f*; entendido *m*, -da *f*

connotation [ˌkɑnə'teɪʃən] *n* : connotación *f*

connote [kə'no:t] *vt* **-noted; -noting** : connotar

conquer ['kɑŋkər] *vt* : conquistar, vencer

conqueror ['kɑŋkərər] *n* : conquistador *m*, -dora *f*

conquest ['kɑn̩kwɛst, 'kɑŋ-] *n* : conquista *f*

conscience ['kɑntʃənts] *n* : conciencia *f*, consciencia *f* ⟨to have a clear conscience : tener la conciencia limpia⟩

conscientious [ˌkɑntʃi'ɛntʃəs] *adj* : concienzudo — **conscientiously** *adv*

conscious ['kɑntʃəs] *adj* **1** AWARE : consciente ⟨to become conscious of : darse cuenta de⟩ **2** ALERT, AWAKE : consciente **3** INTENTIONAL : intencional, deliberado

consciously ['kɑntʃəsli] *adv* INTENTIONALLY : intencionalmente, deliberadamente, a propósito

consciousness ['kɑntʃəsnəs] *n* **1** AWARENESS : conciencia *f*, consciencia *f* **2** : conocimiento *m* ⟨to lose consciousness : perder el conocimiento⟩

conscript[1] [kən'skrɪpt] *vt* : reclutar, alistar, enrolar

conscript[2] ['kɑn̩skrɪpt] *n* : conscripto *m*, -ta *f*; recluta *mf*

conscription [kən'skrɪpʃən] *n* : conscripción *f*

consecrate ['kɑntsə̩kreɪt] *vt* **-crated; -crating** : consagrar

consecration [ˌkɑntsə'kreɪʃən] *n* : consagración *f*, dedicación *f*

consecutive [kən'sɛkjətɪv] *adj* : consecutivo, seguido ⟨on five consecutive days : cinco días seguidos⟩

consecutively [kən'sɛkjətɪvli] *adv* : consecutivamente

consensus [kən'sɛntsəs] *n* : consenso *m*

consent[1] [kən'sɛnt] *vi* **1** AGREE : acceder, ponerse de acuerdo **2 to consent to do something** : consentir en hacer algo

consent[2] *n* : consentimiento *m*, permiso *m* ⟨by common consent : de común acuerdo⟩

consequence ['kɑntsə̩kwɛnts, -wənts] *n* **1** RESULT : consecuencia *f*, secuela *f* **2** IMPORTANCE : importancia *f*, trascendencia *f*

consequent ['kɑntsə'kwɛnt, -ˌkwɛnt] *adj* : consiguiente

consequential [ˌkɑntsə'kwɛntʃəl] *adj* **1** CONSEQUENT : consiguiente **2** IMPORTANT : importante, trascendente, trascendental

consequently ['kɑntsəkwəntli, -ˌkwɛnt-] *adv* : por consiguiente, por ende, por lo tanto

conservation [ˌkɑntsər'veɪʃən] *n* : conservación *f*, protección *f*

conservationist [ˌkɑntsər'veɪʃənɪst] *n* : conservacionista *f*

conservatism [kən'sərvə̩tɪzəm] *n* : conservadurismo *m*

conservative[1] [kən'sərvə̩tɪv] *adj* **1** : conservador **2** CAUTIOUS : moderado, cauteloso ⟨a conservative estimate : un cálculo moderado⟩

conservative[2] *n* : conservador *m*, -dora *f*

conservatory [kən'sərvə̩tori] *n, pl* **-ries** : conservatorio *m*

conserve[1] [kən'sərv] *vt* **-served; -serving** : conservar, preservar

conserve[2] ['kɑn̩sərv] *n* PRESERVES : confitura *f*

consider [kən'sɪdər] *vt* **1** CONTEMPLATE : considerar, pensar en ⟨we'd considered attending : habíamos pensado en asistir⟩ **2** : considerar, tener en cuenta ⟨consider the consequences : considera las consecuencias⟩ **3** JUDGE, REGARD : considerar, estimar

considerable [kən'sɪdərəbəl] *adj* : considerable — **considerably** [-bli] *adv*

considerate [kən'sɪdərət] *adj* : considerado, atento

consideration [kən̩sɪdə'reɪʃən] *n* : consideración *f* ⟨to take into consideration : tener en cuenta⟩

considering [kən'sɪdərɪŋ] *prep* : teniendo en cuenta, visto

consign [kən'saɪn] *vt* **1** COMMIT, ENTRUST : confiar, encomendar **2** TRANSFER : consignar, transferir **3** SEND : consignar, enviar (mercancía)

consignment [kən'saɪnmənt] *n* **1** : envío *m*, remesa *f* **2 on ~** : en consignación

consist [kən'sɪst] *vi* **1** LIE : consistir ⟨success consists in hard work : el éxito consiste en trabajar duro⟩ **2** : constar, componerse ⟨the set consists of 5 pieces : el juego se compone de 5 piezas⟩

consistency [kən'sɪstəntsi] *n, pl* **-cies** **1** : consistencia *f* (de una mezcla o sustancia) **2** COHERENCE : coherencia *f* **3** UNIFORMITY : regularidad *f*, uniformidad *f*

consistent [kən'sɪstənt] *adj* **1** COMPATIBLE : compatible, coincidente ⟨consistent with policy : coincidente con la política⟩ **2** UNIFORM : uniforme, constante, regular — **consistently** [kən'sɪstəntli] *adv*

consolation [ˌkɑnsəˈleɪʃə n] n 1 : consuelo m 2 **consolation prize** : premio m de consolación
console[1] [kənˈsoːl] vt -soled; -soling : consolar
console[2] [ˈkɑnˌsoːl] n : consola f
consolidate [kənˈsɑləˌdeɪt] vt -dated; -dating : consolidar, unir
consolidation [kɑnˌsɑləˈdeɪʃən] n : consolidación f
consommé [ˌkɑnsəˈmeɪ] n : consomé m
consonant [ˈkɑnsənənt] n : consonante m
consort[1] [kənˈsɔrt] vi : asociarse, relacionarse, tener trato ⟨to consort with criminals : tener trato con criminales⟩
consort[2] [ˈkɑnˌsɔrt] n : consorte mf
consortium [kənˈsɔrʃəm] n, pl **-tia** [-ʃə] or **-tiums** [-ʃəmz] : consorcio m
conspicuous [kənˈspɪkjuəs] adj 1 OBVIOUS : visible, evidente 2 STRIKING : llamativo
conspicuously [kənˈspɪkjuəsli] adv : de manera llamativa
conspiracy [kənˈspɪrəsi] n, pl **-cies** : conspiración f, complot m, confabulación f
conspirator [kənˈspɪrətər] n : conspirador m, -dora f
conspire [kənˈspaɪr] vi -spired; -spiring : conspirar, confabularse
constable [ˈkɑnstəbəl, ˈkʌnstə-] n : agente mf de policía (en un pueblo)
constancy [ˈkɑnstənsi] n, pl **-cies** : constancia f
constant[1] [ˈkɑnstənt] adj 1 FAITHFUL : leal, fiel 2 INVARIABLE : constante, invariable 3 CONTINUAL : constante, continuo
constant[2] n : constante f
constantly [ˈkɑnstəntli] adv : constantemente, continuamente
constellation [ˌkɑnstəˈleɪʃən] n : constelación f
consternation [ˌkɑnstərˈneɪʃən] n : consternación f
constipate [ˈkɑnstəˌpeɪt] vt -pated; -pating : estreñir
constipated [ˈkɑnstəˌpeɪtəd] adj : estreñido
constipation [ˌkɑnstəˈpeɪʃən] n : estreñimiento m, constipación f (de vientre)
constituency [kənˈstɪtʃuənsi] n, pl **-cies** 1 : distrito m electoral 2 : residentes mpl de un distrito electoral
constituent[1] [kənˈstɪtʃuənt] adj 1 COMPONENT : constituyente, componente 2 : constituyente, constitutivo ⟨a constituent assembly : una asamblea constituyente⟩
constituent[2] n 1 COMPONENT : componente m 2 VOTER : elector m, -tora f; votante mf
constitute [ˈkɑnstəˌtuːt, -ˌtjuːt] vt -tuted; -tuting 1 ESTABLISH : constituir, establecer 2 COMPOSE, FORM : constituir, componer
constitution [ˌkɑnstəˈtuːʃən, -ˈtjuː-] n : constitución f
constitutional [ˌkɑnstəˈtuːʃənəl, -ˈtjuː-] adj : constitucional

constitutionality [ˌkɑnstəˌtuːʃəˈnæ-ləti, -ˌtjuː-] n : constitucionalidad f
constrain [kənˈstreɪn] vt 1 COMPEL : constreñir, obligar 2 CONFINE : constreñir, limitar, restringir 3 RESTRAIN : contener, refrenar
constraint [kənˈstreɪnt] n : restricción f, limitación f
constrict [kənˈstrɪkt] vt : estrechar, apretar, comprimir
constriction [kənˈstrɪkʃən] n : estrechamiento m, compresión f
construct [kənˈstrʌkt] vt : construir
construction [kənˈstrʌkʃən] n : construcción f
constructive [kənˈstrʌktɪv] adj : constructivo
construe [kənˈstruː] vt -strued; -struing : interpretar
consul [ˈkɑnsəl] n : cónsul mf
consular [ˈkɑnsələr] adj : consular
consulate [ˈkɑnsələt] n : consulado m
consult [kənˈsʌlt] vt : consultar — vi to **consult with** : consultar con, solicitar la opinión de
consultancy [kənˈsʌltənsi] n, pl **-cies** : consultoría f
consultant [kənˈsʌltənt] n : consultor m, -tora f; asesor m, -sora f
consultation [ˌkɑnsəlˈteɪʃən] n : consulta f
consumable [kənˈsuːməbəl] adj : consumible
consume [kənˈsuːm] vt -sumed; -suming : consumir, usar, gastar
consumer [kənˈsuːmər] n : consumidor m, -dora f
consumerism [kənˈsuːməˌrɪzəm] n : consumismo m
consummate[1] [ˈkɑnsəˌmeɪt] vt -mated; -mating : consumar
consummate[2] [kənˈsʌmət, ˈkɑnsə-mət] adj : consumado, perfecto
consummation [ˌkɑnsəˈmeɪʃən] n : consumación f
consumption [kənˈsʌmpʃən] n USE : consumo m, uso m ⟨consumption of electricity : consumo de electricidad⟩
contact[1] [ˈkɑnˌtækt, kənˈ-] vt : ponerse en contacto con, contactar (con)
contact[2] [ˈkɑnˌtækt] n 1 TOUCHING : contacto m ⟨to come into contact with : entrar en contacto con⟩ 2 TOUCH : contacto m, comunicación f ⟨to lose contact with : perder contacto con⟩ 3 CONNECTION : contacto m (en negocios) 4 → contact lens
contact lens [ˈkɑnˌtæktˈlɛnz] n : lente mf de contacto, pupilente m Mex
contagion [kənˈteɪdʒən] n : contagio m
contagious [kənˈteɪdʒəs] adj : contagioso
contain [kənˈteɪn] vt 1 : contener 2 to **contain oneself** : contenerse
container [kənˈteɪnər] n : recipiente m, envase m
containment [kənˈteɪnmənt] n : contención f
contaminant [kənˈtæmənənt] n : contaminante m
contaminate [kənˈtæməˌneɪt] vt -nated; -nating : contaminar

contamination [kən‚tæmə'neɪʃən] *n* : contaminación *f*

contemplate ['kɑntəm‚pleɪt] *v* **-plated; -plating** *vt* **1** VIEW : contemplar **2** PONDER : contemplar, considerar **3** CONSIDER, PROPOSE : proponerse, proyectar, pensar en ⟨to contemplate a trip : pensar en viajar⟩ — *vi* MEDITATE : meditar

contemplation [‚kɑntəm'pleɪʃən] *n* : contemplación *f*

contemplative [kən'templətɪv, 'kɑntəm‚pleɪtɪv] *adj* : contemplativo

contemporaneous [kən‚tempə'reɪniəs] *adj* → **contemporary**[1]

contemporary[1] [kən'tempə‚reri] *adj* : contemporáneo

contemporary[2] *n, pl* **-raries** : contemporáneo *m*, -nea *f*

contempt [kən'tempt] *n* **1** DISDAIN : desprecio *m*, desdén *m* ⟨to hold in contempt : despreciar⟩ **2** : desacato *m* (ante un tribunal)

contemptible [kən'temptəbəl] *adj* : despreciable, vil

contemptuous [kən'temptʃuəs] *adj* : despectivo, despreciativo, desdeñoso

contemptuously [kən'temptʃuəsli] *adv* : despectivamente, con desprecio

contend [kən'tend] *vi* **1** STRUGGLE : luchar, lidiar, contender ⟨to contend with a problem : lidiar con un problema⟩ **2** COMPETE : competir ⟨to contend for a position : competir por un puesto⟩ — *vt* **1** ARGUE, MAINTAIN : argüir, sostener, afirmar ⟨he contended that he was right : afirmó que tenía razón⟩ **2** CONTEST : protestar contra (una decisión, etc.), disputar

contender [kən'tendər] *n* : contendiente *mf*; aspirante *mf*; competidor *m*, -dora *f*

content[1] [kən'tent] *vt* SATISFY : contentar, satisfacer

content[2] *adj* : conforme, contento, satisfecho

content[3] *n* CONTENTMENT : contento *m*, satisfacción *f* ⟨to one's heart's content : hasta quedar satisfecho, a más no poder⟩

content[4] ['kɑn‚tent] *n* **1** MEANING : contenido *m*, significado *m* **2** PROPORTION : contenido *m*, proporción *f* ⟨fat content : contenido de grasa⟩ **3 contents** *npl* : contenido *m*, sumario *m* (de un libro) ⟨table of contents : índice de materias⟩

contented [kən'tentəd] *adj* : conforme, satisfecho ⟨a contented smile : una sonrisa de satisfacción⟩

contentedly [kən'tentədli] *adv* : con satisfacción

contention [kən'tentʃən] *n* **1** DISPUTE : disputa *f*, discusión *f* **2** COMPETITION : competencia *f*, contienda *f* **3** OPINION : argumento *m*, opinión *f*

contentious [kən'tentʃəs] *adj* **1** CONTROVERSIAL : controvertido **2** DEBATED : discutido **3** ARGUMENTATIVE : discutidor

contentment [kən'tentmənt] *n* : satisfacción *f*, contento *m*

contest[1] [kən'test] *vt* : disputar, cuestionar, impugnar ⟨to contest a will : impugnar un testamento⟩

contest[2] [kən'test] *n* **1** STRUGGLE : lucha *f*, contienda *f* **2** GAME : concurso *m*, competencia *f*

contestable [kən'testəbəl] *adj* : discutible, cuestionable

contestant [kən'testənt] *n* : concursante *mf*; competidor *m*, -dora *f*

context ['kɑn‚tekst] *n* : contexto *m*

contiguous [kən'tɪgjuəs] *adj* : contiguo

continent[1] ['kɑntənənt] *adj* : continente

continent[2] *n* : continente *m* — **continental** [‚kɑntən'entəl] *adj*

contingency [kən'tɪndʒəntsi] *n, pl* **-cies** : contingencia *f*, eventualidad *f* ⟨contingency plan : plan de emergencia⟩

contingent[1] [kən'tɪndʒənt] *adj* **1** POSSIBLE : contingente, eventual **2** ACCIDENTAL : fortuito, accidental **3 to be contingent on** : depender de, estar sujeto a

contingent[2] *n* : contingente *m*

continual [kən'tɪnjuəl] *adj* : continuo, constante — **continually** [kən'tɪnjuəli, -'tɪnjəli] *adv*

continuance [kən'tɪnjuənts] *n* **1** CONTINUATION : continuación *f* **2** DURATION : duración *f* **3** : aplazamiento *m* (de un proceso)

continuation [kən‚tɪnju'eɪʃən] *n* : continuación *f*, prolongación *f*

continue [kən'tɪnju:] *v* **-tinued; -tinuing** *vi* **1** CARRY ON : continuar, seguir, proseguir ⟨please continue : continúe, por favor⟩ **2** ENDURE, LAST : continuar, prolongarse, durar **3** RESUME : continuar, reanudarse — *vt* **1** : continuar, seguir ⟨she continued writing : continuó escribiendo⟩ **2** RESUME : continuar, reanudar **3** EXTEND, PROLONG : continuar, prolongar

continuity [‚kɑntə'nu:əʈi, -'nju:-] *n, pl* **-ties** : continuidad *f*

continuous [kən'tɪnjuəs] *adj* : continuo — **continuously** *adv*

contort [kən'tɔrt] *vt* : torcer, retorcer, contraer (el rostro) — *vi* : contraerse, demudarse

contortion [kən'tɔrʃən] *n* : contorsión *f*

contour ['kɑn‚tur] *n* **1** OUTLINE : contorno *m* **2 contours** *npl* SHAPE : forma *f*, curvas *fpl* **3 contour map** : mapa *m* topográfico

contraband ['kɑntrə‚bænd] *n* : contrabando *m*

contraception [‚kɑntrə'sepʃən] *n* : anticoncepción *f*, contracepción *f*

contraceptive[1] [‚kɑntrə'septɪv] *adj* : anticonceptivo, contraceptivo

contraceptive[2] *n* : anticonceptivo *m*, contraceptivo *m*

contract[1] [kən'trækt, 1 usu 'kɑn‚trækt] *vt* **1** : contratar (servicios profesionales) **2** : contraer (una enfermedad, una deuda) **3** TIGHTEN : contraer (un músculo) **4** SHORTEN : contraer (una palabra) — *vi* : contraerse, reducirse

contract[2] ['kɑn‚trækt] *n* : contrato *m*

contraction [kən'trækʃən] n : contracción f

contractor ['kɑn,træktər, kən'træk-] n : contratista mf

contractual [kən'træktʃuəl] adj : contractual — **contractually** adv

contradict [,kɑntrə'dɪkt] vt : contradecir, desmentir

contradiction [,kɑntrə'dɪkʃən] n : contradicción f

contradictory [,kɑntrə'dɪktəri] adj : contradictorio

contralto [kən'træl,to:] n, pl **-tos** : contralto m (voz), contralto mf (vocalista)

contraption [kən'træpʃən] n DEVICE : aparato m, artefacto m

contrary[1] ['kɑn,treri, 2 often kən-'treri] adj **1** OPPOSITE : contrario, opuesto **2** BALKY, STUBBORN : terco, testarudo **3** **contrary to** : al contrario de, en contra de ⟨contrary to the facts : en contra de los hechos⟩

contrary[2] ['kɑn,treri] n, pl **-traries 1** OPPOSITE : lo contrario, lo opuesto **2** on **the contrary** : al contrario, todo lo contrario

contrast[1] [kən'træst] vi DIFFER : contrastar, diferir — vt COMPARE : contrastar, comparar

contrast[2] ['kɑn,træst] n : contraste m

contravene [,kɑntrə'vi:n] vt **-vened; -vening** : contravenir, infringir

contribute [kən'trɪbjət] v **-uted; -uting** vt : contribuir, aportar (dinero, bienes, etc.) — vi : contribuir

contribution [,kɑntrə'bju:ʃən] n : contribución f

contributor [kən'trɪbjətər] n : contribuidor m, -dora f; colaborador m, -dora f (en periodismo)

contrite ['kɑn,traɪt, kən'traɪt] adj REPENTANT : contrito, arrepentido

contrition [kən'trɪʃən] n : contrición f, arrepentimiento m

contrivance [kən'traɪvənts] n **1** DEVICE : aparato m, artefacto m **2** SCHEME : artimaña f, treta f, ardid m

contrive [kən'traɪv] vt **-trived; -triving 1** DEVISE : idear, ingeniar, maquinar **2** MANAGE : lograr, ingeniárselas para ⟨she contrived a way out of the mess : se las ingenió para salir del enredo⟩

control[1] [kən'tro:l] vt **-trolled; -trolling** : controlar — **controllable** [kən'tro:ləbəl] adj

control[2] n **1** : control m, dominio m, mando m ⟨to be under control : estar bajo control⟩ ⟨to be out of control : estar fuera de control⟩ ⟨he likes to be in control : le gusta mandar⟩ ⟨to be in control of : controlar⟩ ⟨to lose control : perder el control⟩ ⟨it's beyond my control : no está en mis manos⟩ ⟨for reasons beyond our control : por causas ajenas a nuestra voluntad⟩ **2** RESTRAINT : control m, limitación f ⟨birth control : control natal⟩ ⟨gun control : control de armas⟩ **3** : control m, dispositivo m de mando ⟨remote control : control remoto⟩

controller [kən'tro:lər, 'kɑn,-] n **1** → **comptroller 2** : controlador m, -dora f ⟨air traffic controller : controlador aéreo⟩

controversial [,kɑntrə'vərʃəl, -siəl] adj : controvertido ⟨a controversial decision : una decisión controvertida⟩

controversy ['kɑntrə,vərsi] n, pl **-sies** : controversia f

controvert ['kɑntrə,vərt, ,kɑntrə'-] vt : controvertir, contradecir

contusion [kən'tu:ʒən, -tju:-] n BRUISE : contusión f, moretón m

conundrum [kə'nʌndrəm] n RIDDLE : acertijo m, adivinanza f

convalesce [,kɑnvə'lɛs] vi **-lesced; -lescing** : convalecer

convalescence [,kɑnvə'lɛsənts] n : convalecencia f

convalescent[1] [,kɑnvə'lɛsənt] adj : convaleciente

convalescent[2] n : convaleciente mf

convection [kən'vɛkʃən] n : convección f

convene [kən'vi:n] v **-vened; -vening** vt : convocar — vi : reunirse

convenience [kən'vi:njənts] n **1** : conveniencia f ⟨at your convenience : cuando le resulte conveniente⟩ **2** AMENITY : comodidad f ⟨modern conveniences : comodidades modernas⟩

convenience store n : tienda f de conveniencia

convenient [kən'vi:njənt] adj : conveniente, cómodo — **conveniently** adv

convent ['kɑnvənt, -,vɛnt] n : convento m

convention [kən'vɛntʃən] n **1** PACT : convención f, convenio m, pacto m ⟨the Geneva Convention : la Convención de Ginebra⟩ **2** MEETING : convención f, congreso m **3** CUSTOM : convención f

conventional [kən'vɛntʃənəl] adj : convencional — **conventionally** adv

converge [kən'vərdʒ] vi **-verged; -verging** : converger, convergir

convergence [kən'vərdʒənts] n : convergencia f

convergent [kən'vərdʒənt] adj : convergente

conversant [kən'vərsənt] adj **conversant with** : versado con, experto en

conversation [,kɑnvər'seɪʃən] n : conversación f

conversational [,kɑnvər'seɪʃənəl] adj : familiar ⟨a conversational style : un estilo familiar⟩

conversationalist [,kɑnvər'seɪʃənəlɪst] n : conversador m, -dora f

converse[1] [kən'vərs] vi **-versed; -versing** : conversar

converse[2] [kən'vərs, 'kɑn,vərs] adj : contrario, opuesto, inverso

conversely [kən'vərsli, 'kɑn,vərs-] adv : a la inversa

conversion [kən'vərʒən] n **1** CHANGE : conversión f, transformación f, cambio m **2** : conversión f (a una religión)

convert[1] [kən'vərt] vt **1** : convertir (a una religión o un partido) **2** CHANGE : convertir, cambiar — vi : convertirse

convert² ['kɑn,vərt] n : converso m, -sa f

converter or **convertor** [kən'vərtər] n : convertidor m

convertible¹ [kən'vərtəbəl] adj : convertible

convertible² n : convertible m, descapotable m

convex [kɑn'vɛks, 'kɑn,-, kən'-] adj : convexo

convey [kən'veɪ] vt **1** TRANSPORT : transportar, conducir **2** TRANSMIT : transmitir, comunicar, expresar (noticias, ideas, etc.)

conveyance [kən'veɪənts] n **1** TRANSPORT : transporte m, transportación f **2** COMMUNICATION : transmisión f, comunicación f **3** TRANSFER : transferencia f, traspaso m (de una propiedad)

conveyor [kən'veɪər] n : transportador m, -dora f ⟨conveyor belt : cinta transportadora⟩

convict¹ [kən'vɪkt] vt : declarar culpable

convict² ['kɑn,vɪkt] n : preso m, -sa f; presidiario m, -ria f; recluso m, -sa f

conviction [kən'vɪkʃən] n **1** : condena f (de un acusado) **2** BELIEF : convicción f, creencia f

convince [kən'vɪnts] vt **-vinced; -vincing** : convencer

convincing [kən'vɪntsɪŋ] adj : convincente, persuasivo

convincingly [kən'vɪntsɪŋli] adv : de forma convincente

convivial [kən'vɪvjəl, -'vɪvjəl] adj : jovial, festivo, alegre

conviviality [kən,vɪvi'æləti] n, pl **-ties** : jovialidad f

convoke [kən'voːk] vt **-voked; -voking** : convocar

convoluted ['kɑnvə,luːtəd] adj : intrincado, complicado

convoy ['kɑn,vɔɪ] n : convoy m

convulse [kən'vʌls] v **-vulsed; -vulsing** vt : convulsionar ⟨convulsed with laughter : muerto de risa⟩ — vi : sufrir convulsiones

convulsion [kən'vʌlʃən] n : convulsión f

convulsive [kən'vʌlsɪv] adj : convulsivo — **convulsively** adv

coo¹ ['kuː] vi : arrullar

coo² n : arrullo m (de una paloma)

cook¹ ['kʊk] vi : cocinar — vt **1** : preparar (comida) **2 to cook up** CONCOCT : inventar, tramar

cook² n : cocinero m, -ra f

cookbook ['kʊk,bʊk] n : libro m de cocina

cookery ['kʊkəri] n, pl **-eries** : cocina f

cookie or **cooky** ['kʊki] n, pl **-ies** : galleta f (dulce)

cooking ['kʊkɪŋ] n **1** COOKERY : cocina f **2** : cocción f, cocimiento m ⟨cooking time : tiempo de cocción⟩

cookout ['kʊk,aʊt] n : comida f al aire libre

cool¹ ['kuːl] vt : refrescar, enfriar — vi **1** : refrescarse, enfriarse ⟨the pie is cooling : el pastel se está enfriando⟩ **2** : calmarse, tranquilizarse ⟨his anger cooled : su ira se calmó⟩

cool² adj **1** : fresco, frío ⟨cool weather : tiempo fresco⟩ **2** CALM : tranquilo, sereno **3** ALOOF : frío, distante **4** fam EXCELLENT, TRENDY : muy en la onda fam; chévere fam; bacán Chile, Ecua, Uru fam; bacano Col fam; guay Spain fam; chido Mex fam

cool³ n **1** : fresco m ⟨the cool of the evening : el fresco de la tarde⟩ **2** COMPOSURE : calma f, serenidad f

coolant ['kuːlənt] n : refrigerante m

cooler ['kuːlər] n : nevera f portátil

coolly ['kuːlli] adv **1** CALMLY : con calma, tranquilamente **2** COLDLY : fríamente, con frialdad

coolness ['kuːlnəs] n **1** : frescura f, frescor m ⟨the coolness of the evening : el frescor de la noche⟩ **2** CALMNESS : tranquilidad f, serenidad f **3** COLDNESS, INDIFFERENCE : frialdad f, indiferencia f

coop¹ ['kuːp, 'kʊp] vt or **to coop up** : encerrar ⟨cooped up in the house : encerrado en la casa⟩

coop² n : gallinero m

co–op ['koː,ɑp] n → **cooperative²**

cooperate [koˈɑpə,reɪt] vi **-ated; -ating** : cooperar, colaborar

cooperation [ko,ɑpə'reɪʃən] n : cooperación f, colaboración f

cooperative¹ [koˈɑpərətɪv] adj : cooperativo

cooperative² n : cooperativa f

co–opt [koˈɑpt] vt **1** : nombrar como miembro, cooptar **2** APPROPRIATE : apropiarse de

coordinate¹ [koˈɔrdən,eɪt] v **-nated; -nating** vt : coordinar — vi : coordinarse, combinar, acordar

coordinate² [koˈɔrdənət] adj **1** COORDINATED : coordinado **2** EQUAL : igual, semejante

coordinate³ [koˈɔrdənət] n : coordenada f

coordination [ko,ɔrdən'eɪʃən] n : coordinación f

coordinator [koˈɔrdən,eɪtər] n : coordinador m, -dora f

cop ['kɑp] n → **police officer**

cope ['koːp] vi **coped; coping 1** : arreglárselas **2 to cope with** : hacer frente a, poder con ⟨I can't cope with all this! : ¡no puedo con todo esto!⟩

copier ['kɑpiər] n : copiadora f, fotocopiadora f

copilot ['koː,paɪlət] n : copiloto m

copious ['koːpiəs] adj : copioso, abundante — **copiously** adv

copiousness ['koːpiəsnəs] n : abundancia f

copper ['kɑpər] n : cobre m

coppery ['kɑpəri] adj : cobrizo

copse ['kɑps] n THICKET : soto m, matorral m

copulate ['kɑpjə,leɪt] vi **-lated; -lating** : copular

copulation [,kɑpjə'leɪʃən] n : cópula f, relaciones fpl sexuales

copy¹ ['kɑpi] vt **copied; copying 1** DUPLICATE : hacer una copia de, duplicar, reproducir **2** IMITATE : copiar, imitar

copy² *n*, *pl* **copies** 1 : copia *f*, duplicado *m* (de un documento), reproducción *f* (de una obra de arte) 2 : ejemplar *m* (de un libro), número *m* (de una revista) 3 TEXT : manuscrito *m*, texto *m*

copycat ['kɑpi,kæt] *n* : copión *m*, -piona *f*

copyright¹ ['kɑpi,raɪt] *vt* : registrar los derechos de

copyright² *n* : derechos *mpl* de autor

coral¹ ['kɔrəl] *adj* : de coral ⟨a coral reef : un arrecife de coral⟩

coral² *n* : coral *m*

coral snake *n* : serpiente *f* de coral

cord ['kɔrd] *n* 1 ROPE, STRING : cuerda *f*, cordón *m*, cordel *m* 2 : cuerda *f*, cordón *m*, médula *f* (en la anatomía) ⟨vocal cords : cuerdas vocales⟩ 3 : cuerda *f* ⟨a cord of firewood : una cuerda de leña⟩ 4 *or* **electric cord** : cable *m* eléctrico

cordial¹ ['kɔrdʒəl] *adj* : cordial — **cordially** *adv*

cordial² *n* : cordial *m*

cordiality [,kɔrdʒi'æləti] *n* : cordialidad *f*

cordless ['kɔrdləs] *adj* : inalámbrico

córdoba ['kɔrdəbə] *n* : córdoba *f* (unidad monetaria)

cordon¹ ['kɔrdən] *vt* **to cordon off** : acordonar

cordon² *n* : cordón *m*

corduroy ['kɔrdə,rɔɪ] *n* 1 : pana *f* 2 **corduroys** *npl* : pantalones *mpl* de pana

core¹ ['kor] *vt* **cored; coring** : quitar el corazón a (una fruta)

core² *n* 1 : corazón *m*, centro *m* (de algunas frutas) 2 CENTER : núcleo *m*, centro *m* 3 ESSENCE : núcleo *m*, meollo *m* ⟨to the core : hasta la médula⟩

coriander ['kɔri,ændər] *n* : cilantro *m*

cork¹ ['kɔrk] *vt* : ponerle un corcho a

cork² *n* : corcho *m*

corkscrew ['kɔrk,skru:] *n* : tirabuzón *m*, sacacorchos *m*

cormorant ['kɔrmərənt, -,rænt] *n* : cormorán *m*

corn¹ ['kɔrn] *vt* : conservar en salmuera ⟨corned beef : carne en conserva⟩

corn² *n* 1 GRAIN : grano *m* 2 : maíz *m*, choclo *m*, elote *m* Mex ⟨corn tortillas : tortillas de maíz⟩ 3 : callo *m* ⟨corn plaster : emplasto para callos⟩

corncob ['kɔrn,kɑb] *n* : mazorca *f* (de maíz), choclo *m*, elote *m* CA, Mex

cornea ['kɔrniə] *n* : córnea *f*

corner¹ ['kɔrnər] *vt* 1 TRAP : acorralar, arrinconar 2 MONOPOLIZE : monopolizar, acaparar (un mercado) — *vi* : tomar una curva, doblar una esquina (en un automóvil)

corner² *n* 1 ANGLE : rincón *m*, esquina *f* (de una mesa, etc.), ángulo *m* (de una página) ⟨the corner of a room : el rincón de una habitación⟩ ⟨all corners of the world : todos los rincones del mundo⟩ 2 INTERSECTION : esquina *f* 3 BEND : curva *f* (en una carretera) 4 PREDICAMENT, IMPASSE : aprieto *m*, impasse *m* ⟨to be backed into a corner : estar acorralado⟩ 5 **corner of the eye** : lagrimal *m*, rabillo *m* 6 **corner of the mouth** : comisura *f* de los labios 7 **to cut corners** : economizar esfuerzos

corner kick *n* : córner *m*

cornerstone ['kɔrnər,sto:n] *n* : piedra *f* angular

cornet [kɔr'nɛt] *n* : corneta *f*

cornfield ['kɔrn,fi:ld] *n* : maizal *m*; milpa *f* CA, Mex

cornflakes ['kɔrn,fleɪks] *npl* : copos *mpl* de maíz

cornice ['kɔrnɪs] *n* : cornisa *f*

cornmeal ['kɔrn,mi:l] *n* : harina *f* de maíz

cornstalk ['kɔrn,stɔk] *n* : tallo *m* del maíz

cornstarch ['kɔrn,stɑrtʃ] *n* : maicena *f*, almidón *m* de maíz

cornucopia [,kɔrnə'ko:piə, -njə-] *n* : cornucopia *f*

corny ['kɔrni] *adj* **cornier; -est** 1 SENTIMENTAL : sentimental, cursi 2 SILLY : tonto (dícese de un chiste, etc.)

corolla [kə'rɑlə] *n* : corola *f*

corollary ['kɔrə,lɛri] *n*, *pl* **-laries** : corolario *m*

corona [kə'ro:nə] *n* : corona *f* (del sol)

coronary¹ ['kɔrə,nɛri] *adj* : coronario

coronary² *n*, *pl* **-naries** 1 : trombosis *f* coronaria 2 HEART ATTACK : infarto *m*, ataque *m* al corazón

coronation [,kɔrə'neɪʃən] *n* : coronación *f*

coroner ['kɔrənər] *n* : médico *m* forense

corporal¹ ['kɔrpərəl] *adj* : corporal ⟨corporal punishment : castigos corporales⟩

corporal² *n* : cabo *m*

corporate ['kɔrpərət] *adj* : corporativo, empresarial

corporation [,kɔrpə'reɪʃən] *n* : sociedad *f* anónima, corporación *f*, empresa *f*

corporeal [kɔr'poriəl] *adj* 1 PHYSICAL : corpóreo 2 MATERIAL : material, tangible — **corporeally** *adv*

corps ['kor] *n*, *pl* **corps** ['korz] : cuerpo *m* ⟨medical corps : cuerpo médico⟩ ⟨diplomatic corps : cuerpo diplomático⟩

corpse ['korps] *n* : cadáver *m*

corpulence ['kɔrpjələnts] *n* : obesidad *f*, gordura *f*

corpulent ['kɔrpjələnt] *adj* : obeso, gordo

corpuscle ['kɔr,pʌsəl] *n* : corpúsculo *m*, glóbulo *m* (sanguíneo)

corral¹ [kə'ræl] *vt* **-ralled; -ralling** : acorralar (ganado)

corral² *n* : corral *m*

correct¹ [kə'rɛkt] *vt* 1 RECTIFY : corregir, rectificar 2 REPRIMAND : corregir, reprender

correct² *adj* 1 ACCURATE, RIGHT : correcto, exacto ⟨to be correct : estar en lo cierto⟩ 2 PROPER : correcto, apropiado

correction [kə'rɛkʃən] *n* : corrección *f*

corrective [kə'rɛktɪv] *adj* : correctivo

correctly [kə'rɛktli] *adv* : correctamente

correctness [kə'rɛkt(n)nəs] *n* 1 ACCURACY : exactitud *f* 2 PROPRIETY : corrección *f*

correlate ['kɔrə,leɪt] *vt* **-lated; -lating** : relacionar, poner en correlación

correlation [,kɔrə'leɪʃən] *n* : correlación *f*

correspond [,kɔrə'spand] *vi* 1 MATCH : corresponder, concordar, coincidir 2 WRITE : corresponderse, escribirse

correspondence [ˌkɔrə'spandənts] *n* : correspondencia *f*

correspondent [ˌkɔrə'spandənt] *n* : corresponsal *mf*

corresponding [kɔrə'spandɪŋ, kar-] *adj* : correspondiente

correspondingly [ˌkɔrə'spandɪŋli] *adv* : en consecuencia, de la misma manera

corridor ['kɔrədər, -ˌdɔr] *n* : corredor *m*, pasillo *m*

corroborate [kə'rabəˌreɪt] *vt* **-rated; -rating** : corroborar

corroboration [kəˌrabə'reɪʃən] *n* : corroboración *f*

corrode [kə'ro:d] *v* **-roded; -roding** *vt* : corroer — *vi* : corroerse

corrosion [kə'ro:ʒən] *n* : corrosión *f*

corrosive [kə'ro:sɪv] *adj* : corrosivo

corrugate ['kɔrəˌgeɪt] *vt* **-gated; -gating** : ondular, acanalar, corrugar

corrugated ['kɔrəˌgeɪtəd] *adj* : ondulado, acanalado ⟨corrugated cardboard : cartón ondulado⟩

corrupt¹ [kə'rʌpt] *vt* **1** PERVERT : corromper, pervertir, degradar (información) **2** BRIBE : sobornar

corrupt² *adj* : corrupto, corrompido

corruptible [kə'rʌptəbəl] *adj* : corruptible

corruption [kə'rʌpʃən] *n* : corrupción *f*

corsage [kɔr'saʒ, -'saʤ] *n* : ramillete *m* que se lleva como adorno

corset ['kɔrsət] *n* : corsé *m*

cortex ['kɔrˌteks] *n*, *pl* **-tices** ['kɔrtəˌsi:z] *or* **-texes** : corteza *f* ⟨cerebral cortex : corteza cerebral⟩

cortisone ['kɔrtəˌso:n, -zo:n] *n* : cortisona *f*

cosmetic¹ [kaz'metɪk] *adj* : cosmético ⟨cosmetic surgery : cirugía estética⟩

cosmetic² *n* : cosmético *m*

cosmic ['kazmɪk] *adj* **1** : cósmico ⟨cosmic ray : rayo cósmico⟩ **2** VAST : grandioso, inmenso, vasto

cosmonaut ['kazməˌnɔt] *n* : cosmonauta *mf*

cosmopolitan¹ [ˌkazmə'palətən] *adj* : cosmopolita

cosmopolitan² *n* : cosmopolita *mf*

cosmos ['kazməs, -ˌmo:s, -ˌmas] *n* : cosmos *m*, universo *m*

cost¹ ['kɔst] *v* **cost; costing** *vt* : costar ⟨how much does it cost? : ¿cuánto cuesta?, ¿cuánto vale?⟩ — *vi* : costar ⟨these cost more : éstos cuestan más⟩

cost² *n* : costo *m*, precio *m*, coste *m* ⟨cost of living : costo de vida⟩ ⟨victory at all costs : victoria a toda costa⟩

co-star ['ko:ˌstar] *n* : coprotagonista *mf*

Costa Rican¹ [ˌkɔstə'ri:kən] *adj* : costarricense

Costa Rican² *n* : costarricense *mf*

costly ['kɔstli] *adj* : costoso, caro

costume ['kasˌtu:m, -ˌtju:m] *n* **1** : traje *m* ⟨national costume : traje típico⟩ **2** : disfraz *m* ⟨costume party : fiesta de disfraces⟩ **3** OUTFIT : vestimenta *f*, traje *m*, conjunto *m*

costume jewelry *n* : bisutería *f*

cosy ['ko:zi] → **cozy**

cot ['kat] *n* : catre *m*

coterie ['ko:təˌri, ˌko:ʦə'-] *n* : tertulia *f*, círculo *m* (social)

cottage ['kaʧ] *n* : casita *f* (de campo)

cottage cheese *n* : requesón *m*

cotton ['katən] *n* : algodón *m*

cotton batting → **batting**

cotton candy *n* : algodón *m* de azúcar

cottonmouth ['katənˌmaʊθ] → **moccasin**

cottonseed ['katənˌsi:d] *n* : semilla *f* de algodón

cotton swab → **swab**

cottontail ['katənˌteɪl] *n* : conejo *m* de cola blanca

couch¹ ['kaʊʧ] *vt* : expresar, formular ⟨couched in strong language : expresado en lenguaje enérgico⟩

couch² *n* SOFA : sofá *m*

couch potato *n* : haragán *m*, -gana *f*; vago *m*, -ga *f*

cougar ['ku:gər] *n* : puma *m*

cough¹ ['kɔf] *vi* : toser

cough² *n* : tos *f*

could ['kʊd] → **can**

council ['kaʊntsəl] *n* **1** : concejo *m* ⟨city council : concejo municipal, ayuntamiento⟩ **2** MEETING : concejo *m*, junta *f* **3** BOARD : consejo *m* **4** : concilio *m* (eclesiástico)

councillor *or* **councilor** ['kaʊntsələr] *n* : concejal *m*, -jala *f*

councilman ['kaʊntsəlmən] *n*, *pl* **-men** [-mən, -ˌmɛn] : concejal *m*

councilwoman ['kaʊntsəlˌwʊmən] *n*, *pl* **-women** [-ˌwɪmən] : concejala *f*

counsel¹ ['kaʊntsəl] *v* **-seled** *or* **-selled; -seling** *or* **-selling** *vt* ADVISE : aconsejar, asesorar, recomendar — *vi* CONSULT : consultar

counsel² *n* **1** ADVICE : consejo *m*, recomendación *f* **2** CONSULTATION : consulta *f* **3** counsel *ns & pl* LAWYER : abogado *m*, -da *f*

counselor *or* **counsellor** ['kaʊntsələr] *n* : consejero *m*, -ra *f*; consultor *m*, -tora *f*; asesor *m*, -sora *f*

count¹ ['kaʊnt] *vt* **1** : contar **2** INCLUDE : contar **3** CONSIDER : considerar ⟨count yourself (as) lucky : considérate afortunado⟩ **4** to **count down** : contar los días (etc.) que faltan **5** to **count in/out** ⟨count me in : cuenta conmigo, yo me apunto⟩ ⟨count me out : no cuentes conmigo⟩ — *vi* **1** : contar ⟨to count out loud : contar en voz alta⟩ **2** MATTER : contar, valer, importar ⟨that's what counts : eso es lo que cuenta⟩ **3** to **count on** : contar con **4** to **count towards** : contar para

count² *n* **1** COMPUTATION : cómputo *m*, recuento *m*, cuenta *f* ⟨to lose count : perder la cuenta⟩ **2** CHARGE : cargo *m* ⟨two counts of robbery : dos cargos de robo⟩ **3** POINT : punto *m*, aspecto *m* ⟨you're wrong on all counts : se equivoca en todo lo que dice⟩ **4** : conde *m* (noble)

countable ['kaʊntəbəl] *adj* : numerable

countdown ['kaʊntˌdaʊn] *n* : cuenta *f* atrás

countenance¹ ['kaʊntənənts] *vt* **-nanced; -nancing** : permitir, tolerar

countenance² *n* FACE : semblante *m*, rostro *m*

counter¹ [ˈkaʊntər] *vt* **1** → counteract **2** OPPOSE : oponerse a, resistir — *vi* RETALIATE : responder, contraatacar

counter² *adv* **counter to** : contrario a, en contra de

counter³ *adj* : contrario, opuesto

counter⁴ *n* **1** PIECE : ficha *f* (de un juego), **2** : mostrador *m* (de un negocio), ventanilla *f* (en un banco) **3** : contador *m* (aparato) **4** COUNTERBALANCE : fuerza *f* opuesta, contrapeso *m*

counter- *pref* : contra- ⟨counterattack : contraataque⟩

counteract [ˌkaʊntərˈækt] *vt* : contrarrestar

counterattack [ˈkaʊntərəˌtæk] *n* : contraataque *m*

counterbalance¹ [ˌkaʊntərˈbælənts] *vt* **-anced; -ancing** : contrapesar

counterbalance² [ˈkaʊntərˌbælənts] *n* : contrapeso *m*

counterclockwise [ˌkaʊntərˈklɑk-ˌwaɪz] *adv & adj* : en el sentido opuesto al de las manecillas del reloj

counterfeit¹ [ˈkaʊntərˌfɪt] *vt* **1** : falsificar (dinero) **2** PRETEND : fingir, aparentar

counterfeit² *adj* : falso, inauténtico

counterfeit³ *n* : falsificación *f*

counterfeiter [ˈkaʊntərˌfɪt̬ər] *n* : falsificador *m*, -dora *f*

countermand [ˌkaʊntərˈmænd, ˈkaʊntər-] *vt* : contramandar

countermeasure [ˈkaʊntərˌmeʒər] *n* : contramedida *f*

counterpart [ˈkaʊntərˌpɑrt] *n* : homólogo *m*, contraparte *f Mex*

counterpoint [ˈkaʊntərˌpɔɪnt] *n* : contrapunto *m*

counterproductive [ˌkaʊntərprəˈdʌktɪv] *adj* : contraproducente

counterrevolution [ˌkaʊntərˌrevə-ˈluːʃən] *n* : contrarrevolución *f*

counterrevolutionary¹ [ˌkaʊntərˌrevə-ˈluːʃənˌeri] *adj* : contrarrevolucionario

counterrevolutionary² *n, pl* **-ries** : contrarrevolucionario *m*, -ria *f*

countersign [ˈkaʊntərˌsaɪn] *n* : contraseña *f*

countess [ˈkaʊntɪs] *n* : condesa *f*

countless [ˈkaʊntləs] *adj* : incontable, innumerable

country¹ [ˈkʌntri] *adj* : campestre, rural

country² *n, pl* **-tries 1** NATION : país *m*, nación *f*, patria *f* ⟨country of origin : país de origen⟩ ⟨love of one's country : amor a la patria⟩ **2** : campo *m* ⟨they left the city for the country : se fueron de la ciudad al campo⟩

countryman [ˈkʌntrimən] *n, pl* **-men** [-mən, -ˌmɛn] : compatriota *mf*; paisano *m*, -na *f*

countryside [ˈkʌntriˌsaɪd] *n* : campo *m*, campiña *f*

county [ˈkaʊnti] *n, pl* **-ties** : condado *m*

coup [ˈkuː] *n, pl* **coups** [ˈkuːz] **1** : golpe *m* maestro **2** → coup d'état

coup de grâce *or* **coup de grace** [ˌkuːdəˈgrɑs] *ns & pl* : tiro *m* de gracia, golpe *m* de gracia

coup d'état *or* **coup d'etat** [ˌkuːˈdeɪˈtɑ] *n, pl* **coups d'état** *or* **coups d'etat** [ˌkuːˈdeɪˈtɑ] : golpe *m* (de estado), cuartelazo *m*

coupe [ˈkuːp] *n* : cupé *m*

couple¹ [ˈkʌpəl] *vt* **-pled; -pling** : acoplar, enganchar, conectar

couple² *n* **1** PAIR : par *m* ⟨a couple of hours : un par de horas, unas dos horas⟩ **2** : pareja *f* ⟨a young couple : una pareja joven⟩

coupling [ˈkʌpliŋ] *n* : acoplamiento *m*

coupon [ˈkuːˌpɑn, ˈkjuː-] *n* : cupón *m*

courage [ˈkərɪdʒ] *n* : valor *m*, valentía *f*, coraje *m*

courageous [kəˈreɪdʒəs] *adj* : valiente, valeroso

courageously [kəˈreɪdʒəsli] *adv* : con valor, con coraje

courier [ˈkʊriər, ˈkəriər] *n* : mensajero *m*, -ra *f*

course¹ [ˈkors] *vi* **coursed; coursing** : correr (a toda velocidad)

course² *n* **1** PROGRESS : curso *m*, transcurso *m* ⟨to run its course : seguir su curso⟩ ⟨to follow the normal course : seguir su curso normal⟩ ⟨in due course : a su debido tiempo⟩ ⟨in/during the course of : en/durante el transcurso de⟩ **2** DIRECTION : rumbo *m* (de un avión), derrota *f*, derrotero *m* (de un barco) ⟨to stay on course : mantener el rumbo⟩ ⟨to go off course : desviarse de su rumbo⟩ **3** PATH, WAY : camino *m*, vía *f* **4** : plato *m* (de una cena) ⟨the main course : el plato principal⟩ **5** : curso *m* (académico) **6** : pista *f* (de carreras, de esquí, de obstáculos), campo *m* (de golf) **7** **course of action** : línea *f* de conducta **8** **of course** : desde luego, por supuesto ⟨yes, of course! : ¡sí como que sí!⟩

court¹ [ˈkort] *vt* WOO : cortejar, galantear

court² *n* **1** PALACE : palacio *m* **2** RETINUE : corte *f*, séquito *m* **3** COURTYARD : patio *m* **4** : cancha *f* (de tenis, baloncesto, etc.) **5** TRIBUNAL : corte *f*, tribunal *m* ⟨the Supreme Court : la Corte Suprema⟩

courteous [ˈkərtiəs] *adj* : cortés, atento, educado — **courteously** *adv*

courtesan [ˈkortəzən, ˈkər-] *n* : cortesana *f*

courtesy [ˈkortəsi] *n, pl* **-sies** : cortesía *f*

courthouse [ˈkortˌhaʊs] *n* : palacio *m* de justicia, juzgado *m*

courtier [ˈkortiər, ˈkortjər] *n* : cortesano *m*, -na *f*

courtly [ˈkortli] *adj* **courtlier; -est** : distinguido, elegante, cortés

court-martial¹ [ˈkortˌmarʃəl] *vt* : someter a consejo de guerra

court-martial² *n, pl* **courts-martial** [ˈkortsˌmarʃəl] : consejo *m* de guerra

court order *n* : mandamiento *m* judicial

courtroom [ˈkortˌruːm] *n* : tribunal *m*, corte *f*

courtship [ˈkortˌʃɪp] *n* : cortejo *m*, noviazgo *m*

courtyard [ˈkortˌjɑrd] *n* : patio *m*

cousin [ˈkʌzən] *n* : primo *m*, -ma *f*

couture [ku:'tʊr] *n* : industria *f* de la moda ⟨haute couture : alta costura⟩

cove ['ko:v] *n* : ensenada *f*, cala *f*

covenant ['kʌvənənt] *n* : pacto *m*, contrato *m*

cover¹ ['kʌvər] *vt* **1** : cubrir, tapar ⟨cover your head : cúbrete la cabeza⟩ ⟨cover your eyes : tápate los ojos⟩ ⟨cover the pot : tapa la olla, ponle la tapa a la olla⟩ ⟨covered with mud : cubierto de lodo⟩ **2** : tratar (un tema), cubrir (noticias) **3** INSURE : cubrir, asegurar **4** GUARD, PROTECT : cubrir **5** : cubrir (gastos) **6** TRAVEL : recorrer, cubrir **7 to cover one's ass/butt** *fam* : cubrirse las espaldas **8 to cover up** : cubrir, tapar **9 to cover up** HIDE : ocultar — *vi* **1 to cover for** REPLACE : sustituir a **2 to cover for** PROTECT : encubrir a

cover² *n* **1** SHELTER : cubierta *f*, abrigo *m*, refugio *m* ⟨to take cover : ponerse a cubierto⟩ ⟨under cover of darkness : al amparo de la oscuridad⟩ **2** LID, TOP : cubierta *f*, tapa *f* **3** : cubierta *f* (de un libro), portada *f* (de una revista) ⟨to read from cover to cover : leer de principio a fin⟩ **4** : funda *f* (protectora) **5** FRONT, FACADE : fachada *f* **6 covers** *npl* BEDCLOTHES : ropa *f* de cama, cobijas *fpl*, mantas *fpl*

coverage ['kʌvərɪdʒ] *n* : cobertura *f*

coveralls ['kʌvər,ɔlz] *npl* : overol *m* (con mangas)

covering ['kʌvərɪŋ] *n* : cubierta *f*

coverlet ['kʌvərlət] *n* : cobertor *m*

cover letter *n* : carta *f* de presentación

covert¹ ['ko:,vərt, 'kʌvərt] *adj* : encubierto, secreto ⟨covert operations : operaciones encubiertas⟩

covert² ['kʌvərt, 'ko:-] *n* THICKET : espesura *f*, maleza *f*

cover-up ['kʌvər,ʌp] *n* : encubrimiento *m* (de algo ilícito)

covet ['kʌvət] *vt* : codiciar

covetous ['kʌvətəs] *adj* : codicioso

covey ['kʌvi] *n, pl* **-eys** **1** : bandada *f* pequeña (de codornices, etc.) **2** GROUP : grupo *m*

cow¹ ['kaʊ] *vt* : intimidar, acobardar

cow² *n* : vaca *f*, hembra *f* (de ciertas especies)

coward ['kaʊərd] *n* : cobarde *mf*

cowardice ['kaʊərdɪs] *n* : cobardía *f*

cowardly ['kaʊərdli] *adj* : cobarde

cowbell ['kaʊ,bɛl] *n* : cencerro *m*, esquila *f*

cowboy ['kaʊ,bɔɪ] *n* : vaquero *m*, cowboy *m*

cower ['kaʊər] *vi* : encogerse (de miedo), acobardarse

cowgirl ['kaʊ,gərl] *n* : vaquera *f*

cowherd ['kaʊ,hərd] *n* : vaquero *m*, -ra *f*

cowhide ['kaʊ,haɪd] *n* : cuero *m*, piel *f* de vaca

cowl ['kaʊl] *n* : capucha *f* (de un monje)

cowlick ['kaʊ,lɪk] *n* : remolino *m*

coworker ['ko:,wərkər] *n* : colega *mf*; compañero *m*, -ra *f* de trabajo

cowpuncher ['kaʊ,pʌntʃər] → **cowboy**

cowslip ['kaʊ,slɪp] *n* : prímula *f*, primavera *f*

coxswain ['kɑksən, -,sweɪn] *n* : timonel *m*

coy ['kɔɪ] *adj* **1** SHY : tímido, cohibido **2** FLIRTATIOUS : coqueto

coyote [kaɪ'o:ti, 'kaɪ,o:t] *n, pl* **coyotes** *or* **coyote** : coyote *m*

cozy ['ko:zi] *adj* **cozier; -est** : acogedor, cómodo

CPR [,si:,pi:'ɑr] *n* (cardiopulmonary resuscitation) : resucitación *f* cardiopulmonar

CPU [,si:,pi:'ju:] *n* (central processing unit) : CPU *mf*, UPC *mf*, UCP *mf*

crab ['kræb] *n* : cangrejo *m*, jaiba *f*

crabby ['kræbi] *adj* **crabbier; -est** : gruñón, malhumorado

crabgrass ['kræb,græs] *n* : digitaria *f*, gramilla *f*

crack¹ ['kræk] *vt* **1** : chasquear, hacer restallar (un látigo, etc.) ⟨to crack one's knuckles : hacer crujir los nudillos⟩ **2** SPLIT : rajar, agrietar, resquebrajar **3** BREAK : romper (un huevo), cascar (nueces), forzar (una caja fuerte) **4** OPEN : abrir (un libro), dejar entreabierta (una puerta, etc.) **5** SOLVE : resolver, descifrar (un código) **6 to crack a smile** : sonreír — *vi* **1** : restallar ⟨the whip cracked : el látigo restalló⟩ **2** SPLIT : rajarse, resquebrajarse, agrietarse **3** : quebrarse (dícese de la voz) **4** : dejar de resistirse (en un interrogatorio, etc.) ⟨he cracked under the strain : sufrió una crisis nerviosa⟩ **5 to crack down on** : tomar medidas severas contra **6 to crack up** : echarse a reír **7 to get cracking** : ponerse manos a la obra

crack² *adj* FIRST-RATE : buenísimo, de primera

crack³ *n* **1** : chasquido *m*, restallido *m*, estallido *m* (de un arma de fuego), crujido *m* (de huesos) ⟨a crack of thunder : un trueno⟩ **2** WISECRACK : chiste *m*, ocurrencia *f*, salida *f* **3** CREVICE : raja *f*, grieta *f*, fisura *f* **4** BLOW : golpe *m* **5** ATTEMPT : intento *m*

crackdown ['kræk,daʊn] *n* : medidas *fpl* enérgicas

crack down *vt* : tomar medidas enérgicas

cracker ['krækər] *n* : galleta *f* (de soda, etc.)

crackle¹ ['krækəl] *vi* **-led; -ling** : chisporrotear, crujir

crackle² *n* : crujido *m*

crackpot ['kræk,pɑt] *n* : excéntrico *m*, -ca *f*; chiflado *m*, -da *f*

crack-up ['kræk,ʌp] *n* **1** CRASH : choque *m*, estrellamiento *m* **2** BREAKDOWN : crisis *f* nerviosa

crack up *vt* **1** : estrellar (un vehículo) **2** : hacer reír **3** : elogiar ⟨it isn't all that it's cracked up to be : no es tan bueno como se dice⟩ — *vi* **1** : estrellarse **2** LAUGH : echarse a reír

cradle¹ ['kreɪdəl] *n* **-dled; -dling** : acunar, mecer (a un niño)

cradle² *n* : cuna *f*

craft ['kræft] *n* **1** TRADE : oficio *m* ⟨the craft of carpentry : el oficio de carpintero⟩ **2** CRAFTSMANSHIP, SKILL : arte *m*, artesanía *f*, destreza *f* **3** CRAFTINESS

: astucia f, maña f 4 pl usually craft BOAT : barco m, embarcación f 5 pl usually craft AIRCRAFT : avión m, aeronave f

craftiness [ˈkræftinəs] n : astucia f, maña f

craftsman [ˈkræftsmən] n, pl -men [-mən, -ˌmɛn] : artesano m, -na f

craftsmanship [ˈkræftsmənˌʃɪp] n : artesanía f, destreza f

crafty [ˈkræfti] adj craftier; -est : astuto, taimado

crag [ˈkræg] n : peñasco m

craggy [ˈkrægi] adj craggier; -est : peñascoso

cram [ˈkræm] v crammed; cramming vt 1 JAM : embutir, meter 2 STUFF : atiborrar, abarrotar ⟨crammed with people : atiborrado de gente⟩ — vi : estudiar a última hora, memorizar (para un examen)

cramp[1] [ˈkræmp] vt 1 : dar calambre en 2 RESTRICT : limitar, restringir, entorpecer ⟨to cramp someone's style : cortarle el vuelo a alguien⟩ — vi or to cramp up : acalambrarse

cramp[2] n 1 SPASM : calambre m, espasmo m (de los músculos) 2 cramps npl : retorcijones mpl ⟨stomach cramps : retorcijones de estómago⟩

cranberry [ˈkrænˌberi] n, pl -berries : arándano m (rojo y agrio)

crane[1] [ˈkreɪn] v craned; craning ⟨to crane one's neck : estirar el cuello⟩

crane[2] n 1 : grulla f (ave) 2 : grúa f (máquina)

cranial [ˈkreɪniəl] adj : craneal, craneano

cranium [ˈkreɪniəm] n, pl -niums or -nia [-niə] : cráneo m

crank[1] [ˈkræŋk] vt or to crank up : arrancar (con una manivela)

crank[2] n 1 : manivela f, manubrio m 2 ECCENTRIC : excéntrico m, -ca f

cranky [ˈkræŋki] adj crankier; -est : irritable, malhumorado

cranny [ˈkræni] n, pl -nies : grieta f ⟨every nook and cranny : todos los rincones⟩

crash[1] [ˈkræʃ] vi 1 SMASH : caerse con estrépito, estrellarse 2 COLLIDE : estrellarse, chocar 3 BOOM, RESOUND : retumbar, resonar — vt 1 SMASH : estrellar 2 to crash a party : colarse en una fiesta 3 to crash one's car : tener un accidente

crash[2] n 1 DIN : estrépito m 2 COLLISION : choque m, colisión f ⟨car crash : accidente automovilístico⟩ 3 FAILURE : quiebra f (de un negocio), crac m (de la bolsa)

crash course n : curso m intensivo

crash helmet n : casco m

crass [ˈkræs] adj : grosero, de mal gusto

crate[1] [ˈkreɪt] vt crated; crating : empacar en un cajón

crate[2] n : cajón m (de madera)

crater [ˈkreɪtər] n : cráter m

cravat [krəˈvæt] n : corbata f

crave [ˈkreɪv] vt craved; craving : ansiar, apetecer, tener muchas ganas de

craven [ˈkreɪvən] adj : cobarde, pusilánime

craving [ˈkreɪvɪŋ] n : ansia f, antojo m, deseo m

crawfish [ˈkrɔˌfɪʃ] → crayfish

crawl[1] [ˈkrɔl] vi 1 CREEP : arrastrarse, gatear (dícese de un bebé) 2 TEEM : estar plagado

crawl[2] n 1 : paso m lento 2 : crol m (en natación)

crayfish [ˈkreɪˌfɪʃ] n 1 : ástaco m (de agua dulce) 2 : langostino m (de mar)

crayon [ˈkreɪˌɑn, -ən] n : crayón m

craze [ˈkreɪz] n : moda f pasajera, manía f

crazed [ˈkreɪzd] adj : enloquecido

crazily [ˈkreɪzəli] adv : locamente, erráticamente, insensatamente

craziness [ˈkreɪzinəs] n : locura f, demencia f

crazy [ˈkreɪzi] adj crazier; -est 1 usu offensive INSANE : loco, demente ⟨to go crazy : volverse loco⟩ 2 ABSURD, FOOLISH : loco, insensato, absurdo 3 WEIRD, OUTLANDISH : extraño, raro 4 WILD : loco ⟨the team won and the crowd went crazy : el equipo ganó y el público se enloqueció⟩ 5 like crazy : como loco 6 to be crazy about : estar loco por 7 to drive someone crazy : sacar a alguien de quicio

creak[1] [ˈkrik] vi : chirriar, rechinar, crujir

creak[2] n : chirrido m, crujido m

creaky [ˈkriki] adj creakier; -est : chirriante, que cruje

cream[1] [ˈkrim] vt 1 BEAT, MIX : batir, mezclar (azúcar y mantequilla, etc.) 2 : preparar (alimentos) con crema

cream[2] n 1 : crema f, nata f Spain (de leche) ⟨whipped cream : crema batida, nata montada⟩ 2 LOTION : crema f, loción f 3 ELITE : crema f, elite f ⟨the cream of the crop : la crema y nata, lo mejor⟩

cream cheese n : queso m crema

creamery [ˈkriməri] n, pl -eries : fábrica f de productos lácteos

creamy [ˈkrimi] adj creamier; -est : cremoso

crease[1] [ˈkris] vt creased; creasing 1 : plegar, poner una raya en (pantalones) 2 WRINKLE : arrugar

crease[2] n : pliegue m, doblez m, raya f (de pantalones)

create [kriˈeɪt] vt -ated; -ating : crear, hacer

creation [kriˈeɪʃən] n : creación f

creative [kriˈeɪtɪv] adj : creativo, original ⟨creative people : personas creativas⟩ ⟨a creative work : un obra original⟩

creatively [kriˈeɪtɪvli] adv : creativamente, con originalidad

creativity [ˌkriˌeɪˈtɪvəti] n : creatividad f

creator [kriˈeɪtər] n : creador m, -dora f

creature [ˈkritʃər] n : ser m viviente, criatura f, animal m

crèche [ˈkrɛʃ, ˈkreɪʃ] n : nacimiento m

credence [ˈkridənts] n : crédito m

credentials [krɪˈdɛntʃəlz] npl : referencias fpl oficiales, cartas fpl credenciales

credibility [ˌkrɛdəˈbɪləti] n : credibilidad f

credible ['krɛdəbəl] *adj* : creíble

credit[1] ['krɛdɪt] *vt* **1** BELIEVE : creer, dar crédito a **2** : ingresar, abonar ⟨to credit $100 to an account : ingresar $100 en (una) cuenta⟩ **3** ATTRIBUTE : atribuir ⟨they credit the invention to him : a él se le atribuye el invento⟩

credit[2] *n* **1** : saldo *m* positivo, saldo *m* a favor (de una cuenta) **2** : crédito *m* ⟨to buy on credit : comprar a crédito⟩ ⟨credit card : tarjeta de crédito⟩ ⟨credit limit : límite de crédito⟩ ⟨credit history : historial crediticio⟩ **3** CREDENCE : crédito *m* ⟨I gave credit to everything he said : di crédito a todo lo que dijo⟩ **4** RECOGNITION : reconocimiento *m* ⟨he deserves all the credit : todo el mérito es suyo⟩ ⟨to get/take the credit for : llevarse/atribuirse el mérito de⟩ **5** : orgullo *m*, honor *m* ⟨she's a credit to the school : ella es el orgullo de la escuela⟩ **6** : crédito *m* ⟨a course worth three credits : un curso de tres créditos⟩ ⟨extra credit : puntos extras⟩ **7 credits** *npl* : créditos *mpl* (de una película)

creditable ['krɛdətəbəl] *adj* : encomiable, loable — **creditably** [-bli] *adv*

credit card *n* : tarjeta de crédito

creditor ['krɛdɪt̬ər] *n* : acreedor *m*, -dora *f*

credo ['kri:do:, 'kreɪ-] *n* : credo *m*

credulity [krɪ'du:lət̬i, -'dju:-] *n* : credulidad *f*

credulous ['krɛdʒələs] *adj* : crédulo

creed ['kri:d] *n* : credo *m*

creek ['kri:k, 'krɪk] *n* : arroyo *m*, riachuelo *m*

creel ['kri:l] *n* : nasa *f*, cesta *f* (de pescador)

creep[1] ['kri:p] *vi* **crept** ['krɛpt]; **creeping 1** CRAWL : arrastrarse, gatear **2** : moverse lentamente o sigilosamente ⟨he crept out of the house : salió sigilosamente de la casa⟩ **3** SPREAD : trepar (dícese de una planta)

creep[2] *n* **1** CRAWL : paso *m* lento **2** : asqueroso *m*, -sa *f* **3 creeps** *npl* : escalofríos *mpl* ⟨that gives me the creeps : eso me da escalofríos⟩

creeper ['kri:pər] *n* : planta *f* trepadora, trepadora *f*

creepy ['kri:pi] *adj* **1** SPOOKY : que da miedo, espeluznante **2** UNPLEASANT : asqueroso

cremate ['kri:ˌmeɪt] *vt* **-mated; -mating** : cremar

cremation [krɪ'meɪʃən] *n* : cremación *f*

crematorium [ˌkri:mə'toriəm, ˌkrɛ-] *n* : crematorio *m*

Creole ['kri:ˌo:l] *n* **1** : criollo *m*, criolla *f* **2** : criollo *m* (idioma) — **Creole** *adj*

crepe *or* **crêpe** ['kreɪp] *n* **1** : crespón *m* (tela) **2** PANCAKE : crepe *mf*, crepa *f* Mex

crepe paper *n* : papel *m* crepé

crescendo [krɪ'ʃɛnˌdo:] *n*, *pl* **-dos** *or* **-does** : crescendo *m*

crescent ['krɛsənt] *n* : creciente *m*

crest ['krɛst] *n* **1** : cresta *f*, penacho *m* (de un ave) **2** PEAK, TOP : cresta *f* (de una ola), cima *f* (de una colina) **3** : emblema *m* (sobre un escudo de armas)

crestfallen ['krɛstˌfɔlən] *adj* : alicaído, abatido

cretin ['kri:t̬ən] *n* **1** *often offensive* : cretino *m*, -na *f* (en medicina) **2** : cretino *m*, -na *f*; imbécil *mf*

crevasse [krɪ'væs] *n* : grieta *f*, fisura *f*

crevice ['krɛvɪs] *n* : grieta *f*, hendidura *f*

crew ['kru:] *n* **1** : tripulación *f* (de una nave) **2** TEAM : equipo *m* (de trabajadores o atletas)

crew cut *n* : pelo *m* al rape, casquete *m* corto Mex

crib ['krɪb] *n* **1** MANGER : pesebre *m* **2** GRANARY : granero *m* **3** : cuna *f* (de un bebé)

crick ['krɪk] *n* : calambre *m*, espasmo *m* muscular

cricket ['krɪkət] *n* **1** : grillo *m* (insecto) **2** : críquet *m* (juego)

crime ['kraɪm] *n* **1** : crimen *m*, delito *m* ⟨to commit a crime : cometer un delito⟩ **2** : crimen *m*, delincuencia *f* ⟨organized crime : crimen organizado⟩

criminal[1] ['krɪmənəl] *adj* : criminal

criminal[2] *n* : criminal *mf*, delincuente *mf*

crimp ['krɪmp] *vt* : ondular, rizar (el pelo), arrugar (una tela, etc.)

crimson ['krɪmzən] *n* : carmesí *m*

cringe ['krɪndʒ] *vi* **cringed; cringing** : encogerse

crinkle[1] ['krɪŋkəl] *v* **-kled; -kling** *vt* : arrugar — *vi* : arrugarse

crinkle[2] *n* : arruga *f*

crinkly ['krɪŋkəli] *adj* : arrugado

cripple[1] ['krɪpəl] *vt* **-pled; -pling 1** DISABLE : lisiar, dejar inválido **2** INCAPACITATE : inutilizar, incapacitar

cripple[2] *n* *offensive* : lisiado *m*, -da *f* offensive

crisis ['kraɪsɪs] *n*, *pl* **crises** [-ˌsi:z] : crisis *f*

crisp[1] ['krɪsp] *vt* : tostar, hacer crujiente

crisp[2] *adj* **1** CRUNCHY : crujiente, crocante **2** FIRM, FRESH : firme, fresco ⟨crisp lettuce : lechuga fresca⟩ **3** LIVELY : vivaz, alegre ⟨a crisp tempo : un ritmo alegre⟩ **4** INVIGORATING : fresco, vigorizante ⟨the crisp autumn air : el fresco aire otoñal⟩ — **crisply** *adv*

crisp[3] *n* : postre *m* de fruta (con pedacitos de masa dulce por encima)

crispy ['krɪspi] *adj* **crispier; -est** : crujiente ⟨crispy potato chips : papitas crujientes⟩

crisscross ['krɪsˌkrɔs] *vt* : entrecruzar

criterion [kraɪ'tɪriən] *n*, *pl* **-ria** [-iə] : criterio *m*

critic ['krɪtɪk] *n* **1** : crítico *m*, -ca *f* (de las artes) **2** FAULTFINDER : detractor *m*, -tora *f*; criticón *m*, -cona *f*

critical ['krɪtɪkəl] *adj* : crítico

critically ['krɪtɪkli] *adv* : críticamente ⟨critically ill : gravemente enfermo⟩

criticism ['krɪt̬əˌsɪzəm] *n* : crítica *f*

criticize ['krɪt̬əˌsaɪz] *vt* **-cized; -cizing 1** EVALUATE, JUDGE : criticar, analizar, evaluar **2** CENSURE : criticar, reprobar

critique [krɪ'ti:k] *n* : crítica *f*, evaluación *f*

croak[1] ['kro:k] *vi* : croar

croak[2] *n* : croar *m*, canto *m* (de la rana)

Croatian [kro'eɪʃən] n : croata mf — **Croatian** adj

crochet[1] [kro:'ʃeɪ] v : tejer al croché

crochet[2] n : croché m, crochet m

crock ['krak] n : vasija f de barro

crockery ['krakəri] n : vajilla f (de barro)

crocodile ['krakə‚daɪl] n : cocodrilo m

crocus ['kro:kəs] n, pl -cuses : azafrán m

croissant [krə'sant] n : croissant m

crone ['kro:n] n : vieja f bruja

crony ['kro:ni] n, pl -nies : amigote m fam; compinche mf fam

crook[1] ['kruk] vt : doblar (el brazo o el dedo)

crook[2] n 1 STAFF : cayado m (de pastor), báculo m (de obispo) 2 THIEF : ratero m, -ra f; ladrón m, -drona f

crooked ['krukəd] adj 1 BENT : chueco, torcido 2 DISHONEST : deshonesto

crookedness ['krukədnəs] n 1 : lo torcido, lo chueco 2 DISHONESTY : falta f de honradez

croon ['kru:n] v : cantar suavemente

crop[1] ['krap] v cropped; cropping vt TRIM : recortar, cortar — vi to crop up : aparecer, surgir ⟨these problems keep cropping up : estos problemas no cesan de surgir⟩

crop[2] n 1 : buche m (de un ave o insecto) 2 WHIP : fusta f (de jinete) 3 HARVEST : cosecha f, cultivo m

croquet [‚kro:'keɪ] n : croquet m

croquette [kro:'ket] n : croqueta f

cross[1] ['krɔs] vt 1 : cruzar, atravesar ⟨to cross the street : cruzar la calle⟩ ⟨several canals cross the city : varios canales atraviesan la ciudad⟩ 2 : cruzar (los brazos, los dedos, las piernas) 3 INTERBREED : cruzar (en genética) 4 cross my heart : te lo juro 5 to cross off/out : tachar ⟨he crossed his name off the list : tachó su nombre de la planilla⟩ ⟨he crossed off his name : tachó su nombre⟩ 6 to cross one's mind : ocurrírsele a uno 7 to cross paths : cruzarse con alguien ⟨I crossed paths with him, we crossed paths : me crucé con él⟩

cross[2] adj 1 : que atraviesa ⟨cross ventilation : ventilación que atraviesa un cuarto⟩ 2 CONTRARY : contrario, opuesto ⟨cross purposes : objetivos opuestos⟩ 3 ANGRY : enojado, de mal humor

cross[3] n 1 : cruz f ⟨the sign of the cross : la señal de la cruz⟩ 2 : cruza f (en biología)

crossbar ['krɔs‚bar] n : travesaño m, tranca f

crossbones ['krɔs‚bo:nz] npl 1 : huesos mpl cruzados 2 → skull

crossbow ['krɔs‚bo:] n : ballesta f

crossbreed ['krɔs‚bri:d] vt -bred [-‚bred]; -breeding : cruzar

cross–country ['krɔs'kʌntri] n : cross m

crosscurrent ['krɔs‚kərənt] n : contracorriente f

cross–examination [‚krɔsɪg‚zæmə'neɪʃən] n : repreguntas fpl, interrogatorio m

cross–examine [‚krɔsɪg'zæmən] vt -ined; -ining : repreguntar

cross–eyed ['krɔs‚aɪd] adj : bizco

crossfire ['krɔs‚faɪr] n : fuego m cruzado

crossing ['krɔsɪŋ] n 1 INTERSECTION : cruce m, paso m ⟨pedestrian crossing : paso de peatones⟩ 2 VOYAGE : travesía f (del mar)

cross–legged ['krɔs‚legəd] adv : con las piernas cruzadas

crossly ['krɔsli] adv : con enojo, con enfado

crosspiece ['krɔs‚pi:s] n : travesaño m

cross–reference ['krɔs'refrənts, -‚refə'rənts] n : referencia f, remisión f

crossroads ['krɔs‚ro:dz] n : cruce m, encrucijada f, crucero m Mex

cross section n 1 SECTION : corte m transversal 2 SAMPLE : muestra f representativa ⟨a cross section of the population : una muestra representativa de la población⟩

crosswalk ['krɔs‚wɔk] n : cruce m peatonal, paso m de peatones

crossways ['krɔs‚weɪz] → crosswise

crosswise[1] ['krɔs‚waɪz] adv : transversalmente, diagonalmente

crosswise[2] adj : transversal, diagonal

crossword ['krɔs‚wərd] or crossword puzzle n : crucigrama m

crotch ['kratʃ] n : entrepierna f

crotchety ['kratʃəti] adj CRANKY : malhumorado, irritable, enojadizo

crouch ['krautʃ] vi : agacharse, ponerse de cuclillas

croup ['kru:p] n : crup m

crouton ['kru:‚tan] n : crutón m

crow[1] ['kro:] vi 1 : cacarear, cantar (como un cuervo) 2 BRAG : alardear, presumir

crow[2] n 1 : cuervo m (ave) 2 : cantar m (del gallo)

crowbar ['kro:‚bar] n : palanca f

crowd[1] ['kraud] vi : aglomerarse, amontonarse — vt : atestar, atiborrar, llenar

crowd[2] n : multitud f, muchedumbre f, gentío m

crowded ['kraudəd] adj : repleto, atestado, abarrotado

crown[1] ['kraun] vt : coronar

crown[2] n : corona f

crow's–feet npl : patas fpl de gallo

crucial ['kru:ʃəl] adj : crucial, decisivo

crucible ['kru:səbəl] n : crisol m

crucifix ['kru:sə‚fɪks] n : crucifijo m

crucifixion [‚kru:sə'fɪkʃən] n : crucifixión f

crucify ['kru:sə‚faɪ] vt -fied; -fying : crucificar

crude ['kru:d] adj cruder; -est 1 RAW, UNREFINED : crudo, sin refinar ⟨crude oil : petróleo crudo⟩ 2 VULGAR : grosero, de mal gusto 3 ROUGH : tosco, burdo, rudo

crudely ['kru:dli] adv 1 VULGARLY : groseramente 2 ROUGHLY : burdamente, de manera rudimentaria

crudity ['kru:dəti] n, pl -ties 1 VULGARITY : grosería f 2 COARSENESS, ROUGHNESS : tosquedad f, rudeza f

cruel ['kru:əl] adj crueler or crueller; cruelest or cruellest : cruel

cruelly ['kru:əli] *adv* : cruelmente
cruelty ['kru:əlti] *n, pl* -**ties** : crueldad *f*
⟨the tyrant's cruelty : la crueldad del tirano⟩ ⟨the cruelties of war : las crueldades de la guerra⟩
cruet ['kru:ɪt] *n* : vinagrera *f*, aceitera *f*
cruise[1] ['kru:z] *vi* **cruised; cruising** 1 : hacer un crucero 2 : navegar o conducir a una velocidad constante ⟨cruising speed : velocidad de crucero⟩
cruise[2] *n* : crucero *m*
cruiser ['kru:zər] *n* 1 WARSHIP : crucero *m*, buque *m* de guerra 2 : patrulla *f* (de policía)
crumb ['krʌm] *n* : miga *f*, migaja *f* ⟨bread crumbs : migas de pan, pan rallado⟩
crumble ['krʌmbəl] *v* -**bled; -bling** *vt* : desmigajar, desmenuzar — *vi* : desmigajarse, desmoronarse, desmenuzarse
crumbly ['krʌmbli] *adj* : que se desmenuza fácilmente
crummy ['krʌmi] *adj* **crummier; -est** *fam* : malo
crumple ['krʌmpəl] *v* -**pled; -pling** *vt* RUMPLE : arrugar — *vi* 1 WRINKLE : arrugarse 2 COLLAPSE : desplomarse
crunch[1] ['krʌntʃ] *vt* 1 : ronzar (con los dientes) 2 : hacer crujir (con los pies, etc.) — *vi* : crujir
crunch[2] *n* : crujido *m*
crunchy ['krʌntʃi] *adj* **crunchier; -est** : crujiente
crusade[1] [kru:'seɪd] *vi* -**saded; -sading** : hacer una campaña (a favor de o contra algo)
crusade[2] *n* 1 : campaña *f* (de reforma, etc.) 2 Crusade : cruzada *f*
crusader [kru:'seɪdər] *n* 1 : cruzado *m* (en la Edad Media) 2 : campeón, -peona *f* (de una causa)
crush[1] ['krʌʃ] *vt* 1 SQUASH : aplastar, apachurrar 2 GRIND, PULVERIZE : triturar, machacar 3 SUPPRESS : suprimir 4 DEFEAT : darle una paliza a
crush[2] *n* 1 CROWD, MOB : gentío *m*, multitud *f*, aglomeración *f* 2 INFATUATION : enamoramiento *m*
crushing ['krʌʃɪŋ] *adj* : aplastante, abrumador
crust ['krʌst] *n* 1 : corteza *f*, costra *f* (de pan) 2 : tapa *f* de masa, pasta *f* (de un pastel) 3 LAYER : capa *f*, corteza *f* ⟨the earth's crust : la corteza terrestre⟩
crustacean [ˌkrʌs'teɪʃən] *n* : crustáceo *m*
crusty ['krʌsti] *adj* **crustier; -est** 1 : de corteza dura 2 CROSS, GRUMPY : enojado, malhumorado
crutch ['krʌtʃ] *n* : muleta *f*
crux ['krʌks, 'krʊks] *n, pl* **cruxes** : quid *m*, esencia *f*, meollo *m* ⟨the crux of the problem : el quid del problema⟩
cry[1] ['kraɪ] *v* **cried; crying** 1 SHOUT : gritar 2 WEEP : llorar 3 **to cry for** MAND : pedir a gritos, clamar por 4 **to cry out** : gritar (de dolor, etc.) 5 **to cry out against** : clamar contra 6 **to cry over** : llorar por
cry[2] *n, pl* **cries** 1 SHOUT : grito *m* 2 WEEPING : llanto *m* 3 : chillido *m* (de un animal)

crybaby ['kraɪˌbeɪbi] *n, pl* -**bies** : llorón *m*, -rona *f*
crypt ['krɪpt] *n* : cripta *f*
cryptic ['krɪptɪk] *adj* : enigmático, críptico
cryptocurrency [ˌkrɪptoʊ'kərənsi] *n, pl* -**cies** : criptomoneda *f*, criptodivisa *f*
crystal ['krɪstəl] *n* : cristal *m*
crystalline ['krɪstələn] *adj* : cristalino
crystallize ['krɪstəˌlaɪz] *v* -**lized; -lizing** *vt* : cristalizar, materializar ⟨to crystallize one's thoughts : cristalizar uno sus pensamientos⟩ — *vi* : cristalizarse
C–section ['si:ˌsekʃən] → **cesarean**[2]
cub ['kʌb] *n* : cachorro *m*
Cuban ['kju:bən] *n* : cubano *m*, -na *f* — **Cuban** *adj*
cubbyhole ['kʌbiˌho:l] *n* : chiribitil *m*
cube[1] ['kju:b] *vt* **cubed; cubing** 1 : elevar (un número) al cubo 2 : cortar en cubos
cube[2] *n* 1 : cubo *m* 2 **ice cube** : cubito *m* de hielo 3 **sugar cube** : terrón *m* de azúcar
cubic ['kju:bɪk] *adj* : cúbico
cubicle ['kju:bɪkəl] *n* : cubículo *m*
cuckoo[1] ['ku:ˌku:, 'kʊ-] *adj* : loco, chiflado
cuckoo[2] *n, pl* -**oos** : cuco *m*, cuclillo *m*
cucumber ['kju:ˌkʌmbər] *n* : pepino *m*
cud ['kʌd] *n* **to chew the cud** : rumiar
cuddle[1] ['kʌdəl] *v* -**dled; -dling** *vi* : abrazarse tiernamente, acurrucarse — *vt* : abrazar
cuddle[2] *n* : abrazo *m*
cudgel[1] ['kʌdʒəl] *vt* -**geled** *or* -**gelled; -geling** *or* -**gelling** : apalear, aporrear
cudgel[2] *n* : garrote *m*, porra *f*
cue[1] ['kju:] *vt* **cued; cuing** *or* **cueing** : darle el pie a, darle la señal a
cue[2] *n* 1 SIGNAL : señal *f*, pie *m* (en teatro), entrada *f* (en música) 2 : taco *m* (de billar)
cuff[1] ['kʌf] *vt* : bofetear, cachetear
cuff[2] *n* 1 : puño *m* (de una camisa), vuelta *f* (de pantalones) 2 SLAP : bofetada *f*, cachetada *f* 3 **cuffs** *npl* HANDCUFFS : esposas *fpl*
cuff link *n* : gemelo *m*
cuisine [kwɪ'zi:n] *n* : cocina *f* ⟨Mexican cuisine : la cocina mexicana⟩
cul–de–sac ['kʌldɪˌsæk] *n* : calle *f* sin salida
culinary ['kʌləˌneri, 'kju:lə-] *adj* : culinario
cull ['kʌl] *vt* : seleccionar
culminate ['kʌlməˌneɪt] *vi* -**nated; -nating** : culminar
culmination [ˌkʌlmə'neɪʃən] *n* : culminación *f*, punto *m* culminante
culpable ['kʌlpəbəl] *adj* : culpable
culprit ['kʌlprɪt] *n* : culpable *mf*
cult ['kʌlt] *n* : culto *m*
cultivate ['kʌltəˌveɪt] *vt* -**vated; -vating** 1 TILL : cultivar, labrar 2 FOSTER : cultivar, fomentar 3 REFINE : cultivar, refinar ⟨to cultivate the mind : cultivar la mente⟩
cultivation [ˌkʌltə'veɪʃən] *n* 1 : cultivo *m* ⟨under cultivation : en cultivo⟩ 2 CUL-

TURE, REFINEMENT : cultura *f*, refinamiento *m*

cultural [ˈkʌltʃərəl] *adj* : cultural — **culturally** *adv*

culture [ˈkʌltʃər] *n* 1 CULTIVATION : cultivo *m* 2 REFINEMENT : cultura *f*, educación *f*, refinamiento *m* 3 CIVILIZATION : cultura *f*, civilización *f* ⟨the Incan culture : la cultura inca⟩

cultured [ˈkʌltʃərd] *adj* 1 EDUCATED, REFINED : culto, educado, refinado 2 : de cultivo, cultivado ⟨cultured pearls : perlas de cultivo⟩

culvert [ˈkʌlvərt] *n* : alcantarilla *f*

cumbersome [ˈkʌmbərsəm] *adj* : torpe y pesado, difícil de manejar

cumin [ˈkəmən] *n* : comino *m*

cumulative [ˈkjuːmjələtɪv, -ˌleɪtɪv] *adj* : acumulativo

cumulus [ˈkjuːmjələs] *n, pl* **-li** [-ˌlaɪ, -ˌliː] : cúmulo *m*

cunning[1] [ˈkʌnɪŋ] *adj* 1 CRAFTY : astuto, taimado 2 CLEVER : ingenioso, hábil 3 CUTE : mono, gracioso, lindo

cunning[2] *n* 1 SKILL : habilidad *f* 2 CRAFTINESS : astucia *f*, maña *f*

cup[1] [ˈkʌp] *vt* **cupped; cupping** : ahuecar (las manos)

cup[2] *n* 1 : taza *f* ⟨a cup of coffee : una taza de café⟩ 2 CUPFUL : taza *f* 3 : media pinta *f* (unidad de medida) 4 GOBLET : copa *f* 5 TROPHY : copa *f*, trofeo *m*

cupboard [ˈkʌbərd] *n* : alacena *f*, armario *m*

cupcake [ˈkʌpˌkeɪk] *n* : pastelito *m*

cupful [ˈkʌpˌfʊl] *n* : taza *f*

cupola [ˈkjuːpələ, -ˌloː] *n* : cúpula *f*

cur [ˈkər] *n* : perro *m* callejero, perro *m* corriente *Mex*

curate [ˈkjʊrət] *n* : cura *m*, párroco *m*

curator [ˈkjʊrˌeɪtər, kjuˈreɪtər] *n* : conservador *m*, -dora *f* (de un museo); director *m*, -tora *f* (de un zoológico)

curb[1] [ˈkərb] *vt* : refrenar, restringir, controlar

curb[2] *n* 1 RESTRAINT : freno *m*, control *m* 2 : borde *m* de la acera

curd [ˈkərd] *n* : cuajada *f*

curdle [ˈkərdəl] *v* **-dled; -dling** *vi* : cuajarse — *vt* : cuajar ⟨to curdle one's blood : helarle la sangre a uno⟩

curdled [ˈkərdəld] *adj* : cortado (dícese de la leche, etc.)

cure[1] [ˈkjʊr] *vt* **cured; curing** 1 HEAL : curar, sanar 2 REMEDY : remediar 3 PROCESS : curar (alimentos, etc.)

cure[2] *n* 1 RECOVERY : curación *f*, recuperación *f* 2 REMEDY : cura *f*, remedio *m*

curfew [ˈkərˌfjuː] *n* : toque *m* de queda

curio [ˈkjʊriˌoː] *n, pl* **-rios** : curiosidad *f*, objeto *m* curioso

curiosity [ˌkjʊriˈɑsəti] *n, pl* **-ties** : curiosidad *f*

curious [ˈkjʊriəs] *adj* 1 INQUISITIVE : curioso 2 STRANGE : curioso, raro

curl[1] [ˈkərl] *vt* 1 : rizar, ondular (el pelo) 2 COIL : enrollar 3 TWIST : torcer ⟨to curl one's lip : hacer una mueca⟩ —

vi 1 : rizarse, ondularse 2 **to curl up** : acurrucarse (con un libro, etc.)

curl[2] *n* 1 RINGLET : rizo *m* 2 COIL : espiral *f*, rosca *f*

curler [ˈkərlər] *n* : rulo *m*

curlew [ˈkərˌluː, ˈkərlˌjuː] *n, pl* **-lews** *or* **-lew** : zarapito *m*

curly [ˈkərli] *adj* **curlier; -est** : rizado, crespo

curly brace *or* **curly bracket** *n* : llave *f* (signo de puntuación)

currant [ˈkərənt] *n* 1 : grosella *f* (fruta) ⟨black currant : grosella negra⟩ ⟨red currant : grosella roja⟩ 2 RAISIN : pasa *f* de Corinto

currency [ˈkərəntsi] *n, pl* **-cies** 1 PREVALENCE, USE : uso *m*, aceptación *f*, difusión *f* ⟨to be in currency : estar en uso⟩ 2 MONEY : moneda *f*, dinero *m*

current[1] [ˈkərənt] *adj* 1 PRESENT : actual ⟨current events : actualidades⟩ 2 PREVALENT : corriente, común — **currently** *adv*

current[2] *n* : corriente *f*

curriculum [kəˈrɪkjələm] *n, pl* **-la** [-lə] : currículum *m*, currículo *m*, programa *m* de estudio

curriculum vitae [ˈviːˌtaɪ, ˈvaɪtiː] *n, pl* **curricula vitae** : currículum *m*, currículo *m*

curry[1] [ˈkəri] *vt* **-ried; -rying** 1 GROOM : almohazar (un caballo) 2 : condimentar con curry 3 **to curry favor** : congraciarse (con alguien)

curry[2] *n, pl* **-ries** : curry *m*

curse[1] [ˈkərs] *v* **cursed; cursing** *vt* 1 DAMN : maldecir 2 INSULT : injuriar, insultar, decir malas palabras a 3 AFFLICT : afligir — *vi* : maldecir, decir malas palabras

curse[2] *n* 1 : maldición *f* ⟨to put a curse on someone : echarle una maldición a alguien⟩ 2 AFFLICTION : maldición *f*, aflicción *f*, cruz *f*

cursor [ˈkərsər] *n* : cursor *m*

cursory [ˈkərsəri] *adj* : rápido, superficial, somero

curt [ˈkərt] *adj* : cortante, brusco, seco — **curtly** *adv*

curtail [kərˈteɪl] *vt* : acortar, limitar, restringir

curtailment [kərˈteɪlmənt] *n* : restricción *f*, limitación *f*

curtain [ˈkərtən] *n* : cortina *f* (de una ventana), telón *m* (en un teatro)

curtness [ˈkərtnəs] *n* : brusquedad *f*, sequedad *f*

curtsy[1] *or* **curtsey** [ˈkərtsi] *vi* **-sied** *or* **-seyed; -sying** *or* **-seying** : hacer una reverencia

curtsy[2] *or* **curtsey** *n, pl* **-sies** *or* **-seys** : reverencia *f*

curvature [ˈkərvəˌtʃər] *n* : curvatura *f*

curve[1] [ˈkərv] *v* **curved; curving** *vi* : torcerse, describir una curva — *vt* : encorvar

curve[2] *n* : curva *f*

curvy [ˈkərvi] *adj* **curvier; -est** *adj* 1 : con muchas curvas, sinuoso 2 SHAPELY : curvilíneo

cushion[1] [ˈkʊʃən] *vt* 1 : poner cojines o almohadones a 2 SOFTEN : amortiguar, mitigar, suavizar ⟨to cushion a blow : amortiguar un golpe⟩

cushion² *n* 1 : cojín *m*, almohadón *m* 2 PROTECTION : colchón *m*, protección *f*

cusp [ˈkʌsp] *n* : cúspide *f* (de un diente), cuerno *m* (de la luna)

cuspid [ˈkʌspɪd] *n* : diente *m* canino, colmillo *m*

custard [ˈkʌstərd] *n* : natillas *fpl*

custodian [ˌkʌˈstoːdiən] *n* : custodio *m*, -dia *f*; guardián, -diana *f*

custody [ˈkʌstədi] *n, pl* **-dies** : custodia *f*, cuidado *m* ⟨to be in custody : estar detenido⟩

custom¹ [ˈkʌstəm] *adj* : a la medida, a la orden

custom² *n* 1 : costumbre *f*, tradición *f* 2 **customs** *npl* : aduana *f* ⟨customs officer : agente de aduanas⟩

customarily [ˌkʌstəˈmerəli] *adv* : habitualmente, normalmente, de costumbre

customary [ˈkʌstəˌmeri] *adj* 1 TRADITIONAL : tradicional 2 USUAL : habitual, de costumbre

customer [ˈkʌstəmər] *n* : cliente *m*, -ta *f*

customize [ˈkʌstəˌmaɪz] *vt* **-ized; -izing** : adaptar (algo) a los requisitos de alguien, personalizar — **customization** [ˌkʌstəməˈzeɪʃən] *n*

custom–made [ˈkʌstəmˈmeɪd] *adj* : hecho a la medida

cut¹ [ˈkʌt] *v* **cut; cutting** *vt* 1 : cortar ⟨to cut paper : cortar papel⟩ ⟨cut the meat into strips : cortar la carne en tiras⟩ ⟨cut the apple in half : cortar la manzana por la mitad⟩ ⟨to cut a hole in : hacer un agujero en⟩ ⟨to cut (off) a piece : cortar un trozo⟩ 2 : cortarse ⟨to cut one's finger : cortarse uno el dedo⟩ 3 TRIM : cortar, recortar ⟨to have one's hair cut : cortarse el pelo⟩ 4 INTERSECT : cruzar, atravesar 5 SHORTEN : acortar, abreviar 6 REDUCE : reducir, rebajar ⟨to cut prices : rebajar los precios⟩ 7 : cortar (en informática) ⟨to cut and paste : cortar y pegar⟩ 8 : cortar (una baraja) 9 : sacar (de un equipo, etc.) 10 SKIP : faltar a (clase) 11 TURN OFF : apagar 12 DILUTE : cortar (drogas) 13 **cut it out!** : ¡basta ya! 14 **not to cut it** : no ser lo suficientemente bueno 15 **to cut a deal** : hacer/cerrar un trato 16 **to cut away** : cortar 17 **to cut back** PRUNE : podar 18 **to cut back** REDUCE : reducir (gastos, etc.) 19 **to cut down** FELL : cortar, talar 20 **to cut down** REDUCE : reducir 21 **to cut down** KILL : matar 22 **to cut in** : cortar y mezclar (mantequilla, etc.) 23 **to cut off** : cortar (una rama, una pierna, etc.) 24 **to cut off** : cortar (el acceso, etc.) 25 **to cut off** INTERRUPT : interrumpir 26 **to cut off** ISOLATE : aislar 27 **to cut off** : cortarle el paso a (un vehículo, etc.) 28 **to cut one's teeth** : salirle los dientes a uno 29 **to cut out** CLIP : recortar 30 **to cut out** EXCLUDE : excluir 31 **to cut up** : cortar en pedazos — *vi* 1 : cortar, cortarse 2 **to cut back** : hacer economías 3 **to cut down**

: moderarse 4 **to cut in** : entrometerse 5 **to cut in line** : colarse 6 **to cut up** CLOWN AROUND : hacer payasadas

cut² *n* 1 : corte *m* ⟨a cut of meat : un corte de carne⟩ 2 SLASH : tajo *m*, corte *m*, cortadura *f* 3 REDUCTION : rebaja *f*, reducción *f* ⟨a cut in the rates : una rebaja en las tarifas⟩

cutaneous [kjuˈteɪniəs] *adj* : cutáneo

cutback [ˈkʌtˌbæk] *n* : recorte *m*, reducción *f*

cute [ˈkjuːt] *adj* **cuter; cutest** : mono *fam*, lindo

cuticle [ˈkjuːtɪkəl] *n* : cutícula *f*

cutlass [ˈkʌtləs] *n* : alfanje *m*

cutlery [ˈkʌtləri] *n* : cubiertos *mpl*

cutlet [ˈkʌtlət] *n* : chuleta *f*

cutoff [ˈkʌtˌɔf] *n* 1 INTERRUPTION : corte *m*, interrupción *f* 2 DEADLINE : fecha *f* límite, fecha *f* tope 3 **cutoffs** *npl* : shorts *mpl* de mezclilla

cut–rate [ˈkʌtˌreɪt] *adj* : a precio rebajado

cutter [ˈkʌtər] *n* 1 : cortadora *f* (implemento) 2 : cortador *m*, -dora *f* (persona) 3 : cúter *m* (embarcación)

cutthroat [ˈkʌtˌθroːt] *adj* : despiadado, desalmado ⟨cutthroat competition : competencia feroz⟩

cutting¹ [ˈkʌtɪŋ] *adj* 1 : cortante ⟨a cutting wind : un viento cortante⟩ 2 CAUSTIC : mordaz

cutting² *n* : esqueje *m* (de una planta)

cuttlefish [ˈkʌtəlˌfɪʃ] *n, pl* **-fish** *or* **-fishes** : jibia *f*, sepia *f*

cyanide [ˈsaɪəˌnaɪd, -nɪd] *n* : cianuro *m*

cyber- [ˈsaɪbər-] *pref* : ciber- *m*

cyberbullying [ˈsaɪbərˌbuliŋ] *n* : ciberacoso *m*

cybernetic [ˌsaɪbərˈnetɪk] *adj* : cibernético

cycle¹ [ˈsaɪkəl] *vi* **-cled; -cling** : andar en bicicleta, ir en bicicleta

cycle² *n* 1 : ciclo *m* ⟨life cycle : ciclo de vida, ciclo vital⟩ 2 BICYCLE : bicicleta *f* 3 MOTORCYCLE : motocicleta *f*

cyclic [ˈsaɪklɪk, ˈsɪ-] *or* **cyclical** [-klɪkəl] *adj* : cíclico

cycling [ˈsaɪklɪŋ] *n* : ciclismo *m*

cyclist [ˈsaɪklɪst] *n* : ciclista *mf*

cyclone [ˈsaɪˌkloːn] *n* 1 : ciclón *m* 2 TORNADO : tornado *m*

cyclopedia *or* **cyclopaedia** [ˌsaɪkləˈpiːdiə] → **encyclopedia**

cylinder [ˈsɪləndər] *n* : cilindro *m*

cylindrical [səˈlɪndrɪkəl] *adj* : cilíndrico

cymbal [ˈsɪmbəl] *n* : platillo *m*, címbalo *m*

cynic [ˈsɪnɪk] *n* : cínico *m*, -ca *f*

cynical [ˈsɪnɪkəl] *adj* : cínico

cynicism [ˈsɪnəˌsɪzəm] *n* : cinismo *m*

cypress [ˈsaɪprəs] *n* : ciprés *m*

cyst [ˈsɪst] *n* : quiste *m*

czar [ˈzɑr, ˈsɑr] *n* : zar *m*

czarina [zɑˈriːnə, sɑ-] *n* : zarina *f*

Czech [ˈtʃɛk] *n* 1 : checo *m*, -ca *f* 2 : checo *m* (idioma) — **Czech** *adj*

Czechoslovak [ˌtʃɛkoˈsloːˌvɑk, -ˌvæk] *or* **Czechoslovakian** [-sloˈvɑkiən, -ˈvæ-] *n* : checoslovaco *m*, -ca *f* — **Czechoslovak** *or* **Czechoslovakian** *adj*

D

d ['di:] *n, pl* **d's** *or* **ds** ['di:z] **1** : cuarta letra del alfabeto inglés **2** : re *m* ⟨D sharp/flat : re sostenido/bemol⟩

dab¹ ['dæb] *vt* **dabbed; dabbing** : darle toques ligeros a, aplicar suavemente

dab² *n* **1** BIT : toque *m*, pizca *f*, poco *m* ⟨a dab of ointment : un toque de ungüento⟩ **2** PAT : toque *m* ligero, golpecito *m*

dabble ['dæbəl] *v* **-bled; -bling** *vt* SPATTER : salpicar — *vi* **1** SPLASH : chapotear **2** TRIFLE : jugar, interesarse superficialmente

dabbler ['dæblər] *n* : diletante *mf*

dachshund ['dɑks,hʊnt, -,hʊnd; 'dɑksənt, -sənd] *n* : perro *m* salchicha

dad ['dæd] *n* : papá *m fam*

daddy ['dædi] *n, pl* **-dies** : papi *m fam*

daddy longlegs [-'lɔŋ,lɛgz] *n, pl* **daddy longlegs** : segador *m* (insecto)

daffodil ['dæfə,dɪl] *n* : narciso *m*

daft ['dæft] *adj* : tonto, bobo

dagger ['dægər] *n* : daga *f*, puñal *m*

dahlia ['dæljə, 'dɑl-, 'deɪl-] *n* : dalia *f*

daily¹ ['deɪli] *adv* : a diario, diariamente

daily² *adj* : diario, cotidiano

daily³ *n, pl* **-lies** : diario *m*, periódico *m*

daintily ['deɪntəli] *adv* : delicadamente, con delicadeza

daintiness ['deɪntinəs] *n* : delicadeza *f*, finura *f*

dainty¹ ['deɪnti] *adj* **daintier; -est 1** DELICATE : delicado **2** FASTIDIOUS : remilgado, melindroso **3** DELICIOUS : exquisito, sabroso

dainty² *n, pl* **-ties** DELICACY : exquisitez *f*, manjar *m*

dairy¹ ['dæri] *adj* : lácteo ⟨dairy products : productos lácteos⟩

dairy² *n, pl* **-ries 1** *or* **dairy store** : lechería *f* **2** *or* **dairy farm** : granja *f* lechera **3** : (productos *mpl*) lácteos *mpl* ⟨she stopped eating dairy : dejó los lácteos⟩

dairymaid ['dæri,meɪd] *n* : lechera *f*

dairyman ['dærimən, -,mæn] *n, pl* **-men** [-mən, -,mɛn] : lechero *m*

dais ['deɪəs] *n* : tarima *f*, estrado *m*

daisy ['deɪzi] *n, pl* **-sies** : margarita *f*

dale ['deɪl] *n* : valle *m*

dally ['dæli] *vi* **-lied; -lying 1** TRIFLE : juguetear **2** DAWDLE : entretenerse, perder tiempo

dalmatian [dæl'meɪʃən, dɔl-] *n* : dálmata *m*

dam¹ ['dæm] *vt* **dammed; damming** : represar

dam² *n* **1** : represa *f*, dique *m* **2** : madre *f* (de animales domésticos)

damage¹ ['dæmɪʤ] *vt* **-aged; -aging** : dañar (un objeto o una máquina), perjudicar (la salud o una reputación)

damage² *n* **1** : daño *m*, perjuicio *m* ⟨to cause damage to : ocasionar daños a⟩ **2** **damages** *npl* : daños y perjuicios *mpl*

damaging ['dæməʤɪŋ] *adj* : perjudicial

damask ['dæməsk] *n* : damasco *m*

dame ['deɪm] *n* LADY : dama *f*, señora *f*

damn¹ ['dæm] *vt* **1** CONDEMN : condenar **2** CURSE : maldecir

damn² *or* **damned** ['dæmd] *adj* : condenado *fam*, maldito *fam*

damn³ *n* : pito *m*, bledo *m*, comino *m* ⟨it's not worth a damn : no vale un pito⟩ ⟨I don't give a damn : me importa un comino⟩

damnable ['dæmnəbəl] *adj* : condenable, detestable

damnation [dæm'neɪʃən] *n* : condenación *f*

damned¹ ['dæmd] *adv* VERY : muy

damned² *adj* **1** → **damnable 2** REMARKABLE : extraordinario

damning ['dæmɪŋ] *adj* : condenatorio

damp¹ ['dæmp] *vt* → **dampen**

damp² *adj* : húmedo

damp³ *n* MOISTURE : humedad *f*

dampen ['dæmpən] *vt* **1** MOISTEN : humedecer **2** DISCOURAGE : desalentar, desanimar

damper ['dæmpər] *n* **1** : regulador *m* de tiro (de una chimenea) **2** : sordina *f* (de un piano) **3 to put a damper on** : desanimar, apagar (el entusiasmo), enfriar

dampness ['dæmpnəs] *n* : humedad *f*

damsel ['dæmzəl] *n* : damisela *f*

dance¹ ['dænʦ] *v* **danced; dancing** : bailar

dance² *n* : baile *m*

dancer ['dænʦər] *n* : bailarín *m*, -rina *f*

dandelion ['dændəl,aɪən] *n* : diente *m* de león

dandruff ['dændrəf] *n* : caspa *f*

dandy¹ ['dændi] *adj* **dandier; -est** : excelente, magnífico, macanudo *fam*

dandy² *n, pl* **-dies 1** : dandi *m* **2** : algo *m* excelente ⟨this new program is a dandy : este programa nuevo es algo excelente⟩

Dane ['deɪn] *n* : danés *m*, -nesa *f*

danger ['deɪnʤər] *n* : peligro *m*

dangerous ['deɪnʤərəs] *adj* : peligroso

dangle ['dæŋgəl] *v* **-gled; -gling** *vi* HANG : colgar, pender — *vt* **1** SWING : hacer oscilar **2** PROFFER : ofrecer (como incentivo) **3 to keep someone dangling** : dejar a alguien en suspenso

Danish¹ ['deɪnɪʃ] *adj* : danés

Danish² *n* : danés *m* (idioma)

dank ['dæŋk] *adj* : frío y húmedo

dapper ['dæpər] *adj* : pulcro, atildado

dappled ['dæpəld] *adj* : moteado ⟨a dappled horse : un caballo rodado⟩

dare¹ ['dær] *v* **dared; daring** *vi* : osar, atreverse ⟨how dare you! : ¡cómo te atreves!⟩ — *vt* **1** CHALLENGE : desafiar, retar **2 to dare to do something** : atreverse a hacer algo, osar hacer algo

dare² *n* : desafío *m*, reto *m*

daredevil ['dær,dɛvəl] *n* : persona *f* temeraria

daring¹ ['dærɪŋ] *adj* : osado, atrevido, audaz

daring² *n* : arrojo *m*, coraje *m*, audacia *f*

dark¹ ['dɑrk] *adj* **1** : oscuro (dícese del ambiente o de los colores), moreno (dícese del pelo o de la piel) ⟨it's getting dark : está oscureciendo⟩ **2** SOMBER : sombrío, triste

dark² *n* **1** : oscuridad *f*, tinieblas *f* ⟨to be afraid of the dark : tenerle miedo a la oscuridad⟩ **2** NIGHT : noche ⟨before dark : antes del anochecer⟩

dark chocolate *n* : chocolate *m* oscuro, chocolate *m* amargo, chocolate *m* negro

darken ['dɑrkən] *vt* **1** DIM : oscurecer **2** SADDEN : entristecer — *vi* : ensombrecerse, nublarse

darkly ['dɑrkli] *adv* **1** DIMLY : oscuramente **2** GLOOMILY : tristemente **3** MYSTERIOUSLY : misteriosamente, enigmáticamente

darkness ['dɑrknəs] *n* : oscuridad *f*, tinieblas *f*

darkroom ['dɑrk,ru:m, -,rʊm] *n* : cuarto *m* oscuro

darling¹ ['dɑrlɪŋ] *adj* **1** BELOVED : querido, amado **2** CHARMING : encantador, mono *fam*

darling² *n* **1** BELOVED : querido *m*, -da *f*; amado *m*, -da *f*; cariño *m*; -ña *f* **2** FAVORITE : preferido *m*, -da *f*; favorito *m*, -ta *f*

darn¹ ['dɑrn] *vt* : zurcir

darn² *n* : zurcido *m* **2** → damn³

dart¹ ['dɑrt] *vt* THROW : lanzar, tirar — *vi* DASH : lanzarse, precipitarse

dart² *n* **1** : dardo *m* **2 darts** *npl* : juego *m* de dardos

dash¹ ['dæʃ] *vt* **1** SMASH : romper, estrellar **2** HURL : arrojar, lanzar **3** SPLASH : salpicar **4** FRUSTRATE : frustrar **5 to dash off** : hacer (algo) rápidamente — *vi* **1** SMASH : romperse, estrellarse **2** DART : lanzarse, irse apresuradamente

dash² *n* **1** BURST, SPLASH : arranque *m*, salpicadura *f* (de aguas) **2** : guión *m* largo (signo de puntuación) **3** DROP : gota *f*, pizca *f* **4** VERVE : brío *m* **5** RACE : carrera *f* ⟨a 100-meter dash : una carrera de 100 metros⟩ **6 to make a dash for it** : precipitarse (hacia), echarse a correr **7** → dashboard

dashboard ['dæʃ,bord] *n* : tablero *m* de instrumentos

dashing ['dæʃɪŋ] *adj* : gallardo, apuesto

data ['deɪt̬ə, 'dæ-, 'dɑ-] *ns & pl* : datos *mpl*, información *f*

data bank *n* : banco *m* de datos

database ['deɪt̬ə,beɪs, 'dæ-, 'dɑ-] *n* : base *f* de datos

data processing *n* : procesamiento *m* de datos

date¹ ['deɪt] *v* **dated; dating** *vt* **1** : fechar (una carta, etc.), datar (un objeto) ⟨it was dated June 9 : estaba fechada el 9 de junio⟩ **2** : salir con ⟨she's dating my brother : sale con mi hermano⟩ — *vi* : datar

date² *n* **1** : fecha *f* ⟨to date : hasta la fecha⟩ **2** EPOCH, PERIOD : época *f*, período *m* **3** APPOINTMENT : cita *f* **4** COMPANION : acompañante *mf* **5** : dátil *m* (fruta)

dated ['deɪt̬əd] *adj* OUT-OF-DATE : anticuado, pasado de moda

datum ['deɪt̬əm, 'dæ-, 'dɑ-] *n*, *pl* **-ta** [-t̬ə] *or* **-tums** : dato *m*

daub¹ ['dɔb] *vt* : embadurnar

daub² *n* : mancha *f*

daughter ['dɔt̬ər] *n* : hija *f*

daughter–in–law ['dɔt̬ərɪn,lɔ] *n*, *pl* **daughters–in–law** : nuera *f*, hija *f* política

daunt ['dɔnt] *vt* : amilanar, acobardar, intimidar

daunting ['dɔntɪŋ] *adj* : desalentador

dauntless ['dɔntləs] *adj* : intrépido, impávido

dawdle ['dɔdəl] *vi* **-dled; -dling 1** DALLY : demorarse, entretenerse, perder tiempo **2** LOITER : vagar, holgazanear, haraganear

dawn¹ ['dɔn] *vi* **1** : amanecer, alborear, despuntar ⟨Saturday dawned clear and bright : el sábado amaneció claro y luminoso⟩ **2 to dawn on** : hacerse obvio ⟨it dawned on me that she was right : me di cuenta de que tenía razón⟩

dawn² *n* **1** DAYBREAK : amanecer *m*, alba *f* **2** BEGINNING : albor *m*, comienzo *m* ⟨the dawn of history : los albores de la historia⟩ **3 from dawn to dusk** : de sol a sol

day ['deɪ] *n* **1** : día *m* ⟨the day after tomorrow : pasado mañana⟩ ⟨the day before yesterday : anteayer⟩ ⟨the other day : el otro día⟩ ⟨twice a day, two times a day : dos veces al día⟩ ⟨every day : todos los días⟩ ⟨all day : todo el día⟩ **2** DATE : fecha *f* ⟨what day is (it) today? : ¿qué día es hoy?⟩ **3** TIME : día *m*, tiempo *m* ⟨in those days : en aquellos tiempos⟩ ⟨in my day : en mis tiempos⟩ ⟨to the present day : hasta nuestros días⟩ ⟨to this day : hasta el día de hoy⟩ **4** WORKDAY : jornada *f* laboral **5 any day now** SOON : cualquier día de estos **6 in this day and age** : hoy (en) día **7 one day** SOMEDAY : algún día **8 the good old days** : los viejos tiempos **9 these days** : hoy (en) día **10 to make someone's day** : alegrarle el día a alguien

daybreak ['deɪ,breɪk] *n* : alba *f*, amanecer *m*

day care *n* : servicio *m* de guardería infantil

daydream¹ ['deɪ,dri:m] *vi* : soñar despierto, fantasear

daydream² *n* : ensueño *m*, ensoñación *f*, fantasía *f*

daylight ['deɪ,laɪt] *n* **1** : luz *f* del día ⟨in broad daylight : a plena luz del día⟩ **2** → daytime **3** → daybreak

daylight saving time *n* : hora *f* de verano

daytime ['deɪ,taɪm] *n* : horas *fpl* diurnas, día *m*

day–to–day *adj* : diario, cotidiano

daze¹ ['deɪz] *vt* **dazed; dazing 1** STUN : aturdir **2** DAZZLE : deslumbrar, ofuscar

daze² *n* **1** : aturdimiento *m* **2 in a daze** : aturdido, atontado

dazzle¹ ['dæzəl] *vt* **-zled; -zling** : deslumbrar, ofuscar

dazzle² *n* : resplandor *m*, brillo *m*

dazzling ['dæzəlɪŋ] *adj* : deslumbrante

de- *pref* : des-
deacon ['di:kən] *n* : diácono *m*
deaconess ['di:kənəs] *n* : diaconisa *f*
deactivate [di'æktə,veɪt] *vt* **-vated; -vating** : desactivar
dead¹ ['dɛd] *adv* **1** ABRUPTLY : repentinamente, súbitamente ⟨to stop dead : parar en seco⟩ **2** ABSOLUTELY : absolutamente ⟨I'm dead certain : estoy absolutamente seguro⟩ **3** DIRECTLY : justo ⟨dead ahead : justo adelante⟩
dead² *adj* **1** LIFELESS : muerto ⟨to drop dead : caerse muerto⟩ **2** NUMB : entumecido, dormido **3** INDIFFERENT : indiferente, frío **4** INACTIVE : inactivo ⟨a dead volcano : un volcán inactivo⟩ **5** : desconectado (dícese de un teléfono), descargado (dícese de una batería) **6** EXHAUSTED : agotado, derrengado, muerto **7** OBSOLETE : obsoleto, muerto ⟨a dead language : una lengua muerta⟩ **8** EXACT : exacto ⟨(in the) dead center : justo en el blanco⟩ **9** QUIET, SLOW : muerto (dícese de una fiesta, etc.), de poco movimiento (comercial) **10** : perdido ⟨if she catches you, you're dead : si te agarra, te mata⟩ **11 drop dead!** : ¡vete al infierno! **12 to be caught dead in** ⟨I wouldn't be caught dead in that outfit : no me pondría ese conjunto ni muerta⟩
dead³ *n* **1 the dead** : los muertos **2 in the dead of night** : a las altas horas de la noche **3 in the dead of winter** : en pleno invierno
deadbeat ['dɛd,bi:t] *n* **1** LOAFER : vago *m*, -ga *f*; holgazán *m*, -zana *f* **2** FREELOADER : gorrón *m*, -rrona *f fam*; gorrero *m*, -ra *f fam*
deaden ['dɛdən] *vt* **1** : atenuar (un dolor), entorpecer (sensaciones) **2** DULL : deslustrar **3** DISPIRIT : desanimar **4** MUFFLE : amortiguar, reducir (sonidos)
dead–end ['dɛd'ɛnd] *adj* **1** : sin salida ⟨dead-end street : calle sin salida⟩ **2** : sin futuro ⟨a dead-end job : un trabajo sin porvenir⟩
dead end *n* : callejón *m* sin salida
dead heat *n* : empate *m*
deadline ['dɛd,laɪn] *n* : fecha *f* límite, fecha *f* tope, plazo *m* (determinado)
deadlock¹ ['dɛd,lɑk] *vt* : estancar — *vi* : estancarse, llegar a punto muerto
deadlock² *n* : punto *m* muerto, impasse *m*
deadly¹ ['dɛdli] *adv* : extremadamente, sumamente ⟨deadly serious : muy en serio⟩
deadly² *adj* **deadlier; -est 1** LETHAL : mortal, letal, mortífero **2** ACCURATE : certero, preciso ⟨with deadly aim : con puntería infalible⟩ **3** CAPITAL : capital ⟨the seven deadly sins : los siete pecados capitales⟩ **4** DULL : funesto, aburrido **5** EXTREME : extremo, absoluto ⟨a deadly calm : una calma absoluta⟩
deadpan¹ ['dɛd,pæn] *adv* : de manera inexpresiva, sin expresión
deadpan² *adj* : inexpresivo, impasible
deaf ['dɛf] *adj* : sordo
deafen ['dɛfən] *vt* **-ened; -ening** : ensordecer

deafening ['dɛfənɪŋ] *adj* : ensordecedor
deaf–mute ['dɛf'mju:t] *n often offensive* : sordomudo *m*, -da *f offensive*
deafness ['dɛfnəs] *n* : sordera *f*
deal¹ ['di:l] *v* **dealt; dealing** *vt* **1** *or to* **deal out** APPORTION : repartir ⟨to deal justice : repartir la justicia⟩ **2** DISTRIBUTE : repartir, dar (naipes) **3** DELIVER : asestar, propinar ⟨to deal a blow : asestar un golpe⟩ — *vi* **1** : dar, repartir (en juegos de naipes) **2 to deal in** : comerciar en, traficar con (drogas) **3 to deal with** CONCERN : tratar de, tener que ver con ⟨the book deals with poverty : el libro trata de la pobreza⟩ **4 to deal with** HANDLE : tratar (con), encargarse de **5 to deal with** TREAT : tratar ⟨the judge dealt with him severely : el juez lo trató con severidad⟩ **6 to deal with** ACCEPT : aceptar (una situación o desgracia)
deal² *n* **1** : reparto *m* (de naipes) **2** AGREEMENT, TRANSACTION : trato *m*, acuerdo *m*, transacción *f* ⟨to cut/make/strike a deal : hacer un trato⟩ **3** TREATMENT : trato *m* ⟨he got a raw deal : le hicieron una injusticia⟩ **4** BARGAIN : ganga *f*, oferta *f* ⟨she got a good deal on the car : consiguió el coche a un precio barato⟩ **5 a good/great deal** : mucho, una gran cantidad **6 big deal** : cosa *f* importante ⟨don't worry, it's no big deal : no te preocupes, no tiene importancia⟩ ⟨so what? big deal! : ¿a quién le importa?⟩ **7 the real deal** ⟨to be the real deal : ser auténtico, ser de verdad⟩
dealer ['di:lər] *n* : comerciante *mf*, traficante *mf*
dealership ['di:lər,ʃɪp] *n* : concesión *f*
dealings ['di:lɪŋz] *npl* **1** : relaciones *fpl* (personales) **2** TRANSACTIONS : negocios *mpl*, transacciones *fpl*
dean ['di:n] *n* **1** : deán *m* (del clero) **2** : decano *m*, -na *f* (de una facultad o profesión)
dear¹ ['dɪr] *adj* **1** ESTEEMED, LOVED : querido, estimado ⟨a dear friend : un amigo querido⟩ ⟨Dear Sir : Estimado Señor⟩ **2** COSTLY : caro, costoso
dear² *n* : querido *m*, -da *f*; amado *m*, -da *f*
dearly ['dɪrli] *adv* **1** : mucho ⟨I love them dearly : los quiero mucho⟩ **2** : caro (to pay dearly : pagar caro)
dearth ['dərθ] *n* : escasez *f*, carestía *f*
death ['dɛθ] *n* **1** : muerte *f*, fallecimiento *m* ⟨to be the death of : matar⟩ **2** FATALITY : víctima *f* (mortal); muerto *m*, -ta *f* **3** END : fin *m* ⟨the death of civilization : el fin de la civilización⟩
deathbed ['dɛθ,bɛd] *n* : lecho *m* de muerte
deathblow ['dɛθ,blo:] *n* : golpe *m* mortal
death certificate *n* : certificado *m* de defunción, acta *f* de defunción
deathless ['dɛθləs] *adj* : eterno, inmortal
deathly ['dɛθli] *adj* : de muerte, sepulcral (dícese del silencio), cadavérico (dícese de la palidez)
death penalty *n* : pena *f* de muerte
death trap *n* : trampa *f* mortal, vehículo *m* (o edificio *m*, etc.) peligroso

debacle [dɪˈbɑkəl, -ˈbæ-] *n* : desastre *m*, debacle *m*, fiasco *m*

debar [dɪˈbɑr] *vt* **-barred; -barring** : excluir, prohibir

debase [dɪˈbeɪs] *vt* **-based; -basing** : degradar, envilecer

debatable [dɪˈbeɪtəbəl] *adj* : discutible

debate¹ [dɪˈbeɪt] *vt* **-bated; -bating** : debatir, discutir

debate² *n* : debate *m*, discusión *f*

debauch [dɪˈbɔtʃ] *vt* : pervertir, corromper

debauchery [dɪˈbɔtʃəri] *n, pl* **-eries** : libertinaje *m*, intemperancia *f*

debilitate [dɪˈbɪləˌteɪt] *vt* **-tated; -tating** : debilitar

debility [dɪˈbɪləti] *n, pl* **-ties** : debilidad *f*

debit¹ [ˈdɛbɪt] *vt* : adeudar, cargar, debitar

debit² *n* : débito *m*, cargo *m*, debe *m*

debit card *n* : tarjeta *f* de débito

debonair [ˌdɛbəˈnær] *adj* : elegante y desenvuelto, apuesto

debris [dəˈbri, deɪ-, ˈdeɪˌbri] *n, pl* **-bris** [-ˈbriz, -ˌbriz] **1** RUBBLE, RUINS : escombros *mpl*, ruinas *fpl*, restos *mpl* **2** RUBBISH : basura *f*, desechos *mpl*

debt [ˈdɛt] *n* **1** : deuda *f* ⟨to pay a debt : saldar una deuda⟩ **2** INDEBTEDNESS : endeudamiento *m*

debtor [ˈdɛtər] *n* : deudor *m*, -dora *f*

debunk [dɪˈbʌŋk] *vt* DISCREDIT : desacreditar, desprestigiar

debut¹ [deɪˈbju, ˈdeɪˌbju] *vi* : debutar

debut² *n* **1** : debut *m* (de un actor), estreno *m* (de una obra) **2** : debut *m*, presentación *f* (en sociedad)

debutante [ˈdɛbjuˌtɑnt] *n* : debutante *f*

decade [ˈdɛˌkeɪd, dɛˈkeɪd] *n* : década *f*

decadence [ˈdɛkədənts] *n* : decadencia *f*

decadent [ˈdɛkədənt] *adj* : decadente

decaf¹ [ˈdiˌkæf] → **decaffeinated**

decaf² *n* : café *m* descafeinado

decaffeinated [diˈkæfəˌneɪtəd] *adj* : descafeinado

decal [ˈdiˌkæl, dɪˈkæl] *n* : calcomanía *f*

decamp [dɪˈkæmp] *vi* : irse, largarse *fam*

decanter [dɪˈkæntər] *n* : licorera *f*, garrafa *f*

decapitate [dɪˈkæpəˌteɪt] *vt* **-tated; -tating** : decapitar

decay¹ [dɪˈkeɪ] *vi* **1** DECOMPOSE : descomponerse, pudrirse **2** DETERIORATE : deteriorarse **3** : cariarse (dícese de los dientes)

decay² *n* **1** DECOMPOSITION : descomposición *f* **2** DECLINE, DETERIORATION : decadencia *f*, deterioro *m* **3** : caries *f* (de los dientes)

decease¹ [dɪˈsis] *vi* **-ceased; -ceasing** : morir, fallecer

decease² *n* : fallecimiento *m*, defunción *f*, deceso *m*

deceased *n* : difunto *m*, -ta *f*

deceit [dɪˈsit] *n* **1** DECEPTION : engaño *m* **2** DISHONESTY : deshonestidad *f*

deceitful [dɪˈsitfəl] *adj* : falso, embustero, engañoso, mentiroso

deceitfully [dɪˈsitfəli] *adv* : con engaño, con falsedad

deceitfulness [dɪˈsitfəlnəs] *n* : falsedad *f*, engaño *m*

deceive [dɪˈsiv] *vt* **-ceived; -ceiving** : engañar, burlar

deceiver [dɪˈsivər] *n* : impostor *m*, -tora *f*

decelerate [diˈsɛləˌreɪt] *vi* **-ated; -ating** : reducir la velocidad, desacelerar

December [dɪˈsɛmbər] *n* : diciembre *m* ⟨they arrived on the 18th of December, they arrived on December 18th : llegaron el 18 de diciembre⟩

decency [ˈdisəntsi] *n, pl* **-cies** : decencia *f*, decoro *m*

decent [ˈdisənt] *adj* **1** CORRECT, PROPER : decente, decoroso, correcto **2** CLOTHED : vestido, presentable **3** MODEST : púdico, modesto **4** ADEQUATE : decente, adecuado ⟨decent wages : paga adecuada⟩

decently [ˈdisəntli] *adv* : decentemente

decentralize [diˈsɛntrəˌlaɪz] *v* **-lized [-ˌlaɪzd]; -lizing [-ˌlaɪzɪŋ]** *vt* : descentralizar — *vi* : descentralizarse

deception [dɪˈsɛpʃən] *n* : engaño *m*

deceptive [dɪˈsɛptɪv] *adj* : engañoso, falaz — **deceptively** *adv*

decibel [ˈdɛsəˌbəl, -ˌbɛl] *n* : decibelio *m*

decide [dɪˈsaɪd] *v* **-cided; -ciding** *vt* **1** CONCLUDE : decidir, llegar a la conclusión de ⟨he decided what to do : decidió qué iba a hacer⟩ **2** DETERMINE : decidir, determinar ⟨one blow decided the fight : un solo golpe determinó la pelea⟩ **3** CONVINCE : decidir ⟨her pleas decided me to help : sus súplicas me decidieron a ayudarla⟩ **4** RESOLVE : resolver — *vi* : decidirse

decided [dɪˈsaɪdəd] *adj* **1** UNQUESTIONABLE : indudable **2** RESOLUTE : decidido, resuelto — **decidedly** *adv*

deciduous [dɪˈsɪdʒuəs] *adj* : caduco, de hoja caduca

decimal¹ [ˈdɛsəməl] *adj* : decimal

decimal² *n* : número *m* decimal

decimal point *n* : punto *m* decimal, coma *f* decimal

decipher [dɪˈsaɪfər] *vt* : descifrar — **decipherable** [-əbəl] *adj*

decision [dɪˈsɪʒən] *n* : decisión *f*, determinación *f* ⟨to make a decision : tomar una decisión⟩

decisive [dɪˈsaɪsɪv] *adj* **1** DECIDING : decisivo ⟨the decisive vote : el voto decisivo⟩ **2** CONCLUSIVE : decisivo, concluyente, contundente ⟨a decisive victory : una victoria contundente⟩ **3** RESOLUTE : decidido, resuelto, firme

decisively [dɪˈsaɪsɪvli] *adv* : con decisión, de manera decisiva

decisiveness [dɪˈsaɪsɪvnəs] *n* **1** FORCEFULNESS : contundencia *f* **2** RESOLUTION : firmeza *f*, decisión *f*, determinación *f*

deck¹ [ˈdɛk] *vt* **1** FLOOR : tumbar, derribar ⟨she decked him with one blow : lo tumbó de un solo golpe⟩ **2 to deck out** : adornar, engalanar

deck² *n* **1** : cubierta *f* (de un barco) **2 or deck of cards** : baraja *f* (de naipes)

deck chair *n* : silla *f* de playa

declaim [dɪˈkleɪm] *v* : declamar

declaration [ˌdɛkləˈreɪʃən] *n* : declaración *f*, pronunciamiento *m* (oficial)

declare [dɪ'klær] *vt* **-clared; -claring** : declarar, manifestar ⟨to declare war : declarar la guerra⟩ ⟨they declared their support : manifestaron su apoyo⟩

declassify [dɪ'klæsə,faɪ] *vt* **-fied; -fying** : desclasificar

decline¹ [dɪ'klaɪn] *v* **-clined; -clining** *vi* **1** DESCEND : descender **2** DETERIORATE : deteriorarse, decaer ⟨her health is declining : su salud se está deteriorando⟩ **3** DECREASE : disminuir, decrecer, decaer **4** REFUSE : rehusar — *vt* **1** INFLECT : declinar **2** REFUSE, TURN DOWN : declinar, rehusar

decline² *n* **1** DETERIORATION : decadencia *f*, deterioro *m* **2** DECREASE : disminución *f*, descenso *m* **3** SLOPE : declive *m*, pendiente *f*

decode [dɪ'ko:d] *vt* **-coded; -coding** : descifrar (un mensaje), descodificar (una señal)

decoder [dɪ'ko:dər] *n* : decodificador *m*

decompose [,di:kəm'po:z] *v* **-posed; -posing** *vt* **1** BREAK DOWN : descomponer **2** ROT : descomponer, pudrir — *vi* : descomponerse, pudrirse

decomposition [,di:,kɑmpə'zɪʃən] *n* : descomposición *f*

decongestant [,di:kən'dʒɛstənt] *n* : descongestionante *m*

decontaminate [,di:kən'tæmə,neɪt] *vt* **-nated; -nating** : descontaminar — **decontamination** [,di:kən,tæmə'neɪʃən] *n* : descontaminación *f*

decor *or* **décor** [deɪ'kɔr, 'deɪ,kɔr] *n* : decoración *f*

decorate ['dɛkə,reɪt] *vt* **-rated; -rating 1** ADORN : decorar, adornar **2** : condecorar ⟨he was decorated for bravery : lo condecoraron por valor⟩

decoration [,dɛkə'reɪʃən] *n* **1** ADORNMENT : decoración *f*, adorno *m* **2** : condecoración *f* (de honor)

decorative ['dɛkərətɪv, -,reɪ-] *adj* : decorativo, ornamental, de adorno

decorator ['dɛkə,reɪtər] *n* : decorador *m*, -dora *f*

decorum [dɪ'korəm] *n* : decoro *m*

decoy¹ ['di:,kɔɪ, dɪ'-] *vt* : atraer (con señuelo)

decoy² *n* : señuelo *m*, reclamo *m*

decrease¹ [dɪ'kri:s] *v* **-creased; -creasing** *vi* : decrecer, disminuir, bajar — *vt* : reducir, disminuir

decrease² ['di:,kri:s] *n* : disminución *f*, descenso *m*, bajada *f*

decree¹ [dɪ'kri:] *vt* **-creed; -creeing** : decretar

decree² *n* : decreto *m*

decrepit [dɪ'krɛpɪt] *adj* **1** FEEBLE : decrépito, débil **2** DILAPIDATED : deteriorado, ruinoso

decry [dɪ'kraɪ] *vt* **-cried; -crying** : censurar, criticar

dedicate ['dɛdɪ,keɪt] *vt* **-cated; -cating 1** : dedicar ⟨she dedicated the book to Carlos : le dedicó el libro a Carlos⟩ **2** : consagrar, dedicar ⟨to dedicate one's life : consagrar uno su vida⟩

dedication [,dɛdɪ'keɪʃən] *n* **1** DEVOTION : dedicación *f*, devoción *f* **2** : dedicatoria *f* (de un libro, una canción, etc.) **3** CONSECRATION : dedicación *f*

deduce [dɪ'du:s, -'dju:s] *vt* **-duced; -ducing** : deducir, inferir

deduct [dɪ'dʌkt] *vt* : deducir, descontar, restar

deductible [dɪ'dʌktəbəl] *adj* : deducible

deduction [dɪ'dʌkʃən] *n* : deducción *f*

deed¹ ['di:d] *vt* : ceder, transferir

deed² *n* **1** ACT : acto *m*, acción *f*, hecho *m* ⟨a good deed : una buena acción⟩ **2** FEAT : hazaña *f*, proeza *f* **3** TITLE : escritura *f*, título *m*

deem ['di:m] *vt* : considerar, juzgar

deep¹ ['di:p] *adv* : hondo, profundamente ⟨to dig deep : cavar hondo⟩

deep² *adj* **1** : hondo, profundo ⟨the deep end : la parte honda⟩ ⟨a deep wound : una herida profunda⟩ ⟨take a deep breath : respire hondo⟩ **2** : de fondo, de profundidad ⟨the shelf is six inches deep : el estante mide seis pulgadas de fondo⟩ ⟨the lake is 50 meters deep : el lago tiene 50 metros de profundidad⟩ **3** INTENSE : profundo, intenso ⟨with deep regret : con profundo pesar⟩ **4** SERIOUS : grave, serio ⟨to be in deep trouble : estar en serios aprietos⟩ **5** DARK : intenso, subido ⟨deep red : rojo subido⟩ **6** LOW : profundo ⟨a deep tone : un tono profundo⟩ **7** ABSORBED : absorto ⟨deep in thought : absorto en la meditación⟩

deep³ *n* **1** : the deep : lo profundo, el piélago **2** : the deep of night : lo más profundo de la noche

deepen ['di:pən] *v* **-ened; -ening** *vt* **1** : ahondar, profundizar **2** INTENSIFY : intensificar — *vi* **1** : hacerse más profundo **2** INTENSIFY : intensificarse

deeply ['di:pli] *adv* : hondo, profundamente ⟨I'm deeply sorry : lo siento sinceramente⟩

deep-rooted ['di:p'ru: təd, -'ru-] *adj* : profundamente arraigado, enraizado

deep-seated ['di:p'si:təd] *adj* **1** → **deep-rooted** **2** : profundo ⟨dícese de un miedo, etc.⟩

deer ['dɪr] *ns & pl* : ciervo *m*, venado *m*

deerskin ['dɪr,skɪn] *n* : piel *f* de venado

deface [dɪ'feɪs] *vt* **-faced; -facing** MAR : desfigurar

defamation [,dɛfə'meɪʃən] *n* : difamación *f*

defamatory [dɪ'fæmə,tori] *adj* : difamatorio

defame [dɪ'feɪm] *vt* **-famed; -faming** : difamar, calumniar

default¹ [dɪ'fɔlt, 'di:,fɔlt] *vi* **1** : no cumplir (con una obligación), no pagar **2** : no presentarse (en un tribunal)

default² *n* **1** NEGLECT : omisión *f*, negligencia *f* **2** NONPAYMENT : impago *m*, falta *f* de pago **3** to win by default : ganar por abandono

defaulter [dɪ'fɔltər] *n* : moroso *m*, -sa *f*; rebelde *mf* (en un tribunal)

defeat¹ [dɪ'fi:t] *vt* **1** FRUSTRATE : frustrar **2** BEAT : vencer, derrotar

defeat² *n* : derrota *f*, rechazo *m* (de legislación), fracaso *m* (de planes, etc.)

defeatist [dɪ'fiːtɪst] *n* : derrotista *mf* — **defeatist** *adj*

defecate ['dɛfɪˌkeɪt] *vi* **-cated; -cating** : defecar

defect¹ [dɪ'fɛkt] *vi* : desertar

defect² ['diːˌfɛkt, dɪ'fɛkt] *n* : defecto *m*

defection [dɪ'fɛkʃən] *n* : deserción *f*

defective [dɪ'fɛktɪv] *adj* **1** FAULTY : defectuoso **2** DEFICIENT : deficiente

defector [dɪ'fɛktər] *n* : desertor *m*, -tora *f*

defend [dɪ'fɛnd] *vt* : defender

defendant [dɪ'fɛndənt] *n* : acusado *m*, -da *f*; demandado *m*, -da *f*

defender [dɪ'fɛndər] *n* **1** ADVOCATE : defensor *m*, -sora *f* **2** : defensa *mf* (en deportes)

defense [dɪ'fɛnts, 'diːˌfɛnts] *n* : defensa *f*

defenseless [dɪ'fɛntsləs] *adj* : indefenso

defenselessness [dɪ'fɛntsləsnəs] *n* : indefensión *f*

defensive¹ [dɪ'fɛntsɪv] *adj* : defensivo

defensive² *n* **on the defensive** : a la defensiva

defer [dɪ'fər] *v* **-ferred; -ferring** *vt* POSTPONE : diferir, aplazar, posponer — *vi* **to defer to** : deferir a

deference ['dɛfərənts] *n* : deferencia *f*

deferential [ˌdɛfə'rɛntʃəl] *adj* : respetuoso

deferment [dɪ'fərmənt] *n* : aplazamiento *m*

defiance [dɪ'faɪənts] *n* : desafío *m*

defiant [dɪ'faɪənt] *adj* : desafiante, insolente

deficiency [dɪ'fɪʃəntsi] *n, pl* **-cies** : deficiencia *f*, carencia *f*

deficient [dɪ'fɪʃənt] *adj* : deficiente, carente

deficit ['dɛfəsɪt] *n* : déficit *m*

defile [dɪ'faɪl] *vt* **-filed; -filing** **1** DIRTY : ensuciar, manchar **2** CORRUPT : corromper **3** DESECRATE, PROFANE : profanar **4** DISHONOR : deshonrar

defilement [dɪ'faɪlmənt] *n* **1** DESECRATION : profanación *f* **2** CORRUPTION : corrupción *f* **3** CONTAMINATION : contaminación *f*

define [dɪ'faɪn] *vt* **-fined; -fining** **1** BOUND : delimitar, demarcar **2** CLARIFY : aclarar, definir **3** : definir ⟨to define a word : definir una palabra⟩

definite ['dɛfənɪt] *adj* **1** CERTAIN : definido, determinado **2** CLEAR : claro, explícito **3** UNQUESTIONABLE : seguro, incuestionable

definite article *n* : artículo *m* definido

definitely ['dɛfənɪtli] *adv* **1** DOUBTLESSLY : indudablemente, sin duda **2** DEFINITIVELY : definitivamente, seguramente

definition [ˌdɛfə'nɪʃən] *n* : definición *f*

definitive [dɪ'fɪnətɪv] *adj* **1** CONCLUSIVE : definitivo, decisivo **2** AUTHORITATIVE : de autoridad, autorizado — **definitively** *adv*

deflate [dɪ'fleɪt] *v* **-flated; -flating** *vt* **1** : desinflar (una llanta, etc.) **2** REDUCE : rebajar ⟨to deflate one's ego : bajarle los humos a uno⟩ — *vi* : desinflarse

deflation [dɪ'fleɪʃən] *n* : deflación *f* (económica)

deflect [dɪ'flɛkt] *vt* : desviar — *vi* : desviarse

deforestation [diˌfɔrə'steɪʃən] *n* : deforestación *f*

deform [dɪ'fɔrm] *vt* : deformar

deformation [ˌdiːˌfɔr'meɪʃən] *n* : deformación *f*

deformed [dɪ'fɔrmd] *adj* : deforme

deformity [dɪ'fɔrməti] *n, pl* **-ties** : deformidad *f*

defraud [dɪ'frɔd] *vt* : estafar, defraudar

defray [dɪ'freɪ] *vt* : sufragar, costear

defrost [dɪ'frɔst] *vt* : descongelar, deshelar — *vi* : descongelarse, deshelarse

deft [dɛft] *adj* : hábil, diestro — **deftly** *adv*

defunct [dɪ'fʌŋkt] *adj* **1** DECEASED : difunto, fallecido **2** EXTINCT : extinto, fenecido

defuse [dɪ'fjuːz] *vt* : desactivar ⟨to defuse the situation : reducir las tensiones⟩

defy [dɪ'faɪ] *vt* **-fied; -fying** **1** CHALLENGE : desafiar, retar **2** DISOBEY : desobedecer **3** RESIST : resistir, hacer imposible, hacer inútil ⟨to defy understanding/explanation : ser incomprensible/inexplicable⟩ ⟨to defy all reason : ir en contra de toda lógica⟩

degenerate¹ [dɪ'dʒɛnəˌreɪt] *vi* **-ated; -ating** : degenerar

degenerate² [dɪ'dʒɛnərət] *adj* : degenerado

degeneration [dɪˌdʒɛnə'reɪʃən] *n* : degeneración *f*

degenerative [dɪ'dʒɛnərətɪv] *adj* : degenerativo

degradation [ˌdɛgrə'deɪʃən] *n* : degradación *f*

degrade [dɪ'greɪd] *vt* **-graded; -grading** **1** : degradar, envilecer **2** **to degrade oneself** : rebajarse

degrading [dɪ'greɪdɪŋ] *adj* : degradante

degree [dɪ'griː] *n* **1** EXTENT : grado *m* ⟨a third degree burn : una quemadura de tercer grado⟩ **2** : título *m* (de enseñanza superior) **3** : grado *m* (de un círculo, de la temperatura) **4** **by degrees** : gradualmente, poco a poco

dehydrate [dɪ'haɪˌdreɪt] *v* **-drated; -drating** *vt* : deshidratar — *vi* : deshidratarse

dehydration [ˌdiːhaɪ'dreɪʃən] *n* : deshidratación *f*

deice [ˌdiː'aɪs] *vt* **-iced; -icing** : deshelar, descongelar

deify ['diːəˌfaɪ, 'deɪ-] *vt* **-fied; -fying** : deificar

deign [deɪn] *vi* : dignarse, condescender

deity ['diːəti, 'deɪ-] *n, pl* **-ties** **1** **the Deity** : Dios *m* **2** GOD, GODDESS : deidad *f*; dios *m*, diosa *f*

dejected [dɪ'dʒɛktəd] *adj* : abatido, desalentado, desanimado

dejection [dɪ'dʒɛkʃən] *n* : abatimiento *m*, desaliento *m*, desánimo *m*

delay¹ [dɪ'leɪ] *vt* **1** POSTPONE : posponer, postergar **2** HOLD UP : retrasar, demorar — *vi* : tardar, demorar

delay² *n* **1** LATENESS : tardanza *f* **2** HOLDUP : demora *f*, retraso *m*

delectable [dɪ'lɛktəbəl] *adj* **1** DELICIOUS : delicioso, exquisito **2** DELIGHTFUL : encantador

delegate[1] [ˈdɛlɪˌgeɪt] v **-gated; -gating** : delegar

delegate[2] [ˈdɛlɪgət, -ˌgeɪt] n : delegado m, -da f

delegation [ˌdɛlɪˈgeɪʃən] n : delegación f

delete [dɪˈliːt] vt **-leted; -leting** 1 : suprimir, tachar, eliminar 2 : borrar (en informática)

delete key n : tecla f de borrar, tecla f de borrado

deletion [dɪˈliːʃən] n : supresión f, tachadura f, eliminación f

deli [ˈdɛli] → **delicatessen**

deliberate[1] [dɪˈlɪbəˌreɪt] v **-ated; -ating** vt : deliberar sobre, reflexionar sobre, considerar — vi : deliberar

deliberate[2] [dɪˈlɪbərət] adj 1 CONSIDERED : reflexionado, premeditado 2 INTENTIONAL : deliberado, intencional 3 SLOW : lento, pausado

deliberately [dɪˈlɪbərətli] adv 1 INTENTIONALLY : adrede, a propósito 2 SLOWLY : pausadamente, lentamente

deliberation [dɪˌlɪbəˈreɪʃən] n 1 CONSIDERATION : deliberación f, consideración f 2 SLOWNESS : lentitud f

delicacy [ˈdɛlɪkəsi] n, pl **-cies** 1 : manjar m, exquisitez f ⟨caviar is a real delicacy : el caviar es un verdadero manjar⟩ 2 FINENESS : delicadeza f 3 FRAGILITY : fragilidad f

delicate [ˈdɛlɪkət] adj 1 SUBTLE : delicado ⟨a delicate fragrance : una fragancia delicada⟩ 2 DAINTY : delicado, primoroso, fino 3 FRAGILE : frágil 4 SENSITIVE : delicado ⟨a delicate matter : un asunto delicado⟩

delicately [ˈdɛlɪkətli] adv : delicadamente, con delicadeza

delicatessen [ˌdɛlɪkəˈtɛsən] n : charcutería f, fiambrería f, salchichonería f Mex

delicious [dɪˈlɪʃəs] adj : delicioso, exquisito, rico — **deliciously** adv

delight[1] [dɪˈlaɪt] vt : deleitar, encantar — vi **to delight in** : deleitarse con, complacerse en

delight[2] n 1 JOY : placer m, deleite m, gozo m 2 : encanto m ⟨your garden is a delight : su jardín es un encanto⟩

delighted [dɪˈlaɪtəd] adj : encantado ⟨I'm delighted to meet you : estoy encantada de conocerlo⟩

delightful [dɪˈlaɪtfəl] adj : delicioso, encantador

delightfully [dɪˈlaɪtfəli] adv : de manera encantadora, de maravilla

delineate [dɪˈlɪniˌeɪt] vt **-eated; -eating** : delinear, trazar, bosquejar

delinquency [dɪˈlɪŋkwənsi] n, pl **-cies** : delincuencia f

delinquent[1] [dɪˈlɪŋkwənt] adj 1 : delincuente 2 OVERDUE : vencido y sin pagar, moroso

delinquent[2] n : delincuente mf ⟨juvenile delinquent : delincuente juvenil⟩

delirious [dɪˈlɪriəs] adj : delirante ⟨delirious with joy : loco de alegría⟩

delirium [dɪˈlɪriəm] n : delirio m, desvarío m

deliver [dɪˈlɪvər] vt 1 FREE : liberar, librar 2 DISTRIBUTE : entregar, repartir

(periódicos, etc.) 3 : asistir en el parto de (un niño) 4 : pronunciar ⟨to deliver a speech : pronunciar un discurso⟩ 5 PROJECT : despachar, lanzar ⟨he delivered a fast ball : lanzó una pelota rápida⟩ 6 DEAL : propinar, asestar ⟨to deliver a blow : asestar un golpe⟩ — vi 1 : hacer entregas 2 : cumplir ⟨to deliver on one's promise : cumplir (con) su promesa⟩

deliverance [dɪˈlɪvərənts] n : liberación f, rescate m, salvación f

deliverer [dɪˈlɪvərər] n RESCUER : libertador m, -dora f; salvador m, -dora f

delivery [dɪˈlɪvəri] n, pl **-eries** 1 LIBERATION : liberación f 2 : entrega f, reparto m ⟨cash on delivery : entrega contra reembolso⟩ ⟨home delivery : servicio a domicilio⟩ 3 CHILDBIRTH : parto m, alumbramiento m 4 SPEECH : expresión f oral, modo m de hablar 5 THROW : lanzamiento m

dell [ˈdɛl] n : hondonada f, valle m pequeño

delta [ˈdɛltə] n : delta m

delude [dɪˈluːd] vt **-luded; -luding** 1 : engañar 2 **to delude oneself** : engañarse

deluge[1] [ˈdɛljuːdʒ, -ˌjuːʒ] vt **-uged; -uging** 1 FLOOD : inundar 2 OVERWHELM : abrumar ⟨deluged with requests : abrumado de pedidos⟩

deluge[2] n 1 FLOOD : inundación f 2 DOWNPOUR : aguacero m 3 BARRAGE : aluvión m

delusion [dɪˈluːʒən] n 1 : ilusión f (falsa) 2 **delusions of grandeur** : delirios mpl de grandeza

deluxe [dɪˈlʌks, -ˈluks] adj : de lujo

delve [ˈdɛlv] vi **delved; delving** 1 DIG : escarbar 2 **to delve into** PROBE : cavar en, ahondar en

demagogue [ˈdɛməˌgɑg] n : demagogo m, demagoga f

demand[1] [dɪˈmænd] vt : demandar, exigir, reclamar

demand[2] n 1 REQUEST : petición f, pedido m, demanda f ⟨by popular demand : a petición del público⟩ 2 CLAIM : reclamación f, exigencia f 3 MARKET : demanda f ⟨supply and demand : la oferta y la demanda⟩

demanding [dɪˈmændɪŋ] adj : exigente

demarcate [ˈdiˌmɑrˌkeɪt, dɪˈmɑr-] vt **-cated; -cating** : demarcar, delimitar

demarcation [ˌdiːˌmɑrˈkeɪʃən] n : demarcación f, deslinde m

demean [dɪˈmiːn] vt : degradar, rebajar

demeaning [dɪˈmiːnɪŋ] adj : degradante

demeanor [dɪˈmiːnər] n : comportamiento m, conducta f

demented [dɪˈmɛntəd] adj : demente, loco

dementia [dɪˈmɛntʃə] n : demencia f

demerit [dɪˈmɛrət] n : demérito m

demigod [ˈdɛmiˌgɑd, -ˌgɔd] n : semidiós m

demilitarize [dɪˈmɪlɪtəˌraɪz] vt **-rized; -rizing** : desmilitarizar

demise [dɪˈmaɪz] n 1 DEATH : fallecimiento m, deceso m 2 END : hundimiento m, desaparición f (de una institución, etc.)

demitasse ['dɛmɪˌtæs, -ˌtɑs] *n* : taza *f* pequeña (de café)

demo ['dɛmo] *n* **1** DEMONSTRATION : demostración *f* (de productos, etc.) **2** *or* **demo product/version** (etc.) : demo *f*, producto *m* (o versión *f*, etc.) de demostración **3** *or* **demo tape** : demo *f*, cinta *f* de demostración

demobilization [diˌmoːbələˈzeɪʃən] *n* : desmovilización *f*

demobilize [diˈmoːbəˌlaɪz] *vt* **-lized; -lizing** : desmovilizar

democracy [dɪˈmɑkrəsi] *n, pl* **-cies** : democracia *f*

democrat ['dɛməˌkræt] *n* : demócrata *mf*

democratic [ˌdɛməˈkrætɪk] *adj* : democrático — **democratically** [-ˌtɪkli] *adv*

democratize [dɪˈmɑkrəˌtaɪz] *vt* **-tized; -tizing** : democratizar — **democratization** [dɪˈmɑkrətəˈzeɪʃən] *n*

demographic¹ [ˌdɛməˈɡræfɪk] *adj* : demográfico

demographic² *n* **1** : perfil *m* demográfico **2 demographics** *npl* : estadísticas *fpl* demográficas, demografía *f*

demography [dɪˈmɑɡrəfi] *n* : demografía *f*

demolish [dɪˈmɑlɪʃ] *vt* **1** RAZE : demoler, derribar, arrasar **2** DESTROY : destruir, destrozar

demolition [ˌdɛməˈlɪʃən, ˌdiː-] *n* : demolición *f*, derribo *m*

demon ['diːmən] *n* : demonio *m*, diablo *m*

demoniac [dɪˈmoːniˌæk] *or* **demoniacal** [diːməˈnaɪəkəl] → **demonic**

demonic [dɪˈmɑnɪk] *adj* : demoníaco

demonstrably [dɪˈmɑnstrəbli] *adv* : manifiestamente, claramente

demonstrate ['dɛmənˌstreɪt] *vt* **-strated; -strating 1** SHOW : demostrar **2** PROVE : probar, demostrar **3** EXPLAIN : explicar, ilustrar — *vi* : manifestarse ⟨to demonstrate for something : manifestarse a favor de algo⟩ ⟨to demonstrate against something : manifestarse en contra de algo⟩

demonstration [ˌdɛmənˈstreɪʃən] *n* **1** SHOW : muestra *f*, demostración *f* **2** RALLY : manifestación *f*

demonstrative [dɪˈmɑnstrətɪv] *adj* **1** EFFUSIVE : efusivo, expresivo, demostrativo **2** : demostrativo (en lingüística) ⟨demonstrative pronoun : pronombre demostrativo⟩

demonstrator ['dɛmənˌstreɪtər] *n* PROTESTER : manifestante *mf*

demoralize [dɪˈmɔrəˌlaɪz] *vt* **-ized; -izing** : desmoralizar

demoralizing [dɪˈmɔrəˌlaɪzɪŋ] *adj* : desmoralizador, desmoralizante

demote [dɪˈmoːt] *vt* **-moted; -moting** : degradar, bajar de categoría

demotion [dɪˈmoːʃən] *n* : degradación *f*, descenso *m* de categoría

demur [dɪˈmər] *vi* **-murred; -murring** OBJECT : oponerse ⟨to demur at : ponerle objeciones a (algo)⟩

demure [dɪˈmjʊr] *adj* : recatado, modesto — **demurely** *adv*

demystify [dɪˈmɪstəˌfaɪ] *vi* **-fied; -fying** : desmitificar

den ['dɛn] *n* **1** LAIR : cubil *m*, madriguera *f* **2** HIDEOUT : guarida *f* **3** STUDY : estudio *m*, gabinete *m*

denature [diˈneɪtʃər] *vt* **-tured; -turing** : desnaturalizar

dengue ['dɛŋɡi, -ˌɡeɪ] *n* : dengue *m*

denial [dɪˈnaɪəl] *n* **1** REFUSAL : rechazo *m*, denegación *f*, negativa *f* **2** REPUDIATION : negación *f* (de una creencia, etc.), rechazo *m*

denigrate ['dɛnɪˌɡreɪt] *vt* **-grated; -grating** : denigrar

denim ['dɛnəm] *n* **1** : tela *f* vaquera, mezclilla *f* Chile, Mex **2 denims** *npl* → **jeans**

denizen ['dɛnəzən] *n* : habitante *mf*; morador *m*, -dora *f*

denomination [dɪˌnɑməˈneɪʃən] *n* **1** FAITH : confesión *f*, fe *f* **2** VALUE : denominación *f*, valor *m* (de una moneda)

denominator [dɪˈnɑməˌneɪtər] *n* : denominador *m*

denote [dɪˈnoːt] *vt* **-noted; -noting 1** INDICATE, MARK : indicar, denotar, señalar **2** MEAN : significar

denouement [ˌdeɪnuːˈmɑ] *n* : desenlace *m*

denounce [dɪˈnaʊnts] *vt* **-nounced; -nouncing 1** CENSURE : denunciar, censurar **2** ACCUSE : denunciar, acusar, delatar

dense ['dɛnts] *adj* **denser; -est 1** THICK : espeso, denso ⟨dense vegetation : vegetación densa⟩ ⟨a dense fog : una niebla espesa⟩ **2** STUPID : estúpido, burro *fam*

densely ['dɛntsli] *adv* **1** THICKLY : densamente **2** STUPIDLY : torpemente

denseness ['dɛntsnəs] *n* **1** → **density 2** STUPIDITY : estupidez *f*

density ['dɛntsəti] *n, pl* **-ties** : densidad *f*

dent¹ ['dɛnt] *vt* : abollar, mellar

dent² *n* : abolladura *f*, mella *f*

dental ['dɛntəl] *adj* : dental

dental floss *n* : hilo *m* dental

dental surgeon *n* : odontólogo *m*, -ga *f*

dentifrice ['dɛntəfrɪs] *n* : dentífrico *m*, pasta *f* de dientes

dentist ['dɛntɪst] *n* : dentista *mf*

dentistry ['dɛntɪstri] *n* : odontología *f*

dentures ['dɛntʃərz] *npl* : dentadura *f* postiza

denude [dɪˈnuːd, -ˈnjuːd] *vt* **-nuded; -nuding** STRIP : desnudar, despojar

denunciation [dɪˌnʌntsiˈeɪʃən] *n* : denuncia *f*, acusación *f*

deny [dɪˈnaɪ] *vt* **-nied; -nying 1** REFUTE : desmentir, negar **2** DISOWN, REPUDIATE : negar, renegar de **3** REFUSE : denegar **4 to deny oneself** : privarse, sacrificarse

deodorant [diˈoːdərənt] *n* : desodorante *m*

deodorize [diˈoːdəˌraɪz] *vt* **-ized; -izing** : eliminar los malos olores

depart [dɪˈpɑrt] *vt* : salirse de — *vi* **1** LEAVE : salir, partir, irse **2** DIE : morir

department [dɪˈpɑrtmənt] *n* **1** DIVISION : sección *f* (de una tienda, una organización, etc.), departamento *m* (de una empresa, una universidad, etc.), ministerio *m* (del gobierno) **2** PROVINCE,

SPHERE : esfera *f*, campo *m*, competencia *f*

departmental [di‚part'mɛntəl, ‚di:-] *adj* : departamental

department chair → chair²

department store *n* : grandes almacenes *mpl*

departure [di'partʃər] *n* ‚1 LEAVING : salida *f*, partida *f* 2 DEVIATION : desviación *f*

depend [di'pɛnd] *vi* 1 RELY : contar (con), confiar (en) ⟨depend on me! : ¡cuenta conmigo!⟩ 2 to depend on : depender de ⟨success depends on hard work : el éxito depende de trabajar duro⟩ 3 that depends : según, eso depende

dependable [di'pɛndəbəl] *adj* : responsable, digno de confianza, fiable

dependence [di'pɛndənts] *n* : dependencia *f*

dependency [di'pɛndəntsi] *n, pl* -cies 1 → dependence 2 : posesión *f* (de una unidad política)

dependent¹ [di'pɛndənt] *adj* : dependiente

dependent² *n* : persona *f* a cargo de alguien

depict [di'pɪkt] *vt* 1 PORTRAY : representar 2 DESCRIBE : describir

depiction [di'pɪkʃən] *n* : representación *f*, descripción *f*

deplete [di'pli:t] *vt* -pleted; -pleting 1 EXHAUST : agotar 2 REDUCE : reducir

depletion [di'pli:ʃən] *n* 1 EXHAUSTION : agotamiento *m* 2 REDUCTION : reducción *f*, disminución *f*

deplorable [di'plorəbəl] *adj* 1 CONTEMPTIBLE : deplorable, despreciable 2 LAMENTABLE : lamentable

deplore [di'plor] *vt* -plored; -ploring 1 REGRET : deplorar, lamentar 2 CONDEMN : condenar, deplorar

deploy [di'plɔɪ] *vt* : desplegar

deployment [di'plɔɪmənt] *n* : despliegue *m*

deport [di'port] *vt* 1 EXPEL : deportar, expulsar (de un país) 2 to deport oneself BEHAVE : comportarse

deportation [‚di:‚por'teɪʃən] *n* : deportación *f*

depose [di'po:z] *vt* -posed; -posing : deponer

deposit¹ [di'pazət] *vt* -ited; -iting : depositar

deposit² *n* 1 : depósito *m* (en el banco) 2 DOWN PAYMENT : entrega *f* inicial 3 : depósito *m*, yacimiento *m* (en geología)

deposition [‚dɛpə'zɪʃən] *n* TESTIMONY : deposición *f*

depository [di'pazə‚tori] *n, pl* -ries : almacén *m*, depósito *m*

depot [in sense 1 usu 'dɛ‚po:, 2 usu 'di:-] *n* 1 STOREHOUSE : almacén *m*, depósito *m* 2 STATION, TERMINAL : terminal *mf*, estación *f* (de autobuses, ferrocarriles, etc.)

deprave [di'preɪv] *vt* -praved; -praving : depravar, pervertir

depraved [di'preɪvd] *adj* : depravado, degenerado

depravity [di'prævəti] *n, pl* -ties : depravación *f*

depreciate [di'pri:ʃi‚eɪt] *v* -ated; -ating *vt* 1 DEVALUE : depreciar, devaluar 2 DISPARAGE : menospreciar, despreciar — *vi* : depreciarse, devaluarse

depreciation [di‚pri:ʃi'eɪʃən] *n* : depreciación *f*, devaluación *f*

depress [di'prɛs] *vt* 1 PRESS, PUSH : apretar, presionar, pulsar 2 REDUCE : reducir, hacer bajar (precios, ventas, etc.) 3 SADDEN : deprimir, abatir, entristecer 4 DEVALUE : depreciar

depressant *n* : depresivo *m*

depressed [di'prɛst] *adj* 1 DEJECTED : deprimido, abatido 2 : deprimido, en crisis (dícese de la economía)

depressing [di'prɛsɪŋ] *adj* : deprimente, triste

depression [di'prɛʃən] *n* 1 DESPONDENCY : depresión *f*, abatimiento *m* 2 : depresión (en una superficie) 3 RECESSION : depresión *f* económica, crisis *f*

deprivation [‚dɛprə'veɪʃən] *n* : privación *f*

deprive [di'praɪv] *vt* -prived; -priving : privar

depth [dɛpθ] *n, pl* **depths** ['dɛpθs, 'dɛps] 1 : profundidad *f* 2 **depths** *npl* ⟨in the depths of winter : en pleno invierno⟩ ⟨in the depths of despair : en la más profunda desesperación⟩ 3 in depth : a fondo 4 out of one's depth : perdido ⟨I'm out of my depth : esto es demasiado difícil/especializado (etc.) para mí⟩

deputation [‚dɛpjə'teɪʃən] *n* : diputación *f*

deputize ['dɛpju‚taɪz] *vt* -tized; -tizing : nombrar como segundo

deputy ['dɛpjuti] *n, pl* -ties : suplente *mf*; sustituto *m*, -ta *f*

derail [di'reɪl] *v* : descarrilar

derailment [di'reɪlmənt] *n* : descarrilamiento *m*

derange [di'reɪndʒ] *vt* -ranged; -ranging 1 DISARRANGE : desarreglar, desordenar 2 DISTURB, UPSET : trastornar, perturbar 3 MADDEN : enloquecer, volver loco

deranged [di'reɪndʒd] *adj* DISTURBED, INSANE : trastornado, perturbado

derangement [di'reɪndʒmənt] *n* 1 DISTURBANCE, UPSET : trastorno *m* 2 INSANITY : locura *f*, perturbación *f* mental

derby ['dərbi] *n, pl* -bies 1 : derby *m* ⟨the Kentucky Derby : el Derby de Kentucky⟩ 2 : sombrero *m* hongo, bombín *m*

deregulate [di'rɛgju‚leɪt] *vt* -lated; -lating : desregular

deregulation [di‚rɛgju'leɪʃən] *n* : desregulación *f*

derelict¹ ['dɛrə‚lɪkt] *adj* 1 ABANDONED : abandonado, en ruinas 2 REMISS : negligente, remiso

derelict² *n* 1 : propiedad *f* abandonada 2 VAGRANT : vagabundo *m*, -da *f*

deride [di'raɪd] *vt* -rided; -riding : ridiculizar, burlarse de

derision [dɪˈrɪʒən] *n* : escarnio *m*, irrisión *f*, mofa *f*

derisive [dɪˈraɪsɪv] *adj* : burlón

derisory [dɪˈraɪsəri, -zə-] *adj* 1 → **derisive** 2 PALTRY, MEAGER : irrisorio, mísero ⟨a derisory price : un precio irrisorio⟩

derivation [ˌdɛrəˈveɪʃən] *n* : derivación *f*

derivative¹ [dɪˈrɪvətɪv] *adj* 1 DERIVED : derivado 2 BANAL : carente de originalidad, banal

derivative² *n* : derivado *m*

derive [dɪˈraɪv] *v* -rived; -riving *vt* 1 OBTAIN : obtener, sacar 2 DEDUCE : deducir, inferir — *vi* : provenir, derivar, proceder

dermatologist [ˌdərməˈtɑlədʒɪst] *n* : dermatólogo *m*, -ga *f*

dermatology [ˌdərməˈtɑlədʒi] *n* : dermatología *f*

derogatory [dɪˈrɑgəˌtori] *adj* : despectivo, despreciativo

derrick [ˈdɛrɪk] *n* 1 CRANE : grúa *f* 2 : torre *f* de perforación (sobre un pozo de petróleo)

descend [dɪˈsɛnd] *vt* : descender, bajar — *vi* 1 : descender, bajar ⟨he descended from the platform : descendió del estrado⟩ 2 DERIVE : descender, provenir 3 STOOP : rebajarse ⟨I descended to his level : me rebajé a su nivel⟩ 4 to descend upon : caer sobre, invadir

descendant¹ [dɪˈsɛndənt] *adj* : descendente

descendant² *n* : descendiente *mf*

descent [dɪˈsɛnt] *n* 1 : bajada *f*, descenso *m* ⟨the descent from the mountain : el descenso de la montaña⟩ 2 ANCESTRY : ascendencia *f*, linaje *m* 3 SLOPE : pendiente *f*, cuesta *f* 4 FALL : caída *f* 5 ATTACK : incursión *f*, ataque *m*

describe [dɪˈskraɪb] *vt* -scribed; -scribing : describir

description [dɪˈskrɪpʃən] *n* : descripción *f*

descriptive [dɪˈskrɪptɪv] *adj* : descriptivo ⟨descriptive adjective : adjetivo calificativo⟩

desecrate [ˈdɛsɪˌkreɪt] *vt* -crated; -crating : profanar

desecration [ˌdɛsɪˈkreɪʃən] *n* : profanación *f*

desegregate [diˈsɛgrəˌgeɪt] *vt* -gated; -gating : eliminar la segregación racial de

desegregation [diˌsɛgrəˈgeɪʃən] *n* : eliminación *f* de la segregación racial

desert¹ [ˈdɛzərt] *vt* : abandonar (una persona o un lugar), desertar de (una causa, etc.) — *vi* : desertar

desert² [ˈdɛzərt] *adj* : desierto ⟨a desert island : una isla desierta⟩

desert³ *n* 1 [ˈdɛzərt] : desierto *m* (en geografía) 2 [dɪˈzərt] → **deserts**

deserted [dɪˈzərtəd] *adj* : desierto

deserter [dɪˈzərtər] *n* : desertor *m*, -tora *f*

desertion [dɪˈzərʃən] *n* : abandono *m*, deserción *f* (military)

deserts [dɪˈzərts] *npl* : merecido *m* ⟨to get one's just deserts : llevarse uno su merecido⟩

deserve [dɪˈzərv] *vt* -served; -serving : merecer

deservedly [dɪˈzərvədli] *adv* : merecidamente

deserving [dɪˈzərvɪŋ] *adj* : meritorio ⟨deserving of : digno de⟩

desiccate [ˈdɛsɪˌkeɪt] *vt* -cated; -cating : desecar, deshidratar

design¹ [dɪˈzaɪn] *vt* 1 DEVISE : diseñar, concebir, idear 2 PLAN : proyectar 3 SKETCH : trazar, bosquejar

design² *n* 1 PLAN, SCHEME : plan *m*, proyecto *m* ⟨by design : a propósito, intencionalmente⟩ 2 SKETCH : diseño *m*, bosquejo *m* 3 PATTERN, STYLE : diseño *m*, estilo *m* 4 **designs** *npl* INTENTIONS : propósitos *mpl*, designios *mpl*

designate [ˈdɛzɪgˌneɪt] *vt* -nated; -nating 1 INDICATE, SPECIFY : indicar, especificar 2 APPOINT : nombrar, designar

designation [ˌdɛzɪgˈneɪʃən] *n* 1 NAMING : designación *f* 2 NAME : denominación *f*, nombre *m* 3 APPOINTMENT : designación *f*, nombramiento *m*

designer¹ [dɪˈzaɪnər] *adj* : de diseño, de marca

designer² *n* : diseñador *m*, -dora *f*

desirability [dɪˌzaɪrəˈbɪləti] *n, pl* -ties 1 ADVISABILITY : conveniencia *f* 2 ATTRACTIVENESS : atractivo *m*

desirable [dɪˈzaɪrəbəl] *adj* 1 ADVISABLE : conveniente, aconsejable 2 ATTRACTIVE : deseable, atractivo

desire¹ [dɪˈzaɪr] *vt* -sired; -siring 1 WANT : desear 2 REQUEST : rogar, solicitar

desire² *n* : deseo *m*, anhelo *m*, ansia *m*

desist [dɪˈsɪst, -ˈzɪst] *vi* to desist from : desistir de, abstenerse de

desk [ˈdɛsk] *n* : escritorio *m*, pupitre *m* (en la escuela)

desktop¹ [ˈdɛskˌtɑp] *adj* : de escritorio

desktop² *or* desktop computer *n* : computadora *f*, computador *m*, ordenador *m* *Spain* (no portátil)

desktop publishing *n* : autoedición *f*

desolate¹ [ˈdɛsəˌleɪt, -zə-] *vt* -lated; -lating : devastar, desolar

desolate² [ˈdɛsələt, -zə-] *adj* 1 BARREN : desolado, desierto, yermo 2 DISCONSOLATE : desconsolado, desolado

desolation [ˌdɛsəˈleɪʃən, -zə-] *n* : desolación *f*

despair¹ [dɪˈspær] *vi* : desesperar, perder las esperanzas

despair² *n* : desesperación *f*, desesperanza *f*

despairing *adj* : desesperado

desperate [ˈdɛspərət] *adj* 1 HOPELESS : desesperado, sin esperanzas 2 RASH : desesperado, precipitado 3 SERIOUS, URGENT : grave, urgente, apremiante ⟨a desperate need : una necesidad apremiante⟩

desperately [ˈdɛspərətli] *adv* : desesperadamente, urgentemente

desperation [ˌdɛspəˈreɪʃən] *n* : desesperación *f*

despicable [dɪˈspɪkəbəl, ˈdɛspɪ-] *adj* : vil, despreciable, infame

despise [dɪˈspaɪz] vt **-spised; -spising** : despreciar

despite [dəˈspaɪt] prep : a pesar de, aún con

despoil [dɪˈspɔɪl] vt : saquear

despondency [dɪˈspɑndənʦi] n : desaliento m, desánimo m, depresión f

despondent [dɪˈspɑndənt] adj : desalentado, desanimado

despot [ˈdespət, -ˌpɑt] n : déspota mf; tirano m, -na f

despotic [dɛsˈpɑtɪk] adj : despótico

despotism [ˈdespəˌtɪzəm] n : despotismo m

dessert [dɪˈzərt] n : postre m

dessertspoon [dɪˈzərtˌspuːn] n : cuchara f de postre

destination [ˌdestəˈneɪʃən] n : destino m, destinación f

destined [ˈdestənd] adj **1** FATED : predestinado **2** BOUND : destinado, con destino (a), con rumbo (a)

destiny [ˈdestəni] n, pl **-nies** : destino m

destitute [ˈdestəˌtuːt, -ˌtjuːt] adj **1** LACKING : carente, desprovisto **2** POOR : indigente, en miseria

destitution [ˌdestəˈtuːʃən, -ˈtjuː-] n : indigencia f, miseria f

destroy [dɪˈstrɔɪ] vt **1** KILL : matar **2** DEMOLISH : destruir, destrozar

destroyer [dɪˈstrɔɪər] n : destructor m (buque)

destruction [dɪˈstrʌkʃən] n : destrucción f, ruina f

destructive [dɪˈstrʌktɪv] adj : destructor, destructivo

desultory [ˈdesəlˌtori] adj **1** AIMLESS : sin rumbo, sin objeto **2** DISCONNECTED : inconexo

detach [dɪˈtæʧ] vt : separar, quitar, desprender

detached [dɪˈtæʧt] adj **1** SEPARATE : separado, suelto **2** ALOOF : distante, indiferente **3** IMPARTIAL : imparcial, objetivo

detachment [dɪˈtæʧmənt] n **1** SEPARATION : separación f **2** DETAIL : destacamento m (de tropas) **3** ALOOFNESS : reserva f, indiferencia f **4** IMPARTIALITY : imparcialidad f

detail¹ [dɪˈteɪl, ˈdiːˌteɪl] vt : detallar, exponer en detalle

detail² n **1** : detalle m, pormenor m ⟨to go into detail : entrar en detalles⟩ ⟨in detail : con/en detalle, detalladamente⟩ **2** : destacamento m (de tropas)

detailed [dɪˈteɪld, ˈdiːˌteɪld] adj : detallado, minucioso

detain [dɪˈteɪn] vt **1** HOLD : detener **2** DELAY : entretener, demorar, retrasar

detect [dɪˈtekt] vt : detectar, descubrir

detection [dɪˈtekʃən] n : descubrimiento m

detective [dɪˈtektɪv] n : detective mf ⟨private detective : detective privado⟩ ⟨detective novel : novela policial/policíaca⟩ ⟨detective work : investigación⟩

detector [dɪˈtektər] n : detector m

detention [dɪˈtenʧən] n : detención m

deter [dɪˈtər] vt **-terred; -terring** : disuadir, impedir

detergent [dɪˈtərʤənt] n : detergente m

deteriorate [dɪˈtɪriəˌreɪt] vi **-rated; -rating** : deteriorarse, empeorar

deterioration [dɪˌtɪriəˈreɪʃən] n : deterioro m, empeoramiento m

determinant¹ [dɪˈtərmənənt] adj : determinante

determinant² n **1** : factor m determinante **2** : determinante m (en matemáticas)

determination [dɪˌtərməˈneɪʃən] n **1** DECISION : determinación f, decisión f **2** RESOLUTION : resolución f, determinación f ⟨with grim determination : con una firme resolución⟩

determine [dɪˈtərmən] vt **-mined; -mining** **1** ESTABLISH : determinar, establecer **2** SETTLE : decidir **3** FIND OUT : averiguar **4** BRING ABOUT : determinar

determined [dɪˈtərmənd] adj RESOLUTE : decidido, resuelto

deterrence [dɪˈtərənʦ] n : disuasión f

deterrent [dɪˈtərənt] n : medida f disuasiva

detest [dɪˈtest] vt : detestar, odiar, aborrecer

detestable [dɪˈtestəbəl] adj : detestable, odioso, aborrecible

dethrone [dɪˈθroːn] vt **-throned; -throning** : destronar

detonate [ˈdetənˌeɪt] v **-nated; -nating** vt : hacer detonar — vi : detonar, estallar

detonation [ˌdetəˈneɪʃən] n : detonación f

detonator [ˈdetənˌeɪtər] n : detonador m

detour¹ [ˈdiːˌtur, dɪˈtur] vi : desviarse

detour² n : desvío m, rodeo m

detox¹ [ˈdiːˌtɑks, dɪˈtɑks] vt fam : desintoxicar — vi fam : desintoxicarse

detox² n fam : desintoxicación f ⟨she's in detox : está en el proceso de desintoxicación (de drogas, etc.)⟩

detoxify [dɪˈtɑksəˌfaɪ] vt **-fied; -fying** : desintoxicar — **detoxification** [dɪˌtɑksəfəˈkeɪʃən] n

detract [dɪˈtrækt] vi to detract from : restarle valor a, quitarle méritos a

detractor [dɪˈtræktər] n : detractor m, -tora f

detriment [ˈdetrəmənt] n : detrimento m, perjuicio m

detrimental [ˌdetrəˈmentəl] adj : perjudicial — **detrimentally** adv

devaluation [dɪˌvæljuˈeɪʃən] n : devaluación f

devalue [dɪˈvælˌjuː] vt **-ued; -uing** : devaluar, depreciar

devastate [ˈdevəˌsteɪt] vt **-tated; -tating** : devastar, arrasar, asolar

devastating [ˈdevəˌsteɪtɪŋ] adj **1** DESTRUCTIVE, PAINFUL : devastador **2** CUTTING, POWERFUL : demoledor, aplastante, arrollador

devastation [ˌdevəˈsteɪʃən] n : devastación f, estragos mpl

develop [dɪˈveləp] vt **1** FORM, MAKE : desarrollar, elaborar, formar **2** : revelar (en fotografía) **3** FOSTER : desarrollar, fomentar **4** EXPLOIT : explotar (recursos), urbanizar (un área) **5** ACQUIRE : adquirir ⟨to develop an interest : adquirir un interés⟩ **6** CONTRACT : contraer (una enfermedad) — *vi* **1** GROW : desarrollarse **2** ARISE : aparecer, surgir

developed [dɪ'vɛləpt] *adj* : avanzado, desarrollado

developer [dɪ'vɛləpər] *n* **1** : inmobiliaria *f*, urbanizadora *f* **2** : revelador *m* (en fotografía)

developing [dɪ'vɛləpɪŋ] *adj* : en vías de desarrollo (dícese de países)

development [dɪ'vɛləpmənt] *n* **1** : desarrollo *m* ⟨physical development : desarrollo físico⟩ **2** : urbanización *f* (de un área), explotación *f* (de recursos), creación *f* (de inventos) **3** EVENT : acontecimiento *m*, suceso *m* ⟨to await developments : esperar acontecimientos⟩

deviant [di'viənt] *adj* : desviado, anormal

deviate [di'vi,eɪt] *v* -**ated**; -**ating** *vi* : desviarse, apartarse — *vt* : desviar

deviation [di'vi'eɪʃən] *n* : desviación *f*

device [dɪ'vaɪs] *n* **1** MECHANISM : dispositivo *m*, aparato *m*, mecanismo *m* **2** EMBLEM : emblema *m*

devil [ˈdɛvəl] *vt* -**iled** *or* -**illed**; -**iling** *or* -**illing** **1** : sazonar con picante y especias **2** PESTER : molestar

devil[2] *n* **1** SATAN : el diablo, Satanás *m* **2** DEMON : diablo *m*, demonio *m* **3** FIEND : persona *f* diabólica; malvado *m*, -da *f* **4** FELLOW : persona *f* ⟨you lucky devil! : ¡vaya suerte que tienes!⟩ ⟨poor devil : pobre diablo⟩

devilish [ˈdɛvəlɪʃ] *adj* : diabólico

devilry [ˈdɛvəlri] *n, pl* -**ries** : diabluras *fpl*, travesuras *fpl*

devious [ˈdi:viəs] *adj* **1** CRAFTY : taimado, artero **2** WINDING : tortuoso, sinuoso

devise [dɪ'vaɪz] *vt* -**vised**; -**vising** **1** INVENT : idear, concebir, inventar **2** PLOT : tramar

devoid [dɪ'vɔɪd] *adj* ~ **of** : carente de, desprovisto de

devote [dɪ'vo:t] *vt* -**voted**; -**voting** **1** DEDICATE : consagrar, dedicar ⟨to devote one's life : dedicar uno su vida⟩ **2 to devote oneself** : dedicarse

devoted [dɪ'vo:təd] *adj* **1** FAITHFUL : leal, fiel **2 to be devoted to someone** : tenerle mucho cariño a alguien

devotee [ˌdɛvə'ti:, -'teɪ] *n* : devoto *m*, -ta *f*

devotion [dɪ'vo:ʃən] *n* **1** DEDICATION : dedicación *f*, devoción *f* **2 devotions** PRAYERS : oraciones *fpl*, devociones *fpl*

devour [dɪ'vaʊər] *vt* : devorar

devout [dɪ'vaʊt] *adj* **1** PIOUS : devoto, piadoso **2** EARNEST, SINCERE : sincero, ferviente — **devoutly** *adv*

devoutness [dɪ'vaʊtnəs] *n* : devoción *f*, piedad *f*

dew [ˈdu:, 'dju:] *n* : rocío *m*

dewlap [ˈdu,læp, 'dju-] *n* : papada *f*

dew point *n* : punto *m* de condensación

dewy [ˈdu:i, 'dju:i] *adj* **dewier**; -**est** : cubierto de rocío

dexterity [dɛk'stɛrəṭi] *n, pl* -**ties** : destreza *f*, habilidad *f*

dexterous [ˈdɛkstrəs] *adj* : diestro, hábil

dexterously [ˈdɛkstrəsli] *adv* : con destreza, con habilidad, hábilmente

diabetes [ˌdaɪə'bi:ṭiz] *n* : diabetes *f*

diabetic[1] [ˌdaɪə'bɛṭɪk] *adj* : diabético

diabetic[2] *n* : diabético *m*, -ca *f*

diabolic [ˌdaɪə'bɑlɪk] *or* **diabolical** [-lɪkəl] *adj* : diabólico, satánico

diacritic [ˌdaɪə'krɪṭɪk] *n* : diacrítico *m*

diacritical [ˌdaɪə'krɪṭɪkəl] *or* **diacritic** *adj* : diacrítico

diadem [ˈdaɪə,dɛm, -dəm] *n* : diadema *f*

diagnose [ˈdaɪəg,no:s, ˌdaɪəg'no:s] *vt* -**nosed**; -**nosing** : diagnosticar

diagnosis [ˌdaɪəg'no:sɪs] *n, pl* -**noses** [-'no:,si:z] : diagnóstico *m*

diagnostic [ˌdaɪəg'nɑstɪk] *adj* : diagnóstico

diagonal[1] [daɪ'ægənəl] *adj* : diagonal, en diagonal

diagonal[2] *n* : diagonal *f*

diagonally [daɪ'ægənəli] *adv* : diagonalmente, en diagonal

diagram[1] [ˈdaɪə,græm] *vt* -**gramed** *or* -**grammed**; -**graming** *or* -**gramming** : hacer un diagrama de

diagram[2] *n* : diagrama *m*, gráfico *m*, esquema *m*

dial[1] [ˈdaɪl] *v* **dialed** *or* **dialled**; **dialing** *or* **dialling** **1** : marcar, discar

dial[2] *n* : esfera *f* (de un reloj), dial *m* (de un radio), disco *m* (de un teléfono)

dialect [ˈdaɪə,lɛkt] *n* : dialecto *m*

dialogue [ˈdaɪə,lɔg] *n* : diálogo *m*

dial tone *n* : tono *m* (de marcar/marcado/discar)

diameter [daɪ'æmətər] *n* : diámetro *m*

diamond [ˈdaɪmənd, 'daɪə-] *n* **1** : diamante *m*, brillante *m* ⟨a diamond necklace : un collar de brillantes⟩ **2** : rombo *m*, forma *f* de rombo **3** : diamante *m* (naipe) **4** INFIELD : cuadro *m*, diamante *m* (en béisbol)

diaper [ˈdaɪpər, 'daɪə-] *n* : pañal *m*

diaphragm [ˈdaɪə,fræm] *n* : diafragma *m*

diarrhea [ˌdaɪə'ri:ə] *n* : diarrea *f*

diary [ˈdaɪəri] *n, pl* -**ries** : diario *m*

diatribe [ˈdaɪə,traɪb] *n* : diatriba *f*

dice[1] [ˈdaɪs] *vt* **diced**; **dicing** : cortar en cubos

dice[2] *ns & pl* **1** → **die**[2] **2** : dados *mpl* (juego)

dicker [ˈdɪkər] *vt* : regatear

dictate[1] [ˈdɪk,teɪt, dɪk'teɪt] *v* -**tated**; -**tating** *vt* **1** : dictar ⟨to dictate a letter : dictar una carta⟩ **2** ORDER : mandar, ordenar — *vi* : dar órdenes

dictate[2] [ˈdɪk,teɪt] *n* **1** : mandato *m*, orden *f* **2 dictates** *npl* : dictados *mpl* ⟨the dictates of conscience : los dictados de la conciencia⟩

dictation [dɪk'teɪʃən] *n* : dictado *m*

dictator [ˈdɪk,teɪṭər] *n* : dictador *m*, -dora *f*

dictatorial [ˌdɪktə'toriəl] *adj* : dictatorial — **dictatorially** *adv*

dictatorship [dɪk'teɪṭər,ʃɪp, 'dɪk,-] *n* : dictadura *f*

diction [ˈdɪkʃən] *n* **1** : lenguaje *m*, estilo *m* **2** ENUNCIATION : dicción *f*, articulación *f*

dictionary ['dɪkʃə,neri] *n, pl* **-naries** : diccionario *m*

did → **do**

didactic [daɪ'dæktɪk] *adj* : didáctico

die¹ ['daɪ] *vi* **died** ['daɪd]; **dying** ['daɪɪŋ] **1** : morir, morirse ⟨a dying civilization : una civilización moribunda⟩ **3** STOP : apagarse, dejar de funcionar ⟨the motor died : el motor se apagó⟩ **4 to be dying for/to** : morirse por ⟨I'm dying for a coffee : me muero por un café⟩ ⟨I'm dying to leave : me muero por irme⟩ **5 to die away** FADE : irse apagando, disminuir (dícese de un sonido) **6 to die down** SUBSIDE : disminuir, amainar (dícese del viento, etc.), irse apagando (dícese de los aplausos, las llamas, etc.), calmarse (dícese de un escándalo, etc.) **7 to die laughing** : morirse de risa **8 to die of** : morir de, morirse de ⟨he died of old age : murió de viejo⟩ **9 to die out** : extinguirse

die² ['daɪ] *n, pl* **dice** ['daɪs] : dado *m*

die³ *n, pl* **dies** ['daɪz] **1** STAMP : troquel *m*, cuño *m* **2** MOLD : matriz *f*, molde *m*

diehard ['daɪ,hɑrd] *adj* : fanático

diesel ['diːzəl, -səl] *n* : diesel *m*

diet¹ ['daɪət] *vi* : ponerse a régimen, hacer dieta

diet² *n* : régimen *m*, dieta *f*

dietary ['daɪə,teri] *adj* : alimenticio, dietético

dietitian *or* **dietician** [,daɪə'tɪʃən] *n* : dietista *mf*

differ ['dɪfər] *vi* **-ferred; -ferring** **1** : diferir, diferenciarse **2** VARY : variar **3** DISAGREE : discrepar, diferir, no estar de acuerdo

difference ['dɪfrənts, 'dɪfərənts] *n* **1** : diferencia *f* ⟨to tell/notice the difference : notar/ver la diferencia⟩ **2** DISCREPANCY : diferencia *f* ⟨to split the difference : dividirse la diferencia (en partes iguales)⟩ **3** DISAGREEMENT : diferencia *f*, desacuerdo *m* ⟨to resolve/settle one's differences : resolver/saldar sus diferencias⟩ **4 same difference!** : ¡es casi lo mismo! **5 to make a difference** MATTER : importar ⟨what difference does it make? : ¿qué importa?⟩ ⟨it makes no difference to me : me da igual⟩ **6 to make a difference in** AFFECT : afectar, influir en

different ['dɪfrənt, 'dɪfərənt] *adj* : distinto, diferente

differential¹ [,dɪfə'rentʃəl] *adj* : diferencial

differential² *n* : diferencial *m*

differentiate [,dɪfə'rentʃi,eɪt] *v* **-ated; -ating** *vt* **1** : hacer diferente **2** DISTINGUISH : distinguir, diferenciar — *vi* : distinguir

differentiation [,dɪfə,rentʃi'eɪʃən] *n* : diferenciación *f*

differently ['dɪfrəntli, 'dɪfərənt-] *adv* : de otra manera, de otro modo, distintamente

difficult ['dɪfɪ,kʌlt] *adj* : difícil

difficulty ['dɪfɪ,kʌlti] *n, pl* **-ties** **1** : dificultad *f* **2** PROBLEM : problema *f*, dificultad *f*

diffidence ['dɪfədənts] *n* **1** SHYNESS : retraimiento *m*, timidez *f*, apocamiento *m* **2** RETICENCE : reticencia *f*

diffident ['dɪfədənt] *adj* **1** SHY : tímido, apocado, inseguro **2** RESERVED : reservado

diffuse¹ [dɪ'fjuːz] *v* **-fused; -fusing** *vt* : difundir, esparcir — *vi* : difundirse, esparcirse

diffuse² [dɪ'fjuːs] *adj* **1** WORDY : prolijo, verboso **2** WIDESPREAD : difuso

diffusion [dɪf'juːʒən] *n* : difusión *f*

dig¹ ['dɪg] *v* **dug** ['dʌg]; **digging** *vt* **1** : cavar, excavar ⟨to dig a hole : cavar un hoyo⟩ **2** EXTRACT : sacar ⟨to dig up potatoes : sacar papas del suelo⟩ **3** POKE, THRUST : clavar, hincar ⟨he dug me in the ribs : me dio un codazo en las costillas⟩ **4 to dig out** RETRIEVE, EXTRACT : sacar **5 to dig up** DISCOVER : descubrir, sacar a luz — *vi* **1** : cavar, excavar **2** *or* **to dig around** RUMMAGE : hurgar (en los bolsillos, etc.) ⟨I dig (around) in my purse for my keys : hurgué en el bolso buscando las llaves⟩ **3 to dig for** : buscar ⟨to dig for gold : buscar oro (cavando en el suelo)⟩ ⟨to dig for clues : buscar pistas, investigar⟩ **4 to dig in** : atrincherarse **5 to dig in** : empezar a comer ⟨dig in! : ¡a comer!⟩ **6 to dig into** POKE : clavarse en **7 to dig into** INVESTIGATE : investigar

dig² *n* **1** POKE : codazo *m* **2** GIBE : pulla *f* **3** EXCAVATION : excavación *f*

digest¹ [daɪ'dʒest, dɪ-] *vt* **1** ASSIMILATE : digerir, asimilar **2** : digerir (comida) **3** SUMMARIZE : compendiar, resumir

digest² ['daɪ,dʒest] *n* : compendio *m*, resumen *m*

digestible [daɪ'dʒestəbəl, dɪ-] *adj* : digerible

digestion [daɪ'dʒestʃən, dɪ-] *n* : digestión *f*

digestive [daɪ'dʒestɪv, dɪ-] *adj* : digestivo ⟨the digestive system : el sistema digestivo⟩

digit ['dɪdʒət] *n* **1** NUMERAL : dígito *m*, número *m* **2** FINGER, TOE : dedo *m*

digital ['dɪdʒətəl] *adj* : digital ⟨digital camera : cámara digital⟩ — **digitally** *adv*

digitalize ['dɪdʒətə,laɪz] *vt* **-ized; -izing** : digitalizar

dignified ['dɪgnə,faɪd] *adj* : digno, decoroso

dignify ['dɪgnə,faɪ] *vt* **-fied; -fying** : dignificar, honrar

dignitary ['dɪgnə,teri] *n, pl* **-taries** : dignatario *m*, -ria *f*

dignity ['dɪgnəti] *n, pl* **-ties** : dignidad *f*

digress [daɪ'gres, də-] *vi* : desviarse del tema, divagar

digression [daɪ'greʃən, də-] *n* : digresión *f*

dike *or* **dyke** ['daɪk] *n* : dique *m*

dilapidated [də'læpə,deɪtəd] *adj* : ruinoso, desvencijado, destartalado

dilapidation [də,læpə'deɪʃən] *n* : deterioro *m*, estado *m* ruinoso

dilate [daɪ'leɪt, 'daɪ,leɪt] *v* **-lated; -lating** *vt* : dilatar — *vi* : dilatarse

dilemma [dɪˈlɛmə] *n* : dilema *m*

dilettante [ˈdɪləˌtɑnt, -ˌtænt] *n*, *pl* **-tantes** [-ˌtɑnts, -ˌtænts] *or* **-tanti** [ˌdɪləˈtɑnti, -ˈtæn-] : diletante *mf*

diligence [ˈdɪlədʒənts] *n* : diligencia *f*, aplicación *f*

diligent [ˈdɪlədʒənt] *adj* : diligente ⟨a diligent search : una búsqueda minuciosa⟩ — **diligently** *adv*

dill [ˈdɪl] *n* : eneldo *m*

dillydally [ˈdɪliˌdæli] *vi* **-lied; -lying** : demorarse, perder tiempo

dilute [daɪˈluːt, də-] *vt* **-luted; -luting** : diluir, aguar

dilution [daɪˈluːʃən, də-] *n* : dilución *f*

dim¹ [ˈdɪm] *v* **dimmed; dimming** *vt* : atenuar (la luz), nublar (la vista), borrar (la memoria), opacar (una superficie) — *vi* : oscurecerse, apagarse

dim² *adj* **dimmer; dimmest** **1** FAINT : oscuro, tenue (dícese de la luz), nublado (dícese de la vista), borrado (dícese de la memoria) **2** STUPID : tonto, torpe **3** **to take a dim view of** : ver con malos ojos

dime [ˈdaɪm] *n* : moneda *f* de diez centavos

dimension [dəˈmɛntʃən, daɪ-] *n* **1** : dimensión *f* **2 dimensions** *npl* EXTENT, SCOPE : dimensiones *fpl*, extensión *f*, medida *f*

diminish [dəˈmɪnɪʃ] *vt* LESSEN : disminuir, reducir, amainar — *vi* DWINDLE, WANE : menguar, reducirse

diminutive [dəˈmɪnjʊtɪv] *adj* : diminutivo, minúsculo

dimly [ˈdɪmli] *adv* : indistintamente, débilmente

dimmer [ˈdɪmər] *n* : potenciómetro *m*, conmutador *m* de luces (en automóviles)

dimness [ˈdɪmnəs] *n* : oscuridad *f*, debilidad *f* (de la vista), imprecisión *f* (de la memoria)

dimple [ˈdɪmpəl] *n* : hoyuelo *m*

din [ˈdɪn] *n* : estrépito *m*, estruendo *m*

dine [ˈdaɪn] *vi* **dined; dining** : cenar

diner [ˈdaɪnər] *n* **1** : comensal *mf* (persona) **2** : vagón *m* restaurante (en un tren) **3** : cafetería *f*, restaurante *m* barato

dinghy [ˈdɪŋi, ˈdɪŋgi, ˈdɪŋki] *n*, *pl* **-ghies** : bote *m*

dinginess [ˈdɪndʒinəs] *n* **1** DIRTINESS : suciedad *f* **2** SHABBINESS : lo gastado, lo deslucido

dingy [ˈdɪndʒi] *adj* **dingier; -est** **1** DIRTY : sucio **2** SHABBY : gastado, deslucido

dining car *n* : coche *m* comedor (de un tren)

dining room *n* : comedor *m*

dinner [ˈdɪnər] *n* **1** : cena *f*, comida *f* **2** BANQUET : cena *f*, banquete *m*

dinner jacket *n* : esmoquin *m* (chaqueta)

dinosaur [ˈdaɪnəˌsɔr] *n* : dinosaurio *m*

dint [ˈdɪnt] *n* **by dint of** : a fuerza de

diocese [ˈdaɪəsəs, -ˌsiːz, -ˌsiːs] *n*, *pl* **-ceses** [ˈdaɪəsəsəz] : diócesis *f*

dip¹ [ˈdɪp] *v* **dipped; dipping** *vt* **1** DUNK, PLUNGE : sumergir, mojar, meter **2** LADLE : servir con cucharón **3** LOWER : bajar, arriar (una bandera) — *vi* **1** DESCEND, DROP : bajar en picada, descender **2** SLOPE : bajar, inclinarse

dip² *n* **1** SWIM : chapuzón *m* **2** DROP : descenso *m*, caída *f* **3** SLOPE : cuesta *f*, declive *m* **4** SAUCE : salsa *f*

diphtheria [dɪfˈθɪriə] *n* : difteria *f*

diphthong [ˈdɪfˌθɔŋ] *n* : diptongo *m*

diploma [dəˈploːmə] *n*, *pl* **-mas** : diploma *m*

diplomacy [dəˈploːməsi] *n* **1** : diplomacia *f* **2** TACT : tacto *m*, discreción *f*

diplomat [ˈdɪpləˌmæt] *n* **1** : diplomático *m*, -ca *f* (en relaciones internacionales) **2** : persona *f* diplomática

diplomatic [ˌdɪpləˈmætɪk] *adj* : diplomático ⟨diplomatic immunity : inmunidad diplomática⟩

dipper [ˈdɪpər] *n* **1** LADLE : cucharón *m*, cazo *m* **2 Big Dipper** : Osa *f* Mayor **3 Little Dipper** : Osa *f* Menor

dipstick [ˈdɪpˌstɪk] *n* : varilla *f* de medición (del aceite)

dire [ˈdaɪr] *adj* **direr; direst** **1** HORRIBLE : espantoso, terrible, horrendo **2** EXTREME : extremo ⟨dire poverty : pobreza extrema⟩

direct¹ [dəˈrɛkt, daɪ-] *vt* **1** ADDRESS : dirigir, mandar **2** AIM, POINT : dirigir **3** GUIDE : indicarle el camino (a alguien), orientar **4** MANAGE : dirigir ⟨to direct a film : dirigir una película⟩ **5** COMMAND : ordenar, mandar

direct² *adv* : directamente

direct³ *adj* **1** STRAIGHT : directo **2** FRANK : franco

direct debit *n* : débito *m* automático

direct current *n* : corriente *f* continua

direction [dəˈrɛkʃən, daɪ-] *n* **1** SUPERVISION : dirección *f* **2** INSTRUCTION, ORDER : instrucción *f*, orden *f* **3** COURSE : dirección *f*, rumbo *m* ⟨to change direction : cambiar de dirección⟩ **4 to ask directions** : pedir indicaciones

directional [dəˈrɛkʃənəl, daɪ-] *adj* : direccional

directive [dəˈrɛktɪv, daɪ-] *n* : directiva *f*

directly [dəˈrɛktli, daɪ-] *adv* **1** STRAIGHT : directamente ⟨directly north : directamente al norte⟩ **2** FRANKLY : francamente **3** EXACTLY : exactamente, justo ⟨directly opposite : justo enfrente⟩ **4** IMMEDIATELY : en seguida, inmediatamente

directness [dəˈrɛktnəs, daɪ-] *n* : franqueza *f*

director [dəˈrɛktər, daɪ-] *n* **1** : director *m*, -tora *f* **2 board of directors** : junta *f* directiva, directorio *m*

directory [dəˈrɛktəri, daɪ-] *n*, *pl* **-ries** : guía *f*, directorio *m* ⟨telephone directory : directorio telefónico⟩ ⟨directory assistance : servicio de información (telefónica)⟩

dirge [ˈdərdʒ] *n* : canto *m* fúnebre

dirigible [ˈdɪrədʒəbəl, dəˈrɪdʒə-] *n* : dirigible *m*, zepelín *m*

dirt [ˈdərt] *n* **1** FILTH : suciedad *f*, mugre *f*, porquería *f* **2** SOIL : tierra *f*

dirt cheap *adj* : baratísimo, regalado

dirtiness [ˈdərtinəs] *n* : suciedad *f*

dirty¹ [ˈdərti] *vt* **dirtied; dirtying** : ensuciar, manchar

dirty² *adj* **dirtier; -est** **1** SOILED, STAINED : sucio, manchado **2** DISHONEST : sucio, deshonesto ⟨a dirty player : un jugador tramposo⟩ ⟨a dirty trick : una mala pasada⟩ **3** INDECENT : indecente, cochino ⟨a dirty joke : un chiste verde⟩

dis- *pref* : des-

disability [ˌdɪsəˈbɪləti] *n*, *pl* **-ties** : minusvalía *f*, discapacidad *f*, invalidez *f*

disable [dɪsˈeɪbəl] *vt* **-abled; -abling** : dejar inválido, inutilizar, incapacitar

disabled [dɪsˈeɪbəld] *adj* : minusválido, discapacitado

disabuse [ˌdɪsəˈbjuːz] *vt* **-bused; -busing** : desengañar, sacar del error

disadvantage [ˌdɪsədˈvæntɪdʒ] *n* : desventaja *f*

disadvantageous [ˌdɪsˌædˌvænˈteɪdʒəs] *adj* : desventajoso, desfavorable

disagree [ˌdɪsəˈgriː] *vi* **1** DIFFER : discrepar, no coincidir **2** DISSENT : disentir, discrepar, no estar de acuerdo ⟨I disagree (with you) : no estoy de acuerdo (contigo)⟩ **3** to disagree with someone : sentarle mal a alguien (dícese de comida, etc.)

disagreeable [ˌdɪsəˈgriːəbəl] *adj* : desagradable

disagreement [ˌdɪsəˈgriːmənt] *n* **1** : desacuerdo *m* **2** DISCREPANCY : discrepancia *f* **3** ARGUMENT : discusión *f*, altercado *m*, disputa *f*

disallow [ˌdɪsəˈlaʊ] *vt* **1** : rechazar, desestimar **2** : anular (en deportes)

disappear [ˌdɪsəˈpɪr] *vi* : desaparecer, desvanecerse ⟨to disappear from view : perderse de vista⟩

disappearance [ˌdɪsəˈpɪrənts] *n* : desaparición *f*

disappoint [ˌdɪsəˈpɔɪnt] *vt* : decepcionar, defraudar, fallar

disappointing [ˌdɪsəˈpɔɪntɪŋ] *adj* : decepcionante

disappointment [ˌdɪsəˈpɔɪntmənt] *n* : decepción *f*, desilusión *f*, chasco *m*

disapproval [ˌdɪsəˈpruːvəl] *n* : desaprobación *f*

disapprove [ˌdɪsəˈpruːv] *vi* **-proved; -proving** : desaprobar, estar en contra

disapprovingly [ˌdɪsəˈpruːvɪŋli] *adv* : con desaprobación

disarm [dɪsˈɑrm] *vt* : desarmar

disarmament [dɪsˈɑrməmənt] *n* : desarme *m* ⟨nuclear disarmament : desarme nuclear⟩

disarrange [ˌdɪsəˈreɪndʒ] *vt* **-ranged; -ranging** : desarreglar, desordenar

disarray [ˌdɪsəˈreɪ] *n* : desorden *m*, confusión *f*, desorganización *f*

disassemble [ˌdɪsəˈsɛmbəl] *v* **-bled; -bling** *vt* : desarmar, desmontar — *vi* : desarmarse, desmontarse

disassociate → dissociate

disaster [dɪˈzæstər] *n* : desastre *m*, catástrofe *f*

disastrous [dɪˈzæstrəs] *adj* : desastroso

disband [dɪsˈbænd] *vt* : disolver — *vi* : disolverse, dispersarse

disbar [dɪsˈbɑr] *vt* **-barred; -barring** : prohibir de ejercer la abogacía

disbelief [ˌdɪsbɪˈliːf] *n* : incredulidad *f*

disbelieve [ˌdɪsbɪˈliːv] *v* **-lieved; -lieving** : no creer, dudar

disburse [dɪsˈbərs] *vt* **-bursed; -bursing** : desembolsar

disbursement [dɪsˈbərsmənt] *n* : desembolso *m*

disc → disk

discard [dɪsˈkɑrd, ˈdɪsˌkɑrd] *vt* : desechar, deshacerse de, botar — *vi* : descartarse (en juegos de naipes)

discern [dɪˈsərn, -ˈzərn] *vt* : discernir, distinguir, percibir

discernible [dɪˈsərnəbəl, -ˈzər-] *adj* : perceptible, visible

discerning [dɪˈsərnɪŋ, -ˈzər-] *adj* : refinado (dícese del gusto), perspicaz, sagaz

discernment [dɪˈsərnmənt, -ˈzərn-] *n* : discernimiento *m*, criterio *m*

discharge¹ [dɪsˈtʃɑrdʒ, ˈdɪsˌ-] *v* **-charged; -charging** **1** UNLOAD : descargar (carga), desembarcar (pasajeros) **2** SHOOT : descargar, disparar **3** FREE : liberar, poner en libertad **4** DISMISS : despedir **5** EMIT : despedir (humo, etc.), descargar (electricidad) **6** : cumplir con (una obligación), saldar (una deuda) — *vi* **1** : descargarse (dícese de una batería) **2** OOZE : supurar

discharge² [ˈdɪsˌtʃɑrdʒ, dɪsˈ-] *n* **1** EMISSION : descarga *f* (de electricidad), emisión *f* (de gases) **2** DISMISSAL : despido *m* (del empleo), baja *f* (del ejército) **3** SECRETION : secreción *f*

disciple [dɪˈsaɪpəl] *n* : discípulo *m*, -la *f*

discipline¹ [ˈdɪsəplən] *vt* **-plined; -plining** **1** PUNISH : castigar, sancionar (a los empleados) **2** CONTROL : disciplinar **3** to discipline oneself : disciplinarse

discipline² *n* **1** FIELD : disciplina *f*, campo *m* **2** TRAINING : disciplina *f* **3** PUNISHMENT : castigo *m* **4** SELF-CONTROL : dominio *m* de sí mismo

disc jockey *n* : disc jockey *mf*

disclaim [dɪsˈkleɪm] *vt* DENY : negar

disclose [dɪsˈkloːz] *vt* **-closed; -closing** : revelar, poner en evidencia

disclosure [dɪsˈkloːʒər] *n* : revelación *f*

disco [ˈdɪskoː] *n* **1** → discotheque **2** *or* **disco music** : disco *f*, música *f* disco

discolor [dɪsˈkʌlər] *vt* **1** BLEACH : decolorar **2** FADE : desteñir **3** STAIN : manchar — *vi* : decolorarse, desteñirse

discoloration [dɪsˌkʌləˈreɪʃən] *n* STAIN : mancha *f*

discomfort [dɪsˈkʌmfərt] *n* **1** PAIN : molestia *f*, malestar *m* **2** UNEASINESS : inquietud *f*

disconcert [ˌdɪskənˈsərt] *vt* : desconcertar

disconcerting [ˌdɪskənˈsərtɪŋ] *adj* : desconcertante

disconnect [ˌdɪskəˈnɛkt] *vt* : desconectar

disconnected [ˌdɪskəˈnɛktəd] *adj* : inconexo

disconsolate [dɪsˈkɑntsələt] *adj* : desconsolado

discontent [ˌdɪskənˈtɛnt] *n* : descontento *m*

discontented [ˌdɪskənˈtɛntəd] *adj* : descontento

discontinue [ˌdɪskənˈtɪnˌjuː] *vt* **-ued; -uing** : suspender, descontinuar

discontinuity [dɪsˌkɑntəˈnuːəti, -ˈnjuː-] *n, pl* **-ties** : discontinuidad *f*

discontinuous [ˌdɪskənˈtɪnjəwəs] *adj* : discontinuo

discord [ˈdɪsˌkɔrd] *n* **1** STRIFE : discordia *f*, discordancia *f* **2** : disonancia *f* (en música)

discordant [dɪsˈkɔrdənt] *adj* : discordante — **discordantly** *adv*

discotheque [ˈdɪskəˌtɛk, ˌdɪskəˈtɛk] *n* : discoteca *f*

discount[1] [ˈdɪsˌkaʊnt, dɪsˈ-] *vt* **1** REDUCE : descontar, rebajar (precios) **2** DISREGARD : descartar, ignorar

discount[2] [ˈdɪsˌkaʊnt] *n* : descuento *m*, rebaja *f*

discourage [dɪsˈkərɪdʒ] *vt* **-aged; -aging 1** DISHEARTEN : desalentar, desanimar **2** DISSUADE : disuadir **3** DETER : impedir

discouragement [dɪsˈkərɪdʒmənt] *n* : desánimo *m*, desaliento *m*

discouraging [dɪsˈkərədʒɪŋ] *adj* : desalentador

discourse[1] [ˈdɪsˈkors] *vi* **-coursed; -coursing** : disertar, conversar

discourse[2] [ˈdɪsˌkors] *n* **1** TALK : conversación *f* **2** SPEECH, TREATISE : discurso *m*, tratado *m*

discourteous [dɪsˈkərtiəs] *adj* : descortés — **discourteously** *adv*

discourtesy [dɪsˈkərtəsi] *n, pl* **-sies** : descortesía *f*

discover [dɪsˈkʌvər] *vt* : descubrir

discoverer [dɪsˈkʌvərər] *n* : descubridor *m*, -dora *f*

discovery [dɪsˈkʌvəri] *n, pl* **-ries** : descubrimiento *m*

discredit[1] [dɪsˈkrɛdət] *vt* **1** DISBELIEVE : no creer, dudar **2** : desacreditar, desprestigiar, poner en duda ⟨they discredited his research : desacreditaron sus investigaciones⟩

discredit[2] *n* **1** DISREPUTE : descrédito *m*, desprestigio *m* **2** DOUBT : duda *f*

discreet [dɪsˈkriːt] *adj* : discreto — **discreetly** *adv*

discrepancy [dɪsˈkrɛpəntsi] *n, pl* **-cies** : discrepancia *f*

discretion [dɪsˈkrɛʃən] *n* **1** : discreción *f* **2** JUDGMENT : discernimiento *m*, criterio *m*

discretionary [dɪsˈkrɛʃəˌneri] *adj* : discrecional

discriminate [dɪsˈkrɪməˌneɪt] *v* **-nated; -nating** *vt* DISTINGUISH : distinguir, discriminar, diferenciar — *vi* : discriminar ⟨to discriminate against women : discriminar a las mujeres⟩

discriminating [dɪsˈkrɪməˌneɪtɪŋ] *adj* : refinado (dícese del gusto), entendido (dícese de personas)

discrimination [dɪsˌkrɪməˈneɪʃən] *n* **1** PREJUDICE : discriminación *f* **2** DISCERNMENT : discernimiento *m*

discriminatory [dɪsˈkrɪmənəˌtori] *adj* : discriminatorio

discus [ˈdɪskəs] *n, pl* **-cuses** [-kəsəz] : disco *m*

discuss [dɪsˈkʌs] *vt* : hablar de, discutir, tratar (de)

discussion [dɪsˈkʌʃən] *n* : discusión *f*, debate *m*, conversación *f*

disdain[1] [dɪsˈdeɪn] *vt* : desdeñar, despreciar ⟨they disdained to reply : no se dignaron a responder⟩

disdain[2] *n* : desdén *m*

disdainful [dɪsˈdeɪnfəl] *adj* : desdeñoso — **disdainfully** *adv*

disease [dɪˈziːz] *n* : enfermedad *f*, mal *m*, dolencia *f*

diseased [dɪˈziːzd] *adj* : enfermo

disembark [ˌdɪsɪmˈbɑrk] *v* : desembarcar

disembarkation [dɪsˌɛmˌbɑrˈkeɪʃən] *n* : desembarco *m*, desembarque *m*

disembodied [ˌdɪsɪmˈbadid] *adj* : incorpóreo

disenchant [ˌdɪsɪnˈtʃænt] *vt* : desilusionar, desencantar, desengañar

disenchanted [ˌdɪsɪnˈtʃæntəd] *adj* : desilusionado, desencantado

disenchantment [ˌdɪsɪnˈtʃæntmənt] *n* : desencanto *m*, desilusión *f*

disenfranchise [dɪsɪnˈfrænˌtʃaɪz] *vt* **-chised; -chising** : privar del derecho a votar

disengage [ˌdɪsɪnˈgeɪdʒ] *vt* **-gaged; -gaging** : soltar, desconectar (un mecanismo)

disentangle [ˌdɪsɪnˈtæŋgəl] *vt* **-gled; -gling** UNTANGLE : desenredar, desenmarañar

disfavor [dɪsˈfeɪvər] *n* : desaprobación *f*

disfigure [dɪsˈfɪgjər] *vt* **-ured; -uring** : desfigurar (a una persona), afear (un edificio, un área)

disgrace[1] [dɪsˈskreɪs] *vt* **-graced; -gracing** : deshonrar

disgrace[2] *n* **1** DISHONOR : desgracia *f*, deshonra *f* **2** SHAME : vergüenza *f* ⟨he's a disgrace to his family : es una vergüenza para su familia⟩

disgraceful [dɪsˈskreɪsfəl] *adj* : vergonzoso, deshonroso, ignominioso

disgracefully [dɪsˈskreɪsfəli] *adv* : vergonzosamente

disgruntle [dɪsˈgrʌntəl] *vt* **-tled; -tling** : enfadar, contrariar

disgruntled [dɪsˈgrʌntəld] *adj* : descontento, contrariado

disguise[1] [dɪsˈkaɪz] *vt* **-guised; -guising 1** : disfrazar, enmascarar (el aspecto) **2** CONCEAL : encubrir, disimular

disguise[2] *n* : disfraz *m*

disgust[1] [dɪsˈkʌst] *vt* : darle asco (a alguien), asquear, repugnar ⟨that disgusts me : eso me da asco⟩

disgust[2] *n* : asco *m*, repugnancia *f*

disgusting [dɪsˈkʌstɪŋ] *adj* : asqueroso, repugnante — **disgustingly** *adv*

dish[1] [ˈdɪʃ] *vt* **1** *or* **to dish out/up** SERVE : servir **2** *or* **to dish out** DISPENSE : repartir (dinero, etc.), dar (consejos) **3 to dish it out** : criticar

dish[2] *n* **1** : plato *m* ⟨the national dish : el plato nacional⟩ **2** PLATE : plato *m* ⟨to wash the dishes : lavar los platos⟩ **serving dish** : fuente *f*

dishcloth [ˈdɪʃˌklɔθ] *n* : paño *m* de cocina (para secar), trapo *m* de fregar (para lavar)

dishearten [dɪsˈhɑrtən] *vt* : desanimar, desalentar

dishevel [dɪˈʃɛvəl] *vt* **-eled** *or* **-elled; -eling** *or* **-elling** : desarreglar, despeinar (el pelo)

disheveled *or* **dishevelled** [dɪˈʃɛvəld] *adj* : despeinado (dícese del pelo), desarreglado, desaliñado

dishonest [dɪˈsɑnəst] *adj* : deshonesto, fraudulento — **dishonestly** *adv*

dishonesty [dɪˈsɑnəsti] *n, pl* **-ties** : deshonestidad *f*, falta *f* de honradez

dishonor¹ [dɪˈsɑnər] *vt* : deshonrar

dishonor² *n* : deshonra *f*

dishonorable [dɪˈsɑnərəbəl] *adj* : deshonroso — **dishonorably** [-bli] *adv*

dishrag [ˈdɪʃˌræg] → **dishcloth**

dishtowel [ˈdɪʃˌtaʊəl] → **dishcloth**

dishwasher [ˈdɪʃˌwɔʃər] *n* : lavaplatos *m*, lavavajillas *m*

disillusion [ˌdɪsəˈluːʒən] *vt* : desilusionar, desencantar, desengañar

disillusionment [ˌdɪsəˈluːʒənmənt] *n* : desilusión *f*, desencanto *m*

disinclination [dɪsˌɪnkləˈneɪʃən, -ˌɪŋ-] *n* : aversión *f*

disinclined [ˌdɪsɪnˈklaɪnd] *adj* : poco dispuesto

disinfect [ˌdɪsɪnˈfɛkt] *vt* : desinfectar

disinfectant¹ [ˌdɪsɪnˈfɛktənt] *adj* : desinfectante

disinfectant² *n* : desinfectante *m*

disinherit [ˌdɪsɪnˈhɛrət] *vt* : desheredar

disintegrate [dɪsˈɪntəˌgreɪt] *v* **-grated; -grating** *vt* : desintegrar, deshacer — *vi* : desintegrarse, deshacerse

disintegration [dɪsˌɪntəˈgreɪʃən] *n* : desintegración *f*

disinterested [dɪsˈɪntərəstəd, -ˌrɛs-] *adj* **1** INDIFFERENT : indiferente **2** IMPARTIAL : imparcial, desinteresado

disinterestedness [dɪsˈɪntərəstədnəs, -ˌrɛs-] *n* : desinterés *m*

disjointed [dɪsˈdʒɔɪntəd] *adj* : inconexo, incoherente

disk *or* **disc** [ˈdɪsk] *n* : disco *m*

diskette [ˌdɪsˈkɛt] *n* : diskette *m*, disquete *m*

dislike¹ [dɪsˈlaɪk] *vt* **-liked; -liking** : tenerle aversión a (algo), tenerle antipatía (a alguien), no gustarle (algo a uno)

dislike² *n* : aversión *f*, antipatía *f* ⟨to take a dislike to : tomarle antipatía a⟩

dislocate [ˈdɪsloˌkeɪt, dɪsˈloː-] *vt* **-cated; -cating** : dislocar

dislocation [ˌdɪsloˈkeɪʃən] *n* : dislocación *f*

dislodge [dɪsˈlɑdʒ] *vt* **-lodged; -lodging** : sacar, desalojar, desplazar

disloyal [dɪsˈlɔɪəl] *adj* : desleal

disloyalty [dɪsˈlɔɪəlti] *n, pl* **-ties** : deslealtad *f*

dismal [ˈdɪzməl] *adj* **1** GLOOMY : sombrío, lúgubre, tétrico **2** DEPRESSING : deprimente, triste

dismantle [dɪsˈmæntəl] *vt* **-tled; -tling** : desmantelar, desmontar, desarmar

dismay¹ [dɪsˈmeɪ] *vt* : consternar

dismay² *n* : consternación *f*

dismember [dɪsˈmɛmbər] *vt* : desmembrar

dismiss [dɪsˈmɪs] *vt* **1** : dejar salir, darle permiso (a alguien) para retirarse **2** DISCHARGE : despedir, destituir **3** REJECT : descartar, desechar, rechazar

dismissal [dɪsˈmɪsəl] *n* **1** : permiso *m* para retirarse **2** DISCHARGE : despido *m* (de un empleado), destitución *f* (de un funcionario) **3** REJECTION : rechazo *m*

dismount [dɪsˈmaʊnt] *vi* : desmontar, bajarse, apearse

disobedience [ˌdɪsəˈbiːdiənts] *n* : desobediencia *f* — **disobedient** [-ənt] *adj*

disobey [ˌdɪsəˈbeɪ] *v* : desobedecer

disorder¹ [dɪsˈɔrdər] *vt* : desordenar, desarreglar

disorder² *n* **1** DISARRAY : desorden *m* **2** UNREST : disturbios *mpl*, desórdenes *mpl* **3** AILMENT : afección *f*, indisposición *f*, dolencia *f*

disorderly [dɪsˈɔrdərli] *adj* **1** UNTIDY : desordenado, desarreglado **2** UNRULY : indisciplinado, alborotado **3** disorderly conduct : conducta *f* escandalosa

disorganization [dɪsˌɔrgənəˈzeɪʃən] *n* : desorganización *f*

disorganize [dɪsˈɔrgəˌnaɪz] *vt* **-nized; -nizing** : desorganizar

disorient [dɪsˈɔriˌɛnt] *vt* : desorientar

disown [dɪsˈoːn] *vt* : renegar de, repudiar

disparage [dɪsˈpærɪdʒ] *vt* **-aged; -aging** : menospreciar, denigrar

disparagement [dɪsˈpærɪdʒmənt] *n* : menosprecio *m*

disparate [ˈdɪspərət, dɪsˈpærət] *adj* : dispar, diferente

disparity [dɪsˈpærəti] *n, pl* **-ties** : disparidad *f*

dispassionate [dɪsˈpæʃənət] *adj* : desapasionado, imparcial — **dispassionately** *adv*

dispatch¹ [dɪsˈpætʃ] *vt* **1** SEND : despachar, enviar **2** KILL : despachar, matar **3** HANDLE : despachar

dispatch² *n* **1** SENDING : envío *m*, despacho *m* **2** MESSAGE : despacho *m*, reportaje *m* (de un periodista), parte *m* (en el ejército) **3** PROMPTNESS : prontitud *f*, rapidez *f*

dispel [dɪsˈpɛl] *vt* **-pelled; -pelling** : disipar, desvanecer

dispensable [dɪˈspɛnsəbəl] *adj* : prescindible

dispensary [dɪˈspɛnsəri] *n, pl* **-ries** : dispensario *m*

dispensation [ˌdɪspɛnˈseɪʃən] *n* EXEMPTION : exención *m*, dispensa *f*

dispense [dɪsˈpɛns] *v* **-pensed; -pensing** *vt* **1** DISTRIBUTE : repartir, distribuir, dar **2** ADMINISTER, BESTOW : administrar (justicia), conceder (favores, etc.) **3** : preparar y despachar (medicamentos) — *vi* to dispense with : prescindir de

dispenser [dɪsˈpɛntsər] *n* : dispensador *m*, distribuidor *m* automático

dispersal [dɪsˈpərsəl] *n* : dispersión *f*

disperse [dɪsˈpərs] *v* **-persed; -persing** *vt* : dispersar, diseminar — *vi* : dispersarse

dispersion [dɪˈspɜrʒən] *n* : dispersión *f*
dispirit [dɪˈspɪrət] *vt* : desalentar, desanimar
dispirited [dɪˈspɪrətəd] *adj* : desanimado
displace [dɪsˈpleɪs] *vt* **-placed; -placing 1** : desplazar (un líquido, etc.) **2** REPLACE : reemplazar
displacement [dɪsˈpleɪsmənt] *n* **1** : desplazamiento *m* (de personas) **2** REPLACEMENT : sustitución *f*, reemplazo *m*
display¹ [dɪsˈpleɪ] *vt* : exponer, exhibir, mostrar
display² *n* **1** : muestra *f*, exposición *f*, alarde *m* **2** : visualizador *m* (de un aparato)
displease [dɪsˈpliːz] *vt* **-pleased; -pleasing** : desagradar a, disgustar, contrariar
displeasure [dɪsˈplɛʒər] *n* : desagrado *m*
disposable [dɪsˈpoːzəbəl] *adj* **1** : desechable ⟨disposable diapers : pañales desechables⟩ **2** AVAILABLE : disponible
disposal [dɪsˈpoːzəl] *n* **1** PLACEMENT : disposición *f*, colocación *f* **2** REMOVAL : eliminación *f* **3** → garbage disposal **4 to have at one's disposal** : disponer de, tener a su disposición
dispose [dɪsˈpoːz] *v* **-posed; -posing** *vt* **1** ARRANGE : disponer, colocar **2** INCLINE : predisponer — *vi* **1 to dispose of** DISCARD : desechar, deshacerse de **2 to dispose of** HANDLE : despachar **3 to be disposed to do something** : estar dispuesto a hacer algo
disposition [ˌdɪspəˈzɪʃən] *n* **1** ARRANGEMENT : disposición *f* **2** TENDENCY : predisposición *f*, inclinación *f* **3** TEMPERAMENT : temperamento *m*, carácter *m*
dispossess [ˌdɪspəˈzɛs] *vt* : desposeer
disproportion [ˌdɪsprəˈpɔrʃən] *n* : desproporción *f*
disproportionate [ˌdɪsprəˈpɔrʃənət] *adj* : desproporcionado — **disproportionately** *adv*
disprove [dɪsˈpruːv] *vt* **-proved; -proving** : rebatir, refutar
disputable [dɪsˈpjuːtəbəl, ˈdɪspjʊtəbəl] *adj* : discutible
dispute¹ [dɪsˈpjuːt] *v* **-puted; -puting** *vt* **1** QUESTION : discutir, cuestionar **2** OPPOSE : combatir, resistir — *vi* ARGUE, DEBATE : discutir
dispute² *n* **1** DEBATE : debate *m*, discusión *f* **2** QUARREL : disputa *f*, discusión *f*
disqualification [dɪsˌkwɑləfəˈkeɪʃən] *n* : descalificación *f*
disqualify [dɪsˈkwɑləˌfaɪ] *vt* **-fied; -fying** : descalificar, inhabilitar
disquiet¹ [dɪsˈkwaɪət] *vt* : inquietar
disquiet² *n* : ansiedad *f*, inquietud *f*
disregard¹ [ˌdɪsrɪˈɡɑrd] *vt* : ignorar, no prestar atención a
disregard² *n* : indiferencia *f*
disrepair [ˌdɪsrɪˈpær] *n* : mal estado *m*
disreputable [dɪsˈrɛpjʊtəbəl] *adj* : de mala fama ⟨dícese de una persona o un lugar⟩, vergonzoso ⟨dícese de la conducta⟩
disreputably [dɪsˈrɛpjʊtəbli] *adv* : vergonzosamente

disrepute [ˌdɪsrɪˈpjuːt] *n* : descrédito *m*, mala fama *f*, deshonra *f*
disrespect [ˌdɪsrɪˈspɛkt] *n* : falta *f* de respeto
disrespectful [ˌdɪsrɪˈspɛktfəl] *adj* : irrespetuoso — **disrespectfully** *adv*
disrobe [dɪsˈroːb] *v* **-robed; -robing** *vt* : desvestir, desnudar — *vi* : desvestirse, desnudarse
disrupt [dɪsˈrʌpt] *vt* : trastornar, perturbar
disruption [dɪsˈrʌpʃən] *n* : trastorno *m*
disruptive [dɪsˈrʌptɪv] *adj* : perjudicial, perturbador — **disruptively** *adv*
dissatisfaction [ˌdɪsˌsætəsˈfækʃən] *n* : descontento *m*, insatisfacción *f*
dissatisfied [dɪsˈsætəsˌfaɪd] *adj* : descontento, insatisfecho
dissatisfy [dɪsˈsætəsˌfaɪ] *vt* **-fied; -fying** : no contentar, no satisfacer
dissect [dɪˈsɛkt] *vt* : disecar
dissection [dɪˈsɛkʃən] *n* : disección *f*
dissemble [dɪˈsɛmbəl] *v* **-bled; -bling** *vt* HIDE : ocultar, disimular — *vi* PRETEND : fingir, disimular
disseminate [dɪˈsɛməˌneɪt] *vt* **-nated; -nating** : diseminar, difundir, divulgar
dissemination [dɪˌsɛməˈneɪʃən] *n* : diseminación *f*, difusión *f*
dissension [dɪˈsɛntʃən] *n* : disensión *f*, desacuerdo *m*
dissent¹ [dɪˈsɛnt] *vi* : disentir
dissent² *n* : disentimiento *m*, disensión *f*, disenso *m*
dissertation [ˌdɪsərˈteɪʃən] *n* **1** DISCOURSE : disertación *f*, discurso *m* **2** THESIS : tesis *f*
disservice [dɪsˈsərvɪs] *n* : perjuicio *m*
dissident¹ [ˈdɪsədənt] *adj* : disidente
dissident² *n* : disidente *mf*
dissimilar [dɪˈsɪmələr] *adj* : distinto, diferente, disímil
dissipate [ˈdɪsəˌpeɪt] *vt* **-pated; -pating 1** DISPERSE : disipar, dispersar **2** SQUANDER : malgastar, desperdiciar, derrochar, disipar
dissipation [ˌdɪsəˈpeɪʃən] *n* : libertinaje *m*
dissociate [dɪˈsoːʃiˌeɪt, -si-] *or* **disassociate** [ˌdɪsəˈsoːʃiˌeɪt, -si-] *v* **-ated** [-ˌeɪtəd]; **-ating** [-ˌeɪtɪŋ] *vt* : disociar ⟨to dissociate oneself : disociarse⟩ — *vi* : disociarse
dissociation [dɪˌsoːʃiˈeɪʃən, -si-] *n* : disociación *f*
dissolute [ˈdɪsəˌluːt] *adj* : disoluto
dissolution [ˌdɪsəˈluːʃən] *n* : disolución *f*
dissolve [dɪˈzɑlv] *v* **-solved; -solving** *vt* : disolver — *vi* : disolverse
dissonance [ˈdɪsənənts] *n* : disonancia *f*
dissuade [dɪˈsweɪd] *vt* **-suaded; -suading** : disuadir
distance¹ [ˈdɪstənts] *vt* **-tanced** [-təntst]; **-tancing** [-təntsɪŋ] **to distance oneself** : distanciarse
distance² *n* **1** : distancia *f* ⟨the distance between two points : la distancia entre dos puntos⟩ ⟨in the distance : a lo lejos⟩ **2** RESERVE : actitud *f* distante, reserva *f* ⟨to keep one's distance : guardar las distancias⟩

distant ['dɪstənt] *adj* **1** FAR : distante, lejano **2** REMOTE : distante, lejano, remoto **3** ALOOF : distante, frío

distantly ['dɪstəntli] *adv* **1** LOOSELY : aproximadamente, vagamente **2** COLDLY : fríamente, con frialdad

distaste [dɪs'teɪst] *n* : desagrado *m*, aversión *f*

distasteful [dɪs'teɪstfəl] *adj* : desagradable, de mal gusto

distemper [dɪs'tɛmpər] *n* : moquillo *m*

distend [dɪs'tɛnd] *vt* : dilatar, hinchar — *vi* : dilatarse, hincharse

distill [dɪ'stɪl] *vt* : destilar

distillation [dɪstə'leɪʃən] *n* : destilación *f*

distiller [dɪ'stɪlər] *n* : destilador *m*, -dora *f*

distillery [dɪ'stɪləri] *n, pl* -ries [-riz] : destilería *f*

distinct [dɪ'stɪŋkt] *adj* **1** DIFFERENT : distinto, diferente **2** CLEAR, UNMISTAKABLE : marcado, claro, evidente ⟨a distinct possibility : una clara posibilidad⟩

distinction [dɪ'stɪŋkʃən] *n* **1** DIFFERENTIATION : distinción *f* **2** DIFFERENCE : diferencia *f* **3** EXCELLENCE : distinción *f*, excelencia *f* ⟨a writer of distinction : un escritor destacado⟩

distinctive [dɪ'stɪŋktɪv] *adj* : distintivo, característico — **distinctively** *adv*

distinctiveness [dɪ'stɪŋktɪvnəs] *n* : peculiaridad *f*

distinctly [dɪ'stɪŋktli] *adv* : claramente, con claridad

distinguish [dɪs'tɪŋgwɪʃ] *vt* **1** DIFFERENTIATE : distinguir, diferenciar **2** DISCERN : distinguir ⟨he distinguished the sound of the piano : distinguió el sonido del piano⟩ **3 to distinguish oneself** : señalarse, distinguirse — *vi* DISCRIMINATE : distinguir

distinguishable [dɪs'tɪŋgwɪʃəbəl] *adj* : distinguible

distinguished [dɪs'tɪŋgwɪʃt] *adj* : distinguido

distinguishing [dɪs'tɪŋgwɪʃɪŋ] *adj* : distintivo

distort [dɪ'stɔrt] *vt* **1** MISREPRESENT : distorsionar, tergiversar **2** DEFORM : distorsionar, deformar

distortion [dɪ'stɔrʃən] *n* : distorsión *f*, deformación *f*, tergiversación *f*

distract [dɪ'strækt] *vt* : distraer, entretener

distracted [dɪ'stræktəd] *adj* : distraído

distraction [dɪ'strækʃən] *n* **1** INTERRUPTION : distracción *f*, interrupción *f* **2** CONFUSION : confusión *f* **3** AMUSEMENT : diversión *f*, entretenimiento *m*, distracción *f*

distraught [dɪ'strɔt] *adj* : afligido, turbado

distress¹ [dɪ'strɛs] *vt* : afligir, darle pena (a alguien), hacer sufrir

distress² *n* **1** SORROW : dolor *m*, angustia *f*, aflicción *f* **2** PAIN : dolor *m* **3 in ∼** : en peligro

distressful [dɪ'strɛsfəl] *adj* : doloroso, penoso

distressing [dɪ'strɛsɪŋ] *adj* : angustioso

distribute [dɪ'strɪ,bjuːt, -bjut] *vt* **-uted; -uting** : distribuir, repartir

distribution [,dɪstrə'bjuːʃən] *n* : distribución *f*, reparto *m*

distributive [dɪ'strɪbjutɪv] *adj* : distributivo

distributor [dɪ'strɪbjutər] *n* : distribuidor *m*, -dora *f*

district ['dɪs,trɪkt] *n* **1** REGION : región *f*, zona *f*, barrio *m* (de una ciudad) **2** : distrito *m* (zona política)

district attorney *n* : fiscal *mf* (del distrito)

distrust¹ [dɪs'trʌst] *vt* : desconfiar de

distrust² *n* : desconfianza *f*, recelo *m*

distrustful [dɪs'trʌstfəl] *adj* : desconfiado, receloso, suspicaz

disturb [dɪ'stɔrb] *vt* **1** BOTHER : molestar, perturbar ⟨sorry to disturb you : perdone la molestia⟩ **2** DISARRANGE : desordenar **3** WORRY : inquietar, preocupar **4 to disturb the peace** : alterar el orden público

disturbance [dɪ'stɔrbənts] *n* **1** COMMOTION : alboroto *m*, disturbio *m* **2** INTERRUPTION : interrupción *f*

disturbed [dɪ'stɔrbd] *adj* **1** : trastornado ⟨mentally/emotionally disturbed : con trastornos mentales/emocionales⟩ **2** WORRIED, UNSETTLED : inquieto, agitado

disturbing [dɪ'stɔrbɪŋ] *adj* : inquietante

disuse [dɪs'juːs] *n* : desuso *m*

disused [dɪs'juːzd] *adj* **1** ABANDONED : abandonado **2** ANTIQUATED : desusado

ditch¹ ['dɪtʃ] *vt* **1** : cavar zanjas en **2** DISCARD : deshacerse de, botar

ditch² *n* : zanja *f*, fosa *f*, cuneta *f* (en una carretera)

dither ['dɪðər] *n* **to be in a dither** : estar nervioso, ponerse como loco

ditto ['dɪto] *n, pl* -tos **1** : lo mismo, ídem *m* **2 ditto marks** : comillas *fpl*

ditty ['dɪti] *n, pl* -ties : canción *f* corta y simple

diurnal [daɪ'ərnəl] *adj* **1** DAILY : diario, cotidiano **2** : diurno ⟨a diurnal animal : un animal diurno⟩

diva ['diːvə] *n* : diva *f*

divan ['daɪ,væn, dɪ'-] *n* : diván *m*

dive¹ ['daɪv] *vi* **dived** *or* **dove** ['do:v]; **dived; diving 1** PLUNGE : tirarse al agua, zambullirse, dar un clavado **2** SUBMERGE : sumergirse **3** DROP : bajar en picada (dícese de un avión), caer en picada **4** : bucear, hacer submarinismo ⟨to dive for pearls : bucear buscando perlas⟩

dive² *n* **1** PLUNGE : zambullida *f*, clavado *m* (en el agua) **2** DESCENT : descenso *m* en picada **3** BAR, JOINT : antro *m*

diver ['daɪvər] *n* **1** : saltador *m*, -dora *f*; clavadista *mf* **2** : buceador *m*, -dora *f*; buzo *mf*; submarinista *mf*

diverge [də'vərdʒ, daɪ-] *vi* **-verged; -verging 1** SEPARATE : divergir, separarse **2** DIFFER : divergir, discrepar

divergence [də'vərdʒənts, daɪ-] *n* : divergencia *f* — **divergent** [-ənt] *adj*

diverse [daɪ'vərs, də-, 'daɪ,vərs] *adj* : diverso, variado

diversification [daɪˌvərsəfə'keɪʃən, də-] *n* : diversificación *f*

diversify [daɪ'vərsəˌfaɪ, də-] *vt* **-fied; -fy-ing** : diversificar, variar

diversion [daɪ'vərʒən, də-] *n* **1** DEVIATION : desviación *f* **2** AMUSEMENT, DISTRACTION : diversión *f*, distracción *f*, entretenimiento *m*

diversity [daɪ'vərsəṭi, də-] *n, pl* **-ties** : diversidad *f*

divert [də'vərt, daɪ-] *vt* **1** DEFLECT : desviar **2** DISTRACT : distraer **3** AMUSE : divertir, entretener

divest [daɪ'vest, də-] *vt* **1** UNDRESS : desnudar, desvestir **2 to divest of** : despojar de

divide [də'vaɪd] *v* **-vided; -viding** *vt* **1** HALVE : dividir, partir por la mitad **2** SHARE : repartir, dividir ⟨to divide between/among : dividir entre⟩ **3** : dividir (números) ⟨to divide by : dividir por⟩ — *vi* : dividirse, dividir (en matemáticas)

dividend ['dɪvəˌdend, -dənd] *n* **1** : dividendo *m* (en finanzas) **2** ADVANTAGE, BENEFIT : beneficio *m*, provecho *m* ⟨to pay dividends : reportar beneficios⟩ **3** : dividendo *m* (en matemáticas)

divider [dɪ'vaɪdər] *n* **1** : separador *m* (para ficheros, etc.) **2 or room divider** : mampara *f*, biombo *m*

divination [ˌdɪvə'neɪʃən] *n* : adivinación *f*

divine[1] [də'vaɪn] *adj* **diviner; -est 1** : divino **2** SUPERB : divino, espléndido — **divinely** *adv*

divine[2] *n* : clérigo *m*, eclesiástico *m*

diving ['daɪvɪŋ] *n* **1** : clavados *mpl* **2** : buceo *m*, submarinismo *m*

diving board *n* : trampolín *m*

divinity [də'vɪnəṭi] *n, pl* **-ties** : divinidad *f*

divisible [də'vɪzəbəl] *adj* : divisible

division [dɪ'vɪʒən] *n* **1** DISTRIBUTION : división *f*, reparto *m* ⟨division of labor : distribución del trabajo⟩ **2** PART : división *f*, sección *f* **3** : división *f* (en matemáticas)

divisive [də'vaɪsɪv] *adj* : divisivo

divisor [dɪ'vaɪzər] *n* : divisor *m*

divorce[1] [də'vors] *v* **-vorced; -vorcing** *vt* : divorciar — *vi* : divorciarse

divorce[2] *n* : divorcio *m*

divorcé [dɪˌvor'seɪ, -'si:ˌ, -'vorˌ-] *n* : divorciado *m*

divorcée [dɪˌvor'seɪ, -'si:ˌ, -'vorˌ-] *n* : divorciada *f*

divorced *adj* : divorciado

divulge [də'vʌldʒ, daɪ-] *vt* **-vulged; -vulging** : revelar, divulgar

DIY[1] [ˌdiːˌaɪ'waɪ] → **do-it-yourself**[1]

DIY[2] → **do-it-yourself**[2]

dizzily ['dɪzəli] *adv* : vertiginosamente

dizziness ['dɪzinəs] *n* : mareo *m*, vahído *m*, vértigo *m*

dizzy ['dɪzi] *adj* **dizzier; -est 1** : mareado ⟨I feel dizzy : estoy mareado⟩ **2** DIZZYING : vertiginoso ⟨a dizzy speed : una velocidad vertiginosa⟩

dizzying ['dɪziɪŋ] *adj* : vertiginoso

DNA [ˌdiːˌɛn'eɪ] *n* (*d*eoxyribo*n*ucleic *a*cid) : ADN *m*

do[1] ['duː] *v* **did** ['dɪd]; **done** ['dʌn]; **doing; does** ['dʌz] *vt* **1** CARRY OUT, PERFORM : hacer, realizar, llevar ʻa cabo ⟨she did her best : hizo todo lo posible⟩ ⟨I didn't do it! : ¡no fui yo!⟩ ⟨do something! : ¡haz algo!⟩ ⟨I did something to my knee : me lastimé la rodilla⟩ ⟨she did nothing to help : no hizo nada para ayudar⟩ ⟨I have nothing to do : no tengo nada que hacer⟩ ⟨are you doing anything tonight? : ¿haces algo esta noche?⟩ ⟨what can I do for you? : ¿en qué puedo servirle?⟩ ⟨to do the chores : hacer los quehaceres⟩ ⟨to do the right thing : hacer lo correcto⟩ ⟨to do someone a favor : hacerle un favor a alguien⟩ **2** : dedicarse a, trabajar en ⟨what do you do (for a living)? : ¿a qué te dedicas?⟩ **3** COMPLETE : hacer ⟨did you do your homework? : ¿hiciste la tarea?⟩ **4** PREPARE : hacer, preparar (comida) **5** ARRANGE : arreglar, peinar (el pelo) ⟨to do one's hair : peinarse⟩ ⟨to do one's makeup/face : maquillarse⟩ **6** GO : ir a (una velocidad) ⟨he was doing 90 (miles per hour) : iba a 90 millas por hora⟩ **7** VISIT : visitar (un lugar) **8** : hacer ⟨the change will do you good : el cambio te hará bien⟩ ⟨that color does nothing for you : ese color no te queda bien⟩ ⟨that song does nothing for me : esa canción no me dice nada⟩ **9** CREATE, PRODUCE : hacer **10** WASH, CLEAN : lavar, limpiar ⟨to do laundry : lavar la ropa⟩ **11** DECORATE : pintar, decorar **12 to do in** RUIN : estropear, arruinar **13 to do in** KILL : matar, liquidar *fam* **14 to do in** TIRE, EXHAUST : agotar **15 to do lunch/dinner (etc.)** : juntarse a almorzar/cenar (etc.) **16 to do over** : volver a hacer **17 to do up** FASTEN : atar, abrochar **18 what is/are . . . doing . . . ?** (*expressing surprise or annoyance*) ⟨what are you doing here? : ¿qué haces aquí?⟩ ⟨what is my coat doing on the floor? : ¿qué hace mi abrigo en el suelo?⟩ — *vi* **1** : hacer ⟨you did well : hiciste bien⟩ **2** FARE : estar, ir, andar ⟨how are you doing? : ¿cómo estás?, ¿cómo te va?⟩ **3** SERVE : servir, ser suficiente, alcanzar ⟨this will do for now : esto servirá por el momento⟩ **4 could do with** ⟨I could do with a cup of coffee : un café no me vendría mal⟩ **5 to do away with** ABOLISH : abolir, suprimir **6 to do away with** KILL : eliminar, matar **7 to do by** TREAT : tratar ⟨he does well by her : él la trata bien⟩ **8 to do well to** : hacer bien en **9 to do without** MANAGE : arreglárselas **10 to do without something** : pasar sin algo, prescindir de algo **11 to have to do with** : tener que ver con ⟨that has nothing to do with it : eso no tiene nada que ver (con el asunto)⟩ ⟨I didn't have anything to do with it : no tuve nada que ver con eso⟩ **12 to want nothing to do with** : hacerle la cruz a — *v aux* **1** (*used in questions and negative statements*) ⟨do you know her? : ¿la conoces?⟩ ⟨I don't like that : a mí no me gusta eso⟩ ⟨I don't know : no sé ⟨do not touch : no tocar⟩ **2** (used for emphasis) ⟨I do hope you'll come : espero que vengas⟩ **3** (used as a substitute verb to avoid repetition) ⟨do you speak English? — yes, I do : ¿habla inglés? — sí⟩ ⟨so do I : yo también⟩

do² ['do:] n : do m (en el canto)

docile ['dɑsəl] adj : dócil, sumiso

dock¹ ['dɑk] vt **1** CUT : cortar **2** : descontar dinero de (un sueldo) — vi ANCHOR, LAND : fondear, atracar

dock² n **1** PIER : atracadero m **2** WHARF : muelle m **3** : banquillo m de los acusados (en un tribunal)

dockworker ['dɑk,wərkər] n : estibador m, -dora f

dockyard ['dɑk,jɑrd] n : astillero m

doctor¹ ['dɑktər] vt **1** TREAT : tratar, curar **2** ALTER : adulterar, alterar, falsificar (un documento)

doctor² n **1** : doctor m, -tora f ⟨Doctor of Philosophy : doctor en filosofía⟩ **2** PHYSICIAN : médico m, -ca f; doctor m, -tora f

doctorate ['dɑktərət] n : doctorado m

doctrine ['dɑktrɪn] n : doctrina f

document¹ ['dɑkjə,mɛnt] vt : documentar

document² ['dɑkjumənt] n : documento m

documentary¹ [,dɑkju'mɛntəri] adj : documental

documentary² n, pl -ries : documental m

documentation [,dɑkjumən'teɪʃən] n : documentación f

dodge¹ ['dɑdʒ] v dodged; dodging vt : esquivar, eludir, evadir (impuestos) — vi : echarse a un lado

dodge² n **1** RUSE : truco m, treta f, artimaña f **2** EVASION : regate m, evasión f

doe ['do:] n, pl does or doe : gama f, cierva f

doer ['du:ər] n : hacedor m, -dora f

does → do

doesn't ['dʌzənt] contraction of DOES NOT → do

doff ['dɑf, 'dɔf] vt : quitarse ⟨to doff one's hat : quitarse el sombrero⟩

dog¹ ['dɔg, 'dɑg] vt dogged; dogging : seguir de cerca, perseguir, acosar ⟨to dog someone's footsteps : seguir los pasos de alguien⟩ ⟨dogged by bad luck : perseguido por la mala suerte⟩

dog² n **1** : perro m, -rra f **2** → hot dog **3** (offensive) : mujer f fea **4** sick as a dog : muy enfermo **5** to let sleeping dogs lie : no remover el avispero

dogcatcher ['dɔg,kætʃər] n : perrero m, -ra f

dog-eared ['dɔg,ɪrd] adj : con las esquinas dobladas

dogged ['dɔgəd] adj : tenaz, terco, obstinado

doggy ['dɔgi] n, pl doggies : perrito m, -ta f

doghouse ['dɔg,haʊs] n : casita f de perro

dogma ['dɔgmə] n : dogma m

dogmatic [dɔg'mætɪk] adj : dogmático

dogmatism ['dɔgmə,tɪzəm] n : dogmatismo m

dogwood ['dɔg,wʊd] n : cornejo m

doily ['dɔɪli] n, pl -lies : pañito m

doings ['du:ɪŋz] npl : eventos mpl, actividades fpl

do-it-yourself¹ n : bricolaje m

do-it-yourself² adj : de bricolaje

doldrums ['do:ldrəmz, 'dɑl-] npl **1** : zona f de las calmas ecuatoriales **2** to be in the doldrums : estar abatido (dícese de una persona), estar estancado (dícese de una empresa)

dole ['do:l] n **1** ALMS : distribución f a los necesitados, limosna f **2** : subsidios mpl de desempleo

doleful ['do:lfəl] adj : triste, lúgubre

dolefully ['do:lfəli] adv : con pesar, de manera triste

dole out vt doled out; doling out : repartir

doll ['dɑl, 'dɔl] n : muñeco m, -ca f

dollar ['dɑlər] n : dólar m

dolly ['dɑli] n, pl -lies **1** → doll **2** : plataforma f rodante

dolphin ['dɑlfən, 'dɔl-] n : delfín m

dolt ['do:lt] n : imbécil mf; tonto m, -ta f

domain [do'meɪn, də-] n **1** TERRITORY : dominio m, territorio m **2** FIELD : campo m, esfera f, ámbito m ⟨the domain of art : el ámbito de las artes⟩

dome ['do:m] n : cúpula f, bóveda f

domestic¹ [də'mɛstɪk] adj **1** HOUSEHOLD : doméstico, casero **2** : nacional, interno ⟨domestic policy : política interna⟩ **3** TAME : domesticado

domestic² n : empleado m doméstico, empleada f doméstica

domestically [də'mɛstɪkli] adv : domésticamente

domesticate [də'mɛstɪ,keɪt] vt -cated; -cating : domesticar

domicile ['dɑmə,saɪl, 'do:-,; 'dɑmɪsɪl] n : domicilio m

dominance ['dɑmənənts] n : dominio m, dominación f

dominant ['dɑmənənt] adj : dominante

dominate ['dɑmə,neɪt] v -nated; -nating : dominar

domination [,dɑmə'neɪʃən] n : dominación f

domineer [,dɑmə'nɪr] vt : dominar sobre, avasallar, tiranizar

domineering [,dɑmə'nɪrɪŋ] adj : dominante

Dominican¹ [də'mɪnɪkən] adj **1** : dominicano **2** : dominico (en religión)

Dominican² n **1** : dominicano m, -na f **2** : dominico m, -ca f (en religión)

dominion [də'mɪnjən] n **1** POWER : dominio m **2** DOMAIN, TERRITORY : dominio m, territorio m

domino ['dɑmə,no:] n, pl -noes or -nos **1** : dominó m **2** dominoes npl : dominó m (juego)

don ['dɑn] vt donned; donning : ponerse

donate ['do:,neɪt, do:'-] vt -nated; -nating : donar, hacer un donativo de

donation [do:'neɪʃən] n : donación f, donativo m

done¹ ['dʌn] → do

done² adj **1** FINISHED : terminado, acabado, concluido ⟨now I'm done : ya

terminé〉 **2** COOKED : cocinado **3**
done in : agotado, derrengado **4 done
for** : perdido, frito *Arg, Chile, Peru, Uru
fam*

donkey ['dɑŋki, 'dʌŋ-] *n, pl* **-keys** : burro
m, asno *m*

donor ['do:nər] *n* : donante *mf*; donador
m, -dora *f*

don't ['do:nt] *contraction of* DO NOT → **do**

donut → **doughnut**

doodle[1] ['du:dəl] *v* **-dled; -dling** : garabatear

doodle[2] *n* : garabato *m*

doom[1] ['du:m] *vt* : condenar 〈to be
doomed (to failure) : estar condenado al
fracaso〉

doom[2] *n* **1** JUDGMENT : sentencia *f*, condena *f* **2** DEATH : muerte *f* **3** FATE
: destino *m* **4** RUIN : perdición *f*, ruina *f*

door ['dor] *n* **1** : puerta *f* 〈there's someone at the door : llaman a la puerta〉 〈to
answer the door : abrir la puerta〉 〈can
you get the door for me? : ¿me abres/
cierras la puerta?〉 〈garage/refrigerator
door : puerta del garaje/refrigerador〉 **2**
ENTRANCE : entrada *f*

doorbell ['dor,bɛl] *n* : timbre *m*

doorknob ['dor,nɑb] *n* : pomo *m*, perilla *f*

doorman ['dormən] *n, pl* **-men** [-mən,
-,mɛn] : portero *m*

doormat ['dor,mæt] *n* : felpudo *m*

doorstep ['dor,stɛp] *n* : umbral *m*

doorstop ['dor,stɑp] *n* : tope *m* de puerta

doorway ['dor,weɪ] *n* : entrada *f*, portal *m*

do–over ['du:,o:vər] *n* : otra oportunidad
f, otro intento *m*

dope[1] ['do:p] *vt* **doped; doping** : drogar,
narcotizar

dope[2] *n* **1** DRUG : droga *f*, estupefaciente
m, narcótico *m* **2** IDIOT : idiota *mf*;
tonto *m*, -ta *f* **3** INFORMATION : información *f*

dopey ['do:pi] *adj* **1** GROGGY : atontado,
grogui *fam* **2** FOOLISH : tonto **3**
DRUGGED : drogado

doping *n* : doping *m* (en deportes)

dormant ['dormənt] *adj* : inactivo, latente

dormer ['dormər] *n* : buhardilla *f*

dormitory ['dormə,tori] *n, pl* **-ries** : dormitorio *m*, residencia *f* de estudiantes

dormouse ['dor,maʊs] *n* : lirón *m*

dorsal ['dorsəl] *adj* : dorsal — **dorsally**
adv

dory ['dori] *n, pl* **-ries** : bote *m* de fondo
plano

dosage ['do:sɪʤ] *n* : dosis *f*

dose[1] ['do:s] *vt* **dosed; dosing** : medicinar

dose[2] *n* : dosis *f*

dossier ['dɑs,jeɪ, 'dɑs-] *n* : dossier *m*

dot[1] ['dɑt] *vt* **dotted; dotting** **1** : poner el
punto sobre (una letra) **2** SCATTER : esparcir, salpicar

dot[2] *n* : punto *m* 〈at six on the dot : a las
seis en punto〉 〈dots and dashes : puntos
y rayas〉

dot–com ['dɑt,kɑm] *n* : puntocom *m*

dote ['do:t] *vi* **doted; doting** : chochear

double[1] ['dʌbəl] *v* **-bled; -bling** *vt* **1**
: doblar, duplicar (una cantidad), redob-

lar (esfuerzos) **2** FOLD : doblar, plegar **3 to double one's fist** : apretar el
puño — *vi* **1** : doblarse, duplicarse **2
to double over** : retorcerse

double[2] *adj* : doble — **doubly** *adv*

double[3] *n* : doble *mf*

double–barreled *or* **double–barrelled**
[,dʌbəl'bærəld] *adj* **1** : de dos cañones
(dícese de un arma de fuego) **2** TWO-
FOLD : doble

double bass *n* : contrabajo *m*

double bed *n* : cama *f* de matrimonio

double–breasted [,dʌbəl'brɛstəd] *adj*
: cruzado

double–check [,dʌbəl'tʃɛk] *vt* : verificar
dos veces

double chin *n* : papada *f*

double–click [,dʌbəl'klɪk] *vi* : hacer doble
clic

double–cross [,dʌbəl'krɔs] *vt* : traicionar

double–crosser [,dʌbəl'krɔsər] *n* : traidor
m, -dora *f*

double entendre ['dʌbələn'tɑndrə] *n*
: doble sentido *m*

double–glazed [,dʌbəl'gleɪzd] *n* : con
doble acristalamiento

double–jointed [,dʌbəl'ʤɔɪntəd] *adj* : con
articulaciones dobles

double–spaced [,dʌbəl'speɪst] *n* : a doble
espacio

double–talk ['dʌbəl,tɔk] *n* : ambigüedades
fpl, lenguaje *m* con doble sentido

doubt[1] ['daʊt] *vt* **1** QUESTION : dudar de,
cuestionar **2** DISTRUST : desconfiar
de **3** : dudar, creer poco probable 〈I
doubt it very much : lo dudo mucho〉

doubt[2] *n* **1** UNCERTAINTY : duda *f*, incertidumbre *f* 〈to cast/throw doubt on, to
cast/throw/call into doubt, to raise doubts
about : poner en duda/cuestión〉 **2** DIS-
TRUST : desconfianza *f* **3** SKEPTICISM
: duda *f*, escepticismo *m* **4 beyond doubt**
: sin lugar a duda 〈beyond any/all doubt
: fuera de toda duda〉 〈beyond a reasonable doubt : más allá de toda duda razo-
nable〉 **5 in doubt** : en duda 〈if/when in
doubt : en/ante la duda〉 〈the outcome
remains in doubt : aún no se conoce el
resultado〉 **6 no doubt** DOUBTLESS : sin
duda 〈there's no doubt about it : no hay/
cabe duda〉 **7 without (a) doubt** : sin
duda 〈without a shadow of a doubt : sin el
menor asomo de duda〉

doubtful ['daʊtfəl] *adj* **1** QUESTIONABLE
: dudoso **2** UNCERTAIN : dudoso, incierto

doubtfully ['daʊtfəli] *adv* : dudosamente,
sin estar convencido

doubtless ['daʊtləs] *or* **doubtlessly** *adv*
: sin duda

douche[1] ['du:ʃ] *vt* **douched; douching**
: irrigar

douche[2] *n* : ducha *f*, irrigación *f*

dough ['do:] *n* : masa *f*

doughnut *or* **donut** ['do:,nʌt] *n* : rosquilla
f, dona *f* *Mex*

doughty ['daʊti] *adj* **doughtier; -est**
: fuerte, valiente

doughy ['do:i] *adj* **doughier; -est** **1**
: pastoso **2** PALE : pálido

dour ['daʊər, 'dʊr] *adj* **1** STERN : severo, adusto **2** SULLEN : hosco, taciturno — **dourly** *adv*

douse ['daʊs, 'daʊz] *vt* **doused; dousing 1** DRENCH : empapar, mojar **2** EXTINGUISH : extinguir, apagar

dove[1] ['do:v] → **dive**

dove[2] ['dʌv] *n* : paloma *f*

dovetail ['dʌv,teɪl] *vi* : encajar, enlazar

dowdy ['daʊdi] *adj* **dowdier; -est** : sin gracia, poco elegante

dowel ['daʊəl] *n* : clavija *f*

down[1] ['daʊn] *vt* **1** FELL : tumbar, derribar, abatir **2** DEFEAT : derrotar

down[2] *adv* **1** DOWNWARD : hacia abajo ⟨to bend down : agacharse⟩ ⟨to fall down : caer, caerse⟩ ⟨to look down : mirar (hacia) abajo⟩ ⟨she came down to say hello : bajó a saludarnos⟩ ⟨put it down on the table : ponlo en la mesa⟩ ⟨they knocked the wall down : tiraron abajo la pared⟩ **2** BELOW : abajo ⟨we keep it down in the basement : lo guardamos abajo en el sótano⟩ ⟨what's going on down there? : ¿qué pasa allí abajo?⟩ **3** LOWERED : bajado ⟨keep down! : ¡no te levantes!⟩ **4** : a, hacia ⟨he went down to the store : fue a la tienda⟩ ⟨come down and see us! : ¡ven a visitarnos!⟩ **5** : hacia el sur ⟨we went down to Florida : fuimos a Florida⟩ **6** AWAY, OVER : hacia el fondo/lado (etc.) ⟨move down so I can sit : córrete un poco para que pueda sentarme⟩ **7** (*indicating reduction*) ⟨she turned the volume down : bajó el volumen⟩ **8** THOROUGHLY : bien, completamente ⟨to hose down : lavar (con manguera)⟩ **9** (*indicating restriction of motion*) ⟨tie it down : átalo⟩ **10** (*indicating following to a place or source*) ⟨were you able to track her down? : ¿pudiste localizarla?⟩ ⟨they couldn't pin down the cause : no pudieron averiguar la causa⟩ **11** (*indicating lesser importance in a series, etc.*) ⟨it's pretty far/low down on my list : no es muy importante para mí⟩ **12** : en el estómago ⟨to keep food down : retener comida⟩ **13 down to** INCLUDING : hasta ⟨down to the last detail : hasta el último detalle⟩ **14 down with . . . !** : abajo . . . ! ⟨down with racism! : ¡abajo el racismo!⟩ **15 to hand/pass down** : transmitir (cuentos, etc.), pasar ⟨it was handed down to me by my grandmother : lo heredé de mi abuela⟩ **16 to lie down** : acostarse, echarse **17 to put down** ⟨to put down money, to put down a deposit : pagar un depósito⟩ **18 to sit down** : sentarse **19 to take/write down** : apuntar, anotar

down[3] *adj* **1** DESCENDING : de bajada ⟨the down elevator : el ascensor de bajada⟩ **2** : abajo ⟨it's down on the bottom shelf : está en el estante de abajo⟩ ⟨it's further down : está más abajo⟩ ⟨I'm down here : estoy aquí abajo⟩ **3** LOWERED : bajado **4** REDUCED : reducido, rebajado ⟨attendance is down : la concurrencia ha disminuido⟩ ⟨to keep

prices down : mantener los precios bajos⟩ **5** DOWNCAST : abatido, deprimido ⟨to feel down : andar deprimido⟩ **6** INOPERATIVE : inoperante ⟨the system is down : el sistema no funciona⟩ **7** BEHIND : perdiendo ⟨they're down (by) ten points : van perdiendo por diez puntos⟩ **8** COMPLETED : hecho, acabado ⟨two down, one to go : dos menos, falta uno⟩

down[4] *n* **1** : plumón *m* **2 ups and downs** : altibajos *mpl*

down[5] *prep* **1** : (hacia) abajo ⟨down the mountain : montaña abajo⟩ ⟨I walked down the stairs : bajé por la escalera⟩ **2** ALONG : por, a lo largo de ⟨we ran down the beach : corrimos por la playa⟩ **3** : a través de ⟨down the years : a través de los años⟩

down–and–out *adj* : indigente

downcast ['daʊn,kæst] *adj* **1** SAD : triste, abatido **2 with downcast eyes** : con los ojos bajos, con los ojos mirando al suelo

downfall ['daʊn,fɔl] *n* : ruina *f*, perdición *f*

downgrade[1] ['daʊn,greɪd] *vt* **-graded; -grading** : bajar de categoría

downgrade[2] *n* : bajada *f*

downhearted ['daʊn'hɑrtəd] *adj* : desanimado, descorazonado

downhill ['daʊn'hɪl] *adv & adj* : cuesta abajo

download[1] ['daʊn,lo:d] *vt* : descargar, bajar (en informática)

download[2] *n* : descarga *f* (de archivos, etc.)

downloadable *adj* : descargable

down payment *n* : entrega *f* inicial

downplay ['daʊn,pleɪ] *vt* : minimizar

downpour ['daʊn,por] *n* : aguacero *m*, chaparrón *m*

downright[1] ['daʊn,raɪt] *adv* THOROUGHLY : absolutamente, completamente

downright[2] *adj* : patente, manifiesto, absoluto ⟨a downright refusal : un rechazo categórico⟩

downside ['daʊn,saɪd] *n* : desventaja *f*

downsize ['daʊn,saɪz] *vt* **-sized; -sizing** : recortar, reducir

downstairs[1] ['daʊn'stærz] *adv* : abajo

downstairs[2] ['daʊn'stærz] *adj* : del piso de abajo

downstairs[3] ['daʊn'stærz, -,stærz] *n* : planta *f* baja

downstream ['daʊn'stri:m] *adv* : río abajo

Down syndrome *or* **Down's syndrome** *n* : síndrome *m* de Down

down–to–earth [,daʊntu'ərth] *adj* : práctico, realista

downtown[1] [,daʊn'taʊn] *adv* : hacia el centro, al centro, en el centro (de la ciudad)

downtown[2] *adj* : del centro (de la ciudad) ⟨downtown Chicago : el centro de Chicago⟩

downtown[3] [,daʊn'taʊn, 'daʊn,taʊn] *n* : centro *m* (de la ciudad)

downtrodden ['daʊn,trɑdən] *adj* : oprimido

downward ['daʊnwərd] *or* **downwards** [-wərdz] *adv & adj* : hacia abajo

downwind ['daʊn'wɪnd] *adv & adj* : en la dirección del viento

downy ['daʊni] *adj* **downier; -est** 1 : cubierto de plumón, plumoso 2 VELVETY : aterciopelado, velloso

dowry ['daʊri] *n, pl* **-ries** : dote *f*

doze¹ ['do:z] *vi* **dozed; dozing** : dormitar

doze² *n* : sueño *m* ligero, cabezada *f*

dozen ['dʌzən] *n, pl* **dozens** *or* **dozen** : docena *f* ⟨a dozen eggs : una docena de huevos⟩ ⟨ten dozen : diez docenas⟩ ⟨dozens (and dozens) : decenas, montones⟩

drab ['dræb] *adj* **drabber; drabbest** 1 BROWNISH : pardo 2 DULL, LACKLUSTER : monótono, gris, deslustrado

draft¹ ['dræft, 'draft] *vt* 1 CONSCRIPT : reclutar 2 COMPOSE, SKETCH : hacer el borrador de, redactar

draft² *adj* 1 : de barril ⟨draft beer : cerveza de barril⟩ 2 : de tiro ⟨draft horses : caballos de tiro⟩

draft³ *n* 1 HAULAGE : tiro *m* 2 DRINK, GULP : trago *m* 3 OUTLINE, SKETCH : bosquejo *m*, borrador *m*, versión *f* 4 : corriente *f* de aire, chiflón *m*, tiro *m* (de una chimenea) 5 CONSCRIPTION : conscripción *f* 6 **bank draft** : giro *m* bancario, letra *f* de cambio

draftee [dræf'ti:] *n* : recluta *mf*

draftsman ['dræftsmən] *n, pl* **-men** [-mən, -ˌmɛn] : dibujante *mf*

draftswoman ['dræfts,wʊmən] *n, pl* **-women** [-ˌwɪmən] : dibujante *f*

drafty ['dræfti] *adj* **draftier; -est** : con corrientes de aire

drag¹ ['dræg] *v* **dragged; dragging** *vt* 1 HAUL, TRAIL : arrastrar ⟨I could barely drag myself out of bed : me costó levantarme de la cama⟩ 2 DREDGE : dragar 3 INVOLVE : meter, involucrar ⟨don't drag me into this : no me metas en esto⟩ 4 **to drag one's feet/heels** : dar largas a algo ⟨they're still dragging their feet (on the issue) : siguen dando largas al asunto⟩ 5 **to drag out** PROLONG : alargar, dilatar — *vi* 1 TRAIL : arrastrarse 2 LAG : rezagarse 3 : hacerse pesado/largo ⟨the day dragged on : el día se hizo largo⟩

drag² *n* 1 RESISTANCE : resistencia *f* (aerodinámica) 2 HINDRANCE : traba *f*, estorbo *m* 3 BORE : pesadez *f*, plomo *m* *fam* 4 : chupada *f* (de un cigarrillo)

dragnet ['dræg,nɛt] *n* 1 : red *f* barredera (en pesca) 2 : operativo *m* policial de captura

dragon ['drægən] *n* : dragón *m*

dragonfly ['drægən,flaɪ] *n, pl* **-flies** : libélula *f*

drain¹ ['dreɪn] *vt* 1 EMPTY : vaciar, drenar 2 EXHAUST : agotar, consumir — *vi* 1 : escurrir, escurrirse ⟨the dishes are draining : los platos están escurriéndose⟩ 2 EMPTY : desaguar 3 **to drain away** : irse agotando

drain² *n* 1 : desagüe *m* 2 SEWER : alcantarilla *f* 3 GRATING : sumidero *m*, resumidero *m*, rejilla *f* 4 EXHAUSTION : agotamiento *m*, disminución *f* (de

energía, etc.) ⟨to be a drain on : agotar, consumir⟩ 5 **to throw down the drain** : tirar por la ventana

drainage ['dreɪnɪʤ] *n* : desagüe *m*, drenaje *m*

drainpipe ['dreɪn,paɪp] *n* : tubo *m* de desagüe, caño *m*

drake ['dreɪk] *n* : pato *m* (macho)

drama ['drɑmə, 'dræ-] *n* 1 THEATER : drama *m*, teatro *m* 2 PLAY : obra *f* de teatro, drama *m*

dramatic [drə'mætɪk] *adj* : dramático — **dramatically** [-tɪkli] *adv*

dramatist ['dræmətɪst, 'drɑ-] *n* : dramaturgo *m*, -ga *f*

dramatization [ˌdræmətə'zeɪʃən, ˌdrɑ-] *n* : dramatización *f*

dramatize ['dræmə,taɪz, 'drɑ-] *vt* **-tized; -tizing** : dramatizar

drank → **drink**

drape¹ ['dreɪp] *vt* **draped; draping** 1 COVER : cubrir (con tela) 2 HANG : disponer los pliegues de

drape² *n* 1 HANG : caída *f* 2 **drapes** *npl* : cortinas *fpl*

drapery ['dreɪpəri] *n, pl* **-eries** 1 CLOTH : pañería *f*, tela *f* para cortinas 2 **draperies** *npl* : cortinas *fpl*

drastic ['dræstɪk] *adj* 1 HARSH, SEVERE : drástico, severo 2 EXTREME : radical, excepcional — **drastically** [-tɪkli] *adv*

draught ['dræft, 'draft] *n* → **draft³**

draughty ['drɑfti] → **drafty**

draw¹ ['drɔ] *v* **drew** ['dru:]; **drawn** ['drɔn]; **drawing** *vt* 1 PULL : tirar de, jalar, correr (cortinas) 2 ATTRACT : atraer ⟨to feel drawn to : sentirse atraído por⟩ ⟨to draw attention : llamar la atención⟩ 3 PROVOKE, ELICIT : provocar, suscitar (críticas, etc.) ⟨to draw cheers/applause : arrancar vítores/aplausos⟩ 4 INHALE : aspirar ⟨to draw breath : respirar⟩ 5 EXTRACT : sacar (agua, sangre, etc.) ⟨to draw a gun : sacar una pistola⟩ 6 TAKE : sacar ⟨to draw a number : sacar un número⟩ 7 WITHDRAW : retirar, sacar (dinero) ⟨he drew a hundred dollars from his account : sacó cien dólares de su cuenta⟩ 8 WRITE : hacer, extender (un cheque) 9 COLLECT : cobrar, percibir (un sueldo, etc.) 10 BEND : tensar (un arco) 11 SKETCH : dibujar, trazar ⟨to draw a picture : dibujar algo, hacer un dibujo⟩ 12 FORMULATE : sacar, formular, llegar a ⟨to draw a conclusion : llegar a una conclusión⟩ 13 MAKE : hacer (una distinción, una comparación) 14 **to draw oneself up** : erguirse 15 **to draw out** : hacer hablar (sobre algo), hacer salir de sí mismo 16 **to draw out** PROLONG : prolongar, alargar, extender 17 **to draw up** DRAFT : redactar — *vi* 1 SKETCH : dibujar 2 TUG : tirar, jalar 3 **to draw away** : alejarse 4 **to draw near** : acercarse 5 **to draw on/upon** USE : hacer uso de (información, etc.) 6 **to draw to a close** : terminar, finalizar 7 **to draw up** STOP : parar

draw² *n* 1 DRAWING, RAFFLE : sorteo *m* 2 TIE : empate *m* 3 ATTRACTION

: atracción *f* 4 PUFF : chupada *f* (de un cigarrillo, etc.)

drawback ['drɔ,bæk] *n* : desventaja *f*, inconveniente *m*

drawbridge ['drɔ,brɪʤ] *n* : puente *m* levadizo

drawer ['drɔr, 'drɔər] *n* 1 ILLUSTRATOR : dibujante *mf* 2 : gaveta *f*, cajón *m* (en un mueble) 3 **drawers** *npl* UNDERPANTS : calzones *mpl*

drawing ['drɔɪŋ] *n* 1 LOTTERY : sorteo *m*, lotería *f* 2 SKETCH : dibujo *m*, bosquejo *m*

drawing room *n* : salón *m*

drawl[1] ['drɔl] *vi* : hablar arrastrando las palabras

drawl[2] *n* : habla *f* lenta y con vocales prolongadas

dread[1] ['drɛd] *vt* : tenerle pavor a, temer

dread[2] *adj* : pavoroso, aterrado

dread[3] *n* : pavor *m*, temor *m*

dreadful ['drɛdfəl] *adj* 1 DREAD : pavoroso 2 TERRIBLE : espantoso, atroz, terrible — **dreadfully** *adv*

dream[1] ['dri:m] *v* **dreamed** ['drɛmpt, 'dri:md] *or* **dreamt** ['drɛmpt]; **dreaming** *vi* 1 : soñar ⟨to dream about : soñar con⟩ 2 FANTASIZE : fantasear — *vt* 1 : soñar 2 IMAGINE : imaginarse 3 to **dream up** : inventar, idear

dream[2] *n* 1 : sueño *m*, ensueño *m* 2 **bad dream** NIGHTMARE : pesadilla *f*

dreamer ['dri:mər] *n* : soñador *m*, -dora *f*

dreamlike ['dri:m,laɪk] *adj* : de ensueño

dreamy ['dri:mi] *adj* **dreamier; -est** 1 DISTRACTED : soñador, distraído 2 DREAMLIKE : de ensueño 3 MARVELOUS : maravilloso

drearily ['drɪrəli] *adv* : sombríamente

dreary ['drɪri] *adj* **drearier; -est** : deprimente, lóbrego, sombrío

dredge[1] ['drɛʤ] *vt* **dredged; dredging** 1 DIG : dragar 2 COAT : espolvorear, enharinar

dredge[2] *n* : draga *f*

dredger ['drɛʤər] *n* : draga *f*

dregs ['drɛgz] *npl* 1 LEES : posos *mpl*, heces *fpl* (de un líquido) 2 : heces *fpl*, escoria *f* ⟨the dregs of society : la escoria de la sociedad⟩

drench ['drɛntʃ] *vt* : empapar, mojar, calar

dress[1] ['drɛs] *vt* 1 CLOTHE : vestir ⟨she was dressed in red : iba (vestida) de rojo⟩ 2 DECORATE : decorar, adornar 3 : preparar (pollo o pescado), aliñar (ensalada) 4 : curar, vendar (una herida) 5 FERTILIZE : abonar (la tierra) 6 to **dress down** SCOLD : regañar 7 to **dress up** EMBELLISH : adornar, engalanar 8 to **dress up** DISGUISE : disfrazar — *vi* 1 : vestirse ⟨to dress well/badly : vestir bien/mal⟩ 2 to **dress down** : vestirse informalmente 3 to **dress up** : ataviarse, engalanarse, ponerse de etiqueta 4 to **dress up** : disfrazarse, vestirse ⟨we dressed up as ghosts : nos disfrazamos de fantasmas⟩

dress[2] *n* 1 APPAREL : indumentaria *f*, ropa *f* 2 : vestido *m*, traje *m* (de mujer)

dresser ['drɛsər] *n* : cómoda *f* con espejo

dressing ['drɛsɪŋ] *n* 1 : vestirse *m* 2 *or* **salad dressing** : aderezo *m*, aliño *m* 3 STUFFING : relleno *m* (de pollo, etc.) 4 : apósito *m*, vendaje *m*, gasa *f* (para una herida)

dressing gown *n* : bata *f*

dressing room *n* 1 FITTING ROOM : probador *m* 2 : camerino *m* (en un teatro)

dressing table *n* : tocador *m*

dressmaker ['drɛs,meɪkər] *n* : modista *mf*

dressmaking ['drɛs,meɪkɪŋ] *n* : costura *f*

dress rehearsal *n* : ensayo *m* general

dressy ['drɛsi] *adj* **dressier; -est** : de mucho vestir, elegante

drew → draw

dribble[1] ['drɪbəl] *vi* **-bled; -bling** 1 DRIP : gotear 2 DROOL : babear 3 : driblar (en basquetbol)

dribble[2] *n* 1 TRICKLE : goteo *m*, hilo *m* 2 DROOL : baba *f* 3 : drible *m* (en basquetbol)

drier → dry[2], **dryer**

driest → dry[2]

drift[1] ['drɪft] *vi* 1 : dejarse llevar por la corriente, ir a la deriva (dícese de un bote), ir sin rumbo (dícese de una persona) 2 ACCUMULATE : amontonarse, acumularse, apilarse

drift[2] *n* 1 DRIFTING : deriva *f* 2 HEAP, MASS : montón *m* (de arena, etc.), ventisquero *m* (de nieve) 3 MEANING : sentido *m*

drifter ['drɪftər] *n* : vagabundo *m*, -da *f*

driftwood ['drɪft,wʊd] *n* : madera *f* flotante

drill[1] ['drɪl] *vt* 1 BORE : perforar, taladrar 2 INSTRUCT : instruir por repetición — *vi* 1 TRAIN : entrenarse 2 to **drill for oil** : perforar en busca de petróleo

drill[2] *n* 1 : taladro *m*, barrena *f* 2 EXERCISE, PRACTICE : ejercicio *m*, instrucción *f*

drily → dryly

drink[1] ['drɪŋk] *v* **drank** ['dræŋk]; **drunk** ['drʌŋk] *or* **drank; drinking** *vt* 1 IMBIBE : beber, tomar 2 to **drink up** ABSORB : absorber — *vi* 1 : beber 2 : beber alcohol, tomar

drink[2] *n* 1 : bebida *f* ⟨food and drink : comida y bebida⟩ 2 : bebida *f* alcohólica ⟨to drink someone to drink : llevar a alguien a la bebida⟩

drinkable ['drɪŋkəbəl] *adj* : potable

drinker ['drɪŋkər] *n* : bebedor *m*, -dora *f*

drinking water *n* : agua *f* potable

drinking straw → **straw**

drip[1] ['drɪp] *vi* **dripped; dripping** : gotear, chorrear

drip[2] *n* 1 DROP : gota *f* 2 DRIPPING : goteo *m*

drip-dry ['drɪp,draɪ] *adj* : de lavar y poner

drippings *npl* : pringue *m*, jugo *m*

drive[1] ['draɪv] *v* **drove** ['dro:v]; **driven** ['drɪvən]; **driving** *vt* 1 : manejar, conducir (un vehículo) 2 : llevar (en un automóvil) ⟨she drove me home : me llevó a casa⟩ 3 IMPEL : llevar, impulsar, impeler ⟨to drive someone to do something : llevar a alguien a hacer algo⟩ 4

COMPEL : obligar, forzar **5** : arrear (ganado) **6** POWER : hacer funcionar **7** PROPEL : impeler, impulsar **8** : clavar, hincar ⟨to drive a stake into : clavar una estaca en⟩ **9** : hacer trabajar mucho, exigir mucho ⟨he drives himself too hard : se exige demasiado⟩ **10** : lanzar (una pelota) **11 to drive away/off/out** : ahuyentar, echar, expulsar **12 to drive back** REPEL : hacer retroceder **13 to drive crazy** : volver loco **14 to drive up/down** : hacer subir/bajar (dícese de precios, etc.) — *vi* **1** : manejar, conducir ⟨do you know how to drive? : ¿sabes manejar?⟩ **2** : viajar (en auto) **3 to drive at** : querer decir, insinuar **4 to drive away/off** : alejarse (en un auto) ⟨they drove off : su auto se alejó⟩

drive² *n* **1** RIDE : viaje *m*, paseo *m* (en un automóvil) ⟨a two-hour drive : un viaje de dos horas⟩ **2** CAMPAIGN : campaña *f* ⟨fund-raising drive : campaña para recaudar fondos⟩ **3** DRIVEWAY : camino *m* de entrada, entrada *f* **4** TRANSMISSION : transmisión *f* ⟨front-wheel drive : tracción delantera⟩ **5** ENERGY : dinamismo *m*, energía *f* **6** INSTINCT, NEED : instinto *m*, necesidad *f* básica **7** AMBITION, INITIATIVE : empuje *m*, iniciativa *f* **8** : disparo *m* fuerte, tiro *m* fuerte (en deportes) **9** : ofensiva *f* (militar) **10** STREET : calle *f* ⟨she lives on Oak Drive : vive en la calle Oak⟩ **11** : marcha *f* ⟨to put a car in/into drive : poner en marcha un auto⟩ **12** : unidad *f* ⟨flash drive : unidad (de memoria) flash⟩

drive-in *n* : autocine *m*

drivel¹ ['drɪvəl] *n* : tontería *f*, estupidez *f*

driver ['draɪvər] *n* : conductor *m*, -tora *f*; chofer *m*

driveway ['draɪv,weɪ] *n* : camino *m* de entrada, entrada *f* (para coches)

driving ['draɪvɪŋ] *adj* : torrencial (dícese de la lluvia), que azota (dícese del viento) ⟨the driving force behind the reform : el principal impulsor de la reforma⟩

drizzle¹ ['drɪzəl] *vi* **-zled; -zling** : lloviznar, garuar

drizzle² *n* : llovizna *f*, garúa *f*

droll ['droːl] *adj* : cómico, gracioso, chistoso — **drolly** *adv*

dromedary ['droməˌdɛri] *n, pl* **-daries** : dromedario *m*

drone¹ ['droːn] *vi* **droned; droning 1** BUZZ : zumbar **2** MURMUR : hablar con monotonía, murmurar

drone² *n* **1** : zángano *m* (abeja) **2** BUZZ, HUM : zumbido *m*, murmullo *m*

drool¹ ['druːl] *vi* : babear

drool² *n* : baba *f*

droop¹ ['druːp] *vi* **1** HANG : inclinarse (dícese de la cabeza), encorvarse (dícese de los escombros), marchitarse (dícese de las flores) **2** FLAG : decaer, flaquear ⟨his spirits drooped : se desanimó⟩

droop² *n* : inclinación *f*, caída *f*

drop¹ ['drɑp] *v* **dropped; dropping** *vt* **1** : dejar caer, soltar ⟨she dropped the glass : se le cayó el vaso⟩ **2** SEND : man-

dar ⟨drop me a line : mándame unas líneas⟩ **3** ABANDON : abandonar, dejar ⟨to drop the subject : cambiar de tema⟩ **4** LOWER : bajar ⟨he dropped his voice : bajó la voz⟩ **5** OMIT : omitir **6** REDUCE : reducir, rebajar (precios, etc.) **7** *fam* : perder (peso) **8** *fam* SPEND : gastar **9** : dejar caer (una noticia, etc.) ⟨to drop a hint : lanzar una indirecta⟩ **10 to drop off** : dejar ⟨I dropped her off at the store : la dejé en la tienda⟩ — *vi* **1** DRIP : gotear **2** FALL : caer(se) ⟨to drop to the ground : caer al suelo⟩ ⟨to drop out of sight : perderse de vista⟩ **3** *or* **to drop off** DECREASE, DESCEND : bajar, descender ⟨the wind dropped off : amainó el viento⟩ **4 to drop back/behind** : rezagarse, quedarse atrás **5 to drop by/in** : pasar ⟨he dropped by for a visit : pasó a visitarnos⟩ **6 to drop off** : quedarse dormido **7 to drop out (of something)** : abandonar algo ⟨he dropped out (of school) : abandonó los estudios⟩

drop² *n* **1** : gota *f* (de líquido) **2** DECLINE : caída *f*, bajada *f*, descenso *m* **3** INCLINE : caída *f*, pendiente *f* ⟨a 20-foot drop : una caída de 20 pies⟩ **4** SWEET : pastilla *f*, dulce *m* **5 drops** *npl* : gotas *fpl* (de medicina)

droplet ['drɑplət] *n* : gotita *f*

dropper ['drɑpər] *n* : gotero *m*, cuentagotas *m*

dross ['drɑs, 'drɔs] *n* : escoria *f*

drought ['draʊt] *n* : sequía *f*

drove¹ → **drive**

drove² ['droːv] *n* : multitud *f*, gentío *m*, manada *f* (de ganado) ⟨in droves : en manada⟩

drown ['draʊn] *vt* **1** : ahogar **2** INUNDATE : anegar, inundar **3 to drown out** : ahogar — *vi* : ahogarse

drowse¹ ['draʊz] *vi* **drowsed; drowsing** DOZE : dormitar

drowse² *n* : sueño *m* ligero, cabezada *f*

drowsiness ['draʊzinəs] *n* : somnolencia *f*, adormecimiento *m*

drowsy ['draʊzi] *adj* **drowsier; -est** : somnoliento, soñoliento

drub ['drʌb] *vt* **drubbed; drubbing 1** BEAT, THRASH : golpear, apalear **2** DEFEAT : derrotar por completo

drudge¹ ['drʌdʒ] *vi* **drudged; drudging** : trabajar como esclavo, trabajar duro

drudge² *n* : esclavo *m*, -va *f* del trabajo

drudgery ['drʌdʒəri] *n, pl* **-eries** : trabajo *m* pesado

drug¹ ['drʌg] *vt* **drugged; drugging** : drogar, narcotizar

drug² *n* **1** MEDICATION : droga *f*, medicina *f*, medicamento *m* **2** NARCOTIC : narcótico *m*, estupefaciente *m*, droga *f*

drug addict → **addict**

druggist ['drʌgɪst] *n* : farmacéutico *m*, -ca *f*

drug pusher → **pusher**

drugstore ['drʌgˌstor] *n* : farmacia *f*, botica *f*, droguería *f*

drum¹ ['drʌm] *v* **drummed; drumming** *vt* **1** : meter a fuerza ⟨he drummed it

into my head : me lo metió en la cabeza a fuerza⟩ **2 to drum up** : conseguir, obtener (apoyo, etc.) — *vi* : tocar el tambor
drum² *n* **1** : tambor *m* **2** : bidón *m* ⟨oil drum : bidón de petróleo⟩
drummer ['drʌmər] *n* : baterista *mf*
drumstick ['drʌmˌstɪk] *n* **1** : palillo *m* (de tambor), baqueta *f* **2** : muslo *m* de pollo
drunk¹ *pp* → **drink¹**
drunk² ['drʌŋk] *adj* : borracho, embriagado, ebrio
drunk³ *n* : borracho *m*, -cha *f*
drunkard ['drʌŋkərd] *n* : borracho *m*, -cha *f*
drunken ['drʌŋkən] *adj* : borracho, ebrio ⟨drunken driver : conductor ebrio⟩ ⟨drunken brawl : pleito de borrachos⟩
drunkenly ['drʌŋkənli] *adv* : como un borracho
drunkenness ['drʌŋkənnəs] *n* : borrachera *f*, embriaguez *f*, ebriedad *f*
dry¹ ['draɪ] *v* **dried; drying** *vt* : secar ⟨to dry the dishes : secar los platos⟩ ⟨to dry one's eyes : secarse las lágrimas⟩ — *vi* **1** *or* **to dry out/up** : secarse **2 to dry up** RUN OUT : agotarse
dry² *adj* **drier; driest 1** : seco ⟨the well went dry : el pozo se secó⟩ ⟨to have a dry mouth : tener la boca seca⟩ ⟨there was not a dry eye in the house : no hubo quien no llorara⟩ **2** THIRSTY : sediento **3** : donde la venta de bebidas alcohólicas está prohibida ⟨a dry county : un condado seco⟩ **4** : seco, sin alcohol ⟨a dry party : una fiesta seca⟩ **5** DULL : aburrido, árido ⟨a dry class : una clase aburrida⟩ **6** : sutil e irónico (dícese de un sentido de humor)
dry-clean ['draɪˌkliːn] *v* : limpiar en seco
dry cleaner *n* : tintorería *f* (servicio) ⟨the dry cleaner/cleaner's/cleaners : la tintorería⟩
dry cleaning *n* : limpieza *f* en seco
dryer ['draɪər] *n* **1** *or* **hair dryer** : secador *m*, secadora *f* Mex **2** *or* **clothes dryer** : secadora *f*
dry goods *npl* : artículos *mpl* de confección
dry ice *n* : hielo *m* seco
dryly ['draɪli] *adv* : secamente
dryness ['draɪnəs] *n* : sequedad *f*, aridez *f*
dual ['duːəl, 'djuː-] *adj* : doble
dualism ['duːəˌlɪzəm] *n* : dualismo *m*
duality [duːˈæləti] *n, pl* **-ties** : dualidad *f*
dub ['dʌb] *vt* **dubbed; dubbing 1** CALL : apodar (una película), mezclar (una grabación)
dubious ['duːbiəs, 'djuː-] *adj* **1** UNCERTAIN : dudoso, indeciso **2** QUESTIONABLE : sospechoso, dudoso, discutible
dubiously ['duːbiəsli, 'djuː-] *adv* **1** UNCERTAINLY : dudosamente, con desconfianza **2** SUSPICIOUSLY : de modo sospechoso, con recelo
duchess ['dʌtʃəs] *n* : duquesa *f*
duck¹ ['dʌk] *vt* **1** LOWER : agachar, bajar (la cabeza) **2** PLUNGE : zambullir **3** EVADE : eludir, evadir — *vi* **to duck down** : agacharse
duck² *n, pl* **duck** *or* **ducks** : pato *m*, -ta *f*

duckling ['dʌklɪŋ] *n* : patito *m*, -ta *f*
duct ['dʌkt] *n* : conducto *m*
dud¹ ['dʌd] *adj* : que fracasa, que no funciona ⟨a dud movie : un fracaso de taquilla⟩ ⟨a dud grenade : una granada que no estalla⟩
dud² *n* **1** : fracaso *m* ⟨a box-office dud : un fracaso de taquilla⟩ **2** : cosa *f* que no funciona ⟨this match is a dud : este fósforo no prende⟩ **3** **duds** *npl fam* : trapos *mpl fam*, ropa *f*
dude ['duːd, 'djuːd] *n* GUY : tipo *m*
due¹ ['duː, 'djuː] *adv* : justo a, derecho hacia ⟨due north : derecho hacia al norte⟩
due² *adj* **1** PAYABLE : pagadero, sin pagar ⟨the rent is due : hay que pagar el alquiler⟩ **2** APPROPRIATE : debido, apropiado ⟨after due consideration : con las debidas consideraciones⟩ ⟨with all due respect : con el debido respeto⟩ **3** EXPECTED : esperado ⟨the train is due soon : esperamos el tren muy pronto, el tren debe llegar pronto⟩ ⟨the movie is due out in April : la película sale en abril⟩ **4 due to** : debido a, por
due³ *n* **1** **to give someone his** (her) **due** : darle a alguien su merecido **2 dues** *npl* : cuota *f*
duel¹ ['duːəl, 'djuː-] *vi* : batirse en duelo
duel² *n* : duelo *m*
duet [duˈɛt, dju-] *n* : dúo *m*
due to *prep* : debido a
duffel bag *or* **duffle bag** *n* : bolso *m* (deportivo)
duffle coat *or* **duffel coat** *n* : chaqueta *f* de lana (con capucha), trenca *f* Spain
dug → **dig**
dugout ['dʌɡˌaʊt] *n* **1** CANOE : piragua *f* **2** SHELTER : refugio *m* subterráneo
duke ['duːk, 'djuːk] *n* : duque *m*
dull¹ ['dʌl] *vt* **1** DIM : opacar, quitarle el brillo a, deslustrar **2** BLUNT : desafilar (un filo), despuntar (un lápiz, etc.) **3** BLUNT : entorpecer (los sentidos), embotar (la mente), aliviar (el dolor), amortiguar (sonidos)
dull² *adj* **1** STUPID : torpe, lerdo, lento **2** BLUNT : desafilado, despuntado **3** LACKLUSTER : sin brillo, deslustrado **4** BORING : aburrido, soso, pesado — **dully** *adv*
dullness ['dʌlnəs] *n* **1** STUPIDITY : estupidez *f* **2** MONOTONY : monotonía *f*, lo aburrido **3** : falta *f* de brillo **4** BLUNTNESS : falta *f* de filo
duly ['duːli, 'djuː-] *adv* PROPERLY : debidamente, a su debido tiempo
dumb ['dʌm] *adj* **1** *now often offensive* MUTE : mudo **2** STUPID : estúpido, tonto, bobo — **dumbly** *adv*
dumbbell ['dʌmˌbɛl] *n* **1** WEIGHT : pesa *f* **2** : estúpido *m*, -da *f*
dumbfound *or* **dumfound** [ˌdʌm-ˈfaʊnd] *vt* : dejar atónito, dejar sin habla
dummy¹ ['dʌmi] *adj* : falso, de imitación, artificial
dummy² *n, pl* **-mies 1** SHAM : imitación *f*, sustituto *m* **2** PUPPET : muñeco *m* **3** MANNEQUIN : maniquí *m* **4** IDIOT : tonto *m*, -ta *f*; idiota *mf*

dump¹ ['dʌmp] *vt* : descargar, verter

dump² *n* **1** : vertedero *m*, basural *m*, basurero *m*, botadero *m*, tiradero *m* *Mex* **2 down in the dumps** : triste, deprimido

dumpling ['dʌmplɪŋ] *n* : bola *f* de masa hervida

Dumpster *trademark* se usa para un contenedor de basura

dumpy ['dʌmpi] *adj* **dumpier; -est** : rechoncho, regordete

dun¹ ['dʌn] *vt* **dunned; dunning** : apremiar (a un deudor)

dun² *adj* : pardo (color)

dunce ['dʌns] *n* : estúpido *m*, -da *f*; burro *m*, -rra *f fam*

dune ['du:n, 'dju:n] *n* : duna *f* (de arena)

dung ['dʌŋ] *n* **1** FECES : excrementos *mpl* **2** MANURE : estiércol *m*

dungarees [ˌdʌŋgəˈri:z] *n* **1** → **jeans 2** → **overalls**

dungeon ['dʌndʒən] *n* : mazmorra *f*, calabozo *m*

dunk ['dʌŋk] *vt* : mojar, ensopar

duo ['du:o:, 'dju:-] *n, pl* **duos** : dúo *m*, par *m*

dupe¹ ['du:p, dju:p] *vt* **duped; duping** : engañar, embaucar

dupe² *n* : inocentón *m*, -tona *f*; simple *mf*

duplex¹ ['du:ˌplɛks, 'dju:-] *adj* : doble

duplex² *n* : casa *f* de dos viviendas, dúplex *m*

duplicate¹ ['du:plɪˌkeɪt, 'dju:-] *vt* **-cated; -cating 1** COPY : duplicar, hacer copias de **2** REPEAT : repetir, reproducir

duplicate² ['du:plɪkət, 'dju:-] *adj* : duplicado ⟨a duplicate invoice : una factura por duplicado⟩

duplicate³ ['du:plɪkət, 'dju:-] *n* : duplicado *m*, copia *f*

duplication [ˌdu:plɪˈkeɪʃən, ˌdju:-] *n* **1** DUPLICATING : duplicación *f*, repetición *f* (de esfuerzos) **2** DUPLICATE : copia *f*, duplicado *m*

duplicity [duˈplɪsəti, ˌdju:-] *n, pl* **-ties** : duplicidad *f*

durability [ˌdʊrəˈbɪləti, ˌdjʊr-] *n* : durabilidad *f* (de un producto), permanencia *f*

durable ['dʊrəbəl, 'djʊr-] *adj* : duradero

duration [dʊˈreɪʃən, dju-] *n* : duración *f*

duress [dʊˈrɛs, dju-] *n* : coacción *f*

during ['dʊrɪŋ, 'djʊr-] *prep* : durante

dusk ['dʌsk] *n* : anochecer *m*, crepúsculo *m*

dusky ['dʌski] *adj* **duskier; -est** : oscuro (dícese de los colores)

dust¹ ['dʌst] *vt* **1** : quitar el polvo de **2** SPRINKLE : espolvorear

dust² *n* : polvo *m*

dustcover ['dʌstˌkʌvər] *n* **1** : guardapolvo *m*, funda *f* **2** → **dust jacket**

duster ['dʌstər] *n* **1** *or* **dust cloth** : trapo

m de polvo 2 HOUSECOAT : guardapolvo *m* **3 feather duster** : plumero *m*

dust jacket *n* : sobrecubierta *f*

dustpan ['dʌstˌpæn] *n* : recogedor *m*

dusty ['dʌsti] *adj* **dustier; -est** : cubierto de polvo, polvoriento

Dutch¹ ['dʌtʃ] *adj* : holandés

Dutch² *n* **1** : holandés *m* (idioma) **2 the Dutch** (*used with a plural verb*) : los holandeses

Dutchman ['dʌtʃmən] *n, pl* **-men** [-mən, -ˌmɛn] : holandés *m* (persona)

Dutch treat *n* : invitación o pago a escote

Dutchwoman ['dʌtʃˌwʊmən] *n, pl* **-women** [-ˌwɪmən] : holandesa *f* (persona)

dutiful ['du:tɪfəl, 'dju:-] *adj* : motivado por sus deberes, responsable

duty ['du:ti, 'dju:-] *n, pl* **-ties 1** OBLIGATION : deber *m*, obligación *f*, responsabilidad *f* **2** TAX : impuesto *m*, arancel *m*

duty-free [ˌdu:ti'fri:-, ˌdju:-] *adj* : libre de impuestos

duvet [du'veɪ, 'du:ˌveɪ] *n* : edredón *m*, cobertor *m*

DVD [ˌdi:ˌvi:'di:] *n* : DVD *m* ⟨DVD player/recorder : reproductor/grabador de DVD⟩

dwarf¹ ['dwɔrf] *vt* **1** STUNT : arrestar el crecimiento de **2** : hacer parecer pequeño

dwarf² *n, pl* **dwarfs** ['dwɔrfs] *or* **dwarves** ['dwɔrvz] **1** : enano *m*, -na *f* (en cuentos) **2** *sometimes offensive* : enano *m*, -na *feminine sometimes offensive*

dwell ['dwɛl] *vi* **dwelled** *or* **dwelt** ['dwɛlt]; **dwelling 1** RESIDE : residir, morar, vivir **2 to dwell on** : pensar demasiado en, insistir en

dweller ['dwɛlər] *n* : habitante *mf*

dwelling ['dwɛlɪŋ] *n* : morada *f*, vivienda *f*, residencia *f*

dwindle ['dwɪndəl] *vi* **-dled; -dling** : menguar, reducirse, disminuir

dye¹ ['daɪ] *vt* **dyed; dyeing** : teñir

dye² *n* : tintura *f*, tinte *m*

dying → die

dyke → dike

dynamic [daɪ'næmɪk] *adj* : dinámico

dynamics [daɪ'næmɪks] *npl* : dinámica *f*

dynamite¹ ['daɪnəˌmaɪt] *vt* **-mited; -miting** : dinamitar

dynamite² *n* : dinamita *f*

dynamo ['daɪnəˌmo:] *n, pl* **-mos** : dínamo *m*, generador *m* de electricidad

dynasty ['daɪnəsti, -ˌnæs-] *n, pl* **-ties** : dinastía *f*

dysentery ['dɪsənˌteri] *n, pl* **-teries** : disentería *f*

dysfunction [dɪs'fʌŋkʃən] *n* : disfunción *f* — **dysfunctional** [dɪs'fʌŋkʃənəl] *adj*

dyslexia [dɪs'lɛksiə] *n* : dislexia *f* — **dyslexic** [dɪs'lɛksɪk] *adj*

dystrophy ['dɪstrəfi] *n, pl* **-phies 1** : distrofia *f* **2** → **muscular dystrophy**

E

e [ˈiː] n, pl e's or es [ˈiːz] 1 : quinta letra del alfabeto inglés 2 E : mi m ⟨E sharp/flat : mi sostenido/bemol⟩

e- pref : electrónico ⟨e-mail : email, correo electrónico⟩

each¹ [ˈiːtʃ] adv : cada uno ⟨they cost $10 each : cuestan $10 cada uno⟩

each² adj : cada ⟨each student : cada estudiante⟩ ⟨each and every one : todos sin excepción⟩

each³ pron 1 : cada uno, cada una ⟨each of us : cada uno de nosotros⟩ ⟨each of the cities : cada una de las ciudades⟩ 2 each other : el uno al otro ⟨we are helping each other : nos ayudamos el uno al otro⟩ ⟨they all looked at each other : todos se miraron unos a otros⟩ ⟨they love each other : se quieren⟩

eager [ˈiːgər] adj 1 ENTHUSIASTIC : entusiasta, ávido, deseoso 2 ANXIOUS : ansioso, impaciente ⟨she's eager to meet you : está ansiosa de/por conocerte⟩ ⟨to be eager for change : tener deseos de cambio⟩

eagerly [ˈiːgərli] adv : con entusiasmo, ansiosamente

eagerness [ˈiːgərnəs] n : entusiasmo m, deseo m, impaciencia f

eagle [ˈiːgəl] n : águila f

ear [ˈɪr] n 1 : oído m, oreja f ⟨inner ear : oído interno⟩ ⟨big ears : orejas grandes⟩ 2 ear of corn : mazorca f, choclo m 3 to play by ear : tocar de oído 4 to play it by ear : improvisar

earache [ˈɪrˌeɪk] n : dolor m de oído(s)

earbud [ˈɪrˌbʌd] n : auricular m de tapón

eardrum [ˈɪrˌdrʌm] n : tímpano m

earl [ˈərl] n : conde m

earldom [ˈərldəm] n : condado m

earliest [ˈərliəst] n at the earliest ⟨it won't happen until next year at the earliest : lo más pronto que podría ocurrir sería el año que viene⟩

earliness [ˈərlinəs] n : lo temprano

earlobe [ˈɪrˌloːb] n : lóbulo m de la oreja, perilla f de la oreja

early¹ [ˈərli] adv adj earlier; -est 1 : temprano ⟨he arrived early : llegó temprano, llegó antes de la hora⟩ ⟨she bought the tickets a month early : compró las entradas con un mes de antelación⟩ 2 SOON : pronto ⟨why didn't you tell me earlier? : ¿por qué no me lo dijiste antes?⟩ ⟨as early as possible : lo más pronto posible, cuanto antes⟩ 3 (long ago) ⟨as early as the 1960's : ya en los años sesenta⟩ 4 or ~ on : al principio ⟨early (on) in his career : al principio de su carrera⟩

early² adj earlier; -est 1 (referring to a beginning) : primero ⟨the early stages/hours : las primeras etapas/horas⟩ ⟨the earliest example : el primer ejemplo⟩ ⟨in early May : a principios de mayo⟩ ⟨early in the morning : por la mañana temprano⟩ 2 (referring to antiquity) : primitivo, antiguo ⟨early man : el hombre primitivo⟩ ⟨early painting : la pintura antigua⟩ ⟨in earlier times : antiguamente, en épocas anteriores⟩ 3 (referring to a designated time) : temprano, antes de la hora, prematuro ⟨he was early : llegó temprano⟩ ⟨early fruit : frutas tempraneras⟩ ⟨an early death : una muerte prematura⟩ ⟨early retirement : jubilación anticipada⟩ ⟨an earlier version : una versión anterior⟩

earmark [ˈɪrˌmɑrk] vt : destinar ⟨funds earmarked for education : fondos destinados a la educación⟩

earn [ˈərn] vt 1 : ganar ⟨to earn money : ganar dinero⟩ 2 DESERVE : ganarse

earner [ˈərnər] n or wage earner : asalariado m, -da f

earnest¹ [ˈərnəst] adj : serio, sincero

earnest² n in ~ : en serio, de verdad ⟨we began in earnest : empezamos de verdad⟩

earnestly [ˈərnəstli] adv 1 SERIOUSLY : con seriedad, en serio 2 FERVENTLY : de todo corazón

earnestness [ˈərnəstnəs] n : seriedad f, sinceridad f

earnings [ˈərnɪŋz] npl : ingresos mpl, ganancias fpl, utilidades fpl

earphone [ˈɪrˌfoːn] n : audífono m, auricular m

earplug [ˈɪrˌplʌg] n : tapón m para el oído

earring [ˈɪrˌrɪŋ] n : zarcillo m, arete m, aro m Arg, Chile, Uru, pendiente m Spain

earshot [ˈɪrˌʃɑt] n : alcance m del oído ⟨out of earshot : demasiado lejos para oír⟩

earth [ˈərθ] n 1 LAND, SOIL : tierra f, suelo m 2 the Earth : la Tierra 3 on ~ : en el mundo ⟨what on earth . . . ? : ¿qué demonios/diablos . . . ?⟩

earthen [ˈərθən, -ðən] adj : de tierra, de barro

earthenware [ˈərθənˌwær, -ðən-] n : loza f, vajilla f de barro

earthly [ˈərθli] adj : terrenal, mundano

earthquake [ˈərθˌkweɪk] n : terremoto m, sismo m

earthworm [ˈərθˌwərm] n : lombriz f (de tierra)

earthy [ˈərθi] adj earthier; -est 1 : terroso ⟨earthy colors : colores terrosos⟩ 2 DOWN-TO-EARTH : realista, práctico, llano 3 COARSE, CRUDE : basto, grosero, tosco ⟨earthy jokes : chistes groseros⟩

earwax [ˈɪrˌwæks] n → wax²

earwig [ˈɪrˌwɪg] n : tijereta f

ease¹ [ˈiːz] v eased; easing vt 1 ALLEVIATE : aliviar, calmar ⟨it eased her mind : la tranquilizó⟩ 2 REDUCE : paliar (un problema), reducir (tensiones), aligerar (una carga) 3 LOOSEN, RELAX : aflojar (una cuerda), relajar (restricciones) 4 : mover con cuidado ⟨I eased myself into the chair : me senté con cuidado en la silla⟩ — vi 1 : moverse con cuidado 2 to ease off/up : calmarse (dícese del dolor), amainar (dícese del viento) **3 to ease up on** : aflojar (una cuerda), moderarse con (la comida, etc.), no ser tan duro con (alguien)

ease² *n* **1** CALM, RELIEF : tranquilidad *f*, comodidad *f*, desahogo *m* **2** FACILITY : facilidad *f* ⟨with ease : con facilidad⟩ **3** at ~ : relajado, cómodo ⟨to put someone at ease : tranquilizar a alguien⟩ ⟨at ease! : ¡descansen!⟩

easel ['izəl] *n* : caballete *m*

easily ['izəli] *adv* **1** : fácilmente, con facilidad **2** UNQUESTIONABLY : con mucho, de lejos

easiness ['izinəs] *n* : facilidad *f*, soltura *f*

east¹ ['ist] *adv* : al este ⟨to travel east : viajar hacia el este⟩

east² *adj* : este, del este, oriental ⟨east winds : vientos del este⟩

east³ *n* **1** : este *m* **2 the East** : el Oriente

Easter ['istər] *n* **1** : Pascua *f* (de Resurrección) **2** *or* **Easter Sunday** : Domingo *m* de Pascua, Domingo *m* de Resurrección

Easter egg *n* : huevo *m* de Pascua (pintado)

easterly ['istərli] *adv & adj* : del este

eastern ['istərn] *adj* **1** : Oriental, del Este ⟨Eastern Europe : Europa del Este⟩ **2** : oriental, este

Easterner ['istərnər] *n* : habitante *mf* del este

eastward ['istwərd] *adv & adj* : hacia el este

easy¹ ['izi] *adj* **easier; -est** : fácil ⟨easy to use : fácil de usar⟩ ⟨it's easy to see why : es fácil ver por qué⟩ ⟨to make something easier : facilitar algo⟩ **2** COMFORTABLE : fácil, cómodo **3** RELAXED : relajado **4 to be easy on the eye(s)** : ser agradable a la vista

easy² *adv* **easier; -est 1 to come easy** : ser fácil de conseguir **2 to go easy on** : no ser muy duro con (alguien), no pasarse con (algo) **3 to take it easy** RELAX : relajarse **4 to take it easy** CALM DOWN : tranquilizarse, calmarse

easy chair *n* : sillón *m*, butaca *f*

easygoing [,izi'goiŋ] *adj* : tolerante, poco exigente

eat ['it] *v* **ate** ['eit]; **eaten** ['itən]; **eating** *vt* **1** : comer ⟨eat it up! : ¡cómetelo!⟩ **2** CORRODE : corroer **3** *or* **to eat up** CONSUME : comerse (comida, ganancias), consumir (tiempo, recursos), gastar (combustible) — *vi* **1** : comer **2 to eat away at** *or* **to eat into** : comerse, consumir, corroer **3 to eat out** : comer fuera

eatable¹ ['itəbəl] *adj* : comestible, comible *fam*

eatable² *n* **1** : algo para comer **2 eatables** *npl* : comestibles *mpl*, alimentos *mpl*

eater ['itər] *n* : persona *f* o animal *m* que come ⟨a big eater : un comelón⟩ ⟨meat/plant eaters : carnívoros/herbívoros⟩

eaves ['ivz] *npl* : alero *m*

eavesdrop ['ivz,drɑp] *vi* **-dropped; -dropping** : escuchar a escondidas ⟨he was eavesdropping on us : nos escuchaba a escondidas⟩

eavesdropper ['ivz,drɑpər] *n* : persona *f* que escucha a escondidas

ebb¹ ['ɛb] *vi* **1** : bajar (dícese de la marea) **2** DECLINE : menguar, decaer, disminuir

ebb² *n* **1** : reflujo *m* (de la marea) **2** DECLINE : decadencia *f*, declive *m*, disminución *f* ⟨to be at a low ebb : tocar fondo⟩ **3 the ebb and flow** : el flujo y reflujo

ebony¹ ['ɛbəni] *adj* **1** : de ébano **2** BLACK : de color ébano, negro

ebony² *n*, *pl* **-nies** : ébano *m*

e-book ['i,bʊk] *n* : libro *m* electrónico, e-book *m*

ebullience [ɪ'bʊljənts, -'bʌl-] *n* : efervescencia *f*, vivacidad *f*

ebullient [ɪ'bʊljənt, -'bʌl-] *adj* : efervescente, vivaz

eccentric¹ [ɪk'sɛntrɪk] *adj* **1** : excéntrico ⟨an eccentric wheel : una rueda excéntrica⟩ **2** ODD, SINGULAR : excéntrico, extraño, raro — **eccentrically** [-trɪkli] *adv*

eccentric² *n* : excéntrico *m*, -ca *f*

eccentricity [,ɛk,sɛn'trɪsəti] *n*, *pl* **-ties** : excentricidad *f*

ecclesiastic [ɪ,kli:zi'æstɪk] *n* : eclesiástico *m*, clérigo *m*

ecclesiastical [ɪ,kli:zi'æstɪkəl] *or* **ecclesiastic** *adj* : eclesiástico — **ecclesiastically** *adv*

echelon ['ɛʃə,lɑn] *n* **1** : escalón *m* (de tropas o aviones) **2** LEVEL : nivel *m*, esfera *f*, estrato *m*

echo¹ ['ɛ,ko:] *v* **echoed; echoing** *vi* : hacer eco, resonar — *vt* : repetir, hacerse eco de

echo² *n*, *pl* **echoes** : eco *m*

e-cigarette ['i:,sɪgə'rɛt] → **electronic cigarette**

éclair [eɪ'klær, i-] *n* : pastel *m* relleno de crema

eclectic [ɛ'klɛktɪk, ɪ-] *adj* : ecléctico

eclipse¹ [ɪ'klɪps] *vt* **eclipsed; eclipsing** : eclipsar

eclipse² *n* : eclipse *m*

eco- ['iko] *pref* : eco-, ecológico, ecológicamente

eco–friendly ['iko,frɛndli] *adj* : ecológico

ecological [,iːkə'lɑdʒɪkəl, ,ɛkə-] *adj* : ecológico — **ecologically** *adv*

ecologist [i'kɑlədʒɪst, ɛ-] *n* : ecólogo *m*, -ga *f*

ecology [i'kɑlədʒi, ɛ-] *n*, *pl* **-gies** : ecología *f*

e–commerce ['i,kɑmərs] *n* : comercio *m* electrónico

economic [,iːkə'nɑmɪk, ,ɛkə-] *adj* : económico

economical [,iːkə'nɑmɪkəl, ,ɛkə-] *adj* : económico — **economically** *adv*

economics [,iːkə'nɑmɪks, ,ɛkə-] *n* **1** : economía *f* **2 the economics of** : el aspecto *m* económico de

economist [i'kɑnəmɪst] *n* : economista *mf*

economize [i'kɑnə,maɪz] *v* **-mized; -mizing** : economizar, ahorrar ⟨to economize on something : economizar algo⟩

economy [i'kɑnəmi] *n, pl* **-mies** 1 : economía *f*, sistema *m* económico 2 THRIFT : economía *f*, ahorro *m*

ecosystem ['i:ko,sɪstəm] *n* : ecosistema *m*

ecotourism [,i:ko'tʊr,ɪzəm] *n* : ecoturismo *m*

ecru ['ɛ,kru:, 'eɪ-] *n* : color *m* crudo

ecstasy ['ɛkstəsi] *n, pl* **-sies** 1 : éxtasis *m* 2 **Ecstasy** : éxtasis *m* (droga)

ecstatic [ɛk'stætɪk, ɪk-] *adj* : extático ⟨to be ecstatic about : estar muy entusiasmado con⟩

ecstatically [ɛk'stætɪkli, ɪk-] *adv* : con éxtasis, con gran entusiasmo

Ecuadoran [,ɛkwə'dorən] *or* **Ecuadorean** *or* **Ecuadorian** [-'dorɪən] *n* : ecuatoriano *m*, -na *f* — **Ecuadoran** *or* **Ecuadorian** *adj*

ecumenical [,ɛkju'mnɪkəl] *adj* : ecuménico

eczema [ɪg'zi:mə, 'ɛgzəmə, 'ɛksə-] *n* : eczema *m*

edamame [,ɛdə'mɑmeɪ] *n* : edamame *m*, habas *fpl* de soya/soja

eddy¹ ['ɛdi] *vi* **eddied; eddying** : arremolinarse, formar remolinos

eddy² *n, pl* **-dies** : remolino *m*

edema [ɪ'di:mə] *n* : edema *m*

Eden ['i:dən] *n* : Edén *m*

edge¹ ['ɛdʒ] *v* **edged; edging** *vt* 1 BORDER : bordear, ribetear, orlar ⟨edged with lace : con borde de encaje⟩ 2 SHARPEN : afilar, aguzar 3 *or* to **edge one's way** : avanzar poco a poco 3 to **edge away/closer** : alejarse/acercarse poco a poco 4 to **edge out** : derrotar por muy poco — *vi* ADVANCE : ir avanzando (poco a poco)

edge² *n* 1 : borde *m* (de una cama, etc.), filo *m* (de un cuchillo), margen *m* (de una página) 2 BORDER : borde *m*, orilla *f*, margen *f* ⟨at the water's edge : a la orilla del agua⟩ 3 ADVANTAGE : ventaja *f* 4 to be on edge : tener los nervios de punta 5 to be on the edge of : estar al borde de (la guerra, etc.)

edgewise ['ɛdʒ,waɪz] *adv* SIDEWAYS : de lado, de canto

edginess ['ɛdʒinəs] *n* : tensión *f*, nerviosismo *m*

edging ['ɛdʒɪŋ] *n* : borde *m*

edgy ['ɛdʒi] *adj* **edgier; -est** : tenso, nervioso

edible ['ɛdəbəl] *adj* : comestible, comible *fam*

edict ['i:,dɪkt] *n* : edicto *m*, mandato *m*, orden *f*

edification [,ɛdəfə'keɪʃən] *n* : edificación *f*, instrucción *f*

edifice ['ɛdəfɪs] *n* : edificio *m*

edify ['ɛdə,faɪ] *vt* **-fied; -fying** : edificar

edit ['ɛdɪt] *vt* 1 : editar (un texto, una película, etc.), corregir (un texto) 2 MANAGE : dirigir (un periódico, etc.) 3 *or* to **edit out** DELETE : recortar, cortar

edition [ɪ'dɪʃən] *n* : edición *f*

editor ['ɛdɪtər] *n* 1 : editor *m*, -tora *f* (de libros, artículos, etc.); redactor *m*, -tora *f* (de artículos) 2 : director *m*, -tora *f* (de un periódico, etc.) 3 : editor *m*, -tora *f* (de una película, etc.) 4 : editor *m* (software)

editorial¹ [,ɛdɪ'torɪəl] *adj* 1 : de redacción 2 : editorial ⟨an editorial comment : un comentario editorial⟩

editorial² *n* : editorial *m*

editorship ['ɛdɪtər,ʃɪp] *n* : dirección *f*

educate ['ɛdʒə,keɪt] *vt* **-cated; -cating** 1 TEACH : educar, enseñar 2 INSTRUCT : formar, educar, instruir 3 INFORM : informar, concientizar

educated ['ɛdʒə,keɪtəd] *adj* : culto

education [,ɛdʒə'keɪʃən] *n* : educación *f*

educational [,ɛdʒə'keɪʃənəl] *adj* 1 : docente, de enseñanza ⟨an educational institution : una institución docente⟩ 2 PEDAGOGICAL : pedagógico 3 INSTRUCTIONAL : educativo, instructivo ⟨an educational film : una película educativa⟩

educator ['ɛdʒə,keɪtər] *n* : educador *m*, -dora *f*

eel ['i:l] *n* : anguila *f*

eerie ['ɪri] *adj* **eerier; -est** 1 SPOOKY : que da miedo, espeluznante 2 GHOSTLY : fantasmagórico

eerily ['ɪrəli] *adv* : de manera extraña y misteriosa

efface [ɪ'feɪs, ɛ-] *vt* **-faced; -facing** : borrar

effect¹ [ɪ'fɛkt] *vt* 1 CARRY OUT : efectuar, llevar a cabo 2 ACHIEVE : lograr, realizar

effect² *n* 1 RESULT : efecto *m*, resultado *m*, consecuencia *f* ⟨to no effect : sin resultado⟩ ⟨to have an effect : producir/surtir efecto⟩ 2 MEANING : sentido *m* ⟨something to that effect : algo por el estilo⟩ 3 INFLUENCE : efecto *m*, influencia *f* 4 **effects** *npl* : efectos *mpl* ⟨sound effects : efectos de sonido⟩ 5 **effects** *npl* BELONGINGS : efectos *mpl*, pertenencias *fpl* 6 to **come/go into effect** *or* to **take effect** : entrar en vigor 7 for ~ : para impresionar ⟨he paused for effect : hizo una pausa dramática⟩ 8 in ~ REALLY : en realidad, de hecho

effective [ɪ'fɛktɪv] *adj* 1 EFFECTUAL : efectivo, eficaz 2 OPERATIVE : vigente 3 REAL : efectivo

effectively [ɪ'fɛktɪvli] 1 : eficazmente, con eficacia 2 IN EFFECT : en realidad, de hecho

effectiveness [ɪ'fɛktɪvnəs] *n* : eficacia *f*, efectividad *f*

effectual [ɪ'fɛktʃuəl] *adj* : eficaz, efectivo — **effectually** *adv*

effeminate [ə'fɛmənət] *adj* : afeminado

effervesce [,ɛfər'vɛs] *vi* **-vesced; -vescing** 1 : estar en efervescencia, burbujear (dícese de líquidos) 2 : estar eufórico, estar muy animado (dícese de las personas)

effervescence [,ɛfər'vɛsənts] *n* : efervescencia *f* — **effervescent** [,ɛfər'vɛsənt] *adj*

effete ['ɛfi:t, ɪ-] *adj* 1 WORN-OUT : desgastado, agotado 2 DECADENT : decadente 3 EFFEMINATE : afeminado

efficacious [,ɛfə'keɪʃəs] *adj* : eficaz, efectivo

efficacy ['ɛfɪkəsi] *n, pl* **-cies** : eficacia *f*

efficiency [ɪ'fɪʃənsi] *n, pl* **-cies** 1 : eficiencia *f* 2 YIELD : rendimiento *m*

efficient [ɪ'fɪʃənt] *adj* 1 : eficiente 2 : de alto rendimiento (dícese de una máquina) — **efficiently** *adv*

effigy ['ɛfədʒi] *n, pl* **-gies** : efigie *f*

effluent ['ɛ,flu:ənt, ɛ'flu:-] *n* : efluentes *mpl*

effort ['ɛfərt] *n* 1 EXERTION : esfuerzo *m* 2 ATTEMPT : tentativa *f*, intento *m* ⟨it's not worth the effort : no vale la pena⟩ ⟨to make an/the effort to do something : hacer un/el esfuerzo para hacer algo⟩ ⟨to make no effort to do something : no molestarse en hacer algo⟩

effortless ['ɛfərtləs] *adj* : sin esfuerzo, natural

effortlessly ['ɛfərtləsli] *adv* : sin esfuerzo

effrontery [ɪ'frʌntəri] *n, pl* **-teries** : insolencia *f*, desfachatez *f*, descaro *m*

effusive [ɪ'fju:sɪv, ɛ-] *adj* : efusivo — **effusively** *adv*

effusiveness [ɪ'fju:sɪvnəs, ɛ-] *n* : efusión *f*

EFL [ˌiː'ɛf'ɛl] *n* (*E*nglish as a *f*oreign *l*anguage) : inglés *m* como lengua extranjera

egalitarian [ɪˌgælə'tæriən] *adj* : igualitario

egg¹ ['ɛg] *vt* **to egg on** : incitar, azuzar

egg² *n* 1 : huevo *m* ⟨egg white/yolk : clara/yema de huevo⟩ 2 OVUM : óvulo *m*

eggbeater ['ɛg,bi:tər] *n* : batidor *m* (de huevos)

eggnog ['ɛg,nɑg] *n* : ponche *m* de huevo, rompope *m* CA, Mex

eggplant ['ɛg,plænt] *n* : berenjena *f*

eggshell ['ɛg,ʃɛl] *n* : cascarón *m*

ego ['iː,goː] *n, pl* **egos** 1 SELF-ESTEEM : amor *m* propio, ego *m* 2 SELF : ego *m*, yo *m*

egocentric [ˌiːgo'sɛntrɪk] *adj* : egocéntrico

egoism ['iːgo,wɪzəm] *n* : egoísmo *m*

egoist ['iːgowɪst] *n* : egoísta *mf*

egoistic [ˌiːgo'wɪstɪk] *adj* : egoísta

egotism ['iːgə,tɪzəm] *n* : egotismo *m*

egotist ['iːgətɪst] *n* : egotista *mf*

egotistic [ˌiːgə'tɪstɪk] *or* **egotistical** [-'tɪstɪkəl] *adj* : egotista — **egotistically** *adv*

egregious [ɪ'gri:dʒəs] *adj* : atroz, flagrante, mayúsculo — **egregiously** *adv*

egress ['iː,grɛs] *n* : salida *f*

egret ['iːgrət, -,grɛt] *n* : garceta *f*

Egyptian [ɪ'dʒɪpʃən] *n* 1 : egipcio *m*, -cia *f* 2 : egipcio *m* (idioma) — **Egyptian** *adj*

eh ['eɪ, 'ɛ] *interj* 1 WHAT : ¿eh?, ¿qué? 2 : ¿eh?, ¿no? ⟨pretty clever, eh? : qué listo, ¿no?⟩

eiderdown ['aɪdər,daʊn] *n* 1 : plumón *m* 2 COMFORTER : cdredón *m*

eight¹ ['eɪt] *adj* : ocho ⟨she's eight (years old) : tiene ocho años⟩

eight² *n* : ocho *m* ⟨the eight of hearts : el ocho de corazones⟩

eight³ *pron* : ocho ⟨there are eight of us : somos ocho⟩ ⟨it's eight (o'clock) : son las ocho⟩

eighteen¹ [eɪt'ti:n] *adj & pron* : dieciocho

eighteen² *n* : dieciocho *m*

eighteenth¹ [eɪt'ti:nθ] *adj* : decimoctavo

eighteenth² *n* 1 : decimoctavo *m*, -va *f* (en una serie) 2 : dieciochoavo *m*, dieciochoava parte *f*

eighth¹ ['eɪtθ] *adv* : en octavo lugar

eighth² *adj* : octavo

eighth³ *n* 1 : octavo *m*, -va *f* (en una serie) ⟨(on) the eighth of May : el ocho de mayo⟩ 2 : octavo *m*, octava parte *f*

eight hundred¹ *adj* : ochocientos

eight hundred² *n* : ochocientos

eightieth¹ ['eɪtɪəθ] *adj* : octogésimo

eightieth² *n* 1 : octogésimo *m*, -ma *f* (en una serie) 2 : ochentavo *m*, ochentava parte *f*

eighty¹ ['eɪti] *adj & pron* : ochenta

eighty² *n, pl* **eighties** 1 : ochenta *m* 2 **the eighties** : los ochenta

either¹ ['iːðər, 'aɪ-] *adv* : tampoco ⟨she doesn't believe it and he doesn't, either : ella no lo cree y él tampoco⟩ ⟨me either! : ¡yo tampoco!⟩

either² *adj* 1 : cualquiera (de los dos) ⟨we can watch either movie : podemos ver cualquiera de las dos películas⟩ 2 : ninguno de los dos ⟨she wasn't in either room : no estaba en ninguna de las dos salas⟩ 3 EACH : cada ⟨on either side of : a cada lado de, a ambos lados de⟩

either³ *pron* 1 : cualquiera (de los dos) ⟨either of the answers is correct : cualquiera de las dos respuestas es correcta⟩ 2 : ninguno (de los dos) ⟨which of the two do you want? I don't like either : ¿cuál de los dos quieres? no me gusta ninguna⟩ 3 : alguno ⟨is either of you interested? : ¿está alguno de ustedes (dos) interesado?⟩

either⁴ *conj* 1 : o, u ⟨either David or Daniel could go : puede ir (o) David o Daniel⟩ 2 : ni ⟨he didn't call either yesterday or today : no llamó ni ayer ni hoy⟩

ejaculate [ɪ'dʒækjə,leɪt] *v* **-lated; -lating** *vt* 1 : eyacular 2 EXCLAIM : exclamar — *vi* : eyacular

ejaculation [iˌdʒækjə'leɪʃən] *n* 1 : eyaculación *f* (en fisiología) 2 EXCLAMATION : exclamación *f*

eject [ɪ'dʒɛkt] *vt* 1 : expulsar (a alguien) 2 : expulsar (un CD, etc.), expeler (un gas) — *vi* : expulsarse

ejection [ɪ'dʒɛkʃən] *n* : expulsión *f*

eke ['iːk-] *vt* **eked out; eking out** 1 STRETCH : estirar (provisiones, etc.) 2 **to eke out a living** : ganarse la vida a duras penas

EKG [ˌiː'keɪ'dʒiː] *n, pl* **EKGs** 1 → electrocardiogram 2 → electrocardiograph

elaborate¹ [i'læbə,reɪt] *v* **-rated; -rating** *vt* : elaborar (una teoría, etc.) — *vi* **to elaborate on** : ampliar, entrar en detalles sobre

elaborate² [i'læbərət] *adj* 1 DETAILED : detallado, minucioso, muy elaborado 2 COMPLICATED : complicado, muy elaborado — **elaborately** *adv*

elaboration [iˌlæbə'reɪʃən] *n* : elaboración *f*

elapse [i'læps] *vi* **elapsed; elapsing** : transcurrir, pasar

elastic¹ [i'læstɪk] *adj* **1** : elástico **2** : (de) elástico, elastizado (dícese de una cintura, etc.)

elastic² *n* **1** : elástico *m* **2** *or* **elastic band → rubber band**

elasticity [i,læs'tɪsəṭi, ,i:,læs-] *n, pl* **-ties** : elasticidad *f*

elated [i'leɪṭəd] *adj* : eufórico

elation [i'leɪʃən] *n* : euforia *f*, júbilo *m*, alborozo *m*

elbow¹ ['ɛl,bo:] *vt* : darle un codazo a

elbow² *n* : codo *m*

elder¹ ['ɛldər] *adj* : mayor

elder² *n* **1** : anciano *m*, -na *f* ⟨the tribal elders : los ancianos de la tribu⟩ **2** : miembro *m* del consejo (en varias religiones) **3** : mayor *mf* ⟨she's my elder by one year : es un año mayor que yo⟩

elderberry ['ɛldər,bɛri] *n, pl* **-berries** : baya *f* de saúco (fruta), saúco *m* (árbol)

elderly ['ɛldərli] *adj* : mayor, de edad, anciano ⟨the elderly : las personas mayores, los ancianos⟩

eldest ['ɛldəst] *adj* : mayor ⟨the eldest : el/la mayor, el/la de más edad⟩

elect¹ [i'lɛkt] *vt* **1** : elegir ⟨she was elected President : la eligieron Presidenta⟩ **2** : elegir (hacer algo)

elect² *adj* : electo ⟨the president-elect : el presidente electo⟩

elect³ *npl* **the elect** : los elegidos *mpl*

election [i'lɛkʃən] *n* : elección *f* ⟨an election campaign : una campaña electoral⟩

elective¹ [i'lɛktɪv] *adj* **1** : electivo **2** OPTIONAL : facultativo, optativo

elective² *n* : asignatura *f* electiva

electoral [i'lɛktərəl] *adj* : electoral

electorate [i'lɛktərət] *n* : electorado *m*

electric [i'lɛktrɪk] *adj* **1** *or* **electrical** [-trɪkəl] : eléctrico **2** THRILLING : electrizante, emocionante

electric cord → cord

electrician [i,lɛk'trɪʃən] *n* : electricista *mf*

electricity [i,lɛk'trɪsəṭi] *n, pl* **-ties** **1** : electricidad *f* **2** CURRENT : corriente *m* eléctrica

electric razor → razor

electric shock → shock²

electric socket → socket

electrification [i,lɛktrəfə'keɪʃən] *n* : electrificación *f*

electrify [i'lɛktrə,faɪ] *vt* **-fied; -fying** **1** : electrificar **2** THRILL : electrizar, emocionar

electrocardiogram [i,lɛktro'kɑrdiə,græm] *n* : electrocardiograma *m*

electrocardiograph [i,lɛktro'kɑrdiə,græf] *n* : electrocardiógrafo *m*

electrocute [i'lɛktrə,kju:t] *vt* **-cuted; -cuting** : electrocutar

electrocution [i,lɛktrə'kju:ʃən] *n* : electrocución *f*

electrode [i'lɛk,tro:d] *n* : electrodo *m*

electrolysis [i,lɛk'trɑləsɪs] *n* : electrólisis *f*

electrolyte [i'lɛktrə,laɪt] *n* : electrolito *m*

electromagnet [i,lɛktro'mægnət] *n* : electroimán *m*

electromagnetic [i,lɛktromæg'nɪṭɪk] *adj* : electromagnético — **electromagnetically** [-'ṭɪkli] *adv*

electromagnetism [i,lɛktro'mægnə,-tɪzəm] *n* : electromagnetismo *m*

electron [i'lɛk,trɑn] *n* : electrón *m*

electronic [i,lɛk'trɑnɪk] *adj* : electrónico ⟨electronic devices : aparatos electrónicos⟩ — **electronically** [-nɪkli] *adv*

electronic cigarette *n* : cigarrillo *m* electrónico, vaporizador *m*, vaporeador *m*

electronic mail *n* : correo *m* electrónico

electronics [i,lɛk'trɑnɪks] *n* **1** : electrónica *f* **2** : sistema *m* electrónico (de un aparato)

electroplate [i'lɛktrə,pleɪt] *vt* **-plated; -plating** : galvanizar mediante electrólisis

elegance ['ɛləgənts] *n* : elegancia *f*

elegant ['ɛləgənt] *adj* : elegante — **elegantly** *adv*

elegiac [,ɛlə'dʒaɪək] *adj* : elegíaco

elegy ['ɛlədʒi] *n, pl* **-gies** : elegía *f*

element ['ɛləmənt] *n* **1** COMPONENT : elemento *m*, factor *m* ⟨the element of surprise : el factor sorpresa⟩ **2** : elemento *m* (en la química) **3** MILIEU : elemento *m*, medio *m* ⟨to be in one's element : estar en su elemento⟩ **4** GROUP : elemento *m*, grupo *m* ⟨criminal elements : elementos criminales⟩ **5 elements** *npl* RUDIMENTS : elementos *mpl* (básicos), rudimentos *mpl* **6 the elements** WEATHER : los elementos *mpl* **7** *or* **heating element** : resistencia *f*

elemental [,ɛlə'mɛntəl] *adj* **1** BASIC : elemental, primario **2** : elemental (dícese de los elementos químicos)

elementary [,ɛlə'mɛntri] *adj* **1** SIMPLE : elemental **2** : de enseñanza primaria ⟨elementary (school) teachers : maestros de enseñanza primaria⟩ ⟨elementary school/education : escuela/educación primaria⟩

elephant ['ɛləfənt] *n* : elefante *m*, -ta *f*

elevate ['ɛlə,veɪt] *vt* **-vated; -vating** **1** RAISE : elevar, levantar, alzar **2** PROMOTE : elevar, ascender **3** UPLIFT : elevar, levantar (el espíritu, etc.) **4** INCREASE : aumentar, elevar (niveles, etc.)

elevation [,ɛlə'veɪʃən] *n* **1** : elevación *f* **2** ALTITUDE : altura *f*, altitud *f* **3** PROMOTION : ascenso *m*

elevator ['ɛlə,veɪṭər] *n* **1** : ascensor *m*, elevador *m* **2** *or* **freight elevator** : montacargas *m*

eleven¹ [i'lɛvən] *adj & pron* : once

eleven² *n* : once *m*

eleventh¹ [i'lɛvənθ] *adj* : undécimo

eleventh² *n* **1** : undécimo *m*, -ma *f* (en una serie) **2** : onceavo *m*, onceava parte *f*

elf ['ɛlf] *n, pl* **elves** ['ɛlvz] : elfo *m*, duende *m*

elfin ['ɛlfən] *adj* **1** : de elfo, menudo **2** ENCHANTING, MAGIC : mágico, encantador

elfish ['ɛlfɪʃ] *adj* **1** : de elfo **2** MISCHIEVOUS : travieso

elicit [i'lɪsət] *vt* : provocar (una reacción), obtener (una respuesta)

eligibility [ˌɛləʤə'bɪləti] *n*, *pl* **-ties** : elegibilidad *f*

eligible ['ɛləʤəbəl] *adj* **1** QUALIFIED : que reúne los requisitos, elegible ⟨to be eligible for benefits : tener derecho a recibir prestaciones⟩ ⟨eligible voters : votantes habilitados⟩ **2** SUITABLE : idóneo ⟨an eligible bachelor : un buen partido⟩

eliminate [i'lɪmə,neɪt] *vt* **-nated; -nating 1** : eliminar **2** RULE OUT : eliminar, descartar

elimination [i,lɪmə'neɪʃən] *n* : eliminación *f*

elite¹ [eɪ'li:t, i-] *n* : elite *f*, élite *f*

elite² *n* : de elite, de élite

elitist [eɪ'li:tɪst, i-] *n* : elitista *mf* — **elitist** *adj*

elixir [i'lɪksər] *n* : elixir *m*

elk ['ɛlk] *n* : alce *m* (de Europa), uapití *m* (de América)

ellipse [i'lɪps, ɛ-] *n* : elipse *f*

ellipsis [i'lɪpsəs, ɛ-] *n*, *pl* **-lipses** [-,si:z] **1** : elipsis *f* **2** : puntos *mpl* suspensivos (en la puntuación)

elliptical [i'lɪptɪkəl, ɛ-] *or* **elliptic** [-tɪk] *adj* : elíptico

elm ['ɛlm] *n* : olmo *m*

elocution [ˌɛlə'kju:ʃən] *n* : elocución *f*

elongate [i'lɔŋ,geɪt] *vt* **-gated; -gating** : alargar

elongation [ˌi:,lɔŋ'geɪʃən] *n* : alargamiento *m*

elope [i'lo:p] *vi* **eloped; eloping** : fugarse

elopement [i'lo:pmənt] *n* : fuga *f*

eloquence ['ɛləkwənts] *n* : elocuencia *f*

eloquent ['ɛləkwənt] *adj* : elocuente — **eloquently** *adv*

El Salvadoran [ˌɛlˌsælvə'dorən] *n* : salvadoreño *m*, -ña *f* — **El Salvadoran** *adj*

else¹ ['ɛls] *adv* **1** (*indicating an alternative or addition*) ⟨how else? : ¿de qué otro modo?⟩ ⟨when else? : ¿a qué otra hora?, ¿en qué otro día? (etc.)⟩ ⟨where else? : ¿en qué otro lugar?⟩ ⟨to go someplace else : ir a otro sitio⟩ **2 or else** OTHERWISE : si no, de lo contrario

else² *adj* **1** OTHER : otro ⟨anyone else : cualquier otro⟩ ⟨someone else : otro, otra persona⟩ ⟨everyone else : todos los demás⟩ ⟨everything else : todo lo demás⟩ ⟨nobody else : ningún otro, nadie más⟩ ⟨somebody else : otra persona⟩ **2** MORE : más ⟨nothing else : nada más⟩ ⟨anything else? : ¿algo más?⟩ ⟨what else? : ¿qué más?⟩

elsewhere ['ɛls,hwɛr] *adv* : en/a otra parte, en/a otro sitio/lugar ⟨to go elsewhere : ir a otro lugar⟩ ⟨elsewhere in the book : en otra parte del libro⟩

elucidate [i'lu:sə,deɪt] *vt* **-dated; -dating** : dilucidar, elucidar, esclarecer

elucidation [i,lu:sə'deɪʃən] *n* : elucidación *f*, esclarecimiento *m*

elude [i'lu:d] *vt* **eluded; eluding** : eludir, evadir

elusive [i'lu:sɪv] *adj* **1** : esquivo, escurridizo (dícese de una presa, etc.) ⟨an elusive goal : una meta difícil de alcan-

zar⟩ **2** : difícil de precisar (dícese de una cualidad, etc.)

elusively [i'lu:sɪvli] *adv* : de manera esquiva

elves → **elf**

em- → **en-**

'em [əm] → **them**

emaciate [i'meɪʃi,eɪt] *vt* **-ated; -ating** : enflaquecer

e–mail¹ *or* **email** ['i:,meɪl] *vt* : enviarle/mandarle un email a (alguien), enviarle/mandarle un correo electrónico a (alguien), enviar/mandar (algo) por email, enviar/mandar (algo) por correo electrónico — *vi* : enviar/mandar un email, enviar/mandar un correo electrónico

e–mail² *or* **email** *n* : email *m*, correo *m* electrónico ⟨e-mail address : dirección de correo electrónico, dirección de email⟩

emanate ['ɛmə,neɪt] *v* **-nated; -nating** *vi* : emanar, provenir, proceder — *vt* : emanar

emanation [ˌɛmə'neɪʃən] *n* : emanación *f*

emancipate [i'mæntsə,peɪt] *vt* **-pated; -pating** : emancipar

emancipation [i,mæntsə'peɪʃən] *n* : emancipación *f*

embalm [ɪm'bɑm, ɛm-, -'bɑlm] *vt* : embalsamar

embankment [ɪm'bæŋkmənt, ɛm-] *n* : terraplén *m*, muro *m* de contención

embargo¹ [ɪm'bɑrgo, ɛm-] *vt* **-goed; -going** : imponer un embargo sobre

embargo² *n*, *pl* **-goes** : embargo *m*

embark [ɪm'bɑrk, ɛm-] *vt* : embarcar — *vi* **1** : embarcarse **2 to embark on** START : emprender, embarcarse en

embarkation [ˌɛmbɑr'keɪʃən] *n* : embarque *m*, embarco *m*

embarrass [ɪm'bæros, ɛm-] *vt* : avergonzar, abochornar ⟨you embarrassed me : me hiciste pasar vergüenza⟩

embarrassed [ɪm'bærəst ɛm-] *adj* : embarazoso, violento ⟨I'm embarrassed (about it) : me da vergüenza⟩ ⟨an embarrassed silence : un silencio embarazoso⟩

embarrassing [ɪm'bærəsɪŋ, ɛm-] *adj* : embarazoso, violento ⟨how embarrassing! : ¡qué vergüenza!⟩

embarrassment [ɪm'bærəsmənt, ɛm-] *n* : vergüenza *f*, bochorno *m*, pena *f* ⟨to be an embarrassment to someone : ser una vergüenza para alguien⟩

embassy ['ɛmbəsi] *n*, *pl* **-sies** : embajada *f*

embed [ɪm'bɛd, ɛm-] *vt* **-bedded; -bedding** : incrustar, empotrar (en una pared, etc.), grabar (en la memoria) ⟨a firmly embedded belief : una creencia arraigada⟩

embellish [ɪm'bɛlɪʃ, ɛm-] *vt* : adornar, embellecer

embellishment [ɪm'bɛlɪʃmənt, ɛm-] *n* : adorno *m*

ember ['ɛmbər] *n* : ascua *f*, brasa *f*

embezzle [ɪm'bɛzəl, ɛm-] *vt* **-zled; -zling** : desfalcar, malversar

embezzlement [ɪm'bɛzəlmənt, ɛm-] *n* : desfalco *m*, malversación *f*

embezzler [ɪm'bɛzələr, ɛm-] *n* : desfalcador *m*, -dora *f*; malversador *m*, -dora *f*

embitter [ɪm'bɪtər, ɛm-] *vt* : amargar

emblem ['ɛmbləm] *n* : emblema *m*, símbolo *m*

emblematic [ˌɛmblə'mætɪk] *adj* : emblemático, simbólico

embodiment [ɪm'bɑdimənt, ɛm-] *n* : encarnación *f*, personificación *f*

embody [ɪm'bɑdi, ɛm-] *vt* **-bodied; -bodying 1** PERSONIFY : encarnar, personificar **2** INCLUDE : incorporar

embolism ['ɛmbəˌlɪzəm] *n* : embolia *f*

emboss [ɪm'bɑs, ɛm-, -'bɔs] *vt* : repujar (metal o cuero), grabar en relieve ⟨embossed lettering : caracteres en relieve⟩

embrace¹ [ɪm'breɪs, ɛm-] *v* **-braced; -bracing** *vt* **1** HUG : abrazar **2** ADOPT : adoptar, abrazar (una causa), aceptar (un cambio) **3** WELCOME : aprovechar (una oportunidad) **4** INCLUDE : abarcar — *vi* : abrazarse

embrace² *n* : abrazo *m*

embroider [ɪm'brɔɪdər, ɛm-] *vt* : bordar (una tela), adornar (una historia)

embroidery [ɪm'brɔɪdəri, ɛm-] *n, pl* **-deries** : bordado *m*

embroil [ɪm'brɔɪl, ɛm-] *vt* : enredar ⟨to become embroiled in something : enredarse en algo⟩

embryo ['ɛmbriˌoː] *n, pl* **embryos** : embrión *m*

embryonic [ˌɛmbri'ɑnɪk] *adj* : embrionario

emend [i'mɛnd] *vt* : enmendar, corregir

emendation [ˌiˌmɛn'deɪʃən] *n* : enmienda *f*

emerald¹ ['ɛmrəld, 'ɛmə-] *adj* : verde esmeralda

emerald² *n* : esmeralda *f*

emerge [i'mərdʒ] *vi* **emerged; emerging 1** : salir, emerger ⟨to emerge from : salir de⟩ **2** ARISE, DEVELOP : surgir **3** : revelarse (dícese de la verdad, etc.) **4** **to emerge victorious** : salir victorioso

emergence [i'mərdʒənts] *n* : aparición *f*, surgimiento *m*

emergency [i'mərdʒəntsi] *n, pl* **-cies 1** : emergencia *f* ⟨in case of emergency : en caso de emergencia⟩ ⟨emergency exit/landing/vehicle : salida/aterrizaje/vehículo de emergencia⟩ **2** : urgencia *f*, emergencia *f* (en medicina)

emergency brake *n* HANDBRAKE : freno *m* de mano

emergency room *n* : sala *f* de urgencia(s), sala *f* de emergencia(s)

emergent [i'mərdʒənt] *adj* : emergente

emery ['ɛməri] *n, pl* **-eries** : esmeril *m*

emery board *n* : lima *f* de uñas (de esmeril)

emigrant ['ɛmɪgrənt] *n* : emigrante *mf*

emigrate ['ɛməˌgreɪt] *vi* **-grated; -grating** : emigrar

emigration [ˌɛmə'greɪʃən] *n* : emigración *f*

eminence ['ɛmənənts] *n* **1** PROMINENCE : eminencia *f*, prestigio *m*, renombre *m* **2** DIGNITARY : eminencia *f*; dignatario *m*, -ria *f* ⟨Your Eminence : Su Eminencia⟩

eminent ['ɛmənənt] *adj* : eminente, ilustre

eminently ['ɛmənəntli] *adv* : sumamente

emissary ['ɛməˌsɛri] *n, pl* **-saries** : emisario *m*, -ria *f*

emission [i'mɪʃən] *n* : emisión *f*

emit [i'mɪt] *vt* **emitted; emitting** : emitir, despedir, producir

emoji [i'moːdʒi] *n, pl* **emoji** *or* **emojis** : emoji *m*

emote [i'moːt] *vi* **emoted; emoting** : exteriorizar las emociones

emoticon [i'moːtiˌkɑn] *n* : emoticono *m*, emoticón *m*

emotion [i'moːʃən] *n* : emoción *f*, sentimiento *m*

emotional [i'moːʃənəl] *adj* **1** : emocional, afectivo ⟨an emotional reaction : una reacción emocional⟩ **2** SENSITIVE : emotivo, sensible **3** MOVING : emotivo, conmovedor, emocionante **4 to get emotional** : emocionarse

emotionally [i'moːʃənəli] *adv* : emocionalmente

empathize ['ɛmpəˌθaɪz] *vi* **-thized; -thizing** : sentir empatía ⟨to empathize with : identificarse con⟩

empathy ['ɛmpəθi] *n* : empatía *f*

emperor ['ɛmpərər] *n* : emperador *m*

emphasis ['ɛmfəsɪs] *n, pl* **-phases** [-ˌsiːz] **1** : énfasis *m*, hincapié *m* ⟨to put/place/lay emphasis on : poner énfasis en, hacer hincapié en⟩ **2** : acento *m*, énfasis *m* (en lingüística)

emphasize ['ɛmfəˌsaɪz] *vt* **-sized; -sizing 1** : enfatizar, subrayar, recalcar **2** : acentuar, enfatizar (en lingüística) **3** ACCENTUATE : acentuar, (hacer) resaltar

emphatic [ɪm'fætɪk, ɛm-] *adj* **1** : enfático, enérgico, categórico ⟨an emphatic "no" : un "no" rotundo⟩ ⟨an emphatic victory : una victoria aplastante⟩ **2 to be emphatic about** : poner mucho énfasis en — **emphatically** [-ɪkli] *adv*

empire ['ɛmˌpaɪr] *n* : imperio *m*

empirical [ɪm'pɪrɪkəl, ɛm-] *adj* : empírico — **empirically** [-ɪkli] *adv*

employ¹ [ɪm'plɔɪ, ɛm-] *vt* **1** USE : usar, utilizar, emplear **2** HIRE : contratar, emplear **3** : emplear, dar empleo a ⟨they employ 20 people : emplean a 20 personas⟩ **4** OCCUPY : ocupar, dedicar, emplear

employ² [ɪm'plɔɪ, ɛm-:, 'ɪmˌ-, 'ɛmˌ-] *n* **1** : puesto *m*, cargo *m*, ocupación *f* **2 to be in the employ of** : estar al servicio de, trabajar para

employee [ɪmˌplɔɪ'iː-, ɛm-, -'plɔɪˌiː] *n* : empleado *m*, -da *f*

employer [ɪm'plɔɪər, ɛm-] *n* : patrón *m*, -trona *f*; empleador *m*, -dora *f*

employment [ɪm'plɔɪmənt, ɛm-] *n* : trabajo *m*, empleo *m*

employment agency *n* : agencia *f* de colocación, agencia *f* de trabajo

empower [ɪm'paʊər, ɛm-] *vt* : facultar, autorizar, conferirle poder a

empowerment [ɪm'paʊərmənt, ɛm-] *n* : autorización *f*

empress ['ɛmprəs] *n* : emperatriz *f*

emptiness ['ɛmptinəs] *n* : vacío *m*, vacuidad *f*

empty[1] ['εmpti] v **-tied; -tying** vt : vaciar ⟨to empty (out) your pockets : vaciar sus bolsillos⟩ — vi **1** or **to empty out** : vaciarse (dícese de un lugar) **2 to empty into** : desaguar en (dícese de un río)

empty[2] adj **emptier; -est 1** : vacío **2** VACANT : desocupado, libre **3** MEANINGLESS : vacío, hueco, vano

empty[3] n, pl **-ties** : envase m vacío

empty–handed [ˌεmpti'hændəd] adj : con las manos vacías

empty–headed [ˌεmpti'hεdəd] adj : cabeza hueca, tonto

emu ['iː,mjuː] n : emú m

emulate ['εmjə,leɪt] vt **-lated; -lating** : emular

emulation [ˌεmjə'leɪʃən] n : emulación f

emulsifier [ɪ'mʌlsə,faɪər] n : emulsionante m

emulsify [ɪ'mʌlsə,faɪ] vt **-fied; -fying** : emulsionar

emulsion [ɪ'mʌlʃən] n : emulsión f

en– or **em– pref** : en-, em- ⟨entangle : enredar⟩ ⟨empathy : empatía⟩

enable [ɪ'neɪbəl, ε-] vt **-abled; -abling 1** PERMIT : permitir, hacer posible, posibilitar ⟨to enable someone to do something : permitirle a alguien hacer algo⟩ **2** ACTIVATE : activar, habilitar

enact [ɪ'nækt, ε-] vt **1** : promulgar (un ley o decreto) **2** : representar (un papel en el teatro)

enactment [ɪ'næktmənt, ε-] n : promulgación f

enamel[1] [ɪ'næməl] vt **-eled** or **-elled; -eling** or **-elling** : esmaltar

enamel[2] n : esmalte m

enamor [ɪ'næmər] vt **1** : enamorar **2 to be enamored of** : estar enamorado de (una persona), estar entusiasmado con (algo)

encamp [ɪn'kæmp, εn-] vi : acampar

encampment [ɪn'kæmpmənt, εn-] n : campamento m

encase [ɪn'keɪs, εn-] vt **-cased; -casing** : encerrar, revestir

-ence suf : -encia ⟨independence : independencia⟩

encephalitis [ɪnˌsεfə'laɪtəs, εn-] n, pl **-litides** ['lɪtəˌdiːz] : encefalitis f

enchant [ɪn'tʃænt, εn-] vt **1** BEWITCH : hechizar, encantar, embrujar **2** CHARM, FASCINATE : cautivar, fascinar, encantar

enchanting [ɪn'tʃæntɪŋ, εn-] adj : encantador

enchanter [ɪn'tʃæntər, εn-] n SORCERER : mago m, encantador m

enchantment [ɪn'tʃæntmənt, εn-] n **1** SPELL : encanto m, hechizo m **2** CHARM : encanto m

enchantress [ɪn'tʃæntrəs, εn-] n **1** SORCERESS : maga f, hechicera f **2** CHARMER : mujer f cautivadora

enchilada [εntʃə'lɑdə] n : enchilada f

encircle [ɪn'sərkəl, εn-] vt **-cled; -cling** : rodear, ceñir, cercar

enclose [ɪn'kloːz, εn-] vt **-closed; -closing 1** SURROUND : encerrar, cercar, rodear **2** INCLUDE : incluir, adjuntar,

acompañar ⟨please find enclosed : le(s) envío adjunto⟩

enclosure [ɪn'kloːʒər, εn-] n **1** ENCLOSING : encierro m **2** : cercado m (de terreno), recinto m ⟨an enclosure for the press : un recinto para la prensa⟩ **3** : anexo m (de una carta), documento m adjunto

encode [ɪn'koːd, εn-] vt **1** : cifrar (mensajes, etc.) **2** : codificar (datos, etc.) **3** : codificar (tarjetas de crédito, etc.)

encompass [ɪn'kʌmpəs, εn-, -'kɑm-] vt **1** SURROUND : circundar, rodear **2** INCLUDE : abarcar, comprender

encore ['ɑn,kor] n : bis m ⟨encore! : ¡otra!⟩

encounter[1] [ɪn'kaʊntər, εn-] vt **1** MEET : encontrar, encontrarse con, toparse con, tropezar con **2** FIGHT : combatir, luchar contra

encounter[2] n : encuentro m

encourage [ɪn'kərɪdʒ, εn-] vt **-aged; -aging 1** : animar, alentar ⟨she encouraged me to participate : me animó a participar⟩ **2** FOSTER : fomentar, promover

encouragement [ɪn'kərɪdʒmənt, εn-] n : ánimo m, aliento m

encouraging [ɪn'kərədʒɪŋ, εn-] adj : alentador, esperanzador

encroach [ɪn'kroːtʃ, εn-] vi **to encroach on/upon** : invadir (territorio), abusar (derechos), quitar (tiempo)

encroachment [ɪn'kroːtʃmənt, εn-] n : invasión f, usurpación f

encrust [ɪn'krʌst, εn-] vt **1** : recubrir con una costra **2** INLAY : incrustar ⟨encrusted with gems : incrustado de gemas⟩

encrypt [ɪn'krɪpt, εn-] vt : cifrar, encriptar (datos, etc.)

encumber [ɪn'kʌmbər, εn-] vt **1** BLOCK : obstruir, estorbar **2** BURDEN : cargar, gravar

encumbrance [ɪn'kʌmbrənts, εn-] n : estorbo m, carga f, gravamen m

encyclopedia [ɪnˌsaɪklə'piːdiə, εn-] n : enciclopedia f

encyclopedic [ɪnˌsaɪklə'piːdɪk, εn-] adj : enciclopédico

end[1] ['εnd] vt **1** STOP : terminar, poner fin a, acabar con **2** CONCLUDE : concluir, terminar — vi **1** : terminar(se), acabar, concluir(se) **2 to end up doing something** : acabar/terminar haciendo algo, acabar/terminar por hacer algo

end[2] n **1** : extremo m (de una cuerda, etc.), punta f (de un lápiz, etc.), final m (de una calle, etc.) ⟨I'm at the end of my rope : no puedo aguantar más⟩ **2** CONCLUSION : fin m, final m ⟨to bring something to an end : terminar algo, poner fin a algo⟩ ⟨to come to an end : llegar a su fin⟩ ⟨to put an end to : acabar con, poner fin a⟩ **3** AIM : fin m, objetivo m **4** : ala f (en fútbol americano) ⟨tight end : ala cerrada⟩ **5 at the end** : al fin, al final ⟨at the end of April : a fines/finales de abril⟩ **6 end to end** : juntados por los extremos **7 in the end** : al final **8 on end** : parado, (en posición) vertical ⟨my hair stood on end : se me pusieron los pelos de punta⟩ **9 on end** : sin parar ⟨he read for hours on end : pasaba horas enteras leyendo⟩

endanger [ɪn'deɪndʒər, ɛn-] *vt* : poner en peligro

endangered [ɪn'deɪndʒərd, ɛn-] *adj* : en peligro

endear [ɪn'dɪr, ɛn-] *vt* **to endear oneself to** : ganarse la simpatía de, granjearse el cariño de

endearing [ɪn'dɪrɪŋ, ɛn-] *adj* : encantador

endearment [ɪn'dɪrmənt, ɛn-] *n* : expresión *f* de cariño

endeavor¹ [ɪn'dɛvər, ɛn-] *vt* : intentar, esforzarse por ⟨he endeavored to improve his work : intentó mejorar su trabajo⟩

endeavor² *n* : intento *m*, esfuerzo *m*

ending ['ɛndɪŋ] *n* **1** CONCLUSION : final *m*, desenlace *m* **2** SUFFIX : sufijo *m*, terminación *f*

endive ['ɛn,daɪv, ,ɑn'di:v] *n* : endibia *f*, endivia *f*

endless ['ɛndləs] *adj* **1** INTERMINABLE : interminable, inacabable, sin fin ⟨endless hours : horas interminables⟩ ⟨endless prairie : praderas interminables⟩ ⟨an endless source of : una fuente inagotable de⟩ ⟨with endless patience : con paciencia infinita⟩ **2** COUNTLESS : innumerable, incontable ⟨endless possibilities : posibilidades infinitas⟩ ⟨endless questions : preguntas incesantes⟩

endlessly ['ɛndləsli] *adv* : interminablemente, eternamente, sin parar

endocrine ['ɛndəkrən, -,kraɪn, -,kri:n] *adj* : endocrino

endorse [ɪn'dɔrs, ɛn-] *vt* **-dorsed; -dorsing** **1** SIGN : endosar, firmar **2** APPROVE, SUPPORT : aprobar, respaldar **3** PROMOTE : promocionar

endorsement [ɪn'dɔrsmənt, ɛn-] *n* **1** SIGNATURE : endoso *m*, firma *f* **2** APPROVAL, SUPPORT : aprobación *f*, aval *m*

endow [ɪn'daʊ, ɛn-] *vt* : dotar ⟨to be endowed with : estar dotado de⟩

endowment [ɪn'daʊmənt, ɛn-] *n* **1** FUNDING : dotación *f* **2** DONATION : donación *f*, legado *m* **3** ATTRIBUTE, GIFT : atributo *m*, dotes *fpl*

endurable [ɪn'dʊrəbəl, ɛn-, -'djʊr-] *adj* : tolerable, soportable

endurance [ɪn'dʊrənts, ɛn-, -'djʊr-] *n* : resistencia *f*, aguante *m*

endure [ɪn'dʊr, ɛn-, -'djʊr] *v* **-dured; -during** *vt* **1** BEAR : resistir, soportar, aguantar **2** TOLERATE : tolerar, soportar — *vi* LAST : durar, perdurar

enema ['ɛnəmə] *n* : enema *m*, lavativa *f*

enemy ['ɛnəmi] *n, pl* **-mies** : enemigo *m*, -ga *f*

energetic [,ɛnər'dʒɛtɪk] *adj* : enérgico, vigoroso — **energetically** [-ɪkli] *adv*

energize ['ɛnər,dʒaɪz] *vt* **-gized; -gizing** **1** ACTIVATE : activar **2** INVIGORATE : vigorizar

energy ['ɛnərdʒi] *n, pl* **-gies** **1** : energía *f* **2** EFFORT : energías *fpl*, esfuerzo *m*

enervate ['ɛnər,veɪt] *vt* **-vated; -vating** : enervar, debilitar

enfold [ɪn'fo:ld, ɛn-] *vt* : envolver

enforce [ɪn'fɔrs, ɛn-] *vt* **-forced; -forcing** **1** : hacer respetar, hacer cumplir (una ley, etc.) **2** IMPOSE : imponer ⟨to enforce one's will : imponer su voluntad⟩

enforcement [ɪn'fɔrsmənt, ɛn-] *n* : imposición *f*

enfranchise [ɪn'fræn,tʃaɪz, ɛn-] *vt* **-chised; -chising** : conceder el voto a

enfranchisement [ɪn'fræn,tʃaɪzmənt, ɛn-] *n* : concesión *f* del voto

engage [ɪn'geɪdʒ, ɛn-] *v* **-gaged; -gaging** *vt* **1** ABSORB : captar (la atención, etc.) ⟨to engage someone in conversation : entablar conversación con alguien⟩ **2** : engranar ⟨to engage the clutch : embragar⟩ **3** HIRE : contratar **4** : entablar combate con (un enemigo) — *vi* **1** MESH, INTERLOCK : engranar **2 to engage in** PURSUE : dedicarse a (una actividad) **3 to engage in** INITIATE : entablar

engaged [ɪn'geɪdʒd, ɛn-] *adj* **1** BETROTHED : comprometido, prometido ⟨to get engaged (to someone) : comprometerse (con alguien), prometerse (a alguien)⟩ **2 to be engaged in** : dedicarse a (una actividad)

engagement [ɪn'geɪdʒmənt, ɛn-] *n* **1** APPOINTMENT : compromiso *m*, cita *f* **2** BETROTHAL : compromiso *m* (acto), noviazgo *m* (período) ⟨engagement ring : anillo de compromiso⟩

engaging [ɪn'geɪdʒɪŋ, ɛn-] *adj* : atractivo, encantador, interesante

engender [ɪn'dʒɛndər, ɛn-] *vt* **-dered; -dering** : engendrar

engine ['ɛndʒən] *n* **1** MOTOR : motor *m* **2** LOCOMOTIVE : locomotora *f*, máquina *f*

engineer¹ [,ɛndʒə'nɪr] *vt* **1** : diseñar, construir (un sistema, un mecanismo, etc.) **2** CONTRIVE : maquinar, tramar, fraguar

engineer² *n* **1** : ingeniero *m*, -ra *f* **2** : maquinista *mf* (de locomotoras)

engineering [,ɛndʒə'nɪrɪŋ] *n* : ingeniería *f*

English¹ ['ɪŋglɪʃ, 'ɪŋlɪʃ] *adj* : inglés ⟨the English language : la lengua inglesa⟩ ⟨an English teacher : un profesor de inglés⟩

English² *n* **1** : inglés *m* (idioma) **2 the English** (*used with a plural verb*) : los ingleses

Englishman ['ɪŋglɪʃmən, 'ɪŋlɪʃ-] *n, pl* **-men** [-mən, -,mɛn] : inglés *m*

English muffin *n* : panecillo *m* (que se parte en dos y se come tostado)

Englishwoman ['ɪŋglɪʃ,wʊmən, 'ɪŋlɪʃ-] *n, pl* **-women** [-,wɪmən] : inglesa *f*

engrave [ɪn'greɪv, ɛn-] *vt* **-graved; -graving** : grabar

engraver [ɪn'greɪvər, ɛn-] *n* : grabador *m*, -dora *f*

engraving [ɪn'greɪvɪŋ, ɛn-] *n* : grabado *m*

engross [ɪn'gro:s, ɛn-] *vt* : absorber ⟨to be engrossed in something : estar absorto en algo⟩

engrossed [ɪn'gro:st, ɛn-] *adj* : absorto

engrossing [ɪn'gro:sɪŋ, ɛn-] *adj* : fascinante, absorbente

engulf [ɪn'gʌlf, ɛn-] *vt* : envolver, sepultar

enhance [ɪn'hænts, ɛn-] *vt* **-hanced; -hancing** : realzar, aumentar, mejorar

enhancement [ɪn'hæntsmənt, ɛn-] *n* : mejora *f*, realce *m*, aumento *m*

enigma [ɪ'nɪgmə] *n* : enigma *m*

enigmatic [ˌɛnɪg'mætɪk, ˌɛn-] *adj* : enigmático — **enigmatically** [-tɪkli] *adv*

enjoin [ɪn'dʒɔɪn, ɛn-] *vt* **1** COMMAND : ordenar, imponer **2** FORBID : prohibir, vedar

enjoy [ɪn'dʒɔɪ, ɛn-] *vt* **1** : disfrutar, gozar de ⟨did you enjoy the book? : ¿te gustó el libro?⟩ ⟨to enjoy good health : gozar de buena salud⟩ **2 to enjoy oneself** : divertirse, pasarlo bien

enjoyable [ɪn'dʒɔɪəbəl, ɛn-] *adj* : agradable, placentero

enjoyment [ɪn'dʒɔɪmənt, ɛn-] *n* : placer *m*, goce *m*, disfrute *m*, deleite *m*

enlarge [ɪn'lɑrdʒ, ɛn-] *v* **-larged; -larging** *vt* : ampliar (una foto, etc.), agrandar (un espacio) — *vi* **1** : ampliarse **2 to enlarge upon** : extenderse sobre, entrar en detalles sobre

enlargement [ɪn'lɑrdʒmənt, ɛn-] *n* : expansión *f*, ampliación *f* (dícese de fotografías)

enlighten [ɪn'laɪtən, ɛn-] *vt* **1** INSTRUCT : ilustrar **2** : iluminar (en religión)

enlightenment [ɪn'laɪtənmənt, ɛn-] *n* **1** : ilustración *f* ⟨the Enlightenment : la Ilustración⟩ **2** CLARIFICATION : aclaración *f*

enlist [ɪn'lɪst, ɛn-] *vt* **1** ENROLL : alistar, reclutar **2** SECURE : conseguir ⟨to enlist the support of : conseguir el apoyo de⟩ — *vi* : alistarse

enlisted man [ɪn'lɪstəd, ɛn-] *n* : soldado *m* raso

enlistment [ɪn'lɪstmənt, ɛn-] *n* : alistamiento *m*, reclutamiento *m*

enliven [ɪn'laɪvən, ɛn-] *vt* : animar, alegrar, darle vida a

en masse [ɑn'mæs, -'mɑs, ɛn-] *adv* : en masa, masivamente

enmity ['ɛnməti] *n, pl* **-ties** : enemistad *f*, animadversión *f*

ennoble [ɪ'noːbəl, ɛ-] *vt* **-bled; -bling** : ennoblecer

ennui [ˌɑn'wiː] *n* : hastío *m*, tedio *m*, fastidio *m*, aburrimiento *m*

enormity [ɪ'nɔrməti] *n, pl* **-ties 1** ATROCITY : atrocidad *f*, barbaridad *f* **2** IMMENSITY : enormidad *f*, inmensidad *f*

enormous [ɪ'nɔrməs] *adj* : enorme, inmenso, tremendo — **enormously** *adv*

enough¹ [ɪ'nʌf] *adv* **1** : bastante, suficientemente ⟨it's small enough to fit in a briefcase : es lo bastante pequeño como para caber en un maletín⟩ **2** QUITE : bastante ⟨it seems simple enough : parece bastante sencillo⟩ **3 fair enough!** : ¡está bien!, ¡de acuerdo! **4 strangely/ oddly enough** : por extraño que parezca **5 sure enough** : en efecto, sin duda alguna **6 well enough** : muy bien, bastante bien

enough² *adj* : bastante, suficiente ⟨do we

have enough chairs? : ¿tenemos suficientes sillas?⟩

enough³ *pron* : (lo) suficiente, (lo) bastante ⟨enough to eat : lo suficiente para comer⟩ ⟨it's more than enough : basta y sobra, es más que suficiente⟩ ⟨it's not enough : no basta⟩ ⟨I've had enough! : ¡estoy harto!, ¡está bueno ya!⟩ ⟨(that's) enough! : ¡basta ya!⟩

enquire [ɪn'kwaɪr, ɛn-], **enquiry** ['ɪnˌkwaɪri, 'ɛn-, -kwəri; ɪn'kwaɪri, ɛn'-] → **inquire, inquiry**

enrage [ɪn'reɪdʒ, ɛn-] *vt* **-raged; -raging** : enfurecer, encolerizar

enraged [ɪn'reɪdʒd, ɛn-] *adj* : enfurecido, furioso

enrapture [ɪn'ræptʃər, ɛn-] *vt* **-tured; -turing** : cautivar, arrobar

enrich [ɪn'rɪtʃ, ɛn-] *vt* : enriquecer

enrichment [ɪn'rɪtʃmənt, ɛn-] *n* : enriquecimiento *m*

enroll *or* **enrol** [ɪn'roːl, ɛn-] *v* **-rolled; -rolling** *vt* : matricular, inscribir — *vi* : matricularse, inscribirse

enrollment [ɪn'roːlmənt, ɛn-] *n* : matrícula *f*, inscripción *f*

en route [ɑ'ruːt, ɛn'raʊt] *adv* : de camino, por el camino

ensconce [ɪn'skɑnts, ɛn-] *vt* **-sconced; -sconcing** : acomodar, instalar, establecer cómodamente

ensemble [ɑn'sɑmbəl] *n* : conjunto *m*

enshrine [ɪn'ʃraɪn, ɛn-] *vt* **-shrined; -shrining** : conservar religiosamente, preservar

ensign ['ɛntsən, 'ɛnˌsaɪn] *n* **1** FLAG : enseña *f*, pabellón *m* **2** : alférez *mf* (de fragata)

enslave [ɪn'sleɪv, ɛn-] *vt* **-slaved; -slaving** : esclavizar

enslavement [ɪn'sleɪvmənt, ɛn-] *n* : esclavización *f*

ensnare [ɪn'snær, ɛn-] *vt* **-snared; -snaring** : atrapar

ensue [ɪn'suː, ɛn-] *vi* **-sued; -suing** : seguir, resultar ⟨in the ensuing weeks : en las semanas siguientes⟩

ensure [ɪn'ʃʊr, ɛn-] *vt* **-sured; -suring** : asegurar, garantizar

entail [ɪn'teɪl, ɛn-] *vt* : implicar, suponer, conllevar

entangle [ɪn'tæŋgəl, ɛn-] *vt* **-gled; -gling** : enredar

entanglement [ɪn'tæŋgəlmənt, ɛn-] *n* : enredo *m*

enter ['ɛntər] *vt* **1** : entrar en/a **2** JOIN : entrar en/a, incorporarse a, ingresar a **3** : entrar en/a (un debate, una profesión, etc.) **4** BEGIN : entrar en (una etapa, etc.) **5** RECORD : anotar, inscribir **6** INPUT : introducir, dar entrada a **7** : presentar (una queja, etc.) ⟨she entered a guilty plea : se declaró culpable⟩ **8** : presentarse a (un concurso, etc.), inscribirse en (una carrera, etc.) — *vi* **1** : entrar **2 to enter into** : entrar en, establecer (un acuerdo), entablar (negociaciones, etc.) **3 to enter into** AFFECT, INFLUENCE : incidir en, influir en

enterprise [ˈɛntərˌpraɪz] n 1 UNDER-TAKING : empresa f 2 BUSINESS : empresa f, firma f 3 INITIATIVE : iniciativa f, empuje m

enterprising [ˈɛntərˌpraɪzɪŋ] adj : emprendedor

entertain [ˌɛntərˈteɪn] vt 1 : recibir, agasajar ⟨to entertain guests : tener invitados⟩ 2 CONSIDER : considerar, contemplar 3 AMUSE : entretener, divertir — vi : tener invitados

entertainer [ˌɛntərˈteɪnər] n : artista mf

entertaining [ˌɛntərˈteɪnɪŋ] adj : entretenido, divertido

entertainment [ˌɛntərˈteɪnmənt] n 1 : entretenimiento m, diversión f 2 SHOW : espectáculo m

enthrall or **enthral** [ɪnˈθrɔl, ɛn-] vt -thralled; -thralling : cautivar, embelesar

enthuse [ɪnˈθuːz, ɛn-] v -thused; -thusing vt 1 EXCITE : entusiasmar 2 : decir con entusiasmo — vi to enthuse over : hablar con entusiasmo sobre

enthusiasm [ɪnˈθuːziˌæzəm, ɛn-, -ˈθjuː-] n : entusiasmo m

enthusiast [ɪnˈθuːziˌæst, ɛn-, -ˈθjuː-, -əst] n : entusiasta mf; aficionado m, -da f

enthusiastic [ɪnˌθuːziˈæstɪk, ɛn-, -ˌθjuː-] adj : entusiasta, aficionado ⟨to be enthusiastic about something : estar entusiasmado con algo⟩

enthusiastically [ɪnˌθuːziˈæstɪkli, ɛn-, -ˌθjuː-] adv : con entusiasmo

entice [ɪnˈtaɪs, ɛn-] vt -ticed; -ticing : atraer, tentar

enticement [ɪnˈtaɪsmənt, ɛn-] n : tentación f, atracción f, señuelo m

entire [ɪnˈtaɪr, ɛn-] adj : entero, completo ⟨the entire family : toda la familia⟩

entirely [ɪnˈtaɪrli, ɛn-] adv : completamente, totalmente

entirety [ɪnˈtaɪrti, ɛn-, -ˈtaɪrəti] n, pl -ties : totalidad f ⟨in its entirety : en su totalidad⟩

entitle [ɪnˈtaɪtəl, ɛn-] vt -tled; -tling 1 : titular, intitular ⟨a book entitled "My Life" : un libro titulado "Mi vida"⟩ 2 : dar derecho a ⟨it entitles you to participate : le da derecho a participar⟩ 3 **to be entitled to** : tener derecho a

entitlement [ɪnˈtaɪtəlmənt, ɛn-] n RIGHT : derecho m

entity [ˈɛntəti] n, pl -ties : entidad f, ente m

entomologist [ˌɛntəˈmɑlədʒɪst] n : entomólogo m, -ga f

entomology [ˌɛntəˈmɑlədʒi] n : entomología f

entourage [ˌɑntuˈrɑʒ] n : séquito m

entrails [ˈɛnˌtreɪlz, -trəlz] npl : entrañas fpl, vísceras fpl

entrance¹ [ɪnˈtræns, ɛn-] vt -tranced; -trancing : encantar, embelesar, fascinar

entrance² [ˈɛntrənts, ɛn-] n 1 ENTERING : entrada f ⟨to make an entrance : entrar en escena⟩ 2 ENTRY : entrada f ⟨the main entrance : la entrada principal⟩ 3 ADMISSION : entrada f, ingreso m ⟨entrance examination : examen de ingreso⟩

entrant [ˈɛntrənt] n : candidato m, -ta f (en un examen); participante mf (en un concurso)

entrap [ɪnˈtræp, ɛn-] vt -trapped; -trapping : atrapar, entrampar, hacer caer en una trampa

entrapment [ɪnˈtræpmənt, ɛn-] n : captura f

entreat [ɪnˈtriːt, ɛn-] vt : suplicar, rogar

entreaty [ɪnˈtriːti, ɛn-] n, pl -treaties : ruego m, súplica f

entrée or **entree** [ˈɑnˌtreɪ, ˌɑn¹-] n : plato m principal

entrench [ɪnˈtrɛntʃ, ɛn-] vt 1 FORTIFY : atrincherar (una posición militar) 2 : consolidar, afianzar ⟨firmly entrenched in his job : afianzado en su puesto⟩

entrepreneur [ˌɑntrəprəˈnər, -ˈnjʊr] n : empresario m, -ria f

entrust [ɪnˈtrʌst, ɛn-] vt **to entrust something to someone** or **to entrust someone with something** : confiarle/encomendarle algo a alguien

entry [ˈɛntri] n, pl -tries 1 ENTRANCE : entrada f ⟨a side entry : una entrada lateral⟩ 2 ENTERING : entrada f ⟨after her entry into politics : después de su entrada en política⟩ 3 ADMISSION : entrada f, ingreso m 4 : entrada f (en un diccionario, etc.), anotación f (en un diario), partida f (en contabilidad) 5 PARTICIPANT : participante mf

entwine [ɪnˈtwaɪn, ɛn-] vt -twined; -twining : entrelazar, entretejer, entrecruzar

enumerate [iˈnuːməˌreɪt, ɛ-, -ˈnjuː-] vt -ated; -ating 1 LIST : enumerar 2 COUNT : contar, enumerar

enumeration [ɪˌnuːməˈreɪʃən, ɛ-, -ˌnjuː-] n : enumeración f, lista f

enunciate [iˈnʌnsiˌeɪt, ɛ-] vt -ated; -ating 1 STATE : enunciar, decir 2 PRONOUNCE : articular, pronunciar

enunciation [ɪˌnʌnsiˈeɪʃən, ɛ-] n 1 STATEMENT : enunciación f, declaración f 2 ARTICULATION : articulación f, pronunciación f, dicción f

envelop [ɪnˈvɛləp, ɛn-] vt : envolver, cubrir

envelope [ˈɛnvəˌloːp, ˈɑn-] n : sobre m

enviable [ˈɛnviəbəl] adj : envidiable

envious [ˈɛnviəs] adj : envidioso ⟨an envious look : una mirada de envidia⟩ ⟨to be envious of : envidiar⟩ — **enviously** adv

environment [ɪnˈvaɪrənmənt, ɛn-, -ˈvaɪərn-] n 1 : ambiente m, entorno m ⟨her home environment : su ambiente/entorno familiar⟩ 2 **the environment** : el medio m ambiente

environmental [ɪnˌvaɪrənˈmɛntəl, ɛn-, -ˌvaɪərn-] adj : ambiental, medioambiental ⟨environmental protection : protección del medio ambiente⟩

environmentalism [-ˌlɪzəm] n : ecologismo m

environmentalist [ɪnˌvaɪrənˈmɛntəlɪst, ɛn-, -ˌvaɪərn-] n : ecologista mf

environmentally [ɪnˌvaɪrənˈmɛntəli, ɛn-, -ˌvaɪərn-] adv : ecológicamente ⟨environmentally friendly : verde, ecológico⟩

environs [ɪnˈvaɪrənz, ɛn-, -ˈvaɪərnz] npl

: alrededores *mpl*, entorno *m*, inmediaciones *fpl*

envisage [ɪnˈvɪzɪʤ, ɛn-] *vt* **-aged; -aging 1** IMAGINE : imaginarse, concebir **2** FORESEE : prever

envision [ɪnˈvɪʒən, ɛn-] *vt* : imaginar

envoy [ˈɛn‚vɔɪ, ˈɑn-] *n* : enviado *m*, -da *f*

envy¹ [ˈɛnvi] *vt* **-vied; -vying** : envidiar

envy² *n*, *pl* **envies** : envidia *f*

enzyme [ˈɛn‚zaɪm] *n* : enzima *f*

eon [ˈiːən, iː‚ɑn] → **aeon**

epaulet [‚ɛpəˈlɛt] *n* : charretera *f*

ephemeral [ɪˈfɛmərəl, -ˈfiː-] *adj* : efímero, fugaz

epic¹ [ˈɛpɪk] *adj* : épico ⟨an epic film : una película épica⟩

epic² *n* : poema *m* épico, epopeya *f*

epicenter [ˈɛpɪ‚sɛntər] *n* : epicentro *m*

epicure [ˈɛpɪ‚kjʊr] *n* : epicúreo *m*, -rea *f*; gastrónomo *m*, -ma *f*

epicurean [‚ɛpɪkjʊˈriːən, -ˈkjʊriən] *adj* : epicúreo

epidemic¹ [‚ɛpəˈdɛmɪk] *adj* : epidémico

epidemic² *n* : epidemia *f*

epidemiology [‚ɛpə‚diːmiˈɑləʤi] *n* : epidemiología *f* — **epidemiologic** [‚ɛpə‚diːmiəˈlɑʤɪk] *or* **epidemiological** [-ˈlɑʤɪkəl] *adj*

epigram [ˈɛpə‚græm] *n* : epigrama *m*

epilepsy [ˈɛpə‚lɛpsi] *n*, *pl* **-sies** : epilepsia *f*

epileptic¹ [‚ɛpəˈlɛptɪk] *adj* : epiléptico

epileptic² *n* : epiléptico *m*, -ca *f*

epilogue [ˈɛpə‚lɔg, -‚lɑg] *n* : epílogo *m*

epiphany [ɪˈpɪfəni] *n*, *pl* **-nies 1 Epiphany** : Epifanía *f* **2 to have an epiphany** : tener una revelación

episcopal [ɪˈpɪskəpəl] *adj* : episcopal

Episcopalian [ɪ‚pɪskəˈpeɪljən] *n* : episcopaliano *m*, -na *f*

episode [ˈɛpə‚soːd] *n* : episodio *m*

episodic [‚ɛpəˈsɑdɪk] *adj* : episódico

epistle [ɪˈpɪsəl] *n* : epístola *f*, carta *f*

epitaph [ˈɛpə‚tæf] *n* : epitafio *m*

epithet [ˈɛpə‚θɛt, -ðət] *n* : epíteto *m*

epitome [ɪˈpɪtəmi] *n* **1** SUMMARY : epítome *m*, resumen *m* **2** EMBODIMENT : personificación *f*

epitomize [ɪˈpɪtə‚maɪz] *vt* **-mized; -mizing 1** SUMMARIZE : resumir **2** EMBODY : ser la personificación de (dícese de una persona), ser representativo de

epoch [ˈɛpək, ˈɛ‚pɑk, ˈiː‚pɑk] *n* : época *f*, era *f*

epoxy [ɪˈpɑksi] *n*, *pl* **epoxies** : resina *f* epoxídica

equable [ˈɛkwəbəl, ˈiː-] *adj* **1** CALM, STEADY : ecuánime **2** UNIFORM : estable (dícese de la temperatura), constante (dícese del clima), uniforme

equably [ˈɛkwəbli, ˈiː-] *adv* : con ecuanimidad

equal¹ [ˈiːkwəl] *vt* **equaled** *or* **equalled; equaling** *or* **equalling 1** : ser igual a ⟨two plus three equals five : dos más tres es igual a cinco⟩ **2** MATCH : igualar

equal² *adj* **1** SAME : igual **2** ADEQUATE : adecuado, capaz ⟨she's equal to the task : es capaz de hacerlo⟩

equal³ *n* : igual *mf*

equality [ɪˈkwɑləti] *n*, *pl* **-ties** : igualdad *f*

equalize [ˈiːkwə‚laɪz] *v* **-ized; -izing** *vt* **1** : igualar (oportunidades), equiparar (salarios) **2** : igualar (la presión) — *vi* **1** : igualar **2** *Brit* TIE : empatar (en deportes)

equalizer [ˈiːkwə‚laɪzər] *n* : gol *m* del empate

equally [ˈiːkwəli] *adv* **1** : igualmente, por igual ⟨to treat everyone equally : tratar a todos (por) igual⟩ ⟨equally quickly : con la misma rapidez⟩ **2** EVENLY : por igual ⟨to divide equally : dividir en/a partes iguales⟩

equal opportunity employer *n* : empresa *f* con una política de igualdad de oportunidades

equal sign *n* : signo *m* de igual

equanimity [‚iːkwəˈnɪməti, ‚ɛ-] *n*, *pl* **-ties** : ecuanimidad *f*

equate [ɪˈkweɪt] *vt* **equated; equating 1** : equiparar, identificar **2 to equate to** : equivaler a, ser igual a

equation [ɪˈkweɪʒən] *n* : ecuación *f*

equator [ɪˈkweɪtər] *n* **the Equator** : el ecuador

equatorial [‚iːkwəˈtoriəl, ‚ɛ-] *adj* : ecuatorial

equestrian¹ [ɪˈkwɛstriən, ɛ-] *adj* : ecuestre

equestrian² *n* : jinete *mf*, caballista *mf*

equilateral [‚iːkwəˈlætərəl, ‚ɛ-] *adj* : equilátero

equilibrium [‚iːkwəˈlɪbriəm, ‚ɛ-] *n*, *pl* **-riums** *or* **-ria** [-briə] : equilibrio *m*

equine [ˈiː‚kwaɪn, ˈɛ-] *adj* : equino, hípico

equinox [ˈiːkwə‚nɑks, ˈɛ-] *n* : equinoccio *m*

equip [ɪˈkwɪp] *vt* **equipped; equipping 1** FURNISH : equipar ⟨to equip someone with something : proveer a alguien de algo⟩ **2** PREPARE : preparar

equipment [ɪˈkwɪpmənt] *n* : equipo *m* ⟨sports equipment : artículos deportivos⟩

equitable [ˈɛkwətəbəl] *adj* : equitativo, justo, imparcial

equity [ˈɛkwəti] *n*, *pl* **-ties 1** FAIRNESS : equidad *f*, imparcialidad *f* **2** VALUE : valor *m* líquido

equivalence [ɪˈkwɪvələnts] *n* : equivalencia *f*

equivalent¹ [ɪˈkwɪvələnt] *adj* : equivalente ⟨to be equivalent to : equivaler a⟩

equivalent² *n* : equivalente *m*

equivocal [ɪˈkwɪvəkəl] *adj* **1** AMBIGUOUS : equívoco, ambiguo **2** QUESTIONABLE : incierto, dudoso, sospechoso

equivocate [ɪˈkwɪvə‚keɪt] *vi* **-cated; -cating** : usar lenguaje equívoco, contestar con evasivas

equivocation [ɪ‚kwɪvəˈkeɪʃən] *n* : evasiva *f*, subterfugio *m*

-er *suf* **1** : -ador *m*, -adora *f* ⟨worker : trabajador(a)⟩ ⟨adapter : adaptador⟩ **2** : más ⟨hotter : más caliente⟩

era [ˈɪrə, ˈɛrə, ˈiːrə] *n* : era *f*, época *f*

eradicate [ɪˈrædə‚keɪt] *vt* **-cated; -cating** : erradicar

erase [ɪˈreɪs] *vt* **erased; erasing** : borrar

eraser [ɪˈreɪsər] *n* : goma *f* de borrar, borrador *m*

erasure [ɪ'reɪʃər] n : tachadura f
ere¹ ['ɛr] conj : antes de que
ere² prep 1 : antes de 2 ere long : dentro de poco
e–reader ['iː,riːdər] n : lector m electrónico, lector m de libros electrónicos
erect¹ [ɪ'rɛkt] vt 1 CONSTRUCT : levantar, erigir (un monumento, etc.) 2 RAISE : levantar, armar
erect² adj : erguido, derecho, erecto
erection [ɪ'rɛkʃən] n 1 : erección f (en fisiología) 2 BUILDING : construcción f
ergonomics [,ərgə'namɪks] npl : ergonomía f
ermine ['ərmən] n : armiño m
erode [ɪ'roːd] v eroded; eroding vt : erosionar (el suelo), corroer (metales) ⟨to erode someone's confidence : minar la confianza de alguien⟩ — vi : erosionarse, corroerse ⟨his popular support eroded : perdió el apoyo popular⟩
erosion [ɪ'roːʒən] n 1 : erosión f, corrosión f 2 DETERIORATION : deterioro m
erotic [ɪ'ratɪk] adj : erótico — erotically [-tɪkli] adv
eroticism [ɪ'ratə,sɪzəm] n : erotismo m
err ['ɛr, 'ər] vi : equivocarse, errar
errand ['ɛrənd] n : mandado m, encargo m, recado m Spain ⟨to run an errand (for somebody) : hacer(le) un mandado (a alguien)⟩
errant ['ɛrənt] adj 1 WANDERING : errante 2 ASTRAY : descarriado
erratic [ɪ'rætɪk] adj 1 INCONSISTENT : errático, irregular, inconsistente 2 ECCENTRIC : excéntrico, raro
erratically [ɪ'rætɪkli] adv : erráticamente, de manera irregular
erroneous [ɪ'roːniəs, ɛ-] adj : erróneo — erroneously adv
error ['ɛrər] n : error m, equivocación f ⟨to be in error : estar en un error⟩ ⟨to do something in error : hacer algo por equivocación⟩ ⟨to make an error : cometer un error⟩ ⟨spelling error : falta de ortografía⟩
ersatz ['ɛr,sats, 'ər,sæts] adj : artificial, sustituto
erstwhile ['ərst,ʰwaɪl] adj : antiguo
erudite ['ɛrə,daɪt, 'ɛrjʊ-] adj : erudito, letrado
erudition [,ɛrə'dɪʃən, ,ɛrjʊ-] n : erudición f
erupt [ɪ'rʌpt] vi 1 : hacer erupción, entrar en erupción (dícese de un volcán) 2 : estallar (dícese de la violencia, etc.)
eruption [ɪ'rʌpʃən] n 1 : erupción f 2 OUTBREAK : estallido m, brote m
eruptive [ɪ'rʌptɪv] adj : eruptivo
escalate ['ɛskə,leɪt] v -lated; -lating vt : intensificar (un conflicto), aumentar (precios) — vi : intensificarse, aumentarse
escalation [,ɛskə'leɪʃən] n : intensificación f, escalada f, aumento m, subida f
escalator ['ɛskə,leɪtər] n : escalera f mecánica
escapade ['ɛskə,peɪd] n : aventura f
escape¹ [ɪ'skeɪp, ɛ-] v -caped; -caping vt 1 : escaparse de (la policía, etc.) ⟨the

name escapes me : el nombre se me escapa⟩ ⟨nothing escapes her (notice) : nada se le escapa⟩ 2 AVOID : escapar a, librarse de (un castigo), salvarse de (la muerte) — vi 1 : escaparse 2 SURVIVE : salvarse
escape² n 1 FLIGHT : fuga f, huida f, escapada f 2 LEAKAGE : escape m, fuga f 3 : escapatoria f, evasión f ⟨to have no escape : no tener escapatoria⟩ ⟨escape from reality : evasión de la realidad⟩
escapee [ɪ,skeɪ'piː, ,ɛ-] n : fugitivo m, -va f
escapism [ɪ'skeɪp,ɪzəm] n : escapismo m — escapist [ɪ'skeɪpɪst] adj
escarole ['ɛskə,roːl] n : escarola f
escarpment [ɪs'karpmənt, ɛs-] n : escarpa f
eschew [ɛ'ʃuː, ɪs'tʃuː] vt : evitar, rehuir, abstenerse de
escort¹ [ɪ'skɔrt, ɛ-] vt 1 : escoltar 2 : llevar (a un prisionero) 3 ACCOMPANY : acompañar
escort² ['ɛs,kɔrt] n 1 : escolta f ⟨under armed/police escort : con escolta armada/policial⟩ 2 COMPANION : acompañante mf
escrow ['ɛs,kroː] n in escrow : en depósito, en custodia de un tercero
Eskimo ['ɛskə,moː] n 1 now sometimes offensive : esquimal mf 2 : esquimal m (idioma) — Eskimo adj
ESL [,iː,ɛs'ɛl] n (English as a second language) : inglés m como lengua extranjera
esophagus [ɪ'safəgəs, iː-] n, pl -gi [-,gaɪ, -,dʒaɪ] : esófago m
esoteric [,ɛsə'tɛrɪk] adj : esotérico, hermético
espadrille ['ɛspə,drɪl] n : alpargata f Arg, Spain, Uru, Ven; sandalia f
especially [ɪ'spɛʃəli] adv 1 : especialmente, particularmente 2 SPECIFICALLY : expresamente, especialmente
espionage ['ɛspiə,naʒ, -,nadʒ] n : espionaje m
espouse [ɪ'spauz, ɛ-] vt espoused; espousing 1 MARRY : casarse con 2 ADOPT, ADVOCATE : apoyar, adherirse a, adoptar
espresso [ɛ'sprɛ,soː] n, pl -sos : café m exprés
essay¹ ['ɛseɪ, 'ɛ,seɪ] vt : intentar, tratar
essay² ['ɛ,seɪ] n 1 : ensayo m (publicado) 2 COMPOSITION, PAPER : redacción f, trabajo m 3 ATTEMPT : intento m
essayist ['ɛ,seɪɪst] n : ensayista mf
essence ['ɛsənts] n 1 CORE : esencia f, núcleo m, meollo m ⟨in essence : esencialmente⟩ 2 EXTRACT : esencia f, extracto m 3 PERFUME : esencia f, perfume m
essential¹ [ɪ'sɛntʃəl] adj : esencial ⟨to be essential to : ser esencial para⟩ — essentially adv
essential² n : elemento m esencial ⟨the (bare) essentials : lo imprescindible⟩
-est suf : (el/la/los/las) más ⟨the biggest : el/la más grande, los/las más grandes⟩
establish [ɪ'stæblɪʃ, ɛ-] vt 1 FOUND : establecer, fundar 2 SET UP : establecer,

instaurar, instituir **3** PROVE : establecer, demostrar

established [ɪˈstæblɪʃt, ɛ-] *adj* **1** ACCEPTED : establecido **2** : de amplia trayectoria (dícese de una empresa, etc.) **3** OFFICIAL : oficial

establishment [ɪˈstæblɪʃmənt, ɛ-] *n* **1** ESTABLISHING : establecimiento *m*, fundación *f*, instauración *f* **2** BUSINESS : negocio *m*, establecimiento *m* **3** the Establishment : la clase dirigente

estate [ɪˈsteɪt, ɛ-] *n* **1** POSSESSIONS : bienes *mpl*, propiedad *f*, patrimonio *m* ⟨the estate of the deceased : la sucesión del difunto⟩ **2** PROPERTY : hacienda *f*, finca *f*, propiedad *f*

esteem[1] [ɪˈstiːm, ɛ-] *vt* : estimar, apreciar

esteem[2] *n* : estima *f*, aprecio *m*

esthetic [ɛsˈθɛtɪk] → **aesthetic**

estimable [ˈɛstəməbəl] *adj* : estimable

estimate[1] [ˈɛstəˌmeɪt] *vt* **-mated; -mating** : calcular, estimar

estimate[2] [ˈɛstəmət] *n* **1** : cálculo *m* aproximado ⟨to make an estimate : hacer un cálculo⟩ **2** ASSESSMENT : valoración *f*, estimación *f* **3** QUOTE : presupuesto *m*

estimation [ˌɛstəˈmeɪʃən] *n* **1** JUDGMENT : juicio *m*, opinión *f* ⟨in my estimation : en mi opinión, a mi juicio⟩ **2** ESTIMATE : cálculo *m* aproximado

estimator [ˈɛstəˌmeɪtər] *n* : tasador *m*, -dora *f*

Estonian [ɛˈstoːniən] *n* : estonio *m*, -nia *f* — **Estonian** *adj*

estrange [ɪˈstreɪndʒ, ɛ-] *vt* **-tranged; -tranging** : enajenar, apartar, alejar ⟨he is estranged from his wife : está separado de su mujer⟩

estrangement [ɪˈstreɪndʒmənt, ɛ-] *n* : alejamiento *m*, distanciamiento *m*

estrogen [ˈɛstrədʒən] *n* : estrógeno *m*

estrus [ˈɛstrəs] *n* : celo *m*

estuary [ˈɛstʃʊˌwɛri] *n, pl* **-aries** : estuario *m*

et cetera [ɛtˈsɛtərə, -ˈsɛtrə] : etcétera

etch [ˈɛtʃ] *v* : grabar al aguafuerte

etching [ˈɛtʃɪŋ] *n* : aguafuerte *m*, grabado *m* al aguafuerte

eternal [ɪˈtərnəl, iː-] *adj* **1** EVERLASTING : eterno **2** INTERMINABLE : constante, incesante

eternally [ɪˈtərnəli, iː-] *adv* : eternamente, para siempre

eternity [ɪˈtərnəti, iː-] *n, pl* **-ties** : eternidad *f*

ethanol [ˈɛθəˌnɔl, -ˌnoːl] *n* : etanol *m*

ether [ˈiːθər] *n* : éter *m*

ethereal [ɪˈθɪriəl, iː-] *adj* **1** CELESTIAL : etéreo, celeste **2** DELICATE : delicado

ethical [ˈɛθɪkəl] *adj* : ético ⟨ethical code/question : código/cuestión de ética⟩ — **ethically** *adv*

ethics [ˈɛθɪks] *ns & pl* **1** : ética *f* **2** MORALITY : ética *f*, moralidad *f*

Ethiopian [ˌiːθiˈoːpiən] *n* : etíope *mf* — **Ethiopian** *adj*

ethnic [ˈɛθnɪk] *adj* : étnico ⟨ethnic group : etnia, grupo étnico⟩ ⟨ethnic cleansing : limpieza étnica⟩

etiquette [ˈɛtɪkət, -ˌkɛt] *n* : etiqueta *f*, protocolo *m*

etymological [ˌɛtəməˈlɑdʒɪkəl] *adj* : etimológico

etymology [ˌɛtəˈmɑlədʒi] *n, pl* **-gies** : etimología *f*

eucalyptus [ˌjuːkəˈlɪptəs] *n, pl* **-ti** [-ˌtaɪ] *or* **-tuses** [-təsəz] : eucalipto *m*

Eucharist [ˈjuːkərɪst] *n* : Eucaristía *f*

eulogize [ˈjuːləˌdʒaɪz] *vt* **-gized; -gizing** : elogiar, encomiar

eulogy [ˈjuːlədʒi] *n, pl* **-gies** : panegírico *m* (pronunciado en los funerales)

eunuch [ˈjuːnək] *n* : eunuco *m*

euphemism [ˈjuːfəˌmɪzəm] *n* : eufemismo *m*

euphemistic [ˌjuːfəˈmɪstɪk] *adj* : eufemístico

euphoria [jʊˈforiə] *n* : euforia *f*

euphoric [jʊˈforɪk] *adj* : eufórico

euro [ˈjʊrˌoː] *n, pl* **euros** *or* **euro** : euro *m*

European[1] [ˌjʊrəˈpiən] *adj* : europeo ⟨European Union : Unión Europea⟩

European[2] *n* : europeo *m*, -pea *f*

euthanasia [ˌjuːθəˈneɪʒə, -ʒiə] *n* : eutanasia *f*

euthanize [ˈjuːθəˌnaɪz] *n* **-nized; -nizing** : sacrificar (un perro, etc.)

evacuate [ɪˈvækjuˌeɪt] *v* **-ated; -ating** *vt* VACATE : evacuar, desalojar — *vi* WITHDRAW : retirarse

evacuation [ɪˌvækjuˈeɪʃən] *n* : evacuación *f*, desalojo *m*

evade [ɪˈveɪd] *vt* **evaded; evading** : eludir ⟨to evade taxes : evadir impuestos⟩

evaluate [ɪˈvæljuˌeɪt] *vt* **-ated; -ating** : evaluar, valorar, tasar

evaluation [ɪˌvæljuˈeɪʃən] *n* : evaluación *f*, valoración *f*, tasación *f*

evangelical [ˌiːˌvænˈdʒɛlɪkəl, ˌɛvən-] *adj* : evangélico

evangelism [ɪˈvændʒəˌlɪzəm] *n* : evangelismo *m*

evangelist [ɪˈvændʒəlɪst] *n* **1** : evangelista *m* **2** PREACHER : predicador *m*, -dora *f*

evaporate [ɪˈvæpəˌreɪt] *vi* **-rated; -rating** **1** VAPORIZE : evaporarse **2** VANISH : evaporarse, desvanecerse, esfumarse

evaporated milk *n* : leche *f* evaporada

evaporation [ɪˌvæpəˈreɪʃən] *n* : evaporación *f*

evasion [ɪˈveɪʒən] *n* : evasión *f*

evasive [ɪˈveɪsɪv] *adj* : evasivo

evasiveness [ɪˈveɪsɪvnəs] *n* : carácter *m* evasivo

eve [ˈiːv] *n* **1** : víspera *f* ⟨on the eve of the festivities : en vísperas de las festividades⟩ **2** → **evening**

even[1] [ˈiːvən] *vt* **1** LEVEL : allanar, nivelar, emparejar **2** EQUALIZE : igualar, equilibrar **3 to even out** : nivelar, emparejar — *vi* **to even out** : nivelarse, emparejarse

even[2] *adv* **1** : hasta, incluso ⟨even a child can do it : hasta un niño puede hacerlo⟩ ⟨he looked content, even happy : se le veía satisfecho, incluso feliz⟩ **2** (*in negative constructions*) : ni siquiera ⟨he didn't even try : ni siquiera lo intentó⟩ **3**

(*in comparisons*) : aún, todavía ⟨even better : aún mejor, todavía mejor⟩ **4 even if** : aunque **5 even so** : aun así **6 even though** : aun cuando, a pesar de que, aunque

even³ *adj* **1** SMOOTH : uniforme, liso, parejo **2** FLAT : plano, llano **3** EQUAL : igual, igualado ⟨an even score : un marcador igualado⟩ **4** REGULAR : regular, constante ⟨an even pace : un ritmo constante⟩ **5** EXACT : exacto, justo **6** : par ⟨even number : número par⟩ **7 to be even** : estar en paz, estar a mano **8 to get even** : desquitarse, vengarse

evening [ˈiːvnɪŋ] *n* **1** : tarde *f*, noche *f* ⟨good evening : buenas tardes/noches⟩ ⟨in the evening : por la noche⟩ ⟨evening class : clase nocturna⟩ **2** : velada *f* ⟨an evening of music : una velada musical⟩

evening gown *or* **evening dress** *n* : traje *m* de noche

evenings [ˈiːvnɪŋz] *adv* : por las noches

evenly [ˈiːvənli] *adv* **1** UNIFORMLY : de modo uniforme, de manera constante **2** FAIRLY : igualmente, equitativamente

evenness [ˈiːvənnəs] *n* : uniformidad *f*, igualdad *f*, regularidad *f*

event [ɪˈvɛnt] *n* **1** : acontecimiento *m*, suceso *m*, prueba *f* (en deportes) **2 in any event** *or* **at all events** : de cualquier modo **3 in the event that** : en caso de que

even–tempered [ˈiːvənˈtɛmpərd] *adj* : ecuánime

eventful [ɪˈvɛntfəl] *adj* : lleno de incidentes, memorable

eventual [ɪˈvɛntʃuəl] *adj* : final, consiguiente

eventuality [ɪˌvɛntʃuˈæləti] *n, pl* **-ties** : eventualidad *f*

eventually [ɪˈvɛntʃuəli] *adv* : finalmente, al fin, con el tiempo

ever [ˈɛvər] *adv* **1** ALWAYS : siempre ⟨as ever : como siempre⟩ ⟨ever since (then) : desde entonces⟩ ⟨ever since we met : desde que nos conocimos⟩ **2** (*in questions*) : alguna vez, algún día ⟨have you ever been to Mexico? : ¿has estado en México alguna vez?⟩ ⟨do you ever plan to go back? : ¿piensas volver algún día?⟩ **3** (*in negative constructions*) : nunca ⟨doesn't he ever work? : ¿es que nunca trabaja?⟩ ⟨nobody ever helps me : nadie nunca me ayuda⟩ ⟨we hardly ever speak : casi nunca hablamos⟩ **4** (*in comparisons*) : nunca ⟨better than ever : mejor que nunca⟩ ⟨the best song I ever heard : la mejor canción que oí de nunca⟩ **5** (*as intensifier*) ⟨I'm ever so happy! : ¡estoy tan y tan feliz!⟩ ⟨he looks ever so angry : parece estar muy enojado⟩

evergreen¹ [ˈɛvərˌɡriːn] *adj* : de hoja perenne

evergreen² *n* : planta *f* de hoja perenne

everlasting [ˌɛvərˈlæstɪŋ] *adj* : eterno, perpetuo, imperecedero

evermore [ˌɛvərˈmor] *adv* : eternamente

every [ˈɛvri] *adj* **1** EACH : cada ⟨every time : cada vez⟩ ⟨every other house

: cada dos casas⟩ **2** ALL : todo ⟨every month : todos los meses⟩ ⟨every other year : un año sí y otro no, cada dos años⟩ ⟨every woman : toda mujer, todas las mujeres⟩ **3** COMPLETE : pleno, entero ⟨to have every confidence : tener plena confianza⟩ **4 every now and then** *or* **every once in a while** *or* **every so often** : de vez en cuando

everybody [ˈɛvriˌbɑdi, -ˌbʌ-] *pron* : todos, todo el mundo

everyday [ˌɛvriˈdeɪ, ˈɛvri-] *adj* : cotidiano, diario, corriente ⟨everyday clothes : ropa de todos los días⟩

everyone [ˈɛvriˌwʌn] → **everybody**

everything [ˈɛvriˌθɪŋ] *pron* : todo

everywhere [ˈɛvriˌhwɛr] *adv* : en todas partes, por todas partes, dondequiera ⟨I looked everywhere : busqué en/por todas partes⟩ ⟨everywhere we go : dondequiera que vayamos⟩

evict [ɪˈvɪkt] *vt* : desalojar, desahuciar

eviction [ɪˈvɪkʃən] *n* : desalojo *m*, desahucio *m*

evidence [ˈɛvədəns] *n* **1** INDICATIONS : indicios *mpl*, señales *mpl* ⟨to be in evidence : estar a la vista⟩ **2** PROOF : evidencia *f*, prueba *f* **3** TESTIMONY : testimonio *m*, declaración *f* ⟨to give evidence : declarar como testigo, prestar declaración⟩

evident [ˈɛvədənt] *adj* : evidente, patente, manifiesto

evidently [ˈɛvədəntli, ˌɛviˈdɛntli] *adv* **1** CLEARLY : claramente, obviamente **2** APPARENTLY : aparentemente, evidentemente, al parecer

evil¹ [ˈiːvəl, -vɪl] *adj* **eviler** *or* **eviller; evilest** *or* **evillest** : malvado (dícese de las personas), maligno (dícese de los espíritus), maléfico (dícese de las influencias) ⟨evil deeds : malas acciones, maldades⟩ ⟨an evil spell : una maldición⟩

evil² *n* **1** WICKEDNESS : mal *m*, maldad *f* **2** MISFORTUNE : desgracia *f*, mal *m*

evildoer [ˌiːvəlˈduːər, ˌiːvɪl-] *n* : malhechor *m*, -chora *f*; malvado *m*, -da *f*

evil eye *n* **the evil eye** : el mal de ojo

evince [ɪˈvɪnts] *vt* **evinced; evincing** : mostrar, manifestar, revelar

eviscerate [ɪˈvɪsəˌreɪt] *vt* **-ated; -ating** : eviscerar

evocation [ˌiːvoˈkeɪʃən, ˌɛ-] *n* : evocación *f*

evocative [ɪˈvɑkətɪv] *adj* : evocador

evoke [ɪˈvoːk] *vt* **evoked; evoking** : evocar, provocar

evolution [ˌɛvəˈluːʃən, ˌiː-] *n* : evolución *f*, desarrollo *m*

evolutionary [ˌɛvəˈluːʃəˌnɛri, ˌiː-] *adj* : evolutivo

evolve [ɪˈvɑlv] *vi* **evolved; evolving** : evolucionar, desarrollarse

ewe [ˈjuː] *n* : oveja *f* (hembra)

ex [ˈɛks] *n* : ex *mf*

ex- [ˈɛks] *pref* : ex-, ex ⟨ex-wife : exesposa, ex esposa⟩

exacerbate [ɪɡˈzæsərˌbeɪt] *vt* **-bated; -bating** : exacerbar

exact¹ [ɪɡˈzækt, ɛ-] *vt* : exigir, imponer, arrancar

exact² [ig'zækt, εg-] *adj* : exacto, preciso

exacting [i'zæktiŋ, εg-] *adj* : exigente, riguroso

exactitude [ig'zæktə,tu:d, εg-, -,tju:d] *n* : exactitud *f*, precisión *f*

exactly [ig'zæktli, ε-] *adv* : exactamente ⟨it's exactly six o'clock : son las seis en punto⟩ ⟨exactly! : ¡exacto!⟩

exaggerate [ig'zædʒə,reit, εg-] *v* -ated; -ating : exagerar

exaggerated [ig'zædʒə,reitəd, εg-] *adj* : exagerado — **exaggeratedly** *adv*

exaggeration [ig,zædʒə'reiʃən, εg-] *n* : exageración *f*

exalt [ig'zɔlt, εg-] *vt* : exaltar, ensalzar, glorificar

exaltation [,εg,zɔl'teiʃən, ,εk,sɔl-] *n* : exaltación *f*

exam [ig'zæm, εg-] → **examination**

examination [ig,zæmə'neiʃən, εg-] *n* 1 TEST : examen *m* 2 INSPECTION : inspección *f*, revisión *f* 3 reconocimiento *m*, examen *m* (en medicina) 4 INVESTIGATION : examen *m*, estudio *m*

examine [ig'zæmən, εg-] *vt* -ined; -ining 1 TEST : examinar 2 INSPECT : inspeccionar, revisar 3 : examinar, revisar (en medicina) 4 STUDY : examinar

example [ig'zæmpəl, εg-] *n* : ejemplo *m* ⟨for example : por ejemplo⟩ ⟨to set an example : dar ejemplo⟩ ⟨to make an example of someone : darle un castigo ejemplar a alguien⟩

exasperate [ig'zæspə,reit, εg-] *vt* -ated; -ating : exasperar, sacar de quicio

exasperation [ig,zæspə'reiʃən, εg-] *n* : exasperación *f*

excavate ['εkskə,veit] *vt* -vated; -vating : excavar

excavation [,εkskə'veiʃən] *n* : excavación *f*

excavator ['εkskə,veitər] *n* : excavadora *f*

exceed [ik'si:d, εk-] *vt* 1 : exceder de, sobrepasar (un límite, etc.) 2 **to exceed expectations** : superar las expectativas 3 **to exceed one's authority** : excederse en sus facultades

exceedingly [ik'si:diŋli, εk-] *adv* : extremadamente, sumamente

excel [ik'sεl, εk-] *v* -celled; -celling *vi* : destacar, sobresalir ⟨to excel at/in something : destacar(se) en algo⟩ — *vt* : superar

excellence ['εksələnts] *n* : excelencia *f*

excellency ['εksələntsi] *n, pl* -cies : excelencia *f* ⟨His Excellency : Su Excelencia⟩

excellent ['εksələnt] *adj* : excelente, sobresaliente — **excellently** *adv*

except¹ [ik'sεpt] *vt* : exceptuar, excluir

except² *conj* : pero, si no fuera por

except³ *prep* : excepto, menos, salvo ⟨everyone except Carlos : todos menos Carlos⟩

except for → **except³**

exception [ik'sεpʃən] *n* 1 : excepción *f* 2 **to take exception to** : ofenderse por, objetar a 3 **with the exeption of** : a/con excepción de

exceptional [ik'sεpʃənəl] *adj* : excepcional, extraordinario — **exceptionally** *adv*

excerpt¹ [εk'sərpt, εg'zərpt, 'εk,-, 'g,-] *vt* : escoger, seleccionar

excerpt² ['εk,sərpt, 'εg,zərpt] *n* : pasaje *m*, selección *f*

excess¹ ['εk,sεs, ik'sεs] *adj* 1 : excesivo, de sobra 2 **excess baggage** : exceso *m* de equipaje

excess² [ik'sεs, 'εk,sεs] *n* 1 SUPERFLUITY : exceso *m*, superfluidad *f* ⟨an excess of energy : un exceso de energía⟩ 2 SURPLUS : excedente *m*, sobrante *m* ⟨in excess of : superior a⟩

excessive [ik'sεsiv, εk-] *adj* : excesivo, exagerado, desmesurado — **excessively** *adv*

exchange¹ [iks'tʃeindʒ, εks-;, 'εks-,tʃeindʒ] *vt* -changed; -changing : cambiar, intercambiar, canjear ⟨to exchange something for something : cambiar algo por algo⟩

exchange² *n* 1 : cambio *m*, intercambio *m*, canje *m* ⟨in exchange for : a cambio de⟩ 2 **stock exchange** : bolsa *f* (de valores) 3 *or* **telephone exchange** : central *f* telefónica

exchangeable [iks'tʃeindʒəbəl, εks-] *adj* : canjeable

exchange rate *n* : tasa *f* de cambio

exchequer ['εks,tʃεkər, iks'tʃεkər] *n* TREASURY : erario *m*, tesoro *m*, fisco *m*

excise¹ [ik'saiz, εk-] *vt* -cised; -cising : extirpar

excise² ['εk,saiz] *n* **excise tax** : impuesto *m* interno, impuesto *m* sobre el consumo

excitability [ik,saitə'biləti, εk-] *n* : excitabilidad *f*

excitable [ik'saitəbəl, εk-] *adj* : nervioso

excitation [,εk,sai'teiʃən, -sə-] *n* : excitación *f*

excite [ik'sait, εk-] *vt* -cited; -citing 1 AROUSE, STIMULATE : excitar, mover, estimular 2 ANIMATE : entusiasmar, animar 3 EVOKE, PROVOKE : provocar, despertar, suscitar ⟨to excite curiosity : despertar la curiosidad⟩

excited [ik'saitəd, εk-] *adj* 1 STIMULATED : excitado 2 ENTHUSIASTIC : entusiasmado, emocionado

excitedly [ik'saitədli, εk-] *adv* : con excitación, con entusiasmo

excitement [ik'saitmənt, εk-] *n* 1 ENTHUSIASM : entusiasmo *m*, emoción *f* 2 AGITATION : agitación *f*, alboroto *m*, conmoción *f* 3 AROUSAL : excitación *f*

exciting [ik'saitiŋ, εk-] *adj* 1 : emocionante 2 AROUSING : excitante

exclaim [iks'kleim, εks-] *v* : exclamar

exclamation [,εkskslə'meiʃən] *n* : exclamación *f*

exclamation point *n* : signo *m* de admiración

exclude [iks'klu:d, εks-] *vt* -cluded; -cluding 1 LEAVE OUT : excluir 2 RULE OUT : excluir, descartar 3 BAR : no admitir

excluding [iks'klu:diŋ, εks-] *prep* : excluyendo, sin incluir

exclusion [iks'klu:ʒən, εks-] *n* : exclusión *f*

exclusive¹ [iks'klu:siv, εks-] *adj* 1 SOLE : exclusivo, único 2 SELECT : exclusivo, selecto 3 **exclusive of** → **excluding**

exclusive² n : exclusiva f
exclusively [ɪksˈkluːsɪvli, ɛks-] adv : exclusivamente, únicamente
exclusiveness [ɪksˈkluːsɪvnəs, ɛks-] n : exclusividad f
excommunicate [ˌɛkskəˈmjuːnəˌkeɪt] vt -cated; -cating : excomulgar
excommunication [ˌɛkskəˌmjuːnəˈkeɪʃən] n : excomunión f
excrement [ˈɛkskrəmənt] n : excremento m
excrete [ɪkˈskriːt, ɛk-] vt -creted; -creting : excretar
excretion [ɪkˈskriːʃən, ɛk-] n : excreción f
excruciating [ɪkˈskruːʃiˌeɪtɪŋ, ɛk-] adj : insoportable, atroz, terrible — **excruciatingly** adv
exculpate [ˈɛkskəlˌpeɪt] vt -pated; -pating : exculpar
excursion [ɪkˈskərʒən, ɛk-] n 1 OUTING : excursión f, paseo m 2 DIGRESSION : digresión f
excusable [ɪkˈskjuːzəbəl, ɛk-] adj : disculpable
excuse¹ [ɪkˈskjuːz, ɛk-] vt -cused; cusing 1 PARDON : disculpar, perdonar ⟨excuse me : con permiso, perdóneme, perdón⟩ 2 DISMISS : dejar salir ⟨may I be excused? : ¿puedo ir?⟩ 3 EXEMPT : disculpar, eximir 4 JUSTIFY : excusar, justificar 5 to excuse yourself : excusarse
excuse² [ɪkˈskjuːs, ɛk-] n 1 JUSTIFICATION : excusa f, justificación f 2 PRETEXT : pretexto m 3 to make excuses : poner excusas 4 to make one's excuses to someone : pedirle disculpas a alguien
execute [ˈɛksɪˌkjuːt] vt -cuted; -cuting 1 CARRY OUT : ejecutar, llevar a cabo, desempeñar 2 ENFORCE : ejecutar, cumplir (un testamento, etc.) 3 KILL : ejecutar, ajusticiar
execution [ˌɛksɪˈkjuːʃən] n 1 PERFORMANCE : ejecución f, desempeño m 2 IMPLEMENTATION : cumplimiento m 3 : ejecución f (por un delito)
executioner [ˌɛksɪˈkjuːʃənər] n : verdugo m
executive¹ [ɪgˈzɛkjətɪv, ɛg-] adj : ejecutivo
executive² n : ejecutivo m, -va f
executor [ɪgˈzɛkjətər, ɛg-] n : albacea m/f, testamentario m, -ria f
executrix [ɪgˈzɛkjəˌtrɪks, ɛg-] n, pl **executrices** [-ˌzɛkjəˈtraɪˌsiːz] or **executrixes** [-ˈzɛkjəˌtrɪksəz] : albacea f, testamentaria f
exemplary [ɪgˈzɛmpləri, ɛg-] adj : ejemplar
exemplify [ɪgˈzɛmpləˌfaɪ, ɛg-] vt -fied; -fying : ejemplificar, ilustrar, demostrar
exempt¹ [ɪgˈzɛmpt, ɛg-] vt : eximir ⟨to exempt someone from something : eximir a alguien de algo⟩
exempt² adj : exento ⟨to be exempt from : estar exento de⟩
exemption [ɪgˈzɛmpʃən, ɛg-] n : exención f
exercise¹ [ˈɛksərˌsaɪz] v -cised; -cising vt 1 : ejercitar (el cuerpo) 2 : ejercitar

(un caballo), sacar a pasear (un perro) 3 USE : ejercer, hacer uso de ⟨to exercise caution/restraint : obrar con cautela/moderación⟩ — vi : hacer ejercicio
exercise² n 1 : ejercicio m ⟨to get exercise : hacer ejercicio⟩ ⟨arm exercises : ejercicios para los brazos⟩ 2 : ejercicio m ⟨math exercises : ejercicios de matemáticas⟩ 3 MANEUVER : ejercicio m, maniobra f 4 USE : ejercicio m 5 **exercises** npl CEREMONY : ceremonia f
exert [ɪgˈzərt, ɛg-] vt 1 : ejercer, emplear 2 to exert oneself : esforzarse
exertion [ɪgˈzərʃən, ɛg-] n 1 USE : ejercicio m (de autoridad, etc.), uso m (de fuerza, etc.) 2 EFFORT : esfuerzo m, empeño m
exhalation [ˌɛksəˈleɪʃən, ˌɛkshə-] n : exhalación f
exhale [ɛksˈheɪl] v -haled; -haling vt 1 : exhalar, espirar 2 EMIT : exhalar, despedir, emitir — vi : espirar
exhaust¹ [ɪgˈzɔst, ɛg-] vt 1 DEPLETE : agotar 2 TIRE : cansar, fatigar, agotar 3 EMPTY : vaciar
exhaust² n 1 or **exhaust fumes** : gases mpl de escape 2 or **exhaust pipe** : tubo m de escape, caño m de escape Arg, Uru 3 or **exhaust system** : sistema m de escape
exhausted [ɪgˈzɔstəd, ɛg-] adj : agotado, derrengado
exhausting [ɪgˈzɔstɪŋ, ɛg-] adj : extenuante, agotador
exhaustion [ɪgˈzɔstʃən, ɛg-] n : agotamiento m
exhaustive [ɪgˈzɔstɪv, ɛg-] adj : exhaustivo
exhibit¹ [ɪgˈzɪbət, ɛg-] vt 1 DISPLAY : exhibir, exponer 2 PRODUCE, SHOW : mostrar, presentar
exhibit² n 1 OBJECT : objeto m expuesto 2 EXHIBITION : exposición f, exhibición f 3 EVIDENCE : prueba f instrumental 4 to be on exhibit : estar expuesto
exhibition [ˌɛksəˈbɪʃən] n 1 : exposición f, exhibición f 2 to make an exhibition of oneself : dar el espectáculo, hacer el ridículo
exhibitor [ɪgˈzɪbətər] n : expositor m, -tora f
exhilarate [ɪgˈzɪləˌreɪt, ɛg-] vt -rated; -rating 1 : animar mucho, llenar de alegría 2 STIMULATE : estimular
exhilaration [ɪgˌzɪləˈreɪʃən, ɛg-] n : alegría f, regocijo m, júbilo m
exhort [ɪgˈzɔrt, ɛg-] vt : exhortar
exhortation [ˌɛkˌsɔrˈteɪʃən, -sər-;, ˌɛgˌzɔr-] n : exhortación f
exhumation [ˌɛksjuˈmeɪʃən, -hju-;, ˌɛgzu-, -zju-] n : exhumación f
exhume [ɪgˈzuːm, -ˈzjuːm;, ɪksˈjuːm, -ˈhjuːm] vt -humed; -huming : exhumar, desenterrar
ex-husband [ˈɛksˈhʌzbənd] n : ex marido m
exigencies [ˈɛksɪdʒənˌsiːz, ɪgˈzɪdʒənˌsiːz] npl : exigencias fpl
exile¹ [ˈɛgˌzaɪl, ˈɛkˌsaɪl] vt exiled; exiling : exiliar, desterrar

exile² *n* **1** BANISHMENT : exilio *m*, destierro *m* **2** OUTCAST : exiliado *m*, -da *f*; desterrado *m*, -da *f*

exist [ɪgˈzɪst, ɛg-] *vi* **1** BE : existir **2** LIVE : subsistir, vivir

existence [ɪgˈzɪstənts, ɛg-] *n* : existencia *f*

existent [ɪgˈzɪstənt, ɛg-] *adj* : existente

existing [ɪgˈzɪstɪŋ] *adj* : existente

exit¹ [ˈɛgzət, ˈɛksət] *vi* : salir, hacer mutis (en el teatro) — *vt* : salir de ⟨to exit the building : salir del edificio⟩ ⟨to exit a program : salir de un programa⟩

exit² *n* **1** DEPARTURE : salida *f*, partida *f* **2** EGRESS : salida *f* ⟨emergency exit : salida de emergencia⟩

exodus [ˈɛksədəs] *n* : éxodo *m*

exonerate [ɪgˈzɑnəˌreɪt, ɛg-] *vt* -ated; -ating : exonerar, disculpar, absolver

exoneration [ɪgˌzɑnəˈreɪʃən, ɛg-] *n* : exoneración *f*

exorbitant [ɪgˈzɔrbətənt, ɛg-] *adj* : exorbitante, excesivo

exorcise [ˈɛkˌsɔrˌsaɪz, -sər-] *vt* -cised; -cising : exorcizar

exorcism [ˈɛksɔrˌsɪzəm] *n* : exorcismo *m*

exotic¹ [ɪgˈzɑtɪk, ɛg-] *adj* : exótico — **exotically** [-ɪkli] *adv*

exotic² *n* : planta *f* exótica

expand [ɪkˈspænd, ɛk-] *vt* **1** ENLARGE : expandir, ampliar **2** BROADEN, EXTEND : ampliar, extender — *vi* **1** ENLARGE : ampliarse, extenderse **2** : expandirse, dilatarse (dícese de los metales, gases, etc.) **3 to expand on/upon** : extenderse en/sobre, explayarse en/sobre

expanse [ɪkˈspænts, ɛk-] *n* : extensión *f*

expansion [ɪkˈspæntʃən, ɛk-] *n* **1** ENLARGEMENT : expansión *f*, ampliación *f* **2** EXPANSE : extensión *f*

expansive [ɪkˈspæntsɪv, ɛk-] *adj* **1** : expansivo **2** OUTGOING : expansivo, comunicativo **3** AMPLE : ancho, amplio — **expansively** *adv*

expatriate¹ [ɛksˈpeɪtriˌeɪt] *vt* -ated; -ating : expatriar

expatriate² [ɛksˈpeɪtriət, -ˌeɪt] *adj* : expatriado

expatriate³ [ɛksˈpeɪtriət, -ˌeɪt] *n* : expatriado *m*, -da *f*

expect [ɪkˈspɛkt, ɛk-] *vt* **1** SUPPOSE : suponer, imaginarse ⟨I expect so : supongo que sí⟩ **2** ANTICIPATE : esperar ⟨we're expecting company : esperamos visita⟩ ⟨rain is expected : se pronostican lluvias⟩ ⟨I expect to win : espero ganar⟩ **3** COUNT ON, REQUIRE : contar con, esperar ⟨I expect you to come : cuento con que vengas⟩ ⟨we expected more of/from you : esperábamos otra cosa de ti⟩ — *vi* **to be expecting** : estar embarazada

expectancy [ɪkˈspɛktəntsi, ɛk-] *n, pl* **-cies** **1** : expectación *f*, expectativa *f* **2** → **life expectancy**

expectant [ɪkˈspɛktənt, ɛk-] *adj* **1** ANTICIPATING : expectante **2** EXPECTING : futuro ⟨expectant mother : futura madre⟩

expectantly [ɪkˈspɛktəntli, ɛk-] *adv* : con expectación

expectation [ˌɛkˌspɛkˈteɪʃən] *n* **1** ANTICI-

PATION : expectación *f* ⟨to have every expectation of : tener muchas esperanzas de⟩ **2** EXPECTANCY : expectativa *f* ⟨it didn't live up to expectations : no estaba a la altura de las expectativas⟩

expedient¹ [ɪkˈspiːdiənt, ɛk-] *adj* : conveniente, oportuno

expedient² *n* : expediente *m*, recurso *m*

expedite [ˈɛkspəˌdaɪt] *vt* -dited; -diting **1** FACILITATE : facilitar, dar curso a **2** HASTEN : acelerar

expedition [ˌɛkspəˈdɪʃən] *n* : expedición *f*

expeditious [ˌɛkspəˈdɪʃəs] *adj* : pronto, rápido

expel [ɪkˈspɛl, ɛk-] *vt* -pelled; -pelling **1** : expulsar (a alguien) **2** : expulsar, expeler (aire, etc.)

expend [ɪkˈspɛnd, ɛk-] *vt* **1** DISBURSE : gastar, desembolsar **2** CONSUME : consumir, agotar

expendable [ɪkˈspɛndəbəl, ɛk-] *adj* : prescindible

expenditure [ɪkˈspɛndɪtʃər, ɛk-, -ˌtʃur] *n* : gasto *m*

expense [ɪkˈspɛnts, ɛk-] *n* **1** COST : gasto *m* **2 expenses** *npl* : gastos *mpl*, expensas *fpl* **3 at the expense of** : a costa de, a expensas de

expensive [ɪkˈspɛntsɪv, ɛk-] *adj* : costoso, caro — **expensively** *adv*

experience¹ [ɪkˈspɪriənts, ɛk-] *vt* -enced; -encing : experimentar (sentimientos), tener (dificultades), sufrir (una pérdida)

experience² *n* : experiencia *f*

experienced [ɪkˈspɪriəntst, ɛk-] *adj* : con experiencia, experimentado

experiment¹ [ɪkˈspɛrəmənt, ɛk-, -ˈspɪr-] *vi* **to experiment on/with** : experimentar con, hacer experimentos con

experiment² *n* : experimento *m*

experimental [ɪkˌspɛrəˈmntəl, ɛk-, -ˌspɪr-] *adj* : experimental — **experimentally** *adv*

experimentation [ɪkˌspɛrəmənˈteɪʃən, ɛk-, -ˌspɪr-] *n* : experimentación *f*

expert¹ [ˈɛkˌspərt, ɪkˈspərt] *adj* : experto, de experto ⟨expert testimony : testimonio pericial⟩ ⟨expert at (doing) something : experto en (hacer) algo⟩ — **expertly** *adv*

expert² [ˈɛkˌspərt] *n* : experto *m*, -ta *f*; perito *m*, -ta *f*

expertise [ˌɛkspərˈtiːz] *n* : pericia *f*, competencia *f*

expiate [ˈɛkspiˌeɪt] *vt* -ated; -ating : expiar

expiation [ˌɛkspiˈeɪʃən] *n* : expiación *f*

expiration [ˌɛkspəˈreɪʃən] *n* **1** EXHALATION : exhalación *f*, espiración *f* **2** DEATH : muerte *f* **3** TERMINATION : vencimiento *m*, caducidad *f*

expire [ɪkˈspaɪr, ɛk-] *vi* -pired; -piring **1** EXHALE : espirar **2** DIE : expirar, morir **3** TERMINATE : caducar, vencer

explain [ɪkˈspleɪn, ɛk-] *vt* **1** : explicar **2 to explain yourself** : explicarse — **explainable** [ɪkˈspleɪnəbəl, ɛk-] *adj*

explanation [ˌɛkspləˈneɪʃən] *n* : explicación *f*

explanatory [ɪkˈsplænəˌtori, ɛk-] *adj* : explicativo, aclaratorio expletive [ˈɛksplətɪv] n : improperio m, palabrota f fam, grosería f

explicable [ɛkˈsplɪkəbəl, ˈɛkspli-] adj : explicable

explicit [ɪkˈsplɪsət, ɛk-] adj : explícito, claro, categórico, rotundo — explicitly adv

explicitness [ɪkˈsplɪsətnəs, ɛk-] n : claridad f, carácter m explícito

explode [ɪkˈsploːd, ɛk-] v -ploded; -ploding vt 1 BURST : hacer explosionar, hacer explotar 2 REFUTE : rebatir, refutar, desmentir — vi 1 BURST : explotar, estallar, reventar 2 SKYROCKET : dispararse

exploit¹ [ɪkˈsplɔɪt, ɛk-] vt : explotar, aprovecharse de

exploit² [ˈɛkˌsplɔɪt] n : hazaña f, proeza f

exploitation [ˌɛkˌsplɔɪˈteɪʃən] n : explotación f

exploration [ˌɛksploˈreɪʃən] n : exploración f

exploratory [ɪkˈsploːrəˌtori, ɛk-] adj : exploratorio

explore [ɪkˈsploːr, ɛk-] vt -plored; -ploring : explorar, investigar, examinar

explorer [ɪkˈsploːrər, ɛk-] n : explorador m, -dora f

explosion [ɪkˈsploːʒən, ɛk-] n : explosión f, estallido m

explosive¹ [ɪkˈsploːsɪv, ɛk-] adj : explosivo, fulminante — explosively adv

explosive² n : explosivo m

exponent [ɪkˈspoːnənt, ˈɛkˌspoː-] n 1 : exponente m 2 ADVOCATE : defensor m, -sora f; partidario m, -ria f

exponential [ˌɛkspəˈnɛntʃəl] adj : exponencial — exponentially adv

export¹ [ɛkˈsport, ˈɛkˌsport] vt : exportar

export² [ˈɛkˌsport] n 1 : artículo m de exportación 2 → exportation

exportation [ˌɛkˌsporˈteɪʃən] n : exportación f

exporter [ɛkˈsportər, ˈɛkˌspor-] n : exportador m, -dora f

expose [ɪkˈspoːz, ɛk-] vt -posed; -posing 1 : exponer (al peligro, a los elementos, a una enfermedad) 2 : exponer (una película a la luz) 3 DISCLOSE : revelar, develar, sacar a la luz 4 UNMASK : desenmascarar ⟨to expose someone as a fraud : demostrar que alguien es un farsante⟩

exposé or expose [ˌɛkspoˈzeɪ] n : exposición f (de hechos), revelación f (de un escándalo)

exposed [ɪkˈspoːzd, ɛk-] adj : expuesto, al descubierto ⟨exposed brick : ladrillo a la vista⟩

exposition [ˌɛkspəˈzɪʃən] n : exposición f

exposure [ɪkˈspoːʒər, ɛk-] n 1 : exposición f (a la luz, a enfermedades, etc.) 2 : congelación f (en medicina) 3 DISCLOSURE : revelación f 4 PUBLICITY : publicidad f 5 ORIENTATION : orientación f ⟨a room with a northern exposure : una sala orientada al norte⟩ 6 : exposición f (en fotografía)

expound [ɪkˈspaʊnd, ɛk-] vt : exponer, explicar — vi : hacer comentarios detallados

express¹ [ɪkˈsprɛs, ɛk-] vt 1 : expresar ⟨to express oneself : expresarse⟩ 2 : mandar/enviar (una carta, etc.) por correo expreso

express² adv : por correo expreso, por correo urgente

express³ adj 1 EXPLICIT : expreso, explícito 2 SPECIFIC : específico ⟨for that express purpose : con ese fin específico⟩ 3 RAPID : expreso, rápido — expressly adv

express⁴ n 1 or express mail : expreso m, correo m expreso/urgente 2 : expreso m, tren m expreso

expression [ɪkˈsprɛʃən, ɛk-] n 1 UTTERANCE : expresión f ⟨freedom of expression : libertad de expresión⟩ 2 : expresión f (en la matemática) 3 PHRASE : frase f, expresión f 4 LOOK : expresión f, cara f, gesto m ⟨with a sad expression : con un gesto de tristeza⟩

expressionless [ɪkˈsprɛʃənləs, ɛk-] adj : inexpresivo

expressive [ɪkˈsprɛsɪv, ɛk-] adj : expresivo

expressway [ɪkˈsprɛsˌweɪ, ɛk-] n : autopista f

expropriate [ɛkˈsproːpriˌeɪt] vt -ated; -ating : expropiar

expulsion [ɪkˈspʌlʃən, ɛk-] n : expulsión f

expurgate [ˈɛkspərˌgeɪt] vt -gated; -gating : expurgar

exquisite [ɛkˈskwɪzət, ˈɛkˌskwɪ-] adj 1 FINE : exquisito, primoroso ⟨in exquisite detail : con todo lujo de detalles⟩ 2 EXTREME : intenso (dícese del dolor, etc.), exquisito

exquisiteness [ɛkˈskwɪzətnəs, ˈɛkˌskwɪ-] n : exquisitez f

extant [ˈɛkstənt, ɛkˈstænt] adj : existente

extemporaneous [ɛkˌstɛmpəˈreɪniəs] adj : improvisado — extemporaneously adv

extend [ɪkˈstɛnd, ɛk-] vt 1 STRETCH : extender, tender 2 PROLONG : prolongar (una visita, etc.), prorrogar (un plazo) 3 ENLARGE : agrandar, ampliar 4 PROFFER : dar (una bienvenida), presentar (disculpas) ⟨to extend an invitation : invitar⟩ — vi : extenderse

extendable adj : extensible

extended [ɪkˈstɛndəd, ɛk-] adj LENGTHY : prolongado, largo ⟨extended warranty : garantía extendida⟩

extension [ɪkˈstɛntʃən, ɛk-] n 1 EXTENDING : extensión f, ampliación f (de un edificio), prórroga f (de un plazo), prolongación f (de una visita) 2 ADDITION, ANNEX : ampliación f, anexo m 3 LINE : extensión f, interno m

extension cord n : extensión f; alargador m; alargue m Arg, Uru

extensive [ɪkˈstɛntsɪv, ɛk-] adj 1 BROAD : extenso, amplio ⟨extensive damage : cuantiosos daños⟩ 2 THOROUGH : exhaustivo — extensively adv

extent [ɪkˈstɛnt, ɛk-] n 1 SIZE : extensión f, magnitud f 2 DEGREE, SCOPE : alcance m, grado m ⟨to a certain extent : hasta cierto punto⟩ ⟨to a great extent : en gran parte⟩

extenuate [ɪkˈstɛnjəˌweɪt, ɛk-] *vt* **-ated; -ating** : atenuar, aminorar, mitigar ⟨extenuating circumstances : (circunstancias) atenuantes⟩

exterior¹ [ɛkˈstɪriər] *adj* : exterior

exterior² *n* : exterior *m*

exterminate [ɪkˈstərməˌneɪt, ɛk-] *vt* **-nated; -nating** : exterminar

extermination [ɪkˌstərməˈneɪʃən, ɛk-] *n* : exterminación *f*, exterminio *m*

exterminator [ɪkˈstərməˌneɪtər, ɛk-] *n* : exterminador *m*, -dora *f* de plagas; fumigador *m*, -dora *f*

external [ɪkˈstərnəl, ɛk-] *adj* : externo, exterior — **externally** *adv*

extinct [ɪkˈstɪŋkt, ɛk-] *adj* : extinto

extinction [ɪkˈstɪŋkʃən, ɛk-] *n* : extinción *f*

extinguish [ɪkˈstɪŋgwɪʃ, ɛk-] *vt* : extinguir, apagar

extinguisher [ɪkˈstɪŋgwɪʃər, ɛk-] *n* : extinguidor *m*, extintor *m*

extirpate [ˈɛkstərˌpeɪt] *vt* **-pated; -pating** : extirpar, exterminar

extol [ɪkˈstoːl, ɛk-] *vt* **-tolled; -tolling** : exaltar, ensalzar, alabar

extort [ɪkˈstɔrt, ɛk-] *vt* : extorsionar

extortion [ɪkˈstɔrʃən, ɛk-] *n* : extorsión *f*

extra¹ [ˈɛkstrə] *adv* **1** : extra, más, super ⟨extra special : super especial⟩ ⟨to pay extra for : pagar más/extra por⟩ **2** : excepcionalmente ⟨to be extra careful : tener especial cuidado⟩

extra² *adj* **1** ADDITIONAL : adicional, suplementario, de más ⟨to be/cost extra : no estar incluido en el precio⟩ ⟨at no extra charge : sin costo adicional⟩ **2** SUPERIOR : superior

extra³ *n* **1** : extra *m* **2** : extra *mf* (en películas)

extra- *pref* : extra-

extract¹ [ɪkˈstrækt, ɛk-] *vt* : extraer, sacar

extract² [ˈɛkˌstrækt] *n* **1** EXCERPT : pasaje *m*, selección *f*, trozo *m* **2** : extracto *m* ⟨vanilla extract : extracto de vainilla⟩

extraction [ɪkˈstrækʃən, ɛk-] *n* : extracción *f*

extractor [ɪkˈstræktər, ɛk-] *n* : extractor *m*

extracurricular [ˌɛkstrəkəˈrɪkjələr] *adj* : extracurricular

extradite [ˈɛkstrəˌdaɪt] *vt* **-dited; -diting** : extraditar

extradition [ˌɛkstrəˈdɪʃən] *n* : extradición *f*

extramarital [ˌɛkstrəˈmærətəl] *adj* : extramatrimonial

extraneous [ɛkˈstreɪniəs] *adj* **1** OUTSIDE : externo **2** SUPERFLUOUS : superfluo, ajeno — **extraneously** *adv*

extraordinary [ɪkˈstrɔrdənˌɛri, ˌɛkstrəˈɔrd-] *adj* : extraordinario, excepcional — **extraordinarily** [ɪkˌstrɔrdənˈɛrəli, ˌɛkstrəˌɔrd-] *adv*

extrapolate [ɪkˈstræpəˌleɪt] *v* **-lated; -lating** *vt* : extrapolar — *vi* : hacer una extrapolación — **extrapolation** [ɪkˌstræpəˈleɪʃən] *n*

extrasensory [ˌɛkstrəˈsɛnsəri] *adj* : extrasensorial

extraterrestrial¹ [ˌɛkstrətəˈrɛstriəl] *adj* : extraterrestre

extraterrestrial² *n* : extraterrestre *mf*

extravagance [ɪkˈstrævɪgənts, ɛk-] *n* **1** EXCESS : exceso *m*, extravagancia *f* **2** WASTEFULNESS : derroche *m*, despilfarro *m* **3** LUXURY : lujo *m*

extravagant [ɪkˈstrævɪgənt, ɛk-] *adj* **1** EXCESSIVE : excesivo, exagerado, extravagante **2** WASTEFUL : despilfarrador, derrochador, gastador **3** EXORBITANT : costoso, exorbitante

extravagantly [ɪkˈstrævɪgəntli, ɛk-] *adv* **1** LAVISHLY : a lo grande **2** EXCESSIVELY : exageradamente, desmesuradamente

extravaganza [ɪkˌstrævəˈgænzə, ɛk-] *n* : gran espectáculo *m*

extreme¹ [ɪkˈstriːm, ɛk-] *adj* **1** : extremo ⟨extreme cold : frío extremo⟩ ⟨of extreme importance : de suma importancia⟩ **2** : extremo, extremista ⟨extreme views : opiniones extremas⟩ **3** SEVERE, DRASTIC : extremo ⟨extreme conditions : condiciones extremas⟩ ⟨extreme measures : medidas excepcionales, medidas drásticas⟩ **4** : más lejos ⟨the extreme north : el extremo norte/septentrional⟩ **5** : extremo ⟨extreme sports : deportes extremos⟩

extreme² *n* **1** : extremo *m* **2 in the extreme** : en extremo, en sumo grado

extremely [ɪkˈstriːmli, ɛk-] *adv* : sumamente, extremadamente, terriblemente ⟨extremely large : grandísimo⟩

extremist [ɪkˈstriːmɪst, ɛk-] *n* : extremista *mf* — **extremist** *adj*

extremity [ɪkˈstrɛməti, ɛk-] *n, pl* **-ties 1** EXTREME : extremo *m* **2 extremities** *npl* LIMBS : extremidades *fpl*

extricate [ˈɛkstrəˌkeɪt] *vt* **-cated; -cating** : librar, sacar

extrovert [ˈɛkstrəˌvərt] *n* : extrovertido *m*, -da *f*

extroverted [ˈɛkstrəˌvərtəd] *adj* : extrovertido

extrude [ɪkˈstruːd, ɛk-] *vt* **-truded; -truding** : extrudir, expulsar

exuberance [ɪgˈzuːbərənts, ɛg-] *n* **1** JOYOUSNESS : euforia *f*, exaltación *f* **2** VIGOR : exuberancia *f*, vigor *m*

exuberant [ɪgˈzuːbərənt, ɛg-] *adj* **1** JOYOUS : eufórico **2** LUSH : exuberante — **exuberantly** *adv*

exude [ɪgˈzuːd, ɛg-] *vt* **-uded; -uding 1** OOZE : rezumar, exudar **2** EMANATE : emanar, irradiar

exult [ɪgˈzʌlt, ɛg-] *vi* : exultar, regocijarse

exultant [ɪgˈzʌltənt, ɛg-] *adj* : exultante, jubiloso — **exultantly** *adv*

exultation [ˌɛksəlˈteɪʃən, ˌɛgzəl-] *n* : exultación *f*, júbilo *m*, alborozo *m*

ex-wife [ˈɛksˈwaɪf] *n* : ex esposa *f*

eye¹ [ˈaɪ] *vt* **eyed; eyeing** *or* **eying** : mirar, observar

eye² *n* **1** : ojo *m* **2** VISION : visión *f*, vista *f*, ojo *m* ⟨to have a good eye for bargains : tener un buen ojo para las gangas⟩ **3** GAZE : mirada *f*, ojeada *f* ⟨before my (very) eyes : ante mis propios ojos⟩ ⟨keep an eye on him : vigílalo⟩ ⟨keep an eye out for her : fíjate a ver si la ves⟩ ⟨don't take your eyes off the road : no

apartes la vista de la carretera⟩ 4 AT-
TENTION : atención f ⟨to catch one's eye
: llamar la atención⟩ 5 POINT OF VIEW
: punto m de vista ⟨in the eyes of the law
: según la ley⟩ 6 : ojo m (de una aguja,
una papa, una tormenta)

eyeball ['aɪˌbɔl] n : globo m ocular

eyebrow ['aɪˌbraʊ] n : ceja f ⟨to raise an
eyebrow at : asombrarse ante⟩

eye-catching ['aɪˌkatʃɪŋ, -ˌke-] adj : llamativo

eyed ['aɪd] adj (used in combination) : de
ojos ⟨blue-eyed : de ojos azules⟩ ⟨wide-
eyed : con los ojos muy abiertos⟩ ⟨cross-
eyed : bizco⟩ ⟨one-eyed : tuerto⟩

eyedropper ['aɪˌdrɑpər] n : cuentagotas f

eyedrops ['aɪˌdrɑps] n : colirio m

eyeglasses ['aɪˌglæsəz] npl : anteojos
mpl, lentes mpl, espejuelos mpl, gafas fpl

eyelash ['aɪˌlæʃ] n : pestaña f

eyelet ['aɪlət] n : ojete m

eyelid ['aɪˌlɪd] n : párpado m

eyeliner ['aɪˌlaɪnər] n : delineador m (de
ojos)

eye-opener ['aɪˌoːpənər] n : revelación f,
sorpresa f

eye-opening ['aɪˌoːpənɪŋ] adj : revelador

eyepiece ['aɪˌpiːs] n : ocular m

eye shadow n : sombra f de ojos

eyesight ['aɪˌsaɪt] n : vista f, visión f

eyesore ['aɪˌsor] n : monstruosidad f, adefesio m

eyestrain ['aɪˌstreɪn] n : fatiga f visual,
vista f cansada

eyetooth ['aɪˌtuːθ] n : colmillo m

eyewitness ['aɪˌwɪtnəs] n : testigo mf ocular, testigo mf presencial

eyrie ['aɪri] → aerie

F

f ['ɛf] n, pl **f's** or **fs** ['ɛfs] 1 : sexta letra del
alfabeto inglés 2 **F** : fa m ⟨F sharp/flat
: fa sostenido/bemol⟩ 3 **F** : insuficiente
m (calificación)

fa ['fɛ] n : fa m (en el canto)

fable ['feɪbəl] n : fábula f

fabled ['feɪbəld] adj : legendario, fabuloso

fabric ['fæbrɪk] n 1 MATERIAL : tela f,
tejido m 2 STRUCTURE : estructura f
⟨the fabric of society : la estructura de la
sociedad⟩

fabricate ['fæbrɪˌkeɪt] vt -cated; -cat-
ing 1 CONSTRUCT, MANUFACTURE
: construir, fabricar 2 INVENT : inventar (excusas o mentiras)

fabrication [ˌfæbrɪˈkeɪʃən] n 1 LIE
: mentira f, invención f 2 MANUFAC-
TURE : fabricación f

fabulous ['fæbjələs] adj 1 LEGENDARY
: fabuloso, legendario 2 INCREDIBLE
: increíble, fabuloso ⟨fabulous wealth
: riqueza fabulosa⟩ 3 WONDERFUL
: magnífico, estupendo, fabuloso — **fab-
ulously** adv

facade [fəˈséd] n : fachada f

face¹ ['feɪs] v **faced; facing** vt 1 LINE : recubrir (una superficie), forrar (ropa) 2
CONFRONT : enfrentarse a, afrontar,
hacer frente a ⟨to face the music : afrontar las consecuencias⟩ ⟨to face the facts
: aceptar la realidad⟩ 3 : estar de cara a,
estar enfrente de ⟨she's facing her
brother : está de cara a su hermano⟩ 4
OVERLOOK : dar a — vi : mirar (hacia),
estar orientado (a) 5 **to face up to** CON-
FRONT : hacer frente a

face² n 1 : cara f, rostro m ⟨he told me to
my face : me lo dijo a la cara⟩ ⟨face to
face : cara a cara⟩ 2 EXPRESSION : cara
f, expresión f ⟨to make a face : poner
mala cara⟩ ⟨he couldn't keep a straight
face : no pudo aguantarse la risa⟩ ⟨to
put on a brave face : no demostrar uno
el miedo que tiene⟩ 3 GRIMACE : mueca

f ⟨to make faces : hacer muecas⟩ 4 AP-
PEARANCE : fisonomía f, aspecto m ⟨the
face of society : la fisonomía de la socie-
dad⟩ ⟨on the face of it : aparentemente,
a primera vista⟩ 5 PERSON : cara f 6
PRESTIGE : prestigio m ⟨to lose face : des-
prestigiarse⟩ ⟨to save face : salvar las
apariencias⟩ 7 FRONT, SIDE : cara f (de
una moneda), esfera f (de un reloj),
fachada f (de un edificio), pared f (de
una montaña) 8 SURFACE : superficie f,
faz f (de la tierra), cara f (de la luna) 9
in the face of DESPITE : en medio de, en
visto de, ante 10 **to be/get in
someone's face** fam : gritarle a alguien,
regañarle a alguien 11 **to fly in the face
of** : hacer caso omiso de algo

facedown ['feɪsˌdaʊn] adv : boca abajo

face-first [ˌfeɪsˈfərst] adv : de bruces

faceless ['feɪsləs] adj ANONYMOUS
: anónimo

face-lift ['feɪsˌlɪft] n 1 : estiramiento m
facial 2 RENOVATION : renovación f,
remozamiento m

face-off ['feɪsˌɔf] n : confrontación f,
careo m

facet ['fæsət] n 1 : faceta f (de una piedra) 2 ASPECT : faceta f, aspecto m

facetious [fəˈsiːʃəs] adj : gracioso, burlón,
bromista

facetiously [fəˈsiːʃəsli] adv : en tono de
burla

facetiousness [fəˈsiːʃəsnəs] n : jocosidad
f

face-to-face adv & adj : cara a cara

faceup ['feɪsˌʌp] adv : boca arriba

face value n : valor m nominal

facial¹ ['feɪʃəl] adj : de la cara, facial

facial² n : tratamiento m facial, limpieza f
de cutis

facile ['fæsəl] adj SUPERFICIAL : superficial, simplista

facilitate [fəˈsɪləˌteɪt] vt -tated; -tating
: facilitar — **facilitator** [fəˈsɪləˌteɪtər] n

facility [fə'sɪləṭi] *n, pl* **-ties** 1 EASE : facilidad *f* 2 CENTER, COMPLEX : centro *m*, complejo *m* 3 **facilities** *npl* AMENITIES : comodidades *fpl*, servicios *mpl*

facing ['feɪsɪŋ] *n* 1 LINING : entretela *f* (de una prenda) 2 : revestimiento *m* (de un edificio)

facsimile [fæk'sɪməli] *n* : facsímil *m*

fact ['fækt] *n* 1 : hecho *m* ⟨as a matter of fact : de hecho⟩ 2 INFORMATION : información *f*, datos *mpl* ⟨facts and figures : datos y cifras⟩ 3 REALITY : realidad *f* ⟨in fact : en realidad⟩

faction ['fækʃən] *n* : facción *m*, bando *m*

factional ['fækʃənəl] *adj* : entre facciones

factor ['fæktər] *n* : factor *m*

factory ['fæktəri] *n, pl* **-ries** : fábrica *f*

factual ['fæktʃuəl] *adj* : basado en hechos, objetivo

factually ['fæktʃuəli] *adv* : en cuanto a los hechos

faculty ['fækəlti] *n, pl* **-ties** 1 : facultad *f* ⟨the faculty of sight : las facultades visuales, el sentido de la vista⟩ 2 APTITUDE : aptitud *f*, facilidad *f* 3 TEACHERS : cuerpo *m* docente

fad ['fæd] *n* : moda *f* pasajera, manía *f*

fade ['feɪd] *v* **faded; fading** *vi* 1 WITHER : debilitarse (dícese de las personas), marchitarse (dícese de las flores y las plantas) 2 DISCOLOR : desteñirse, decolorarse (dícese de la tez) 3 DIM : apagarse (dícese de la luz), perderse (dícese de los sonidos), fundirse (dícese de las imágenes) 4 VANISH : desvanecerse, decaer — *vt* DISCOLOR : desteñir

fag ['fæg] *vt* **fagged; fagging** EXHAUST : cansar, fatigar

fagot *or* **faggot** ['fægət] *n* : haz *m* de leña

Fahrenheit ['færən,haɪt] *adj* : Fahrenheit

fail¹ ['feɪl] *vi* 1 WEAKEN : fallar, deteriorarse 2 STOP : fallar, detenerse ⟨his heart failed : le falló el corazón⟩ 3 : fracasar, fallar ⟨her plan failed : su plan fracasó⟩ ⟨the crops failed : se perdió la cosecha⟩ ⟨if all else fails : como último recurso⟩ 4 : quebrar ⟨a business about to fail : una empresa a punto de quebrar⟩ 5 **to fail in** : faltar a, no cumplir con ⟨to fail in one's duties : faltar a sus deberes⟩ — *vt* 1 FLUNK : reprobar (un examen) 2 : fallar ⟨words fail me : las palabras me fallan, no encuentro palabras⟩ 3 DISAPPOINT : fallar, decepcionar ⟨don't fail me! : ¡no me falles!⟩

fail² *n* : fracaso *m*

failing ['feɪlɪŋ] *n* : defecto *m*

failure ['feɪljər] *n* 1 : fracaso *m*, malogro *m* ⟨crop failure : pérdida de la cosecha⟩ ⟨heart failure : insuficiencia cardíaca⟩ ⟨engine failure : falla mecánica⟩ 2 BANKRUPTCY : bancarrota *f*, quiebra *f* 3 : fracaso *m* (persona) ⟨he was a failure as a manager : como gerente, fue un fracaso⟩

faint¹ ['feɪnt] *vi* : desmayarse

faint² *adj* 1 COWARDLY, TIMID : cobarde, tímido 2 DIZZY : mareado ⟨faint with hunger : desfallecido de hambre⟩ 3 SLIGHT : leve, ligero, vago ⟨I

haven't the faintest idea : no tengo la más mínima idea⟩ 4 INDISTINCT : tenue, indistinto, apenas perceptible

faint³ *n* : desmayo *m*

fainthearted [feɪnt'hɑrṭəd] *adj* : cobarde, pusilánime

faintly ['feɪntli] *adv* : débilmente, ligeramente, levemente

faintness ['feɪntnəs] *n* 1 INDISTINCTNESS : lo débil, falta *f* de claridad 2 FAINTING : desmayo *m*, desfallecimiento *m*

fair¹ ['fær] *adj* 1 ATTRACTIVE, BEAUTIFUL : bello, hermoso, atractivo 2 (*relating to weather*) : bueno, despejado 3 JUST : justo (dícese de personas, precios, etc.) ⟨fair elections : elecciones limpias⟩ ⟨one's fair share : lo que a uno le corresponde⟩ ⟨give her a fair chance : dale una oportunidad⟩ ⟨to be fair, . . . : en honor a la verdad, . . .⟩ 4 ADEQUATE : adecuado, aceptable ⟨fair to middling : mediano, regular⟩ ⟨he's in fair condition : se encuentra en estado estable⟩ ⟨a fair number : un buen número⟩ ⟨I have a fair idea of how it works : tengo una idea de como funciona⟩ ⟨they have a fair chance of winning : tienen (bastantes) posibilidades de ganar⟩ 5 BLOND, LIGHT : rubio (dícese del pelo), blanco (dícese de la tez) 6 **all's fair in love and war** : en el amor y en la guerra todo vale 7 **fair and square** : con todas las de la ley, en buena ley 8 **fair enough** : de acuerdo, me parece razonable 9 **fair's fair** : lo justo es justo 10 **fair game** : presa *f* fácil 11 **to play fair** : jugar limpio

fair² *n* : feria *f*

fairground ['fær,graʊnd] *n* : parque *m* de diversiones

fair-haired ['fær'hærd] *adj* : rubio

fairly ['færli] *adv* 1 IMPARTIALLY : imparcialmente, limpiamente, equitativamente 2 QUITE : bastante 3 MODERATELY : medianamente

fairness ['færnəs] *n* 1 IMPARTIALITY : imparcialidad *f*, justicia *f* 2 LIGHTNESS : blancura *f* (de la piel), lo rubio (del pelo)

fairy ['færi] *n, pl* **fairies** 1 : hada *f* 2 **fairy tale** : cuento *m* de hadas

fairyland ['færi,lænd] *n* 1 : país *m* de las hadas 2 : lugar *m* encantador

faith ['feɪθ] *n, pl* **faiths** ['feɪθs, 'feɪðz] 1 BELIEF : fe *f* 2 ALLEGIANCE : lealtad *f* 3 CONFIDENCE, TRUST : confianza *f*, fe *f* 4 RELIGION : religión *f*

faithful ['feɪθfəl] *adj* : fiel — **faithfully** *adv*

faithfulness ['feɪθfəlnəs] *n* : fidelidad *f*

faithless ['feɪθləs] *adj* 1 DISLOYAL : desleal 2 : infiel (en la religión) — **faithlessly** *adv*

faithlessness ['feɪθləsnəs] *n* : deslealtad *f*

fake¹ ['feɪk] *v* **faked; faking** *vt* 1 FALSIFY : falsificar, falsear 2 FEIGN : fingir — *vi* 1 PRETEND : fingir 2 : hacer un engaño, hacer una finta (en deportes)

fake² *adj* : falso, fingido, postizo

fake³ *n* 1 IMITATION : imitación *f*, falsificación *f* 2 IMPOSTOR : impostor *m*,

-tora *f*; charlatán *m*, -tana *f*; farsante *mf* 3 FEINT : engaño *m*, finta *f* (en deportes)

faker ['feɪkər] *n* : impostor *m*, -tora *f*; charlatán *m*, -tana *f*; farsante *mf*

falcon ['fælkən, 'fɔl-] *n* : halcón *m*

fall¹ ['fɔl] *vi* **fell** ['fɛl]; **fallen** ['fɔlən]; **falling** 1 : caer, caerse ⟨the rain was falling : caía la lluvia⟩ ⟨a vase fell off the shelf : un jarrón se cayó del estante⟩ 2 : caerse, caer ⟨she tripped and fell down the stairs : tropezó y se cayó por las escaleras⟩ 3 HANG : caer 4 : caer (dícese de la noche) 5 DROP, LOWER : caer (dícese de los ingresos, etc.), bajar (dícese de los precios, las temperaturas, etc.), reducirse (dícese de la voz) ⟨her face fell : se le descompuso la cara⟩ 6 BECOME : volverse, quedarse ⟨to fall silent : callarse, quedarse callado⟩ ⟨to fall in love : enamorarse⟩ 7 : caer (ante un enemigo), rendirse ⟨the city fell : la ciudad se rindió⟩ 8 : caer ⟨to fall in battle : caer en combate⟩ 9 OCCUR : caer ⟨Christmas falls on a Friday : la Navidad cae en viernes⟩ **10 to fall down** : caerse **11 to fall apart** : deshacerse **12 to fall asleep** : dormirse, quedarse dormido **13 to fall away** : decaer, disminuir **14 to fall back** RETREAT : retirarse **15 to fall behind** : quedarse atrás **16 to fall behind on/with** : atrasarse en, retrasarse en **17 to fall down** : caerse **18 to fall down on the job** : no cumplir con su deber **19 to fall flat** : no ser bien recibido (dícese de un chiste, etc.), no dar resultado **20 to fall for** : enamorarse de **21 to fall for** BELIEVE : tragarse **22 to fall in** COLLAPSE : hundirse **23 to fall in** : formar filas **24 to fall into place** : ir bien, aclararse **25 to fall into the hands of** : caer en manos de **26 to fall in with** : juntarse con **27 to fall off** LESSEN : disminuir **28 to fall off** DETACH : desprenderse, caerse **29 to fall on** ATTACK : atacar, caer sobre **30 to fall out** : caerse (dícese del pelo, etc.) **31 to fall out** ARGUE : pelearse **32 to fall out** : romper filas **33 to fall out of favor** : caer en desgracia **34 to fall out of use** : caer en desuso **35 to fall over** : caerse **36 to fall sick** : caer enfermo, enfermarse **37 to fall through** : fracasar, caer en la nada **38 to fall to** : tocar a, corresponder a ⟨the task fell to him : le tocó a él hacerlo⟩

fall² *n* 1 TUMBLE : caída *f* ⟨to break one's fall : frenar uno su caída⟩ ⟨a fall of three feet : una caída de tres pies⟩ 2 FALLING : derrumbe *m* (de rocas), aguacero *m* (de lluvia), nevada *f* (de nieve), bajada *f* (de precios), disminución *f* (de cantidades) 3 AUTUMN : otoño *m* 4 DOWNFALL : caída *f*, ruina *f* 5 **falls** *npl* WATERFALL : cascada *f*, catarata *f*

fallacious [fə'leɪʃəs] *adj* : erróneo, engañoso, falaz

fallacy ['fæləsi] *n, pl* **-cies** : falacia *f*

fall back *vi* 1 RETREAT : retirarse, replegarse 2 **to fall back on** : recurrir a

fall guy *n* SCAPEGOAT : chivo *m* expiatorio

fallible ['fæləbəl] *adj* : falible

fallout ['fɔl,aʊt] *n* 1 : lluvia *f* radioactiva 2 CONSEQUENCES : secuelas *fpl*, consecuencias *fpl*

fallow¹ ['fælo:] *adj* to lie fallow : estar en barbecho

fallow² *n* : barbecho *m*

false ['fɔls] *adj* **falser**; **falsest** 1 UNTRUE : falso ⟨true or false? : ¿verdadero o falso?⟩ ⟨a false name : un nombre falso/ficticio⟩ 2 ERRONEOUS, MISTAKEN : erróneo, equivocado ⟨false hopes : falsas expectativas⟩ ⟨false alarm : falsa alarma⟩ 3 FAKE : falso, postizo ⟨false teeth : dentadura postiza⟩ 4 UNFAITHFUL : infiel 5 INSINCERE, FEIGNED : falso 6 FRAUDULENT : fraudulento ⟨under false pretenses : por fraude⟩ 7 **false move** : movimiento *m* en falso

falsehood ['fɔls,hʊd] *n* : mentira *f*, falsedad *f*

falsely ['fɔlsli] *adv* : falsamente, con falsedad

falseness ['fɔlsnəs] *n* : falsedad *f*

falsetto [fɔl'sɛto:] *n, pl* **-tos** : falsete *m*

falsification [,fɔlsəfə'keɪʃən] *n* : falsificación *f*

falsify ['fɔlsə,faɪ] *vt* **-fied**; **-fying** : falsificar, falsear

falsity ['fɔlsəti] *n, pl* **-ties** : falsedad *f*

falter ['fɔltər] *vi* **-tered**; **-tering** 1 TOTTER : tambalearse 2 STAMMER : titubear, tartamudear 3 WAVER : vacilar

faltering ['fɔltərɪŋ] *adj* : titubeante, vacilante — **falteringly** *adv*

fame ['feɪm] *n* : fama *f*

famed ['feɪmd] *adj* : famoso, célebre, afamado

familial [fə'mɪljəl, -liəl] *adj* : familiar

familiar¹ [fə'mɪljər] *adj* 1 KNOWN : familiar, conocido ⟨to be familiar with : estar familiarizado con⟩ 2 INFORMAL : familiar, informal 3 INTIMATE : íntimo, de confianza 4 FORWARD : confianzudo, atrevido — **familiarly** *adv*

familiar² *n* : espíritu *m* guardián

familiarity [fə,mɪli'ærəti, -,mɪl'jær-] *n, pl* **-ties** 1 KNOWLEDGE : conocimiento *m*, familiaridad *f* 2 INFORMALITY, INTIMACY : confianza *f*, familiaridad *f* 3 FORWARDNESS : exceso *m* de confianza, descaro *m*

familiarize [fə'mɪljə,raɪz] *vt* **-ized**; **-izing** 1 : familiarizar 2 **to familiarize oneself** : familiarizarse

family ['fæmli, 'fæmə-] *n, pl* **-lies** : familia *f*

family name *n* SURNAME : apellido *m*

family room *n* : living *m*, sala *f* (informal)

family tree *n* : árbol *m* genealógico

famine ['fæmən] *n* : hambre *f*, hambruna *f*

famish ['fæmɪʃ] *vi* to be famished : estar famélico, estar hambriento, morir de hambre

famous ['feɪməs] *adj* : famoso

famously ['feɪməsli] *adv* to get on famously : llevarse de maravilla

fan¹ [ˈfæn] *vt* **fanned; fanning** **1** : abanicar (a una persona), avivar (un fuego) **2** STIMULATE : avivar, estimular

fan² *n* **1** : ventilador *m*, abanico *m* **2** ADMIRER, ENTHUSIAST : aficionado *m*, -da *f*; entusiasta *mf*; admirador *m*, -dora *f*

fanatic¹ [fəˈnætɪk] *or* **fanatical** [-tɪ-kəl] *adj* : fanático

fanatic² *n* : fanático *m*, -ca *f*

fanaticism [fəˈnætəˌsɪzəm] *n* : fanatismo *m*

fan belt *n* : correa *f* del ventilador

fanciful [ˈfæntsɪfəl] *adj* **1** CAPRICIOUS : caprichoso, fantástico, extravagante **2** IMAGINATIVE : imaginativo — **fancifully** *adv*

fancy¹ [ˈfæntsi] *vt* **-cied; -cying** **1** IMAGINE : imaginarse, figurarse ⟨fancy that! : ¡figúrate!, ¡imagínate!⟩ **2** CRAVE : apetecer, tener ganas de

fancy² *adj* **fancier; -est** **1** ELABORATE : elaborado **2** LUXURIOUS : lujoso, elegante — **fancily** [ˈfæntsəli] *adv*

fancy³ *n*, *pl* **-cies** **1** LIKING : gusto *m*, afición *f* **2** WHIM : antojo *m*, capricho *m* **3** IMAGINATION : fantasía *f*, imaginación *f*

fandango [fænˈdæŋgo] *n*, *pl* **-gos** : fandango *m*

fanfare [ˈfænˌfær] *n* : fanfarria *f*

fang [ˈfæŋ] *n* : colmillo *m* (de un animal), diente *m* (de una serpiente)

fanlight [ˈfænˌlaɪt] *n* : tragaluz *m*

fantasia [fænˈteɪʒə, -ziə,, ˌfæntə-ˈzi:ə] *n* : fantasía *f*

fantasize [ˈfæntəˌsaɪz] *vi* **-sized; -sizing** : fantasear

fantastic [fænˈtæstɪk] *adj* **1** UNBELIEVABLE : fantástico, increíble, extraño **2** ENORMOUS : fabuloso, inmenso ⟨fantastic sums : sumas fabulosas⟩ **3** WONDERFUL : estupendo, fantástico, bárbaro *fam*, macanudo *fam* — **fantastically** [-tɪkli] *adv*

fantasy [ˈfæntəsi] *n*, *pl* **-sies** : fantasía *f*

FAQ [ˈfæk, ˌɛfˌeɪˈkju:] *n*, *pl* **FAQs** (frequently asked question, frequently asked questions) : FAQ *m* (lista de preguntas)

far¹ [ˈfɑr] *adv* **farther** [ˈfɑrðər] *or* **further** [ˈfər-]; **farthest** *or* **furthest** [-ðəst] **1** : lejos ⟨far from here : lejos de aquí⟩ ⟨to go far : llegar lejos⟩ ⟨far away : a lo lejos⟩ ⟨in the far distant future : en un futuro lejano⟩ ⟨her birthday isn't far off/away : falta poco para su cumpleaños⟩ **2** MUCH : muy, mucho ⟨far bigger : mucho más grande⟩ ⟨far better : mucho mejor⟩ ⟨far different : muy distinto/diferente⟩ ⟨far too expensive : demasiado caro⟩ **3** (*indicating a particular point, degree, or extent*) ⟨we got as far as Chicago : llegamos hasta Chicago⟩ ⟨as far north as Toronto : tan al norte como Toronto⟩ ⟨to go so far as to say : decir tanto como⟩ ⟨as far as I know : que yo sepa⟩ **4** (*indicating an advanced point or extent*) : lejos ⟨to go far (in life) : llegar lejos (en la vida)⟩ ⟨not to go far enough : quedarse corto⟩ ⟨we've come too far to quit now

: hemos llegado demasiado lejos para dejarlo ahora⟩ ⟨we still have far to go : aún nos queda un largo camino por recorrer⟩ ⟨to take something too far : llevar algo demasiado lejos⟩ **5 as/so far as** WITH REGARD TO : en lo que respecta a **6 as/so far as** (*expressing an opinion*) ⟨as far as I'm concerned : en lo que a mí respecta, por mí⟩ **7 by far** : con mucho, de lejos ⟨it's by far the best : es con mucho el mejor⟩ **8 far and wide** : por todas partes **9 far from it!** : ¡todo lo contrario! **10 far off** : muy errado **11 so far** : hasta ahora, todavía

far² *adj* **farther** *or* **further; farthest** *or* **furthest** **1** DISTANT, REMOTE : lejano, remoto ⟨the far horizon : el horizonte lejano⟩ ⟨the far reaches of outer space : los confines del espacio exterior⟩ ⟨the Far East : el Lejano Oriente, el Extremo Oriente⟩ ⟨in the far future : en el/un futuro lejano/remoto⟩ **2** : más lejano ⟨on the far side of the lake : en el otro lado del lago⟩ ⟨at the far end of the room : en el otro extremo de la sala⟩ **3 the far left/right** : la extrema izquierda/derecha (en la política)

faraway [ˈfɑrəˌweɪ] *adj* : remoto, lejano

farce [ˈfɑrs] *n* : farsa *f*

farcical [ˈfɑrsɪkəl] *adj* : absurdo, ridículo

fare¹ [ˈfær] *vi* : ir, salir ⟨how did you fare? : ¿cómo te fue?⟩

fare² *n* **1** : pasaje *m*, billete *m*, boleto *m* ⟨half fare : medio pasaje⟩ **2** FOOD : comida *f*

farewell¹ [ˌfærˈwɛl] *adj* : de despedida

farewell² *n* : despedida *f*

far-fetched [ˈfɑrˈfɛtʃt] *adj* : improbable, exagerado

farina [fəˈri:nə] *n* : harina *f*

farm¹ [ˈfɑrm] *vt* **1** : cultivar, labrar **2** : criar (animales) — *vi* : ser agricultor

farm² *n* : granja *f*, hacienda *f*, finca *f*, estancia *f*

farmer [ˈfɑrmər] *n* : agricultor *m*, granjero *m*

farmhand [ˈfɑrmˌhænd] *n* : peón *m*

farmhouse [ˈfɑrmˌhaʊs] *n* : granja *f*, vivienda *f* del granjero, casa *f* de hacienda

farming [ˈfɑrmɪŋ] *n* : labranza *f*, cultivo *m*, crianza *f* (de animales)

farmland [ˈfɑrmˌlænd] *n* : tierras *fpl* de labranza

farmyard [ˈfɑrmˌjɑrd] *n* : corral *m*

far-off [ˈfɑrˌɔf, -ˈɔf] *adj* : remoto, distante, lejano

far-reaching [ˈfɑrˈri:tʃɪŋ] *adj* : de gran alcance

farsighted [ˈfɑrˌsaɪtəd] *adj* **1** : hipermétrope **2** JUDICIOUS : con visión de futuro, previsor, precavido

farsightedness [ˈfɑrˌsaɪtədnəs] *n* **1** : hipermetropía *f* **2** PRUDENCE : previsión *f*

fart¹ [ˈfɑrt] *vi often vulgar* : tirarse un pedo *fam*

fart² *n often vulgar* **1** : pedo *m fam* **2 old fart** : viejo *m*, -ja *f*

farther¹ [ˈfɑrðər] *adv* **1** AHEAD : más lejos (en el espacio), más adelante (en el tiempo) **2** MORE : más

farther² adj : más lejano, más remoto

farthermost ['farðər,moːst] adj : (el) más lejano

farthest¹ ['farðəst] adv 1 : lo más lejos ⟨I jumped farthest : salté lo más lejos⟩ 2 : lo más avanzado ⟨he progressed farthest : progresó al punto más avanzado⟩ 3 : más ⟨the farthest developed plan : el plan más desarrollado⟩

farthest² adj : más lejano

fascinate ['fæsən,eɪt] vt -nated; -nating : fascinar, cautivar

fascinating ['fæsən,eɪtɪŋ] adj : fascinante

fascination [,fæsən'eɪʃən] n : fascinación f

fascism ['fæʃɪzəm] n : fascismo m

fascist¹ ['fæʃɪst] adj : fascista

fascist² n : fascista mf

fashion¹ ['fæʃən] vt : formar, moldear

fashion² n 1 MANNER : manera f, modo m 2 CUSTOM : costumbre f 3 STYLE : moda f

fashionable ['fæʃənəbəl] adj : de moda, chic

fashionably ['fæʃənəbli] adv : a la moda

fashion show n : desfile m de modelos

fast¹ ['fæst] vi : ayunar

fast² adv 1 SECURELY : firmemente, seguramente ⟨to hold fast : agarrarse bien⟩ 2 RAPIDLY : rápidamente, rápido, de prisa 3 to run fast : ir adelantado ⟨dícese de un reloj⟩ 4 SOUNDLY : profundamente ⟨fast asleep : profundamente dormido⟩

fast³ adj 1 SECURE : firme, seguro ⟨to make fast : amarrar (un barco)⟩ 2 FAITHFUL : leal ⟨fast friends : amigos leales⟩ 3 RAPID : rápido, veloz 4 : adelantado ⟨my watch is fast : tengo el reloj adelantado⟩ 5 DEEP : profundo ⟨a fast sleep : un sueño profundo⟩ 6 COLORFAST : inalterable, que no destiñe 7 DISSOLUTE : extravagante, disipado, disoluto

fast⁴ n : ayuno m

fasten ['fæsən] vt 1 ATTACH : sujetar, atar 2 FIX : fijar ⟨to fasten one's eyes on : fijar los ojos en⟩ 3 SECURE : abrochar (ropa o cinturones), atar (cordones), cerrar (una maleta) — vi : abrocharse, cerrar

fastener ['fæsənər] n : cierre m, sujetador m

fastening ['fæsənɪŋ] n : cierre m, sujetador m

fast food n : comida f rápida

fastidious [fæs'tɪdiəs] adj : quisquilloso, exigente — **fastidiously** adv

fat¹ ['fæt] adj fatter; fattest 1 OBESE : gordo, obeso 2 THICK : grueso

fat² n : grasa f

fatal ['feɪtəl] adj 1 DEADLY : mortal 2 ILL-FATED : malhadado, fatal 3 MOMENTOUS : fatídico

fatalism ['feɪtəl,ɪzəm] n : fatalismo m

fatalist ['feɪtəlɪst] n : fatalista mf

fatalistic [,feɪtəl'ɪstɪk] adj : fatalista

fatality [feɪ'tæləti, fə-] n, pl -ties : víctima f mortal

fatally ['feɪtəli] adv : mortalmente

fate ['feɪt] n 1 DESTINY : destino m 2 END, LOT : final m, suerte f

fated ['feɪtəd] adj : predestinado

fateful ['feɪtfəl] adj 1 MOMENTOUS : fatídico, aciago 2 PROPHETIC : profético — **fatefully** adv

father¹ ['faðər] vt : engendrar

father² n 1 : padre m ⟨my father and my mother : mi padre y mi madre⟩ ⟨Father Smith : el padre Smith⟩ 2 the Father GOD : el Padre, Dios m

fatherhood ['faðər,hʊd] n : paternidad f

father-in-law ['faðərɪn,lɔ] n, pl fathers-in-law : suegro m

fatherland ['faðər,lænd] n : patria f

fatherless ['faðərləs] adj : huérfano de padre, sin padre

fatherly ['faðərli] adj : paternal

fathom¹ ['fæðəm] vt UNDERSTAND : entender, comprender

fathom² n : braza f

fatigue¹ [fə'tiːg] vt -tigued; -tiguing : fatigar, cansar

fatigue² n : fatiga f

fatness ['fætnəs] n : gordura f (de una persona o un animal), grosor m (de un objeto)

fatten ['fætən] vt : engordar, cebar

fattening ['fætnɪŋ] adj : que engorda

fatty ['fæti] adj fattier; -est : graso, grasoso

fatuous ['fætʃuəs] adj : necio, fatuo — **fatuously** adv

faucet ['fɔsət] n : llave f, canilla f Arg, Uru, grifo m

fault¹ ['fɔlt] vt : encontrar defectos a

fault² n 1 SHORTCOMING : defecto m, falta f 2 DEFECT : falta f, defecto m, falla f ⟨to find fault with : encontrarle defectos a, criticar⟩ 3 BLAME : culpa f ⟨to be at fault : tener la culpa⟩ 4 FRACTURE : falla f (geológica)

faultfinder ['fɔlt,faɪndər] n : criticón m, -cona f

faultfinding ['fɔlt,faɪndɪŋ] n : crítica f

faultless ['fɔltləs] adj : sin culpa, sin imperfecciones, impecable

faultlessly ['fɔltləsli] adv : impecablemente, perfectamente

faulty ['fɔlti] adj faultier; -est : defectuoso, imperfecto — **faultily** ['fɔltəli] adv

fauna ['fɔnə] n : fauna f

faux ['foː] adj : de imitación

faux pas [,foː'pɑ] n, pl faux pas [same or -'pɑz] : metedura f de pata fam

favor¹ ['feɪvər] vt 1 SUPPORT : estar a favor de, ser partidario de, apoyar 2 OBLIGE : hacerle un favor a 3 PREFER : preferir 4 RESEMBLE : parecerse a, salir a

favor² n : favor m ⟨in favor of : a favor de⟩ ⟨an error in his favor : un error a su favor⟩

favorable ['feɪvərəbəl] adj : favorable, propicio

favorably ['feɪvərəbli] adv : favorablemente, bien

favorite¹ ['feɪvərət] adj : favorito, preferido

favorite² n : favorito m, -ta f; preferido m, -da f

favoritism ['feɪvərə,tɪzəm] n : favoritismo m

fawn¹ ['fɔn] vi : adular, lisonjear

fawn² n : cervato m

fax¹ ['fæks] n : facsímil m, facsímile m

fax² vt 1 : mandarle un fax a 2 : enviar por fax

faze ['feɪz] vt fazed; fazing : desconcertar, perturbar

fear¹ ['fɪr] vt : temer, tener miedo de — vi : temer

fear² n : miedo m, temor m ⟨for fear of : por temor a⟩

fearful ['fɪrfəl] adj 1 FRIGHTENING : espantoso, aterrador, horrible 2 FRIGHTENED : temeroso, miedoso

fearfully ['fɪrfəli] adv 1 EXTREMELY : extremadamente, terriblemente 2 TIMIDLY : con temor

fearless ['fɪrləs] adj : intrépido, impávido

fearlessly ['fɪrləsli] adv : sin temor

fearlessness ['fɪrləsnəs] n : intrepidez f, impavidez f

fearsome ['fɪrsəm] adj : aterrador

feasibility [ˌfiːzə'bɪləʈi] n : viabilidad f, factibilidad f

feasible ['fiːzəbəl] adj : viable, factible, realizable

feast¹ ['fiːst] vi : banquetear — vt 1 : agasajar, festejar 2 to feast one's eyes on : regalarse la vista con

feast² n 1 BANQUET : banquete m, festín m 2 FESTIVAL : fiesta f

feat ['fiːt] n : proeza f, hazaña f

feather¹ ['fɛðər] vt to feather one's nest : hacer su agosto

feather² n 1 : pluma f 2 a feather in one's cap : un triunfo personal

feathered ['fɛðərd] adj : con plumas

feathery ['fɛðəri] adj 1 DOWNY : plumoso 2 LIGHT : liviano

feature¹ ['fiːʈʃər] v -tured; -turing vt 1 IMAGINE : imaginarse 2 PRESENT : presentar — vi : figurar

feature² n 1 CHARACTERISTIC : característica f, rasgo m 2 : largometraje m (en el cine), artículo m (en un periódico), documental m (en la televisión) 3 features npl : rasgos mpl, facciones fpl ⟨delicate features : facciones delicadas⟩

February ['fɛbjuˌri, 'fɛbu-, 'fɛbru-] n : febrero m ⟨they arrived on the 21st of February, they arrived on February 21st : llegaron el 21 de febrero⟩

fecal ['fiːkəl] adj : fecal

feces ['fiːˌsiːz] npl : heces fpl, excrementos mpl

feckless ['fɛkləs] adj : irresponsable

fecund ['fɛkənd, 'fiː-] adj : fecundo

fecundity [fɪ'kʌndəʈi, fɛ-] n : fecundidad f

federal ['fɛdrəl, -dərəl] adj : federal

federalism ['fɛdrəˌlɪzəm, -dərə-] n : federalismo m

federalist¹ ['fɛdrəlɪst, -dərə-] adj : federalista

federalist² n : federalista mf

federate ['fɛdəˌreɪt] vt -ated; -ating : federar

federation [ˌfɛdə'reɪʃən] n : federación f

fedora [fɪ'dorə] n : sombrero m flexible de fieltro

fed up adj : harto

fee ['fiː] n 1 : honorarios mpl (a un médico, un abogado, etc.) 2 entrance fee : entrada f

feeble ['fiːbəl] adj feebler; feeblest 1 WEAK : débil, endeble 2 INEFFECTIVE : flojo, pobre, poco convincente

feebleminded [ˌfiːbəl'maɪndəd] adj 1 often offensive : débil mental 2 FOOLISH, STUPID : imbécil, tonto

feebleness ['fiːbəlnəs] n : debilidad f

feebly ['fiːbli] adv : débilmente

feed¹ ['fiːd] v fed ['fɛd]; feeding vt 1 : dar de comer a, nutrir, alimentar (a una persona) 2 : alimentar (un fuego o una máquina), proveer (información), introducir (datos) — vi : comer, alimentarse

feed² n 1 NOURISHMENT : alimento m 2 FODDER : pienso m 3 : alimentación f ⟨paper feed : (mecanismo de) alimentación de papel⟩ 4 : transmisión f (de video, etc.) 5 : fuente f (de noticias), canal m (en una red social)

feedback ['fiːdˌbæk] n 1 : retroalimentación f (electrónica) 2 RESPONSE : reacción f

feeder ['fiːdər] n : comedero m (para animales)

feel¹ ['fiːl] v felt ['fɛlt]; feeling vi 1 : sentirse, encontrarse ⟨I feel tired : me siento cansada⟩ ⟨he feels hungry/cold : tiene hambre/frío⟩ ⟨she feels like a fool : se siente como una idiota⟩ ⟨to feel like doing something : tener ganas de hacer algo⟩ 2 SEEM : parecer ⟨it feels like spring : parece primavera⟩ ⟨it feels like rain : parece que va a llover⟩ ⟨it feels smooth : es suave al tacto⟩ 3 THINK : parecerse, opinar, pensar ⟨how does he feel about that? : ¿qué opina él de eso?⟩ 4 to feel (around) for : buscar a tientas 5 to feel for PITY : compadecer — vt 1 TOUCH : tocar, palpar ⟨to feel one's way : tantear, ir a tientas⟩ 2 SENSE : sentir ⟨to feel the cold : sentir el frío⟩ 3 CONSIDER : sentir, creer, considerar ⟨I didn't feel it necessary to inform him : no creí necesario informarle⟩ 4 to feel out : tantear 5 to feel up fam : manosear, meterle mano a fam

feel² n 1 SENSATION, TOUCH : sensación f, tacto m 2 ATMOSPHERE : ambiente m, atmósfera f 3 to have a feel for : tener un talento especial para

feeler ['fiːlər] n : antena f, tentáculo m

feeling ['fiːlɪŋ] n 1 SENSATION : sensación f, sensibilidad f 2 EMOTION : sentimiento m 3 HUNCH, INTUITION : sensación f 4 OPINION : opinión f 5 feelings npl SENSIBILITIES : sentimientos mpl ⟨to hurt/spare someone's feelings : herir/no herir los sentimientos de alguien⟩ ⟨no hard feelings, right? : no me guardas rencor, ¿verdad?⟩ ⟨to have feelings for someone : tener sentimientos por alguien⟩

feet → foot

feign ['feɪn] vt : simular, aparentar, fingir

feint¹ ['feɪnt] vi : fintar, fintear

feint² n : finta f

felicitate [fɪ'lɪsəˌteɪt] vt -tated; -tating : felicitar, congratular

felicitation [fɪ‚lɪsə'teɪʃən] n : felicitación f
felicitous [fɪ'lɪsətəs] adj : acertado, oportuno
feline¹ ['fiː‚laɪn] adj : felino
feline² n : felino m, -na f
fell¹ ['fɛl] vt : talar (un árbol), derribar (a una persona)
fell² → fall
fellow¹ ['fɛ‚loː] adj ⟨his fellow students : sus compañeros de estudios⟩ ⟨fellow citizen : conciudadano, paisano⟩
fellow² n 1 COMPANION : compañero m, -ra f; camarada mf 2 ASSOCIATE : socio m, -cia f 3 MAN : tipo m, hombre m
fellowman [‚fɛlo'mæn] n, pl -men : prójimo m, semejante m
fellowship ['fɛlo‚ʃɪp] n 1 COMPANIONSHIP : camaradería f, compañerismo m 2 ASSOCIATION : fraternidad f 3 GRANT : beca f (de investigación)
felon ['fɛlən] n : malhechor m, -chora f; criminal mf
felonious [fə'loːniəs] adj : criminal
felony ['fɛloni] n, pl -nies : delito m grave
felt¹ ['fɛlt] n : fieltro m
felt² → feel
felt–tip ['fɛlt‚tɪp] or felt–tip pen n : marcador m, rotulador m Spain
female¹ ['fiː‚meɪl] adj : femenino
female² n 1 : hembra f (de animal) 2 WOMAN : mujer f
feminine ['fɛmənən] adj : femenino
femininity [‚fɛmə'nɪnəti] n : feminidad f, femineidad f
feminism ['fɛmə‚nɪzəm] n : feminismo m
feminist¹ ['fɛmənɪst] adj : feminista
feminist² n : feminista mf
femoral ['fɛmərəl] adj : femoral
femur ['fiː‚mər] n, pl femurs or femora ['fɛmərə] : fémur m
fence¹ ['fɛns] v fenced; fencing vt : vallar, cercar — vi : hacer esgrima
fence² n : cerca f, valla f, cerco m, barda f Mex
fencer ['fɛnsər] n : esgrimista mf
fencing ['fɛnsɪŋ] n 1 : esgrima m (deporte) 2 : materiales mpl para cercas 3 ENCLOSURE : cercado m
fend ['fɛnd] vt to fend off : rechazar (un enemigo), parar (un golpe), eludir (una pregunta) — vi to fend for oneself : arreglárselas sólo, valerse por sí mismo
fender ['fɛndər] n : guardabarros mpl, salpicadera f Mex
fennel ['fɛnəl] n : hinojo m
ferment¹ [fər'mɛnt] v : fermentar
ferment² ['fər‚mɛnt] n 1 : fermento m (en la química) 2 TURMOIL : agitación f, conmoción f
fermentation [‚fərmən'teɪʃən, -‚mɛn-] n : fermentación f
fern ['fərn] n : helecho m
ferocious [fə'roːʃəs] adj : feroz — ferociously adv
ferociousness [fə'roːʃəsnəs] n : ferocidad f
ferocity [fə'rɑsəti] n : ferocidad f
ferret¹ ['fɛrət] vi SNOOP : hurgar, husmear — vt to ferret out : descubrir
ferret² n : hurón m

Ferris wheel ['fɛrɪs] n : noria f
ferry¹ ['fɛri] vt -ried; -rying : llevar, transportar
ferry² n, pl -ries : transbordador m, ferry m
ferryboat ['fɛri‚boːt] n : transbordador m, ferry m
fertile ['fərtəl] adj : fértil, fecundo
fertility [fər'tɪləti] n : fertilidad f
fertilization [‚fərtələ'zeɪʃən] n : fertilización f (del suelo), fecundación f (de un huevo)
fertilize ['fərtəl‚aɪz] vt -ized; -izing 1 : fecundar (un huevo) 2 : fertilizar, abonar (el suelo)
fertilizer ['fərtəl‚aɪzər] n : fertilizante m, abono m
fervent ['fərvənt] adj : ferviente, fervoroso, ardiente — fervently adv
fervid ['fərvɪd] adj : ardiente, apasionado — fervidly adv
fervor ['fərvər] n : fervor m, ardor m
fester ['fɛstər] vi : enconarse, supurar
festival ['fɛstəvəl] n : fiesta f, festividad f, festival m
festive ['fɛstɪv] adj : festivo — festively adv
festivity [fɛs'tɪvəti] n, pl -ties : festividad f, celebración f
festoon¹ [fɛs'tuːn] vt : adornar, engalanar
festoon² n GARLAND : guirnalda f
fetal ['fiː‚təl] adj : fetal
fetch ['fɛtʃ] vt 1 BRING : traer, recoger, ir a buscar 2 REALIZE : realizar, venderse por ⟨the jewelry fetched $10,000 : las joyas se vendieron por $10,000⟩
fetching ['fɛtʃɪŋ] adj : atractivo, encantador
fête¹ ['feɪt, 'fɛt] vt : fêted; fêting : festejar, agasajar
fête² n : fiesta f
fetid ['fɛtəd] adj : fétido
fetish ['fɛtɪʃ] n : fetiche m
fetlock ['fɛt‚lɑk] n : espolón m
fetter ['fɛtər] vt : encadenar, poner grillos a
fetters ['fɛtərz] npl : grillos mpl, grilletes mpl, cadenas fpl
fettle ['fɛtəl] n in fine fettle : en buena forma, en plena forma
fetus ['fiː‚təs] n : feto m
feud¹ ['fjuːd] vi : pelear, contender
feud² n : contienda f, enemistad f (heredada)
feudal ['fjuːdəl] adj : feudal
feudalism ['fjuːdəl‚ɪzəm] n : feudalismo m
fever ['fiː‚vər] n : fiebre f, calentura f
feverish ['fiː‚vərɪʃ] adj 1 : afiebrado, con fiebre, febril 2 FRANTIC : febril, frenético
few¹ ['fjuː] adj fewer; fewest : pocos ⟨with few exceptions : con pocas excepciones⟩ ⟨a few times : varias veces⟩ ⟨fewer people : menos gente⟩ ⟨the fewest (number of) points : el menor número de puntos⟩
few² pron fewer; fewest 1 : pocos ⟨few (of them) were ready : pocos estaban listos⟩ ⟨the fewer, the better : cuantos menos mejor⟩ ⟨our group is the fewest in number : nuestro grupo tiene el menor

número de personas⟩ 2 a few : algunos, unos cuantos ⟨a few of the women came : algunas de las mujeres vinieron⟩ ⟨I read a few (of them) : leí algunos, leí unos cuantos⟩ **3 few and far between** : contados

fiancé [ˌfiːˌɑnˈseɪ, ˌfiːˈɑnˌseɪ] *n* : prometido *m*, novio *m*

fiancée [ˌfiːˌɑnˈseɪ, ˌfiːˈɑnˌseɪ] *n* : prometida *f*, novia *f*

fiasco [fiˈæsˌkoː] *n, pl* **-coes** : fiasco *m*, fracaso *m*

fiat [ˈfiːˌɑt, -ˌæt, -ˌɑt;, ˈfaɪət, -ˌæt] *n* : decreto *m*, orden *m*

fib¹ [ˈfɪb] *vi* **fibbed; fibbing** *fam* : decir bolas

fib² *n fam* : bola *f fam*, mentira *f*

fibber [ˈfɪbər] *n* : mentirosillo *m*, -lla *f*; cuentista *mf fam*

fiber *or* **fibre** [ˈfaɪbər] *n* : fibra *f*

fiberboard [ˈfaɪbərˌbord] *n* : cartón *m* madera

fiberglass [ˈfaɪbərˌglæs] *n* : fibra *f* de vidrio

fibrous [ˈfaɪbrəs] *adj* : fibroso

fibula [ˈfɪbjələ] *n, pl* **-lae** [-ˌliː, -ˌlaɪ] *or* **-las** : peroné *m*

fickle [ˈfɪkəl] *adj* : inconstante, voluble, veleidoso

fickleness [ˈfɪkəlnəs] *n* : volubilidad *f*, inconstancia *f*, veleidad *f*

fiction [ˈfɪkʃən] *n* : ficción *f*

fictional [ˈfɪkʃənəl] *adj* : ficticio

fictitious [fɪkˈtɪʃəs] *adj* **1** IMAGINARY : ficticio, imaginario **2** FALSE : falso, ficticio

fiddle¹ [ˈfɪdəl] *vi* **-dled; -dling 1** : tocar el violín **2 to fiddle with** : juguetear con, toquetear

fiddle² *n* : violín *m*

fiddler [ˈfɪdlər, ˈfɪdələr] *n* : violinista *mf*

fiddlesticks [ˈfɪdəlˌstɪks] *interj* : ¡tonterías!

fidelity [fəˈdɛləti, faɪ-] *n, pl* **-ties** : fidelidad *f*

fidget¹ [ˈfɪdʒət] *vi* **1** : moverse, estarse inquieto **2 to fidget with** : juguetear con

fidget² *n* **1** : persona *f* inquieta **2 fidgets** *npl* RESTLESSNESS : inquietud *f*

fidgety [ˈfɪdʒəti] *adj* : inquieto

fiduciary¹ [fəˈduːʃiˌɛri, -ˈdjuː-, -ˌʃəri] *adj* : fiduciario

fiduciary² *n, pl* **-ries** : fiduciario *m*, -ria *f*

field¹ [ˈfiːld] *vt* : interceptar y devolver (una pelota), presentar (un candidato), sortear (una pregunta)

field² *adj* : de campaña, de campo ⟨field hospital : hospital de campaña⟩ ⟨field goal : gol de campo⟩ ⟨field trip : viaje de estudio⟩

field³ *n* **1** : campo *m* (de cosechas, de batalla, de magnetismo) **2** : campo *m*, cancha *f* (en deportes) ⟨baseball field : campo de beisbol⟩ ⟨left/right/center field : jardín izquierdo/derecho/central⟩ **3** : campo *m* (de trabajo), esfera *f* (de actividades) ⟨the field of economics : el campo de la economía⟩

fielder [ˈfiːldər] *n* : jugador *m*, -dora *f* de campo; fildeador *m*, -dora *f*

field glasses *n* : binoculares *mpl*, gemelos *mpl*

field hockey *n* : hockey *m* sobre césped

fiend [ˈfiːnd] *n* **1** DEMON : demonio *m* **2** EVILDOER : persona *f* maligna; malvado *m*, -da *f* **3** FANATIC : fanático *m*, -ca *f*

fiendish [ˈfiːndɪʃ] *adj* : diabólico — **fiendishly** *adv*

fierce [ˈfɪrs] *adj* **fiercer; -est 1** FEROCIOUS : fiero, feroz **2** HEATED : acalorado **3** INTENSE : intenso, violento, fuerte — **fiercely** *adv*

fierceness [ˈfɪrsnəs] *n* **1** FEROCITY : ferocidad *f*, fiereza *f* **2** INTENSITY : intensidad *f*, violencia *f*

fieriness [ˈfaɪərinəs] *n* : pasión *f*, ardor *m*

fiery [ˈfaɪəri] *adj* **fierier; -est 1** BURNING : ardiente, llameante **2** GLOWING : encendido **3** PASSIONATE : acalorado, ardiente, fogoso

fiesta [fiˈɛstə] *n* : fiesta *f*

fife [ˈfaɪf] *n* : pífano *m*

fifteen¹ [fɪfˈtiːn] *adj & pron* : quince

fifteen² *n* : quince *m*

fifteenth¹ [fɪfˈtiːnθ] *adj* : decimoquinto

fifteenth² *n* **1** : decimoquinto *m*, -ta *f* (en una serie) **2** : quinceavo *m*, quinceava parte *f*

fifth¹ [ˈfɪfθ] *adv* : en quinto lugar

fifth² *adj* : quinto ⟨(on) the fifth of June : el cinco de junio⟩

fifth³ *n* **1** : quinto *m*, -ta *f* (en una serie) **2** : quinto *m*, quinta parte *f* **3** : quinta *f* (en la música) **4** *or* **fifth gear** : quinta *f*

fiftieth¹ [ˈfɪftiəθ] *adj* : quincuagésimo

fiftieth² *n* **1** : quincuagésimo *m*, -ma *f* (en una serie) **2** : cincuentavo *m*, cincuentava parte *f*

fifty¹ [ˈfɪfti] *adj & pron* : cincuenta

fifty² *n, pl* **-ties** : cincuenta *m*

fifty-fifty¹ [ˌfɪftiˈfɪfti] *adv* : a medias, mitad y mitad

fifty-fifty² *adj* **to have a fifty-fifty chance** : tener un cincuenta por ciento de posibilidades

fig [ˈfɪg] *n* : higo *m*

fight¹ [ˈfaɪt] *v* **fought** [ˈfɔt]; **fighting** *vi* **1** : luchar, combatir, pelear ⟨to fight to the death : pelear a muerte⟩ ⟨to fight for one's life : debatirse entre la vida y la muerte⟩ **2 to fight back** : defenderse **3 to fight about/over** : discutir por **4 to fight on** : seguir luchando — *vt* **1** : luchar contra, combatir contra **2 to fight back** SUPPRESS : reprimir, contener **3 to fight off** : rechazar, combatir

fight² *n* **1** COMBAT : lucha *f*, pelea *f*, combate *m* **2** MATCH : pelea *f*, combate *m* (en boxeo) **3** QUARREL : disputa *f*, pelea *f*, pleito *m*

fighter [ˈfaɪtər] *n* **1** COMBATANT : luchador *m*, -dora *f*; combatiente *mf* **2** BOXER : boxeador *m*, -dora *f*

figment [ˈfɪgmənt] *n* **figment of the imagination** : producto *m* de la imaginación

figurative [ˈfɪgjərətɪv, -gə-] *adj* : figurado, metafórico

figuratively [ˈfɪgjərətɪvli, -gə-] *adv* : en sentido figurado, de manera metafórica

figure¹ ['fɪgjər, -gər] v **-ured; -uring** vt **1** CALCULATE : calcular **2** ESTIMATE : figurarse, calcular ⟨he figured it was possible : se figuró que era posible⟩ **3** to figure in : incluir en los cálculos **4** to figure out : entender — vi **1** FEATURE, STAND OUT : figurar, destacar **2** that figures! : ¡obvio!, ¡no me extraña nada! **3** to figure on : contar con, tener en cuenta **4** to figure on doing something : pensar hacer algo

figure² n **1** DIGIT : número m, cifra f **2** PRICE : precio m, cifra f **3** PERSONAGE : figura f, personaje m **4** : figura f, tipo m, físico m ⟨to have a good figure : tener buen tipo, tener un buen físico⟩ **5** DESIGN, OUTLINE : figura f **6** figures npl : aritmética f

figurehead ['fɪgjər,hɛd, -gər-] n : testaferro m, líder mf sin poder

figure of speech n : figura f retórica, figura f de hablar

figure out vt **1** UNDERSTAND : entender **2** RESOLVE : resolver (un problema, etc.)

figurine [,fɪgjə'ri:n] n : estatuilla f

filament ['fɪləmənt] n : filamento m

filbert ['fɪlbərt] n : avellana f

filch ['fɪltʃ] vt : hurtar, birlar fam

file¹ ['faɪl] v **filed; filing** vt **1** CLASSIFY : clasificar **2** : archivar (documentos) **3** SUBMIT : presentar ⟨to file charges : presentar cargos⟩ **4** SMOOTH : limar — vi : desfilar, entrar (o salir) en fila

file² n **1** : lima f ⟨nail file : lima de uñas⟩ **2** DOCUMENTS : archivo m **3** LINE : fila f **4** : archivo m (de una computadora)

filial ['fɪliəl, 'fɪljəl] adj : filial

filibuster¹ ['fɪlə,bʌstər] vi : practicar el obstruccionismo

filibuster² n : obstruccionismo m

filibusterer ['fɪlə,bʌstərər] n : obstruccionista mf

filigree ['fɪlə,gri:] n : filigrana f

filing cabinet n : archivador m

Filipino [,fɪlə'pi:no:] n : filipino m, -na f — **Filipino** adj

fill¹ ['fɪl] vt **1** : llenar, ocupar ⟨to fill a cup : llenar una taza⟩ ⟨to fill a room : ocupar una sala⟩ **2** STUFF : rellenar **3** PLUG : tapar, rellenar, empastar (un diente) **4** SATISFY : cumplir con, satisfacer **5** or to fill in/out : rellenar, llenar ⟨fill (in) the blanks : rellene los espacios⟩ ⟨to fill out a form : rellenar un formulario⟩ **6** to fill someone in on : poner a alguien al corriente de **7** to fill up : llenar (hasta arriba) — vi or to fill up : llenarse ⟨her eyes filled with tears : se le llenaron los ojos de lágrimas⟩

fill² n **1** FILLING, STUFFING : relleno m **2** to eat one's fill : comer lo suficiente **3** to have one's fill of : estar harto de

filler ['fɪlər] n : relleno m

fillet¹ ['fɪlət, fɪ'leɪ, 'fɪ,leɪ] vt : cortar en filetes

fillet² n : filete m

fill in vt INFORM : informar, poner al corriente — vi to fill in for : reemplazar a

filling ['fɪlɪŋ] n **1** : relleno m **2** : empaste m (de un diente)

filling station n → gas station

filly ['fɪli] n, pl **-lies** : potra f, potranca f

film¹ ['fɪlm] vt : filmar — vi : rodar

film² n **1** COATING : capa f, película f **2** : película f (fotográfica) **3** MOVIE : película f, filme m

filmmaker ['fɪlm,meɪkər] n : cineasta mf

filmy ['fɪlmi] adj **filmier; -est 1** GAUZY : diáfano, vaporoso **2** : cubierto de una película

filter¹ ['fɪltər] vt : filtrar

filter² n : filtro m

filth ['fɪlθ] n : mugre f, porquería f, roña f

filthiness ['fɪlθinəs] n : suciedad f

filthy ['fɪlθi] adj **filthier; -est 1** DIRTY : mugriento, sucio **2** OBSCENE : obsceno, indecente

filtration [fɪl'treɪʃən] n : filtración f

fin ['fɪn] n **1** : aleta f **2** : alerón m (de un automóvil o un avión)

finagle [fə'neɪgəl] vt **-gled; -gling** : arreglárselas para conseguir

final¹ ['faɪnəl] adj **1** DEFINITIVE : definitivo, final, inapelable **2** ULTIMATE : final **3** LAST : último, final

final² n **1** : final f (en deportes) **2** finals npl : exámenes mpl finales

finale [fɪ'næli, -'na-] n : final m ⟨grand finale : final triunfal⟩

finalist ['faɪnəlɪst] n : finalista mf

finality [faɪ'næləti, fə-] n, pl **-ties** : finalidad f

finalize ['faɪnəl,aɪz] vt **-ized; -izing** : finalizar

finally ['faɪnəli] adv **1** LASTLY : por último, finalmente **2** EVENTUALLY : por fin, al final **3** DEFINITIVELY : definitivamente

finance¹ [fə'nænts, 'faɪ,nænts] vt **-nanced; -nancing** : financiar

finance² n **1** : finanzas fpl **2** finances npl RESOURCES : recursos mpl financieros

financial [fə'næntʃəl, faɪ-] adj : financiero, económico

financially [fə'næntʃəli, faɪ-] adv : económicamente

financier [,fɪnən'sɪr, ,faɪ,næn-] n : financiero m, -ra f; financista mf

financing [fə'næntsɪŋ, 'fæɪ,næntsɪŋ] n : financiación f, financiamiento m

finch ['fɪntʃ] n : pinzón m

find¹ ['faɪnd] vt **found** ['faʊnd]; **finding 1** LOCATE : encontrar ⟨I can't find it : no lo encuentro⟩ ⟨he was nowhere to be found : no se lo encontraba por ninguna parte⟩ **2** CHANCE UPON : encontrar (por casualidad) ⟨I found a dollar : encontré un dólar⟩ **3** LEARN : encontrar, descubrir ⟨to find the answer : encontrar la solución⟩ ⟨we found that . . . : descubrimos que . . .⟩ **4** GET : encontrar, obtener ⟨to find the time to do something : encontrar el tiempo para hacer algo⟩ ⟨to find satisfaction in : obtener satisfacción de⟩ **5** PERCEIVE : encontrar ⟨I find it strange/difficult : lo encuentro raro/difícil, me resulta raro/difícil⟩ **6** DECLARE : declarar, hallar ⟨they found him guilty : lo declararon culpable⟩ **7 to find fault** : criticar **8 to find favor/approval** : ser bien recibido **9 to find oneself** ⟨she found herself in an unfamiliar place : se encontró en un lugar desconocido⟩ ⟨he found himself in a bad situation : se vio en apuros⟩ ⟨I found myself thinking about her : me di cuenta de que estaba pensando en ella⟩ **10 to find oneself** ⟨he left to find himself : se fue para encontrarse a sí mismo⟩ **11 to find one's way** : encontrar el camino, orientarse **12 to find out** : descubrir, averiguar

find² *n* : hallazgo *m*

finder ['faɪndər] *n* : descubridor *m*, -dora *f*

finding ['faɪndɪŋ] *n* **1** FIND : hallazgo *m* **2 findings** *npl* : conclusiones *fpl*

find out *vt* DISCOVER : descubrir, averiguar — *vi* LEARN : enterarse

fine¹ ['faɪn] *vt* **fined; fining** : multar

fine² *adj* **finer; finest 1** PURE : puro (dícese del oro y de la plata) **2** THIN : fino, delgado **3** : fino ⟨fine sand : arena fina⟩ **4** SMALL : pequeño, minúsculo ⟨fine print : letras minúsculas⟩ **5** SUBTLE : sutil, delicado **6** EXCELLENT : excelente, magnífico, selecto **7** FAIR : bueno ⟨it's a fine day : hace buen tiempo⟩ **8** EXQUISITE : exquisito, delicado, fino **9 fine arts** : bellas artes *fpl*

fine³ *n* : multa *f*

finely ['faɪnli] *adv* **1** EXCELLENTLY : con arte **2** ELEGANTLY : elegantemente **3** PRECISELY : con precisión **4 to chop finely** : picar muy fino, picar en trozos pequeños

fineness ['faɪnnəs] *n* **1** EXCELLENCE : excelencia *f* **2** ELEGANCE : elegancia *f*, refinamiento *m* **3** DELICACY : delicadeza *f*, lo fino **4** PRECISION : precisión *f* **5** SUBTLETY : sutileza *f* **6** PURITY : ley *f* (de oro y plata)

finery ['faɪnəri] *n* : galas *fpl*, adornos *mpl*

finesse¹ [fə'nɛs] *vt* **-nessed; -nessing** : ingeniar

finesse² *n* **1** REFINEMENT : refinamiento *m*, finura *f* **2** TACT : delicadeza *f*, tacto *m*, diplomacia *f* **3** CRAFTINESS : astucia *f*

fine–tune ['faɪn'tuːn] *vt* **1** : poner a punto (un motor), ajustar **2** REFINE : afinar, ajustar

finger¹ ['fɪŋgər] *vt* **1** HANDLE : tocar, toquetear **2** ACCUSE : acusar, delatar

finger² *n* : dedo *m* ⟨to lay a finger on someone : ponerle a alguien la mano encima⟩ ⟨not to lift a finger : no mover un dedo, no hacer nada⟩ ⟨to point a finger at someone : culpar a alguien⟩ ⟨to put one's finger on it : dar en el clavo⟩ ⟨to work one's fingers to the bone : deslomarse trabajando⟩

fingerling ['fɪŋgərlɪŋ] *n* : pez *m* pequeño y joven

fingernail ['fɪŋgər,neɪl] *n* : uña *f*

fingerprint¹ ['fɪŋgər,prɪnt] *vt* : tomar las huellas digitales a

fingerprint² *n* : huella *f* digital

fingertip ['fɪŋgər,tɪp] *n* : punta *f* del dedo, yema *f* del dedo

finicky ['fɪnɪki] *adj* : maniático, melindroso, mañoso

finish¹ ['fɪnɪʃ] *vt* **1** COMPLETE : acabar, terminar **2** : aplicar un acabado a (muebles, etc.) **3** RUIN, DESTROY : acabar con **4 to finish off** : terminar **5 to finish up** : terminar — *vi* **1** : terminar **2 to finish up** : terminar, acabar

finish² *n* **1** END : fin *m*, final *m* **2** REFINEMENT : refinamiento *m* **3** : acabado *m* ⟨a glossy finish : un acabado brillante⟩

finish line *n* : línea *f* de meta

finite ['faɪ,naɪt] *adj* : finito

fink¹ ['fɪŋk] *vi fam* **to fink on someone** : delatar a alguien

fink² *n fam* : mequetrefe *mf fam*

Finn ['fɪn] *n* : finlandés *m*, -desa *f*

Finnish¹ ['fɪnɪʃ] *adj* : finlandés

Finnish² *n* : finlandés *m* (idioma)

fiord [fi'ɔrd] → **fjord**

fir ['fər] *n* : abeto *m*

fire¹ ['faɪr] *vt* **fired; firing 1** IGNITE, KINDLE : encender **2** ENLIVEN : animar, avivar **3** DISMISS : despedir ⟨I was fired : me despidieron⟩ **4** SHOOT : disparar ⟨to fire a gun at someone : dispararle a alguien (con un arma de fuego)⟩ **5** BAKE : cocer (cerámica) **6 to fire off** : disparar (un arma, etc.) **7 to fire off** : lanzar (preguntas) **8 to fire up** ENERGIZE, MOTIVATE : entusiasmar **9 to fire up** START : arrancar, poner en marcha (un motor, etc.) — *vi* SHOOT : disparar ⟨to fire at someone : dispararle a alguien, disparar contra alguien⟩

fire² *n* **1** : fuego *m* **2** BURNING : incendio *m* ⟨forest fire : incendio forestal⟩ ⟨fire alarm : alarma contra incendios⟩ ⟨to be on fire : estar en llamas⟩ ⟨to catch (on) fire : prender fuego⟩ ⟨to set fire to : prenderle fuego a⟩ **3** ENTHUSIASM : ardor *m*, entusiasmo *m* **4** SHOOTING : fuego *m*, disparos *mpl* ⟨to open fire : abrir fuego⟩ ⟨to hold one's fire : hacer alto el fuego⟩ ⟨to come under enemy fire : ser sometido al fuego enemigo⟩ **5 to come under fire** : ser blanco de críticas

firearm ['faɪr,ɑrm] *n* : arma *f* de fuego

fireball ['faɪr,bɔl] *n* **1** : bola *f* de fuego **2** METEOR : bólido *m*

firebreak ['faɪr,breɪk] *n* : cortafuegos *m*

firebug ['faɪr,bʌg] *n* : pirómano *m*, -na *f*; incendiario *m*, -ria *f*

firecracker ['faɪr,krækər] *n* : petardo *m*

fire door *n* : puerta *f* cortafuegos

fire engine *n* : coche *m* de bomberos, autobomba *f*

fire escape *n* : escalera *f* de incendios

fire exit *n* : salida *f* de incendios

fire extinguisher *n* : extinguidor *m* de incendios

firefighter ['faɪr,faɪtər] *n* : bombero *m*, -ra *f*

firefly ['faɪr,flaɪ] *n*, *pl* **-flies** : luciérnaga *f*

fireman ['faɪrmən] *n*, *pl* **-men** [-mən, -,mɛn] FIREFIGHTER : bombero *m*

fireplace ['faɪr,pleɪs] *n* : hogar *m*, chimenea *f*

fireproof[1] ['faɪr,pru:f] *vt* : hacer incombustible

fireproof[2] *adj* : incombustible, ignífugo

fireside[1] ['faɪr,saɪd] *adj* : informal ⟨fireside chat : charla informal⟩

fireside[2] *n* **1** HEARTH : chimenea *f*, hogar *m* **2** HOME : hogar *m*, casa *f*

fire station *n* : estación *f* de bomberos

fire truck → **fire engine**

firewall ['faɪr,wɔl] *n* : cortafuegos *m*

firewood ['faɪr,wʊd] *n* : leña *f*

fireworks ['faɪr,wərks] *npl* : fuegos *mpl* artificiales, pirotecnia *f*

firing squad *n* : pelotón *m* de ejecución

firm[1] ['fərm] *vt* or **to firm up** : endurecer

firm[2] *adj* **1** VIGOROUS : fuerte, vigoroso **2** SOLID, UNYIELDING : firme, duro, sólido **3** UNCHANGING : firme, inalterable **4** RESOLUTE : firme, resuelto

firm[3] *n* : empresa *f*, firma *f*, compañía *f*

firmament ['fərməmənt] *n* : firmamento *m*

firmly ['fərmli] *adv* : firmemente

firmness ['fərmnəs] *n* : firmeza *f*

first[1] ['fərst] *adv* **1** : primero ⟨finish your homework first : primero termina tu tarea⟩ ⟨first and foremost : ante todo⟩ ⟨first of all : en primer lugar⟩ **2** : por primera vez ⟨I saw it first in Boston : lo vi por primera vez en Boston⟩

first[2] *adj & pron* **1** : primero ⟨the first time : la primera vez⟩ ⟨the first of many : el primero de muchos, la primera de muchas⟩ ⟨at first sight : a primera vista⟩ ⟨in the first place : en primer lugar⟩ ⟨the first ten applicants : los diez primeros candidatos⟩ ⟨that's the first I've heard of it! : ¡(es la) primera noticia (que tengo)!, ¡ahora me entero!⟩ **2** FOREMOST : principal, primero ⟨first tenor : tenor principal⟩

first[3] *n* **1** : primero *m*, -ra *f* ⟨the first of April : el primero/uno de abril⟩ **2** or **first base** : primera base *f* **3** or **first gear** : primera *f* **4** at ~ : al principio

first aid *n* : primeros auxilios *mpl* ⟨first aid kit : botiquín⟩

firstborn *n* : primogénito *m*, -ta *f* — **firstborn** *adj*

first–class[1] ['fərst'klæs] *adv* : en primera ⟨to travel first-class : viajar en primera⟩

first–class[2] *adj* : de primera

first class *n* : primera clase *f*

firsthand[1] ['fərst'hænd] *adv* : directamente

firsthand[2] *adj* : de primera mano

first lady *n* : primera dama *f*

first lieutenant *n* : teniente *mf*; teniente primero *m*, teniente primera *f*

firstly ['fərstli] *adv* : primeramente, principalmente, en primer lugar

first name *n* : nombre *m* de pila

first–rate[1] ['fərst'reɪt] *adv* : muy bien

first–rate[2] *adj* : de primera, de primera clase

first sergeant *n* : sargento *mf*

firth ['fərθ] *n* : estuario *m*

fiscal ['fɪskəl] *adj* : fiscal — **fiscally** *adv*

fish[1] ['fɪʃ] *vi* **1** : pescar **2** **to fish for** SEEK : buscar, rebuscar ⟨to fish for compliments : andar a la caza de cumplidos⟩ — *vt* : pescar

fish[2] *n*, *pl* **fish** or **fishes** : pez *m* (vivo), pescado *m* (para comer)

fishbowl ['fɪʃ,bo:l] *n* : pecera *f*

fisherman ['fɪʃərmən] *n*, *pl* **-men** [-mən, -,mɛn] : pescador *m*

fisherwoman ['fɪʃər,wʊmən] *n*, *pl* **-women** [-,wɪmən] : pescadora *f*

fishery ['fɪʃəri] *n*, *pl* **-eries** **1** → **fishing** **2** : zona *f* pesquera, pesquería *f*

fishhook ['fɪʃ,hʊk] *n* : anzuelo *m*

fishing ['fɪʃɪŋ] *n* : pesca *f*, industria *f* pesquera

fishing pole or **fishing rod** *n* : caña *f* de pescar

fish market *n* : pescadería *f*

fish sticks *npl* : palitos *mpl* de pescado

fishy ['fɪʃi] *adj* **fishier; -est** **1** : a pescado ⟨a fishy taste : un sabor a pescado⟩ **2** QUESTIONABLE : dudoso, sospechoso ⟨there's something fishy going on : aquí hay gato encerrado⟩

fission ['fɪʃən, -ʒən] *n* : fisión *f*

fissure ['fɪʃər] *n* : fisura *f*, hendidura *f*

fist ['fɪst] *n* : puño *m*

fist bump *n* : choque *m* de puños

fistful ['fɪst,fʊl] *n* : puñado *m*

fisticuffs ['fɪstɪ,kʌfs] *npl* : lucha *f* a puñetazos

fist pump *n* : acto *m* de batir un puño en el aire (para celebrar una victoria, etc.)

fit[1] ['fɪt] *v* **fitted; fitting** *vt* **1** MATCH : corresponder a, coincidir con ⟨the punishment fits the crime : el castigo corresponde al crimen⟩ **2** : quedar ⟨the dress doesn't fit me : el vestido no me queda⟩ **3** GO : caber, encajar en ⟨her key fits the lock : su llave encaja en la cerradura⟩ **4** INSERT, INSTALL : poner, colocar **5** ADAPT : adecuar, ajustar, adaptar **6** or **to fit out** EQUIP : equipar **7** **to fit in** : acomodar — *vi* **1** : quedar, entallar ⟨these pants don't fit : estos pantalones no me quedan⟩ **2** CONFORM : encajar, cuadrar **3** **to fit in** : encajar, estar integrado **4** **to fit in** : adaptarse (dícese de una persona)

fit[2] *adj* **fitter; fittest** **1** SUITABLE : adecuado, apropiado, conveniente ⟨do as you see/think fit : haz lo que creas conveniente⟩ ⟨she didn't see fit to mention it : no juzgó necesario mencionarlo⟩ **2** QUALIFIED : calificado, competente **3** HEALTHY : sano, en forma ⟨to get/keep fit : ponerse/mantenerse en forma⟩

fit[3] *n* **1** ATTACK : ataque *m*, acceso *m*, arranque *m* **2** **to be a good fit** : quedar bien **3** **to be a tight fit** : ser muy entallado (de ropa), estar apretado (de espacios)

fitful ['fɪtfəl] *adj* : irregular, intermitente — **fitfully** *adv*

fitness ['fɪtnəs] *n* **1** HEALTH : salud *f*, buena forma *f* (física) **2** SUITABILITY : idoneidad *f*

fitting¹ ['fɪtɪŋ] *adj* : adecuado, apropiado

fitting² *n* : accesorio *m*

fitting room *n* : probador *m*

five¹ ['faɪv] *adj* : cinco ⟨the child is five (years old) : el niño tiene cinco años⟩

five² *n* : cinco *m* ⟨the five of hearts : el cinco de corazones⟩ ⟨it's five (o'clock) : son las cinco⟩

five³ *pron* : cinco ⟨there are five of us : somos cinco⟩

five hundred¹ *adj & pron* : quinientos

five hundred² *n* : quinientos

fiver ['faɪvər] *n fam* : billete *m* de cinco dólares

fix¹ ['fɪks] *vt* **1** ATTACH, SECURE : sujetar, asegurar, fijar **2** ESTABLISH, SET : fijar (precios, fechas, etc.), concretar (planes, etc.) **3** : fijar (los ojos, la mirada, etc.) **4** REPAIR : arreglar, reparar **5** SOLVE : resolver, solucionar **6** PREPARE : preparar ⟨to fix dinner : preparar la cena⟩ **7** RIG : arreglar, amañar ⟨to fix a race : arreglar una carrera⟩ **8** ARRANGE : arreglar ⟨to fix one's hair/face : peinarse/maquillarse⟩ ⟨she fixed it so we won't have to pay : lo arregló para que no tengamos que pagar⟩ **9** PUNISH : castigar ⟨I'll fix him! : ¡se las verá conmigo!⟩ **10 to fix oneself up** : arreglarse **11 to fix someone up** : arreglarle una cita a alguien **12 to fix someone up** ⟨I'll fix you up : te lo arreglaré todo⟩ ⟨they fixed us up with a rental car : nos consiguió un auto/carro/coche de alquiler⟩ **13 to fix up** : arreglar (una casa, etc.)

fix² *n* **1** PREDICAMENT : aprieto *m*, apuro *m* **2** : posición *f* ⟨to get a fix on : establecer la posición de⟩

fixate ['fɪkˌseɪt] *vi* **-ated; -ating** : obsesionarse

fixation [fɪk'seɪʃən] *n* : fijación *f*, obsesión *f*

fixed ['fɪkst] *adj* **1** STATIONARY : estacionario, inmóvil **2** UNCHANGING : fijo, inalterable **3** INTENT : fijo ⟨a fixed stare : una mirada fija⟩ **4 to be comfortably fixed** : estar en posición acomodada

fixedly ['fɪksədli] *adv* : fijamente

fixedness ['fɪksədnəs, 'fɪkst-] *n* : rigidez *f*

fixture ['fɪkstʃər] *n* **1** : parte *f* integrante, elemento *m* fijo **2 fixtures** *npl* : instalaciones *fpl* (de una casa)

fizz¹ ['fɪz] *vi* : burbujear

fizz² *n* : efervescencia *f*

fizzle¹ ['fɪzəl] *vi* **-zled; -zling** **1** FIZZ : burbujear **2** FAIL : fracasar

fizzle² *n* : fracaso *m*, fiasco *m*

fizzy ['fɪzi] *adj* **fizzier; -est** : gaseoso, efervescente

fjord ['fiˈɔrd] *n* : fiordo *m*

flab ['flæb] *n* : gordura *f*

flabbergast ['flæbərˌgæst] *vt* : asombrar, pasmar, dejar atónito

flabby ['flæbi] *adj* **flabbier; -est** : blando, fofo, aguado *CA, Col, Mex*

flaccid ['flæksəd, 'flæsəd] *adj* : fláccido

flag¹ ['flæg] *vi* **flagged; flagging** **1** : hacer señales con banderas **2** WEAKEN : flaquear, desfallecer

flag² *n* : bandera *f*, pabellón *m*, estandarte *m*

flagon ['flægən] *n* : jarra *f* grande

flagpole ['flægˌpoːl] *n* : asta *f*, mástil *m*

flagrant ['fleɪgrənt] *adj* : flagrante — **flagrantly** *adv*

flagship ['flægˌʃɪp] *n* : buque *m* insignia

flagstaff ['flægˌstæf] → **flagpole**

flagstone ['flægˌstoːn] *n* : losa *f*, piedra *f*

flail ['fleɪl] *vt* **1** : trillar (grano) **2** : sacudir, agitar (los brazos)

flair ['flær] *n* : don *m*, facilidad *f*

flak ['flæk] *ns & pl* **1** : fuego *m* antiaéreo **2** CRITICISM : críticas *fpl*

flake¹ ['fleɪk] *vi* **flaked; flaking** : desmenuzarse, pelarse (dícese de la piel)

flake² *n* : copo *m* (de nieve), escama *f* (de la piel), astilla *f* (de madera)

flamboyance [flæm'bɔɪəns] *n* : extravagancia *f*

flamboyant [flæm'bɔɪənt] *adj* : exuberante, extravagante, rimbombante

flame¹ ['fleɪm] *vi* **flamed; flaming** **1** BLAZE : arder, llamear **2** GLOW : brillar, encenderse

flame² *n* BLAZE : llama *f* ⟨to burst into flames : estallar en llamas⟩ ⟨to go up in flame : incendiarse⟩

flamenco [flə'mɛŋko] *n* : flamenco *m* (música o baile) — **flamenco** *adj*

flamethrower ['fleɪmˌθroːər] *n* : lanzallamas *m*

flamingo [flə'mɪŋgo] *n, pl* **-gos** : flamenco *m*

flammable ['flæməbəl] *adj* : inflamable, flamable

flan ['flæn, 'flɑn] *n* : flan *m*

flange ['flændʒ] *n* : reborde *m*, pestaña *f*

flank¹ ['flæŋk] *vt* **1** : flanquear (para defender o atacar) **2** BORDER, LINE : bordear

flank² *n* : ijada *f* (de un animal), costado *m* (de una persona), falda *f* (de una colina), flanco *m* (de un cuerpo de soldados)

flannel ['flænəl] *n* : franela *f*

flap¹ ['flæp] *v* **flapped; flapping** *vi* **1** : aletear ⟨the bird was flapping (its wings) : el pájaro aleteaba⟩ **2** FLUTTER : ondear, agitarse — *vt* : batir, agitar

flap² *n* **1** FLAPPING : aleteo *m* **2** : solapa *f* (de un sobre), hoja *f* (de una mesa), faldón *m* (de una chaqueta)

flapjack ['flæpˌdʒæk] → **pancake**

flare¹ ['flær] *vi* **flared; flaring** **1** FLAME, SHINE : llamear, brillar **2** *or* **to flare up** : estallar, explotar (de cólera) ⟨tempers flared : se encendieron los ánimos⟩ **3 to flare up** : recrudecerse (dícese de una enfermedad)

flare² *n* **1** FLASH : destello *m* **2** SIGNAL : (luz *f* de) bengala *f* **3 solar flare** : erupción *f* solar

flare–up ['flærˌʌp] *n* **1** : llamarada *f* **2** OUTBREAK : estallido *m*, brote *m* **3** : empeoramiento *m* (de una enfermedad)

flash¹ ['flæʃ] *vi* **1** SHINE, SPARKLE : destellar, brillar, relampaguear **2** : pasar como un relámpago ⟨an idea flashed through my mind : una idea me cruzó la mente como un relámpago) — *vt* : despedir, lanzar (una luz), transmitir (un mensaje)

flash² *adj* SUDDEN : repentino

flash³ *n* **1** : destello *m* (de luz), fogonazo *m* (de una explosión) **2 flash of lightning** : relámpago *m* **3 in a flash** : de repente, de un abrir y cerrar los ojos

flashback ['flæʃ,bæk] *n* : flashback *m*

flash drive *n* : unidad *f* (de memoria) flash

flashiness ['flæʃinəs] *n* : ostentación *f*

flashlight ['flæʃ,laɪt] *n* : linterna *f*

flash memory *n* : memoria *f* flash

flashy ['flæʃi] *adj* **flashier; -est** : llamativo, ostentoso

flask ['flæsk] *n* : frasco *m*

flat¹ ['flæt] *vt* **flatted; flatting 1** FLATTEN : aplanar, achatar **2** : bajar de tono (en música)

flat² *adv* **1** EXACTLY : exactamente ⟨in ten minutes flat : en diez minutos exactos⟩ **2** : desafinado, demasiado bajo (en la música) ⟨to sing flat : cantar desafinado⟩ **3** HORIZONTALLY : ⟨she fell flat on her back/face : cayó de espaldas/ bruces⟩ ⟨lay the map flat on the desk : extiende el mapa sobre el escritorio⟩ **4** COMPLETELY : completamente ⟨I'm flat broke : estoy pelado⟩

flat³ *adj* **flatter; flattest 1** EVEN, LEVEL : plano, llano **2** SMOOTH : liso **3** LOW : bajo ⟨dícese de los zapatos, etc.⟩ **4** SPREAD : tendido ⟨dícese de una persona⟩, extendido ⟨dícese de una cosa⟩ **5** DEFINITE : categórico, rotundo, explícito ⟨a flat refusal : una negativa categórica⟩ **6** : plano ⟨flat rate : tarifa plana⟩ **7** DULL : aburrido, soso, monótono ⟨dícese de la voz⟩ **8** DEFLATED : desinflado, pinchado, ponchado *Mex* **9** : bemol (en música) **10** : sin efervescencia **11** MATTE : mate

flat⁴ *n* **1** PLAIN : llano *m*, terreno *m* llano **2** : bemol *m* (en la música) **3** APARTMENT : apartamento *m*, departamento *m* **4 or flat tire** : pinchazo *m*, ponchadura *f Mex* **5 flats** *npl* : zapatos *mpl* bajos

flatbed ['flæt,bɛd] *n* : camión *m* de plataforma

flatcar ['flæt,kɑr] *n* : vagón *m* abierto

flatfish ['flæt,fɪʃ] *n* : platija *f*

flat-footed ['flæt,fʊtəd, ,flæt'-] *adj* : de pies planos

flatly ['flætli] *adv* DEFINITELY : categóricamente, rotundamente

flatness ['flætnəs] *n* **1** EVENNESS : lo llano, lisura *f*, uniformidad *f* **2** DULLNESS : monotonía *f*

flat-out ['flæt'aut] *adj* **1** : frenético, a toda máquina ⟨a flat-out effort : un esfuerzo frenético⟩ **2** CATEGORICAL : descarado, rotundo, categórico

flatten ['flætən] *vt* : aplanar, achatar

flatter ['flætər] *vt* **1** OVERPRAISE : adular **2** COMPLIMENT : halagar **3** : favorecer ⟨the photo flatters you : la foto te favorece⟩

flatterer ['flætərər] *n* : adulador *m*, -dora *f*

flattering ['flætərɪŋ] *adj* **1** COMPLIMENTARY : halagador **2** BECOMING : favorecedor

flattery ['flætəri] *n, pl* **-ries** : halagos *mpl*

flatulence ['flætʃələnts] *n* : flatulencia *f*, ventosidad *f*

flatulent ['flætʃələnt] *adj* : flatulento

flatware ['flæt,wær] *n* : cubertería *f*, cubiertos *mpl*

flaunt¹ ['flɔnt] *vt* : alardear, hacer alarde de

flaunt² *n* : alarde *m*, ostentación *f*

flavor¹ ['fleɪvər] *vt* : dar sabor a, sazonar

flavor² *n* **1** : gusto *m*, sabor *m* **2** → flavoring

flavored ['fleɪvərd] *adj* : con sabor

flavorful ['fleɪvərfəl] *adj* : sabroso

flavoring ['fleɪvərɪŋ] *n* : condimento *m*, sazón *f* ⟨artificial flavoring : saborizante artificial⟩

flavorless ['fleɪvərləs] *adj* : sin sabor

flaw ['flɔ] *n* : falla *f*, defecto *m*, imperfección *f*

flawed ['flɔd] *adj* : imperfecto, con defectos

flawless ['flɔləs] *adj* : impecable, perfecto — **flawlessly** *adv*

flax ['flæks] *n* : lino *m*

flaxen ['flæksən] *adj* : rubio, blondo ⟨dícese del pelo⟩

flay ['fleɪ] *vt* **1** SKIN : desollar, despellejar **2** VILIFY : criticar con dureza, vilipendiar

flea ['fliː] *n* : pulga *f*

flea market *n* : mercado *m* de pulgas, tianguis *m Mex*, mercadillo *m Spain*

fleck¹ ['flɛk] *vt* : salpicar

fleck² *n* : mota *f*, pinta *f*

fledgling ['flɛdʒlɪŋ] *n* : polluelo *m*, pollito *m*

flee ['fliː] *v* **fled** ['flɛd]; **fleeing** *vi* : huir, escapar(se) — *vt* : huir de

fleece¹ ['fliːs] *vt* **fleeced; fleecing 1** SHEAR : esquilar, trasquilar **2** SWINDLE : estafar, defraudar

fleece² *n* : lana *f*, vellón *m*

fleet¹ ['fliːt] *vi* : moverse con rapidez

fleet² *adj* SWIFT : rápido, veloz

fleet³ *n* : flota *f*

fleet admiral *n* : almirante *mf*

fleeting ['fliːtɪŋ] *adj* : fugaz, breve

Fleming ['flɛmɪŋ] *n* : flamenco *m*, -ca *f*

Flemish ['flɛmɪʃ] *n* **1 the Flemish** (used with a plural verb) : los flamencos *mpl* — **2** : flamenco *m* (idioma) — **Flemish** *adj*

flesh ['flɛʃ] *n* **1** : carne *f* (de seres humanos y animales) **2** : pulpa *f* (de frutas)

flesh out *vt* : desarrollar, darle cuerpo a

fleshy ['flɛʃi] *adj* **fleshier; -est** : gordo ⟨dícese de las personas⟩, carnoso ⟨dícese de la fruta⟩

flew → fly

flex ['flɛks] *vt* : doblar, flexionar

flexibility [,flɛksə'bɪləti] *n, pl* **-ties** : flexibilidad *f*, elasticidad *f*

flexible ['flɛksəbəl] *adj* : flexible — **flexibly** [-bli] *adv*

flextime ['flɛks,taɪm] *n* : horario *m* flexible

flick¹ ['flɪk] *vt* : dar un capirotazo a (con el

dedo⟩ ⟨to flick a switch : darle al interruptor⟩ — vi 1 FLIT : revolotear 2 **to flick through** : hojear (un libro)

flick² n : coletazo m (de una cola), capirotazo m (de un dedo)

flicker¹ ['flɪkər] vi 1 FLUTTER : revolotear, aletear 2 BLINK, TWINKLE : parpadear, titilar

flicker² n 1 : parpadeo m, titileo m 2 HINT, TRACE : indicio m, rastro m ⟨a flicker of hope : un rayo de esperanza⟩

flier ['flaɪər] n 1 AVIATOR : aviador m, -dora f 2 CIRCULAR : folleto m publicitario, circular f

flight ['flaɪt] n 1 : vuelo m (de aves o aviones), trayectoria f (de proyectiles) 2 TRIP : vuelo m 3 FLOCK, SQUADRON : bandada f (de pájaros), escuadrilla f (de aviones) 4 ESCAPE : huida f, fuga f 5 **flight of fancy** : ilusiones fpl, fantasía f 6 **flight of stairs** : tramo m

flight attendant n : auxiliar mf de vuelo

flightless ['flaɪtləs] adj : no volador

flighty ['flaɪti] adj **flightier; -est** : caprichoso, frívolo

flimsy [flɪmzi] adj **flimsier; -est** 1 LIGHT, THIN : ligero, fino 2 WEAK : endeble, poco sólido 3 IMPLAUSIBLE : pobre, flojo, poco convincente ⟨a flimsy excuse : una excusa floja⟩

flinch ['flɪntʃ] vi 1 WINCE : estremecerse 2 RECOIL : recular, retroceder

fling¹ ['flɪŋ] vt flung ['flʌŋ]; **flinging** 1 THROW : lanzar, tirar, arrojar 2 **to fling oneself** : lanzarse, tirarse, precipitarse

fling² n 1 THROW : lanzamiento m 2 ATTEMPT : intento m 3 AFFAIR : aventura f 4 BINGE : juerga f

flint ['flɪnt] n : pedernal m

flinty ['flɪnti] adj **flintier; -est** 1 : de pedernal 2 STERN, UNYIELDING : severo, inflexible

flip¹ ['flɪp] v flipped; **flipping** 1 TOSS : tirar ⟨to flip a coin : echar a cara o cruz⟩ 2 OVERTURN : dar la vuelta a, voltear — vi 1 : moverse bruscamente 2 **to flip through** : hojear (un libro)

flip² adj : insolente, descarado

flip³ n 1 FLICK : capirotazo m, golpe m ligero 2 SOMERSAULT : voltereta f

flip-flop ['flɪp,flɑp] n 1 REVERSAL : giro m radical 2 THONG : chancla f, chancleta f

flippancy ['flɪpəntsi] n, pl **-cies** : ligereza f, falta f de seriedad

flippant ['flɪpənt] adj : ligero, frívolo, poco serio

flipper ['flɪpər] n : aleta f

flirt¹ ['flərt] vi 1 : coquetear, flirtear 2 TRIFLE : jugar ⟨to flirt with death : jugar con la muerte⟩

flirt² n : coqueto m, -ta f

flirtation [ˌflər'teɪʃən] n : devaneo m, coqueteo m

flirtatious [ˌflər'teɪʃəs] adj : insinuante, coqueto

flit ['flɪt] vi flitted; **flitting** 1 : revolotear 2 **to flit about** : ir y venir rápidamente

float¹ ['floːt] vi 1 : flotar 2 WANDER : vagar, errar — vt 1 : poner a flote, hacer flotar (un barco) 2 LAUNCH : hacer flotar (una empresa) 3 ISSUE : emitir (acciones en la bolsa)

float² n 1 : flotador m, corcho m (para pescar) 2 BUOY : boya f 3 : carroza f (en un desfile)

floating ['floːtɪŋ] adj : flotante

flock¹ ['flɑk] vi : moverse en rebaño 2 CONGREGATE : congregarse, reunirse

flock² n : rebaño m (de ovejas), bandada f (de pájaros)

floe ['floː] n : témpano m de hielo

flog ['flɑg] vt flogged; **flogging** : azotar, fustigar

flood¹ ['flʌd] vt : inundar, anegar

flood² n 1 INUNDATION : inundación f 2 TORRENT : avalancha f, diluvio m, torrente m ⟨a flood of tears : un mar de lágrimas⟩

floodgate ['flʌd,geɪt] n : compuerta f, esclusa f ⟨to open the floodgates for/to : abrirle las puertas a, desatar una ola de⟩

flooding ['flʌdɪŋ] n : inundación f

floodlight ['flʌd,laɪt] n : foco m

floodwater ['flʌd,wɔtər] n : crecida f, creciente f

floor¹ ['flor] vt 1 : solar, poner suelo a (una casa o una sala) 2 KNOCK DOWN : derribar, echar al suelo 3 NONPLUS : desconcertar, confundir, dejar perplejo

floor² n 1 : suelo m, piso m ⟨dance floor : pista de baile⟩ 2 STORY : piso m, planta f ⟨ground floor : planta baja⟩ ⟨second floor : primer piso⟩ 3 : mínimo m (de sueldos, precios, etc.)

floorboard ['flor,bord] n : tabla f del suelo, suelo m, piso m

flooring ['florɪŋ] n : entarimado m

floor show n : espectáculo m (en un cabaret, etc.)

floor tile → **tile²**

flop¹ ['flɑp] vi flopped; **flopping** 1 FLAP : golpearse, agitarse 2 COLLAPSE : dejarse caer, desplomarse 3 FAIL : fracasar

flop² n 1 FAILURE : fracaso m 2 **to take a flop** : caerse

floppy ['flɑpi] adj **floppier; -est** 1 : blando, flexible 2 **floppy disk** : diskette m, disquete m

flora ['florə] n : flora f

floral ['florəl] adj : floral, floreado

florid ['florɪd] adj 1 FLOWERY : florido 2 REDDISH : rojizo

florist ['florɪst] n : florista mf

floss¹ ['flɔs] vi : limpiarse los dientes con hilo dental

floss² n 1 : hilo m de seda (de bordar) 2 → **dental floss**

flotation [floː'teɪʃən] n : flotación f

flotilla [floː'tɪlə] n : flotilla f

flotsam ['flɑtsəm] n 1 : restos mpl flotantes (en el mar) 2 **flotsam and jetsam** : desechos mpl, restos mpl

flounce ['flaʊnts] vi **flounced; flouncing** : moverse haciendo aspavientos ⟨she flounced into the room : entró en la sala haciendo aspavientos⟩

flounce² n **1** RUFFLE : volante m **2** FLOURISH : aspaviento m

flounder¹ ['flaundər] vi **1** STRUGGLE : forcejear **2** STUMBLE : no saber qué hacer o decir, perder el hilo (en un discurso)

flounder² n, pl **flounder** or **flounders** : platija f

flour¹ ['flauər] vt : enharinar

flour² n : harina f

flourish¹ ['flərɪʃ] vi THRIVE : florecer, prosperar, crecer (dícese de las plantas) — vt BRANDISH : blandir

flourish² n : floritura f, floreo m

flourishing ['flərɪʃɪŋ] adj : floreciente, próspero

flout ['flaut] vt : desobedecer (una regla, etc.) descaradamente

flow¹ ['floː] vi **1** COURSE : fluir, manar, correr **2** CIRCULATE : circular, correr ⟨traffic is flowing smoothly : el tránsito está circulando con fluidez⟩

flow² n **1** FLOWING : flujo m, circulación f **2** STREAM : corriente f, chorro m

flow chart n : diagrama m, organigrama m

flower¹ ['flauər] vi : florecer, florear

flower² n : flor f

flowerbed ['flauər,bɛd] n : arriate m Mex, Spain; cantero m

flowered ['flauərd] adj : florido, floreado

floweriness ['flauərinəs] n : floritura f

flowering¹ ['flauərɪŋ] adj : floreciente

flowering² n : floración f, florecimiento m

flowerpot ['flauər,pat] n : maceta f, tiesto m, macetero m

flowery ['flauəri] adj **1** : florido **2** FLOWERED : floreado, de flores

flowing ['floːɪŋ] adj : fluido, corriente

flown → **fly**

flu ['fluː] n : gripe f, gripa f Col, Mex

fluctuate ['flʌktʃʊˌeɪt] vi -ated; -ating : fluctuar

fluctuation [ˌflʌktʃʊˈeɪʃən] n : fluctuación f

flue ['fluː] n : tiro m, salida f de humos

fluency ['fluːənsi] n : fluidez f, soltura f

fluent ['fluːənt] adj : fluido

fluently ['fluːəntli] adv : con soltura, con fluidez

fluff¹ ['flʌf] vt **1** : ahuecar (una almohada, etc.) **2** BUNGLE : echar a perder, equivocarse

fluff² n **1** FUZZ : pelusa f **2** DOWN : plumón m

fluffy ['flʌfi] adj **fluffier; -est 1** DOWNY : lleno de pelusa, velloso **2** SPONGY : esponjoso

fluid¹ ['fluːɪd] adj : fluido

fluid² n : fluido m, líquido m

fluidity [fluˈɪdəti] n : fluidez f

fluid ounce n : onza f líquida (29.57 mililitros)

fluke ['fluːk] n : golpe m de suerte, chiripa f, casualidad f

flummox ['flʌməks] vt CONFUSE : desconcertar

flung → **fling**

flunk ['flʌŋk] vt FAIL : reprobar — vi : salir reprobando

fluorescence [ˌflʊrˈɛsənts, ˌflɔr-] n : fluorescencia — **fluorescent** [ˌflʊrˈɛsənt, ˌflɔr-] adj ⟨fluorescent light : (luz) fluorescente⟩

fluoride ['flɔrˌaɪd, 'flʊr-] n : fluoruro m

fluorine ['flɔrˌiːn] n : flúor m

flurry ['flɔri] n, pl **-ries 1** GUST : ráfaga f **2** SNOWFALL : nevisca f **3** BUSTLE : frenesí m, bullicio m **4** BARRAGE : aluvión m, oleada f ⟨a flurry of questions : un aluvión de preguntas⟩

flush¹ ['flʌʃ] vt **1** : limpiar con agua ⟨to flush the toilet : jalar la cadena⟩ **2** RAISE : hacer salir, levantar (en la caza) — vi BLUSH : ruborizarse, sonrojarse

flush² adv : al mismo nivel, a ras

flush³ adj **1** or **flushed** ['flʌʃt] : colorado, rojo, encendido (dícese de la cara) **2** FILLED : lleno a rebosar **3** ABUNDANT : copioso, abundante **4** AFFLUENT : adinerado **5** ALIGNED, SMOOTH : alineado, liso **6 flush against** : pegado a, contra

flush⁴ n **1** FLOW, JET : chorro m, flujo m rápido **2** SURGE : arrebato m, arranque m ⟨a flush of anger : un arrebato de cólera⟩ **3** BLUSH : rubor m, sonrojo m **4** GLOW : resplandor m, flor f ⟨the flush of youth : la flor de la juventud⟩ ⟨in the flush of victory : en la euforia del triunfo⟩

fluster¹ ['flʌstər] vt : poner nervioso, aturdir

fluster² n : agitación f, confusión f

flute ['fluːt] n : flauta f

fluted ['fluːtəd] adj **1** GROOVED : acanalado **2** WAVY : ondulado

fluting ['fluːtɪŋ] n : estrías fpl

flutist ['fluːtɪst] n : flautista mf

flutter¹ ['flʌtər] vi **1** : revolotear (dícese de un pájaro), ondear (dícese de una bandera), palpitar con fuerza (dícese del corazón) **2 to flutter about** : ir y venir, revolotear — vt : sacudir, batir

flutter² n **1** FLUTTERING : revoloteo m, aleteo m **2** COMMOTION, STIR : revuelo m, agitación f

flux ['flʌks] n **1** : flujo m (en física y medicina) **2** CHANGE : cambio m ⟨to be in a state of flux : estar cambiando continuamente⟩

fly¹ ['flaɪ] v **flew** ['fluː]; **flown** ['floːn]; **flying** vi **1** : volar ⟨the birds flew off/away : los pájaros se echaron a volar⟩ **2** TRAVEL : volar ⟨we flew to Europe : volamos a Europa, fuimos en avión a Europa⟩ **3** SOAR, SAIL : volar ⟨he tripped and went flying : se tropezó y salió volando⟩ ⟨clouds flew across the sky : las nubes pasaban rápido por el cielo⟩ ⟨bullets were flying in all directions : las balas silbaban en todas direcciones⟩ **4** : ondear (dícese de una bandera, etc.) **5** FLEE : huir, escapar **6** RUSH : correr, irse volando **7** : correr (dícese de rumores), lanzarse (dícese de insultos) **8** PASS : pasar (volando) ⟨how time flies! : ¡cómo pasa el tiempo!⟩ ⟨our vacation flew by : las vacaciones se nos pasaron volando⟩ **9 to fly open** : abrir de golpe

— vt 1 : pilotar (un avión), hacer volar (una cometa) 2 : transportar, llevar (en avión)

fly² n, pl flies 1 : mosca f ⟨to drop like flies : caer como moscas⟩ 2 : bragueta f (de pantalones, etc.)

flyer → flier

flying saucer n : platillo m volador

flypaper ['flaɪ,peɪpər] n : papel m matamoscas

flyswatter ['flaɪ,swɑtər] n : matamoscas m

flywheel ['flaɪ,ʰwiːl] n : volante m

foal¹ ['foːl] vi : parir

foal² n : potro m, -tra f

foam¹ ['foːm] vi : hacer espuma

foam² n : espuma f

foam rubber n : goma f espuma, hule m espuma Mex

foamy ['foːmi] adj foamier; -est : espumoso

focal ['foːkəl] adj 1 : focal, central 2 focal point : foco m, punto m de referencia

fo'c'sle ['foːksəl] → forecastle

focus¹ ['foːkəs] v -cused or -cussed; -cusing or -cussing vt 1 : enfocar (un instrumento) 2 CONCENTRATE : concentrar, centrar — vi : enfocar, fijar la vista

focus² n, pl -ci ['foː,saɪ, -,kaɪ] 1 : foco m ⟨to be in focus : estar enfocado⟩ 2 FOCUSING : enfoque m 3 CENTER : centro m, foco m

fodder ['fɑdər] n : pienso m, forraje m

foe ['foː] n : enemigo m, -ga f

fog¹ ['fɑg, 'fɔg] v fogged; fogging vt : empañar — vi to fog up : empañarse

fog² n : niebla f, neblina f

foggy ['fɑgi, 'fɔ-] adj foggier; -est : nebuloso, brumoso

foghorn ['fɑg,hɔrn, 'fɔg-] n : sirena f de niebla

fogy ['foːgi] n, pl -gies : carca mf fam, persona f chapada a la antigua

foible ['fɔɪbəl] n : flaqueza f, debilidad f

foil¹ ['fɔɪl] vt : frustrar, hacer fracasar

foil² n 1 : lámina f de metal, papel m de aluminio 2 CONTRAST : contraste m, complemento m 3 SWORD : florete m (en esgrima)

foist ['fɔɪst] vt : encajar, endilgar fam, colocar

fold¹ ['foːld] vt 1 BEND : doblar, plegar 2 CLASP : cruzar (brazos), enlazar (manos), plegar (alas) 3 EMBRACE : estrechar, abrazar 4 to fold in : incorporar ⟨fold in the cream : incorpore la crema⟩ 5 to fold up : doblar, plegar — vi 1 FAIL : fracasar, venirse abajo 2 to fold up : doblarse, plegarse

fold² n 1 SHEEPFOLD : redil m (para ovejas) 2 FLOCK : rebaño m ⟨to return to the fold : volver al redil⟩ 3 CREASE : pliegue m, doblez m

-fold ['foːld] suf 1 : (multiplicado) por ⟨to increase fourfold : multiplicarse por cuatro, cuadruplicarse⟩ ⟨there's been a tenfold increase in thefts : el número de robos se ha multiplicado por diez⟩ 2 (indicating a number of parts) ⟨a three-fold problem : un problema que tiene tres aspectos⟩

folder ['foːldər] n 1 CIRCULAR : circular f, folleto m 2 BINDER : carpeta f 3 : carpeta f, directorio m (en informática)

foliage ['foːliɪdʒ, -lɪdʒ] n : follaje m

folio ['foːliˌoː] n, pl -lios : folio m

folk¹ ['foːk] adj : popular, folklórico ⟨folk customs : costumbres populares⟩ ⟨folk dance : danza folklórica⟩ ⟨folk music : (música) folk⟩

folk² n, pl folk or folks 1 PEOPLE : gente f 2 : folk m, música f folk 3 folks npl : familia f, padres mpl

folklore ['foːk,lɔr] n : folklore m

folksy ['foːksi] adj folksier; -est : campechano

follicle ['fɑlɪkəl] n : folículo m

follow ['fɑloː] vt 1 : seguir (un camino, a una persona, etc.) 2 PURSUE : seguir, perseguir 3 : venir después de, seguir a (en una serie, etc.) 4 OBEY : seguir (instrucciones, etc.), cumplir (la ley, etc.) 5 MONITOR : seguir 6 UNDERSTAND : entender ⟨I don't follow you : no (te) entiendo⟩ 7 to follow suit : hacer lo mismo 8 to follow up : darle seguimiento a (un caso, etc.), seguir (una pista) — vi 1 : seguir 2 UNDERSTAND : entender ⟨as follows ⟨it reads as follows . . . : dice lo siguiente . . . , dice así . . .⟩ 4 it follows that . . . : se deduce que . . . 5 to follow through : continuar con algo 6 to follow through on/with : continuar con (un plan, etc.), cumplir (una promesa, etc.) 7 to follow up : dar seguimiento ⟨to follow up (on) a lead : seguir una pista⟩ ⟨he followed up with us later : nos contactó después⟩ ⟨she followed up with another best seller : después sacó otro best-seller⟩

follower ['fɑloːər] n : seguidor m, -dora f

following¹ ['fɑloːɪŋ] adj NEXT : siguiente

following² n FOLLOWERS : seguidores mpl

following³ prep AFTER : después de

follow-up ['fɑloːˌʌp] n : continuación f, seguimiento m

folly ['fɑli] n, pl -lies : locura f, desatino m

foment [foˈmɛnt] vt : fomentar

fond ['fɑnd] adj 1 LOVING : cariñoso, tierno 2 PARTIAL : aficionado 3 FERVENT : ferviente, fervoroso

fondle ['fɑndəl] vt -dled; -dling : acariciar

fondly ['fɑndli] adv : cariñosamente, afectuosamente

fondness ['fɑndnəs] n 1 LOVE : cariño m 2 LIKING : afición f

fondue [fɑnˈduː, -ˈdjuː] n : fondue f

font ['fɑnt] n 1 or baptismal font : pila f bautismal 2 FOUNTAIN : fuente f

food ['fuːd] n : comida f, alimento m

food chain n : cadena f alimenticia

food poisoning n : intoxicación f alimenticia

food processor n : robot m de cocina

foodstuff ['fuːd,stʌf] n : comestible m, producto m alimenticio

fool¹ ['fuːl] vi 1 JOKE : bromear, hacer el tonto ⟨I was only fooling : sólo estaba bromeando⟩ 2 or to fool around TOY

fool · for

: jugar, juguetear ⟨don't fool (around) with the computer : no juegues con la computadora⟩ **3 to fool around** : perder el tiempo ⟨he fools around instead of working : pierde el tiempo en vez de trabajar⟩ **4 to fool around** : tener líos (amorosos) — *vt* DECEIVE : engañar, burlar ⟨he had me fooled : me tenía convencido⟩ ⟨he fooled me into thinking that . . . : me hizo creer que . . .⟩ ⟨stop fooling yourself! : ¡desengáñate!⟩

fool² *n* **1** IDIOT : idiota *mf*; tonto *m*, -ta *f*; bobo *m*, -ba *f* **2** JESTER : bufón *m*, -fona *f* **3 to make a fool of** : poner/dejar en ridículo, hacer quedar en ridículo ⟨to make a fool of oneself : hacer el ridículo, quedar en ridículo⟩

foolhardiness [ˈfuːlˌhɑrdinəs] *n* : imprudencia *f*

foolhardy [ˈfuːlˌhɑrdi] *adj* RASH : imprudente, temerario, precipitado

foolish [ˈfuːlɪʃ] *adj* **1** STUPID : insensato, estúpido **2** SILLY : idiota, tonto

foolishly [ˈfuːlɪʃli] *adv* : tontamente

foolishness [ˈfuːlɪʃnəs] *n* : insensatez *f*, estupidez *f*, tontería *f*

foolproof [ˈfuːlˌpruːf] *adj* : infalible

foot [ˈfʊt] *n, pl* **feet** [ˈfiːt] **1** : pie *m* ⟨to go on foot : ir a pie⟩ ⟨to be on one's feet : estar de pie⟩ **2 to get/start off on the wrong foot** : empezar con mal pie **3 to put one's best foot forward** : tratar de dejar una buena impresión **4 to put one's foot down** : no ceder **5 to put one's foot in one's mouth** : meter la pata **6 to stand on one's own two feet** : valerse por sí mismo **7 to think on one's feet** : pensar con rapidez

footage [ˈfʊtɪdʒ] *n* : medida *f* en pies, metraje *m* (en el cine)

football [ˈfʊtˌbɔl] *n* : futbol *m* americano, fútbol *m* americano

footbridge [ˈfʊtˌbrɪdʒ] *n* : pasarela *f*, puente *m* peatonal

foothills [ˈfʊtˌhɪlz] *npl* : estribaciones *fpl*

foothold [ˈfʊtˌhoːld] *n* **1** : punto *m* de apoyo **2 to gain a foothold** : afianzarse en una posición

footing [ˈfʊtɪŋ] *n* **1** BALANCE : equilibrio *m* **2** FOOTHOLD : punto *m* de apoyo **3** BASIS : base *f* ⟨on an equal footing : en igualdad⟩

footlights [ˈfʊtˌlaɪts] *npl* : candilejas *fpl*

footlocker [ˈfʊtˌlɑkər] *n* : baúl *m* pequeño, cofre *m*

footloose [ˈfʊtˌluːs] *adj* : libre y sin compromiso

footman [ˈfʊtmən] *n, pl* **-men** [-mən, -ˌmɛn] : lacayo *m*

footnote [ˈfʊtˌnoːt] *n* : nota *f* al pie de la página

footpath [ˈfʊtˌpæθ] *n* : sendero *m*, senda *f*, vereda *f*

footprint [ˈfʊtˌprɪnt] *n* : huella *f*

footrace [ˈfʊtˌreɪs] *n* : carrera *f* pedestre

footrest [ˈfʊtˌrɛst] *n* : apoyapiés *m*, reposapiés *m*

footstep [ˈfʊtˌstɛp] *n* **1** STEP : paso *m* **2** FOOTPRINT : huella *f*

footstool [ˈfʊtˌstuːl] *n* : taburete *m*, escabel *m*

footwear [ˈfʊtˌwær] *n* : calzado *m*

footwork [ˈfʊtˌwərk] *n* : juego *m* de piernas, juego *m* de pies

for¹ [ˈfɔr] *conj* : puesto que, porque

for² *prep* **1** (*indicating purpose*) : para, de, por ⟨the food for the party : la comida para la fiesta⟩ ⟨clothes for children : ropa para niños⟩ ⟨it's time for dinner : es la hora de comer⟩ ⟨to travel for pleasure : viajar por placer⟩ ⟨what's that for? : ¿para qué es/sirve eso?⟩ **2** (*indicating a recipient*) : para ⟨a gift for you : un regalo para ti⟩ **3** (*indicating an object of thoughts or feelings*) : por ⟨his admiration for her : su admiración por ella⟩ ⟨I feel sorry for him : le tengo lástima⟩ **4** BECAUSE OF : por ⟨for fear of : por miedo de⟩ ⟨to jump for joy : saltar de alegría⟩ **5** : por, en beneficio de ⟨he fought for his country : luchó por su patria⟩ ⟨I did it for you : lo hice por ti⟩ ⟨for your own good : por tu propio bien⟩ **6** (*indicating to whom a statement applies*) : para ⟨it's difficult for me : me es difícil, es difícil para mí⟩ ⟨it's time for us to go : es hora de irnos⟩ ⟨I'd hate for you to miss it : sería una lástima que te lo perdieras⟩ **7** IN FAVOR OF : a favor de **8** (*indicating a goal*) : para ⟨to study for a test : estudiar para un examen⟩ ⟨a cure for cancer : una cura para el cáncer⟩ ⟨for more information, call . . . : para más información, llame al . . .⟩ ⟨they ran for safety : corrieron para ponerse a salvo⟩ **9** TOWARDS, TO : para ⟨he left for the office : salió para la oficina⟩ ⟨the train for London : el tren para Londres⟩ **10** (*indicating correspondence or exchange*) : por, para ⟨I bought it for $5 : lo compré por $5⟩ ⟨a lot of trouble for nothing : mucha molestia para nada⟩ **11** AS FOR : para, con respecto a **12** (*indicating duration*) : por, durante ⟨he's going for two years : se va por dos años⟩ ⟨I spoke for ten minutes : hablé (durante) diez minutos⟩ ⟨she has known it for three months : lo sabe desde hace tres meses⟩ ⟨they won't arrive for hours yet : tardarán horas en llegar⟩ ⟨he drove for 100 miles : hizo 100 millas⟩ **13** (*indicating a particular time*) : para, por ⟨the wedding is planned for April : la boda está prevista para abril⟩ ⟨that's enough for now : basta por ahora⟩ **14** INSTEAD OF, ON BEHALF OF : por ⟨to speak for someone : hablar por alguien⟩ ⟨say hello for me : dales saludos de mi parte⟩ **15** (*indicating association*) : para ⟨he works for the university : trabaja para la universidad⟩ **16** (*used in listing items*) : para ⟨for one thing . . . : para empezar . . .⟩ **17** : para (una enfermedad) ⟨for colds and flu : para resfriados y gripe⟩ **18** (*indicating amount or value*) : por, de ⟨a check for $100 : un cheque por/de $100⟩ **19** (*indicating meaning*) ⟨The French word for "good" is "bon" : en francés la palabra "bon" significa "bueno") ⟨what's the word for "taxi" in Japanese? : ¿cómo se dice "taxi" en japonés?⟩ **20** (*used in comparisons*) : para ⟨he's tall for his age : es alto para su edad⟩ **21** (*used in comparing numbers or amounts*) : por ⟨for every dollar invested, there's a return of five dollars : por cada dólar invertido, hay un retorno de cinco dólares⟩ **22** (*used for emphasis*) : por ⟨for crying out loud! : ¡por el amor de Dios!⟩ **23** : para, con ocasión de ⟨a gift for his birthday : un regalo para su cumpleaños⟩ **24 for all IN SPITE OF** : a pesar de **25 for all** : por ⟨she can go now for all I care : por mí que se vaya ahora⟩ ⟨for all I know : que yo sepa⟩ **26 for breakfast/lunch/dinner (etc.)** ⟨we had eggs for breakfast : desayunamos huevos⟩ ⟨what's for dinner/ dessert? : ¿qué hay de comer/ postre?⟩ **27 in for** ⟨he's in for a surprise : se va a llevar una sorpresa⟩ **28 in for it** ⟨if mom finds out, you're in for it : si mamá se entera, te mata⟩ **29 not for** ⟨it's not for you to say she can't go : no te corresponde a ti decir que no vaya⟩

forage [ˈfɔrɪdʒ] *v* **-aged; -aging** *vi* : hurgar (en busca de alimento) — *vt* : buscar (provisiones)

foray [ˈfɔrˌeɪ] *n* : incursión *f*

forbear[1] [fɔrˈbær] *vi* **-bore** [-ˈbor]; **-borne** [-ˈborn]; **-bearing** **1** ABSTAIN : abstenerse **2** : tener paciencia

forbear[2] → **forbear**

forbearance [fɔrˈbærəns] *n* **1** ABSTAINING : abstención *f* **2** PATIENCE : paciencia *f*

forbid [fərˈbɪd] *vt* **-bade** [-ˈbæd, -ˈbeɪd]; **-bidden** [-ˈbɪdən]; **-bidding** **1** PROHIBIT : prohibir **2** PREVENT : impedir

forbidden [fərˈbɪdən] *adj* : prohibido

forbidding [fərˈbɪdɪŋ] *adj* **1** IMPOSING : imponente **2** DISAGREEABLE : desagradable, ingrato **3** GRIM : severo

force[1] [ˈfors] *vt* **forced; forcing** **1** COMPEL : obligar, forzar **2** : forzar ⟨to force open the window : forzar la ventana⟩ ⟨to force a lock : forzar una cerradura⟩ **3** IMPOSE : imponer, obligar

force[2] *n* **1** : fuerza *f* ⟨brute force : fuerza bruta⟩ ⟨the force of gravity : la fuerza de la gravedad⟩ ⟨force of habit : la fuerza de la costumbre⟩ ⟨security forces : fuerzas de seguridad⟩ **2 by force** : por la fuerza **3 in force** : en vigor/vigencia

forced [ˈforst] *adj* : forzado, forzoso

forceful [ˈforsfəl] *adj* : fuerte, enérgico, contundente

forcefully [ˈforsfəli] *adv* : con energía, con fuerza

forcefulness [ˈforsfəlnəs] *n* : contundencia *f*, fuerza *f*

forceps [ˈforsəps, -ˌseps] *ns & pl* : fórceps *m*

forcible [ˈforsəbəl] *adj* **1** FORCED : forzoso **2** CONVINCING : contundente, convincente — **forcibly** [-bli] *adv*

ford[1] [ˈford] *vt* : vadear

ford[2] *n* : vado *m*

fore[1] [ˈfor] *adv* **1** FORWARD : hacia adelante **2 fore and aft** : de popa a proa

fore[2] *adj* **1** FORWARD : delantero, de adelante **2** FORMER : anterior

fore[3] *n* **1** : frente *m*, delantera *f* **2 to come to the fore** : empezar a destacar, saltar a primera plana

fore-and-aft [ˈforənˈæft, -ənd-] *adj* : longitudinal

forearm [ˈforˌarm] *n* : antebrazo *m*

forebear [ˈforˌbær] *n* : antepasado *m*, -da *f*

foreboding [forˈbodɪŋ] *n* : premonición *f*, presentimiento *m*

forecast[1] [ˈforˌkæst] *vt* **-cast; -casting** : pronosticar, predecir

forecast[2] *n* : predicción *f*, pronóstico *m* ⟨weather forecast : pronóstico del tiempo, parte meteorológico⟩

forecastle [ˈfoˌksəl] *n* : castillo *m* de proa

foreclose [forˈkloz] *vt* **-closed; -closing** : ejecutar (una hipoteca)

forefather [ˈforˌfaðər] *n* : antepasado *m*, ancestro *m*

forefinger [ˈforˌfɪŋɡər] *n* : índice *m*, dedo *m* índice

forefoot [ˈforˌfʊt] *n* : pata *f* delantera

forefront [ˈforˌfrʌnt] *n* : frente *m*, vanguardia *f* ⟨in the forefront : a la vanguardia⟩

forego [forˈɡo] *vt* **-went; -gone; -going** **1** PRECEDE : preceder **2** → **forgo**

foregoing [forˈɡoɪŋ] *adj* : precedente, anterior

foregone [forˈɡɔn] *adj* : previsto ⟨a foregone conclusion : un resultado inevitable⟩

foreground [ˈforˌɡraʊnd] *n* : primer plano *m*

forehand[1] [ˈforˌhænd] *adj* : directo, derecho

forehand[2] *n* : golpe *m* del derecho

forehead [ˈforəd, ˈforˌhed] *n* : frente *f*

foreign [ˈfɔrən] *adj* **1** : extranjero, exterior ⟨foreign countries : países extranjeros⟩ ⟨foreign trade : comercio exterior⟩ **2** ALIEN : ajeno, extraño ⟨foreign to their nature : ajeno a su carácter⟩ ⟨a foreign body : un cuerpo extraño⟩

foreigner [ˈforənər] *n* : extranjero *m*, -ra *f*

foreknowledge [forˈnalɪdʒ] *n* : conocimiento *m* previo

foreleg [ˈforˌleɡ] *n* : pata *f* delantera

foreman [ˈformən] *n, pl* **-men** [-mən, -ˌmen] : capataz *mf* ⟨foreman of the jury : presidente del jurado⟩

foremost[1] [ˈforˌmoːst] *adj* : en primer lugar

foremost[2] *adj* : más importante, principal, grande

forenoon [ˈforˌnuːn] *n* : mañana *m*

forensic [fəˈrɛnsɪk] *adj* **1** RHETORICAL : retórico, de argumentación **2** : forense ⟨forensic medicine : medicina forense⟩

foreordain [ˌforərˈdeɪn] *vt* : predestinar, predeterminar

forequarter [ˈforˌkwortər] *n* : cuarto *m* delantero

forerunner [ˈforˌrʌnər] *n* : precursor *m*, -sora *f*

foresee [forˈsiː] *vt* **-saw; -seen; -seeing** : prever

foreseeable [forˈsiːəbəl] *adj* : previsible ⟨in the foreseeable future : en el futuro inmediato⟩

foreshadow [for'ʃædo:] *vt* : anunciar, prefigurar

foresight ['for,saɪt] *n* : previsión *f*

foresighted ['for,saɪtəd] *adj* : previsto

forest ['forəst] *n* : bosque *m* (en zonas templadas), selva *f* (en zonas tropicales)

forestall [for'stɔl] *vt* 1 PREVENT : prevenir, impedir 2 PREEMPT : adelantarse a

forested ['forəstəd] *adj* : arbolado

forester ['forəstər] *n* : silvicultor *m*, -tora *f*

forestland ['forəst,lænd] *n* : zona *f* boscosa

forest ranger → ranger

forestry ['forəstri] *n* : silvicultura *f*, ingeniería *f* forestal

foreswear → forswear

foretaste¹ ['for,teɪst] *vt* **-tasted; -tasting** : anticipar

foretaste² *n* : anticipo *m*

foretell [for'tɛl] *vt* **-told; -telling** : predecir, pronosticar, profetizar

forethought ['for,θɔt] *n* : previsión *f*, reflexión *f* previa

forever [for'ɛvər] *adv* 1 PERPETUALLY : para siempre, eternamente 2 CONTINUALLY : siempre, constantemente

forevermore [for,ɛvər'mor] *adv* : por siempre jamás

forewarn [for'worn] *vt* : prevenir, advertir

forewoman ['for,wumən] *n*, *pl* **-women** [-,wimən] : capataz *f*, capataza *f* ⟨forewoman of the jury : presidente/presidenta del jurado⟩

foreword ['forwərd] *n* : prólogo *m*

forfeit¹ ['forfət] *vt* : perder el derecho a

forfeit² *n* 1 FINE, PENALTY : multa *f* 2 : prenda *f* (en un juego)

forge¹ ['forʤ] *v* **forged; forging** *vt* 1 : forjar (metal o un plan) 2 COUNTERFEIT : falsificar — *vi* **to forge ahead** : avanzar, seguir adelante

forge² *n* : forja *f*

forger ['forʤər] *n* : falsificador *m*, -dora *f*

forgery ['forʤəri] *n*, *pl* **-eries** : falsificación *f*

forget [fər'gɛt] *v* **-got** [-'gɑt]; **-gotten** [-'gɑtən] *or* **-got; -getting** *vt* : olvidar — *vi* **to forget about** : olvidarse de, no acordarse de

forgetful [fər'gɛtfəl] *adj* : olvidadizo

forgetfulness [fər'gɛtfəlnəs] *n* : olvido *m*, mala memoria *f*

forget-me-not [fər'gɛtmi,nɑt] *n* : nomeolvides *m*

forgettable [fər'gɛtəbəl] *adj* : poco memorable

forgivable [fər'gɪvəbəl] *adj* : perdonable

forgive [fər'gɪv] *vt* **-gave** [-'geɪv]; **-given** [-'gɪvən]; **-giving** : perdonar

forgiveness [fər'gɪvnəs] *n* : perdón *m*

forgiving [fər'gɪvɪŋ] *adj* : indulgente, comprensivo, clemente

forgo *or* **forego** [for'go:] *vt* **-went; -gone; -going** : privarse de, renunciar a

fork¹ ['fork] *vi* : ramificarse, bifurcarse — *vt* 1 : levantar (con un tenedor, una horca, etc.) 2 **to fork out/over** : desembolsar

fork² *n* 1 : tenedor *m* (utensilio de cocina) 2 PITCHFORK : horca *f*, horquilla

f 3 : bifurcación *f* (de un río o camino), horqueta *f* (de un árbol)

forked ['forkt, 'forkəd] *adj* : bífido, ahorquillado

forklift ['fork,lɪft] *n* : carretilla *f* elevadora

forlorn [for'lorn] *adj* 1 DESOLATE : abandonado, desolado, desamparado 2 SAD : triste 3 DESPERATE : desesperado

forlornly [for'lornli] *adv* 1 SADLY : con tristeza 2 HALFHEARTEDLY : sin ánimo

form¹ ['form] *vt* 1 FASHION, MAKE : formar 2 DEVELOP : moldear, desarrollar 3 CONSTITUTE : constituir, formar 4 ACQUIRE : adquirir (un hábito), formar (una idea) — *vi* : tomar forma, formarse

form² *n* 1 SHAPE : forma *f*, figura *f* ⟨in the form of : en forma de⟩ 2 MANNER : manera *f*, forma *f* 3 DOCUMENT : formulario *m* ⟨tax form : formulario de declaración de renta⟩ ⟨to fill out a form : rellenar/llenar un formulario⟩ 4 : forma *f* ⟨in good form : en buena forma⟩ ⟨true to form : fiel a su costumbre⟩ 5 MOLD : molde *m* 6 KIND, VARIETY : clase *f*, tipo *m* ⟨some form of : algún tipo de⟩ 7 : forma *f* (en gramática) ⟨plural forms : formas plurales⟩

formal¹ ['forməl] *adj* 1 CEREMONIOUS : formal, de etiqueta, ceremonioso 2 OFFICIAL : formal, oficial, de forma

formal² *n* 1 BALL : baile *m* formal, baile *m* de etiqueta 2 *or* **formal dress** : traje *m* de etiqueta

formaldehyde [for'mældə,haɪd] *n* : formaldehído *m*

formality [for'mæləti] *n*, *pl* **-ties** : formalidad *f*

formalize ['formə,laɪz] *vt* **-ized; -izing** : formalizar

formally ['forməli] *adv* : formalmente

format¹ ['for,mæt] *vt* **-matted; -matting** : formatear

format² *n* : formato *m*

formation [for'meɪʃən] *n* 1 FORMING : formación *f* 2 SHAPE : forma *f* 3 **in formation** : en formación

formative ['formətɪv] *adj* : formativo

former ['formər] *adj* 1 PREVIOUS : antiguo, anterior ⟨the former president : el antiguo presidente⟩ 2 : primero (de dos)

formerly ['formərli] *adv* : anteriormente, antes

formidable ['formədəbəl, for'mɪdə-] *adj* : formidable — **formidably** *adv*

formless ['formləs] *adj* : informe, amorfo

formula ['formjələ] *n*, *pl* **-las** *or* **-lae** [-,li:, -,laɪ] 1 : fórmula *f* 2 **baby formula** : preparado *m* para biberón

formulate ['formjə,leɪt] *vt* **-lated; -lating** : formular, hacer

formulation [,formjə'leɪʃən] *n* : formulación *f*

fornicate ['fornə,keɪt] *vi* **-cated; -cating** : fornicar

fornication [,fornə'keɪʃən] *n* : fornicación *f*

forsake [fər'seɪk] *vt* **-sook** [-'sʊk]; **-saken** [-'seɪkən]; **-saking** 1 ABANDON : abandonar, desamparar **2** RELINQUISH : renunciar a

forswear [fɔr'swær] v **-swore**; **-sworn**; **-swearing** vt RENOUNCE : renunciar a — vi : perjurar

forsythia [far'sɪθiə] n : forsitia f

fort ['fɔrt] n **1** STRONGHOLD : fuerte m, fortaleza f, fortín m **2** BASE : base f militar

forte ['fɔrt, 'fɔr,teɪ] n : fuerte m

forth ['fɔrθ] adv **1** : adelante ⟨from this day forth : de hoy en adelante⟩ **2** and so forth : etcétera

forthcoming [forθ'kʌmɪŋ, 'forθˌ-] adj **1** COMING : próximo **2** DIRECT, OPEN : directo, franco, comunicativo

forthright ['forθ,raɪt] adj : directo, franco — **forthrightly** adv

forthrightness ['forθ,raɪtnəs] n : franqueza f

forthwith [forθ'wɪθ, -'wɪð] adv : inmediatamente, en el acto, enseguida

fortieth[1] ['fɔrtiəθ] adj : cuadragésimo

fortieth[2] n **1** : cuadragésimo m, -ma f (en una serie) **2** : cuarentavo m, cuarentava parte f

fortification [ˌfortəfə'keɪʃən] n : fortificación f

fortify ['fortəˌfaɪ] vt **-fied**; **-fying** : fortificar

fortitude ['fortəˌtu:d, -ˌtju:d] n : fortaleza f, valor m

fortnight ['fort,naɪt] n : quince días mpl, dos semanas fpl

fortnightly[1] ['fort,naɪtli] adv : cada quince días

fortnightly[2] adj : quincenal

fortress ['fortrəs] n : fortaleza f

fortuitous [for'tu:ətəs, -'tju:-] adj : fortuito, accidental

fortunate ['fortʃənət] adj : afortunado

fortunately ['fortʃənətli] adv : afortunadamente, con suerte

fortune ['fortʃən] n **1** : fortuna f ⟨to seek one's fortune : buscar uno su fortuna⟩ **2** LUCK : suerte f, fortuna f **3** DESTINY, FUTURE : destino m, buenaventura f **4** : dineral m, platal m ⟨she spent a fortune : se gastó un dineral⟩

fortune–teller ['fortʃənˌtelər] n : adivino m, -na f

fortune–telling ['fortʃənˌtelɪŋ] n : adivinación f

forty[1] ['fɔrti] adj & pron : cuarenta

forty[2] n, pl **forties** : cuarenta m

forum ['forəm] n, pl **-rums** : foro m

forward[1] ['forwərd] vt **1** PROMOTE : promover, adelantar, fomentar **2** SEND : remitir, enviar

forward[2] adv **1** : adelante, hacia adelante ⟨to go forward : irse adelante⟩ **2** from this day forward : de aquí en adelante

forward[3] adj **1** : hacia adelante, delantero **2** BRASH : atrevido, descarado

forward[4] n : delantero m, -ra f (en deportes)

forwardness ['forwədnəs] n : atrevimiento m, descaro m

forwards ['forwədz] adv → **forward**[2]

fossil[1] ['fasəl] adj : fósil

fossil[2] n : fósil m

fossilize ['fasəˌlaɪz] vt **-ized**; **-izing** : fosilizar — vi : fosilizarse

foster[1] ['fɔstər] vt : promover, fomentar

foster[2] adj : adoptivo ⟨foster child : niño adoptivo⟩

fought → **fight**

foul[1] ['faul] vi : cometer faltas (en deportes) — vt **1** DIRTY, POLLUTE : contaminar, ensuciar **2** TANGLE : enredar

foul[2] adv **1** → **foully 2** : contra las reglas

foul[3] adj **1** REPULSIVE : asqueroso, repugnante **2** CLOGGED : atascado, obstruido **3** TANGLED : enredado **4** OBSCENE : obsceno **5** BAD : malo ⟨foul weather : mal tiempo⟩ **6** : antirreglamentario (en deportes)

foul[4] n : falta f, faul m

foully ['faulli] adv : asquerosamente

foulmouthed ['faul,mæu:ðd, -,mauθt] adj : malhablado

foulness ['faulnəs] n **1** DIRTINESS : suciedad f **2** INCLEMENCY : inclemencia f **3** OBSCENITY : obscenidad f, grosería f

foul play n : actos mpl criminales

foul shot n → **free throw**

foul–up ['faulˌʌp] n : lío m, confusión f, desastre m

foul up vt SPOIL : estropear, arruinar — vi BUNGLE : echar todo a perder

found[1] → **find**

found[2] ['faund] vt : fundar, establecer

foundation [faun'deɪʃən] n **1** FOUNDING : fundación f **2** BASIS : fundamento m, base f **3** INSTITUTION : fundación f **4** : cimientos mpl (de un edificio) **5** or foundation makeup : base f de maquillaje

founder[1] ['faundər] vi SINK : hundirse, irse a pique

founder[2] n : fundador m, -dora f

founding ['faundɪŋ] adj : fundador ⟨the founding fathers : los fundadores⟩

foundling ['faundlɪŋ] n : expósito m, -ta f

foundry ['faundri] n, pl **-dries** : fundición f

fount ['faunt] n SOURCE : fuente f, origen m

fountain ['fauntən] n **1** SPRING : fuente f, manantial m **2** SOURCE : fuente f, origen m **3** JET : chorro m (de agua), surtidor m

fountain pen n : pluma f fuente, estilográfica f

four[1] ['for] adj : cuatro ⟨the child is four (years old) : la niña tiene cinco años⟩

four[2] n **1** : cuatro m ⟨the four of hearts : el cuatro de corazones⟩ ⟨it's four o'clock : son las cuatro⟩ **2** on all fours : a gatas

four[3] pron : cuatro ⟨there are four of us : somos cuatro⟩

four hundred[1] adj & pron : cuatrocientos

four hundred[2] n : cuatrocientos m

four–poster [ˌfor'postər] n : cama f de (cuatro) columnas

fourscore ['for'skor] adj EIGHTY : ochenta

fourteen[1] [for'ti:n] adj & pron : catorce

fourteen[2] n : catorce m

fourteenth[1] [forˈtiːnθ] *adj* : decimocuarto

fourteenth[2] *n* 1 : decimocuarto *m*, -ta *f* (en una serie) 2 : catorceavo *m*, catorceava parte *f*

fourth[1] [ˈforθ] *adv* : en cuarto lugar

fourth[2] *adj* : cuarto

fourth[3] *n* 1 : cuarto *m*, -ta *f* (en una serie) ⟨(on) the fourth of August : el cuatro de agosto⟩ 2 : cuarto *m*, cuarta parte *f* 3 *or* **fourth gear** : cuarta *f*

fowl [ˈfaʊl] *n, pl* **fowl** *or* **fowls** 1 BIRD : ave *f* 2 CHICKEN : pollo *m*

fox[1] [ˈfɑks] *vt* 1 TRICK : engañar 2 BAFFLE : confundir

fox[2] *n, pl* **foxes** : zorro *m*, -ra *f*

foxglove [ˈfɑks,glʌv] *n* : dedalera *f*, digital *f*

foxhole [ˈfɑks,hoːl] *n* : hoyo *m* para atrincherarse, trinchera *f* individual

foxy [ˈfɑksi] *adj* **foxier; -est** SHREWD : astuto

foyer [ˈfɔɪər, ˈfɔɪˌjeɪ] *n* : vestíbulo *m*

fracas [ˈfreɪkəs, ˈfræ-] *n, pl* **-cases** [-kəsəz] : altercado *m*, pelea *f*, reyerta *f*

fracking [ˈfrækɪŋ] *n* : fracking *m*; fractura *f* hidráulica; fracturación *f* hidráulica; estimulación *f* hidráulica *Arg, Col*

fraction [ˈfrækʃən] *n* 1 : fracción *f*, quebrado *m* 2 PORTION : porción *f*, parte *f*

fractional [ˈfrækʃənəl] *adj* 1 : fraccionario *m* 2 TINY : minúsculo, mínimo, insignificante

fractious [ˈfrækʃəs] *adj* 1 UNRULY : rebelde 2 IRRITABLE : malhumorado, irritable

fracture[1] [ˈfræktʃər] *vt* **-tured; -turing** : fracturar

fracture[2] *n* 1 : fractura *f* (de un hueso) 2 CRACK : fisura *f*, grieta *f*, falla *f* (geológica)

fragile [ˈfrædʒəl, -ˌdʒaɪl] *adj* : frágil

fragility [frəˈdʒɪləti] *n, pl* **-ties** : fragilidad *f*

fragment[1] [ˈfrægˌment] *vi* : fragmentarse, hacerse añicos

fragment[2] [ˈfrægmənt] *n* : fragmento *m*, trozo *m*, pedazo *m*

fragmentary [ˈfrægmənˌteri] *adj* : fragmentario, incompleto

fragmentation [ˌfrægmənˈteɪʃən, -ˌmn-] *n* : fragmentación *f*

fragrance [ˈfreɪgrənts] *n* : fragancia *f*, aroma *m*

fragrant [ˈfreɪgrənt] *adj* : fragante, aromático — **fragrantly** *adv*

frail [ˈfreɪl] *adj* : frágil, delicado

frailty [ˈfreɪlti] *n, pl* **-ties** : debilidad *f*, flaqueza *f*

frame[1] [ˈfreɪm] *vt* **framed; framing** 1 FORMULATE : formular, elaborar 2 BORDER : enmarcar, encuadrar 3 INCRIMINATE : incriminar

frame[2] *n* 1 BODY : cuerpo *m* 2 : armazón *f* (de un edificio, un barco, o un avión), bastidor *m* (de un automóvil), cuadro *m* (de una bicicleta), marco *m* (de un cuadro, una ventana, una puerta, etc.) 3 **frames** *npl* : armazón *m*f, montura *f* (para anteojos) 4 **frame of mind** : estado *m* de ánimo

framework [ˈfreɪm,wərk] *n* 1 SKELETON,

STRUCTURE : armazón *f*, estructura *f* 2 BASIS : marco *m*

franc [ˈfræŋk] *n* : franco *m*

franchise [ˈfræn,tʃaɪz] *n* 1 LICENSE : licencia *f* exclusiva, concesión *f* (en comercio) 2 SUFFRAGE : sufragio *m*

franchisee [ˌfræn,tʃaɪˈziː-, -tʃə-] *n* : concesionario *m*, -ria *f*

Franciscan [frænˈsɪskən] *n* : franciscano *m*, -na *f* — **Franciscan** *adj*

frank[1] [ˈfræŋk] *vt* : franquear

frank[2] *adj* : franco, sincero, cándido — **frankly** *adv*

frank[3] *n* : franqueo *m* (de correo)

frankfurter [ˈfræŋkˌfərtər, -ˌfər-] *or* **frankfurt** [-fərt] *n* : salchicha *f* (de Frankfurt, de Viena), perro *m* caliente

frankincense [ˈfræŋkən,sents] *n* : incienso *m*

frankness [ˈfræŋknəs] *n* : franqueza *f*, sinceridad *f*, candidez *f*

frantic [ˈfræntɪk] *adj* : frenético, desesperado — **frantically** *adv*

fraternal [frəˈtərnəl] *adj* : fraterno, fraternal

fraternity [frəˈtərnəti] *n, pl* **-ties** : fraternidad *f*

fraternization [ˌfrætərnəˈzeɪʃən] *n* : fraternización *f*, confraternización *f*

fraternize [ˈfrætərˌnaɪz] *vi* **-nized; -nizing** : fraternizar, confraternizar

fraud [ˈfrɔd] *n* 1 DECEPTION, SWINDLE : fraude *m*, estafa *f*, engaño *m* 2 IMPOSTOR : impostor *m*, -tora *f*; farsante *m*f

fraudulent [ˈfrɔdʒələnt] *adj* : fraudulento — **fraudulently** *adv*

fraught [ˈfrɔt] *adj* **fraught with** : lleno de, cargado de

fray[1] [ˈfreɪ] *vt* 1 WEAR : desgastar, deshilachar 2 IRRITATE : crispar, irritar (los nervios) — *vi* : desgastarse, deshilacharse

fray[2] *n* : pelea *f* ⟨to join the fray : salir a la palestra⟩ ⟨to return to the fray : volver a la carga⟩

frazzle[1] [ˈfræzəl] *vt* **-zled; -zling** 1 FRAY : desgastar, deshilachar 2 EXHAUST : agotar, fatigar

frazzle[2] *n* EXHAUSTION : agotamiento *m*

freak [ˈfriːk] *n* 1 ODDITY : ejemplar *m* anormal, fenómeno *m*, rareza *f* 2 ENTHUSIAST : entusiasta *m*f

freakish [ˈfriːkɪʃ] *adj* : extraño, estrafalario, raro

freak out *vi* : ponerse como loco — *vt* : darle un ataque (a alguien)

freckle[1] [ˈfrɛkəl] *vi* **-led; -ling** : cubrirse de pecas

freckle[2] *n* : peca *f*

free[1] [ˈfriː] *vt* **freed; freeing** 1 LIBERATE : libertar, liberar, poner en libertad 2 RELIEVE, RID : librar, eximir 3 RELEASE, UNTIE : desatar, soltar 4 UNCLOG : desatascar, destapar

free[2] *adv* 1 FREELY : libremente 2 GRATIS : gratuitamente, gratis

free[3] *adj* **freer; freest** 1 : gratuito, gratis ⟨free tickets : entradas gratuitas⟩ ⟨it's free : es gratis⟩ 2 : libre ⟨to set free : liberar, dejar/poner en libertad⟩ ⟨to get free : escaparse⟩ **3** PERMITTED : libre ⟨to be free to do something : ser libre de hacer algo⟩ **4** : libre (dícese de un país, etc.) ⟨free speech : libertad de expresión⟩ ⟨free trade : libre comercio⟩ **5** EXEMPT : libre ⟨tax-free : libre de impuestos⟩ **6** VOLUNTARY : espontáneo, voluntario, libre **7** UNOCCUPIED : libre, desocupado ⟨I'm free tomorrow : mañana estoy libre⟩ ⟨a free seat : un asiento libre⟩ ⟨he waved with his free hand : nos saludó con su mano libre⟩ **8** LOOSE : suelto **9** : generoso ⟨they were very free with their money : fueron muy generosos con su dinero⟩ **10 for free** : gratis **11 free from/of** : libre de

freeborn ['fri:'bɔrn] *adj* : nacido libre
freedom ['fri:dəm] *n* : libertad *f*
free enterprise *n* : libre empresa *f*
free–for–all ['fri:fər,ɔl] *n* : pelea *f*, batalla *f* campal
free gift *n* : obsequio *m*
freehand ['fri:,hænd] *adj* : a pulso, a mano alzada
free kick *n* : tiro *m* libre
freelance[1] ['fri:,læns] *vi* -lanced; -lancing : trabajar por cuenta propia
freelance[2] *adj* : por cuenta propia, freelance
freelancer ['fri:,lænsər] *n* : trabajador *m*, -dora *f* por cuenta propia; freelance *mf*
freeload ['fri:,lo:d] *vi* : gorronear *fam*, gorrear *fam*
freeloader ['fri:,lo:dər] *n* : gorrón *m*, -rrona *f*; gorrero *m*, -ra *f*; vividor *m*, -dora *f*
freely ['fri:li] *adv* **1** FREE : libremente **2** GRATIS : gratis, gratuitamente
Freemason ['fri:'meɪsən] *n* : francmasón *m*, masón *m*
Freemasonry ['fri:'meɪsənri] *n* : francmasonería *f*, masonería *f*
free–range ['fri:,reɪndʒ] *adj* : de granja
freestanding ['fri:'stændɪŋ] *adj* : de pie, no empotrado, independiente
free throw *n* : tiro *m* libre (en baloncesto)
freeway ['fri:,weɪ] *n* : autopista *f*
freewill ['fri:,wɪl] *adj* : de propia voluntad
free will *n* : libre albedrío *m*, propia voluntad *f*
freeze[1] ['fri:z] *v* **froze** ['fro:z]; **frozen** ['fro:zən]; **freezing** *vi* **1** : congelarse, helarse ⟨the water froze in the lake : el agua se congeló en el lago⟩ ⟨my blood froze : se me heló la sangre⟩ ⟨I'm freezing : me estoy helando⟩ **2** STOP : quedarse inmóvil **3** : bloquearse (dícese de una computadora) — *vt* : helar, congelar (líquidos), congelar (alimentos, precios, activos), bloquear (cuentas, etc.)
freeze[2] *n* **1** FROST : helada *f* **2** FREEZING : congelación *f*, congelamiento *m*
freeze–dried ['fri:z'draɪd] *adj* : liofilizado
freeze–dry ['fri:z'draɪ] *vt* -dried; -drying : liofilizar
freezer ['fri:zər] *n* : congelador *m*
freezing ['fri:zɪŋ] *adj* : helando ⟨it's freezing! : ¡hace un frío espantoso!⟩
freezing point *n* : punto *m* de congelación
freight[1] ['freɪt] *vt* : enviar como carga

freight[2] *n* **1** SHIPPING, TRANSPORT : transporte *m*, porte *m*, flete *m* **2** GOODS : mercancías *fpl*, carga *f*
freighter ['freɪtər] *n* : carguero *m*, buque *m* de carga
freight train *n* : tren *m* de carga, tren *m* de mercancías
French[1] ['frɛntʃ] *adj* : francés
French[2] *n* **1** : francés *m* (idioma) **2 the French** (*used with a plural verb*) : los franceses
French doors *npl* : puerta *f* ventana
French dressing *n* **1** : aderezo *m* cremoso con sabor a tomate **2** *Brit* VINAIGRETTE : vinagreta *f*
french fries ['frɛntʃ,fraɪz] *npl* : papas *fpl* fritas, papas *fpl* a la francesa *Mexico, Colombia*
Frenchman ['frɛntʃmən] *n, pl* -men [-mən, -,mɛn] : francés *m*
French toast *n* : torreja *f*, torrija *f* *Spain*
French windows *npl* → **French doors**
Frenchwoman ['frɛntʃ,wʊmən] *n, pl* -women [-,wɪmən] : francesa *f*
frenemy ['frɛnəmi] *n, pl* -mies : amienemigo *m*, -ga *f* *fam*
frenetic [frɪ'nɛtɪk] *adj* : frenético — **frenetically** [-ţɪkli] *adv*
frenzied ['frɛnzid] *adj* : frenético
frenzy ['frɛnzi] *n, pl* -zies : frenesí *m*
frequency ['fri:kwənsi] *n, pl* -cies : frecuencia *f*
frequent[1] ['fri:kwɛnt, 'fri:,kwɛnt] *vt* : frecuentar
frequent[2] ['fri:kwənt] *adj* : frecuente — **frequently** *adv*
fresco ['frɛs,ko:] *n, pl* -coes : fresco *m*
fresh ['frɛʃ] *adj* **1** : dulce ⟨freshwater : agua dulce⟩ **2** PURE : puro **3** : fresco ⟨fresh fruits : frutas frescas⟩ **4** CLEAN, NEW : limpio, nuevo ⟨fresh clothes : ropa limpia⟩ ⟨fresh evidence : evidencia nueva⟩ **5** REFRESHED : fresco, descansado **6** IMPERTINENT : descarado, impertinente
freshen ['frɛʃən] *vt* : refrescar, arreglar — *vi* **to freshen up** : arreglarse, lavarse
freshet ['frɛʃət] *n* : arroyo *m* desbordado
freshly ['frɛʃli] *adv* : recientemente, recién
freshman ['frɛʃmən] *n, pl* -men [-mən, -,mɛn] : estudiante *mf* de primer año universitario
freshness ['frɛʃnəs] *n* : frescura *f*
freshwater ['frɛʃ,wɔţər] *n* : agua *f* dulce
fret[1] ['frɛt] *vi* **fretted; fretting** : preocuparse, inquietarse
fret[2] *n* **1** VEXATION : irritación *f*, molestia *f* **2** WORRY : preocupación *f* **3** : traste *m* (de un instrumento musical)
fretful ['frɛtfəl] *adj* : fastidioso, quejoso, neurótico
fretfully ['frɛtfəli] *adv* : ansiosamente, fastidiosamente, inquieto
fretfulness ['frɛtfəlnəs] *n* : inquietud *f*, irritabilidad *f*
friar ['fraɪər] *n* : fraile *m*
friction ['frɪkʃən] *n* **1** RUBBING : fricción *f* **2** CONFLICT : fricción *f*, roce *m*
Friday ['fraɪ,deɪ, -di] *n* : viernes *m* ⟨today is Friday : hoy es viernes⟩ ⟨(on) Friday

: el viernes⟩ ⟨(on) Fridays : los viernes⟩ ⟨last Friday : el viernes pasado⟩ ⟨next Friday : el viernes que viene⟩ ⟨every other Friday : cada dos viernes⟩ ⟨Friday afternoon/morning : viernes por la tarde/mañana⟩

fridge [ˈfrɪdʒ] → **refrigerator**

fried [ˈfraɪd] *adj* : frito

friend¹ [ˈfrend] *n* : amigo *m*, -ga *f* ⟨to be/make friends with : ser/hacerse amigo de⟩

friend² *vt* : agregar (a alguien) a su lista de amigos ⟨he friended me on Facebook : me agregó (como amigo) en Facebook⟩

friendless [ˈfrendləs] *adj* : sin amigos

friendliness [ˈfrendlinəs] *n* : simpatía *f*, amabilidad *f*

friendly [ˈfrendli] *adj* **friendlier; -est** **1** : simpático, amable, de amigo ⟨a friendly child : un niño simpático⟩ ⟨friendly advice : consejo de amigo⟩ **2** : agradable, acogedor ⟨a friendly atmosphere : un ambiente agradable⟩ **3** GOOD-NATURED : amigable, amistoso ⟨friendly competition : competencia amistosa⟩

friendship [ˈfrendˌʃɪp] *n* : amistad *f*

frieze [ˈfriːz] *n* : friso *m*

frigate [ˈfrɪgət] *n* : fragata *f*

fright [ˈfraɪt] *n* : miedo *m*, susto *m*

frighten [ˈfraɪtən] *vt* : asustar, espantar

frightened [ˈfraɪtənd] *adj* : asustado, temeroso

frightening [ˈfraɪtənɪŋ] *adj* : espantoso, aterrador

frightful [ˈfraɪtfəl] *adj* **1** → **frightening** **2** TREMENDOUS : espantoso, tremendo

frightfully [ˈfraɪtfəli] *adv* : terriblemente, tremendamente

frigid [ˈfrɪdʒɪd] *adj* : glacial, extremadamente frío

frigidity [frɪˈdʒɪdəti] *n* **1** COLDNESS : frialdad *f* **2** : frigidez *f* (sexual)

frill [ˈfrɪl] *n* **1** RUFFLE : volante *m* **2** EMBELLISHMENT : floritura *f*, adorno *m*

frilly [ˈfrɪli] *adj* **frillier; -est** **1** RUFFLY : con volantes **2** OVERDONE : recargado

fringe¹ [ˈfrɪndʒ] *vt* **fringed; fringing** : orlar, bordear

fringe² *n* **1** BORDER : fleco *m*, orla *f* **2** EDGE : periferia *f*, margen *m* **3** **fringe benefits** : incentivos *mpl*, extras *mpl*

Frisbee [ˈfrɪzbi] *trademark* se usa para un disco volador que se lanza de un jugador a otro

frisk [ˈfrɪsk] *vi* FROLIC : retozar, juguetear — *vt* SEARCH : cachear, registrar

friskiness [ˈfrɪskinəs] *n* : vivacidad *f*

frisky [ˈfrɪski] *adj* **friskier; -est** : retozón, juguetón

fritter¹ [ˈfrɪtər] *vt* : desperdiciar, malgastar ⟨I frittered away the money : malgasté el dinero⟩

fritter² *n* : buñuelo *m*

frivolity [frɪˈvɑləti] *n*, *pl* **-ties** : frivolidad *f*

frivolous [ˈfrɪvələs] *adj* : frívolo, de poca importancia

frivolously [ˈfrɪvələsli] *adv* : frívolamente, a la ligera

frizz¹ [ˈfrɪz] *vi* : rizarse, encresparse, ponerse chino *Mex*

frizz² *n* : rizos *mpl* muy apretados

frizzy [ˈfrɪzi] *adj* **frizzier; -est** : rizado, crespo, chino *Mex*

fro [ˈfroː] *adv* **to and fro** : de aquí para allá, de un lado para otro

frock [ˈfrɑk] *n* DRESS : vestido *m*

frog [ˈfrɔg, ˈfrɑg] *n* **1** : rana *f* **2 to have a frog in one's throat** : tener carraspera

frogman [ˈfrɔgˌmæn, ˈfrɑg-, -mən] *n*, *pl* **-men** [-mən, -ˌmen] : hombre *m* rana, submarinista *mf*

frolic¹ [ˈfrɑlɪk] *vi* **-icked; -icking** : retozar, juguetear

frolic² *n* FUN : diversión *f*

frolicsome [ˈfrɑlɪksəm] *adj* : juguetón

from [ˈfrʌm, ˈfrɑm] *prep* **1** (*indicating a starting, central, or lowest point*) : desde, de, a partir de ⟨from Cali to Bogota : de Cali a Bogotá⟩ ⟨where are you from? : ¿de dónde eres?⟩ ⟨he watched us from above : nos miraba desde arriba⟩ ⟨from that time onward : desde entonces⟩ ⟨from January to March : de enero a marzo, desde enero hasta marzo⟩ ⟨from tomorrow : a partir de mañana⟩ ⟨they cost from 5 to 10 dollars : cuestan entre 5 y 10 dólares⟩ ⟨to speak from the heart : hablar con el corazón⟩ **2** OFF, OUT OF : de ⟨she took it from the drawer : lo sacó del cajón⟩ **3** (*indicating a source or sender*) : de ⟨a letter from my friend : una carta de mi amiga⟩ ⟨a quote from Shakespeare : una cita de Shakespeare⟩ **4** (*indicating distance*) : de ⟨10 feet from the entrance : a 10 pies de la entrada⟩ ⟨we got separated from the group : nos vimos separados del grupo⟩ **5** (*indicating a cause*) : de ⟨red from crying : rojos de llorar⟩ ⟨he died from the cold : murió del frío⟩ **6** (*indicating material*) : de ⟨made from wood : (hecho) de madera⟩ **7** (*indicating blocking, removal, etc.*) : de ⟨to protect from : proteger de⟩ ⟨to provide relief from : aliviar⟩ ⟨to refrain from : abstenerse de⟩ ⟨to omit from : omitir de⟩ ⟨she was excluded from the club : no la admitieron en el club⟩ **8** (*indicating a change*) : de ⟨from bad to worse : de mal en peor⟩ **9** (*in mathematics*) : de ⟨to deduct something from something : deducir/descontar algo de algo⟩ ⟨to subtract 10 from 30 : restarle 10 a 30, restar 10 de 30⟩ **10** (*indicating alternatives*) : de ⟨to choose from (among) : elegir de (entre)⟩

frond [ˈfrɑnd] *n* : fronda *f*, hoja *f*

front¹ [ˈfrʌnt] *vi* **1** FACE : dar, estar orientado ⟨the house fronts north : la casa da al norte⟩ **2** : servir de pantalla ⟨he fronts for his boss : sirve de pantalla para su jefe⟩

front² *adj* : delantero, de adelante, primero ⟨the front row : la primera fila⟩ ⟨the front door : la puerta principal⟩ ⟨it appeared on the front page : salió en primera plana⟩

front³ *n* **1** : frente *m*, parte *f* de adelante, delantera *f* ⟨the front of the class : el frente de la clase⟩ ⟨at the front of the

train : en la parte delantera del tren⟩ **2**
AREA, ZONE : frente *m*, zona *f* ⟨the
Eastern front : el frente oriental⟩ ⟨on
the educational front : en el frente de la
enseñanza⟩ **3** FACADE : fachada *f* ⟨de
un edificio o una persona⟩ **4** : frente *m*
(en meteorología)

frontage ['frʌntɪʤ] *n* : fachada *f*, frente *m*

frontal ['frʌntəl] *adj* : frontal, de frente

frontier [.frʌn'tɪr] *n* : frontera *f*

frontiersman [.frʌn'tɪrzmən] *n, pl* **-men**
[-mən, -.mɛn] : hombre *m* de la frontera

front–wheel drive ['frʌnt'hwiːl] *n* : tracción *f* delantera

frost¹ ['frɔst] *vt* **1** FREEZE : helar **2** ICE
: bañar (pasteles)

frost² *n* **1** : helada *f* (en meteorología) **2**
: escarcha *f* ⟨frost on the window : escarcha en la ventana⟩

frostbite ['frɔst.baɪt] *n* : congelación *f*

frostbitten ['frɔst.bɪtən] *adj* : congelado
(dícese de una persona), quemado
(dícese de una planta)

frosting ['frɔstɪŋ] *n* ICING : baño *m*, glaseado *m*, betún *m* *Mex*

frosty ['frɔsti] *adj* **frostier; -est 1** CHILLY
: helado, frío **2** COOL, UNFRIENDLY
: frío, glacial

froth ['frɔθ] *n, pl* **froths** ['frɔθs, 'frɔðz]
: espuma *f*

frothy ['frɔθi] *adj* **frothier; -est** : espumoso

frown¹ ['fraʊn] *vi* **1** : fruncir el ceño,
fruncir el entrecejo **2 to frown at** : mirar (algo) con ceño, mirar a (alguien)
con ceño **2 to frown on/upon** : desaprobar

frown² *n* : ceño *m* (fruncido)

froze → freeze

frozen → freeze

frugal ['fruːgəl] *adj* : frugal, ahorrativo,
parco — **frugally** *adv*

frugality [fruˈgæləti] *n* : frugalidad *f*

fruit¹ ['fruːt] *vi* : dar fruto

fruit² *n* **1** : fruta *f* (término genérico),
fruto *m* (término particular) **2 fruits**
npl REWARDS : frutos *mpl* ⟨the fruits of
his labor : los frutos de su trabajo⟩

fruitcake ['fruːt.keɪk] *n* : pastel *m* de frutas

fruitful ['fruːtfəl] *adj* : fructífero, provechoso

fruition [fruˈɪʃən] *n* **1** : cumplimiento *m*,
realización *f* **2 to bring to fruition** : realizar

fruitless ['fruːtləs] *adj* : infructuoso, inútil
— **fruitlessly** *adv*

fruit salad *n* : ensalada *f* de frutas

fruity ['fruːti] *adj* **fruitier; -est** : (con sabor) a fruta

frumpy ['frʌmpi] *adj* **frumpier; -est** : anticuado y sin atractivo

frustrate ['frʌs.treɪt] *vt* **-trated; -trating**
: frustrar

frustrating ['frʌs.treɪtɪŋ] *adj* : frustrante
— **frustratingly** *adv*

frustration [.frʌs'treɪʃən] *n* : frustración *f*

fry¹ ['fraɪ] *vt* **fried; frying** : freír

fry² *n, pl* **fries 1** : fritura *f*, plato *m*
frito **2** : fiesta *f* en que se sirven fritu

ras **3** *pl* **fry** : alevín *m* (pez) **4 fries** *npl*
→ **French fries**

frying pan *n* : sartén *mf*

fuchsia ['fjuːʃə] *n* **1** : fucsia *f* (planta) **2**
: fucsia *m* (color)

fuddle ['fʌdəl] *vt* **-dled; -dling** : confundir,
atontar

fuddy–duddy ['fʌdi.dʌdi] *n, pl* **-dies** : persona *f* chapada a la antigua, carca *mf*

fudge¹ ['fʌʤ] *vt* **fudged; fudging 1** FAL
SIFY : amañar, falsificar **2** DODGE : esquivar

fudge² *n* : dulce *m* blando de chocolate y
leche

fuel¹ ['fjuːəl] *vt* **-eled** *or* **-elled; -eling** *or*
-elling 1 : abastecer de combustible **2**
STIMULATE : estimular

fuel² *n* : combustible *m*, carburante *m*
(para motores)

fugitive¹ ['fjuːʤətɪv] *adj* **1** RUNAWAY
: fugitivo **2** FLEETING : efímero, pasajero, fugaz

fugitive² *n* : fugitivo *m*, -va *f*

fugue ['fjuːg] *n* : fuga *f*

fulcrum ['fʊlkrəm, 'fʌl-] *n, pl* **-crums** *or*
-cra [-krə] : fulcro *m*

fulfill *or* **fulfil** [fʊl'fɪl] *vt* **-filled; -filling 1**
PERFORM : cumplir con, realizar, llevar
a cabo **2** SATISFY : satisfacer

fulfillment [fʊl'fɪlmənt] *n* **1** PERFOR
MANCE : cumplimiento *m*, ejecución *f* **2**
SATISFACTION : satisfacción *f*, realización *f*

full¹ ['fʊl, 'fʌl] *adv* **1** VERY : muy ⟨full
well : muy bien, perfectamente⟩ **2** EN
TIRELY : completamente ⟨she swung full
around : giró completamente⟩ **3** DI
RECTLY : de lleno, directamente ⟨he
looked me full in the face : me miró directamente a la cara⟩

full² *adj* **1** FILLED : lleno ⟨a full glass
: un vaso lleno⟩ ⟨I'm full : estoy lleno⟩
⟨full of holes : lleno de agujeros⟩ **2**
COMPLETE : completo, detallado ⟨two
full weeks : dos semanas completas⟩ ⟨a
full report : un informe detallado⟩ **3**
MAXIMUM : todo, pleno ⟨at full speed : a
toda velocidad⟩ ⟨in full bloom : en plena
flor⟩ **4** PLUMP : redondo, llenito *fam*,
regordete *fam* ⟨a full face : una cara redonda⟩ ⟨a full figure : un cuerpo
llenito⟩ **5** AMPLE : amplio ⟨a full skirt
: una falda amplia⟩

full³ *n* **1 to pay in full** : pagar en su totalidad **2 to the full** : al máximo

full–fledged ['fʊl'flɛʤd] *adj* : hecho y
derecho

full–length ['fʊl.lɛŋkθ] *adj* **1** : de cuerpo
entero (dícese de un espejo, etc.) **2**
: largo (dícese de un vestido, etc.) **3** : de
extensión normal ⟨full-length film : largometraje⟩

full moon *n* : luna *f* llena

fullness ['fʊlnəs] *n* **1** ABUNDANCE : plenitud *f*, abundancia *f* **2** : amplitud *f* (de
una falda)

full–scale ['fʊl.skeɪl] *adj* **1** : a escala natural **2** COMPLETE : total ⟨full-scale war
: guerra total⟩ ⟨a full-scale investigation
: una investigación rigurosa⟩

full–time[1] ['fʊl,taɪm] *adv* : a/de tiempo completo

full–time[2] *adj* : de tiempo completo

fully ['fʊli] *adv* **1** COMPLETELY : completamente, totalmente **2** : al menos, por lo menos ⟨fully half of them : al menos la mitad de ellos⟩

fulsome ['fʊlsəm] *adj* : excesivo, exagerado, efusivo

fumble[1] ['fʌmbəl] *v* -bled; -bling *vt* : dejar caer, fumblear **2 to fumble one's way** : ir a tientas — *vi* **1** GROPE : hurgar, tantear **2 to fumble with** : manejar con torpeza

fumble[2] *n* : fumble *m* (en futbol americano)

fume[1] ['fju:m] *vi* fumed; fuming **1** SMOKE : echar humo, humear **2** : estar furioso

fume[2] *n* : gas *m*, humo *m*, vapor *m*

fumigate ['fju:mə,geɪt] *vt* -gated; -gating : fumigar

fumigation [,fju:mə'geɪʃən] *n* : fumigación *m*

fun[1] ['fʌn] *adj* : divertido, entretenido

fun[2] *n* **1** AMUSEMENT : diversión *f*, entretenimiento *m* ⟨the party was really fun : la fiesta fue muy divertida⟩ ⟨for fun : por diversión⟩ **2** ENJOYMENT : disfrute *m* **3 to have fun** : divertirse **4 to make fun of** : reírse de, burlarse de

function[1] ['fʌŋkʃən] *vi* : funcionar, desempeñarse, servir

function[2] *n* **1** PURPOSE : función *f* **2** GATHERING : reunión *f* social, recepción *f* **3** CEREMONY : ceremonia *f*, acto *m*

functional ['fʌŋkʃənəl] *adj* : funcional — **functionally** *adv*

functionary ['fʌŋkʃə,nɛri] *n*, *pl* -aries : funcionario *m*, -ria *f*

fund[1] ['fʌnd] *vt* : financiar

fund[2] *n* **1** SUPPLY : reserva *f*, cúmulo *m* **2** : fondo *m* ⟨investment fund : fondo de inversiones⟩ **3 funds** *npl* RESOURCES : fondos *mpl*

fundamental[1] [,fʌndə'mɛntəl] *adj* **1** BASIC : fundamental, básico **2** PRINCIPAL : esencial, principal **3** INNATE : innato, intrínseco

fundamental[2] *n* : fundamento *m*

fundamentalism [,fʌndə'mɛntəl,ɪzəm] *n* : integrismo *m*, fundamentalismo *m*

fundamentalist [,fʌndə'mɛntəlɪst] *n* : integrista *mf*, fundamentalista *mf* — **fundamentalist** *adj*

fundamentally [,fʌndə'mɛntəli] *adv* : fundamentalmente, básicamente

funding ['fʌndɪŋ] *n* : financiación *f*

fund–raiser ['fʌnd,reɪzər] *n* : función *f* para recaudar fondos

funeral[1] ['fju:nərəl] *adj* **1** : funeral, funerario, fúnebre ⟨funeral procession : cortejo fúnebre⟩ **2 funeral home/parlor** : funeraria *f*

funeral[2] *n* : funeral *m*, funerales *mpl*

funereal [fju'nɪriəl] *adj* : fúnebre

fungicide ['fʌndʒə,saɪd, 'fʌŋgə-] *n* : fungicida *m*

fungus ['fʌŋgəs] *n*, *pl* **fungi** ['fʌn,dʒaɪ, 'fʌŋ,gaɪ] : hongo *m*

funk ['fʌŋk] *n* **1** FEAR : miedo *m* **2** DEPRESSION : depresión *f*

funky ['fʌŋki] *adj* **funkier; -est** ODD, QUAINT : raro, extraño, original

funnel[1] ['fʌnəl] *vt* -neled; -neling CHANNEL : canalizar, encauzar

funnel[2] *n* **1** : embudo *m* **2** SMOKESTACK : chimenea *f* (de un barco o vapor)

funnies ['fʌniz] *npl* : tiras *fpl* cómicas

funny ['fʌni] *adj* **funnier; -est 1** AMUSING : divertido, cómico **2** STRANGE : extraño, raro

fur[1] ['fər] *adj* : de piel

fur[2] *n* **1** : pelaje *m*, piel *f* **2** : prenda *f* de piel

furbish ['fərbɪʃ] *vt* : pulir, limpiar

furious ['fjʊriəs] *adj* **1** ANGRY : furioso **2** FRANTIC : violento, frenético, vertiginoso (dícese de la velocidad)

furiously ['fjʊriəsli] *adv* **1** ANGRILY : furiosamente **2** FRANTICALLY : frenéticamente

furlong ['fər,lɔŋ] *n* : estadio *m* (201.2 m)

furlough[1] ['fər,lo:] *vt* : dar permiso a, dar licencia a

furlough[2] *n* LEAVE : permiso *m*, licencia *f*

furnace ['fərnəs] *n* : horno *m*

furnish ['fərnɪʃ] *vt* **1** SUPPLY : proveer, suministrar **2** : amueblar ⟨furnished apartment : departamento amueblado⟩

furnishings ['fərnɪʃɪŋz] *npl* **1** ACCESSORIES : accesorios *mpl* **2** FURNITURE : muebles *mpl*, mobiliario *m*

furniture ['fərnɪtʃər] *n* : muebles *mpl*, mobiliario *m*

furor ['fjʊr,ɔr, -ər] *n* **1** RAGE : furia *f*, rabia *f* **2** UPROAR : escándalo *m*, jaleo *m*, alboroto *m*

furrier ['fəriər] *n* : peletero *m*, -ra *f*

furrow[1] ['fəro:] *vt* **1** : surcar **2 to furrow one's brow** : fruncir el ceño

furrow[2] *n* **1** GROOVE : surco *m* **2** WRINKLE : arruga *f*, surco *m*

furry ['fəri] *adj* **furrier; -est** : peludo (dícese de un animal), peluche (dícese de un objeto)

further[1] ['fərðər] *vt* : promover, fomentar

further[2] *adv* **1** FARTHER : más lejos, más adelante **2** MOREOVER : además **3** MORE : más ⟨I'll consider it further in the morning : lo consideraré más en la mañana⟩

further[3] *adj* **1** FARTHER : más lejano **2** ADDITIONAL : adicional, más

furtherance ['fərðərəns] *n* : promoción *f*, fomento *m*, adelantamiento *m*

furthermore ['fərðər,mor] *adv* : además

furthermost ['fərðər,mo:st] *adj* : más lejano, más distante

furthest ['fərðəst] → **farthest**[1], **farthest**[2]

furtive ['fərtɪv] *adj* : furtivo, sigiloso — **furtively** *adv*

furtiveness ['fərtɪvnəs] *n* STEALTH : sigilo *m*

fury ['fjʊri] *n*, *pl* -ries **1** RAGE : furia *f*, ira *f* **2** VIOLENCE : furia *f*, furor *m*

fuse[1] ['fju:z] *or* **fuze** *vt* **fused** *or* **fuzed; fusing** *or* **fuzing** : equipar con un fusible

fuse[2] *v* **fused; fusing** *vt* **1** SMELT : fundir **2** MERGE : fusionar, fundir — *vi* : fundirse, fusionarse

fuse³ *n* : fusible *m*

fuselage ['fju:sə,lɑʒ, -zə-] *n* : fuselaje *m*

fusillade ['fju:sə,lɑd, -,leɪd, ,fju:sə'-, -zə-] *n* : descarga *f* de fusilería

fusion ['fju:ʒən] *n* : fusión *f*

fuss¹ ['fʌs] *vi* **1** WORRY : preocuparse **2 to fuss with** : juguetear con, toquetear **3 to fuss over** : mimar

fuss² *n* **1** COMMOTION : alboroto *m*, escándalo *m* **2** ATTENTION : atenciones *fpl* **3** COMPLAINT : quejas *fpl*

fussbudget ['fʌs,bʌdʒət] *n* : quisquilloso *m*, -sa *f*; melindroso *m*, -sa *f*

fussiness ['fʌsinəs] *n* **1** IRRITABILITY : irritabilidad *f* **2** : lo recargado (dícese de la decoración, etc.) **3** METICULOUSNESS : meticulosidad *f*

fussy ['fʌsi] *adj* **fussier; -est** **1** IRRITABLE : irritable, nervioso **2** OVERELABO-

RATE : recargado **3** METICULOUS : meticuloso **4** FASTIDIOUS : quisquilloso, exigente

futile ['fju:təl, 'fju:,taɪl] *adj* : inútil, vano

futility [fju:'tɪləti] *n, pl* **-ties** : inutilidad *f*

futon ['fu:,tɑn] *n* : futón *m*

future¹ ['fju:tʃər] *adj* : futuro

future² *n* **1** : futuro *m* ⟨in the future : en el futuro⟩ ⟨a job with a future : un trabajo con futuro⟩

futuristic [,fju:tʃə'rɪstɪk] *adj* : futurista

fuze → fuse¹

fuzz ['fʌz] *n* : pelusa *f*

fuzziness ['fʌzinəs] *n* **1** : vellosidad *f* **2** INDISTINCTNESS : falta *f* de claridad

fuzzy ['fʌzi] *adj* **fuzzier; -est** **1** FLUFFY, FURRY : con pelusa, peludo **2** INDISTINCT : indistinto, borroso ⟨a fuzzy image : una imagen borrosa⟩

G

g ['dʒi:] *n, pl* **g's** *or* **gs** ['dʒi:z] **1** : séptima letra del alfabeto inglés — **2** : sol *m* ⟨G sharp/flat : sol sostenido/bemol⟩

gab¹ ['gæb] *vi* **gabbed; gabbing** : charlar, cotorrear *fam*, parlotear *fam*

gab² *n* CHATTER : cotorreo *m fam*, parloteo *m fam*

gabardine ['gæbər,di:n] *n* : gabardina *f*

gabby ['gæbi] *adj* **gabbier; -est** : hablador, parlanchín

gable ['geɪbəl] *n* : gablete *m*, aguilón *m*

Gabonese [,gæbə'ni:z, -'ni:s] *n* : gabonés *m*, -nesa *f* — **Gabonese** *adj*

gad ['gæd] *vi* **gadded; gadding** WANDER : deambular, vagar, callejear

gadfly ['gæd,flaɪ] *n, pl* **-flies** **1** : tábano *m* (insecto) **2** FAULTFINDER : criticón *m*, -cona *f fam*

gadget ['gædʒət] *n* : artilugio *m*, aparato *m*

gadgetry ['gædʒətri] *n* : artilugios *mpl*, aparatos *mpl*

Gaelic ['geɪlɪk, 'gæ] *n* : gaélico *m* (idioma) — **Gaelic** *adj*

gaff ['gæf] *n* **1** : garfio *m* **2 → gaffe**

gaffe ['gæf] *n* : metedura *f* de pata *fam*

gag¹ ['gæg] *v* **gagged; gagging** *vt* : amordazar ⟨to tie up and gag : atar y amordazar⟩ — *vi* **1** CHOKE : atragantarse **2** RETCH : hacer arcadas

gag² *n* **1** : mordaza *f* (para la boca) **2** JOKE : chiste *m*

gage → gauge

gaggle ['gægəl] *n* : bandada *f*, manada *f* (de gansos)

gaiety ['geɪəti] *n, pl* **-eties** **1** MERRYMAKING : juerga *f* **2** MERRIMENT : alegría *f*, regocijo *m*

gaily ['geɪli] *adv* : alegremente

gain¹ ['geɪn] *vt* **1** ACQUIRE, OBTAIN : ganar, obtener, adquirir, conseguir ⟨to gain knowledge : adquirir conocimientos⟩ ⟨to gain a victory : obtener una victoria⟩ **2** REACH : alcanzar, llegar a **3** INCREASE

: ganar, aumentar ⟨to gain weight : aumentar de peso⟩ **4** : adelantarse, ganar ⟨the watch gains two minutes a day : el reloj se adelanta dos minutos por día⟩ **5 to gain on someone** : ganarle terreno a alguien — *vi* **1** PROFIT : beneficiarse **2** INCREASE : aumentar

gain² *n* **1** PROFIT : beneficio *m*, ganancia *f*, lucro *m*, provecho *m* **2** INCREASE : aumento *m*

gainful ['geɪnfəl] *adj* : lucrativo, beneficioso, provechoso ⟨gainful employment : trabajo remunerado⟩

gait ['geɪt] *n* : paso *m*, andar *m*, manera *f* de caminar

gal ['gæl] *n* : muchacha *f*

gala¹ ['geɪlə, 'gæ-, 'gɑ-] *adj* : de gala

gala² *n* : gala *f*, fiesta *f*

galactic [gə'læktɪk] *adj* : galáctico

galaxy ['gæləksi] *n, pl* **-axies** : galaxia *f*

gale ['geɪl] *n* **1** WIND : vendaval *f*, viento *m* fuerte **2 gales of laughter** : carcajadas *fpl*

Galician [gə'lɪʃən] *n* : gallego *m*, -ga *f* — **Galician** *adj*

gall¹ ['gɔl] *vt* **1** CHAFE : rozar **2** IRRITATE, VEX : irritar, molestar

gall² *n* **1** BILE : bilis *f*, hiel *f* **2** INSOLENCE : audacia *f*, insolencia *f*, descaro *m* **3** SORE : rozadura *f* (de un caballo) **4** : agalla *f* (de una planta)

gallant ['gælənt] *adj* **1** BRAVE : valiente, gallardo **2** CHIVALROUS, POLITE : galante, cortés

gallantry ['gæləntri] *n, pl* **-ries** : galantería *f*, caballerosidad *f*

gallbladder ['gɔl,blædər] *n* : vesícula *f* biliar

galleon ['gæljən] *n* : galeón *m*

gallery ['gæləri] *n, pl* **-leries** **1** BALCONY : galería *f* (para espectadores) **2** CORRIDOR : pasillo *m*, galería *f*, corredor *m* **3** *or* **art gallery** : galería *f* (para exposiciones)

galley ['gæli] *n, pl* **-leys** : galera *f*

gallium ['gæliəm] *n* : galio *m*

gallivant ['gælə,vænt] *vi* : callejear

gallon ['gælən] *n* : galón *m*

gallop¹ ['gæləp] *vi* : galopar

gallop² *n* : galope *m*

gallows ['gæ,lo:z] *n, pl* **-lows** *or* **-lowses** [-,lo:zəz] : horca *f*

gallstone ['gɔl,sto:n] *n* : cálculo *m* biliar

galore [gə'lor] *adj* : en abundancia ⟨bargains galore : muchísimas gangas⟩

galoshes [gə'laʃəz] *npl* : galochas *fpl*, chanclos *mpl*

galvanize ['gælvən,aɪz] *vt* **-nized; -nizing** 1 STIMULATE : estimular, excitar, impulsar 2 : galvanizar (metales)

Gambian ['gæmbiən] *n* : gambiano *m*, -na *f* — **Gambian** *adj*

gambit ['gæmbɪt] *n* 1 : gambito *m* (en ajedrez) 2 STRATAGEM : estratagema *f*, táctica *f*

gamble¹ ['gæmbəl] *v* **-bled; -bling** *vi* : jugar, arriesgarse — *vt* 1 BET, WAGER : apostar, jugarse 2 RISK : arriesgar

gamble² *n* 1 BET : apuesta *f* 2 RISK : riesgo *m*

gambler ['gæmbələr] *n* : jugador *m*, -dora *f*

gambling ['gæmbəlɪŋ] *n* : juego *m*

gambol ['gæmbəl] *vi* **-boled** *or* **-bolled; -boling** *or* **-bolling** FROLIC : retozar, juguetear

game¹ ['geɪm] *adj* 1 READY : listo, dispuesto ⟨we're game for anything : estamos listos para lo que sea⟩ 2 LAME : cojo

game² *n* 1 : juego *m* ⟨card game : juego de cartas/naipes⟩ ⟨board game : juego de mesa⟩ ⟨video game : videojuego⟩ 2 MATCH : partido *m* (de fútbol, ajedrez, etc.), partida *f* (de ajedrez, etc.) 3 ROUND : juego *m* 4 : caza *f* ⟨big game : caza mayor⟩ 5 early in the game : al principio 6 late in the game : tarde ⟨it's a little late in the game for that : ya es tarde para eso⟩ 7 to be ahead of the game : llevar la delantera 8 to beat someone at their own game : vencer a alguien con sus propias armas 9 to be on/off one's game : estar/no estar en forma 10 to play games (with someone) : jugar con alguien, manipular a alguien

gamecock ['geɪm,kɑk] *n* : gallo *m* de pelea

gamekeeper ['geɪm,ki:pər] *n* : guardabosque *mf*

gamely ['geɪmli] *adv* : animosamente

gamer ['geɪmər] *n* : videojugador *m*, -dora *f*

gaming ['geɪmɪŋ] *n* 1 GAMBLING : juego *m* 2 : juegos *mpl* ⟨online gaming : juegos en línea⟩

gamma ray ['gæmə] *n* : rayo *m* gamma

gamut ['gæmət] *n* : gama *f*, espectro *m* ⟨to run the gamut : pasar por toda la gama⟩

gamy *or* **gamey** ['geɪmi] *adj* **gamier; -est** : con sabor de animal de caza, fuerte

gander ['gændər] *n* 1 : ganso *m* (animal) 2 GLANCE : mirada *f*, vistazo *m*, ojeada *f*

gang¹ ['gæŋ] *vi* **to gang up** : agruparse, unirse

gang² *n* : banda *f*, pandilla *f*

gangland ['gæŋ,lænd] *n* : hampa *f*

gangling ['gæŋglɪŋ] *adj* LANKY : larguirucho *fam*

ganglion ['gæŋgliən] *n, pl* **-glia** [-gliə] : ganglio *m*

gangplank ['gæŋ,plæŋk] *n* : pasarela *f*

gangrene ['gæŋ,gri:n, 'gæn-;, gæŋ'-, gæn'-] *n* : gangrena *f*

gangster ['gæŋstər] *n* : gángster *mf*

gangway ['gæŋ,weɪ] *n* 1 : pasarela *f* 2 **gangway!** : ¡abran paso!

gap ['gæp] *n* 1 BREACH, OPENING : espacio *m*, brecha *f*, abertura *f* 2 GORGE : desfiladero *m*, barranco *m* 3 : laguna *f* ⟨a gap in my education : una laguna en mi educación⟩ 4 INTERVAL : pausa *f*, intervalo *m* 5 DISPARITY : brecha *f*, disparidad *f*

gape¹ ['geɪp] *vi* **gaped; gaping** 1 OPEN : abrirse, estar abierto 2 STARE : mirar fijamente con la boca abierta, mirar boquiabierto

gape² *n* 1 OPENING : abertura *f*, brecha *f* 2 STARE : mirada *f* boquiabierta

garage¹ [gə'rɑʒ, -'rɑdʒ] *vt* **-raged; -raging** : dejar en un garaje

garage² *n* : garaje *m*, cochera *f*

garb¹ ['gɑrb] *vt* : vestir, ataviar

garb² *n* : vestimenta *f*, atuendo *f*

garbage ['gɑrbɪdʒ] *n* : basura *f*, desechos *mpl*

garbage can *n* : bote *m* de basura *CA, Mex*; basurero *m Mex*; caneca *f Col*; cubo *m* de (la) basura *Spain*; tacho *m* de basura *Arg, Chile, Ecua, Peru, Uru*; tarro *m* de (la) basura *Arg, Chile, CoRi, Uru*

garbage disposal *n* : trituradora *f* de basura

garbageman ['gɑrbɪdʒ,mən] *n, pl* **-men** [-mən, -,mɛn] : basurero *m*

garbage truck *n* : camión *m* de la basura

garble ['gɑrbəl] *vt* **-bled; -bling** : tergiversar, distorsionar

garbled ['gɑrbəld] *adj* : incoherente, incomprensible

garden¹ ['gɑrdən] *vi* : trabajar en el jardín

garden² *n* : jardín *m* ⟨vegetable garden : huerto⟩

garden center *n* : centro *m* de jardinería *f*

gardener ['gɑrdənər] *n* : jardinero *m*, -ra *f*

gardenia [gɑr'di:njə] *n* : gardenia *f*

gardening ['gɑrdənɪŋ] *n* : jardinería *f*

gargantuan [gɑr'gæntʃuən] *adj* : gigantesco, colosal

gargle¹ ['gɑrgəl] *vi* **-gled; -gling** : hacer gárgaras, gargarizar

gargle² *n* : gárgara *f*

gargoyle ['gɑr,gɔɪl] *n* : gárgola *f*

garish ['gærɪʃ] *adj* GAUDY : llamativo, chillón, charro — **garishly** *adv*

garland¹ ['gɑrlənd] *vt* : adornar con guirnaldas

garland² *n* : guirnalda *f*

garlic ['gɑrlɪk] *n* : ajo *m*

garment ['gɑrmənt] *n* : prenda *f*

garner ['gɑrnər] *vt* : recoger, cosechar

garnet ['gɑrnət] *n* : granate *m*

garnish¹ [ˈgɑrnɪʃ] *vt* : aderezar, guarnecer
garnish² *n* : aderezo *m*, guarnición *f*
garret [ˈgærət] *n* : buhardilla *f*, desván *m*
garrison¹ [ˈgærəsən] *vt* **1** QUARTER : acuartelar (tropas) **2** OCCUPY : guarnecer, ocupar (con tropas)
garrison² *n* **1** : guarnición *f* (ciudad) **2** FORT : fortaleza *f*, poste *m* militar
garrulous [ˈgærələs] *adj* : charlatán, parlanchín
garter [ˈgɑrtər] *n* : liga *f*
gas¹ [ˈgæs] *v* **gassed; gassing** *vt* : gasear — *vi* **to gas up** : llenar el tanque con gasolina
gas² *n, pl* **gases** [ˈgæsəz] **1** : gas *m* ⟨tear gas : gas lacrimógeno⟩ **2** → **gasoline**
gaseous [ˈgæʃəs, ˈgæsiəs] *adj* : gaseoso
gash¹ [ˈgæʃ] *vt* : hacer un tajo en, cortar
gash² *n* : cuchillada *f*, tajo *m*
gasket [ˈgæskət] *n* : junta *f*
gas mask *n* : máscara *f* antigás
gasoline [ˈgæsəˌliːn, ˌgæsəˈ-] *n* : gasolina *f*, nafta *f*, bencina *f* Chile
gasp¹ [ˈgæsp] *vi* **1** : boquear ⟨to gasp with surprise : gritar de asombro⟩ **2** PANT : jadear, respirar con dificultad
gasp² *n* **1** : boqueada *f* ⟨a gasp of surprise : un grito sofocado⟩ **2** PANTING : jadeo *m*
gas pedal *n* : acelerador *m*
gas station *n* : estación *f* de servicio; gasolinera *f*; bencinera *f* Chile; bomba *f* Chile, CoRi, Ven
gas tank *n* : tanque *m*, depósito *m* (de gasolina/bencina/nafta)
gastric [ˈgæstrɪk] *adj* : gástrico ⟨gastric juice : jugo gástrico⟩
gastronomic [ˌgæstrəˈnɑmɪk] *adj* : gastronómico
gastronomy [gæsˈtrɑnəmi] *n* : gastronomía *f*
gate [ˈgeɪt] *n* : portón *m*, verja *f*, puerta *f*
gatekeeper [ˈgeɪtˌkiːpər] *n* : guarda *mf*; guardián *m*, -diana *f*
gateway [ˈgeɪtˌweɪ] *n* : puerta *f* (de acceso), entrada *f*
gather [ˈgæðər] *vt* **1** ASSEMBLE, COLLECT : juntar, recoger, reunir ⟨to gather dust : acumular polvo⟩ **2** HARVEST : recoger, cosechar **3** : fruncir (una tela) **4** INFER : deducir, suponer — *vi* : reunirse, congregarse, acumularse
gathering [ˈgæðərɪŋ] *n* : reunión *f*
gauche [ˈgoːʃ] *adj* : torpe, falto de tacto
gaucho [ˈgaʊtʃo] *n* : gaucho *m*
gaudy [ˈgodi] *adj* **gaudier; -est** : chillón, llamativo
gauge¹ [ˈgeɪdʒ] *vt* **gauged; gauging** **1** MEASURE : medir **2** ESTIMATE, JUDGE : estimar, evaluar, juzgar
gauge² *n* **1** : indicador *m* ⟨pressure gauge : indicador de presión⟩ **2** CALIBER : calibre *m* **3** INDICATION : indicio *m*, muestra *f*
gaunt [ˈgɔnt] *adj* : demacrado, descarnado
gauntlet [ˈgɔntlət] *n* : guante *m* ⟨to run the gauntlet of : exponerse a⟩
gauze [ˈgoz] *n* : gasa *f*
gauzy [ˈgozi] *adj* **gauzier; -est** : diáfano, vaporoso

gave → **give**
gavel [ˈgævəl] *n* : martillo *m* (de un juez, un subastador, etc.)
gawk [ˈgɔk] *vi* GAPE : mirar boquiabierto
gawker [ˈgɔkər] *n* : mirón *m*, -rona *f*
gawky [ˈgɔki] *adj* **gawkier; -est** : desmañado, torpe, desgarbado
gay¹ [ˈgeɪ] *adj* **1** MERRY : alegre **2** BRIGHT, COLORFUL : vistoso, vivo **3** HOMOSEXUAL : homosexual
gay² *n* HOMOSEXUAL : homosexual *mf*
gaze¹ [ˈgeɪz] *vi* **gazed; gazing** : mirar (fijamente)
gaze² *n* : mirada *f* (fija)
gazebo [gəˈziːbo] *n* : pabellón *m*, cenador *m*, glorieta *f*
gazelle [gəˈzɛl] *n* : gacela *f*
gazette [gəˈzɛt] *n* : gaceta *f*
gazetteer [ˌgæzəˈtɪr] *n* : diccionario *m* geográfico
gazpacho [gəzˈpɑtʃo, gəˈspɑ-] *n* : gazpacho *m*
gear¹ [ˈgɪr] *vt* ADAPT, ORIENT : adaptar, ajustar, orientar ⟨a book geared to children : un libro adaptado a los niños⟩ — *vi* **to gear up** : prepararse
gear² *n* **1** CLOTHING : ropa *f* **2** BELONGINGS : efectos *mpl* personales **3** EQUIPMENT, TOOLS : equipo *m*, aparejo *m*, herramientas *fpl* ⟨fishing gear : aparejo de pescar⟩ ⟨landing gear : tren de aterrizaje⟩ **4** COGWHEEL : rueda *f* dentada **5** : marcha *f*, velocidad *f* (de un vehículo) ⟨to put in gear : poner en marcha⟩ ⟨to change gear(s) : cambiar de velocidad⟩
gearbox [ˈgɪrˌbɑks] *n* : caja *f* de cambios
gearshift [ˈgɪrˌʃɪft] *n* TRANSMISSION : palanca *f* de cambio, palanca *f* de velocidad
geek [ˈgiːk] *n fam* **1** : intelectual *mf* (en general); fanático *m* -ca *f* (de algo específico) ⟨a computer geek : un genio informático⟩ **2** MISFIT : inadaptado *m*, -da *f*
geese → **goose**
Geiger counter [ˈgaɪgərˌkaʊntər] *n* : contador *m* Geiger
gel [ˈdʒɛl] *n* : gel *m*
gelatin [ˈdʒɛlətən] *n* : gelatina *f*
gem [ˈdʒɛm] *n* : joya *f*, gema *f*, alhaja *f*
Gemini [ˈdʒɛməˌnaɪ] *n* **1** : Géminis *m* (signo o constelación) **2** : Géminis *mf* (persona)
gemstone [ˈdʒɛmˌstoːn] *n* : piedra *f* (semipreciosa o preciosa), gema *f*
gender [ˈdʒɛndər] *n* **1** SEX : sexo *m*, género *m* (de una persona) **2** : género *m* (en la gramática)
gender identity *n* : identidad *f* de género
gender–neutral *adj* : de género neutro
gene [ˈdʒiːn] *n* : gen *m*, gene *m*
genealogical [ˌdʒiːniəˈlɑdʒɪkəl] *adj* : genealógico
genealogy [ˌdʒiːniˈɑlədʒi, ˌdʒɛ-, -ˈæ-] *n, pl* **-gies** : genealogía *f*
genera → **genus**
general¹ [ˈdʒɛnrəl, ˈdʒɛnə-] *adj* : general ⟨in general : en general, por lo general⟩ ⟨general election : elecciones generales⟩ ⟨general knowledge : cultura general⟩

general² n : general mf

generality [ˌʤɛnəˈrælət̬i] n, pl **-ties** : generalidad f

generalization [ˌʤɛnərələˈzeiʃən, ˌʤɛnərə-] n : generalización f

generalize [ˈʤɛnrəˌlaɪz, ˈʤɛnərə-] v **-ized; -izing** : generalizar

generally [ˈʤɛnrəli, ˈʤɛnərə-] adv : generalmente, por lo general, en general

general practitioner n : médico m, -ca f de cabecera

generate [ˈʤɛnəˌreɪt] vt **ated; -ating** : generar, producir

generation [ˌʤɛnəˈreɪʃən] n : generación f — **generational** [ˌʤɛnəˈreɪʃənəl] adj

generator [ˈʤɛnəˌreɪtər] n : generador m

generic [ʤəˈnɛrɪk] adj : genérico

generosity [ˌʤɛnəˈrasət̬i] n, pl **-ties** : generosidad f

generous [ˈʤɛnərəs] adj **1** OPENHANDED : generoso, dadivoso, desprendido **2** ABUNDANT, AMPLE : abundante, amplio, generoso — **generously** adv

genetic [ʤəˈnɛt̬ɪk] adj : genético — **genetically** [-t̬ɪkli] adv

genetically modified adj : transgénico

geneticist [ʤəˈnɛt̬əsɪst] n : genetista m

genetics [ʤəˈnɛt̬ɪks] n : genética f

genial [ˈʤiːnjəl] adj GRACIOUS : simpático, cordial, afable — **genially** adv

geniality [ˌʤiːniˈælət̬i] n : simpatía f, afabilidad f

genie [ˈʤiːni] n : genio m

genital [ˈʤɛnət̬əl] adj : genital

genitals [ˈʤɛnət̬əlz] npl : genitales mpl

genius [ˈʤiːnjəs] n : genio m

genocide [ˈʤɛnəˌsaɪd] n : genocidio m

genre [ˈʒɑnrə, ˈʤɑn-] n : género m

genteel [ʤɛnˈtiːl] adj : cortés, fino, refinado

gentile¹ [ˈʤɛnˌtaɪl] adj : gentil

gentile² n : gentil mf

gentility [ʤɛnˈtɪlət̬i] n, pl **-ties 1** : nobleza f (de nacimiento) **2** POLITENESS, REFINEMENT : cortesía f, refinamiento m

gentle [ˈʤɛnt̬əl] adj gentler; gentlest **1** NOBLE : bien nacido, noble **2** DOCILE : dócil, manso **3** KINDLY : bondadoso, amable **4** MILD : suave, apacible ⟨a gentle breeze : una brisa suave⟩ **5** SOFT : suave (dícese de un sonido), ligero (dícese del tacto) **6** MODERATE : moderado, gradual ⟨a gentle slope : una cuesta gradual⟩

gentleman [ˈʤɛnt̬əlmən] n, pl **-men** [-mən, -ˌmɛn] : caballero m, señor m

gentlemanly [ˈʤɛnt̬əlmənli] adj : caballeroso

gentleness [ˈʤɛnt̬əlnəs] n : delicadeza f, suavidad f, ternura f

gentlewoman [ˈʤɛnt̬əlˌwʊmən] n, pl **-women** [-ˌwɪmən] : dama f, señora f

gently [ˈʤɛnt̬li] adv **1** CAREFULLY, SOFTLY : con cuidado, suavemente, ligeramente **2** KINDLY : amablemente, con delicadeza

gentry [ˈʤɛntri] n, pl **-tries** : aristocracia f

genuflect [ˈʤɛnjuˌflɛkt] vi : doblar la rodilla, hacer una genuflexión

genuflection [ˌʤɛnjuˈflɛkʃən] n : genuflexión f

genuine [ˈʤɛnjuwən] adj **1** AUTHENTIC, REAL : genuino, verdadero, auténtico **2** SINCERE : sincero — **genuinely** adv

genus [ˈʤiːnəs] n, pl **genera** [ˈʤɛnərə] : género m

geographer [ʤiˈɑgrəfər] n : geógrafo m, -fa f

geographical [ˌʤiːəˈgræfɪkəl] or **geographic** [-fɪk] adj : geográfico — **geographically** [-fɪkli] adv

geography [ʤiˈɑgrəfi] n, pl **-phies** : geografía f

geologic [ˌʤiːəˈlɑʤɪk] or **geological** [-ʤɪkəl] adj : geológico — **geologically** [-ʤɪkli] adv

geologist [ʤiˈɑləʤɪst] n : geólogo m, -ga f

geology [ʤiˈɑləʤi] n : geología f

geometric [ˌʤiːəˈmɛtrɪk] or **geometrical** [-trɪkəl] adj : geométrico

geometry [ʤiˈɑmətri] n, pl **-tries** : geometría f

geopolitical [ˌʤiːopəˈlɪt̬ɪkəl] adj : geopolítico

Georgian [ˈʤɔrʤən] n **1** : georgiano m (idioma) **2** : georgiano m, -na f — **Georgian** adj

geranium [ʤəˈreɪniəm] n : geranio m

gerbil [ˈʤɔrbəl] n : jerbo m, gerbo m

geriatric [ˌʤɛriˈætrɪk] adj : geriátrico

geriatrics [ˌʤɛriˈætrɪks] n : geriatría f

germ [ˈʤɔrm] n **1** MICROORGANISM : microbio m, germen m **2** BEGINNING : germen m, principio m

German [ˈʤɔrmən] n **1** : alemán m, -mana f **2** : alemán m (idioma) — **German** adj

germane [ʤɔrˈmeɪn] adj : relevante, pertinente

Germanic [ʤɔrˈmænɪk] adj : germano

germanium [ʤɔrˈmeɪniəm] n : germanio m

German measles n : rubéola f

German shepherd n : pastor m alemán

germ cell n : célula f germen

germicide [ˈʤɔrməˌsaɪd] n : germicida m

germinate [ˈʤɔrməˌneɪt] v **-nated; -nating** vi : germinar — vt : hacer germinar

germination [ˌʤɔrməˈneɪʃən] n : germinación f

gerund [ˈʤɛrənd] n : gerundio m

gestation [ʤɛˈsteɪʃən] n : gestación f

gesticulate [ʤɛˈstɪkjəˌleɪt] vi **-lated; -lating** : gesticular — **gesticulation** [ʤɛˌstɪkjəˈleɪʃən] n

gesture¹ [ˈʤɛstʃər] vi **-tured; -turing** : gesticular, hacer gestos

gesture² n **1** : gesto m, ademán m **2** SIGN, TOKEN : gesto m, señal f ⟨a gesture of friendship : una señal de amistad⟩

get [ˈgɛt] v got [ˈgɑt]; got or gotten [ˈgɑt̬ən]; getting vt **1** OBTAIN : conseguir, obtener, adquirir ⟨to get a job : conseguir trabajo⟩ ⟨she got the dress on sale : compró el vestido rebajado⟩ ⟨to get someone's attention : atraer la atención de alguien⟩ ⟨to get a good night's sleep : dormir bien⟩ **2** RECEIVE : recibir ⟨to get a letter : recibir una carta⟩

⟨we've been getting a lot of rain : ha llovido mucho⟩ **3** EARN : ganar ⟨he gets $10 an hour : gana $10 por hora⟩ **4** FETCH : traer ⟨get me my book : tráeme el libro⟩ ⟨go (and) get your coat : vete a buscar tu abrigo⟩ **5** CATCH : tomar (un tren, etc.), agarrar (una pelota, etc.) **6** SEIZE, GRASP : agarrar ⟨he got me by the arm : me agarró del brazo⟩ **7** CAPTURE : agarrar, capturar **8** SEND : mandar, hacer llegar ⟨we got a message to her : le hicimos llegar un mensaje⟩ **9** TAKE : llevar ⟨we got him to the hospital : lo llevamos al hospital⟩ **10** : hacer ir/mover (etc.) ⟨he got them out of bed : los sacó de la cama⟩ ⟨we got ourselves through customs : pasamos por la aduana⟩ **11** : hacer progresar ⟨flattery will get you nowhere : con halagos no conseguirás nada⟩ **12** FIT : hacer entrar/pasar (etc.) ⟨can you get it into this box? : ¿puedes meterlo en esta caja?⟩ ⟨I can't get the key into the lock : la llave no entra en la cerradura⟩ ⟨can you get it through the door? : ¿va a pasar por la puerta?⟩ **13** CONTRACT : contagiarse, contraer ⟨she got the measles from him : (a ella) le dio el sarampión⟩ **14** SUFFER, SUSTAIN : sufrir (una herida, etc.) **15** PREPARE : preparar (una comida) **16** : tener (una impresión, etc.) ⟨where did you get that idea? : ¿de dónde sacaste esa idea?⟩ **17** CAUSE, ELICIT : causar, provocar ⟨to get a laugh : hacer reír⟩ **18** (*to cause to do something*) ⟨I can't get them to behave : no puedo hacer que se porten bien⟩ ⟨I got him to agree : logré convencerlo⟩ ⟨she got the computer working, she got the computer to work : hizo funcionar la computadora⟩ **19** (*to cause to be*) ⟨I got my feet wet : me mojé los pies⟩ ⟨to get one's hair cut : cortarse el pelo⟩ ⟨he got himself ready to go : se preparó para ir⟩ ⟨let me get this straight : a ver si te entiendo⟩ **20** ANSWER : contestar (el teléfono), abrir (la puerta) **21** *fam* BOTHER : molestar, irritar ⟨what really gets me is . . . : lo que más me molesta es . . .⟩ **22** UNDERSTAND : entender ⟨now I get it! : ¡ya entiendo!⟩ ⟨I didn't get your name : no oí su nombre⟩ **23** NOTICE : notar, ver **24** STUMP : agarrar, pillar **25** TRICK : engañar **26** MOVE, SADDEN : conmover **27** RECEIVE : captar, recibir (un canal, etc.) **28** HIT : dar ⟨it got him in the leg : le dio en la pierna⟩ **29** KILL : matar, acabar con **30** **to get across** : comunicar, hacer entender **31** **to get back** : recuperar (dinero, etc.) **32** **to get someone back** : vengarse de alguien **33** **to get down** : bajar (de un estante, etc.) **34** **to get down** SWALLOW : tragar **35** **to get down** DEPRESS, SADDEN : deprimir **36** **to get down** WRITE DOWN : anotar **37** **to get in** SUBMIT, DELIVER : entregar **38** **to get in** : hacer (un comentario, etc.), dar (un golpe, etc.) ⟨to get a word in edgewise : meter baza⟩ **39** **to get in** : arreglárselas

para hacer ⟨we got in a visit to the museum : pudimos visitar el museo⟩ **40** **to get into** : meter (a alguien) en (un asunto) ⟨to get oneself into trouble : meterse en un lío⟩ **41** **to get off** REMOVE : quitar **42** **to get off** : librar de, salvar de (un castigo) **43** **to get off** SEND : mandar, enviar **44** **to get out** EXTRACT, REMOVE : sacar, quitar **45** **to get something out of someone** : sacarle algo a alguien **46** **to get something over with** : quitarse algo de encima **47** **to get through** : hacer llegar (un mensaje, etc.) **48** **to get through** SUSTAIN : mantener, sustentar **49** **to get through** LAST : alcanzar **50** **to get together** COLLECT : juntar, reunir ⟨to get oneself together : organizar⟩ **51** **to get up** RAISE, LIFT : subir **52** **to get up** MUSTER : armarse de (valor), cobrar (fuerzas) **53** **to get up** : organizar (una petición, etc.) **54** **to have got** : tener ⟨I've got a headache : tengo un dolor de cabeza⟩ **55** **to have got to** : tener que ⟨you've got to come : tienes que venir⟩ — *vi* **1** BECOME : ponerse, volverse, hacerse ⟨to get angry : ponerse furioso, enojarse⟩ ⟨to get wet/dirty : mojarse/ensuciarse⟩ ⟨to get dressed : vestirse⟩ ⟨to get used to something : acostumbrarse a algo⟩ ⟨to get lost : perderse⟩ ⟨it's getting late : se hace tarde⟩ **2** GO, MOVE : ir, avanzar ⟨he didn't get far : no avanzó mucho⟩ **3** PROGRESS : progresar, avanzar ⟨now we're getting somewhere! : ¡ahora sí que estamos progresando!⟩ **4** ARRIVE : llegar ⟨to get home : llegar a casa⟩ ⟨she got to the last page : llegó a la última página⟩ **5** **get out (of here)!** (*expressing surprise or disbelief*) : ¡anda!, ¡qué va! **6** **to get across** COMMUNICATE : comunicarse, hacerse entender **7** **to get after** *fam* NAG : estar encima de/a **8** **to get ahead** : adelantarse, progresar **9** **to get along** : llevarse bien (con alguien), congeniar **10** **to get along** MANAGE : arreglárselas **11** **to get along** PROGRESS : marchar, progresar **12** **to get around** SPREAD, CIRCULATE : difundirse ⟨word got around that . . . : se corrió la voz de que . . .⟩ **13** **to get around** CIRCUMVENT : evitar, vencer **14** **to get around** WALK : caminar, andar **15** **to get around** TRAVEL : viajar **16** **to get around to doing something** : encontrar el tiempo para hacer algo **17** **to get at** REACH : llegar a, alcanzar **18** **to get at** DISCOVER : descubrir **19** **to get at** IMPLY : insinuar **20** **to get away** : salir ⟨I can't get away until later : no puedo salir hasta más tarde⟩ **21** **to get away** ESCAPE : escaparse **22** **to get away** : ir de vacaciones **23** **to get away** MANAGE : arreglárselas (con/sin algo) **24** **to get away with** ⟨to get away with a crime : salir impune de un delito⟩ ⟨how does he get away with being so rude? : ¿cómo se le permite ser tan grosero?⟩ **25** **to get back** RETURN : volver **26** **to get** back RETREAT : echarse atrás **27 to get back at someone** : vengarse de alguien **28 to get back to** : volver a, reanudar (una actividad) **29 to get back to** : volver a contactar **30 to get behind** : atrasarse **31 to get behind** SUPPORT : apoyar **32 to get by** MANAGE : arreglárselas **33 to get down to something** : ponerse a hacer algo **34 to get going** LEAVE : irse **35 to get going** : ponerse a hablar **36 to get going on something** : ponerse a hacer algo **37 to get in** ENTER : entrar ⟨it got in through the window : entró por la ventana⟩ **38 to get in** ARRIVE : llegar **39 to get in** : entrar, ser aceptado **40 to get into** : entrar en/a (una universidad, etc.) **41 to get into** : meterse en (una situación) ⟨to get into trouble : meterse en un lío⟩ ⟨to get into an argument : empezar a discutir⟩ **42 to get into** : entusiasmarse con, interesarse en **43 to get into** : afectar a ⟨what's gotten into him? : ¿qué le pasa?⟩ **44 to get into** : llegar a (un lugar) **45 to get into** : ponerse ⟨I can't get into these jeans : estos jeans no me entran⟩ **46 to get in/into** BOARD : subir (a) **47 to get it** ⟨when mom finds out, you're going to get it! : cuando mamá se entere, ¡te mata!⟩ **48 to get off** : quedar impune ⟨to get off with a warning : librarse con sólo una amonestación⟩ **49 to get off** : salir (del trabajo) **50 to get off** : salirse de (un tema, etc.) **51 to get off (of)** EXIT : bajarse (de) **52 to get on** : llevarse bien (con alguien) **53 to get on** ⟨how are you getting on? : ¿qué tal te va?⟩ **54 to get on** SUCCEED : tener éxito **55 to get on** : ocuparse de ⟨I'll get right on it : lo haré ahora mismo⟩ **56 to get on/onto** MOUNT : montarse (a) **57 to get on/onto** BOARD : subirse (a) **58 to get onto** : empezar a hablar de (un tema) **59 to get on with** : seguir con (una actividad) **60 to get out** LEAVE : salir **61 to get out** LEAK : difundirse, filtrarse **62 to get out (of)** EXIT : bajarse (de) **63 to get out of** : escapar de **64 to get out of** : salvarse de **65 to get over** : recuperarse de (una enfermedad, etc.), superar (el miedo, etc.), aceptar (una situación), no guardar (rencor), olvidar a (un amante), consolarse de (una pérdida) **66 to get through** : sobrevivir (el invierno), superar (una crisis, etc.) **67 to get through** : aprobar (un examen) **68 to get through** : comunicar (por teléfono) **69 to get through** : hacer entender ⟨I think I finally got through (to him) : creo que por fin lo hice entender⟩ **70 to get through (with)** FINISH : terminar, acabar **71 to get to** BOTHER : molestar, irritar **72 to get to be** BECOME : llegar a ser **73 to get together** MEET : reunirse **74 to get together** UNITE : unirse, juntarse **75 to get up** : levantarse **76 to get up on** : subirse a **77 to get up to** : hacer (travesuras, etc.) **78 to get up to** REACH : alcanzar, llegar hasta — *v aux* ⟨I got

paid : me pagaron⟩ ⟨they got married : se casaron⟩

getaway [ˈgɛtəˌweɪ] *n* ESCAPE : fuga *f*, huida *f*, escapada *f*

get-go [ˈgɪtˌgoː, ˈgɛt-] *n* **from the get-go** : desde el primer momento

get-together [ˈgɛttəˌgɛðər] *n* : reunión *f* (informal)

geyser [ˈgaɪzər] *n* : géiser *m*

Ghanaian [ˈgɑniən, ˈgæ-] *n* : ghanés *m*, -nesa *f* — **Ghanaian** *adj*

ghastly [ˈgæstli] *adj* **ghastlier; -est 1** HORRIBLE : horrible, espantoso **2** PALE : pálido, cadavérico

gherkin [ˈgərkən] *n* : pepinillo *m*

ghetto [ˈgɛtoː] *n, pl* **-tos** *or* **-toes** : gueto *m*

ghost [ˈgoːst] *n* **1** : fantasma *m*, espectro *m* **2 the Holy Ghost** : el Espíritu Santo

ghostly [ˈgoːstli] *adv* : fantasmal

ghoul [ˈguːl] *n* **1** : demonio *m* (que come cadáveres) **2** : persona *f* de gustos macabros

GI [ˌdʒiːˈaɪ] *n, pl* **GI's** *or* **GIs** : soldado *m* estadounidense

qiant¹ [ˈdʒaɪənt] *adj* : gigante, gigantesco, enorme

giant² *n* : gigante *m*, -ta *f*

gibberish [ˈdʒɪbərɪʃ] *n* : galimatías *m*, jerigonza *f*

gibbon [ˈgɪbən] *n* : gibón *m*

gibe¹ [ˈdʒaɪb] *vi* **gibed; gibing** : mofarse, burlarse

gibe² *n* : pulla *f*, burla *f*, mofa *f*

giblets [ˈdʒɪbləts] *npl* : menudos *mpl*, menudencias *fpl*

giddiness [ˈgɪdinəs] *n* **1** DIZZINESS : vértigo *m*, mareo *m* **2** SILLINESS : frivolidad *f*, estupidez *f*

giddy [ˈgɪdi] *adj* **giddier; -est 1** DIZZY : mareado, vertiginoso **2** FRIVOLOUS, SILLY : frívolo, tonto

gift [ˈgɪft] *n* **1** TALENT : don *m*, talento *m*, dotes *fpl* **2** PRESENT : regalo *m*, obsequio *m*

gift card *n* : tarjeta *f* de regalo, tarjeta *f* regalo

gift certificate *n* : certificado *m* de regalo

gifted [ˈgɪftəd] *adj* TALENTED : talentoso

gig¹ [ˈgɪg] *n* : trabajo *m* (de duración limitada) ⟨to play a gig : tocar en un concierto⟩

gig² *n fam* : giga *mf fam*, gigabyte *m*

gigabyte [ˈdʒɪgəˌbaɪt, ˈgɪ-] *n* : gigabyte *m*

gigantic [dʒaɪˈgæntɪk] *adj* : gigantesco, enorme, colosal

giggle¹ [ˈgɪgəl] *vi* **-gled; -gling** : reírse tontamente

giggle² *n* : risita *f*, risa *f* tonta

gild [ˈgɪld] *vt* **gilded** *or* **gilt** [ˈgɪlt]; **gilding** : dorar

gill [ˈgɪl] *n* : agalla *f*, branquia *f*

gilt¹ [ˈgɪlt] *adj* : dorado

gilt² *n* : dorado *m*

gimlet [ˈgɪmlət] *n* **1** : barrena *f* (herramienta) **2** : bebida *f* de vodka o ginebra y limón

gimmick [ˈgɪmɪk] *n* **1** GADGET : artilugio *m* **2** CATCH : engaño *m*, trampa *f* **3** SCHEME, TRICK : ardid *m*, truco *m* gin ['dʒɪn] n : ginebra f (bebida alcohólica)

ginger ['dʒɪndʒər] n : jengibre m

ginger ale n : gaseosa f de jengibre

gingerbread ['dʒɪndʒər,brɛd] n : pan m de jengibre

gingerly ['dʒɪndʒərli] adv : con cuidado, cautelosamente

gingham ['gɪŋəm] n : guinga f

ginseng ['dʒɪn,sɪŋ, -ˌsɛŋ] n : ginseng m

giraffe [dʒə'ræf] n : jirafa f

gird ['gərd] vt girded or girt ['gərt]; girding 1 BIND : ceñir, atar 2 ENCIRCLE : rodear 3 to gird oneself : prepararse

girder ['gərdər] n : viga f

girdle¹ ['gərdəl] vt -dled; -dling 1 GIRD : ceñir, atar 2 SURROUND : rodear, circundar

girdle² n : faja f

girl ['gərl] n 1 : chica f, muchacha f 2 or little girl : niña f, chica f 3 SWEETHEART : novia f 4 DAUGHTER : hija f

girlfriend ['gərl,frɛnd] n : novia f, amiga f

girlhood ['gərl,hʊd] n : niñez f, juventud f (de una muchacha)

girlish ['gərlɪʃ] adj : de niña

girth ['gərθ] n 1 : circunferencia f (de un árbol, etc.), cintura f (de una persona) 2 CINCH : cincha f (para caballos, etc.)

gist ['dʒɪst] n : quid m, meollo m

give¹ ['gɪv] v gave ['geɪv]; given ['gɪvən]; giving vt 1 HAND : dar, entregar ⟨give it to me : dámelo⟩ 2 PRESENT : dar, regalar ⟨they gave him a gold watch : le regalaron un reloj de oro⟩ 3 DONATE : dar, donar ⟨to give blood : dar sangre⟩ ⟨to give money to charity : dar dinero a organizaciones benéficas⟩ 4 PAY : dar, pagar ⟨I'll give you $10 for the blue one : te daré $10 por el azul⟩ 5 dar ⟨un grito, un salto, etc.⟩ ⟨she gave me a kiss : me dio un beso⟩ ⟨he gave us the signal : nos dio la señal⟩ 6 ADMINISTER : dar (un castigo, una inyección, etc.) 7 OFFER : dar ⟨he gave me his hand : me dio la mano⟩ ⟨she didn't give a reason : no dijo por qué⟩ 8 PROVIDE : dar ⟨to give one's word : dar uno su palabra⟩ ⟨she gave me a ride to work : me llevó a la oficina⟩ ⟨cows give milk : las vacas dan leche⟩ 9 ATTRIBUTE : dar ⟨to give credit to someone : darle el mérito a alguien⟩ 10 PRONOUNCE : dictar (una sentencia) 11 CAUSE : dar, causar, ocasionar ⟨to give trouble : causar problemas⟩ ⟨to give someone to understand : darle a entender algo⟩ 12 GRANT : dar, otorgar ⟨to give permission : dar permiso⟩ 13 to give away : regalar 14 to give away REVEAL : revelar 15 to give away : llevar (una novia) al altar 16 to give away BETRAY : delatar 17 to give back RETURN : devolver 18 to give in (to) : ceder (a) 19 to give off EMIT : despedir 20 to give oneself (over) to : entregarse a 21 to give out DISTRIBUTE : distribuir 22 to give up : dejar, renunciar a, abandonar ⟨to give up smoking : dejar de fumar⟩ — vi 1 : hacer regalos 2 or to give way YIELD : ceder, romperse ⟨it gave under

the weight of the crowd : cedió bajo el peso de la muchedumbre⟩ 3 to give in/up SURRENDER : rendirse, entregarse 4 to give out RUN OUT : agotarse, acabarse

give² n FLEXIBILITY : flexibilidad f, elasticidad f

give–and–take n : toma y daca f

giveaway ['gɪvə,weɪ] n 1 : revelación f involuntaria 2 GIFT : regalo m, obsequio m

given ['gɪvən] adj 1 INCLINED : dado, inclinado ⟨he's given to quarreling : es muy dado a discutir⟩ 2 SPECIFIC : dado, determinado ⟨at a given time : en un momento dado⟩

given name n : nombre m de pila

give or take adv APPROXIMATELY : más o menos

gizzard ['gɪzərd] n : molleja f

glacial ['gleɪʃəl] adj : glacial — glacially adv

glacier ['gleɪʃər] n : glaciar m

glad ['glæd] adj gladder; gladdest 1 PLEASED : alegre, contento ⟨she was glad I came : se alegró de que haya venido⟩ ⟨glad to meet you! : ¡mucho gusto!⟩ 2 HAPPY, PLEASING : feliz, agradable ⟨glad tidings : buenas nuevas⟩ 3 WILLING : dispuesto, gustoso ⟨I'll be glad to do it : lo haré con mucho gusto⟩

gladden ['glædən] vt : alegrar

glade ['gleɪd] n : claro m

gladiator ['glædi,eɪtər] n : gladiador m

gladiolus [ˌglædi'oːləs] n, pl -li [-li, -ˌlaɪ] : gladiolo m, gladíolo m

gladly ['glædli] adv : con mucho gusto

gladness ['glædnəs] n : alegría f, gozo m

glamor or glamour ['glæmər] n : atractivo m, hechizo m, encanto m

glamorous ['glæmərəs] adj : atractivo, encantador

glamping ['glæmpɪŋ] n : glamping m fam, camping m de lujo

glance¹ ['glænts] vi glanced; glancing 1 RICOCHET : rebotar ⟨it glanced off the wall : rebotó en la pared⟩ 2 to glance at : mirar, echar un vistazo a 3 to glance away : apartar los ojos

glance² n : mirada f, vistazo m, ojeada f

gland ['glænd] n : glándula f

glandular ['glændʒʊlər] adj : glandular

glare¹ ['glær] vi glared; glaring 1 SHINE : brillar, relumbrar 2 STARE : mirar con ira, lanzar una mirada feroz

glare² n 1 BRIGHTNESS : resplandor m, luz f deslumbrante 2 : mirada f feroz

glaring ['glærɪŋ] adj 1 BRIGHT : deslumbrante, brillante 2 FLAGRANT, OBVIOUS : flagrante, manifiesto ⟨a glaring error : un error que salta a la vista⟩

glaringly ['glærɪŋli] adv ⟨to be glaringly obvious : saltar a la vista⟩

glass ['glæs] n 1 : vidrio m, cristal m (de una ventana, etc.) 2 vaso m ⟨a glass of milk : un vaso de leche⟩ 3 glasses npl SPECTACLES : gafas fpl, anteojos mpl, lentes mpl, espejuelos mpl

glassblowing ['glæs,bloːɪŋ] n : soplado m del vidrio

glassful ['glæs‚fʊl] n : vaso m, copa f

glassware ['glæs‚wær] n : cristalería f

glassy ['glæsi] adj **glassier; -est** 1 : vítreo 2 : vidrioso ⟨glassy eyes : ojos vidriosos⟩

glaucoma [glaʊ'ko:mə, glɔ-] n : glaucoma m

glaze[1] ['gleɪz] vt **glazed; glazing** 1 : ponerle vidrios a (una ventana, etc.) 2 : vidriar (cerámica) 3 : glasear (papel, verduras, etc.)

glaze[2] n : vidriado m, glaseado m, barniz m

glazier ['gleɪʒər] n : vidriero m, -ra f

glazing ['gleɪzɪŋ] n : vidrios mpl, acristalamiento m Spain ⟨double-glazing : doble vidrio, doble acristalamiento⟩

gleam[1] ['gli:m] vi : brillar, destellar, relucir

gleam[2] n 1 LIGHT : luz f (oscura) 2 GLINT : destello m 3 GLIMMER : rayo m, vislumbre f ⟨a gleam of hope : un rayo de esperanza⟩

glean ['gli:n] vt : recoger, espigar

glee ['gli:] n : alegría f, júbilo m, regocijo m

gleeful ['gli:fəl] adj : lleno de alegría

glen ['glɛn] n : cañada f

glib ['glɪb] adj **glibber; glibbest** 1 : simplista ⟨a glib reply : una respuesta simplista⟩ 2 : con mucha labia (dícese de una persona)

glibly ['glɪbli] adv : con mucha labia

glide[1] ['glaɪd] vi **glided; gliding** : deslizarse (en una superficie), planear (en el aire)

glide[2] n : planeo m

glider ['glaɪdər] n 1 : planeador m (aeronave) 2 : mecedor m (tipo de columpio)

glimmer[1] ['glɪmər] vi : brillar con luz trémula

glimmer[2] n 1 : luz f trémula, luz f tenue 2 GLEAM : rayo m, vislumbre f ⟨a glimmer of understanding : un rayo de entendimiento⟩

glimpse[1] ['glɪmps] vt **glimpsed; glimpsing** : vislumbrar, entrever

glimpse[2] n : mirada f breve ⟨to catch a glimpse of : alcanzar a ver, vislumbrar⟩

glint[1] ['glɪnt] vi GLEAM, SPARKLE : destellar

glint[2] n 1 SPARKLE : destello m, centelleo m 2 to have a glint in one's eye : chispearle los ojos a uno

glisten[1] ['glɪsən] vi : brillar, centellear

glisten[2] n : brillo m, centelleo m

glitch ['glɪtʃ] n 1 MALFUNCTION : mal funcionamiento m 2 SNAG : problema m, complicación f

glitter[1] ['glɪtər] vi 1 SPARKLE : destellar, relucir, brillar 2 FLASH : relampaguear ⟨his eyes glittered in anger : le relampagueaban los ojos de ira⟩

glitter[2] n 1 BRIGHTNESS : brillo m 2 : purpurina f (para decoración)

glitz ['glɪts] n : oropel m

gloat ['glo:t] vi to gloat over : regodearse en

glob ['glɑb] n : plasta f, masa f, grumo m

global ['glo:bəl] adj 1 FULL, COMPREHENSIVE : global 2 WORLDWIDE : global, mundial — **globally** adv —

globalization [‚glo:bələ'zeɪʃən] n

global warming n : calentamiento m global

globe ['glo:b] n 1 SPHERE : esfera f, globo m 2 EARTH : globo m, Tierra f 3 : globo m terráqueo (modelo de la Tierra)

globe–trotter ['glo:b‚trɑtər] n : trotamundos mf

globule ['glɑ‚bju:l] n : glóbulo m

gloom ['glu:m] n 1 DARKNESS : penumbra f, oscuridad f 2 MELANCHOLY : melancolía f, tristeza f

gloomily ['glu:məli] adv : tristemente

gloomy ['glu:mi] adj **gloomier; -est** 1 DARK : oscuro, tenebroso ⟨gloomy weather : tiempo gris⟩ 2 MELANCHOLY : melancólico 3 PESSIMISTIC : pesimista 4 DEPRESSING : deprimente, lúgubre

glorification [‚glorəfə'keɪʃən] n : glorificación f

glorify ['glorə‚faɪ] vt **-fied; -fying** : glorificar

glorious ['gloriəs] adj 1 ILLUSTRIOUS : glorioso, ilustre 2 MAGNIFICENT : magnífico, espléndido, maravilloso — **gloriously** adv

glory[1] ['glori] vi **-ried; -rying** EXULT : exultar, regocijarse

glory[2] n, pl **-ries** 1 RENOWN : gloria f, fama f, honor m 2 PRAISE : gloria f ⟨glory to God : gloria a Dios⟩ 3 MAGNIFICENCE : magnificencia f, esplendor m, gloria f 4 to be in one's glory : estar uno en su gloria

gloss[1] ['glɔs, 'glɑs] vt 1 EXPLAIN : glosar, explicar 2 POLISH : lustrar, pulir 3 to gloss over : quitarle importancia a, minimizar

gloss[2] n 1 SHINE : lustre m, brillo m 2 EXPLANATION : glosa f, explicación f breve 3 → glossary

glossary ['glɔsəri, 'glɑ-] n, pl **-ries** : glosario m

glossy ['glɔsi, 'glɑ-] adj **glossier; -est** : brillante, lustroso, satinado (dícese del papel)

glove ['glʌv] n : guante m ⟨boxing glove : guante de boxeo⟩

glove compartment n : guantera f

glow[1] ['glo:] vi 1 SHINE : brillar, resplandecer 2 BRIM : rebosar ⟨to glow with health : rebosar de salud⟩

glow[2] n 1 BRIGHTNESS : resplandor m, brillo m, luminosidad f 2 FEELING : sensación f (de bienestar), oleada f (de sentimiento) 3 INCANDESCENCE : incandescencia f

glower ['glaʊər] vi : fruncir el ceño

glowworm ['glo:‚wərm] n : luciérnaga f

glucose ['glu:‚ko:s] n : glucosa f

glue[1] ['glu:] vt **glued; gluing** or **glueing** : pegar con cola

glue[2] n : pegamento m, cola f

gluey ['glu:i] adj **gluier; -est** : pegajoso

glum ['glʌm] adj **glummer; glummest** 1 SULLEN : hosco, sombrío 2 DREARY, GLOOMY : sombrío, triste, melancólico

glut¹ ['glʌt] *vt* **glutted; glutting 1** SATIATE : saciar, hartar **2** : inundar (el mercado)

glut² *n* : exceso *m*, superabundancia *f*

glutinous ['glu:tənəs] *adj* STICKY : pegajoso, glutinoso

glutton ['glʌtən] *n* : glotón *m*, -tona *f*

gluttonous ['glʌtənəs] *adj* : glotón

gluttony ['glʌtəni] *n, pl* **-tonies** : glotonería *f*, gula *f*

glycerin *or* **glycerine** ['glɪsrən, 'glɪ-] *n* : glicerina *f*

gnarled ['nɑrld] *adj* **1** KNOTTY : nudoso **2** TWISTED : retorcido

gnash ['næʃ] *vt* : hacer rechinar (los dientes)

gnat ['næt] *n* : jején *m*

gnaw ['nɔ] *vt* : roer

gnome ['no:m] *n* : gnomo *m*

gnu ['nu:, 'nju:] *n, pl* **gnu** *or* **gnus** : ñu *m*

go¹ ['go:] *v* **went** ['wɛnt]; **gone** ['gɔn 'gɑn]; **going; goes** ['go:z] *vi* **1** : ir ⟨to go slow : ir despacio⟩ ⟨to go shopping : ir de compras⟩ ⟨to go to work : ir a trabajar⟩ ⟨to go to school : ir a la escuela⟩ ⟨we went to Spain : fuimos a España⟩ ⟨we went to see a movie : fuimos a ver una película⟩ ⟨you should go (to/and) see her : deberías ir a verla⟩ ⟨we went up/down to the mountains : fuimos a las montañas, fuimos al norte/sur a ver las montañas⟩ ⟨to go for a drive : ir a dar una vuelta en coche⟩ ⟨to go on foot : ir a pie⟩ **2** (*used figuratively*) : ir ⟨she'll go far : llegará lejos⟩ ⟨I wouldn't go so far as to say that . . . : no diría tanto como que . . .⟩ ⟨this time he's gone too far : esta vez se ha pasado⟩ ⟨to go a long way towards : ayudar en gran medida a⟩ **3** LEAVE : irse, marcharse, salir ⟨let's go! : ¡vámonos!⟩ ⟨the train went on time : el tren salió a tiempo⟩ **4** DISAPPEAR : pasarse, irse ⟨her fear is gone : se le ha pasado el miedo⟩ ⟨those days have gone : esos días ya pasaron⟩ **5** DIE : morir **6** EXTEND : ir, extenderse, llegar ⟨this road goes to the river : este camino se extiende hasta el río⟩ ⟨to go from top to bottom : ir de arriba abajo⟩ **7** LEAD, CONNECT : dar ⟨that door goes to the cellar : esa puerta da al sótano⟩ **8** FUNCTION : funcionar, marchar ⟨the car won't go : el coche no funciona⟩ ⟨to get something going : poner algo en marcha⟩ **9** SELL : venderse ⟨it goes for $15 : se vende por $15⟩ **10** (*to be disposed of*) ⟨that one can go : podemos deshacernos de ése⟩ **11** FAIL : fallarse (dícese de la vista, etc.), gastarse (dícese de pilas, etc.), estropearse (dícese de un motor, etc.) **12** GIVE WAY : ceder, romperse (dícese de un dique, etc.) **13** PROGRESS : ir, andar, seguir ⟨my exam went well : me fue bien en el examen⟩ ⟨how did the meeting go? : ¿qué tal la reunión?⟩ **14** BECOME : volverse, quedarse ⟨to go crazy : volverse loco⟩ ⟨he's going bald : se está quedando calvo⟩ ⟨the tire went flat : la llanta se desinfló⟩ **15** (*describing a condition*) ⟨to go

hungry : pasar hambre⟩ ⟨to go barefoot : ir descalzo⟩ ⟨to go unnoticed : pasar desapercibido⟩ **16** (*describing a story, song, etc.*) ⟨how does the story go? : ¿qué pasa en el cuento?⟩ ⟨how does the song go? — it goes like this: . . . : ¿cómo es la canción? — es así: . . .⟩ ⟨the legend goes that . . . : cuenta la leyenda que . . . , según (dice) la leyenda . . .⟩ **17** FIT : caber ⟨it will go through the door : cabe por la puerta⟩ **18** : pasar (dícese del tiempo) ⟨the time went quickly : el tiempo pasó rápidamente⟩ **19** SOUND : sonar **20 anything goes!** : ¡todo vale! **21 to be good/ready to go** : estar listo **22 to go** : faltar ⟨only 10 days to go : faltan sólo 10 días⟩ ⟨we still have a long way to go : aún nos queda mucho camino por recorrer⟩ **23 to go** : para llevar (dícese de comida, etc.) **24 to go about** DO : hacer **25 to go about** APPROACH, TACKLE : abordar, emprender **26 to go after** PURSUE : perseguir **27 to go against** : ir en contra **28 to go against** : jugar contra (en deportes) **29 to go ahead** (*to proceed without delay or hesitation*) ⟨go ahead and start without me : empiecen sin mí⟩ ⟨I went ahead and bought it : me decidí y lo compré⟩ ⟨sure, go (right) ahead! : ¡por supuesto!⟩ **30 to go ahead** (**with**) : seguir adelante (con) **31 to go all out** : hacer lo máximo ⟨he went all out for his wife's birthday : en el cumpleaños de su esposa tiró la casa por la ventana⟩ **32 to go along** PROCEED : ir, marchar **33 to go along** ACQUIESCE : acceder ⟨to go along with something : acceder a algo, aceptar algo⟩ ⟨to go along with someone : cooperar con alguien⟩ **34 to go along with** ⟨the stress that goes along with the job : el estrés que conlleva el trabajo⟩ **35 to go around** : correr (dícese de un rumor, etc.), circular ⟨there's a bug going around : hay un virus dando vueltas por ahí⟩ **36 to go around** ⟨there's enough/plenty to go around : hay para todos⟩ **37 to go at** ATTACK : atacar **38 to go at** : atacar, abordar (un problema, etc.) **39 to go at it** ARGUE, FIGHT : discutir, pelearse **40 to go away** LEAVE : irse **41 to go away** DISAPPEAR : desaparecer **42 to go back** RETURN : volver (a un lugar, un tema, etc.) ⟨he never went back : nunca volvió⟩ ⟨to go back to school : volver a la escuela⟩ **43 to go back** : remontarse ⟨the records go back to 1900 : los registros se remontan a 1900⟩ ⟨we go back a long way : nos conocemos desde hace muchos años⟩ **44 to go back on** : faltar uno a (su promesa) **45 to go back to** (**doing**) **something** : volver a hacer algo, reanudar algo ⟨to go back to sleep : volver a dormir⟩ ⟨she went back to work : reanudó el trabajo⟩ ⟨afterwards he went back to reading : después siguió leyendo⟩ **46 to go bad** SPOIL : estropearse, echarse a perder **47 to go beyond** : ir más allá de **48 to go by** PASS

: pasar **49 to go by** : guiarse por (una regla, etc.), juzgar por (las apariencias, etc.) **50 to go by** : hacerse llamar ⟨he goes by "Ed" : se hace llamar "Ed"⟩ **51 to go by** STOP BY : pasar por **52 to go down** : hundirse (dícese de un barco), caer (dícese de un avión), caerse (dícese de una persona) **53 to go down** DE-CREASE : bajar, disminuir **54 to go down** : dejar de funcionar (dícese de un sistema, etc.) **55 to go down** : caer (dícese de un gobierno, etc.) **56 to go down** SET : ponerse (dícese del sol) **57 to go down** : pasar (dícese de comida) ⟨it went down the wrong way : se me atragantó, se me fue por mal camino⟩ **58 to go down in history → history 59 to go down well/badly** : caer bien/mal, tener una buena/mala acogida **60 to go for** : interesarse uno en, gustarle a uno (algo, alguien) ⟨I don't go for that : eso no me interesa⟩ **61 to go for** SELECT : decidirse por **62 to go for** ACCEPT : aceptar **63 to go for** ATTACK : atacar **64 to go for** PURSUE : ir tras, ir a por *Spain* **65 to go for** : ir por ⟨that goes for you, too! : ¡también va por ti!⟩ **66 to go in** : esconderse (dícese del sol o de la luna) **67 to go in on** ⟨we both/all went in on the gift together : el regalo lo compramos a medias/entre todos⟩ **68 to go in for** LIKE : interesarse uno en, gustarle a uno (algo) **69 to go into** : entrar en ⟨to go into action/effect : entrar en acción/vigor⟩ ⟨to go into hid-ing : esconderse⟩ **70 to go into** DISCUSS : entrar en **71 to go into** LOOK INTO : investigar **72 to go into** : dedicarse a (una profesión) **73 to go off** : estallar, explotar (dícese de una bomba, etc.), dispararse (dícese de una pistola, etc.) **74 to go off** SOUND : sonar **75 to go off** : echarse a perder (dícese de la comida, etc.) **76 to go off** TURN OFF : apagarse **77 to go off on** *fam* SCOLD : regañar **78 to go on** CONTINUE : se-guir, continuar ⟨life goes on : la vida sigue⟩ ⟨we can't go on like this : no podemos seguir así⟩ ⟨we went on to Chi-cago : seguimos el viaje a Chicago, con-tinuamos nuestro camino a Chicago⟩ ⟨she went on working : siguió traba-jando⟩ ⟨she went on to say that . . . : pasó a decir que . . .⟩ ⟨to go on to be-come : llegar/pasar a ser⟩ **79 to go on** LAST : durar **80 to go on** HAPPEN : pasar, ocurrir ⟨what's going on? : ¿qué pasa?⟩ **81 to go on** RAMBLE : no parar de hablar **82 to go on** : guiarse por (pruebas, etc.) **83 to go on (ahead)** : ir adelante, adelantarse **84 to go out** LEAVE : salir **85 to go out** : apagarse ⟨the power went out : se fue la electri-cidad⟩ **86 to go out** : bajar (dícese de la marea) **87 to go out** : emitirse (dícese de un anuncio, etc.) **88 to go out with** DATE : salir con **89 to go over** EX-AMINE, REVIEW : examinar, repasar **90 to go over to** : pasarse a (la competen-cia, etc.) **91 to go over to** APPROACH

: acercarse a **92 to go over well/badly** : caer bien/mal, tener una buena/mala acogida **93 to go there** *fam* ⟨let's not go there : no quiero hablar/pensar de eso⟩ **94 to go through** PIERCE : pene-trar, atravesar **95 to go through** USE UP : gastar, agotar **96 to go through** SEARCH : registrar, revolver en **97 to go through** : pasar por (dificultades, etapas, etc.) **98 to go through** PER-FORM : hacer **99 to go through** : ser aprobado (dícese de un proyecto de ley, etc.) **100 to go through someone's head/mind** : pasársele por la cabeza/ mente a alguien **101 to go through with** : llevar a cabo **102 to go to** : otor-garse a, transmitirse a ⟨the prize went to . . . : el premio se lo llevó . . .⟩ **103 to go to** *(to begin to be in)* ⟨to go to sleep : dormirse⟩ ⟨to go to war : entrar en guerra⟩ **104 to go together** MATCH : combinar, hacer juego, armonizar **105 to go to show/prove** : demostrar **106 to go to trouble/expense (etc.)** ⟨he went to a lot of trouble : se esmeró mucho⟩ ⟨they went to great expense : gastaron mucho⟩ **107 to go towards** : contribuir a **108 to go under** FOUN-DER : hundirse **109 to go up** RISE, IN-CREASE : subir **110 to go up** : levan-tarse (dícese de un edificio) **111 to go with** MATCH : armonizar con, hacer juego con, ir bien con **112 to go with** CHOOSE : elegir, decidirse por **113 to go without** MAKE DO : arreglárselas (sin algo) **114 to go without something** : prescindir de algo — *v aux* **to be going to** : ir a ⟨I'm going to write a letter : voy a escribir una carta⟩ ⟨it's not going to last : no va a durar⟩

go² *n, pl* **goes 1** ATTEMPT : intento *m* ⟨to have a go at : intentar, probar⟩ **2** SUC-CESS : éxito *m* **3** ENERGY : energía *f*, empuje *m* ⟨to be on the go : no parar, no descansar⟩

goad¹ [ˈgoːd] *vt* : aguijonear (un animal), incitar (a una persona)

goad² *n* : aguijón *m*

go-ahead *n* APPROVAL : luz *f* verde

goal [ˈgoːl] *n* **1** : portería *f*, arco *m*, marco *m* (en deportes) **2** : gol *m* (en de-portes) ⟨to score a goal : anotar un gol⟩ **3** AIM, OBJECTIVE : meta *m*, objeti-vo *m*

goalie [ˈgoːli] → **goalkeeper**

goalkeeper [ˈgoːlˌkiːpər] *n* : portero *m*, -ra *f*; guardameta *mf*; arquero *m*, -ra *f*

goalpost [ˈgoːlˌpoːst] *n* : poste *m* (de la portería)

goaltender [ˈgoːlˌtɛndər] → **goalkeeper**

goat [ˈgoːt] *n* **1** : cabra *f* (hembra) **2** bil-ly goat : macho *m* cabrío, chivo *m*

goatee [goˈtiː] *n* : barbita *f* de chivo; pe-rilla *f*; pera *f* *Arg, Chile, Uru*; piocha *f* *Mex*

goatskin [ˈgoːtˌskɪn] *n* : piel *f* de cabra

gob [ˈgɑb] *n* : masa *f*, grumo *m*

gobble [ˈgɑbəl] *v* **-bled; -bling** *vt* to gob-ble up/down : tragar, engullir — *vi* : hacer ruidos de pavo

gobbledygook ['gabəldɪ,guk, -,gu:k] n
GIBBERISH : jerigonza f
go–between ['go:bɪ,twi:n] n : intermediario m, -ria f; mediador m, -dora f
goblet ['gablət] n : copa f
goblin ['gablən] n : duende m, trasgo m
god ['gad, 'gɔd] n 1 : dios m 2 **God**
: Dios m
godchild ['gad,tʃaɪld, 'gɔd-] n, pl -children : ahijado m, -da f
goddaughter ['gad,dɔtər, 'gɔd-] n : ahijada f
goddess ['gadəs, 'gɔ-] n : diosa f
godfather ['gad,faðər, 'gɔd-] n : padrino
m
godless ['gadləs, 'gɔd-] adj : ateo
godlike ['gad,laɪk, 'gɔd-] adj : divino
godly ['gadli, 'gɔd-] adj **godlier; -est 1**
DIVINE : divino 2 DEVOUT, PIOUS
: piadoso, devoto, beato
godmother ['gad,mʌðər, 'gɔd-] n : madrina f
godparent ['gad,pærənt, 'gɔd-] n : padrino m, madrina f ⟨her godparents : sus
padrinos⟩
godsend ['gad,sɛnd, 'gɔd-] n : bendición
f, regalo m divino
godson ['gad,sʌn, 'gɔd-] n : ahijado m
goes → go
go–getter ['go:,gɛtər] n : persona f ambiciosa, buscavidas mf fam
goggle ['gagəl] vi -gled; -gling : mirar
con ojos desorbitados
goggles ['gagəlz] npl : gafas fpl (protectoras), anteojos mpl
going [,go:ɪŋ] n 1 DEPARTURE : salida f,
partida f 2 (describing progress) : ⟨it's
been slow going : las cosas van despacio⟩
⟨it's going to be tough going : va a ser
difícil⟩ 3 **comings and goings** → coming²
goings–on [,go:ɪŋz'an, -'ɔn] npl : sucesos
mpl, ocurrencias fpl
goiter ['gɔɪtər] n : bocio m
gold¹ ['go:ld] adj 1 : (hecho) de oro 2
: dorado, de color oro
gold² n : oro m
golden ['go:ldən] adj 1 : (hecho) de
oro 2 : dorado, de color oro ⟨golden
hair : pelo rubio⟩ 3 FLOURISHING,
PROSPEROUS : dorado, próspero ⟨golden
years : años dorados⟩ 4 FAVORABLE
: favorable, excelente ⟨a golden opportunity : una excelente oportunidad⟩
goldenrod ['go:ldən,rad] n : vara f de oro
golden rule n : regla f de oro
goldfinch ['go:ld,fɪntʃ] n : jilguero m
goldfish ['go:ld,fɪʃ] n : pez m de colores
gold mine n : mina f de oro
goldsmith ['go:ld,smɪθ] n : orífice mf, orfebre mf
golf¹ ['galf, 'gɔlf] vi : jugar (al) golf
golf² n : golf m
golf ball n : pelota f de golf
golf cart n : carrito m de golf
golf club n 1 : palo m de golf (implemento) 2 : club m de golf (organización)
golf course n : campo m de golf, cancha f
de golf

golfer ['galfər, 'gɔl-] n : golfista mf
gondola ['gandələ, gan'do:lə] n : góndola
f
gone ['gɔn] adj 1 DEAD : muerto 2 PAST
: pasado, ido ⟨those days are gone : esos
días ya pasaron⟩ ⟨her fear is gone : se le
ha pasado el miedo⟩ 3 LOST : perdido,
desaparecido ⟨my car is gone! : ¡mi coche no está!⟩ 4 **to be far gone** : estar
muy avanzado 5 **to be gone on** : estar
loco por
goner ['gɔnər] n **to be a goner** : estar en
las últimas
gong ['gɔŋ, 'gaŋ] n : gong m
gonorrhea [,ganə'ri:ə] n : gonorrea f
good¹ ['gud] adv 1 (used as an intensifier)
: bien ⟨a good strong rope : una cuerda
bien fuerte⟩ 2 WELL : bien
good² adj better ['bɛtər]; best ['bɛst] 1
(of high quality) : bueno ⟨a good restaurant : un buen restaurante⟩ ⟨the book is
no good : el libro es malísimo⟩ ⟨in good
condition : en buenas condiciones⟩
⟨keep up the good work! : ¡buen trabajo!
sigue así⟩ 2 ACCEPTABLE : aceptable 3
PLEASANT : bueno, agradable ⟨good
weather : buen tiempo⟩ ⟨the sauce is
good : la salsa está buena⟩ ⟨that dress
looks good on you : ese vestido te queda
bien⟩ ⟨to have a good time : divertirse⟩
⟨have a good day! : ¡qué te vaya bien!⟩ 4
FORTUNATE : bueno ⟨good news : buenas noticias⟩ ⟨good luck : buena suerte⟩
⟨it's a good thing that . . . : menos mal
que . . .⟩ 5 SUITABLE : bueno ⟨a good
day for a picnic : un buen día para ir de
picnic⟩ ⟨these tires are no good : estas
llantas no sirven⟩ 6 SOUND : bueno,
sensato ⟨good advice : un buen consejo⟩ ⟨with good reason : con razón⟩ 7 PROM
ISING : bueno ⟨a good deal : un buen
negocio⟩ ⟨a good bet : una apuesta segura⟩ 8 HEALTHY : bueno ⟨good for a
cold : bueno para los resfriados⟩ ⟨it's
good for you : es bueno para uno⟩ ⟨a
good diet : una buena alimentación⟩ ⟨to
be in good health : estar bien de salud⟩
⟨I'm not feeling very good : no me siento
bien⟩ 9 FULL : completo, entero ⟨a
good hour : una hora entera⟩ ⟨to get a
good night's sleep : dormir por la
noche⟩ 10 THOROUGH : bueno ⟨a good
kick : una buena patada⟩ ⟨take a good
look at it : míralo bien⟩ ⟨we had a good
laugh : nos reímos mucho⟩ 11 CON
SIDERABLE : bueno, bastante ⟨a good
many people : muchísima gente, un
buen número de gente⟩ 12 ATTRAC
TIVE, DESIRABLE : bueno ⟨a good salary/
price : un buen sueldo/precio⟩ 13 (referring to status) : bueno ⟨a good family
: una buena familia⟩ 14 APPROVING
: bueno ⟨good reviews : buena
crítica⟩ 15 KIND, VIRTUOUS : bueno,
amable ⟨she's a good person : es buena
gente⟩ ⟨that's good of you! : ¡qué amable!⟩ ⟨good deeds : buenas obras⟩ ⟨the
good guys : los buenos⟩ 16 CLOSE : íntimo ⟨we're good friends : somos muy
amigos⟩ 17 WELL-BEHAVED : bueno

⟨be good : sé bueno⟩ **18** LOYAL, FAITHFUL : bueno, fiel **19** (*within bounds*) : bueno (en deportes) **20** SKILLED : bueno, hábil ⟨to be good at : tener facilidad para⟩ ⟨a good cook : un buen cocinero⟩ ⟨he's good with children : es bueno con los niños⟩ **21** PLEASED, CHEERFUL : bueno ⟨in a good mood : de buen humor⟩ ⟨helping others makes me feel good : me siento bien ayudando a los demás⟩ **22** SATISFIED : satisfecho ⟨no thanks — I'm good : no, gracias — estoy bien⟩ **23** FRESH : fresco **24** FUNNY : gracioso ⟨she's always good for a laugh : es muy divertida⟩ ⟨he said he didn't know? that's a good one : ¿dijo que no lo sabía? no me hagas reír⟩ **25** (*in greetings*) : bueno ⟨good morning : buenos días⟩ ⟨good afternoon/evening : buenas tardes⟩ ⟨good night : buenas noches⟩ **26** (*used as a response*) ⟨I'm ready — good, let's go : estoy listo — bueno, vamos⟩ **27 as good as** NEARLY : casi **28 as good as it gets** *fam* ⟨this is as good as it gets : mejor imposible, no hay mejor⟩ **29 good and** (*used for emphasis*) ⟨good and hot : muy caliente⟩ ⟨I hit him good and hard : le pegué bien duro⟩ ⟨when I'm good and ready : cuando me dé la gana⟩ **30 good God/heavens!** : ¡Dios mío! **31 good old** : el bueno de, la buena de ⟨good old Carl : el bueno de Carl⟩ **32 to be good about** ⟨she's very good about calling us : nunca se olvida de llamarnos⟩ ⟨I'm trying to be better about exercising : estoy tratando de hacer más ejercicio⟩ **33 to be good for** *fam* ⟨he's good for the money : seguro que le pagará⟩ **34 to be good (for/until)** : valer (por/hasta) ⟨good for one free meal : vale por una comida gratis⟩ ⟨the car is good for a few more years : al carro le quedan unos años más⟩ **35 to be good to go** *fam* : estar listo **36 too good to be true** : demasiado bueno para ser cierto **37 to make good** : tener éxito **38 to make good on** : cumplir con

good³ *n* **1** RIGHT : bien *m* ⟨to do good : hacer el bien⟩ ⟨to be up to no good : estar tramando algo⟩ **2** GOODNESS : bondad *f* **3** BENEFIT : bien *m*, provecho *m* ⟨it's for your own good : es por tu propio bien⟩ ⟨for the common good : por el bien común⟩ **4 goods** *npl* PROPERTY : efectos *mpl* personales, posesiones *fpl* **5 goods** *npl* WARES : mercancía *f*, mercadería *f*, artículos *mpl* ⟨consumer goods : bienes de consumo⟩ **6 for ~** : para siempre **7 the good** : los buenos **8 to be in good with someone** *fam* : estar a bien con alguien **9 to be no good** : no servir (para nada) **10 to deliver the goods** *fam* : cumplir con lo prometido **11 to get/have the goods on** *fam* : obtener/tener pruebas contra

good–bye *or* **good–by** [gʊd'baɪ] *n* : adiós *m*

good–for–nothing [ˈgʊdfərˌnʌθɪŋ] *n*

: inútil *mf*; haragán *m*, -gana *f*; holgazán *m*, -zana *f*

Good Friday *n* : Viernes *m* Santo

good–hearted [ˈgʊdˈhɑrtəd] *adj* : bondadoso, benévolo, de buen corazón

good–looking [ˈgʊdˈlʊkɪŋ] *adj* : bello, bonito, guapo

goodly [ˈgʊdli] *adj* **goodlier; -est** : considerable, importante ⟨a goodly number : un número considerable⟩

good–natured [ˈgʊdˈneɪtʃərd] *adj* : amigable, amistoso, bonachón *fam*

goodness [ˈgʊdnəs] *n* **1** : bondad *f* **2 thank goodness!** : ¡gracias a Dios!, ¡menos mal!

good–tempered [ˈgʊdˈtɛmpərd] *adj* : de buen genio

goodwill [ˌgʊdˈwɪl] *n* **1** BENEVOLENCE : benevolencia *f*, buena voluntad *f* **2** : buen nombre *m* (de comercios), renombre *m* comercial

goody [ˈgʊdi] *n, pl* **goodies** : cosa *f* rica para comer, golosina *f*

gooey [ˈguːi] *adj* **gooier; gooiest** : pegajoso

goof¹ [ˈguːf] *vi fam* **1** *or* **to goof up** BLUNDER : cometer un error, equivocarse **2 to goof off** : holgazanear **3 to goof around** : hacer tonterías

goof² *n* **1** *fam* : bobo *m*, -ba *f*; tonto *m*, -ta *f* **2** BLUNDER : error *m*, planchazo *m fam*

goofy [ˈguːfi] *adj* **goofier; -est** SILLY : tonto, bobo

google *or* **Google** [ˈguːgəl] *vt* **-gled; -gling** (*Google*, trademark) : googlear

goose [ˈguːs] *n, pl* **geese** [ˈgiːs] : ganso *m*, -sa *f*; ánsar *m*; oca *f*

gooseberry [ˈguːsˌbɛriː; ˈguːzˌ-] *n, pl* **-ries** : grosella *f* espinosa

goose bumps *npl* : carne *f* de gallina

gooseflesh [ˈguːsˌflɛʃ] → **goose bumps**

goose pimples → **goose bumps**

gopher [ˈgoːfər] *n* : taltuza *f*

gore¹ [ˈgor] *vt* **gored; goring** : cornear

gore² *n* BLOOD : sangre *f*

gorge¹ [ˈgɔrdʒ] *vt* **gorged; gorging 1** SATIATE : saciar, hartar **2 to gorge oneself** : hartarse, atiborrarse, atracarse *fam*

gorge² *n* RAVINE : desfiladero *m*

gorgeous [ˈgɔrdʒəs] *adj* : hermoso, espléndido, magnífico

gorilla [gəˈrɪlə] *n* : gorila *m*

gory [ˈgori] *adj* **gorier; -est** BLOODY : sangriento

gosh [ˈgɑʃ, ˈgɔʃ] *interj* : ¡caramba!

gosling [ˈgɑzlɪŋ, ˈgɔz-] *n* : ansarino *m*

gospel [ˈgɑspəl] *n* **1** *or* **Gospel** : evangelio *m* ⟨the four Gospels : los cuatro evangelios⟩ **2 the gospel truth** : el evangelio, la pura verdad

gossamer [ˈgɑsəmər, ˈgɑzə-] *adj* : tenue, sutil ⟨gossamer wings : alas tenues⟩

gossip¹ [ˈgɑsɪp] *vi* : chismear, contar chismes

gossip² *n* **1** : chismoso *m*, -sa *f*; cotilla *mf Spain fam* (persona) **2** RUMOR : chisme *m*, rumor *m*

gossiper [ˈgɑsɪpər] *n* GOSSIP : chismoso *m*, -sa *f*; cotilla *mf Spain fam*

gossipy ['gɑsɪpi] *adj* : chismoso
got → **get**
Gothic ['gɑθɪk] *adj* : gótico
gotten → **get**
gouge¹ ['gaʊdʒ] *vt* **gouged; gouging 1**
: excavar **2** SWINDLE : estafar, extorsionar
gouge² *n* **1** CHISEL : formón *m* **2**
GROOVE : ranura *f*, hoyo *m* (hecho por
un formón)
goulash ['gu:,lɑʃ, -,læʃ] *n* : estofado *m*,
guiso *m* al estilo húngaro
gourd ['gord, 'gʊrd] *n* : calabaza *f*
gourmand ['gʊr,mɑnd] *n* **1** GLUTTON
: glotón *m*, -tona *f* **2** → **gourmet**
gourmet ['gʊr,meɪ, gʊr'meɪ] *n* : gourmet
mf; gastrónomo *m*, -ma *f*
gout ['gaʊt] *n* : gota *f*
govern ['gʌvərn] *vt* **1** RULE : gobernar **2** CONTROL, DETERMINE : determinar, controlar, guiar **3** RESTRAIN
: dominar (las emociones, etc.) — *vi*
: gobernar
governess ['gʌvərnəs] *n* : institutriz *f*
government ['gʌvərmənt] *n* : gobierno *m*
governmental [,gʌvər'mentəl] *adj* : gubernamental, gubernativo
governor ['gʌvənər, 'gʌvərnər] *n* **1**
: gobernador *m*, -dora *f* (de un estado,
etc.) **2** : regulador *m* (de una máquina)
governorship ['gʌvənər,ʃɪp, 'gʌvərnər-] *n*
: cargo *m* de gobernador
gown ['gaʊn] *n* **1** : vestido *m* ⟨evening
gown : traje de fiesta⟩ **2** : toga *f* (de
magistrados, clérigos, etc.)
GPS [,dʒi:'pi:'ɛs] *n* (*Global Positioning
System*) : GPS *m*
grab¹ ['græb] *v* **grabbed; grabbing** *vt*
SNATCH : agarrar, arrebatar — *vi* : agarrarse
grab² *n* **1 to make a grab for** : tratar de
agarrar **2 up for grabs** : disponible, libre
grace¹ ['greɪs] *vt* **graced; gracing 1** HONOR : honrar **2** ADORN : adornar, embellecer
grace² *n* **1** : gracia *f* ⟨by the grace of
God : por la gracia de Dios⟩ **2** BLESSING : bendición *f* (de la mesa) **3** RESPITE : plazo *m*, gracia *f* ⟨a five days'
grace (period) : un plazo de cinco días,
un período de gracia de cinco días⟩ **4**
GRACIOUSNESS : gentileza *f*, cortesía *f* **5**
ELEGANCE : elegancia *f*, gracia *f* **6 to be
in the good graces of** : estar en buenas
relaciones con **7 with good grace** : de
buena gana
graceful ['greɪsfəl] *adj* : lleno de gracia,
garboso, grácil
gracefully ['greɪsfəli] *adv* : con gracia, con
garbo
gracefulness ['greɪsfəlnəs] *n* : gracilidad
f, apostura *f*, gallardía *f*
graceless ['greɪsləs] *adj* **1** DISCOURTEOUS : descortés **2** CLUMSY, INELEGANT : torpe, desgarbado, poco elegante
gracious ['greɪʃəs] *adj* : cortés, gentil,
cordial
graciously ['greɪʃəsli] *adv* : gentilmente
graciousness ['greɪʃəsnəs] *n* : gentileza *f*

gradation [greɪ'deɪʃən, grə-] *n* : gradación
f
grade¹ ['greɪd] *vt* **graded; grading 1**
SORT : clasificar **2** LEVEL : nivelar **3**
: calificar (exámenes, alumnos)
grade² *n* **1** QUALITY : categoría *f*, calidad
f **2** RANK : grado *m*, rango *m* (militar) **3** YEAR : grado *m*, curso *m*, año *m*
⟨sixth grade : el sexto grado⟩ **4** MARK
: nota *f*, calificación *f* (en educación) **5**
SLOPE : cuesta *f*, pendiente *f*, gradiente *f*
grade school → **elementary school**
gradient ['greɪdiənt] *n* : gradiente *f*
gradual ['grædʒuəl] *adj* : gradual, paulatino
gradually ['grædʒuəli, 'grædʒəli] *adv*
: gradualmente, poco a poco
graduate¹ ['grædʒu,eɪt] *v* **-ated; -ating** *vi*
: graduarse, licenciarse — *vt* : graduar ⟨a
graduated thermometer : un termómetro graduado⟩
graduate² ['grædʒuət] *adj* : de postgrado
⟨graduate course : curso de postgrado⟩
graduate³ *n* **1** : licenciado *m*, -da *f*; graduado *m*, -da *f* (de la universidad) **2**
: bachiller *mf* (de la escuela secundaria)
graduate student *n* : postgraduado *m*,
-da *f*
graduation [,grædʒu'eɪʃən] *n* : graduación
f
graffiti [grə'fi:ti, græ-] *npl* : pintadas *fpl*,
graffiti *mpl*
graft¹ ['græft] *vt* : injertar
graft² *n* **1** : injerto *m* ⟨skin graft : injerto
cutáneo⟩ **2** CORRUPTION : soborno *m*
(político), ganancia *f* ilegal
grain ['greɪn] *n* **1** : grano *m* ⟨a grain of
corn : un grano de maíz⟩ ⟨like a grain of
sand : como grano de arena⟩ **2** CEREALS
: cereales *mpl* **3** : veta *f*, vena *f*, grano *m*
(de madera) **4** SPECK, TRACE : pizca *f*,
ápice *m* ⟨a grain of truth : una pizca de
verdad⟩ **5** : grano *m* (unidad de peso) **6**
to go against the grain ir a contrapelo
grainy ['greɪni] *adj* **grainier; -est** : granuloso, granulado, granular
gram ['græm] *n* : gramo *m*
grammar ['græmər] *n* : gramática *f*
grammar school → **elementary school**
grammatical [grə'mætɪkəl] *adj* : gramatical — **grammatically** [-kli] *adv*
gran ['græn] → **grandma**
granary ['greɪnəri, 'græ-] *n*, *pl* **-ries** : granero *m*
grand ['grænd] *adj* **1** FOREMOST
: grande **2** IMPRESSIVE : impresionante,
magnífico ⟨a grand view : una vista magnífica⟩ **3** LAVISH : grandioso, suntuoso,
lujoso ⟨to live in a grand manner : vivir
a lo grande⟩ **4** FABULOUS : fabuloso,
magnífico ⟨to have a grand time : pasarlo estupendamente, pasarlo en
grande⟩ **5 grand total** : total *m*, suma *f*
total
grandchild ['grænd,tʃaɪld] *n*, *pl* **-children**
: nieto *m*, -ta *f*
granddad ['grænd,dæd] → **grandpa**
granddaughter ['grænd,dɔtər] *n* : nieta *f*
grandeur ['grændʒər] *n* : grandiosidad *f*,
esplendor *m*

grandfather ['grænd,faðər] n : abuelo m
grandiose ['grændi,o:s, ,grændi'-] adj 1 IMPOSING : imponente, grandioso 2 POMPOUS : pomposo, presuntuoso
grandma ['græn,ma, -,mɔ] n fam : abuelita f fam, nana f fam, yaya f fam
grandmother ['græn,maðər] n : abuela f
grandpa ['græm,pa, -,pɔ] n fam : abuelito m fam, yayo m fam
grandparents ['grænd,pærənts] npl : abuelos mpl
grand piano n : piano m de cola
grandson ['grænd,sʌn] n : nieto m
grandstand ['grænd,stænd] n : tribuna f
granite ['grænit] n : granito m
granny ['græni] n, pl -nies → grandma
grant¹ ['grænt] vt 1 ALLOW : conceder ⟨to grant a request : conceder una petición⟩ 2 BESTOW : conceder, dar, otorgar ⟨to grant a favor : otorgar un favor⟩ 3 ADMIT : reconocer, admitir ⟨I'll grant that he's clever : reconozco que es listo⟩ 4 to take for granted : dar (algo) por sentado
grant² n 1 GRANTING : concesión f, otorgamiento m 2 SCHOLARSHIP : beca f 3 SUBSIDY : subvención f
granular ['grænjulər] adj : granular
granulated ['grænju,leɪtəd] adj : granulado
grape ['greɪp] n : uva f
grapefruit ['greɪp,fru:t] n : toronja f, pomelo m
grapevine ['greɪp,vaɪn] n 1 : vid f, parra f 2 through the grapevine : por vías secretas ⟨I heard it through the grapevine : me lo contaron⟩
graph ['græf] n : gráfica f, gráfico m
graphic¹ ['græfɪk] adj : VIVID : vívido, gráfico
graphic² n 1 GRAPH, CHART : gráfica f, gráfico m 2 graphics npl : gráficos mpl, infografía f
graphically ['græfɪkli] adv : gráficamente
graphic arts npl : artes fpl gráficas
graphite ['græ,faɪt] n : grafito m
grapple ['græpəl] v -pled; -pling vt GRIP : agarrar (con un garfio) — vi 1 STRUGGLE : forcejear, luchar (con un problema, etc.)
grasp¹ ['græsp] vt 1 GRIP, SEIZE : agarrar, asir 2 COMPREHEND : entender, comprender — vi to grasp at : aprovechar
grasp² n 1 GRIP : agarre m 2 CONTROL : control m, garras fpl 3 REACH : alcance m ⟨within your grasp : a su alcance⟩ 4 UNDERSTANDING : comprensión f, entendimiento m
grasping ['græspɪŋ] adj : avaricioso
grass ['græs] n 1 : hierba f (planta) 2 PASTURE : pasto m, zacate m CA, Mex 3 LAWN : césped m, pasto m
grasshopper ['græs,hapər] n : saltamontes m
grassland ['græs,lænd] n : pradera f
grassroots ['græs,ru:ts, -,ruts] adj : de base ⟨at the grassroots level : a nivel de base⟩ ⟨a grassroots movement : un movimiento de base⟩

grass roots npl : las bases ⟨the party's grass roots : las bases del partido⟩
grassy ['græsi] adj grassier; -est : cubierto de hierba
grate¹ ['greɪt] v grated; -ing vt 1 : rallar (en cocina) 2 SCRAPE : rascar 3 to grate one's teeth : hacer rechinar los dientes — vi 1 RASP, SQUEAK : chirriar 2 IRRITATE : irritar ⟨it grates on me : me crispa⟩ ⟨to grate on one's nerves : crisparle los nervios a uno⟩
grate² n 1 : parrilla f (para cocinar) 2 GRATING : reja f, rejilla f, verja f (en una ventana)
grateful ['greɪtfəl] adj : agradecido
gratefully ['greɪtfəli] adv : con agradecimiento
gratefulness ['greɪtfəlnəs] n : gratitud f, agradecimiento m
grater ['greɪtər] n : rallador m
gratification [,grætəfə'keɪʃən] n : gratificación f
gratify ['grætə,faɪ] vt -fied; -fying 1 PLEASE : complacer 2 SATISFY : satisfacer, gratificar
grating ['greɪtɪŋ] n : reja f, rejilla f
gratis ['grætəs, 'greɪ-] adv : gratis, gratuitamente
gratis² adj : gratis, gratuito
gratitude ['grætə,tu:d, -,tju:d] n : gratitud f, agradecimiento m
gratuitous [grə'tu:ətəs] adj UNWARRANTED : gratuito, injustificado — gratuitously [grə'tu:ətəsli] adv
gratuity [grə'tu:əti] n, pl -ities TIP : propina f
grave¹ ['greɪv] adj graver; gravest 1 IMPORTANT : grave, de mucha gravedad 2 SERIOUS, SOLEMN : grave, serio
grave² n : tumba f, sepultura f
gravel ['grævəl] n : grava f, gravilla f
gravelly ['grævəli] adj 1 : de grava 2 HARSH : áspero (dícese de la voz)
gravely ['greɪvli] adv : gravemente
gravestone ['greɪv,sto:n] n : lápida f
graveyard ['greɪv,jɑrd] n CEMETERY : cementerio m, panteón m, camposanto m
gravitate ['grævə,teɪt] vi -tated; -tating : gravitar
gravitation [,grævə'teɪʃən] n : gravitación f
gravitational [,grævə'teɪʃənəl] adj : gravitacional
gravity ['grævəti] n, pl -ties 1 SERIOUSNESS : gravedad f, seriedad f 2 : gravedad f ⟨the law of gravity : la ley de la gravedad⟩
gravy ['greɪvi] n, pl -vies : salsa f (preparada con el jugo de la carne asada)
gray¹ ['greɪ] vt : hacer gris — vi : encanecer, ponerse gris
gray² adj : gris (dícese del color) 2 : cano, canoso ⟨gray hair : pelo canoso⟩ ⟨to go gray : volverse cano⟩ 3 DISMAL, GLOOMY : gris, triste
gray³ n : gris m
grayish ['greɪɪʃ] adj : grisáceo
graze ['greɪz] v grazed; grazing vi : pastar, pacer — vt 1 : pastorear (ganado) 2 BRUSH : rozar 3 SCRATCH : raspar

grease[1] ['griːs, 'griːz] *vt* **greased; greasing** : engrasar, lubricar

grease[2] ['griːs] *n* : grasa *f*

greasy ['griːsi, -zi] *adj* **greasier; -est** 1 : grasiento 2 OILY : graso, grasoso

great ['greɪt] *adj* 1 LARGE : grande ⟨a great mountain : una montaña grande⟩ ⟨a great crowd : una gran muchedumbre⟩ ⟨a great big house : una casa grandísima⟩ ⟨a great success : un gran éxito⟩ 2 EXTREME, INTENSE : grande, intenso, fuerte ⟨with great care/difficulty : con gran cuidado/dificultad⟩ ⟨in great pain : muy dolorido⟩ ⟨there's no great hurry : no hay prisa⟩ ⟨a great admirer of : un gran admirador de⟩ 3 IMPORTANT : grande ⟨a great poet : un gran poeta⟩ ⟨great works of art : grandes obras de arte⟩ 4 EXCELLENT, TERRIFIC : excelente, estupendo, fabuloso ⟨to have a great time : pasarlo en grande⟩ ⟨a great movie : una película estupenda⟩ ⟨he's great at soccer : juega muy bien al fútbol⟩ ⟨you look great! : ¡te ves muy bien!⟩ 5 : bis- ⟨great-grandson : bisabuelo/bisnieto⟩ ⟨great niece : sobrina nieta⟩ ⟨great-great-grandmother : tatarabuela⟩ 6 a great deal (of) : mucho, un montón (de) 7 a great while : mucho tiempo 8 great! : ¡qué bien!

great-aunt [ˌgreɪt'ænt, -'ɑnt] *n* : tía *f* abuela

greater ['greɪtər] (*comparative of* GREAT) : mayor

greatest ['greɪtəst] (*superlative of* GREAT) : el mayor, la mayor

great-grandchild [ˌgreɪt'grænd-ˌtʃaɪld] *n*, *pl* **-children** [-ˌtʃɪldrən] : bisnieto *m*, -ta *f*

great-grandfather [ˌgreɪt'grænd-ˌfɑðər] *n* : bisabuelo *m*

great-grandmother [ˌgreɪt'grænd-ˌmʌðər] *n* : bisabuela *f*

greatly ['greɪtli] *adv* 1 MUCH : mucho, sumamente ⟨to be greatly improved : haber mejorado mucho⟩ 2 VERY : muy ⟨greatly superior : muy superior⟩

greatness ['greɪtnəs] *n* : grandeza *f*

great-uncle [ˌgreɪt'ʌŋkəl] *n* : tío *m* abuelo

grebe ['griːb] *n* : somorgujo *m*

greed ['griːd] *n* 1 AVARICE : avaricia *f*, codicia *f* 2 GLUTTONY : glotonería *f*, gula *f*

greedily ['griːdəli] *adv* : con avaricia, con gula

greediness ['griːdinəs] → **greed**

greedy ['griːdi] *adj* **greedier; -est** 1 AVARICIOUS : codicioso, avaricioso 2 GLUTTONOUS : glotón

Greek ['griːk] *n* 1 : griego *m*, -ga *f* 2 : griego *m* (idioma) — **Greek** *adj*

green[1] ['griːn] *adj* 1 : verde (dícese del color) 2 UNRIPE : verde, inmaduro 3 INEXPERIENCED : verde, novato

green[2] *n* 1 : verde *m* 2 **greens** *npl* VEGETABLES : verduras *fpl*

greenback ['griːnˌbæk] *n fam* : billete *m* (dinero)

green card *n* : permiso *m* de residencia y trabajo

greenery ['griːnəri] *n*, *pl* **-eries** : plantas *fpl* verdes, vegetación *f*

greengrocer ['griːnˌgroʊsər] *n* : verdulero *m*, -ra *f*

greenhorn ['griːnˌhorn] *n* : novato *m*, -ta *f*

greenhouse ['griːnˌhaʊs] *n* : invernadero *m*

greenhouse effect : efecto *m* invernadero

greenish ['griːnɪʃ] *adj* : verdoso

Greenlander ['griːnləndər, -ˌlæn-] *n* : groenlandés *m*, -desa *f*

greenness ['griːnnəs] *n* 1 : verdor *m* 2 INEXPERIENCE : inexperiencia *f*

green thumb *n* **to have a green thumb** : tener buena mano para las plantas

greet ['griːt] *vt* 1 : saludar ⟨to greet a friend : saludar a un amigo⟩ 2 : acoger, recibir ⟨they greeted him with boos : lo recibieron con abucheos⟩

greeting ['griːtɪŋ] *n* 1 : saludo *m* 2 **greetings** *npl* REGARDS : saludos *mpl*, recuerdos *mpl*

greeting card *n* : tarjeta *f* de felicitación

gregarious [grɪ'gæriəs] *adj* : gregario (dícese de los animales), sociable (dícese de las personas) — **gregariously** *adv*

gregariousness [grɪ'gæriəsnəs] *n* : sociabilidad *f*

gremlin ['gremlən] *n* : duende *m*

grenade [grə'neɪd] *n* : granada *f*

Grenadian [grə'neɪdiən] *n* : granadino *m*, -na *f* — **Grenadian** *adj*

grew → **grow**

grey → **gray**

greyhound ['greɪˌhaʊnd] *n* : galgo *m*

grid ['grɪd] *n* 1 GRATING : rejilla *f* 2 NETWORK : red *f* (de electricidad, etc.) 3 : cuadriculado *m* (de un mapa)

griddle ['grɪdəl] *n* : plancha *f*

griddle cake → **pancake**

gridiron ['grɪdˌaɪərn] *n* 1 GRILL : parrilla *f* 2 : campo *m* de fútbol americano

gridlock ['grɪdˌlɑk] *n* : atasco *m* completo (de una red de calles)

grief ['griːf] *n* 1 SORROW : dolor *m*, pena *f* 2 ANNOYANCE, TROUBLE : problemas *mpl*, molestia *f*

grief-stricken *adj* : afligido, desconsolado

grievance ['griːvəns] *n* COMPLAINT : queja *f*

grieve ['griːv] *v* **grieved; grieving** *vt* DISTRESS : afligir, entristecer, apenar — *vi* 1 : sufrir, afligirse 2 **to grieve for** *or* **to grieve over** : llorar, lamentar

grievous ['griːvəs] *adj* 1 OPPRESSIVE : gravoso, opresivo, severo 2 GRAVE, SERIOUS : grave, severo, doloroso

grievously ['griːvəsli] *adv* : gravemente, de gravedad

grill[1] ['grɪl] *vt* 1 : asar (a la parrilla) 2 INTERROGATE : interrogar

grill[2] *n* 1 : parrilla *f* (para cocinar) 2 : parrillada *f* (comida) 3 : parrilla *f* (restaurante)

grille *or* **grill** ['grɪl] *n* : reja *f*, enrejado *m*

grim ['grɪm] *adj* **grimmer; grimmest** 1 CRUEL : cruel, feroz 2 STERN : adusto, severo ⟨a grim expression : un gesto severo⟩ 3 GLOOMY : sombrío, deprimente 4 SINISTER : macabro, siniestro 5 UNYIELDING : inflexible, persistente ⟨with grim determination : con una voluntad de hierro⟩

grimace¹ [ˈɡrɪməs, ɡrɪˈmeɪs] vi -maced; -macing : hacer muecas

grimace² n : mueca f

grime [ˈɡraɪm] n : mugre f, suciedad f

grimly [ˈɡrɪmli] adv 1 STERNLY : severamente 2 RESOLUTELY : inexorablemente

grimy [ˈɡraɪmi] adj grimier; -est : mugriento, sucio

grin¹ [ˈɡrɪn] vi grinned; grinning : sonreír abiertamente

grin² n : sonrisa f abierta

grind¹ [ˈɡraɪnd] v ground [ˈɡraʊnd]; grinding vt 1 CRUSH : moler, machacar, triturar 2 SHARPEN : afilar 3 POLISH : pulir 4 to grind one's teeth : rechinar los dientes a uno 5 to grind down OPPRESS : oprimir, agobiar — vi 1 : funcionar con dificultad, rechinar ⟨to grind to a halt : pararse poco a poco, llegar a un punto muerto⟩ 2 STUDY : estudiar mucho

grind² n : trabajo m pesado ⟨the daily grind : la rutina diaria⟩

grinder [ˈɡraɪndər] n : molinillo m ⟨coffee grinder : molinillo de café⟩

grindstone [ˈɡraɪndˌstoːn] n : piedra f de afilar

gringo [ˈɡrɪŋɡo] n often disparaging : gringo m, -ga feminine often disparaging

grip¹ [ˈɡrɪp] vt gripped; gripping 1 GRASP : agarrar, asir 2 HOLD, INTEREST : captar el interés de

grip² n 1 GRASP : agarre m, asidero m ⟨to have a firm grip on something : agarrarse bien de algo⟩ 2 CONTROL, HOLD : control m, dominio m ⟨to lose one's grip on : perder el control de⟩ ⟨inflation tightened its grip on the economy : la inflación se afianzó en su dominio de la economía⟩ ⟨to get a grip on oneself : controlarse, calmarse⟩ 3 UNDERSTANDING : comprensión f, entendimiento m ⟨to come to grips with : llegar a entender⟩ 4 HANDLE : asidero m, empuñadura f (de un arma)

gripe¹ [ˈɡraɪp] vt griped; griping vt IRRITATE, VEX : irritar, fastidiar, molestar — vi COMPLAIN : quejarse, rezongar

gripe² n : queja f

grippe [ˈɡrɪp] n : influenza f, gripe f, gripa f Col, Mex

gripping [ˈɡrɪpɪŋ] adj : apasionante

grisly [ˈɡrɪzli] adj grislier; -est : horripilante, horroroso, truculento

grist [ˈɡrɪst] n : molienda f ⟨it's all grist for the mill : todo ayuda, todo es provechoso⟩

gristle [ˈɡrɪsəl] n : cartílago m

gristly [ˈɡrɪsli] adj gristlier; -est : duro, con mucho cartílago

grit¹ [ˈɡrɪt] vt gritted; gritting : hacer rechinar (los dientes, etc.)

grit² n 1 SAND : arena f 2 GRAVEL : grava f 3 COURAGE : valor m, coraje m 4 grits npl : sémola f de maíz

gritty [ˈɡrɪti] adj grittier; -est 1 : arenoso ⟨a gritty surface : una superficie arenosa⟩ 2 PLUCKY : valiente

grizzled [ˈɡrɪzəld] adj : entrecano

grizzly bear [ˈɡrɪzli] n : oso m pardo

groan¹ [ˈɡroːn] vi 1 MOAN : gemir, quejarse 2 CREAK : crujir

groan² n 1 MOAN : gemido m, quejido m 2 CREAK : crujido m

grocer [ˈɡroːsər] n : tendero m, -ra f

grocery [ˈɡroːsəri, -ʃəri] n, pl -ceries 1 or grocery store : tienda f de comestibles, tienda f de abarrotes 2 groceries npl : comestibles mpl, abarrotes mpl

groggy [ˈɡrɑɡi] adj groggier; -est : atontado, grogui, tambaleante

groin [ˈɡrɔɪn] n : ingle f

grommet [ˈɡrɑmət, ˈɡrʌ-] n : arandela f

groom¹ [ˈɡruːm, ˈɡrʊm] vt 1 : cepillar, almohazar (un animal) 2 : arreglar, cuidar ⟨well-groomed : bien arreglado⟩ 3 PREPARE : preparar

groom² n 1 : mozo m, -za f de cuadra 2 BRIDEGROOM : novio m

groove¹ [ˈɡruːv] vt grooved; grooving : acanalar, hacer ranuras en, surcar

groove² n 1 FURROW, SLOT : ranura f, surco m 2 RUT : rutina f

grope [ˈɡroːp] v groped; groping vi : andar a tientas, tantear ⟨he groped for the switch : buscó el interruptor a tientas⟩ — vt to grope one's way : avanzar a tientas

gross¹ [ˈɡroːs] vt : tener entrada bruta de, recaudar en bruto

gross² adj 1 FLAGRANT : flagrante, grave ⟨a gross error : un error flagrante⟩ ⟨a gross injustice : una injusticia grave⟩ 2 FAT : muy gordo, obeso 3 : bruto ⟨gross national product : producto nacional bruto⟩ 4 COARSE, VULGAR : grosero, basto 5 fam DISGUSTING : asqueroso

gross³ n 1 pl gross : gruesa f (12 docenas) 2 or gross income : ingresos mpl brutos

grossly [ˈɡroːsli] adv 1 EXTREMELY : extremadamente ⟨grossly unfair : totalmente injusto⟩ 2 CRUDELY : groseramente

grotesque [ɡroːˈtɛsk] adj : grotesco

grotesquely [ɡroːˈtɛskli] adv : de forma grotesca

grotto [ˈɡrɑtoː] n, pl -toes : gruta f

grouch¹ [ˈɡraʊtʃ] vi : refunfuñar, rezongar

grouch² n 1 COMPLAINT : queja f 2 GRUMBLER : gruñón m, -ñona f; cascarrabias mf fam

grouchy [ˈɡraʊtʃi] adj grouchier; -est : malhumorado, gruñón

ground¹ [ˈɡraʊnd] vt 1 BASE : fundar, basar 2 INSTRUCT : enseñar los conocimientos básicos a ⟨to be well grounded in : ser muy entendido en⟩ 3 : conectar a tierra (un aparato eléctrico) 4 : varar, hacer encallar (un barco) 5 : restringir (un avión o un piloto) a la tierra 6 fam : no dejar salir (como castigo)

ground² n 1 EARTH, SOIL : suelo m, tierra f ⟨to dig (in) the ground : cavar la tierra⟩ ⟨to fall to the ground : caerse al suelo⟩ 2 LAND, TERRAIN : terreno m ⟨high ground : terreno alto⟩ ⟨to be on solid/firm ground : pisar terreno firme⟩ **3** BASIS, REASON : razón *f*, motivo *m* ⟨grounds for complaint : motivos de queja⟩ **4** INFORMATION : información *f* ⟨we've covered a lot of ground : hemos abarcado muchos temas/puntos⟩ ⟨familiar ground : terreno conocido⟩ **5** VIEWS : terreno *m* ⟨to find a common/middle ground : encontrar un terreno común⟩ **6** BACKGROUND : fondo *m* **7** FIELD : campo *m*, plaza *f* ⟨parade ground : plaza de armas⟩ **8** : tierra *f* (para electricidad) **9 grounds** *npl* PREMISES : recinto *m*, terreno *m* **10 grounds** *npl* DREGS : posos *mpl* (de café) **11 from the ground up** COMPLETELY : completamente, radicalmente **12 from the ground up** FRESH : de cero ⟨to build/start from the ground up : construir/empezar de cero⟩ **13 into the ground** ⟨he ran the business into the ground : llevó la empresa a la ruina⟩ ⟨she's working herself into the ground : se mata trabajando⟩ **14 to break new ground** : abrir nuevos caminos **15 to gain/lose ground** : ganar/perder terreno **16 to get off the ground** : llegar a concretarse **17 to hold/stand one's ground** : no ceder terreno

ground³ → grind

groundhog ['graʊnd,hɔg] *n* : marmota *f* (de América)

grounding ['graʊndɪŋ] *n* : conocimientos *mpl* básicos

groundless ['graʊndləs] *adj* : infundado

groundwork ['graʊnd,wərk] *n* **1** FOUNDATION : fundamento *m*, base *f* **2** PREPARATION : trabajo *m* preparatorio

group¹ ['gru:p] *vt* : agrupar

group² *n* : grupo *m*, agrupación *f*, conjunto *m*, compañía *f*

grouper ['gru:pər] *n* : mero *m*

grouse¹ ['graʊs] *vi* **groused; grousing** : quejarse, rezongar, refunfuñar

grouse² *n, pl* **grouse** *or* **grouses** : urogallo *m* (ave)

grout ['graʊt] *n* : lechada *f*

grove ['gro:v] *n* : bosquecillo *m*, arboleda *f*, soto *m*

grovel ['grʌvəl, 'grɑ-] *vi* **-eled** *or* **-elled; -eling** *or* **-elling** **1** CRAWL : arrastrarse **2** : humillarse, postrarse ⟨to grovel before someone : postrarse ante alguien⟩

grow ['gro:] *v* **grew** ['gru:]; **grown** ['gro:n]; **growing** *vi* **1** : crecer ⟨palm trees grow on the islands : en las islas crecen palmas⟩ ⟨my hair grows very fast : mi pelo crece muy rápido⟩ **2** DEVELOP, MATURE : desarrollarse, madurar **3** INCREASE : crecer, aumentar **4** BECOME : hacerse, volverse, ponerse ⟨she was growing angry : se estaba poniendo furiosa⟩ ⟨to grow dark : oscurecerse⟩ **5 to grow apart** : distanciarse **6 to grow from** : nacer de **7 to grow into** BECOME : convertirse en **8 to grow on someone** : empezar a gustarle a alguien **9 to grow out of** : dejar atrás (las cosas de la niñez) **10 to grow to** : llegar a ⟨I grew

to love the city : aprendí a amar la ciudad⟩ **11 to grow up** : hacerse mayor ⟨grow up! : ¡no seas niño!⟩ — *vt* **1** CULTIVATE, RAISE : cultivar **2** : dejar crecer ⟨to grow one's hair : dejarse crecer el pelo⟩ **3** EXPAND, DEVELOP : expansionar, desarrollar (una empresa, etc.)

grower ['gro:ər] *n* : cultivador *m*, -dora *f*

growl¹ ['graʊl] *vi* : gruñir (dícese de un animal), refunfuñar (dícese de una persona)

growl² *n* : gruñido *m*

grown ['gro:n] → **grown-up¹**

grown–up¹ ['gro:n,əp] *adj* : adulto, mayor

grown–up² *n* : adulto *m*, -ta *f*; persona *f* mayor

growth ['gro:θ] *n* **1** : crecimiento *m* ⟨to stunt one's growth : detener el crecimiento⟩ **2** INCREASE : aumento *m*, crecimiento *m*, expansión *f* **3** DEVELOPMENT : desarrollo *m* ⟨economic growth : desarrollo económico⟩ ⟨a five days' growth of beard : una barba de cinco días⟩ **4** LUMP, TUMOR : bulto *m*, tumor *m*

grub¹ ['grʌb] *vi* **grubbed; grubbing 1** DIG : escarbar **2** RUMMAGE : hurgar, buscar **3** DRUDGE : trabajar duro

grub² *n* **1** : larva *f* ⟨beetle grub : larva del escarabajo⟩ **2** DRUDGE : esclavo *m*, -va *f* del trabajo **3** FOOD : comida *f*

grubby ['grʌbi] *adj* **grubbier; -est** : mugriento, sucio

grudge¹ ['grʌdʒ] *vt* **grudged; grudging** : dar/hacer (etc.) de mala gana ⟨I don't grudge the money I spent : no me molesta el dinero que gasté⟩

grudge² *n* : rencor *m*, resentimiento *m* ⟨to hold a grudge : guardar rencor⟩ ⟨to hold a grudge against someone for something : guardarle rencor a alguien por algo⟩

grueling *or* **gruelling** ['gru:lɪŋ, 'gru:ə-] *adj* : extenuante, agotador, duro

gruesome ['gru:səm] *adj* : horripilante, truculento, horroroso

gruff ['grʌf] *adj* **1** BRUSQUE : brusco ⟨a gruff reply : una respuesta brusca⟩ **2** HOARSE : ronco — **gruffly** *adv*

grumble¹ ['grʌmbəl] *vi* **-bled; -bling 1** COMPLAIN : refunfuñar, rezongar, quejarse **2** RUMBLE : hacer un ruido sordo, retumbar (dícese del trueno)

grumble² *n* **1** COMPLAINT : queja *f* **2** RUMBLE : ruido *m* sordo, estruendo *m*

grumbler ['grʌmbələr] *n* : gruñón *m*, -ñona *f*

grumpy ['grʌmpi] *adj* **grumpier; -est** : malhumorado, gruñón

grungy ['grʌndʒi] *adj* : sucio

grunt¹ ['grʌnt] *vi* : gruñir

grunt² *n* : gruñido *m*

guacamole [ˌgwɑkə'mo:li] *n* : guacamole *m*, guacamol *m*

guanaco [gwə'nɑko] *n* : guanaco *m*

guano ['gwɑno] *n* : guano *m*

guarani [ˌgwɑrɑ'ni:] *n, pl* **-nies** *or* **-nis** : guaraní *m* (unidad monetaria)

Guarani [ˌgwɑrɑ'ni:] *n* **1** : guaraní *m* (idioma) **2** *pl* **-ni** *or* **-nis** : guaraní *mf* (persona)

guarantee¹ [ˌgærən'tiː] vt **-teed; -teeing 1** PROMISE : asegurar, prometer **2** : poner bajo garantía, garantizar (un producto o servicio)

guarantee² n **1** PROMISE : garantía f, promesa f ⟨lifetime guarantee : garantía de por vida⟩ **2** → **guarantor**

guarantor [ˌgærən'tɔr] n : garante mf; fiador m, -dora f

guaranty [ˌgærən'tiː] → **guarantee**

guard¹ ['gɑrd] vt **1** DEFEND, PROTECT : defender, proteger **2** : guardar, vigilar, custodiar ⟨to guard the frontier : vigilar la frontera⟩ ⟨she guarded my secret well : guardó bien mi secreto⟩ — vi **to guard against** : protegerse contra, evitar

guard² n **1** WATCHMAN : guarda mf ⟨security guard : guarda de seguridad⟩ **2** SOLDIERS : guardia f **3** VIGILANCE : guardia f, vigilancia f ⟨to be on guard : estar en guardia⟩ ⟨to let one's guard down : bajar la guardia⟩ ⟨to catch someone off guard : agarrar a alguien desprevenido⟩ ⟨to keep under guard : vigilar⟩ **4** SAFEGUARD : salvaguardia f, dispositivo m de seguridad (en una máquina) **5** PRECAUTION : precaución f, protección f **6** : guardia mf (en deportes)

guard dog n : perro m guardián

guarded ['gɑrdəd] adj : cauteloso

guardhouse ['gɑrd,haus] n : cuartel m de la guardia

guardian ['gɑrdiən] n **1** PROTECTOR : guardián m, -diana f; custodio m, -dia f ⟨guardian angel : ángel de la guarda⟩ **2** : tutor m, -tora f (de un niño)

guardianship ['gɑrdiən,ʃip] n : custodia f, tutela f

guardrail ['gɑrd,reil] n **1** : antepecho m (de un puente, etc.) **2** : barrera f de contención (de una carretera)

Guatemalan [ˌgwɑtə'mɑlən] n : guatemalteco m, -ca f — **Guatemalan** adj

guava ['gwɑvə] n : guayaba f

gubernatorial [ˌguːbənə'tɔriːəl, ˌgjuː-] adj : del gobernador

guerrilla or **guerilla** [gə'rilə] n : guerrillero m, -ra f

guess¹ ['gɛs] vt **1** CONJECTURE : adivinar, conjeturar ⟨guess what happened! : ¡adivina lo que pasó!⟩ **2** SUPPOSE : pensar, creer, suponer ⟨I guess so : supongo que sí⟩ **3** : adivinar correctamente, acertar ⟨to guess the answer : acertar la respuesta⟩ — vi : adivinar

guess² n : conjetura f, suposición f

guesswork ['gɛs,wərk] n : suposiciones fpl, conjeturas fpl

guest ['gɛst] n : huésped mf; invitado m, -da f

guffaw¹ [gə'fɔ] vi : reírse a carcajadas, carcajearse fam

guffaw² [gə'fɔ, 'gʌ,fɔ] n : carcajada f, risotada f

guidance ['gaidənts] n : orientación f, consejos mpl

guide¹ ['gaid] vt **guided; guiding 1** DIRECT, LEAD : guiar, dirigir, conducir **2** ADVISE, COUNSEL : aconsejar, orientar

guide² n : guía f

guidebook ['gaid,buk] n : guía f (para viajeros)

guide dog n : perro m guía, perro m lazarillo

guideline ['gaid,lain] n : pauta f, directriz f

guild ['gild] n : gremio m, sindicato m, asociación f

guile ['gail] n : astucia f, engaño m

guileless ['gailləs] adj : inocente, cándido, sin malicia

guillotine¹ ['gilə,tiːn, 'giːjə,-] vt **-tined; -tining** : guillotinar

guillotine² n : guillotina f

guilt ['gilt] n : culpa f, culpabilidad f

guilty ['gilti] adj **guiltier; -est** : culpable

guinea fowl ['gini] n : gallina f de Guinea

guinea pig n : conejillo m de Indias, cobaya f

guise ['gaiz] n : apariencia f, aspecto m, forma f

guitar [gə'tɑr, gi-] n : guitarra f

guitarist [gə'tɑrist, gi-] n : guitarrista mf

gulch ['gʌltʃ] n : barranco m, quebrada f

gulf ['gʌlf] n **1** : golfo m ⟨the Gulf of Mexico : el Golfo de México⟩ **2** GAP : brecha f ⟨the gulf between generations : la brecha entre las generaciones⟩ **3** CHASM : abismo m

gull ['gʌl] n : gaviota f

gullet ['gʌlət] n : garganta f

gullible ['gʌlibəl] adj : crédulo

gully ['gʌli] n, pl **-lies** : barranco m, hondonada f

gulp¹ ['gʌlp] vt **1** : engullir, tragar ⟨he gulped down the whiskey : engulló el whisky⟩ **2** SUPPRESS : suprimir, reprimir, tragar ⟨to gulp down a sob : reprimir un sollozo⟩ — vi : tragar saliva, tener un nudo en la garganta

gulp² n : trago m

gum ['gʌm] n **1** CHEWING GUM : goma f de mascar, chicle m **2 gums** npl : encías fpl

gumbo ['gʌm,boː] n : sopa f de quingombó

gumdrop ['gʌm,drɑp] n : pastilla f de goma

gummy ['gʌmi] adj **gummier; -est** : gomoso

gumption ['gʌmpʃən] n : iniciativa f, agallas fpl fam

gun¹ ['gʌn] vt **gunned; gunning 1** or **to gun down** : matar a tiros, asesinar **2** : acelerar (rápidamente) ⟨to gun the engine : acelerar el motor⟩

gun² n **1** CANNON : cañón m **2** FIREARM : arma f de fuego **3** SPRAY GUN : pistola f **4 to jump the gun** : adelantarse, salir antes de tiempo

gunboat ['gʌn,boːt] n : cañonero m

gunfight ['gʌn,fait] n : tiroteo m, balacera f

gunfire ['gʌn,fair] n : disparos mpl

gunman ['gʌnmən] n, pl **-men** [-mən, -ˌmɛn] : pistolero m, gatillero m Mex

gunner ['gʌnər] n : artillero m, -ra f

gunnysack ['gʌni,sæk] n : saco m de yute

gunpoint ['gʌn,pɔint] n **at ~** : a punta de pistola

gunpowder ['gʌn,paudər] n : pólvora f

gunshot ['gʌn,ʃɑt] *n* : disparo *m*, tiro *m*, balazo *m*

gunsmith ['gʌn,smiθ] *n* : armero *m*, -ra *f*

gunwale ['gʌnəl] *n* : borda *f*

guppy ['gʌpi] *n, pl* **-pies** : guppy *m*

gurgle[1] ['gərgəl] *vi* **-gled; -gling** 1 : borbotar, gorgotear (dícese de un líquido) 2 : gorjear (dícese de un niño)

gurgle[2] *n* 1 : borboteo *m*, gorgoteo *m* (de un líquido) 2 : gorjeo *m* (de un niño)

gush ['gʌʃ] *vi* 1 SPOUT : surgir, salir a chorros, chorrear 2 : hablar con entusiasmo efusivo ⟨she gushed with praise : se deshizo en elogios⟩

gust ['gʌst] *n* : ráfaga *f*, racha *f*

gusto ['gʌs,to:] *n, pl* **gustoes** : entusiasmo *m* ⟨with gusto : con deleite, con ganas⟩

gusty ['gʌsti] *adj* **gustier; -est** : racheado

gut[1] ['gʌt] *vt* **gutted; gutting** 1 EVISCERATE : limpiar (un pollo, un pescado, etc.) 2 : destruir el interior de (un edificio)

gut[2] *n* 1 INTESTINE : intestino *m* 2 **guts** *npl* INNARDS : tripas *fpl fam*, entrañas *fpl* 3 **guts** *npl* COURAGE : valentía *f*, agallas *fpl*

gutter ['gʌtər] *n* 1 : canal *mf*, canaleta *f* (de un techo) 2 : cuneta *f*, arroyo *m* (de una calle)

guttural ['gʌtərəl] *adj* : gutural

guy ['gaɪ] *n* 1 → **guyline** 2 FELLOW : tipo *m*, hombre *m*

guyline ['gaɪ,laɪn] *n* : cable *m* tensor

guzzle ['gʌzəl] *vt* **-zled; -zling** : chupar, tragarse

gym ['dʒɪm] → **gymnasium**

gymnasium [dʒɪm'neɪziəm, -ʒəm] *n, pl* **-siums** *or* **-sia** [-ziːə, -ʒə] : gimnasio *m*

gymnast ['dʒɪmnəst, -,næst] *n* : gimnasta *mf*

gymnastic [dʒɪm'næstɪk] *adj* : gimnástico

gymnastics [dʒɪm'næstɪks] *ns & pl* : gimnasia *f*

gynecologic [,gaɪnəkə'lɑdʒɪk, ,dʒɪnə-] *or* **gynecological** [,gaɪnəkə'lɑdʒɪkəl, ,dʒɪnə-] *adj* : ginecológico

gynecologist [,gaɪnə'kɑlədʒɪst, ,dʒɪnə-] *n* : ginecólogo *m*, -ga *f*

gynecology [,gaɪnə'kɑlədʒi, ,dʒɪnə-] *n* : ginecología *f*

gypsum ['dʒɪpsəm] *n* : yeso *m*

Gypsy ['dʒɪpsi] *n, pl* **-sies** *sometimes offensive* : gitano *m*, -na *f*

gyrate ['dʒaɪ,reɪt] *vi* **-rated; -rating** : girar, rotar

gyration [dʒaɪ'reɪʃən] *n* : giro *m*, rotación *f*

gyroscope ['dʒaɪrə,sko:p] *n* : giroscopio *m*, giróscopo *m*

H

h ['eɪtʃ] *n, pl* **h's** *or* **hs** ['eɪtʃəz] : octava letra del alfabeto inglés

ha ['hɑ] *interj* : ¡ja!

haberdashery ['hæbər,dæʃəri] *n, pl* **-eries** : tienda *f* de ropa para caballeros

habit ['hæbɪt] *n* 1 CUSTOM : hábito *m*, costumbre *f* ⟨to break/kick a bad habit : perder una mala costumbre⟩ ⟨to be in the habit of doing something : acostumbrar/soler hacer algo, tener la costumbre de hacer algo⟩ ⟨she got into the habit of sleeping in : se le hizo costumbre dormir hasta tarde⟩ ⟨to make a habit of doing something : tomar el costumbre de hacer algo⟩ ⟨don't make a habit of it : que no se repita⟩ 2 : hábito *m* (de un monje o una religiosa) 3 ADDICTION : dependencia *f*, adicción *f* ⟨to have a drug habit : ser drogadicto⟩ ⟨to kick the habit : dejar el vicio⟩

habitable ['hæbɪtəbəl] *adj* : habitable

habitat ['hæbɪ,tæt] *n* : hábitat *m*

habitation [,hæbɪ'teɪʃən] *n* 1 OCCUPANCY : habitación *f* 2 RESIDENCE : residencia *f*, morada *f*

habit-forming ['hæbɪt,fɔrmɪŋ] *adj* : que crea dependencia

habitual [hə'bɪtʃuəl] *adj* 1 CUSTOMARY : habitual, acostumbrado 2 INVETERATE : incorregible, empedernido — **habitually** *adv*

habituate [hə'bɪtʃu,eɪt] *vt* **-ated; -ating** : habituar, acostumbrar

hack[1] ['hæk] *vt* 1 : cortar, tajear (a hachazos, etc.) ⟨to hack one's way : abrirse paso⟩ 2 : entrar en, hackear *fam* (un sistema, etc.) — *vi* 1 : hacer tajos 2 COUGH : toser 3 **to hack into** : entrar en, hackear *fam*

hack[2] *n* 1 CHOP : hachazo *m*, tajo *m* 2 HORSE : caballo *m* de alquiler 3 WRITER : escritor *m*, -tora *f* a sueldo; escritorzuelo *m*, -la *f* 4 COUGH : tos *f* seca

hacker ['hækər] *n* : pirata *m* informático, pirata *f* informática; hacker *mf fam*

hackles ['hækəlz] *npl* 1 : pluma *f* erizada (de un ave), pelo *m* erizado (de un perro, etc.) 2 **to get one's hackles up** : ponerse furioso

hackney ['hækni] *n, pl* **-neys** : caballo *m* de silla, caballo *m* de tiro

hackneyed ['hæknid] *adj* TRITE : trillado, gastado

hacksaw ['hæk,sɔ] *n* : sierra *f* para metales

had → **have**

haddock ['hædək] *ns & pl* : eglefino *m*

hadn't ['hædənt] *contraction of* HAD NOT → **have**

hag ['hæg] *n offensive* : bruja *f*, vieja *f* fea

haggard ['hægərd] *adj* : demacrado, macilento — **haggardly** *adv*

haggle ['hægəl] *vi* **-gled; -gling** : regatear

ha–ha *or* **ha ha** [,hɑ'hɑ, 'hɑ'hɑ] *interj* : ¡ja, ja!

hail¹ ['heɪl] *vt* **1** GREET : saludar **2** SUMMON : llamar ⟨to hail a taxi : llamar un taxi⟩ **3** WELCOME : aclamar — *vi* : granizar (en meteorología)

hail² *n* **1** : granizo *m* **2** BARRAGE : aluvión *m*, lluvia *f*

hail³ *interj* : ¡salve!

hailstone ['heɪl,stoːn] *n* : granizo *m*, piedra *f* de granizo

hailstorm ['heɪl,storm] *n* : granizada *f*

hair ['hær] *n* **1** : pelo *m*, cabello *m* ⟨to get one's hair cut : cortarse el pelo⟩ **2** : vello *m* (en las piernas, etc.)

hairbreadth ['hær,bredθ] *or* **hairsbreadth** ['hærz-] *n* **by a hairbreadth** : por un pelo

hairbrush ['hær,brʌʃ] *n* : cepillo *m* (para el pelo)

haircut ['hær,kʌt] *n* : corte *m* de pelo

hairdo ['hær,duː] *n, pl* **-dos** : peinado *m*

hairdresser ['hær,drɛsər] *n* **1** : peluquero *m*, -ra *f* **2 the hairdresser's** : la peluquería

hairdressing ['hær,drɛsɪŋ] *n* : peluquería *f* (profesión o actividad)

haired ['hærd] *adj* (*used in combination*) : de pelo ⟨long-haired : de pelo largo⟩ ⟨red-haired : pelirrojo⟩

hairiness ['hærinəs] *n* : vellosidad *f*

hairless ['hærləs] *adj* : sin pelo, calvo, pelón

hairline ['hær,laɪn] *n* **1** : línea *f* delgada **2** : nacimiento *m* del pelo ⟨to have a receding hairline : tener entradas⟩

hairpiece ['hær,piːs] *n* : bisoñé *m*, peluquín *m*

hairpin ['hær,pɪn] *n* : horquilla *f*

hair–raising ['hær,reɪzɪŋ] *adj* : espeluznante

hair spray *n* : laca *f*, fijador *m* (para el pelo)

hairstyle ['hær,staɪl] *n* : peinado *m*

hairy ['hæri] *adj* **hairier; -est** : peludo, velludo

Haitian ['heɪʃən, 'heɪtiən] *n* : haitiano *m*, -na *f* — **Haitian** *adj*

hake ['heɪk] *n* : merluza *f*

hale¹ ['heɪl] *vt* **haled; haling** : arrastrar, halar ⟨to hale to court : arrastrar al tribunal⟩

hale² *adj* : saludable, robusto

half¹ ['hæf, 'haf] *adv* **1** PARTIALLY : medio, a medias ⟨half cooked : medio cocido⟩ ⟨half closed/open : entreabierto⟩ ⟨she was half asleep : estaba medio dormida⟩ **2** : medio ⟨half full : medio lleno⟩ ⟨it's half past eleven (o'clock) : son las once y media⟩ ⟨she's half Mexican : es medio mexicana⟩ **3 half off** : a mitad de precio

half² *adj* : medio, a medias ⟨a half hour : una media hora⟩ ⟨a half truth : una verdad a medias⟩

half³ *n, pl* **halves** ['hævz, 'havz] **1** : mitad *f* ⟨to cut in half, to cut into halves : cortar por la mitad⟩ **2** : tiempo *m* (en deportes)

half⁴ *pron* : la mitad ⟨half of my friends : la mitad de mis amigos⟩ ⟨do you want

half? : ¿quieres la mitad?⟩ ⟨half a million people : medio millón de personas⟩

half brother *n* : medio hermano *m*, hermanastro *m*

halfhearted ['hæf'hɑrtəd] *adj* : sin ánimo, poco entusiasta

halfheartedly ['hæf'hɑrtədli] *adv* : con poco entusiasmo, sin ánimo

half–life ['hæf,laɪf] *n, pl* **half–lives** : media vida *f*

half–mast ['hæf'mæst] *n* **at ~** : a media asta

half–moon ['hæf,muːn] *n, pl* **half–moons** : media luna *f*

half note *n* : blanca *f* (en música)

half–price ['hæf,praɪs] *adj & adv* : a mitad de precio ⟨a half-price sale : rebajas de 50 por ciento⟩

half price *n* : mitad *f* de precio ⟨to buy at half price, to pay half price for : comprar a mitad de precio⟩

half sister *n* : media hermana *f*, hermanastra *f*

halftime ['hæf,taɪm] *n* : descanso *m*, medio tiempo *m* (en deportes)

half–truth ['hæf,truːθ] *n* : verdad *f* a medias

halfway¹ ['hæf'weɪ] *adv* : a medio camino, a mitad de camino

halfway² *adj* : medio, intermedio ⟨a halfway point : un punto intermedio⟩

half–wit ['hæf,wɪt] *n* : tonto *m*, -ta *f*; imbécil *mf*

half–witted ['hæf,wɪtəd] *adj* : estúpido

halibut ['hælɪbət] *ns & pl* : halibut *m*

hall ['hɔl] *n* **1** BUILDING : residencia *f* estudiantil, facultad *f* (de una universidad) **2** VESTIBULE : entrada *f*, vestíbulo *m*, zaguán *m* **3** CORRIDOR : corredor *m*, pasillo *m* **4** AUDITORIUM : sala *f*, salón *m* ⟨concert hall : sala de conciertos⟩ **5 city hall** : ayuntamiento *m*

hallelujah [,hælə'luːjə, ,hɑ-] *interj* : ¡aleluya!

hallmark ['hɔl,mɑrk] *n* : sello *m* (distintivo)

hallow ['hæ,loː] *vt* : santificar, consagrar

hallowed ['hæ,loːd, 'hæ,loːəd, 'hɑ,loːd] *adj* : sagrado

Halloween [,hælə'wiːn, ,hɑ-] *n* : víspera *f* de Todos los Santos

hallucinate [hæ'luːsən,eɪt] *vi* **-nated; -nating** : alucinar

hallucination [hə,luːsən'eɪʃən] *n* : alucinación *f*

hallucinatory [hə'luːsənə,tori] *adj* : alucinante

hallucinogen [hə'luːsənədʒən] *n* : alucinógeno *m*

hallucinogenic [hə,luːsənə'dʒɛnɪk] *adj* : alucinógeno

hallway ['hɔl,weɪ] *n* **1** ENTRANCE : entrada *f* **2** CORRIDOR : corredor *m*, pasillo *m*

halo ['heɪ,loː] *n, pl* **-los** *or* **-loes** : aureola *f*, halo *m*

halt¹ ['hɔlt] *vi* : detenerse, pararse — *vt* **1** STOP : detener, parar (a una persona) **2** INTERRUPT : interrumpir (una actividad)

halt² *n* **1** : alto *m*, parada *f* **2 to come to a halt** : pararse, detenerse

halter [ˈhɔltər] n 1 : cabestro m, ronzal m (para un animal) 2 : blusa f sin espalda

halting [ˈhɔltɪŋ] adj HESITANT : vacilante, titubeante — **haltingly** adv

halve [ˈhæv, ˈhav] vt **halved; halving** 1 DIVIDE : partir por la mitad 2 REDUCE : reducir a la mitad

halves → **half**

ham [ˈhæm] n 1 : jamón m 2 : payaso m, -sa f; persona f graciosa 3 or **ham radio operator** : radioaficionado m, -da f 4 **hams** npl HAUNCHES : ancas fpl

hamburger [ˈhæm,bərgər] or **hamburg** [-,bərg] n 1 : carne f molida 2 : hamburguesa f (emparedado)

hamlet [ˈhæmlət] n VILLAGE : aldea f, poblado m

hammer[1] [ˈhæmər] vt 1 STRIKE : clavar, golpear 2 NAIL : clavar, martillar 3 DEFEAT : darle una paliza a 4 to **hammer out** NEGOTIATE : elaborar, negociar, llegar a — vi : martillar, golpear

hammer[2] n 1 : martillo m 2 : percusor m, percutor m (de un arma de fuego)

hammock [ˈhæmək] n : hamaca f

hamper[1] [ˈhæmpər] vt : obstaculizar, dificultar

hamper[2] n : cesto m, canasta f

hamster [ˈhæmpstər] n : hámster m

hamstring [ˈhæm,strɪŋ] vt **-strung** [-,strʌŋ]; **-stringing** 1 : cortarle el tendón del corvejón a (un animal) 2 INCAPACITATE : incapacitar, inutilizar

hand[1] [ˈhænd] vt 1 : pasar, dar, entregar 2 to **hand back** RETURN : devolver 3 to **hand down** : dejar en herencia 4 to **hand in** SUBMIT : entregar, presentar 5 to **hand it to** fam : aplaudir, felicitar ⟨I've got to hand it to you — you did a great job! : ¡tengo que reconocer que hiciste muy bien!⟩ 6 to **hand out** DISTRIBUTE : distribuir 7 to **hand over** SURRENDER : entregar

hand[2] n 1 : mano f ⟨made by hand : hecho a mano⟩ ⟨hand in hand : tomados de la mano⟩ ⟨to hold hands : ir tomados de la mano⟩ ⟨to raise one's hand : levantar la mano⟩ ⟨to join hands : darse las manos⟩ 2 POINTER : manecilla f, aguja f (de un reloj o instrumento) 3 SIDE : lado m ⟨on the one hand . . . on the other hand . . . : por un lado . . . por otro lado . . .⟩ 4 HANDWRITING : letra f, escritura f 5 APPLAUSE : aplauso m ⟨let's give them all a hand! : ¡aplausos para todos!⟩ 6 : mano f, cartas fpl (en juegos de naipes) 7 WORKER : obrero m, -ra f; trabajador m, -dora f 8 **hands** npl CONTROL : manos fpl ⟨to fall into the hands of : caer en manos de⟩ ⟨it's out of my hands : no está en mis manos⟩ 9 at hand NEAR : a mano ⟨to keep close at hand : tener a mano⟩ ⟨the problem at hand : el problema más acuciante⟩ 10 on hand AVAILABLE : a mano, disponible 11 on hand PRESENT, NEAR : presente, cerca 12 on one's hands ⟨I had some time on my hands : tenía un rato libre⟩ ⟨she has all that work on her hands : tiene tanto trabajo

que hacer⟩ 13 on one's hands and knees : a gatas 14 out of hand : descontrolado ⟨the situation is getting out of hand : la situación se les/nos (etc.) va de las manos⟩ 15 out of hand IMMEDIATELY : sin miramientos 16 to ask for someone's hand (in marriage) : pedir la mano de alguien 17 to give/lend a hand : echar una mano 18 to go hand in hand : ir de la mano 19 to have a hand in : tener parte en 20 to have one's hands full : estar muy ocupado 21 to have one's hands tied : tener las manos atadas 22 to live from hand to mouth : vivir al día 23 to try one's hand at : probar a hacer 24 to wait on someone hand and foot : hacerle de sirviente/sirvienta a alguien

handbag [ˈhænd,bæg] n : cartera f, bolso m, bolsa f Mex

handball [ˈhænd,bɔl] n : frontón m, pelota f

handbill [ˈhænd,bɪl] n : folleto m, volante m

handbook [ˈhænd,bʊk] n : manual m

handbrake [ˈhænd,breɪk] n : freno m de mano

handcuff [ˈhænd,kʌf] vt : esposar, ponerle esposas (a alguien)

handcuffs [ˈhænd,kʌfs] npl : esposas fpl

handful [ˈhænd,fʊl] n : puñado m

handgun [ˈhænd,gʌn] n : pistola f, revólver m

handheld [ˈhænd,held] adj : de mano

handicap[1] [ˈhændi,kæp] vt **-capped; -capping** 1 : asignar un handicap a (en deportes) 2 HAMPER : obstaculizar, poner en desventaja

handicap[2] n 1 sometimes offensive DISABILITY : minusvalía f, discapacidad f 2 DISADVANTAGE : desventaja f, handicap m (en deportes)

handicapped [ˈhændi,kæpt] adj sometimes offensive DISABLED : minusválido, discapacitado

handicraft [ˈhændi,kræft] n : artesanía f

handily [ˈhændəli] adv EASILY : fácilmente, con facilidad

handiwork [ˈhændi,wərk] n 1 WORK : trabajo m 2 CRAFTS : artesanías fpl

handkerchief [ˈhæŋkərtʃəf, -,tʃiːf] n, pl **-chiefs** : pañuelo m

handle[1] [ˈhændəl] v **-dled; -dling** vt 1 TOUCH : tocar 2 MANAGE : tratar, manejar, despachar 3 SELL : comerciar con, vender — vi : responder, conducirse (dícese de un vehículo)

handle[2] n : asa m, asidero m, mango m (de un cuchillo, etc.), pomo m (de una puerta), tirador m (de un cajón)

handlebars [ˈhændəl,bɑrz] npl : manubrio m, manillar m

handler [ˈhændələr] n : cuidador m, -dora f

handling [ˈhændəlɪŋ] n 1 MANAGEMENT : manejo m 2 TOUCHING : manoseo m 3 shipping and handling : porte m, transporte m

handmade [ˈhænd,meɪd] adj : hecho a mano

hand–me–downs ['hænd₁miˌdaʊnz] npl : ropa f usada

handout ['hændˌaʊt] n 1 AID : dádiva f, limosna f 2 LEAFLET : folleto m

handpick ['hændˈpɪk] vt : seleccionar con cuidado

handrail ['hændˌreɪl] n : pasamanos m, barandilla f, barandal m

handsaw ['hændˌsɔ] n : serrucho m

hands down adv 1 EASILY : con facilidad 2 UNQUESTIONABLY : con mucho, de lejos

hands–free ['hændzˈfriː] adj : (de) manos libres

handshake ['hændˌʃeɪk] n : apretón m de manos

handsome ['hæntsəm] adj handsomer; -est 1 ATTRACTIVE : apuesto, guapo, atractivo 2 GENEROUS : generoso 3 SIZABLE : considerable

handsomely ['hæntsəmli] adv 1 ELEGANTLY : elegantemente 2 GENEROUSLY : con generosidad

handspring ['hændˌsprɪŋ] n : voltereta f

handstand ['hændˌstænd] n to do a handstand : pararse de manos

hand–to–hand ['hændtəˈhænd] adj : cuerpo a cuerpo

hand truck → **truck²**

handwriting ['hændˌraɪtɪŋ] n : letra f, escritura f

handwritten ['hændˌrɪtən] adj : escrito a mano

handy ['hændi] adj handier; -est 1 NEARBY : a mano, cercano 2 USEFUL : útil, práctico 3 DEXTEROUS : hábil

handyman ['hændiˌmæn] n, pl -men [-mən, -ˌmɛn] : hombre m que hace pequeños arreglos del hogar, manitas m Spain

handywoman ['hændiˌwʊmən] n, pl -women [-ˌwɪmən] : mujer f que hace pequeños arreglos del hogar, manitas f Spain

hang¹ ['hæŋ] v hung ['hʌŋ]; hanging vt 1 SUSPEND : colgar, tender (ropa lavada), colocar (una pintura, etc.) 2 past tense often hanged EXECUTE : colgar, ahorcar 3 to hang one's head : bajar la cabeza — vi 1 FALL : caer (dícese de las telas y la ropa) 2 DANGLE : colgar 3 HOVER : flotar, sostenerse en el aire 4 : ser ahorcado 5 DROOP : inclinarse 6 to hang around fam : pasar el rato 7 to hang back : quedar atrás 8 to hang in there : seguir adelante 9 to hang on : WAIT esperar 10 to hang on (to) : agarrarse (a) 6 to hang out fam : pasar el rato 11 to hang out with someone : andar con alguien 12 to be hanging over one or to be hanging over one's head : tener pendiente, quedarle a alguien por resolver/terminar (etc.) ⟨I can't relax with this test hanging over me : no puedo relajarme hasta que me quite de encima este examen⟩ 13 to hang tight : seguir adelante 14 to hang tough : mantenerse firme 15 to hang up : colgar ⟨he hung up on me : me colgó⟩

hang² n 1 DRAPE : caída f 2 to get the hang of something : agarrarle la onda a algo

hangar ['hæŋər, 'hæŋgər] n : hangar m

hanger ['hæŋər] n : percha f, gancho m (para ropa)

hang glider ['hæŋˌglaɪdər] n : ala f delta (vehículo), deslizador m Mex

hang gliding ['hæŋˌglaɪdɪŋ] n : ala f delta (deporte), vuelo m

hangman ['hæŋmən] n, pl -men [-mən, -ˌmɛn] : verdugo m

hangnail ['hæŋˌneɪl] n : padrastro m

hangout ['hæŋˌaʊt] n : lugar m popular, sitio m muy frecuentado

hangover ['hæŋˌoːvər] n : resaca f

hank ['hæŋk] n : madeja f

hanker ['hæŋkər] vi to hanker for : tener ansias de, tener ganas de

hankering ['hæŋkərɪŋ] n : ansia f, anhelo m

hankie or **hanky** ['hæŋki] n, pl -kies : pañuelo m

Hanukkah ['xɑnəkə, 'hɑ-] n : Janucá, Janucá, Hanukkah

haphazard [hæpˈhæzərd] adj : casual, fortuito, al azar — **haphazardly** adv

hapless ['hæpləs] adj UNFORTUNATE : desafortunado, desventurado — **haplessly** adv

happen ['hæpən] vi 1 OCCUR : pasar, ocurrir, suceder, tener lugar 2 BEFALL : pasar, acontecer ⟨what happened to her? : ¿qué le ha pasado?⟩ 3 CHANCE : resultar, ocurrir por casualidad ⟨it happened that I wasn't home : resulta que estaba fuera de casa⟩ ⟨he happens to be right : da la casualidad de que tiene razón⟩

happening ['hæpənɪŋ] n : suceso m, acontecimiento m

happiness ['hæpinəs] n : felicidad f, dicha f

happy ['hæpi] adj happier; -est 1 JOYFUL : feliz, contento, alegre ⟨I'm happy for you : me alegro por ti⟩ ⟨a happy smile : una sonrisa de alegría⟩ 2 FORTUNATE : afortunado, feliz — **happily** [-pəli] adv

happy–go–lucky ['hæpigoːˈlʌki] adj : despreocupado

harangue¹ [həˈræŋ] vt -rangued; -ranguing : arengar

harangue² n : arenga f

harass [həˈræs, 'hærəs] vt 1 BESIEGE, HOUND : acosar, asediar, hostigar 2 ANNOY : molestar

harassment [həˈræsmənt, 'hærəsmənt] n : acoso m, hostigamiento m ⟨sexual harassment : acoso sexual⟩

harbinger ['hɑrbɪnʤər] n 1 HERALD : heraldo m, precursor m 2 OMEN : presagio m

harbor¹ ['hɑrbər] vt 1 SHELTER : dar refugio a, albergar 2 CHERISH, KEEP : abrigar, guardar, albergar ⟨to harbor doubts : guardar dudas⟩

harbor² n 1 REFUGE : refugio m 2 PORT : puerto m

hard¹ ['hɑrd] adv 1 FORCEFULLY : fuerte, con fuerza ⟨the wind blew hard : el viento sopló fuerte⟩ 2 STRENUOUSLY : duro, mucho ⟨to work hard : trabajar duro⟩ 3 to take something hard : tomarse algo muy mal, estar muy afectado por algo

hard² *adj* 1 FIRM, SOLID : duro, firme, sólido 2 DIFFICULT : difícil, arduo 3 SEVERE : severo, duro ⟨a hard winter : un invierno severo⟩ 4 UNFEELING : insensible, duro 5 DILIGENT : diligente ⟨to be a hard worker : ser muy trabajador⟩ 6 FORCEFUL : fuerte (dícese de un golpe, etc.) 7 HARSH : fuerte (dícese de una luz), definido (dícese de una línea) 8 hard liquor : bebidas *fpl* fuertes 9 hard water : agua *f* dura 10 to be hard on *fam* CRITICIZE, PUNISH : ser duro con 11 to be hard on *fam* HARM : ser malo para 12 to be hard on *fam* STRESS : ser difícil para 13 to be hard up *fam* : estar/andar mal de dinero 14 to be hard up for *fam* : andar escaso de 15 to have a hard time *fam* : pasarlo mal 16 to have a hard time with/doing something *fam* : costarle a uno hacer algo 17 to learn the hard way *fam* : aprender a las malas 18 to do something the hard way *fam* : complicar las cosas

hardback ['hɑrd,bæk] *n* : libro *m* de tapa dura

hardball ['hɑrd,bɔl] *n* 1 → baseball 2 to play hardball : ser agresivo, jugar sucio

hard–boiled ['hɑrd'bɔɪld] *adj* : duro (dícese de un huevo)

hard copy *n* : copia *f* impresa

hardcover¹ ['hɑrd,kʌvər] *adj* : de pasta dura, de tapa dura

hardcover² *n* : libro *m* de pasta/tapa dura

hard disk *n* : disco *m* duro

hard drive 1 → hard disk 2 : (unidad *f* de) disco *m* duro

harden ['hɑrdən] *vt* 1 SOLIDIFY, CONGEAL : endurecer 2 : endurecer, hacer duro (a una persona) ⟨to harden someone's heart : endurecerle el corazón a alguien⟩ 3 : reforzar, fortalecer (la determinación, etc.) — *vi* 1 SOLIDIFY, CONGEAL : endurecerse 2 : reforzarse, fortalecerse 3 : endurecerse, hacerse duro (dícese de la voz, etc.)

hard–fought ['hɑrd'fɔt] *adj* : muy reñido

hardheaded [,hɑrd'hɛdəd] *adj* 1 STUBBORN : testarudo, terco 2 REALISTIC : realista, práctico — **hardheadedly** *adv*

hard–hearted [,hɑrd'hɑrtəd] *adj* : despiadado, insensible — **hard–heartedly** *adv*

hard–heartedness [,hɑrd'hɑrtədnəs] *n* : dureza *f* de corazón

hardly ['hɑrdli] *adv* 1 SCARCELY : apenas, casi ⟨I hardly knew her : apenas la conocía⟩ ⟨hardly ever : casi nunca⟩ 2 NOT : difícilmente, poco, no ⟨they can hardly blame me! : ¡difícilmente pueden echarme la culpa!⟩ ⟨it's hardly likely : es poco probable⟩

hardness ['hɑrdnəs] *n* 1 FIRMNESS : dureza *f* 2 DIFFICULTY : dificultad *f* 3 SEVERITY : severidad *f*

hardship ['hɑrd,ʃɪp] *n* : dificultad *f*, privación *f*

hardware ['hɑrd,wær] *n* 1 : ferretería *f* 2 : hardware *m* (de una computadora)

hardware store *n* : ferretería *f*

hardwired ['hɑrd,waɪrd] *adj* 1 : integrado (dícese de un sistema, etc.) 2 : mentalmente programado

hardwood ['hɑrd,wʊd] *n* : madera *f* dura, madera *f* noble

hardworking ['hɑrd'wɔrkɪŋ] *adj* : trabajador

hardy ['hɑrdi] *adj* **hardier; -est** : fuerte, robusto, resistente (dícese de las plantas) — **hardily** [-dəli] *adv*

hare ['hær] *n, pl* **hare** *or* **hares** : liebre *f*

harebrained ['hær,breɪnd] *adj* : estúpido, absurdo, disparatado

harem ['hærəm] *n* : harén *m*

hark ['hɑrk] *vi* 1 (*used only in the imperative*) LISTEN : escuchar 2 **hark back** RETURN : volver 3 **hark back** RECALL : recordar

harlequin ['hɑrlɪkən, -kwən] *n* : arlequín *m*

harlot ['hɑrlət] *n* : ramera *f*

harm¹ ['hɑrm] *vt* : hacerle daño a, perjudicar

harm² *n* 1 : daño *m*, perjuicio *m* ⟨I meant no harm : no lo dije/hice (etc.) con mala intención⟩ ⟨to do more harm than good : hacer más mal/daño que bien⟩ ⟨there's no harm in asking : con preguntar no se pierde nada⟩ 2 in harm's way : en peligro 3 no harm done *fam* : no fue nada, no pasó nada

harmful ['hɑrmfəl] *adj* : dañino, perjudicial — **harmfully** *adv*

harmless ['hɑrmləs] *adj* : inofensivo, inocuo — **harmlessly** *adv*

harmlessness ['hɑrmləsnəs] *n* : inocuidad *f*

harmonic [hɑr'mɑnɪk] *adj* : armónico — **harmonically** [-nɪkli] *adv*

harmonica [hɑr'mɑnɪkə] *n* : armónica *f*

harmonious [hɑr'moːniəs] *adj* : armonioso — **harmoniously** *adv*

harmonize ['hɑrmə,naɪz] *v* **-nized; -nizing** : armonizar

harmony ['hɑrməni] *n, pl* **-nies** : armonía *f*

harness¹ ['hɑrnəs] *vt* 1 : enjaezar (un animal) 2 UTILIZE : utilizar, aprovechar

harness² *n* : arreos *mpl*, guarniciones *fpl*, arnés *m*

harp ['hɑrp] *vi* **to harp on** : insistir sobre, machacar sobre

harp² *n* : arpa *m*

harpist ['hɑrpɪst] *n* : arpista *mf*

harpoon¹ [hɑr'puːn] *vt* : arponear

harpoon² *n* : arpón *m*

harpsichord ['hɑrpsɪ,kɔrd] *n* : clavicémbalo *m*

harrow¹ ['hær,oː] *vt* 1 CULTIVATE : gradar, labrar (la tierra) 2 TORMENT : atormentar

harrow² *n* : grada *f*, rastra *f*

harry ['hæri] *vt* **-ried; -rying** HARASS : acosar, hostigar

harsh ['hɑrʃ] *adj* 1 ROUGH : áspero 2 SEVERE : duro, severo 3 : discordante (dícese de los sonidos) — **harshly** *adv*

harshness ['hɑrʃnəs] n 1 ROUGHNESS : aspereza f 2 SEVERITY : dureza f, severidad f

harvest¹ ['hɑrvəst] v : cosechar

harvest² n 1 HARVESTING : siega f, recolección f 2 CROP : cosecha f

harvester ['hɑrvəstər] n : segador m, -dora f; cosechadora f (máquina)

has → **have**

has-been ['hæz‚bɪn, -‚bɛn] n : vieja gloria f

hash¹ ['hæʃ] vt 1 MINCE : picar 2 to **hash over** DISCUSS : discutir, repasar

hash² n 1 : picadillo m (comida) 2 JUMBLE : revoltijo m, fárrago m

hashish ['hæ‚ʃiːʃ, hæ'ʃiːʃ] n : hachís m

hashtag ['hæʃ‚tæg] n : hashtag m, etiqueta f (en las redes sociales)

hasn't ['hæzənt] contraction of HAS NOT → **has**

hasp ['hæsp] n : picaporte m, pestillo m

hassle¹ ['hæsəl] vt -sled; -sling : fastidiar, molestar

hassle² n 1 ARGUMENT : discusión f, disputa f, bronca f 2 FIGHT : pelea f, riña f 3 BOTHER, TROUBLE : problemas mpl, lío m

hassock ['hæsək] n 1 CUSHION : almohadón m, cojín m 2 FOOTSTOOL : escabel m

haste ['heɪst] n 1 : prisa f, apuro m 2 to **make haste** : darse prisa, apurarse

hasten ['heɪsən] vt : acelerar, precipitar — vi : apresurarse, apurarse

hasty ['heɪsti] adj hastier; -est 1 HURRIED, QUICK : rápido, apresurado, apurado 2 RASH : precipitado — hastily ['-təli] adv

hat ['hæt] n : sombrero m

hatch¹ ['hætʃ] vt 1 : incubar, empollar (huevos) 2 DEVISE : idear, tramar — vi 1 : salir del cascarón

hatch² n : escotilla f

hatchback ['hætʃ‚bæk] n 1 : hatchback m (automóvil) 2 : puerta f trasera

hatchery ['hætʃəri] n, pl -ries : criadero m

hatchet ['hætʃət] n : hacha f

hatchway ['hætʃ‚weɪ] n : escotilla f

hate¹ ['heɪt] vt hated; hating : odiar, aborrecer, detestar

hate² n : odio m

hateful ['heɪtfəl] adj : odioso, aborrecible, detestable — hatefully adv

hatred ['heɪtrəd] n : odio m

hatter ['hætər] n : sombrerero m, -ra f

haughtiness ['hɔtinəs] n : altanería f, altivez f

haughty ['hɔti] adj haughtier; -est 1 : altanero, altivo — haughtily ['-təli] adv

haul¹ ['hɔl] vt 1 DRAG, PULL : arrastrar, jalar 2 TRANSPORT : transportar

haul² n 1 PULL : tirón m, jalón m 2 CATCH : redada f 3 JOURNEY : viaje m, trayecto m ⟨it's a long haul : es un trayecto largo⟩

haulage ['hɔlɪdʒ] n : transporte m, tiro m

hauler ['hɔlər] n : transportista mf

haunch ['hɔntʃ] n 1 : cadera f 2 **haunches** npl HINDQUARTERS : ancas fpl, cuartos mpl traseros

haunt¹ ['hɔnt] vt 1 : rondar, habitar (dícese de un fantasma) 2 FREQUENT : frecuentar, rondar 3 PREOCCUPY : perseguir, obsesionar

haunt² n : guarida f (de animales o ladrones), lugar m predilecto

haunted ['hɔntəd] adj : embrujado, encantado (dícese de una casa, etc.)

haunting ['hɔntɪŋ] adj : inolvidable (por ser hermoso o triste) — **hauntingly** adv

haute ['oːt] adj 1 : de moda, de categoría 2 **haute couture** [‚oːtkuˈtʊr] : alta costura f 3 **haute cuisine** [‚oːkwiˈziːn] : alta cocina f

have ['hæv, in sense 7 as an auxiliary verb usu 'hæf] v had ['hæd]; having; has ['hæz, in sense 7 as an auxiliary verb usu 'hæz] vt 1 POSSESS : tener ⟨she has long hair : tiene el pelo largo⟩ ⟨they have three children : tienen tres hijos⟩ ⟨do you have change? : ¿tienes cambio?⟩ ⟨you can have it : te lo doy⟩ 2 OBTAIN : conseguir ⟨I must have it! : ¡no puedo sin ello!⟩ 3 (indicating availability) : tener ⟨when you have a minute : cuando tengas un momento⟩ 4 : tener (en casa) ⟨we have guests : tenemos visita⟩ 5 EXPERIENCE, UNDERGO : tener ⟨I have a toothache : tengo un dolor de muelas⟩ ⟨to have surgery : operarse⟩ ⟨to have a good time : pasarlo bien⟩ 6 : tener (una idea, una opinión, etc.) 7 INCLUDE : tener, incluir ⟨April has 30 days : abril tiene 30 días⟩ 8 CONSUME : comer, tomar 9 RECEIVE : tener, recibir ⟨he had my permission : tenía mi permiso⟩ 10 ALLOW : permitir, tolerar ⟨I won't have it! : ¡no lo permitiré!⟩ 11 HOLD : hacer ⟨to have a party : dar una fiesta⟩ ⟨to have a meeting : celebrar una reunión⟩ 12 DO : hacer ⟨to have a nap : echarse una siesta⟩ ⟨to have a look at : mirar⟩ ⟨I'll have a talk with him : hablaré con él⟩ 13 HOLD : tener ⟨he had me in his power : me tenía en su poder⟩ ⟨she had me by the arm : me tenía agarrado del brazo⟩ 14 BEAR : tener (niños) 15 (indicating causation) ⟨she had a dress made : mandó hacer un vestido⟩ ⟨to have one's hair cut : cortarse el pelo⟩ ⟨have her call me : dile que me llame⟩ ⟨he had it ready : lo tenía listo⟩ 16 (indicating loss, damage, etc.) ⟨she had her car stolen : le robaron el auto⟩ 17 **to be had** : ser engañado ⟨I've been had! : ¡me han engañado!⟩ 18 **to be had** ⟨there were none to be had : no había disponibles⟩ 19 **to have back** ⟨can I have my book back? : ¿me puedes devolver el libro?⟩ 20 **to have back** : volver a invitar ⟨we must have you back : tienes que volver a visitarnos⟩ 21 **to have back** ⟨it's good to have you back! : ¡qué gusto volver a verte por aquí!⟩ 22 **to have it easy/rough** (etc.) : tenerlo todo muy fácil/difícil (etc.) 23 **to have it in for** : tenerle manía a 24 **to have it in one** : ser capaz ⟨she doesn't have it in her to be cruel : no es capaz de ser cruel⟩ 25 **to have it out** (with)

: aclarar(le) las cosas (a) **26 to have off**
: tener (un día, etc.) libre **27 to have on**
WEAR : llevar **28 to have over** : invitar
(a casa) **29 to have on one** : tener/llevar encima ⟨I don't have it on me : no lo tengo encima⟩ **30 to have with one**
: traer (a alguien), tener/llevar (algo) encima — *v aux* **1** : haber ⟨she has been very busy : ha estado muy ocupada⟩ ⟨I've lived here three years : hace tres años que vivo aquí⟩ **2** (*used in tags*) ⟨you've finished, haven't you? : ha terminado, ¿no?⟩ **3 to have got** (*used in the present tense*) *fam* : tener ⟨I've got an idea : tengo una idea⟩ ⟨we've got to leave : tenemos que salir⟩ **4 you've got me!** : ¡no sé!, ¡ni idea! **5 to have had it** : no dar para más (dícese de una cosa) **6 to have had it (with someone/something)** : estar harto (de alguien/algo) **7 to have to** : deber, tener que ⟨we have to leave : tenemos que salir⟩

haven ['heɪvən] *n* : refugio *m*
havoc ['hævək] *n* **1** DESTRUCTION : estragos *mpl*, destrucción *f* **2** CHAOS, DISORDER : desorden *m*, caos *m*
Hawaiian[1] [hə'waɪən] *adj* : hawaiano
Hawaiian[2] *n* : hawaiano *m*, -na *f*
hawk[1] ['hɔk] *vt* : pregonar, vender (mercancías) en la calle
hawk[2] *n* : halcón *m*
hawker ['hɔkər] *n* : vendedor *m*, -dora *f* ambulante
hawthorn ['hɔ,θɔrn] *n* : espino *m*
hay ['heɪ] *n* : heno *m*
hay fever *n* : fiebre *f* del heno
hayloft ['heɪ,lɔft] *n* : pajar *m*
hayseed ['heɪ,si:d] *n* : palurdo *m*, -da *f*
haystack ['heɪ,stæk] *n* : almiar *m*
haywire ['heɪ,waɪr] *adj* : descompuesto, desbaratado ⟨to go haywire : estropearse⟩
hazard[1] ['hæzərd] *vt* : arriesgar, aventurar
hazard[2] *n* **1** DANGER : peligro *m*, riesgo *m* **2** CHANCE : azar *m*
hazardous ['hæzərdəs] *adj* : arriesgado, peligroso
haze[1] ['heɪz] *vt* **hazed; hazing** : abrumar, acosar
haze[2] *n* : bruma *f*, neblina *f*
hazel ['heɪzəl] *n* **1** : avellano *m* (árbol) **2** : color *m* avellana
hazelnut ['heɪzəl,nʌt] *n* : avellana *f*
haziness ['heɪzinəs] *n* **1** MISTINESS : nebulosidad *f* **2** VAGUENESS : vaguedad *f*
hazy ['heɪzi] *adj* **hazier; -est** **1** MISTY : brumoso, neblinoso, nebuloso **2** VAGUE : vago, confuso
he ['hi:] *pron* : él
head[1] ['hɛd] *vt* **1** LEAD : encabezar **2** DIRECT : dirigir — *vi* : dirigirse
head[2] *adj* MAIN : principal ⟨the head office : la oficina central, la sede⟩ ⟨head of state/government : jefe dè estado/gobierno⟩
head[3] *n* **1** : cabeza *f* ⟨from head to foot : de pies a cabeza⟩ ⟨to stand on one's head : pararse de cabeza⟩ ⟨to nod one's head : asentir con la cabeza⟩ **2** MIND

: mente *f*, cabeza *f* ⟨use your head! : ¡usa la cabeza!⟩ ⟨to add in one's head : sumar mentalmente⟩ ⟨it's all in your head : es pura imaginación tuya⟩ ⟨to come into one's head : venirle a la cabeza⟩ ⟨to enter one's head : pasársele por la cabeza⟩ ⟨to put something out of your head : sacarse algo de la cabeza⟩ ⟨don't put ideas in his head! : ¡no le metas ideas a la cabeza!⟩ ⟨she's gotten it into her head that . . . : se le ha metido en la cabeza que . . .⟩ **3** TIP, TOP : cabeza *f* (de un clavo, un martillo, etc.), cabecera *f* (de una mesa o un río), punta *f* (de una flecha), flor *m* (de un repollo, etc.), encabezamiento *m* (de una carta, etc.), espuma *f* (de cerveza) **4** DIRECTOR, LEADER : director *m*, -tora *f*; jefe *m*, -fa *f*; cabeza *f* (de una familia) ⟨head of state/government : jefe de Estado/gobierno⟩ **5** : cara *f* (de una moneda) ⟨heads or tails : cara o cruz⟩ **6** : cabeza *f* ⟨500 head of cattle : 500 cabezas de ganado⟩ ⟨$10 a head : $10 por cabeza⟩ **7 to come to a head** : llegar a un punto crítico **8 heads or/nor tails** ⟨I can't make heads nor tails of it : para mí no tiene ni pies ni cabeza⟩ **9 heads will roll** : van a rodar cabezas **10 over one's head** ⟨it's over my head : no alcanzo a entenderlo⟩ ⟨the joke went over his head : no entendió el chiste⟩ **11 to be head over heels (in love)** : estar perdidamente enamorado **12 to be out of one's head** : estar como una cabra **13 to go to someone's head** : subírsele a la cabeza a alguien **14 to have a good head on one's shoulders** : tener cabeza **15 to hold one's head high** : ir con la cabeza bien alta **16 to keep/lose one's head** : mantener/perder la calma **17 to keep one's head above water** : mantenerse a flote **18 to keep one's head down** : mantenerse al margen **19 to rear its (ugly) head** : aparecer

headache ['hɛd,eɪk] *n* : dolor *m* de cabeza, jaqueca *f*
headband ['hɛd,bænd] *n* : cinta *f* del pelo
headboard ['hɛd,bɔrd] *n* : cabecera *f*
headdress ['hɛd,drɛs] *n* : tocado *m*
headfirst ['hɛd'fərst] *adv* : de cabeza
headgear ['hɛd,gɪr] *n* : gorro *m*, casco *m*, sombrero *m*
heading ['hɛdɪŋ] *n* **1** DIRECTION : dirección *f* **2** TITLE : encabezamiento *m*, título *m* **3** : membrete *m* (de una carta)
headland ['hɛdlənd, -,lænd] *n* : cabo *m*
headlight ['hɛd,laɪt] *n* : faro *m*, foco *m*, farol *m* Mex
headline ['hɛd,laɪn] *n* : titular *m*
headlong[1] ['hɛd'lɔŋ] *adv* **1** HEADFIRST : de cabeza **2** HASTILY : precipitadamente
headlong[2] ['hɛd,lɔŋ] *adj* : precipitado
headmaster ['hɛd,mæstər] *n* : director *m*
headmistress ['hɛd,mɪstrəs, -'mɪs-] *n* : directora *f*
head-on ['hɛd'ɑn, -'ɔn] *adv & adj* : de frente

headphones ['hɛdˌfoːnz] npl : audífonos mpl, cascos mpl

headquarters ['hɛdˌkwɔrtərz] ns & pl 1 SEAT : oficina f central, sede f 2 : cuartel m general (de los militares)

headrest ['hɛdˌrɛst] n : apoyacabezas m

headroom ['hɛdˌruːm, -ˌrʊm] n : espacio m libre entre la cabeza y el techo (de un coche, etc.)

headset ['hɛdˌsɛt] n : audífonos mpl, cascos mpl

headship ['hɛdˌʃɪp] n : dirección f

head start n : ventaja f

headstone ['hɛdˌstoːn] n : lápida f

headstrong ['hɛdˌstrɔŋ] adj : testarudo, obstinado, empecinado

heads-up ['hɛdzˈʌp] n fam WARNING : aviso m ⟨to give someone a heads-up : avisarle/advertirle a alguien⟩

headwaiter ['hɛdˌweɪtər] n : jefe m, -fa f de comedor

headwaters ['hɛdˌwɔtərz, -ˌwɑ-] npl : cabecera f

headway ['hɛdˌweɪ] n : progreso m ⟨to make headway against : avanzar contra⟩

heady ['hɛdi] adj **headier; -est** 1 INTOXICATING : embriagador, excitante 2 SHREWD : astuto, sagaz

heal ['hiːl] vt : curar, sanar — vi 1 : sanar, curarse ⟨to heal up : cicatrizarse⟩

healer ['hiːlər] n 1 : curandero m, -dera f 2 : curador m, -dora f (cosa)

health ['hɛlθ] n : salud f ⟨health care : asistencia médica⟩ ⟨health center : centro sanitario⟩ ⟨health food : alimentos naturales⟩

healthful ['hɛlθfəl] adj : saludable, salubre — **healthfully** adv

healthiness ['hɛlθinəs] n : lozanía f

healthy ['hɛlθi] adj **healthier; -est** : sano, bien — **healthily** [-θəli] adv

heap¹ ['hiːp] vt 1 PILE : amontonar, apilar 2 SHOWER : colmar

heap² n : montón m, pila f

hear ['hɪr] v **heard** ['hərd]; **hearing** vt 1 : oír ⟨do you hear me? : ¿me oyes?⟩ ⟨I can't hear myself think : no puedo pensar con tanto ruido⟩ 2 HEED : oír, prestar atención a 3 LEARN : oír, enterarse de 4 **to hear out** : escuchar hasta el final — vi 1 : oír ⟨to hear about : oír hablar de⟩ 2 **to hear from** : tener noticias de 3 **to hear of** : oír hablar de ⟨I've heard of him : lo conozco de oídas⟩ 4 **not to hear of** : no permitir ⟨I won't hear of it! : ¡no lo permitiré!, ¡no hablar!⟩ 5 **not/never to hear the end of** ⟨I'll never hear the end of it, she'll never let me hear the end of it : nunca me lo dejará olvidar⟩

hearing ['hɪrɪŋ] n 1 : oído m ⟨hard of hearing : duro de oído⟩ 2 : vista f (en un tribunal) 3 ATTENTION : consideración f, oportunidad f de expresarse 4 EARSHOT : alcance m del oído

hearing aid n : audífono m

hearken ['hɑrkən] vt : escuchar

hearsay ['hɪrˌseɪ] n : rumores mpl

hearse ['hərs] n : coche m fúnebre

heart ['hɑrt] n 1 : corazón m ⟨heart rate : ritmo cardíaco⟩ ⟨heart disease : enfermedades cardíacas⟩ ⟨heart surgery : cirugía cardíaca⟩ ⟨heart murmur : soplo en el corazón⟩ 2 CENTER, CORE : corazón m, centro m ⟨the heart of the matter : el meollo del asunto⟩ 3 FEELINGS : corazón m, sentimientos mpl ⟨a broken heart : un corazón destrozado⟩ ⟨to have a good heart : tener buen corazón⟩ ⟨to take something to heart : tomarse algo a pecho⟩ ⟨from the heart : con toda sinceridad⟩ ⟨to be close to one's heart : significar mucho a alguien⟩ ⟨with a light heart : con el corazón alegre⟩ ⟨with a heavy heart : deprimido, acongojado⟩ ⟨my heart sank : se me cayó el alma a los pies⟩ 4 COURAGE : valor m, corazón m ⟨to take heart : animarse, cobrar ánimos⟩ 5 : corazón m (naipe) 6 **at heart** : en el fondo 7 **by heart** : de memoria 8 **to one's heart's content** : a voluntad, todo lo que quiere

heartache ['hɑrtˌeɪk] n : pena f, angustia f

heart attack n : infarto m, ataque m al corazón

heartbeat ['hɑrtˌbiːt] n : latido m (del corazón)

heartbreak ['hɑrtˌbreɪk] n : congoja f, angustia f

heartbreaker ['hɑrtˌbreɪkər] n : rompecorazones mf

heartbreaking ['hɑrtˌbreɪkɪŋ] adj : desgarrador, que parte el corazón

heartbroken ['hɑrtˌbroːkən] adj : desconsolado, destrozado

heartburn ['hɑrtˌbərn] n : acidez f estomacal

hearten ['hɑrtən] vt : alentar, animar

heartfelt ['hɑrtˌfɛlt] adj : sentido

hearth ['hɑrθ] n : hogar m, chimenea f

heartily ['hɑrtəli] adv 1 ENTHUSIASTICALLY : de buena gana, con entusiasmo 2 TOTALLY : totalmente, completamente

heartless ['hɑrtləs] adj : desalmado, despiadado, cruel

heart of palm n : palmito m

heartsick ['hɑrtˌsɪk] adj : abatido, desconsolado

heartstrings ['hɑrtˌstrɪŋz] npl : fibras fpl del corazón

heartwarming ['hɑrtˌwɔrmɪŋ] adj : conmovedor, emocionante

hearty ['hɑrti] adj **heartier; -est** 1 CORDIAL, WARM : cordial, caluroso 2 STRONG : fuerte ⟨to have a hearty appetite : ser de buen comer⟩ 3 SUBSTANTIAL : abundante, sustancioso ⟨a hearty breakfast : un desayuno abundante⟩

heat¹ ['hiːt] vt : calentar

heat² n 1 WARMTH : calor m 2 HEATING : calefacción f 3 EXCITEMENT : calor m, entusiasmo m ⟨in the heat of the moment : en el calor del momento⟩ 4 ESTRUS : celo m

heated ['hiːtəd] adj 1 WARMED : calentado 2 IMPASSIONED : acalorado, apasionado

heater ['hiːtər] n : calentador m, estufa f, calefactor m

heath ['hiːθ] n 1 MOOR : páramo m 2 HEATHER : brezo m

heathen[1] ['hiːðən] *adj often offensive* : pagano

heathen[2] *n, pl* **-thens** *or* **-then** *often offensive* : pagano *m*, -na *f*; infiel *mf*

heather ['hɛðər] *n* : brezo *m*

heating ['hiːtɪŋ] *n* : calefacción *f*

heat wave *n* : ola *f* de calor

heave[1] ['hiːv] *v* **heaved** *or* **hove** ['hoːv]; **heaving** *vt* **1** LIFT, RAISE : levantar con esfuerzo **2** HURL : lanzar, tirar **3 to heave a sigh** : echar un suspiro, suspirar — *vi* **1** : subir y bajar, palpitar (dícese del pecho) **2 to heave up** RISE : levantarse

heave[2] *n* **1** EFFORT : gran esfuerzo *m* (para levantar algo) **2** THROW : lanzamiento *m*

heaven ['hɛvən] *n* **1** : cielo *m* ⟨for heaven's sake : por Dios⟩ **2 heavens** *npl* SKY : cielo *m* ⟨the heavens opened up : empezó a llover a cántaros⟩

heavenly ['hɛvənli] *adj* **1** : celestial, celeste **2** DELIGHTFUL : divino, encantador

heavily ['hɛvəli] *adv* **1** : mucho, muy ⟨heavily salted foods : comidas muy saladas⟩ ⟨he relies heavily on her : depende mucho de ella⟩ ⟨to smoke/drink heavily : fumar/beber mucho⟩ **2** LABORIOUSLY : pesadamente

heaviness ['hɛvinəs] *n* : peso *m*, pesadez *f*

heavy ['hɛvi] *adj* **heavier; -est** **1** WEIGHTY : pesado ⟨to be heavy : pesar mucho, ser pesado⟩ ⟨how heavy is it? : ¿cuánto pesa?⟩ **2** DENSE, THICK : denso, espeso, grueso ⟨a heavy coat : un grueso abrigo⟩ ⟨a heavy beard : una barba poblada⟩ **3** LARGE, HIGH : grande, alto ⟨heavy turnout : alta concurrencia⟩ **4** INTENSE : intenso ⟨heavy traffic : denso tráfico⟩ ⟨heavy trading : mucha actividad (en la bolsa, etc.)⟩ **5** FORCEFUL : fuerte **6** SEVERE : severo ⟨heavy losses : grandes pérdidas⟩ **7** SERIOUS, IMPORTANT : serio, importante **8** PROFOUND : profundo ⟨to be a heavy sleeper : tener el sueño pesado⟩ **9** FILLING : pesado, fuerte **10** SLUGGISH : lento, tardo **11** STOUT : corpulento

heavy–duty ['hɛvi'duːṭi, -'djuː-] *adj* : muy resistente, fuerte

heavyweight ['hɛvi,weɪt] *n* : peso *m* pesado (en deportes)

Hebrew[1] ['hiː,bruː] *adj* : hebreo

Hebrew[2] *n* **1** : hebreo *m*, -brea *f* **2** : hebreo *m* (idioma)

heck ['hɛk] *n* : ¡caramba!, ¡caray! ⟨a heck of a lot : un montón⟩ ⟨what the heck is . . . ? : ¿que diablos es . . . ?⟩

heckle ['hɛkəl] *vt* **-led; -ling** : interrumpir (a un orador)

hectare ['hɛk,tær] *n* : hectárea *f*

hectic ['hɛktɪk] *adj* : agitado, ajetreado — **hectically** [-tɪkli] *adv*

he'd ['hiːd] *contraction of* HE HAD *or* HE WOULD → **have, would**

hedge[1] ['hɛdʒ] *v* **hedged; hedging** *vt* **1** : cercar con un seto **2 to hedge one's bet** : cubrirse — *vi* **1** : dar rodeos, contestar con evasivas **2 to hedge against** : cubrirse contra, protegerse contra

hedge[2] *n* **1** : seto *m* vivo **2** SAFEGUARD : salvaguardia *f*, protección *f*

hedgehog ['hɛdʒ,hɔg, -hɑg] *n* : erizo *m*

heed[1] ['hiːd] *vt* : prestar atención a, hacer caso de

heed[2] *n* : atención *f*

heedless ['hiːdləs] *adj* : descuidado, despreocupado, inconsciente ⟨to be heedless of : hacer caso omiso de⟩ — **heedlessly** *adv*

heel[1] ['hiːl] *vi* : inclinarse

heel[2] *n* **1** : talón *m* (del pie), tacón *m* (de calzado) **2 to be close/hard/hot on the heels of** : ir pisándole los talones (a alguien), seguir (algo) inmediatamente **3 to cool one's heels** *fam* : esperar **4 to dig one's heels in** : no ceder

heft ['hɛft] *vt* : sopesar

hefty ['hɛfti] *adj* **heftier; -est** : robusto, fornido, pesado

hegemony [hɪ'dʒɛməni] *n, pl* **-nies** : hegemonía *f*

heifer ['hɛfər] *n* : novilla *f*

height ['haɪt] *n* **1** PEAK : cumbre *f*, cima *f*, punto *m* alto ⟨at the height of her career : en la cumbre de su carrera⟩ ⟨the height of stupidity : el colmo de la estupidez⟩ **2** : estatura *f* (de una persona), altura *f* (de un objeto) **3** ALTITUDE : altura *f*

heighten ['haɪtən] *vt* **1** : hacer más alto **2** INTENSIFY : aumentar, intensificar — *vi* : aumentarse, intensificarse

heinous ['heɪnəs] *adj* : atroz, abominable, nefando

heir ['ær] *n* : heredero *m*, -ra *f*

heiress ['ærəs] *n* : heredera *f*

heirloom ['ær,luːm] *n* : reliquia *f* de familia

heist ['haɪst] *n* : golpe *m*, asalto *m*, atraco *m* ⟨to pull a heist : dar un golpe⟩

held → **hold**

helicopter ['hɛlə,kɑptər] *n* : helicóptero *m*

heliport ['hɛlə,pɔrt] *n* : helipuerto *m*

helium ['hiːliəm] *n* : helio *m*

helix ['hiːlɪks] *n, pl* **helices** ['hɛlə,siːz, 'hiː-] *or* **helixes** ['hiːlɪksəz] : hélice *f*

hell ['hɛl] *n* **1** : infierno *m* **2** *(referring to a bad situation)* : a living hell : un auténtico infierno ⟨to go through hell : vivir un infierno, pasar las de Caín⟩ ⟨all hell broke loose : se armó la gorda⟩ **3** *fam (used for emphasis)* ⟨she was mad as hell : estaba que echaba chispas⟩ ⟨a/one hell of a (nice) guy : un tipo genial⟩ ⟨it hurts like hell : duele muchísimo⟩ ⟨to run like hell : correr como loco⟩ ⟨what the hell . . . ? : ¿que diablos/demonios . . . ?⟩ ⟨you scared the hell out of me! : ¡qué susto me pegaste!⟩ **4 come hell or high water** *fam* : sea como sea, pase lo que pase **5 go to hell!** *fam* : ¡vete al infierno! **6 (just) for the hell of it** *fam* : sólo por divertirse **7 like hell** *fam* : malísimo ⟨you look like hell : tienes muy mala cara⟩ ⟨I did/will (etc.)!⟩ *fam* : ¡y un cuerno! **8 there will be hell to pay** *fam* : se va a armar la gorda **10 to catch hell** *fam* ⟨she caught hell from the boss : el jefe le echó la bronca⟩ **11 to give someone hell** 12 **to raise hell** *fam* : armar un buen lío, armar jarana

he'll ['hi:l, 'hɪl] *contraction of* HE SHALL *or* HE WILL → **shall, will**

hellhole ['hɛl,ho:l] *n* : infierno *m*

hellish ['hɛlɪʃ] *adj* : horroroso, infernal

hello [hə'lo:, hɛ-] *interj* : ¡hola!

helm ['hɛlm] *n* 1 : timón *m* 2 **to take the helm** : tomar el mando

helmet ['hɛlmət] *n* : casco *m*

help¹ ['hɛlp] *vt* 1 : ayudar ⟨can I help you? : ¿en qué puedo servirle?⟩ 2 ALLEVIATE : aliviar 3 SERVE : servir ⟨help yourself! : ¡sírvete!⟩ 4 AVOID : evitar ⟨it can't be helped : no lo podemos evitar, no hay más remedio⟩ ⟨I couldn't help smiling : no pude menos que sonreír⟩ 5 **to help out** : echarle una mano a — *vi* 1 : ayudar ⟨I was only trying to help : sólo quería ayudar⟩ 2 **to help out** : echar una mano

help² *n* 1 ASSISTANCE : ayuda *f* ⟨help! : ¡socorro!, ¡auxilio!⟩ ⟨to call for help : pedir ayuda⟩ ⟨to go for help : ir a buscar ayuda⟩ ⟨she was a big help : me ayudó mucho⟩ ⟨she's no help : no me ayuda en absoluto⟩ ⟨thanks for your help : gracias por ayudarme⟩ ⟨help menu/screen : menú/pantalla de ayuda⟩ 2 STAFF : personal *m* (en una oficina), servicio *m* doméstico ⟨help wanted : se necesita personal⟩

help desk *n* : servicio *m* de asistencia (técnica), soporte *m* técnico

helper ['hɛlpər] *n* : ayudante *mf*

helpful ['hɛlpfəl] *adj* 1 OBLIGING : servicial, amable, atento 2 USEFUL : útil, práctico — **helpfully** *adv*

helpfulness ['hɛlpfəlnəs] *n* 1 KINDNESS : bondad *f*, amabilidad *f* 2 USEFULNESS : utilidad *f*

helping ['hɛlpɪŋ] *n* : porción *f*

helpless ['hɛlpləs] *adj* 1 POWERLESS : incapaz, impotente 2 DEFENSELESS : indefenso

helplessly ['hɛlpləsli] *adv* : en vano, inútilmente

helplessness ['hɛlpləsnəs] *n* POWERLESSNESS : incapacidad *f*, impotencia *f*

helter-skelter [,hɛltər'skɛltər] *adv* : atropelladamente, precipitadamente

hem¹ ['hɛm] *vt* **hemmed; hemming** 1 : hacerle el dobladillo a 2 **to hem in** : encerrar

hem² *n* : dobladillo *m*

he-man ['hi:,mæn] *n, pl* -**men** [-mən, -,mɛn] : macho *m*, machote *m*

hematoma [,hi:mə'to:mə] *n* : hematoma *m*

hemisphere ['hɛmə,sfɪr] *n* : hemisferio *m*

hemispheric [,hɛmə'sfɪrɪk, -'sfɛr-] *or* **hemispherical** [-ɪkəl] *adj* : hemisférico

hemline ['hɛm,laɪn] *n* : bajo *m* (de un vestido, etc.)

hemlock ['hɛm,lɑk] *n* : cicuta *f*

hemoglobin ['hi:mə,glo:bən] *n* : hemoglobina *f*

hemophilia [,hi:mə'fɪliə] *n* : hemofilia *f*

hemophiliac [,hi:mə'fɪli,æk] *n* : hemofílico *m*, -ca *f* — **hemophiliac** *adj*

hemorrhage¹ ['hɛmərɪdʒ] *vi* -**rhaged; -rhaging** : sufrir una hemorragia

hemorrhage² *n* : hemorragia *f*

hemorrhoids ['hɛmə,rɔɪdz, 'hɛm-,rɔɪdz] *npl* : hemorroides *fpl*, almorranas *fpl*

hemp ['hɛmp] *n* : cáñamo *m*

hen ['hɛn] *n* : gallina *f*

hence ['hɛnts] *adv* 1 : de aquí, de ahí ⟨10 years hence : de aquí a 10 años⟩ ⟨a dog bit me, hence my dislike of animals : un perro me mordió, de ahí mi aversión a los animales⟩ 2 THEREFORE : por lo tanto, por consiguiente

henceforth ['hɛnts,forθ, ,hɛnts'-] *adv* : de ahora en adelante

henchman ['hɛntʃmən] *n, pl* -**men** [-mən, -,mɛn] : secuaz *mf*, esbirro *m*

henpeck ['hɛn,pɛk] *vt* : dominar (al marido)

hepatitis [,hɛpə'taɪtəs] *n, pl* -**titides** [-'tɪt̬ə,di:z] : hepatitis *f*

her¹ ['hər, ər] *adj* : su, sus, de ella ⟨her house : su casa, la casa de ella⟩

her² *pron* 1 (*used as direct object*) : la ⟨I saw her yesterday : la vi ayer⟩ ⟨I like her : me gusta⟩ 2 (*used as indirect object*) : le, se ⟨he gave her the book : le dio el libro⟩ ⟨he sent it to her : se lo mandó⟩ 3 (*used as object of a preposition*) : ella ⟨we did it for her : lo hicimos por ella⟩ ⟨taller than her : más alto que ella⟩

herald¹ ['hɛrəld] *vt* ANNOUNCE : anunciar, proclamar

herald² *n* 1 MESSENGER : heraldo *m* 2 HARBINGER : precursor *m*

heraldic [hɛ'rældɪk, hə-] *adj* : heráldico

heraldry ['hɛrəldri] *n, pl* -**ries** : heráldica *f*

herb ['ərb, 'hərb] *n* : hierba *f*

herbal ['ərbəl, 'hər-] *adj* : herbario

herbicide ['ərbə,saɪd, 'hər-] *n* : herbicida *m*

herbivore ['ərbə,vor, 'hər-] *n* : herbívoro *m*

herbivorous [,ər'bɪvərəs, ,hər-] *adj* : herbívoro

herculean [,hərkjə'li:ən, ,hər'kju:-liən] *adj* : hercúleo, sobrehumano

herd¹ ['hərd] *vt* : reunir en manada, conducir en manada — *vi* : ir en manada (dícese de los animales), apiñarse (dícese de la gente)

herd² *n* : manada *f*

herder ['hərdər] → **herdsman**

herdsman ['hərdzmən] *n, pl* -**men** [-mən, -,mɛn] : vaquero *m* (de ganado), pastor *m* (de ovejas)

here ['hɪr] *adv* 1 : aquí, acá ⟨come here! : ¡ven acá!⟩ ⟨right here : aquí mismo⟩ ⟨she's not here : no está⟩ 2 NOW : en este momento, ahora, ya ⟨here he comes : ya viene⟩ ⟨here it's three o'clock (already) : ahora son las tres⟩ 3 : en este punto ⟨here we agree : estamos de acuerdo en este punto⟩ 4 **here and now** : ahora mismo, en este mismo momento 5 **here and there** : aquí y allá 6 **here (you are/go)!** : ¡toma! 7 **the here**

and now : el presente, el momento **8 to be neither here nor there** : no venir al caso

hereabouts [ˈhɪrəˌbaʊts] *or* **hereabout** [-ˌbaʊt] *adv* : por aquí (cerca)

hereafter[1] [hɪrˈæftər] *adv* **1** : de aquí en adelante, a continuación **2** : en el futuro

hereafter[2] *n* **the hereafter** : el más allá

hereby [hɪrˈbaɪ] *adv* : por este medio

hereditary [həˈrɛdəˌtɛri] *adj* : hereditario

heredity [həˈrɛdəti] *n* : herencia *f*

herein [hɪrˈɪn] *adv* : aquí

hereof [hɪrˈʌv] *adv* : de aquí

hereon [hɪrˈɑn, -ˈɔn] *adv* : sobre esto

heresy [ˈhɛrəsi] *n*, *pl* **-sies** : herejía *f*

heretic [ˈhɛrəˌtɪk] *n* : hereje *mf*

heretical [həˈrɛtɪkəl] *adj* : herético

hereto [hɪrˈtu] *adv* : a esto

heretofore [ˈhɪrtəˌfor] *adv* HITHERTO : hasta ahora

hereunder [hɪrˈʌndər] *adv* : a continuación, abajo

hereupon [hɪrəˈpɑn, -ˈpɔn] *adv* : con esto, en ese momento

herewith [hɪrˈwɪθ] *adv* : adjunto

heritage [ˈhɛrətɪdʒ] *n* : patrimonio *m* (nacional)

hermaphrodite [hərˈmæfrəˌdaɪt] *n* : hermafrodita *mf*

hermetic [hərˈmɛtɪk] *adj* : hermético — **hermetically** [-tɪkli] *adv*

hermit [ˈhərmət] *n* : ermitaño *m*, -ña *f*; eremita *mf*

hernia [ˈhərniə] *n*, *pl* **-nias** *or* **-niae** [-ni,i:, -ni,aɪ] : hernia *f*

hero [ˈhiːˌroː, ˈhɪrˌoː] *n*, *pl* **-roes 1** : héroe *m* **2** PROTAGONIST : protagonista *m*

heroic [hɪˈroːɪk] *adj* : heroico — **heroically** [-ɪkli] *adv*

heroics [hɪˈroːɪks] *npl* : actos *mpl* heroicos

heroin [ˈhɛroən] *n* : heroína *f*

heroine [ˈhɛroən] *n* **1** : heroína *f* **2** PROTAGONIST : protagonista *f*

heroism [ˈhɛroˌɪzəm] *n* : heroísmo *m*

heron [ˈhɛrən] *n* : garza *f*

herpes [ˈhərˌpiːz] *n* : herpes *m*

herring [ˈhɛrɪŋ] *n*, *pl* **-ring** *or* **-rings** : arenque *m*

hers [ˈhərz] *pron* : suyo, de ella ⟨these suitcases are hers : estas maletas son suyas⟩ ⟨hers are bigger : los de ella son más grandes⟩

herself [hərˈsɛlf] *pron* **1** (*used reflexively*) : se ⟨she dressed herself : se vistió⟩ **2** (*used emphatically*) : ella misma ⟨she fixed it herself : lo arregló ella misma, lo arregló por sí sola⟩

hertz [ˈhərts, ˈhrts] *ns & pl* : hercio *m*

he's [ˈhiːz] *contraction of* HE IS *or* HE HAS → **have**

hesitancy [ˈhɛzətənsi] *n*, *pl* **-cies** : vacilación *f*, titubeo *m*, indecisión *f*

hesitant [ˈhɛzətənt] *adj* : titubeante, vacilante — **hesitantly** *adv*

hesitate [ˈhɛzəˌteɪt] *vi* **-tated; -tating** : vacilar, titubear

hesitation [ˌhɛzəˈteɪʃən] *n* : vacilación *f*, indecisión *f*, titubeo *m*

heterogeneous [ˌhɛtərəˈdʒiːniəs, -njəs] *adj* : heterogéneo

heterosexual[1] [ˌhɛtəroˈsɛkʃʊəl] *adj* : heterosexual

heterosexual[2] *n* : heterosexual *mf*

heterosexuality [ˌhɛtəroˌsɛkʃʊˈæləti] *n* : heterosexualidad *f*

hew [ˈhjuː] *v* **hewed; hewed** *or* **hewn** [ˈhjuːn]; **hewing** *vt* **1** CUT : cortar, talar (árboles) **2** SHAPE : labrar, tallar — *vi* CONFORM : conformarse, ceñirse

hex[1] [ˈhɛks] *vt* : hacerle un maleficio (a alguien)

hex[2] *n* : maleficio *m*

hexagon [ˈhɛksəˌɡɑn] *n* : hexágono *m*

hexagonal [hɛkˈsæɡənəl] *adj* : hexagonal

hey [ˈheɪ] *interj* : ¡eh!, ¡oye!

heyday [ˈheɪˌdeɪ] *n* : auge *m*, apogeo *m*

hi [ˈhaɪ] *interj* : ¡hola!

hiatus [haɪˈeɪtəs] *n* **1** : hiato *m* **2** PAUSE : pausa *f*

hibernate [ˈhaɪbərˌneɪt] *vi* **-nated; -nating** : hibernar, invernar

hibernation [ˌhaɪbərˈneɪʃən] *n* : hibernación *f*

hiccup[1] [ˈhɪkəp] *vi* **-cuped; -cuping** : hipar, tener hipo

hiccup[2] *n* : hipo *m* ⟨to have the hiccups : tener hipo⟩

hick [ˈhɪk] *n* BUMPKIN : palurdo *m*, -da *f*

hickory [ˈhɪkəri] *n*, *pl* **-ries** : nogal *m* americano

hidden [ˈhɪdən] *adj* : oculto

hide[1] [ˈhaɪd] *v* **hid** [ˈhɪd]; **hidden** [ˈhɪdən] *or* **hid; hiding** *vt* **1** : esconder ⟨to be in hiding : estar escondido⟩ **2** : ocultar (los sentimientos, etc.) **3** SCREEN : tapar, no dejar ver — *vi* : esconderse

hide[2] *n* : piel *f*, cuero *m* ⟨to save one's hide : salvar el pellejo⟩

hide-and-seek [ˈhaɪdəndˈsiːk] *n* **to play hide-and-seek** : jugar a las escondidas

hidebound [ˈhaɪdˌbaʊnd] *adj* : rígido, conservador

hideous [ˈhɪdiəs] *adj* : horrible, horroroso, espantoso — **hideously** *adv*

hideout [ˈhaɪdˌaʊt] *n* : guarida *f*, escondrijo *m*

hiding [ˈhaɪdɪŋ] *n* **1** *chiefly Brit fam* : paliza *f* **2 to be in hiding** : estar escondido

hierarchical [ˌhaɪəˈrɑrkɪkəl] *adj* : jerárquico

hierarchy [ˈhaɪəˌrɑrki] *n*, *pl* **-chies** : jerarquía *f*

hieroglyphic [ˌhaɪərəˈɡlɪfɪk] *n* : jeroglífico *m*

hi-fi [ˈhaɪˈfaɪ] *n* **1** → **high fidelity 2** : equipo *m* de alta fidelidad

high[1] [ˈhaɪ] *adv* **1** : alto ⟨to aim high : apuntar alto⟩ **2 high and low** : por todas partes **3 to leave high and dry** : dejar tirado

high[2] *adj* **1** TALL : alto ⟨a high wall : un muro alto⟩ ⟨it's two feet high : tiene dos pies de altura⟩ ⟨waist-high : que llega hasta la cintura⟩ ⟨the highest mountain : la montaña más alta⟩ **2** ELEVATED : alto, elevado ⟨high ground : terreno elevado⟩ ⟨high prices : precios elevados⟩ ⟨high blood pressure : presión alta⟩ ⟨at a

high rate of speed : a gran velocidad⟩ **3**
GREAT : grande ⟨a high number : un
número grande⟩ ⟨high hopes : grandes
esperanzas⟩ **4** GOOD, FAVORABLE
: bueno, favorable ⟨in high esteem : en
gran estima⟩ ⟨on a high note : con una
nota de optimismo⟩ ⟨the high point of
the trip : el mejor momento del viaje⟩ **5**
STRONG : fuerte ⟨high winds : fuertes
vientos⟩ **6** : alto ⟨high society : alta so-
ciedad⟩ ⟨high-ranking : alto, de alto
rango⟩ ⟨the high life : la gran vida⟩ **7**
: alto (en música) **8** : pleno ⟨in high
summer : en pleno verano⟩ **9** INTOXI-
CATED : borracho, drogado

high³ n **1** : récord m, punto m máximo
⟨to reach an all-time high : batir el ré-
cord⟩ **2** : zona f de alta presión (en meteorología) **3 or high gear** : directa f **4
on high** : en las alturas

highbrow ['haɪˌbraʊ] n : intelectual mf

high chair n : silla f alta (para bebé), periquera f Mex, trona f Spain

high-definition ['haɪˌdɛfə'nɪʃən] adj :
alta definición (dícese de una televisión)

high-end ['haɪ'ɛnd] : de lujo

higher ['haɪər] adj : superior ⟨higher education : enseñanza f superior⟩

high fidelity n : alta fidelidad f

high-flown ['haɪ'floːn] adj : altisonante

high-handed ['haɪ'hændəd] adj : arbitrario

high-heeled ['haɪ'hiːld] adj : de tacón alto

highlands ['haɪləndz] npl : tierras fpl
altas, altiplano m

high-level ['haɪ'lɛvəl] adj : de alta nivel

highlight¹ ['haɪˌlaɪt] vt **1** EMPHASIZE : destacar, poner en relieve, subrayar **2** : ser
el punto culminante de

highlight² n : punto m culminante

highlighter ['haɪˌlaɪtər] n : marcador m,
rotulador m Spain

highly ['haɪli] adv **1** VERY : muy, sumamente **2** FAVORABLY : muy bien ⟨to
speak highly of : hablar muy bien de⟩
⟨to think highly of : tener en mucho a⟩

highness ['haɪnəs] n **1** HEIGHT : altura
f **2 Highness** : Alteza f ⟨Your Royal
Highness : Su Alteza Real⟩

high-pitched ['haɪ'pɪtʃt] adj : agudo

high-rise ['haɪˌraɪz] adj : alto, de muchas
plantas

high school n : escuela f superior, escuela
f secundaria

high seas npl : alta mar f

high-speed ['haɪ'spiːd] adj : de alta veloci-
cidad

high-spirited ['haɪ'spɪrətəd] adj : vivaz,
muy animado, brioso

high-strung [ˌhaɪ'strʌŋ] adj : nervioso

high-tech ['haɪ'tɛk] adj : de alta tecnología

high-tension ['haɪ'tɛntʃən] adj : de alta
tensión

high-voltage ['haɪ'voːltɪdʒ] adj : de alto
voltaje

highway ['haɪˌweɪ] n : carretera f

highwayman ['haɪˌweɪmən] n, pl **-men**
[-mən, -ˌmɛn] : salteador m (de caminos), bandido m

hijab [hɪ'dʒɑb] n : hiyab m, hijab m

hijack¹ ['haɪˌdʒæk] vt : secuestrar

hijack² n : secuestro m

hijacker ['haɪˌdʒækər] n : secuestrador m,
-dora f

hike¹ ['haɪk] v **hiked; hiking** vi : hacer una
caminata — vt RAISE : subir

hike² n **1** : caminata f, excursión f **2** IN-
CREASE : subida f (de precios)

hiker ['haɪkər] n : excursionista mf

hilarious [hɪ'læriəs, haɪ-] adj : muy divertido, hilarante

hilarity [hɪ'lærəti, haɪ-] n : hilaridad f

hill ['hɪl] n **1** : colina f, cerro m **2** SLOPE
: cuesta f, pendiente f

hillbilly ['hɪlˌbɪli] n, pl **-lies** often disparaging + offensive : palurdo m, -da f (de las
montañas)

hillock ['hɪlək] n : loma f, altozano m,
otero m

hillside ['hɪlˌsaɪd] n : ladera f, cuesta f

hilltop ['hɪlˌtɑp] n : cima f, cumbre f

hilly ['hɪli] adj **hillier; -est** : montañoso,
accidentado

hilt ['hɪlt] n : puño m, empuñadura f

him ['hɪm, əm] pron **1** (used as direct object) : lo ⟨I found him : lo encontré⟩ **2**
(used as indirect object) : le, se ⟨we gave
him a present : le dimos un regalo⟩ ⟨I
sent it to him : se lo mandé⟩ **3** (used as
object of a preposition) : él ⟨she was
thinking of him : pensaba en él⟩
⟨younger than him : más joven que él⟩

himself [hɪm'sɛlf, əm-] pron **1** (used reflexively) : se ⟨he washed himself : se
lavó⟩ **2** (used emphatically) : él mismo
⟨he did it himself : lo hizo él mismo, lo
hizo por sí solo⟩

hind¹ ['haɪnd] adj : trasero, posterior
⟨hind legs : patas traseras⟩

hind² n : cierva f

hinder ['hɪndər] vt : dificultar, impedir,
estorbar

Hindi ['hɪndiː] n : hindi m

hindquarters ['haɪndˌkwɔrtərz] npl : cuartos mpl traseros

hindrance ['hɪndrəns] n : estorbo m,
obstáculo m, impedimento m

hindsight ['haɪndˌsaɪt] n : retrospectiva f
⟨with the benefit of hindsight : en retrospectiva, con la perspectiva que da la
experiencia⟩

Hindu¹ ['hɪnˌduː] adj : hindú

Hindu² n : hindú mf

Hinduism ['hɪnduˌɪzəm] n : hinduismo m

hinge¹ ['hɪndʒ] v **hinged; hinging** vt : unir
con bisagras — vi **to hinge on/upon**
: depender de

hinge² n : bisagra f, gozne m

hint¹ ['hɪnt] vt : insinuar, dar a entender —
vi : soltar indirectas

hint² n **1** INSINUATION : insinuación f,
indirecta f **2** TIP : consejo m, sugerencia
f **3** TRACE : pizca f, indicio m

hinterland ['hɪntərˌlænd, -lənd] n : interior m (de un país)

hip ['hɪp] n : cadera f

hip-hop ['hɪpˌhɑp] n : hip-hop m

hippie ['hɪpi] n : hippie mf, hippy mf

hippo ['hɪpoː] n, pl **hippos** → **hippopotamus**

hippopotamus [ˌhɪpəˈpɑṭəməs] *n, pl* **-muses** *or* **-mi** [-ˌmaɪ] : hipopótamo *m*

hire¹ [ˈhaɪr] *vt* **hired; hiring** **1** EMPLOY : contratar, emplear **2** RENT : alquilar, arrendar

hire² *n* **1** RENT : alquiler *m* ⟨for hire : se alquila⟩ **2** WAGES : paga *f*, sueldo *m* **3** EMPLOYEE : empleado *m*, -da *f*

his¹ [ˈhɪz, ɪz] *adj* : su, sus, de él ⟨his hat : su sombrero, el sombrero de él⟩

his² *pron* : suyo, de él ⟨the decision is his : la decisión es suya⟩ ⟨it's his, not hers : es de él, no de ella⟩

Hispanic¹ [hɪˈspænɪk] *adj* : hispano, hispánico

Hispanic² *n* : hispano *m*, -na *f*; hispánico *m*, -ca *f*

hiss¹ [ˈhɪs] *vi* : sisear, silbar — *vt* : decir entre dientes

hiss² *n* : siseo *m*, silbido *m*

historian [hɪˈstɔriən] *n* : historiador *m*, -dora *f*

historic [hɪˈstɔrɪk] *or* **historical** [-ɪkəl] *adj* : histórico — **historically** [-kli] *adv*

history [ˈhɪstəri] *n, pl* **-ries** **1** : historia *f* **2** RECORD : historial *m* ⟨family history : historial personal⟩ **3 to go down in history** : pasar a la historia **4 to go down in history** : hacer historia

histrionics [ˌhɪstriˈɑnɪks] *ns & pl* : histrionismo *m*

hit¹ [ˈhɪt] *v* **hit; hitting** *vt* **1** STRIKE : golpear (algo), pegarle a (alguien), batear (una pelota) ⟨he hit the dog : le pegó al perro⟩ **2** : chocar contra, dar con, dar en (el blanco) ⟨the car hit a tree : el coche chocó contra un árbol⟩ ⟨it hit me in the face : me dio en la cara⟩ ⟨he hit his head against the door : se dio con la cabeza contra la puerta⟩ **3** *fam* OPERATE : apretar (un botón), darle a (un freno, un interruptor, etc.) **4** ATTACK : atacar **5** AFFECT : afectar ⟨the news hit us hard : la noticia nos afectó mucho⟩ **6** ENCOUNTER : tropezar con, toparse con ⟨to hit a snag : tropezar con un obstáculo⟩ **7** : ocurrírsele a uno ⟨it hit me that . . . : se me ocurrió que . . . , me di cuenta de que . . .⟩ **8** REACH : llegar a, alcanzar ⟨the price hit $10 a pound : el precio alcanzó los $10 dólares por libra⟩ ⟨to hit the headlines : ser noticia⟩ **9** ARRIVE AT : llegar a ⟨to hit town : llegar a la ciudad⟩ ⟨let's hit the beach! : ¡vamos a la playa!⟩ **10** MAKE : hacer ⟨to hit a home run : hacer un jonrón⟩ **11 to hit it off (with)** : congeniar (con) **12 to hit someone up for something** : pedirle algo a alguien **13 to hit the ceiling/roof** *fam* : poner el grito en el cielo **14 to hit the hay/sack** *fam* : irse al catre, acostarse **15 to hit the nail on the head** *fam* : dar en el clavo **16 to hit the road** *fam* : ponerse en marcha — *vi* **1** : golpear **2 to hit back** : devolver el golpe **3 to hit on** *fam* : tratar de ligarse a **4 to hit on/upon** : dar con (una solución, etc.)

hit² *n* **1** BLOW : golpe *m* **2** : impacto *m* (de un arma) **3** SUCCESS : éxito *m* **4** : visita *f* (a un sitio Web)

hit-and-run [ˌhɪtənˈrʌn] *adj* **1** : en que el conductor culpable se da a la fuga (dícese de un accidente de tránsito) **2** : fugitivo (dícese de un conductor)

hitch¹ [ˈhɪtʃ] *vt* **1** : mover con sacudidas **2** ATTACH : enganchar, atar, amarrar **3 to hitch up** : subirse (los pantalones, etc.) — *vi → **hitchhike**

hitch² *n* **1** JERK : tirón *m*, jalón *m* **2** OBSTACLE : obstáculo *m*, impedimento *m*, tropiezo *m*

hitchhike [ˈhɪtʃˌhaɪk] *vi* **-hiked; -hiking** : hacer autostop, ir de aventón *Col, Mex fam*

hitchhiker [ˈhɪtʃˌhaɪkər] *n* : autostopista *mf*

hither [ˈhɪðər] *adv* : acá, por aquí

hitherto [ˈhɪðərˌtuː, ˌhɪðərˈ-] *adv* : hasta ahora

hit man *n* : sicario *m*, -ria *f*; asesino *m*, -na *f*

hitter [ˈhɪṭər] *n* BATTER : bateador *m*, -dora *f*

HIV [ˌeɪtʃˌaɪˈviː] *n* (*human immunodeficiency virus*) : VIH *m*, virus *m* del sida ⟨HIV negative/positive : VIH negativo/positivo⟩

hive [ˈhaɪv] *n* **1** : colmena *f* **2** SWARM : enjambre *m* **3** : lugar *m* muy activo ⟨a hive of activity : un hervidero de actividad⟩

hives [ˈhaɪvz] *ns & pl* : urticaria *f*

hoard¹ [ˈhord] *vt* : acumular, atesorar

hoard² *n* : tesoro *m*, reserva *f*, provisión *f*

hoarfrost [ˈhorˌfrɔst] *n* : escarcha *f*

hoarse [ˈhors] *adj* **hoarser; hoarsest** : ronco — **hoarsely** *adv*

hoarseness [ˈhorsnəs] *n* : ronquera *f*

hoary [ˈhori] *adj* **hoarier; -est** **1** : cano, canoso **2** OLD : vetusto, antiguo

hoax¹ [ˈhoːks] *vt* : engañar, embaucar, bromear

hoax² *n* : engaño *m*, broma *f*

hobble¹ [ˈhɑbəl] *v* **-bled; -bling** *vi* LIMP : cojear, renguear

hobble² *n* LIMP : cojera *f*, rengo *m*

hobby [ˈhɑbi] *n, pl* **-bies** : pasatiempo *m*, afición *f*

hobgoblin [ˈhɑbˌgɑblən] *n* : duende *m*

hobnail [ˈhɑbˌneɪl] *n* : tachuela *f*

hobnob [ˈhɑbˌnɑb] *vi* **-nobbed; -nobbing** : codearse

hobo [ˈhoːˌboː] *n, pl* **-boes** : vagabundo *m*, -da *f*

hock¹ [ˈhɑk] *vt* PAWN : empeñar

hock² *n* **in hock** : empeñado

hockey [ˈhɑki] *n* : hockey *m*

hodgepodge [ˈhɑdʒˌpɑdʒ] *n* : mezcolanza *f*

hoe¹ [ˈhoː] *vt* **hoed; hoeing** : remover con una azada

hoe² *n* : azada *f*

hog¹ [ˈhɔg, ˈhɑg] *vt* **hogged; hogging** : acaparar, monopolizar

hog² *n* **1** PIG : cerdo *m*, -da *f* GLUTTON : glotón *m*, -tona *f*

hogshead [ˈhɔgzˌhed, ˈhɑgz-] *n* : tonel *m*

hoist¹ [ˈhɔɪst] *vt* : levantar, alzar, izar (una bandera, una vela)

hoist² *n* : grúa *f*

hold¹ ['hoːld] *v* **held** ['hɛld]; **holding** *vt* **1**
POSSESS : tener ⟨to hold office : ocupar
un puesto⟩ **2** RESTRAIN : detener, controlar ⟨to hold one's temper : controlar
su mal genio⟩ **3** CLASP, GRASP : agarrar, coger ⟨to hold hands : agarrarse de
la mano⟩ ⟨hold it tightly : agárralo
fuerte⟩ **4** CARRY : llevar, tener (en la
mano o las manos) **5** : sujetar, mantener fijo ⟨hold this nail for me : su-
jétame este clavo⟩ ⟨hold it upright
: mantenlo derecho⟩ ⟨hold the door
: sostén la puerta⟩ **6** CONTAIN : dar cabida a, tener capacidad para (personas,
etc.), tener una capacidad de (litros,
etc.) **7** *or* **to hold in store** : deparar **8**
SUPPORT : aguantar, sostener **9** RE-
GARD : considerar, tener ⟨he held me
responsible : me consideró respon-
sable⟩ **10** CONDUCT : celebrar (una reunión, una elección), realizar (un
evento), mantener (una conversación) **11** KEEP, RESERVE : guardar **12** MAINTAIN : mantener **13** DE-
TAIN : detener **14** **to hold against**
: tomar en cuenta, guardar rencor
por **15** **to hold back** REPRESS, CONTAIN
: reprimir, contener **16** **to hold back**
WITHHOLD : retener, ocultar (información) **17** **to hold down** : conservar
(un trabajo) **18** **to hold in** CONTAIN
: contener **19** **to hold off** RESIST : resistir **20** **to hold one's liquor** : ser de
buen beber **21** **to hold one's tongue**
: callarse **22** **to hold out** : extender, tender (la mano, etc.), dar (esperanzas) **23**
to hold over POSTPONE : postergar, aplazar **24** **to hold up** DELAY : retrasar **25**
to hold up LIFT : levantar **26** **to hold
up** *fam* ROB : robarle (a alguien), atracar, asaltar — *vi* **1** : aguantar, resistir
⟨the rope will hold : la cuerda re-
sistirá⟩ **2** : ser válido, valer ⟨my offer
still holds : mi oferta todavía es
válida⟩ **3** **to hold forth** : perorar, arén-
gar **4** **to hold off** WAIT : esperar, aguantar **5** **to hold off (on)** DELAY : retrasar **6** **to hold on** WAIT : esperar,
aguantar **7** **to hold on to** : agarrarse
a **8** **to hold out** LAST : aguantar, durar **9** **to hold out** RESIST : resistir **10** **to
hold out for** AWAIT : esperar (algo me-
jor) **11** **to hold to** : mantenerse firme
en **12** **to hold together** : mantenerse
unidos **13** **to hold up** : aguantar ⟨how
are you holding up? : ¿cómo estás?,
¿cómo lo estás llevando?⟩ **14** **to hold
with** : estar de acuerdo con

hold² *n* **1** GRIP : agarre *m*, llave *f* (en deportes) **2** CONTROL : control *m*, dominio
m ⟨to get hold of oneself : controlarse⟩ **3**
DELAY : demora *f* **4** : bodega *f* (en un
barco o un avión) **5** **on hold** DELAYED
: suspendido ⟨to put on hold : suspender
temporalmente⟩ **6** **on hold** : en espera
(en el teléfono) ⟨to be/put on hold : estar/
poner en espera⟩ **7** **no holds barred** : sin
restricciones **8** **to get hold of** : conseguir,
localizar **9** **to take hold** : establecerse **10**
to take hold of GRASP : agarrar

holder ['hoːldər] *n* : poseedor *m*, -dora *f*;
titular *mf*

holdings ['hoːldɪŋz] *npl* : propiedades *fpl*

holdup ['hoːldˌʌp] *n* **1** ROBBERY : atraco
m **2** DELAY : retraso *m*, demora *f*

hole ['hoːl] *n* : agujero *m*, hoyo *m*

holiday ['hɑːləˌdeɪ] *n* **1** : día *m* feriado,
fiesta *f* ⟨happy holidays : felices fies-
tas⟩ **2** VACATION : vacaciones *fpl*

holiness ['hoːlinəs] *n* **1** : santidad *f* **2**
His Holiness : Su Santidad

holistic [hoːˈlɪstɪk] *adj* : holístico

holler¹ ['hɑːlər] *vi* : gritar, chillar

holler² *n* : grito *m*, chillido *m*

hollow¹ ['hɑːloː] *vt* *or* **to hollow out**
: ahuecar

hollow² *adj* **hollower; -est 1** : hueco,
hundido (dícese de las mejillas, etc.),
cavernoso (dícese de un sonido) **2**
EMPTY, FALSE : vacío, falso

hollow³ *n* **1** CAVITY : hueco *m*, depresión
f, cavidad *f* **2** VALLEY : hondonada *f*,
valle *m*

hollowness ['hɑːloːnəs] *n* **1** HOLLOW
: hueco *m*, cavidad *f* **2** FALSENESS
: falsedad *f* **3** EMPTINESS : vacuidad *f*

holly ['hɑːli] *n, pl* **-lies** : acebo *m*

holocaust ['hɑːləˌkɔːst, 'hoː-, 'hɔː-] *n* : holocausto *m*

hologram ['hoːləˌgræm, 'hɑː-] *n* : holograma *m*

holster ['hoːlstər] *n* : pistolera *f*

holy ['hoːli] *adj* **holier; -est** : santo, sagrado

Holy Ghost → Holy Spirit

holy orders → order²

Holy Spirit *n* **the Holy Spirit** : el Espíritu
Santo

homage ['ɑːmɪdʒ, 'hɑː-] *n* : homenaje *m*

home ['hoːm] *n* **1** : hogar *m*, casa *f* ⟨home
sweet home : hogar dulce hogar⟩ ⟨there's
no place like home : como en casa no se
está en ningún sitio⟩ ⟨to leave home : irse
de casa⟩ ⟨to hit close to home : tocar muy
de cerca⟩ **2** HOUSE, RESIDENCE : casa *f*,
domicilio *m* ⟨to own one's own home
: tener casa propia⟩ ⟨a home away from
home : una segunda casa⟩ **3** SEAT : sede
f **4** HABITAT : hábitat *m* **5** INSTITUTION
: residencia *f*, asilo *m* **6** → **home plate** **7**
at home : en casa ⟨is Julia at home? : ¿está
Julia (en casa)?⟩ **8** **at home** : cómodo
⟨make yourself at home : estás en tu
casa⟩ **9** **to play at home** : jugar en casa

homebody ['hoːmˌbɑːdi] *n, pl* **-dies** : persona *f* hogareña

homecoming ['hoːmˌkʌmɪŋ] *n* : regreso *m*
(a casa)

home game *n* : partido *m* en casa

homegrown ['hoːmˈɡroːn] *adj* **1** : de cosecha propia **2** LOCAL : local

homeland ['hoːmˌlænd] *n* : patria *f*, tierra
f natal, terruño *m*

homeless ['hoːmləs] *adj* : sin hogar, sin
techo

homely ['hoːmli] *adj* **homelier; -est 1**
DOMESTIC : casero, hogareño **2** UGLY
: feo, poco atractivo

homemade ['hoːmˈmeɪd] *adj* : casero,
hecho en casa

homemaker ['ho:m,meɪkər] n : ama f de casa, persona f que se ocupa de la casa
homeopathy [,ho:mi'apəθi] n : homeopatía f — **homeopathic** adj
home page n : página f de inicio
home plate n : base f del bateador
home run n : jonrón m
homesick ['ho:m,sɪk] adj : nostálgico ⟨to be homesick : echar de menos a la familia⟩
homesickness ['ho:m,sɪknəs] n : nostalgia f, morriña f
homespun ['ho:m,spʌn] adj : simple, sencillo
homestead ['ho:m,sted] n : estancia f, hacienda f
hometown ['ho:m,taʊn] n : ciudad f natal, pueblo m natal
homeward[1] ['ho:mwərd] or **homewards** [-wərdz] adv : de vuelta a casa, hacia casa
homeward[2] adj : de vuelta, de regreso
homework ['ho:m,wərk] n : tarea f, deberes mpl Spain, asignación f PRi
homey ['ho:mi] adj **homier; -est** : hogareño
homicidal [,homə'saɪdəl, ,ho:-] adj : homicida
homicide ['homə,saɪd, 'ho:-] n : homicidio m
homily ['homəli] n, pl **-lies** : homilía f
hominy ['homəni] n : maíz m descascarado
homogeneity [,ho:mədʒə'ni:əti, -'neɪ-] n, pl **-ties** : homogeneidad f
homogeneous [,ho:mə'dʒi:niəs, -njəs] adj : homogéneo — **homogeneously** adv
homogenize [ho:'madʒə,naɪz, hə-] vt **-nized; -nizing** : homogeneizar
homograph ['homə,græf, 'ho:-] n : homógrafo m
homologous [ho:'maləgəs, hə-] adj : homólogo
homonym ['homə,nɪm, 'ho:-] n : homónimo m
homophone ['homə,fo:n, 'ho:-] n : homófono m
homosexual[1] [,ho:mə'sɛkʃuəl] adj : homosexual
homosexual[2] n : homosexual mf
homosexuality [,ho:mə,sɛkʃu'æləti] n : homosexualidad f
honcho ['han,tʃo:] n : pez m gordo ⟨the head honcho : el jefe⟩
Honduran [han'dʊrən, -'djʊr-] n : hondureño m, -ña f — **Honduran** adj
hone ['ho:n] vt **honed; honing** : afilar
honest ['anəst] adj : honesto, honrado — **honestly** adv
honesty ['anəsti] n, pl **-ties** : honestidad f, honradez f
honey ['hʌni] n, pl **-eys** : miel f
honeybee ['hʌni,bi:] n : abeja f
honeycomb ['hʌni,ko:m] n : panal m
honeymoon[1] ['hʌni,mu:n] vi : pasar la luna de miel
honeymoon[2] n : luna f de miel
honeysuckle ['hʌni,sʌkəl] n : madreselva f
honk[1] ['haŋk, 'hɔŋk] vi **1** : graznar

(dícese del ganso) **2** : tocar la bocina (dícese de un vehículo), pitar
honk[2] n : graznido m (del ganso), bocinazo m (de un vehículo)
honor[1] ['anər] vt **1** RESPECT : honrar **2** : cumplir con ⟨to honor one's word : cumplir con su palabra⟩ **3** : aceptar (un cheque, etc.)
honor[2] n **1** : honor m ⟨in honor of : en honor de⟩ ⟨a man of honor : un hombre de honor/palabra⟩ ⟨guest of honor : invitado de honor⟩ **2 honors** npl AWARDS : honores mpl, condecoraciones fpl **3 on my honor** : juro por mi honor **4 to do someone the honor of** : hacerle a alguien el honor de **5 to do the honors** : hacer los honores **6 Your Honor** : Su Señoría
honorable ['anərəbəl] adj : honorable, honroso — **honorably** [-bli] adv
honorary ['anə,rɛri] adj : honorario
hood ['hʊd] n **1** : capucha f **2** : capó m, bonete m Car (de un automóvil)
hooded ['hʊdəd] adj : encapuchado
hoodie ['hʊdi] n **1** : sudadera f (con capucha); buzo m Arg, Col
hoodlum ['hʊdləm, 'hu:d-] n THUG : maleante mf, matón m
hoodwink ['hʊd,wɪŋk] vt : engañar
hoof ['hʊf, 'hu:f] n, pl **hooves** ['hʊvz, 'hu:vz] or **hoofs** : pezuña f, casco m
hoofed ['hʊft, 'hu:ft] adj : ungulado
hook[1] ['hʊk] vt **1** : enganchar **2** CATCH : pescar **3 to hook up** CONNECT : conectar (algo a algo) **4 to hook up** fam ⟨don't worry — I'll hook you up : no te preocupes, te lo arreglaré todo⟩ — vi **1** : abrocharse, engancharse **2 to hook up** fam MEET : reunirse **3 to hook up** fam JOIN, UNITE : juntarse, unirse **4 to hook up** fam : tener sexo
hook[2] n **1** : gancho m, percha f **2 to let someone off the hook** : dejar a alguien ir sin castigo
hooked ['hʊkt] adj **1** : en forma de gancho **2 to be hooked on** : estar enganchado a
hooker ['hʊkər] n : prostituta f, fulana f fam
hookworm ['hʊk,wərm] n : anquilostoma m
hooligan ['hu:lɪgən] n : gamberro m, -rra f
hoop ['hu:p] n : aro m
hooray [hʊ'reɪ] → **hurrah**
hoot[1] ['hu:t] vi **1** SHOUT : gritar **2** : ulular (dícese de un búho), tocar la bocina (dícese de un vehículo), silbar (dícese de un tren o un barco) **3** or **to hoot with laughter** : reírse a carcajadas
hoot[2] n **1** : ululato m (de un búho), silbido m (de un tren), bocinazo m (de un vehículo) **2** GUFFAW : carcajada f, risotada f **3 I don't give a hoot** : me vale un comino, me importa un pito
hop[1] ['hap] vi **hopped; hopping** : brincar, saltar
hop[2] n **1** LEAP : salto m, brinco m **2** FLIGHT : vuelo m corto **3** : lúpulo m (planta)

hope[1] ['ho:p] v **hoped; hoping** vi : esperar — vt : esperar que ⟨we hope she comes : esperamos que venga⟩ ⟨I hope so/not : espero que sí/no⟩

hope[2] n : esperanza f ⟨to have high hopes of : tener muchas esperanzas de⟩ ⟨to get one's hopes up : hacerse ilusiones⟩ ⟨in the hope of : con la esperanza de⟩ ⟨in the hope that : con la esperanza de que⟩

hopeful ['ho:pfəl] adj : esperanzado

hopefully ['ho:pfəli] adj **1** : con esperanza ⟨"it's a good sign," she said hopefully : "es buena señal," dijo esperanzada⟩ **2** ⟨hopefully, it won't rain : ojalá no llueva, espero que no llueva⟩ ⟨the rain will hopefully continue : se espera que las lluvias continúen⟩

hopeless ['ho:pləs] adj **1** DESPAIRING : desesperado **2** IMPOSSIBLE : imposible ⟨a hopeless case : un caso perdido⟩

hopelessly ['ho:pləsli] adv **1** : sin esperanzas, desesperadamente **2** COMPLETELY : totalmente, completamente **3** IMPOSSIBLY : imposiblemente

hopelessness ['ho:pləsnəs] n : desesperanza f

hopper ['hɑpər] n : tolva f

hopping[1] adv to be hopping mad : estar furioso

hopping[2] adj BUSY : animado, concurrido

hopscotch ['hɑp,skɑtʃ] n : tejo m

horde ['hɔrd] n : horda f, multitud f

horizon [hə'raɪzən] n : horizonte m

horizontal [,hɔrə'zɑntəl] adj : horizontal — **horizontally** adv

hormone ['hɔr,mo:n] n : hormona f — **hormonal** [hɔr'mo:nəl] adj

horn ['hɔrn] n **1** : cuerno m (de un toro, una vaca, etc.) **2** : cuerno m, trompa f (instrumento musical) **3** : bocina f, claxon m (de un vehículo)

horned ['hɔrnd, 'hɔrnəd] adj : cornudo, astado, con cuernos

hornet ['hɔrnət] n : avispón m

horny ['hɔrni] adj **hornier; -est 1** CALLOUS : calloso **2** LUSTFUL fam : caliente fam

horoscope ['hɔrə,sko:p] n : horóscopo m

horrendous [hə'rendəs] adj : horrendo, horroroso, atroz

horrible ['hɔrəbəl] adj : horrible, espantoso, horroroso — **horribly** [-bli] adv

horrid ['hɔrəd] adj : horroroso, horrible — **horridly** adv

horrific [hə'rɪfɪk] adj : terrorífico, horroroso

horrify ['hɔrə,faɪ] vt **-fied; -fying** : horrorizar

horrifying ['hɔrə,faɪɪŋ] adj : horripilante, horroroso

horror ['hɔrər] n : horror m

hors d'oeuvre [ɔr'dərv] n, pl **hors d'oeuvres** [-'dərvz] : entremés m

horse ['hɔrs] n **1** : caballo m **2 a horse of a different color** : harina de otro costal **3 from the horse's mouth** ⟨I heard it straight from the horse's mouth : me lo dijo él mismo, me lo dijo ella misma⟩ **4 hold your horses** : un momentito

horseback ['hɔrs,bæk] n **on ~** : a caballo

horseback riding n : equitación f

horse chestnut n : castaña f de Indias

horsefly ['hɔrs,flaɪ] n, pl **-flies** : tábano m

horsehair ['hɔrs,hær] n : crin f

horseman ['hɔrsmən] n, pl **-men** [-mən, -,mɛn] : jinete m, caballista m

horsemanship ['hɔrsmən,ʃɪp] n : equitación f

horseplay ['hɔrs,pleɪ] n : payasadas fpl

horsepower ['hɔrs,paʊər] n : caballo m de fuerza

horse racing n : carreras fpl de caballos

horseradish ['hɔrs,rædɪʃ] n : rábano m picante

horseshoe ['hɔrs,ʃu:] n : herradura f

horsewhip ['hɔrs,ʍɪp] vt **-whipped; -whipping** : azotar

horsewoman ['hɔrs,wʊmən] n, pl **-women** [-,wɪmən] : amazona f, jinete f, caballista f

horsey or **horsy** ['hɔrsi] adj **horsier; -est** : relacionado a los caballos, caballar

horticultural [,hɔrtə'kʌltʃərəl] adj : hortícola

horticulture ['hɔrtə,kʌltʃər] n : horticultura f

hose[1] ['ho:z] vt **hosed; hosing** : regar o lavar con manguera

hose[2] n **1** pl **hose** SOCKS : calcetines mpl, medias fpl **2** pl **hose** STOCKINGS : medias fpl **3** pl **hoses** : manguera f, manga f

hosiery ['ho:ʒəri, 'ho:zə-] n : calcetería f, medias fpl

hospice ['hɑspəs] n : centro m de cuidados paliativos

hospitable [hɑ'spɪtəbəl, 'hɑs,pɪ-] adj : hospitalario — **hospitably** [-bli] adv

hospital ['hɑs,pɪtəl] n : hospital m

hospitality [,hɑspə'tæləti] n, pl **-ties** : hospitalidad f

hospitalization [,hɑs,pɪtələ'zeɪʃən] n : hospitalización f

hospitalize ['hɑs,pɪtəl,aɪz] vt **-ized; -izing** : hospitalizar

host[1] ['ho:st] vt : presentar (un programa de televisión, etc.)

host[2] n **1** : anfitrión m, -triona f (en la casa, a un evento); presentador m, -dora f (de un programa de televisión, etc.) **2** or **host organism** : huésped m **3** TROOPS : huestes fpl **4** MULTITUDE : multitud f ⟨for a host of reasons : por muchas razones⟩ **5** EUCHARIST : hostia f, Eucaristía f

hostage ['hɑstɪdʒ] n : rehén m

hostel ['hɑstəl] n : albergue m juvenil

hostess ['ho:stɪs] n : anfitriona f (en la casa), presentadora f (de un programa)

hostile ['hɑstəl, -,taɪl] adj : hostil — **hostilely** adv

hostility [hɑs'tɪləti] n, pl **-ties** : hostilidad f

hot ['hɑt] adj **hotter; hottest 1** : caliente, cálido, caluroso ⟨hot water : agua caliente⟩ ⟨a hot climate : un clima cálido⟩ ⟨a hot day : un día caluroso⟩ ⟨it's hot in here : hace calor aquí dentro⟩ **2** ARDENT, FIERY : ardiente, acalorado ⟨to

have a hot temper : tener mal genio⟩ **3**
SPICY : picante **4** FRESH : reciente,
nuevo ⟨hot news : noticias de última
hora⟩ ⟨hot off the press : de último momento⟩ **5** EAGER : ávido **6** STOLEN
: robado **7** *fam* SEXY : guapo, bueno
fam **8 hot and bothered** *or* **hot under
the collar** : enojado — **hotly** *adv*

hot air *n* : palabrería *f*

hotbed [ˈhɑtˌbɛd] *n* **1** : semillero *m* (de
plantas) **2** : hervidero *m*, semillero *m*
(de crimen, etc.)

hot chocolate *n* COCOA : chocolate *m*,
cocoa *f*, cacao *m* (bebida)

hot dog *n* : perro *m* caliente; pancho *m*
Arg, Uru

hotel [hoˈtɛl] *n* : hotel *m*

hotelier [hoːˈtɛljər, ˌoːtəlˈjeɪ] *n* : hotelero
m, -ra *f*

hot flash *n* : bochorno *m*, sofoco *m* (de la
menopausia)

hothead [ˈhɑtˌhɛd] *n* : exaltado *m*, -da *f*

hotheaded [ˈhɑtˈhɛdəd] *adj* : exaltado

hothouse [ˈhɑtˌhaʊs] *n* : invernadero *m*

hot plate *n* : placa *f* (de cocina)

hot rod *n* : coche *m* con motor modificado

hot tub *n* : bañera *f* de hidromasaje

hot water *n* **to get into hot water** : meterse en un lío

hot–water bottle *n* : bolsa *f* de agua caliente

hound[1] [ˈhaʊnd] *vt* : acosar, perseguir

hound[2] *n* : perro *m* (de caza)

hour [ˈaʊər] *n* **1** : hora *f* ⟨on the hour : a
la hora en punto⟩ ⟨60 miles an/per hour
: 60 millas por hora⟩ ⟨by the hour : por
hora(s)⟩ ⟨at all hours : a todas horas⟩
⟨until all hours : hasta las tantas, hasta
muy tarde⟩ ⟨open 24 hours (a day)
: abierto 24 horas (al día)⟩ **2 hours** *npl*
: horas *pl*, horario *m* (de una empresa,
etc.) **3 the wee hours** ⟨in/until the wee
hours (of the morning/night) : a/hasta
las altas horas de la madrugada/noche⟩

hourglass [ˈaʊərˌglæs] *n* : reloj *m* de
arena

hourly [ˈaʊərli] *adv & adj* : cada hora, por
hora

house[1] [ˈhaʊz] *vt* **housed; housing** : albergar, alojar, hospedar

house[2] [ˈhaʊs] *n, pl* **houses** [ˈhaʊzəz,
-səz] **1** HOME : casa *f* ⟨come (over) to my
house : ven a mi casa⟩ ⟨house pet : animal doméstico⟩ ⟨house painter : pintor
de casas⟩ **2** : cámara *f* (del gobierno) **3**
BUSINESS : casa *f*, empresa *f* **4 on the
house** : gratis ⟨it's on the house : invita
la casa⟩ **5 to bring the house down**
: ser muy aplaudido **6 to clean house**
: limpiar la casa **7 to get/put/set one's
house in order** : poner sus asuntos en
orden, ordenar sus asuntos **8 to keep
house** : ocuparse de la casa **9 to play
house** : jugar a las casitas **10 to set up
house** : poner casa

houseboat [ˈhaʊsˌboːt] *n* : casa *f* flotante

housebroken [ˈhaʊsˌbroːkən] *adj*
: enseñada

housecoat [ˈhaʊsˌkoːt] *n* : bata *f*,
guardapolvo *m*

housefly [ˈhaʊsˌflaɪ] *n, pl* **-flies** : mosca *f*
común

household[1] [ˈhaʊsˌhoːld] *adj* **1** DOMESTIC : doméstico, de la casa **2** FAMILIAR
: conocido por todos

household[2] *n* : casa *f*, familia *f*

householder [ˈhaʊsˌhoːldər] *n* : dueño *m*,
-ña *f* de casa

housekeeper [ˈhaʊsˌkiːpər] *n* : ama *f* de
llaves

housekeeping [ˈhaʊsˌkiːpɪŋ] *n* : gobierno
m de la casa, quehaceres *mpl* domésticos

housemaid [ˈhaʊsˌmeɪd] *n* : criada *f*, mucama *f*, muchacha *f*, sirvienta *f*

houseplant [ˈhaʊsˌplænt] *n* : planta *f* de
interior

housewarming [ˈhaʊsˌwɔrmɪŋ] *n* : fiesta *f*
de estreno de una casa

housewife [ˈhaʊsˌwaɪf] *n, pl* **-wives** : ama
f de casa

housework [ˈhaʊsˌwɔrk] *n* : faenas *fpl*
domésticas, quehaceres *mpl* domésticos

housing [ˈhaʊzɪŋ] *n* **1** HOUSES : vivienda
f **2** COVERING : caja *f* protectora

hove → **heave**

hovel [ˈhʌvəl, ˈhɑ-] *n* : casucha *f*, tugurio
m

hover [ˈhʌvər, ˈhɑ-] *vi* **1** : cernerse, sostenerse en el aire **2 to hover about**
: rondar

hovercraft [ˈhʌvərˌkræft] *n* : aerodeslizador *m*

how [ˈhaʊ] *adv* **1** : cómo ⟨how are you?
: ¿cómo estás?⟩ ⟨I don't know how to fix
it : no sé cómo arreglarlo⟩ ⟨how do I
look? : ¿cómo estoy?⟩ ⟨how big is it?
: ¿cómo es de grande?, ¿qué tan grande
es?⟩ ⟨how bad is it? : ¿de qué gravedad
es?, ¿qué tan grave es?⟩ ⟨how do you do
: mucho gusto⟩ **2** (*used for emphasis*)
: qué ⟨how beautiful! : ¡qué bonito!⟩
⟨how right you are! : ¡cuánta razón
tiene!⟩ ⟨I can't tell you how grateful I
am : no puedo decirle lo agradecida que
estoy⟩ **3** : cuánto ⟨how old are you?
: ¿cuántos años tienes?⟩ ⟨how many
people are here? : ¿cuánta gente está
aquí?⟩ **4 and how!** : ¡y cómo! **5 how
about . . . ?** : ¿qué te parece . . . ? **6 how
come?** *fam* : ¿cómo es eso?, ¿por
qué? **7 how come . . . ?** *fam* : ¿cómo es
que . . . ?, ¿por qué . . . ? **8 how much**
: cuánto **9 how so?** : ¿por qué dice(s)
eso? **10 how's that?** *fam* : ¿qué?,
¿cómo?

however[1] [haʊˈɛvər] *adv* **1** : por mucho
que, por más que ⟨however hot it is : por
mucho calor que haga⟩ **2** NEVERTHELESS : sin embargo, no obstante

however[2] *conj* : comoquiera que, de cualquier manera que

howl[1] [ˈhaʊl] *vi* : aullar

howl[2] *n* : aullido *m*, alarido *m*

hub [ˈhʌb] *n* **1** CENTER : centro *m* **2**
: cubo *m* (de una rueda)

hubbub [ˈhʌˌbʌb] *n* : algarabía *f*, alboroto
m, jaleo *m*

hubcap [ˈhʌbˌkæp] *n* : tapacubos *m*

huckster [ˈhʌkstər] *n* : buhonero *m*, -ra *f*;
vendedor *m*, -dora *f* ambulante

huddle[1] ['hʌdəl] vi **-dled; -dling** 1 : apiñarse, amontonarse 2 **to huddle together** : acurrucarse

huddle[2] n : grupo m (cerrado) ⟨to go into a huddle : discutir en secreto⟩

hue ['hju:] n : color m, tono m

huff ['hʌf] n : enojo m, enfado m ⟨to be in a huff : estar enojado⟩

huffy ['hʌfi] adj **huffier; -est** : enojado, enfadado

hug[1] ['hʌg] vt **hugged; hugging** 1 EMBRACE : abrazar 2 : ir pegado a ⟨the road hugs the river : el camino está pegado al río⟩

hug[2] n : abrazo m

huge ['hju:ʤ] adj **huger; hugest** : inmenso, enorme — **hugely** adv

hugeness ['hju:ʤnəs] n : lo grande

huh ['hʌ] interj 1 WHAT : ¿eh?, ¿qué? 2 : ¿eh?, ¿no? ⟨not bad, huh? : no está mal, ¿eh?⟩ 3 (expressing surprise or disbelief) : ¡vaya!, ¡anda! 4 (expressing disapproval) : ¡bah!

hulk ['hʌlk] n 1 : persona f fornida 2 : casco m (barco), armatoste m (edificio, etc.)

hulking ['hʌlkɪŋ] adj : grande, pesado

hull[1] ['hʌl] vt : pelar

hull[2] n 1 HUSK : cáscara f 2 : casco m (de un barco, un avión, etc.)

hullabaloo ['hʌləbə,lu:] n, pl **-loos** : alboroto m, jaleo m

hum[1] ['hʌm] v **hummed; humming** vi 1 BUZZ : zumbar 2 : estar muy activo, moverse ⟨to hum with activity : bullir de actividad⟩ — vt : tararear (una melodía)

hum[2] n : zumbido m, murmullo m

human[1] ['hju:mən, 'ju:-] adj : humano ⟨human rights : derechos humanos⟩ — **humanly** adv

human[2] n : humano m

human being n : ser m humano

humane [hju:'meɪn, ju:-] adj : humano, humanitario — **humanely** adv

humanism ['hju:mə,nɪzəm, 'ju:-] n : humanismo m

humanist[1] ['hju:mənɪst, 'ju:-] n : humanista mf

humanist[2] or **humanistic** [,hju:mə'nɪstɪk, ,ju:-] adj : humanístico

humanitarian[1] [hju:,mænə'triən, ju:-] : humanitario

humanitarian[2] n : humanitario m, -ria f

humanity [hju:'mænəṭi, ju:-] n, pl **-ties** : humanidad f

humanize ['hju:mə,naɪz, 'ju:-] vt **-ized; -izing** : humanizar

humankind ['hju:mən'kaɪnd, 'ju:-] n : género m humano

humble[1] ['hʌmbəl] vt **-bled; -bling** 1 : humillar 2 **to humble oneself** : humillarse

humble[2] adj **humbler; humblest** : humilde, modesto — **humbly** ['hʌmbli] adv

humbug ['hʌm,bʌg] n 1 FRAUD : charlatán m, -tana f; farsante mf 2 NONSENSE : patrañas fpl, tonterías fpl

humdrum ['hʌm,drʌm] adj : monótono, rutinario

humid ['hju:məd, 'ju:-] adj : húmedo

humidifier [hju:'mɪdə,faɪər, ju:-] n : humidificador m

humidify [hju:'mɪdə,faɪ, ju:-] vt **-fied; -fying** : humidificar

humidity [hju:'mɪdəṭi, ju:-] n, pl **-ties** : humedad f

humiliate [hju:'mɪli,eɪt, ju:-] vt **-ated; -ating** : humillar

humiliating [hju:'mɪli,eɪtɪŋ, ju:-] adj : humillante

humiliation [hju:,mɪli'eɪʃən, ju:-] n : humillación f

humility [hju:'mɪləṭi, ju:-] n : humildad f

hummingbird ['hʌmɪŋ,bərd] n : colibrí m, picaflor m

hummock ['hʌmək] n : montículo m

humor[1] ['hju:mər, 'ju:-] vt : seguir el humor a, complacer

humor[2] n : humor m

humorist ['hju:mərɪst, 'ju:-] n : humorista mf

humorless ['hju:mərləs, 'ju:-] adj : sin sentido del humor ⟨a humorless smile : una sonrisa forzada⟩

humorous ['hju:mərəs, 'ju:-] adj : humorístico, cómico — **humorously** adv

hump ['hʌmp] n : joroba f, giba f

humpback ['hʌmp,bæk] n 1 HUMP, HUNCHBACK : joroba f, giba f 2 offensive HUNCHBACK : jorobado m, -da f; giboso m, -sa f (persona) 3 or **humpback whale** : ballena f jorobada, yubarta f

humpbacked ['hʌmp,bækt] adj : jorobado, giboso

humus ['hju:məs, 'ju:-] n : humus m

hunch[1] ['hʌntʃ] vi : encorvar — vi or **to hunch up** : encorvarse

hunch[2] n PREMONITION : presentimiento m

hunchback ['hʌntʃ,bæk] n 1 HUMP, HUMPBACK : joroba f, giba f 2 offensive HUMPBACK : jorobado m, -da f; giboso m, -sa f (persona)

hunchbacked ['hʌntʃ,bækt] adj : jorobado, giboso

hundred[1] ['hʌndrəd] adj : cien, ciento

hundred[2] n, pl **-dreds** or **-dred** 1 : cien m, ciento m ⟨a/one hundred : cien⟩ ⟨a/one hundred (and) one : ciento uno⟩ ⟨hundreds of people : cientos de personas⟩ ⟨hundreds of times : cientos de veces⟩ 2 : billete m de cien dólares

hundredth[1] ['hʌndrədθ] adv : en centésimo lugar

hundredth[2] adj : centésimo

hundredth[3] n 1 : centésimo m, -ma f (en una serie) 2 : centésimo m, centésima parte f

hundredweight ['hʌndrəd,weɪt] n : quintal m

hung → hang

Hungarian [hʌŋ'gæriən] n 1 : húngaro m, -ra f 2 : húngaro m (idioma) — **Hungarian** adj

hunger[1] ['hʌŋgər] vi 1 : tener hambre 2 **to hunger after/for** : ansiar, anhelar

hunger[2] n : hambre m

hungrily ['hʌŋgrəli] adv : ávidamente

hungry ['hʌŋgri] adj **hungrier; -est** 1 : hambriento 2 **to be hungry** : tener hambre

hunk ['hʌŋk] *n* : trozo *m*, pedazo *m*
hunt[1] ['hʌnt] *vt* 1 PURSUE : cazar 2 **to hunt for** : buscar
hunt[2] *n* 1 PURSUIT : caza *f*, cacería *f* 2 SEARCH : búsqueda *f*, busca *f*
hunter ['hʌntər] *n* : cazador *m*, -dora *f*
hunting ['hʌntɪŋ] *n* : caza *f* ⟨to go hunting : ir de caza⟩
hurdle[1] ['hərdəl] *v* -**dled; -dling** : saltar, salvar (un obstáculo)
hurdle[2] *n* : valla *f* (en deportes), obstáculo *m*
hurl ['hərl] *vt* : arrojar, tirar, lanzar
hurrah [hu'ra, -'rɔ] *interj* : ¡hurra!
hurricane ['hərə,keɪn] *n* : huracán *m*
hurried ['hərid] *adj* : apresurado, precipitado
hurriedly ['hərədli] *adv* : apresuradamente, de prisa
hurry[1] ['həri] *v* -**ried; -rying** *vi* : apurarse, darse prisa, apresurarse — *vt* : apurar, darle prisa a (alguien)
hurry[2] *n* : prisa *f*, apuro *f*
hurt[1] ['hərt] *v* **hurt; hurting** *vt* 1 INJURE : hacer daño a, herir, lastimar ⟨to hurt oneself : hacerse daño⟩ 2 DISTRESS, OFFEND : hacer sufrir, ofender, herir — *vi* : doler ⟨my foot hurts : me duele el pie⟩
hurt[2] *n* 1 INJURY : herida *f* 2 DISTRESS, PAIN : dolor *m*, pena *f*
hurtful ['hərtfəl] *adj* : hiriente, doloroso
hurtle ['hərtəl] *vi* -**tled; -tling** : lanzarse, precipitarse
husband[1] ['hʌzbənd] *vt* : economizar, bien administrar
husband[2] *n* : esposo *m*, marido *m*
husbandry ['hʌzbəndri] *n* 1 MANAGEMENT, THRIFT : economía *f*, buena administración *f* 2 AGRICULTURE : agricultura *f* ⟨animal husbandry : cría de animales⟩
hush[1] ['hʌʃ] *vt* 1 SILENCE : hacer callar, acallar 2 CALM : calmar, apaciguar
hush[2] *n* : silencio *m*
hush-hush [hʌʃ,hʌʃ, ,hʌʃ'hʌʃ] *adj* : muy secreto, confidencial
husk[1] ['hʌsk] *vt* : descascarar
husk[2] *n* : cáscara *f*
huskily ['hʌskəli] *adv* : con voz ronca
husky[1] ['hʌski] *adj* **huskier; -est** 1 HOARSE : ronco 2 BURLY : fornido
husky[2] *n, pl* -**kies** : perro *m*, -rra *f* esquimal
hustle[1] ['hʌsəl] *v* -**tled; -tling** *vt* : darle prisa (a alguien), apurar ⟨they hustled me in : me hicieron entrar a empujones⟩ — *vi* : apurarse, ajetrearse
hustle[2] *n or* **hustle and bustle** : bullicio *m*, ajetreo *m*
hut ['hʌt] *n* : cabaña *f*, choza *f*, barraca *f*, bohío *m*
hutch ['hʌtʃ] *n* 1 CUPBOARD : alacena *f* 2 **rabbit hutch** : conejera *f*
hyacinth ['haɪə,sɪnθ] *n* : jacinto *m*
hybrid[1] ['haɪbrɪd] *adj* : híbrido
hybrid[2] *n* : híbrido *m*
hydrant ['haɪdrənt] *n* : boca *f* de riego, hidrante *m CA, Col* ⟨fire hydrant : boca de incendios⟩

hydraulic [haɪ'drɔlɪk] *adj* : hidráulico — **hydraulically** *adv*
hydrocarbon [,haɪdro'karbən] *n* : hidrocarburo *m*
hydrochloric acid [,haɪdro'klorɪk] *n* : ácido *m* clorhídrico
hydroelectric [,haɪdroɪ'lɛktrɪk] *adj* : hidroeléctrico
hydrofoil ['haɪdrə,fɔɪl] *n* : hidroala *m*, aliscafo *m*
hydrogen ['haɪdrədʒən] *n* : hidrógeno *m*
hydrogen bomb *n* : bomba *f* de hidrógeno
hydrogen peroxide *n* : agua *f* oxigenada, peróxido *m* de hidrógeno
hydrophobia [,haɪdro'fo:biə] *n* : hidrofobia *f*, rabia *f*
hydroplane ['haɪdrə,pleɪn] *n* : hidroplano *m*
hyena [haɪ'i:nə] *n* : hiena *f*
hygiene ['haɪ,dʒi:n] *n* : higiene *f*
hygienic [haɪ'dʒɛnɪk, -'dʒi:-, ,haɪ-dʒi'nɪk] *adj* : higiénico — **hygienically** [-nɪkli] *adv*
hygienist [haɪ'dʒi:nɪst, -'dʒɛ-; 'haɪ-,dʒi:-] *n* : higienista *mf*
hygrometer [haɪ'gramətər] *n* : higrómetro *m*
hymn ['hɪm] *n* : himno *m*
hymnal ['hɪmnəl] *n* : himnario *m*
hype[1] ['haɪp] *n* : bombo *m* publicitario
hype[2] *vt* **hyped; hyping** : promocionar con bombos y platillos
hyperactive [,haɪpər'æktɪv] *adj* : hiperactivo
hyperactivity [,haɪpər,æk'tɪvəti] *n, pl* -**ties** : hiperactividad *f*
hyperbole [haɪ'pərbəli] *n* : hipérbole *f*
hyperbolic [,haɪpər'balɪk] *adj* : hiperbólico
hypercritical [,haɪpər'krɪtɪkəl] *adj* : hipercrítico
hyperlink ['haɪpər,lɪŋk] *n* : hiperenlace *m*
hypermarket ['haɪpər,markət] *n* : hipermercado *m*
hypersensitivity [,haɪpər,sɛnɪsə'tɪ-vəti] *n* : hipersensibilidad *f*
hypertension ['haɪpər,tɛntʃən] *n* : hipertensión *f*
hyphen ['haɪfən] *n* : guión *m*
hyphenate ['haɪfən,eɪt] *vt* -**ated; -ating** : escribir con guión
hypnosis [hɪp'no:sɪs] *n, pl* -**noses** [-,si:z] : hipnosis *f*
hypnotic [hɪp'natɪk] *adj* : hipnótico, hipnotizador
hypnotism ['hɪpnə,tɪzəm] *n* : hipnotismo *m*
hypnotist ['hɪpnə,tɪst] *n* : hipnotizador *m*, -dora *f*
hypnotize ['hɪpnə,taɪz] *vt* -**tized; -tizing** : hipnotizar
hypochondria [,haɪpə'kandriə] *n* : hipocondría *f*
hypochondriac [,haɪpə'kandri,æk] *n* : hipocondríaco *m*, -ca *f*
hypocrisy [hɪp'akrəsi] *n, pl* -**sies** : hipocresía *f*
hypocrite ['hɪpə,krɪt] *n* : hipócrita *mf*
hypocritical [,hɪpə'krɪtɪkəl] *adj* : hipócrita
hypodermic[1] [,haɪpə'dərmɪk] *adj* : hipodérmico
hypodermic[2] *n* : aguja *f* hipodérmica

hypotenuse [haɪˈpɑtənˌuːs, -ˌuːz, -ˌjuːs, -juːz] *n, pl* **-nuses** : hipotenusa *f*

hypothermia [ˌhaɪpoˈθɜrmiə] *n* : hipotermia *f*

hypothesis [haɪˈpɑθəsɪs] *n, pl* **-eses** [-ˌsiːz] : hipótesis *f*

hypothetical [ˌhaɪpoˈθεtɪkəl] *adj* : hipotético — **hypothetically** [-ˌtɪkli] *adv*

hysterectomy [ˌhɪstəˈrεktəmi] *n, pl* **-mies** : histerectomía *f*

hysteria [hɪsˈtεriə, -tɪr-] *n* : histeria *f*, histerismo *m*

hysterical [hɪsˈtεrɪkəl] *adj* : histérico — **hysterically** [-ɪkli] *adv*

hysterics [hɪsˈtεrɪks] *n* : histeria *f*, histerismo *m*

I

i [ˈaɪ] *n, pl* **i's** *or* **is** [ˈaɪz] : novena letra del alfabeto inglés

I [ˈaɪ] *pron* : yo

Iberian [aɪˈbɪriən] *adj* : ibérico

-ible *suf* : -ible

ice¹ [ˈaɪs] *v* **iced; icing** *vt* **1** FREEZE : congelar, helar **2** CHILL : enfriar **3 to ice a cake** : bañar un pastel — *vi* : helarse, congelarse

ice² *n* **1** : hielo *m* ⟨ice cube : cubito de hielo⟩ **2** SHERBET : sorbete *m*; nieve *f* *Cuba, Mex, PRi*

iceberg [ˈaɪsˌbərg] *n* : iceberg *m*

icebox [ˈaɪsˌbɑks] → **refrigerator**

icebreaker [ˈaɪsˌbreɪkər] *n* : rompehielos *m*

ice cap *n* : casquete *m* glaciar ⟨polar ice cap : casquete polar⟩

ice–cold [ˈaɪsˈkoːld] *adj* : helado

ice cream *n* : helado *m*, mantecado *m* PRi

ice–cream soda → **soda**

ice hockey *n* : hockey *m* sobre hielo

Icelander [ˈaɪsˌlændər, -lən-] *n* : islandés *m*, -desa *f*

Icelandic¹ [aɪsˈlændɪk] *adj* : islandés

Icelandic² *n* : islandés *m* (idioma)

ice–skate [ˈaɪsˌskeɪt] *vi* **-skated; -skating** : patinar

ice skater *n* : patinador *m*, -dora *f*

icicle [ˈaɪsɪkəl] *n* : carámbano *m*

icily [ˈaɪsəli] *adv* : fríamente, con frialdad ⟨he stared at me icily : me fijó la mirada con mucha frialdad⟩

icing [ˈaɪsɪŋ] *n* : baño *m*, glaseado *m*, betún *m* Mex

icon [ˈaɪˌkɑn, -kən] *n* : icono *m*

iconoclasm [aɪˈkɑnəˌklæzəm] *n* : iconoclasia *f*

iconoclast [aɪˈkɑnəˌklæst] *n* : iconoclasta *mf*

icy [ˈaɪsi] *adj* **icier; -est 1** : cubierto de hielo ⟨an icy road : una carretera cubierta de hielo⟩ **2** FREEZING : helado, gélido, glacial **3** ALOOF : frío, distante

id [ˈɪd] *n* : id *m*

I'd [ˈaɪd] *contraction of* I SHOULD *or* I HAD *or* I WOULD → **should, have, would**

ID [ˈaɪˈdiː] *n, pl* **ID's** *or* **IDs** → **identification**

ID card → **identification card**

idea [aɪˈdiːə] *n* : idea *f* ⟨to have an idea about something : tener idea de algo⟩ ⟨to have no idea : no tener (ni) idea⟩ ⟨to get the idea : captar la idea⟩ ⟨that's not a bad idea : no es mala idea⟩

ideal¹ [aɪˈdiːəl] *adj* : ideal

ideal² *n* : ideal *m*

idealism [aɪˈdiːəˌlɪzəm] *n* : idealismo *m*

idealist [aɪˈdiːəlɪst] *n* : idealista *mf*

idealistic [aɪˌdiːəˈlɪstɪk] *adj* : idealista

idealistically [aɪˌdiːəˈlɪstɪkli] *adv* : con idealismo

idealization [aɪˌdiːələˈzeɪʃən] *n* : idealización *f*

idealize [aɪˈdiːəˌlaɪz] *vt* **-ized; -izing** : idealizar

ideally [aɪˈdiːəli] *adv* : perfectamente

identical [aɪˈdεntɪkəl] *adj* : idéntico — **identically** [-ɪkli] *adv*

identifiable [aɪˌdεntəˈfaɪəbəl] *adj* : identificable

identification [aɪˌdεntəfəˈkeɪʃən] *n* : identificación *f*

identification card *n* : carnet *m* (de identidad), cédula *f* de identidad, tarjeta *f* de identificación/identidad

identify [aɪˈdεntəˌfaɪ] *v* **-fied; -fying** *vt* : identificar — *vi* **to identify with** : identificarse con

identity [aɪˈdεntəti] *n, pl* **-ties** : identidad *f*

identity card → **identification card**

identity theft *n* : robo *m* de identidad, suplantación *f* de identidad

ideological [ˌaɪdiəˈlɑdʒɪkəl, ˌɪ-] *adj* : ideológico — **ideologically** [-dʒɪkli] *adv*

ideologue [ˈaɪdiəˌlɔg, -ˌlɑg] *n* : ideólogo *m*, -ga *f*

ideology [ˌaɪdiˈɑlədʒi, ˌɪ-] *n, pl* **-gies** : ideología *f*

idiocy [ˈɪdiəsi] *n, pl* **-cies 1** *dated, now offensive* : idiotez *f* **2** NONSENSE : estupidez *f*, tontería *f*

idiom [ˈɪdiəm] *n* **1** LANGUAGE : lenguaje *m* **2** EXPRESSION : modismo *m*, expresión *f* idiomática

idiomatic [ˌɪdiəˈmætɪk] *adj* : idiomático

idiosyncrasy [ˌɪdioˈsɪŋkrəsi] *n, pl* **-sies** : idiosincrasia *f*

idiosyncratic [ˌɪdiosɪnˈkrætɪk] *adj* : idiosincrásico — **idiosyncratically** [-ˌtɪkli] *adv*

idiot [ˈɪdiət] *n* **1** *dated, now offensive* : idiota *mf* (en medicina) *dated, now offensive* **2** FOOL : idiota *mf*; tonto *m*, -ta *f*; imbécil *mf* fam

idiotic [ˌɪdiˈɑtɪk] *adj* : estúpido, idiota

idiotically [ˌɪdiˈɑtɪkli] *adv* : estúpidamente

idle¹ [ˈaɪdəl] *v* **idled; idling** *vi* **1** LOAF : holgazanear, flojear, haraganear **2** : andar al ralentí (dícese de un automóvil), marchar en vacío (dícese de una máquina) — vt : dejar sin trabajo

idle² adj **idler; idlest** 1 VAIN : frívolo, vano, infundado ⟨idle curiosity : pura curiosidad⟩ 2 INACTIVE : inactivo, parado, desocupado 3 LAZY : holgazán, haragán, perezoso

idleness ['aɪdlnəs] n 1 INACTIVITY : inactividad f, ociosidad f 2 LAZINESS : holgazanería f, flojera f, pereza f

idler ['aɪdlər] n : haragán m, -gana f; holgazán m, -zana f

idly ['aɪdli] adv : ociosamente

idol ['aɪdəl] n : ídolo m

idolater or **idolator** [aɪ'dɑlətər] n : idólatra mf

idolatrous [aɪ'dɑlətrəs] adj : idólatra

idolatry [aɪ'dɑlətri] n, pl **-tries** : idolatría f

idolize ['aɪdə,laɪz] vt **-ized; -izing** : idolatrar

idyll ['aɪdəl] n : idilio m

idyllic [aɪ'dɪlɪk] adj : idílico

if ['ɪf] conj 1 : si ⟨I would do it if I could : lo haría si pudiera⟩ ⟨if so : si es así⟩ ⟨as if : como si⟩ ⟨if I were you : yo que tú⟩ ⟨if not : si no, de lo contrario⟩ ⟨if only it were true! : ¡si fuera verdad!⟩ 2 WHETHER : si ⟨I don't know if they're ready : no sé si están listos⟩ 3 THOUGH : aunque, si bien ⟨it's pretty, if somewhat old-fashioned : es lindo aunque algo anticuado⟩

igloo ['ɪ,glu:] n, pl **-loos** : iglú m

ignite [ɪg'naɪt] v **-nited; -niting** vt : prenderle fuego a, encender — vi : prender, encenderse

ignition [ɪg'nɪʃən] n 1 IGNITING : ignición f, encendido m 2 or **ignition switch** : encendido m, arranque m ⟨to turn on the ignition : arrancar el motor⟩

ignoble [ɪg'no:bəl] adj : innoble — **ignobly** adv

ignominious [,ɪgnə'mɪniəs] adj : ignominioso, deshonroso — **ignominiously** adv

ignominy ['ɪgnə,mɪni] n, pl **-nies** : ignominia f

ignoramus [,ɪgnə'reɪməs] n : ignorante mf; bestia mf; bruto m, -ta f

ignorance ['ɪgnərəns] n : ignorancia f

ignorant ['ɪgnərənt] adj 1 : ignorante ⟨to be ignorant of : no ser consciente de, desconocer, ignorar⟩

ignorantly ['ɪgnərəntli] adv : ignorantemente, con ignorancia

ignore [ɪg'nor] vt **-nored; -noring** : ignorar, hacer caso omiso de (algo), no hacer caso de (algo), no hacerle caso a (alguien)

iguana [ɪ'gwɑnə] n : iguana f, garrobo f CA

il- → **in-**

ilk ['ɪlk] n : tipo m, clase f, índole f

ill¹ ['ɪl] adv **worse** ['wərs], **worst** ['wərst] : mal ⟨to speak ill of : hablar mal de⟩ ⟨he can ill afford to fail : mal puede permitirse el lujo de fracasar⟩

ill² adj **worse; worst** 1 SICK : enfermo 2 BAD : malo ⟨ill luck : mala suerte⟩

ill³ n 1 EVIL : mal m 2 MISFORTUNE : mal m, desgracia f 3 AILMENT : enfermedad f

I'll ['aɪl] contraction of I SHALL or I WILL → **shall, will**

ill-advised ['ɪləd'vaɪzd] adj : poco aconsejable, imprudente

ill at ease adj : incómodo

ill-bred ['ɪl'brɛd] adj : malcriado

illegal [ɪl'li:gəl] adj : ilegal — **illegally** adv

illegality [ɪli'gæləti] n : ilegalidad f

illegibility [ɪl,lɛdʒə'bɪləti] n, pl **-ties** : ilegibilidad f

illegible [ɪl'lɛdʒəbəl] adj : ilegible — **illegibly** [-bli] adv

illegitimacy [,ɪlɪ'dʒɪtəməsi] n : ilegitimidad f

illegitimate [,ɪlɪ'dʒɪtəmət] adj 1 BASTARD : ilegítimo, bastardo 2 UNLAWFUL : ilegítimo, ilegal — **illegitimately** adv

ill-fated ['ɪl'feɪtəd] adj : malhadado, infortunado, desventurado

ill-gotten ['ɪl'gɑtən] adj : mal habido

illicit [ɪl'lɪsət] adj : ilícito — **illicitly** adv

illiteracy [ɪl'lɪtərəsi] n, pl **-cies** : analfabetismo m

illiterate¹ [ɪl'lɪtərət] adj : analfabeto

illiterate² n : analfabeto m, -ta f

ill-mannered [,ɪl'mænərd] adj : descortés, maleducado

ill-natured [,ɪl'neɪtʃərd] adj : desagradable, de mal genio

ill-naturedly [,ɪl'neɪtʃərdli] adv : desagradablemente

illness ['ɪlnəs] n : enfermedad f

illogical [ɪl'lɑdʒɪkəl] adj : ilógico — **illogically** [-kli] adv

ill-tempered [,ɪl'tɛmpərd] → **ill-natured**

ill-treat [,ɪl'tri:t] vt : maltratar

ill-treatment [,ɪl'tri:tmənt] n : maltrato m

illuminate [ɪ'lu:mə,neɪt] vt **-nated; -nating** 1 : iluminar, alumbrar 2 ELUCIDATE : esclarecer, elucidar

illumination [ɪ,lu:mə'neɪʃən] n 1 LIGHTING : iluminación f, luz f 2 ELUCIDATION : esclarecimiento m, elucidación f

ill-use ['ɪl'ju:z] → **ill-treat**

illusion [ɪ'lu:ʒən] n : ilusión f

illusory [ɪ'lu:səri, -zəri] adj : engañoso, ilusorio

illustrate ['ɪlə,streɪt] v **-trated; -trating** : ilustrar

illustration [,ɪlə'streɪʃən] n 1 PICTURE : ilustración f 2 EXAMPLE : ejemplo m, ilustración f

illustrative [ɪ'lʌstrətɪv, 'ɪlə,streɪtɪv] adj : ilustrativo — **illustratively** adv

illustrator ['ɪlə,streɪtər] n : ilustrador m, -dora f; dibujante mf

illustrious [ɪ'lʌstriəs] adj : ilustre, eminente, glorioso

illustriousness [ɪ'lʌstriəsnəs] n : eminencia f, prestigio m

ill will n : animosidad f, malquerencia f, mala voluntad f

IM ['aɪ'ɛm] v **IM'd; IM'ing** (instant message) vt : enviarle un mensaje instantáneo a — vi : enviar un mensaje instantáneo

I'm ['aɪm] contraction of I AM → **be**

im- → **in-**

image¹ ['ɪmɪdʒ] vt **-aged; -aging** : imaginar, crear una imagen de

image² n : imagen f

imagery ['ɪmɪʤri] *n, pl* **-eries 1** IMAGES : imágenes *fpl* **2** : imaginería *f* (en el arte)

imaginable [ɪ'mæʤənəbəl] *adj* : imaginable — **imaginably** [-bli] *adv*

imaginary [ɪ'mæʤə,neri] *adj* : imaginario

imagination [ɪ,mæʤə'neɪʃən] *n* : imaginación *f*

imaginative [ɪ'mæʤənətɪv, -ə,neɪtɪv] *adj* : imaginativo — **imaginatively** *adv*

imagine [ɪ'mæʤən] *vt* **-ined; -ining 1** : imaginar(se) ⟨try to imagine it : trata de imaginarlo⟩ ⟨imagine that! : ¡imagínate!⟩ ⟨I can't imagine why : no me imagino por qué⟩ **2** : imaginar, creer (equivocadamente) ⟨she imagines herself to be charming : se cree encantadora⟩ ⟨you're imagining things : son imaginaciones tuyas⟩ **3** BELIEVE : imaginarse, creer ⟨I imagine so : me imagino que sí⟩

imbalance [ɪm'bæləns] *n* : desajuste *m*, desbalance *m*, desequilibrio *m*

imbecile[1] ['ɪmbəsəl, -,sɪl] *or* **imbecilic** [,ɪmbə'sɪlɪk] *adj* : imbécil, estúpido

imbecile[2] *n* **1** *dated, now offensive* : imbécil *mf* (en medicina) *dated, now offensive* **2** FOOL : idiota *mf*; imbécil *mf fam*; estúpido *m*, -da *f*

imbecility [,ɪmbə'sɪləti] *n, pl* **-ties 1** *dated, now offensive* : imbecilidad *f* (en medicina) **2** FOOLISHNESS: imbecilidad

imbibe [ɪm'baɪb] *v* **-bibed; -bibing** *vt* **1** DRINK : beber **2** ABSORB : absorber, embeber — *vi* : beber

imbue [ɪm'bju:] *vt* **-bued; -buing** : imbuir

imitate ['ɪmə,teɪt] *vt* **-tated; -tating** : imitar, remedar

imitation[1] [,ɪmə'teɪʃən] *adj* : de imitación, artificial

imitation[2] *n* : imitación *f*

imitative ['ɪmə,teɪtɪv] *adj* : imitativo, imitador, poco original

imitator ['ɪmə,teɪtər] *n* : imitador *m*, -dora *f*

immaculate [ɪ'mækjələt] *adj* **1** PURE : inmaculado, puro **2** FLAWLESS : impecable, intachable — **immaculately** *adv*

immaterial [,ɪmə'tɪriəl] *adj* **1** INCORPOREAL : incorpóreo **2** UNIMPORTANT : irrelevante, sin importancia

immature [,ɪmə'tʃʊr, -'tjʊr, -'tʊr] *adj* : inmaduro, verde (dícese de la fruta)

immaturity [,ɪmə'tʃʊrəti, -'tjʊr-, -'tʊr-] *n, pl* **-ties** : inmadurez *f*, falta *f* de madurez

immeasurable [ɪ'mɛʒərəbəl] *adj* : inconmensurable, incalculable — **immeasurably** [-bli] *adv*

immediacy [ɪ'mi:diəsi] *n* : inmediatez *f*

immediate [ɪ'mi:diət] *adj* **1** INSTANT : inmediato, instantáneo ⟨immediate relief : alivio instantáneo⟩ **2** DIRECT : inmediato, directo ⟨the immediate cause of death : la causa directa de la muerte⟩ **3** URGENT : urgente, apremiante **4** CLOSE : cercano, próximo, inmediato ⟨her immediate family : sus familiares más cercanos⟩ ⟨in the immediate vicinity : en los alrededores, en las inmediaciones⟩

immediately [ɪ'mi:diətli] *adv* : inmediatamente, enseguida

immemorial [,ɪmə'moriəl] *adj* : inmemorial

immense [ɪ'mɛnts] *adj* : inmenso, enorme — **immensely** *adv*

immensity [ɪ'mɛntsəti] *n, pl* **-ties** : inmensidad *f*

immerse [ɪ'mərs] *vt* **-mersed; -mersing** SUBMERGE : sumergir **2 to immerse oneself in** : enfrascarse en

immersion [ɪ'mərʒən] *n* **1** : inmersión *f* (en un líquido) **2** : absorción *f* (en una actividad)

immigrant ['ɪmɪgrənt] *n* : inmigrante *mf*

immigrate ['ɪmə,greɪt] *vi* **-grated; -grating** : inmigrar

immigration [,ɪmə'greɪʃən] *n* : inmigración *f*

imminence ['ɪmənənts] *n* : inminencia *f*

imminent ['ɪmənənt] *adj* : inminente — **imminently** *adv*

immobile [ɪ'mo:bəl] *adj* **1** FIXED, IMMOVABLE : inmovible, fijo **2** MOTIONLESS : inmóvil

immobility [,ɪmo'bɪləti] *n, pl* **-ties** : inmovilidad *f*

immobilize [ɪ'mo:bə,laɪz] *vt* **-lized; -lizing** : inmovilizar, paralizar — **immobilization** *n*

immoderate [ɪ'mɑdərət] *adj* : inmoderado, desmesurado, desmedido, excesivo — **immoderately** *adv*

immodest [ɪ'mɑdəst] *adj* **1** INDECENT : inmodesto, indecente, impúdico **2** CONCEITED : inmodesto, presuntuoso, engreído — **immodestly** *adv*

immodesty [ɪ'mɑdəsti] *n* : inmodestia *f*

immoral [ɪ'morəl] *adj* : inmoral

immorality [,ɪmo'ræləti, ,ɪmə-] *n, pl* **-ties** : inmoralidad *f*

immorally [ɪ'morəli] *adv* : de manera inmoral

immortal[1] [ɪ'mortəl] *adj* : inmortal

immortal[2] *n* : inmortal *mf*

immortality [,ɪ,mor'tæləti] *n* : inmortalidad *f*

immortalize [ɪ'mortəl,aɪz] *vt* **-ized; -izing** : inmortalizar

immovable [ɪ'mu:vəbəl] *adj* **1** FIXED : fijo, inmovible **2** UNYIELDING : inflexible

immune [ɪ'mju:n] *adj* **1** : inmune ⟨immune to smallpox : inmune a la viruela⟩ **2** EXEMPT : exento, inmune

immune system *n* : sistema *m* inmunológico

immunity [ɪ'mju:nəti] *n, pl* **-ties 1** : inmunidad *f* **2** EXEMPTION : exención *f*

immunization [,ɪmjunə'zeɪʃən] *n* : inmunización *f*

immunize ['ɪmju,naɪz] *vt* **-nized; -nizing** : inmunizar

immunology [,ɪmju'nɑləʤi] *n* : inmunología *f*

immutable [ɪ'mju:təbəl] *adj* : inmutable

imp ['ɪmp] *n* RASCAL : diablillo *m*; pillo *m*, -lla *f*

impact[1] [ɪm'pækt] *vt* **1** STRIKE : chocar con, impactar **2** AFFECT : afectar, impactar, impresionar — *vi* **1** STRIKE : hacer impacto, golpear **2 to impact on** : tener un impacto sobre

impact² [ˈɪmˌpækt] *n* **1** COLLISION : impacto *m*, choque *m*, colisión *f* **2** EFFECT : efecto *m*, impacto *m*, consecuencias *fpl*

impacted [ɪmˈpæktəd] *adj* : impactado, incrustado (dícese de los dientes)

impair [ɪmˈpær] *vt* : perjudicar, dañar, afectar

impairment [ɪmˈpærmənt] *n* : perjuicio *m*, daño *m*

impala [ɪmˈpɑlə, -ˈpæ-] *n, pl* **impalas** *or* **impala** : impala *m*

impale [ɪmˈpeɪl] *vt* **-paled; -paling** : empalar

impalpable [ɪmˈpælpəbəl] *adj* : impalpable, intangible

impanel [ɪmˈpænəl] *vt* **-eled** *or* **-elled; -eling** *or* **-elling** : elegir (un jurado)

impart [ɪmˈpɑrt] *vt* **1** CONVEY : impartir, dar, conferir **2** DISCLOSE : revelar, divulgar

impartial [ɪmˈpɑrʃəl] *adj* : imparcial — **impartially** *adv*

impartiality [ɪmˌpɑrʃiˈæləti] *n, pl* **-ties** : imparcialidad *f*

impassable [ɪmˈpæsəbəl] *adj* : infranqueable, intransitable — **impassably** [-bli] *adv*

impasse [ˈɪmˌpæs] *n* **1** DEADLOCK : impasse *m*, punto *m* muerto **2** DEAD END : callejón *m* sin salida

impassioned [ɪmˈpæʃənd] *adj* : apasionado, vehemente

impassive [ɪmˈpæsɪv] *adj* : impasible, indiferente

impassively [ɪmˈpæsɪvli] *adv* : impasiblemente, sin emoción

impatience [ɪmˈpeɪʃənts] *n* : impaciencia *f*

impatient [ɪmˈpeɪʃənt] *adj* : impaciente — **impatiently** *adv*

impeach [ɪmˈpiːtʃ] *vt* : destituir (a un funcionario) de su cargo

impeachment [ɪmˈpiːtʃmənt] *n* **1** ACCUSATION : acusación *f* **2** DISMISSAL : destitución *f*

impeccable [ɪmˈpɛkəbəl] *adj* : impecable — **impeccably** [-bli] *adv*

impecunious [ˌɪmpɪˈkjuːniəs] *adj* : falto de dinero

impede [ɪmˈpiːd] *vt* **-peded; -peding** : impedir, dificultar, obstaculizar

impediment [ɪmˈpɛdəmənt] *n* **1** HINDRANCE : impedimento *m*, obstáculo *m* **2** speech impediment : defecto *m* del habla

impel [ɪmˈpɛl] *vt* **-pelled; -pelling** : impeler

impending [ɪmˈpɛndɪŋ] *adj* : inminente

impenetrable [ɪmˈpɛnətrəbəl] *adj* **1** : impenetrable ⟨an impenetrable forest : una selva impenetrable⟩ **2** INSCRUTABLE : incomprensible, inescrutable, impenetrable — **impenetrably** [-bli] *adv*

imperative¹ [ɪmˈpɛrətɪv] *adj* **1** AUTHORITATIVE : imperativo, imperioso **2** NECESSARY : imprescindible — **imperatively** *adv*

imperative² *n* : imperativo *m*

imperceptible [ˌɪmpərˈsɛptəbəl] *adj* : imperceptible — **imperceptibly** [-bli] *adv*

imperfect [ɪmˈpərfɪkt] *adj* : imperfecto, defectuoso — **imperfectly** *adv*

imperfection [ˌɪmpərˈfɛkʃən] *n* : imperfección *f*, defecto *m*

imperial [ɪmˈpɪriəl] *adj* **1** : imperial **2** SOVEREIGN : soberano **3** IMPERIOUS : imperioso, señorial

imperialism [ɪmˈpɪriəˌlɪzəm] *n* : imperialismo *m*

imperialist¹ [ɪmˈpɪriəlɪst] *adj* : imperialista

imperialist² *n* : imperialista *mf*

imperialistic [ɪmˌpɪriəˈlɪstɪk] *adj* : imperialista

imperil [ɪmˈpɛrəl] *vt* **-iled** *or* **-illed; -iling** *or* **-illing** : poner en peligro

imperious [ɪmˈpɪriəs] *adj* : imperioso — **imperiously** *adv*

imperishable [ɪmˈpɛrɪʃəbəl] *adj* : imperecedero

impermanent [ɪmˈpərmənənt] *adj* : pasajero, inestable, efímero — **impermanently** *adv*

impermeable [ɪmˈpərmiəbəl] *adj* : impermeable

impersonal [ɪmˈpərsənəl] *adj* : impersonal — **impersonally** *adv*

impersonate [ɪmˈpərsənˌeɪt] *vt* **-ated; -ating** : hacerse pasar por, imitar

impersonation [ɪmˌpərsəˈneɪʃən] *n* : imitación *f*

impersonator [ɪmˈpərsənˌeɪtər] *n* : imitador *m*, -dora *f*

impertinence [ɪmˈpərtənənts] *n* : impertinencia *f*

impertinent [ɪmˈpərtənənt] *adj* **1** IRRELEVANT : impertinente, irrelevante **2** INSOLENT : impertinente, insolente

impertinently [ɪmˈpərtənəntli] *adv* : con impertinencia, impertinentemente

imperturbable [ˌɪmpərˈtərbəbəl] *adj* : imperturbable

impervious [ɪmˈpərviəs] *adj* **1** IMPENETRABLE : impermeable **2** INSENSITIVE : insensible ⟨impervious to criticism : insensible a la crítica⟩

impetuous [ɪmˈpɛtʃuəs] *adj* : impetuoso, impulsivo

impetuously [ɪmˈpɛtʃuəsli] *adv* : de manera impulsiva, impetuosamente

impetus [ˈɪmpətəs] *n* : ímpetu *m*, impulso *m*

impiety [ɪmˈpaɪəti] *n, pl* **-ties** : impiedad *f*

impinge [ɪmˈpɪndʒ] *vi* **-pinged; -pinging** **1 to impinge on** AFFECT : afectar a, incidir en **2 to impinge on** VIOLATE : violar, vulnerar

impious [ˈɪmpiəs, ɪmˈpaɪəs] *adj* : impío, irreverente

impish [ˈɪmpɪʃ] *adj* MISCHIEVOUS : pícaro, travieso

impishly [ˈɪmpɪʃli] *adv* : con picardía

implacable [ɪmˈplækəbəl] *adj* : implacable — **implacably** [-bli] *adv*

implant¹ [ɪmˈplænt] *vt* **1** INCULCATE, INSTILL : inculcar, implantar **2** INSERT : implantar, insertar

implant² [ˈɪmˌplænt] *n* : implante *m* (de pelo), injerto *m* (de piel)

implantation [ˌɪmˌplænˈteɪʃən] *n* : implantación *f*

implausibility [ɪmˌplɔːzəˈbɪləʧi] n, pl **-ties** : inverosimilitud f

implausible [ɪmˈplɔːzəbəl] adj : inverosímil, poco convincente

implement¹ [ˈɪmpləˌmɪnt] vt : poner en práctica, implementar

implement² [ˈɪmpləmənt] n : utensilio m, instrumento m, implemento m

implementation [ˌɪmpləmənˈteɪʃən] n : implementación f, ejecución f, cumplimiento m

implicate [ˈɪmpləˌkeɪt] vt **-cated; -cating** : implicar, involucrar

implication [ˌɪmpləˈkeɪʃən] n **1** CONSEQUENCE : implicación f, consecuencia f **2** INFERENCE : insinuación f, inferencia f

implicit [ɪmˈplɪsət] adj **1** IMPLIED : implícito, tácito **2** ABSOLUTE : absoluto, completo ⟨implicit faith : fe ciega⟩ — **implicitly** adv

implied [ɪmˈplaɪd] adj : implícito, tácito

implode [ɪmˈploːd] vi **-ploded; -ploding** : implosionar

implore [ɪmˈplor] vt **-plored; -ploring** : implorar, suplicar

implosion [ɪmˈploːʒən] n : implosión f

imply [ɪmˈplaɪ] vt **-plied; -plying 1** SUGGEST : insinuar, dar a entender **2** INVOLVE : implicar, suponer ⟨rights imply obligations : los derechos implican unas obligaciones⟩

impolite [ˌɪmpəˈlaɪt] adj : descortés, maleducado

impoliteness [ˌɪmpəˈlaɪtnəs] n : descortesía f, falta f de educación

impolitic [ɪmˈpɑləˌtɪk] adj : imprudente, poco político

imponderable¹ [ɪmˈpɑndərəbəl] adj : imponderable

imponderable² n : imponderable m

import¹ [ɪmˈport] vt **1** SIGNIFY : significar **2** importar ⟨to import foreign cars : importar autos extranjeros⟩ **3** : importar (en informática)

import² [ˈɪmˌport] n **1** SIGNIFICANCE : importancia f, significación f **2** → portation

importance [ɪmˈportənts] n : importancia f

important [ɪmˈportənt] adj : importante

importantly [ɪmˈportəntli] adv **1** : con importancia **2** more importantly : lo que es más importante

importation [ˌɪmˌporˈteɪʃən] n : importación f

importer [ɪmˈportər] n : importador m, -dora f

importune [ˌɪmpərˈtuːn, -ˈtjuːn; ɪmˈportʃən] vt **-tuned; -tuning** : importunar, implorar

impose [ɪmˈpoːz] v **-posed; -posing** vt : imponer ⟨to impose a tax : imponer un impuesto⟩ — vi to impose on : abusar de, molestar ⟨to impose on her kindness : abusar de su bondad⟩

imposing [ɪmˈpoːzɪŋ] adj : imponente, impresionante

imposition [ˌɪmpəˈzɪʃən] n : imposición f

impossibility [ɪmˌpɑsəˈbɪləʧi] n, pl **-ties** : imposibilidad f

impossible [ɪmˈpɑsəbəl] adj **1** : imposible ⟨an impossible task : una tarea imposible⟩ ⟨to make life impossible for : hacerle la vida imposible a⟩ **2** UNACCEPTABLE : inaceptable

impossibly [ɪmˈpɑsəbli] adv : imposiblemente, increíblemente

impostor or **imposter** [ɪmˈpastər] n : impostor m, -tora f

impotence [ˈɪmpətənts] n : impotencia f

impotency [ˈɪmpətəntsi] → **impotence**

impotent [ˈɪmpətənt] adj : impotente

impound [ɪmˈpaʊnd] vt : incautar, embargar, confiscar

impoverish [ɪmˈpɑvərɪʃ] vt : empobrecer

impoverished [ɪmˈpɑvərɪʃt] adj : empobrecido

impoverishment [ɪmˈpɑvərɪʃmənt] n : empobrecimiento m

impracticable [ɪmˈpræktɪkəbəl] adj : impracticable

impractical [ɪmˈpræktɪkəl] adj : poco práctico

imprecise [ˌɪmprɪˈsaɪs] adj : impreciso

imprecisely [ˌɪmprɪˈsaɪsli] adv : con imprecisión

impreciseness [ˌɪmprɪˈsaɪsnəs] → **imprecision**

imprecision [ˌɪmprɪˈsɪʒən] n : imprecisión f, falta de precisión f

impregnable [ɪmˈprɛgnəbəl] adj : inexpugnable, impenetrable, inconquistable

impregnate [ɪmˈprɛgˌneɪt] vt **-nated; -nating 1** FERTILIZE : fecundar **2** PERMEATE, SATURATE : impregnar, empapar, saturar

impresario [ˌɪmprəˈsɑriˌo, -ˈsær-] n, pl **-rios** : empresario m, -ria f

impress [ɪmˈprɛs] vt **1** IMPRINT : imprimir, estampar **2** : impresionar, causar impresión a ⟨I was not impressed : no me hizo buena impresión⟩ **3** to **impress (something) on someone** : recalcarle (algo) a alguien — vi : impresionar, hacer una impresión

impression [ɪmˈprɛʃən] n **1** IMPRINT : marca f, huella f, molde m (de los dientes) **2** EFFECT : impresión f, efecto m, impacto m ⟨to make a good/bad impression on someone : causarle (una) buena/mala impresión a alguien⟩ **3** PRINTING : impresión f **4** NOTION : impresión f, noción f ⟨to give the impression that : dar la impresión de que⟩ ⟨to have the impression that, to be under the impression that : tener la impresión de que⟩

impressionable [ɪmˈprɛʃənəbəl] adj : impresionable

impressionism [ɪmˈprɛʃəˌnɪzəm] n : impresionismo m

impressionist [ɪmˈprɛʃənɪst] n : impresionista mf — **impressionist** adj

impressive [ɪmˈprɛsɪv] adj : impresionante — **impressively** adv

impressiveness [ɪmˈprɛsɪvnəs] n : calidad de ser impresionante

imprint¹ [ɪmˈprɪnt, ˈɪmˌ-] vt : imprimir, estampar

imprint² [ˈɪmˌprɪnt] n : marca f, huella f

imprison [ɪmˈprɪzən] *vt* **1** JAIL : encarcelar, aprisionar **2** CONFINE : recluir, encerrar

imprisonment [ɪmˈprɪzənmənt] *n* : encarcelamiento *m*

improbability [ɪmˌprɑbəˈbɪləṭi] *n*, *pl* **-ties** : improbabilidad *f*, inverosimilitud *f*

improbable [ɪmˈprɑbəbəl] *adj* : improbable, inverosímil

impromptu¹ [ɪmˈprɑmp,tu:, -ˌtju:] *adv* : sin preparación, espontáneamente

impromptu² *adj* : espontáneo, improvisado

impromptu³ *n* : improvisación *f*

improper [ɪmˈprɑpər] *adj* **1** INCORRECT : incorrecto, impropio **2** INDECOROUS : indecoroso

improperly [ɪmˈprɑpərli] *adv* : incorrectamente, indebidamente

impropriety [ˌɪmprəˈpraɪəṭi] *n*, *pl* **-eties** INDECOROUSNESS : indecoro *m*, falta *f* de decoro **2** ERROR : impropiedad *f*, incorrección *f*

improve [ɪmˈpru:v] *v* **-proved; -proving** : mejorar

improvement [ɪmˈpru:vmənt] *n* : mejoramiento *m*, mejora *f*

improvidence [ɪmˈprɑvədən̬ts] *n* : improvisión *f*

improvisation [ɪmˌprɑvəˈzeɪʃən, ˌɪmprəvə-] *n* : improvisación *f*

improvise [ˈɪmprəˌvaɪz] *v* **-vised; -vising** : improvisar

imprudence [ɪmˈpru:dən̬ts] *n* : imprudencia *f*, indiscreción *f*

imprudent [ɪmˈpru:dənt] *adj* : imprudente, indiscreto

impudence [ˈɪmpjədən̬ts] *n* : insolencia *f*, descaro *m*

impudent [ˈɪmpjədənt] *adj* : insolente, descarado — **impudently** *adv*

impugn [ɪmˈpju:n] *vt* : impugnar

impulse [ˈɪm,pʌls] *n* **1** : impulso *m* **2 on impulse** : sin reflexionar

impulsive [ɪmˈpʌlsɪv] *adj* : impulsivo — **impulsively** *adv*

impulsiveness [ɪmˈpʌlsɪvnəs] *n* : impulsividad *f*

impunity [ɪmˈpju:nəṭi] *n* **1** : impunidad *f* **2 with impunity** : impunemente

impure [ɪmˈpjʊr] *adj* **1** : impuro ⟨impure thoughts : pensamientos impuros⟩ **2** CONTAMINATED : con impurezas, impuro

impurity [ɪmˈpjʊrəṭi] *n*, *pl* **-ties** : impureza *f*

impute [ɪmˈpju:t] *vt* **-puted; -puting** ATTRIBUTE : imputar, atribuir

in¹ [ˈɪn] *adv* **1** INSIDE : dentro, adentro ⟨let's go in : vamos adentro⟩ ⟨the burglars broke in through the window : los ladrones entraron por la ventana⟩ **2** (*to or towards a place*) ⟨they flew in yesterday : llegaron ayer (en avión)⟩ ⟨she leaned farther in : se inclinó más (hacia adelante)⟩ **3** (*indicating a union*) ⟨mix the flour in : añade la harina⟩ **4** (*indicating containment*) ⟨to shut in : encerrar⟩ **5** PARTICIPATING ⟨count me in : yo me apunto⟩ **6** (*to a job or position*)

⟨she was voted in : fue elegida, ganó las elecciones⟩ **7** COLLECTED ⟨the crops are in : las cosechas ya están recogidas⟩ ⟨are all the votes in? : ¿tenemos todos los votos?⟩ ⟨the results are in : se conocen los resultados⟩ **8** (*within bounds*) : dentro (en deportes) **9** in that : en el sentido de que **10 to be in** : estar ⟨is Linda in? : ¿está Linda?⟩ ⟨is the train in? : ¿ha llegado el tren?⟩ **11 to be in** : estar en poder ⟨the Democrats are in : los demócratas están en el poder⟩ **12 to be in for** ⟨they're in for a treat : les va a encantar⟩ ⟨he's in for a surprise : se va a llevar una sorpresa⟩ **13 to be in on** : participar en, tomar parte en **14 to be in with someone** : ser muy amigo de alguien **15 to get in good/bad with someone** : quedar bien/mal con alguien

in² *adj* **1** INSIDE : interior ⟨the in part : la parte interior⟩ **2** FASHIONABLE : de moda

in³ *prep* **1** (*indicating location or position*) ⟨in the lake : en el lago⟩ ⟨a pain in the leg : un dolor en la pierna⟩ ⟨in the sun : al sol⟩ ⟨in the rain : bajo la lluvia⟩ **2** (*with superlatives*) : de ⟨the best in the world : el mejor del mundo⟩ **3** INTO : en, a ⟨he broke it in pieces : lo rompió en pedazos⟩ ⟨she went in the house : se metió a la casa⟩ **4** DURING : por, en, durante ⟨in the afternoon : por la tarde⟩ **5** WITHIN : dentro de ⟨I'll be back in a week : vuelvo dentro de una semana⟩ **6** (*indicating belonging*) : en, de ⟨she plays in a band : toca en una banda⟩ ⟨the first scene in the movie : la primera escena de la película⟩ **7** (*indicating manner or form*) : en, con, de ⟨in Spanish : en español⟩ ⟨written in pencil : escrito con lápiz⟩ ⟨in this way : de esta manera⟩ ⟨in some respects : en algún sentido⟩ ⟨in a circle : en un círculo⟩ ⟨in height : de altura⟩ ⟨in theory : en teoría⟩ ⟨she was in uniform : llevaba uniforme⟩ ⟨she was (dressed) in blue : iba (vestido) de azul⟩ **8** (*indicating states or circumstances*) ⟨to be in luck : tener suerte⟩ ⟨to be in love : estar enamorado⟩ ⟨to be in a hurry : tener prisa⟩ ⟨to be/get in trouble : estar/meterse en un lío⟩ **9** (*indicating purpose*) ⟨in reply : en respuesta, como réplica⟩ **10** (*with regard to*) : en ⟨do you believe in ghosts? : ¿crees en los fantasmas?⟩ **11** : en (un campo) ⟨he works in insurance : trabaja en seguros⟩ **12** (*in approximations*) ⟨she's in her thirties : tiene treinta y tantos años⟩ ⟨in the 1940's : en los años cuarenta⟩ **13** (*indicating a ratio*) : de ⟨one in five : uno de cada cinco⟩

in⁴ *n* **ins and outs** : pormenores *mpl*

in- *or* **im-** *or* **il-** *pref* : in-, im-, i- ⟨inexact : inexacto⟩ ⟨imperfect : imperfecto⟩ ⟨illegal : ilegal⟩

inability [ˌɪnəˈbɪləṭi] *n*, *pl* **-ties** : incapacidad *f*

inaccessibility [ˌɪnɪkˌsesəˈbɪləṭi] *n*, *pl* **-ties** : inaccesibilidad *f*

inaccessible [ˌɪnɪkˈsesəbəl] *adj* : inaccesible

inaccuracy [ɪn'ækjərəsi] *n, pl* **-cies** 1 : inexactitud *f* 2 MISTAKE : error *m*

inaccurate [ɪn'ækjərət] *n* : inexacto, erróneo, incorrecto

inaccurately [ɪn'ækjərətli] *adv* : incorrectamente, con inexactitud

inaction [ɪn'ækʃən] *n* : inactividad *f*, inacción *f*

inactive [ɪn'æktɪv] *adj* : inactivo

inactivity [ˌɪnˌæk'tɪvəti] *n, pl* **-ties** : inactividad *f*, ociosidad *f*

inadequacy [ɪn'ædɪkwəsi] *n, pl* **-cies** 1 INSUFFICIENCY : insuficiencia *f* 2 INCOMPETENCE : ineptitud *f*, incompetencia *f*

inadequate [ɪn'ædɪkwət] *adj* 1 INSUFFICIENT : insuficiente, inadecuado 2 INCOMPETENT : inepto, incompetente

inadmissible [ˌɪnəd'mɪsəbəl] *adj* : inadmisible

inadvertent [ˌɪnəd'vərtənt] *adj* : inadvertido, involuntario — **inadvertently** *adv*

inadvisable [ˌɪnæd'vaɪzəbəl] *adj* : desaconsejable

inalienable [ɪn'eɪljənəbəl, -'eɪliənə-] *adj* : inalienable

inane [ɪ'neɪn] *adj* **inaner; -est** : estúpido, idiota, necio

inanimate [ɪn'ænəmət] *adj* : inanimado, exánime

inanity [ɪ'nænəti] *n, pl* **-ties** 1 STUPIDITY : estupidez *f* 2 NONSENSE : idiotez *f*, disparate *m*

inapplicable [ɪn'æplɪkəbəl, ˌɪnə-'plɪkəbəl] *adj* IRRELEVANT : inaplicable, irrelevante

inappropriate [ˌɪnə'proːpriət] *adj* : inapropiado, inadecuado, impropio

inappropriateness [ˌɪnə'proːpriətnəs] *n* : lo inapropiado, impropiedad *f*

inapt [ɪn'æpt] *adj* 1 UNSUITABLE : inadecuado, inapropiado 2 INEPT : inepto

inarticulate [ˌɪnɑr'tɪkjələt] *adj* : inarticulado, incapaz de expresarse

inarticulately [ˌɪnɑr'tɪkjələtli] *adv* : inarticuladamente

inasmuch as [ˌɪnæz'mʌtʃˌæz] *conj* : ya que, dado que, puesto que

inattention [ˌɪnə'tentʃən] *n* : falta *f* de atención, distracción *f*

inattentive [ˌɪnə'tentɪv] *adj* : distraído, despistado

inattentively [ˌɪnə'tentɪvli] *adv* : distraídamente, sin prestar atención

inaudible [ɪn'ɔdəbəl] *adj* : inaudible

inaudibly [ɪn'ɔdəbli] *adv* : de forma inaudible

inaugural¹ [ɪ'nɔgjərəl, -gərəl] *adj* : inaugural, de investidura

inaugural² *n* **or inaugural address** : discurso *m* de investidura 2 INAUGURATION : investidura *f* (de una persona)

inaugurate [ɪ'nɔgjəˌreɪt, -gə-] *vt* **-rated; -rating** 1 BEGIN : inaugurar 2 INDUCT : investir ⟨to inaugurate the president : investir al presidente⟩

inauguration [ɪˌnɔgjə'reɪʃən, -gə-] *n* 1 : inauguración *f* (de un edificio, un sistema, etc.) 2 : investidura *f* (de una persona)

inauspicious [ˌɪnɔ'spɪʃəs] *adj* : desfavorable, poco propicio

inauthentic [ˌɪnɔ'θɛntɪk] *adj* : inauténtico

inborn ['ɪnˌbɔrn] *adj* 1 CONGENITAL, INNATE : innato, congénito 2 HEREDITARY : hereditario

inbound ['ɪnˌbaʊnd] *adj* : que llega, de llegada

in-box ['ɪnˌbɑks] *n* : bandeja *f* de entrada

inbred ['ɪnˌbred] *adj* 1 : engendrado por endogamia 2 INNATE : innato

inbreed ['ɪnˌbriːd] *vt* **-bred; -breeding** : engendrar por endogamia

inbreeding ['ɪnˌbriːdɪŋ] *n* : endogamia *f*

Inca ['ɪŋkə] *n* : inca *mf*

incalculable [ɪn'kælkjələbəl] *adj* : incalculable — **incalculably** [-bli] *adv*

Incan ['ɪŋkən] *adj* : incaico

incandescence [ˌɪnkən'dɛsənts] *n* : incandescencia *f*

incandescent [ˌɪnkən'dɛsənt] *adj* 1 : incandescente 2 BRILLIANT : brillante

incantation [ˌɪnˌkæn'teɪʃən] *n* : conjuro *m*, ensalmo *m*

incapable [ɪn'keɪpəbəl] *adj* : incapaz

incapacitate [ˌɪnkə'pæsəˌteɪt] *vt* **-tated; -tating** : incapacitar

incapacity [ˌɪnkə'pæsəti] *n, pl* **-ties** : incapacidad *f*

incarcerate [ɪn'kɑrsəˌreɪt] *vt* **-ated; -ating** : encarcelar

incarceration [ɪnˌkɑrsə'reɪʃən] *n* : encarcelamiento *m*, encarcelación *f*

incarnate¹ [ɪn'kɑrˌneɪt] *vt* **-nated; -nating** : encarnar

incarnate² [ɪn'kɑrnət, -ˌneɪt] *adj* : encarnado

incarnation [ˌɪnˌkɑr'neɪʃən] *n* : encarnación *f*

incendiary¹ [ɪn'sɛndiˌri] *adj* : incendiario

incendiary² *n, pl* **-aries** : incendiario *m*, -ria *f*; pirómano *m*, -na *f*

incense¹ [ɪn'sɛnts] *vt* **-censed; -censing** : indignar, enfadar, enfurecer

incense² ['ɪnˌsɛnts] *n* : incienso *m*

incentive [ɪn'sɛntɪv] *n* : incentivo *m*, aliciente *m*, motivación *f*, acicate *m*

inception [ɪn'sɛpʃən] *n* : comienzo *m*, principio *m*

incessant [ɪn'sɛsənt] *adj* : incesante, continuo — **incessantly** *adv*

incest ['ɪnˌsɛst] *n* : incesto *m*

incestuous [ɪn'sɛstʃuəs] *adj* : incestuoso

inch¹ ['ɪntʃ] *v* : avanzar poco a poco

inch² *n* 1 : pulgada *f* 2 **every inch** : absoluto, seguro ⟨every inch a winner : un seguro ganador⟩ 3 **within an inch of** : a punto de

incidence ['ɪnˌsədənts] *n* 1 FREQUENCY : frecuencia *f*, índice *m* ⟨a high incidence of crime : un alto índice de crímenes⟩ 2 **angle of incidence** : ángulo *m* de incidencia

incident¹ ['ɪntsədənt] *adj* : incidente

incident² *n* : incidente *m*, incidencia *f*, episodio *m* (en una obra de ficción)

incidental¹ [ˌɪntsə'dɛntəl] *adj* 1 SECONDARY : incidental, secundario 2 ACCIDENTAL : casual, fortuito

incidental² *n* **1** : algo incidental **2 incidentals** *npl* : imprevistos *mpl*

incidentally [ˌɪntsə'dɛntəli, -'dɛntli] *adv* **1** BY CHANCE : incidentalmente, casualmente **2** BY THE WAY : a propósito, por cierto

incinerate [ɪn'sɪnə,reɪt] *vt* -ated; -ating : incinerar

incinerator [ɪn'sɪnə,reɪtər] *n* : incinerador *m*

incipient [ɪn'sɪpiənt] *adj* : incipiente, naciente

incise [ɪn'saɪz] *vt* -cised; -cising **1** ENGRAVE : grabar, cincelar, inscribir **2** : hacer una incisión en

incision [ɪn'sɪʒən] *n* : incisión *f*

incisive [ɪn'saɪsɪv] *adj* : incisivo, penetrante

incisively [ɪn'saɪsɪvli] *adv* : con agudeza

incisor [ɪn'saɪzər] *n* : incisivo *m*

incite [ɪn'saɪt] *vt* -cited; -citing : incitar, instigar

incitement [ɪn'saɪtmənt] *n* : incitación *f*

inclemency [ɪn'klɛməntsi] *n, pl* -cies : inclemencia *f*

inclement [ɪn'klɛmənt] *adj* : inclemente, tormentoso

inclination [ˌɪnklə'neɪʃən] *n* **1** PROPENSITY : inclinación *f*, tendencia *f* **2** DESIRE : deseo *m*, ganas *fpl* **3** BOW : inclinación *f*

incline¹ [ɪn'klaɪn] *v* -clined; -clining *vi* **1** SLOPE : inclinarse **2** TEND : inclinarse, tender ⟨he is inclined to be late : tiende a llegar tarde⟩ — *vt* **1** LOWER : inclinar, bajar ⟨to incline one's head : bajar la cabeza⟩ **2** SLANT : inclinar **3** PREDISPOSE : predisponer

incline² [ˈɪn,klaɪn] *n* : inclinación *f*, pendiente *f*

inclined [ɪn'klaɪnd] *adj* **1** SLOPING : inclinado **2** PRONE : prono, dispuesto, dado

inclose, inclosure → enclose, enclosure

include [ɪn'klu:d] *vt* -cluded; -cluding : incluir, comprender

including [ɪn'klu:dɪŋ] *prep* : incluyendo ⟨including tax : (con) impuestos incluidos⟩ ⟨without including expenses : sin incluir los gastos⟩ ⟨up to and including . . . : hasta . . . inclusive⟩

inclusion [ɪn'klu:ʒən] *n* : inclusión *f*

inclusive [ɪn'klu:sɪv] *adj* : inclusivo

incognito [ˌɪn,kɑg'ni:to, ɪn'kɑgnə,to:] *adv & adj* : de incógnito

incoherence [ˌɪnko'hɪrənts, -'hɛr-] *n* : incoherencia *f*

incoherent [ˌɪnko'hɪrənt, -'hɛr-] *adj* : incoherente — **incoherently** *adv*

incombustible [ˌɪnkəm'bʌstəbəl] *adj* : incombustible

income [ˈɪn,kʌm] *n* : ingresos *mpl*, entradas *fpl*

income tax *n* : impuesto *m* sobre la renta

incoming [ˈɪn,kʌmɪŋ] *adj* **1** ARRIVING : que se recibe (dícese del correo), que llega (dícese de las personas), ascendente (dícese de la marea) **2** NEW : nuevo, entrante ⟨the incoming president : el nuevo presidente⟩ ⟨the incoming year : el año entrante⟩

incommunicado [ˌɪnkə,mju:nə'kɑdo] *adj* : incomunicado

incomparable [ɪn'kɑmpərəbəl] *adj* : incomparable, sin igual

incompatibility [ˌɪnkəm,pætə'bɪləti] *n, pl* -ties : incompatibilidad *f*

incompatible [ˌɪnkəm'pætəbəl] *adj* : incompatible

incompetence [ɪn'kɑmpətənts] *n* : incompetencia *f*, impericia *f*, ineptitud *f*

incompetent [ɪn'kɑmpətənt] *n* : incompetente *mf*; inepto *m*, -ta *f* — **incompetent** *adj*

incomplete [ˌɪnkəm'pli:t] *adj* : incompleto — **incompletely** *adv*

incomprehensible [ˌɪn,kɑmprɪ'hɛntsəbəl] *adj* : incomprensible

incomprehension [ˌɪn,kɑmprɪ'hɛntʃən] *n* : incomprensión *f*

inconceivable [ˌɪnkən'si:vəbəl] *adj* **1** INCOMPREHENSIBLE : incomprensible **2** UNBELIEVABLE : inconcebible, increíble

inconceivably [ˌɪnkən'si:vəbli] *adv* : inconcebiblemente, increíblemente

inconclusive [ˌɪnkən'klu:sɪv] *adj* : no concluyente, no decisivo

incongruity [ˌɪnkən'gru:əti, -,kɑn-] *n, pl* -ties : incongruencia *f*

incongruous [ɪn'kɑŋgruəs] *adj* : incongruente, inapropiado, fuera de lugar

incongruously [ɪn'kɑŋgruəsli] *adv* : de manera incongruente, inapropiadamente

inconsequential [ˌɪn,kɑnsə'kwɛntʃəl] *adj* : intrascendente, de poco importancia

inconsiderable [ˌɪnkən'sɪdərəbəl] *adj* : insignificante

inconsiderate [ˌɪnkən'sɪdərət] *adj* : desconsiderado, sin consideración — **inconsiderately** *adv*

inconsistency [ˌɪnkən'sɪstəntsi] *n, pl* -cies : inconsecuencia *f*, inconsistencia *f*

inconsistent [ˌɪnkən'sɪstənt] *adj* : inconsecuente, inconsistente

inconsolable [ˌɪnkən'so:ləbəl] *adj* : inconsolable — **inconsolably** [-bli] *adv*

inconspicuous [ˌɪnkən'spɪkjuəs] *adj* : discreto, no conspicuo, que no llama la atención

inconspicuously [ˌɪnkən'spɪkjuəsli] *adv* : discretamente, sin llamar la atención

incontestable [ˌɪnkən'tɛstəbəl] *adj* : incontestable, indiscutible — **incontestably** [-bli] *adv*

incontinence [ɪn'kɑntənənts] *n* : incontinencia *f*

incontinent [ɪn'kɑntənənt] *adj* : incontinente

inconvenience¹ [ˌɪnkən'vi:njənts] *vt* -nienced; -niencing : importunar, incomodar, molestar

inconvenience² *n* : incomodidad *f*, molestia *f*

inconvenient [ˌɪnkən'vi:njənt] *adj* : inconveniente, importuno, incómodo — **inconveniently** *adv*

incorporate [ɪn'kɔrpə,reɪt] *vt* -rated; -rating **1** INCLUDE : incorporar, incluir **2** : incorporar, constituir en sociedad (dícese de un negocio)

incorporation [ɪn,kɔrpə'reɪʃən] *n* : incorporación *f*

incorporeal [,ɪn,kɔr'poriəl] *adj* : incorpóreo

incorrect [,ɪnkə'rɛkt] *adj* **1** INACCURATE : incorrecto **2** WRONG : equivocado, erróneo **3** IMPROPER : impropio — **incorrectly** *adv*

incorrigible [ɪn'kɔrədʒəbəl] *adj* : incorregible

incorruptible [,ɪnkə'rʌptəbəl] *adj* : incorruptible

increase¹ [ɪn'kri:s, 'ɪn,kri:s] *v* **-creased; -creasing** *vi* GROW : aumentar, crecer, subir (dícese de los precios) — *vt* AUGMENT : aumentar, acrecentar

increase² ['ɪn,kri:s, ɪn'kri:s] *n* : aumento *m*, incremento *m*, subida *f* (de precios)

increasing [ɪn'kri:sɪŋ, 'ɪn,kri:sɪŋ] *adj* : creciente

increasingly [ɪn'kri:sɪŋli] *adv* : cada vez más

incredible [ɪn'krɛdəbəl] *adj* : increíble — **incredibly** [-bli] *adv*

incredulity [,ɪnkrɪ'du:ləti, -'dju:-] *n* : incredulidad *f*

incredulous [ɪn'krɛdʒələs] *adj* : incrédulo, escéptico

incredulously [ɪn'krɛdʒələsli] *adv* : con incredulidad

increment ['ɪŋkrəmənt, 'ɪn-] *n* : incremento *m*, aumento *m*

incremental [,ɪŋkrə'mɛntəl, ,ɪn-] *adj* : de incremento

incriminate [ɪn'krɪmə,neɪt] *vt* **-nated; -nating** : incriminar

incrimination [ɪn,krɪmə'neɪʃən] *n* : incriminación *f*

incriminatory [ɪn'krɪmənə,tori] *adj* : incriminatorio

incubate ['ɪŋkjʊ,beɪt, 'ɪn-] *v* **-bated; -bating** *vt* : incubar, empollar — *vi* : incubar(se), empollar

incubation [,ɪŋkjʊ'beɪʃən, ,ɪn-] *n* : incubación *f*

incubator ['ɪŋkjʊ,beɪtər, 'ɪn-] *n* : incubadora *f*

inculcate [ɪn'kʌl,keɪt, 'ɪn,kʌl-] *vt* **-cated; -cating** : inculcar

incumbency [ɪn'kʌmbəntsi] *n, pl* **-cies 1** OBLIGATION : incumbencia *f* **2** : mandato *m* (en la política)

incumbent¹ [ɪn'kʌmbənt] *adj* : obligatorio

incumbent² *n* : titular *mf*

incur [ɪn'kər] *vt* **incurred; incurring** : provocar (al enojo), incurrir en (gastos, obligaciones)

incurable [ɪn'kjʊrəbəl] *adj* : incurable, sin remedio

incursion [ɪn'kərʒən] *n* : incursión *f*

indebted [ɪn'dɛtəd] *adj* **1** : endeudado **2 to be indebted to** : estar en deuda con, estarle agradecido a

indebtedness [ɪn'dɛtədnəs] *n* : endeudamiento *m*

indecency [ɪn'di:səntsi] *n, pl* **-cies** : indecencia *f*

indecent [ɪn'di:sənt] *adj* : indecente — **indecently** *adv*

indecipherable [,ɪndɪ'saɪfərəbəl] *adj* : indescifrable

indecision [,ɪndɪ'sɪʒən] *n* : indecisión *f*, irresolución *f*

indecisive [,ɪndɪ'saɪsɪv] *adj* **1** INCONCLUSIVE : indeciso, que no es decisivo **2** IRRESOLUTE : indeciso, irresoluto, vacilante **3** INDEFINITE : indefinido — **indecisively** *adv*

indecorous [ɪn'dɛkərəs, ,ɪndɪ'korəs] *adj* : indecoroso — **indecorously** *adv*

indecorousness [ɪn'dɛkərəsnəs, ,ɪndɪ'korəs-] *n* : indecoro *m*

indeed [ɪn'di:d] *adv* **1** (*emphasizing the truth of a statement*) : efectivamente ⟨yes, indeed : sí, efectivamente⟩ ⟨it's a very serious problem indeed : esto sí que es un problema muy grave⟩ ⟨thank you very much indeed : muchísimas gracias⟩ **2** (*expressing surprise or doubt*) ⟨indeed? : ¿ah, sí?, ¿de veras?, ¡no me digas!⟩ **3** (*strengthening a previous statement*) ⟨it is possible — indeed, probable — that . . . : es posible, e incluso probable, que . . .⟩ **4** (*emphasizing that one does not know the answer*) ⟨how can we help them? how, indeed! : ¿cómo podemos ayudarlos? ¡buena pregunta!⟩

indefatigable [,ɪndɪ'fætɪgəbəl] *adj* : incansable, infatigable — **indefatigably** [-bli] *adv*

indefensible [,ɪndɪ'fɛntsəbəl] *adj* **1** VULNERABLE : indefendible, vulnerable **2** INEXCUSABLE : inexcusable

indefinable [,ɪndɪ'faɪnəbəl] *adj* : indefinible

indefinite [ɪn'dɛfənət] *adj* **1** : indefinido, indeterminado **2** : indefinido (en lingüística) ⟨indefinite pronouns/articles : pronombres/artículos indefinidos⟩ **3** VAGUE : vago, impreciso

indefinitely [ɪn'dɛfənətli] *adv* : indefinidamente, por un tiempo indefinido

indelible [ɪn'dɛləbəl] *adj* : indeleble, imborrable — **indelibly** [-bli] *adv*

indelicacy [ɪn'dɛləkəsi] *n* : falta *f* de delicadeza

indelicate [ɪn'dɛlɪkət] *adj* **1** IMPROPER : indelicado, indecoroso **2** TACTLESS : indiscreto, falto de tacto

indemnify [ɪn'dɛmnə,faɪ] *vt* **-fied; -fying 1** INSURE : asegurar **2** COMPENSATE : indemnizar, compensar

indemnity [ɪn'dɛmnəti] *n, pl* **-ties 1** INSURANCE : indemnidad *f* **2** COMPENSATION : indemnización *f*

indent [ɪn'dɛnt] *vt* : sangrar (un párrafo)

indentation [,ɪn,dɛn'teɪʃən] *n* **1** NOTCH : muesca *f*, mella *f* **2** INDENTING : sangría *f* (de un párrafo)

indenture¹ [ɪn'dɛntʃər] *vt* **-tured; -turing** : ligar por contrato

indenture² *n* : contrato de aprendizaje

independence [,ɪndə'pɛndənts] *n* : independencia *f*

Independence Day *n* : día *m* de la Independencia (4 de julio en los EEUU.)

independent¹ [,ɪndə'pɛndənt] *adj* : independiente — **independently** *adv*

independent² *n* : independiente *mf*

in–depth *adj* : a fondo, exhaustivo

indescribable [ˌɪndɪˈskraɪbəbəl] *adj* : indescriptible, incalificable — **indescribably** [-bli] *adv*

indestructible [ˌɪndɪˈstrʌktəbəl] *adj* : indestructible

indeterminate [ˌɪndɪˈtərmənət] *adj* **1** VAGUE : vago, impreciso, indeterminado **2** INDEFINITE : indeterminado, indefinido

index[1] [ˈɪnˌdɛks] *vt* **1** : ponerle un índice a (un libro o una revista) **2** : incluir en un índice ⟨all proper names are indexed : todos los nombres propios están incluidos en el índice⟩ **3** INDICATE : indicar, señalar **4** REGULATE : indexar, indiciar ⟨to index prices : indiciar los precios⟩

index[2] *n, pl* **-dexes** *or* **-dices** [ˈɪndəˌsiːz] **1** : índice *m* (de un libro, de precios) **2** INDICATION : indicio *m*, índice *m*, señal *f* ⟨an index of her character : una señal de su carácter⟩

index finger *n* FOREFINGER : dedo *m* índice

Indian [ˈɪndiən] *n* : indio *m*, -dia *f* **2** *often offensive* → **Native American** — **Indian** *adj*

indicate [ˈɪndəˌkeɪt] *vt* **-cated; -cating** **1** POINT OUT : indicar, señalar **2** SHOW, SUGGEST : ser indicio de, ser señal de **3** EXPRESS : expresar, señalar **4** REGISTER : marcar, poner (una medida, etc.)

indication [ˌɪndəˈkeɪʃən] *n* : indicio *m*, señal *f*

indicative [ɪnˈdɪkətɪv] *adj* : indicativo

indicator [ˈɪndəˌkeɪtər] *n* : indicador *m*

indict [ɪnˈdaɪt] *vt* : acusar, procesar (por un crimen)

indictment [ɪnˈdaɪtmənt] *n* : acusación *f*

indifference [ɪnˈdɪfrənts, -ˈdɪfə-] *n* : indiferencia *f*

indifferent [ɪnˈdɪfrənt, -ˈdɪfə-] *adj* **1** UNCONCERNED : indiferente **2** MEDIOCRE : mediocre

indifferently [ɪnˈdɪfrəntli, -ˈdɪfə-] *adv* **1** : con indiferencia, indiferentemente **2** SO-SO : de modo regular, más o menos

indigence [ˈɪndɪdʒənts] *n* : indigencia *f*

indigenous [ɪnˈdɪdʒənəs] *adj* : indígena, nativo

indigent [ˈɪndɪdʒənt] *adj* : indigente, pobre

indigestible [ˌɪndaɪˈdʒɛstəbəl, -dɪ-] *adj* : difícil de digerir

indigestion [ˌɪndaɪˈdʒɛstʃən, -dɪ-] *n* : indigestión *f*, empacho *m*

indignant [ɪnˈdɪgnənt] *adj* : indignado

indignantly [ɪnˈdɪgnəntli] *adv* : con indignación

indignation [ˌɪndɪgˈneɪʃən] *n* : indignación *f*

indignity [ɪnˈdɪgnəti] *n, pl* **-ties** : indignidad *f*

indigo [ˈɪndɪˌgoː] *n, pl* **-gos** *or* **-goes** : añil *m*, índigo *m*

indirect [ˌɪndəˈrɛkt, -daɪ-] *adj* : indirecto — **indirectly** *adv*

indiscernible [ˌɪndɪˈsərnəbəl, -ˈzər-] *adj* : imperceptible

indiscreet [ˌɪndɪˈskriːt] *adj* : indiscreto — **indiscreetly** *adv*

indiscretion [ˌɪndɪˈskrɛʃən] *n* : indiscreción *f*

indiscriminate [ˌɪndɪˈskrɪmənət] *adj* : indiscriminado

indiscriminately [ˌɪndɪˈskrɪmənətli] *adv* : sin discriminación, sin discernimiento

indispensable [ˌɪndɪˈspɛntsəbəl] *adj* : indispensable, necesario, imprescindible — **indispensably** [-bli] *adv*

indisposed [ˌɪndɪˈspoːzd] *adj* **1** ILL : indispuesto, enfermo **2** AVERSE, DISINCLINED : opuesto, reacio ⟨to be indisposed toward working : no tener ganas de trabajar⟩

indisputable [ˌɪndɪˈspjuːtəbəl, ɪnˈdɪspjʊtə-] *adj* : indiscutible, incuestionable, incontestable — **indisputably** [-bli] *adv*

indistinct [ˌɪndɪˈstɪŋkt] *adj* : indistinto — **indistinctly** *adv*

indistinctness [ˌɪndɪˈstɪŋktnəs] *n* : falta *f* de claridad

indistinguishable [ˌɪndɪˈstɪŋgwɪʃəbəl] *adj* : indistinguible

individual[1] [ˌɪndəˈvɪdʒuəl] *adj* **1** PERSONAL : individual, personal ⟨individual traits : características personales⟩ **2** SEPARATE : individual, separado **3** PARTICULAR : particular, propio

individual[2] *n* : individuo *m*

individualism [ˌɪndəˈvɪdʒəwəˌlɪzəm] *n* : individualismo *m*

individualist [ˌɪndəˈvɪdʒuəlɪst] *n* : individualista *mf*

individualistic [ˌɪndəˌvɪdʒuəˈlɪstɪk] *adj* : individualista

individuality [ˌɪndəˌvɪdʒuˈæləti] *n, pl* **-ties** : individualidad *f*

individualize [ˌɪndəˈvɪdʒuəˌlaɪz] *vt* **-ized; -izing** : individualizar

individually [ˌɪndəˈvɪdʒuəli, -dʒəli] *adv* : individualmente

indivisible [ˌɪndɪˈvɪzəbəl] *adj* : indivisible

indoctrinate [ɪnˈdaktrəˌneɪt] *vt* **-nated; -nating** **1** TEACH : enseñar, instruir **2** PROPAGANDIZE : adoctrinar

indoctrination [ɪnˌdaktrəˈneɪʃən] *n* : adoctrinamiento *m*

indolence [ˈɪndələnts] *n* : indolencia *f*

indolent [ˈɪndələnt] *adj* : indolente

indomitable [ɪnˈdamətəbəl] *adj* : invencible, indomable, indómito — **indomitably** [-bli] *adv*

Indonesian [ˌɪndoˈniːʒən, -ʃən] *n* : indonesio *m*, -sia *f* — **Indonesian** *adj*

indoor [ˈɪnˌdor] *adj* : interior (dícese de las plantas), para estar en casa (dícese de la ropa), cubierto (dícese de las piscinas, etc.), bajo techo (dícese de los deportes)

indoors [ˈɪnˈdorz] *adv* : adentro, dentro

indubitable [ɪnˈduːbətəbəl, -ˈdjuː-] *adj* : indudable, incuestionable, indiscutible

indubitably [ɪnˈduːbətəbli, -ˈdjuː-] *adv* : indudablemente

induce [ɪnˈduːs, -ˈdjuːs] *vt* **-duced; -ducing** **1** PERSUADE : persuadir, inducir **2** CAUSE : inducir, provocar ⟨to induce labor : provocar un parto⟩

inducement [ɪnˈduːsmənt, -ˈdjuːs-] *n* **1** INCENTIVE : incentivo *m*, aliciente *m* **2** : inducción *f*, provocación *f* (de un parto)

induct [ɪn'dʌkt] *vt* **1** INSTALL : instalar, investir **2** ADMIT : admitir (como miembro) **3** CONSCRIPT : reclutar (al servicio militar)

inductee [,ɪn,dʌk'ti:] *n* : recluta *mf*, conscripto *m*, -ta *f*

induction [ɪn'dʌkʃən] *n* **1** INTRODUCTION : iniciación *f*, introducción *f* **2** : inducción *f* (en la lógica o la electricidad)

inductive [ɪn'dʌktɪv] *adj* : inductivo

indulge [ɪn'dʌldʒ] *v* -dulged; -dulging *vt* **1** GRATIFY : gratificar, satisfacer **2** SPOIL : consentir, mimar — *vi* **to indulge in** : permitirse

indulgence [ɪn'dʌldʒənts] *n* **1** SATISFYING : satisfacción *f*, gratificación *f* **2** HUMORING : complacencia *f*, indulgencia *f* **3** SPOILING : consentimiento *m* **4** : indulgencia *f* (en la religión)

indulgent [ɪn'dʌldʒənt] *adj* : indulgente, consentido — **indulgently** *adv*

industrial [ɪn'dʌstriəl] *adj* : industrial — **industrially** *adv*

industrialist [ɪn'dʌstriəlɪst] *n* : industrial *mf*

industrialization [ɪn,dʌstriələ'zeɪ-ʃən] *n* : industrialización *f*

industrialize [ɪn'dʌstriə,laɪz] *vt* -ized; -izing : industrializar

industrious [ɪn'dʌstriəs] *adj* : diligente, industrioso, trabajador

industriously [ɪn'dʌstriəsli] *adv* : con diligencia, con aplicación

industriousness [ɪn'dʌstriəsnəs] *n* : diligencia *f*, aplicación *f*

industry ['ɪndəstri] *n, pl* -tries **1** DILIGENCE : diligencia *f*, aplicación *f* **2** : industria *f* ⟨the steel industry : la industria siderúrgica⟩

inebriated [ɪ'ni:bri,eɪtəd] *adj* : ebrio, embriagado

inebriation [ɪ,ni:bri'eɪʃən] *n* : ebriedad *f*, embriaguez *f*

inedible [ɪn'ɛdəbəl] *adj* : incomible

ineffable [ɪn'ɛfəbəl] *adj* : inefable — **ineffably** [-bli] *adv*

ineffective [,ɪnɪ'fɛktɪv] *adj* **1** INEFFECTUAL : ineficaz, inútil **2** INCAPABLE : incompetente, ineficiente, incapaz

ineffectively [,ɪnɪ'fɛktɪvli] *adv* : ineficazmente, infructuosamente

ineffectual [,ɪnɪ'fɛktʃuəl] *adj* : inútil, ineficaz — **ineffectually** *adv*

inefficiency [,ɪnɪ'fɪʃəntsi] *n, pl* -cies : ineficiencia *f*, ineficacia *f*

inefficient [,ɪnɪ'fɪʃənt] *adj* **1** : ineficiente, ineficaz **2** INCAPABLE, INCOMPETENT : incompetente, incapaz — **inefficiently** *adv*

inelegance [ɪn'ɛləgənts] *n* : inelegancia *f*

inelegant [ɪn'ɛləgənt] *adj* : inelegante, poco elegante

ineligibility [ɪn,ɛlədʒə'bɪləti] *n* : inelegibilidad *f*

ineligible [ɪn'ɛlədʒəbəl] *adj* : inelegible

inept [ɪ'nɛpt] *adj* : inepto ⟨inept at : incapaz para⟩

ineptitude [ɪ'nɛptə,tu:d, -,tju:d] *n* : ineptitud *f*, incompetencia *f*, incapacidad *f*

inequality [,ɪnɪ'kwɑləti] *n, pl* -ties : desigualdad *f*

inequitable [ɪn'ɛkwətəbəl] *adj* : inequitativo

inequity [ɪn'ɛkwəti] *n, pl* -ties : inequidad *f*

inert [ɪ'nərt] *adj* **1** INACTIVE : inerte, inactivo **2** SLUGGISH : lento

inertia [ɪ'nərʃə] *n* : inercia *f*

inescapable [,ɪnɪ'skeɪpəbəl] *adj* : inevitable, ineludible — **inescapably** [-bli] *adv*

inessential [,ɪnɪ'sɛntʃəl] *adj* : que no es esencial, innecesario

inestimable [ɪn'ɛstəməbəl] *adj* : inestimable, inapreciable

inevitability [ɪn,ɛvətə'bɪləti] *n, pl* -ties : inevitabilidad *f*

inevitable [ɪn'ɛvətəbəl] *adj* : inevitable — **inevitably** [-bli] *adv*

inexact [,ɪnɪg'zækt] *adj* : inexacto

inexactly [,ɪnɪg'zæktli] *adv* : sin exactitud

inexcusable [,ɪnɪk'skju:zəbəl] *adj* : inexcusable, imperdonable — **inexcusably** [-bli] *adv*

inexhaustible [,ɪnɪg'zɔstəbəl] *adj* **1** INDEFATIGABLE : infatigable, incansable **2** ENDLESS : inagotable — **inexhaustibly** [-bli] *adv*

inexorable [ɪn'ɛksərəbəl] *adj* : inexorable — **inexorably** [-bli] *adv*

inexpensive [,ɪnɪk'spɛntsɪv] *adj* : barato, económico

inexperience [,ɪnɪk'spɪriənts] *n* : inexperiencia *f*

inexperienced [,ɪnɪk'spɪriəntst] *adj* : inexperto, novato

inexplicable [,ɪnɪk'splɪkəbəl] *adj* : inexplicable — **inexplicably** [-bli] *adv*

inexpressible [,ɪnɪk'sprɛsəbəl] *adj* : inexpresable, inefable

inextricable [,ɪnɪk'strɪkəbəl, ɪn'ɛk-,strɪ-] *adj* : inextricable — **inextricably** [-bli] *adv*

infallibility [ɪn,fæləˈbɪləti] *n* : infalibilidad *f*

infallible [ɪn'fæləbəl] *adj* : infalible — **infallibly** [-bli] *adv*

infamous ['ɪnfəməs] *adj* : infame — **infamously** *adv*

infamy ['ɪnfəmi] *n, pl* -mies : infamia *f*

infancy ['ɪnfəntsi] *n, pl* -cies : infancia *f*

infant ['ɪnfənt] *n* : bebé *m*; niño *m*, -ña *f*

infantile ['ɪnfən,taɪl, -təl, -,ti:l] *adj* : infantil, pueril

infantile paralysis → poliomyelitis

infantry ['ɪnfəntri] *n, pl* -tries : infantería *f*

infatuated [ɪn'fætʃu,eɪtəd] *adj* **to be infatuated with** : estar encaprichado con

infatuation [ɪn,fætʃu'eɪʃən] *n* : encaprichamiento *m*, enamoramiento *m*

infect [ɪn'fɛkt] *vt* : infectar, contagiar

infection [ɪn'fɛkʃən] *n* : infección *f*, contagio *m*

infectious [ɪn'fɛkʃəs] *adj* : infeccioso, contagioso

infer [ɪn'fər] *vt* **inferred; inferring 1** DEDUCE : deducir, inferir **2** SURMISE : concluir, suponer, tener entendido **3** IMPLY : sugerir, insinuar

inference ['ɪnfərənts] *n* : deducción *f*, inferencia *f*, conclusión *f*

inferior[1] [ɪm'fɪriər] *adj* : inferior, malo
inferior[2] *n* : inferior *mf*
inferiority [ɪnˌfɪri'orəti] *n, pl* -ties : inferioridad *f* ⟨inferiority complex : complejo de inferioridad⟩
infernal [ɪn'fərnəl] *adj* 1 : infernal ⟨infernal fires : fuegos infernales⟩ 2 DIABOLICAL : infernal, diabólico 3 DAMNABLE : maldito, condenado
inferno [ɪn'fərˌnoː] *n, pl* -nos : infierno *m*
infertile [ɪn'fərtəl, -ˌtaɪl] *adj* : estéril, infecundo
infertility [ˌɪnfər'tɪləti] *n* : esterilidad *f*, infecundidad *f*
infest [ɪn'fɛst] *vt* : infestar, plagar
infestation [ˌɪnˌfɛs'teɪʃən] *n* : infestación *f*, plaga *f*
infidel ['ɪnfədəl, -ˌdɛl] *n* : infiel *mf*
infidelity [ˌɪnfə'dɛləti, -faɪ-] *n, pl* -ties 1 UNFAITHFULNESS : infidelidad *f* 2 DISLOYALTY : deslealtad *f*
infield ['ɪnˌfiːld] *n* : cuadro *m*, diamante *m*
infighting ['ɪnˌfaɪtɪŋ] *n* : disputas *fpl* internas, luchas *fpl* internas
infiltrate [ɪn'fɪlˌtreɪt, 'ɪnfɪl-] *v* -trated; -trating *vt* : infiltrar — *vi* : infiltrarse
infiltration [ˌɪnfɪl'treɪʃən] *n* : infiltración *f*
infiltrator [ɪn'fɪlˌtreɪtər, 'ɪnfɪl-] *n* : infiltrado *m*, -da *f*
infinite ['ɪnfənət] *adj* 1 LIMITLESS : infinito, sin límites 2 VAST : infinito, vasto, extenso
infinitely ['ɪnfənətli] *adv* : infinitamente
infinitesimal [ˌɪnˌfɪnə'tɛsəməl] *adj* : infinitesimal — **infinitesimally** *adv*
infinitive [ɪn'fɪnətɪv] *n* : infinitivo *m*
infinity [ɪn'fɪnəti] *n, pl* -ties 1 : infinito *m* (en matemáticas, etc.) 2 : infinidad *f* ⟨an infinity of stars : una infinidad de estrellas⟩
infirm [ɪn'fərm] *adj* 1 FEEBLE : enfermizo, endeble 2 INSECURE : inseguro
infirmary [ɪn'fərməri] *n, pl* -ries : enfermería *f*, hospital *m*
infirmity [ɪn'fərməti] *n, pl* -ties 1 FRAILTY : debilidad *f* 2 AILMENT : enfermedad *f*, dolencia *f* ⟨the infirmities of age : los achaques de la vejez⟩
inflame [ɪn'fleɪm] *v* -flamed; -flaming *vt* 1 KINDLE : inflamar, encender 2 : inflamar (una herida) 3 STIR UP : encender, provocar, inflamar — *vi* : inflamarse
inflammable [ɪn'flæməbəl] *adj* 1 FLAMMABLE : inflamable 2 IRASCIBLE : irascible, explosivo
inflammation [ˌɪnflə'meɪʃən] *n* : inflamación *f*
inflammatory [ɪn'flæmətori] *adj* : inflamatorio, incendiario
inflatable [ɪn'fleɪtəbəl] *adj* : inflable
inflate [ɪn'fleɪt] *vt* -flated; -flating : inflar, hinchar
inflation [ɪn'fleɪʃən] *n* : inflación *f*
inflationary [ɪn'fleɪʃəˌneri] *adj* : inflacionario, inflacionista
inflect [ɪn'flɛkt] *vt* 1 CONJUGATE, DECLINE : conjugar, declinar 2 MODULATE : modular (la voz)
inflection [ɪn'flɛkʃən] *n* : inflexión *f*

inflexibility [ɪnˌflɛksə'bɪləti] *n, pl* -ties : inflexibilidad *f*
inflexible [ɪn'flɛksɪbəl] *adj* : inflexible
inflict [ɪn'flɪkt] *vt* 1 : infligir, causar, imponer 2 **to inflict oneself on** : imponer uno su presencia (a alguien)
infliction [ɪn'flɪkʃən] *n* : imposición *f*
influence[1] ['ɪnˌfluːənts, ɪn'fluːənts] *vt* -enced; -encing : influenciar, influir en
influence[2] *n* 1 : influencia *f*, influjo *m* ⟨to exert influence over : ejercer influencia sobre⟩ ⟨the influence of gravity : el influjo de la gravedad⟩ 2 **under the influence** : bajo la influencia del alcohol, embriagado
influential [ˌɪnflu'ɛntʃəl] *adj* : influyente
influenza [ˌɪnflu'ɛnzə] *n* : gripe *f*, influenza *f*, gripa *f* Col, Mex
influx ['ɪnˌflʌks] *n* : afluencia *f* (de gente), entrada *f* (de mercancías), llegada *f* (de ideas)
info ['ɪnfo] *n fam* → information
inform [ɪn'form] *vt* : informar, notificar, avisar — *vi* **to inform on** : delatar, denunciar
informal [ɪn'forməl] *adj* 1 UNCEREMONIOUS : sin ceremonia, sin etiqueta 2 CASUAL : informal, familiar (dícese del lenguaje) 3 UNOFFICIAL : informal, extraoficial
informality [ˌɪnfor'mæləti, -fər-] *n, pl* -ties : informalidad *f*, familiaridad *f*, falta *f* de ceremonia
informally [ɪn'forməli] *adv* : sin ceremonias, de manera informal, informalmente
informant [ɪn'formənt] *n* : informante *mf*; informador *m*, -dora *f*
information [ˌɪnfor'meɪʃən] *n* : información *f*
informational [ˌɪnfor'meɪʃənəl] *adj* : informativo
information technology *n* : informática *f*
informative [ɪn'formətɪv] *adj* : informativo, instructivo
informer [ɪn'formər] *n* : informante *mf*; informador *m*, -dora *f*
infraction [ɪn'frækʃən] *n* : infracción *f*, violación *f*, transgresión *f*
infrared [ˌɪnfrə'rɛd] *adj* : infrarrojo
infrastructure ['ɪnfrəˌstrʌktʃər] *n* : infraestructura *f*
infrequent [ɪn'friːkwənt] *adj* : infrecuente, raro
infrequently [ɪn'friːkwəntli] *adv* : raramente, con poca frecuencia
infringe [ɪn'frɪndʒ] *v* -fringed; -fringing *vt* : infringir, violar — *vi* **to infringe on** : abusar de, violar
infringement [ɪn'frɪndʒmənt] *n* 1 VIOLATION : violación *f* (de la ley), incumplimiento *m* (de un contrato) 2 ENCROACHMENT : usurpación *f* (de derechos, etc.)
infuriate [ɪn'fjuriˌeɪt] *vt* -ated; -ating : enfurecer, poner furioso
infuriating [ɪn'fjuriˌeɪtɪŋ] *adj* : indignante, exasperante
infuse [ɪn'fjuːz] *vt* -fused; -fusing 1 INSTILL : infundir 2 STEEP : hacer una infusión de

infusion [ɪnˈfjuːʒən] *n* : infusión *f*

ingenious [ɪnˈdʒiːnjəs] *adj* : ingenioso — **ingeniously** *adv*

ingenue *or* **ingénue** [ˈɑndʒəˌnuː, ˈæn-, ˈæʒə-, ˈɑ-] *n* : ingenua *f*

ingenuity [ˌɪndʒəˈnuːəti, -ˈnjuː-] *n, pl* **-ities** : ingenio *m*

ingenuous [ɪnˈdʒɛnjuəs] *adj* **1** FRANK : cándido, franco **2** NAIVE : ingenuo — **ingenuously** *adv*

ingenuousness [ɪnˈdʒɛnjuəsnəs] *n* **1** FRANKNESS : candidez *f*, candor *m* **2** NAÏVETÉ : ingenuidad *f*

ingest [ɪnˈdʒɛst] *vt* : ingerir

ingestion [ɪnˈdʒɛstʃən] *n* : ingestión *f*

inglorious [ɪnˈɡlɔriəs] *adj* : deshonroso, ignominioso

ingot [ˈɪŋɡət] *n* : lingote *m*

ingrained [ɪnˈɡreɪnd] *adj* : arraigado

ingrate [ˈɪnˌɡreɪt] *n* : ingrato *m*, -ta *f*

ingratiate [ɪnˈɡreɪʃiˌeɪt] *vt* **-ated; -ating** : conseguir la benevolencia de ⟨to ingratiate oneself with someone : congraciarse con alguien⟩

ingratiating [ɪnˈɡreɪʃiˌeɪtɪŋ] *adj* : halagador, zalamero, obsequioso

ingratitude [ɪnˈɡrætəˌtuːd, -ˌtjuːd] *n* : ingratitud *f*

ingredient [ɪnˈɡriːdiənt] *n* : ingrediente *m*, componente *m*

ingrown [ˈɪnˌɡroːn] *adj* **1** : crecido hacia adentro **2 ingrown toenail** : uña *f* encarnada

inhabit [ɪnˈhæbət] *vt* : vivir en, habitar, ocupar

inhabitable [ɪnˈhæbətəbəl] *adj* : habitable

inhabitant [ɪnˈhæbətənt] *n* : habitante *mf*

inhalant [ɪnˈheɪlənt] *n* : inhalante *m*

inhalation [ˌɪnhəˈleɪʃən, ˌɪnə-] *n* : inhalación *f*

inhale [ɪnˈheɪl] *v* **-haled; -haling** *vt* : inhalar, aspirar — *vi* : inspirar

inhaler [ɪnˈheɪlər] *n* : inhalador *m*

inhere [ɪnˈhɪr] *vi* **-hered; -hering** : ser inherente

inherent [ɪnˈhɪrənt, -ˈhɛr-] *adj* : inherente, intrínseco — **inherently** *adv*

inherit [ɪnˈhɛrət] *vt* : heredar

inheritance [ɪnˈhɛrətənts] *n* : herencia *f*

inheritor [ɪnˈhɛrətər] *n* : heredero *m*, -ra *f*

inhibit [ɪnˈhɪbət] *vt* IMPEDE : inhibir, impedir

inhibition [ˌɪnhəˈbɪʃən, ˌɪnə-] *n* : inhibición *f*, cohibición *f*

inhospitable [ˌɪnhɑˈspɪtəbəl, -ˈhɑsˌpɪ-] *adj* : inhóspito

inhuman [ɪnˈhjuːmən, -ˈjuː-] *adj* : inhumano, cruel — **inhumanly** *adv*

inhumane [ˌɪnhjuˈmeɪn, -juˈ-] *adj* INHUMAN : inhumano, cruel

inhumanity [ˌɪnhjuˈmænəti, -juˈ-] *n, pl* **-ties** : inhumanidad *f*, crueldad *f*

inimical [ɪˈnɪmɪkəl] *adj* **1** UNFAVORABLE : adverso, desfavorable **2** HOSTILE : hostil — **inimically** *adv*

inimitable [ɪˈnɪmətəbəl] *adj* : inimitable

iniquitous [ɪˈnɪkwətəs] *adj* : inicuo, malvado

iniquity [ɪˈnɪkwəti] *n, pl* **-ties** : iniquidad *f*

initial¹ [ɪˈnɪʃəl] *vt* **-tialed** *or* **-tialled; -tialing** *or* **-tialling** : poner las iniciales a, firmar con las iniciales

initial² *adj* : inicial, primero — **initially** *adv*

initial³ *n* : inicial *f*

initiate¹ [ɪˈnɪʃiˌeɪt] *vt* **-ated; -ating** **1** BEGIN : comenzar, iniciar **2** INDUCT : instruir **3** INTRODUCE : introducir, instruir

initiate² [ɪˈnɪʃiət] *n* : iniciado *m*, -da *f*

initiation [ɪˌnɪʃiˈeɪʃən] *n* : iniciación *f*

initiative [ɪˈnɪʃəˌtɪv] *n* : iniciativa *f*

initiatory [ɪˈnɪʃiəˌtori] *adj* **1** INTRODUCTORY : introductorio **2** : de iniciación ⟨initiatory rites : ritos de iniciación⟩

inject [ɪnˈdʒɛkt] *vt* : inyectar

injection [ɪnˈdʒɛkʃən] *n* : inyección *f*

injudicious [ˌɪndʒuˈdɪʃəs] *adj* : imprudente, indiscreto, poco juicioso

injunction [ɪnˈdʒʌŋkʃən] *n* **1** ORDER : orden *f*, mandato *m* **2** COURT ORDER : mandamiento *m* judicial

injure [ˈɪndʒər] *vt* **-jured; -juring** **1** WOUND : herir, lesionar **2** HURT : lastimar, dañar, herir **3 to injure oneself** : hacerse daño

injurious [ɪnˈdʒuriəs] *adj* : perjudicial ⟨injurious to one's health : perjudicial a la salud⟩

injury [ˈɪndʒəri] *n, pl* **-ries** **1** WRONG : mal *m*, injusticia *f* **2** DAMAGE, HARM : herida *f*, daño *m*, perjuicio *m*

injustice [ɪnˈdʒʌstəs] *n* : injusticia *f*

ink¹ [ˈɪŋk] *vt* : entintar

ink² *n* : tinta *f*

inkjet printer [ˈɪŋkˌdʒɛt-] *n* : impresora *f* de inyección de tinta

inkling [ˈɪŋklɪŋ] *n* : presentimiento *m*, indicio *m*, sospecha *f*

ink pad *n* : tampón *m* (para entintar)

inkwell [ˈɪŋkˌwɛl] *n* : tintero *m*

inky [ˈɪŋki] *adj* **1** : manchado de tinta **2** BLACK : negro, impenetrable ⟨inky darkness : negra oscuridad⟩

inland¹ [ˈɪnˌlænd, -lənd] *adv* : hacia el interior, tierra adentro

inland² *adj* : interior

inland³ *n* : interior *m*

in-law [ˈɪnˌlɔ] *n* **1** : pariente *m* político **2 in-laws** *npl* : suegros *mpl*

inlay¹ [ɪnˈleɪ, ˈɪnˌleɪ] *vt* **-laid** [-ˈleɪd, -ˌleɪd]; **-laying** : incrustar

inlay² [ˈɪnˌleɪ] *n* **1** : incrustación *f* **2** : empaste *m* (de un diente)

inlet [ˈɪnˌlɛt, -lət] *n* : cala *f*, ensenada *f*, brazo *m* del mar

in-line skate [ˈɪnˌlaɪn-] *n* : patín *m* en línea

inmate [ˈɪnˌmeɪt] *n* : paciente *mf* (en un hospital); preso *m*, -sa *f* (en una prisión); interno *m*, -na *f* (en un asilo)

in memoriam [ˌɪnməˈmoriəm] *prep* : en memoria de

inmost [ˈɪnˌmoːst] → **innermost**

inn [ˈɪn] *n* **1** : posada *f*, hostería *f*, fonda *f* **2** TAVERN : taberna *f*

innards [ˈɪnərdz] *npl* : entrañas *fpl*, tripas *fpl fam*

innate [ɪˈneɪt] *adj* **1** INBORN : innato **2** INHERENT : inherente

inner ['ɪnər] *adj* : interior, interno
inner city *n* : barrios *mpl* pobres (en el centro de una ciudad)
innermost ['ɪnər,mo:st] *adj* : más íntimo, más profundo
innersole ['ɪnər'so:l] → **insole**
inner tube → **tube**
inning ['ɪnɪŋ] *n* : entrada *f*
innkeeper ['ɪn,ki:pər] *n* : posadero *m*, -ra *f*
innocence ['ɪnəsənts] *n* : inocencia *f*
innocent¹ ['ɪnəsənt] *adj* : inocente — **innocently** *adv*
innocent² *n* : inocente *mf*
innocuous [ɪ'nɑkjəwəs] *adj* **1** HARMLESS : inocuo **2** INOFFENSIVE : inofensivo
innovate ['ɪnə,veɪt] *vi* **-vated; -vating** : innovar
innovation [,ɪnə'veɪʃən] *n* : innovación *f*, novedad *f*
innovative ['ɪnə,veɪtɪv] *adj* : innovador
innovator ['ɪnə,veɪtər] *n* : innovador *m*, -dora *f*
innuendo [,ɪnju'ɛndo] *n*, *pl* **-dos** *or* **-does** : insinuación *f*, indirecta *f*
innumerable [ɪ'nu:mərəbəl, -'nju:-] *adj* : innumerable
inoculate [ɪ'nɑkjə,leɪt] *vt* **-lated; -lating** : inocular
inoculation [ɪ,nɑkjə'leɪʃən] *n* : inoculación *f*
inoffensive [,ɪnə'fɛntsɪv] *adj* : inofensivo
inoperable [ɪn'ɑpərəbəl] *adj* : inoperable
inoperative [ɪn'ɑpərətɪv, -,reɪ-] *adj* : inoperante
inopportune [ɪn,ɑpər'tu:n, -'tju:n] *adj* : inoportuno — **inopportunely** *adv*
inordinate [ɪn'ɔrdənət] *adj* : excesivo, inmoderado, desmesurado — **inordinately** *adv*
inorganic [,ɪnɔr'gænɪk] *adj* : inorgánico
inpatient ['ɪn,peɪʃənt] *n* : paciente *mf* hospitalizado
input¹ ['ɪn,pʊt] *vt* **inputted** *or* **input; inputting** : entrar (datos, información)
input² *n* **1** CONTRIBUTION : aportación *f*, contribución *f* **2** ENTRY : entrada *f* (de datos) **3** ADVICE, OPINION : consejos *mpl*, opinión *f*
inquest ['ɪn,kwɛst] *n* INQUIRY, INVESTIGATION : investigación *f*, pesquisa *f* (judicial), indagatoria *f*
inquire [ɪn'kwaɪr] *v* **-quired; -quiring** *vt* : preguntar, informarse de, inquirir ⟨he inquired how to get in : preguntó como entrar⟩ — *vi* **1** ASK : preguntar, informarse ⟨to inquire about : informarse sobre⟩ ⟨to inquire after (someone) : preguntar por (alguien)⟩ **2 to inquire into** INVESTIGATE : investigar, inquirir sobre
inquiringly [ɪn'kwaɪrɪŋli] *adv* : inquisitivamente
inquiry ['ɪn,kwaɪri, ɪn'kwaɪri;, 'ɪnkwɔri, 'ɪŋ-] *n*, *pl* **-ries 1** QUESTION : pregunta *f* ⟨to make inquiries about : pedir información sobre⟩ **2** INVESTIGATION : investigación *f*, pesquisa *f*
inquisition [,ɪnkwə'zɪʃən, ,ɪŋ-] *n* **1** : inquisición *f*, interrogatorio *m*, investigación *f* **2 the Inquisition** : la Inquisición *f*

inquisitive [ɪn'kwɪzətɪv] *adj* : inquisidor, inquisitivo, curioso — **inquisitively** *adv*
inquisitiveness [ɪn'kwɪzətɪvnəs] *n* : curiosidad *f*
inquisitor [ɪn'kwɪzətər] *n* : inquisidor *m*, -dora *f*; interrogador *m*, -dora *f*
inroad ['ɪn,ro:d] *n* **1** ENCROACHMENT, INVASION : invasión *f*, incursión *f* **2 to make inroads into** : ocupar parte de (un tiempo), agotar parte de (ahorros, recursos), invadir (un territorio)
insane [ɪn'seɪn] *adj* **1** MAD : loco, demente ⟨to go insane : volverse loco⟩ ⟨to drive someone insane : volver loco a alguien⟩ **2** ABSURD : absurdo, insensato ⟨an insane scheme : un proyecto insensato⟩
insanely [ɪn'seɪnli] *adv* : como un loco ⟨insanely suspicious : loco de recelo⟩
insanity [ɪn'sænəti] *n*, *pl* **-ties 1** MADNESS : locura *f* **2** FOLLY : locura *f*, insensatez *f*
insatiable [ɪn'seɪʃəbəl] *adj* : insaciable — **insatiably** [-bli] *adv*
inscribe [ɪn'skraɪb] *vt* **-scribed; -scribing 1** ENGRAVE : inscribir, grabar **2** ENROLL : inscribir **3** DEDICATE : dedicar (un libro)
inscription [ɪn'skrɪpʃən] *n* : inscripción *f* (en un monumento), dedicación *f* (en un libro), leyenda *f* (de una ilustración, etc.)
inscrutable [ɪn'skru:təbəl] *adj* : inescrutable, misterioso — **inscrutably** [-bli] *adv*
inseam ['ɪn,si:m] *n* : entrepierna *f*
insect ['ɪn,sɛkt] *n* : insecto *m*
insecticidal [ɪn,sɛktə'saɪdəl] *adj* : insecticida
insecticide [ɪn'sɛktə,saɪd] *n* : insecticida *m*
insecure [,ɪnsɪ'kjʊr] *adj* : inseguro, poco seguro
insecurely [,ɪnsɪ'kjʊrli] *adv* : inseguramente
insecurity [,ɪnsɪ'kjʊrəti] *n*, *pl* **-ties** : inseguridad *f*
inseminate [ɪn'sɛmə,neɪt] *vt* **-nated; -nating** : inseminar
insemination [ɪn,sɛmə'neɪʃən] *n* : inseminación *f*
insensibility [ɪn,sɛntsə'bɪləti] *n*, *pl* **-ties** : insensibilidad *f*
insensible [ɪn'sɛntsəbəl] *adj* **1** UNCONSCIOUS : inconsciente, sin conocimiento **2** NUMB : insensible, entumecido **3** UNAWARE : inconsciente
insensitive [ɪn'sɛntsətɪv] *adj* : insensible
insensitivity [ɪn,sɛntsə'tɪvəti] *n*, *pl* **-ties** : insensibilidad *f*
inseparable [ɪn'sɛpərəbəl] *adj* : inseparable
insert¹ [ɪn'sərt] *vt* **1** : insertar, introducir, poner, meter ⟨insert your key in the lock : mete tu llave en la cerradura⟩ **2** INTERPOLATE : interpolar, intercalar
insert² ['ɪn,sərt] *n* : inserción *f*, hoja *f* insertada (en una revista, etc.)
insertion [ɪn'sərʃən] *n* : inserción *f*
inshore¹ ['ɪn'ʃor] *adv* : hacia la costa
inshore² *adj* : cercano a la costa, costero ⟨inshore fishing : pesca costera⟩

inside¹ [ɪn'saɪd, 'ɪn,saɪd] adv : adentro, dentro ⟨to run inside : correr para adentro⟩ ⟨inside and out : por dentro y por fuera⟩

inside² adj 1 : interior, de adentro, dentro ⟨the inside lane : el carril interior⟩ 2 : confidencial ⟨inside information : información confidencial⟩

inside³ n 1 : interior m, parte f de adentro ⟨the inside of the house : el interior de la casa⟩ 2 **insides** npl BELLY, GUTS : tripas fpl fam 3 **inside out** : al/del revés ⟨to turn something inside out : darle la vuelta a algo, volver/poner algo al/del revés, voltear algo⟩

inside⁴ prep 1 INTO : al interior de 2 WITHIN : dentro de 3 (referring to time) : en menos de ⟨inside an hour : en menos de una hora⟩

inside of prep INSIDE : dentro de

insider [ɪn'saɪdər] n : persona f enterada

insidious [ɪn'sɪdiəs] adj : insidioso — **insidiously** adv

insidiousness [ɪn'sɪdiəsnəs] n : insidia f

insight ['ɪn,saɪt] n : perspicacia f, penetración f

insightful [ɪn'saɪtfəl] adj : perspicaz

insignia [ɪn'sɪgniə] or **insigne** [-,ni:] n, pl **-nia** or **-nias** : insignia f, enseña f

insignificance [,ɪnsɪg'nɪfɪkəns] n : insignificancia f

insignificant [,ɪnsɪg'nɪfɪkənt] adj : insignificante

insincere [,ɪnsɪn'sɪr] adj : insincero, poco sincero

insincerely [,ɪnsɪn'sɪrli] adv : con poca sinceridad

insincerity [,ɪnsɪn'serəti, -'sɪr-] n, pl **-ties** : insinceridad f

insinuate [ɪn'sɪnjuˌeɪt] vt **-ated; -ating** : insinuar

insinuation [ɪn,sɪnju'eɪʃən] n : insinuación f

insipid [ɪn'sɪpəd] adj : insípido

insist [ɪn'sɪst] v : insistir

insistence [ɪn'sɪstənts] n : insistencia f

insistent [ɪn'sɪstənt] adj : insistente — **insistently** adv

insofar as [,ɪnso'fɑːræz] conj : en la medida en que, en tanto que, en cuanto a

insole ['ɪn,so:l] n : plantilla f

insolence ['ɪntsələnts] n : insolencia f

insolent ['ɪntsələnt] adj : insolente

insolubility [ɪn,sɑljo'bɪləti] n : insolubilidad f

insoluble [ɪn'sɑljʊbəl] adj : insoluble

insolvency [ɪn'sɑlvəntsi] n, pl **-cies** : insolvencia f

insolvent [ɪn'sɑlvənt] adj : insolvente

insomnia [ɪn'sɑmniə] n : insomnio m

insomniac [ɪn'sɑmni,æk] n : insomne mf — **insomniac** adj

insomuch as [,ɪnso'mʌt,sæz] → **inasmuch as**

insomuch that conj SO : así que, de manera que

inspect [ɪn'spɛkt] vt : inspeccionar, examinar, revisar

inspection [ɪn'spɛkʃən] n : inspección f, examen m, revisión f, revista f (de tropas)

inspector [ɪn'spɛktər] n : inspector m, -tora f

inspiration [,ɪnspə'reɪʃən] n : inspiración f

inspirational [,ɪnspə'reɪʃənəl] adj : inspirador

inspire [ɪn'spaɪr] v **-spired; -spiring** vt 1 INHALE : inhalar, aspirar 2 STIMULATE : estimular, animar, inspirar 3 INSTILL : inspirar, infundir — vi : inspirar

instability [,ɪnstə'bɪləti] n, pl **-ties** : inestabilidad f

install [ɪn'stɔl] vt **-stalled; -stalling** 1 : instalar ⟨to install a fan : montar un abanico⟩ 2 INDUCT : instalar, investir ⟨to install the new president : instalar el presidente nuevo⟩ 3 **to install oneself** : instalarse

installation [,ɪnstə'leɪʃən] n : instalación f

installment [ɪn'stɔlmənt] n 1 : plazo m, cuota f ⟨to pay in four installments : pagar a cuatro plazos⟩ 2 : entrega f (de una publicación o telenovela) 3 INSTALLATION : instalación f

instance ['ɪnstənts] n 1 INSTIGATION : instancia f 2 EXAMPLE : ejemplo m ⟨for instance : por ejemplo⟩ 3 OCCASION : instancia f, caso m, ocasión f ⟨he prefers, in this instance, to remain anonymous : en este caso prefiere quedarse anónimo⟩

instant¹ ['ɪnstənt] adj 1 IMMEDIATE : inmediato, instantáneo ⟨an instant reply : una respuesta inmediata⟩ 2 : instantáneo ⟨instant coffee : café instantáneo⟩

instant² n : momento m, instante m

instantaneous [,ɪnstən'teɪniəs] adj : instantáneo

instantaneously [,ɪnstən'teɪniəsli] adv : instantáneamente, al instante

instantly ['ɪnstəntli] adv : al instante, instantáneamente

instant message n : mensaje m instantáneo

instant messaging n : mensajería f instantánea

instead [ɪn'stɛd] adv 1 : en cambio, en lugar de eso, en su lugar ⟨Dad was going, but Mom went instead : papá iba a ir, pero mamá fue en su lugar⟩ 2 RATHER : al contrario

instead of prep : en vez de, en lugar de

instep [ɪn,stɛp] n : empeine m

instigate ['ɪnstəˌgeɪt] vt **-gated; -gating** INCITE, PROVOKE : instigar, incitar, provocar, fomentar

instigation [,ɪnstə'geɪʃən] n : instancia f, incitación f

instigator ['ɪnstəˌgeɪtər] n : instigador m, -dora f; incitador m, -dora f

instill [ɪn'stɪl] vt **-stilled; -stilling** : inculcar, infundir

instinct ['ɪn,stɪŋkt] n 1 TALENT : instinto m, don m ⟨an instinct for the right word : un don para escoger la palabra apropiada⟩ 2 : instinto m ⟨maternal instincts : instintos maternales⟩

instinctive [ɪn'stɪŋktɪv] adj : instintivo

instinctively [ɪn'stɪŋktɪvli] adv : instintivamente, por instinto

instinctual [ɪn'stɪŋkt∫ʊəl] *adj* : instintivo

institute[1] ['ɪntstə,tu:t, -,tju:t] *vt* **-tuted; -tuting 1** ESTABLISH : establecer, instituir, fundar **2** INITIATE : iniciar, empezar, entablar

institute[2] *n* : instituto *m*

institution [,ɪntstə'tu:∫ən, -'tju:-] *n* **1** ESTABLISHING : institución *f*, establecimiento *m* **2** CUSTOM : institución *f*, tradición *f* ⟨the institution of marriage : la institución del matrimonio⟩ **3** ORGANIZATION : institución *f*, organismo *m* **4** ASYLUM : asilo *m*

institutional [,ɪntstə'tu:∫ənəl, -'tju:-] *adj* : institucional

institutionalize [,ɪntstə'tu:∫ənə,laɪz, -'tju:-] *vt* **-ized; -izing 1** : institucionalizar ⟨institutional values : valores institucionalizados⟩ **2** : internar ⟨institutionalized orphans : huérfanos internados⟩

instruct [ɪn'strʌkt] *vt* **1** TEACH, TRAIN : instruir, adiestrar, enseñar **2** COMMAND : mandar, ordenar, dar instrucciones a

instruction [ɪn'strʌk∫ən] *n* **1** TEACHING : instrucción *f*, enseñanza *f* **2** COMMAND : orden *f*, instrucción *f* **3** instructions *npl* DIRECTIONS : instrucciones *fpl*, modo *m* de empleo

instructional [ɪn'strʌk∫ənəl] *adj* : instructivo, educativo

instructive [ɪn'strʌktɪv] *adj* : instructivo

instructor [ɪn'strʌktər] *n* : instructor *m*, -tora *f*

instrument ['ɪntstrəmənt] *n* **1** : instrumento *m* (musical) **2** TOOL, DEVICE : instrumento *m* **3** MEANS : instrumento *m*

instrumental [,ɪntstrə'mɛntəl] *adj* : instrumental

instrumentalist [,ɪntstrə'mɛntəlɪst] *n* : instrumentista *mf*

insubordinate [,ɪnsə'bordənət] *adj* : insubordinado

insubordination [,ɪnsə,bordən'eɪ∫ən] *n* : insubordinación *f*

insubstantial [,ɪnsəb'stæntʃəl] *adj* : insustancial, poco nutritivo (dícese de una comida), poco sólido (dícese de una estructura o un argumento)

insufferable [ɪn'sʌfərəbəl] *adj* UNBEARABLE : insufrible, intolerable, inaguantable, insoportable — **insufferably** [-bli] *adv*

insufficiency [,ɪnsə'fɪ∫əntsi] *n, pl* **-cies** : insuficiencia *f*

insufficient [,ɪnsə'fɪ∫ənt] *adj* : insuficiente — **insufficiently** *adv*

insular ['ɪntsʊlər, -sjʊ-] *adj* **1** : isleño (dícese de la gente), insular (dícese del clima) ⟨insular residents : residentes de la isla⟩ **2** NARROW-MINDED : de miras estrechas

insularity [,ɪntsʊ'lærəti, -sjʊ-] *n* : insularidad *f*

insulate ['ɪntsə,leɪt] *vt* **-lated; -lating** : aislar

insulation [,ɪntsə'leɪ∫ən] *n* : aislamiento *m*

insulator ['ɪntsə,leɪtər] *n* : aislador *m* (pieza), aislante *m* (material)

insulin ['ɪntsələn] *n* : insulina *f*

insult[1] [ɪn'sʌlt] *vt* : insultar, ofender, injuriar

insult[2] ['ɪn,sʌlt] *n* : insulto *m*, injuria *f*, agravio *m*

insulting [ɪn'sʌltɪŋ] *adj* : ofensivo, injurioso, insultante

insultingly [ɪn'sʌltɪŋli] *adv* : ofensivamente, de manera insultante

insurance [ɪn'∫ʊrənts, 'ɪn,∫ʊr-] *n* : seguro *m* ⟨life insurance : seguro de vida⟩ ⟨insurance company/policy : compañía/póliza de seguros⟩

insure [ɪn'∫ʊr] *vt* **-sured; -suring 1** UNDERWRITE : asegurar **2** ENSURE : asegurar, garantizar

insured [ɪn'∫ʊrd] *n* : asegurado *m*, -da *f*

insurer [ɪn'∫ʊrər] *n* : asegurador *m*, -dora *f*

insurgent[1] [ɪn'sərdʒənt] *adj* : insurgente

insurgent[2] *n* : insurgente *mf*

insurmountable [,ɪnsər'maʊntəbəl] *adj* : insuperable, insalvable — **insurmountably** [-bli] *adv*

insurrection [,ɪnsə'rɛk∫ən] *n* : insurrección *f*, levantamiento *m*, alzamiento *m*

intact [ɪn'tækt] *adj* : intacto

intake ['ɪn,teɪk] *n* **1** OPENING : entrada *f*, toma *f* ⟨fuel intake : toma de combustible⟩ **2** : entrada *f* (de agua o aire), consumo *m* (de sustancias nutritivas) **3** intake of breath : inhalación *f*

intangible [ɪn'tændʒəbəl] *adj* : intangible, impalpable — **intangibly** [-bli] *adv*

integer ['ɪntɪdʒər] *n* : entero *m*

integral ['ɪntɪgrəl] *adj* : integral, esencial

integrate ['ɪntə,greɪt] *v* **-grated; -grating** *vt* **1** UNITE : integrar, unir **2** DESEGREGATE : eliminar la segregación de — *vi* : integrarse

integration [,ɪntə'greɪ∫ən] *n* : integración *f*

integrity [ɪn'tɛgrəti] *n* : integridad *f*

intellect ['ɪntəl,ɛkt] *n* : intelecto *m*, inteligencia *f*, capacidad *f* intelectual

intellectual[1] [,ɪntə'lɛkt∫ʊəl] *adj* : intelectual — **intellectually** *adv*

intellectual[2] *n* : intelectual *mf*

intelligence [ɪn'tɛlədʒənts] *n* **1** : inteligencia *f* **2** INFORMATION, NEWS : inteligencia *f*, información *f*, noticias *fpl*

intelligent [ɪn'tɛlədʒənt] *adj* : inteligente — **intelligently** *adv*

intelligentsia [ɪn,tɛlə'dʒɛntsiə, -'gɛn-] *ns & pl* : intelectualidad *f*

intelligibility [ɪn,tɛlədʒə'bɪləti] *n* : inteligibilidad *f*

intelligible [ɪn'tɛlədʒəbəl] *adj* : inteligible, comprensible — **intelligibly** [-bli] *adv*

intemperance [ɪn'tɛmpərənts] *n* : inmoderación *f*, intemperancia *f*

intemperate [ɪn'tɛmpərət] *adj* : excesivo, inmoderado, desmedido

intend [ɪn'tɛnd] *vt* **1** (*indicating goal or purpose*) : querer, tener la intención de ⟨I didn't intend to hurt you : no quería hacerte daño⟩ ⟨no insult was intended : no fue mi intención ofender⟩ ⟨it was intended as a warning : pretendía servir de advertencia⟩ ⟨she intended for him to come : su intención era que viniera ⟨I intended it as a joke : lo dije en broma⟩ ⟨a film intended to educate : una película tendiente a educar⟩ **2** MEAN, SIGNIFY : querer decir **3** PLAN : pensar, tener planeado, proyectar, proponerse ⟨what do you intend to do? : ¿qué piensas hacer?⟩ ⟨I intend to finish by Thursday : me propongo acabar para el jueves⟩ ⟨if all goes as intended : si todo va según lo planeado⟩ **4 to be intended for** : ser para, ir dirigido a (un público, etc.), estar destinado a (un fin), estar diseñado para (un uso)

intended [ɪn'tɛndəd] *adj* **1** PLANNED : previsto, proyectado **2** INTENTIONAL : intencional, deliberado

intense [ɪn'tɛns] *adj* **1** EXTREME : intenso, extremo ⟨intense pain : dolor intenso⟩ **2** : profundo, intenso ⟨to my intense relief : para mi alivio profundo⟩ ⟨intense enthusiasm : entusiasmo ardiente⟩

intensely [ɪn'tɛnsli] *adv* : sumamente, profundamente, intensamente

intensification [ɪn,tɛnsəfə'keɪʃən] *n* : intensificación *f*

intensifier [ɪn'tɛnsə,faɪər] *n* : intensificador *m* (en lingüística)

intensify [ɪn'tɛnsə,faɪ] *v* **-fied; -fying** *vt* **1** STRENGTHEN : intensificar, redoblar ⟨to intensify one's efforts : redoblar unos sus esfuerzos⟩ **2** SHARPEN : intensificar, agudizar (dolor, ansiedad) — *vi* : intensificarse, hacerse más intenso

intensity [ɪn'tɛnsəti] *n, pl* **-ties** : intensidad *f*

intensive [ɪn'tɛnsɪv] *adj* : intensivo ⟨intensive care : cuidados intensivos⟩ — **intensively** *adv*

intent¹ [ɪn'tɛnt] *adj* **1** FIXED : concentrado, fijo ⟨an intent stare : una mirada fija⟩ **2 intent on** *or* **intent upon** : resuelto a, empeñado en

intent² *n* **1** PURPOSE : intención *f*, propósito *m* **2 for all intents and purposes** : a todos los efectos, prácticamente

intention [ɪn'tɛntʃən] *n* : intención *f*, propósito *m*

intentional [ɪn'tɛntʃənəl] *adj* : intencional, deliberado

intentionally [ɪn'tɛntʃənəli] *adv* : a propósito, adrede

intently [ɪn'tɛntli] *adv* : atentamente, fijamente

inter [ɪn'tər] *vt* **-terred; -terring** : enterrar, inhumar

inter- *pref* inter-

interact [,ɪntər'ækt] *vi* : interactuar, actuar recíprocamente, relacionarse

interaction [,ɪntər'ækʃən] *n* : interacción *f*, interrelación *f*

interactive [,ɪntər'æktɪv] *adj* : interactivo

interbreed [,ɪntər'bri:d] *v* **-bred** [-'brɛd]; **-breeding** *vt* : cruzar — *vi* : cruzarse

intercede [,ɪntər'si:d] *vi* **-ceded; -ceding** : interceder

intercept [,ɪntər'sɛpt] *vt* : interceptar

interception [,ɪntər'sɛpʃən] *n* : intercepción *f*

intercession [,ɪntər'sɛʃən] *n* : intercesión *f*

interchange¹ [,ɪntər'tʃeɪndʒ] *vt* **-changed; -changing** : intercambiar

interchange² [ɪn'tər,tʃeɪndʒ] *n* **1** EXCHANGE : intercambio *m*, cambio *m* **2** JUNCTION : empalme *m*, enlace *m* de carreteras

interchangeable [,ɪntər'tʃeɪndʒəbəl] *adj* : intercambiable

intercity [ɪn'tər,sɪti] *adj* : interurbano

intercollegiate [,ɪntərkə'li:dʒət, -dʒiət] *adj* : interuniversitario

intercom [ɪn'tər,kɑm] *n* : interfono *m* *Spain*, interfón *m* *Mex*

interconnect [,ɪntərkə'nɛkt] *vt* **1** : conectar, interconectar (en tecnología) **2** RELATE : interrelacionar — *vi* **1** : conectar **2** : interrelacionarse

intercontinental [,ɪntər,kɑntən'ɛntəl] *adj* : intercontinental

intercourse [ɪn'tər,kors] *n* **1** RELATIONS : relaciones *fpl*, trato *m* **2** COPULATION : acto *m* sexual, relaciones *fpl* sexuales, coito *m*

interdenominational [,ɪntərdɪ,nɑmə'neɪʃənəl] *adj* : interconfesional

interdepartmental [,ɪntərdɪ,pɑrt-'mɛntəl, -,di:-] *adj* : interdepartamental

interdependence [,ɪntərdɪ'pɛndənts] *n* : interdependencia *f*

interdependent [,ɪntərdɪ'pɛndənt] *adj* : interdependiente

interdict [,ɪntər'dɪkt] *vt* **1** PROHIBIT : prohibir **2** : cortar (las líneas de comunicación o provisión del enemigo)

interdisciplinary [,ɪntər'dɪsəplə,nɛri] *adj* : interdisciplinario

interest¹ ['ɪntrəst, -tə,rɛst] *vt* : interesar

interest² *n* **1** SHARE, STAKE : interés *m*, participación *f* **2** BENEFIT : provecho *m*, beneficio *m*, interés *m* ⟨in the public interest : en el interés público⟩ **3** CHARGE : interés *m*, cargo *m* ⟨compound interest : interés compuesto⟩ ⟨interest rate : tasa de interés⟩ **4** CURIOSITY : interés *m*, curiosidad *f* ⟨to take an interest in : interesarse por⟩ ⟨to lose interest : perder interés⟩ **5** COLOR : color *m*, interés *m* ⟨places of local interest : lugares de color local⟩ **6** HOBBY : afición *f*

interested ['ɪntrəstəd, -tə,rɛstəd] *adj* : interesado

interesting ['ɪntrəstɪŋ, -tə,rɛstɪŋ] *adj* : interesante — **interestingly** *adv*

interface ['ɪntər,feɪs] *n* **1** : interfaz *f*, interfase *f* **2** : punto *m* de contacto (en la física, etc.)

interfere [,ɪntər'fɪr] *vi* **-fered; -fering 1** INTERPOSE : interponerse, hacer interferencia ⟨to interfere with a play : obstruir una jugada⟩ **2** MEDDLE : entrometerse, interferir, intervenir **3 to interfere with** DISRUPT : afectar (una actividad), interferir (la transmisión de una señal) **4 to interfere with** TOUCH : tocar ⟨someone interfered with my papers : alguien tocó mis papeles⟩

interference [,ɪntər'fɪrənts] *n* : interferencia *f*, intromisión *f*

intergalactic [ˌɪntərgəˈlæktɪk] *adj* : intergaláctico

intergovernmental [ˌɪntərˌgʌvərˈmentəl, -vərn-] *adj* : intergubernamental

interim[1] [ˈɪntərəm] *adj* : interino, provisional

interim[2] *n* **1** : interín *m*, intervalo *m* **2 in the interim** : en el interín, mientras tanto

interior[1] [ɪnˈtɪriər] *adj* : interior

interior[2] *n* : interior *m*

interject [ˌɪntərˈdʒekt] *vt* : interponer, agregar

interjection [ˌɪntərˈdʒekʃən] *n* **1** : interjección *f* (en lingüística) **2** EXCLAMATION : exclamación *f* **3** INTERRUPTION : interrupción *f*

interlace [ˌɪntərˈleɪs] *vt* **-laced; -lacing 1** INTERWEAVE : entrelazar **2** INTERSPERSE : intercalar

interlock [ˌɪntərˈlɑk] *vt* **1** UNITE : trabar, unir **2** ENGAGE : engranar — *vi* : entrelazarse, trabarse

interloper [ˌɪntərˈloːpər] *n* **1** INTRUDER : intruso *m*, -sa *f* **2** MEDDLER : entrometido *m*, -da *f*

interlude [ˈɪntərˌluːd] *n* **1** INTERVAL : intervalo *m*, intermedio *m* (en el teatro) **2** : interludio *m* (en música)

intermarriage [ˌɪntərˈmærɪdʒ] *n* **1** : matrimonio *m* mixto (entre miembros de distintas razas o religiones) **2** : matrimonio *m* entre miembros del mismo grupo

intermarry [ˌɪntərˈmæri] *vi* **-married; -marrying 1** : casarse (con miembros de otros grupos) **2** : casarse entre sí (con miembros del mismo grupo)

intermediary[1] [ˌɪntərˈmiːdiˌeri] *adj* : intermediario

intermediary[2] *n, pl* **-aries** : intermediario *m*, -ria *f*

intermediate[1] [ˌɪntərˈmiːdiət] *adj* : intermedio

intermediate[2] *n* GO-BETWEEN : intermediario *m*, -ria *f*; mediador *m*, -dora *f*

interment [ɪnˈtərmənt] *n* : entierro *m*

interminable [ɪnˈtərmənəbəl] *adj* : interminable, constante — **interminably** [-bli] *adv*

intermingle [ˌɪntərˈmɪŋgəl] *vt* **-mingled; -mingling** : entremezclar, mezclar — *vi* : entremezclarse

intermission [ˌɪntərˈmɪʃən] *n* : intermisión *f*, intervalo *m*, intermedio *m*

intermittent [ˌɪntərˈmɪtənt] *adj* : intermitente — **intermittently** *adv*

intermix [ˌɪntərˈmɪks] *vt* : entremezclar

intern[1] [ˈɪnˌtərn, ɪnˈtərn] *vt* : confinar (durante la guerra) — *vi* : servir de interno, hacer las prácticas

intern[2] [ˈɪnˌtərn] *n* : interno *m*, -na *f*

internal [ɪnˈtərnəl] *adj* : interno, interior ⟨internal bleeding : hemorragia interna⟩ ⟨internal affairs : asuntos interiores, asuntos domésticos⟩ — **internally** *adv*

international [ˌɪntərˈnæʃənəl] *adj* : internacional — **internationally** *adv*

internationalize [ˌɪntərˈnæʃənəˌlaɪz] *vt* **-ized; -izing** : internacionalizar

internecine [ˌɪntərˈneˌsiːn, ɪnˈtərnəˌsiːn] *adj* : intestino, interno

Internet [ˈɪntərˌnet] *n* : Internet *mf*

Internet café *n* : cibercafé *m*

Internet service provider → **ISP**

internist [ˈɪnˌtərnɪst] *n* : internista *mf*

internment [ɪnˈtərnmənt] *n* : internamiento *m*

interpersonal [ˌɪntərˈpərsənəl] *adj* : interpersonal

interplay [ˈɪntərˌpleɪ] *n* : interacción *f*, juego *m*

interpolate [ɪnˈtərpəˌleɪt] *vt* **-lated; -lating** : interpolar

interpose [ˌɪntərˈpoːz] *vt* **-posed; -posing** *vt* : interponer, interrumpir con — *vi* : interponerse

interpret [ɪnˈtərprət] *vt* : interpretar

interpretation [ɪnˌtərprəˈteɪʃən] *n* : interpretación *f*

interpretative [ɪnˈtərprəˌteɪtɪv] *adj* : interpretativo

interpreter [ɪnˈtərprətər] *n* : intérprete *mf*

interpretive [ɪnˈtərprəṭɪv] *adj* : interpretativo

interracial [ˌɪntərˈreɪʃəl] *adj* : interracial

interrelate [ˌɪntərɪˈleɪt] *v* **-related; -relating** : interrelacionar

interrelationship [ˌɪntərɪˈleɪʃənˌʃɪp] *n* : interrelación *f*

interrogate [ɪnˈtɛrəˌgeɪt] *vt* **-gated; -gating** : interrogar, someter a un interrogatorio

interrogation [ɪnˌtɛrəˈgeɪʃən] *n* : interrogatorio *m*, interrogación *f*

interrogative[1] [ˌɪntəˈrɑgəˌtɪv] *adj* : interrogativo

interrogative[2] *n* : interrogativo *m*

interrogator [ɪnˈtɛrəˌgeɪtər] *n* : interrogador *m*, -dora *f*

interrogatory [ˌɪntəˈrɑgəˌtɔri] *adj* → **interrogative**[1]

interrupt [ˌɪntəˈrʌpt] *v* : interrumpir

interruption [ˌɪntəˈrʌpʃən] *n* : interrupción *f*

intersect [ˌɪntərˈsekt] *vt* : cruzar, cortar — *vi* : cruzarse (dícese de los caminos), intersecarse (dícese de las líneas o figuras), cortarse

intersection [ˌɪntərˈsekʃən] *n* : intersección *f*, cruce *m*

intersperse [ˌɪntərˈspərs] *vt* **-spersed; -spersing** : intercalar, entremezclar

interstate [ˌɪntərˈsteɪt] *adj* : interestatal

interstellar [ˌɪntərˈstelər] *adj* : interestelar

interstice [ɪnˈtərstəs] *n, pl* **-stices** [-stəˌsiːz, -stəsəz] : intersticio *m*

intertwine [ˌɪntərˈtwaɪn] *vi* **-twined; -twining** : entrelazarse

interval [ˈɪntərvəl] *n* : intervalo *m*

intervene [ˌɪntərˈviːn] *vi* **-vened; -vening 1** ELAPSE : transcurrir, pasar ⟨the intervening years : los años intermediarios⟩ **2** INTERCEDE : intervenir, interceder, mediar

intervention [ˌɪntərˈventʃən] *n* : intervención *f*

interview[1] [ˈɪntərˌvjuː] *vt* : entrevistar — *vi* : hacer entrevistas

interview[2] *n* : entrevista *f*

interviewer [ˈɪntərˌvjuːər] n : entrevistador m, -dora f
interweave [ˌɪntərˈwiːv] v -wove [-ˈwoːv]; -woven [-ˈwoːvən]; -weaving vt : entretejer, entrelazar — vi INTERTWINE : entrelazarse, entretejerse
interwoven [ˌɪntərˈwoːvən] adj : entretejido
intestate [ɪnˈtɛsˌteɪt, -tət] adj : intestado
intestinal [ɪnˈtɛstənəl] adj : intestinal
intestine [ɪnˈtɛstən] n 1 : intestino m 2 **small intestine** : intestino m delgado 3 **large intestine** : intestino m grueso
intimacy [ˈɪntəməsi] n, pl -cies 1 CLOSE-NESS : intimidad f 2 FAMILIARITY : familiaridad f
intimate¹ [ˈɪntəˌmeɪt] vt -mated; -mating : insinuar, dar a entender
intimate² [ˈɪntəmət] adj 1 CLOSE : íntimo, de confianza ⟨intimate friends : amigos íntimos⟩ 2 PRIVATE : íntimo, privado ⟨intimate clubs : clubes íntimos⟩ 3 INNERMOST, SECRET : íntimo, secreto ⟨intimate fantasies : fantasías secretas⟩
intimate³ n : amigo m íntimo, amiga f íntima
intimidate [ɪnˈtɪməˌdeɪt] vt -dated; -dating : intimidar
intimidation [ɪnˌtɪməˈdeɪʃən] n : intimidación f
into [ˈɪnˌtuː] prep 1 (indicating motion) : en, a, contra, dentro de ⟨she got into bed : se metió en la cama⟩ ⟨to get into a plane : subir a un avión⟩ ⟨he crashed into the wall : chocó contra la pared⟩ ⟨looking into the sun : mirando al sol⟩ ⟨staring into space : mirando al vacío⟩ 2 (indicating state or condition) : a, en ⟨to burst into tears : echarse a llorar⟩ ⟨the water turned into ice : el agua se convirtió en hielo⟩ ⟨to translate into English : traducir al inglés⟩ 3 (indicating time) ⟨far into the night : hasta bien entrada la noche⟩ ⟨he's well into his eighties : tiene los ochenta bien cumplidos⟩ 4 (in mathematics) ⟨3 into 12 is 4 : 12 dividido por 3 es 4⟩ 5 fam (indicating interest or involvement) ⟨he's really into sports : le ha dado fuerte por los deportes⟩
intolerable [ɪnˈtɑlərəbəl] adj : intolerable — **intolerably** [-bli] adv
intolerance [ɪnˈtɑlərənts] n : intolerancia f
intolerant [ɪnˈtɑlərənt] adj : intolerante
intonation [ˌɪntoˈneɪʃən] n : entonación f
intone [ɪnˈtoːn] vt -toned; -toning : entonar
intoxicant [ɪnˈtɑksɪkənt] n : bebida f alcohólica
intoxicate [ɪnˈtɑksəˌkeɪt] vt -cated; -cating : emborrachar, embriagar
intoxicated [ɪnˈtɑksəˌkeɪtəd] adj : borracho, embriagado
intoxicating [ɪnˈtɑksəˌkeɪtɪŋ] adj : embriagador
intoxication [ɪnˌtɑksəˈkeɪʃən] n : embriaguez f
intractable [ɪnˈtræktəbəl] adj : obstinado, intratable

intramural [ˌɪntrəˈmjʊrəl] adj : interno, dentro de la universidad
intransigence [ɪnˈtræntsədʒənts, -ˈtrænzə-] n : intransigencia f
intransigent [ɪnˈtræntsədʒənt, -ˈtrænzə-] adj : intransigente
intransitive [ɪnˈtræntsəˌtɪv, -ˈtrænzə-] adj : intransitivo
intrauterine device [ˌɪntrəˈjuːtərən-] n : dispositivo m intrauterino, DIU m
intravenous [ˌɪntrəˈviːnəs] adj : intravenoso — **intravenously** adv
intrepid [ɪnˈtrɛpəd] adj : intrépido
intricacy [ˈɪntrɪkəsi] n, pl -cies : complejidad f, lo intrincado
intricate [ˈɪntrɪkət] adj : intrincado, complicado — **intricately** adv
intrigue¹ [ɪnˈtriːg] v -trigued; -triguing : intrigar
intrigue² [ˈɪnˌtriːg, ɪnˈtriːg] n : intriga f
intriguing [ɪnˈtriːgɪŋ] adj : intrigante, fascinante
intrinsic [ɪnˈtrɪnzɪk, -ˈtrɪnˌsɪk] adj : intrínseco, esencial — **intrinsically** [-zɪkli, -sɪ-] adv
intro [ˈɪntro] n fam → introduction
introduce [ˌɪntrəˈduːs, -ˈdjuːs] vt -duced; -ducing 1 : presentar ⟨let me introduce my father : permítame presentar a mi padre⟩ ⟨to introduce oneself : presentarse⟩ 2 : introducir (algo nuevo), lanzar (un producto), presentar (una ley), proponer (una idea o un tema)
introduction [ˌɪntrəˈdʌkʃən] n : introducción f, presentación f
introductory [ˌɪntrəˈdʌktəri] adj : introductorio, preliminar, de introducción
introspection [ˌɪntrəˈspɛkʃən] n : introspección f
introspective [ˌɪntrəˈspɛktɪv] adj : introspectivo — **introspectively** adv
introvert [ˈɪntrəˌvərt] n : introvertido m, -da f
introverted [ˈɪntrəˌvərtəd] adj : introvertido
intrude [ɪnˈtruːd] v -truded; -truding vi 1 INTERFERE : inmiscuirse, entrometerse 2 DISTURB, INTERRUPT : molestar, estorbar, interrumpir — vt : introducir por fuerza
intruder [ɪnˈtruːdər] n : intruso m, -sa f
intrusion [ɪnˈtruːʒən] n : intrusión f
intrusive [ɪnˈtruːsɪv] adj : intrusivo
intuit [ɪnˈtuːɪt, -ˈtjuː-] v : intuir
intuition [ˌɪntuˈɪʃən, -tjuː-] n : intuición f
intuitive [ɪnˈtuːətɪv, -ˈtjuː-] adj : intuitivo — **intuitively** adv
inundate [ˈɪnənˌdeɪt] vt -dated; -dating : inundar
inundation [ˌɪnənˈdeɪʃən] n : inundación f
inure [ɪˈnʊr, -ˈnjʊr] vt -ured; -uring : acostumbrar, habituar
invade [ɪnˈveɪd] vt -vaded; -vading : invadir
invader [ɪnˈveɪdər] n : invasor m, -sora f
invalid¹ [ɪnˈvæləd] adj : inválido, nulo
invalid² [ˈɪnvələd] adj : inválido, discapacitado
invalid³ [ˈɪnvələd] n : inválido m, -da f
invalidate [ɪnˈvæləˌdeɪt] vt -dated; -dating : invalidar

invalidity [ˌɪnvəˈlɪdəṭi] n, pl **-ties** : invalidez f, falta de validez f

invaluable [ɪnˈvæljəbəl, -ˈvæljuə-] adj : invalorable, inestimable, inapreciable

invariable [ɪnˈværiəbəl] adj : invariable, constante — **invariably** [-bli] adv

invasion [ɪnˈveɪʒən] n : invasión f

invasive [ɪnˈveɪsɪv] adj : invasivo

invective [ɪnˈvɛktɪv] n : invectiva f, improperio m

inveigh [ɪnˈveɪ] vi **to inveigh against** : arremeter contra, lanzar invectivas contra

inveigle [ɪnˈveɪɡəl, -ˈviː-] vt **-gled; -gling** : engatusar, embaucar, persuadir con engaños

invent [ɪnˈvɛnt] vt : inventar

invention [ɪnˈvɛntʃən] n : invención f, invento m

inventive [ɪnˈvɛntɪv] adj : inventivo

inventiveness [ɪnˈvɛntɪvnəs] n : ingenio m, inventiva f

inventor [ɪnˈvɛntər] n : inventor m, -tora f

inventory¹ [ˈɪnvənˌtɔri] vt **-ried; -rying** : inventariar

inventory² n, pl **-ries** 1 LIST : inventario m 2 STOCK : existencias fpl

inverse¹ [ɪnˈvərs, ˈɪnˌvərs] adj : inverso — **inversely** adv

inverse² n : inverso m

inversion [ɪnˈvərʒən] n : inversión f

invert [ɪnˈvərt] vt : invertir

invertebrate¹ [ɪnˈvərṭəbrət, -ˌbreɪt] adj : invertebrado

invertebrate² n : invertebrado m

invest [ɪnˈvɛst] vt 1 AUTHORIZE : autorizar 2 CONFER : conferir 3 : invertir, dedicar ⟨he invested his savings in stocks : invirtió sus ahorros en acciones⟩ ⟨to invest one's time : dedicar uno su tiempo⟩

investigate [ɪnˈvɛstəˌɡeɪt] v **-gated; -gating** : investigar

investigation [ɪnˌvɛstəˈɡeɪʃən] n : investigación f, estudio m

investigative [ɪnˈvɛstəˌɡeɪṭɪv] adj : investigador

investigator [ɪnˈvɛstəˌɡeɪṭər] n : investigador m, -dora f

investiture [ɪnˈvɛstəˌtʃʊr, -tʃər] n : investidura f

investment [ɪnˈvɛstmənt] n : inversión f

investor [ɪnˈvɛstər] n : inversor m, -sora f; inversionista mf

inveterate [ɪnˈvɛṭərət] adj 1 DEEP-SEATED : inveterado, enraizado 2 HABITUAL : empedernido, incorregible

invidious [ɪnˈvɪdiəs] adj 1 OBNOXIOUS : repugnante, odioso 2 UNJUST : injusto — **invidiously** adv

invigorate [ɪnˈvɪɡəˌreɪt] vt **-rated; -rating** : vigorizar, animar

invigorating [ɪnˈvɪɡəˌreɪṭɪŋ] adj : vigorizante, estimulante

invincibility [ɪnˌvɪntsəˈbɪləṭi] n : invencibilidad f

invincible [ɪnˈvɪntsəbəl] adj : invencible — **invincibly** [-bli] adv

inviolable [ɪnˈvaɪələbəl] adj : inviolable

inviolate [ɪnˈvaɪələt] adj : inviolado, puro

invisibility [ɪnˌvɪzəˈbɪləṭi] n : invisibilidad f

invisible [ɪnˈvɪzəbəl] adj : invisible — **invisibly** [-bli] adv

invitation [ˌɪnvəˈteɪʃən] n : invitación f

invite [ɪnˈvaɪt] vt **-vited; -viting** 1 ATTRACT : atraer, tentar ⟨a book that invites interest : un libro que atrae el interés⟩ 2 PROVOKE : provocar, buscar ⟨to invite trouble : buscarse problemas⟩ 3 ASK : invitar ⟨we invited them for dinner : los invitamos a cenar⟩ 4 SOLICIT : solicitar, buscar (preguntas, comentarios, etc.)

inviting [ɪnˈvaɪṭɪŋ] adj : atractivo, atrayente

invocation [ˌɪnvəˈkeɪʃən] n : invocación f

invoice¹ [ˈɪnˌvɔɪs] vt **-voiced; -voicing** : facturar

invoice² n : factura f

invoke [ɪnˈvoːk] vt **-voked; -voking** 1 : invocar, apelar a ⟨she invoked our aid : apeló a nuestra ayuda⟩ 2 CITE : invocar, citar ⟨to invoke a precedent : invocar un precedente⟩ 3 CONJURE UP : hacer aparecer, invocar

involuntary [ɪnˈvɑlənˌtɛri] adj : involuntario — **involuntarily** [ɪnˌvɑlənˈtrɛli] adv

involve [ɪnˈvɑlv] vt **-volved; -volving** 1 ENGAGE : ocupar (con una tarea, etc.) 2 IMPLICATE : involucrar, enredar, implicar ⟨to be involved in a crime : estar involucrado en un crimen⟩ 3 CONCERN : concernir, afectar 4 CONNECT : conectar, relacionar 5 ENTAIL, INCLUDE : suponer, incluir, consistir en ⟨what does the job involve? : ¿en qué consiste el trabajo?⟩ 6 **to be involved with someone** : tener una relación (amorosa) con alguien

involved [ɪnˈvɑlvd] adj 1 COMPLEX, INTRICATE : complicado, complejo 2 CONCERNED : interesado, afectado

involvement [ɪnˈvɑlvmənt] n 1 PARTICIPATION : participación f, complicidad f 2 RELATIONSHIP : relación f

invulnerable [ɪnˈvʌlnərəbəl] adj : invulnerable

inward¹ [ˈɪnwərd] or **inwards** [-wərdz] adv : hacia adentro, hacia el interior

inward² adj INSIDE : interior, interno

inwardly [ˈɪnwərdli] adv 1 MENTALLY, SPIRITUALLY : por dentro 2 INTERNALLY : internamente, interiormente 3 PRIVATELY : para sus adentros, para sí

iodine [ˈaɪəˌdaɪn, -dən] n : yodo m, tintura f de yodo

ion [ˈaɪən, ˈaɪˌɑn] n : ion m

ionic [aɪˈɑnɪk] adj : iónico

ionize [ˈaɪəˌnaɪz] v **ionized; ionizing** : ionizar

ionosphere [aɪˈɑnəˌsfɪr] n : ionosfera f

iota [aɪˈoːṭə] n : pizca f, ápice m

IOU [ˌaɪˌoˈjuː] n : pagaré m, vale m

IPA [ˌaɪˌpiːˈeɪ] n (International Phonetic Alphabet) : AFI m

IQ [ˌaɪˈkjuː] n (intelligence quotient) : CI m, coeficiente m intelectual

Iranian [ɪˈreɪniən, -ˈræ-, -ˈrɑ-; aɪ-] n : iraní mf — **Iranian** adj

Iraqi [ɪ'rɑːkiː] n : iraquí mf — **Iraqi** adj
irascibility [ɪˌræsə'bɪlət̬i] n : irascibilidad f
irascible [ɪ'ræsəbəl] adj : irascible
irate [aɪ'reɪt] adj : furioso, airado, iracundo — **irately** adv
ire ['aɪr] n : ira f, cólera f
iridescence [ˌɪrə'dɛsənts] n : iridiscencia f
iridescent [ˌɪrə'dɛsənt] adj : iridiscente
iridium [ɪ'rɪdiəm] n : iridio m
iris ['aɪrəs] n, pl **irises** or **irides** ['aɪrəˌdiːz, 'ɪr-] 1 : iris m (del ojo) 2 : lirio m (planta)
Irish¹ ['aɪrɪʃ] adj : irlandés
Irish² n 1 : irlandés m (idioma) 2 **the Irish** (used with a plural verb) : los irlandeses
Irishman ['aɪrɪʃmən] n, pl **-men** : irlandés m
Irishwoman ['aɪrɪʃˌwʊmən] n, pl **-women** : irlandesa f
irk ['ərk] vt : fastidiar, irritar, preocupar
irksome ['ərksəm] adj : irritante, fastidioso — **irksomely** adv
iron¹ ['aɪərn] v 1 : planchar **2 to iron out** : resolver
iron² n 1 : hierro m, fierro m ⟨a will of iron : una voluntad de hierro, una voluntad férrea⟩ 2 : plancha f (para planchar la ropa)
ironclad ['aɪərnˌklæd] adj 1 : acorazado, blindado 2 STRICT : riguroso, estricto
ironic [aɪ'rɑːnɪk] or **ironical** [-nɪkəl] adj : irónico — **ironically** [-kli] adv
ironing ['aɪərnɪŋ] n 1 PRESSING : planchada f 2 : ropa f para planchar
ironing board n : tabla f (de planchar)
ironwork ['aɪərnˌwərk] n 1 : obra f de hierro 2 **ironworks** npl : fundición f
irony ['aɪrəni] n, pl **-nies** : ironía f
irradiate [ɪ'reɪdiˌeɪt] vt **-ated; -ating** : irradiar, radiar
irradiation [ɪˌreɪdi'eɪʃən] n : irradiación f, radiación f
irrational [ɪ'ræʃənəl] adj : irracional — **irrationally** adv
irrationality [ɪˌræʃə'næləti] n, pl **-ties** : irracionalidad f
irreconcilable [ɪˌrɛkən'saɪləbəl] adj : irreconciliable
irrecoverable [ˌɪrɪ'kʌvərəbəl] adj : irrecuperable — **irrecoverably** [-bli] adv
irredeemable [ˌɪrɪ'diːməbəl] adj 1 : irredimible (dícese de un bono) una **2** HOPELESS : irremediable, irreparable
irrefutable [ˌɪrɪ'fjuːtəbəl, ɪ'rɛfjə-] adj : irrefutable
irregular¹ [ɪ'rɛgjələr] adj : irregular — **irregularly** adv
irregular² n 1 : soldado m irregular 2 **irregulars** npl : artículos mpl defectuosos
irregularity [ˌɪrɛgjə'lærət̬i] n, pl **-ties** : irregularidad f
irrelevance [ɪ'rɛləvənts] n : irrelevancia f
irrelevant [ɪ'rɛləvənt] adj : irrelevante
irreligious [ˌɪrɪ'lɪdʒəs] adj : irreligioso
irreparable [ɪ'rɛpərəbəl] adj : irreparable
irreplaceable [ˌɪrɪ'pleɪsəbəl] adj : irreemplazable, insustituible
irrepressible [ˌɪrɪ'prɛsəbəl] adj : incontenible, incontrolable

irreproachable [ˌɪrɪ'proːtʃəbəl] adj : irreprochable, intachable
irresistible [ˌɪrɪ'zɪstəbəl] adj : irresistible — **irresistibly** [-bli] adv
irresolute [ɪ'rɛzəˌluːt] adj : irresoluto, indeciso
irresolutely [ɪ'rɛzəˌluːtli, -ˌrzə'luːt-] adv : de manera indecisa
irresolution [ɪˌrɛzə'luːʃən] n : irresolución f
irrespective of [ˌɪrɪ'spɛktɪvəv] prep : sin tomar en consideración, sin tener en cuenta
irresponsibility [ˌɪrɪˌspantsə'bɪləti] n, pl **-ties** : irresponsabilidad f, falta f de responsabilidad
irresponsible [ˌɪrɪ'spantsəbəl] adj : irresponsable — **irresponsibly** [-bli] adv
irretrievable [ˌɪrɪ'triːvəbəl] adj IRRECOVERABLE : irrecuperable
irreverence [ɪ'rɛvərənts] n : irreverencia f, falta f de respeto
irreverent [ɪ'rɛvərənt] adj : irreverente, irrespetuoso
irreversible [ˌɪrɪ'vərsəbəl] adj : irreversible
irrevocable [ɪ'rɛvəkəbəl] adj : irrevocable — **irrevocably** [-bli] adv
irrigate ['ɪrəˌgeɪt] vt **-gated; -gating** : irrigar, regar
irrigation [ˌɪrə'geɪʃən] n : irrigación f, riego m
irritability [ˌɪrət̬ə'bɪləti] n, pl **-ties** : irritabilidad f
irritable ['ɪrət̬əbəl] adj : irritable, colérico
irritably ['ɪrət̬əbli] adv : con irritación
irritant¹ ['ɪrət̬ənt] adj : irritante
irritant² n : agente m irritante
irritate ['ɪrəˌteɪt] vt **-tated; -tating** 1 ANNOY : irritar, molestar 2 : irritar (en medicina)
irritating ['ɪrəˌteɪt̬ɪŋ] adj : irritante
irritatingly ['ɪrəˌteɪt̬ɪŋli] adv : de modo irritante, fastidiosamente
irritation [ˌɪrə'teɪʃən] n : irritación f
is → be
-ish [ɪʃ] suf ALMOST, APPROXIMATELY ⟨grayish : grisáceo⟩ ⟨she's fiftyish : tiene unos cincuenta años⟩
Islam [ɪs'lɑːm, ɪz-, -'læm;, 'ɪsˌlɑm, 'ɪz-, -ˌlæm] n : el Islam
Islamic [ɪs'lɑmɪk, ɪz-, -'læ-] adj : islámico
Islamism [ɪs'lɑˌmɪzəm, ɪz-, -'læ-;, 'ɪzlə-] n : islamismo m — **Islamist** n
island ['aɪlənd] n : isla f
islander ['aɪləndər] n : isleño m, -ña f
isle ['aɪl] n : isla f, islote m
islet ['aɪlət] n : islote m
isn't ['ɪzənt] contraction of IS NOT → be
isolate ['aɪsəˌleɪt] vt **-lated; -lating** : aislar
isolated ['aɪsəˌleɪt̬əd] adj : aislado, solo
isolation [ˌaɪsə'leɪʃən] n : aislamiento m
isometric [ˌaɪsə'mɛtrɪk] adj : isométrico
isometrics [ˌaɪsə'mɛtrɪks] ns & pl : isometría f
isosceles [aɪ'sɑsəˌliːz] adj : isósceles
isotope ['aɪsəˌtoːp] n : isótopo m
ISP [ˌaɪˌɛs'piː] n (Internet service provider) : PSI m, proveedor m de servicios de Internet

Israeli [ɪz'reɪli] n : israelí mf — **Israeli** adj
issue¹ ['ɪˌʃuː] v **-sued; -suing** vi 1
EMERGE : emerger, salir, fluir 2 DES-
CEND : descender (dícese de los padres o
antepasados específicos) 3 EMANATE,
RESULT : emanar, surgir, resultar —
vt 1 EMIT : emitir 2 DISTRIBUTE
: emitir, distribuir ⟨to issue a new stamp
: emitir un sello nuevo⟩ 3 PUBLISH
: publicar
issue² n 1 EMERGENCE, FLOW : emergencia f, flujo m 2 PROGENY : descendencia f, progenie f 3 OUTCOME, RE-
SULT : desenlace m, resultado m, consecuencia f 4 MATTER, QUESTION
: asunto m, cuestión f ⟨to avoid the issue
: evitar el tema⟩ ⟨to make an issue of
something : darle demasiada importancia a algo⟩ 5 PUBLICATION : publicación f, distribución f, emisión f 6
: número m (de un periódico o una revista)
isthmus ['ɪsməs] n : istmo m
it ['ɪt] pron 1 (as subject; generally omitted) : él, ella, ello ⟨it's a big building : es
un edificio grande⟩ ⟨who was it? : ¿quién
era?⟩ ⟨one more and that's it : uno más y
se acabó⟩ 2 (as indirect object) : le ⟨I'll
give it some water : voy a darle agua⟩
⟨give it time : dale tiempo⟩ 3 (as direct
object) : lo, la ⟨give it to me : dámelo⟩ ⟨I
don't understand it : no lo entiendo⟩
⟨stop it! : ¡basta!⟩ 4 (as object of a preposition; generally omitted) : él, ella, ello
⟨behind it : detrás, detrás de él⟩ 5 (in
impersonal constructions) : está llo-
viendo⟩ ⟨what time is it? : ¿qué
hora es?⟩ ⟨it's 8 o'clock : son las ocho⟩
⟨it's hot/cold : hace calor/frío⟩ 6 (as the
implied subject or object of a verb) ⟨it is
necessary to study : es necesario estu-
diar⟩ ⟨it's good to see you : (me) da gusto
verte⟩ ⟨it is known/said that . . . : se
sabe/dice que . . .⟩ ⟨it would seem to
: eso parece⟩ ⟨to give it all one's got : dar
lo mejor de sí⟩
Italian [ɪ'tæliən, aɪ-] n 1 : italiano m, -na
f 2 : italiano m (idioma) — **Italian** adj
italic¹ [ɪ'tælɪk, aɪ-] adj : en cursiva, en bastardilla

italic² n : cursiva f, bastardilla f
italicize [ɪ'tælə,saɪz, aɪ-] vt **-cized; -cizing**
: poner en cursiva
itch¹ ['ɪtʃ] vi 1 : picar ⟨her arm itched : le
pica el brazo⟩ 2 : morirse ⟨they were
itching to go outside : se morían por
salir⟩ — vt : dar picazón, hacer picar
itch² n 1 ITCHING : picazón f, picor m,
comezón f 2 RASH : sarpullido m, erupción f 3 DESIRE : ansia f, deseo m
itchiness ['ɪtʃinəs] n ITCHING : picazón f,
picor m, comezón f
itchy ['ɪtʃi] adj **itchier; -est** : que pica, que
da comezón
it'd ['ɪtəd] contraction of IT HAD or IT
WOULD → have, would
item ['aɪtəm] n 1 OBJECT : artículo m,
pieza f ⟨item of clothing : prenda de ves-
tir⟩ 2 : punto m (en una agenda),
número m (en el teatro), ítem m (en un
documento) 3 news item : noticia f
itemization [ˌaɪtəmə'zeɪʃən] n : desglose
m
itemize ['aɪtə,maɪz] vt **-ized; -izing** : detallar, enumerar, listar
itinerant [aɪ'tɪnərənt] adj : itinerante, ambulante
itinerary [aɪ'tɪnə,reri] n, pl **-aries** : itinerario m
it'll ['ɪtəl] contraction of IT SHALL or IT
WILL → shall, will
its ['ɪts] adj : su, sus ⟨its kennel : su pe-
rrera⟩ ⟨a city and its inhabitants : una
ciudad y sus habitantes⟩
it's ['ɪts] contraction of IT IS or IT HAS →
be, have
itself [ɪt'self] pron 1 (used reflexively) : se
⟨the cat gave itself a bath : el gato se
bañó⟩ 2 (used for emphasis) : (él)
mismo, (ella) misma, sí (mismo), solo
⟨he is courtesy itself : es la misma cor-
tesía⟩ ⟨in and of itself : por sí mismo⟩ ⟨it
opened by itself : se abrió solo⟩
IUD [ˌaɪˌjuː'diː] n (intrauterine device)
: DIU m, dispositivo m intrauterino
I've ['aɪv] contraction of I HAVE → have
ivory ['aɪvəri] n, pl **-ries** 1 : marfil m 2
: color m de marfil
ivy ['aɪvi] n, pl **ivies** 1 : hiedra f, yedra
f 2 → poison ivy

J

j ['dʒeɪ] n, pl **j's** or **js** ['dʒeɪz] : décima letra
del alfabeto inglés
jab¹ ['dʒæb] v **jabbed; jabbing** vt 1
PUNCTURE : clavar, pinchar 2 POKE
: dar, golpear (con la punta de algo) ⟨he
jabbed me in the ribs : me dio un codazo
en las costillas⟩ — vi to jab at : dar, golpear
jab² n 1 PRICK : pinchazo m 2 POKE
: golpe m abrupto
jabber ['dʒæbər] v : farfullar
jack¹ ['dʒæk] vt to jack up 1 : levantar (con
un gato) 2 INCREASE : subir, aumentar

jack² n 1 : gato m, cric m ⟨hydraulic
jack : gato hidráulico⟩ 2 FLAG : pabellón m 3 SOCKET : enchufe m hembra 4 : jota f, valet m ⟨jack of hearts
: jota de corazones⟩ 5 jacks npl : cantillos mpl
jackal ['dʒækəl] n : chacal m
jackass ['dʒæk,æs] n : asno m, burro m
jacket ['dʒækət] n 1 : chaqueta f 2 COVER
: sobrecubierta f (de un libro), carátula f
(de un disco)
jackhammer ['dʒæk,hæmər] n : martillo
m neumático

jack–in–the–box ['dʒækɪndə,baks] *n* : caja *f* de sorpresa

jackknife¹ ['dʒæk,naɪf] *vi* -knifed; -knifing : doblarse como una navaja, plegarse

jackknife² *n* : navaja *f*

jack–of–all–trades *n* : persona *f* que sabe un poco de todo, persona *f* de muchos oficios

jack–o'–lantern ['dʒækə,læntərn] *n* : linterna *f* hecha de una calabaza

jackpot ['dʒæk,pat] *n* **1** : primer premio *m*, gordo *m* **2 to hit the jackpot** : sacarse la lotería, sacarse el gordo

jackrabbit ['dʒæk,ræbət] *n* : liebre *f* grande de Norteamérica

Jacuzzi [dʒə'ku:zi] *trademark* se usa para una bañera de hidromasaje

jade ['dʒeɪd] *n* : jade *m*

jaded ['dʒeɪdəd] *adj* **1** TIRED : agotado **2** BORED : hastiado

jagged ['dʒægəd] *adj* : dentado, mellado

jaguar ['dʒæg,war, 'dʒægju,war] *n* : jaguar *m*

jai alai ['haɪ,laɪ] *n* : jai alai *m*, pelota *f* vasca

jail¹ ['dʒeɪl] *vt* : encarcelar

jail² *n* : cárcel *f*

jailbreak ['dʒeɪl,breɪk] *n* : fuga *f*, huida *f* (de la cárcel)

jailer *or* **jailor** ['dʒeɪlər] *n* : carcelero *m*, -ra *f*

jalapeño [,halə'peɪnjo, ,hæ-, -'pi:no] *n* : jalapeño *m*

jalopy [dʒə'lapi] *n, pl* -lopies : cacharro *m* fam, carro *m* destartalado

jalousie ['dʒæləsi] *n* : celosía *f*

jam¹ ['dʒæm] *v* jammed; jamming *vt* **1** CRAM : apiñar, embutir, atiborrar ⟨jammed with people : atestado de gente⟩ **2** STICK, THRUST : meter **3** BLOCK : atascar, atorar **4** : interferir (una señal, etc.) **5 to jam on the brakes** : frenar en seco — *vi* **1** : atascarse, atrancarse, bloquearse (dícese de un mecanismo) ⟨the copier has jammed : la fotocopiadora se ha bloqueado/atascado⟩ **2** PLAY fam : tocar

jam² *n* **1** *or* **traffic jam** : atasco *m*, embotellamiento *m* (de tráfico) **2** PREDICAMENT : lío *m*, aprieto *m*, apuro *m* **3** : mermelada *f* ⟨strawberry jam : mermelada de fresa⟩

Jamaican [dʒə'meɪkən] *n* : jamaiquino *m*, -na *f*; jamaicano *m*, -na *f* — **Jamaican** *adj*

jamb ['dʒæm] *n* : jamba *f*

jamboree [,dʒæmbə'ri:] *n* : fiesta *f* grande

jam–packed *adj* : repleto, hasta el tope (dícese de un recipiente), atestado (de gente)

jangle¹ ['dʒæŋgəl] *v* -gled; -gling *vi* : hacer un ruido metálico — *vt* **1** : hacer sonar **2 to jangle one's nerves** : irritar, crispar

jangle² *n* : ruido *m* metálico

janitor ['dʒænətər] *n* : portero *m*, -ra *f*; conserje *mf*

January ['dʒænju,eri] *n* : enero *m* ⟨they arrived on January 12th, they arrived on the 12th of January : llegaron el 12 de enero⟩

Japanese¹ [,dʒæpə'ni:z, -'ni:s] *adj* : japonés

Japanese² *n* **1** : japonés *m* (idioma) **2 the Japanese** (*used with a plural verb*) : los japoneses

jar¹ ['dʒar] *v* jarred; jarring *vi* **1** GRATE : chirriar **2** CLASH : desentonar **3** SHAKE : sacudirse **4 to jar on** : crispar, enervar — *vt* JOLT : sacudir

jar² *n* **1** GRATING : chirrido *m* **2** JOLT : vibración *f*, sacudida *f* **3** : tarro *m*, bote *m*, pote *m* ⟨a jar of honey : un tarro de miel⟩

jargon ['dʒargən] *n* : jerga *f*

jasmine ['dʒæzmən] *n* : jazmín *m*

jasper ['dʒæspər] *n* : jaspe *m*

jaundice ['dʒɔndɪs] *n* : ictericia *f*

jaundiced ['dʒɔndɪst] *adj* **1** : ictérico **2** EMBITTERED, RESENTFUL : amargado, resentido, negativo ⟨with a jaundiced eye : con una actitud de cinismo⟩

jaunt ['dʒɔnt] *n* : excursión *f*, paseo *m*

jauntily ['dʒɔntəli] *adv* : animadamente

jauntiness ['dʒɔntinəs] *n* : animación *f*, vivacidad *f*

jaunty ['dʒɔnti] *adj* **jauntier; -est** SPRIGHTLY : animado, alegre ? RAKISH ; desenvuelto, desenfadado

java ['dʒævə] *n* fam → coffee

Javanese [,dʒævə'ni:z, ,dʒa-, -'ni:s] *n* **1** : javanés *m* (idioma) **2** : javanés *m*, -nesa *f* — **Javanese** *adj*

javelin ['dʒævələn] *n* : jabalina *f*

jaw¹ ['dʒɔ] *vi* GAB : cotorrear *fam*, parlotear *fam*

jaw² *n* **1** : mandíbula *f*, quijada *f* **2** : mordaza *f* (de una herramienta) **3 the jaws of death** : las garras *f* de la muerte

jawbone ['dʒɔ,bo:n] *n* : mandíbula *f*

jay ['dʒeɪ] *n* : arrendajo *m*, chara *f* Mex, azulejo *m* Mex

jaybird ['dʒeɪ,bərd] *n* → jay

jaywalk ['dʒeɪ,wɔk] *vi* : cruzar la calle sin prudencia

jaywalker ['dʒeɪ,wɔkər] *n* : peatón *m* imprudente

jazz¹ ['dʒæz] *vt* **to jazz up** : animar, alegrar

jazz² *n* : jazz *m*

jazzy ['dʒæzi] *adj* jazzier; -est **1** : con ritmo de jazz **2** FLASHY, SHOWY : llamativo, ostentoso

jealous ['dʒɛləs] *adj* : celoso, envidioso — **jealously** *adv*

jealousy ['dʒɛləsi] *n* : celos *mpl*, envidia *f*

jeans ['dʒi:nz] *npl* : jeans *mpl*; vaqueros *mpl*; tejanos *mpl*; pantalones *mpl* de mezclilla Chile, Mex

jeep ['dʒi:p] *n* : jeep *m* (vehículo militar)

Jeep *trademark* se usa para un camión pequeño

jeer¹ ['dʒɪr] *vi* **1** BOO : abuchear **2** SCOFF : mofarse, burlarse — *vt* RIDICULE : mofarse de, burlarse de

jeer² *n* **1** : abucheo *m* **2** TAUNT : mofa *f*, burla *f*

Jehovah [dʒɪ'ho:və] *n* : Jehová *m*

jell ['dʒɛl] *vi* **1** SET : gelificarse, cuajar **2** FORM : cuajar, formarse (una idea, etc.)

Jell–O ['dʒɛ,lo:] *trademark* se usa para gelatina con sabor a frutas, etc.

jelly *n*, *pl* **-lies** 1 : jalea *f* 2 GELATIN : gelatina *f*

jellyfish ['dʒɛli,fɪʃ] *n* : medusa *f*

jeopardize ['dʒɛpər,daɪz] *vt* **-dized; -dizing** : arriesgar, poner en peligro

jeopardy ['dʒɛpərdi] *n* : peligro *m*, riesgo *m*

jerk¹ ['dʒərk] *vt* 1 JOLT : sacudir 2 TUG, YANK : darle un tirón — *vi* JOLT : dar sacudidas ⟨the train jerked along : el tren iba moviéndose a sacudidas⟩

jerk² *n* 1 TUG : tirón *m*, jalón *m* 2 JOLT : sacudida *f* brusca 3 FOOL : estúpido *m*, -da *f*; idiota *mf*

jerkin ['dʒərkən] *n* : chaqueta *f* sin mangas, chaleco *m*

jerky¹ ['dʒərki] *adj* **jerkier; -est** 1 : espasmódico (dícese de los movimientos) 2 CHOPPY : inconexo (dícese de la prosa) — **jerkily** [-kəli] *adv*

jerky² *n* : cecina *f*; tasajo *m*; charqui *m* Chile, Peru

jerry–built ['dʒeri,bɪlt] *adj* : mal construido, chapucero

jersey ['dʒərzi] *n*, *pl* **-seys** : jersey *m*

jest¹ ['dʒɛst] *vi* : bromear

jest² *n* : broma *f*, chiste *m*

jester ['dʒɛstər] *n* : bufón *m*, -fona *f*

Jesuit ['dʒɛzuət] *n* : jesuita *m* — **Jesuit** *adj*

Jesus ['dʒiːzəs, -zəz] *n* 1 : Jesús *m* 2 **Jesus Christ** : Jesucristo *m* 3 **Jesus (Christ)**! *fam* : ¡por Dios!

jet¹ ['dʒɛt] *vi* **jetted; jetting** *vt* SPOUT : arrojar a chorros — *vi* 1 GUSH : salir a chorros, chorrear 2 FLY : viajar en avión, volar

jet² *n* 1 STREAM : chorro *m* 2 **jet airplane** : avión *m* a reacción, reactor *m* 3 : azabache *m* (mineral)

jet–black *adj* : negro azabache

jet black *n* : negro *m* azabache

jet engine *n* : reactor *m*, motor *m* a reacción

jet lag *n* : desfase *m* (de) horario

jet–propelled *adj* : a reacción

jetsam ['dʒɛtsəm] *n* flotsam and jetsam : restos *mpl*, desechos *mpl*

jettison ['dʒɛtəsən] *vt* 1 : echar al mar 2 DISCARD : desechar, deshacerse de

jetty ['dʒɛti] *n*, *pl* **-ties** 1 PIER, WHARF : embarcadero *m*, muelle *m* 2 BREAKWATER : malecón *m*, rompeolas *m*

Jew ['dʒuː] *n* : judío *m*, -día *f*

jewel ['dʒuːəl] *n* 1 : joya *f*, alhaja *f* 2 GEM : piedra *f* preciosa, gema *f* 3 : rubí *m* (de un reloj) 4 TREASURE : joya *f*, tesoro *m*

jeweler *or* **jeweller** ['dʒuːələr] *n* : joyero *m*, -ra *f*

jewelry ['dʒuːəlri] *n* : joyas *fpl*, alhajas *fpl* ⟨jewelry store : joyería⟩ ⟨jewelry box : alhajero, joyero⟩

Jewish ['dʒuːɪʃ] *adj* : judío

jibe ['dʒaɪb] *vi* **jibed; jibing** AGREE : concordar

jicama ['hiːkəmə] *n* : jícama *f*

jiffy ['dʒɪfi] *n*, *pl* **-fies** : santiamén *m*, segundo *m*, momento *m*

jig¹ ['dʒɪg] *vi* **jigged; jigging** : bailar la giga

jig² *n* 1 : giga *f* 2 **the jig is up** : se acabó la fiesta

jigger ['dʒɪgər] *n* : medida de 1 a 2 onzas (para licores)

jiggle¹ ['dʒɪgəl] *v* **-gled; -gling** *vt* : agitar o sacudir ligeramente — *vi* : agitarse, vibrar

jiggle² *n* : sacudida *f*, vibración *f*

jigsaw ['dʒɪg,sɔ] *n* 1 : sierra *f* de vaivén 2 **jigsaw puzzle** : rompecabezas *m*

jihad [dʒɪˈhɑd] *n* : yihad *mf*, jihad *mf* — **jihadist** [dʒɪˈhɑdɪst] *n*

jilt ['dʒɪlt] *vt* : dejar plantado, dar calabazas a

jimmy¹ ['dʒɪmi] *vt* **-mied; -mying** : forzar con una palanqueta

jimmy² *n*, *pl* **-mies** : palanqueta *f*

jingle¹ ['dʒɪŋgəl] *v* **-gled; -gling** *vi* : tintinear — *vt* : hacer sonar

jingle² *n* 1 TINKLE : tintineo *m*, retintín *m* 2 : canción *f* rimada

jingoism ['dʒɪŋgo,ɪzəm] *n* : jingoísmo *m*, patriotería *f*

jingoistic [,dʒɪŋgoˈɪstɪk] *or* **jingoist** ['dʒɪŋgoɪst] *adj* : jingoísta, patriotero

jinx¹ ['dʒɪŋks] *vt* : traer mala suerte a, salar CoRi, Mex

jinx² *n* 1 : cenizo *m*, -za *f* 2 **to put a jinx on** : echarle el mal de ojo a

jitters ['dʒɪtərz] *npl* : nervios *mpl* ⟨he got the jitters : se puso nervioso⟩

jittery ['dʒɪtəri] *adj* : nervioso

Jivaro ['hiːvə,ro] *n* : jíbaro *m*, -ra *f*

job ['dʒab] *n* 1 : trabajo *m* ⟨he did odd jobs for her : le hizo algunos trabajos⟩ 2 CHORE, TASK : tarea *f*, quehacer *m* 3 EMPLOYMENT : trabajo *m*, empleo *m*, puesto *m*

jobber ['dʒabər] *n* MIDDLEMAN : intermediario *m*, -ria *f*

jobless ['dʒabləs] *adj* : desempleado

jock ['dʒak] *n* : deportista *mf*, atleta *mf*

jockey¹ ['dʒaki] *v* **-eyed; -eying** *vt* 1 MANIPULATE : manipular 2 MANEUVER : maniobrar — *vi* **to jockey for position** : maniobrar para conseguir algo

jockey² *n*, *pl* **-eys** : jockey *mf*

jocose [dʒoˈkoːs] *adj* : jocoso

jocular ['dʒakjələr] *adj* : jocoso — **jocularly** *adv*

jocularity [,dʒakjuˈlærəti] *n* : jocosidad *f*

jodhpurs ['dʒadpərz] *npl* : pantalones *mpl* de montar

joe ['dʒoː] *n* *fam* 1 GUY, FELLOW : tipo *m* *fam* ⟨an average joe : un hombre cualquiera⟩ 2 → **coffee**

jog¹ ['dʒag] *v* **jogged; jogging** *vt* 1 NUDGE : dar, empujar, codear 2 **to jog one's memory** : refrescar la memoria — *vi* 1 RUN : correr despacio, trotar, hacer footing (como ejercicio) 2 TRUDGE : andar a trote corto

jog² *n* 1 PUSH, SHAKE : empujoncito *m*, sacudida *f* leve 2 TROT : trote *m* corto, footing *m* (en deportes) 3 TWIST : recodo *m*, vuelta *f*, curva *f*

jogger ['dʒagər] *n* : persona *f* que hace footing

jogging ['dʒagɪŋ] *n* : footing *m*, jogging *m*

john ['dʒɑn] n fam TOILET : inodoro m

join¹ ['dʒɔɪn] vt **1** CONNECT, LINK : unir, juntar ⟨to join in marriage : unir en matrimonio⟩ ⟨to join hands : tomarse de la mano⟩ **2** ADJOIN : lindar con, colindar con **3** MEET : reunirse con, encontrarse con ⟨we joined them for lunch : nos reunimos con ellos para almorzar⟩ ⟨may I join you? : ¿puedo sentarme aquí?⟩ **4** ACCOMPANY : acompañar **5** : hacerse socio de (una organización), afiliarse a (un partido), entrar en (una empresa) ⟨to join the ranks of : sumarse a las filas de⟩ — vi **1** UNITE : unirse **2** MERGE : empalmar (dícese de las carreteras), confluir (dícese de los ríos) **3** : hacerse socio, afiliarse, entrar **4 to join in** PARTICIPATE : participar, tomar parte **5 to join up** ENLIST : enrolarse, alistarse

join² n JUNCTURE : juntura f, unión f

joiner ['dʒɔɪnər] n **1** CARPENTER : carpintero m, -ra f **2** : persona f que se une a varios grupos

joint¹ ['dʒɔɪnt] adj : conjunto, colectivo, mutuo ⟨a joint effort : un esfuerzo conjunto⟩ ⟨a joint account : una cuenta conjunta⟩ — **jointly** adv

joint² n **1** : articulación f, coyuntura f ⟨out of joint : dislocado⟩ **2** ROAST : asado m **3** JUNCTURE : juntura f, unión f **4** DIVE : antro m, tasca f **5** fam : porro m

joist ['dʒɔɪst] n : viga f

joke¹ ['dʒo:k] vi **joked; joking** : bromear

joke² n **1** STORY : chiste m **2** PRANK : broma f

joker ['dʒo:kər] n **1** PRANKSTER : bromista mf **2** : comodín m (en los naipes)

jokingly ['dʒo:kɪŋli] adv : en broma

jollity ['dʒɑləti] n, pl **-ties** MERRIMENT : alegría f, regocijo m

jolly ['dʒɑli] adj **jollier; -est** : alegre, jovial

jolt¹ ['dʒo:lt] vi JERK : dar tumbos, dar sacudidas — vt : sacudir

jolt² n **1** JERK : sacudida f brusca **2** SHOCK : golpe m (emocional)

jonquil ['dʒɑŋkwɪl] n : junquillo m

Jordanian [dʒɔr'deɪniən] n : jordano m, -na f — **Jordanian** adj

josh ['dʒɑʃ] vt TEASE : tomarle el pelo (a alguien) — vi JOKE : bromear

jostle ['dʒɑsəl] v **-tled; -tling** vi **1** SHOVE : empujar, dar empellones **2** CONTEND : competir — vt **1** SHOVE : empujar **2 to jostle one's way** : abrirse paso a empellones

jot¹ ['dʒɑt] vt **jotted; jotting** : anotar, apuntar ⟨jot it down : apúntalo⟩

jot² n BIT : ápice m, jota f, pizca f

jounce¹ ['dʒaʊns] v **jounced; jouncing** vi JOLT : sacudir — vi : dar tumbos, dar sacudidas

jounce² n JOLT : sacudida f, tumbo m

journal ['dʒərnəl] n **1** DIARY : diario m **2** PERIODICAL : revista f, publicación f periódica **3** NEWSPAPER : periódico m, diario m

journalism ['dʒərnəl,ɪzəm] n : periodismo m

journalist ['dʒərnəlɪst] n : periodista mf

journalistic [,dʒərnəl'ɪstɪk] adj : periodístico

journey¹ ['dʒərni] vi **-neyed; -neying** : viajar

journey² n, pl **-neys** : viaje m

journeyman ['dʒərnimən] n, pl **-men** [-mən, -,mɛn] : oficial m

joust¹ ['dʒaʊst] vi : justar

joust² n : justa f

jovial ['dʒo:viəl] adj : jovial — **jovially** adv

joviality [,dʒo:vi'æləti] n : jovialidad f

jowl ['dʒaʊl] n **1** JAW : mandíbula f **2** CHEEK : mejilla f, cachete m

joy ['dʒɔɪ] n **1** HAPPINESS : gozo m, alegría f, felicidad f **2** DELIGHT : placer m, deleite m ⟨the child is a real joy : el niño es un verdadero placer⟩

joyful ['dʒɔɪfəl] adj : gozoso, alegre, feliz — **joyfully** adv

joyless ['dʒɔɪləs] adj : sin alegría, triste

joyous ['dʒɔɪəs] adj : alegre, feliz, eufórico — **joyously** adv

joyousness ['dʒɔɪəsnəs] n : alegría f, felicidad f, euforia f

joyride ['dʒɔɪ,raɪd] n **1** : paseo m en coche a alta velocidad **2** : paseo m en un coche robado

joyriding ['dʒɔɪ,raɪdɪŋ] n **to go joyriding 1** : pasear en coche a alta velocidad (por diversión) **2** : pasear en un coche robado

joystick ['dʒɔɪ,stɪk] n : joystick m

jubilant ['dʒu:bələnt] adj : jubiloso, alborozado — **jubilantly** adv

jubilation [,dʒu:bə'leɪʃən] n : júbilo m

jubilee ['dʒu:bə,li:] n **1** : quincuagésimo aniversario m **2** CELEBRATION : celebración f, festejos mpl

Judaic [dʒu'deɪɪk] adj : judaico

Judaism ['dʒu:də,ɪzəm, 'dʒu:di-, 'dʒu:,deɪ-] n : judaísmo m

judge¹ ['dʒʌdʒ] vt **judged; judging 1** ASSESS : evaluar, juzgar **2** DEEM : juzgar, considerar **3** TRY : juzgar (ante el tribunal) **4 judging by** : a juzgar por ⟨judging by the results : a juzgar por los resultados⟩

judge² n **1** : juez mf, jueza f **2** : jurado mf (en una competencia) **3 to be a good judge of** : saber juzgar a, entender mucho de

judge's chambers → chamber

judgment or **judgement** ['dʒʌdʒmənt] n **1** RULING : fallo m, sentencia f **2** OPINION : opinión f **3** DISCERNMENT : juicio m, discernimiento m ⟨against my better judgment, I agreed to go : aunque me pareció mala idea, consentí en ir⟩

judgmental [,dʒʌdʒ'mntəl] adj : crítico — **judgmentally** adv

judicature ['dʒu:dɪkə,tʃʊr] n : judicatura f

judicial [dʒu'dɪʃəl] adj : judicial — **judicially** adv

judiciary¹ [dʒu'dɪʃi,ri, -'dɪʃəri] adj : judicial

judiciary² n **1** JUDICATURE : judicatura f **2** : poder m judicial

judicious [dʒu'dɪʃəs] adj SOUND WISE : juicioso, sensato — **judiciously** adv

judo ['dʒu:,do:] n : judo m

jug ['dʒʌg] *n* **1** : jarra *f*, jarro *m*, cántaro *m* **2** JAIL : cárcel *f*, chirona *f fam*

juggernaut ['dʒʌgərˌnɔt] *n* : gigante *m*, fuerza *f* irresistible ⟨a political juggernaut : un gigante político⟩

juggle ['dʒʌgəl] *v* **-gled; -gling** *vt* **1** : hacer juegos malabares con **2** MANIPULATE : manipular, jugar con — *vi* : hacer juegos malabares

juggler ['dʒʌglər] *n* : malabarista *mf*

jugular ['dʒʌgjələr] *adj* : yugular ⟨jugular vein : vena yugular⟩

juice ['dʒuːs] *n* **1** : jugo *m* (de carne, de frutas) *m*, zumo *m* (de frutas) **2** ELECTRICITY : electricidad *f*, luz *f*

juicer ['dʒuːsər] *n* : exprimidor *m*

juiciness ['dʒuːsinəs] *n* : jugosidad *f*

juicy ['dʒuːsi] *adj* **juicier; -est 1** SUCCULENT : jugoso, suculento **2** PROFITABLE : jugoso, lucrativo **3** RACY : picante

jukebox ['dʒuːkˌbɑks] *n* : rocola *f*, máquina *f* de discos

julep ['dʒuːləp] *n* : bebida *f* hecha con whisky americano y menta

July ['dʒuːlaɪ] *n* **1** : julio *m* ⟨they arrived on July 29th, they arrived on the 29th of July : llegaron el 29 de julio⟩ **2 the Fourth of July** INDEPENDENCE DAY : el 4 de julio (día festivo en los EEUU)

jumble¹ ['dʒʌmbəl] *vt* **-bled; -bling** : mezclar, revolver

jumble² *n* : revoltijo *m*, fárrago *m*, embrollo *m*

jumbo¹ ['dʒʌmˌboʊ] *adj* : gigante, enorme, de tamaño extra grande

jumbo² *n*, *pl* **-bos** : coloso *m*, cosa *f* de tamaño extra grande

jump¹ ['dʒʌmp] *vi* **1** LEAP : saltar, brincar **2** START : levantarse de un salto, sobresaltarse **3** MOVE, SHIFT : moverse, pasar ⟨to jump from job to job : pasar de un empleo a otro⟩ **4** INCREASE, RISE : dar un salto, aumentarse de golpe, subir bruscamente **5** BUSTLE : animarse, ajetrearse **6 to jump at** : no dejar escapar (una oportunidad) **7 to jump in** : meterse (en una conversación, etc.) **8 to jump on** ATTACK, CRITICIZE : atacar, criticar **9 to jump on** SCOLD : regañar, reprender, reñir **10 to jump out at** POUNCE ON : abalanzarse sobre **11 to jump out at** : llamar la atención de ⟨it jumps out at you : salta a la vista⟩ **12 to jump to conclusions** : sacar conclusiones precipitadas — *vt* **1** : saltar ⟨to jump a fence : saltar una valla⟩ **2** SKIP : saltarse **3** ATTACK : atacar, asaltar **5 to jump the gun** : precipitarse

jump² *n* **1** LEAP : salto *m* **2** START : sobresalto *m*, respingo *m* **3** INCREASE : subida *f* brusca, aumento *m* **4** ADVANTAGE : ventaja *f* ⟨we got the jump on them : les llevamos la ventaja⟩

jumper ['dʒʌmpər] *n* **1** : saltador *m*, -dora *f* (en deportes) **2** : jumper *m*, vestido *m* sin mangas

jumper cables *npl* : cables *mpl* de arranque, cables *mpl* pasacorriente *Mex*

jump–start *vt* : arrancar haciendo puente

jumpy ['dʒʌmpi] *adj* **jumpier; -est** : asustadizo, nervioso

junction ['dʒʌŋkʃən] *n* **1** JOINING : unión *f* **2** : cruce *m* (de calles), empalme *m* (de un ferrocarril), confluencia *f* (de ríos)

juncture ['dʒʌŋktʃər] *n* **1** UNION : juntura *f*, unión *f* **2** MOMENT POINT : coyuntura *f* ⟨at this juncture : en esta coyuntura, en este momento⟩

June ['dʒuːn] *n* : junio *m* ⟨they arrived on the 15th of June, they arrived on June 15th : llegaron el 15 de junio⟩

jungle ['dʒʌŋgəl] *n* : jungla *f*, selva *f*

junior¹ ['dʒuːnjər] *adj* **1** YOUNGER : más joven ⟨John Smith, Junior : John Smith, hijo⟩ **2** SUBORDINATE : subordinado, subalterno

junior² *n* **1** : persona *f* de menor edad ⟨she's my junior : es menor que yo⟩ **2** SUBORDINATE : subalterno *m*, -na *f*; subordinado *m*, -da *f* **3** : estudiante *mf* de penúltimo año

junior high school *n* : primer ciclo *m* de la educación secundaria en los EEUU

juniper ['dʒuːnəpər] *n* : enebro *m*

junk¹ ['dʒʌŋk] *vt* : echar a la basura

junk² *n* **1** RUBBISH : desechos *mpl*, desperdicios *mpl* **2** STUFF : trastos *mpl fam*, cachivaches *mpl fam* **3 piece of junk** : cacharro *m*, porquería *f*

junket ['dʒʌŋkət] *n* : viaje *m* (pagado con dinero público)

junk food *n* : comida *f* basura, comida *f* chatarra

junkie ['dʒʌŋki] *n* : drogadicto *m*, -ta *f*

junk mail *n* : correo *m* basura, propaganda *f*

junta ['hʊntə, 'dʒʌn-, 'hʌn-] *n* : junta *f* militar

Jupiter ['dʒuːpətər] *n* : Júpiter *m*

jurisdiction [ˌdʒʊrəs'dɪkʃən] *n* : jurisdicción *f* — **jurisdictional** [ˌdʒʊrəs'dɪkʃənəl] *adj*

jurisprudence [ˌdʒʊrəs'pruːdənts] *n* : jurisprudencia *f*

jurist ['dʒʊrɪst] *n* : jurista *mf*; magistrado *m*, -da *f*

juror ['dʒʊrər] *n* : jurado *m*, -da *f*

jury ['dʒʊri] *n*, *pl* **-ries** : jurado *m*

just¹ ['dʒʌst] *adv* **1** EXACTLY : justo, precisamente, exactamente ⟨it was just what she hoped for : fue exactamente lo que esperaba⟩ ⟨it is just what I need : es justo lo que necesito⟩ ⟨just as/when : justo cuando⟩ **2** POSSIBLY : posiblemente ⟨it just might work : tal vez resulte⟩ **3** BARELY : justo, apenas ⟨just in time : justo a tiempo⟩ ⟨I had just enough time : tenía el tiempo justo⟩ ⟨just over an hour : una hora larga, una hora y pico⟩ ⟨we just missed the plane : perdimos el avión por un pelo⟩ ⟨we just missed each other : no nos vimos por poco⟩ ⟨it's just around the corner : está a la vuelta de la esquina⟩ **4** ONLY : sólo, solamente, nada más ⟨just us : sólo nosotros⟩ ⟨just one more : sólo uno más⟩ ⟨she's just a child : es sólo una niña⟩ ⟨just for fun : sólo por diversión⟩ ⟨just a moment/minute, please : un momento, por favor⟩

⟨I'm just kidding : (sólo) estoy bromeando⟩ ⟨she's not just my friend, she's my lawyer : además de ser mi amiga, es mi abogada⟩ **5** (*used for emphasis*) ⟨it's just horrible! : ¡qué horrible!⟩ ⟨I just don't understand it : simplemente no lo entiendo⟩ ⟨I just knew it! : ¡ya me lo sospechaba!⟩ ⟨just imagine! : ¡imagínate!⟩ ⟨just tell him how you feel! : ¡por qué no le dices lo que sientes?⟩ ⟨don't just stand there — do something! : no te quedes ahí parado — ¡haz algo!⟩ **6 to have just done something** : acabar de hacer algo ⟨he just called : acaba de llamar⟩ **7 just about** ALMOST : casi **8 just about to** : al punto de **9 just as ... as** : tan ... como ⟨just as good as : tan bueno como⟩ **10 just as soon** RATHER ⟨I'd just as soon stay home : prefiero quedarme en casa⟩ **11 just as well (that)** : menos mal (que) **12 just like that** : de repente **13 just now** : hace un momento ⟨I saw him just now : acabo de verlo⟩ **14 just now** RIGHT NOW : ahora mismo **15 just so** PERFECT : perfecto **16 just the thing** ⟨just the thing for

you : justo lo que necesitas⟩ **17 just yet** ⟨are you ready? — not just yet : ¿estás lista? — casi⟩ ⟨don't buy it just yet : no lo compres ahora mismo⟩

just² adj : justo — **justly** adv
justice ['dʒʌstɪs] n **1** : justicia f ⟨to do justice to : hacerle justicia a⟩ **2** JUDGE : juez mf, jueza f
justice of the peace n : juez mf de paz, jueza f de paz
justification [ˌdʒʌstəfə'keɪʃən] n : justificación f
justify ['dʒʌstəˌfaɪ] vt **-fied; -fying** : justificar — **justifiable** [ˌdʒʌstə-'faɪəbəl] adj
jut ['dʒʌt] vi **jutted; jutting** : sobresalir
jute ['dʒuːt] n : yute m
juvenile¹ ['dʒuːvəˌnaɪl, -vənəl] adj **1** : juvenil ⟨juvenile delinquent : delincuente juvenil⟩ ⟨juvenile court : tribunal de menores⟩ **2** CHILDISH : infantil
juvenile² n : menor mf
juxtapose ['dʒʌkstəˌpoːz] vt **-posed; -posing** : yuxtaponer
juxtaposition [ˌdʒʌkstəpə'zɪʃən] n : yuxtaposición f

K

k ['keɪ] n, pl **k's** or **ks** ['keɪz] : undécima letra del alfabeto inglés
kabob [kə'bab] → kebab
kaiser ['kaɪzər] n : káiser m
kale ['keɪl] n : col f rizada
kaleidoscope [kə'laɪdəˌskoːp] n : calidoscopio m
kamikaze [ˌkɑmɪ'kɑzi] n : kamikaze m — **kamikaze** adj
kangaroo [ˌkæŋgə'ruː] n, pl **-roos** : canguro m
karaoke [ˌkæri'oːki] n : karaoke m
karat ['kærət] n : quilate m
karate [kə'rɑti] n : karate m
katydid ['keɪtiˌdɪd] n : saltamontes m
kayak ['kaɪˌæk] n : kayac m, kayak m
kebab [kə'bab] n : kebab m
keel¹ ['kiːl] vi **to keel over** : volcar (dícese de un barco), desplomarse (dícese de una persona)
keel² n : quilla f
keen ['kiːn] adj **1** SHARP : afilado, filoso ⟨a keen blade : una hoja afilada⟩ **2** PENETRATING : cortante, penetrante ⟨a keen wind : un viento cortante⟩ **3** ENTHUSIASTIC : entusiasta **4** ACUTE : agudo, fino ⟨keen hearing : oído fino⟩ ⟨keen intelligence : inteligencia aguda⟩
keenly ['kiːnli] adv **1** ENTHUSIASTICALLY : con entusiasmo **2** INTENSELY : vivamente, profundamente ⟨keenly aware of : muy consciente de⟩
keenness ['kiːnnəs] n **1** SHARPNESS : lo afilado, lo filoso **2** ENTHUSIASM : entusiasmo m **3** ACUTENESS : agudeza f
keep¹ ['kiːp] v **kept** ['kɛpt]; **keeping** vt **1** RETAIN : guardar, conservar, quedarse con ⟨do you want to keep these papers?

: ¿quieres guardar estos papeles?⟩ ⟨he kept the money : se quedó con el dinero⟩ ⟨to keep one's cool : mantener la calma⟩ **2** : mantener ⟨keep me informed : manténme informado⟩ ⟨she keeps herself fit : se mantiene en forma⟩ ⟨he kept his coat on : se quedó con el abrigo puesto⟩ ⟨to keep something a secret : mantener algo en secreto⟩ **3** DETAIN : retener, detener ⟨I won't keep you any longer : no te entretengo más⟩ ⟨what kept you? : ¿por qué tardaste?⟩ **4** (*with a present participle*) ⟨don't keep her waiting : no la hagas esperar⟩ ⟨he kept the company going : mantuvo la compañía a flote⟩ **5** : cumplir (su palabra), acudir (a una cita) **6** PRESERVE : guardar ⟨to keep a secret : guardar un secreto⟩ ⟨he kept it to himself : no se lo contó a nadie⟩ **7** HIDE : ocultar ⟨he kept it from her : se lo ocultó, no se lo dijo⟩ **8** OBSERVE : observar (una fiesta) **9** STORE : guardar **10** RESERVE : guardar **11** GUARD : guardar, cuidar **12** : llevar, escribir (un diario, etc.) **13** SUPPORT : mantener (una familia) **14** RAISE : criar (animales) **15** : mantener (a un amante) **16 to keep after** (school) : hacer quedar después de clase **17 to keep back** : no dejar acercarse **18 to keep back** : hacer repetir un año (a un estudiante) **19 to keep back** HIDE, REPRESS : ocultar, retener **20 to keep company** : hacerle compañía a **21 to keep company with** : andar en compañía de **22 to keep down** : mantener bajo ⟨to keep prices down : mantener los precios bajos⟩ **23** to keep down : retener (en el estómago) 24 to keep in : no dejar salir 25 to keep in CONTAIN : contener 26 to keep it down : no hacer tanto ruido 27 to keep off : no dejar pisar, tocar, etc. ⟨keep the dog off the sofa : no dejes que el perro se suba al sofá⟩ 28 to keep off : hacer evitar (un tema) 29 to keep weight off ⟨he has kept the weight off : ha mantenido el peso (tras adelgazar)⟩ 30 to keep on : mantener (a un empleado) en puesto 31 to keep out BLOCK : no dejar pasar 32 to keep up CONTINUE : seguir con 33 to keep up MAINTAIN : mantener 34 to keep up one's end of something : cumplir (con) su parte de algo — vi 1 REMAIN, STAY : mantener ⟨to keep quiet : mantener silencio⟩ ⟨to keep still : estarse quieto⟩ ⟨to keep calm : mantener la calma⟩ ⟨she likes to keep busy : le gusta estar ocupada⟩ 2 : conservarse (dícese de los alimentos) ⟨the soup will keep for a week : la sopa se conserva una semana⟩ 3 or to keep on (with a present participle) CONTINUE : seguir, no dejar de ⟨keep going straight : sigue todo recto⟩ ⟨he keeps on pestering us : no deja de molestarnos⟩ 4 to keep after NAG : estarle encima a ⟨he kept after me to quit smoking : me estaba encima para que deje de fumar⟩ 5 to keep at it PERSIST : seguir dándole 6 to keep back : no acercarse 7 to keep down : no levantarse 8 to keep from : abstenerse de ⟨I couldn't keep from laughing : no pude contener la risa⟩ 9 to keep off : no pisar (el césped, etc.) 10 to keep off AVOID : evitar (un tema) 11 to keep on CONTINUE : seguir, continuar ⟨the rain kept on : seguía lloviendo⟩ 12 to keep out (of) : no entrar (en) ⟨the sign says "keep out" : el letrero dice "prohibido el paso"⟩ ⟨to keep out of an argument : no meterse en una discusión⟩ 13 to keep to : no apartarse de (un camino, etc.), quedarse dentro de (una casa, etc.) 14 to keep to : ceñirse a (las reglas, un tema, etc.) 15 to keep to oneself : ser muy reservado 16 to keep up CONTINUE : seguir, continuar ⟨the rain kept up : seguía lloviendo⟩ 17 to keep up : mantenerse al tanto/corriente (de las noticias, etc.) 18 to keep up (with) : seguir/mantener el ritmo (de) ⟨I can't keep up (with him) : no puedo seguir su ritmo, no puedo seguirle el ritmo ⟨to keep up with the Joneses : no ser menos que el vecino⟩ 19 to keep up with someone : mantener contacto con alguien

keep² n 1 TOWER : torreón m (de un castillo), torre f del homenaje 2 SUSTENANCE : manutención f, sustento m 3 for keeps : para siempre

keeper ['ki:pər] n 1 : guarda mf (en un zoológico); conservador m, -dora f (en un museo) 2 GAMEKEEPER : guardabosque mf

keeping ['ki:piŋ] n 1 CONFORMITY : conformidad f, acuerdo m ⟨in keeping with

: de acuerdo con⟩ 2 CARE : cuidado m ⟨in the keeping of : al cuidado de⟩

keepsake ['ki:p,seik] n : recuerdo m

keg ['kɛg] n : barril m

kelp ['kɛlp] n : alga f marina

ken ['kɛn] n 1 SIGHT : vista f, alcance m de la vista 2 UNDERSTANDING : comprensión f, alcance m del conocimiento ⟨it's beyond his ken : no lo puede entender⟩

kennel ['kɛnəl] n : caseta f para perros, perrera f

Kenyan ['kɛnjən, 'ki:n-] n : keniano m, -na f — Kenyan adj

kept → keep

kerchief ['kərtʃəf, -,tʃi:f] n : pañuelo m

kernel ['kərnəl] n 1 : almendra f (de semillas y nueces) 2 : grano m (de cereales) 3 CORE : meollo m ⟨a kernel of truth : un fondo de verdad⟩

kerosene or kerosine ['kɛrə,si:n, ,kɛrə'-] n : queroseno m, kerosén m, kerosene m

ketchup ['kɛtʃəp, 'kæ-] n : salsa f catsup

kettle ['kɛtəl] n 1 : hervidor m, pava f Arg, Bol, Chile 2 → teakettle

kettledrum ['kɛtəl,drʌm] n : timbal m

key¹ ['ki:] vt 1 ATTUNE : adaptar, adecuar 2 to key up : poner nervioso, inquietar

key² adj : clave, fundamental

key³ n 1 : llave f 2 SOLUTION : clave f, soluciones fpl 3 : tecla f (de un piano o una máquina) 4 : tono m, tonalidad f (en la música) 5 ISLET, REEF : cayo m, islote m

keyboard ['ki:,bord] n : teclado m

key chain n : llavero m

keyhole ['ki:,ho:l] n : bocallave f, ojo m (de una cerradura)

keynote¹ ['ki:,no:t] vt -noted; -noting 1 : establecer la tónica de (en música) 2 : pronunciar el discurso principal de

keynote² n 1 : tónica f (en música) 2 : idea f fundamental

keypad ['ki:,pæd] n : teclado m numérico

key ring n : llavero m

keystroke ['ki:,stro:k] n : pulsación f (de tecla)

khaki ['kæki, 'kɑ-] n : caqui m

khan ['kɑn, 'kæn] n : kan m

kibbutz [kə'buts, -'bu:ts] n, pl -butzim [-,but'si:m, -,bu:t-] : kibutz m

kibitz ['kɪbɪts] vi : dar consejos molestos

kibitzer ['kɪbɪtsər, kɪ'bɪt-] n : persona f que da consejos molestos

kick¹ ['kɪk] vi 1 : dar patadas (dícese de una persona), cocear (dícese de un animal) 2 PROTEST : patalear, protestar 3 RECOIL : dar un culatazo (dícese de un arma de fuego) 4 to kick around fam : andar dando vueltas (por), viajar (por) 5 to kick back fam : relajarse 6 to kick in fam : arrancar (dícese de un motor, etc.), hacer efecto (dícese de drogas), tener efecto (dícese de una ley) 7 to kick off BEGIN : empezar, iniciar 8 to kick off : hacer el saque inicial (en deportes) — vt 1 : patear, darle una patada (a alguien) ⟨to kick someone when they're down : pegarle a alguien en el suelo⟩ **2** : dejar, perder (un vicio) **3 to kick around** *fam* : considerar, barajar (ideas, etc.) **4 to kick in** *fam* CONTRIBUTE : contribuir, poner **5 to kick off** : empezar **6 to kick oneself** *fam* : castigarse, culparse **7 to kick out** EJECT : echar **8 to kick up** : levantar (polvo, etc.) **9 to kick up a fuss** *fam* : armar una bronca

kick² *n* **1** : patada *f*, puntapié *m*, coz *f* (de un animal) **2** RECOIL : culatazo *m* (de un arma de fuego) **3** : fuerza *f* ⟨a drink with a kick : una bebida fuerte⟩ **4 to get a kick out of** : disfrutar de, deleitarse con

kicker ['kɪkər] *n* : pateador *m*, -dora *f* (en deportes)

kickoff ['kɪk,ɔf] *n* : saque *m* (inicial)

kid¹ ['kɪd] *v* **kidded; kidding** *vt* **1** FOOL : engañar **2** TEASE : tomarle el pelo (a alguien) **3 to kid oneself** : hacerse ilusiones — *vi* JOKE : bromear ⟨I'm only kidding : lo digo en broma⟩

kid² *n* **1** : chivo *m*, -va *f*; cabrito *m*, -ta *f* **2** CHILD : chico *m*, -ca *f*; niño *m*, -ña *f*

kidder ['kɪdər] *n* : bromista *mf*

kiddingly ['kɪdɪŋli] *adv* : en broma

kidnap ['kɪd,næp] *vt* **-napped** *or* **-naped** [-,næpt]; **-napping** *or* **-naping** [-,næpɪŋ] : secuestrar, raptar

kidnapper *or* **kidnaper** ['kɪd,næpər] *n* : secuestrador *m*, -dora *f*; raptor *m*, -tora *f*

kidnapping ['kɪd,næpɪŋ] *n* : secuestro *m*

kidney ['kɪdni] *n, pl* **-neys** : riñón *m*

kidney bean *n* : frijol *m*

kill¹ ['kɪl] *vt* **1** : matar **2** END : acabar con, poner fin a **3 to kill off** : matar **4 to kill time** : matar el tiempo

kill² *n* **1** KILLING : matanza *f* **2** PREY : presa *f*

killer ['kɪlər] *n* : asesino *m*, -na *f*

killer whale *n* : orca *f*

killing ['kɪlɪŋ] *n* : asesinato *m* (de alguien), matanza *f* (de un animal) **2 to make a killing** : enriquecerse, hacer una fortuna

killjoy ['kɪl,dʒɔɪ] *n* : aguafiestas *mf*

kiln ['kɪl, 'kɪln] *n* : horno *m*

kilo ['kiː,loː] *n, pl* **-los** : kilo *m*

kilobyte ['kɪlə,baɪt] *n* : kilobyte *m*

kilocycle ['kɪlə,saɪkəl] *n* : kilociclo *m*

kilogram ['kɪlə,græm, 'kiː-] *n* : kilogramo *m*

kilohertz ['kɪlə,hərts] *n* : kilohertzio *m*

kilometer [kɪ'lɑmətər, 'kɪlə,miː-] *n* : kilómetro *m*

kilowatt ['kɪlə,wɑt] *n* : kilovatio *m*

kilt ['kɪlt] *n* : falda *f* escocesa

kilter ['kɪltər] *n* **1** ORDER : buen estado *m* **2 out of kilter** : descompuesto, estropeado

kimono [kə'moː,no, -nə] *n, pl* **-nos** : kimono *m*, quimono *f*

kin ['kɪn] *n* : familiares *mpl*, parientes *mpl*

kind¹ ['kaɪnd] *adj* : amable, bondadoso, benévolo

kind² *n* **1** ESSENCE : esencia *f* ⟨a difference in degree, not in kind : una diferencia cuantitativa y no cualitativa⟩ **2** CAT-

EGORY : especie *f*, género *m* **3** TYPE : clase *f*, tipo *m*, índole *f* ⟨they're two of a kind : son tal para cual⟩ ⟨of all kinds : de todo tipo⟩

kindergarten ['kɪndər,gɑrtn, -dən] *n* : kinder *m*, kindergarten *m*, jardín *m* de infantes, jardín *m* de niños *Mex*

kindhearted [,kaɪnd'hɑrtəd] *adj* : bondadoso, de buen corazón

kindle ['kɪndəl] *v* **-dled; -dling** *vt* **1** IGNITE : encender **2** AROUSE : despertar, suscitar — *vi* : encenderse

kindliness ['kaɪndlinəs] *n* : bondad *f*

kindling ['kɪndlɪŋ, 'kɪndlən] *n* : astillas *fpl*, leña *f*

kindly¹ ['kaɪndli] *adv* **1** AMIABLY : amablemente, bondadosamente **2** COURTEOUSLY : cortésmente, con cortesía ⟨we kindly ask you not smoke : les rogamos que no fumen⟩ **3** PLEASE : por favor **4 to take kindly to** : aceptar de buena gana

kindly² *adj* **kindlier; -est** : bondadoso, amable

kindness ['kaɪndnəs] *n* : bondad *f*

kind of *adv* SOMEWHAT : un tanto, algo

kindred¹ ['kɪndrəd] *adj* SIMILAR : similar, afín ⟨kindred spirits : almas gemelas⟩

kindred² *n* **1** FAMILY : familia *f*, parentela *f* **2** → **kin**

kinfolk ['kɪn,foːk] *or* **kinfolks** [-,foːks] *npl* → **kin**

king ['kɪŋ] *n* : rey *m*

kingdom ['kɪŋdəm] *n* : reino *m*

kingfisher ['kɪŋ,fɪʃər] *n* : martín *m* pescador

kingly ['kɪŋli] *adj* **kinglier; -est** : regio, real

king-size ['kɪŋ,saɪz] *or* **king-sized** [-,saɪzd] *adj* : de tamaño muy grande, extra largo (dícese de cigarrillos)

kink ['kɪŋk] *n* **1** : rizo *m* (en el pelo), vuelta *f* (en una cuerda) **2** CRAMP : calambre *m* ⟨to have a kink in the neck : tener tortícolis⟩

kinky ['kɪŋki] *adj* **kinkier; -est** : rizado (dícese del pelo), enroscado (dícese de una cuerda)

kinship ['kɪn,ʃɪp] *n* : parentesco *m*

kinsman ['kɪnzmən] *n, pl* **-men** [-mən, -,mɛn] : familiar *m*, pariente *m*

kinswoman ['kɪnz,wumən] *n, pl* **-women** [-,wɪmən] : familiar *f*, pariente *f*

kiosk ['kiː,ɑsk] *n* : quiosco *m*

kipper ['kɪpər] *n* : arenque *m* ahumado

kiss¹ ['kɪs] *vt* : besar — *vi* : besarse

kiss² *n* : beso *m* ⟨to blow someone a kiss : tirarle un beso a alguien⟩

kit ['kɪt] *n* **1** SET : juego *m*, kit *m* **2** CASE : estuche *m*, caja *f* **3** first-aid kit : botiquín *m* **4** → **tool kit** **5** travel kit : neceser *m*

kitchen ['kɪtʃən] *n* : cocina *f*

kitchenette [,kɪtʃə'nɛt] *n* : cocineta *f*

kite ['kaɪt] *n* : cometa *f*, papalote *m* *Mex* ⟨to fly a kite : hacer volar una cometa⟩

kith ['kɪθ] *n* : amigos *mpl* ⟨kith and kin : amigos y parientes⟩

kitten ['kɪtən] *n* : gatito *m*, -ta *f*

kitty ['kɪti] *n, pl* **-ties** **1** FUND, POOL

: bote *m*, fondo *m* común **2** CAT : gato *m*, gatito *m*

kitty–corner [ˈkɪti̱ˌkɔrnər] *or* **kitty–cornered** [-nərd] → **catercorner**

kiwi [ˈkiːˌwiː] *or* **kiwifruit** [ˈkiːˌwiːˌfruːt] *n* : kiwi *m*

Kleenex [ˈkliːˌnɛks] *trademark* se usa para un pañuelo de papel

kleptomania [ˌklɛptəˈmeɪniə] *n* : cleptomanía *f*

kleptomaniac [ˌklɛptəˈmeɪniˌæk] *n* : cleptómano *m*, -na *f*

klutz [ˈklʌts] *n* : torpe *mf*

knack [ˈnæk] *n* : maña *f*, facilidad *f* ⟨to have a knack for something : tener habilidad para algo⟩ ⟨to get the knack of something : agarrarle la onda a algo⟩

knapsack [ˈnæpˌsæk] *n* : mochila *f*, morral *m*

knave [ˈneɪv] *n* : bellaco *m*, pícaro *m*

knead [ˈniːd] *vt* **1** : amasar, sobar **2** MASSAGE : masajear

knee [ˈniː] *n* : rodilla *f*

kneecap [ˈniːˌkæp] *n* : rótula *f*

kneel [ˈniːl] *vi* **knelt** [ˈnɛlt] *or* **kneeled** [ˈniːld]; **kneeling** : arrodillarse, ponerse de rodillas

knell [ˈnɛl] *n* : doble *m*, toque *m* ⟨death knell : toque de difuntos⟩

knew → **know**

knickers [ˈnɪkərz] *npl* : pantalones *mpl* bombachos de media pierna

knickknack [ˈnɪkˌnæk] *n* : chuchería *f*, baratija *f*

knife¹ [ˈnaɪf] *vt* **knifed** [ˈnaɪft]; **knifing** : acuchillar, apuñalar

knife² *n, pl* **knives** [ˈnaɪvz] : cuchillo *m*

knight¹ [ˈnaɪt] *vt* : conceder el título de *Sir* a

knight² *n* **1** : caballero *m* ⟨knight errant : caballero andante⟩ **2** : caballo *m* (en ajedrez) **3** : uno que tiene el título de *Sir*

knighthood [ˈnaɪtˌhʊd] *n* **1** : caballería *f* **2** : título *m* de *Sir*

knightly [ˈnaɪtli] *adj* : caballeresco

knit¹ [ˈnɪt] *v* **knit** *or* **knitted** [ˈnɪtəd]; **knitting** *vt* **1** UNITE : unir, enlazar **2** : tejer ⟨to knit a sweater : tejer un suéter⟩ ⟨to knit one's brows : fruncir el ceño⟩ — *vi* **1** : tejer **2** : soldarse (dícese de los huesos)

knit² *n* : prenda *f* tejida

knitter [ˈnɪtər] *n* : tejedor *m*, -dora *f*

knitwear [ˈnɪtˌwær] *n* : ropa *f* de punto

knob [ˈnɑb] *n* **1** LUMP : bulto *m*, protuberancia *f* **2** HANDLE : perilla *f*, tirador *m*, botón *m*

knobbed [ˈnɑbd] *adj* **1** KNOTTY : nudoso **2** : que tiene perilla o botón

knobby [ˈnɑbi] *adj* **knobbier; -est 1** KNOTTY : nudoso **2 knobby knees** : rodillas *fpl* huesudas

knock¹ [ˈnɑk] *vt* **1** HIT, RAP : golpear, golpetear **2** : hacer chocar ⟨they knocked heads : se dieron en la cabeza⟩ **3** CRITICIZE : criticar **4 to knock around** *fam* BEAT : pegarle a **5 to knock back** *fam* DRINK : beberse, tomarse **6 to knock dead** *fam* STUN : dejar boquiabierto **7**

to knock down : derribar, echar abajo (una puerta, etc.), tirar al suelo (a una persona) **8 to knock off** *fam* KILL : asesinar, liquidar *fam* **9 to knock off** *fam* : quitar (puntos, etc.) ⟨he knocked 10% off the price : rebajó el precio un 10%⟩ **10 to knock off** *fam* RIP OFF : copiar (un diseño, etc.) ilegalmente **11 knock it off!** *fam* : ¡basta ya!, ¡déjala! **12 to knock out** : dejar sin sentido, dejar fuera de combate (en el boxeo) **13 to knock out** ELIMINATE : eliminar **14 to knock out** DESTROY : destruir (un edificio, etc.) ⟨the storm knocked out the power : la tormenta nos dejó sin luz⟩ **15 to knock oneself out** *fam* : matarse (trabajando, etc.) ⟨go ahead — knock yourself out! : ¡adelante!, ¡disfruta!⟩ **16 to knock over** OVERTURN : tirar, volcar **17 to knock over** *fam* ROB : robar **18 to knock up** *fam* : dejar embarazada — *vi* **1** RAP : dar un golpe, llamar (a la puerta) **2** COLLIDE : darse, chocar **3 to knock around in** *fam* : viajar por **4 to knock off** *fam* : salir del trabajo ⟨to knock off early : salir temprano⟩

knock² *n* : golpe *m*, llamada *f* (a la puerta), golpeteo *m* (de un motor)

knocker [ˈnɑkər] *n* : aldaba *f*, llamador *m*

knock–kneed [ˈnɑkˈniːd] *adj* : patizambo

knockout [ˈnɑkˌaʊt] *n* **1** : nocaut *m*, knockout *m* (en deportes) **2 to be a knockout** *fam* : estar bueno *fam*, ser muy guapo

knoll [ˈnoːl] *n* : loma *f*, otero *m*, montículo *m*

knot¹ [ˈnɑt] *v* **knotted; knotting** *vt* : anudar — *vi* : anudarse

knot² *n* **1** : nudo *m* (en cordel o madera), nódulo *m* (en los músculos) **2** CLUSTER : grupo *m* **3** : nudo *m* (unidad de velocidad)

knotty [ˈnɑti] *adj* **knottier; -est 1** GNARLED : nudoso **2** COMPLEX : espinoso, enredado, complejo

know [ˈnoː] *v* **knew** [ˈnuː, ˈnjuː]; **known** [ˈnoːn]; **knowing** *vt* **1** : saber ⟨he knows French/the answer : sabe francés/la respuesta⟩ ⟨I might/should have known that . . . : debería haber sabido que . . .⟩ ⟨he made it known that . . . : hizo saber que . . .⟩ ⟨she let me know that . . . : me avisó que . . .⟩ ⟨to know something for a fact : constarle que algo es así⟩ **2** : conocer (a una persona, un lugar) ⟨do you know Julia? : ¿conoces a Julia?⟩ ⟨she knows the city well : conoce bien la ciudad⟩ ⟨he's better known as . . . : es más conocido por el nombre de . . .⟩ ⟨to be known for : conocerse por⟩ **3** RECOGNIZE : reconocer **4** DISCERN, DISTINGUISH : distinguir, discernir **5 before you know it** : antes de que te des cuenta **6 for all I know** : que yo sepa **7 God/heaven (only) knows** : quién sabe **8 if you know what I mean** : si me entiendes **9 not to know the first thing about** : no saber nada de, no tener ni idea de **10 to know how to do something**

: saber hacer algo **11 to know something inside out** *or* **to know something like the back of your hand** : saberse algo al dedillo **12 to know what's best** : saber lo que es lo mejor — *vi* **1** : saber ⟨yes, I know : sí, lo sé⟩ ⟨how should I know? : ¿qué sé yo?⟩ **2 to know best** : saber lo que es lo mejor **3 to know better** ⟨you're old enough to know better : a tu edad no debes hacer eso⟩ ⟨she doesn't know any better : es demasiado joven/novata (etc.) para saber lo que hace⟩ ⟨you know better than to ask : ya deberías saber que es mejor no preguntar⟩ **4 you know** (*used for emphasis*) ⟨you know, we really have to go : bueno, ya es hora de irnos⟩ ⟨it's cold out, you know : hace frío, ¿eh?⟩ **5 you know** (*expressing uncertainty*) ⟨we're going to, you know, hang out : vamos a . . . pues nada, pasar el rato⟩ **6 you never know** : nunca se sabe

knowable ['noːəbəl] *adj* : conocible

know–how ['noːˌhaʊ] *n* EXPERTISE : pericia *f*

knowing ['noːɪŋ] *adj* **1** KNOWLEDGEABLE : informado ⟨a knowing look : una mirada de complicidad⟩ **2** ASTUTE : astuto **3** DELIBERATE : deliberado, intencional

knowingly ['noːɪŋli] *adv* **1** : con complicidad ⟨she smiled knowingly : sonrió con una mirada de complicidad⟩ **2** DE-

LIBERATELY : a sabiendas, adrede, a propósito

know–it–all ['noːɪtˌɔl] *n* : sabelotodo *mf fam*

knowledge ['nɑlɪdʒ] *n* **1** AWARENESS : conocimiento *m* **2** LEARNING : conocimientos *mpl*, saber *m*

knowledgeable ['nɑlɪdʒəbəl] *adj* : informado, entendido, enterado

known ['noːn] *adj* : conocido, familiar

knuckle ['nʌkəl] *n* : nudillo *m*

KO[1] [ˌkeɪˈoː, ˈkeɪˌoː] *vt* **KO'd; KO'ing** KNOCK OUT : noquear (en deportes)

KO[2] *n* KNOCKOUT : nocaut *m*, knockout *m* (en deportes)

koala [koˈwɑlə] *n* : koala *m*

Koran [kəˈrɑn, -ˈræn] *n* **the Koran** : el Corán

Korean [kəˈriːən] *n* **1** : coreano *m*, -na *f* **2** : coreano *m* (idioma) — **Korean** *adj*

kosher ['koːʃər] *adj* : aprobado por la ley judía

kowtow [ˌkaʊˈtaʊ, ˈkaʊˌtaʊ] *vi* **to kowtow to** : humillarse ante, doblegarse ante

krypton ['krɪpˌtɑn] *n* : criptón *m*

kudos ['kjuːˌdɑs, 'kuː-, -ˌdoːz] *n* : fama *f*, renombre *m*

kumquat ['kʌmˌkwɑt] *n* : naranjita *f* china

Kurd ['kʊrd, 'kərd] *n* : kurdo *m*, -da *f*

Kurdish ['kʊrdɪʃ, 'kər-] *adj* : kurdo

Kuwaiti [kʊˈweɪti] *n* : kuwaití *mf* — **Kuwaiti** *adj*

L

l ['el] *n*, *pl* **l's** *or* **ls** ['lz] : duodécima letra del alfabeto inglés

la ['lɑ] *n* : la *m* (en el canto)

lab ['læb] → **laboratory**

label[1] ['leɪbəl] *vt* **-beled** *or* **-belled; -beling** *or* **-belling** **1** : etiquetar, poner etiqueta a **2** BRAND, CATEGORIZE : calificar, tildar, tachar ⟨they labeled him as a fraud : lo calificaron de farsante⟩

label[2] *n* **1** : etiqueta *f*, rótulo *m* **2** DESCRIPTION : calificación *f*, descripción *f* **3** BRAND : marca *f*

labial ['leɪbiəl] *adj* : labial

labor[1] ['leɪbər] *vi* **1** WORK : trabajar **2** STRUGGLE : avanzar penosamente (dícese de una persona), funcionar con dificultad (dícese de un motor) **3 to labor under a delusion** : hacerse ilusiones, tener una falsa impresión — *vt* BELABOR : insistir en, extenderse sobre

labor[2] *n* **1** EFFORT, WORK : trabajo *m*, esfuerzos *mpl* **2** : parto *m* ⟨to be in labor : estar de parto⟩ **3** TASK : tarea *f*, labor *m* **4** WORKERS : mano *f* de obra

laboratory ['læbrəˌtori, ləˈbɑrə-] *n*, *pl* **-ries** : laboratorio *m*

Labor Day *n* : Día *m* del Trabajo

laborer ['leɪbərər] *n* : peón *m*; trabajador *m*, -dora *f*

laborious [ləˈboriəs] *adj* : laborioso, difícil

laboriously [ləˈboriəsli] *adv* : laboriosamente, trabajosamente

labor union → **union**

labyrinth ['læbəˌrɪnθ] *n* : laberinto *m*

labyrinthine [ˌlæbəˈrɪnθən, -ˌθaɪn, -ˌθiːn] *adj* : laberíntico

lace[1] ['leɪs] *vt* **laced; lacing 1** TIE : acordonar, atar los cordones de **2** : adornar de encaje ⟨I laced the dress in white : adorné el vestido de encaje blanco⟩ **3** SPIKE : echar licor a

lace[2] *n* **1** : encaje *m* **2** SHOELACE : cordón *m* (de zapatos), agujeta *f* Mex

lacerate ['læsəˌreɪt] *vt* **-ated; -ating** : lacerar

laceration [ˌlæsəˈreɪʃən] *n* : laceración *f*

lack[1] ['læk] *vt* : carecer de, no tener ⟨she lacks patience : carece de paciencia⟩ — *vi* : faltar ⟨they lack for nothing : no les falta nada⟩

lack[2] *n* : falta *f*, carencia *f*

lackadaisical [ˌlækəˈdeɪzɪkəl] *adj* : apático, indiferente, lánguido — **lackadaisically** [-kli] *adv*

lackey ['læki] *n*, *pl* **-eys 1** FOOTMAN : lacayo *m* **2** TOADY : adulador *m*, -dora *f*

lackluster ['lækˌlʌstər] *adj* **1** DULL : sin brillo, apagado, deslustrado **2** MEDIOCRE : deslucido, mediocre

laconic [ləˈkɑnɪk] *adj* : lacónico — **laconically** [-nɪkli] *adv*

lacquer¹ [ˈlækər] vt : laquear, pintar con laca

lacquer² n : laca f

lacrosse [ləˈkrɔs] n : lacrosse m

lacy [ˈleɪsi] adj **lacier; -est** : de encaje, como de encaje

lad [ˈlæd] n : muchacho m, niño m

ladder [ˈlædər] n : escalera f

laden [ˈleɪdən] adj : cargado

ladle¹ [ˈleɪdəl] vt **-died; -dling** : servir con cucharón

ladle² n : cucharón m, cazo m

lady [ˈleɪdi] n, pl **-dies** 1 : señora f, dama f 2 WOMAN : mujer f

ladybird [ˈleɪdiˌbərd] → **ladybug**

ladybug [ˈleɪdiˌbʌɡ] n : mariquita f

lag¹ [ˈlæɡ] vi **lagged; lagging to lag behind** 1 : quedarse atrás, quedarse rezagado, ir a la zaga ⟨she lagged behind the group⟩ : se quedó atrás (del grupo), iba a la zaga (del grupo)⟩ ⟨we lag behind other countries : quedamos rezagados con respecto a otros países, vamos a la zaga de los otros países⟩ 2 : atrasarse, retrasarse (con respecto a un programa, etc.)

lag² n 1 DELAY : retraso m, demora f 2 INTERVAL : lapso m, intervalo m

lager [ˈlɑɡər] n : cerveza f rubia

laggard¹ [ˈlæɡərd] adj : retardado, retrasado

laggard² n : rezagado m, -da f

lagoon [ləˈɡuːn] n : laguna f

laid → **lay¹**

laid-back [ˈleɪdˈbæk] adj : tranquilo, relajado

lain pp → **lie¹**

lair [ˈlær] n : guarida f, madriguera f

laissez-faire [ˌlɛˌseɪˈfær, ˌleɪˌzeɪ-] n : liberalismo m económico

laity [ˈleɪəti] n **the laity** : los laicos, el laicado

lake [ˈleɪk] n : lago m

lama [ˈlɑmə] n : lama m

lamb [ˈlæm] n 1 : cordero m, borrego m (animal) 2 : carne f de cordero

lambaste [læmˈbeɪst] or **lambast** [-ˈbæst] vt **-basted; -basting** 1 BEAT, THRASH : golpear, azotar, darle una paliza (a alguien) 2 CENSURE : arremeter contra, censurar

lame¹ [ˈleɪm] vt **lamed; laming** : lisiar, hacer cojo

lame² adj **lamer; lamest** 1 : cojo, renco, rengo 2 WEAK : pobre, débil, poco convincente ⟨a lame excuse : una excusa débil⟩

lame duck n : persona f sin poder ⟨a lame-duck President : un presidente saliente⟩

lamely [ˈleɪmli] adv : sin convicción

lameness [ˈleɪmnəs] n 1 : cojera f, renquera f 2 : falta f de convicción, debilidad f, pobreza f ⟨the lameness of her response : la pobreza de su respuesta⟩

lament¹ [ləˈmɛnt] vt 1 MOURN : llorar, llorar por 2 DEPLORE : lamentar, deplorar — vi : llorar

lament² n : lamento m

lamentable [ˈlæməntəbəl, ləˈmɛntə-] adj : lamentable, deplorable — **lamentably** [-bli] adv

lamentation [ˌlæmənˈteɪʃən] n : lamentación f, lamento m

laminate¹ [ˈlæməˌneɪt] vt **-nated; -nating** : laminar

laminate² [ˈlæmənət] n : laminado m

laminated [ˈlæməˌneɪtəd] adj : laminado

lamp [ˈlæmp] n : lámpara f

lampoon¹ [læmˈpuːn] vt : satirizar

lampoon² n : sátira f

lamppost [ˈlæmpˌpoːst] n : farol m, farola f

lamprey [ˈlæmpri] n, pl **-preys** : lamprea f

lampshade [ˈlæmpˌʃeɪd] n : pantalla f (de lámpara)

lance¹ [ˈlænts] vt **lanced; lancing** : sajar

lance² n : lanza f

lance corporal n : cabo m interino, soldado m de primera clase

land¹ [ˈlænd] vt 1 : desembarcar (pasajeros de un barco), hacer aterrizar (un avión) 2 CATCH : pescar, sacar (un pez) del agua 3 GAIN, SECURE : conseguir, ganar ⟨to land a job : conseguir empleo⟩ 4 DELIVER : dar, asestar ⟨he landed a punch : asestó un puñetazo⟩ — vi 1 : aterrizar, tomar tierra, atracar ⟨the plane just landed : el avión acaba de aterrizar⟩ ⟨the ship landed an hour ago : el barco atracó hace una hora⟩ 2 ALIGHT : posarse, aterrizar ⟨to land on one's feet : caer de pie⟩ 3 FALL : caer 4 END UP, WIND UP : ir a parar

land² n 1 GROUND : tierra f ⟨dry land : tierra firme⟩ 2 TERRAIN : terreno m 3 NATION : país m, nación f 4 DOMAIN : mundo m, dominio m ⟨the land of dreams : el mundo de los sueños⟩

landfill [ˈlændˌfɪl] n : vertedero m (de basuras)

landing [ˈlændɪŋ] n 1 : aterrizaje m (de aviones), desembarco m (de barcos) 2 : descanso m, descansillo m Spain (de una escalera)

landing field n : campo m de aterrizaje

landing pad n : plataforma f de aterrizaje

landing strip → **airstrip**

landlady [ˈlændˌleɪdi] n, pl **-dies** : casera f, dueña f, arrendadora f

landless [ˈlændləs] adj : sin tierra

landlocked [ˈlændˌlɑkt] adj : sin salida al mar

landlord [ˈlændˌlɔrd] n : dueño m, casero m, arrendador m

landlubber [ˈlændˌlʌbər] n : marinero m de agua dulce

landmark [ˈlændˌmɑrk] n 1 : señal f (geográfica), punto m de referencia 2 MILESTONE : hito m ⟨a landmark in our history : un hito en nuestra historia⟩ 3 MONUMENT : monumento m histórico

landowner [ˈlændˌoːnər] n : hacendado m, -da f; terrateniente mf

landscape¹ [ˈlændˌskeɪp] vt **-scaped; -scaping** : ajardinar

landscape² n : paisaje m

landscaper [ˈlændˌskeɪpər] n : paisajista mf

landscaping [ˈlændˌskeɪpɪŋ] n : paisajismo m

landslide ['lænd,slaɪd] n 1 : desprendimiento m de tierras, derrumbe m 2 **landslide victory** : victoria f arrolladora
landward ['lændwərd] adv : en dirección de la tierra, hacia tierra
lane ['leɪn] n 1 PATH, WAY : camino m, sendero m 2 : carril m (de una carretera)
language ['læŋgwɪdʒ] n 1 : idioma m, lengua f ⟨the English language : el idioma inglés⟩ 2 : lenguaje m ⟨body language : lenguaje corporal⟩
languid ['læŋgwɪd] adj : lánguido — **languidly** adv
languish ['læŋgwɪʃ] vi 1 WEAKEN : languidecer, debilitarse 2 PINE : consumirse, suspirar (por) ⟨to languish for love : suspirar por el amor⟩ ⟨he languished in prison : estuvo pudriéndose en la cárcel⟩
languor ['læŋgər] n : languidez f
languorous ['læŋgərəs] adj : lánguido — **languorously** adv
lank ['læŋk] adj 1 THIN : delgado, larguirucho fam 2 LIMP : lacio
lanky ['læŋki] adj **lankier; -est** : delgado, larguirucho fam
lanolin ['lænələn] n : lanolina f
lantern ['læntərn] n : linterna f, farol m
Laotian [leɪ'oʃən, 'lauʃən] n : laosiano m, -na f — **Laotian** adj
lap¹ ['læp] v **lapped; lapping** vt 1 FOLD : plegar, doblar 2 WRAP : envolver 3 : lamer, besar ⟨waves were lapping the shore : las olas lamían la orilla⟩ 4 **to lap up** : beber a lengüetadas (como un gato) — vi OVERLAP : traslaparse
lap² n 1 : falda f, regazo m (del cuerpo) 2 OVERLAP : traslapo m 3 : vuelta f (en deportes) 4 STAGE : etapa f (de un viaje)
lapdog ['læp,dɔg] n : perro m faldero
lapel [lə'pɛl] n : solapa f
lapp ['læp] n : lapón m, -pona f — **Lapp** adj
lapse¹ ['læps] vi **lapsed; lapsing** 1 FALL, SLIP : caer ⟨to lapse into bad habits : caer en malos hábitos⟩ ⟨to lapse into unconsciousness : perder el conocimiento⟩ ⟨to lapse into silence : quedarse callado⟩ 2 FADE : decaer, desvanecerse ⟨her dedication lapsed : su dedicación se desvaneció⟩ 3 CEASE : cancelarse, perderse 4 ELAPSE : transcurrir, pasar 5 EXPIRE : caducar
lapse² n 1 SLIP : lapsus m, desliz m, falla f ⟨a lapse of memory : una falla de memoria⟩ 2 INTERVAL : lapso m, intervalo m, período m 3 EXPIRATION : caducidad f
laptop¹ ['læp,tɑp] adj : portátil, laptop
laptop² n : laptop m
larcenous ['lɑrsənəs] adj : de robo
larceny ['lɑrsəni] n, pl **-nies** : robo m, hurto m
larch ['lɑrtʃ] n : alerce m
lard ['lɑrd] n : manteca f de cerdo
larder ['lɑrdər] n : despensa f, alacena f
large ['lɑrdʒ] adj **larger; largest** 1 BIG : grande 2 COMPREHENSIVE : amplio, extenso 3 **by and large** : por lo general 4 **at large** : en general ⟨society at large : la sociedad en general⟩ 5 **at large** FREE : prófugo, suelto ⟨the criminal is still at large : el criminal permanece prófugo⟩ 6 **at large** : general, que habla/escribe (etc.) de diversos temas
largely ['lɑrdʒli] adv : en gran parte, en su mayoría
largeness ['lɑrdʒnəs] n : lo grande
largesse or **largess** [lɑr'ʒɛs, -'dʒɛs] n : generosidad f, largueza f
lariat ['læriət] n : lazo m
lark ['lɑrk] n 1 FUN : diversión f ⟨what a lark! : ¡qué divertido!⟩ 2 : alondra f (pájaro)
larva ['lɑrvə] n, pl **-vae** [-,viː, -,vaɪ] : larva f — **larval** [-vəl] adj
laryngitis [,lærən'dʒaɪtəs] n : laringitis f
larynx ['lærɪŋks] n, pl **-rynges** [lə'rɪn,dʒiːz] or **-ynxes** ['lærɪŋksəz] : laringe f
lasagna [lə'zɑnjə] n : lasaña f
lascivious [lə'sɪviəs] adj : lascivo
lasciviousness [lə'sɪviəsnəs] n : lascivia f, lujuria f
laser ['leɪzər] n : láser m
laser disc n : disco m láser
laser printer n : impresora f láser
lash¹ ['læʃ] vt 1 WHIP : azotar 2 BIND : atar, amarrar
lash² n 1 WHIP : látigo m 2 STROKE : latigazo m 3 EYELASH : pestaña f
lass ['læs] or **lassie** ['læsi] n : muchacha f, chica f
lasso¹ ['læ,so, læ'suː] vt : lazar
lasso² n, pl **-sos** or **-soes** : lazo m, reata f Mex
last¹ ['læst] vi 1 CONTINUE : durar ⟨how long will it last? : ¿cuánto durará?⟩ 2 ENDURE : aguantar, durar 3 SURVIVE : durar, sobrevivir 4 SUFFICE : durar, bastar — vt 1 : durar ⟨it will last you a lifetime : te durará toda la vida⟩ 2 **to last out** : aguantar
last² adv 1 : en último lugar, al último ⟨we came in last : llegamos en último lugar⟩ 2 : por última vez, la última vez ⟨I saw him last in Bogota : lo vi por última vez en Bogotá⟩ 3 FINALLY : por último, en conclusión ⟨last but not least : por último, pero no por ello menos importante⟩
last³ adj 1 FINAL : último, final 2 PREVIOUS : pasado ⟨last year : el año pasado⟩
last⁴ n 1 : el último, la última, lo último ⟨at last : por fin, al fin, finalmente⟩ 2 : horma f (de zapatero)
last-ditch ['læst'dɪtʃ] adj : desesperado, último
lasting ['læstɪŋ] adj : perdurable, duradero, estable
lastly ['læstli] adv : por último, finalmente
last-minute ['læst'mɪnət] adj : de última hora
latch¹ ['lætʃ] vt 1 : cerrar con picaporte 2 **to latch on to** or **to latch onto** GRAB : agarrarse de 3 **to latch on to** or **to latch onto** : pegarse a (alguien), abrazar (una costumbre, etc.)

latch[2] n : picaporte m, pestillo m, pasador m

late[1] ['leɪt] adv later; latest 1 : tarde ⟨to arrive late : llegar tarde⟩ ⟨to sleep late : dormir hasta tarde⟩ ⟨I'm running late : voy a llegar tarde⟩ 2 : a última hora, a finales ⟨late in the evening : a últimas horas de la tarde⟩ ⟨late in the month : a finales del mes⟩ 3 RECENTLY : recién, últimamente ⟨as late as last year : todavía en el año pasado⟩ 4 of late → lately

late[2] adj later; latest 1 TARDY : tardío ⟨I'm sorry I'm late : perdón por llegar tarde⟩ ⟨I was two hours late : llegué dos horas tarde⟩ ⟨the plane was two hours late : el avión llegó con dos horas de retraso⟩ ⟨we had a late start : salimos tarde⟩ ⟨the train's late arrival/departure : el retraso en la llegada/salida del tren⟩ 2 : avanzado ⟨because of the late hour : a causa de la hora avanzada⟩ ⟨he's in his late thirties : tiene cerca de cuarenta años⟩ 3 DECEASED : difunto, fallecido 4 RECENT : reciente, último ⟨our late quarrel : nuestra última pelea⟩ 5 it's getting late : se hace tarde 6 late in the day : tarde ⟨it's a little late in the day for an apology : ya es un poco tarde para pedir disculpas⟩

latecomer ['leɪt,kʌmər] n : rezagado m, -da f

lately ['leɪtli] adv : recientemente, últimamente

lateness ['leɪtnəs] n 1 DELAY : retraso m, atraso m, tardanza f 2 : lo avanzado (de la hora)

latent ['leɪtənt] adj : latente — **latently** adv

later[1] ['leɪtər] adv 1 : más tarde, después ⟨she returned later : volvió más tarde⟩ ⟨later in the week : a finales de la semana⟩ 2 later on : más tarde, después 3 no later than : a más tardar 4 see you later! : ¡hasta luego!

later[2] adj : posterior, ulterior ⟨his later works : sus obras posteriores⟩ ⟨in her later years : en su madurez⟩ 2 at a later time/date : más tarde, más adelante

lateral ['læṱərəl] adj : lateral — **laterally** adv

latest[1] ['leɪṱəst] adj : último

latest[2] n 1 : lo último 2 at the latest : a más tardar

latex ['leɪ,tɛks] n, pl **-tices** ['leɪṱə,si:z, 'læṱə-] or **-texes** : látex m

lath ['læθ, 'læð] n, pl **laths** or **lath** : listón m

lathe ['leɪð] n : torno m

lather[1] ['læðər] vt : enjabonar — vi : espumar, hacer espuma

lather[2] n 1 : espuma f (de jabón) 2 : sudor m (de caballo) 3 to get into a lather : ponerse histérico

Latin[1] adj : latino

Latin[2] n 1 : latín m (idioma) 2 → Latin American

Latin–American ['læṱənə'mrɪkən] adj : latinoamericano

Latin American n : latinoamericano m, -na f

latitude ['læṱə,tu:d, -,tju:d] n : latitud f

latrine [lə'tri:n] n : letrina f

latte ['lɑ,teɪ] n : café m con leche

latter ['læṱər] adj 1 SECOND : segundo 2 LAST : último 3 the latter : éste, ésta, éstos pl, éstas pl

lattice ['læṱəs] n : enrejado m, celosía f

Latvian ['lætviən] n : letón m, -tona f — **Latvian** adj

laud[1] ['lɔd] vt : alabar, loar

laud[2] n : alabanza f, loa f

laudable ['lɔdəbəl] adj : loable — **laudably** [-bli] adv

laugh[1] ['læf] vi 1 : reír, reírse 2 to laugh at : reírse de — vt to laugh off : tomar en/a broma

laugh[2] n 1 LAUGHTER : risa f 2 JOKE : chiste m, broma f ⟨he did it for a laugh : lo hizo en broma, lo hizo para divertirse⟩

laughable ['læfəbəl] adj : risible, de risa

laughingstock ['læfɪŋ,stɑk] n : hazmerreír m

laughter ['læftər] n : risa f, risas fpl

launch[1] ['lɔntʃ] vt 1 HURL : lanzar 2 : botar (un barco) 3 START : iniciar, empezar 4 : lanzar, abrir (un programa)

launch[2] n 1 : lancha f(bote) 2 LAUNCHING : lanzamiento m

launchpad ['lɔntʃ,pæd] n : plataforma f de lanzamiento

launder ['lɔndər] vt 1 : lavar y planchar (ropa) 2 : blanquear, lavar (dinero)

launderer ['lɔndərər] n : lavandero m, -ra f

laundress ['lɔndrəs] n : lavandera f

laundry ['lɔndri] n, pl **laundries** 1 : ropa f sucia, ropa f para lavar ⟨to do the laundry : lavar la ropa⟩ 2 : lavandería f(servicio de lavar)

laureate ['lɔriət] n : laureado m, -da f ⟨poet laureate : poeta laureado⟩

laurel ['lɔrəl] n 1 : laurel m (planta) 2 **laurels** npl : laureles mpl ⟨to rest on one's laurels : dormirse uno en sus laureles⟩

lava ['lɑvə, 'læ-] n : lava f

lavatory ['lævə,tori] n, pl **-ries** : baño m, cuarto m de baño

lavender ['lævəndər] n : lavanda f, espliego m

lavish[1] ['lævɪʃ] vt : prodigar (a), colmar (de)

lavish[2] adj 1 EXTRAVAGANT : pródigo, generoso, derrochador 2 ABUNDANT : abundante 3 LUXURIOUS : lujoso, espléndido

lavishly ['lævɪʃli] adv : con generosidad, espléndidamente ⟨to live lavishly : vivir a lo grande⟩

lavishness ['lævɪʃnəs] n : generosidad f, esplendidez f

law ['lɔ] n 1 : ley f ⟨to break the law : violar la ley⟩ 2 : derecho m ⟨criminal law : derecho criminal⟩ ⟨to study law : estudiar derecho⟩ ⟨law school : facultad de Derecho⟩ 3 : abogacía f ⟨to practice law : ejercer la abogacía⟩ 4 PRINCIPLE : ley f ⟨the laws of physics : las leyes de la física⟩ 5 RULE : ley f (en religión, etc.) **6 the law** POLICE : policía f ⟨to be in trouble with the law : tener problemas con la ley⟩

law–abiding ['lɔ,baɪdɪŋ] adj : observante de la ley

lawbreaker ['lɔ,breɪkər] n : infractor m, -tora f de la ley

lawful ['lɔfəl] adj : legal, legítimo, lícito — **lawfully** adv

lawgiver ['lɔ,gɪvər] n : legislador m, -dora f

lawless ['lɔləs] adj : anárquico, ingobernable — **lawlessly** adv

lawlessness ['lɔləsnəs] n : anarquía f, desorden m

lawmaker ['lɔ,meɪkər] n : legislador m, -dora f

lawman ['lɔmən] n, pl -men [-mən, -,mɛn] : agente m del orden

lawn ['lɔn] n : césped m, pasto m

lawn mower n : cortadora f de césped

lawsuit ['lɔ,suːt] n : pleito m, litigio m, demanda f

lawyer ['lɔɪər, 'lɔjər] n : abogado m, -da f

lax ['læks] adj : laxo, relajado — **laxly** adv

laxative ['læksətɪv] n : laxante m

laxity ['læksəti] n : relajación f, descuido m, falta f de rigor

lay¹ ['leɪ] v **laid** ['leɪd]; **laying** vt **1** PLACE PUT : poner, colocar ⟨she laid it on the table : lo puso en la mesa⟩ ⟨to lay a hand/finger on someone : ponerle a alguien la mano encima⟩ **2** INSTALL : poner, colocar (ladrillos, etc.), tender (vías, cables, etc.) ⟨to lay the foundation : poner los cimientos⟩ **3** PREPARE : preparar ⟨to lay a trap : tender una trampa⟩ ⟨the best-laid plans : los planes mejor trazados⟩ **4** BET : apostar **5** PLACE : poner (énfasis, etc.) ⟨to lay the blame on : echarle la culpa a⟩ **6 to be laid over** : hacer escala **7 to be laid up** : estar enfermo, tener que guardar cama **8 to lay aside** : dejar a un lado **9 to lay aside/by** SAVE : guardar, ahorrar **10 to lay down** IMPOSE ESTABLISH : imponer, establecer **11 to lay down** : dejar, deponer (armas) **12 to lay eggs** : poner huevos **13 to lay in** STOCK : comprar, proveerse de **14 to lay it on (thick)** : exagerar, cargar las tintas **15 to lay out** PRESENT : presentar, exponer ⟨he laid out his plan : presentó su proyecto⟩ **16 to lay off** : despedir (a un empleado) **17 to lay out** DESIGN : diseñar (el trazado de) **18 to lay up** STORE : guardar, almacenar — vi **1 to lay into** ATTACK : arremeter contra **2 to lay off** : dejar (un vicio) **3 to lay off** : dejar en paz ⟨lay off him! : ¡déjalo en paz!⟩ ⟨lay off! : ¡basta ya!⟩ **4 to lay over** : hacer escala

lay² → **lie¹**

lay³ adj SECULAR : laico, lego

lay⁴ n **1** : disposición f, configuración f ⟨the lay of the land : la configuración del terreno⟩ **2** BALLAD : romance m, balada f

layer ['leɪər] n **1** : capa f (de pintura, etc.), estrato m (de roca) **2** : gallina f ponedora

layman ['leɪmən] n, pl -men [-mən, -,mɛn] **1** : laico m, lego m, seglar mf (en religión) **2** : profano m, -na f; lego m, -ga f ⟨in layman's terms : en lenguaje sencillo⟩

layoff ['leɪ,ɔf] n : despido m

layout ['leɪ,aʊt] n : disposición f, distribución f (de una casa, etc.), trazado m (de una ciudad)

layover ['leɪ,oːvər] n STOPOVER : escala f

layperson ['leɪ,pərsən] n **1** : laico m, -ca f; lego m, -ga f; seglar mf (en religión) **2** : profano m, -na f; lego m, -ga f

laywoman ['leɪ,wʊmən] n, pl -women [-,wɪmən] : laica f, lega f

laziness ['leɪzinəs] n : pereza f, flojera f

laze ['leɪz] v **lazed**; **lazing** vi or **to laze around** : holgazanear — vt **to laze away** ⟨she lazed away the afternoon : pasó la tarde holgazaneando⟩

lazy ['leɪzi] adj **lazier; -est** : perezoso, holgazán — **lazily** ['leɪzəli] adv

lazybones ['leɪzi,boːnz] n : gandul m, -dula f

LCD [,el,siː'diː] n (liquid crystal display) : LCD m, pantalla f de cristal líquido

leach ['liːtʃ] vt : filtrar

lead¹ ['liːd] v **led** ['lɛd]; **leading** vt **1** GUIDE : conducir, llevar, guiar **2** DIRECT : dirigir **3** HEAD : encabezar, ir al frente de **4** : llevar (una vida) **5 to lead on** : engañar — vi **1 to lead to** : conducir a, llevar a **2 to lead to** : dar a (dícese de una puerta) **3** : ir a la cabeza, ir en cabeza (en una competición, etc.) ⟨they're leading by 20 points : van ganando por 20 puntos, tienen 20 puntos de ventaja⟩ **4 to lead to** : resultar en, llevar a ⟨it only leads to trouble : sólo resulta en problemas⟩ **5 to lead up to** PRECEDE : preceder a **6 to lead up to** INTRODUCE : introducir

lead² n **1** : delantera f, primer lugar m ⟨to take the lead : tomar la delantera⟩ ⟨to be in the lead : ir a la cabeza, ir en cabeza⟩ ⟨to follow someone's lead : seguir el ejemplo de alguien⟩ **2** or **lead actor** : primer actor m, primera actriz f **3** or **lead guitarist** : guitarrista mf principal **4** or **lead role** : papel m principal **5** or **lead singer** : cantante mf principal **6** or **lead story** : artículo m principal **7** CLUE : pista f **8** : correa f (de un perro)

lead³ ['lɛd] n **1** : plomo m (metal) **2** : mina f (de lápiz) **3 lead poisoning** : saturnismo m

leaden ['lɛdən] adj **1** : plomizo ⟨a leaden sky : un cielo plomizo⟩ **2** HEAVY : pesado

leader ['liːdər] n : jefe m, -fa f; líder mf; dirigente mf; gobernante mf

leadership ['liːdər,ʃɪp] n : mando m, dirección f

leading ['liːdɪŋ] adj **1** IMPORTANT : principal, importante ⟨a leading expert : un destacado experto⟩ **2** FOREMOST : principal, más importante ⟨the leading cause of death : la principal causa de muerte⟩

leaf¹ ['liːf] vi **1** : echar hojas (dícese de un

árbol) **2 to leaf through** : hojear (un libro)

leaf² *n*, *pl* **leaves** [ˈliːvz] **1** : hoja *f* (de plantas o libros) **2 to turn over a new leaf** : hacer borrón y cuenta nueva

leafless [ˈliːfləs] *adj* : sin hojas, pelado

leaflet [ˈliːflət] *n* : folleto *m*

leafy [ˈliːfi] *adj* **leafier; -est** : frondoso

league¹ [ˈliːg] *v* **leagued; leaguing** *vt* : aliar, unir — *vi* : aliarse, unirse

league² *n* **1** : legua *f* (medida de distancia) **2** ASSOCIATION : alianza *f*, sociedad *f*, liga *f*

leak¹ [ˈliːk] *vt* **1** : perder, dejar escapar (un líquido o un gas) **2** : filtrar (información) — *vi* **1** : gotear, escaparse, fugarse (dícese de un líquido o un gas) **2** : hacer agua (dícese de un bote) **3** : filtrarse, divulgarse (dícese de información)

leak² *n* **1** HOLE : agujero *m* (en recipientes), gotera *f* (en un tejado) **2** ESCAPE : fuga *f*, escape *m* **3** : filtración *f* (de información)

leakage [ˈliːkɪdʒ] *n* : escape *m*, fuga *f*

leaky [ˈliːki] *adj* **leakier; -est** : agujereado (dícese de un recipiente), que hace agua (dícese de un bote), con goteras (dícese de un tejado)

lean¹ [ˈliːn] *vi* **1** BEND : inclinarse, ladearse **2** RECLINE : reclinarse **3** RELY : apoyarse (en), depender (de) **4** INCLINE TEND : inclinarse, tender — *vt* : apoyar

lean² *adj* **1** THIN : delgado, flaco **2** : sin grasa, magro (dícese de la carne)

leaning [ˈliːnɪŋ] *n* TENDENCY : inclinación *f*

leanness [ˈliːnnəs] *n* : delgadez *f*

lean–to [ˈliːnˌtuː] *n* : cobertizo *m*

leap¹ [ˈliːp] *vi* **leaped** [ˈliːpt, ˈlɛpt] *or* **leapt** [ˈliːpt, ˈlɛpt]; **leaping** : saltar, brincar

leap² *n* : salto *m*, brinco *m*

leap year *n* : año *m* bisiesto

learn [ˈlɜrn] *vt* **1** : aprender ⟨to learn to sing : aprender a cantar⟩ **2** MEMORIZE : aprender de memoria **3** DISCOVER : saber, enterarse de — *vi* **1** : aprender ⟨to learn from experience : aprender por experiencia⟩ **2** FIND OUT : enterarse, saber

learned [ˈlɜrnəd] *adj* : erudito

learner [ˈlɜrnər] *n* : principiante *mf*, estudiante *mf*

learning [ˈlɜrnɪŋ] *n* : erudición *f*, saber *m*

lease¹ [ˈliːs] *vt* **leased; leasing** : arrendar

lease² *n* : contrato *m* de arrendamiento

leash *n* : traílla *f*

least¹ [ˈliːst] *adv* : menos ⟨when least expected : cuando menos se espera⟩

least² *adj* (*superlative of* LITTLE) : menor, más mínimo

least³ *n* **1 at least** : al menos, por lo menos **2 the least** : lo menos ⟨it's the least I can do : es lo menos que puedo hacer⟩ ⟨it doesn't bother me in the least : no me molesta para nada⟩ **3 to say the least** : por no decir más

leather [ˈlɛðər] *n* : cuero *m*

leathery [ˈlɛðəri] *adj* : curtido (dícese de la piel), correoso (dícese de la carne)

leave¹ [ˈliːv] *v* **left** [ˈlɛft]; **leaving** *vt* **1** DEPART : salir(se) de, ir(se) de ⟨she left the office/party : salió de la oficina/fiesta⟩ ⟨I left home after high school : me fui de casa después de terminar el colegio⟩ **2** : dejar ⟨we left her doing her work : la dejamos trabajando⟩ **3** : dejar (que alguien haga algo) ⟨leave the dishes for me : deja los trastes, los lavaré después⟩ ⟨we left all the arrangements to him : dejamos que él lo arreglara todo⟩ ⟨I'll leave it (up) to you (to decide) : te dejo a ti decidir⟩ ⟨leave it to me! : ¡yo me encargo!⟩ ⟨leave it to her to arrive early : llegó temprano, como siempre⟩ **4** ABANDON : dejar (uno a su familia, etc.) ⟨they left me to clean up : se fueron y me tocó a mí limpiar⟩ **5** QUIT, GIVE UP : dejar (un trabajo, etc.) **6** *or* **to leave behind** FORGET : dejar, olvidarse (en casa, etc.) **7** *or* **to leave behind** : dejar ⟨she left her home/family (behind) : dejó (atrás) su hogar/a su familia⟩ ⟨to leave the past behind : dejar atrás el pasado⟩ **8** DEPOSIT : dejar ⟨leave it on the table/with me : déjalo en la mesa/conmigo⟩ ⟨I left him at the airport : lo dejé en el aeropuerto⟩ ⟨to leave a message : dejar un mensaje⟩ **9** : dejar (en un estado) ⟨I left the lights on : dejé las luces encendidas⟩ ⟨he was left paralyzed : se quedó paralizado⟩ **10** ALLOW, RESERVE : dejar (espacio, etc.) **11** : dejar (una marca, etc.) **12** BEQUEATH : dejar, legar **13** : dejar ⟨he left (behind) a wife and child : dejó esposa y un hijo⟩ **14 to be left** : quedar ⟨it's all I have left : es todo lo que me queda⟩ **15 to be left over** : sobrar **16 to be left behind** : quedarse atrás **17 to leave off** : dejar de, parar de **18 to leave off/on** OMIT : omitir, excluir — *vi* : irse, salir, partir, marcharse ⟨she left yesterday morning : se fue ayer por la mañana⟩ ⟨they left for Paris : salieron para París⟩

leave² *n* **1** PERMISSION : permiso *m* ⟨by your leave : con su permiso⟩ **2** *or* **leave of absence** : permiso *m*, licencia *f* ⟨maternity leave : licencia por maternidad⟩ **3 to take one's leave** : despedirse

leaven [ˈlɛvən] *n* : levadura *f*

leaves → **leaf²**

leaving [ˈliːvɪŋ] *n* **1** : salida *f*, partida *f* **2 leavings** *npl* : restos *mpl*, sobras *fpl*

Lebanese [ˌlɛbəˈniːz, -ˈniːs] *n* : libanés *m*, -nesa *f* — **Lebanese** *adj*

lecherous [ˈlɛtʃərəs] *adj* : lascivo, libidinoso — **lecherously** *adv*

lechery [ˈlɛtʃəri] *n* : lascivia *f*, lujuria *f*

lectern [ˈlɛktərn] *n* : atril *m*

lecture¹ [ˈlɛktʃər] *v* **-tured; -turing** *vi* : dar clase, dictar clase, dar una conferencia — *vt* SCOLD : sermonear, echar una reprimenda a, regañar

lecture² *n* **1** : conferencia *f* **2** REPRIMAND : reprimenda *f*

lecturer [ˈlɛktʃərər] *n* **1** SPEAKER : conferenciante *mf* **2** TEACHER : profesor *m*, -sora *f*

led → **lead¹**

LED [ˌɛl.iˈdiː] n (*light-emitting diode*) : LED m, led m

ledge [ˈlɛʤ] n : repisa f (de una pared), antepecho m (de una ventana), saliente m (de una montaña)

ledger [ˈlɛʤər] n : libro m mayor, libro m de contabilidad

lee[1] [ˈliː] adj : de sotavento

lee[2] n : sotavento m

leech [ˈliːtʃ] n : sanguijuela f

leek [ˈliːk] n : puerro m

leer[1] [ˈlɪr] vi : mirar con lascivia

leer[2] n : mirada f lasciva

leery [ˈlɪri] adj : receloso

lees [ˈliːz] npl : posos mpl, heces fpl

leeward[1] [ˈliːwərd, ˈluːərd] adj : de sotavento

leeward[2] n : sotavento m

leeway [ˈliːˌweɪ] n : libertad f, margen m

left[1] [ˈlɛft] adj : hacia la izquierda

left[2] → **leave**[1]

left[3] adj : izquierdo

left[4] n : izquierda f ⟨on the left : a la izquierda⟩

left-click [ˈlɛftˈklɪk] vi : hacer clic/click izquierdo — vt : hacer clic/click izquierdo en

left-hand [ˈlɛftˈhænd] adj **1** : de la izquierda **2** → **left-handed**

left-handed [ˈlɛftˈhændəd] adj **1** : zurdo (dícese de una persona) **2** : con doble sentido ⟨a left-handed compliment : un cumplido a medias⟩

leftist [ˈlɛftɪst] n : izquierdista mf — **leftist** adj

leftover [ˈlɛftˌoːvər] adj : sobrante, que sobra

leftovers [ˈlɛftˌoːvərz] npl : restos mpl, sobras fpl

left wing n **the left wing** : la izquierda

left-winger [ˈlɛftˈwɪŋər] n : izquierdista mf

leg [ˈlɛg] n **1** : pierna f (de una persona, de carne, de ropa), pata f (de un animal, de muebles) **2** STAGE : etapa f (de un viaje), vuelta f (de una carrera)

legacy [ˈlɛgəsi] n, pl **-cies** : legado m, herencia f

legal [ˈliːgəl] adj **1** : legal, jurídico ⟨legal advisor : asesor jurídico⟩ ⟨the legal profession : la abogacía⟩ **2** LAWFUL : legítimo, legal ⟨legal tender : moneda de curso legal⟩

legalistic [ˌliːgəˈlɪstɪk] adj : legalista

legality [liˈgæləti] n, pl **-ties** : legalidad f

legalize [ˈliːgəˌlaɪz] vt **-ized; -izing** : legalizar

legally [ˈliːgəli] adv : legalmente

legate [ˈlɛgət] n : legado m

legation [lɪˈgeɪʃən] n : legación f

legend [ˈlɛʤənd] n **1** STORY : leyenda f **2** INSCRIPTION : leyenda f, inscripción f **3** : signos mpl convencionales (en un mapa)

legendary [ˈlɛʤənˌderi] adj : legendario

legerdemain [ˌlɛʤərdəˈmeɪn] → **sleight of hand**

leggings [ˈlɛgɪŋz, ˈlɛgənz] npl : mallas fpl

legibility [ˌlɛʤəˈbɪləti] n : legibilidad f

legible [ˈlɛʤəbəl] adj : legible

legibly [ˈlɛʤəbli] adv : de manera legible

legion [ˈliːʤən] n : legión f

legionnaire [ˌliːʤəˈnær] n : legionario m, -ria f

legislate [ˈlɛʤəsˌleɪt] vi **-lated; -lating** : legislar

legislation [ˌlɛʤəsˈleɪʃən] n : legislación f

legislative [ˈlɛʤəsˌleɪtɪv] adj : legislativo, legislador

legislator [ˈlɛʤəsˌleɪtər] n : legislador m, -dora f

legislature [ˈlɛʤəsˌleɪtʃər] n : asamblea f legislativa

legitimacy [lɪˈʤɪtəməsi] n : legitimidad f

legitimate [lɪˈʤɪtəmət] adj **1** VALID : legítimo, válido, justificado **2** LAWFUL : legítimo, legal

legitimately [lɪˈʤɪtəmətli] adv : legítimamente

legitimize [lɪˈʤɪtəˌmaɪz] vt **-mized; -mizing** : legitimar, hacer legítimo

legume [ˈlɛˌgjuːm, lɪˈgjuːm] n : legumbre f

leisure [ˈliːʒər, ˈlɛ-] n **1** : ocio m, tiempo m libre ⟨a life of leisure : una vida de ocio⟩ **2 to take one's leisure** : reposar **3 at your leisure** : cuando te venga bien, cuando tengas tiempo

leisurely [ˈliːʒərli, ˈlɛ-] adj & adv : lento, sin prisas

lemming [ˈlɛmɪŋ] n : lemming m

lemon [ˈlɛmən] n : limón m

lemonade [ˌlɛməˈneɪd] n : limonada f

lemony [ˈlɛməni] adj : a limón

lempira [lɛmˈpɪrə] n : lempira f (unidad monetaria)

lend [ˈlɛnd] vt **lent** [ˈlɛnt]; **lending 1** : prestar ⟨to lend money : prestar dinero⟩ **2** GIVE : dar ⟨it lends force to his criticism : da fuerza a su crítica⟩ ⟨to lend a hand to someone : echarle una mano a alguien⟩ **3 to lend oneself to** : prestarse a

length [ˈlɛŋkθ] n **1** : longitud f, largo m ⟨10 feet in length : 10 pies de largo⟩ **2** DURATION : duración f **3** : trozo m (de madera), corte m (de tela) **4 to go to any lengths** : hacer todo lo posible **5 at ~** : extensamente ⟨to speak at length : hablar largo y tendido⟩ **6 at ~ FINALLY** : por fin

lengthen [ˈlɛŋkθən] vt **1** : alargar ⟨can they lengthen the dress? : ¿se puede alargar el vestido?⟩ **2** EXTEND, PROLONG : prolongar, extender — vi : alargarse, crecer ⟨the days are lengthening : los días están creciendo⟩

lengthways [ˈlɛŋkθˌweɪz] → **lengthwise**

lengthwise [ˈlɛŋkθˌwaɪz] adv : a lo largo, longitudinalmente

lengthy [ˈlɛŋkθi] adj **lengthier; -est 1** OVERLONG : largo y pesado **2** EXTENDED : prolongado, largo

leniency [ˈliːniənsi] n, pl **-cies** : lenidad f, indulgencia f

lenient [ˈliːniənt] adj : indulgente, poco severo

leniently [ˈliːniəntli] adv : con lenidad, con indulgencia

lens [ˈlɛnz] n **1** : cristalino m (del ojo) **2** : lente mf (de un instrumento o una cámara) **3** → **contact lens**

lent → lend

Lent [ˈlɛnt] *n* : Cuaresma *f*

lentil [ˈlɛntəl] *n* : lenteja *f*

Leo [ˈliːoː] *n* **1** : Leo *m* (signo o constelación) **2** : Leo *mf* (persona)

leopard [ˈlɛpərd] *n* : leopardo *m*

leotard [ˈliːəˌtɑrd] *n* : leotardo *m*, malla *f*

leper [ˈlɛpər] *n* : leproso *m*, -sa *f*

leprechaun [ˈlɛprəˌkɑn] *n* : duende *m* (irlandés)

leprosy [ˈlɛprəsi] *n* : lepra *f* — **leprous** [ˈlɛprəs] *adj*

lesbian¹ [ˈlɛzbiən] *adj* : lesbiano

lesbian² *n* : lesbiana *f*

lesbianism [ˈlɛzbiəˌnɪzəm] *n* : lesbianismo *m*

lesion [ˈliːʒən] *n* : lesión *f*

less¹ [ˈlɛs] *adv* (*comparative of* LITTLE¹) : menos ⟨the less you know, the better : cuanto menos sepas, mejor⟩ ⟨less and less : cada vez menos⟩

less² *adj* (*comparative of* LITTLE²) : menos ⟨less than three : menos de tres⟩ ⟨less money : menos dinero⟩ ⟨nothing less than perfection : nada menos que la perfección⟩

less³ *pron* : menos ⟨I'm earning less : estoy ganando menos⟩

less⁴ *prep* : menos ⟨one month less two days : un mes menos dos días⟩

-less [ləs] *suf* : sin

lessee [lɛˈsiː] *n* : arrendatario *m*, -ria *f*

lessen [ˈlɛsən] *vt* : disminuir, reducir — *vi* : disminuir, reducirse

lesser [ˈlɛsər] *adj* : menor ⟨to a lesser degree : en menor grado⟩

lesson [ˈlɛsən] *n* **1** CLASS : clase *f*, curso *m* **2** : lección *f* ⟨the lessons of history : las lecciones de la historia⟩

lessor [ˈlɛˌsɔr, lˈsɔr] *n* : arrendador *m*, -dora *f*

lest [ˈlɛst] *conj* : para (que) no ⟨lest we forget : para que no olvidemos⟩

let [ˈlɛt] *v* **let; letting** *vt* **1** ALLOW : dejar, permitir ⟨let me see it : déjame verlo⟩ ⟨let it chill : déjalo enfriar⟩ ⟨let him in/out : déjalo entrar/salir⟩ **2** MAKE : hacer ⟨let me know : házmelo saber, avísame⟩ ⟨let them wait! : ¡que esperen!⟩ **3** RENT : alquilar **4** (*used in the first person plural imperative*) ⟨let's go! : ¡vamos!, ¡vámonos!⟩ ⟨let us pray : oremos⟩ **5 let alone** : ni mucho menos, (y) menos aún ⟨I can barely understand it, let alone explain it : apenas puedo entenderlo, ni mucho menos explicarlo⟩ **6 to let down** LOWER : bajar **7 to let down** DISAPPOINT : fallar ⟨to let someone down gently : suavizarle el golpe a alguien⟩ **8 to let go** RELEASE, FREE : soltar ⟨let me go! : ¡suéltame!⟩ **9 to let oneself go** : dejarse, abandonarse **10 to let in on** : to let someone in on a secret : contarle un secreto a alguien **11 to let off** FORGIVE : perdonar ⟨they let him off the hook : lo dejaron ir sin castigo⟩ ⟨they let her off lightly : la dieron un leve castigo⟩ **12 to let off** : echar (vapor), hacer estallar (un petardo, etc.) **13 to let oneself in for** : exponerse a (críticas), buscarse (problemas) ⟨I didn't know what I was letting myself in for : no sabía en la que me estaba metiendo⟩ **14 to let out** REVEAL : revelar **15 to let out** : soltar (un grito, etc.) **16 to let out** : ensanchar (un vestido, etc.) — *vi* **1 to let go** RELAX : soltarse el pelo **2 to let go (of)** : soltar ⟨let go (of me)! : ¡suélta(me)!⟩ **3 to let on** REVEAL, SHOW : revelar, demostrar ⟨don't let on! : ¡no digas nada!⟩ ⟨he didn't let on that he knew : hizo como si no lo supiera⟩ **4 to let on** PRETEND, SEEM : fingir, parecer **5 to let out** END : terminar ⟨school lets out in June : el año escolar termina en junio⟩ **6 to let up** ABATE : amainar, disminuir ⟨the pace never lets up : el ritmo nunca disminuye⟩ **7 to let up** STOP : parar **8 to let up on** : soltar (un freno, etc.), no ser tan duro con (alguien)

letdown [ˈlɛtˌdaʊn] *n* : chasco *m*, decepción *f*

lethal [ˈliːθəl] *adj* : letal — **lethally** *adv*

lethargic [lɪˈθɑrdʒɪk] *adj* : letárgico

lethargy [ˈlɛθərdʒi] *n* : letargo *m*

let's [ˈlɛts] *contraction of* LET US → **let**

letter¹ [ˈlɛtər] *vt* : marcar con letras, inscribir letras en

letter² *n* **1** : letra *f* (del alfabeto) **2** : carta *f* ⟨a letter to my mother : una carta a mi madre⟩ **3 letters** *npl* ARTS : letras *fpl* **4 to the letter** : al pie de la letra

letter bomb *n* : carta *f* bomba

letterhead [ˈlɛtərˌhɛd] *n* **1** : membrete *m* (de una carta) **2** : papel *m* con membrete

lettering [ˈlɛtərɪŋ] *n* : letra *f*

lettuce [ˈlɛtəs] *n* : lechuga *f*

letup [ˈlɛtˌʌp] *n* LULL : pausa *f*, respiro *m*

leukemia [luːˈkiːmiə] *n* : leucemia *f*

levee [ˈlɛvi] *n* : dique *m*

level¹ [ˈlɛvəl] *v* **-eled** *or* **-elled; -eling** *or* **-elling** *vt* **1** *or* **to level off** FLATTEN : nivelar, aplanar **2** AIM : apuntar (una pistola), dirigir (una acusación) **3** RAZE : rasar, arrasar — *vi* **1 to level off/out** : estabilizarse ⟨dícese de los precios, etc.), nivelarse (dícese de un avión), allanarse (dícese del paisaje) **2 to level with someone** : ser sincero con alguien

level² *adj* **1** EVEN : llano, plano, parejo **2** CALM : tranquilo ⟨to keep a level head : no perder la cabeza⟩

level³ *n* : nivel *m*

leveler [ˈlɛvələr] *n* : nivelador *m*, -dora *f*

levelheaded [ˈlɛvəlˈhɛdəd] *adj* : sensato, equilibrado

levelly [ˈlɛvəli] *adv* CALMLY : con ecuanimidad *f*, con calma

levelness [ˈlɛvəlnəs] *n* : uniformidad *f*

lever [ˈlɛvər, ˈliː-] *n* : palanca *f*

leverage [ˈlɛvərɪdʒ, ˈliː-] *n* **1** : apalancamiento *m* (en física) **2** INFLUENCE : influencia *f*, palanca *f* *fam*

leviathan [lɪˈvaɪəθən] *n* : leviatán *m*, gigante *m*

levitate [ˈlɛvəˌteɪt] *vi* **-tated; -tating** : levitar — *vt* : hacer levitar

levity ['lɛvəṭi] *n* : ligereza *f*, frivolidad *f*

levy[1] ['lɛvi] *vt* **levied; levying 1** IMPOSE : imponer, exigir, gravar (un impuesto) **2** COLLECT : recaudar (un impuesto)

levy[2] *n, pl* **levies** : impuesto *m*, gravamen *m*

lewd ['lu:d] *adj* : lascivo — **lewdly** *adv*

lewdness ['lu:dnəs] *n* : lascivia *f*

lexical ['lɛksɪkəl] *adj* : léxico

lexicographer [,lɛksə'kagrəfər] *n* : lexicógrafo *m*, -fa *f*

lexicographical [,lɛksəko'græfɪkəl] *or* **lexicographic** [-'græfɪk] *adj* : lexicográfico

lexicography [,lɛksə'kagrəfi] *n* : lexicografía *f*

lexicon ['lɛksɪkan] *n, pl* **-ica** [-kə] *or* **-icons** : léxico *m*

liability [,laɪə'bɪləṭi] *n, pl* **-ties 1** RESPONSIBILITY : responsabilidad *f* **2** SUSCEPTIBILITY : propensión *f* **3** DRAWBACK : desventaja *f* **4 liabilities** *npl* DEBTS : deudas *fpl*, pasivo *m*

liable ['laɪəbəl] *adj* **1** RESPONSIBLE : responsable **2** SUSCEPTIBLE : propenso **3** PROBABLE : probable ⟨it's liable to happen : es probable que suceda⟩

liaison ['li:ə,zan, li'eɪ-] *n* **1** CONNECTION : enlace *m*, relación *f* **2** AFFAIR : amorío *m*, aventura *f*

liar ['laɪər] *n* : mentiroso *m*, -sa *f*; embustero *m*, -ra *f*

libel[1] ['laɪbəl] *vt* **-beled** *or* **-belled; -beling** *or* **-belling** : difamar, calumniar

libel[2] *n* : difamación *f*, calumnia *f*

libelous *or* **libellous** ['laɪbələs] *adj* : difamatorio, calumnioso, injurioso

liberal[1] ['lɪbrəl, 'lɪbərəl] *adj* **1** TOLERANT : liberal, tolerante **2** GENEROUS : generoso **3** ABUNDANT : abundante — **liberal arts** : humanidades *fpl*, artes *fpl* liberales

liberal[2] *n* : liberal *mf*

liberalism ['lɪbrə,lɪzəm, 'lɪbərə-] *n* : liberalismo *m*

liberality [,lɪbə'ræləṭi] *n, pl* **-ties** : liberalidad *f*, generosidad *f*

liberalize ['lɪbrə,laɪz, 'lɪbərə-] *vt* **-ized; -izing** : liberalizar

liberally ['lɪbrəli, 'lɪbərə-] *adv* **1** GENEROUSLY : generosamente **2** ABUNDANTLY : abundantemente **3** FREELY : libremente

liberate ['lɪbə,reɪt] *vt* **-ated; -ating** : liberar, libertar

liberation [,lɪbə'reɪʃən] *n* : liberación *f*

liberator ['lɪbə,reɪṭər] *n* : libertador *m*, -dora *f*

Liberian [laɪ'bɪriən] *n* : liberiano *m*, -na *f* — **Liberian** *adj*

libertarian [,lɪbər'tɛriən] *adj & n* : libertario *m*, -ria *f*

libertine ['lɪbər,ti:n] *n* : libertino *m*, -na *f*

liberty ['lɪbərṭi] *n, pl* **-ties 1** : libertad *f* **2 to take the liberty of** : tomarse la libertad de **3 to take liberties with** : tomarse confianzas con, tomarse libertades con

libido [lə'bi:do:, -'baɪ-] *n, pl* **-dos** : libido *f* — **libidinous** [lə'bɪdənəs] *adj*

Libra ['li:brə] *n* **1** : Libra *m* (signo o constelación) **2** : Libra *mf* (persona)

librarian [laɪ'brɛriən] *n* : bibliotecario *m*, -ria *f*

library ['laɪ,brɛri] *n, pl* **-braries** : biblioteca *f*

librettist [lɪ'brɛṭɪst] *n* : libretista *mf*

libretto [lɪ'brɛṭo] *n, pl* **-tos** *or* **-ti** [-ṭi:] : libreto *m*

Libyan ['lɪbiən] *n* : libio *m*, -bia *f* — **Libyan** *adj*

lice → **louse**

license[1] ['laɪsənts] *vt* **licensed; licensing** : licenciar, autorizar, dar permiso a

license[2] *or* **licence** *n* **1** PERMISSION : licencia *f*, permiso *m* **2** PERMIT : licencia *f*, carnet *m Spain* ⟨driver's license : licencia de conducir⟩ **3** FREEDOM : libertad *f* **4** LICENTIOUSNESS : libertinaje *m*

licensed *adj* CERTIFIED : autorizado, certificado, licenciado ⟨a licensed physician : un médico certificado⟩ ⟨a licensed driver : un conductor con licencia⟩

license plate *n* : placa *f* de matrícula; chapa *f Arg, Uru*; patente *f Arg, Chile, Uru*

licentious [laɪ'sɛntʃəs] *adj* : licencioso, disoluto — **licentiously** *adv*

licentiousness [laɪ'sɛntʃəsnəs] *n* : libertinaje *m*

lichen ['laɪkən] *n* : liquen *m*

licit ['lɪsɪt] *adj* : lícito

lick[1] ['lɪk] *vt* **1** : lamer **2** BEAT : darle una paliza (a alguien)

lick[2] *n* **1** : lamida *f*, lengüetada *f* ⟨a lick of paint : una mano de pintura⟩ **2** BIT : pizca *f*, ápice *m* **3 a lick and a promise** : una lavada a la carrera

licorice ['lɪkərɪʃ, -rəs] *n* : regaliz *m*, dulce *m* de regaliz

lid ['lɪd] *n* **1** COVER : tapa *f* **2** EYELID : párpado *m*

lie[1] ['laɪ] *vi* **lay** ['leɪ]; **lain** ['leɪn]; **lying** ['laɪɪŋ] **1** *or* **to lie down** : acostarse, echarse, tumbarse, tenderse ⟨I lay down on the bed : me acosté en la cama⟩ ⟨lie on your back : acuéstate boca arriba⟩ ⟨he was lying unconscious on the floor : estaba tendido en el suelo sin sentido⟩ ⟨to take something lying down : dejar pasar algo sin protestar⟩ **2** : estar, estar situado, encontrarse ⟨the book lay on the table : el libro estaba en la mesa⟩ ⟨the city lies to the south : la ciudad se encuentra al sur⟩ ⟨there were papers lying around : había papeles tirados por todos lados⟩ **3** CONSIST : consistir **4 to lie ahead** AWAIT : estar por venir **5 to lie around** RELAX : holgazanear **6 to lie back** : reclinarse **7 to lie down on the job** : no cumplir **8 to lie in/with** : residir en ⟨the power lies in the people : el poder reside en el pueblo⟩ **9 to lie low** : tratar de no llamar la atención

lie[2] *vi* **lied; lying** ['laɪɪŋ] : mentir

lie[3] *n* **1** UNTRUTH : mentira *f* ⟨to tell lies : decir mentiras⟩ **2** POSITION : posición *f*

liege ['li:dʒ] *n* : señor *m* feudal

lien ['li:n, 'li:ən] *n* : derecho *m* de retención

lieu ['lu:] n in lieu of : en lugar de
lieutenant [lu:'tɛnənt] n : teniente mf
life ['laɪf] n, pl **lives** ['laɪvz] 1 : vida f ⟨plant life : la vida vegetal⟩ 2 EXISTENCE : vida f ⟨early/late in life : en la juventud/vejez⟩ ⟨later in life : a una edad más avanzada⟩ ⟨I've lived here my whole/entire life, I've lived here all my life : siempre he vivido aquí⟩ ⟨never in my life : (jamás) en la vida⟩ ⟨life of crime : vida delictiva⟩ ⟨way of life : estilo de vida⟩ 3 BIOGRAPHY : biografía f, vida f 4 DURATION : duración f, vida f 5 LIVELINESS : vivacidad f, animación f 6 or **life imprisonment** : cadena f perpetua 7 **a matter of life and death** : una cuestión de vida o muerte 8 **as big as life** : en carne y hueso 9 **for dear life** : desesperadamente 10 **for the life of me** : por nada del mundo 11 **not on your life** : ni pensarlo 12 **that's life** : así es la vida 13 **the life of the party** : el alma de la fiesta 14 **to bring back to life** : resucitar 15 **to come to life** : animarse 16 **to claim/take someone's life** : matar a alguien 17 **to frighten/scare the life out of** : darle/pegarle un susto mortal a 18 **to lose one's life** : perder la vida 19 **to risk life and limb** : arriesgar la vida 20 **to save someone's life** : salvarse la vida 21 **to take one's own life** : suicidarse 22 **true to life** : verosímil
lifeblood ['laɪf,blʌd] n : parte f vital, sustento m
lifeboat ['laɪf,bo:t] n : bote m salvavidas
life cycle n : ciclo m vital
life expectancy n : esperanza f de vida, expectativa f de vida, expectativas fpl de vida
lifeguard ['laɪf,gɑrd] n : socorrista mf; salvavidas mf; bañero m, -ra f Arg, Uru
life insurance n : seguro m de vida
life jacket n : chaleco m salvavidas
lifeless ['laɪfləs] adj : sin vida, muerto
lifelike ['laɪf,laɪk] adj : que parece vivo, natural, verosímil
lifeline ['laɪf,laɪn] n 1 : cuerda f de salvamento 2 : sustento m
lifelong ['laɪf'lɔŋ] adj : de toda la vida ⟨a lifelong friend : un amigo de toda la vida⟩
life preserver n : salvavidas m
lifesaver ['laɪf,seɪvər] n 1 : salvación f 2 → lifeguard
lifesaving ['laɪf,seɪvɪŋ] n : socorrismo m
life sentence n : cadena f perpetua
life-size ['laɪf'saɪz] or **life-sized** ['laɪf'saɪzd] adj : de tamaño natural
lifespan ['laɪf,spæn] n : vida f
lifestyle ['laɪf,staɪl] n : estilo m de vida
lifetime ['laɪf,taɪm] n : vida f, curso m de la vida
lift¹ ['lɪft] vt 1 RAISE : levantar, alzar, subir 2 END : levantar ⟨to lift a ban : levantar una prohibición⟩ — vi 1 RISE : levantarse, alzarse 2 CLEAR UP : despejar ⟨the fog lifted : se disipó la niebla⟩
lift² n 1 LIFTING : levantamiento m, alzamiento m 2 BOOST : impulso m, estímulo m 3 **to give someone a lift** : llevar en coche a alguien
liftoff ['lɪft,ɔf] n : despegue m
ligament ['lɪgəmənt] n : ligamento m
ligature ['lɪgə,tʃʊr, -tʃər] n : ligadura f
light¹ ['laɪt] v lit ['lɪt] or **lighted**; **lighting** vt 1 ILLUMINATE : iluminar, alumbrar 2 IGNITE : encender, prenderle fuego a — vi : encenderse, prender
light² vi **lighted** or lit ['lɪt]; **lighting** 1 LAND, SETTLE : posarse 2 DISMOUNT : bajarse, apearse
light³ ['laɪt] adv 1 LIGHTLY : suavemente, ligeramente 2 **to travel light** : viajar con poco equipaje
light⁴ adj 1 LIGHTWEIGHT : ligero, liviano, poco pesado 2 EASY : fácil, ligero, liviano ⟨light reading : lectura fácil⟩ ⟨light work : trabajo liviano⟩ 3 GENTLE, MILD : fino, suave, leve ⟨a light breeze : una brisa suave⟩ ⟨a light rain : una lluvia fina⟩ 4 DELICATE : leve, ligero ⟨she wore light makeup : llevaba poco maquillaje⟩ 5 LOW : bajo ⟨light turnout : baja asistencia⟩ ⟨light trading : poco movimiento (en los mercados)⟩ ⟨traffic was light : había poco tráfico⟩ 6 MINOR, SUPERFICIAL : de poca importancia, superficial 7 BRIGHT : brillante (dícese de una luz), luminosa (dícese de una habitación) ⟨to be light out : ser de día⟩ ⟨to get light out : amanecer⟩ 8 PALE : claro (dícese de los colores), rubio (dícese del pelo) 9 or **lite** : light
light⁵ n 1 ILLUMINATION : luz f 2 DAYLIGHT : luz f del día 3 DAWN : amanecer m, madrugada f 4 LAMP : lámpara f ⟨to turn off the light : apagar la luz⟩ 5 ASPECT : aspecto m ⟨in a new light : con otros ojos⟩ ⟨to show in a good/bad light : dar una imagen positiva/negativa a⟩ ⟨in (the) light of : en vista de, a la luz de⟩ 6 MATCH : fósforo m, cerillo m 7 **the light at the end of the tunnel** : la luz al final del túnel 8 **the light of someone's life** : la niña de los ojos de alguien 9 **to be out like a light** : dormirse como un tronco 10 **to bring to light** : sacar a (la) luz 11 **to cast/shed/throw light on** : arrojar luz sobre 12 **to come to light** : salir a (la) luz 13 **to see the light** : abrir los ojos
lightbulb ['laɪt,bʌlb] n 1 : bombilla f; foco m; bombillo m CA, Col, Ven; bombita f Arg, Uru
lighten ['laɪtən] vt 1 ILLUMINATE : iluminar, dar más luz a 2 : aclararse (el pelo) 3 : aligerar (una carga, etc.) 4 RELIEVE : aliviar 5 GLADDEN : alegrar ⟨it lightened his heart : alegró su corazón⟩
lighter ['laɪtər] n : encendedor m
light-headed ['laɪt'hɛdəd] adj : mareado
lighthearted ['laɪt'hɑrtəd] adj : alegre, despreocupado, desenfadado — **lightheartedly** adv
lightheartedness ['laɪt'hɑrtədnəs] n : desenfado m, alegría f
lighthouse ['laɪt,haʊs] n : faro m
lighting ['laɪtɪŋ] n : iluminación f

lightly [ˈlaɪtli] *adv* **1** GENTLY : suavemente **2** SLIGHTLY : ligeramente **3** FRIVOLOUSLY : a la ligera **4 to let off lightly** : tratar con indulgencia

lightness [ˈlaɪtnəs] *n* **1** BRIGHTNESS : luminosidad *f*, claridad *f* **2** GENTLENESS : ligereza *f*, suavidad *f*, delicadeza *f* **3** : ligereza *f*, liviandad *f* (de peso)

lightning [ˈlaɪtnɪŋ] *n* : relámpago *m*, rayo *m*

lightning bug → firefly

lightproof [ˈlaɪtˌpruːf] *adj* : impenetrable por la luz, opaco

lightweight¹ [ˈlaɪtˌweɪt] *adj* : ligero, liviano, de poco peso

lightweight² *n* : peso *m* ligero (en deportes)

light–year [ˈlaɪtˌjɪr] *n* : año *m* luz

likable *or* **likeable** [ˈlaɪkəbəl] *adj* : simpático, agradable

like¹ [ˈlaɪk] *v* **liked; liking** *vt* **1** : gustarle (algo a uno) ⟨he likes rice : le gusta el arroz⟩ ⟨she doesn't like flowers : a ella no le gustan las flores⟩ ⟨I like you : me caes bien⟩ **2** WANT : querer, desear ⟨I'd like a hamburger : quiero una hamburguesa⟩ ⟨he would like more help : le gustaría tener más ayuda⟩ ⟨I'd like to *some* : quiero *venir*⟩ ⟨I'd like to think (that) . . . : quiero creer que . . .⟩ — *vi* : querer ⟨do as you like : haz lo que quieras⟩ ⟨if you like : si quieres, si te parece⟩ ⟨whenever you like : cuando quieras⟩

like² *adj* : parecido, semejante, similar

like³ *n* **1** PREFERENCE : preferencia *f*, gusto *m* **2 the like** : cosa *f* parecida, cosas *fpl* por el estilo ⟨I've never seen the like : nunca he visto cosa parecida⟩

like⁴ *conj* **1** AS IF : como si ⟨they looked at me like I was crazy : se me quedaron mirando como si estuviera loca⟩ **2** AS : como, igual que ⟨she doesn't love you like I do : ella no te quiere como yo⟩

like⁵ *prep* **1** : como, parecido a ⟨she acts like my mother : se comporta como mi madre⟩ ⟨he looks like me : se parece a mí⟩ **2** : propio de, típico de ⟨that's just like her : eso es muy típico de ella⟩ **3** : como ⟨animals like cows : animales como vacas⟩ **4 like this like that** : así ⟨do it like that : hazlo así⟩

-like [ˈlaɪk] *suf* **1** : como, parecido a ⟨cat-like : como un gato, parecido a un gato, felino⟩ **2** : propio de ⟨ladylike : propio de una dama⟩

likelihood [ˈlaɪkliˌhʊd] *n* : probabilidad *f* ⟨in all likelihood : con toda probabilidad⟩

likely¹ [ˈlaɪkli] *adv* : probablemente ⟨most likely he's sick : lo más probable es que esté enfermo⟩ ⟨they're likely to come : es probable que vengan⟩

likely² *adj* **likelier; -est 1** PROBABLE : probable ⟨to be likely to : ser muy probable que⟩ **2** SUITABLE : apropiado, adecuado **3** BELIEVABLE : verosímil, creíble **4** PROMISING : prometedor

liken [ˈlaɪkən] *vt* : comparar

likeness [ˈlaɪknəs] *n* **1** SIMILARITY : semejanza *f*, parecido *m* **2** PORTRAIT : retrato *m*

likewise [ˈlaɪkˌwaɪz] *adv* **1** SIMILARLY : de la misma manera, asimismo **2** ALSO : también, además, asimismo

liking [ˈlaɪkɪŋ] *n* **1** FONDNESS : afición *f* (por una cosa), simpatía *f* (por una persona) **2** TASTE : gusto *m* ⟨is it to your liking? : ¿te gusta?⟩ ⟨to take a liking to : tomarle el gusto a algo⟩

lilac [ˈlaɪˌlɑk, -ˌlæk, -ˌlɑk] *n* : lila *f* — **lilac** *adj*

lilt [ˈlɪlt] *n* : cadencia *f*, ritmo *m* alegre

lily [ˈlɪli] *n, pl* **lilies 1** : lirio *m*, azucena *f* **2 lily of the valley** : lirio *m* de los valles, muguete *m*

lily pad *n* : hoja *f* grande (de un nenúfar)

lima bean [ˈlaɪmə] *n* : frijol *m* de media luna

limb [ˈlɪm] *n* **1** APPENDAGE : miembro *m*, extremidad *f* **2** BRANCH : rama *f*

limber¹ [ˈlɪmbər] *vi* **or to limber up** : calentarse, prepararse

limber² *adj* : ágil (dícese de las personas), flexible (dícese de los objetos)

limbo [ˈlɪmˌboː] *n, pl* **-bos 1** : limbo *m* (en religión) **2** OBLIVION : olvido *m* ⟨the project is in limbo : el proyecto ha caído en el olvido⟩

lime [ˈlaɪm] *n* **1** : cal *f* (óxido) **2** : lima *f* (fruta), limón *m* verde *Mex*

limelight [ˈlaɪmˌlaɪt] *n* **to be in the limelight** : ser el centro de atención, estar en el candelero

limerick [ˈlɪmərɪk] *n* : poema *m* jocoso de cinco versos

limestone [ˈlaɪmˌstoːn] *n* : piedra *f* caliza, caliza *f*

limit¹ [ˈlɪmət] *vt* : limitar, restringir

limit² *n* **1** MAXIMUM : límite *m*, máximo *m* ⟨speed limit : límite de velocidad⟩ **2 limits** *npl* : límites *mpl*, confines *mpl* ⟨city limits : límites de la ciudad⟩ **3 that's the limit!** : ¡eso es el colmo!

limitation [ˌlɪməˈteɪʃən] *n* : limitación *f*, restricción *f*

limited [ˈlɪmətəd] *adj* : limitado, restringido

limitless [ˈlɪmətləs] *adj* : ilimitado, sin límites

limousine [ˈlɪməˌziːn, ˌlɪməˈ-] *n* : limusina *f*

limp¹ [ˈlɪmp] *vi* : cojear

limp² *adj* **1** FLACCID : fláccido **2** LANK : lacio (dícese del pelo) **3** WEAK : débil ⟨to feel limp : sentirse desfallecer, sentirse sin fuerzas⟩

limp³ *n* : cojera *f*

limpet [ˈlɪmpət] *n* : lapa *f*

limpid [ˈlɪmpəd] *adj* : límpido, claro

limply [ˈlɪmpli] *adv* : sin fuerzas

limpness [ˈlɪmpnəs] *n* : flaccidez *f*, debilidad *f*

limy [ˈlaɪmi] *adj* : calizo

linden [ˈlɪndən] *n* : tilo *m*

line¹ [ˈlaɪn] *v* **lined; lining** *vt* **1** : forrar, cubrir ⟨to line a dress : forrar un vestido⟩ ⟨to line the walls : cubrir las paredes⟩ **2** MARK : rayar, trazar líneas en **3** BORDER : bordear **4** *or* **to line up** ALIGN : alinear **5 to line up** : organizar — *vi* **to line up** : ponerse en fila, hacer cola

line² *n* **1** MARK : línea *f*, raya *f* ⟨straight line : (línea) recta⟩ ⟨dotted line : línea de puntos⟩ **2** BOUNDARY : línea *f*, límite *m* ⟨dividing line : línea divisoria⟩ ⟨property line : límite de la propiedad⟩ ⟨to draw the line : fijar límites⟩ ⟨to draw the line at something : no tolerar algo⟩ **3** ROW : fila *f*, hilera *f* **4** QUEUE : cola *f* ⟨to wait in line : hacer cola⟩ **5 lines** *npl* SILHOUETTE : líneas *fpl* **6** CORD, ROPE : cuerda *f* **7** → **pipeline** **8** WIRE : cable *m* ⟨power line : cable eléctrico⟩ **9** : línea *f* (de teléfono) ⟨the line is busy : está ocupado⟩ ⟨the boss is on the line : te llama el jefe⟩ **10** : línea *f* (de texto), verso *m* (de poesía) **11** NOTE : nota *f*, líneas *fpl* ⟨drop me a line : mándame unas líneas⟩ **12 lines** *npl* : diálogo *m* (de un actor) **13** COMMENT : comentario *m* **14** WRINKLE : línea *f*, arruga *f* (de la cara) **15** PATH : línea *f* ⟨line of fire : línea de fuego⟩ **16** SERVICE : línea *f* ⟨bus line : línea de autobuses⟩ **17** : línea *f*, cadena *f* ⟨production line : línea de producción⟩ **18** SERIES : serie *f* (de problemas, etc.) **19** LINEAGE : línea *f*, linaje *m* **20** MANNER : línea *f* ⟨line of inquiry : línea de investigación⟩ ⟨to take a firm line on : ponerse firme sobre⟩ **21** POSITION : línea *f* ⟨the party line : la línea del partido⟩ **22** OCCUPATION : ocupación *f*, rama *f*, especialidad *f* **23 lines** *npl* RANKS : líneas *fpl*, filas *fpl* ⟨behind enemy lines : tras las líneas enemigas⟩ **24** RANGE : línea *f* ⟨product line : línea de productos⟩ **25** AGREEMENT : conformidad *f* ⟨to be in line with : estar conforme con⟩ ⟨to fall into line : conformarse⟩ **26 along the line** ⟨somewhere along the line : en algún momento⟩ **27 along the lines of** : por el estilo de **28 down the line** : en el futuro **29 in line** ⟨he's in line for a promotion : lo consideran para un ascenso⟩ ⟨first/next in line to succeed the President : primero en la línea de sucesión a la presidencia⟩ **30 in line** ⟨to keep someone in line : mantener a alguien en raya⟩ **31 on the line** ENDANGERED : en peligro **32 out of line** DISRESPECTFUL : fuera de lugar (dícese de un comentario) ⟨you're out of line : te has pasado de la raya⟩ **33 to lay it on the line** : no andarse con rodeos **34 to read between the lines** : leer entre líneas

lineage [ˈlɪnɪʤ] *n* : linaje *m*, abolengo *m*

lineal [ˈlɪniəl] *adj* : en línea directa

lineaments [ˈlɪniəmənts] *npl* : facciones *fpl* (de la cara), rasgos *mpl*

linear [ˈlɪniər] *adj* : lineal

lined [ˈlaɪnd] *adj* **1** : de rayas (dícese de papel, etc.) **2** WRINKLY : arrugado (dícese de la cara)

linen [ˈlɪnən] *n* **1** : lino *m* **2** *or* **bed linen** : ropa *f* de cama **3** *or* **table linen** : mantelería *f*

liner [ˈlaɪnər] *n* **1** LINING : forro *m* **2** SHIP : buque *m*, transatlántico *m*

lineup [ˈlaɪnˌəp] *n* **1** : fila *f* de sospechosos **2** : formación *f* (en deportes) **3** ALIGNMENT : alineación *f*

linger [ˈlɪŋɡər] *vi* **1** TARRY : quedarse, entretenerse, rezagarse **2** PERSIST : persistir, sobrevivir

lingerie [ˌlɑnʤəˈreɪ, ˌlɑnʒˈriː] *n* : ropa *f* íntima femenina, lencería *f*

lingo [ˈlɪŋɡo] *n, pl* **-goes** **1** LANGUAGE : idioma *m* **2** JARGON : jerga *f*

linguist [ˈlɪŋɡwɪst] *n* : lingüista *mf*

linguistic [lɪŋˈɡwɪstɪk] *adj* : lingüístico

linguistics [lɪŋˈɡwɪstɪks] *n* : lingüística *f*

liniment [ˈlɪnəmənt] *n* : linimento *m*

lining [ˈlaɪnɪŋ] *n* : forro *m*

link¹ [ˈlɪŋk] *vt* : unir, enlazar, conectar — *vi* **to link up** : unirse, conectar

link² *n* **1** : eslabón *m* (de una cadena) **2** BOND : conexión *f*, lazo *m*, vínculo *m* **3** HYPERLINK : enlace *m*, vínculo *m*

linkage [ˈlɪŋkɪʤ] *n* : conexión *f*, unión *f*, enlace *m*

links [ˈlɪŋks] *n* : campo *m* de golf, cancha *f* de golf

linoleum [ləˈnoːliəm] *n* : linóleo *m*

lint [ˈlɪnt] *n* : pelusa *f*

lintel [ˈlɪntəl] *n* : dintel *m*

lion [ˈlaɪən] *n* : león *m*

lioness [ˈlaɪənɪs] *n* : leona *f*

lionize [ˈlaɪəˌnaɪz] *vt* **-ized; -izing** : tratar a una persona como muy importante

lip [ˈlɪp] *n* **1** : labio *m* **2** : pico *m* (de una jarra), borde *m* (de una taza)

lip–read [ˈlɪpˌriːd] *vi* : leer los labios

lipreading [ˈlɪpˌriːdɪŋ] *n* : lectura *f* de los labios

lipstick [ˈlɪpˌstɪk] *n* : lápiz *m* labial, barra *f* de labios

liquefy [ˈlɪkwəˌfaɪ] *v* **-fied; -fying** *vt* : licuar — *vi* : licuarse

liqueur [lɪˈkʊr, -ˈkər, -ˈkjʊr] *n* : licor *m*

liquid¹ [ˈlɪkwəd] *adj* : líquido

liquid² *n* : líquido *m*

liquidate [ˈlɪkwəˌdeɪt] *vt* **-dated; -dating** : liquidar

liquidation [ˌlɪkwəˈdeɪʃən] *n* : liquidación *f*

liquidity [lɪkˈwɪdəti] *n* : liquidez *f*

liquor [ˈlɪkər] *n* : alcohol *m*, bebidas *fpl* alcohólicas, licor *m*

lisp¹ [ˈlɪsp] *vi* : cecear

lisp² *n* : ceceo *m*

lissome [ˈlɪsəm] *adj* **1** FLEXIBLE : flexible **2** LITHE : ágil y grácil

list¹ [ˈlɪst] *vt* **1** ENUMERATE : hacer una lista de, enumerar **2** INCLUDE : poner en una lista, incluir — *vi* : escorar (dícese de un barco)

list² *n* : lista *f* ⟨he's first/last on the list : es el primero/último de la lista⟩

listen [ˈlɪsən] *vi* **1** : escuchar, oír **2 to listen to** HEED : escuchar, prestar atención a, hacer caso de (algo), hacerle caso (a alguien) **3 to listen to reason** : atender a razones

listener [ˈlɪsənər] *n* : oyente *mf*, persona *f* que sabe escuchar

listless [ˈlɪstləs] *adj* : lánguido, apático **listlessly** *adv*

listlessness [ˈlɪstləsnəs] *n* : apatía *f*, languidez *f*, desgana *f*

lit [ˈlɪt] → **light**
litany [ˈlɪtəni] n, pl **-nies** : letanía f
liter [ˈliːt̬ər] n : litro m
literacy [ˈlɪt̬ərəsi] n : alfabetismo m
literal [ˈlɪt̬ərəl] adj : literal — **literally** adv
literary [ˈlɪt̬əˌrɪri] adj : literario
literate [ˈlɪt̬ərət] adj : alfabetizado
literature [ˈlɪt̬ərəˌt̬ʃʊr, -t̬ʃər] n : literatura f
lithe [ˈlaɪð, ˈlaɪθ] adj : ágil y grácil
lithesome [ˈlaɪðsəm, ˈlaɪθ-] → **lissome**
lithium [ˈlɪθiəm] n : litio m
lithograph [ˈlɪθəˌgræf] n : litografía f
lithographer [lɪˈθɑgrəfər, ˈlɪθəˌgræfər] n
: litógrafo m, -fa f
lithography [lɪˈθɑgrəfi] n : litografía f
lithosphere [ˈlɪθəˌsfɪr] n : litosfera f
Lithuanian [ˌlɪθəˈweiniən] n 1 : lituano
m (idioma) 2 : lituano m, -na f — **Lithuanian** adj
litigant [ˈlɪt̬ɪgənt] n : litigante mf
litigate [ˈlɪt̬əˌgeɪt] vi **-gated; -gating** : litigar
litigation [ˌlɪt̬əˈgeɪʃən] n : litigio m
litmus [ˈlɪtməs] n : tornasol m
litmus paper n : papel m de tornasol
litmus test n : prueba f decisiva
litter¹ [ˈlɪt̬ər] vt : tirar basura en, ensuciar
— vi : tirar basura
litter² n 1 : camada f, cría f ⟨a litter of
kittens : una cría de gatitos⟩ 2 STRETCHER : camilla f 3 RUBBISH : basura f 4
: arena f higiénica (para gatos)
little¹ [ˈlɪt̬əl] adv **less** [ˈlɛs]; **least** [ˈliːst] 1
: poco ⟨she sings very little : canta muy
poco⟩ 2 **little did I know that . . .** : no
tenía la menor idea de que . . . 3 **as little
as possible** : lo menos posible
little² adj **littler** or **less** [ˈlɛs] or **lesser**
[ˈlɛsər]; **littlest** or **least** [ˈliːst] 1 SMALL
: pequeño ⟨poco ⟨they speak little
Spanish : hablan poco español⟩ ⟨little by
little : poco a poco⟩ ⟨a little bit : un
poco⟩ ⟨a little while : un ratito⟩ 3 TRIVIAL : sin importancia, trivial
little³ n 1 : poco m ⟨little has changed
: poco ha cambiado⟩ 2 **a little** : un
poco, algo ⟨it's a little surprising : es algo
sorprendente⟩
Little Dipper → **dipper**
little person n, pl **little people** 1 : persona f pequeña; enano m, -na f 2 **the
little people** : la gente común
liturgical [ləˈtərdʒɪkəl] adj : litúrgico —
liturgically [-kli] adv
liturgy [ˈlɪt̬ərdʒi] n, pl **-gies** : liturgia f
livable [ˈlɪvəbəl] adj : habitable
live¹ [ˈlɪv] v **lived; living** vi 1 EXIST : vivir
⟨as long as I live : mientras viva⟩ ⟨to live
from day to day : vivir al día⟩ ⟨long live
the Queen/King! : ¡viva el rey/la
reina!⟩ 2 : llevar una vida, vivir ⟨he
lived simply : llevó una vida sencilla⟩
⟨they lived happily ever after : vivieron
felices (y comieron perdices)⟩ 3 SUBSIST : vivir, mantenerse ⟨to live within/
beyond one's means : vivir dentro/fuera
de sus posibilidades⟩ 4 RESIDE : vivir,
residir ⟨where do you live? : ¿dónde
vives?⟩ 5 **live and let live** : vive y deja
vivir a los demás 6 **to live down** ⟨they'll

never let you live it down, you'll never
live it down : nunca te dejarán olvidarlo⟩ 7 **to live off** : vivir de (algo), vivir a costa de (alguien) 8 **to live on** : vivir de (un sueldo, etc.), alimentarse de
(comida) ⟨they live on less than a dollar
a day : viven con menos de un dólar por
día⟩ 9 **to live on** PERSIST : permanecer 10 **to live out one's life** : vivir
toda su vida 11 **to live through** SURVIVE : sobrevivir 12 **to live together**
: vivir juntos 13 **to live up to** : estar a la
altura de (las expectativas, etc.) 14 **to
live up to** : cumplir (su palabra, etc.) 15
to live with : vivir con (alguien) 16 **to
live with** ACCEPT : aceptar — vt : llevar,
vivir ⟨he lived a simple life : llevó una
vida sencilla⟩ ⟨to live the good life : vivir
la buena vida⟩
live² [ˈlaɪv] adj 1 LIVING : vivo 2 BURNING : encendido ⟨a live coal : una
brasa⟩ 3 : con corriente ⟨live wires
: cables con corriente⟩ 4 : cargado, sin
estallar ⟨a live bomb : una bomba sin
estallar⟩ 5 CURRENT : de actualidad ⟨a
live issue : un asunto de actualidad⟩ 6
: en vivo, en directo ⟨a live interview
: una entrevista en vivo⟩
livelihood [ˈlaɪvliˌhʊd] n : sustento m, vida
f, medio m de vida
liveliness [ˈlaɪvlinəs] n : animación f, vivacidad f
livelong [ˈlɪvˈlɔŋ] adj : entero, completo
lively [ˈlaɪvli] adj **livelier; -est** : animado,
vivaz, vivo, enérgico
liven [ˈlaɪvən] vt : animar — vi : animarse
liver [ˈlɪvər] n : hígado m
livery [ˈlɪvəri] n, pl **-eries** : librea f
lives → **life**
livestock [ˈlaɪvˌstɑk] n : ganado m
livestream¹ [ˈlaɪvˌstriːm] v : hacer (un)
streaming en vivo
livestream² n : streaming m en vivo
live wire n : persona f vivaz y muy activa
livid [ˈlɪvəd] adj 1 BLACK-AND-BLUE
: amoratado 2 PALE : lívido 3 ENRAGED : furioso
living¹ [ˈlɪvɪŋ] adj : vivo
living² n **to make a living** : ganarse la vida
living room n : living m, sala f de estar
lizard [ˈlɪzərd] n : lagarto m
llama [ˈlɑmə, ˈja-] n : llama f
load¹ [ˈloːd] vt 1 : cargar, embarcar (vehículos, cargamento, etc.) 2 : embarcar
(pasajeros) 3 : cargar (una pistola,
etc.) 4 : cargar (un programa, etc.) 5
: cargar, sobrecargar ⟨she loaded (up)
her plate with food : llenó el plato de
comida⟩ 6 **to load down with** BURDEN
: cargar de ⟨to be loaded down with debt
: estar agobiado por las deudas⟩ — vi 1
: cargar 2 **to load up on** : pasarse con
(la comida, etc.)
load² n 1 CARGO : carga f 2 WEIGHT
: peso m 3 BURDEN : carga f, peso m 4
loads npl : montón m, pila f, cantidad f
⟨loads of work : un montón de trabajo⟩
loaded [ˈloːdəd] adj 1 : cargado (dícese
de una pistola, una cámara, etc.) 2
WEIGHTED : cargado ⟨loaded dice : da-

dos cargados⟩ **3** : cargado (de conotaciones) ⟨a loaded question : una pregunta capciosa⟩ **4 RICH** : muy rico **5** *fam* **DRUNK** : borracho, chupado *fam* **6 to be loaded with** : estar repleto de

loaf¹ [ˈloːf] *vi* : holgazanear, flojear, haraganear

loaf² *n, pl* **loaves** [ˈloːvz] **1** : pan *m*, pan *m* de molde, barra *f* de pan **2 meat loaf** : pan *m* de carne

loafer [ˈloːfər] *n* : holgazán *m*, -zana *f*; haragán *m*, -gana *f*; vago *m*, -ga *f*

loan¹ [ˈloːn] *vt* : prestar

loan² *n* : préstamo *m*, empréstito *m* (del banco)

loanword [ˈloːnˌwərd] *n* : préstamo *m*, barbarismo *m*

loath [ˈloːθ, ˈloːð] *adj* : poco dispuesto ⟨I am loath to say it : me resisto a decirlo⟩

loathe [ˈloːð] *vt* **loathed; loathing** : odiar, aborrecer

loathing [ˈloːðɪŋ] *n* : aversión *f*, odio *m*, aborrecimiento *m*

loathsome [ˈloːθsəm, ˈloːð-] *adj* : odioso, repugnante

lob¹ [ˈlab] *vt* **lobbed; lobbing** : hacerle un globo (a otro jugador)

lob² *n* : globo *m* (en deportes)

lobby¹ [ˈlabi] *v* **-bied; -bying** *vt* : presionar, ejercer presión sobre — *vi* **to lobby for** : presionar para (lograr algo)

lobby² *n, pl* **-bies** **1 FOYER** : vestíbulo *m* **2 LOBBYISTS** : grupo *m* de presión, lobby *m*

lobbyist [ˈlabiɪst] *n* : miembro *m* de un lobby

lobe [ˈloːb] *n* : lóbulo *m*

lobed [ˈloːbd] *adj* : lobulado

lobotomy [ləˈbatəmi, loː-] *n, pl* **-mies** : lobotomía *f*

lobster [ˈlabstər] *n* : langosta *f*

local¹ [ˈloːkəl] *adj* : local

local² *n* **1** : anestesia *f* local **2 the locals** : los vecinos del lugar, los habitantes

locale [loːˈkæl] *n* : lugar *m*, escenario *m*

locality [loːˈkæləţi] *n, pl* **-ties** : localidad *f*

localization [ˌloːkələˈzeɪʃən] *n* **POSITION** : localización *f*

localize [ˈloːkəˌlaɪz] *vt* **-ized; -izing** : localizar

locally [ˈloːkəli] *adv* : en la localidad, en la zona

locate [ˈloːˌkeɪt, loːˈkeɪt] *v* **-cated; -cating** *vt* **1 POSITION** : situar, ubicar **2 FIND** : localizar, ubicar — *vi* **SETTLE** : establecerse

location [loːˈkeɪʃən] *n* **1 POSITION** : posición *f*, emplazamiento *m*, ubicación *f* **2 PLACE** : lugar *m*, sitio *m*

loch [ˈlak] *n* : lago *m*

lock¹ [ˈlak] *vt* **1 FASTEN** : cerrar (con llave) **2 CONFINE** : encerrar ⟨they locked me in the room : me encerraron en la habitación⟩ **3 IMMOBILIZE** : bloquear (una rueda) **4 to lock away/up** : encerrar (a alguien), guardar (algo) bajo llave **5 to lock out** : dejar fuera a, cerrar la puerta a ⟨I locked myself out : me quedé fuera (sin llaves)⟩ — *vi* **1** *or* **to lock up** : cerrar (con llave) **2** : ce-

rrarse (dícese de una puerta) **3** : trabarse, bloquearse (dícese de una rueda) **4 to lock horns** : chocar, pelearse **5 to lock on/onto TARGET** : fijar (el blanco)

lock² *n* **1** : mechón *m* (de pelo) **2 FASTENER** : cerradura *f*, cerrojo *m*, chapa *f* **3** : esclusa *f* (de un canal)

locker [ˈlakər] *n* : armario *m*, cajón *m* con llave, lócker *m*

locker room *n* : vestuario *m*; camarín *m* *Chile, Peru, Uru*

locket [ˈlakət] *n* : medallón *m*, guardapelo *m*, relicario *m*

lockjaw [ˈlakˌjɔ] *n* : tétano *m*

lockout [ˈlakˌaʊt] *n* : cierre *m* patronal

locksmith [ˈlakˌsmɪθ] *n* : cerrajero *m*, -ra *f*

lockup [ˈlakˌʌp] *n* **JAIL** : cárcel *f*

locomotion [ˌloːkəˈmoːʃən] *n* : locomoción *f*

locomotive¹ [ˌloːkəˈmoːţɪv] *adj* : locomotor

locomotive² *n* : locomotora *f*

locust [ˈloːkəst] *n* **1** : langosta *f*, chapulín *m* *CA, Mex* **2 CICADA** : cigarra *f*, chicharra *f* **3** : acacia *f* blanca (árbol)

locution [loːˈkjuːʃən] *n* : locución *f*

lode [ˈloːd] *n* : veta *f*, vena *f*, filón *m*

lodestar [ˈloːdˌstar] *n* : estrella *f* polar

lodestone [ˈloːdˌstoːn] *n* : piedra *f* imán

lodge¹ [ˈladʒ] *v* **lodged; lodging** *vt* **1 HOUSE** : hospedar, alojar **2 FILE** : presentar ⟨to lodge a complaint : presentar una demanda⟩ — *vi* **1** : posarse, meterse ⟨the bullet lodged in the door : la bala se incrustó en la puerta⟩ **2 STAY** : hospedarse, alojarse

lodge² *n* **1** : pabellón *m*, casa *f* de campo ⟨hunting lodge : refugio de caza⟩ **2** : madriguera *f* (de un castor) **3** : logia *f* ⟨Masonic lodge : logia masónica⟩

lodger [ˈladʒər] *n* : inquilino *m*, -na *f*; huésped *m*, -peda *f*

lodging [ˈladʒɪŋ] *n* **1** : alojamiento *m* **2 lodgings** *npl* **ROOMS** : habitaciones *fpl*

loft [ˈlɔft] *n* **1 ATTIC** : desván *m*, ático *m*, buhardilla *f* **2** : piso *m* superior (de un depósito comercial) ⟨a converted loft : un depósito convertido en apartamentos⟩ **3 HAYLOFT** : pajar *m* **4** : galería *f* ⟨choir loft : galería del coro⟩

loftily [ˈlɔftəli] *adv* : altaneramente, con altivez

loftiness [ˈlɔftinəs] *n* **1 NOBILITY** : nobleza *f* **2 ARROGANCE** : altanería *f*, arrogancia *f* **3 HEIGHT** : altura *f*, elevación *f*

lofty [ˈlɔfti] *adj* **loftier; -est 1 NOBLE** : noble, elevado **2 HAUGHTY** : altivo, arrogante, altanero **3 HIGH** : majestuoso, elevado

log¹ [ˈlɔg, ˈlag] *vi* **logged; logging 1** : talar (árboles) **2 RECORD** : registrar, anotar **3 to log in** *or* **to log on** : entrar (al sistema), iniciar (la) sesión **4 to log off** *or* **to log out** : salir (del sistema), cerrar (la) sesión

log² *n* **1** : tronco *m*, leño *m* **2 RECORD** : diario *m*

logarithm [ˈlɔgə,rɪðəm, ˈlɑ-] n : logaritmo m

logger [ˈlɔgər, ˈlɑ-] n : leñador m, -dora f

loggerhead [ˈlɔgərˌhd, ˈlɑ-] n 1 : tortuga f boba 2 to be at loggerheads : estar en pugna, estar en desacuerdo

logic [ˈlɑdʒɪk] n : lógica f — **logical** [ˈlɑdʒɪkəl] adj — **logically** [-kli] adv

login [ˈlɔg,ɪn, ˈlag-] n 1 or **logon** [ˈlɔg,ɔn, ˈlag,ɑn] : inicio m de sesión, login m 2 or **login credentials** : login m, credenciales fpl de acceso/usuario

logistic [ləˈdʒɪstɪk, lo-] adj : logístico

logistics [ləˈdʒɪstɪks, lo-] ns & pl : logística f

logo [ˈlo:,go:] n, pl **logos** [-,go:z] : logotipo m

loin [ˈlɔɪn] n 1 : pork loin : lomo de cerdo 2 **loins** npl : lomos mpl ⟨to gird one's loins : prepararse para la lucha⟩

loincloth [ˈlɔɪn,klɔθ] n : taparrabos m

loiter [ˈlɔɪtər] vi : vagar, perder el tiempo

loll [ˈlɑl] vi 1 SLOUCH : repantigarse 2 IDLE : holgazanear, hacer el vago

lollipop or **lollypop** [ˈlali,pap] n : dulce m en palito, chupete m Chile, Peru, paleta f CA, Mex

Londoner [ˈlʌndənər] n : londinense mf

lone [ˈlo:n] adj 1 SOLITARY : solitario 2 ONLY : único

loneliness [ˈlo:nlinəs] n : soledad f

lonely [ˈlo:nli] adj lonelier; -est 1 SOLITARY : solitario, aislado 2 LONESOME : solo ⟨to feel lonely : sentirse muy solo⟩

loner [ˈlo:nər] n : solitario m, -ria f; recluso m, -sa f

lonesome [ˈlo:nsəm] adj : solo, solitario

long¹ [ˈlɔŋ] vi 1 to long for : añorar, desear, anhelar 2 to long to : anhelar, estar deseando ⟨they longed to see her : estaban deseando verla, tenían muchas ganas de verla⟩

long² adv 1 : mucho, mucho tiempo ⟨it didn't take long : no llevó mucho tiempo⟩ ⟨will it last long? : ¿va a durar mucho?⟩ ⟨will you be long? : ¿tardarás mucho?⟩ ⟨a (little) bit longer : un poco más (tiempo)⟩ ⟨I didn't have long enough to visit : no me alcanzó el tiempo para visitar⟩ 2 all day long : todo el día 3 as/so long as : IF : mientras, con tal (de) que 4 as/so long as SINCE : ya que 5 as/so long as WHILE : mientras 6 before long : antes de poco 7 long ago : hace mucho tiempo 8 long before/after : hace mucho antes/después 9 long gone ⟨that building is long gone : ese edificio se desapareció hace mucho⟩ 10 long since : hace mucho 11 no longer or (not) any longer ⟨it's no longer needed : ya no hace falta⟩ ⟨I can't wait any longer : no puedo esperar más⟩ 12 so long! : ¡hasta luego!, ¡adiós!

long³ adj longer [ˈlɔŋgər]; longest [ˈlɔŋgəst] 1 (indicating length) : largo ⟨long hair : pelo largo⟩ ⟨the dress is too long : el vestido es demasiado largo⟩ ⟨the book is two hundred pages long : el libro tiene doscientas páginas⟩ ⟨a long way

from : bastante lejos de⟩ 2 (indicating time) : largo, prolongado ⟨a long illness : una enfermedad prolongada⟩ ⟨a long walk : un paseo largo⟩ ⟨a long time ago : hace mucho (tiempo)⟩ ⟨I've known him for a long time : lo conozco desde hace mucho⟩ ⟨the drive is five hours long : el viaje dura cinco horas⟩ ⟨a long last : por fin⟩ ⟨in the long run : a la larga⟩ 3 to be long on : estar cargado de

long⁴ n 1 before long : dentro de poco 2 the long and (the) short of it : lo esencial, lo fundamental

long–distance [ˈlɔŋˈdɪstənts] adj 1 : de larga distancia ⟨long-distance call : llamada de larga distancia, llamada interurbana⟩ ⟨long-distance trip : viaje de largo recorrido⟩ ⟨long-distance runner : fondista⟩ 2 : a larga distancia ⟨a long-distance romance : una relación a (larga) distancia⟩

longevity [lɑnˈdʒvəti] n : longevidad f

long–haired [ˈlɔŋˈhærd] adj : melenudo

longhand [ˈlɔŋ,hænd] n : escritura f a mano, escritura f cursiva

long–haul [ˈlɔŋˈhɔl] adj : de larga distancia

longing [ˈlɔŋɪŋ] n : vivo deseo m, ansia f, anhelo m

longingly [ˈlɔŋɪŋli] adv : ansiosamente, con ansia

longitude [ˈlɑndʒə,tu:d, -,tju:d] n : longitud f

longitudinal [,lɑndʒəˈtu:dənəl, -ˈtju:-] adj : longitudinal — **longitudinally** adv

long jump n : salto m de longitud, salto m (en) largo

long–lived [ˈlɔŋˈlɪvd, -ˈlaɪvd] adj : longevo

long–range [ˈlɔŋˈreɪndʒ] adj 1 : de largo alcance (dícese de un avión, etc.) 2 : a largo plazo (dícese de un plan, etc.)

longshoreman [ˈlɔŋˈʃormən] n, pl -men [-mən, -ˌmɛn] : estibador m, -dora f

longshorewoman [ˈlɔŋˈʃorˌwʊmən] n, pl -women [-ˌwɪmən] : cargadora f

long–standing [ˈlɔŋˈstændɪŋ] adj : de larga data

long–suffering [ˈlɔŋˈsʌfərɪŋ] adj : paciente, sufrido

long–term [ˈlɔŋˈtərm] adj : a largo plazo (dícese de un plan, etc.)

long–winded [,lɔŋˈwɪndəd] adj : prolijo

look¹ [ˈlʊk] vi 1 : mirar ⟨to look out the window : mirar por la ventana⟩ ⟨to look ahead/back : mirar hacia adelante/atrás⟩ ⟨look around you : mira a tu alrededor⟩ ⟨look! there he is : ¡mira! ahí está⟩ 2 INVESTIGATE : buscar, mirar ⟨look in the closet : busca en el clóset⟩ ⟨look before you leap : mira lo que haces⟩ 3 SEEM : parecer ⟨he looks happy : parece estar contento⟩ ⟨you look very nice! : ¡estás guapísima!⟩ ⟨she looked (to be) about forty : parecía tener alrededor de cuarenta años⟩ 4 (used to warn, express anger, etc.) ⟨look, it's not going to work : mira, no va a funcionar⟩ ⟨now look what you've done! : ¡mira lo que has hecho!⟩ ⟨(now) look here! : ¡oye!⟩ 5 FACE, POINT : dar a 6 to look after TAKE CARE OF : cuidar, cuidar de (personas o animales), encargarse de (una empresa, etc.) **7 to look ahead** : mirar hacia el futuro **8 to look around** EXPLORE : mirar, echar un vistazo a **9 to look around for** : buscar **10 to look as if/though** : parecer que ⟨it looks as if it will rain : parece que va a llover⟩ **11 to look at** : mirar **12 to look at** CONSIDER : considerar **13 to look at** EXAMINE : examinar **14 to look at** FACE : estar frente a, enfrentarse a ⟨problemas, etc.⟩ **15 to look back** : mirar hacia el pasado **16 to look down on** : despreciar, menospreciar **17 to look for** EXPECT : esperar **18 to look for** SEEK : buscar **19 to look forward to** ANTICIPATE : estar ansioso de (hacer algo), estar ansioso de que llegue(n) ⟨una fecha, etc.⟩ **20 to look in on** : ir a ver (a alguien) **21 to look into** INVESTIGATE : investigar **22 to look like** : parecer, parecerse ⟨it looks like a large bird : parece un pájaro grande⟩ ⟨it looks like it will rain : parece que va a llover⟩ ⟨I look like my mother : me parezco a mi madre⟩ **23 to look on** WATCH : mirar **24 to look on** CONSIDER : considerar ⟨I look on her as a friend : la considero una amiga⟩ ⟨he looked on his accomplishments with pride : sus logros le llenaba de orgullo⟩ **25 to look out** : tener cuidado **26 to look out for** WATCH FOR : estar alerta por **27 to look out for** PROTECT : mirar por ⟨she only looks out for number one : sólo piensa en sí misma⟩ **28 to look the other way** : hacer la vista gorda **29 to look through** : hojear (una revista, etc.) **30 to look to . . . for . . .** ⟨to look to someone for something : recurrir a alguien para hacer algo⟩ ⟨they looked to history for an answer : buscaron la solución en la historia⟩ **31 to look up** IMPROVE : mejorar **32 to look up to** ADMIRE : respetar, admirar — *vt* **1** : mirar ⟨look what I found! : ¡mira lo que encontré!⟩ **2** HOPE, EXPECT : esperar ⟨we look to have a good year, we're looking to have a good year : esperamos tener un buen año⟩ **3 to look over/through** EXAMINE : revisar **4 to look up** : buscar (en un diccionario, etc.) **5 to look up** CALL, VISIT : llamar, visitar

look² *n* **1** GLANCE : mirada *f* ⟨to take a look at : mirar⟩ **2** EXPRESSION : cara *f* ⟨a look of disapproval : una cara de desaprobación⟩ **3** ASPECT : aspecto *m*, apariencia *f*, aire *m* **4 looks** *npl* : belleza *f*

looker [ˈlʊkər] *n* **to be a looker** : ser guapísimo

looking [ˈlʊkɪŋ] *adj (used in combination)* : de aspecto ⟨nice-looking : (de aspecto) atractivo⟩

lookout [ˈlʊkˌaʊt] *n* **1** : centinela *mf*, vigía *mf* **2 to be on the lookout for** : estar al acecho de, andar a la caza de

loom¹ [ˈluːm] *vi* **1** : aparecer, surgir ⟨the city loomed up in the distance : la ciu-

dad surgió en la distancia⟩ **2** MENACE, APPROACH : amenazar, ser inminente **3 to loom large** : cobrar mucha importancia

loom² *n* : telar *m*

loon [ˈluːn] *n* : somorgujo *m*, somormujo *m*

loony *or* **looney** [ˈluːni] *adj* **loonier; -est** : loco, chiflado *fam*

loop¹ [ˈluːp] *vt* **1** : hacer lazadas con **2 to loop around** : pasar alrededor de — *vi* **1** : rizar el rizo (dícese de un avión) **2** : serpentear (dícese de una carretera)

loop² *n* **1** : lazada *f* (en hilo o cuerda) **2** BEND : curva *f* **3** CIRCUIT : circuito *m* cerrado **4** : rizo *m* (en la aviación) ⟨to loop the loop : rizar el rizo⟩

loophole [ˈluːpˌhoːl] *n* : escapatoria *f*, pretexto *m*

loose¹ [ˈluːs] *vt* **loosed; loosing 1** RELEASE : poner en libertad, soltar **2** UNTIE : deshacer, desatar **3** DISCHARGE, UNLEASH : descargar, desatar

loose² → **loosely**

loose³ *adj* **looser; -est 1** INSECURE : flojo, suelto, poco seguro ⟨a loose tooth : un diente flojo⟩ **2** ROOMY : suelto, holgado ⟨loose clothing : ropa holgada⟩ **3** OPEN : suelto, abierto ⟨loose soil : suelo suelto⟩ ⟨a loose weave : una tejida abierta⟩ **4** FREE : suelto ⟨to break loose : soltarse⟩ ⟨to let loose : soltar⟩ ⟨loose sheets of paper : papeles sueltos⟩ ⟨loose change : dinero suelto⟩ **5** SLACK : flojo, flexible **6** APPROXIMATE : libre, aproximado ⟨a loose translation : una traducción aproximada⟩

loosely [ˈluːsli] *adv* **1** : sin apretar **2** ROUGHLY : aproximadamente, más o menos

loose–leaf [ˈluːsˈliːf] *adj* : de hojas sueltas

loosen [ˈluːsən] *vt* **1** : aflojar **2 to loosen up** RELAX : relajar — *vi* **1** : aflojarse **2 to loosen up** RELAX : relajarse

looseness [ˈluːsnəs] *n* **1** : holgura *f* (de ropa) **2** IMPRECISION : imprecisión *f*

loot¹ [ˈluːt] *vt* : saquear, robar

loot² *n* : botín *m*

looter [ˈluːtər] *n* : saqueador *m*, -dora *f*

lop [ˈlɑp] *vt* **lopped; lopping** : cortar, podar

lope¹ [ˈloːp] *vi* **loped; loping** : correr a paso largo

lope² *n* : paso *m* largo

lopsided [ˈlɑpˌsaɪdəd] *adj* **1** CROOKED : torcido, chueco, ladeado **2** ASYMMETRICAL : asimétrico

loquacious [loˈkweɪʃəs] *adj* : locuaz

lord [ˈlɔrd] *n* **1** : señor *m*, noble *m* **2** : lord *m* (en la Gran Bretaña) **3 the Lord** : el Señor **4 (good) Lord!** : ¡Dios mío!

lordly [ˈlɔrdli] *adj* **lordlier; -est** HAUGHTY : arrogante, altanero

lordship [ˈlɔrdˌʃɪp] *n* : señoría *f*

Lord's Supper *n* : Eucaristía *f*

lore [ˈlɔr] *n* : saber *m* popular, tradición *f*

lose [ˈluːz] *v* **lost** [ˈlɔst]; **losing** [ˈluːzɪŋ] *vt* **1** MISLAY : perder ⟨I lost my umbrella : perdí mi paraguas⟩ 2 : perder (un partido, etc.) 3 (*to fail to keep*) : perder ⟨to lose blood : perder sangre⟩ ⟨to lose one's appetite : perder el apetito⟩ ⟨to lose track of the time : perder la noción del tiempo⟩ ⟨to have nothing to lose : no tener nada que perder⟩ ⟨to lose sight of : perder de vista⟩ 4 : perder (dinero) 5 (*to be deprived of*) : perder ⟨they lost everything : lo perdieron todo⟩ ⟨we lost power : se cortó la luz⟩ ⟨to lose one's voice : quedarse afónico⟩ ⟨she lost her husband : perdió a su esposo⟩ ⟨we're sorry to lose you! : ¡qué pena que te vayas!⟩ 6 (*to gradually have less of*) : perder (peso, interés, etc.) 7 : perder (valor) 8 WASTE : perder ⟨there's no time to lose : no hay tiempo que perder⟩ 9 : perder (la calma, el control, etc.) ⟨to lose one's temper : perder los estribos, enojarse, enfadarse⟩ ⟨to lose one's nerve : perder el valor⟩ 10 : costar, hacer perder ⟨the errors lost him his job : los errores le costaron su empleo⟩ 11 : atrasar ⟨my watch loses 5 minutes a day : mi reloj se atrasa 5 minutos por día⟩ 12 CONFUSE : confundir 13 GET RID OF : deshacerse de 14 GET AWAY FROM : deshacerse de 15 **to lose oneself** : perderse, ensimismarse 16 **to lose one's way** : perderse — *vi* : perder ⟨we lost to the other team : perdimos contra el otro equipo⟩

loser ['luːzər] *n* : perdedor *m*, -dora *f*

loss ['lɔs] *n* 1 LOSING : pérdida *f* ⟨loss of memory : pérdida de memoria⟩ ⟨to sell at a loss : vender con pérdida⟩ ⟨to cut one's losses : reducir las pérdidas (económicas)⟩ ⟨to be at a loss to : no saber cómo⟩ ⟨to be at a loss for words : no saber qué decir⟩ 2 DEFEAT : derrota *f*, juego *m* perdido 3 **losses** *npl* DEATHS : muertos *mpl*

lost ['lɔst] *adj* 1 : perdido ⟨a lost cause : una causa perdida⟩ ⟨lost in thought : absorto⟩ 2 **to get lost** : perderse 3 **to make up for lost time** : recuperar el tiempo perdido

lot ['lɑt] *n* 1 DRAWING : sorteo *m* ⟨by lot : por sorteo⟩ 2 SHARE : parte *f*, porción *f* 3 FATE : suerte *f* 4 LAND, PLOT : terreno *m*, solar *m*, lote *m*, parcela *f* ⟨parking lot : estacionamiento⟩ 5 **a lot** : mucho ⟨I liked it a lot : me gustó mucho⟩ ⟨she doesn't travel a lot : no viaja mucho⟩ 6 **a lot** *or* **lots** : mucho ⟨a lot better : mucho mejor⟩ ⟨thanks a lot : muchas gracias⟩ ⟨there's lots to do : hay mucho que hacer⟩ 7 **a lot of** *or* **lots of** : mucho, un montón de, bastante ⟨lots of books : un montón de libros, muchos libros⟩ ⟨a lot of people : mucha gente⟩

loth ['loːθ, 'loːð] → **loath**

lotion ['loːʃən] *n* : loción *f*

lottery ['lɑtəri] *n, pl* **-teries** : lotería *f*

lotus ['loːtəs] *n* : loto *m*

loud¹ ['laʊd] *adv* : alto, fuerte ⟨out loud : en voz alta⟩

loud² *adj* 1 : alto, fuerte ⟨a loud voice : una voz alta⟩ 2 NOISY : ruidoso ⟨a loud party : una fiesta ruidosa⟩ 3 FLASHY : llamativo, chillón

loudly ['laʊdli] *adv* : alto, fuerte, en voz alta

loudmouth ['laʊd,maʊθ] *n* : bocón *m*, -cona *f*

loudness ['laʊdnəs] *n* : volumen *m*, fuerza *f* (del ruido)

loudspeaker ['laʊd,spiːkər] *n* : altavoz *m*, altoparlante *m*

lounge¹ ['laʊndʒ] *vi* **lounged; lounging** : holgazanear, gandulear

lounge² *n* : salón *m*, sala *f* de estar

louse ['laʊs] *n, pl* **lice** ['laɪs] : piojo *m*

lousy ['laʊzi] *adj* **lousier; -est** 1 : piojoso, lleno de piojos 2 BAD : pésimo, muy malo

lout ['laʊt] *n* : bruto *m*, patán *m*

louver *or* **louvre** ['luːvər] *n* : persiana *f*, listón *m* de persiana

lovable ['lʌvəbəl] *adj* : adorable, amoroso, encantador

love¹ ['lʌv] *v* **loved; loving** *vt* 1 : querer, amar ⟨I love you : te quiero⟩ 2 ENJOY : encantarle a alguien, ser (muy) aficionado a, gustarle mucho a uno (algo) ⟨she loves flowers : le encantan las flores⟩ ⟨he loves golf : es muy aficionado al golf⟩ ⟨I'd love to go with you : me gustaría mucho acompañarte⟩ — *vi* : querer, amar

love² *n* 1 : amor *m*, cariño *m* ⟨to be in love with : estar enamorado de⟩ ⟨to fall in love with : enamorarse de⟩ ⟨to fall out of love with : dejar de querer a⟩ ⟨love affair : aventura⟩ ⟨love life : vida amorosa⟩ 2 ENTHUSIASM, INTEREST : amor *m*, afición *f*, gusto *m* ⟨love of music : afición a la música⟩ 3 BELOVED : amor *m*; amado *m*, -da *f*; enamorado *m*, -da *f* ⟨yes, my love : sí, mi amor⟩ 4 REGARDS : recuerdos *mpl* ⟨Love, Brian : cariños, Brian⟩ 5 **love at first sight** : amor a primera vista 6 **no/little love lost** ⟨there is no love lost between them : no se pueden ver⟩ 7 **not for love or money** : por nada del mundo 8 **to make love** : hacer el amor

loveless ['lʌvləs] *adj* : sin amor

loveliness ['lʌvlinəs] *n* : belleza *f*, hermosura *f*

lovelorn ['lʌv,lɔrn] *adj* : herido de amor, perdidamente enamorado

lovely ['lʌvli] *adj* **lovelier; -est** : hermoso, bello, lindo, precioso

lover ['lʌvər] *n* : amante *mf* (de personas); aficionado *m*, -da *f* (a alguna actividad)

loving ['lʌvɪŋ] *adj* : amoroso, cariñoso

lovingly ['lʌvɪŋli] *adv* : cariñosamente

low¹ ['loː] *vi* : mugir

low² *adv* : bajo, profundo ⟨to aim low : apuntar bajo⟩ ⟨to lie low : mantenerse escondido⟩ ⟨to turn the lights down low : bajar las luces⟩

low³ *adj* **lower** ['loːər]; **lowest** 1 : bajo ⟨a low building : un edificio bajo⟩ ⟨a low bow : una profunda reverencia⟩ 2 : bajo ⟨low temperatures/speeds : bajas temperaturas/velocidades⟩ ⟨low-calorie/low-

fat : bajo en calorías/grasas) **3** SHALLOW
: bajo, poco profundo **4** WEAK, GENTLE
: flojo (dícese del viento), tenue (dícese
de la luz) 〈over low heat : a fuego
lento〉 **5** SOFT : bajo, suave 〈in a low
voice : en voz baja〉 **6** DEEP : grave, profundo (dícese de la voz, etc.) **7** HUMBLE
: humilde, modesto **8** DEPRESSED : deprimido, bajo de moral **9** INFERIOR
: bajo, inferior **10** UNFAVORABLE : mal
〈she has a low opinion of him : tiene un
mal concepto de él〉 **11** LOW-CUT : escotado **12 to be low on** : tener poco de,
estar escaso de 〈we're low on gas : nos
queda muy poca gasolina〉

low⁴ n **1** : punto m bajo 〈to reach an all-
time low : estar más bajo que nunca〉 **2**
or **low gear** : primera velocidad f **3**
: mugido m (de una vaca)
lowbrow [¹loː‚braʊ] n : persona f inculta
low-class [¹loː¹klæs] adj → **lower-class**
low-cut [¹loː¹kʌt] adj : escotado
lower¹ [¹loːər] vt **1** DROP : bajar 〈to lower
one's voice : bajar la voz〉 **2** : arriar, bajar 〈to lower the flag : arriar la ban-
dera〉 **3** REDUCE : reducir, bajar **4 to
lower oneself** : rebajarse
lower² [¹loːər] adj : inferior, más bajo, de
abajo
lowercase¹ [‚loːər¹keɪs] adj : minúsculo
lowercase² n **in lowercase** : en
minúsculas
lower-class [‚loːər¹klæs] adj : de clase
baja
lower class n : clase f baja
low-key [¹loː¹kiː] adj : informal, sin ceremonias
lowland [¹loːlənd, -‚lænd] n : tierras fpl bajas
lowliness [¹loːlinəs] n : humildad f, bajeza
f
lowly [¹loːli] adj **lowlier; -est** : humilde,
modesto
loyal [¹lɔɪəl] adj : leal, fiel — **loyally** adv
loyalist [¹lɔɪəlɪst] n : partidario m, -ria f
del régimen
loyalty [¹lɔɪəlti] n, pl **-ties** : lealtad f, fidelidad f
loyalty card n : tarjeta f de cliente
lozenge [¹lɑzənʤ] n : pastilla f
LSD [‚ɛl‚es¹diː] n : LSD m
lubricant [¹luːbrɪkənt] n : lubricante m
lubricate [¹luːbrɪ‚keɪt] vt **-cated; -cating**
: lubricar — **lubrication** [‚luːbrɪ¹keɪʃən] n
lucid [¹luːsəd] adj : lúcido, claro — **lu-
cidly** adv
lucidity [luː¹sɪdəti] n : lucidez f
luck¹ [¹lʌk] n **1** : suerte f 〈hard luck
: mala suerte〉 **2 as luck would have it**
: quiso la suerte que **3 good luck!**
: ¡(buena) suerte! **4 the luck of the
draw** 〈to depend on the luck of the
draw : ser cuestión de suerte〉 **5 to be down
on one's luck** : estar de mala racha **6 to
be in luck** : estar de suerte **7 to be out
of luck** : no estar de suerte **8 to have
bad luck** : tener mala suerte **9 to press/
push one's luck** : desafiar a la suerte **10
to try one's luck** : probar suerte **11
with any luck** : con un poco de suerte

luckily [¹lʌkəli] adv : afortunadamente,
por suerte
luckless [¹lʌkləs] adj : desafortunado
lucky [¹lʌki] adj **luckier; -est 1** : afortunado, que tiene suerte 〈a lucky woman
: una mujer afortunada〉 **2** FORTUITOUS
: fortuito, de suerte **3** OPPORTUNE
: oportuno **4** : de (la) suerte 〈lucky
number : número de la suerte〉
lucrative [¹luːkrətɪv] adj : lucrativo, provechoso — **lucratively** adv
ludicrous [¹luːdəkrəs] adj : ridículo, absurdo — **ludicrously** adv
ludicrousness [¹luːdəkrəsnəs] n : ridiculez f, absurdo m
lug [¹lʌg] vt **lugged; lugging** : arrastrar,
transportar con dificultad
luggage [¹lʌgɪʤ] n : equipaje m
lugubrious [lʊ¹guːbriəs] adj : lúgubre —
lugubriously adv
lukewarm [¹luːk¹wɔrm] adj **1** TEPID
: tibio **2** HALFHEARTED : poco entusiasta
lull¹ [¹lʌl] vt **1** CALM, SOOTHE : calmar,
sosegar **2 to lull to sleep** : arrullar,
adormecer
lull² n : calma f, pausa f
lullaby [¹lʌlə‚baɪ] n, pl **-bies** : canción f de
cuna, arrullo m, nana f
lumbago [‚lʌm¹beɪgo] n : lumbago m
lumbar [¹lʌmbər, -‚bɑr] adj : lumbar
lumber¹ [¹lʌmbər] vt : aserrar (madera) —
vi : moverse pesadamente
lumber² n : madera f
lumberjack [¹lʌmbər‚ʤæk] n : leñador m,
-dora f
lumberyard [¹lʌmbər‚jɑrd] n : almacén m
de maderas
luminary [¹luːmə‚neri] n, pl **-naries** : lumbrera f, luminaria f
luminescence [‚luːmə¹nesənts] n : luminiscencia f — **luminescent** [-¹nɛs-ənt]
adj
luminosity [‚luːmə¹nɑsəti] n, pl **-ties** : luminosidad f
luminous [¹luːmənəs] adj : luminoso —
luminously adv
lump¹ [¹lʌmp] vt or **to lump together**
: juntar, agrupar, amontonar — vi
CLUMP : agruparse, aglutinarse
lump² n **1** GLOB : grumo m **2** PIECE
: pedazo m, trozo m, terrón m 〈a lump
of coal : un trozo de carbón〉 〈a lump of
sugar : un terrón de azúcar〉 **3** SWELL-
ING : bulto m, hinchazón f, protuberancia f **4 to have a lump in one's throat**
: tener un nudo en la garganta
lump sum n : cantidad f global, pago m
único
lumpy [¹lʌmpi] adj **lumpier; -est 1**
: lleno de grumos (dícese de una salsa) **2**
UNEVEN : desigual, disparejo
lunacy [¹luːnəsi] n, pl **-cies** : locura f
lunar [¹luːnər] adj : lunar
lunatic¹ [¹luːnə‚tɪk] adj sometimes offensive
: lunático, loco
lunatic² n sometimes offensive : loco m,
-ca f
lunch¹ [¹lʌntʃ] vi : almorzar, comer
lunch² n : almuerzo m, comida f, lonche
m Mex

luncheon ['lʌntʃən] n 1 : comida f, almuerzo m 2 **luncheon meat** : fiambres fpl

lunchroom ['lʌntʃˌruːm, -ˌrʊm] n : merendero m, cafetería f

lunchtime ['lʌntʃˌtaɪm] n : hora f del almuerzo

lung ['lʌŋ] n : pulmón m

lunge¹ ['lʌndʒ] vi **lunged; lunging** 1 THRUST : atacar (en la esgrima) 2 to **lunge forward** : arremeter, lanzarse

lunge² n 1 : arremetida f, embestida f 2 : estocada f (en la esgrima)

lurch¹ ['lərtʃ] vi 1 PITCH : cabecear, dar bandazos, dar sacudidas 2 STAGGER : tambalearse

lurch² n 1 : sacudida f, bandazo m (de un vehículo) 2 : tambaleo m (de una persona)

lure¹ ['lʊr] vt **lured; luring** : atraer

lure² n 1 ATTRACTION : atractivo m 2 ENTICEMENT : señuelo m, aliciente m 3 BAIT : cebo m artificial (en la pesca)

lurid ['lʊrəd] adj 1 GRUESOME : espeluznante, horripilante 2 SENSATIONAL : sensacionalista, chocante 3 GAUDY : chillón

lurk ['lərk] vi : estar al acecho

luscious ['lʌʃəs] adj 1 DELICIOUS : delicioso, exquisito 2 SEDUCTIVE : seductor, saturador

lush ['lʌʃ] adj 1 LUXURIANT : exuberante, lozano 2 LUXURIOUS : suntuoso, lujoso — **lushness** ['lʌʃnəs] n

lust¹ ['lʌst] vi to **lust after** : desear (a una persona), codiciar (riquezas, etc.)

lust² n 1 LASCIVIOUSNESS : lujuria f, lascivia f 2 CRAVING : deseo m, ansia f, anhelo m

luster or **lustre** ['lʌstər] n 1 GLOSS, SHEEN : lustre m, brillo m 2 SPLENDOR : lustre m, esplendor m

lusterless ['lʌstərləs] adj : deslustrado, sin brillo

lustful ['lʌstfəl] adj : lujurioso, lascivo, lleno de deseo

lustrous ['lʌstrəs] adj : brillante, brilloso, lustroso

lusty ['lʌsti] adj **lustier; -est** : fuerte, robusto, vigoroso — **lustily** ['lʌstəli] adv

lute ['luːt] n : laúd m

luxuriance [ˌlʌgˈʒʊriənts, ˌlʌkˈʃʊr-] n : lozanía f, exuberancia f

luxuriant [ˌlʌgˈʒʊriənt, ˌlʌkˈʃʊr-] adj 1 : exuberante, lozano (dícese de las plantas) 2 : abundante y hermoso (dícese del pelo) — **luxuriantly** adv

luxuriate [ˌlʌgˈʒʊriˌeɪt, ˌlʌkˈʃʊr-] vi **-ated; -ating** 1 : disfrutar 2 to **luxuriate in** : deleitarse con

luxurious [ˌlʌgˈʒʊriəs, ˌlʌkˈʃʊr-] adj : lujoso, suntuoso — **luxuriously** adv

luxury ['lʌkʃəri, 'lʌgʒə-] n, pl **-ries** : lujo m

-ly [li] suf : -mente ⟨frequently : frecuentemente⟩

lye ['laɪ] n : lejía f

lying → **lie¹, lie²**

lymph ['lɪmpf] n : linfa f

lymphatic [lɪmˈfætɪk] adj : linfático

lynch ['lɪntʃ] vt : linchar

lynx ['lɪŋks] n, pl **lynx** or **lynxes** : lince m

lyre ['laɪr] n : lira f

lyric¹ ['lɪrɪk] adj : lírico

lyric² n 1 : poema m lírico 2 **lyrics** npl : letra f (de una canción)

lyrical ['lɪrɪkəl] adj : lírico, elocuente

lyricist ['lɪrɪsɪst] n : letrista mf

M

m ['ɛm] n, pl **m's** or **ms** ['ɛmz] : decimotercera letra del alfabeto inglés

ma'am ['mæm] → **madam**

macabre [məˈkɑb, -ˈkɑbər, -ˈkɑbrə] adj : macabro

macadam [məˈkædəm] n : macadán m

macaroni [ˌmækəˈroːni] n : macarrones mpl

macaroon [ˌmækəˈruːn] n : macarrón m, mostachón m

macaw [məˈkɔ] n : guacamayo m

mace ['meɪs] n 1 : maza f (arma o símbolo) 2 : macis f (especia)

machete [məˈʃɛti] n : machete m

machination [ˌmækəˈneɪʃən, ˌmæʃə-] n : maquinación f, intriga f

machine¹ [məˈʃiːn] vt **-chined; -chining** : trabajar a máquina

machine² n 1 : máquina f ⟨machine shop : taller de máquinas⟩ 2 : aparato m, maquinaria f (en política)

machine gun n : ametralladora f

machinery [məˈʃiːnəri] n, pl **-eries** 1 : maquinaria f 2 WORKS : mecanismo m

machinist [məˈʃiːnɪst] n : maquinista mf

machismo [məˈtʃiːzmoː] n : machismo m, masculinidad f

macho ['mɑtʃoː] adj : machote, macho

mackerel ['mækərəl] n, pl **-el** or **-els** : caballa f

mad ['mæd] adj **madder; maddest** 1 INSANE : loco, demente 2 RABID : rabioso 3 FOOLISH : tonto, insensato 4 ANGRY : enojado, furioso 5 CRAZY : loco ⟨I'm mad about you : estoy loco por ti⟩

Madagascan [ˌmædəˈgæskən] n : malgache mf — **Madagascan** adj

madam ['mædəm] n, pl **mesdames** [meɪˈdɑm, -ˈdæm] : señora f

madcap¹ ['mædˌkæp] adj ZANY : alocado, disparatado

madcap² n : alocado m, -da f

madden ['mædən] vt : enloquecer, enfurecer

maddening ['mædənɪŋ] adj : enloquecedor, exasperante ⟨I find it maddening : me saca de quicio⟩

made → make[1]
made–to–measure *adj* : hecho a la medida
made–up *adj* 1 : maquillado 2 INVENTED : inventado
madhouse ['mæd,haʊs] *n fam* 1 : INSANE ASYLUM *now often offensive* : manicomio *m fam* 2 (*used figuratively*) : manicomio *m fam*, casa *f* de locos
madly ['mædli] *adv* : como un loco, locamente
madman ['mæd,mæn, -mən] *n, pl* -men [-mən, -,mɛn] : loco *m*, demente *m*
madness ['mædnəs] *n* : locura *f*, demencia *f*
madwoman ['mæd,wʊmən] *n, pl* -women [-,wɪmən] : loca *f*, demente *f*
maelstrom ['meɪlstrəm] *n* : remolino *m*, vorágine *f*
maestro ['maɪ,stro:] *n, pl* -stros *or* -stri [-,stri:] : maestro *m*
Mafia ['mɑfiə] *n* : Mafia *f*
mafioso [,mɑfi'o:so] *n* : mafioso *m*, -sa *f*
magazine ['mægə,zi:n] *n* 1 STOREHOUSE : almacén *m*, polvorín *m* (de explosivos) 2 PERIODICAL : revista *f* 3 : cargador *m* (de un arma de fuego)
magenta [mə'dʒɛntə] *n* : magenta *f*, color *m* magenta
maggot ['mægət] *n* : gusano *m*
Magi ['meɪ,dʒaɪ, 'mæ-] *npl* the Magi : los Reyes Magos
magic[1] ['mædʒɪk] *or* magical ['mædʒɪkəl] *adj* : mágico
magic[2] *n* : magia *f*
magically ['mædʒɪkli] *adv* : mágicamente (they magically appeared : aparecieron como por arte de magia)
magician [mə'dʒɪʃən] *n* 1 SORCERER : mago *m*, -ga *f* 2 CONJURER : prestidigitador *m*, -dora *f*; mago *m*, -ga *f*
magistrate ['mædʒə,streɪt] *n* : magistrado *m*, -da *f*
magma ['mægmə] *n* : magma *m*
magnanimity [,mægnə'nɪməṭi] *n, pl* -ties : magnanimidad *f*
magnanimous [mæg'nænəməs] *adj* : magnánimo, generoso — magnanimously *adv*
magnate ['mæg,neɪt, -nət] *n* : magnate *mf*
magnesium [mæg'ni:ziəm, -ʒəm] *n* : magnesio *m*
magnet ['mægnət] *n* : imán *m*
magnetic [mæg'nɛṭɪk] *adj* : magnético — magnetically [-ɪkli] *adv*
magnetic field *n* : campo *m* magnético
magnetism ['mægnə,tɪzəm] *n* : magnetismo *m*
magnetize ['mægnə,taɪz] *vt* -tized; -tizing 1 : magnetizar, imantar 2 ATTRACT : magnetizar, atraer
magnification [,mægnəfə'keɪʃən] *n* : aumento *m*, ampliación *f*
magnificence [mæg'nɪfəsənts] *n* : magnificencia *f*
magnificent [mæg'nɪfəsənt] *adj* : magnífico — magnificently *adv*
magnify ['mægnə,faɪ] *vt* -fied; -fying 1 ENLARGE : ampliar 2 EXAGGERATE : magnificar, exagerar

magnifying glass *n* : lupa *f*
magnitude ['mægnə,tu:d, -,tju:d] *n* 1 GREATNESS : magnitud *f*, grandeza *f* 2 QUANTITY : cantidad *f* 3 IMPORTANCE : magnitud *f*, envergadura *f*
magnolia [mæg'no:ljə] *n* : magnolia *f* (flor), magnolio *m* (árbol)
magpie ['mæg,paɪ] *n* : urraca *f*
maguey [mə'geɪ] *n* : maguey *m*
mahogany [mə'hɑgəni] *n, pl* -nies : caoba *f*
maid ['meɪd] *n* 1 MAIDEN : doncella *f* 2 *or* maidservant ['meɪd,sərvənt] : sirvienta *f*, muchacha *f*, mucama *f*, criada *f*
maiden[1] ['meɪdən] *adj* 1 UNMARRIED : soltera 2 FIRST : primero (maiden voyage : primera travesía)
maiden[2] *n* : doncella *f*
maiden name *n* : nombre *m* de soltera
mail[1] ['meɪl] *vt* : enviar por correo, echar al correo
mail[2] *n* 1 : correo *m* 2 : malla *f* (coat of mail : cota de malla)
mailbox ['meɪl,bɑks] *n* : buzón *m*
mailing list *n* : lista *f* de correo(s), lista *f* de direcciones
mailman ['meɪl,mæn, -mən] *n, pl* -men [-mən, -,mɪn] : cartero *m*
mail order *n* : venta *f* por correo
maim ['meɪm] *vt* : mutilar, desfigurar, lisiar
main[1] ['meɪn] *adj* : principal, central (the main office : la oficina central) (main course : plato principal/fuerte) (main road : carretera principal)
main[2] *n* 1 HIGH SEAS : alta mar *f* 2 : tubería *f* principal (de agua o gas), cable *m* principal (de un circuito) 3 with might and main : con todas sus fuerzas
mainframe ['meɪn,freɪm] *n* : mainframe *m*, computadora *f* central
mainland ['meɪn,lænd, -lənd] *n* : continente *m*
mainly ['meɪnli] *adv* 1 PRINCIPALLY : principalmente, en primer lugar 2 MOSTLY : principalmente, en la mayor parte
mainstay ['meɪn,steɪ] *n* : pilar *m*, sostén *m* principal
mainstream[1] ['meɪn,stri:m] *adj* : dominante, corriente, convencional
mainstream[2] *n* : corriente *f* principal
maintain [meɪn'teɪn] *vt* 1 SERVICE : dar mantenimiento a (una máquina) 2 PRESERVE : mantener, conservar (to maintain silence : guardar silencio) 3 SUPPORT : mantener, sostener 4 ASSERT : mantener, sostener, afirmar
maintenance ['meɪntənənts] *n* : mantenimiento *m*
maize ['meɪz] *n* : maíz *m*
majestic [mə'dʒɛstɪk] *adj* : majestuoso — majestically [-tɪkli] *adv*
majesty ['mædʒəsti] *n, pl* -ties 1 : majestad *f* (Your Majesty : su Majestad) 2 SPLENDOR : majestuosidad *f*, esplendor *m*
major[1] ['meɪdʒər] *vi* -jored; -joring : especializarse
major[2] *adj* 1 GREATER : mayor 2 NOTEWORTHY : mayor, notable 3 SERIOUS : grave 4 : mayor (en la música)

major³ *n* 1 : mayor *mf*, comandante *mf* (en las fuerzas armadas) 2 : especialidad *f* (universitaria)

Majorcan [mə'ʤɔrkən, mɔ-, -'jɔr-] *n* : mallorquín *m*, -quina *f* — **Majorcan** *adj*

major general *n* : general *mf* de división

majority [mə'ʤɔrəṭi] *n*, *pl* -**ties** 1 ADULTHOOD : mayoría *f* de edad 2 : mayoría *f*, mayor parte *f* ⟨the vast majority : la inmensa mayoría⟩

make¹ ['meɪk] *v* **made** ['meɪd]; **making** *vt* 1 CREATE, PRODUCE : hacer, fabricar (máquinas, etc.), promulgar (leyes) ⟨she made a dress : hizo un vestido⟩ ⟨to make a fire : hacer un fuego⟩ ⟨to make a movie : hacer una película⟩ ⟨the milk is made into cheese : con la leche se hace queso⟩ ⟨to be made from : hacerse de⟩ ⟨made (out) of stone : hecho de piedra⟩ 2 CAUSE, PRODUCE : hacer (ruido, etc.) ⟨to make trouble : hacer problemas⟩ ⟨to make a mistake : cometer un error⟩ ⟨to make room for : hacer lugar para⟩ 3 ARRANGE : hacer (planes, etc.) ⟨to make an appointment : hacer/pedir/concertar una cita, pedir hora⟩ 4 PREPARE : hacer (una cama, etc.), preparar (una comida, etc.) 5 RENDER : hacer, poner ⟨it makes him nervous : lo pone nervioso⟩ ⟨it made me happy : me hizo feliz, me alegró⟩ ⟨it made me sad : me dio pena⟩ ⟨it made her famous : la hizo famosa⟩ 6 : hacer, convertir en ⟨it'll make a man of you : te hará hombre⟩ ⟨to make a fool of : hacer en ridículo⟩ ⟨to make a big deal of : hacer un problema por⟩ ⟨to make a mess of things : meter la pata⟩ ⟨wait — make that a cheeseburger : o mejor, dame una hamburguesa con queso⟩ 7 BE, BECOME : ser ⟨you'll make a fine doctor : serás una médica buenísima⟩ 8 EQUAL : ser ⟨two plus two makes four : dos y dos son cuatro⟩ ⟨that makes two of us! : ¡ya somos dos!⟩ 9 SCORE : hacer, marcar 10 PERFORM : hacer ⟨to make a gesture : hacer un gesto⟩ ⟨to make a speech : pronunciar un discurso⟩ 11 : no perder (un vuelo, etc.), cumplir con (una fecha de entrega) 12 REACH : llegar a (un lugar, etc.) ⟨they made the finals : llegaron a las finales⟩ 13 ATTEND : asistir a 14 COMPEL : hacer, forzar, obligar 15 EARN : hacer (dinero, amigos) ⟨to make a living : ganarse la vida⟩ 16 to make do (with something) : arreglárselas (con algo) 17 to make into : convertir en 18 to make it SUCCEED : tener éxito en la vida 19 to make it SURVIVE : vivir, sobrevivir 20 to make it : llegar ⟨we made it home safely : llegamos bien a casa⟩ ⟨I'm glad you could make it! : ¡me alegro de que hayas podido venir!⟩ 21 to make it up to someone ⟨I'll make it up to you : te lo compensaré⟩ 22 to make of : pensar de ⟨I don't know what to make of him/it : no sé qué pensar de él/ello⟩ ⟨I can't make anything of it : no lo entiendo⟩ 23 to make or break : ser el éxito o la ruina de 24 to make out DISCERN : distin-

guir 25 to make out : comprender, entender (a alguien) 26 to make out WRITE : hacer (una lista, etc.) ⟨to make a check out to : extender un cheque a nombre de⟩ 27 to make out PORTRAY : pintar, hacer parecer 28 to make over : transformar, maquillar (a alguien), redecorar (una habitación) 29 to make someone's day : alegrarle el día a alguien 30 to make up INVENT : inventar 31 to make up PREPARE : preparar 32 to make up FORM : formar, constituir 33 to make up : compensar (tiempo) 34 to make up one's mind : decidirse — *vi* 1 HEAD : ir, dirigirse ⟨we made for home : nos fuimos a casa⟩ 2 to make away with : escaparse con 3 to make do : arreglárselas 4 to make for HEAD FOR : dirigirse a 5 to make for PROMOTE : contribuir a 6 to make good REPAY : pagar 7 to make good SUCCEED : tener éxito 8 to make off : salir corriendo 9 to make off with : escaparse con 10 to make out *fam* : besuquearse ⟨to make out with someone : besar y acariciar a alguien⟩ 11 to make up for : compensar

make² *n* BRAND : marca *f*

make–believe¹ [,meɪkbə'li:v] *adj* : imaginario

make–believe² *n* : fantasía *f*, invención *f* ⟨a world of make-believe : un mundo de ensueño⟩

make out *vt* 1 WRITE : hacer (un cheque) 2 DISCERN : distinguir, divisar 3 UNDERSTAND : comprender, entender — *vi* : arreglárselas ⟨how did you make out? : ¿qué tal te fue?⟩

makeover ['meɪk,o:vər] *n* 1 : cambio *m* de imagen 2 REMODELING : reformas *fpl*, remodelación *f*

maker ['meɪkər] *n* : fabricante *mf*

makeshift ['meɪk,ʃɪft] *adj* : provisional, improvisado

makeup ['meɪk,ʌp] *n* 1 COMPOSITION : composición *f* 2 CHARACTER : carácter *m*, temperamento *m* 3 COSMETICS : maquillaje *m*

make up *vt* 1 INVENT : inventar 2 : recuperar ⟨she made up the time : recuperó las horas perdidas⟩ — *vi* RECONCILE : hacer las paces, reconciliarse

making ['meɪkɪŋ] *n* 1 : creación *f*, producción *f* ⟨in the making : en ciernes⟩ 2 to have the makings of : tener madera de (dícese de personas), tener los ingredientes para

maladjusted [,mælə'ʤʌstəd] *adj* : inadaptado

maladjustment [,mælə'ʤʌstmənt] *n* : desajuste *m*

malady ['mælədi] *n*, *pl* -**dies** : dolencia *f*, enfermedad *f*, mal *m*

malaise [mə'leɪz, mæ-] *n* : malestar *m*

malaria [mə'lɛriə] *n* : malaria *f*, paludismo *m*

Malawian [mə'lɑwiən] *n* : malauiano *m*, -na *f* — **Malawian** *adj*

Malay [mə'leɪ, 'meɪ,leɪ] *n* 1 *or* **Malayan** [mə'leɪən, meɪ-, 'meɪ,leɪən] : malayo *m*,

-ya f **2** : malayo m (idioma) — **Malay** or **Malayan** adj

Malaysian [məˈleɪʒən, -ʃən] n : malasio m, -sia f; malaisio m, -sia f — **Malaysian** adj

male¹ [ˈmeɪl] adj **1** : macho **2** MASCULINE : masculino

male² n : macho m (de animales o plantas), varón m (de personas)

malefactor [ˈmæləˌfæktər] n : malhechor m, -chora f

maleness [ˈmeɪlnəs] n : masculinidad f

malevolence [məˈlɛvələnts] n : malevolencia f

malevolent [məˈlɛvələnt] adj : malévolo

malformation [ˌmælfɔrˈmeɪʃən] n : malformación f

malformed [mælˈfɔrmd] adj : mal formado, deforme

malfunction¹ [mælˈfʌŋkʃən] vi : funcionar mal

malfunction² n : mal funcionamiento m

malice [ˈmæləs] n **1** : malicia f, malevolencia f **2 with malice aforethought** : con premeditación

malicious [məˈlɪʃəs] adj : malicioso, malévolo — **maliciously** adv

malign¹ [məˈlaɪn] vt : calumniar, difamar

malign² adj : maligno

malignancy [məˈlɪgnəntsi] n, pl **-cies** : malignidad f

malignant [məˈlɪgnənt] adj : maligno

malinger [məˈlɪŋgər] vi : fingirse enfermo

malingerer [məˈlɪŋgərər] n : uno que se finge enfermo

mall [ˈmɔl] n **1** PROMENADE : alameda f, paseo m (arbolado) **2** : centro m comercial ⟨shopping mall : galería comercial⟩

mallard [ˈmælərd] n, pl **-lard** or **-lards** : pato m real, ánade mf real

malleable [ˈmæliəbəl] adj : maleable

mallet [ˈmælət] n : mazo m

malnourished [mælˈnərɪʃt] adj : desnutrido, malnutrido

malnutrition [ˌmælnuˈtrɪʃən, -njuˈ-] n : desnutrición f, malnutrición f

malodorous [mælˈoːdərəs] adj : maloliente

malpractice [ˌmælˈpræktəs] n : mala práctica f, negligencia f

malt [ˈmɔlt] n : malta f

maltreat [mælˈtriːt] vt : maltratar

malware [ˈmælˌwær] n : malware m

mama or **mamma** [ˈmɑmə] n : mamá f

mambo [ˈmɑmbo] n : mambo m

mammal [ˈmæməl] n : mamífero m

mammalian [məˈmeɪliən, mæ-] adj : mamífero

mammary [ˈmæməri] adj **1** : mamario **2 mammary gland** : glándula mamaria

mammogram [ˈmæməˌgræm] n : mamografía f

mammoth¹ [ˈmæməθ] adj : colosal, gigantesco

mammoth² n : mamut m

man¹ [ˈmæn] vt **manned; manning** : tripular (un barco o avión), encargarse de (un servicio)

man² n, pl **men** [ˈmɛn] **1** PERSON : hombre m, persona f ⟨the man in the street

: el hombre de la calle⟩ ⟨to a man : todos sin excepción⟩ ⟨every man for himself : sálvese quien pueda⟩ ⟨to be one's own man : ser independiente⟩ **2** MALE : hombre m **3** MANKIND : humanidad f **4** HUSBAND, BOYFRIEND : marido m, novio m **5 men** npl : trabajadores mpl (de una empresa), soldados mpl (en el ejército) **6 hey, man** fam : hola amigo

manacles [ˈmænɪkəlz] npl HANDCUFFS : esposas fpl

manage [ˈmænɪʤ] v **-aged; -aging** vt **1** HANDLE : controlar, manejar **2** DIRECT : administrar, dirigir ⟨to manage one's life : organizar uno su vida⟩ **3** CONTRIVE : lograr, ingeniárselas para ⟨I managed to do it : pude hacerlo⟩ — vi COPE : arreglárselas

manageable [ˈmænɪʤəbəl] adj : manejable

management [ˈmænɪʤmənt] n **1** DIRECTION : administración f, gestión f, dirección f **2** HANDLING : manejo m **3** MANAGERS : dirección f, gerencia f

manager [ˈmænɪʤər] n : director m, -tora f; gerente mf; administrador m, -dora f

managerial [ˌmænəˈʤɪriəl] adj : directivo, gerencial

managing director n : director m gerente, directora f gerente

manatee [ˈmænəˌtiː] n : manatí m

mandarin [ˈmændərən] n **1** : mandarín m **2** or **mandarin orange** : mandarina f

mandate [ˈmænˌdeɪt] n : mandato m

mandatory [ˈmændəˌtori] adj : obligatorio

mandible [ˈmændəbəl] n : mandíbula f

mandolin [ˈmændəˈlɪn, ˈmændələn] n : mandolina f

mane [ˈmeɪn] n : crin f (de un caballo), melena f (de un león o una persona)

maneuver¹ [məˈnuːvər, -ˈnjuː-] vt **1** PLACE, POSITION : maniobrar, posicionar, colocar **2** MANIPULATE : manipular, maniobrar — vi : maniobrar

maneuver² n : maniobra f

manfully [ˈmænfəli] adj : valientemente

manganese [ˈmæŋgəˌniːz, -ˌniːs] n : manganeso m

mange [ˈmeɪnʤ] n : sarna f

manger [ˈmeɪnʤər] n : pesebre m

mangle [ˈmæŋgəl] vt **-gled; -gling 1** CRUSH, DESTROY : aplastar, despedazar, destrozar **2** MUTILATE : mutilar ⟨to mangle a text : mutilar un texto⟩

mango [ˈmæŋˌgoː] n, pl **-goes** : mango m

mangrove [ˈmænˌgroːv, ˈmæŋ-] n : mangle m

mangy [ˈmeɪnʤi] adj **mangier; -est 1** : sarnoso **2** SHABBY : gastado

manhandle [ˈmænˌhændəl] vt **-dled; -dling** : maltratar, tratar con poco cuidado

manhole [ˈmænˌhoːl] n : boca f de alcantarilla

manhood [ˈmænˌhʊd] n **1** : madurez f (de un hombre) **2** COURAGE, MANLINESS : hombría f, valor m **3** MEN : hombres mpl

manhunt [ˈmænˌhʌnt] n : búsqueda f (de un criminal)

mania [ˈmeɪniə, -njə] *n* : manía *f*
maniac [ˈmeɪniˌæk] *n* : maníaco *m*, -ca *f*; maniático *m*, -ca *f*
maniacal [məˈnaɪəkəl] *adj fam* : maníaco, maniaco
manic [ˈmænɪk] *adj* : maníaco, maniaco
manicure[1] [ˈmænəˌkjʊr] *vt* -cured; -curing 1 : hacer la manicura a 2 TRIM : recortar
manicure[2] *n* : manicura *f*
manicurist [ˈmænəˌkjʊrɪst] *n* : manicuro *m*, -ra *f*
manifest[1] [ˈmænəˌfɛst] *vt* : manifestar
manifest[2] *adj* : manifiesto, patente — **manifestly** *adv*
manifestation [ˌmænəfəˈsteɪʃən] *n* : manifestación *f*
manifesto [ˌmænəˈfɛsˌtoː] *n, pl* -tos *or* -toes : manifiesto *m*
manifold[1] [ˈmænəˌfoːld] *adj* : diverso, variado
manifold[2] *n* : colector *m* (de escape)
manioc [ˈmæniˌɑk] *n* : mandioca *f*, yuca *f*
manipulate [məˈnɪpjəˌleɪt] *vt* -lated; -lating : manipular
manipulation [məˌnɪpjəˈleɪʃən] *n* : manipulación *f*
manipulative [məˈnɪpjəˌleɪtɪv, -lətɪv] *adj* : manipulador
manipulator [məˈnɪpjəˌleɪtər] *n* : manipulador *m*, -dora *f*
mankind [ˈmænˈkaɪnd, -ˌkaɪnd] *n* : género *m* humano, humanidad *f*
manliness [ˈmænlinəs] *n* : hombría *f*, masculinidad *f*
manly [ˈmænli] *adj* **manlier; -est** : varonil, viril
man-made [ˈmænˈmeɪd] *adj* : artificial ⟨man-made fabrics : telas sintéticas⟩
manna [ˈmænə] *n* : maná *m*
mannequin [ˈmænɪkən] *n* 1 DUMMY : maniquí *m* 2 MODEL : modelo *mf*
manner [ˈmænər] *n* 1 KIND, SORT : tipo *m*, clase *f* 2 WAY : manera *f*, modo *m* 3 STYLE : estilo *m* (artístico) 4 **manners** *npl* CUSTOMS : costumbres *fpl* 5 **manners** *npl* ETIQUETTE : modales *mpl*, educación *f*, etiqueta *f* ⟨good manners : buenos modales⟩
mannered [ˈmænərd] *adj* 1 AFFECTED, ARTIFICIAL : amanerado, afectado 2 **well-mannered** : educado, cortés 3 → **ill-mannered**
mannerism [ˈmænəˌrɪzəm] *n* : peculiaridad *f*, gesto *m* particular
mannish [ˈmænɪʃ] *adj* : masculino, hombruno
man-of-war [ˌmænəˈwɔr, -əvˈwɔr] *n, pl* **men-of-war** [ˌmɛn-] WARSHIP : buque *m* de guerra
manor [ˈmænər] *n* 1 : casa *f* solariega, casa *f* señorial 2 ESTATE : señorío *m*
manpower [ˈmænˌpaʊər] *n* : personal *m*, mano *f* de obra
mansion [ˈmæntʃən] *n* : mansión *f*
manslaughter [ˈmænˌslɔtər] *n* : homicidio *m* sin premeditación
mantel [ˈmæntəl] *n* : repisa *f* de chimenea
mantelpiece [ˈmæntəlˌpiːs] → **mantel**

mantis [ˈmæntəs] *n, pl* -tises *or* -tes [ˈmænˌtiːz] : mantis *f* religiosa
mantle [ˈmæntəl] *n* : manto *m*
manual[1] [ˈmænjʊəl] *adj* : manual — **manually** *adv*
manual[2] *n* : manual *m*
manufacture[1] [ˌmænjəˈfæktʃər] *vt* -tured; -turing : fabricar, manufacturar, confeccionar (ropa), elaborar (comestibles)
manufacture[2] *n* : manufactura *f*, fabricación *f*, confección *f* (de ropa), elaboración *f* (de comestibles)
manufacturer [ˌmænjəˈfæktʃərər] *n* : fabricante *m*; manufacturero *m*, -ra *f*
manure [məˈnʊr, -ˈnjʊr] *n* : estiércol *m*
manuscript [ˈmænjəˌskrɪpt] *n* : manuscrito *m*
many[1] [ˈmɛni] *adj* **more** [ˈmor]; **most** [ˈmoːst] 1 : muchos ⟨for many years : durante muchos años⟩ ⟨many years ago : hace muchos años⟩ ⟨so/too many ideas : tantas/demasiadas ideas⟩ ⟨I don't have that many employees : no tengo tantos empleados⟩ ⟨a good/great many people : muchísima gente⟩ ⟨one of her many interests : uno de sus muchos intereses⟩ 2 **as many** ⟨I have as many books as she does : tengo tantos libros como ella⟩ ⟨take as many books as you want : llévate cuantos libros quieras⟩ ⟨we saw three plays in as many days : vimos tres obras en el mismo número de días⟩ 3 **how many** : cuántos, cuántas ⟨how many people were there? : ¿cuánta gente había?⟩
many[2] *pron* 1 : muchos ⟨many of them : muchos de ellos⟩ ⟨many of the novels : muchas de las novelas⟩ ⟨some stayed, but many left : algunos se quedaron, pero muchos se fueron⟩ ⟨I don't have that many : no tengo tantos⟩ 2 **as many as** ⟨I have as many as she does : tengo tantos como ella⟩ ⟨as many as a hundred people : hasta cien personas⟩ ⟨take as many as you want : llévate cuantos quieras⟩ 3 **many a/an** ⟨many a time : muchas veces⟩ 4 **the many** : la mayoría
map[1] [ˈmæp] *vt* **mapped; mapping** 1 : trazar el mapa de 2 PLAN : planear, proyectar ⟨to map out a program : planear un programa⟩
map[2] *n* : mapa *m*
maple [ˈmeɪpəl] *n* : arce *m*
mar [ˈmar] *vt* **marred; marring** 1 SPOIL : estropear, echar a perder 2 DEFACE : desfigurar
maraca [məˈrɑkə] *n* : maraca *f*
maraschino [ˌmærəˈskiːˌnoː, -ˈʃiː-] *n, pl* -nos : cereza *f* al marrasquino
marathon [ˈmærəˌθɑn] *n* 1 RACE : maratón *m* 2 CONTEST : competencia *f* de resistencia
maraud [məˈrɑd] *vi* : merodear
marauder [məˈrɑdər] *n* : merodeador *m*, -dora *f*
marble [ˈmɑrbəl] *n* 1 : mármol *m* 2 : canica *f*, bolita *f* ⟨to play marbles : jugar a las canicas⟩
march[1] [ˈmɑrtʃ] *vi* 1 : marchar, desfilar ⟨they marched past the grandstand

: desfilaron ante la tribuna⟩ **2** : caminar con resolución ⟨she marched right up to him : se le acercó sin vacilación⟩

march[2] *n* **1** MARCHING : marcha *f* **2** PASSAGE : paso *m* (del tiempo) **3** PROGRESS : avance *m*, progreso *m* **4** : marcha *f* (en música)

March ['mɑrtʃ] *n* : marzo *m* ⟨they arrived on the 13th of March, they arrived on March 13th : llegaron el trece de marzo⟩

marchioness ['mɑrʃənɪs] *n* : marquesa *f*

Mardi Gras ['mɑrdi,grɑ] *n* : martes *m* de Carnaval

mare ['mær] *n* : yegua *f*

margarine ['mɑrdʒərən] *n* : margarina *f*

margarita [,mɑrgə'ri:tə] *n* : margarita *f* (cóctel)

margin ['mɑrdʒən] *n* : margen *m*

marginal ['mɑrdʒənəl] *adj* **1** : marginal **2** MINIMAL : mínimo — **marginally** *adv*

marginalization [,mɑrdʒənələ'zeɪʃən] *n* : marginación *f*

mariachi [,mɑri'ɑtʃi, ,mæ-] *n* **1** *or* **mariachi band** : mariachi *m* (grupo) **2** *or* **mariachi musician** : mariachi *m* (músico) **3** **mariachi music** : mariachi *m*, música *f* de mariachi

marigold ['mærə,go:ld] *n* : maravilla *f*, caléndula *f*

marijuana *or* **marihuana** [,mærə'hwɑnə] *n* : marihuana *f*

marimba [mə'rɪmbə] *n* : marimba *f*

marina [mə'ri:nə] *n* : puerto *m* deportivo

marinade [,mærə'nɑd] *n* : adobo *m*, marinada *f*

marinate ['mærə,neɪt] *vt* **-nated; -nating** : marinar

marine[1] [mə'ri:n] *adj* **1** : marino ⟨marine life : vida marina⟩ **2** NAUTICAL : náutico, marítimo **3** : de la infantería de marina

marine[2] *n* : soldado *m* de marina

mariner ['mærɪnər] *n* : marinero *m*, marino *m*

marionette [,mæriə'nɛt] *n* : marioneta *f*, títere *m*

marital ['mærətəl] *adj* **1** : matrimonial **2** **marital status** : estado *m* civil

maritime ['mærə,taɪm] *adj* : marítimo

marjoram ['mɑrdʒərəm] *n* : mejorana *f*

mark[1] ['mɑrk] *vt* **1** : marcar **2** MAR : dejar marca en **3** CHARACTERIZE : caracterizar **4** SIGNAL : señalar, marcar **5** GRADE : corregir (exámenes, etc.) **6** **mark my words!** : ¡acuérdate de lo que te digo! **7** **to mark down** : rebajar **8** **to mark off** : demarcar, delimitar **9** **to mark up** : anotar, (un manuscrito, etc.) **10** **to mark up** : aumentar el precio de

mark[2] *n* **1** TARGET : blanco *m* ⟨to miss the mark, to be wide of the mark : no dar en el blanco⟩ **2** : marca *f*, señal *f* ⟨put a mark where you left off : pon una señal donde terminaste⟩ **3** INDICATION : señal *f*, indicio *m* ⟨a mark of respect : una señal de respeto⟩ **4** GRADE : nota *f* **5** LEVEL : nivel *m* ⟨to reach the halfway mark : llegar al ecuador⟩ ⟨we've

topped the one million dollar mark : hemos superado el millón de dólares⟩ **6** IMPRINT : huella *f*, marca *f* **7** BLEMISH : marca *f*, imperfección *f* **8** **on your mark(s), get set, go!** : en sus marcas, listos, ¡ya!; en sus marcas, listos, ¡fuera! *Mex*; preparados, listos, ¡ya! *Spain* **9** **to fall short of the mark** : quedarse corto **10** **to make/leave one's mark** : dejar su impronta **11** **to miss the mark** ERR, FAIL : errar, fracasar

marked ['mɑrkt] *adj* : marcado, notable — **markedly** ['mɑrkədli] *adv*

marker ['mɑrkər] *n* : marcador *m*

market[1] ['mɑrkət] *vt* : poner en venta, comercializar

market[2] *n* **1** MARKETPLACE : mercado *m* ⟨the open market : el mercado libre⟩ **2** DEMAND : demanda *f*, mercado *m* **3** STORE : tienda *f* **4** → **stock market**

marketable ['mɑrkətəbəl] *adj* : vendible

marketing ['mɑrkətɪŋ] *n* : mercadotecnia *f*, mercadeo *m*

marketplace ['mɑrkət,pleɪs] *n* : mercado *m*

market research *n* : estudio *m* de mercado

marking *n* **1** : corrección *f* (de exámenes, etc.) **2** : marca *f*, señal *f* **3** : pinta *f*, mancha *f* (de un animal) **4** **to have all the markings of** : tener madera de (dícese de personas), tener los ingredientes para

marksman ['mɑrksmən] *n*, *pl* **-men** [-mən, -,mɛn] : tirador *m*

marksmanship ['mɑrksmən,ʃɪp] *n* : puntería *f*

markswoman ['mɑrks,wʊmən] *n*, *pl* **-women** [-,wɪmən] : tiradora *f*

marmalade ['mɑrmə,leɪd] *n* : mermelada *f*

marmoset ['mɑrmə,set] *n* : tití *m*

marmot ['mɑrmət] *n* : marmota *f*

maroon[1] [mə'ru:n] *vt* : abandonar, aislar

maroon[2] *n* : rojo *m* oscuro, granate *m*

marquee [mɑr'ki:] *n* : marquesina *f*

marquess ['mɑrkwɪs] *or* **marquis** ['mɑrkwɪs, mɑr'ki:] *n*, *pl* **-quesses** *or* **-quises** [-'ki:z, -'ki:zəz] *or* **-quis** [-'ki:, -'ki:z] : marqués *m*

marquise [mɑr'ki:z] → **marchioness**

marriage ['mærɪdʒ] *n* **1** : matrimonio *m* **2** WEDDING : casamiento *m*, boda *f*

marriageable ['mærɪdʒəbəl] *adj* **of marriageable age** : de edad de casarse

marriage certificate *n* : certificado *m* de matrimonio, acta *f* de matrimonio

married ['mærid] *adj* **1** : casado **2** **to get married** : casarse

marrow ['mæro] *n* : médula *f*, tuétano *m*

marry ['mæri] *vt* **-ried; -rying** **1** : casar ⟨the priest married them : el cura los casó⟩ **2** : casarse con ⟨she married John : se casó con John⟩

Mars ['mɑrz] *n* : Marte *m*

marsh ['mɑrʃ] *n* **1** : pantano *m* **2** **salt marsh** : marisma *f*

marshal[1] ['mɑrʃəl] *vt* **-shaled** *or* **-shalled; -shaling** *or* **-shalling** **1** : poner en orden, reunir **2** USHER : conducir

marshal[2] *n* **1** : maestro *m* de ceremonias **2** : mariscal *m* (en el ejército); jefe *m*, -fa *f* (de la policía, de los bomberos, etc.)

marshmallow ['mɑrʃ,mɛlo:, -,mælo:] *n* : malvavisco *m*

marshy ['mɑrʃi] *adj* **marshier; -est** : pantanoso

marsupial [mɑr'su:piəl] *n* : marsupial *m*

mart ['mɑrt] *n* MARKET : mercado *m*

marten ['mɑrtən] *n*, *pl* **-ten** *or* **-tens** : marta *f*

martial ['mɑrʃəl] *adj* : marcial ⟨martial arts : artes marciales⟩ ⟨martial law : ley marcial⟩

Martian ['mɑrʃən] *n* : marciano *m*, -na *f* — **Martian** *adj*

martin ['mɑrtən] *n* **1** SWALLOW : golondrina *f* **2** SWIFT : vencejo *m*

martyr[1] ['mɑrtər] *n* : martirizar

martyr[2] *n* : mártir *mf*

martyrdom ['mɑrtərdəm] *n* : martirio *m*

marvel[1] ['mɑrvəl] *vi* **-veled** *or* **-velled; -veling** *or* **-velling** : maravillarse

marvel[2] *n* : maravilla *f*

marvelous ['mɑrvələs] *or* **marvellous** *adj* : maravilloso — **marvelously** *adv*

Marxism ['mɑrk,sɪzəm] *n* : marxismo *m*

Marxist[1] ['mɑrksɪst] *adj* : marxista

Marxist[2] *n* : marxista *mf*

marzipan ['mɑrtsə,pɑn, 'mɑrzə,pæn] *n* : mazapán *m*

mascara [mæs'kærə] *n* : rímel *m*, rimel *m*

mascot ['mæs,kɑt, -kɑt] *n* : mascota *f*

masculine ['mæskjələn] *adj* : masculino

masculinity [,mæskjə'lɪnəṭi] *n* : masculinidad *f*

mash[1] ['mæʃ] *vt* **1** : hacer puré de (papas, etc.) **2** CRUSH : aplastar, majar

mash[2] *n* **1** FEED : afrecho *m* **2** : malta *f* (para hacer bebidas alcohólicas) **3** PASTE, PULP : papilla *f*, pasta *f*

mask[1] ['mæsk] *vt* **1** CONCEAL, DISGUISE : enmascarar, ocultar **2** COVER : cubrir, tapar

mask[2] *n* **1** : máscara *f*, careta *f*, mascarilla *f* (de un cirujano o dentista) **2** *or* **facial mask** : mascarilla *f* (facial)

masochism ['mæsə,kɪzəm, 'mæzə-] *n* : masoquismo *m*

masochist ['mæsə,kɪst, 'mæzə-] *n* : masoquista *mf*

masochistic [,mæsə'kɪstɪk, ,mæzə-] *adj* : masoquista

mason ['meɪsən] *n* **1** BRICKLAYER : albañil *mf* **2** *or* **stonemason** ['sto:n,-] : mampostero *m*, cantero *m* **3** **Mason** → **freemason**

Masonic [mə'sɑnɪk] *adj* : masónico

masonry ['meɪsənri] *n*, *pl* **-ries 1** BRICKLAYING : albañilería *f* **2** *or* **stonemasonry** ['sto:n,-] : mampostería *f*

masquerade[1] [,mæskə'reɪd] *vi* **-aded; -ading 1** : disfrazarse (de), hacerse pasar (por) **2** : asistir a una mascarada

masquerade[2] *n* **1** : mascarada *f*, baile *m* de disfraces **2** FACADE : farsa *f*, fachada *f*

mass[1] ['mæs] *vi* : concentrarse, juntarse en masa — *vt* : concentrar

mass[2] *n* **1** : masa *f* ⟨atomic mass : masa atómica⟩ **2** BULK : mole *f*, volumen *m* **3** MULTITUDE : cantidad *f*, montón *m*

(de cosas), multitud *f* (de gente) **4 the masses** : las masas, el pueblo, el populacho

Mass ['mæs] *n* : misa *f*

massacre[1] ['mæsɪkər] *vt* **-cred; -cring** : masacrar

massacre[2] *n* : masacre *f*

massage[1] [mə'sɑʒ, -'sɑdʒ] *vt* **-saged; -saging** : masajear

massage[2] *n* : masaje *m*

masseur [mæ'sər] *n* : masajista *m*

masseuse [mæ'søz, -'su:z] *n* : masajista *f*

massive ['mæsɪv] *adj* **1** BULKY : voluminoso, macizo **2** HUGE : masivo, enorme — **massively** *adv*

mass media *npl* : medios *mpl* de comunicación masiva, medios *mpl* de comunicación de masas

mass–produce *vt* : producir en masa, fabricar en serie

mass production *n* : producción *f* en masa, fabricación *f* en serie

mass transit *n* : transporte *m* público

mast ['mæst] *n* : mástil *m*, palo *m*

master[1] ['mæstər] *vt* **1** SUBDUE : dominar **2** : llegar a dominar ⟨she mastered French : llegó a dominar el francés⟩

master[2] *n* **1** TEACHER : maestro *m*, profesor *m* **2** EXPERT : experto *m*, -ta *f*; maestro *m*, -tra *f* **3** : amo *m* (de animales o esclavos), señor *m* (de la casa) **4 master's degree** : maestría *f*

masterful ['mæstərfəl] *adj* **1** IMPERIOUS : autoritario, imperioso, dominante **2** SKILLFUL : magistral — **masterfully** *adv*

masterly ['mæstərli] *adj* : magistral

mastermind[1] ['mæstər,maɪnd] *n* : cerebro *m*, artífice *mf*

mastermind[2] *vt* : ser el cerebro de, planear, organizar

masterpiece ['mæstər,pi:s] *n* : obra *f* maestra

masterwork ['mæstər,wərk] → **masterpiece**

mastery ['mæstəri] *n* **1** DOMINION : dominio *m*, autoridad *f* **2** SUPERIORITY : superioridad *f* **3** EXPERTISE : maestría *f*

masticate ['mæstə,keɪt] *v* **-cated; -cating** : masticar

mastiff ['mæstɪf] *n* : mastín *m*

mastodon ['mæstə,dɑn] *n* : mastodonte *m*

masturbate ['mæstər,beɪt] *vi* **-bated; -bating** : masturbarse

masturbation [,mæstər'beɪʃən] *n* : masturbación *f*

mat[1] ['mæt] *v* **matted; matting** *vt* TANGLE : enmarañar — *vi* : enmarañarse

mat[2] *n* **1** : estera *f* **2** TANGLE : maraña *f* **3** PAD : colchoneta *f* (de gimnasia) **4** *or* **matt** *or* **matte** ['mæt] FRAME : marco *m* (de cartón)

mat[3] → **matte**

matador ['mæṭə,dɔr] *n* : matador *m*

match[1] ['mætʃ] *vt* **1** PIT : enfrentar, oponer **2** EQUAL, FIT : igualar, corresponder a, coincidir con **3** : combinar con, hacer juego con ⟨her shoes match her dress : sus zapatos hacen juego con su vestido⟩ — *vi* **1** CORRESPOND : concordar, coincidir **2** : hacer juego ⟨with a tie to match : con una corbata que hace juego⟩

match² n **1** EQUAL : igual mf ⟨he's no match for her : no puede competir con ella⟩ **2** FIGHT, GAME : partido m, combate m (en boxeo) **3** MARRIAGE : matrimonio m, casamiento m **4** : fósforo m, cerilla f, cerillo m (in various countries) ⟨he lit a match : encendió un fósforo⟩ **5 to be a good match** : hacer buena pareja (dícese de las personas), hacer juego (dícese de la ropa)

matchbox ['mætʃ,bɑks] n : caja f de cerillas

matchless ['mætʃləs] adj : sin igual, sin par

matchmaker ['mætʃ,meɪkər] n : casamentero m, -ra f

mate¹ ['meɪt] v **mated; mating** vi **1** FIT : encajar **2** PAIR : emparejarse **3** (relating to animals) : aparearse, copular — vt : aparear, acoplar (animales)

mate² n **1** COMPANION : compañero m, -ra f; camarada mf **2** : macho m, hembra f (de animales) **3** : oficial mf (de un barco) ⟨first mate : primer oficial⟩ **4** : compañero m, -ra f; pareja f (de un zapato, etc.)

maté ['mɑ,teɪ] n : yerba f, mate m

material¹ [mə'tɪriəl] adj **1** PHYSICAL : material, físico ⟨the material world : el mundo material⟩ ⟨material needs : necesidades materiales⟩ **2** IMPORTANT : importante, esencial **3 material evidence** : prueba f sustancial

material² n **1** : material m **2** CLOTH : tejido m, tela f

materialism [mə'tɪriə,lɪzəm] n : materialismo m

materialist [mə'tɪriəlɪst] n : materialista mf

materialistic [mə,tɪriə'lɪstɪk] adj : materialista

materialize [mə'tɪriə,laɪz] v **-ized; -izing** vt : materializar, hacer aparecer — vi : materializarse, aparecer

maternal [mə'tərnəl] adj MOTHERLY : maternal — **maternally** adv

maternity¹ [mə'tərnəti] n : de maternidad ⟨maternity clothes : ropa de futura mamá⟩ ⟨maternity leave : licencia por maternidad⟩

maternity² n, pl **-ties** : maternidad f

math ['mæθ] → mathematics

mathematical [,mæθə'mætɪkəl] adj : matemático — **mathematically** adv

mathematician [,mæθəmə'tɪʃən] n : matemático m, -ca f

mathematics [,mæθə'mætɪks] ns & pl : matemáticas fpl, matemática f

matinee or **matinée** [mætən'eɪ] n : matiné f

matriarch ['meɪtri,ɑrk] n : matriarca f

matriarchy ['meɪtri,ɑrki] n, pl **-chies** : matriarcado m

matriculate [mə'trɪkjə,leɪt] v **-lated; -lating** vt : matricular — vi : matricularse

matriculation [mə,trɪkjə'leɪʃən] n : matrícula f, matriculación f

matrimony ['mætrə,moːni] n : matrimonio m — **matrimonial** [,mætrə'moːniəl] adj

matrix ['meɪtrɪks] n, pl **-trices** ['meɪtrə,siːz, 'mæ-] or **-trixes** ['meɪtrɪksəz] : matriz f

matron ['meɪtrən] n : matrona f

matronly ['meɪtrənli] adj : de matrona, matronal

matte ['mæt] adj : mate, de acabado mate

matter¹ ['mætər] vi : importar ⟨it doesn't matter : no importa⟩

matter² n **1** QUESTION : asunto m, cuestión f ⟨a matter of taste/opinion/time : una cuestión de gusto/opiniones/tiempo⟩ **2** SUBSTANCE : materia f, sustancia f **3 matters** npl CIRCUMSTANCES : situación f, cosas fpl ⟨to make matters worse : para colmo de males⟩ **4 as a matter of course** : automáticamente **5 as a matter of fact** : en efecto, en realidad **6 for that matter** : de hecho **7 no matter how much** : por mucho que **8 the fact/truth of the matter** : la verdad **9 to be no laughing matter** : no ser motivo de risa **10 to be the matter** : pasar ⟨what's the matter? : ¿qué pasa?⟩

matter-of-fact ['mætərəv'fækt] adj : práctico, realista

mattress ['mætrəs] n : colchón m

mature¹ [mə'tʊr, -'tjʊr, -'tʃʊr] vi **-tured; -turing 1** : madurar **2** : vencer ⟨when does the loan mature? : ¿cuándo vence el préstamo?⟩

mature² adj **maturer; -est 1** : maduro **2** DUE : vencido

maturity [mə'tʊrəti, -'tjʊr-, -'tʃʊr-] n : madurez f

maudlin ['mɔdlɪn] adj : sensiblero

maul ['mɔl] vt **1** BEAT : golpear, pegar **2** MANGLE : mutilar **3** MANHANDLE : maltratar

maul² n MALLET : mazo m

Mauritanian [,mɔrə'teɪniən] n : mauritano m, -na f — **Mauritanian** adj

mausoleum [,mɔsə'liːəm, ,mɔzə-] n, pl **-leums** or **-lea** [-'liːə] : mausoleo m

mauve ['moːv, 'mɔv] n : malva f

maven or **mavin** ['meɪvən] n EXPERT : experto m, -ta f

maverick ['mævrɪk, 'mævə-] n **1** : ternero m sin marcar **2** NONCONFORMIST : inconformista mf, disidente mf

maw ['mɔ] n : fauces fpl

mawkish ['mɔkɪʃ] adj : sensiblero

maxim ['mæksəm] n : máxima f

maximize ['mæksə,maɪz] vt **-mized; -mizing 1** : maximizar, llevar al máximo **2** : maximizar (en informática)

maximum¹ ['mæksəməm] adj : máximo

maximum² n, pl **-ma** ['mæksəmə] or **-mums** : máximo m

may ['meɪ] v aux, past **might** ['maɪt] present s & pl **may 1** (expressing permission) : poder ⟨you may go : puedes ir⟩ ⟨if I may : si me lo permites⟩ **2** (expressing possibility or probability) : poder ⟨you may be right : puede que tengas razón⟩ ⟨it may happen occasionally : puede pasar de vez en cuando⟩ ⟨be that as it may : sea como sea⟩ **3** (*expressing desires, intentions, or contingencies*) ⟨may the best man win : que gane el mejor⟩ ⟨I laugh that I may not weep : me río para no llorar⟩ ⟨come what may : pase lo que pase⟩

May ['meɪ] *n* : mayo *m* ⟨they arrived on the 20th of May, they arrived on May 20th : llegaron el 20 de mayo⟩

Maya ['maɪə] *or* **Mayan** ['maɪən] *n* : maya *mf* — **Maya** *or* **Mayan** *adj*

maybe ['meɪbi] *adv* PERHAPS : quizás, tal vez

mayfly ['meɪ,flaɪ] *n, pl* **-flies** : efímera *f*

mayhem ['meɪ,hɛm, 'meɪəm] *n* **1** MUTILATION : mutilación *f* **2** DEVASTATION : estragos *mpl*

mayonnaise [,meɪə'neɪz] *n* : mayonesa *f*

mayor ['meɪər, 'mɛr] *n* : alcalde *m*, -desa *f*

mayoral ['meɪərəl, 'mɛrəl] *adj* : de alcalde

maze ['meɪz] *n* : laberinto *m*

me ['mi] *pron* **1** *me* ⟨she called me : me llamó⟩ ⟨give it to me : dámelo⟩ **2** (*after a preposition*) : mí ⟨for me : para mí⟩ ⟨with me : conmigo⟩ **3** (*after conjunctions and verbs*) : yo ⟨it's me : soy yo⟩ ⟨as big as me : tan grande como yo⟩ **4** (*emphatic use*) : yo ⟨me, too! : ¡yo también!⟩ ⟨who, me? : ¿quién, yo?⟩

meadow ['mɛdo] *n* : prado *m*, pradera *f*

meadowland ['mɛdo,lænd] *n* : pradera *f*

meadowlark ['mɛdo,lɑrk] *n* : pájaro *m* cantor con el pecho amarillo

meager *or* **meagre** ['migər] *adj* **1** THIN : magro, flaco **2** POOR, SCANTY : exiguo, escaso, pobre

meagerly ['migərli] *adv* : pobremente

meagerness ['migərnəs] *n* : escasez *f*, pobreza *f*

meal ['mil] *n* **1** : comida *f* ⟨a hearty meal : una comida sustanciosa⟩ **2** : harina *f* (de maíz, etc.)

mealtime ['mil,taɪm] *n* : hora *f* de comer

mean¹ ['min] *vt* **meant** ['mɛnt]; **meaning 1** INTEND : querer, pensar, tener la intención de ⟨I didn't mean to do it : lo hice sin querer⟩ ⟨what do you mean to do? : ¿qué piensas hacer?⟩ ⟨I don't mean you any harm : no quiero hacerte daño⟩ ⟨she meant for him to come : su intención era que viniera⟩ **2** : querer decir ⟨what do you mean? : ¿qué quieres decir?⟩ ⟨if you know what I mean : si me entiendes⟩ ⟨I meant it : lo dije en serio⟩ ⟨she meant it as a compliment : lo dijo como un cumplido⟩ **3** SIGNIFY : querer decir, significar ⟨what does that mean? : ¿qué quiere decir eso?⟩ ⟨that means nothing to me : no significa nada para mí⟩ ⟨that means trouble : eso supone problemas⟩ **4** : importar ⟨health means everything : lo que más importa es la salud⟩ ⟨she means the world to me : ella es muy importante para mí⟩ **5 to mean well** : tener buenas intenciones

mean² *adj* **1** HUMBLE : humilde **2** NEGLIGIBLE : despreciable ⟨it's no mean feat : no es poca cosa⟩ **3** STINGY : mezquino, tacaño **4** CRUEL : malo, cruel ⟨to be mean to someone : tratar mal a alguien⟩ **5** AVERAGE, MEDIAN : medio

mean³ *n* **1** MIDPOINT : término *m* medio **2** AVERAGE : promedio *m*, media *f* aritmética **3 means** *npl* WAY : medio *m*, manera *f*, vía *f* **4 means** *npl* RESOURCES : medios *mpl*, recursos *mpl* **5 by all means** : por supuesto, cómo no **6 by means of** : por medio de **7 by no means** : de ninguna manera, de ningún modo

meander [mi'ændər] *vi* **-dered; -dering 1** WIND : serpentear **2** WANDER : vagar, andar sin rumbo fijo

meaning ['minɪŋ] *n* **1** : significado *m*, sentido *m* ⟨double meaning : doble sentido⟩ **2** INTENT : intención *f*, propósito *m*

meaningful ['minɪŋfəl] *adj* : significativo — **meaningfully** *adv*

meaningless ['minɪŋləs] *adj* : sin sentido

meanness ['minnəs] *n* **1** CRUELTY : crueldad *f*, mezquindad *f* **2** STINGINESS : tacañería *f*

meantime¹ ['min,taɪm] *adv* → **meanwhile¹**

meantime² *n* **1** : interín *m* **2 in the meantime** : entretanto, mientras tanto

meanwhile¹ ['min,hwaɪl] *adv* : entretanto, mientras tanto

meanwhile² *n* → **meantime²**

measles ['mizəlz] *ns & pl* : sarampión *m*

measly ['mizli] *adj* **measlier; -est** : miserable, mezquino

measurable ['mɛʒərəbəl, 'meɪ-] *adj* : mensurable — **measurably** [-bli] *adv*

measure¹ ['mɛʒər, 'meɪ-] *v* **-sured; -suring** : medir ⟨he measured the table : midió la mesa⟩ ⟨it measures 15 feet tall : mide 15 pies de altura⟩

measure² *n* **1** AMOUNT : medida *f*, cantidad *f* ⟨in large measure : en gran medida⟩ ⟨a full measure : una cantidad exacta⟩ ⟨a measure of proficiency : una cierta competencia⟩ ⟨for good measure : de ñapa, por añadidura⟩ **2** DIMENSIONS, SIZE : medida *f*, tamaño *m* **3** RULER : regla *f* ⟨tape measure : cinta métrica⟩ **4** MEASUREMENT : medida *f* ⟨cubic measure : medida de capacidad⟩ **5** MEASURING : medición *f* **6 measures** *npl* : medidas *fpl* ⟨security measures : medidas de seguridad⟩

measureless ['mɛʒərləs, 'meɪ-] *adj* : inmensurable

measurement ['mɛʒərmənt, 'meɪ-] *n* **1** MEASURING : medición *f* **2** DIMENSION : medida *f*

measure up *vi* **to measure up to** : estar a la altura de

meat ['mit] *n* **1** FOOD : comida *f* **2** : carne *f* ⟨meat and fish : carne y pescado⟩ **3** SUBSTANCE : sustancia *f*, esencia *f* ⟨the meat of the story : la sustancia del cuento⟩

meatball ['mit,bɔl] *n* : albóndiga *f*

meaty ['miti] *adj* **meatier; -est** : con mucha carne, carnoso

mechanic [mɪ'kænɪk] *n* : mecánico *m*, -ca *f*

mechanical [mɪ'kænɪkəl] *adj* : mecánico — **mechanically** *adv*

mechanics [mɪ'kænɪks] *ns & pl* **1** : mecánica *f* ⟨fluid mechanics : la mecánica de fluidos⟩ **2** MECHANISMS : mecanismos *mpl*, aspectos *mpl* prácticos

mechanism ['mɛkə,nɪzəm] *n* : mecanismo *m*

mechanization [,mɛkənə'zeɪʃən] *n* : mecanización *f*

mechanize ['mɛkə,naɪz] *vt* **-nized; -nizing** : mecanizar

medal ['mɛdəl] *n* : medalla *f*, condecoración *f*

medalist ['mɛdəlɪst] *or* **medallist** *n* : medallista *mf*

medallion [mə'dæljən] *n* : medallón *m*

meddle ['mɛdəl] *vi* **-dled; -dling** : meterse, entrometerse

meddler ['mɛdələr] *n* : entrometido *m*, -da *f*

meddlesome ['mɛdəlsəm] *adj* : entrometido

media ['mi:diə] *npl* : medios *mpl* de comunicación ⟨social media : redes/medios sociales⟩

median[1] ['mi:diən] *adj* : medio

median[2] *n* : valor *m* medio

mediate ['mi:di,eɪt] *vi* **-ated; -ating** : mediar

mediation [,mi:di'eɪʃən] *n* : mediación *f*

mediator ['mi:di,eɪtər] *n* : mediador *m*, -dora *f*

medical ['mɛdɪkəl] *adj* : médico

medicate ['mɛdə,keɪt] *vt* **-cated; -cating** : medicar ⟨medicated powder : polvos medicinales⟩

medication [,mɛdə'keɪʃən] *n* **1** TREATMENT : tratamiento *m*, medicación *f* **2** MEDICINE : medicamento *m* ⟨to be on medication : estar medicado⟩

medicinal [mə'dɪsənəl] *adj* : medicinal

medicine ['mɛdəsən] *n* **1** MEDICATION : medicina *f*, medicamento *m* **2** : medicina *f* ⟨he's studying medicine : estudia medicina⟩

medicine man *n* : hechicero *m*

medieval *or* **mediaeval** [mɪ'di:vəl, ,mi:-, ,m-, -di'i:vəl] *adj* : medieval

mediocre [,mi:di'o:kər] *adj* : mediocre

mediocrity [,mi:di'ɑkrəti] *n, pl* **-ties** : mediocridad *f*

meditate ['mɛdə,teɪt] *vi* **-tated; -tating** : meditar

meditation [,mɛdə'teɪʃən] *n* : meditación *f*

meditative ['mɛdə,teɪtɪv] *adj* : meditabundo

Mediterranean [,mɛdətə'reɪniən] *adj* : mediterráneo

medium[1] ['mi:diəm] *adj* : mediano ⟨of medium height : de estatura mediana, de estatura regular⟩ ⟨medium-sized : de tamaño mediano⟩

medium[2] *n, pl* **-diums** *or* **-dia** ['mi:diə] **1** MEAN : punto *m* medio, término *m* medio ⟨happy medium : justo medio⟩ **2** MEANS : medio *m* **3** SUBSTANCE : medio *m*, sustancia *f* ⟨a viscous medium : un medio viscoso⟩ **4** : medio *m* de comunicación **5** : medio *m* (artístico) **6** *pl* **mediums** : médium *mf* (persona)

medley ['mɛdli] *n, pl* **-leys** : popurrí *m* (de canciones)

meek ['mi:k] *adj* **1** LONG-SUFFERING : paciente, sufrido **2** SUBMISSIVE : sumiso, dócil, manso

meekly ['mi:kli] *adv* : dócilmente

meekness ['mi:knəs] *n* : mansedumbre *f*, docilidad *f*

meet[1] ['mi:t] *v* **met** ['mɛt]; **meeting** *vt* **1** ENCOUNTER : encontrarse con ⟨he met me at the park : nos encontramos en el parque⟩ **2** JOIN : unirse con **3** CONFRONT : enfrentarse a **4** ENCOUNTER : encontrar **5** SATISFY : satisfacer, cumplir con ⟨to meet costs : cubrir los gastos⟩ **6** REACH : alcanzar (una meta, etc.) **7** MATCH : igualar **8** : conocer ⟨I met his sister : conocí a su hermana⟩ **9 to meet someone halfway** : llegar a un arreglo con alguien **10 to meet someone's eyes/gaze** : mirarlo a la cara a alguien — *vi* **1** : encontrarse ⟨I hope we meet again : espero que nos volvamos a encontrar⟩ **2** ASSEMBLE : reunirse, congregarse **3** COMPETE, BATTLE : enfrentarse **4** : conocerse **5** JOIN : unirse **6** : encontrarse (dícese de los ojos) **7** : cerrarse (dícese de una chaqueta, etc.), tocar (dícese de dos extremos) **8 to meet up** : encontrarse **9 to meet with** : reunirse con **10 to meet with** RECEIVE : ser recibido con

meet[2] *n* : encuentro *m*

meeting ['mi:tɪŋ] *n* **1** : reunión *f* ⟨to open the meeting : abrir la sesión⟩ **2** ENCOUNTER : encuentro *m* **3** : entrevista *f* (formal)

meetinghouse ['mi:tɪŋ,haʊs] *n* : iglesia *f* (de ciertas confesiones protestantes)

megabyte ['mɛgə,baɪt] *n* : megabyte *m*

megahertz ['mɛgə,hərts, -,hrts] *n* : megahercio *m*

megaphone ['mɛgə,fo:n] *n* : megáfono *m*

megaton ['mɛgə,tʌn] *n* : megatón *m*

megawatt ['mɛgə,wɑt] *n* : megavatio *m*

melancholy[1] ['mɛlən,kɑli] *adj* : melancólico, triste, sombrío

melancholy[2] *n, pl* **-cholies** : melancolía *f*

melanoma [,mɛlə'no:mə] *n, pl* **-mas** : melanoma *m*

meld ['mɛld] *vt* : fusionar, unir — *vi* : fusionarse, unirse

melee ['meɪ,leɪ, meɪ'leɪ] *n* BRAWL : reyerta *f*, riña *f*, pelea *f*

meliorate ['mi:ljə,reɪt, 'mi:liə-] → **ameliorate**

mellow[1] ['mɛlo:] *vt* : suavizar, endulzar — *vi* : suavizarse, endulzarse

mellow[2] *adj* **1** RIPE : maduro **2** MILD : apacible ⟨a mellow character : un carácter apacible⟩ ⟨mellow wines : vinos añejos⟩ **3** : suave, dulce ⟨mellow colors : colores suaves⟩ ⟨mellow tones : tonos dulces⟩

mellowness ['mɛlonəs] *n* : suavidad *f*, dulzura *f*

melodic [mə'lɑdɪk] *adj* : melódico — **melodically** [-dɪkli] *adv*

melodious [mə'lo:diəs] *adj* : melodioso — **melodiously** *adv*

melodiousness [mə'lo:diəsnəs] *n* : calidad *f* de melódico

melodrama [ˈmɛləˌdrɑmə, -ˌdræ-] *n* : melodrama *m*

melodramatic [ˌmɛlədrəˈmætɪk] *adj* : melodramático — **melodramatically** [-tɪkli] *adv*

melody [ˈmɛlədi] *n, pl* **-dies** : melodía *f*, tonada *f*

melon [ˈmɛlən] *n* : melón *m*

melt [ˈmɛlt] *vt* **1** : derretir, disolver **2** SOFTEN : ablandar ⟨it melted his heart : ablandó su corazón⟩ **3 to melt down** : fundir — *vi* **1** : derretirse, disolverse **2** SOFTEN : ablandarse **3** DISAPPEAR : desvanecerse, esfumarse ⟨the clouds melted away : las nubes se desvanecieron⟩

melting point *n* : punto *m* de fusión

member [ˈmɛmbər] *n* **1** LIMB : miembro *m* **2** : miembro *m* (de un grupo); socio *m*, -cia *f* (de un club) **3** PART : miembro *m*, parte *f*

membership [ˈmɛmbərˌʃɪp] *n* **1** : membresía *f* ⟨application for membership : solicitud de entrada⟩ **2** MEMBERS : membresía *f*, miembros *mpl*, socios *mpl*

membrane [ˈmɛmˌbreɪn] *n* : membrana *f* — **membranous** [ˈmɛmbrə-nəs] *adj*

memento [mɪˈmɛnˌtoː] *n, pl* **-tos** *or* **-toes** : recuerdo *m*

memo [ˈmɛmoː] *n, pl* **memos** : memorándum *m*

memoirs [ˈmɛmˌwɑrz] *npl* : memorias *fpl*, autobiografía *f*

memorabilia [ˌmɛmərəˈbiliə, -ˈbiljə] *npl* **1** : objetos *mpl* de interés histórico **2** MEMENTOS : recuerdos *mpl*

memorable [ˈmɛmərəbəl] *adj* : memorable, notable — **memorably** [-bli] *adv*

memorandum [ˌmɛməˈrændəm] *n, pl* **-dums** *or* **-da** [-də] : memorándum *m*

memorial¹ [məˈmoriəl] *adj* : conmemorativo

memorial² *n* : monumento *m* conmemorativo

Memorial Day *n* : el último lunes de mayo (observado en Estados Unidos como día feriado para conmemorar a los caídos en guerra)

memorialize [məˈmoriəˌlaɪz] *vt* **-ized; -izing** COMMEMORATE : conmemorar

memorization [ˌmɛmərəˈzeɪʃən] *n* : memorización *f*

memorize [ˈmɛməˌraɪz] *vt* **-rized; -rizing** : memorizar, aprender de memoria

memory [ˈmɛmri, ˈmɛmə-] *n, pl* **-ries** **1** : memoria *f* ⟨he has a good memory : tiene buena memoria⟩ **2** RECOLLECTION : recuerdo *m* **3** COMMEMORATION : memoria *f*, conmemoración *f* **4** : memoria *f* (en informática)

men → man²

menace¹ [ˈmɛnəs] *vt* **-aced; -acing** **1** THREATEN : amenazar **2** ENDANGER : poner en peligro

menace² *n* : amenaza *f*

menacing [ˈmɛnəsɪŋ] *adj* : amenazador, amenazante

menagerie [məˈnæʤəri, -ˈnæʒəri] *n* : colección *f* de animales salvajes

mend¹ [ˈmɛnd] *vt* **1** CORRECT : enmendar, corregir ⟨to mend one's ways : en-

mendarse⟩ **2** REPAIR : remendar, arreglar, reparar — *vi* HEAL : curarse

mend² *n* : remiendo *m*

mendicant [ˈmɛndɪkənt] *n* BEGGAR : mendigo *m*, -ga *f*

menhaden [mɛnˈheɪdən, mən-] *ns & pl* : pez *m* de la misma familia que los arenques

menial¹ [ˈmiːniəl] *adj* : servil, bajo

menial² *n* : sirviente *m*, -ta *f*

meningitis [ˌmɛnənˈʤaɪtəs] *n, pl* **-gitides** [-ˈʤɪtəˌdiːz] : meningitis *f*

menopausal [ˌmɛnəˈpɔzəl] *adj* : menopáusico

menopause [ˈmɛnəˌpɔz] *n* : menopausia *f*

menorah [məˈnorə] *n* : candelabro *m* (usado en los oficios religiosos judíos)

men's room *n* : servicios *mpl* de caballeros

menstrual [ˈmɛnstruəl] *adj* : menstrual

menstruate [ˈmɛnstruˌeɪt] *vi* **-ated; -ating** : menstruar

menstruation [ˌmɛnstruˈeɪʃən] *n* : menstruación *f*

menswear [ˈmɛnzˌwær] *n* : ropa *f* de caballero

-ment [mənt] *suf* : -miento ⟨entertainment : entretenimiento⟩

mental [ˈmɛntəl] *adj* : mental ⟨mental hospital : hospital psiquiátrico⟩ ⟨mental block : bloqueo mental⟩ — **mentally** *adv*

mentality [mɛnˈtæləti] *n, pl* **-ties** : mentalidad *f*

mental retardation [ˌriːˌtɑrˈdeɪʃən] *n* *dated, now sometimes offensive* : retraso *m* mental *dated, now sometimes offensive*

menthol [ˈmɛnˌθɔl, -ˌθoːl] *n* : mentol *m* — **mentholated** [ˌmɛnˈθəˌleɪtəd] *adj*

mention¹ [ˈmɛntʃən] *vt* : mencionar, mentar, referirse a ⟨don't mention it! : ¡de nada!, ¡no hay de qué!⟩

mention² *n* : mención *f*

mentor [ˈmɛnˌtor, ˈmɛntər] *n* : mentor *m*

menu [ˈmɛnˌjuː] *n* **1** : menú *m*, carta *f* (en un restaurante) **2** : menú *m* (en informática)

meow¹ [miˈaʊ] *vi* : maullar

meow² *n* : maullido *m*, miau *m*

mercantile [ˈmərkənˌtiːl, -ˌtaɪl] *adj* : mercantil

mercenary¹ [ˈmərsənəˌri] *adj* : mercenario

mercenary² *n, pl* **-naries** : mercenario *m*, -ria *f*

merchandise [ˈmərtʃənˌdaɪz, -ˌdaɪs] *n* : mercancía *f*, mercadería *f*

merchandiser [ˈmərtʃənˌdaɪzər] *n* : comerciante *mf*; vendedor *m*, -dora *f*

merchant [ˈmərtʃənt] *n* : comerciante *mf*

merchant marine *n* : marina *f* mercante

merciful [ˈmərsɪfəl] *adj* : misericordioso, clemente

mercifully [ˈmərsɪfli] *adv* **1** : con misericordia, con compasión **2** FORTUNATELY : afortunadamente

merciless [ˈmərsɪləs] *adj* : despiadado — **mercilessly** *adv*

mercurial [ˌmərˈkjuriəl] *adj* TEMPERAMENTAL : temperamental, volátil

mercury [ˈmərkjəri] *n, pl* **-ries** : mercurio *m*

Mercury n : Mercurio m

mercy ['mərsi] n, pl **-cies** 1 CLEMENCY : misericordia f, clemencia f 2 BLESSING : bendición f

mere ['mɪr] adj, superlative **merest** : mero, simple

merely ['mɪrli] adv : solamente, simplemente

merengue [mə'rɛŋ₁geɪ] n : merengue m (música o baile)

merge ['mərdʒ] v **merged; merging** vi : unirse, fusionarse (dícese de las compañías), confluir (dícese de los ríos, las calles, etc.) — vt : unir, fusionar, combinar

merger ['mərdʒər] n : unión f, fusión f

meridian [mə'rɪdiən] n : meridiano m

meringue [mə'ræŋ] n : merengue m

merit[1] ['mɛrət] vt : merecer, ser digno de

merit[2] n : mérito m, valor m

meritorious [₁mɛrə'toriəs] adj : meritorio

mermaid ['mər₁meɪd] n : sirena f

merriment ['mɛrimənt] n : alegría f, júbilo m, regocijo m

merry ['mɛri] adj **merrier; -est** : alegre — **merrily** ['mɛrəli] adv

merry-go-round ['mɛriɡo₁raʊnd] n : carrusel m, tiovivo m

merrymaker ['mɛri₁meɪkər] n : juerguista mf

merrymaking ['mɛri₁meɪkɪŋ] n : juerga f

mesa ['meɪsə] n : mesa f

mesdames → **madam, Mrs.**

mesh[1] ['mɛʃ] vi 1 ENGAGE : engranar (dícese de las piezas mecánicas) 2 TANGLE : enredarse 3 COORDINATE : coordinarse, combinar

mesh[2] n 1 : malla f ⟨wire mesh : malla metálica⟩ 2 NETWORK : red f 3 MESHING : engranaje m ⟨in mesh : engranado⟩

mesmerize ['mɛzmə₁raɪz] vt **-ized; -izing** 1 HYPNOTIZE : hipnotizar 2 FASCINATE : cautivar, embelesar, fascinar

mess[1] ['mɛs] vt 1 to mess up DISARRANGE : desordenar, desarreglar 2 to mess up BUNGLE : echar a perder — vi 1 to mess around HANG OUT : pasar el rato, entretenerse 2 to mess around : tener líos (amorosos) 3 to mess (around) with : tocar, jugar con ⟨don't mess with my things! : ¡no toques mis cosas!⟩ 4 to mess with PROVOKE : meterse con

mess[2] n 1 : rancho m (para soldados, etc.) 2 DISORDER : desorden m ⟨your room is a mess : tienes el cuarto hecho un desastre⟩ 3 CONFUSION, TURMOIL : confusión f, embrollo m, lío m ⟨a mess of⟩

message[1] ['mɛsɪdʒ] v **-saged; -saging** : mensajear

message[2] n : mensaje m, recado m

messaging ['mɛsɪdʒɪŋ] n : mensajería f

messenger ['mɛsəndʒər] n : mensajero m, -ra f

Messiah [mə'saɪə] n : Mesías m

Messrs. → **Mr.**

messy ['mɛsi] adj **messier; -est** UNTIDY : desordenado, sucio — **messily** adv

mestizo [mɛ'sti:zo] n : mestizo m, -za f; ladino m, -na f CA, Mex — **mestizo** adj

met → **meet**

metabolic [₁mɛtə'bɑlɪk] adj : metabólico

metabolism [mə'tæbə₁lɪzəm] n : metabolismo m

metabolize [mə'tæbə₁laɪz] vt **-lized; -lizing** : metabolizar

metal ['mɛtəl] n : metal m

metallic [mə'tælɪk] adj : metálico

metallurgical [₁mɛtəl'ərdʒɪkəl] adj : metalúrgico

metallurgy ['mɛtəl₁ərdʒi] n : metalurgia f

metalwork ['mɛtəl₁wərk] n : objeto m de metal

metalworker ['mɛtəl₁wərkər] n : metalúrgico m, -ca f

metalworking ['mɛtəl₁wərkɪŋ] n : metalistería f

metamorphosis [₁mɛtə'mɔrfəsɪs] n, pl **-phoses** [-₁si:z] : metamorfosis f

metaphor ['mɛtə₁fɔr, -fər] n : metáfora f

metaphoric [₁mɛtə'fɔrɪk] or **metaphorical** [-ɪkəl] adj : metafórico

metaphysical [₁mɛtə'fɪzɪkəl] adj : metafísico

metaphysics [₁mɛtə'fɪzɪks] n : metafísica f

mete ['mi:t] vt **meted; meting** ALLOT : repartir, distribuir ⟨to mete out punishment : imponer castigos⟩

meteor ['mi:tiər, -ti:₁ɔr] n : meteoro m

meteoric [₁mi:ti'ɔrɪk] adj : meteórico

meteorite ['mi:tiə₁raɪt] n : meteorito m

meteorologic [₁mi:ti₁ɔrə'lɑdʒɪk] or **meteorological** [-'lɑdʒɪkəl] adj : meteorológico

meteorologist [₁mi:ti'ɔrələdʒɪst] n : meteorólogo m, -ga f

meteorology [₁mi:ti'ɔrələdʒi] n : meteorología f

meter ['mi:tər] n 1 : metro m ⟨it measures 2 meters : mide 2 metros⟩ 2 : contador m, medidor m (de electricidad, etc.) ⟨parking meter : parquímetro⟩ 3 : metro m (en literatura o música)

methane ['mɛ₁θeɪn] n : metano m

method ['mɛθəd] n : método m

methodical [mə'θɑdɪkəl] adj : metódico — **methodically** adv

Methodist ['mɛθədɪst] n : metodista mf — **Methodist** adj

methodology [₁mɛθə'dɑlədʒi] n, pl **-gies** : metodología f

meticulous [mə'tɪkjələs] adj : meticuloso — **meticulously** adv

meticulousness [mə'tɪkjələsnəs] n : meticulosidad f

metric ['mɛtrɪk] or **metrical** [-trɪkəl] adj : métrico

metric system n : sistema m métrico

metro ['mɛtro] n SUBWAY : metro m; subterráneo m Arg, Uru

metronome ['mɛtrə₁no:m] n : metrónomo m

metropolis [mə'trɑpələs] n : metrópoli f, metrópolis f

metropolitan [₁mɛtrə'pɑlətən] adj : metropolitano

mettle ['mɛtəl] n : temple m, valor m ⟨on one's mettle : dispuesto a mostrar su valía⟩

Mexican ['mɛksɪkən] n : mexicano m, -na f — **Mexican** adj

mezzanine ['mɛzə,niːn, ,mɛzə'niːn] n 1 : entrepiso m 2 : primer piso m (de un teatro)

mi ['miː] n : mi m (en el canto)

miasma [maɪ'æzmə] n : miasma m

mica ['maɪkə] n : mica f

mice → **mouse**

micro ['maɪkro] adj : muy pequeño, microscópico

micro- pref : micro-

microbe ['maɪ,kroːb] n : microbio m

microbiology [,maɪkrobaɪ'ɑlədʒi] n : microbiología f

microchip ['maɪkro,tʃɪp] n : microchip m

microcomputer ['maɪkrokəm,pjuːtər] n : microcomputadora f

microcosm ['maɪkro,kɑzəm] n : microcosmos m

microfilm ['maɪkro,fɪlm] n : microfilm m

micrometer ['maɪkro,miːtər] n : micrómetro m

microorganism [,maɪkro'ɔrgə,nɪzəm] n : microorganismo m, microbio m

microphone ['maɪkrə,foːn] n : micrófono m

microprocessor [,maɪkro,prɑ'sɛsər] n : microprocesador m

microscope ['maɪkrə,skoːp] n : microscopio m

microscopic [,maɪkrə'skɑpɪk] adj : microscópico

microwave ['maɪkrə,weɪv] n 1 : microonda f 2 or **microwave oven** : microondas m

mid ['mɪd] adj : medio ⟨mid morning : a media mañana⟩ ⟨in mid-August : a mediados de agosto⟩ ⟨in mid ocean : en alta mar⟩

midair ['mɪd'ær] n in ~ : en el aire ⟨to catch in midair : agarrar al vuelo⟩

midday ['mɪd'deɪ] n NOON : mediodía m

middle[1] ['mɪdəl] adj 1 CENTRAL : medio, del medio, de en medio 2 INTERMEDIATE : intermedio, mediano ⟨middle age : la mediana edad⟩

middle[2] n 1 CENTER : medio m, centro m ⟨fold it down the middle : dóblalo por la mitad⟩ 2 in the middle of : en medio de (un espacio), a mitad de (una actividad) ⟨in the middle of the month : a mediados del mes⟩

Middle Ages npl : Edad f Media

middle-class adj : de clase media

middle class n : clase f media

middleman ['mɪdəl,mæn] n, pl -men [-mən, -,mɛn] : intermediario m, -ria f

middle school n : colegio m para niños de 10 a 14 años

middling ['mɪdlɪŋ, -lən] adj 1 MEDIUM, MIDDLE : mediano 2 MEDIOCRE : mediocre, regular

midfielder ['mɪd,fiːldər] n : mediocampista mf

midge ['mɪdʒ] n : mosca f pequeña

midget ['mɪdʒət] n 1 sometimes offensive : enano m, -na f (persona) sometimes offensive 2 : cosa f diminuta

midland ['mɪdlənd, -,lænd] n : región f central (de un país)

midnight ['mɪd,naɪt] n : medianoche f

midpoint ['mɪd,pɔɪnt] n : punto m medio, término m medio

midriff ['mɪd,rɪf] n : diafragma m

midshipman ['mɪdʃɪpmən, ,mɪd'ʃɪp-] n, pl -men [-mən, -,mɛn] : guardiamarina m

midst[1] ['mɪdst] n : medio m ⟨in our midst : entre nosotros⟩ ⟨in the midst of : en medio de⟩

midst[2] prep : entre

midstream ['mɪd'striːm, -,striːm] n : medio m de la corriente ⟨in the midstream of his career : en medio de su carrera⟩

midsummer ['mɪd'sʌmər, -,sʌ-] n : pleno verano m

midtown ['mɪd,taʊn] n : centro m (de una ciudad)

midway ['mɪd,weɪ] adv HALFWAY : a mitad de camino

midweek ['mɪd,wiːk] n : medio m de la semana ⟨in midweek : a media semana⟩

midwife ['mɪd,waɪf] n, pl -wives [-,waɪvz] : partera f, comadrona f

midwinter ['mɪd'wɪntər, -,wɪn-] n : pleno invierno m

midyear ['mɪd,jɪr] n : medio m del año ⟨at midyear : a mediados del año⟩

mien ['miːn] n : aspecto m, porte m, semblante m

miff ['mɪf] vt : ofender

might[1] ['maɪt] (used to express permission or possibility or as a polite alternative to may) → may : it might be true : podría ser verdad ⟨might I speak with Sarah? : ¿se puede hablar con Sarah?⟩

might[2] n : fuerza f, poder m

mightily ['maɪtɪli] adv : con mucha fuerza, poderosamente

mighty[1] ['maɪti] adv VERY : muy ⟨mighty good : muy bueno, buenísimo⟩

mighty[2] adj mightier; -est 1 POWERFUL : poderoso, potente 2 GREAT : grande, imponente

migraine ['maɪ,greɪn] n : jaqueca f, migraña f

migrant ['maɪgrənt] n : trabajador m, -dora f ambulante

migrate ['maɪ,greɪt] vi -grated; -grating : emigrar, migrar

migration [maɪ'greɪʃən] n : migración f

migratory ['maɪgrə,tori] adj : migratorio

mike ['maɪk] n fam → **microphone**

mild ['maɪld] adj 1 GENTLE : apacible, suave ⟨a mild disposition : un temperamento suave⟩ 2 LIGHT : leve, ligero ⟨a mild punishment : un castigo leve, un castigo poco severo⟩ 3 TEMPERATE : templado (dícese del clima) — **mildly** adv

mildew[1] ['mɪl,duː, -,djuː] vi : enmohecerse

mildew[2] n : moho m

mildness ['maɪldnəs] n : suavidad f

mile ['maɪl] n : milla f

mileage ['maɪlɪdʒ] n 1 ALLOWANCE : viáticos mpl (pagados por milla recorrida) 2 : distancia f recorrida (en millas), kilometraje m

milestone ['maɪl,stoːn] n LANDMARK : hito m, jalón m ⟨a milestone in his life : un hito en su vida⟩

milieu [miːl'juː, -'jø] n, pl -lieus or -lieux

[-'ju:z, -'jə] SURROUNDINGS : entorno m, medio m, ambiente m

militancy ['mɪlətəntsi] n, pl **-cies** : militancia f

militant¹ ['mɪlətənt] adj : militante, combativo

militant² n : militante mf

militarism ['mɪlətə,rɪzəm] n : militarismo m

militaristic [,mɪlətə'rɪstɪk] adj : militarista

militarize ['mɪlətə,raɪz] vt **-rized; -rizing** : militarizar

military¹ ['mɪlə,teri] adj : militar

military² n **the military** : las fuerzas armadas

militia [mə'lɪʃə] n : milicia f

milk¹ ['mɪlk] vt **1** : ordeñar (una vaca, etc.) **2** EXPLOIT : explotar

milk² n **1** : leche f **2** : leche f (de una planta)

milk chocolate n : chocolate m con leche

milkman ['mɪlk,mæn, -mən] n, pl **-men** [-mən, -,mɛn] : lechero m

milk of magnesia n : leche f de magnesia

milk shake n : batido m, licuado m

milkweed ['mɪlk,wi:d] n : algodoncillo m

milky ['mɪlki] adj **milkier; -est** : lechoso

Milky Way n : Vía f Láctea

mill¹ ['mɪl] vt : moler (granos), acordonar (monedas) — vi **to mill about/around** : arremolinarse

mill² n **1** : molino m (para moler granos) **2** FACTORY : fábrica f ⟨textile mill : fábrica textil⟩ **3** GRINDER : molinillo m

millennial¹ [mə'lɛniəl] adj : milenario

millennial² n : milenario m, -ria f : milenial mf (persona nacida entre 1980 y 2000)

millennium [mə'lɛniəm] n, pl **-nia** [-niə] or **-niums** : milenio m

miller ['mɪlər] n : molinero m, -ra f

millet ['mɪlət] n : mijo m

milligram ['mɪlə,græm] n : miligramo m

milliliter ['mɪlə,li:tər] n : mililitro m

millimeter ['mɪlə,mi:tər] n : milímetro m

milliner ['mɪlənər] n : sombrerero m, -ra f (de señoras)

millinery ['mɪlə,nɛri] n : sombreros mpl de señora

million¹ ['mɪljən] adj **a million** : un millón de

million² n, pl **millions** or **million** : millón m

millionaire [,mɪljə'nær, 'mɪljə,nær] n : millonario m, -ria f

millionth¹ ['mɪljənθ] adj : millonésimo

millionth² n : millonésimo m

millipede ['mɪlə,pi:d] n : milpiés m

millstone ['mɪl,sto:n] n : rueda f de molino, muela f

mime¹ ['maɪm] v **mimed; miming** vt MIMIC : imitar, remedar — vi PANTOMIME : hacer la mímica

mime² n **1** : mimo mf **2** PANTOMIME : pantomima f

mimeograph ['mɪmiə,græf] n : mimeógrafo m

mimic¹ ['mɪmɪk] vt **-icked; -icking** : imitar, remedar

mimic² n : imitador m, -dora f

mimicry ['mɪmɪkri] n, pl **-ries** : mímica f, imitación f

minaret ['mɪnə'ret] n : alminar m, minarete m

mince ['mɪnts] v **minced; mincing** vt **1** CHOP : picar, moler (carne) **2 not to mince one's words** : no tener un pelos en la lengua — vi : caminar de manera afectada

mincemeat ['mɪnts,mi:t] n : mezcla f de fruta picada, sebo, y especias

mind¹ ['maɪnd] vt **1** TEND : cuidar, atender ⟨mind the children : cuida a los niños⟩ **2** OBEY : obedecer **3** : preocuparse por, sentirse molestado por ⟨I don't mind his jokes : sus bromas no me molestan⟩ ⟨if you don't mind my saying so : si me permites⟩ ⟨never mind him : no le hagas caso⟩ **4** : tener cuidado con ⟨mind the ladder! : ¡cuidado con la escalera!⟩ **5 never mind** LET ALONE : ni mucho menos, (y) menos aún ⟨I can barely understand it, never mind explain it : apenas puedo entenderlo, ni mucho menos explicarlo⟩ — vi **1** OBEY : obedecer **2** CARE : importarle a uno ⟨I don't mind : no me importa, me es igual⟩ — **3 never mind** : no importa, no se preocupe

mind² n **1** : mente f ⟨the mind and the body : la mente y el cuerpo⟩ ⟨it's all in your mind : es pura imaginación tuya⟩ ⟨what's on your mind? : ¿qué te preocupa?⟩ **2** INTENTION : intención f, propósito m **3** : razón f ⟨he's out of his mind : está loco⟩ **4** OPINION : opinión f ⟨in/to my mind : a mi parecer⟩ **5** INTELLECT : mente f ⟨she has a brilliant mind : tiene una mente brillante⟩ **6** ATTENTION : atención f ⟨pay him no mind : no le hagas caso⟩ **7 at/in the back of one's mind** : en el fondo **8 great minds think alike** : los genios pensamos igual **9 state of mind** : estado m de ánimo **10 to be of one mind** or **to be of the same mind** : estar de acuerdo **11 to be of two minds about** : estar indeciso sobre **12 to blow someone's mind** fam : maravillar a alguien **13 to call/bring to mind** : recordar, traer a la memoria **14 to change one's mind** : cambiar de opinión **15 to change someone's mind** : hacerle a alguien cambiar de opinión **16 to come/leap/spring to mind** : ocurrírsele a alguien **17 to cross someone's mind** : pasársele a alguien por la cabeza **18 to give someone a piece of one's mind** : cantarle las cuarentas a alguien **19 to have a good mind to** or **to have half a mind to** : tener ganas de (regañar a alguien, etc.) **20 to have a mind of one's own** : ser independiente **21 to have in mind** : tener (algo, a alguien) en mente, tener pensado (hacer algo) ⟨what did you have in mind? : ¿qué tenías en mente?⟩ **22 to have one's mind set on** : estar empeñado en **23 to keep an open mind** : mantener la mente abierta **24 to keep/bear in mind** : tener en cuenta **25 to keep**

one's mind on : concentrarse en **26 to lose one's mind** : perder la razón **27 to make up one's mind** : decidirse **28 to put/set one's mind to** : poner empeño en **29 to put someone in mind of something** : recordarle algo a alguien **30 to speak one's mind** : hablar sin rodeos **31 to take a load/weight off one's mind** : quitarse un peso de encima

minded ['maɪndəd] *adj* (*used in combination*) ⟨narrow-minded : de mentalidad cerrada⟩ ⟨health-minded : preocupado por la salud⟩ **2** INCLINED : inclinado

mindful ['maɪndfəl] *adj* AWARE : consciente — **mindfully** *adv*

mindless ['maɪndləs] *adj* **1** SENSELESS : estúpido, sin sentido ⟨mindless violence : violencia sin sentido⟩ **2** HEEDLESS : inconsciente

mindlessly ['maɪndləsli] *adv* **1** SENSELESSLY : sin sentido **2** HEEDLESSLY : inconscientemente

mine¹ ['maɪn] *vt* **mined; mining 1** : extraer (oro, etc.) **2** : minar (con artefactos explosivos)

mine² *n* : mina *f* ⟨gold mine : mina de oro⟩

mine³ *pron* : mío ⟨that one's mine : ése es el mío, ésa es la mía⟩ ⟨some friends of mine : unos amigos míos⟩

minefield ['maɪn,fi:ld] *n* : campo *m* de minas

miner ['maɪnər] *n* : minero *m*, -ra *f*

mineral ['mɪnərəl] *n* : mineral *m* — **mineral** *adj*

mineralogy [,mɪnə'rɑlədʒi, -'ræ-] *n* : mineralogía *f*

mine shaft → **shaft**

mingle ['mɪŋgəl] *v* **-gled; -gling** *vt* MIX : mezclar — *vi* **1** MIX : mezclarse **2** CIRCULATE : circular

mini- *pref* : mini-

miniature¹ ['mɪniə,tʃʊr, 'mɪnɪ,tʃʊr, -tʃər] *adj* : en miniatura, diminuto

miniature² *n* : miniatura *f*

minibus ['mɪni,bʌs] *n* : microbús *m*; pesera *f Mex*; buseta *f Col, CoRi, Ecua, Ven*

minicomputer ['mɪnikəm,pju:tər] *n* : minicomputadora *f*

minimal ['mɪnəməl] *adj* : mínimo

minimally ['mɪnəməli] *adv* : en grado mínimo

minimize ['mɪnə,maɪz] *vt* **-mized; -mizing 1** : minimizar (un riesgo, etc.) **2** : minimizar (en informática)

minimum¹ ['mɪnəməm] *adj* : mínimo

minimum² *n, pl* **-ma** ['mɪnəmə] *or* **-mums** : mínimo *m*

mining ['maɪnɪŋ] *n* : minería *f*

miniseries ['mɪni,sɪri:z] *n* : miniserie *f*

miniskirt ['mɪni,skərt] *n* : minifalda *f*

minister¹ ['mɪnəstər] *vi* **to minister to** : cuidar (de), atender a

minister² *n* **1** : pastor *m*, -tora *f* (de una iglesia) **2** : ministro *m*, -tra *f* (en política)

ministerial [,mɪnə'stɪriəl] *adj* : ministerial

ministry ['mɪnəstri] *n, pl* **-tries 1** : ministerio *m* (en política) **2** : sacerdocio *m*

(en el catolicismo), clerecía *f* (en el protestantismo)

minivan ['mɪni,væn] *n* : minivan *f*

mink ['mɪŋk] *n, pl* **mink** *or* **minks** : visón *m*

minnow ['mɪno:] *n, pl* **-nows** : pececillo *m* de agua dulce

minor¹ ['maɪnər] *adj* : menor

minor² *n* **1** : menor *mf* (de edad) **2** : asignatura *f* secundaria (de estudios)

minority [mə'nɔrəti, maɪ-] *n, pl* **-ties** : minoría *f*

minstrel ['mɪnstrəl] *n* : juglar *m*, trovador *m* (en el medioevo)

mint¹ ['mɪnt] *vt* : acuñar

mint² *adj* : sin usar ⟨in mint condition : como nuevo⟩

mint³ *n* **1** : menta *f* ⟨mint tea : té de menta⟩ **2** : pastilla *f* de menta **3** : casa *f* de la moneda ⟨the U.S. Mint : la casa de la moneda de los EEUU⟩ **4** FORTUNE : dineral *m*, fortuna *f*

minuet [,mɪnju'et] *n* : minué *m*

minus¹ ['maɪnəs] *n* **1** : cantidad *f* negativa **2 minus sign** : signo *m* de menos

minus² *prep* **1** : menos ⟨four minus two : cuatro menos dos⟩ **2** WITHOUT : sin ⟨minus his hat : sin su sombrero⟩

minuscule *or* **miniscule** ['mɪnəs,kju:l, mɪ'nʌs-] *adj* : minúsculo

minute¹ [maɪ'nu:t, mɪ-, -'nju:t] *adj* **minuter; -est 1** TINY : diminuto, minúsculo **2** DETAILED : minucioso

minute² ['mɪnət] *n* **1** : minuto *m* **2** MOMENT : momento *m* ⟨at any minute : en cualquier momento⟩ **3 minutes** *npl* : actas *fpl* (de una reunión) **4 at the last minute** : a último momento, a última hora **5 hang/hold on a minute** *or* **wait a minute** : espera un momento **6 just a minute** : un momento **7 this minute** : ahora mismo, inmediatamente

minute hand *n* : minutero *m*

minutely [maɪ'nu:tli, mɪ-, -'nju:t-] *adv* : minuciosamente

miracle ['mɪrɪkəl] *n* : milagro *m*

miraculous [mə'rækjələs] *adj* : milagroso — **miraculously** *adv*

mirage [mɪ'rɑʒ, *chiefly Brit* 'mɪr,ɑʒ] *n* : espejismo *m*

mire¹ ['maɪr] *vi* **mired; miring** : atascarse

mire² *n* **1** MUD : barro *m*, lodo *m* **2** : atolladero *m* ⟨stuck in a mire of debt : agobiado por la deuda⟩

mirror¹ ['mɪrər] *vt* : reflejar

mirror² *n* : espejo *m*

mirth ['mərθ] *n* : alegría *f*, regocijo *m*

mirthful ['mərθfəl] *adj* : alegre, regocijado

misadventure [,mɪsəd'vɛntʃər] *n* : malaventura *f*, desventura *f*

misanthrope ['mɪsən,θro:p] *n* : misántropo *m*, -pa *f*

misanthropic [,mɪsən'θrɑpɪk] *adj* : misantrópico

misanthropy [mɪ'sænθrəpi] *n* : misantropía *f*

misapprehend [,mɪs,æprə'hɛnd] *vt* : entender mal

misapprehension [,mɪs,æprə'hɛntʃən] *n* : malentendido *m*

misappropriate [ˌmɪsəˈproːpriˌeɪt] *vt* -ated; -ating : malversar

misappropriation [ˌmɪsəˌproːpriˈeɪʃən] *n* : malversación *f*

misbegotten [ˌmɪsbɪˈgatən] *adj* **1** ILLEGITIMATE : ilegítimo **2** : mal concebido ⟨misbegotten laws : leyes mal concebidas⟩

misbehave [ˌmɪsbɪˈheɪv] *vi* -haved; -having : portarse mal

misbehavior [ˌmɪsbɪˈheɪvjər] *n* : mala conducta *f*

miscalculate [mɪsˈkælkjəˌleɪt] *v* -lated; -lating : calcular mal

miscalculation [mɪsˌkælkjəˈleɪʃən] *n* : error *m* de cálculo, mal cálculo *m*

miscarriage [ˌmɪsˈkærɪʤ, ˈmɪsˌkærɪʤ] *n* **1** : aborto *m* **2** FAILURE : fracaso *m*, malogro *m* ⟨a miscarriage of justice : una injusticia, un error judicial⟩

miscarry [ˌmɪsˈkæri, ˈmɪsˌkæri] *vi* -ried; -rying **1** ABORT : abortar **2** FAIL : malograrse, fracasar

miscellaneous [ˌmɪsəˈleɪniəs] *adj* : misceláneo

miscellany [ˈmɪsəˌleɪni] *n*, *pl* -nies : miscelánea *f*

mischance [mɪsˈtʃænts] *n* : desgracia *f*, infortunio *m*, mala suerte *f*

mischief [ˈmɪstʃəf] *n* : diabluras *fpl*, travesuras *fpl*

mischievous [ˈmɪstʃəvəs] *adj* : travieso, pícaro

mischievously [ˈmɪstʃəvəsli] *adv* : de manera traviesa

misconception [ˌmɪskənˈsɛpʃən] *n* : concepto *m* erróneo, idea *f* falsa

misconduct [mɪsˈkɑndəkt] *n* : mala conducta *f*

misconstrue [ˌmɪskənˈstruː] *vt* -strued; -struing : malinterpretar

misdeed [mɪsˈdiːd] *n* : fechoría *f*

misdemeanor [ˌmɪsdɪˈmiːnər] *n* : delito *m* menor

miser [ˈmaɪzər] *n* : avaro *m*, -ra *f*; tacaño *m*, -ña *f*

miserable [ˈmɪzərəbəl] *adj* **1** UNHAPPY : triste, desdichado **2** WRETCHED : miserable, desgraciado ⟨a miserable hut : una choza miserable⟩ **3** UNPLEASANT : desagradable, malo ⟨miserable weather : tiempo malísimo⟩ **4** CONTEMPTIBLE : despreciable, mísero ⟨for a miserable $10 : por unos míseros diez dólares⟩

miserably [ˈmɪzərəbli] *adv* **1** SADLY : tristemente **2** WRETCHEDLY : miserablemente, lamentablemente **3** UNFORTUNATELY : desgraciadamente

miserly [ˈmaɪzərli] *adj* : avaro, tacaño

misery [ˈmɪzəri] *n*, *pl* -eries : miseria *f*, sufrimiento *m*

misfire [mɪsˈfaɪr] *vi* -fired; -firing : fallar

misfit [ˈmɪsˌfɪt] *n* : inadaptado *m*, -da *f*

misfortune [mɪsˈfɔrtʃən] *n* : desgracia *f*, desventura *f*, infortunio *m*

misgiving [mɪsˈgɪvɪŋ] *n* : duda *f*, recelo *m*

misguided [mɪsˈgaɪdəd] *adj* : desacertado, equivocado, mal informado

mishap [ˈmɪsˌhæp] *n* : contratiempo *m*, percance *m*, accidente *m*

misinform [ˌmɪsɪnˈfɔrm] *vt* : informar mal

misinterpret [ˌmɪsɪnˈtərprət] *vt* : malinterpretar

misinterpretation [ˌmɪsɪnˌtərprəˈteɪʃən] *n* : mala interpretación *f*, malentendido *m*

misjudge [mɪsˈʤʌʤ] *vt* -judged; -judging : juzgar mal

mislay [mɪsˈleɪ] *vt* -laid [-ˈleɪd]; -laying : extraviar, perder

mislead [mɪsˈliːd] *vt* -led [-ˈlɛd]; -leading : engañar

misleading [mɪsˈliːdɪŋ] *adj* : engañoso

mismanage [mɪsˈmænɪʤ] *vt* -aged; -aging : administrar mal

mismanagement [mɪsˈmænɪʤmənt] *n* : mala administración *f*

misnomer [mɪsˈnoːmər] *n* : nombre *m* inapropiado

misogynist [mɪˈsɑʤənɪst] *n* : misógino *m*

misogyny [məˈsɑʤəni] *n* : misoginia *f*

misplace [mɪsˈpleɪs] *vt* -placed; -placing : extraviar, perder

misprint [ˈmɪsˌprɪnt, mɪsˈ-] *n* : errata *f*, error *m* de imprenta

mispronounce [ˌmɪsprəˈnaʊnts] *vt* -nounced; -nouncing : pronunciar mal

mispronunciation [ˌmɪsprəˌnʌntsiˈeɪʃən] *n* : pronunciación *f* incorrecta

misquote [mɪsˈkwoːt] *vt* -quoted; -quoting : citar incorrectamente

misread [mɪsˈriːd] *vt* -read [-ˈrɛd]; -reading **1** : leer mal ⟨she misread the sentence : leyó mal la frase⟩ **2** MISUNDERSTAND : malinterpretar ⟨they misread his intention : malinterpretaron su intención⟩

misrepresent [ˌmɪsˌrɛprɪˈzɛnt] *vt* : distorsionar, falsear, tergiversar

miss¹ [ˈmɪs] *vt* **1** : errar, faltar ⟨to miss the target : no dar en el blanco⟩ **2** : no encontrar, perder ⟨they missed each other : no se encontraron⟩ ⟨I missed the plane : perdí el avión⟩ **3** : echar de menos, extrañar ⟨we miss him a lot : lo echamos mucho de menos⟩ **4** OVERLOOK : pasar por alto ⟨to miss the point : no entender algo⟩ ⟨you can't miss it : no puedes dejar de verlo⟩ **5** : no enterarse de (una noticia), no oír (palabras habladas) **6** : perderse (una oportunidad, etc.) **7** PASS UP : pasar por alto **8** : faltar a (una reunión, etc.) **9** AVOID : evitar ⟨they just missed hitting the tree : por muy poco chocan contra el árbol⟩ **10** OMIT : saltarse ⟨he missed breakfast : se saltó el desayuno⟩ **11 to be missing** : faltarle (algo a uno) ⟨he's missing two teeth : le faltan dos dientes⟩ **12 to miss out on** : perderse (una oportunidad, etc.)

miss² *n* **1** : fallo *m* (de un tiro, etc.) **2** FAILURE : fracaso *m* **3** : señorita *f* ⟨Miss Jones called us : nos llamó la señorita Jones⟩ ⟨excuse me, miss : perdone, señorita⟩

misshapen [mɪsˈʃeɪpən] *adj* : deforme

missile [ˈmɪsəl] *n* **1** : misil *m* ⟨guided missile : misil guiado⟩ **2** PROJECTILE : proyectil *m*

missing [ˈmɪsɪŋ] *adj* **1** ABSENT : ausente ⟨who's missing? : ¿quién falta?⟩ **2** LOST

: perdido, desaparecido ⟨missing persons : los desaparecidos⟩

mission ['mɪʃən] *n* **1** : misión *f* (mandada por una iglesia) **2** DELEGATION : misión *f*, delegación *f*, embajada *f* **3** TASK : misión *f*

missionary¹ ['mɪʃəˌnɛri] *adj* : misionero

missionary² *n, pl* **-aries** : misionero *m*, -ra *f*

missive ['mɪsɪv] *n* : misiva *f*

misspell [mɪs'spɛl] *vt* : escribir mal

misspelling [mɪs'spɛlɪŋ] *n* : falta *f* de ortografía

misstep ['mɪsˌstɛp] *n* : traspié *m*, tropezón *m*

mist ['mɪst] *n* **1** HAZE : neblina *f*, niebla *f* **2** SPRAY : rocío *m*

mistake¹ [mɪ'steɪk] *vt* **-took** [-'stʊk]; **-taken** [-'steɪkən]; **-taking 1** MISINTERPRET : malinterpretar **2** CONFUSE : confundir ⟨he mistook her for Clara : la confundió con Clara⟩

mistake² *n* **1** MISUNDERSTANDING : malentendido *m*, confusión *f* **2** ERROR : error *m* ⟨I made a mistake : me equivoqué, cometí un error⟩

mistaken [mɪ'steɪkən] *adj* WRONG : equivocado — **mistakenly** *adv*

mister ['mɪstər] *n* : señor *m* ⟨watch out, mister : cuidado, señor⟩

mistiness [ˈmɪstinəs] *n* 1 : nebulosidad *f*

mistletoe ['mɪsəlˌtoː] *n* : muérdago *m*

mistreat [mɪs'triːt] *vt* : maltratar

mistreatment [mɪs'triːtmənt] *n* : maltrato *m*, abuso *m*

mistress ['mɪstrəs] *n* **1** : dueña *f*, señora *f* (de una casa) **2** LOVER : amante *f*

mistrust¹ [mɪs'trʌst] *vt* : desconfiar de

mistrust² *n* : desconfianza *f*

mistrustful [mɪs'trʌstfəl] *adj* : desconfiado

misty ['mɪsti] *adj* **mistier; -est 1** : neblinoso, nebuloso **2** TEARFUL : lloroso

misunderstand [ˌmɪsˌʌndərˈstænd] *vt* **-stood** [-'stʊd]; **-standing 1** : entender mal **2** MISINTERPRET : malinterpretar ⟨don't misunderstand me : no me malinterpretes⟩

misunderstanding [ˌmɪsˌʌndərˈstændɪŋ] *n* **1** MISINTERPRETATION : malentendido *m* **2** DISAGREEMENT, QUARREL : disputa *f*, discusión *f*

misuse¹ [mɪs'juːz] *vt* **-used; -using 1** : emplear mal **2** ABUSE, MISTREAT : abusar de, maltratar

misuse² [mɪs'juːs] *n* **1** : mal empleo *m*, mal uso *m* **2** WASTE : derroche *m*, despilfarro *m* **3** ABUSE : abuso *m*

mite ['maɪt] *n* **1** : ácaro *m* **2** BIT : poco *m* ⟨a mite tired : un poquito cansado⟩

miter *or* **mitre** ['maɪtər] *n* **1** : mitra *f* (de un obispo) **2** *or* **miter joint** : inglete *m*

mitigate ['mɪtəˌgeɪt] *vt* **-gated; -gating** : mitigar, aliviar

mitigation [ˌmɪtəˈgeɪʃən] *n* : mitigación *f*, alivio *m*

mitosis [maɪ'toːsɪs] *n, pl* **-toses** [-ˌsiːz] : mitosis *f*

mitt ['mɪt] *n* **1** : manopla *f*, guante *m* (de béisbol) **2** HAND : mano *f*, manaza *f*

mitten ['mɪtən] *n* : manopla *f*

mix¹ ['mɪks] *vt* **1** COMBINE : mezclar **2** STIR : remover, revolver **3 to mix up** CONFUSE : confundir **4 to mix up** COMBINE : mezclar — *vi* : mezclarse

mix² *n* : mezcla *f*

mixed *adj* : mezclado, variado

mixed–up *adj* **1** CONFUSED, TROUBLED : confundido, con problemas **2** CONFUSING : confuso

mixer ['mɪksər] *n* **1** : batidora *f* (de la cocina) **2 cement mixer** : hormigonera *f*

mixture ['mɪkstʃər] *n* : mezcla *f*

mix–up ['mɪksˌʌp] *n* CONFUSION : confusión *f*, lío *m fam*

mnemonic [nɪ'manɪk] *adj* : mnemónico

moan¹ ['moːn] *vi* : gemir

moan² *n* : gemido *m*

moat ['moːt] *n* : foso *m*

mob¹ ['mab] *vt* **mobbed; mobbing 1** ATTACK : atacar en masa **2** HOUND : acosar, rodear

mob² *n* **1** THRONG : multitud *f*, turba *f*, muchedumbre *f* **2** GANG : pandilla *f*

mobile¹ ['moːbəl, -,biːl, -,baɪl] *adj* : móvil ⟨mobile home : caravana, casa rodante⟩

mobile² ['moːˌbiːl] *n* : móvil *m*

mobile phone → **cell phone**

mobility [moˈbɪlət͡ʃi] *n* : movilidad *f*

mobilize ['moːbəˌlaɪz] *vt* **-lized; -lizing** : movilizar

moccasin ['makəsən] *n* **1** : mocasín *m* **2** *or* **water moccasin** : serpiente *f* venenosa de Norteamérica

mocha ['moːkə] *n* **1** : mezcla *f* de café y chocolate **2** : color *m* chocolate

mock¹ ['mak, 'mɔk] *vt* **1** RIDICULE : burlarse de, mofarse de **2** MIMIC : imitar, remedar (de manera burlona)

mock² *adj* **1** SIMULATED : simulado **2** PHONY : falso

mockery ['makəri, 'mɔ-] *n, pl* **-eries 1** JEER TAUNT : burla *f*, mofa *f* ⟨to make a mockery of : burlarse de⟩ **2** FAKE : imitación *f* (burlona)

mockingbird ['makɪŋˌbərd, 'mɔ-] *n* : sinsonte *m*

mode ['moːd] *n* **1** FORM : modo *m*, forma *f* **2** MANNER : modo *m*, manera *f*, estilo *m* **3** FASHION : moda *f*

model¹ ['madəl] *v* **-eled** *or* **-elled; -eling** *or* **-elling** *vt* SHAPE : modelar — *vi* : trabajar de modelo

model² *adj* **1** EXEMPLARY : modelo, ejemplar ⟨a model student : un estudiante modelo⟩ **2** MINIATURE : en miniatura

model³ *n* **1** PATTERN : modelo *m* **2** MINIATURE : modelo *m*, miniatura *f* **3** EXAMPLE : modelo *m*, ejemplo *m* **4** MANNEQUIN : modelo *mf* **5** DESIGN : modelo *m* ⟨the '97 model : el modelo '97⟩

modem ['moːdəm, -ˌdɛm] *n* : módem *m*

moderate¹ ['madəˌreɪt] *v* **-ated; -ating** *vt* **1** : moderar, temperar — *vi* CALM : moderarse, calmarse **2** : fungir como moderador (en un debate, etc.)

moderate² ['madərət] *adj* : moderado

moderate³ ['madərət] *n* : moderado *m*, -da *f*

moderately ['madərətli] *adv* 1 : con moderación 2 FAIRLY : medianamente

moderation [,madə'reɪʃən] *n* : moderación *f*

moderator ['madə,reɪtər] *n* : moderador *m*, -dora *f*

modern ['madərn] *adj* : moderno

modernism ['madər,nɪzəm] *n* : modernismo *m*

modernist ['madərnɪst] *n* : modernista *mf* — **modernist** *adj*

modernity [mə'dərnəti] *n* : modernidad *f*

modernization [,madərnə'zeɪʃən] *n* : modernización *f*

modernize ['madər,naɪz] *v* -ized; -izing *vt* : modernizar — *vi* : modernizarse

modest ['madəst] *adj* 1 HUMBLE : modesto 2 DEMURE : recatado, pudoroso 3 MODERATE : modesto, moderado — **modestly** *adv*

modesty ['madəsti] *n* : modestia *f*

modicum ['madɪkəm] *n* : mínimo *m*, pizca *f*

modification [,madəfə'keɪʃən] *n* : modificación *f*

modifier ['madə,faɪər] *n* : modificante *m*, modificador *m*

modify ['madə,faɪ] *vt* -fied; -fying : modificar, calificar (en gramática)

modish ['mo:dɪʃ] *adj* STYLISH : a la moda, de moda

modular ['madʒələr] *adj* : modular

modulate ['madʒə,leɪt] *vt* -lated; -lating : modular

modulation [,madʒə'leɪʃən] *n* : modulación *f*

module ['madʒu:l] *n* : módulo *m*

mogul ['mo:gəl] *n* : magnate *mf*; potentado *m*, -da *f*

moist ['mɔɪst] *adj* : húmedo

moisten ['mɔɪsən] *vt* : humedecer

moistness ['mɔɪstnəs] *n* : humedad *f*

moisture ['mɔɪstʃər] *n* : humedad *f*

moisturize ['mɔɪstʃə,raɪz] *vt* -ized; -izing : humedecer (el aire), hidratar (la piel)

moisturizer ['mɔɪstʃə,raɪzər] *n* : crema *f* hidratante, crema *f* humectante

molar ['mo:lər] *n* : muela *f*, molar *m*

molasses [mə'læsəz] *n* : melaza *f*

mold[1] ['mo:ld] *vt* : moldear, formar (carácter, etc.) — *vi* : enmohecerse ⟨the bread will mold : el pan se enmohecerá⟩

mold[2] *n* 1 FORM : molde *m* ⟨to break the mold : romper el molde⟩ 2 FUNGUS : moho *m*

molder ['mo:ldər] *vi* CRUMBLE : desmoronarse

molding ['mo:ldɪŋ] *n* : moldura *f* (en arquitectura)

moldy ['mo:ldi] *adj* **moldier; -est** : mohoso

mole ['mo:l] *n* 1 : lunar *m* (en la piel) 2 : topo *m* (animal)

molecule ['malɪ,kju:l] *n* : molécula *f* — **molecular** [mə'lɛkjələr] *adj*

molehill ['mo:l,hɪl] *n* **to make a mountain out of a molehill** : ahogarse en un vaso de agua

molest [mə'lɛst] *vt* 1 ANNOY, DISTURB : molestar 2 : abusar (sexualmente)

mollify ['malə,faɪ] *vt* -fied; -fying : apaciguar, aplacar

mollusk *or* **mollusc** ['maləsk] *n* : molusco *m*

mollycoddle ['mali,kadəl] *vt* -dled; -dling PAMPER : consentir, mimar

molt ['mo:lt] *vi* : mudar, hacer la muda

molten ['mo:ltən] *adj* : fundido

mom ['mam, 'mʌm] *n* : mamá *f*

moment ['mo:mənt] *n* 1 INSTANT : momento *m* ⟨one moment, please : un momento, por favor⟩ 2 TIME : momento *m* ⟨from that moment : desde entonces⟩ 3 **at any moment** : de un momento a otro 4 **at the moment** : de momento, actualmente 5 **for the moment** : de momento, por el momento 6 **the moment of truth** : la hora de la verdad

momentarily [,mo:mən'tɛrəli] *adv* 1 : momentáneamente 2 SOON : dentro de poco, pronto

momentary ['mo:mən,tɛri] *adj* : momentáneo

momentous [mo'mɛntəs] *adj* : de suma importancia, fatídico

momentum [mo'mɛntəm] *n, pl* -ta [-tə] *or* -tums 1 : momento *m* (en física) 2 IMPETUS : ímpetu *m*, impulso *m*

mommy ['mami, 'mʌ-] *n* : mami *f*

monarch ['ma,nark, -,nərk] *n* : monarca *mf*

monarchist ['ma,narkɪst, -nər-] *n* : monárquico *m*, -ca *f*

monarchy ['ma,narki, -nər-] *n, pl* -chies : monarquía *f*

monastery ['manə,stɛri] *n, pl* -teries : monasterio *m*

monastic [mə'næstɪk] *adj* : monástico — **monastically** [-tɪkli] *adv*

Monday ['mʌn,deɪ, -di] *n* : lunes *m* ⟨today is Monday : hoy es lunes⟩ ⟨(on) Monday : el lunes⟩ ⟨(on) Mondays : los lunes⟩ ⟨last Monday : el lunes pasado⟩ ⟨next Monday : el lunes que viene⟩ ⟨every other Monday : cada dos lunes⟩ ⟨Monday afternoon/morning : lunes por la tarde/mañana⟩

monetary ['manə,tɛri, 'mʌnə-] *adj* : monetario

money ['mʌni] *n, pl* -eys *or* -ies ['mʌniz] 1 : dinero *m*, plata *f* ⟨to make/lose money : ganar/perder dinero⟩ 2 **monies** *npl* : sumas *fpl* de dinero 3 **for my money** : en mi opinión, para mí 4 **money talks** : poderoso caballero es don Dinero 5 **on the money** : exacto, correcto

money changer [-'tʃeɪndʒər] *n* : cambista *mf* (de dinero)

moneyed ['mʌnid] *adj* : adinerado

moneylender ['mʌni,lɛndər] *n* : prestamista *mf*

money order *n* : giro *m* postal

Mongol ['maŋgəl, -,go:l] → **Mongolian**

Mongolian [man'go:liən, maŋ-] *n* : mongol *m*, -gola *f* — **Mongolian** *adj*

mongoose ['maŋ,gu:s, 'man-] *n, pl* -gooses : mangosta *f*

mongrel ['maŋgrəl, 'man-] *n* 1 : perro *m* mestizo, perro *m* corriente *Mex* 2 HYBRID : híbrido *m*

monitor · more

monitor¹ ['mɑnətər] *vt* : controlar, monitorear

monitor² *n* **1** : ayudante *mf* (en una escuela) **2** : monitor *m* (de una computadora, etc.)

monk ['mʌŋk] *n* : monje *m*

monkey¹ ['mʌŋki] *vi* **-keyed; -keying 1 to monkey around** : hacer payasadas, payasear **2 to monkey with** : juguetear con

monkey² *n, pl* **-keys** : mono *m*, -na *f*

monkeyshines ['mʌŋki,ʃaɪnz] *npl* PRANKS : picardías *fpl*, travesuras *fpl*

monkey wrench *n* → **wrench²**

monocle ['mɑnɪkəl] *n* : monóculo *m*

monogamous [mə'nɑgəməs] *adj* : monógamo

monogamy [mə'nɑgəmi] *n* : monogamia *f*

monogram¹ ['mɑnə,græm] *vt* **-grammed; -gramming** : marcar con monograma ⟨monogrammed towels : toallas con monograma⟩

monogram² *n* : monograma *m*

monograph ['mɑnə,græf] *n* : monografía *f*

monolingual [,mɑnə'lɪŋgwəl] *adj* : monolingüe

monolith ['mɑnə,lɪθ] *n* : monolito *m*

monolithic [,mɑnə'lɪθɪk] *adj* : monolítico

monologue ['mɑnə,lɔg] *n* : monólogo *m*

monopolize [mə'nɑpə,laɪz] *vt* **-lized; -lizing** : monopolizar

monopoly [mə'nɑpəli] *n, pl* **-lies** : monopolio *m*

monosyllabic [,mɑnəsə'læbɪk] *adj* : monosilábico

monosyllable ['mɑnə,sɪləbəl] *n* : monosílabo *m*

monotheism ['mɑnəθi:,ɪzəm] *n* : monoteísmo *m* — **monotheist** *n*

monotheistic [,mɑnəθi:'ɪstɪk] *adj* : monoteísta

monotone ['mɑnə,to:n] *n* : voz *f* monótona

monotonous [mə'nɑtənəs] *adj* : monótono — **monotonously** *adv*

monotony [mə'nɑtəni] *n* : monotonía *f*, uniformidad *f*

monsignor [mɑn'si:njər] *n* : monseñor *m*

monsoon [mɑn'su:n] *n* : monzón *m*

monster ['mɑnstər] *n* : monstruo *m*

monstrosity [mɑn'strɑsəti] *n, pl* **-ties** : monstruosidad *f*

monstrous ['mɑnstrəs] *adj* : monstruoso — **monstrously** *adv*

montage [mɑn'tɑʒ] *n* : montaje *m*

month ['mʌnθ] *n* : mes *m*

monthly¹ ['mʌnθli] *adv* : mensualmente

monthly² *adj* : mensual

monthly³ *n, pl* **-lies** : publicación *f* mensual

monument ['mɑnjəmənt] *n* : monumento *m*

monumental [,mɑnjə'mɛntəl] *adj* : monumental — **monumentally** *adv*

moo¹ ['mu:] *vi* : mugir

moo² *n* : mugido *m*

mood ['mu:d] *n* : humor *m* ⟨to be in a good mood : estar de buen humor⟩ ⟨to be in the mood for : tener ganas de⟩ ⟨to be in no mood for : no estar para⟩

moodiness ['mu:dinəs] *n* **1** SADNESS : melancolía *f*, tristeza *f* **2** : cambios *mpl* de humor, carácter *m* temperamental

moody ['mu:di] *adj* **moodier; -est 1** GLOOMY : melancólico, deprimido **2** TEMPERAMENTAL : temperamental, de humor variable

moon ['mu:n] *n* : luna *f*

moonbeam ['mu:n,bi:m] *n* : rayo *m* de luna

moonlight¹ ['mu:n,laɪt] *vi* : estar pluriempleado

moonlight² *n* : claro *m* de luna, luz *f* de la luna

moonlit ['mu:n,lɪt] *adj* : iluminado por la luna ⟨a moonlit night : una noche de luna⟩

moonshine ['mu:n,ʃaɪn] *n* **1** MOONLIGHT : luz *f* de la luna **2** NONSENSE : disparates *mpl*, tonterías *fpl* **3** : whisky *m* destilado ilegalmente

moor¹ ['mʊr, 'mɔr] *vt* : amarrar

moor² *n* : páramo *m*

Moor ['mʊr] *n* : moro *m*, -ra *f*

mooring ['mʊrɪŋ, 'mɔr-] *n* DOCK : atracadero *m*

Moorish ['mʊrɪʃ] *adj* : moro

moose ['mu:s] *ns & pl* : alce *m* (norteamericano)

moot ['mu:t] *adj* DEBATABLE : discutible

mop¹ ['mɑp] *v* **mopped; mopping** *vt* **1** : trapear **2 to mop up** : limpiar (un líquido) **3 to mop up** FINISH : terminar, acabar — *vi* **1** : trapear el suelo **2 to mop up** FINISH : terminar, acabar

mop² *n* : trapeador *m*

mope ['mo:p] *vi* **moped; moping** : andar deprimido, quedar abatido

moped ['mo:,pɛd] *n* : ciclomotor *m*

moraine [mə'reɪn] *n* : morena *f*

moral¹ ['mɔrəl] *adj* : moral ⟨moral judgment : juicio moral⟩ ⟨moral support : apoyo moral⟩ — **morally** *adv*

moral² *n* **1** : moraleja *f* (de un cuento, etc.) **2 morals** *npl* : moral *f*, moralidad *f*

morale [mə'ræl] *n* : moral *f*

moralist ['mɔrəlɪst] *n* : moralista *mf*

moralistic [,mɔrə'lɪstɪk] *adj* : moralista

morality [mə'ræləti] *n, pl* **-ties** : moralidad *f*

morass [mə'ræs] *n* **1** SWAMP : ciénaga *f*, pantano *m* **2** CONFUSION, MESS : lío *m* *fam*, embrollo *m*

moratorium [,mɔrə'tɔriəm] *n, pl* **-riums** *or* **-ria** [-iə] : moratoria *f*

moray ['mɔr,eɪ, mə'reɪ] *n* : morena *f*

morbid ['mɔrbɪd] *adj* **1** : mórbido, morboso (en medicina) **2** GRUESOME : morboso, horripilante

morbidity [mɔr'bɪdəti] *n, pl* **-ties** : morbosidad *f*

more¹ ['mor] *adv* **1** : más ⟨what more can I say? : ¿qué más puedo decir?⟩ ⟨you need to exercise more : debes hacer más ejercicio⟩ ⟨more important : más importante⟩ ⟨once more : una vez más⟩ ⟨more and more difficult : cada vez más difícil⟩ **2 more or less** : más o menos **3 more than** VERY : muy, bastante ⟨I'm more than happy to help you : te ayudo encantado⟩ **4 more than a little** ⟨I was more than a little surprised : me sorprendió bastante⟩

more² *adj* : más ⟨nothing more than that : nada más que eso⟩ ⟨more than a hundred : más de cien⟩ ⟨more work : más trabajo⟩

more³ *n* : más *m* ⟨the more you eat, the more you want : cuanto más comes, tanto más quieres⟩

more⁴ *pron* **1** : más ⟨more were found : se encontraron más⟩ ⟨I don't want any more : no quiero más⟩ ⟨it costs more : cuesta más⟩ ⟨no more, no less : ni más ni menos⟩ ⟨more and more of them : un número cada vez mayor de ellos⟩ ⟨and what's more : y lo que es más⟩ ⟨we see more of each other now : ahora nos vemos más⟩ **2 more of** : más bien ⟨it's more of a maroon than a red : es más bien granate que rojo⟩

morello [mə'rɛlo] *n* : guinda *f*

moreover [mor'o:vər] *adv* : además

mores ['mor,eɪz, -i:z] *npl* CUSTOMS : costumbres *fpl*, tradiciones *fpl*

morgue ['mɔrg] *n* : morgue *f*

moribund ['mɔrə,bʌnd] *adj* : moribundo

Mormon ['mɔrmən] *n* : mormón *m*, -mona *f* — **Mormon** *adj*

morn ['mɔrn] → **morning**

morning ['mɔrnɪŋ] *n* : mañana *f* ⟨good morning! : ¡buenos días!⟩

morning sickness *n* : náuseas *fpl* matutinas (del embarazo)

Moroccan [mə'rɑkən] *n* : marroquí *mf* — **Moroccan** *adj*

moron ['mɔr,ɑn] *n* **1** *dated, now offensive* : retrasado *m*, -da *f* mental *dated, now offensive* **2** DUNCE : estúpido *m*, -da *f*; tonto *m*, -ta *f*

morose [mə'ro:s] *adj* : hosco, sombrío — **morosely** *adv*

moroseness [mə'ro:snəs] *n* : malhumor *m*

morphine ['mɔr,fi:n] *n* : morfina *f*

morphology [mɔr'fɑlədʒi] *n, pl* **-gies** : morfología *f*

morrow ['mɑro:] *n* : día *m* siguiente

Morse code ['mɔrs] *n* : código *m* morse

morsel ['mɔrsəl] *n* **1** BITE : bocado *m* **2** FRAGMENT : pedazo *m*

mortadella [,mɔrtə'dɛlə] *n* : mortadela *f*

mortal¹ ['mɔrtəl] *adj* : mortal ⟨mortal blow : golpe mortal⟩ ⟨mortal fear : miedo mortal⟩ — **mortally** *adv*

mortal² *n* : mortal *mf*

mortality [mɔr'tæləti] *n* : mortalidad *f*

mortar ['mɔrtər] *n* **1** : mortero *m*, molcajete *m Mex* ⟨mortar and pestle : mortero y maja⟩ **2** : mortero *m* ⟨mortar shell : granada de mortero⟩ **3** CEMENT : mortero *m*, argamasa *f*

mortarboard ['mɔrtər,bord] *n* : bonete *m*, birrete *m*

mortgage¹ ['mɔrgɪdʒ] *vt* **-gaged; -gaging** : hipotecar

mortgage² *n* : hipoteca *f*

mortification [,mɔrtəfə'keɪʃən] *n* **1** : mortificación *f* **2** HUMILIATION : humillación *f*, vergüenza *f*

mortify ['mɔrtə,faɪ] *vt* **-fied; -fying 1** : mortificar (en religión) **2** HUMILIATE : humillar, avergonzar

mortuary ['mɔrtʃə,wɛri] *n, pl* **-aries** FUNERAL HOME : funeraria *f*

mosaic [mo'zeɪk] *n* : mosaico *m*

Moslem ['mɑzləm] → **Muslim**

mosque ['mɑsk] *n* : mezquita *f*

mosquito [mə'ski:to] *n, pl* **-toes** : mosquito *m*, zancudo *m*

moss ['mɔs] *n* : musgo *m*

mossy ['mɔsi] *adj* **mossier; -est** : musgoso

most¹ ['mo:st] *adv* : más ⟨the most interesting book : el libro más interesante⟩ ⟨most certainly : con toda seguridad⟩ ⟨most often : más a menudo⟩

most² *adj* **1** : la mayoría de, la mayor parte de ⟨most people : la mayoría de la gente⟩ **2** GREATEST : más (dícese de los números), mayor (dícese de las cantidades) ⟨the most ability : la mayor capacidad⟩

most³ *n* : más *m*, máximo *m* ⟨the most I can do : lo más que puedo hacer⟩ ⟨he did the most : hizo más que nadie⟩ ⟨three weeks at (the) most : tres semanas como máximo⟩ ⟨to make the most of something : sacar el mejor provecho/partido posible de algo⟩

most⁴ *pron* : la mayoría, la mayor parte ⟨most will go : la mayoría irá⟩ ⟨most of : la mayoría de⟩ ⟨most of the time : la mayor parte del tiempo⟩

mostly ['mo:stli] *adv* MAINLY : en su mayor parte, principalmente

mote ['mo:t] *n* SPECK : mota *f*

motel [mo'tɛl] *n* : motel *m*

moth ['mɔθ] *n* : palomilla *f*, polilla *f*

mothball ['mɔθ,bɔl] *n* : bola *f* de naftalina

mother¹ ['mʌðər] *vt* **1** BEAR : dar a luz **2** PROTECT : cuidar de, proteger

mother² *n* : madre *f*

motherhood ['mʌðər,hʊd] *n* : maternidad *f*

mother-in-law ['mʌðərɪn,lɔ] *n, pl* **mothers-in-law** : suegra *f*

motherland ['mʌðər,lænd] *n* : patria *f*

motherly ['mʌðərli] *adj* : maternal

mother-of-pearl [,mʌðərəv'pərl] *n* : nácar *m*, madreperla *f*

mother-to-be *n* : futura madre *f*

mother tongue *n* : lengua *f* materna

motif [mo'ti:f] *n* : motivo *m*

motion¹ ['mo:ʃən] *vt* : hacerle señas (a alguien) ⟨she motioned us to come in : nos hizo señas para que entráramos⟩

motion² *n* **1** MOVEMENT : movimiento *m* ⟨to set in motion : poner en marcha⟩ **2** PROPOSAL : moción *f* ⟨to second a motion : apoyar una moción⟩

motionless ['mo:ʃənləs] *adj* : inmóvil, quieto

motion picture *n* MOVIE : película *f*

motivate ['mo:tə,veɪt] *vt* **-vated; -vating** : motivar, mover, inducir

motivation [,mo:tə'veɪʃən] *n* : motivación *f*

motive¹ ['mo:tɪv] *adj* : motor ⟨motive power : fuerza motriz⟩

motive² n : motivo m, móvil m

motley ['matli] adj : abigarrado, variopinto

motor¹ ['mo:tər] vi : viajar en coche

motor² n : motor m

motorbike ['mo:tər,baɪk] n : motocicleta f (pequeña), moto f

motorboat ['mo:tər,bo:t] n : bote m a motor, lancha f motora

motorcar ['mo:tər,kɑr] n : automóvil m

motorcycle ['mo:tər,saɪkəl] n : motocicleta f

motorcycling ['mo:tər,saɪklɪŋ] n : motociclismo m

motorcyclist ['mo:tər,saɪklɪst] n : motociclista mf

motorist ['mo:tərɪst] n : automovilista mf, motorista mf

motorized ['mo:tə,raɪzd] adj : motorizado

motor racing n : carreras fpl de coches

motor vehicle → vehicle

mottled ['matəld] adj : manchado, moteado ⟨mottled skin : piel manchada⟩ ⟨a mottled surface : una superficie moteada⟩

motto ['mato] n, pl **-toes** : lema m

mould ['mo:ld] → **mold**

mound ['maund] n 1 PILE : montón m 2 KNOLL : montículo m 3 **burial mound** : túmulo m

mount¹ ['maunt] vt 1 : montar a (un caballo), montar en (una bicicleta), subir a 2 : montar (artillería, etc.) — vi INCREASE : aumentar

mount² n 1 SUPPORT : soporte m 2 HORSE : caballería f, montura f 3 MOUNTAIN : monte m, montaña f

mountain ['mauntən] n 1 : montaña f 2 **to make a mountain out of a molehill → molehill**

mountain bike n : bicicleta f de montaña

mountaineer [,mauntən'ɪr] n : alpinista mf, montañero m, -ra f

mountaineering [,mauntən'ɪrɪŋ] n : montañismo m, alpinismo m

mountainous ['mauntənəs] adj : montañoso

mountaintop ['mauntən,tap] n : cima f, cumbre f

mourn ['morn] vt : llorar (por), lamentar ⟨to mourn the death of : llorar la muerte de⟩ — vi : llorar, estar de luto

mourner ['mornər] n : doliente mf

mournful ['mornfəl] adj 1 SORROWFUL : lloroso, plañidero, triste 2 GLOOMY : deprimente — **mournfully** adv

mourning ['mornɪŋ] n : duelo m, luto m

mouse ['maus] n, pl **mice** ['maɪs] 1 : ratón m, -tona f 2 : ratón m (de una computadora)

mouse pad n : alfombrilla f de/para ratón, almohadilla f de/para ratón

mousetrap ['maus,træp] n : ratonera f

mousse ['mu:s] n : mousse mf

moustache ['mʌ,stæf, mə'stæf] → **mustache**

mouth¹ ['mauð] vt 1 : decir con poca sinceridad, repetir sin comprensión 2 : articular en silencio ⟨she mouthed the words : formó las palabras con los labios⟩

mouth² ['mauθ] n : boca f (de una persona o un animal), entrada f (de un túnel), desembocadura f (de un río)

mouthed ['mauðd, 'mauθt] adj (used in combination) : de boca ⟨a large-mouthed jar : un tarro de boca grande⟩

mouthful ['mauθ,ful] n : bocado m (de comida), bocanada f (de líquido o humo)

mouth organ n → **harmonica**

mouthpiece ['mauθ,pi:s] n : boquilla f (de un instrumento musical)

mouth–to–mouth resuscitation or **mouth–to–mouth** n : respiración f boca a boca, el boca a boca

mouthwash ['mauθ,wɔʃ, -,waʃ] n : enjuague m bucal

mouth–watering ['mauθ,wɔtərɪŋ, -,wɑ-] n : delicioso

movable ['mu:vəbəl] or **moveable** adj : movible, móvil

move¹ ['mu:v] v **moved; moving** vi 1 GO : ir ⟨to move closer : acercarse⟩ ⟨to move forward/back : echarse (hacia adelante/atrás⟩ 2 RELOCATE : mudarse, trasladarse 3 STIR : moverse ⟨don't move! : ¡no te muevas!⟩ 4 ACT : actuar 5 **to move aside** : hacerse a un lado 6 **to move along** PROCEED : circular 7 **to move away** LEAVE : marcharse 8 **to move away** STEP BACK : apartarse 9 **to move heaven and earth** : hacer todo lo posible 10 **to move in** : mudarse (a un lugar) ⟨to move in with someone : irse a vivir con alguien⟩ 11 **to move on** LEAVE : marcharse 12 **to move on** CONTINUE : pasar 13 **to move out** : mudarse (de un lugar) 14 **to move over** : hacer sitio 15 **to move up** : subir — vt 1 : mover ⟨he kept moving his feet : no dejaba de mover los pies⟩ ⟨move it forward/back : muévalo hacia adelante/atrás⟩ ⟨move it over there : ponlo allí⟩ 2 RELOCATE : trasladar 3 INDUCE, PERSUADE : inducir, persuadir, mover 4 TOUCH : conmover ⟨it moved him to tears : lo hizo llorar⟩ 5 PROPOSE : proponer 6 **to move along** : dispersar, hacer circular 7 **to move up** : adelantar (una fecha)

move² n 1 MOVEMENT : movimiento m 2 RELOCATION : mudanza f (de casa), traslado m 3 STEP : paso m ⟨a good move : un paso acertado⟩

movement ['mu:vmənt] n : movimiento m

mover ['mu:vər] n : persona f que hace mudanzas

movie ['mu:vi] n 1 : película f 2 **movies** npl : cine m

movie theater n : cine m

moving ['mu:vɪŋ] adj 1 : en movimiento ⟨a moving target : un blanco móvil⟩ 2 TOUCHING : conmovedor, emocionante

mow¹ ['mo:] vt **mowed; mowed** or **mown** ['mo:n]; **mowing** 1 : cortar (la hierba) 2 **mow down** SHOOT : acribillar

mow² ['mau] n : pajar m

mower ['mo:ər] → **lawn mower**

MP3 [,ɛm,pi:'θri:] n : MP3 m

Mr. ['mɪstər] n, pl **Messrs.** ['mɛsərz] : señor m

Mrs. ['mɪsəz, -səs, esp South 'mɪzəz, -zəs] n, pl **Mesdames** [meɪ'dɑm, -'dæm] : señora f

Ms. ['mɪz] n : señora f, señorita f

much¹ ['mʌtʃ] adv **more** ['mor]; **most** ['mo:st] **1** : mucho ⟨I'm much happier : estoy mucho más contenta⟩ ⟨she talks as much as I do : habla tanto como yo⟩ ⟨do you travel much? : ¿viajas mucho?⟩ ⟨I like it very much : me gusta mucho⟩ ⟨thank you very much : muchas gracias⟩ **2** VERY : muy ⟨he's not much good at golf : no es muy bueno para el golf⟩ **3** NEARLY : casi ⟨the town looks much the same : el pueblo no ha cambiado mucho, el pueblo es casi igual que antes⟩ **4** LONG : mucho ⟨not much before noon : poco antes del mediodía⟩ **5 as much** : lo mismo ⟨she'd do as much for me : haría lo mismo para mí⟩ ⟨I thought as much : ya me lo imaginaba⟩ **6 as much as** : tanto como **7 as much as** NEARLY : casi **8 much as** ALTHOUGH : aunque **9 very much** (used for emphasis) ENTIRELY, UNQUESTIONABLY : totalmente, indudablemente

much² adj **more; most** : mucho ⟨there isn't much difference : no hay mucha diferencia⟩ ⟨he doesn't know much French : no sabe mucho francés⟩ ⟨she wasn't much help : no nos ayudó mucho⟩ ⟨was there much food? : ¿había mucha comida?⟩ ⟨we spent so much money : gastamos tanto dinero⟩ ⟨too much time : demasiado tiempo⟩ ⟨it was all too much for him : no podía con todo⟩

much³ pron **1** : mucho ⟨I don't need much : no necesito mucho⟩ ⟨there was food, but not much : había comida, pero poca cantidad⟩ ⟨I don't see much of them : no los veo mucho⟩ ⟨it doesn't amount to much : no es gran cosa⟩ ⟨much of the time : una buena parte del tiempo⟩ ⟨too much : demasiado⟩ **2 as much as** : tanto como **3 not much of a** ⟨he's not much of a cook : no cocina muy bien⟩ ⟨it wasn't much of a vacation : mis vacaciones no fueron nada especial⟩ **4 not much on** ⟨she's not much on studying : no estudia mucho⟩ ⟨he's not much on looks : no es muy guapo⟩

mucilage ['mju:səlɪdʒ] n : mucílago m

muck ['mʌk] n **1** MANURE : estiércol m **2** DIRT, FILTH : mugre f, suciedad f **3** MIRE, MUD : barro m, fango m, lodo m

mucous ['mju:kəs] adj : mucoso ⟨mucous membrane : membrana mucosa⟩

mucus ['mju:kəs] n : mucosidad f

mud ['mʌd] n : barro m, fango m, lodo m

muddle¹ ['mʌdəl] v **-dled; -dling** vt **1** CONFUSE : confundir (a alguien) **2** to **muddle up** MIX UP : confundir ⟨I always get them muddled up in my mind : siempre los confundo⟩ — vi : andar confundido ⟨to muddle through : arreglárselas⟩

muddle² n : confusión f, embrollo m, lío m

muddleheaded [ˌmʌdəl'hedəd, 'mʌdəlˌ-] adj CONFUSED : confuso, despistado

muddy¹ ['mʌdi] vt **-died; -dying** : llenar de barro

muddy² adj **muddier; -est** : barroso, fangoso, lodoso, enlodado ⟨you're all muddy : estás cubierto de barro⟩

mudguard ['mʌdˌgɑrd] n : guardabarros m

muff¹ ['mʌf] vt BUNGLE : echar a perder, fallar (un tiro, etc.)

muff² n : manguito m

muffin ['mʌfən] n : magdalena f

muffle ['mʌfəl] vt **-fled; -fling 1** ENVELOP : cubrir, tapar **2** DEADEN : amortiguar (un sonido)

muffler ['mʌflər] n **1** SCARF : bufanda f **2** : silenciador m; mofle m CA, Mex (de un automóvil)

mug¹ ['mʌg] v **mugged; mugging** vi : posar (con afectación), hacer muecas ⟨mugging for the camera : haciendo muecas para la cámara⟩ — vt ASSAULT : asaltar, atracar

mug² n CUP : tazón m

mugger ['mʌgər] n : atracador m, -dora f

mugginess ['mʌginəs] n : bochorno m

mugging ['mʌgɪŋ] n : atraco m

muggy ['mʌgi] adj **muggier; -est** : bochornoso

mulatto [mu'lɑto, -'læ-] n, pl **-toes** or **-tos** now sometimes offensive : mulato m, -ta f

mulberry ['mʌlˌbɛri] n, pl **-ries** : morera f (árbol), mora f (fruta)

mulch¹ ['mʌltʃ] vt : cubrir con pajote

mulch² n : pajote m

mule ['mju:l] n **1** : mula f **2** : obstinado m, -da f; terco m, -ca f

mulish ['mju:lɪʃ] adj : obstinado, terco

mull ['mʌl] vt to **mull over** : reflexionar sobre

mullet ['mʌlət] n, pl **-let** or **-lets** : mújol m

multi- [ˌmʌlti-, ˌmʌltaɪ-] pref : multi-

multicolored [ˌmʌlti'kʌlərd, ˌmʌltaɪ-] adj : multicolor, abigarrado

multicultural [ˌmʌlti'kʌltʃərəl] adj : multicultural — **multiculturalism** [ˌmʌlti'kʌltʃərəˌlɪzəm] n

multidisciplinary [ˌmʌlti'dɪsəpləˌnɛri] adj : multidisciplinario

multifaceted [ˌmʌlti'fæsətəd, ˌmʌltaɪ-] adj : multifacético

multifamily [ˌmʌlti'fæmli, ˌmʌltaɪ-] adj : multifamiliar

multifarious [ˌmʌltə'færiəs] adj DIVERSE : diverso, variado

multilateral [ˌmʌlti'lætərəl, ˌmʌltaɪ-] adj : multilateral

multimedia [ˌmʌlti'mi:diə, ˌmʌltaɪ-] adj : multimedia

multimillionaire [ˌmʌlti,mɪljə'nær, ˌmʌltaɪ-, -'mɪljəˌnær] adj : multimillonario

multinational [ˌmʌlti'næʃənəl, ˌmʌltaɪ-] adj : multinacional

multiple¹ ['mʌltəpəl] adj : múltiple

multiple² n : múltiplo m

multiple sclerosis [skləˈro:sɪs] n : esclerosis f múltiple

multiplex ['mʌltəˌplɛks] n : multicine m

multiplication [ˌmʌltəplə'keɪʃən] n : multiplicación f

multiplicity [ˌmʌltə'plɪsəti] n, pl **-ties** : multiplicidad f

multiply ['mʌltə,plaɪ] v **-plied; -plying** vt : multiplicar — vi : multiplicarse

multipurpose [,mʌltɪ'pərpəs, ,mʌltaɪ-] adj : multiuso

multistory [,mʌlti'stori, ,mʌltaɪ-] adj : de varias plantas, de varios pisos

multitask ['mʌlti,tæsk] vi : hacer multitarea

multitasking ['mʌlti,tæskɪŋ] n : multitarea f

multitude ['mʌltə,tu:d, -,tju:d] n 1 CROWD : multitud f, muchedumbre f 2 HOST : multitud f, gran cantidad f ⟨a multitude of ideas : numerosas ideas⟩

multivitamin [,mʌlti'vaɪtəmən, ,mʌltaɪ-] adj : multivitamínico

mum¹ ['mʌm] adj SILENT : callado

mum² n → **chrysanthemum**

mumble¹ ['mʌmbəl] v **-bled; -bling** vt : mascullar, musitar — vi : mascullar, hablar entre dientes, murmurar

mumble² n **to speak in a mumble** : hablar entre dientes

mumbo jumbo [,mʌmbo'dʒʌmbo] n : jerigonza f

mummy ['mʌmi] n, pl **-mies** : momia f

mumps ['mʌmps] ns & pl : paperas fpl

munch ['mʌntʃ] v : mascar, masticar

mundane [,mʌn'deɪn, 'mʌn,-] adj 1 EARTHLY, WORLDLY : mundano, terrenal 2 COMMONPLACE : rutinario, ordinario

municipal [mju'nɪsəpəl] adj : municipal

municipality [mju,nɪsə'pælət̬i] n, pl **-ties** : municipio m

munitions [mju'nɪʃənz] npl : municiones fpl

mural¹ ['mjʊrəl] adj : mural

mural² n : mural m

murder¹ ['mərdər] vt : asesinar, matar — vi : matar

murder² n : asesinato m, homicidio m

murderer ['mərdərər] n : asesino m, -na f; homicida mf

murderess ['mərdərəs] n : asesina f, homicida f

murderous ['mərdərəs] adj : asesino, homicida

murk ['mərk] n DARKNESS : oscuridad f, tinieblas fpl

murkiness ['mərkinəs] n : oscuridad f, tenebrosidad f

murky ['mərki] adj **murkier; -est** : oscuro, tenebroso

murmur¹ ['mərmər] vi 1 DRONE : murmurar 2 GRUMBLE : refunfuñar, regañar, rezongar — vt MUMBLE : murmurar

murmur² n 1 COMPLAINT : queja f 2 DRONE : murmullo m, rumor m

muscle¹ ['mʌsəl] vi **-cled; -cling** : meterse ⟨to muscle in on : meterse por la fuerza en, entrometerse en⟩

muscle² n 1 : músculo m 2 STRENGTH : fuerza f

muscular ['mʌskjələr] adj 1 : muscular ⟨muscular tissue : tejido muscular⟩ 2 BRAWNY : musculoso

muscular dystrophy n : distrofia f muscular

musculature ['mʌskjələ,tʃʊr, -tʃər] n : musculatura f

muse¹ ['mju:z] vi **mused; musing** PONDER, REFLECT : cavilar, meditar, reflexionar

muse² n : musa f

museum [mju'zi:əm] n : museo m

mush ['mʌʃ] n 1 : gachas fpl (de maíz) 2 SENTIMENTALITY : sensiblería f

mushroom¹ ['mʌʃ,ru:m, -,rʊm] vi GROW, MULTIPLY : crecer rápidamente, multiplicarse

mushroom² n : hongo m, champiñón m, seta f, callampa f Chile

mushy ['mʌʃi] adj **mushier; -est** 1 SOFT : blando 2 MAWKISH : sensiblero

music ['mju:zɪk] n : música f

musical¹ ['mju:zɪkəl] adj : musical, de música ⟨musical instrument : instrumento musical⟩ — **musically** adv

musical² n : comedia f musical

music box n : cajita f de música

musician [mju'zɪʃən] n : músico m, -ca f

musk ['mʌsk] n : almizcle m

musket ['mʌskət] n : mosquete m

musketeer [,mʌskə'tɪr] n : mosquetero m

muskrat ['mʌsk,ræt] n, pl **-rat** or **-rats** : rata f almizclera

Muslim¹ ['mʌzləm, 'mʊs-, 'mʊz-] adj : musulmán

Muslim² n : musulmán m, -mana f

muslin ['mʌzlən] n : muselina f

muss¹ ['mʌs] vt : desordenar, despeinar (el pelo)

muss² n : desorden m

mussel ['mʌsəl] n : mejillón m

must¹ ['mʌst] v aux 1 (expressing obligation or necessity) : deber, tener que ⟨you must stop : debes parar⟩ ⟨we must obey : tenemos que obedecer⟩ 2 (expressing probability) : deber (de), haber de ⟨you must be tired : debes de estar cansado⟩ ⟨it must be late : ha de ser tarde⟩

must² n 1 : necesidad f ⟨to be a must : ser imprescindible⟩ 2 : mosto m

mustache ['mʌ,stæʃ, mʌ'stæʃ] n : bigote m, bigotes mpl

mustang ['mʌ,stæŋ] n : caballo m mesteño

mustard ['mʌstərd] n : mostaza f

muster¹ ['mʌstər] vt 1 ASSEMBLE : reunir 2 **to muster up** : armarse de, cobrar (valor, fuerzas, etc.)

muster² n 1 INSPECTION : revista f (de tropas) ⟨it didn't pass muster : no resistió un examen minucioso⟩ 2 COLLECTION : colección f

mustiness ['mʌstinəs] n : lo mohoso

musty ['mʌsti] adj **mustier; -est** : mohoso, que huele a moho, que huele a encerrado

mutant¹ ['mju:tənt] adj : mutante

mutant² n : mutante m

mutate ['mju:,teɪt] vi **-tated; -tating** 1 : mutar (genéticamente) 2 CHANGE : transformarse

mutation [mju'teɪʃən] n : mutación f (genética)

mute¹ ['mju:t] vt **muted; muting** MUFFLE : amortiguar, ponerle sordina a (un instrumento musical)

mute² adj **muter; mutest** : mudo — **mutely** adv

mute³ n 1 *sometimes offensive* : mudo m, -da f (persona) 2 : sordina f (para un instrumento musical)

muted adj 1 : apagado (dícese de colores, la voz, etc.), sordo (dícese de sonidos) 2 RESTRAINED, WEAK : contenido, débil

mutilate ['mju:t̬ə.leɪt] vt -lated; -lating : mutilar

mutilation [.mju:t̬ə'leɪʃən] n : mutilación f

mutineer [.mju:t̬ən'ɪr] n : amotinado m, -da f

mutinous ['mju:t̬ənəs] adj : amotinado

mutiny¹ ['mju:t̬əni] vi -nied; -nying : amotinarse

mutiny² n, pl -nies : amotinamiento m, motín m

mutt ['mʌt] n MONGREL : perro m mestizo, perro m corriente Mex

mutter ['mʌt̬ər] vi 1 MUMBLE : mascullar, hablar entre dientes, murmurar 2 GRUMBLE : refunfuñar, regañar, rezongar

mutton ['mʌt̬ən] n : carne f de carnero

mutual ['mju:tʃuəl] adj 1 : mutuo ⟨mutual respect : respeto mutuo⟩ 2 COMMON : común ⟨a mutual friend : un amigo común⟩

mutually ['mju:tʃuəli, -tʃəli] adv 1 : mutuamente ⟨mutually beneficial : mutuamente beneficioso⟩ 2 JOINTLY : conjuntamente

muzzle¹ ['mʌzəl] vt -zled; -zling : ponerle un bozal a (un animal), amordazar

muzzle² n 1 SNOUT : hocico m 2 : bozal m (para un perro, etc.) 3 : boca f (de un arma de fuego)

my¹ ['maɪ] adj : mi ⟨my parents : mis padres⟩

my² interj : ¡caramba!, ¡Dios mío!

myopia [maɪ'o:piə] n : miopía f

myopic [maɪ'o:pɪk, -'a-] adj : miope

myriad¹ ['mɪriəd] adj INNUMERABLE : innumerable

myriad² n : miríada f

myrrh ['mər] n : mirra f

myrtle ['mərt̬əl] n : mirto m, arrayán m

myself [maɪ'sɛlf] pron 1 (*used reflexively*) : me ⟨I washed myself : me lavé⟩ 2 (*used for emphasis*) : yo mismo, yo misma ⟨I did it myself : lo hice yo mismo⟩

mysterious [mɪ'stɪriəs] adj : misterioso — **mysteriously** adv

mysteriousness [mɪ'strɪriəsnəs] n : lo misterioso

mystery ['mɪstəri] n, pl -teries : misterio m

mystic¹ ['mɪstɪk] adj : místico

mystic² n : místico m, -ca f

mystical ['mɪstɪkəl] adj : místico — **mystically** adv

mysticism ['mɪstə.sɪzəm] n : misticismo m

mystify ['mɪstə.faɪ] vt -fied; -fying : dejar perplejo, confundir

mystique [mɪ'sti:k] n : aura f de misterio

myth ['mɪθ] n : mito m

mythic ['mɪθɪk] adj : mítico

mythical ['mɪθɪkəl] adj : mítico

mythological [.mɪθə'lɑdʒɪkəl] adj : mitológico

mythology [mɪ'θɑlədʒi] n, pl -gies : mitología f

N

n ['ɛn] n, pl **n's** or **ns** ['ɛnz] : decimocuarta letra del alfabeto inglés

nab ['næb] vt **nabbed; nabbing** : prender, pillar fam, pescar fam

nadir ['neɪdər, 'neɪ.dɪr] n : nadir m, punto m más bajo

nag¹ ['næg] v **nagged; nagging** vi 1 COMPLAIN : quejarse, rezongar 2 to nag at HASSLE : molestar, darle (la) lata (a alguien) — vt 1 PESTER : molestar, fastidiar 2 SCOLD : regañar, estarle encima a fam

nag² n 1 GRUMBLER : gruñón m, -ñona f 2 HORSE : jamelgo m

nail¹ ['neɪl] vt : clavar, sujetar con clavos

nail² n 1 FINGERNAIL : uña f ⟨nail file : lima (de uñas)⟩ ⟨nail polish : laca de uñas⟩ 2 : clavo m ⟨to hit the nail on the head : dar en el clavo⟩

naive or **naïve** [na'i:v] adj **naiver; -est** 1 INGENUOUS : ingenuo, cándido 2 GULLIBLE : crédulo

naively [na'i:vli] adv : ingenuamente

naïveté [.na.i:və'teɪ, na'i:və.-] n : ingenuidad f

naked ['neɪkəd] adj 1 UNCLOTHED : desnudo 2 UNCOVERED : desenvainado (dícese de una espada), pelado (dícese de los árboles), expuesto al aire (dícese de una llama) 3 OBVIOUS, PLAIN : manifiesto, puro, desnudo ⟨the naked truth : la pura verdad⟩ 4 to the naked eye : a simple vista

nakedly ['neɪkədli] adv : manifiestamente

nakedness ['neɪkədnəs] n : desnudez f

name¹ ['neɪm] vt **named; naming** 1 CALL : llamar, bautizar, ponerle nombre a ⟨they named the baby after his father : le pusieron al niño el nombre de su padre⟩ 2 MENTION : mentar, mencionar, dar el nombre de ⟨they have named a suspect : han dado el nombre de un sospechoso⟩ 3 APPOINT : nombrar 4 to name a price : fijar un precio

name² adj PROMINENT : de renombre, de prestigio

name³ n 1 : nombre m ⟨what is your name? : ¿cómo se llama?⟩ ⟨my name is Ted : me llamo Ted⟩ ⟨first name : nombre de pila⟩ ⟨middle name : segundo nombre⟩ ⟨last name : apellido⟩ ⟨full name : nombre completo, nombre y apellido(s)⟩ ⟨she wasn't mentioned by name : no dieron su nombre⟩ 2 EPITHET : epíteto m ⟨to call somebody names : insultar a alguien⟩ 3 REPUTA-

TION : fama f, reputación f ⟨to make a name for oneself : darse a conocer, hacerse famoso⟩ ⟨to have a good name : tener buena fama⟩ **5 in all/everything but name** : a todos los efectos **6 in name only** : sólo de nombre **7 in the name of** : en nombre de **8 to drop names** : mencionar a gente importante

name–brand [ˈneɪm,brænd] *adj* : de marca conocida

name brand *n* : marca f conocida

nameless [ˈneɪmləs] *adj* **1** ANONYMOUS : anónimo **2** INDESCRIBABLE : indecible, indescriptible

namelessly [ˈneɪmləsli] *adv* : anónimamente

namely [ˈneɪmli] *adv* : a saber

namesake [ˈneɪm,seɪk] *n* : tocayo *m*, -ya f; homónimo *m*, -ma f

Namibian [nəˈmɪbiən] *n* : namibio *m*, -bia f — **Namibian** *adj*

nanny [ˈnæni] *n*, *pl* **nannies** : niñera f; nana f CA, Col, Mex, Ven

nanotechnology [ˌnænotek'nɑləʤi] *n*, *pl* **-gies** : nanotecnología f

nap¹ [ˈnæp] *vi* **napped; napping 1** : dormir, dormir la siesta **2 to be caught napping** : estar desprevenido

nap² *n* **1** SLEEP : siesta f ⟨to take a nap : echarse una siesta⟩ **2** FUZZ, PILE : pelo *m*, pelusa f (de telas)

nape [ˈneɪp, ˈnæp] *n* : nuca f, cerviz f, cogote *m*

naphtha [ˈnæfθə] *n* : nafta f

napkin [ˈnæpkɪn] *n* : servilleta f

narcissism [ˈnɑrsə,sɪzəm] *n* : narcisismo *m*

narcissist [ˈnɑrsəsɪst] *n* : narcisista *mf*

narcissistic [ˌnɑrsəˈsɪstɪk] *adj* : narcisista

narcissus [nɑrˈsɪsəs] *n*, *pl* **-cissus** or **-cissuses** or **-cissi** [-ˈsɪsaɪ, -ˌsiː] : narciso *m*

narcotic¹ [nɑrˈkɑtɪk] *adj* : narcótico

narcotic² *n* : narcótico *m*, estupefaciente *m*

narrate [ˈnær,eɪt] *vt* **-rated; -rating** : narrar, relatar

narration [næˈreɪʃən] *n* : narración f

narrative¹ [ˈnærətɪv] *adj* : narrativo

narrative² *n* : narración f, narrativa f, relato *m*

narrator [ˈnær,eɪtər] *n* : narrador *m*, -dora f

narrow¹ [ˈnær,oː] *vi* : estrecharse, angostarse ⟨the river narrowed : el río se estrechó⟩ — *vt* **1** : estrechar, angostar **2** LIMIT : restringir, limitar ⟨to narrow the search : limitar la búsqueda⟩

narrow² *adj* **1** : estrecho, angosto **2** LIMITED : estricto, limitado ⟨in the narrowest sense of the word : en el sentido más estricto de la palabra⟩ **3 to have a narrow escape** : escapar por un pelo

narrowly [ˈnæroli] *adv* **1** BARELY : por poco **2** CLOSELY : de cerca

narrow–minded [ˌnæro'maɪndəd] *adj* : de miras estrechas

narrowness [ˈnæronəs] *n* : estrechez f

narrows [ˈnæro:z] *npl* STRAIT : estrecho *m*

nasal [ˈneɪzəl] *adj* : nasal

nasally [ˈneɪzəli] *adv* **1** : por la nariz **2** : con voz nasal

nastily [ˈnæstəli] *adv* : con maldad, cruelmente

nastiness [ˈnæstinəs] *n* : porquería f

nasty [ˈnæsti] *adj* **nastier; -est 1** FILTHY : sucio, mugriento **2** OBSCENE : obsceno **3** MEAN, SPITEFUL : malo, malicioso **4** UNPLEASANT : desagradable, feo **5** REPUGNANT : asqueroso, repugnante ⟨a nasty smell : un olor asqueroso⟩

natal [ˈneɪtəl] *adj* : natal

nation [ˈneɪʃən] *n* : nación f

national¹ [ˈnæʃənəl] *adj* : nacional

national² *n* : ciudadano *m*, -na f; nacional *mf*

national anthem *n* : himno *m* nacional

nationalism [ˈnæʃənə,lɪzəm] *n* : nacionalismo *m*

nationalist¹ [ˈnæʃənəlɪst] *adj* : nacionalista

nationalist² *n* : nacionalista *mf*

nationalistic [ˌnæʃənəˈlɪstɪk] *adj* : nacionalista

nationality [ˌnæʃəˈnæləti] *n*, *pl* **-ties** : nacionalidad f

nationalization [ˌnæʃənələˈzeɪʃən] *n* : nacionalización f

nationalize [ˈnæʃənə,laɪz] *vt* **-ized; -izing** : nacionalizar

nationally [ˈnæʃənəli] *adv* : a escala nacional, a nivel nacional

national park *n* = parque *m* nacional

nationwide [ˈneɪʃən'waɪd] *adj* : en toda la nación, por todo el país

native¹ [ˈneɪtɪv] *adj* **1** INNATE : innato **2** : natal ⟨her native city : su ciudad natal⟩ ⟨native speaker : hablante nativo/nativa⟩ ⟨native language : lengua materna⟩ **3** INDIGENOUS : indígena, autóctono

native² *n* **1** ABORIGINE : nativo *m*, -va f; indígena *mf* **2** : natural *m* ⟨he's a native of Mexico : es natural de México⟩

Native American *n* : nativo *m* americano, nativa f americana; indígena *m* (americano), indígena f (americana) — **Native American** *adj*

nativity [nəˈtɪvəti, neɪ-] *n*, *pl* **-ties 1** BIRTH : navidad f **2 the Nativity** : la Natividad, la Navidad

natty [ˈnæti] *adj* **nattier; -est** : elegante, garboso

natural¹ [ˈnætʃərəl] *adj* **1** : natural, de la naturaleza ⟨natural woodlands : bosques naturales⟩ ⟨natural childbirth : parto natural⟩ **2** INNATE : innato, natural **3** UNAFFECTED : natural, sin afectación **4** LIFELIKE : natural, vivo

natural² *n* **to be a natural** : tener un talento innato (para algo)

natural gas *n* : gas *m* natural

natural history *n* : historia f natural

naturalism [ˈnætʃərə,lɪzəm] *n* : naturalismo *m*

naturalist [ˈnætʃərəlɪst] *n* : naturalista *mf* — **naturalist** *adj*

naturalistic [ˌnætʃərəˈlɪstɪk] *adj* : naturalista

naturalization [ˌnætʃərələˈzeɪʃən] *n* : naturalización f

naturalize [ˈnætʃərə,laɪz] *vt* **-ized; -izing** : naturalizar

naturally [ˈnætʃərəli] *adv* **1** INHERENTLY : naturalmente, intrínsecamente **2** UNAFFECTEDLY : de manera natural **3** OF COURSE : por supuesto, naturalmente

naturalness [ˈnætʃərəlnəs] *n* : naturalidad *f*

natural science *n* : ciencias *fpl* naturales

nature [ˈneɪtʃər] *n* **1** : naturaleza *f* ⟨the laws of nature : las leyes de la naturaleza⟩ **2** KIND, SORT : índole *f*, clase *f* ⟨things of this nature : cosas de esta índole⟩ **3** DISPOSITION : carácter *m*, natural *m*, naturaleza *f* ⟨it is his nature to be friendly : es de natural simpático⟩ ⟨human nature : la naturaleza humana⟩

naught [ˈnɔt] *n* **1** : nada *f* ⟨to come to naught : reducirse a nada, fracasar⟩ **2** ZERO : cero *m*

naughtily [ˈnɔtəli] *adv* : traviesamente, con malicia

naughtiness [ˈnɔtinəs] *n* : mala conducta *f*, travesuras *fpl*, malicia *f*

naughty [ˈnɔti] *adj* **naughtier; -est 1** MISCHIEVOUS : travieso, pícaro **2** RISQUÉ : picante, subido de tono

nausea [ˈnɔziə, ˈnɔʃə] *n* **1** SICKNESS : náuseas *fpl* **2** DISGUST : asco *m*

nauseate [ˈnɔziˌeɪt, -ʒi-, -si-, -ʃi-] *vt* **-ated; -ating 1** SICKEN : darle náuseas (a alguien) **2** DISGUST : asquear, darle asco (a alguien)

nauseating *adj* : nauseabundo, repugnante

nauseatingly [ˈnɔziˌeɪtɪŋli, -ʒi-, -si-, -ʃi-] *adv* : hasta el punto de dar asco ⟨nauseatingly sweet : tan dulce que da asco⟩

nauseous [ˈnɔʃəs, -ziəs] *adj* **1** SICK : mareado, con náuseas **2** SICKENING : nauseabundo

nautical [ˈnɔtɪkəl] *adj* : náutico

nautilus [ˈnɔtələs] *n, pl* **-luses** *or* **-li** [-ˌlaɪ, -ˌliː] : nautilo *m*

Navajo [ˈnævəˌhoː, ˈnɑ-] *n* : navajo *m*, -ja *f* — **Navajo** *adj*

naval [ˈneɪvəl] *adj* : naval

nave [ˈneɪv] *n* : nave *f*

navel [ˈneɪvəl] *n* : ombligo *m*

navigability [ˌnævɪɡəˈbɪlət̬i] *n* : navegabilidad *f*

navigable [ˈnævɪɡəbəl] *adj* : navegable

navigate [ˈnævəˌɡeɪt] *v* **-gated; -gating** *vi* : navegar — *vt* **1** STEER : gobernar (un barco), pilotar (un avión) **2** : navegar por (un río, etc.)

navigation [ˌnævəˈɡeɪʃən] *n* : navegación *f*

navigator [ˈnævəˌɡeɪtər] *n* : navegante *mf*

navy [ˈneɪvi] *n, pl* **-vies 1** FLEET : flota *f* **2** : marina *f* de guerra, armada *f* ⟨the United States Navy : la armada de los Estados Unidos⟩ **3** *or* **navy blue** : azul *m* marino

nay[1] [ˈneɪ] *adv* : no

nay[2] *n* : no *m*, voto *m* en contra

Nazi [ˈnɑtsi, ˈnæt-] *n* : nazi *mf*

Nazism [ˈnɑtˌsɪzəm, ˈnæt-] *or* **Naziism** [ˈnɑtsiˌɪzəm, ˈnæt-] *n* : nazismo *m*

Neanderthal [niˈændərˌθɔl, -ˌtɔl] *n* **1** *or* **Neanderthal man** : Neandertal *m*, hombre *m* de Neandertal **2** *fam* : neandertal *m*

near[1] [ˈnɪr] *vt* **1** : acercarse a ⟨the ship is nearing port : el barco se está acercando al puerto⟩ **2** : estar a punto de ⟨she is nearing graduation : está a punto de graduarse⟩

near[2] *adv* **1** CLOSE : cerca ⟨my family lives quite near : mi familia vive muy cerca⟩ ⟨the day of the wedding was drawing near : se acercaba el día de la boda⟩ **2** NEARLY : casi ⟨near perfect/impossible : casi perfecto/imposible⟩ **3** (as) near as I can tell/figure : según parece, por lo visto **4** nowhere near → nowhere[1]

near[3] *adj* **1** CLOSE : cercano, próximo ⟨the nearest pharmacy : la farmacia más cercana/próxima⟩ ⟨in the near future : en un/el futuro próximo/cercano⟩ **2** CLOSER : más cercano, más próximo ⟨the near side/end : el lado/extremo más cercano/próximo, el lado/extremo de acá⟩ **3** (close to or similar to being) : ⟨they had a near win : perdieron por poco⟩ ⟨a near miracle : casi un milagro⟩ ⟨the nearest thing to : lo más parecido a⟩ **4** : cercano (dícese de un pariente) **5** : cercano (de grado, etc.) ⟨his nearest rival : su más cercano rival⟩ **6** near and dear ⟨my nearest and dearest friend : mi amigo más íntimo⟩ **7** to the nearest ⟨it's rounded to the nearest dollar : se redondea al dólar más cercano⟩

near[4] *prep* : cerca de ⟨near the store : cerca de la tienda⟩ ⟨she lives near here : vive cerca de aquí, vive aquí cerca⟩ ⟨it was near midnight : era casi medianoche⟩ ⟨near the end : casi al final⟩ ⟨near death : al borde de la muerte⟩ ⟨to go near someone/something : acercarse a alguien/algo⟩

nearby[1] [ˈnɪrˈbaɪ, ˈnɪrˌbaɪ] *adv* : cerca

nearby[2] *adj* : cercano

nearly [ˈnɪrli] *adv* **1** ALMOST : casi ⟨nearly asleep : casi dormido⟩ **2** not nearly : ni con mucho, ni mucho menos ⟨it was not nearly so bad as I had expected : no fue ni con mucho tan malo como esperaba⟩

nearness [ˈnɪrnəs] *n* : proximidad *f*

nearsighted [ˈnɪrˌsaɪtəd] *adj* : miope, corto de vista

nearsightedly [ˈnɪrˌsaɪtədli] *adv* : con miopía

nearsightedness [ˈnɪrˌsaɪtədnəs] *n* : miopía *f*

neat [ˈniːt] *adj* **1** CLEAN, ORDERLY : ordenado, pulcro, limpio **2** UNDILUTED : solo, sin diluir **3** SIMPLE, TASTEFUL : sencillo y de buen gusto **4** CLEVER : hábil, ingenioso ⟨a neat trick : un truco ingenioso⟩ **5** GREAT, TERRIFIC : genial, estupendo

neaten [ˈniːtən] *vt* : arreglar, ordenar, poner en orden — *vi* to neaten up : poner las cosas en orden

neatly [ˈniːtli] *adv* **1** TIDILY : ordenadamente **2** CLEVERLY : ingeniosamente

neatness [ˈniːtnəs] *n* : pulcritud *f*, limpieza *f*, orden *m*

nebula [ˈnɛbjʊlə] *n, pl* **-lae** [-ˌliː, -ˌlaɪ] : nebulosa *f*

nebulous [ˈnɛbjʊləs] *adj* : nebuloso, vago

necessarily [ˌnɛsəˈsɛrəli] *adv* : necesariamente, forzosamente

necessary[1] [ˈnɛsəˌsɛri] *adj* **1** INEVITABLE : inevitable **2** COMPULSORY : necesario, obligatorio **3** ESSENTIAL : imprescindible, preciso, necesario

necessary[2] *n, pl* **-saries** : lo esencial, lo necesario

necessitate [nɪˈsɛsəˌteɪt] *vt* **-tated; -tating** : necesitar, requerir

necessity [nɪˈsɛsəti] *n, pl* **-ties 1** NEED : necesidad *f* **2** REQUIREMENT : requisito *m* indispensable **3** POVERTY : indigencia *f*, necesidad *f* **4** INEVITABILITY : inevitabilidad *f*

neck[1] [ˈnɛk] *vi* : besuquearse

neck[2] *n* **1** : cuello *m* (de una persona), pescuezo *m* (de un animal) **2** COLLAR : cuello *m* **3** : cuello *m* (de una botella), mástil *m* (de una guitarra)

necklace [ˈnɛkləs] *n* : collar *m*

neckline [ˈnɛkˌlaɪn] *n* : escote *m*

necktie [ˈnɛkˌtaɪ] *n* : corbata *f*

nectar [ˈnɛktər] *n* : néctar *m*

nectarine [ˌnɛktəˈriːn] *n* : nectarina *f*

née *or* **nee** [ˈneɪ] *adj* : de soltera ⟨Mrs. Smith, née Whitman : la señora Smith, de soltera Whitman⟩

need[1] [ˈniːd] *vt* **1** : necesitar ⟨I need your help : necesito su ayuda⟩ ⟨I need money : me falta dinero⟩ **2** REQUIRE : requerir, exigir ⟨that job needs patience : ese trabajo exige paciencia⟩ **3 to need to** : tener que ⟨he needs to study : tiene que estudiar⟩ ⟨they need to be scolded : hay que reprenderlos⟩ — *v aux* **1** MUST : tener que, deber ⟨need you shout? : ¿tienes que gritar?⟩ **2 to be needed** : hacer falta ⟨you needn't worry : no hace falta que te preocupes, no hay por qué preocuparse⟩

need[2] *n* **1** NECESSITY : necesidad *f* ⟨in case of need : en caso de necesidad⟩ **2** LACK : falta *f* ⟨the need for better training : la falta de mejor capacitación⟩ ⟨to be in need : necesitar⟩ **3** POVERTY : necesidad *f*, indigencia *f* **4 needs** *npl* : requisitos *mpl*, carencias *fpl*

needful [ˈniːdfəl] *adj* : necesario

needle[1] [ˈniːdəl] *vt* **-dled; -dling** : pinchar

needle[2] *n* **1** : aguja *f* ⟨to thread a needle : enhebrar una aguja⟩ ⟨knitting needle : aguja de tejer⟩ **2** POINTER : aguja *f*, indicador *m*

needlepoint [ˈniːdəlˌpɔɪnt] *n* **1** LACE : encaje *m* de mano **2** EMBROIDERY : bordado *m*

needless [ˈniːdləs] *adj* : innecesario

needlessly [ˈniːdləsli] *adv* : sin ninguna necesidad, innecesariamente

needlework [ˈniːdəlˌwərk] *n* : bordado *m*

needn't [ˈniːdənt] *contraction of* NEED NOT → need

needy[1] [ˈniːdi] *adj* **needier; -est** : necesitado

needy[2] *n* **the needy** : los necesitados *mpl*

nefarious [nɪˈfæriəs] *adj* : nefario, nefando, infame

negate [nɪˈgeɪt] *vt* **-gated; -gating 1** DENY : negar **2** NULLIFY : invalidar, anular

negation [nɪˈgeɪʃən] *n* : negación *f*

negative[1] [ˈnɛgətɪv] *adj* : negativo

negative[2] *n* **1** : negación *f* (en lingüística) **2** : negativa *f* ⟨to answer in the negative : contestar con una negativa⟩ **3** : término *m* negativo (en matemáticas) **4** : negativo *m*, imagen *f* en negativo (en fotografía)

negatively [ˈnɛgətɪvli] *adv* : negativamente

neglect[1] [nɪˈglɛkt] *vt* **1** : desatender, descuidar ⟨to neglect one's health : descuidar la salud⟩ **2** : no cumplir con, faltar a ⟨to neglect one's obligations : faltar uno a sus obligaciones⟩ ⟨he neglected to tell me : omitió decírmelo⟩

neglect[2] *n* **1** : negligencia *f*, descuido *m*, incumplimiento *m* ⟨through neglect : por negligencia⟩ ⟨neglect of duty : incumplimiento del deber⟩ **2 in a state of neglect** : abandonado, descuidado

neglected [nɪˈglɛktəd] *adj* : abandonado, descuidado

neglectful [nɪˈglɛktfəl] *adj* : descuidado *m*

negligee [ˌnɛgləˈʒeɪ] *n* : negligé *m*

negligence [ˈnɛglɪʤəns] *n* : descuido *m*, negligencia *f*

negligent [ˈnɛglɪʤənt] *adj* : negligente, descuidado — **negligently** *adv*

negligible [ˈnɛglɪʤəbəl] *adj* : insignificante, despreciable

negotiable [nɪˈgoːʃəbəl, -ʃiə-] *adj* : negociable

negotiate [nɪˈgoːʃiˌeɪt] *vt* **-ated; -ating** *vi* : negociar — *vt* **1** : negociar, gestionar ⟨to negotiate a treaty : negociar un trato⟩ **2** : salvar, franquear ⟨they negotiated the obstacles : salvaron los obstáculos⟩ ⟨to negotiate a turn : tomar una curva⟩

negotiation [nɪˌgoːʃiˈeɪʃən, -siˈeɪ-] *n* : negociación *f*

negotiator [nɪˈgoːʃiˌeɪtər, -siˌeɪ-] *n* : negociador *m*, -dora *f*

Negro [ˈniːˌgroː] *n, pl* **-groes** *dated, now sometimes offensive* : negro *m*, -gra *f*

neigh[1] [ˈneɪ] *vi* : relinchar

neigh[2] *n* : relincho *m*

neighbor[1] [ˈneɪbər] *vt* : ser vecino de, estar junto a ⟨her house neighbors mine : su casa está junto a la mía⟩ — *vi* : estar cercano, lindar, colindar ⟨her land neighbors on mine : sus tierras lindan con las mías⟩

neighbor[2] *n* **1** : vecino *m*, -na *f* **2 love thy neighbor** : ama a tu prójimo

neighborhood [ˈneɪbərˌhʊd] *n* **1** : barrio *m*, vecindad *f*, vecindario *m* **2 in the neighborhood of** : alrededor de, cerca de

neighboring [ˈneɪbərɪŋ] *adj* : vecino

neighborly [ˈneɪbərli] *adv* : amable, de buena vecindad

neither[1] [ˈniːðər, ˈnaɪ-] *adj* : ninguno (de los dos)

neither² *conj* **1** : ni ⟨neither asleep nor awake : ni dormido ni despierto⟩ **2** NOR : ni (tampoco) ⟨I'm not asleep — neither am I : no estoy dormido — ni yo tampoco⟩

neither³ *pron* : ninguno ⟨which do you want? neither : ¿cuál quieres? ninguno⟩ ⟨neither of the two sisters : ninguna de las dos hermanas⟩

nemesis [ˈnɛməsɪs] *n, pl* **-eses** [-ˌsiːz] **1** RIVAL : rival *mf* **2** RETRIBUTION : justo castigo *m*

neologism [niˈɑləˌdʒɪzəm] *n* : neologismo *m*

neon¹ [ˈniːˌɑn] *adj* : de neón ⟨neon sign : letrero de neón⟩

neon² *n* : neón *m*

neophyte [ˈniːəˌfaɪt] *n* : neófito *m*, -ta *f*

Nepali [nəˈpɑli, -ˈpɑ-, -ˈpæ-] *n* : nepalés *m*, -lesa *f* — **Nepali** *adj*

nephew [ˈnɛˌfjuː, *chiefly Brit* ˈnɛˌvjuː] *n* : sobrino *m*

nepotism [ˈnɛpəˌtɪzəm] *n* : nepotismo *m*

Neptune [ˈnɛpˌtuːn, -ˌtjuːn] *n* : Neptuno *m*

nerd [ˈnɚd] *n* : ganso *m*, -sa *f*

nerve [ˈnɚv] *n* **1** : nervio *m* **2** COURAGE : coraje *m*, valor *m*, fuerza *f* de la voluntad ⟨to lose one's nerve : perder el valor⟩ **3** AUDACITY, GALL : atrevimiento *m*, descaro *m* ⟨of all the nerve!, some/what nerve! : ¡qué descaro!⟩ ⟨you have a lot of nerve! : ¡qué cara tienes!⟩ **4 nerves** *npl* : nervios *mpl* ⟨to be a bag/bundle of nerves : ser un manojo de nervios⟩ ⟨to calm one's nerves : calmarse (los nervios)⟩ ⟨to get on someone's nerves : crisparle los nervios a alguien⟩ ⟨to have a (bad) case of nerves : estar nerviosísimo⟩ ⟨to have nerves of steel : tener nervios de acero⟩ ⟨to have one's nerves on edge : tener los nervios de punta⟩ ⟨a war of nerves : una guerra de nervios⟩ **5** to hit/touch/strike a nerve : poner el dedo en la llaga

nerve–racking *or* **nerve–wracking** [ˈnɚvˌrækɪŋ] *adj* : estresante, desesperante, angustioso

nervous [ˈnɚvəs] *adj* **1** : nervioso ⟨the nervous system : el sistema nervioso⟩ **2** EXCITABLE : nervioso ⟨to get nervous : excitarse, ponerse nervioso⟩ **3** FEARFUL : miedoso, temeroso

nervous breakdown *n* → **breakdown**

nervously [ˈnɚvəsli] *adv* : nerviosamente

nervousness [ˈnɚvəsnəs] *n* : nerviosismo *m*, nerviosidad *f*, ansiedad *f*

nervy [ˈnɚvi] *adj* **nervier; -est 1** COURAGEOUS : valiente **2** IMPUDENT : atrevido, descarado, fresco *fam* **3** NERVOUS : nervioso

nest¹ [ˈnɛst] *vi* : anidar

nest² *n* **1** : nido *m* (de un ave), avispero *m* (de una avispa), madriguera *f* (de un animal) **2** REFUGE : nido *m*, refugio *m* **3** SET : juego *m* ⟨a nest of tables : un juego de mesitas⟩

nestle [ˈnɛsəl] *vi* **-tled; -tling** : acurrucarse, arrimarse cómodamente

net¹ [ˈnɛt] *vt* **netted; netting 1** CATCH : pescar, atrapar con una red **2** CLEAR : ganar neto ⟨they netted $5000 : ganaron $5000 netos⟩ **3** YIELD : producir neto

net² *adj* : neto ⟨net weight : peso neto⟩ ⟨net gain : ganancia neta⟩

net³ *n* : red *f*, malla *f*

nether [ˈnɛðər] *adj* **1** : inferior, más bajo **2 the nether regions** : el infierno

nettle¹ [ˈnɛtəl] *vt* **-tled; -tling** : irritar, provocar, molestar

nettle² *n* : ortiga *f*

network [ˈnɛtˌwɚk] *n* **1** SYSTEM : red *f* ⟨social network : red social⟩ **2** CHAIN : cadena *f* ⟨a network of supermarkets : una cadena de supermercados⟩

neural [ˈnʊrəl, ˈnjʊr-] *adj* : neural

neuralgia [nʊˈrældʒə, njʊ-] *n* : neuralgia *f*

neuritis [nʊˈraɪtəs, njʊ-] *n, pl* **-ritides** [-ˈrɪtəˌdiːz] *or* **-ritises** : neuritis *f*

neurological [ˌnʊrəˈlɑdʒɪkəl, ˌnjʊr-] *or* **neurologic** [ˌnʊrəˈlɑdʒɪk, ˌnjʊr-] *adj* : neurológico

neurologist [nʊˈrɑlədʒɪst, njʊ-] *n* : neurólogo *m*, -ga *f*

neurology [nʊˈrɑlədʒi, njʊ-] *n* : neurología *f*

neurosis [nʊˈroːsɪs, njʊ-] *n, pl* **-roses** [-ˌsiːz] : neurosis *f*

neurotic¹ [nʊˈrɑtɪk, njʊ-] *adj* : neurótico

neurotic² *n* : neurótico *m*, -ca *f*

neuter¹ [ˈnuːtər, ˈnjuː-] *vt* : castrar

neuter² *adj* : neutro

neutral¹ [ˈnuːtrəl, ˈnjuː-] *adj* **1** IMPARTIAL : neutral, imparcial ⟨to remain neutral : permanecer neutral⟩ **2** : neutro ⟨a neutral color : un color neutro⟩ **3** : neutro (en la química o la electricidad)

neutral² *n* : punto *m* muerto (de un automóvil)

neutrality [nuːˈtrælətiː, njuː-] *n* : neutralidad *f*

neutralization [ˌnuːtrələˈzeɪʃən, ˌnjuː-] *n* : neutralización *f*

neutralize [ˈnuːtrəˌlaɪz, ˈnjuː-] *vt* **-ized; -izing** : neutralizar

neutron [ˈnuːˌtrɑn, ˈnjuː-] *n* : neutrón *m*

never [ˈnɛvər] *adv* **1** : nunca, jamás ⟨he never studies : nunca estudia⟩ **2 never again** : nunca más, nunca jamás **3 never mind** : no importa

never–ending [ˈnɛvərˈɛndɪŋ] *adj* ENDLESS : interminable, inacabable, sin fin

nevermore [ˌnɛvərˈmor] *adv* : nunca más

nevertheless [ˌnɛvərðəˈlɛs] *adv* : sin embargo, no obstante

new [ˈnuː, ˈnjuː] *adj* **1** : nuevo ⟨a new dress : un vestido nuevo⟩ **2** RECENT : nuevo, reciente ⟨what's new? : ¿qué hay de nuevo?⟩ ⟨a new arrival : un recién llegado⟩ **3** DIFFERENT : nuevo, distinto ⟨this problem is new : este problema es distinto⟩ ⟨new ideas : ideas nuevas⟩ **4 like new** : como nuevo

newborn [ˈnuːˌbɔrn, ˈnjuː-] *adj* : recién nacido

newcomer [ˈnuːˌkʌmər, ˈnjuː-] *n* : recién llegado *m*, recién llegada *f*

newfangled [ˈnuːˈfæŋɡəld, ˈnjuː-] *adj* : novedoso

newfound [ˈnuːˈfaʊnd, ˈnjuː-] *adj* : recién descubierto

newly ['nu:li, 'nju:-] *adv* : recién, recientemente

newlywed ['nu:li,wɛd, 'nju:-] *n* : recién casado *m*, -da *f*

new moon *n* : luna *f* nueva

newness ['nu:nəs, 'nju:-] *n* : novedad *f*

news ['nu:z, 'nju:z] *n* 1 INFORMATION : noticias *fpl* ⟨good/bad news : buenas/malas noticias⟩ ⟨to break the news to someone : darle la noticia a alguien⟩ ⟨further news : más noticias⟩ ⟨that's news to me! : ¡(es la) primera noticia (que tengo)!⟩ ⟨no news is good news : (el) que no haya noticias es (una) buena noticia⟩ 2 : noticias *fpl* ⟨local/international news : noticias locales/internacionales⟩ ⟨to be in the news : salir en las noticias⟩ 3 NEWSCAST : noticias *fpl*, noticiero *m*, informativo *m*, noticiario *m* ⟨the nightly news : el noticiero nocturno⟩ ⟨I saw it on the news : lo vi en las noticias⟩

newscast ['nu:z,kæst, 'nju:z-] *n* : noticiero *m*, informativo *m*, noticiario *m*

newscaster ['nu:z,kæstər, 'nju:z-] *n* : presentador *m*, -dora *f*; locutor *m*, -tora *f*

newsgroup ['nu:z,gru:p, 'nju:z-] *n* : grupo *m* de noticias

newsletter ['nu:z,lɛtər, 'nju:z-] *n* : boletín *m* informativo

newsman ['nu:zmən, 'nju:z-, -,mæn] *n, pl* **-men** [-mən, -,mɛn] : periodista *m*, reportero *m*

newspaper ['nu:z,peɪpər, 'nju:z-] *n* 1 : periódico *m*, diario *m* ⟨newspaper articles : artículos periodísticos⟩ ⟨newspaper reporter : periodista⟩ 2 : papel *m* de periódico

newspaperman ['nu:z,peɪpər,mæn, 'nju:z-] *n, pl* **-men** [-mən, -,mɛn] 1 REPORTER : periodista *m*, reportero *m* 2 : dueño *m* de un periódico

newsprint ['nu:z,prɪnt, 'nju:z-] *n* : papel *m* de prensa

newsstand ['nu:z,stænd, 'nju:z-] *n* : quiosco *m*, puesto *m* de periódicos

newswoman ['nu:z,wʊmən, 'nju:z-] *n, pl* **-women** [-,wɪmən] : periodista *f*, reportera *f*

newsworthy ['nu:z,wərði, 'nju:z-] *adj* : de interés periodístico

newsy ['nu:zi:, 'nju:-] *adj* **newsier; -est** : lleno de noticias

newt ['nu:t, 'nju:t] *n* : tritón *m*

New Testament *n* : Nuevo Testamento *m*

New Year *n* : Año *m* Nuevo

New Year's Day *n* : día *m* del Año Nuevo

New Year's Eve *n* : noche *f* de Fin de Año, Nochevieja *f*

New Yorker [nu:'jɔrkər, nju:-] *n* : neoyorquino *m*, -na *f*

New Zealander [nu:'zi:ləndər, nju:-] *n* : neozelandés *m*, -desa *f*

next¹ ['nɛkst] *adv* 1 AFTERWARD : después, luego ⟨what will you do next? : ¿qué harás después?⟩ 2 NOW : después, ahora, entonces ⟨next I will sing a song : ahora voy a cantar una canción⟩ 3 : la próxima vez ⟨when next we meet : la próxima vez que nos encontremos⟩

next² *adj* 1 ADJACENT : contiguo, de al lado 2 COMING : que viene, próximo ⟨next Friday : el viernes que viene⟩ 3 FOLLOWING : siguiente ⟨the next year : el año siguiente⟩

next–door ['nɛkst'dor] *adj* : de al lado

next–of–kin *n, pl* **next–of–kin** : familiar *m* más cercano, pariente *m* más cercano

next to¹ *adv* ALMOST : casi, prácticamente ⟨next to impossible : casi imposible⟩

next to² *prep* : junto a, al lado de

nexus ['nɛksəs] *n* : nexo *m*

nib ['nɪb] *n* : plumilla *f*

nibble¹ ['nɪbəl] *v* **-bled; -bling** *vt* : pellizcar, mordisquear, picar — *vi* : picar

nibble² *n* : mordisco *m*

Nicaraguan [,nɪkə'rɑgwən] *n* : nicaragüense *mf* — **Nicaraguan** *adj*

nice ['naɪs] *adj* **nicer; nicest** 1 REFINED : pulido, refinado 2 SUBTLE : fino, sutil 3 PLEASING : agradable, bueno, lindo ⟨nice weather : buen tiempo⟩ 4 RESPECTABLE : bueno, decente 5 **nice and** : bien, muy ⟨nice and hot : bien caliente⟩ ⟨nice and slow : despacito⟩

nicely ['naɪsli] *adv* 1 KINDLY : amablemente 2 POLITELY : con buenos modales 3 ATTRACTIVELY : de buen gusto

niceness ['naɪsnəs] *n* : simpatía *f*, amabilidad *f*

nicety ['naɪsəti] *n, pl* **-ties** 1 DETAIL, SUBTLETY : sutileza *f*, detalle *m* 2 **niceties** *npl* : lujos *mpl*, detalles *mpl*

niche ['nɪtʃ] *n* 1 RECESS : nicho *m*, hornacina *f* 2 : nicho *m*, hueco *m* ⟨to make a niche for oneself : hacerse un hueco, encontrarse una buena posición⟩

nick¹ ['nɪk] *vt* : cortar, hacer una muesca en

nick² *n* 1 CUT : corte *m*, muesca *f* 2 **in the nick of time** : en el momento crítico, justo a tiempo

nickel ['nɪkəl] *n* 1 : níquel *m* 2 : moneda *f* de cinco centavos

nickname¹ ['nɪk,neɪm] *vt* **-named; -naming** : apodar

nickname² *n* : apodo *m*, mote *m*, sobrenombre *m*

nicotine ['nɪkə,ti:n] *n* : nicotina *f*

niece ['ni:s] *n* : sobrina *f*

Nigerian [naɪ'dʒɪriən] *n* : nigeriano *m*, -na *f* — **Nigerian** *adj*

niggardly ['nɪɡərdli] *adj* : mezquino, tacaño

niggling ['nɪɡəlɪŋ] *adj* 1 PETTY : insignificante 2 PERSISTENT : constante, persistente ⟨a niggling doubt : una duda constante⟩

nigh¹ ['naɪ] *adv* 1 NEARLY : casi 2 **to draw nigh** : acercarse, avecinarse

nigh² *adj* : cercano, próximo

night¹ ['naɪt] *adj* : nocturno, de la noche ⟨the night sky : el cielo nocturno⟩ ⟨night shift : turno de la noche⟩

night² *n* 1 EVENING : noche *f* ⟨at night : de noche⟩ ⟨last night : anoche⟩ ⟨tomorrow night : mañana por la noche⟩ 2 DARKNESS : noche *f*, oscuridad *f* ⟨night fell : cayó la noche⟩

nightclothes ['naɪt,kloːðz, -,kloːz] *npl* : ropa *f* de dormir

nightclub ['naɪt,klʌb] *n* : cabaret *m*; club *m* nocturno; boliche *m* *Arg*, *Uru*

night crawler ['naɪt,krɔlər] *n* EARTHWORM : lombriz *f* (de tierra)

nightdress ['naɪt,drɛs] → **nightgown**

nightfall ['naɪt,fɔl] *n* : anochecer *m*

nightgown ['naɪt,gaʊn] *n* : camisón *m* (de noche)

nightie ['naɪti] *n* : camisón *m* corto (de noche)

nightingale ['naɪtən,geɪl, 'naɪtɪŋ-] *n* : ruiseñor *m*

nightlife ['naɪt,laɪf] *n* : vida *f* nocturna

nightly[1] ['naɪtli] *adv* : cada noche, todas las noches

nightly[2] *adj* : de todas las noches

nightmare ['naɪt,mær] *n* : pesadilla *f*

nightmarish ['naɪt,mærɪʃ] *adj* : de pesadilla

night owl *n* : noctámbulo *m*, -la *f*

night school *n* : escuela *f* nocturna, clases *fpl* nocturnas

nightshade ['naɪt,ʃeɪd] *n* : hierba *f* mora

nightshirt ['naɪt,ʃərt] *n* : camisa *f* de dormir

nightstick ['naɪt,stɪk] *n* : porra *f*

night table *or* **nightstand** ['naɪt,stænd] *n* : mesita *f*, mesilla *f* *Spain* (de noche)

nighttime ['naɪt,taɪm] *n* : noche *f*

nihilism ['naɪə,lɪzəm] *n* : nihilismo *m*

nil ['nɪl] *n* : nada *f*, cero *m*

nimble ['nɪmbəl] *adj* **nimbler**; **-blest** **1** AGILE : ágil **2** CLEVER : hábil, ingenioso

nimbleness ['nɪmbəlnəs] *n* : agilidad *f*

nimbly ['nɪmbli] *adv* : con agilidad, ágilmente

nincompoop ['nɪnkəm,pu:p, 'nɪŋ-] *n* FOOL : tonto *m*, -ta *f*; bobo *m*, -ba *f*

nine[1] ['naɪn] *adj* **1** : nueve ⟨he's nine (years old) : tiene nueve años⟩ **2** **nine times out of ten** : casi siempre

nine[2] *n* : nueve *m* ⟨the nine of hearts : el nueve de corazones⟩

nine[3] *pron* : nueve ⟨it's nine (o'clock) : son las nueve⟩ ⟨there are nine of us : somos nueve⟩

nine hundred[1] *adj* : novecientos

nine hundred[2] *n* : novecientos *m*

ninepins ['naɪn,pɪnz] *n* : bolos *mpl*

nineteen[1] [naɪn'ti:n] *adj & pron* : diecinueve

nineteen[2] *n* : diecinueve *m*

nineteenth[1] [naɪn'ti:nθ] *adj* : decimonoveno, decimonono ⟨the nineteenth century : el siglo diecinueve⟩

nineteenth[2] *n* **1** : decimonoveno *m*, -na *f*; decimonono *m*, -na *f* (en una serie) **2** : diecinueveavo *m*, diecinueveava parte *f*

ninetieth[1] ['naɪntiəθ] *adj* : nonagésimo

ninetieth[2] *n* **1** : nonagésimo *m*, -ma *f* (en una serie) **2** : noventavo *m*, noventava parte *f*

ninety[1] ['naɪnti] *adj & pron* : noventa

ninety[2] *n*, *pl* **-ties** : noventa *m*

ninny ['nɪni] *n*, *pl* **ninnies** FOOL : tonto *m*, -ta *f*; bobo *m*, -ba *f*

ninth[1] ['naɪnθ] *adv* : en noveno lugar

ninth[2] *adj* : noveno

ninth[3] *n* **1** : noveno *m*, -na *f* (en una serie) ⟨(on) the ninth of June : el nueve de junio⟩ **2** : noveno *m*, novena parte *f*

nip[1] ['nɪp] *vt* **nipped**; **nipping** **1** PINCH : pellizcar **2** BITE : morder, mordisquear **3 to nip in the bud** : cortar de raíz

nip[2] *n* **1** TANG : sabor *m* fuerte **2** PINCH : pellizco *m* **3** NIBBLE : mordisco *m* **4** SWALLOW : trago *m*, traguito *m* **5 there's a nip in the air** : hace fresco

nipple ['nɪpəl] *n* : pezón *m* (de una mujer), tetilla *f* (de un hombre)

nippy ['nɪpi] *adj* **nippier**; **-est** **1** SHARP : fuerte, picante **2** CHILLY : frío ⟨it's nippy today : hoy hace frío⟩

nit ['nɪt] *n* : liendre *f*

nitrate ['naɪ,treɪt] *n* : nitrato *m*

nitric acid ['naɪtrɪk] *n* : ácido *m* nítrico

nitrogen ['naɪtrədʒən] *n* : nitrógeno *m*

nitroglycerin *or* **nitroglycerine** [,naɪtro-'glɪsərən] *n* : nitroglicerina *f*

nitwit ['nɪt,wɪt] *n* : zonzo *m*, -za *f*; bobo *m*, -ba *f*

no[1] ['no:] *adv* : no ⟨are you leaving? — no : ¿te vas? — no⟩ ⟨no less than : no menos de⟩ ⟨to say no : decir que no⟩ ⟨like it or no : quieras o no quieras⟩

no[2] *adj* **1** : ninguno ⟨it's no trouble : no es ningún problema⟩ ⟨she has no money : no tiene dinero⟩ ⟨with little or no experience : con poca o ninguna experiencia⟩ ⟨the sign says "no smoking" : el letrero dice "no fumar"⟩ ⟨there's no arguing with him : no se puede discutir con él⟩ **2** (*indicating a small amount*) ⟨we'll be there in no time : enseguida llegamos⟩ **3** (*expressing that someone or something is not the kind of person or thing being described*) ⟨he's no liar : no es mentiroso⟩ ⟨that's no excuse : eso no es ninguna excusa⟩

no[3] *n*, *pl* **noes** *or* **nos** ['no:z] **1** DENIAL : no *m* ⟨I won't take no for an answer : no aceptaré un no por respuesta⟩ **2** : voto *f* en contra ⟨the noes have it : se ha rechazado la moción⟩

nobility [no'bɪlət̬i] *n* : nobleza *f*

noble[1] ['no:bəl] *adj* **nobler**; **-blest** **1** ILLUSTRIOUS : noble, glorioso **2** ARISTOCRATIC : noble **3** STATELY : majestuoso, magnífico **4** LOFTY : noble; elevado ⟨noble sentiments : sentimientos elevados⟩

noble[2] *n* : noble *mf*, aristócrata *mf*

nobleman ['no:bəlmən] *n*, *pl* **-men** [-mən, -,mɛn] : noble *m*, aristócrata *m*

nobleness ['no:bəlnəs] *n* : nobleza *f*

noblewoman ['no:bəl,wʊmən] *n*, *pl* **-women** [-,wɪmən] : noble *f*, aristócrata *f*

nobly ['no:bli] *adv* : noblemente

nobody[1] ['no:,bɑdi, -,bʌdi] *n*, *pl* **-bodies** : don nadie *m* ⟨he's a mere nobody : es un don nadie⟩

nobody[2] *pron* : nadie

nocturnal [nɑk'tərnəl] *adj* : nocturno

nocturne ['nɑk,tərn] *n* : nocturno *m*

nod[1] ['nɑd] *v* **nodded**; **nodding** *vi* **1** : saludar con la cabeza, asentir con la cabeza **2 to nod off** : dormirse, quedarse dormido — *vt* : inclinar (la cabeza) ⟨to nod one's head in agreement : asentir con la cabeza⟩

nod[2] *n* : saludo *m* con la cabeza, señal *m* con la cabeza, señal *m* de asentimiento

node ['no:d] *n* : nudo *m* (de una planta)
nodule ['na₁dʒu:l] *n* : nódulo *m*
noel [no'ɛl] *n* **1** CAROL : villancico *m* de Navidad **2** Noel CHRISTMAS : Navidad *f*
noes → **no³**
noise *n* : ruido *m*
noiseless ['nɔızləs] *adj* : silencioso, sin ruido
noiselessly ['nɔızləsli] *adv* : silenciosamente
noisemaker ['nɔız₁meıkər] *n* : matraca *f*
noisiness ['nɔızinəs] *n* : ruido *m*
noisy ['nɔızi] *adj* noisier; -est : ruidoso — **noisily** ['nɔızəli] *adv*
nomad¹ ['no:₁mæd] → **nomadic**
nomad² *n* : nómada *mf*
nomadic [no'mædık] *adj* : nómada
nomenclature ['no:mən₁kleıtʃər] *n* : nomenclatura *f*
nominal ['namənəl] *adj* **1** : nominal (the nominal head of his party : el jefe nominal de su partido) **2** TRIFLING : insignificante
nominally ['namənəli] *adv* : sólo de nombre, nominalmente
nominate ['namə₁neıt] *vt* -nated; -nating **1** PROPOSE : proponer (como candidato), nominar **2** APPOINT : nombrar
nomination [₁namə'neıʃən] *n* **1** PROPOSAL : propuesta *f*, postulación *f* **2** APPOINTMENT : nombramiento *m*
nominative¹ ['namənətıv] *adj* : nominativo
nominative² *n or* **nominative case** : nominativo *m*
nominee [₁namə'ni:] *n* : candidato *m*, -ta *f*
non- [₁nan] *pref* : no ⟨non-smoker : no fumador⟩
nonaddictive [₁nanə'dıktıv] *adj* : que no crea dependencia
nonalcoholic [₁nan₁ælkə'hɔlık] *adj* : sin alcohol, no alcohólico
nonaligned [₁nanə'laınd] *adj* : no alineado
nonbeliever [₁nanbə'li:vər] *n* : no creyente *mf*
nonbreakable [₁nan'breıkəbəl] *adj* : irrompible
nonce ['nants] *n* **for the nonce** : por el momento
nonchalance [₁nanʃə'lants] *n* : indiferencia *f*, despreocupación *f*
nonchalant [₁nanʃə'lant] *adj* : indiferente, despreocupado, impasible
nonchalantly [₁nanʃə'lantli] *adv* : con aire despreocupado, con indiferencia
noncombatant [₁nankəm'bætənt, -'kambə-] *n* : no combatiente *mf*
noncommissioned officer [₁nankə-'mıʃənd] *n* : suboficial *mf*
noncommittal [₁nankə'mıtəl] *adj* : evasivo, que no se compromete
nonconductor [₁nankən'dʌktər] *n* : aislante *m*
nonconformist [₁nankən'fɔrmıst] *n* : inconformista *mf*, inconforme *mf*
nonconformity [₁nankən'fɔrməti] *n* : inconformidad *f*, no conformidad *f*
noncontagious [₁nankən'teıdʒəs] *adj* : no contagioso

nondenominational [₁nandı₁namə-'neıʃənəl] *adj* : no sectario
nondescript [₁nandı'skrıpt] *adj* : anodino, soso
nondiscriminatory [₁nandı'skrımənə-₁tori] *adj* : no discriminatorio
nondrinker [₁nan'drınkər] *n* : abstemio *m*, -mia *f*
none¹ ['nʌn] *adv* : de ninguna manera, de ningún modo, nada ⟨he was none too happy : no se sintió nada contento⟩ ⟨I'm none the worse for it : no estoy peor por ello⟩ ⟨none too soon : a buena hora⟩
none² *pron* **1** (*not one*) : ninguno ⟨there's none left : no queda ninguno/ninguna⟩ ⟨none of the cities : ninguna de las ciudades⟩ ⟨do you have any ideas? none whatsoever : ¿se te ocurre algo? no, nada⟩ **2** (*no amount or part*) : nada, ninguna parte ⟨there's none left : no queda nada⟩ ⟨none of it makes any sense : no tiene ningún sentido⟩ ⟨it's none of your business : no es asunto tuyo⟩ **3 to have none of** : no permitir, no aceptar **4 ~ but** : sólo, solamente **5 none other than** : ni más ni menos que **6 second to none** : insuperable
nonentity [₁nan'ɛntəti] *n*, *pl* -ties : persona *f* insignificante, nulidad *f*
nonessential [₁nanı'sɛntʃəl] *adj* : secundario, no esencial
nonessentials [₁nanı'sɛntʃəlz] *npl* : cosas *fpl* secundarias, cosas *fpl* accesorias
nonetheless [₁nʌnðə'lɛs] *adv* : sin embargo, no obstante
nonexistence [₁nanıg'zıstənts] *n* : inexistencia *f*
nonexistent [₁nanıg'zıstənt] *adj* : inexistente
nonfat [₁nan'fæt] *adj* : sin grasa
nonfattening [₁nan'fætənıŋ] *adj* : que no engorda
nonfiction [₁nan'fıkʃən] *n* : no ficción *f*
nonflammable [₁nan'flæməbəl] *adj* : no inflamable
nonintervention [₁nan₁ıntər'vɛntʃən] *n* : no intervención *f*
noninvasive [₁nanın'veısıv] *adj* : no invasivo
nonmalignant [₁nanmə'lıgnənt] *adj* : no maligno, benigno
nonnegotiable [₁nannı'go:ʃəbəl, -ʃiə-] *adj* : no negociable
nonpareil¹ [₁nanpə'rɛl] *adj* : sin parangón, sin par
nonpareil² *n* : persona *f* sin igual, cosa *f* sin par
nonpartisan [₁nan'pɑrtəzən, -sən] *adj* : imparcial
nonpaying [₁nan'peııŋ] *adj* : que no paga
nonpayment [₁nan'peımənt] *n* : impago *m*, falta *f* de pago
nonperson [₁nan'pərsən] *n* : persona *f* sin derechos
nonplus [₁nan'plʌs] *vt* -plussed; -plussing : confundir, desconcertar, dejar perplejo
nonprescription [₁nanpri'skrıpʃən] *adj* : disponible sin receta del médico
nonproductive [₁nanprə'dʌktıv] *adj* : improductivo

nonprofit [ˌnɑnˈprɑfət] *adj* : sin fines lucrativos

nonproliferation [ˌnɑnprəˌlɪfəˈreɪʃən] *adj* : no proliferación

nonresident [ˌnɑnˈrɛzədənt, -ˌdɛnt] *n* : no residente *mf*

nonscheduled [ˌnɑnˈskɛˌdʒuːld] *adj* : no programado, no regular

nonsectarian [ˌnɑnˌsɛkˈtæriən] *adj* : no sectario

nonsense [ˈnɑnˌsɛns, ˈnɑnˌsəns] *n* : tonterías *fpl*, disparates *mpl*

nonsensical [nɑnˈsɛnsɪkəl] *adj* ABSURD : absurdo, disparatado — **nonsensically** [-kli] *adv*

nonsmoker [ˌnɑnˈsmoːkər] *n* : no fumador *m*, -dora *f*; persona *f* que no fuma

nonsmoking [ˌnɑnˈsmoːkɪŋ] *adj* **1 → no-smoking 2** : que no fuma, no fumador (dícese de una persona)

nonstandard [ˌnɑnˈstændərd] *adj* : no regular, no estándar

nonstick [ˌnɑnˈstɪk] *adj* : antiadherente

nonstop¹ [ˌnɑnˈstɑp] *adv* : sin parar ⟨he talked nonstop : habló sin parar⟩

nonstop² *adj* : directo, sin escalas ⟨nonstop flight : vuelo directo⟩

nonsupport [ˌnɑnsəˈpɔrt] *n* : falta *f* de manutención

nontaxable [ˌnɑnˈtæksəbəl] *adj* : exento de impuestos

nontoxic [ˌnɑnˈtɑksɪk] *adj* : no tóxico

nontransferable [ˌnɑnˌtrænsˈfərəbəl] *adj* : intransferible

nonviolence [ˌnɑnˈvaɪlənts, -ˈvaɪə-] *n* : no violencia *f*

nonviolent [ˌnɑnˈvaɪlənt, -ˈvaɪə-] *adj* : pacífico, no violento

noodle [ˈnuːdəl] *n* : fideo *m*, tallarín *m*

nook [ˈnʊk] *n* : rincón *m*, recoveco *m*, escondrijo *m* ⟨in every nook and cranny : en todos los rincones⟩

noon [ˈnuːn] *n* : mediodía *m*

noonday [ˈnuːnˌdeɪ] *n* : mediodía *m* ⟨the noonday sun : el sol de mediodía⟩

no one *pron* NOBODY : nadie

noontime [ˈnuːnˌtaɪm] *n* : mediodía *m*

noose [ˈnuːs] *n* **1** LASSO : lazo *m*, cuerda *f* (con un nudo corredizo) **2 hangman's noose** : soga *f*

nope [ˈnoːp] *adv fam* → **no¹**

nor [ˈnɔr] *conj* : ni ⟨neither good nor bad : ni bueno ni malo⟩ ⟨nor I! : ¡ni yo tampoco!⟩

Nordic [ˈnɔrdɪk] *adj* : nórdico

norm [ˈnɔrm] *n* **1** STANDARD : norma *f*, modelo *m* **2** CUSTOM, RULE : regla *f* general, lo normal

normal [ˈnɔrməl] *adj* : normal — **normally** *adv*

normalcy [ˈnɔrməlsi] *n* : normalidad *f*

normality [nɔrˈmæləti] *n* : normalidad *f*

normalization [ˌnɔrmələˈzeɪʃən] *n* : normalización *f*, regularización *f*

normalize [ˈnɔrməˌlaɪz] *vt* : normalizar

Norse [ˈnɔrs] *adj* : nórdico

north¹ [ˈnɔrθ] *adv* : al norte

north² *adj* : norte, del norte ⟨the north coast : la costa del norte⟩

north³ *n* **1** : norte *m* **2 the North** : el Norte *m*

North American *n* : norteamericano *m*, -na *f* — **North American** *adj*

northbound¹ [ˈnɔrθˌbaʊnd] *adv* : con rumbo al norte

northbound² *adj* : que va hacia el norte

northeast¹ [nɔrˈθiːst] *adv* : hacia el nordeste

northeast² *adj* : nordeste, del nordeste

northeast³ *n* : nordeste *m*, noreste *m*

northeasterly¹ [nɔrˈθiːstərli] *adv* : hacia el nordeste

northeasterly² *adj* : nordeste, del nordeste

northeastern [nɔrˈθiːstərn] *adj* : nordeste, del nordeste

northerly¹ [ˈnɔrðərli] *adv* : hacia el norte

northerly² *adj* : del norte ⟨a northerly wind : un viento del norte⟩

northern [ˈnɔrðərn] *adj* : norte, norteño, septentrional

Northerner [ˈnɔrðərnər] *n* : norteño *m*, -ña *f*

northern lights → aurora borealis

North Pole : Polo *m* Norte

North Star *n* : estrella *f* polar

northward [ˈnɔrθwərd] *adv & adj* : hacia el norte

northwest¹ [nɔrˈθwɛst] *adv* : hacia el noroeste

northwest² *adj* : del noroeste

northwest³ *n* : noroeste *m*

northwesterly¹ [nɔrˈθwɛstərli] *adv* : hacia el noroeste

northwesterly² *adj* : del noroeste

northwestern [nɔrˈθwɛstərn] *adj* : noroeste, del noroeste

Norwegian [nɔrˈwiːdʒən] *n* **1** : noruego *m*, -ga *f* **2** : noruego *m* (idioma) — **Norwegian** *adj*

nose¹ [ˈnoːz] *v* **nosed; nosing** *vt* **1** SMELL : olfatear **2** : empujar con el hocico ⟨the dog nosed open the bag : el perro abrió el saco con el hocico⟩ **3** EDGE, MOVE : mover poco a poco — *vi* **1** PRY : entrometerse, meter las narices **2** EDGE : avanzar poco a poco

nose² *n* **1** : nariz *f* (de una persona), hocico *m* (de un animal) ⟨to blow one's nose : sonarse las narices⟩ **2** SMELL : olfato *m*, sentido *m* del olfato **3** FRONT : parte *f* delantera, nariz *f* (de un avión), proa *f* (de un barco) **4 to be right on the nose** : dar en el clavo **5 to follow one's nose** : dejarse guiar por el instinto **6 to look down one's nose at someone** : mirar a alguien por encima del hombro **7 to pay through the nose** : pagar un ojo de la cara **8 to poke/stick one's nose in** : meter las narices en **9 to turn up one's nose at** : hacerle ascos a **10 to win by a nose** : ganar por un pelo **11 under one's nose** : delante de las narices

nosebleed [ˈnoːzˌbliːd] *n* : hemorragia *f* nasal

nosed [ˈnoːzd] *adj* : de nariz ⟨big-nosed : de nariz grande, narigón⟩

nosedive [ˈnoːzˌdaɪv] *n* **1** : descenso *m* en picada (de un avión) **2** : caída *f* súbita (de precios, etc.)

nose–dive ['no:z,daɪv] vi : descender en picada, caer en picada

no–smoking adj : de no fumar, de/para no fumadores (dícese de un área, etc.)

nostalgia [nɑ'stældʒə, nɔ-] n : nostalgia f

nostalgic [nɑ'stældʒɪk, nɔ-] adj : nostálgico

nostril ['nɑstrəl] n : ventana f de la nariz

nostrum ['nɑstrəm] n : panacea f

nosy or **nosey** ['no:zi] adj **nosier; -est** : entrometido

not ['nɑt] adv 1 (used to form a negative) : no ⟨she is not tired : no está cansada⟩ ⟨not many came : no vinieron muchos⟩ ⟨not to say something would be wrong : no decir algo sería injusto⟩ ⟨not at all : en absoluto⟩ ⟨not a chance : de ninguna manera⟩ ⟨not only . . . but also . . . : no sólo . . . sino también . . .⟩ 2 (used to replace a negative clause) : no ⟨are we going or not? : ¿vamos a ir o no?⟩ ⟨of course not! : ¡claro que no!⟩ ⟨I hope/think not : espero/creo que no⟩ ⟨believe it or not : aunque no lo creas⟩ 3 : menos de ⟨not six inches away : a menos de seis pulgadas⟩ ⟨not all of us agree : no todos estamos de acuerdo⟩

notable[1] ['no:təbəl] adj 1 NOTEWORTHY : notable, de notar 2 DISTINGUISHED, PROMINENT : distinguido, destacado

notable[2] n : persona f importante, personaje m

notably ['no:təbli] adv : notablemente, particularmente

notarize ['no:tə,raɪz] vt **-rized; -rizing** : autenticar, autorizar

notary ['no:təri] or **notary public** n, pl **notaries** or **notaries public** or **notary publics** : notario m, -ria f; escribano m, -na f

notation [no'teɪʃən] n 1 NOTE : anotación f, nota f 2 : notación f ⟨musical notation : notación musical⟩

notch[1] ['nɑtʃ] vt : hacer una muesca en, cortar

notch[2] n : muesca f, corte m

note[1] ['no:t] vt **noted; noting** 1 NOTICE : notar, observar, tomar nota de 2 RECORD : anotar, apuntar

note[2] n 1 : nota f (musical) 2 COMMENT : nota f, comentario m 3 ANNOTATION : nota f, apunte m ⟨to take notes : tomar notas/apuntes⟩ ⟨to compare notes : cambiar impresiones⟩ ⟨I'll make a note of it : lo apuntaré⟩ 4 LETTER : nota f, cartita f ⟨to leave a note : dejar una nota⟩ 5 PROMINENCE : prestigio m ⟨a musician of note : un músico destacado⟩ 6 ATTENTION : atención f ⟨to take note of : tomar nota de, prestar atención a⟩ 7 TOUCH : nota f, dejo m 8 **on a high note** : con una nota de optimismo

notebook ['no:t,bʊk] n 1 : libreta f, cuaderno m 2 : notebook m (computadora)

noted ['no:təd] adj EMINENT : renombrado, eminente, celebrado

notepad ['no:t,pæd] n : bloc m de notas

notepaper ['no:t,peɪpər] n : papel m de escribir

noteworthy ['no:t,wərði] adj : notable, de notar, de interés

nothing[1] ['nʌθɪŋ] adv 1 : de ninguna manera ⟨nothing daunted, we carried on : sin amilanarnos, seguimos adelante⟩ 2 **nothing like** : no . . . en nada ⟨he's nothing like his brother : no se parece en nada a su hermano⟩

nothing[2] n 1 NOTHINGNESS : nada f 2 ZERO : cero m 3 : persona f de poca importancia, cero m 4 TRIFLE : nimiedad f

nothing[3] pron : nada ⟨there's nothing better : no hay nada mejor⟩ ⟨there's nothing like . . . : no hay nada como . . .⟩ ⟨there's nothing to it : es facilísimo⟩ ⟨nothing else : nada más⟩ ⟨nothing but : solamente⟩ ⟨they're nothing but trouble : no traen más que problemas⟩ ⟨they mean nothing to me : ellos me son indiferentes⟩ ⟨I got it for nothing : me lo dieron gratis⟩ ⟨it was all for nothing : todo fue en vano⟩ ⟨are you hurt? it's nothing : ¿te hiciste daño? no es nada⟩ ⟨he's nothing if not polite : es muy cortés⟩

nothingness ['nʌθɪŋnəs] n 1 VOID : vacío m, nada f 2 NONEXISTENCE : inexistencia f 3 TRIFLE : nimiedad f

notice[1] ['no:tɪs] vt **-ticed; -ticing** : notar, observar, advertir, darse cuenta de

notice[2] n 1 NOTIFICATION : aviso m, notificación f ⟨at/on short notice, at a moment's notice : con poca antelación⟩ ⟨until further notice : hasta nuevo aviso⟩ ⟨without notice : sin previo aviso⟩ ⟨to give notice : presentar la renuncia⟩ 2 ATTENTION : atención f ⟨to take notice of : prestar atención a⟩ ⟨to make someone sit up and take notice : hacer que alguien preste atención⟩

noticeable ['no:tɪsəbəl] adj : evidente, perceptible — **noticeably** [-bli] adv

notification [,no:təfə'keɪʃən] n : notificación f, aviso m

notify ['no:tə,faɪ] vt **-fied; -fying** : notificar, avisar

notion ['no:ʃən] n 1 IDEA : idea f, noción f 2 WHIM : capricho m, antojo m 3 **notions** npl : artículos mpl de mercería

notoriety [,no:tə'raɪəti] n : mala fama f, notoriedad f

notorious [no'to:riəs] adj : de mala fama, célebre, bien conocido

notwithstanding[1] [,nɑtwɪθ'stændɪŋ, -wɪð-] adv NEVERTHELESS : no obstante, sin embargo

notwithstanding[2] conj : a pesar de que

notwithstanding[3] prep : a pesar de, no obstante

nougat ['nu:gət] n : turrón m

nought ['nɔt, 'nɑt] → **naught**

noun ['naʊn] n : nombre m, sustantivo m

nourish ['nərɪʃ] vt 1 FEED : alimentar, nutrir, sustentar 2 FOSTER : fomentar, alentar

nourishing ['nərɪʃɪŋ] adj : alimenticio, nutritivo

nourishment ['nərɪʃmənt] n : nutrición f, alimento m, sustento m

novel¹ ['navəl] *adj* : original, novedoso

novel² *n* : novela *f*

novelist ['navəlɪst] *n* : novelista *mf*

novelty ['navəlti] *n, pl* **-ties** **1** : novedad *f* **2 novelties** *npl* TRINKETS : baratijas *fpl*, chucherías *fpl*

November [no'vɛmbər] *n* : noviembre *m* ⟨they arrived on the 18th of November, they arrived on November 18th : llegaron el 18 de noviembre⟩

novena [no'vi:nə] *n* : novena *f*

novice ['navɪs] *n* : novato *m*, -ta *f*; principiante *mf*; novicio *m*, -cia *f*

novocaine ['no:və,keɪn] *n* : novocaína *f*

now¹ ['nau] *adv* **1** PRESENTLY : ahora, ya, actualmente ⟨from now on : de ahora en adelante⟩ ⟨for now : por ahora⟩ ⟨for several months now : desde hace varios meses⟩ ⟨between now and . . . , from now until . . . : de aquí a . . .⟩ ⟨long before now : ya hace tiempo⟩ ⟨now or never : ahora o nunca⟩ **2** SOON : dentro de poco, pronto ⟨any day now : cualquier día de estos⟩ ⟨they'll be here any minute now : estarán por caer⟩ **3** : ahora, como están las cosas ⟨do you believe me now? : ¿ahora me crees?⟩ **4** IMMEDIATELY : ahora (mismo), inmediatamente ⟨do it right now! : ¡hazlo ahora mismo!⟩ **5** THEN : ya, entonces ⟨now they were ready : ya estaban listos⟩ **6** (*used to introduce a statement, a question, a command, or a transition*) ⟨now hear this! : ¡presten atención!⟩ ⟨now what do you think of that? : ¿qué piensas de eso?⟩ **7 now and then** : de vez en cuando **8 now, now** : vamos, vamos

now² *n* (*indicating the present time*) ⟨until now : hasta ahora⟩ ⟨by now : ya⟩ ⟨ten years from now : dentro de 10 años⟩

now³ *conj* ahora que, ya que

nowadays ['nauə,deɪz] *adv* : hoy en día, actualmente, en la actualidad

nowhere¹ ['no:,hwɛr] *adv* **1** : en ninguna parte, a ningún lado ⟨nowhere to be found : en ninguna parte, por ningún lado⟩ ⟨you're going nowhere : no estás yendo a ningún lado, no estás yendo a ninguna parte⟩ **2 nowhere near** : ni con mucho, nada cerca ⟨it's nowhere near here : no está nada cerca de aquí⟩ ⟨it's nowhere near finished : no está terminado ni mucho menos⟩

nowhere² *n* **1** : ninguna parte *f* **2 out of nowhere** : de la nada

noxious ['nakʃəs] *adj* : nocivo, dañino, tóxico

nozzle ['nazəl] *n* : boca *f*, boquilla *f*

nth ['ɛnθ] *adj* **1** : enésimo ⟨for the nth time : por enésima vez⟩ **2 to the nth degree** EXTREMELY : al máximo, sumamente

nuance ['nu:,ɑnts, 'nju:-] *n* : matiz *m*

nub ['nʌb] *n* **1** KNOB, LUMP : protuberancia *f*, nudo *m* **2** GIST : quid *m*, meollo *m*

nuclear ['nu:kliər, 'nju:-] *adj* : nuclear

nucleus ['nu:kliəs, 'nju:-] *n, pl* **-clei** [-kli,aɪ] : núcleo *m*

nude¹ ['nu:d, 'nju:d] *adj* **nuder; nudest** : desnudo

nude² *n* : desnudo *m*

nudge¹ ['nʌdʒ] *vt* **nudged; nudging** : darle con el codo (a alguien)

nudge² *n* : toque *m* que se da con el codo

nudism ['nu:,dɪzəm, 'nju:-] *n* : nudismo *m*

nudist ['nu:dɪst, 'nju:-] *n* : nudista *mf*

nudity ['nu:dəti, 'nju:-] *n* : desnudez *f*

nugget ['nʌgət] *n* : pepita *f*

nuisance ['nu:sənts, 'nju:-] *n* **1** BOTHER : fastidio *m*, molestia *f*, lata *f* **2** PEST : pesado *m*, -da *f fam*

nuke¹ ['nu:k, 'nju:k] *vt* **nuked; nuking** *fam* **1** : atacar con armas nucleares **2** : cocinar en el microondas

nuke² *n fam* : arma *m* nuclear

null ['nʌl] *adj* : nulo ⟨null and void : nulo y sin efecto⟩

nullify ['nʌlə,faɪ] *vt* **-fied; -fying** : invalidar, anular

nullity ['nʌləti] *n, pl* **-ties** : nulidad *f*

numb¹ ['nʌm] *vt* : entumecer, adormecer

numb² *adj* : entumecido, dormido ⟨numb with fear : paralizado de miedo⟩

number¹ ['nʌmbər] *vt* **1** COUNT, INCLUDE : contar, incluir **2** : numerar ⟨number the pages : numera las páginas⟩ **3** TOTAL : ascender a, sumar

number² *n* **1** : número *m* ⟨in round numbers : en números redondos⟩ **2 or telephone number** *or* **phone number** : número *m* (de teléfono) **3 a number of** : varios, unos pocos, unos cuantos **4 any number of** : una cantidad de **5 to look out for number one** : pensar ante todo en el propio interés

numberless ['nʌmbərləs] *adj* : innumerable, sin número

numbness ['nʌmnəs] *n* : entumecimiento *m*

numeral ['nu:mərəl, 'nju:-] *n* : número *m* ⟨Roman numeral : número romano⟩

numerator ['nu:mə,reɪtər, 'nju:-] *n* : numerador *m*

numeric [nu'mɛrɪk, nju-] *adj* : numérico

numerical [nu'mɛrɪkəl, nju-] *adj* : numérico — **numerically** [-kli] *adv*

numerous ['nu:mərəs, 'nju:-] *adj* : numeroso

numismatics [,nu:məz'mætɪks, ,nju:-] *n* : numismática *f*

numskull ['nʌm,skʌl] *n* : tonto *m*, -ta *f*; mentecato *m*, -ta *f*; zoquete *m fam*

nun ['nʌn] *n* : monja *f*

nuptial ['nʌpʃəl] *adj* : nupcial

nuptials ['nʌpʃəlz] *npl* WEDDING : nupcias *fpl*, boda *f*

nurse¹ ['nərs] *vt* **nursed; nursing** **1** SUCKLE : amamantar **2** : cuidar (de), atender ⟨to nurse the sick : cuidar a los enfermos⟩ ⟨to nurse a cold : curarse de un resfriado⟩

nurse² *n* **1** : enfermero *m*, -ra *f* **2** → **nursemaid**

nursemaid ['nərs,meɪd] *n* : niñera *f*

nursery ['nərsəri] *n, pl* **-eries** **1** *or* **day nursery** : guardería *f* **2** : vivero *m* (de plantas)

nursery rhyme *n* : canción *f* infantil

nursery school *n* : parvulario *m*

nursing ['nərsɪŋ] *n* : profesión *f* de enfermero

nursing home *n* : hogar *m* de ancianos, clínica *f* de reposo

nurture[1] [ˈnərtʃər] *vt* -**tured**; -**turing** 1 FEED, NOURISH : nutrir, alimentar 2 EDUCATE : criar, educar 3 FOSTER : alimentar, fomentar

nurture[2] *n* 1 UPBRINGING : crianza *f*, educación *f* 2 FOOD : alimento *m*

nut [ˈnʌt] *n* 1 : nuez *f* 2 : tuerca *f* ⟨nuts and bolts : tuercas y tornillos⟩ 3 LUNATIC : loco *m*, -ca *f*; chiflado *m*, -da *f* *fam* 4 ENTHUSIAST : fanático *m*, -ca *f*; entusiasta *mf*

nutcracker [ˈnʌtˌkrækər] *n* : cascanueces *m*

nuthatch [ˈnʌtˌhætʃ] *n* : trepador *m*

nutmeg [ˈnʌtˌmɛg] *n* : nuez *f* moscada

nutria [ˈnuːtriə, ˈnjuː-] *n* : nutria *f*

nutrient [ˈnuːtriənt, ˈnjuː-] *n* : nutriente *m*, alimento *m* nutritivo

nutriment [ˈnuːtrəmənt, ˈnjuː-] *n* : nutrimento *m*

nutrition [nʊˈtrɪʃən, njuː-] *n* : nutrición *f*

nutritional [nʊˈtrɪʃənəl, njuː-] *adj* : alimenticio

nutritionist [nʊˈtrɪʃənɪst, njuː-] *n* : nutricionista *mf*

nutritious [nʊˈtrɪʃəs, njuː-] *adj* : nutritivo, alimenticio

nuts [ˈnʌts] *adj* 1 FANATICAL : fanático 2 CRAZY : loco, chiflado *fam*

nutshell [ˈnʌtˌʃɛl] *n* 1 : cáscara *f* de nuez 2 **in a nutshell** : en pocas palabras

nutty [ˈnʌti] *adj* **nuttier**; **-est** : loco, chiflado *fam*

nuzzle [ˈnʌzəl] *v* -**zled**; -**zling** *vi* NESTLE : acurrucarse, arrimarse — *vt* : acariciar con el hocico

nylon [ˈnaɪˌlɑn] *n* 1 : nilón *m* 2 **nylons** *npl* : medias *fpl* de nilón

nymph [ˈnɪmpf] *n* : ninfa *f*

O

o [ˈoː] *n*, *pl* **o's** *or* **os** [ˈoːz] 1 : decimoquinta letra del alfabeto inglés 2 ZERO : cero *m*

O [ˈoː] → **oh**

oaf [ˈoːf] *n* : zoquete *m*; bruto *m*, -ta *f*

oafish [ˈoːfɪʃ] *adj* : torpe, lerdo

oak [ˈoːk] *n*, *pl* **oaks** *or* **oak** : roble *m*

oaken [ˈoːkən] *adj* : de roble

oar [ˈor] *n* : remo *m*

oarlock [ˈorˌlɑk] *n* : tolete *m*

oasis [oˈeɪsɪs] *n*, *pl* **oases** [-ˌsiːz] : oasis *m*

oat [ˈoːt] *n* : avena *f*

oath [ˈoːθ] *n*, *pl* **oaths** [ˈoːðz, ˈoːθs] 1 : juramento *m* ⟨to take an oath : prestar juramento⟩ 2 SWEARWORD : mala palabra *f*, palabrota *f*

oatmeal [ˈoːtˌmiːl] *n* : avena *f* ⟨instant oatmeal : avena instantánea⟩

obdurate [ˈɑbdʊrət, -djʊ-] *adj* : inflexible, firme, obstinado

obedience [oˈbiːdiənts] *n* : obediencia *f*

obedient [oˈbiːdiənt] *adj* : obediente — **obediently** *adv*

obelisk [ˈɑbəˌlɪsk] *n* : obelisco *m*

obese [oˈbiːs] *adj* : obeso

obesity [oˈbiːsəti] *n* : obesidad *f*

obey [oˈbeɪ] *v* **obeyed**; **obeying** : obedecer ⟨to obey the law : cumplir la ley⟩

obfuscate [ˈɑbfəˌskeɪt] *vt* -**cated**; -**cating** : ofuscar, confundir

obituary [əˈbɪtʃuˌeri] *n*, *pl* -**aries** : obituario *m*, necrología *f*

object[1] [ˈɑbˌdʒɛkt] *vt* : objetar — *vi* : oponerse, poner reparos, hacer objeciones

object[2] [ˈɑbdʒɪkt] *n* 1 : objeto *m* 2 OBJECTIVE, PURPOSE : objetivo *m*, propósito *m* 3 : complemento *m* (en gramática)

objection [əbˈdʒɛkʃən] *n* : objeción *f*

objectionable [əbˈdʒɛkʃənəbəl] *adj* : ofensivo, indeseable — **objectionably** [-bli] *adv*

objective[1] [əbˈdʒɛktɪv] *adj* 1 IMPARTIAL : objetivo, imparcial 2 : de complemento, directo (en gramática)

objective[2] *n* 1 : objetivo *m* 2 *or* **objective case** : acusativo *m*

objectively [əbˈdʒɛktɪvli] *adv* : objetivamente

objectivity [ˌɑbˌdʒɛkˈtɪvəti] *n*, *pl* -**ties** : objetividad *f*

objector [əbˈdʒɛktər] *n* : objetor *m*, -tora *f* ⟨conscientious objector : objetor de conciencia⟩

obligate [ˈɑbləˌgeɪt] *vt* -**gated**; -**gating** : obligar

obligation [ˌɑbləˈgeɪʃən] *n* : obligación *f*

obligatory [əˈblɪgəˌtori] *adj* : obligatorio

oblige [əˈblaɪdʒ] *vt* **obliged**; **obliging** 1 COMPEL : obligar 2 : hacerle un favor (a alguien), complacer ⟨to oblige a friend : hacerle un favor a un amigo⟩ 3 **to be much obliged** : estar muy agradecido

obliging [əˈblaɪdʒɪŋ] *adj* : servicial, complaciente — **obligingly** *adv*

oblique [oˈbliːk] *adj* 1 SLANTING : oblicuo 2 INDIRECT : indirecto — **obliquely** *adv*

obliterate [əˈblɪtəˌreɪt] *vt* -**ated**; -**ating** 1 ERASE : obliterar, borrar 2 DESTROY : destruir, eliminar

obliteration [əˌblɪtəˈreɪʃən] *n* : obliteración *f*

oblivion [əˈblɪviən] *n* : olvido *m*

oblivious [əˈblɪviəs] *adj* : inconsciente — **obliviously** *adv*

oblong[1] [ˈɑˌblɑŋ] *adj* : oblongo

oblong[2] *n* : figura *f* oblonga, rectángulo *m*

obnoxious [ɑbˈnɑkʃəs, əb-] *adj* : repugnante, odioso — **obnoxiously** *adv*

oboe [ˈoːˌboː] *n* : oboe *m*

oboist [ˈoːˌboɪst] *n* : oboe *mf*

obscene [ɑbˈsiːn, əb-] *adj* : obsceno, indecente — **obscenely** *adv*

obscenity [ab'sɛnəti, əb-] *n*, *pl* **-ties** : obscenidad *f*

obscure¹ [ab'skjʊr, əb-] *vt* **-scured; -scuring** 1 CLOUD, DIM : oscurecer, nublar 2 HIDE : ocultar

obscure² *adj* 1 DIM : oscuro 2 REMOTE, SECLUDED : recóndito 3 VAGUE : oscuro, confuso, vago 4 UNKNOWN : desconocido ⟨an obscure poet : un poeta desconocido⟩ — **obscurely** *adv*

obscurity [ab'skjʊrəti, əb-] *n*, *pl* **-ties** : oscuridad *f*

obsequious [əb'si:kwiəs] *adj* : servil, excesivamente atento

observable [əb'zərvəbəl] *adj* : observable, perceptible

observance [əb'zərvənts] *n* 1 FULFILLMENT : observancia *f*, cumplimiento *m* 2 PRACTICE : práctica *f*

observant [əb'zərvənt] *adj* : observador

observation [ˌabsər'veɪʃən, -zər-] *n* : observación *f*

observatory [əb'zərvəˌtori] *n*, *pl* **-ries** : observatorio *m*

observe [əb'zərv] *v* **-served; -serving** *vt* 1 OBEY : observar, obedecer 2 CELEBRATE : celebrar, guardar (una práctica religiosa) 3 WATCH : observar, mirar 4 REMARK : observar, comentar — *vi* LOOK : mirar

observer [əb'zərvər] *n* : observador *m*, -dora *f*

obsess [əb'sɛs] *vt* : obsesionar

obsession [ab'sɛʃən, əb-] *n* : obsesión *f*

obsessive [ab'sɛsɪv, əb-] *adj* : obsesivo — **obsessively** *adv*

obsolescence [ˌabsə'lɛsənts] *n* : obsolescencia *f*

obsolescent [ˌabsə'lɛsənt] *adj* : obsolescente ⟨to become obsolescent : caer en desuso⟩

obsolete [ˌabsə'li:t, 'absə-] *adj* : obsoleto, anticuado

obstacle ['abstɪkəl] *n* : obstáculo *m*, impedimento *m*

obstetric [əb'stɛtrɪk] *or* **obstetrical** [-trɪkəl] *adj* : obstétrico

obstetrician [ˌabstə'trɪʃən] *n* : obstetra *mf*; tocólogo *m*, -ga *f*

obstetrics [əb'stɛtrɪks] *ns & pl* : obstetricia *f*, tocología *f*

obstinacy ['abstənəsi] *n*, *pl* **-cies** : obstinación *f*, terquedad *f*

obstinate ['abstənət] *adj* : obstinado, terco — **obstinately** *adv*

obstreperous [əb'strɛpərəs] *adj* 1 CLAMOROUS : ruidoso, clamoroso 2 UNRULY : rebelde, indisciplinado

obstruct [əb'strʌkt] *vt* : obstruir, bloquear

obstruction [əb'strʌkʃən] *n* : obstrucción *f*, bloqueo *m*

obstructive [əb'strʌktɪv] *adj* : obstructor

obtain [əb'teɪn] *vt* : obtener, conseguir — *vi* PREVAIL : imperar, prevalecer

obtainable [əb'teɪnəbəl] *adj* : obtenible, asequible

obtrusive [əb'tru:sɪv] *adj* 1 IMPERTINENT, MEDDLESOME : impertinente, entrometido 2 PROTRUDING : prominente

obtuse [ab'tu:s, əb-, -'tju:s] *adj* : obtuso, torpe

obtuse angle *n* : ángulo obtuso

obvious ['abviəs] *adj* : obvio, evidente, manifiesto

obviously ['abviəsli] *adv* 1 CLEARLY : obviamente, evidentemente 2 OF COURSE : claro, por supuesto

occasion¹ [ə'keɪʒən] *vt* : ocasionar, causar

occasion² *n* 1 OPPORTUNITY : oportunidad *f*, ocasión *f* 2 CAUSE : motivo *m*, razón *f* 3 INSTANCE : ocasión *f* 4 EVENT : ocasión *f*, acontecimiento *m* 5 **on ~** : de vez en cuando, ocasionalmente

occasional [ə'keɪʒənəl] *adj* : ocasional

occasionally [ə'keɪʒənəli] *adv* : de vez en cuando, ocasionalmente

occult¹ [ə'kʌlt, 'aˌkʌlt] *adj* 1 HIDDEN, SECRET : oculto, secreto 2 ARCANE : arcano, esotérico

occult² *n* **the occult** : las ciencias ocultas

occupancy ['akjəpəntsi] *n*, *pl* **-cies** : ocupación *f*, habitación *f*

occupant ['akjəpənt] *n* : ocupante *mf*

occupation [ˌakjə'peɪʃən] *n* : ocupación *f*, profesión *f*, oficio *m*

occupational [ˌakjə'peɪʃənəl] *adj* : ocupacional

occupier ['akjəˌpaɪər] *n* : ocupante *mf*

occupy ['akjəˌpaɪ] *vt* **-pied; -pying** : ocupar

occur [ə'kər] *vi* **occurred; occurring** 1 EXIST : encontrarse, existir 2 HAPPEN : ocurrir, acontecer, suceder, tener lugar 3 : ocurrirse ⟨it occurred to him that . . . : se le ocurrió que . . .⟩

occurrence [ə'kərənts] *n* : acontecimiento *m*, suceso *m*, ocurrencia *f*

ocean ['oːʃən] *n* : océano *m*

oceanic [ˌoːʃiˈænɪk] *adj* : oceánico

oceanography [ˌoːʃəˈnagrəfi] *n* : oceanografía *f* — **oceanographic** *adj*

ocelot ['asəˌlat, 'oːsəˌ-] *n* : ocelote *m*

ocher *or* **ochre** ['oːkər] *n* : ocre *m*

o'clock [ə'klak] *adv* (*used in telling time*) ⟨it's ten o'clock : son las diez⟩ ⟨at six o'clock : a las seis⟩

octagon ['aktəˌgan] *n* : octágono *m*

octagonal [ak'tægənəl] *adj* : octagonal

octave ['aktɪv] *n* : octava *f*

October [ak'toːbər] *n* : octubre *m* ⟨they arrived on the 13th of October, they arrived on October 13th : llegaron el 13 de octubre⟩

octopus ['aktəˌpʊs, -pəs] *n*, *pl* **-puses** *or* **-pi** [-ˌpaɪ] : pulpo *m*

ocular ['akjələr] *adj* : ocular

oculist ['akjəlɪst] *n* 1 OPHTHALMOLOGIST : oftalmólogo *m*, -ga *f*; oculista *mf* 2 OPTOMETRIST : optometrista *mf*

odd ['ad] *adj* 1 : sin pareja, suelto ⟨an odd sock : un calcetín sin pareja⟩ 2 UNEVEN : impar ⟨odd numbers : números impares⟩ 3 : y pico, y tantos ⟨forty-odd years ago : hace cuarenta y pico años⟩ 4 : alguno, uno que otro ⟨odd jobs : algunos trabajos⟩ 5 STRANGE : extraño, raro

oddball ['adˌbɔl] *n* : excéntrico *m*, -ca *f*; persona *f* rara

oddity ['ɑdəṱi] *n, pl* **-ties** : rareza *f*, cosa *f* rara

oddly ['ɑdli] *adv* : de manera extraña

oddness ['ɑdnəs] *n* : rareza *f*, excentricidad *f*

odds ['ɑdz] *npl* **1** CHANCES : probabilidades *fpl* ⟨against all odds : contra viento y marea⟩ **2** : puntos *mpl* de ventaja (de una apuesta) **3 to be at odds** : estar en desacuerdo

odds and ends *npl* : costillas *fpl*, cosas *fpl* sueltas, cachivaches *mpl*

ode ['o:d] *n* : oda *f*

odious ['o:diəs] *adj* : odioso — **odiously** *adv*

odometer [o'dɑmətər] *n* : cuentakilómetros *m*, odómetro *m*

odor ['o:dər] *n* : olor *m*

odorless ['o:dərləs] *adj* : inodoro, sin olor

odyssey ['ɑdəsi] *n, pl* **-seys** : odisea *f*

o'er ['or] → **over**

of ['ʌv, 'əv] *prep* **1** FROM : de ⟨a man of the city : un hombre de la ciudad⟩ **2** (*indicating a quality or characteristic*) : de ⟨a woman of great ability : una mujer de gran capacidad⟩ ⟨a boy of twelve : un niño de doce años⟩ ⟨her husband of 30 years : su marido, con quien lleva 30 años de casada⟩ **3** (*describing behavior*) : de parte de (alguien) ⟨that was very nice of you : fue muy amable de tu parte⟩ **4** (*indicating cause*) : de ⟨he died of the flu : murió de la gripe⟩ **5** BY : de ⟨the works of Shakespeare : las obras de Shakespeare⟩ **6** (*indicating contents, material, or quantity*) : de ⟨a house of wood : una casa de madera⟩ ⟨a glass of water : un vaso de agua⟩ ⟨thousands of people : miles de personas⟩ **7** (*indicating belonging or connection*) : de ⟨the front of the house : el frente de la casa⟩ ⟨a friend of mine : un amigo mío⟩ ⟨the President of the United States : el presidente de los Estados Unidos⟩ ⟨the best of intentions : las mejores intenciones⟩ **8** (*indicating belonging to a group*) : de ⟨one of my friends : uno de mis amigos⟩ ⟨the four of us went : fuimos los cuatro⟩ ⟨two of which : dos de los/las cuales⟩ **9** ABOUT : sobre, de ⟨tales of the West : los cuentos del Oeste⟩ **10** (*indicating a particular example*) : de ⟨the city of Caracas : la ciudad de Caracas⟩ **11** FOR : por, a ⟨love of country : amor por la patria⟩ **12** (*indicating time or date*) ⟨five minutes of ten : las diez menos cinco⟩ ⟨the eighth of April : el ocho de abril⟩

off¹ ['ɔf] *adv* **1** (*indicating change of position or state*) ⟨to march off : marcharse⟩ ⟨he dozed off : se puso a dormir⟩ **2** (*indicating distance in space or time*) ⟨some miles off : a varias millas⟩ ⟨the holiday is three weeks off : faltan tres semanas para la fiesta⟩ **3** (*indicating removal*) ⟨the knob came off : se le cayó el pomo⟩ ⟨he took off his coat : se quitó el abrigo⟩ **4** (*indicating termination*) ⟨shut the television off : apaga la televisión⟩ ⟨to finish off : terminar, acabar⟩ **5** (*indicating suspension of work*) ⟨to take a

day off : tomarse un día de descanso⟩ **6 off and on** : de vez en cuando

off² *adj* **1** FARTHER : más remoto, distante ⟨the off side of the building : el lado distante del edificio⟩ **2** STARTED : empezado ⟨to be off on a spree : irse de juerga⟩ **3** OUT : apagado ⟨the light is off : la luz está apagada⟩ **4** CANCELED : cancelado, suspendido **5** INCORRECT : erróneo, incorrecto **6** REMOTE : remoto, lejano ⟨an off chance : una posibilidad remota⟩ **7** FREE : libre ⟨I'm off today : hoy estoy libre⟩ **8** SPOILED : estropeado, cortado **9 to be well off** : vivir con desahogo, tener bastante dinero

off³ *prep* **1** (*indicating physical separation*) : de ⟨she took it off the table : lo tomó de la mesa⟩ ⟨a shop off the main street : una tienda al lado de la calle principal⟩ **2** : a la costa de, a expensas de ⟨he lives off his sister : vive a expensas de su hermana⟩ **3** (*indicating the suspension of an activity*) ⟨to be off duty : estar libre⟩ ⟨he's off liquor : ha dejado el alcohol⟩ **4** BELOW : por debajo de ⟨he's off his game : está por debajo de su juego normal⟩

offal ['ɔfəl] *n* **1** RUBBISH, WASTE : desechos *mpl*, desperdicios *mpl* **2** VISCERA : vísceras *fpl*, asaduras *fpl*

off-balance ['ɔf'bæləns] *adj* : desequilibrado

off-color ['ɔf'kʌlər] *adj* : subido de tono, pícaro, picante

offend [ə'fɛnd] *vt* **1** VIOLATE : violar, atentar contra **2** HURT : ofender ⟨to be easily offended : ser muy susceptible⟩

offender [ə'fɛndər] *n* : delincuente *mf*; infractor *m*, -tora *f*

offense *or* **offence** [ə'fɛnts, 'ɔ,fɛnts] *n* **1** INSULT : ofensa *f*, injuria *f*, agravio *m* ⟨to take offense : ofenderse⟩ **2** ASSAULT : ataque *m* **3** : ofensiva *f* (en deportes) **4** CRIME, INFRACTION : infracción *f*, delito *m*

offensive¹ [ə'fɛntsɪv, 'ɔ,fɛnt-] *adj* : ofensivo — **offensively** *adv*

offensive² *n* : ofensiva *f*

offer¹ ['ɔfər] *vt* **1** : ofrecer ⟨they offered him the job : le ofrecieron el puesto⟩ **2** PROPOSE : proponer, sugerir **3** SHOW : ofrecer, mostrar ⟨to offer resistance : ofrecer resistencia⟩

offer² *n* : oferta *f*, ofrecimiento *m*, propuesta *f*

offering ['ɔfərɪŋ] *n* : ofrenda *f*

offhand¹ ['ɔf'hænd] *adv* : sin preparación, sin pensarlo

offhand² *adj* **1** IMPROMPTU : improvisado **2** ABRUPT : brusco

office ['ɔfəs] *n* **1** : cargo *m* ⟨to run for office : presentarse como candidato⟩ **2** : oficina *f*, despacho *m*, gabinete *m* (en la casa)

officeholder ['ɔfəs,ho:ldər] *n* : titular *mf*

office hours *n* : horas *fpl* de oficina

officer ['ɔfəsər] *n* **1** → **police officer 2** OFFICIAL : oficial *mf*; funcionario *m*, -ria *f*; director *m*, -tora *f* (en una empresa) **3** COMMISSIONED OFFICER : oficial *mf*

office worker n : oficinista mf
official¹ [ə'fɪʃəl] adj : oficial — **officially** adv
official² n : funcionario m, -ria f; oficial mf
officiate [ə'fɪʃi,eɪt] v -ated; -ating vi 1 : arbitrar (en deportes) 2 **to officiate at** : oficiar, celebrar — vt 2 : arbitrar
officious [ə'fɪʃəs] adj : oficioso
offing ['ɔfɪŋ] n **in the offing** : en perspectiva
off–key ['ɔf'ki] adj : desafinado
off–line ['ɔf'laɪn] adj : fuera de línea
off–peak ['ɔf'pi:k] adj : fuera de las horas pico
off–putting ['ɔf,pʊtɪŋ] adj : desagradable, repelente
offset ['ɔf,sɛt] vt -set; -setting : compensar
offshoot ['ɔf,ʃu:t] n 1 OUTGROWTH : producto m, resultado m 2 BRANCH, SHOOT : retoño m, rama f, vástago m (de una planta)
offshore¹ ['ɔf'ʃor] adv : a una distancia de la costa
offshore² adj 1 : de (la) tierra ⟨an offshore wind : un viento que sopla de tierra⟩ 2 : (de) costa afuera, cercano a la costa ⟨an offshore island : una isla costera⟩
offside ['ɔf'saɪd] adj : fuera de juego (en deportes)
offspring ['ɔf,sprɪŋ] ns & pl 1 YOUNG : crías fpl (de los animales) 2 PROGENY : prole f, progenie f
off–white ['ɔf'hwaɪt] adj : blancuzco
often ['ɔfən, 'ɔftən] adv : muchas veces, a menudo, seguido
oftentimes ['ɔfən,taɪmz, 'ɔftən-] or **ofttimes** ['ɔft,taɪmz] → **often**
ogle ['o:gəl] vt ogled; ogling : comerse con los ojos, quedarse mirando a
ogre ['o:gər] n : ogro m
oh ['o:] interj : ¡oh!, ¡ah!, ¡ay! ⟨oh, of course : ah, por supuesto⟩ ⟨oh no! : ¡ay no!⟩ ⟨oh really? : ¿de veras?⟩
ohm ['o:m] n : ohm m, ohmio m
oil¹ ['ɔɪl] vt : lubricar, engrasar, aceitar
oil² n 1 : aceite m 2 PETROLEUM : petróleo m 3 or **oil painting** : óleo m, pintura f al óleo 4 or **oil paint(s)** : óleo m
oilcan ['ɔɪl,kæn] n : aceitera f
oilcloth ['ɔɪl,klɔθ] n : hule m
oiliness ['ɔɪlinəs] n : lo aceitoso
oil rig → **rig²**
oilskin ['ɔɪl,skɪn] n 1 : hule m 2 **oilskins** npl : impermeable m
oil slick n : marea f negra
oil well n : pozo m petrolero
oily ['ɔɪli] adj **oilier; -est** : aceitoso, grasiento, grasoso ⟨oily fingers : dedos grasientos⟩
ointment ['ɔɪntmənt] n : ungüento m, pomada f
OK¹ [,o:'keɪ] vt **OK'd** or **okayed** [,o:'keɪd]; **OK'ing** or **okaying** APPROVE, AUTHORIZE : dar el visto bueno a, autorizar, aprobar
OK² or **okay** [,o:'keɪ] adv 1 WELL : bien 2 YES : sí, por supuesto

OK³ adj : bien ⟨he's OK : está bien⟩ ⟨it's OK with me : estoy de acuerdo⟩
OK⁴ n : autorización f, visto m bueno
okra ['o:krə, South also -kri] n : quingombó m
old¹ ['o:ld] adj 1 ANCIENT : antiguo ⟨old civilizations : civilizaciones antiguas⟩ 2 FAMILIAR : viejo ⟨old friends : viejos amigos⟩ ⟨the same old story : la misma historia de siempre⟩ 3 (indicating a certain age) ⟨how old is he? : ¿cuántos años tiene?⟩ ⟨he's ten years old : tiene diez años (de edad)⟩ ⟨he's a year older than I am : es un año mayor que yo⟩ ⟨she's my older sister : es mi hermana mayor⟩ ⟨our oldest daughter : nuestra hija mayor⟩ 4 AGED : viejo, anciano ⟨an old woman : una anciana⟩ 5 FORMER : antiguo ⟨her old neighborhood : su antiguo barrio⟩ 6 WORN-OUT : viejo, gastado 7 **any old** fam : cualquier
old² n 1 **the old** : los viejos, los ancianos 2 **in the days of old** : antaño, en los tiempos antiguos
old age n : vejez f
olden ['o:ldən] adj : de antaño, de antigüedad
old–fashioned ['o:ld'fæʃənd] adj : anticuado, pasado de moda
old maid n offensive SPINSTER : solterona f
Old Testament n : Antiguo Testamento m
old–time ['o:ld'taɪm] adj : antiguo
old–timer ['o:ld'taɪmər] n 1 VETERAN : veterano m, -na f 2 or **oldster** : anciano m, -na f
old–world ['o:ld'wərld] adj : pintoresco (de antaño)
oleander ['o:li,ændər] n : adelfa f
oleomargarine [,o:lio'mɑrdʒərən] → **margarine**
olfactory [ɑl'fæktəri, ol-] adj : olfativo
oligarchy ['ɑlə,gɑrki, 'o:lə-] n, pl -chies : oligarquía f
olive ['ɑlɪv, -ləv] n 1 : aceituna f, oliva f (fruta) 2 : olivo m (árbol) 3 or **olive green** : color m aceituna, verde m oliva
olive oil n : aceite m de oliva
Olmec ['ɑl,mɛk, 'o:l-] n : olmeca mf — **Olmec** adj
Olympiad [ə'lɪmpi,æd, o-] n : olimpiada f
Olympic [ə'lɪmpɪk, o-] adj : olímpico
Olympic Games npl : Juegos mpl Olímpicos
Olympics [ə'lɪmpɪks, o-] npl : olimpiadas fpl
Omani [o'mɑni, -'mæ-] n : omaní mf — **Omani** adj
ombudsman ['ɑm,bʊdzmən, ɑm-'bʊdz-] n, pl -men [-mən, -,mɛn] : ombudsman m
omelet or **omelette** ['ɑmlət, 'ɑmə-] n : omelette mf, tortilla f (de huevo)
omen ['o:mən] n : presagio m, augurio m, agüero m
ominous ['ɑmənəs] adj : ominoso, agorero, de mal agüero
ominously ['ɑmənəsli] adv : de manera amenazadora
omission [o'mɪʃən] n : omisión f
omit [o'mɪt] vt omitted; omitting 1 LEAVE OUT : omitir, excluir 2 NEGLECT

: omitir ⟨they omitted to tell us : omitieron decírnoslo⟩

omnipotence [ɑm'nɪpətəns] *n* : omnipotencia *f* — **omnipotent** [ɑm-'nɪpətənt] *adj*

omnipresence [ˌɑmnɪ'prezəns] *n* : omnipresencia *f*

omnipresent [ˌɑmnɪ'prezənt] *adj* : omnipresente

omniscient [ɑm'nɪʃənt] *adj* : omnisciente

omnivorous [ɑm'nɪvərəs] *adj* **1** : omnívoro **2** AVID : ávido, voraz

on¹ ['ɑn, 'ɔn] *adv* **1** (*indicating contact with a surface*) ⟨put the top on : pon la tapa⟩ ⟨he has a hat on : lleva un sombrero puesto⟩ **2** (*taking movement*) ⟨from that moment on : a partir de ese momento⟩ ⟨farther on : más adelante⟩ **3** (*indicating operation or an operating position*) ⟨turn the light on : prende la luz⟩

on² *adj* **1** (*being in operation*) ⟨the radio is on : el radio está prendido⟩ **2** (*taking place*) ⟨the game is on : el juego ha comenzado⟩ **3 to be on to** : estar enterado de

on³ *prep* **1** (*indicating location or position*) : en, sobre, encima de ⟨on the table : en/sobre la mesa, encima de la mesa⟩ ⟨shadows on the wall : sombras en la pared⟩ ⟨on foot/horseback : a pie/caballo⟩ ⟨on one's hands and knees : a gatas⟩ ⟨she kissed him on the cheek : lo besó en la mejilla⟩ ⟨on page 102 : en la página 102⟩ ⟨on a Web site : en un sitio web⟩ **2** BY, BESIDE : junto a, al lado de ⟨a house on the lake : una casa junto al lago⟩ **3** AT, TO : a ⟨it's on the right : está a la derecha⟩ **4** ABOARD IN : en, a ⟨on the plane : en el avión⟩ ⟨he got on the train : subió al tren⟩ **5** (*indicating time*) ⟨she worked on Saturdays : trabajaba los sábados⟩ ⟨every hour on the hour : cada hora en punto⟩ **6** (*indicating means or agency*) : por ⟨he cut himself on a tin can : se cortó con una lata⟩ ⟨to talk on the telephone : hablar por teléfono⟩ **7** (*indicating source*) : de ⟨to live on a salary : vivir de un sueldo⟩ ⟨it runs on diesel : funciona con diesel⟩ ⟨based on fact : basado en hechos reales⟩ **8** ACCORDING TO : de, según ⟨on good authority : de buena fuente⟩ **9** (*indicating a state or process*) : en ⟨on fire : en llamas⟩ ⟨on the increase : en aumento⟩ ⟨on sale : rebajado⟩ **10** (*indicating connection or membership*) : en ⟨on a committee : en una comisión⟩ **11** (*indicating an activity*) ⟨on vacation : de vacaciones⟩ ⟨on a diet : a dieta⟩ **12** ABOUT, CONCERNING : sobre ⟨a book on insects : un libro sobre insectos⟩ ⟨reflect on that : reflexiona sobre eso⟩ **13** : tomando ⟨to be on medication : tomar medicamentos⟩ ⟨to be on drugs : drogarse⟩ **14 on it** *fam* ⟨don't worry — I'm on it : no te preocupes, yo me encargo de eso⟩ **15 on one** : encima ⟨I don't have it on me : no lo llevo/tengo encima⟩ **16 on someone** : por cuenta de alguien ⟨drinks are on the house : invita la casa⟩

once¹ ['wʌnts] *adv* **1** : una vez ⟨once a month : una vez al mes⟩ ⟨once and for all : de una vez por todas⟩ ⟨once in a while : de vez en cuando⟩ ⟨once or twice : alguna que otra vez⟩ ⟨for once : por una vez⟩ **2** EVER : alguna vez **3** FORMERLY : antes, anteriormente

once² *adj* FORMER : antiguo

once³ *n* **1** : una vez **2 (all) at ~** : de una vez, de un golpe, de un tirón **3 at ~** SIMULTANEOUSLY : al mismo tiempo, simultáneamente **4 at ~** IMMEDIATELY : inmediatamente, en seguida

once⁴ *conj* : una vez que, tan pronto como

once–over [wʌnts'o:vər, 'wʌnts,-] *n* **to give someone the once-over** : echarle un vistazo a alguien

oncoming ['ɑn,kʌmɪŋ, 'ɔn-] *adj* : que viene

one¹ ['wʌn] *adj* **1** (*being a single unit*) : un, una ⟨he only wants one apple : sólo quiere una manzana⟩ **2** (*being a particular one*) : un, una ⟨he arrived early one morning : llegó temprano una mañana⟩ **3** (*being the same*) : mismo, misma ⟨they're all members of one team : todos son miembros del mismo equipo⟩ ⟨one and the same thing : la misma cosa⟩ **4** SOME : alguno, alguna; un, una ⟨I'll see you again one day : algún día te veré otra vez⟩ ⟨at one time or another : en una u otra ocasión⟩

one² *n* **1** : uno *m* (número) **2** (*indicating the first of a set or series*) ⟨from day one : desde el primer momento⟩ **3** (*indicating a single person or thing*) ⟨the one (girl) on the right : la de la derecha⟩ ⟨he has the one but needs the other : tiene uno pero necesita el otro⟩

one³ *pron* **1** : uno ⟨it's one (o'clock) : es la una⟩ ⟨one of his friends : una de sus amigas⟩ ⟨one never knows : uno nunca sabe, nunca se sabe⟩ ⟨to cut one's finger : cortarse el dedo⟩ **2 one and all** : todos, todo el mundo **3 one another** : el uno al otro, se ⟨they loved one another : se amaban⟩ **4 that one** : aquél, aquella **5 which one?** : ¿cuál?

one–handed [wʌn'hændəd] *adj & adv* : con una sola mano

one–on–one [wʌnɑn'wʌn, -ɑn-] *adj* : uno a uno — **one–on–one** *adv*

onerous ['ɑnərəs, 'o:nə-] *adj* : oneroso, gravoso

oneself [wʌn'sɛlf] *pron* **1** (*used reflexively or for emphasis*) : se, sí mismo, uno mismo ⟨to control oneself : controlarse⟩ ⟨to talk to oneself : hablarse a sí mismo⟩ ⟨to do it oneself : hacérselo uno mismo⟩ **2 by ~** : solo

one–sided [wʌn'saɪdəd] *adj* **1** : de un solo lado **2** LOPSIDED : asimétrico **3** BIASED : parcial, tendencioso **4** UNILATERAL : unilateral

onetime ['wʌn,taɪm] *adj* FORMER : antiguo

one–way ['wʌn'weɪ] *adj* **1** : de sentido único, de una sola dirección ⟨a one-way street : una calle de sentido único⟩ **2**

: de ida, sencillo ⟨a one-way ticket : un boleto de ida⟩

one–way mirror *n* : espejo *m* polarizado

ongoing [ˈɑnˌgoːɪŋ] *adj* 1 CONTINUING : en curso, corriente 2 DEVELOPING : en desarrollo

onion [ˈʌnjən] *n* : cebolla *f*

online [ˈɔnˌlaɪn, ˈɑn-] *adj & adv* : en línea, online

onlooker [ˈɔnˌlʊkər, ˈɑn-] *n* : espectador *m*, -dora *f*, circunstante *mf*

only[1] [ˈoːnli] *adv* 1 MERELY : sólo, solamente, nomás ⟨for only two dollars : por tan sólo dos dólares⟩ ⟨only once : sólo una vez, no más de una vez⟩ ⟨I only did it to help : lo hice por ayudar nomás⟩ 2 SOLELY : únicamente, sólo, solamente ⟨only he knows it : solamente él lo sabe⟩ ⟨only because you asked me to : sólo porque tú me lo pediste⟩ 3 ASSUMING : sólo, solamente ⟨I'll go only if he goes with me : iré sólo si él me acompaña⟩ 4 (*indicating a result*) ⟨it will only cause him problems : no hará más que crearle problemas⟩ 5 (*used for emphasis*) ⟨I only hope it will work! : ¡espero que resulte!⟩ 6 (*indicating that something was recent*) ⟨it seems like only yesterday : parece que fue ayer⟩ 7 **if only** : ojalá, por lo menos ⟨if only it were true! : ¡ojalá sea cierto!⟩ ⟨if he could only dance : si por lo menos pudiera bailar⟩ 8 **not only . . . but also . . .** : no sólo . . . sino también 9 **only just** BARELY : apenas ⟨we've only just begun : acabamos de empezar⟩ ⟨I only just missed the flight : perdí el vuelo por un pelo⟩

only[2] *adj* : único ⟨an only child : un hijo único⟩ ⟨the only chance : la única oportunidad⟩

only[3] *conj* BUT : pero ⟨I would go, only I'm sick : iría, pero estoy enfermo⟩

onset [ˈɑnˌsɛt] *n* : comienzo *m*, llegada *f*

onslaught [ˈɑnˌslɔt, ˈɔn-] *n* : arremetida *f*, embestida *f*, embate *m*

onto [ˈɑnˌtuː, ˈɔn-] *prep* 1 : sobre 2 (*indicating knowledge or awareness*) ⟨the police are onto them : la policía anda tras ellos⟩ ⟨I think you're onto something : creo que han dado con algo interesante/importante⟩ ⟨the scientists were onto something big : los científicos estaban a punto de descubrir algo importante⟩

onus [ˈoːnəs] *n* : responsabilidad *f*, carga *f*

onward[1] [ˈɑnwərd, ˈɔn-] *or* **onwards** *adv* FORWARD : adelante, hacia adelante

onward[2] *adj* : hacia adelante

onyx [ˈɑnɪks] *n* : ónix *m*

oops [ˈʊps, ˈwʊps] *interj* : ¡huy! ⟨oops! I goofed : ¡huy! me equivoqué⟩

ooze[1] [ˈuːz] *v* **oozed; oozing** *vi* : rezumar — *vt* 1 : rezumar 2 EXUDE : irradiar, rebosar ⟨to ooze confidence : irradiar confianza⟩

ooze[2] *n* SLIME : cieno *m*, limo *m*

opacity [oˈpæsəti] *n, pl* **-ties** : opacidad *f*

opal [ˈoːpəl] *n* : ópalo *m*

opaque [oˈpeɪk] *adj* 1 : opaco 2 UNCLEAR : poco claro

open[1] [ˈoːpən] *vt* 1 : abrir ⟨open the door : abre la puerta⟩ ⟨open your books : abran sus libros⟩ 2 UNCOVER : abrir, destapar (una botella, etc.) 3 UNFOLD : abrir, desplegar 4 CLEAR : abrir (un camino, etc.) 5 INAUGURATE : abrir (una tienda), inaugurar (una exposición, etc.) 6 INITIATE : iniciar, entablar, abrir ⟨to open the meeting : abrir la sesión⟩ ⟨to open a discussion : entablar un debate⟩ ⟨to open a document : abrir un documento⟩ 7 **to open fire (on)** : abrir fuego (sobre) 8 **to open up** : abrir — *vi* 1 : abrirse 2 BEGIN : empezar, comenzar 3 **to open onto** : dar a 4 **to open up** : abrirse 5 **to open up** : abrir (dícese de una empresa, etc.)

open[2] *adj* 1 : abierto ⟨an open window : una ventana abierta⟩ 2 FRANK : abierto, franco, directo ⟨to be open with : ser sincero/franco con⟩ 3 UNCOVERED : abierto, descubierto ⟨an open box : una caja abierta⟩ 4 EXTENDED : abierto, extendido ⟨with open arms : con los brazos abiertos⟩ 5 UNRESTRICTED : libre, abierto ⟨in the open air : al aire libre⟩ ⟨open to the public : abierto al público⟩ ⟨open admission : entrada libre⟩ ⟨an open letter : una carta abierta⟩ 6 : abierto (dícese de una tienda, etc.) 7 UNDECIDED : pendiente, por decidir, sin resolver ⟨an open question : una cuestión pendiente⟩ 8 AVAILABLE : vacante, libre ⟨the job is open : el puesto está vacante⟩ 9 EXPOSED, VULNERABLE : expuesto, vulnerable ⟨he has left himself open to criticism : se ha expuesto a las críticas⟩ ⟨to be open to abuse : prestarse al abuso⟩ ⟨to be open to doubt/question : ser discutible⟩

open[3] *n* **in the open** 1 OUTDOORS : al aire libre 2 KNOWN : conocido, sacado a la luz

open–air [ˈoːpənˌær] *adj* OUTDOOR : al aire libre

open–and–shut [ˈoːpənəndˈʃʌt] *adj* : claro, evidente ⟨an open-and-shut case : un caso muy claro⟩

opener [ˈoːpənər] *n* : destapador *m*, abrelatas *m*, abridor *m*

openhanded [ˌoːpənˈhændəd] *adj* : generoso, liberal

open–heart [ˈoːpənˌhɑrt] *adj* : de corazón abierto

openhearted [ˌoːpənˈhɑrtəd] *adj* 1 FRANK : franco, sincero 2 : generoso, de gran corazón

opening [ˈoːpənɪŋ] *n* 1 BEGINNING : comienzo *m*, principio *m*, apertura *f* 2 APERTURE : abertura *f*, brecha *f*, claro *m* (en el bosque) 3 OPPORTUNITY : oportunidad *f*

openly [ˈoːpənli] *adv* 1 FRANKLY : abiertamente, francamente 2 PUBLICLY : públicamente, declaradamente

open–minded [ˌoːpənˈmaɪndəd] *adj* : sin prejuicios, de actitud abierta

open–mouthed [ˌoːpənˈmaʊðd, -ˈmaʊθt] *adj* : boquiabierto

openness [ˈoːpənnəs] *n* : franqueza *f*

opera ['ɑprə, 'ɑprə] *n* 1 : ópera *f* 2 → **opus**

opera glasses *npl* : gemelos *mpl* de teatro

operate ['ɑpə,reɪt] *v* -ated; -ating *vi* 1 ACT, FUNCTION : operar, funcionar, actuar 2 **to operate on (someone)** : operar a (alguien) — *vt* 1 WORK : operar, manejar, hacer funcionar (una máquina) 2 MANAGE : manejar, administrar (un negocio)

operatic [,ɑpə'rætɪk] *adj* : operístico

operating room *n* : quirófano *m*

operation [,ɑpə'reɪʃən] *n* 1 FUNCTIONING : funcionamiento *m* 2 USE : uso *m*, manejo *m* (de máquinas) 3 SURGERY : operación *f*, intervención *f* quirúrgica

operational [,ɑpə'reɪʃənəl] *adj* : operacional, de operación

operative ['ɑpərətɪv, -,reɪ-] *adj* 1 OPERATING : vigente, en vigor 2 WORKING : operativo 3 SURGICAL : quirúrgico

operator ['ɑpə,reɪtər] *n* : operador *m*, -dora *f*

operetta [,ɑpə'rɛtə] *n* : opereta *f*

ophthalmologist [,ɑf,θæl'mɑlədʒɪst, -θə'mɑ-] *n* : oftalmólogo *m*, -ga *f*

ophthalmology [,ɑf,θæl'mɑlədʒi, -θə'mɑ-] *n* : oftalmología *f*

opiate ['o,piət, pi,ːt] *n* : opiato *m*

opine [o'paɪn] *v* : opinar

opinion [ə'pɪnjən] *n* : opinión *f*

opinionated [ə'pɪnjə,neɪtəd] *adj* : testarudo, dogmático

opinion poll *n* SURVEY : sondeo *m*, encuesta *f* de opinión

opium ['o,piəm] *n* : opio *m*

opossum [ə'pɑsəm] *n* : zarigüeya *f*, oposum *m*

opponent [ə'po,nənt] *n* : oponente *mf*; opositor *m*, -tora *f*; contrincante *mf* (en deportes)

opportune [,ɑpər'tu:n, -'tju:n] *adj* : oportuno — **opportunely** *adv*

opportunism [,ɑpər'tu:,nɪzəm, -'tju:-] *n* : oportunismo *m*

opportunist [,ɑpər'tu:nɪst, -'tju:-] *n* : oportunista *mf*

opportunistic [,ɑpərtu'nɪstɪk, -tju-] *adj* : oportunista *mf*

opportunity [,ɑpər'tu:nəti, -'tju:-] *n, pl* -ties : oportunidad *f*, ocasión *f*, chance *m*, posibilidades *fpl*

oppose [ə'po:z] *vt* -posed; -posing 1 : ir en contra de, oponerse a ⟨good opposes evil : el bien se opone al mal⟩ 2 COMBAT : luchar contra, combatir, resistir

opposite¹ ['ɑpəzət] *adv* : enfrente

opposite² *adj* 1 FACING : de enfrente ⟨the opposite side : el lado de enfrente⟩ 2 CONTRARY : opuesto, contrario ⟨in opposite directions : en direcciones contrarias⟩ ⟨the opposite sex : el sexo opuesto, el otro sexo⟩

opposite³ *n* : lo contrario, lo opuesto

opposite⁴ *prep* : enfrente de, frente a

opposition [,ɑpə'zɪʃən] *n* : oposición *f*, resistencia *f* 2 **in opposition to** AGAINST : en contra de

oppress [ə'prɛs] *vt* 1 PERSECUTE : oprimir, perseguir 2 BURDEN : oprimir, agobiar

oppression [ə'prɛʃən] *n* : opresión *f*

oppressive [ə'prɛsɪv] *adj* 1 HARSH : opresivo, severo 2 STIFLING : agobiante, sofocante ⟨oppressive heat : calor sofocante⟩

oppressor [ə'prɛsər] *n* : opresor *m*, -sora *f*

opprobrium [ə'pro:briəm] *n* : oprobio *m*

opt ['ɑpt] *vi* 1 : optar 2 **to opt for** : optar por 3 **to opt in** : decidir participar 4 **to opt into** : decidir participar en 5 **to opt out (of)** : decidir no participar (en)

optic ['ɑptɪk] *or* **optical** [-tɪkəl] *adj* : óptico

optical disk *n* : disco *m* óptico

optician [ɑp'tɪʃən] *n* : óptico *m*, -ca *f*

optics ['ɑptɪks] *npl* : óptica *f*

optimal ['ɑptəməl] *adj* : óptimo

optimism ['ɑptə,mɪzəm] *n* : optimismo *m*

optimist ['ɑptəmɪst] *n* : optimista *mf*

optimistic [,ɑptə'mɪstɪk] *adj* : optimista

optimistically [,ɑptə'mɪstɪkli] *adv* : con optimismo, positivamente

optimum¹ ['ɑptəməm] *adj* → **optimal**

optimum² *n, pl* -ma ['ɑptəmə] : lo óptimo, lo ideal

option ['ɑpʃən] *n* : opción *f* ⟨she has no option : no tiene más remedio⟩

optional ['ɑpʃənəl] *adj* : facultativo, optativo

optometrist [ɑp'tɑmətrɪst] *n* : optometrista *mf*

optometry [ɑp'tɑmətri] *n* : optometría *f*

opulence ['ɑpjələnts] *n* : opulencia *f*

opulent ['ɑpjələnt] *adj* : opulento

opus ['o:pəs] *n, pl* **opera** [o:'pərə, 'ɑpə-] : opus *m*, obra *f* (de música)

or ['ɔr] *conj* 1 (*indicating an alternative*) : o (*u before words beginning with o or ho*) ⟨coffee or tea : café o té⟩ ⟨one day or another : un día u otro⟩ 2 (*following a negative*) : ni ⟨he didn't have his keys or his wallet : no llevaba ni sus llaves ni su billetera⟩

oracle ['ɔrəkəl] *n* : oráculo *m*

oral ['ɔrəl] *adj* : oral — **orally** *adv*

orange ['ɔrɪndʒ] *n* 1 : naranja *f*, china *f* PRi (fruto) 2 : naranja *m* (color), color *m* de china PRi

orangeade [,ɔrɪndʒ'eɪd] *n* : naranjada *f*

orangutan [ə'ræŋə,tæŋ, -'ræŋgə-, -,tæŋ] *n* : orangután *m*

oration [ə'reɪʃən] *n* : oración *f*, discurso *m*

orator ['ɔrətər] *n* : orador *m*, -dora *f*

oratorio [,ɔrə'tori,o:] *n, pl* -rios : oratorio *m*

oratory ['ɔrə,tori] *n, pl* -ries : oratoria *f*

orb ['ɔrb] *n* : orbe *m*

orbit¹ ['ɔrbət] *vt* 1 CIRCLE : girar alrededor de, orbitar 2 : poner en órbita (un satélite, etc.) — *vi* : orbitar

orbit² *n* : órbita *f*

orbital ['ɔrbətəl] *adj* : orbital

orca ['ɔrkə] *n* : orca *f*

orchard ['ɔrtʃərd] *n* : huerto *m*

orchestra ['ɔrkəstrə] *n* : orquesta *f*

orchestral [ɔr'kɛstrəl] *adj* : orquestal

orchestrate [ˈɔrkəˌstreɪt] vt -trated; -trating 1 : orquestar, instrumentar (en música) 2 ORGANIZE : arreglar, organizar
orchestration [ˌɔrkəˈstreɪʃən] n : orquestación f
orchid [ˈɔrkɪd] n : orquídea f
ordain [ɔrˈdeɪn] vt 1 : ordenar (en religión) 2 DECREE : decretar, ordenar
ordeal [ɔrˈdiːl, ˈɔrˌdiːl] n : prueba f dura, experiencia f terrible
order¹ [ˈɔrdər] vt 1 ORGANIZE : arreglar, ordenar, poner en orden 2 COMMAND : ordenar, mandar 3 REQUEST : pedir, encargar ⟨to order a meal : pedir algo de comer⟩ — vi : hacer un pedido
order² n 1 : orden f ⟨a religious order : una orden religiosa⟩ 2 COMMAND : orden f, mandato m ⟨to give an order : dar una orden⟩ ⟨to give the order to do something : dar orden de hacer algo⟩ ⟨by order of : por orden de⟩ 3 REQUEST : orden f, pedido m ⟨purchase order : orden de compra⟩ ⟨to place/take an order : hacer/tomar un pedido⟩ ⟨to be on order : estar pedido⟩ 4 SERVING : porción f, ración f ⟨an order of fries : una porción de papas fritas⟩ 5 ARRANGEMENT : orden m ⟨in chronological order : por orden cronológico⟩ ⟨out of order : desordenado⟩ ⟨everything seems to be in order : parece que todo está en orden⟩ 6 DISCIPLINE : orden m ⟨law and order : el orden público⟩ ⟨to keep order : mantener el orden⟩ 7 in order for : para que ⟨in order for this to work : para que esto funcione⟩ 8 in order that : para que ⟨in order that others might live : para que otros puedan vivir⟩ 9 in order to : para 10 in (working) order : funcionando 11 out of order BROKEN : descompuesto, averiado 12 orders npl or holy orders : órdenes fpl sagradas
orderliness [ˈɔrdərlinəs] n : orden m
orderly¹ [ˈɔrdərli] adj 1 METHODICAL : ordenado, metódico 2 PEACEFUL : pacífico, disciplinado
orderly² n, pl -lies 1 : ordenanza m (en el ejército) 2 : camillero m (en un hospital)
ordinal [ˈɔrdənəl] n or ordinal number : ordinal m, número m ordinal
ordinance [ˈɔrdənənts] n : ordenanza f, reglamento m
ordinarily [ˌɔrdənˈerəli] adv : ordinariamente, por lo general
ordinary [ˈɔrdənˌeri] adj 1 NORMAL, USUAL : normal, usual 2 AVERAGE : común y corriente, normal 3 MEDIOCRE : mediocre, ordinario
ordination [ˌɔrdənˈeɪʃən] n : ordenación f
ordnance [ˈɔrdnənts] n : artillería f
ore [ˈor] n : mineral m (metálico), mena f
oregano [əˈregəˌnoː] n : orégano m
organ [ˈɔrgən] n 1 : órgano m (instrumento) 2 : órgano m (del cuerpo) 3 PERIODICAL : publicación f periódica, órgano m
organic [ɔrˈgænɪk] adj : orgánico — organically adv

organism [ˈɔrgəˌnɪzəm] n : organismo m
organist [ˈɔrgənɪst] n : organista mf
organization [ˌɔrgənəˈzeɪʃən] n 1 ORGANIZING : organización f 2 BODY : organización f, organismo m
organizational [ˌɔrgənəˈzeɪʃənəl] adj : organizativo
organize [ˈɔrgəˌnaɪz] vt -nized; -nizing : organizar, arreglar, poner en orden
organizer [ˈɔrgəˌnaɪzər] n : organizador m, -dora f
orgasm [ˈɔrˌgæzəm] n : orgasmo m
orgy [ˈɔrdʒi] n, pl -gies : orgía f
orient [ˈoriˌent] vt : orientar
Orient n the Orient : el Oriente
oriental [ˌoriˈentəl] adj dated, now usu offensive when used of people : del Oriente, oriental dated, now sometimes offensive when used of people
Oriental n dated, now usu offensive : oriental masculine or feminine dated, now sometimes offensive
orientation [ˌoriənˈteɪʃən] n : orientación f
orifice [ˈɔrəfəs] n : orificio m
origin [ˈɔrədʒən] n 1 ANCESTRY : origen m, ascendencia f 2 SOURCE : origen m, raíz f, fuente f
original¹ [əˈrɪdʒənəl] adj : original
original² n : original m
originality [əˌrɪdʒəˈnæləti] n : originalidad f
originally [əˈrɪdʒənəli] adv 1 AT FIRST : al principio, originariamente 2 CREATIVELY : originalmente, con originalidad
originate [əˈrɪdʒəˌneɪt] v -nated; -nating vt : originar, iniciar, crear — vi 1 BEGIN : originarse, empezar 2 COME : provenir, proceder, derivarse
originator [əˈrɪdʒəˌneɪtər] n : creador m, -dora f; inventor m, -tora f
oriole [ˈoriˌoːl, -iəl] n : oropéndola f
ornament¹ [ˈɔrnəmənt] vt : adornar, decorar, ornamentar
ornament² n : ornamento m, adorno m, decoración f
ornamental [ˌɔrnəˈmentəl] adj : ornamental, de adorno, decorativo
ornamentation [ˌɔrnəmənˈteɪʃən, -men-] n : ornamentación f
ornate [ɔrˈneɪt] adj : elaborado, recargado
ornery [ˈɔrnəri, ˈɑrnəri] adj ornerier; -est : de mal genio, malhumorado
ornithologist [ˌɔrnəˈθɑlədʒɪst] n : ornitólogo m, -ga f
ornithology [ˌɔrnəˈθɑlədʒi] n, pl -gies : ornitología f
orphan¹ [ˈɔrfən] vt : dejar huérfano
orphan² n : huérfano m, -na f
orphanage [ˈɔrfənɪdʒ] n : orfelinato m, orfanato m
orthodontics [ˌɔrθəˈdɑntɪks] n : ortodoncia f
orthodontist [ˌɔrθəˈdɑntɪst] n : ortodoncista m
orthodox [ˈɔrθəˌdɑks] adj : ortodoxo
orthodoxy [ˈɔrθəˌdɑksi] n, pl -doxies : ortodoxia f
orthographic [ˌɔrθəˈgræfɪk] adj : ortográfico

orthography [ɔr'θɑgrəfi] *n*, *pl* **-phies** SPELL-ING : ortografía *f*

orthopedic [ˌɔrθə'pidɪk] *adj* : ortopédico

orthopedics [ˌɔrθə'pidɪks] *ns & pl* : ortopedia *f*

orthopedist [ˌɔrθə'pidɪst] *n* : ortopedista *mf*

oscillate ['ɑsəˌleɪt] *vi* **-lated; -lating** : oscilar

oscillation [ˌɑsə'leɪʃən] *n* : oscilación *f*

osmosis [ɑz'mosɪs, ɑs-] *n* : ósmosis *f*, osmosis *f*

osprey ['ɑspri, -ˌpreɪ] *n* : pigargo *m*

ostensible [ɑ'stɛnsəbəl] *adj* APPARENT : aparente, ostensible — **ostensibly** [-bli] *adv*

ostentation [ˌɑstən'teɪʃən] *n* : ostentación *f*, boato *m*

ostentatious [ˌɑstən'teɪʃəs] *adj* : ostentoso — **ostentatiously** *adv*

osteopath ['ɑstiəˌpæθ] *n* : osteópata *f*

osteopathy [ˌɑsti'ɑpəθi] *n* : osteopatía *f*

osteoporosis [ˌɑstiopə'rosɪs] *n*, *pl* **-roses** [-ˌsiːz] : osteoporosis *f*

ostracism ['ɑstrəˌsɪzəm] *n* : ostracismo *m*

ostracize ['ɑstrəˌsaɪz] *vt* **-cized; -cizing** : condenar al ostracismo, marginar, aislar

ostrich ['ɑstrɪtʃ, 'ɔs-] *n* : avestruz *m*

other[1] ['ʌðər] *adv* **other than** : aparte de, fuera de

other[2] *adj* **1** : otro ⟨the other boys : los otros muchachos⟩ ⟨smarter than other people : más inteligente que los demás⟩ ⟨on the other hand : por otra parte, por otro lado⟩ **2 every other** : cada dos ⟨every other day : cada dos días⟩

other[3] *pron* **1** : otro ⟨one in front of the other : uno tras otro⟩ ⟨either one or the other : uno u otro⟩ ⟨myself and three others : yo y tres otros/más⟩ ⟨this class and three others : esta clase y tres otras/más⟩ ⟨from one extreme to the other : de un extremo al otro⟩ ⟨somewhere or other : en alguna parte⟩ ⟨somehow or other : de alguna manera⟩ **2 the others** : los otros, los demás ⟨this class and the others : esta clase y las otras⟩

otherwise[1] ['ʌðərˌwaɪz] *adv* **1** DIFFERENTLY : de otro modo, de manera distinta ⟨he could not act otherwise : no pudo actuar de manera distinta⟩ **2** : eso aparte, por lo demás ⟨I'm dizzy, but otherwise I'm fine : estoy mareado pero, por lo demás, estoy bien⟩ **3** OR ELSE : de lo contrario, si no ⟨do what I tell you, otherwise you'll be sorry : haz lo que te digo, de lo contrario, te arrepentirás⟩

otherwise[2] *adj* : diferente, distinto ⟨the facts are otherwise : la realidad es diferente⟩

otitis [o'taɪtəs] *n* : otitis *f*

otter ['ɑtər] *n* : nutria *f*

Ottoman ['ɑtəmən] *n* **1** : otomano *m*, -na *f* **2** : otomana *f* (mueble) — **Ottoman** *adj*

ouch ['aʊtʃ] *interj* : ¡ay!, ¡huy!

ought ['ɔt] *v aux* : deber ⟨you ought to take care of yourself : deberías cuidarte⟩

oughtn't ['ɔtənt] *contraction of* OUGHT NOT → **ought**

ounce ['aʊn/ts] *n* : onza *f*

our ['ɑr, 'aʊr] *adj* : nuestro

ours ['aʊrz, 'ɑrz] *pron* : nuestro ⟨a cousin of ours : un primo nuestro, una prima nuestra⟩

ourselves [ɑr'sɛlvz, aʊr-] *pron* **1** (*used reflexively*) : nos, nosotros, nosotras ⟨we amused ourselves : nos divertimos⟩ ⟨we were always thinking of ourselves : siempre pensábamos en nosotros⟩ **2** (*used for emphasis*) : nosotros mismos, nosotras mismas ⟨we did it ourselves : lo hicimos nosotros mismos⟩

oust ['aʊst] *vt* : desbancar, expulsar

ouster ['aʊstər] *n* : expulsión *f* (de un país, etc.), destitución *f* (de un puesto)

out[1] ['aʊt] *vi* : revelarse, hacerse conocido

out[2] *adv* **1** (*indicating direction or movement*) OUTSIDE : para afuera ⟨she opened the door and looked out : abrió la puerta y miró para afuera⟩ ⟨he went out to the garden : salió al jardín⟩ ⟨she took the dog out : sacó al perro⟩ **2** (*indicating location*) OUTSIDE : fuera, afuera ⟨out in the garden : afuera en el jardín⟩ ⟨it's sunny out : hace sol⟩ ⟨your shirt is hanging out : tienes la camisa afuera⟩ **3** (*indicating outward movement*) ⟨they flew out yesterday : salieron ayer (en avión)⟩ ⟨out to sea : mar adentro⟩ **4** (*indicating distance*) ⟨they live out in the country : viven en el campo⟩ **5** (*indicating omission*) ⟨you left out a comma : omitiste 'una coma⟩ ⟨count me out : no cuentes conmigo⟩ **6** (*indicating removal, loss, or incorrect placement*) ⟨they voted him out : no lo reeligieron⟩ ⟨his hair is falling out : se está cayendo el pelo⟩ ⟨she threw out her shoulder : se lastimó el hombro⟩ **7** (*indicating drawing from a group*) ⟨she picked out a shirt : escogió una camisa⟩ **8** (*indicating a location away from home or work*) : fuera, afuera ⟨to eat out : comer afuera⟩ ⟨he asked her out : la invitó a salir⟩ **9** (*indicating loss of control or possession*) ⟨they let the secret out : sacaron el secreto a la luz⟩ **10** (*indicating ending or stopping*) ⟨his money ran out : se acabó el dinero⟩ ⟨to turn out the light : apagar la luz⟩ **11** (*indicating completion*) ⟨to fill out a form : rellenar un formulario⟩ **12** ALOUD : en voz alta, en alto ⟨to cry out : gritar⟩ **13** UNCONSCIOUS : inconsciente **14** : abiertamente homosexual **15** → **out-of-bounds 16 to be out for** : estar buscando (venganza, etc.) **17 to be out to** : querer (vengarse, etc.) ⟨he's out to get me : me la tiene jurada⟩

out[3] *adj* **1** EXTERNAL : externo, exterior **2** OUTLYING : alejado, distante ⟨the out islands : las islas distantes⟩ **3** ABSENT : ausente **4** UNFASHIONABLE : fuera de moda **5** EXTINGUISHED : apagado **6 to be out and about** : estar andando por ahí

out[4] *prep* **1** (*used to indicate an outward movement*) : por ⟨I looked out the window : miré por la ventana⟩ ⟨she ran out the door : corrió por la puerta⟩ 2 → **out of**

out–and–out [ˈaʊtənˈaʊt] *adj* UTTER : redomado, absoluto

outback [ˈaʊtˌbæk] *n* **the outback** : el interior (de Australia)

outboard motor [ˈaʊtˌbord] *n* : motor *m* fuera de borde

outbound [ˈaʊtˌbaʊnd] *adj* : que sale, de salida

out–box [ˈaʊtˌbɑks] *n* : bandeja *f* de salida

outbreak [ˈaʊtˌbreɪk] *n* : brote *m* (de una enfermedad), comienzo *m* (de guerra), ola *f* (de violencia), erupción *f* (de granos)

outbuilding [ˈaʊtˌbɪldɪŋ] *n* : edificio *m* anexo

outburst [ˈaʊtˌbərst] *n* : arranque *m*, arrebato *m*

outcast [ˈaʊtˌkæst] *n* : marginado *m*, -da *f*; paria *mf*

outcome [ˈaʊtˌkʌm] *n* : resultado *m*, desenlace *m*, consecuencia *f*

outcry [ˈaʊtˌkraɪ] *n, pl* **-cries** : clamor *m*, protesta *f*

outdated [ˌaʊtˈdeɪtəd] *adj* : anticuado, fuera de moda

outdistance [ˌaʊtˈdɪstən*t*s] *vt* **-tanced; -tancing** : aventajar, dejar atrás

outdo [ˌaʊtˈduː] *vt* **-did** [-ˈdɪd]; **-done** [-ˈdʌn]; **-doing; -does** [-ˈdʌz] : superar

outdoor [ˈaʊtˈdor] *adj* : al aire libre ⟨outdoor sports : deportes al aire libre⟩ ⟨outdoor clothing : ropa de calle⟩

outdoors[1] [ˈaʊtˈdorz] *adv* : afuera, al aire libre

outdoors[2] *n* : aire *m* libre

outer [ˈaʊtər] *adj* 1 : exterior, externo 2 **outer space** : espacio *m* exterior

outermost [ˈaʊtərˌmoːst] *adj* : más remoto, más exterior, extremo

outfield [ˈaʊtˌfiːld] *n* **the outfield** : los jardines

outfielder [ˈaʊtˌfiːldər] *n* : jardinero *m*, -ra *f*

outfit[1] [ˈaʊtˌfɪt] *vt* **-fitted; -fitting** EQUIP : equipar

outfit[2] *n* 1 EQUIPMENT : equipo *m* 2 COSTUME, ENSEMBLE : traje *m*, conjunto *m* 3 GROUP : conjunto *m*

outgo [ˈaʊtˌgoː] *n, pl* **outgoes** : gasto *m*

outgoing [ˈaʊtˌgoːɪŋ] *adj* 1 OUTBOUND : que sale 2 DEPARTING : saliente ⟨an outgoing president : un presidente saliente⟩ 3 EXTROVERTED : extrovertido, expansivo

outgrow [ˌaʊtˈgroː] *vt* **-grew** [-ˈgruː]; **-grown** [-ˈgroːn]; **-growing** 1 : crecer más que ⟨that tree outgrew all the others : ese árbol creció más que todos los otros⟩ 2 **to outgrow one's clothes** : quedarle pequeña la ropa a uno

outgrowth [ˈaʊtˌgroːθ] *n* 1 OFFSHOOT : brote *m*, vástago *m* (de una planta) 2 CONSEQUENCE : consecuencia *f*, producto *m*, resultado *m*

outing [ˈaʊtɪŋ] *n* : excursión *f*

outlandish [aʊtˈlændɪʃ] *adj* : descabellado, muy extraño

outlast [ˌaʊtˈlæst] *vt* : durar más que

outlaw[1] [ˈaʊtˌlɔ] *vt* : hacerse ilegal, declarar fuera de la ley, prohibir

outlaw[2] *n* : bandido *m*, -da *f*; bandolero *m*, -ra *f*; forajido *m*, -da *f*

outlay [ˈaʊtˌleɪ] *n* : gasto *m*, desembolso *m*

outlet [ˈaʊtˌlet, -lət] *n* 1 EXIT : salida *f*, escape *m* ⟨electrical outlet : toma de corriente⟩ 2 RELIEF : desahogo *m* 3 MARKET : mercado *m*, salida *f*

outline[1] [ˈaʊtˌlaɪn] *vt* **-lined; -lining** 1 SKETCH : diseñar, esbozar, bosquejar 2 DEFINE EXPLAIN : perfilar, delinear, explicar ⟨she outlined our responsibilities : delineó nuestras responsabilidades⟩

outline[2] *n* 1 PROFILE : perfil *m*, silueta *f*, contorno *m* 2 SKETCH : bosquejo *m*, boceto *m* 3 SUMMARY : esquema *m*, resumen *m*, sinopsis *m* ⟨an outline of world history : un esquema de la historia mundial⟩

outlive [ˌaʊtˈlɪv] *vt* **-lived; -living** : sobrevivir a

outlook [ˈaʊtˌlʊk] *n* 1 VIEW : vista *f*, panorama *f* 2 POINT OF VIEW : punto *m* de vista 3 PROSPECTS : perspectivas *fpl*

outlying [ˈaʊtˌlaɪɪŋ] *adj* : alejado, distante, remoto ⟨the outlying areas : las afueras⟩

outmoded [ˌaʊtˈmoːdəd] *adj* : pasado de moda, anticuado

outnumber [ˌaʊtˈnʌmbər] *vt* : superar en número a, ser más numeroso de

out of *prep* 1 (*indicating direction or movement from within*) : de, por ⟨we ran out of the house : salimos corriendo de la casa⟩ ⟨to look out of the window : mirar por la ventana⟩ 2 (*being beyond the limits of*) ⟨out of control : fuera de control⟩ ⟨to be out of sight : desaparecer de vista⟩ 3 OF : de ⟨one out of four : uno de cada cuatro⟩ 4 (*indicating absence or loss*) : sin ⟨out of money : sin dinero⟩ ⟨we're out of matches : nos hemos quedado sin fósforos⟩ 5 BECAUSE OF : por ⟨out of curiosity : por curiosidad⟩ 6 FROM : de ⟨made out of plastic : hecho de plástico⟩

out–of–bounds [ˌaʊtəvˈbaʊndz] *adj* : fuera de juego

out–of–date [ˌaʊtəvˈdeɪt] *adj* : anticuado, obsoleto, pasado de moda

out–of–door [ˌaʊtəvˈdor] *or* **out–of–doors** [-ˈdorz] → **outdoor**

out–of–doors *n* → **outdoors**[2]

out–of–the–way [ˌaʊtəvðəˈweɪ] *adj* : alejado, distante, remoto

outpatient [ˈaʊtˌpeɪʃənt] *n* : paciente *m* externo, paciente *f* externa

outpost [ˈaʊtˌpoːst] *n* : puesto *m* avanzado

output[1] [ˈaʊtˌpʊt] *vt* **-putted** *or* **-put; -putting** : producir

output[2] *n* : producción *f* (de una fábrica), rendimiento *m* (de una máquina), productividad *f* (de una persona)

outrage[1] [ˈaʊtˌreɪdʒ] *vt* **-raged; -raging** 1 INSULT : ultrajar, injuriar 2 INFURIATE : indignar, enfurecer

outrage[2] *n* 1 ATROCITY : atropello *m*, atrocidad *f*, atentado *m* 2 SCANDAL : escándalo *m* 3 ANGER : ira *f*, furia *f*

outrageous [ˌaʊtˈreɪdʒəs] *adj* 1 SCANDALOUS : escandaloso, ofensivo, atroz 2

UNCONVENTIONAL : poco convencional, extravagante **3** EXORBITANT : exorbitante, excesivo (dícese de los precios, etc.)

outright¹ [ˌaʊtˈraɪt] *adv* **1** COMPLETELY : por completo, totalmente ⟨to sell outright : vender por completo⟩ ⟨he refused it outright : lo rechazó rotundamente⟩ **2** DIRECTLY : directamente, sin reserva **3** INSTANTLY : al instante, en el acto

outright² [ˈaʊtˌraɪt] *adj* **1** COMPLETE : completo, absoluto, categórico ⟨an outright lie : una mentira absoluta⟩ **2** : sin reservas ⟨an outright gift : un regalo sin reservas⟩

outset [ˈaʊtˌsɛt] *n* : comienzo *m*, principio *m*

outshine [ˌaʊtˈʃaɪn] *vt* **-shone** [-ˈʃoːn, -ˈʃɑn] *or* **-shined; -shining** : eclipsar

outside¹ [ˌaʊtˈsaɪd, ˈaʊtˌ-] *adv* : fuera, afuera

outside² *adj* **1** : exterior, externo ⟨the outside edge : el borde exterior⟩ ⟨outside influences : influencias externas⟩ **2** REMOTE : remoto ⟨an outside chance : una posibilidad remota⟩

outside³ *n* **1** EXTERIOR : parte *f* de afuera, exterior *m* **2** MOST : máximo *m* ⟨three weeks at the outside : tres semanas como máximo⟩ **3 from the outside** : desde afuera, desde fuera

outside⁴ *prep* : fuera de, afuera de ⟨outside my window : fuera de mi ventana⟩ ⟨outside regular hours : fuera del horario normal⟩ ⟨outside the law : afuera de la ley⟩

outside of *prep* **1** → outside⁴ **2** → besides²

outsider [ˌaʊtˈsaɪdər] *n* : forastero *m*, -ra *f*

outsize [ˈaʊtˌsaɪz] *also* **outsized** [ˈaʊtˌsaɪzd] *adj* : enorme

outskirts [ˈaʊtˌskərts] *npl* : afueras *fpl*, alrededores *mpl*

outsmart [ˌaʊtˈsmɑrt] → outwit

outsource [ˈaʊtˌsors] *vt* : externalizar

outsourcing [ˈaʊtˌsorsɪŋ] *n* : externalización *f*

outspoken [ˌaʊtˈspoːkən] *adj* : franco, directo

outstanding [ˌaʊtˈstændɪŋ] *adj* **1** UNPAID : pendiente **2** NOTABLE : destacado, notable, excepcional, sobresaliente

outstandingly [ˌaʊtˈstændɪŋli] *adv* : excepcionalmente

outstretched [ˌaʊtˈstrɛtʃt] *adj* : extendido

outstrip [ˌaʊtˈstrɪp] *vt* **-stripped** *or* **-stript** [-ˈstrɪpt]; **-stripping 1** : aventajar, dejar atrás ⟨he outstripped the other runners : aventajó a los otros corredores⟩ **2** SURPASS : aventajar, sobrepasar

outward¹ [ˈaʊtwərd] *or* **outwards** [-wərdz] *adv* : hacia afuera, hacia el exterior

outward² *adj* **1** : hacia afuera ⟨an outward flow : un flujo hacia afuera⟩ **2** : externo ⟨outward beauty : belleza externa⟩

outwardly [ˈaʊtwərdli] *adv* **1** EXTERNALLY : exteriormente **2** APPARENTLY : aparentemente ⟨outwardly friendly : aparentemente simpático⟩

outweigh [ˌaʊtˈweɪ] *vt* **1** : pesar más que **2** : ser mayor que ⟨the benefit outweighs the risk : el beneficio es mayor que el riesgo⟩

outwit [ˌaʊtˈwɪt] *vt* **-witted; -witting** : ser más listo que

ova → ovum

oval¹ [ˈoːvəl] *adj* : ovalado, oval

oval² *n* : óvalo *m*

ovarian [oˈværiən] *adj* : ovárico

ovary [ˈoːvəri] *n, pl* **-ries** : ovario *m*

ovation [oˈveɪʃən] *n* : ovación *f*

oven [ˈʌvən] *n* : horno *m*

over¹ [ˈoːvər] *adv* **1** (*indicating movement across*) ⟨he flew over to London : voló a Londres⟩ ⟨come on over! : ¡ven acá!⟩ ⟨we crossed over to the other side : cruzamos al otro lado⟩ **2** (*indicating movement from an upright position*) ⟨to fall over : caerse⟩ ⟨to push someone over : tirar a alguien al suelo⟩ **3** (*indicating reversal of position*) ⟨to turn/flip something over : darle la vuelta a algo, voltear algo⟩ ⟨roll over, please : date la vuelta, por favor⟩ **4** (*indicating an additional amount*) ⟨the show ran 10 minutes over : el espectáculo terminó 10 minutos tarde⟩ ⟨there's a lot of food left over : sobra/queda mucha comida⟩ ⟨women 65 and over : mujeres de 65 años en adelante⟩ ⟨parties of six or over : grupos de seis o más⟩ **5** (*indicating a later time*) ⟨to sleep over : quedarse a dormir⟩ ⟨some money to tide him over : un poco de dinero para sacarlo del apuro⟩ **6** (*indicating covering*) ⟨the sky clouded over : se nubló⟩ **7** THOROUGHLY : bien ⟨read it over : léelo bien⟩ **8** ABOVE, OVERHEAD : por encima **9** (*indicating repetition*) ⟨over and over : una y otra vez⟩ ⟨to start over : volver a empezar⟩ ⟨twice over : dos veces⟩ ⟨many times over : muchas veces⟩ **10 all over** EVERYWHERE : por todas partes **11 over (and done) with** ⟨I want to get this over (and done) with : quiero quitarme esto de encima⟩ **12 over and out** (*in radio transmissions*) : cambio y corto/fuera, corto y cambio

over² *adj* **1** HIGHER, UPPER : superior **2** REMAINING : sobrante, que sobra **3** ENDED : terminado, acabado ⟨the work is over : el trabajo está terminado⟩

over³ *prep* **1** ABOVE : encima de, arriba de, sobre ⟨over the fireplace : encima de la chimenea⟩ ⟨the hawk flew over the hills : el halcón voló sobre los cerros⟩ **2** : más de ⟨over $50 : más de $50⟩ **3** ALONG : por, sobre ⟨to glide over the ice : deslizarse sobre el hielo⟩ **4** (*indicating motion through a place or thing*) ⟨they showed me over the house : me mostraron la casa⟩ **5** ACROSS : por encima de, sobre ⟨he jumped over the ditch : saltó por encima de la zanja⟩ ⟨we crossed over the border : cruzamos la frontera⟩ **6** BEYOND : más allá de ⟨just over that hill : un poco más allá de esa colina⟩ **7** OFF : por ⟨she fell over the side of the boat : se cayó por la borda del

barco〉 **8** (*indicating direction*) : por
〈it's over here somewhere : está por acá〉
〈look over there! : ¡mira allí!〉 **9** UPON
: sobre 〈a cape over my shoulders : una
capa sobre los hombros〉 〈she hit him
over the head : le dio en la cabeza〉 **10**
ON : por 〈to speak over the phone
: hablar por teléfono〉 〈over the radio
: por la radio〉 **11** DURING : en, durante
〈over the past 25 years : durante los últimos 25 años〉 **12** PAST, THROUGH : terminado con 〈we're over the worst of it
: hemos pasado lo peor〉 **13** BECAUSE
OF : por 〈they fought over the money
: se pelearon por el dinero〉 〈to laugh
over something : reírse por algo〉 **14**
CONCERNING : sobre **15** (*indicating
comparison*) 〈to be an improvement
over : ser mejor que〉 〈to choose one
thing over another : elegir una cosa en
lugar de otra〉 〈to have an advantage
over : tener una ventaja sobre〉 **16** DE-
SPITE : a pesar de (objeciones, etc.) **17**
(*indicating omission*) 〈to skip over something : saltarse algo〉 **18** (*referring to
power or authority*) : por encima de, sobre 〈those over you : los que están por
encima de ti〉 〈to have control over
: tener control sobre〉 **19** all over 〈there
was water all over the floor : había agua
por todo el suelo〉 〈all over the place
: por todas partes〉 **20** over and above
: además de

over- *pref* : demasiado, excesivamente
overabundance [ˌoːvərˈbʌndənts] *n* : superabundancia *f*
overabundant [ˌoːvərˈbʌndənt] *adj* : superabundante
overactive [ˌoːvərˈæktɪv] *adj* : hiperactivo
overall [ˌoːvərˈɔl] *adj* : total, global, de
conjunto
overalls [ˈoːvərˌɔlz] *npl* : overol *m*
overawe [ˌoːvərˈɔ] *vt* **-awed; -awing** : intimidar, impresionar
overbearing [ˌoːvərˈbærɪŋ] *adj* : dominante, imperioso, prepotente
overblown [ˌoːvərˈbloːn] *adj* **1** INFLATED
: inflado, exagerado **2** BOMBASTIC
: grandilocuente, rimbombante
overboard [ˈoːvərˌbord] *adv* : por la
borda, al agua
overburden [ˌoːvərˈbərdən] *vt* : sobrecargar, agobiar
overcast [ˈoːvərˌkæst] *adj* CLOUDY
: nublado
overcharge [ˌoːvərˈtʃɑrdʒ] *vt* **-charged;
-charging** : cobrarle de más (a alguien)
overcoat [ˈoːvərˌkoːt] *n* : abrigo *m*
overcome [ˌoːvərˈkʌm] *v* **-came** [-ˈkeɪm];
-come; -coming *vt* **1** CONQUER : vencer,
derrotar, superar **2** OVERWHELM : abrumar, agobiar — *vi* : vencer
overconfidence [ˌoːvərˈkɑnfədənts] *n*
: exceso *m* de confianza
overconfident [ˌoːvərˈkɑnfədənt] *adj* : demasiado confiado
overcook [ˌoːvərˈkʊk] *vt* : recocer, cocer
demasiado
overcrowded [ˌoːvərˈkraʊdəd] *adj* **1** PAC-

KED : abarrotado, atestado de gente **2**
OVERPOPULATED : superpoblado
overcrowding [ˌoːvərˈkraʊdɪŋ] *n* **1**
: hacinamiento *m*, masificación *f*
Spain **2** OVERPOPULATION : superpoblación *f*
overdo [ˌoːvərˈduː] *vt* **-did** [-ˈdɪd]; **-done** [-
ˈdʌn]; **-doing; -does** [-ˈdʌz] **1** : hacer
demasiado **2** EXAGGERATE : exagerar **3** OVERCOOK : recocer
overdose [ˈoːvərˌdoːs] *n* : sobredosis *f*
overdraft [ˈoːvərˌdræft] *n* : sobregiro *m*,
descubierto *m*
overdraw [ˌoːvərˈdrɔ] *vt* **-drew** [-ˈdruː];
-drawn [-ˈdrɔn]; **-drawing 1** : sobregirar 〈my account is overdrawn : tengo la
cuenta en descubierto〉 **2** EXAGGERATE
: exagerar
overdue [ˌoːvərˈduː] *adj* **1** UNPAID : vencido y sin pagar **2** TARDY : de retraso,
tardío
overeat [ˌoːvərˈiːt] *vi* **-ate** [-ˈeɪt]; **-eaten**
[-ˈiːtən]; **-eating** : comer demasiado
overelaborate [ˌoːvərɪˈlæbərət] *adj* : recargado
overestimate [ˌoːvərˈɛstəˌmeɪt] *vt* **-mated;
-mating** : sobreestimar
overexcited [ˌoːvərɪkˈsaɪtəd] *adj* : sobreexcitado
overexpose [ˌoːvərɪkˈspoːz] *vt* **-posed;
-posing** : sobreexponer
overfeed [ˌoːvərˈfiːd] *vt* **-fed** [-ˈfɛd]; **-feed-
ing** : sobrealimentar
overflow¹ [ˌoːvərˈfloː] *vt* **1** : desbordar **2**
INUNDATE : inundar — *vi* : desbordarse,
rebosar
overflow² [ˈoːvərˌfloː] *n* **1** : derrame *m*,
desbordamiento *m* (de un río) **2** SUR-
PLUS : exceso *m*, excedente *m*
overfly [ˌoːvərˈflaɪ] *vt* **-flew** [-ˈfluː]; **-flown**
[-ˈfloːn]; **-flying** : sobrevolar
overgrown [ˌoːvərˈgroːn] *adj* **1** : cubierto
〈overgrown with weeds : cubierto de
malas hierbas〉 **2** : demasiado grande
overhand¹ [ˈoːvərˌhænd] *adv* : por encima
de la cabeza
overhand² *adj* : por lo alto (tirada)
overhang¹ [ˈoːvərˌhæŋ] *v* **-hung** [-ˈhʌŋ];
-hanging *vt* **1** : sobresalir por encima
de **2** THREATEN : amenazar — *vi* : sobresalir
overhang² [ˈoːvərˌhæŋ] *n* : saliente *mf*
overhaul [ˌoːvərˈhɔl] *vt* **1** : revisar 〈to
overhaul an engine : revisar un mo-
tor〉 **2** OVERTAKE : adelantar
overhead¹ [ˌoːvərˈhɛd] *adv* : por encima,
arriba, por lo alto
overhead² [ˈoːvərˌhɛd] *adj* : de arriba
overhead³ [ˈoːvərˌhɛd] *n* : gastos *mpl* generales
overhear [ˌoːvərˈhɪr] *vt* **-heard** [-ˈhərd];
-hearing : oír por casualidad
overheat [ˌoːvərˈhiːt] *vt* : recalentar, sobrecalentar, calentar demasiado
overjoyed [ˌoːvərˈdʒɔɪd] *adj* : rebosante de
alegría
overkill [ˌoːvərˌkɪl] *n* : exceso *m*, excedente *m*
overland¹ [ˈoːvərˌlænd, -lənd] *adv* : por
tierra

overland² [ˌoːvərˈlænd] *adj* : terrestre, por tierra

overlap¹ [ˌoːvərˈlæp] *v* **-lapped; -lapping** *vt* : traslapar — *vi* : traslaparse, solaparse

overlap² [ˈoːvərˌlæp] *n* : traslapo *m*

overlay¹ [ˌoːvərˈleɪ] *vt* **-laid** [-ˈleɪd]; **-laying** : recubrir, revestir

overlay² [ˈoːvərˌleɪ] *n* : revestimiento *m*

overload [ˌoːvərˈloːd] *vt* : sobrecargar

overlong [ˌoːvərˈlɔŋ] *adj* : excesivamente largo, largo y pesado

overlook [ˌoːvərˈlʊk] *vt* **1** INSPECT : inspeccionar, revisar **2** : tener vista a, dar a ⟨a house overlooking the valley : una casa que tiene vista al valle⟩ **3** MISS : pasar por alto **4** EXCUSE : dejar pasar, disculpar

overly [ˈoːvərli] *adv* : demasiado

overnight¹ [ˌoːvərˈnaɪt] *adv* **1** : por la noche, durante la noche **2** : de la noche a la mañana ⟨we can't do it overnight : no podemos hacerlo de la noche a la mañana⟩

overnight² [ˈoːvərˌnaɪt] *adj* **1** : de noche ⟨an overnight stay : una estancia de una noche⟩ ⟨an overnight bag : una bolsa de viaje⟩ **2** SUDDEN : repentino

overpass [ˈoːvərˌpæs] *n* : paso *m* elevado, paso *m* a desnivel *Mex*

overpay [ˌoːvərˈpeɪ] *v* **-paid** [-ˈpeɪd]; **-paying** *vt* : pagarle demasiado a (alguien) — *vi* : pagar demasiado

overpopulated [ˌoːvərˈpɑpjəˌleɪtəd] *adj* : superpoblado, sobrepoblado

overpopulation [ˌoːvərˌpɑpjəˈleɪʃən] *n* : superpoblación *f*, sobrepoblación *f*

overpower [ˌoːvərˈpaʊər] *vt* **1** CONQUER, SUBDUE : vencer, superar **2** OVERWHELM : abrumar, agobiar ⟨overpowered by the heat : sofocado por el calor⟩

overpraise [ˌoːvərˈpreɪz] *vt* **-praised; -praising** : adular

overprotective [ˌoːvərprəˈtɛktɪv] *adj* : sobreprotector

overrate [ˌoːvərˈreɪt] *vt* **-rated; -rating** : sobrevalorar, sobrevaluar

overreact [ˌoːvərriˈækt] *vi* : reaccionar de forma exagerada

override [ˌoːvərˈraɪd] *vt* **-rode** [-ˈroːd]; **-ridden** [-ˈrɪdən]; **-riding** **1** : predominar sobre, contar más que ⟨hunger overrode our manners : el hambre predominó sobre los modales⟩ **2** ANNUL : anular, invalidar ⟨to override a veto : anular un veto⟩

overripe [ˌoːvərˈraɪp] *adj* : pasado

overrule [ˌoːvərˈruːl] *vt* **-ruled; -ruling** : anular (una decisión), desautorizar (una persona), denegar (un pedido)

overrun [ˌoːvərˈrʌn] *v* **-ran** [-ˈræn]; **-running** *vt* **1** INVADE : invadir **2** INFEST : infestar, plagar **3** EXCEED : exceder, rebasar — *vi* : rebasar el tiempo previsto

overseas¹ [ˈoːvərˌsiːz] *adv* : en el extranjero ⟨to travel overseas : viajar al extranjero⟩

overseas² [ˈoːvərˌsiːz] *adj* : extranjero, exterior

oversee [ˌoːvərˈsiː] *vt* **-saw** [-ˈsɔ]; **-seen** [-ˈsiːn]; **-seeing** SUPERVISE : supervisar

overseer [ˈoːvərˌsiːər] *n* : supervisor *m*, -sora *f*; capataz *mf*

oversell [ˌoːvərˈsɛl] *vt* : sobrevender

overshadow [ˌoːvərˈʃæˌdoː] *vt* **1** DARKEN : oscurecer, ensombrecer **2** ECLIPSE, OUTSHINE : eclipsar

overshoe [ˈoːvərˌʃuː] *n* : chanclo *m*

overshoot [ˌoːvərˈʃuːt] *vt* **-shot** [-ˈʃɑt]; **-shooting** : pasarse de ⟨to overshoot the mark : pasarse de la raya⟩

oversight [ˈoːvərˌsaɪt] *n* : descuido *m*, inadvertencia *f*

oversleep [ˌoːvərˈsliːp] *vi* **-slept** [-ˈslɛpt]; **-sleeping** : no despertarse a tiempo, quedarse dormido

overspread [ˌoːvərˈsprɛd] *vt* **-spread; -spreading** : extenderse sobre

overstaffed [ˌoːvərˈstæft] *adj* : con exceso de personal

overstate [ˌoːvərˈsteɪt] *vt* **-stated; -stating** EXAGGERATE : exagerar

overstatement [ˌoːvərˈsteɪtmənt] *n* : exageración *f*

overstep [ˌoːvərˈstɛp] *vt* **-stepped; -stepping** EXCEED : sobrepasar, traspasar, exceder

overt [oːˈvərt, ˈoːˌvərt] *adj* : evidente, manifiesto, patente

overtake [ˌoːvərˈteɪk] *vt* **-took** [-ˈtʊk]; **-taken** [-ˈteɪkən]; **-taking** : pasar, adelantar, rebasar *Mex*

overthrow¹ [ˌoːvərˈθroː] *vt* **-threw** [-ˈθruː]; **-thrown** [-ˈθroːn]; **-throwing** **1** OVERTURN : dar la vuelta a, volcar **2** DEFEAT, TOPPLE : derrocar, derribar, deponer

overthrow² [ˈoːvərˌθroː] *n* : derrocamiento *m*, caída *f*

overtime [ˈoːvərˌtaɪm] *n* **1** : horas *fpl* extras (de trabajo) **2** : prórroga *f*; alargue *m Arg, Chile, Uru* (en deportes)

overtly [oːˈvərtli, ˈoːˌvərt-] *adv* OPENLY : abiertamente

overtone [ˈoːvərˌtoːn] *n* **1** : armónico *m* (en música) **2** HINT, SUGGESTION : tinte *m*, insinuación *f*

overture [ˈoːvərˌtʃʊr, -tʃər] *n* **1** PROPOSAL : propuesta *f* **2** : obertura *f* (en música)

overturn [ˌoːvərˈtərn] *vt* **1** UPSET : dar la vuelta a, volcar **2** NULLIFY : anular, invalidar — *vi* TURN OVER : volcar, dar un vuelco

overuse [ˌoːvərˈjuːz] *vt* **-used; -using** : abusar de

overview [ˈoːvərˌvjuː] *n* : resumen *m*, visión *f* general

overweening [ˌoːvərˈwiːnɪŋ] *adj* **1** ARROGANT : arrogante, soberbio **2** IMMODERATE : desmesurado

overweight [ˌoːvərˈweɪt] *adj* : demasiado gordo, demasiado pesado

overwhelm [ˌoːvərˈhwɛlm] *vt* **1** CRUSH, DEFEAT : aplastar, arrollar **2** SUBMERGE : inundar, sumergir **3** OVERPOWER : abrumar, agobiar ⟨overwhelmed by remorse : abrumado de remordimiento⟩

overwhelming [ˌoːvərˈhwɛlmɪŋ] *adj* **1** CRUSHING : abrumador, apabullante **2** SWEEPING : arrollador, aplastante ⟨an overwhelming majority : una mayoría aplastante⟩

overwork [ˌoːvərˈwərk] *vt* **1** : hacer trabajar demasiado **2** OVERUSE : abusar de — *vi* : trabajar demasiado

overwrought [ˌoːvərˈrɔt] *adj* : alterado, sobreexcitado

ovoid ['oːˌvɔid] *or* **ovoidal** [oˈvɔidəl] *adj* : ovoide

ovulate ['ɑvjəˌleɪt, 'oː-] *vi* -lated; -lating : ovular

ovulation [ˌɑvjəˈleɪʃən, ˌoː-] *n* : ovulación *f*

ovum ['oːvəm] *n, pl* **ova** [-və] : óvulo *m*

ow ['aʊ] *interj* : ¡ay!, ¡huy!, ¡uy!

owe ['oː] *vt* **owed; owing** : deber ⟨you owe me $10 : me debes $10⟩ ⟨he owes his wealth to his father : le debe su riqueza a su padre⟩

owing to *prep* : debido a

owl ['aʊl] *n* : búho *m*, lechuza *f*, tecolote *m Mex*

own¹ ['oːn] *vt* **1** POSSESS : poseer, tener, ser dueño de **2** ADMIT : reconocer, admitir — *vi* **to own up** : reconocer (algo), admitir (algo)

own² *adj* : propio, personal, particular ⟨his own car : su propio coche⟩

own³ *pron* **1** (*used with a possessive*) ⟨the book is his own : el libro es suyo, el libro lo escribió él⟩ ⟨money of your own : tu/ su propio dinero⟩ ⟨I want an apartment to call my own : quiero un apartamento para mí solo⟩ ⟨she has a style all her own : tiene un estilo muy particular⟩ ⟨to each his own : cada uno a lo suyo⟩ **2 on one's own** : solo ⟨we did it on our own : lo hicimos solos⟩ ⟨they left her on her own : la dejaron sola⟩

owner ['oːnər] *n* : dueño *m*, -ña *f*; propietario *m*, -ria *f*

ownership ['oːnərˌʃip] *n* : propiedad *f*

ox ['ɑks] *n, pl* **oxen** ['ɑksən] : buey *m*

oxidation [ˌɑksəˈdeɪʃən] *n* : oxidación *f*

oxide ['ɑkˌsaɪd] *n* : óxido *m*

oxidize ['ɑksəˌdaɪz] *vt* -dized; -dizing : oxidar

oxygen ['ɑksɪdʒən] *n* : oxígeno *m*

oxygenate ['ɑksɪdʒəˌneɪt] *vt* -nated; -nating : oxigenar

oyster ['ɔɪstər] *n* : ostra *f*, ostión *m Mex*

ozone ['oːˌzoːn] *n* : ozono *m* ⟨ozone layer : capa de ozono⟩

P

p ['piː] *n, pl* **p's** *or* **ps** ['piːz] : decimosexta letra del alfabeto inglés

PA [ˌpiːˈeɪ] *n* (*public address system*) : altavoces *mpl*, altoparlantes *mpl*

pace¹ ['peɪs] *v* **paced; pacing** *vi* : caminar, ir y venir — *vt* **1** : caminar por ⟨she paced the floor : caminaba de un lado a otro del cuarto⟩ **2 to pace a runner** : marcarle el ritmo a un corredor

pace² *n* **1** STEP : paso *m* **2** RATE : paso *m*, ritmo *m* ⟨to set the pace : marcar el paso, marcar la pauta⟩

pacemaker ['peɪsˌmeɪkər] *n* : marcapasos *m*

pacific [pəˈsɪfɪk] *adj* : pacífico

pacifier ['pæsəˌfaɪər] *n* : chupete *m*, chupón *m*, mamila *f Mex*

pacifism ['pæsəˌfɪzəm] *n* : pacifismo *m*

pacifist ['pæsəfɪst] *n* : pacifista *mf*

pacify ['pæsəˌfaɪ] *vt* -fied; -fying **1** SOOTHE : apaciguar, pacificar **2** : pacificar (un país, una región, etc.) — **pacification** *n*

pack¹ ['pæk] *vt* **1** PACKAGE : empaquetar, embalar, envasar **2** : empacar, meter (en una maleta) ⟨to pack one's bags : hacer las maletas⟩ **3** FILL : llenar, abarrotar ⟨a packed theater : un teatro abarrotado⟩ **4** TAMP : apisonar (tierra), compactar (nieve) ⟨firmly packed brown sugar : azúcar morena bien compacta⟩ **5 to pack in** LEAVE : dejar **6 to pack in/into** : meter en ⟨they packed us all into one room : nos metieron a todos en una sala⟩ ⟨to pack them in : atraer una multitud⟩ **7 to pack it in** *fam* QUIT, STOP : parar **8 to pack off** SEND : mandar **9 to pack up** : recoger, guardar

(para llevar) — *vi or* **to pack up** : empacar, hacer las maletas

pack² *n* **1** BUNDLE : bulto *m*, fardo *m* **2** BACKPACK : mochila *f* **3** PACKAGE : paquete *m*, cajetilla *f* (de cigarrillos, etc.) **4** : manada *f* (de lobos, etc.), jauría *f* (de perros) ⟨a pack of thieves : una pandilla de ladrones⟩ **5** : baraja *f* (de naipes)

package¹ ['pækɪdʒ] *vt* -aged; -aging : empaquetar, embalar

package² *n* : paquete *m*, bulto *m*

packaging ['pækɪdʒɪŋ] *n* **1** : embalaje *m* **2** WRAPPING : envoltorio *m*

packer ['pækər] *n* : empacador *m*, -dora *f*

packet ['pækət] *n* : paquete *m*

packing ['pækɪŋ] *n* : embalaje *m*

pact ['pækt] *n* : pacto *m*, acuerdo *m*

pad¹ ['pæd] *vt* **padded; padding 1** FILL, STUFF : rellenar, acolchar (una silla, una pared) **2** : meter paja en, rellenar ⟨to pad a speech : rellenar un discurso⟩

pad² *n* **1** CUSHION : almohadilla *f* ⟨a shoulder pad : una hombrera⟩ **2** TABLET : bloc *m* (de papel) **3** → **lily pad 4** → **ink pad 5** → **launchpad 6** → **landing pad**

padding ['pædɪŋ] *n* **1** FILLING : relleno *m* **2** : paja *f* (en un discurso, etc.)

paddle¹ ['pædəl] *v* -dled; -dling *vt* **1** : hacer avanzar (una canoa) con canalete **2** HIT : azotar, darle nalgadas a (con una pala o paleta) — *vi* **1** : remar (en una canoa) **2** SPLASH : chapotear, mojarse los pies

paddle² *n* **1** : canalete *m*, zagual *m* (de una canoa, etc.) **2** : pala *f*, paleta *f* (en deportes)

paddock ['pædək] *n* **1** PASTURE : potrero *m* **2** : paddock *m*, cercado *m* (en un hipódromo)

paddy ['pædi] n, pl -dies : arrozal m
padlock¹ ['pæd,lɑk] vt : cerrar con candado
padlock² n : candado m
paella [pɑ'ɛlɑ, -'eɪljɑ, -'eɪɑ] n : paella f
pagan¹ ['peɪɡən] adj : pagano
pagan² n : pagano m, -na f
paganism ['peɪɡən,ɪzəm] n : paganismo m
page¹ ['peɪdʒ] vt paged; paging : llamar por altavoz
page² n 1 BELLHOP : botones m 2 : página f (de un libro, etc.) ⟨page six : la página seis⟩
pageant ['pædʒənt] n 1 SPECTACLE : espectáculo m 2 PROCESSION : desfile m
pageantry ['pædʒəntri] n : pompa f, fausto m
pager ['peɪdʒər] n BEEPER : buscapersonas m
pagoda [pə'ɡoːdə] n : pagoda f
paid → pay
pail ['peɪl] n : balde m, cubo m, cubeta f Mex
pailful ['peɪl,fʊl] n : balde m, cubo m, cubeta f Mex
pain¹ ['peɪn] vt : doler
pain² n 1 PENALTY : pena f ⟨under pain of death : so pena de muerte⟩ 2 SUFFERING : dolor m, malestar m, pena f (mental) 3 pains npl EFFORT : esmero m, esfuerzo m ⟨to take pains : esmerarse⟩ 4 ANNOYANCE : molestia f, fastidio m ⟨he's a pain in the neck : es un pesado⟩
painful ['peɪnfəl] adj : doloroso — painfully adv
painkiller ['peɪn,kɪlər] n : analgésico m
painless ['peɪnləs] adj : indoloro, sin dolor
painlessly ['peɪnləsli] adv : sin dolor
painstaking ['peɪn,steɪkɪŋ] adj : esmerado, cuidadoso, meticuloso — painstakingly adv
paint¹ ['peɪnt] v : pintar
paint² n : pintura f
paintbrush ['peɪnt,brʌʃ] n : pincel m (de un artista), brocha f (para pintar casas, etc.)
painter ['peɪntər] n : pintor m, -tora f
painting ['peɪntɪŋ] n : pintura f
pair¹ ['pær] vt : emparejar, poner en parejas — vi : emparejarse
pair² n : par m (de objetos), pareja f (de personas o animales) ⟨a pair of scissors : unas tijeras⟩
pajamas [pə'dʒɑməz, -'dʒæ-] npl : pijama m, piyama mf
Pakistani [,pæki'stɑni, ,pɑki'stɑni] n : paquistaní mf — Pakistani adj
pal ['pæl] n : amigo m, -ga f; compinche mf fam; chamo m, -ma f Venezuela familiar; cuate m, -ta f Mex
palace ['pæləs] n : palacio m
palatable ['pælətəbəl] adj : sabroso
palate ['pælət] n 1 : paladar m (de la boca) 2 TASTE : paladar m, gusto m
palatial [pə'leɪʃəl] adj : suntuoso, espléndido
palaver [pə'lævər, -'lɑ-] n : palabrería f

pale¹ ['peɪl] v paled; paling vi : palidecer — vt : hacer pálido
pale² adj paler; palest 1 : pálido ⟨to turn pale : palidecer, ponerse pálido⟩ 2 : claro (dícese de los colores)
paleness ['peɪlnəs] n : palidez f
paleontologist [,peɪli,ɑn'tɑlədʒɪst] n : paleontólogo m, -ga f
paleontology [,peɪli,ɑn'tɑlədʒi] n : paleontología f
Palestinian [,pælə'stɪniən] n : palestino m, -na f — Palestinian adj
palette ['pælət] n : paleta f (para mezclar pigmentos)
palisade [,pælə'seɪd] n 1 FENCE : empalizada f, estacada f 2 CLIFFS : acantilado m
pall¹ ['pɔl] vi : perder su sabor, dejar de gustar
pall² n 1 : paño m funerario (sobre un ataúd) 2 COVER : cortina f (de humo, etc.) 3 to cast a pall over : ensombrecer
pallbearer ['pɔl,bɛrər] n : portador m, -dora f del féretro
pallet ['pælət] n 1 BED : camastro m 2 PLATFORM : plataforma f de carga
palliative ['pæli,eɪtɪv, 'pælijətɪv] adj : paliativo ⟨palliative care : cuidados paliativos⟩
pallid ['pæləd] adj : pálido
pallor ['pælər] n : palidez f
palm¹ ['pɑm, 'pɑlm] vt 1 CONCEAL : escamotear (un naipe, etc.) 2 to palm off : encajar, endilgar fam ⟨he palmed it off on me : me lo endilgó⟩
palm² n 1 or palm tree : palmera f 2 : palma f (de la mano)
palmistry ['pɑməstri, 'pɑlmə-] n : quiromancia f
Palm Sunday n : Domingo m de Ramos
palomino [,pælə'miː,noː] n, pl -nos : caballo m de color dorado
palpable ['pælpəbəl] adj : palpable — palpably [-bli] adv
palpitate ['pælpə,teɪt] vi -tated; -tating : palpitar
palpitation [,pælpə'teɪʃən] n : palpitación f
palsy ['pɔlzi] n, pl -sies 1 : parálisis f 2 → cerebral palsy
paltry ['pɔltri] adj paltrier; -est : mísero, mezquino, insignificante ⟨a paltry excuse : una mala excusa⟩
pampas ['pæmpəz, 'pɑmpəs] npl : pampa f
pamper ['pæmpər] vt : mimar, consentir, chiquear Mex
pamphlet ['pæmpflət] n : panfleto m, folleto m
pan¹ ['pæn] vt panned; panning CRITICIZE : poner por los suelos — vi 1 to pan for gold : cribar el oro con batea, lavar oro 2 to pan out : resultar, salir
pan² n 1 : cacerola f, cazuela f 2 frying pan : sartén mf, freidera f Mex
pan- pref : pan- ⟨panacea : panacea⟩
panacea [,pænə'siːə] n : panacea f
Panamanian [,pænə'meɪniən] n : panameño m, -ña f — Panamanian adj

pancake ['pæn,keɪk] n : panqueque m

pancreas ['pæŋkriəs, 'pæn-] n : páncreas m

panda ['pændə] n : panda mf

pandemonium [,pændə'mo:niəm] n : pandemonio m, pandemónium m

pander ['pændər] vi to pander to : satisfacer, complacer (a alguien) ⟨to pander to popular taste : satisfacer el gusto popular⟩

pane ['peɪn] n : cristal m, vidrio m

panel¹ ['pænəl] vt -eled or -elled; -eling or -elling : adornar con paneles

panel² n 1 : lista f de nombres (de un jurado, etc.) 2 GROUP : grupo m, panel m (de discusión), jurado m (de un concurso, etc.) 3 : panel m (de una pared, etc.) 4 : tablero m ⟨control panel : tablero de control⟩

paneling ['pænəlɪŋ] n : paneles mpl

pang ['pæŋ] n : puntada f, punzada f

panhandler ['pæn,hændlər] n : mendigo m, -ga f

panic¹ ['pænɪk] v -icked; -icking vt : llenar de pánico — vi : ser presa de pánico

panic² n : pánico m

panicky ['pænɪki] adj : presa del pánico

panic-stricken adj : presa del pánico ⟨to be panic-stricken : ser presa del pánico⟩

panini [pə'ni:ni] n, pl -ni or -nis : panini m

panorama [,pænə'ræmə, -'rɑ-] n : panorama m

panoramic [,pænə'ræmɪk, -'rɑ-] adj : panorámico

pansexual [,pæn'sɛk{ʃʊəl] adj : pansexual ⟨pansexual people : las personas pansexuales⟩

pansy ['pænzi] n, pl -sies : pensamiento m

pant¹ ['pænt] vi : jadear, resoplar

pant² adj : del pantalón

pant³ n : jadeo m, resoplo m

pantaloons [,pæntə'lu:nz] npl → pants

pantheon ['pænθi,ɑn, -ən] n : panteón m

panther ['pænθər] n : pantera f

panties ['pæntiz] npl : calzones mpl; pantaletas fpl Mex, Ven; bombacha f Arg, Uru; panties mfpl CA, Car; bragas fpl Spain

pantomime¹ ['pæntə,maɪm] v -mimed; -miming vt : representar mediante la pantomima — vi : hacer la mímica

pantomime² n : pantomima f

pantry ['pæntri] n, pl -tries : despensa f

pants ['pænts] npl 1 TROUSERS : pantalón m, pantalones mpl 2 → panties

pantsuit ['pænt,su:t] n : traje m pantalón

panty hose ['pænti] ns & pl : medias fpl, panties mfpl Spain, pantimedias fpl Mex

pap ['pæp] n : papilla f (para bebés, etc.)

papa ['pɑpə] n : papá m

papal ['peɪpəl] adj : papal

papaya [pə'paɪə] n : papaya f (fruta)

paper¹ ['peɪpər] vt WALLPAPER : empapelar

paper² adj : de papel

paper³ n 1 : papel m ⟨a piece of paper : un papel⟩ 2 DOCUMENT : papel m, documento m 3 NEWSPAPER : periódico m, diario m 4 ESSAY : ensayo m

paperback ['peɪpər,bæk] n : libro m en rústica

paper clip n : clip m, sujetapapeles m

paperweight ['peɪpər,weɪt] n : pisapapeles m

paperwork ['peɪpər,wərk] n : papeleo m

papery ['peɪpəri] adj : parecido al papel

papier-mâché [,peɪpərmə'ʃeɪ, ,pæ,pjeɪmæ'ʃeɪ] n : papel m maché

paprika [pə'pri:kə, pæ-] n : pimentón m, paprika f

Pap smear ['pæp-] n : Papanicolau m

papyrus [pə'paɪrəs] n, pl -ruses or -ri [-ri, -,raɪ] : papiro m

par ['pɑr] n 1 VALUE : valor m (nominal), par f ⟨below par : debajo de la par⟩ 2 EQUALITY : igualdad f ⟨to be on a par with : estar al mismo nivel que⟩ 3 : par m (en golf)

parable ['pærəbəl] n : parábola f

parabola [pə'ræbələ] n : parábola f (en matemáticas)

parachute¹ ['pærə,ʃu:t] vi -chuted; -chuting : lanzarse en paracaídas

parachute² n : paracaídas m

parachutist ['pærə,ʃu:tɪst] n : paracaidista mf

parade¹ [pə'reɪd] vi -raded; -rading 1 MARCH : desfilar 2 SHOW OFF : pavonearse, lucirse

parade² n 1 PROCESSION : desfile m 2 DISPLAY : alarde m

paradigm ['pærə,daɪm] n : paradigma m

paradise ['pærə,daɪs, -,daɪz] n : paraíso m

paradox ['pærə,dɑks] n : paradoja f

paradoxical [,pærə'dɑksɪkəl] adj : paradójico — paradoxically adv

paraffin ['pærəfən] n : parafina f

paragliding ['pærə,glaɪdɪŋ] n : parapente m

paragon ['pærə,gɑn, -gən] n : dechado m

paragraph¹ ['pærə,græf] vt : dividir en párrafos

paragraph² n : párrafo m, acápite m

Paraguayan [,pærə'gwaɪən, -'gweɪ-] n : paraguayo m, -ya f — Paraguayan adj

parakeet ['pærə,ki:t] n : periquito m

paralegal [,pærə'li:gəl] n : asistente mf de abogado

parallel¹ ['pærə,lɛl, -ləl] vt 1 MATCH, RESEMBLE : ser paralelo a, ser análogo a, corresponder con 2 : extenderse en línea paralela con ⟨the road parallels the river : el camino se extiende a lo largo del río⟩

parallel² adj : paralelo

parallel³ n 1 : línea f paralela, superficie f paralela 2 : paralelo m (en geografía) 3 SIMILARITY : paralelismo m, semejanza f

parallelogram [,pærə'lɛlə,græm] n : paralelogramo m

paralysis [pə'ræləsɪs] n, pl -yses [-,si:z] : parálisis f

paralyze ['pærə,laɪz] vt -lyzed; -lyzing : paralizar

paramedic [,pærə'mɛdɪk] n : paramédico m, -ca f

parameter [pə'ræmətər] n : parámetro m

paramount ['pærə,maʊnt] adj : supremo ⟨of paramount importance : de suma importancia⟩

paranoia [ˌpærəˈnɔɪə] n : paranoia f

paranoid [ˈpærəˌnɔɪd] adj : paranoico

paranormal [ˌpærəˈnɔrməl] adj : paranormal

parapet [ˈpærəpət, -ˌpet] n : parapeto m

paraphernalia [ˌpærəfəˈneɪljə, -fər-] ns & pl : parafernalia f

paraphrase¹ [ˈpærəˌfreɪz] vt -phrased; -phrasing : parafrasear

paraphrase² n : paráfrasis f

paraplegic¹ [ˌpærəˈpliːdʒɪk] adj : parapléjico

paraplegic² n : parapléjico m, -ca f

parasite [ˈpærəˌsaɪt] n : parásito m

parasitic [ˌpærəˈsɪtɪk] adj : parasitario

parasol [ˈpærəˌsɔl] n : sombrilla f, quitasol m, parasol m

paratrooper [ˈpærəˌtruːpər] n : paracaidista m (militar)

parboil [ˈpɑrˌbɔɪl] vt : sancochar, cocer a medias

parcel¹ [ˈpɑrsəl] vt -celed or -celled; -celing or -celling or to parcel out : repartir, parcelar (tierras)

parcel² n 1 LOT : parcela f, lote m 2 PACKAGE : paquete m, bulto m

parch [ˈpɑrtʃ] vt : resecar

parched adj 1 DRY : muy seco, quemado 2 THIRSTY : seco

parchment [ˈpɑrtʃmənt] n : pergamino m

pardon¹ [ˈpɑrdən] vt 1 FORGIVE : perdonar, disculpar ⟨pardon me! : ¡perdone!, ¡disculpe la molestia!⟩ 2 REPRIEVE : indultar (a un delincuente)

pardon² n 1 FORGIVENESS : perdón m 2 REPRIEVE : indulto m

pardonable [ˈpɑrdənəbəl] adj : perdonable

pare [ˈpær] vt pared; paring 1 PEEL : pelar 2 TRIM : recortar 3 REDUCE : reducir ⟨he pared it (down) to 50 pages : lo redujo a 50 páginas⟩

parent [ˈpærənt] n 1 : madre f, padre m 2 parents npl : padres mpl

parentage [ˈpærəntɪdʒ] n : linaje m, abolengo m, origen m

parental [pəˈrɛntəl] adj : de los padres

parenthesis [pəˈrɛnθəsɪs] n, pl -theses [-ˌsiːz] : paréntesis m

parenthetic [ˌpærənˈθɛtɪk] or parenthetical [-tɪkəl] adj : parentético — parenthetically [-tɪkli] adv

parenthood [ˈpærəntˌhʊd] n : paternidad f

parfait [pɑrˈfeɪ] n : postre m elaborado con frutas y helado

pariah [pəˈraɪə] n : paria mf

parish [ˈpærɪʃ] n : parroquia f

parishioner [pəˈrɪʃənər] n : feligrés m, -gresa f

parity [ˈpærəti] n, pl -ties : paridad f

park¹ [ˈpɑrk] vt : estacionar, parquear, aparcar Spain — vi : estacionarse, parquearse, aparcar Spain

park² n : parque m

parka [ˈpɑrkə] n : parka f

parking [ˈpɑrkɪŋ] n : estacionamiento m, aparcamiento m Spain

parking lot n : estacionamiento m, parking m, aparcamiento m Spain (lugar)

parking meter n : parquímetro m

parking ticket n : multa f (de parquímetro o por estacionarse mal)

parkour [pɑrˈkur] n : parkour m

parkway [ˈpɑrkˌweɪ] n : carretera f ajardinada, bulevar m

parley¹ [ˈpɑrli] vi : parlamentar, negociar

parley² n, pl -leys : negociación f, parlamento m

parliament [ˈpɑrləmənt, ˈpɑrljə-] n : parlamento m

parliamentary [ˌpɑrləˈmɛntəri, ˌpɑrljə-] adj : parlamentario

parlor [ˈpɑrlər] n 1 : sala f, salón m (en una casa) 2 : salón m ⟨beauty parlor : salón de belleza⟩ 3 funeral parlor : funeraria f

parochial [pəˈroːkiəl] adj 1 : parroquial 2 PROVINCIAL : pueblerino, de miras estrechas

parody¹ [ˈpærədi] vt -died; -dying : parodiar

parody² n, pl -dies : parodia f

parole [pəˈroːl] n : libertad f condicional

paroxysm [ˈpærəkˌsɪzəm, pəˈrɑk-] n : paroxismo m

parquet [pɑrˈkeɪ, pɑrˈkeɪ] n : parquet m, parqué m

parrakeet → parakeet

parrot [ˈpærət] n : loro m, papagayo m

parry¹ [ˈpæri] v -ried; -rying vi : parar un golpe — vt EVADE : esquivar (una pregunta, etc.)

parry² n, pl -ries : parada f

parsimonious [ˌpɑrsəˈmoːniəs] adj : tacaño, mezquino

parsley [ˈpɑrsli] n : perejil m

parsnip [ˈpɑrsnɪp] n : chirivía f

parson [ˈpɑrsən] n : pastor m, -tora f; clérigo m

parsonage [ˈpɑrsənɪdʒ] n : rectoría f, casa f del párroco

part¹ [ˈpɑrt] vi 1 SEPARATE : separarse, despedirse ⟨we should part as friends : debemos separarnos amistosamente⟩ 2 OPEN : abrirse ⟨the curtains parted : las cortinas se abrieron⟩ 3 to part with : deshacerse de — vt 1 SEPARATE : separar 2 to part one's hair : hacerse la raya, peinarse con raya

part² n 1 SECTION, SEGMENT : parte f, sección f ⟨for the better part of a year : durante casi un año⟩ ⟨in the latter part of the century : hacia finales de siglo⟩ ⟨the western part of the state : la parte oeste del estado⟩ ⟨the best/worst part is that . . . : lo mejor/peor es que . . .⟩ 2 PIECE : pieza f (de una máquina, etc.) 3 ROLE : papel m (en teatro, etc.) ⟨to play a part : hacer un papel⟩ ⟨to look the part : tener el aspecto para el papel⟩ 4 ROLE, INFLUENCE : papel m ⟨to play a part : jugar un papel⟩ ⟨to want no part of/in : no querer tener nada que ver con⟩ 5 : raya f (del pelo) 6 for my/his (etc.) part : por mi/su (etc.) parte 7 for the most part MOSTLY : en su mayoría, en su mayor parte 8 for the most part USUALLY : en general 9 in part : en parte 10 in these parts : por aquí 11 on the part of : de/por parte de 12 to take part (in) : tomar parte (en), participar (en)

partake [par'teɪk, pər-] vi -took [-'tʊk]; -taken [-'teɪkən]; -taking 1 to partake of CONSUME : comer, beber, tomar 2 to partake in : participar en (una actividad, etc.)

partial ['parʃəl] adj 1 BIASED : parcial, tendencioso 2 INCOMPLETE : parcial, incompleto 3 to be partial to : ser aficionado a

partiality [ˌparʃi'æləti] n, pl -ties : parcialidad f

partially ['parʃəli] adv : parcialmente

participant [pər'tɪsəpənt, par-] n : participante mf

participate [pər'tɪsəˌpeɪt, par-] vi -pated; -pating : participar

participation [pərˌtɪsə'peɪʃən, par-] n : participación f

participle ['partəˌsɪpəl] n : participio m

particle ['partɪkəl] n : partícula f

particular¹ [pər'tɪkjələr] adj 1 SPECIFIC : particular, en particular ⟨this particular person : esta persona en particular⟩ 2 SPECIAL : particular, especial ⟨with particular emphasis : con un énfasis especial⟩ 3 FUSSY : exigente, maniático ⟨to be very particular : ser muy especial⟩ ⟨I'm not particular : me da igual⟩

particular² n 1 DETAIL : detalle m, sentido m 2 in particular : en particular, en especial

particularly [pər'tɪkjələrli] adv 1 ESPECIALLY : particularmente, especialmente 2 SPECIFICALLY : específicamente, en especial

partisan ['partəzən, -sən] n 1 ADHERENT : partidario m, -ria f 2 GUERRILLA : partisano m, -na f; guerrillero m, -ra f

partition¹ [pər'tɪʃən, par-] vt : dividir ⟨to partition off (a room) : dividir (una habitación) con un tabique⟩

partition² n 1 DISTRIBUTION : partición f, división f, reparto m 2 DIVIDER : tabique m, mampara f, biombo m

partly ['partli] adv : en parte, parcialmente

partner ['partnər] n 1 COMPANION : compañero m, -ra f 2 : pareja f (en un juego, etc.) ⟨dancing partner : pareja de baile⟩ 3 MATE : pareja f; compañero m, -ra f ⟨(marital) partner : cónyuge⟩ 4 : socio m, -cia f; asociado m, -da f ⟨business/senior partner : socio comercial/mayoritario⟩

partnership ['partnərˌʃɪp] n 1 ASSOCIATION : asociación f, compañerismo m 2 : sociedad f (de negociantes) ⟨to form a partnership : asociarse⟩

part of speech : categoría f gramatical

partridge ['partrɪdʒ] n, pl -tridge or -tridges : perdiz f

part-time¹ ['part'taɪm] adv : medio tiempo, a tiempo parcial

part-time² adj : de medio tiempo, a tiempo parcial

party ['parti] n, pl -ties 1 : partido m (político) 2 PARTICIPANT : parte f, participante mf 3 GROUP : grupo m (de personas) 4 GATHERING : fiesta f ⟨to throw a party : dar una fiesta⟩

parvenu ['parvəˌnu:, -ˌnju:] n : advenedizo m, -za f

pass¹ ['pæs] vi 1 : pasar, cruzarse ⟨a plane passed overhead : pasó un avión⟩ ⟨we passed in the hallway : nos cruzamos en el pasillo⟩ 2 CEASE : pasarse ⟨the pain passed : se pasó el dolor⟩ 3 ELAPSE : pasar, transcurrir 4 PROCEED : pasar ⟨let me pass : déjame pasar⟩ 5 HAPPEN : pasar, ocurrir 6 : pasar, aprobar (en un examen) 7 or to pass down : pasar ⟨the throne passed to his son : el trono pasó a su hijo⟩ 8 to pass as : pasar por 9 to pass away/on DIE : fallecer, morir 10 to pass by : pasar 11 to pass out FAINT : desmayarse — vt 1 : pasar por (un lugar) 2 OVERTAKE : pasar, adelantar 3 SPEND : pasar (tiempo) 4 HAND : pasar ⟨pass me the salt : pásame la sal⟩ 5 : aprobar (un examen) 6 : aprobar (a un estudiante) 7 : aprobar (una ley) 8 to let pass OVERLOOK, IGNORE : pasar por alto, dejar pasar 9 to pass by : escapársele a (alguien) ⟨don't let life pass you by : no dejes que la vida se te pase⟩ 10 to pass off as : hacer pasar por ⟨to pass oneself off as : hacerse pasar por⟩ 11 to pass on TRANSMIT, RELAY : pasar 12 to pass over SKIP, OMIT : pasar por alto 13 to pass up DECLINE : dejar pasar 14 to pass the time : pasar el rato

pass² n 1 CROSSING, GAP : paso m, desfiladero m, puerto m ⟨mountain pass : puerto de montaña⟩ 2 PERMIT : pase m, permiso m 3 : pase m (en deportes) 4 SITUATION : situación f (difícil) ⟨how did we come to such a pass? : ¿cómo llegamos a tal extremo?⟩

passable ['pæsəbəl] adj 1 ADEQUATE : adecuado, pasable 2 : transitable (dícese de un camino, etc.)

passably ['pæsəbli] adv : pasablemente

passage ['pæsɪdʒ] n 1 PASSING : paso m ⟨the passage of time : el paso del tiempo⟩ 2 PASSAGEWAY : pasillo m (dentro de un edificio), pasaje m (entre edificios) 3 VOYAGE : travesía f (por el mar), viaje m ⟨to grant safe passage : dar un salvoconducto⟩ 4 SECTION : pasaje m (en música o literatura) 5 APPROVAL : aprobación f (de un proyecto de ley, etc.)

passageway ['pæsɪdʒˌweɪ] n : pasillo m, pasadizo m, corredor m

passbook ['pæsˌbʊk] n BANKBOOK : libreta f de ahorros

passé [pæ'seɪ] adj : pasado de moda

passenger ['pæsəndʒər] n : pasajero m, -ra f

passerby [ˌpæsər'baɪ, 'pæsərˌ-] n, pl passersby : transeúnte mf

passing¹ adj 1 : que pasa ⟨he saw a passing train : vio un tren que pasaba⟩ ⟨with each passing day/year : con cada día/año que pasa⟩ 2 TRANSIENT : pasajero 3

CURSORY : somero ⟨to make a passing reference to : referirse de pasada a⟩ 4 SLIGHT, SUPERFICIAL : ligero (dícese de un parecido), superficial (dícese de un conocimiento, un interés, etc.) 5 SATISFACTORY : satisfactorio ⟨to get a passing grade : aprobar (un examen, etc.)⟩

passing² ['pæsɪŋ] n 1 DEATH : fallecimiento m 2 PASSAGE, MOVEMENT : paso m (del tiempo, etc.) 3 PASSAGE, APPROVAL : aprobación f 4 in passing : de pasada

passion ['pæʃən] n : pasión f, ardor m

passionate ['pæʃənət] adj 1 IRASCIBLE : irascible, iracundo 2 ARDENT : apasionado, ardiente, ferviente, fogoso

passionately ['pæʃənətli] adv : apasionadamente, fervientemente, con pasión

passionflower ['pæʃən,flaʊər] n : pasionaria f, pasiflora f

passive¹ ['pæsɪv] adj : pasivo — **passively** adv

passive² n : voz f pasiva (en gramática)

Passover ['pæs,o:vər] n : Pascua f (en el judaísmo)

passport ['pæs,port] n : pasaporte m

password ['pæs,wərd] n : contraseña f

past¹ ['pæst] adv : por delante ⟨he drove past : pasamos en coche⟩

past² adj 1 AGO : hace ⟨10 years past : hace 10 años⟩ 2 LAST : último ⟨the past few months : los últimos meses⟩ 3 BYGONE : pasado ⟨in past times : en tiempos pasados⟩ 4 : pasado (en gramática)

past³ n : pasado m

past⁴ prep 1 BY : por, por delante de ⟨he ran past the house : pasó por la casa corriendo⟩ 2 BEYOND : más allá de ⟨just past the corner : un poco más allá de la esquina⟩ ⟨we went past the exit : pasamos la salida⟩ 3 AFTER : después de ⟨past noon : después del mediodía⟩ ⟨half past two : las dos y media⟩

pasta ['pɑstə, 'pæs-] n : pasta f

paste¹ ['peɪst] vt **pasted; pasting** 1 : pegar (con engrudo) 2 : pegar (en un documento electrónico)

paste² n 1 : pasta f ⟨tomato paste : pasta de tomate⟩ 2 : engrudo m (para pegar)

pasteboard ['peɪst,bord] n : cartón m, cartulina f

pastel [pæ'stɛl] n : pastel m — **pastel** adj

pasteurization [,pæstʃərə'zeɪʃən, ,pæstjə-] n : pasteurización f

pasteurize ['pæstʃə,raɪz, 'pæstjə-] vt **-ized; -izing** : pasteurizar

pastime ['pæs,taɪm] n : pasatiempo m

pastor ['pæstər] n : pastor m, -tora f

pastoral ['pæstərəl] adj : pastoral

past participle n : participio m pasado

pastry ['peɪstri] n, pl **-ries** 1 DOUGH : pasta f, masa f 2 **pastries** npl : pasteles mpl

pasture¹ ['pæstʃər] v **-tured; -turing** vi GRAZE : pacer, pastar — vt : apacentar, pastar

pasture² n : pastizal m, potrero m, pasto m

pasty ['peɪsti] adj **pastier; -est** 1 : pastoso (en consistencia) 2 PALLID : pálido

pat¹ ['pæt] vt **patted; patting** : dar palmaditas a, tocar

pat² adv : de memoria ⟨to have down pat : saberse de memoria⟩

pat³ adj 1 APT : apto, apropiado 2 GLIB : fácil 3 UNYIELDING : firme ⟨to stand pat : mantenerse firme⟩

pat⁴ n 1 TAP : golpecito m, palmadita f ⟨a pat on the back : una palmadita en la espalda⟩ 2 CARESS : caricia f 3 : porción f ⟨a pat of butter : una porción de mantequilla⟩

patch¹ ['pætʃ] vt 1 MEND, REPAIR : remendar, parchar, ponerle un parche a 2 **to patch together** IMPROVISE : confeccionar, improvisar 3 **to patch up** : arreglar ⟨they patched things up : hicieron las paces⟩

patch² n 1 : parche m, remiendo m (para la ropa) ⟨eye patch : parche para el ojo⟩ 2 PIECE : mancha f, trozo m ⟨a patch of sky : un trozo de cielo⟩ 3 PLOT : parcela f, terreno m ⟨cabbage patch : parcela de repollos⟩ 4 : período m ⟨to go through a bad/rough patch : pasar una mala racha⟩ 5 : parche m (para el software)

patchwork ['pætʃ,wərk] n : labor f de retazos

patchy ['pætʃi] adj **patchier; -est** 1 IRREGULAR : irregular, desigual 2 INCOMPLETE : parcial, incompleto

pâté [pɑ'teɪ, pæ-] n : paté m

patent¹ ['pætənt] vt : patentar

patent² ['pætənt, 'peɪt-] adj 1 OBVIOUS : patente, evidente 2 ['pæt-] PATENTED : patentado

patent³ ['pætənt] n : patente f

patent leather ['pætənt-] n : charol m

patently ['pætəntli] adv : patentemente, evidentemente

paternal [pə'tərnəl] adj 1 FATHERLY : paternal 2 : paterno ⟨paternal grandfather : abuelo paterno⟩

paternity [pə'tərnəti] n : paternidad f ⟨paternity leave : licencia por paternidad⟩

path ['pæθ, 'pɑθ] n 1 TRACK, TRAIL : camino m, sendero m, senda f 2 COURSE, ROUTE : recorrido m, trayecto m, trayectoria f

pathetic [pə'θɛtɪk] adj : patético — **pathetically** [-tɪkli] adv

pathological [,pæθə'lɑdʒɪkəl] adj : patológico

pathologist [pə'θɑlədʒɪst] n : patólogo m, -ga f

pathology [pə'θɑlədʒi] n, pl **-gies** : patología f

pathos ['peɪ,θɑs, 'pæ-, -,θɔs] n : patetismo m

pathway ['pæθ,weɪ] n : camino m, sendero m, senda f, vereda f

patience ['peɪʃənts] n : paciencia f

patient¹ ['peɪʃənt] adj : paciente — **patiently** adv

patient² n : paciente mf

patina [pə'ti:nə, 'pætənə] n : pátina f

patio ['pæti,o:] n, pl **-tios** : patio m

patriarch ['peɪtri,ɑrk] n : patriarca m

patriarchy ['peɪtri,ɑrki] n, pl **-chies** : patriarcado m

patrimony [ˈpætrəˌmoːni] n, pl **-nies** : patrimonio m
patriot [ˈpeɪtriət] n : patriota mf
patriotic [ˌpeɪtriˈɑtɪk] adj : patriótico — **patriotically** adv
patriotism [ˈpeɪtriəˌtɪzəm] n : patriotismo m
patrol¹ [pəˈtroːl] v **-trolled; -trolling** : patrullar
patrol² n : patrulla f
patrol car n : patrulla f, patrullero m (automóvil)
patrolman [pəˈtroːlmən] n, pl **-men** [-mən, -ˌmɛn] : policía mf, guardia mf
patron [ˈpeɪtrən] n 1 SPONSOR : patrocinador m, -dora f 2 CUSTOMER : cliente m, -ta f 3 or **patron saint** : patrono m, -na f
patronage [ˈpeɪtrənɪdʒ, ˈpæ-] n 1 SPONSORSHIP : patrocinio m 2 CLIENTELE : clientela f 3 : influencia f (política)
patronize [ˈpeɪtrəˌnaɪz, ˈpæ-] vt **-ized; -izing** 1 SPONSOR : patrocinar 2 : ser cliente de (un negocio) 3 : tratar con condescendencia
patronizing adj : condescendiente
patter¹ [ˈpætər] vi TAP : golpetear, tamborilear (dícese de la lluvia)
patter² n 1 TAPPING : golpeteo m, tamborileo m (de la lluvia), correteo m (de pies) 2 CHATTER : palabrería f, parloteo m fam
pattern¹ [ˈpætərn] vt 1 BASE : basar (en un modelo) 2 to **pattern after** : hacer imitación de
pattern² n 1 MODEL : modelo m, patrón m (de costura) 2 DESIGN : diseño m, dibujo m, estampado m (de tela) 3 NORM, STANDARD : pauta f, norma f, patrón m
patty [ˈpæti] n, pl **-ties** : porción f de carne picada (u otro alimento) en forma de ruedita ⟨a hamburger patty : una hamburguesa⟩ ⟨a turkey patty : una hamburguesa de pavo⟩
paucity [ˈpɔsəti] n : escasez f
paunch [ˈpɔntʃ] n : panza f, barriga f
pauper [ˈpɔpər] n : pobre mf, indigente mf
pause¹ [ˈpɔz] vi **paused; pausing** : hacer una pausa, pararse (brevemente)
pause² n : pausa f
pave [ˈpeɪv] vt **paved; paving** : pavimentar ⟨to pave with stones : empedrar⟩
pavement [ˈpeɪvmənt] n : pavimento m, empedrado m
pavilion [pəˈvɪljən] n : pabellón m
paving [ˈpeɪvɪŋ] → **pavement**
paw¹ [ˈpɔ] vt : tocar, manosear, sobar
paw² n : pata f, garra f, zarpa f
pawn¹ [ˈpɔn] vt : empeñar, prendar
pawn² n 1 PLEDGE, SECURITY : prenda f 2 PAWNING : empeño m 3 : peón m (en ajedrez)
pawnbroker [ˈpɔnˌbroːkər] n : prestamista mf
pawnshop [ˈpɔnˌʃɑp] n : casa f de empeños, monte m de piedad
pay¹ [ˈpeɪ] v **paid** [ˈpeɪd]; **paying** vt 1 : pagar ⟨she paid the bill/rent : pagó la cuenta/renta⟩ ⟨he paid $200 for the bike

: pagó $200 por la bici⟩ ⟨they paid her to mow the lawn : la pagaron para cortar el pasto⟩ 2 to **pay attention** : poner atención, prestar atención, hacer caso 3 to **pay a visit** : hacer una visita 4 to **pay back** : pagar (un préstamo), devolver (dinero) ⟨she paid them back : les devolvió el dinero⟩ ⟨I'll pay you back for what you did! : ¡me las pagarás!⟩ 5 to **pay off** SETTLE : saldar, cancelar (una deuda, etc.) 6 to **pay one's respects** : presentar uno sus respetos — vi 1 : pagar ⟨to pay in cash : pagar en efectivo⟩ ⟨the job pays well : el trabajo está bien pagado⟩ 2 : valer la pena ⟨crime doesn't pay : no hay crimen sin castigo⟩ 3 to **pay for** : pagar ⟨he paid for our dinner : nos pagó la comida⟩ ⟨she paid dearly for her mistakes : pagó caro sus errores⟩ ⟨you'll pay for this! : ¡me las pagarás!⟩ 4 to **pay one's (own) way** ⟨she paid her way through college : se pagó los estudios⟩ ⟨he paid his own way at dinner : pagó su parte de la cena⟩ 5 to **pay up** : pagar
pay² n : paga f
payable [ˈpeɪəbəl] adj DUE : pagadero
paycheck [ˈpeɪˌtʃɛk] n : sueldo m, cheque m del sueldo
payday [ˈpeɪˌdeɪ] n : día m de pago/paga
payee [peɪˈiː] n : beneficiario m, -ria f (de un cheque, etc.)
payer [ˈpeɪər] n : pagador m, -dora f
payment [ˈpeɪmənt] n 1 : pago m 2 INSTALLMENT : plazo m, cuota f 3 REWARD : recompensa f
payoff [ˈpeɪˌɔf] n 1 REWARD : recompensa f 2 PROFIT : ganancia f 3 BRIBE : soborno m
pay phone n : teléfono m público
payroll [ˈpeɪˌroːl] n : nómina f
PC [ˌpiːˈsiː] n, pl **PCs** or **PC's** : PC mf, computadora f personal
PDA [ˌpiːˌdiːˈeɪ] n, pl **PDAs** or **PDA's** (*personal digital assistant*) : PDA m
pea [ˈpiː] n : chícharo m, guisante m, arveja f
peace [ˈpiːs] n 1 : paz f ⟨peace treaty : tratado de paz⟩ ⟨peace and tranquillity : paz y tranquilidad⟩ 2 ORDER : orden m (público)
peaceable [ˈpiːsəbəl] adj : pacífico — **peaceably** [-bli] adv
peaceful [ˈpiːsfəl] adj 1 PEACEABLE : pacífico 2 CALM, QUIET : tranquilo, sosegado — **peacefully** adv
peacemaker [ˈpiːsˌmeɪkər] n : conciliador m, -dora f; mediador m, -dora f
peacetime [ˈpiːsˌtaɪm] n : tiempos mpl de paz
peach [ˈpiːtʃ] n : durazno m, melocotón m
peacock [ˈpiːˌkɑk] n : pavo m real
peak¹ [ˈpiːk] vi : alcanzar su nivel máximo
peak² adj : máximo
peak³ n 1 POINT : punta f 2 CREST, SUMMIT : cima f, cumbre f 3 APEX : cúspide f, apogeo m, nivel m máximo
peaked [ˈpiːkəd] adj SICKLY : pálido
peal¹ [ˈpiːl] vi : repicar
peal² n : repique m, tañido m (de campanada) ⟨peals of laughter : carcajadas⟩

peanut ['piː,nʌt] n : maní m, cacahuate m Mex, cacahuete m Spain

peanut butter n : mantequilla/crema f de maní, manteca f de maní Arg, crema/ mantequilla f de cacahuate Mex, mantequilla/crema f de cacahuete Spain

pear ['pær] n : pera f

pearl ['pərl] n : perla f

pearly ['pərli] adj **pearlier; -est** : nacarado

peasant ['pezənt] n : campesino m, -na f

peat ['piːt] n : turba f

pebble ['pɛbəl] n : guijarro m, piedrecita f, piedrita f

pecan [pɪ'kɑn, -'kæn, 'piː,kæn] n : pacana f, nuez f Mex

peccary ['pɛkəri] n, pl **-ries** : pécari m, pecarí m

peck[1] ['pɛk] vt : picar, picotear

peck[2] n 1 : medida f de áridos equivalente a 8.810 litros 2 : picotazo m (de un pájaro) ⟨a peck on the cheek : un besito en la mejilla⟩

pectoral ['pɛktərəl] adj : pectoral

peculiar [pɪ'kjuːljər] adj 1 DISTINCTIVE : propio, peculiar, característico ⟨peculiar to this area : propio de esta zona⟩ 2 STRANGE : extraño, raro — **peculiarly** adv

peculiarity [pɪ,kjuːl'iːærəti, -,kjuːli'ær-] n, pl **-ties** 1 DISTINCTIVENESS : peculiaridad f 2 ODDITY, QUIRK : rareza f, idiosincrasia f, excentricidad f

pecuniary [pɪ'kjuːni,ɛri] adj : pecuniario

pedagogical [,pɛdə'gɑdʒɪkəl, -'goː-] or **pedagogic** [,pɛdə'gɑdʒɪk, -'goː-] adj : pedagógico

pedagogy ['pɛdə,goːdʒi, -,gɑ-] n : pedagogía f

pedal[1] ['pɛdəl] v **-aled** or **-alled; -aling** or **-alling** vi : pedalear — vt : darle a los pedales de

pedal[2] n : pedal m

pedant ['pɛdənt] n : pedante mf

pedantic [pɪ'dæntɪk] adj : pedante

pedantry ['pɛdəntri] n, pl **-ries** : pedantería f

peddle ['pɛdəl] vt **-dled; -dling** : vender (en las calles)

peddler ['pɛdlər] n : vendedor m, -dora f ambulante; mercachifle m

pedestal ['pɛdəstəl] n : pedestal m

pedestrian[1] [pə'dɛstriən] adj 1 COMMONPLACE : pedestre, ordinario 2 : de peatón, peatonal ⟨pedestrian crossing : paso de peatones⟩

pedestrian[2] n : peatón m, -tona f

pediatric [,piːdi'ætrɪk] adj : pediátrico

pediatrician [,piːdiə'trɪʃən] n : pediatra mf

pediatrics [,piːdi'ætrɪks] ns & pl : pediatría f

pedigree ['pɛdə,griː] n 1 FAMILY TREE : árbol m genealógico 2 LINEAGE : pedigrí m (de un animal), linaje m (de una persona)

pee[1] ['piː] vi fam URINATE : hacer pipí fam

pee[2] n fam : pipí m fam ⟨to take a pee : hacer pipí⟩

peek[1] ['piːk] vi 1 PEEP : espiar, mirar furtivamente 2 GLANCE : echar un vistazo

peek[2] n 1 : miradita f (furtiva) 2 GLANCE : vistazo m, ojeada f

peel[1] ['piːl] vt 1 : pelar (fruta, etc.) 2 or **to peel away** : quitar — vi : pelarse (dícese de la piel), desconcharse (dícese de la pintura)

peel[2] n : cáscara f

peeler ['piːlər] n : pelador m, pelapapas mpl

peep[1] ['piːp] vi 1 PEEK : espiar, mirar furtivamente 2 CHEEP : piar 3 **to peep out** SHOW : asomarse

peep[2] n 1 CHEEP : pío m (de un pajarito) 2 GLANCE : vistazo m, ojeada f

peer[1] ['pɪr] vi : mirar detenidamente, mirar con atención

peer[2] n 1 EQUAL : par m, igual mf ⟨peer group : grupo paritario⟩ 2 NOBLE : noble mf

peerage ['pɪrɪdʒ] n : nobleza f

peerless ['pɪrləs] adj : sin par, incomparable

peeve[1] ['piːv] vt **peeved; peeving** : fastidiar, irritar, molestar

peeve[2] n : queja f

peevish ['piːvɪʃ] adj : quejoso, fastidioso — **peevishly** adv

peevishness ['piːvɪʃnəs] n : irritabilidad f

peg[1] ['pɛg] vt **pegged; pegging** 1 PLUG : tapar (con una clavija) 2 FASTEN, FIX : sujetar (con estaquillas) 3 **to peg out** MARK : marcar (con estaquillas)

peg[2] n : estaquilla f (para clavar), clavija f (para tapar)

pejorative [pɪ'dʒɔrətɪv] adj : peyorativo — **pejoratively** adv

pelican ['pɛlɪkən] n : pelícano m

pellagra [pə'lægrə, -'leɪ-] n : pelagra f

pellet ['pɛlət] n 1 BALL : bolita f ⟨food pellet : bolita de comida⟩ 2 SHOT : perdigón m

pell-mell ['pɛl'mɛl] adv : desordenadamente, atropelladamente

pelt[1] ['pɛlt] vt 1 THROW : lanzar, tirar (algo a alguien) 2 **to pelt with stones** : apedrear — vi 1 BEAT : golpear con fuerza ⟨the rain was pelting down : llovía a cántaros⟩ 2 : ir a todo correr

pelt[2] n : piel f, pellejo m

pelvic ['pɛlvɪk] adj : pélvico

pelvis ['pɛlvɪs] n, pl **-vises** or **-ves** ['pɛl,viːz] : pelvis f

pen[1] ['pɛn] vt **penned; penning** 1 or **pen in** : encerrar (animales) 2 WRITE : escribir

pen[2] n 1 CORRAL : corral m, redil m (para ovejas) 2 : pluma f ⟨fountain pen : pluma fuente⟩ ⟨ballpoint pen : bolígrafo⟩

penal ['piːnəl] adj : penal

penalize ['piːnəl,aɪz, 'pɛn-] vt **-ized; -izing** : penalizar, sancionar

penalty ['pɛnəlti] n, pl **-ties** 1 PUNISHMENT : pena f, castigo m 2 DISADVANTAGE : desventaja f, castigo m, penalty m (en deportes) 3 FINE : multa f

penance ['pɛnənts] n : penitencia f

pence → penny

penchant ['pɛntʃənt] n : inclinación f, afición f

pencil[1] ['pɛntsəl] *vt* **-ciled** *or* **-cilled; -ciling** *or* **-cilling** : escribir con lápiz, dibujar con lápiz
pencil[2] *n* : lápiz *m*
pencil case *n* : estuche *m* (para lápices)
pencil sharpener *n* : sacapuntas *m*
pencil skirt *n* : falda *f* de tubo
pendant ['pɛndənt] *n* : colgante *m*
pending[1] ['pɛndɪŋ] *adj* : pendiente
pending[2] *prep* **1** DURING : durante **2** AWAITING : en espera de
pendulum ['pɛndʒələm, -djʊləm] *n* : péndulo *m*
penetrate ['pɛnə,treɪt] *vt* **-trated; -trating** : penetrar
penetrating ['pɛnə,treɪtɪŋ] *adj* : penetrante, cortante
penetration [,pɛnə'treɪʃən] *n* : penetración *f*
penguin ['pɛŋgwɪn, 'pɛn-] *n* : pingüino *m*
penicillin [,pɛnə'sɪlən] *n* : penicilina *f*
peninsula [pə'nɪntsələ, -'nɪntʃʊlə] *n* : península *f*
penis ['pi:nəs] *n, pl* **-nes** [-,ni:z] *or* **-nises** : pene *m*
penitence ['pɛnətənts] *n* : arrepentimiento *m*, penitencia *f*
penitent[1] ['pɛnətənt] *adj* : arrepentido, penitente
penitent[2] *n* : penitente *mf*
penitentiary [,pɛnə'tɛntʃəri] *n, pl* **-ries** : penitenciaría *f*, prisión *m*, presidio *m*
penknife ['pɛn,naɪf] *n* : navaja *f*
penmanship ['pɛnmən,ʃɪp] *n* : escritura *f*, caligrafía *f*
pen name *n* : seudónimo *m*
pennant ['pɛnənt] *n* : gallardete *m* (de un barco), banderín *m*
penniless ['pɛniləs] *adj* : sin un centavo
penny ['pɛni] *n, pl* **-nies** *or* **pence** ['pɛnts] **1** : penique *m* (del Reino Unido) **2** *pl* **-nies** CENT : centavo *m* (de los Estados Unidos)
pen pal *n* : amigo *m*, -ga *f* por correspondencia
pension[1] ['pɛntʃən] *vt or* **to pension off** : jubilar
pension[2] *n* : pensión *m*, jubilación *f*
pensioner ['pɛntʃənər] *n* : pensionista *mf*
pensive ['pɛntsɪv] *adj* : pensativo, meditabundo — **pensively** *adv*
pentagon ['pɛntə,gɑn] *n* : pentágono *m*
pentagonal [pɛn'tægənəl] *adj* : pentagonal
penthouse ['pɛnt,haʊs] *n* : ático *m*, penthouse *m*
pent–up ['pɛnt'ʌp] *adj* : encerrado ⟨pent-up feelings : emociones reprimidas⟩
penultimate [pɪ'nʌltəmət] *adj* : penúltimo
penury ['pɛnjəri] *n* : penuria *f*, miseria *f*
peon ['pi:,ɑn, -ən] *n, pl* **-ons** *or* **-ones** [pe'o:ni:z] : peón *m*
peony ['pi:əni] *n, pl* **-nies** : peonía *f*
people[1] ['pi:pəl] *vt* **-pled; -pling** : poblar
people[2] *ns & pl* **1 people** *npl* : gente *f*, personas *fpl* ⟨people like him : él le cae bien a la gente⟩ ⟨many people : mucha gente, muchas personas⟩ ⟨young/old people : los jóvenes/ancianos⟩ **2** *pl* **peoples** : pueblo *m* ⟨the Cuban people : el pueblo cubano⟩

pep[1] ['pɛp] *vt* **pepped; pepping** *or* **to pep up** : animar
pep[2] *n* : energía *f*, vigor *m*
pepper[1] ['pɛpər] *vt* **1** : añadir pimienta a **2** RIDDLE : acribillar (a balazos) **3** SPRINKLE : salpicar ⟨peppered with quotations : salpicado de citas⟩
pepper[2] *n* **1** : pimienta *f* (condimento) **2** : pimiento *m*, pimentón *m* (fruta) **3** → **chili**
peppermint ['pɛpər,mɪnt] *n* : menta *f*
pepper shaker → **shaker**
peppery ['pɛpəri] *adj* : picante
peppy ['pɛpi] *adj* **peppier; -est** : lleno de energía, vivaz
pep rally *n* : reunión *f* (para animar a un equipo antes de un partido)
pep talk *n* : plática *f*, charla *f* (para animar a un equipo, etc.) ⟨to give someone a pep talk : animar a alguien⟩
peptic ['pɛptɪk] *adj* **peptic ulcer** : úlcera *f* estomacal
per ['pər] *prep* **1** : por ⟨miles per hour : millas por hora⟩ **2** ACCORDING TO : según ⟨per his specifications : según sus especificaciones⟩
per annum [pər'ænəm] *adv* : al año, por año
percale [,pər'keɪl, 'pər-,, ,pər'kæl] *n* : percal *m*
per capita [pər'kæpɪtə] *adv & adj* : per cápita
perceive [pər'si:v] *vt* **-ceived; -ceiving 1** REALIZE : percatarse de, concientizarse de, darse cuenta de **2** NOTE : percibir, notar
percent[1] [pər'sɛnt] *adv* : por ciento
percent[2] *n, pl* **-cent** *or* **-cents 1** : por ciento ⟨10 percent of the population : el 10 por ciento de la población⟩ **2** → **percentage**
percentage [pər'sɛntɪdʒ] *n* : porcentaje *m*
perceptible [pər'sɛptəbəl] *adj* : perceptible — **perceptibly** [-bli] *adv*
perception [pər'sɛpʃən] *n* **1** : percepción *f* ⟨color perception : la percepción de los colores⟩ **2** INSIGHT : perspicacia *f* **3** IDEA : idea *f*, imagen *f*
perceptive [pər'sɛptɪv] *adj* : perspicaz
perceptively [pər'sɛptɪvli] *adv* : con perspicacia
perch[1] ['pərtʃ] *vi* **1** ROOST : posarse **2** SIT : sentarse (en un sitio elevado) — *vt* PLACE : posar, colocar
perch[2] *n* **1** ROOST : percha *f* (para los pájaros) **2** *pl* **perch** *or* **perches** : perca *f* (pez)
percolate ['pərkə,leɪt] *vi* **-lated; -lating** : colarse, filtrarse ⟨percolated coffee : café filtrado⟩
percolator ['pərkə,leɪtər] *n* : cafetera *f* de filtro
percussion [pər'kʌʃən] *n* **1** STRIKING : percusión *f* **2** *or* **percussion instruments** : instrumentos *mpl* de percusión
peremptory [pə'rɛmptəri] *adj* : perentorio
perennial[1] [pə'rɛniəl] *adj* **1** : perenne, vivaz ⟨perennial flowers : flores perennes⟩ **2** RECURRENT : perenne, con-

tinuo ⟨a perennial problem : un problema eterno⟩
perennial[2] *n* : planta *f* perenne, planta *f* vivaz
perfect[1] [pər'fɛkt] *vt* : perfeccionar
perfect[2] ['pərfɪkt] *adj* : perfecto — **perfectly** *adv*
perfection [pər'fɛkʃən] *n* : perfección *f*
perfectionism [pər'fɛkʃə,nɪzəm] *n* : perfeccionismo *m*
perfectionist [pər'fɛkʃənɪst] *n* : perfeccionista *mf*
perfidious [pər'fɪdiəs] *adj* : pérfido
perforate ['pərfə,reɪt] *vt* -rated; -rating : perforar
perforation [,pərfə'reɪʃən] *n* : perforación *f*
perform [pər'form] *vt* 1 CARRY OUT : realizar, hacer, desempeñar 2 PRESENT : representar, dar (una obra teatral, etc.) — *vi* 1 : actuar (en una obra teatral), cantar (en una ópera, etc.), tocar (en un concierto, etc.), bailar (en un ballet, etc.) 2 : funcionar
performance [pər'formənts] *n* 1 EXECUTION : ejecución *f*, realización *f*, desempeño *m*, rendimiento *m* 2 INTERPRETATION : interpretación *f* ⟨his performance of Hamlet : su interpretación de Hamlet⟩ 3 PRESENTATION : representación *f* (de una obra teatral), función *f*
performer [pər'formər] *n* : artista *mf*; actor *m*, -triz *f*; intérprete *mf* (de música)
perfume[1] [pər'fju:m, 'pər,-] *vt* -fumed; -fuming : perfumar
perfume[2] ['pər,fju:m, pər'-] *n* : perfume *m*
perfunctory [pər'fʌŋktəri] *adj* : mecánico, superficial, somero
perhaps [pər'hæps] *adv* : tal vez, quizá, quizás, a lo mejor ⟨perhaps so/not : tal vez sí/no⟩ ⟨perhaps he didn't know : quizá(s) no lo sabía⟩ ⟨perhaps I'm wrong : a lo mejor me equivoco⟩ ⟨perhaps I can go tomorrow : quizá(s) pueda ir mañana⟩
peril ['pɛrəl] *n* : peligro *m*
perilous ['pɛrələs] *adj* : peligroso — **perilously** *adv*
perimeter [pə'rɪmətər] *n* : perímetro *m*
period ['pɪriəd] *n* 1 : punto *m* (en puntuación) 2 : período *m* ⟨a two-hour period : un período de dos horas⟩ 3 STAGE : época *f* (histórica), fase *f*, etapa *f* 4 MENSTRUATION : período *m*, regla *f* ⟨to have one's period : tener el período, tener la regla⟩ 5 : hora *f* (de clase)
periodic [,pɪri'ɑdɪk] *or* **periodical** [-dɪkəl] *adj* : periódico — **periodically** [-dɪkli] *adv*
periodical [,pɪri'ɑdɪkəl] *n* : publicación *f* periódica, revista *f*
peripheral [pə'rɪfərəl] *adj* : periférico
periphery [pə'rɪfəri] *n*, *pl* -eries : periferia *f*
periscope ['pɛrə,sko:p] *n* : periscopio *m*
perish ['pɛrɪʃ] *vi* DIE : perecer, morirse
perishable[1] ['pɛrɪʃəbəl] *adj* : perecedero
perishable[2] *n* : producto *m* perecedero
perjure ['pərdʒər] *vt* -jured; -juring (*used in law*) to perjure oneself ⟨: perjurar, perjurarse

perjury ['pərdʒəri] *n* : perjurio *m*
perk[1] ['pərk] *vt* 1 : levantar (las orejas, etc.) 2 *or* to perk up FRESHEN : arreglar — *vi* to perk up : animarse, reanimarse
perk[2] *n* : extra *m*
perky ['pərki] *adj* perkier; -est : animado, alegre, lleno de vida
perm ['pərm] *n* : permanente *f*
permanence ['pərmənənts] *n* : permanencia *f*
permanent[1] ['pərmənənt] *adj* : permanente — **permanently** *adv*
permanent[2] *n* : permanente *f*
permeability [,pərmiə'bɪləti] *n* : permeabilidad *f*
permeable ['pərmiəbəl] *adj* : permeable
permeate ['pərmi,eɪt] *v* -ated; -ating *vt* 1 PENETRATE : penetrar, impregnar 2 PERVADE : penetrar, difundirse por — *vi* : penetrar
permissible [pər'mɪsəbəl] *adj* : permisible, lícito
permission [pər'mɪʃən] *n* : permiso *m*
permissive [pər'mɪsɪv] *adj* : permisivo
permissiveness [pər'mɪsɪvnəs] *adj* : permisividad *f*
permit[1] [pər'mɪt] *vt* -mitted; -mitting : permitir, dejar ⟨weather permitting : si el tiempo lo permite⟩
permit[2] ['pər,mɪt, pər'-] *n* : permiso *m*, licencia *f*
permutation [,pərmju'teɪʃən] *n* : permutación *f*
pernicious [pər'nɪʃəs] *adj* : pernicioso
peroxide [pə'rɑk,saɪd] *n* 1 : peróxido *m* 2 → **hydrogen peroxide**
perpendicular[1] [,pərpən'dɪkjələr] *adj* 1 VERTICAL : vertical 2 : perpendicular ⟨perpendicular lines : líneas perpendiculares⟩ — **perpendicularly** *adv*
perpendicular[2] *n* : perpendicular *f*
perpetrate ['pərpə,treɪt] *vt* -trated; -trating : perpetrar, cometer (un delito)
perpetrator ['pərpə,treɪtər] *n* : autor *m*, -tora *f* (de un delito)
perpetual [pər'pɛtʃuəl] *adj* 1 EVERLASTING : perpetuo, eterno 2 CONTINUAL : perpetuo, continuo, constante
perpetually [pər'pɛtʃuəli, -tʃəli] *adv* : para siempre, eternamente
perpetuate [pər'pɛtʃu,eɪt] *vt* -ated; -ating : perpetuar
perpetuity [,pərpə'tu:əti, -'tju:-] *n*, *pl* -ties : perpetuidad *f*
perplex [pər'plɛks] *vt* : dejar perplejo, confundir
perplexed [pər'plɛkst] *adj* : perplejo
perplexity [pər'plɛksəti] *n*, *pl* -ties : perplejidad *f*, confusión *f*
per se [pər'seɪ] *adv* : per se, de por sí, en sí
persecute ['pərsɪ,kju:t] *vt* -cuted; -cuting : perseguir
persecution [,pərsɪ'kju:ʃən] *n* : persecución *f*
persecutor ['pərsɪ,kju:tər] *n* : perseguidor *m*, -dora *f*
perseverance [,pərsə'vɪrənts] *n* : perseverancia *f*

persevere [ˌpərsə'vɪr] vi **-vered; -vering**
: perseverar

Persian ['pərʒən] n **1** : persa mf **2**
: persa m (idioma) — **Persian** adj

persist [pər'sɪst] vi : persistir

persistence [pər'sɪstənts] n **1** CONTI-
NUATION : persistencia f **2** TENACITY
: perseverancia f, tenacidad f

persistent [pər'sɪstənt] adj : persistente
— **persistently** adv

person ['pərsən] n **1** pl **people** or **persons** HUMAN, INDIVIDUAL : persona f,
individuo m, ser m humano **2** : persona
f (en gramática) **3 in person** : en persona

personable ['pərsənəbəl] adj : agradable

personage ['pərsənɪʤ] n : personaje m

personal ['pərsənəl] adj **1** OWN, PRIVATE
: personal, particular, privado ⟨for personal reasons : por razones personales⟩ **2**
: en persona ⟨to make a personal appearance : presentarse en persona, hacer
acto de presencia⟩ **3** : íntimo, personal
⟨personal hygiene : higiene personal⟩ **4**
INDISCREET, PRYING : indiscreto, personal

personal assistant n : secretario m, -ria f
personal

personal computer n : computadora f
personal, ordenador m personal Spain

personality [ˌpərsən'æləti] n, pl **-ties 1**
DISPOSITION : personalidad f, temperamento m **2** CELEBRITY : personalidad f,
personaje m, celebridad f

personalize ['pərsənəˌlaɪz] vt **-ized; -izing**
: personalizar

personally ['pərsənəli] adv **1** : personalmente, en persona ⟨I'll do it personally
: lo haré personalmente⟩ **2** : como persona ⟨personally she's very amiable
: como persona es muy amable⟩ **3**
: personalmente ⟨personally, I don't believe it : yo, personalmente, no me lo
creo⟩

personification [pərˌsɑnəfə'keɪʃən] n
: personificación f

personify [pər'sɑnəˌfaɪ] vt **-fied; -fying**
: personificar

personnel [ˌpərsən'ɛl] n : personal m

perspective [pər'spɛktɪv] n : perspectiva f

perspicacious [ˌpərspə'keɪʃəs] adj : perspicaz

perspicacity [ˌpərspə'kæsəti] n : clarividencia f, perspicacia f

perspiration [ˌpərspə'reɪʃən] n : transpiración f, sudor m

perspire [pər'spaɪr] vi **-spired; -spiring**
: transpirar, sudar

persuade [pər'sweɪd] vt **-suaded; -suad-
ing** : persuadir, convencer

persuasion [pər'sweɪʒən] n : persuasión f

persuasive [pər'sweɪsɪv, -zɪv] adj : persuasivo — **persuasively** adv

persuasiveness [pər'sweɪsɪvnəs, -zɪv-] n
: persuasión f

pert ['pərt] adj **1** SAUCY : descarado, impertinente **2** JAUNTY : alegre, animado
⟨a pert little hat : un sombrero coqueto⟩

pertain [pər'teɪn] vi **1** BELONG
: pertenecer (a) **2** RELATE : estar relacionado (con)

pertinence ['pərtənənts] n : pertinencia f

pertinent ['pərtənənt] adj : pertinente

perturb [pər'tərb] vt : perturbar

perusal [pə'ruːzəl] n : lectura f cuidadosa

peruse [pə'ruːz] vt **-rused; -rusing 1**
READ : leer con cuidado **2** SCAN : recorrer con la vista ⟨he perused the newspaper : echó un vistazo al periódico⟩

Peruvian [pə'ruːviən] n : peruano m, -na f
— **Peruvian** adj

pervade [pər'veɪd] vt **-vaded; -vading**
: penetrar, difundirse por

pervasive [pər'veɪsɪv, -zɪv] adj : penetrante

perverse [pər'vərs] adj **1** CORRUPT : perverso, corrompido **2** STUBBORN : obstinado, porfiado, terco (sin razón) — **per-
versely** adv

perversion [pər'vərʒən] n : perversión f

perversity [pər'vərsəti] n, pl **-ties 1** COR-
RUPTION : corrupción f **2** STUBBORN-
NESS : obstinación f, terquedad f

pervert¹ [pər'vərt] vt **1** DISTORT : pervr-
tir, distorsionar **2** CORRUPT : pervertir,
corromper

pervert² ['pərˌvərt] n : pervertido m, -da f

peseta [pə'seɪt̬ə] n : peseta f

pesky ['pɛski] adj : molestoso, molesto

peso ['peɪˌsoː] n, pl **-sos** : peso m (unidad
monetaria)

pessimism ['pɛsəˌmɪzəm] n : pesimismo
m

pessimist ['pɛsəmɪst] n : pesimista mf

pessimistic [ˌpɛsə'mɪstɪk] adj : pesimista

pest ['pɛst] n **1** NUISANCE : peste f, la-
toso m, -sa f fam ⟨to be a pest : dar (la)
lata⟩ **2** : insecto m nocivo, animal m
nocivo ⟨the squirrels were pests : las ar-
dillas eran una plaga⟩

pester ['pɛstər] vt **-tered; -tering** : molestar, fastidiar

pesticide ['pɛstəˌsaɪd] n : pesticida m

pestilence ['pɛstələnts] n : pestilencia f,
peste f

pestle ['pɛsəl, 'pɛstəl] n : mano f de
mortero, mazo m, maja f

pet¹ ['pɛt] vt **petted; petting** : acariciar

pet² n **1** : animal m doméstico, mascota f
⟨pet store : tienda de mascotas⟩ ⟨pet food
: alimento para mascotas⟩ **2** FAVORITE
: favorito m, -ta f

pet³ adj : preferido, favorito ⟨her pet theory : su teoría preferida⟩ ⟨his pet project
: su proyecto favorito⟩ ⟨pet name
: apodo (cariñoso)⟩

petal ['pɛt̬əl] n : pétalo m

peter ['piːt̬ər] vi **to peter out** : agotarse,
apagarse, disminuir (poco a poco)

petite [pə'tiːt] adj : pequeña, menuda,
chiquita

petition¹ [pə'tɪʃən] vt : peticionar

petition² n : petición f

petitioner [pə'tɪʃənər] n : peticionario m,
-ria f

petrify ['pɛtrəˌfaɪ] vt **-fied; -fying** : petrificar

petroleum [pə'troːliəm] n : petróleo m

petroleum jelly n : vaselina f

petticoat ['pɛt̬iˌkoːt] n : enagua f, fondo m
Mex

pettiness [ˈpɛṭinəs] n 1 INSIGNIFICANCE : insignificancia f 2 MEANNESS : mezquindad f

petty [ˈpɛṭi] adj **pettier; -est** 1 MINOR : menor ⟨petty cash : dinero para gastos menores⟩ 2 INSIGNIFICANT : insignificante, trivial, nimio 3 MEAN : mezquino

petty officer n : suboficial mf

petulance [ˈpɛtʃələns] n : irritabilidad f, mal genio m

petulant [ˈpɛtʃələnt] adj : irritable, de mal genio

petunia [pɪˈtuːnjə, -ˈtjuː-] n : petunia f

pew [ˈpjuː] n : banco m (de iglesia)

pewter [ˈpjuːṭər] n : peltre m

pH [ˌpiːˈeɪtʃ] n : pH m

phallic [ˈfælɪk] adj : fálico

phallus [ˈfæləs] n, pl **-li** [ˈfæˌlaɪ] or **-luses** : falo m

phantasy [ˈfæntəsi] → **fantasy**

phantom [ˈfæntəm] n : fantasma m

pharaoh [ˈfɛrˌoː, ˈfeɪˌroː] n : faraón m

pharmaceutical [ˌfɑrməˈsuːṭɪkəl] adj : farmacéutico

pharmacist [ˈfɑrməsɪst] n : farmacéutico m, -ca f

pharmacology [ˌfɑrməˈkɑlədʒi] n : farmacología f

pharmacy [ˈfɑrməsi] n, pl **-cies** : farmacia f

pharynx [ˈfærɪŋks] n, pl **pharynges** [fəˈrɪnˌdʒiːz] : faringe f

phase¹ [ˈfeɪz] vt **phased; phasing** 1 SYNCHRONIZE : sincronizar, poner en fase 2 STAGGER : escalonar 3 **to phase in** : introducir progresivamente 4 **to phase out** : retirar progresivamente, dejar de producir

phase² n 1 : fase f (de la luna, etc.) 2 STAGE : fase f, etapa f

pheasant [ˈfɛzənt] n, pl **-ant** or **-ants** : faisán m

phenomenal [fɪˈnɑmənəl] adj : extraordinario, excepcional

phenomenon [fɪˈnɑməˌnɑn, -nən] n, pl **-na** [-nə] or **-nons** 1 : fenómeno m 2 pl **-nons** PRODIGY : fenómeno m, prodigio m

phew [ˈfjuː] interj : ¡uf!

philanthropic [ˌfɪlənˈθrɑpɪk] adj : filantrópico

philanthropist [fəˈlænθrəpɪst] n : filántropo m, -pa f

philanthropy [fəˈlænθrəpi] n, pl **-pies** : filantropía f

philately [fəˈlæṭəli] n : filatelia f

philharmonic [ˌfɪlɑrˈmɑnɪk] n : filarmónica f

philosopher [fəˈlɑsəfər] n : filósofo m, -fa f

philosophic [ˌfɪləˈsɑfɪk] or **philosophical** [-fɪkəl] adj : filosófico — **philosophically** [-kli] adv

philosophize [fəˈlɑsəˌfaɪz] vi **-phized; -phizing** : filosofar

philosophy [fəˈlɑsəfi] n, pl **-phies** : filosofía f

phishing [ˈfɪʃɪŋ] n : phishing m, suplantación f de identidad (en Internet)

phlegm [ˈflɛm] n : flema f

phlegmatic [flɛɡˈmæṭɪk] adj : flemático

phlox [ˈflɑks] n, pl **phlox** or **phloxes** : polemonio m

phobia [ˈfoːbiə] n : fobia f

phoenix [ˈfiːnɪks] n : fénix m

phone¹ [ˈfoːn] v → **telephone¹**

phone² n → **telephone²**

phone book n : guía f telefónica

phone call → **call²**

phone card n : tarjeta f telefónica

phoneme [ˈfoːˌniːm] n : fonema m

phone number → **number²**

phonetic [fəˈnɛṭɪk] adj : fonético

phonetics [fəˈnɛṭɪks] n : fonética f

phonics [ˈfɑnɪks] n : método m fonético de aprender a leer

phony¹ or **phoney** [ˈfoːni] adj **phonier; -est** : falso

phony² or **phoney** n, pl **-nies** : farsante mf; charlatán m, -tana f

phosphate [ˈfɑsˌfeɪt] n : fosfato m

phosphorescence [ˌfɑsfəˈrɛsənts] n : fosforescencia f

phosphorescent [ˌfɑsfəˈrɛsənt] adj : fosforescente — **phosphorescently** adv

phosphorus [ˈfɑsfərəs] n : fósforo m

photo [ˈfoːˌtoː] n, pl **-tos** : foto f

photocopier [ˈfoːṭoˌkɑpiər] n : fotocopiadora f

photocopy¹ [ˈfoːṭoˌkɑpi] vt **-copied; -copying** : fotocopiar

photocopy² n, pl **-copies** : fotocopia f

photoelectric [ˌfoːṭoɪˈlɛktrɪk] adj : fotoeléctrico

photogenic [ˌfoːṭoˈdʒɛnɪk] adj : fotogénico

photograph¹ [ˈfoːṭəˌgræf] vt : fotografiar

photograph² n : fotografía f, foto f ⟨to take a photograph of : tomarle una fotografía a, tomar una fotografía de⟩

photographer [fəˈtɑgrəfər] n : fotógrafo m, -fa f

photographic [ˌfoːṭəˈgræfɪk] adj : fotográfico — **photographically** [-fɪkli] adv

photography [fəˈtɑgrəfi] n : fotografía f

photojournalist [ˌfoːṭoˈdʒərnəlɪst] n : reportero m gráfico, reportera f gráfica

photoshop or **Photoshop** [ˈfoːṭoˌʃɑp] vt (**Photoshop**, trademark) : editar (con un editor de imágenes)

photosynthesis [ˌfoːṭoˈsɪnθəsɪs] n : fotosíntesis f

phrasal verb n : verbo m con partícula(s)

phrase¹ [ˈfreɪz] vt **phrased; phrasing** : expresar

phrase² n : frase f, locución f ⟨to coin a phrase : para decirlo así⟩

phrase book n : guía f de conversación

phylum [ˈfaɪləm] n, pl **-la** [-lə] : phylum m

phys ed [ˈfɪzˈɛd] n fam → **physical education**

physical¹ [ˈfɪzɪkəl] adj 1 : físico ⟨physical laws : leyes físicas⟩ 2 MATERIAL : material, físico 3 BODILY : físico, corpóreo — **physically** [-kli] adv

physical² n CHECKUP : chequeo m, reconocimiento m médico

physical education n : educación f física

physical therapist n : fisioterapeuta mf

physical therapy *n* : fisioterapia *f*
physician [fə'zɪʃən] *n* : médico *m*, -ca *f*
physicist ['fɪzəsɪst] *n* : físico *m*, -ca *f*
physics ['fɪzɪks] *ns & pl* : física *f*
physiognomy [,fɪzi'agnəmi] *n, pl* **-mies**
: fisonomía *f*
physiological ['fɪziə'ladʒɪkəl] *or* **physio-logic** [-dʒɪk] *adj* : fisiológico
physiologist [,fɪzi'alədʒɪst] *n* : fisiólogo
m, -ga *f*
physiology [,fɪzi'alədʒi] *n* : fisiología *f*
physique [fə'zi:k] *n* : físico *m*
pi ['paɪ] *n, pl* **pis** ['paɪz] : pi *f*
pianist [pi'ænɪst, 'pi:ənɪst] *n* : pianista *mf*
piano [pi'æno:] *n, pl* **-anos** : piano *m*
piazza [pi'æzə, -'ɑtsə] *n, pl* **-zas** *or* **-ze**
[-'ɑt,seɪ] : plaza *f*
picador ['pɪkə,dɔr] *n* : picador *m*, -dora *f*
picaresque [,pɪkə'rɛsk, ,pi:-] *adj* : pi-caresco
picayune [,pɪki'ju:n] *adj* : trivial, nimio,
insignificante
piccolo ['pɪkə,lo:] *n, pl* **-los** : flautín *m*
pick¹ ['pɪk] *vt* **1** SELECT : escoger, elegir
⟨pick a card : elige una carta⟩ **2** : qui-tar,
sacar (poco a poco) ⟨to pick meat
off the bones : quitar pedazos de carne
de los huesos⟩ **3** : recoger, arrancar
(frutas, flores, etc.) **4** PROVOKE : provo-car
⟨to pick a fight : buscar pelea⟩ **5**
: hurgarse (la nariz), escarbarse (los dien-tes)
6 to pick a lock : forzar una cerra-dura
7 to pick out CHOOSE : escoger **8
to pick out** IDENTIFY : identificar, distin-guir
9 to pick someone's pocket
: robarle a alguien la cartera (etc.) del
bolsillo **10 to pick up** LIFT : levan-tar
11 to pick up TIDY : ordenar (una
habitación, etc.), recoger (juguetes,
etc.) **12 to pick up** FETCH : (ir a) reco-ger
13 to pick up LOAD : recoger (pasa-jeros),
cargar **14 to pick up** BUY, GET
: comprar, conseguir **15 to pick up**
LEARN : aprender (un idioma, etc.), ad-quirir
(una costumbre) **16 to pick up**
RESUME : continuar **17 to pick up**
: captar (una señal) **18 to pick up** DE-TECT
: detectar **19 to pick up speed**
: ganar velocidad **20 to pick up the
pace** : ir/trabajar (etc.) más rápido **21
to pick up the tab/bill/check** : cargar
con la cuenta — *vi* **1** NIBBLE : picar,
picotear **2 to pick and choose** : ser
exigente **3 to pick at** : tocar, rascarse
(una herida, etc.) **4 to pick on** TEASE
: mofarse de, atormentar **5 to pick up**
IMPROVE : mejorar **6 to pick up** : le-vantarse
(dícese del viento), acelerarse
(dícese de un ritmo, etc.) **7 to pick up**
ANSWER : contestar (el teléfono) **8 to
pick up** TIDY : ordenar ⟨pick up after
yourself : ordena lo que has desorde-nado⟩
9 to pick up RESUME : continuar
⟨let's pick up where we left off : re-tomemos
donde lo dejamos⟩ **10 to pick
up on** : darse cuenta de
pick² *n* **1** CHOICE : selección *f* **2** BEST
: lo mejor ⟨the pick of the crop : la
crema y nata⟩ **3** → **pickax** **4** : púa *f*
(para una guitarra, etc.)

pickax ['pɪk,æks] *n* : pico *m*, zapapico *m*,
piqueta *f*
pickerel ['pɪkərəl] *n, pl* **-el** *or* **-els** : lucio
m pequeño
picket¹ ['pɪkət] *v* : piquetear
picket² *n* **1** STAKE : estaca *f* **2** STRIKER
: huelguista *mf*, integrante *mf* de un pi-quete
picketer ['pɪkətər] *n* : piquete mm
pickle¹ ['pɪkəl] *vt* **-led; -ling** : encurtir, es-cabechar
pickle² *n* **1** BRINE : escabeche *m* **2**
GHERKIN : pepinillo *m* (encurtido) **3**
JAM, TROUBLE : lío *m*, apuro *m*
pickpocket ['pɪk,pakət] *n* : carterista *mf*
pickup ['pɪk,əp] *n* **1** IMPROVEMENT : me-jora
f **2** *or* **pickup truck** : camioneta *f*
picky ['pɪki] *adj* : quisquilloso, melin-droso,
mañoso ⟨he's a picky eater : es
muy quisquilloso para comer⟩
picnic¹ ['pɪk,nɪk] *vi* **-nicked; -nicking** : ir
de picnic
picnic² *n* : picnic *m*
pictorial [pɪk'tɔriəl] *adj* : pictórico
picture¹ ['pɪktʃər] *vt* **-tured; -turing** **1**
DEPICT : representar **2** IMAGINE : ima-ginarse
⟨can you picture it? : ¿te lo pue-des
imaginar?⟩
picture² *n* **1** : cuadro *m* (pintado o dibu-jado),
ilustración *f*, fotografía *f* **2** DE-SCRIPTION
: descripción *f* **3** IMAGE
: imagen *f* ⟨he's the picture of his father
: es la viva imagen de su padre⟩ **4**
MOVIE : película *f* **5** IMAGE : imagen *f*
(de una pantalla) **6** : idea *f* ⟨now I get
the picture : ahora lo entiendo⟩ **7** : situ-ación
f ⟨the economic picture : la situa-ción
económica⟩ ⟨marriage never
entered the picture : nunca pensaron en
casarse⟩ ⟨her old boyfriend is back in
the picture : ha vuelto a salir con su
antiguo novio⟩ **8** → **big picture**
picturesque [,pɪktʃə'rɛsk] *adj* : pin-toresco
pie ['paɪ] *n* : pastel *m* (con fruta o carne),
empanada *f* (con carne)
piece¹ ['pi:s] *vt* **pieced; piecing** **1** PATCH
: parchar, arreglar **2 to piece together**
: construir pieza por pieza
piece² *n* **1** FRAGMENT : pedazo *m* ⟨to
rip/tear something to pieces : hacer pe-dazos
algo, romper algo en pedazos⟩ ⟨to
fall to pieces : hacerse pedazos⟩ ⟨in
pieces : en pedazos⟩ ⟨one piece : in-tacto⟩
2 SEGMENT : pedazo *m*, trozo *m*
(de pan, carne, cordel, etc.) **3** COMPO-NENT
: pieza *f* ⟨a three-piece suit : un
traje de tres piezas⟩ **4** UNIT : pieza *f* ⟨a
piece of fruit : una (pieza de) fruta⟩ ⟨a
piece of clothing : una prenda⟩ ⟨a piece
of paper : un papel⟩ **5** (*indicating an
instance of something*) ⟨a piece of advice
: un consejo⟩ ⟨a piece of news : una no-ticia⟩
⟨a nice piece of work : un buen
trabajo⟩ **6** WORK : obra *f*, pieza *f* (de
música, etc.) **7** (*in board games*) : ficha
f, pieza *f*, figura *f* (en ajedrez) **8** ARTI-CLE
: artículo *m* **9** COIN : moneda *f*,
pieza *f* **10** *fam* GUN : pistola *f* **11** *fam*
DISTANCE : trecho *m* **12 in one piece**

SAFE : sano y salvo **13 to fall/go to pieces** : venirse abajo **14 to give someone a piece of one's mind** : cantarle las cuarenta a alguien **15 to pick up the pieces** : sacarse las castañas del fuego **16 to pieces** : mucho, muy ⟨she was thrilled to pieces : estaba contentísima⟩ ⟨he loves her to pieces : la quiere muchísimo⟩

piecemeal[1] [ˈpi:s,mi:l] *adv* : poco a poco, por partes

piecemeal[2] *adj* : hecho poco a poco, poco sistemático

piecework [ˈpi:s,wərk] *n* : trabajo *m* a destajo

pied [ˈpaɪd] *adj* : pío

pier [ˈpɪr] *n* **1** : pila *f* (de un puente) **2** WHARF : muelle *m*, atracadero *m*, embarcadero *m* **3** PILLAR : pilar *m*

pierce [ˈpɪrs] *vt* **pierced; piercing 1** PENETRATE : atravesar, traspasar, penetrar (en) ⟨the bullet pierced his leg : la bala le atravesó la pierna⟩ ⟨to pierce one's heart : traspasarle el corazón a uno⟩ **2** PERFORATE : perforar, agujerear (las orejas, etc.) **3 to pierce the silence** : desgarrar el silencio

piety [ˈpaɪəti] *n, pl* **-eties** : piedad *f*

pig [ˈpɪɡ] *n* **1** HOG, SWINE : cerdo *m*, -da *f*; puerco *m*, -ca *f* **2** SLOB : persona *f* desaliñada; cerdo *m*, -da *f* **3** GLUTTON : glotón *m*, -tona *f* **4** *or* **pig iron** : lingote *m* de hierro

pigeon [ˈpɪdʒən] *n* : paloma *f*

pigeonhole [ˈpɪdʒən,ho:l] *n* : casilla *f*

piggish [ˈpɪɡɪʃ] *adj* **1** GREEDY : glotón **2** DIRTY : cochino, sucio

piggyback [ˈpɪɡi,bæk] *adv & adj* : a cuestas

piggy bank *n* : alcancía *f*

pigheaded [ˈpɪɡ,hɛdəd] *adj* : terco, obstinado

piglet [ˈpɪɡlət] *n* : cochinillo *m*; lechón *m*, -chona *f*

pigment [ˈpɪɡmənt] *n* : pigmento *m*

pigmentation [ˌpɪɡmənˈteɪʃən] *n* : pigmentación *f*

pigmy → **pygmy**

pig out *vi* **to pig out (on)** : darse un atracón (de)

pigpen [ˈpɪɡ,pɛn] *n* : chiquero *m*, pocilga *f*

pigsty [ˈpɪɡ,staɪ] → **pigpen**

pigtail [ˈpɪɡ,teɪl] *n* : coleta *f*, trenza *f*

pike [ˈpaɪk] *n, pl* **pike** *or* **pikes 1** : lucio *m* (pez) **2** LANCE : pica *f* **3** → **turnpike**

pile[1] [ˈpaɪl] *v* **piled; piling** *vt* : amontonar, apilar — *vi* **to pile up** : amontonarse, acumularse

pile[2] *n* **1** STAKE : pilote *m* **2** HEAP : montón *m*, pila *f* **3** NAP : pelo *m* (de telas)

pileup [ˈpaɪl,ʌp] *n* : choque *m* en cadena

piles [ˈpaɪlz] *npl* HEMORRHOIDS : hemorroides *fpl*, almorranas *fpl*

pilfer [ˈpɪlfər] *vt* : robar (cosas pequeñas), ratear

pilgrim [ˈpɪlɡrəm] *n* : peregrino *m*, -na *f*

pilgrimage [ˈpɪlɡrəmɪdʒ] *n* : peregrinación *f*

pill [ˈpɪl] *n* : pastilla *f*, píldora *f* ⟨to be on the pill, to be on birth control pills : tomar la píldora (anticonceptiva)⟩

pillage[1] [ˈpɪlɪdʒ] *vt* **-laged; -laging** : saquear

pillage[2] *n* : saqueo *m*

pillar [ˈpɪlər] *n* : pilar *m*, columna *f*

pillory [ˈpɪləri] *n, pl* **-ries** : picota *f*

pillow [ˈpɪ,lo:] *n* : almohada *f*

pillowcase [ˈpɪ,lo:,keɪs] *n* : funda *f*

pilot[1] [ˈpaɪlət] *vt* : pilotar, pilotear

pilot[2] *n* : piloto *mf*

pilot light *n* : piloto *m*

pimento [pəˈmɛn,to:] → **pimiento**

pimiento [pəˈmɛn,to:, -ˈmjɛn-] *n, pl* **-tos** : pimiento *m* morrón

pimp [ˈpɪmp] *n* : proxeneta *m*

pimple [ˈpɪmpəl] *n* : grano *m*

pimply [ˈpɪmpəli] *adj* **pimplier; -est** : cubierto de granos

pin[1] [ˈpɪn] *vt* **pinned; pinning 1** FASTEN : prender, sujetar (con alfileres) **2** HOLD, IMMOBILIZE : inmovilizar, sujetar **3 to pin one's hopes on** : poner sus esperanzas en **4 to pin down** : identificar, determinar, definir

pin[2] *n* **1** : alfiler *m* ⟨safety pin : alfiler de gancho⟩ ⟨a bobby pin : una horquilla⟩ **2** BROOCH : alfiler *m*, broche *m*, prendedor *m* **3** → **bowling pin**

pinafore [ˈpɪnə,fɔr] *n* : delantal *m*

piñata [pɪnˈjɑtə] *n* : piñata *f*

pinball [ˈpɪn,bɔl] *n* : pinball *m*

pincer [ˈpɪntsər] *n* **1** CLAW : pinza *f* (de una langosta, etc.) **2 pincers** *npl* : pinzas *fpl*, tenazas *fpl*, tenaza *f*

pinch[1] [ˈpɪntʃ] *vt* **1** : pellizcar ⟨she pinched my cheek : me pellizcó el cachete⟩ **2** STEAL : robar — *vi* : apretar ⟨my shoes pinch : me aprietan los zapatos⟩

pinch[2] *n* **1** EMERGENCY : emergencia *f* ⟨in a pinch : en caso necesario⟩ **2** PAIN : dolor *m*, tormento *m* **3** SQUEEZE : pellizco *m* (con los dedos) **4** BIT : pizca *f*, pellizco *m* ⟨a pinch of cinnamon : una pizca de canela⟩

pinch hitter *n* **1** SUBSTITUTE : sustituto *m*, -ta *f* **2** : bateador *m* emergente (en beisbol)

pincushion [ˈpɪn,kʊʃən] *n* : acerico *m*, alfiletero *m*

pine[1] [ˈpaɪn] *vi* **pined; pining 1 to pine away** : languidecer, consumirse **2 to pine for** : añorar, suspirar por

pine[2] *n* **1** : pino *m* (árbol) **2** : madera *f* de pino

pineapple [ˈpaɪn,æpəl] *n* : piña *f*, ananá *m*, ananás *m*

pine cone *n* : piña *f*

ping [ˈpɪŋ] *n* : sonido *m* metálico

Ping-Pong [ˈpɪŋ,pɑŋ, -,pɔŋ] *trademark* se usa para tenis de mesa

pinion[1] [ˈpɪnjən] *vt* : sujetar los brazos de, inmovilizar

pinion[2] *n* : piñón *m*

pink[1] [ˈpɪŋk] *adj* : rosa, rosado

pink[2] *n* **1** : clavelito *m* (flor) **2** : rosa *m*, rosado *m* (color) **3 to be in the pink** : estar en plena forma, rebosar de salud

pinkeye ['pɪŋk,aɪ] *n* : conjuntivitis *f* aguda

pinkie *or* **pinky** ['pɪŋki] *n* : meñique *m*

pinkish ['pɪŋkɪʃ] *adj* : rosáceo

pinnacle ['pɪnɪkəl] *n* **1** : pináculo *m* (de un edificio) **2** PEAK : cima *f*, cumbre *f* (de una montaña) **3** ACME : pináculo *m*, cúspide *f*, apogeo *m*

pinpoint ['pɪn,pɔɪnt] *vt* : precisar, localizar con precisión

pint ['paɪnt] *n* : pinta *f*

pinto ['pɪn,to:] *n, pl* **pintos** : caballo *m* pinto

pinworm ['pɪn,wərm] *n* : oxiuro *m*

pioneer[1] [,paɪə'nɪr] *vt* : promover, iniciar, introducir

pioneer[2] *n* : pionero *m*, -ra *f*

pious ['paɪəs] *adj* **1** DEVOUT : piadoso, devoto **2** SANCTIMONIOUS : beato, santurrón — **piously** ['paɪəsli] *adv*

pip ['pɪp] *n* : pepita *f*

pipe[1] ['paɪp] *v* **piped; piping** *vi* : hablar en voz chillona — *vt* **1** PLAY : tocar (el caramillo o la flauta) **2** : conducir por tuberías ⟨to pipe water : transportar el agua por tubería⟩

pipe[2] *n* **1** : caramillo *m* (instrumento musical) **2** BAGPIPE : gaita *f* **3** : tubo *m*, caño *m* ⟨gas pipes : tubería de gas⟩ **4** : pipa *f* (para fumar)

pipe dream *n* : quimera *f*, sueño *m* imposible

pipeline ['paɪp,laɪn] *n* **1** : conducto *m*, oleoducto *m* (para petróleo), gasoducto *m* (para gas) **2** CONDUIT : vía *f* (de información, etc.)

piper ['paɪpər] *n* : músico *m*, -ca *f* que toca el caramillo o la gaita

piping ['paɪpɪŋ] *n* **1** : música *f* del caramillo o de la gaita **2** TRIM : cordoncillo *m*, ribete *m* con cordón

piping hot *adj* : muy caliente

piquant ['pi:kənt, 'pɪkwənt] *adj* **1** SPICY : picante **2** INTRIGUING : intrigante, estimulante

pique[1] ['pi:k] *vt* **piqued; piquing 1** IRRITATE : picar, irritar **2** AROUSE : despertar (la curiosidad, etc.)

pique[2] *n* : pique *m*, resentimiento *m*

piracy ['paɪrəsi] *n, pl* **-cies** : piratería *f*

piranha [pə'rɑnə, -'rɑnjə, -'rænjə] *n* : piraña *f*

pirate[1] ['paɪrət] *n* : pirata *mf*

pirate[2] *vt* **-rated; -rating** : piratear (software, etc.)

pirouette [,pɪrə'wɛt] *n* : pirueta *f*

pis → **pi**

Pisces ['paɪ,si:z, 'pɪ-,; 'pɪs,keɪs] *n* **1** : Piscis *m* (signo o constelación) **2** : Piscis *mf* (persona)

piss[1] ['pɪs] *vi usu vulgar* : mear *usu vulgar* — *vt fam* **to piss off** ANGER : enojar, enfadar

piss[2] *n usu vulgar* **1** URINE : meados *mpl, usu vulgar*; pipí *m fam*; pis *m fam* **2 to take a piss** : mear *usu vulgar*, hacer pipí/pis *fam*

pistachio [pə'stæʃi,o:, -'stɑ-] *n, pl* **-chios** : pistacho *m*

pistil ['pɪstəl] *n* : pistilo *m*

pistol ['pɪstəl] *n* : pistola *f*

piston ['pɪstən] *n* : pistón *m*, émbolo *m*

pit[1] ['pɪt] *v* **pitted; pitting** *vt* **1** : marcar de hoyos, picar (una superficie) **2** : deshuesar (una fruta) **3 to pit against** : enfrentar a, oponer a — *vi* : quedar marcado

pit[2] *n* **1** HOLE : fosa *f*, hoyo *m* ⟨a bottomless pit : un pozo sin fondo⟩ **2** MINE : mina *f* **3** : foso *m* ⟨orchestra pit : foso orquestal⟩ **4** POCKMARK : marca *f* (en la cara), cicatriz *f* de viruela **5** STONE : hueso *m*, pepa *f* (de una fruta) **6 pit of the stomach** : boca *f* del estómago

pita ['pi:tə] *or* **pita bread** *n* : pita *f*; pan *m* pita; pan *m* árabe *Arg, Ven, Uru*

pitch[1] ['pɪtʃ] *vt* **1** SET UP : montar, armar (una tienda) **2** THROW : lanzar, arrojar **3** ADJUST, SET : dar el tono de (un discurso, un instrumento musical) — *vi* **1** *or* **to pitch forward** FALL : caerse **2** LURCH : cabecear (dícese de un barco o un avión), dar bandazos **3 to pitch in** : arrimar el hombro

pitch[2] *n* **1** LURCHING : cabezada *f*, cabeceo *m* (de un barco o un avión) **2** SLOPE : (grado de) inclinación *f*, pendiente *f* **3** : tono *m* (en música) ⟨perfect pitch : oído absoluto⟩ **4** THROW : lanzamiento *m* **5** DEGREE : grado *m*, nivel *m*, punto *m* ⟨the excitement reached a high pitch : la excitación llegó a un punto culminante⟩ **6** *or* **sales pitch** : presentación *f* (de un vendedor) **7** TAR : pez *f*, brea *f*

pitch–black ['pɪtʃ'blæk] *adj* : muy oscuro, oscuro como boca de lobo *fam*

pitcher ['pɪtʃər] *n* **1** JUG : jarra *f*, jarro *m*, cántaro *m*, pichel *m* **2** : lanzador *m*, -dora *f* (en béisbol, etc.)

pitchfork ['pɪtʃ,fɔrk] *n* : horquilla *f*, horca *f*

piteous ['pɪtiəs] *adj* : lastimoso, lastimero — **piteously** *adv*

pitfall ['pɪt,fɔl] *n* : peligro *m* (poco obvio), dificultad *f*

pith ['pɪθ] *n* **1** : médula *f* (de una planta) **2** CORE : meollo *m*, entraña *f*

pithy ['pɪθi] *adj* **pithier; -est** : conciso y sustancioso ⟨pithy comments : comentarios sucintos⟩

pitiable ['pɪtiəbəl] → **pitiful**

pitiful ['pɪtɪfəl] *adj* **1** LAMENTABLE : lastimero, lastimoso, lamentable **2** CONTEMPTIBLE : despreciable, lamentable — **pitifully** [-fli] *adv*

pitiless ['pɪtiləs] *adj* : despiadado — **pitilessly** *adv*

pittance ['pɪtənts] *n* : miseria *f*

pituitary [pə'tu:ə,tɛri, -'tju:-] *adj* : pituitario

pity[1] ['pɪti] *vt* **pitied; pitying** : compadecer, compadecerse de

pity[2] *n, pl* **pities 1** COMPASSION : compasión *f*, piedad *f* **2** SHAME : lástima *f*, pena *f* ⟨what a pity! : ¡qué lástima!⟩

pivot[1] ['pɪvət] *vi* **1** : girar sobre un eje **2 to pivot on** : girar sobre, depender de

pivot[2] *n* : pivote *m*

pivotal ['pɪvətəl] *adj* : fundamental, central

pixie or **pixy** ['pɪksi] n, pl **pixies** : elfo m, hada f

pizza ['pi:tsə] n : pizza f

pizzazz or **pizazz** [pə'zæz] n **1** GLAMOR : encanto m **2** VITALITY : animación f, vitalidad f

pizzeria [ˌpi:tsə'ri:ə] n : pizzería f

placard ['plækərd, -ˌkɑrd] n POSTER : cartel m, póster m, afiche m

placate ['pleɪˌkeɪt, 'plæ-] vt -**cated**; -**cating** : aplacar, apaciguar

place¹ ['pleɪs] vt **placed**; **placing** **1** PUT, SET : poner, colocar ⟨she carefully placed the book on the table : colocó el libro con cuidado sobre la mesa⟩ **2** SITUATE : situar, ubicar, emplazar ⟨to be well placed : estar bien situado⟩ ⟨to place in a job : colocar en un trabajo⟩ **3** IDENTIFY RECALL : identificar, ubicar, recordar ⟨I can't place him : no lo ubico⟩ **4 to place an order** : hacer un pedido

place² n **1** SPACE : sitio m, lugar m ⟨there's no place to sit : no hay sitio para sentarse⟩ **2** LOCATION : lugar m, sitio m, parte f ⟨place of work : lugar de trabajo⟩ ⟨faraway places : lugares remotos⟩ ⟨all over the place : por todas partes⟩ **3** HOME : casa f ⟨our summer place : nuestra casa de verano⟩ **4** POSITION, SPOT : lugar m, sitio m ⟨everything in its place : todo en su lugar⟩ ⟨to hold in place : sujetar⟩ ⟨I got distracted and lost my place : me distraje y ya no sé por donde iba⟩ **5** SEAT, SPOT : asiento m, sitio m ⟨she changed places with him : le cambió el asiento⟩ ⟨would you hold/save my place? : ¿me guardas el asiento?⟩ **6** or **place setting** : cubierto m **7** RANK : lugar m, puesto m ⟨he took first place : ganó el primer lugar⟩ **8** JOB : puesto m **9** ROLE : lugar m, papel m ⟨to trade places with someone : cambiarse por alguien, cambiarle el lugar a alguien⟩ ⟨put yourself in my place : ponte en mi lugar⟩ ⟨she put him in his place : lo puso en su lugar⟩ **10** : lugar m ⟨the ones/tens place : el lugar de las unidades/decenas⟩ ⟨a decimal place : un decimal⟩ **11 in place** : en marcha ⟨to put a plan/system in place : poner en marcha un plan/sistema⟩ **12 in place of** : en lugar de **13 in the first place** : para empezar **14 in the first/second place** : en primer/segundo lugar **15 out of place** : fuera de lugar **16 to go places** : tener éxito, llegar lejos **17 to take place** : tener lugar **18 to take the place of** : sustituir a

placebo [plə'si:ˌbo:] n, pl **-bos** : placebo m

place mat n : individual m, mantel m individual

placement ['pleɪsmənt] n : colocación f

placenta [plə'sɛntə] n, pl **-tas** or **-tae** [-ti, -ˌtaɪ] : placenta f

placid ['plæsəd] adj : plácido, tranquilo — **placidly** adv

plagiarism ['pleɪdʒəˌrɪzəm] n : plagio m

plagiarist ['pleɪdʒərɪst] n : plagiario m, -ria f

plagiarize ['pleɪdʒəˌraɪz] vt -**rized**; -**rizing** : plagiar

plague¹ ['pleɪg] vt **plagued**; **plaguing** **1** AFFLICT : plagar, afligir ⟨plagued with problems : plagado de problemas⟩ **2** DISTRESS : acosar, atormentar ⟨plagued by doubts : acosado por dudas⟩

plague² n **1** : plaga f ⟨de insectos, etc.⟩ **2** : peste f ⟨en medicina⟩

plaid¹ ['plæd] adj : escocés, de cuadros ⟨a plaid skirt : una falda escocesa⟩

plaid² n TARTAN : tela f escocesa, tartán m

plain¹ ['pleɪn] adj **1** SIMPLE, UNADORNED : liso, sencillo, sin adornos **2** CLEAR : claro ⟨in plain language : en palabras claras⟩ ⟨to make something plain : dejar algo (en) claro⟩ **3** FRANK : franco, puro ⟨the plain truth : la pura verdad⟩ **4** HOMELY : ordinario, poco atractivo **5 in plain sight** : a la vista de todos

plain² n : llanura f, llano m, planicie f

plainclothes ['pleɪn'klo:z, -'klo:ðz] adj : de civil; de paisano; de particular Arg, Uru (dícese de un policía, etc.)

plainly ['pleɪnli] adv **1** CLEARLY : claramente **2** FRANKLY : francamente, con franqueza **3** SIMPLY : sencillamente

plaintiff ['pleɪntɪf] n : demandante mf

plaintive ['pleɪntɪv] adj MOURNFUL : lastimero, plañidero

plait¹ ['pleɪt, 'plæt] vt **1** PLEAT : plisar **2** BRAID : trenzar

plait² n **1** PLEAT : pliegue m **2** BRAID : trenza f

plan¹ ['plæn] v **planned**; **planning** vt **1** : planear, proyectar, planificar ⟨to plan a trip : planear un viaje⟩ ⟨to plan a city : planificar una ciudad⟩ **2** INTEND : tener planeado, proyectar — vi : hacer planes

plan² n **1** DIAGRAM : plano m, esquema m **2** SCHEME : plan m, proyecto m, programa m ⟨to draw up a plan : elaborar un proyecto⟩

plane¹ ['pleɪn] vt **planed**; **planing** : cepillar (madera)

plane² adj : plano

plane³ n **1** : plano m (en matemáticas, etc.) **2** LEVEL : nivel m **3** : cepillo m (de carpintero) **4** → **airplane**

planet ['plænət] n : planeta f

planetarium [ˌplænə'teriəm] n, pl -**iums** or -**ia** [-iə] : planetario m

planetary ['plænəˌteri] adj : planetario

plank ['plæŋk] n **1** BOARD : tablón m, tabla f **2** : artículo m, punto m (de una plataforma política)

plankton ['plæŋktən] n : plancton m

planner ['plænər] n : planificador m, -dora f ⟨wedding planner : organizador de bodas⟩ ⟨financial planner : asesor financiero⟩

plant¹ ['plænt] vt **1** : plantar, sembrar (semillas) ⟨planted with flowers : plantado de flores⟩ **2** PLACE : plantar, colocar ⟨to plant an idea : inculcar una idea⟩

plant² n **1** : planta f ⟨leafy plants : plantas frondosas⟩ **2** FACTORY : planta f, fábrica f ⟨hydroelectric plant : planta hidroeléctrica⟩ **3** MACHINERY : maquinaria f, equipo m

plantain ['plæntən] n   1 : llantén m (mala hierba)   2 : plátano m, plátano m macho Mex (fruta)

plantation [plæn'teɪʃən] n : plantación f, hacienda f ⟨a coffee plantation : un cafetal⟩

planter ['plæntər] n   1 : hacendado m, -da f (de una hacienda)   2 FLOWERPOT : tiesto m, maceta f

plaque ['plæk] n   1 TABLET : placa f   2 : placa f (dental)

plasma ['plæzmə] n : plasma m

plaster[1] ['plæstər] vt   1 : enyesar, revocar (con yeso)   2 COVER : cubrir, llenar ⟨a wall plastered with notices : una pared cubierta de avisos⟩

plaster[2] n   1 : yeso m, revoque m (para paredes, etc.)   2 : escayola f, yeso m (en medicina)   3 plaster of Paris ['pærɪs] : yeso m mate

plastered ['plæstərd] adj INTOXICATED : colocado

plastic[1] ['plæstɪk] adj   1 : de plástico   2 PLIABLE : plástico, flexible

plastic[2] n : plástico m

plasticity [plæ'stɪsəṭi] n, pl -ties : plasticidad f

plastic surgery n : cirugía f plástica

plastic wrap n : papel m film

plate[1] ['pleɪt] vt plated; plating : chapar (en metal)

plate[2] n   1 PLAQUE, SHEET : placa f ⟨a steel plate : una placa de acero⟩   2 UTENSILS : vajilla f (de metal) ⟨silver plate : vajilla de plata⟩   3 DISH : plato m   4 DENTURES : dentadura f postiza   5 ILLUSTRATION : lámina f (en un libro)   6 **license plate** : matrícula f, placa f de matrícula

plateau [plæ'to:] n, pl -teaus or -teaux [-'to:z] : meseta f

platform ['plæt,fɔrm] n   1 STAGE : plataforma f, estrado m, tribuna f   2 : andén m (de una estación de ferrocarril)   3 **political platform** : plataforma f política, programa m electoral

plating ['pleɪṭɪŋ] n   1 : enchapado m   2 **silver plating** : plateado m

platinum ['plæṭənəm] n : platino m

platitude ['plæṭə,tu:d, -,tju:d] n : lugar m común, perogrullada f

platonic [plə'tɑnɪk] adj : platónico

platoon [plə'tu:n] n : sección f (en el ejército)

platter ['plæṭər] n : fuente f

platypus ['plæṭɪpəs, -,pʊs] n, pl platypuses or platypi [-,paɪ, -,pi:] : ornitorrinco m

plausibility [,plɔzə'bɪləṭi] n, pl -ties : credibilidad f, verosimilitud f

plausible ['plɔzəbəl] adj : creíble, convincente, verosímil — **plausibly** [-bli] adv

play[1] ['pleɪ] vi   1 : jugar ⟨the children were playing in the yard : los niños jugaban en el jardín⟩ ⟨she plays on the basketball team : juega con el equipo de baloncesto⟩ ⟨he plays for the Red Sox : juega para los Red Sox⟩ ⟨we play for fun : jugamos por diversión⟩ ⟨they're playing against the Yankees : juegan

contra los Yanquis⟩ ⟨it's your turn to play : te toca a ti jugar⟩ ⟨to play with a doll : jugar con una muñeca⟩ ⟨to play with an idea : darle vueltas a una idea⟩   2 or **to play around** FIDDLE, TOY : jugar, juguetear ⟨don't play (around) with your food : no juegues con la comida⟩   3 or **to play around** JOKE : bromear, hacer el tonto ⟨I was only playing (around) : sólo estaba bromeando⟩   4 : tocar ⟨to play in a band : tocar en un grupo⟩   5 : sonar (en la radio, etc.)   6 : actuar (en una obra de teatro)   7 SHOW : ⟨what's playing at the movies/theatre? : ¿qué dan/ponen en el cine?⟩   8 BEHAVE ⟨to play fair/dirty : jugar limpio/sucio⟩ ⟨to play by the rules : respetar las reglas⟩   9 ACT : hacerse ⟨to play dumb/dead : hacerse el tonto/muerto⟩   10 **to play along** with someone⟩ : seguirle la corriente a alguien, hacerle el juego a alguien   11 **to play around** : perder el tiempo ⟨he plays around instead of working : pierde el tiempo en vez de trabajar⟩   12 **to play around** : tener líos (amorosos)   13 **to play for time** STALL : tratar de ganar tiempo   14 **to play hard to get** : hacerse (de) rogar   15 **to play into** SUPPORT : dar crédito a   16 **to play into the hands of** : dárselo en bandeja a   17 **to play off** COMPLEMENT : complementar   18 **to play on** EXPLOIT : explotar, aprovecharse de   19 **to play out** DEVELOP, UNFOLD : desarrollarse, desenvolverse — vt   1 : jugar (un deporte, etc.), jugar a (un juego), jugar contra (un contrincante) ⟨he wouldn't play her at chess : no quiso jugar al ajedrez con ella⟩ ⟨the Yankees are playing the Red Sox : los Yanquis juegan contra los Red Sox⟩ ⟨he plays shortstop : juega de/ como torpedero⟩ ⟨to play house : jugar a las casitas, jugar a papás y mamás⟩   2 : tirar (una carta), mover (una pieza), tirar/patear (etc.) (una pelota) ⟨to play a shot : hacer un tiro⟩   3 : tocar (música u un instrumento), tocar en (un lugar)   4 : poner (un DVD, etc.), poner/pasar (una canción en la radio, etc.) ⟨he plays his music too loud : pone la música demasiado alta/fuerte⟩   5 SHOW : dar, poner (una película)   6 : jugar a (la lotería, etc.)   7 PERFORM : interpretar, hacer el papel de (un carácter), representar (una obra de teatro) ⟨she plays the lead : hace el papel principal⟩   8 CARRY OUT : jugar, desempeñar ⟨she played an important role in the negotiations : jugó un papel importante en las negociaciones⟩   9 ACT : hacerse ⟨to play the fool : hacerse el tonto⟩   10 BEHAVE ⟨to play it cool : (actuar) como si nada⟩ ⟨to play it safe : ir a la segura, ir a lo seguro⟩   11 MANIPULATE : manipular ⟨to play someone for a fool : engañar a alguien⟩   12 : hacer, gastar ⟨he played a joke on her : le hizo/gastó una broma⟩ ⟨to play a dirty trick on : jugarle una mala pasada a⟩   13 **to play back** : poner (una grabación) **14 to play down** : minimizar **15 to play God** : jugar a ser Dios **16 to play out** : realizar, vivir (un sueño, etc.) ⟨this scene plays itself out every day : esta situación ocurre cada día⟩ **17 to play up** EMPHASIZE : resaltar

play² n **1** GAME, RECREATION : juego m ⟨children at play : niños jugando⟩ ⟨a play on words : un juego de palabras⟩ **2** ACTION : juego m ⟨rain held up play for an hour : el partido tuvo una hora de retraso por lluvia⟩ ⟨the ball is in play : la pelota está en juego⟩ ⟨to bring into play : poner en juego⟩ **3** DRAMA : obra f de teatro, pieza f (de teatro) ⟨to put on a play : presentar/representar una obra⟩ **4** MOVEMENT : juego m (de la luz, una brisa, etc.) **5** SLACK : juego m ⟨there's not enough play in the wheel : la rueda no da lo suficiente⟩

playacting [ˈpleɪˌæktɪŋ] n : actuación f, teatro m

playboy [ˈpleɪˌbɔɪ] n : playboy m

player [ˈpleɪər] n **1** : jugador m, -dora f (en un juego) **2** ACTOR : actor m, actriz f **3** MUSICIAN : músico m, -ca f **4** : reproductor m (de DVD, etc.)

playful [ˈpleɪfəl] adj **1** FROLICSOME . juguetón **2** JOCULAR : jocoso — **playfully** adv

playfulness [ˈpleɪfəlnəs] n : lo juguetón, jocosidad f, alegría f

playground [ˈpleɪˌɡraʊnd] n : patio m de recreo, jardín m para jugar

playgroup [ˈpleɪˌɡruːp] n : grupo m de recreo para niños

playhouse [ˈpleɪˌhaʊs] n **1** THEATER : teatro m **2** : casita f de juguete

playing card n : naipe m, carta f

playing field n : campo m de juego

playmate [ˈpleɪˌmeɪt] n : compañero m, -ra f de juego

play-off [ˈpleɪˌɔf] n : desempate m

playpen [ˈpleɪˌpɛn] n : corral m (para niños)

playroom [ˈpleɪˌruːm] n : cuarto m de juegos

plaything [ˈpleɪˌθɪŋ] n : juguete m

playtime [ˈpleɪˌtaɪm] n : hora f de recreo

playwright [ˈpleɪˌraɪt] n : dramaturgo m, -ga f

plaza [ˈplæzə, ˈplɑ-] n **1** SQUARE : plaza f **2** shopping plaza MALL : centro m comercial

plea [ˈpliː] n **1** : acto m de declararse ⟨he entered a plea of guilty : se declaró culpable⟩ **2** APPEAL : ruego m, súplica f

plead [ˈpliːd] v **pleaded** or **pled** [ˈplɛd]; **pleading** vi **1** : declararse (culpable o inocente) **2 to plead for** : suplicar, implorar **3 to plead with** : implorarle, suplicarle (a alguien) — vt **1** : alegar, pretextar ⟨he pleaded illness : pretextó la enfermedad⟩ **2 to plead a case** : defender un caso

pleasant [ˈplɛzənt] adj : agradable, grato, bueno — **pleasantly** adv

pleasantness [ˈplɛzəntnəs] n : lo agradable, amenidad f

pleasantries [ˈplɛzəntriz] npl : cumplidos mpl, cortesías fpl ⟨to exchange pleasantries : intercambiar cumplidos⟩

please¹ [ˈpliːz] v **pleased; pleasing** vt **1** GRATIFY : complacer ⟨please yourself! : ¡cómo quieras!⟩ **2** SATISFY : contentar, satisfacer — vi **1** SATISFY : complacer, agradar ⟨anxious to please : deseoso de complacer⟩ **2** LIKE : querer ⟨do as you please : haz lo que quieras, haz lo que te parezca⟩

please² adv : por favor

pleased [ˈpliːzd] adj : contento, satisfecho, alegre ⟨to be pleased about/with : estar contento con/por⟩ ⟨pleased to meet you! : ¡mucho gusto!⟩

pleasing [ˈpliːzɪŋ] adj : agradable — **pleasingly** adv

pleasurable [ˈplɛʒərəbəl] adj PLEASANT : agradable

pleasure [ˈplɛʒər] n **1** WISH : deseo m, voluntad f ⟨at your pleasure : cuando guste⟩ **2** ENJOYMENT : placer m, disfrute m, goce m ⟨with pleasure : con mucho gusto⟩ **3** : placer m, gusto m ⟨it's a pleasure to be here : me da gusto estar aquí⟩ ⟨the pleasures of reading : los placeres de leer⟩

pleat¹ [ˈpliːt] vt : plisar

pleat² n : pliegue m

plebeian [plɪˈbiən] adj : ordinario, plebeyo

pledge¹ [ˈplɛʤ] vt **pledged; pledging 1** PAWN : empeñar, prendar **2** PROMISE : prometer, jurar

pledge² n **1** SECURITY : garantía f, prenda f **2** PROMISE : promesa f

plenteous [ˈplɛntiəs] adj : copioso, abundante

plentiful [ˈplɛntɪfəl] adj : abundante — **plentifully** [-fli] adv

plenty [ˈplɛnti] n : abundancia f ⟨plenty of time : tiempo de sobra⟩ ⟨plenty of visitors : muchos visitantes⟩

plethora [ˈplɛθərə] n : plétora f

pleurisy [ˈplʊrəsi] n : pleuresía f

plexiglass [ˈplɛksɪˌɡlæs] n (Plexiglas, trademark) : acrílico m, plexiglás m Spain

pliable [ˈplaɪəbəl] adj : flexible, maleable

pliant [ˈplaɪənt] adj → **pliable**

pliers [ˈplaɪərz] npl : alicates mpl, pinzas fpl

plight [ˈplaɪt] n : situación f difícil, apuro m

plod [ˈplɑd] vi **plodded; plodding 1** TRUDGE : caminar pesadamente y lentamente **2** DRUDGE : trabajar laboriosamente

plonk → **plunk**

plot¹ [ˈplɑt] v **plotted; plotting** vt **1** DEVISE : tramar **2 to plot out** : trazar, determinar (una posición, etc.) — vi CONSPIRE : conspirar

plot² n **1** LOT : terreno m, parcela f, lote m **2** STORY : argumento m (en el teatro), trama f (en un libro, etc.) **3** CONSPIRACY, INTRIGUE : complot m, intriga f

plotter [ˈplɑtər] n : conspirador m, -dora f; intrigante mf

plow¹ *or* **plough** [ˈplaʊ] *vt* **1** : arar (la tierra) **2 to plow the seas** : surcar los mares

plow² *or* **plough** *n* **1** : arado *m* **2** → **snowplow**

plowshare [ˈplaʊˌʃɛr] *n* : reja *f* del arado

ploy [ˈplɔɪ] *n* : estratagema *f*, maniobra *f*

pluck¹ [ˈplʌk] *vt* **1** PICK : arrancar **2** : desplumar (un pollo, etc.) — *vi* **to pluck at** : tirar de

pluck² *n* **1** TUG : tirón *m* **2** COURAGE, SPIRIT : valor *m*, ánimo *m*

plucky [ˈplʌki] *adj* **pluckier; -est** : valiente, animoso

plug¹ [ˈplʌg] *vt* **plugged; plugging 1** BLOCK : tapar **2** PROMOTE : hacerle publicidad a, promocionar **3 to plug in** : enchufar

plug² *n* **1** STOPPER : tapón *m* **2** : enchufe *m* (eléctrico) **3** ADVERTISEMENT : publicidad *f*, propaganda *f*

plum [ˈplʌm] *n* **1** : ciruela *f* (fruta) **2** : color *m* ciruela **3** PRIZE : premio *m*, algo muy atractivo

plumage [ˈpluːmɪdʒ] *n* : plumaje *m*

plumb¹ [ˈplʌm] *vt* **1** : aplomar ⟨to plumb a wall : aplomar una pared⟩ **2** SOUND : sondar, sondear

plumb² *adv* **1** VERTICALLY : a plomo, verticalmente **2** EXACTLY : justo, exactamente **3** COMPLETELY : completamente, absolutamente ⟨plumb crazy : loco de remate⟩

plumb³ *adj* : a plomo

plumb⁴ *n* *or* **plumb line** : plomada *f*

plumber [ˈplʌmər] *n* : plomero *m*, -ra *f*; fontanero *m*, -ra *f*

plumbing [ˈplʌmɪŋ] *n* **1** : plomería *f*, fontanería *f* (trabajo del plomero) **2** PIPES : cañería *f*, tubería *f*

plume [ˈpluːm] *n* **1** FEATHER : pluma *f* **2** TUFT : penacho *m* (en un sombrero, etc.)

plumed [ˈpluːmd] *adj* : con plumas ⟨white-plumed birds : aves de plumaje blanco⟩

plummet [ˈplʌmət] *vi* : caer en picada, desplomarse

plump¹ [ˈplʌmp] *vi* *or* **to plump down** : dejarse caer (pesadamente)

plump² *adv* **1** STRAIGHT : a plomo **2** DIRECTLY : directamente, sin rodeos ⟨he ran plump into the door : dio de cara con la puerta⟩

plump³ *adj* : llenito *fam*, regordete *fam*, rechoncho *fam*

plumpness [ˈplʌmpnəs] *n* : gordura *f*

plunder¹ [ˈplʌndər] *vi* : saquear, robar

plunder² *n* : botín *m*

plunderer [ˈplʌndərər] *n* : saqueador *m*, -dora *f*

plunge¹ [ˈplʌndʒ] *v* **plunged; plunging** *vt* **1** IMMERSE : sumergir **2** THRUST : hundir, clavar — *vi* **1** DIVE : zambullirse (en el agua) **2** : meterse precipitadamente o violentamente ⟨they plunged into war : se enfrascaron en una guerra⟩ ⟨he plunged into depression : cayó en la depresión⟩ **3** DESCEND : descender en picada ⟨the road plunges dizzily : la calle desciende vertiginosamente⟩

plunge² *n* **1** DIVE : zambullida *f* **2** DROP : descenso *m* abrupto ⟨the plunge in prices : el desplome de los precios⟩

plunger [ˈplʌndʒər] *n* : desatorador *m*, desatascador *m* *Spain*, destapacaños *m* *Mex*, bomba *f* (destapacaños) *Mex*, sopapa *f* *Arg*

plunk [ˈplʌŋk] *or* **plonk** [ˈplɑŋk] *vt* **1** : dejar caer **2 to plunk down** : gastar (dinero) — *vi* **to plunk down** : dejarse caer

pluperfect [ˌpluːˈpərfɪkt] *n* : pluscuamperfecto *m*

plural¹ [ˈplʊrəl] *adj* : plural

plural² *n* : plural *m*

plurality [plʊˈræləti] *n*, *pl* **-ties** : pluralidad *f*

pluralize [ˈplʊrəˌlaɪz] *vt* **-ized; -izing** : pluralizar

plus¹ [ˈplʌs] *adj* **1** POSITIVE : positivo ⟨a plus factor : un factor positivo⟩ **2** (*indicating a quantity in addition*) ⟨a grade of C plus : una calificación entre C y B⟩ ⟨a salary of $30,000 plus : un sueldo de más de $30,000⟩

plus² *n* **1** *or* **plus sign** : más *m*, signo *m* de más **2** ADVANTAGE : ventaja *f*

plus³ *prep* : más (en matemáticas)

plus⁴ *conj* AND : y

plush¹ [ˈplʌʃ] *adj* **1** : afelpado **2** LUXURIOUS : lujoso

plush² *n* : felpa *f*, peluche *m*

plushy [ˈplʌʃi] *adj* **plushier; -est** : lujoso

plus–size [ˈplʌsˌsaɪz] *adj* : de talla grande

Pluto [ˈpluːtoː] *n* : Plutón *m*

plutocracy [pluːˈtɑkrəsi] *n*, *pl* **-cies** : plutocracia *f*

plutonium [pluːˈtoːniəm] *n* : plutonio *m*

ply¹ [ˈplaɪ] *v* **plied; plying** *vt* **1** USE, WIELD : manejar ⟨to ply an ax : manejar un hacha⟩ **2** PRACTICE : ejercer ⟨to ply a trade : ejercer un oficio⟩ **3 to ply with questions** : acosar con preguntas

ply² *n*, *pl* **plies 1** LAYER : chapa *f* (de madera), capa *f* (de papel) **2** STRAND : capa *f* (de hilo, etc.)

plywood [ˈplaɪˌwʊd] *n* : contrachapado *m*

PMS [ˌpiːˌɛmˈɛs] → **premenstrual syndrome**

pneumatic [nʊˈmætɪk, njʊ-] *adj* : neumático

pneumonia [nʊˈmoːnjə, njʊ-] *n* : pulmonía *f*, neumonía *f*

poach [ˈpoːtʃ] *vt* **1** : cocer a fuego lento ⟨to poach an egg : escalfar un huevo⟩ **2 to poach game** : cazar ilegalmente — *vi* : cazar ilegalmente

poacher [ˈpoːtʃər] *n* : cazador *m* furtivo, cazadora *f* furtiva

P.O. Box *n* (*Post Office Box*) : apartado *m* postal, casilla *f* de correos *Arg*

pock [ˈpɑk] *n* **1** PUSTULE : pústula *f* **2** → **pockmark**

pocket¹ [ˈpɑkət] *vt* **1** : meterse en el bolsillo ⟨he pocketed the pen : se metió la pluma en el bolsillo⟩ **2** STEAL : embolsarse

pocket² *n* **1** : bolsillo *m*, bolsa *f* *Mex* ⟨a coat pocket : el bolsillo de un abrigo⟩ ⟨air pockets : bolsas/baches de aire⟩ **2**

CENTER : foco *m*, centro *m* ⟨a pocket of resistance : un foco de resistencia⟩
pocketbook [ˈpakət,bʊk] *n* **1** PURSE : cartera *f*, bolso *m*, bolsa *f* *Mex* **2** MEANS : recursos *mpl*
pocketknife [ˈpakət,naɪf] *n, pl* -knives : navaja *f*
pocket money *n* : dinero *m* de bolsillo
pocket–size [ˈpakət,saɪz] *adj* : de bolsillo
pockmark [ˈpak,mark] *n* : cicatriz *f* de viruela, viruela *f*
pod [ˈpad] *n* : vaina *f* ⟨pea pod : vaina de guisantes⟩
podcast [ˈpad,kæst] *n* : podcast *m*
podiatrist [pəˈdaɪətrɪst, po-] *n* : podólogo *m*, -ga *f*
podiatry [pəˈdaɪətri, po-] *n* : podología *f*, podiatría *f*
podium [ˈpoːdiəm] *n, pl* -diums *or* -dia [-diə] : podio *m*, estrado *m*, tarima *f*
poem [ˈpoːəm] *n* : poema *m*, poesía *f*
poet [ˈpoːət] *n* : poeta *mf*
poetess [ˈpoːətəs] *n* : poetisa *f*
poetic [poˈɛtɪk] *or* **poetical** [-tɪkəl] *adj* : poético
poetry [ˈpoːətri] *n* : poesía *f*
pogrom [ˈpoːgrəm, pəˈgram, ˈpagrəm] *n* : pogrom *m*
poignancy [ˈpɔɪnjəntsi] *n, pl* -cies : lo conmovedor
poignant [ˈpɔɪnjənt] *adj* **1** PAINFUL : penoso, doloroso ⟨poignant grief : profundo dolor⟩ **2** TOUCHING : conmovedor, emocionante
poinsettia [pɔɪnˈsɛtiə, -ˈsɛtə] *n* : flor *f* de Nochebuena
point¹ [ˈpɔɪnt] *vt* **1** : apuntar (una pistola, etc.), señalar con (el dedo) **2** DIRECT : encaminar ⟨can you point me towards the highway? : ¿me puedes indicar cómo llegar a la carretera?⟩ **3** INDICATE : señalar, indicar ⟨to point the way : señalar el camino⟩ **4** SHARPEN : afilar (la punta de) **5 to point out** : señalar, indicar — *vi* **1** : señalar (con el dedo) **2** : apuntar ⟨the needle points north : la aguja apunta hacia el norte⟩ **3** : apuntar (en una pantalla, etc.) ⟨to point and click : apuntar y hacer clic⟩ **4 to point at/to** : señalar (con el dedo) **5 to point to** REFERENCE : señalar **6 to point to/toward** INDICATE : señalar, indicar
point² *n* **1** ITEM : punto *m* ⟨the main points : los puntos principales⟩ **2** : argumento *m*, observación *f* ⟨what's your point? : ¿qué quieres decir?⟩ ⟨that's a good point : es cierto⟩ ⟨point taken : te entiendo⟩ ⟨to have a point : tener razón⟩ ⟨to make a point : hacer una observación⟩ ⟨to get one's point across : hacerse entender⟩ **3 the point** (*indicating the chief idea or meaning*) ⟨to get to the point : ir al grano⟩ ⟨to be beside the point : no venir al caso⟩ ⟨to stick to the point : no salirse del tema⟩ **4** PURPOSE : fin *m*, propósito *m* ⟨there's no point to it : no vale la pena, no sirve para nada⟩ ⟨to make a point of doing something : proponerse hacer algo⟩ **5** QUALITY : cualidad *f* ⟨her good points : sus buenas cualidades⟩ ⟨it's not his strong point : no es su (punto) fuerte⟩ **6** PLACE : punto *m*, lugar *m* ⟨points of interest : puntos interesantes⟩ **7** : punto *m* (en una escala) ⟨boiling point : punto de ebullición⟩ **8** MOMENT : momento *m*, coyuntura *f* ⟨at this point : en este momento⟩ **9** TIP : punta *f* **10** HEADLAND : punta *f*, cabo *m* **11** PERIOD : punto *m* (marca de puntuación) **12** UNIT : punto *m* ⟨he scored 15 points : ganó 15 puntos⟩ ⟨shares fell 10 points : las acciones bajaron 10 enteros⟩ **13** → decimal point **14 compass points** : puntos *mpl* cardinales **15 sore point** : asunto *m* delicado
point–blank¹ [ˈpɔɪntˈblæŋk] *adv* **1** : a quemarropa ⟨to shoot point-blank : disparar a quemarropa⟩ **2** BLUNTLY, DIRECTLY : a bocajarro, sin rodeos, francamente
point–blank² *adj* **1** : a quemarropa ⟨point-blank shots : disparos a quemarropa⟩ **2** BLUNT DIRECT : directo, franco
pointed [ˈpɔɪntəd] *adj* **1** POINTY : puntiagudo **2** PERTINENT : atinado **3** CONSPICUOUS : marcado, manifiesto
pointedly [ˈpɔɪntədli] *adv* : intencionadamente, directamente
pointer [ˈpɔɪntər] *n* **1** STICK : puntero *m* (para maestros, etc.) **2** INDICATOR, NEEDLE : indicador *m*, aguja *f* **3** : perro *m* de muestra **4** HINT, TIP : consejo *m*
pointless [ˈpɔɪntləs] *adj* : inútil, ocioso, vano ⟨it's pointless to continue : no tiene sentido continuar⟩
point of view *n* : perspectiva *f*, punto *m* de vista
pointy [ˈpɔɪnti] *adj* : puntiagudo
poise¹ [ˈpɔɪz] *vt* **poising** BALANCE : equilibrar, balancear
poise² *n* : aplomo *m*, compostura *f*
poison¹ [ˈpɔɪzən] *vt* **1** : envenenar, intoxicar **2** CORRUPT : corromper
poison² *n* : veneno *m*
poisoning *n* : envenenamiento *m*
poison ivy *n* : hiedra *f* venenosa
poisonous [ˈpɔɪzənəs] *adj* : venenoso, tóxico, ponzoñoso
poke¹ [ˈpoːk] *v* **poked; poking** *vt* **1** JAB : golpear (con la punta de algo), dar ⟨he poked me with his finger : me dio con el dedo⟩ **2** THRUST : introducir, asomar ⟨I poked my head out the window : asomé la cabeza por la ventana⟩ — *vi* **1 to poke around** RUMMAGE : hurgar **2 to poke along** DAWDLE : demorarse, entretenerse **3 to poke out of** : asomar por, sobresalir por
poke² *n* : golpe *m* abrupto (con la punta de algo)
poker [ˈpoːkər] *n* **1** : atizador *m* (para el fuego) **2** : póker *m*, poker *m* (juego de naipes)
poky [ˈpoːki] *adj fam* **1** SLOW : lento **2** TINY : diminuto
polar [ˈpoːlər] *adj* : polar
polar bear *n* : oso *m* blanco
Polaris [poˈlærɪs, -ˈlɑr-] → North Star
polarize [ˈpoːlə,raɪz] *vt* **-ized; -izing** : polarizar

Polaroid ['poːlə‚rɔɪd] *trademark* se usa para una cámara que produce fotos reveladas o para las fotos así producidas

pole ['poːl] *n* 1 : palo *m*, poste *m*, vara *f* ⟨telephone pole : poste de teléfonos⟩ 2 : polo *m* ⟨the South Pole : el Polo Sur⟩ 3 : polo *m* (eléctrico o magnético)

Pole ['poːl] *n* : polaco *m*, -ca *f*

polecat ['poːl‚kæt] *n, pl* **polecats** or **polecat** 1 : turón *m* (de Europa) 2 SKUNK : mofeta *f*, zorrillo *m*

polemical [pə'lɛmɪkəl] *adj* : polémico

polemics [pə'lɛmɪks] *ns & pl* : polémica *f*

polestar ['poːl‚stɑr] → **North Star**

pole vault *n* : salto *m* con/de pértiga, salto *m* con/de garrocha

police¹ [pə'liːs] *vt* **-liced; -licing** : mantener el orden en ⟨to police the streets : patrullar las calles⟩

police² *ns & pl* 1 : policía *f* (organización) 2 POLICE OFFICERS : policías *mfpl*

police car *n* : patrulla *f*, patrullero *m*

police force *n* : fuerza *f* policial, cuerpo *m* policial

policeman [pə'liːsmən] *n, pl* **-men** [-mən, -‚mɛn] : policía *m*

police officer *n* : policía *mf*, agente *mf* de policía

police station *n* : comisaría *f*

policewoman [pə'liːs‚wʊmən] *n, pl* **-women** [-‚wɪmən] : policía *f*, mujer *f* policía

policy ['pɑləsi] *n, pl* **-cies** 1 : política *f* ⟨foreign policy : política exterior⟩ 2 or **insurance policy** : póliza *f* de seguros, seguro *m*

polio¹ ['poːli‚oː] *adj* : de polio ⟨polio vaccine : vacuna contra la polio⟩

polio² *n* → **poliomyelitis**

poliomyelitis [‚poːli‚oːmaɪə'laɪtəs] *n* : poliomielitis *f*, polio *f*

polish¹ ['pɑlɪʃ] *vt* 1 : pulir, lustrar, sacar brillo a ⟨to polish one's nails : pintarse las uñas⟩ 2 REFINE : pulir, perfeccionar 3 **to polish off** : despacharse (comida)

polish² *n* 1 LUSTER : brillo *m*, lustre *m* 2 REFINEMENT : refinamiento *m* 3 : betún *m* (para zapatos), cera *f* (para suelos y muebles), esmalte *m* (para las uñas)

Polish¹ ['poːlɪʃ] *adj* : polaco

Polish² *n* : polaco *m* (idioma)

polite [pə'laɪt] *adj* **politer; -est** : cortés, correcto, educado

politely [pə'laɪtli] *adv* : cortésmente, correctamente, con buenos modales

politeness [pə'laɪtnəs] *n* : cortesía *f*

politic ['pɑlə‚tɪk] *adj* : diplomático, prudente

political [pə'lɪtɪkəl] *adj* : político — **politically** [-tɪkli] *adv*

politically correct *adj* : políticamente correcto

politician [‚pɑlə'tɪʃən] *n* : político *m*, -ca *f*

politics ['pɑlə‚tɪks] *ns & pl* : política *f*

polka ['poːlkə, 'poːkə] *n* : polka *f*

polka dot ['poːkə‚dɑt] *n* : lunar *m* (en un diseño)

poll¹ ['poːl] *vt* 1 : obtener (votos) ⟨she polled over 1000 votes : obtuvo más de 1000 votos⟩ 2 CANVASS : encuestar, sondear — *vi* : obtener votos

poll² *n* 1 SURVEY : encuesta *f*, sondeo *m* 2 **polls** *npl* : urnas *fpl* ⟨to go to the polls : acudir a las urnas, ir a votar⟩

pollen ['pɑlən] *n* : polen *m*

pollinate ['pɑlə‚neɪt] *vt* **-nated; -nating** : polinizar

pollination [‚pɑlə'neɪʃən] *n* : polinización *f*

polling place *n* : centro *m* de votación

pollster ['poːlstər] *n* : encuestador *m*, -dora *f*

pollutant [pə'luːtənt] *n* : contaminante *m*

pollute [pə'luːt] *vt* **-luted; -luting** : contaminar

pollution [pə'luːʃən] *n* : contaminación *f*

pollywog or **polliwog** ['pɑli‚wɑg] *n* TADPOLE : renacuajo *m*

polo ['poːl‚loː] *n* 1 : polo *m* (deporte) 2 or **polo shirt** : polo *m*

poltergeist ['poːltər‚gaɪst] *n* : fantasma *m* travieso

polyester ['pɑli‚ɛstər, ‚pɑli'-] *n* : poliéster *m*

polygamist [pə'lɪgəmɪst] *n* : polígamo *m*, -ma *f*

polygamous [pə'lɪgəməs] *adj* : polígamo

polygamy [pə'lɪgəmi] *n* : poligamia *f*

polygon ['pɑli‚gɑn] *n* : polígono *m* — **polygonal** [pə'lɪgənəl] *adj*

polymer ['pɑləmər] *n* : polímero *m*

Polynesian [‚pɑlə'niːʒən, -ʃən] *n* : polinesio *m*, -sia *f* — **Polynesian** *adj*

polytheism ['pɑli‚θiː‚ɪzəm] *n* : politeísmo *m*

polyunsaturated [‚pɑli‚ʌn'sætʃə-‚reɪtəd] *adj* : poliinsaturado

pomegranate ['pɑmə‚grænət, 'pɑm-‚grænət] *n* : granada *f* (fruta)

pommel¹ ['pʌməl] *vt* → **pummel**

pommel² ['pʌməl, 'pɑ-] *n* 1 : pomo *m* (de una espada) 2 : perilla *f* (de una silla de montar)

pomp ['pɑmp] *n* 1 SPLENDOR : pompa *f*, esplendor *m* 2 OSTENTATION : boato *m*, ostentación *f*

pom–pom ['pɑm‚pɑm] *n* : borla *f*, pompón *m*

pomposity [pɑm'pɑsəṭi] *n, pl* **-ties** : pomposidad *f*

pompous ['pɑmpəs] *adj* : pomposo — **pompously** *adv*

poncho ['pɑn‚tʃoː] *n, pl* **-chos** : poncho *m*

pond ['pɑnd] *n* : charca *f* (natural), estanque *m* (artificial)

ponder ['pɑndər] *vt* : reflexionar, considerar — *vi* **to ponder over** : reflexionar sobre, sopesar

ponderous ['pɑndərəs] *adj* : pesado

pontiff ['pɑntɪf] *n* POPE : pontífice *m*

pontificate [pɑn'tɪfə‚keɪt] *vi* **-cated; -cating** : pontificar

pontoon [pɑn'tuːn] *n* : pontón *m*

pony ['poːni] *n, pl* **-nies** : poni *m*, poney *m*, jaca *f*

ponytail ['poːni‚teɪl] *n* : cola *f* de caballo, coleta *f*

poodle ['puːdəl] n : caniche m

pool¹ ['puːl] vt : mancomunar (recursos), hacer un fondo común de (dinero) — vi : encharcarse

pool² n 1 : charca f ⟨a swimming pool : una piscina⟩ 2 PUDDLE : charco m 3 RESERVE SUPPLY : fondo m común (de recursos), reserva f 4 : billar m (juego)

poop¹ ['puːp] vi fam : hacerse caca — vt fam to poop one's pants/diaper (etc.) : hacerse caca

poop² n fam : caca f

poor ['pur, 'por] adj 1 : pobre ⟨poor people : los pobres⟩ 2 SCANTY : pobre, escaso ⟨poor attendance : baja asistencia⟩ 3 UNFORTUNATE : pobre ⟨poor thing! : ¡pobrecito!⟩ 4 BAD : malo ⟨to be in poor health : estar mal de salud⟩

poorly ['purli, 'por-] adv : mal

pop¹ ['pɑp] v popped; popping vi 1 BURST : reventarse, estallar 2 : saltar (dícese de un corcho) 3 : ir, venir, o aparecer abruptamente ⟨he popped into the house : se metió en la casa⟩ ⟨a menu pops up : aparece un menú⟩ 4 to pop out PROTRUDE : salirse, saltarse ⟨my eyes popped out of my head : se me saltaban los ojos⟩ 5 to pop the question fam : proponerle matrimonio a alguien — vt 1 BURST : reventar 2 : sacar o meter abruptamente ⟨he popped it in his mouth : se lo metió en la boca⟩ ⟨she popped her head out the window : sacó la cabeza por la ventana⟩

pop² adj : popular ⟨pop music : música popular⟩ ⟨pop star : estrella de música popular⟩

pop³ n 1 : estallido m pequeño (de un globo, etc.) 2 SODA : refresco m, gaseosa f

popcorn ['pɑp,kɔrn] n : palomitas fpl (de maíz)

pope ['poːp] n : papa m ⟨Pope John : el Papa Juan⟩

poplar ['pɑplər] n : álamo m

poplin ['pɑplɪn] n : popelín m, popelina f

poppy ['pɑpi] n, pl -pies : amapola f

Popsicle ['pɑp,sɪkəl] trademark se usa para una paleta helada

populace ['pɑpjələs] n 1 MASSES : pueblo m 2 POPULATION : población f

popular ['pɑpjələr] adj 1 : popular ⟨the popular vote : el voto popular⟩ 2 COMMON : generalizado, común ⟨popular beliefs : creencias generalizadas⟩ 3 : popular, de gran popularidad ⟨a popular singer : un cantante popular⟩

popularity [ˌpɑpjə'lærəti] n : popularidad f

popularize ['pɑpjələˌraɪz] vt -ized; -izing : popularizar

popularly ['pɑpjələrli] adv : popularmente, vulgarmente

populate ['pɑpjəˌleɪt] vt -lated; -lating : poblar

population [ˌpɑpjə'leɪʃən] n : población f

populist ['pɑpjəlɪst] n : populista mf — populist adj

populous ['pɑpjələs] adj : populoso

pop–up ['pɑp,ʌp] n : ventana f emergente (de una página web)

porcelain ['pɔrsələn] n : porcelana f

porch ['pɔrtʃ] n : porche m

porcupine ['pɔrkjəˌpaɪn] n : puerco m espín

pore¹ ['por] vi pored; poring 1 GAZE : mirar (con atención) 2 to pore over : leer detenidamente, estudiar

pore² n : poro m

pork ['pork] n : carne f de cerdo, carne f de puerco ⟨pork chop : chuleta de cerdo⟩

pornographic [ˌpɔrnə'græfɪk] adj : pornográfico

pornography [pɔr'nɑgrəfi] n : pornografía f

porous ['porəs] adj : poroso

porpoise ['pɔrpəs] n 1 : marsopa f 2 DOLPHIN : delfín m

porridge ['pɔrɪdʒ] n : sopa f espesa de harina, gachas fpl

port¹ ['port] adj : de babor ⟨on the port side : a babor⟩

port² n 1 HARBOR : puerto m 2 ORIFICE : orificio m (de una válvula, etc.) 3 : puerto m (de una computadora) 4 PORTHOLE : portilla f 5 or port side : babor m (de un barco) 6 : oporto m (vino)

portable ['portəbəl] adj : portátil

portal ['pɔrtəl] n : portal m

portend [pɔr'tend] vt : presagiar, augurar

portent ['pɔrˌtent] n : presagio m, augurio m

portentous [pɔr'tentəs] adj : profético, que presagia

porter ['pɔrtər] n : maletero m, mozo m (de estación)

portfolio [pɔrt'foːliˌo] n, pl -lios 1 FOLDER : cartera f (para llevar papeles), carpeta f 2 : cartera f (diplomática) 3 investment portfolio : cartera de inversiones

porthole ['pɔrtˌhoːl] n : portilla f (de un barco), ventanilla f (de un avión)

portico ['pɔrtiˌko] n, pl -coes or -cos : pórtico m

portion¹ ['pɔrʃən] vt DISTRIBUTE : repartir

portion² n PART, SHARE : porción f, parte f

portly ['pɔrtli] adj portlier; -est : corpulento

portrait ['pɔrtrət, -ˌtreɪt] n : retrato m

portray [pɔr'treɪ] vt 1 DEPICT : representar, retratar 2 DESCRIBE : describir 3 PLAY : interpretar (un personaje)

portrayal [pɔr'treɪəl] n 1 REPRESENTATION : representación f 2 PORTRAIT : retrato m

Portuguese¹ [ˌpɔrtʃə'giːz, -'giːs] adj : portugués

Portuguese² n 1 : portugués m (idioma) 2 the Portuguese (used with a plural verb) : los portugueses

pose¹ ['poːz] v posed; posing vt PRESENT : plantear (una pregunta, etc.), representar (una amenaza) — vi 1 : posar (para una foto, etc.) 2 to pose as : hacerse pasar por

pose[2] *n* 1 : pose *f* ⟨to strike a pose : asumir una pose⟩ 2 PRETENSE : pose *f*, afectación *f*

posh ['pɑʃ] *adj* : elegante, de lujo

position[1] [pə'zɪʃən] *vt* : colocar, situar, ubicar

position[2] *n* 1 LOCATION : posición *f*, ubicación *f* 2 : posición *f*, postura *f* (del cuerpo) 3 OPINION, STANCE : posición *f*, postura *f*, planteamiento *m* 4 STATUS : posición *f* (en una jerarquía) 5 JOB : puesto *m* 6 : posición *f* (en un equipo) 7 SITUATION : situación *f* ⟨to be in no position to do something : no estar en condiciones de hacer algo⟩

positive ['pɑzətɪv] *adj* 1 DEFINITE : incuestionable, inequívoco ⟨positive evidence : pruebas irrefutables⟩ 2 CONFIDENT : seguro 3 : positivo (en gramática, matemáticas, y física) 4 AFFIRMATIVE : positivo, afirmativo ⟨a positive response : una respuesta positiva⟩

positively ['pɑzətɪvli] *adv* 1 FAVORABLY : favorablemente 2 OPTIMISTICALLY : positivamente 3 DEFINITELY : definitivamente, en forma concluyente 4 (*used for emphasis*) : realmente, verdaderamente ⟨it's really awful! : ¡es verdaderamente malo!⟩

posse ['pɑsi] *n* 1 : partida *f*, patrulla *f* 2 *fam* GANG, ENTOURAGE : grupo *m* de amigos/seguidores (etc.) 3 *fam* GROUP : grupo *m*

possess [pə'zɛs] *vt* 1 HAVE, OWN : poseer, tener 2 SEIZE : apoderarse de ⟨he was possessed by fear : el miedo se apoderó de él⟩

possession [pə'zɛʃən] *n* 1 POSSESSING : posesión *f* 2 : posesión *f* (por un demonio, etc.) 3 **possessions** *npl* PROPERTY : bienes *mpl*, propiedad *f*

possessive[1] [pə'zɛsɪv] *adj* 1 : posesivo (en gramática) 2 JEALOUS : posesivo, celoso

possessive[2] *n or* **possessive case** : posesivo *m*

possessor [pə'zɛsər] *n* : poseedor *m*, -dora *f*

possibility [ˌpɑsə'bɪləti] *n*, *pl* **-ties** : posibilidad *f*

possible ['pɑsəbəl] *adj* : posible ⟨as soon as possible : lo antes posible⟩ ⟨as much as possible : lo más posible⟩ ⟨if possible : si es posible⟩

possibly ['pɑsəbli] *adv* 1 CONCEIVABLY : posiblemente ⟨it can't possibly be true! : ¡no puede ser!⟩ ⟨I can't possibly do that : me es imposible, no puedo hacerlo de ninguna manera⟩ 2 PERHAPS : quizás, posiblemente

possum ['pɑsəm] → **opossum**

post[1] ['po:st] *vt* 1 MAIL : echar al correo, mandar por correo 2 : postear *fam*, publicar en la red 3 ANNOUNCE : anunciar ⟨they've posted the grades : han anunciado las notas⟩ 4 AFFIX : fijar, poner (noticias, etc.) 5 STATION : apostar 6 **to keep (someone) posted** : tener al corriente (a alguien)

post[2] *n* 1 POLE : poste *m*, palo *m* 2 STATION : puesto *m* 3 CAMP : puesto *m* (militar) 4 JOB, POSITION : puesto *m*, empleo *m*, cargo *m* 5 : post *m*, posteo *m*, mensaje *m* en Internet

post- ['po:st] *pref* : pos-, post- ⟨postpone : posponer⟩ ⟨postgraduate : postgraduado⟩

postage ['po:stɪʤ] *n* : franqueo *m*

postage stamp → **stamp**[2]

postal ['po:stəl] *adj* : postal

postcard ['po:st,kard] *n* : postal *f*, tarjeta *f* postal

postdate ['po:st'deɪt] *vt* **-dated; -dating** : posfechar

poster ['po:stər] *n* : póster *m*, cartel *m*, afiche *m*

posterior[1] [pɑ'stɪriər, po-] *adj* : posterior

posterior[2] *n* BUTTOCKS : trasero *m*, nalgas *fpl*, asentaderas *fpl*

posterity [pɑ'stɛrəti] *n* : posteridad *f*

postgraduate[1] [ˌpo:st'græʤuət] *adj* : de postgrado

postgraduate[2] *n* : postgraduado *m*, -da *f*

posthaste ['po:st'heɪst] *adv* : a toda prisa

posthumous ['pɑstʃəməs] *adj* : póstumo — **posthumously** *adv*

Post-it ['po:st,ɪt] *trademark* se usa para un papelito con borde adhesivo

postman ['po:stmən, -ˌmæn] *n*, *pl* **-men** [-mən, -ˌmɛn] → **mailman**

postmark[1] ['po:st,mark] *vt* : matasellar

postmark[2] *n* : matasellos *m*

postmaster ['po:st,mæstər] *n* : administrador *m*, -dora *f* de correos

postmodern [ˌpo:st'mɑdərn] *adj* : posmoderno

postmortem [ˌpo:st'mɔrtəm] *n* : autopsia *f*

postnatal [ˌpo:st'neɪtəl] *adj* : postnatal

postnatal depression → **postpartum depression**

post office *n* : correo *m*, oficina *f* de correos

post office box → **P.O. Box**

postoperative [ˌpo:st'ɑpərətɪv, -ˌreɪ-] *adj* : posoperatorio

postpaid [ˌpo:st'peɪd] *adv* : con franqueo pagado

postpartum depression [ˌpo:st'pɑrtəm-] *n* : depresión *f* posparto

postpone [ˌpo:st'po:n] *vt* **-poned; -poning** : postergar, aplazar, posponer

postponement [ˌpo:st'po:nmənt] *n* : postergación *f*, aplazamiento *m*

postscript ['po:st,skrɪpt] *n* : postdata *f*, posdata *f*

postulate ['pɑstʃə,leɪt] *vt* **-lated; -lating** : postular

posture[1] ['pɑstʃər] *vi* **-tured; -turing** : posar, asumir una pose

posture[2] *n* : postura *f*

postwar [ˌpo:st'wɔr] *adj* : de (la) posguerra

posy ['po:zi] *n*, *pl* **-sies** 1 FLOWER : flor *f* 2 BOUQUET : ramo *m*, ramillete *m*

pot[1] ['pɑt] *vt* **potted; potting** : plantar (en una maceta)

pot[2] *n* 1 : olla *f* (de cocina) 2 **pots and pans** : cacharros *mpl* 3 **to go to pot** : echarse a perder

potable ['poːṭəbəl] *adj* : potable

potash ['pɑt̬ˌæʃ] *n* : potasa *f*

potassium [pəˈtæsiəm] *n* : potasio *m*

potato [pəˈteɪt̬o] *n, pl* **-toes** : papa *f*, patata *f Spain*

potato chips *npl* : papas *fpl* fritas (de bolsa)

potbellied ['pɑt̬ˌbɛlid] *adj* : panzón, barrigón *fam*

potbelly ['pɑt̬ˌbeli] *n* : panza *f*, barriga *f*

potency ['poːt̬əntsi] *n, pl* **-cies** **1** POWER : fuerza *f*, potencia *f* **2** EFFECTIVENESS : eficacia *f*

potent ['poːt̬ənt] *adj* **1** POWERFUL : potente, poderoso **2** EFFECTIVE : eficaz ⟨a potent medicine : una medicina bien fuerte⟩

potential[1] [pəˈtɛntʃəl] *adj* : potencial, posible

potential[2] *n* **1** : potencial *m* ⟨growth potential : potencial de crecimiento⟩ ⟨a child with potential : un niño que promete⟩ **2** : potencial *m* (eléctrico) — **potentially** *adv*

potful ['pɑt̬ˌfʊl] *n* : contenido *m* de una olla ⟨a potful of water : una olla de agua⟩

pothole ['pɑt̬ˌhoːl] *n* : bache *m*

potion ['poːʃən] *n* : brebaje *m*, poción *f*

potluck ['pɑt̬ˌlʌk] *n* **to take potluck** : tomar lo que haya

potpourri [ˌpoːpʊˈriː] *n* : popurrí *m*

potshot ['pɑt̬ˌʃɑt] *n* **1** : tiro *m* al azar ⟨to take potshots at : disparar al azar⟩ **2** CRITICISM : crítica *f* (hecha al azar)

potter[1] ['pɑt̬ər] *n* : alfarero *m*, -ra *f*

potter[2] → **putter**

pottery ['pɑt̬əri] *n, pl* **-teries** : cerámica *f*

potty ['pɑt̬i] *n fam* **1** : bacinica *f* (para niños) **2 to go potty** : hacer pipí, hacer popó

pouch ['paʊtʃ] *n* **1** BAG : bolsa *f* pequeña **2** : bolsa *f* (de un animal)

poultice ['poːlt̬əs] *n* : emplasto *m*, cataplasma *f*

poultry ['poːltri] *n* : aves *fpl* de corral

pounce ['paʊnts] *vi* **pounced; pouncing** : abalanzarse

pound[1] ['paʊnd] *vt* **1** CRUSH : machacar, machucar, majar **2** BEAT : golpear, machacar ⟨she pounded the lessons into them : les machacaba las lecciones⟩ ⟨he pounded home his point : les hizo entender su razonamiento⟩ — *vi* **1** BEAT : palpitar (dícese del corazón) **2** RESOUND : retumbar, resonar **3** : andar con paso pesado ⟨we pounded through the mud : caminamos pesadamente por el barro⟩

pound[2] *n* **1** : libra *f* (unidad de peso) **2** : libra *f* (unidad monetaria) **3 dog pound** : perrera *f*

pour ['por] *vt* **1** : echar, verter, servir (bebidas) ⟨pour it into a pot : viértalo en una olla⟩ **2** : proveer con abundancia ⟨they poured money into it : le invirtieron mucho dinero⟩ **3 to pour out** : dar salida a ⟨he poured out his feelings to her : se desahogó con ella⟩ — *vi* **1** FLOW : manar, fluir, salir ⟨blood was pouring from the wound : la sangre le manaba de la herida⟩ ⟨people poured out of the subway : la gente salía del metro a raudales⟩ ⟨the orders came pouring in : había un aluvión de pedidos⟩ **2 it's pouring (outside)** : está lloviendo a cántaros

pout[1] ['paʊt] *vi* : hacer pucheros

pout[2] *n* : pucheros *m*

poverty ['pɑvərt̬i] *n* : pobreza *f*, indigencia *f*

poverty–stricken *adj* : necesitado, paupérrimo

powder[1] ['paʊdər] *vt* **1** : empolvar ⟨to powder one's face : empolvarse la cara⟩ **2** PULVERIZE : pulverizar

powder[2] *n* : polvo *m*, polvos *mpl*

powdery ['paʊdəri] *adj* : polvoriento, como polvo

power[1] ['paʊər] *vt* : impulsar, propulsar

power[2] *n* **1** CONTROL, AUTHORITY : poder *m*, autoridad *f* ⟨executive powers : poderes ejecutivos⟩ ⟨power struggle : lucha por el poder⟩ ⟨to have power over somebody : tener poder sobre alguien⟩ ⟨to come to power : llegar al poder⟩ ⟨to be in power : estar en el poder⟩ **2** ABILITY : capacidad *f*, poder *m* ⟨the power of speech : el habla⟩ ⟨I'll do everything in my power : haré todo lo que pueda⟩ ⟨it's not within my power : no está en mis manos⟩ **3** : potencia *f* (política) ⟨foreign powers : potencias extranjeras⟩ **4** STRENGTH : fuerza *f*, poder *m* ⟨the power of love : la fuerza del amor⟩ **5** : potencia *f* (en física y matemáticas) **6** : electricidad *f*, luz *f* ⟨power failure : corte de luz, corte de energía eléctrica, apagón⟩

powerboat ['paʊərˌboːt] *n* **1** → **motorboat** **2** → **speedboat**

powerful ['paʊərfəl] *adj* : poderoso, potente — **powerfully** *adv*

powerhouse ['paʊərˌhaʊs] *n* : persona *f* dinámica

powerless ['paʊərləs] *adj* : impotente

powerlessness ['paʊərləsnəs] *n* : impotencia *f*

power plant *n* : central *f* eléctrica

powwow ['paʊˌwaʊ] *n* : conferencia *f*

pox ['pɑks] *n, pl* **pox** *or* **poxes** **1** CHICKEN POX : varicela *f* **2** SYPHILIS : sífilis *f*

PR ['piːˈɑr] → **public relations**

practicable ['præktɪkəbəl] *adj* : practicable, viable, factible

practical ['præktɪkəl] *adj* : práctico

practicality [ˌpræktɪˈkæləṭi] *n, pl* **-ties** : factibilidad *f*, viabilidad *f*

practical joke *n* : broma *f* (pesada)

practically ['præktɪkli] *adv* **1** : de manera práctica **2** ALMOST : casi, prácticamente

practice[1] *or* **practise** ['præktəs] *vt* **-ticed** *or* **-tised; -ticing** *or* **-tising** **1** : practicar, ensayar, entrenar ⟨he practiced his German on us : practicó el alemán con nosotros⟩ ⟨to practice politeness : practicar la cortesía⟩ **2** : ejercer ⟨to practice medicine : ejercer la medicina⟩

practice[2] *n* **1** USE : práctica *f* ⟨to put into practice : poner en práctica⟩ **2**

CUSTOM : costumbre *f* ⟨it's a common practice here : por aquí se acostumbra hacerlo⟩ **3** TRAINING : práctica *f* ⟨she's out of practice : le falta práctica⟩ ⟨practice makes perfect : la práctica hace al maestro⟩ **4** : ejercicio *m* (de una profesión)

practitioner [præk'tɪʃənər] *n* **1** : profesional *mf* **2 general practitioner** : médico *m*, -ca *f*

pragmatic [præg'mætɪk] *adj* : pragmático — **pragmatically** *adv*

pragmatism ['prægmə,tɪzəm] *n* : pragmatismo

prairie ['preri] *n* : pradera *f*, llanura *f*

praise¹ ['preɪz] *vt* **praised; praising** : elogiar, alabar ⟨to praise God : alabar a Dios⟩

praise² *n* : elogio *m*, alabanza *f*

praiseworthy ['preɪz,wərði] *adj* : digno de alabanza, loable

prance¹ ['præns] *vi* **pranced; prancing** **1** : hacer cabriolas, cabriolar ⟨a prancing horse : un caballo haciendo cabriolas⟩ **2** SWAGGER : pavonearse

prance² *n* : cabriola *f*

prank ['præŋk] *n* : broma *f*, travesura *f*

prankster ['præŋkstər] *n* : bromista *mf*

prattle¹ ['prætəl] *vi* **-tled; -tling** : parlotear *fam*, cotorrear *fam*, balbucear (como un niño)

prattle² *n* : parloteo *m fam*, cotorreo *m fam*, cháchara *f fam*

prawn ['prɔn] *n* : langostino *m*, camarón *m*, gamba *f*

pray ['preɪ] *vt* ENTREAT : rogar, suplicar — *vi* : rezar

prayer ['prer] *n* **1** : plegaria *f*, oración *f* ⟨to say one's prayers : orar, rezar⟩ ⟨the Lord's Prayer : el Padrenuestro⟩ **2** PRAYING : rezo *m*, oración *f* ⟨to kneel in prayer : arrodillarse para rezar⟩

praying mantis → mantis

pre- [,pri] *pref* **1** : antes de **2** : con antelación

preach ['pritʃ] *vi* : predicar — *vt* ADVOCATE : abogar por ⟨to preach cooperation : promover la cooperación⟩

preacher ['pritʃər] *n* **1** : predicador *m*, -dora *f* **2** MINISTER : pastor *m*, -tora *f*

preamble ['pri,æmbəl] *n* : preámbulo *m*

prearrange [,priːə'reɪndʒ] *vt* **-ranged; -ranging** : arreglar de antemano

precarious [prɪ'kæriəs] *adj* : precario — **precariously** *adv*

precariousness [prɪ'kæriəsnəs] *n* : precariedad *f*

precaution [prɪ'kɔʃən] *n* : precaución *f*

precautionary [prɪ'kɔʃə,neri] *adj* : preventivo, cautelar, precautorio

precede [prɪ'siːd] *v* **-ceded; -ceding** : preceder a

precedence ['presədənts, prɪ'siːdənts] *n* : precedencia *f*

precedent ['presədənt] *n* : precedente *m*

precept ['pri,sept] *n* : precepto *m*

precinct ['pri,sɪŋkt] *n* **1** DISTRICT : distrito *m* (policial, electoral, etc.) **2 precincts** *npl* PREMISES : recinto *m*, predio *m*, límites *mpl* (de una ciudad)

precious ['preʃəs] *adj* **1** : precioso ⟨precious gems : piedras preciosas⟩ **2** DEAR : querido **3** AFFECTED : afectado

precipice ['presəpəs] *n* : precipicio *m*

precipitate [prɪ'sɪpə,teɪt] *v* **-tated; -tating** *vt* **1** HASTEN, PROVOKE : precipitar, provocar **2** HURL : arrojar **3** : precipitar (en química) — *vi* : precipitarse (en química), condensarse (en meteorología)

precipitation [prɪ,sɪpə'teɪʃən] *n* **1** HASTE : precipitación *f*, prisa *f* **2** : precipitaciones *fpl* (en meteorología)

precipitous [prɪ'sɪpətəs] *adj* **1** HASTY, RASH : precipitado **2** STEEP : escarpado, empinado ⟨a precipitous drop : una caída vertiginosa⟩

précis [preɪ'siː] *n, pl* **précis** [-'siːz] : resumen *m*

precise [prɪ'saɪs] *adj* **1** DEFINITE : preciso, explícito **2** EXACT : exacto, preciso ⟨precise calculations : cálculos precisos⟩ — **precisely** *adv*

preciseness [prɪ'saɪsnəs] *n* : precisión *f*, exactitud *f*

precision [prɪ'sɪʒən] *n* : precisión *f*

preclude [prɪ'kluːd] *vt* **-cluded; -cluding** : evitar, impedir, excluir (una posibilidad, etc.)

precocious [prɪ'koːʃəs] *adj* : precoz — **precociously** *adv*

precocity [prɪ'kasəti] *n* : precocidad *f*

preconceived [,priːkən'siːvd] *adj* : preconcebido

preconception [,priːkən'spʃən] *n* : idea *f* preconcebida

precondition [,priːkən'dɪʃən] *n* : precondición *f*, condición *f* previa

precook [,priː'kʊk] *vt* : precocinar

precursor [prɪ'kərsər] *n* : precursor *m*, -sora *f*

predator ['predətər] *n* : depredador *m*, -dora *f*

predatory ['predə,tori] *adj* : depredador

predecessor ['predə,sesər, 'prɛ:-] *n* : antecesor *m*, -sora *f*; predecesor *m*, -sora *f*

predestination [prɪ,destə'neɪʃən] *n* : predestinación *f*

predestine [prɪ'destən] *vt* **-tined; -tining** : predestinar

predetermine [,priːdɪ'tərmən] *vt* **-mined; -mining** : predeterminar

predicament [prɪ'dɪkəmənt] *n* : apuro *m*, aprieto *m*

predicate¹ ['predə,keɪt] *vt* **-cated; -cating** **1** AFFIRM : afirmar, aseverar **2 to be predicated on** : estar basado en

predicate² ['predɪkət] *n* : predicado *m*

predict [prɪ'dɪkt] *vt* : pronosticar, predecir

predictable [prɪ'dɪktəbəl] *adj* : previsible — **predictably** [-bli] *adv*

prediction [prɪ'dɪkʃən] *n* : pronóstico *m*, predicción *f*

predilection [,predəl'ekʃən, ,prɪ:-] *n* : predilección *f*

predispose [,priːdɪ'spoːz] *vt* **-posed; -posing** : predisponer

predisposition [,priː,dɪspə'zɪʃən] *n* : predisposición *f*

predominance [prɪ'damənənts] *n* : predominio *m*

predominant [pri'dɑmənənt] *adj* : predominante — **predominantly** *adv*

predominate [pri'dɑmə,neɪt] *vi* -nated; -nating **1** : predominar (en cantidad) **2** PREVAIL : prevalecer

preeminence [pri'emənənts] *n* : preeminencia *f*

preeminent [pri'emənənt] *adj* : preeminente

preeminently [pri'emənəntli] *adv* : especialmente

preempt [pri'empt] *vt* **1** APPROPRIATE : apoderarse de, apropiarse de **2** : reemplazar (un programa de televisión, etc.) **3** FORESTALL : adelantarse a (un ataque, etc.)

preemptive [pri'emptɪv] *adj* : preventivo

preen ['pri:n] *vt* : arreglarse (el pelo, las plumas, etc.)

prefabricated [,pri:'fæbrə,keɪtəd] *adj* : prefabricado

preface ['prɛfəs] *n* : prefacio *m*, prólogo *m*

prefatory ['prɛfə,tori] *adj* : preliminar

prefect ['pri:,fɛkt] *n* **1** : prefecto *m* (oficial) **2** : monitor *m*, -tora *f* (estudiante)

prefer [pri'fər] *vt* -ferred; -ferring **1** : preferir ⟨I prefer coffee : prefiero café⟩ **2** to prefer charges against : presentar cargos contra

preferable ['prɛfərəbəl] *adj* : preferible

preferably ['prɛfərəbli] *adv* : preferentemente, de preferencia

preference ['prɛfrənts, 'prɛfər-] *n* : preferencia *f*, gusto *m*

preferential [,prɛfə'rɛntʃəl] *adj* : preferencial, preferente

prefigure [pri'fɪɡjər] *vt* -ured; -uring FORESHADOW : prefigurar, anunciar

prefix ['pri:,fɪks] *n* : prefijo *m*

pregnancy ['prɛɡnəntsi] *n, pl* -cies : embarazo *m*, preñez *f*

pregnant ['prɛɡnənt] *adj* **1** : embarazada (dícese de una mujer), preñada (dícese de un animal) **2** MEANINGFUL : significativo

preheat [,pri:'hi:t] *vt* : precalentar

prehensile [pri'hentsəl, -'hɛn,saɪl] *adj* : prensil

prehistoric [,pri:his'tɔrɪk] *or* **prehistorical** [-ɪkəl] *adj* : prehistórico

prejudge [,pri:'ʤʌʤ] *vt* -judged; -judging : prejuzgar

prejudice¹ ['prɛʤədəs] *vt* -diced; -dicing **1** DAMAGE : perjudicar **2** BIAS : predisponer, influir en

prejudice² *n* **1** DAMAGE : perjuicio *m* (en derecho) **2** BIAS : prejuicio *m*

prelate ['prɛlət] *n* : prelado *m*

preliminary¹ [pri'lɪmə,nɛri] *adj* : preliminar

preliminary² *n, pl* -naries **1** : preámbulo *m*, preludio *m* **2** **preliminaries** *npl* : preliminares *mpl*

prelude ['prɛ,lu:d, 'prɛl,ju:d;, 'preɪ,lu:d, 'pri:-] *n* : preludio *m*

premarital [,pri:'mærətəl] *adj* : prematrimonial

premature [,pri:mə'tʊr, -'tjʊr, -'tʃʊr] *adj* : prematuro — **prematurely** *adv*

premeditate [pri'mɛdə,teɪt] *vt* -tated; -tating : premeditar

premeditation [pri,mɛdə'teɪʃən] *n* : premeditación *f*

premenstrual [pri'mɛntstruəl] *adj* : premenstrual

premenstrual syndrome *n* : síndrome *m* premenstrual, SPM *m*

premier¹ [pri'mɪr, -'mjɪr;, 'pri:miər] *adj* : principal

premier² *n* PRIME MINISTER : primer ministro *m*, primera ministra *f*

premiere¹ [pri'mjɛr, -'mɪr] *vt* -miered; -miering : estrenar

premiere² *n* : estreno *m*

premise ['prɛmɪs] *n* **1** : premisa *f* ⟨the premise of his arguments : la premisa de sus argumentos⟩ **2 premises** *npl* : recinto *m*, local *m*

premium ['pri:miəm] *n* **1** BONUS : prima *f* **2** SURCHARGE : recargo *m* ⟨to sell at a premium : vender (algo) muy caro⟩ **3 insurance premium** : prima *f* (de seguros) **4 to set a premium on** : darle un gran valor (a algo)

premonition [,pri:mə'nɪʃən, ,prɛmə-] *n* : presentimiento *m*, premonición *f*

prenatal [,pri:'neɪtəl] *adj* : prenatal

preoccupation [pri,ɑkjə'peɪʃən] *n* : preocupación *f*

preoccupied [pri'ɑkjə,paɪd] *adj* : abstraído, ensimismado, preocupado

preoccupy [pri'ɑkjə,paɪ] *vt* -pied; -pying : preocupar

preparation [,prɛpə'reɪʃən] *n* **1** PREPARING : preparación *f* **2** MIXTURE : preparado *m* ⟨a preparation for burns : un preparado para quemaduras⟩ **3 preparations** *npl* ARRANGEMENTS : preparativos *mpl*

preparatory [pri'pærə,tori] *adj* : preparatorio

preparatory school → prep school

prepare [pri'pær] *v* -pared; -paring *vt* : preparar — *vi* : prepararse

prepay [,pri:'peɪ] *vt* -paid; -paying : pagar por adelantado

preponderance [pri'pɑndərənts] *n* : preponderancia *f*

preponderant [pri'pɑndərənt] *adj* : preponderante — **preponderantly** *adv*

preposition [,prɛpə'zɪʃən] *n* : preposición *f*

prepositional [,prɛpə'zɪʃənəl] *adj* : preposicional

prepossessing [,pri:pə'zɛsɪŋ] *adj* : atractivo, agradable

preposterous [pri'pɑstərəs] *adj* : absurdo, ridículo

prep school [,prɛp-] *n* : escuela *f* secundaria privada

prerecorded [,pri:rɪ'kɔrdəd] *adj* : pregrabado

prerequisite¹ [pri'rɛkwəzət] *adj* : necesario, esencial

prerequisite² *n* : condición *f* necesario, requisito *m* previo

prerogative [pri'rɑɡətɪv] *n* : prerrogativa *f*

presage ['prɛsɪʤ, pri'seɪʤ] *vt* -saged; -saging : presagiar

preschool ['pri:ˌskuːl] *adj* : preescolar
preschooler ['pri:ˌskuːlər] *n* : párvulo *m*, -la *f*; estudiante *mf* de preescolar
prescient ['prɛʃənt] *adj* : profético
prescribe [pri'skraɪb] *vt* -**scribed**; -**scribing** **1** ORDAIN : prescribir, ordenar **2** : recetar (medicinas, etc.)
prescription [pri'skrɪpʃən] *n* : receta *f*
presence ['prɛzənts] *n* : presencia *f*
presence of mind *n* : aplomo *m*
present[1] [pri'zɛnt] *vt* **1** INTRODUCE : presentar ⟨to present oneself : presentarse⟩ **2** : presentar (una obra de teatro, etc.) **3** GIVE : entregar (un regalo, etc.), regalar, obsequiar **4** SHOW : presentar, ofrecer ⟨it presents a lovely view : ofrece una vista muy linda⟩
present[2] ['prɛzənt] *adj* **1** : actual ⟨present conditions : condiciones actuales⟩ **2** : presente ⟨all the students were present : todos los estudiantes estaban presentes⟩
present[3] ['prɛzənt] *n* **1** GIFT : regalo *m*, obsequio *m* **2** : presente *m* ⟨at present : en este momento⟩ **3** *or* **present tense** : presente *m*
presentable [pri'zɛntəbəl] *adj* : presentable
presentation [ˌpri:ˌzɛn'teɪʃən, ˌprɛzən-] *n* : presentación *f* ⟨presentation ceremony : ceremonia de entrega⟩
present–day ['prɛzənt'deɪ] *adj* : actual, de hoy en día
presenter [pri'zɛntər] *n* : presentador *m*, -dora *f*
presentiment [pri'zɛntəmənt] *n* : presentimiento *m*, premonición *f*
presently ['prɛzəntli] *adv* **1** SOON : pronto, dentro de poco **2** NOW : actualmente, ahora
present participle *n* : participio *m* presente, participio *m* activo
preservation [ˌprɛzər'veɪʃən] *n* : conservación *f*, preservación *f*
preservative [pri'zərvətɪv] *n* : conservante *m*
preserve[1] [pri'zərv] *vt* -**served**; -**serving** **1** PROTECT : proteger, preservar **2** : conservar (los alimentos, etc.) **3** MAINTAIN : conservar, mantener
preserve[2] *n* **1** *or* **preserves** *npl* : conserva *f* ⟨peach preserves : duraznos en conserva⟩ **2** : coto *m* ⟨game preserve : coto de caza⟩
preside [pri'zaɪd] *vi* -**sided**; -**siding** **1 to preside over** : presidir ⟨he presided over the meeting : presidió la reunión⟩ **2 to preside over** : supervisar ⟨she presides over the department : dirige el departamento⟩
presidency ['prɛzədəntsi] *n*, *pl* -**cies** : presidencia *f*
president ['prɛzədənt] *n* : presidente *m*, -ta *f*
presidential [ˌprɛzə'dɛntʃəl] *adj* : presidencial
press[1] ['prɛs] *vt* **1** PUSH : apretar (un botón, etc.) **2** SQUEEZE : apretar, prensar (frutas, flores, etc.) **3** IRON : planchar (ropa) **4** URGE : instar, apremiar ⟨he pressed me to come : insistió en

que viniera⟩ **5** STRESS : recalcar ⟨to press the point/issue : insistir⟩ **6** IMPOSE : imponer **7 to press charges against** : demandar a **8 to press the flesh** *fam* : estrechar manos — *vi* **1** PUSH : apretar ⟨press hard : aprieta con fuerza⟩ **2** CROWD : apiñarse **3** : abrirse paso ⟨I pressed through the crowd : me abrí paso entre el gentío⟩ **4** URGE : presionar **5 to press ahead/on/forward** : seguir adelante **6 to press for** DEMAND : exigir, presionar para
press[2] *n* **1** CROWD : multitud *f* **2** : imprenta *f*, prensa *f* ⟨to go to press : entrar en prensa⟩ **3** URGENCY : urgencia *f*, prisa *f* **4** PRINTER, PUBLISHER : imprenta *f*, editorial *f* **5 the press** : la prensa ⟨freedom of the press : libertad de prensa⟩
press conference *n* : conferencia *f* de prensa, rueda *f* de prensa
pressing ['prɛsɪŋ] *adj* URGENT : urgente
press release *n* : boletín *m* de prensa
pressure[1] ['prɛʃər] *vt* -**sured**; -**suring** : presionar, apremiar
pressure[2] *n* **1** : presión *f* ⟨to be under pressure : estar bajo presión⟩ **2** → **blood pressure**
pressure cooker *n* : olla *f* a presión
pressure group *n* : grupo *m* de presión
pressurize ['prɛʃəˌraɪz] *vt* -**ized**; -**izing** : presurizar
prestige [prɛ'stiːʒ, -'stiːdʒ] *n* : prestigio *m*
prestigious [prɛ'stɪdʒəs] *adj* : prestigioso
presto ['prɛsˌtoː] *adv* : de pronto
presumably [pri'zuːməbli] *adv* : es de suponer, supuestamente ⟨presumably, he's guilty : supone que es culpable⟩
presume [pri'zuːm] *vt* -**sumed**; -**suming** **1** ASSUME, SUPPOSE : suponer, asumir, presumir **2 to presume to** : atreverse a, osar
presumption [pri'zʌmpʃən] *n* **1** AUDACITY : atrevimiento *m*, osadía *f* **2** ASSUMPTION : presunción *f*, suposición *f*
presumptuous [pri'zʌmptʃʊəs] *adj* : descarado, atrevido
presuppose [ˌpri:sə'poːz] *vt* -**posed**; -**posing** : presuponer
preteen ['pri:ˌtiːn] *n* : preadolescente *nmf*
pretend [pri'tɛnd] *vt* **1** CLAIM : pretender ⟨I won't pretend to understand it : no voy a pretender comprenderlo⟩ **2** FEIGN : fingir, simular ⟨to pretend to do something : fingir hacer algo⟩ ⟨he pretended everything was fine : fingía que todo estaba bien⟩ ⟨she pretended not to hear me : hacía como si no me oyera⟩ — *vi* : fingir
pretender [pri'tɛndər] *n* : pretendiente *mf* (al trono, etc.)
pretense *or* **pretence** ['pri:ˌtɛnts, pri'tɛnts] *n* **1** CLAIM : afirmación *f* (falsa), pretensión *f* **2** FEIGNING : fingimiento *m*, simulación *f* ⟨to make a pretense of doing something : fingir hacer algo⟩ ⟨a pretense of order : una apariencia de orden⟩ **3** PRETEXT : pretexto *m* ⟨under false pretenses : con pretextos falsos, de manera fraudulenta⟩

pretension [pri'tentʃən] n 1 CLAIM : pretensión f, afirmación f 2 ASPIRATION : aspiración f, ambición f 3 PRETENTIOUSNESS : pretensiones fpl, presunción f

pretentious [pri'tentʃəs] adj : pretencioso

pretentiousness [pri'tentʃənəs] n : presunción f, pretensiones fpl

preterit ['preterət] nm : pretérito m

pretext ['pri:ˌtekst] n : pretexto m, excusa f

prettily ['pritəli] adv : atractivamente

prettiness ['pritinəs] n : lindeza f

pretty¹ ['priti] adv : bastante, bien ⟨it's pretty obvious : está bien claro⟩ ⟨it's pretty much the same : es más o menos igual⟩

pretty² adj prettier; -est : bonito, lindo, guapo ⟨a pretty girl : una muchacha guapa⟩ ⟨what a pretty dress! : ¡qué vestido más lindo!⟩

pretzel ['pretsəl] n : galleta f salada (en forma de nudo)

prevail [pri'veɪl] vi 1 TRIUMPH : prevalecer 2 PREDOMINATE : predominar 3 **to prevail upon** : persuadir, convencer ⟨I prevailed upon her to sing : la convencí para que cantara⟩

prevailing [pri'veɪlɪŋ] adj : imperante, prevaleciente

prevalence ['prevələns] n : preponderancia f, predominio m

prevalent ['prevələnt] adj 1 COMMON : común y corriente, general 2 WIDESPREAD : extendido

prevaricate [pri'værəˌkeɪt] vi -cated; -cating LIE : mentir

prevarication [priˌværə'keɪʃən] n : mentira f

prevent [pri'vent] vt 1 AVOID : prevenir, evitar ⟨steps to prevent war : medidas para evitar la guerra⟩ 2 HINDER : impedir

preventable [pri'ventəbəl] adj : evitable

preventative [pri'ventətɪv] → preventive

prevention [pri'ventʃən] n : prevención f

preventive [pri'ventɪv] adj : preventivo

preview ['pri:ˌvju] n : preestreno m

previous ['pri:viəs] adj : previo, anterior ⟨previous knowledge : conocimientos previos⟩ ⟨the previous day : el día anterior⟩ ⟨in the previous year : en el año pasado⟩

previously ['pri:viəsli] adv : antes

prewar [ˌpri:'wɔr] adj : de antes de la guerra

prey¹ ['preɪ] n, pl **preys** : presa f

prey² vi 1 : cazar, alimentarse de ⟨it preys on fish : se alimenta de peces⟩ 2 **to prey on one's mind** : hacer presa en alguien, atormentar a alguien

price¹ ['praɪs] vt **priced; pricing** : poner un precio a ⟨to be reasonably/competitively priced : tener precios razonables/competitivos⟩

price² n 1 : precio m ⟨to pay the price for something : pagar el precio de algo⟩ ⟨price tag : etiqueta de precio⟩ ⟨price range : gama de precios⟩ ⟨to go up/down in price : subir/bajar de precio⟩

⟨price cut : rebaja en el precio⟩ 2 **at any price** : a toda costa

priceless ['praɪsləs] adj : inestimable, inapreciable

pricey ['praɪsi] adj : caro

prick¹ ['prɪk] vt 1 : pinchar 2 **to prick up one's ears** : levantar las orejas — vi : pinchar

prick² n 1 STAB : pinchazo m ⟨a prick of conscience : un remordimiento⟩ 2 → **pricker**

pricker ['prɪkər] n THORN : espina f

prickle¹ ['prɪkəl] vi -led; -ling : sentir un cosquilleo, tener un hormigueo

prickle² n 1 : espina f (de una planta) 2 TINGLE : cosquilleo m, hormigueo m

prickly ['prɪkəli] adj 1 THORNY : espinoso 2 : que pica ⟨a prickly sensation : un hormigueo⟩

prickly pear n 1 : nopal m, tuna f (planta) 2 : tuna f, higo m chumbo (fruta)

pride¹ ['praɪd] vt **prided; priding** : estar orgulloso de ⟨to pride oneself on : preciarse de, enorgullecerse de⟩

pride² n : orgullo m

priest ['pri:st] n : sacerdote m, cura m

priestess ['pri:stɪs] n : sacerdotisa f

priesthood ['pri:stˌhud] n : sacerdocio m

priestly ['pri:stli] adj : sacerdotal

prig ['prɪg] n : mojigato m, -ta f; gazmoño m, -ña f

prim ['prɪm] adj **primmer; primmest** 1 PRISSY : remilgado 2 PRUDISH : mojigato, gazmoño

prima ballerina ['pri:mə-] n : prima ballerina f

prima donna [ˌprɪmə'danə, ˌpri:-] n : divo m, diva f

primarily [praɪ'merəli] adv : principalmente, fundamentalmente

primary¹ ['praɪˌmeri, 'praɪməri] adj 1 FIRST : primario 2 PRINCIPAL : principal 3 BASIC : fundamental

primary² n, pl -ries : elección f primaria

primary color n : color m primario

primary school n : elementary school

primate n 1 ['praɪˌmeɪt, -mət] : primado m (obispo) 2 [-ˌmeɪt] : primate m (animal)

prime¹ ['praɪm] vt **primed; priming** 1 : cebar ⟨to prime a pump : cebar una bomba⟩ 2 PREPARE : preparar (una superficie para pintar) 3 COACH : preparar (a un testigo, etc.)

prime² adj 1 CHIEF, MAIN : principal, primero 2 EXCELLENT : de primera (categoría), excelente

prime³ n **the prime of one's life** : la flor de la vida

prime minister n : primer ministro m, primera ministra f

prime number n : número m primo

primer¹ ['prɪmər] n 1 READER : cartilla f 2 MANUAL : manual m

primer² ['praɪmər] n 1 : cebo m (para explosivos) 2 : base f (de pintura)

prime time n : horas fpl de mayor audiencia

primeval [praɪ'mi:vəl] adj : primitivo, primigenio

primitive [ˈprɪmətɪv] *adj* : primitivo

primly [ˈprɪmli] *adv* : mojigatamente

primness [ˈprɪmnəs] *n* : mojigatería *f*, gazmoñería *f*

primordial [praɪˈmɔrdiəl] *adj* : primordial, fundamental

primp [ˈprɪmp] *vi* : arreglarse, acicalarse

primrose [ˈprɪmˌroːz] *n* : primavera *f*, prímula *f*

prince [ˈprɪnts] *n* : príncipe *m*

princely [ˈprɪntsli] *adj* : principesco

princess [ˈprɪntsəs, ˈprɪnˌses] *n* : princesa *f*

principal¹ [ˈprɪntsəpəl] *adj* : principal — **principally** *adv*

principal² *n* **1** PROTAGONIST : protagonista *mf* **2** : director *m*, -tora *f* (de una escuela) **3** CAPITAL : principal *m*, capital *m* (en finanzas)

principality [ˌprɪntsəˈpælətɪ] *n, pl* **-ties** : principado *m*

principle [ˈprɪntsəpəl] *n* **1** : principio *m* ⟨it's against my principles : va en contra de mis principios⟩ ⟨it's a matter of principle : es una cuestión de principios⟩ **2 as a matter of principle** : por principio **3 in principle** : en principio **4 on principle** : por principio

print¹ [ˈprɪnt] *vt* **1** : imprimir (libros, etc.) **2** : publicar **3** : estampar (tela) **4 to print out** : imprimir — *vi* : escribir con letra de molde/imprenta

print² *n* **1** IMPRESSION : marca *f*, huella *f*, impresión *f* **2** : texto *m* impreso ⟨to be out of print : estar agotado⟩ **3** LETTERING : letra *f* **4** ENGRAVING : grabado *m* **5** : copia *f* (en fotografía) **6** : estampado *m* (de tela)

printer [ˈprɪntər] *n* **1** : impresor *m*, -sora *f* (persona) **2** : impresora *f* (máquina)

printing [ˈprɪntɪŋ] *n* **1** : impresión *f* (acto) ⟨the third printing : la tercera tirada⟩ **2** : imprenta *f* (profesión) **3** LETTERING : letras *fpl* de molde

printing press *n* : prensa *f*

print out *vt* : imprimir (de una computadora)

printout [ˈprɪntˌaʊt] *n* : copia *f* impresa (de una computadora)

prior¹ [ˈpraɪər] *adj* **1** : previo ⟨prior engagement/commitment : compromiso previo⟩ ⟨without prior notice : sin previo aviso⟩ **2 prior to** : antes de

prior² *n* : prior *m*

prioress [ˈpraɪərəs] *n* : priora *f*

priority [praɪˈɔrətɪ] *n, pl* **-ties** : prioridad *f*

priory [ˈpraɪərɪ] *n, pl* **-ries** : priorato *m*

prism [ˈprɪzəm] *n* : prisma *m*

prison [ˈprɪzən] *n* : prisión *f*, cárcel *f* ⟨he's in prison : está preso, está en la cárcel⟩ ⟨they put him in prison : lo encarcelaron, lo metieron en la cárcel⟩ ⟨a prison sentence : una pena de prisión⟩ ⟨she was sentenced to ten years in prison : fue condenada a diez años de prisión⟩

prisoner [ˈprɪzənər] *n* : preso *m*, -sa *f*; recluso *m*, -sa *f* ⟨prisoner of war : prisionero de guerra⟩

prison warden → **warden**

prissy [ˈprɪsi] *adj* **prissier; -est** : remilgado, melindroso

pristine [ˈprɪsˌtiːn, prɪsˈ-] *adj* : puro, prístino

privacy [ˈpraɪvəsi] *n, pl* **-cies** : privacidad *f*

private¹ [ˈpraɪvət] *adj* **1** PERSONAL : privado, particular ⟨private property : propiedad privada⟩ **2** INDEPENDENT : privado, independiente ⟨private studies : estudios privados⟩ **3** SECRET : secreto **4** SECLUDED : aislado, privado **5** SHY : reservado — **privately** *adv*

private² *n* : soldado *m* raso

private detective → **private investigator**

private enterprise → **free enterprise**

private eye *fam* → **private investigator**

private investigator *n* : investigador *m* privado, investigadora *f* privada, detective *m* privado, detective *f* privada

private school *n* : escuela *f* privada

privation [praɪˈveɪʃən] *n* : privación *f*

privatize [ˈpraɪvəˌtaɪz] *vt* **-ized; -izing** : privatizar

privilege [ˈprɪvlɪdʒ, ˈprɪvə-] *n* : privilegio *m*

privileged [ˈprɪvlɪdʒd, ˈprɪvə-] *adj* : privilegiado

privy¹ [ˈprɪvi] *adj* **to be privy to** : estar enterado de

privy² *n, pl* **privies** : excusado *m*, retrete *m* (exterior)

prize¹ [ˈpraɪz] *vt* **prized; prizing** : valorar, apreciar

prize² *adj* **1** : premiado ⟨a prize stallion : un semental premiado⟩ **2** OUTSTANDING : de primera, excepcional

prize³ *n* **1** AWARD : premio *m* ⟨third prize : el tercer premio⟩ **2** : joya *f*, tesoro *m* ⟨he's a real prize : es un tesoro⟩

prizefighter [ˈpraɪzˌfaɪtər] *n* : boxeador *m*, -dora *f* profesional

prizewinner [ˈpraɪzˌwɪnər] *n* : premiado *m*, -da *f*

prizewinning [ˈpraɪzˌwɪnɪŋ] *adj* : premiado, galardonado

pro¹ [ˈproː] *adv* : a favor

pro² *adj* → **professional¹**

pro³ *n* **1** : pro *m* ⟨the pros and cons : los pros y los contras⟩ **2** → **professional²**

pro- *pref* : pro-

probability [ˌprɑbəˈbɪlətɪ] *n, pl* **-ties** : probabilidad *f*

probable [ˈprɑbəbəl] *adj* : probable — **probably** [-blɪ] *adv*

probate¹ [ˈproːˌbeɪt] *vt* **-bated; -bating** : autenticar (un testamento)

probate² *n* : autenticación *f* (de un testamento)

probation [proːˈbeɪʃən] *n* **1** : período *m* de prueba (para un empleado, etc.) **2** : libertad *f* condicional (para un preso) ⟨to put someone on probation : dejar/poner a alguien en libertad condicional⟩

probationary [proːˈbeɪʃəˌneri] *adj* : de prueba

probe¹ [ˈproːb] *vt* **probed; probing 1** : sondar (en medicina y tecnología) **2** INVESTIGATE : investigar, sondear

probe² *n* **1** : sonda *f* (en medicina, etc.) ⟨space probe : sonda espacial⟩ **2** INVESTIGATION : investigación *f*, sondeo *m*

probity ['proːbət̬i] n : probidad f

problem¹ ['prɑbləm] adj : difícil

problem² n : problema m

problematic [ˌprɑbləˈmæt̬ɪk] or problematical [-t̬ɪkəl] adj : problemático

proboscis [prəˈbɑsɪs] n, pl -cises also -cides [-səˌdiːz] : trompa f, probóscide f

procedural [prəˈsiːd͡ʒərəl] adj : de procedimiento

procedure [prəˈsiːd͡ʒər] n : procedimiento m ⟨administrative procedures : trámites administrativos⟩

proceed [proˈsiːd] vi 1 : proceder ⟨to proceed to do something : proceder a hacer algo⟩ 2 CONTINUE : continuar, proseguir, seguir ⟨he proceeded to the next phase : pasó a la segunda fase⟩ 3 ADVANCE : avanzar ⟨as the conference proceeded : mientras seguía avanzando la conferencia⟩ ⟨the road proceeds south : la calle sigue hacia el sur⟩

proceeding [proˈsiːdɪŋ] n 1 PROCEDURE : procedimiento m 2 proceedings npl EVENTS : acontecimientos mpl 3 proceedings npl MINUTES : actas fpl (de una reunión, etc.)

proceeds ['proːˌsiːdz] npl : ganancias fpl

process¹ ['prɑˌsɛs, 'proː-] vt : procesar, tratar

process² n, pl -cesses ['prɑˌsɛsəz, 'proː-, -səsəz, -səˌsiːz] 1 : proceso m ⟨the process of elimination : el proceso de eliminación⟩ 2 METHOD : proceso m, método m ⟨manufacturing processes : procesos industriales⟩ 3 : acción f judicial ⟨due process of law : el debido proceso (de la ley)⟩ 4 SUMMONS : citación f 5 PROJECTION : protuberancia f (anatómica) 6 in the process of : en vías de ⟨in the process of repair : en reparaciones⟩

processing n : procesamiento m (en informática)

procession [prəˈsɛʃən] n : procesión f, desfile m ⟨a funeral procession : un cortejo fúnebre⟩

processional [prəˈsɛʃənəl] n : himno m para una procesión

processor ['prɑˌsɛsər, 'proː-, -səsər] n 1 : procesador m (de una computadora) 2 food processor : procesador m de alimentos

proclaim [proˈkleɪm] vt : proclamar

proclamation [ˌprɑkləˈmeɪʃən] n : proclamación f

proclivity [proˈklɪvət̬i] n, pl -ties : proclividad f

procrastinate [prəˈkræstəˌneɪt] vi -nated; -nating : demorar, aplazar las responsabilidades

procrastination [prəˌkræstəˈneɪʃən] n : aplazamiento m, demora f, dilación f

procreate ['proːkriˌeɪt] vi -ated; -ating : procrear

procreation [ˌproːkriˈeɪʃən] n : procreación f

proctor¹ ['prɑktər] vt : supervisar (un examen)

proctor² n : supervisor m, -sora f (de un examen)

procure [prəˈkjʊr] vt -cured; -curing 1 OBTAIN : procurar, obtener 2 BRING ABOUT : provocar, lograr, conseguir

procurement [prəˈkjʊrmənt] n : obtención f

prod¹ ['prɑd] vt prodded; prodding 1 JAB, POKE : pinchar, golpear (con la punta de algo) 2 GOAD : incitar, estimular

prod² n 1 JAB, POKE : golpe m (con la punta de algo), pinchazo m 2 STIMULUS : estímulo m 3 cattle prod : picana f, aguijón m

prodigal¹ ['prɑdɪgəl] adj SPENDTHRIFT : pródigo, despilfarrador, derrochador

prodigal² n : pródigo m, -ga f; derrochador m, -dora f

prodigious [prəˈdɪd͡ʒəs] adj 1 MARVELOUS : prodigioso, maravilloso 2 HUGE : enorme, vasto ⟨prodigious sums : muchísimo dinero⟩ — prodigiously adv

prodigy ['prɑdəd͡ʒi] n, pl -gies : prodigio m ⟨child prodigy : niño prodigio⟩

produce¹ [prəˈduːs, -ˈdjuːs] vt -duced; -ducing 1 EXHIBIT : presentar, mostrar 2 YIELD : producir 3 CAUSE : producir, causar 4 CREATE : producir ⟨to produce a poem : escribir un poema⟩ 5 : poner en escena (una obra de teatro), producir (una película)

produce² ['prɑˌduːs, 'proː-, -ˌdjuːs] n : productos mpl agrícolas

producer [prəˈduːsər, -ˈdjuː-] n : productor m, -tora f

product ['prɑˌdʌkt] n : producto m

production [prəˈdʌkʃən] n : producción f

productive [prəˈdʌktɪv] adj : productivo

productivity [ˌproːˌdʌkˈtɪvət̬i, ˌprɑ-] n : productividad f

profane¹ [proˈfeɪn] vt -faned; -faning : profanar

profane² adj 1 SECULAR : profano 2 IRREVERENT : irreverente, impío

profanity [proˈfænət̬i] n, pl -ties 1 IRREVERENCE : irreverencia f, impiedad f 2 : blasfemias fpl, obscenidades fpl ⟨don't use profanity : no digas blasfemias⟩

profess [prəˈfɛs] vt 1 DECLARE : declarar, manifestar 2 CLAIM : pretender 3 : profesar (una religión, etc.)

professedly [prəˈfɛsədli] adv 1 OPENLY : declaradamente 2 ALLEGEDLY : supuestamente

profession [prəˈfɛʃən] n : profesión f

professional¹ [prəˈfɛʃənəl] adj : profesional — professionally adv

professional² n : profesional mf

professionalism [prəˈfɛʃənəˌlɪzəm] n : profesionalismo m

professor [prəˈfɛsər] n : profesor m (universitario), profesora f (universitaria); catedrático m, -ca f

professorship [prəˈfɛsərˌʃɪp] n : cátedra f

proffer ['prɑfər] vt -fered; -fering : ofrecer, dar

proficiency [prəˈfɪʃəntsi] n : competencia f, capacidad f

proficient [prəˈfɪʃənt] adj : competente, experto — proficiently adv

profile ['pro:ˌfaɪl] n : perfil m ⟨a portrait in profile : un retrato de perfil⟩ ⟨to keep a low profile : no llamar la atención, hacerse pasar desapercibido⟩

profit¹ ['prɑfət] vi : sacar provecho (de), beneficiarse (de)

profit² n 1 ADVANTAGE : provecho m, partido m, beneficio m 2 GAIN : beneficio m, utilidad f, ganancia f ⟨to make a profit : sacar beneficios⟩

profitability [ˌprɑfətəˈbɪləti] n : rentabilidad f

profitable ['prɑfətəbəl] adj : rentable, lucrativo — **profitably** [-bli] adv

profitless ['prɑfətləs] adj : infructuoso, inútil

profligate ['prɑflɪɡət, -ˌɡeɪt] adj 1 DISSOLUTE : disoluto, licencioso 2 SPENDTHRIFT : despilfarrador, derrochador, pródigo

profound [prəˈfaʊnd] adj : profundo

profoundly [prəˈfaʊndli] adv : profundamente, en profundidad

profundity [prəˈfʌndəti] n, pl **-ties** : profundidad f

profuse [prəˈfjuːs] adj 1 COPIOUS : profuso, copioso 2 LAVISH : pródigo — **profusely** adv

profusion [prəˈfjuːʒən] n : abundancia f, profusión f

progenitor [proˈdʒɛnətər] n : progenitor m, -tora f

progeny ['prɑdʒəni] n, pl **-nies** : progenie f

progesterone [proˈdʒɛstəˌroːn] n : progesterona f

prognosis [prɑɡˈnoːsɪs] n, pl **-noses** [-ˌsiːz] : pronóstico m (médico)

program¹ ['proːˌɡræm, -ɡrəm] vt **-grammed** or **-gramed; -gramming** or **-graming** : programar

program² n : programa m

programmable ['proːˌɡræməbəl] adj : programable

programmer ['proːˌɡræmər] n : programador m, -dora f

programming ['proːˌɡræmɪŋ] n : programación f

progress¹ [prəˈɡrɛs] vi 1 PROCEED : progresar, adelantar 2 IMPROVE : mejorar

progress² ['prɑɡrəs, -ˌɡrɛs] n 1 ADVANCE : progreso m, adelanto m, avance m ⟨to make progress : hacer progresos⟩ 2 BETTERMENT : mejora f, mejoramiento m

progression [prəˈɡrɛʃən] n 1 ADVANCE : avance m 2 SEQUENCE : desarrollo m (de eventos)

progressive [prəˈɡrɛsɪv] adj 1 : progresista ⟨a progressive society : una sociedad progresista⟩ 2 : progresivo ⟨a progressive disease : una enfermedad progresiva⟩ 3 or **Progressive** : progresista (en política) 4 : progresivo (en gramática)

progressively [prəˈɡrɛsɪvli] adv : progresivamente, poco a poco

prohibit [proˈhɪbət] vt : prohibir

prohibition [ˌproːəˈbɪʃən, ˌproːhə-] n : prohibición f

prohibitive [proˈhɪbətɪv] adj : prohibitivo

project¹ [prəˈdʒɛkt] vt 1 PLAN : proyectar, planear 2 : proyectar (imágenes, misiles, etc.) — vi PROTRUDE : sobresalir, salir

project² ['prɑˌdʒɛkt, -dʒɪkt] n : proyecto m, trabajo m (de un estudiante) ⟨research project : proyecto de investigación⟩

projectile [prəˈdʒɛktəl, -ˌtaɪl] n : proyectil m

projection [prəˈdʒɛkʃən] n 1 PLAN : plan m, proyección f 2 : proyección f (de imágenes, misiles, etc.) 3 PROTRUSION : saliente m

projectionist [prəˈdʒɛkʃənɪst] n : proyeccionista mf; operador m, -dora f

projector [prəˈdʒɛktər] n : proyector m

proletarian¹ [ˌproːləˈtɛriən] adj : proletario

proletarian² n : proletario m, -ria f

proletariat [ˌproːləˈtɛriət] n : proletariado m

proliferate [prəˈlɪfəˌreɪt] vi **-ated; -ating** : proliferar

proliferation [prəˌlɪfəˈreɪʃən] n : proliferación f

prolific [prəˈlɪfɪk] adj : prolífico

prologue ['proːˌlɔɡ] n : prólogo m

prolong [prəˈlɔŋ] vt : prolongar

prolongation [ˌproːˌlɔŋˈɡeɪʃən] n : prolongación f

prom ['prɑm] n : baile m formal (de un colegio)

promenade¹ [ˌprɑməˈneɪd, -ˈnɑd] vi **-naded; -nading** : pasear, pasearse, dar un paseo

promenade² n : paseo m

prominence ['prɑmənənts] n 1 PROJECTION : prominencia f 2 EMINENCE : eminencia f, prestigio m

prominent ['prɑmənənt] adj 1 OUTSTANDING : prominente, destacado 2 PROJECTING : prominente, saliente

prominently ['prɑmənəntli] adv : destacadamente, prominentemente

promiscuity [ˌprɑmɪsˈkjuːəti] n, pl **-ties** : promiscuidad f

promiscuous [prəˈmɪskjuəs] adj : promiscuo — **promiscuously** adv

promise¹ ['prɑməs] v **-ised; -ising** : prometer

promise² n 1 : promesa f ⟨he kept his promise : cumplió su promesa⟩ 2 **to show promise** : prometer

promising ['prɑməsɪŋ] adj : prometedor

promissory ['prɑməˌsori] adj : que promete ⟨a promissory note : un pagaré⟩

promontory ['prɑmənˌtori] n, pl **-ries** : promontorio m

promote [prəˈmoːt] vt **-moted; -moting** 1 : ascender (a un alumno o un empleado) 2 ADVERTISE : promocionar, hacerle publicidad a 3 FURTHER : promover, fomentar

promoter [prəˈmoːtər] n : promotor m, -tora f; empresario m, -ria f (en deportes)

promotion [prəˈmoːʃən] n 1 : ascenso m (de un alumno o un empleado) 2 FURTHERING : promoción f, fomento m 3

ADVERTISING : publicidad *f*, propaganda *f*

promotional [prə'moːʃənəl] *adj* : promocional

prompt¹ ['prɑmpt] *vt* 1 INDUCE : provocar (una cosa), inducir (a una persona) ⟨curiosity prompted me to ask you : la curiosidad me indujo a preguntarle⟩ 2 : apuntar (a un actor, etc.)

prompt² *adj* : pronto, rápido ⟨prompt payment : pago puntual⟩

prompter ['prɑmptər] *n* : apuntador *m*, -dora *f* (en teatro)

promptly ['prɑmptli] *adv* : inmediatamente, rápidamente

promptness ['prɑmptnəs] *n* : prontitud *f*, rapidez *f*

promulgate ['prɑməl,geɪt] *vt* -gated; -gating : promulgar

prone ['proːn] *adj* 1 LIABLE : propenso, proclive ⟨accident-prone : propenso a los accidentes⟩ 2 : boca abajo, decúbito prono ⟨in a prone position : en decúbito prono⟩

prong ['prɔŋ] *n* : punta *f*, diente *m*

pronoun ['proː,naʊn] *n* : pronombre *m*

pronounce [prə'naʊnts] *vt* -nounced; -nouncing 1 : pronunciar ⟨how do you pronounce your name? : ¿cómo se pronuncia su nombre?⟩ 2 DECLARE : declarar 3 to pronounce sentence : dictar sentencia, pronunciar un fallo

pronounced [prə'naʊntst] *adj* MARKED : pronunciado, marcado

pronouncement [prə'naʊntsmənt] *n* : declaración *f*

pronunciation [prə,nʌntsi'eɪʃən] *n* : pronunciación *f*

proof¹ ['pruːf] *adj* : a prueba ⟨proof against tampering : a prueba de manipulación⟩

proof² *n* : prueba *f*

proofread ['pruːf,riːd] *v* -read; -reading *vt* : corregir — *vi* : corregir pruebas

proofreader ['pruːf,riːdər] *n* : corrector *m*, -tora *f* (de pruebas)

prop¹ ['prɑp] *vt* propped; propping 1 to prop against : apoyar contra 2 to prop up SUPPORT : apoyar, apuntalar, sostener 3 to prop up SUSTAIN : alentar (a alguien), darle ánimo (a alguien)

prop² *n* 1 SUPPORT : puntal *m*, apoyo *m*, soporte *m* 2 : accesorio *m* (en teatro)

propaganda [,prɑpə'gændə, ,proː-] *n* : propaganda *f*

propagandize [,prɑpə'gæn,daɪz, ,proː-] *v* -dized; -dizing *vt* : someter a propaganda — *vi* : hacer propaganda

propagate ['prɑpə,geɪt] *v* -gated; -gating *vi* : propagarse — *vt* : propagar

propagation [,prɑpə'geɪʃən] *n* : propagación *f*

propane ['proː,peɪn] *n* : propano *m*

propel [prə'pɛl] *vt* -pelled; -pelling : impulsar, propulsar, impeler

propellant *or* **propelent** [prə'pɛlənt] *n* : propulsor *m*

propeller [prə'pɛlər] *n* : hélice *f*

propensity [prə'pɛntsəti] *n*, *pl* -ties : propensión *f*, tendencia *f*, inclinación *f*

proper ['prɑpər] *adj* 1 RIGHT, SUITABLE : apropiado, adecuado 2 : propio, mismo ⟨the city proper : la propia ciudad⟩ 3 CORRECT : correcto 4 GENTEEL : fino, refinado, cortés 5 OWN, SPECIAL : propio — **properly** *adv*

proper noun *or* **proper name** *n* : nombre *m* propio

property ['prɑpərti] *n*, *pl* -ties 1 CHARACTERISTIC : característica *f*, propiedad *f* 2 POSSESSIONS : propiedad *f* 3 BUILDING : inmueble *m* 4 LAND, LOT : terreno *m*, lote *m*, parcela *f* 5 PROP : accesorio *m* (en teatro)

prophecy ['prɑfəsi] *n*, *pl* -cies : profecía *f*, vaticinio *m*

prophesy ['prɑfə,saɪ] *v* -sied; -sying *vt* 1 FORETELL : profetizar (como profeta) 2 PREDICT : profetizar, predecir, vaticinar — *vi* : hacer profecías

prophet ['prɑfət] *n* : profeta *m*

prophetic [prə'fɛtɪk] *or* **prophetical** [-tɪkəl] *adj* : profético — **prophetically** [-ɪkli] *adv*

propitiate [proː'pɪʃi,eɪt] *vt* -ated; -ating : propiciar

propitious [prə'pɪʃəs] *adj* : propicio

proponent [prə'poːnənt] *n* : defensor *m*, -sora *f*; partidario *m*, -ria *f*

proportion¹ [prə'porʃən] *vt* : proporcionar ⟨well-proportioned : de buenas proporciones⟩

proportion² *n* 1 RATIO : proporción *f* 2 SYMMETRY : proporción *f*, simetría *f* ⟨out of proportion : desproporcionado⟩ ⟨to keep things in proportion : no exagerar⟩ ⟨you're blowing things out of proportion : estás exagerando⟩ 3 PART, SHARE : parte *f* 4 **proportions** *npl* SIZE : dimensiones *fpl*

proportional [prə'porʃənəl] *adj* : proporcional — **proportionally** *adv*

proportionate [prə'porʃənət] *adj* : proporcional — **proportionately** *adv*

proposal [prə'poːzəl] *n* 1 PROPOSITION : propuesta *f*, proposición *f* ⟨marriage proposal : propuesta de matrimonio⟩ 2 PLAN : proyecto *m*, propuesta *f*

propose [prə'poːz] *v* -posed; -posing *vi* : proponer matrimonio — *vt* 1 INTEND : pensar, proponerse 2 SUGGEST : proponer

proposition [,prɑpə'zɪʃən] *n* 1 PROPOSAL : proposición *f*, propuesta *f* 2 STATEMENT : proposición *f*

propound [prə'paʊnd] *vt* : proponer, exponer

proprietary [prə'praɪə,tɛri] *adj* : propietario, patentado

proprietor [prə'praɪətər] *n* : propietario *m*, -ria *f*

propriety [prə'praɪəti] *n*, *pl* -eties 1 DECORUM : decencia *f*, decoro *m* 2 **proprieties** *npl* CONVENTIONS : convenciones *fpl*, cánones *mpl* sociales

propulsion [prə'pʌlʃən] *n* : propulsión *f*

prosaic [proː'zeɪɪk] *adj* : prosaico

proscribe [proː'skraɪb] *vt* -scribed; -scribing : proscribir

prose ['proːz] *n* : prosa *f*

prosecute [ˈprɑsɪˌkjuːt] vt **-cuted; -cuting 1** CARRY OUT : llevar a cabo **2** : procesar, enjuiciar ⟨prosecuted for fraud : procesado por fraude⟩

prosecution [ˌprɑsɪˈkjuːʃən] n **1** : procesamiento m ⟨the prosecution of forgers : el procesamiento de falsificadores⟩ **2** PROSECUTORS : acusación f ⟨witness for the prosecution : testigo de cargo⟩

prosecutor [ˈprɑsɪˌkjuːtər] n : acusador m, -dora f; fiscal mf

prospect¹ [ˈprɑˌspɛkt] vi : prospectar (el terreno) ⟨to prospect for gold : buscar oro⟩

prospect² n **1** VISTA : vista f, panorama m **2** OPPORTUNITY : posibilidad f, perspectiva f ⟨he has few prospects for employment : tiene pocas posibilidades/ perspectivas de empleo⟩ **3** POSSIBILITY : posibilidad f ⟨the prospect of going to war : la posibilidad de entrar en guerra⟩ **4** CANDIDATE : candidato m, -ta f **5 in próspect** : en perspectiva

prospective [prəˈspɛktɪv, ˈprɑˌspɛk-] adj **1** EXPECTANT : futuro ⟨prospective mother : futura madre⟩ **2** POTENTIAL : potencial, posible ⟨prospective employee : posible empleado⟩

prospector [ˈprɑˌspɛktər, prəˈspɛk-] n : prospector m, -tora f; explorador m, -dora f

prospectus [prəˈspɛktəs] n : prospecto m

prosper [ˈprɑspər] vi : prosperar

prosperity [prɑˈspɛrɪti] n : prosperidad f

prosperous [ˈprɑspərəs] adj : próspero

prostate [ˈprɑˌsteɪt] n : próstata f

prosthesis [prɑsˈθiːsɪs, ˈprɑsθə-] n, pl **-theses** [-ˌsiːz] : prótesis f

prostitute¹ [ˈprɑstəˌtuːt, -ˌtjuːt] vt **-tuted; -tuting 1** : prostituir **2 to prostitute oneself** : prostituirse

prostitute² n : prostituto m, -ta f

prostitution [ˌprɑstəˈtuːʃən, -ˈtjuː-] n : prostitución f

prostrate¹ [ˈprɑˌstreɪt] vt **-trated; -trating 1** : postrar **2 to prostrate oneself** : postrarse

prostrate² adj : postrado

prostration [prɑˈstreɪʃən] n : postración f

protagonist [proˈtægənɪst] n : protagonista m

protect [prəˈtɛkt] vt : proteger

protection [prəˈtɛkʃən] n : protección f

protective [prəˈtɛktɪv] adj : protector

protector [prəˈtɛktər] n **1** : protector m, -tora f (persona) **2** GUARD : protector m (aparato)

protectorate [prəˈtɛktərət] n : protectorado m

protégé [ˈproːtəˌʒeɪ] n : protegido m, -da f

protein [ˈproːˌtiːn] n : proteína f

protest¹ [proˈtɛst, prə-] vt **1** ASSERT : afirmar, declarar **2** : protestar ⟨they protested the decision : protestaron (por) la decisión⟩ — vi **to protest against** : protestar contra

protest² [ˈproːˌtɛst] n **1** DEMONSTRATION : manifestación f (de protesta) ⟨a public protest : una manifestación pública⟩ **2** COMPLAINT : queja f, protesta f

Protestant [ˈprɑtəstənt] n : protestante mf

Protestantism [ˈprɑtəstənˌtɪzəm] n : protestantismo m

protester [proˈtɛstər, prə-] n : manifestante mf

protocol [ˈproːtəˌkɔl] n : protocolo m

proton [ˈproːˌtɑn] n : protón m

protoplasm [ˈproːtəˌplæzəm] n : protoplasma m

prototype [ˈproːtəˌtaɪp] n : prototipo m

protract [proˈtrækt] vt : prolongar

protractor [proˈtræktər] n : transportador m (instrumento)

protrude [proˈtruːd] vi **-truded; -truding** : salir, sobresalir

protrusion [proˈtruːʒən] n : protuberancia f, saliente m

protuberance [proˈtuːbərənts, -ˈtjuː-] n : protuberancia f

proud [ˈpraʊd] adj **1** HAUGHTY : altanero, orgulloso, arrogante **2** : orgulloso ⟨she was proud of her work : estaba orgullosa de su trabajo⟩ ⟨too proud to beg : demasiado orgulloso para rogar⟩ **3** GLORIOUS : glorioso — **proudly** adv

provable [ˈpruːvəbəl] adj : comprobable

prove [ˈpruːv] v **proved; proved** or **proven** [ˈpruːvən]; **proving** vt **1** TEST : probar **2** DEMONSTRATE : probar, demostrar ⟨this proves her guilt, this proves that she is guilty : esto prueba/demuestra que es culpable⟩ ⟨you've already proven your point : ya sé que tienes razón⟩ **3** (show someone/something to be) ⟨can you prove him wrong? : ¿puedes demostrar que está equivocado?⟩ ⟨evidence that proves her guilty : pruebas que demuestran que es culpable⟩ ⟨it has been proven effective : se ha demostrado ser eficaz⟩ — vi **1** : resultar ⟨it proved effective : resultó eficaz⟩ **2 to prove oneself** : demóstrar sus cualidades

Provençal [ˌproːvɑnˈsɑl, ˌprɑvɑn-] n **1** : provenzal mf **2** : provenzal m (idioma) — **Provençal** adj

proverb [ˈprɑˌvərb] n : proverbio m, refrán m

proverbial [prəˈvərbiəl] adj : proverbial

provide [prəˈvaɪd] v **-vided; -viding** vt **1** STIPULATE : estipular **2 to provide with** : proveer de, proporcionar — vi **1** : proveer ⟨the Lord will provide : el Señor proveerá⟩ **2 to provide for** SUPPORT : mantener **3 to provide for** ANTICIPATE : hacer previsiones para, prever

provided [prəˈvaɪdəd] or **provided that** conj : con tal (de) que, siempre que

providence [ˈprɑvədənts] n **1** PRUDENCE : previsión f, prudencia f **2** or **Providence** : providencia f ⟨divine providence : la Divina Providencia⟩ **3** Providence GOD : Providencia f

provident [ˈprɑvədənt] adj **1** PRUDENT : prévisor, prudente **2** FRUGAL : frugal, ahorrativo

providential [ˌprɑvəˈdɛntʃəl] adj : providencial

provider [prəˈvaɪdər] n **1** PURVEYOR : proveedor m, -dora f **2** BREADWINNER : sostén m (económico)

providing that → provided

province ['prɑvɪnʃs] n 1 : provincia f (de un país) ⟨to live in the provinces : vivir en las provincias⟩ 2 FIELD, SPHERE : campo m, competencia f ⟨it's not in my province : no es de mi competencia⟩

provincial [prə'vɪntʃəl] adj 1 : provincial ⟨provincial government : gobierno provincial⟩ 2 : provinciano, pueblerino ⟨a provincial mentality : una mentalidad provinciana⟩

provision¹ [prə'vɪʒən] vt : aprovisionar, abastecer

provision² n 1 PROVIDING : provisión f, suministro m 2 STIPULATION : condición f, salvedad f, estipulación f 3 **provisions** npl : despensa f, víveres mpl, provisiones fpl

provisional [prə'vɪʒənəl] adj : provisional, provisorio — **provisionally** adv

proviso [prə'vaɪˌzo] n, pl **-sos** or **-soes** : condición f, salvedad f, estipulación f

provocation [ˌprɑvə'keɪʃən] n : provocación f

provocative [prə'vɑkətɪv] adj 1 INCITING : provocador 2 SUGGESTIVE : provocativo, insinuante 3 INTRIGUING : que hace pensar

provoke [prə'voːk] vt **-voked; -voking** : provocar

prow ['praʊ] n : proa f

prowess ['praʊəs] n 1 VALOR : valor m, valentía f 2 SKILL : habilidad f, destreza f

prowl ['praʊl] vi : merodear, rondar — vt : rondar por

prowler ['praʊlər] n : merodeador m, -dora f

proximity [prɑk'sɪmət̬i] n : proximidad f

proxy ['prɑksi] n, pl **proxies** 1 : poder m (de actuar en nombre de alguien) ⟨by proxy : por poder⟩ 2 AGENT : apoderado m, -da f; representante m

prude ['pruːd] n : mojigato m, -ta f; gazmoño m, -ña f

prudence ['pruːdənts] n 1 SHREWDNESS : prudencia f, sagacidad f 2 CAUTION : prudencia f, cautela f 3 THRIFT : frugalidad f

prudent ['pruːdənt] adj 1 SHREWD : prudente, sagaz 2 CAUTIOUS, FARSIGHTED : prudente, previsor, precavido 3 THRIFTY : frugal, ahorrativo — **prudently** adv

prudery ['pruːdəri] n, pl **-eries** : mojigatería f, gazmoñería f

prudish ['pruːdɪʃ] adj : mojigato, gazmoño

prune¹ ['pruːn] vt **pruned; pruning** : podar (arbustos, etc.), acortar (un texto), recortar (gastos, etc.)

prune² n : ciruela f pasa

prurient ['prʊriənt] adj : lascivo

pry ['praɪ] v **pried; prying** vi : curiosear, huronear ⟨to pry into other people's business : meterse uno en lo que no le importa⟩ — vt or **to pry open** : abrir (con una palanca), apalancar

psalm ['sɑm, 'sɑlm] n : salmo m

pseudonym ['suːdəˌnɪm] n : seudónimo m

psoriasis [sə'raɪəsɪs] n : soriasis f, psoriasis f

psyche ['saɪki] n : psique f, psiquis f

psychedelic¹ [ˌsaɪkə'dɛlɪk] adj : psicodélico

psychedelic² n : droga f psicodélica

psychiatric [ˌsaɪki'ætrɪk] adj : psiquiátrico, siquiátrico

psychiatrist [sə'kaɪətrɪst, saɪ-] n : psiquiatra mf, siquiatra mf

psychiatry [sə'kaɪətri, saɪ-] n : psiquiatría f, siquiatría f

psychic¹ ['saɪkɪk] adj 1 : psíquico, síquico (en psicología) 2 CLAIRVOYANT : clarividente

psychic² n : vidente mf, clarividente mf

psychoanalysis [ˌsaɪkoʊ'næləsɪs] n, pl **-yses** : psicoanálisis m, sicoanálisis m

psychoanalyst [ˌsaɪko'ænəlɪst] n : psicoanalista mf, sicoanalista mf

psychoanalytic [ˌsaɪkoˌænəl'ɪt̬ɪk] adj : psicoanalítico, sicoanalítico

psychoanalyze [ˌsaɪko'ænəlˌaɪz] vt **-lyzed; -lyzing** : psicoanalizar, sicoanalizar

psychological [ˌsaɪkə'lɑdʒɪkəl] adj : psicológico, sicológico — **psychologically** adv

psychologist [saɪ'kɑlədʒɪst] n : psicólogo m, -ga f; sicólogo m, -ga f

psychology [saɪ'kɑlədʒi] n, pl **-gies** : psicología f, sicología f

psychopath ['saɪkəˌpæθ] n : psicópata mf, sicópata mf

psychopathic [ˌsaɪkə'pæθɪk] adj : psicopático, sicopático

psychosis [saɪ'koːsɪs] n, pl **-choses** [-'koːˌsiːz] : psicosis f, sicosis f

psychosomatic [ˌsaɪkoʊsə'mæt̬ɪk] adj : psicosomático, sicosomático

psychotherapist [ˌsaɪko'θɛrəpɪst] n : psicoterapeuta mf, sicoterapeuta mf

psychotherapy [ˌsaɪko'θɛrəpi] n, pl **-pies** : psicoterapia f, sicoterapia f

psychotic¹ [saɪ'kɑt̬ɪk] adj : psicótico, sicótico

psychotic² n : psicótico m, -ca f; sicótico m, -ca f

pub ['pʌb] n : cervecería f, taberna m, bar m

puberty ['pjuːbərt̬i] n : pubertad f

pubic ['pjuːbɪk] adj : pubiano, púbico

public¹ ['pʌblɪk] adj 1 : público ⟨public opinion : opinión pública⟩ ⟨a public figure : un personaje público⟩ 2 **to go public** : salir a la bolsa, comenzar/empezar a cotizar en (la) bolsa (dícese de una empresa) 3 **to go public with** REVEAL : revelar — **publicly** adv

public² n : público m

publication [ˌpʌblə'keɪʃən] n : publicación f

publicist ['pʌbləsɪst] n : publicista mf

publicity [pə'blɪsət̬i] n : publicidad f

publicize ['pʌbləˌsaɪz] vt **-cized; -cizing** : publicitar

public relations npl : relaciones fpl públicas

public school n : escuela f pública

public–spirited adj : de espíritu cívico

public transit *n* : transporte *m* público
publish [ˈpʌblɪʃ] *vt* : publicar
publisher [ˈpʌblɪʃər] *n* : casa *f* editorial (compañía); editor *m*, -tora *f* (persona)
publishing [ˈpʌblɪʃɪŋ] *n* : industria *f* editorial
pucker[1] [ˈpʌkər] *vt* : fruncir, arrugar — *vi* : arrugarse
pucker[2] *n* : arruga *f*, fruncido *m*
pudding [ˈpʊdɪŋ] *n* : budín *m*, pudín *m*
puddle [ˈpʌdəl] *n* : charco *m*
pudgy [ˈpʌdʒi] *adj* **pudgier; -est** : regordete *fam*, rechoncho *fam*, gordinflón *fam*
puerile [ˈpjʊrəl] *adj* : pueril
Puerto Rican[1] [ˌpwɛrtəˈriːkən, ˌpɔrtə-] *adj* : puertorriqueño
Puerto Rican[2] *n* : puertorriqueño *m*, -ña *f*
puff[1] [ˈpʌf] *vi* **1** BLOW : soplar **2** PANT : resoplar, jadear **3 to puff up** SWELL : hincharse — *vt* **1** BLOW : soplar ⟨to puff smoke : echar humo⟩ **2** INFLATE : inflar, hinchar ⟨to puff out one's cheeks : inflar las mejillas⟩
puff[2] *n* **1** GUST : soplo *m*, ráfaga *f*, bocanada *f* (de humo) **2** DRAW : chupada *f* (a un cigarrillo) **3** SWELLING : hinchazón *f* **4 cream puff** : pastelito *m* de crema **5 powder puff** : borla *f*
puff pastry *n* : hojaldre *m*
puffy [ˈpʌfi] *adj* **puffier; -est 1** SWOLLEN : hinchado, inflado **2** SPONGY : esponjoso, suave
pug [ˈpʌɡ] *n* **1** : doguillo *m* (perro) **2** *or* **pug nose** : nariz *f* achatada
pugnacious [ˌpʌɡˈneɪʃəs] *adj* : pugnaz, agresivo
pug–nosed [ˈpʌɡˌnoːzd] *adj* : de nariz chata
puke [ˈpjuːk] *vi* **puked; puking** *fam* : vomitar, devolver
pull[1] [ˈpʊl, ˈpʌl] *vt* **1** DRAW, TUG : tirar de, jalar **2** EXTRACT : sacar, extraer ⟨to pull teeth : sacar muelas⟩ ⟨to pull a gun on someone : amenazar a alguien con una pistola⟩ **3** TEAR : desgarrarse (un músculo, etc.) **4** DO : hacer (una broma, un turno, etc.) ⟨to pull a heist : dar un golpe⟩ ⟨to pull an all-nighter : trasnochar (estudiando, etc.)⟩ **5 to pull a fast one on** DECEIVE : engañar, jugarle una mala pasada a **6 to pull apart** SEPARATE, TEAR : separar, hacer pedazos **7 to pull aside** : llevar aparte, llevar a un lado **8 to pull down** : bajar, echar abajo, derribar (un edificio) **9 to pull in** ATTRACT : atraer (clientes, etc.) ⟨to pull in votes : conseguir votos⟩ **10 to pull off** REMOVE : sacar, quitar **11 to pull off** ACHIEVE : conseguir, lograr **12 to pull oneself together** : calmarse, tranquilizarse **13 to pull out** EXTRACT : sacar, arrancar **14 to pull out** RECALL, WITHDRAW : retirar **15 to pull over** : parar ⟨he was pulled over for speeding : lo pararon por exceso de velocidad⟩ **16 to pull through** SUSTAIN : sacar adelante **17 to pull up** RAISE : levantar, subir **18 to pull up** STOP : parar (un vehículo) — *vi* **1** DRAW, TUG : tirar, ja-

lar **2** (*indicating movement of a vehicle in a specific direction*) ⟨he pulled off the highway : salió de la carretera⟩ ⟨they pulled in front of us : se nos metieron delante⟩ ⟨to pull to a stop : pararse⟩ **3 to pull ahead** : tomar la delantera **4 to pull at** : tirar, dar tirones de **5 to pull away** : alejarse **6 to pull back** : echarse atrás **7 to pull for** : apoyar, alentar **8 to pull on** : tirar de, jalar **9 to pull on** DON : ponerse **10 to pull out** LEAVE : salir, arrancar (en un vehículo) **11 to pull out** WITHDRAW : retirarse **12 to pull over** : hacerse a un lado (en un vehículo) **13 to pull through** SURVIVE, ENDURE : sobrevivir, salir adelante **14 to pull together** COOPERATE : trabajar juntos, cooperar **15 to pull up** STOP : parar (en un vehículo)
pull[2] *n* **1** TUG : tirón *m*, jalón *m* ⟨he gave it a pull : le dio un tirón⟩ **2** ATTRACTION : atracción *f*, fuerza *f* ⟨the pull of gravity : la fuerza de la gravedad⟩ **3** INFLUENCE : influencia *f* **4** HANDLE : tirador *m* (de un cajón, etc.) **5 bell pull** : cuerda *f*
pullet [ˈpʊlət] *n* : polla *f*, gallina *f* (joven)
pulley [ˈpʊli] *n*, *pl* **-leys** : polea *f*
pullover [ˈpʊlˌoːvər] *n* : suéter *m*
pulmonary [ˈpʊlməˌnɛri, ˈpʌl-] *adj* : pulmonar
pulp [ˈpʌlp] *n* **1** : pulpa *f* (de una fruta, etc.) **2** MASH : papilla *f*, pasta *f* ⟨wood pulp : pasta de papel, pulpa de papel⟩ ⟨to beat to a pulp : hacer papilla (a alguien)⟩ **3** : pulpa *f* (de los dientes)
pulpit [ˈpʊlˌpɪt] *n* : púlpito *m*
pulsate [ˈpʌlˌseɪt] *vi* **-sated; -sating 1** BEAT : latir, palpitar **2** VIBRATE : vibrar
pulsation [ˌpʌlˈseɪʃən] *n* : pulsación *f*
pulse [ˈpʌls] *n* : pulso *m*
pulverize [ˈpʌlvəˌraɪz] *vt* **-ized; -izing** : pulverizar
puma [ˈpuːmə, ˈpjuː-] *n* : puma *m*; león *m*, leona *f* (*in various countries*)
pumice [ˈpʌməs] *n* : piedra *f* pómez
pummel [ˈpʌməl] *vt* **-meled; -meling** : aporrear, apalear
pump[1] [ˈpʌmp] *vt* **1** : bombear ⟨to pump water : bombear agua⟩ ⟨to pump (up) a tire : inflar una llanta⟩ **2** : mover (una manivela, un pedal, etc.) de arriba abajo ⟨to pump someone's hand : darle un fuerte apretón de manos a alguien⟩ **3 to pump iron** : hacer pesas **4 to pump out** : sacar, vaciar (con una bomba) **5 to pump out** CHURN OUT : producir (en masa) — *vi* : bombear
pump[2] *n* **1** : bomba *f* ⟨water pump : bomba de agua⟩ **2** SHOE : zapato *m* de tacón
pumpernickel [ˈpʌmpərˌnɪkəl] *n* : pan *m* negro de centeno
pumpkin [ˈpʌmpkɪn, ˈpʌŋkən] *n* : calabaza *f*, zapallo *m* *Arg, Chile, Peru, Uru*
pun[1] [ˈpʌn] *vi* **punned; punning** : hacer juegos de palabras
pun[2] *n* : juego *m* de palabras, albur *m* *Mex*
punch[1] [ˈpʌntʃ] *vt* **1** HIT : darle un puñetazo (a alguien), golpear ⟨she

punched him in the nose : le dio un puñetazo en la nariz⟩ 2 PERFORATE : perforar (papel, etc.), picar (un boleto)

punch² n 1 : perforadora f ⟨paper punch : perforadora de papel⟩ 2 BLOW : golpe m, puñetazo m 3 : ponche m ⟨fruit punch : ponche de frutas⟩

punch line n : remate m

punctilious [pəŋk'tɪliəs] adj : puntilloso

punctual ['pʌŋktʃuəl] adj : puntual

punctuality [ˌpʌŋktʃu'æləti] n : puntualidad f

punctually ['pʌŋktʃuəli] adv : puntualmente, a tiempo

punctuate ['pʌŋktʃu,eɪt] vt -ated; -ating : puntuar

punctuation [ˌpʌŋktʃu'eɪʃən] n : puntuación f

punctuation mark n : signo m de puntuación

puncture¹ ['pʌŋktʃər] vt -tured; -turing : pinchar, punzar, perforar, ponchar Mex

puncture² n : pinchazo m, ponchadura f Mex

pundit ['pʌndɪt] n : experto m, -ta f

pungency ['pʌndʒəntsi] n : acritud f, acrimonia f

pungent ['pʌndʒənt] adj : acre

punish ['pʌnɪʃ] vt : castigar

punishable ['pʌnɪʃəbəl] adj : punible

punishment ['pʌnɪʃmənt] n : castigo m

punitive ['pju:nətɪv] adj : punitivo

punk¹ ['pʌŋk] adj : punk

punk² n 1 or **punk rock** : punk m (música) 2 or **punk rocker** : punk mf 3 HOODLUM : matón m, maleante mf

punt¹ ['pʌnt] vi : impulsar (un barco) con una pértiga — vi : despejar (en deportes)

punt² n 1 : batea f (barco) 2 : patada f de despeje (en deportes)

puny ['pju:ni] adj **punier; -est** : enclenque, endeble

pup ['pʌp] n 1 : cachorro m, -rra f (de un perro); cría f (de otros animales)

pupa ['pju:pə] n, pl **-pae** [-pi, -ˌpaɪ] or **-pas** : crisálida f, pupa f

pupil ['pju:pəl] n, 1 : alumno m, -na f (de colegio) 2 : pupila f (del ojo)

puppet ['pʌpət] n : títere m, marioneta f

puppeteer [ˌpʌpə'tɪr] n : titiritero m, -ra f

puppy ['pʌpi] n, pl **-pies** : cachorro m, -rra f

purchase¹ ['pərtʃəs] vt **-chased; -chasing** : comprar — **purchaser** n

purchase² n 1 PURCHASING : compra f, adquisición f 2 : compra f ⟨last-minute purchases : compras de última hora⟩ 3 GRIP : agarre m, asidero m ⟨she got a firm purchase on the wheel : se agarró bien del volante⟩

purchase order n : orden f de compra

pure ['pjur] adj **purer; purest** : puro

purebred ['pjur,brɛd] adj : de pura raza

puree¹ [pju'reɪ, -'ri:] vt **-reed; -reeing** : hacer un puré con

puree² n : puré m

purely ['pjurli] adv 1 WHOLLY : puramente, completamente ⟨purely by

chance : por pura casualidad⟩ 2 SIMPLY : sencillamente, meramente

purgative ['pərgətɪv] n : purgante m

purgatory ['pərgə,tori] n, pl **-ries** : purgatorio m

purge¹ ['pərdʒ] vt **purged; purging** : purgar

purge² n : purga f

purification [ˌpjurəfə'keɪʃən] n : purificación f

purifier ['pjurə,faɪər] n : purificador m

purify ['pjurə,faɪ] vt **-fied; -fying** : purificar

puritan ['pjurətən] n : puritano m, -na f — **puritan** adj

puritanical [ˌpjurə'tænɪkəl] adj : puritano

purity ['pjurəti] n : pureza f

purl¹ ['pərl] v : tejer al revés, tejer del revés

purl² n : punto m del revés

purloin [pər'lɔɪn, 'pər,lɔɪn] vt : hurtar, robar

purple ['pərpəl] n : morado m, color m púrpura

purport [pər'port] vt : pretender ⟨to purport to be : pretender ser⟩

purpose ['pərpəs] n 1 INTENTION : propósito m, intención f ⟨on purpose : a propósito, adrede⟩ ⟨for a purpose : por una razón⟩ ⟨for all practical purposes : a efectos prácticos⟩ 2 FUNCTION : función f ⟨to serve a purpose : servir de algo⟩ 3 RESOLUTION : resolución f, determinación f ⟨to have a sense of purpose : tener un norte en la vida⟩

purposeful ['pərpəsfəl] adj : determinado, decidido, resuelto

purposefully ['pərpəsfəli] adv : decididamente, resueltamente

purposely ['pərpəsli] adv : intencionadamente, a propósito, adrede

purr¹ ['pər] vi : ronronear

purr² n : ronroneo m

purse¹ ['pərs] vt **pursed; pursing** : fruncir ⟨to purse one's lips : fruncir la boca⟩

purse² n 1 HANDBAG : cartera f, bolso m, bolsa f Mex ⟨a change purse : un monedero⟩ 2 FUNDS : fondos mpl 3 PRIZE : premio m

purser ['pərsər] n : sobrecargo mf

pursue [pər'su:] vt **-sued; -suing** 1 CHASE : perseguir 2 SEEK : buscar, tratar de encontrar ⟨to pursue pleasure : buscar el placer⟩ 3 FOLLOW : seguir ⟨the road pursues a northerly course : el camino sigue hacia el norte⟩ 4 : dedicarse a ⟨to pursue a hobby : dedicarse a un pasatiempo⟩

pursuer [pər'su:ər] n : perseguidor m, -dora f

pursuit [pər'su:t] n 1 CHASE : persecución f 2 SEARCH : búsqueda f, busca f 3 ACTIVITY : actividad f, pasatiempo m

purveyor [pər'veɪər] n : proveedor m, -dora f

pus ['pʌs] n : pus m

push¹ ['puʃ] vt 1 : empujar ⟨he pushed the chair back/forward : empujó la silla hacia atrás/adelante⟩ ⟨she pushed him aside : lo apartó (de un empujón) **2** PRESS : apretar, pulsar (un botón, etc.) **3** PRESSURE, URGE : presionar ⟨to push someone to do something : empujar a alguien a hacer algo⟩ ⟨to push someone too hard : exigir demasiado de alguien⟩ **4** STRESS : recalcar ⟨to push the point/issue : insistir⟩ **5** PROVOKE, PESTER : provocar, fastidiar ⟨don't push him too far : no lo provoques⟩ **6** FORCE : hacer cambiar ⟨to push prices up/down : hacer subir/bajar los precios⟩ **7** PROMOTE : promocionar **8** : pasar (drogas) **9** APPROACH : rayar, rozar (una edad, un número, un límite) **10 to push around** BULLY : intimidar, mangonear **11 to push back** : aplazar, postergar (una fecha) **12 to push it (too far)** : pasarse **13 to push through** : conseguir que se apruebe **14 to push one's luck** : tentar a la suerte **15 to push over** : echar abajo, tirar al suelo — *vi* **1** : empujar **2** INSIST : insistir, presionar **3 to push ahead/forward/on** : seguir adelante **4 to push for** DEMAND : exigir, presionar para **5 to push off** LEAVE : marcharse, irse, largarse *fam*

push² *n* **1** SHOVE : empujón *m* **2** DRIVE : empuje *m*, energía *f*, dinamismo *m* **3** EFFORT : esfuerzo *m*

push–button [ˈpʊʃˈbʌtən] *adj* : de botones

pusher [ˈpʊʃər] *n* : camello *m fam*

push-up [ˈpʊʃˌʌp] *n* : flexión *f*

pushy [ˈpʊʃi] *adj* **pushier; -est** : mandón, prepotente

pussy [ˈpʊsi] *n, pl* **pussies** : gatito *m*, -ta *f*; minino *m*, -na *f*

pussy willow *n* : sauce *m* blanco

pustule [ˈpʌsˌtʃuːl] *n* : pústula *f*

put [ˈpʊt] *v* **put; putting** *vt* **1** PLACE : poner, colocar ⟨put it on the table : ponlo en la mesa⟩ ⟨put the car in the garage : guarda el auto en el garaje⟩ ⟨she put her arms around me : me abrazó⟩ **2** INSERT : meter **3** : poner (en cierto estado) ⟨it put her in a good mood : la puso de buen humor⟩ ⟨to put into effect : poner en práctica⟩ **4** IMPOSE : imponer ⟨they put a tax on it : lo gravaron con un impuesto⟩ **5** SUBJECT : someter, poner ⟨to put to the test : poner a prueba⟩ ⟨to put to death : ejecutar⟩ **6** EXPRESS : expresar, decir ⟨he put it simply : lo dijo sencillamente⟩ **7** APPLY : aplicar ⟨to put one's mind to something : proponerse hacer algo⟩ **8** SET : poner ⟨I put him to work : lo puse a trabajar⟩ **9** ATTACH : dar ⟨to put a high value on : dar gran valor a⟩ **10** PRESENT : presentar, exponer ⟨to put a question to someone : hacerle una pregunta a alguien⟩ **11 to put across/over** : comunicar (un mensaje, etc.) **12 to put oneself across/over as** : dar la impresión de ser **13 to put aside** : dejar a un lado **14 to put aside** RESERVE : guardar, reservar **15 to put at** : calcular en ⟨they put the number of deaths at 3,000 : calculan en 3000 la cifra de muertos⟩ **16 to put away** SAVE : guardar **17 to put back/**

away : volver a su sitio **18 to put before** : presentar a **19 to put behind one** : olvidar ⟨to put the past behind you : olvidar el pasado⟩ **20 to put down** DEPOSIT : dejar (en el suelo, etc.) **21 to put down** SUPPRESS : aplastar, suprimir **22 to put down** *fam* DISPARAGE : menospreciar **23 to put down** ATTRIBUTE : atribuir ⟨she put it down to luck : lo atribuyó a la suerte⟩ **24 to put down** : dejar (un depósito) **25 to put down** WRITE DOWN : escribir, apuntar **26 to put down** INSTALL, LAY : poner, colocar **27 to put down** EUTHANIZE : sacrificar **28 to put forth/forward** PROPOSE : proponer, presentar **29 to put in** INVEST : dedicar (tiempo), invertir (dinero) ⟨to put in a lot of effort : esforzarse mucho⟩ **30 to put in** DO : hacer, trabajar (horas extras, etc.) ⟨to put in one's time : cumplir su condena⟩ **31 to put in** PRESENT : presentar, hacer (una oferta, etc.) **32 to put in** INSTALL : instalar **33 to put in** MAKE : hacer (una llamada, etc.) ⟨to put in an appearance : hacer acto de presencia⟩ **34 to put in** INTERJECT : hacer (un comentario) **35 to put in a good word for** RECOMMEND, PRAISE : recomendar, hablar bien de **36 to put into** INVEST : dedicar (tiempo) a, invertir (dinero) en ⟨to put effort into something : esforzarse en algo⟩ ⟨to put thought into something : pensar algo⟩ **37 to put off** DEFER : aplazar, posponer **38 to put off** STALL, DISTRACT : hacer esperar, distraer **39 to put off** DISSUADE, DISCOURAGE : disuadir, desalentar ⟨it put him off his food : le quitó las ganas de comer⟩ **40 to put on** DON : ponerse (ropa, etc.) **41 to put on** ASSUME : afectar, adoptar ⟨to put on a brave face : ponerle buena cara a algo/alguien⟩ **42 to put on** ADD, INCREASE : añadir, aumentar ⟨to put on weight : engordar, ganar peso⟩ **43 to put on** PRODUCE : presentar (una obra de teatro, etc.) **44 to put on** TURN ON, START : encender (luces, etc.), poner (música) ⟨to put the water on (to boil) : poner el agua a calentar⟩ **45 to put money (etc.) on** : apostar dinero (etc.) por **46 to put on** : poner en (una lista, un menú, etc.) **47 to put on** : poner a (régimen, etc.), recetarle (medicina) a **48 to put on (the phone)** ⟨put Dad on (the phone) : pásame a papá⟩ **49 to put someone on** *fam* TEASE : tomarle el pelo a alguien **50 to put out** : apagar (llamas, luces, etc.) **51 to put out** BOTHER, INCONVENIENCE : molestar, incomodar **52 to put out** DISPLAY : disponer **53 to put out** EXTEND : extender, tender (la mano) **54 to put out** PRODUCE : producir **55 to put out** RELEASE, ISSUE : sacar (un álbum, etc.), publicar (un estudio, etc.), emitir (un aviso, etc.) ⟨to put word out that . . . : hacer correr la voz que . . .⟩ **57 to put something/one over on** TRICK : engañar **58 to put through**

: pasar (una llamada) **59 to put through** : hacer pasar (dificultades, etc.) ⟨she put us through hell : nos hizo pasar las de Caín⟩ **60 to put someone through college** : pagarle los estudios a alguien **61 to put together** COMBINE : reunir, juntar **62 to put together** PREPARE : preparar, hacer **63 to put together** ASSEMBLE : armar, montar **64 to put up** RAISE : subir, levantar (la mano, etc.), izar (una bandera) ⟨to put up one's hair : recoger el pelo⟩ **65 to put up** PRESERVE : hacer conserva de **66 to put up** LODGE : alojar **67 to put up** BUILD, ERECT, ASSEMBLE : construir, levantar, montar **68 to put up** HANG : poner, colgar **69 to put up** : oponer ⟨to put up a fight/struggle : oponer resistencia⟩ ⟨to put up a fuss : armar un lío⟩ **70 to put up** OFFER UP : ofrecer ⟨to put up for sale : poner a la venta⟩ ⟨to put up for adoption : dar en adopción⟩ **71 to put up** PRESENT : presentar (argumentos), hacer (una propuesta) **72 to put up** PROVIDE : poner (dinero), ofrecer (una recompensa) **73 to put someone up to something** : incitar a alguien a algo, animar a alguien a hacer algo — *vi* **1 to put forth** : echar, extender **2 to put in for** REQUEST : solicitar (una promoción, etc.) **3 to put to sea** : hacerse a la mar **4 to put up with** : aguantar, soportar

putrefy [ˈpjuːtrəˌfaɪ] *v* **-fied; -fying** *vt* : pudrir — *vi* : pudrirse

putrid [ˈpjuːtrɪd] *adj* : putrefacto, pútrido

putter [ˈpʌt̬ər] *vi or* **to putter around** : entretenerse

putty[1] [ˈpʌti] *vt* **-tied; -tying** : poner masilla en

putty[2] *n, pl* **-ties** : masilla *f*

puzzle[1] [ˈpʌzəl] *vt* **-zled; -zling 1** CONFUSE : confundir, dejar perplejo **2 to puzzle out** : dar vueltas a, tratar de resolver

puzzle[2] *n* **1** : rompecabezas *m* ⟨a crossword puzzle : un crucigrama⟩ **2** MYSTERY : misterio *m*, enigma *m*

puzzlement [ˈpʌzəlmənt] *n* : desconcierto *m*, perplejidad *f*

puzzling *adj* : desconcertante

pygmy [ˈpɪgmi] *adj* : enano, pigmeo

Pygmy *n, pl* **-mies** : pigmeo *m*, -mea *f*

pylon [ˈpaɪˌlɑn, -lən] *n* **1** : torre *f* de conducta eléctrica **2** : pilón *m* (de un puente)

pyramid [ˈpɪrəˌmɪd] *n* : pirámide *f*

pyre [ˈpaɪr] *n* : pira *f*

pyromania [ˌpaɪroˈmeɪniə] *n*·: piromanía *f*

pyromaniac [ˌpaɪroˈmeɪniˌæk] *n* : pirómano *m*, -na *f*

pyrotechnics [ˌpaɪrəˈtekniks] *npl* **1** FIREWORKS : fuegos *mpl* artificiales **2** DISPLAY, SHOW : espectáculo *m*, muestra *f* de virtuosismo ⟨computer pyrotechnics : efectos especiales hechos por computadora⟩ — **pyrotechnic** *adj*

Pyrrhic [ˈpɪrɪk] *adj* : pírrico

python [ˈpaɪˌθɑn, -θən] *n* : pitón *f*, serpiente *f* pitón

Q

q [ˈkjuː] *n, pl* **q's** *or* **qs** [ˈkjuːz] : decimoséptima letra del alfabeto inglés

Q–tips [ˈkjuːˌtɪps] *trademark* : se usa para hisopos

quack[1] [ˈkwæk] *vi* : graznar

quack[2] *n* **1** : graznido *m* (de pato) **2** CHARLATAN : curandero *m*, -ra *f*; matasanos *m fam*

quad [ˈkwɑd] → **quadrangle 1**

quadrangle [ˈkwɑˌdræŋgəl] *n* **1** COURTYARD : patio *m* interior (de una universidad, etc.) **2** → **quadrilateral**

quadrant [ˈkwɑdrənt] *n* : cuadrante *m*

quadrilateral [ˌkwɑdrəˈlæt̬ərəl] *n* : cuadrilátero *m*

quadruple[1] [kwɑˈdruːpəl, -ˈdrʌ-; ˈkwɑdrə-] *v* **-pled; -pling** *vt* : cuadruplicar — *vi* : cuadruplicarse

quadruple[2] *adj* : cuádruple

quadruplet [kwɑˈdruːplət, -ˈdrʌ-; ˈkwɑdrə-] *n* : cuatrillizo *m*, -za *f*

quagmire [ˈkwægˌmaɪr, ˈkwɑg-] *n* **1** : lodazal *m*, barrizal *m* **2** PREDICAMENT : atolladero *m*

quail [ˈkweɪl] *n, pl* **quail** *or* **quails** : codorniz *f*

quaint [ˈkweɪnt] *adj* **1** ODD : extraño, curioso **2** PICTURESQUE : pintoresco — **quaintly** *adv*

quake[1] [ˈkweɪk] *vi* **quaked; quaking** : temblar

quake[2] *n* : temblor *m*, terremoto *m*

Quaker [ˈkweɪkər] *n* : cuáquero *m*, -ra *f* — **Quaker** *adj*

qualification [ˌkwɑləfəˈkeɪʃən] *n* **1** LIMITATION, RESERVATION : reserva *f*, limitación *f* ⟨without qualification : sin reservas⟩ **2** REQUIREMENT : requisito *m* **3** **qualifications** *npl* ABILITY : aptitud *f*, capacidad *f*

qualified [ˈkwɑləˌfaɪd] *adj* **1** : capacitado, habilitado ⟨to be qualified to : ser capacitado para⟩ ⟨she's qualified for the job : cumple los requisitos para el puesto⟩ **2** LIMITED : limitado

qualifier [ˈkwɑləˌfaɪər] *n* **1** : clasificado *m*, -da *f* (en deportes) **2** : calificativo *m* (en gramática)

qualify [ˈkwɑləˌfaɪ] *v* **-fied; -fying** *vt* **1** : matizar ⟨to qualify a statement : matizar una declaración⟩ **2** : calificar (en gramática) **3** : habilitar, capacitar ⟨the certificate qualified her to teach : el certificado la habilitó para enseñar⟩ — *vi* **1** : obtener el título, recibirse ⟨to qualify as an engineer : recibirse de ingeniero⟩ **2** : tener derecho ⟨to qualify for assistance : tener derecho a recibir ayuda⟩ **3** : clasificarse (en deportes)

qualitative [ˈkwɑlǝˌteɪtɪv] *adj* : cualitativo

quality [ˈkwɑlǝti] *n, pl* **-ties** 1 NATURE : carácter *m* 2 ATTRIBUTE : cualidad *f* 3 GRADE : calidad *f* ⟨of good quality : de buena calidad⟩

qualm [ˈkwɑm, ˈkwɑlm, ˈkwɔm] *n* 1 MISGIVING : duda *f*, aprensión *f* 2 RESERVATION, SCRUPLE : escrúpulo *m*, reparo *m*

quandary [ˈkwɑndri] *n, pl* **-ries** : dilema *m*

quantify [ˈkwɑntǝfaɪ] *vt* **-fied; -fying** : cuantificar

quantitative [ˈkwɑntǝˌteɪtɪv] *adj* : cuantitativo

quantity [ˈkwɑntǝti] *n, pl* **-ties** : cantidad *f*

quantum¹ [ˈkwɑntǝm] *n* : cuanto *m* (en física)

quantum² *adj* : cuántico ⟨quantum theory : teoría cuántica⟩

quarantine¹ [ˈkwɔrǝnˌtiːn] *vt* **-tined; -tining** : poner en cuarentena

quarantine² *n* : cuarentena *f*

quarrel¹ [ˈkwɔrǝl] *vi* **-reled** *or* **-relled; -reling** *or* **-relling** : pelearse, reñir, discutir

quarrel² *n* : pelea *f*, riña *f*, disputa *f*

quarrelsome [ˈkwɔrǝlsǝm] *adj* : pendenciero, discutidor

quarry¹ [ˈkwɔri] *vt* **quarried; quarrying** 1 EXTRACT : extraer (mármol, etc.) 2 EXCAVATE : excavar (un cerro, etc.)

quarry² *n, pl* **quarries** 1 : cantera *f* 2 PREY : presa *f*

quart [ˈkwɔrt] *n* : cuarto *m* de galón

quarter¹ [ˈkwɔrtǝr] *vt* 1 : dividir en cuatro partes 2 LODGE : alojar, acuartelar (tropas)

quarter² *adj* : cuarto ⟨a quarter hour/mile : un cuarto de hora/milla⟩

quarter³ *n* 1 : cuarto *m*, cuarta parte *f* ⟨a foot and a quarter : un pie y cuarto⟩ ⟨a quarter after three : las tres y cuarto⟩ 2 : moneda *f* de 25 centavos, cuarto *m* de dólar 3 DISTRICT : barrio *m* ⟨business quarter : barrio comercial⟩ 4 PLACE : parte *f* ⟨from all quarters : de todas partes⟩ ⟨at close quarters : de muy cerca⟩ 5 MERCY : clemencia *f*, cuartel *m* ⟨to give no quarter : no dar cuartel⟩ 6 **quarters** *npl* LODGING : alojamiento *m*, cuartel *m* (militar)

quarterback [ˈkwɔrtǝrˌbæk] *n* : mariscal *m* de campo

quarterfinal [ˌkwɔrtǝrˈfaɪnǝl] *n* : cuarto *m* de final

quarterly¹ [ˈkwɔrtǝrli] *adv* : cada tres meses, trimestralmente

quarterly² *adj* : trimestral

quarterly³ *n, pl* **-lies** : publicación *f* trimestral

quartermaster [ˈkwɔrtǝrˌmæstǝr] *n* : intendente *m*

quarter note *n* : negra *f* (en música)

quartet [kwɔrˈtɛt] *n* : cuarteto *m*

quartz [ˈkwɔrts] *n* : cuarzo *m*

quash [ˈkwɑʃ, ˈkwɔʃ] *vt* 1 ANNUL : anular 2 QUELL : sofocar, aplastar

quasi- [ˈkweɪˌzaɪ, ˈkwɑzi] *pref* : cuasi-

quaver¹ [ˈkweɪvǝr] *vi* 1 SHAKE : temblar ⟨her voice was quavering : le temblaba la voz⟩ 2 TRILL : trinar

quaver² *n* : temblor *m* (de la voz)

quay [ˈkiː, ˈkeɪ, ˈkweɪ] *n* : muelle *m*

queasiness [ˈkwiːzinǝs] *n* : mareo *m*, náusea *f*

queasy [ˈkwiːzi] *adj* **queasier; -est** : mareado

quebracho *or* **quebracho tree** [keɪˈbrɑtʃoː, kɪ-] *n* : quebracho *m*

queen [ˈkwiːn] *n* : reina *f*

queenly [ˈkwiːnli] *adj* **queenlier; -est** : de reina, regio

queer¹ [ˈkwɪr] *adj* 1 : extraño, raro, curioso 2 *sometimes disparaging + offensive* : queer

queer² *n sometimes disparaging + offensive* : queer *mf*

quell [ˈkwɛl] *vt* : aplastar, sofocar

quench [ˈkwɛntʃ] *vt* 1 EXTINGUISH : apagar, sofocar 2 SATISFY : saciar, satisfacer (la sed)

query¹ [ˈkwɪri, ˈkwɛr-] *vt* **-ried; -rying** 1 ASK : preguntar, interrogar ⟨to query someone about something : preguntarle a alguien sobre algo⟩ 2 QUESTION, CHALLENGE : cuestionar

query² *n, pl* **-ries** 1 QUESTION : pregunta *f* 2 DOUBT : duda *f*

quesadilla [ˌkeɪsǝˈdiːǝ] *n* : quesadilla *f*

quest¹ [ˈkwɛst] *v* : buscar

quest² *n* : búsqueda *f*

question¹ [ˈkwɛstʃǝn] *vt* 1 ASK : preguntar 2 DOUBT : poner en duda, cuestionar 3 INTERROGATE : interrogar — *vi* INQUIRE : inquirir, preguntar

question² *n* 1 QUERY : pregunta *f* ⟨to ask a question : hacer una pregunta⟩ 2 ISSUE : cuestión *f*, asunto *m*, problema *f* 3 POSSIBILITY : posibilidad *f* ⟨it's out of the question : es absolutamente imposible⟩ 4 DOUBT : duda *f* ⟨without question : sin duda⟩ ⟨to call into question : poner en duda⟩ ⟨there's no question about it : no cabe duda⟩ 5 **in question** : en cuestión ⟨the book in question : el libro en cuestión⟩

questionable [ˈkwɛstʃǝnǝbǝl] *adj* : cuestionable

questioner [ˈkwɛstʃǝnǝr] *n* : interrogador *m*, -dora *f*

questioning¹ [ˈkwɛstʃǝnɪŋ] *adj* : inquisitivo

questioning² *n* INTERROGATION : interrogatorio *m*, interrogación *f*

question mark *n* : signo *m* de interrogación

questionnaire [ˌkwɛstʃǝˈnær] *n* : cuestionario *m*

quetzal [kɛtˈsɑl] *n, pl* **-zals** *or* **-zales** 1 : quetzal *m* (pájaro) 2 : quetzal *m* (unidad monetaria)

queue¹ [ˈkjuː] *vi* **queued; queuing** *or* **queueing** : hacer cola

queue² *n* LINE : cola *f*, fila *f*

quibble¹ [ˈkwɪbǝl] *vi* **-bled; -bling** : quejarse por nimiedades ⟨to quibble about : quejarse por⟩ ⟨to quibble over : discutir sobre⟩

quibble² *n* : queja *f* (menor)

quiche [ˈkiːʃ] *n* : quiche *f* (pastel)

quick¹ [ˈkwɪk] *adv* : rápidamente

quick² *adj* **1** RAPID : rápido ⟨make it quick : date prisa⟩ ⟨a quick fix : una solución rápida⟩ ⟨she was quick to criticize us : se apresuró a criticarnos⟩ **2** ALERT, CLEVER : listo, vivo, agudo ⟨to have a quick wit/mind : ser muy agudo⟩ **3 a quick temper** : un genio vivo

quick³ *n* **1** FLESH : carne *f* viva **2 to cut someone to the quick** : herir a alguien en lo más vivo

quicken ['kwɪkən] *vt* **1** REVIVE : resucitar **2** AROUSE : estimular, despertar **3** HASTEN : acelerar (el paso, etc.)

quickly ['kwɪkli] *adv* : rápidamente, rápido

quickness ['kwɪknəs] *n* : rapidez *f*

quicksand ['kwɪk,sænd] *n* : arena *f* movediza

quick–tempered ['kwɪk'tɛmpərd] *adj* : de genio vivo

quick–witted ['kwɪk'wɪtəd] *adj* : agudo

quid ['kwɪd] *n fam* POUND : libra *f* (unidad monetaria)

quiet¹ ['kwaɪət] *vt* **1** SILENCE : hacer callar, acallar **2** CALM : calmar, tranquilizar — *vi* **to quiet down** : calmarse, tranquilizarse

quiet² *adv* : silenciosamente

quiet³ *adj* **1** : silencioso ⟨a quiet voice : una voz baja⟩ **2** CALM : tranquilo ⟨a quiet life : una vida tranquila⟩ **3** : callado ⟨be quiet! : ¡cállate!⟩ ⟨to keep quiet about : no decir nada de⟩ **4** MILD : sosegado, suave ⟨a quiet disposition : un temperamento sosegado⟩ **5** UNOBTRUSIVE : discreto **6** SECLUDED : aislado ⟨a quiet nook : un rincón aislado⟩ — **quietly** *adv*

quiet⁴ *n* **1** CALM : calma *f*, tranquilidad *f* **2** SILENCE : silencio *m*

quietness ['kwaɪətnəs] *n* : suavidad *f* (de la voz, etc.), quietud *f* (de un lugar, etc.)

quietude ['kwaɪə,tu:d, -'tju:d] *n* : quietud *f*, reposo *m*

quill ['kwɪl] *n* **1** : púa *f* (de un puerco espín) **2** : pluma *f* de ave (para escribir)

quilt¹ ['kwɪlt] *vt* : acolchar

quilt² *n* : colcha *f*, edredón *m*

quince ['kwɪnts] *n* : membrillo *m*

quinine ['kwaɪ,naɪn] *n* : quinina *f*

quintessence [kwɪn'tɛsənts] *n* : quintaesencia *f*

quintessential [,kwɪntə'sɛtʃəl] *adj* : arquetípico

quintet [kwɪn'tɛt] *n* : quinteto *m*

quintuple [kwɪn'tu:pəl, -'tju:-, -'tʌ-; 'kwɪntə-] *adj* : quíntuplo

quintuplet [kwɪn'tʌplət, -'tu:-, -'tju:-; 'kwɪntə-] *n* : quintillizo *m*, -za *f*

quip¹ ['kwɪp] *vi* quipped; quipping : bromear

quip² *n* : ocurrencia *f*, salida *f*

quirk ['kwərk] *n* : peculiaridad *f*, rareza *f* ⟨a quirk of fate : un capricho del destino⟩

quirky ['kwərki] *adj* quirkier; -est : peculiar, raro

quit ['kwɪt] *v* quit; quitting *vt* : dejar, abandonar ⟨to quit smoking : dejar de fumar⟩ ⟨quit complaining! : ¡deja de quejarte!⟩ ⟨quit it! : ¡basta ya!⟩ — *vi* **1** STOP : parar **2** RESIGN : dimitir, renunciar

quite ['kwaɪt] *adv* **1** VERY : muy, bastante ⟨quite near : bastante cerca⟩ ⟨quite ill : muy enfermo⟩ **2** COMPLETELY : completamente, totalmente ⟨I'm not quite sure : no estoy del todo seguro⟩ **3** EXACTLY : exactamente ⟨there's nothing quite like Paris : no hay como París⟩ **4** (*used as an intensifier*) ⟨that's quite enough! : ¡basta ya!⟩ ⟨that's quite all right : no fue nada⟩ ⟨I haven't seen her in quite a while : hace bastante tiempo que no la veo⟩ ⟨quite a few things : muchas cosas⟩ ⟨quite a lot/bit of money : bastante dinero⟩ ⟨quite a surprise : una gran sorpresa⟩ ⟨quite an experience : toda una experiencia⟩

quits ['kwɪts] *adj* **to call it quits** : quedar en paz

quitter ['kwɪtər] *n* : derrotista *mf*

quiver¹ ['kwɪvər] *vi* : temblar, estremecerse, vibrar

quiver² *n* **1** : carcaj *m*, aljaba *f* (para flechas) **2** TREMBLING : temblor *m*, estremecimiento *m*

quixotic [kwɪk'saɪk] *adj* : quijotesco

quiz¹ ['kwɪz] *vt* quizzed; quizzing **1** QUESTION : interrogar **2** TEST : hacerle una prueba a, examinar

quiz² *n, pl* quizzes : examen *m* corto, prueba *f*

quizzical ['kwɪzɪkəl] *adj* CURIOUS : curioso, interrogativo

quorum ['kworəm] *n* : quórum *m*

quota ['kwo:tə] *n* : cuota *f*, cupo *m*

quotable ['kwo:təbəl] *adj* : citable

quotation [kwo'teɪʃən] *n* **1** CITATION : cita *f* **2** ESTIMATE : presupuesto *m*, estimación *f* **3** PRICE : cotización *f*

quotation marks *npl* : comillas *fpl*

quote¹ ['kwo:t] *vt* quoted; quoting **1** CITE : citar (un pasaje, a un autor, etc.) ⟨don't quote me on that : no lo repitas⟩ ⟨he said, (and I) quote, . . . : dijo textualmente: . . .⟩ **2** : cotizar (en finanzas)

quote² *n* **1** → quotation **2 quotes** *npl* → quotation marks **3** ESTIMATE : presupuesto *m*

quotient ['kwo:ʃənt] *n* : cociente *m*

quotidian [kwo'tɪdiən] *adj* : cotidiano

Quran *or* **Qur'an** → Koran

R

r ['ɑr] n, pl r's or rs ['ɑrz] : decimoctava letra del alfabeto inglés

rabbi ['ræ,baɪ] n : rabino m, -na f

rabbit ['ræbət] n, pl -bit or -bits : conejo m, -ja f

rabble ['ræbəl] n 1 MASSES : populacho m 2 RIFFRAFF : chusma f, gentuza f

rabid ['ræbɪd] adj 1 : rabioso, afectado con la rabia 2 FURIOUS : furioso 3 FANATIC : fanático

rabies ['reɪbi:z] ns & pl : rabia f

raccoon [ræ'ku:n] n, pl -coon or -coons : mapache m

race¹ ['reɪs] vi raced; racing 1 : correr, competir (en una carrera) 2 RUSH : ir a toda prisa, ir corriendo

race² n 1 CURRENT : corriente f (de agua) 2 : carrera f ⟨dog race : carrera de perros⟩ ⟨the presidential race : la carrera presidencial⟩ 3 : raza f ⟨all races and creeds : todas las razas y religiones⟩ ⟨the human race : el género humano⟩

race car n : carro/auto/coche m de carreras

race course n : pista f (de carreras)

racehorse ['reɪs,hɔrs] n : caballo m de carreras

racer ['reɪsər] n : corredor m, -dora f

racetrack ['reɪs,træk] n : pista f (de carreras)

racial ['reɪʃəl] adj : racial ⟨racial discrimination : discriminación racial⟩ — racially adv

racing ['reɪsɪŋ] n : carreras fpl

racing shell → shell²

racism ['reɪ,sɪzəm] n : racismo m

racist ['reɪsɪst] n : racista mf

rack¹ ['ræk] vt 1 : atormentar ⟨racked with pain : atormentado por el dolor⟩ 2 to rack one's brains : devanarse los sesos

rack² n SHELF, STAND : estante m ⟨a luggage/roof rack : un portaequipajes, una baca⟩ ⟨a coatrack : un perchero, una percha⟩

racket ['rækət] n 1 or racquet : raqueta f (en deportes) 2 DIN : estruendo m, bulla f, jaleo m fam 3 SWINDLE : estafa f, timo m fam

racketeer [,rækə'tɪr] n : estafador m, -dora f

racy ['reɪsi] adj racier; -est : subido de tono, picante

radar ['reɪ,dɑr] n : radar m

radial ['reɪdiəl] adj : radial

radiance ['reɪdiəns] n : resplandor m

radiant ['reɪdiənt] adj : radiante — radiantly adv

radiate ['reɪdi,eɪt] v -ated; -ating vt : irradiar (calor), emitir (luz) ⟨to radiate happiness : rebosar de alegría⟩ — vi : irradiar 2 or to radiate out SPREAD : extenderse, salir (de un centro)

radiation [,reɪdi'eɪʃən] n : radiación f

radiator ['reɪdi,eɪtər] n : radiador m

radical¹ ['rædɪkəl] adj : radical — radically [-kli] adv

radical² n : radical mf

radicalism ['rædɪkə,lɪzəm] n : radicalismo m

radii → radius

radio¹ ['reɪdi,oː] v : llamar por radio, transmitir por radio

radio² n, pl -dios : radio m (aparato), radio f (emisora, radiodifusión)

radioactive ['reɪdio'æktɪv] adj : radiactivo, radioactivo

radioactivity [,reɪdio,æk'tɪvəti] n, pl -ties : radiactividad f, radioactividad f

radio-controlled adj : teledirigido

radiologist [,reɪdi'ɑlədʒɪst] n : radiólogo m, -ga f

radiology [,reɪdi'ɑlədʒi] n : radiología f

radio station n : emisora f

radish ['rædɪʃ] n : rábano m

radium ['reɪdiəm] n : radio m

radius ['reɪdiəs] n, pl radii [-di,aɪ] : radio m

radon ['reɪ,dɑn] n : radón m

raffle¹ ['ræfəl] vt -fled; -fling : rifar, sortear

raffle² n : rifa f, sorteo m

raft ['ræft] n 1 : balsa f ⟨rubber rafts : balsas de goma⟩ 2 LOT, SLEW : montón m

rafter ['ræftər] n : par m, viga f

rafting ['ræftɪŋ] n : rafting m

rag ['ræg] n 1 CLOTH : trapo m ⟨rag doll : muñeca de trapo⟩ 2 rags npl TATTERS : harapos mpl, andrajos mpl

ragamuffin ['rægə,mʌfən] n : pilluelo m, -la f

rage¹ ['reɪdʒ] vi raged; raging 1 : estar furioso, rabiar ⟨to rage against : clamar contra⟩ 2 : seguir de manera violenta ⟨the wind was raging : el viento bramaba⟩ ⟨the debate raged on : el debate continuaba desenfrenado⟩

rage² n 1 ANGER : furia f, ira f, cólera f ⟨to fly into a rage : enfurecerse⟩ 2 FAD : moda f, furor m

ragged ['rægəd] adj 1 UNEVEN : irregular, desigual 2 TORN : hecho jirones 3 TATTERED : andrajoso, harapiento

ragtime ['ræg,taɪm] n : ragtime m

raid¹ ['reɪd] vt 1 : invadir, hacer una incursión en ⟨raided by enemy troops : invadido por tropas enemigas⟩ 2 : asaltar, atracar ⟨the gang raided the warehouse : la pandilla asaltó el almacén⟩ 3 : allanar, hacer una redada en ⟨police raided the house : la policía allanó la vivienda⟩

raid² n 1 : invasión f (militar) 2 : asalto m (por delincuentes) 3 : redada f, batida f, allanamiento m (por la policía)

raider ['reɪdər] n 1 ATTACKER : asaltante mf; invasor m, -sora f 2 corporate raider : tiburón m

rail¹ ['reɪl] vi 1 to rail against REVILE : denostar contra 2 to rail at SCOLD : regañar, reprender

rail² n 1 BAR : barra f, barrera f 2 HANDRAIL : pasamanos m, barandilla f 3

TRACK : riel *m* (para ferrocarriles) 4
RAILROAD : ferrocarril *m*
railing ['reɪlɪŋ] *n* 1 : baranda *f* (de un balcón, etc.) 2 RAILS : verja *f*
raillery ['reɪləri] *n*, *pl* **-leries** : bromas *fpl*
railroad ['reɪl,ro:d] *n* : ferrocarril *m*
railroad tie → tie²
railroad track → track²
railway ['reɪl,weɪ] → **railroad**
raiment ['reɪmənt] *n* : vestiduras *fpl*
rain¹ ['reɪn] *vi* : llover ⟨it's raining : está lloviendo⟩ 2 **to rain down** : llover ⟨insults rained down on him : le llovieron los insultos⟩
rain² *n* : lluvia *f*
rainbow ['reɪn,bo:] *n* : arco *m* iris
raincoat ['reɪn,ko:t] *n* : impermeable *m*
raindrop ['reɪn,drɑp] *n* : gota *f* de lluvia
rainfall ['reɪn,fɔl] *n* : lluvia *f*, precipitación *f*
rain forest *n* : bosque *m* tropical
rainstorm ['reɪn,stɔrm] *n* : temporal *m* (de lluvia)
rainwater ['reɪn,wɔtər] *n* : agua *f* de lluvia
rainy ['reɪni] *adj* **rainier; -est** : lluvioso
raise¹ ['reɪz] *vt* **raised; raising** 1 LIFT : levantar, subir, alzar ⟨to raise someone's spirits : levantarle el ánimo a alguien⟩ 2 ERECT : levantar, erigir 3 COLLECT : recaudar ⟨to raise money : recaudar dinero⟩ 4 REAR : criar ⟨she raised her two children : crió a sus dos niños⟩ 5 GROW : cultivar 6 INCREASE : aumentar, subir ⟨to raise one's voice : levantar la voz⟩ 7 PROMOTE : ascender 8 PROVOKE : provocar ⟨it raised a laugh : provocó una risa⟩ 9 BRING UP : sacar (temas, objeciones, etc.)
raise² *n* : aumento *m*
raisin ['reɪzən] *n* : pasa *f*
raja *or* **rajah** ['rɑdʒə, -,dʒɑ, -,ʒɑ] *n* : rajá *m*
rake¹ ['reɪk] *v* **raked; raking** *vt* 1 : rastrillar ⟨to rake (up) leaves : rastrillar las hojas⟩ 2 SWEEP : barrer ⟨raked with gunfire : barrido con balas⟩ 3 **to rake it in** : hacer mucho dinero — *vi* **to rake through** : revolver, hurgar en
rake² *n* 1 : rastrillo *m* 2 LIBERTINE : libertino *m*, -na *f*; calavera *m*
rakish ['reɪkɪʃ] *adj* 1 JAUNTY : desenvuelto, desenfadado 2 DISSOLUTE : libertino, disoluto
rally¹ ['ræli] *v* **-lied; -lying** *vi* 1 MEET, GATHER : reunirse, congregarse 2 RECOVER : recuperarse 3 **to rally against** : unirse en contra de 4 **to rally around** : juntarse para apoyar (algo/a alguien) 5 **to rally for/behind** : unirse a favor de — *vt* 1 ASSEMBLE : reunir (tropas, etc.) 2 RECOVER : recobrar (la fuerza, el ánimo, etc.)
rally² *n*, *pl* **-lies** : reunión *f*, mitin *m*, manifestación *f*
ram¹ ['ræm] *v* **rammed; ramming** *vt* 1 DRIVE : hincar, clavar ⟨he rammed it into the ground : lo hincó en la tierra⟩ 2 SMASH : estrellar, embestir — *vi* COLLIDE : chocar (contra), estrellarse
ram² *n* 1 : carnero *m* (animal) 2 **battering ram** : ariete *m*

RAM ['ræm] *n* : RAM *f*, memoria *f* de acceso aleatorio
Ramadan ['rɑmə,dɑn] *n* : Ramadán *m*
ramble¹ ['ræmbəl] *vi* **-bled; -bling** 1 WANDER : pasear, deambular 2 **to ramble on** : divagar, perder el hilo 3 SPREAD : trepar (dícese de una planta)
ramble² *n* : paseo *m*, excursión *f*
rambler ['ræmblər] *n* 1 WALKER : excursionista *mf* 2 ROSE : rosa *f* trepadora
rambling ['ræmblɪŋ] *adj* 1 : laberíntico 2 DISJOINTED : inconexo, incoherente
rambunctious [ræm'bʌŋkʃəs] *adj* UNRULY : alborotado
ramification [,ræməfə'keɪʃən] *n* : ramificación *f*
ramp ['ræmp] *n* : rampa *f*
rampage¹ ['ræm,peɪdʒ, ræm'peɪdʒ] *vi* **-paged; -paging** : andar arrasando todo, correr destrozando
rampage² ['ræm,peɪdʒ] *n* : alboroto *m*, frenesí *m* (de violencia)
rampant ['ræmpənt] *adj* : desenfrenado
rampart ['ræm,pɑrt] *n* : terraplén *m*, muralla *f*
ramrod ['ræm,rɑd] *n* : baqueta *f*
ramshackle ['ræm,ʃækəl] *adj* : destartalado
ran → run
ranch¹ ['ræntʃ] *vi* : trabajar en una hacienda *f* — *vi* : criar (ganado)
ranch² *n* 1 : hacienda *f*, rancho *m*, finca *f* ganadera 2 *or* **ranch house** : casa *f* (en una hacienda) 3 *or* **ranch house** : casa *f* de una sola planta
ranch dressing *n* : aderezo *m* a base de leche de manteca, mayonesa, y hierbas
rancher ['ræntʃər] *n* : estanciero *m*, -ra *f*; ranchero *m*, -ra *f*
rancid ['ræn(t)səd] *adj* : rancio
rancor ['ræŋkər] *n* : rencor *m* — **rancorous** ['ræŋkərəs] *adj*
random ['rændəm] *adj* 1 : fortuito, aleatorio 2 **at ∼** : al azar — **randomly** *adv*
random–access memory *n* : memoria *f* de acceso aleatorio, RAM *f*
rang → ring
range¹ ['reɪndʒ] *v* **ranged; ranging** *vt* ARRANGE : alinear, ordenar, arreglar — *vi* 1 ROAM : deambular 2 EXTEND : extenderse ⟨the results range widely : los resultados se extienden mucho⟩ 3 VARY : variar ⟨discounts range from 20% to 40% : los descuentos varían entre 20% y 40%⟩
range² *n* 1 ROW : fila *f*, hilera *f* ⟨a mountain range : una cordillera⟩ 2 GRASSLAND : pradera *f*, pampa *f* 3 STOVE : cocina *f* 4 VARIETY : variedad *f*, gama *f* 5 SPHERE : ámbito *m*, esfera *f*, campo *m* 6 REACH : registro *m* (de la voz), alcance *m* (de un arma de fuego) ⟨out of range : fuera del alcance⟩ ⟨at close range : de cerca⟩ 7 **shooting range** : campo *m* de tiro
ranger ['reɪndʒər] *n* *or* **forest ranger** : guardabosque *mf*
rangy ['reɪndʒi] *adj* **rangier; -est** : alto y delgado

rank¹ ['ræŋk] vt 1 RANGE : alinear, ordenar, poner en fila 2 CLASSIFY : clasificar — vi 1 to rank above : ser superior a 2 to rank among : encontrarse entre, figurar entre

rank² adj 1 SMELLY : fétido, maloliente 2 OUTRIGHT : completo, absoluto ⟨a rank injustice : una injusticia manifiesta⟩

rank³ n 1 LINE, ROW : fila f ⟨to close ranks : cerrar filas⟩ 2 GRADE, POSITION : grado m, rango m (militar) ⟨to pull rank : abusar de su autoridad⟩ 3 CLASS : categoría f, clase f 4 ranks npl : soldados mpl rasos

rank and file n 1 RANKS : soldados mpl rasos 2 : bases fpl (de un partido, etc.)

rankle ['ræŋkəl] v -kled; -kling vi : doler — vt : irritar, herir

ransack ['ræn‚sæk] vt : revolver, desvalijar, registrar de arriba abajo

ransom¹ ['rænsəm] vt : rescatar, pagar un rescate por

ransom² n : rescate m

ransomware ['rænsəm‚wær] n : ransomware m, virus m de secuestro de datos

rant ['rænt] vi or to rant and rave : despotricar, desvariar

rap¹ ['ræp] v rapped; rapping vt 1 KNOCK : golpetear, dar un golpe en 2 CRITICIZE : criticar — vi 1 CHAT : charlar, cotorrear fam 2 KNOCK : dar un golpe

rap² n 1 BLOW, KNOCK : golpe m, golpecito m 2 CHAT : charla f 3 or rap music : rap m 4 to take the rap : pagar el pato fam

rapacious [rə'peɪʃəs] adj GREEDY : avaricioso, codicioso

rape¹ ['reɪp] vt raped; raping : violar

rape² n 1 : colza f (planta) 2 : violación f (de una persona)

rapid ['ræpɪd] adj : rápido — rapidly adv

rapidity [rə'pɪdəti] n : rapidez f

rapids ['ræpɪdz] npl : rápidos mpl

rapier ['reɪpiər] n : estoque m

rapist ['reɪpɪst] n : violador m, -dora f

rapper ['ræpər] n : cantante mf de rap; rapero m, -ra f

rapport [ræ'pɔr] n : relación f armoniosa, entendimiento m

rapprochement [‚ræ‚proːʃ'mɑnt] n : acercamiento m, aproximación f

rapt ['ræpt] adj : absorto, embelesado

rapture ['ræptʃər] n : éxtasis m

rapturous ['ræptʃərəs] adj : extasiado, embelesado

rare ['rær] adj rarer; rarest 1 FINE : excelente, excepcional ⟨a rare talent : un talento excepcional⟩ 2 UNCOMMON : raro, poco común 3 : poco cocido (dícese de la carne)

rarefy ['ræro‚faɪ] vt -fied; -fying : enrarecer

rarely ['rærli] adv SELDOM : pocas veces, rara vez

raring ['ræron, -ɪŋ] adj : lleno de entusiasmo, con muchas ganas

rarity ['ræroti] n, pl -ties : rareza f

rascal ['ræskəl] n : pillo m, -lla f; pícaro m, -ra f

rash¹ ['ræʃ] adj : imprudente, precipitado — rashly adv

rash² n : sarpullido m, erupción f

rashness ['ræʃnəs] n : precipitación f

rasp¹ ['ræsp] vt 1 SCRAPE : raspar 2 : decir en voz áspera — vi : hacer un ruido áspero

rasp² n : escofina f

raspberry ['ræz‚beri] n, pl -ries : frambuesa f

rat ['ræt] n : rata f

ratchet ['rætʃət] n : trinquete m

rate¹ ['reɪt] vt rated; rating 1 CONSIDER, REGARD : considerar, estimar 2 DESERVE : merecer

rate² n 1 SPEED, PACE : velocidad f, ritmo m ⟨at this rate : a este paso⟩ 2 : índice m, tasa f ⟨birth rate : índice de natalidad⟩ ⟨interest rate : tasa de interés⟩ 3 CHARGE, PRICE : precio m, tarifa f 4 at any rate ANYWAY : de todos modos 5 at any rate AT LEAST : al menos, por lo menos

rather ['ræðər, 'rʌ-, 'rɑ-] adv 1 (indicating preference) ⟨she would rather stay : preferiría quedarse⟩ ⟨I'd rather not : mejor que no⟩ 2 (indicating preciseness) ⟨my father, or rather, my stepfather : mi padre, o mejor dicho mi padrastro⟩ 3 INSTEAD : sino que, más que, al contrario ⟨I'm not pleased; rather, I'm disappointed : no estoy satisfecho, sino desilusionado⟩ 4 SOMEWHAT : algo, un tanto ⟨rather strange : un poco extraño⟩ 5 QUITE : bastante ⟨rather difficult : bastante difícil⟩ 6 — than INSTEAD OF : en vez de

ratification [‚rætəfə'keɪʃən] n : ratificación f

ratify ['rætə‚faɪ] vt -fied; -fying : ratificar

rating ['reɪtɪŋ] n 1 STANDING : clasificación f, posición f 2 ratings npl : índice m de audiencia

ratio ['reɪʃio] n, pl -tios : proporción f, relación f

ration¹ ['ræʃən, 'reɪʃən] vt : racionar

ration² n 1 : ración f 2 rations npl PROVISIONS : víveres mpl

rational ['ræʃənəl] adj 1 : racional 2 REASONABLE : razonable, racional — rationally adv — rationality [‚ræʃə'næləti] n

rationale [‚ræʃə'næl] n 1 EXPLANATION : explicación f 2 BASIS : base f, razones fpl

rationalize ['ræʃənə‚laɪz] vt -ized; -izing : racionalizar — rationalization [‚ræʃənələ'zeɪʃən] n

rat race n : competencia f laboral (excesiva)

rattle¹ ['rætəl] v -tled; -tling vi 1 CLATTER : traquetear, hacer ruido 2 to rattle on CHATTER : parlotear fam — vt 1 : hacer sonar, agitar ⟨the wind rattled the door : el viento sacudió la puerta⟩ 2 DISCONCERT, WORRY : desconcertar, poner nervioso 3 to rattle off : despachar, recitar, decir de corrido

rattle² n 1 CLATTER : traqueteo m, ruido m 2 : sonajero m (para bebés) 3 : cascabel m (de una culebra)

rattler ['rætələr] → rattlesnake

rattlesnake ['ræt̮əl,sneɪk] *n* : serpiente *f* de cascabel

ratty ['ræt̮i] *adj* **rattier; -est** : raído, andrajoso

raucous ['rɔkəs] *adj* **1** HOARSE : ronco **2** BOISTEROUS : escandaloso, bullicioso — **raucously** *adv*

ravage¹ ['rævɪdʒ] *vt* **-aged; -aging** : devastar, arrasar, hacer estragos

ravage² *n* : destrozo *m*, destrucción *f* ⟨the ravages of war : los estragos de la guerra⟩

rave ['reɪv] *vi* **raved; raving 1** : delirar, desvariar **2 to rave about** : hablar con entusiasmo sobre, entusiasmarse por

ravel ['rævəl] *v* **-eled** *or* **-elled; -eling** *or* **-elling** *vt* UNRAVEL : desenredar, desenmarañar — *vi* FRAY : deshilacharse

raven ['reɪvən] *n* : cuervo *m*

ravenous ['rævənəs] *adj* : hambriento, voraz — **ravenously** *adv*

ravine [rə'viːn] *n* : barranco *m*, quebrada *f*

ravings ['reɪvɪŋz] *npl* : desvaríos *mpl*, delirios *mpl*

ravioli [,rævi'oːli] *ns & pl* : raviolis *mpl*, ravioles *mpl*

ravish ['rævɪʃ] *vt* **1** PLUNDER : saquear **2** ENCHANT : embelesar, cautivar, encantar

ravishing ['rævɪʃɪŋ] *adj* : deslumbrante, impresionante (dícese de la belleza, etc.)

raw ['rɔ] *adj* **rawer; rawest 1** : crudo ⟨raw meat : carne cruda⟩ **2** UNTREATED : sin tratar, sin refinar, puro ⟨raw data : datos en bruto⟩ ⟨raw materials : materias primas⟩ **3** INEXPERIENCED : novato, inexperto **4** SORE, CHAFED : en carne viva **5** : frío y húmedo ⟨a raw day : un día crudo⟩ **6** UNFAIR : injusto ⟨a raw deal : un trato injusto, una injusticia⟩

rawhide ['rɔ,haɪd] *n* : cuero *m* sin curtir

ray ['reɪ] *n* **1** : rayo *m* (de la luz, etc.) ⟨a ray of hope : un resquicio de esperanza⟩ **2** : raya *f* (pez)

rayon ['reɪ,ɑn] *n* : rayón *m*

raze ['reɪz] *vt* **razed; razing** : arrasar, demoler

razor ['reɪzər] *n* **1** *or* **straight razor** : navaja *f* (de afeitar) **2** *or* **safety razor** : maquinilla *f* de afeitar, rastrillo *m* *Mex* **3** *or* **electric razor** SHAVER : afeitadora *f*, rasuradora *f* **4** *or* **razor blade** : hoja *f* de afeitar, cuchilla *f* de afeitar

re ['reɪ] *n* : re *m* (en el canto)

re- [,ri:] *pref* : re-

reach¹ ['riːtʃ] *vt* **1** EXTEND : extender, alargar ⟨to reach out one's hand : extender la mano⟩ **2** : alcanzar ⟨I couldn't reach the apple : no pude alcanzar la manzana⟩ **3** : llegar a/hasta ⟨the shadow reached the wall : la sombra llegó hasta la pared⟩ **4** CONTACT : contactar, ponerse en contacto con — *vi* **1** *or* **to reach out** : extender la mano **2** STRETCH : extenderse **3 to reach for** : tratar de agarrar

reach² *n* : alcance *m*, extensión *f* ⟨within reach : a mi/tu (etc.) alcance⟩ ⟨within reach of : al alcance de⟩ ⟨out of reach : fuera de mi/tu (etc.) alcance⟩

react [ri'ækt] *vi* : reaccionar

reaction [ri'ækʃən] *n* : reacción *f*

reactionary¹ [ri'ækʃə,neri] *adj* : reaccionario

reactionary² *n, pl* **-ries** : reaccionario *m*, -ria *f*

reactivate [ri'æktə,veɪt] *vt* **-vated; -vating** : reactivar — **reactivation** *n*

reactor [ri'æktər] *n* : reactor *m* ⟨nuclear reactor : reactor nuclear⟩

read¹ ['riːd] *v* **read** ['rɛd]; **reading** *vt* **1** : leer ⟨to read a story : leer un cuento⟩ **2** INTERPRET : interpretar ⟨it can be read two ways : se puede interpretar de dos maneras⟩ **3** : decir, poner ⟨the sign read "No smoking" : el letrero decía "No Fumar"⟩ **4** : marcar ⟨the thermometer reads 70° : el termómetro marca 70°⟩ **5 to read aloud/out** : leer en voz alta **6 to read between the lines** : leer entre las líneas **7 to read into something** : buscarle el significado a algo ⟨don't read too much into it : no le des demasiada importancia⟩ **8 to read through/over** : leer (del principio al fin) **9 to read up on** : documentarse sobre — *vi* **1** : leer ⟨he can read : sabe leer⟩ **2** SAY : decir ⟨the list reads as follows : la lista dice lo siguiente⟩

read² *n* **to be a good read** : ser una lectura amena

readable ['riːdəbəl] *adj* : legible

reader ['riːdər] *n* : lector *m*, -tora *f*

readership ['riːdər,ʃɪp] *n* : lectores *mpl*

readily ['redəli] *adv* **1** WILLINGLY : de buena gana, con gusto **2** EASILY : fácilmente, con facilidad

readiness ['redinəs] *n* **1** WILLINGNESS : buena disposición *f* **2 to be in readiness** : estar preparado

reading ['riːdɪŋ] *n* : lectura *f*

readjust [,riːə'dʒʌst] *vt* : reajustar — *vi* : volverse a adaptar

readjustment [,riːə'dʒʌstmənt] *n* : reajuste *m*

readout ['riːd,aʊt] *n* : lectura *f* (en informática)

ready¹ ['redi] *vt* **readied; readying** : preparar

ready² *adj* **readier; -est 1** PREPARED : listo, preparado ⟨they'll be ready soon : enseguida están listos⟩ ⟨to be ready to : estar listo para⟩ ⟨to make ready : prepararse⟩ **2** WILLING : dispuesto ⟨ready and willing : dispuesto a todo⟩ **3** : a punto de ⟨ready to cry : a punto de llorar⟩ **4** AVAILABLE : disponible ⟨ready cash/money : efectivo⟩ **5** QUICK : vivo, agudo ⟨a ready wit : un ingenio agudo⟩

ready–made ['redi'meɪd] *adj* : preparado, confeccionado

reaffirm [,riːə'fərm] *vt* : reafirmar

real¹ ['riːl] *adv fam* VERY : muy ⟨we had a real good time : lo pasamos muy bien⟩

real² *adj* **1** : inmobiliario ⟨real property : bien inmueble, bien raíz⟩ **2** GENUINE : auténtico, genuino **3** ACTUAL, TRUE : real, verdadero ⟨a real friend : un verdadero amigo⟩ **4 for real** SERIOUSLY : de veras, de verdad **5 for real** GEN-

UINE, TRUE : auténtico, verdadero **6 for real** SINCERE : sincero ⟨is that guy for real? : ¿nos está tomando el pelo?⟩ **7 get real!** *fam* : ¡no te engañes! **8 to keep it real** *fam* : ser sincero, no darse aires

real[3] [ˈreɪˈɑl] *n, pl* **reais** [ˈreɪʃ] *or* **reis** [ˈreɪʃ] : real *m* (unidad monetaria)

real estate *n* : propiedad *f* inmobiliaria, bienes *mpl* raíces

real estate agent *n* : agente *m* inmobiliario, agente *f* inmobiliaria

realign [ˌriːəˈlaɪn] *vt* : realinear — **realignment** [ˌriːəˈlaɪnmənt] *n*

realism [ˈriːəˌlɪzəm] *n* : realismo *m*

realist [ˈriːəlɪst] *n* : realista *mf*

realistic [ˌriːəˈlɪstɪk] *adj* : realista

realistically [ˌriːəˈlɪstɪkli] *adv* : de manera realista

reality [riˈæləti] *n, pl* **-ties** : realidad *f*

reality TV *or* **reality television** *n* : telerrealidad *f*

realizable [ˌriːəˈlaɪzəbəl] *adj* : realizable, asequible

realization [ˌriːələˈzeɪʃən] *n* : realización *f*

realize [ˈriːəˌlaɪz] *vt* **-ized; -izing 1** UNDERSTAND : darse cuenta de, saber **2** FULFILL : realizar (sueños, etc.) ⟨my worst fears were realized : mis mayores temores se hicieron realidad⟩ **3** ACCOMPLISH : realizar, llevar a cabo **4** EARN : obtener, realizar

really [ˈriːli, ˈrɪ-] *adv* **1** ACTUALLY : de verdad, en realidad ⟨really good : buenísimo⟩ **2** TRULY : verdaderamente, realmente ⟨I really don't care : la verdad es que no me importa⟩ **3** FRANKLY : francamente, en serio

realm [ˈrɛlm] *n* **1** KINGDOM : reino *m* **2** SPHERE : esfera *f*, campo *m*

Realtor [ˈriːəltər, -ˌtɔr] *service mark* se usa para un agente inmobiliario autorizado

ream [ˈriːm] *n* **1** : resma *f* (de papel) **2 reams** *npl* LOADS : montones *mpl*

reap [ˈriːp] *vi* : cosechar

reaper [ˈriːpər] *n* **1** : cosechador *m*, -dora *f* (persona) ⟨the Grim Reaper : la muerte⟩ **2** : cosechadora *f* (máquina)

reappear [ˌriːəˈpɪr] *vi* : reaparecer

reappearance [ˌriːəˈpɪrənts] *n* : reaparición *f*

rear[1] [ˈrɪr] *vt* **1** LIFT, RAISE : levantar **2** BREED, BRING UP : criar — *vi or* **to rear up** : encabritarse

rear[2] *adj* : trasero, posterior, de atrás

rear[3] *n* **1** BACK : parte *f* de atrás ⟨to bring up the rear : cerrar la marcha⟩ **2** *or* **rear end** : trasero *m*

rear admiral *n* : contraalmirante *mf*

rearrange [ˌriːəˈreɪndʒ] *vt* **-ranged; -ranging** : colocar de otra manera, volver a arreglar, reorganizar

rearview mirror [ˈrɪrˌvjuː-] *n* : retrovisor *m*

reason[1] [ˈriːzən] *vt* THINK : pensar — *vi* : razonar ⟨I can't reason with her : no puedo razonar con ella⟩ — **reasoned** [ˈriːzənd] *adj*

reason[2] *n* **1** CAUSE, GROUND : razón *f*, motivo *m* ⟨the reason for his trip : el mo-

tivo de su viaje⟩ ⟨for this reason : por esta razón, por lo cual⟩ ⟨for no (good) reason : sin razón⟩ ⟨he's the champion for a reason : por algo es el campeón⟩ ⟨the reason why : la razón por la cual, el porqué⟩ ⟨to have reason to : tener motivos para⟩ **2** SENSE : razón *f* ⟨to listen to reason, to see reason : avenirse a razones⟩ ⟨to stand to reason : ser lógico⟩ ⟨within reason : dentro de lo razonable⟩

reasonable [ˈriːzənəbəl] *adj* **1** SENSIBLE : razonable **2** INEXPENSIVE : barato, económico

reasonably [ˈriːzənəbli] *adv* **1** SENSIBLY : razonablemente **2** FAIRLY : bastante

reasoning [ˈriːzənɪŋ] *n* : razonamiento *m*, raciocinio *m*, argumentos *mpl*

reassess [ˌriːəˈsɛs] *vt* : revaluar, reconsiderar

reassurance [ˌriːəˈʃʊrənts] *n* : consuelo *m*, palabras *fpl* alentadoras

reassure [ˌriːəˈʃʊr] *vt* **-sured; -suring** : tranquilizar

reassuring [ˌriːəˈʃʊrɪŋ] *adj* : tranquilizador

reawaken [ˌriːəˈweɪkən] *vt* : volver a despertar, reavivar

rebate [ˈriːˌbeɪt] *n* : reembolso *m*, devolución *f*

rebel[1] [rɪˈbɛl] *vi* **-belled; -belling** : rebelarse, sublevarse

rebel[2] [ˈrɛbəl] *adj* : rebelde

rebel[3] [ˈrɛbəl] *n* : rebelde *mf*

rebellion [rɪˈbɛljən] *n* : rebelión *f*

rebellious [rɪˈbɛljəs] *adj* : rebelde

rebelliousness [rɪˈbɛljəsnəs] *n* : rebeldía *f*

rebirth [ˌriːˈbərθ] *n* : renacimiento *m*

reboot [ˈriːˈbuːt] *vt* : reiniciar (una computadora)

reborn [riːˈbɔrn] *adj* **to be reborn** : renacer

rebound[1] [ˈriːˌbaʊnd, rɪˈbaʊnd] *vi* : rebotar

rebound[2] [ˈriːˌbaʊnd] *n* : rebote *m*

rebuff[1] [rɪˈbʌf] *vt* : desairar, rechazar

rebuff[2] *n* : desaire *m*, rechazo *m*

rebuild [ˈriːˈbɪld] *vt* **-built** [-ˈbɪlt]; **-building** : reconstruir

rebuke[1] [rɪˈbjuːk] *vt* **-buked; -buking** : reprender, regañar

rebuke[2] *n* : reprimenda *f*, reproche *m*

rebut [rɪˈbʌt] *vt* **-butted; -butting** : rebatir, refutar

rebuttal [rɪˈbʌtəl] *n* : refutación *f*

recalcitrant [rɪˈkælsɪtrənt] *adj* : recalcitrante

recall[1] [rɪˈkɔl] *vt* **1** : llamar, retirar ⟨recalled to active duty : llamado al servicio activo⟩ **2** REMEMBER : recordar, acordarse de **3** REVOKE : revocar

recall[2] [rɪˈkɔl, ˈriːˌkɔl] *n* **1** : retirada *f* (de personas o mercancías) **2** MEMORY : memoria *f* ⟨to have total recall : poder recordar todo⟩

recant [rɪˈkænt] *vt* : retractarse de — *vi* : retractarse, renegar

recap[1] [ˈriːˌkæp] *v* **-capped; -capping** *fam* → **recapitulate**

recap[2] *n* SUMMARY : resumen *m*

recapitulate [ˌriːkəˈpɪtʃəˌleɪt] *v* **-lated; -lating** : resumir, recapitular

recapture [ˌriːˈkæptʃər] vt **-tured; -turing 1** : volver a capturar **2** REGAIN : recuperar

recast [riːˈkæst] vt **-cast; -casting 1** : cambiar el reparto de (una película, etc.), cambiarle el papel a (un actor) **2** REWRITE : refundir

recede [rɪˈsiːd] vi **-ceded; -ceding 1** WITHDRAW : retirarse, retroceder **2** FADE : desvanecerse, alejarse **3** SLANT : inclinarse **4 to have a receding hairline** : tener entradas

receipt [rɪˈsiːt] n **1** : recibo m, boleta f, ticket m **2 receipts** npl : ingresos mpl, entradas fpl

receivable [rɪˈsiːvəbəl] adj **accounts receivable** : cuentas por cobrar

receive [rɪˈsiːv] vt **-ceived; -ceiving 1** GET : recibir (una carta, un golpe, etc.) **2** WELCOME : acoger, recibir ⟨to receive guests : tener invitados⟩ **3** : recibir, captar (señales de radio)

receiver [rɪˈsiːvər] n **1** : receptor m, -tora f (en futbol americano) **2** : receptor m (de radio o televisión) **3** or **telephone receiver** : auricular m

recent [ˈriːsənt] adj : reciente — **recently** adv

receptacle [rɪˈseptɪkəl] n : receptáculo m, recipiente m

reception [rɪˈsepʃən] n : recepción f ⟨reception desk : recepción⟩ ⟨reception area : vestíbulo⟩

receptionist [rɪˈsepʃənɪst] n : recepcionista mf

receptive [rɪˈseptɪv] adj : receptivo — **receptivity** [ˌriːˌsepˈtɪvəti] n

receptiveness [rɪˈseptɪvnəs] n : receptividad f

recess[1] [ˈriːˌses, rɪˈses] vt ADJOURN : suspender, levantar

recess[2] n **1** ALCOVE : hueco m, nicho m **2** BREAK : receso m, descanso m, recreo m (en el colegio)

recessed [ˈriːˌsest, rɪˈsest] adj : empotrado

recession [rɪˈseʃən] n : recesión f, depresión f económica

recessive [rɪˈsesɪv] adj : recesivo

recharge [ˌriːˈtʃɑːrdʒ] vt **-charged; -charging** : recargar

rechargeable [ˌriːˈtʃɑːrdʒəbəl] adj : recargable

recidivism [rɪˈsɪdəˌvɪzəm] n : reincidencia f

recidivist [rɪˈsɪdəvɪst] n : reincidente mf — **recidivist** adj

recipe [ˈresəˌpiː] n : receta f

recipient [rɪˈsɪpiənt] n : recipiente mf

reciprocal [rɪˈsɪprəkəl] adj : recíproco

reciprocate [rɪˈsɪprəˌkeɪt] vi **-cated; -cating** : reciprocar

reciprocity [ˌresəˈprɑːsəti] n, pl **-ties** : reciprocidad f

recital [rɪˈsaɪtəl] n **1** PERFORMANCE : recital m **2** ENUMERATION : relato m, enumeración f

recitation [ˌresəˈteɪʃən] n : recitación f —

recite [rɪˈsaɪt] vt **-cited; -citing 1** : recitar (un poema, etc.) **2** LIST : enumerar

reckless [ˈrekləs] adj : imprudente, temerario — **recklessly** adv

recklessness [ˈrekləsnəs] n : imprudencia f, temeridad f

reckon [ˈrekən] vt **1** fam THINK, SUPPOSE : creer ⟨I reckon so : creo que sí⟩ **2** CALCULATE : calcular, contar **3** CONSIDER : considerar **4 to reckon on/with** : contar con **5 to reckon with** : enfrentarse a ⟨they'll have me to reckon with : se las verán conmigo⟩ ⟨to be a force to be reckoned with : ser algo/alguien de temer⟩

reckoning [ˈrekənɪŋ] n **1** CALCULATION : cálculo m **2** SETTLEMENT : ajuste m de cuentas ⟨day of reckoning : día del juicio final⟩

reclaim [rɪˈkleɪm] vt **1** : ganar (tierra) ⟨to reclaim marshy land : sanear las tierras pantanosas⟩ **2** RECOVER : recobrar, reciclar ⟨to reclaim old tires : reciclar llantas desechadas⟩ **3** REGAIN : reclamar, recuperar ⟨to reclaim one's rights : reclamar uno sus derechos⟩

recline [rɪˈklaɪn] vi **-clined; -clining 1** LEAN : reclinarse **2** REPOSE : recostarse

reclining [rɪˈklaɪnɪŋ] adj : reclinable

recluse [ˈreˌkluːs, rɪˈkluːs] n : solitario m, -ria f

recognition [ˌrekɪɡˈnɪʃən] n : reconocimiento m

recognizable [ˈrekəɡˌnaɪzəbəl] adj : reconocible

recognize [ˈrekɪɡˌnaɪz] vt **-nized; -nizing** : reconocer

recoil[1] [rɪˈkɔɪl] vi : retroceder, dar un culatazo

recoil[2] [ˈriːˌkɔɪl, rɪˈ-] n : retroceso m, culatazo m

recollect [ˌrekəˈlekt] v : recordar

recollection [ˌrekəˈlekʃən] n : recuerdo m

recommend [ˌrekəˈmend] vt **1** : recomendar **2** ADVISE, COUNSEL : aconsejar, recomendar

recommendation [ˌrekəmənˈdeɪʃən] n : recomendación f

recompense[1] [ˈrekəmˌpens] vt **-pensed; -pensing** : indemnizar, recompensar

recompense[2] n : indemnización f, compensación f

reconcile [ˈrekənˌsaɪl] v **-ciled; -ciling** vt **1** : reconciliar (personas), conciliar (ideas, etc.) **2 to reconcile oneself to** : resignarse a — vi MAKE UP : reconciliarse, hacer las paces

reconciliation [ˌrekənˌsɪliˈeɪʃən] n : reconciliación f (con personas), conciliación f (con ideas, etc.)

recondition [ˌriːkənˈdɪʃən] vt : reacondicionar

reconnaissance [rɪˈkɑːnəzənts, -sənts] n : reconocimiento m

reconnoiter or **reconnoitre** [ˌriːkəˈnɔɪtər, ˌrekə-] v **-tered** or **-tred; -tering** or **-tring** vt : reconocer — vi : hacer un reconocimiento

reconquer [ˌriːˈkɑːŋkər] vt : reconquistar

reconquest [ˌriːˈkɑːnˌkwest, -ˈkɑːŋ-] n : reconquista f

reconsider [ˌriːkənˈsɪdər] vt : reconsiderar, repensar

reconsideration [ˌriːkənˌsɪdəˈreɪʃən] n
: reconsideración f

reconstruct [ˌriːkənˈstrʌkt] vt : reconstruir

reconstruction [ˌriːkənˈstrʌkʃən] n : reconstrucción f

reconstructive [ˌriːkənˈstrʌktɪv] adj : reconstructivo

record¹ [rɪˈkɔrd] vt 1 WRITE DOWN : anotar, apuntar 2 REGISTER : registrar,
hacer constar 3 INDICATE : marcar
(una temperatura, etc.) 4 : grabar (audio o video)

record² [ˈrɛkərd] adj : récord

record³ [ˈrɛkərd] n 1 DOCUMENT : registro m, documento m oficial 2 HISTORY
: historial m ⟨a good academic record
: un buen historial académico⟩ ⟨crimi-
nal record : antecedentes penales⟩ 3
: récord m ⟨the world record : el récord
mundial⟩ 4 : disco m (de música,
etc.) 5 for the record : que conste 6
off the record : extraoficialmente 7 on
record ⟨he is on record as saying . . .
: dijo públicamente que . . .⟩ 8 on record : registrado ⟨the highest on record : el más alto registrado⟩ 9 on the record : oficialmente 10 to set the record straight : poner las cosas en su
lugar

recorder [rɪˈkɔrdər] n 1 : flauta f dulce
(instrumento de viento) 2 tape recorder : grabadora f

recording [rɪˈkɔrdɪŋ] n : grabación f

record player n : tocadiscos m

recount¹ [rɪˈkaʊnt] vt 1 NARRATE : narrar, relatar 2 : volver a contar (votos,
etc.)

recount² [ˈriːˌkaʊnt, ˌriː-] n : recuento m

recoup [rɪˈkuːp] vt : recuperar, recobrar

recourse [ˈriːˌkors, rɪ-] n : recurso m ⟨to
have recourse to : recurrir a⟩

recover [rɪˈkʌvər] vt 1 REGAIN : recobrar, recuperar 2 : rescatar (algo robado o perdido) 3 RECOUP : recuperar
— vi RECUPERATE : recuperarse

recovery [rɪˈkʌvəri] n, pl -eries : recuperación f

re–create [ˌriːkriˈeɪt] vt -ated; -ating : recrear — re–creation [ˌriːkriˈeɪʃən] n

recreation [ˌrɛkriˈeɪʃən] n : recreo m, esparcimiento m, diversión f

recreational [ˌrɛkriˈeɪʃənəl] adj : recreativo, de recreo

recreational vehicle n : vehículo m de
recreo

recrimination [rɪˌkrɪməˈneɪʃən] n : recriminación f

recruit¹ [rɪˈkruːt] vt : reclutar

recruit² n : recluta mf

recruitment [rɪˈkruːtmənt] n : reclutamiento m, alistamiento m

rectal [ˈrɛktəl] adj : rectal

rectangle [ˈrɛkˌtæŋɡəl] n : rectángulo m

rectangular [rɛkˈtæŋɡjələr] adj : rectangular

rectify [ˈrɛktəˌfaɪ] vt -fied; -fying : rectificar — rectification [ˌrɛktəfəˈkeɪʃən] n

rectitude [ˈrɛktəˌtuːd, -ˌtjuːd] n : rectitud f

rector [ˈrɛktər] n : rector m, -tora f

rectory [ˈrɛktəri] n, pl -ries : rectoría f

rectum [ˈrɛktəm] n, pl -tums or -ta [-tə]
: recto m

recuperate [rɪˈkuːpəˌreɪt, -ˈkjuː-] v -ated;
-ating vt : recuperar — vi : recuperarse,
restablecerse

recuperation [rɪˌkuːpəˈreɪʃən, -ˌkjuː-] n
: recuperación f

recur [rɪˈkər] vi -curred; -curring : volver
a ocurrir, volver a producirse, repetirse

recurrence [rɪˈkərənts] n : repetición f,
reaparición f

recurrent [rɪˈkərənt] adj : recurrente, que
se repite

recyclable [riːˈsaɪkələbəl] adj : reciclable

recycle [riːˈsaɪkəl] vt -cled; -cling : reciclar

recycling [riːˈsaɪkəlɪŋ] n : reciclaje m

red¹ [ˈrɛd] adj 1 : rojo, colorado ⟨to be
red in the face : ponerse colorado⟩ ⟨to
have red hair : ser pelirrojo⟩ 2 COMMU-
NIST : rojo, comunista

red² n 1 : rojo m, colorado m 2 Red
COMMUNIST : comunista mf

red blood cell n : glóbulo m rojo

red–blooded [ˈrɛdˈblʌdəd] adj : vigoroso

redden [ˈrɛdən] vt : enrojecer — vi BLUSH
: enrojecerse, ruborizarse

reddish [ˈrɛdɪʃ] adj : rojizo

redecorate [ˌriːˈdɛkəˌreɪt] vt -rated; -rat-
ing : renovar, pintar de nuevo

redeem [rɪˈdiːm] vt 1 RESCUE, SAVE : rescatar, salvar 2 : desempeñar ⟨she re-
deemed it from the pawnshop : lo desem-
peñó de la casa de empeños⟩ 3 : redimir
(en religión) 4 : canjear, vender ⟨to redeem coupons : canjear cupones⟩

redeemer [rɪˈdiːmər] n : redentor m, -tora f

redeeming [rɪˈdiːmɪŋ] adj : positivo ⟨re-
deeming qualities : cualidades positivas⟩

redefine [ˌriːdɪˈfaɪn] vt : redefinir

redemption [rɪˈdɛmpʃən] n : redención f

redesign [ˌriːdɪˈzaɪn] vt : rediseñar

red–eye [ˈrɛdˌaɪ] or red–eye flight n
: vuelo m nocturno

red–haired [ˈrɛdˈhærd] adj : pelirrojo

red–handed [ˈrɛdˈhændəd] adv : in fraganti

redhead [ˈrɛdˌhɛd] n : pelirrojo m, -ja f

redheaded [ˈrɛdˌhɛdəd] → red–haired

red herring [ˈrɛdˈlɛtər-] n : trampa f (para distraer la
atención)

red–hot [ˈrɛdˈhɑt] adj 1 : al rojo vivo,
candente 2 CURRENT : de candente actualidad 3 POPULAR : de gran popularidad

redirect [ˌriːdəˈrɛkt, -daɪ-] vt : desviar
(tráfico, dinero, etc.)

rediscover [ˌriːdɪˈskʌvər] vt : redescubrir

redistribute [ˌriːdɪˈstrɪˌbjuːt] vt -uted; -ut-
ing : redistribuir

red–letter day [ˈrɛdˈlɛtər-] n : día m memorable

redness [ˈrɛdnəs] n : rojez f

redo [riːˈduː] vt -did [-ˈdɪd]; -done [-ˈdʌn];
-doing 1 : hacer de nuevo 2 → redecorate

redolence [ˈrɛdələnts] n : fragancia f

redolent [ˈrɛdələnt] adj 1 FRAGRANT
: fragante, oloroso 2 SUGGESTIVE : evocador

redouble [riˈdʌbəl] *vt* -**bled**; -**bling** : redoblar, intensificar (esfuerzos, etc.)

redress [riˈdrɛs] *vt* : reparar, remediar, enmendar

red snapper *n* : pargo *m*, huachinango *m Mex*

red tape *n* : papeleo *m*

reduce [riˈduːs, -ˈdjuːs] *v* -**duced**; -**ducing** *vt* **1** LESSEN : reducir, disminuir, rebajar (precios) **2** DEMOTE : bajar de categoría, degradar **3** : dejar reducir (un líquido) **4 to be reduced to** : quedar reducido a (escombros, etc.) **5 to be reduced to** : verse rebajado/forzado a **6 to reduce someone to tears** : hacer llorar a alguien — *vi* SLIM : adelgazar

reduction [riˈdʌkʃən] *n* : reducción *f*, rebaja *f*

redundancy [riˈdʌndəntsi] *n, pl* -**cies** **1** : superfluidad *f* **2** REPETITION : redundancia *f*

redundant [riˈdʌndənt] *adj* : superfluo, redundante

redwood [ˈrɛdˌwʊd] *n* : secoya *f*

reed [ˈriːd] *n* **1** : caña *f*, carrizo *m*, junco *m* **2** : lengüeta *f* (para instrumentos de viento)

reef [ˈriːf] *n* : arrecife *m*, escollo *m*

reek¹ [ˈriːk] *vi* : apestar

reek² *n* : hedor *m*

reel¹ [ˈriːl] *vt* **1 to reel in** : enrollar, sacar (un pez) del agua **2 to reel off** : recitar de un tirón — *vi* **1** SPIN, WHIRL : girar, dar vueltas **2** STAGGER : tambalearse

reel² *n* **1** : carrete *m* (de película, etc.) ⟨fishing reel : carrete de pesca⟩ **2** : baile *m* escocés **3** STAGGER : tambaleo *m*

reelect [ˌriːˈlɛkt] *vt* : reelegir

reenact [ˌriːɪˈnækt] *vt* : representar de nuevo, reconstruir

reenter [ˌriːˈɛntər] *vt* : volver a entrar

reestablish [ˌriːɪˈstæblɪʃ] *vt* : restablecer — **reestablishment** [ˌriːɪˈstæblɪʃmənt] *n*

reevaluate [ˌriːɪˈvæljuˌeɪt] *vt* -**ated**; -**ating** : revaluar

reevaluation [ˌriːɪˌvæljuˈeɪʃən] *n* : revaluación *f*

reexamine [ˌriːɪgˈzæmən, -g-] *vt* -**ined**; -**ining** : volver a examinar, reexaminar

ref → **referee**

refer [riˈfər] *v* -**ferred**; -**ferring** *vt* DIRECT, SEND : remitir, enviar ⟨to refer a patient to a specialist : enviar a un paciente a un especialista⟩ — *vi* **to refer to** MENTION : referirse a, aludir a

referee¹ [ˌrɛfəˈriː] *v* -**eed**; -**eeing** : arbitrar

referee² *n* : árbitro *m*, -tra *f*; réferi *mf*

reference [ˈrɛfrənts, ˈrɛfə-] *n* **1** ALLUSION : referencia *f*, alusión *f* ⟨to make reference to : hacer referencia a⟩ **2** CONSULTATION : consulta *f* ⟨for future reference : para futuras consultas⟩ **3** or **reference book** : libro *m* de consulta **4** TESTIMONIAL : informe *m*, referencia *f*, recomendación *f* **5 in/with reference to** : con referencia a

referendum [ˌrɛfəˈrɛndəm] *n, pl* -**da** [-də] *or* -**dums** : referéndum *m*

refill¹ [ˌriːˈfɪl] *vt* : rellenar

refill² [ˈriːˌfɪl] *n* : recambio *m*

refinance [ˌriːfaɪˈnænts] *vt* -**nanced**; -**nancing** : refinanciar

refine [riˈfaɪn] *vt* -**fined**; -**fining** **1** : refinar (azúcar, petróleo, etc.) **2** PERFECT : perfeccionar, pulir

refined [riˈfaɪnd] *adj* **1** : refinado (dícese del azúcar, etc.) **2** CULTURED : culto, educado, refinado

refinement [riˈfaɪnmənt] *n* : refinamiento *m*, fineza *f*, finura *f*

refinery [riˈfaɪnəri] *n, pl* -**eries** : refinería *f*

reflect [riˈflɛkt] *vt* **1** : reflejar **2 to be reflected in** : reflejarse en **3 to reflect that** : pensar que, considerar que — *vi* **1** : reflejarse **2 to reflect on** : reflexionar sobre **3 to reflect badly on** : desacreditar, dejar mal parado

reflection [riˈflɛkʃən] *n* **1** : reflexión *f*, reflejo *m* (de la luz, de imágenes, etc.) **2** THOUGHT : reflexión *f*, meditación *f*

reflective [riˈflɛktɪv] *adj* **1** THOUGHTFUL : reflexivo, pensativo **2** : reflectante (en física)

reflector [riˈflɛktər] *n* : reflector *m*

reflex [ˈriːˌflɛks] *n* : reflejo *m*

reflexive [riˈflɛksɪv] *adj* : reflexivo ⟨a reflexive verb : un verbo reflexivo⟩

reform¹ [riˈfɔrm] *vt* : reformar — *vi* : reformarse

reform² *n* : reforma *f*

reformation [ˌrɛfərˈmeɪʃən] *n* : reforma *f* ⟨the Reformation : la Reforma⟩

reform school *n* : reformatorio *m*

reformer [riˈfɔrmər] *n* : reformador *m*, -dora *f*

refract [riˈfrækt] *vt* : refractar — *vi* : refractarse

refraction [riˈfrækʃən] *n* : refracción *f*

refrain¹ [riˈfreɪn] *vi* **to refrain from** : abstenerse de

refrain² *n* : estribillo *m* (en música)

refresh [riˈfrɛʃ] *vt* : refrescar ⟨to refresh one's memory : refrescarle la memoria a uno⟩

refreshing [riˈfrɛʃɪŋ] *adj* : refrescante ⟨a refreshing sleep : un sueño reparador⟩

refreshment [riˈfrɛʃmənt] *n* **1** : refresco *m* **2 refreshments** *npl* : refrigerio *m*

refried [ˈriːˌfraɪd] *adj* : refrito

refrigerate [riˈfrɪdʒəˌreɪt] *vt* -**ated**; -**ating** : refrigerar

refrigeration [riˌfrɪdʒəˈreɪʃən] *n* : refrigeración *f*

refrigerator [riˈfrɪdʒəˌreɪtər] *n* : refrigerador *m*, -dora *f*; nevera *f*

refuel [riːˈfjuːəl] *v* -**eled** *or* -**elled**; -**eling** *or* -**elling** *vi* : repostar — *vt* : llenar de combustible

refuge [ˈrɛˌfjuːdʒ] *n* : refugio *m*

refugee [ˌrɛfjuˈdʒiː] *n* : refugiado *m*, -da *f*

refund¹ [riˈfʌnd, ˈriːˌfʌnd] *vt* : reembolsar, devolver

refund² [ˈriːˌfʌnd] *n* : reembolso *m*, devolución *f*

refundable [riˈfʌndəbəl] *adj* : reembolsable

refurbish [riˈfərbɪʃ] *vt* : renovar, restaurar

refusal [riˈfjuːzəl] *n* : negativa *f*, rechazo *m*, denegación *f* (de una petición)

refuse¹ [rɪˈfjuːz] *vt* **-fused; -fusing 1** RE-JECT : rechazar, rehusar **2** DENY : negar, rehusar, denegar ⟨to refuse permission : negar el permiso⟩ **3 to refuse to** : negarse a

refuse² [ˈrɛˌfjuːs, -ˌfjuːz] *n* : basura *f*, desechos *mpl*, desperdicios *mpl*

refutation [ˌrɛfjʊˈteɪʃən] *n* : refutación *f*

refute [rɪˈfjuːt] *vt* **-futed; -futing 1** DENY : desmentir, negar **2** DISPROVE : refutar, rebatir

regain [riːˈɡeɪn] *vt* **1** RECOVER : recuperar, recobrar **2** REACH : alcanzar ⟨to regain the shore : llegar a la tierra⟩

regal [ˈriːɡəl] *adj* : real, regio

regale [rɪˈɡeɪl] *vt* **-galed; -galing 1** ENTERTAIN : agasajar, entretener **2** AMUSE, DELIGHT : deleitar, divertir

regalia [rɪˈɡeɪljə] *n* : ropaje *m*, vestiduras *fpl*, adornos *fpl*

regard¹ [rɪˈɡɑrd] *vt* **1** OBSERVE : observar, mirar ⟨he regarded me with suspicion : me miró con recelo⟩ **2** HEED : tener en cuenta, hacer caso de **3** CONSIDER : considerar ⟨I regard her as a friend : la considero una amiga⟩ **4** RESPECT : respetar ⟨highly regarded : muy estimado⟩ **5 as regards** : en cuanto a, en lo que se refiere a

regard² *n* **1** CONSIDERATION : consideración *f* ⟨with no regard for : sin ninguna consideración por⟩ **2** ESTEEM : respeto *m*, estima *f* ⟨to hold someone in high regard : tener a alguien en gran estima⟩ **3** PARTICULAR : aspecto *m*, sentido *m* ⟨in this regard : en este sentido⟩ **4 regards** *npl* : saludos *mpl*, recuerdos *mpl* **5 with regard to** : con relación a, con respecto a

regarding [rɪˈɡɑrdɪŋ] *prep* : con respecto a, en cuanto a

regardless [rɪˈɡɑrdləs] *adv* : a pesar de todo

regardless of *prep* : a pesar de, sin tener en cuenta ⟨regardless of our mistakes : a pesar de nuestros errores⟩ ⟨regardless of age : sin tener en cuenta la edad⟩

regatta [rɪˈɡɑtə] *n* : regata *f*

regency [ˈriːdʒəntsi] *n, pl* **-cies** : regencia *f*

regenerate [rɪˈdʒɛnəˌreɪt] *v* **-ated; -ating** *vt* : regenerar — *vi* : regenerarse

regeneration [rɪˌdʒɛnəˈreɪʃən] *n* : regeneración *f*

regent [ˈriːdʒənt] *n* **1** RULER : regente *mf* **2** : miembro *m* de la junta directiva (de una universidad)

reggae [ˈrɛˌɡeɪ, ˈreɪ-] *n* : reggae *m*

regime [reɪˈʒiːm, rɪ-] *n* : régimen *m*

regimen [ˈrɛdʒəmən] *n* : régimen *m*

regiment¹ [ˈrɛdʒəˌment] *vt* : reglamentar

regiment² [ˈrɛdʒəmənt] *n* : regimiento *m*

region [ˈriːdʒən] *n* **1** : región *f* **2 in the region of** : alrededor de

regional [ˈriːdʒənəl] *adj* : regional — **regionally** *adv*

register¹ [ˈrɛdʒəstər] *vt* **1** RECORD : registrar, inscribir, matricular (un vehículo) **2** INDICATE : marcar (temperatura, medidas, etc.) **3** SHOW : manifestar, acusar ⟨to register surprise : acusar sor-

presa⟩ **4** : certificar (correo) — *vi* ENROLL : inscribirse, matricularse ⟨to register to vote : inscribirse para votar⟩

register² *n* : registro *m*

registrar [ˈrɛdʒəˌstrɑr] *n* : registrador *m*, -dora *f* oficial

registration [ˌrɛdʒəˈstreɪʃən] *n* **1** REGISTERING : inscripción *f*, matriculación *f*, registro *m* **2 or registration number** : matrícula *f*, número *m* de matrícula

registry [ˈrɛdʒəstri] *n, pl* **-tries** : registro *m*

regress [rɪˈɡrɛs] *vi* : retroceder

regression [rɪˈɡrɛʃən] *n* : retroceso *m*, regresión *f*

regressive [rɪˈɡrɛsɪv] *adj* : regresivo

regret¹ [rɪˈɡrɛt] *vt* **-gretted; -gretting** : arrepentirse de, lamentar ⟨he regrets nothing : no se arrepiente de nada⟩ ⟨I regret to tell you : lamento decirle⟩

regret² *n* **1** REMORSE : arrepentimiento *m*, remordimientos *mpl* **2** SADNESS : pesar *m*, dolor *m* **3 regrets** *npl* : excusas *fpl* ⟨to send one's regrets : excusarse⟩

regretful [rɪˈɡrɛtfəl] *adj* : arrepentido, pesaroso

regretfully [rɪˈɡrɛtfəli] *adv* : con pesar

regrettable [rɪˈɡrɛtəbəl] *adj* : lamentable — **regrettably** [-bli] *adv*

regroup [riˈɡruːp] *vi* **1** : reagruparse **2** : tomarse un respiro (para prepararse, etc.)

regular¹ [ˈrɛɡjələr] *adj* **1** NORMAL : normal ⟨regular-sized⟩ : de tamaño normal⟩ ⟨at the regular time : a la hora de siempre⟩ **2** ORDINARY : normal **3** : regular ⟨a regular pace/pattern : un ritmo/dibujo regular⟩ ⟨on a regular basis : regularmente, con regularidad⟩ **4** : habitual ⟨a regular customer : un cliente habitual⟩ **5** : regular (en gramática) **6** REAL : verdadero

regular² *n* : cliente *mf* habitual

regularity [ˌrɛɡjəˈlærəti] *n, pl* **-ties** : regularidad *f*

regularly [ˈrɛɡjələrli] *adv* : regularmente, con regularidad

regulate [ˈrɛɡjəˌleɪt] *vt* **-lated; -lating** : regular

regulation [ˌrɛɡjəˈleɪʃən] *n* **1** REGULATING : regulación *f* **2** RULE : regla *f*, reglamento *m*, norma *f* ⟨safety regulations : reglas de seguridad⟩

regulator [ˈrɛɡjəˌleɪtər] *n* **1** : regulador *m* (mecanismo) **2** : persona *f* que regula

regulatory [ˈrɛɡjələˌtori] *adj* : regulador

regurgitate [rɪˈɡərdʒəˌteɪt] *v* **-tated; -tating** : regurgitar, vomitar

rehab [ˈriːˌhæb] → **rehabilitate, rehabilitation**

rehabilitate [ˌriːhəˈbɪləˌteɪt, ˌriːə-] *vt* **-tated; -tating** : rehabilitar

rehabilitation [ˌriːhəˌbɪləˈteɪʃən, ˌriːə-] *n* : rehabilitación *f*

rehearsal [rɪˈhərsəl] *n* : ensayo *m*

rehearse [rɪˈhərs] *v* **-hearsed; -hearsing** : ensayar

reheat [ˌriːˈhiːt] *vt* : recalentar

reign¹ [ˈreɪn] *vi* **1** : reinar **2** PREVAIL : reinar, predominar ⟨the reigning champion : el actual campeón⟩

reign[2] *n* : reinado *m*
reimburse [ˌriːəmˈbərs] *vt* **-bursed; -bursing** : reembolsar
reimbursement [ˌriːəmˈbərsmənt] *n* : reembolso *m*
rein[1] [ˈreɪn] *vt* : refrenar (un caballo)
rein[2] *n* **1** : rienda *f* ⟨to give free rein to : dar rienda suelta a⟩ **2** CHECK : control *m* ⟨to keep a tight rein on : llevar un estricto control de⟩
reincarnation [ˌriːɪnˌkɑrˈneɪʃən] *n* : reencarnación *f*
reindeer [ˈreɪnˌdɪr] *n* : reno *m*
reinforce [ˌriːənˈfors] *vt* **-forced; -forcing** : reforzar
reinforcement [ˌriːənˈforsmənt] *n* : refuerzo *m*
reinstall [ˌriːənˈstɔl] *vt* **-stalled; -stalling** : reinstalar
reinstate [ˌriːənˈsteɪt] *vt* **-stated; -stating 1** : reintegrar, restituir (una persona) **2** RESTORE : restablecer (un servicio, etc.)
reinstatement [ˌriːənˈsteɪtmənt] *n* : reintegración *f*, restitución *f*, restablecimiento *m*
reintegrate [riˈɪntəˌgreɪt] *vt* **-ated; -ating** : reintegrar — **reintegration** [riˌɪntəˈgreɪʃən] *n*
reintroduce [riˌɪntrəˈduːs, -ˈdjuːs] *vt* **-duced; -ducing** : reintroducir (un animal, una política, etc.)
reiterate [riˈɪtəˌreɪt] *vt* **-ated; -ating** : reiterar, repetir
reiteration [riˌɪtəˈreɪʃən] *n* : reiteración *f*, repetición *f*
reject[1] [rɪˈʤɛkt] *vt* : rechazar
reject[2] [ˈriːˌʤɛkt] *n* : desecho *m* (cosa), persona *f* rechazada
rejection [rɪˈʤɛkʃən] *n* : rechazo *m*
rejoice [rɪˈʤɔɪs] *vi* **-joiced; -joicing** : alegrarse, regocijarse
rejoin [ˌriːˈʤɔɪn] *vt* **1** : reincorporarse a, reintegrarse a ⟨he rejoined the firm : se reincorporó a la firma⟩ **2** [riˈ-] REPLY, RETORT : replicar
rejoinder [rɪˈʤɔɪndər] *n* : réplica *f*
rejuvenate [rɪˈʤuːvəˌneɪt] *vt* **-nated; -nating** : rejuvenecer
rejuvenation [rɪˌʤuːvəˈneɪʃən] *n* : rejuvenecimiento *m*
rekindle [ˌriːˈkɪndəl] *vt* **-dled; -dling** : reavivar
relapse[1] [rɪˈlæps] *vi* **-lapsed; -lapsing** : recaer, volver a caer
relapse[2] [ˈriːˌlæps, rɪˈlæps] *n* : recaída *f*
relate [rɪˈleɪt] *v* **-lated; -lating** *vt* **1** TELL : relatar, contar **2** ASSOCIATE : relacionar, asociar ⟨to relate crime to poverty : relacionar la delincuencia con la pobreza⟩ — *vi* **1** INTERACT : relacionarse (con), llevarse bien (con) **2** relating to : relacionado con **3** to be related (to) : estar relacionado (con) **4** to relate to UNDERSTAND : identificarse con, simpatizar con
related [rɪˈleɪtəd] *adj* : emparentado ⟨to be related to : ser pariente de⟩
relation [rɪˈleɪʃən] *n* **1** NARRATION : relato *m*, narración *f* **2** RELATIVE : pa-

riente *mf*, familiar *mf* **3** RELATIONSHIP : relación *f* ⟨in relation to : en relación con, con relación a⟩ ⟨to have/bear no relation to : no tener nada que ver con⟩ **4** relations *npl* : relaciones *fpl* ⟨public relations : relaciones públicas⟩
relationship [rɪˈleɪʃənˌʃɪp] *n* **1** CONNECTION : relación *f* **2** KINSHIP : parentesco *m*
relative[1] [ˈrɛlətɪv] *adj* **1** : relativo **2** relative to CONCERNING : con relación a **3** relative to : en comparación a — **relatively** *adv*
relative[2] *n* : pariente *mf*, familiar *mf*
relativism [ˈrɛlətɪˌvɪzəm] *n* : relativismo *m*
relativity [ˌrɛləˈtɪvəti] *n*, *pl* **-ties** : relatividad *f*
relaunch [riˈlɔntʃ] *v* : relanzar
relax [rɪˈlæks] *vt* : relajar, aflojar — *vi* : relajarse
relaxation [ˌriːˌlækˈseɪʃən] *n* **1** RELAXING : relajación *f* **2** DIVERSION : esparcimiento *m*, distracción *f*
relaxing [rɪˈlæksɪŋ] *adj* : relajante
relay[1] [ˈriːˌleɪ, rɪˈleɪ] *vt* **-layed; -laying** : transmitir
relay[2] [ˈriːˌleɪ] *n* **1** : relevo *m* **2** *or* relay race : carrera de relevos
release[1] [rɪˈliːs] *vt* **-leased; -leasing 1** FREE : liberar, poner en libertad **2** LOOSEN : soltar, aflojar ⟨to release the brake : soltar el freno⟩ **3** GIVE OFF : despedir, emitir **4** DIVULGE : divulgar **5** RELINQUISH : renunciar a, ceder **6** ISSUE : publicar (un libro), estrenar (una película), sacar (un disco)
release[2] *n* **1** LIBERATION : liberación *f*, puesta *f* en libertad **2** RELINQUISHING : cesión *f* (de propiedad, etc.) **3** ISSUE : estreno *m* (de una película), puesta *f* en venta (de un disco), publicación *f* (de un libro) **4** ESCAPE : escape *m*, fuga *f* (de un gas)
relegate [ˈrɛləˌgeɪt] *vt* **-gated; -gating** : relegar
relent [rɪˈlɛnt] *vi* : ablandarse, ceder
relentless [rɪˈlɛntləs] *adj* : implacable, sin tregua
relentlessly [rɪˈlɛntləsli] *adv* : implacablemente
relevance [ˈrɛləvənts] *n* : pertinencia *f*, relación *f*
relevant [ˈrɛləvənt] *adj* : pertinente — **relevantly** *adv*
reliability [rɪˌlaɪəˈbɪləti] *n*, *pl* **-ties 1** : fiabilidad *f*, seguridad *f* (de una cosa) **2** : formalidad *f*, seriedad *f* (de una persona)
reliable [rɪˈlaɪəbəl] *adj* : confiable, fiable, fidedigno, seguro
reliably [rɪˈlaɪəbli] *adv* : sin fallar ⟨to be reliably informed : saber (algo) de fuentes fidedignas⟩
reliance [rɪˈlaɪənts] *n* **1** DEPENDENCE : dependencia *f* **2** CONFIDENCE : confianza *f*
reliant [rɪˈlaɪənt] *adj* : dependiente
relic [ˈrɛlɪk] *n* **1** : reliquia *f* **2** VESTIGE : vestigio *m*
relief [rɪˈliːf] *n* **1** : alivio *m*, desahogo *m*

⟨what a relief! : ¡qué alivio!⟩ ⟨pain relief : alivio del dolor⟩ **2** AID, WELFARE : ayuda *f* (benéfica), asistencia *f* social **3** : relieve *m* ⟨relief map : mapa en relieve⟩ **4** REPLACEMENT : relevo *m*

relieve [rɪ'liːv] *vt* **-lieved; -lieving 1** ALLEVIATE : aliviar, mitigar ⟨to feel relieved : sentirse aliviado⟩ **2** FREE : liberar **3** EXEMPT : eximir **4** REPLACE : relevar (a un centinela, etc.) **5** BREAK : romper ⟨to relieve the monotony : romper la monotonía⟩ **6 to relieve someone of** : relevar a alguien de (su cargo, etc.)

religion [rɪ'lɪdʒən] *n* : religión *f*

religious [rɪ'lɪdʒəs] *adj* : religioso — **religiously** *adv*

relinquish [rɪ'lɪŋkwɪʃ, -'lɪn-] *vt* **1** GIVE UP : renunciar a, abandonar **2** RELEASE : soltar

relish[1] ['rɛlɪʃ] *vt* : saborear (comida), disfrutar con (un reto, etc.) ⟨I don't relish the idea : no me entusiasma la idea⟩

relish[2] *n* **1** ENJOYMENT : gusto *m*, deleite *m* **2** : salsa *f* de pepinillos en vinagre

relive [ˌriː'lɪv] *vt* **-lived; -living** : revivir

reload [ˌriː'loːd] *vt* : recargar

relocate [ˌriː'loːˌkeɪt, ˌriːloː'keɪt] *v* **-cated; -cating** *vt* : reubicar, trasladar — *vi* : trasladarse

relocation [ˌriːloː'keɪʃən] *n* : reubicación *f*, traslado *m*

reluctance [rɪ'lʌktənts] *n* : renuncia *f*, reticencia *f*, desgana *f*

reluctant [rɪ'lʌktənt] *adj* : renuente, reacio, reticente

reluctantly [rɪ'lʌktəntli] *adv* : a regañadientes

rely [rɪ'laɪ] *vi* **-lied; -lying 1** DEPEND : depender (de), contar (con) **2** TRUST : confiar (en)

remain [rɪ'meɪn] *vi* **1** : quedar ⟨very little remains : queda muy poco⟩ ⟨there's remaining 10 minutes : los 10 minutos que quedan⟩ **2** STAY : quedarse, permanecer **3** CONTINUE : seguir, continuar ⟨to remain the same : seguir siendo igual⟩ **4 to remain to** : quedar por ⟨to remain to be done : quedar por hacer⟩ ⟨it remains to be seen : está por ver⟩

remainder [rɪ'meɪndər] *n* : resto *m*, remanente *m*

remains [rɪ'meɪnz] *npl* : restos *mpl* ⟨mortal remains : restos mortales⟩

remake[1] [ˌriː'meɪk] *vt* **-made; -making 1** TRANSFORM : rehacer **2** : hacer una nueva versión de (una película, etc.)

remake[2] ['riːˌmeɪk] *n* : nueva versión *f*

remand [rɪ'mænd] *vt* **1** : devolver (un juicio) a otro tribunal **2 to remand someone into custody** : dictarle a alguien la prisión preventiva

remark[1] [rɪ'mɑrk] *vt* **1** NOTICE : observar **2** SAY : comentar, observar — *vi* **to remark on** : hacer observaciones sobre

remark[2] *n* : comentario *m*, observación *f*

remarkable [rɪ'mɑrkəbəl] *adj* : extraordinario, notable — **remarkably** [-bli] *adv*

remarry [ˌriː'mæri] *v* **-ried; -rying** *vi* : volver a casarse — *vt* : volver a casarse con

rematch ['riːˌmætʃ] *n* : revancha *f*

remedial [rɪ'miːdiəl] *adj* : correctivo ⟨remedial classes : clases para alumnos atrasados⟩

remedy[1] ['rɛmədi] *vt* **-died; -dying** : remediar

remedy[2] *n*, *pl* **-dies** : remedio *m*, medicamento *m*

remember [rɪ'mɛmbər] *vt* **1** RECOLLECT : acordarse de, recordar **2** : no olvidar ⟨remember my words : no olvides mis palabras⟩ ⟨to remember to : acordarse de⟩ **3** : dar saludos, dar recuerdos ⟨remember me to her : dale saludos de mi parte⟩ **4** COMMEMORATE : recordar, conmemorar

remembrance [rɪ'mɛmbrənts] *n* **1** RECOLLECTION : recuerdo *m* ⟨in remembrance of : en conmemoración de⟩ **2** MEMENTO : recuerdo *m*

remind [rɪ'maɪnd] *vt* : recordar ⟨remind me to do it : recuérdame que lo haga⟩ ⟨she reminds me of Clara : me recuerda de Clara⟩

reminder [rɪ'maɪndər] *n* : recuerdo *m*

reminisce [ˌrɛmə'nɪs] *vi* **-nisced; -niscing** : rememorar los viejos tiempos

reminiscence [ˌrɛmə'nɪsənts] *n* : recuerdo *m*, reminiscencia *f*

reminiscent [ˌrɛmə'nɪsənt] *adj* **1** NOSTALGIC : nostálgico **2** SUGGESTIVE : evocador, que recuerda — **reminiscently** *adv*

remiss [rɪ'mɪs] *adj* : negligente, descuidado, remiso

remission [rɪ'mɪʃən] *n* : remisión *f*

remit [rɪ'mɪt] *vt* **-mitted; -mitting 1** PARDON : perdonar **2** SEND : remitir, enviar (dinero)

remittance [rɪ'mɪtənts] *n* : remesa *f*

remnant ['rɛmnənt] *n* : restos *mpl*, vestigio *m*

remodel [rɪ'mɑdəl] *vt* **-eled** *or* **-elled; -eling** *or* **-elling** : remodelar, reformar

remonstrate [rɪ'mɑnˌstret] *vi* **-strated; -strating** : protestar ⟨to remonstrate with someone : quejarse a alguien⟩

remorse [rɪ'mɔrs] *n* : remordimiento *m*

remorseful [rɪ'mɔrsfəl] *adj* : arrepentido, lleno de remordimiento

remorseless [rɪ'mɔrsləs] *adj* **1** PITILESS : despiadado **2** RELENTLESS : implacable

remote[1] [rɪ'moːt] *adj* **remoter; -est 1** FAR-OFF : lejano, remoto ⟨remote countries : países remotos⟩ ⟨in the remote past : en el pasado lejano⟩ **2** SECLUDED : recóndito **3** : a distancia, remoto **4** SLIGHT : remoto **5** ALOOF : distante

remote[2] *or* **remote control** *n* : control *m* remoto

remote-controlled *adj* : teledirigido

remotely [rɪ'moːtli] *adv* **1** SLIGHTLY : remotamente **2** DISTANTLY : en un lugar remoto, muy lejos

remoteness [rɪ'moːtnəs] *n* : lejanía *f*

removable [rɪ'muːvəbəl] *adj* : removible

removal [rɪ'muːvəl] *n* : separación *f*, extracción *f*, supresión *f* (en algo escrito), eliminación *f* (de problemas, etc.)

remove [rɪ'muːv] vt **-moved; -moving 1** : quitar, quitarse ⟨remove the lid : quite la tapa⟩ ⟨to remove one's hat : quitarse el sombrero⟩ **2** EXTRACT : sacar, extraer ⟨to remove the contents of : sacar el contenido de⟩ **3** ELIMINATE : eliminar, disipar

remover [rɪ'muːvər] n **1** nail polish remover : quitaesmalte m **2** stain remover : quitamanchas m

remunerate [rɪ'mjuːnə,reɪt] vt **-ated; -ating** : remunerar

remuneration [rɪ,mjuːnə'reɪʃən] n : remuneración f

renaissance [,rɛnə'sɑːnts, -'zɑːnts;, 'rɛnə,-] n : renacimiento m ⟨the Renaissance : el Renacimiento⟩

renal ['riːnəl] adj : renal

rename [,riː'neɪm] vt **-named; -naming** : ponerle un nombre nuevo a

rend ['rɛnd] vt **rent** ['rɛnt]; **rending** : desgarrar

render ['rɛndər] vt **1** : derretir (manteca, etc.) **2** GIVE : prestar, dar ⟨to render aid : prestar ayuda⟩ **3** MAKE : hacer, volver, dejar ⟨it rendered him helpless : lo dejó incapacitado⟩ **4** TRANSLATE : traducir, verter ⟨to render into English : traducir al inglés⟩

rendezvous ['rɑːndɪ,vuː, -deɪ-] ns & pl : encuentro m, cita f

rendition [rɛn'dɪʃən] n : interpretación f

renegade ['rɛnɪ,geɪd] n : renegado m, -da f

renege [rɪ'nɪg, -'nɛg] vi **-neged; -neging to renege on** : incumplir, no cumplir (una promesa, etc.)

renew [rɪ'nuː, -'njuː] vt **1** REVIVE : renovar (esperanzas, etc.) **2** RESUME : reanudar **3** EXTEND : renovar ⟨to renew a subscription : renovar una suscripción⟩

renewable [rɪ'nuːəbəl, -'njuː-] adj : renovable

renewal [rɪ'nuːəl, -'njuː-] n : renovación f

renounce [rɪ'naʊnts] vt **-nounced; -nouncing** : renunciar a

renovate ['rɛnə,veɪt] vt **-vated; -vating** : restaurar, renovar

renovation [,rɛnə'veɪʃən] n : restauración f, renovación f

renown [rɪ'naʊn] n : renombre m, fama f, celebridad f

renowned [rɪ'naʊnd] adj : renombrado, célebre, famoso

rent¹ ['rɛnt] vt : rentar, alquilar

rent² n **1** : renta f, alquiler m ⟨for rent : se alquila⟩ **2** RIP : rasgadura f

rental¹ ['rɛntəl] adj RENT : de alquiler

rental² n : alquiler m

renter ['rɛntər] n : arrendatario m, -ria f

renunciation [rɪ,nʌntsi'eɪʃən] n : renuncia f

reopen [,riː'oːpən] vt : volver a abrir

reorganization [,riː,ɔrgənə'zeɪʃən] n : reorganización f

reorganize [,riː'ɔrgən,aɪz] vt **-nized; -nizing** : reorganizar

rep ['rɛp] n → representative²

repair¹ [rɪ'pær] vt : reparar, arreglar, refaccionar

repair² n **1** : reparación f, arreglo m **2** CONDITION : estado m ⟨in bad repair : en mal estado⟩

repairman [rɪ'pær,mæn, -mən] n, pl **-men** [-mən, -,mɛn] : mecánico m, técnico m

reparation [,rɛpə'reɪʃən] n **1** AMENDS : reparación f **2 reparations** npl COMPENSATION : indemnización f

repartee [,rɛpər'tiː, -,pɑr-, -'teɪ] n : intercambio m de réplicas ingeniosas

repast [rɪ'pæst, 'riː,pæst] n : comida f

repatriate [riː'peɪtri,eɪt] vt **-ated; -ating** : repatriar

repay [ri'peɪ] vt **-paid; -paying 1** : pagar (una deuda), devolver (dinero) **2** : pagar (un favor)

repayment [ri'peɪmənt] n : pago m

repeal¹ [rɪ'piːl] vt : abrogar, revocar

repeal² n : abrogación f, revocación f

repeat¹ [rɪ'piːt] vt : repetir

repeat² n : repetición f

repeatedly [rɪ'piːtədli] adv : repetidamente, repetidas veces

repel [rɪ'pɛl] vt **-pelled; -pelling 1** REPULSE : repeler (un enemigo, etc.) **2** RESIST : repeler **3** REJECT : rechazar, repeler **4** DISGUST : repugnar, darle asco (a alguien)

repellent or **repellant** [rɪ'pɛlənt] n : repelente m

repent [rɪ'pɛnt] vi : arrepentirse

repentance [rɪ'pɛntənts] n : arrepentimiento m

repentant [rɪ'pɛntənt] adj : arrepentido

repercussion [,riːpər'kʌʃən, ,rɛpər-] n : repercusión f

repertoire ['rɛpər,twɑr] n : repertorio m

repertory ['rɛpər,tori] n, pl **-ries** : repertorio m

repetition [,rɛpə'tɪʃən] n : repetición f

repetitious [,rɛpə'tɪʃəs] adj : repetitivo, reiterativo — **repetitiously** adv

repetitive [rɪ'pɛtətɪv] adj : repetitivo, reiterativo

repetitive stress or **repetitive strain** n : esfuerzo m repetitivo ⟨repetitive stress injury : lesión por esfuerzo repetitivo⟩

rephrase [riː'freɪz] vt **-phrased; -phrasing** REWORD : expresar de otra forma

replace [rɪ'pleɪs] vt **-placed; -placing 1** : volver a poner (en un lugar) **2** SUBSTITUTE : reemplazar, sustituir **3** : reponer ⟨to replace the worn carpet : reponer la alfombra raída⟩

replaceable [rɪ'pleɪsəbəl] adj : reemplazable

replacement [rɪ'pleɪsmənt] n **1** SUBSTITUTION : reemplazo m, sustitución f **2** SUBSTITUTE : sustituto m, -ta f; suplente mf (persona) **3 replacement part** : repuesto m, pieza f de recambio

replay¹ [ri'pleɪ] vt **1** : volver a poner (un video, etc.) **2** : volver a jugar (un partido)

replay² ['riː,pleɪ] n : repetición f

replenish [rɪ'plɛnɪʃ] vt : rellenar, llenar de nuevo

replenishment [rɪ'plɛnɪʃmənt] n : reabastecimiento m

replete [rɪ'pliːt] adj : repleto, lleno

replica [ˈrɛplɪkə] *n* : réplica *f*, reproducción *f*

replicate [ˈrɛpləˌkeɪt] *v* -cated; -cating *vt* : duplicar, repetir — *vi* : duplicarse

replication [ˌrɛpləˈkeɪʃən] *n* 1 REPRODUCTION : reproducción *f* 2 REPETITION : repetición *f* 3 : replicación *f* (celular)

reply¹ [rɪˈplaɪ] *vi* -plied; -plying : contestar, responder

reply² *n, pl* -plies : respuesta *f*, contestación *f*

report¹ [rɪˈport] *vt* 1 : informar sobre (una noticia, etc.) 2 ANNOUNCE : anunciar 3 : decir, afirmar ⟨35% reported having voted : el 35% dijo haber votado⟩ 4 : dar parte de, reportar (un accidente, etc.), denunciar (un delito) — *vi* 1 : informar ⟨to report on : informar sobre⟩ 2 to report back RETURN : volver (a la base, etc.) 3 to report back : dar parte (a un jefe) 4 to report for duty : presentarse, reportarse 5 to report to someone : reportar a alguien

report² *n* 1 ACCOUNT : informe *m*, reportaje *m* (en un periódico, etc.) 2 RUMOR : rumor *m* 3 BANG : estallido *m* (de un arma de fuego)

report card *n* : boletín *m* de calificaciones, boletín *m* de notas, boleta *f* de calificaciones *Mex*

reportedly [rɪˈportədli] *adv* : según se dice, según se informa

reporter [rɪˈportər] *n* : periodista *mf*; reportero *m*, -ra *f*

repose¹ [rɪˈpoːz] *vi* -posed; -posing : reposar, descansar

repose² *n* 1 : reposo *m*, descanso *m* 2 CALM : calma *f*, tranquilidad *f*

repository [rɪˈpazəˌtori] *n, pl* -ries : depósito *m*

repossess [ˌriːpəˈzɛs] *vt* : recuperar, recobrar la posesión de

repost [riˈpoːst] *vt* : repostear

reprehensible [ˌrɛprɪˈhɛntsəbəl] *adj* : reprensible — **reprehensibly** [-bli] *adv*

represent [ˌrɛprɪˈzɛnt] *vt* 1 SYMBOLIZE, EXEMPLIFY : representar 2 CONSTITUTE : representar 3 : representar (a un cliente, etc.), ser un representante de (una compañía, etc.) 4 PORTRAY : presentar ⟨he represents himself as a friend : se presenta como amigo⟩

representation [ˌrɛprɪˌzɛnˈteɪʃən, -zən-] *n* : representación *f*

representative¹ [ˌrɛprɪˈzɛntətɪv] *adj* : representativo

representative² *n* 1 : representante *mf* 2 : diputado *m*, -da *f* (en la política)

repress [rɪˈprɛs] *vt* : reprimir

repression [rɪˈprɛʃən] *n* : represión *f*

repressive [rɪˈprɛsɪv] *adj* : represivo

reprieve¹ [rɪˈpriːv] *vt* -prieved; -prieving : indultar

reprieve² *n* : indulto *m*

reprimand¹ [ˈrɛprəˌmænd] *vt* : reprender

reprimand² *n* : reprimenda *f*

reprint¹ [riˈprɪnt] *vt* : reimprimir

reprint² [ˈriːˌprɪnt, riˈprɪnt] *n* : reedición *f*

reprisal [rɪˈpraɪzəl] *n* : represalia *f*

reproach¹ [rɪˈproːtʃ] *vt* : reprochar

reproach² *n* 1 DISGRACE : deshonra *f* 2 REBUKE : reproche *m*, recriminación *f*

reproachful [rɪˈproːtʃfəl] *adj* : de reproche

reproduce [ˌriːprəˈduːs, -ˈdjuːs] *v* -duced; -ducing *vt* : reproducir — *vi* BREED : reproducirse

reproduction [ˌriːprəˈdʌkʃən] *n* : reproducción *f*

reproductive [ˌriːprəˈdʌktɪv] *adj* : reproductor

reproof [rɪˈpruːf] *n* : reprobación *f*, reprimenda *f*, reproche *m*

reprove [rɪˈpruːv] *vt* -proved; -proving : reprender, censurar

reptile [ˈrɛpˌtaɪl] *n* : reptil *m*

reptilian [rɛpˈtɪliən] *n* : reptil

republic [rɪˈpʌblɪk] *n* : república *f*

republican¹ [rɪˈpʌblɪkən] *adj* : republicano

republican² *n* : republicano *m*, -na *f* — **Republicanism** [rɪˈpʌblɪkəˌnɪzəm] *n*

repudiate [rɪˈpjuːdiˌeɪt] *vt* -ated; -ating 1 REJECT : rechazar 2 DISOWN : repudiar, renegar de

repudiation [rɪˌpjuːdiˈeɪʃən] *n* : rechazo *m*, repudio *m*

repugnance [rɪˈpʌɡnənts] *n* : repugnancia *f*

repugnant [rɪˈpʌɡnənt] *adj* : repugnante, asqueroso

repulse¹ [rɪˈpʌls] *vt* -pulsed; -pulsing 1 REPEL : repeler 2 REBUFF : desairar, rechazar

repulse² *n* : rechazo *m*

repulsive [rɪˈpʌlsɪv] *adj* : repulsivo, repugnante, asqueroso — **repulsively** *adv*

reputable [ˈrɛpjətəbəl] *adj* : acreditado, de buena reputación

reputation [ˌrɛpjəˈteɪʃən] *n* : reputación *f*, fama *f*

repute [rɪˈpjuːt] *n* : reputación *f*, fama *f*

reputed [rɪˈpjuːtəd] *adj* : reputado, supuesto ⟨she's reputed to be the best : tiene fama de ser la mejor⟩

reputedly [rɪˈpjuːtədli] *adv* : supuestamente, según se dice

request¹ [rɪˈkwɛst] *vt* : pedir, solicitar, rogar ⟨to request information : solicitar/pedir información⟩ ⟨as requested : conforme a lo solicitado⟩

request² *n* : petición *f*, solicitud *f*, pedido *m*

require [rɪˈkwaɪr] *vt* -quired; -quiring 1 CALL FOR, DEMAND : requerir, exigir ⟨if required : si se requiere⟩ ⟨to require that something be done : exigir que algo se haga⟩ 2 NEED : necesitar, requerir

requirement [rɪˈkwaɪrmənt] *n* 1 NECESSITY : necesidad *f* 2 DEMAND : requisito *m*, demanda *f*

requisite¹ [ˈrɛkwəzɪt] *adj* : esencial, necesario

requisite² *n* : requisito *m*, necesidad *f*

requisition¹ [ˌrɛkwəˈzɪʃən] *vt* : requisar

requisition² *n* : requisa *f*

reread [ˌriːˈriːd] *vt* -read [-ˈrɛd]; -reading : releer

reroute [ˌriːˈruːt, -ˈraʊt] *vt* -routed; -routing : desviar

rerun¹ [ˌriːˈrʌn] vt **-ran; -run; -running** : reponer (un programa televisivo)

rerun² [ˈriːˌrʌn] n 1 : reposición f (de un programa televisivo) 2 REPEAT : repetición f

resale [ˈriːˌseɪl, ˌriːˈseɪl] n : reventa f

reschedule [riːˈskɛˌdʒuːl, -dʒəl, esp Brit -ˈʃedˌjuːl] vt **-duled; -duling** : cambiar la hora/fecha de (una cita, etc.)

rescind [rɪˈsɪnd] vt 1 CANCEL : rescindir, cancelar 2 REPEAL : abrogar, revocar

rescue¹ [ˈrɛsˌkjuː] vt **-cued; -cuing** : rescatar, salvar

rescue² n : rescate m

rescuer [ˈrɛsˌkjuːər] n : salvador m, -dora f

research¹ [rɪˈsərtʃ, ˈriːˌsərtʃ] v : investigar

research² n : investigación f

researcher [rɪˈsərtʃər, ˈriːˌ-] n : investigador m, -dora f

resell [riːˈsɛl] vt **-sold** [-ˈsoːld]; **-selling** : revender

resemblance [rɪˈzɛmbləns] n : semejanza f, parecido m

resemble [rɪˈzɛmbəl] vt **-sembled; -sembling** : parecerse a, asemejarse a

resent [rɪˈzɛnt] vt : molestarse por (algo), ofenderse por (algo), guardarle rencor a (alguien)

resentful [rɪˈzɛntfəl] adj : resentido, rencoroso — **resentfully** adv

resentment [rɪˈzɛntmənt] n : resentimiento m

reservation [ˌrɛzərˈveɪʃən] n 1 : reservación f, reserva f ⟨to make a reservation : hacer una reservación⟩ 2 DOUBT, MISGIVING : reserva f, duda f ⟨without reservations : sin reservas⟩ 3 : reserva f (de indios americanos)

reserve¹ [rɪˈzərv] vt **-served; -serving** : reservar

reserve² n 1 STOCK : reserva f ⟨to keep in reserve : guardar en reserva⟩ 2 RESTRAINT : reserva f, moderación f 3 **reserves** npl : reservas fpl (militares)

reserved [rɪˈzərvd] adj : reservado

reservoir [ˈrɛzərˌvwɑr, -ˌvwɔr, -ˌvɔr] n : embalse m

reset [ˌriːˈsɛt] vt **-set; -setting** : poner en hora (un reloj), poner a cero (un temporizador), reiniciar (una computadora), borrar (una contraseña)

reside [rɪˈzaɪd] vi **-sided; -siding** 1 DWELL : residir 2 LIE : radicar, residir ⟨the power resides in the presidency : el poder radica en la presidencia⟩

residence [ˈrɛzədənts] n : residencia f

resident¹ [ˈrɛzədənt] adj : residente

resident² n : residente mf

residential [ˌrɛzəˈdɛntʃəl] adj : residencial

residual [rɪˈzɪdʒuəl] adj : residual

residue [ˈrɛzəˌduː, -ˌdjuː] n : residuo m, resto m

resign [rɪˈzaɪn] vt 1 QUIT : dimitir, renunciar 2 **to resign oneself** : aguantarse, resignarse

resignation [ˌrɛzɪɡˈneɪʃən] n : resignación f

resilience [rɪˈzɪljənts] n 1 : capacidad f de recuperación, adaptabilidad f 2 ELASTICITY : elasticidad f

resiliency [rɪˈzɪljənsi] → **resilience**

resilient [rɪˈzɪljənt] adj 1 STRONG : resistente, fuerte 2 ELASTIC : elástico

resin [ˈrɛzən] n : resina f

resist [rɪˈzɪst] vt 1 : resistir (el calor, la tentación, etc.) 2 OPPOSE : oponerse a — vi 1 OPPOSE : resistir 2 : resistirse ⟨I couldn't resist : no me pude resistir⟩

resistance [rɪˈzɪstənts] n : resistencia f

resistant [rɪˈzɪstənt] adj : resistente

resolute [ˈrɛzəˌluːt] adj : firme, resuelto, decidido

resolutely [ˈrɛzəˌluːtli, ˌrɛzə-] adv : resueltamente, firmemente

resolution [ˌrɛzəˈluːʃən] n 1 SOLUTION : solución f 2 RESOLVE : resolución f, determinación f 3 DECISION : propósito m, decisión f ⟨New Year's resolutions : propósitos para el Año Nuevo⟩ 4 MOTION, PROPOSAL : moción f, resolución f (legislativa)

resolve¹ [rɪˈzɑlv] vt **-solved; -solving** 1 SOLVE : resolver, solucionar 2 DECIDE : resolver ⟨she resolved to get more sleep : resolvió dormir más⟩

resolve² n : resolución f, determinación f

resonance [ˈrɛzənənts] n : resonancia f

resonant [ˈrɛzənənt] adj : resonante

resort¹ [rɪˈzɔrt] vi **to resort to** : recurrir a ⟨to resort to force : recurrir a la fuerza⟩

resort² n 1 RECOURSE : recurso m ⟨as a last resort : como último recurso⟩ 2 HANGOUT : lugar m popular, lugar m muy frecuentado 3 : lugar m de vacaciones ⟨tourist resort : centro turístico⟩

resound [rɪˈzaʊnd] vi : retumbar, resonar

resounding [rɪˈzaʊndɪŋ] adj 1 RESONANT : resonante 2 ABSOLUTE, CATEGORICAL : rotundo, tremendo ⟨a resounding success : un éxito rotundo⟩

resource [ˈriːˌsɔrs, rɪˈsɔrs] n 1 RESOURCEFULNESS : ingenio m, recursos mpl 2 **resources** npl : recursos mpl ⟨natural resources : recursos naturales⟩ 3 **resources** npl MEANS : recursos mpl, medios mpl, fondos mpl

resourceful [rɪˈsɔrsfəl, -ˈzɔrs-] adj : ingenioso

resourcefulness [rɪˈsɔrsfəlnəs, -ˈzɔrs-] n : ingenio m, recursos mpl, inventiva f

respect¹ [rɪˈspɛkt] vt : respetar, estimar

respect² n 1 REFERENCE : relación f, respecto m ⟨with respect to : en lo que respecta a⟩ 2 ESTEEM : respeto m 3 DETAIL, PARTICULAR : aspecto m, sentido m, respecto m ⟨in some respects : en algunos aspectos⟩ ⟨in this/that respect : en este/ese sentido⟩ 4 **respects** npl : respetos mpl ⟨to pay one's respects : presentar uno sus respetos⟩

respectability [rɪˌspɛktəˈbɪləti] n : respetabilidad f

respectable [rɪˈspɛktəbəl] adj 1 PROPER : respetable, decente 2 CONSIDERABLE : considerable, respetable ⟨a respectable amount : una cantidad respetable⟩ — **respectably** [-bli] adv

respectful [rɪ'spɛktfəl] *adj* : respetuoso — **respectfully** *adv*

respectfulness [rɪ'spɛktfəlnəs] *n* : respetuosidad *f*

respective [rɪ'spɛktɪv] *adj* : respectivo ⟨their respective homes : sus casas respectivas⟩ — **respectively** *adv*

respiration [ˌrɛspə'reɪʃən] *n* : respiración *f*

respirator ['rɛspə,reɪtər] *n* : respirador *m*

respiratory ['rɛspərə,tori, rɪ'spaɪrə-] *adj* : respiratorio

respite ['rɛspɪt, rɪ'spaɪt] *n* : respiro *m*, tregua *f*

resplendent [rɪ'splɛndənt] *adj* : resplandeciente — **resplendently** *adv*

respond [rɪ'spand] *vi* 1 ANSWER : contestar, responder 2 REACT : responder, reaccionar ⟨to respond to treatment : responder al tratamiento⟩

response [rɪ'spans] *n* : respuesta *f*

responsibility [rɪ,spansə'bɪləti] *n, pl* **-ties** : responsabilidad *f*

responsible [rɪ'spansəbəl] *adj* 1 : responsable 2 **to be responsible for** CAUSE : ser el/la responsable de (dícese de una persona), ser la causa de 3 **to be responsible for** MANAGE : ser responsable de (algo), tener (a alguien) a su cargo 4 **to be responsible to** : ser responsable ante 5 **to hold someone responsible for** : hacer responsable a alguien de — **responsibly** [-bli] *adv*

responsive [rɪ'spansɪv] *adj* 1 ANSWERING : que responde 2 SENSITIVE : sensible, receptivo

responsiveness [rɪ'spansɪvnəs] *n* : receptividad *f*, sensibilidad *f*

rest¹ ['rɛst] *vi* 1 : descansar ⟨to rest comfortably : descansar cómodamente⟩ 2 STOP : pararse, detenerse 3 DEPEND : basarse (en), descansar (sobre), depender (de) ⟨the decision rests with her : la decisión pesa sobre ella⟩ 4 **to rest easy** : quedarse tranquilo 5 **to rest on** : apoyarse en, descansar sobre ⟨to rest on one's arm : apoyarse en el brazo⟩ — *vt* 1 RELAX : descansar 2 SUPPORT : apoyar 3 **to rest one's eyes on** : fijar la mirada en

rest² *n* 1 RELAXATION : descanso *m*, reposo *m* ⟨to get some rest : descansar⟩ 2 BREAK : descanso *m* 3 SUPPORT : soporte *m*, apoyo *m* 4 : silencio *m* (en música) 5 REMAINDER : resto *m* ⟨the rest (of us/them) : los demás⟩ 6 **to come to rest** : pararse

rest area → **rest stop**

restart [ri'start] *vt* 1 : volver a empezar 2 RESUME : reanudar 3 : volver a arrancar (un motor), reiniciar (una computadora) — *vi* 1 : reanudarse 2 : volver a arrancar

restate [ˌri:'steɪt] *vt* **-stated; -stating** : replantear (una pregunta, etc.), repetir

restatement [ˌri:'steɪtmənt] *n* : repetición *f*

restaurant ['rɛstə,rɑnt, -rənt] *n* : restaurante *m*

restful ['rɛstfəl] *adj* 1 RELAXING : relajante 2 PEACEFUL : tranquilo, sosegado

rest home → **nursing home**

restitution [ˌrɛstə'tu:ʃən, -'tju:-] *n* : restitución *f*

restive ['rɛstɪv] *adj* : inquieto, nervioso

restless ['rɛstləs] *adj* 1 FIDGETY : inquieto, agitado 2 IMPATIENT : impaciente 3 SLEEPLESS : desvelado ⟨a restless night : una noche en blanco⟩

restlessly ['rɛstləsli] *adv* : nerviosamente

restlessness ['rɛstləsnəs] *n* : inquietud *f*, agitación *f*

restoration [ˌrɛstə'reɪʃən] *n* : restauración *f*, restablecimiento *m*

restore [rɪ'stor] *vt* **-stored; -storing** 1 RETURN, GIVE BACK : devolver, restituir 2 REESTABLISH : restablecer (el orden, etc.), recuperar (la confianza, la salud, etc.), restaurar (una monarquía, etc.) 3 REPAIR : restaurar

restrain [rɪ'streɪn] *vt* 1 : refrenar, contener 2 **to restrain oneself** : contenerse

restrained [rɪ'streɪnd] *adj* : comedido, templado, contenido

restraint [rɪ'streɪnt] *n* 1 RESTRICTION : restricción *f*, limitación *f*, control *m* 2 CONFINEMENT : encierro *m* 3 RESERVE : reserva *f*, control *m* de sí mismo

restrict [rɪ'strɪkt] *vt* : restringir, limitar, constreñir

restricted [rɪ'strɪktəd] *adj* 1 LIMITED : limitado, restringido 2 CLASSIFIED : secreto, confidencial

restriction [rɪ'strɪkʃən] *n* : restricción *f*

restrictive [rɪ'strɪktɪv] *adj* : restrictivo — **restrictively** *adv*

restroom ['rɛst,ru:m, -,rum] *n* : servicios *mpl*, baño *m*

restructure [rɪ'strʌktʃər] *vt* **-tured; -turing** : reestructurar

rest stop *n* : área *f* de descanso (en una carretera)

result¹ [rɪ'zʌlt] *vi* : resultar ⟨to result in : resultar en, tener por resultado⟩ ⟨to result from : resultar de⟩

result² *n* : resultado *m*, consecuencia *f* ⟨as a result of : como consecuencia de⟩

resultant [rɪ'zʌltənt] *adj* : resultante

resume [rɪ'zu:m] *v* **-sumed; -suming** *vt* : reanudar — *vi* : reanudarse

résumé *or* **resume** *or* **resumé** ['rɛzə,meɪ, ,rɛzə'-] *n* 1 SUMMARY : resumen *m* 2 CURRICULUM VITAE : currículum *m*, currículo *m*

resumption [rɪ'zʌmpʃən] *n* : reanudación *f*

resurface [ˌri:'sərfəs] *v* **-faced; -facing** *vt* : pavimentar (una carretera) de nuevo — *vi* 1 : volver a salir a la superficie 2 REAPPEAR : resurgir, reaparecer

resurgence [rɪ'sərdʒənts] *n* : resurgimiento *m*

resurrect [ˌrɛzə'rɛkt] *vt* : resucitar, desempolvar

resurrection [ˌrɛzə'rɛkʃən] *n* : resurrección *f*

resuscitate [rɪ'sʌsə,teɪt] *vt* **-tated; -tating** : resucitar, revivir

resuscitation [rɪ,sʌsə'teɪʃən] *n* : reanimación *f*, resucitación *f*

retail¹ ['ri:,teɪl] *vt* : vender al por menor, vender al detalle

retail² adv : al por menor, al detalle
retail³ adj : detallista, minorista ⟨retail price : precio de venta al público⟩
retail⁴ n : venta f al detalle, venta f al por menor
retailer [ˈriːˌteɪlər] n : detallista mf, minorista mf
retain [rɪˈteɪn] vt : retener, conservar, guardar
retainer [rɪˈteɪnər] n 1 SERVANT : criado m, -da f 2 ADVANCE : anticipo m
retaliate [rɪˈtæliˌeɪt] vi -ated; -ating : responder, contraatacar, tomar represalias
retaliation [rɪˌtæliˈeɪʃən] n : represalia f, retaliación f
retard [rɪˈtɑrd] vt : retardar, retrasar
retardation → mental retardation
retarded [rɪˈtɑrdəd] adj dated, now usu offensive : retrasado dated, now usu offensive
retch [ˈrɛtʃ] vi : hacer arcadas
retention [rɪˈtɛntʃən] n : retención f
retentive [rɪˈtɛntɪv] adj : retentivo
rethink [riːˈθɪŋk] vt -thought; -thinking : reconsiderar, repensar
reticence [ˈrɛtəsənts] n : reticencia f
reticent [ˈrɛtəsənt] adj : reticente
retina [ˈrɛtənə] n, pl -nas or -nae [-əˌni, -ənˌaɪ] : retina f
retinue [ˈrɛtənˌuː, -ˌjuː] n : séquito m, comitiva f, cortejo m
retire [rɪˈtaɪr] v -tired; -tiring 1 RETREAT, WITHDRAW : retirarse, retraerse 2 : retirarse, jubilarse (de su trabajo) 3 : acostarse, irse a dormir
retiree [rɪˌtaɪˈriː] n : jubilado m, -da f
retirement [rɪˈtaɪrmənt] n : jubilación f
retiring [rɪˈtaɪrɪŋ] adj SHY : retraído
retort¹ [rɪˈtɔrt] vt : replicar
retort² n : réplica f
retrace [riːˈtreɪs] vt -traced; -tracing : volver sobre, desandar ⟨to retrace one's steps : volver uno sobre sus pasos⟩
retract [rɪˈtrækt] vt 1 TAKE BACK, WITHDRAW : retirar, retractarse de 2 : retraer (las garras) — vi : retractarse
retractable [rɪˈtræktəbəl] adj : retractable
retraction [rɪˈtrækʃən] n : retracción f, retractación f
retrain [ˌriːˈtreɪn] vt : reciclar, reconvertir
retreat¹ [rɪˈtriːt] vi : retirarse, batirse en retirada
retreat² n 1 : retirada f ⟨to beat a hasty retreat : salir huyendo⟩ 2 REFUGE : retiro m (espiritual), refugio m
retrial [ˌriːˈtraɪəl] n : nuevo juicio m
retribution [ˌrɛtrəˈbjuːʃən] n : castigo m
retrieval [rɪˈtriːvəl] n : recuperación f ⟨beyond retrieval : irrecuperable⟩ ⟨data retrieval : recuperación de datos⟩
retrieve [rɪˈtriːv] vt -trieved; -trieving 1 RECOVER : recuperar 2 FETCH : ir a buscar, cobrar (la caza)
retriever [rɪˈtriːvər] n : perro m cobrador
retroactive [ˌrɛtroˈæktɪv] adj : retroactivo — **retroactively** adv
retrograde [ˈrɛtrəˌɡreɪd] adj : retrógrado
retrospect [ˈrɛtrəˌspɛkt] n in retrospect : mirando hacia atrás, retrospectivamente

retrospective [ˌrɛtrəˈspɛktɪv] adj : retrospectivo
return¹ [rɪˈtɔrn] vi 1 : volver, regresar ⟨to return home : regresar a casa⟩ 2 REAPPEAR : reaparecer, resurgir 3 REVERT : volver (a un estado anterior) 4 : volver (a una actividad, un tema, etc.) 5 ANSWER : responder 6 : emitir (un veredicto) — vt 1 REPLACE, RESTORE : devolver, volver (a poner), restituir ⟨to return something to its place : volver a poner algo en su lugar⟩ 2 YIELD : producir, redituar 3 REPAY : devolver, corresponder a ⟨to return a compliment : devolver un cumplido⟩
return² adj : de vuelta
return³ n 1 RETURNING : regreso m, vuelta f, retorno m 2 or tax return : declaración f de impuestos, declaración f de la renta 3 YIELD : rédito m, rendimiento m, ganancia f 4 returns npl DATA, RESULTS : resultados mpl, datos mpl 5 in return (for) : a cambio (de)
retweet [riːˈtwiːt] vt : retuitear
reunion [riːˈjuːnjən] n : reunión f, reencuentro m
reunite [ˌriːjuˈnaɪt] v -nited; -niting : (volver a) reunir — vi : (volver a) reunirse
reusable [riːˈjuːzəbəl] adj : reutilizable
reuse [riːˈjuːz] vt -used; -using : reutilizar, usar de nuevo
rev¹ [ˈrɛv] v -revved; -revving vt 1 or to rev up : acelerar (un motor) 2 to rev up : impulsar (la economía), acelerar (un proceso, etc.) — vi to rev up : prepararse
rev² n : revolución f (de un motor)
revamp [riːˈvæmp] vt : renovar
reveal [rɪˈviːl] vt 1 DIVULGE : revelar, divulgar ⟨to reveal a secret : revelar un secreto⟩ 2 SHOW : manifestar, mostrar, dejar ver
revealing [rɪˈviːlɪŋ] adj : revelador
reveille [ˈrɛvəli] n : toque m de diana
revel¹ [ˈrɛvəl] vi -eled or -elled; -eling or -elling 1 CAROUSE : ir de juerga 2 to revel in : deleitarse en
revel² n : juerga f, parranda f fam
revelation [ˌrɛvəˈleɪʃən] n : revelación f
reveler or **reveller** [ˈrɛvələr] n : juerguista mf
revelry [ˈrɛvəlri] n, pl -ries : juerga f, parranda f fam, jarana f fam
revenge¹ [rɪˈvɛndʒ] vt -venged; -venging to revenge oneself on : vengarse de
revenge² n : venganza f ⟨to take (one's) revenge on : vengarse de⟩ ⟨in revenge for : como venganza por⟩
revenue [ˈrɛvəˌnuː, -ˌnjuː] n : ingresos mpl, rentas fpl
reverberate [rɪˈvɔrbəˌreɪt] vi -ated; -ating : reverberar
reverberation [rɪˌvɔrbəˈreɪʃən] n : reverberación f
revere [rɪˈvɪr] vt -vered; -vering : reverenciar, venerar
reverence [ˈrɛvərənts] n : reverencia f, veneración f
reverend [ˈrɛvərənd] adj : reverendo ⟨the

Reverend John Chapin : el reverendo John Chapin⟩
reverent [ˈrɛvərənt] *adj* : reverente — **reverently** *adv*
reverie [ˈrɛvəri] *n, pl* **-eries** : ensueño *m*
reversal [rɪˈvərsəl] *n* **1** INVERSION : inversión *f* (del orden normal) **2** CHANGE : cambio *m* total **3** SETBACK : revés *m*, contratiempo *m*
reverse¹ [rɪˈvərs] *v* **-versed; -versing** *vt* **1** INVERT : invertir (el orden, los roles, etc.) **2** CHANGE : cambiar totalmente **3** UNDO : reparar (daño, etc.), revertir ⟨to reverse a trend : revertir una tendencia⟩ **4** ANNUL : revocar, revertir — *vi* : dar marcha atrás
reverse² *adj* **1** : inverso ⟨in reverse order : en orden inverso⟩ ⟨the reverse side : el reverso⟩ **2** OPPOSITE : contrario, opuesto
reverse³ *n* **1** BACK : reverso *m*, dorso *m*, revés *m* **2** SETBACK : revés *m*, contratiempo *m* **3 the reverse** : lo contrario, lo opuesto **4** *or* **reverse gear** : marcha *f* atrás; reversa *f* Col, Mex ⟨to put a car in reverse : dar marcha atrás, dar reversa⟩
reversible [rɪˈvərsəbəl] *adj* : reversible
reversion [rɪˈvərʒən] *n* : reversión *f*, vuelta *f*
revert [rɪˈvərt] *vi* **1** : revertir (a un propietario) **2** : volver (a un estado anterior)
review¹ [rɪˈvjuː] *vt* **1** REEXAMINE : volver a examinar, repasar (una lección) **2** CRITICIZE : reseñar, hacer una crítica de **3** EXAMINE : examinar, analizar ⟨to review one's life : examinar su vida⟩ **4 to review the troops** : pasar revista a las tropas
review² *n* **1** INSPECTION : revista *f* (de tropas) **2** ANALYSIS, OVERVIEW : resumen *m*, análisis *m* ⟨a review of current affairs : un análisis de las actualidades⟩ **3** CRITICISM : reseña *f*, crítica *f* (de un libro, etc.) **4** : repaso *m* (para un examen) **5** REVUE : revista *f* (musical)
reviewer [rɪˈvjuːər] *n* : crítico *m*, -ca *f*
revile [rɪˈvaɪl] *vt* **-viled; -viling** : injuriar, denostar
revise [rɪˈvaɪz] *vt* **-vised; -vising** : revisar, corregir, refundir ⟨to revise a dictionary : corregir un diccionario⟩
revision [rɪˈvɪʒən] *n* : revisión *f*
revitalize [ˌriːˈvaɪtəˌlaɪz] *vt* **-ized; -izing** : resucitar, revitalizar
revival [rɪˈvaɪvəl] *n* **1** : renacimiento *m* (de ideas, etc.), restablecimiento *m* (de costumbres, etc.), reactivación *f* (de la economía) **2** : reanimación *f*, resucitación *f* (en medicina) **3** *or* **revival meeting** : asamblea *f* evangelista
revive [rɪˈvaɪv] *v* **-vived; -viving** *vt* **1** REAWAKEN : reavivar, reanimar, reactivar (la economía), resucitar (a un paciente) **2** REESTABLISH : restablecer — *vi* **1** : renacer, reanimarse, reactivarse **2** COME TO : recobrar el sentido, volver en sí
revoke [rɪˈvoːk] *vt* **-voked; -voking** : revocar — **revocation** [ˌrɛvəˈkeɪʃən, rɪˌvoː-] *n*
revolt¹ [rɪˈvoːlt] *vi* **1** REBEL : rebelarse,

sublevarse **2 to revolt at** : sentir repugnancia por — *vt* DISGUST : darle asco (a alguien), repugnar
revolt² *n* REBELLION : rebelión *f*, revuelta *f*, sublevación *f*
revolting [rɪˈvoːltɪŋ] *adj* : asqueroso, repugnante
revolution [ˌrɛvəˈluːʃən] *n* : revolución *f*
revolutionary¹ [ˌrɛvəˈluːʃəˌnɛri] *adj* : revolucionario
revolutionary² *n, pl* **-aries** : revolucionario *m*, -ria *f*
revolutionize [ˌrɛvəˈluːʃəˌnaɪz] *vt* **-ized; -izing** : cambiar radicalmente, revolucionar
revolve [rɪˈvalv] *v* **-volved; -volving** *vt* ROTATE : hacer girar — *vi* **1** ROTATE : girar ⟨to revolve around : girar alrededor de⟩ **2 to revolve in one's mind** : darle vueltas en la cabeza a alguien
revolver [rɪˈvalvər] *n* : revólver *m*
revolving [rɪˈvalvɪŋ] *adj* : giratorio ⟨revolving door : puerta giratoria⟩
revue [rɪˈvjuː] *n* : revista *f* (musical)
revulsion [rɪˈvʌlʃən] *n* : repugnancia *f*
reward¹ [rɪˈwɔrd] *vt* : recompensar, premiar
reward² *n* : recompensa *f*
rewarding [rɪˈwɔrdɪŋ] *adj* **1** : gratificante **2** PROFITABLE : rentable
rewarm [riˈwɔrm] *vt* : recalentar
rewind [ˌriˈwaɪnd] *vt* : rebobinar
reword [ˌriˈwərd] *vt* REPHRASE : expresar de otra forma
rewrite [ˌriˈraɪt] *vt* **-wrote; -written; -writing** : escribir de nuevo, volver a escribir
rhapsody [ˈræpsədi] *n, pl* **-dies** **1** : elogio *m* excesivo ⟨to go into rhapsodies over : extasiarse por⟩ **2** : rapsodia *f* (en música)
rhea [ˈriːə] *n* : ñandú *m*
rhetoric [ˈrɛtərɪk] *n* : retórica *f*
rhetorical [rɪˈtɔrɪkəl] *adj* : retórico ⟨rhetorical question : pregunta retórica⟩
rheumatic [ruˈmætɪk] *adj* : reumático
rheumatism [ˈruːməˌtɪzəm, ˈrʊ-] *n* : reumatismo *m*
rhinestone [ˈraɪnˌstoːn] *n* : diamante *m* de imitación
rhino [ˈraɪˌnoː] *n, pl* **rhino** *or* **rhinos** → rhinoceros
rhinoceros [raɪˈnasərəs] *n, pl* **-eroses** *or* **-eros** *or* **-eri** [-ˌraɪ] : rinoceronte *m*
rhododendron [ˌroːdəˈdɛndrən] *n* : rododendro *m*
rhombus [ˈrɑmbəs] *n, pl* **-buses** *or* **-bi** [-ˌbaɪ, -bi] : rombo *m*
rhubarb [ˈruːˌbɑrb] *n* : ruibarbo *m*
rhyme¹ [ˈraɪm] *vi* **rhymed; rhyming** : rimar
rhyme² *n* **1** : rima *f* **2** VERSE : verso *m* (en rima)
rhythm [ˈrɪðəm] *n* : ritmo *m*
rhythmic [ˈrɪðmɪk] *or* **rhythmical** [-mɪkəl] *adj* : rítmico — **rhythmically** [-mɪkli] *adv*
rib¹ [ˈrɪb] *vt* **ribbed; ribbing** **1** : hacer en canalé ⟨a ribbed sweater : un suéter en canalé⟩ **2** TEASE : tomarle el pelo (a alguien)

rib² *n* **1** : costilla *f* (de una persona o un animal) **2** : nervio *m* (de una bóveda o una hoja), varilla *f* (de un paraguas), canalé *m* (de una prenda tejida)

ribald ['rɪbəld] *adj* : escabroso, procaz

ribbon ['rɪbən] *n* **1** : cinta *f* **2 to tear to ribbons** : hacer jirones

rib cage *n* : caja *f* torácica

rice ['raɪs] *n* : arroz *m*

rich ['rɪtʃ] *adj* **1** WEALTHY : rico **2** SUMPTUOUS : suntuoso, lujoso **3** : pesado ⟨rich foods : comidas pesadas⟩ **4** ABUNDANT : abundante **5** : vivo, intenso ⟨rich colors : colores vivos⟩ **6** FERTILE : fértil, rico

riches ['rɪtʃəz] *npl* : riquezas *fpl*

richly ['rɪtʃli] *adv* **1** SUMPTUOUSLY : suntuosamente, ricamente **2** ABUNDANTLY : abundantemente **3 richly deserved** : bien merecido

richness ['rɪtʃnəs] *n* : riqueza *f*

rickets ['rɪkəts] *n* : raquitismo *m*

rickety ['rɪkəti] *adj* : desvencijado, destartalado

rickshaw ['rɪk,ʃɔ] *n* : rickshaw *m*

ricochet¹ ['rɪkə,ʃeɪ] *vi* **-cheted** [-,ʃeɪd] *or* **-chetted** [-,ʃɛtəd]; **-cheting** [-,ʃeɪɪŋ] *or* **-chetting** [-,ʃɛtɪŋ] : rebotar

ricochet² *n* : rebote *m*

rid ['rɪd] *vt* **rid; ridding 1** FREE : librar ⟨to rid the city of thieves : librar la ciudad de ladrones⟩ **2 to get rid of** *or* **to rid oneself of** : deshacerse de, desembarazarse de

riddance ['rɪdənts] *n* : libramiento *m* ⟨good riddance! : ¡adiós y buen viaje!, ¡vete con viento fresco!⟩

riddle¹ ['rɪdəl] *vt* **-dled; -dling** : acribillar ⟨riddled with bullets : acribillado a balazos⟩ ⟨riddled with errors : lleno de errores⟩

riddle² *n* : acertijo *m*, adivinanza *f*

ride¹ ['raɪd] *v* **rode** ['roːd]; **ridden** ['rɪdən]; **riding** *vt* **1** : montar, ir, andar ⟨to ride a horse : montar a caballo⟩ ⟨to ride a bicycle : montar/andar en bicicleta⟩ ⟨to ride the bus/train : ir en autobús/tren⟩ **2** : recorrer ⟨he rode 5 miles : recorrió 5 millas⟩ ⟨we rode the trails : recorrimos los senderos⟩ **3** TEASE : burlarse de, ridiculizar **4 to ride out** WEATHER : capear ⟨they rode out the storm : capearon el temporal⟩ **5 to ride the waves** : surcar los mares — *vi* **1** : montar a caballo, cabalgar **2** TRAVEL : ir, viajar (en coche, en bicicleta, etc.) **3** RUN : andar, marchar ⟨the car rides well : el coche anda bien⟩ **4 to be riding high** : estar encantado de la vida **5 to be riding on** : depender de **6 to be riding for a fall** : ir camino al desastre **7 to let something ride** *fam* : dejar pasar algo **8 to ride herd on** *fam* : vigilar **9 to ride shotgun** *fam* : ir en el asiento del pasajero delantero **10 to ride up** : subírsele (dícese de la ropa)

ride² *n* **1** : paseo *m*, vuelta *f* (en coche, en bicicleta, a caballo) ⟨to go for a ride : dar una vuelta⟩ ⟨to give someone a ride : llevar en coche a alguien⟩ **2** : aparato

m, juego *m* (en un parque de diversiones)

rider ['raɪdər] *n* **1** : jinete *mf* ⟨the rider fell off his horse : el jinete se cayó de su caballo⟩ **2** CYCLIST : ciclista *mf* **3** MOTORCYCLIST : motociclista *mf* **4** CLAUSE : cláusula *f* añadida

ridge ['rɪdʒ] *n* **1** CHAIN : cadena *f* (de montañas o cerros) **2** : caballete *m* (de un techo), cresta *f* (de una ola o una montaña), cordoncillo *m* (de telas)

ridicule¹ ['rɪdə,kjuːl] *vt* **-culed; -culing** : burlarse de, mofarse de, ridiculizar

ridicule² *n* : burlas *fpl*

ridiculous [rə'dɪkjələs] *adj* : ridículo, absurdo

ridiculously [rə'dɪkjələsli] *adv* : de forma ridícula

rife ['raɪf] *adj* : abundante, común ⟨to be rife with : estar plagado de⟩

riffraff ['rɪf,ræf] *n* : chusma *f*, gentuza *f*

rifle¹ ['raɪfəl] *v* **-fled; -fling** *vt* RANSACK : desvalijar, saquear — *vi* **to rifle through** : revolver

rifle² *n* : rifle *m*, fusil *m*

rift ['rɪft] *n* **1** FISSURE : grieta *f*, fisura *f* **2** BREAK : ruptura *f* (entre personas), división *f* (dentro de un grupo)

rig¹ ['rɪg] *vt* **rigged; rigging 1** : aparejar (un barco) **2** EQUIP : equipar **3** FIX : amañar (una elección, etc.) **4 to rig up** CONSTRUCT : construir, erigir **5 to rig oneself out as** : vestirse de

rig² *n* **1** : aparejo *m* (de un barco) **2** *or* **oil rig** : torre *f* de perforación, plataforma *f* petrolífera

rigamarole → rigmarole

rigging ['rɪgɪŋ, -gən] *n* : jarcia *f*, aparejo *m*

right¹ ['raɪt] *vt* **1** FIX, RESTORE : reparar **2** STRAIGHTEN : enderezar

right² *adv* **1** PRECISELY : justo ⟨right here : aquí mismo⟩ ⟨right on time : a la hora exacta⟩ **2** DIRECTLY, STRAIGHT : derecho, directamente ⟨to go right home : ir derecho a casa⟩ ⟨come right this way : pase por aquí⟩ **3** CORRECTLY : correctamente ⟨to guess right : acertar⟩ **4** WELL : bien ⟨to eat right : comer bien⟩ ⟨nothing is going right : nada está saliendo bien⟩ **5** IMMEDIATELY : inmediatamente ⟨right after class : inmediatamente después de la clase⟩ ⟨I'll be right with you : enseguida lo atiendo⟩ **6** COMPLETELY : completamente ⟨to feel right at home : sentirse completamente cómodo⟩ ⟨right from the start : desde el principio⟩ **7** : a la derecha ⟨to turn right : girar a la derecha⟩ **8 ~ away** : enseguida **9 ~ now** IMMEDIATELY : ahora mismo **10 ~ now** PRESENTLY : en este momento

right³ *adj* **1** MORAL : justo ⟨to be right : ser justo⟩ ⟨to do the right thing : hacer lo correcto⟩ ⟨you were right to forgive him : hiciste bien en perdonarlo⟩ **2** CORRECT : correcto ⟨the right answer : la respuesta correcta⟩ ⟨you're right : tienes razón⟩ ⟨you know him, right? : lo conoces, ¿verdad?⟩ ⟨that's right : así es⟩ **3** APPROPRIATE : apropiado, adecuado

⟨the right man for the job : el hombre indicado para el trabajo⟩ ⟨the right moment : el momento oportuno⟩ ⟨if the price is right : si está bien de precio⟩ **4** *(used for emphasis)* : bien, bueno ⟨right — let's go : bueno, vamos⟩ **5** *(used ironically)* ⟨it's true! yeah, right : ¡es verdad! sí, claro⟩ **6** : derecho ⟨the right hand : la mano derecha⟩ **7** : bien ⟨I don't feel right : no me siento bien⟩ ⟨he's not in his right mind : no está bien de la cabeza⟩ **8 right side** : derecho *m* ⟨right side up : con la derecha para arriba⟩ ⟨right side out : del/al derecho⟩

right⁴ *n* **1** GOOD : bien *m* ⟨you did right : hiciste bien⟩ ⟨to know right from wrong : saber la diferencia entre el bien y el mal⟩ **2** : derecha *f* ⟨on the right : a la derecha⟩ **3** : derecho *m* ⟨to have a right to : tener derecho a⟩ ⟨the right to vote : el derecho a votar⟩ ⟨women's rights : los derechos de la mujer⟩ **4 rights** *npl* : derechos *mpl* ⟨television rights : derechos televisivos⟩ **5 to take/make a right** : girar a la derecha ⟨take the next right : gire en la próxima a la derecha⟩ **6 the Right** : la derecha (en la política)

right angle *n* : ángulo *m* recto

right-click [ˈraɪtˈklɪk] *vi* : hacer clic/click derecho — *vt* : hacer clic/click derecho en

righteous [ˈraɪtʃəs] *adj* : recto, honrado — **righteously** *adv*

righteousness [ˈraɪtʃəsnəs] *n* : rectitud *f*, honradez *f*

rightful [ˈraɪtfəl] *adj* **1** JUST : justo **2** LAWFUL : legítimo — **rightfully** *adv*

right-hand [ˈraɪtˈhænd] *adj* **1** : situado a la derecha **2** RIGHT-HANDED : para la mano derecha, con la mano derecha **right-hand man** : brazo *m* derecho

right-handed [ˈraɪtˈhændəd] *adj* **1** : diestro ⟨a right-handed pitcher : un lanzador diestro⟩ **2** : para la mano derecha, con la mano derecha **3** CLOCKWISE : en la dirección de las manecillas del reloj

rightist [ˈraɪtɪst] *n* : derechista *mf* — **rightist** *adj*

rightly [ˈraɪtli] *adv* **1** JUSTLY : justamente, con razón **2** PROPERLY : debidamente, apropiadamente **3** CORRECTLY : correctamente

right-of-way [ˈraɪtəˈweɪ, -əv-] *n*, *pl* **rights-of-way** **1** : preferencia (del tráfico) **2** ACCESS : derecho *m* de paso

right triangle *n* : triángulo *m* rectángulo

rightward [ˈraɪtwərd] *adj* : a la derecha, hacia la derecha

right-wing [ˈraɪtˈwɪŋ] *adj* : derechista

right wing *n* **the right wing** : la derecha

right-winger [ˈraɪtˈwɪŋər] *n* : derechista *mf*

rigid [ˈrɪdʒɪd] *adj* : rígido — **rigidly** *adv*

rigidity [rɪˈdʒɪdəti] *n*, *pl* **-ties** : rigidez *f*

rigmarole [ˈrɪgməˌroːl, ˈrɪgə-] *n* **1** NONSENSE : galimatías *m*, disparates *mpl* **2** PROCEDURES : trámites *mpl*

rigor [ˈrɪgər] *n* : rigor *m*

rigor mortis [ˌrɪgərˈmɔrtəs] *n* : rigidez *f* cadavérica

rigorous [ˈrɪgərəs] *adj* : riguroso — **rigorously** *adv*

rile [ˈraɪl] *vt* **riled**; **riling** : irritar

rill [ˈrɪl] *n* : riachuelo *m*

rim [ˈrɪm] *n* **1** EDGE : borde *m* **2** : llanta *f*, rin *m* Col, Mex (de una rueda) **3** FRAME : montura *f* (de anteojos)

rime [ˈraɪm] *n* : escarcha *f*

rind [ˈraɪnd] *n* : corteza *f*

ring¹ [ˈrɪŋ] *v* **rang** [ˈræŋ]; **rung** [ˈrʌŋ]; **ringing** *vi* **1** : sonar ⟨the doorbell rang : sonó el timbre⟩ ⟨to ring for : llamar⟩ **2** RESOUND : resonar **3** SEEM : parecer ⟨to ring true : parecer cierto⟩ **4 to ring out** : sonar, oírse — *vt* **1** : tocar, hacer sonar (un timbre, una alarma, etc.) ⟨the name rings a bell : el nombre me suena⟩ **2** SURROUND : cercar, rodear **3 to ring up** : cobrar (compras) **4 to ring in the New Year** : recibir el Año Nuevo

ring² *n* **1** : anillo *m*, sortija *f* ⟨wedding ring : anillo de matrimonio⟩ **2** BAND : aro *m*, anillo *m* ⟨key ring : llavero⟩ **3** CIRCLE : círculo *m* **4** ARENA : arena *f*, ruedo *m* ⟨a boxing ring : un cuadrilátero, un ring⟩ **5** GANG : banda *f* (de ladrones, etc.) **6** SOUND : timbre *m*, sonido *m* **7** CALL : llamada *f* (por teléfono)

ringer [ˈrɪŋər] *n* **to be a dead ringer for** : ser un vivo retrato de

ringing [ˈrɪŋɪŋ] *adj* **1** : de timbre, de campana (dícese de un sonido) **2** LOUD : sonoro **3** RESOUNDING : categórico

ringleader [ˈrɪŋˌliːdər] *n* : cabecilla *mf*

ringlet [ˈrɪŋlət] *n* : sortija *f*, rizo *m*

ringtone [ˈrɪŋˌtoːn] *n* : tono *m* de llamada, ringtone *m*

ringworm [ˈrɪŋˌwərm] *n* : tiña *f*

rink [ˈrɪŋk] *n* : pista *f* ⟨skating rink : pista de patinaje⟩

rinse¹ [ˈrɪnts] *vt* **rinsed**; **rinsing** : enjuagar ⟨to rinse out one's mouth : enjuagarse la boca⟩

rinse² *n* : enjuague *m*

riot¹ [ˈraɪət] *vi* : amotinarse

riot² *n* : motín *m*, tumulto *m*, alboroto *m*

rioter [ˈraɪətər] *n* : alborotador *m*, -dora *f*

riotous [ˈraɪətəs] *adj* **1** UNRULY, WILD : desenfrenado, alborotado **2** ABUNDANT : abundante

rip¹ [ˈrɪp] *v* **ripped**; **ripping** *vt* **1** : rasgar, arrancar, desgarrar **2 to rip apart** : destruir **3 to rip up** : hacer pedazos — *vi* : rasgarse, desgarrarse

rip² *n* : rasgón *m*, desgarrón *m*

ripe [ˈraɪp] *adj* **riper**; **ripest** **1** MATURE : maduro ⟨ripe fruit : fruta madura⟩ **2** READY : listo, preparado

ripen [ˈraɪpən] *v* : madurar

ripeness [ˈraɪpnəs] *n* : madurez *f*

rip-off [ˈrɪpˌɔf] *n* **1** THEFT : robo *m* **2** SWINDLE : estafa *f*, timo *m* fam **3** COPY : copia *f* (plagiada)

rip off *vt* **1** : rasgar, arrancar, desgarrar **2** SWINDLE fam : estafar, timar

ripple¹ [ˈrɪpəl] *v* **-pled**; **-pling** *vi* : rizarse, ondear, ondular — *vt* : rizar

ripple² *n* : onda *f*, ondulación *f*

rise¹ [ˈraɪz] *vi* **rose** [ˈroːz]; **risen** [ˈrɪzən]; **rising** **1** GET UP : levantarse ⟨to rise to one's feet : ponerse de pie⟩ **2** : elevarse, alzarse ⟨the mountains rose to the west : las montañas se elevaron al oeste⟩ **3** : salir (dícese del sol y de la luna) **4** : subir (dícese de las aguas, del humo, etc.) ⟨the river rose : las aguas del río subieron de nivel⟩ ⟨let the dough rise : dejar subir la masa⟩ ⟨my spirits rose : me animé⟩ **5** INCREASE : aumentar, subir **6** ORIGINATE : nacer, proceder **7 to rise in rank** : ascender **8 to rise to the occasion** : estar a la altura de las circunstancias **9 to rise up** REBEL : sublevarse, rebelarse

rise² n **1** ASCENT : ascensión f, subida f **2** ORIGIN : origen m **3** ELEVATION : elevación f **4** INCREASE : subida f, aumento m, alzamiento m ⟨on the rise : en alza, en ascenso⟩ **5** SLOPE : pendiente f, cuesta f **6 to get a rise out of** PROVOKE : provocar, fastidiar **7 to give rise to** CAUSE : causar, dar origen a

riser ['raɪzər] n **1** : contrahuella f (de una escalera) **2 early riser** : madrugador m, -dora f **3 late riser** : dormilón m, -lona f

risk¹ ['rɪsk] vt : arriesgar, arriesgarse ⟨to risk one's life : arriesgar la vida⟩ ⟨to risk losing : arriesgarse a perder⟩ ⟨I won't risk it : no me arriesgo⟩

risk² n : riesgo m, peligro m ⟨at risk : en peligro⟩ ⟨at your own risk : por su cuenta y riesgo⟩ ⟨to take a risk : arriesgarse⟩ ⟨to run the risk of : arriesgarse a, correr el riesgo de⟩ ⟨at the risk of : a riesgo de⟩

risky ['rɪski] adj **riskier; -est** : arriesgado, peligroso, riesgoso

risqué [rɪ'skeɪ] adj : escabroso, picante, subido de tono

rite ['raɪt] n : rito m

ritual¹ ['rɪtʃuəl] adj : ritual — **ritually** adv

ritual² n : ritual m

rival¹ ['raɪvəl] vt **-valed** or **-valled; -valing** or **-valling** : rivalizar con, competir con

rival² adj : competidor, rival

rival³ n : rival mf; competidor m, -dora f

rivalry ['raɪvəlri] n, pl **-ries** : rivalidad f

river ['rɪvər] n : río m

riverbank ['rɪvər,bæŋk] n : ribera f, orilla f

riverbed ['rɪvər,bɛd] n : cauce m, lecho m

riverside ['rɪvər,saɪd] n : ribera f, orilla f

rivet¹ ['rɪvət] vt **1** : remachar **2** FIX : fijar (los ojos, etc.) **3** FASCINATE : fascinar, cautivar

rivet² n : remache m

riveting ['rɪvətɪŋ] adj : fascinante

rivulet ['rɪvjələt] n : arroyo m, riachuelo m ⟨rivulets of sweat : gotas de sudor⟩

roach ['roʊtʃ] → **cockroach**

road ['roʊd] n **1** : carretera f, calle f, camino m ⟨road map : mapa de rutas⟩ ⟨road rage : agresividad al volante⟩ ⟨road safety : seguridad vial⟩ ⟨road trip : viaje en coche (de larga distancia)⟩ ⟨to hit the road : ponerse en marcha⟩ ⟨I've been on the road since six : llevo viajando desde las seis⟩ **2** PATH : camino m, sendero m, vía f ⟨on the road to a solution : en vías de una solución⟩

roadblock ['roʊd,blɑk] n : control m

roadrunner ['roʊd,rʌnər] n : correcaminos m

roadside ['roʊd,saɪd] n : borde m de la carretera

road sign n : señal f de tráfico, señal f de tránsito

roadway ['roʊd,weɪ] n : carretera f, calzada f

roadwork ['roʊd,wərk] n : obras fpl (viales)

roam ['roʊm] vi : vagar, deambular, errar — vt : vagar por

roar¹ ['ror] vi : rugir, bramar ⟨to roar with laughter : reírse a carcajadas⟩ — vt : decir a gritos

roar² n **1** : rugido m, bramido m (de un animal) **2** DIN : clamor m (de gente), fragor m (del trueno), estruendo m (del tráfico, etc.)

roaring ['rorɪŋ] adj **1** THUNDEROUS : estruendoso, atronador **2** ACTIVE, STRONG : vivo (dícese de un fuego), caudaloso (dícese de un río), pujante (dícese de la economía) ⟨a roaring success : un gran éxito⟩

roast¹ ['rost] vt : asar (carne, papas), tostar (café, nueces) — vi : asarse

roast² adj **1** : asado ⟨roast chicken : pollo asado⟩ **2 roast beef** : rosbif m

roast³ n : asado m

roaster ['rostər] n **1** : asador m (para carne), tostador m (para café) **2** : pollo m (para asar)

rob ['rɑb] v **robbed; robbing** vt **1** STEAL : robar **2** DEPRIVE : privar, quitar — vi : robar

robber ['rɑbər] n : ladrón m, -drona f

robbery ['rɑbəri] n, pl **-beries** : robo m

robe¹ ['rob] vt **robed; robing** : vestirse

robe² n **1** : toga f (de magistrados, etc.), sotana f (de eclesiásticos) ⟨robe of office : traje de ceremonias⟩ **2** BATHROBE : bata f

robin ['rɑbən] n : petirrojo m

robot ['ro,bɑt, -bət] n : robot m — **robotic** [ro'bɑtɪk] adj

robotics [ro'bɑtɪks] ns & pl : robótica f

robust [ro'bʌst, 'ro,bʌst] adj : robusto, fuerte — **robustly** adv

robustness [ro'bʌstnəs, 'ro,bʌst-] n : robustez f, lozanía f

rock¹ ['rɑk] vt **1** : acunar (a un niño), mecer (una cuna) **2** SHAKE : sacudir **3** SHOCK : sacudir, conmocionar — vi SWAY : mecerse, balancearse

rock² n **1** : roca f (sustancia) ⟨rock climbing : escalada en roca⟩ **2** STONE : piedra f **3** ROCKING : balanceo m. **4** or **rock music** : rock m, música f rock ⟨a rock band : una banda de rock⟩ **5 on the rocks** : con hielo **6 to be on the rocks** : andar mal

rock and roll n : rock and roll m

rock bottom n **to hit/reach rock bottom** : tocar fondo

rocker ['rɑkər] n **1** : balancín m **2** or **rocking chair** : mecedora f, balancín m **3 to be off one's rocker** : estar chiflado, estar loco

rocket[1] ['rɑkət] *vi* : dispararse, subir rápidamente

rocket[2] *n* : cohete *m*

rocking horse *n* : caballito *m* (de balancín)

rock salt *n* : sal *f* gema

rocky ['rɑki] *adj* **rockier; -est** **1** : rocoso, pedregoso **2** UNSTEADY : inestable

rod ['rɑd] *n* **1** BAR : barra *f*, varilla *f*, vara *f* (de madera) ⟨a fishing rod : una caña (de pescar)⟩ **2** : medida *f* de longitud equivalente a 5.03 metros (5 yardas)

rode → **ride**[1]

rodent ['ro:dənt] *n* : roedor *m*

rodeo ['ro:di,o:, ro'dei,o:] *n, pl* **-deos** : rodeo *m*

roe ['ro:] *n* : hueva *f*

rogue ['ro:g] *n* SCOUNDREL : pícaro *m*, -ra *f*; pillo *m*, -lla *f*

roguish ['ro:gɪʃ] *adj* : pícaro, travieso

role ['ro:l] *n* : papel *m*, función *f*, rol *m*

role model *n* : modelo *m* de conducta

roll[1] ['ro:l] *vi* **1** : rodar (dícese de una pelota, etc.) **2** SLIP : resbalar **3** : ir (en un vehículo) ⟨to roll to a stop : detenerse poco a poco⟩ ⟨to roll up : llegar⟩ **4** SWAY : balancearse **5** : tronar (dícese del trueno), redoblar (dícese de un tambor) **6** FILM : rodar **7** *or* **to get rolling** : ponerse en marcha **8** *or* **to roll over** : darse la vuelta ⟨to roll (over) onto one's back/stomach : ponerse boca arriba/abajo⟩ **9** *or* **to roll over** OVERTURN : volcarse **10** *or* **to roll up** CURL : enrollarse ⟨he rolled up into a ball : se hizo una bola⟩ **11 to be rolling in it** : ser ricachón **12 to roll around** THRASH : revolcarse **13 to roll around** : llegar (dícese de una fecha, etc.) **14 to roll by/past** : pasar — *vt* **1** : hacer rodar (una pelota, etc.) ⟨to roll the dice : echar los dados⟩ ⟨to roll one's eyes : poner los ojos en blanco⟩ **2** *fam* : hacer volcar ⟨he rolled his car : se volcó en su auto⟩ **3** : liar (un cigarrillo) **4** *or* **to roll up** : enrollar ⟨to roll something (up) into a ball : hacer una bola de algo⟩ **5** *or* **to roll out** FLATTEN : estirar (masa), laminar (metales) **6 to roll back** : rebajar (precios) **7 to roll back** : revertir (cambios, etc.) ⟨to roll back the clock : volver atrás⟩ **8 to roll down/up** : bajar/subir (una ventanilla, etc.) **9 to roll out** : lanzar (un producto) **10 to roll the cameras** : rodar **11 to roll up one's sleeves** : arremangarse

roll[2] *n* **1** LIST : lista *f* ⟨to call the roll : pasar lista⟩ ⟨to have on the roll : tener inscrito⟩ **2** BUN : panecito *m*, bolillo *m* Mex **3** : rollo *m* (de papel, de tela, etc.) ⟨a roll of film : un carrete⟩ ⟨a roll of bills : un fajo⟩ **4** : redoble *m* (de tambores), retumbo *m* (del trueno, etc.) **5** ROLLING, SWAYING : balanceo *m*

roller ['ro:lər] *n* **1** : rodillo *m* **2** CURLER : rulo *m*

Rollerblade ['ro:lər,bleɪd] *trademark* se usa para patines en línea

roller coaster ['ro:lər,ko:stər] *n* : montaña *f* rusa

roller-skate ['ro:lər,skeɪt] *vi* **-skated; -skating** : patinar (sobre ruedas)

roller skate *n* : patín *m* (de ruedas)

rollicking ['rɑlɪkɪŋ] *adj* : animado, alegre

rolling ['ro:lɪŋ] *adj* : ondulante

rolling pin *n* : rodillo *m*

ROM ['rɑm] *n* : ROM *f*

Roman[1] ['ro:mən] *adj* : romano

Roman[2] *n* : romano *m*, -na *f*

Roman Catholic *n* : católico *m*, -ca *f* — **Roman Catholic** *adj*

Roman Catholicism *n* : catolicismo *m*

romance[1] [ro'mæns, 'ro:,mæns] *vi* **-manced; -mancing** FANTASIZE : fantasear

romance[2] *n* **1** : romance *m*, novela *f* de caballerías **2** : novela *f* de amor, novela *f* romántica **3** AFFAIR : romance *m*, amorío *m*

Romanian [ro'meɪniən, ro-] *n* **1** : rumano *m*, -na *f* **2** : rumano *m* (idioma) — **Romanian** *adj*

Roman numeral *n* : número *m* romano

romantic [ro'mæntɪk] *adj* : romántico — **romantic** *n* — **romantically** [-tɪkli] *adv*

romanticism [ro'mæntə,sɪzəm] *n* : romanticismo *m*

romp[1] ['rɑmp] *vi* FROLIC : retozar, juguetear

romp[2] *n* : retozo *m*

roof[1] ['ru:f, 'rʊf] *vt* : techar

roof[2] *n, pl* **roofs** ['ru:fs, 'rʊfs;, 'ru:vz, 'rʊvz] **1** : techo *m*, tejado *m*, techado *m* **2 roof of the mouth** : paladar *m*

roofing ['ru:fɪŋ, 'rʊfɪŋ] *n* : techumbre *f*

roof rack *n* : portaequipajes *m*

rooftop ['ru:f,tɑp, 'rʊf-] *n* ROOF : tejado *m*

rook[1] ['rʊk] *vt* CHEAT : defraudar, estafar, timar

rook[2] *n* **1** : grajo *m* (ave) **2** : torre *f* (en ajedrez)

rookie ['rʊki] *n* : novato *m*, -ta *f*

room[1] ['ru:m, 'rʊm] *vi* LODGE : alojarse, hospedarse

room[2] *n* **1** SPACE : espacio *m*, sitio *m*, lugar *m* ⟨to make room for : hacer lugar para⟩ **2** : cuarto *m*, habitación *f* (en una casa), sala *f* (para reuniones, etc.) **3** BEDROOM : dormitorio *m*, habitación *f*, pieza *f* **4** (*indicating possibility or opportunity*) ⟨room for improvement : posibilidad de mejorar⟩ ⟨there's no room for error : no hay lugar para errores⟩

room divider → **divider**

roomer ['ru:mər, 'rʊmər] *n* : inquilino *m*, -na *f*

roomie ['ru:mi] *n fam* → **roommate**

rooming house *n* : pensión *f*

roommate ['ru:m,meɪt, 'rʊm-] *n* : compañero *m*, -ra *f* de cuarto

room service *n* : servicio *m* de habitaciones, servicio *m* a la habitación

roomy ['ru:mi, 'rʊmi] *adj* **roomier; -est 1** SPACIOUS : espacioso, amplio **2** LOOSE : suelto, holgado ⟨a roomy blouse : una blusa holgada⟩

roost[1] ['ru:st] *vi* : posarse, dormir (en una percha)

roost[2] *n* : percha *f*

rooster ['ru:stər, 'rʊs-] *n* : gallo *m*

root[1] [ˈruːt, ˈrʊt] *vi* **1** : arraigar (en botánica) **2** : hozar (dícese de los cerdos) ⟨to root around in : hurgar en⟩ **3 to be rooted in** : estar basado en, tener su origen en **4 to be rooted to** : no poder moverse de (su silla, etc.) **5 to root for** : apoyar a, alentar — *vt* **to root out** : desarraigar (plantas), extirpar (problemas, etc.)

root[2] *n* **1** : raíz *f* (de una planta) **2** ORIGIN : origen *m*, raíz *f* **3** CORE : centro *m*, núcleo *m* ⟨to get to the root of the matter : ir al centro del asunto⟩ **4 to put down roots** SETTLE : afincarse **5 to take root** : arraigar, enraizar, echar raíces

root beer *n* : refresco *m* hecho de raíces y hierbas

rootless [ˈruːtləs, ˈrʊt-] *adj* : desarraigado

rope[1] [ˈroːp] *vt* **roped; roping 1** TIE : amarrar, atar **2** LASSO : lazar **3 to rope in/into** ⟨they roped me into driving : me agarraron para manejar⟩ ⟨I didn't want to go, but I was roped in : no quería ir, pero me arrastraron⟩ **4 to rope off** : acordonar

rope[2] *n* : soga *f*, cuerda *f*

rosary [ˈroːzəri] *n, pl* **-ries** : rosario *m*

rose[1] → **rise**

rose[2] [ˈroːz] *adj* : rosa, color de rosa

rose[3] *n* **1** : rosal *m* (planta), rosa *f* (flor) **2** : rosa *m* (color)

rosé [roːˈzeɪ] *n* : vino *m* rosado

rosebush [ˈroːzˌbʊʃ] *n* : rosal *m*

rosemary [ˈroːzˌmeri] *n, pl* **-maries** : romero *m*

rosette [roːˈzɛt] *n* : escarapela *f* (hecho de cintas), roseta *f* (en arquitectura)

Rosh Hashanah [ˌrɑʃəˈʃɑːnə, ˌroːʃ-] *n* : el Año Nuevo judío

rosin [ˈrɑzən] *n* : colofonia *f*

roster [ˈrɑstər] *n* : lista *f*

rostrum [ˈrɑstrəm] *n, pl* **-trums** *or* **-tra** [-trə] : tribuna *f*, estrado *m*

rosy [ˈroːzi] *adj* **rosier; -est 1** : sonrosado, de color rosa **2** PROMISING : prometedor

rot[1] [ˈrɑt] *v* **rotted; rotting** *vi* : pudrirse, descomponerse — *vt* : pudrir, descomponer

rot[2] *n* : putrefacción *f*, descomposición *f*, podredumbre *f*

rotary[1] [ˈroːtəri] *adj* : rotativo, rotatorio

rotary[2] *n, pl* **-ries 1** : máquina *f* rotativa **2** TRAFFIC CIRCLE : rotonda *f*, glorieta *f*

rotate [ˈroːˌteɪt] *v* **-tated; -tating** *vi* REVOLVE : girar, rotar — *vt* **1** TURN : hacer girar, darle vueltas a **2** ALTERNATE : alternar

rotation [roːˈteɪʃən] *n* : rotación *f*

rote [ˈroːt] *n* **to learn by rote** : aprender de memoria

rotisserie [roːˈtɪsri, -ˈtɪsəri] *n* SPIT : asador *m*

rotor [ˈroːtər] *n* : rotor *m*

rotten [ˈrɑtən] *adj* **1** PUTRID : podrido, putrefacto **2** CORRUPT : corrompido **3** BAD : malo ⟨a rotten day : un día malísimo⟩

rottenness [ˈrɑtənnəs] *n* : podredumbre *f*

rotund [roːˈtʌnd] *adj* **1** ROUNDED : redondeado **2** PLUMP : regordete *fam*, llenito *fam*

rotunda [roːˈtʌndə] *n* : rotonda *f*

rouge [ˈruːʒ, ˈruːdʒ] *n* : colorete *m*

rough[1] [ˈrʌf] *vt* **1** ROUGHEN : poner áspero **2 to rough out** SKETCH : esbozar, bosquejar **3 to rough up** BEAT : darle una paliza (a alguien) **4 to rough it** : vivir sin comodidades

rough[2] *adj* **1** COARSE : áspero, basto **2** UNEVEN : desigual, escabroso, accidentado (dícese del terreno) **3** : agitado (dícese del mar), tempestuoso (dícese del tiempo), violento (dícese del viento) **4** VIOLENT : violento, brutal ⟨a rough neighborhood : un barrio peligroso⟩ **5** DIFFICULT : duro, difícil **6** CRUDE : rudo, tosco, burdo ⟨a rough cottage : una casita tosca⟩ ⟨a rough draft : un borrador⟩ ⟨a rough sketch : un bosquejo⟩ **7** APPROXIMATE : aproximado ⟨a rough idea : una idea aproximada⟩

rough[3] *n* **1 the rough** : el rough (en golf) **2 in the rough** : en borrador

roughage [ˈrʌfɪdʒ] *n* : fibra *f* (dietética)

roughen [ˈrʌfən] *vt* : poner áspero — *vi* : ponerse áspero

roughly [ˈrʌfli] *adv* **1** : bruscamente ⟨to treat roughly : maltratar⟩ **2** CRUDELY : burdamente **3** APPROXIMATELY : aproximadamente, más o menos

roughneck [ˈrʌfˌnɛk] *n* : matón *m*

roughness [ˈrʌfnəs] *n* : rudeza *f*, aspereza *f*

roulette [ruːˈlɛt] *n* : ruleta *f*

round[1] [ˈraʊnd] *vt* **1** TURN : doblar ⟨to round the corner : dar la vuelta a la esquina⟩ **2** : redondear ⟨she rounded the edges : redondeó los bordes⟩ **3 to round off** : redondear (un número) **4 to round off/out** COMPLETE : rematar, terminar **5 to round up** GATHER : reunir (a personas), rodear (ganado), hacer una redada de (delincuentes) ⟨to round up suspects : detener a los sospechosos⟩ **6 to round up/down** : redondear (un número) por exceso/defecto

round[2] *adv* → **around**[1]

round[3] *adj* **1** CIRCULAR, SPHERICAL : redondo ⟨a round table/face : una mesa/cara redonda⟩ **2** CYLINDRICAL : circular, cilíndrico **3** CURVED : redondeado ⟨round shoulders : espaldas cargadas⟩ **4 round number** : número *m* redondo **5 round trip** : viaje *m* de ida y vuelta

round[4] *n* **1** CIRCLE : círculo *m* ⟨cucumber rounds : rodajas de pepino⟩ **2** SERIES : serie *f*, sucesión *f* ⟨a round of talks : una ronda de negociaciones⟩ **3** : asalto *m* (en boxeo), recorrido *m* (en golf), vuelta *f* (en varios juegos) **4** : salva *f* (de aplausos) **5** : ronda *f* (de bebidas) **6** *or* **round of ammunition** : disparo *m*, cartucho *m* **7 rounds** *npl* : recorridos *mpl* (de un cartero), rondas *fpl* (de un vigilante), visitas *fpl* (de un médico) ⟨to make the rounds : hacer visitas⟩

round⁵ *prep* → **around²**

roundabout ['raʊndə,baʊt] *adj* : indirecto ⟨to speak in a roundabout way : hablar con rodeos⟩

roundly ['raʊndli] *adv* **1** THOROUGHLY : completamente **2** BLUNTLY : francamente, rotundamente **3** VIGOROUSLY : con vigor

roundness ['raʊndnəs] *n* : redondez *f*

round–shouldered ['raʊnd,ʃoːldərd] *adj* : cargado de hombros

round–trip ['raʊnd,trɪp] *adj* : de ida y vuelta

roundup ['raʊnd,ʌp] *n* **1** : rodeo *m* (de animales), redada *f* (de delincuentes, etc.) **2** SUMMARY : resumen *m*

roundworm ['raʊnd,wərm] *n* : lombriz *f* intestinal

rouse ['raʊz] *vt* **roused**; **rousing** **1** AWAKE : despertar **2** EXCITE : excitar ⟨it roused him to fury : lo enfureció⟩

rout¹ ['raʊt] *vt* **1** DEFEAT : derrotar, aplastar **2 to rout out** : hacer salir

rout² *n* **1** DISPERSAL : desbandada *f*, dispersión *f* **2** DEFEAT : derrota *f* aplastante

route¹ ['ru:t, 'raʊt] *vt* **routed**; **routing** : dirigir, enviar, encaminar

route² *n* : camino *m*, ruta *f*, recorrido *m*

router ['raʊtər] *n* : router *m* (en informática)

routine¹ [ru:'ti:n] *adj* : rutinario — **routinely** *adv*

routine² *n* : rutina *f*

rove ['ro:v] *v* **roved**; **roving** *vi* : vagar, errar — *vt* : errar por

rover ['ro:vər] *n* **1** : vagabundo *m*, -da *f* **2** : explorador *m* (robot)

row¹ ['ro:] *vt* **1** : avanzar a remo ⟨to row a boat : remar⟩ **2** : llevar a remo ⟨he rowed me to shore : me llevó hasta la orilla⟩ — *vi* : remar

row² ['raʊ] *n* **1** : paseo *m* en barca ⟨to go for a row : salir a remar⟩ **2** LINE, RANK : fila *f*, hilera *f* **3** SERIES : serie *f* ⟨three days in a row : tres días seguidos⟩ **4** RACKET : estruendo *m*, bulla *f* **5** QUARREL : pelea *f*, riña *f*

rowboat ['ro:,bo:t] *n* : bote *m* de remos

rowdiness ['raʊdinəs] *n* : bulla *f*

rowdy¹ ['raʊdi] *adj* **rowdier**; **-est** : escandaloso, alborotador

rowdy² *n, pl* **-dies** : alborotador *m*, -dora *f*

rower ['ro:ər] *n* : remero *m*, -ra *f*

row house *n* : casa *f* adosada

royal¹ ['rɔɪəl] *adj* : real — **royally** *adv*

royal² *n* : persona *f* de linaje real, miembro de la familia real

royalist ['rɔɪəlɪst] *n* : realista *mf* — **royalism** ['rɔɪə,lɪzəm] *n* — **royalist** *adj*

royalty ['rɔɪəlti] *n, pl* **-ties** **1** : realeza *f* (posición) **2** : miembros *mpl* de la familia real **3 royalties** *npl* : derechos *mpl* de autor

rub¹ ['rʌb] *v* **rubbed**; **rubbing** *vt* **1** : frotar, restregar, friccionar ⟨to rub one's hands together : frotarse las manos⟩ ⟨rub the lotion into your skin : frote la loción en la piel⟩ **2** CHAFE

: rozar **3** POLISH : frotar, pulir **4** SCRUB : fregar **5 to rub elbows with** : codearse con **6 to rub off on** ⟨the ink rubbed off on my fingers : se me mancharon los dedos de tinta⟩ ⟨his enthusiasm rubbed off on me : me contagió con su entusiasmo⟩ **7 to rub someone the wrong way** *fam* : crispar a alguien **8 to rub something in** (**someone's face**) *fam* : restregarle (en la cara) algo a alguien ⟨you don't have to rub it in : no tienes que restregármelo⟩ — *vi* **to rub against** : rozar

rub² *n* **1** RUBBING : fricción *f*, friega *f* **2 the rub** : el problema

rubber ['rʌbər] *n* **1** : goma *f*, caucho *m*, hule *m Mex* **2 rubbers** *npl* OVERSHOES : chanclos *mpl*

rubber band *n* : goma *f* (elástica), gomita *f*

rubber–stamp ['rʌbər'stæmp] *vt* **1** APPROVE : aprobar, autorizar **2** STAMP : sellar

rubber stamp *n* : sello *m* (de goma)

rubbery ['rʌbəri] *adj* : gomoso

rubbish ['rʌbɪʃ] *n* : basura *f*, desechos *mpl*, desperdicios *mpl*

rubble ['rʌbəl] *n* : escombros *mpl*, ripio *m*

rubella [ru:'bɛlə] *n* : rubéola *f*

ruble ['ru:bəl] *n* : rublo *m*

ruby ['ru:bi] *n, pl* **-bies** **1** : rubí *m* (gema) **2** : color *m* de rubí

rucksack ['rʌk,sæk, 'rʊk-] *n* BACKPACK : mochila *f*

ruckus ['rʌkəs] *n* COMMOTION : alboroto *m*, bullicio *m*

rudder ['rʌdər] *n* : timón *m*

ruddy ['rʌdi] *adj* **ruddier**; **-est** : rubicundo (dícese del rostro, etc.), sanguíneo (dícese de la complexión)

rude ['ru:d] *adj* **ruder**; **rudest** **1** CRUDE : tosco, rústico **2** IMPOLITE : grosero, descortés, maleducado **3** ABRUPT : brusco ⟨a rude awakening : una sorpresa desagradable⟩

rudely ['ru:dli] *adv* : groseramente

rudeness ['ru:dnəs] *n* **1** IMPOLITENESS : grosería *f*, descortesía *f*, falta *f* de educación **2** ROUGHNESS : tosquedad *f* **3** SUDDENNESS : brusquedad *f*

rudiment ['ru:dəmənt] *n* : rudimento *m*, noción *f* básica ⟨the rudiments of Spanish : los rudimentos del español⟩

rudimentary [,ru:də'mɛntəri] *adj* : rudimentario, básico

rue ['ru:] *vt* **rued**; **ruing** : lamentar, arrepentirse de

rueful ['ru:fəl] *adj* **1** PITIFUL : lastimoso **2** REGRETFUL : arrepentido, pesaroso

ruffian ['rʌfiən] *n* : matón *m*

ruffle¹ ['rʌfəl] *vt* **-fled**; **-fling** **1** AGITATE : agitar, rizar (agua) **2** RUMPLE : arrugar (ropa), despeinar (pelo) **3** ERECT : erizar (plumas) **4** VEX : alterar, irritar, perturbar **5** : fruncir volantes en (tela)

ruffle² *n* FLOUNCE : volante *m*

ruffly ['rʌfəli] *adj* : con volantes

rug ['rʌg] *n* : alfombra *f*, tapete *m*

rugby ['rʌgbi] *n* : rugby *m*

rugged ['rʌgəd] *adj* **1** ROUGH, UNEVEN : accidentado, escabroso ⟨rugged mountains : montañas accidentadas⟩ **2** HARSH : duro, severo **3** ROBUST, STURDY : robusto, fuerte

ruin¹ ['ru:ən] *vt* **1** DESTROY : destruir, arruinar **2** BANKRUPT : arruinar, hacer quebrar

ruin² *n* **1** : ruina *f* ⟨to fall into ruin : caer en ruinas⟩ **2** : ruina *f*, perdición *f* ⟨to be the ruin of : ser la perdición de⟩ **3 ruins** *npl* : ruinas *fpl*, restos *mpl* ⟨the ruins of the ancient temple : las ruinas del templo antiguo⟩

ruinous ['ru:ənəs] *adj* : ruinoso

rule¹ ['ru:l] *v* **ruled; ruling** *vt* **1** CONTROL, GOVERN : gobernar (un país), controlar (las emociones) **2** DECIDE : decidir, fallar ⟨the judge ruled that . . . : el juez falló que . . .⟩ **3** DRAW : trazar con una regla **4 to rule out** EXCLUDE : descartar — *vi* **1** GOVERN : gobernar, reinar **2** PREVAIL : prevalecer, imperar **3 to rule against** : fallar en contra de **4 to rule in favor of** : fallar a favor de **5 to rule on** : fallar en

rule² *n* **1** REGULATION : regla *f*, norma *f* ⟨to follow/break the rules : seguir/violar las reglas⟩ ⟨to be against the rules : ir en contra de las reglas⟩ **2** CUSTOM, HABIT : regla *f* general ⟨as a rule : por lo general⟩ **3** GOVERNMENT : gobierno *m*, dominio *m* ⟨to be under the rule of : estar bajo el dominio de⟩ **4** RULER : regla *f* (para medir)

ruler ['ru:lər] *n* **1** LEADER, SOVEREIGN : gobernante *mf*; soberano *m*, -na *f* **2** : regla *f* (para medir)

ruling ['ru:lɪŋ] *n* : resolución *f*, fallo *m*

Rumanian [ru'meɪniən] → **Romanian**

rumba ['rʌmbə, 'rʊm-, 'ru:m-] *n* : rumba *f*

rumble¹ ['rʌmbəl] *vi* **-bled; -bling** : retumbar, hacer ruidos (dícese del estómago)

rumble² *n* : estruendo *m*, ruido *m* sordo, retumbo *m*

ruminant¹ ['ru:mənənt] *adj* : rumiante

ruminant² *n* : rumiante *m*

ruminate ['ru:mə,neɪt] *vi* **-nated; -nating** **1** : rumiar (en zoología) **2** REFLECT : reflexionar, rumiar

rummage ['rʌmɪdʒ] *vi* **-maged; -maging** : hurgar ⟨to rummage (around) in, to rummage through : hurgar en⟩

rummage sale *n* : venta *f* de beneficencia (de objetos de segunda mano)

rummy ['rʌmi] *n* : rummy *m* (juego de naipes)

rumor¹ ['ru:mər] *vt* : rumorear ⟨it is rumored that . . . : se rumorea que . . . , se dice que . . .⟩ ⟨her rumored resignation : su rumoreada dimisión⟩

rumor² *n* : rumor *m*

rump ['rʌmp] *n* **1** : ancas *fpl*, grupa *f* (de un animal) **2** : cadera *f* ⟨rump steak : filete de cadera⟩

rumple ['rʌmpəl] *vt* **-pled; -pling** : arrugar (ropa, etc.), despeinar (pelo)

run¹ ['rʌn] *v* **ran** ['ræn]; **run; running** *vi* **1** : correr ⟨she ran to catch the bus : co-

rrió para alcanzar el autobús⟩ ⟨run and fetch the doctor : corre a buscar al médico⟩ ⟨he ran to the store : salió rápido a la tienda⟩ ⟨to run after someone/something : correr tras alguien/algo⟩ **2** : circular, correr ⟨the train runs between Detroit and Chicago : el tren circula entre Detroit y Chicago⟩ ⟨to run on time : ser puntual⟩ **3** FUNCTION : funcionar, ir ⟨the engine runs on gasoline : el motor funciona con gasolina⟩ ⟨with the motor running : con el motor en marcha⟩ ⟨to run smoothly : ir bien⟩ **4** FLOW : correr, ir **5** LAST : durar ⟨the movie runs for two hours : la película dura dos horas⟩ ⟨the contract runs for three years : el contrato es válido por tres años⟩ **6** : desteñir, despintar (dícese de los colores) **7** EXTEND : correr, extenderse ⟨the path runs along the lake : el sendero bordea el lago⟩ **8** TRAVEL, SPREAD : correr, extenderse **9 to run away** : salir corriendo ⟨to run away from : fugarse de⟩ ⟨to run away from home : escaparse de casa⟩ **10 to run down** : agotarse, gastarse (dícese de pilas, etc.) **11 to run for office** : postularse, presentarse (como candidato) **12 to run out** : acabarse ⟨time is running out : se acaba el tiempo⟩ ⟨I ran out of money : se me acabó el dinero⟩ **13 to run over** OVERFLOW : rebosar — *vt* **1** : correr ⟨to run 10 miles : correr 10 millas⟩ ⟨to run errands : hacer los mandados⟩ ⟨to run out of town : hacer salir del pueblo⟩ **2** PASS : pasar ⟨she ran her fingers through her hair : se pasó la mano por el pelo⟩ **3** DRIVE : llevar (en coche) **4** OPERATE : hacer funcionar (un motor, etc.) **5** PERFORM : realizar (un análisis, etc.) **6** : echar ⟨to run water over : echarle agua a⟩ ⟨to run the water/faucet : abrir la llave (del agua)⟩ **7** MANAGE : dirigir, llevar (un negocio, etc.) **8** EXTEND : tender (un cable, etc.) **9 to run across** : encontrarse con **10 to run a risk** : correr un riesgo **11 to run down** USE UP : gastar, agotar **12 to run down/over** : atropellar **13 to run into** : encontrar **14 to run off** PRINT : tirar, sacar **15 to run through** : repasar, ensayar **16 to run up** : incurrir en **17 to run up against** : tropezar con

run² *n* **1** : carrera *f* ⟨at a run : a la carrera, corriendo⟩ ⟨to go for a run : ir a correr⟩ ⟨to make a run for it : huir corriendo⟩ ⟨to be on the run : estar fugitivo⟩ **2** TRIP : vuelta *f*, paseo *m* (en coche), viaje *m* (en avión) **3** SERIES : serie *f* ⟨a run of disappointments : una serie de desilusiones⟩ ⟨in the long run : a la larga⟩ ⟨in the short run : a corto plazo⟩ **4** DEMAND : gran demanda *f* ⟨a run on the banks : una corrida bancaria⟩ **5** (*used for theatrical productions and films*) ⟨to have a long run : mantenerse mucho tiempo en la cartelera⟩ **6** TYPE : tipo *m* ⟨the average run of students : el tipo más común de estudiante⟩ **7** : carrera *f* (en béisbol) **8** : carrera *f* (en una media) **9 to have the run of** : tener libre acceso de (una casa, etc.) **10 ski run** : pista *f* (de esquí)

runaway¹ [ˈrʌnəˌweɪ] *adj* **1** FUGITIVE : fugitivo **2** UNCONTROLLABLE : incontrolable, fuera de control ⟨runaway inflation : inflación desenfrenada⟩ ⟨a runaway success : un éxito aplastante⟩

runaway² *n* : fugitivo *m*, -va *f*

rundown [ˈrʌnˌdaʊn] *n* SUMMARY : resumen *m*

run-down [ˈrʌnˈdaʊn] *adj* **1** DILAPIDATED : ruinoso, destartalado **2** SICKLY, TIRED : cansado, débil

rung¹ *pp* → **ring¹**

rung² [ˈrʌŋ] *n* : peldaño *m*, escalón *m*

run-in [ˈrʌnˌɪn] *n* : disputa *f*, altercado *m*

runner [ˈrʌnər] *n* **1** RACER : corredor *m*, -dora *f* **2** MESSENGER : mensajero *m*, -ra *f* **3** TRACK : riel *m* (de un cajón, etc.) **4** : patín *m* (de un trineo), cuchilla *f* (de un patín) **5** : estolón *m* (planta)

runner-up [ˌrʌnərˈʌp] *n, pl* **runners-up** : subcampeón *m*, -peona *f*

running [ˈrʌnɪŋ] *adj* **1** FLOWING : corriente ⟨running water : agua corriente⟩ **2** CONTINUOUS : continuo ⟨a running battle : una lucha continua⟩ **3** CONSECUTIVE : seguido ⟨six days running : por seis días seguidos⟩

runny [ˈrʌni] *adj* **runnier; -est 1** WATERY : caldoso **2 to have a runny nose** : moquear

run-of-the-mill [ˌrʌnəvðəˈmɪl] *adj* : normal y corriente, común

runt [ˈrʌnt] *n* : animal *m* pequeño ⟨the runt of the litter : el más pequeño de la camada⟩

runway [ˈrʌnˌweɪ] *n* : pista *f* de aterrizaje

rupee [ruːˈpiː, ˈruːˌ-] *n* : rupia *f*

rupture¹ [ˈrʌptʃər] *v* **-tured; -turing** *vt* **1** BREAK, BURST : romper, reventar **2** : causar una hernia en — *vi* : reventarse

rupture² *n* **1** BREAK : ruptura *f* **2** HERNIA : hernia *f*

rural [ˈrʊrəl] *adj* : rural, campestre

ruse [ˈruːs, ˈruːz] *n* : treta *f*, ardid *m*, estratagema *f*

rush¹ [ˈrʌʃ] *vi* **1** : correr, ir de prisa ⟨to rush around : correr de un lado a otro⟩ ⟨to rush off/in/out : irse/entrar/salir corriendo⟩ ⟨let's not rush into it : no nos precipitemos⟩ **2** FLOW : correr con fuerza — *vt* **1** HURRY : apresurar, apurar ⟨don't rush me : no me apures⟩ ⟨to rush something : hacer algo apresuradamente⟩ ⟨she rushed me into making a decision : me hizo tomar una decisión apresurada⟩ **2** : llevar o enviar urgentemente ⟨he was rushed to the hospital : fue trasladado de urgencia al hospital⟩ **3** ATTACK : abalanzarse sobre, asaltar

rush² *adj* : urgente

rush³ *n* **1** HASTE : prisa *f*, apuro *m* ⟨there's no rush : no hay ninguna prisa⟩ ⟨to be in a rush : tener prisa, estar/ir apurado⟩ **2** SURGE : ráfaga *f* (de aire), torrente *m* (de aguas), avalancha *f* (de gente) **3** DEMAND : demanda *f* ⟨a rush on sugar : una gran demanda para el azúcar⟩ **4** : carga *f* (en futbol americano) **5** : junco *m* (planta)

rush hour *n* : hora *f* pico

russet [ˈrʌsət] *n* : color *m* rojizo

Russian [ˈrʌʃən] *n* **1** : ruso *m*, -sa *f* **2** : ruso *m* (idioma) — **Russian** *adj*

rust¹ [ˈrʌst] *vi* : oxidarse — *vt* : oxidar

rust² *n* **1** : herrumbre *f*, orín *m*, óxido *m* (en los metales) **2** : roya *f* (en las plantas)

rustic¹ [ˈrʌstɪk] *adj* : rústico, campestre

rustic² *n* : rústico *m*, -ca *f*; campesino *m*, -na *f*

rustle¹ [ˈrʌsəl] *v* **rustled; rustling** *vt* **1** : hacer susurrar, hacer crujir ⟨to rustle a newspaper : hacer crujir un periódico⟩ **2** STEAL : robar (ganado) **3 to rustle up** : improvisar (una comida), conseguir (información, etc.) — *vi* : susurrar, crujir

rustle² *n* : murmullo *m*, susurro *m*, crujido *m*

rustler [ˈrʌslər] *n* : ladrón *m*, -drona *f* de ganado

rustproof [ˈrʌstˌpruːf] *adj* : inoxidable

rusty [ˈrʌsti] *adj* **rustier; -est** : oxidado, herrumbroso

rut [ˈrʌt] *n* **1** GROOVE, TRACK : rodada *f*, surco *m* **2 to be in a rut** : ser esclavo de la rutina

ruthless [ˈruːθləs] *adj* : despiadado, cruel — **ruthlessly** *adv*

ruthlessness [ˈruːθləsnəs] *n* : crueldad *f*, falta *f* de piedad

RV [ˌɑrˈviː] → **recreational vehicle**

Rwandan [ruˈɑndən] *n* : ruandés *m*, -desa *f* — **Rwandan** *adj*

rye [ˈraɪ] *n* **1** : centeno *m* **2** *or* **rye bread** : pan *m* de centeno **3** *or* **rye whiskey** : whisky *m* de centeno

S

s [ˈɛs] *n, pl* **s's** *or* **ss** [ˈɛsəz] : decimonovena letra del alfabeto inglés

Sabbath [ˈsæbəθ] *n* **1** : sábado *m* (en el judaísmo) **2** : domingo *m* (en el cristianismo)

sabbatical [səˈbætɪkəl] *n* : sabático *m*

saber [ˈseɪbər] *n* : sable *m*

sable [ˈseɪbəl] *n* **1** BLACK : negro *m* **2** : marta *f* cebellina (animal)

sabotage¹ [ˈsæbəˌtɑːʒ] *vt* **-taged; -taging** : sabotear

sabotage² *n* : sabotaje *m*

saboteur [ˌsæbəˈtər] *n* : saboteador *m*, -dora *f*

sac [ˈsæk] *n* : saco *m* (anatómico)

saccharin ['sækərən] n : sacarina f
saccharine ['sækərən, -ˌriːn, -ˌraɪn] adj : meloso, empalagoso
sachet [sæ'ʃeɪ] n : bolsita f (perfumada)
sack¹ ['sæk] vt **1** FIRE : echar (del trabajo), despedir **2** PLUNDER : saquear
sack² n BAG : saco m
sacrament ['sækrəmənt] n : sacramento m
sacramental [ˌsækrə'mɛntəl] adj : sacramental
sacred ['seɪkrəd] adj **1** RELIGIOUS : sagrado, sacro ⟨sacred texts : textos sagrados⟩ **2** HOLY : sagrado **3** sacred to : consagrado a
sacrifice¹ ['sækrəˌfaɪs] vt **-ficed; -ficing 1** : sacrificar **2 to sacrifice oneself** : sacrificarse
sacrifice² n : sacrificio m
sacrilege ['sækrəlɪdʒ] n : sacrilegio m
sacrilegious [ˌsækrə'lɪdʒəs, -'liː-] adj : sacrílego
sacrosanct ['sækroˌsæŋkt] adj : sacrosanto
sad ['sæd] adj **sadder; saddest** : triste — **sadly** adv
sadden ['sædən] vt : entristecer
saddle¹ ['sædəl] vt **-dled; -dling 1** : ensillar **2 to saddle someone with something** : cargar a alguien con algo, endilgarle algo a alguien
saddle² n : silla f (de montar)
saddlebag ['sædəlˌbæg] n : alforja f
sadism ['seɪˌdɪzəm, 'sæ-] n : sadismo m
sadist ['seɪdɪst, 'sæ-] n : sádico m, -ca f
sadistic [sə'dɪstɪk] adj : sádico — **sadistically** [-tɪkli] adv
sadness ['sædnəs] n : tristeza f
safari [sə'fɑri, -'fær-] n : safari m
safe¹ ['seɪf] adj **safer; safest 1** UNHARMED : ileso ⟨safe and sound : sano y salvo⟩ **2** SECURE, PROTECTED : seguro **3** : seguro (dícese de vehículos, actividades, etc.) ⟨have a safe trip! : ¡(que tengas un) buen viaje!⟩ **4** : seguro (dícese de medicamentos, etc.) ⟨safe to eat/drink : comestible/potable⟩ **5** PROTECTIVE : seguro ⟨a safe place : un lugar seguro⟩ ⟨at a safe distance : a una distancia prudencial⟩ **6** : seguro (dícese de inversiones, etc.) **7** CAREFUL : prudente ⟨a safe driver : un conductor responsable⟩ **8 (it's) better (to be) safe than sorry** : más vale prevenir que curar **9 it's safe to say that . . .** or **it's a safe bet that . . .** : se puede decir, sin temor a equivocarse, que . . . **10 to be on the safe side** : para mayor seguridad **11 to play it safe** : ir a la segura
safe² n : caja f fuerte
safe–conduct ['seɪf'kɑnˌdʌkt] n : salvoconducto m
safe–deposit box n : caja f de seguridad
safeguard¹ ['seɪfˌgɑrd] vt : salvaguardar, proteger
safeguard² n : salvaguarda f, protección f
safekeeping ['seɪf'kiːpɪŋ] n : custodia f, protección f ⟨to put into safekeeping : poner en buen recaudo⟩
safely ['seɪfli] adv **1** UNHARMED : sin in-

cidentes, sin novedades ⟨they landed safely : aterrizaron sin novedades⟩ **2** SECURELY : con toda seguridad, sin peligro **3** : sin temor a equivocarse ⟨one can safely say that . . . : se puede decir, sin temor a equivocarse, que . . .⟩
safety ['seɪfti] n, pl **-ties** : seguridad f
safety belt n : cinturón m de seguridad
safety net n **1** : red f de seguridad **2** : protección f
safety pin n : alfiler m de gancho, alfiler m de seguridad, imperdible m Spain
safety razor → razor
saffron ['sæfrən] n : azafrán m
sag¹ ['sæg] vi **sagged; sagging 1** DROOP, SINK : combarse, hundirse, inclinarse **2** : colgar, caer ⟨his jowls sagged : le colgaban las mejillas⟩ **3** FLAG : flaquear, decaer ⟨his spirits sagged : se le flaqueó el ánimo⟩
sag² n : comba f
saga ['sɑgə, 'sæ-] n : saga f
sagacious [sə'geɪʃəs] adj : sagaz
sage¹ ['seɪdʒ] adj **sager; sagest** : sabio — **sagely** adv
sage² n **1** : sabio m, -bia f **2** : salvia f (planta)
sagebrush ['seɪdʒˌbrʌʃ] n : artemisa f
Sagittarius [ˌsædʒə'tɛriəs] n **1** : Sagitario m (signo o constelación) **2** : Sagitario mf (persona)
said → say
sail¹ ['seɪl] vi **1** : navegar (en un barco) **2** : ir/marchar (etc.) fácilmente ⟨we sailed right in : entramos sin ningún problema⟩ ⟨she sailed through the exam : aprobó/pasó el examen sin problemas⟩ — vt **1** : gobernar (un barco) **2 to sail the seas** : cruzar los mares
sail² n **1** : vela f (de un barco) **2** : viaje m en velero ⟨to go for a sail : salir a navegar⟩
sailboat ['seɪlˌboːt] n : velero m, barco m de vela
sailfish ['seɪlˌfɪʃ] n : pez m vela
sailing ['seɪlɪŋ] n **1** : navegación f (de un barco de vela) **2** : vela f (deporte)
sailing ship n : barco m de vela
sailor ['seɪlər] n : marinero m
saint ['seɪnt, before a name ˌseɪnt, or sənt] n : santo m, -ta f ⟨Saint Francis : San Francisco⟩ ⟨Saint Rose : Santa Rosa⟩
saintliness ['seɪntlinəs] n : santidad f
saintly ['seɪntli] adj **saintlier; -est** : santo
sake ['seɪk] n **1** BENEFIT : bien m ⟨for the children's sake : por el bien de los niños⟩ **2** (indicating an end or a purpose) ⟨art for art's sake : el arte por el arte⟩ ⟨let's say, for argument's sake, . . . : pongamos que . . .⟩ **3 for goodness' sake!** : ¡por (el amor de) Dios!
salable or **saleable** ['seɪləbəl] adj : vendible
salacious [sə'leɪʃəs] adj : salaz — **salaciously** adv
salad ['sæləd] n : ensalada f
salad dressing → dressing
salamander ['sæləˌmændər] n : salamandra f
salami [sə'lɑmi] n : salami m

salary ['sæləri] n, pl **-ries** : sueldo m
sale ['seɪl] n **1** SELLING : venta f **2** : liquidación f, rebajas fpl ⟨on sale : de rebaja⟩ **3 sales** npl : ventas fpl ⟨to work in sales : trabajar en ventas⟩
salesman ['seɪlzmən] n, pl **-men** [-mən, -ˌmɛn] **1** : vendedor m, dependiente m (en una tienda) **2 traveling salesman** : viajante m, representante m
salesperson ['seɪlzˌpərsən] n : vendedor m, -dora f; dependiente m, -ta f (en una tienda)
sales pitch → **pitch²**
saleswoman ['seɪlzˌwʊmən] n, pl **-women** [-ˌwɪmən] **1** : vendedora f, dependienta f (en una tienda) **2 traveling saleswoman** : viajante f, representante f
salient ['seɪljənt] adj : saliente, sobresaliente
saline ['seɪˌli:n, -ˌlaɪn] adj : salino
salinity [ˌseɪˈlɪnəti, sə-] n : salinidad f
saliva [səˈlaɪvə] n : saliva f
salivary ['sæləˌvɛri] adj : salival ⟨salivary gland : glándula salival⟩
salivate ['sæləˌveɪt] vi **-vated; -vating** : salivar
sallow ['sæloː] adj : amarillento
sally¹ ['sæli] vi **-lied; -lying** SET OUT : salir, hacer una salida
sally² n, pl **-lies** **1** : salida f (militar), misión f **2** QUIP : salida f, ocurrencia f
salmon ['sæmən] ns & pl **1** : salmón m (pez) **2** : color m salmón
salon [səˈlɑn, ˈsæˌlɑn, sæˈlɔ̃] n : salón m ⟨beauty salon : salón de belleza⟩
saloon [səˈlu:n] n **1** HALL : salón m (en un barco) **2** BARROOM : bar m
salsa ['sɔlsə, 'sɑl-] n : salsa f mexicana, salsa f picante
salt¹ ['sɔlt] vt : salar, echarle sal a
salt² adj : salado
salt³ n : sal f
saltiness ['sɔltinəs] n : lo salado, salinidad f
salt shaker → **shaker**
saltwater ['sɔltˌwɒtər, -ˌwɑ-] adj : de agua salada
salty ['sɔlti] adj **saltier; -est** : salado
salubrious [səˈlu:briəs] adj : salubre
salutary ['sæljəˌtɛri] adj : saludable, salubre
salutation [ˌsæljəˈteɪʃən] n : saludo m, salutación f
salute¹ [səˈlu:t] v **-luted; -luting** vt **1** : saludar (con gestos o ademanes) **2** ACCLAIM : reconocer, aclamar — vi : hacer un saludo
salute² n **1** : saludo m (gesto), salva f (de cañonazos) **2** TRIBUTE : reconocimiento m, homenaje m
Salvadoran [ˌsælvəˈdorən] → **El Salvadoran**
salvage¹ ['sælvɪʤ] vt **-vaged; -vaging** : salvar, rescatar
salvage² n **1** SALVAGING : salvamento m, rescate m **2** : objetos mpl salvados
salvation [sælˈveɪʃən] n : salvación f
salve¹ ['sæv, 'sav] vt **salved; salving** : calmar, apaciguar ⟨to salve one's conscience : aliviarse la conciencia⟩

salve² n : ungüento m
salvo ['sælˌvoː] n, pl **-vos** or **-voes** : salva f
samba ['sæmbə, 'sɑ-] n : samba f
same¹ ['seɪm] adj **1** : mismo ⟨he and I are from the same town : él y yo somos del mismo pueblo⟩ ⟨the same exact day, the exact/very same day : el mismísimo día⟩ ⟨they're one and the same person : son la misma persona⟩ **2** ALIKE, IDENTICAL : igual ⟨I have the same shirt : tengo una camisa igual a la tuya⟩ ⟨they're spelled the same way : se escriben igual⟩ **3** (indicating repetition) : mismo ⟨the same thing happened yesterday : ayer pasó lo mismo⟩ **4** (indicating a shared characteristic) : mismo ⟨they're the same age : tienen la misma edad⟩ ⟨she has the same eyes as her father : tiene los mismos ojos de su padre⟩ **5 the same old** ⟨it's always the same old thing : siempre pasa lo mismo⟩ ⟨the same old story : la misma historia de siempre⟩ **6 the same thing** ⟨it amounts to the same thing : viene a ser lo mismo⟩
same² pron **1 the same** : lo mismo ⟨it's all the same to me : me da lo mismo, me da igual⟩ ⟨the same to you! : ¡igualmente!⟩ ⟨the same goes for you : también va por ti⟩ ⟨you should do the same : deberías hacer lo mismo⟩ ⟨they're one and the same : son la misma persona/cosa⟩ ⟨I could say the same : podría decir lo mismo⟩ **2 the same** : igual ⟨the two cars are the same : los dos coches son iguales⟩ **3 the same** : igual (que antes) ⟨things are still the same : las cosas siguen igual⟩ ⟨he was never quite the same again : ya no era el mismo de antes⟩ **4 all/just the same** : de todos modos **5 same here** fam : yo también, a mí también
sameness ['seɪmnəs] n **1** SIMILARITY : identidad f, semejanza f **2** MONOTONY : monotonía f
same-sex ['seɪmˈsɛks] adj : del mismo sexo ⟨same-sex marriage : el matrimonio entre personas del mismo sexo⟩
sample¹ ['sæmpəl] vt **-pled; -pling** : probar
sample² n : muestra f, prueba f
sampler ['sæmplər] n **1** : dechado m (de bordado) **2** COLLECTION : colección f **3** ASSORTMENT : surtido m
sanatorium [ˌsænəˈtoriəm] n, pl **-riums** or **-ria** [-iə] : sanatorio m
sanctify ['sæŋktəˌfaɪ] vt **-fied; -fying** : santificar
sanctimonious [ˌsæŋktəˈmoːniəs] adj : beato, santurrón
sanction¹ ['sæŋkʃən] vt : sancionar, aprobar
sanction² n **1** AUTHORIZATION : sanción f, autorización f **2 sanctions** npl : sanciones fpl ⟨to impose sanctions on : imponer sanciones a⟩
sanctity ['sæŋktəti] n, pl **-ties** : santidad f
sanctuary ['sæŋktʃuˌɛri] n, pl **-aries** **1** : presbiterio m (en una iglesia) **2** REFUGE : refugio m, asilo m

sand¹ ['sænd] *vt* : lijar (madera)
sand² *n* : arena *f*
sandal ['sændəl] *n* : sandalia *f*
sandalwood ['sændəl,wʊd] *n* : sándalo *m*
sandbank ['sænd,bæŋk] *n* : banco *m* de arena
sandbar ['sænd,bɑr] *n* : banco *m* de arena
sandbox ['sænd,bɑks] *n* : cajón *m* de arena
sand castle *n* : castillo *m* de arena
sand dune *n* → dune
sandpaper ['sænd,peɪpər] *n* : papel *m* de lija
sandstone ['sænd,sto:n] *n* : arenisca *f*
sandstorm ['sænd,stɔrm] *n* : tormenta *f* de arena
sandwich¹ ['sænd,wɪtʃ] *vt* : intercalar, encajonar, meter (entre dos cosas)
sandwich² *n* : sandwich *m*, emparedado *m*, bocadillo *m* Spain
sandy ['sændi] *adj* sandier; -est : arenoso
sane ['seɪn] *adj* saner; sanest 1 : cuerdo 2 SENSIBLE : sensato, razonable
sang → sing
sangria ['sæŋˈgriːə, ˌsæn-] *n* : sangría *f*
sanguine ['sæŋgwən] *adj* 1 RUDDY : sanguíneo, rubicundo 2 HOPEFUL : optimista
sanitarium [ˌsænəˈteriəm] *n, pl* -iums *or* -ia [-iə] → sanatorium
sanitary ['sænətɛri] *adj* 1 : sanitario ⟨sanitary measures : medidas sanitarias⟩ 2 HYGIENIC : higiénico 3 sanitary napkin : compresa *f*, paño *m* higiénico
sanitation [ˌsænəˈteɪʃən] *n* : sanidad *f*
sanitize ['sænə,taɪz] *vt* -tized; -tizing 1 : desinfectar 2 EXPURGATE : expurgar
sanity ['sænəti] *n* : cordura *f*, razón *f* ⟨to lose one's sanity : perder el juicio⟩
sank → sink
Santa Claus ['sæntə,klɔz] *n* : Papá Noel, San Nicolás
sap¹ ['sæp] *vt* sapped; sapping 1 UNDERMINE : socavar 2 WEAKEN : minar, debilitar
sap² *n* 1 : savia *f* (de una planta) 2 SUCKER : inocentón *m*, -tona *f*
sapling ['sæplɪŋ] *n* : árbol *m* joven
sapphire ['sæ,faɪr] *n* : zafiro *m*
Saran Wrap [səˈræn-] *trademark* se usa para papel film
sarcasm ['sɑr,kæzəm] *n* : sarcasmo *m*
sarcastic [sɑrˈkæstɪk] *adj* : sarcástico — sarcastically [-tɪkli] *adv*
sarcophagus [sɑrˈkɑfəgəs] *n, pl* -gi [-ˌgaɪ, -ˌdʒaɪ] : sarcófago *m*
sardine [sɑrˈdiːn] *n* : sardina *f*
sardonic [sɑrˈdɑnɪk] *adj* : sardónico — sardonically [-nɪkli] *adv*
sari ['sɑri] *n* : sari *m*
sarsaparilla [ˌsæspəˈrɪlə, ˌsɑrs-] *n* : zarzaparrilla *f*
sash ['sæʃ] *n* 1 : faja *f* (de un vestido), fajín *m* (de un uniforme) 2 *pl* sash : marco *m* (de una ventana)
sassafras ['sæsə,fræs] *n* : sasafrás *m*
sassy ['sæsi] *adj* sassier; -est 1 *fam* IMPERTINENT : fresco, descarado, impertinente 2 STYLISH : moderno, llamativo 3 VIVACIOUS : vivaz

sat → sit
Satan ['seɪtən] *n* : Satanás *m*, Satán *m*
satanic [səˈtænɪk, seɪ-] *adj* : satánico — satanically [-nɪkli] *adv*
satchel ['sætʃəl] *n* : cartera *f*, saco *m*
sate ['seɪt] *vt* sated; sating : saciar
satellite ['sætə,laɪt] *n* : satélite *m* ⟨spy satellite : satélite espía⟩
satellite dish *n* : antena *m* parabólica
satiate ['seɪʃi,eɪt] *vt* -ated; -ating : saciar, hartar
satin ['sætən] *n* : raso *m*, satín *m*, satén *m*
satire ['sæ,taɪr] *n* : sátira *f*
satiric [səˈtɪrɪk] *or* satirical [-ɪkəl] *adj* : satírico
satirize ['sætə,raɪz] *vt* -rized; -rizing : satirizar
satisfaction [ˌsætəsˈfækʃən] *n* : satisfacción *f*
satisfactory [ˌsætəsˈfæktəri] *adj* : satisfactorio, bueno — satisfactorily [-rəli] *adv*
satisfy ['sætəs,faɪ] *v* -fied; -fying *vt* 1 PLEASE : satisfacer, contentar 2 CONVINCE : convencer 3 FULFILL : satisfacer, cumplir con, llenar 4 SETTLE : pagar, saldar (una cuenta) — *vi* SUFFICE : bastar
satisfying ['sætəs,faɪɪŋ] *adj* : satisfactorio
saturate ['sætʃə,reɪt] *vt* -rated; -rating 1 SOAK : empapar 2 FILL : saturar
saturation [ˌsætʃəˈreɪʃən] *n* : saturación *f*
Saturday ['sætər,deɪ, -di] *n* : sábado *m* ⟨today is Saturday : hoy es sábado⟩ ⟨on Saturday : el sábado⟩ ⟨(on) Saturdays : los sábados⟩ ⟨last Saturday : el sábado pasado⟩ ⟨next Saturday : el sábado que viene⟩ ⟨every other Saturday : cada dos sábados⟩ ⟨Saturday afternoon/morning : sábado por la tarde/mañana⟩
Saturn ['sætərn] *n* : Saturno *m*
satyr ['seɪtər, 'sæ-] *n* : sátiro *m*
sauce ['sɔs] *n* : salsa *f*
saucepan ['sɔs,pæn] *n* : cacerola *f*, cazo *m*, cazuela *f*
saucer ['sɔsər] *n* : platillo *m*
sauciness ['sɔsinəs] *n* : descaro *m*, frescura *f*
saucy ['sɔsi] *adj* saucier; -est IMPUDENT : descarado, fresco *fam* — saucily *adv*
Saudi ['saʊdi, 'sɔ-] → Saudi Arabian
Saudi Arabian *n* : saudita *mf*, saudí *mf* — Saudi Arabian *adj*
sauna ['sɔnə, 'saʊnə] *n* : sauna *mf*
saunter ['sɔntər, 'sɑn-] *vi* : pasear, pasearse
sausage ['sɔsɪdʒ] *n* : salchicha *f*, embutido *m*
sauté [sɔˈteɪ, soː-] *vt* -téed *or* -téd; -téing : saltear, sofreír
savage¹ ['sævɪdʒ] *adj* 1 *offensive* PRIMITIVE : salvaje 2 : salvaje, feroz — savagely *adv*
savage² *n* 1 *offensive* : salvaje *mf* 2 BEAST, BRUTE : salvaje *mf*
savagery ['sævɪdʒri, -dʒəri] *n, pl* -ries 1 FEROCITY : ferocidad *f* 2 ATROCITY : salvajada *f*, atrocidad *f*, crueldad *f* ⟨the savageries of war : las atrocidades de la guerra⟩

savanna [sə'vænə] *n* : sabana *f*

save¹ ['seɪv] *v* **saved; saving** *vt* **1** RESCUE : salvar, rescatar ⟨she saved him from drowning : lo salvó de morir ahogado⟩ ⟨you really saved my bacon/hide/neck/skin! : ¡me salvaste el pellejo!⟩ **2** PRESERVE : salvar, preservar, conservar ⟨he hopes to save his job : espera salvar su trabajo⟩ **3** KEEP : guardar, ahorrar (dinero), almacenar (alimentos) ⟨to save one's strength : guardarse las fuerzas⟩ **4** : guardar (en informática) **5** ECONOMIZE : ahorrar (tiempo, espacio, combustible, etc.) **6** SPARE : ahorrar ⟨you saved me a trip : me ahorraste el viaje⟩ **7 to save someone's life** : salvarle la vida a alguien **8 to save the day** : salvar la situación — *vi* : ahorrar ⟨to save for the future : ahorrar para el futuro⟩ ⟨you'll save on insurance : ahorrarás dinero en tu seguro⟩

save² *prep* EXCEPT : salvo, excepto, menos

savings ['seɪvɪŋz] *n* : ahorros *mpl*

savings account *n* : cuenta *f* de ahorro(s)

savings bank *n* : caja *f* de ahorros

savior ['seɪvjər] *n* **1** : salvador *m*, -dora *f* **2 the Savior** : el Salvador *m*

savor¹ ['seɪvər] *vt* : saborear

savor² *n* : sabor *m*

savory ['seɪvəri] *adj* : sabroso

saw¹ → **see**

saw² ['sɔ] *vt* **sawed; sawed** *or* **sawn** ['sɔn]; **sawing** : serrar, cortar (con sierra)

saw³ *n* : sierra *f*

sawdust ['sɔˌdʌst] *n* : aserrín *m*, serrín *m*

sawhorse ['sɔˌhɔrs] *n* : caballete *m*, burro *m* (en carpintería)

sawmill ['sɔˌmɪl] *n* : aserradero *m*

sax ['sæks] *n* : saxo *m fam* (instrumento)

saxophone ['sæksəˌfoːn] *n* : saxofón *m* — **saxophonist** ['sæksəˌfoːnɪst] *n*

say¹ ['seɪ] *v* **said** ['sɛd]; **saying; says** ['sɛz] *vt* **1** EXPRESS, UTTER : decir, expresar ⟨to say yes/no : decir que sí/no⟩ ⟨to say again : repetir⟩ ⟨to say one's prayers : rezar⟩ ⟨she didn't say a word : no dijo ni una palabra⟩ **2** INDICATE : marcar ⟨dícese de un reloj⟩, poner (dícese de un letrero, etc.) **3** EXPRESS, REVEAL : decir, revelar ⟨her face says it all : su cara lo dice todo⟩ **4** OPINE : decir ⟨so they say : eso dicen⟩ **5** KNOW : decir, saber ⟨it's hard to say why : es difícil decir por qué⟩ **6** COMMAND : decir, mandar ⟨what he says goes : lo que ella dice va a misa⟩ ⟨do as I say : haz lo que te digo⟩ ⟨whatever you say : lo que tú digas⟩ **7** PRONOUNCE : decir, pronunciar **8** SUPPOSE : suponer, decir **9 if I say so myself** : modestia aparte **10 no sooner said than done** : dicho y hecho **11 that goes without saying** : ni que decir tiene **12 that is to say** : es decir **13 that said, . . .** : dicho esto, . . . **14 to say the least** : y me quedo corto **15 when all is said and done** : al fin y al cabo **16 you can say that again!** *fam* : ¡y tanto! **17 you said

it! : ¡de acuerdo! — *vi* **1** : decir ⟨I couldn't say : no podría decirle⟩ **2 I'll say!** : ¡y tanto! **3 you don't say!** : ¡no me digas!

say² *n, pl* **says** : voz *f*, opinión *f* ⟨to have no say : no tener ni voz ni voto⟩ ⟨to have one's say : dar uno su opinión⟩

saying ['seɪɪŋ] *n* : dicho *m*, refrán *m*

scab ['skæb] *n* **1** : costra *f*, postilla *f* (en una herida) **2** STRIKEBREAKER : rompehuelgas *mf*, esquirol *mf*

scabbard ['skæbərd] *n* : vaina *f* (de una espada), funda *f* (de un puñal, etc.)

scabby ['skæbi] *adj* **scabbier; -est** : lleno de costras

scaffold ['skæfəld, -ˌfoːld] *n* **1** *or* **scaffolding** : andamio *m* (para obreros, etc.) **2** : patíbulo *m*, cadalso *m* (para ejecuciones)

scald ['skɔld] *vt* **1** BURN : escaldar **2** HEAT : calentar (hasta el punto de ebullición)

scale¹ ['skeɪl] *v* **scaled; scaling** *vt* **1** : escamar (un pescado) **2** CLIMB : escalar (un muro, etc.) **3 to scale down** : reducir — *vi* WEIGH : pesar ⟨he scaled in at 200 pounds : pesó 200 libras⟩

scale² *n* **1** *or* **scales** *npl* : balanza *f*, báscula *f* (para pesar), baremo *m* ⟨bathroom scale : báscula de baño⟩ ⟨kitchen scale : balanza de cocina⟩ ⟨to tip the scales in one's favor : inclinar la balanza a su favor⟩ **2** : escama *f* (de un pez, etc.) **3** EXTENT : escala *f*, proporción *f* ⟨on a worldwide scale : a escala mundial⟩ ⟨large-scale production : producción a gran escala⟩ **4** RANGE : escala *f* ⟨wage scale : escala salarial⟩ **5** : escala *f* (en cartografía, etc.) ⟨to draw to scale : dibujar a escala⟩ **6** : escala *f* (en música)

scallion ['skæljən] *n* : cebollino *m*, cebolleta *f*

scallop ['skɑləp, 'skæ-] *n* **1** : vieira *f* (molusco) **2** : festón *m* (decoración)

scalp¹ ['skælp] *vt* **1** : arrancar la cabellera a **2** : revender (ilegalmente)

scalp² *n* : cuero *m* cabelludo

scalpel ['skælpəl] *n* : bisturí *m*, escalpelo *m*

scalper ['skælpər] *n* : revendedor *m*, -dora *f* (de entradas)

scaly ['skeɪli] *adj* **scalier; -est** : escamoso

scam ['skæm] *n* : estafa *f*, timo *m fam*, chanchullo *m fam*

scamp ['skæmp] *n* : bribón *m*, -bona *f*; granuja *mf*; travieso *m*, -sa *f*

scamper ['skæmpər] *vi* : corretear

scan¹ ['skæn] *vt* **scanned; scanning** **1** : escandir (versos) **2** SCRUTINIZE : escudriñar, escrutar ⟨to scan the horizon : escudriñar el horizonte⟩ **3** PERUSE : echarle un vistazo a (un periódico, etc.) **4** EXPLORE : explorar (con radar), hacer un escáner de (en ecografía) **5** : escanear (una imagen)

scan² *n* **1** : ecografía *f*, examen *m* ultrasónico, escáner *m* (en medicina) **2** : imagen *f* escaneada (en una computadora)

scandal ['skændəl] *n* **1** DISGRACE, OUTRAGE : escándalo *m* **2** GOSSIP : habladurías *fpl*, chismes *mpl*

scandalize ['skændəl,aɪz] vt -ized; -izing : escandalizar

scandalous ['skændələs] adj : de escándalo

Scandinavian¹ [,skændə'neɪviən] adj : escandinavo

Scandinavian² n : escandinavo m, -va f

scanner ['skænər] n : escáner m, scanner m

scant ['skænt] adj : escaso

scanty ['skænti] adj scantier; -est : exiguo, escaso ⟨a scanty meal : una comida insuficiente⟩ — **scantily** [-təli] adv

scapegoat ['skeɪp,ɡoːt] n : chivo m expiatorio, cabeza f de turco

scapula ['skæpjələ] n, pl -lae [-,liː, -,laɪ] or -las → shoulder blade

scar¹ ['skɑr] v scarred; scarring vt : dejar una cicatriz en — vi : cicatrizar

scar² n : cicatriz f, marca f

scarab ['skærəb] n : escarabajo m

scarce ['skɛrs] adj scarcer; -est : escaso

scarcely ['skɛrsli] adv 1 BARELY : apenas 2 : ni mucho menos, ni nada que se le parezca ⟨he's scarcely an expert : ciertamente no es experto⟩

scarcity ['skɛrsəti] n, pl -ties : escasez f

scare¹ ['skɛr] vt scared; scaring 1 : asustar, espantar 2 to scare away/off : ahuyentar

scare² n 1 FRIGHT : susto m, sobresalto m 2 ALARM : pánico m

scarecrow ['skɛr,kroː] n : espantapájaros m, espantajo m

scared ['skɛrd] n : asustado ⟨to be scared stiff, to be scared to death : estar muerto de miedo⟩ ⟨I'm scared of snakes : las culebras me dan miedo⟩

scarf ['skɑrf] n, pl scarves ['skɑrvz] or scarfs 1 MUFFLER : bufanda f 2 KERCHIEF : pañuelo m

scarlet ['skɑrlət] n : escarlata f — **scarlet** adj

scarlet fever n : escarlatina f

scary ['skɛri] adj scarier; -est : espantoso, pavoroso

scathing ['skeɪðɪŋ] adj : mordaz, cáustico

scatter ['skæt̬ər] vt : esparcir, desparramar — vi DISPERSE : dispersarse

scatterbrained ['skæt̬ər,breɪnd] adj : atolondrado, despistado, alocado

scavenge ['skævəndʒ] v -venged; -venging vt : rescatar (de la basura); penepar CA, Mex — vi : rebuscar, hurgar en la basura ⟨to scavenge for food : andar buscando comida⟩

scavenger ['skævəndʒər] n 1 : persona f que rebusca en las basuras; penepador m, -dora f CA, Mex 2 : carroñero m, -ra f (animal)

scenario [sə'næri,oː, -'nɑr-] n, pl -ios 1 PLOT : argumento m (en teatro), guión m (en cine) 2 SITUATION : situación f hipotética ⟨in the worst-case scenario : en el peor de los casos⟩

scene ['siːn] n 1 : escena f (en una obra de teatro) 2 SCENERY : decorado m (en el teatro) ⟨behind the scenes : entre bastidores⟩ 3 VIEW : escena f 4 LOCALE, LOCATION : escena f, escenario m ⟨the

scene where the movie was filmed : el lugar donde la película se filmó⟩ ⟨the scene of the crime : la escena del crimen⟩ ⟨police are on/at the scene : los policías están en el lugar⟩ 5 COMMOTION, FUSS : escándalo m, escena f ⟨to make a scene : armar un escándalo⟩ 6 to set the scene : describir el escenario (de un cuento, etc.) 7 to set the scene for : crear un ambiente propicio para

scenery ['siːnəri] n, pl -eries 1 : decorado m (en el teatro) 2 LANDSCAPE : paisaje m

scenic ['siːnɪk] adj : pintoresco

scent¹ ['sɛnt] vt 1 SMELL : oler, olfatear 2 PERFUME : perfumar 3 SENSE : sentir, percibir

scent² n 1 ODOR : olor m, aroma m 2 : olfato m ⟨a dog with a keen scent : un perro con un buen olfato⟩ 3 PERFUME : perfume m

scented ['sɛntəd] adj : perfumado

scepter ['sɛptər] n : cetro m

sceptic ['skɛptɪk] → **skeptic**

schedule¹ ['skɛ,dʒuːl, -dʒəl, esp Brit 'ʃɛd,juːl] vt -uled; -uling : planear, programar

schedule² n 1 PLAN : programa m, plan m ⟨on schedule : según lo previsto⟩ ⟨behind schedule : atrasado, con retraso⟩ 2 TIMETABLE : horario m

schematic¹ [skɪ'mæt̬ɪk] adj : esquemático

schematic² n : plano m, esquema m

scheme¹ ['skiːm] vi schemed; scheming : intrigar, conspirar

scheme² n 1 PLAN : plan m, proyecto m 2 PLOT, TRICK : intriga f, ardid m 3 FRAMEWORK : esquema m ⟨a color scheme : una combinación de colores⟩

schemer ['skiːmər] n : intrigante mf

schism ['sɪzəm, 'skɪ-] n : cisma m

schizophrenia [,skɪtsə'friːniə, ,skɪzə-, -'frɛ-] n : esquizofrenia f

schizophrenic [,skɪtsə'frɛnɪk, ,skɪzə-] n : esquizofrénico m, -ca f — **schizophrenic** adj

scholar ['skɑlər] n 1 STUDENT : escolar mf; alumno m, -na f 2 EXPERT : especialista mf

scholarly ['skɑlərli] adj : erudito

scholarship ['skɑlər,ʃɪp] n 1 LEARNING : erudición f 2 GRANT : beca f

scholastic [skə'læstɪk] adj : académico

school¹ ['skuːl] vt : instruir, enseñar

school² n 1 : escuela f, colegio m (institución) ⟨to go to school : ir a la escuela⟩ ⟨school district : distrito escolar⟩ ⟨law/medical school : facultad de derecho/medicina⟩ 2 : estudiantes y profesores (de una escuela) 3 : escuela f (en pintura, etc.) ⟨the Flemish school : la escuela flamenca⟩ 4 school of fish : banco m, cardumen m

schoolbook ['skuːl,bʊk] n : libro m de texto

schoolboy ['skuːl,bɔɪ] n : escolar m, colegial m

schoolchild ['skuːl,tʃaɪld] n : colegial m, -giala f; escolar mf

schoolgirl ['skuːl,ɡərl] n : escolar f, colegiala f

schoolhouse ['sku:l,haʊs] n : escuela f

schooling ['sku:lɪŋ] n : educación f escolar

schoolmate ['sku:l,meɪt] n : compañero m, -ra f de escuela

schoolroom ['sku:l,ru:m, -,rʊm] → classroom

schoolteacher ['sku:l,ti:tʃər] n : maestro m, -tra f; profesor m, -sora f

schoolwork ['sku:l,wərk] n : trabajo m escolar

schooner ['sku:nər] n : goleta f

science ['saɪənts] n : ciencia f

science fiction n : ciencia ficción f

scientific [,saɪən'tɪfɪk] adj : científico — scientifically [-fɪkli] adv

scientist ['saɪəntɪst] n : científico m, -ca f

sci-fi ['saɪ'faɪ] fam → science fiction

scintillating ['sɪntə,leɪtɪŋ] adj : chispeante, brillante

scissors ['sɪzərz] npl : tijeras fpl

sclerosis [sklə'ro:səs] n, pl -roses : esclerosis f

scoff ['skɑf] vi to scoff at : burlarse de, mofarse de

scold ['sko:ld] vt : regañar, reprender, reñir

scoop¹ ['sku:p] vt 1 : sacar (con pala o cucharón) 2 to scoop out HOLLOW : vaciar, ahuecar

scoop² n 1 : pala f (para harina, etc.), cucharón m (para helado, etc.) 2 : bola f (de helado), cucharada f

scoot ['sku:t] vi : ir rápidamente ⟨she scooted around the corner : volvió a la esquina a toda prisa⟩

scooter ['sku:tər] n : patineta f, monopatín m, patinete m

scope ['sko:p] n 1 RANGE : alcance m, ámbito m, extensión f 2 OPPORTUNITY : posibilidades fpl, libertad f

scorch ['skɔrtʃ] vt : chamuscar, quemar — vi : chamuscarse, quemarse

score¹ ['skor] v scored; scoring vt 1 RECORD : anotar 2 MARK, SCRATCH : marcar, rayar 3 : marcar, meter (en deportes) 4 GAIN : ganar, apuntarse 5 GRADE : calificar (exámenes, etc.) 6 : instrumentar, orquestar (música) — vi 1 : marcar (en deportes) 2 : obtener una puntuación (en un examen)

score² n, pl scores 1 or pl score TWENTY : veintena f 2 LINE, SCRATCH : línea f, marca f 3 : resultado m (en deportes) ⟨what's the score? : ¿cómo va el marcador?⟩ ⟨to keep score : anotar los tantos⟩ 4 GRADE, POINTS : calificación f (en un examen), puntuación f (en un concurso) 5 ACCOUNT : cuenta f ⟨to settle a score : ajustar una cuenta⟩ ⟨on that score : a ese respecto⟩ 6 : partitura f (musical)

scoreboard ['skor,bord] n : marcador m, tanteador m, pizarra f

scorer ['skorər] n : anotador m, -dora f; goleador m, -dora f (de fútbol, etc.) ⟨the team's top scorer : el máximo anotador del equipo⟩

scorn¹ ['skɔrn] vt : despreciar, menospreciar, desdeñar

scorn² n : desprecio m, menosprecio m, desdén m

scornful ['skɔrnfəl] adj : desdeñoso, despreciativo — scornfully adv

Scorpio ['skɔrpi,o:] n 1 : Escorpio m, Escorpión m (signo o constelación) 2 : Escorpio mf, Escorpión mf (persona)

scorpion ['skɔrpiən] n : alacrán m, escorpión m

Scot ['skɑt] n : escocés m, -cesa f

Scotch¹ ['skɑtʃ] adj → Scottish¹

Scotch² npl the Scotch (used with a plural verb) : los escoceses

Scotch³ trademark se usa para un tipo de cinta adhesiva

scot-free ['skɑt'fri:] adj to get off scot-free : salir impune, quedar sin castigo

Scots ['skɑts] n : escocés m (idioma)

Scottish¹ ['skɑtɪʃ] adj : escocés

Scottish² n → Scots

scoundrel ['skaʊndrəl] n : sinvergüenza mf; bellaco m, -ca f

scour ['skaʊər] vt 1 EXAMINE, SEARCH : registrar (un área), revisar (documentos, etc.) 2 SCRUB : fregar, restregar

scourge¹ ['skərdʒ] vt scourged; scourging : azotar

scourge² n : azote m

scout¹ ['skaʊt] vi 1 RECONNOITER : reconocer 2 to scout around for : explorar en busca de

scout² n 1 : explorador m, -dora f 2 or talent scout : cazatalentos mf

scowl¹ ['skaʊl] vi : fruncir el ceño

scowl² n : ceño m fruncido

scrabble ['skræbəl] vi scrabbled; -bling : escarbar/hurgar (etc.) frenéticamente ⟨they scrabbled in the dirt : escarbaban en el suelo⟩ ⟨she scrabbled around in her handbag : hurgaba en el bolso⟩ ⟨he scrabbled at the rock : intentó agarrarse a la roca⟩

scram ['skræm] vi scrammed; scramming : largarse

scramble¹ ['skræmbəl] v scrambled; -bling vi 1 : trepar, gatear (apresuradamente) ⟨he scrambled over the fence : se trepó a la cerca con rapidez⟩ 2 : hacer/ir (etc.) frenéticamente ⟨we scrambled for cover : corrimos a ponernos a cubierto⟩ 3 STRUGGLE : pelearse (por) ⟨they scrambled for seats : se pelearon por los asientos⟩ — vt 1 JUMBLE : mezclar 2 ENCODE, ENCRYPT : codificar, cifrar, encriptar 3 to scramble eggs : hacer huevos revueltos

scramble² n : rebatiña f, pelea f

scrambled eggs npl : huevos mpl revueltos

scrap¹ ['skræp] v scrapped; scrapping vt DISCARD : desechar — vi FIGHT : pelearse

scrap² n 1 FRAGMENT : pedazo m, trozo m ⟨a scrap of paper : un pedacito de papel, un papelito⟩ ⟨scraps of fabric : retazos⟩ 2 FIGHT : pelea f 3 or scrap metal : chatarra f 4 scraps npl LEFTOVERS : restos mpl, sobras fpl

scrapbook ['skræp,bʊk] n : álbum m de recortes

scrape¹ ['skreɪp] v **scraped; scraping** vt **1** GRAZE, SCRATCH : rozar, rascar ⟨to scrape one's knee : rasparse la rodilla⟩ **2** CLEAN : raspar (con un cuchillo, etc.) **3 to scrape off** : raspar (pintura, etc.) **4 to scrape up/together** : juntar, reunir poco a poco — vi **1** RUB : rozar **2 to scrape by/along** : arreglárselas, ir tirando **3 to scrape by/through** ⟨he just barely scraped by on the exam : aprobó el examen por los pelos⟩

scrape² n **1** SCRAPING : raspadura f **2** SCRATCH : rasguño m **3** PREDICAMENT : apuro m, aprieto m

scraping ['skreɪpɪŋ] n SHAVING : raspadura f

scrap paper n : papel para borrador, papel usado

scratch¹ ['skrætʃ] vt **1** : rascarse (la cabeza, etc.) ⟨to scratch an itch : rascarse⟩ **2** : arañar, rasguñar (con las uñas, etc.) **3** MARK : rayar, marcar **4 to scratch out** : tachar — vi **1** : rascarse **2** : arañar **3** : rayar **4 to scratch at** : arañar, rasguñar (una puerta, etc.)

scratch² n **1** : rasguño m, arañazo m (en la piel) **2** MARK : raya f, rayón m (en un mueble, etc.) **3** : sonido m rasposo ⟨I heard a scratch at the door : oí cómo que raspaban a la puerta⟩ **4 from ~** ⟨to start from scratch : empezar desde cero⟩ ⟨I made the cake from scratch : el pastel lo hice yo⟩ **5 to be up to scratch** : dar la talla

scratchy ['skrætʃi] adj **scratchier; -est** : áspero, que pica ⟨a scratchy sweater : un suéter que pica⟩

scrawl¹ ['skrɔl] v : garabatear

scrawl² n : garabato m

scrawny ['skrɔni] adj **scrawnier; -est** : flaco, escuálido

scream¹ ['skri:m] vi : chillar, gritar

scream² n : chillido m, grito m

screech¹ ['skri:tʃ] vi : chillar (dícese de las personas o de los animales), chirriar (dícese de los frenos, etc.)

screech² n **1** : chillido m, grito m (de una persona o un animal) **2** : chirrido m (de frenos, etc.)

screen¹ ['skri:n] vt **1** SHIELD : proteger **2** CONCEAL : tapar, ocultar **3** TEST : someter (a un paciente) a pruebas preventivas o de detección ⟨to screen for drugs/cancer : someter a una prueba de (detección de) drogas/cáncer⟩ **4** INSPECT : revisar (equipaje, etc.) **5** SELECT : seleccionar (candidatos, etc.), filtrar (llamadas, etc.) **6** SIEVE : cribar **7** : emitir (un programa de televisión), proyectar (una película)

screen² n **1** PARTITION : biombo m, pantalla f **2** SIEVE : criba f **3** : pantalla f (de un televisor, una computadora, etc.) **4** MOVIES : cine m **5 or window screen** : ventana f de tela metálica

screening ['skri:nɪŋ] n **1** : proyección f (de una película), emisión f (de un programa de televisión) **2** TESTING : acto m de hacer pruebas médicas (preventivas o

de drogas) **3** INSPECTION : control m (de pasajeros, equipaje), selección f (de candidatos)

screenplay ['skri:n,pleɪ] n SCRIPT : guión m

screen saver n : protector m de pantalla, salvapantallas m

screw¹ ['skru] vt **1** : atornillar (un tornillo) **2** : atornillar, sujetar (con tornillos) **3** : enroscar (una tapa) **4 or to screw over** fam CHEAT, DECEIVE : estafar, engañar **5 to screw someone out of something** fam : quitarle algo a alguien (injustamente) — vi **1 to screw around** TOY : jugar, juguetear **2 to screw around** fam : perder el tiempo **3 to screw around** fam : tener líos (amorosos) **4 to screw in** : atornillarse **5 to screw up** fam : meter la pata

screw² n **1** : tornillo m (para fijar algo) **2** TWIST : vuelta f **3** PROPELLER : hélice f

screwdriver ['skru,draɪvər] n : destornillador m, desarmador m Mex

scribble¹ ['skrɪbəl] v **-bled; -bling** : garabatear

scribble² n : garabato m

scribe ['skraɪb] n : escriba m

scrimmage ['skrɪmɪdʒ] n : escaramuza f

scrimp ['skrɪmp] vi **1 to scrimp on** : escatimar **2 to scrimp and save** : hacer economías

script ['skrɪpt] n **1** HANDWRITING : letra f, escritura f **2** : guión m (de una película, etc.)

scriptural ['skrɪptʃərəl] adj : bíblico

scripture ['skrɪptʃər] n **1** : escritos mpl sagrados (de una religión) **2 the Scriptures** npl : las Sagradas Escrituras

scriptwriter ['skrɪpt,raɪtər] n : guionista mf, libretista mf

scroll¹ ['skro:l] n **1** : rollo m (de pergamino, etc.) **2** : voluta f (adorno en arquitectura)

scroll² vi : desplazarse (en informática) — vt : desplazar (en informática)

scrotum ['skro:təm] n, pl **scrota** [-tə] or **scrotums** : escroto m

scrounge ['skraʊndʒ] v **scrounged; scrounging** vt **1** BUM, SPONGE : gorrear fam, sablear fam (dinero) **2 or to scrounge up** : conseguir, encontrar — vi **1 to scrounge off** : vivir a costa de **2 to scrounge around for** : buscar, andar a la busca de

scrounger ['skraʊndʒər] n : gorrón m, -rrona f

scrub¹ ['skrʌb] vt **scrubbed; scrubbing** : restregar, fregar

scrub² n **1** THICKET, UNDERBRUSH : maleza f, matorral m, matorrales mpl **2** SCRUBBING : fregado m, restregadura f

scrubby ['skrʌbi] adj **scrubbier; -est 1** STUNTED : achaparrado **2** : cubierto de maleza

scruff ['skrʌf] n **by the scruff of the neck** : por el cogote, por el pescuezo

scruffy ['skrʌfi] adj **scruffier; -est** : dejado, desaliñado

scrumptious ['skrʌmpʃəs] *adj* : delicioso, muy rico

scruple ['skru:pəl] *n* : escrúpulo *m*

scrupulous ['skru:pjələs] *adj* : escrupuloso — **scrupulously** *adv*

scrutinize ['skru:tən,aɪz] *vt* -**nized; -nizing** : escrutar, escudriñar

scrutiny ['skru:təni] *n, pl* -**nies** : escrutinio *m*, inspección *f*

scuba ['sku:bə] *n* **1** *or* **scuba gear** : equipo *m* de submarinismo **2 scuba diver** : submarinista *mf* **3 scuba diving** : submarinismo *m*

scuff ['skʌf] *vt* : rayar, raspar ⟨to scuff one's feet : arrastrar los pies⟩

scuffle[1] ['skʌfəl] *vi* -**fled; -fling 1** TUSSLE : pelearse **2** SHUFFLE : caminar arrastrando los pies

scuffle[2] *n* **1** TUSSLE : refriega *f*, pelea *f* **2** SHUFFLE : arrastre *m* de los pies

sculpt ['skʌlpt] *v* : esculpir

sculptor ['skʌlptər] *n* : escultor *m*, -tora *f*

sculptural ['skʌlptʃərəl] *adj* : escultórico

sculpture[1] ['skʌlptʃər] *vt* -**tured; -turing** : esculpir

sculpture[2] *n* : escultura *f*

scum ['skʌm] *n* **1** FROTH : espuma *f*, nata *f* **2** : verdín *m* (encima de un líquido)

scurrilous ['skərələs] *adj* : difamatorio, calumnioso, injurioso

scurry ['skəri] *vi* -**ried; -rying** : corretear

scurvy ['skərvi] *n* : escorbuto *m*

scuttle[1] ['skʌtəl] *v* -**tled; -tling** *vt* : hundir (un barco) — *vi* SCAMPER : corretear

scuttle[2] *n* : cubo *m* (para carbón)

scythe ['saɪð] *n* : guadaña *f*

sea[1] ['si:] *adj* : del mar

sea[2] *n* **1** : mar *mf* ⟨the Black Sea : el Mar Negro⟩ ⟨on the high seas : en alta mar⟩ ⟨heavy seas : mar gruesa, mar agitada⟩ **2** MASS : mar *m*, multitud *f* ⟨a sea of faces : un mar de rostros⟩

sea bass ['bæs] *n* : lubina *f*

seabed ['si:,bɛd] *n* : fondo *m* del mar

seabird ['si:,bərd] *n* : ave *f* marina

seaboard ['si:,bɔrd] *n* : litoral *m*

seacoast ['si:,ko:st] *n* : costa *f*, litoral *m*

seafarer ['si:,færər] *n* : marinero *m*

seafaring[1] ['si:,færɪŋ] *adj* : marinero

seafaring[2] *n* : navegación *f*

seafood ['si:,fu:d] *n* : mariscos *mpl*

seafront ['si:,frʌnt] *n* : paseo *m* marítimo ⟨a restaurant on the seafront : un restaurante frente al mar⟩

seagull ['si:,gʌl] *n* : gaviota *f*

sea horse ['si:,hɔrs] *n* : hipocampo *m*, caballito *m* de mar

seal[1] ['si:l] *vt* **1** CLOSE : sellar, cerrar ⟨to seal a letter : cerrar una carta⟩ ⟨to seal an agreement : sellar un acuerdo⟩ **2** to **seal off** : acordonar, cerrar **3** to **seal up** : tapar, rellenar (una grieta, etc.)

seal[2] *n* **1** : foca *f* (animal) **2** : sello *m* ⟨seal of approval : sello de aprobación⟩ **3** CLOSURE : cierre *m*, precinto *m*

sea level *n* : nivel *m* del mar

sea lion *n* : león *m* marino

sealskin ['si:l,skɪn] *n* : piel *f* de foca

seam[1] ['si:m] *vt* **1** STITCH : unir con costuras **2** MARK : marcar

seam[2] *n* **1** STITCHING : costura *f* **2** LODE, VEIN : veta *f*, filón *m*

seaman ['si:mən] *n, pl* -**men** [-mən, -,mɛn] **1** SAILOR : marinero *m* **2** : marino *m* (en la armada)

seamless ['si:mləs] *adj* **1** : sin costuras, de una pieza **2** : perfecto ⟨a seamless transition : una transición fluida⟩

seamstress ['si:mpstrəs] *n* : costurera *f*

seamy ['si:mi] *adj* **seamier; -est** : sórdido

séance ['seɪ,ɑːns] *n* : sesión *f* de espiritismo

seaplane ['si:,pleɪn] *n* : hidroavión *m*

seaport ['si:,pɔrt] *n* : puerto *m* marítimo

sear ['sɪr] *vt* **1** PARCH, WITHER : secar, resecar **2** SCORCH : chamuscar, quemar

search[1] ['sərtʃ] *vt* : registrar (un edificio, un área), cachear (a una persona), buscar en — *vi* to **search for** : buscar

search[2] *n* **1** : búsqueda *f*, registro *m* (de un edificio, etc.), cacheo *m* (de una persona) **2** in **search of** : en busca de

search engine *n* : buscador *m*

searching ['sərtʃɪŋ] *adj* : inquisitivo, penetrante

searchlight ['sərtʃ,laɪt] *n* : reflector *m*

seashell ['si:,ʃɛl] *n* : concha *f* (marina)

seashore ['si:,ʃɔr] *n* : orilla *f* del mar

seasick ['si:,sɪk] *adj* : mareado ⟨to get seasick : marearse⟩

seasickness ['si:,sɪknəs] *n* : mareo *m*

seaside → **seacoast**

season[1] ['si:zən] *vt* **1** FLAVOR, SPICE : sazonar, condimentar **2** CURE : curar, secar (madera)

season[2] *n* **1** : estación *f* (del año) **2** : temporada *f* ⟨baseball season : la temporada de beisbol⟩ ⟨the holiday season : las fiestas⟩ ⟨in season : en temporada⟩ ⟨out of season : fuera de temporada⟩ **3** HEAT, ESTRUS : celo *m*

seasonable ['si:zənəbəl] *adj* **1** : propio de la estación (dícese del tiempo, de las temperaturas, etc.) **2** TIMELY : oportuno

seasonal ['si:zənəl] *adj* : estacional — **seasonally** *adv*

seasoned ['si:zənd] *adj* **1** SPICED : condimentado, sazonado **2** EXPERIENCED : veterano ⟨a seasoned veteran : un veterano avezado⟩ **3** : curado, seco ⟨seasoned wood : madera curada/seca⟩

seasoning ['si:zənɪŋ] *n* : condimento *m*, sazón *f*

season ticket *n* : abono *m*

seat[1] ['si:t] *vt* **1** SIT : sentar ⟨please be seated : siéntense, por favor⟩ **2** HOLD : tener cabida para ⟨the stadium seats 40,000 : el estadio tiene 40,000 asientos⟩

seat[2] *n* **1** : asiento *m*, plaza *f* (en un vehículo) ⟨take a seat : tome asiento⟩ **2** : asiento *m* (de una silla) **3** BOTTOM : fondillos *mpl* (de la ropa), trasero *m* (del cuerpo) **4** : sede *f* (de un gobierno, del poder, etc.), centro *m* (de enseñanza, etc.)

seat belt *n* : cinturón *m* de seguridad

seating ['si:tɪŋ] *n* **1** : asientos *mpl* ⟨is there enough seating for everyone? : ¿hay asientos para todos?⟩ ⟨seating ca-

pacity : aforo⟩ ⟨the seating plan/ar-
rangement for the wedding reception : el
plano de mesas para el banquete de bo-
das⟩ **2** SITTING : turno m
sea urchin n : erizo m de mar
seawall ['si:ˌwɔl] n : rompeolas m, dique
m marítimo
seawater ['si:ˌwɔt̬ər, -ˌwɑ-] n : agua f de
mar
seaweed ['si:ˌwi:d] n : alga f marina
seaworthy ['si:ˌwərði] adj : en condiciones de navegar
secede [sɪ'si:d] vi **-ceded; -ceding** : separarse (de una nación, etc.)
seclude [sɪ'klu:d] vt **-cluded; -cluding**
: aislar
seclusion [sɪ'klu:ʒən] n : aislamiento m
second¹ ['sɛkənd] vt : secundar, apoyar
(una moción)
second² or **secondly** ['sɛkəndli] adv : en
segundo lugar
second³ adj **1** : segundo ⟨her second husband : su segundo marido⟩ ⟨the second
house on the left : la segunda casa a la
izquierda⟩ ⟨he took second place : ganó
el segundo lugar⟩ **2** : otro ⟨a second
chance/time : otra oportunidad/vez⟩ **3**
every second EVERY OTHER : cada dos
⟨every second month : cada dos meses⟩
second⁴ n **1** : segundo m, -da f (en una
serie) ⟨the second of July : el dos de ju-
lio⟩ **2** : segundo m, ayudante m (en deportes) **3** MOMENT : segundo m, momento m **4** or **second base** : segunda
base f **5** or **second gear** : segunda (de
un automóvil) **6 seconds** npl : segunda
ración ⟨to have seconds : repetir⟩ ⟨who
wants seconds? : ¿quién quiere más?⟩
secondary ['sɛkənˌdri] adj : secundario
secondary school n : escuela f de
enseñanza secundaria
second–class ['sɛkəndˈklæs] adj : de segunda clase/categoría, mediocre
secondhand ['sɛkəndˈhænd] adj : de segunda mano
second lieutenant n : alférez mf, subteniente mf
second–rate ['sɛkəndˈreɪt] adj : mediocre, de segunda categoría
second thought n **1** : duda f ⟨later he
had second thoughts about going : luego
le entró la duda sobre si ir o no⟩ ⟨don't
give it a second thought : no tiene importancia, no te preocupes⟩ **2 on second thought** : pensándolo bien **3
without a second thought** : sin pensarlo
dos veces
secrecy ['si:krəsi] n, pl **-cies** : secreto m
secret¹ ['si:krət] adj **1** : secreto ⟨to keep
a secret : guardar un secreto⟩ ⟨to make
no secret of something : no ocultar/es-
conder algo⟩ ⟨in secret : en secreto⟩ **2**
→ secretive — **secretly** adv
secret² n : secreto m
secretarial [ˌsɛkrə'triəl] adj : de secretario, de oficina
secretariat [ˌsɛkrə'triət] n : secretaría f,
secretariado m
secretary ['sɛkrəˌtri] n, pl **-taries** : secretario m, -ria f (en una oficina, etc.) **2**

: ministro m, -tra f; secretario m, -ria f
⟨Secretary of State : Secretario de Es-
tado⟩
secrete [sɪ'kri:t] vt **-creted; -creting 1**
: secretar, segregar (en fisiología) **2**
HIDE : ocultar
secretion [sɪ'kri:ʃən] n : secreción f
secretive ['si:krətɪv, sɪ'kri:tɪv] adj : reservado, callado, secreto
sect ['sɛkt] n : secta f
sectarian [sɛk'triən] adj : sectario
section¹ ['sɛkʃən] vt **1** : dividir **2 to section off** : separar
section² n : sección f, parte f (de un mueble, etc.), sector m (de la población),
barrio m (de una ciudad)
sectional ['sɛkʃənəl] adj **1** : en sección,
en corte ⟨a sectional diagram : un
gráfico en corte⟩ **2** FACTIONAL : de
grupo, entre facciones **3** : modular
⟨sectional furniture : muebles modula-
res⟩
sector ['sɛktər] n : sector m
secular ['sɛkjələr] adj **1** : secular, laico
⟨secular life : la vida secular⟩ **2** : seglar
(dícese de los sacerdotes, etc.)
secure¹ [sɪ'kjʊr] vt **-cured; -curing 1**
FASTEN : asegurar (una puerta, etc.), sujetar **2** GET : conseguir
secure² adj securer; **-est** : seguro — **securely** adv
security [sɪ'kjʊrət̬i] n, pl **-ties 1** SAFETY
: seguridad f **2** GUARANTEE : garantía
f **3 securities** npl : valores mpl
security guard n : guardia mf de seguridad, guarda mf de seguridad
sedan [sɪ'dæn] n **1** or **sedan chair** : silla
f de manos **2** : sedán m (automóvil)
sedate¹ [sɪ'deɪt] vt **-dated; -dating** : sedar
sedate² adj : sosegado — **sedately** adv
sedation [sɪ'deɪʃən] n : sedación f
sedative¹ ['sɛdət̬ɪv] adj : sedante
sedative² n : sedante m, calmante m
sedentary ['sɛdənˌteri] adj : sedentario
sedge ['sɛdʒ] n : juncia f
sediment ['sɛdəmənt] n : sedimento m
(geológico), poso m (en un líquido) —
sedimentary [ˌsɛdə'mentəri] adj — **sed-
imentation** [ˌsɛdəmən'teɪʃən] n
sedition [sɪ'dɪʃən] n : sedición f
seditious [sɪ'dɪʃəs] adj : sedicioso
seduce [sɪ'du:s, -'dju:s] vt **-duced; -duc-
ing** : seducir
seduction [sɪ'dʌkʃən] n : seducción f
seductive [sɪ'dʌktɪv] adj : seductor, seductivo
seducer [sɪ'du:sər, -'dju:-] n : seductor m,
-tora f
see¹ ['si:] v **saw** ['sɔ]; **seen** ['si:n]; **seeing**
vt **1** : ver ⟨I saw a dog : vi un perro⟩
⟨see you later! : ¡hasta luego!⟩ ⟨I'll believe it when I see it : hasta que no lo
vea, no lo creo⟩ ⟨so I see : ya veo⟩ ⟨did
you see the game? : ¿viste el partido?⟩
⟨see below : ver más abajo, véase más
abajo⟩ **2** ASCERTAIN : ver ⟨see who's at
the door : ve a abrir (la puerta)⟩ ⟨let's
wait and see what happens : esperemos a
ver qué pasa⟩ **3** READ : leer **4** EXPE-
RIENCE : ver, conocer **5** UNDERSTAND

: ver, entender **6** CONSIDER : ver ⟨as I see it : a mi entender⟩ **7** IMAGINE : imaginar **8** FORESEE : ver **9** ENSURE : asegurarse ⟨see that it's correct : asegúrese de que sea correcto⟩ **10** MEET, VISIT : ver **11** CONSULT : ver **12** ACCOMPANY : acompañar ⟨to see someone to the door : acompañar a alguien a la puerta⟩ **13** to be seeing someone : salir con alguien **14** to see in someone ⟨what does she see in him? : ¿qué le ve?⟩ **15** to see off : despedir, despedirse de **16** to see out/through COMPLETE : terminar **17** to see through HELP : sacar adelante — *vi* **1** : ver ⟨seeing is believing : ver para creer⟩ **2** UNDERSTAND : entender, ver ⟨now I see! : ¡ya entiendo!⟩ **3** ASCERTAIN : ver ⟨can I go? we'll see : ¿puedo ir? vamos a ver⟩ ⟨you'll see : ya verás⟩ **4** CONSIDER : ver ⟨let's see : vamos a ver⟩ **5** see here! : ¡oye!, ¡mira! **6** to see about : ocuparse de (algo) **7** we'll see about that! : ¡ya veremos! **8** to see after/to : ocuparse de **9** to see through : calar (a alguien)

see² *n* : sede *f* ⟨the Holy See : la Santa Sede⟩

seed¹ [ˈsiːd] *vt* **1** SOW : sembrar **2** : quitarle las semillas a

seed² *n*, *pl* seed *or* seeds **1** : semilla *f*, pepita *f* (de una fruta) **2** SOURCE : germen *m*, semilla *f*

seedless [ˈsiːdləs] *adj* : sin semillas

seedling [ˈsiːdlɪŋ] *n* : plantón *m*

seedpod [ˈsiːdˌpɑd] → pod

seedy [ˈsiːdi] *adj* seedier; -est **1** : lleno de semillas **2** SHABBY : raído (dícese de la ropa) **3** RUN-DOWN : ruinoso (dícese de los edificios, etc.), sórdido

Seeing Eye *trademark* se usa para un perro guía

seek [ˈsiːk] *v* sought [ˈsɔt]; seeking *vt* **1** : buscar ⟨to seek an answer : buscar una solución⟩ **2** REQUEST : solicitar, pedir **3** to seek to : tratar de, intentar de — *vi* SEARCH : buscar

seem [ˈsiːm] *vi* : parecer

seeming [ˈsiːmɪŋ] *adj* : aparente, ostensible

seemingly [ˈsiːmɪŋli] *adv* : aparentemente, según parece

seemly [ˈsiːmli] *adj* seemlier; -est : apropiado, decoroso

seep [ˈsiːp] *vi* : filtrarse

seer [ˈsiːr] *n* : vidente *mf*, clarividente *mf*

seesaw¹ [ˈsiːˌsɔ] *vi* **1** : jugar en un subibaja **2** VACILLATE : vacilar, oscilar

seesaw² *n* : balancín *m*, subibaja *m*

seethe [ˈsiːð] *vi* seethed; seething **1** : bullir, hervir **2** to seethe with anger : rabiar, estar furioso

segment [ˈsɛgmənt] *n* : segmento *m*

segmented [ˈsɛgˌmɛntəd, sɛgˈmɛn-] *adj* : segmentado

segregate [ˈsɛgrɪˌgeɪt] *vt* -gated; -gating : segregar

segregation [ˌsɛgrɪˈgeɪʃən] *n* : segregación *f*

seismic [ˈsaɪzmɪk, ˈsaɪs-] *adj* : sísmico

seismograph [ˈsaɪzməˌgræf, ˈsaɪs-] *n* : sismógrafo *m*

seize [ˈsiːz] *v* seized; seizing *vt* **1** CAPTURE : capturar, tomar, apoderarse de **2** ARREST : detener **3** CLUTCH, GRAB : agarrar, coger, aprovechar (una oportunidad) **4** to be seized with : estar sobrecogido por — *vi* or to seize up : agarrotarse

seizure [ˈsiːʒər] *n* **1** CAPTURE : toma *f*, captura *f* **2** ARREST : detención *f* **3** : ataque *m* ⟨an epileptic seizure : un ataque epiléptico⟩

seldom [ˈsɛldəm] *adv* : pocas veces, rara vez, casi nunca

select¹ [səˈlɛkt] *vt* : escoger, elegir, seleccionar (a un candidato, etc.)

select² *adj* : selecto

selection [səˈlɛkʃən] *n* : selección *f*, elección *f*

selective [səˈlɛktɪv] *adj* : selectivo

selenium [səˈliːniəm] *n* : selenio *m*

self [ˈsɛlf] *n*, *pl* selves [ˈsɛlvz] **1** : ser *m*, persona *f* ⟨the self : el yo⟩ ⟨with his whole self : con todo su ser⟩ ⟨her own self : su propia persona⟩ **2** SIDE : lado (de la personalidad) ⟨his better self : su lado bueno⟩

self- [ˈsɛlf] *pref* : auto-

self-addressed [ˌsɛlfəˈdrɛst] *adj* : con la dirección del remitente ⟨include a self-addressed envelope : incluya un sobre con su nombre y dirección⟩

self-appointed [ˌsɛlfəˈpɔɪntəd] *adj* : autoproclamado, autonombrado

self-assurance [ˌsɛlfəˈʃurənts] *n* : seguridad *f* en sí mismo

self-assured [ˌsɛlfəˈʃurd] *adj* : seguro de sí mismo

self-care [ˌsɛlfˈkær] *n* : cuidado *m* personal

self-centered [ˌsɛlfˈsɛntərd] *adj* : egocéntrico

self-confidence [ˌsɛlfˈkɑnfədənts] *n* : confianza *f* en sí mismo

self-confident [ˌsɛlfˈkɑnfədənt] *adj* : seguro de sí mismo

self-conscious [ˌsɛlfˈkɑntʃəs] *adj* : cohibido, tímido

self-consciously [ˌsɛlfˈkɑntʃəsli] *adv* : de manera cohibida

self-consciousness [ˌsɛlfˈkɑntʃəsnəs] *n* : vergüenza *f*, timidez *f*

self-contained [ˌsɛlfkənˈteɪnd] *adj* **1** INDEPENDENT : independiente **2** RESERVED : reservado

self-control [ˌsɛlfkənˈtroːl] *n* : autocontrol *m*, control *m* de sí mismo

self-defense [ˌsɛlfdɪˈfɛnts] *n* : defensa *f* propia, defensa *f* personal ⟨to act in self-defense : actuar en defensa propia⟩ ⟨self-defense class : clase de defensa personal⟩

self-denial [ˌsɛlfdɪˈnaɪəl] *n* : abnegación *f*

self-destructive [ˌsɛlfdɪˈstrʌktɪv] *adj* : autodestructivo — **self-destruction** *n*

self-determination [ˌsɛlfdɪˌtərməˈneɪʃən] *n* : autodeterminación *f*

self-discipline [ˌsɛlfˈdɪsəplən] *n* : autodisciplina *f*

self–employed [ˌsɛlfɪmˈplɔɪd] *adj* : que trabaja por cuenta propia, autónomo

self–esteem [ˌsɛlfɪˈstiːm] *n* : autoestima *f*, amor *m* propio

self–evident [ˌsɛlfˈɛvədənt] *adj* : evidente, manifiesto

self–explanatory [ˌsɛlfɪkˈsplænəˌtori] *adj* : fácil de entender, evidente

self–expression [ˌsɛlfɪkˈsprɛʃən] *n* : expresión *f* personal

self–government [ˌsɛlfˈgʌvərmənt, -vərn-] *n* : autogobierno *m*

self–help [ˌsɛlfˈhɛlp] *n* : autoayuda *f*

selfie [ˈsɛlfi] *n, pl* **-fies** : selfie *m*, selfi *m*, autofoto *f*

self–important [ˌsɛlfɪmˈpɔrtənt] *adj* **1** VAIN : vanidoso, presumido **2** ARROGANT : arrogante

self–indulgent [ˌsɛlfɪnˈdʌlʤənt] *adj* : que se permite excesos

self–inflicted [ˌsɛlfɪnˈflɪktəd] *adj* : autoinfligido

self–interest [ˌsɛlfˈɪntrəst, -təˌrɪst] *n* : interés *m* personal

selfish [ˈsɛlfɪʃ] *adj* : egoísta

selfishly [ˈsɛlfɪʃli] *adv* : de manera egoísta

selfishness [ˈsɛlfɪʃnəs] *n* : egoísmo *m*

selfless [ˈsɛlfləs] *adj* UNSELFISH : desinteresado

self–made [ˌsɛlfˈmeɪd] *adj* : próspero gracias a sus propios esfuerzos

self–pity [ˌsɛlfˈpɪti] *n, pl* **-ties** : autocompasión *f*

self–portrait [ˌsɛlfˈpɔrtrət] *n* : autorretrato *f*

self–proclaimed [ˌsɛlfproˈkleɪmd] *adj* : autoproclamado

self–propelled [ˌsɛlfproˈpɛld] *adj* : autopropulsado

self–reliance [ˌsɛlfrɪˈlaɪənts] *n* : independencia *f*, autosuficiencia *f*

self–respect [ˌsɛlfrɪˈspɛkt] *n* : autoestima *f*, amor *m* propio

self–restraint [ˌsɛlfrɪˈstreɪnt] *n* : autocontrol *m*, moderación *f*

self–righteous [ˌsɛlfˈraɪtʃəs] *adj* : santurrón, moralista

self–sacrifice [ˌsɛlfˈsækrəˌfaɪs] *n* : abnegación *f*

self–sacrificing [ˌsɛlfˈsækrəˌfaɪsɪŋ] *adj* : abnegado

selfsame [ˈsɛlfˌseɪm] *adj* : mismo

self–satisfaction [ˌsɛlfˌsætəsˈfækʃən] *n* : suficiencia *f*

self–satisfied [ˌsɛlfˈsætəsˌfaɪd] *adj* : ufano *fam*

self–seeking [ˌsɛlfˈsiːkɪŋ] *adj* : interesado

self–service [ˌsɛlfˈsərvɪs] *adj* **1** : de autoservicio **2 self–service restaurant** : autoservicio *m*

self–sufficiency [ˌsɛlfsəˈfɪʃəntsi] *n* : autosuficiencia *f*

self–sufficient [ˌsɛlfsəˈfɪʃənt] *adj* : autosuficiente

self–taught [ˌsɛlfˈtɔt] *adj* : autodidacta

sell [ˈsɛl] *v* **sold** [ˈsoːld]; **selling** *vt* **1** : vender ⟨to sell to someone something, to sell something to someone : venderle algo a alguien⟩ **2 to sell at a loss** : vender con pérdidas **3 to sell off** : li-

quidar **4 to sell on** ⟨can you sell them on the project? : ¿puedes convencerles de los méritos del proyecto?⟩ ⟨she's not sold on the idea : la idea no la convence⟩ **5 to sell out** BETRAY : vender, traicionar a **6 to sell short** UNDERESTIMATE : subestimar, menospreciar — *vi* **1** : venderse ⟨this car sells well : este coche se vende bien⟩ **2 to sell out** : agotarse (dícese de entrada, etc.) **3 to sell out** : venderse (dícese de un músico, etc.)

seller [ˈsɛlər] *n* : vendedor *m*, -dora *f*

selves → **self**

semantic [sɪˈmæntɪk] *adj* : semántico

semantics [sɪˈmæntɪks] *ns & pl* : semántica *f*

semaphore [ˈsɛməˌfor] *n* : semáforo *m*

semblance [ˈsɛmbləns] *n* : apariencia *f*

semen [ˈsiːmən] *n* : semen *m*

semester [səˈmɛstər] *n* : semestre *m*

semi- [ˈsɛmi, ˈsɛmaɪ] *pref* : semi-

semiannual [ˌsɛmiˈænjuəl, ˌsɛmaɪ-] *adj* : semestral

semicircle [ˈsɛmiˌsərkəl, ˈsɛˌmaɪ-] *n* : semicírculo *m*

semicolon [ˈsɛmiˌkoːlən, ˈsɛˌmaɪ-] *n* : punto y coma *m*

semiconductor [ˈsɛmikənˌdʌktər, ˈsɛˌmaɪ-] *n* : semiconductor *m*

semifinal [ˈsɛmiˌfaɪnəl, ˈsɛˌmaɪ-] *n* : semifinal *f*

semimonthly [ˈsɛmiˌmʌnθli, ˈsɛˌmaɪ-] *adj* : bimensual, quincenal

seminar [ˈsɛməˌnɑr] *n* : seminario *m*

seminary [ˈsɛməˌnɛri] *n, pl* **-naries** : seminario *m*

semiprecious [ˈsɛmiˈprɛʃəs, ˈsɛˌmaɪ-] *adj* : semiprecioso

Semite [ˈsɛˌmaɪt] *n* : semita *mf* — **Semitic** [səˈmɪtɪk] *adj*

semolina [ˌsɛməˈliːnə] *n* : sémola *f*

senate [ˈsɛnət] *n* : senado *m*

senator [ˈsɛnəˌtər] *n* : senador *m*, -dora *f*

send [ˈsɛnd] *vt* **sent** [ˈsɛnt]; **sending** **1** : mandar, enviar ⟨to send a letter : mandar una carta⟩ ⟨to send word : avisar, mandar decir⟩ ⟨he was sent to prison : lo mandaron a la cárcel, lo encarcelaron⟩ **2** PROPEL : mandar, lanzar ⟨he sent it into left field : lo mandó al jardín izquierdo⟩ ⟨it sent a shiver down my spine : me dio un escalofrío⟩ ⟨to send up dust : levantar polvo⟩ **3 to send away for** : pedir (por correo) **4 to send back** RETURN : devolver, mandar de vuelta **5 to send for** SUMMON : mandar llamar **6 to send for** REQUEST : pedir (ayuda, refuerzos, etc.) **7 to send in** SUBMIT : enviar, mandar, presentar **8 to send in** : enviar, mandar (tropas, etc.) **9 to send into a rage** : poner furioso **10 to send off** : mandar, enviar (por correo, etc.) **11 to send on** : enviar por adelantado **12 to send out** : enviar, mandar (invitaciones, etc.) **13 to send out** EMIT : emitir

sender [ˈsɛndər] *n* : remitente *mf* (de una carta, etc.)

send–off [ˈsɛndˌɔf] *n* FAREWELL : despedida *f*

Senegalese [ˌsɛnəgəˈliːz, -ˈliːs] n : senegalés m, -lesa f — **Senegalese** adj
senile [ˈsiːˌnaɪl] adj : senil
senility [sɪˈnɪləti] n : senilidad f
senior¹ [ˈsiːnjər] adj **1** ELDER : mayor ⟨John Doe, Senior : John Doe, padre⟩ **2** : superior (en rango), más antiguo (en años de servicio) ⟨a senior official : un alto oficial⟩
senior² n **1** : superior m (en rango) **2 to be someone's senior** : ser mayor que alguien ⟨she's two years my senior : me lleva dos años⟩
senior citizen n : persona f de la tercera edad
seniority [ˌsiːˈnjɔrəti] n : antigüedad f (en años de servicio)
sensation [sɛnˈseɪʃən] n : sensación f
sensational [sɛnˈseɪʃənəl] adj : que causa sensación ⟨sensational stories : historias sensacionalistas⟩
sensationalism [sɛnˈseɪʃənəˌlɪzəm] n : sensacionalismo m
sensationalist [sɛnˈseɪʃənəlɪst] or **sensationalistic** [sɛnˌseɪʃənəˈlɪstɪk] adj : sensacionalista
sense¹ [ˈsɛns] vt sensed; sensing : sentir ⟨he sensed danger : se dio cuenta del peligro⟩
sense² n **1** MEANING : sentido m, significado m **2** : sentido m ⟨the sense of smell : el sentido del olfato⟩ **3** : sentido m ⟨sense of humor : sentido del humor⟩ ⟨sense of duty : sentido del deber⟩ ⟨sense of direction : sentido de la orientación⟩ **4** FEELING : sensación f ⟨a huge sense of relief : un gran alivio⟩ ⟨his sense of accomplishment : su satisfacción (por haber logrado algo)⟩ **5** WISDOM : sensatez f, tino m ⟨he had the (good) sense to leave : tuvo la sensatez de retirarse⟩ ⟨common sense : sentido común⟩ ⟨to come to one's senses : entrar en razón⟩ ⟨there's no sense in arguing : no tiene sentido discutir⟩ **6 to make sense** : tener sentido **7 to make sense of** : entender
senseless [ˈsɛnsləs] adj **1** MEANINGLESS : sin sentido, sin razón **2** UNCONSCIOUS : inconsciente
senselessly [ˈsɛnsləsli] adv : sin sentido
sensibility [ˌsɛnsəˈbɪləti] n, pl -ties : sensibilidad f
sensible [ˈsɛnsəbəl] adj **1** PERCEPTIBLE : sensible, perceptible **2** AWARE : consciente **3** REASONABLE : sensato ⟨a sensible man : un hombre sensato⟩ ⟨sensible shoes : zapatos prácticos⟩ — **sensibly** [-bli] adv
sensibleness [ˈsɛnsəbəlnəs] n : sensatez f, solidez f
sensitive [ˈsɛnsətɪv] adj **1** : sensible, delicado ⟨sensitive skin : piel sensible⟩ **2** TOUCHY : susceptible, sensible ⟨to be sensitive to criticism : ser susceptible a las críticas⟩ ⟨to be sensitive about something : tener complejo por algo, preocuparse mucho por algo⟩ **3** AWARE : sensibilizado ⟨sensitive to something : sensibilizado sobre/con algo, sensibilizado frente a algo⟩ **4** : de mucha sensi-

bilidad (dícese de un artista, una interpretación, etc.) **5** DELICATE : delicado **6** CONTROVERSIAL : controvertido **7** CONFIDENTIAL : confidencial
sensitiveness [ˈsɛnsətɪvnəs] → **sensitivity**
sensitivity [ˌsɛnsəˈtɪvəti] n, pl -ties : sensibilidad f
sensitize [ˈsɛnsəˌtaɪz] vt -tized; -tizing : sensibilizar
sensor [ˈsɛnˌsɔr, ˈsɛnsər] n : sensor m
sensory [ˈsɛnsəri] adj : sensorial
sensual [ˈsɛnʃʊəl] adj : sensual — **sensually** adv
sensuality [ˌsɛnʃəˈwæləti] n, pl -ties : sensualidad f
sensuous [ˈsɛnʃʊəs] adj : sensual
sent → **send**
sentence¹ [ˈsɛntəns, -ənz] vt -tenced; -tencing : sentenciar
sentence² n **1** JUDGMENT : sentencia f **2** : oración f, frase f (en gramática)
sentient [ˈsɛntʃənt, -ʃiənt] adj : sensitivo, sensible
sentiment [ˈsɛntəmənt] n **1** BELIEF : opinión f **2** FEELING : sentimiento m **3** → **sentimentality**
sentimental [ˌsɛntəˈmɛntəl] adj : sentimental
sentimentality [ˌsɛntəˌmɛnˈtæləti] n, pl -ties : sentimentalismo m, sensiblería f
sentinel [ˈsɛntənəl] n : centinela mf, guardia mf
sentry [ˈsɛntri] n, pl -tries : centinela mf
separate¹ [ˈsɛpəˌreɪt] v -rated; -rating vt **1** DETACH, SEVER : separar **2** DISTINGUISH : diferenciar, distinguir — vi PART : separarse
separate² [ˈsɛprət, ˈsɛpə-] adj **1** INDIVIDUAL : separado, aparte ⟨a separate state : un estado separado⟩ ⟨in a separate envelope : en un sobre aparte⟩ **2** DISTINCT : distinto
separately [ˈsɛprətli, ˈsɛpə-] adv : por separado, separadamente, aparte
separation [ˌsɛpəˈreɪʃən] n : separación f
sepia [ˈsiːpiə] n : color m sepia
September [sɛpˈtɛmbər] n : septiembre m, setiembre m ⟨they arrived on the 30th of September, they arrived on September 30th : llegaron el 30 de septiembre⟩
septic [ˈsɛptɪk] adj : séptico ⟨septic tank : fosa séptica⟩
sepulchre [ˈsɛpəlkər] n : sepulcro m
sequel [ˈsiːkwəl] n **1** CONSEQUENCE : secuela f, consecuencia f **2** : continuación f (de una película, etc.)
sequence [ˈsiːkwəns] n **1** SERIES : serie f, sucesión f, secuencia f (matemática o música) **2** ORDER : orden m
sequester [sɪˈkwɛstər] vt : aislar
sequin [ˈsiːkwən] n : lentejuela f
sequoia [sɪˈkwɔɪə] n : secoya f, secuoya f
sera → **serum**
Serb [ˈsɔrb] or **Serbian** [ˈsɔrbiən] n **1** : serbio m, -bia f **2** : serbio m (idioma) — **Serb** or **Serbian** adj
Serbo–Croatian [ˌsɔrbokroˈeɪʃən] n : serbocroata m (idioma) — **Serbo–Croatian** adj

serenade¹ [ˌsɛrəˈneɪd] vt **-naded; -nading** : darle una serenata (a alguien)

serenade² n : serenata f

serene [səˈriːn] adj : sereno — **serenely** adv

serendipity [ˌsɛrənˈdɪpəţi] n : suerte f, fortuna f (de descubrir algo bueno por pura casualidad)

serenity [səˈrɛnəţi] n : serenidad f

serf [ˈsərf] n : siervo m, -va f

serge [ˈsərdʒ] n : sarga f

sergeant [ˈsɑrdʒənt] n : sargento mf

serial¹ [ˈsɪriəl] adj : seriado

serial² n : serie f, serial m (de radio o televisión), publicación f por entregas

serially [ˈsɪriəli] adv : en serie

serial number n : número m de serie

series [ˈsɪrˌiːz] n, pl **series** : serie f, sucesión f

serious [ˈsɪriəs] adj **1** SOBER : serio **2** DEDICATED, EARNEST : serio, dedicado ⟨to be serious about something : tomar algo en serio⟩ **3** GRAVE : serio, grave ⟨serious problems : problemas graves⟩

seriously [ˈsɪriəsli] adv **1** EARNESTLY : seriamente, con seriedad, en serio ⟨to take seriously : tomar en serio⟩ **2** SEVERELY : gravemente ⟨seriously ill : gravemente enfermo⟩

seriousness [ˈsɪriəsnəs] n : seriedad f, gravedad f

sermon [ˈsərmən] n : sermón m

serpent [ˈsərpənt] n : serpiente f

serrated [səˈreɪţəd, ˈsɛrˌeɪţəd] adj : dentado, serrado

serum [ˈsɪrəm] n, pl **serums** or **sera** [ˈsɪrə] : suero m

servant [ˈsərvənt] n : criado m, -da f; sirviente m, -ta f

serve [ˈsərv] v **served; serving** vi **1** : servir ⟨to serve in the navy : servir en la armada⟩ ⟨to serve on a jury : ser miembro de un jurado⟩ **2** DO, FUNCTION : servir ⟨to serve as : servir de, servir como⟩ **3** : sacar (en deportes) — vt **1** : servir ⟨to serve God : servir a Dios⟩ **2** HELP : servir ⟨it serves no purpose : no sirve para nada⟩ ⟨it serves you right : te lo mereces⟩ **3** : servir (comida o bebida) ⟨dinner is served : la cena está servida⟩ **4** SUPPLY : abastecer **5** CARRY OUT : cumplir, hacer ⟨to serve time : servir una pena⟩ **6 to serve a summons** : entregar una citación

server [ˈsərvər] n **1** : camarero m, -ra f; mesero m, -ra f (en un restaurante) **2** or **serving dish** : fuente f (para servir comida) **3** : servidor m (en informática)

service¹ [ˈsərvəs] vt **-viced; -vicing 1** MAINTAIN : darle mantenimiento a (una máquina), revisar **2** REPAIR : arreglar, reparar

service² n **1** HELP, USE : servicio m ⟨to do someone a service : hacerle un servicio a alguien⟩ ⟨at your service : a sus órdenes⟩ ⟨to be out of service : no funcionar⟩ **2** CEREMONY : oficio m (religioso) **3** DEPARTMENT, SYSTEM : servicio m ⟨social services : servicios sociales⟩ ⟨train service : servicio de trenes⟩ **4** SET

: juego m, servicio m ⟨tea service : juego de té⟩ **5** MAINTENANCE : mantenimiento m, revisión f, servicio m **6** : servicio m (en un restaurante, etc.) ⟨customer service : atención al cliente⟩ **7** : saque m (en deportes) **8 armed services** : fuerzas fpl armadas

serviceable [ˈsərvəsəbəl] adj **1** USEFUL : útil **2** DURABLE : duradero

service charge n : servicio m

serviceman [ˈsərvəsˌmæn, -mən] n, pl **-men** [-mən, -ˌmɛn] : militar m

service station → **gas station**

servicewoman [ˈsərvəsˌwʊmən] n, pl **-women** [-ˌwɪmən] : militar f

servile [ˈsərvəl, -ˌvaɪl] adj : servil

servility [sərˈvɪləţi] n : servilismo m

serving [ˈsərvɪŋ] n HELPING : porción f, ración f

servitude [ˈsərvəˌtuːd, -ˌtjuːd] n : servidumbre f

sesame [ˈsɛsəmi] n : ajonjolí m, sésamo m

session [ˈsɛʃən] n : sesión f

set¹ [ˈsɛt] v set; **setting** vt **1** or **set down** PLACE : poner, colocar ⟨set the books (down) on the table : pon los libros en la mesa⟩ **2** INSTALL : poner, colocar (ladrillos, etc.) **3** MOUNT : engarzar, montar (un diamante, etc.) **4** ESTABLISH : fijar (una fecha, un precio, etc.), establecer (reglas, un récord, etc.) ⟨to set (oneself) a goal : fijarse una meta⟩ ⟨to set a precedent : sentar precedente⟩ ⟨to set a good/bad example : dar buen/mal ejemplo⟩ **5** PREPARE : tender (una trampa), poner (un freno de mano, etc.) ⟨to set the table : poner la mesa⟩ **6** ADJUST : poner (un reloj, etc.) **7** (indicating the causing of a certain condition) ⟨to set fire to : prenderle fuego a⟩ ⟨she set it free : la soltó⟩ **8** MAKE, START : poner, hacer ⟨I set them working : los puse a trabajar⟩ ⟨it set me (to) thinking : me hizo pensar⟩ ⟨to set something in motion : poner algo en marcha⟩ **9** : ambientar (the book is set in Chicago : el libro está ambientado en Chicago⟩ **10** : componer (un hueso roto, etc.) **11** : tensar (la mandíbula, la boca, etc.) **12** : marcar (el pelo) **13** : componer (texto) **14 to set about** BEGIN : comenzar **15 to set aside** RESERVE : reservar, dejar de lado **16 to set back** DELAY : retrasar, atrasar **17 to set off** PROVOKE : provocar **18 to set off** EXPLODE : hacer estallar (una bomba, etc.) **19 to set out** INTEND : proponerse **20 to set up** ASSEMBLE : montar, armar **21 to set up** ERECT : levantar, erigir **22 to set up** ESTABLISH : establecer, fundar, montar (un negocio) **23 to set up** CAUSE : armar ⟨they set up a clamor : armaron un alboroto⟩ — vi **1** SOLIDIFY : fraguar (dícese del cemento, etc.), cuajar (dícese de la gelatina, etc.) **2** : ponerse (dícese del sol o de la luna) **3 to set in** BEGIN : comenzar, empezar **4 to set off/forth** : salir **5 to set out** : salir (de viaje)

set² adj **1** ESTABLISHED, FIXED : fijo, establecido **2** RIGID : inflexible ⟨to be set in one's ways : tener costumbres muy arraigadas⟩ **3** READY : listo, preparado

set³ n **1** COLLECTION : juego m ⟨a set of dishes : un juego de platos, una vajilla⟩ ⟨a tool set : una caja de herramientas⟩ **2** or **stage set** : decorado m (en el teatro), plató m (en el cine) **3** APPARATUS : aparato m ⟨a television set : un televisor⟩ **4** : conjunto m (en matemáticas)

setback ['sɛt,bæk] n : revés m, contratiempo m

settee [sɛ'ti:] n : sofá m

setter ['sɛtər] n **1** : setter mf ⟨Irish setter : setter irlandés⟩ **2** (one that establishes) ⟨record setter : persona que establece un récord⟩ ⟨style setter : persona que inicia una moda⟩

setting ['sɛtɪŋ] n **1** : posición f, ajuste m (de un control) **2** : montura f (de una gema) **3** SCENE : escenario m (de una novela, etc.) **4** SURROUNDINGS : ambiente m, entorno m, marco m

settle ['sɛtəl] v **settled; settling** vi **1** ALIGHT, LAND : posarse (dícese de las aves, una mirada, etc.), depositarse (dícese del polvo) **2** SINK : asentarse (dícese de los edificios) **3** : acomodarse ⟨he settled into the chair : se arrellanó en la silla⟩ **4** : resolver una disputa ⟨they settled out of court : resolvieron extrajudicialmente su disputa⟩ **5** DECIDE : decidir (un asunto) ⟨that settles it : ya está decidido⟩ **6** : instalarse (en una casa), establecerse (en una ciudad o región) **7 to settle down** : calmarse, tranquilizarse ⟨settle down! : ¡tranquilízate!, ¡cálmate!⟩ **8 to settle down** : sentar cabeza, hacerse sensato ⟨to marry and settle down : casarse y sentar cabeza⟩ **9 to settle for** : conformarse con **10 to settle in** : instalarse (en una casa, etc.), adaptarse (a un trabajo, etc.) **11 to settle up** : arreglar las cuentas — vt **1** ARRANGE, DECIDE : fijar, decidir, acordar (planes, etc.) **2** RESOLVE : resolver, solucionar ⟨to settle an argument : resolver una discusión⟩ **3** PAY : pagar ⟨to settle an account : saldar una cuenta⟩ **4** CALM : calmar (los nervios), asentar (el estómago) **5** : acomodar, poner ⟨he settled the baby into its crib : puso al bebé en su cuna⟩ **6** COLONIZE : colonizar **7 to settle oneself** : acomodarse, hacerse cómodo

settlement ['sɛtəlmənt] n **1** PAYMENT : pago m, liquidación f **2** COLONY : asentamiento m **3** RESOLUTION : acuerdo m

settler ['sɛtələr] n : poblador m, -dora f; colono m, -na f

setup ['sɛt,ʌp] n **1** ASSEMBLY : montaje m, ensamblaje m **2** ARRANGEMENT : disposición f **3** PREPARATION : preparación f **4** TRAP, TRICK : encerrona f

seven¹ ['sɛvən] adj : siete ⟨he's seven (years old) : tiene siete años⟩

seven² n : siete m ⟨the seven of hearts : el siete de corazones⟩

seven³ pron : siete ⟨there are seven of us : somos siete⟩ ⟨it's seven (o'clock) : son las siete⟩

seven hundred¹ adj & pron : setecientos

seven hundred² n : setecientos m

seventeen¹ [,sɛvən'ti:n] adj & pron : diecisiete

seventeen² n : diecisiete m

seventeenth¹ [,sɛvən'ti:nθ] adj : decimoséptimo

seventeenth² n **1** : decimoséptimo m, -ma f (en una serie) **2** : diecisieteavo m, diecisieteava parte f

seventh¹ ['sɛvənθ] adv : en séptimo lugar

seventh² adj : séptimo

seventh³ n **1** : séptimo m, -ma f (en una serie) **2** : séptimo m, séptima parte f

seventieth¹ ['sɛvəntiəθ] adj : septuagésimo

seventieth² n **1** : septuagésimo m, -ma f (en una serie) **2** : setentavo m, setentava parte f, septuagésima parte f

seventy¹ ['sɛvənti] adj & pron : setenta

seventy² n, pl **-ties** : setenta m

sever ['sɛvər] vt **-ered; -ering** : cortar, romper

several¹ ['sɛvrəl, 'sɛvə-] adj **1** DISTINCT : distinto **2** SOME : varios ⟨several weeks : varias semanas⟩

several² pron : varios ⟨several of the novels : varias de las novelas⟩

severance ['sɛvrəns, 'sɛvə-] n **1** : ruptura f (de relaciones, etc.) **2 severance pay** : indemnización f (por despido)

severe [sə'vɪr] adj **severer; -est 1** STRICT : severo **2** AUSTERE : sobrio, austero **3** SERIOUS : grave ⟨a severe wound : una herida grave⟩ ⟨severe aches : dolores fuertes⟩ **4** DIFFICULT : duro, difícil — **severely** adv

severity [sə'vɛrəti] n **1** HARSHNESS : severidad f **2** AUSTERITY : sobriedad f, austeridad f **3** SERIOUSNESS : gravedad f (de una herida, etc.)

sew ['so:] v **sewed; sewn** ['so:n] or **sewed; sewing** : coser

sewage ['su:ɪdʒ] n : aguas fpl negras, aguas fpl residuales

sewer¹ ['so:ər] n : uno que cose

sewer² ['su:ər] n : alcantarilla f, cloaca f

sewing ['so:ɪŋ] n : costura f

sewing machine n : máquina f de coser

sex ['sɛks] n **1** : sexo m ⟨the opposite sex : el sexo opuesto⟩ **2** COPULATION : relaciones fpl sexuales ⟨sex education : educación sexual⟩

sexism ['sɛk,sɪzəm] n : sexismo m

sexist¹ ['sɛksɪst] adj : sexista

sexist² n : sexista mf

sextant ['sɛkstənt] n : sextante m

sextet [sɛk'stɛt] n : sexteto m

sexton ['sɛkstən] n : sacristán m

sexual ['sɛkʃuəl] adj : sexual ⟨sexual intercourse : relaciones sexuales⟩ ⟨sexual discrimination/harassment : discriminación/acoso sexual⟩ — **sexually** adv

sexuality [,sɛkʃu'æləti] n : sexualidad f

sexy ['sɛksi] adj **sexier; -est** : sexy

sh or **ssh** or **sssh** [ʃ, often prolonged] interj : chis!, chist!

shabbily ['ʃæbəli] *adv* 1 : pobremente ⟨shabbily dressed : pobremente vestido⟩ 2 UNFAIRLY : mal, injustamente

shabbiness ['ʃæbinəs] *n* 1 : lo gastado (de ropa, etc.) 2 : lo mal vestido (de personas) 3 UNFAIRNESS : injusticia *f*

shabby ['ʃæbi] *adj* **shabbier; -est** 1 : gastado (dícese de la ropa, etc.) 2 : mal vestido (dícese de las personas) 3 UNFAIR : malo, injusto ⟨shabby treatment : mal trato⟩

shack ['ʃæk] *n* : choza *f*, rancho *m*

shackle[1] ['ʃækəl] *vt* **-led; -ling** : ponerle grilletes (a alguien)

shackle[2] *n* : grillete *m*

shad ['ʃæd] *n* : sábalo *m*

shade[1] ['ʃeɪd] *v* **shaded; shading** *vt* 1 SHELTER : proteger (del sol o de la luz) 2 **or to shade in** : matizar los colores de — *vi* : convertirse gradualmente ⟨his irritation shaded into rage : su irritación iba convirtiéndose en furia⟩

shade[2] *n* 1 : sombra *f* ⟨to give shade : dar sombra⟩ 2 : tono *m* (de un color) 3 NUANCE : matiz *m* 4 : pantalla *f* (de una lámpara), persiana *f* (de una ventana)

shadow[1] ['ʃædo:] *vt* 1 DARKEN : ensombrecer 2 TRAIL : seguir de cerca, seguirle la pista (a alguien)

shadow[2] *n* 1 : sombra *f* 2 DARKNESS : oscuridad *f* 3 TRACE : sombra *f*, atisbo *m*, indicio *m* ⟨without a shadow of a doubt : sin sombra de duda, sin lugar a dudas⟩ 4 **to cast a shadow over** : ensombrecer

shadowy ['ʃædowi] *adj* 1 INDISTINCT : vago, indistinto 2 DARK : oscuro

shady ['ʃeɪdi] *adj* **shadier, -est** 1 : sombreado (dícese de un lugar), que da sombra (dícese de un árbol) 2 DISREPUTABLE : sospechoso (dícese de una persona), turbio (dícese de un negocio, etc.)

shaft ['ʃæft] *n* 1 : asta *f* (de una lanza), astil *m* (de una flecha), mango *m* (de una herramienta) 2 **or mine shaft** : pozo *m*

shaggy ['ʃægi] *adj* **shaggier, -est** 1 HAIRY : peludo ⟨a shaggy dog : un perro peludo⟩ 2 UNKEMPT : enmarañado, despeinado (dícese del pelo, de las barbas, etc.)

shake[1] ['ʃeɪk] *v* **shook** ['ʃʊk]; **shaken** ['ʃeɪkən]; **shaking** *vt* 1 : sacudir, agitar, hacer temblar ⟨he shook his head : negó con la cabeza⟩ 2 WEAKEN : debilitar, hacer flaquear ⟨it shook her faith : debilitó su confianza⟩ 3 UPSET : afectar, alterar 4 **to shake hands with someone** : darle/estrecharle la mano a alguien 5 **to shake off** : deshacer 6 **to shake up** : reestructurar, reorganizar — *vi* : temblar, sacudirse ⟨to shake with fear : temblar de miedo⟩

shake[2] *n* : sacudida *f*, apretón *m* (de manos)

shaker ['ʃeɪkər] *n* 1 **salt shaker** : salero *m* 2 **pepper shaker** : pimentero *m* 3 **cocktail shaker** : coctelera *f*

shake–up ['ʃeɪk,ʌp] *n* : reorganización *f*

shakily ['ʃeɪkəli] *adv* : temblorosamente

shaky ['ʃeɪki] *adj* **shakier; -est** 1 SHAKING : tembloroso 2 UNSTABLE : poco firme, inestable 3 PRECARIOUS : precario, incierto 4 QUESTIONABLE : dudoso, cuestionable ⟨shaky arguments : argumentos discutibles⟩

shale ['ʃeɪl] *n* : esquisto *m*

shall ['ʃæl] *v aux, past* **should** ['ʃʊd] *present s & pl* **shall** 1 (*used formally to express a command*) ⟨you shall do as I say : harás lo que te digo⟩ ⟨there shall be no talking during the test : se prohíbe hablar durante el examen⟩ 2 (*used formally to request an opinion*) ⟨shall I call a taxi? : ¿quiere que llame un taxi?⟩ 3 (*used formally to express futurity*) ⟨we shall see : ya veremos⟩ ⟨when shall we expect you? : ¿cuándo te podemos esperar?⟩ ⟨I shall not mention it, I shan't mention it : no lo mencionaré⟩ 4 (*used formally to express determination*) ⟨you shall have the money : tendrás el dinero⟩

shallow ['ʃælo:] *adj* 1 : poco profundo (dícese del agua, etc.) 2 SUPERFICIAL : superficial

shallows ['ʃælo:z] *npl* : bajío *m*, bajos *mpl*

sham[1] ['ʃæm] *v* **shammed; shamming** : fingir

sham[2] *adj* : falso, fingido

sham[3] *n* 1 FAKE, PRETENSE : farsa *f*, simulación *f*, imitación *f* 2 FAKER : impostor *m*, -tora *f*; farsante *mf*

shamble ['ʃæmbəl] *vi* **-bled; -bling** : caminar arrastrando los pies

shambles ['ʃæmbəlz] *ns & pl* : caos *m*, desorden *m*, confusión *f*

shame[1] ['ʃeɪm] *vt* **shamed; shaming** 1 : avergonzar ⟨he was shamed by their words : sus palabras le dieron vergüenza⟩ 2 DISGRACE : deshonrar

shame[2] *n* 1 : vergüenza *f* ⟨to have no shame : no tener vergüenza⟩ 2 DISGRACE : vergüenza *f*, deshonra *f* 3 PITY : lástima *f*, pena *f* ⟨what a shame! : ¡qué pena!⟩

shamefaced ['ʃeɪm,feɪst] *adj* : avergonzado

shameful ['ʃeɪmfəl] *adj* : vergonzoso — **shamefully** *adv*

shameless ['ʃeɪmləs] *adj* : descarado, desvergonzado — **shamelessly** *adv*

shampoo[1] ['ʃæm'pu:] *vt* : lavar (el pelo)

shampoo[2] *n, pl* **-poos** : champú *m*

shamrock ['ʃæm,rɑk] *n* : trébol *m*

shank ['ʃæŋk] *n* : parte *f* baja de la pierna

shan't ['ʃænt] *contraction of* SHALL NOT → **shall**

shanty ['ʃænti] *n, pl* **-ties** : choza *f*, rancho *m*

shantytown ['ʃænti,taʊn] *n* : barriada *f*, cinturón *m* de miseria, ciudad *f* perdida *Mex*, villa *f* miseria *Arg*, villa *f* de emergencia *Arg*, pueblo *m* joven *Peru*, población *f* callampa *Chile*, barrio *m* de invasión *Col*, barrio *m* de chabolas *Spain*

shape[1] ['ʃeɪp] *v* **shaped; shaping** *vt* 1 : dar forma a, modelar (arcilla, etc.), tallar (madera, piedra), formar (carácter) ⟨to be shaped like : tener forma de⟩ 2

DETERMINE : decidir, determinar — *vi* or **to shape up** : tomar forma

shape² *n* **1** : forma *f*, figura *f* ⟨in the shape of a circle : en forma de círculo⟩ ⟨to take shape : tomar forma⟩ **2** CONDITION : estado *m*, condiciones *fpl*, forma *f* (física) ⟨to be in good shape : estar en forma⟩ ⟨to be in bad shape : no estar en forma⟩ ⟨to get in shape : ponerse en forma⟩

-shaped [ˌʃeɪpt] *suf* : en forma de

shapeless [ˈʃeɪpləs] *adj* : informe

shapely [ˈʃeɪpli] *adj* **shapelier, -est** : curvilíneo, bien proporcionado

shard [ˈʃɑrd] *n* : fragmento *m*, casco *m* (de cerámica, etc.)

share¹ [ˈʃɛr] *v* **shared; sharing** *vt* **1** APPORTION : dividir, repartir **2** : compartir ⟨they share a room : comparten una habitación⟩ — *vi* : compartir

share² *n* **1** PORTION : parte *f*, porción *f* ⟨one's fair share : lo que le corresponde a uno⟩ **2** : acción *f* (en una compañía) ⟨to hold shares : tener acciones⟩

sharecropper [ˈʃɛrˌkrɑpər] *n* : aparcero *m*, -ra *f*

shareholder [ˈʃɛrˌhoːldər] *n* : accionista *mf*

shark [ˈʃɑrk] *n* : tiburón *m*

sharp¹ [ˈʃɑrp] *adv* : en punto ⟨at two o'clock sharp : a las dos en punto⟩

sharp² *adj* **1** : afilado, filoso ⟨a sharp knife : un cuchillo afilado⟩ **2** PENETRATING : cortante, fuerte **3** CLEVER : agudo, listo, perspicaz **4** ACUTE : agudo ⟨sharp eyesight : vista aguda⟩ **5** HARSH, SEVERE : duro, severo, agudo ⟨a sharp rebuke : una reprimenda mordaz⟩ ⟨to have a sharp tongue : tener una lengua afilada⟩ **6** STRONG : fuerte ⟨sharp cheese : queso fuerte⟩ **7** ABRUPT : brusco, repentino **8** DISTINCT : nítido, definido ⟨a sharp image : una imagen bien definida⟩ **9** ANGULAR : anguloso (dícese de la cara)· **10** : sostenido (en música)

sharp³ *n* : sostenido *m* (en música)

sharpen [ˈʃɑrpən] *vt* : afilar, aguzar ⟨to sharpen a pencil : sacarle punta a un lápiz⟩ ⟨to sharpen one's wits : aguzar el ingenio⟩

sharpener [ˈʃɑrpənər] *n* : afilador *m* (para cuchillos, etc.), sacapuntas *m* (para lápices)

sharply [ˈʃɑrpli] *adv* **1** ABRUPTLY : bruscamente **2** DISTINCTLY : claramente, marcadamente

sharpness [ˈʃɑrpnəs] *n* **1** : lo afilado (de un cuchillo, etc.) **2** ACUTENESS : agudeza *f* (de los sentidos o de la mente) **3** INTENSITY : intensidad *f*, agudeza *f* (de dolores, etc.) **4** HARSHNESS : dureza *f*, severidad *f* **5** ABRUPTNESS : brusquedad *f* **6** CLARITY : nitidez *f*

sharpshooter [ˈʃɑrpˌʃuːtər] *n* : tirador *m*, -dora *f* de primera

shatter [ˈʃætər] *vt* **1** : hacer añicos ⟨to shatter the silence : romper el silencio⟩ **2 to be shattered by** : quedar destrozado por — *vi* : hacerse añicos, romperse en pedazos

shave¹ [ˈʃeɪv] *v* **shaved; shaved** *or* **shaven** [ˈʃeɪvən]; **shaving** *vt* **1** : afeitar, rasurar ⟨she shaved her legs : se rasuró las piernas⟩ ⟨they shaved (off) his beard : le afeitaron la barba⟩ **2** SLICE : cortar (en pedazos finos) — *vi* : afeitarse, rasurarse

shave² *n* : afeitada *f*, rasurada *f*

shaver [ˈʃeɪvər] *n* : afeitadora *f*, máquina *f* de afeitar, rasuradora *f*

shaving [ˈʃeɪvɪŋ] *n* : viruta *f* ⟨wood shavings : virutas de madera⟩

shaving cream *n* : crema *f* de afeitar

shawl [ˈʃɔl] *n* : chal *m*, mantón *m*, rebozo *m*

she [ˈʃiː] *pron* : ella

sheaf [ˈʃiːf] *n, pl* **sheaves** [ˈʃiːvz] : gavilla *f* (de cereales), haz *m* (de flechas), fajo *m* (de papeles)

shear [ˈʃɪr] *vt* **sheared; sheared** *or* **shorn** [ˈʃɔrn]; **shearing 1** : esquilar, trasquilar ⟨to shear sheep : trasquilar ovejas⟩ **2** CUT : cortar (el pelo, etc.)

shears [ˈʃɪrz] *npl* : tijeras *fpl* (grandes)

sheath [ˈʃiːθ] *n, pl* **sheaths** [ˈʃiːðz, ˈʃiːθs] : funda *f*, vaina *f*

sheathe [ˈʃiːð] *vt* **sheathed; sheathing** : envainar, enfundar

shed¹ [ˈʃɛd] *vt* **shed; shedding 1** : derramar (sangre o lágrimas) **2** EMIT : emitir (luz) ⟨to shed light on : aclarar⟩ **3** DISCARD : mudar (la piel, etc.) ⟨to shed one's clothes : quitarse una la ropa⟩

shed² *n* : cobertizo *m*

she'd [ˈʃiːd] *contraction of* SHE HAD *or* SHE WOULD → **have, would**

sheen [ˈʃiːn] *n* : brillo *m*, lustre *m*

sheep [ˈʃiːp] *ns & pl* : oveja *f*

sheepdog [ˈʃiːpˌdɔg] *n* : perro *m* pastor

sheepfold [ˈʃiːpˌfoːld] *n* : redil *m*

sheepish [ˈʃiːpɪʃ] *adj* : avergonzado

sheepskin [ˈʃiːpˌskɪn] *n* : piel *f* de oveja, piel *f* de borrego

sheer¹ [ˈʃɪr] *adv* **1** COMPLETELY : completamente, totalmente **2** VERTICALLY : verticalmente

sheer² *adj* **1** TRANSPARENT : vaporoso, transparente **2** ABSOLUTE, UTTER : puro ⟨by sheer luck : por pura suerte⟩ **3** STEEP : escarpado, vertical

sheet [ˈʃiːt] *n* **1** *or* **bedsheet** [ˈbɛdˌʃiːt] : sábana *f* **2** : hoja *f* (de papel) **3** : capa *f* (de hielo, etc.) **4** : lámina *f*, placa *f* (de vidrio, metal, etc.), plancha *f* (de metal, madera, etc.) ⟨baking sheet : placa de horno⟩

sheikh *or* **sheik** [ˈʃiːk, ˈʃeɪk] *n* : jeque *m*

shelf [ˈʃɛlf] *n, pl* **shelves** [ˈʃɛlvz] **1** : estante *m*, anaquel *m* (en una pared) **2** : banco *m*, arrecife *m* (en geología) ⟨continental shelf : plataforma continental⟩

shell¹ [ˈʃɛl] *vt* **1** : pelar (nueces, etc.) **2** BOMBARD : bombardear

shell² *n* **1** SEASHELL : concha *f* **2** : cáscara *f* (de huevos, nueces, etc.), vaina *f* (de chícharos, etc.), caparazón *m* (de crustáceos, tortugas, etc.) **3** : cartucho *m*, casquillo *m* ⟨a .45 caliber shell : un cartucho calibre .45⟩ **4** *or* **racing shell** : bote *m* (para hacer regatas de remos)

she'll ['ʃiːl, 'ʃɪl] *contraction of* SHE SHALL *or* SHE WILL → **shall, will**

shellac¹ [ʃə'læk] *vt* **-lacked; -lacking** 1 : laquear (madera, etc.) 2 DEFEAT : darle una paliza (a alguien), derrotar

shellac² *n* : laca *f*

shellfish ['ʃɛl,fɪʃ] *n* : marisco *m*

shelter¹ ['ʃɛltər] *vt* 1 PROTECT : proteger, abrigar 2 HARBOR : dar refugio a, albergar

shelter² *n* : refugio *m*, abrigo *m* ⟨to take shelter : refugiarse⟩

shelve ['ʃɛlv] *vt* **shelved; shelving** 1 : poner en estantes 2 DEFER : dar carpetazo a

shenanigans [ʃə'nænɪɡənz] *npl* 1 TRICKERY : artimañas *fpl* 2 MISCHIEF : travesuras *fpl*

shepherd¹ ['ʃɛpərd] *vt* 1 : cuidar (ovejas, etc.) 2 GUIDE : conducir, guiar

shepherd² *n* : pastor *m*

shepherdess ['ʃɛpərdəs] *n* : pastora *f*

sherbet ['ʃərbət] *or* **sherbert** [-bərt] *n* : sorbete *m*; nieve *f* Cuba, Mex, PRi

sheriff ['ʃɛrɪf] *n* : sheriff *m*

sherry ['ʃɛri] *n, pl* **-ries** : jerez *m*

she's ['ʃiːz] *contraction of* SHE IS *or* SHE HAS → **be, have**

Shia *or* **Shi'a** ['ʃiːˌɑ] *n* 1 : chiismo *m* 2 *pl* **Shia** *or* **Shi'a** *or* **Shias** *or* **Shi'as** SHIITE : chií *mf*, chiita *mf*

shield¹ ['ʃiːld] *vt* 1 PROTECT : proteger 2 CONCEAL : ocultar ⟨to shield one's eyes : taparse los ojos⟩

shield² *n* : escudo *m* (armadura), PROTECTION : protección *f*, blindaje *m* (de un cable)

shier, shiest → **shy**

shift¹ ['ʃɪft] *vt* 1 CHANGE : cambiar ⟨to shift gears : cambiar de velocidad⟩ 2 MOVE : mover 3 TRANSFER : transferir ⟨to shift the blame : echarle la culpa a otro⟩ — *vi* 1 CHANGE : cambiar 2 MOVE : moverse 3 **to shift for oneself** : arreglárselas solo

shift² *n* 1 CHANGE, TRANSFER : cambio *m* ⟨a shift in priorities : un cambio de prioridades⟩ 2 : turno *m* ⟨night shift : turno de noche⟩ 3 DRESS : vestido *m* (suelto) 4 → **gearshift**

shiftless ['ʃɪftləs] *adj* : perezoso, vago, holgazán

shifty ['ʃɪfti] *adj* **shiftier; -est** : taimado, artero ⟨a shifty look : una mirada huidiza⟩

Shiite *or* **Shi'ite** ['ʃiːˌaɪt] *n* SHIA : chií *mf*, chiita *mf* — **Shiite** *or* **Shi'ite** *adj*

shilling ['ʃɪlɪŋ] *n* : chelín *m*

shimmer ['ʃɪmər] *vi* GLIMMER : brillar con luz trémula

shin¹ ['ʃɪn] *vi* **shinned; shinning** : trepar, subir ⟨she shinned up the pole : subió al poste⟩

shin² *n* : espinilla *f*, canilla *f*

shine¹ ['ʃaɪn] *v* **shone** ['ʃoːn] *or* **shined; shining** *vi* 1 : brillar, relucir ⟨the stars were shining : las estrellas brillaban⟩ 2 EXCEL : brillar, lucirse — *vt* 1 : alumbrar ⟨he shined the flashlight at it : lo alumbró con la linterna⟩ 2 POLISH : sacarle brillo a, lustrar

shine² *n* : brillo *m*, lustre *m*

shingle¹ ['ʃɪŋɡəl] *vt* **-gled; -gling** : techar

shingle² *n* : tablilla *f* (para techar)

shingles ['ʃɪŋɡəlz] *npl* : herpes *m*

shinny ['ʃɪni] *vi* **-nied; -nying** → **shin¹**

shiny ['ʃaɪni] *adj* **shinier; -est** : brillante

ship¹ ['ʃɪp] *vt* **shipped; shipping** 1 LOAD : embarcar (en un barco) 2 SEND : transportar (en barco), enviar ⟨to ship by air : enviar por avión⟩

ship² *n* 1 : barco *m*, buque *m* 2 → **spaceship**

shipboard ['ʃɪpˌbord] *n* **on** ~ : a bordo

shipbuilder ['ʃɪpˌbɪldər] *n* : constructor *m*, -tora *f* naval

shipment ['ʃɪpmənt] *n* 1 SHIPPING : transporte *m*, embarque *m* 2 : envío *m*, remesa *f* ⟨a shipment of medicine : un envío de medicina⟩

shipper ['ʃɪpər] *n* : exportador *m*, -dora *f*

shipping ['ʃɪpɪŋ] *n* 1 SHIPS : barcos *mpl*, embarcaciones *fpl* 2 TRANSPORTATION : transporte *m* (de mercancías)

shipshape ['ʃɪpˌʃeɪp] *adj* : ordenado

shipwreck¹ ['ʃɪpˌrɛk] *vt* **to be shipwrecked** : naufragar

shipwreck² *n* : naufragio *m*

shipyard ['ʃɪpˌjɑrd] *n* : astillero *m*

shirk ['ʃərk] *vt* : eludir, rehuir ⟨to shirk one's responsibilities : esquivar uno sus responsabilidades⟩

shirt ['ʃərt] *n* : camisa *f*

shiver¹ ['ʃɪvər] *vi* 1 : tiritar (de frío) 2 TREMBLE : estremecerse, temblar

shiver² *n* : escalofrío *m*, estremecimiento *m*

shoal ['ʃoːl] *n* : banco *m*, bajío *m*

shock¹ ['ʃɑk] *vt* 1 UPSET : conmover, conmocionar 2 STARTLE : asustar, sobresaltar 3 SCANDALIZE : escandalizar 4 : darle una descarga eléctrica a

shock² *n* 1 COLLISION, JOLT : choque *m*, sacudida *f* 2 UPSET : shock *m*, choque *m*, golpe *m* (emocional) ⟨she's in for a shock : se va a llevar un shock⟩ ⟨it came as a shock to me : me sorprendió/afectó mucho⟩ 3 : shock *m*, choque *m* (en medicina) ⟨to be in shock : estar en estado de shock⟩ 4 *or* **electric shock** : descarga *f* eléctrica, calambre *m* 5 SHEAVES : gavillas *fpl* 6 **shock of hair** : mata *f* de pelo

shock absorber *n* : amortiguador *m*

shocker ['ʃɑkər] *n* : bomba *f*, bombazo *m*

shocking ['ʃɑkɪŋ] *adj* 1 : chocante 2 **shocking pink** : rosa *m* estridente

shoddy ['ʃɑdi] *adj* **shoddier; -est** : de mala calidad ⟨a shoddy piece of work : un trabajo chapucero⟩

shoe¹ ['ʃuː] *vt* **shod** ['ʃɑd]; **shoeing** : herrar (un caballo)

shoe² *n* 1 : zapato *m* ⟨the shoe industry : la industria del calzado⟩ 2 HORSESHOE : herradura *f* 3 **brake shoe** : zapata *f*

shoehorn ['ʃuːˌhɔrn] *n* : calzador *m*

shoelace ['ʃuːˌleɪs] *n* : cordón *m* (de zapatos)

shoemaker ['ʃuːˌmeɪkər] *n* : zapatero *m*, -ra *f*

shoe polish n : betún m, grasa f Mex
shoeshine ['ʃuːˌʃaɪn] n : acto m de limpiar o lustrar los zapatos ⟨shoeshine boy/girl : limpiabotas, lustrabotas, bolero/bolera⟩
shoe store n : zapatería f
shone → **shine**
shoo ['ʃuː] vt **to shoo away/off/out** (etc.) : espantar, mandar a otra parte
shook → **shake**
shoot¹ ['ʃuːt] v **shot** ['ʃɑt]; **shooting** vt **1** : disparar, tirar ⟨to shoot a bullet/pistol : disparar una bala/pistola⟩ **2** : pegarle un tiro a, darle un balazo a, balacear, balear ⟨he shot her : le pegó un tiro⟩ ⟨to shoot oneself : pegarse un tiro⟩ ⟨to shoot and kill, to shoot dead/down : matar a balazos⟩ **3** THROW : lanzar (una pelota, una mirada, etc.) **4** SCORE : anotar ⟨to shoot a basket : encestar⟩ **5** PLAY : jugar a (los dados, etc.) **6** PHOTOGRAPH : fotografiar **7** FILM : filmar **8 to shoot down** : derribar (un avión) **9 to shoot down** DEFEAT : echar por tierra **10 to shoot oneself in the foot** fam : crearse problemas — vi **1** : disparar (con un arma de fuego) **2** DART : ir rápidamente ⟨it shot past : pasó como una bala⟩ **3** : disparar (en deportes) **4 to shoot for** : poner como objetivo ⟨let's shoot for Monday : intentémoslo para el lunes⟩ **5 to shoot up** : pincharse, inyectarse **6 to shoot up** INCREASE : dispararse
shoot² n : brote m, retoño m, vástago m
shooting ['ʃuːtɪŋ] n : baleo m, tiroteo m ⟨shooting death : asesinato (con arma de fuego)⟩
shooting star n : estrella f fugaz
shoot–out ['ʃuːtˌaʊt] n : balacera f, baleo m, tiroteo m
shop¹ ['ʃɑp] vi **shopped; shopping** : hacer compras ⟨to go shopping : ir de compras⟩
shop² n **1** WORKSHOP : taller m **2** STORE : tienda f
shopkeeper ['ʃɑpˌkiːpər] n : tendero m, -ra f
shoplift ['ʃɑpˌlɪft] vi : hurtar mercancía (de una tienda) — vt : hurtar (de una tienda)
shoplifter ['ʃɑpˌlɪftər] n : ladrón m, -drona f (que roba en una tienda)
shopper ['ʃɑpər] n : comprador m, -dora f
shopping bag n : bolsa f (para las compras)
shopping cart n : carrito/carro m de compras; carrito m de la compra Mex, Spain; carro m de la compra Spain
shopping center or **shopping plaza** n : centro m comercial
shopping mall n : centro m comercial
shop window n : vitrina f, escaparate m, aparador m
shore¹ ['ʃor] vt **shored; shoring** : apuntalar ⟨they shored up the wall : apuntalaron la pared⟩
shore² n **1** : orilla f (del mar, etc.) **2** PROP : puntal m

shoreline ['ʃorˌlaɪn] n : orilla f
shorn → **shear**
short¹ ['ʃort] v → **short-circuit**
short² adv **1** ABRUPTLY : repentinamente, súbitamente ⟨the car stopped short : el carro se paró en seco⟩ ⟨the sight of it brought me up short : lo que vi me hizo parar en seco⟩ **2 to be running short** ⟨the food is running short, we're running short on food : se nos está acabando la comida⟩ **3 to cut short** : interrumpir **4 to fall short** : no alcanzar, quedarse corto ⟨to fall short of expectations : no estar a la altura de las expectativas⟩ **5 to stop short of doing something** : no llegar a hacer algo
short³ adj **1** : corto (de medida), bajo (de estatura) ⟨a short distance away : a poca distancia⟩ **2** BRIEF : corto ⟨short and sweet : corto y bueno⟩ ⟨a short time ago : hace poco⟩ ⟨a short delay : una pequeña demora⟩ ⟨on short notice : con poca antelación⟩ **3** ABBREVIATED : abreviado ⟨to be short for : ser una forma breve de⟩ **4** CURT : brusco, cortante, seco **5** : corto (de dinero, etc.) ⟨I'm one dollar short : me falta un dólar⟩ ⟨to be short on/of time : andar corto de tiempo⟩ ⟨to be short of breath : quedarse sin aliento⟩ **6 nothing short of** : nada menos que, ni más ni menos que
short⁴ n **1 shorts** npl : shorts mpl, pantalones mpl cortos **2** → **short circuit 3** : cortometraje m (en el cine) **4 for short** : para abreviar **5 in short** : en resumen
shortage ['ʃortɪʤ] n : falta f, escasez f, carencia f
shortbread ['ʃortˌbred] n : galleta f dulce de mantequilla, harina, y azúcar
shortcake ['ʃortˌkeɪk] n : tarta f de fruta
shortchange ['ʃortˌʧeɪnʤ] vt **-changed; -changing** : darle mal el cambio a (alguien)
short–circuit vt : provocar un cortocircuito en — vi **1** : provocar un cortocircuito **2** : hacer cortocircuito ⟨the lamp short-circuited : la lámpara hizo cortocircuito⟩
short circuit n : cortocircuito m, corto m (eléctrico)
shortcoming ['ʃortˌkʌmɪŋ] n : defecto m
shortcut ['ʃortˌkʌt] n **1** : atajo m ⟨to take a shortcut : cortar camino⟩ **2** : alternativa f fácil, método m rápido
shorten ['ʃortən] vt : acortar — vi : acortarse
shortfall ['ʃortˌfol] n : déficit m
shorthand ['ʃortˌhænd] n : taquigrafía f
short list n : lista f de candidatos finales
short–lived ['ʃortˈlɪvd, -ˈlaɪvd] adj : efímero
shortly ['ʃortli] adv **1** BRIEFLY : brevemente ⟨to put it shortly : para decirlo en pocas palabras⟩ **2** SOON : dentro de poco
shortness ['ʃortnəs] n **1** : lo corto ⟨shortness of stature : estatura baja⟩ **2** BREVITY : brevedad f **3** CURTNESS : brusquedad f **4** SHORTAGE : falta f, escasez f, carencia f

shortsighted ['ʃɔrt,saɪtəd] → **nearsighted**
short–sleeved ['ʃɔrt,sli:vd] *adj* : de manga corta
short–staffed ['ʃɔrt,stæft] *adj* **to be short–staffed** : faltarle personal a
shortstop ['ʃɔrt,stɑp] *n* : torpedero *m*, -ra *f*; parador *m*, -dora *f* en corto *Car, Mex, Ven*
short story *n* : cuento *m*
short–tempered ['ʃɔrt,tɛmpərd] *adj* : de mal genio
short–term ['ʃɔrt,tərm] *adj* : a corto plazo
shorty ['ʃɔrti] *n* : enano *m*, -na *f*, *often disparaging*; petiso *m*, -sa *f* (persona)
shot ['ʃɑt] *n* **1** : disparo *m*, tiro *m* ⟨to fire a shot : disparar⟩ **2** PELLETS : perdigones *mpl* **3** : tiro *m* (en deportes) **4** ATTEMPT : intento *m*, tentativa *f* ⟨to have/take a shot at : hacer un intento por⟩ **5** CHANCE : posibilidad *f*, chance *m* ⟨we have a shot at winning : tenemos posibilidades de ganar⟩ ⟨a long shot : una posibilidad remota⟩ **6** PHOTOGRAPH : foto *f* **7** INJECTION : inyección *f* **8** : trago *m* (de licor) **9** MARKSMAN : tirador *m*, -dora *f* ⟨a good/poor shot : un buen/mal tirador⟩
shotgun ['ʃɑt,gʌn] *n* : escopeta *f*
shot put *n* : lanzamiento *m* de bala
should ['ʃʊd] *v aux (past of* shall*)* **1** (*expressing a condition*) ⟨he should die : si muriera⟩ ⟨if they should call, tell me : si llaman, dímelo⟩ **2** (*indicating what is proper, required, or desirable*) ⟨they should be punished : deberían ser castigados⟩ ⟨what time should we meet? : ¿a qué hora nos encontramos?⟩ **3** (*indicating a preferred thing that did not happen*) ⟨I should have realized : tendría que haberme dado cuenta⟩ ⟨he shouldn't have said it : no debería haberlo dicho⟩ **4** (*expressing polite thanks*) ⟨you shouldn't have gone to all that trouble! : ¡no deberías haberte molestado tanto!⟩ **5** (*expressing a wish*) ⟨you should have seen her face! : ¡tendrías que haber visto la cara que puso!⟩ **6** (*requesting an opinion*) ⟨what should I do? : ¿qué hago?⟩ **7** (*expressing a feeling about someone's words or behavior*) ⟨(it's funny you should say that — I was just thinking the same thing : ¡qué casualidad! estaba pensando lo mismo⟩ **8** (*emphasizing a belief, thought, or hope*) ⟨I should hope so/not! : ¡faltaría más!⟩ **9** (*expressing probability*) ⟨they should arrive soon : deben (de) llegar pronto⟩ ⟨why should he lie? : ¿porqué ha de mentir?⟩
shoulder[1] ['ʃo:ldər] *vt* **1** JOSTLE : empujar (con el hombro) **2** : ponerse al hombro (una mochila, etc.) **3** : cargar con (la responsabilidad, etc.)
shoulder[2] *n* **1** : hombro *m* ⟨to shrug one's shoulders : encogerse los hombros⟩ **2** : arcén *m*; banquina *f Arg, Uru*; berma *f Chile, Col, Ecua, Peru* (de una carretera)
shoulder bag *n* HANDBAG : cartera *f*, bolso *m*, bolsa *f Mex* (con correa)

shoulder blade *n* : omóplato *m*, omoplato *m*, escápula *f*
shoulder–length *n* : hasta los hombros
shoulder strap *n* : tirante *m*
shouldn't ['ʃʊdənt] *contraction of* SHOULD NOT → **should**
shout[1] ['ʃaʊt] *v* : gritar, vocear
shout[2] *n* : grito *m*
shove[1] ['ʃʌv] *v* **shoved; shoving** : empujar bruscamente
shove[2] *n* : empujón *m*, empellón *m*
shovel[1] ['ʃʌvəl] *vt* **-veled** *or* **-velled; -veling** *or* **-velling 1** : mover con (una) pala ⟨they shoveled the dirt out : sacaron la tierra con palas⟩ **2** DIG : cavar (con una pala)
shovel[2] *n* : pala *f*
show[1] ['ʃo:] *v* **showed; shown** ['ʃo:n] *or* **showed; showing** *vt* **1** PRESENT, DISPLAY : mostrar, enseñar ⟨I showed him the photo : le mostré la foto⟩ **2** REVEAL : demostrar, manifestar, revelar ⟨he showed himself to be a coward : se reveló como cobarde⟩ ⟨to show signs of : dar muestras/señales/indicios de⟩ ⟨to show one's feelings : demostrar uno sus emociones⟩ **3** TEACH : enseñar ⟨show me how to do it : enséñame cómo hacerlo⟩ ⟨to show someone who's boss : demostrarle a alguien quién manda⟩ ⟨I'll show him! ; ¡ya lo verá!⟩ **4** PROVE : demostrar, probar ⟨it just goes to show that . . . : esto demuestra que . . .⟩ **5** DEPICT : representar ⟨the photo shows children playing : la foto es de unos niños jugando⟩ **6** DISPLAY, READ : marcar **7** INDICATE : indicar **8** CONDUCT, LEAD : llevar, conducir ⟨to show someone the way : conducir a alguien⟩ ⟨to show someone out : acompañar a alguien a la puerta⟩ ⟨they showed us around their house : nos mostraron su casa⟩ **9** : proyectar (una película), dar (un programa de televisión) **10 to show off** : lucirse con **11 to show off** ACCENTUATE : hacer resaltar **12 to show up** EMBARRASS : hacer quedar mal — *vi* **1** : notarse, verse ⟨the stain doesn't show : la mancha no se ve⟩ **2** APPEAR : aparecer, dejarse ver **3 to show off** : lucirse
show[2] *n* **1** : demostración *f* ⟨a show of force/strength : una demostración de fuerza⟩ **2** EXHIBITION : exposición *f*, exhibición *f* ⟨flower show : exposición de flores⟩ ⟨to be on show : estar expuesto⟩ **3** : espectáculo *m* (teatral), programa *m* (de televisión, etc.) ⟨to go to a show : ir al teatro⟩ **4** APPEARANCE : apariencia *f* ⟨she put on a show of sympathy : fingió compasión⟩ ⟨his friendliness was all show : su simpatía era puro teatro⟩ **5 to run the show** : ser el/la que manda
show business *n* : mundo *m* del espectáculo
showcase ['ʃo:,keɪs] *n* : vitrina *f*
showdown ['ʃo:,daʊn] *n* : confrontación *f* (decisiva)
shower[1] ['ʃaʊər] *vt* **1** SPRAY : regar, mojar **2** HEAP : colmar ⟨they showered

him with gifts : lo colmaron de regalos, le llovieron los regalos⟩ — *vi* **1** BATHE : ducharse, darse una ducha **2** RAIN : llover

shower² *n* **1** : chaparrón *m*, chubasco *m* ⟨a chance of showers : una posibilidad de chaparrones⟩ **2** : ducha *f* ⟨to take a shower : ducharse⟩ **3** PARTY : fiesta *f* ⟨a bridal shower : una despedida de soltera⟩

shower cap *n* : gorro *m* de ducha

showing [ˈʃoʊɪŋ] *n* : exposición *f*

show-off [ˈʃoʊˌɔf] *n* : fanfarrón *m*, -rrona *f*

show off *vt* : hacer alarde de, ostentar — *vi* : lucirse

showroom [ˈʃoʊˌruːm, -ˌrʊm] *n* : sala *f* de exposición

show up *vi* APPEAR : aparecer — *vt* EXPOSE : revelar

showy [ˈʃoːi] *adj* **showier; -est** : llamativo, ostentoso — **showily** *adv*

shrank → shrink

shrapnel [ˈʃræpnəl] *ns & pl* : metralla *f*

shred¹ [ˈʃrɛd] *vt* **shredded; shredding** : hacer trizas, desmenuzar (con las manos), triturar (con una máquina) ⟨to shred vegetables : cortar verduras en tiras⟩

shred² *n* **1** STRIP : tira *f*, jirón *m* (de tela) ⟨to tear to shreds : hacer trizas⟩ **2** BIT : pizca *f* ⟨not a shred of evidence : ni la más mínima prueba⟩ ⟨not a shred of truth : ni pizca de verdad⟩

shredder *n* : trituradora *f* ⟨paper shredder : trituradora de papel⟩

shrew [ˈʃruː] *n* **1** : musaraña *f* (animal) **2** : mujer *f* regañona

shrewd [ˈʃruːd] *adj* : astuto, inteligente, sagaz — **shrewdly** *adv*

shrewdness [ˈʃruːdnəs] *n* : astucia *f*

shriek¹ [ˈʃriːk] *vi* : chillar, gritar

shriek² *n* : chillido *m*, alarido *m*, grito *m*

shrill [ˈʃrɪl] *adj* : agudo, estridente

shrilly [ˈʃrɪli] *adv* : agudamente

shrimp [ˈʃrɪmp] *n* **1** : camarón *m*; langostino *m*; gamba *f* *Arg, Uru, Spain* **2** *usu disparaging* : enano *m*, -na *f*, *often disparaging*; petiso *m*, -sa *f* (persona)

shrine [ˈʃraɪn] *n* **1** TOMB : sepulcro *m* (de un santo) **2** SANCTUARY : lugar *m* sagrado, santuario *m*

shrink [ˈʃrɪŋk] *vi* **shrank** [ˈʃræŋk] or **shrunk** [ˈʃrʌŋk]; **shrunk** or **shrunken** [ˈʃrʌŋkən]; **shrinking 1** RECOIL : retroceder ⟨he shrank back : se echó para atrás⟩ **2** : encogerse (dícese de la ropa) **3 to shrink from** AVOID : eludir

shrinkage [ˈʃrɪŋkɪdʒ] *n* : encogimiento *m* (de ropa, etc.), contracción *f*, reducción *f*

shrivel [ˈʃrɪvəl] *vi* **-veled** or **-velled; -veling** or **-velling** : arrugarse, marchitarse

shroud¹ [ˈʃraʊd] *vt* : envolver

shroud² *n* **1** : sudario *m*, mortaja *f* **2** VEIL : velo *m* ⟨wrapped in a shroud of mystery : envuelto en un aura de misterio⟩

shrub [ˈʃrʌb] *n* : arbusto *m*, mata *f*

shrubbery [ˈʃrʌbəri] *n*, *pl* **-beries** : arbustos *mpl*, matas *fpl*

shrug [ˈʃrʌɡ] *vi* **shrugged; shrugging** : encogerse de hombros — *vt* **to shrug off** DISMISS : hacer caso omiso de

shrunk → shrink

shuck [ˈʃʌk] *vt* : pelar (mazorcas, etc.), abrir (almejas, etc.)

shudder¹ [ˈʃʌdər] *vi* : estremecerse

shudder² *n* : estremecimiento *m*, escalofrío *m*

shuffle¹ [ˈʃʌfəl] *v* **-fled; -fling** *vt* MIX : mezclar, revolver, barajar (naipes) — *vi* : caminar arrastrando los pies

shuffle² *n* **1** : acto *m* de revolver ⟨each player gets a shuffle : a cada jugador le toca barajar⟩ **2** JUMBLE : revoltijo *m* **3** : el arrastrar los pies

shun [ˈʃʌn] *vi* **shunned; shunning** : evitar, esquivar, eludir

shunt [ˈʃʌnt] *vt* : desviar, cambiar de vía (un tren)

shut [ˈʃʌt] *v* **shut; shutting** *vt* **1** CLOSE : cerrar (una puerta, los ojos, un libro, etc.) ⟨shut the lid : tápalo⟩ **2 to shut away/in** : encerrar **3 to shut down** CLOSE : cerrar (un negocio, etc.) **4 to shut off** TURN OFF : cortar (la electricidad), apagar (las luces, etc.) **6 to shut off** ISOLATE : aislar **7 to shut out** EXCLUDE : excluir, dejar fuera a (personas), no dejar que entre (luz, ruido, etc.) **8 to shut up** CLOSE : cerrar **9 to shut up** CONFINE : encerrar **10 to shut up** *fam* SILENCE : callar — *vi* **1** : cerrarse **2 to shut down** : cerrar, cerrar sus puertas (dícese de una empresa) **3 to shut up** *fam* : callarse ⟨shut up! : ¡cállate (la boca)!⟩

shut-in [ˈʃʌtˌɪn] *n* : inválido *m*, -da *f* (que no puede salir de casa)

shutter [ˈʃʌtər] *n* **1** : contraventana *f*, postigo *m* (de una ventana o puerta) **2** : obturador *m* (de una cámara)

shuttle¹ [ˈʃʌtəl] *v* **-tled; -tling** *vt* : transportar ⟨she shuttled him back and forth : lo llevaba de acá para allá⟩ — *vi* : ir y venir

shuttle² *n* **1** : lanzadera *f* (para tejer) **2** : vehículo *m* que hace recorridos cortos **3** → **space shuttle**

shuttlecock [ˈʃʌtəlˌkɑk] *n* : volante *m*

shy¹ [ˈʃaɪ] *vi* **shied; shying** : retroceder, asustarse

shy² *adj* **shier** or **shyer** [ˈʃaɪər]; **shiest** or **shyest** [ˈʃaɪəst] **1** TIMID : tímido **2** WARY : cauteloso ⟨he's not shy about asking : no vacila en preguntar⟩ **3** SHORT : corto (de dinero, etc.) ⟨I'm two dollars shy : me faltan dos dólares⟩

shyly [ˈʃaɪli] *adv* : tímidamente

shyness [ˈʃaɪnəs] *n* : timidez *f*

Siamese¹ [ˌsaɪəˈmiːz, -ˈmiːs] *adj* : siamés ⟨Siamese twins : hermanos siameses⟩

Siamese² *n* **1** : siamés *m*, -mesa *f* **2** : siamés *m* (idioma) **3** or **Siamese cat** : gato *m* siamés

sibling [ˈsɪblɪŋ] *n* : hermano *m*, hermana *f*

Sicilian [səˈsɪljən] *n* : siciliano *m*, -na *f* — **Sicilian** *adj*

sick ['sɪk] *adj* 1 : enfermo ⟨the baby is sick : el bebé está enfermo⟩ 2 NAUSEOUS : mareado, con náuseas ⟨to get sick : vomitar⟩ 3 : para uso de enfermos ⟨sick day : día de permiso (por enfermedad)⟩ 4 to be sick (and tired) of : estar harto de, estar hasta la coronilla de

sickbed ['sɪk,bɛd] *n* : lecho *m* de enfermo

sicken ['sɪkən] *vt* 1 : poner enfermo 2 REVOLT : darle asco (a alguien) — *vi* : enfermar(se), caer enfermo

sickening ['sɪkənɪŋ] *adj* : asqueroso, repugnante, nauseabundo

sickle ['sɪkəl] *n* : hoz *f*

sick leave *n* : baja *f* por enfermedad

sickly ['sɪkli] *adj* **sicklier; -est** 1 : enfermizo 2 → **sickening**

sickness ['sɪknəs] *n* 1 : enfermedad *f* 2 NAUSEA : náuseas *fpl*

side¹ ['saɪd] *n* 1 : lado *m* (de un lago, una cama, una frontera, etc.) ⟨by the side of the road : al lado de la calle⟩ ⟨the far side : el otro lado⟩ ⟨on the left-hand side : a mano izquierda⟩ ⟨on both sides : a ambos lados⟩ ⟨on either side : a cada lado⟩ ⟨from side to side : de un lado a otro⟩ ⟨side by side : uno al lado del otro⟩ ⟨they attacked from all sides : los atacaron desde todos los frentes⟩ ⟨there are mountains on all sides : todo alrededor hay montañas⟩ 2 : lado *m*, cara *f* (de una moneda, una caja, etc.) ⟨this side up : este lado hacia arriba⟩ 3 : falda *f* (de una montaña) 4 : lado *m*, costado *m* (de una persona), ijada *f* (de un animal) 5 *or* side dish : guarnición *f*, acompañamiento *m* ⟨with a side of fries : con papas fritas como guarnición⟩ 6 : lado *m*, parte *f* ⟨he's on my side : está de mi parte⟩ ⟨to take sides : tomar partido⟩ ⟨to listen to both sides (of the story) : escuchar las dos campanas⟩ 7 : aspecto *m* ⟨to look on the bright side : ver el aspecto positivo⟩ 8 on the side SEPARATELY : aparte 9 on the side : como segundo trabajo 10 on the side ⟨a lover on the side : un/una amante (de una persona casada)⟩

side² *v* **sided; siding** *vt* : instalar revestimiento exterior en — *vi* 1 to side against : ponerse en contra de 2 to side with : ponerse de parte de

sideboard ['saɪd,bord] *n* : aparador *m*

sideburns ['saɪd,bərnz] *npl* : patillas *fpl*

sided ['saɪdəd] *adj* : que tiene lados (one-sided : de un lado)

side effect *n* : efecto *m* secundario

sideline ['saɪd,laɪn] *n* 1 : línea *f* de banda (en deportes) 2 : actividad *f* suplementaria (en negocios) 3 to be on the sidelines : estar al margen

sidelong ['saɪd,lɔŋ] *adj* : de reojo, de soslayo

sideshow ['saɪd,ʃoː] *n* : espectáculo *m* secundario, atracción *f* secundaria

sidestep ['saɪd,stɛp] *v* **-stepped; -stepping** *vi* : dar un paso hacia un lado — *vt* AVOID : esquivar, eludir

side street *n* : calle *f* lateral

sidetrack ['saɪd,træk] *vt* : desviar (una conversación, etc.), distraer (a una persona)

sidewalk ['saɪd,wɔk] *n* : acera *f*; vereda *f*; andén *m CA, Col*; banqueta *f Mex*

sideways¹ ['saɪd,weɪz] *adv* 1 : hacia un lado ⟨it leaned sideways : se inclinaba hacia un lado⟩ 2 : de lado, de costado ⟨lie sideways : acuéstese de costado⟩

sideways² *adj* : hacia un lado ⟨a sideways glance : una mirada de reojo⟩

siding ['saɪdɪŋ] *n* : revestimiento *m* exterior (de un edificio)

sidle ['saɪdəl] *vi* **-dled; -dling** : moverse furtivamente

siege ['siːʤ, 'siːʒ] *n* : sitio *m* ⟨to be under siege : estar sitiado⟩

siesta [si'ɛstə] *n* : siesta *f*

sieve ['sɪv] *n* : tamiz *m*, cedazo *m*, criba *f* (en mineralogía)

sift ['sɪft] *vt* 1 : tamizar, cerner ⟨sift the flour : tamice la harina⟩ 2 *or* to sift through : examinar cuidadosamente, pasar por el tamiz

sifter ['sɪftər] *n* : tamiz *m*, cedazo *m*

sigh¹ ['saɪ] *vi* : suspirar

sigh² *n* : suspiro *m*

sight¹ ['saɪt] *vt* : ver (a una persona), divisar (la tierra, un barco)

sight² *n* 1 EYESIGHT : vista *f* (facultad) 2 VIEW : vista *f* ⟨out of sight : fuera de vista⟩ ⟨to come into sight : aparecer⟩ ⟨in plain sight : a plena vista⟩ 3 : algo visto ⟨it's a familiar sight : se ve con frecuencia⟩ ⟨she's a sight for sore eyes : da gusto verla⟩ 4 : lugar *m* de interés (para turistas, etc.) 5 : mira *f* (de un rifle, etc.) 6 GLIMPSE : mirada *f* breve ⟨at first sight : a primera vista⟩ ⟨I know him by sight : lo conozco de vista⟩ ⟨I caught sight of her : la divisé, alcancé a verla⟩ ⟨to lose sight of : perder de vista⟩ ⟨he faints at the sight of blood : cuando ve sangre se desmaya⟩ ⟨to shoot on sight : disparar sin previo aviso⟩

sighting ['saɪtɪŋ] *n* : avistamiento *m*

sightless ['saɪtləs] *adj* : invidente, ciego

sightseeing ['saɪt,siːɪŋ] *n* : acto *m* de visitar los lugares de interés ⟨to go sightseeing : hacer turismo⟩ ⟨sightseeing tour : excursión, tour⟩

sightseer ['saɪt,siːər] *n* : turista *mf*

sign¹ ['saɪn] *vt* 1 : firmar ⟨to sign a check : firmar un cheque⟩ 2 *or* to sign on/up HIRE : contratar (a un empleado), fichar (a un jugador) 3 to sign in/out : registrar la entrada/salida de — *vi* 1 : hacer una seña ⟨she signed for him to stop : le hizo una seña para que se parara⟩ 2 : comunicarse por señas 3 to sign for : firmar el recibo de 4 to sign in/out : firmar el registro (al entrar/salir), registrar la entrada/salida 5 to sign off : despedirse (en una carta, etc.) 6 to sign off (on) APPROVE : dar el visto bueno a 7 to sign up : inscribirse, matricularse

sign² *n* 1 SYMBOL : símbolo *m*, signo *m* ⟨minus sign : signo de menos⟩ ⟨sign of the zodiac : signo del zodíaco⟩ 2 GES-

TURE : seña *f*, señal *f*, gesto *m* **3** : letrero *m*, cartel *m* ⟨neon sign : letrero de neón⟩ **4** TRACE : señal *f*, indicio *m*

signage ['saɪnɪdʒ] *n* : señalización *f*

signal[1] ['sɪgnəl] *vt* **-naled** *or* **-nalled; -naling** *or* **-nalling** **1** : hacerle señas (a alguien) ⟨she signaled me to leave : me hizo señas para que saliera⟩ **2** INDICATE : señalar, indicar — *vi* : hacer señas, comunicar por señas

signal[2] *adj* NOTABLE : señalado, notable

signal[3] *n* : señal *f*

signatory ['sɪgnə,tori] *n, pl* **-ries** : firmante *mf*; signatario *m*, -ria *f*

signature ['sɪgnə,tʃʊr] *n* : firma *f*

signer ['saɪnər] *n* : firmante *mf*

signet ['sɪgnət] *n* : sello *m*

significance [sɪg'nɪfɪkəns] *n* **1** MEANING : significado *m* **2** IMPORTANCE : importancia *f*

significant [sɪg'nɪfɪkənt] *adj* **1** IMPORTANT : importante **2** MEANINGFUL : significativo — **significantly** *adv*

signify ['sɪgnə,faɪ] *vt* **-fied; -fying** **1** : indicar ⟨he signified his desire for more : haciendo señas indicó que quería más⟩ **2** MEAN : significar

sign language *n* : lenguaje *m* por señas

signpost ['saɪn,post] *n* : poste *m* indicador

silence[1] ['saɪləns] *vt* **-lenced; -lencing** : silenciar, acallar

silence[2] *n* : silencio *m*

silencer ['saɪlənsər] *n* : silenciador *m*

silent ['saɪlənt] *adj* **1** : callado ⟨to remain silent : quedarse callado, guardar silencio⟩ **2** QUIET, STILL : silencioso **3** MUTE : mudo ⟨a silent letter : una letra muda⟩

silently ['saɪləntli] *adv* : silenciosamente, calladamente

silhouette[1] [,sɪlə'wɛt] *vt* **-etted; -etting** : destacar la silueta de ⟨it was silhouetted against the sky : se perfilaba contra el cielo⟩

silhouette[2] *n* : silueta *f*

silica ['sɪlɪkə] *n* : sílice *f*

silicon ['sɪlɪkən, -,kɑn] *n* : silicio *m* ⟨silicon chip : chip de silicio⟩

silk ['sɪlk] *n* : seda *f*

silk-cotton tree *n* : ceiba *f*

silken ['sɪlkən] *adj* **1** : de seda ⟨a silken veil : un velo de seda⟩ **2** SILKY : sedoso ⟨silken hair : cabellos sedosos⟩

silkworm ['sɪlk,wərm] *n* : gusano *m* de seda

silky ['sɪlki] *adj* **silkier; -est** : sedoso

sill ['sɪl] *n* : alféizar *m* (de una ventana), umbral *m* (de una puerta)

silliness ['sɪlinəs] *n* : tontería *f*, estupidez *f*

silly ['sɪli] *adj* **sillier; -est** : tonto, estúpido, ridículo

silo ['saɪ,lo:] *n, pl* **silos** : silo *m*

silt ['sɪlt] *n* : cieno *m*

silver[1] ['sɪlvər] *adj* **1** : de plata ⟨a silver spoon : una cuchara de plata⟩ **2** → silvery

silver[2] *n* **1** : plata *f* **2** COINS : monedas *fpl* **3** → silverware **4** : color *m* plata

silver-plated ['sɪlvər'pleɪtəd] *adj* : plateado

silversmith ['sɪlvər,smɪθ] *n* : orfebre *mf*

silverware ['sɪlvər,wær] *n* **1** : artículos *mpl* de plata, platería *f* **2** FLATWARE : cubertería *f*

silvery ['sɪlvəri] *adj* : plateado

similar ['sɪmələr] *adj* : similar, parecido, semejante

similarity [,sɪmə'lærəti] *n, pl* **-ties** : semejanza *f*, parecido *m*

similarly ['sɪmələrli] *adv* : de manera similar

simile ['sɪmə,li:] *n* : símil *m*

simmer ['sɪmər] *v* : hervir a fuego lento

simper[1] ['sɪmpər] *vi* : sonreír como un tonto

simper[2] *n* : sonrisa *f* tonta

simple ['sɪmpəl] *adj* **simpler; simplest** **1** INNOCENT : inocente **2** PLAIN : sencillo, simple **3** EASY : simple, sencillo, fácil **4** STRAIGHTFORWARD : puro, simple ⟨the simple truth : la pura verdad⟩ **5** NAIVE : ingenuo, simple

simpleminded [,sɪmpəl'maɪndəd] *adj* : simple (dícese de una persona)

simpleton ['sɪmpəltən] *n* : bobo *m*, -ba *f*; tonto *m*, -ta *f*

simplicity [sɪm'plɪsəti] *n* : simplicidad *f*, sencillez *f*

simplification [,sɪmpləfə'keɪʃən] *n* : simplificación *f*

simplify ['sɪmplə,faɪ] *vt* **-fied; -fying** : simplificar

simplistic [sɪm'plɪstɪk] *n* : simplista

simply ['sɪmpli] *adv* **1** PLAINLY : sencillamente **2** SOLELY : simplemente, sólo **3** REALLY : absolutamente

simulate ['sɪmjə,leɪt] *vt* **-lated; -lating** : simular

simulation [,sɪmjə'leɪʃən] *n* : simulación *f*

simultaneous [,saɪməl'teɪniəs] *adj* : simultáneo — **simultaneously** *adv*

sin[1] ['sɪn] *vi* **sinned; sinning** : pecar

sin[2] *n* : pecado *m*

since[1] ['sɪnts] *adv* **1** : desde entonces ⟨they've been friends ever since : desde entonces han sido amigos⟩ ⟨she's since become mayor : más tarde se hizo alcalde⟩ **2** AGO : hace ⟨he's long since dead : murió hace mucho⟩

since[2] *conj* **1** : desde que ⟨since he was born : desde que nació⟩ **2** INASMUCH AS : ya que, puesto que, dado que

since[3] *prep* : desde

sincere [sɪn'sɪr] *adj* **-cerer; -est** : sincero — **sincerely** *adv*

sincerity [sɪn'serəti] *n* : sinceridad *f*

sinew ['sɪn,ju:, 'sɪn,nu:] *n* **1** TENDON : tendón *m*, nervio *m* (en la carne) **2** POWER : fuerza *f*

sinewy ['sɪnjui, 'sɪnui] *adj* **1** STRINGY : fibroso **2** STRONG, WIRY : fuerte, nervudo

sinful ['sɪnfəl] *adj* : pecador (dícese de las personas), pecaminoso

sing ['sɪŋ] *v* **sang** ['sæŋ] *or* **sung** ['sʌŋ]; **sung; singing** : cantar

singe ['sɪndʒ] *vt* **singed; singeing** : chamuscar, quemar

singer ['sɪŋər] n : cantante mf
singer–songwriter ['sɪŋər'sɔŋ,raɪtər] n : cantautor m, -tora f
single¹ ['sɪŋɡəl] vt -gled; -gling or to single out 1 SELECT : escoger 2 DISTINGUISH : señalar
single² adj 1 UNMARRIED : soltero ⟨a single parent : un padre soltero, una madre soltera⟩ 2 SOLE : solo ⟨a single survivor : un solo sobreviviente⟩ ⟨every single one : cada uno, todos⟩
single³ n 1 : soltero m, -ra f ⟨for married couples and singles : para los matrimonios y los solteros⟩ 2 or single room : habitación f individual 3 DOLLAR : billete m de un dólar
single file¹ adv : en fila india
single file² n in single file : en fila india
single–handed ['sɪŋɡəl'hændəd] adj : sin ayuda, solo
single–minded ['sɪŋɡəl'maɪndəd] adj : resuelto
singly ['sɪŋɡli] adv : individualmente, uno por uno
singular¹ ['sɪŋɡjələr] adj 1 : singular (en gramática) 2 OUTSTANDING : singular, sobresaliente 3 STRANGE : singular, extraño
singular² n : singular m
singularity [,sɪŋɡjə'lærəti] n, pl -ties : singularidad f
singularly ['sɪŋɡjələrli] adv : singularmente
sinister ['sɪnəstər] adj : siniestro
sink¹ ['sɪŋk] v sank ['sæŋk] or sunk ['sʌŋk]; sunk; sinking vi 1 : hundirse (dícese de un barco, etc.) ⟨his foot sank into the mud : su pie se hundió en el barro⟩ 2 DROP, FALL : descender, caer ⟨to sink into a chair : dejarse caer en una silla⟩ ⟨her heart sank : se le cayó el alma a los pies⟩ ⟨I had the sinking feeling that . . . : tenía un mal presentimiento de que . . .⟩ 3 DECREASE : bajar ⟨the company's stock sank : las acciones de la compañía cayeron en picada⟩ ⟨his voice sank to a whisper : su voz se redujo a un susurro⟩ 4 FOUNDER : hundirse, irse a pique (dícese de una compañía, etc.) 5 STOOP : rebajarse (a hacer algo) ⟨to sink so/that low : caer tan bajo⟩ 6 to sink in : hacer mella — vt 1 : hundir (un barco, etc.) 2 EXCAVATE : excavar (un pozo para minar), perforar (un pozo de agua) 3 PLUNGE, STICK : clavar, hincar 4 INVEST : invertir (fondos) 5 : meter (en deportes) ⟨to sink a basket : encestar⟩
sink² n 1 or kitchen sink : fregadero m; lavaplatos m Chile, Col, Mex 2 or bathroom sink : lavabo m, lavamanos m 3 WEIGHT : plomo m, plomada f
sinker ['sɪŋkər] n WEIGHT : plomada f, plomo m
sinner ['sɪnər] n : pecador m, -dora f
sinuous ['sɪnjuəs] adj : sinuoso — sinuously adv
sinus ['saɪnəs] n : seno m
sip¹ ['sɪp] v sipped; sipping vt : sorber — vi : beber a sorbos

sip² n : sorbo m
siphon¹ ['saɪfən] vt : sacar con sifón
siphon² n : sifón m
sir ['sər] n 1 (in titles) : sir m 2 (as a form of address) : señor m ⟨Dear Sir : Muy señor mío⟩ ⟨yes sir! : ¡sí, señor!⟩
sire¹ ['saɪr] vt sired; siring : engendrar, ser el padre de
sire² n : padre m
siren ['saɪrən] n : sirena f
sirloin ['sər,lɔɪn] n : solomillo m
sirup → syrup
sissy ['sɪsi] n, pl -sies fam + disparaging : mariquita f fam + disparaging
sister ['sɪstər] n 1 : hermana f 2 Sister : hermana f, Sor f ⟨Sister Mary : Sor María⟩
sisterhood ['sɪstər,hʊd] n 1 : condición f de ser hermana 2 : sociedad f de mujeres
sister–in–law ['sɪstərɪn,lɔ] n, pl sisters–in–law : cuñada f
sisterly ['sɪstərli] adj : de hermana
sit ['sɪt] v sat ['sæt]; sitting vi 1 : sentarse ⟨he sat down : se sentó⟩ ⟨he sat (down) in the chair : se sentó en la silla⟩ 2 : estar sentado ⟨she was sitting in the chair : estaba sentada en la silla⟩ ⟨they sat across from me : estaban sentados frente a mí⟩ 3 ROOST : posarse 4 : sesionar ⟨the legislature is sitting : la legislatura está en sesión⟩ 5 POSE : posar (para un retrato) 6 LIE, REST : estar (ubicado) ⟨the house sits on a hill : la casa está en una colina⟩ ⟨it was sitting right in front of me : lo tenía delante de las narices⟩ 7 to sit around : relajarse, no hacer nada 8 to sit back : relajarse 9 to sit in for : sustituir a 10 to sit in on : asistir a (como observador) 11 to sit on : darle largas a (algo) 12 to sit out ENDURE : aguantar 13 to sit out : no participar en ⟨I'll sit this one out : no voy a bailar/jugar (etc.) esta vez⟩ 14 to sit through : aguantar (un discurso, etc.) 15 to sit tight : esperar 16 to sit up : incorporarse 17 to sit up : quedarse levantado ⟨we sat up talking : nos quedamos hablando hasta muy tarde⟩ — vt SEAT : sentar, colocar ⟨I sat him on the sofa : lo senté en el sofá⟩
sitcom ['sɪt,kɑm] n : situation comedy
site ['saɪt] n 1 : sitio m, lugar m (en general), emplazamiento m, ubicación f (de un edificio, etc.) ⟨construction/building site : obra⟩ 2 SCENE : lugar m, escena f (de un accidente, etc.), escenario m (de una batalla) 3 → Web site
sitter ['sɪtər] → baby-sitter
sitting ['sɪtɪŋ] n 1 : turno m (de cena, etc.) 2 : sesión f
sitting room → living room
situate ['sɪtʃu,eɪt] vt -ated; -ating 1 ESTABLISH, LOCATE : situar, ubicar 2 PLACE : poner, colocar
situated ['sɪtʃu,eɪtəd] adj LOCATED : ubicado, situado
situation [,sɪtʃu'eɪʃən] n 1 LOCATION : situación f, ubicación f, emplazamiento m 2 CIRCUMSTANCES : situación f 3 JOB : empleo m

situation comedy n : comedia f de situación

six¹ ['sɪks] adj : seis ⟨she's six (years old) : tiene seis años⟩

six² n : seis m ⟨the six of hearts : el seis de corazones⟩

six³ pron : seis ⟨there are six of us : somos seis⟩ ⟨it's six (o'clock) : son las seis⟩

six–gun ['sɪks,gʌn] n : revólver m (con seis cámaras)

six hundred¹ adj & pron : seiscientos

six hundred² n : seiscientos m

six–shooter ['sɪks,ʃuːtər] → six-gun

sixteen¹ [sɪks'tiːn] adj & pron : dieciséis

sixteen² n : dieciséis m

sixteenth¹ [sɪks'tiːnθ] adj : decimosexto

sixteenth² n 1 : decimosexto m, -ta f (en una serie) 2 : dieciseisavo m, dieciseisava parte f

sixth¹ ['sɪksθ, 'sɪkst] adv : en sexto lugar

sixth² adj : sexto

sixth³ n 1 : sexto m, -ta f (en una serie) 2 : sexto m, sexta parte f

sixtieth¹ ['sɪkstiəθ] adj : sexagésimo

sixtieth² n 1 : sexagésimo m, -ma f (en una serie) 2 : sesentavo m, sesentava parte f

sixty¹ ['sɪksti] adj & pron : sesenta

sixty² n, pl -ties : sesenta m

sizable or **sizeable** ['saɪzəbəl] adj : considerable

size¹ ['saɪz] vt **sized; sizing** 1 : clasificar según el tamaño 2 **to size up** : evaluar, apreciar

size² n 1 DIMENSIONS : tamaño m, talla f (de ropa), número m (de zapatos) 2 MAGNITUDE : magnitud f

sized ['saɪzd] adj (used in combination) : de tamaño ⟨large-sized : de tamaño grande⟩

sizzle ['sɪzəl] vi **-zled; -zling** : chisporrotear

skate¹ ['skeɪt] vi **skated; skating** : patinar

skate² n 1 : patín m ⟨roller skate : patín de ruedas⟩ 2 : raya f (pez)

skateboard ['skeɪt,bord] n : monopatín m, patineta f, skateboard m

skateboarding ['skeɪt,bordɪŋ] n : monopatinaje m, skateboarding m

skater ['skeɪtər] n : patinador m, -dora f

skating ['skeɪtɪŋ] n : patinaje m

skating rink n : pista f de patinaje

skein ['skeɪn] n : madeja f

skeletal ['skɛlətəl] adj 1 : óseo (en anatomía) 2 EMACIATED : esquelético

skeleton ['skɛlətən] n 1 : esqueleto m (anatómico) 2 FRAMEWORK : armazón mf

skeleton key n : llave f maestra

skeptic ['skɛptɪk] n : escéptico m, -ca f

skeptical ['skɛptɪkəl] adj : escéptico

skepticism ['skɛptə,sɪzəm] n : escepticismo m

sketch¹ ['skɛtʃ] vt : bosquejar — vi : hacer bosquejos

sketch² n 1 DRAWING, OUTLINE : esbozo m, bosquejo m 2 ESSAY : ensayo m

sketchy ['skɛtʃi] adj **sketchier; -est** : incompleto, poco detallado

skewer¹ ['skjuːər] vt : ensartar (carne, etc.)

skewer² n : brocheta f, broqueta f

ski¹ ['skiː] vi **skied; skiing** : esquiar

ski² n, pl **skis** : esquí m

ski boot n : bota f de esquiar

skid¹ ['skɪd] vi **skidded; skidding** : derrapar, patinar

skid² n : derrape m, patinazo m

skier ['skiːər] n : esquiador m, -dora f

skiing ['skiːɪŋ] n : esquí m

ski jump n : trampolín m (de esquí)

ski lift n : telesquí m, telesilla f

skill ['skɪl] n 1 DEXTERITY : habilidad f, destreza f 2 CAPABILITY : capacidad f, arte m, técnica f ⟨organizational skills : la capacidad para organizar⟩

skilled ['skɪld] adj : hábil, experto

skillet ['skɪlət] n : sartén mf

skillful ['skɪlfəl] adj : hábil, diestro

skillfully ['skɪlfəli] adv : con habilidad, con destreza

skim¹ ['skɪm] v **skimmed; skimming** vt 1 : espumar (sopa, etc.), quitar (grasa, etc.) ⟨I skimmed the broth to remove the fat, I skimmed the fat off/from the broth : le quité la grasa al caldo⟩ 2 : echarle un vistazo a (un libro, etc.) 3 : pasar rozando (una superficie) 4 or **to skim off** : embolsarse (dinero) — vi **to skim through/over** : echarle un vistazo a (un libro, etc.)

skim² adj : descremado ⟨skim milk : leche descremada⟩

ski mask n : pasamontañas m

skimp ['skɪmp] vi **to skimp on** : escatimar

skimpy ['skɪmpi] adj **skimpier; -est** : exiguo, escaso, raquítico

skin¹ ['skɪn] vt **skinned; skinning** : despellejar, desollar

skin² n 1 : piel f, cutis m (de la cara) ⟨dark skin : piel morena⟩ 2 RIND : piel f

skin–deep ['skɪn'diːp] adj : superficial

skin diving n : buceo m, submarinismo m

skinflint ['skɪn,flɪnt] n : tacaño m, -ña f

skinhead ['skɪn,hɛd] n : cabeza mf rapada

skinned ['skɪnd] adj (used in combination) : de piel ⟨tough-skinned : de piel dura⟩

skinny ['skɪni] adj **skinnier; -est** : flaco

skip¹ ['skɪp] v **skipped; skipping** vi : ir dando brincos — vt : saltarse

skip² n : brinco m, salto m

skipper ['skɪpər] n : capitán m, -tana f

ski pole n : bastón m (de esquí)

skirmish¹ ['skərmɪʃ] vi : escaramuzar

skirmish² n : escaramuza f, refriega f

skirt¹ ['skərt] vt 1 BORDER : bordear 2 EVADE : evadir, esquivar

skirt² n : falda f, pollera f

skit ['skɪt] n : sketch m (teatral)

skittish ['skɪtɪʃ] adj : asustadizo, nervioso

skulk ['skʌlk] vi : merodear

skull ['skʌl] n 1 : cráneo m, calavera f 2 **skull and crossbones** : calavera f (bandera pirata)

skullcap ['skʌl,kæp] n : casquete m

skunk ['skʌŋk] n : zorrillo m, mofeta f

sky ['skaɪ] n, pl **skies** : cielo m

skylark ['skaɪ,lɑrk] n : alondra f

skylight [ˈskaɪˌlaɪt] n : claraboya f, traga-luz m

skyline [ˈskaɪˌlaɪn] n : horizonte m

skyrocket [ˈskaɪˌrɑkət] vi : dispararse

skyscraper [ˈskaɪˌskreɪpər] n : rascacielos m

slab [ˈslæb] n : losa f (de piedra), tabla f (de madera), pedazo m grueso (de pan, etc.)

slack¹ [ˈslæk] adj 1 CARELESS : descuidado, negligente 2 LOOSE : flojo 3 SLOW : de poco movimiento

slack² n 1 : parte f floja ⟨to take up the slack : tensar (una cuerda, etc.)⟩ 2 **slacks** npl : pantalones mpl

slacken [ˈslækən] vt : aflojar — vi : aflojarse

slacker [ˈslækər] n : vago m, -ga f; holgazán m, -zana f

slackness [ˈslæknəs] n 1 LOOSENESS : soltura f 2 LAXITY : laxitud f

slag [ˈslæɡ] n : escoria f

slain → slay

slake [ˈsleɪk] vt **slaked; slaking** : saciar (la sed), satisfacer (la curiosidad)

slam¹ [ˈslæm] v **slammed; slamming** vt 1 : cerrar de golpe ⟨he slammed the door : dio un portazo⟩ 2 : tirar o dejar caer de golpe ⟨he slammed down the book : dejó caer el libro de un golpe⟩ — vi 1 : cerrarse de golpe 2 **to slam into** : chocar contra

slam² n : golpe m, portazo m (de una puerta)

slam dunk n : clavada f, mate m, donqueo m

slander¹ [ˈslændər] vt : calumniar, difamar

slander² n : calumnia f, difamación f

slanderous [ˈslændərəs] adj : difamatorio, calumnioso

slang [ˈslæŋ] n : argot m, jerga f

slant¹ [ˈslænt] vi : inclinarse, ladearse — vt 1 SLOPE : inclinar 2 ANGLE : sesgar, orientar, dirigir ⟨a story slanted towards youth : un artículo dirigido a los jóvenes⟩

slant² n 1 INCLINE : inclinación f 2 PERSPECTIVE : perspectiva f, enfoque m

slap¹ [ˈslæp] vt **slapped; slapping** 1 : bofetear, cachetear ⟨she slapped him in/across the face, she slapped his face : le dio una bofetada⟩ ⟨to slap someone on the back : darle una palmada a alguien en la espalda⟩ 2 : golpear (dícese de las olas, etc.) 3 : tirar (con fuerza) ⟨she slapped the book (down) on the desk : tiró el libro en el escritorio⟩ 4 : poner (rápidamente) ⟨he slapped some butter on the bread : le puso mantequilla al pan⟩ ⟨she slapped some paint on it : le dio una pasada rápida de pintura⟩ 5 **to slap around** : darle palizas a 6 **to slap together** : preparar de prisa 7 **to slap with** : ponerle (una multa, etc.) a

slap² n 1 : bofetada f, cachetada f, palmada f 2 **slap in the face** INSULT : bofetada f

slapdash [ˈslæpˌdæʃ] adj : chapucero

slapstick [ˈslæpˌstɪk] n : payasadas fpl, bufonadas fpl

slash¹ [ˈslæʃ] vt 1 GASH : cortar, hacer un tajo en 2 REDUCE : reducir, rebajar (precios)

slash² n 1 : tajo m, corte m 2 or **forward slash** : diagonal f, barra f (oblicua)

slat [ˈslæt] n : tablilla f, listón m

slate [ˈsleɪt] n 1 : pizarra f ⟨a slate roof : un techo de pizarra⟩ 2 : lista f de candidatos (políticos)

slaughter¹ [ˈslɔtər] vt 1 BUTCHER : matar (animales) 2 MASSACRE : masacrar (personas)

slaughter² n 1 : matanza f (de animales) 2 MASSACRE : masacre f, carnicería f

slaughterhouse [ˈslɔtərˌhaʊs] n : matadero m

Slav [ˈslɑv, ˈslæv] n : eslavo m, -va f

slave¹ [ˈsleɪv] vi **slaved; slaving** : trabajar como un burro

slave² n : esclavo m, -va f

slaver [ˈslævər, ˈsleɪ-] vi : babear

slavery [ˈsleɪvəri] n : esclavitud f

Slavic [ˈslɑvɪk, ˈslæ-] adj : eslavo

slavish [ˈsleɪvɪʃ] adj 1 SERVILE : servil 2 IMITATIVE : poco original

slay [ˈsleɪ] vt **slew** [ˈsluː]; **slain** [ˈsleɪn]; **slaying** : asesinar, matar

slayer [ˈsleɪər] n : asesino m, -na f

sleazy [ˈsliːzi] adj **sleazier; -est** 1 SHODDY : chapucero, de mala calidad 2 DILAPIDATED : ruinoso 3 DISREPUTABLE : de mala fama

sled¹ [ˈsled] v **sledded; sledding** vi : ir en trineo — vt : transportar en trineo

sled² n : trineo m

sledge [ˈsledʒ] n 1 : trineo m (grande) 2 → sledgehammer

sledgehammer [ˈsledʒˌhæmər] n : almádena f; combo m Chile, Peru

sleek¹ [ˈsliːk] vt SLICK : alisar

sleek² adj : liso y brillante

sleep¹ [ˈsliːp] vi **slept** [ˈslept]; **sleeping** 1 : dormir 2 **to sleep in** : levantarse tarde 3 **to sleep together** : acostarse, tener relaciones 4 **to sleep with** : acostarse con

sleep² n 1 : sueño m 2 : legañas fpl (en los ojos) 3 **to go to sleep** : dormirse

sleeper [ˈsliːpər] n 1 : durmiente mf ⟨to be a light sleeper : tener el sueño ligero⟩ 2 or **sleeping car** : coche m cama, coche m dormitorio

sleepily [ˈsliːpəli] adv : de manera somnolienta

sleepiness [ˈsliːpinəs] n : somnolencia f

sleeping bag n : saco m de dormir

sleeping pill n : pastilla f para dormir

sleepless [ˈsliːpləs] adj : sin dormir, desvelado ⟨to have a sleepless night : pasar la noche en blanco⟩

sleepwalk [ˈsliːpˌwɔk] vi : caminar dormido

sleepwalker [ˈsliːpˌwɔkər] n : sonámbulo m, -la f

sleepwalking [ˈsliːpˌwɔkɪŋ] n : sonambulismo m

sleepy [ˈsliːpi] adj **sleepier; -est** 1 DROWSY : somnoliento, soñoliento ⟨to

be sleepy : tener sueño **2** LETHARGIC
: aletargado, letárgico

sleet¹ ['sli:t] *vi* **to be sleeting** : caer aguanieve

sleet² *n* : aguanieve *f*

sleeve ['sli:v] *n* : manga *f* (de una camisa,
etc.)

sleeveless ['sli:vləs] *adj* : sin mangas

sleigh¹ ['sleɪ] *vi* : ir en trineo

sleigh² *n* : trineo *m* (tirado por caballos)

sleight of hand [ˌslaɪtəvˈhænd] : prestidigitación *f*, juegos *mpl* de manos

slender ['slɛndər] *adj* **1** SLIM : esbelto,
delgado **2** SCANTY : exiguo, escaso ⟨a
slender hope : una esperanza lejana⟩

sleuth ['slu:θ] *n* : detective *mf*, sabueso *m*

slew → slay

slice¹ ['slaɪs] *vt* **sliced; slicing** : cortar

slice² *n* : rebanada *f*, tajada *f*, lonja *f* (de
carne, etc.), rodaja *f* (de una verdura,
fruta, etc.), trozo *m* (de pastel, etc.)

slicer ['slaɪsər] *n* : cortadora *f* (de fiambres, etc.), rebanadora *f* (de pan)

slick¹ ['slɪk] *vt* : alisar

slick² *adj* **1** SLIPPERY : resbaladizo, resbaloso **2** CRAFTY : astuto, taimado

slicker ['slɪkər] *n* : impermeable *m*

slide¹ ['slaɪd] *v* **slid** ['slɪd]; **sliding**
['slaɪdɪŋ] *vi* **1** SLIP : resbalar **2** GLIDE
: deslizarse **3** DECLINE : bajar ⟨to let
things slide : dejar pasar las cosas⟩ — *vt*
: correr, deslizar

slide² *n* **1** SLIDING : deslizamiento *m* **2**
SLIP : resbalón *m* **3** : tobogán *m* (para
niños) **4** TRANSPARENCY : diapositiva *f*
(fotográfica) **5** DECLINE : descenso *m*

slider ['slaɪdər] *n* **1** (*in baseball*) : slider
m **2** : hamburguesa *f* pequeña, sandwich *m* pequeño

slier, sliest → sly

slight¹ ['slaɪt] *vt* : desairar, despreciar

slight² *adj* **1** SLENDER : esbelto, delgado **2** FLIMSY : endeble **3** TRIFLING
: leve, insignificante ⟨a slight pain : un
leve dolor⟩ **4** SMALL : pequeño, ligero
⟨not in the slightest : en absoluto⟩

slight³ *n* SNUB : desaire *m*

slightly ['slaɪtli] *adv* : ligeramente, un
poco

slim¹ ['slɪm] *v* **slimmed; slimming** : adelgazar

slim² *adj* **slimmer; slimmest 1** SLENDER
: esbelto, delgado **2** SCANTY : exiguo,
escaso

slime ['slaɪm] *n* **1** : baba *f* (secretada por
un animal) **2** MUD, SILT : fango *m*, cieno *m*

slimy ['slaɪmi] *adj* **slimier; -est** : viscoso

sling¹ ['slɪŋ] *vt* **slung** ['slʌŋ]; **slinging 1**
THROW : lanzar, tirar **2** HANG : colgar

sling² *n* **1** : honda *f* (arma) **2** : cabestrillo *m* ⟨my arm is in a sling : llevo el
brazo en cabestrillo⟩

slingshot ['slɪŋˌʃɑt] *n* : tiragomas *m*, resortera *f Mex*

slink ['slɪŋk] *vi* **slunk** ['slʌŋk]; **slinking**
: caminar furtivamente

slip¹ ['slɪp] *v* **slipped; slipping** *vi* **1** STEAL
: ir sigilosamente ⟨to slip away : escabullirse⟩ ⟨to slip out the door : escaparse

por la puerta⟩ ⟨an error slipped through
: se deslizó un error⟩ **2** SLIDE : resbalarse, deslizarse ⟨he slipped and fell
: se resbaló y se cayó⟩ **3** FALL, LAPSE
: caer ⟨she slipped into a coma : cayó en
coma⟩ **4** WORSEN, DECLINE : empeorar, bajar ⟨I must be slipping : voy
perdiendo facultades⟩ **5 to let slip** : dejar escapar **6 to slip off** *or* **to slip out of**
TAKE OFF : quitarse (una prenda) **7 to**
slip on/into PUT ON : ponerse (una
prenda) **8 to slip through one's fin**
gers : escaparse de las manos **9 to slip**
up : meter la pata — *vt* **1** PUT : meter,
poner **2** PASS : pasar ⟨she slipped me a
note : me pasó una nota⟩ **3** ESCAPE : escaparse de **4 to slip one's mind**
: olvidársele a uno

slip² *n* **1** PIER : atracadero *m* **2** MISHAP
: percance *m*, contratiempo *m* **3** MIS
TAKE : error *m*, desliz *m* ⟨a slip of the
tongue : un lapsus⟩ **4** PETTICOAT : enagua *f* **5** : injerto *m*, esqueje *m* (de una
planta) **6** RECEIPT, TICKET : recibo *m*,
boleta *f*, ticket *m* **7** slip of paper : papelito *m* **8 to give someone the slip**
: dar esquinazo a alguien

slipknot ['slɪpˌnɑt] *n* : nudo *m* corredizo

slipper ['slɪpər] *n* : zapatilla *f*, pantufla *f*

slipperiness ['slɪpərinəs] *n* **1** : lo resbaloso, lo resbaladizo **2** CRAFTINESS : astucia *f*

slippery ['slɪpəri] *adj* **slipperier; -est 1**
: resbaloso, resbaladizo ⟨a slippery road
: un camino resbaloso⟩ **2** TRICKY : artero, astuto, taimado **3** ELUSIVE : huidizo, escurridizo

slipshod ['slɪpˌʃɑd] *adj* : descuidado, chapucero

slip up *vi* : equivocarse

slit¹ ['slɪt] *vt* **slit; slitting** : cortar, abrir por
lo largo

slit² *n* **1** OPENING : abertura *f*, rendija
f **2** CUT : corte *m*, raja *f*, tajo *m*

slither ['slɪðər] *vi* : deslizarse

sliver ['slɪvər] *n* : astilla *f*

slob ['slɑb] *n* : persona *f* desaliñada ⟨what
a slob! : ¡qué cerdo!⟩

slobber¹ ['slɑbər] *vi* : babear

slobber² *n* : baba *f*

slog¹ ['slɑg] *vi* : trabajar duro

slog² *n* : trabajo *m* largo y arduo

slogan ['sloːgən] *n* : lema *m*, eslogan *m*

sloop ['slu:p] *n* : balandra *f*

slop¹ ['slɑp] *v* **slopped; slopping** *vt* : derramar — *vi* : derramarse

slop² *n* : bazofia *f*

slope¹ ['sloːp] *vi* **sloped; sloping** : inclinarse ⟨the road slopes upward : el
camino sube (en pendiente)⟩

slope² *n* : inclinación *f*, pendiente *f*, declive *m*

sloppiness ['slɑpinəs] *n* **1** : falta *f* de cuidado (en el trabajo, etc.), desaliño *m* (de
aspecto)

sloppy ['slɑpi] *adj* **sloppier; -est 1** : que
chorrea ⟨a sloppy kiss : un beso baboso⟩ **2** : descuidado (en el trabajo,
etc.), desaliñado (de aspecto)

slot ['slɑt] *n* 1 : ranura *f* 2 *or* time slot : espacio *m* (de un programa de televisión, etc.)

sloth ['slɔθ, 'slo:θ] *n* 1 LAZINESS : pereza *f* 2 : perezoso *m* (animal)

slot machine *n* : tragamonedas *mf*, tragaperras *mf Spain*

slotted spoon ['slɑt̬əd-] *n* : espumadera *f*

slouch¹ ['slaʊtʃ] *vi* : andar con los hombros caídos, repantigarse (en un sillón)

slouch² *n* 1 SLUMPING : mala postura *f* 2 BUNGLER, IDLER : haragán *m*, -gana *f*; inepto *m*, -ta *f* ⟨to be no slouch : no quedarse atrás⟩

slough¹ ['slʌf] *vt* : mudar de (piel)

slough² ['slu:, 'slaʊ] *n* SWAMP : ciénaga *f*

Slovak ['slo:vɑk, -,væk] *or* **Slovakian** [slo:'vɑkiən, -'væ-] *n* : eslovaco *m*, -ca *f* — **Slovak** *or* **Slovakian** *adj*

Slovene ['slo:,vi:n] *or* **Slovenian** [slo:'vi:niən] *n* : esloveno *m*, -na *f* — **Slovene** *or* **Slovenian** *adj*

slovenliness ['slʌvənlinəs, 'slʌv-] *adj* : falta *f* de cuidado (en el trabajo, etc.), desaliño *m* (de aspecto)

slovenly ['slʌvənli, 'slʌv-] *adj* : descuidado (en el trabajo, etc.), desaliñado (de aspecto)

slow¹ ['slo:] *vt* : retrasar, reducir la marcha de — *vi* : ir más despacio

slow² *adv* : despacio, lentamente

slow³ *adj* 1 : lento ⟨a slow process : un proceso lento⟩ 2 : atrasado ⟨my watch is slow : mi reloj está atrasado, mi reloj se atrasa⟩ 3 SLUGGISH : lento, poco activo 4 STUPID : lento, torpe, corto de alcances

slow cooker [-'kʊkər] *n* : olla *f* de cocción lenta, olla *f* de cocimiento lento

slowly ['slo:li] *adv* : lentamente, despacio

slow motion *n* : cámara *f* lenta ⟨in slow motion : a cámara lenta⟩

slowness ['slo:nəs] *n* : lentitud *f*, torpeza *f*

slow-witted ['slo:'wɪt̬əd] *adj* : limitado, lento, lerdo

sludge ['slʌdʒ] *n* : aguas *fpl* negras, aguas *fpl* residuales

slug¹ ['slʌg] *vt* **slugged; slugging** : pegarle un porrazo (a alguien)

slug² *n* 1 : babosa *f* (molusco) 2 BULLET : bala *f* 3 TOKEN : ficha *f* 4 BLOW : porrazo *m*, puñetazo *m*

sluggish ['slʌgɪʃ] *adj* : aletargado, lento

sluice¹ ['slu:s] *vt* **sluiced; sluicing** : lavar en agua corriente

sluice² *n* : canal *m*

slum ['slʌm] *n* : barriada *f*, barrio *m* bajo

slumber¹ ['slʌmbər] *vi* : dormir

slumber² *n* : sueño *m*

slump¹ ['slʌmp] *vi* 1 DECLINE, DROP : disminuir, bajar 2 SLOUCH : encorvarse, dejarse caer (en una silla, etc.)

slump² *n* : bajón *m*, declive *m* (económico)

slung → sling

slunk → slink

slur¹ ['slər] *vt* **slurred; slurring** : ligar (notas musicales), tragarse (las palabras)

slur² *n* 1 : ligado *m* (en música), mala pronunciación *f* (de las palabras) 2 ASPERSION : calumnia *f*, difamación *f*

slurp¹ ['slərp] *vi* : beber o comer haciendo ruido — *vt* : sorber ruidosamente

slurp² *n* : sorbo *m* (ruidoso)

slush ['slʌʃ] *n* : nieve *f* medio derretida

slut ['slʌt] *n disparaging + offensive* : fulana *f disparaging*, ramera *f*

sly ['slaɪ] *adj* **slier** ['slaɪər]; **sliest** ['slaɪəst] 1 CUNNING : astuto, taimado 2 UNDERHANDED : solapado — **slyly** *adv*

slyness ['slaɪnəs] *n* : astucia *f*

smack¹ ['smæk] *vi* to smack of : oler a, saber a — *vt* 1 KISS : besar, plantarle un beso (a alguien) 2 SLAP : pegarle una bofetada (a alguien) 3 to smack one's lips : relamerse

smack² *adv* : justo, exactamente ⟨smack in the face : en plena cara⟩

smack³ *n* 1 TASTE, TRACE : sabor *m*, indicio *m* 2 : chasquido *m* (de los labios) 3 SLAP : bofetada *f* 4 KISS : beso *m*

small ['smɔl] *adj* 1 : pequeño, chico ⟨a small house : una casa pequeña⟩ ⟨small change : monedas de poco valor⟩ 2 TRIVIAL : pequeño, insignificante

smallness ['smɔlnəs] *n* : pequeñez *f*

smallpox ['smɔl,pɑks] *n* : viruela *f*

small talk *n* to make small talk : hablar de cosas sin importancia

smart¹ ['smɑrt] *vi* 1 STING : escocer, ~~tingle~~ arder 2 HURT : dolerse, resentirse ⟨to smart under a rejection : dolerse ante un rechazo⟩

smart² *adj* 1 BRIGHT : listo, vivo, inteligente 2 STYLISH : elegante — **smartly** *adv*

smart³ *n* 1 PAIN : escozor *m*, dolor *m* 2 **smarts** *npl* : inteligencia *f*

smarten up ['smɑrtən'ʌp] *vt* : atildar, arreglar — *vi* : atildarse, arreglarse

smartness ['smɑrtnəs] *n* 1 INTELLIGENCE : inteligencia *f* 2 ELEGANCE : elegancia *f*

smartphone ['smɑrt,fo:n] *n* : smartphone *m*, teléfono *m* inteligente

smash¹ ['smæʃ] *vt* 1 BREAK : romper, quebrar, hacer pedazos 2 WRECK : destrozar, arruinar 3 CRASH : estrellar, chocar — *vi* 1 SHATTER : hacerse pedazos, hacerse añicos 2 COLLIDE, CRASH : estrellarse, chocar ⟨to smash against/into something : chocar contra algo⟩

smash² *n* 1 BLOW : golpe *m* 2 COLLISION : choque *m* 3 BANG, CRASH : estrépito *m* 4 HIT, SUCCESS : exitazo *m*

smattering ['smæt̬ərɪŋ] *n* 1 : nociones *fpl* ⟨she has a smattering of programming : tiene nociones de programación⟩ 2 : un poco, unos cuantos ⟨a smattering of spectators : unos cuantos espectadores⟩

smear¹ ['smɪr] *vt* 1 DAUB : embadurnar, untar (mantequilla, etc.) 2 SMUDGE : emborronar 3 SLANDER : calumniar, difamar

smear² *n* 1 SMUDGE : mancha *f* 2 SLANDER : calumnia *f*

smell¹ ['smɛl] *v* **smelled** *or* **smelt** ['smɛlt]; **smelling** *vt* : oler, olfatear ⟨to smell danger : olfatear el peligro⟩ — *vi* : oler ⟨to smell good : oler bien⟩

smell[2] *n* **1** : olfato *m*, sentido *m* del olfato **2** ODOR : olor *m*

smelly ['smɛli] *adj* **smellier; -est** : maloliente

smelt[1] ['smɛlt] *vt* : fundir

smelt[2] *n, pl* **smelts** *or* **smelt** : eperlano *m* (pez)

smidgen ['smɪdʒən] *or* **smidge** ['smɪdʒ] *or* **smidgeon** ['smɪdʒən] *n* BIT : poquito *m*

smile[1] ['smaɪl] *vi* **smiled; smiling** : sonreír

smile[2] *n* : sonrisa *f*

smiley face ['smaɪli-] *n* : carita *f* sonriente (emoticono o dibujo)

smirk[1] ['smərk] *vi* : sonreír con suficiencia

smirk[2] *n* : sonrisa *f* satisfecha

smite ['smaɪt] *vt* **smote** ['smoːt]; **smitten** ['smɪtən] *or* **smote; smiting 1** STRIKE : golpear **2** AFFLICT : afligir

smith ['smɪθ] *n* : herrero *m*, -ra *f*

smithereens [ˌsmɪðəˈriːnz] *npl* : añicos *mpl*

smithy ['smɪθi] *n, pl* **smithies** : herrería *f*

smock ['smɑk] *n* : bata *f*, blusón *m*

smog ['smɑɡ, 'smɔɡ] *n* : smog *m*

smoke[1] ['smoːk] *v* **smoked; smoking** *vi* **1** : echar humo, humear ⟨a smoking chimney : una chimenea que echa humo⟩ **2** : fumar ⟨I don't smoke : no fumo⟩ — *vt* : ahumar (carne, etc.)

smoke[2] *n* : humo *m*

smoked ['smoːkt] *adj* : ahumado

smoke detector [dɪˈtɛktər] *n* : detector *m* de humo

smoker ['smoːkər] *n* : fumador *m*, -dora *f*

smokescreen ['smoːkˌskriːn] *n* : cortina *f* de humo

smoke signal *n* : señal *f* de humo

smokestack ['smoːkˌstæk] *n* : chimenea *f*

smoky ['smoːki] *adj* **smokier; -est 1** SMOKING : humeante **2** : a humo ⟨a smoky flavor : un sabor a humo⟩ **3** : lleno de humo ⟨a smoky room : un cuarto lleno de humo⟩

smolder ['smoːldər] *vi* **1** : arder sin llama **2** : arder (en el corazón) ⟨his anger smoldered : su rabia ardía⟩

smooch ['smuːtʃ] *vi* : besuquearse

smooth[1] ['smuːð] *vt* **1** : alisar ⟨she smoothed (down/back) her hair : alisó el pelo⟩ ⟨he smoothed (out) the tablecloth : alisó los pliegues del mantel⟩ **2** SPREAD : extender ⟨smooth the cream on/onto/over your skin : extienda la crema sobre la piel⟩ **3 to smooth away/over** REMOVE : allanar (dificultades, etc.) ⟨to smooth things over : limar asperezas⟩ **4 to smooth the way for** *or* **to smooth a path for** : allanarle el camino a

smooth[2] *adj* **1** : liso (dícese de una superficie) ⟨smooth skin : piel lisa⟩ **2** : suave (dícese de un movimiento) ⟨a smooth landing : un aterrizaje suave⟩ **3** : sin grumos ⟨a smooth sauce : una salsa sin grumos⟩ **4** : fluido ⟨smooth writing : escritura fluida⟩

smoothly ['smuːðli] *adv* **1** GENTLY, SOFTLY : suavemente **2** EASILY : con facilidad, sin problemas

smoothness ['smuːðnəs] *n* : suavidad *f*

smother ['smʌðər] *vt* **1** SUFFOCATE : ahogar, sofocar **2** COVER : cubrir **3** SUPPRESS : contener — *vi* : asfixiarse

smudge[1] ['smʌdʒ] *v* **smudged; smudging** *vt* : emborronar — *vi* : correrse

smudge[2] *n* : mancha *f*, borrón *m*

smug ['smʌɡ] *adj* **smugger; smuggest** : suficiente, pagado de sí mismo

smuggle ['smʌɡəl] *vt* **-gled; -gling** : contrabandear, pasar de contrabando

smuggler ['smʌɡələr] *n* : contrabandista *mf*

smuggling ['smʌɡəlɪŋ] *n* : contrabando *m* (acto)

smugly ['smʌɡli] *adv* : con suficiencia

smut ['smʌt] *n* **1** SOOT : tizne *m*, hollín *m* **2** OBSCENITY : obscenidad *f*, inmundicia *f*

smutty ['smʌti] *adj* **smuttier; -est 1** SOOTY : tiznado **2** OBSCENE : obsceno, indecente

snack ['snæk] *n* : refrigerio *m*, bocado *m*, tentempié *m* *fam* ⟨an afternoon snack : una merienda⟩

snack bar *n* : cafetería *f*

snag[1] ['snæɡ] *v* **snagged; snagging** *vt* : enganchar — *vi* : engancharse

snag[2] *n* : problema *m*, inconveniente *m*

snail ['sneɪl] *n* : caracol *m*

snake ['sneɪk] *n* : culebra *f*, serpiente *f*

snakebite ['sneɪkˌbaɪt] *n* : mordedura *f* de serpiente

snap[1] ['snæp] *v* **snapped; snapping** *vi* **1** BREAK : romperse, quebrarse (haciendo un chasquido) ⟨the branch snapped : la rama se rompió⟩ **2** : intentar morder (dícese de un perro, etc.) **3** : hablar con severidad ⟨he snapped at me! : ¡me gritó!⟩ **4** : moverse de un golpe ⟨the trap snapped shut : la trampa se cerró de golpe⟩ ⟨the branch snapped back : la rama se volvió de golpe⟩ ⟨the pieces snap together : las piezas se encajan⟩ **5 to snap out of** *fam* : salir de (la depresión, el ensueño, etc.) ⟨snap out of it! : ¡anímate!, ¡espabílate!⟩ **6 to snap to it** *fam* : moverse, apurarse — *vt* **1** BREAK : partir (en dos), quebrar **2** : hacer (algo) de un golpe ⟨she snapped it open : lo abrió de golpe⟩ **3** RETORT : decir bruscamente **4** CLICK : chasquear ⟨to snap one's fingers : chasquear los dedos⟩ **5 to snap up** : no dejar escapar

snap[2] *n* **1** CLICK, CRACK : chasquido *m* **2** FASTENER : broche *m* **3** CINCH : cosa *f* fácil ⟨it's a snap : es facilísimo⟩

snapdragon ['snæpˌdræɡən] *n* : dragón *m* (flor)

snapper ['snæpər] → **red snapper**

snappy ['snæpi] *adj* **snappier; -est 1** FAST : rápido ⟨make it snappy! : ¡date prisa!⟩ **2** LIVELY : vivaz **3** CHILLY : frío **4** STYLISH : elegante

snapshot ['snæpˌʃɑt] *n* : instantánea *f*

snare[1] ['snær] *vt* **snared; snaring** : atrapar

snare[2] *n* : trampa *f*, red *f*

snare drum *n* : tambor *m* con bordón

snarl[1] ['snɑrl] *vi* **1** TANGLE : enmarañar, enredar **2** GROWL : gruñir

snarl² *n* **1** TANGLE : enredo *m*, maraña *f* **2** GROWL : gruñido *m*

snatch¹ [ˈsnætʃ] *vt* : arrebatar

snatch² *n* : fragmento *m*

sneak¹ [ˈsniːk] *vi* : ir a hurtadillas ⟨to sneak in/out : entrar/salir a escondidas⟩ ⟨to sneak away : escabullirse⟩ — *vt* : hacer furtivamente ⟨to sneak a look : mirar con disimulo⟩ ⟨he sneaked a smoke : fumó un cigarrillo a escondidas⟩

sneak² *n* : soplón *m*, -plona *f*

sneaker [ˈsniːkər] *npl* : tenis *m*, zapatilla *f* ⟨a pair of sneakers : un par de tenis/zapatillas⟩

sneaky [ˈsniːki] *adj* sneakier; -est : solapado

sneer¹ [ˈsnɪr] *vi* : sonreír con desprecio

sneer² *n* : sonrisa *f* de desprecio

sneeze¹ [ˈsniːz] *vi* sneezed; sneezing : estornudar

sneeze² *n* : estornudo *m*

snicker¹ [ˈsnɪkər] *vi* : reírse (disimuladamente)

snicker² *n* : risita *f*

snide [ˈsnaɪd] *adj* : sarcástico

sniff¹ [ˈsnɪf] *vi* **1** SMELL : oler, husmear (dícese de los animales) **2** to sniff at : despreciar, desdeñar — *vt* **1** SMELL : oler **2** to sniff out : olerse, husmear

sniff² *n* **1** SNIFFING : aspiración *f* por la nariz **2** SMELL : olor *m*

sniffle [ˈsnɪfəl] *vi* -fled; -fling : respirar con la nariz congestionada

sniffles [ˈsnɪfəlz] *npl* : resfriado *m*

snigger¹ [ˈsnɪɡər] → **snicker¹**

snigger² → **snicker²**

snip¹ [ˈsnɪp] *vt* snipped; snipping : cortar (con tijeras)

snip² *n* : tijeretada *f*, recorte *m*

snipe¹ [ˈsnaɪp] *vi* sniped; sniping : disparar

snipe² *n*, *pl* snipes *or* snipe : agachadiza *f*

sniper [ˈsnaɪpər] *n* : francotirador *m*, -dora *f*

snippet [ˈsnɪpət] *n* : fragmento *m* (de un texto, etc.)

snitch¹ [ˈsnɪtʃ] *v fam vi* : cantar (a la policía, etc.) ⟨to snitch on someone : acusar/delatar a alguien⟩ — *vt* STEAL : robar

snitch² *n fam* : chivato *m*, -ta *f*

snivel [ˈsnɪvəl] *vi* -veled *or* -velled; -veling *or* -velling **1** → **snuffle 2** WHINE : lloriquear

snob [ˈsnɑb] *n* : esnob *mf*, snob *mf*

snobbery [ˈsnɑbəri] *n*, *pl* -beries : esnobismo *m*

snobbish [ˈsnɑbɪʃ] *adj* : esnob, snob

snobbishness [ˈsnɑbɪʃnəs] *n* : esnobismo *m*

snoop¹ [ˈsnuːp] *vi* : husmear, curiosear

snoop² *n* : fisgón *m*, -gona *f*

snooty [ˈsnuːti] *adj* snootier; -est HAUGHTY : esnob, snob, altanero, altivo

snooze¹ [ˈsnuːz] *vi* snoozed; snoozing : dormitar

snooze² *n* : siestecita *f*, siestita *f*

snore¹ [ˈsnor] *vi* snored; snoring : roncar

snore² *n* : ronquido *m*

snorkel¹ [ˈsnorkəl] *vi* : bucear con esnórquel

snorkel² *n* : esnórquel *m*, snorkel *m*, tubo *m* respiratorio/respirador

snort¹ [ˈsnort] *vi* : bufar, resoplar

snort² *n* : bufido *m*, resoplo *m*

snot [ˈsnɑt] *n* : mocos *mpl*

snotty [ˈsnɑti] *adj* snottier; -est **1** → **snooty 2** : lleno de mocos

snout [ˈsnaʊt] *n* : hocico *m*, morro *m*

snow¹ [ˈsnoː] *vi* **1** : nevar ⟨I'm snowed in : estoy aislado por la nieve⟩ **2** to be snowed under : estar inundado

snow² *n* : nieve *f*

snowball¹ [ˈsnoːˌbɔl] *vi* : aumentar, agravarse (rápidamente)

snowball² *n* : bola *f* de nieve

snowboard [ˈsnoːˌbord] *n* : snowboard *m*

snowboarding [ˈsnoːˌbordɪŋ] *n* : snowboard *m* (deporte)

snowcapped [ˈsnoːˌkæpt] *adj* : nevado

snowdrift [ˈsnoːˌdrɪft] *n* : ventisquero *m*

snowdrop [ˈsnoːˌdrɑp] *n* : campanilla *f* blanca

snowfall [ˈsnoːˌfɔl] *n* : nevada *f*

snowflake [ˈsnoːˌfleɪk] *n* : copo *m* de nieve

snowman [ˈsnoːˌmæn] *n*, *pl* -men [-mən, -ˌmɛn] : muñeco *m* de nieve

snowplow [ˈsnoːˌplaʊ] *n* : quitanieves *m*

snowshoe [ˈsnoːˌʃuː] *n* : raqueta *f* (para nieve)

snowstorm [ˈsnoːˌstorm] *n* : tormenta *f* de nieve, ventisca *f*

snow–white *adj* : blanco como la nieve

snowy [ˈsnoːi] *adj* snowier; -est : nevoso ⟨a snowy road : un camino nevado⟩

snub¹ [ˈsnʌb] *vt* snubbed; snubbing : desairar

snub² *n* : desaire *m*

snub–nosed [ˈsnʌbˌnoːzd] *adj* : de nariz respingada

snuff¹ [ˈsnʌf] *vt* **1** : apagar (una vela) **2** : sorber (algo) por la nariz

snuff² *n* : rapé *m*

snuffle [ˈsnʌfəl] *vi* -fled; -fling : respirar con la nariz congestionada

snug [ˈsnʌɡ] *adj* snugger; snuggest **1** COMFORTABLE : cómodo **2** TIGHT : ajustado, ceñido ⟨snug pants : pantalones ajustados⟩

snuggle [ˈsnʌɡəl] *vi* -gled; -gling : acurrucarse ⟨to snuggle up to someone : arrimársele a alguien⟩

snugly [ˈsnʌɡli] *adv* **1** COMFORTABLY : cómodamente **2** : de manera ajustada ⟨the shirt fits snugly : la camisa queda ajustada⟩

so¹ [ˈsoː] *adv* **1** (indicating a stated or suggested degree) : tan, tanto ⟨he'd never been so happy : nunca había estado tan contento⟩ ⟨she was so tired that she almost fell asleep : estaba tan cansada que casi se durmió⟩ ⟨would you be so kind as to help me? : ¿tendría la amabilidad de ayudarme?⟩ ⟨it's not so much a science as an art : no es tanto una ciencia como un arte⟩ ⟨all the more so because : tanto más cuanto que⟩ ⟨never more so than : nunca más que⟩ **2** VERY : tan, tanto ⟨it's so much fun : es tan divertido⟩ ⟨I'm so glad to meet you : me alegro tanto de conocerte⟩ ⟨he loves her so : la quiere tanto⟩ ⟨not so long ago : no hace mucho tiempo⟩ ⟨thank you so much : muchísimas gracias⟩ **3** ALSO : también ⟨so do I : yo también⟩ **4** THUS : así, de esta manera ⟨and so it began : y así empezó⟩ ⟨it so happened that . . . : resultó que . . .⟩ **5** *(used for emphasis)* *fam* ⟨it's so not fair : es totalmente injusto⟩ ⟨I so wanted to go : tenía tantas ganas de ir⟩ **6** CONSEQUENTLY : por lo tanto **7 and so forth/on** : etcétera **8 so much for** *(indicating that something has ended)* ⟨so much for that idea : hasta ahí llegó esa idea⟩ **9 so much so (that)** : tanto es así que **10 without so much as** : sin siquiera

so² *adj* : cierto, verdad ⟨it's not so : no es cierto, no es verdad⟩ ⟨is that so? : ¿ah, sí?⟩

so³ *conj* **1** THEREFORE : así que ⟨he didn't answer, so I called again : no contestó, así que lo llamé otra vez⟩ **2 so that** : para que, así que, de manera que ⟨move over so I can sit down : córrete para que pueda sentarme⟩ ⟨we left early so that we would arrive on time : salimos temprano para llegar a tiempo⟩ **3 so what?** : ¿y qué?

so⁴ *pron* **1** *(referring to something indicated or suggested)* ⟨do you think so? : ¿tú crees?⟩ ⟨so it would seem : eso/así parece⟩ ⟨I told her so : se lo dije⟩ ⟨he's ready, or so he says : según dice, está listo⟩ ⟨do it like so : hazlo así⟩ ⟨so be it : así sea⟩ ⟨if so : si es así⟩ ⟨I'm afraid so : me temo que sí⟩ **2 or so** : más o menos ⟨a week or so : una semana, más o menos⟩

soak¹ [ˈsoːk] *vi* : estar en remojo — *vt* **1** : poner en remojo **2** DRENCH : empapar **3 to soak up** ABSORB : absorber

soak² *n* : remojo *m*

so-and-so *n* : fulano *m*, -na *f*

soap¹ [ˈsoːp] *vt* : enjabonar

soap² *n* **1** : jabón *m* **2** → **soap opera**

soap opera *n* : culebrón *m*, telenovela *f*

soapsuds [ˈsoːpˌsʌdz] → **suds**

soapy [ˈsoːpi] *adj* **soapier; -est** : jabonoso ⟨a soapy taste : un gusto a jabón⟩ ⟨a soapy texture : una textura de jabón⟩

soar [ˈsor] *vi* **1** FLY : volar **2** RISE : remontar el vuelo (dícese de las aves) ⟨her hopes soared : su esperanza renació⟩ ⟨prices are soaring : los precios están subiendo vertiginosamente⟩

sob¹ [ˈsab] *vi* **sobbed; sobbing** : sollozar

sob² *n* : sollozo *m*

sober¹ [ˈsoːbər] *adj* **1** : sobrio ⟨he's not sober enough to drive : está demasiado borracho para manejar⟩ **2** SERIOUS : serio

sober² *vi* **1** SADDEN : entristecer **2 to sober up** : pasársele la borrachera

soberly [ˈsoːbərli] *adv* **1** : sobriamente **2** SERIOUSLY : seriamente

sobriety [səˈbraɪəti, soː-] *n* **1** : sobriedad *f*

⟨sobriety test : prueba de alcoholemia⟩ **2** SERIOUSNESS : seriedad *f*

so-called [ˈsoːˈkɔld] *adj* : supuesto, presunto ⟨the so-called experts : los expertos, así llamados⟩

soccer [ˈsakər] *n* : futbol *m*, fútbol *m*

sociability [ˌsoːʃəˈbɪləti] *n* : sociabilidad *f*

sociable [ˈsoːʃəbəl] *adj* : sociable

social¹ [ˈsoːʃəl] *adj* : social — **socially** *adv*

social² *n* : reunión *f* social

socialism [ˈsoːʃəˌlɪzəm] *n* : socialismo *m*

socialist¹ [ˈsoːʃəlɪst] *adj* : socialista

socialist² *n* : socialista *mf*

socialize [ˈsoːʃəˌlaɪz] *v* **-ized; -izing** *vt* **1** NATIONALIZE : nacionalizar **2** : socializar (en psicología) — *vi* : alternar, circular ⟨to socialize with friends : alternar con amigos⟩

social media *ns & pl* : redes *fpl* sociales, medios *mpl* sociales

social networking *n* : establecimiento *m* y mantenimiento *m* de una red de contactos en línea ⟨a social networking site : un sitio de redes sociales⟩

social security *n* : seguridad *f* social

social work *n* : asistencia *f* social

social worker *n* : asistente *m*, -ta *f* social

society [səˈsaɪəti] *n*, *pl* **-eties 1** COMPANIONSHIP : compañía *f* **2** : sociedad *f* ⟨a democratic society : una sociedad democrática⟩ ⟨high society : alta sociedad⟩ **3** ASSOCIATION : sociedad *f*, asociación *f*

socioeconomic [ˌsoːsioːˌiːkəˈnɑmɪk, -ˌɛkə-] *adj* : socioeconómico

sociological [ˌsoːsiəˈlɑdʒɪkəl] *adj* : sociológico

sociologist [ˌsoːsiˈɑlədʒɪst] *n* : sociólogo *m*, -ga *f*

sociology [ˌsoːsiˈɑlədʒi] *n* : sociología *f*

sock¹ [ˈsak] *vt* : pegar, golpear, darle un puñetazo a

sock² *n* **1** *pl* **socks** *or* **sox** [ˈsaks] : calcetín *m*, media *f* ⟨shoes and socks : zapatos y calcetines⟩ **2** *pl* **socks** [ˈsaks] PUNCH : puñetazo *m*

socket [ˈsakət] *n* **1** *or* **electric socket** : enchufe *m*, toma *f* de corriente **2** : glena *f* (de una articulación) ⟨shoulder socket : glena del hombro⟩ **3 eye socket** : órbita *f*, cuenca *f*

sod¹ [ˈsad] *vt* **sodded; sodding** : cubrir de césped

sod² *n* TURF : césped *m*, tepe *m*

soda [ˈsoːdə] *n* **1** *or* **soda water** : soda *f* **2** *or* **soda pop** : gaseosa *f*; refresco *m*; fresco *m*; soda *f* *CA*, *Car* **3** *or* **ice–cream soda** : refresco *m* con helado

sodden [ˈsadən] *adj* SOGGY : empapado

sodium [ˈsoːdiəm] *n* : sodio *m*

sodium bicarbonate *n* : bicarbonato *m* de soda

sodium chloride → **salt**

sofa [ˈsoːfə] *n* : sofá *m*

soft [ˈsɔft] *adj* **1** : blando ⟨a soft pillow : una almohada blanda⟩ **2** SMOOTH : suave (dícese de las texturas, de los sonidos, etc.) **3** NONALCOHOLIC : no alcohólico ⟨a soft drink : un refresco⟩

softball [ˈsɔftˌbɔl] *n* : softbol *m*

soft–boiled ['soft'boɪld] *adj* : pasado por agua

soften ['sofən] *vt* : ablandar (algo sólido), suavizar (la piel, un golpe, etc.), amortiguar (un impacto) — *vi* : ablandarse, suavizarse

softener ['sofənər] *n* : suavizante *m*

softly ['softli] *adv* : suavemente ⟨she spoke softly : habló en voz baja⟩

softness ['softnəs] *n* **1** : blandura *f*, lo blando (de una almohada, de la mantequilla, etc.) **2** SMOOTHNESS : suavidad *f*

soft–spoken ['soft'spo:kən] *adj* : de voz suave

software ['soft,wær] *n* : software *m*

soggy ['sagi] *adj* **soggier; -est** : empapado

soil[1] ['soɪl] *vt* : ensuciar — *vi* : ensuciarse

soil[2] *n* **1** DIRTINESS : suciedad *f* **2** DIRT, EARTH : suelo *m*, tierra *f* **3** COUNTRY : patria *f* ⟨her native soil : su tierra natal⟩

sojourn[1] ['so:,dʒərn, so:'dʒərn] *vi* : pasar una temporada

sojourn[2] *n* : estadía *f*, estancia *f*, permanencia *f*

sol ['so:l] *n* **1** : sol *m* (en el canto) **2** : sol *m* (unidad monetaria)

solace ['saləs] *n* : consuelo *m*

solar ['so:lər] *adj* : solar ⟨the solar system : el sistema solar⟩ ⟨solar energy : energía solar⟩

sold → **sell**

solder[1] ['sadər, 'so-] *vt* : soldar

solder[2] *n* : soldadura *f*

soldier[1] ['so:ldʒər] *vi* : servir como soldado

soldier[2] *n* : soldado *mf*

sole[1] ['so:l] *adj* : único

sole[2] *n* **1** : suela *f* (de un zapato) **2** : lenguado *m* (pez)

solely ['so:li] *adv* : únicamente, sólo

solemn ['saləm] *adj* : solemne, serio — **solemnly** *adv*

solemnity [sə'lɛmnəti] *n, pl* **-ties** : solemnidad *f*

sol–fa [,so:l'fa] *n* : solfeo *m*

solicit [sə'lɪsət] *vt* : solicitar

solicitous [sə'lɪsətəs] *adj* : solícito

solicitude [sə'lɪsə,tu:d, -,tju:d] *n* : solicitud *f*

solid[1] ['saləd] *adj* **1** : macizo ⟨a solid rubber ball : una bola maciza de caucho⟩ **2** CUBIC : tridimensional **3** COMPACT : compacto, denso **4** STURDY : sólido **5** CONTINUOUS : seguido, continuo ⟨two solid hours : dos horas seguidas⟩ ⟨a solid line : una línea continua⟩ **6** UNANIMOUS : unánime **7** DEPENDABLE : serio, fiable **8** PURE : macizo, puro ⟨solid gold : oro macizo⟩

solid[2] *n* : sólido *m*

solidarity [,salə'dærəti] *n* : solidaridad *f*

solidify [sə'lɪdə,faɪ] *v* **-fied; -fying** *vt* : solidificar — *vi* : solidificarse

solidity [sə'lɪdəti] *n, pl* **-ties** : solidez *f*

solidly ['salədli] *adv* **1** : sólidamente **2** UNANIMOUSLY : unánimemente

soliloquy [sə'lɪləkwi] *n, pl* **-quies** : soliloquio *m*

solitaire ['salə,tær] *n* : solitario *m*

solitary ['salə,teri] *adj* **1** ALONE : solitario **2** SECLUDED : apartado, retirado **3** SINGLE : solo

solitude ['salə,tu:d, -,tju:d] *n* : soledad *f*

solo[1] ['so:,lo:] *vi* : volar en solitario (dícese de un piloto)

solo[2] *adv & adj* : en solitario, a solas

solo[3] *n, pl* **solos** : solo *m*

soloist ['so:loɪst] *n* : solista *mf*

solstice ['salstɪs] *n* : solsticio *m*

soluble ['saljəbəl] *adj* : soluble

solution [sə'lu:ʃən] *n* : solución *f*

solve ['salv] *vt* **solved; solving** : resolver, solucionar

solvency ['salvəntsi] *n* : solvencia *f*

solvent ['salvənt] *n* : solvente *m*

somber ['sambər] *adj* **1** DARK : sombrío, oscuro ⟨somber colors : colores oscuros⟩ **2** GRAVE : sombrío, serio **3** MELANCHOLY : sombrío, lúgubre

sombrero [səm'brer,o:] *n, pl* **-ros** : sombrero *m* (mexicano)

some[1] ['sʌm] *adv* **1** : unos, unas ⟨some 80 people came, 80-some people came : unas 80 personas vinieron⟩ **2** : un poco ⟨he helped me some *fam* : me ayudó un poco⟩ ⟨I need to work on it some more : necesito pulirlo un poco más⟩

some[2] *adj* **1** : un, algún ⟨some lady stopped me : una mujer me detuvo⟩ ⟨some distant galaxy : alguna galaxia lejana⟩ ⟨there must be some mistake : debe de haber algún error⟩ **2** : algo de, un poco de ⟨he drank some water : tomó (un poco de) agua⟩ **3** : unos ⟨do you want some apples? : ¿quieres unas manzanas?⟩ ⟨some years ago : hace varios años⟩ **4** *fam* (*expressing approval*) ⟨that was some game! : ¡vaya partido!⟩ **5** *fam* (*expressing disapproval*) ⟨you've got some nerve! : ¡qué cara tienes!⟩ ⟨some friend he is! : ¡qué clase de amigo!⟩

some[3] *pron* **1** : algunos ⟨some went, others stayed : algunos se fueron, otros se quedaron⟩ ⟨some of my friends : algunos de mis amigos⟩ ⟨some of the movies : algunas de las películas⟩ **2** : un poco, algo ⟨there's some left : queda un poco⟩ ⟨some of the cake : parte del pastel⟩ ⟨I have gum; do you want some? : tengo chicle, ¿quieres?⟩

somebody ['sʌmbədi, -,badi] *pron* : alguien

someday ['sʌm,deɪ] *adv* : algún día

somehow ['sʌm,haʊ] *adv* **1** : de alguna manera, de algún modo ⟨I'll do it somehow : lo haré de alguna manera⟩ **2** : por alguna razón ⟨somehow I don't trust her : por alguna razón no me fío de ella⟩

someone ['sʌm,wʌn] *pron* : alguien

someplace ['sʌm,pleɪs] → **somewhere**

somersault[1] ['sʌmər,solt] *vi* : dar volteretas, dar un salto mortal

somersault[2] *n* : voltereta *f*, salto *m* mortal

something ['sʌmθɪŋ] *pron* : algo ⟨I want something else : quiero otra cosa⟩ ⟨she's writing a novel or something : está escribiendo una novela o no sé qué⟩

sometime ['sʌm,taɪm] *adv* : algún día, en algún momento ⟨sometime next month : durante el mes que viene⟩

sometimes ['sʌm,taɪmz] *adv* : a veces, algunas veces, de vez en cuando

somewhat ['sʌm,hwʌt, -,hwɑt] *adv* : algo, un tanto

somewhere ['sʌm,hwer] *adv* **1** (*indicating location*) : en algún lugar ⟨it must be somewhere else : estará en otra parte⟩ **2** (*indicating destination*) : a algún lugar ⟨she went somewhere else : fue a otra parte⟩ **3** APPROXIMATELY : alrededor de ⟨somewhere around a thousand dollars : alrededor de mil dólares⟩ ⟨he's somewhere in his thirties : tiene unos treinta años, tiene treinta y tantos/pico⟩

son ['sʌn] *n* : hijo *m*

sonar ['so:,nɑr] *n* : sonar *m*

sonata [sə'nɑtə] *n* : sonata *f*

song ['sɔŋ] *n* : canción *f*, canto *m* (de un pájaro)

songbird ['sɔŋ,bərd] *n* : pájaro *m* cantor

songbook ['sɔŋ,bʊk] *n* : cancionero *m*

songwriter ['sɔŋ,raɪtər] *n* : compositor *m*, -tora *f*

sonic ['sɑnɪk] *adj* **1** : sónico **2 sonic boom** : estampido *m* sónico

son-in-law ['sʌnɪn,lɔ] *n, pl* **sons-in-law** : yerno *m*, hijo *m* político

sonnet ['sɑnət] *n* : soneto *m*

son of a bitch *n, pl* **sons of bitches** *sometimes offensive* : hijo *m* de puta *sometimes offensive*

sonorous ['sɑnərəs, sə'nɔrəs] *adj* : sonoro

soon ['su:n] *adv* **1** : pronto, dentro de poco ⟨he'll arrive soon : llegará pronto⟩ **2** QUICKLY : pronto ⟨as soon as possible : lo más pronto posible⟩ ⟨the sooner the better : cuanto antes mejor⟩ **3** : de buena gana ⟨I'd sooner walk : prefiero caminar⟩

soot ['sʊt, 'su:t, 'sʌt] *n* : hollín *m*, tizne *m*

soothe ['su:ð] *vt* **soothed; soothing 1** CALM : calmar, tranquilizar **2** RELIEVE : aliviar

soothsayer ['su:θ,seɪər] *n* : adivino *m*, -na *f*

sooty ['sʊti, 'su:-, 'sʌ-] *adj* **sootier; -est** : cubierto de hollín, tiznado

sop¹ ['sɑp] *vt* **sopped; sopping 1** DIP : mojar **2** SOAK : empapar **3 to sop up** : rebañar, absorber

sop² *n* **1** CONCESSION : concesión *f* **2** BRIBE : soborno *m*

sophisticated [sə'fɪstə,keɪtəd] *adj* **1** : sofisticado **2** COMPLEX : complejo

sophistication [sə,fɪstə'keɪʃən] *n* **1** COMPLEXITY : complejidad *f* **2** : sofisticación *f*

sophomore ['sɑf,mor, 'sɑfə,mor] *n* : estudiante *mf* de segundo año

sophistry ['sɑfəstri] *n* : sofistería *f*

soporific [,sɑpə'rɪfɪk, ,so:-] *adj* : soporífero

soprano [sə'præ,no:] *n, pl* **-nos** : soprano *mf*

sorbet [,sɔr'beɪ] *n* : sorbete *m*

sorcerer ['sɔrsərər] *n* : hechicero *m*, brujo *m*, mago *m*

sorceress ['sɔrsərəs] *n* : hechicera *f*, bruja *f*, maga *f*

sorcery ['sɔrsəri] *n* : hechicería *f*, brujería *f*

sordid ['sɔrdɪd] *adj* : sórdido

sore¹ ['sor] *adj* **sorer; sorest 1** PAINFUL : dolorido, doloroso ⟨I have a sore throat : me duele la garganta⟩ **2** ACUTE, SEVERE : extremo, grande ⟨in sore straits : en grandes apuros⟩ **3** ANGRY : enojado, enfadado

sore² *n* : llaga *f*

sorely ['sorli] *adv* : muchísimo ⟨it was sorely needed : se necesitaba urgentemente⟩ ⟨she was sorely missed : la echaban mucho de menos⟩

soreness ['sornəs] *n* : dolor *m*

sorghum ['sɔrgəm] *n* : sorgo *m*

sorority [sə'rɔrəti] *n, pl* **-ties** : hermandad *f* (de estudiantes femeninas)

sorrel ['sɔrəl] *n* **1** : alazán *m* (color o animal) **2** : acedera *f* (hierba)

sorrow ['sar,o:] *n* : pesar *m*, dolor *m*, pena *f*

sorrowful ['sarofəl] *adj* : triste, afligido, apenado

sorrowfully ['sarofəli] *adv* : con tristeza

sorry ['sari] *adj* **sorrier; -est 1** PITIFUL : lastimero, lastimoso ⟨to be a sorry sight : tener un aspecto lamentable/horrible⟩ **2 to be sorry** : lamentar ⟨I'm sorry : lo siento⟩ ⟨I'm sorry to have to tell you that . . . : siento tener que decirte que . . .⟩ ⟨I'm sorry, but I disagree : lo siento, pero no estoy de acuerdo⟩ ⟨I'm sorry to disturb you : siento molestarlo⟩ **3 to feel sorry for** : compadecer ⟨I feel sorry for him : me da pena⟩ ⟨to feel sorry for oneself : lamentarse de su suerte⟩

sort¹ ['sort] *vt* **1** : dividir en grupos **2** CLASSIFY : clasificar **3 to sort out** ORGANIZE : poner en orden **4 to sort out** RESOLVE : resolver

sort² *n* **1** KIND : tipo *m*, clase *f* ⟨a sort of writer : una especie de escritor⟩ ⟨all sorts of : todo tipo de⟩ **2** NATURE : índole *f* **3 of the sort** ⟨I said nothing of the sort : no dije nada semejante⟩ **4 of sorts** *or* **of a sort** ⟨he's a poet of sorts : es poeta, si se le puede llamar así⟩ **5 out of sorts** : de mal humor **6 sort of** : más o menos **7 sort of a** : una especie de

sortie ['sorti, sor'ti:] *n* : salida *f*

SOS [,ɛs,o:'ɛs] *n* : SOS *m*

so-so ['so:'so:] *adj & adv* : así así, de modo regular

soufflé [su:'fleɪ] *n* : suflé *m*

sought → seek

soul ['so:l] *n* **1** SPIRIT : alma *f* **2** ESSENCE : esencia *f* **3** PERSON : persona *f*, alma *f*

soulful ['so:lfəl] *adj* : conmovedor, lleno de emoción

sound¹ ['saʊnd] *vt* **1** : sondar (en navegación) **2** *or* **to sound out** PROBE : sondear **3** : hacer sonar, tocar (una trompeta, etc.) — *vi* **1** : sonar ⟨the alarm sounded : la alarma sonó⟩ **2** SEEM : parecer

sound² *adj* **1** HEALTHY : sano ⟨safe and sound : sano y salvo⟩ ⟨of sound mind and body : en pleno uso de sus facultades⟩ **2** FIRM, SOLID : sólido **3** SENSIBLE : lógico, sensato **4** DEEP : profundo ⟨a sound sleep : un sueño profundo⟩

sound³ *adv* : profundamente ⟨sound asleep : profundamente dormido⟩

sound⁴ *n* **1** : sonido *m* ⟨the speed of sound : la velocidad del sonido⟩ **2** NOISE : sonido *m*, ruido *m* ⟨I heard a sound : oí un sonido⟩ **3** CHANNEL : brazo *m* de mar, canal *m* (ancho)

soundless ['saʊndləs] *adj* : sordo

soundlessly ['saʊndləsli] *adv* : silenciosamente

soundly ['saʊndli] *adv* **1** SOLIDLY : sólidamente **2** SENSIBLY : lógicamente, sensatamente **3** DEEPLY : profundamente ⟨sleeping soundly : durmiendo profundamente⟩

soundness ['saʊndnəs] *n* **1** SOLIDITY : solidez *f* **2** SENSIBLENESS : sensatez *f*, solidez *f*

soundproof ['saʊnd,pru:f] *adj* : insonorizado

sound system *n* : equipo *m* de sonido

soundtrack ['saʊnd,træk] *n* : banda *f* sonora

sound wave *n* : onda *f* sonora

soup ['su:p] *n* : sopa *f*

sour¹ ['saʊər] *vi* : agriarse, cortarse (dícese de la leche) — *vt* : agriar, cortar (leche)

sour² *adj* **1** ACID : agrio, ácido (dícese de la fruta, etc.), cortado (dícese de la leche) **2** DISAGREEABLE : desagradable, agrio

source ['sors] *n* : fuente *f*, origen *m*, nacimiento *m* (de un río)

sourness ['saʊərnəs] *n* : acidez *f*

soursop ['saʊər,sɑp] *n* : guanábana *f*

south¹ ['saʊθ] *adv* : al sur, hacia el sur ⟨the window looks south : la ventana mira al sur⟩ ⟨she continued south : continuó hacia el sur⟩

south² *adj* : sur, del sur ⟨the south entrance : la entrada sur⟩ ⟨South America : Sudamérica, América del Sur⟩

south³ *n* : sur *m*

South African *n* : sudafricano *m*, -na *f* — **South African** *adj*

South American¹ *adj* : sudamericano, suramericano

South American² *n* : sudamericano *m*, -na *f*; suramericano *m*, -na *f*

southbound ['saʊθ,baʊnd] *adj* : con rumbo al sur

southeast¹ [saʊ'θi:st] *adj* : sureste, sudeste, del sureste

southeast² *n* : sureste *m*, sudeste *m*

southeasterly [saʊ'θi:stərli] *adv & adj* **1** : del sureste (dícese del viento) **2** : hacia el sureste

southeastern [saʊ'θi:stərn] *adj* → **southeast¹**

southerly ['sʌðərli] *adv & adj* : del sur

southern ['sʌðərn] *adj* : sur, sureño, meridional, austral ⟨a southern city : una ciudad del sur del país, una ciudad meridional⟩ ⟨the southern side : el lado sur⟩

Southerner ['sʌðərnər] *n* : sureño *m*, -ña *f*

South Pole : Polo *m* Sur

southward ['saʊθwərd] *or* **southwards** [-wərdz] *adv & adj* : hacia el sur

southwest¹ [saʊθ'wɛst, as a nautical term often saʊ'wɛst] *adj* : suroeste, sudoeste, del suroeste

southwest² *n* : suroeste *m*, sudoeste *m*

southwesterly [saʊθ'wɛstərli] *adv & adj* **1** : del suroeste (dícese del viento) **2** : hacia el suroeste

southwestern [saʊθ'wɛstərn] *adj* → **southwest¹**

souvenir [,su:və'nɪr, 'su:və,-] *n* : recuerdo *m*, souvenir *m*

sovereign¹ ['sɑvərən] *adj* : soberano

sovereign² *n* **1** : soberano *m*, -na *f* (monarca) **2** : soberano *m* (moneda)

sovereignty ['sɑvərənti] *n*, *pl* **-ties** : soberanía *f*

Soviet ['so:vi,ɛt, 'sɑ-, -viət] *adj* : soviético

sow¹ ['so:] *vt* **sowed; sown** ['so:n] *or* **sowed; sowing 1** PLANT : sembrar **2** SCATTER : esparcir

sow² ['saʊ] *n* : cerda *f*

sox → sock

soy ['sɔɪ] *n* : soya *f*, soja *f*

soybean ['sɔɪ,bi:n] *n* : soya *f*, soja *f*

spa ['spɑ] *n* : balneario *m*

space¹ ['speɪs] *vt* **spaced; spacing** : espaciar

space² *n* **1** PERIOD : espacio *m*, lapso *m*, período *m* **2** ROOM : espacio *m*, sitio *m*, lugar *m* ⟨is there space for me? : ¿hay sitio para mí?⟩ **3** : espacio *m* ⟨blank space : espacio en blanco⟩ **4** : espacio *m* (en física) **5** PLACE : plaza *f*, sitio *m* ⟨to reserve space : reservar plazas⟩ ⟨parking space : sitio para estacionarse⟩

spacecraft ['speɪs,kræft] *n* : nave *f* espacial

spaceflight ['speɪs,flaɪt] *n* : vuelo *m* espacial

spaceman ['speɪsmən, -,mæn] *n*, *pl* **-men** [-mən, -,mɛn] : astronauta *m*, cosmonauta *m*

spaceship ['speɪs,ʃɪp] *n* : nave *f* espacial

space shuttle *n* : transbordador *m* espacial

space station *n* : estación *f* espacial

space suit *n* : traje *m* espacial

spacious ['speɪʃəs] *adj* : espacioso, amplio

spade¹ ['speɪd] *v* **spaded; spading** *vt* : palear — *vi* : usar una pala

spade² *n* **1** SHOVEL : pala *f* **2** : pica *f* (naipe)

spaghetti [spə'gɛtɪ] *n* : espagueti *m*, espaguetis *mpl*, spaghetti *mpl*

spam¹ ['spæm] *vt* **spammed; spamming** : enviarle spam a

spam² *n* : spam *m*, correo *m* electrónico no solicitado

Spam *trademark* se usa para un tipo de carne enlatada

span¹ ['spæn] *vt* **spanned; spanning** : abarcar (un período de tiempo), extenderse sobre (un espacio)

span² *n* **1** : lapso *m*, espacio *m* (de tiempo) ⟨life span : duración de la vida⟩ **2** : luz *f* (entre dos soportes)

spangle ['spæŋgəl] n : lentejuela f
Spaniard ['spænjərd] n : español m, -ñola f
spaniel ['spænjəl] n : spaniel m
Spanish¹ ['spænɪʃ] adj : español
Spanish² n 1 : español m (idioma) 2 the Spanish (used with a plural verb) : los españoles
spank ['spæŋk] vt : darle nalgadas (a alguien)
spar¹ ['spar] vi sparred; sparring : entrenarse (en boxeo)
spar² n : palo m, verga f (de un barco)
spare¹ ['spær] vt spared; sparing 1 : perdonar ⟨to spare someone's life : perdonarle la vida a alguien⟩ ⟨to spare someone's feelings : no herir los sentimientos de alguien⟩ ⟨the fire spared their house : su casa se salvó del fuego⟩ 2 SAVE : ahorrar, evitar ⟨he spared us the trouble/embarrassment : nos ahorró la molestia/vergüenza⟩ ⟨spare me the details : ahórrate los detalles⟩ ⟨she was spared (from) punishment : se libró del castigo⟩ 3 : prescindir de ⟨I can't spare her : no puedo prescindir de ella⟩ ⟨I can't spare the time : no me da el tiempo⟩ ⟨can you spare a dollar? : ¿me das un dólar?⟩ ⟨can you spare a minute? : ¿tienes un momento?⟩ 4 STINT : escatimar ⟨they spared no expense : no repararon en gastos⟩ 5 to spare : de sobra
spare² adj sparer; sparest 1 : de repuesto, de recambio ⟨spare tire : llanta de repuesto⟩ 2 EXCESS, EXTRA : de más, de sobra, libre ⟨spare time : tiempo libre⟩ ⟨spare room : cuarto de huéspedes⟩ 3 LEAN : delgado
spare³ n or spare part : repuesto m, recambio m
sparing ['spærɪŋ] adj : parco, económico — **sparingly** adv
spark¹ ['spark] vi : chispear, echar chispas — vt PROVOKE : despertar, provocar ⟨to spark interest : despertar interés⟩
spark² n 1 : chispa f ⟨to throw off sparks : echar chispas⟩ 2 GLIMMER, TRACE : destello m, pizca f
sparkle¹ ['sparkəl] vi -kled; -kling 1 FLASH, SHINE : destellar, centellear, brillar 2 : estar muy animado (dícese de una conversación, etc.)
sparkle² n : destello m, centelleo m
sparkler ['sparklər] n : luz f de bengala
spark plug n : bujía f
sparrow ['spæro:] n : gorrión m
sparse ['spars] adj sparser; sparsest : escaso — **sparsely** adv
spasm ['spæzəm] n 1 : espasmo m (muscular) 2 BURST, FIT : arrebato m
spasmodic [spæz'madɪk] adj 1 : espasmódico 2 SPORADIC : irregular, esporádico — **spasmodically** [-dɪkli] adv
spastic ['spæstɪk] adj : espástico
spat¹ → spit¹
spat² ['spæt] n : discusión f, disputa f, pelea f
spate ['speɪt] n : avalancha f, torrente m

spatial ['speɪʃəl] adj : espacial
spatter¹ ['spætər] v : salpicar
spatter² n : salpicadura f
spatula ['spætʃələ] n : espátula f, paleta f (para servir)
spawn¹ ['spɔn] vi : desovar — vt GENERATE : generar, producir
spawn² n : hueva f
spay ['speɪ] vt : esterilizar (una perra, etc.)
speak ['spi:k] v spoke ['spo:k]; spoken ['spo:kən]; speaking vi 1 TALK : hablar ⟨to speak to/with someone : hablar con alguien⟩ ⟨who's speaking? : ¿de parte de quien?⟩ ⟨so to speak : por así decirlo⟩ ⟨generally speaking : por lo general, generalmente⟩ ⟨they're not speaking (to each other) : no se hablan⟩ ⟨she spoke at the conference : habló en el congreso⟩ ⟨she spoke well of you : habló bien de ti⟩ 2 to be spoken for : estar reservado (dícese de un asiento, etc.), estar comprometido (dícese de una persona) 3 to speak for : hablar en nombre de ⟨speak for yourself! : ¡habla por ti mismo!⟩ 4 to speak of SIGNIFICANT : significante, que merece comentario ⟨there's been no progress to speak of : no han avanzado nada⟩ 5 to speak of MENTION : mencionar ⟨(and) speaking of which . . . : a propósito . . .⟩ 6 to speak out : hablar claramente 7 to speak out against : denunciar 8 to speak up : hablar en voz alta 9 to speak up for : defender — vt 1 SAY : decir ⟨she spoke her mind : habló con franqueza⟩ 2 : hablar (un idioma)
speaker ['spi:kər] n 1 : hablante mf ⟨a native speaker : un hablante nativo⟩ 2 : orador m, -dora f ⟨the keynote speaker : el orador principal⟩ 3 LOUDSPEAKER : altavoz m, altoparlante m
spear¹ ['spɪr] vt : atravesar con una lanza
spear² n : lanza f
spearhead¹ ['spɪr,hɛd] vt : encabezar
spearhead² n : punta f de lanza
spearmint ['spɪrmɪnt] n : menta f verde
special ['spɛʃəl] adj : especial ⟨nothing special : nada en especial, nada en particular⟩ — **specially** adv
special delivery n : correo m urgente
special effects npl : efectos mpl especiales
specialist ['spɛʃəlɪst] n : especialista mf
specialization [,spɛʃələ'zeɪʃən] n : especialización f
specialize ['spɛʃə,laɪz] vi -ized; -izing : especializarse
specialty ['spɛʃəlti] n, pl -ties : especialidad f
species ['spi:,ʃi:z, -,si:z] ns & pl : especie f
specific [spɪ'sɪfɪk] adj : específico, determinado — **specifically** [-fɪkli] adv
specification [,spɛsəfə'keɪʃən] n : especificación f
specify ['spɛsə,faɪ] vt -fied; -fying : especificar
specimen ['spɛsəmən] n 1 SAMPLE : espécimen m, muestra f 2 EXAMPLE : espécimen m, ejemplar m
speck ['spɛk] n 1 SPOT : manchita f 2 BIT, TRACE : mota f, pizca f, ápice m

speckled ['spɛkəld] *adj* : moteado
spectacle ['spɛktɪkəl] *n* **1** : espectáculo *m* **2 spectacles** *npl* GLASSES : lentes *fpl*, gafas *fpl*, anteojos *mpl*, espejuelos *mpl*
spectacular [spɛk'tækjələr] *adj* : espectacular
spectator ['spɛk,teɪtər] *n* : espectador *m*, -dora *f*
specter *or* **spectre** ['spɛktər] *n* : espectro *m*, fantasma *m*
spectrum ['spɛktrəm] *n*, *pl* **spectra** [-trə] *or* **spectrums** **1** : espectro *m* (de colores, etc.) **2** RANGE : gama *f*, abanico *m*
speculate ['spɛkjə,leɪt] *vi* **-lated; -lating** **1** : especular (en finanzas) **2** WONDER : preguntarse, hacer conjeturas
speculation [,spɛkjə'leɪʃən] *n* : especulación *f*
speculative ['spɛkjə,leɪtɪv] *adj* : especulativo
speculator ['spɛkjə,leɪtər] *n* : especulador *m*, -dora *f*
speech ['spiːtʃ] *n* **1** : habla *f*, modo *m* de hablar, expresión *f* **2** ADDRESS : discurso *m*
speechless ['spiːtʃləs] *adj* : enmudecido, estupefacto
speed¹ ['spiːd] *v* **sped** ['spɛd] *or* **speeded; speeding** *vi* **1** : ir a toda velocidad, correr a toda velocidad ⟨he sped off : se fue a toda velocidad⟩ **2** : conducir a excesiva velocidad — *vt* **to speed up** : acelerar
speed² *n* **1** SWIFTNESS : rapidez *f* **2** VELOCITY : velocidad *f*
speedboat ['spiːd,boːt] *n* : lancha *f* motora (rápida), deslizador *m*
speed bump *n* : badén *m*
speeding ['spiːdɪŋ] *n* : exceso *m* de velocidad ⟨he was stopped/ticketed for speeding : lo pararon/multaron por exceso de velocidad⟩
speed limit *n* : velocidad *f* máxima, límite *m* de velocidad
speedometer [spɪ'dɑmətər] *n* : velocímetro *m*
speedup ['spiːd,ʌp] *n* : aceleración *f*
speedy ['spiːdi] *adj* **speedier; -est** : rápido — **speedily** [-dəli] *adv*
spell¹ ['spɛl] *vt* **1** : escribir, deletrear (verbalmente) ⟨how do you spell it? : ¿cómo se escribe?, ¿cómo se deletrea?⟩ **2** MEAN : significar ⟨that could spell trouble : eso puede significar problemas⟩ **3** RELIEVE : relevar **4 to spell out** EXPLAIN : explicar en detalle — *vi* : escribir correctamente, deletrear (verbalmente)
spell² *n* **1** TURN : turno *m* **2** PERIOD, TIME : período *m* (de tiempo) ⟨a dry spell : un período de sequía⟩ ⟨a cold spell : una ola de frío⟩ **3** : condición *f* pasajera ⟨a fainting spell : un desmayo⟩ ⟨a dizzy spell : un mareo⟩ **4** ENCHANTMENT : encanto *m*, hechizo *m*, maleficio *m*
spellbinding ['spɛl,baɪndɪŋ] *adj* : hipnotizador
spellbound ['spɛl,baʊnd] *adj* : embelesado
spell–check¹ ['spɛl,tʃɛk] *vt* : corregir (la ortografía de), pasar el corrector ortográfico a

spell–check² *n* : corrección *f* ortográfica
spellchecker ['spɛl,tʃɛkər] *n* : corrector *m* ortográfico
speller ['spɛlər] *n* : persona *f* que escribe ⟨she's a good speller : tiene buena ortografía⟩
spelling ['spɛlɪŋ] *n* : ortografía *f*
spend ['spɛnd] *vt* **spent** ['spɛnt]; **spending** **1** : gastar (dinero, etc.) **2** PASS : pasar (el tiempo) ⟨to spend time on : dedicar tiempo a⟩
spendthrift ['spɛnd,θrɪft] *n* : derrochador *m*, -dora *f*; despilfarrador *m*, -dora *f*
sperm ['spərm] *n*, *pl* **sperm** *or* **sperms** : esperma *mf*
sperm whale *n* : cachalote *m*
spew ['spjuː] *vi* : salir a chorros — *vt* : vomitar, arrojar (lava, etc.)
sphere ['sfɪr] *n* : esfera *f*
spherical ['sfɪrɪkəl, 'sfɛr-] *adj* : esférico
sphinx ['sfɪŋks] *n* : esfinge *f*
spice¹ ['spaɪs] *vt* **spiced; spicing** **1** SEASON : condimentar, sazonar **2** *or* **to spice up** : salpimentar, hacer más interesante
spice² *n* **1** : especia *f* **2** FLAVOR, INTEREST : sabor *m* ⟨the spice of life : la sal de la vida⟩
spick–and–span ['spɪkænd'spæn] *adj* : limpio y ordenado
spiciness ['spaɪsinəs] *n* : picante *m*, lo picante
spicy ['spaɪsi] *adj* **spicier; -est** **1** FLAVORED : condimentado, sazonado **2** HOT : picante **3** RACY : picante
spider ['spaɪdər] *n* : araña *f*
spiderweb ['spaɪdər,wɛb] *n* : telaraña *f*, tela *f* de araña
spiel ['spiːl] *n* : rollo *m*, perorata *f*
spigot ['spɪɡət, -ɡɑt] *n* : llave *f*; grifo *m*; canilla *f* Arg, Uru
spike¹ ['spaɪk] *vt* **spiked; spiking** **1** FASTEN : clavar (con clavos grandes) **2** PIERCE : atravesar **3** : añadir alcohol a ⟨he spiked her drink with rum : le puso ron a la bebida⟩
spike² *n* **1** : clavo *m* grande **2** CLEAT : clavo *m* **3** : remache *m* (en voleibol) **4** PEAK : pico *m*
spill¹ ['spɪl] *vt* **1** SHED : derramar, verter ⟨to spill blood : derrame sangre⟩ **2** DIVULGE : revelar, divulgar — *vi* : derramarse
spill² *n* **1** SPILLING : derrame *m*, vertido *m* ⟨oil spill : derrame de petróleo⟩ **2** FALL : caída *f*
spin¹ ['spɪn] *v* **spun** ['spʌn]; **spinning** *vi* **1** : hilar **2** TURN : girar ⟨the car spun out of control : el auto giró fuera de control⟩ ⟨he spun around to look at me : se dio la vuelta para mirarme⟩ **3** REEL : dar vueltas ⟨my head is spinning : la cabeza me está dando vueltas⟩ — *vt* **1** : hilar (hilo, etc.) **2** : tejer ⟨to spin a web : tejer una telaraña⟩ **3** TWIRL : hacer girar **4** : darle un sesgo positivo a (en política) **5 to spin a yarn/tale** : contar un cuento **6 to spin one's wheels** *fam* STAGNATE : estancarse
spin² *n* : vuelta *f*, giro *m* ⟨to go for a spin : dar una vuelta (en coche)⟩

spinach ['spɪnɪtʃ] n : espinacas fpl, espinaca f

spinal ['spaɪnəl] adj : espinal

spinal column n BACKBONE : columna f vertebral

spinal cord n : médula f espinal

spindle ['spɪndəl] n 1 : huso m (para hilar) 2 : eje m (de un mecanismo)

spindly ['spɪndli] adj : larguirucho fam, largo y débil (dícese de una planta)

spin doctor n : portavoz mf

spine ['spaɪn] n 1 BACKBONE : columna f vertebral, espina f dorsal 2 QUILL : púa f (de un animal) 3 THORN : espina f 4 : lomo m (de un libro)

spineless ['spaɪnləs] adj 1 : sin púas, sin espinas 2 INVERTEBRATE : invertebrado 3 WEAK : débil (de carácter)

spinster ['spɪnstər] n : soltera f

spiny ['spaɪni] adj **spinier; -est** : con púas (dícese de los animales), espinoso (dícese de las plantas)

spiral¹ ['spaɪrəl] vi **-raled** or **-ralled; -raling** or **-ralling** : ir en espiral

spiral² adj : espiral, en espiral ⟨a spiral staircase : una escalera de caracol⟩

spiral³ n : espiral f

spire ['spaɪr] n : aguja f

spirit¹ ['spɪrət] vt **to spirit away** : hacer desaparecer

spirit² n 1 : espíritu m ⟨body and spirit : cuerpo y espíritu⟩ 2 GHOST : espíritu m, fantasma m 3 MOOD : espíritu m, humor m ⟨in the spirit of friendship : en el espíritu de amistad⟩ ⟨to be in good spirits : estar de buen humor⟩ 4 ENTHUSIASM, VIVACITY : espíritu m, ánimo m, brío m 5 **spirits** npl : licores mpl

spirited ['spɪrətəd] adj : animado, enérgetico

spiritless ['spɪrətləs] adj : desanimado

spiritual¹ ['spɪrɪtʃuəl, -tʃəl] adj : espiritual — **spiritually** adv

spiritual² n : espiritual m (canción)

spiritualism ['spɪrɪtʃuəˌlɪzəm, -tʃə-] n : espiritismo m

spiritualist ['spɪrɪtʃuəlɪst, -tʃə-] n : médium mf, espiritista mf

spirituality [ˌspɪrɪtʃuˈæləti] n, pl **-ties** : espiritualidad f

spit¹ ['spɪt] v **spit** or **spat** ['spæt] **spitting** : escupir

spit² n 1 SALIVA : saliva f 2 ROTISSERIE : asador m 3 POINT : lengua f (de tierra)

spite¹ ['spaɪt] vt **spited; spiting** : fastidiar, molestar

spite² n 1 : despecho m, rencor m 2 **in spite of** : a pesar de (que), pese a ⟨spiteful ['spaɪtfəl] adj : malicioso, rencoroso

spitting image n **to be the spitting image of** : ser el vivo retrato de

spittle ['spɪtəl] n : saliva f

splash¹ ['splæʃ] vt : salpicar — vi 1 : salpicar 2 **to splash around** : chapotear

splash² n 1 SPLASHING : salpicadura f 2 SQUIRT : chorrito m 3 SPOT : mancha f

splatter ['splætər] → **spatter**

splay ['spleɪ] vt : extender (hacia afuera)

⟨to splay one's fingers : abrir los dedos⟩ — vi : extenderse (hacia afuera)

spleen ['spli:n] n 1 : bazo m (órgano) 2 ANGER, SPITE : ira f, rencor m

splendid ['splɛndəd] adj : espléndido — **splendidly** adv

splendor ['splɛndər] n : esplendor m

splice¹ ['splaɪs] vt **spliced; splicing** : empalmar, unir

splice² n : empalme m, unión f

splint ['splɪnt] n : tablilla f

splinter¹ ['splɪntər] vt : astillar — vi : astillarse

splinter² n : astilla f

split¹ ['splɪt] v **split; splitting** vt 1 CLEAVE : partir, hender ⟨to split wood : partir madera⟩ 2 BURST : romper, rajar ⟨to split open : abrir⟩ 3 DIVIDE, SHARE : dividir, repartir — vi 1 : partirse (dícese de la madera, etc.) 2 BURST, CRACK : romperse, rajarse 3 or **to split up** : dividirse

split² n 1 CRACK : rajadura f 2 TEAR : rotura f 3 DIVISION : división f, escisión f

splurge¹ ['splərdʒ] v **splurged; splurging** vt : derrochar — vi : derrochar dinero

splurge² n : derroche m

splutter ['splʌtər] vi 1 : balbucear (dícese de una persona) 2 SPUTTER : petardear (dícese de un motor)

spoil¹ ['spɔɪl] v 1 PILLAGE : saquear 2 RUIN : estropear, arruinar 3 PAMPER : consentir, mimar — vi : estropearse, echarse a perder

spoil² n PLUNDER : botín m

spoiled ['spɔɪld, 'spɔɪlt] adj 1 : estropeado, cortado (dícese de la comida) 2 PAMPERED : consentido

spoilsport ['spɔɪlˌsport] n : aguafiestas mf

spoke¹ → **speak**

spoke² ['spo:k] n : rayo m (de una rueda)

spoken → **speak**

spokesman ['spo:ksmən] n, pl **-men** [-mən, -ˌmɛn] : portavoz mf; vocero m, -ra f

spokesperson ['spo:ksˌpərsən] n : portavoz mf; vocero m, -ra f

spokeswoman ['spo:ksˌwʊmən] n, pl **-women** [-ˌwɪmən] : portavoz f, vocera f

sponge¹ ['spʌndʒ] vt **sponged; sponging** 1 : limpiar con una esponja 2 BUM, SCROUNGE : gorrear fam, sablear fam (dinero) — vi **to sponge off someone** : vivir a costa de alguien

sponge² n : esponja f

sponge cake n : bizcocho m

sponger ['spʌndʒər] n : gorrero m, -ra f fam; vividor m, -dora f; sanguijuela f; arrimado m, -da f Mex fam

spongy ['spʌndʒi] adj **spongier; -est** : esponjoso

sponsor¹ ['spɑntsər] vt : patrocinar, auspiciar, apadrinar (a una persona)

sponsor² n : patrocinador m, -dora f; padrino m, madrina f

sponsorship ['spɑntsərˌʃɪp] n : patrocinio m

spontaneity [ˌspɑntəˈni:əti, -ˈneɪ-] n : espontaneidad f

spontaneous [spɑn'teɪnɪəs] *adj*
: espontáneo — **spontaneously** *adv*
spoof ['spu:f] *n* : burla *f*, parodia *f*
spook¹ ['spu:k] *vt* : asustar
spook² *n* : fantasma *m*, espíritu *m*, espectro *m*
spooky ['spu:ki] *adj* **spookier; -est** : que da miedo, espeluznante
spool ['spu:l] *n* : carrete *m*, bobina *f*
spoon¹ ['spu:n] *vt* : comer, servir, o echar con cuchara
spoon² *n* : cuchara *f*
spoonful ['spu:n,fʊl] *n* : cucharada *f* ⟨by the spoonful : a cucharadas⟩
spoor ['spʊr, 'spɔr] *n* : rastro *m*, pista *f*
sporadic [spə'rædɪk] *adj* : esporádico — **sporadically** [-dɪkli] *adv*
spore ['spɔr] *n* : espora *f*
sport¹ ['spɔrt] *vi* to FROLIC : retozar, juguetear — *vt* SHOW OFF : lucir, ostentar
sport² *n* **1** : deporte *m* ⟨outdoor sports : deportes al aire libre⟩ **2** JEST : broma *f* **3 to be a good sport** : tener espíritu deportivo
sporting ['spɔrtɪŋ] *adj* : deportivo ⟨a sporting chance : buenas posibilidades⟩
sports car *n* : carro *m* sport, auto *m* sport, coche *m* deportivo
sports center *n* : centro *m* deportivo
sportsman ['spɔrtsmən] *n, pl* **-men** [-mən, -ˌmɛn] : deportista *m*
sportsmanship ['spɔrtsmən,ʃɪp] *n* : espíritu *m* deportivo, deportividad *f* Spain
sportswear ['spɔrts,wær] *n* : ropa *f* deportiva
sportswoman ['spɔrts,wʊmən] *n, pl* **-women** [-,wɪmən] : deportista *f*
sport–utility vehicle *n* → **SUV**
sporty ['spɔrti] *adj* **sportier; -est** : deportivo
spot¹ ['spɑt] *v* **spotted; spotting** *vt* **1** STAIN : manchar **2** RECOGNIZE, SEE : ver, reconocer ⟨to spot an error : descubrir un error⟩ — *vi* : mancharse
spot² *adj* : hecho al azar ⟨a spot check : un vistazo, un control aleatorio⟩
spot³ *n* **1** STAIN : mancha *f* **2** DOT : punto *m* **3** PIMPLE : grano *m* ⟨to break out in spots : salirle granos a alguien⟩ **4** PREDICAMENT : apuro *m*, aprieto *m*, lío *m* ⟨in a tight spot : en apuros⟩ **5** PLACE : lugar *m*, sitio *m* ⟨to be on the spot : estar en el lugar⟩
spotless ['spɑtləs] *adj* : impecable, inmaculado — **spotlessly** *adv*
spotlight¹ ['spɑt,laɪt] *vt* **-lighted** *or* **-lit** [-,lɪt]; **-lighting 1** LIGHT : iluminar (con un reflector) **2** HIGHLIGHT : destacar, poner en relieve
spotlight² *n* **1** : reflector *m*, foco *m* **2 to be in the spotlight** : ser el centro de atención
spotty ['spɑti] *adj* **spottier; -est** : irregular, desigual
spouse ['spaʊs] *n* : cónyuge *mf*
spout¹ ['spaʊt] *vt* **1** : lanzar chorros de **2** DECLAIM : declamar — *vi* : salir a chorros
spout² *n* **1** : pico *m* (de una jarra, etc.) **2** STREAM : chorro *m*

sprain¹ ['spreɪn] *vt* : sufrir un esguince en
sprain² *n* : esguince *m*, torcedura *f*
sprawl¹ ['sprɔl] *vi* **1** LIE : tumbarse, echarse, despatarrarse **2** EXTEND : extenderse
sprawl² *n* **1** : postura *f* despatarrada **2** SPREAD : extensión *f*, expansión *f*
spray¹ ['spreɪ] *vt* : rociar (una superficie), pulverizar (un líquido)
spray² *n* **1** BOUQUET : ramillete *m* **2** MIST : rocío *m* **3** ATOMIZER : atomizador *m*, pulverizador *m*
spray gun *n* : pistola *f*
spread¹ ['spred] *v* **spread; spreading** *vt* **1** *or* to spread out : desplegar, extender **2** SCATTER, STREW : esparcir **3** SMEAR : untar (mantequilla, etc.) **4** DISSEMINATE : difundir, sembrar, propagar — *vi* **1** : difundirse, correr, propagarse **2** EXTEND : extenderse
spread² *n* **1** EXTENSION : extensión *f*, difusión *f* (de noticias, etc.), propagación *f* (de enfermedades, etc.) **2** : colcha *f* (para una cama), mantel *m* (para una mesa) **3** PASTE : pasta *f* ⟨cheese spread : pasta de queso⟩
spreadsheet ['spred,ʃi:t] *n* : hoja *f* de cálculo
spree ['spri] *n* **1** : acción *f* desenfrenada ⟨to go on a shopping spree : comprar como loco⟩ **2** BINGE : parranda *f*, juerga *f* ⟨on a spree : de parranda, de juerga⟩
sprig ['sprɪg] *n* : ramita *f*, ramito *m*
sprightly ['spraɪtli] *adj* **sprightlier; -est** : vivo, animado ⟨with a sprightly step : con paso ligero⟩
spring¹ ['sprɪŋ] *v* **sprang** ['spræŋ] *or* **sprung** ['sprʌŋ]; **sprung; springing** *vi* **1** LEAP : saltar **2** : mover rápidamente ⟨the lid sprang shut : la tapa se cerró de un golpe⟩ ⟨he sprang to his feet : se paró de un salto⟩ **3 to spring up** : brotar (dícese de las plantas), surgir **4 to spring from** : surgir de — *vt* **1** RELEASE : soltar (de repente) ⟨to spring the news on someone : sorprender a alguien con las noticias⟩ ⟨to spring a trap : hacer saltar una trampa⟩ **2** ACTIVATE : accionar (un mecanismo) **3 to spring a leak** : hacer agua
spring² *n* **1** SOURCE : fuente *f*, origen *m* **2** : manantial *m*, fuente *f* ⟨hot spring : fuente termal⟩ **3** : primavera *f* ⟨spring and summer : la primavera y el verano⟩ **4** : resorte *m*, muelle *m* (de metal, etc.) **5** LEAP : salto *m*, brinco *m* **6** RESILIENCE : elasticidad *f*
springboard ['sprɪŋ,bɔrd] *n* : trampolín *m*
spring cleaning *n* : limpieza *f* a fondo
springtime ['sprɪŋ,taɪm] *n* : primavera *f*
springy ['sprɪŋi] *adj* **springier; -est 1** RESILIENT : elástico **2** LIVELY : enérgico
sprinkle¹ ['sprɪŋkəl] *vt* **-kled; -kling** : rociar (con agua), espolvorear (con azúcar, etc.), salpicar
sprinkle² *n* : llovizna *f*
sprinkler ['sprɪŋkələr] *n* : rociador *m*, aspersor *m*

sprint[1] ['sprɪnt] *vi* : echar la carrera, esprintar (en deportes)

sprint[2] *n* : esprint *m* (en deportes)

sprinter ['sprɪntər] *n* : esprínter *mf*

sprite ['sprait] *n* : hada *f*, elfo *m*

sprocket ['sprɑkət] *n* : diente *m* (de una rueda dentada)

sprout[1] ['spraʊt] *vi* : brotar

sprout[2] *n* : brote *m*, retoño *m*, vástago *m*

spruce[1] ['spru:s] *v* **spruced; sprucing** *vt* : arreglar — *vi* or **to spruce up** : arreglarse, acicalarse

spruce[2] *adj* **sprucer; sprucest** : pulcro, arreglado

spruce[3] *n* : picea *f* (árbol)

spun → **spin**

spunk ['spʌŋk] *n* : valor *m*, coraje *m*, agallas *fpl fam*

spunky ['spʌŋki] *adj* **spunkier; -est** : animoso, corajudo

spur[1] ['spər] *vt* **spurred; spurring** *or* **to spur on** : espolear (un caballo), motivar (a una persona, etc.)

spur[2] *n* **1** : espuela *f*, acicate *m* **2** STIMULUS : acicate *m* **3** : espolón *m* (de un gallo) **4** : ramal *m* (de una línea de ferrocarril)

spurious ['spjʊriəs] *adj* : espurio

spurn ['spərn] *vt* : desdeñar, rechazar

spurt[1] ['spərt] *vt* SQUIRT : lanzar un chorro de — *vi* SPOUT : salir a chorros

spurt[2] *n* **1** : actividad *f* repentina ⟨a spurt of energy : una explosión de energía⟩ ⟨to do in spurts : hacer por rachas⟩ **2** JET : chorro *m* (de agua, etc.)

sputter[1] ['spʌtər] *vi* JABBER : farfullar **2** : petardear (dícese de un motor)

sputter[2] *n* : petardeo *m* (de un motor)

spy[1] ['spai] *v* **spied; spying** *vt* SEE : ver, divisar — *vi* : espiar ⟨to spy on someone : espiar a alguien⟩

spy[2] *n* : espía *mf*

squab ['skwɑb] *n, pl* **squabs** *or* **squab** : pichón *m*

squabble[1] ['skwɑbəl] *vi* **-bled; -bling** : reñir, pelearse, discutir

squabble[2] *n* : riña *f*, pelea *f*, discusión *f*

squad ['skwɑd] *n* : pelotón *m* (militar), brigada *f* (de policías), cuadrilla *f* (de obreros, etc.)

squadron ['skwɑdrən] *n* : escuadrón *m* (de militares), escuadrilla *f* (de aviones), escuadra *f* (de naves)

squalid ['skwɑlɪd] *adj* : miserable

squall ['skwɔl] *n* **1** : aguacero *m* tormentoso, chubasco *m* tormentoso **2** **snow squall** : tormenta *f* de nieve

squalor ['skwɑlər] *n* : miseria *f*

squander ['skwɑndər] *vt* : derrochar (dinero, etc.), desaprovechar (una oportunidad, etc.), desperdiciar (talentos, energías, etc.)

square[1] ['skwær] *vt* **squared; squaring 1** : cuadrar **2** : elevar al cuadrado (en matemáticas) **3** CONFORM : conciliar (con), ajustar (con) **4** SETTLE : saldar (una cuenta) ⟨I squared it with him : lo arreglé con él⟩

square[2] *adj* **squarer; -est 1** : cuadrado ⟨a square house : una casa cuadrada⟩ **2** : a escuadra, en ángulo recto (en carpintería, etc.) **3** : cuadrado (en matemáticas) ⟨a square mile : una milla cuadrada⟩ **4** HONEST : justo ⟨a square deal : un buen acuerdo⟩ ⟨fair and square : en buena lid⟩

square[3] *n* **1** : escuadra *f* (instrumento) **2** : cuadrado *m*, cuadro *m* ⟨to fold into squares : plegar en cuadrados⟩ **3** : plaza *f* (de una ciudad) **4** : cuadrado *m* (en matemáticas)

squarely ['skwærli] *adv* **1** EXACTLY : exactamente, directamente, justo **2** HONESTLY : honradamente, justamente

square root *n* : raíz *f* cuadrada

squash[1] ['skwɑʃ, 'skwɔʃ] *vt* **1** CRUSH : aplastar **2** SUPPRESS : acallar (protestas), sofocar (una rebelión)

squash[2] *n* **1** *pl* **squashes** *or* **squash** : calabaza *f* (vegetal) **2** *or* **squash racquets** : squash *m* (deporte)

squat[1] ['skwɑt] *vi* **squatted; squatting 1** CROUCH : agacharse, ponerse en cuclillas **2** : ocupar un lugar sin derecho

squat[2] *adj* **squatter; squattest** : bajo y ancho, rechoncho *fam* (dícese de una persona)

squat[3] *n* **1** : posición *f* en cuclillas, flexión *f* (en deportes) **2** : ocupación *f* ilegal (de un lugar)

squatter ['skwɑtər] *n* : okupa *mf*

squawk[1] ['skwɔk] *vi* : graznar (dícese de las aves), chillar

squawk[2] *n* : graznido *m* (de un ave), chillido *m*

squeak[1] ['skwi:k] *vi* : chillar (dícese de un animal), chirriar (dícese de un objeto)

squeak[2] *n* : chillido *m*, chirrido *m*

squeaky ['skwi:ki] *adj* **squeakier; -est** : chirriante ⟨a squeaky voice : una voz chillona⟩

squeal[1] ['skwi:l] *vi* **1** : chillar (dícese de las personas o los animales), chirriar (dícese de los frenos, etc.) **2** PROTEST : quejarse **3** *fam* SNITCH : cantar (a la policía, etc.) ⟨to squeal on someone : acusar/delatar a alguien⟩

squeal[2] *n* **1** : chillido *m* (de una persona o un animal) **2** SCREECH : chirrido *m* (de frenos, etc.)

squeamish ['skwi:mɪʃ] *adj* : impresionable, sensible ⟨he's squeamish about cockroaches : las cucarachas le dan asco⟩

squeeze[1] ['skwi:z] *vt* **squeezed; squeezing 1** PRESS : apretar, exprimir (naranjas, etc.) **2** EXTRACT : extraer (jugo, etc.) **3** : meter

squeeze[2] *n* : apretón *m*

squelch ['skwɛltʃ] *vt* : aplastar (una rebelión, etc.)

squid ['skwɪd] *n, pl* **squid** *or* **squids** : calamar *m*

squint[1] ['skwɪnt] *vi* : mirar con los ojos entornados

squint[2] *adj* *or* **squint–eyed** ['skwɪnt,aɪd] : bizco

squint³ *n* : estrabismo *m*
squire [ˈskwaɪr] *n* : hacendado *m*, -da *f*; terrateniente *mf*
squirm [ˈskwərm] *vi* : retorcerse
squirrel [ˈskwərəl] *n* : ardilla *f*
squirt¹ [ˈskwərt] *vt* : lanzar un chorro de — *vi* SPURT : salir a chorros
squirt² *n* : chorrito *m*
stab¹ [ˈstæb] *vt* **stabbed; stabbing 1** KNIFE : acuchillar, apuñalar **2** STICK : clavar (con una aguja, etc.), golpear (con el dedo, etc.)
stab² *n* **1** : puñalada *f*, cuchillada *f* **2** JAB : pinchazo *m* (con una aguja, etc.), golpe *m* (con un dedo, etc.) **3 to take a stab at** : intentar
stability [stəˈbɪləti] *n*, *pl* **-ties** : estabilidad *f*
stabilize [ˈsteɪbəˌlaɪz] *v* **-lized; -lizing** *vt* : estabilizar — *vi* : estabilizarse — **stabilization** *n* — **stabilizer** *n*
stable¹ [ˈsteɪbəl] *vt* **-bled; -bling** : poner (ganado) en un establo, poner (caballos) en una caballeriza
stable² *adj* **stabler; -blest 1** FIXED, STEADY : fijo, sólido, estable **2** LASTING : estable, perdurable ⟨a stable government : un gobierno estable⟩ **3** : estacionario (en medicina), equilibrado (en psicología)
stable³ *n* : establo *m* (para ganado), caballeriza *f* o cuadra *f* (para caballos)
staccato [stəˈkɑtoː] *adj* : staccato
stack¹ [ˈstæk] *vt* **1** PILE : amontonar, apilar **2** COVER : cubrir, llenar ⟨he stacked the table with books : cubrió la mesa de libros⟩
stack² *n* **1** PILE : montón *m*, pila *f* **2** SMOKESTACK : chimenea *f*
stadium [ˈsteɪdiəm] *n*, *pl* **-dia** [-diə] *or* **-diums** : estadio *m*
staff¹ [ˈstæf] *vt* : proveer de personal
staff² *n*, *pl* **staffs** [ˈstæfs, ˈstævz] *or* **staves** [ˈstævz, ˈstɛrvz] **1** : bastón *m* (de mando), báculo *m* (de obispo) **2** *pl* **staffs** PERSONNEL : personal *m* **3** *or* **stave** : pentagrama *m* (en música)
stag¹ [ˈstæg] *adv* : solo, sin pareja ⟨to go stag : ir solo⟩
stag² *adj* : sólo para hombres
stag³ *n*, *pl* **stags** *or* **stag** : ciervo *m*, venado *m*
stage¹ [ˈsteɪdʒ] *vt* **staged; staging** : poner en escena (una obra de teatro)
stage² *n* **1** PLATFORM : estrado *m*, tablado *m*, escenario *m* (de un teatro) **2** PHASE, STEP : fase *f*, etapa *f* ⟨stage of development : fase de desarrollo⟩ ⟨in stages : por etapas⟩ **3 the stage** : el teatro *m*
stagecoach [ˈsteɪdʒˌkoːtʃ] *n* : diligencia *f*
stage fright *n* : miedo *m* escénico, pánico *m* escénico
stage set → set³
stagger¹ [ˈstægər] *vi* TOTTER : tambalearse — *vt* **1** ALTERNATE : alternar, escalonar (turnos de trabajo) **2** : hacer tambalear ⟨to be staggered by : quedarse estupefacto por⟩
stagger² *n* : tambaleo *m*

staggering [ˈstægərɪŋ] *adj* : asombroso
stagnant [ˈstægnənt] *adj* : estancado
stagnate [ˈstægˌneɪt] *vi* **-nated; -nating** : estancarse
stagnation [stægˈneɪʃən] *n* : estancamiento *m*
staid [ˈsteɪd] *adj* : serio, sobrio
stain¹ [ˈsteɪn] *vt* **1** DISCOLOR : manchar **2** DYE : teñir (madera, etc.) **3** SULLY : manchar, empañar
stain² *n* **1** SPOT : mancha *f* **2** DYE : tinte *m*, tintura *f* **3** BLEMISH : mancha *f*, mácula *f*
stained glass *n* : vidrio *m* de color ⟨stained-glass window : vidriera, vitral⟩
stainless [ˈsteɪnləs] *adj* : sin mancha ⟨stainless steel : acero inoxidable⟩
stair [ˈstær] *n* **1** STEP : escalón *m*, peldaño *m* **2 stairs** *npl* : escalera *f*, escaleras *fpl*
staircase [ˈstærˌkeɪs] *n* : escalera *f*, escaleras *fpl*
stairway [ˈstærˌweɪ] *n* : escalera *f*, escaleras *fpl*
stairwell [ˈstærˌwel] *n* : caja *f*, hueco *m* (de la escalera)
stake¹ [ˈsteɪk] *vt* **staked; staking 1** : estacar, marcar con estacas (una propiedad) **2** BET : jugarse, apostar **3 to stake a claim to** : reclamar, reivindicar
stake² *n* **1** POST : estaca *f* **2** BET : apuesta *f* ⟨to be at stake : estar en juego⟩ **3** INTEREST, SHARE : interés *m*, participación *f*
stalactite [stəˈlækˌtaɪt] *n* : estalactita *f*
stalagmite [stəˈlægˌmaɪt] *n* : estalagmita *f*
stale [ˈsteɪl] *adj* **staler; stalest** : viejo ⟨stale bread : pan duro⟩ ⟨stale news : viejas noticias⟩
stalemate [ˈsteɪlˌmeɪt] *n* : punto *m* muerto, impasse *m*
stalk¹ [ˈstɔk] *vt* : acechar — *vi* : caminar rígidamente (por orgullo, ira, etc.)
stalk² *n* : tallo *m* (de una planta)
stall¹ [ˈstɔl] *vt* **1** : parar (un motor) **2** DELAY : entretener (a una persona), demorar — *vi* **1** : pararse (dícese de un motor) **2** DELAY : demorar, andar con rodeos ⟨to stall for time : tratar de ganar tiempo⟩
stall² *n* **1** : compartimiento *m* (de un establo) **2** : puesto *m* (en un mercado, etc.)
stallion [ˈstæljən] *n* : caballo *m* semental
stalwart [ˈstɔlwərt] *adj* **1** STRONG : fuerte ⟨a stalwart supporter : un firme partidario⟩ **2** BRAVE : valiente, valeroso
stamen [ˈsteɪmən] *n* : estambre *m*
stamina [ˈstæmənə] *n* : resistencia *f*
stammer¹ [ˈstæmər] *vi* : tartamudear, titubear
stammer² *n* : tartamudeo *m*, titubeo *m*
stamp¹ [ˈstæmp] *vt* **1** : pisotear (con los pies) ⟨to stamp one's feet : patear, dar una patada⟩ **2** IMPRESS, IMPRINT : sellar (una factura, etc.), acuñar (monedas) **3** : franquear, ponerle estampillas a (correo) **4 to stamp out** : aplastar, sofocar, erradicar
stamp² *n* **1** : sello *m* (para documentos, etc.) **2** DIE : cuño *m* (para monedas) **3**

or **postage stamp** : sello *m*, estampilla *f*, timbre *m CA, Mex*

stampede¹ [stæmˈpiːd] *vi* -peded; -peding : salir en estampida

stampede² *n* : estampida *f*

stance [ˈstænts] *n* : postura *f*

stanch [ˈstɔntʃ, ˈstantʃ] *vt* : detener, estancar (un líquido)

stand¹ [ˈstænd] *v* stood [ˈstʊd]; standing *vi* 1 : estar de pie, estar parado ⟨I was standing on the corner : estaba parada en la esquina⟩ ⟨to stand still : estarse quieto⟩ ⟨to stand in line : hacer cola⟩ ⟨to stand around waiting/watching : quedarse esperando/mirando (sin hacer nada)⟩ 2 MOVE : ponerse, pararse ⟨stand beside me : ponte a mi lado⟩ ⟨stand aside/back! : ¡apártate!⟩ 3 *or* to **stand up** : levantarse, pararse, ponerse de pie ⟨she stood up and left : se paró y se fue⟩ ⟨to stand up straight : ponerse derecho⟩ 4 *(indicating a specified position or location)* ⟨they stand third in the country : ocupan el tercer lugar en el país⟩ 5 *(referring to an opinion)* ⟨how does he stand on the matter? : ¿cuál es su postura respecto al asunto?⟩ 6 BE : estar ⟨the house stands on a hill : la casa está en una colina⟩ ⟨I won't stand in your way : no te lo voy a impedir⟩ 7 REMAIN : estar ⟨the machines are standing idle : las máquinas están paradas⟩ ⟨as things stand : tal (y) como están las cosas⟩ 8 CONTINUE : seguir ⟨the order still stands : el mandato sigue vigente⟩ 9 MEASURE : medir ⟨he stands six feet two (inches tall) : mide seis pies y dos pulgadas⟩ 10 to **stand by** : estar listo, estar disponible 11 to **stand by** SUPPORT : apoyar 12 to **stand by** HONOR : cumplir con (una promesa, etc.) 13 to **stand down** : bajar las armas (dícese de un soldado), retirarse (dícese de un ejército) 14 to **stand firm** : mantenerse firme 15 to **stand for** SIGNIFY, REPRESENT : significar, representar 16 to **stand for** ALLOW : permitir 17 to **stand guard** : hacer la guardia 18 to **stand in (for)** : sustituir (a) 19 to **stand on end** : ponerse de punta, pararse (dícese de los pelos) 20 to **stand out** : resaltar 21 to **stand out** EXCEL : destacarse 22 to **stand up for** DEFEND : defender 23 to **stand up to** WITHSTAND : resistir 24 to **stand up to** CONFRONT : hacerle frente a — *vt* 1 PLACE : poner, colocar ⟨he stood them in a row : los colocó en hilera⟩ 2 TOLERATE : aguantar, soportar ⟨she can't stand her : no la puede tragar⟩ 3 WITHSTAND : resistir 4 USE : beneficiarse de ⟨you could stand a nap : una siesta te vendría bien⟩ 5 to **stand someone up** : dejar plantado a alguien

stand² *n* 1 RESISTANCE : resistencia *f* ⟨to make a stand against : resistir a⟩ 2 BOOTH, STALL : stand *m*, puesto *m*, quiosco *m* (para vender periódicos, etc.) 3 BASE : pie *m*, base *f* 4 : grupo *m* (de árboles, etc.) 5 POSITION : posición *f*, postura *f* 6 **stands** *npl* GRANDSTAND : tribuna *f*

standard¹ [ˈstændərd] *adj* 1 ESTABLISHED : estándar, oficial ⟨standard measures : medidas oficiales⟩ ⟨standard English : el inglés estándar⟩ 2 NORMAL : normal, estándar, común 3 CLASSIC : estándar, clásico ⟨a standard work : una obra clásica⟩

standard² *n* 1 BANNER : estandarte *m* 2 CRITERION : criterio *m* 3 RULE : estándar *m*, norma *f*, regla *f* 4 LEVEL : nivel *m* ⟨standard of living : nivel de vida⟩ 5 SUPPORT : poste *m*, soporte *m*

standard–bearer [ˈstændərdˌbærər] *n* : abanderado *m*, -da *f*

standardization [ˌstændərdəˈzeɪʃən] *n* : estandarización *f*

standardize [ˈstændərˌdaɪz] *vt* -ized; -izing : estandarizar

standard time *n* : hora *f* oficial

standby [ˈstændˌbaɪ] *n* 1 BACKUP ⟨we bought another as a standby : compramos otro de reserva/emergencia⟩ 2 to **be on standby** : estar a la espera de órdenes, etc. ⟨the passengers who are on standby : los pasajeros que están en la lista de espera⟩

stand by *vt* : atenerse a, cumplir con (una promesa, etc.) — *vi* 1 : mantenerse aparte ⟨to stand by and do nothing : mirar sin hacer nada⟩ 2 : estar preparado, estar listo (para un anuncio, un ataque, etc.)

stand for *vt* 1 REPRESENT : significar 2 PERMIT, TOLERATE : permitir, tolerar

stand-in [ˈstændˌɪn] *n* : doble *m*, sustituto *m*, -ta *f*

standing¹ [ˈstændɪŋ] *adj* 1 : de pie, parado ⟨in a standing position : en posición parada, (en posición) de pie⟩ 2 STAGNANT : estancado 3 ACTIVE : en pie (dícese de una oferta, etc.), fijo (dícese de un pedido) 4 PERMANENT : permanente

standing² *n* 1 POSITION, RANK : posición *f* 2 DURATION : duración *f*

stand out *vi* 1 : destacar(se) ⟨she stands out from the rest : se destaca entre los otros⟩ 2 to **stand out against** RESIST : oponerse a

standpoint [ˈstændˌpɔɪnt] *n* : punto *m* de vista

standstill [ˈstændˌstɪl] *n* 1 STOP : detención *f*, paro *m* ⟨to come to a standstill : pararse⟩ 2 DEADLOCK : punto *m* muerto, impasse *m*

stand up *vt* : dejar plantado ⟨he stood me up again : otra vez me dejó plantado⟩ — *vi* 1 ENDURE : durar, resistir 2 to **stand up for** : defender 3 to **stand up to** : hacerle frente (a alguien)

stank → stink

stanza [ˈstænzə] *n* : estrofa *f*

staple¹ [ˈsteɪpəl] *vt* -pled; -pling : engrapar, grapar

staple² *adj* : principal, básico ⟨a staple food : un alimento básico⟩

staple³ *n* 1 : producto *m* principal, producto *m* de primera necesidad 2 : grapa *f*, broche *m Arg* (para engrapar papeles)

stapler [ˈsteɪplər] *n* : engrapadora *f*, grapadora *f*

star¹ [ˈstɑr] v **starred; starring** vt 1 : marcar con una estrella o un asterisco 2 FEATURE : estar protagonizada por — vi : tener el papel principal ⟨to star in : protagonizar⟩

star² n 1 : estrella f (en astronomía) 2 : estrella f (medalla, etc.), asterisco m (símbolo) 3 CELEBRITY : estrella f ⟨rock/movie star : estrella de rock/cine⟩ ⟨the star of the movie : el protagonista de la película⟩ ⟨our star player : la estrella de nuestro equipo⟩

starboard [ˈstɑrbərd] n : estribor m

starch¹ [ˈstɑrtʃ] vt : almidonar

starch² n : almidón m, fécula f (comida)

starchy [ˈstɑrtʃi] adj **starchier, -est** : lleno de almidón

stardom [ˈstɑrdəm] n : estrellato m

stare¹ [ˈstær] vi **stared; staring** : mirar fijamente

stare² n : mirada f fija

starfish [ˈstɑr,fɪʃ] n : estrella f de mar

stark¹ [ˈstɑrk] adv : completamente ⟨stark raving mad : loco de remate⟩ ⟨stark naked : completamente desnudo⟩

stark² adj 1 ABSOLUTE : absoluto 2 BARREN, DESOLATE : desolado, desierto 3 BARE : desnudo 4 HARSH : duro

starlight [ˈstɑrlaɪt] n : luz f de las estrellas

starling [ˈstɑrlɪŋ] n : estornino m

starry [ˈstɑri] adj **starrier, -est** : estrellado

start¹ [ˈstɑrt] vi 1 JUMP : sobresaltarse, dar un respingo 2 BEGIN : empezar, comenzar ⟨let's get started : empecemos⟩ ⟨she started (off/out) by thanking us : empezó por agradecernos⟩ ⟨he started (off/out) as a receptionist : empezó como recepcionista⟩ ⟨young couples who are just starting off/out : parejas jóvenes que acaban de casarse⟩ 3 or to start off/out SET OUT : salir (de viaje, etc.) 4 or to start up : arrancar (dícese de un motor, etc.) 5 to start from scratch : empezar desde cero 6 to start in : empezar ⟨after a break he started in again : tras un descanso empezó otra vez⟩ 7 to start over : volver a empezar, empezar de nuevo — vt 1 BEGIN : empezar, comenzar, iniciar ⟨I started cleaning, I started to clean : empecé a limpiar⟩ ⟨she started (off/out) her speech with a joke : empezó su discurso con una broma⟩ 2 CAUSE : empezar (una discusión, etc.), provocar (un incendio, etc.), causar 3 SET : hacer, poner ⟨her questions started me thinking : sus preguntas me hicieron pensar⟩ ⟨I started them working : los puse a trabajar⟩ ⟨he started us (off) with some questions : para empezar nos hizo unas preguntas⟩ 4 ESTABLISH : fundar, montar, establecer ⟨to start (up) a business : montar un negocio⟩ 5 : arrancar, poner en marcha, encender ⟨to start (up) the car : arrancar el auto/carro/coche⟩ 6 to start a family : tener hijos 7 to start over : volver a empezar, empezar de nuevo

start² n 1 JUMP : sobresalto m, respingo m 2 BEGINNING : principio m, comienzo m ⟨to get an early start : salir temprano⟩

starter [ˈstɑrtər] n 1 : participante mf (en una carrera, etc.); jugador m titular, jugadora f titular (en beisbol, etc.) 2 APPETIZER : entremés m, aperitivo m 3 or starter motor : motor m de arranque

starting point n : punto m de partida

startle [ˈstɑrtəl] vt **-tled; -tling** : asustar, sobresaltar

start–up [ˈstɑrtˌʌp] adj : de puesta en marcha

starvation [stɑrˈveɪʃən] n : inanición f, hambre f

starve [ˈstɑrv] v **starved; starving** vi 1 : morirse de hambre ⟨starving children : niños hambrientos/famélicos⟩ 2 to be starved/starving fam ⟨I'm starved/starving! : ¡me muero de hambre!⟩ 3 to be starved/starving for or to be starved of : estar hambriento/sediento de (atención, cariño, etc.) — vt : privar de comida

stash [ˈstæʃ] vt : esconder, guardar (en un lugar secreto)

stat [ˈstæt] → **statistic**

state¹ [ˈsteɪt] vt **stated; stating** 1 REPORT : puntualizar, exponer (los hechos, etc.) ⟨state your name : diga su nombre⟩ 2 ESTABLISH, FIX : establecer, fijar

state² n 1 CONDITION : estado m, condición f ⟨a liquid state : un estado líquido⟩ ⟨state of mind : estado de ánimo⟩ ⟨in a bad state : en malas condiciones⟩ 2 NATION : estado m, nación f 3 : estado m (dentro de un país) ⟨the States : los Estados Unidos⟩

stateliness [ˈsteɪtlinəs] n : majestuosidad f

stately [ˈsteɪtli] adj **statelier, -est** : majestuoso

statement [ˈsteɪtmənt] n 1 DECLARATION : declaración f, afirmación f 2 or bank statement : estado m de cuenta

stateroom [ˈsteɪtˌruːm, -ˌrʊm] n : camarote m

statesman [ˈsteɪtsmən] n, pl **-men** [-mən, -ˌmɛn] : estadista m

static¹ [ˈstætɪk] adj : estático

static² n : estática f, interferencia f

station¹ [ˈsteɪʃən] vt : apostar, estacionar

station² n 1 : estación f (de trenes, etc.) 2 RANK, STANDING : condición f (social) 3 : canal m (de televisión), estación f o emisora f (de radio) 4 → police station 5 → fire station

stationary [ˈsteɪʃəˌnɛri] adj 1 IMMOBILE : estacionario, inmovible 2 UNCHANGING : inmutable, inalterable

stationery [ˈsteɪʃəˌnɛri] n : papel y sobres (para correspondencia) ⟨stationery store : papelería⟩

station wagon n : camioneta f ranchera, camioneta f guayín Mex

statistic [stəˈtɪstɪk] n : estadística f ⟨according to statistics : según las estadísticas⟩

statistical [stəˈtɪstɪkəl] adj : estadístico

statistician [ˌstætəˈstɪʃən] n : estadístico m, -ca f

statue [ˈstæˌtʃuː] n : estatua f

statuesque [ˌstætʃʊˈɛsk] *adj* : escultural
statuette [ˌstætʃʊˈɛt] *n* : estatuilla *f*
stature [ˈstætʃər] *n* **1** HEIGHT : estatura *f*, talla *f* **2** PRESTIGE : talla *f*, prestigio *m*
status [ˈsteɪt̬əs, ˈstæ-] *n* : condición *f*, situación *f*, estatus *m* (social) ⟨marital status : estado civil⟩
status quo [-ˈkwoː] *n* : statu quo *m*
status symbol *n* : símbolo *m* de estatus
statute [ˈstæˌtʃuːt] *n* : ley *f*, estatuto *m*
statutory [ˈstæˌtʃəˌtori] *adj* : estatutorio
staunch [ˈstɔntʃ] *adj* : acérrimo, incondicional, leal ⟨a staunch supporter : un partidario incondicional⟩ — **staunchly** *adv*
stave [ˈsteɪv] *vt* **staved** *or* **stove** [ˈstoːv]; **staving 1** to stave in : romper **2** to stave off : evitar (un ataque), prevenir (un problema)
staves → **staff**
stay¹ [ˈsteɪ] *vi* **1** REMAIN : quedarse, permanecer ⟨she stayed after class : se quedó después de clase⟩ ⟨stay out of my room! : ¡no entres a/en mi cuarto!⟩ ⟨stay off the grass : no pisar el césped⟩ ⟨he stayed in the city : permaneció en la ciudad⟩ **2** CONTINUE : seguir, quedarse ⟨it stayed cloudy : seguía nublado⟩ ⟨stay awake : mantenerse despierto⟩ ⟨stay in touch! : ¡mantente en contacto!⟩ ⟨they stayed friends : siguieron siendo amigos⟩ **3** LODGE : hospedarse, alojarse (en un hotel, etc.) **4 to stay away from** : no acercarse a (una persona, un lugar) ⟨I stay away from coffee : no puedo tomar café⟩ **5 to stay in** : quedarse en casa **6 to stay off** AVOID : evitar (un tema, etc.) ⟨to stay off drugs : no volver a tomar drogas⟩ **7 to stay on** : permanecer, quedarse (en un trabajo, etc.) **8 to stay out** : quedarse fuera **9 to stay out of** : no meterse en (problemas, una discusión, etc.) **10 to stay over** : quedarse a dormir **11 to stay up (late)** : quedarse levantado (hasta tarde) — *vt* **1** HALT : detener, suspender (una ejecución, etc.) **2 to stay the course** : aguantar hasta el final
stay² *n* **1** SOJOURN : estadía *f*, estancia *f*, permanencia *f* **2** SUSPENSION : suspensión *f* (de una sentencia) **3** SUPPORT : soporte *m*
stead [ˈstɛd] *n* **1** : lugar *m* ⟨she went in his stead : fue en su lugar⟩ **2 to stand (someone) in good stead** : ser muy útil a, servir de mucho a
steadfast [ˈstɛdˌfæst] *adj* : firme, resuelto ⟨a steadfast friend : un fiel amigo⟩ ⟨a steadfast refusal : una negativa categórica⟩
steadily [ˈstɛdəli] *adv* **1** CONSTANTLY : continuamente, sin parar **2** FIRMLY : con firmeza **3** FIXEDLY : fijamente
steady¹ [ˈstɛdi] *v* **steadied; steadying** *vt* : sujetar ⟨she steadied herself : recobró el equilibrio⟩ — *vi* : estabilizarse
steady² *adj* **steadier; -est 1** FIRM, SURE : seguro, firme ⟨to have a steady hand : tener buen pulso⟩ **2** FIXED, REGULAR : fijo ⟨a steady income : ingresos fi-

jos⟩ **3** CALM : tranquilo, ecuánime ⟨she has steady nerves : es imperturbable⟩ **4** DEPENDABLE : responsable, fiable **5** CONSTANT : constante
steak [ˈsteɪk] *n* : bistec *m*; filete *m*; churrasco *m*; bife *m Arg, Chile, Uru*
steal [ˈstiːl] *v* **stole** [ˈstoːl]; **stolen** [ˈstoːlən]; **stealing** *vt* : robar, hurtar — *vi* **1** : robar, hurtar **2** : ir sigilosamente ⟨to steal away : escabullirse⟩
stealth [ˈstɛlθ] *n* : sigilo *m*
stealthily [ˈstɛlθəli] *adv* : furtivamente
stealthy [ˈstɛlθi] *adj* **stealthier; -est** : furtivo, sigiloso
steam¹ [ˈstiːm] *vi* **1** : echar vapor ⟨to steam away/along (etc.) : moverse echando vapor⟩ **2 to steam up** : empañarse — *vt* **1** : cocer al vapor (en cocina) **2 to steam open** : abrir con vapor **3 to steam up** : empañar
steam² *n* **1** : vapor *m* **2 to let off steam** : desahogarse
steamboat [ˈstiːmˌboːt] → **steamship**
steamed *adj* **1** : cocido al vapor **2** IRATE : furioso
steam engine *n* : motor *m* de vapor
steamer [ˈstiːmər] *n* **1** → **steamship 2** : vaporera, olla vaporera (en cocina) **3** : almeja *f* de Nueva Inglaterra
steaming *adj* **1** *or* **steaming hot** : muy caliente **2** *or* **steaming mad** : furioso
steamroller [ˈstiːmˌroːlər] *n* : apisonadora *f*
steamship [ˈstiːmˌʃɪp] *n* : vapor *m*, barco *m* de vapor
steamy [ˈstiːmi] *adj* **steamier; -est 1** : lleno de vapor **2** EROTIC : erótico ⟨a steamy romance : un tórrido romance⟩
steed [ˈstiːd] *n* : corcel *m*
steel¹ [ˈstiːl] *vt* **to steel oneself** : armarse de valor
steel² *adj* : de acero
steel³ *n* : acero *m*
steely [ˈstiːli] *adj* **steelier; -est** : como acero ⟨a steely gaze : una mirada fría⟩ ⟨steely determination : determinación férrea⟩
steep¹ [ˈstiːp] *vt* : remojar, dejar (té, etc.) en infusión
steep² *adj* **1** : empinado, escarpado ⟨a steep cliff : un precipicio escarpado⟩ **2** CONSIDERABLE : considerable, marcado **3** EXCESSIVE : excesivo ⟨steep prices : precios muy altos⟩
steeple [ˈstiːpəl] *n* : aguja *f*, campanario *m*
steeplechase [ˈstiːpəlˌtʃeɪs] *n* : carrera *f* de obstáculos
steeply [ˈstiːpli] *adv* : abruptamente
steer¹ [ˈstɪr] *vt* **1** : manejar, conducir (un automóvil), gobernar (un barco) **2** GUIDE : dirigir, guiar — *vi* **to steer clear of** : evitar (algo, a alguien)
steer² *n* : buey *m*
steering [ˈstɪrɪŋ] *n* : dirección *f*
steering wheel → **wheel**
stein [ˈstaɪn] *n* : jarra *f* (para cerveza)
stellar [ˈstɛlər] *adj* : estelar
stem¹ [ˈstɛm] *v* **stemmed; stemming** *vt* : detener, contener, parar ⟨to stem the

tide : detener el curso⟩ — *vi* **to stem from** : provenir de, ser el resultado de

stem² *n* : tallo *m* (de una planta)

stem cell *n* : célula *f* madre

stench ['stɛntʃ] *n* : hedor *m*, mal olor *m*

stencil¹ ['stɛntsəl] *vt* **-ciled** *or* **-cilled; -ciling** *or* **-cilling** : marcar utilizando una plantilla

stencil² *n* : plantilla *f* (para marcar)

stenographer [stə'nɑgrəfər] *n* : taquígrafo *m*, -fa *f*

stenographic [ˌstɛnə'græfɪk] *adj* : taquigráfico

stenography [stə'nɑgrəfi] *n* : taquigrafía *f*

step¹ ['stɛp] *v* **stepped; stepping** *vi* **1** : dar un paso ⟨step this way, please : pase por aquí, por favor⟩ ⟨step aside : apártate⟩ ⟨to step forward/back : dar un paso (hacia) adelante/atrás⟩ ⟨he stepped outside : salió⟩ ⟨step right up! : ¡acérquense!⟩ **2 to step back** : distanciarse **3 to step down** RESIGN : renunciar **4 to step in** INTERVENE : intervenir **5 to step on** : pisar **6 to step out** *fam* : salir **7 to step up** INCREASE : aumentar **8 to step up** *fam* : mejorarse, esforzarse más — *vt* **1 to step up** INCREASE : aumentar **2 to step up** *fam* IMPROVE : mejorar

step² *n* **1** : paso *m* ⟨to take a step : dar un paso⟩ **2** : paso *m* (distancia) ⟨a few steps away : a unos pasos⟩ **3** : paso *m* (sonido) **4** FOOTPRINT : huella *f* **5** STAIR : escalón *m*, peldaño *m* **6** RUNG : escalón *m*, travesaño *m* **7** RANK, DEGREE : peldaño *m*, escalón *m* ⟨a step up : un ascenso⟩ **8** MEASURE, MOVE : medida *f*, paso *m* ⟨to take steps : tomar medidas⟩ **9** STAGE : paso *m* ⟨step by step : paso a paso⟩ **10** STRIDE : paso *m* ⟨with a quick step : con paso rápido⟩ **11 to be a/one step ahead of** : llevarle ventaja a **12 to be in step** : llevar el paso **13 to watch one's step** : mirar uno donde camina **14 to watch one's step** BEWARE : andarse con cuidado

stepbrother ['stɛpˌbrʌðər] *n* : hermanastro *m*

stepchild ['stɛpˌtʃaɪld] *n* : hijastro *m*, -tra *f*; entenado *m*, -da *f* *Mex*

stepdaughter ['stɛpˌdɔtər] *n* : hijastra *f*

stepfather ['stɛpˌfɑðər, -ˌfɑ-] *n* : padrastro *m*

stepladder ['stɛpˌlædər] *n* : escalera *f* de tijera

stepmother ['stɛpˌmʌðər] *n* : madrastra *f*

steppe ['stɛp] *n* : estepa *f*

stepping-stone ['stɛpɪŋˌstoːn] *n* : **1** : piedra *f* (para cruzar un arroyo, etc.) **2** : trampolín *m* (al éxito)

stepsister ['stɛpˌsɪstər] *n* : hermanastra *f*

stepson ['stɛpˌsʌn] *n* : hijastro *m*

step up *vt* INCREASE : aumentar

stereo¹ ['stɛriˌoː, 'stɪr-] *adj* : estéreo

stereo² *n*, *pl* **stereos** : estéreo *m*

stereophonic [ˌstɛrioˈfɑnɪk, ˌstɪr-] *adj* : estereofónico

stereotype¹ ['stɛrioˌtaɪp, 'stɪr-] *vt* **-typed; -typing** : estereotipar

stereotype² *n* : estereotipo *m*

sterile ['stɛrəl] *adj* : estéril

sterility [stə'rɪləti] *n* : esterilidad *f*

sterilization [ˌstɛrələ'zeɪʃən] *n* : esterilización *f*

sterilize ['stɛrəˌlaɪz] *vt* **-ized; -izing** : esterilizar

sterling ['stɜrlɪŋ] *adj* **1** : de ley ⟨sterling silver : plata de ley⟩ **2** EXCELLENT : excelente

stern¹ ['stɜrn] *adj* : severo, adusto — **sternly** *adv*

stern² *n* : popa *f*

sternness ['stɜrnnəs] *n* : severidad *f*

sternum ['stɜrnəm] *n*, *pl* **sternums** *or* **sterna** [-nə] : esternón *m*

steroid ['stɪrˌɔɪd, 'stɛr-] *n*, *pl* **steroids** : esteroide *m*

stethoscope ['stɛθəˌskoːp] *n* : estetoscopio *m*

stevedore ['stiːvəˌdor] *n* : estibador *m*, -dora *f*

stew¹ ['stuː, 'stjuː] *vt* : estofar, guisar — *vi* **1** : cocer (dícese de la carne, etc.) **2** FRET : preocuparse

stew² *n* **1** : estofado *m*, guiso *m* **2 to be in a stew** : estar agitado

steward ['stuːərd, 'stjuː-] *n* **1** MANAGER : administrador *m* **2** : auxiliar *m* de vuelo (en un avión), camarero *m* (en un barco)

stewardess ['stuːərdəs, 'stjuː-] *n* **1** MANAGER : administradora *f* **2** : camarera *f* (en un barco) **3** : auxiliar *f* de vuelo, azafata *f*, aeromoza *f* (en un avión)

stick¹ ['stɪk] *v* **stuck** ['stʌk]; **sticking** *vt* **1** STAB : clavar **2** ATTACH : pegar **3** PUT : poner, meter ⟨she stuck the letter under the door : metió la carta por debajo de la puerta⟩ ⟨stick 'em up! : ¡manos arriba!, ¡arriba las manos!⟩ **4 to stick it to** : darle duro a **5 to stick out** : sacar (la lengua, etc.), extender (la mano) **6 to stick out** ENDURE : aguantar an **7 to stick someone with** : endilgarle (una responsabilidad) a alguien, dejar a alguien solo con (una persona) — *vi* **1** ADHERE : pegarse, adherirse **2** JAM : atascarse ⟨the door sticks : la puerta se atasca⟩ ⟨the song stuck in my head/mind : la canción se me grabó en la cabeza/mente⟩ **3 to stick around** : quedarse **4 to stick by** : no abandonar **5 to stick out** PROJECT : sobresalir (de una superficie), asomar (por detrás o debajo de algo) **6 to stick out** STAND OUT : resaltar **7 to stick to** : no abandonar, no desviarse de ⟨stick to your guns : manténgase firme⟩ ⟨to stick to the rules : atenerse a las reglas⟩ ⟨to stick to one's word : cumplir uno con su palabra⟩ **8 to stick up** : estar parado (dícese del pelo, etc.), sobresalir (de una superficie) **9 to stick up for** : defender **10 to stick with** : serle fiel a (una persona), seguir con (una cosa) ⟨I'll stick with what I know : prefiero lo conocido⟩

stick² *n* **1** BRANCH, TWIG : ramita *f* **2** : palo *m*, vara *f* ⟨a walking stick : un bastón⟩

sticker ['stɪkər] *n* : etiqueta *f* adhesiva

stick–in–the–mud n : aguafiestas mf
stickler ['stɪklər] n : persona f exigente ⟨to be a stickler for : insistir mucho en⟩
sticky ['stɪki] adj **stickier; -est 1** ADHESIVE : pegajoso, adhesivo **2** MUGGY : bochornoso **3** DIFFICULT : difícil
stiff ['stɪf] adj **1** RIGID : rígido, tieso ⟨a stiff dough : una masa firme⟩ **2** : agarrotado, entumecido ⟨stiff muscles : músculos entumecidos⟩ **3** STILTED : acartonado, poco natural **4** STRONG : fuerte (dícese del viento, etc.) **5** DIFFICULT, SEVERE : severo, difícil, duro
stiffen ['stɪfən] vt **1** STRENGTHEN : fortalecer, reforzar (tela, etc.) **2** : hacer más duro (un castigo, etc.) — vi **1** HARDEN : endurecerse **2** : entumecerse (dícese de los músculos)
stiffly ['stɪfli] adv **1** RIGIDLY : rígidamente **2** COLDLY : con frialdad
stiffness ['stɪfnəs] n **1** RIGIDITY : rigidez f **2** COLDNESS : frialdad f **3** SEVERITY : severidad f
stifle ['staɪfəl] vt **-fled; -fling** SMOTHER, SUPPRESS : sofocar, reprimir, contener ⟨to stifle a yawn : reprimir un bostezo⟩
stifling ['staɪfəlɪŋ] adj : sofocante
stigma ['stɪgmə] n, pl **stigmata** [stɪg'mɑtə, 'stɪgmətə] or **stigmas** : estigma m
stigmatize ['stɪgmə,taɪz] vt **-tized; -tizing** : estigmatizar
stile ['staɪl] n : escalones mpl para cruzar un cerco
stiletto [stə'lɛ,to:] n, pl **-tos** or **-toes** : estilete m
still¹ ['stɪl] vt CALM : pacificar, apaciguar — vi : pacificarse, apaciguarse
still² adv **1** QUIETLY : quieto ⟨sit still! : ¡quédate quieto!⟩ **2** : de todos modos, aún, todavía ⟨she still lives there : aún vive allí⟩ ⟨it's still the same : sigue siendo lo mismo⟩ **3** IN ANY CASE : de todos modos, aún así ⟨he still has doubts : aún así le quedan dudas⟩ ⟨I still prefer that you stay : de todos modos prefiero que te quedes⟩
still³ adj **1** MOTIONLESS : quieto, inmóvil **2** SILENT : callado
still⁴ n **1** SILENCE : quietud f, calma f **2** : alambique m (para destilar alcohol)
stillborn ['stɪl,bɔrn] adj : nacido muerto
still life n : naturaleza f muerta, bodegón m
stillness ['stɪlnəs] n : calma f, silencio m
stilt ['stɪlt] n : zanco m
stilted ['stɪltəd] adj : afectado, poco natural
stimulant ['stɪmjələnt] n : estimulante m — **stimulant** adj
stimulate ['stɪmjə,leɪt] vt **-lated; -lating** : estimular
stimulation [,stɪmjə'leɪʃən] n **1** STIMULATING : estimulación f **2** STIMULUS : estímulo m
stimulus ['stɪmjələs] n, pl **-li** [-,laɪ] **1** : estímulo m **2** INCENTIVE : acicate m
sting¹ ['stɪŋ] v **stung** ['stʌŋ]; **stinging** vt **1** : picar ⟨a bee stung him : le picó una abeja⟩ **2** HURT : hacer escocer (físicamente), herir (emocionalmente) — vi **1**

: picar (dícese de las abejas, etc.) **2** SMART : escocer, arder
sting² n **1** : picadura f (herida), escozor m (sensación)
stinger ['stɪŋər] n : aguijón m (de una abeja, etc.)
stinginess ['stɪndʒinəs] n : tacañería f
stingy ['stɪndʒi] adj **stingier; -est 1** MISERLY : tacaño, avaro **2** PALTRY : mezquino, mísero
stink¹ ['stɪŋk] vi **stank** ['stæŋk] or **stunk** ['stʌŋk]; **stunk; stinking** : apestar, oler mal
stink² n : hedor m, mal olor m, peste f
stint¹ ['stɪnt] vt : escatimar ⟨to stint oneself of : privarse de⟩ — vi **to stint on** : escatimar
stint² n : período m
stipend ['staɪ,pend, -pənd] n : estipendio m
stipulate ['stɪpjə,leɪt] vt **-lated; -lating** : estipular
stipulation [,stɪpjə'leɪʃən] n : estipulación f
stir¹ ['stər] v **stirred; stirring** vt **1** AGITATE : mover, agitar **2** MIX : revolver, remover **3** INCITE : incitar, impulsar, motivar **4** or **to stir up** AROUSE : despertar (memorias, etc.), provocar (ira, etc.) — vi : moverse, agitarse
stir² n **1** MOTION : movimiento m **2** COMMOTION : revuelo m
stirrup ['stərəp, 'stɪr-] n : estribo m
stitch¹ ['stɪtʃ] vt : coser, bordar (para decorar) — vi : coser
stitch² n **1** : puntada f **2** TWINGE : punzada f, puntada f
stock¹ ['stɑk] vt : surtir, abastecer, vender — vi **to stock up** : abastecerse
stock² n **1** SUPPLY : reserva f, existencias fpl (en comercio) ⟨to be out of stock : estar agotadas las existencias⟩ **2** SECURITIES : acciones fpl, valores mpl **3** LIVESTOCK : ganado m **4** ANCESTRY : linaje m, estirpe f **5** BROTH : caldo m **6** **to take stock (of)** : evaluar
stockade [stɑ'keɪd] n : estacada f
stockbroker ['stɑk,bro:kər] n : corredor m, -dora f de bolsa
stock exchange n : bolsa f
stockholder ['stɑk,ho:ldər] n : accionista mf
stocking ['stɑkɪŋ] n : media f ⟨a pair of stockings : unas medias⟩
stock market n : mercado m de valores, bolsa f de valores
stockpile¹ ['stɑk,paɪl] vt **-piled; -piling** : acumular, almacenar
stockpile² n : reservas fpl
stocky ['stɑki] adj **stockier; -est** : robusto, fornido
stockyard ['stɑk,jɑrd] n : corral m
stodgy ['stɑdʒi] adj **stodgier; -est 1** DULL : aburrido, pesado **2** OLD-FASHIONED : anticuado
stoic¹ ['sto:ɪk] or **stoical** [-ɪkəl] adj : estoico — **stoically** [-ɪkli] adv
stoic² n : estoico m, -ca f
stoicism ['sto:ə,sɪzəm] n : estoicismo m
stoke ['sto:k] vt **stoked; stoking** : atizar (un fuego), echarle carbón a (un horno)

stole¹ → steal

stole² ['stoːl] n : estola f

stolen → steal

stolid ['stɑlɪd] adj : impasible, imperturbable — **stolidly** adv

stomach¹ ['stʌmɪk] vt : aguantar, soportar

stomach² n 1 : estómago m 2 BELLY : vientre m, barriga f, panza f 3 DESIRE : ganas fpl ⟨he had no stomach for a fight : no quería pelea⟩

stomachache ['stʌmɪk,eɪk] n : dolor m de estómago

stomp ['stɑmp, 'stɔmp] vt : pisotear — vi : pisar fuerte

stone¹ ['stoːn] vt stoned; stoning : apedrear, lapidar

stone² n 1 : piedra f 2 PIT : hueso m, pepa f (de una fruta)

Stone Age n : Edad f de Piedra

stoned ['stoːnd] adj fam : drogado

stonemason → mason

stonemasonry → masonry

stony ['stoːni] adj stonier; -est 1 ROCKY : pedregoso 2 UNFEELING : insensible, frío ⟨a stony stare : una mirada glacial⟩

stood → stand

stool ['stuːl] n 1 SEAT : taburete m, banco m 2 FOOTSTOOL : escabel m 3 FECES : deposición f de heces

stoop ['stuːp] vi 1 CROUCH : agacharse 2 to stoop to : rebajarse a

stoop² n 1 : espaldas fpl encorvadas ⟨to have a stoop : ser encorvado⟩ 2 : entrada f (de una casa)

stop¹ ['stɑp] v stopped; stopping vt 1 or to stop up PLUG : tapar 2 PREVENT : impedir, evitar ⟨she stopped me from leaving : me impidió que saliera⟩ 3 HALT : parar, detener ⟨I was stopped by the police : me paró un policía⟩ ⟨he stopped the car : paró el carro⟩ 4 CEASE, QUIT : dejar de ⟨he stopped talking : dejó de hablar⟩ ⟨stop it! : ¡basta!⟩ 5 END : terminar (una pelea, etc.), detener (una hemorragia) ⟨we must stop the violence : tenemos que poner fin a la violencia⟩ 6 to stop (payment on) a check : dar orden de no pago (a un cheque) — vi 1 HALT : detenerse, parar ⟨she stopped to watch : se detuvo a mirar⟩ ⟨we stopped for gas : paramos a poner gasolina⟩ ⟨he stopped dead : paró en seco⟩ ⟨stop! who goes there? : ¡alto! ¿quién va?⟩ 2 : detenerse, parar ⟨let's stop and take a break : paremos para descansar⟩ ⟨to stop to consider something : detenerse a pensar en algo⟩ 3 : pararse (dícese de un motor, etc.) ⟨his heart stopped : se le paró el corazón⟩ 4 CEASE, END : cesar, terminar ⟨the rain won't stop : no deja de llover⟩ 5 STAY : quedarse ⟨I can't stop for long : no puedo quedarme mucho tiempo⟩ 6 to stop by/in : pasar a ver, visitar 7 to stop off : hacer una parada 8 to stop over : parar, quedarse 9 to stop over : hacer escala (dícese de un avión)

stop² n 1 STOPPER : tapón m 2 HALT : parada f, alto m ⟨to come to a stop : pararse, detenerse⟩ ⟨to put a stop to : poner fin a⟩ 3 : parada f ⟨bus stop : parada de autobús⟩

stopgap ['stɑp,gæp] n : arreglo m provisorio

stoplight ['stɑp,laɪt] n : semáforo m

stopover ['stɑp,oːvər] n LAYOVER : escala f

stoppage ['stɑpɪdʒ] n : acto m de parar ⟨a work stoppage : un paro⟩

stopper ['stɑpər] n : tapón m

stopwatch ['stɑp,wɑtʃ] n : cronómetro m

storage ['storɪdʒ] n : almacenamiento m, almacenaje m

storage battery n : acumulador m

store¹ ['stor] vt stored; storing : guardar, almacenar

store² n 1 RESERVE, SUPPLY : reserva f 2 SHOP : tienda f ⟨grocery store : tienda de comestibles⟩

storehouse ['stor,haʊs] n : almacén m, depósito m

storekeeper ['stor,kiːpər] n : tendero m, -ra f

storeroom ['stor,ruːm, -,rʊm] n : almacén m, depósito m

stork ['stork] n : cigüeña f

storm¹ ['storm] vi 1 : llover o nevar tormentosamente 2 RAGE : ponerse furioso, vociferar 3 to storm out : salir echando pestes — vt ATTACK : asaltar

storm² n 1 : tormenta f, tempestad f 2 UPROAR : alboroto m, escándalo m ⟨a storm of abuse : un torrente de abusos⟩

stormy ['stormi] adj stormier; -est : tormentoso — stormily adv

story ['stori] n, pl stories 1 NARRATIVE, TALE : cuento m, relato m ⟨a bedtime story : un cuento para dormir⟩ 2 ACCOUNT : historia f, relato m ⟨it's a long story : es largo de contar⟩ ⟨to make a long story short : en pocas palabras⟩ 3 ARTICLE : artículo m 4 TALE, LIE : cuento m, mentira f 5 INFORMATION : información f ⟨what's his story? : ¿qué me puedes contar de él?⟩ ⟨the story behind the changes : la razón de los cambios⟩ 6 : piso m, planta f (de un edificio) ⟨first story : planta baja⟩

stout ['staʊt] adj 1 FIRM, RESOLUTE : firme, resuelto 2 STURDY : fuerte, robusto, sólido 3 FAT : corpulento, gordo

stoutness ['staʊtnəs] n 1 FIRMNESS : firmeza f 2 STURDINESS : fuerza f, robustez f, solidez f 3 FATNESS : corpulencia f, gordura f

stove¹ ['stoːv] n : cocina f (para cocinar), estufa f (para calentar)

stove² → stave¹

stow ['stoː] vt 1 STORE : poner, meter, guardar 2 LOAD : cargar — vi to stow away : viajar de polizón

stowaway ['stoːə,weɪ] n : polizón m

straddle ['strædəl] vt -dled; -dling : sentarse a horcajadas sobre

straggle ['strægəl] vi -gled; -gling : rezagarse, quedarse atrás

straggler ['stræglər] n : rezagado m, -da f

straight[1] ['streɪt] *adv* **1** : derecho, directamente ⟨go straight, then turn right : sigue derecho, luego gira a la derecha⟩ **2** HONESTLY : honestamente ⟨to go straight : enmendarse⟩ **3** CLEARLY : con claridad **4** FRANKLY : francamente, con franqueza

straight[2] *adj* **1** : recto (dícese de las líneas, etc.), derecho (dícese de algo vertical), lacio (dícese del pelo) **2** HONEST, JUST : honesto, justo **3** NEAT, ORDERLY : arreglado, ordenado **4** : solo (dícese de una bebida alcohólica)

straightaway [,streɪtə'weɪ] *adv* : inmediatamente

straighten ['streɪtən] *vt* **1** *or* to straighten out : enderezar, poner derecho **2** to straighten out/up NEATEN : arreglar, ordenar ⟨he straightened up the house : arregló la casa⟩ ⟨I straightened out my papers : ordené los papeles⟩ **3** to straighten out FIX : arreglar, resolver (problemas, etc.), poner (la vida) en orden **4** to straighten out : enderezar, meter en vereda (a un niño rebelde, etc.) **5** to straighten out ENLIGHTEN : aclararle las dudas (a alguien) — *vi* **1** to straighten up : ponerse derecho **2** to straighten up/out IMPROVE : enderezarse

straightforward [streɪt'fɔrwərd] *adj* **1** FRANK : franco, sincero **2** CLEAR, PRECISE : puro, simple, claro

straight razor → razor

strain[1] ['streɪn] *vt* **1** EXERT : forzar (la vista, la voz) ⟨to strain oneself : hacer un gran esfuerzo⟩ **2** FILTER : colar, filtrar **3** INJURE : lastimarse, hacerse daño en ⟨to strain a muscle : sufrir un esguince⟩ — *vi* to strain to do something : esforzarse por hacer algo

strain[2] *n* **1** LINEAGE : linaje *m*, abolengo *m* **2** STREAK, TRACE : veta *f* **3** VARIETY : tipo *m*, variedad *f* **4** STRESS : tensión *f*, presión *f* **5** SPRAIN : esguince *m*, torcedura *f* (del tobillo, etc.) **6** strains *npl* TUNE : melodía *f*, acordes *mpl*, compases *fpl*

strained ['streɪnd] *adj* **1** FORCED : forzado **2** ANXIOUS : preocupado **3** TIRED : cansado **4** TENSE : tenso

strainer ['streɪnər] *n* : colador *m*

strait ['streɪt] *n* **1** : estrecho *m* **2** straits *npl* DISTRESS : aprietos *mpl*, apuros *mpl* ⟨in dire straits : en serios aprietos⟩

straitened ['streɪtənd] *adj* in straitened circumstances : en apuros económicos

straitjacket [streɪt,ʤækət] *n* : camisa *f* de fuerza

strand[1] ['strænd] *vt* **1** : varar **2** to be left stranded : quedar(se) varado, quedar colgado ⟨they left me stranded : me dejaron abandonado⟩

strand[2] *n* **1** : hebra *f* (de hilo, etc.) ⟨a strand of hair : un pelo⟩ **2** BEACH : playa *f*

strange ['streɪnʤ] *adj* **stranger; -est 1** QUEER, UNUSUAL : extraño, raro **2** UNFAMILIAR : desconocido, nuevo

strangely ['streɪnʤli] *adv* ODDLY : de manera extraña ⟨to behave strangely : portarse de una manera rara⟩ ⟨strangely, he didn't call : curiosamente, no llamó⟩

strangeness ['streɪnʤnəs] *n* **1** ODDNESS : rareza *f* **2** UNFAMILIARITY : lo desconocido

stranger ['streɪnʤər] *n* : desconocido *m*, -da *f*; extraño *m*, -ña *f*

strangle ['stræŋgəl] *vt* **-gled; -gling** : estrangular

strangler ['stræŋglər] *n* : estrangulador *m*, -dora *f*

strangulation [,stræŋgjə'leɪʃən] *n* : estrangulamiento *m*

strap[1] ['stræp] *vt* **strapped; strapping 1** FASTEN : sujetar con una correa **2** FLOG : azotar (con una correa)

strap[2] *n* **1** : correa *f* **2** shoulder strap : tirante *m*

strapless ['stræpləs] *n* : sin tirantes

strapping ['stræpɪŋ] *adj* : robusto, fornido

stratagem ['stræɪtəʤəm, -,ʤɛm] *n* : estratagema *f*, artimaña *f*

strategic [strə'tiːʤɪk] *adj* : estratégico

strategist ['stræɪtəʤɪst] *n* : estratega *mf*

strategy ['stræɪtəʤi] *n, pl* **-gies** : estrategia *f*

stratified ['stræɪtə,faɪd] *adj* : estratificado

stratosphere ['stræɪtə,sfɪr] *n* : estratosfera *f*

stratospheric [,stræɪtə'sfɪrɪk, -'sfɛr-] *adj* : estratosférico

stratum ['streɪtəm, 'stræ-] *n, pl* **strata** [-ə] : estrato *m*, capa *f*

straw ['strɔ] *n* **1** : paja *f* ⟨the last straw : el colmo⟩ **2** *or* drinking straw : pajita *f*, popote *m* Mex

strawberry ['strɔ,beri] *n, pl* **-ries** : fresa *f*

stray[1] ['streɪ] *vi* **1** WANDER : alejarse, extraviarse ⟨the cattle strayed away : el ganado se descarrió⟩ **2** DIGRESS : desviarse, divagar

stray[2] *adj* : perdido, callejero (dícese de un perro o un gato), descarriado (dícese del ganado)

stray[3] *n* : animal *m* perdido, animal *m* callejero

streak[1] ['striːk] *vt* : hacer rayas en ⟨hair streaked with grey : azul veteado con gris⟩ — *vi* : ir como una flecha

streak[2] *n* **1** : raya *f*, veta *f* (en mármol, queso, etc.), mechón *m* (en el pelo) **2** : rayo *m* (de luz) **3** TRACE : veta *f* **4** : racha *f* ⟨a streak of luck : una racha de suerte⟩

stream[1] ['striːm] *vi* : correr, salir a chorros ⟨tears streamed from his eyes : las lágrimas brotaban de sus ojos⟩ — *vt* **1** : derramar, dejar correr ⟨to stream blood : derramar sangre⟩ **2** : transmitir (audio o video) en streaming **3** : ver (video) o escuchar (audio) en streaming

stream[2] *n* **1** BROOK : arroyo *m*, riachuelo *m* **2** RIVER : río *m* **3** FLOW : corriente *f*, chorro *m* **4** SERIES : serie *f*, sarta *f*

streamer ['striːmər] *n* **1** PENNANT : banderín *m* **2** RIBBON : serpentina *f* (de papel), cinta *f* (de tela)

streaming[1] ['striːmɪŋ] adj : de streaming ⟨streaming video : video en streaming⟩
streaming[2] n : streaming m
streamline ['striːmˌlaɪn] vt : racionalizar (un proceso, etc.)
streamlined ['striːmˌlaɪnd] adj 1 : aerodinámico (dícese de los automóviles, etc.) 2 EFFICIENT : eficiente, racionalizado
street ['striːt] n : calle f
streetcar ['striːtˌkɑr] n : tranvía m
streetlight ['striːtˌlaɪt] or **streetlamp** ['striːtˌlæmp] n : farol m, farola f
strength ['strɛŋkθ] n 1 : fuerza f ⟨with all her strength : con toda(s) su(s) fuerza(s)⟩ ⟨to save one's strength : reservar uno sus energías⟩ 2 POWER : poder m, fuerza f ⟨economic/military strength : poder económico/military⟩ ⟨there is strength in numbers : la unión hace la fuerza⟩ 3 FORTITUDE : fortaleza f ⟨strength of character : fortaleza/fuerza de carácter⟩ 4 SOLIDITY, TOUGHNESS : solidez f, resistencia f, dureza f (de un material) 5 INTENSITY : intensidad f (de emociones, etc.), fuerza f (del viento, etc.), lo fuerte (de un sabor, etc.) 6 CONCENTRATION : concentración f ⟨full strength : sin diluir⟩ 7 POTENCY : potencia f (de un medicamento) ⟨full/maximum strength : máxima potencia⟩ 8 : fuerte m, punto m fuerte ⟨strengths and weaknesses : virtudes y defectos⟩ 9 NUMBER : número m, complemento m ⟨in full strength : en gran número⟩
strengthen ['strɛŋkθən] vt 1 : fortalecer (los músculos, el espíritu, etc.) 2 REINFORCE : reforzar 3 INTENSIFY : intensificar, redoblar (esfuerzos, etc.) — vi 1 : fortalecerse, hacerse más fuerte 2 INTENSIFY : intensificarse
strenuous ['strɛnjuəs] adj 1 VIGOROUS : vigoroso, enérgico 2 ARDUOUS : duro, riguroso
strenuously ['strɛnjuəsli] adv : vigorosamente, duro
stress[1] ['strɛs] vt 1 : someter a tensión (física) 2 EMPHASIZE : enfatizar, recalcar 3 to stress out : estresar
stress[2] n 1 : tensión f (en un material) 2 EMPHASIS : énfasis m, acento m (en lingüística) 3 TENSION : tensión f (nerviosa), estrés m
stressful ['strɛsfəl] adj : estresante
stretch[1] ['strɛtʃ] vt 1 : estirar (un suéter, un cable, etc.), extender (un lienzo, etc.), desplegar (alas) ⟨to stretch one's legs : estirar las piernas, caminar⟩ 2 to stretch the truth : forzar la verdad, exagerar — vi 1 or to stretch out : estirarse 2 REACH : extenderse 3 to stretch back (in time) : remontarse
stretch[2] n 1 STRETCHING : extensión f, estiramiento m (de músculos) 2 ELASTICITY : elasticidad f 3 EXPANSE : tramo m, trecho m ⟨the home stretch : la recta final⟩ 4 PERIOD : período m (de tiempo)
stretcher ['strɛtʃər] n : camilla f
strew ['struː] vt strewed; strewed or strewn ['struːn]; strewing 1 SCATTER

: esparcir (semillas, etc.), desparramar (papeles, etc.) 2 to strew with : cubrir de
stricken ['strɪkən] adj stricken with : aquejado de (una enfermedad), afligido por (tristeza, etc.)
strict ['strɪkt] adj : estricto — **strictly** adv
strictness ['strɪktnəs] n : severidad f, lo estricto
stricture ['strɪktʃər] n : crítica f, censura f
stride[1] ['straɪd] vi strode ['stroːd]; stridden ['strɪdən]; striding : ir a trancos, ir dando zancadas
stride[2] n : tranco m, zancada f
strident ['straɪdənt] adj : estridente
strife ['straɪf] n : conflictos mpl, disensión f
strike[1] ['straɪk] v struck ['strʌk]; striking vt 1 HIT : golpear, pegarle (a una persona) ⟨the bullet struck him in the leg : la bala lo alcanzó en la pierna⟩ 2 HIT : chocar contra, dar contra ⟨the car struck a tree : el carro chocó contra un árbol⟩ 3 DELETE : suprimir, tachar 4 COIN, MINT : acuñar (monedas) 5 : dar (la hora) 6 AFFLICT : sobrevenir ⟨he was stricken with a fever : le sobrevino una fiebre⟩ 7 IMPRESS : impresionar, parecer ⟨her voice struck me : su voz me impresionó⟩ ⟨it struck him as funny : le pareció chistoso⟩ 8 : ocurrírsele a ⟨it struck me that . . . : se me ocurrió que . . .⟩ 9 : encender (un fósforo) 10 FIND : descubrir (oro, petróleo) 11 ADOPT : adoptar (una pose, etc.) 12 : tocar (en música) 13 REACH : llegar a, alcanzar (un acuerdo, etc.) 14 to strike a blow : pegar un golpe 15 to strike down : fulminar 16 to strike out : tachar (palabras, etc.) 17 to strike up : entablar (una conversación, una amistad), empezar a tocar (una canción) — vi 1 HIT : golpear ⟨to strike against : chocar contra⟩ 2 ATTACK : atacar 3 : declararse en huelga 4 to strike back at : devolverle el golpe a 5 to strike out : poncharse (en beisbol) 6 to strike out FAIL : fracasar 7 to strike out at ATTACK : arremeter contra 8 to strike out for : emprender el camino hacia 9 to strike out on one's own : emprender algo solo
strike[2] n 1 BLOW : golpe m 2 : huelga f, paro m ⟨to be on strike : estar en huelga⟩ 3 ATTACK : ataque m
strikebreaker ['straɪkˌbreɪkər] n : rompehuelgas mf, esquirol mf
strike out vi 1 HEAD : salir (para) 2 : ser ponchado (en béisbol) ⟨the batter struck out : poncharon al bateador⟩
striker ['straɪkər] n : huelguista mf
strike up vt START : entablar, empezar
striking ['straɪkɪŋ] adj : notable, sorprendente, llamativo ⟨a striking beauty : una belleza imponente⟩ — **strikingly** adv
string[1] ['strɪŋ] vt strung ['strʌŋ]; stringing 1 THREAD : ensartar ⟨to string beads : ensartar cuentas⟩ 2 HANG : colgar (con un cordel)
string[2] n 1 : cordel m, cuerda f 2 SERIES : serie f, sarta f (de insultos, etc.) 3

strings *npl* : cuerdas *fpl* (en música) 4
strings *npl* : influencias *fpl* ⟨to pull strings : utilizar sus influencias⟩ 5
strings *npl* : compromisos *mpl* ⟨with no strings attached : sin compromiso(s)⟩
string bean *n* : judía *f*, ejote *m Mex*
stringent ['strɪndʒənt] *adj* : estricto, severo
stringy ['strɪŋi] *adj* **stringier; -est** : fibroso
strip¹ ['strɪp] *v* **stripped; stripping** *vt* : quitar (ropa, pintura, etc.), desnudar, despojar — *vi* UNDRESS : desnudarse
strip² *n* : tira *f* ⟨a strip of land : una faja⟩
stripe¹ ['straɪp] *vt* **striped** ['straɪpt]; **striping** : marcar con rayas o listas
stripe² *n* 1 : raya *f*, lista *f* 2 BAND : franja *f*
striped ['straɪpt, 'straɪpəd] *adj* : a rayas, de rayas, rayado, listado
strive ['straɪv] *vi* **strove** ['stroːv], **striven** ['strɪvən] *or* **strived; striving** 1 **to strive for** : luchar por lograr 2 **to strive to** : esforzarse por
strode → **stride**
stroke¹ ['stroːk] *vt* **stroked; stroking** : acariciar
stroke² *n* 1 : apoplejía *f*, derrame *m* cerebral (en medicina) 2 : pincelada *f*, trazo *m* (en el arte) 3 : estilo *m* (de nadar) 4 : movimiento *m*, batir *m* (de alas), brazada *f* (al nadar), remada *f* (al remar) 5 CARESS : caricia *f* 6 : golpe *m* (en beisbol, etc.) 7 ACT : golpe *m* ⟨in one stroke : de un golpe⟩ ⟨a stroke of genius/inspiration : una genialidad/inspiración⟩ 8 : golpe *m* ⟨a stroke of luck : un golpe de suerte⟩ 9 : campanada *f* (de un reloj)
stroll¹ ['stroːl] *vi* : pasear, pasearse, dar un paseo
stroll² *n* : paseo *m*
stroller ['stroːlər] *n* : cochecito *m* (para niños)
strong ['strɔŋ] *adj* 1 : fuerte ⟨strong arms : brazos fuertes⟩ ⟨strong winds : vientos fuertes⟩ ⟨a strong odor : un olor fuerte⟩ ⟨strong coffee/medicine : café/medicina fuerte⟩ ⟨strong language : lenguaje fuerte⟩ ⟨a strong candidate/leader : un candidato/líder fuerte⟩ ⟨strong opposition : fuerte oposición⟩ ⟨of strong character : de carácter fuerte⟩ ⟨his strong point : su (punto) fuerte⟩ 2 DURABLE : resistente, fuerte 3 HEALTHY : sano 4 NOTICEABLE : marcado 5 FIRM : firme (dícese de convicciones, etc.) 6 PERSUASIVE : poderoso, convincente 7 CONCENTRATED : concentrado (dícese de detergente, etc.) 8 : con mucho aumento (dícese de lentes) 9 (*with numbers*) ⟨an organization five hundred people strong : una organización de quinientas personas⟩
strongbox ['strɔŋ,bɑks] *n* : caja *f* fuerte
stronghold ['strɔŋ,hoːld] *n* : fortaleza *f*, fuerte *m*, bastión *m* ⟨a cultural stronghold : un baluarte de la cultura⟩
strongly ['strɔŋli] *adv* 1 POWERFULLY : fuerte, con fuerza 2 STURDILY

: fuertemente, sólidamente 3 INTENSELY : intensamente, profundamente : to feel strongly about something : tener ideas muy claras sobre algo⟩ ⟨to feel/believe strongly that . . . : estar totalmente convencido de que . . . , tener la convicción de que . . .⟩ ⟨I am strongly tempted· : me siento muy tentada⟩ 4 WHOLEHEARTEDLY : totalmente ⟨I strongly agree : estoy totalmente de acuerdo⟩ ⟨I strongly disagree : estoy totalmente en desacuerdo⟩ 5 EMPHATICALLY : enérgicamente ⟨to criticize strongly : criticar duramente⟩ ⟨a strongly worded letter : una carta muy dura⟩ ⟨I strongly advise that you see a doctor : le recomiendo encarecidamente que vaya a un médico⟩ 6 **to smell/taste strongly of** : oler/saber fuertemente a
struck → **strike**¹
structural ['strʌktʃərəl] *adj* : estructural
structure¹ ['strʌktʃər] *vt* **-tured; -turing** : estructurar
structure² *n* 1 BUILDING : construcción *f* 2 ARRANGEMENT, FRAMEWORK : estructura *f*
struggle¹ ['strʌgəl] *vi* **-gled; -gling** 1 CONTEND : forcejear (físicamente), luchar, contender 2 : hacer con dificultad ⟨she struggled forward : avanzó con dificultad⟩
struggle² *n* : lucha *f*, pelea *f* (física)
strum ['strʌm] *vt* **strummed; strumming** : rasguear
strung → **string**¹
strut¹ ['strʌt] *vi* **strutted; strutting** : pavonearse
strut² *n* 1 : pavoneo *m* ⟨he walked with a strut : se pavoneaba⟩ 2 : puntal *m* (en construcción, etc.)
stub¹ ['stʌb] *vt* **stubbed; stubbing** 1 **to stub one's toe** : darse en el dedo (del pie) 2 **to stub out** : apagarse
stub² *n* : colilla *f* (de un cigarrillo), cabo *m* (de un lápiz, etc.), talón *m* (de un cheque)
stubble ['stʌbəl] *n* 1 : rastrojo *m* (de plantas) 2 BEARD : barba *f*
stubborn ['stʌbərn] *adj* 1 OBSTINATE : terco, obstinado, empecinado 2 PERSISTENT : pertinaz, persistente — **stubbornly** *adv*
stubbornness ['stʌbərnnəs] *n* 1 OBSTINACY : terquedad *f*, obstinación *f* 2 PERSISTENCE : persistencia *f*
stubby ['stʌbi] *adj* **stubbier; -est** : corto y grueso ⟨stubby fingers : dedos regordetes⟩
stucco ['stʌkoː] *n, pl* **stuccos** *or* **stuccoes** : estuco *m*
stuck → **stick**¹
stuck–up ['stʌk'ʌp] *adj* : engreído, creído *fam*
stud¹ ['stʌd] *vt* **studded; studding** : tachonar, salpicar
stud² *n* 1 *or* **stud horse** : semental *m* 2 : montante *m* (en construcción) 3 HOBNAIL : tachuela *f*, tachón *m*
student ['stuːdənt, 'stjuː-] *n* : estudiante *mf*; alumno *m*, -na *f* (de un colegio)

studied ['stʌdid] *adj* : intencionado, premeditado

studio ['stu:di,o:, 'stju:-] *n, pl* **studios** : estudio *m*

studious ['stu:diəs, 'stju:-] *adj* : estudioso — **studiously** *adv*

study¹ ['stʌdi] *v* **studied; studying 1** : estudiar **2** EXAMINE : examinar, estudiar

study² *n, pl* **studies 1** STUDYING : estudio *m* **2** OFFICE : estudio *m*, gabinete *m* (en una casa) **3** RESEARCH : investigación *f*, estudio *m*

stuff¹ ['stʌf] *vt* : rellenar, llenar, atiborrar ⟨a stuffed toy : un juguete de peluche⟩

stuff² *n* **1** POSSESSIONS : cosas *fpl* ⟨my stuff : mis cosas⟩ **2** SUPPLIES, EQUIPMENT : cosas *fpl* ⟨baby stuff : cosas para bebés⟩ **3** *fam* : cosa *f*, cosas *fpl* ⟨some sticky stuff : una cosa pegajosa⟩ ⟨this stuff really works! : ¡esto funciona de maravilla!⟩ ⟨they're giving away free stuff : están regalando cosas⟩ ⟨and stuff (like that) : y cosas por el estilo⟩ **4** *(referring to something heard, read, etc.) fam* ⟨this is fascinating stuff : esto es fascinante⟩ ⟨the stuff he said isn't true : lo que dijo no es verdad⟩ **5** *(referring to behavior) fam* : cosas *fpl* ⟨she does stuff to bug me : hace cosas para fastidiarme⟩ ⟨how can he get away with that stuff? : ¿cómo es que siempre se sale con la suya?⟩ **6** ESSENCE : esencia *f* ⟨to know your stuff : ser experto⟩

stuffing ['stʌfiŋ] *n* : relleno *m*

stuffy ['stʌfi] *adj* **stuffier; -est 1** CLOSE : viciado, cargado ⟨a stuffy room : una sala mal ventilada⟩ ⟨stuffy weather : tiempo bochornoso⟩ **2** : tapado (dícese de la nariz) **3** STODGY : pesado, aburrido

stumble¹ ['stʌmbəl] *vi* **-bled; -bling 1** TRIP : tropezar, dar un traspié **2** FLOUNDER : quedarse sin saber qué hacer o decir ⟨to stumble across *or* to stumble upon : dar con, tropezar con

stumble² *n* : tropezón *m*, traspié *m*

stumbling block *n* : obstáculo *m*

stump¹ ['stʌmp] *vt* : dejar perplejo ⟨to be stumped : no tener respuesta⟩

stump² *n* **1** : muñón *m* (de un brazo o una pierna) **2** *or* **tree stump** : cepa *f*, tocón *m* **3** STUB : cabo *m*

stun ['stʌn] *vt* **stunned; stunning 1** : aturdir (con un golpe) **2** ASTONISH, SHOCK : dejar estupefacto, dejar atónito, aturdir

stung → **sting¹**

stunk → **stink¹**

stunning ['stʌnɪŋ] *adj* **1** ASTONISHING : asombroso, pasmoso, increíble **2** STRIKING : imponente, impresionante (dícese de la belleza)

stunt¹ ['stʌnt] *vt* : atrofiar

stunt² *n* : proeza *f* (acrobática)

stupefy ['stu:pə,faɪ, 'stju:-] *vt* **-fied; -fying 1** : aturdir, atontar (con drogas, etc.) **2** AMAZE : dejar estupefacto, dejar atónito

stupendous [stu'pɛndəs, stju-] *adj* **1** MARVELOUS : estupendo, maravilloso **2** TREMENDOUS : tremendo — **stupendously** *adv*

stupid ['stu:pəd, 'stju:-] *adj* **1** IDIOTIC, SILLY : tonto, bobo, estúpido **2** DULL, OBTUSE : lento, torpe, lerdo

stupidity [stu'pɪdəti, stju:-] *n* : tontería *f*, estupidez *f*

stupidly ['stu:pədli, 'stju:-] *adv* **1** IDIOTICALLY : estúpidamente, tontamente **2** DENSELY : torpemente

stupor ['stu:pər, 'stju:-] *n* : estupor *m*

sturdily ['stərdəli] *adv* : sólidamente

sturdiness ['stərdinəs] *n* : solidez *f* (de muebles, etc.), robustez *f* (de una persona)

sturdy ['stərdi] *adj* **sturdier; -est** : fuerte, robusto, sólido

sturgeon ['stərdʒən] *n* : esturión *m*

stutter¹ ['stʌtər] *vi* : tartamudear

stutter² *n* STAMMER : tartamudeo *m*

sty ['staɪ] *n* **1** *pl* **sties** PIGPEN : chiquero *m*, pocilga *f* **2** *or* **stye** *pl* **sties** *or* **styes** : orzuelo *m* (en el ojo)

style¹ ['staɪl] *vt* **styled; styling 1** NAME : llamar **2** : peinar (pelo), diseñar (vestidos, etc.) ⟨carefully styled prose : prosa escrita con gran esmero⟩

style² *n* **1** : estilo *m* ⟨that's just his style : él es así⟩ ⟨to live in style : vivir a lo grande⟩ **2** FASHION : moda *f*

stylish ['staɪlɪʃ] *adj* : de moda, elegante, chic

stylishly ['staɪlɪʃli] *adv* : con estilo

stylishness ['staɪlɪʃnəs] *n* : estilo *m*

stylist ['staɪlɪst] *n* : estilista *mf*

stylize ['staɪ,laɪz, 'staɪə-] *vt* : estilizar

stylus ['staɪləs] *n, pl* **styli** ['staɪ,laɪ] **1** PEN : estilo *m* **2** NEEDLE : aguja *f* (de un tocadiscos)

stymie ['staɪmi] *vt* **-mied; -mieing** : obstacular

suave ['swɑv] *adj* : fino, urbano

sub¹ ['sʌb] *vi* **subbed; subbing** → **substitute¹**

sub² *n* **1** → **substitute²** **2** → **submarine**

sub- [ˌsʌb] *pref* : sub-

subcommittee ['sʌbkə,mɪti] *n* : subcomité *m*

subconscious¹ [sʌb'kɑntʃəs] *adj* : subconsciente — **subconsciously** *adv*

subconscious² *n* : subconsciente *m*

subcontract [ˌsʌb'kɑn,trækt] *vt* : subcontratar

subcontractor [ˌsʌb'kɑn,træktər] *n* : subcontratista *mf*

subculture ['sʌb,kʌltʃər] *n* : subcultura *f*

subdivide [ˌsʌbdə'vaɪd, 'sʌbdə,vaɪd] *vt* **-vided; -viding** : subdividir

subdivision ['sʌbdə,vɪʒən] *n* : subdivisión *f*

subdue [səb'du:, -'dju:] *vt* **-dued; -duing 1** OVERCOME : sojuzgar (a un enemigo), vencer, superar **2** CONTROL : dominar **3** SOFTEN : suavizar, atenuar (luz, etc.), moderar (lenguaje)

subgroup ['sʌb,gru:p] *n* : subgrupo *m*

subhead ['sʌb,hɛd] *or* **subheading** [-,hɛdɪŋ] *n* : subtítulo *m*

subhuman [ˌsʌb'hju:mən, -'ju:-] *adj* : infrahumano

subject[1] [səb'dʒɛkt] *vt* **1** CONTROL, DOMINATE : controlar, dominar **2** : someter ⟨they subjected him to pressure : lo sometieron a presiones⟩

subject[2] ['sʌbdʒɪkt] *adj* **1** : subyugado, sometido ⟨a subject nation : una nación subyugada⟩ **2** PRONE : sujeto, propenso ⟨subject to colds : sujeto a resfriarse⟩ **subject to** : sujeto a ⟨subject to congressional approval : sujeto a la aprobación del congreso⟩

subject[3] ['sʌbdʒɪkt] *n* **1** : súbdito *m*, -ta *f* (de un gobierno) **2** *or* **subject matter** TOPIC : tema *m* **3** : sujeto *m* (en gramática)

subjection [səb'dʒɛkʃən] *n* : sometimiento *m*

subjective [səb'dʒɛktɪv] *adj* : subjetivo — **subjectively** *adv*

subjectivity [,sʌb,dʒɛk'tɪvəti] *n* : subjetividad *f*

subjugate ['sʌbdʒɪ,geɪt] *vt* **-gated; -gating** : subyugar, someter, sojuzgar

subjunctive [səb'dʒʌŋktɪv] *n* : subjuntivo *m* — **subjunctive** *adj*

sublet ['sʌb,lɛt] *vt* **-let; -letting** : subarrendar

sublimate ['sʌblə,meɪt] *vt* **-mated; -mating** : sublimar — **sublimation** [,sʌblə'meɪʃən] *n*

sublime [sə'blaɪm] *adj* : sublime

sublimely [sə'blaɪmli] *adv* **1** : de manera sublime **2** UTTERLY : absolutamente, completamente

submarine[1] ['sʌbmə,riːn, ,sʌbmə'-] *adj* : submarino

submarine[2] *n* : submarino *m*

submachine gun [,sʌbmə'ʃiːn-] *n* : metralleta *f*

submerge [səb'mərdʒ] *v* **-merged; -merging** *vt* : sumergir — *vi* : sumergirse

submission [səb'mɪʃən] *n* **1** YIELDING : sumisión *f* **2** PRESENTATION : presentación *f*

submissive [səb'mɪsɪv] *adj* : sumiso, dócil

submissiveness [səb'mɪsɪvnəs] *n* : sumisión *f*

submit [səb'mɪt] *v* **-mitted; -mitting** *vi* YIELD : rendirse ⟨to submit to : someterse a⟩ — *vt* PRESENT : presentar

subnormal [,sʌb'nɔrməl] *adj* : por debajo de lo normal

subordinate[1] [sə'bɔrdən,eɪt] *vt* **-nated; -nating** : subordinar

subordinate[2] [sə'bɔrdənət] *adj* : subordinado ⟨a subordinate clause : una oración subordinada⟩

subordinate[3] *n* : subordinado *m*, -da *f*; subalterno *m*, -na *f*

subordination [sə,bɔrdən'eɪʃən] *n* : subordinación *f*

subpoena[1] [sə'piːnə] *vt* **-naed; -naing** : citar

subpoena[2] *n* : citación *f*, citatorio *m*

subscribe [səb'skraɪb] *vi* **-scribed; -scribing 1** : suscribirse (a una revista, etc.) **2 to subscribe to** : suscribir (una opinión, etc.), estar de acuerdo con

subscriber [səb'skraɪbər] *n* : suscriptor *m*, -tora *f* (de una revista, etc.); abonado *m*, -da *f* (de un servicio)

subscription [səb'skrɪpʃən] *n* : suscripción *f*

subsection ['sʌb,sɛkʃən] *n* : inciso *m* (de un artículo, etc.)

subsequent ['sʌbsɪkwənt, -sə,kwɛnt] *adj* : subsiguiente ⟨subsequent to : posterior a⟩

subsequently ['sʌbsɪkwəntli, -kwɛnt-] *adv* : posteriormente

subservient [səb'sərviənt] *adj* : servil

subside [səb'saɪd] *vi* **-sided; -siding 1** SINK : hundirse, descender **2** ABATE : calmarse (dícese de las emociones), amainar (dícese del viento, etc.)

subsidiary[1] [səb'sɪdi,ɛri] *adj* : secundario

subsidiary[2] *n, pl* **-ries** : filial *f*, subsidiaria *f*

subsidize ['sʌbsə,daɪz] *vt* **-dized; -dizing** : subvencionar, subsidiar

subsidy ['sʌbsədi] *n, pl* **-dies** : subvención *f*, subsidio *m*

subsist [səb'sɪst] *vi* : subsistir, mantenerse, vivir

subsistence [səb'sɪstənts] *n* : subsistencia *f*

substance ['sʌbstənts] *n* **1** ESSENCE : sustancia *f*, esencia *f* **2** : sustancia *f* ⟨a toxic substance : una sustancia tóxica⟩ **3** WEALTH : riqueza *f* ⟨a woman of substance : una mujer acaudalada⟩

substandard [,sʌb'stændərd] *adj* : inferior, deficiente

substantial [səb'stæntʃəl] *adj* **1** ABUNDANT : sustancioso ⟨a substantial meal : una comida sustanciosa⟩ **2** CONSIDERABLE : considerable, apreciable **3** SOLID, STURDY : sólido

substantially [səb'stæntʃəli] *adv* : considerablemente

substantiate [səb'stæntʃi,eɪt] *vt* **-ated; -ating** : confirmar, probar, justificar

substitute[1] ['sʌbstə,tuːt, -,tjuːt] *v* **-tuted; -tuting** *vt* : sustituir — *vi* **to substitute for** : sustituir

substitute[2] *n* **1** : sustituto *m*, -ta *f*; suplente *mf* (persona) **2** : sucedáneo *m* ⟨sugar substitute : sucedáneo de azúcar⟩

substitute teacher *n* : profesor *m*, -sora *f* suplente

substitution [,sʌbstə'tuːʃən, -'tjuː-] *n* : sustitución *f*

subterfuge ['sʌbtər,fjuːdʒ] *n* : subterfugio *m*

subterranean [,sʌbtə'reɪniən] *adj* : subterráneo

subtitle ['sʌb,taɪtəl] *n* : subtítulo *m*

subtle ['sʌtəl] *adj* **subtler; subtlest 1** DELICATE, ELUSIVE : sutil, delicado **2** CLEVER : sutil, ingenioso

subtlety ['sʌtəlti] *n, pl* **-ties** : sutileza *f*

subtly ['sʌtəli] *adv* : sutilmente

subtotal ['sʌb,toːtəl] *n* : subtotal *m*

subtract [səb'trækt] *vt* : restar, sustraer

subtraction [səb'trækʃən] *n* : resta *f*, sustracción *f*

suburb ['sʌ,bərb] *n* : municipio *m* periférico, suburbio *m*

suburban [sə'bərbən] *adj* : de las afueras (de una ciudad), suburbano

suburbia [sə'bərbiə] *n* : municipios *mpl* periféricos, suburbios *mpl*

subversion [səb'vərʒən] n : subversión f
subversive [səb'vərsɪv] adj : subversivo
subvert [səb'vərt] vt : subvertir
subway ['sʌb,weɪ] n : metro m; subterráneo m Arg, Uru
succeed [sək'si:d] vt FOLLOW : suceder a — vi 1 : tener éxito (dícese de las personas), dar resultado (dícese de los planes, etc.) ⟨she succeeded in finishing : logró terminar⟩ ⟨to succeed in life : triunfar en la vida⟩ 2 : subir, acceder ⟨to succeed to the throne : subir/acceder al trono⟩ — vt 1 : suceder a (algo) 2 : suceder (a alguien)
success [sək'sɛs] n : éxito m
successful [sək'sɛsfəl] adj : exitoso, logrado — **successfully** adv
succession [sək'sɛʃən] n : sucesión f ⟨in succession : sucesivamente⟩
successive [sək'sɛsɪv] adj : sucesivo, consecutivo — **successively** adv
successor [sək'sɛsər] n : sucesor m, -sora f
succinct [sək'sɪŋkt, sə'sɪŋkt] adj : sucinto — **succinctly** adv
succor[1] ['sʌkər] vt : socorrer
succor[2] n : socorro m
succotash ['sʌkə,tæʃ] n : guiso m de maíz y frijoles
succulent[1] ['sʌkjələnt] adj : suculento, jugoso
succulent[2] n : suculenta f (planta)
succumb [sə'kʌm] vi : sucumbir
such[1] ['sʌtʃ] adv 1 (used for emphasis) : tan ⟨she's such a nice person! : ¡es tan amable!⟩ ⟨it's been such a long time! : ¡(hace) tanto tiempo!⟩ ⟨it's such a long trip : es un viaje tan largo, es un viaje larguísimo⟩ ⟨such tall buildings! : ¡qué edificios más grandes!⟩ ⟨he's not in such good shape : anda un poco mal⟩ 2 (indicating degree) : tan ⟨I've never seen such a large cat! : ¡nunca he visto un gato tan grande como ése!⟩ 3 **such as** : como ⟨animals such as cows and sheep : animales como vacas y ovejas⟩
such[2] adj 1 : tal ⟨there's no such thing : no existe tal cosa⟩ ⟨there's no such person here : no hay nadie aquí con ese nombre⟩ ⟨in such cases : en tales casos⟩ ⟨to such a degree : hasta tal punto⟩ 2 (indicating degree) : tal . . . que, tanto . . . que ⟨where are you off to in such a rush? : ¿adónde vas con tanta prisa?⟩ ⟨I'm such a fool! : ¡qué tonto soy!⟩ 3 **such that** : tal . . . que, tanto . . . que ⟨her excitement was such that . . . : tal/tanto era su entusiasmo que . . .⟩
such[3] pron 1 : tal ⟨such was the result : tal fue el resultado⟩ ⟨he's a child, and acts as such : es un niño, y se porta como tal⟩ 2 : algo o alguien semejante ⟨books, papers and such : libros, papeles y cosas por el estilo⟩
such–and–such adj : tal, cual ⟨at such-and-such (a) time : a tal tiempo⟩
suck ['sʌk] vi 1 : chupar 2 : aspirar (dícese de las máquinas) 3 SUCKLE : mamar 4 fam : apestar, ser una lata ⟨this sucks : qué lata⟩ 5 fam : ser malísimo ⟨I

suck at sports : soy malísimo en los deportes⟩ 6 **to suck on** : chupar 7 **to suck up to** : dar coba a — vt 1 : sorber (bebidas), chupar (dulces, etc.) 2 PULL, DRAG : arrastrar 3 or **to suck up** ABSORB : absorber 4 **to suck in** : meter (la panza), aspirar (aire) 5 **to be/get sucked in** : dejarse engañar 6 **to be/get sucked into** : verse envuelto en (un asunto)
sucker ['sʌkər] n 1 : ventosa f (de un insecto, etc.) 2 : chupón m (de una planta) 3 → **lollipop** 4 FOOL : tonto m, -ta f; idiota mf
suckle ['sʌkəl] v **-led; -ling** vt : amamantar — vi : mamar
suckling ['sʌklɪŋ] n : lactante mf
sucrose ['su:,kro:s, -,kro:z] n : sacarosa f
suction ['sʌkʃən] n : succión f
Sudanese[1] [,su:dən'i:z, -'i:s] adj : sudanés
Sudanese[2] n **the Sudanese** (used with a plural verb) : los sudaneses
sudden ['sʌdən] adj 1 : repentino, súbito ⟨all of a sudden : de pronto, de repente⟩ 2 UNEXPECTED : inesperado, improviso 3 ABRUPT, HASTY : precipitado, brusco
suddenly ['sʌdənli] adv 1 : de repente, de pronto 2 ABRUPTLY : bruscamente
suddenness ['sʌdənnəs] n 1 : lo repentino 2 ABRUPTNESS : brusquedad f 3 HASTE : lo precipitado
suds ['sʌdz] npl : espuma f (de jabón)
sue ['su:] v **sued; suing** vt : demandar — vi **to sue for** : demandar por (daños, etc.)
suede ['sweɪd] n : ante m, gamuza f
suet ['su:ət] n : sebo m
suffer ['sʌfər] vi : sufrir — vt 1 : sufrir, padecer (dolores, etc.) 2 PERMIT : permitir, dejar
sufferer ['sʌfərər] n : persona f que padece (una enfermedad, etc.)
suffering ['sʌfərɪŋ] n : sufrimiento m
suffice [sə'faɪs] vi **-ficed; -ficing** : ser suficiente, bastar
sufficient [sə'fɪʃənt] adj : suficiente
sufficiently [sə'fɪʃəntli] adv : (lo) suficientemente, bastante
suffix ['sʌ,fɪks] n : sufijo m
suffocate ['sʌfə,keɪt] v **-cated; -cating** vt : asfixiar, ahogar — vi : asfixiarse, ahogarse
suffocation [,sʌfə'keɪʃən] n : asfixia f, ahogo m
suffrage ['sʌfrɪdʒ] n : sufragio m, derecho m al voto
suffuse [sə'fju:z] vt **-fused; -fusing** : impregnar (de olores, etc.), bañar (de luz), teñir (de colores), llenar (de emociones)
sugar[1] ['ʃʊgər] vt : azucarar
sugar[2] n : azúcar mf
sugarcane ['ʃʊgər,keɪn] n : caña f de azúcar
sugary ['ʃʊgəri] adj 1 : azucarado ⟨sugary desserts : postres azucarados⟩ 2 SACCHARINE : empalagoso
suggest [səg'dʒɛst, sə-] vt 1 PROPOSE : sugerir 2 IMPLY : indicar, dar a entender
suggestible [səg'dʒɛstəbəl, sə-] adj : influenciable

suggestion [səg'dʒɛstʃən, sə-] *n* **1** PRO-POSAL : sugerencia *f* **2** INDICATION : indicio *m* **3** INSINUATION : insinuación *f*

suggestive [səg'dʒɛstɪv, sə-] *adj* : insinuante — **suggestively** *adv*

suicidal [ˌsuːə'saɪdəl] *adj* : suicida

suicide ['suːəˌsaɪd] *n* **1** : suicidio *m* (acto) **2** : suicida *mf* (persona)

suit¹ ['suːt] *vt* **1** ADAPT : adaptar **2** BEFIT : convenir a, ser apropiado a **3** BECOME : favorecer, quedarle bien (a alguien) ⟨the dress suits you : el vestido te queda bien⟩ **4** PLEASE : agradecer, satisfacer, convenirle bien (a alguien) ⟨does Friday suit you? : ¿le conviene el viernes?⟩ ⟨suit yourself! : ¡como quieras!⟩

suit² *n* **1** LAWSUIT : pleito *m*, litigio *m* **2** : traje *m* (ropa) **3** : palo *m* (de naipes)

suitability [ˌsuːtə'bɪlət̬i] *n* : idoneidad *f*, lo apropiado

suitable ['suːt̬əbəl] *adj* : apropiado, idóneo — **suitably** [-bli] *adv*

suitcase ['suːtˌkeɪs] *n* : maleta *f*, valija *f*, petaca *f* Mex

suite ['swiːt, for 2 also 'suːt] *n* **1** : suite *f* (de habitaciones) **2** SET : juego *m* (de muebles)

suitor ['suːt̬ər] *n* : pretendiente *m*

sulfur ['sʌlfər] *n* : azufre *m*

sulfuric acid [ˌsʌl'fjʊrɪk] *adj* : ácido *m* sulfúrico

sulk¹ ['sʌlk] *vi* : estar de mal humor, enfurruñarse *fam*

sulk² *n* : mal humor *m*

sulky ['sʌlki] *adj* **sulkier; -est** : malhumorado, taimado *Chile*

sullen ['sʌlən] *adj* **1** MOROSE : hosco, taciturno **2** DREARY : sombrío, deprimente

sullenly ['sʌlənli] *adv* **1** MOROSELY : hoscamente **2** GLOOMILY : sombríamente

sully ['sʌli] *vt* **sullied; sullying** : manchar, empañar

sultan ['sʌltən] *n* : sultán *m*

sultry ['sʌltri] *adj* **sultrier; -est 1** : bochornoso ⟨sultry weather : tiempo sofocante, tiempo bochornoso⟩ **2** SENSUAL : sensual, seductor

sum¹ ['sʌm] *vt* **summed; summing 1** : sumar (números) **2 → sum up**

sum² *n* **1** AMOUNT : suma *f*, cantidad *f* **2** TOTAL : suma *f*, total *f* **3** : suma *f*, adición *f* (en matemáticas)

sumac ['ʃuːˌmæk, 'suː-] *n* : zumaque *m*

summarize ['sʌməˌraɪz] *v* **-rized; -rizing** : resumir, compendiar

summary¹ ['sʌməri] *adj* **1** CONCISE : breve, conciso **2** IMMEDIATE : inmediato ⟨a summary dismissal : un despido inmediato⟩ — **summarily** *adv*

summary² *n*, *pl* **-ries** : resumen *m*, compendio *m*

summation [sʌ'meɪʃən] *n* : resumen *m*

summer ['sʌmər] *n* : verano *m*

summertime ['sʌmərˌtaɪm] *n* : verano *m*, estío *m*

summery ['sʌməri] *adj* : veraniego

summit ['sʌmət] *n* **1** : cumbre *f*, cima *f* (de una montaña) **2** *or* **summit conference** : cumbre *f*

summon ['sʌmən] *vt* **1** CALL : convocar (una reunión, etc.), llamar (a una persona) **2** : citar (en derecho) **3 to summon up** : armarse (de valor, etc.) ⟨to summon up one's strength : reunir fuerzas⟩

summons ['sʌmənz] *n*, *pl* **summonses 1** SUBPOENA : citación *f*, citatorio *m* Mex **2** CALL : llamada *f*, llamamiento *m*

sumptuous ['sʌmptʃuəs] *adj* : suntuoso — **sumptuously** *adv*

sum up *vt* **1** SUMMARIZE : resumir **2** EVALUATE : evaluar — *vi* : recapitular

sun¹ ['sʌn] *vt* **sunned; sunning 1** : poner al sol **2 to sun oneself** : asolearse, tomar el sol

sun² *n* **1** : sol *m* **2** SUNSHINE : luz *f* del sol

sunbathe ['sʌnˌbeɪð] *vi* **-bathed; -bathing** : asolearse, tomar el sol

sunbeam ['sʌnˌbiːm] *n* : rayo *m* de sol

sunblock ['sʌnˌblɑk] *n* : filtro *m* solar

sunburn¹ ['sʌnˌbərn] *vi* **-burned** [-ˌbərnd] *or* **-burnt** [-ˌbərnt]; **-burning** : quemarse

sunburn² *n* : quemadura *f* de sol

sundae ['sʌnˌdeɪ, -di] *n* : postre *m* de helado (con jarabe, crema batida, etc.)

Sunday ['sʌnˌdeɪ, -di] *n* : domingo *m* ⟨today is Sunday : hoy es domingo⟩ ⟨(on) Sunday : el domingo⟩ ⟨(on) Sundays : los domingos⟩ ⟨last Sunday : el domingo pasado⟩ ⟨next Sunday : el domingo que viene⟩ ⟨every other Sunday : cada dos domingos⟩ ⟨Sunday afternoon/morning : domingo por la tarde/mañana⟩

sundial ['sʌnˌdaɪl] *n* : reloj *m* de sol

sundown ['sʌnˌdaʊn] *n* → **sunset**

sundries ['sʌndriz] *npl* : artículos *mpl* diversos

sundry ['sʌndri] *adj* : varios, diversos

sunflower ['sʌnˌflaʊər] *n* : girasol *m*, mirasol *m*

sung → sing

sunglasses ['sʌnˌglæsəz] *npl* : gafas *fpl* de sol, lentes *mpl* de sol

sunk → sink¹

sunken ['sʌŋkən] *adj* : hundido

sunlight ['sʌnˌlaɪt] *n* : sol *m*, luz *f* del sol

Sunni ['sʊni] *n* : sunita *mf*

sunny ['sʌni] *adj* **sunnier; -est** : soleado

sunrise ['sʌnˌraɪz] *n* : salida *f* del sol

sunroof ['sʌnˌruːf] *n* : techo *m* corredizo

sunscreen ['sʌnˌskriːn] *n* : filtro *m* solar

sunset ['sʌnˌsɛt] *n* : puesta *f* del sol

sunshine ['sʌnˌʃaɪn] *n* : sol *m*, luz *f* del sol

sunspot ['sʌnˌspɑt] *n* : mancha *f* solar

sunstroke ['sʌnˌstroːk] *n* : insolación *f*

suntan ['sʌnˌtæn] *n* : bronceado *m* ⟨suntan lotion : bronceador⟩

suntanned ['sʌnˌtænd] *adj* : bronceado

sup ['sʌp] *vi* **supped; supping** : cenar

super ['suːpər] *adj* : súper ⟨super! : ¡fantástico!⟩

super- ['suːpər] *pref* : super-

superb [su'pərb] *adj* : magnífico, espléndido — **superbly** *adv*

supercilious [ˌsuːpərˈsɪliəs] *adj* : altivo, altanero, desdeñoso

supercomputer [ˈsuːpərkəmˌpjuːtər] *n* : supercomputadora *f*

superficial [ˌsuːpərˈfɪʃəl] *adj* : superficial — **superficially** *adv* — **superficiality** *n*

superfluous [suˈpərfluəs] *adj* : superfluo — **superfluity** *n*

superhighway [ˈsuːpərˌhaɪˌweɪ, ˌsuːpərˈ-] *n* : autopista *f*

superhuman [ˌsuːpərˈhjuːmən] *adj* **1** SUPERNATURAL : sobrenatural **2** HERCULEAN : sobrehumano

superimpose [ˌsuːpərɪmˈpoːz] *vt* **-posed; -posing** : superponer, sobreponer

superintend [ˌsuːpərɪnˈtend] *vt* : supervisar

superintendent [ˌsuːpərɪnˈtendənt] *n* : portero *m*, -ra *f* (de un edificio); director *m*, -tora *f* (de una escuela, etc.); superintendente *mf* (de policía)

superior¹ [suˈpɪriər] *adj* **1** BETTER : superior **2** HAUGHTY : altivo, altanero

superior² *n* : superior *m*

superiority [suˌpɪriˈɔrəti] *n, pl* **-ties** : superioridad *f*

superlative¹ [suˈpərlətɪv] *adj* **1** : superlativo (en gramática) **2** SUPREME : supremo **3** EXCELLENT : excelente, excepcional

superlative² *n* : superlativo *m*

supermarket [ˈsuːpərˌmɑrkət] *n* : supermercado *m*

supernatural [ˌsuːpərˈnætʃərəl] *adj* : sobrenatural

supernaturally [ˌsuːpərˈnætʃərəli] *adv* : de manera sobrenatural

superpower [ˈsuːpərˌpaʊər] *n* : superpotencia *f*

supersede [ˌsuːpərˈsiːd] *vt* **-seded; -seding** : suplantar, reemplazar, sustituir

supersonic [ˌsuːpərˈsɑnɪk] *adj* : supersónico

superstar [ˈsuːpərˌstɑr] *n* : superestrella *f*

superstition [ˌsuːpərˈstɪʃən] *n* : superstición *f*

superstitious [ˌsuːpərˈstɪʃəs] *adj* : supersticioso

superstore [ˈsuːpərˌstɔr] *n* : hipermercado *m*

superstructure [ˈsuːpərˌstrʌktʃər] *n* : superestructura *f*

supervise [ˈsuːpərˌvaɪz] *vt* **-vised; -vising** : supervisar, dirigir

supervision [ˌsuːpərˈvɪʒən] *n* : supervisión *f*, dirección *f*

supervisor [ˈsuːpərˌvaɪzər] *n* : supervisor *m*, -sora *f*

supervisory [ˌsuːpərˈvaɪzəri] *adj* : de supervisor

supine [suˈpaɪn] *adj* **1** : en decúbito supino, en decúbito dorsal **2** ABJECT, INDIFFERENT : indiferente, apático

supper [ˈsʌpər] *n* : cena *f*, comida *f*

supplant [səˈplænt] *vt* : suplantar

supple [ˈsʌpəl] *adj* **suppler; supplest** : flexible

supplement¹ [ˈsʌpləˌment] *vt* : complementar, completar

supplement² [ˈsʌpləmənt] *n* **1** : complemento *m* ⟨dietary supplement : complemento alimenticio⟩ **2** : suplemento *m* (de un libro o periódico)

supplementary [ˌsʌpləˈmentəri] *adj* : suplementario

supplicate [ˈsʌpləˌkeɪt] *v* **-cated; -cating** *vi* : rezar — *vt* : suplicar

supplier [səˈplaɪər] *n* : proveedor *m*, -dora *f*; abastecedor *m*, -dora *f*

supply¹ [səˈplaɪ] *vt* **-plied; -plying** : suministrar, proveer de, proporcionar

supply² *n, pl* **-plies** **1** PROVISION : provisión *f*, suministro *m* ⟨supply and demand : la oferta y la demanda⟩ **2** STOCK : reserva *f*, existencias *fpl* (de un negocio) **3** supplies *npl* PROVISIONS : provisiones *fpl*, víveres *mpl*, despensa *f*

support¹ [səˈpɔrt] *vt* **1** BACK : apoyar, respaldar **2** MAINTAIN : mantener, sostener, sustentar **3** PROP UP : sostener, apoyar, apuntalar, soportar

support² *n* **1** : apoyo *m* (moral), ayuda *f* (económica) **2** PROP : soporte *m*, apoyo *m*

supporter [səˈpɔrtər] *n* : partidario *m*, -ria *f*

supportive [səˈpɔrtɪv] *adj* : que apoya ⟨his family is very supportive : su familia lo apoya mucho⟩

suppose [səˈpoːz] *vt* **posed; -posing** **1** ASSUME : suponer, imaginarse ⟨let's suppose that . . . : supongamos que . . .⟩ **2** BELIEVE : suponer, creer ⟨I suppose so/not : supongo que sí/no⟩ **3** (*used in polite requests*) ⟨I don't suppose you could help me? : ¿tú no podrías ayudarme?⟩ **4 to be supposed to** (*indicating expectation or intention*) ⟨he's supposed to arrive today : se supone que llegue hoy⟩ ⟨it was supposed to be a surprise : se suponía que iba a ser una sorpresa⟩ ⟨what's that supposed to mean? : ¿qué quieres decir con eso?⟩ **5 to be supposed to** (*indicating obligation or permission*) ⟨I'm supposed to study : (se supone que) tengo que estudiar⟩ ⟨you're not supposed to go : no deberías ir⟩ **6 to be supposed to** (*indicating what others say*) ⟨she's supposed to be the best : dicen que es la mejor⟩

supposed [səˈpoːzd, -ˈpoːzəd] *adj* : supuesto — **supposedly** [səˈpoːzədli] *adv*

supposition [ˌsʌpəˈzɪʃən] *n* : suposición *f*

suppository [səˈpɑzəˌtori] *n, pl* **-ries** : supositorio *m*

suppress [səˈpres] *vt* **1** SUBDUE : sofocar, suprimir, reprimir (una rebelión, etc.) **2** : suprimir, ocultar (información) **3** REPRESS : reprimir, contener ⟨to suppress a yawn : reprimir un bostezo⟩

suppression [səˈpreʃən] *n* **1** SUBDUING : represión *f* **2** : supresión *f* (de información) **3** REPRESSION : represión *f*, inhibición *f*

supremacy [suˈpreməsi] *n, pl* **-cies** : supremacía *f*

supreme [suˈpriːm] *adj* : supremo

Supreme Being *n* : Ser *m* Supremo

supremely [su'pri:mli] *adv* : totalmente, sumamente

surcharge ['sər,tʃɑrdʒ] *n* : recargo *m*

sure¹ ['ʃur] *adv* **1** ALL RIGHT : por supuesto, claro **2** (*used as an intensifier*) ⟨it sure is hot! : ¡hace tanto calor!⟩ ⟨she sure is pretty! : ¡qué linda es!⟩

sure² *adj* **surer; -est** **1** : seguro ⟨a sure sign : una clara señal⟩ ⟨a sure method : un método seguro⟩ ⟨it's a sure thing that . . . : seguro que . . .⟩ **2 for sure** ⟨to know for sure : saber a ciencia cierta, saber con certeza⟩ ⟨for sure! : ¡ya lo creo!⟩ ⟨that's for sure : eso es seguro⟩ **3 to be sure** ⟨to be sure (about/of something) : estar seguro (de algo)⟩ ⟨to be sure that . . . : estar seguro de que . . .⟩ ⟨to be sure of oneself : estar seguro de sí mismo⟩ ⟨I'm not sure why : no sé por qué⟩ ⟨be sure to call! : ¡no dejes de llamar!⟩ **4 to make sure** ⟨he made sure (that) the door was locked : se aseguró de que la puerta estaba cerrada con llave⟩ ⟨make sure to call! : ¡no dejes de llamar!⟩ ⟨make sure it doesn't happen again : que no vuelva a pasar⟩

surely ['ʃurli] *adv* **1** CERTAINLY : seguramente **2** (*used as an intensifier*) ⟨you surely don't mean that! : ¡no me digas que estás hablando en serio!⟩

sureness ['ʃurnəs] *n* : certeza *f*, seguridad *f*

surety ['ʃurəti] *n*, *pl* **-ties** : fianza *f*, garantía *f*

surf¹ ['sərf] *vi* : hacer surf — *vt* : navegar ⟨to surf the Web : navegar por/en la web⟩

surf² *n* **1** WAVES : oleaje *m* **2** FOAM : espuma *f*

surface¹ ['sərfəs] *v* **-faced; -facing** *vi* : salir a la superficie — *vt* : revestir (una carretera)

surface² *n* **1** : superficie *f* **2 on the surface** : en apariencia

surfboard ['sərf,bord] *n* : tabla *f* de surf, tabla *f* de surfing

surfeit ['sərfət] *n* : exceso *m*

surfer ['sərfər] *n* : surfista *mf* ⟨Internet surfers : internautas⟩

surfing ['sərfɪŋ] *n* : surf *m*, surfing *m*

surge¹ ['sərdʒ] *vi* **surged; surging** **1** : hincharse (dícese del mar), levantarse (dícese de las olas) **2** SWARM : salir en tropel (dícese de la gente, etc.)

surge² *n* **1** : oleaje *m* (del mar), oleada *f* (de gente) **2** FLUSH : arranque *m*, arrebato *m* (de ira, etc.) **3** INCREASE : aumento *m* (súbito)

surgeon ['sərdʒən] *n* : cirujano *m*, -na *f*

surgery ['sərdʒəri] *n*, *pl* **-geries** : cirugía *f*

surgical ['sərdʒɪkəl] *adj* : quirúrgico — **surgically** [-kli] *adv*

surly ['sərli] *adj* **surlier; -est** : hosco, arisco

surmise¹ [sər'maɪz] *vt* **-mised; -mising** : conjeturar, suponer, concluir

surmise² *n* : conjetura *f*

surmount [sər'maunt] *vt* **1** OVERCOME : superar, vencer, salvar **2** CLIMB : escalar **3** CAP, TOP : coronar

surname ['sər,neɪm] *n* : apellido *m*

surpass [sər'pæs] *vt* : superar, exceder, rebasar, sobrepasar

surplus ['sər,pləs] *n* : excedente *m*, sobrante *m*, superávit *m* (de dinero)

surprise¹ [sə'praɪz, sər-] *vt* **-prised; -prising** : sorprender

surprise² *n* : sorpresa *f* ⟨to take by surprise : sorprender⟩

surprising [sə'praɪzɪŋ, sər-] *adj* : sorprendente — **surprisingly** *adv*

surreal [sə'ri:l] *adj* : surrealista

surrealism [sə'ri:ə,lɪzəm] *n* : surrealismo *m*

surrealist [sə'ri:əlɪst] *n* : surrealista *mf*

surrealistic [sə,ri:ə'lɪstɪk] *adj* : surrealista

surrender¹ [sə'rendər] *vt* **1** : entregar, rendir **2 to surrender oneself** : entregarse — *vi* : rendirse

surrender² *n* : rendición *m* (de una ciudad, etc.), entrega *f* (de posesiones)

surreptitious [,sərəp'tɪʃəs] *adj* : subrepticio — **surreptitiously** *adv*

surrogate ['sərəgət, -,geɪt] *n* **1** : sustituto *m* **2 or surrogate mother** : madre *f* de alquiler

surround [sə'raund] *vt* : rodear

surroundings [sə'raundɪŋz] *npl* : ambiente *m*, entorno *m*

surveillance [sər'veɪləns, -'veɪljəns, -'veɪəns] *n* : vigilancia *f*

survey¹ [sər'veɪ] *vt* **-veyed; -veying** **1** : medir (un terreno) **2** EXAMINE : inspeccionar, examinar, revisar **3** POLL : hacer una encuesta de, sondear

survey² ['sər,veɪ] *n*, *pl* **-veys** **1** INSPECTION : inspección *f*, revisión *f* **2** : medición *f* (de un terreno) **3** POLL : encuesta *f*, sondeo *m*

surveyor [sər'veɪər] *n* : agrimensor *m*, -sora *f*

survival [sər'vaɪvəl] *n* : supervivencia *f*, sobrevivencia *f*

survive [sər'vaɪv] *v* **-vived; -viving** *vi* : sobrevivir — *vt* OUTLIVE : sobrevivir a

survivor [sər'vaɪvər] *n* : superviviente *mf*, sobreviviente *mf*

susceptibility [sə,septə'bɪləti] *n*, *pl* **-ties** : vulnerabilidad *f*, propensión *f* (a enfermedades, etc.)

susceptible [sə'septəbəl] *adj* **1** VULNERABLE : vulnerable, sensible ⟨susceptible to flattery : sensible a halagos⟩ **2** PRONE : propenso ⟨susceptible to colds : propenso a resfriarse⟩

suspect¹ [sə'spekt] *vt* **1** DISTRUST : dudar de **2** : sospechar (algo), sospechar de (una persona) **3** IMAGINE, THINK : imaginarse, creer

suspect² [sʌs,pekt, sə'spekt] *adj* : sospechoso, dudoso, cuestionable

suspect³ ['sʌs,pekt] *n* : sospechoso *m*, -sa *f*

suspend [sə'spend] *vt* : suspender

suspenders [sə'spendərz] *npl* : tirantes *mpl*

suspense [sə'spens] *n* : incertidumbre *f*, suspenso *m* (en una película, etc.)

suspenseful [sə'spensfəl] *adj* : de suspenso

suspension [sə'spɛntʃən] n : suspensión f

suspension bridge n : puente m colgante

suspicion [sə'spɪʃən] n 1 : sospecha f 2 TRACE : pizca f, atisbo m

suspicious [sə'spɪʃəs] adj 1 QUESTIONABLE : sospechoso, dudoso 2 DISTRUSTFUL : suspicaz, desconfiado

suspiciously [sə'spɪʃəsli] adv : de modo sospechoso, con recelo

sustain [sə'steɪn] vt 1 NOURISH : sustentar 2 PROLONG : sostener 3 SUFFER : sufrir 4 SUPPORT, UPHOLD : apoyar, respaldar, sostener

sustainable [sə'steɪnəbəl] adj : sostenible

sustenance ['sʌstənənts] n 1 NOURISHMENT : sustento m 2 SUPPORT : sostén m

suture ['suːtʃər] n : sutura f

SUV [,ɛsˌjuː'viː] n : SUV m, vehículo m deportivo utilitario

svelte ['sfɛlt] adj : esbelto

swab¹ ['swɑb] vt swabbed; swabbing 1 CLEAN : lavar, limpiar 2 : aplicar a (con hisopo)

swab² n or cotton swab : hisopo m, bastoncillo m, cotonete m Mex

swaddle ['swɑdəl] vt -dled; -dling ['swɑdəlɪŋ] : envolver (en pañales)

swagger¹ ['swæɡər] vi : pavonearse

swagger² n : pavoneo m

swallow¹ ['swɑloʊ] vt 1 : tragar (comida, etc.) 2 ENGULF : tragarse, envolver 3 REPRESS : tragarse (insultos, etc.) — vi : tragar

swallow² n 1 : golondrina f (pájaro) 2 GULP : trago m

swam → swim¹

swamp¹ ['swɑmp] vt : inundar ⟨to swamp with : inundar de⟩

swamp² n : pantano m, ciénaga f

swampy ['swɑmpi] adj swampier; -est : pantanoso, cenagoso

swan ['swɑn] n : cisne f

swap¹ ['swɑp] vt swapped; swapping : cambiar, intercambiar ⟨to swap places : cambiarse de sitio⟩

swap² n : cambio m, intercambio m

swarm¹ ['swɔrm] vi : enjambrar

swarm² n : enjambre m

swarthy ['swɔrði, -θi] adj swarthier; -est : moreno

swashbuckling ['swɑʃˌbʌklɪŋ] adj : de aventurero

swastika ['swɑstɪkə] n : esvástica f

swat¹ ['swɑt] vt swatted; swatting : aplastar (un insecto), darle una palmada (a alguien)

swat² n : palmada f (con la mano), golpe m (con un objeto)

swatch ['swɑtʃ] n : muestra f

swath ['swɑθ, 'swɔθ] or swathe ['swɑð, 'swɔð, 'sweɪð] n : franja f (de grano segado)

swathe ['swɑð, 'swɔð, 'sweɪð] vt swathed; swathing : envolver

swatter ['swɑtər] → flyswatter

sway¹ ['sweɪ] vi : balancearse, mecerse — vt INFLUENCE : influir en, convencer

sway² n 1 SWINGING : balanceo m 2 INFLUENCE : influjo m

swear ['swær] v swore ['swor]; sworn ['sworn]; swearing vi 1 VOW : jurar ⟨I could have sworn it was true : habría jurado que era verdad⟩ 2 CURSE : decir palabrotas — vt 1 : jurar ⟨I couldn't swear to it : no me atrevería a jurarlo⟩ 2 to swear in : juramentar (a un testigo), investir (a un oficial)

swearword ['swær,wərd] n : mala palabra f, palabrota f

sweat¹ ['swɛt] vi sweat or sweated; sweating 1 PERSPIRE : sudar, transpirar 2 OOZE : rezumar 3 to sweat over : sudar la gota gorda por

sweat² n : sudor m, transpiración f

sweater ['swɛtər] n : suéter m, buzo m Uru

sweatpants ['swɛt,pænts] n : pantalón m de ejercicio, jogging m Arg, pants m Mex

sweatshirt ['swɛt,ʃərt] n : sudadera f, buzo m Arg, Col; polerón m Chile (camisa)

sweatsuit ['swɛt,suːt] n : sudadera f, buzo m Chile, Peru; jogging m Arg; pants m Mex; chándal m Spain (traje)

sweaty ['swɛti] adj sweatier; -est : sudoroso, sudado, transpirado

Swede ['swiːd] n : sueco m, -ca f

Swedish¹ ['swiːdɪʃ] adj : sueco

Swedish² n 1 : sueco m (idioma) 2 the Swedish (used with a plural verb) : los suecos

sweep¹ ['swiːp] v swept ['swɛpt]; sweeping vt 1 : barrer (el suelo), limpiar (la suciedad, etc.) ⟨he swept the books aside : apartó los libros de un manotazo⟩ 2 or to sweep through : extenderse por (dícese del fuego, etc.), azotar (dícese de una tormenta) ⟨a craze that's sweeping the nation : una moda que está haciendo furor en todo el país⟩ 3 DRAG : barrer, arrastrar 4 : recorrer ⟨her gaze swept the class : recorrió la clase con la mirada⟩ 5 SEARCH : barrer 6 : ir (dramáticamente) ⟨she swept into the room : entró a lo grande en la habitación⟩ 7 DEFEAT : barrer con (un rival, etc.) 8 : barrer en, arrasar (elecciones, etc.) ⟨the team swept the series : el equipo barrió en la serie⟩ 9 to sweep aside DISMISS : desechar 10 to sweep up : recoger — vi 1 : barrer, limpiar 2 : extenderse (en una curva), describir una curva ⟨the sun swept across the sky : el sol describía una curva en el cielo⟩ 3 to sweep up : barrer

sweep² n 1 : barrido m, barrida f (con una escoba) 2 : movimiento m circular 3 SCOPE : alcance m

sweeper ['swiːpər] n : barrendero m, -ra f

sweeping ['swiːpɪŋ] adj 1 WIDE : amplio (dícese de un movimiento) 2 EXTENSIVE : extenso, radical 3 INDISCRIMINATE : indiscriminado, demasiado general 4 OVERWHELMING : arrollador, aplastante

sweepstakes ['swiːp,steɪks] ns & pl 1 : carrera f (en que el ganador se lleva el premio entero) 2 LOTTERY : lotería f

sweet¹ ['swi:t] *adj* **1** : dulce ⟨sweet desserts : postres dulces⟩ **2** FRESH : fresco **3** : sin sal (dícese de la mantequilla, etc.) **4** PLEASANT : dulce, agradable **5** DEAR : querido

sweet² *n* : dulce *m*

sweet–and–sour *adj* : agridulce

sweeten ['swi:tən] *vt* : endulzar

sweetener ['swi:tənər] *n* : endulzante *m*

sweetheart ['swi:t,hɑrt] *n* : novio *m*, -via *f* ⟨thanks, sweetheart : gracias, cariño⟩

sweetly ['swi:tli] *adv* : dulcemente

sweetness ['swi:tnəs] *n* : dulzura *f*

sweet potato *n* : batata *f*, boniato *m*

swell¹ ['swɛl] *vi* **swelled; swelled** *or* **swollen** ['swo:lən, 'swʌl-]; **swelling 1** *or* **to swell up** : hincharse ⟨her ankle swelled : se le hinchó el tobillo⟩ **2** *or* **to swell out** : inflarse, hinchase (dícese de las velas, etc.) **3** INCREASE : aumentar, crecer

swell² *n* **1** : oleaje *m* (del mar) **2** → **swelling**

swelling ['swɛlɪŋ] *n* : hinchazón *f*

swelter ['swɛltər] *vi* : sofocarse de calor

swept → **sweep¹**

swerve¹ ['swərv] *vi* **swerved; swerving** : virar bruscamente

swerve² *n* : viraje *m* brusco

swift¹ ['swɪft] *adj* **1** FAST : rápido, veloz **2** SUDDEN : repentino, súbito — **swiftly** *adv*

swift² *n* : vencejo *m* (pájaro)

swiftness ['swɪftnəs] *n* : rapidez *f*, velocidad *f*

swig¹ ['swɪg] *vi* **swigged; swigging** : tomar a tragos, beber a tragos

swig² *n* : trago *m*

swill¹ ['swɪl] *vt* : chupar, beber a tragos grandes

swill² *n* **1** SLOP : bazofia *f* **2** GARBAGE : basura *f*

swim¹ ['swɪm] *vi* **swam** ['swæm]; **swum** ['swʌm]; **swimming 1** : nadar **2** FLOAT : flotar **3** REEL : dar vueltas ⟨his head was swimming : la cabeza le daba vueltas⟩

swim² *n* : baño *m*, chapuzón *m* ⟨to go for a swim : ir a nadar⟩

swimmer ['swɪmər] *n* : nadador *m*, -dora *f*

swimming ['swɪmɪŋ] *n* : natación *f* ⟨to go swimming : ir a nadar⟩

swimming pool *n* : piscina *f*

swimming trunks *n* : traje *m* de baño; malla *f* de baño *Arg, Uru*; bañador *m* *Spain* (de hombre)

swimsuit ['swɪm,su:t] *n* : traje *m* de baño; malla *f* de baño *Arg, Uru*; bañador *m* *Spain*

swindle¹ ['swɪndəl] *vt* **-dled; -dling** : estafar, timar

swindle² *n* : estafa *f*, timo *m* *fam*

swindler ['swɪndlər] *n* : estafador *m*, -dora *f*; timador *m*, -dora *f*

swine ['swaɪn] *ns & pl* : cerdo *m*, -da *f*

swing¹ ['swɪŋ] *v* **swung** ['swʌŋ]; **swinging** *vt* **1** : describir una curva con ⟨she swung the ax at the tree : le dio al árbol con el hacha⟩ ⟨he swung himself (up) into the truck : se subió al camión⟩ **2** : balancear (los brazos, etc.), hacer oscilar **3** SUSPEND : colgar **4** MANAGE : arreglar ⟨he'll come if he can swing it : vendrá si puede arreglarlo⟩ ⟨I can't swing a new car : no me alcanza para comprar un auto nuevo⟩ — *vi* **1** SWAY : balancearse (dícese de los brazos, etc.), oscilar (dícese de un objeto), columpiarse, mecerse (en un columpio) **2** SWIVEL : girar (en un pivote) ⟨the door swung shut : la puerta se cerró⟩ **3** CHANGE : virar, cambiar (dícese de las opiniones, etc.) **4** : intentar darle a algo/alguien ⟨he swung at me : intentó pegarme⟩ ⟨she swung (at the ball) but missed : bateó pero no conectó⟩ **5 to swing by** *fam* : pasar (por) ⟨I'll swing by later : pasaré a verte luego⟩ ⟨he'll swing by the store on his way home : pasará por la tienda de camino a casa⟩ **6 to swing into action** : entrar en acción

swing² *n* **1** SWINGING : vaivén *m*, balanceo *m* **2** CHANGE, SHIFT : viraje *m*, movimiento *m* **3** : columpio *m* (para niños) **4 to take a swing at someone** : intentar pegarle a alguien

swipe¹ ['swaɪp] *v* **swiped; swiping 1** STRIKE : dar, pegar (con un movimiento amplio) **2** WIPE : limpiar **3** STEAL : birlar *fam*, robar

swipe² *n* BLOW : golpe *m*

swirl¹ ['swərl] *vi* : arremolinarse

swirl² *n* **1** EDDY : remolino *m* **2** SPIRAL : espiral *f*

swish¹ ['swɪʃ] *vt* : mover (produciendo un sonido) ⟨she swished her skirt : movía la falda⟩ — *vi* : moverse (produciendo un sonido) ⟨the cars swished by : se oían pasar los coches⟩

swish² *n* : silbido *m* (de un látigo, etc.), susurro *m* (de agua), crujido *m* (de ropa, etc.)

Swiss¹ ['swɪs] *adj* : suizo

Swiss² *n* **the Swiss** (*used with a plural verb*) : los suizos

swiss chard *n* : acelga *f*

switch¹ ['swɪtʃ] *vt* **1** LASH, WHIP : azotar **2** CHANGE : cambiar de **3** EXCHANGE : intercambiar **4 to switch on** : encender, prender **5 to switch off** : apagar — *vi* **1** : moverse de un lado al otro **2** CHANGE : cambiar **3** SWAP : intercambiarse

switch² *n* **1** WHIP : vara *f* **2** CHANGE, SHIFT : cambio *m* **3** : interruptor *m*, llave *f* (de la luz, etc.)

switchblade ['swɪtʃ,bleɪd] *n* : navaja *f* de muelle

switchboard ['swɪtʃ,bord] *n* : conmutador *m*, centralita *f*

swivel¹ ['swɪvəl] *vi* **-veled** *or* **-velled; -veling** *or* **-velling** : girar (sobre un pivote)

swivel² *n* : base *f* giratoria

swollen *pp* → **swell¹**

swoon¹ ['swu:n] *vi* : desvanecerse, desmayarse

swoon² *n* : desvanecimiento *m*, desmayo *m*

swoop¹ ['swu:p] *vi* : abatirse (dícese de las aves), descender en picada (dícese de un avión)

swoop² *n* : descenso *m* en picada
sword ['sɔrd] *n* : espada *f*
swordfish ['sɔrd,fɪʃ] *n* : pez *m* espada
swore, sworn → swear
swum *pp →* **swim¹**
swung → swing¹
sycamore ['sɪkə,mor] *n* : sicomoro *m*
sycophant ['sɪkəfənt, -,fænt] *n* : adulador *m*, -dora *f*
syllabic [sə'læbɪk] *adj* : silábico
syllable ['sɪləbəl] *n* : sílaba *f*
syllabus ['sɪləbəs] *n*, *pl* **-bi** [-,baɪ] *or* **-buses** : programa *m* (de estudios)
symbol ['sɪmbəl] *n* : símbolo *m*
symbolic [sɪm'bɑlɪk] *adj* : simbólico — **symbolically** [-kli] *adv*
symbolism ['sɪmbə,lɪzəm] *n* : simbolismo *m*
symbolize ['sɪmbə,laɪz] *vt* **-ized; -izing** : simbolizar
symmetrical [sə'mɛtrɪkəl] *or* **symmetric** [-trɪk] *adj* : simétrico — **symmetrically** [-trɪkli] *adv*
symmetry ['sɪmətri] *n*, *pl* **-tries** : simetría *f*
sympathetic [,sɪmpə'θɛtɪk] *adj* **1** PLEASING : agradable **2** RECEPTIVE : receptivo, favorable **3** COMPASSIONATE, UNDERSTANDING : comprensivo, compasivo
sympathetically [,sɪmpə'θɛtɪkli] *adv* : con compasión, con comprensión
sympathize ['sɪmpə,θaɪz] *vi* **-thized; -thizing** : compadecer ⟨I sympathize with you : te compadezco⟩
sympathizer ['sɪmpə,θaɪzər] *n* : simpatizante *mf*
sympathy ['sɪmpəθi] *n*, *pl* **-thies 1** COMPASSION : compasión *f* **2** UNDERSTANDING : comprensión *f* **3** AGREEMENT : solidaridad *f* ⟨in sympathy with : de acuerdo con⟩ **4** CONDOLENCES : pésame *m*, condolencias *fpl*
symphonic [sɪm'fɑnɪk] *adj* : sinfónico
symphony ['sɪmfəni] *n*, *pl* **-nies 1** : sinfonía *f* **2** *or* **symphony orchestra** : orquesta *f* sinfónica
symposium [sɪm'poːziəm] *n*, *pl* **-sia** [-ziə] *or* **-siums** : simposio *m*
symptom ['sɪmptəm] *n* : síntoma *m*
symptomatic [,sɪmptə'mætɪk] *adj* : sintomático

synagogue ['sɪnə,gɑg, -,gɔg] *n* : sinagoga *f*
sync ['sɪŋk] *n* : sincronización *f* ⟨in sync : sincronizado⟩
synchronize ['sɪŋkrə,naɪz, 'sɪn-] *v* **-nized; -nizing** *vi* : estar sincronizado — *vt* : sincronizar
syncopate ['sɪŋkə,peɪt, 'sɪn-] *vt* **-pated; -pating** : sincopar
syncopation [,sɪŋkə'peɪʃən, ,sɪn-] *n* : síncopa *f*
syndicate¹ ['sɪndə,keɪt] *vi* **-cated; -cating** : formar una asociación
syndicate² ['sɪndɪkət] *n* : asociación *f*, agrupación *f*
syndrome ['sɪn,droːm] *n* : síndrome *m*
synonym ['sɪnə,nɪm] *n* : sinónimo *m*
synonymous [sə'nɑnəməs] *adj* : sinónimo
synopsis [sə'nɑpsɪs] *n*, *pl* **-opses** [-,siːz] : sinopsis *f*
syntactic [sɪn'tæktɪk] *adj* : sintáctico
syntax ['sɪn,tæks] *n* : sintaxis *f*
synthesis ['sɪnθəsɪs] *n*, *pl* **-theses** [-,siːz] : síntesis *f*
synthesize ['sɪnθə,saɪz] *vt* **-sized; -sizing** : sintetizar
synthesizer ['sɪnθə,saɪzər] *n* : sintetizador *m*
synthetic¹ [sɪn'θɛtɪk] *adj* : sintético, artificial — **synthetically** [-tɪkli] *adv*
synthetic² *n* : producto *m* sintético
syphilis ['sɪfələs] *n* : sífilis *f*
Syrian ['sɪriən] *n* : sirio *m*, -ria *f* — **Syrian** *adj*
syringe [sə'rɪndʒ, 'sɪrɪndʒ] *n* : jeringa *f*, jeringuilla *f*
syrup ['sərəp, 'sɪrəp] *n* : jarabe *m*, almíbar *m* (de azúcar y agua)
system ['sɪstəm] *n* **1** METHOD : sistema *m*, método *m* **2** APPARATUS : sistema *m*, instalación *f*, aparato *m* ⟨electrical system : instalación eléctrica⟩ ⟨digestive system : aparato digestivo⟩ **3** BODY : organismo *m*, cuerpo *m* ⟨diseases that affect the whole system : enfermedades que afectan el organismo entero⟩ **4** NETWORK : red *f*
systematic [,sɪstə'mætɪk] *adj* : sistemático — **systematically** [-tɪkli] *adv*
systematize ['sɪstəmə,taɪz] *vt* **-tized; -tizing** : sistematizar
systemic [sɪs'tɛmɪk] *adj* : sistémico
systems analyst *n* : analista *mf* de sistemas (en informática)

T

t ['tiː] *n*, *pl* **t's** *or* **ts** ['tiːz] : vigésima letra del alfabeto inglés
tab¹ ['tæb] *n* **1** FLAP, TAG : lengüeta *f* (de un sobre, una caja, etc.), etiqueta *f* (de ropa) : pestaña *f* (de un navegador, etc.) **3** BILL, CHECK : cuenta *f* **4** *or* **tab key** : tabulador *m*, tecla *f* Tab **5 to keep tabs on** : tener bajo vigilancia
tab² *vi* **tabbed; tabbing** : usar el tabulador, usar la tecla Tab
tabby ['tæbi] *n*, *pl* **-bies 1** *or* **tabby cat** : gato *m* atigrado **2** : gata *f*

tabernacle ['tæbər,nækəl] *n* : tabernáculo *m*
table ['teɪbəl] *n* **1** : mesa *f* ⟨a table for two : una mesa para dos⟩ ⟨table lamp : lámpara de mesa⟩ **2** LIST : tabla *f* ⟨multiplication table : tabla de multiplicar⟩ **3 table of contents** : tabla de materias
tableau [tæ'bloː, 'tæ,-] *n*, *pl* **-leaux** [-'bloːz, -,bloːz] : retablo *m*, cuadro *m* vivo (en teatro)
tablecloth ['teɪbəl,klɔθ] *n* : mantel *m*

tablespoon ['teɪbəl,spu:n] *n* **1** : cuchara *f* (de mesa) **2** → **tablespoonful**

tablespoonful ['teɪbəl,spu:n,fʊl] *n* : cucharada *f*

tablet ['tæblət] *n* **1** PLAQUE : placa *f* **2** PAD : bloc *m* (de papel) **3** PILL : tableta *f*, pastilla *f*, píldora *f* ⟨an aspirin tablet : una tableta de aspirina⟩ **4** : tableta *f*, tablet *f* (computadora)

table tennis *n* : tenis *m* de mesa

tableware ['teɪbəl,wær] *n* : vajillas *fpl*, cubiertos *mpl* (de mesa)

tabloid ['tæ,blɔɪd] *n* : tabloide *m*

taboo¹ [tə'bu:, tæ-] *adj* : tabú

taboo² *n* : tabú *m*

tabular ['tæbjələr] *adj* : tabular

tabulate ['tæbjə,leɪt] *vt* -**lated**; -**lating** : tabular

tabulator ['tæbjə,leɪtər] *n* : tabulador *m*

tacit ['tæsɪt] *adj* : tácito, implícito — **tacitly** *adv*

taciturn ['tæsɪ,tərn] *adj* : taciturno

tack¹ ['tæk] *vt* **1** : sujetar con tachuelas **2 to tack on** ADD : añadir, agregar

tack² *n* **1** : tachuela *f* **2** COURSE : rumbo *m* ⟨to change tack : cambiar de rumbo⟩

tackle¹ ['tækəl] *vt* -**led**; -**ling 1** : taclear (en futbol americano) **2** CONFRONT : abordar, enfrentar, emprender (un problema, un trabajo, etc.)

tackle² *n* **1** EQUIPMENT, GEAR : equipo *m*, aparejo *m* **2** : aparejo *m* (de un buque) **3** : tacleada *f* (en futbol americano)

tacky ['tæki] *adj* **tackier; -est 1** STICKY : pegajoso **2** CHEAP, GAUDY : de mal gusto, naco *Mex*

taco ['tako] *n, pl* **tacos** : taco *m*

tact ['tækt] *n* : tacto *m*, delicadeza *f*, discreción *f*

tactful ['tæktfəl] *adj* : discreto, diplomático, de mucho tacto

tactfully ['tæktfəli] *adv* : discretamente, con mucho tacto

tactic ['tæktɪk] *n* : táctica *f*

tactical ['tæktɪkəl] *adj* : táctico, estratégico

tactics ['tæktɪks] *ns & pl* : táctica *f*, estrategia *f*

tactile ['tæktəl, -,taɪl] *adj* : táctil

tactless ['tæktləs] *adj* : indiscreto, poco delicado

tactlessly ['tæktləsli] *adv* : rudamente, sin tacto

tadpole ['tæd,po:l] *n* : renacuajo *m*

taffeta ['tæfəɡə] *n* : tafetán *m*; tafeta *f Arg, Mex, Uru*

taffy ['tæfi] *n, pl* -**fies** : caramelo *m* de melaza, chicloso *m Mex*

tag¹ ['tæg] *v* **tagged; tagging** *vt* **1** LABEL : etiquetar **2** TAIL : seguir de cerca **3** TOUCH : tocar (en varios juegos) — *vi* **to tag along** : pegarse, acompañar

tag² *n* **1** LABEL : etiqueta *f* **2** SAYING : dicho *m*, refrán *m*

tail¹ ['teɪl] *vt* FOLLOW : seguir de cerca, pegarse

tail² *n* **1** : cola *f*, rabo *m* (de un animal) **2** : cola *f*, parte *f* posterior ⟨a comet's tail : la cola de un cometa⟩ **3 tails**

npl : cruz *f* (de una moneda) ⟨heads or tails : cara o cruz⟩ **4 tails** *npl* → **tailcoat**

tailcoat ['teɪl,ko:t] *n* : frac *m*

tailed ['teɪld] *adj* **1** : que tiene cola **2** (*used in combination*) : de cola ⟨longtailed : de cola larga⟩

tail end *n* : final *m*, últimos momentos *mpl* (de un espectáculo, etc.), cola *f* (de un grupo, etc.)

tailgate¹ ['teɪl,geɪt] *vi* -**gated**; -**gating** : seguir a un vehículo demasiado de cerca

tailgate² *n* : puerta *f* trasera (de un vehículo)

taillight ['teɪl,laɪt] *n* : luz *f* trasera (de un vehículo), calavera *f Mex*

tailor¹ ['teɪlər] *vt* **1** : confeccionar o alterar (ropa) **2** ADAPT : adaptar, ajustar

tailor² *n* : sastre *m*, -tra *f*

tailor-made *adj* : hecho a la medida

tailpipe ['teɪl,paɪp] *n* : tubo *m* de escape

tailspin ['teɪl,spɪn] *n* : barrena *f*

taint¹ ['teɪnt] *vt* : contaminar, corromper

taint² *n* : corrupción *f*, impureza *f*

take¹ ['teɪk] *v* **took** ['tʊk], **taken** ['teɪkən]; **taking** *vt* **1** GRASP : tomar, agarrar ⟨to take by the hand : tomar de la mano⟩ ⟨to take the bull by the horns : tomar al toro por los cuernos⟩ **2** BRING, CARRY : llevar, sacar, cargar ⟨take them with you : llévalos contigo⟩ ⟨take this note to your teacher : lleva esta nota a tu maestro⟩ ⟨I took her to school : la llevé a la escuela⟩ ⟨she took him aside : lo llevó aparte⟩ **3** REMOVE, EXTRACT : sacar, extraer ⟨take a beer from the fridge : saca una cerveza de la nevera⟩ ⟨to take blood : sacar sangre⟩ **4** CATCH : tomar, agarrar ⟨taken by surprise : tomado por sorpresa⟩ **5** CAPTURE, SEIZE : tomar ⟨to take someone prisoner : hacer/tomar a alguien prisionero⟩ ⟨to take someone hostage : tomar a alguien como rehén⟩ ⟨to take control : tomar el control de⟩ **6** CAPTIVATE : encantar, fascinar **7** REMOVE, STEAL : llevarse ⟨someone took the painting : alguien se llevó la pintura⟩ ⟨he took it from her : se lo quitó⟩ ⟨to take someone's life : quitarle la vida a alguien⟩ **8** (*indicating selection*) ⟨I'll take the fish : dame el pescado⟩ ⟨I'll take it : me lo llevo⟩ ⟨take your pick : escoge el que quieras⟩ ⟨do you take cream in your coffee? : ¿le pones crema al café?⟩ **9** NEED, REQUIRE : tomar, requerir ⟨it will take a month to complete : llevará un mes terminarlo⟩ ⟨these things take time : estas cosas toman tiempo⟩ ⟨will it take long? : ¿tardará mucho (tiempo)?⟩ ⟨what size do you take? : ¿qué talla usas?⟩ ⟨it takes diesel : usa diesel⟩ **10** BORROW : tomar (una frase, etc.) ⟨to take one's inspiration from : inspirarse en⟩ **11** OCCUPY : ocupar ⟨to take a seat : tomar asiento⟩ ⟨this seat is taken : este asiento está ocupado⟩ ⟨to take the place of : ocupar el lugar de⟩ **12** INGEST : tomar, ingerir ⟨to take two pills : tome dos píldoras⟩ ⟨to take drugs : drogarse⟩ **13** : tomar, coger (un tren, un autobús, etc.) **14** TRAVEL : tomar (un camino) **15** BEAR, ENDURE : soportar, aguantar (dolores, etc.), resistir (el frío, etc.) ⟨I can't take it anymore : no puedo más⟩ ⟨she can't take a joke : no sabe aguantar una broma⟩ ⟨to take something well/badly : llevar algo bien/mal⟩ **16** ACCEPT : aceptar (un cheque, un cliente, un trabajo, etc.), seguir (consejos), cargar con (la culpa, la responsabilidad) ⟨take it or leave it : tómalo o déjalo⟩ ⟨take it from me : hazme caso⟩ **17** ADOPT : adoptar (una perspectiva, etc.) **18** INTERPRET : tomar, interpretar ⟨don't take it the wrong way : no te lo tomes a mal, no me malinterpretes⟩ **19** FEEL : sentir ⟨to take offense : ofenderse⟩ ⟨to take pride in : sentirse orgulloso de⟩ **20** SUPPOSE : suponer ⟨I take it that . . . : supongo que . . .⟩ **21** CONSIDER : mirar (como ejemplo) **22** (indicating an action or an undertaking) ⟨to take a walk : dar un paseo⟩ ⟨to take a class : tomar una clase⟩ ⟨to take a picture : sacar una foto⟩ ⟨to take a right/left : girar a la derecha/izquierda⟩ **23** MEASURE, RECORD : tomar ⟨to take someone's temperature : tomarle la temperatura a alguien⟩ ⟨to take notes : tomar apuntes⟩ **24** EXACT ⟨to take a toll on : afectar⟩ **25** WIN : ganar **26** to be taken sick/ill : caer enfermo **27** to take aback : sorprender, desconcertar **28** to take a lot out of someone : agotar a alguien **29** to take apart : desmontar **30** to take away REMOVE : quitar **31** take it away! : ¡adelante!, ¡vamos! (dícese a un cantante, etc.) **32** to take back : retirar (palabras, etc.) **33** to take back RETURN : devolver **34** to take back RECLAIM : llevarse **35** to take back : aceptar la devolución de (mercancía), dejar regresar (a un amante) **36** to take down NOTE : tomar nota de **37** to take down DISASSEMBLE : desmontar **38** to take down REMOVE : quitar **39** to take down LOWER : bajar **40** to take for : tomar por **41** to take in : recoger (a un perro, etc.) **42** to take in : detener, llevar a la comisaría **43** to take in : hacer (dinero) **44** to take in : tomarle a, achicar (un vestido, etc.) **45** to take in INCLUDE : incluir, abarcar **46** to take in ATTEND, VISIT : ir a (una película, etc.), visitar (un museo, etc.) **47** to take in GRASP, UNDERSTAND : captar, entender **48** to take in DECEIVE : engañar **49** to take it upon oneself (to do something) : encargarse (de hacer algo) **50** to take note/notice of : notar, prestarle atención a **51** to take off REMOVE : quitar ⟨take off your hat : quítate el sombrero⟩ ⟨take your hands off me! : ¡quítame las manos de encima!⟩ **52** to take off : tomar (el día, etc.), libre **53** to take someone off (of) : hacerle a alguien dejar (un proyecto, etc.) **54** to take on TACKLE : abordar, enfrentar (problemas, etc.) **55** to take on UNDERTAKE : encargarse de, emprender (una tarea), asumir

(una responsabilidad) **56** to take on ACCEPT : tomar (como a un cliente, etc.) **57** to take on CONTRACT : contratar (trabajadores) **58** to take on ASSUME : adoptar, asumir, adquirir ⟨the neighborhood took on a dingy look : el barrio asumió una apariencia deprimente⟩ **59** to take out REMOVE, WITHDRAW, EXTRACT : sacar ⟨take the trash out : saca la basura⟩ ⟨they took her tonsils out : la operaron de las amígdalas⟩ **60** to take out OBTAIN : sacar **61** to take out : sacar (libros, etc.) **62** to take out : llevar (a cenar, etc.), sacar (a pasear, etc.) **63** to take out DESTROY : eliminar **64** to take it out on someone : desquitarse con alguien, agarrársela con alguien **65** to take over SEIZE : apoderarse de **66** to take over : hacerse cargo de (una compañía, etc.), asumir (una responsabilidad) **67** to take over RELIEVE : sustituir, relevar **68** to take place HAPPEN : tener lugar, suceder, ocurrir **69** to take shape/form : tomar forma **70** to take something to something ⟨he took an axe to the tree : empezó a cortar el árbol con un hacha⟩ **71** to take up LIFT : levantar **72** to take up SHORTEN : acortar (una falda, etc.) **73** to take up BEGIN : empezar, dedicarse a (un pasatiempo, etc.) **74** to take up OCCUPY : ocupar (espacio), llevar (tiempo) **75** to take up PURSUE : volver a (una cuestión, un asunto) **76** to take up CONTINUE : seguir con **77** to take someone up on : aceptarle la invitación (etc.) a alguien — vi **1** : agarrar (dícese de un tinte), prender (dícese de una vacuna) **2** to take after : parecerse a, salir a **3** to take away from : restarle valor/atractivo (etc.) a **4** to take off : despegar (dícese de un avión, etc.) **5** to take off fam LEAVE : irse **6** to take over : asumir el mando **7** to take to : aficionarse a (un pasatiempo), adaptarse a (una situación), tomarle simpatía a (alguien) ⟨he doesn't take kindly to criticism : no le gusta nada que lo critiquen⟩ **8** to take to START : empezar a, acostumbrarse a (hacer algo)

take² n **1** PROCEEDS : recaudación f, ingresos mpl, ganancias fpl **2** : toma f (de un rodaje o una grabación)

takeoff ['teɪk,ɔf] n **1** PARODY : parodia f **2** : despegue m (de un avión o cohete)

takeout ['teɪk,aʊt] n : comida f para llevar

takeover ['teɪk,oːvər] n : toma f (de poder o de control), adquisición f (de una empresa por otra)

taker ['teɪkər] n : persona f interesada ⟨available to all takers : disponible a cuantos estén interesados⟩

takings ['teɪkɪŋz] n EARNINGS : recaudación f

talc ['tælk] n : talco m

talcum powder ['tælkəm] n : talco m, polvos mpl de talco

tale ['teɪl] n **1** ANECDOTE, STORY : cuento m, relato m, anécdota f **2** FALSEHOOD : cuento m, mentira f

talent ['tælənt] *n* : talento *m*, don *m*

talented ['tæləntəd] *adj* : talentoso

talent scout → scout²

talisman ['tæləsmən, -līz-] *n, pl* **-mans** : talismán *m*

talk¹ ['tɔk] *vi* **1** : hablar ⟨he talks for hours : se pasa horas hablando⟩ **2** CHAT : charlar, platicar **3 to talk about/of** : hablar de **4 to talk back** : contestar (de manera impertinente) **5 to talk down to** : hablarle en tono condescendiente a — *vt* **1** SPEAK : hablar ⟨to talk French : hablar francés⟩ ⟨to talk business : hablar de negocios⟩ **2 to talk into** ⟨I talked him into coming : lo convencí de que viniera⟩ **3 to talk out of** ⟨she talked me out of it : me convenció de que no lo hiciera⟩ **4 to talk over** DISCUSS : hablar de, discutir

talk² *n* **1** CONVERSATION : charla *f*, plática *f*, conversación *f* **2** GOSSIP, RUMOR : chisme *m*, rumores *mpl* **3** SPEECH : charla *f*

talkative ['tɔkətɪv] *adj* : locuaz, parlanchín, charlatán

talker ['tɔkər] *n* : conversador *m*, -dora *f*; hablador *m*, -dora *f*

talk show *n* : programa *m* de entrevistas

tall ['tɔl] *adj* : alto ⟨how tall is he? : ¿cuánto mide?⟩

tallow ['tælo:] *n* : sebo *m*

tall tale *adj* : cuento *m* chino

tally¹ ['tæli] *v* **-lied; -lying** *vt* RECKON : contar, hacer una cuenta de — *vi* MATCH : concordar, corresponder, cuadrar

tally² *n, pl* **-lies** : cuenta *f* ⟨to keep a tally : llevar la cuenta⟩

talon ['tælən] *n* : garra *f* (de un ave de rapiña)

tamale [tə'mɑli] *n* : tamal *m*

tamarind ['tæmərənd] *n* : tamarindo *m*

tambourine [ˌtæmbə'riːn] *n* : pandero *m*, pandereta *f*

tame¹ ['teɪm] *vt* **tamed; taming** : domar, amansar, domesticar

tame² *adj* **tamer; -est 1** DOMESTICATED : domesticado, manso **2** DOCILE : manso, dócil **3** DULL : aburrido, soso

tamely ['teɪmli] *adv* : mansamente, dócilmente

tamer ['teɪmər] *n* : domador *m*, -dora *f*

tamp ['tæmp] *vt* : apisonar

tamper ['tæmpər] *vi* **to tamper with** : adulterar (una sustancia), forzar (un sello, una cerradura), falsear (documentos), manipular (una máquina)

tampon ['tæm.pɑn] *n* : tampón *m*

tan¹ ['tæn] *v* **tanned; tanning** *vt* **1** : curtir (pieles) **2** : broncear — *vi* : broncearse

tan² *n* **1** SUNTAN : bronceado *m* ⟨to get a tan : broncearse⟩ **2** : color *m* canela, color *m* café con leche

tandem¹ ['tændəm] *adv or* **in tandem** : en tándem

tandem² *n* : tándem *m* (bicicleta)

tang ['tæŋ] *n* : sabor *m* fuerte

tangent ['tændʒənt] *n* : tangente *f* ⟨to go off on a tangent : irse por la tangente⟩

tangerine ['tændʒəˌriːn, ˌtændʒə'-] *n* : mandarina *f*

tangible ['tændʒəbəl] *adj* : tangible, palpable — **tangibly** [-bli] *adv*

tangle¹ ['tæŋgəl] *v* **-gled; -gling** *vt* : enredar, enmarañar — *vi* : enredarse

tangle² *n* : enredo *m*, maraña *f*

tango¹ ['tæŋˌgoː] *vi* : bailar el tango

tango² *n, pl* **-gos** : tango *m*

tangy ['tæŋi] *adj* **tangier; -est** : que tiene un sabor fuerte

tank ['tæŋk] *n* : tanque *m*; depósito *m*; bombona *f Spain, Ven* ⟨fuel tank : depósito de combustibles⟩

tankard ['tæŋkərd] *n* : jarra *f*

tanker ['tæŋkər] *n* : buque *m* cisterna, camión *m* cisterna, avión *m* cisterna ⟨an oil tanker : un petrolero⟩

tanner ['tænər] *n* : curtidor *m*, -dora *f*

tannery ['tænəri] *n, pl* **-neries** : curtiduría *f*, tenería *f*

tannin ['tænən] *n* : tanino *m*

tantalize ['tæntəˌlaɪz] *vt* **-lized; -lizing** : tentar, atormentar (con algo inase--quible)

tantalizing ['tæntəˌlaɪzɪŋ] *adj* : tentador, seductor

tantamount ['tæntəˌmaʊnt] *adj* : equivalente

tantrum ['tæntrəm] *n* : rabieta *f*, berrinche *m* ⟨to throw a tantrum : hacer un berrinche⟩

tap¹ ['tæp] *vt* **tapped; tapping 1** : ponerle una espita a, sacar líquido de (un barril, un tanque, etc.) **2** : intervenir, pinchar *fam* (un teléfono) **3** PAT, TOUCH : tocar, golpear ligeramente ⟨he tapped me on the shoulder : me tocó en el hombro⟩

tap² *n* **1** FAUCET : llave *f*, grifo *m* ⟨beer on tap : cerveza de barril⟩ **2** : extracción *f* (de líquido) ⟨a spinal tap : una punción lumbar⟩ **3** PAT, TOUCH : golpecito *m*, toque *m*

tape¹ ['teɪp] *vt* **taped; taping 1** : sujetar o arreglar con cinta adhesiva **2** RECORD : grabar (en cinta)

tape² *n* **1** : cinta *f* (adhesiva, magnética, etc.) **2 → tape measure**

tape measure *n* : cinta *f* métrica

taper¹ ['teɪpər] *vi* **1** : estrecharse gradualmente ⟨its tail tapers towards the tip : su cola va estrechándose hacia la punta⟩ **2** *or* **to taper off** : disminuir gradualmente

taper² *n* **1** CANDLE : vela *f* larga y delgada **2** TAPERING : estrechamiento *m* gradual

tape recorder *n* : grabadora *f*, grabador *m* (de cinta)

tapestry ['tæpəstri] *n, pl* **-tries** : tapiz *m*

tapeworm ['teɪpˌwərm] *n* : solitaria *f*, tenia *f*

tapioca [ˌtæpi'oːkə] *n* : tapioca *f*

tapir ['teɪpər] *n* : tapir *m*

tar¹ ['tɑr] *vt* **tarred; tarring** : alquitranar

tar² *n* : alquitrán *m*, brea *f*, chapopote *m Mex*

tarantula [tə'ræntʃələ, -'ræntələ] *n* : tarántula *f*

tardiness ['tɑrdinəs] *n* : tardanza *f*, retraso *m*

tardy ['tɑrdi] *adj* **tardier; -est** LATE : tardío, de retraso

target¹ ['tɑrgət] *vt* : fijar como objetivo, dirigir, destinar

target² *n* **1** : blanco *m* ⟨target practice : tiro al blanco⟩ **2** GOAL, OBJECTIVE : meta *f*, objetivo *m*

tariff ['tærɪf] *n* DUTY : tarifa *f*, arancel *m*

tarmac ['tɑr,mæk] *n* pista *f* (de un aeropuerto)

Tarmac ['tɑr,mæk] *trademark* se usa para un tipo de pavimento

tarnish¹ ['tɑrnɪʃ] *vt* **1** DULL : deslustrar **2** SULLY : empañar, manchar (una reputación, etc.) — *vi* : deslustrarse

tarnish² *n* : deslustre *m*

taro ['tɑro, 'ter-] *n* : taro *m*, malanga *f*

tarpaulin [tɑr'pɔlən, 'tɑrpə-] *n* : lona *f* (impermeable)

tarragon ['tærə,gɑn, -gən] *n* : estragón *m*

tarry¹ ['tæri] *vi* -ried; -rying : demorarse, entretenerse

tarry² ['tɑri] *adj* **1** : parecido al alquitrán **2** : cubierto de alquitrán

tart¹ ['tɑrt] *adj* **1** SOUR : ácido, agrio **2** CAUSTIC : mordaz, acrimonioso — **tartly** *adv*

tart² *n* : tartaleta *f*

tartan ['tɑrtən] *n* : tartán *m*

tartar ['tɑrtər] *n* **1** : tártaro *m* ⟨tartar sauce : salsa tártara⟩ **2** : sarro *m* (dental)

tartness [tʌrtnəs] *n* **1** DULLNESS : acidez *f* **2** ACRIMONY, SHARPNESS : mordacidad *f*, acrimonia *f*, acritud *f*

task ['tæsk] *n* : tarea *f*, trabajo *m*

taskmaster ['tæsk,mæstər] *n* **to be a hard taskmaster** : ser exigente, ser muy estricto

tassel ['tæsəl] *n* : borla *f*

taste¹ ['teɪst] *v* **tasted; tasting** *vt* : probar (alimentos), degustar, catar (vinos) ⟨taste this soup : prueba esta sopa⟩ — *vi* : saber ⟨this tastes good : esto sabe bueno⟩

taste² *n* **1** SAMPLE : prueba *f*, bocado *m* (de comida), trago *m* (de bebidas) **2** FLAVOR : gusto *m*, sabor *m* **3** : gusto *m* ⟨she has good taste : tiene buen gusto⟩ ⟨in bad taste : de mal gusto⟩

taste bud *n* : papila *f* gustativa

tasteful ['teɪstfəl] *adj* : de buen gusto

tastefully ['teɪstfəli] *adv* : con buen gusto

tasteless ['teɪstləs] *adj* **1** FLAVORLESS : sin sabor, soso, insípido **2** : de mal gusto ⟨a tasteless joke : un chiste de mal gusto⟩

taster ['teɪstər] *n* : degustador *m*, -dora *f*; catador *m*, -dora *f* (de vinos)

tastiness ['teɪstinəs] *n* : lo sabroso

tasty ['teɪsti] *adj* **tastier; -est** : sabroso, gustoso

tatter ['tætər] *n* **1** SHRED : tira *f*, jirón *m* (de tela) **2 tatters** *npl* : andrajos *mpl*, harapos *mpl* ⟨to be in tatters : estar por los suelos⟩

tattered ['tætərd] *adj* : andrajoso, en jirones

tattle ['tætəl] *vi* -tled; -tling **1** CHATTER : parlotear *fam*, cotorrear *fam* **2 to tattle on someone** : acusar a alguien

tattletale ['tætəl,teɪl] *n* : soplón *m*, -plona *f fam*

tattoo¹ [tæ'tu:] *vt* : tatuar

tattoo² *n* : tatuaje *m* ⟨to get a tattoo : tatuarse⟩

tatty ['tæti] *adj* **tattier; -est** SHABBY, WORN : gastado

taught → teach

taunt¹ ['tɔnt] *vt* MOCK : mofarse de, burlarse de

taunt² *n* : mofa *f*, burla *f*

Taurus ['tɔrəs] *n* **1** : Tauro *m* (signo o constelación) **2** : Tauro *mf* (persona)

taut ['tɔt] *adj* : tirante, tenso — **tautly** *adv*

tautness ['tɔtnəs] *n* : tirantez *f*, tensión *f*

tavern ['tævərn] *n* : taberna *f*

tawdry ['tɔdri] *adj* **tawdrier; -est** : chabacano, vulgar

tawny ['tɔni] *adj* **tawnier; -est** : leonado

tax¹ ['tæks] *vt* **1** : gravar, cobrar un impuesto sobre **2** CHARGE : acusar ⟨they taxed him with neglect : fue acusado de incumplimiento⟩ **3 to tax someone's strength** : ponerle a prueba las fuerzas (a alguien)

tax² *n* **1** : impuesto *m*, tributo *m* ⟨tax collector : recaudador de impuestos⟩ ⟨tax evasion : evasión de impuestos⟩ **2** BURDEN : carga *f*

taxable ['tæksəbəl] *adj* : sujeto a un impuesto

taxation [tæk'seɪʃən] *n* : impuestos *mpl*

tax-exempt ['tæks,ɪg'zɛmpt, -ɛg-] *adj* : libre de impuestos

taxi¹ ['tæksi] *vi* **taxied; taxiing** *or* **taxying; taxis** *or* **taxies 1** : ir en taxi **2** : rodar sobre la pista de aterrizaje (dícese de un avión)

taxi² *n, pl* **taxis** : taxi *m*, libre *m Mex*

taxicab ['tæksi,kæb] *n* → **taxi²**

taxidermist ['tæksə,dərmɪst] *n* : taxidermista *mf*

taxidermy ['tæksə,dərmi] *n* : taxidermia *f*

taxi driver *n* : taxista *mf*

taxpayer ['tæks,peɪər] *n* : contribuyente *mf*, causante *mf Mex*

tax return → return³

TB [,ti:'bi:] → **tuberculosis**

tea ['ti:] *n* **1** : té *m* (planta y bebida) **2** : merienda *f*, té *m* (comida)

tea bag *n* : bolsita *f* de té

teach ['ti:tʃ] *v* **taught** ['tɔt] **teaching** *vt* : enseñar, dar clases de ⟨she teaches math : da clases de matemáticas⟩ ⟨she taught me everything I know : me enseñó todo lo que sé⟩ — *vi* : enseñar, dar clases

teacher ['ti:tʃər] *n* : maestro *m*, -tra *f* (de enseñanza primaria); profesor *m*, -sora *f* (de enseñanza secundaria)

teaching ['ti:tʃɪŋ] *n* : enseñanza *f*

teacup ['ti:,kʌp] *n* : taza *f* para té

teak ['ti:k] *n* : teca *f*

teakettle ['ti:,kɛtəl] *n* : tetera *f*

teal ['ti:l] *n, pl* **teal** *or* **teals 1** : cerceta *f* (pato) **2** *or* **teal blue** : azul *m* verdoso oscuro

team¹ ['ti:m] *vi or* **to team up 1** : formar un equipo (en deportes) **2** COLLABORATE : asociarse, juntarse, unirse

team² *adj* : de equipo

team³ *n* **1** : tiro *m* (de caballos), yunta *f*

(de bueyes o mulas) **2** : equipo *m* (en deportes, etc.)

teammate ['tiːmˌmeɪt] *n* : compañero *m*, -ra *f* de equipo

teamster ['tiːmstər] *n* : camionero *m*, -ra *f*

teamwork ['tiːmˌwərk] *n* : trabajo *m* en equipo, cooperación *f*

teapot ['tiːˌpɑt] *n* : tetera *f*

tear¹ ['tær] *v* **tore** ['tor]; **torn** ['torn]; **tearing** *vt* **1** RIP : desgarrar, romper, rasgar (tela) ⟨to tear to pieces : hacer pedazos⟩ ⟨to tear apart : desgarrar⟩ **2** *or* **to tear apart** DIVIDE : dividir **3** REMOVE : arrancar ⟨torn from his family : arrancado de su familia⟩ **4 to tear down** : derribar **5 to tear off** : arrancar (un pedazo, etc.) **6 to tear out** : arrancar (una página, etc.) **7 to tear up** : hacer pedazos — *vi* **1** RIP : desgarrarse, romperse **2** RUSH : ir a gran velocidad ⟨she went tearing down the street : se fue como rayo por la calle⟩ **3 to tear into** ATTACK : arremeter contra

tear² *n* : desgarradura *f*, rotura *f*, desgarro *m* (muscular)

tear³ ['tɪr] *n* : lágrima *f*

teardrop ['tɪrˌdrɑp] *n* → **tear³**

tearful ['tɪrfəl] *adj* : lloroso, triste — **tearfully** *adv*

tear gas *n* : gas *m* lacrimógeno

tearoom ['tiːˌruːm, -ˌrʊm] *n* : salón *m* de té, confitería *f*

tease¹ ['tiːz] *vt* **teased; teasing 1** MOCK : burlarse de, mofarse de **2** ANNOY : irritar, fastidiar

tease² *n* **1** TEASING : burla *f*, mofa *f* **2** : bromista *mf*; guasón *m*, -sona *f*

teaspoon ['tiːˌspuːn] *n* **1** : cucharita *f* **2** → **teaspoonful**

teaspoonful ['tiːˌspuːnˌfʊl] *n*, *pl* **-spoonfuls** [-ˌfʊlz] *or* **-spoonsful** [-ˌspuːnzˌfʊl] : cucharadita *f*

teat ['tiːt] *n* : tetilla *f*

technical ['tɛknɪkəl] *adj* : técnico — **technically** [-kli] *adv*

technicality [ˌtɛknə'kæləti] *n*, *pl* **-ties** : detalle *m* técnico

technician [tɛk'nɪʃən] *n* : técnico *m*, -ca *f*

technique [tɛk'niːk] *n* : técnica *f*

technological [ˌtɛknə'lɑʤɪkəl] *adj* : tecnológico

technology [tɛk'nɑləʤi] *n*, *pl* **-gies** : tecnología *f*

teddy bear ['tɛdi] *n* : oso *m* de peluche

tedious ['tiːdiəs] *adj* : aburrido, pesado, monótono — **tediously** *adv*

tediousness ['tiːdiəsnəs] *n* : lo aburrido, lo pesado

tedium ['tiːdiəm] *n* : tedio *m*, pesadez *f*

tee ['tiː] *n* : tee *m* (en golf)

teem ['tiːm] *vi* : estar repleto de, estar lleno de

teen ['tiːn] → **teenager**

teenage ['tiːnˌeɪʤ] *or* **teenaged** [-eɪʤd] *adj* : adolescente, de adolescencia

teenager ['tiːnˌeɪʤər] *n* : adolescente *mf*

teens ['tiːnz] *npl* : adolescencia *f*

teepee → **tepee**

teeter¹ ['tiːtər] *vi* : balancearse, tambalearse

teeter² *or* **teeter–totter** ['tiːtər-ˌtɑtər] *n* → **seesaw**

teeth → **tooth**

teethe ['tiːð] *vi* **teethed; teething** : formársele a uno los dientes ⟨the baby's teething : le están saliendo los dientes al niño⟩

teetotal ['tiːˌtoːtəl] *adj* : abstemio

teetotaler ['tiːˌtoːtələr] *n* : abstemio *m*, -mia *f*

Teflon ['tɛˌflɑn] *trademark* se usa para un revestimiento antiadherente

telecast¹ ['tɛləˌkæst] *vt* **-cast; -casting** : televisar, transmitir por televisión

telecast² *n* : transmisión *f* por televisión

telecommunication [ˌtɛləkəˌmjuːnə'keɪʃən] *n* : telecomunicación *f*

teleconference ['tɛliˌkɑnfrənts, -fərənts] *n* : teleconferencia *f*

telegram ['tɛləˌgræm] *n* : telegrama *m*

telegraph¹ ['tɛləˌgræf] *v* : telegrafiar

telegraph² *n* : telégrafo *m*

telemarketing [ˌtɛlə'mɑrkətɪŋ] *n* : telemárketing *m*

telepathic [ˌtɛlə'pæθɪk] *adj* : telepático — **telepathically** [-θɪkli] *adv*

telepathy [tə'lɛpəθi] *n* : telepatía *f*

telephone¹ ['tɛləˌfoːn] *v* **-phoned; -phoning** *vt* : llamar por teléfono a, telefonear — *vi* : telefonear

telephone² *n* : teléfono *m*

telephone book → **phone book**

telephone call → **call²**

telephone directory → **phone book**

telephone exchange → **exchange²**

telephone number → **number²**

telephone receiver → **receiver**

telescope¹ ['tɛləˌskoːp] *vi* **-scoped; -scoping** : plegarse (como un telescopio)

telescope² *n* : telescopio *m*

telescopic [ˌtɛlə'skɑpɪk] *adj* : telescópico

televise ['tɛləˌvaɪz] *vt* **-vised; -vising** : televisar

television ['tɛləˌvɪʒən] *n* : televisión *f*

tell ['tɛl] *v* **told** ['toːld]; **telling** *vt* **1** : decir, contar ⟨he told us the story : nos contó la historia⟩ ⟨he told us what happened : nos contó qué pasó⟩ ⟨she told me the news : me dio la noticia⟩ ⟨tell me all about it : cuéntamelo todo⟩ ⟨tell her that . . . : dile que . . .⟩ ⟨tell her hello for me : dale saludos de mi parte⟩ **2** INFORM : decir ⟨tell me when they get here : dime cuando lleguen⟩ ⟨I won't tell anyone : no se lo diré a nadie⟩ ⟨I'm telling Mom! : ¡se lo voy a decir a mamá!⟩ **3** INSTRUCT : decir ⟨do what I tell you : haz lo que te digo⟩ ⟨they told her to wait : le dijeron que esperara⟩ **4** RELATE : contar ⟨to tell a story : contar una historia⟩ ⟨to tell a lie : decir una mentira⟩ **5** DISCERN : discernir, notar ⟨I can't tell the difference : no noto la diferencia⟩ ⟨I could tell that she was lying : me di cuenta de que estaba mintiendo⟩ **6** : indicar, señalar ⟨the evidence tells us that . . . : las pruebas nos indican que . . .⟩ **7 all told** : en total **8**

don't tell me : no me digas 9 **I'll tell you what** *(introducing a suggestion)* : hagamos así 10 **I told you so** : te lo dije 11 **to tell apart** : distinguir 12 **to tell it like it is** *fam* : contar/decir las cosas como son 13 **to tell off** *fam* : regañar 14 **to tell (you) the truth** : a decir verdad 15 **you're telling me!** : ¡a mí me lo vas a decir! — *vi* 1 SAY : decir ⟨I won't tell : no voy a decírselo a nadie⟩ 2 KNOW : saber ⟨you never can tell : nunca se sabe⟩ ⟨as far as I can tell : según parece⟩ 3 SHOW : notarse, hacerse sentir ⟨the strain is beginning to tell : la tensión se empieza a notar⟩ 4 **to tell on** : denunciar

teller ['tɛlər] *n* 1 NARRATOR : narrador *m*, -dora *f* 2 *or* **bank teller** : cajero *m*, -ra *f*

telltale ['tɛl,teɪl] *adj* : revelador

temerity [tə'mɛrəti] *n, pl* -**ties** : temeridad *f*

temp¹ ['tɛmp] *n* : empleado *m*, -da *f* temporal

temp² *vi* : hacer trabajo temporal

temper¹ ['tɛmpər] *vt* 1 MODERATE : moderar, temperar 2 ANNEAL : templar (acero, etc.)

temper² *n* 1 DISPOSITION : carácter *m*, genio *m* 2 HARDNESS : temple *m*, dureza *f* (de un metal) 3 COMPOSURE : calma *f*, serenidad *f* ⟨to lose one's temper : perder los estribos⟩ 4 RAGE : furia *f* ⟨to fly into a temper : ponerse furioso⟩

temperament ['tɛmpərmənt, -prə-, -pərə-] *n* : temperamento *m*

temperamental [,tɛmpər'mɛntəl, -prə-, -pərə-] *adj* : temperamental

temperance ['tɛmprəns] *n* : templanza *f*, temperancia *f*

temperate ['tɛmpərət] *adj* : templado (dícese del clima, etc.), moderado

temperature ['tɛmpər,tʃʊr, -prə-, -pərə-, -tʃər] *n* 1 : temperatura *f* 2 FEVER : calentura *f*, fiebre *f*

tempest ['tɛmpəst] *n* 1 : tempestad *f* 2 **a tempest in a teapot** : una tormenta en un vaso de agua

tempestuous [tɛm'pɛstʃʊəs] *adj* : tempestuoso

template ['tɛmplət] *n* : plantilla *f*

temple ['tɛmpəl] *n* 1 : templo *m* (en religión) 2 : sien *f* (en anatomía)

tempo ['tɛm,poʊ] *n, pl* -**pi** [-,pi] *or* -**pos** : ritmo *m*, tempo *m* (en música)

temporal ['tɛmpərəl] *adj* : temporal

temporarily [,tɛmpə'rɛrəli] *adv* : temporalmente, provisionalmente

temporary ['tɛmpə,rɛri] *adj* : temporal, provisional, provisorio

tempt ['tɛmpt] *vt* : tentar

temptation [tɛmp'teɪʃən] *n* : tentación *f*

tempter ['tɛmptər] *n* : tentador *m*

temptress ['tɛmptrəs] *n* : tentadora *f*

ten¹ ['tɛn] *adj* : diez ⟨she's ten (years old) : tiene diez años⟩

ten² *n* 1 : diez *m* (número) ⟨the ten of hearts : el diez de corazones⟩ 2 : decena *f* ⟨tens of thousands : decenas de millares⟩

ten³ *pron* : diez ⟨there are ten of us : somos diez⟩ ⟨it's ten (o'clock) : son las diez⟩

tenable ['tɛnəbəl] *adj* : sostenible, defendible

tenacious [tə'neɪʃəs] *adj* : tenaz — **tenaciously** [tə'neɪʃəsli] *adv*

tenacity [tə'næsəti] *n* : tenacidad *f*

tenancy ['tɛnəntsi] *n, pl* -**cies** : tenencia *f*, inquilinato *m* (de un inmueble)

tenant ['tɛnənt] *n* : inquilino *m*, -na *f*; arrendatario *m*, -ria *f*

tend ['tɛnd] *vt* : atender, cuidar (de), ocuparse de — *vi* : tender ⟨it tends to benefit the consumer : tiende a beneficiar al consumidor⟩

tendency ['tɛndəntsi] *n, pl* -**cies** : tendencia *f*, proclividad *f*, inclinación *f*

tender¹ ['tɛndər] *vt* : entregar, presentar ⟨I tendered my resignation : presenté mi renuncia⟩

tender² *adj* 1 : tierno, blando ⟨tender steak : bistec tierno⟩ 2 AFFECTIONATE, LOVING : tierno, cariñoso, afectuoso 3 DELICATE : tierno, sensible, delicado

tender³ *n* 1 OFFER : propuesta *f*, oferta *f* (en negocios) 2 **legal tender** : moneda *f* de curso legal

tenderize ['tɛndə,raɪz] *vt* -**ized**; -**izing** : ablandar (carnes)

tenderloin ['tɛndr,lɔɪn] *n* : lomo *f* (de res o de puerco)

tenderly ['tɛndərli] *adv* : tiernamente, con ternura

tenderness ['tɛndərnəs] *n* : ternura *f*

tendon ['tɛndən] *n* : tendón *m*

tendril ['tɛndrɪl] *n* : zarcillo *m*

tenement ['tɛnəmənt] *n* : casa *f* de vecindad

tenet ['tɛnət] *n* : principio *m*

tennis ['tɛnəs] *n* : tenis *m* ⟨tennis ball/court/match/racket : pelota/cancha/partido/raqueta de tenis⟩ ⟨tennis player : tenista⟩

tenor ['tɛnər] *n* 1 PURPORT : tenor *m*, significado *m* 2 : tenor *m* (en música)

tenpins ['tɛn,pɪnz] *npl* : bolos *mpl*, boliche *m*

tense¹ ['tɛnts] *v* **tensed**; **tensing** *vt* : tensar — *vi* : tensarse, ponerse tenso

tense² *adj* **tenser**; **tensest** 1 TAUT : tenso, tirante 2 NERVOUS : tenso, nervioso

tense³ *n* : tiempo *m* (de un verbo)

tensely ['tɛntsli] *adv* : tensamente

tenseness ['tɛntsnəs] → **tension**

tension ['tɛntʃən] *n* 1 TAUTNESS : tensión *f*, tirantez *f* 2 STRESS : tensión *f*, nerviosismo *m*, estrés *m*

tent ['tɛnt] *n* : tienda *f* de campaña

tentacle ['tɛntɪkəl] *n* : tentáculo *m*

tentative ['tɛntətɪv] *adj* 1 HESITANT : indeciso, vacilante 2 PROVISIONAL : sujeto a cambios, provisional

tentatively ['tɛntətɪvli] *adv* : provisionalmente

tenth¹ ['tɛnθ] *adv* : en décimo lugar

tenth² *adj* : décimo

tenth³ *n* 1 : décimo *m*, -ma *f* (en una serie) 2 : décimo *m*, décima parte *f*

tenuous [ˈtɛnjʊəs] *adj* : tenue, débil ⟨tenuous reasons : razones poco convincentes⟩

tenuously [ˈtɛnjʊəsli] *adv* : ligeramente, débilmente

tenure [ˈtɛnjər] *n* : tenencia *f* (de un cargo o una propiedad), titularidad *f* (de un puesto académico)

tepee [ˈtiːˌpiː] *n* : tipi *m*

tepid [ˈtɛpɪd] *adj* : tibio

tequila [təˈkiːlə] *n* : tequila *m*

term¹ [ˈtərm] *vt* : calificar de, llamar, nombrar

term² *n* **1** PERIOD : término *m*, plazo *m*, período *m* **2** : término *m* (en matemáticas) **3** WORD : término *m*, vocablo *m* ⟨a term of endearment : un apelativo cariñoso⟩ ⟨medical terms : términos médicos⟩ **4 terms** *npl* CONDITIONS : términos *mpl*, condiciones *fpl* **5 terms** *npl* RELATIONS : relaciones *fpl* ⟨to be on good terms with : tener buenas relaciones con⟩ **6 in terms of** : con respecto a, en cuanto a **7 to come to terms with** : aceptar

terminal¹ [ˈtərmənəl] *adj* : terminal

terminal² *n* **1** : terminal *m*, polo *m* (en electricidad) **2** : terminal *m* (de una computadora) **3** STATION : terminal *f*, estación *f* (de transporte público)

terminate [ˈtərməˌneɪt] *v* **-nated; -nating** *vi* : terminar(se), concluirse — *vt* : terminar, poner fin a

termination [ˌtərməˈneɪʃən] *n* : cese *m*, terminación *f*

terminology [ˌtərməˈnɑləʤi] *n*, *pl* **-gies** : terminología *f*

terminus [ˈtərmənəs] *n*, *pl* **-ni** [-ˌnaɪ] *or* **-nuses 1** END : término *m*, fin *m* **2** : terminal *f* (de transporte público)

termite [ˈtərˌmaɪt] *n* : termita *f*

tern [ˈtərn] *n* : golondrina *f* de mar

terrace¹ [ˈtɛrəs] *vt* **-raced; -racing** : formar en terrazas, disponer en bancales

terrace² *n* **1** PATIO : terraza *f*, patio *m* **2** : terraplén *m*, terraza *f*, bancal *m* (en agricultura)

terra-cotta [ˌtɛrəˈkɑtə] *n* : terracota *f*

terrain [təˈreɪn] *n* : terreno *m*

terrapin [ˈtɛrəpɪn] *n* : galápago *m* norteamericano

terrestrial [təˈrɛstriəl] *adj* : terrestre

terrible [ˈtɛrəbəl] *adj* : atroz, horrible, terrible

terribly [ˈtɛrəbli] *adv* **1** BADLY : muy mal **2** EXTREMELY : terriblemente, extremadamente

terrier [ˈtɛriər] *n* : terrier *mf*

terrific [təˈrɪfɪk] *adj* **1** FRIGHTFUL : aterrador **2** EXTRAORDINARY : extraordinario, excepcional **3** EXCELLENT : excelente, estupendo

terrify [ˈtɛrəˌfaɪ] *vt* **-fied; -fying** : aterrorizar, aterrar, espantar

terrifying [ˈtɛrəˌfaɪɪŋ] *adj* : espantoso, aterrador

territory [ˈtɛrəˌtori] *n*, *pl* **-ries** : territorio *m* — **territorial** [ˌtɛrəˈtoriəl] *adj*

terror [ˈtɛrər] *n* : terror *m*

terrorism [ˈtɛrərˌɪzəm] *n* : terrorismo *m*

terrorist¹ [ˈtɛrərɪst] *adj* : terrorista

terrorist² *n* : terrorista *mf*

terrorize [ˈtɛrərˌaɪz] *vt* **-ized; -izing** : aterrorizar

terry [ˈtɛri] *n*, *pl* **-ries** *or* **terry cloth** : (tela de) toalla *f*

terse [ˈtərs] *adj* **terser; tersest** : lacónico, conciso, seco — **tersely** *adv*

tertiary [ˈtərʃiˌɛri] *adj* : terciario

test¹ [ˈtɛst] *vt* **1** : examinar (estudiantes, etc.), evaluar (conocimientos, etc.) **2** : hacerle un análisis a, hacerle una prueba a, someter a pruebas ⟨to test someone for drugs/cancer : hacerle a alguien pruebas de drogas/cáncer⟩ **3** : analizar ⟨to test soil for lead : analizar tierra para detectar la presencia de plomo⟩ **4** : probar, experimentar (productos, etc.) **5** CHALLENGE, TRY : poner a prueba ⟨you're testing my patience : estás poniendo a prueba mi paciencia⟩ — *vi* : hacer pruebas

test² *n* : prueba *f*, examen *m*, test *m* ⟨to put to the test : poner a prueba⟩

testament [ˈtɛstəmənt] *n* **1** WILL : testamento *m* **2** : Testamento *m* (en la Biblia) ⟨the Old Testament : el Antiguo Testamento⟩

tester [ˈtɛstər] *n* **1** : probador *m*, -dora *f*; verificador *m*, -dora *f* (persona) **2** : verificador *m* (aparato)

testicle [ˈtɛstɪkəl] *n* : testículo *m*

testify [ˈtɛstəˌfaɪ] *v* **-fied; -fying** *vi* : testificar, atestar, testimoniar — *vt* : testificar

testimonial [ˌtɛstəˈmoːniəl] *n* **1** REFERENCE : recomendación *f* **2** TRIBUTE : homenaje *m*, tributo *m*

testimony [ˈtɛstəˌmoːni] *n*, *pl* **-nies** : testimonio *m*, declaración *f*

test tube *n* : probeta *f*, tubo *m* de ensayo

testy [ˈtɛsti] *adj* **testier; -est** : irritable

tetanus [ˈtɛtənəs] *n* : tétano *m*, tétanos *m*

tête-à-tête [ˌtɛtəˈtɛt, ˌteɪtəˈteɪt] *n* : conversación *f* en privado

tether¹ [ˈtɛðər] *vt* : atar (con una cuerda), amarrar

tether² *n* : atadura *f*, cadena *f*, correa *f*

text¹ [ˈtɛkst] *n* **1** : texto *m* **2** TOPIC : tema *m* **3** → **textbook 4** *or* **text message** : mensaje *m* de texto, SMS *m*

text² *vi* : mandar un mensaje de texto, mensajear *fam*, textear *fam* — *vt* : mandarle un mensaje de texto a, mensajear *fam*, textear *fam*

textbook [ˈtɛkstˌbʊk] *n* : libro *m* de texto

texting [ˈtɛkstɪŋ] *or* **text messaging** *n* : mensajería *f* de texto

textile [ˈtɛkˌstaɪl, ˈtɛkstəl] *n* : textil *m*, tela *f* ⟨the textile industry : la industria textil⟩

textual [ˈtɛkstʃuəl] *adj* : textual

texture [ˈtɛkstʃər] *n* : textura *f*

Thai [ˈtaɪ] *n* **1** : tailandés *m*, -desa *f* **2** : tailandés *m* (idioma) — **Thai** *adj*

than¹ [ˈðæn] *conj* : que, de ⟨it's worth more than that : vale más que eso⟩ ⟨more than you think : más de lo que piensas⟩

than² *prep* : que, de ⟨you're better than he is : eres mejor que él⟩ ⟨more than once : más de una vez⟩

thank ['θæŋk] vt : agradecer, darle (las) gracias (a alguien) ⟨thank you! : ¡gracias!⟩ ⟨I thanked her for the present : le di las gracias por el regalo⟩ ⟨I thank you for your help : le agradezco su ayuda⟩

thankful ['θæŋkfəl] adj : agradecido

thankfully ['θæŋkfəli] adv **1** GRATEFULLY : con agradecimiento **2** FORTUNATELY : afortunadamente, por suerte ⟨thankfully, it's over : se acabó, gracias a Dios⟩

thankfulness ['θæŋkfəlnəs] n : agradecimiento m, gratitud f

thankless ['θæŋkləs] adj : ingrato ⟨a thankless task : un trabajo ingrato⟩

thanks ['θæŋks] npl **1** : agradecimiento m **2 thanks!** : ¡gracias!

Thanksgiving [θæŋks'gɪvɪŋ, 'θæŋks-] n : el día de Acción de Gracias (fiesta estadounidense)

that¹ ['ðæt] adv (in negative constructions) : tan ⟨it's not that expensive : no es tan caro⟩ ⟨not that much : no tanto⟩

that² adj, pl **those** : ese, esa, aquel, aquella ⟨do you see those children? : ¿ves a aquellos niños?⟩

that³ conj & pron : que ⟨he said that he was afraid : dijo que tenía miedo⟩ ⟨the book that he wrote : el libro que escribió⟩

that⁴ pron, pl **those** ['ðo:z] **1** : ese/ese, esa/ésa, eso ⟨that's my father : ése/ése es mi padre⟩ ⟨those are the ones he likes : esos/ésos son los que le gustan⟩ ⟨what's that? : ¿qué es eso?⟩ ⟨why did you do that? : ¿por qué hiciste eso?⟩ ⟨that's impossible : (eso) es imposible⟩ ⟨is that so? : ¿de veras?, ¿ah, sí?⟩ ⟨after that : después, luego⟩ **2 those** pl (referring to a group of people) ⟨those who came : los que vinieron⟩ ⟨there are those who say . . . : hay quien dice . . .⟩ **3** (referring to more distant objects or items) : aquel/aquél, aquella/aquélla, aquello ⟨those are maples and these are elms : aquellos/aquéllos son arces y estos/éstos son olmos⟩ ⟨that came to an end : aquello se acabó⟩ **4 at that** ALSO, MOREOVER : además **5 at that** THEREUPON : al decir/oír (eso), eso **6 at that** : sin decir más ⟨let's leave it at that : dejémoslo ahí⟩ **7 for all that** : a pesar de ello **8 that is (to say)** : o sea, es decir **9 that's it** ⟨that's it — it's finished : ya está (terminado)⟩ ⟨that's it — I'm leaving! : ¡se acabó! ¡me voy!⟩ ⟨do it like this — that's it! : hazlo así — ¡eso es!⟩

thatch¹ ['θætʃ] vt : cubrir o techar con paja, hojas, etc.

thatch² n : paja f, hojas fpl (para techos)

thaw¹ ['θɔ] vt : descongelar — vi : derretirse (dícese de la nieve), descongelarse (dícese de los alimentos)

thaw² n : deshielo m

the¹ [ðə, before vowel sounds usu ði:] adv **1** (used to indicate comparison) ⟨the sooner the better : cuanto más pronto, mejor⟩ ⟨she likes this one the best : éste es el que más le gusta⟩ **2** (used as a conjunction) : cuanto ⟨the more I learn, the less I understand : cuanto más aprendo, menos entiendo⟩

the² art : el, la, los, las, lo ⟨the gloves : los guantes⟩ ⟨the girl : la chica⟩ ⟨the winter : el invierno⟩ ⟨the worst part : lo peor⟩ ⟨forty cookies to the box : cuarenta galletas por caja⟩ ⟨today is the ninth : hoy es nueve⟩ ⟨the 18th of august : el 18 de agosto⟩ ⟨William the Conqueror : Guillermo el Conquistador⟩ ⟨the French : los franceses⟩ ⟨the Smiths : los Smith⟩ ⟨the Mississippi River : el río Mississippi⟩ ⟨the English language : la lengua inglesa, el idioma inglés⟩

theater or **theatre** ['θi:ətər] n **1** : teatro m (edificio) **2** DRAMA : teatro m, drama m

theatrical [θi'ætrɪkəl] adj : teatral, dramático

thee ['ði:] pron : te, ti

theft ['θɛft] n : robo m, hurto m

their ['ðer] adj : su ⟨their friends : sus amigos⟩

theirs ['ðerz] pron : (el) suyo, (la) suya, (los) suyos, (las) suyas ⟨they came for theirs : vinieron por el suyo⟩ ⟨theirs is bigger : la suya es más grande, la de ellos es más grande⟩ ⟨a brother of theirs : un hermano suyo, un hermano de ellos⟩

them ['ðem] pron **1** (as a direct object) : los Spain sometimes les, las ⟨I know them : los conozco⟩ **2** (as indirect object) : les, se ⟨I sent them a letter : les mandé una carta⟩ ⟨give it to them : dáselo (a ellos)⟩ **3** (as object of a preposition) : ellos, ellas ⟨go with them : ve con ellos⟩ **4** (for emphasis) : ellos, ellas ⟨I wasn't expecting them : no los esperaba a ellos⟩

thematic [θi'mætɪk] adj : temático

theme ['θi:m] n **1** SUBJECT, TOPIC : tema m **2** COMPOSITION : composición f, trabajo m (escrito) **3** : tema m (en música)

theme park n : parque m temático

themselves [ðəm'sɛlvz, ðem-] pron **1** (as a reflexive) : se, sí ⟨they enjoyed themselves : se divirtieron⟩ ⟨they divided it among themselves : lo repartieron entre sí, se lo repartieron⟩ **2** (for emphasis) : ellos mismos, ellas mismas ⟨they built it themselves : ellas mismas lo construyeron⟩

then¹ ['ðen] adv **1** : entonces, en ese tiempo ⟨I was sixteen then : tenía entonces dieciséis años⟩ ⟨by/since/until then : para/desde/hasta entonces⟩ **2** NEXT : después, luego ⟨we'll go to Toronto, then to Winnipeg : iremos a Toronto, y luego a Winnipeg⟩ **3** BESIDES, FURTHERMORE : además, aparte ⟨then there's the tax : y aparte está el impuesto⟩ **4** : entonces, en ese caso ⟨if you like music, then you should attend : si te gusta la música, entonces deberías asistir⟩ ⟨it's true, then? : ¿entonces es cierto?⟩ ⟨OK, then, I'll see you later : hasta luego, entonces⟩ ⟨you're sure? all right, then : ¿estás seguro? bueno, está bien⟩ **5 then and there** : en el momento

then² adj : entonces ⟨the then governor of Georgia : el entonces gobernador de Georgia⟩

thence ['ðɛnts, 'θɛnts] *adv* : de ahí, de ahí en adelante

theologian [ˌθiːə'loːdʒən] *n* : teólogo *m*, -ga *f*

theological [ˌθiːə'lɑdʒɪkəl] *adj* : teológico

theology [θi'ɑlədʒi] *n, pl* **-gies** : teología *f*

theorem ['θiːərəm, 'θɪrəm] *n* : teorema *m*

theoretical [ˌθiːə'rɛtɪkəl] *adj* : teórico — **theoretically** *adv*

theorist ['θiːərɪst] *n* : teórico *m*, -ca *f*

theorize ['θiːəˌraɪz] *vi* **-rized; -rizing** : teorizar

theory ['θiːəri, 'θɪri] *n, pl* **-ries** : teoría *f*

therapeutic [ˌθɛrə'pjuːtɪk] *adj* : terapéutico — **therapeutically** *adv*

therapist ['θɛrəpɪst] *n* : terapeuta *mf*

therapy ['θɛrəpi] *n, pl* **-pies** : terapia *f*

there¹ ['ðær] *adv* **1** : ahí, allí, allá ⟨stand over there : párate ahí⟩ ⟨we can walk there : podemos ir a pie⟩ ⟨over there : por allí/allá⟩ ⟨out/in there : ahí fuera/dentro⟩ ⟨who's there? : ¿quién es?⟩ ⟨is Mom there? : ¿está mamá?⟩ ⟨there it is : ahí está⟩ ⟨there you are/go : aquí tienes, toma⟩ ⟨. . . and there you have it! : ¡ . . . y ya está!⟩ ⟨that clock there : ese reloj que ves allí⟩ ⟨you there! : ¡oye, tú!⟩ ⟨hello there! : ¡hola!⟩ **2** : ahí, en esto, en eso ⟨there is where we disagree : en eso es donde no estamos de acuerdo⟩ **3** THEN : entonces ⟨from there : de ahí, a partir de ese momento⟩ **4 to be our there** EXIST : existir **5 to have been there** (*referring to an experience*) ⟨I've been there myself : yo también he pasado por eso⟩

there² *pron* **1** (*introducing a sentence or clause*) ⟨there comes a time to decide : llega un momento en que uno tiene que decidir⟩ **2 there is/are** : hay ⟨there are many children here : aquí hay muchos niños⟩ ⟨are there a lot of errors? : ¿hay muchos errores?⟩ ⟨there's a good hotel downtown : hay un buen hotel en el centro⟩ ⟨there was no way to know : no había manera de saberlo⟩

thereabouts [ˌðærə'baʊts, 'ðærəˌ-] *or* **thereabout** [-'baʊt, -ˌbaʊt] *adv or* **thereabouts** : por ahí, más o menos ⟨at five o'clock or thereabouts : por ahí de las cinco⟩

thereafter [ðær'æftər] *adv* : después ⟨shortly thereafter : poco después⟩

thereby [ðær'baɪ, 'ðærˌbaɪ] *adv* : de tal modo, de esa manera, así

therefore ['ðærˌfor] *adv* : por lo tanto, por consiguiente

therein [ðær'ɪn] *adv* **1** : allí adentro, ahí adentro ⟨the contents therein : lo que allí se contiene⟩ **2** : allí, en ese aspecto ⟨therein lies the problem : allí está el problema⟩

thereof [ðær'ʌv, -'ɑv] *adv* : de eso, de esto

thereupon ['ðærəˌpɑn, -ˌpɔn;, ˌðærə'pɑn, -'pɔn] *adv* : acto seguido, inmediatamente (después)

therewith [ðær'wɪð, -'wɪθ] *adv* : con eso, con ello

thermal ['θərməl] *adj* **1** : térmico (en física) **2** HOT : termal

thermodynamics [ˌθərmodaɪ'næmɪks] *ns & pl* : termodinámica *f*

thermometer [θər'mɑmətər] *n* : termómetro *m*

thermos ['θərməs] *n* : termo *m*

thermostat ['θərməˌstæt] *n* : termostato *m*

thesaurus [θɪ'sɔrəs] *n, pl* **-sauri** [-'sɔrˌaɪ] *or* **-sauruses** [-'sɔrəsəz] : diccionario *m* de sinónimos

these → **this**

thesis ['θiːsɪs] *n, pl* **theses** ['θiːˌsiːz] : tesis *f*

they ['ðeɪ] *pron* : ellos, ellas ⟨they are here : están aquí⟩ ⟨they don't know : ellos no saben⟩

they'd ['ðeɪd] *contraction of* THEY HAD *or* THEY WOULD → **have, would**

they'll ['ðeɪl, 'ðɛl] *contraction of* THEY SHALL *or* THEY WILL → **shall, will**

they're ['ðɔr] *contraction of* THEY ARE → **be**

they've ['ðeɪv] *contraction of* THEY HAVE → **have**

thiamine ['θaɪəmɪn, -ˌmiːn] *n* : tiamina *f*

thick¹ ['θɪk] *adj* **1** : grueso ⟨a thick plank : una tabla gruesa⟩ **2** : espeso, denso ⟨thick syrup : jarabe espeso⟩ — **thickly** *adv*

thick² *n* **1 in the thick of** : en medio de ⟨in the thick of the battle : en lo más reñido de la batalla⟩ **2 through thick and thin** : a las duras y a las maduras

thicken ['θɪkən] *vt* : espesar (un líquido) — *vi* : espesarse

thickener ['θɪkənər] *n* : espesante *m*

thicket ['θɪkət] *n* : matorral *m*, maleza *f*, espesura *f*

thickness ['θɪknəs] *n* : grosor *m*, grueso *m*, espesor *m*

thickset ['θɪk'sɛt] *adj* STOCKY : robusto, fornido

thick-skinned ['θɪk'skɪnd] *adj* : poco sensible, que no se ofende fácilmente

thief ['θiːf] *n, pl* **thieves** ['θiːvz] : ladrón *m*, -drona *f*

thieve ['θiːv] *v* **thieved; thieving** : hurtar, robar

thievery ['θiːvəri] *n* : hurto *m*, robo *m*, latrocinio *m*

thigh ['θaɪ] *n* : muslo *m*

thighbone ['θaɪˌboːn] *n* : fémur *m*

thimble ['θɪmbəl] *n* : dedal *m*

thin¹ ['θɪn] *v* **thinned; thinning** *vt* : hacer menos denso, diluir, aguar (un líquido), enrarecer (un gas) — *vi* : diluirse, aguarse (dícese de un líquido), enrarecerse (dícese de un gas)

thin² *adj* **thinner; thinnest** **1** LEAN, SLIM : delgado, esbelto, flaco **2** SPARSE : ralo, escaso ⟨a thin beard : una barba rala⟩ **3** WATERY : claro, aguado, diluido **4** FINE : delgado, fino ⟨thin slices : rebanadas finas⟩

thing ['θɪŋ] *n* **1** MATTER, FACT, IDEA : cosa *f* ⟨don't talk about those things : no hables de esas cosas⟩ ⟨how are things? : ¿cómo van las cosas?⟩ ⟨the main thing : lo principal⟩ ⟨the thing is . . . : el caso es que . . .⟩ ⟨to think things over : pensarlo (bien)⟩ ⟨for one thing, . . . : para empezar, . . .⟩ ⟨I said no such thing! : ¡no dije tal/semejante cosa!⟩ **2** ACT, EVENT : cosa *f* ⟨the flood was a terrible thing : la inundación fue una cosa terrible⟩ ⟨it's a good thing that . . . : menos mal que . . .⟩ ⟨to do the right thing : hacer lo correcto⟩ **3** OBJECT : cosa *f* ⟨don't forget your things : no olvides tus cosas⟩ ⟨baby things : cosas para bebés⟩ ⟨there's no such thing : no existe (tal cosa)⟩ ⟨I can't see a thing : no puedo ver nada⟩ ⟨I have just the thing for you : tengo justo lo que necesitas⟩ **4 as things stand** : tal como están las cosas **5 a thing or two** : unas cuantas cosas **6 first/last thing** : a primera/última hora ⟨I'll do it first thing tomorrow : lo haré mañana a primera hora⟩ **7 it's (just) one of those things** : son cosas de la vida **8 of all things** ⟨he's learning jousting, of all things! : ¡está aprendiendo a justar! ¿te lo imaginas?⟩ **9 to have another thing coming** : estar muy equivocado

thingamajig [ˈθɪŋəmə͵dʒɪg] *or* **thingamabob** [ˈθɪŋəmə͵bab] *n fam* : cosa *f*, vaina *f fam*, chisme *m Spain fam*

think[1] [ˈθɪŋk] *v* **thought** [ˈθɔt]; **thinking** *vt* **1** PLAN : pensar, creer ⟨he thinks (that) he'll return early : piensa regresar temprano⟩ ⟨I think (that) I'll call her : creo que la llamaré⟩ **2** BELIEVE : creer, opinar ⟨I think (that) I can go : creo que puedo ir⟩ ⟨I think so : creo que sí⟩ ⟨I don't think so : creo que no⟩ ⟨what do you think? : ¿qué opinas?⟩ ⟨who does she think she is? : ¿quién se cree?⟩ **3** PONDER : pensar ⟨"how odd," he thought : qué raro — pensó⟩ ⟨what were you thinking? : ¿en qué pensabas?⟩ **4** REMEMBER : acordarse de ⟨I didn't think to ask : no se me ocurrió preguntar⟩ **5 to think better of** : cambiar de idea **6 to think nothing of** ⟨she thinks nothing of running 10 miles : correr 10 millas no le parece nada extraño⟩ ⟨think nothing of it : de nada, no hay de qué⟩ **7 to think out/through** : pensar bien, estudiar **8 to think over** CONSIDER : pensar **9 to think up** : idear, inventar ⟨we've thought up a plan : se nos ha ocurrido un plan⟩ — *vi* **1** : pensar ⟨let me think : déjame pensar⟩ **2 to think about/of** : pensar en ⟨I was just thinking about/of you when you called : pensaba en ti justo cuando llamaste⟩ **3 to think about/of** WEIGH : pensar (en) ⟨think about it : piénsalo⟩ ⟨I'm thinking about/of buying it : estoy pensando en comprarlo⟩ **4 to think about/of** : pensar en ⟨think about/of your family! : ¡piensa en tu familia!⟩ **5 to think about/of** : pensar de ⟨what did you think about/of the book? : ¿qué pensaste del libro?, ¿qué te pareció el libro?⟩ **6 to think again** : pensar dos veces **7 to think ahead** : ser previsor **8 to think aloud** : pensar en voz alta **9 to think back** : recordar **10 to think of** REMEMBER : acordarse de **11 to think of** : idear,

inventar ⟨we'll think of something : algo se nos ocurrirá⟩ **12 to think poorly of** : pensar mal de **13 to think twice** : pensárselo dos veces **14 to think well of** : tener buena opinión de

think[2] *n* **1 to have a think about** : pensar **2 to have another think coming** : estar muy equivocado

thinker [ˈθɪŋkər] *n* : pensador *m*, -dora *f*

thinly [ˈθɪnli] *adv* **1** LIGHTLY : ligeramente **2** SPARSELY : escasamente ⟨thinly populated : poco poblado⟩ **3** BARELY : apenas

thinness [ˈθɪnnəs] *n* : delgadez *f*

thin–skinned [ˈθɪnˈskɪnd] *adj* : susceptible, muy sensible

third[1] *or* **thirdly** [-li] *adv* : en tercer lugar ⟨she came in third : llegó en tercer lugar⟩

third[2] *adj* : tercero ⟨the third day : el tercer día⟩

third[3] *n* **1** : tercero *m*, -ra *f* (en una serie) ⟨the third of June : el tres de junio⟩ **2** : tercero *m*, tercera parte *f* **3** *or* **third base** : tercera base *f* **4** *or* **third gear** : tercera *f*

third world *n sometimes offensive* **Third World** : el Tercer Mundo *m*

thirst[1] [ˈθərst] *vi* **1** : tener sed **2 to thirst for** DESIRE : tener sed de, estar sediento de

thirst[2] *n* : sed *f*

thirsty [ˈθərsti] *adj* **thirstier, -est** : sediento, que tiene sed ⟨I'm thirsty : tengo sed⟩

thirteen[1] [͵θərˈtiːn] *adj & pron* : trece

thirteen[2] *n* : trece *m*

thirteenth[1] [͵θərˈtiːnθ] *adj* : décimo tercero

thirteenth[2] *n* **1** : decimotercero *m*, -ra *f* (en una serie) **2** : treceavo *m*, treceava parte *f*

thirtieth[1] [ˈθərtiəθ] *adj* : trigésimo

thirtieth[2] *n* **1** : trigésimo *m*, -ma *f* (en una serie) **2** : treintavo *m*, treintava parte *f*

thirty[1] [ˈθərti] *adj & pron* : treinta

thirty[2] *n, pl* **thirties** : treinta *m*

this[1] [ˈðɪs] *adv* : así, a tal punto ⟨this big : así de grande⟩

this[2] *adj, pl* **these** [ˈðiːz] : este ⟨these things : estas cosas⟩ ⟨read this book : lee este libro⟩

this[3] *pron, pl* **these** : este/éste, esta/ésta, esto ⟨what's this? : ¿qué es esto?⟩ ⟨this wasn't here yesterday : esto no estaba aquí ayer⟩ ⟨this is for you : esto es para ti⟩ ⟨those magazines and these : aquellas revistas y estas/éstas⟩ ⟨these aren't the files I need : estos/éstos no son los archivos que necesito⟩

thistle [ˈθɪsəl] *n* : cardo *m*

thong [ˈθɔŋ] *n* **1** STRAP : correa *f*, tira *f* **2** FLIP-FLOP : chancla *f*, chancleta *f*

thorax [ˈθɔr͵æks] *n, pl* **-raxes** *or* **-races** [ˈθɔrə͵siːz] : tórax *m*

thorn [ˈθɔrn] *n* : espina *f*

thorny [ˈθɔrni] *adj* **thornier, -est** : espinoso

thorough [ˈθɔroː] *adj* **1** CONSCIENTIOUS

: concienzudo, meticuloso **2** COMPLETE : absoluto, completo — **thoroughly** adv

thoroughbred ['θəro,bred] adj : de pura sangre (dícese de un caballo)

Thoroughbred n or **Thoroughbred horse** : pura sangre mf

thoroughfare ['θəro,fær] n : vía f pública, carretera f

thoroughness ['θəronəs] n : esmero m, meticulosidad f

those → **that**

thou ['ðaʊ] pron : tú

though¹ ['ðo:] adv **1** HOWEVER, NEVERTHELESS : sin embargo, no obstante **2 as ~** : como si ⟨as though nothing had happened : como si nada hubiera pasado⟩

though² conj : aunque, a pesar de ⟨though it was raining, we went out : salimos a pesar de la lluvia⟩

thought¹ → **think**

thought² ['θɔt] n **1** THINKING : pensamiento m, ideas fpl ⟨Western thought : el pensamiento occidental⟩ **2** COGITATION : pensamiento m, reflexión f, raciocinio m **3** IDEA : idea f, ocurrencia f ⟨it was just a thought : fue sólo una idea⟩

thoughtful ['θɔtfəl] adj **1** PENSIVE : pensativo, meditabundo **2** CONSIDERATE : considerado, atento, cortés — **thoughtfully** adv

thoughtfulness ['θɔtfəlnəs] n : consideración f, atención f, cortesía f

thoughtless ['θɔtləs] adj **1** CARELESS : descuidado, negligente **2** INCONSIDERATE : desconsiderado — **thoughtlessly** adv

thoughtlessness n **1** CARELESSNESS : descuido m, irreflexión f, imprevisión f **2** : falta f de consideración

thousand¹ ['θaʊzənd] adj & pron : mil

thousand² n, pl **-sands** or **-sand** : mil m

thousandth¹ ['θaʊzənθ] adj : milésimo

thousandth² n **1** : milésimo m, -ma f (en una serie) **2** : milésimo m, milésima parte f

thrash ['θræʃ] vt **1** → **thresh 2** BEAT : golpear, azotar, darle una paliza (a alguien) **3** FLAIL : sacudir, agitar bruscamente

thread¹ ['θred] vt **1** : enhilar, enhebrar (una aguja) **2** STRING : ensartar (cuentas en un hilo) **3 to thread one's way** : abrirse paso

thread² n **1** : hilo m, hebra f ⟨needle and thread : aguja e hilo⟩ ⟨the thread of an argument : el hilo de un debate⟩ **2** : rosca f, filete m (de un tornillo)

threadbare ['θred,bær] adj **1** SHABBY, WORN : raído, gastado **2** TRITE : trillado, tópico, manido

threat ['θret] n : amenaza f

threaten ['θretən] v : amenazar

threatening ['θretənɪŋ] adj : amenazador — **threateningly** adv

three¹ ['θri:] adj : tres ⟨he's three (years old) : tiene tres años⟩

three² n : tres m ⟨the three of hearts : el tres de corazones⟩

three³ pron : tres ⟨there are three of us

: somos tres⟩ ⟨it's three (o'clock) : son las tres⟩

3–D ['θri:'di:] adj → **three-dimensional**

three–dimensional ['θri:də'mentʃənəl] adj : tridimensional

threefold ['θri:,fo:ld] adj TRIPLE : triple

three hundred¹ adj & pron : trescientos

three hundred² n : trescientos m

three–piece suit n : terno m, tresillo m

threescore ['θri:'skor] adj SIXTY : sesenta

thresh ['θreʃ] vt : trillar (grano)

thresher ['θreʃər] n : trilladora f

threshold ['θreʃ,ho:ld, -,o:ld] n : umbral m

threw → **throw¹**

thrice ['θraɪs] adv : tres veces

thrift ['θrɪft] n : economía f, frugalidad f

thriftless ['θrɪftləs] adj : despilfarrador, manirroto

thrifty ['θrɪfti] adj **thriftier; -est** : económico, frugal — **thriftily** ['θrɪftəli] adv

thrill¹ ['θrɪl] vt : emocionar — vi **to thrill to** : dejarse conmover por, estremecerse con

thrill² n : emoción f

thriller ['θrɪlər] n **1** : evento m emocionante **2** : obra f de suspenso

thrilling ['θrɪlɪŋ] adj : emocionante, excitante

thrive ['θraɪv] vi **throve** or **thrived; thriven** ['θrɪvən] **1** FLOURISH : florecer, crecer abundantemente **2** PROSPER : prosperar

throat ['θro:t] n : garganta f

throaty ['θro:ti] adj **throatier; -est** : ronco (dícese de la voz)

throb¹ ['θrɑb] vi **throbbed; throbbing** : palpitar, latir (dícese del corazón), vibrar (dícese de un motor, etc.)

throb² n : palpitación f, latido m, vibración f

throe ['θro:] n **1** PAIN, SPASM : espasmo m, dolor m ⟨the throes of childbirth : los dolores de parto⟩ **2 throes** npl : lucha f larga y ardua ⟨in the throes of : en el medio de⟩

thrombosis [θrɑm'bo:səs] n : trombosis f

throne ['θro:n] n : trono m

throng¹ ['θrɔŋ] vt CROWD : atestar, atiborrar, llenar — vi : aglomerarse, amontonarse

throng² n : muchedumbre f, gentío m, multitud f

throttle¹ ['θrɑtəl] vt **-tled; -tling 1** STRANGLE : estrangular, ahogar **2 to throttle down** : desacelerar (un motor)

throttle² n **1** : válvula f reguladora **2 at full throttle** : a toda máquina

through¹ ['θru:] adv **1** : a través, de un lado a otro ⟨let them through : déjenlos pasar⟩ **2** : de principio a fin ⟨she read the book through : leyó el libro de principio a fin⟩ **3** COMPLETELY : completamente ⟨soaked through : completamente empapado⟩

through² adj **1** DIRECT : directo ⟨a through train : un tren directo⟩ **2** FINISHED : terminado, acabado ⟨we're through : hemos terminado⟩

through³ *prep* **1** : a través de, por ⟨through the door : por la puerta⟩ ⟨a road through the woods : un camino que atraviesa el bosque⟩ **2** BETWEEN : entre ⟨a path through the trees : un sendero entre los árboles⟩ **3** BECAUSE OF : a causa de, como consecuencia de **4** DURING : por, durante ⟨through the night : durante la noche⟩ **5** : a, hasta ⟨from Monday through Friday : de lunes a viernes⟩ **6** (*indicating completion*) ⟨she's been through a lot : ha pasado muchas dificultades⟩ ⟨we're through the worst of it : hemos pasado lo peor⟩ **7** VIA : a través de, por ⟨I got the job through her cousin : conseguí el trabajo a través de su primo⟩

throughout¹ *adv* **1** EVERYWHERE : por todas partes **2** THROUGH : desde el principio hasta el fin de (algo)

throughout² *prep* **1** : en todas partes de, a través de ⟨throughout the United States : en todo Estados Unidos⟩ **2** : de principio a fin de, durante ⟨throughout the winter : durante todo el invierno⟩

throve → **thrive**

throw¹ ['θroː] *v* **threw** ['θruː]; **thrown** ['θroːn]; **throwing** *vt* **1** TOSS : tirar; lanzar; echar; arrojar; aventar *Col, Mex* ⟨to throw a ball : tirar una pelota⟩ **2** : desmontar (a un jinete) 〈 cast : proyectar 〈it threw a long shadow : proyectó una sombra larga⟩ **4** to throw a party : dar una fiesta **5** to throw in : dar de ñapa **6** to throw into confusion : desconcertar **7** to throw away/out DISCARD : botar, tirar (a la basura) **8** to throw out REJECT : rechazar **9** to throw out EJECT : echar **10** to throw up VOMIT : vomitar, devolver (comida, etc.) — *vi* to throw up VOMIT : vomitar, devolver

throw² *n* TOSS : tiro *m*, tirada *f*, lanzamiento *m*, lance *m* (de dados)

thrower ['θroːər] *n* : lanzador *m*, -dora *f*

thrush ['θrʌʃ] *n* : tordo *m*, zorzal *m*

thrust¹ ['θrʌst] *v* **thrust**; **thrusting** **1** SHOVE : empujar bruscamente **2** PLUNGE, STAB : apuñalar, clavar ⟨he thrust a dagger into her heart : la apuñaló en el corazón⟩ **3** to thrust one's way : abrirse paso **4** to thrust upon : imponer a

thrust² *n* **1** PUSH, SHOVE : empujón *m*, empellón *m* **2** LUNGE : estocada *f* (en esgrima) **3** IMPETUS : ímpetu *m*, impulso *m*, propulsión *f* (de un motor)

thud¹ ['θʌd] *vi* **thudded**; **thudding** : producir un ruido sordo

thud² *n* : ruido *m* sordo (que produce un objeto al caer)

thug ['θʌɡ] *n* : matón *m*

thumb¹ ['θʌm] *vt* : hojear (con el pulgar)

thumb² *n* : pulgar *m*, dedo *m* pulgar

thumbnail ['θʌm,neɪl] *n* **1** : uña *f* del pulgar **2** : thumbnail *m*, miniatura *f*

thumbtack ['θʌm,tæk] *n* : tachuela *f*, chinche *f*

thump¹ ['θʌmp] *vt* POUND : golpear, aporrear — *vi* : latir con vehemencia (dícese del corazón)

thump² *n* THUD : ruido *m* sordo

thunder¹ ['θʌndər] *vi* **1** : tronar ⟨it rained and thundered all night : llovió y tronó durante la noche⟩ **2** BOOM : retumbar, bramar, resonar — *vt* ROAR, SHOUT : decir a gritos, vociferar

thunder² *n* : truenos *mpl*

thunderbolt ['θʌndər,boːlt] *n* : rayo *m*

thunderclap ['θʌndər,klæp] *n* : trueno *m*

thunderous ['θʌndərəs] *adj* : atronador, ensordecedor, estruendoso

thundershower ['θʌndər,ʃaʊər] *n* : lluvia *f* con truenos y relámpagos

thunderstorm ['θʌndər,stɔrm] *n* : tormenta *f* con truenos y relámpagos

thunderstruck ['θʌndər,strʌk] *adj* : atónito

Thursday ['θərz,deɪ, -di] *n* : jueves *m* ⟨today is Thursday : hoy es jueves⟩ ⟨(on) Thursday : el jueves⟩ ⟨(on) Thursdays : los jueves⟩ ⟨last Thursday : el jueves pasado⟩ ⟨next Thursday : el jueves que viene⟩ ⟨every other Thursday : cada dos jueves⟩ ⟨Thursday afternoon/morning : jueves por la tarde/mañana⟩

thus ['ðʌs] *adv* **1** : así, de esta manera **2** SO : hasta (cierto punto) ⟨the weather's been nice thus far : hasta ahora ha hecho buen tiempo⟩ **3** HENCE : por consiguiente, por lo tanto

thwart ['θwɔrt] *vt* FRUSTRATE : frustrar

thy ['ðaɪ] *adj* : tu

thyme ['taɪm, 'θaɪm] *n* : tomillo *m*

thyroid ['θaɪ,rɔɪd] *n or* **thyroid gland** : tiroides *mf*, glándula *f* tiroidea ⟨thyroid hormone : hormona tiroidea⟩

thyself [ðaɪ'sɛlf] *pron* : ti, ti mismo

ti ['tiː] *n* : si *m* (en el canto)

tiara [ti'ærə, -'ɑr-] *n* : diadema *f*

Tibetan [tə'bɛtən] *n* **1** : tibetano *m*, -na *f* **2** : tibetano *m* (idioma) — **Tibetan** *adj*

tibia ['tɪbiə] *n, pl* **-iae** [-bi,iː] : tibia *f*

tic ['tɪk] *n* : tic *m*

tick¹ ['tɪk] *vi* **1** : hacer tictac **2** OPERATE, RUN : operar, andar (dícese de un mecanismo) ⟨what makes him tick? : ¿qué es lo que lo mueve?⟩ — *vt or* **to tick off** CHECK : marcar

tick² *n* **1** : tictac *m* (de un reloj) **2** CHECK : marca *f* **3** : garrapata *f* (insecto)

ticket¹ ['tɪkət] *vt* LABEL : etiquetar

ticket² *n* **1** : boleto *m*, boleta *f*, entrada *f* (de un espectáculo), pasaje *m* (de avión, tren, etc.) **2** SLATE : lista *f* de candidatos

ticket collector *n* : revisor *m*, -sora *f*

ticket office *n* : taquilla *f*

tickle¹ ['tɪkəl] *v* **-led**; **-ling** *vt* **1** AMUSE : divertir, hacerle gracia (a alguien) **2** : hacerle cosquillas (a alguien) ⟨don't tickle me! : ¡no me hagas cosquillas!⟩ — *vi* : picar

tickle² *n* : cosquilleo *m*, cosquillas *fpl*, picor *m* (en la garganta)

ticklish ['tɪkəlɪʃ] *adj* **1** : cosquilloso (dícese de una persona) **2** DELICATE, TRICKY : delicado, peliagudo

tick–tock *n* : tictac *m*

tidal ['taɪdəl] *adj* : de marea, relativo a la marea

tidal wave *n* : maremoto *m*

tidbit ['tɪd,bɪt] *n* **1** BITE, SNACK : bocado *m*, golosina *f* **2** : dato *m* o noticia *f* interesante ⟨useful tidbits of information : informaciones útiles⟩

tide¹ ['taɪd] *vt* **tided; tiding** *or* **to tide over** : proveer lo necesario para aguantar una dificultad ⟨this money will tide you over until you find work : este dinero te mantendrá hasta que encuentres empleo⟩

tide² *n* **1** : marea *f* **2** CURRENT : corriente *f* (de eventos, opiniones, etc.)

tidily ['taɪdəli] *adv* : ordenadamente

tidiness ['taɪdinəs] *n* : aseo *m*, limpieza *f*, orden *m*

tidings ['taɪdɪŋz] *npl* : nuevas *fpl*

tidy¹ ['taɪdi] *vt* **-died; -dying** : asear, limpiar, poner en orden — *vi* **to tidy up** : poner las cosas en orden

tidy² *adj* **tidier; -est** **1** CLEAN, NEAT : limpio, aseado, en orden **2** SUBSTANTIAL : grande, considerable ⟨a tidy sum : una suma considerable⟩

tie¹ ['taɪ] *v* **tied; tying** *or* **tieing** *vt* **1** : atar, amarrar ⟨to tie a knot : atar un nudo⟩ ⟨to tie one's shoelaces : atarse los cordones⟩ **2** BIND, UNITE : ligar, atar **3** : empatar ⟨they tied the score : empataron el marcador⟩ **4 to be fit to be tied** : estar hecho una furia **5 to tie down/up** : atar **6 to tie in with** : relacionar con **7 to tie up** : ocupar (a alguien), inmovilizar (dinero), atascar (tráfico) — *vi* **1** : empatar ⟨the two teams were tied : los dos equipos empataron⟩ **2 to tie in with** : relacionarse con

tie² *n* **1** : ligadura *f*, cuerda *f*, cordón *m* (para atar algo) **2** BOND, LINK : atadura *f*, ligadura *f*, vínculo *m*, lazo *m* ⟨family ties : lazos familiares⟩ **3** *or* **railroad tie** : traviesa *f* **4** DRAW : empate *m* (en deportes) **5** NECKTIE : corbata *f*

tiebreaker ['taɪ,breɪkər] *n* : desempate *m*

tier ['tɪr] *n* : hilera *f*, escalón *m*

tiff ['tɪf] *n* : disgusto *m*, disputa *f*

tiger ['taɪgər] *n* : tigre *m*

tight¹ ['taɪt] *adv* TIGHTLY : bien, fuerte ⟨shut it tight : ciérralo bien⟩

tight² *adj* **1** : bien cerrado, hermético ⟨a tight seal : un cierre hermético⟩ **2** STRICT : estricto, severo **3** TAUT : tirante, tenso **4** SNUG : apretado, ajustado, ceñido ⟨a tight dress : un vestido ceñido⟩ **5** DIFFICULT : difícil ⟨to be in a tight spot : estar en un aprieto⟩ **6** STINGY : apretado, avaro, agarrado *fam* **7** CLOSE : reñido ⟨a tight game : un juego reñido⟩ **8** SCARCE : escaso ⟨money is tight : escasea el dinero⟩

tighten ['taɪtən] *vt* : tensar (una cuerda, etc.), apretar (un nudo, un tornillo, etc.), apretarse (el cinturón), reforzar (las reglas)

tightfisted ['taɪt'fɪstəd] *adj* STINGY : apretado, avaro, agarrado *fam*

tightly ['taɪtli] *adv* : bien, fuerte

tightness ['taɪtnəs] *n* : lo apretado, lo tenso, tensión *f*

tightrope ['taɪt,ro:p] *n* : cuerda *f* floja

tights ['taɪts] *npl* : leotardo *m*, malla *f*

tightwad ['taɪt,wɑd] *n* : avaro *m*, -ra *f*; tacaño *m*, -ña *f*

tigress ['taɪgrəs] *n* : tigresa *f*

tilde ['tɪldə] *n* : tilde *mf*

tile¹ ['taɪl] *vt* **tiled; tiling** : embaldosar (un piso), revestir de azulejos (una pared), tejar (un techo)

tile² *n* **1** *or* **floor tile** : losa *f*, baldosa *f*, mosaico *m* Mex (de un piso) **2** : azulejo *m* (de una pared) **3** : teja *f* (de un techo)

till¹ ['tɪl] *vt* : cultivar, labrar

till² *n* : caja *f*, caja *f* registradora

till³ *prep & conj* → **until**

tiller ['tɪlər] *n* **1** : cultivador *m*, -dora *f* (de la tierra) **2** : caña *f* del timón (de un barco)

tilt¹ ['tɪlt] *vt* : ladear, inclinar — *vi* : ladearse, inclinarse

tilt² *n* **1** SLANT : inclinación *f* **2 at full tilt** : a toda velocidad

timber ['tɪmbər] *n* **1** : madera *f* (para construcción) **2** BEAM : viga *f*

timberland ['tɪmbər,lænd] *n* : bosque *m* maderero

timbre ['tæmbər, 'tɪm-] *n* : timbre *m*

time¹ ['taɪm] *vt* **timed; timing** **1** SCHEDULE : fijar la hora de, calcular el momento oportuno para **2** CLOCK : cronometrar, medir el tiempo de (una competencia, etc.)

time² *n* **1** : tiempo *m* ⟨the passing of time : el paso del tiempo⟩ ⟨she doesn't have time : no tiene tiempo⟩ **2** MOMENT : tiempo *m*, momento *m* ⟨this is not the time to bring it up : no es el momento de sacar el tema⟩ ⟨it can wait until another time : podemos dejarlo para otro momento⟩ ⟨since that time : desde entonces⟩ **3** : vez *f* ⟨he called you three times : te llamó tres veces⟩ ⟨three times greater : tres veces mayor⟩ ⟨this time : esta vez⟩ ⟨one more time : una vez más⟩ **4** AGE : tiempo *m*, era *f* ⟨in your grandparents' time : en el tiempo de tus abuelos⟩ ⟨it was before your time : fue antes de que nacieras⟩ **5** TEMPO : tiempo *m*, ritmo *m* (en música) **6** : hora *f* (del día), época *f* (del año) ⟨what time is it? : ¿qué hora es?⟩ ⟨do you have the time? : ¿tienes hora?⟩ ⟨it's time for dinner : es hora de comer⟩ ⟨at the usual time : a la hora acostumbrada⟩ ⟨during work time : en horas de trabajo⟩ ⟨local time : hora local⟩ ⟨arrival/departure time : hora de llegada/salida⟩ **7** WHILE : tiempo *m*, rato *m* ⟨a short/long time ago : hace poco/mucho tiempo⟩ ⟨for (quite) some time now : desde hace mucho tiempo⟩ ⟨he watched us the whole/entire time : nos miraba (durante) todo el tiempo⟩ **8** EXPERIENCE : rato *m*, experiencia *f* ⟨we had a nice time together : pasamos juntos un rato agradable⟩ ⟨to have a rough time : pasarlo mal⟩ ⟨have a good time! : ¡que se diviertan!⟩ **9 against time** : contra el reloj **10 ahead of one's time** ⟨she was ahead of her time : se adelantó a su época⟩ **11 ahead of time** ⟨I prepared it ahead of time : lo preparé con ante-

lación⟩ ⟨she handed it in ahead of time : lo entregó antes de tiempo⟩ ⟨he showed up ahead of time : apareció antes de la hora⟩ **12 all in good time** : todo a su debido tiempo **13 all the time** ALWAYS, OFTEN : todo el tiempo **14 all the time** THROUGHOUT : (durante) todo el tiempo **15 at all times** : siempre, en todo momento **16 (at) any time** : en cualquier momento **17 at a time** SIMULTANEOUSLY : al mismo tiempo, a la vez ⟨one at a time : uno por uno, de a uno⟩ ⟨two at a time : de dos en dos⟩ ⟨one thing at a time : una cosa por vez⟩ ⟨one step at a time : paso por paso⟩ **18 at a time** : sin parar ⟨he read for hours at a time : pasaba horas enteras leyendo⟩ ⟨she disappears for months at a time : desaparece por meses⟩ **19 at no time** : en ningún momento **20 at the same time** CONVERSELY : al mismo tiempo **21 at the same time** SIMULTANEOUSLY : al mismo tiempo, a la vez **22 at times** SOMETIMES : a veces **23 behind the times** OUTDATED : anticuado **24 each and every time** : cada vez **25 each/ every time** : cada vez **26 for a time** : (por) un tiempo **27 for the time being** : por el momento, de momento **28 from time to time** OCCASIONALLY : de vez en cuando **29 in good time** : con tiempo **30 in no time** : enseguida, en un santiamén **31 in time** PUNCTUALLY : a tiempo **32 in time** EVENTUALLY : con el tiempo **33 it's about time** : ya es hora, ya va siendo hora ⟨it was about time (that) you got here : ya era hora de que llegaras⟩ **34 most of the time** : la mayor parte del tiempo **35 on time** : a tiempo **36 over time** : con el paso del tiempo **37 time after time** : una y otra vez **38 time flies** : el tiempo pasa volando **39 time marches on** : el tiempo pasa **40 time off** : tiempo *m* libre, vacaciones *fpl* **41 to buy time** : ganar tiempo **42 to give someone a hard time** : mortificar a alguien **43 to have time on one's hands** : sobrarle el tiempo a uno **44 to keep time** : marcar la hora (dícese de un reloj) **45 to keep time** : seguir/marcar el ritmo (en música) **46 to lose time** : atrasar (dícese de un reloj) **47 to make good time** : ir adelantando (en un viaje, etc.) **48 to make time for** : encontrar tiempo para **49 to pass the time** : pasar el rato **50 to serve/do time** : cumplir una condena **51 to take one's time** : tomarse tiempo ⟨take your time : tómate todo el tiempo que necesites⟩ ⟨you sure took your time! : tardaste mucho⟩ **52 to take the time to** : tomar el tiempo para/de **53 to take time** : tomar tiempo, tomarse tiempo ⟨these things take time : estas cosas toman tiempo⟩ ⟨take all the time you need : tómate todo el tiempo que necesites⟩ **54 to waste time** : perder el tiempo
time bomb *n* : bomba *f* de tiempo, bomba *f* de relojería *Spain*

timekeeper ['taɪm,kiːpər] *n* : cronometrador *m*, -dora *f*
timeless ['taɪmləs] *adj* : eterno
time limit *n* : plazo *m*
timely ['taɪmli] *adj* **timelier; -est** : oportuno
timepiece ['taɪm,piːs] *n* : reloj *m*
timer ['taɪmər] *n* : temporizador *m*, cronómetro *m*
times ['taɪmz] *prep* : por ⟨3 times 4 is 12 : 3 por 4 son 12⟩
timeshare ['taɪm,ʃɛr] *n* : multipropiedad *f*, tiempo *m* compartido
time slot → slot
timetable ['taɪm,teɪbəl] *n* : horario *m*
time zone *n* : huso *m* horario
timid ['tɪmɪd] *adj* : tímido — **timidly** *adv*
timidity [tə'mɪdəti] *n* : timidez *f*
timorous ['tɪmərəs] *adj* : timorato, miedoso
timpani ['tɪmpəni] *npl* : timbales *mpl*
tin ['tɪn] *n* **1** : estaño *m* (elemento), hojalata *f* (metal) **2** CAN, BOX : lata *f*, bote *m*, envase *m*
tincture ['tɪŋktʃər] *n* : tintura *f*
tinder ['tɪndər] *n* : yesca *f*
tine ['taɪn] *n* : diente *m* (de un tenedor, etc.)
tinfoil ['tɪn,fɔɪl] *n* : papel *m* (de) aluminio
tinge¹ ['tɪndʒ] *vt* **tinged; tingeing** or **tinging** TINT : matizar, teñir ligeramente
tinge² *n* **1** TINT : matiz *m*, tinte *m* sutil **2** TOUCH : dejo *m*, sensación *f* ligera
tingle¹ ['tɪŋɡəl] *vi* **-gled; -gling** : sentir (un) hormigueo, sentir (un) cosquilleo
tingle² *n* : hormigueo *m*, cosquilleo *m*
tinker ['tɪŋkər] *vi* to tinker with : arreglar con pequeños ajustes, toquetear (con intento de arreglar)
tinkle¹ ['tɪŋkəl] *vi* **-kled; -kling** : tintinear
tinkle² *n* : tintineo *m*
tinplate ['tɪn'pleɪt] *n* : hojalata *f*
tinsel ['tɪntsəl] *n* : oropel *m*
tint¹ ['tɪnt] *vt* : teñir, colorear
tint² *n* : tinte *m*
tiny ['taɪni] *adj* **tinier; -est** : diminuto, minúsculo
tip¹ ['tɪp] *v* **tipped; tipping** *vt* **1** or to tip over : volcar, voltear, hacer caer **2** TILT : ladear, inclinar ⟨to tip one's hat : saludar con el sombrero⟩ **3** TAP : tocar, golpear ligeramente **4** : darle una propina (a un mesero, etc.) ⟨I tipped him $5 : le di $5 de propina⟩ **5** : adornar o cubrir la punta de ⟨wings tipped in red : alas que tienen las puntas rojas⟩ **6 to tip off** : avisar a, dar información a (la policía, etc.) — *vi* **1** TILT : ladearse, inclinarse **2 to tip over** : volcarse, caerse
tip² *n* **1** END, POINT : punta *f*, extremo *m* ⟨on the tip of one's tongue : en la punta de la lengua⟩ **2** GRATUITY : propina *f* **3** ADVICE, INFORMATION : consejo *m*, información *f* (confidencial)
tip-off ['tɪp,ɔf] *n* **1** SIGN : indicación *f*, señal *f* **2** TIP : información *f* (confidencial)
tipple ['tɪpəl] *vi* **-pled; -pling** : tomarse unas copas

tipsy ['tɪpsi] *adj* **tipsier; -est** : achispado

tiptoe¹ ['tɪp,to:] *vi* **-toed; -toeing** : caminar de puntillas

tiptoe² *adv* : de puntillas

tiptoe³ *n* : punta *f* del pie

tip-top¹ ['tɪp'tɑp, -,tɑp] *adj* EXCELLENT : excelente

tip-top² *n* SUMMIT : cumbre *f*, cima *f*

tirade ['taɪ,reɪd] *n* : diatriba *f*

tire¹ ['taɪr] *v* **tired; tiring** *vt* : cansar — *vi* : cansarse

tire² *n* : llanta *f*, neumático *m*, goma *f*

tired ['taɪrd] *adj* : cansado ⟨to get tired : cansarse⟩

tiredness *n* : cansancio *m*

tireless ['taɪrləs] *adj* : incansable, infatigable — **tirelessly** *adv*

tiresome ['taɪrsəm] *adj* : fastidioso, pesado, tedioso — **tiresomely** *adv*

tissue ['tɪ,ʃu:] *n* **1** : pañuelo *m* de papel **2** : tejido *m* ⟨lung tissue : tejido pulmonar⟩

tissue paper *n* : papel *m* de seda

titanic [taɪ'tænɪk, tə-] *adj* GIGANTIC : titánico, gigantesco

titanium [taɪ'teɪniəm, tə-] *n* : titanio *m*

titillate ['tɪtəl,eɪt] *vt* **-lated; -lating** : excitar, estimular placenteramente

title¹ ['taɪtəl] *vt* **-tled; -tling** : titular, intitular

title² *n* : título *m*

titter¹ ['tɪtər] *vi* GIGGLE : reírse tontamente

titter² *n* : risita *f*, risa *f* tonta

titular ['tɪtʃələr] *adj* : titular

tizzy ['tɪzi] *n, pl* **tizzies** : estado *m* agitado o nervioso ⟨I'm all in a tizzy : estoy todo alterado⟩

TNT [,ti:,ɛn'ti:] *n* : TNT *m*

to¹ ['tu:] *adv* **1** : a un estado consciente ⟨to come to : volver en sí⟩ **2 to and fro** : de aquí para allá, de un lado para otro

to² *prep* **1** (*indicating a place or activity*) : a ⟨to go to the doctor : ir al médico⟩ ⟨I'm going to John's : voy a casa de John⟩ ⟨we went to lunch : fuimos a almorzar⟩ **2** TOWARD : a, hacia ⟨two miles to the south : dos millas hacia el sur⟩ ⟨to the right : a la derecha⟩ ⟨she ran to her mother : corrió a su mamá⟩ **3** UP TO : hasta, a ⟨to a degree : hasta cierto grado⟩ ⟨from head to toe : de pies a cabeza⟩ ⟨the water was up to my waist : el agua me llegaba a la cintura⟩ **4** (*in expressions of time*) ⟨it's quarter to seven : son las siete menos cuarto⟩ **5** UNTIL : a, hasta ⟨from May to December : de mayo a diciembre⟩ **6** (*indicating belonging or association*) : de, con ⟨the key to the lock : la llave del candado⟩ ⟨he's married to my sister : está casado con mi hermana⟩ **7** (*indicating recipient*) : a ⟨I gave it to the boss : se lo di a la jefa⟩ ⟨she spoke to his parents : habló con sus padres⟩ ⟨listen to me : escúchame⟩ **8** (*indicating response or result*) : a ⟨dancing to the rhythm : bailando al compás⟩ ⟨to my surprise : para mi sorpresa⟩ ⟨the answer to your question : la respuesta a su pregunta⟩ ⟨to my sur-

presa⟩ **9** (*indicating comparison or proportion*) : a ⟨it's similar to mine : es parecido al mío⟩ ⟨they won 4 to 2 : ganaron 4 a 2⟩ **10** (*indicating agreement or conformity*) : a, de acuerdo con ⟨made to order : hecho a la orden⟩ ⟨to my knowledge : a mi saber⟩ **11** (*indicating opinion or viewpoint*) : a, para ⟨it's agreeable to all of us : nos parece bien a todos⟩ ⟨it seemed odd to us : nos pareció raro⟩ ⟨it's news to me : no lo sabía⟩ ⟨it means nothing to him : para él no significa nada⟩ **12** (*indicating inclusion*) : en cada, por ⟨twenty to the box : veinte por caja⟩ **13** (*indicating joining or touching*) : a ⟨he tied it to a tree : lo ató a un árbol⟩ ⟨apply salve to the wound : póngale ungüento a la herida⟩ **14** (*used to form the infinitive*) ⟨to understand : entender⟩ ⟨to go away : irse⟩ ⟨I didn't mean to (do it) : lo hice sin querer⟩ **15** (**all**) **to oneself** : para sí sólo

toad ['to:d] *n* : sapo *m*

toadstool ['to:d,stu:l] *n* : hongo *m* (no comestible)

toady ['to:di] *n, pl* **toadies** : adulador *m*, -dora *f*

toast¹ ['to:st] *vt* **1** : tostar (pan) **2** : brindar por ⟨to toast the victors : brindar por los vencedores⟩ **3** WARM : calentar ⟨to toast oneself : calentarse⟩

toast² *n* **1** : pan *m* tostado, tostadas *fpl* **2** : brindis *m* ⟨to propose a toast : proponer un brindis⟩

toaster ['to:stər] *n* : tostador *m*

tobacco [tə'bæko:] *n, pl* **-cos** : tabaco *m*

toboggan¹ [tə'bagən] *vi* : deslizarse en tobogán

toboggan² *n* : tobogán *m*

today¹ [tə'deɪ] *adv* **1** : hoy ⟨she arrives today : hoy llega⟩ **2** NOWADAYS : hoy en día

today² *n* : hoy *m* ⟨today is a holiday : hoy es día de fiesta⟩

toddle ['tadəl] *vi* **-dled; -dling** : hacer pininos, hacer pinitos

toddler ['tadələr] *n* : niño *m* pequeño, niña *f* pequeña (que comienza a caminar)

to-do [tə'du:] *n, pl* **to-dos** [-'du:z] FUSS : lío *m*, alboroto *m*

toe¹ ['to:] *vt* **toed; toeing** to toe the line : acatar la disciplina

toe² *n* : dedo *m* del pie

TOEFL ['to:fəl] *trademark* se usa para un examen que evalúa el dominio del inglés de personas que estudian este idioma como lengua extranjera

toenail ['to:,neɪl] *n* : uña *f* del pie

toffee *or* **toffy** ['tɔfi, 'tɑ-] *n, pl* **toffees** *or* **toffies** : caramelo *m* elaborado con azúcar y mantequilla

toga ['to:gə] *n* : toga *f*

together [tə'gɛðər] *adv* **1** : juntamente, juntos (el uno con el otro) ⟨Susan and Sarah work together : Susan y Sarah trabajan juntas⟩ **2** ~ **with** : junto con

togetherness [tə'gɛðərnəs] *n* : unión *f*, compañerismo *m*

togs ['tagz, 'tɔgz] *npl* : ropa *f*

toil[1] ['tɔɪl] vi : trabajar arduamente

toil[2] n : trabajo m arduo

toilet ['tɔɪlət] n 1 : arreglo m personal 2 BATHROOM : (cuarto de) baño m, servicios mpl (públicos), sanitario m Col, Mex, Ven 3 : inodoro m ⟨to flush the toilet : jalar la cadena⟩

toilet paper n : papel m higiénico

toiletries ['tɔɪlətriz] npl : artículos mpl de tocador

token[1] ['to:kən] adj : simbólico

token[2] n 1 PROOF, SIGN : prueba f, muestra f, señal f 2 SYMBOL : símbolo m 3 SOUVENIR : recuerdo m 4 : ficha f (para transporte público, etc.) 5 by the same token : del mismo modo

told → **tell**

tolerable ['tɑlərəbəl] adj : tolerable — **tolerably** [-bli] adv

tolerance ['tɑlərənts] n : tolerancia f

tolerant ['tɑlərənt] adj : tolerante — **tolerantly** adv

tolerate ['tɑlə,reɪt] vt **-ated; -ating** 1 ACCEPT : tolerar, aceptar 2 BEAR, ENDURE : tolerar, aguantar, soportar

toleration [,tɑlə'reɪʃən] n : tolerancia f

toll[1] ['to:l] vt : tañer, sonar (una campana) — vi : sonar, doblar (dícese de las campanas)

toll[2] n 1 : peaje m (de una carretera, un puente, etc.) 2 CASUALTIES : pérdida f, número m de víctimas 3 TOLLING : tañido m (de campanas)

tollbooth ['to:l,bu:θ] n : caseta f de peaje; caseta f de cobro CA, Mex

toll–free ['to:l'fri:] adj : gratuito

tollgate ['to:l,geɪt] n : barrera f de peaje

tomahawk ['tɑmə,hɔk] n : hacha f de guerra (de los indígenas norteamericanos)

tomato [tə'meɪto, -'mɑ-] n, pl **-toes** : tomate m

tomb ['tu:m] n : sepulcro m, tumba f

tomboy ['tɑm,bɔɪ] n : marimacho mf; niña f que se porta como muchacho

tombstone ['tu:m,sto:n] n : lápida f

tomcat ['tɑm,kæt] n : gato m (macho)

tome ['to:m] n : tomo m

tomorrow[1] [tə'mɑro] adv : mañana

tomorrow[2] n : mañana m

tom–tom ['tɑm,tɑm] n : tam-tam m

ton ['tʌn] n : tonelada f

tone[1] ['to:n] vt **toned; toning** 1 or **to tone down** : atenuar, suavizar, moderar 2 or **to tone up** STRENGTHEN : tonificar, vigorizar

tone[2] n : tono m ⟨in a friendly tone : en tono amistoso⟩ ⟨a grayish tone : un tono grisáceo⟩

tongs ['tɑŋz, 'tɔŋz] npl : tenazas fpl

tongue ['tʌŋ] n 1 : lengua f 2 LANGUAGE : lengua f, idioma m

tongue–tied ['tʌŋ,taɪd] adj **to get tongue-tied** : trabársele la lengua a uno

tongue–twister ['tʌŋ,twɪstər] n : trabalenguas m

tonic[1] ['tɑnɪk] adj : tónico

tonic[2] n 1 : tónico m 2 or **tonic water** : tónica f

tonight[1] [tə'naɪt] adv : esta noche

tonight[2] n : esta noche f

tonnage ['tʌnɪdʒ] n : tonelaje m

tonsil ['tɑntsəl] n : amígdala f, angina f Mex

tonsillitis [,tɑntsə'laɪtəs] n : amigdalitis f, anginas fpl Mex

too ['tu:] adv 1 ALSO : también 2 EXCESSIVELY : demasiado ⟨it's too hot in here : aquí hace demasiado calor⟩

took → **take**[1]

tool[1] ['tu:l] vt 1 : fabricar, confeccionar (con herramientas) 2 EQUIP : instalar maquinaria en (una fábrica)

tool[2] n : herramienta f

toolbar ['tu:l,bɑr] n : barra f de herramientas

toolbox ['tu:l,bɑks] n : caja f de herramientas

tool kit n : juego m de herramientas

toot[1] ['tu:t] vt : sonar (un claxon o un pito)

toot[2] n : pitido m, bocinazo m (de un claxon)

tooth ['tu:θ] n, pl **teeth** ['ti:θ] 1 : diente m 2 **like pulling teeth** : casi imposible 3 **long in the tooth** : viejo 4 **to grit one's teeth** : apretar los dientes, aguantarse 5 **to have a sweet tooth** : ser goloso, gustarle mucho los dulces a uno 6 **to lie through one's teeth** : mentir descaradamente 7 **tooth and nail** : a ultranza, a capa y espada 8 **to set someone's teeth on edge** : crispar/erizar a alguien 9 **to sink one's teeth into** : clavar los dientes en 10 **to sink/get one's teeth into** : hincarle el diente a (una actividad, etc.)

toothache ['tu:θ,eɪk] n : dolor m de muelas

toothbrush ['tu:θ,brʌʃ] n : cepillo m de dientes

toothed ['tu:θt] adj 1 : dentado 2 (used in combination) : de dientes ⟨bucktoothed : de dientes salientes⟩

toothless ['tu:θləs] adj : desdentado

toothpaste ['tu:θ,peɪst] n : pasta f de dientes, crema f dental, dentífrico m

toothpick ['tu:θ,pɪk] n : palillo m (de dientes), mondadientes m

top[1] ['tɑp] vt **topped; topping** 1 COVER : cubrir, coronar 2 SURPASS : sobrepasar, superar 3 CLEAR : pasar por encima de 4 : encabezar (una lista, etc.) ⟨to top the charts : ser el número uno en las listas de éxitos⟩ 5 **to top off** END : terminar ⟨to top it all off : para colmo⟩ 6 **to top off** : llenar hasta arriba (un depósito, un vaso, etc.)

top[2] adj : superior ⟨the top shelf : la repisa superior⟩ ⟨one of the top lawyers : uno de los mejores abogados⟩

top[3] n 1 : parte f superior, cumbre f, cima f (de un monte, etc.) ⟨to climb to the top : subir a la cumbre⟩ ⟨from top to bottom : de arriba abajo⟩ 2 COVER : tapa f, cubierta f 3 : trompo m (juguete) 4 **at the top of one's lungs/voice** : a voz en grito/cuello, a grito pelado 5 **on top of** : encima de 6 **on top of** BESIDES : además de 7 **on top of the world** : muy alegre 8 **over the top** : exagerado 9 **to be on top of** CONTROL

: controlar, tener controlado **10 to be/ stay on top of** : estar/mantenerse al día en (las noticias, etc.) **11 to come out on top** : salir ganando

topaz ['to:ˌpæz] *n* : topacio *m*

topcoat ['tɑpˌko:t] *n* : sobretodo *m*, abrigo *m*

top hat *n* : sombrero *m* de copa

topic ['tɑpɪk] *n* : tema *m*, tópico *m*

topical ['tɑpɪkəl] *adj* : de interés actual

topless ['tɑpləs] *adj* : sin camisa

topmost ['tɑpˌmo:st] *adj* : más alto

top–notch ['tɑp'nɑtʃ] *adj* : de lo mejor, de primera categoría

topographic [ˌtɑpə'græfɪk] *or* **topographical** [-fɪkəl] *adj* : topográfico

topography [tə'pɑgrəfi] *n, pl* **-phies** : topografía *f*

topple ['tɑpəl] *v* **-pled; -pling** *vi* : caerse, venirse abajo — *vt* : volcar, derrocar (un gobierno, etc.)

top secret *adj* : ultrasecreto

topsoil ['tɑpˌsɔɪl] *n* : capa *f* superior del suelo

topsy–turvy [ˌtɑpsi'tərvi] *adv & adj* : patas arriba, al revés

torch ['tɔrtʃ] *n* : antorcha *f*

tore → tear¹

torment¹ [tɔr'mɛnt, 'tɔr-] *vt* : atormentar, torturar, martirizar

torment² ['tɔrˌmɛnt] *n* : tormento *m*, suplicio *m*, martirio *m*

tormentor [tɔr'mɛntər] *n* : atormentador *m*, -dora *f*

torn *pp* → **tear¹**

tornado [tɔr'neɪdo] *n, pl* **-does** *or* **-dos** : tornado *m*

torpedo¹ [tɔr'pi:do] *vt* : torpedear

torpedo² *n, pl* **-does** : torpedo *m*

torpid ['tɔrpɪd] *adj* **1** SLUGGISH : aletargado **2** APATHETIC : apático

torpor ['tɔrpər] *n* : letargo *m*, apatía *f*

torrent ['tɔrənt] *n* : torrente *m*

torrential [tɔ'rɛntʃəl, tə-] *adj* : torrencial

torrid ['tɔrɪd] *adj* : tórrido

torso ['tɔrˌso:] *n, pl* **-sos** *or* **-si** [-ˌsi:] : torso *m*

tortilla [tɔr'tijə] *n* : tortilla *f* (de maíz)

tortoise ['tɔrtəs] *n* : tortuga *f* (terrestre)

tortoiseshell ['tɔrtəsˌʃɛl] *n* : carey *m*, concha *f*

tortuous ['tɔrtʃuəs] *adj* : tortuoso

torture¹ ['tɔrtʃər] *vt* **-tured; -turing** : torturar, atormentar

torture² *n* : tortura *f*, tormento *m* ⟨it was sheer torture! : ¡fue un verdadero suplicio!⟩

torturer ['tɔrtʃərər] *n* : torturador *m*, -dora *f*

toss¹ ['tɔs, 'tɑs] *vt* **1** AGITATE, SHAKE : sacudir, agitar ⟨to toss a salad : mezclar una ensalada⟩ **2** THROW : tirar, echar, lanzar ⟨to toss a coin : echarlo a cara o cruz⟩ **3 to toss away/out** DISCARD : botar, tirar (a la basura) **4 to toss back** *fam* : tomarse **5 to toss off** : escribir (rápidamente) **6 to toss out** REJECT : rechazar **7 to toss out** EJECT : echar — *vi* : sacudirse ⟨to toss and turn : dar vueltas⟩

toss² *n* THROW : lanzamiento *m*, tiro *m*, tirada *f*, lance *m* (de dados, etc.)

toss–up ['tɔsˌʌp] *n* : posibilidad *f* igual ⟨it's a toss-up : quizá sí, quizá no⟩

tot ['tɑt] *n* : pequeño *m*, -ña *f*

total¹ ['to:təl] *vt* **-taled** *or* **-talled; -taling** *or* **-talling 1** *or* **to total up** ADD : sumar, totalizar **2** AMOUNT TO : ascender a, llegar a **3** *fam* WRECK : destrozar (un automóvil)

total² *adj* : total, completo, absoluto — **totally** *adv*

total³ *n* : total *m*

totalitarian [toˌtælə'tɛriən] *adj* : totalitario

totalitarianism [toˌtælə'tɛriəˌnɪzəm] *n* : totalitarismo *m*

totality [to'tæləti] *n, pl* **-ties** : totalidad *f*

tote ['to:t] *vt* **toted; toting** : cargar, llevar

totem ['to:təm] *n* : tótem *m*

totter ['tɑtər] *vi* : tambalearse

touch¹ ['tʌtʃ] *vt* **1** FEEL, HANDLE : tocar, tentar **2** AFFECT, MOVE : conmover, afectar, tocar ⟨his gesture touched our hearts : su gesto nos tocó el corazón⟩ **3 to touch up** — *vi* **1** : retocar ⟨do not touch : no tocar⟩ **2** : tocarse ⟨our hands touched : nuestras manos se tocaron⟩ **3 to touch down** : aterrizar **4 to touch on** : tocar (un tema)

touch² *n* **1** : tacto *m* (sentido) **2** DETAIL : toque *m*, detalle *m* ⟨a touch of color/ humor : un toque de color/humor⟩ ⟨the finishing touches : los toques finales⟩ **3** BIT : pizca *f*, gota *f*, poco *m* **4** ABILITY : habilidad *f* ⟨to lose one's touch : perder la habilidad⟩ **5** CONTACT : contacto *m*, comunicación *f* ⟨to keep/stay in touch : mantenerse en contacto⟩ ⟨to lose touch : perder el contacto⟩ **6 out of touch** : desconectado (de la realidad, etc.)

touchdown ['tʌtʃˌdaun] *n* : touchdown *m* (en futbol americano)

touching ['tʌtʃɪŋ] *adj* MOVING : conmovedor

touchline ['tʌtʃˌlaɪn] *n* : banda *f*, línea *f* de banda (en fútbol)

touchscreen ['tʌtʃˌskri:n] *n* : pantalla *f* táctil

touchstone ['tʌtʃˌsto:n] *n* : piedra *f* de toque

touch–up ['tʌtʃˌʌp] *n* : retoque *m*

touchy ['tʌtʃi] *adj* **touchier; -est 1** : sensible, susceptible (dícese de una persona) **2** : delicado ⟨a touchy subject : un tema delicado⟩

tough¹ ['tʌf] *adj* **1** STRONG : fuerte, resistente (dícese de materiales) **2** LEATHERY : correoso ⟨a tough steak : un bistec duro⟩ **3** HARDY : fuerte, robusto (dícese de una persona) **4** STRICT : severo, exigente **5** DIFFICULT : difícil **6** STUBBORN : terco, obstinado

tough² *n* : matón *m*, persona *f* ruda y brusca

toughen ['tʌfən] *vt* : fortalecer, endurecer — *vi* : endurecerse, hacerse más fuerte

toughness ['tʌfnəs] *n* : dureza *f*

toupee [tu'peɪ] *n* : peluquín *m*, bisoñé *m*

tour¹ ['tʊr] *vi* : tomar una excursión, viajar — *vt* : recorrer, hacer una gira por

tour² *n* **1** : gira *f*, tour *m*, excursión *f* **2 tour of duty** : período *m* de servicio

tourism ['tʊr,ɪzəm] *n* : turismo *m*

tourist ['tʊrɪst, 'tʊr-] *n* : turista *mf*

tournament ['tɔrnəmənt, 'tʊr-] *n* : torneo *m*

tourniquet ['tɔrnɪkət, 'tʊr-] *n* : torniquete *m*

tousle ['taʊzəl] *vt* **-sled; -sling** : desarreglar, despeinar (el cabello)

tout ['taʊt] *vt* : promocionar, elogiar (con exageración)

tow¹ ['to:] *vt* : remolcar

tow² *n* : remolque *m*

toward ['tord, tə'word] *or* **towards** ['tordz, tə'wordz] *prep* **1** *(indicating direction)* : hacia, rumbo a ⟨heading toward town : dirigiéndose rumbo al pueblo⟩ ⟨efforts towards peace : esfuerzos hacia la paz⟩ **2** *(indicating time)* : alrededor de ⟨toward midnight : alrededor de la medianoche⟩ **3** REGARDING : hacia, con respecto a ⟨his attitude toward life : su actitud hacia la vida⟩ **4** FOR : para, como pago parcial de (una compra o deuda)

towel ['taʊəl] *n* : toalla *f* ⟨to throw in the towel : tirar la toalla⟩

tower¹ ['taʊər] *vi* **to tower over** : descollar sobre, elevarse sobre, dominar

tower² *n* : torre *f*

towering ['taʊərɪŋ] *adj* : altísimo, imponente

town ['taʊn] *n* : pueblo *m*, ciudad *f* (pequeña)

town hall *n* : ayuntamiento *m*

township ['taʊn,ʃɪp] *n* : municipio *m*

tow truck ['to:,trʌk] *n* : grúa *f*

toxic ['tɑksɪk] *adj* : tóxico

toxicity [tɑk'sɪsəti] *n*, *pl* **-ties** : toxicidad *f*

toxin ['tɑksɪn] *n* : toxina *f*

toy¹ ['tɔɪ] *vi* : juguetear, jugar

toy² *adj* : de juguete ⟨a toy rifle : un rifle de juguete⟩

toy³ *n* : juguete *m*

trace¹ ['treɪs] *vt* **traced; tracing** **1** : calcar (un dibujo, etc.) **2** OUTLINE : delinear, trazar (planes, etc.) **3** TRACK : describir (un curso, una historia) **4** FIND : localizar, ubicar

trace² *n* **1** SIGN, TRACK : huella *f*, rastro *m*, indicio *m*, vestigio *m* ⟨he disappeared without a trace : desapareció sin dejar rastro⟩ **2** BIT, HINT : pizca *f*, ápice *m*, dejo *m*

trachea ['treɪkiə] *n*, *pl* **-cheae** [-ki,i:] : tráquea *f*

tracing paper *n* : papel *m* de calcar

track¹ ['træk] *vt* **1** TRAIL : seguir la pista de, rastrear **2** : dejar huellas de ⟨he tracked mud all over : dejó huellas de lodo por todas partes⟩ **3 to track down** : localizar

track² *n* **1** : rastro *m*, huella *f* (de animales), pista *f* (de personas) **2** PATH : pista *f*, sendero *m*, camino *m* **3** *or* rail-

road track : vía *f* (férrea) **4** → racetrack **5** : oruga *f* (de un tanque, etc.) **6** : atletismo *m* (deporte) **7 the wrong side of the tracks** : los barrios bajos **8 to be on the right/wrong track** : ir bien/mal encaminado **9 to be on track** : ir bien encaminado **10 to cover one's tracks** : no dejar rastros **11 to get back on track** : volver a encarrilarse **12 to get/go off track** : desviarse del tema/plan (etc.) **13 to keep track of** : llevar la cuenta de **14 to lose track of** : perder la cuenta de ⟨I lost track of the time : no me di cuenta de la hora⟩ **15 to throw someone off the track** : despistar a alguien

track–and–field ['trækənd'fi:ld] *adj* : de pista y campo

tracksuit ['træk,su:t] *n* : sudadera *f*; buzo *m* *Chile, Peru*; jogging *m* *Arg*; pants *m* *Mex*; chándal *m* *Spain* (traje)

tract ['trækt] *n* **1** AREA : terreno *m*, extensión *f*, área *f* **2** : tracto *m* ⟨digestive tract : tracto digestivo⟩ **3** PAMPHLET : panfleto *m*, folleto *m*

traction ['trækʃən] *n* : tracción *f*

tractor ['træktər] *n* **1** : tractor *m* (vehículo agrícola) **2** TRUCK : camión *m* (con remolque)

trade¹ ['treɪd] *vi* **traded; trading** **1** : comerciar, negociar **2** EXCHANGE : hacer un cambio **3 to trade on** : explotar — *vt* **1** EXCHANGE : cambiar, intercambiar, canjear ⟨we traded seats : nos cambiamos de asiento⟩ ⟨I'll trade (you) a cookie for a chocolate : te cambio una galleta por un chocolate⟩ **2 to trade in** : entregar en/como parte de pago

trade² *n* **1** OCCUPATION : oficio *m*, profesión *f*, ocupación *f* ⟨a carpenter by trade : carpintero de oficio⟩ **2** COMMERCE : comercio *m*, industria *f* ⟨free trade : libre comercio⟩ ⟨the book trade : la industria del libro⟩ **3** EXCHANGE : intercambio *m*, canje *m*

trade–in ['treɪd,ɪn] *n* : artículo *m* que se canjea por otro

trademark ['treɪd,mɑrk] *n* **1** : marca *f* ⟨registered trademark : marca registrada⟩ **2** : sello *m* característico (de un grupo, una persona, etc.)

trader ['treɪdər] *n* : negociante *mf*, tratante *mf*, comerciante *mf*

tradesman ['treɪdzmən] *n*, *pl* **-men** [-mən, -,men] **1** CRAFTSMAN : artesano *m*, -na *f* **2** SHOPKEEPER : tendero *m*, -ra *f*; comerciante *mf*

tradition [trə'dɪʃən] *n* : tradición *f*

traditional [trə'dɪʃənəl] *adj* : tradicional — **traditionally** *adv*

traffic¹ ['træfɪk] *vi* **trafficked; trafficking** : traficar (con)

traffic² *n* **1** COMMERCE : tráfico *m*, comercio *m* ⟨the drug traffic : el narcotráfico⟩ **2** : tráfico *m*, tránsito *m*, circulación *f* (de vehículos, etc.)

traffic circle *n* : rotonda *f*, glorieta *f*

traffic jam → **jam²**

trafficker ['træfɪkər] *n* : traficante *mf*

traffic light *n* : semáforo *m*, luz *f* (de tránsito)

tragedy ['trædʒədi] *n*, *pl* **-dies** : tragedia *f*

tragic ['trædʒɪk] *adj* : trágico — **tragically** *adv*

trail¹ ['treɪl] *vi* 1 DRAG : arrastrarse 2 LAG : quedarse atrás, retrasarse 3 to **trail away** *or* to **trail off** : disminuir, menguar, desvanecerse — *vt* 1 DRAG : arrastrar 2 PURSUE : perseguir, seguir la pista de

trail² *n* 1 TRACK : rastro *m*, huella *f*, pista *f* ⟨a trail of blood : un rastro de sangre⟩ 2 : cola *f*, estela *f* (de un meteoro) 3 PATH : sendero *m*, camino *m*, vereda *f*

trailer ['treɪlər] *n* 1 : remolque *m*, tráiler *m* (de un camión) 2 : caravana *f* (vivienda ambulante)

train¹ ['treɪn] *vt* 1 : adiestrar, entrenar (atletas), capacitar (trabajadores), amaestrar (animales) 2 POINT : apuntar (un arma, etc.) — *vi* 1 : entrenar(se) (físicamente), prepararse (profesionalmente) ⟨she's training at the gym : se está entrenando en el gimnasio⟩

train² *n* 1 : cola *f* (de un vestido) 2 RETINUE : cortejo *m*, séquito *m* 3 SERIES : serie *f* (de eventos) 4 : tren *m* ⟨passenger train : tren de pasajeros⟩ 5 : tren *m* (mecanismo) ⟨drive train : tren motriz⟩ 6 **train of thought** : hilo *m* de razonamiento

trainee [treɪ'ni:] *n* : aprendiz *m*, -diza *f*

trainer ['treɪnər] *n* : entrenador *m*, -dora *f*

training ['treɪnɪŋ] *n* : adiestramiento *m*, entrenamiento *m* (físico), capacitación *f* (de trabajadores)

traipse ['treɪps] *vi* **traipsed; traipsing** : andar de un lado para otro, vagar

trait ['treɪt] *n* : rasgo *m*, característica *f*

traitor ['treɪtər] *n* : traidor *m*, -dora *f*

traitorous ['treɪtərəs] *adj* : traidor

trajectory [trə'dʒɛktəri] *n*, *pl* **-ries** : trayectoria *f*

tramp¹ ['træmp] *vi* : caminar (a paso pesado) — *vt* : deambular por, vagar por ⟨to tramp the streets : vagar por las calles⟩

tramp² *n* 1 VAGRANT : vagabundo *m*, -da *f* 2 HIKE : caminata *f*

trample ['træmpəl] *vt* **-pled; -pling** : pisotear, hollar

trampoline [₁træmpə'li:n, 'træmpə₁-] *n* : trampolín *m*, cama *f* elástica

trance ['trænts] *n* : trance *m*

tranquil ['træŋkwəl] *adj* : calmo, tranquilo, sereno — **tranquilly** *adv*

tranquilize ['træŋkwə₁laɪz] *vt* **-ized; -izing** : tranquilizar

tranquilizer ['træŋkwə₁laɪzər] *n* : tranquilizante *m*

tranquillity *or* **tranquility** [træŋ'kwɪləti] *n* : sosiego *m*, tranquilidad *f*

trans ['trænts, 'trænz] *adj* 1 TRANSGENDER : trans, transgénero 2 TRANSSEXUAL : trans, transexual

transact [træn'zækt] *vt* : negociar, gestionar, hacer (negocios)

transaction [træn'zækʃən] *n* 1 : transac-

ción *f*, negocio *m*, operación *f* 2 **transactions** *npl* RECORDS : actas *fpl*

transatlantic [₁træntsət'læntɪk, ₁trænz-] *adj* : transatlántico

transcend [træn'sɛnd] *vt* : trascender, sobrepasar

transcendent [træn'sɛndənt] *adj* : trascendente — **transcendence** [træn'sɛndənts] *n*

transcendental [₁trænt₁sɛn'dɛntəl, -sən-] *adj* : trascendental ⟨transcendental meditation : meditación trascendental⟩

transcribe [træn'skraɪb] *vt* **-scribed; -scribing** : transcribir

transcript ['træn₁skrɪpt] *n* : copia *f* oficial

transcription [træn'skrɪpʃən] *n* : transcripción *f*

transfer¹ [trænts'fər, 'trænts₁fər] *v* **-ferred; -ferring** *vt* 1 : trasladar (a una persona), transferir (fondos) 2 : transferir, traspasar, ceder (propiedad) 3 PRINT : imprimir (un diseño) — *vi* 1 MOVE : trasladarse, cambiarse 2 CHANGE : transbordar, cambiar (de un transporte a otro) ⟨he transfers at E Street : hace transbordo en la calle E⟩

transfer² ['trænts₁fər] *n* 1 TRANSFERRING : transferencia *f* (de fondos, de propiedad, etc.), traslado *m* (de una persona) 2 DECAL : calcomanía *f* 3 : boleto *m* (para cambiar de un avión, etc., a otro)

transferable [trænts'fərəbəl] *adj* : transferible

transference [trænts'fərənts] *n* : transferencia *f*

transfigure [trænts'fɪgjər] *vt* **-ured; -uring** : transfigurar, transformar

transfix [trænts'fɪks] *vt* 1 PIERCE : traspasar, atravesar 2 IMMOBILIZE : paralizar

transform [trænts'fɔrm] *vt* : transformar

transformation [₁træntsfər'meɪʃən] *n* : transformación *f*

transformer [trænts'fɔrmər] *n* : transformador *m*

transfusion [trænts'fju:ʒən] *n* : transfusión *f*

transgender [trænts'dʒɛndər, trænz-] *adj* : transgénero ⟨transgender people : las personas transgénero⟩

transgress [trænts'grɛs, trænz-] *vt* : transgredir, infringir — **transgression** [trænts'grɛʃən, trænz-] *n* — **transgressor** [trænts'grɛsər, trænz-] *n*

transient¹ ['trænt₃ənt, 'træntsiənt] *adj* : pasajero, transitorio — **transiently** *adv*

transient² *n* : transeúnte *mf*

transistor [træn'zɪstər, -'sɪs-] *n* : transistor *m*

transit ['trænt₃ɪt, 'træntzɪt] *n* 1 PASSAGE : pasaje *m*, tránsito *m* ⟨in transit : en tránsito⟩ 2 TRANSPORTATION : transporte *m* (público)

transition [træn'sɪʒən, -'zɪʃ-] *n* : transición *f*

transitional [træn'sɪʒənəl, -'zɪʃ-] *adj* : de transición

transitive ['træntsətɪv, 'trænzə-] *adj* : transitivo

transitory [ˈtrænsəˌtori, ˈtrænzə-] *adj* : transitorio

translatable [trænsˈleɪtəbəl, trænz-] *adj* : traducible

translate [trænsˈleɪt, trænz-; ˈtrænsˌ-, ˈtrænzˌ-] *vt* -lated; -lating : traducir

translation [trænsˈleɪʃən, trænz-] *n* : traducción *f*

translator [trænsˈleɪtər, trænz-; ˈtrænsˌ-, ˈtrænzˌ-] *n* : traductor *m*, -tora *f*

translucent [trænsˈluːsənt, trænz-] *adj* : translúcido

transmissible [trænsˈmɪsəbəl, trænz-] *adj* : transmisible

transmission [trænsˈmɪʃən, trænz-] *n* : transmisión *f*

transmit [trænsˈmɪt, trænz-] *vt* -mitted; -mitting : transmitir

transmitter [trænsˈmɪtər, trænz-; ˈtrænsˌ-, ˈtrænzˌ-] *n* : transmisor *m*, emisor *m*

transom [ˈtrænsəm] *n* : montante *m* (de una puerta), travesaño *m* (de una ventana)

transparency [trænsˈpærənsi] *n*, *pl* -cies : transparencia *f*

transparent [trænsˈpærənt] *adj* 1 : transparente, traslúcido ⟨a transparent fabric : una tela transparente⟩ 2 OBVIOUS : transparente, obvio, claro — **transparently** *adv*

transpiration [ˌtrænspəˈreɪʃən] *n* : transpiración *f*

transpire [trænsˈpaɪr] *vi* -spired; -spiring 1 : transpirar (en biología y botánica) 2 TURN OUT : resultar 3 HAPPEN : suceder, ocurrir, tener lugar

transplant¹ [trænsˈplænt] *vt* : trasplantar

transplant² [ˈtrænsˌplænt] *n* : trasplante *m*

transport¹ [trænsˈport, ˈtrænsˌ-] *vt* 1 CARRY : transportar, acarrear 2 ENRAPTURE : transportar

transport² [ˈtrænsˌport] *n* 1 TRANSPORTATION : transporte *m*, transportación *f* 2 RAPTURE : éxtasis *m* 3 *or* **transport ship** : buque *m* de transporte (de personal militar)

transportation [ˌtrænspərˈteɪʃən] *n* : transporte *m*, transportación *f*

transpose [trænsˈpoːz] *vt* -posed; -posing : trasponer, trasladar, transportar (una composición musical)

transsexual [trænsˈsɛkʃuəl] *n* : transexual *mf* — **transsexual** *adj*

transverse [trænsˈvərs, trænz-] *adj* : transversal, transverso, oblicuo — **transversely** *adv*

transvestite [trænsˈvɛstaɪt, trænz-] *n* : travesti *mf*, travestí *mf* — **transvestite** *adj*

trap¹ [ˈtræp] *vt* **trapped; trapping** : atrapar, apresar (en una trampa)

trap² *n* : trampa *f* ⟨to set a trap : tender una trampa⟩

trapdoor [ˈtræpˈdor] *n* : trampilla *f*

trapeze [træˈpiːz] *n* : trapecio *m*

trapezoid [ˈtræpəˌzɔɪd] *n* : trapezoide *m*, trapecio *m*

trapper [ˈtræpər] *n* : trampero *m*, -ra *f*; cazador *m*, -dora *f* (que usa trampas)

trappings [ˈtræpɪŋz] *npl* 1 : arreos *mpl*, jaeces *mpl* (de un caballo) 2 ADORNMENTS : adornos *mpl*, pompa *f*

trash [ˈtræʃ] *n* : basura *f*

trash can → **garbage can**

trashy [ˈtræʃi] *adj* : de pacotilla

trauma [ˈtrɔmə, ˈtraʊ-] *n* : trauma *m*

traumatic [trəˈmætɪk, trɔ-, traʊ-] *adj* : traumático

travel¹ [ˈtrævəl] *vi* **-eled** *or* **-elled; -eling** *or* **-elling** 1 JOURNEY : viajar 2 GO, MOVE : desplazarse, moverse, ir ⟨the waves travel at uniform speed : las ondas se desplazan a una velocidad uniforme⟩

travel² *n or* **travels** *npl* : viajes *mpl*

travel agency *n* : agencia *f* de viajes

travel agent *n* : agente *mf* de viajes

traveler *or* **traveller** [ˈtrævələr] *n* : viajero *m*, -ra *f*

traveler's check *or* **traveller's check** *n* : cheque *m* de viajero

traverse [trəˈvərs, træˈvərs, ˈtrævərs] *vt* -versed; -versing CROSS : atravesar, extenderse a través de, cruzar

travesty [ˈtrævəsti] *n*, *pl* -ties : parodia *f*

trawl¹ [ˈtrɔl] *vi* : pescar con red de arrastre, rastrear

trawl² *n or* **trawl net** : red *f* de arrastre

trawler [ˈtrɔlər] *n* : barco *m* de pesca (utilizado para rastrear)

tray [ˈtreɪ] *n* : bandeja *f*, charola *f* Bol, Mex, Peru

treacherous [ˈtrɛtʃərəs] *adj* 1 TRAITOROUS : traicionero, traidor 2 DANGEROUS : peligroso

treacherously [ˈtrɛtʃərəsli] *adv* : a traición

treachery [ˈtrɛtʃəri] *n*, *pl* -eries : traición *f*

tread¹ [ˈtrɛd] *v* **trod** [ˈtrɑd]; **trodden** [ˈtrɑdən] *or* **trod; treading** *vt* TRAMPLE : pisotear, hollar — *vi* 1 WALK : caminar, andar 2 **to tread on** : pisar

tread² *n* 1 STEP : paso *m*, andar *m* 2 : banda *f* de rodadura (de un neumático, etc.) 3 : escalón *m* (de una escalera)

treadle [ˈtrɛdəl] *n* : pedal *m* (de una máquina)

treadmill [ˈtrɛdˌmɪl] *n* 1 : rueda *f* de andar 2 ROUTINE : rutina *f*

treason [ˈtriːzən] *n* : traición *f* (a la patria, etc.)

treasure¹ [ˈtrɛʒər, ˈtreɪ-] *vt* -sured; -suring : apreciar, valorar

treasure² *n* : tesoro *m*

treasurer [ˈtrɛʒərər, ˈtreɪ-] *n* : tesorero *m*, -ra *f*

treasury [ˈtrɛʒəri, ˈtreɪ-] *n*, *pl* -suries : tesorería *f*, tesoro *m*

treat¹ [ˈtriːt] *vt* 1 DEAL WITH : tratar (un asunto) ⟨the article treats of poverty : el artículo trata de la pobreza⟩ 2 HANDLE : tratar (a una persona), manejar (un objeto) ⟨to treat something as a joke : tomar(se) algo a broma⟩ 3 INVITE : invitar, convidar ⟨he treated me to a meal : me invitó a comer⟩ 4 : tratar, atender (en medicina) 5 PROCESS : tratar ⟨to treat sewage : tratar las aguas negras⟩ — **treatable** ['tri:ţəbəl] *adj*

treat² *n* : gusto *m*, placer *m* ⟨it was a treat to see you : fue un placer verte⟩ ⟨it's my treat : yo invito⟩

treatise ['tri:ţıs] *n* : tratado *m*, estudio *m*

treatment ['tri:tmənt] *n* : trato *m*, tratamiento *m* (médico)

treaty ['tri:ţi] *n, pl* **-ties** : tratado *m*, convenio *m*

treble¹ ['trɛbəl] *vt* **-bled; -bling** : triplicar

treble² *adj* **1 →** **triple** **2** : de tiple, soprano (en música) **3 treble clef** : clave *f* de sol

treble³ *n* : tiple *m*, parte *f* de soprano

tree ['tri:] *n* : árbol *m*

treeless ['tri:ləs] *adj* : carente de árboles

tree–lined ['tri:,laınd] *adj* : bordeado de árboles

tree stump → **stump²**

trek¹ ['trɛk] *vi* **trekked; trekking** : hacer un viaje largo y difícil

trek² *n* : viaje *m* largo y difícil

trellis ['trɛlıs] *n* : enrejado *m*, celosía *f*

tremble ['trɛmbəl] *vi* **-bled; -bling** : temblar

tremendous [trı'mɛndəs] *adj* : tremendo — **tremendously** *adv*

tremor ['trɛmər] *n* : temblor *m*

tremulous ['trɛmjələs] *adj* : trémulo, tembloroso

trench ['trɛntʃ] *n* **1** DITCH : zanja *f* **2** : trinchera *f* (militar)

trenchant ['trɛntʃənt] *adj* : cortante, mordaz

trend¹ ['trɛnd] *vi* : tender, inclinarse

trend² *n* **1** TENDENCY : tendencia *f* **2** FASHION : moda *f*

trendy ['trɛndi] *adj* **trendier; -est** : de moda

trepidation [,trɛpə'deıʃən] *n* : inquietud *f*, ansiedad *f*

trespass¹ ['trɛspəs, -,pæs] *vi* **1** SIN : pecar, transgredir **2** : entrar ilegalmente (en propiedad ajena)

trespass² *n* **1** SIN : pecado *m*, transgresión *f* ⟨forgive us our trespasses : perdónanos nuestras deudas⟩ **2** : entrada *f* ilegal (en propiedad ajena)

tress ['trɛs] *n* : mechón *m*

trestle ['trɛsəl] *n* **1** : caballete *m* (armazón) **2 or trestle bridge** : puente *m* de caballete

tri- ['traı] *pref* : tri-

triad ['traı,æd] *n* : tríada *f*

trial¹ ['traıəl] *adj* : de prueba ⟨trial period : período de prueba⟩

trial² *n* **1** : juicio *m*, proceso *m* ⟨to stand trial : ser sometido a juicio⟩ **2** AFFLICTION : aflicción *f*, tribulación *f* **3** TEST : prueba *f*, ensayo *m* ⟨by trial and error : por ensayo y error⟩

triangle ['traı,æŋgəl] *n* : triángulo *m*

triangular [traı'æŋgjələr] *adj* : triangular

tribal ['traıbəl] *adj* : tribal

tribe ['traıb] *n* : tribu *f*

tribesman ['traıbzmən] *n, pl* **-men** [-mən, -,mɛn] : miembro *m* de una tribu

tribulation [,trıbjə'leıʃən] *n* : tribulación *f*

tribunal [traı'bju:nəl, trı-] *n* : tribunal *m*, corte *f*

tributary ['trıbjə,tɛri] *n, pl* **-taries** : afluente *m*

tribute ['trıb,ju:t] *n* : tributo *m*

trick¹ ['trık] *vt* : engañar, embaucar

trick² *n* **1** RUSE : trampa *f*, treta *f*, artimaña *f* **2** PRANK : broma *f* ⟨we played a trick on her : le gastamos una broma⟩ **3** : truco *m* ⟨magic tricks : trucos de magia⟩ ⟨the trick is to wait five minutes : el truco está en esperar cinco minutos⟩ **4** MANNERISM : peculiaridad *f*, manía *f* **5** : baza *f* (en juegos de naipes) **6 to do the trick** *fam* : servir como solución

trickery ['trıkəri] *n* : engaños *mpl*, trampas *fpl*

trickle¹ ['trıkəl] *vi* **-led; -ling** : gotear, chorrear

trickle² *n* : goteo *m*, hilo *m*

trickster ['trıkstər] *n* : estafador *m*, -dora *f*; embaucador *m*, -dora *f*

tricky ['trıki] *adj* **trickier; -est** **1** SLY : astuto, taimado **2** DIFFICULT : delicado, peliagudo, difícil

tricolor ['traı,kʌlər] *adj* : tricolor

tricycle ['traısəkəl, -,sıkəl] *n* : triciclo *m*

trident ['traıdənt] *n* : tridente *m*

triennial [,traı'ɛniəl] *adj* : trienal

trifle¹ ['traıfəl] *vi* **-fled; -fling** : jugar, juguetear

trifle² *n* : nimiedad *f*, insignificancia *f*

trifling ['traıflıŋ] *adj* : trivial, insignificante

trigger¹ ['trıgər] *vt* : causar, provocar

trigger² *n* : gatillo *m*

trigonometry [,trıgə'nɑmətri] *n* : trigonometría *f*

trill¹ ['trıl] *vi* QUAVER : trinar, gorjear — *vt* : vibrar ⟨to trill the r : vibrar la r⟩

trill² *n* **1** QUAVER : trino *m*, gorjeo *m* **2** : vibración *f* (en fonética)

trillion ['trıljən] *n* : billón *m*

trilogy ['trılədʒi] *n, pl* **-gies** : trilogía *f*

trim¹ ['trım] *vt* **trimmed; trimming** **1** DECORATE : adornar, decorar **2** CUT : recortar **3** REDUCE : recortar, reducir ⟨to trim the excess : recortar el exceso⟩

trim² *adj* **trimmer; trimmest** **1** SLIM : esbelto **2** NEAT : limpio y arreglado, bien cuidado

trim³ *n* **1** CONDITION : condición *f*, estado *m* ⟨to keep in trim : mantenerse en buena forma⟩ **2** CUT : recorte *m* **3** TRIMMING : adornos *mpl*

trimester [,traı'mɛstər] *n* : trimestre *m*

trimming ['trımıŋ] *n* : adornos *mpl*, accesorios *mpl*

Trinity ['trınəţi] *n* : Trinidad *f*

trinket ['trıŋkət] *n* : chuchería *f*, baratija *f*

trio ['tri:,o:] *n, pl* **trios** : trío *m*

trip¹ ['trıp] *v* **tripped; tripping** *vi* **1** : caminar (a paso ligero) **2** STUMBLE : tropezar **3 to trip up** ERR : equivocarse, cometer un error — *vt* **1** : hacerle una zancadilla (a alguien) ⟨you tripped me on purpose! : ¡me hiciste la zancadilla a propósito!⟩ **2** ACTIVATE : activar (un mecanismo) **3 to trip up** : hacer equivocar (a alguien)

trip² *n* **1** JOURNEY : viaje *m* ⟨to take a trip : hacer un viaje⟩ **2** STUMBLE : tropiezo *m*, traspié *m*

tripartite [traɪˈpɑr.taɪt] *adj* : tripartito

tripe [ˈtraɪp] *n* **1** : mondongo *m*, callos *mpl*, pancita *f Mex* **2** TRASH : porquería *f*

triple¹ [ˈtrɪpəl] *vt* **-pled; -pling** : triplicar

triple² *adj* : triple

triple³ *n* : triple *m*

triplet [ˈtrɪplət] *n* **1** : terceto *m* (en poesía, música, etc.) **2** : trillizo *m*, -za *f* (persona)

triplicate [ˈtrɪplɪkət] *n* : triplicado *m*

tripod [ˈtraɪˌpɑd] *n* : trípode *m*

trite [ˈtraɪt] *adj* **triter; tritest** : trillado, tópico, manido

triumph¹ [ˈtraɪəmpf] *vi* : triunfar

triumph² *n* : triunfo *m*

triumphal [traɪˈʌmpfəl] *adj* : triunfal

triumphant [traɪˈʌmpfənt] *adj* : triunfante, triunfal — **triumphantly** *adv*

triumvirate [traɪˈʌmvərət] *n* : triunvirato *m*

trivet [ˈtrɪvət] *n* : salvamanteles *m*

trivia [ˈtrɪviə] *ns & pl* : trivialidades *fpl*, nimiedades *fpl*

trivial [ˈtrɪviəl] *adj* : trivial, intrascendente, insignificante

triviality [ˌtrɪviˈæləti] *n, pl* **-ties** : trivialidad *f*

trod, trodden → tread¹

troll [ˈtroːl] *n* : duende *m* o gigante *m* de cuentos folklóricos

trolley [ˈtrɑli] *n, pl* **-leys** : tranvía *m*

trombone [trɑmˈboːn] *n* : trombón *m*

trombonist [trɑmˈboːnɪst] *n* : trombón *m*

troop¹ [ˈtruːp] *vi* : desfilar, ir en tropel

troop² *n* **1** : escuadrón *m* (de caballería) **2** GROUP : grupo *m*, banda *f* (de personas) **3 troops** *npl* SOLDIERS : tropas *fpl*, soldados *mpl*

trooper [ˈtruːpər] *n* **1** : soldado *m* (de caballería) **2** : policía *m* montado **3** : policía *m* (estatal)

trophy [ˈtroːfi] *n, pl* **-phies** : trofeo *m*

tropic¹ [ˈtrɑpɪk] *or* **tropical** [-pɪkəl] *adj* : tropical

tropic² *n* **1** : trópico *m* ⟨tropic of Cancer : trópico de Cáncer⟩ **2 the tropics** : el trópico

trot¹ [ˈtrɑt] *vi* **trotted; trotting** : trotar

trot² *n* : trote *m*

troubadour [ˈtruːbəˌdɔr] *n* : trovador *m*, -dora *f*

trouble¹ [ˈtrʌbəl] *v* **-bled; -bling** *vt* **1** DISTURB, WORRY : molestar, perturbar, inquietar **2** AFFLICT : afligir, afectar — *vi* : molestarse, hacer un esfuerzo ⟨they didn't trouble to come : no se molestaron en venir⟩

trouble² *n* **1** PROBLEMS : problemas *mpl*, dificultades *fpl* ⟨to be in trouble : estar en un aprieto⟩ ⟨heart trouble : problemas de corazón⟩ **2** EFFORT : molestia *f*, esfuerzo *m* ⟨to take the trouble : tomarse la molestia⟩ ⟨it's not worth the trouble : no vale la pena⟩

troublemaker [ˈtrʌbəlˌmeɪkər] *n* : agitador *m*, -dora *f*; alborotador *m*, -dora *f*

troubleshooter [ˈtrʌbəlˌʃuːtər] *n* : persona *f* que resuelve problemas

troublesome [ˈtrʌbəlsəm] *adj* : problemático, dificultoso — **troublesomely** *adv*

trough [ˈtrɔf] *n, pl* **troughs** [ˈtrɔfs, ˈtrɔvz] **1** : comedero *m*, bebedero *m* (de animales) **2** CHANNEL, HOLLOW : depresión *f* (en el suelo), seno *m* (de olas)

trounce [ˈtraʊns] *vt* **trounced; trouncing 1** THRASH : apalear, darle una paliza (a alguien) **2** DEFEAT : derrotar contundentemente

troupe [ˈtruːp] *n* : troupe *f*

trouser [ˈtraʊzər] *adj* : del pantalón

trousers [ˈtraʊzərz] *npl* : pantalón *m*, pantalones *mpl*

trousseau [ˈtruːˌsoː, truːˈsoː] *n* : ajuar *m*

trout [ˈtraʊt] *ns & pl* : trucha *f*

trowel [ˈtraʊəl] *n* **1** : llana *f*, paleta *f* (de albañil) **2** : desplantador *m* (de jardinero)

truant [ˈtruːənt] *n* : alumno *m*, -na *f* que falta a clase sin permiso

truce [ˈtruːs] *n* : tregua *f*, armisticio *m*

truck¹ [ˈtrʌk] *vt* : transportar en camión

truck² *n* **1** : camión *m* (vehículo automóvil), carro *m* (manual) ⟨truck driver : camionero⟩ **2** *or* **hand truck** : carretilla *f*, carro *m* (para llevar cajones, etc.) **3** DEALINGS : tratos *mpl* ⟨to have no truck with : no tener nada que ver con⟩

trucker [ˈtrʌkər] *n* : camionero *m*, -ra *f*

truculent [ˈtrʌkjələnt] *adj* : agresivo, beligerante

trudge [ˈtrʌdʒ] *vi* **trudged; trudging** : caminar a paso pesado

true¹ [ˈtruː] *vt* **trued; trueing** : aplomar (algo vertical), nivelar (algo horizontal), centrar (una rueda)

true² *adv* **1** TRUTHFULLY : lealmente, sinceramente **2** ACCURATELY : exactamente, certeramente

true³ *adj* **truer; truest 1** LOYAL : fiel, leal **2** : cierto, verdadero, verídico ⟨it's true : es cierto, es la verdad⟩ ⟨a true story : una historia verídica⟩ **3** GENUINE : auténtico, genuino — **truly** *adv*

true-blue [ˈtruːˈbluː] *adj* LOYAL : leal, fiel

truffle [ˈtrʌfəl] *n* : trufa *f*

truism [ˈtruːˌɪzəm] *n* : perogrullada *f*, verdad *f* obvia

trump¹ [ˈtrʌmp] *vt* : matar (en juegos de naipes)

trump² *n* : triunfo *m* (en juegos de naipes)

trumped–up [ˈtrʌmptˈʌp] *adj* : inventado, fabricado ⟨trumped-up charges : falsas acusaciones⟩

trumpet¹ [ˈtrʌmpət] *vi* **1** : sonar una trompeta **2** : berrear, bramar (dícese de un animal) — *vt* : proclamar a los cuatro vientos

trumpet² *n* : trompeta *f*

trumpeter [ˈtrʌmpətər] *n* : trompetista *mf*

truncate [ˈtrʌnˌkeɪt, ˈtrʌn-] *vt* **-cated; -cating** : truncar

trundle [ˈtrʌndəl] *v* **-dled; -dling** *vi* : rodar lentamente — *vt* : hacer rodar, empujar lentamente

trunk [ˈtrʌŋk] *n* **1** : tronco *m* (de un árbol o del cuerpo) **2** : trompa *f* (de un elefante) **3** CHEST : baúl *m* **4** : maletero *m*, baúl *m* (*in various countries*), cajuela *f* *Mex* (de un auto) **5 trunks** *npl* → **swimming trunks**

truss¹ [ˈtrʌs] *vt* : atar (con fuerza)

truss² *n* **1** FRAMEWORK : armazón *m* (de una estructura) **2** : braguero *m* (en medicina)

trust¹ [ˈtrʌst] *vi* : confiar, esperar ⟨to trust in God : confiar en Dios⟩ — *vt* **1** ENTRUST : confiar, encomendar **2** : confiar en, tenerle confianza a ⟨I trust you : te tengo confianza⟩

trust² *n* **1** CONFIDENCE : confianza *f* **2** HOPE : esperanza *f*, fe *f* **3** CREDIT : crédito *m* ⟨to sell on trust : fiar⟩ **4** : fideicomiso *m* ⟨to hold in trust : guardar en fideicomiso⟩ **5** : trust *m* (consorcio empresarial) **6** CUSTODY : responsabilidad *f*, custodia *f*

trustee [ˌtrʌsˈtiː] *n* : fideicomisario *m*, -ria *f*; fiduciario *m*, -ria *f*

trustful [ˈtrʌstfəl] *adj* : confiado — **trustfully** *adv*

trustworthiness [ˈtrəstˌwərðinəs] *n* : integridad *f*, honradez *f*

trustworthy [ˈtrəstˌwərði] *adj* : digno de confianza, confiable

trusty [ˈtrəsti] *adj* **trustier; -est** : fiel, confiable

truth [ˈtruːθ] *n, pl* **truths** [ˈtruːðz, ˈtruːθs] : verdad *f*

truthful [ˈtruːθfəl] *adj* : sincero, veraz — **truthfully** *adv*

truthfulness [ˈtruːθfəlnəs] *n* : sinceridad *f*, veracidad *f*

try¹ [ˈtraɪ] *v* **tried; trying** *vt* **1** : enjuiciar, juzgar, procesar ⟨he was tried for murder : fue procesado por homicidio⟩ **2** : probar ⟨did you try the salad? : ¿probaste la ensalada?⟩ **3** TEST : tentar, poner a prueba ⟨to try one's patience : tentarle la paciencia a uno⟩ — *vt* ATTEMPT : tratar (de), intentar **5** or **to try on** : probarse (ropa) **6 to try out** : poner a prueba — *vi* **1** : tratar, intentar **2 to try out (for)** : presentarse a una prueba (para)

try² *n, pl* **tries** : intento *m*, tentativa *f*

tryout [ˈtraɪˌaʊt] *n* : prueba *f*

tsar [ˈzɑr, ˈtsɑr, ˈsɑr] → **czar**

T–shirt [ˈtiːˌʃərt] *n* : camiseta *f*

tub [ˈtʌb] *n* **1** CASK : cuba *f*, barril *m*, tonel *m* **2** CONTAINER : envase *m* (de plástico, etc.) ⟨a tub of margarine : un envase de margarina⟩ **3** BATHTUB : tina *f* (de baño), bañera *f*

tuba [ˈtuːbə, ˈtjuː-] *n* : tuba *f*

tube [ˈtuːb, ˈtjuːb] *n* **1** PIPE : tubo *m* **2** : tubo *m* (de dentífrico, etc.) **3** or **inner tube** : cámara *f* **4** : tubo *m* (de un aparato electrónico) **5** : trompa *f* (en anatomía) **6** (*Brit*) SUBWAY : metro *m*; subterráneo *m* *Arg, Uru* **7 the tube** *fam* : la tele *fam*

tubeless [ˈtuːbləs, ˈtjuːb-] *adj* : sin cámara (dícese de una llanta)

tuber [ˈtuːbər, ˈtjuː-] *n* : tubérculo *m*

tubercular [tʊˈbərkjələr, tjʊ-] → **tuberculous**

tuberculosis [tʊˌbərkjəˈloːsɪs, tjʊ-] *n, pl* **-loses** [-ˌsiːz] : tuberculosis *f*

tuberculous [tʊˈbərkjələs, tjʊ-] *adj* : tuberculoso

tuberous [ˈtuːbərəs, ˈtjuː-] *adj* : tuberoso

tubing [ˈtuːbɪŋ, ˈtjuː-] *n* : tubería *f*

tubular [ˈtuːbjələr, ˈtjuː-] *adj* : tubular

tuck¹ [ˈtʌk] *vt* **1** PLACE, PUT : meter, colocar ⟨tuck in your shirt : métete la camisa⟩ **2** : guardar, esconder ⟨to tuck away one's money : guardar uno bien su dinero⟩ **3** or **to tuck in** COVER : arropar (a un niño en la cama)

tuck² *n* : pliegue *m*, alforza *f*

Tuesday [ˈtuːzˌdeɪ, ˈtjuːz-, -di] *n* : martes *m* ⟨today is Tuesday : hoy es martes⟩ ⟨(on) Tuesday : el martes⟩ ⟨(on) Tuesdays : los martes⟩ ⟨last Tuesday : el martes pasado⟩ ⟨next Tuesday : el martes que viene⟩ ⟨every other Tuesday : cada dos martes⟩ ⟨Tuesday afternoon/morning : martes por la tarde/mañana⟩

tuft [ˈtʌft] *n* : penacho *m* (de plumas), copete *m* (de pelo)

tug¹ [ˈtʌg] *v* **tugged; tugging** *vi* : tirar, jalar, dar un tirón — *vt* : jalar, arrastrar, remolcar (con un barco)

tug² *n* **1** : tirón *m*, jalón *m* **2** → **tugboat**

tugboat [ˈtʌgˌboːt] *n* : remolcador *m*

tug-of-war [ˌtʌgəˈwɔr] *n, pl* **tugs-of-war** **1** : juego *m* de tirar de la cuerda **2** : lucha *f*

tuition [tuˈɪʃən] *n* or **tuition fees** : tasas *fpl* de matrícula, colegiatura *f* *Mex*

tulip [ˈtuːlɪp, ˈtjuː-] *n* : tulipán *m*

tulle [ˈtuːl] *n* : tul *m*

tumble¹ [ˈtʌmbəl] *v* **-bled; -bling** *vi* **1** : dar volteretas (en acrobacia) **2** FALL : caerse, venirse abajo — *vt* **1** TOPPLE : volcar **2** TOSS : hacer girar

tumble² *n* : voltereta *f*, caída *f*

tumbledown [ˈtʌmbəlˌdaʊn] *adj* : en ruinas

tumbler [ˈtʌmblər] *n* **1** ACROBAT : acróbata *mf*, saltimbanqui *mf* **2** GLASS : vaso *m* (de mesa) **3** : clavija *f* (de una cerradura)

tummy [ˈtʌmi] *n, pl* **-mies** BELLY : panza *f*, vientre *m*

tumor [ˈtuːmər, ˈtjuː-] *n* : tumor *m*

tumult [ˈtuːˌmʌlt, ˈtjuː-] *n* : tumulto *m*, alboroto *m*

tumultuous [tʊˈmʌltʃʊəs, tjʊ-] *adj* : tumultuoso

tuna [ˈtuːnə, ˈtjuː-] *n, pl* **-na** or **-nas** : atún *m*

tundra [ˈtʌndrə] *n* : tundra *f*

tune¹ [ˈtuːn, ˈtjuːn] *v* **tuned; tuning** *vt* **1** ADJUST : ajustar, hacer más preciso, afinar (un motor) **2** : afinar (un instrumento musical) **3** : sintonizar (un radio o televisor) — *vi* **to tune in** : sintonizar (con una emisora)

tune² *n* **1** MELODY : tonada *f*, canción *f*, melodía *f* **2 in tune** : afinado (dícese de un instrumento o de la voz), sintonizado, en sintonía

tuneful [ˈtuːnfəl, ˈtjuːn-] *adj* : armonioso, melódico

tuner ['tu:nər, 'tju:-] n : afinador m, -dora f (de instrumentos); sintonizador m (de un radio o un televisor)

tune–up n : afinado m, afinación f, puesta f a punto

tungsten ['tʌŋkstən] n : tungsteno m

tunic ['tu:nɪk, 'tju:-] n : túnica f

tuning fork n : diapasón m

Tunisian [tu:'nɪʒən, tju:'nɪziən] n : tunecino m, -na f — **Tunisian** adj

tunnel[1] ['tʌnəl] vi -neled or -nelled; -neling or -nelling : hacer un túnel

tunnel[2] n : túnel m

turban ['tɜrbən] n : turbante m

turbid ['tɜrbɪd] adj : turbio

turbine ['tɜrbən, -ˌbaɪn] n : turbina f

turbulence ['tɜrbjələnts] n : turbulencia f

turbulent ['tɜrbjələnt] adj : turbulento — **turbulently** adv

tureen [təˈriːn, tju-] n : sopera f

turf ['tɜrf] n SOD : tepe m

turgid ['tɜrdʒɪd] adj 1 SWOLLEN : turgente 2 : ampuloso, hinchado ⟨turgid style : estilo ampuloso⟩

Turk ['tɜrk] n : turco m, -ca f

turkey ['tɜrki] n, pl -keys : pavo m

Turkish[1] ['tɜrkɪʃ] adj : turco

Turkish[2] n : turco m (idioma)

turmoil ['tɜrˌmɔɪl] n : agitación f, desorden m, confusión f

turn[1] ['tɜrn] vt 1 : girar, voltear, volver ⟨to turn one's head : voltear la cabeza⟩ ⟨she turned her chair toward the fire : giró su asiento hacia la hoguera⟩ 2 ROTATE, SPIN : darle vuelta(s) a, hacer girar ⟨turn the handle : dale vuelta a la manivela⟩ 3 FLIP : darle vuelta a, dar vuelta, voltear ⟨to turn the page : darle vuelta a la página/hoja, voltear/pasar la hoja/página⟩ ⟨to turn face up/down : volver boca arriba/abajo⟩ 4 SET : poner (un termostato, etc.) 5 SPRAIN, WRENCH : torcer, dislocar 6 DIRECT : dirigir (los esfuerzos, la atención, etc.) ⟨to turn one's mind/thoughts to : ponerse a pensar en⟩ 7 UPSET : revolver (el estómago) 8 TRANSFORM : convertir ⟨to turn water into wine : convertir el agua en vino⟩ 9 SHAPE : tornear (en carpintería) 10 to turn against : poner (a alguien) en contra de 11 to turn a profit : obtener ganancias/beneficios 12 to turn around SPIN : hacer girar 13 to turn around FLIP : dar la vuelta a, dar vuelta, voltear 14 to turn away : no dejar/permitir entrar 15 to turn back : hacer volver 16 to turn down REFUSE, REJECT : rehusar, rechazar ⟨they turned down our invitation : rehusaron nuestra invitación⟩ 17 to turn down LOWER : bajar (el volumen) 18 to turn in : entregar ⟨to turn in one's work : entregar uno su trabajo⟩ ⟨they turned in the suspect : entregaron al sospechoso⟩ 19 to turn off/out : apagar (la luz, la radio, etc.) 20 to turn on : prender (la luz, etc.), encender (un motor, etc.) 21 to turn on : interesarle el agua 22 to turn on to : despertarle el interés por 23 to turn out EVICT, EXPEL

: expulsar, echar, desalojar 24 to turn out PRODUCE : producir 25 to turn over TRANSFER : entregar, transferir (un cargo, una responsabilidad) 26 to turn over FLIP : voltear, darle la vuelta a ⟨turn the pancake over : voltea el panqueque⟩ 27 to turn over CONSIDER : considerar ⟨I kept turning the problem over in my mind : el problema me estaba dando vueltas en la cabeza⟩ 28 to turn up : subir (el volumen) — vi 1 ROTATE, SPIN : girar, dar vueltas 2 : girar, doblar, dar una vuelta (en un vehículo) ⟨turn left : gira/dobla a la izquierda⟩ ⟨turn onto Main : toma la calle Main⟩ 3 : volverse, darse la vuelta, voltearse ⟨to turn towards : volverse hacia⟩ ⟨I turned (around) and left : di media vuelta y me fui⟩ 4 BECOME : hacerse, volverse, ponerse ⟨it got cold (out) : (el tiempo) se volvió frío⟩ ⟨she turned red : se puso colorado, se sonrojó⟩ ⟨he turned 80 : cumplió los 80⟩ 5 CHANGE : cambiar (dícese de la marea, etc.) 6 SOUR : agriarse, cortarse (dícese de la leche) 7 to turn against : volverse en contra de 8 to turn away : volverse (de espaldas), darse la vuelta, voltearse 9 to turn back RETURN : volverse 10 to turn in : acostarse, irse a la cama 11 to turn into : convertirse en 12 to turn off : salir (de una carretera), desviarse de ⟨turn off at/onto Main : toma la (calle) Main⟩ ⟨turn off (of) First onto Main : sal de First tomando Main⟩ 13 to turn on ATTACK : atacar (inesperadamente) 14 to turn out : concurrir, presentarse ⟨many turned out to vote : muchos concurrieron a votar⟩ 15 to turn out PROVE, RESULT : resultar 16 to turn over : darse (la) vuelta (dícese de una persona), volcarse (dícese de un vehículo) 17 to turn over START : arrancar 18 to turn to : recurrir a ⟨they have no one to turn to : no tienen quien les ayude⟩ ⟨to turn to violence : recurrir a la violencia⟩ 19 to turn up APPEAR : aparecer, presentarse 20 to turn up HAPPEN : ocurrir, suceder (inesperadamente)

turn[2] n 1 : vuelta f, giro m ⟨give it a turn : dale vuelta⟩ ⟨a sudden turn : una vuelta repentina⟩ 2 CHANGE : cambio m ⟨to take a turn for the better/worse : mejorar/empeorar⟩ ⟨turn of events : giro de los acontecimientos⟩ 3 INTERSECTION : bocacalle f ⟨we took a wrong turn : nos equivocamos de calle/salida (etc.), dimos una vuelta equivocada⟩ 4 CURVE : curva f (en un camino) 5 : turno m ⟨they're awaiting their turn : están esperando su turno⟩ ⟨whose turn is it? : ¿a quién le toca?⟩ ⟨to take turns : turnarse⟩ 6 at every turn : a cada paso 7 in turn : sucesivamente 8 in turn LIKEWISE : a su vez 9 one good turn deserves another : favor por favor se paga 10 out of turn : fuera de lugar 11 the turn of the century : el final del siglo

turnaround ['tǝrnǝ‚raʊnd] *n* PROCESSING
: procesamiento *m*

turncoat ['tǝrn‚koːt] *n* : traidor *m*, -dora *f*

turning point *n* : momento *m* decisivo

turnip ['tǝrnǝp] *n* : nabo *m*

turnout ['tǝrn‚aʊt] *n* : concurrencia *f*

turnover ['tǝrn‚oːvǝr] *n* 1 : empanada *f*
(salada o dulce) 2 : volumen *m* (de ventas) 3 : rotación *f* (de personal) ⟨a high
turnover : un alto nivel de rotación⟩

turnpike ['tǝrn‚paɪk] *n* : carretera *f* de
peaje

turnstile ['tǝrn‚staɪl] *n* : torniquete *m* (de
acceso)

turntable ['tǝrn‚teɪbǝl] *n* : tornamesa *mf*

turpentine ['tǝrpǝn‚taɪn] *n* : aguarrás *m*,
trementina *f*

turquoise ['tǝr‚kɔɪz, -‚kwɔɪz] *n* : turquesa *f*

turret ['tǝrǝt] *n* 1 TOWER : torre *f*
pequeña 2 : torreta *f* (de un tanque, un
avión, etc.)

turtle ['tǝrtǝl] *n* : tortuga *f* (marina)

turtledove ['tǝrtǝl‚dʌv] *n* : tórtola *f*

turtleneck ['tǝrtǝl‚nɛk] *n* : cuello *m* de
tortuga, cuello *m* alto

tusk ['tʌsk] *n* : colmillo *m*

tussle¹ ['tʌsǝl] *vi* -**sled; -sling** SCUFFLE
: pelearse, reñir

tussle² *n* : riña *f*, pelea *f*

tutelage ['tuːtl̩ɪdʒ, 'tjuː-] *n* : tutela *f*

tutor¹ ['tuːtǝr, 'tjuː-] *vt* : darle clases particulares (a alguien)

tutor² *n* : tutor *m*, -tora *f*; maestro *m*, -tra
f (particular)

tutorial [‚tuːˈtoːriǝl, ‚tjuː-] *n* 1 : tutorial
m 2 : clase *f* (individual o con un
pequeño grupo de estudiantes)

tuxedo [‚tǝkˈsiː‚doː] *n, pl* -**dos** *or* -**does**
: esmoquin *m*, smoking *m* (traje)

TV [‚tiːˈviː, 'tiː‚viː] → television

twain ['tweɪn] *n* : dos *m*

twang¹ ['twæŋ] *vt* : pulsar la cuerda de
(una guitarra) — *vi* : hablar con tono nasal

twang² *n* 1 : tañido *m* (de una cuerda de
guitarra) 2 : tono *m* nasal (de voz)

tweak¹ ['twiːk] *vt* : pellizcar

tweak² *n* : pellizco *m*

tweed ['twiːd] *n* : tweed *m*

tweet¹ ['twiːt] *vi* 1 : piar 2 : tuitear, twittear (en la red social Twitter) — *vt* : tuitear, twittear (en la red social Twitter)

tweet² *n* 1 : gorjeo *m*, pío *m* 2 : tuit *m*,
tweet *m* (en la red social Twitter)

tweezers ['twiːzǝrz] *npl* : pinzas *fpl*

twelfth¹ ['twɛlfθ] *adj* : duodécimo

twelfth² *n* 1 : duodécimo *m*, -ma *f* (en una
serie) 2 : doceavo *m*, doceava parte *f*

twelve¹ ['twɛlv] *adj & pron* : doce

twelve² *n* : doce *m*

twentieth¹ ['twʌntiǝθ, 'twɛn-] *adj*
: vigésimo

twentieth² *n* 1 : vigésimo *m*, -ma *f* (en una
serie) 2 : veinteavo *m*, veinteava parte *f*

twenty¹ ['twʌnti, 'twɛn-] *adj & pron*
: veinte

twenty² *n, pl* -**ties** : veinte *m*

twice ['twaɪs] *adv* : dos veces ⟨twice a day
: dos veces al día⟩ ⟨it costs twice as
much : cuesta el doble⟩

twig ['twɪg] *n* : ramita *f*

twilight ['twaɪ‚laɪt] *n* : crepúsculo *m*

twill ['twɪl] *n* : sarga *f*, tela *f* cruzada

twin¹ ['twɪn] *adj* 1 : gemelo, mellizo 2
: doble, gemelo ⟨twin city : ciudad her-
mana⟩ ⟨twin-engine plane : avión bimo-
tor⟩

twin² *n* : gemelo *m*, -la *f*; mellizo *m*, -za *f*

twin bed *n* : cama *f* individual

twine¹ ['twaɪn] *v* **twined; twining** *vt* : entrelazar, entrecruzar — *vi* : enroscarse
(alrededor de algo)

twine² *n* : cordel *m*, cuerda *f*, mecate *m*
CA, Mex, Ven

twinge¹ ['twɪndʒ] *vi* **twinged; twinging** *or*
twingeing : sentir punzadas

twinge² *n* : punzada *f*, dolor *m* agudo

twinkle¹ ['twɪŋkǝl] *vi* -**kled; -kling** 1
: centellear, titilar (dícese de las estrellas
o de la luz) 2 : chispear, brillar (dícese
de los ojos)

twinkle² *n* : centelleo *m* (de las estrellas),
brillo *m* (de los ojos)

twirl¹ ['twǝrl] *vt* : girar, darle vueltas a —
vi : girar, dar vueltas (rápidamente)

twirl² *n* : giro *m*, vuelta *f*

twist¹ ['twɪst] *vt* 1 : torcer, retorcer ⟨he
twisted my arm : me torció el brazo⟩ 2
DISTORT : tergiversar — *vi* : retorcerse,
enroscarse, serpentear (dícese de un río,
un camino, etc.)

twist² *n* 1 BEND : vuelta *f*, recodo *m* (en
el camino, el río, etc.) 2 TURN : giro *m*
⟨give it a twist : hazlo girar⟩ 3 SPIRAL
: espiral *f* ⟨a twist of lemon : una rodajita
de limón⟩ 4 : giro *m* inesperado (de
eventos, etc.)

twisted ['twɪstǝd] *adj* : retorcido ⟨a
twisted mind : una mente retorcida⟩

twister ['twɪstǝr] *n* 1 → tornado 2 →
waterspout

twitch¹ ['twɪtʃ] *vi* : moverse nerviosamente, contraerse espasmódicamente
(dícese de un músculo)

twitch² *n* : espasmo *m*, sacudida *f* ⟨a nervous twitch : un tic nervioso⟩

twitter¹ ['twɪtǝr] *vi* CHIRP : gorjear, cantar
(dícese de los pájaros)

twitter² *n* : gorjeo *m*

two¹ ['tuː] *adj* : dos ⟨she's two (years old)
: tiene dos años⟩

two² *n, pl* **twos** : dos *m* ⟨the two of hearts
: el dos de corazones⟩

two³ *pron* : dos ⟨there are two of us : somos dos⟩ ⟨it's two (o'clock) : son las dos⟩

two-faced ['tuːˈfeɪst] *adj* : hipócrita

twofold¹ ['tuːˈfoːld] *adv* : al doble

twofold² ['tuː‚foːld] *adj* : doble

two hundred¹ *adj & pron* : doscientos

two hundred² *n* : doscientos *m*

two-piece ['tuːˈpiːs] *adj* : de dos piezas

twosome ['tuːsǝm] *n* COUPLE : pareja *f*

two-tone ['tuːˈtoːn] *adj* : bicolor

two-way *adj* 1 : de doble sentido, de
doble dirección (dícese de una calle) 2
MUTUAL : mutuo 3 : bidireccional

two-way mirror → one-way mirror

tycoon [taɪˈkuːn] *n* : magnate *mf*

tying → tie¹

type¹ ['taɪp] *v* **typed; typing** *vt* 1 TYPE-
WRITE : escribir a máquina, pasar (un

texto) a máquina **2** CATEGORIZE : categorizar, identificar — *vi* : escribir a máquina

type² *n* **1** KIND : tipo *m*, clase *f*, categoría *f* **2** : tipo *m* (de imprenta) ⟨italic type : bastardilla, cursiva⟩

typeface ['taɪpˌfeɪs] *n* : tipo *m* de imprenta

typewrite ['taɪpˌraɪt] *v* **-wrote; -written** : escribir a máquina

typewriter ['taɪpˌraɪtər] *n* : máquina *f* de escribir

typhoid¹ ['taɪˌfɔɪd, taɪ'-] *adj* : relativo al tifus o a la tifoidea

typhoid² *n or* **typhoid fever** : tifoidea *f*

typhoon [taɪ'fu:n] *n* : tifón *m*

typhus ['taɪfəs] *n* : tifus *m*

typical ['tɪpɪkəl] *adj* : típico, característico — **typically** *adv*

typify ['tɪpəˌfaɪ] *vt* **-fied; -fying** : ser típico o representativo de (un grupo, una clase, etc.)

typing ['taɪpɪŋ] *n* : mecanografía *f*

typist ['taɪpɪst] *n* : mecanógrafo *m*, -fa *f*

typographer [taɪ'pɑgrəfər] *n* : tipógrafo *m*, -fa *f*

typographic [ˌtaɪpə'græfɪk] *or* **typographical** [-fɪkəl] *adj* : tipográfico — **typographically** [-frkli] *adv*

typography [taɪ'pɑgrəfi] *n* : tipografía *f*

tyrannical [tə'rænɪkəl, taɪ-] *adj* : tiránico — **tyrannically** [-nɪkli] *adv*

tyrannize ['tɪrəˌnaɪz] *vt* **-nized; -nizing** : tiranizar

tyranny ['tɪrəni] *n, pl* **-nies** : tiranía *f*

tyrant ['taɪrənt] *n* : tirano *m*, -na *f*

Tyrolean [tə'ro:liən, taɪ-] *adj* : tirolés

tzar ['zɑr, 'tsɑr, 'sɑr] → **czar**

U

u ['ju:] *n, pl* **u's** *or* **us** ['ju:z] : vigésima primera letra del alfabeto inglés

ubiquitous [ju:'bɪkwətəs] *adj* : ubicuo, omnipresente

udder ['ʌdər] *n* : ubre *f*

UFO [ˌju:ˌef'o:, 'ju:ˌfo:] *n, pl* **UFO's** *or* **UFOs** (unidentified *f*lying *o*bject) : ovni *m*, OVNI *m*

Ugandan [ju:'gændən, -'gɑn-; u:'gɑn-] *n* : ugandés *m*, -desa *f* — **Ugandan** *adj*

ugliness ['ʌglinəs] *n* : fealdad *f*

ugly ['ʌgli] *adj* **uglier; -est 1** UNATTRACTIVE : feo **2** DISAGREEABLE : desagradable, feo ⟨ugly weather : tiempo feo⟩ ⟨to have an ugly temper : tener mal genio⟩

Ukrainian [ju:'kreɪniən, -'kraɪ-] *n* **1** : ucraniano *m*, -na *f* **2** : ucraniano *m* (idioma) — **Ukrainian** *adj*

ukulele [ˌju:kə'leɪli] *n* : ukelele *m*

ulcer ['ʌlsər] *n* : úlcera *f* (interna), llaga *f* (externa)

ulcerate ['ʌlsəˌreɪt] *vi* **-ated; -ating** : ulcerarse

ulcerous ['ʌlsərəs] *adj* : ulceroso

ulna ['ʌlnə] *n* : cúbito *m*

ulterior [ˌʌl'tɪriər] *adj* : oculto ⟨ulterior motive : motivo oculto, segunda intención⟩

ultimate ['ʌltəmət] *adj* **1** FINAL : último, final **2** SUPREME : supremo, máximo **3** FUNDAMENTAL : fundamental, esencial

ultimately ['ʌltəmətli] *adv* **1** FINALLY : por último, finalmente **2** EVENTUALLY : a la larga, con el tiempo

ultimatum [ˌʌltə'meɪtəm, -'mɑ-] *n, pl* **-tums** *or* **-ta** [-tə] : ultimátum *m*

ultra- [ˌʌltrə] *pref* : ultra-, super-

ultrasonic [ˌʌltrə'sɑnɪk] *adj* : ultrasónico

ultrasound [ˌʌltrə'saʊnd] *n* **1** : ultrasonido *m* **2** : ecografía *f* (técnica o imagen)

ultraviolet [ˌʌltrə'vaɪələt] *adj* : ultravioleta

umbilical cord [ˌʌm'bɪlɪkəl] *n* : cordón *m* umbilical

umbrage ['ʌmbrɪdʒ] *n* to take umbrage at : ofenderse por

umbrella [ˌʌm'brɛlə] *n* **1** : paraguas *m* **2** **beach umbrella** : sombrilla *f*

umpire¹ ['ʌmˌpaɪr] *v* **-pired; -piring** : arbitrar

umpire² *n* : árbitro *m*, -tra *f*

umpteen [ˌʌmp'ti:n] *adj* : miles de, un millón de

umpteenth [ˌʌmp'ti:nθ] *adj* : enésimo ⟨for the umpteenth time : por enésima vez⟩

un- [ˌʌn] *pref* : in-, im-, ir-, i-, des-, poco, no ⟨uncertain : incierto⟩ ⟨unforeseeable : imprevisible⟩ ⟨unreasonable : irrazonable⟩ ⟨unlimited : ilimitado⟩ ⟨unfavorable : desfavorable⟩ ⟨uncommon : poco común⟩ ⟨unresolved : no resuelto⟩ ⟨to uncurl : desenrollar⟩

unable [ˌʌn'eɪbəl] *adj* : incapaz ⟨to be unable to : no poder⟩

unabridged [ˌʌnə'brɪdʒd] *adj* : íntegro

unacceptable [ˌʌnɪk'sɛptəbəl] *adj* : inaceptable

unaccompanied [ˌʌnə'kʌmpənid] *adj* : solo, sin acompañamiento (en música)

unaccountable [ˌʌnə'kaʊntəbəl] *adj* : inexplicable, incomprensible — **unaccountably** [-bli] *adv*

unaccustomed [ˌʌnə'kʌstəmd] *adj* **1** UNUSUAL : desacostumbrado, inusual **2** UNUSED : inhabituado ⟨unaccustomed to noise : inhabituado al ruido⟩

unacquainted [ˌʌnə'kweɪntəd] *adj* to be unacquainted with : desconocer, ignorar

unadorned [ˌʌnə'dɔrnd] *adj* : sin adornos, puro y simple

unadulterated [ˌʌnə'dʌltəˌreɪtəd] *adj* **1** PURE : puro ⟨unadulterated food : comida pura⟩ **2** ABSOLUTE : completo, absoluto

unaffected [ˌʌnə'fɛktəd] *adj* **1** : no afectado, indiferente **2** NATURAL : sin afectación, natural

unaffectedly [ˌʌnəˈfɛktədli] *adv* : de manera natural

unafraid [ˌʌnəˈfreɪd] *adj* : sin miedo

unaided [ˌʌnˈeɪdəd] *adj* : sin ayuda, solo

unalterable [ˌʌnˈɔltərəbəl] *adj* : inalterable

unambiguous [ˌʌnæmˈbɪgjuəs] *adj* : inequívoco

unanimity [ˌjuːnəˈnɪmətɪ] *n* : unanimidad *f*

unanimous [juˈnænəməs] *adj* : unánime — **unanimously** *adv*

unannounced [ˌʌnəˈnaʊnst] *adj* : sin dar aviso

unanswerable [ˌʌnˈænʦərəbəl] *adj* **1** : incontestable **2** IRREFUTABLE : irrefutable, irrebatible

unanswered [ˌʌnˈænʦərd] *adj* : sin contestar

unappealing [ˌʌnəˈpiːlɪŋ] *adj* : desagradable

unarmed [ˌʌnˈɑrmd] *adj* : sin armas, desarmado

unashamed [ˌʌnəˈʃeɪmd] *adj* : sin vergüenza ⟨he's unashamed of his patriotism : no tiene reparos en demostrar su patriotismo⟩

unassailable [ˌʌnəˈseɪləbəl] *adj* IRREFUTABLE : irrefutable, irrebatible

unassisted [ˌʌnəˈsɪstəd] *adj* : sin ayuda

unassuming [ˌʌnəˈsuːmɪŋ] *adj* : modesto, sin pretensiones

unattached [ˌʌnəˈtæʧt] *adj* **1** LOOSE : suelto **2** INDEPENDENT : independiente **3** : solo (ni casado ni prometido)

unattainable [ˌʌnəˈteɪnəbəl] *adj* : inalcanzable, inasequible

unattended [ˌʌnəˈtɛndəd] *adj* : desatendido

unattractive [ˌʌnəˈtræktɪv] *adj* : poco atractivo

unauthorized [ˌʌnˈɔθəˌraɪzd] *adj* : sin autorización, no autorizado

unavailable [ˌʌnəˈveɪləbəl] *adj* : no disponible

unavoidable [ˌʌnəˈvɔɪdəbəl] *adj* : inevitable, ineludible — **unavoidably** *adv*

unaware¹ [ˌʌnəˈwær] *adv* → **unawares**

unaware² *adj* : inconsciente

unawares [ˌʌnəˈwærz] *adv* **1** : por sorpresa ⟨to catch someone unawares : agarrar a alguien desprevenido⟩ **2** UNINTENTIONALLY : inconscientemente, inadvertidamente

unbalance [ˌʌnˈbæləns] *vt* : desequilibrar

unbalanced [ˌʌnˈbælənʦt] *adj* : desequilibrado

unbearable [ˌʌnˈbærəbəl] *adj* : insoportable, inaguantable — **unbearably** [-bli] *adv*

unbeatable [ˌʌnˈbiːtəbəl] *adj* : insuperable

unbeaten [ˌʌnˈbiːtən] *adj* : invicto

unbecoming [ˌʌnbɪˈkʌmɪŋ] *adj* **1** UNSEEMLY : impropio, indecoroso **2** UNFLATTERING : poco favorecedor

unbeknownst [ˌʌbɪˈnoʊnʦt] *adj* unbeknownst to : sin el conocimiento de

unbelievable [ˌʌnbəˈliːvəbəl] *adj* : increíble — **unbelievably** [-bli] *adv*

unbend [ˌʌnˈbɛnd] *vi* -**bent** [-ˈbɛnt]; -**bending** RELAX : relajarse

unbending [ˌʌnˈbɛndɪŋ] *adj* : inflexible

unbiased [ˌʌnˈbaɪəst] *adj* : imparcial, objetivo

unblock [ˌʌnˈblɑk] *vt* : desatascar, destapar (cañería, etc.)

unbolt [ˌʌnˈboːlt] *vt* : abrir el cerrojo de, descorrer el pestillo de

unborn [ˌʌnˈbɔrn] *adj* : aún no nacido, que va a nacer

unbosom [ˌʌnˈbuːzəm, -ˈbuː-] *vt* : revelar, divulgar

unbreakable [ˌʌnˈbreɪkəbəl] *adj* : irrompible

unbreathable [ˌʌˈbriːðəbəl] *adj* : irrespirable

unbridled [ˌʌnˈbraɪdəld] *adj* : desenfrenado

unbroken [ˌʌnˈbroːkən] *adj* **1** INTACT : intacto, sano **2** CONTINUOUS : continuo, ininterrumpido

unbuckle [ˌʌnˈbʌkəl] *vt* -**led**; -**ling** : desabrochar

unburden [ˌʌnˈbərdən] *vt* **1** UNLOAD : descargar **2 to unburden oneself** : desahogarse

unbutton [ˌʌnˈbʌtən] *vt* : desabrochar, desabotonar

uncalled–for [ˌʌnˈkɔld.fɔr] *adj* : inapropiado, innecesario

uncanny [ənˈkæni] *adj* uncannier; -est **1** STRANGE : extraño **2** EXTRAORDINARY : raro, extraordinario — **uncannily** [-ˈkænəli] *adv*

uncaring [ˌʌnˈkærɪŋ] *adj* : indiferente

unceasing [ˌʌnˈsiːsɪŋ] *adj* : incesante, continuo — **unceasingly** *adv*

unceremonious [ˌʌnˌsɛrəˈmoːniəs] *adj* **1** INFORMAL : sin ceremonia, sin pompa **2** ABRUPT : abrupto, brusco — **unceremoniously** *adv*

uncertain [ˌʌnˈsərtən] *adj* **1** INDEFINITE : indeterminado **2** UNSURE : incierto, dudoso **3** CHANGEABLE : inestable, variable ⟨uncertain weather : tiempo inestable⟩ **4** HESITANT : indeciso **5** VAGUE : poco claro

uncertainly [ˌʌnˈsərtənli] *adv* : dudosamente, con desconfianza

uncertainty [ˌʌnˈsərtənti] *n, pl* -**ties** : duda *f*, incertidumbre *f*

unchain [ˌʌnˈʧeɪn] *vt* : desencadenar

unchangeable [ˌʌnˈʧeɪnʤəbəl] *adj* : inalterable, inmutable

unchanged [ˌʌnˈʧeɪnʤd] *adj* : sin cambiar

unchanging [ˌʌnˈʧeɪnʤɪŋ] *adj* : inalterable, inmutable, firme

uncharacteristic [ˌʌnˌkærɪktəˈrɪstɪk] *adj* : inusual, desacostumbrado

uncharged [ˌʌnˈʧɑrʤd] *adj* : sin carga (eléctrica)

uncharitable [ˌʌnˈʧærətəbəl] *adj* : poco caritativo

unchecked [ˌʌnˈʧɛkt] *adj* : sin freno, sin obsáculos

uncivilized [ˌʌnˈsɪvəˌlaɪzd] *adj* **1** BARBAROUS : incivilizado, bárbaro **2** WILD : salvaje

uncle [ˈʌŋkəl] *n* : tío *m*

unclean [ˌʌnˈkliːn] *adj* **1** IMPURE : impuro **2** DIRTY : sucio

unclear [ˌʌnˈklɪr] *adj* : confuso, borroso, poco claro

Uncle Sam [ˈsæm] *n* : el Tío Sam

unclog [ˌʌnˈklɑg] *vt* **-clogged; -clogging** : desatascar, destapar

unclothed [ˌʌnˈkloːðd] *adj* : desnudo

uncluttered [ˌʌnˈklʌtərd] *adj* : despejado (dícese de una habitación, etc.)

uncoil [ˌʌnˈkɔɪl] *vi* : desenroscarse — *vt* : desenroscar

uncomfortable [ˌʌnˈkʌmpfərtəbəl] *adj* **1** : incómodo (dícese de una silla, etc.) **2** UNEASY : inquieto, incómodo — **uncomfortably** *adv*

uncommitted [ˌʌnkəˈmɪtəd] *adj* : sin compromisos

uncommon [ˌʌnˈkɑmən] *adj* **1** UNUSUAL : raro, poco común **2** REMARKABLE : excepcional, extraordinario

uncommonly [ˌʌnˈkɑmənli] *adv* : extraordinariamente

uncommunicative [ˌʌnkəˈmjuːnɪˌkeɪtɪv, -kətɪv] *adj* : poco comunicativo

uncomplaining [ˌʌnkəmˈpleɪnɪŋ] *adj* : que no se queja

uncomplicated [ˌʌˈkɑmplɪˌkeɪtəd] *adj* : sencillo ⟨he's an uncomplicated person : no es una persona complicada⟩

uncompromising [ˌʌnˈkɑmprəˌmaɪzɪŋ] *adj* : inflexible, intransigente

unconcerned [ˌʌnkənˈsərnd] *adj* : indiferente — **unconcernedly** [-ˈsərnədli] *adv*

unconditional [ˌʌnkənˈdɪʃənəl] *adj* : incondicional — **unconditionally** *adv*

unconnected [ˌʌnkəˈnɛktəd] *adj* **1** UNRELATED : no relacionado, sin conexión **2** DISCONNECTED : desconectado

unconscious¹ [ˌʌnˈkɑntʃəs] *adj* : inconsciente — **unconsciously** *adv*

unconscious² *n* : inconsciente *m*

unconsciousness [ˌʌnˈkɑntʃəsnəs] *n* : inconsciencia *f*

unconstitutional [ˌʌnˌkɑntstəˈtuːʃənəl, -ˈtjuː-] *adj* : inconstitucional — **unconstitutionally** *n*

uncontrollable [ˌʌnkənˈtroːləbəl] *adj* : incontrolable, incontenible — **uncontrollably** [-bli] *adv*

uncontrolled [ˌʌnkənˈtroːld] *adj* : incontrolado

unconventional [ˌʌnkənˈvɛntʃənəl] *adj* : poco convencional

unconvinced [ˌʌnkənˈvɪntst] *adj* : no convencido, escéptico

unconvincing [ˌʌnkənˈvɪntsɪŋ] *adj* : poco convincente

uncoordinated [ˌʌnkoˈɔrdənˌeɪtəd] *adj* **1** : no coordinado **2** CLUMSY : torpe

uncork [ˌʌnˈkɔrk] *vt* : descorchar

uncorroborated [ˌʌnkəˈrɑbəˌreɪtəd] *adj* : no corroborado

uncountable [ˌʌnˈkaʊntəbəl] *adj* : no contable

uncouple [ˌʌnˈkʌpəl] *vt* : desenganchar

uncouth [ˌʌnˈkuːθ] *adj* CRUDE, ROUGH : grosero, rudo

uncover [ˌʌnˈkʌvər] *vt* **1** : destapar (un objeto), dejar al descubierto **2** EXPOSE, REVEAL : descubrir, revelar, exponer

uncultivated [ˌʌnˈkʌltəˌveɪtəd] *adj* : inculto

uncultured [ˌʌnˈkʌltʃərd] *adj* : inculto

uncurl [ˌʌnˈkərl] *vt* UNROLL : desenrollar — *vi* : desenrollarse

uncut [ˌʌnˈkʌt] *adj* **1** : sin cortar ⟨uncut grass : hierba sin cortar⟩ **2** : sin tallar, en bruto ⟨an uncut diamond : un diamante en bruto⟩ **3** UNABRIDGED : completo, íntegro

undamaged [ˌʌnˈdæmɪdʒd] *adj* : intacto, no dañado

undaunted [ˌʌnˈdɔntəd] *adj* : impávido

undecided [ˌʌndiˈsaɪdəd] *adj* **1** IRRESOLUTE : indeciso, irresoluto **2** UNRESOLVED : pendiente, no resuelto

undefeated [ˌʌndiˈfiːtəd] *adj* : invicto

undefined [ˌʌndiˈfaɪnd] *adj* : indefinido

undemanding [ˌʌndiˈmændɪŋ] *adj* : que exige poco

undeniable [ˌʌndiˈnaɪəbəl] *adj* : innegable — **undeniably** [-bli] *adv*

under¹ [ˈʌndər] *adv* **1** LESS : menos ⟨$10 or under : $10 o menos⟩ **2** UNDERWATER : debajo del agua **3** : bajo los efectos de la anestesia

under² *adj* **1** LOWER : (más) bajo, inferior **2** SUBORDINATE : inferior **3** : insuficiente ⟨an under dose of medicine : una dosis insuficiente de medicina⟩

under³ *prep* **1** BELOW, BENEATH : debajo de, abajo de ⟨under the table : abajo de la mesa⟩ ⟨we walked under the arch : pasamos por debajo del arco⟩ ⟨under the sun : bajo el sol⟩ **2** : menos de ⟨in under 20 minutes : en menos de 20 minutos⟩ **3** : bajo (un nombre, una categoría, etc.) **4** (indicating rank or authority) : bajo ⟨under the command of : bajo las órdenes de⟩ **5** SUBJECT TO : bajo ⟨under suspicion : bajo sospecha⟩ ⟨he's under stress : está estresado, sufre de estrés⟩ ⟨under the influence of alcohol : bajo los efectos del alcohol⟩ ⟨under the circumstances : dadas las circunstancias⟩ ⟨I was under the impression that . . . : tenía la impresión de que . . .⟩ **7** : en (una condición) ⟨under arrest : detenido⟩ ⟨under construction : en construcción⟩ ⟨it's under discussion : se está discutiendo⟩ **8** ACCORDING TO : según, de acuerdo con, conforme a ⟨under the present laws : según las leyes actuales⟩

under- [ˌʌndər] *pref* **1** : sub-, abajo ⟨underside : parte de abajo⟩ ⟨underlying : subyacente⟩ **2** : sub-, insuficientemente ⟨underdeveloped : subdesarrollado⟩ ⟨underestimate : subestimar⟩

underage [ˌʌndərˈeɪdʒ] *adj* : menor de edad

underarm¹ [ˈʌndərˌɑrm] *adj* : de axila, para las axilas ⟨underarm deodorant : desodorante⟩

underarm² [ˈʌndərˌɑrm] *n* ARMPIT : axila *f*, sobaco *m*

underbrush [ˈʌndərˌbrʌʃ] *n* : maleza *f*

undercarriage [ˈʌndərˌkærɪdʒ] *n* **1** CHASSIS : chassis *m*, armazón *m* **2** : tren *f* de aterrizaje (de un avión)

undercharge [ˌʌndərˈtʃɑrdʒ] *vt* : cobrarle de menos a

underclass [ˈʌndərˌklæs] *n* : clases *fpl* marginadas

underclothes [ˈʌndərˌkloːz, -ˌkloːðz] → **underwear**

underclothing [ˈʌndərˌkloːðɪŋ] → **underwear**

undercoat [ˈʌndərˌkoːt] *n* : primera capa *f* (de pintura)

undercooked [ˌʌndərˈkʊkt] *adj* : medio crudo, poco cocinado ⟨it's a little undercooked : le falta un poco de cocción⟩

undercover [ˌʌndərˈkʌvər] *adj* : secreto, clandestino

undercurrent [ˈʌndərˌkərənt] *n* 1 : corriente *f* submarina 2 UNDERTONE : corriente *f* oculta, trasfondo *m*

undercut [ˌʌndərˈkʌt] *vt* -cut; -cutting : vender más barato que

underdeveloped [ˌʌndərdɪˈvɛləpt] *adj* : subdesarrollado, atrasado

underdevelopment [ˌʌndərdɪˈvɛləpmənt] *n* : subdesarrollo *m*

underdog [ˈʌndərˌdɔg] *n* : persona *f* que tiene menos posibilidades

underdone [ˌʌndərˈdʌn] *adj* RARE : poco cocido

underestimate [ˌʌndərˈɛstəˌmeɪt] *vt* -mated; -mating : subestimar, menospreciar

underexpose [ˌʌndərɪkˈspoːz] *vt* : subexponer (en fotografía)

underexposure [ˌʌndərɪkˈspoːʒər] *vt* : subexposición *f*

underfoot [ˌʌndərˈfʊt] *adv* 1 : bajo los pies ⟨to trample underfoot : pisotear⟩ 2 to be underfoot : estorbar ⟨they're always underfoot : están siempre estorbando⟩

undergarment [ˈʌndərˌgɑrmənt] *n* : prenda *f* íntima

undergo [ˌʌndərˈgoː] *vt* -went [-ˈwɛnt], -gone [-ˈgɔn]; -going : sufrir, experimentar ⟨to undergo an operation : someterse a una intervención quirúrgica⟩

undergraduate [ˌʌndərˈgrædʒuət] *n* : estudiante *m* universitario, estudiante *f* universitaria

underground¹ [ˌʌndərˈgraʊnd] *adv* 1 : bajo tierra 2 SECRETLY : clandestinamente, en secreto ⟨to go underground : pasar a la clandestinidad⟩

underground² [ˈʌndərˌgraʊnd] *adj* 1 SUBTERRANEAN : subterráneo 2 SECRET : secreto, clandestino

underground³ [ˈʌndərˌgraʊnd] *n* : movimiento *m* o grupo *m* clandestino

undergrowth [ˈʌndərˌgroːθ] *n* : maleza *f*, broza *f*

underhand¹ [ˈʌndərˌhænd] *adv* 1 SECRETLY : de manera clandestina 2 or **underhanded** : sin levantar el brazo por encima del hombro (en deportes)

underhand² *adj* 1 SLY : solapado 2 : por debajo del hombro (en deportes)

underhanded [ˌʌndərˈhændəd] *adj* 1 SLY : solapado 2 SHADY : turbio, poco limpio

underlie [ʌndərˈlaɪ] *vt* -lay; -lain; -lying : subyacer en/a

underline [ˈʌndərˌlaɪn] *vt* -lined; -lining 1 : subrayar 2 EMPHASIZE : subrayar, acentuar, hacer hincapié en

underling [ˈʌndərlɪŋ] *n* : subordinado *m*, -da *f*; inferior *mf*

underlying [ˌʌndərˈlaɪɪŋ] *adj* 1 : subyacente ⟨the underlying rock : la roca subyacente⟩ 2 FUNDAMENTAL : fundamental, esencial

undermine [ˌʌndərˈmaɪn] *vt* -mined; -mining 1 : socavar (una estructura, etc.) 2 SAP, WEAKEN : minar, debilitar

underneath¹ [ˌʌndərˈniːθ] *adv* : debajo, abajo ⟨the part underneath : la parte de abajo⟩

underneath² *prep* : debajo de, abajo de

undernourished [ˌʌndərˈnərɪʃt] *adj* : desnutrido

underpaid [ˌʌndərˈpeɪd] *adj* : mal pagado

underpants [ˈʌndərˌpænts] *npl* : calzoncillos *mpl*, calzones *mpl*

underpass [ˈʌndərˌpæs] *n* : paso *m* a desnivel

underpay [ˌʌndərˈpeɪ] *v* -paid [-ˈpeɪd]; -paying *vt* : pagarle mal a (alguien) — *vi* : pagar mal

underprivileged [ˌʌndərˈprɪvlədʒd] *adj* : desfavorecido

underrate [ˌʌndərˈreɪt] *vt* -rated; -rating : subestimar, menospreciar

underscore [ˌʌndərˈskor] *vt* -scored; -scoring → **underline**

undersea¹ [ˌʌndərˈsiː] *or* **underseas** [-ˈsiːz] *adv* : bajo la superficie del mar

undersea² *adj* : submarino

undersecretary [ˌʌndərˈsɛkrəˌteri] *n, pl* -ries : subsecretario *m*, -ria *f*

undersell [ˌʌndərˈsɛl] *vt* -sold; -selling : vender más barato que

undeserved [ˌʌndɪˈzərvd] *adj* : inmerecido

undershirt [ˈʌndərˌʃərt] *n* : camiseta *f*

undershorts [ˈʌndərˌʃɔrts] *npl* : calzoncillos *mpl*

underside [ˈʌndərˌsaɪd, ˌʌndərˈsaɪd] *n* : parte *f* de abajo

undersigned [ˈʌndərˌsaɪnd] *n* **the undersigned** : el abajo firmante, la abajo firmante, los abajo firmantes, las abajo firmantes

undersized [ˌʌndərˈsaɪzd] *adj* : más pequeño de lo normal

understand [ˌʌndərˈstænd] *v* -stood [-ˈstʊd]; -standing *vt* 1 COMPREHEND : comprender, entender ⟨I don't understand it : no lo entiendo⟩ ⟨that's understood : eso se comprende⟩ ⟨to make oneself understood : hacerse entender⟩ 2 BELIEVE : entender ⟨to give someone to understand : dar a alguien a entender⟩ 3 INFER : tener entendido ⟨I understand that she's leaving : tengo entendido que se va⟩ — *vi* : comprender, entender

understandable [ˌʌndərˈstændəbəl] *adj* : comprensible

understanding¹ [ˌʌndərˈstændɪŋ] *adj* : comprensivo, compasivo

understanding² *n* 1 GRASP : comprensión *f*, entendimiento *m* 2 SYMPATHY

: comprensión f (mutua) **3** INTERPRE-
TATION : interpretación f ⟨it's my understanding that . . . : tengo la impresión de
que . . . , tengo entendido que . . .⟩ **4**
AGREEMENT : acuerdo m, arreglo m
understate [ˌʌndərˈsteɪt] vt **-stated; -stat-**
ing : minimizar, subestimar
understatement [ˌʌndərˈsteɪtmənt] n : atenuación f ⟨that's an understatement
: decir sólo eso es quedarse corto⟩
understudy [ˈʌndərˌstʌdi] n, pl **-dies** : sobresaliente mf, suplente mf (en el teatro)
undertake [ˌʌndərˈteɪk] vt **-took** [-ˈtʊk];
-taken [-ˈteɪkən]; **-taking 1** : emprender
(una tarea), asumir (una responsabilidad) **2** PROMISE : comprometerse (a
hacer algo)
undertaker [ˈʌndərˌteɪkər] n : director m,
-tora f de funeraria
undertaking [ˈʌndərˌteɪkɪŋ, ˌʌndərˈ-] n **1**
ENTERPRISE, TASK : empresa f, tarea f **2**
PLEDGE : promesa f, garantía f
undertone [ˈʌndərˌtoːn] n **1** : voz f baja
⟨to speak in an undertone : hablar en
voz baja⟩ **2** HINT, UNDERCURRENT
: trasfondo m, matiz m
undertow [ˈʌndərˌtoː] n : resaca f
undervalue [ˈʌndərˈvæljuː] vt **-ued; -uing**
: menospreciar, subestimar
underwater[1] [ˌʌndərˈwɔtər, -ˈwɑ-] adv
: debajo (del agua)
underwater[2] adj : submarino
under way [ˌʌndərˈweɪ] adv : en marcha,
en camino ⟨to get under way : ponerse
en marcha⟩
underwear [ˈʌndərˌwær] n : ropa f interior, ropa f íntima
underworld [ˈʌndərˌwɔrld] n **1** HELL : infierno m **2 the underworld** CRIMINALS
: la hampa, los bajos fondos
underwrite [ˈʌndərˌraɪt, ˌʌndərˈ-] vt **-wrote**
[-ˌroːt, -ˈroːt]; **-written** [-ˌrɪtən, -ˈrɪtən];
-writing 1 INSURE : asegurar **2** FI-
NANCE : financiar **3** BACK, ENDORSE
: suscribir, respaldar
underwriter [ˈʌndərˌraɪtər, ˌʌndərˈ-] n IN-
SURER : asegurador m, -dora f
undeserving [ˌʌndɪˈzərvɪŋ] adj : indigno
undesirable[1] [ˌʌndɪˈzaɪrəbəl] adj : indeseable
undesirable[2] n : indeseable mf
undeveloped [ˌʌndɪˈvɛləpt] adj : sin desarrollar, sin revelar (dícese de una
película)
undies [ˈʌndiːz] → **underwear**
undignified [ˌʌnˈdɪɡnəfaɪd] adj : indecoroso
undiluted [ˌʌndərˈluːtəd, -də-] adj : sin diluir, concentrado
undisciplined [ˌʌnˈdɪsəplənd] adj : indisciplinado
undiscovered [ˌʌndɪˈskʌvərd] adj : no
descubierto
undisputed [ˌʌndɪˈspjuːtəd] adj : indiscutible
undisturbed [ˌʌndɪˈstərbd] adj : tranquilo
(dícese de una persona), sin tocar (dícese
de un objeto)
undivided [ˌʌndɪˈvaɪdəd] adj : íntegro,
completo

undo [ˌʌnˈduː] vt **-did** [-ˈdɪd]; **-done**
[-ˈdʌn]; **-doing 1** UNFASTEN : desabrochar, desatar, abrir **2** ANNUL : anular **3** REVERSE : deshacer, reparar
(daños, etc.) **4** RUIN : arruinar, destruir
undoing [ˌʌnˈduːɪŋ] n : ruina f, perdición f
undoubted [ˌʌnˈdautəd] adj : cierto, indudable — **undoubtedly** adv
undress [ˌʌnˈdrɛs] vt : desvestir, desabrigar,
desnudar — vi : desvestirse, desnudarse
undue [ˌʌnˈduː, -ˈdjuː] adj : excesivo, indebido — **unduly** adv
undulate [ˈʌndʒəˌleɪt] vi **-lated; -lating**
: ondular
undulation [ˌʌndʒəˈleɪʃən] n : ondulación f
undying [ˌʌnˈdaɪɪŋ] adj : perpetuo, imperecedero
unearth [ˌʌnˈərθ] vt **1** EXHUME : desenterrar, exhumar **2** DISCOVER : descubrir
unearthly [ˌʌnˈərθli] adj **unearthlier; -est**
: sobrenatural, de otro mundo
unease [ˌʌnˈiːz] n : inquietud f
uneasily [ˌʌnˈiːzəli] adv : inquietamente,
con inquietud
uneasiness [ˌʌnˈiːzinəs] n : inquietud f
uneasy [ˌʌnˈiːzi] adj **uneasier; -est 1**
AWKWARD : incómodo **2** WORRIED
: preocupado, inquieto **3** RESTLESS : inquieto, agitado
uneducated [ˌʌnˈɛdʒəˌkeɪtəd] adj : inculto, sin educación
unemotional [ˌʌniˈmoːʃənəl] adj **1** COLD
: frío, indiferente **2** IMPARTIAL : imparcial, objetivo
unemployed [ˌʌnɪmˈplɔɪd] adj : desempleado
unemployment [ˌʌnɪmˈplɔɪmənt] n : desempleo m
unending [ˌʌnˈɛndɪŋ] adj ENDLESS : interminable, inacabable, sin fin
unenthusiastic [ˌʌnɪmˌθuːziˈæstɪk, -ɛn-,
-ˌθjuː-] adj : poco entusiasta, tibio
unenviable [ˌʌnˈɛnviəbəl] adj : nada envidiable
unequal [ˌʌnˈiːkwəl] adj **1** : desigual **2**
INADEQUATE : incapaz, incompetente
⟨to be unequal to a task : no estar a la
altura de una tarea⟩
unequaled or **unequalled** [ˌʌnˈiːkwəld]
adj : sin igual
unequivocal [ˌʌnɪˈkwɪvəkəl] adj : inequívoco, claro — **unequivocally** adv
unerring [ˌʌnˈɛrɪŋ, -ˈər-] adj : infalible
unethical [ˌʌnˈɛθɪkəl] adj : poco ético
uneven [ˌʌnˈiːvən] adj **1** ODD : impar
(dícese de un número) **2** : desigual, disparejo, desnivelado (dícese de una superficie) ⟨uneven terrain : terreno acciden-
tado⟩ **3** IRREGULAR : irregular,
desigual, disparejo **4** UNEQUAL
: desigual — **unevenly** [ˌʌnˈiːvənli] adv
unevenness [ˌʌnˈiːvənnəs] n **1** : lo
desigual, lo desnivelado (de una superficie) **2** IRREGULARITY : irregularidad
f **3** : lo desigual (de una contienda, etc.)
uneventful [ˌʌnɪˈvɛntfəl] adj : sin incidentes, tranquilo
unexpected [ˌʌnɪkˈspɛktəd] adj : imprevisto, inesperado — **unexpectedly** adv

unexplored [ˌʌnɪk'splɔrd] *adj* : inexplorado

unfailing [ˌʌn'feɪlɪŋ] *adj* **1** CONSTANT : constante **2** INEXHAUSTIBLE : inagotable **3** SURE : a toda prueba, indefectible

unfair [ˌʌn'fær] *adj* : injusto — **unfairly** *adv*

unfairness [ˌʌn'færnəs] *n* : injusticia *f*

unfaithful [ˌʌn'feɪθfəl] *adj* : desleal, infiel — **unfaithfully** *adv*

unfaithfulness [ˌʌn'feɪθfəlnəs] *n* : infidelidad *f*, deslealtad *f*

unfamiliar [ˌʌnfə'mɪljər] *adj* **1** STRANGE : desconocido, extraño ⟨an unfamiliar place : un lugar nuevo⟩ **2 to be unfamiliar with** : no estar familiarizado con, desconocer

unfamiliarity [ˌʌnfəˌmɪli'ærəti] *n* : falta *f* de familiaridad

unfashionable [ˌʌn'fæʃənəbəl] *adj* : fuera de moda

unfasten [ˌʌn'fæsən] *vt* : desabrochar, desatar (una cuerda, etc.), abrir (una puerta)

unfavorable [ˌʌn'feɪvərəbəl] *adj* : desfavorable, mal — **unfavorably** [-bli] *adv*

unfeeling [ˌʌn'fiːlɪŋ] *adj* : insensible — **unfeelingly** *adv*

unfinished [ˌʌn'fɪnɪʃd] *adj* : inacabado, incompleto

unfit [ˌʌn'fɪt] *adj* **1** UNSUITABLE : inadecuado, impropio **2** UNSUITED : no apto, incapaz **3** : incapacitado (físicamente) ⟨to be unfit : no estar en forma⟩

unflagging [ˌʌn'flægɪŋ] *adj* : inagotable

unflappable [ˌʌn'flæpəbəl] *adj* : imperturbable

unflattering [ˌʌn'flætərɪŋ] *adj* : poco favorecedor

unfold [ˌʌn'foːld] *vt* **1** EXPAND : desplegar, desdoblar, extender ⟨to unfold a map : desplegar un mapa⟩ **2** DISCLOSE, REVEAL : revelar, exponer (un plan, etc.) — *vi* **1** DEVELOP : desarrollarse, desenvolverse ⟨the story unfolded : el cuento se desarrolló⟩ **2** EXPAND : extenderse, desplegarse

unforeseeable [ˌʌnfor'siːəbəl] *adj* : imprevisible

unforeseen [ˌʌnfor'siːn] *adj* : imprevisto

unforgettable [ˌʌnfor'ɡeṱəbəl] *adj* : inolvidable, memorable — **unforgettably** [-bli] *adv*

unforgivable [ˌʌnfor'ɡɪvəbəl] *adj* : imperdonable

unfortunate¹ [ˌʌn'fɔrtʃənət] *adj* **1** UNLUCKY : desgraciado, infortunado, desafortunado ⟨how unfortunate! : ¡qué mala suerte!⟩ **2** INAPPROPRIATE : inoportuno ⟨an unfortunate comment : un comentario poco feliz⟩

unfortunate² *n* : desgraciado *m*, -da *f*

unfortunately [ˌʌn'fɔrtʃənətli] *adv* : desafortunadamente

unfounded [ˌʌn'faʊndəd] *adj* : infundado

unfreeze [ˌʌn'friːz] *v* **-froze** [-'froːz]; **-frozen** [-'froːzən]; **-freezing** *vt* : descongelar — *vi* : descongelarse

unfriend [ˌʌn'frɛnd] *vt* : eliminar (a alguien) de sus amigos (en una red social)

unfriendliness [ˌʌn'frɛndlinəs] *n* : hostilidad *f*, antipatía *f*

unfriendly [ˌʌn'frɛndli] *adj* **unfriendlier; -est** : poco amistoso, hostil

unfulfilled [ˌʌnfʊl'fɪld] *adj* **1** UNSATISFIED : insatisfecho **2** : no realizado

unfurl [ˌʌn'fərl] *vt* : desplegar, desdoblar — *vi* : desplegarse

unfurnished [ˌʌn'fərnɪʃt] *adj* : desamueblado

ungainly [ˌʌn'ɡeɪnli] *adj* : desgarbado

ungodly [ˌʌn'ɡɑdli, -'ɡɑd-] *adj* **1** IMPIOUS : impío **2** OUTRAGEOUS : atroz, terrible ⟨at an ungodly hour : a una hora intempestiva⟩

ungovernable [ˌʌn'ɡʌvərnəbəl] *adj* : ingobernable

ungracious [ˌʌn'ɡreɪʃəs] *adj* : descortés

ungrateful [ˌʌn'ɡreɪtfəl] *adj* : desagradecido, ingrato — **ungratefully** *adv*

ungratefulness [ˌʌn'ɡreɪtfəlnəs] *n* : ingratitud *f*

unguarded [ˌʌn'ɡɑrdəd] *adj* **1** CARELESS : irreflexivo, desprevenido **2** UNPROTECTED : sin vigilancia, no vigilado

unhappily [ˌʌn'hæpəli] *adv* **1** SADLY : tristemente **2** UNFORTUNATELY : desafortunadamente, lamentablemente

unhappiness [ˌʌn'hæpinəs] *n* : infelicidad *f*, tristeza *f*, desdicha *f*

unhappy [ˌʌn'hæpi] *adj* **unhappier; -est 1** UNFORTUNATE : desafortunado, desventurado **2** MISERABLE, SAD : infeliz, triste, desdichado **3** INOPPORTUNE : inoportuno, poco feliz

unharmed [ˌʌn'hɑrmd] *adj* : salvo, ileso

unhealthy [ˌʌn'hɛlθi] *adj* **unhealthier; -est 1** UNWHOLESOME : insalubre, malsano, nocivo a la salud ⟨an unhealthy climate : un clima insalubre⟩ **2** SICKLY : de mala salud, enfermizo

unheard-of [ˌʌn'hərdəv] *adj* : sin precedente, inaudito, insólito

unhelpful [ˌʌn'hɛlpfəl] *adj* : poco servicial (dícese de personas), inútil (dícese de consejos, etc.)

unhinge [ˌʌn'hɪndʒ] *vt* **-hinged; -hinging 1** : desquiciar (una puerta, etc.) **2** DISRUPT, UNSETTLE : trastornar, perturbar

unhitch [ˌʌn'hɪtʃ] *vt* : desenganchar

unholy [ˌʌn'hoːli] *adj* **unholier; -est 1** : profano, impío **2** UNGODLY : atroz, terrible

unhook [ˌʌn'hʊk] *vt* **1** : desenganchar, descolgar (de algo) **2** UNDO : desabrochar

unhurried [ˌʌn'hərid] *adj* : lento, sin prisas

unhurt [ˌʌn'hərt] *adj* : ileso

unhygienic [ˌʌnhaɪ'dʒɛnɪk, -'dʒiː-, -ˌhaɪdʒi'ɛnɪk] *adj* : antihigiénico

unicorn ['juːnəˌkɔrn] *n* : unicornio *m*

unidentified [ˌʌnaɪ'dɛntəˌfaɪd] *adj* : no identificado ⟨unidentified flying object : objeto volador no identificado⟩

unification [ˌjuːnəfə'keɪʃən] *n* : unificación *f*

uniform¹ ['juːnəˌfɔrm] *adj* : uniforme, homogéneo, constante — **uniformly** *adv*

uniform[2] *n* : uniforme *m*
uniformed [ˈjuːnəˌfɔrmd] *adj* : uniformado
uniformity [ˌjuːnəˈfɔrməti] *n, pl* **-ties** : uniformidad *f*
unify [ˈjuːnəˌfaɪ] *vt* **-fied; -fying** : unificar, unir
unilateral [ˌjuːnəˈlætərəl] *adj* : unilateral — **unilaterally** *adv*
unimaginable [ˌʌnɪˈmædʒənəbəl] *adj* : inimaginable, inconcebible
unimaginative [ˌʌnɪˈmædʒənətɪv, -ə,neɪtɪv] *adj* : poco imaginativo
unimportant [ˌʌnɪmˈpɔrtənt] *adj* : intrascendente, insignificante, sin importancia
unimpressive [ˌʌnɪmˈprɛsɪv] *adj* : mediocre
uninformed [ˌʌnɪnˈfɔrmd] *adj* : no enterado
uninhabitable [ˌʌnɪnˈhæbətəbəl] *adj* : inhabitable
uninhabited [ˌʌnɪnˈhæbətəd] *adj* : deshabitado, desierto, despoblado
uninhibited [ˌʌnɪnˈhɪbətəd] *adj* : desenfadado, desinhibido, sin reservas
uninjured [ˌʌnˈɪndʒərd] *adj* : ileso
unintelligent [ˌʌnɪnˈtɛlədʒənt] *adj* : poco inteligente
unintelligible [ˌʌnɪnˈtɛlədʒəbəl] *adj* : ininteligible, incomprensible
unintentional [ˌʌnɪnˈtɛntʃənəl] *adj* : no deliberado, involuntario
unintentionally [ˌʌnɪnˈtɛntʃənəli] *adv* : involuntariamente, sin querer
uninterested [ˌʌnˈɪntəˌrɛstəd, -trəstəd] *adj* : indiferente
uninteresting [ˌʌnˈɪntəˌrɛstɪŋ, -trəstɪŋ] *adj* : poco interesante, sin interés
uninterrupted [ˌʌnɪntəˈrʌptəd] *adj* : ininterrumpido, continuo
uninvited [ˌʌnɪnˈvaɪtəd] *adj* : no invitado ⟨she showed up uninvited : vino sin que nadie la invitara⟩
uninviting [ˌʌnɪnˈvaɪtɪŋ] *adj* : poco acogedor (dícese de una casa, etc.), poco atractivo
union [ˈjuːnjən] *n* **1** : unión *f* **2** *or* **labor union** : sindicato *m*, gremio *m*
unionism [ˈjuːnjəˌnɪzəm] *n* : sindicalismo *m* — **unionist** [ˈjuːnjənɪst] *n*
unionize [ˈjuːnjəˌnaɪz] *v* **-ized; -izing** *vt* : sindicalizar, sindicar — *vi* : sindicalizarse
unique [juˈniːk] *adj* **1** SOLE : único, solo **2** UNUSUAL : extraordinario
uniquely [juˈniːkli] *adv* **1** EXCLUSIVELY : exclusivamente **2** EXCEPTIONALLY : excepcionalmente
uniqueness [juˈniːknəs] *n* : singularidad *f*
unison [ˈjuːnəsən, -zən] *n* **1** : unísono *m* (en música) **2** CONCORD : acuerdo *m*, armonía *f*, concordia *f* **3 in ~** SIMULTANEOUSLY : simultáneamente, al unísono
unit [ˈjuːnɪt] *n* **1** : unidad *f* **2** : módulo *m* (de un mobiliario)
unitary [ˈjuːnəˌtɛri] *adj* : unitario
unite [juˈnaɪt] *v* **united; uniting** *vt* : unir, juntar, combinar — *vi* : unirse, juntarse
unity [ˈjuːnəti] *n, pl* **-ties 1** UNION : unidad *f*, unión *f* **2** HARMONY : armonía *f*, acuerdo *m*

universal [ˌjuːnəˈvərsəl] *adj* **1** GENERAL : general, universal ⟨a universal rule : una regla universal⟩ **2** WORLDWIDE : universal, mundial — **universality** *n* — **universally** *adv*
universe [ˈjuːnəˌvərs] *n* : universo *m*
university [ˌjuːnəˈvərsəti] *n, pl* **-ties** : universidad *f*
unjust [ˌʌnˈdʒʌst] *adj* : injusto — **unjustly** *adv*
unjustifiable [ˌʌnˌdʒʌstəˈfaɪəbəl] *adj* : injustificable — **unjustifiably** *adv*
unjustified [ˌʌnˈdʒʌstəˌfaɪd] *adj* : injustificado
unkempt [ˌʌnˈkɛmpt] *adj* : descuidado, desaliñado, despeinado (dícese del pelo)
unkind [ˌʌnˈkaɪnd] *adj* : poco amable, cruel — **unkindly** *adv*
unkindness [ˌʌnˈkaɪndnəs] *n* : crueldad *f*, falta *f* de amabilidad
unknowing [ˌʌnˈnoːɪŋ] *adj* : inconsciente, ignorante — **unknowingly** *adv*
unknown [ˌʌnˈnoːn] *adj* : desconocido
unlawful [ˌʌnˈlɔfəl] *adj* : ilícito, ilegal — **unlawfully** *adv*
unleaded [ˌʌnˈlɛdəd] *adj* : sin plomo
unleash [ˌʌnˈliːʃ] *vt* : soltar, desatar
unless [ənˈlɛs] *conj* : a menos que, salvo que, a no ser que
unlike[1] [ˌʌnˈlaɪk] *adj* **1** DIFFERENT : diferente, distinto **2** UNEQUAL : desigual
unlike[2] *prep* **1** : diferente de, distinto de ⟨unlike the others : distinto a los demás⟩ **2** : a diferencia de ⟨unlike her sister, she is shy : a diferencia de su hermana, es tímida⟩
unlikelihood [ˌʌnˈlaɪkliˌhʊd] *n* : improbabilidad *f*
unlikely [ˌʌnˈlaɪkli] *adj* **unlikelier; -est 1** IMPROBABLE : improbable, poco probable **2** UNPROMISING : poco prometedor
unlimited [ˌʌnˈlɪmətəd] *adj* : ilimitado
unlisted [ˌʌnˈlɪstəd] *adj* : que no aparece en la guía telefónica
unload [ˌʌnˈloːd] *vt* **1** REMOVE : descargar, desembarcar (mercancías o pasajeros) **2** : descargar (un avión, un camión, etc.) **3** DUMP : deshacerse de — *vi* : descargar (dícese de un avión, un camión, etc.)
unlock [ˌʌnˈlɑk] *vt* **1** : abrir (con llave) **2** DISCLOSE, REVEAL : revelar
unluckily [ˌʌnˈlʌkəli] *adv* : desgraciadamente
unlucky [ˌʌnˈlʌki] *adj* **unluckier; -est 1** : de mala suerte, desgraciado, desafortunado ⟨an unlucky year : un año de mala suerte⟩ **2** INAUSPICIOUS : desfavorable, poco propicio **3** REGRETTABLE : lamentable
unmanageable [ˌʌnˈmænɪdʒəbəl] *adj* : difícil de controlar, poco manejable, ingobernable
unmanned [ˌʌnˈmænd] *adj* : no tripulado, sin tripulación
unmarried [ˌʌnˈmærid] *adj* : soltero
unmask [ˌʌnˈmæsk] *vt* EXPOSE : desenmascarar
unmerciful [ˌʌnˈmərsɪfəl] *adj* MERCILESS : despiadado — **unmercifully** *adv*

unmistakable [ˌʌnmɪˈsteɪkəbəl] *adj* : evidente, inconfundible, obvio — **unmistakably** [-bli] *adv*

unmotivated [ˌʌnˈmoːt̬əˌveɪt̬əd] *adj* : inmotivado

unmoved [ˌʌnˈmuːvd] *adj* : impasible ⟨to be unmoved by : permanecer impasible ante⟩

unnatural [ˌʌnˈnætʃərəl] *adj* 1 ABNORMAL, UNUSUAL : anormal, poco natural, poco normal 2 AFFECTED : afectado, forzado ⟨an unnatural smile : una sonrisa forzada⟩ 3 PERVERSE : perverso, antinatural

unnecessary [ˌʌnˈnɛsəˌseri] *adj* : innecesario — **unnecessarily** [-ˌnɛsəˈserəli] *adv*

unnerve [ˌʌnˈnərv] *vt* **-nerved; -nerving** : turbar, desconcertar, poner nervioso

unnoticed [ˌʌnˈnoːt̬əst] *adj* : inadvertido ⟨to go unnoticed : pasar inadvertido⟩

unobjectionable [ˌʌnəbˈdʒɛkʃənəbəl] *adj* : inobjetable

unobstructed [ˌʌnəbˈstrʌktəd] *adj* : libre, despejado

unobtainable [ˌʌnəbˈteɪnəbəl] *adj* : inasequible

unobtrusive [ˌʌnəbˈstruːsɪv] *adj* : discreto

unoccupied [ˌʌnˈɑkjəˌpaɪd] *adj* 1 IDLE : desempleado, desocupado 2 EMPTY : desocupado, libre, deshabitado

unofficial [ˌʌnˈfɪʃəl] *adj* : extraoficial, no oficial, oficioso

unopened [ˌʌnˈoːpənd] *adj* : sin abrir

unorganized [ˌʌnˈɔrɡəˌnaɪzd] *adj* : desorganizado

unorthodox [ˌʌnˈɔrθəˌdɑks] *adj* : poco ortodoxo, poco convencional

unpack [ˌʌnˈpæk] *vt* : desempacar — *vi* : desempacar, deshacer las maletas

unpaid [ˌʌnˈpeɪd] *adj* : no remunerado, no retribuido ⟨an unpaid bill : una cuenta pendiente⟩

unparalleled [ˌʌnˈpærəˌlɛld] *adj* : sin igual

unpatriotic [ˌʌnˌpeɪtriˈɑt̬ɪk] *adj* : antipatriótico

unpayable [ˌʌnˈpeɪəbəl] *adj* : impagable

unpleasant [ˌʌnˈplɛzənt] *adj* : desagradable — **unpleasantly** *adv*

unplug [ˌʌnˈplʌɡ] *vt* **-plugged; -plugging** 1 UNCLOG : destapar, desatascar 2 DISCONNECT : desconectar, desenchufar

unpolished [ˌʌnˈpɑlɪʃt] *adj* IMPERFECT : poco pulido

unpopular [ˌʌnˈpɑpjələr] *adj* : impopular, poco popular

unprecedented [ˌʌnˈprɛsəˌdɛntəd] *adj* : sin precedentes, inaudito, nuevo

unpredictable [ˌʌnpriˈdɪktəbəl] *adj* : impredecible

unprejudiced [ˌʌnˈprɛdʒədəst] *adj* : imparcial, objetivo

unprepared [ˌʌnpriˈpærd] *adj* : no preparado ⟨an unprepared speech : un discurso improvisado⟩

unpretentious [ˌʌnpriˈtɛntʃəs] *adj* : modesto, sin pretensiones

unprincipled [ˌʌnˈprɪntsəpəld] *adj* : sin principios, carente de escrúpulos

unproductive [ˌʌnprəˈdʌktɪv] *adj* : improductivo

unprofessional [ˌʌnprəˈfɛʃənəl] *adj* : poco profesional

unprofitable [ˌʌnˈprɑfət̬əbəl] *adj* : no rentable, poco provechoso

unpromising [ˌʌnˈprɑməsɪŋ] *adj* : poco prometedor

unprotected [ˌʌnprəˈtɛktəd] *adj* : sin protección, desprotegido

unproven [ˌʌnˈpruːvən] *adj* : no demostrado

unprovoked [ˌʌnprəˈvoːkt] *adj* : no provocado

unpublished [ˌʌnˈpʌblɪʃt] *adj* : inédito

unpunished [ˌʌnˈpʌnɪʃt] *adj* : impune ⟨to go unpunished : escapar sin castigo⟩

unqualified [ˌʌnˈkwɑləˌfaɪd] *adj* 1 : no calificado, sin título 2 COMPLETE : completo, absoluto ⟨an unqualified denial : una negación incondicional⟩

unquestionable [ˌʌnˈkwɛstʃənəbəl] *adj* : incuestionable, indudable, indiscutible — **unquestionably** [-bli] *adv*

unquestioning [ˌʌnˈkwɛstʃənɪŋ] *adj* : incondicional, absoluto, ciego

unravel [ˌʌnˈrævəl] *v* **-eled** *or* **-elled; -eling** *or* **-elling** *vt* 1 DISENTANGLE : desenmarañar, desenredar 2 SOLVE : aclarar, desenmarañar, desentrañar — *vi* : deshacerse

unreachable [ˌʌnˈriːtʃəbəl] *adj* : inalcanzable

unreadable [ˌʌnˈriːdəbəl] *adj* 1 ILLEGIBLE : ilegible 2 : difícil de leer

unreal [ˌʌnˈriːl] *adj* : irreal

unrealistic [ˌʌnˌriːəˈlɪstɪk] *adj* : poco realista

unreasonable [ˌʌnˈriːzənəbəl] *adj* 1 IRRATIONAL : poco razonable, irrazonable, irracional 2 EXCESSIVE : excesivo ⟨unreasonable prices : precios excesivos⟩

unreasonably [ˌʌnˈriːzənəbli] *adv* 1 IRRATIONALLY : irracionalmente, de manera irrazonable 2 EXCESSIVELY : excesivamente

unrecognizable [ˌʌnˈrɛkəɡˌnaɪzəbəl] *adj* : irreconocible

unrefined [ˌʌnriˈfaɪnd] *adj* 1 : no refinado, sin refinar (dícese del azúcar, de la harina, etc.) 2 : poco refinado, inculto (dícese de una persona)

unrelated [ˌʌnriˈleɪt̬əd] *adj* : no relacionado, inconexo

unrelenting [ˌʌnriˈlɛntɪŋ] *adj* 1 STERN : severo, inexorable 2 CONSTANT, RELENTLESS : constante, implacable

unreliable [ˌʌnriˈlaɪəbəl] *adj* : que no es de fiar, de poca confianza, inestable (dícese del tiempo)

unrepeatable [ˌʌnriˈpiːt̬əbəl] *adj* : irrepetible

unrepentant [ˌʌnriˈpɛntənt] *adj* : impenitente

unrepresentative [ˌʌnˌrɛprɪˈzɛntət̬ɪv] *adj* : poco representativo

unrequited [ˌʌnriˈkwaɪt̬əd] *adj* : no correspondido

unreserved [ˌʌnrɪˈzərvd] *adv* 1 UNLIMITED : sin reservas 2 : sin reservar

unresolved [ˌʌnri'zɑlvd] *adj* : pendiente, no resuelto

unresponsive [ˌʌnri'spɑntsɪv] *adj* 1 : indiferente 2 : insensible, inconsciente (en medicina)

unrest [ˌʌn'rɛst] *n* : inquietud *f*, malestar *m* ⟨political unrest : disturbios políticos⟩

unrestrained [ˌʌnri'streɪnd] *adj* : desenfrenado, incontrolado

unrestricted [ˌʌnri'strɪktəd] *adj* : sin restricción ⟨unrestricted access : libre acceso⟩

unrewarding [ˌʌnri'wɔrdɪŋ] *adj* THANKLESS : ingrato

unripe [ˌʌn'raɪp] *adj* : inmaduro, verde

unrivaled *or* **unrivalled** [ˌʌn'raɪvəld] *adj* : incomparable

unroll [ˌʌn'ro:l] *vt* : desenrollar — *vi* : desenrollarse

unruffled [ˌʌn'rʌfəld] *adj* 1 SERENE : sereno, tranquilo 2 SMOOTH : tranquilo, liso ⟨unruffled waters : aguas tranquilas⟩

unruliness [ˌʌn'ru:linəs] *n* : indisciplina *f*

unruly [ˌʌn'ru:li] *adj* : indisciplinado, díscolo, rebelde

unsafe [ˌʌn'seɪf] *adj* : inseguro

unsaid [ˌʌn'sɛd] *adj* : sin decir ⟨to leave unsaid : quedar por decir⟩

unsalted [ˌʌn'sɔltəd] *adj* : sin sal

unsanitary [ˌʌn'sænəˌteri] *adj* : antihigiénico

unsatisfactory [ˌʌnˌsætəs'fæktəri] *adj* : insatisfactorio

unsatisfied [ˌʌn'sætəsˌfaɪd] *adj* : insatisfecho

unsavory [ˌʌn'seɪvəri] *adj* : desagradable

unscathed [ˌʌn'skeɪðd] *adj* UNHARMED : ileso

unscheduled [ˌʌn'skɛˌdʒu:ld] *adj* : no programado, imprevisto

unscientific [ˌʌnˌsaɪən'tɪfɪk] *adj* : poco científico

unscramble [ˌʌn'skræmbəl] *vt* : descifrar, descodificar (una señal, etc.)

unscrew [ˌʌn'skru:] *vt* 1 : quitar (una tapa, etc.) 2 : destornillar

unscrupulous [ˌʌn'skru:pjələs] *adj* : inescrupuloso, sin escrúpulos — **unscrupulously** *adv*

unseal [ˌʌn'si:l] *vt* : abrir, quitarle el sello a

unseasonable [ˌʌn'si:zənəbəl] *adj* 1 : extemporáneo ⟨unseasonable rain : lluvia extemporánea⟩ 2 UNTIMELY : extemporáneo, inoportuno

unseat [ˌʌn'si:t] *vt* : derribar, derrocar

unseemly [ˌʌn'si:mli] *adj* **unseemlier; -est** 1 INDECOROUS : indecoroso 2 INAPPROPRIATE : impropio, inapropiado

unseen [ˌʌn'si:n] *adj* 1 UNNOTICED : inadvertido 2 INVISIBLE : oculto, invisible

unselfish [ˌʌn'sɛlfɪʃ] *adj* : generoso, desinteresado — **unselfishly** *adv*

unselfishness [ˌʌn'sɛlfɪʃnəs] *n* : generosidad *f*, desinterés *m*

unsentimental [ˌʌnˌsɛntə'mɛntəl] *adj* : poco sentimental

unsettle [ˌʌn'sɛtəl] *vt* **-tled; -tling** DISTURB : trastornar, alterar, perturbar

unsettled [ˌʌn'sɛtəld] *adj* 1 CHANGEABLE : inestable, variable ⟨unsettled weather : tiempo inestable⟩ 2 DISTURBED : agitado, inquieto ⟨unsettled waters : aguas agitadas⟩ 3 UNDECIDED : pendiente (dícese de un asunto), indeciso (dícese de una persona) 4 UNPAID : sin saldar, pendiente 5 UNINHABITED : despoblado, no colonizado

unsettling [ˌʌn'sɛtəlɪŋ] *adj* : inquietante

unshakable [ˌʌn'ʃeɪkəbəl] *adj* : inquebrantable

unshaped [ˌʌn'ʃeɪpt] *adj* : sin forma, informe

unshaven [ˌʌn'ʃeɪvən] *adj* : sin afeitar, sin rasurar

unsheathe [ˌʌn'ʃi:ð] *vt* : desenvainar

unsightly [ˌʌn'saɪtli] *adj* UGLY : feo, de aspecto malo

unsigned [ˌʌn'saɪnd] *adj* : sin firmar

unskilled [ˌʌn'skɪld] *adj* : no calificado

unsmiling [ˌʌn'smaɪlɪŋ] *adj* : de aspecto serio

unsnap [ˌʌn'snæp] *vt* **-snapped; -snapping** : desabrochar

unsociable [ˌʌn'so:ʃəbəl] *adj* : poco sociable

unsolicited [ˌʌnsə'lɪsətəd] *adj* : no solicitado

unsolved [ˌʌn'sɑlvd] *adj* : no resuelto, sin resolver

unsophisticated [ˌʌnsə'fɪstəˌkeɪtəd] *adj* 1 NAIVE : ingenuo, de poco mundo 2 SIMPLE : simple, poco sofisticado, rudimentario

unsound [ˌʌn'saʊnd] *adj* 1 UNHEALTHY : enfermizo, de mala salud 2 : poco sólido, defectuoso (dícese de una estructura, etc.) 3 INVALID : inválido, erróneo 4 of unsound mind : mentalmente incapacitado

unspeakable [ˌʌn'spi:kəbəl] *adj* 1 INDESCRIBABLE : indecible, inexpresable, incalificable 2 HEINOUS : atroz, nefando, abominable — **unspeakably** [-bli] *adv*

unspecified [ˌʌn'spɛsəˌfaɪd] *adj* : indeterminado, sin especificar

unspoiled [ˌʌn'spɔɪld] *adj* 1 : conservado, sin estropear (dícese de un lugar) 2 : que no está mimado (dícese de un niño)

unspoken [ˌʌn'spo:kən] *adj* TACIT : tácito

unstable [ˌʌn'steɪbəl] *adj* 1 CHANGEABLE : variable, inestable, cambiable ⟨an unstable pulse : un pulso irregular⟩ 2 UNSTEADY : inestable, poco sólido (dícese de una estructura)

unsteadily [ˌʌn'stɛdəli] *adv* : de modo inestable

unsteadiness [ˌʌn'stɛdinəs] *n* : inestabilidad *f*, inseguridad *f*

unsteady [ˌʌn'stɛdi] *adj* 1 UNSTABLE : inestable, variable 2 SHAKY : tembloroso

unstoppable [ˌʌn'stɑpəbəl] *adj* : irrefrenable, incontenible

unsubscribe [ˌʌnsəb'skraɪb] *vi* **-scribed; -scribing** : darse de baja, cancelar la suscripción

unsubstantiated [ˌʌnsəb'stæntʃiˌeɪtəd] *adj* : no corroborado, no demostrado

unsuccessful [ˌʌnsək'sɛsfəl] *adj* : fracasado, infructuoso

unsuitable [ˌʌn'suːtəbəl] *adj* : inadecuado, impropio, inapropiado ⟨an unsuitable time : una hora inconveniente⟩

unsuited [ˌʌn'suːtəd] *adj* : inadecuado, inepto

unsung [ˌʌn'sʌŋ] *adj* : olvidado

unsure [ˌʌn'ʃʊr] *adj* : incierto, dudoso

unsurpassed [ˌʌnsər'pæst] *adj* : sin par, sin igual

unsuspecting [ˌʌnsə'spɛktɪŋ] *adj* : desprevenido, desapercibido, confiado

unsweetened [ˌʌn'swiːtənd] *adj* : sin endulzar

unsympathetic [ˌʌnˌsɪmpə'θɛtɪk] *adj* : poco comprensivo, indiferente

untamed [ˌʌn'teɪmd] *adj* : indómito, agreste

untangle [ˌʌn'tæŋgəl] *vt* **-gled; -gling** : desenmarañar, desenredar

untapped [ˌʌn'tæpt] *adj* : sin explotar

untenable [ˌʌn'tɛnəbəl] *adj* : insostenible

unthinkable [ˌʌn'θɪŋkəbəl] *adj* : inconcebible, impensable

unthinking [ˌʌn'θɪŋkɪŋ] *adj* : irreflexivo, inconsciente — **unthinkingly** *adv*

untidiness [ˌʌn'taɪdinəs] *n* : desarreglo *m*

untidy [ˌʌn'taɪdi] *adj* **1** SLOVENLY : desaliñado **2** DISORDERLY : desordenado, desarreglado — **untidily** *adv*

untie [ˌʌn'taɪ] *vt* **-tied; -tying** *or* **-tieing** : desatar, deshacer

until[1] [ˌʌn'tɪl] *prep* : hasta ⟨until now : hasta ahora⟩

until[2] *conj* : hasta que ⟨until they left : hasta que salieron⟩ ⟨don't answer until you're sure : no contestes hasta que (no) estés seguro⟩

untimely [ˌʌn'taɪmli] *adj* **1** PREMATURE : prematuro ⟨an untimely death : una muerte prematura⟩ **2** INOPPORTUNE : inoportuno, intempestivo

untold [ˌʌn'toːld] *adj* **1** : nunca dicho ⟨the untold secret : el secreto sin contar⟩ **2** INCALCULABLE : incalculable, indecible

untouchable [ˌʌn'tʌtʃəbəl] *adj* : intocable

untouched [ˌʌn'tʌtʃt] *adj* **1** INTACT : intacto, sin tocar, sin probar (dícese de la comida) **2** UNAFFECTED : insensible, indiferente

untoward [ˌʌn'tord, -'toːord, -tə-'word] *adj* **1** : indecoroso, impropio (dícese del comportamiento) **2** ADVERSE, UNFORTUNATE : desafortunado, adverso ⟨untoward effects : efectos perjudiciales⟩ **3** UNSEEMLY : indecoroso

untrained [ˌʌn'treɪnd] *adj* : inexperto, no capacitado

untreated [ˌʌn'triːtəd] *adj* : no tratado (dícese de una enfermedad, etc.), sin tratar (dícese de un material)

untroubled [ˌʌn'trʌbəld] *adj* : tranquilo ⟨to be untroubled by : no estar afectado por⟩

untrue [ˌʌn'truː] *adj* **1** UNFAITHFUL : infiel **2** FALSE : falso

untrustworthy [ˌʌn'trʌstˌwərði] *adj* : de poca confianza (dícese de una persona), no fidedigno (dícese de la información)

untruth [ˌʌn'truːθ, 'ʌnˌ-] *n* : mentira *f*, falsedad *f*

untruthful [ˌʌn'truːθfəl] *adj* : mentiroso, falso

unusable [ˌʌn'juːzəbəl] *adj* : inútil, inservible

unused [ˌʌn'juːzd, in sense 1 usu -'juːst] *adj* **1** UNACCUSTOMED : inhabituado **2** NEW : nuevo **3** IDLE : no utilizado (dícese de la tierra) **4** REMAINING : restante ⟨the unused portion : la porción restante⟩

unusual [ˌʌn'juːʒʊəl] *adj* : inusual, poco común, raro

unusually [ˌʌn'juːʒʊəli, -'juːʒəli] *adv* : excepcionalmente, extraordinariamente, fuera de lo común

unveil [ˌʌn'veɪld] *vt* **1** REVEAL : revelar **2** : develar, descubrir (una estatua, etc.)

unwanted [ˌʌn'wɑntəd] *adj* : superfluo, de sobre

unwarranted [ˌʌn'wɔrəntəd] *adj* : injustificado

unwary [ˌʌn'wæri] *adj* : incauto

unwashed [ˌʌn'wɔʃt, -'wɑʃt] *adj* : sin lavar, sucio

unwavering [ˌʌn'weɪvərɪŋ] *adj* : firme, inquebrantable ⟨an unwavering gaze : una mirada fija⟩

unwed [ˌʌn'wed] *adj* : soltero

unwelcome [ˌʌn'wɛlkəm] *adj* : importuno, molesto

unwell [ˌʌn'wel] *adj* : enfermo, mal

unwholesome [ˌʌn'hoːlsəm] *adj* **1** UNHEALTHY : malsano, insalubre **2** PERNICIOUS : pernicioso **3** LOATHSOME : repugnante, muy desagradable

unwieldy [ˌʌn'wiːldi] *adj* CUMBERSOME : difícil de manejar, torpe y pesado

unwilling [ˌʌn'wɪlɪŋ] *adj* : poco dispuesto ⟨to be unwilling to : no estar dispuesto a⟩

unwillingly [ˌʌn'wɪlɪŋli] *adv* : a regañadientes, de mala gana

unwillingness [ˌʌn'wɪlɪŋnəs] *n* : desgana *f*, renuencia *f*

unwind [ˌʌn'waɪnd] *v* **-wound** [-'waʊnd]; **-winding** *vt* UNROLL : desenrollar — *vi* **1** : desenrollarse **2** RELAX : relajarse

unwise [ˌʌn'waɪz] *adj* : imprudente, desacertado, poco aconsejable

unwisely [ˌʌn'waɪzli] *adv* : imprudentemente

unwitting [ˌʌn'wɪtɪŋ] *adj* **1** UNAWARE : inconsciente **2** INADVERTENT : involuntario, inadvertido ⟨an unwitting mistake : un error inadvertido⟩ — **unwittingly** *adv*

unworkable [ˌʌn'wərkəbəl] *adj* : impracticable

unworthiness [ˌʌn'wərðinəs] *n* : falta *f* de valía

unworthy [ˌʌn'wərði] *adj* **1** UNDESERVING : indigno ⟨to be unworthy of : no ser digno de⟩ **2** UNMERITED : inmerecido

unwrap [ˌʌnˈræp] vt **-wrapped; -wrapping** : desenvolver, deshacer

unwritten [ˌʌnˈrɪtən] adj : no escrito

unyielding [ˌʌnˈjiːldɪŋ] adj : firme, inflexible, rígido

unzip [ˌʌnˈzɪp] vt **-zipped; -zipping** : abrir el cierre de

up¹ [ˈʌp] v **upped** [ˈʌpt]; **upping; ups** vt INCREASE : aumentar, subir ⟨they upped the prices : aumentaron los precios⟩ — vi **to up and** : agarrar y fam ⟨she up and left : agarró y se fue⟩

up² adv **1** ABOVE : arriba, en lo alto ⟨up in the mountains : arriba en las montañas⟩ ⟨put it up on the shelf : ponlo en el estante⟩ ⟨we keep it up in the attic : lo guardamos arriba en el desván⟩ ⟨what's going on up there? : ¿qué pasa allí arriba?⟩ **2** UPWARDS : hacia arriba ⟨push it up : empújalo hacia arriba⟩ ⟨pull up your pants : súbete los pantalones⟩ ⟨the sun came up : el sol salió⟩ ⟨prices went up : los precios subieron⟩ ⟨she called up to me : me llamó desde abajo⟩ ⟨he looked up at the sky : miró al cielo⟩ **3** (indicating an upright position) ⟨to sit up : ponerse derecho⟩ **4** (indicating a waking state) ⟨they got up late : se levantaron tarde⟩ ⟨I stayed up all night : pasé toda la noche sin dormir⟩ **5** (indicating a usable state) ⟨we set up the equipment : instalamos el equipo⟩ **6** (indicating closure) ⟨I sealed up the package : precinté el paquete⟩ **7** (indicating activity or excitement) ⟨they stirred up the crowd : incitaron a la muchedumbre⟩ **8** (indicating greater or higher volume or intensity) ⟨to speak up : hablar más fuerte⟩ ⟨to speed up : acelerar⟩ **9** (indicating a northerly direction) ⟨the climate up north : el clima del norte⟩ ⟨I'm going up to Canada : voy para Canadá⟩ ⟨come up and see us! : ¡ven a visitarnos!⟩ **10** (indicating the appearance or existence of something) ⟨the book turned up : el libro apareció⟩ **11** (indicating consideration) ⟨she brought the matter up : mencionó el asunto⟩ **12** COMPLETELY : completamente ⟨eat it up : cómetelo todo⟩ **13** : en pedazos ⟨he tore it up : lo rompió en pedazos⟩ **14** (indicating approaching and stopping) ⟨the car pulled up to the curb : el carro paró al borde de la acera⟩ ⟨he walked up to her : se le acercó⟩ **15** (indicating advancement or progress) ⟨we moved up to the front of the line : nos pusimos al principio de la fila⟩ ⟨she has moved up in the company : ha ascendido en la compañía⟩ ⟨to grow up : hacerse mayor⟩ **16** (indicating greater importance in a series, etc.) ⟨it's pretty far/high up on my list : es muy importante para mí⟩ **17** (indicating an even score) ⟨the game was 10 up : empataron a 10⟩ **18** **to be one up on someone** : tener ventaja sobre alguien **19** **up and down** : de arriba abajo

up³ adj **1** (above the horizon) ⟨the sun is up : ha salido el sol⟩ **2** (above a surface) ⟨the tulips are up : los tulipanes han sa- lido⟩ **3** (in a high or higher position) ⟨it's up on the top shelf : está en el estante de arriba⟩ ⟨it's further up : está más arriba⟩ ⟨I'm up here : estoy aquí arriba⟩ **4** (in a forward place or position) ⟨we were up near the stage : estábamos cerca del escenario⟩ ⟨the table was up against the wall : la mesa estaba contra la pared⟩ **5** (above a normal or former level) ⟨prices are up : los precios han aumentado⟩ ⟨the river is up : las aguas están altas⟩ **6** (equal to a given level) ⟨it wasn't up to our expectations : no estuvo a la altura de lo que esperábamos⟩ ⟨I've had it up to here with your nonsense! : ¡estoy hasta las narices de tus tonterías!⟩ **7** : despierto, levantado ⟨up all night : despierto toda la noche⟩ **8** BUILT : construido ⟨the house is up : la casa está construida⟩ **9** OPEN : abierto ⟨the windows are up : las ventanas están abiertas⟩ **10** (moving or going upward) ⟨the up staircase : la escalera para subir⟩ **11** ABREAST : enterado, al día, al corriente ⟨to be up on the news : estar al corriente de las noticias⟩ **12** PREPARED : preparado ⟨we were up for the test : estuvimos preparados para el examen⟩ **13** CAPABLE : capaz ⟨she's up to the task : es capaz de hacerlo⟩ **14** FUNCTIONING : funcionando ⟨the system is back up, the system is up and running again : el sistema ha vuelto a funcionar⟩ **15** AHEAD : ganando ⟨they're up (by) ten points : van ganando por diez puntos⟩ **16** FINISHED : terminado, acabado ⟨time is up : se ha terminado el tiempo permitido⟩ **17** **to be up** : pasar ⟨what's up? : ¿qué pasa?⟩ **18** **to be up and about** : estar levantado **19** **to be up against** : enfrentarse a **20** **to be up to** **something** : estar tramando algo

up⁴ prep **1** (to, toward, or at a higher point of) ⟨he went up the stairs : subió la escalera⟩ **2** (to or toward the source of) ⟨to go up the river : ir río arriba⟩ **3** ALONG : a lo largo, por ⟨up the coast : a lo largo de la costa⟩ ⟨just up the way : un poco más adelante⟩ ⟨up and down the city : por toda la ciudad⟩

up–and–coming adj : prometedor

upbraid [ˌʌpˈbreɪd] vt : reprender, regañar

upbringing [ˈʌpˌbrɪŋɪŋ] n : crianza f, educación f

upcoming [ˌʌpˈkʌmɪŋ] adj : próximo

update¹ [ˌʌpˈdeɪt] vt **-dated; -dating** : poner al día, poner al corriente, actualizar

update² [ˈʌpˌdeɪt] n : actualización f, puesta f al día

upend [ˌʌpˈɛnd] vt **1** : poner vertical **2** OVERTURN : volcar

upgrade¹ [ˈʌpˌɡreɪd, ˌʌpˈ-] vt **-graded; -grading 1** PROMOTE : ascender **2** IMPROVE : mejorar

upgrade² [ˈʌpˌɡreɪd] n **1** SLOPE : cuesta f, pendiente f **2** RISE : aumento m de categoría (de un puesto), ascenso m (de un empleado) **3** IMPROVEMENT : mejoramiento m

upheaval [ˌʌpˈhiːvəl] *n* **1** : levantamiento *m* (en geología) **2** DISTURBANCE, UPSET : trastorno *m*, agitación *f*, conmoción *f*

uphill¹ [ˌʌpˈhɪl] *adv* : cuesta arriba

uphill² [ˈʌpˌhɪl] *adj* **1** ASCENDING : en subida **2** DIFFICULT : difícil, arduo

uphold [ˌʌpˈhoːld] *vt* **-held; -holding 1** SUPPORT : sostener, apoyar, mantener **2** RAISE : levantar **3** CONFIRM : confirmar (una decisión judicial)

upholster [ˌʌpˈhoːlstər] *vt* : tapizar

upholsterer [ˌʌpˈhoːlstərər] *n* : tapicero *m*, -ra *f*

upholstery [ˌʌpˈhoːlstəri] *n*, *pl* **-steries** : tapicería *f*

upkeep [ˈʌpˌkiːp] *n* : mantenimiento *m*

upland [ˈʌpˌlənd, -ˌlænd] *n* : altiplanicie *f*, altiplano *m*

uplift [ˌʌpˈlɪft] *vt* **1** RAISE : elevar, levantar **2** ELEVATE : elevar, animar (el espíritu, la mente, etc.)

uplift² [ˈʌpˌlɪft] *n* : elevación *f*

uplifting [ˈʌpˌlɪftɪŋ] *adj* : inspirador

upload [ˌʌpˈloʊd, ˈʌpˌloʊd] *vt* : cargar, subir (un archivo, etc.)

upon [əˈpɔn, əˈpɑn] *prep* : en, sobre ⟨upon the desk : sobre el escritorio⟩ ⟨upon leaving : al salir⟩ ⟨questions upon questions : pregunta tras pregunta⟩

upper¹ [ˈʌpər] *adj* **1** HIGHER : superior **2** : alto (en geografía) ⟨the upper Mississippi : el alto Mississippi⟩

upper² *n* : parte *f* superior (del calzado, etc.)

uppercase¹ [ˌʌpərˈkeɪs] *adj* : mayúsculo

uppercase² *n* **in uppercase** : en mayúsculas

upper–class [ˌʌpərˈklæs] *adj* : de clase alta

upper class *n* : clase *f* alta

upper hand *n* : ventaja *f*, dominio *m*

uppermost [ˈʌpərˌmoʊst] *adj* : más alto ⟨it was uppermost in his mind : era lo que más le preocupaba⟩

upright¹ [ˈʌpˌraɪt] *adj* **1** VERTICAL : vertical **2** ERECT : erguido, derecho **3** JUST : recto, honesto, justo

upright² *n* : montante *m*, poste *m*, soporte *m*

uprising [ˈʌpˌraɪzɪŋ] *n* : insurrección *f*, revuelta *f*, alzamiento *m*

uproar [ˈʌpˌror] *n* COMMOTION : alboroto *m*, jaleo *m*, escándalo *m*

uproarious [ˌʌpˈroriəs] *adj* **1** CLAMOROUS : estrepitoso, clamoroso **2** HILARIOUS : muy divertido, hilarante — **uproariously** *adv*

uproot [ˌʌpˈruːt, -ˈrʊt] *vt* : desarraigar

upset¹ [ˌʌpˈsɛt] *vt* **-set; -setting 1** OVERTURN : volcar **2** SPILL : derramar **3** DISTURB : perturbar, disgustar, inquietar, alterar **4** SICKEN : sentar mal a ⟨it upsets my stomach : me sienta mal al estómago⟩ **5** DISRUPT : trastornar, desbaratar (planes, etc.) **6** DEFEAT : derrotar (en deportes)

upset² *adj* **1** DISPLEASED, DISTRESSED : disgustado, alterado **2 to have an upset stomach** : estar mal del estómago, estar descompuesto (de estómago)

upset³ [ˈʌpˌsɛt] *n* **1** OVERTURNING : vuelco *m* **2** DISRUPTION : trastorno *m* (de planes, etc.) **3** DEFEAT : derrota *f* (en deportes)

upshot [ˈʌpˌʃɑt] *n* : resultado *m* final

upside–down [ˌʌpˌsaɪdˈdaʊn] *adj* : al revés

upside down [ˌʌpˌsaɪdˈdaʊn] *adv* **1** : al revés **2** : en confusión, en desorden

upstairs¹ [ˌʌpˈstærz] *adv* : arriba, en el piso superior

upstairs² [ˈʌpˌstærz, ˌʌpˈ-] *adj* : de arriba

upstairs³ [ˈʌpˌstærz, ˌʌpˈ-] *ns & pl* : piso *m* de arriba, planta *f* de arriba

upstanding [ˌʌpˈstændɪŋ, ˈʌpˌ-] *adj* HONEST, UPRIGHT : honesto, íntegro, recto

upstart [ˈʌpˌstɑrt] *n* : advenedizo *m*, -za *f*

upstream [ˈʌpˈstriːm] *adv* : río arriba

upsurge [ˈʌpˌsərdʒ] *n* : aumento *m* apreciable

upswing [ˈʌpˌswɪŋ] *n* : alza *f*, mejora *f* notable ⟨to be on the upswing : estar mejorándose⟩

uptight [ˌʌpˈtaɪt] *adj* : tenso, nervioso

up to *prep* **1** : hasta ⟨up to a year : hasta un año⟩ ⟨in mud up to my ankles : en barro hasta los tobillos⟩ **2 to be up to** : estar a la altura de ⟨I'm not up to going : no estoy en condiciones de ir⟩ **3 to be up to** : depender de ⟨it's up to the director : depende del director⟩

up–to–date [ˌʌptəˈdeɪt] *adj* **1** CURRENT : corriente, al día ⟨to keep up-to-date : mantenerse al corriente⟩ **2** MODERN : moderno

uptown [ˈʌpˈtaʊn] *adv* : hacia la parte alta de la ciudad, hacia el distrito residencial

upturn [ˈʌpˌtərn] *n* : mejora *f*, auge *m* (económico)

upward¹ [ˈʌpwərd] *or* **upwards** [-wərdz] *adv* **1** : hacia arriba **2 ~ of** : más de

upward² *adj* : ascendente, hacia arriba

upwind [ˈʌpˈwɪnd] *adv & adj* : contra el viento

uranium [jʊˈreɪniəm] *n* : uranio *m*

Uranus [jʊˈreɪnəs, ˈjʊrənəs] *n* : Urano *m*

urban [ˈərbən] *adj* : urbano

urbane [ˌərˈbeɪn] *adj* : urbano, cortés

urchin [ˈərtʃən] *n* **1** SCAMP : granuja *mf*, pillo *m*, -lla *f* **2 sea urchin** : erizo *m* de mar

urethra [jʊˈriːθrə] *n*, *pl* **-thras** *or* **-thrae** [-ˌθriː] : uretra *f*

urge¹ [ˈərdʒ] *vt* **urged; urging 1** PRESS : instar, apremiar, insistir ⟨we urged him to come : insistimos en que viniera⟩ **2** ADVOCATE : recomendar, abogar por **3 to urge on** : animar, alentar

urge² *n* : impulso *m*, ganas *fpl*, compulsión *f*

urgency [ˈərdʒənsi] *n*, *pl* **-cies** : urgencia *f*

urgent [ˈərdʒənt] *adj* **1** PRESSING : urgente, apremiante **2** INSISTENT : insistente **3 to be urgent** : urgir

urgently [ˈərdʒəntli] *adv* : urgentemente

urinal [ˈjʊrənəl, *esp Brit* jʊˈraɪnəl] *n* : orinal *m*

urinary [ˈjʊrəˌneri] *adj* : urinario

urinate [ˈjʊrəˌneɪt] *vi* **-nated; -nating** : orinar

urination [ˌjʊrəˈneɪʃən] n : orinación f
urine [ˈjʊrən] n : orina f
urn [ˈərn] n 1 VASE : urna f 2 : recipiente m (para servir café, etc.)
Uruguayan [ˌʊrəˈgwaɪən, ˌjʊr-, -ˈgweɪ-] n : uruguayo m, -ya f — **Uruguayan** adj
us [ˈʌs] pron 1 (as direct object) : nos ⟨they were visiting us : nos visitaban⟩ 2 (as indirect object) : nos ⟨he gave us a present : nos dio un regalo⟩ 3 (as object of preposition) : nosotros, nosotras ⟨stay with us : quédese con nosotros⟩ ⟨both of us : nosotros dos⟩ ⟨all/some of us : todos/algunos de nosotros⟩ 4 (for emphasis) : nosotros, nosotras ⟨it's us! : ¡somos nosotros!⟩
usable [ˈjuːzəbəl] adj : utilizable
usage [ˈjuːsɪʤ, -zɪʤ] n 1 HABIT : costumbre f, hábito m 2 USE : uso m
use¹ [ˈjuːz] v [ˈjuːzd, in phrase "used to" usually ˈjuːstu]; **using** vt 1 EMPLOY, UTILIZE : usar, utilizar, emplear ⟨can I use your phone? : ¿puedo usar tu teléfono?⟩ ⟨they use traditional methods : utilizan métodos tradicionales⟩ ⟨use your head! : ¡usa la cabeza!⟩ ⟨we used a contractor : contratamos a un contratista⟩ ⟨use this to clean it : usa esto para limpiarlo, límpialo con esto⟩ ⟨he uses it as an office : lo usa de/como oficina⟩ ⟨she used the money for college : usó el dinero para pagar la matrícula (universitaria)⟩ 2 CONSUME : consumir (electricidad, etc.), tomar (drogas, etc.) 3 EXPLOIT : usar, utilizar ⟨he used his friends to get ahead : usó a sus amigos para mejorar su posición⟩ 4 TREAT : tratar ⟨they used the horse cruelly : maltrataron al caballo⟩ 5 STAND : beneficiarse de ⟨you could use a nap : una siesta te vendría bien⟩ 6 to use up : agotar, consumir, gastar — vi (used in the past with to to indicate a former fact or state) : soler, acostumbrar ⟨winters used to be colder : los inviernos solían ser más fríos, los inviernos eran más fríos⟩ ⟨she used to dance : acostumbraba bailar⟩
use² [ˈjuːs] n 1 : uso m, empleo m, utilización f ⟨ready for use : listo para usar⟩ ⟨the use of seat belts : el uso de los cinturones de seguridad⟩ ⟨to wear down from/with use : desgastarse por el uso⟩ 2 USEFULNESS : utilidad f ⟨to be of use : ser útil⟩ ⟨to be of no use : no servir (para nada)⟩ ⟨it's no use! : ¡es inútil!⟩ 3 : uso m ⟨a tool with many uses : una herramienta con muchos usos⟩ ⟨to find a use for : encontrarle uso a⟩ 4 : uso m ⟨to have the use of : poder usar, tener acceso a⟩ ⟨for member use only : para uso exclusivo de los socios⟩ 5 : uso m (de las piernas, etc.) 6 to be in use : usarse, estar en uso (dícese de máquinas, palabras, etc.) ⟨the room is in use : la sala está ocupada⟩ 7 to fall out of use : caer en desuso 8 to have

no use for : no necesitar ⟨she has no use for poetry : a ella no le gusta la poesía⟩ 9 to make use of : servirse de, aprovechar 10 to put to (good) use : hacer (buen) uso de
used [ˈjuːzd] adj 1 SECONDHAND : usado, de segunda mano ⟨used cars : coches usados⟩ 2 ACCUSTOMED : acostumbrado ⟨used to the heat : acostumbrado al calor⟩
useful [ˈjuːsfəl] adj : útil, práctico — **usefully** adv
usefulness [ˈjuːsfəlnəs] n : utilidad f
useless [ˈjuːsləs] adj : inútil — **uselessly** adv
uselessness [ˈjuːsləsnəs] n : inutilidad f
user [ˈjuːzər] n : usuario m, -ria f
user-friendly adj : fácil de usar
user name n : nombre m de usuario
usher¹ [ˈʌʃər] v 1 ESCORT : acompañar, conducir 2 to usher in : hacer pasar (a alguien) ⟨to usher in a new era : anunciar una nueva época⟩
usher² n : acomodador m, -dora f
usherette [ˌʌʃəˈrɛt] n : acomodadora f
usual [ˈjuːʒʊəl] adj 1 NORMAL : usual, normal 2 CUSTOMARY : acostumbrado, habitual, de costumbre 3 ORDINARY : ordinario, típico
usually [ˈjuːʒʊəli, ˈjuːʒəli] adv : usualmente, normalmente
usurp [jʊˈsərp, -ˈzərp] vt : usurpar
usurper [jʊˈsərpər, -ˈzər-] n : usurpador m, -dora f
usury [ˈjuːʒəri] n : usura f
utensil [jʊˈtɛntsəl] n 1 : utensilio m (de cocina) 2 IMPLEMENT : implemento m, útil m (de labranza, etc.)
uterine [ˈjuːtəˌraɪn, -rən] adj : uterino
uterus [ˈjuːtərəs] n, pl **uteri** [-ˌraɪ] : útero m, matriz f
utilitarian [juːˌtɪləˈteriən] adj : utilitario
utility [juːˈtɪləti] n, pl **-ties** 1 USEFULNESS : utilidad f 2 public utility : empresa f de servicio público
utilization [ˌjuːtələˈzeɪʃən] n : utilización f
utilize [ˈjuːtəˌlaɪz] vt **-lized; -lizing** : utilizar, hacer uso de
utmost¹ [ˈʌtˌmoːst] adj 1 FARTHEST : extremo, más lejano 2 GREATEST : sumo, mayor ⟨of the utmost importance : de suma importancia⟩
utmost² n : lo más posible ⟨to the utmost : al máximo⟩
utopia [juːˈtoːpiə] n : utopía f
utopian [juːˈtoːpiən] adj : utópico
utter¹ [ˈʌtər] vt : decir, articular, pronunciar (palabras)
utter² adj : absoluto — **utterly** adv
utterance [ˈʌtərənts] n : declaración f, articulación f
U-turn [ˈjuːˌtərn] n 1 : giro m en U, vuelta f en U, cambio m de sentido 2 fam ABOUT-FACE, REVERSAL : giro m de 180 grados
uvula [ˈjuːvjələ] n : campanilla f

V

v ['vi:] *n*, *pl* **v's** *or* **vs** ['vi:z] : vigésima segunda letra del alfabeto inglés

vacancy ['veɪkənsi] *n*, *pl* **-cies** 1 EMPTINESS : vacío *m*, vacuidad *f* 2 : vacante *f*, puesto *m* vacante ⟨to fill a vacancy : ocupar un puesto⟩ 3 : habitación *f* libre (en un hotel) ⟨no vacancies : completo⟩

vacant ['veɪkənt] *adj* 1 EMPTY : libre, desocupado (dícese de los edificios, etc.) 2 : vacante (dícese de los puestos) 3 BLANK : vacío, ausente ⟨a vacant stare : una mirada ausente⟩

vacate ['veɪˌkeɪt] *vt* **-cated; -cating** : desalojar, desocupar

vacation[1] [veɪˈkeɪʃən, və-] *vi* : pasar las vacaciones, vacacionar *Mex*

vacation[2] *n* : vacaciones *fpl* ⟨to be on vacation : estar de vacaciones⟩

vacationer [veɪˈkeɪʃənər, və-] *n* : turista *mf*, veraneante *mf*, vacacionista *mf CA, Mex*

vaccinate ['væksəˌneɪt] *vt* **-nated; -nating** : vacunar

vaccination [ˌvæksəˈneɪʃən] *n* : vacunación *f*

vaccine [væk'si:n, 'væk-] *n* : vacuna *f*

vacillate ['væsəˌleɪt] *vi* **-lated; -lating** 1 HESITATE : vacilar 2 SWAY : oscilar

vacillation [ˌvæsəˈleɪʃən] *n* : indecisión *f*, vacilación *f*

vacuous ['vækjuəs] *adj* 1 EMPTY : vacío 2 INANE : vacuo, necio, estúpido

vacuousness ['vækjuəsnəs] *n* : vacuidad *f*

vacuum[1] ['væˌkjuːm, -kjəm] *vt* : limpiar con aspiradora, pasar la aspiradora por

vacuum[2] *n*, *pl* **vacuums** *or* **vacua** ['vækjuə] : vacío *m*

vacuum cleaner *n* : aspiradora *f*

vagabond[1] ['væɡəˌbɑnd] *adj* : vagabundo

vagabond[2] *n* : vagabundo *m*, -da *f*

vagary ['veɪɡəri, vəˈɡɛri] *n*, *pl* **-ries** : capricho *m*

vagina [vəˈdʒaɪnə] *n*, *pl* **-nae** [-ˌniː, -ˌnaɪ] *or* **-nas** : vagina *f*

vagrancy ['veɪɡrənsi] *n*, *pl* **-cies** : vagancia *f*

vagrant[1] ['veɪɡrənt] *adj* : vagabundo

vagrant[2] *n* : vagabundo *m*, -da *f*

vague [veɪɡ] *adj* **vaguer; vaguest** 1 IMPRECISE : vago, impreciso ⟨a vague feeling : una sensación indefinida⟩ ⟨I haven't the vaguest idea : no tengo la más remota idea⟩ 2 UNCLEAR : borroso, poco claro ⟨a vague outline : un perfil indistinto⟩ 3 ABSENTMINDED : distraído

vaguely ['veɪɡli] *adv* : vagamente, de manera imprecisa

vagueness ['veɪɡnəs] *n* : vaguedad *f*, imprecisión *f*

vain [veɪn] *adj* 1 WORTHLESS : vano 2 FUTILE : vano, inútil ⟨in vain : en vano⟩ 3 CONCEITED : vanidoso, presumido

vainly ['veɪnli] *adv* : en vano, vanamente, inútilmente

valance ['væləns, 'veɪ-] *n* 1 FLOUNCE : volante *m* (de una cama, etc.) 2 : galería *f* de cortina (sobre una ventana)

vale ['veɪl] *n* : valle *m*

valedictorian [ˌvælədɪkˈtoriən] *n* : estudiante *mf* que pronuncia el discurso de despedida en ceremonia de graduación

valedictory [ˌvæləˈdɪktəri] *adj* : de despedida

valentine ['vælənˌtaɪn] *n* : tarjeta *f* que se manda el Día de los Enamorados (el 14 de febrero)

Valentine's Day *n* : Día *m* de los Enamorados

valet ['væˌleɪ, væˈleɪ, 'vælət] *n* : ayuda *m* de cámara

valiant ['væljənt] *adj* : valiente, valeroso

valiantly ['væljəntli] *adv* : con valor, valientemente

valid ['væləd] *adj* : válido

validate ['væləˌdeɪt] *vt* **-dated; -dating** : validar, dar validez a

validity [vəˈlɪdəti, væ-] *n* : validez *f*

valise [vəˈliːs] *n* : maleta *f* (de mano)

Valium ['væliəm, 'væljəm] *trademark* se usa para una droga que reduce la ansiedad y el estrés

valley ['væli] *n*, *pl* **-leys** : valle *m*

valor ['vælər] *n* : valor *m*, valentía *f*

valuable[1] ['væljuəbəl, 'væljəbəl] *adj* 1 EXPENSIVE : valioso, de valor 2 WORTHWHILE : valioso, apreciable

valuable[2] *n* : objeto *m* de valor

valuation [ˌvæljuˈeɪʃən] *n* 1 APPRAISAL : valoración *f*, tasación *f* 2 VALUE : valuación *f*

value[1] ['væljuː] *vt* **-ued; -uing** 1 APPRAISE : valorar, avaluar, tasar 2 APPRECIATE : valorar, apreciar

value[2] *n* 1 : valor *m* ⟨of little value : de poco valor⟩ ⟨to be a good value : estar bien de precio, tener buen precio⟩ ⟨at face value : en su sentido literal⟩ 2 **values** *npl* : valores *mpl* (morales), principios *mpl*

valueless ['væljuːləs] *adj* : sin valor

valve ['vælv] *n* : válvula *f*

vampire ['væmˌpaɪr] *n* 1 : vampiro *m* 2 *or* **vampire bat** : vampiro *m*

van[1] ['væn] → **vanguard**

van[2] *n* : furgoneta *f*, camioneta *f*

vandal ['vændəl] *n* : vándalo *m*

vandalism ['vændəlˌɪzəm] *n* : vandalismo *m*

vandalize ['vændəlˌaɪz] *vt* : destrozar, destruir, estropear

vane ['veɪn] *n* *or* **weather vane** : veleta *f*

vanguard ['vænˌɡɑrd] *n* : vanguardia *f*

vanilla [vəˈnɪlə, -ˈnɛ-] *n* : vainilla *f*

vanish ['vænɪʃ] *vi* : desaparecer, disiparse, desvanecerse

vanity ['vænəti] *n*, *pl* **-ties** 1 : vanidad *f* 2 *or* **vanity table** : tocador *m*

vanquish ['væŋkwɪʃ, 'væn-] *vt* : vencer, conquistar

vantage point ['væntɪdʒ] *n* : posición *f* ventajosa

vape ['veɪp] v **vaped; vaping** : vapear
vapid ['væpəd, 'veɪ-] adj : insípido, insulso
vapor ['veɪpər] n : vapor m
vaporize ['veɪpə,raɪz] v **-rized; -rizing** vt : vaporizar — vi : vaporizarse, evaporarse
vaporizer ['veɪpə,raɪzər] n : vaporizador m
variability [,vɛriə'bɪləti] n, pl **-ties** : variabilidad f
variable[1] ['vɛriəbəl] adj : variable ⟨variable cloudiness : nubosidad variable⟩
variable[2] n : variable f, factor m
variance ['vɛriənts] n 1 DISCREPANCY : varianza f, discrepancia f 2 DISAGREEMENT : desacuerdo m ⟨at variance with : en desacuerdo con⟩
variant[1] ['vɛriənt] adj : variante, divergente
variant[2] n : variante f
variation [,vɛri'eɪʃən] n : variación f, diferencias fpl
varicose ['vɛrə,koːs] adj : varicoso
varicose veins npl : varices fpl, várices fpl
varied ['vɛrid] adj : variado, dispar, diferente
variegated ['vɛriə,geɪtd] adj : abigarrado, multicolor
variety [və'raɪəti] n, pl **-ties** 1 DIVERSITY : diversidad f, variedad f 2 ASSORTMENT : surtido m ⟨for a variety of reasons : por diversas razones⟩ 3 SORT : clase f 4 BREED : variedad f (de plantas)
various ['vɛriəs] adj : varios, diversos
varnish[1] ['vɑrnɪʃ] vt : barnizar
varnish[2] n : barniz m
varsity ['vɑrsəti] n, pl **-ties** : equipo m universitario
vary ['vɛri] v **varied; varying** vt : variar, diversificar — vi 1 CHANGE : variar, cambiar 2 DEVIATE : desviarse
vascular ['væskjələr] adj : vascular
vase ['veɪs, 'veɪz, 'vɑz] n : jarrón m, florero m
Vaseline ['væsə,liːn, ,væsə'liːn] trademark se usa para vaselina
vassal ['væsəl] n : vasallo m, -lla f
vast ['væst] adj : inmenso, enorme, vasto
vastly ['væstli] adv : enormemente
vastness ['væstnəs] n : vastedad f, inmensidad f
vat ['væt] n : cuba f, tina f
vaudeville ['vɔdvəl, -,vɪl;, 'vɔdə,vɪl] n : vodevil m
vault[1] ['vɔlt] vi LEAP : saltar
vault[2] n 1 JUMP : salto m ⟨pole vault : salto de pértiga, salto con garrocha⟩ 2 DOME : bóveda f 3 : bodega f (para vino), bóveda f de seguridad (de un banco) 4 CRYPT : cripta f
vaulted ['vɔltəd] adj : abovedado
vaunted ['vɔntəd] adj : cacareado, alardeado ⟨a much vaunted wine : un vino muy alardeado⟩
VCR [,vi,si'ɑr] n : video m, videocasetera f
veal ['viːl] n : ternera f, carne f de ternera
veer ['vɪr] vi : virar (dícese de un barco), girar (dícese de un coche), torcer (dícese de un camino)

vegan ['viːgən] n : vegetariano m estricto, vegetariana f estricta
vegetable[1] ['vɛdʒtəbəl, 'vɛdʒətə-] adj : vegetal
vegetable[2] n 1 : vegetal m ⟨the vegetable kingdom : el reino vegetal⟩ 2 : verdura f, hortaliza f (para comer)
vegetarian [,vɛdʒə'tɛriən] n : vegetariano mf — **vegetarian** adj — **vegetarianism** n
vegetate ['vɛdʒə,teɪt] vi **-tated; -tating** : vegetar
vegetation [,vɛdʒə'teɪʃən] n : vegetación f
vegetative ['vɛdʒə,teɪtɪv] adj : vegetativo
veggie ['vɛdʒi] n fam VEGETABLE : verdura f, hortaliza f (para comer)
vehemence ['viːəmənts] n : intensidad f, vehemencia f
vehement ['viːəmənt] adj : intenso, vehemente
vehemently ['viːəməntli] adv : vehementemente, con vehemencia
vehicle ['viːəkəl, 'viː,hɪkəl] n 1 or motor vehicle : vehículo m 2 MEDIUM : vehículo m, medio m
vehicular [vi'hɪkjələr, və-] adj : vehicular ⟨vehicular homicide : muerte por atropello⟩
veil[1] ['veɪl] vt 1 CONCEAL : velar, disimular 2 : cubrir con un velo ⟨to veil one's face : cubrirse con un velo⟩
veil[2] n : velo m ⟨bridal veil : velo de novia⟩
vein ['veɪn] n 1 : vena f (en anatomía, botánica, etc.) 2 LODE : veta f, vena f, filón m 3 STYLE : vena f ⟨in a humorous vein : en vena humorística⟩
veined ['veɪnd] adj : veteado (dícese del queso, de los minerales, etc.)
Velcro ['vɛl,kroː] trademark se usa para un tipo de cierre de nilón
velocity [və'lɑsəti] n, pl **-ties** : velocidad f
velour [və'lʊr] or **velours** [-'lʊrz] n : velour m
velvet[1] ['vɛlvət] adj 1 : de terciopelo 2 → **velvety**
velvet[2] n : terciopelo m
velvety ['vɛlvəti] adj : aterciopelado
venal ['viːnəl] adj : venal
vend ['vɛnd] vt : vender
vendetta [vɛn'dɛtə] n : vendetta f
vending machine n : máquina f expendedora
vendor ['vɛndər] n : vendedor m, -dora f; puestero m, -ra f
veneer n 1 : enchapado m, chapa f 2 APPEARANCE : apariencia f, barniz m ⟨a veneer of culture : un barniz de cultura⟩
venerable ['vɛnərəbəl] adj : venerable
venerate ['vɛnə,reɪt] vt **-ated; -ating** : venerar
veneration [,vɛnə'reɪʃən] n : veneración f
venereal disease [və'nɪriəl] n : enfermedad f venérea
venetian blind [və'niːʃən] n : persiana f (de lamas)
Venezuelan [,vɛnə'zweɪlən, -zu'eɪ-] n : venezolano m, -na f — **Venezuelan** adj
vengeance ['vɛndʒənts] n : venganza f ⟨to take vengeance on : vengarse de⟩

vengeful [ˈvɛndʒfəl] *adj* : vengativo
venial [ˈviːniəl] *adj* : venial ⟨a venial sin : un pecado venial⟩
venison [ˈvɛnəsən, -zən] *n* : venado *m*, carne *f* de venado
venom [ˈvɛnəm] *n* **1** : veneno *m* **2** MALICE : veneno *m*, malevolencia *f*
venomous [ˈvɛnəməs] *adj* : venenoso
vent[1] [ˈvɛnt] *vt* : desahogar, dar salida a ⟨to vent one's feelings : desahogarse⟩
vent[2] *n* **1** OPENING : abertura *f* (de escape), orificio *m* **2** *or* air vent : respiradero *m*, rejilla *f* de ventilación **3** OUTLET : desahogo *m* ⟨to give vent to one's anger : desahogar la ira⟩
ventilate [ˈvɛntəlˌeɪt] *vt* -lated; -lating : ventilar
ventilation [ˌvɛntəlˈeɪʃən] *n* : ventilación *f*
ventilator [ˈvɛntəlˌeɪtər] *n* : ventilador *m*
ventricle [ˈvɛntrɪkəl] *n* : ventrículo *m*
ventriloquism [vɛnˈtrɪləˌkwɪzəm] *n* : ventriloquia *f*
ventriloquist [vɛnˈtrɪləˌkwɪst] *n* : ventrílocuo *m*, -cua *f*
venture[1] [ˈvɛntʃər] *v* -tured; -turing *vt* **1** RISK : arriesgar **2** OFFER : aventurar ⟨to venture an opinion : aventurar una opinión⟩ — *vi* : arriesgarse, atreverse, aventurarse
venture[2] *n* **1** UNDERTAKING : empresa *f* **2** GAMBLE, RISK : aventura *f*, riesgo *m*
venturesome [ˈvɛntʃərsəm] *adj* **1** ADVENTUROUS : audaz, atrevido **2** RISKY : arriesgado
venue [ˈvɛnˌjuː] *n* **1** PLACE : lugar *m* **2** : jurisdicción *f* (en derecho)
Venus [ˈviːnəs] *n* : Venus *m*
veracity [vəˈræsəti] *n*, *pl* -ties : veracidad *f*
veranda *or* **verandah** [vəˈrændə] *n* : terraza *f*, veranda *f*
verb [ˈvərb] *n* : verbo *m*
verbal [ˈvərbəl] *adj* : verbal
verbalize [ˈvərbəˌlaɪz] *vt* -ized; -izing : expresar con palabras, verbalizar
verbally [ˈvərbəli] *adv* : verbalmente, de palabra
verbatim [vərˈbeɪtəm] *adv* : palabra por palabra, textualmente
verbatim[2] *adj* : literal, textual
verbose [vərˈboːs] *adj* : verboso, prolijo
verdant [ˈvərdənt] *adj* : verde, verdeante
verdict [ˈvərdɪkt] *n* **1** : veredicto *m* (de un jurado) **2** JUDGMENT, OPINION : juicio *m*, opinión *f*
verge[1] [ˈvərdʒ] *vi* verged; verging : estar al borde, rayar ⟨it verges on madness : raya en la locura⟩
verge[2] *n* **1** EDGE : borde *m* **2 to be on the verge of** : estar a pique de, estar al borde de, estar a punto de
verification [ˌvɛrəfəˈkeɪʃən] *n* : verificación *f*
verify [ˈvɛrəˌfaɪ] *vt* -fied; -fying : verificar, comprobar, confirmar
veritable [ˈvɛrətəbəl] *adj* : verdadero — **veritably** [-bli] *adv*
vermicelli [ˌvərməˈtʃɛli, -ˈsɛli] *n* : fideos *mpl* finos
vermin [ˈvərmən] *ns & pl* : alimañas *fpl*, bichos *mpl*, sabandijas *fpl*

vermouth [vərˈmuːθ] *n* : vermut *m*
vernacular[1] [vərˈnækjələr] *adj* : vernáculo
vernacular[2] *n* : lengua *f* vernácula
vernal [ˈvərnəl] *adj* : vernal
versatile [ˈvərsətəl] *adj* : versátil
versatility [ˌvərsəˈtɪləti] *n* : versatilidad *f*
verse [ˈvərs] *n* **1** LINE, STANZA : verso *m*, estrofa *f* **2** POETRY : poesía *f* **3** : versículo *m* (en la Biblia)
versed [ˈvərst] *adj* : versado ⟨to be well versed in : ser muy versado en⟩
version [ˈvərʒən] *n* : versión *f*
versus [ˈvərsəs] *prep* : versus
vertebra [ˈvərtəbrə] *n*, *pl* -brae [-ˌbreɪ, -ˌbriː] *or* -bras : vértebra *f*
vertebrate[1] [ˈvərtəbrət, -ˌbreɪt] *adj* : vertebrado
vertebrate[2] *n* : vertebrado *m*
vertex [ˈvərˌtɛks] *n*, *pl* **vertices** [ˈvərtəˌsiːz] **1** : vértice *m* (en matemáticas y anatomía) **2** SUMMIT, TOP : ápice *m*, cumbre *f*, cima *f*
vertical[1] [ˈvərtɪkəl] *adj* : vertical — **vertically** *adv*
vertical[2] *n* : vertical *f*
vertigo [ˈvərtɪˌgoː] *n*, *pl* -goes *or* -gos : vértigo *m*
verve [ˈvərv] *n* : brío *m*
very[1] [ˈvɛri] *adv* **1** EXTREMELY : muy, sumamente ⟨very few : muy pocos⟩ ⟨very much : mucho⟩ ⟨I am very sorry : lo siento mucho⟩ **2** (*used for emphasis*) ⟨at the very least : por lo menos, como mínimo⟩ ⟨the very same dress : el mismo vestido⟩ ⟨a room of my very own : mi propio cuarto⟩ ⟨(on) the very next day : al día siguiente⟩
very[2] *adj* verier; -est **1** EXACT, PRECISE : mismo, exacto ⟨at that very moment : en ese mismo momento⟩ ⟨it's the very thing : es justo lo que hacía falta⟩ **2** BARE, MERE : solo, mero ⟨the very thought of it : sólo pensarlo⟩ **3** EXTREME : extremo, de todo ⟨at the very top : arriba de todo⟩
vesicle [ˈvɛsɪkəl] *n* : vesícula *f*
vespers [ˈvɛspərz] *npl* : vísperas *fpl*
vessel [ˈvɛsəl] *n* **1** CONTAINER : vasija *f*, recipiente *m* **2** BOAT, CRAFT : nave *f*, barco *m*, buque *m* **3** : vaso *m* ⟨blood vessel : vaso sanguíneo⟩
vest[1] [ˈvɛst] *vt* **1** CONFER : conferir ⟨to vest authority in : conferirle la autoridad a⟩ **2** CLOTHE : vestir
vest[2] *n* **1** : chaleco *m* **2** UNDERSHIRT : camiseta *f*
vestibule [ˈvɛstəˌbjuːl] *n* : vestíbulo *m*
vestige [ˈvɛstɪdʒ] *n* : vestigio *m*, rastro *m*
vestments [ˈvɛstmənts] *npl* : vestiduras *fpl*
vestry [ˈvɛstri] *n*, *pl* -tries : sacristía *f*
vet [ˈvɛt] *n* **1** → veterinarian **2** → veteran[2]
veteran[1] [ˈvɛtərən, ˈvɛtrən] *adj* : veterano
veteran[2] *n* : veterano *m*, -na *f*
Veterans Day *n* : día *m* del Armisticio (celebrado el 11 de noviembre en los Estados Unidos)
veterinarian [ˌvɛtərəˈnɛriən, ˌvɛtrə-] *n* : veterinario *m*, -ria *f*

veterinary [ˈvɛtərəˌnɛri] *adj* : veterinario
veto¹ [ˈviːˌto] *vt* **1** FORBID : prohibir **2** : vetar ⟨to veto a bill : vetar un proyecto de ley⟩
veto² *n, pl* **-toes** **1** : veto *m* ⟨the power of veto : el derecho de veto⟩ **2** BAN : veto *m*, prohibición *f*
vex [ˈvɛks] *vt* : contrariar, molestar, irritar
vexation [vɛkˈseɪʃən] *n* : contrariedad *f*, irritación *f*
via [ˈvaɪə, ˈviːə] *prep* : por, vía
viability [ˌvaɪəˈbɪləti] *n* : viabilidad *f*
viable [ˈvaɪəbəl] *adj* : viable
viaduct [ˈvaɪəˌdʌkt] *n* : viaducto *m*
vial [ˈvaɪəl] *n* : frasco *m*
vibrant [ˈvaɪbrənt] *adj* **1** LIVELY : vibrante, animado, dinámico **2** BRIGHT : fuerte, vivo (dícese de los colores)
vibrate [ˈvaɪˌbreɪt] *vi* **-brated; -brating** **1** OSCILLATE : vibrar, oscilar **2** THRILL : bullir ⟨to vibrate with excitement : bullir de emoción⟩
vibration [vaɪˈbreɪʃən] *n* : vibración *f*
vibrator [ˈvaɪˌbreɪtʃər] *n* : vibrador *m*
vicar [ˈvɪkər] *n* : vicario *m*, -ria *f*
vicarious [vaɪˈkæriːəs, vɪ-] *adj* : indirecto — **vicariously** *adv*
vice¹ [ˈvaɪs] *n* : vicio *m*
vice- [ˈvaɪs] *pref* : vice-
vice admiral *n* : vicealmirante *mf*
vice president *n* : vicepresidente *m*, -ta *f*
viceroy [ˈvaɪsˌrɔɪ] *n* : virrey *m*, -reina *f*
vice versa [ˌvaɪsɪˈvərsə, ˌvaɪsˈvər-] *adv* : viceversa
vicinity [vəˈsɪnəti] *n, pl* **-ties** **1** NEIGHBORHOOD : vecindad *f*, inmediaciones *fpl* **2** NEARNESS : proximidad *f*
vicious [ˈvɪʃəs] *adj* **1** DEPRAVED : depravado, malo **2** SAVAGE : malo, fiero, salvaje ⟨a vicious dog : un perro feroz⟩ **3** MALICIOUS : malicioso
vicious circle *n* : círculo *m* vicioso
viciously [ˈvɪʃəsli] *adv* : con saña, brutalmente
viciousness [ˈvɪʃəsnəs] *n* : brutalidad *f*, ferocidad *f* (de un animal), malevolencia *f* (de un comentario, etc.)
vicissitude [vəˈsɪsəˌtuːd, vaɪ-, -ˌtjuːd] *n* : vicisitud *f*
victim [ˈvɪktəm] *n* : víctima *f*
victimize [ˈvɪktəˌmaɪz] *vt* **-mized; -mizing** : tomar como víctima; perseguir; victimizar *Arg, Mex*
victor [ˈvɪktər] *n* : vencedor *m*, -dora *f*
Victorian [vɪkˈtoːriən] *adj* : victoriano
victorious [vɪkˈtoːriəs] *adj* : victorioso — **victoriously** *adv*
victory [ˈvɪktəri] *n, pl* **-ries** : victoria *f*, triunfo *m*
video¹ [ˈvɪdiːˌo] *adj* : de video ⟨video recording : grabación de video⟩
video² *n* : video *m*
video camera *n* : videocámara *f*
videocassette [ˌvɪdiokəˈsɛt] *n* : videocasete *m*, videocinta *f*
videocassette recorder → VCR
videoconferencing [ˌvɪdioˈkɑnfrənˌsɪŋ] *n* : uso *m* de videoconferencias — **videoconference** [ˌvɪdioˈkɑnfrəns, -ˈkɑnfərənts] *n*

video game *n* : videojuego *m*, juego *m* de video
video recorder → VCR
videotape¹ [ˈvɪdioˌteɪp] *vt* **-taped; -taping** : grabar en video, videograbar
videotape² *n* : videocinta *f*
vie [ˈvaɪ] *vi* **vied; vying** [ˈvaɪɪŋ] : competir, rivalizar
Vietnamese [viˌɛtnəˈmiːz, -ˈmiːs] *n* **1** : vietnamita *mf* **2** : vietnamita *m* (idioma) — **Vietnamese** *adj*
view¹ [ˈvjuː] *vt* **1** OBSERVE : mirar, ver, observar **2** CONSIDER : considerar, contemplar
view² *n* **1** SIGHT : vista *f* ⟨to come into view : aparecer⟩ **2** ATTITUDE, OPINION : opinión *f*, parecer *m*, actitud *f* ⟨in my view : en mi opinión⟩ **3** SCENE : vista *f*, panorama *f* **4** INTENTION : idea *f*, vista *f* ⟨with a view to : con vistas a, con la idea de⟩ **5 in view of** : dado que, en vista de (que)
viewer [ˈvjuːər] *n* : televidente *mf*; telespectador *m*, -dora *f* ⟨the show was watched by millions of viewers : el programa fue visto por millones de televidentes⟩
viewfinder [ˈvjuːˌfaɪndər] *n* : visor *m*
viewpoint [ˈvjuːˌpɔɪnt] *n* : punto *m* de vista
vigil [ˈvɪdʒəl] *n* **1** : vigilia *f*, vela *f* **2 to keep vigil** : velar
vigilance [ˈvɪdʒələnts] *n* : vigilancia *f*
vigilant [ˈvɪdʒələnt] *adj* : vigilante
vigilante [ˌvɪdʒəˈlænˌtiː] *n* : integrante *mf* de un comité de vigilancia (que actúa como policía)
vigilantly [ˈvɪdʒələntli] *adv* : con vigilancia
vigor [ˈvɪgər] *n* : vigor *m*, energía *f*, fuerza *f*
vigorous [ˈvɪgərəs] *adj* : vigoroso, enérgico — **vigorously** *adv*
Viking [ˈvaɪkɪŋ] *n* : vikingo *m*, -ga *f*
vile [ˈvaɪl] *adj* **viler; vilest** **1** WICKED : vil, infame **2** REVOLTING : asqueroso, repugnante **3** TERRIBLE : horrible, atroz ⟨vile weather : tiempo horrible⟩ ⟨to be in a vile mood : estar de un humor de perros⟩
vileness [ˈvaɪlnəs] *n* : vileza *f*
vilify [ˈvɪləˌfaɪ] *vt* **-fied; -fying** : vilipendiar, denigrar, difamar
villa [ˈvɪlə] *n* : casa *f* de campo, quinta *f*
village [ˈvɪlɪdʒ] *n* : pueblo *m* (grande), aldea *f* (pequeña)
villager [ˈvɪlɪdʒər] *n* : vecino *m*, -na *f* (de un pueblo); aldeano *m*, -na *f* (de una aldea)
villain [ˈvɪlən] *n* : villano *m*, -na *f*; malo *m*, -la *f* (en ficción, películas, etc.)
villainess [ˈvɪlənəs, -nəs] *n* : villana *f*
villainous [ˈvɪlənəs] *adj* : infame, malvado
villainy [ˈvɪləni] *n, pl* **-lainies** : vileza *f*, maldad *f*
vim [ˈvɪm] *n* : brío *m*, vigor *m*, energía *f*
vinaigrette [ˌvɪniˈgrɛt] *n* : vinagreta *f*
vindicate [ˈvɪndəˌkeɪt] *vt* **-cated; -cating** **1** EXONERATE : vindicar, disculpar **2** JUSTIFY : justificar
vindication [ˌvɪndəˈkeɪʃən] *n* : vindicación *f*, justificación *f*

vindictive [vɪnˈdɪktɪv] *adj* : vengativo

vine [ˈvaɪn] *n* **1** GRAPEVINE : vid *f*, parra *f* **2** : planta *f* trepadora, enredadera *f*

vinegar [ˈvɪnɪɡər] *n* : vinagre *m*

vinegary [ˈvɪnɪɡəri] *adj* : avinagrado

vineyard [ˈvɪnjərd] *n* : viña *f*, viñedo *m*

vintage[1] [ˈvɪntɪdʒ] *adj* **1** : añejo (dícese de un vino) **2** CLASSIC : clásico, de época

vintage[2] *n* **1** : cosecha *f* ⟨the 1947 vintage : la cosecha de 1947⟩ **2** ERA : época *f*, era *f* ⟨slang of recent vintage : argot de la época reciente⟩

vinyl [ˈvaɪnəl] *n* : vinilo *m*

viola [viːˈoːlə] *n* : viola *f*

violate [ˈvaɪəˌleɪt] *vt* -lated; -lating **1** BREAK : infringir, violar, quebrantar ⟨to violate the rules : violar las reglas⟩ **2** RAPE : violar **3** DESECRATE : profanar

violation [ˌvaɪəˈleɪʃən] *n* **1** : violación *f*, infracción *f* (de una ley) **2** DESECRATION : profanación *f*

violator [ˈvaɪəˌleɪtər] *n* : infractor *m*, -tora *f*

violence [ˈvaɪələnts, ˈvaɪə-] *n* : violencia *f*

violent [ˈvaɪələnt, ˈvaɪə-] *adj* : violento

violently [ˈvaɪələntli, ˈvaɪə-] *adv* : violentamente, con violencia

violet [ˈvaɪələt, ˈvaɪə-] *n* : violeta *f*

violin [ˌvaɪəˈlɪn] *n* : violín *m*

violinist [ˌvaɪəˈlɪnɪst] *n* : violinista *mf*

violoncello [ˌvaɪələnˈtʃeloː, ˌviːə-] → **cello**

VIP [ˌviːˌaɪˈpiː] *n, pl* **VIPs** [-ˈpiːz] : VIP *mf*, persona *f* de categoría

viper [ˈvaɪpər] *n* : víbora *f*

viral [ˈvaɪrəl] *adj* : viral, vírico ⟨viral pneumonia : pulmonía viral⟩

virgin[1] [ˈvərdʒən] *adj* **1** CHASTE : virginal ⟨the virgin birth : el alumbramiento virginal⟩ **2** : virgen, intacto ⟨a virgin forest : una selva virgen⟩ ⟨virgin wool : lana virgen⟩

virgin[2] *n* : virgen *mf*

virginal [ˈvərdʒənəl] *adj* : virginal

virginity [vərˈdʒɪnəti] *n* : virginidad *f*

Virgo [ˈvərˌɡoː, ˈvɪr-] *n* **1** : Virgo *m* (signo o constelación) **2** : Virgo *mf* (persona)

virile [ˈvɪrəl, -ˌaɪl] *adj* : viril, varonil

virility [vəˈrɪləti] *n* : virilidad *f*

virtual [ˈvərtʃuəl] *adj* : virtual ⟨a virtual dictator : un virtual dictador⟩ ⟨virtual reality : realidad virtual⟩

virtually [ˈvərtʃuəli, ˈvərtʃəli] *adv* : en realidad, de hecho, casi

virtue [ˈvərˌtʃuː] *n* **1** : virtud *f* **2 by virtue of** : en virtud de, debido a

virtuosity [ˌvərtʃuˈɑsəti] *n, pl* -ties : virtuosismo *m*

virtuoso [ˌvərtʃuˈoːsoː, -zoː] *n, pl* -sos *or* -si [-ˌsiː, -ziː] : virtuoso *m*, -sa *f*

virtuous [ˈvərtʃuəs] *adj* : virtuoso, bueno — **virtuously** *adv*

virulence [ˈvɪrələnts, ˈvɪrjə-] *n* : virulencia *f*

virulent [ˈvɪrələnt, ˈvɪrjə-] *adj* : virulento

virus [ˈvaɪrəs] *n* : virus *m*

visa [ˈviːzə, -sə] *n* : visa *f*

vis-à-vis [ˌviːzɑˈviː, -sə-] *prep* : con relación a, con respecto a

viscera [ˈvɪsərə] *npl* : vísceras *fpl*

visceral [ˈvɪsərəl] *adj* : visceral

viscosity [vɪsˈkɑsəti] *n, pl* -ties : viscosidad *f*

viscous [ˈvɪskəs] *adj* : viscoso

vise [ˈvaɪs] *n* : torno *m* de banco, tornillo *m* de banco

visibility [ˌvɪzəˈbɪləti] *n, pl* -ties : visibilidad *f*

visible [ˈvɪzəbəl] *adj* **1** : visible ⟨the visible stars : las estrellas visibles⟩ **2** OBVIOUS : evidente, patente

visibly [ˈvɪzəbli] *adv* : visiblemente

vision [ˈvɪʒən] *n* **1** EYESIGHT : vista *f*, visión *f* **2** APPARITION : visión *f*, aparición *f* **3** FORESIGHT : visión *f* (del futuro), previsión *f* **4** IMAGE : imagen *f* ⟨she had visions of a disaster : se imaginaba un desastre⟩

visionary[1] [ˈvɪʒəˌneri] *adj* **1** FARSIGHTED : visionario, con visión de futuro **2** UTOPIAN : utópico, poco realista

visionary[2] *n, pl* -ries : visionario *m*, -ria *f*

visit[1] [ˈvɪzət] *vt* **1** : visitar, ir a ver **2** AFFLICT : azotar, afligir ⟨visited by troubles : afligido con problemas⟩ — *vi* : hacer (una) visita ⟨visiting hours : horas de visita⟩

visit[2] *n* : visita *f*

visitor [ˈvɪzətər] *n* : visitante *mf* (a una ciudad, etc.), visita *f* (a una casa)

visor [ˈvaɪzər] *n* : visera *f*

vista [ˈvɪstə] *n* : vista *f*

visual [ˈvɪʒuəl] *adj* : visual ⟨the visual arts : las artes visuales⟩ — **visually** *adv*

visualize [ˈvɪʒuəˌlaɪz] *vt* -ized; -izing : visualizar, imaginarse, hacerse una idea de — **visualization** [ˌvɪʒuələˈzeɪʃən] *n*

vital [ˈvaɪtəl] *adj* **1** : vital ⟨vital organs : órganos vitales⟩ **2** CRUCIAL : esencial, crucial, decisivo ⟨of vital importance : de suma importancia⟩ **3** LIVELY : enérgico, lleno de vida, vital

vitality [vaɪˈtæləti] *n, pl* -ties : vitalidad *f*, energía *f*

vitally [ˈvaɪtəli] *adv* : sumamente

vital statistics *npl* : estadísticas *fpl* demográficas

vitamin [ˈvaɪtəmən] *n* : vitamina *f* ⟨vitamin deficiency : carencia vitamínica⟩

vitriol [ˈvɪtriəl] *n* : vitriolo *m*

vitriolic [ˌvɪtriˈɑlɪk] *adj* : mordaz, virulento

vivacious [vəˈveɪʃəs, vaɪ-] *adj* : vivaz, animado, lleno de vida

vivaciously [vəˈveɪʃəsli, vaɪ-] *adv* : con vivacidad, animadamente

vivacity [vəˈvæsəti, vaɪ-] *n* : vivacidad *f*

vivid [ˈvɪvəd] *adj* **1** LIVELY : lleno de vitalidad **2** BRILLIANT : vivo, intenso ⟨vivid colors : colores vivos⟩ **3** INTENSE, SHARP : vívido, gráfico ⟨a vivid dream : un sueño vívido⟩

vividly [ˈvɪvədli] *adv* **1** BRIGHTLY : con colores vivos **2** SHARPLY : vívidamente

vividness [ˈvɪvədnəs] *n* **1** BRIGHTNESS : intensidad *f*, viveza *f* **2** SHARPNESS : lo gráfico, nitidez *f*

vivisection [ˌvɪvəˈsɛkʃən, ˈvɪvəˌ-] *n* : vivisección *f*

vixen [ˈvɪksən] *n* : zorra *f*, raposa *f*

V-neck ['vi:,nɛk] *n* **1** : escote *m* en V, cuello *m* en V **2** : camisa *f* (etc.) con escote/cuello en V

vocabulary [vo:'kæbjə,lɛri] *n, pl* **-laries 1** : vocabulario *m* **2** LEXICON : léxico *m*

vocal ['vo:kəl] *adj* **1** : vocal **2** LOUD, OUTSPOKEN : ruidoso, muy franco

vocal cords *npl* : cuerdas *fpl* vocales

vocalist ['vo:kəlist] *n* : cantante *mf*, vocalista *mf*

vocalize ['vo:kə,laiz] *vt* **-ized; -izing** : vocalizar

vocation [vo'keiʃən] *n* : vocación *f* ⟨to have a vocation for : tener vocación de⟩

vocational [vo'keiʃənəl] *adj* : profesional ⟨vocational guidance : orientación profesional⟩

vociferous [vo'sifərəs] *adj* : ruidoso, vociferante

vodka ['vadkə] *n* : vodka *m*

vogue ['vo:g] *n* : moda *f*, boga *f* ⟨to be in vogue : estar de moda, estar en boga⟩

voice¹ ['vɔis] *vt* **voiced; voicing** : expresar

voice² *n* **1** : voz *f* ⟨in a low voice : en voz baja⟩ ⟨a high/deep voice : una voz aguda/profunda⟩ ⟨to raise/lower one's voice : hablar más alto/bajo⟩ ⟨to lose one's voice : quedarse sin voz⟩ ⟨his voice is changing : le está cambiando la voz⟩ ⟨to have a good (singing) voice : tener una buena voz, cantar bien⟩ **2** WISH, OPINION : voz *f* ⟨the voice of the people : la voz del pueblo⟩ **3** SAY, INFLUENCE : voz *f* ⟨to have no voice : no tener voz, no tener ni voz ni voto⟩ **4** : voz *f* (en gramática) **5 to make one's voice heard** : hacerse oír

voice box → **larynx**

voiced ['vɔist] *adj* : sonoro

voice mail *n* : correo *m* de voz, buzón *m* de voz

void¹ ['vɔid] *vt* : anular, invalidar ⟨to void a contract : anular un contrato⟩

void² *adj* **1** EMPTY : vacío, desprovisto ⟨void of content : desprovisto de contenido⟩ **2** INVALID : inválido, nulo

void³ *n* : vacío *m*

volatile ['valətəl] *adj* : volátil, inestable

volatility [,valə'tiləti] *n* : volatilidad *f*, inestabilidad *f*

volcanic [val'kænik] *adj* : volcánico

volcano [val'kei,no:] *n, pl* **-noes** *or* **-nos** : volcán *m*

vole ['vo:l] *n* : campañol *m*

volition [vo'liʃən] *n* : volición *f*, voluntad *f* ⟨of one's own volition : por voluntad propia⟩

volley ['vali] *n, pl* **-leys 1** : descarga *f* (de tiros) **2** : torrente *m*, lluvia *f* (de insultos, etc.) **3** : salva *f* (de aplausos) **4** : volea *f* (en deportes)

volleyball ['vali,bɔl] *n* : voleibol *m*; volibol *m Car, Hond, Mex*

volt ['vo:lt] *n* : voltio *m*

voltage ['vo:ltɪʤ] *n* : voltaje *m*

voluble ['valjəbəl] *adj* : locuaz

volume ['valjəm, -ju:m] *n* **1** BOOK : volumen *m*, tomo *m* **2** SPACE : capacidad *f*, volumen *m* (en física) **3** AMOUNT : cantidad *f*, volumen *m* **4** LOUDNESS : volumen *m*

voluminous [və'lu:mənəs] *adj* : voluminoso

voluntary ['valən,tɛri] *adj* : voluntario — **voluntarily** [,valən'tɛrəli] *adv*

volunteer¹ [,valən'tir] *vt* : ofrecer, dar ⟨to volunteer one's assistance : ofrecer la ayuda⟩ — *vi* : ofrecerse, alistarse como voluntario

volunteer² *n* : voluntario *m*, -ria *f*

voluptuous [və'lʌptʃuəs] *adj* : voluptuoso

voluptuousness [və'lʌptʃuəsnəs] *n* : voluptuosidad *f*

vomit¹ ['vamət] *v* : vomitar

vomit² *n* : vómito *m*

voodoo ['vu:,du:] *n, pl* **voodoos** : vudú *m*

voracious [vo'reiʃəs, və-] *adj* : voraz

voraciously [vo'reiʃəsli, və-] *adv* : vorazmente, con voracidad

voracity [vo'ræsəti, və-] *n* : voracidad *f*

vortex ['vɔr,tɛks] *n, pl* **vortices** ['vɔrtə,si:z] : vórtice *m*

vote¹ ['vo:t] *v* **voted; voting** *vi* **1** : votar ⟨to vote Democratic/Republican : votar por los demócratas/republicanos⟩ **2 to vote against** : votar en contra de **3 to vote for** : votar, votar a favor de (una propuesta, etc.) ⟨to vote for a candidate : votar por un candidato⟩ **4 to vote on** : someter a votación, votar sobre — *vt* **1** : votar **2 to vote down** : rechazar **3 to vote in** : elegir **4 to vote out** : no reelegir

vote² *n* **1** : voto *m* **2** SUFFRAGE : sufragio *m*, derecho *m* al voto

voter ['vo:tər] *n* : votante *mf*

voting ['vo:tɪŋ] *n* : votación *f*

vouch ['vautʃ] *vi* **to vouch for** : garantizar (algo), responder de (algo), responder por (alguien)

voucher ['vautʃər] *n* **1** RECEIPT : comprobante *m* **2** : vale *m* ⟨travel voucher : vale de viajar⟩

vow¹ ['vau] *vt* : jurar, prometer, hacer voto de

vow² *n* : promesa *f*, voto *m* (en la religión) ⟨a vow of poverty : un voto de pobreza⟩

vowel ['vauəl] *n* : vocal *m*

voyage¹ ['vɔiʤ] *vi* **-aged; -aging** : viajar

voyage² *n* : viaje *m*

voyager ['vɔiʤər] *n* : viajero *m*, -ra *f*

voyeur [vwa'jər, vɔi'ər] *n* : mirón *m*, -rona *f*

vulgar ['vʌlgər] *adj* **1** COMMON : ordinario, populachero, del vulgo **2** COARSE, CRUDE : grosero, de mal gusto, majadero *Mex* **3** INDECENT : indecente, colorado (dícese de un chiste, etc.)

vulgarity [,vʌl'gærəti] *n, pl* **-ties** : grosería *f*, vulgaridad *f*

vulgarly ['vʌlgərli] *adv* : vulgarmente, groseramente

vulnerability [,vʌlnərə'biləti] *n, pl* **-ties** : vulnerabilidad *f*

vulnerable ['vʌlnərəbəl] *adj* : vulnerable

vulture ['vʌltʃər] *n* : buitre *m*; zopilote *m CA, Mex*

vying → **vie**

W

w ['dʌbəlˌju:] *n*, *pl* **w's** *or* **ws** [-ˌju:z]
: vigésima tercera letra del alfabeto inglés

wad¹ ['wɑd] *vt* **wadded; wadding**
: hacer un taco con, formar en una
masa **2** STUFF : rellenar

wad² *n* : taco *m* (de papel), bola *f* (de algodón, etc.), fajo *m* (de billetes)

waddle¹ ['wɑdəl] *vi* **-dled; -dling** : andar
como un pato

waddle² *n* : andar *m* de pato

wade ['weɪd] *v* **waded; wading** *vi* **1**
: caminar por el agua **2 to wade
through** : leer (algo) con dificultad — *vt
or* **to wade across** : vadear

wading bird *n* : zancuda *f*, ave *f* zancuda

wafer ['weɪfər] *n* : barquillo *m*, galleta *f* de
barquillo

waffle¹ ['wɑfəl] *vi* **waffled; waffling** VAC-
ILLATE : vacilar

waffle² *n* **1** : wafle *m* **2 waffle iron**
: waflera *f*

waft ['wɑft, 'wæft] *vt* : llevar por el aire —
vi : flotar

wag¹ ['wæg] *v* **wagged; wagging** *vt*
: menear — *vi* : menearse, moverse

wag² *n* **1** : meneo *m* (de la cola) **2**
JOKER, WIT : bromista *mf*

wage¹ ['weɪdʒ] *vt* **waged; waging** : hacer,
librar ⟨to wage war : hacer la guerra⟩

wage² *n or* **wages** *npl* : sueldo *m*, salario
m ⟨minimum wage : salario mínimo⟩

wage earner → earner

wager¹ ['weɪdʒər] *v* : apostar

wager² *n* : apuesta *f*

waggish ['wægɪʃ] *adj* : burlón, bromista
(dícese de una persona), chistoso (dícese
de un comentario)

waggle ['wægəl] *vt* **-gled; -gling** : menear,
mover (de un lado a otro)

wagon ['wægən] *n* **1** : carro *m* (tirado
por caballos) **2** CART : carrito *m* **3 →
station wagon**

waif ['weɪf] *n* : niño *m* abandonado, animal *m* sin hogar

wail¹ ['weɪl] *vi* : gemir, lamentarse

wail² *n* : gemido *m*, lamento *m*

wainscot ['weɪnskət, -ˌskɑt, -ˌsko:t] *or*
wainscoting [-skətɪŋ, -ˌskɑ-, -ˌsko:-] *n*
: revestimiento *m* de paneles de madera

waist ['weɪst] *n* : cintura *f* (del cuerpo humano o de ropa), talle *m* (de ropa)

waistband ['weɪstˌbænd] *n* : cinturilla *f*

waistline ['weɪstˌlaɪn] → **waist**

wait¹ ['weɪt] *vi* **1** : esperar ⟨wait and see!
: ¡espera y verás!⟩ ⟨I can't wait : me
muero de ganas⟩ **2 to wait for** : esperar
⟨what are you waiting for? : ¿a qué esperas?⟩ **3 to wait on** : servir **4 to wait up
(for someone)** : quedarse despierto esperando (a alguien) — *vt* **1** AWAIT : esperar ⟨wait your turn : espera a que te
toque⟩ ⟨wait a minute : espere un momento⟩ **2** SERVE : servir, atender ⟨to
wait tables : servir (a la mesa)⟩ **3 to
wait out** : esperar hasta que pase

wait² *n* **1** : espera *f* **2 to lie in wait** : estar al acecho

waiter ['weɪtər] *n* : mesero *m*, camarero
m, mozo *m* Arg, Chile, Col, Peru

waiting list *n* : lista *f* de espera

waiting room *n* : sala *f* de espera

waitress ['weɪtrəs] *n* : mesera *f*, camarera
f, moza *f* Arg, Chile, Col, Peru

waive ['weɪv] *vt* **waived; waiving** : renunciar a ⟨to waive one's rights : renunciar
a sus derechos⟩ ⟨to waive the rules : no
aplicar las reglas⟩

waiver ['weɪvər] *n* : renuncia *f*

wake¹ ['weɪk] *v* **woke** ['wo:k]; **woken**
['wo:kən] *or* **waked; waking** *vi or* **to
wake up** : despertar(se) ⟨he woke at
noon : se despertó al mediodía⟩ ⟨wake
up! : ¡despiértate!⟩ — *vt* : despertar

wake² *n* **1** VIGIL : velatorio *m*, velorio *m*
(de un difunto) **2** TRAIL : estela *f* (de un
barco, un huracán, etc.) **3** AFTERMATH
: consecuencias *fpl* ⟨in the wake of : tras,
como consecuencia de⟩

wakeful ['weɪkfəl] *adj* **1** SLEEPLESS
: desvelado **2** VIGILANT : alerta, vigilante

wakefulness ['weɪkfəlnəs] *n* : vigilia *f*

waken ['weɪkən] → **awake**

walk¹ ['wɔk] *vi* **1** : caminar, andar, pasear
⟨you're walking too fast : estás caminando
demasiado rápido⟩ ⟨to walk around the
city : pasearse por la ciudad⟩ **2** : ir andando, ir a pie ⟨we had to walk home : tuvimos que ir a casa a pie⟩ **3** : recibir una
base por bolas (dícese de un bateador) **4
to walk away** LEAVE : irse **5 to walk
away** : salir ileso (de un accidente, etc.) **6
to walk away from** ABANDON : abandonar, retirarse de (negociaciones, etc.),
rechazar (un acuerdo, etc.) **7 to walk
away with** : ganar fácilmente (un premio,
etc.) **8 to walk in on** INTERRUPT, SUR-
PRISE : interrumpir, sorprender **9 to walk
off** LEAVE : irse **10 to walk off with** : llevarse **11 to walk out** LEAVE : irse **12 to
walk out on** : abandonar — *vt* **1**
: recorrer, caminar ⟨she walked two miles
: caminó dos millas⟩ **2** ACCOMPANY
: acompañar **3** : sacar a pasear (a un
perro) **4** : darle una base por bolas (a un
bateador) **5 to walk off** : caminar para
aliviar (un calambre, etc.)

walk² *n* **1** : paseo *m*, caminata *f* ⟨to go
for a walk : ir a caminar, dar un
paseo⟩ **2** PATH : camino *m* **3** GAIT
: andar *m* **4** : marcha *f* (en beisbol) **5
walk of life** : esfera *f*, condición *f*

walker ['wɔkər] *n* **1** : paseante *mf* **2**
HIKER : excursionista *mf* **3** : andador *m*
(aparato)

walking *n* : (el) caminar, (el) andar ⟨walking is good exercise : (el) caminar es
buen ejercicio⟩

walking stick *n* : bastón *m*

walkout ['wɔkˌaʊt] *n* STRIKE : huelga *f*

walk out *vi* **1** STRIKE : declararse en
huelga **2** LEAVE : salir, irse **3 to walk
out on** : abandonar, dejar

walkway ['wɔk,weɪ] *n* **1** SIDEWALK : acera *f* **2** PATH : sendero *m* **3** PASSAGEWAY : pasadizo *m*

wall¹ ['wɔl] *vt* **1 to wall in** : cercar con una pared o un muro, tapiar, amurallar **2 to wall off** : separar con una pared o un muro **3 to wall up** : tapiar, condenar (una ventana, etc.)

wall² *n* **1** : pared *f* : muro *m*, barda *f Mex* ⟨the walls of the city : las murallas de la ciudad⟩ **3** BARRIER : barrera *f* ⟨a wall of mountains : una barrera de montañas⟩ **4** : pared *f* (en anatomía) **5 to drive someone up the wall** *fam* : volver loco a alguien

walled ['wɔld] *adj* : amurallado

wallet ['wɑlət] *n* : billetera *f*, cartera *f*

wallflower ['wɔl,flaʊər] *n* **1** : alhelí *m* (flor) **2 to be a wallflower** : comer pavo

wallop¹ ['wɑləp] *vt* **1** TROUNCE : darle una paliza (a alguien) **2** SOCK : pegar fuerte

wallop² *n* : golpe *m* fuerte, golpazo *m*

wallow ['wɑ,lo:] *vi* **1** : revolcarse ⟨to wallow in the mud : revolcarse en el lodo⟩ **2** DELIGHT : deleitarse ⟨to wallow in luxury : nadar en lujos⟩

wallpaper¹ ['wɔl,peɪpər] *vt* : empapelar

wallpaper² *n* : papel *m* pintado

wall–to–wall *adj* **1** FILLED : lleno ⟨it was wall-to-wall (with) people : estaba repleto de gente⟩ **2 wall-to-wall carpeting** : alfombra *f* (de pared a pared), moquette *f Arg, Uru*; moqueta *f Spain*

walnut ['wɔl,nʌt] *n* **1** : nuez *f* (fruta) **2** : nogal *m* (árbol y madera)

walrus ['wɔlrəs, 'wɑl-] *n, pl* **-rus** *or* **-ruses** : morsa *f*

waltz¹ ['wɔlts] *vi* **1** : bailar el vals **2** BREEZE : pasar con ligereza ⟨to waltz in : entrar tan campante⟩

waltz² *n* : vals *m*

wan ['wɑn] *adj* **wanner; wannest 1** PALLID : pálido **2** DIM : tenue ⟨wan light : luz tenue⟩ **3** LANGUID : lánguido ⟨a wan smile : una sonrisa lánguida⟩ — **wanly** *adv*

wand ['wɑnd] *n* : varita *f* (mágica)

wander ['wɑndər] *vi* **1** RAMBLE : deambular, vagar, vagabundear **2** STRAY : alejarse, desviarse, divagar ⟨she let her mind wander : dejó vagar la imaginación⟩ — *vt* : recorrer ⟨to wander the streets : vagar por las calles⟩

wanderer ['wɑndərər] *n* : vagabundo *m*, -da *f*; viajero *m*, -ra *f*

wanderlust ['wɑndər,lʌst] *n* : pasión *f* por viajar

wane¹ ['weɪn] *vi* **waned; waning 1** : menguar (dícese de la luna) **2** DECLINE : disminuir, decaer, menguar

wane² *n* **on the wane** : decayendo, en decadencia

wangle ['wæŋgəl] *vt* **-gled; -gling** FINAGLE : arreglárselas para conseguir

wannabe ['wɑnə,bi:] *n* : aspirante *mf* (a algo); imitador *m*, -dora *f* (de alguien)

want¹ ['wɑnt, 'wɔnt] *vt* **1** LACK : faltar **2** REQUIRE : requerir, necesitar **3** DESIRE : querer, desear

want² *n* **1** LACK : falta *f* **2** DESTITUTION : indigencia *f*, miseria *f* **3** DESIRE, NEED : deseo *m*, necesidad *f*

wanting ['wɑntɪŋ, 'wɔn-] *adj* **1** ABSENT : ausente **2** DEFICIENT : deficiente ⟨he's wanting in common sense : le falta sentido común⟩

wanton ['wɑntən, 'wɔn-] *adj* **1** LEWD, LUSTFUL : lascivo, lujurioso, licencioso **2** INHUMANE, MERCILESS : despiadado ⟨wanton cruelty : crueldad despiadada⟩

wapiti ['wɑpəti] *n, pl* **-ti** *or* **-tis** ELK : uapití *m*, wapití *m*

war¹ ['wɔr] *vi* **warred; warring** : combatir, batallar, hacer la guerra

war² *n* : guerra *f* ⟨to go to war : entrar en guerra⟩ ⟨to be at war : estar en guerra⟩

warble¹ ['wɔrbəl] *vi* **-bled; -bling** : gorjear, trinar

warble² *n* : trino *m*, gorjeo *m*

warbler ['wɔrblər] *n* : curruca *f*

ward¹ ['wɔrd] *vt* **to ward off** : desviar, protegerse contra

ward² *n* **1** : sala *f* (de un hospital, etc.) ⟨maternity ward : sala de maternidad⟩ **2** : distrito *m* electoral o administrativo (de una ciudad) **3** : pupilo *m*, -la *f* (de un tutor, etc.)

warden ['wɔrdən] *n* **1** KEEPER : guarda *mf*; guardián *m*, -diana *f* ⟨game warden : guardabosque⟩ **2** *or* **prison warden** : alcaide *m*

wardrobe ['wɔrd,ro:b] *n* **1** CLOSET : armario *m* **2** CLOTHES : vestuario *m*, guardarropa *f*

ware ['wær] *n* **1** POTTERY : cerámica *f* **2 wares** *npl* GOODS : mercancía *f*, mercadería *f*

warehouse ['wær,haʊs] *n* : depósito *m*, almacén *m*, bodega *f Chile, Col, Mex*

warfare ['wɔr,fær] *n* **1** WAR : guerra *f* **2** STRUGGLE : lucha *f* ⟨the warfare against drugs : la lucha contra las drogas⟩

warhead ['wɔr,hɛd] *n* : ojiva *f*, cabeza *f* (de un misil)

warily ['wærəli] *adv* : cautelosamente, con cautela

wariness ['wærinəs] *n* : cautela *f*

warlike ['wɔr,laɪk] *adj* : belicoso, guerrero

warm¹ ['wɔrm] *vt* **1** HEAT : calentar, recalentar **2 to warm one's heart** : reconfortar a uno, alegrar el corazón **3 to warm up** : calentar (los músculos, un automóvil, etc.) — *vi* **1** : calentarse **2 to warm to** : tomarle simpatía (a alguien), entusiasmarse con (algo)

warm² *adj* **1** LUKEWARM : tibio, templado **2** : caliente, cálido, caluroso ⟨a warm wind : un viento cálido⟩ ⟨a warm day : un día caluroso, un día de calor⟩ ⟨warm hands : manos calientes⟩ **3** : caliente, que abriga ⟨warm clothes : ropa de abrigo⟩ ⟨I feel warm : tengo calor⟩ **4** CARING, CORDIAL : cariñoso, cordial **5** : cálido (dícese de colores) **6** FRESH : fresco, reciente ⟨a warm trail : un rastro reciente⟩ **7** (*used for riddles*) : caliente

warm–blooded ['wɔrm'blʌdəd] *adj* : de sangre caliente

warmhearted ['wɔrm'hɑrtəd] *adj* : cariñoso

warmly ['wɔrmli] *adv* **1** AFFECTIONATELY : calurosamente, afectuosamente **2 to dress warmly** : abrigarse

warmonger ['wɔr,mɑŋgər, -,mʌŋ-] *n* : belicista *mf*

warmth ['wɔrmpθ] *n* **1** : calor *m* **2** AFFECTION : cariño *m*, afecto *m* **3** ENTHUSIASM : ardor *m*, entusiasmo *m*

warm–up ['wɔrm,ʌp] *n* : calentamiento *m*

warn ['wɔrn] *vt* **1** CAUTION : advertir, alertar **2** INFORM : avisar, informar

warning ['wɔrniŋ] *n* **1** ADVICE : advertencia *f*, aviso *m* **2** ALERT : alerta *f*, alarma *f*

warp¹ ['wɔrp] *vt* **1** : alabear, combar **2** PERVERT : pervertir, deformar — *vi* : pandearse, alabearse, combarse

warp² *n* **1** : urdimbre *f* ⟨the warp and the weft : la urdimbre y la trama⟩ **2** : alabeo *m* (en la madera, etc.)

warrant¹ ['wɔrənt] *vt* **1** ASSURE : asegurar, garantizar **2** GUARANTEE : garantizar, JUSTIFY, MERIT : justificar, merecer

warrant² *n* **1** AUTHORIZATION : autorización *f*, permiso *m* ⟨an arrest warrant : una orden de detención⟩ **2** JUSTIFICATION : justificación *f*

warranty ['wɔrənti, ,wɔrən'ti:] *n, pl* **-ties** : garantía *f*

warren ['wɔrən] *n* : madriguera *f* (de conejos)

warrior ['wɔriər] *n* : guerrero *m*, -ra *f*

warship ['wɔr,ʃɪp] *n* : buque *m* de guerra

wart ['wɔrt] *n* : verruga *f*

wartime ['wɔr,taɪm] *n* : tiempo *m* de guerra

wary ['wæri] *adj* **warier; -est** : cauteloso, receloso ⟨to be wary of : desconfiar de⟩

was → **be**

wash¹ ['wɔʃ, 'wɑʃ] *vt* **1** CLEAN : lavar(se), limpiar, fregar ⟨to wash the dishes : lavar los platos⟩ ⟨to wash one's hands : lavarse las manos⟩ **2** DRENCH : mojar **3** LAP : bañar ⟨waves were washing the shore : las olas bañaban la orilla⟩ **4** CARRY, DRAG : arrastrar ⟨they were washed out to sea : fueron arrastrados por el mar⟩ **5 to be/get washed out** : cancelarse por lluvia **6 to wash away** : llevarse (un puente, etc.) **7 to wash down** : lavar (paredes, etc.) **8 to wash down** : tragarse (con agua, etc.) **9 to wash off** : lavar **10 to wash off** : quitar (la suciedad, etc.) **11 to wash out** : lavar (un recipiente, etc.) **12 to wash out** : destruir, inundar (una carretera, etc.) **13 to wash out** : quitar (una mancha, etc.) — *vi* **1** : lavar(se) ⟨I'll wash, you dry : yo lavo y tú secas⟩ ⟨wash before dinner : lávate antes de cenar⟩ ⟨the dress washes well : el vestido se lava bien⟩ **2 to wash over** : bañar ⟨relief washed over me : sentí un gran alivio⟩ **3 to wash off/out** : quitarse **4 to wash up** BATHE : lavarse **5 to wash up/ashore** : ser arrojado por el mar

wash² *n* **1** : lavado *m* ⟨to give something a wash : lavar algo⟩ **2** LAUNDRY : artículos *mpl* para lavar, ropa *f* sucia **3** : estela *f* (de un barco)

washable ['wɔʃəbəl, 'wɑ-] *adj* : lavable

washboard ['wɔʃ,bɔrd, 'wɑʃ-] *n* : tabla *f* de lavar

washbowl ['wɔʃ,boːl, 'wɑʃ-] *n* : lavabo *m*, lavamanos *m*

washcloth ['wɔʃ,klɔθ, 'wɑʃ-] *n* : toallita *f* (para lavarse)

washed-out ['wɔʃt'aʊt, 'wɑʃt-] *adj* **1** : desvaído (dícese de colores) **2** EXHAUSTED : agotado, desanimado

washed-up ['wɔʃt'ʌp, 'wɑʃt-] *adj* : acabado (dícese de una persona), fracasado (dícese de un negocio, etc.)

washer ['wɔʃər, 'wɑ-] *n* **1** → **washing machine** : arandela *f* (de una llave, etc.)

washing ['wɔʃɪŋ, 'wɑ-] *n* WASH : ropa *f* para lavar

washing machine *n* : máquina *f* de lavar, lavadora *f*

washout ['wɔʃ,aʊt, 'wɑʃ-] *n* **1** : erosión *f* (de la tierra) **2** FAILURE : fracaso *m* ⟨she's a washout : es un desastre⟩

washroom ['wɔʃ,ruːm, 'wɑʃ-, -,rʊm] *n* : servicios *mpl* (públicos); baño *m*; sanitario *m* Col, Mex, Ven

wasn't ['wʌzənt] *contraction of* WAS NOT → **be**

wasp ['wɑsp] *n* : avispa *f*

WASP *or* **Wasp** ['wɑsp] *n* (white Anglo-Saxon Protestant) *sometimes disparaging* : persona *f* blanca, anglosajona, y protestante

waspish ['wɑspɪʃ] *adj* **1** IRRITABLE : irritable, irascible **2** CAUSTIC : cáustico, mordaz

waste¹ ['weɪst] *v* **wasted; wasting** *vt* **1** DEVASTATE : arrasar, arruinar, devastar **2** SQUANDER : desperdiciar, despilfarrar, malgastar ⟨to waste time : perder tiempo⟩ — *vi or* **to waste away** : consumirse, chuparse

waste² *adj* **1** BARREN : yermo, baldío **2** DISCARDED : de desecho **3** EXCESS : sobrante

waste³ *n* **1** → **wasteland 2** MISUSE : derroche *m*, desperdicio *m*, despilfarro *m* ⟨a waste of time : una pérdida de tiempo⟩ **3** RUBBISH : basura *f*, desechos *mpl*, desperdicios *mpl* **4** EXCREMENT : excremento *m*

wastebasket ['weɪst,bæskət] *or* **wastepaper basket** *n* : cesto *m* (de basura), papelera *f*, zafación *m* Car

wasteful ['weɪstfəl] *adj* : despilfarrador, derrochador, pródigo

wastefulness ['weɪstfəlnəs] *n* : derroche *m*, despilfarro *m*

wasteland ['weɪst,lænd, -lənd] *n* : baldío *m*, yermo *m*, desierto *m*

wastepaper ['weɪst,peɪpər] *n* : papel *m* de desecho

wastepaper basket → **wastebasket**

watch¹ ['wɑtʃ] *vt* **1** OBSERVE : mirar, observar ⟨to watch television : mirar/ver la televisión⟩ ⟨watch this! : ¡mira!⟩ **2** MONITOR : vigilar **3** *or* **to watch over** : vigilar, cuidar (a niños, etc.) ⟨would you

watch my things? : ¿me puedes cuidar/
vigilar las cosas?⟩ **4** : tener cuidado de,
vigilar ⟨watch what you do : ten cuidado
con lo que haces⟩ ⟨I have to watch my
cholesterol : tengo que vigilar el colesterol⟩ — *vi* **1** OBSERVE : mirar, ver, observar **2 to watch for** AWAIT : esperar,
quedar a la espera de **3 to watch out**
: tener cuidado ⟨watch out! : ¡ten cuidado!, ¡ojo!⟩

watch² *n* **1** : guardia *f* ⟨to be on watch,
to stand watch : estar de guardia⟩ **2**
SURVEILLANCE : vigilancia *f* **3**
LOOKOUT : guardia *mf*, centinela *f*, vigía
mf **4** TIMEPIECE : reloj *m* **5 to keep
watch on/over** : vigilar, cuidar

watchdog [ˈwɑtʃˌdɔg] *n* : perro *m*
guardián

watcher [ˈwɑtʃər] *n* : observador *m*, -dora
f

watchful [ˈwɑtʃfəl] *adj* : alerta, vigilante,
atento

watchfulness [ˈwɑtʃfəlnəs] *n* : vigilancia *f*

watchmaker [ˈwɑtʃˌmeɪkər] *n* : relojero
m, -ra *f*

watchmaking [ˈwɑtʃˌmeɪkɪŋ] *n* : relojería
f (actividad)

watchman [ˈwɑtʃmən] *n, pl* **-men** [-mən,
-ˌmɛn] : vigilante *m*, guarda *m*

watchtower [ˈwɑtʃˌtaʊər] *n* : atalaya *f*

watchword [ˈwɑtʃˌwɜrd] *n* **1** PASSWORD
: contraseña *f* **2** SLOGAN : lema *m*, eslogan *m*

water¹ [ˈwɔtər, ˈwɑ-] *vt* **1** : regar (el
jardín, etc.) **2 to water down** DILUTE
: diluir, aguar — *vi* **1** : lagrimear (dícese de
los ojos), hacérsele agua la boca a uno
⟨my mouth is watering : se me hace agua
la boca⟩

water² *n* **1** : agua *f* ⟨drinking water
: agua potable⟩ ⟨running water : agua
corriente⟩ **2 waters** *npl* : aguas *fpl* **3
not to hold water** : hacer agua por todos
lados **4 to pass water** : orinar

water buffalo *n* : búfalo *m* de agua

watercolor [ˈwɔtərˌkʌlər, ˈwɑ-] *n* : acuarela *f*

watercourse [ˈwɔtərˌkors, ˈwɑ-] *n* : curso
m de agua

watercress [ˈwɔtərˌkrɛs, ˈwɑ-] *n* : berro *m*

waterfall [ˈwɔtərˌfɔl, ˈwɑ-] *n* : cascada *f*,
salto *m* de agua, catarata *f*

waterfowl [ˈwɔtərˌfaʊl, ˈwɑ-] *n* : ave *f*
acuática

waterfront [ˈwɔtərˌfrʌnt, ˈwɑ-] *n* **1**
: tierra *f* que bordea un río, un lago, o un
mar **2** WHARF : muelle *m*

water heater *n* : calentador *m* de agua,
bóiler *m Mex*

watering can *n* : regadera *f*

water lily *n* : nenúfar *m*

waterlogged [ˈwɔtərˌlɔgd, ˈwɑtər-ˌlɑgd]
adj : lleno de agua, empapado, inundado
(dícese del suelo)

watermark [ˈwɔtərˌmɑrk, ˈwɑ-] *n* **1**
: marca *f* del nivel de agua **2** : filigrana
f (en el papel)

watermelon [ˈwɔtərˌmɛlən, ˈwɑ-] *n* : sandía *f*

water moccasin → **moccasin**

waterpower [ˈwɔtərˌpaʊər, ˈwɑ-] *n* : energía *f* hidráulica

waterproof¹ [ˈwɔtərˌpruːf, ˈwɑ-] *vt* : hacer
impermeable, impermeabilizar

waterproof² *adj* : impermeable, a prueba
de agua

waterproofing *n* : impermeabilizante *nm*
(sustancia química)

water repellent *n* : impermeabilizante *nm*

water–resistant or **water–repellent** *adj*
: hidrófugo, impermeabilizado

watershed [ˈwɔtərˌʃɛd, ˈwɑ-] *n* **1** : línea *f*
divisoria de aguas **2** BASIN : cuenca *f*
(de un río)

waterskiing [ˈwɔtərˌskiːɪŋ, ˈwɑ-] *n* : esquí
m acuático

waterspout [ˈwɔtərˌspaʊt, ˈwɑ-] *n* WHIRL
WIND : tromba *f* marina

watertight [ˈwɔtərˌtaɪt, ˈwɑ-] *adj* **1** : hermético **2** IRREFUTABLE : irrebatible, irrefutable ⟨a watertight contract : un contrato sin lagunas⟩

waterwheel [ˈwɔtərˌhwiːl, ˈwɑ-] *n* : noria *f*

waterway [ˈwɔtərˌweɪ, ˈwɑ-] *n* : vía *f*
navegable

waterworks [ˈwɔtərˌwɜrks, ˈwɑ-] *npl*
: central *f* de abastecimiento de agua

watery [ˈwɔtəri, ˈwɑ-] *adj* **1** : acuoso,
como agua **2** : aguado, diluido ⟨watery
soup : sopa aguada⟩ **3** : lloroso ⟨watery
eyes : ojos llorosos⟩ **4** WASHED-OUT
: desvaído (dícese de colores)

watt [ˈwɑt] *n* : vatio *m*

wattage [ˈwɑtɪdʒ] *n* : vataje *m*

wave¹ [ˈweɪv] *v* **waved; waving** *vi* **1** : saludar con la mano, hacer señas con la
mano ⟨she waved at him : lo saludó con
la mano⟩ **2** FLUTTER, SHAKE : ondear,
agitarse **3** UNDULATE : ondular — *vt* **1**
SHAKE : agitar **2** BRANDISH : blandir **3**
CURL : ondular, marcar (el pelo) **4** SIG
NAL : hacerle señas a (con la mano) ⟨he
waved farewell : se despidió con la
mano⟩

wave² *n* **1** : ola *f* (de agua) **2** CURL
: onda *f* (en el pelo) **3** : onda *f* (en
física) **4** SURGE : oleada *f* ⟨a wave of
enthusiasm : una oleada de entusiasmo⟩ **5** GESTURE : señal *f* con la
mano, saludo *m* con la mano

wavelength [ˈweɪvˌlɛŋkθ] *n* : longitud *f* de
onda

waver [ˈweɪvər] *vi* **1** VACILLATE : vacilar,
fluctuar **2** FLICKER : parpadear, titilar,
oscilar **3** FALTER : flaquear, tambalearse

wavy [ˈweɪvi] *adj* **wavier; -est** : ondulado

wax¹ [ˈwæks] *vi* **1** : crecer (dícese de la
luna) **2** BECOME : volverse, ponerse ⟨to
wax indignant : indignarse⟩ — *vt*
: encerar

wax² *n* **1** BEESWAX : cera *f* de abejas **2**
: cera *f* ⟨floor wax : cera para el piso⟩ **3**
or **earwax** [ˈɪrˌwæks] : cerilla *f*, cerumen
m

waxen [ˈwæksən] *adj* : de cera

waxy [ˈwæksi] *adj* **waxier; -est** : ceroso

way [ˈweɪ] *n* **1** PATH, ROAD : camino *m*,
vía *f* ⟨they live across the way : viven enfrente⟩ **2** ROUTE : camino *m*, ruta *f* ⟨to

go the wrong way : equivocarse de camino ⟨to lose one's way : perderse⟩ ⟨do you know the way? : ¿sabes el camino?⟩ ⟨can you tell me the way to . . . ? : ¿me puedes indicar cómo llegar a . . . ?⟩ ⟨I'm on my way : estoy de camino⟩ ⟨we should be on our way : tenemos que irnos⟩ ⟨on the way back : en el camino de regreso/vuelta⟩ ⟨the only way in/out : la única entrada/salida⟩ **3** : línea *f* de conducta, camino *m* ⟨he chose the easy way : optó por el camino fácil⟩ **4** MANNER, MEANS : manera *f*, modo *m*, forma *f* ⟨in the same way : del mismo modo, igualmente⟩ ⟨in no way : de ninguna manera⟩ ⟨to my way of thinking : a mi modo de ver⟩ ⟨the way she spends money, you would think she was rich! : gasta dinero como si fuera rica⟩ ⟨their way of life : su modo de vida⟩ **5** (*indicating a wish*) ⟨have it your way : como tú quieras⟩ ⟨to get one's own way : salirse uno con la suya⟩ **6** (*indicating progress*) ⟨we inched our way forward : avanzamos poco a poco⟩ ⟨to talk one's way out of something : librarse de algo (engatusándole a alguien)⟩ **7** (*indicating a condition or situation*) ⟨he's in a bad way : está muy mal de salud⟩ ⟨that's just the way things are : así son las cosas⟩ **8** (*indicating one of two alternatives*) ⟨either way : de cualquier manera⟩ ⟨you can't have it both ways : tienes que elegir⟩ **9** (*indicating a portion*) ⟨we split it three ways : lo dividimos en tres⟩ **10** RESPECT : aspecto *m*, sentido *m* ⟨in a way, it was a relief : en cierto modo fue un alivio⟩ ⟨in every way : en todo⟩ **11** CUSTOM : costumbre *f* ⟨to change/mend one's ways : dejar las malas costumbres, enmendarse⟩ ⟨to be set in one's ways : ser inflexible⟩ **12** PASSAGE : camino *m* ⟨to be/get in the way : estar/meterse en el camino⟩ ⟨get it out of the way! : ¡quítalo de en medio!⟩ ⟨to make way for, to clear the way for : abrirle paso a⟩ **13** DISTANCE : distancia *f* ⟨to come a long way : hacer grandes progresos⟩ ⟨he talked the whole way home : habló durante todo el camino a casa⟩ ⟨she ran all the way there : corrió hasta allí⟩ ⟨it stretches all the way along the beach : se extiende a lo largo de la playa⟩ ⟨we went all the way up : subimos hasta arriba⟩ ⟨we sat all the way at the back : nos sentamos al fondo⟩ ⟨you came all this way just to see me? : ¿viniste desde tan lejos sólo para verme?⟩ **14** DIRECTION : dirección *f* ⟨come this way : venga por aquí⟩ ⟨this way and that : de un lado a otro⟩ ⟨which way did he go? : ¿por dónde fue?⟩ **15 all the way** COMPLETELY : completamente **16 all the way** CONTINUOUSLY : en todo momento ⟨he was with us all the way : nos apoyó en todo momento⟩ ⟨all the way through the concert : durante todo el concierto⟩ **17 by the way** : a propósito, por cierto **18 by way of** VIA : vía, pasando por **19 by way of** *or* **in the way of** AS : a

modo de, a manera de **20 every step of the way** : en todo momento **21 no way** : de ninguna manera, ni hablar **22 out of the way** REMOTE : remoto, recóndito **23 out of the way** FINISHED : acabado ⟨to get a task out of the way : quitar una tarea de en medio⟩ **24 the other way (around)** : al revés **25 there are no two ways about it** : no cabe la menor duda **26 to give way** COLLAPSE : romperse, hundirse, ceder **27 to give way to** : ceder a **28 to go out of one's way (to)** : tomarse muchas molestias (para), desvivirse (por) **29 to go someone's way** : salirle bien a alguien **30 to have a way of** : soler, tender a ⟨things have a way of working out : las cosas suelen arreglarse solas⟩ ⟨she has a way of exaggerating : tiende a exagerar las cosas⟩ **31 to have a way with words** : saber como tratar a (los niños, los animales, etc.) ⟨to have a way with words : tener facilidad de palabra⟩ **32** → **under way 33 way to go!** *fam* : ¡bien hecho!

wayfarer ['weɪ,færər] *n* : caminante *mf*

waylay ['weɪ,leɪ] *vt* **-laid** [-,leɪd]; **-laying** ACCOST : abordar

wayside ['weɪ,saɪd] *n* : borde *m* del camino

wayward ['weɪwərd] *adj* **1** UNRULY : díscolo, rebelde **2** UNTOWARD : adverso

we ['wiː] *pron* : nosotros, nosotras

weak ['wiːk] *adj* **1** : débil ⟨weak arms/eyes : brazos/ojos débiles⟩ ⟨a weak leader/character : un líder/carácter débil⟩ ⟨a weak drug/signal/economy : una droga/señal/economía débil⟩ **2** GENTLE : flojo (dícese de un golpe), leve (dícese de un viento) **3** : flojo (dícese de un estudiante, etc.) **4** : flojo (dícese de una pieza, etc.) **5** : débil, flojo (dícese de un argumento, una excusa, etc.) ⟨a weak attempt : un intento tímido⟩ **6** DILUTED : aguado, diluido ⟨weak tea : té poco cargado⟩ **7** FAINT : tenue (dícese de los colores, las luces, los sonidos, etc.) **8** : poco pronunciado (dícese de la barbilla) **9** : regular (en gramática)

weaken ['wiːkən] *vt* : debilitar — *vi* : debilitarse, flaquear

weakling ['wiːklɪŋ] *n* : alfeñique *m* *fam*; debilucho *m*, -cha *f*

weakly[1] ['wiːkli] *adv* : débilmente

weakly[2] *adj* **weaklier; -est** : débil, enclenque

weakness ['wiːknəs] *n* **1** FEEBLENESS : debilidad *f* **2** FAULT, FLAW : flaqueza *f*, punto *m* débil

wealth ['wɛlθ] *n* **1** RICHES : riqueza *f* **2** PROFUSION : abundancia *f*, profusión *f*

wealthy ['wɛlθi] *adj* **wealthier; -est** : rico, acaudalado, adinerado

wean ['wiːn] *vt* **1** : destetar (a los niños o las crías) **2 to wean someone away from** : quitarle a alguien la costumbre de

weapon ['wɛpən] *n* : arma *f* ⟨biological/chemical weapon : arma biológica/

química⟩ ⟨weapon of mass destruction : arma de destrucción masiva⟩

weaponless ['wepənləs] *adj* : desarmado

weaponry ['wepənri] *n* : armamento *m*

wear¹ ['wær] *v* **wore** ['wor]; **worn** ['worn]; **wearing** *vt* **1** : llevar (ropa, un reloj, etc.), calzar (zapatos) ⟨to wear a smile : sonreír⟩ **2** *or* **to wear away** : gastar, desgastar, erosionar (rocas, etc.) ⟨the carpet was badly worn : la alfombra estaba muy gastada⟩ **3** : hacer (por el uso) ⟨he wore a hole in his pants : se le hizo un agujero en los pantalones⟩ **4 to wear down** DRAIN : agotar **5 to wear down** : convencer por cansancio **6 to wear on** IRRITATE : molestar, irritar **7 to wear one's heart on one's sleeve** : no ocultar uno sus sentimientos **8 to wear out** : gastar ⟨he wore out his shoes : gastó sus zapatos⟩ **9 to wear out** EXHAUST : agotar, fatigar ⟨to wear oneself out : agotarse⟩ **10 to wear through** : gastar (completamente) ⟨he wore through his shoes : se le hizo agujeros en los zapatos⟩ — *vi* **1** LAST : durar **2 to wear away** : desgastarse **3 to wear off** DIMINISH, VANISH : disminuir, desaparecer ⟨the drug wears off in a few hours : los efectos de la droga desaparecen después de unas horas⟩ **4 to wear on** CONTINUE, DRAG : continuar, alargarse **5 to wear out** : gastarse **6 to wear the pants** : llevar los pantalones **7 to wear thin** : gastarse (dícese de la tela, etc.) **8 to wear thin** : agotarse (dícese de la paciencia, etc.), perder la gracia (dícese de un chiste)

wear² *n* **1** USE : uso *m* ⟨for everyday wear : para todos los días⟩ **2** CLOTHING : ropa *f* ⟨children's wear : ropa de niños⟩ **3** DETERIORATION : desgaste *m* ⟨to be the worse for wear : estar deteriorado⟩

wearable ['wærəbəl] *adj* : que puede ponerse (dícese de una prenda)

wear and tear *n* : desgaste *m*

weariness ['wɪrinəs] *n* : fatiga *f*, cansancio *m*

wearisome ['wɪrisəm] *adj* : aburrido, pesado, cansado

weary¹ ['wɪri] *v* **-ried; -rying** *vt* **1** TIRE : cansar, fatigar **2** BORE : hastiar, aburrir — *vi* : cansarse

weary² *adj* **wearier; -est 1** TIRED : cansado **2** FED UP : harto **3** BORED : aburrido

weasel ['wi:zəl] *n* : comadreja *f*

weather¹ ['wɛðər] *vt* **1** WEAR : erosionar, desgastar **2** ENDURE : aguantar, sobrellevar, capear ⟨to weather the storm : capear el temporal⟩

weather² *n* **1** : tiempo *m* ⟨good/bad weather : buen/mal tiempo⟩ ⟨weather permitting : si hace buen tiempo⟩ ⟨weather forecast : pronóstico del tiempo, parte meteorológico⟩ **2 to be under the weather** : estar enfermo, no estar muy bien

weather–beaten ['wɛðər,bi:tən] *adj* : curtido

weatherman ['wɛðər,mæn] *n, pl* **-men** [-mən, -,mɛn] METEOROLOGIST : meteorólogo *m*, -ga *f*

weatherproof ['wɛðər,pru:f] *adj* : que resiste a la intemperie, impermeable

weather vane → **vane**

weave¹ ['wi:v] *v* **wove** ['wo:v] *or* **weaved; woven** ['wo:vən] *or* **weaved; weaving** *vt* **1** : tejer (tela) **2** INTERLACE : entretejer, entrelazar **3 to weave one's way through** : abrirse camino por — *vi* **1** : tejer **2** WIND : serpentear, zigzaguear

weave² *n* : tejido *m*, trama *f*

weaver ['wi:vər] *n* : tejedor *m*, -dora *f*

web¹ ['wɛb] *vt* **webbed; webbing** : cubrir o proveer con una red

web² *n* **1** COBWEB, SPIDERWEB : telaraña *f*, tela *f* de araña **2** ENTANGLEMENT, SNARE : red *f*, enredo *m* ⟨a web of intrigue : una red de intriga⟩ **3** : membrana *f* interdigital (de aves) **4** NETWORK : red *f* ⟨a web of highways : una red de carreteras⟩ **5 the Web** : la web

webbed ['wɛbd] *adj* : palmeado ⟨webbed feet : patas palmeadas⟩

webcam ['wɛb,kæm] *n* : webcam *f*

weblog → **blog**

webmaster *or* **Webmaster** ['wɛb,mæstər] *n* : webmaster *mf*

web site *or* **Web site** *n* : sitio *m* web

wed ['wɛd] *vt* **wedded; wedding 1** MARRY : casarse con **2** UNITE : ligar, unir

we'd ['wi:d] *contraction of* WE HAD, WE SHOULD *or* WE WOULD → **have, should, would**

wedding ['wɛdɪŋ] *n* : boda *f*, casamiento *m* ⟨wedding dress : traje de novia⟩ ⟨wedding ring : anillo de boda⟩

wedge¹ ['wɛdʒ] *vt* **wedged; wedging 1** : apretar (con una cuña) ⟨to wedge open : mantener abierto con una cuña⟩ **2** CRAM : meter, embutir

wedge² *n* **1** : cuña *f* **2** PIECE : porción *f*, trozo *m*

wedlock ['wɛd,lɑk] → **marriage**

Wednesday ['wɛnz,deɪ, -di] *n* : miércoles *m* ⟨today is Wednesday : hoy es miércoles⟩ ⟨(on) Wednesday : el miércoles⟩ ⟨(on) Wednesdays : los miércoles⟩ ⟨last Wednesday : el miércoles pasado⟩ ⟨next Wednesday : el miércoles que viene⟩ ⟨every other Wednesday : cada dos miércoles⟩ ⟨Wednesday afternoon/morning : miércoles por la tarde/mañana⟩

wee ['wi:] *adj* **1** : pequeño, minúsculo **2 the wee hours** → **hour**

weed¹ ['wi:d] *vt* **1** : desherbar **2 to weed out** : eliminar, quitar

weed² *n* : mala hierba *f*

weed killer *n* : herbicida *m*

weedy ['wi:di] *adj* **weedier; -est 1** : cubierto de malas hierbas **2** LANKY, SKINNY : flaco, larguirucho *fam*

week ['wi:k] *n* : semana *f* ⟨last week : la semana pasada⟩ ⟨next week : la semana que viene⟩

weekday ['wi:k,deɪ] *n* : día *m* laborable

weekend [ˈwiːkˌɛnd] *n* : fin *m* de semana
weekly¹ [ˈwiːkli] *adv* : semanalmente
weekly² *adj* : semanal
weekly³ *n, pl* **-lies** : semanario *m*
weep [ˈwiːp] *v* **wept** [ˈwɛpt]; **weeping** : llorar
weeping willow *n* : sauce *m* llorón
weepy [ˈwiːpi] *adj* **weepier; -est** : lloroso, triste
weevil [ˈwiːvəl] *n* : gorgojo *m*
weft [ˈwɛft] *n* : trama *f*
weigh [ˈweɪ] *vt* 1 : pesar 2 CONSIDER : considerar, sopesar 3 **to weigh anchor** : levar anclas 4 **to weigh down** : sobrecargar (con una carga), abrumar (con preocupaciones, etc.) 5 **to weigh up** : hacerse una idea de — *vi* 1 : pesar ⟨it weighs 10 pounds : pesa 10 libras⟩ 2 COUNT : tener importancia, contar ⟨to weigh for/against : favorecer/perjudicar⟩ 3 **to weigh in** : intervenir 4 **to weigh on one's mind** : preocuparle a uno
weight¹ [ˈweɪt] *vt or* **to weight down** 1 : poner peso en, sujetar con un peso 2 BURDEN : cargar, oprimir
weight² *n* 1 HEAVINESS : peso *m* ⟨to lose weight : bajar de peso, adelgazar⟩ 2 : peso *m* ⟨weights and measures : pesos y medidas⟩ 3 : pesa *f* ⟨to lift weights : levantar pesas⟩ 4 SINKER : plomo *m*, plomada *f* 5 BURDEN : peso *m*, carga *f* ⟨to take a weight off one's mind : quitarle un peso de encima a uno⟩ 6 IMPORTANCE : peso *m* 7 INFLUENCE : influencia *f*, autoridad *f* ⟨to throw one's weight around : hacer sentir su influencia⟩ 8 **to pull one's weight** : poner uno de su parte
weightless [ˈweɪtləs] *adj* : ingrávido
weight lifting *n* : halterofilia *f*, levantamiento *m* de pesas
weighty [ˈweɪti] *adj* **weightier; -est** 1 HEAVY : pesado 2 IMPORTANT : importante, de peso
weir [ˈwɛr, ˈwɪr] *n* : dique *m*
weird [ˈwɪrd] *adj* 1 MYSTERIOUS : misterioso 2 STRANGE : extraño, raro — **weirdly** *adv*
weirdo [ˈwɪrˌdoː] *n, pl* **weirdos** : bicho *m* raro
welcome¹ [ˈwɛlkəm] *vt* **-comed; -coming** : darle la bienvenida a, recibir
welcome² *adj* : bienvenido ⟨to make someone welcome : acoger bien a alguien⟩ ⟨you're welcome! : ¡de nada!, ¡no hay de qué!⟩
welcome³ *n* : bienvenida *f*, recibimiento *m*, acogida *f*
weld¹ [ˈwɛld] *v* : soldar
weld² *n* : soldadura *f*
welder [ˈwɛldər] *n* : soldador *m*, -dora *f*
welfare [ˈwɛlˌfær] *n* 1 WELL-BEING : bienestar *m* 2 : asistencia *f* social
well¹ [ˈwɛl] *vi or* **to well up** : brotar, manar
well² *adv* **better** [ˈbɛtər]; **best** [ˈbɛst] 1 RIGHTLY : bien, correctamente 2 SATISFACTORILY : bien ⟨to turn out well : resultar/salir bien⟩ ⟨well done! : ¡muy bien!⟩ 3 SKILLFULLY : bien ⟨she sings well : canta bien⟩ 4 (*indicating benevolence*) : bien ⟨to speak well of : hablar

bien de⟩ ⟨to wish someone well : desearle lo mejor a alguien⟩ ⟨he means well : tiene buenas intenciones⟩ 5 COMPLETELY : completamente ⟨well-hidden : completamente escondido⟩ 6 : bien ⟨I knew him well : lo conocía bien⟩ 7 CONSIDERABLY, FAR : muy, bastante ⟨well ahead : muy adelante⟩ ⟨well before the deadline : bastante antes de la fecha⟩ 8 CERTAINLY : bien ⟨you know very well that . . . : sabes muy bien que . . .⟩ ⟨he can well afford it : bien puede permitírselo⟩ 9 LIKELY : bien ⟨it could/may/might well be true : bien puede/podría/pudiera ser verdad⟩ 10 (*used for emphasis*) ⟨one might well ask if . . . : uno podría preguntarse si . . .⟩ ⟨I couldn't very well refuse! : ¿cómo iba a decir que no?⟩ 11 **as well** ALSO : también 12 **as well** (*indicating advisability*) ⟨we may/might as well get started : más vale que empecemos⟩ 13 **as well** (*indicating equivalence*) ⟨I might as well have stayed home : bien podría haberme quedado en casa⟩ 14 → **as well as** 15 **well and truly** : completamente
well³ *adj* 1 SATISFACTORY : bien ⟨all is well : todo está bien⟩ 2 DESIRABLE : conveniente ⟨it would be well if you left : sería conveniente que te fueras⟩ 3 HEALTHY : bien, sano 4 **it's just as well** : menos mal
well⁴ *n* 1 : pozo *m* (de agua, petróleo, gas, etc.), aljibe *m* (de agua) 2 SOURCE : fuente *f* ⟨a well of information : una fuente de información⟩ 3 → **stairwell**
well⁵ *interj* 1 (*used to introduce a remark*) : bueno 2 (*used to express surprise*) : ¡vaya!
we'll [ˈwiːl, wɪl] *contraction of* WE SHALL *or* WE WILL → **shall, will**
well-adjusted [ˌwɛləˈdʒʌstəd] *adj* : equilibrado (dícese de una persona)
well-balanced [ˈwɛlˈbælənst] *adj* : equilibrado
well-behaved [ˈwɛlbɪˈheɪvd] *adj* : (bien) educado, que se porta bien
well-being [ˈwɛlˈbiːɪŋ] *n* : bienestar *m*
well-bred [ˈwɛlˈbrɛd] *adj* : fino, (bien) educado
well-built [ˈwɛlˈbɪlt] *adj* : fornido
well-defined [ˌwɛldiˈfaɪnd] *adj* : bien definido
well-done [ˈwɛlˈdʌn] *adj* 1 : bien hecho ⟨well-done! : ¡bravo!⟩ 2 : bien cocido
well-dressed [ˈwɛlˈdrɛst] *adj* : bien vestido
well-founded [ˈwɛlˈfaʊndəd] *adj* : bien fundado
well-informed [ˈwɛlɪnˈfɔrmd] *adj* : bien informado
well-kept [ˈwɛlˈkɛpt] *adj* : bien cuidado
well-known [ˈwɛlˈnoːn] *adj* : famoso, bien conocido
well-made [ˈwɛlˈmeɪd] *adj* : sólido
well-mannered [ˈwɛlˈmænərd] *adj* : (bien) educado, de buenos modales
well-meaning [ˈwɛlˈmiːnɪŋ] *adj* : bienintencionado, que tiene buenas intenciones

well–nigh ['wɛl'naɪ] *adv* : casi ⟨well-nigh impossible : casi imposible⟩

well–off ['wɛl'ɔf] **1** → **well-to-do 2** FORTUNATE : afortunado

well–read ['wɛl'rɛd] *adj* : culto

well–rounded ['wɛl'raʊndəd] *adj* : completo, equilibrado

well–to–do [ˌwɛltə'duː] *adj* : próspero, adinerado, rico

well–wisher ['wɛl'wɪʃər] *n* ⟨a group of well-wishers gathered to say goodbye to him : un grupo de amigos/admiradores (etc.) se congregó para despedirlo⟩

well–worn ['wɛl'wɔrn] *adj* : muy gastado

Welsh ['wɛlʃ] *n* **1** : galés *m*, galesa *f* **2** : galés *m* (idioma) — **Welsh** *adj*

Welshman ['wɛlʃmən] *n, pl* **-men** [-mən, -ˌmɛn] : galés *m*

Welshwoman ['wɛlʃˌwʊmən] *n, pl* **-women** [-ˌwɪmən] : galesa *f*

welt ['wɛlt] *n* : verdugón *m*

welter ['wɛltər] *n* : fárrago *m*, revoltijo *m* ⟨a welter of data : un fárrago de datos⟩

wend ['wɛnd] *vi* **to wend one's way** : ponerse en camino, encaminar sus pasos

went → **go¹**

wept → **weep**

were → **be**

we're ['wɪr, 'wɔr, 'wiːr] *contraction of* WE ARE → **be**

~~**weren't** ['wɪrənt] *contraction of* WERE NOT~~ → **be**

werewolf ['wɪrˌwʊlf, 'wɛr-, 'wɔr-, -ˌwʌlf] *n, pl* **-wolves** [-ˌwʊlvz, -ˌwʌlvz] : hombre *m* lobo

west¹ ['wɛst] *adv* : al oeste

west² *adj* : oeste, del oeste, occidental ⟨west winds : vientos del oeste⟩

west³ *n* **1** : oeste *m* **2 the West** : Oeste, el Occidente

westbound ['wɛstˌbaʊnd] *adj* : que va hacia el oeste

westerly ['wɛstərli] *adv & adj* : del oeste

western¹ ['wɛstərn] *adj* **1** : Occidental, del Oeste **2** : occidental, oeste

western² *n* : western *m*

Westerner ['wɛstərnər] *n* : habitante *mf* del oeste

West Indian *n* : antillano *m*, -na *f* — **West Indian** *adj*

westward ['wɛstwərd] *adv & adj* : hacia el oeste

wet¹ ['wɛt] *vt* **wet** *or* **wetted; wetting** : mojar, humedecer

wet² *adj* **wetter; wettest 1** : mojado, húmedo ⟨wet clothes : ropa mojada⟩ ⟨wet paint : pintura fresca⟩ **2** RAINY : lluvioso

wet³ *n* **1** MOISTURE : humedad *f* **2** RAIN : lluvia *f*

wet blanket *n* : aguafiestas *mf*

wet nurse *n* : nodriza *f*

wet suit *n* : traje *m* de neopreno, traje *m* de buzo

we've ['wiːv] *contraction of* WE HAVE → **have**

whack¹ ['hwæk] *vt* : golpear (fuertemente), aporrear

whack² *n* **1** : golpe *m* fuerte, porrazo *m* **2** ATTEMPT : intento *m*, tentativa *f*

whale¹ ['hweɪl] *vi* **whaled; whaling** : cazar ballenas

whale² *n, pl* **whales** *or* **whale** : ballena *f*

whaleboat ['hweɪlˌboːt] *n* : ballenero *m*

whalebone ['hweɪlˌboːn] *n* : barba *f* de ballena

whaler ['hweɪlər] *n* **1** : ballenero *m*, -ra *f* **2** → **whaleboat**

wham ['hwæm] *interj* : zas!

wharf ['hwɔrf] *n, pl* **wharves** ['hwɔrvz] : muelle *m*, embarcadero *m*

what¹ ['hwɑt, 'hwʌt] *adv* **1** HOW : cómo, qué, cuánto ⟨what does it matter? : ¿qué importa?⟩ **2 what with** : entre ⟨what with one thing and another : entre una cosa y otra⟩ **3 so what?** : ¿y qué?

what² *adj* **1** (*used in questions*) : qué ⟨what more do you want? : ¿qué más quieres?⟩ ⟨what color is it? : ¿de qué color es?⟩ **2** (*used in exclamations*) : qué ⟨what an idea! : ¡qué idea!⟩ **3** ANY, WHATEVER : cualquier ⟨give what help you can : da cualquier contribución que puedas⟩

what³ *pron* **1** (*used in direct questions*) : qué ⟨what happened? : ¿qué pasó?⟩ ⟨what does it cost? : ¿cuánto cuesta?⟩ ⟨what does this mean? : ¿qué significa esto?⟩ ⟨what's it called? : ¿cómo se llama?⟩ ⟨what's the problem? : ¿cuál es el problema?⟩ ⟨what (did you mean)? : ¿qué?, ¿cómo?⟩ ⟨what else did she say? : ¿qué más dijo?⟩ **2** : lo que, qué ⟨tell me what happened : dime qué pasó⟩ ⟨I don't know what to do : no sé qué hacer⟩ ⟨do what I tell you : haz lo que te digo⟩ ⟨guess what! : ¿sabes qué?⟩ **3 and/or what have you** : y no sé qué, y cosas por el estilo **4 what about** ⟨we're all going together — what about Kenny? : vamos todos juntos — ¿y Kenny?⟩ ⟨what about if . . . ? : ¿qué te parece si . . . ?⟩ **5 what for** WHY : por qué ⟨what did you do that for? : ¿por qué hiciste eso?⟩ **6 what if** : y si ⟨what if he knows? : ¿y si lo sabe?⟩ **7 what's more** : además **8 what's up?** *fam* : ¿qué pasa? **9 what's up?** (*used as a greeting*) *fam* : ¿qué hay?, ¿qué tal? **10 what's with . . . ?** *fam* : ¿a qué viene/vienen . . . ?

whatever¹ [hwɑt'ɛvər, ˌhwʌt-] *adj* **1** ANY : cualquier, cualquier . . . que ⟨whatever way you prefer : de cualquier manera que prefiera, como prefiera⟩ **2** (*in negative constructions*) ⟨there's no chance whatever : no hay ninguna posibilidad⟩ ⟨nothing whatever : nada en absoluto⟩

whatever² *pron* **1** ANYTHING : (todo) lo que ⟨I'll do whatever I want : haré lo que quiera⟩ **2** (*no matter what*) ⟨whatever it may be : sea lo que sea⟩ ⟨whatever happens : pase lo que pase⟩ **3** WHAT ⟨whatever do you mean? : ¿qué quieres decir?⟩

whatnot ['hwɑtˌnɑt, 'hwʌt-] *pron* : y qué sé yo ⟨diamonds, pearls, and whatnot : diamantes, perlas, y qué sé yo⟩

what's–his–name ['hwɑtsəzˌneɪm, 'hwʌt-] *n* : fulano *m*

what's–her–name ['hwɑtsərˌneɪm, 'hwʌt-] *n* : fulana *f*

whatsoever[1] [ˌʰwɑtsoˈɛvər, ˌʰwʌt-] *adj* →
  whatever[1]
whatsoever[2] *pron* → **whatever**[2]
wheat ['ʰwiːt] *n* : trigo *m* 1
wheaten ['ʰwiːtən] *adj* : de trigo
wheedle ['ʰwiːdəl] *vt* **-dled; -dling** CAJOLE
  : engatusar ⟨to wheedle something out
  of someone : sonsacarle algo a alguien⟩
wheel[1] ['ʰwiːl] *vt* : empujar (una bicicleta,
  etc.), mover (algo sobre ruedas) — *vi* 1
  ROTATE : girar, rotar **2 to wheel around**
  TURN : darse la vuelta
wheel[2] *n* 1 : rueda *f* 2 *or* **steering
  wheel** : volante *m* (de automóviles, etc.),
  timón *m* (de barcos o aviones) **3 wheels**
  npl : maquinaria *f*, fuerza *f* impulsora
  ⟨the wheels of government : la maquinaria del gobierno⟩
wheelbarrow ['ʰwiːlˌbærˌoː] *n* : carretilla
  f
wheelchair ['ʰwiːlˌtʃær] *n* : silla *f* de ruedas
wheeze[1] ['ʰwiːz] *vi* **wheezed; wheezing**
  : resollar, respirar con dificultad
wheeze[2] *n* : resuello *m*
whelp[1] ['ʰwɛlp] *vi* : parir
whelp[2] *n* : cachorro *m*, -rra *f*
when[1] ['ʰwɛn] *adv* : cuándo ⟨when will
  you return? : ¿cuándo volverás?⟩ ⟨he
  asked me when I would be home : me
  preguntó cuándo estaría en casa⟩ ⟨say
  when : di basta/cuándo⟩
when[2] *conj* 1 (*referring to a particular
  time*) : cuando, en que ⟨when you are
  ready : cuando estés listo⟩ ⟨the days
  when I clean the house : los días en que
  limpio la casa⟩ 2 IF : cuando, si ⟨how
  can I go when I have no money? : ¿cómo
  voy a ir si no tengo dinero?⟩ 3
  ALTHOUGH : cuando ⟨you said it was big
  when actually it's small : dijiste que era
  grande cuando en realidad es pequeño⟩
when[3] *pron* : cuándo ⟨since when are you
  the boss? : ¿desde cuándo eres el jefe?⟩
whence ['ʰwɛnts] *adv* : de donde
whenever[1] [ʰwɛnˈɛvər] *adv* 1 : cuando
  sea ⟨tomorrow or whenever : mañana o
  cuando sea⟩ 2 (*in questions*) : cuándo
whenever[2] *conj* 1 : siempre que, cada
  vez que ⟨whenever I go, I'm disappointed : siempre que voy, quedo desilu-
  sionado⟩ 2 WHEN : cuando ⟨whenever
  you like : cuando quieras⟩
where[1] ['ʰwɛr] *adv* : dónde, adónde
  ⟨where is he? : ¿dónde está?⟩ ⟨where did
  they go? : ¿adónde fueron?⟩
where[2] *conj* : donde, adonde ⟨she knows
  where the house is : sabe donde está la
  casa⟩ ⟨she goes where she likes : va
  adonde quiera⟩
where[3] *pron* : donde ⟨Chicago is where I
  live : Chicago es donde vivo⟩
whereabouts[1] ['ʰwɛrəˌbaʊts] *adv* : dónde,
  por dónde ⟨whereabouts is the house? :
  ¿dónde está la casa?⟩
whereabouts[2] *ns & pl* : paradero *m*
whereas [ʰwɛrˈæz] *conj* 1 : conside-
  rando que (usado en documentos lega-
  les) 2 : mientras que ⟨I like the white
  one whereas she prefers the black : me

gusta el blanco mientras que ella prefiere el negro⟩
whereby [ʰwɛrˈbaɪ] *adv* : por lo cual
wherefore ['ʰwɛrˌfor] *adv* : por qué
wherein [ʰwɛrˈɪn] *adv* : en el cual, en el
  que
whereof [ʰwɛrˈʌv, -ˈɑv] *conj* : de lo cual
whereupon ['ʰwɛrəˌpɑn, -ˌpɔn] *conj* : con
  lo cual, después de lo cual
wherever[1] [ʰwɛrˈɛvər] *adv* 1 WHERE
  : dónde, adónde 2 : en cualquier parte
  ⟨or wherever : o donde sea⟩
wherever[2] *conj* : dondequiera que, donde
  sea ⟨wherever you go : dondequiera que
  vayas⟩
wherewithal ['ʰwɛrwɪˌðɔl, -ˌθɔl] *n* : medios *mpl*, recursos *mpl*
whet ['ʰwɛt] *vt* **whetted; whetting** 1
  SHARPEN : afilar 2 STIMULATE : estimular ⟨to whet the appetite : estimular
  el apetito⟩
whether ['ʰwɛðər] *conj* 1 : si ⟨I don't
  know whether it is finished : no sé si está
  acabado⟩ ⟨we doubt whether he'll show
  up : dudamos que aparezca⟩ 2 (*used in
  comparisons*) ⟨whether I like it or not
  : tanto si quiero como si no⟩ ⟨whether
  he comes or he doesn't : venga o no⟩
whetstone ['ʰwɛtˌstoːn] *n* : piedra *f* de afilar
whey ['ʰweɪ] *n* : suero *m* (de la leche)
which[1] ['ʰwɪtʃ] *adj* : qué, cuál ⟨which tie
  do you prefer? : ¿cuál corbata prefieres?⟩ ⟨which ones? : ¿cuáles?⟩ ⟨tell me
  which house is yours : dime qué casa es
  la tuya⟩
which[2] *pron* 1 : cuál ⟨which is the right
  answer? : ¿cuál es la respuesta correcta?⟩ 2 : que, el cual, la cual, los cuales, las cuales ⟨the cup which broke : la
  taza que se quebró⟩ ⟨the houses, which
  are made of brick . . . : las casas, las cuales son de ladrillo . . .⟩
whichever[1] [ʰwɪtʃˈɛvər] *adj* : el (la) que,
  cualquiera que ⟨whichever book you
  like : cualquier libro que te guste⟩
whichever[2] *pron* : el que, la que, cualquiera que ⟨take whichever you want
  : toma el que quieras⟩ ⟨whichever I
  choose : cualquiera que elija⟩
whiff[1] ['ʰwɪf] *v* PUFF : soplar
whiff[2] *n* 1 PUFF : soplo *m*, ráfaga *f* 2
  SNIFF : olor *m* 3 HINT : dejo *m*, pizca *f*
while[1] ['ʰwaɪl] *vt* **whiled; whiling** : pasar
  ⟨to while away the time : matar el
  tiempo⟩
while[2] *n* 1 TIME : rato *m*, tiempo *m* ⟨af-
  ter a while : después de un rato⟩ ⟨in a
  while : dentro de poco⟩ **2 to be worth
  one's while** : valer la pena
while[3] *conj* 1 : mientras ⟨whistle while
  you work : silba mientras trabajas⟩ 2
  WHEREAS : mientras que 3 ALTHOUGH
  : aunque ⟨while it's very good, it's not
  perfect : aunque es muy bueno, no es
  perfecto⟩
whim ['ʰwɪm] *n* : capricho *m*, antojo *m*
whimper[1] ['ʰwɪmpər] *vi* : lloriquear, gimotear
whimper[2] *n* : quejido *m*

whimsical ['ʰwɪmzɪkəl] *adj* **1** CAPRI-
CIOUS : caprichoso, fantasioso **2** ERRA-
TIC : errático — **whimsically** *adv*
whine[1] ['ʰwaɪn] *vi* **whined; whining 1**
: lloriquear, gimotear, gemir **2** COM-
PLAIN : quejarse
whine[2] *n* : quejido *m*, gemido *m*
whiner ['ʰwaɪnər] *n* : llorón *m*, -rona *f*
whiny ['ʰwaɪni] *adj* **whinier; -est** : ñoño
whinny[1] ['ʰwɪni] *vi* **-nied; -nying**
: relinchar
whinny[2] *n, pl* **-nies** : relincho *m*
whip[1] ['ʰwɪp] *v* **whipped; whipping** *vt* **1**
SNATCH : arrebatar ⟨she whipped the
cloth off the table : arrebató el mantel de
la mesa⟩ **2** LASH : azotar **3** MOVE, STIR
: agitar (con fuerza) **4** FLING : lanzar,
tirar (rápidamente) **5** *fam* DEFEAT
: vencer, derrotar **6** INCITE : incitar,
despertar, provocar ⟨to whip up enthusiasm : despertar el entusiasmo⟩ ⟨to whip
up a controversy : provocar una
polémica⟩ ⟨he whipped the crowd into a
frenzy : enardeció a la multitud⟩ **7**
BEAT : batir (huevos, crema, etc.) **8 to
whip into shape** *fam* : poner en forma **9
to whip out** *fam* : sacar (rápidamente) **10
to whip up** *fam* PREPARE : improvisar,
preparar (rápidamente) — *vi* **1** FLAP
: agitarse **2** RACE : ir rápidamente ⟨I
[illegible] :
tareas volando⟩ ⟨to whip past/by : pasar
como una bala⟩
whip[2] *n* **1** : látigo *m*, azote *m*, fusta *f* (de
jinete) **2** : miembro *m* de un cuerpo legislativo encargado de disciplina
whiplash ['ʰwɪp,læʃ] *n or* **whiplash injury**
: traumatismo *m* cervical
whippet ['ʰwɪpət] *n* : galgo *m* pequeño,
galgo *m* inglés
whir[1] ['ʰwər] *vi* **whirred; whirring** : zumbar
whir[2] *n* : zumbido *m*
whirl[1] ['ʰwərl] *vi* **1** SPIN : dar vueltas, girar ⟨my head is whirling : la cabeza me
está dando vueltas⟩ **2 to whirl about**
: arremolinarse, moverse rápidamente
whirl[2] *n* **1** SPIN : giro *m*, vuelta *f*, remolino *m* (dícese del polvo, etc.) **2** BUSTLE
: bullicio *m*, torbellino *m* (de actividad,
etc.) **3 to give it a whirl** : intentar
hacer, probar
whirlpool ['ʰwərl,pu:l] *n* **1** : vorágine *f*,
remolino *m* **2 or whirlpool bath**
: bañera *f* de hidromasaje
whirlwind[1] ['ʰwərl,wɪnd] *n* : remolino *m*,
torbellino *m*, tromba *f*
whirlwind[2] *adj* : muy rápido
whisk[1] ['ʰwɪsk] *vt* **1** : llevar ⟨she whisked
the children off to bed : llevó a los niños
a la cama⟩ **2** : batir ⟨to whisk eggs
: batir huevos⟩ **3 to whisk away** *or* **to
whisk off** : sacudir
whisk[2] *n* **1** WHISKING : sacudida *f* (movimiento) **2** : batidor *m* (para batir huevos, etc.)
whisk broom *n* : escobilla *f*
whisker ['ʰwɪskər] *n* **1** : pelo *m* (de la
barba o el bigote) **2 whiskers** *npl* : bigotes *mpl* (de animales)

whiskey *or* **whisky** ['ʰwɪski] *n, pl* **-keys** *or*
-kies : whisky *m*
whisper[1] ['ʰwɪspər] *vi* : cuchichear, susurrar — *vt* : decir en voz baja, susurrar
whisper[2] *n* **1** WHISPERING : susurro *m*,
cuchicheo *m* **2** RUMOR : rumor *m* **3**
TRACE : dejo *m*, pizca *f*
whistle[1] ['ʰwɪsəl] *v* **-tled; -tling** *vi* : silbar,
chiflar, pitar (dícese de un tren, etc.) —
vt : silbar ⟨to whistle a tune : silbar una
melodía⟩
whistle[2] *n* **1** WHISTLING : chiflido *m*, silbido *m* **2** : silbato *m*, pito *m* (instrumento)
whit ['ʰwɪt] *n* BIT : ápice *m*, pizca *f*
white[1] ['ʰwaɪt] *adj* **whiter; whitest**
: blanco
white[2] *n* **1** : blanco *m* (color) **2** : clara *f*
(de huevos) **3** : blanco *m* (del ojo) **4** *or*
white person : blanco *m*, -ca *f*
white blood cell *n* : glóbulo *m* blanco
white chocolate *n* : chocolate *m* blanco
white–collar ['ʰwaɪt'kɑlər] *adj* **1** : de oficina **2 white–collar worker** : oficinista
mf
whitefish ['ʰwaɪt,fɪʃ] *n* : pescado *m*
blanco
white–hot *adj* : candente
white lie *n* : mentira *f* piadosa
whiten ['ʰwaɪtən] *vt* : blanquear — *vi*
: [illegible]
whitener ['ʰwaɪtənər] *n* : blanqueador *m*
whiteness ['ʰwaɪtnəs] *n* : blancura *f*
white–tailed deer ['ʰwaɪt,wɔʃ] *n* : ciervo
f de Virginia
whitewash[1] ['ʰwaɪt,wɔʃ] *vt* **1** : enjalbegar, blanquear ⟨to whitewash a fence
: enjalbegar una valla⟩ **2** CONCEAL : encubrir (un escándalo), etc.)
whitewash[2] *n* **1** : jalbegue *m*, lechada
f **2** COVER-UP : encubrimiento *m*
whither ['ʰwɪðər] *adv* : adónde
whittle ['ʰwɪtəl] *vt* **-tled; -tling 1** : tallar
(madera) **2 to whittle down** : reducir,
recortar ⟨to whittle down expenses : reducir los gastos⟩
whiz[1] *or* **whizz** ['ʰwɪz] *vi* **whizzed; whi-
zzing 1** BUZZ : zumbar **2 to whiz by**
: pasar muy rápido, pasar volando
whiz[2] *or* **whizz** *n, pl* **whizzes 1** BUZZ
: zumbido *m* **2 to be a whiz** : ser un
prodigio, ser muy hábil
whiz kid *or* **whizz kid** *n* : prodigio *m*,
genio *m*
who ['hu:] *pron* **1** (*used in direct and indirect questions*) : quién ⟨who is that?
: ¿quién es ése?⟩ ⟨who did it? : ¿quién lo
hizo?⟩ ⟨we know who they are : sabemos quiénes son⟩ **2** (*used in relative
clauses*) : que, quien ⟨the lady who lives
there : la señora que vive allí⟩ ⟨for those
who wait : para los que esperan, para
quienes esperan⟩
whodunit [hu:'dʌnɪt] *n* : novela *f* policíaca
whoever [hu:'ɛvər] *pron* **1** : quienquiera
que, quien ⟨whoever did it : quienquiera
que lo hizo⟩ ⟨give it to whoever you
want : dalo a quien quieras⟩ **2** (*used in
questions*) : quién ⟨whoever could that
be? : ¿quién podría ser?⟩

whole¹ ['hoːl] *adj* **1** UNHURT : ileso **2** INTACT : intacto, sano **3** ENTIRE : entero, íntegro ⟨the whole island : toda la isla⟩ ⟨whole milk : leche entera⟩ **4 a whole lot** : muchísimo

whole² *n* **1** : todo *m* **2 as a whole** : en conjunto **3 on the whole** : en general

wholehearted ['hoːl'hɑrtəd] *adj* : sin reservas, incondicional — **wholeheartedly** *adv*

whole note *n* : semibreve *f*, redonda *f*

whole number *n* : entero *m*

wholesale¹ ['hoːlˌseɪl] *v* **-saled; -saling** *vt* : vender al por mayor — *vi* : venderse al por mayor

wholesale² *adv* : al por mayor

wholesale³ *adj* **1** : al por mayor ⟨wholesale grocer : tendero al por mayor⟩ **2** TOTAL : total, absoluto ⟨wholesale slaughter : matanza sistemática⟩

wholesale⁴ *n* : mayoreo *m*

wholesaler ['hoːlˌseɪlər] *n* : mayorista *mf*

wholesome ['hoːlsəm] *adj* **1** : sano ⟨wholesome advice : consejo sano⟩ **2** HEALTHY : sano, saludable

whole wheat *adj* : de trigo integral ⟨whole wheat bread : pan integral⟩

wholly ['hoːli] *adv* **1** COMPLETELY : completamente **2** SOLELY : exclusivamente, únicamente

whom ['huːm] *pron* **1** (*used in direct questions*) : a quién ⟨whom did you choose? : ¿a quién elegiste?⟩ **2** (*used in indirect questions*) : de quién, con quién, en quién ⟨I don't know whom to consult : no sé con quién consultar⟩ **3** (*used in relative clauses*) : que, a quien ⟨the lawyer whom I recommended to you : el abogado que te recomendé⟩

whomever [huːm'evər] *pron* WHOEVER : quienquiera, quien ⟨marry whomever you please : cásate con quien quieras⟩

whoop¹ ['hwuːp, 'hwʊp] *vi* : gritar, chillar

whoop² *n* : grito *m*

whooping cough *n* : tos *f* ferina

whopper ['hwɑpər] *n* **1** : cosa *f* enorme **2** LIE : mentira *f* colosal

whopping ['hwɑpɪŋ] *adj* : enorme

whore ['hoːr] *n* : puta *f* offensive, ramera *f*

whorl ['hwɔrl, 'hwərl] *n* : espiral *f*, línea *f* (de una huella digital)

whose¹ ['huːz] *adj* **1** (*used in questions*) : de quién ⟨whose truck is that? : ¿de quién es ese camión?⟩ **2** (*used in relative clauses*) : cuyo ⟨the person whose work is finished : la persona cuyo trabajo está terminado⟩

whose² *pron* : de quién ⟨tell me whose it was : dime de quién era⟩

why¹ ['hwaɪ] *adv* : por qué ⟨why did you do it? : ¿por qué lo hizo?⟩

why² *n, pl* **whys** REASON : porqué *m*, razón *f*

why³ *conj* : por qué ⟨I know why he left : yo sé por qué salió⟩ ⟨there's no reason why it should exist : no hay razón para que exista⟩

why⁴ *interj* (*used to express surprise*) : ¡vaya!, ¡mira!

Wicca ['wɪkə] *n* : wicca *f*

Wiccan ['wɪkən] *n* : wiccano *m*, -na *f* — **Wiccan** *adj*

wick ['wɪk] *n* : mecha *f*

wicked ['wɪkəd] *adj* **1** EVIL : malo, malvado **2** MISCHIEVOUS : travieso, pícaro ⟨a wicked grin : una sonrisa traviesa⟩ **3** TERRIBLE : terrible, horrible ⟨a wicked storm : una tormenta horrible⟩

wickedly ['wɪkədli] *adv* : con maldad

wickedness ['wɪkədnəs] *n* : maldad *f*

wicker¹ ['wɪkər] *adj* : de mimbre

wicker² *n* **1** : mimbre *m* **2** → **wickerwork**

wickerwork ['wɪkərˌwərk] *n* : artículos *mpl* de mimbre

wicket ['wɪkət] *n* **1** WINDOW : ventanilla *f* **2 or wicket gate** : postigo *m* **3 :** aro *m* (en croquet), palos *mpl* (en críquet)

wide¹ ['waɪd] *adv* **wider; widest 1** WIDELY : por todas partes ⟨to travel far and wide : viajar por todas partes⟩ **2** COMPLETELY : completamente, totalmente ⟨wide open : abierto de par en par⟩ **3 wide apart** : muy separados

wide² *adj* **wider; widest 1** VAST : vasto, extensivo ⟨a wide area : una área extensiva⟩ **2** : ancho ⟨three meters wide : tres metros de ancho⟩ **3** BROAD : ancho, amplio **4 or wide–open** : muy abierto **5 wide of the mark** : desviado, lejos del blanco

wide–awake ['waɪdə'weɪk] *adj* : (completamente) despierto

wide–eyed ['waɪd'aɪd] *adj* **1** : con los ojos muy abiertos **2** NAIVE : inocente, ingenuo

widely ['waɪdli] *adv* : extensivamente, por todas partes

widen ['waɪdən] *vt* : ampliar, ensanchar — *vi* : ampliarse, ensancharse

wide–ranging ['waɪdˌreɪndʒɪŋ] *adj* EXTENSIVE, DIVERSE : amplio, diverso ⟨wide-ranging implications : implicaciones de gran alcance⟩ ⟨a wide-ranging discussion : una discusión que abarca muchos temas⟩

widescreen ['waɪdˌskriːn] *adj* : de pantalla ancha

widespread ['waɪd'sprɛd] *adj* : extendido, extenso, difuso

widow¹ ['wɪˌdoː] *vt* : dejar viuda ⟨to be widowed : enviudar⟩

widow² *n* : viuda *f*

widower ['wɪdoːwər] *n* : viudo *m*

width ['wɪdθ] *n* : ancho *m*, anchura *f*

wield ['wiːld] *vt* **1** USE : usar, manejar ⟨to wield a broom : usar una escoba⟩ **2** EXERCISE : ejercer ⟨to wield influence : influir⟩

wiener ['wiːnər] *n* → **frankfurter**

wife ['waɪf] *n, pl* **wives** ['waɪvz] : esposa *f*, mujer *f*

wifely ['waɪfli] *adj* : de esposa, conyugal

wig ['wɪg] *n* : peluca *f*

wiggle¹ ['wɪɡəl] *v* **-gled; -gling** *vt* **1** : menear ⟨to wiggle one's hips : menear las caderas, menearse, contonearse⟩ **2** : mover (los dedos, etc.) — *vi* **1** : menearse, contonearse **2** SQUIRM, WRIGGLE : retorcerse

wiggle² *n* : meneo *m*, contoneo *m*

wiggly ['wɪɡəli] *adj* **wigglier; -est 1** : que se menea **2** WAVY : ondulado

wigwag ['wɪɡ,wæɡ] *vi* **-wagged; -wagging** : comunicar por señales

wigwam ['wɪɡ,wɑm] *n* : wigwam *m*

wild¹ ['waɪld] *adv* **1** → **wildly 2 to run wild** : descontrolarse

wild² *adj* **1** : salvaje, silvestre, cimarrón ⟨wild horses : caballos salvajes⟩ ⟨wild rice : arroz silvestre⟩ **2** DESOLATE : yermo, agreste **3** UNRULY : desenfrenado **4** CRAZY : loco, fantástico ⟨wild ideas : ideas locas⟩ **5** BARBAROUS : salvaje, bárbaro **6** ERRATIC : errático ⟨a wild throw : un tiro errático⟩ **7** FRENETIC : frenético **8** : extravagante ⟨to take/make a wild guess : adivinar, hacer una conjetura (al azar)⟩ **9 to be wild about** : estar loco por

wild³ *n* → **wilderness**

wild boar *n* : jabalí *m*

wild card *n* **1** : factor *m* desconocido **2** : comodín *m* (carta) **3** *usu* **wildcard** : comodín *m* (símbolo)

wildcat ['waɪld,kæt] *n* **1** : gato *m* montés **2** BOBCAT : lince *m* rojo

wilderness ['wɪldərnəs] *n* : yermo *m*, desierto *m*

wildfire ['waɪld,faɪr] *n* **1** : fuego *m* descontrolado **2 to spread like wildfire** : propagarse como un reguero de pólvora

wildflower ['waɪld,flaʊər] *n* : flor *f* silvestre

wildfowl ['waɪld,faʊl] *n* : ave *f* de caza

wild goose chase *n fam* : misión *f* imposible o inútil ⟨it turned out to be a wild goose chase : resultó ser una pérdida de tiempo⟩

wildlife ['waɪld,laɪf] *n* : fauna *f*

wildly ['waɪldli] *adv* **1** FRANTICALLY : frenéticamente, como un loco **2** EXTREMELY : extremadamente ⟨wildly happy : loco de felicidad⟩

wile¹ ['waɪl] *v*, *past* **wiled; wiling** LURE : atraer

wile² *n* : ardid *m*, artimaña *f*

will¹ ['wɪl] *v*, *past* **would** ['wʊd] *present s & pl* **will** *vt* WISH : querer ⟨do what you will : haz lo que quieras⟩ — *v aux* **1** (*expressing willingness*) : querer ⟨no one would take the job : nadie aceptaría el trabajo⟩ ⟨I won't do it : no lo haré⟩ **2** (*expressing habitual action*) ⟨he will get angry over nothing : se pone furioso por cualquier cosa⟩ **3** (*forming the future tense*) ⟨tomorrow we will go shopping : mañana iremos de compras⟩ **4** (*expressing capacity*) ⟨the couch will hold three people : en el sofá cabrán tres personas⟩ **5** (*expressing determination*) ⟨I will go despite them : iré a pesar de ellos⟩ **6** (*expressing probability*) ⟨that will be the mailman : ese ha de ser el cartero⟩ **7** (*expressing inevitability*) ⟨accidents will happen : los accidentes ocurrirán⟩ **8** (*expressing a command*) ⟨you will do as I say : harás lo que digo⟩

will² *vt* **1** ORDAIN : disponer, decretar ⟨if God wills it : si Dios lo dispone, si Dios quiere⟩ **2** : lograr a fuerza de voluntad ⟨they were willing him to succeed : estaban deseando que tuviera éxito⟩ **3** BEQUEATH : legar

will³ *n* **1** DESIRE : deseo *m*, voluntad *f* **2** VOLITION : voluntad *f* ⟨free will : libre albedrío⟩ **3** WILLPOWER : voluntad *f*, fuerza *f* de voluntad ⟨a will of iron : una voluntad férrea⟩ **4** : testamento *m* ⟨to make a will : hacer testamento⟩

willful *or* **wilful** ['wɪlfəl] *adj* **1** OBSTINATE : obstinado, terco **2** INTENTIONAL : intencionado, deliberado — **willfully** *adv*

willing ['wɪlɪŋ] *adj* **1** INCLINED, READY : listo, dispuesto **2** OBLIGING : servicial, complaciente

willingly ['wɪlɪŋli] *adv* : con gusto

willingness ['wɪlɪŋnəs] *n* : buena voluntad *f*

willow ['wɪ,loː] *n* : sauce *m*

willowy ['wɪlowi] *adj* : esbelto

willpower ['wɪl,paʊər] *n* : voluntad *f*, fuerza *f* de voluntad

willy-nilly [,wɪli'nɪli] *adv fam* : de cualquier manera

wilt ['wɪlt] *vi* **1** : marchitarse (dícese de las flores) **2** LANGUISH : debilitarse, languidecer

wily ['waɪli] *adj* **wilier; -est** : artero, astuto

wimp ['wɪmp] *n* **1** COWARD : gallina *f*, cobarde *mf* **2** WEAKLING : debilucho *m*, -cha *f*, alfeñique *m*

win¹ ['wɪn] *v* **won** ['wʌn]; **winning** *vi* : ganar — *vt* **1** : ganar, conseguir **2 to win over** : ganarse a **3 to win someone's heart** : conquistar a alguien

win² *n* : triunfo *m*, victoria *f*

wince¹ ['wɪnts] *vi* **winced; wincing** : estremecerse, hacer una mueca de dolor

wince² *n* : mueca *f* de dolor

winch ['wɪntʃ] *n* : torno *m*

wind¹ ['wɪnd] *vt* : dejar sin aliento ⟨to be winded : quedarse sin aliento⟩

wind² ['waɪnd] *v* **wound** ['waʊnd]; **winding** *vi* **1** MEANDER : serpentear **2 to wind down** END : acabarse poco a poco **3 to wind down** UNWIND : relajarse **4 to wind up** END : terminar, acabar ⟨the meeting will be winding up soon : la reunión va a terminar pronto⟩ **5 to wind up** END UP : acabar, terminar ⟨to wind up doing something : acabar/terminar haciendo algo, acabar/terminar por hacer algo⟩ — *vt* **1** COIL, ROLL : envolver, enrollar **2** TURN : hacer girar ⟨to wind (up) a clock : darle cuerda a un reloj⟩ **3 to wind up** END : terminar, concluir

wind³ ['wɪnd] *n* **1** : viento *m* ⟨against the wind : contra el viento⟩ **2** BREATH : aliento *m* **3** FLATULENCE : flatulencia *f*, ventosidad *f* **4 to get wind of** : enterarse de

wind⁴ ['waɪnd] *n* **1** TURN : vuelta *f* **2** BEND : recodo *m*, curva *f*

windbreak ['wɪnd,breɪk] *n* : barrera *f* contra el viento, abrigadero *m*

windfall ['wɪnd,fɔl] *n* **1** : fruta *f* caída **2** : beneficio *m* imprevisto

wind instrument *n* : instrumento *m* de viento

windmill [ˈwɪndˌmɪl] *n* : molino *m* de viento

window [ˈwɪndo:] *n* **1** : ventana *f* (de un edificio), ventanilla *f* (de un vehículo o avión), vitrina *f* (de una tienda) **2** → **windowpane 3** : ventana *f* (en informática)

window box *n* : jardinera *f* de ventana

windowpane [ˈwɪndo:ˌpeɪn] *n* : vidrio *m*

window screen → **screen²**

window-shop [ˈwɪndoˌʃɑp] *vi* -**shopped**; -**shopping** : mirar las vitrinas

windowsill [ˈwɪndo:ˌsɪl] *n* : alféizar *m* de la ventana

windpipe [ˈwɪndˌpaɪp] *n* : tráquea *f*

windshield [ˈwɪndˌʃi:ld] *n* **1** : parabrisas *m* **2 windshield wiper** : limpiaparabrisas *m*

windsurfing [ˈwɪndˌsərfɪŋ] *n* : windsurf *m*

windswept [ˈwɪndˌswɛpt] *adj* **1** : azotado por el viento **2** DISHEVELED : despeinado

windup [ˈwaɪndˌʌp] *n* : conclusión *f*

windy [ˈwɪndi] *adj* **windier**; -**est 1** : ventoso ⟨it's windy : hace viento⟩ **2** VERBOSE : verboso, prolijo

wine¹ [ˈwaɪn] *v* **wined**; **wining** *vi* : beber vino — *vt* **to wine and dine** : agasajar

wine² *n* : vino *m*

wineglass [ˈwaɪnˌglæs] *n* : copa *f* (de vino)

winery [ˈwaɪnəri] *n, pl* -**eries** : bodega *f*

wineskin [ˈwaɪnˌskɪn] *n* : odre *m*, bota *f*

wine tasting *n* : degustación *f* de vinos

wing¹ [ˈwɪŋ] *vi* FLY : volar

wing² *n* **1** : ala *f* (de un ave o un avión) ⟨to take wing : levantar vuelo⟩ **2** : ala *f* (de un edificio) **3** FACTION : ala *f* ⟨the right wing of the party : el ala derecha del partido⟩ **4 wings** *npl* : bastidores *mpl* (de un teatro) ⟨to be waiting in the wings : estar esperando su momento⟩ **5 on the wing** : al vuelo, volando **6 under one's wing** : bajo el cargo de uno ⟨to take someone under one's wing : encargarse de alguien⟩

winged [ˈwɪŋd, ˈwɪŋəd] *adj* : alado

wink¹ [ˈwɪŋk] *vi* **1** : guiñar el ojo **2** BLINK : pestañear, parpadear **3** FLICKER : parpadear, titilar

wink² *n* **1** : guiño *m* (del ojo) **2** NAP : siesta *f* ⟨not to sleep a wink : no pegar el ojo⟩

winner [ˈwɪnər] *n* : ganador *m*, -dora *f*

winning [ˈwɪnɪŋ] *adj* **1** VICTORIOUS : ganador **2** CHARMING : encantador

winnings [ˈwɪnɪŋz] *npl* : ganancias *fpl*

winnow [ˈwɪˌno:] *vt* : aventar (el grano, etc.)

winsome [ˈwɪnsəm] *adj* CHARMING : encantador

winter¹ [ˈwɪntər] *adj* : invernal, de invierno

winter² *n* : invierno *m*

wintertime [ˈwɪntərˌtaɪm] *n* : invierno *m*

wintry [ˈwɪntri] *adj* **wintrier**; -**est 1** WINTER : invernal, de invierno **2** COLD : frío ⟨she gave us a wintry greeting : nos saludó fríamente⟩

wipe¹ [ˈwaɪp] *v* **wiped**; **wiping** *vt* **1** *or* **to wipe off** : limpiar, pasarle un trapo a ⟨to wipe one's feet : limpiarse los pies⟩ ⟨to wipe dry : secar⟩ **2** *or* **to wipe off** REMOVE : limpiar, quitar **3** *or* **to wipe clean** ERASE : borrar (un disco, etc.) **4 to wipe away** REMOVE : limpiar (suciedad), secar (lágrimas), borrar (una memoria) **5 to wipe down** : pasarle un trapo a **6 to wipe out** ANNIHILATE : aniquilar, destruir **7 to wipe up** : limpiar, secar (líquido, etc.) — *vi* **to wipe out** *fam* : caerse (violentamente)

wipe² *n* : pasada *f* (con un trapo, etc.)

wire¹ [ˈwaɪr] *vt* **wired**; **wiring 1** : instalar el cableado en (una casa, etc.) **2** BIND : atar con alambre **3** TELEGRAPH : telegrafiar, mandarle un telegrama a (alguien)

wire² *n* **1** : alambre *m* ⟨barbed wire : alambre de púas⟩ **2** : cable *m* (eléctrico o telefónico) **3** TELEGRAM : telegrama *m*, cable *m*

wireless [ˈwaɪrləs] *adj* : inalámbrico ⟨a wireless microphone : un micrófono inalámbrico⟩ ⟨wireless Internet access : acceso inalámbrico a Internet⟩

wiretap¹ [ˈwaɪrˌtæp] *vt* TAP : intervenir, pinchar *fam* (un teléfono)

wiretap² *n* TAP : micrófono *m* oculto (para la intervención telefónica)

wiretapping [ˈwaɪrˌtæpɪŋ] *n* : intervención *f* telefónica

wiring [ˈwaɪrɪŋ] *n* : cableado *m*

wiry [ˈwaɪri] *adj* **wirier**; -**est 1** : hirsuto, tieso (dícese del pelo) **2** : esbelto y musculoso (dícese del cuerpo)

wisdom [ˈwɪzdəm] *n* **1** KNOWLEDGE : sabiduría *f* **2** JUDGMENT, SENSE : sensatez *f*

wisdom tooth *n* : muela *f* de juicio

wise¹ [ˈwaɪz] *adj* **wiser**; **wisest 1** LEARNED : sabio **2** SENSIBLE : sabio, sensato, prudente **3** KNOWLEDGEABLE : entendido, enterado ⟨they're wise to his tricks : conocen muy bien sus mañas⟩

wise² *n* : manera *f*, modo *m* ⟨in no wise : de ninguna manera⟩

wisecrack [ˈwaɪzˌkræk] *n* : broma *f*, chiste *m*

wisely [ˈwaɪzli] *adv* : sabiamente, sensatamente

wish¹ [ˈwɪʃ] *vt* **1** : pedir (como deseo) ⟨I wish I were rich : ojalá fuera rica⟩ ⟨I wish I'd known : ojalá lo hubiera sabido⟩ ⟨I wish you'd be quiet! : ¿quieres callarte?⟩ **2** WANT : desear, querer ⟨I wish to be alone : quiero estar solo⟩ **3** : desear ⟨they wished me well : me desearon lo mejor⟩ ⟨I wish you luck : te deseo suerte⟩ ⟨I wish you a Happy New Year! : ¡que tengas un feliz Año Nuevo!⟩ — *vi* **1** : pedir un deseo ⟨to wish upon a star : pedir un deseo a una estrella⟩ **2** : querer ⟨as you wish : como quiera⟩ **3 to wish for** : pedir (como deseo)

wish² *n* **1** : deseo *m* ⟨to grant a wish : conceder un deseo⟩ **2 wishes** *npl* : saludos *mpl*, recuerdos *mpl* ⟨to send best wishes : mandar muchos recuerdos⟩

wishbone ['wɪʃ,boːn] n : espoleta f
wishful ['wɪʃfəl] adj 1 HOPEFUL : deseoso, lleno de esperanza 2 **wishful thinking** : ilusiones fpl
wishy-washy ['wɪʃi,wɔʃi, -,wɑʃi] adj : insípido, soso
wisp ['wɪsp] n 1 BUNCH : manojo m (de paja) 2 STRAND : mechón m (de pelo) 3 : voluta f (de humo)
wispy ['wɪspi] adj **wispier; -est** : tenue, ralo (dícese del pelo)
wisteria [wɪs'tɪriə] f : glicinia f
wistful ['wɪstfəl] adj : anhelante, melancólico — **wistfully** adv
wistfulness ['wɪstfəlnəs] n : añoranza f, melancolía f
wit ['wɪt] n 1 INTELLIGENCE : inteligencia f 2 CLEVERNESS : ingenio m, gracia f, agudeza f 3 HUMOR : humorismo m 4 JOKER : chistoso m, -sa f 5 **wits** npl : razón f, buen juicio m ⟨scared out of one's wits : muerto de miedo⟩ ⟨to be at one's wits' end : estar desesperado⟩
witch ['wɪtʃ] n 1 bruja f 2 → Wiccan
witchcraft ['wɪtʃ,kræft] n 1 : brujería f, hechicería f 2 → Wicca
witch doctor n : hechicero m, -ra f
witchery ['wɪtʃəri] n, pl **-eries** WITCHCRAFT : brujería f, hechicería f 2 CHARM : encanto m
witch hunt ['wɪtʃ,hʌnt] n : caza f de brujas
with ['wɪð, 'wɪθ] prep 1 : con ⟨I'm going with you : voy contigo⟩ ⟨coffee with milk : café con leche⟩ 2 AGAINST : con ⟨to argue with someone : discutir con alguien⟩ 3 (used in descriptions) : con, de ⟨the girl with red hair : la muchacha de pelo rojo⟩ 4 (indicating manner, means, or cause) : con ⟨to cut with a knife : cortar con un cuchillo⟩ ⟨fix it with tape : arréglalo con cinta⟩ ⟨with luck : con suerte⟩ ⟨trembling with fear : temblando de miedo⟩ 5 DESPITE : a pesar de, aún con ⟨even with all his work, the business failed : a pesar de todo su trabajo, el negocio fracasó⟩ 6 REGARDING : con respecto a, con ⟨the trouble with your plan : el problema con su plan⟩ 7 ACCORDING TO : según ⟨it varies with the season : varía según la estación⟩ 8 (indicating support or understanding) : con ⟨I'm with you all the way : estoy contigo hasta el final⟩
withdraw [wɪð'drɔ, wɪθ-] v **-drew** [-'druː]; **-drawn** [-'drɔn]; **-drawing** vt 1 REMOVE : retirar, apartar, sacar (dinero) 2 RETRACT : retractarse de — vi : retirarse, recluirse (de la sociedad)
withdrawal [wɪð'drɔəl, wɪθ-] n 1 : retirada f, retiro m (de fondos, etc.), retraimiento m (social) 2 RETRACTION : retractación f 3 or **withdrawal symptoms** : síndrome m de abstinencia
withdrawn [wɪð'drɔn, wɪθ-] adj : retraído, reservado, introvertido
wither ['wɪðər] vt : marchitar, agostar — vi 1 WILT : marchitarse 2 WEAKEN : decaer, debilitarse
withhold [wɪθ'hoːld, wɪð-] vt **-held** [-'hld];

-holding : retener (fondos), aplazar (una decisión), negar (permiso, etc.)
within¹ [wɪð'ɪn, wɪθ-] adv : dentro
within² prep 1 : dentro de ⟨within the limits : dentro de los límites⟩ ⟨within sight of : a la vista de⟩ 2 (in expressions of distance) : a menos de ⟨within 10 miles of the ocean : a menos de 10 millas del mar⟩ 3 (in expressions of time) : dentro de ⟨within an hour : dentro de una hora⟩ ⟨within a month of her birthday : a poco menos de un mes de su cumpleaños⟩
without¹ [wɪð'aʊt, wɪθ-] adv 1 OUTSIDE : fuera 2 **to do without** : pasar sin algo
without² prep 1 OUTSIDE : fuera de 2 : sin ⟨without fear : sin temor⟩ ⟨he left without his briefcase : se fue sin su portafolios⟩
withstand [wɪθ'stænd, wɪð-] vt **-stood** [-'stud]; **-standing** 1 BEAR : aguantar, soportar 2 RESIST : resistir, resistirse a
witless ['wɪtləs] adj : estúpido, tonto
witness¹ ['wɪtnəs] vt 1 SEE : presenciar, ver, ser testigo de 2 : atestiguar (una firma, etc.) — vi TESTIFY : atestiguar, testimoniar
witness² n 1 TESTIMONY : testimonio m ⟨to bear witness : atestiguar, testimoniar⟩ 2 : testigo mf ⟨witness for the prosecution : testigo de cargo⟩
witness stand n : estrado m
witticism ['wɪtə,sɪzəm] n : agudeza f, ocurrencia f
witty ['wɪti] adj **wittier; -est** : ingenioso, ocurrente, gracioso
wives → wife
wizard ['wɪzərd] n 1 SORCERER : mago m, brujo m, hechicero m 2 : genio m ⟨a math wizard : un genio en matemáticas⟩
wizened ['wɪzənd, 'wiː-] adj : arrugado, marchito
wobble¹ ['wɑbəl] vi **-bled; -bling** : bambolearse, tambalearse, temblar (dícese de la voz)
wobble² n : tambaleo m, bamboleo m
wobbly ['wɑbəli] adj **wobblier; -est** : que se tambalea, inestable
woe ['woː] n 1 GRIEF, MISFORTUNE : desgracia f, infortunio m, aflicción f 2 **woes** npl TROUBLES : penas fpl, males mpl
woeful ['woːfəl] adj 1 SORROWFUL : afligido, apenado, triste 2 UNFORTUNATE : desgraciado, infortunado 3 DEPLORABLE : lamentable
woke¹, woken → wake¹
woke² ['woːk] adj : consciente de y sensible a los asuntos de justicia racial y social
wolf¹ ['wʊlf] vt or **to wolf down** : engullir
wolf² n, pl **wolves** ['wʊlvz] : lobo m, -ba f
wolfram ['wʊlfrəm] → tungsten
wolverine [,wʊlvə'riːn] n : glotón m (animal)
woman ['wʊmən] n, pl **women** ['wɪmən] : mujer f
womanhood ['wʊmən,hʊd] n 1 : condición f de mujer 2 WOMEN : mujeres fpl

womanizer ['wʊmə,naɪzər] n : picaflor m

womanly ['wʊmənli] adj : femenino

womb ['wu:m] n : útero m, matriz f

won → **win**

wonder¹ ['wʌndər] vi 1 SPECULATE : preguntarse, pensar ⟨to wonder about : preguntarse por⟩ 2 MARVEL : asombrarse, maravillarse — vt : preguntarse ⟨I wonder if/whether they're coming : me pregunto si vendrán⟩

wonder² n 1 MARVEL : maravilla f, milagro m ⟨to work wonders : hacer maravillas⟩ 2 AMAZEMENT : asombro m

wonderful ['wʌndərfəl] adj : maravilloso, estupendo

wonderfully ['wʌndərfəli] adv : maravillosamente, de maravilla

wonderland ['wʌndər,lænd, -lənd] n : país m de las maravillas

wonderment ['wʌndərmənt] n : asombro m

wondrous ['wʌndrəs] → **wonderful**

wont¹ ['wɔnt, 'wo:nt, 'wʌnt] adj : acostumbrado, habituado

wont² n : hábito m, costumbre f

won't ['wo:nt] contraction of WILL NOT → **will¹**

woo ['wu:] vt 1 COURT : cortejar 2 : buscar el apoyo de (clientes, votantes, etc.)

wood¹ ['wʊd] adj : de madera

wood² n 1 or **woods** npl FOREST : bosque m 2 : madera f (materia) 3 FIREWOOD : leña f

woodchuck ['wʊd,tʃʌk] n : marmota f de América

woodcut ['wʊd,kʌt] n 1 : plancha f de madera (para imprimir imágenes) 2 : grabado m en madera

woodcutter ['wʊd,kʌtər] n : leñador m, -dora f

wooded ['wʊdəd] adj : arbolado, boscoso

wooden ['wʊdən] adj 1 : de madera ⟨a wooden cross : una cruz de madera⟩ 2 STIFF : rígido, inexpresivo (dícese del estilo, de la cara, etc.)

woodland ['wʊdlənd, -,lænd] n : bosque m

woodpecker ['wʊd,pɛkər] n : pájaro m carpintero

woodshed ['wʊd,ʃɛd] n : leñera f

woodsman ['wʊdzmən] n, pl **-men** [-mən, -,mɛn] → **woodcutter**

woodwind ['wʊd,wɪnd] n : instrumento m de viento de madera

woodwork ['wʊd,wərk] n : carpintería f

woodworking ['wʊd,wərkɪŋ] n : carpintería f

woody ['wʊdi] adj **woodier; -est** 1 → **wooded** 2 : leñoso ⟨woody plants : plantas leñosas⟩ 3 : leñoso (dícese de la textura), a madera (dícese del aroma, etc.)

woof ['wʊf] → **weft**

wool ['wʊl] n : lana f

woolen¹ or **woollen** ['wʊlən] adj : de lana

woolen² or **woollen** n 1 : lana f (tela) 2 **woolens** npl : prendas fpl de lana

woolly ['wʊli] adj **woollier; -est** 1 : lanudo 2 CONFUSED : confuso, vago

woozy ['wu:zi] adj **woozier; -est** : mareado

word¹ ['wərd] vt : expresar, formular, redactar

word² n 1 : palabra f, vocablo m, voz f ⟨word for word : palabra por palabra⟩ ⟨words fail me : me quedo sin habla⟩ ⟨I can't understand a word she says : no entiendo ni una sola palabra de lo que dice⟩ 2 REMARK : palabra f ⟨by word of mouth : de palabra⟩ ⟨in a word : en una palabra⟩ ⟨in other words : en otras palabras⟩ ⟨in one's own words : en/con sus propias palabras⟩ ⟨in so many words : con esas palabras⟩ ⟨the last word : la última palabra⟩ ⟨to have a word with : hablar (dos palabras) con⟩ ⟨don't believe a word of it : no te creas ni una sola palabra⟩ ⟨don't say/breathe a word of this (to anyone) : de esto ni una palabra (a nadie)⟩ 3 COMMAND : orden f ⟨to give the word : dar la orden⟩ ⟨just say the word : no tienes más que decirlo⟩ 4 MESSAGE, NEWS : noticias fpl ⟨is there any word from her? : ¿hay noticias de ella?⟩ ⟨to send word : mandar un recado⟩ ⟨word has it that . . . : dicen que . . . , corre el rumor de que . . .⟩ 5 PROMISE : palabra f ⟨word of honor : palabra de honor⟩ ⟨to keep one's word : cumplir uno su palabra⟩ ⟨you have my word (on it) : te doy mi palabra⟩ ⟨take my word for it : te lo digo yo⟩ ⟨to take someone at his/her word : confiar en la palabra de alguien, fiarse de la palabra de alguien⟩ 6 **words** npl QUARREL : palabra f, riña f ⟨to have words with : tener unas palabras con, reñir con⟩ 7 **words** npl TEXT : letra f (de una canción, etc.) 8 from the word go : desde el principio 9 to get a word in edgewise : meter la cuchara 10 to have the last word : tener/decir la última palabra 11 to put in a good word for someone : recomendar a alguien 12 to put words into someone's mouth : atribuirle a alguien algo que no dijo 13 to take the words out of someone's mouth : quitarle las palabras de la boca a alguien 14 to waste words : gastar saliva

wordiness ['wərdinəs] n : verbosidad f

wording ['wərdɪŋ] n : redacción f, lenguaje m (de un documento)

word processing n : procesamiento m de textos

word processor n : procesador m de textos

wordy ['wərdi] adj **wordier; -est** : verboso, prolijo

wore → **wear¹**

work¹ ['wərk] v **worked** ['wərkt] or **wrought** ['rɔt]; **working** vi 1 LABOR : trabajar ⟨to work hard : trabajar mucho/duro⟩ ⟨to work full-time : trabajar a tiempo completo⟩ ⟨to work part-time : trabajar a/de medio tiempo⟩ ⟨to work overtime : trabajar horas extras⟩ 2 FUNCTION : funcionar, servir 3 to work around : esquivar (un problema, etc.) 4 to work at : esforzarse para mejorar ⟨she's working at controlling her temper : está tratando de apren-

der a controlar su mal genio⟩ ⟨you'll
have to work harder at it : tendrás que
esforzarte más⟩ **5 to work loose**
: soltarse, desprenderse **6 to work on**
: trabajar en (un proyecto, etc.) ⟨to work
on a cure : trabajar para encontrar una
cura⟩ ⟨she's working on (controlling)
her temper : está tratando de aprender a
controlar su mal genio⟩ **7 to work out**
TURN OUT : resultar, salir **8 to work out**
SUCCEED : dar resultado, salir bien **9 to
work out** EXERCISE : hacer ejercicio **10
to work up to** (*indicating a gradual increase*) ⟨to work up to full speed : ir co-
brando velocidad poco a poco⟩ — *vt* **1**
: trabajar ⟨to work long hours : trabajar
muchas horas⟩ ⟨to work weekends : trabajar los fines de semana⟩ ⟨to work
nights : trabajar de noche⟩ ⟨to work the
night shift : hacer el turno de noche⟩
⟨she works two jobs : tiene dos em-
pleos⟩ **2** : trabajar, labrar (la tierra,
etc.) **3** : hacer trabajar (a alguien) **4**
OPERATE : operar ⟨to work one's way up
: lograr subir por sus propios esfuer-
zos⟩ **6** EFFECT : efectuar, llevar a cabo,
obrar (milagros) **7** MANIPULATE, SHAPE
: trabajar, formar ⟨work the dough : tra-
baje la masa⟩ ⟨a beautifully wrought
vase : un florero bellamente elabo-
rado⟩ **8** HANDLE : manejar (a alguien)
⟨he knows how to work a crowd/room
: sabe conquistar al público⟩ **9 to work
off** : pagar trabajando **10 to work out**
DEVELOP, PLAN : idear, planear, desarrollar **11 to work out** RESOLVE : solucionar, resolver ⟨to work out the answer
: calcular la solución⟩ **12 to work over**
: darle una paliza (a alguien) **13 to work up** : estimular, excitar ⟨don't work yourself up
: no te agites⟩ **14 to work up** PRODUCE
: generar ⟨to work up the courage to
: armarse de valor para⟩ ⟨to work up a
sweat : empezar a sudar⟩

work² *adj* : laboral

work³ *n* **1** : trabajo *m* ⟨work to do : trabajo que hacer⟩ ⟨the quality of his work
: la calidad de su trabajo⟩ ⟨to bring work
home : llevar trabajo a casa⟩ **2** EMPLOY-
MENT : trabajo *m*, empleo *m* ⟨out of
work : desempleado⟩ ⟨line of work
: profesión⟩ **3** : trabajo *m* (lugar) ⟨to go
to work : ir a trabajar⟩ ⟨to leave work
: salir del trabajo⟩ ⟨she's at work : está
en el trabajo⟩ **4** EFFORT : trabajo *m* **5**
DEED : obra *f*, labor *f* ⟨works of charity
: obras de caridad⟩ **6** : obra *f* (de arte o
literatura) **7** : obras *fpl* ⟨road work
: obras viales⟩ **8** → **workmanship** **9
works** *npl* FACTORY : fábrica *f* **10
works** *npl* MECHANISM : mecanismo
m **11 the works** EVERYTHING : absolutamente todo *m* **12 at ~** WORKING
: trabajando **13 at ~** INVOLVED : en
juego **14 in the works** : en trámite **15
it's all in a day's work** : es el pan nuestro
de cada día **16 to have one's work cut**

out for one : tener mucho trabajo por
delante **17 to make short work of**
: hacer rápidamente

workable [ˈwərkəbəl] *adj* **1** : explotable
(dícese de una mina, etc.) **2** FEASIBLE
: factible, realizable

workaday [ˈwərkəˌdeɪ] *adj* : ordinario, banal

workaholic [ˌwərkəˈhɒlɪk] *n* : adicto *m*, -ta
f al trabajo

workbench [ˈwərkˌbɛntʃ] *n* : mesa *f* de
trabajo

workday [ˈwərkˌdeɪ] *n* **1** : jornada *f* laboral **2** WEEKDAY : día *m* hábil, día *m*
laborable

worked up *adj* : agitado ⟨to get (all)
worked up : agitarse⟩

worker [ˈwərkər] *n* : trabajador *m*, -dora *f*;
obrero *m*, -ra *f*

workforce [ˈwərkˌfors] *n* **1** STAFF : mano
f de obra **2** : fuerza *f* de trabajo, fuerza
f laboral

working [ˈwərkɪŋ] *adj* **1** : que trabaja
⟨working mothers : madres que traba-
jan⟩ ⟨the working class : la clase
obrera⟩ **2** : de trabajo ⟨working hours
: horas de trabajo⟩ **3** FUNCTIONING
: que funciona, operativo **4** SUFFICIENT
: suficiente ⟨a working majority : una
mayoría suficiente⟩ ⟨working knowledge : conocimientos básicos⟩

working–class [ˈwərkɪŋˈklæs] *adj* : obrero

workingman [ˈwərkɪŋˌmæn] *n*, *pl* **-men**
[-mən, -ˌmɛn] : obrero *m*

workload [ˈwərkˌloːd] *n* : cantidad *f* de
trabajo

workman [ˈwərkmən] *n*, *pl* **-men** [-mən,
-ˌmɛn] **1** → **workingman 2** ARTISAN
: artesano *m*

workmanlike [ˈwərkmənˌlaɪk] *adj* : bien
hecho, competente

workmanship [ˈwərkmənˌʃɪp] *n* **1** WORK
: ejecución *f*, trabajo *m* **2** CRAFTSMAN-
SHIP : artesanía *f*, destreza *f*

workout [ˈwərkˌaʊt] *n* : ejercicios *mpl* físi-
cos, entrenamiento *m*

workplace [ˈwərkˌples] *n* : lugar *m* de trabajo

workroom [ˈwərkˌruːm, -ˌrʊm] *n* : taller *m*

worksheet [ˈwərkˌʃiːt] *n* **1** : hoja *f* de
ejercicios **2** : hoja *f* de cálculo (de impuestos, etc.)

workshop [ˈwərkˌʃɑp] *n* : taller *m* ⟨ce-
ramics workshop : taller de cerámica⟩

workstation [ˈwərkˌsteʃən] *n* : estación *f*
de trabajo (en informática)

world¹ [ˈwərld] *adj* : mundial, del mundo
⟨world championship : campeonato
mundial⟩

world² *n* **1** : mundo *m* ⟨around the world
: alrededor del mundo⟩ **2** : mundo *m*
⟨the industrialized world : el mundo in-
dustrializado⟩ **3** SOCIETY : mundo *m*
⟨the real world : el mundo real⟩ **4** PEOPLE
: mundo *m*, gente *f* ⟨to watch the world
go by : ver pasar a la gente⟩ **5** REALM
: mundo *m* ⟨the fashion world : el
mundo de la moda⟩ **6** LIFE : mundo *m*,
vida *f* ⟨his world fell apart : su mundo se

derrumbó⟩ **7** PLANET : mundo *m*, planeta *f* **8 the world** EVERYTHING : todo *m* ⟨to mean the world to someone : ser todo para alguien⟩ **9 a world of** ⟨a world of difference : una diferencia enorme⟩ ⟨it'll do you a world of good : te hará la mar de bien⟩ **10 for all the world** *fam* EXACTLY : exactamente **11 (not) for the world** *fam* : por nada del mundo **12 in one's own world** *or* **in a world of one's own** *fam* : en su mundo **13 in the world** *fam* : del mundo ⟨the best in the world : el mejor del mundo⟩ ⟨what in the world . . . ? : ¿qué diablos/demonios . . . ?⟩ **14 out of this world** *fam* : increíble, fantástico **15 the (whole) world over** *fam* : por/en/de todo el mundo **16 to have all the time in the world** : tener todo el tiempo del mundo **17 to come/move up in the world** : prosperar, tener éxito **18 to think the world of someone** *fam* : tener a alguien en alta estima

world–famous *adj* : mundialmente famoso, de fama mundial

worldly [ˈwɔrldli] *adj* **worldlier; -est 1** : mundano ⟨worldly goods : bienes materiales⟩ **2** SOPHISTICATED : sofisticado, de mundo

worldwide¹ [ˈwɔrldˈwaɪd] *adv* : mundialmente, en todo el mundo

worldwide² *adj* : global, mundial

World Wide Web *n* : World Wide Web *f*, Red (informática) mundial

worm¹ [ˈwɔrm] *vi* CRAWL : arrastrarse, deslizarse (como gusano) — *vt* **1** : desparasitar (un animal) **2 to worm one's way into** : introducirse en ⟨he wormed his way into her confidence : se ganó su confianza⟩ **3 to worm something out of someone** : sonsacarle algo a alguien

worm² *n* **1** : gusano *m*, lombriz *f* **2 worms** *npl* : lombrices *fpl* (parásitos)

worm–eaten [ˈwɔrmˌiːtən] *adj* : carcomido

wormy [ˈwɔrmi] *adj* **wormier; -est** : infestado de gusanos

worn *pp* → **wear¹**

worn–out [ˈwornˈaʊt] *adj* **1** USED : gastado, desgastado **2** TIRED : agotado

worried [ˈwɔrid] *adj* : inquieto, preocupado

worrier [ˈwɔriər] *n* : persona *f* que se preocupa mucho

worrisome [ˈwɔrisəm] *adj* **1** DISTURBING : preocupante, inquietante **2** : que se preocupa mucho (dícese de una persona)

worry [ˈwɔri] *v* **-ried; -rying** *vt* : preocupar, inquietar — *vi* : preocuparse, inquietarse, angustiarse

worry² *n*, *pl* **-ries** : preocupación *f*, inquietud *f*, angustia *f*

worrying [ˈwɔriɪŋ] *adj* DISTURBING : preocupante, inquietante

worse¹ [ˈwɔrs] *adv* (*comparative of* BAD *or of* ILL) : peor

worse² *adj* (*comparative of* BAD *or of* ILL) : peor ⟨from bad to worse : de mal en peor⟩ ⟨to get worse : empeorar⟩ ⟨to feel worse : sentirse peor⟩

worse³ *n* : estado *m* peor ⟨to take a turn for the worse : ponerse peor⟩ ⟨so much the worse : tanto peor⟩

worsen [ˈwɔrsən] *vt* : empeorar — *vi* : empeorar(se)

worship¹ [ˈwɔrʃəp] *v* **-shiped** *or* **-shipped; -shiping** *or* **-shipping** *vt* : adorar, venerar ⟨to worship God : adorar a Dios⟩ — *vi* : practicar una religión

worship² *n* : adoración *f*, culto *m*

worshiper *or* **worshipper** [ˈwɔrʃəpər] *n* : devoto *m*, -ta *f*; adorador *m*, -dora *f*

worst¹ [ˈwɔrst] *vt* DEFEAT : derrotar

worst² *adv* (*superlative of* ILL *or of* BAD *or* BADLY) : peor ⟨the worst dressed of all : el peor vestido de todos⟩

worst³ *adj* (*superlative of* BAD *or of* ILL) : peor ⟨the worst movie : la peor película⟩

worst⁴ *n* **the worst** : lo peor, el/la peor ⟨the worst is over : ya ha pasado lo peor⟩ ⟨if worst comes to worst : en el peor de los casos⟩

worst–case *adj* **a/the worst–case scenario** : el peor de los casos

worsted [ˈwʊstəd, ˈwɔrstəd] *n* : estambre *m*

worth¹ [ˈwɔrθ] *n* **1** : valor *m* (monetario) ⟨ten dollars' worth of gas : diez dólares de gasolina⟩ **2** MERIT : valor *m*, mérito *m*, valía *f* ⟨an employee of great worth : un empleado de gran valía⟩

worth² *prep* **to be worth** : valer ⟨her holdings are worth a fortune : sus propiedades valen una fortuna⟩ ⟨it's not worth it : no vale la pena⟩

worthiness [ˈwɔrðinəs] *n* : mérito *m*

worthless [ˈwɔrθləs] *adj* **1** : sin valor ⟨worthless trinkets : chucherías sin valor⟩ **2** USELESS : inútil

worthwhile [ˌwɔrθˈhwaɪl] *adj* : que vale la pena

worthy [ˈwɔrði] *adj* **worthier; -est 1** : digno ⟨worthy of promotion : digno de un ascenso⟩ **2** COMMENDABLE : meritorio, encomiable

would [ˈwʊd] (*past of* WILL) **1** (*expressing preference, desire, or willingness*) ⟨I would rather go alone than with her : preferiría ir sola que con ella⟩ ⟨I would like to help : me gustaría ayudar⟩ ⟨he would do anything for her : haría cualquier cosa por ella⟩ **2** (*expressing intent*) ⟨those who would ban certain books : aquellos que prohibirían ciertos libros⟩ **3** (*expressing habitual action*) ⟨he would often take his kids to the park : solía llevar a sus hijos al parque⟩ **4** (*expressing possibility or contingency*) ⟨I would go if I had the money : iría yo si tuviera el dinero⟩ ⟨I would if I could : lo haría si pudiera⟩ **5** (*offering or requesting advice*) ⟨if I were you, I would do it : yo en tu lugar lo haría⟩ ⟨what would you do? : ¿qué harías tú?⟩ **6** (*expressing probability*) ⟨she would have won if she hadn't tripped : habría ganado si no hubiera tropezado⟩ **7** (*expressing a request*) ⟨would you kindly help me with this? : ¿tendría la bondad de ayudarme con esto?⟩ ⟨would you mind waiting? : ¿le importaría esperar?⟩

would–be ['wʊd'bi:] *adj* : potencial ⟨a would-be celebrity : un aspirante a celebridad⟩

wouldn't ['wʊdənt] *contraction of* WOULD NOT → would

wound[1] ['wu:nd] *vt* : herir

wound[2] *n* : herida *f*

wound[3] ['waʊnd] → **wind**[2]

wove, woven → **weave**[1]

wow ['waʊ] *interj (expressing surprise or pleasure)* : ¡guau!, ¡híjole! *Mex*, ¡hala! *Spain*

wrangle[1] ['ræŋgəl] *vi* -gled; -gling : discutir, reñir ⟨to wrangle over : discutir por⟩

wrangle[2] *n* : riña *f*, disputa *f*

wrap[1] ['ræp] *v* wrapped; wrapping *vt* 1 COVER : envolver, cubrir ⟨to wrap a package : envolver un paquete⟩ ⟨wrapped in mystery : envuelto en misterio⟩ 2 ENCIRCLE : rodear, ceñir ⟨to wrap one's arms around someone : estrechar a alguien⟩ 3 to wrap up FINISH : darle fin a (algo) — *vi* 1 COIL : envolverse, enroscarse 2 to wrap up DRESS : abrigarse ⟨wrap up warmly : abrígate bien⟩

wrap[2] *n* 1 WRAPPER : envoltura *f* 2 : prenda *f* que envuelve (como un chal, una bata, etc.)

wrapper ['ræpər] *n* : envoltura *f*, envoltorio *m*

wrapping ['ræpɪŋ] *n* : envoltura *f*, envoltorio *m*

wrath ['ræθ] *n* : ira *f*, cólera *f*

wrathful ['ræθfəl] *adj* : iracundo

wreak ['ri:k] *vt* : infligir, causar ⟨to wreak havoc : crear caos, causar estragos⟩

wreath ['ri:θ] *n, pl* wreaths ['ri:ðz, 'ri:θs] : corona *f* (de flores, etc.)

wreathe ['ri:ð] *vt* wreathed; wreathing 1 ADORN : coronar (de flores, etc.) 2 ENVELOP : envolver ⟨wreathed in mist : envuelto en niebla⟩

wreck[1] ['rɛk] *vt* : destruir, arruinar, estrellar (un automóvil), naufragar (un barco)

wreck[2] *n* 1 WRECKAGE : restos *mpl* (de un buque naufragado, un avión siniestrado, etc.) 2 RUIN : ruina *f*, desastre *m* ⟨this place is a wreck! : ¡este lugar está hecho un desastre!⟩ ⟨to be a nervous wreck : tener los nervios destrozados⟩

wreckage ['rɛkɪdʒ] *n* : restos *mpl* (de un buque naufragado, un avión siniestrado, etc.), ruinas *fpl* (de un edificio)

wrecker ['rɛkər] *n* TOW TRUCK : grúa *f*

wren ['rɛn] *n* : chochín *m*

wrench[1] ['rɛntʃ] *vt* 1 PULL : arrancar (de un tirón) 2 SPRAIN, TWIST : torcerse (un tobillo, un músculo, etc.)

wrench[2] *n* 1 TUG : tirón *m*, jalón *m* 2 SPRAIN : torcedura *f* 3 *or* **monkey wrench** : llave *f* inglesa

wrest ['rɛst] *vt* : arrancar

wrestle[1] ['rɛsəl] *v* -tled; -tling *vi* 1 : luchar, practicar la lucha (en deportes) 2 STRUGGLE : luchar ⟨to wrestle with a dilemma : lidiar con un dilema⟩ — *vt* : luchar contra

wrestle[2] *n* STRUGGLE : lucha *f*

wrestler ['rɛslər] *n* : luchador *m*, -dora *f*

wrestling ['rɛsəlɪŋ] *n* : lucha *f*

wretch ['rɛtʃ] *n* : infeliz *mf*; desgraciado *m*, -da *f*

wretched ['rɛtʃəd] *adj* 1 MISERABLE, UNHAPPY : desdichado, afligido ⟨I feel wretched : me siento muy mal⟩ 2 UNFORTUNATE : miserable, desgraciado, lastimoso ⟨wretched weather : tiempo espantoso⟩ 3 INFERIOR : inferior, malo

wretchedly ['rɛtʃədli] *adv* : miserablemente, lamentablemente

wriggle ['rɪgəl] *vi* -gled; -gling : retorcerse, menearse

wring ['rɪŋ] *vt* wrung ['rʌŋ]; wringing 1 *or* to wring out : escurrir, exprimir (el lavado) 2 EXTRACT : arrancar, sacar (por la fuerza) 3 TWIST : torcer, retorcer 4 to wring someone's heart : partirle el corazón a alguien

wringer ['rɪŋər] *n* : escurridor *m*

wrinkle[1] ['rɪŋkəl] *v* -kled; -kling *vt* : arrugar — *vi* : arrugarse

wrinkle[2] *n* : arruga *f*

wrinkly ['rɪŋkəli] *adj* wrinklier; -est : arrugado

wrist ['rɪst] *n* 1 : muñeca *f* (en anatomía) 2 *or* **wristband** ['rɪst-,bænd] CUFF : puño *m*

wristwatch ['rɪst,wɑtʃ] *n* : reloj *m* de pulsera

writ ['rɪt] *n* : orden *f* (judicial)

write ['raɪt] *v* wrote ['ro:t]; written ['rɪtən]; writing *vi* 1 : escribir 2 to write back : contestar 3 to write in : escribir — *vt* 1 : escribir 2 to write back : contestar 3 to write down : apuntar, anotar 4 to write in INSERT : escribir, insertar 5 to write into : incluir (en un contrato, etc.) 6 to write off : declarar siniestro total (en contabilidad) 7 to write off DEDUCT : deducir, descontar (de los impuestos) 8 to write off : dar por perdido ⟨he wrote it off as a failure : lo consideró un fracaso⟩ 9 to write out : escribir 10 to write out : hacer (un cheque, una factura) 11 to write someone out of : eliminar a alguien de (un testamento, etc.) 12 to write up : redactar 13 to write up REPORT : ponerle una multa a (un conductor), darle una carta de amonestación a (un empleado)

write–off ['raɪt,ɔf] *n* 1 : cancelación *f* (de una deuda) 2 : siniestro *m* total, pérdida *f* total

writer ['raɪtər] *n* : escritor *m*, -tora *f*

writhe ['raɪð] *vi* writhed; writhing : retorcerse

writing ['raɪtɪŋ] *n* 1 : escritura *f* 2 HANDWRITING : letra *f* 3 **writings** *npl* WORKS : escritos *mpl*, obra *f*

writing paper *n* : papel *m* de carta

wrong[1] ['rɔŋ] *vt* wronged; wronging : ofender, ser injusto con

wrong[2] *adv* : mal, incorrectamente

wrong[3] *adj* wronger ['rɔŋər]; wrongest ['rɔŋəst] 1 EVIL, SINFUL : malo, injusto, inmoral ⟨it's wrong to lie : mentir está mal⟩ ⟨I've done nothing wrong : no he hecho nada malo⟩ **2** IMPROPER, UNSUITABLE : inadecuado, inapropiado, malo ⟨you're asking the wrong guy : no soy la persona indicada para responder⟩ **3** INCORRECT : malo, equivocado, incorrecto, erróneo ⟨a wrong answer : una mala respuesta, una respuesta equivocada⟩ ⟨I dialed the wrong number : me equivoqué de número (al marcar)⟩ ⟨the clock is wrong : el reloj anda mal⟩ **4 to be wrong** : equivocarse, estar equivocado ⟨I could be wrong : puede que esté equivocado⟩

wrong⁴ *n* **1** INJUSTICE : injusticia *f*, mal *m* **2** OFFENSE : ofensa *f*, agravio *m* (en derecho) **3 to be in the wrong** : haber hecho mal, estar equivocado

wrongdoer [ˈrɔŋ₁duːər] *n* : malhechor *m*, -chora *f*

wrongdoing [ˈrɔŋ₁duːɪŋ] *n* : fechoría *f*, maldad *f*

wrongful [ˈrɔŋfəl] *adj* **1** UNJUST : injusto **2** UNLAWFUL : ilegal

wrongly [ˈrɔŋli] *adv* **1** : injustamente **2** INCORRECTLY : erróneamente, incorrectamente

wrote → write

wrought [ˈrɔt] *adj* **1** SHAPED : formado, forjado ⟨wrought iron : hierro forjado⟩ **2** *or* **wrought up** : agitado, excitado

wrung → wring

wry [ˈraɪ] *adj* **wrier** [ˈraɪər]; **wriest** [ˈraɪəst] **1** TWISTED : torcido ⟨a wry neck : un cuello torcido⟩ **2** : irónico, sardónico (dícese del humor)

X

x¹ *n*, *pl* **x's** *or* **xs** [ˈɛksəz] **1** : vigésima cuarta letra del alfabeto inglés **2** : incógnita *f* (en matemáticas)

x² [ˈks] *vt* **x-ed** [ˈekst]; **x-ing** *or* **x'ing** [ˈeksɪŋ] DELETE : tachar

xenon [ˈziːˌnɑn, ˈze-] *n* : xenón *m*

xenophobe [ˈzenəˌfoːb, ˈzi-] *n* : xenófobo *m*, -ba *f*

xenophobia [ˌzenəˈfoːbiə, ˌzi-] *n* : xenofobia *f*

xenophobic [ˌzenəˈfoːbɪk, ˌzi-] *adj* : xenófobo

xerox [ˈzɪrˌɑks] *vt* : xerografiar

Xerox [ˈzɪrˌɑks] *trademark* se usa para una fotocopiadora

Xmas [ˈkrɪsməs] *n* : Navidad *f*

x–ray [ˈeksˌreɪ] *vt* : radiografiar

X ray [ˈeksˌreɪ] *n* **1** : rayo *m* X **2** : radiografía *f* (imagen)

xylophone [ˈzaɪləˌfoːn] *n* : xilófono *m*

Y

y [ˈwaɪ] *n*, *pl* **y's** *or* **ys** [ˈwaɪz] : vigésima quinta letra del alfabeto inglés

yacht¹ [ˈjɑt] *vi* : navegar (a vela), ir en yate ⟨to go yachting : irse a navegar⟩

yacht² *n* : yate *m*

yak [ˈjæk] *n* : yac *m*

yam [ˈjæm] *n* **1** : ñame *m* **2** SWEET POTATO : batata *f*, boniato *m*

yang [ˈjæŋ, ˈjɑŋ] *n* : yang *m* ⟨(the) yin and yang : el yin y el yang⟩

yank¹ [ˈjæŋk] *vt* : tirar de, jalar, darle un tirón a

yank² *n* : tirón *m*

Yankee [ˈjæŋki] *n* : yanqui *mf*

yap¹ [ˈjæp] *vi* **yapped; yapping 1** BARK, YELP : ladrar, gañir **2** CHATTER : cotorrear *fam*, parlotear *fam*

yap² *n* : ladrido *m*, gañido *m*

yard [ˈjɑrd] *n* **1** : yarda *f* (medida) **2** SPAR : verga *f* (de un barco) **3** COURTYARD : patio *m* **4** : jardín *m* (de una casa) **5** : depósito *m* (de mercancías, etc.)

yardage [ˈjɑrdɪdʒ] *n* : medida *f* en yardas

yardarm [ˈjɑrd₁ɑrm] *n* : penol *m*

yardstick [ˈjɑrd₁stɪk] *n* **1** : vara *f* **2** CRITERION : criterio *m*, norma *f*

yarn [ˈjɑrn] *n* **1** : hilado *m* **2** TALE : historia *f*, cuento *m* ⟨to spin a yarn : inventar una historia⟩

yawn¹ [ˈjɔn] *vi* **1** : bostezar **2** OPEN : abrirse

yawn² *n* : bostezo *m*

ye [ˈjiː] *pron* : vosotros, vosotras

ye¹ [ˈjeɪ] *adv* YES : sí

yea² *n* : voto *m* a favor

yeah [ˈjeə, ˈjæə] *adv fam* YES : sí ⟨are you coming? yeah : ¿vienes? sí⟩ ⟨oh, yeah? : ¿ah, sí?⟩ ⟨it's true! yeah, right : ¡es verdad! sí, claro⟩

year [ˈjɪr] *n* **1** : año *m* ⟨last year : el año pasado⟩ ⟨he's ten years old : tiene diez años⟩ **2** : curso *m*, año *m* (escolar) **3 years** *npl* AGES : siglos *mpl*, años *mpl* ⟨I haven't seen them in years : hace siglos que no los veo⟩

yearbook [ˈjɪr₁bʊk] *n* : anuario *m*

year–end [ˈjɪr₁end] *adj* : de fin de año

yearling [ˈjɪrlɪŋ, ˈjɪrlən] *n* : animal *m* menor de dos años

yearly¹ [ˈjɪrli] *adv* : cada año, anualmente

yearly² *adj* : anual

yearn [ˈjɜrn] *vi* : anhelar, ansiar

yearning [ˈjɜrnɪŋ] *n* : anhelo *m*

yeast [ˈjiːst] n : levadura f

yell¹ [ˈjɛl] vi : gritar, chillar — vt : gritar

yell² n : grito m, alarido m ⟨to let out a yell : dar un grito⟩

yellow¹ [ˈjɛloː] vi : ponerse amarillo, volverse amarillo

yellow² adj 1 : amarillo 2 COWARDLY : cobarde

yellow³ n : amarillo m

yellow fever n : fiebre f amarilla

yellowish [ˈjɛloɪʃ] adj : amarillento

yellow jacket n : avispa f (con rayas amarillas)

yelp¹ [ˈjɛlp] vi : dar un gañido (dícese de un animal), dar un grito (dícese de una persona)

yelp² n : gañido m (de un animal), grito m (de una persona)

yen [ˈjɛn] n 1 DESIRE : deseo m, ganas fpl 2 : yen m (moneda japonesa)

yeoman [ˈjoːmən] n, pl -men [-mən, -mɛn] : suboficial mf de marina

yes¹ [ˈjɛs] adv : sí ⟨to say yes : decir que sí⟩

yes² n : sí m

yesterday¹ [ˈjɛstərˌdeɪ, -di] adv : ayer

yesterday² n 1 : ayer m 2 the day before yesterday : anteayer

yesteryear [ˈjɛstərˌjɪr] n of ~ : de antaño

yet¹ [ˈjɛt] adv 1 BESIDES, EVEN : aún ⟨yet more problems : más problemas aún⟩ ⟨yet again : otra vez⟩ 2 SO FAR : aún, todavía ⟨not yet : todavía no⟩ ⟨as yet : hasta ahora, todavía⟩ 3 : ya ⟨has he come yet? : ¿ya ha venido?⟩ 4 EVENTUALLY : todavía, algún día 5 NEVERTHELESS : sin embargo

yet² conj : pero

yew [ˈjuː] n : tejo m

Yiddish [ˈjɪdɪʃ] n : yiddish m, yidis m — **Yiddish** adj

yield¹ [ˈjiːld] vt 1 SURRENDER : ceder ⟨to yield the right of way : ceder el paso⟩ 2 PRODUCE : producir, dar, rendir (en finanzas) — vi 1 GIVE : ceder ⟨to yield under pressure : ceder por la presión⟩ 2 GIVE IN, SURRENDER : ceder, rendirse, entregarse

yield² n : rendimiento m, rédito m (en finanzas)

yin [ˈjɪn] n : yin m ⟨(the) yin and yang : el yin y el yang⟩

yodel¹ [ˈjoːdəl] vi -deled or -delled; -deling or -delling : cantar al estilo tirolés

yodel² n : canción f al estilo tirolés

yoga [ˈjoːgə] n : yoga m

yogurt [ˈjoːgərt] n : yogur m, yogurt m

yoke¹ [ˈjoːk] vt yoked; yoking : uncir (animales)

yoke² n 1 : yugo m (para uncir animales) ⟨the yoke of oppression : el yugo de la opresión⟩ 2 TEAM : yunta f (de bueyes)

yokel [ˈjoːkəl] n : palurdo m, -da f

yolk [ˈjoːk] n : yema f (de un huevo)

Yom Kippur [ˌjoːmkɪˈpʊr, ˌjɑm-, -ˈkɪpər] n : el Día m del Perdón, Yom Kippur

yon [ˈjɑn] → **yonder**

yonder¹ [ˈjɑndər] adv : allá ⟨over yonder : allá lejos⟩

yonder² adj : aquel ⟨yonder hill : aquella colina⟩

yore [ˈjoːr] n in days of yore : antaño

you [ˈjuː] pron 1 (used as subject — familiar) : tú; vos in some Latin American countries; ustedes pl; vosotros, vosotras pl Spain 2 (used as subject — formal) : usted, ustedes pl 3 (used as indirect object — familiar) : te, les pl (se before lo, la, los, las), os pl Spain ⟨he told it to you : te lo contó⟩ ⟨I gave them to (all of, both of) you : se los di⟩ 4 (used as indirect object — formal) : lo Spain sometimes le, la; los Spain sometimes les, las pl 5 (used after a preposition — familiar) : ti; vos in some Latin American countries; ustedes pl; vosotros, vosotras pl Spain 6 (used after a preposition — formal) : usted, ustedes pl 7 (used as an impersonal subject) ⟨you never know : nunca se sabe⟩ ⟨you have to be aware : hay que ser consciente⟩ ⟨you mustn't do that : eso no se hace⟩ 8 with you (familiar) : contigo; con ustedes pl; con vosotros, con vosotras pl Spain 9 with you (formal) : con usted, con ustedes pl

you'd [ˈjuːd, ˈjʊd] contraction of YOU HAD or YOU WOULD → **have, would**

you'll [ˈjuːl, ˈjʊl] contraction of YOU SHALL or YOU WILL → **shall, will**

young¹ [ˈjʌŋ] adj younger [ˈjʌŋgər]; youngest [-gəst] 1 : joven, pequeño, menor ⟨young people : los jóvenes⟩ ⟨my younger brother : mi hermano menor⟩ ⟨she is the youngest : es la más pequeña⟩ 2 FRESH, NEW : tierno (dícese de las verduras), joven (dícese del vino) 3 YOUTHFUL : joven, juvenil

young² npl : jóvenes mfpl (de los humanos), crías fpl (de los animales)

youngster [ˈjʌŋkstər] n 1 YOUTH : joven mf 2 CHILD : chico m, -ca f; niño m, -ña f

your [ˈjʊr, ˈjoːr, jər] adj 1 (familiar singular) : tu ⟨your cat : tu gato⟩ ⟨your books : tus libros⟩ ⟨wash your hands : lávate las manos⟩ 2 (familiar plural) : su, vuestro Spain ⟨your car : su coche, el coche de ustedes⟩ 3 (formal) : su ⟨your houses : sus casas⟩ 4 (impersonal) : el, la, los, las ⟨on your left : a la izquierda⟩

you're [ˈjʊr, ˈjoːr, ˈjər, ˈjuːər] contraction of YOU ARE → **be**

yours [ˈjʊrz, ˈjoːrz] pron 1 (belonging to one person — familiar) : (el) tuyo, (la) tuya, (los) tuyos, (las) tuyas ⟨those are mine; yours are there : ésas son mías; las tuyas están allí⟩ ⟨is this one yours? : ¿éste es tuyo?⟩ 2 (belonging to more than one person — familiar) : (el) suyo, (la) suya, (los) suyos, (las) suyas; (el) vuestro, (la) vuestra, (los) vuestros, (las) vuestras Spain ⟨our house and yours : nuestra casa y la suya⟩ 3 (formal) : (el) suyo, (la) suya, (los) suyos, (las) suyas

yourself [jərˈsɛlf] pron, pl **yourselves** [-ˈsɛlvz] 1 (used reflexively — familiar) : te, se pl, os pl Spain ⟨wash yourself : lávate⟩ ⟨you dressed yourselves : se vistieron, os vestisteis⟩ 2 (used reflexively — formal) : se ⟨did you hurt yourself? : ¿se hizo daño?⟩ ⟨you've gotten yourselves dirty : se ensuciaron⟩ 3 (used for emphasis) : tú mismo, tú misma; usted mismo, usted misma; ustedes mismos, ustedes mismas pl; vosotros mismos, vosotras mismas pl Spain ⟨you did it yourselves? : ¿lo hicieron ustedes mismos?, ¿lo hicieron por sí solos?⟩

youth ['juːθ] n, pl **youths** ['juːðz, 'juːθs] **1** : juventud f ⟨in her youth : en su juventud⟩ **2** BOY : joven m **3** : jóvenes mfpl, juventud f ⟨the youth of our city : los jóvenes de nuestra ciudad⟩

youthful ['juːθfəl] adj **1** : de juventud **2** YOUNG : joven **3** JUVENILE : juvenil

youthfulness ['juːθfəlnəs] n : juventud f

youth hostel → hostel

you've ['juːv] contraction of YOU HAVE → have

yowl¹ ['jaʊl] vi : aullar

yowl² n : aullido m

yo-yo ['joːˌjoː] n, pl **-yos** : yoyo m, yoyó m

yucca ['jʌkə] n : yuca f

Yugoslavian [ˌjuːgoˈslɑviən] n : yugoslavo m, -va f — **Yugoslavian** adj

yule ['juːl] n CHRISTMAS : Navidad f

yuletide ['juːlˌtaɪd] n : Navidades fpl

yup ['jʌp] adv fam → yes¹

yuppie ['jʌpi] n : yuppy mf

Z

z ['ziː] n, pl **z's** or **zs** : vigésima sexta letra del alfabeto inglés

zany¹ ['zeɪni] adj **zanier; -est** : alocado, disparatado

zany² n, pl **-nies** : bufón m, -fona f

zap¹ ['zæp] vt **zapped; zapping 1** ELIMINATE : eliminar **2** : enviar o transportar rápidamente — vi : ir rápidamente

zap² n **1** ZEST : sabor m, sazón f **2** BLAST : golpe m fuerte

zeal ['ziːl] n : fervor m, celo m, entusiasmo m

zealot ['zɛlət] n : fanático m, -ca f

zealous ['zɛləs] adj : celoso — **zealously** adv

zebra ['ziːbrə] n : cebra f

zebu ['ziːˌbuː, -ˌbjuː] n : cebú m

zenith ['ziːnəθ] n **1** : cenit m (en astronomía) **2** PEAK : apogeo m, cenit m ⟨at the zenith of his career : en el apogeo de su carrera⟩

zeppelin ['zɛplən, -pələn] n : zepelín m

zero¹ ['ziːro, 'zɪro] vi **to zero in on** : apuntar hacia, centrarse en (un problema, etc.)

zero² adj : cero, nulo ⟨zero degrees : cero grados⟩ ⟨zero opportunities : oportunidades nulas⟩

zero³ n, pl **-ros** : cero m ⟨below zero : bajo cero⟩

zest ['zɛst] n **1** GUSTO : entusiasmo m, brío m **2** FLAVOR : sabor m, sazón f

zestful ['zɛstfəl] adj : brioso

zesty ['zɛsti] adj **zestier; -est 1** FLAVORFUL : sabroso, gustoso, picante **2** LIVELY : brioso

zigzag¹ ['zɪgˌzæg] vi **-zagged; -zagging** : zigzaguear

zigzag² adv & adj : en zigzag

zigzag³ n : zigzag m

Zimbabwean [zɪmˈbɑbwiən, -bweɪ-] n : zimbabuense mf — **Zimbabwean** adj

zinc ['zɪŋk] n : cinc m, zinc m

zing ['zɪŋ] n **1** HISS, HUM : zumbido m, silbido m **2** ENERGY : brío m

zinnia ['zɪniə, 'ziː-, -njə] n : zinnia f

Zionism ['zaɪəˌnɪzəm] n : sionismo m

Zionist ['zaɪənɪst] n : sionista f

zip¹ ['zɪp] v **zipped; zipping** vt or **to zip up** : cerrar el cierre de — vi **1** SPEED : pasarse volando ⟨the day zipped by : el día se pasó volando⟩ **2** HISS, HUM : silbar, zumbar

zip² n **1** ZING : zumbido m, silbido m **2** ENERGY : brío m

zip code n : código m postal

zipper ['zɪpər] n : cierre m, cremallera f, zíper m CA, Mex

zippy ['zɪpi] adj **zippier; -est** : brioso

zit ['zɪt] n : grano m

zodiac ['zoːdiˌæk] n : zodíaco m

zombie ['zambi] n : zombi mf, zombie mf

zone¹ ['zoːn] vt **zoned; zoning 1** : dividir en zonas **2** DESIGNATE : declarar ⟨to zone for business : declarar como zona comercial⟩

zone² n : zona f

zoo ['zuː] n, pl **zoos** : zoológico m, zoo m

zoological [ˌzoːəˈlɑdʒɪkəl, ˌzuːə-] adj : zoológico

zoologist [zoˈɑlədʒɪst, zuː-] n : zoólogo m, -ga f

zoology [zoˈɑlədʒi, zuː-] n : zoología f

zoom¹ ['zuːm] vi **1** : zumbar, ir volando ⟨to zoom past : pasar volando⟩ **2** CLIMB : elevarse ⟨the plane zoomed up : el avión se elevó⟩

zoom² n **1** : zumbido m ⟨the zoom of an engine : el zumbido de un motor⟩ **2** : subida f vertical (de un avión, etc.) **3** or **zoom lens** : zoom m

zucchini [zuˈkiːni] n, pl **-ni** or **-nis** : calabacín m, calabacita f Mex

Zulu ['zuːluː] n **1** : zulú mf **2** : zulú m (idioma) — **Zulu** adj

zygote ['zaɪˌgoːt] n : zigoto m, cigoto m

Common Spanish Abbreviations

CGT	Confederación General de Trabajadores or del Trabajo	—	confederation of workers, union
CI	coeficiente intelectual or de inteligencia	IQ	intelligence quotient
Cía.	compañía	Co.	Company
cm.	centímetro	cm	centimeter
Cmte.	comandante	Cmdr.	Commander
Cnel.	coronel	Col.	Colonel
col.	columna	col.	column
Col. *Mex*	colonia	—	residential area
Com.	comandante	Cmdr.	Commander
comp.	compárese	comp.	compare
Cor.	coronel	Col.	Colonel
C.P.	código postal	—	zip code
CSF, c.s.f.	coste, seguro y flete	c.i.f.	cost, insurance, and freight
cta.	cuenta	ac., acct.	account
cte.	corriente	cur.	current
CTI	centro de tratamiento intensivo *Uru*	ICU	intensive care unit
c/u	cada uno, cada una	ea.	each
CV	caballo de vapor	hp	horsepower
D.	don	—	—
Da., D.ª	doña	—	—
dB	decibel, decibelio	dB	decibel
d.C.	después de Cristo	AD	anno Domini (in the year of our Lord)
dcha.	derecha	—	right
d. de J.C.	después de Jesucristo	AD	anno Domini (in the year of our Lord)
dep.	departamento	dept.	department
DF, D.F.	Distrito Federal	—	Federal District
dic.	diciembre	Dec.	December
dir.	director, directora	dir.	director
dir.	dirección	—	direction, address
DNI	*Arg, Spain* documento nacional de identidad	—	national identity card
Dña.	doña	—	—
dom., do.	domingo	Sun.	Sunday
dpto.	departamento	dept.	department
Dr.	doctor	Dr.	Doctor
Dra.	doctora	Dr.	Doctor
DSL	línea de abonado digital	DSL	digital subscriber line
dto.	descuento	—	discount
E, E.	Este, este	E	East, east
Ed.	editorial	—	publishing house
Ed., ed.	edición	Ed., ed.	edition
edif.	edificio	Bldg.	building
edo.	estado	st.	state
EEUU, EE.UU.	Estados Unidos	US, U.S.	United States
ej.	por ejemplo	ex.	for example
E.M.	esclerosis múltiple	MS	multiple sclerosis
ene.	enero	Jan.	January

et al.	et alii (y otros)	et al.	et alii (and others)
etc.	etcétera	etc.	et cetera
ext.	extensión	ext.	extension
F	Fahrenheit	F	Fahrenheit
f.a.b.	franco a bordo	f.o.b.	free on board
FAQ	pregunta(s) frecuente(s)	FAQ	frequently asked question(s)
FC	ferrocarril	RR	railroad
feb.	febrero	Feb.	February
FF AA, FF.AA.	Fuerzas Armadas	—	armed forces
FMI	Fondo Monetario Internacional	IMF	International Monetary Fund
g.	gramo	g., gm, gr.	gram
G	(talla) grande	L	large
GMT	tiempo medio de Greenwich, hora del meridiano de Greenwich	GMT	Greenwich Mean Time
G.P.	giro postal	M.O.	money order
gr.	gramo	g., gm, gr.	gram
Gral.	general	Gen.	General
h.	hora	hr.	hour
Hno(s).	hermano(s)	Bro(s).	Brother(s)
ib., ibid.	ibidem (en el mismo lugar)	ibid.	ibidem (in the same place)
I + D, I & D, I y D	investigación y desarrollo	R & D	research and development
i.e.	esto es, es decir	i.e.	that is
incl.	inclusive	incl.	inclusive, inclusively, including
Ing.	ingeniero, ingeniera	eng.	engineer
IPC	índice de precios al consumo	CPI	consumer price index
IVA	impuesto al valor agregado	VAT	value-added tax
izq.; izdo., izda.; izqdo., izqda.	izquierdo; izquierda	l.	Left
JJ.OO., JJ OO	Juegos Olímpicos	—	Olympics, Olympic Games
Jr.	Júnior	Jr., Jun.	Junior
juev.	jueves	Thu., Thur., Thurs.	Thursday
jul.	julio	Jul.	July
jun.	junio	Jun.	June
kg.	kilogramo	kg	kilogram
km.	kilómetro	km	kilometer
km/h	kilómetros por hora	kph	kilometers per hour
kv, kV	kilovatio	kw, kW	kilowatt
l.	litro	l, lit.	liter
lcdo., lcda.	licenciado, licenciada	—	—
ldo., lda.	licenciado, licenciada	—	—

LGBT	lesbianas, gays, bisexuales y transgénero	LGBT	lesbian, gay, bisexual, and transgender
LGBTQ	lesbianas, gays, bisexuales, transgénero y queer	LGBTQ	lesbian, gay, bisexual, transgender, and queer/questioning
Lic.	licenciado, licenciada	—	—
Ltda.	limitada	Ltd.	Limited
lun.	lunes	Mon.	Monday
m	masculino	m	masculine
m	metro	m	meter
m	minuto	m	minute
M	mediano, (talla) mediana	M	medium
mar.	marzo	Mar.	March
mart.	martes	Tue., Tues.	Tuesday
Méx.	mexicano, México	Mex.	Mexican, Mexico
mg.	miligramo	mg	milligram
miérc.	miércoles	Wed.	Wednesday
min	minuto	min.	minute
ml.	mililitro	ml	milliliter
mm.	milímetro	mm	millimeter
MN, M.N., m.n., m/n	moneda nacional	—	national currency
Mons.	monseñor	Msgr.	Monsignor
Mtra.	maestra	—	teacher
Mtro.	maestro	—	teacher
N, N.	Norte, norte	N, no.	North, north
NIP	número de identificación personal	PIN	personal identification number
n/	nuestro	—	our
N. de (la) R.	nota de (la) redacción	Ed.	editor's note
NE	nordeste	NE	northeast
NN.UU.	Naciones Unidas	UN	United Nations
n.º	número	no.	number
NO	noroeste	NW	northwest
nov.	noviembre	Nov.	November
N.T.	Nuevo Testamento	N.T.	New Testament
ntra., ntro.	nuestra, nuestro	—	our
NU	Naciones Unidas	UN	United Nations
núm.	número	no.	number
NY	Nueva York, New York	NY	New York
O, O.	Oeste, oeste	W	West, west
oct.	octubre	Oct.	October
OEA, O.E.A.	Organización de Estados Americanos	OAS	Organization of American States
OMS	Organización Mundial de la Salud	WHO	World Health Organization
ONG	organización no gubernamental	NGO	non-governmental organization
ONU	Organización de las Naciones Unidas	UN	United Nations
OTAN	Organización del Tratado del Atlántico Norte	NATO	North Atlantic Treaty Organization
p.	página	p.	page

P	(talla) pequeña	**S**	small
P, P.	padre	**Fr.**	Father
pág(s).	página(s)	**p(p)., pg(s).**	page(s)
Pat.	patente	**pat.**	patent
PBI	producto bruto interno	**GDP**	gross domestic product
PCL	pantalla de cristal líquido	**LCD**	liquid crystal display
P.D.	post data	**P.S.**	postscript
p. ej.	por ejemplo	**e.g.**	for example
PIB	producto interno bruto, producto interior bruto	**GDP**	gross domestic product
PIN	número de identificación personal	**PIN**	personal identification number
p.m.	post meridiem (de la tarde)	**p.m., PM**	post meridiem (afternoon)
PNB	Producto Nacional Bruto	**GNP**	gross national product
p°	paseo	**Ave.**	Avenue
p.p.	porte pagado	**ppd.**	postpaid
PP, p.p.	por poder, por poderes	**p.p.**	by proxy
PR	Puerto Rico	**PR**	Puerto Rico
prom.	promedio	**av., avg.**	average
pto.	punto	**pt.**	point
ptas., pts.	pesetas	—	—
PYME	Pequeña y Mediana Empresa	—	Small to Medium-Sized Business
Pza.	Plaza	**Sq.**	Square
q.e.p.d.	que en paz descanse	**R.I.P.**	(may he/she) rest in peace
R, R/	remite	—	sender
RAE	Real Academia Española	—	—
R & B	rhythm and blues, rhythm y blues	**R & B**	rhythm and blues
RCP	reanimación cardiopulmonar, resucitación cardiopulmonar	**CPR**	cardiopulmonary resuscitation
Rdo., Rda.	reverendo, reverenda	**Rev.**	Reverend
ref., ref.[a]	referencia	**ref.**	reference
Rep.	República	**Rep.**	Republic
r.p.m.	revoluciones por minuto	**rpm**	revolutions per minute
Rte.	remite, remitente	—	sender
s.	siglo	**c., cent.**	century
s/	su, sus	—	his, her, your, their
S, S.	Sur, sur	**S, so.**	South, south
S.	san, santo	**St.**	Saint
Sr.	Sénior	**Sr.**	Senior
S.A.	Sociedad Anónima	**Inc.**	Incorporated (company)
sáb.	sábado	**Sat.**	Saturday
s/c	su cuenta	—	your account
SE	sudeste, sureste	**SE**	southeast

seg.	segundo, segundos	sec.	second, seconds
sep., sept.	septiembre	Sept.	September
s.e.u.o.	salvo error u omisión	—	errors and omissions excepted
Sgto.	sargento	Sgt.	Sergeant
S.L.	Sociedad Limitada	Ltd.	Limited (corporation)
S.M.	Su Majestad	HM	His Majesty, Her Majesty
SMS	servicio de mensajes cortos	SMS	Short Message Service
s/n	sin número	—	no (street) number
s.n.m.	sobre el nivel de mar	a.s.l.	above sea level
SO	sudoeste/suroeste	SW	southwest
S.R.C.	se ruega contestación	R.S.V.P.	please reply
ss.	siguientes	—	the following ones
SS, S.S.	Su Santidad	H.H.	His Holiness
Sta.	santa	St.	Saint
Sto.	santo	St.	Saint
t, t.	tonelada	t., tn.	ton
TAE	tasa anual efectiva	APR	annual percentage rate
tb.	también	—	also
tel., Tel.	teléfono	tel.	telephone
Tm.	tonelada métrica	MT	metric ton
Tn.	tonelada	t., tn.	ton
TOC	trastorno obsesivo-compulsivo	OCD	obsessive-compulsive disorder
trad.	traducido, traductor, traducción	tr., trans., transl.	translated, translator, translation
UCI	unidad de cuidados intensivos	ICU	intensive care unit
UE	Unión Europea	EU	European Union
Univ.	universidad	Univ., U.	University
Urb.	urbanización	—	residential area
UTI	unidad de terapia intensiva, unidad de tratamiento intensivo *Chile*	ICU	intensive care unit
v	versus	v., vs.	versus
v	verso	v., vs.	verse
v.	véase	viz.	see
Vda.	viuda	—	widow
v.g., v.gr.	verbigracia	e.g.	for example
vier., viern.	viernes	Fri.	Friday
V.M.	Vuestra Majestad	—	Your Majesty
VºBº, V.ºB.º	visto bueno	—	OK, approved
vol, vol.	volumen	vol.	volume
vra., vro.	vuestra, vuestro	—	your
www	world wide web, red mundial	www	World Wide Web

Abreviaturas comunes en inglés

ABREVIATURA INGLESA Y EXPANSIÓN			EQUIVALENTE ESPAÑOL
AAA	American Automobile Association	—	—
AC	alternating current	CA	corriente alterna
AC	air-conditioning	—	aire acondicionado
ac., acct.	account	cta.	cuenta
AD	anno Domini (in the year of our Lord)	A.D., d.C., d. de J.C.	anno Domini, después de Cristo, después de Jesucristo
AK	Alaska	—	Alaska
aka	also known as	—	alias
AL, Ala.	Alabama	—	Alabama
Alas.	Alaska	—	Alaska
a.m., AM	ante meridiem (before noon)	a.m.	ante meridiem (de la mañana)
Am., Amer.	America, American	—	América, americano
amt.	amount	—	cantidad
anon.	anonymous	—	anónimo
ans.	answer	—	respuesta
Apr.	April	abr.	abril
approx.	approximately	aprox.	aproximadamente
APR	annual percentage rate	TAE	tasa anual efectiva
AR	Arkansas	—	Arkansas
arch.	architect	Arq.	arquitecto
Ariz.	Arizona	—	Arizona
Ark.	Arkansas	—	Arkansas
a.s.l.	above sea level	s.n.m.	sobre el nivel de mar
asst.	assistant	ayte.	ayudante
atty.	attorney	—	abogado, -da
Aug.	August	ago.	agosto
av.	average	prom.	promedio
Ave.	Avenue	av., avda.	avenida
avg.	average	prom.	promedio
AZ	Arizona	—	Arizona
BA	Bachelor of Arts	Lic.	Licenciado, -da en Filosofía y Letras
BA	Bachelor of Arts (degree)	—	Licenciatura en Filosofía y Letras
BC	before Christ	a.C., A.C., a. de J.C.	antes de Cristo, antes de Jesucristo
bcc	blind carbon copy	CCO	copia (de carbón) oculta
BCE	before the Christian Era, before the Common Era	—	antes de la era cristiana, antes de la era común
bet.	between	—	entre
Bldg.	Building	edif.	edificio
Blvd.	Boulevard	blvar., br.	bulevar
Br., Brit.	Britain, British	—	Gran Bretaña, británico
Bro(s).	Brother(s)	Hno(s).	hermano(s)
BS	Bachelor of Science	Lic.	Licenciado, -da en Ciencias
BS	Bachelor of Science (degree)	—	Licenciatura en Ciencias
c	carat	—	quilate

c	cent	—	centavo
c	centimeter	cm.	centímetro
c	century	s.	siglo
c	cup	—	taza
C	Celsius, centigrade	C	Celsius, centígrado
CA, Cal., Calif.	California	—	California
Can., Canad.	Canada, Canadian	—	Canadá, canadiense
cap.	capital	—	capital
cap.	capital	—	mayúscula
Capt.	Captain	Cap.	capitán
cc	cubic centimeters	c.c.	centímetros cúbicos
cc	carbon copy	CC	copia de carbón
cent.	century	s.	siglo
CEO	chief executive officer	—	presidente, -ta (de una corporación)
cf.	compare	cf.	compárese
CFO	chief financial officer	—	director financiero, directora financiera
cg	centigram	cg.	centígramo
ch., chap.	chapter	cap.	capítulo
CIA	Central Intelligence Agency	CIA	Agencia Central de Inteligencia
cm	centimeter	cm.	centímetro
Cmdr.	Commander	Com., Cmte.	comandante
Co.	Company	C., Cía.	compañía
co.	county	—	condado
CO	Colorado	—	Colorado
c/o	care of	a/c	a cargo de
COD	cash on delivery, collect on delivery	—	(pago) contra reembolso
col.	column	col.	columna
Col., Colo.	Colorado	—	Colorado
comp.	compare	comp.	compárese
Conn.	Connecticut	—	Connecticut
Corp.	Corporation	—	corporación
CPI	consumer price index	IPC	índice de precios al consumo
CPR	cardiopulmonary resuscitation	RCP	reanimación cardiopulmonar, resucitación cardiopulmonar
ct.	cent	—	centavo
CT	Connecticut	—	Connecticut
cu. cm	cubic centimeters	c.c.	centímetros cúbicos
D.A.	district attorney	—	fiscal (del distrito)
dB	decibel	dB	decibel, decibelio
DC	District of Columbia	—	—
DC	direct current	CC	corriente continua
DDS	Doctor of Dental Surgery	—	doctor de cirugía dental
DE.	Delaware	—	Delaware
Dec.	December	dic.	diciembre
Del.	Delaware	—	Delaware
DHS	Department of Homeland Security	DHS	Departamento de Seguridad Nacional
dir.	director	dir.	director, directora
dir.	direction	dir.	dirección
DJ	disc jockey	—	disc jockey
dept.	department	dep., dpto.	departamento
DMD	Doctor of Dental Medicine	—	doctor de medicina dental

doz.	dozen	—	docena
Dr.	Doctor	Dr., Dra.	doctor, doctora
DSL	digital subscriber line	DSL	línea de abonado digital
DST	daylight saving time	—	—
DVM	Doctor of Veterinary Medicine	—	doctor de medicina veterinaria
E	East, east	E, E.	Este, este
ea.	each	c/u	cada uno, cada una
EC	European Community	CE	Comunidad Europea
EEC	European Economic Community	CEE	Comunidad Económica Europea
Ed., ed.	edition	Ed., ed.	edición
e.g.	for example	v.g., v.gr., p.ej.	verbigracia, por ejemplo
enc., encl.	enclosure	—	anexo
EMT	emergency medical technician	—	técnico, -ca en urgencias médicas
Eng.	England, English	—	Inglaterra, inglés
esp.	especially	—	especialmente
ER	emergency room	—	sala de urgencia(s), sala de emergencia(s)
EST	eastern standard time	—	—
etc.	et cetera	etc.	etcétera
ETA	estimated time of arrival	—	hora aproximada de llegada
et al.	et alii (and others)	et al.	et alii (y otros)
EU	European Union	UE	Unión Europea
ext.	extension	ext.	extensión
f	false	—	falso
f	female	f	femenino
F	Fahrenheit	F	Fahrenheit
FAQ	frequently asked question(s)	FAQ	pregunta(s) frecuente(s)
FBI	Federal Bureau of Investigation	FBI	Buró Federal de Investigaciones
Feb.	February	feb.	febrero
fem.	feminine	—	femenino
FEMA	Federal Emergency Agency	—	Agencia Federal para el Manejo de Emergencias
FL, Fla.	Florida	—	Florida
f.o.b.	free on board	f.a.b.	franco a bordo
Fr.	Father	P, P.	padre
Fri.	Friday	vier., viern.	viernes
ft.	feet, foot	—	pie(s)
FYI	for your information	—	para su información
g	gram	g., gr.	gramo
Ga., GA	Georgia	—	Georgia
gal.	gallon	—	galón
GDP	gross domestic product	PBI, PIB	producto bruto interno, producto interno bruto, producto interior bruto
Gen.	General	Gral.	general
GMT	Greenwich Mean Time	GMT	tiempo medio de Greenwich, hora del meridiano de Greenwich
GNP	gross national product	PNB	producto nacional bruto

gm	gram	g., gr.	gramo
Gov.	Governor	—	gobernador, -dora
govt.	government	—	gobierno
gr.	gram	g., gr.	gramo
H.H.	His Holiness	SS, S.S.	Su Santidad
HI	Hawaii	—	Hawai, Hawaii
hp	horsepower	CV	caballo de vapor
hr.	hour	h.	hora
HM	His Majesty, Her Majesty	S.M.	Su Majestad
HS	high school	—	colegio secundario
ht.	height	—	altura
Ia., IA	Iowa	—	Iowa
ibid.	ibidem (in the same place)	ib., ibid.	ibidem (en el mismo lugar)
ICE	Immigration and Customs Enforcement	ICE	Servicio de Inmigración y Control de Aduanas
ICU	intensive care unit	UCI, UTI, CTI *Uru*	unidad de cuidados intensivos, unidad de terapia intensiva, unidad de tratamiento intensivo *Chile*, centro de tratamiento intensivo *Uru*
ID	Idaho	—	Idaho
i.e.	that is	i.e.	esto es, es decir
IL, Ill.	Illinois	—	Illinois
IM	instant message	—	mensaje instantánea
IMF	International Monetary Fund	FMI	Fondo Monetario Internacional
in.	inch	—	pulgada
IN	Indiana	—	Indiana
Inc.	Incorporated (company)	S.A.	sociedad anónima
incl.	inclusive, inclusively, including	incl.	inclusive
Ind.	Indian, Indiana	—	Indiana
IQ	intelligence quotient	CI	coeficiente intelectual or de inteligencia
IRS	Internal Revenue Service		Servicio de Rentas Internas
ISP	Internet service provider		proveedor de servicios de Internet
Jan.	January	ene.	enero
Jul.	July	jul.	julio
Jun.	June	jun.	junio
Jr., Jun.	Junior	Jr.	Júnior
Kan., Kans.	Kansas		Kansas
kg	kilogram	kg.	kilogramo
km	kilometer	km.	kilómetro
kph	kilometers per hour	km/h	kilómetros por hora
KS	Kansas	—	Kansas
kw, kW	kilowatt	kv, kV	kilovatio
Ky., KY	Kentucky		Kentucky
l	liter	l.	litro
l.	left	izq.	izquierda
L	large	G	(talla) grande
La., LA	Louisiana	—	Luisiana, Louisiana
lb.	pound		libra
LCD	liquid crystal display	PCL	pantalla de cristal líquido

LGBT	lesbian, gay, bisexual, and transgender	**LGBT**	lesbianas, gays, bisexuales y transgénero
LGBTQ	lesbian, gay, bisexual, transgender, and queer/questioning	**LGBTQ**	lesbianas, gays, bisexuales, transgénero y queer
lit.	liter	**l.**	litro
LOL	laugh out loud, laughing out loud	—	reírse a carcajadas, riendo a carcajadas
Ltd.	Limited (corporation)	**S.L.**	Sociedad Limitada
m	male	**m**	masculino
m	meter	**m**	metro
m	mile	—	milla
M	medium	**M**	(talla) mediana
MA	Massachusetts	—	Massachusetts
Maj.	Major	—	mayor
Mar.	March	**mar.**	marzo
masc.	masculine	—	masculino
Mass.	Massachusetts	—	Massachusetts
Md., MD	Maryland	—	Maryland
M.D.	Doctor of Medicine	—	doctor de medicina
Me., ME	Maine	—	Maine
Mex.	Mexican, Mexico	**Méx.**	mexicano, México
mg	milligram	**mg.**	miligramo
mi.	mile	—	milla
MI, Mich.	Michigan	—	Michigan
min.	minute	**min**	minuto
Minn.	Minnesota	—	Minnesota
Miss.	Mississippi	—	Mississippi, Misisipí
ml	milliliter	**ml.**	mililitro
mm	millimeter	**mm.**	milímetro
MN	Minnesota	—	Minnesota
mo.	month	—	mes
M.O.	money order	**G.P.**	giro postal
Mo., MO	Missouri	—	Missouri
Mon.	Monday	**lun.**	lunes
Mont.	Montana	—	Montana
mpg	miles per gallon	—	millas por galón
mph	miles per hour	—	millas por hora
MS	Mississippi	—	Mississippi, Misisipí
MS	multiple sclerosis	**E.M.**	esclerosis múltiple
Msgr.	Monsignor	**Mons.**	monseñor
Mt.	Mount, Mountain	—	monte, montaña
MT	Montana	—	Montana
MT	Mountain Time	—	Hora de la(s) Montaña(s)
Mtn.	Mountain	—	montaña
N	North, north	**N, N.**	Norte, norte
NASA	National Aeronautics and Space Administration	—	—
NATO	North Atlantic Treaty Organization	**OTAN**	Organización del Tratado del Atlántico Norte
NC	North Carolina	—	Carolina del Norte, North Carolina
ND, N. Dak.	North Dakota	—	Dakota del Norte, North Dakota
NE	northeast	**NE**	nordeste
NE, Neb., Nebr.	Nebraska	—	Nebraska
Nev.	Nevada		Nevada

NGO	non-governmental organization	ONG	organización no gubernamental
NH	New Hampshire	—	Nueva Hampshire, Nuevo Hampshire, New Hampshire
NJ	New Jersey	—	Nueva Jersey, New Jersey
NM., N. Mex.	New Mexico	—	Nuevo México, New Mexico
no.	north	N, N.	norte
no.	number	n.º	número
Nov.	November	nov.	noviembre
NSA	National Security Agency	NSA	Agencia de Seguridad Nacional
N.T.	New Testament	N.T.	Nuevo Testamento
NV	Nevada	—	Nevada
NW	northwest	NO	noroeste
NY	New York	NY	Nueva York, New York
O	Ohio	—	Ohio
OAS	Organization of American States	OEA. O.E.A.	Organización de Estados Americanos
OCD	obsessive-compulsive disorder	TOC	trastorno obsesivo-compulsivo
Oct.	October	oct.	octubre
OH	Ohio	—	Ohio
OK, Okla.	Oklahoma	—	Oklahoma
OR, Ore., Oreg.	Oregon	—	Oregon
O.T.	Old Testament	A.T.	Antiguo Testamento
oz.	ounce, ounces	—	onza, onzas
p.	page	p., pág.	página
Pa., PA	Pennsylvania	—	Pennsylvania, Pensilvania
pat.	patent	pat.	patente
PD	police department	—	departamento de policía
PE	physical education	—	educación física
Penn., Penna.	Pennsylvania	—	Pennsylvania, Pensilvania
pg.	page	pág., p.	página
pgs.	pages	págs.	páginas
PhD	Doctor of Philosophy	—	doctor, -tora (en filosofía)
PIN	personal identification number	PIN, NIP	número de identificación personal
pkg.	package	—	paquete
p.m., PM	post meridiem (after noon)	p.m.	post meridiem (de la tarde)
P.O.	post office	—	oficina de correos, correo
pp.	pages	págs.	páginas
p.p.	by proxy	PP, p.p.	por poder, por poderes
ppd.	postpaid	p.p.	porte pagado
PR	Puerto Rico	PR	Puerto Rico
pres.	present	—	presente
Pres.	President	—	presidente, -ta
Prof.	Professor	—	profesor, -sora
P.S.	postscript	P.D.	postdata
P.S.	public school	—	escuela pública
pt.	pint	—	pinta

pt.	point	pto.	punto
PT	part-time, physical therapist, physical therapy	—	(de) medio tiempo, fisioterapeuta, fisioterapia
PTA	Parent-Teacher Association	—	—
PTO	Parent-Teacher Organization	—	—
q, qt.	quart	—	cuarto de galón
r.	right	dcha.	derecha
R & B	rhythm and blues	R & B	rhythm and blues, rhythm y blues
R & D	research and development	I + D, I & D, I y D	investigación y desarrollo
R & R	rest and recreation, rest and recuperation, rest and relaxation	—	descanso y recreo, descanso y recuperación, descanso y relajación
rd.	road	c/, C/	calle
RDA	recommended daily allowance	—	consumo diario recomendado
recd.	received	—	recibido
ref.	reference	ref., ref. a	referencia
Rep.	Republic	Rep.	República
Rev.	Reverend	Rdo., Rda.	reverendo, reverenda
RI	Rhode Island	—	Rhode Island
R.I.P.	(may he/she) rest in peace	q.e.p.d.	que en paz descanse
rpm	revolutions per minute	r.p.m.	revoluciones por minuto
RR	railroad	FC	ferrocarril
R.S.V.P.	please reply (répondez s'il vous plaît)	S.R.C.	se ruega contestación
rt.	right	dcha.	derecha
Rte.	Route	—	ruta
S	small	P	(talla) pequeña
S	South, south	S, S.	Sur, sur
S.A.	South America	—	Sudamérica, América del Sur
Sat.	Saturday	sáb.	sábado
SC	South Carolina	—	Carolina del Sur, South Carolina
SD, S. Dak.	South Dakota	—	Dakota del Sur, South Dakota
SE	southeast	SE	sudeste, sureste
sec.	second, seconds	seg.	segundo, segundos
Sept.	September	sep., sept.	septiembre
Sgt.	Sergeant	Sgto.	sargento
SMS	Short Message Service	SMS	servicio de mensajes cortos
so.	south	S, S.	sur
sq.	square	—	cuadrado
Sq.	Square	Pza.	Plaza
Sr.	Senior	Sr.	Sénior
Sr.	Sister (*in religion*)	—	sor
st.	state	—	estado
St.	Street	c/, C/	calle
St.	Saint	S.; Sto., Sta.	santo, santa

Sun.	Sunday	dom., do.	domingo
SW	southwest	SO	sudoeste, suroeste
t.	teaspoon	—	cucharadita
t.	ton	t, t.	tonelada
T, tb., tbsp.	tablespoon	—	cucharada (grande)
tel.	telephone	tel., Tel.	teléfono
Tenn.	Tennessee	—	Tennessee
Tex.	Texas	—	Texas
Thu., Thur., Thurs.	Thursday	juev.	jueves
TM	trademark	—	marca (de un producto)
tn.	ton	t, t.	tonelada
TN	Tennessee	—	Tennessee
tr., trans., transl.	translated, translator, translation	trad.	traducido, traductor, traducción
TSA	Transportation Security Administration	TSA	Administración de Seguridad en el Transporte
tsp.	teaspoon	—	cucharadita
Tue., Tues.	Tuesday	mart.	martes
TX	Texas	—	Texas
U.	University	Univ.	universidad
UN	United Nations	NU, NN.UU.	Naciones Unidas
Univ.	University	Univ.	universidad
US	United States	EEUU, EE.UU.	Estados Unidos
USA	United States of America	EEUU, EE.UU.	Estados Unidos de América
usu.	usually	—	usualmente
UT	Utah	—	Utah
v.	versus	v	versus
v.	verse	v	verso
Va., VA	Virginia	—	Virginia
VAT	value-added tax	IVA	impuesto al valor agregado
viz.	see	v.	véase
ver.	verse	v	verso
vol.	volume	vol, vol.	volumen
VP	vice president	—	vicepresidente, -ta
vs.	versus	v	versus
vs.	verse	v	verso
Vt., VT	Vermont	—	Vermont
W	West, west	O, O.	Oeste, oeste
WA, Wash.	Washington (state)	—	Washington
Wed.	Wednesday	miérc.	miércoles
WHO	World Health Organization	OMS	Organización Mundial de la Salud
WI, Wis., Wisc.	Wisconsin	—	Wisconsin
wt.	weight	—	peso
WV, W. Va.	West Virginia	—	Virginia del Oeste, West Virginia
www	World Wide Web	www	world wide web, red mundial
WY, Wyo.	Wyoming	—	Wyoming
yd.	yard	—	yarda
yr.	year	—	año

Spanish Numbers

Cardinal Numbers[1]

1	uno	28	veintiocho
2	dos	29	veintinueve
3	tres	30	treinta
4	cuatro	31	treinta y uno
5	cinco	40	cuarenta
6	seis	50	cincuenta
7	siete	60	sesenta
8	ocho	70	setenta
9	nueve	80	ochenta
10	diez	90	noventa
11	once	100	cien
12	doce	101	ciento uno
13	trece	200	doscientos
14	catorce	300	trescientos
15	quince	400	cuatrocientos
16	dieciséis	500	quinientos
17	diecisiete	600	seiscientos
18	dieciocho	700	setecientos
19	diecinueve	800	ochocientos
20	veinte	900	novecientos
21	veintiuno	1000	mil
22	veintidós	1001	mil uno
23	veintitrés	2000	dos mil
24	veinticuatro	100,000	cien mil
25	veinticinco	1,000,000	un millón
26	veintiséis	1,000,000,000	mil millones
27	veintisiete	1,000,000,000,000	un billón

[1]Most Spanish-speaking countries use either a decimal point (e.g., 38.25%) or a decimal comma (e.g., 38,25). In countries that use the decimal point, a different symbol (such as a comma, an apostrophe, or a space) is used as a thousands separator. Similarly, in countries where the decimal comma is preferred, a symbol other than a comma (such as a point, an apostrophe, or a space) is used to separate thousands.

Ordinal Numbers

1.º, 1.ª	primero, -ra[2]
2.º, 2.ª	segundo, -da
3.º, 3.ª	tercero, -ra[2]
4.º, 4.ª	cuarto, -ta
5.º, 5.ª	quinto, -ta
6.º, 6.ª	sexto, -ta
7.º, 7.ª	séptimo, -ma
8.º, 8.ª	octavo, -va
9.º, 9.ª	noveno, -na
10.º, 10.ª	décimo, -ma[3]
11.º, 11.ª	undécimo, -ma
12.º, 12.ª	duodécimo, -ma
13.º, 13.ª	decimotercero, -ra
14.º, 14.ª	decimocuarto, -ta
15.º, 15.ª	decimoquinto, -ta
16.º, 16.ª	decimosexto, -ta
17.º, 17.ª	decimoséptimo, -ma
18.º, 18.ª	decimoctavo, -va
19.º, 19.ª	decimonoveno, -na *or* decimonono, -na
20.º, 20.ª	vigésimo, -ma
21.º, 21.ª	vigésimoprimero, -ra[2]
30.º, 30.ª	trigésimo, -ma
40.º, 40.ª	cuadragésimo, -ma
50.º, 50.ª	quincuagésimo, -ma
60.º, 60.ª	sexagésimo, -ma
70.º, 70.ª	septuagésimo, -ma
80.º, 80.ª	octogésimo, -ma
90.º, 90.ª	nonagésimo, -ma
100.º, 100.ª	centésimo, -ma
1000.º, 1000.ª	milésimo, -ma
1,000,000.º, 1,000,000.ª	millonésimo, -ma
1,000,000,000.º, 1,000,000,000.ª	milmillonésimo, -ma

[2]The shortened forms of *primero* and *tercero* (which are *primer* and *tercer*, respectively) are abbreviated as *1.*er and *3.*er. Higher ordinals that end in these forms follow the same pattern (e.g., *vigésimoprimer → 21.*er).

[3]In informal Spanish speech and writing, higher ordinals are often replaced with their corresponding cardinal number: *el 35 aniversario de la compañía*, the company's 35th anniversary.

Números ingleses

Números cardinales

1	one	50	fifty
2	two	60	sixty
3	three	70	seventy
4	four	80	eighty
5	five	90	ninety
6	six	100	one hundred
7	seven	101	one hundred (and) one
8	eight	200	two hundred
9	nine	300	three hundred
10	ten	400	four hundred
11	eleven	500	five hundred
12	twelve	600	six hundred
13	thirteen	700	seven hundred
14	fourteen	800	eight hundred
15	fifteen	900	nine hundred
16	sixteen	1,000	one thousand
17	seventeen	1,001	one thousand (and) one
18	eighteen	2,000	two thousand
19	nineteen	10,000	ten thousand
20	twenty	100,000	one hundred thousand
21	twenty-one	1,000,000	one million
30	thirty	1,000,000,000	one billion
40	forty	1,000,000,000,000	one trillion

Números ordinales

1st	first	17th	seventeenth
2nd	second	18th	eighteenth
3rd	third	19th	nineteenth
4th	fourth	20th	twentieth
5th	fifth	21st	twenty-first
6th	sixth	30th	thirtieth
7th	seventh	40th	fortieth
8th	eighth	50th	fiftieth
9th	ninth	60th	sixtieth
10th	tenth	70th	seventieth
11th	eleventh	80th	eightieth
12th	twelfth	90th	ninetieth
13th	thirteenth	100th	hundredth
14th	fourteenth	1,000th	thousandth
15th	fifteenth	1,000,000th	millionth
16th	sixteenth	1,000,000,000th	billionth

Nations of the World
(Naciones del mundo)

Africa/África

Algeria	Argelia
Angola	Angola
Benin	Benin
Botswana	Botswana, Botsuana
Burkina Faso	Burkina Faso
Burundi	Burundi
Cameroon	Camerún
Cape Verde	Cabo Verde
Central African Republic	República Centroafricana
Chad	Chad
Comoros	Comores, Comoras
Congo, Democratic Republic of the	Congo, República Democrática del
Congo, Republic of the	Congo, República del
Côte d'Ivoire (Ivory Coast)	Costa de Marfil
Djibouti	Yibuti, Djibouti
Egypt	Egipto
Equatorial Guinea	Guinea Ecuatorial
Eritrea	Eritrea
Eswatini (Swaziland)	Esuatini (Suazilandia)
Ethiopia	Etiopía
Gabon	Gabón
Gambia	Gambia
Ghana	Ghana
Guinea	Guinea
Guinea-Bissau	Guinea-Bissau
Kenya	Kenya, Kenia
Lesotho	Lesotho, Lesoto
Liberia	Liberia
Libya	Libia
Madagascar	Madagascar
Malawi	Malawi, Malaui
Mali	Malí
Mauritania	Mauritania
Mauritius	Mauricio
Morocco	Marruecos
Mozambique	Mozambique
Namibia	Namibia
Niger	Níger
Nigeria	Nigeria
Rwanda	Ruanda
São Tomé and Principe	Santo Tomé y Príncipe
Senegal	Senegal
Seychelles	Seychelles
Sierra Leone	Sierra Leona
Somalia	Somalia

South Africa, Republic of	Sudáfrica, República de
South Sudan	Sudán del Sur
Sudan	Sudán
Tanzania	Tanzania, Tanzanía
Togo	Togo
Tunisia	Túnez
Uganda	Uganda
Zambia	Zambia
Zimbabwe	Zimbabwe, Zimbabue

Antarctica/Antártida

No independent countries

Asia/Asia

Afghanistan	Afganistán
Armenia	Armenia
Azerbaijan	Azerbaiyán, Azerbaiján
Bahrain	Bahrein
Bangladesh	Bangladesh
Bhutan	Bután, Bhután
Brunei	Brunei
Cambodia	Camboya
China	China
East Timor (Timor-Leste)	Timor Oriental
Georgia	Georgia
India	India
Indonesia	Indonesia
Iran	Irán
Iraq	Iraq, Irak
Israel	Israel
Japan	Japón
Jordan	Jordania
Kazakhstan	Kazajistán, Kazajstán
Korea, North	Corea del Norte
Korea, South	Corea del Sur
Kuwait	Kuwait
Kyrgyzstan	Kirguizistán, Kirguistán
Laos	Laos
Lebanon	Líbano
Malaysia	Malasia
Maldives	Maldivas
Mongolia	Mongolia
Myanmar (Burma)	Myanmar (Birmania)
Nepal	Nepal
Oman	Omán
Pakistan	Pakistán, Paquistán

Philippines	Filipinas
Qatar	Qatar
Saudi Arabia	Arabia Saudí, Arabia Saudita
Singapore	Singapur
Sri Lanka	Sri Lanka
Syria	Siria
Taiwan	Taiwán, Taiwan
Tajikistan	Tayikistán
Thailand	Tailandia
Turkey	Turquía
Turkmenistan	Turkmenistán
United Arab Emirates	Emiratos Árabes Unidos
Uzbekistan	Uzbekistán
Vietnam	Vietnam
Yemen	Yemen

Europe/Europa

Albania	Albania
Andorra	Andorra
Austria	Austria
Belarus	Belarús
Belgium	Bélgica
Bosnia and Herzegovina	Bosnia-Herzegovina
Bulgaria	Bulgaria
Croatia	Croacia
Cyprus	Chipre
Czech Republic	República Checa
Denmark	Dinamarca
Estonia	Estonia
Finland	Finlandia
France	Francia
Germany	Alemania
Greece	Grecia
Hungary	Hungría
Iceland	Islandia
Ireland	Irlanda
Italy	Italia
Kosovo	Kosovo
Latvia	Letonia
Liechtenstein	Liechtenstein
Lithuania	Lituania
Luxembourg	Luxemburgo
Macedonia	Macedonia
Malta	Malta
Moldova	Moldova
Monaco	Mónaco
Montenegro	Montenegro
Netherlands	Países Bajos

Norway	Noruega
Poland	Polonia
Portugal	Portugal
Romania	Rumanía, Rumania
Russia	Rusia
San Marino	San Marino
Serbia	Serbia
Slovakia	Eslovaquia
Slovenia	Eslovenia
Spain	España
Sweden	Suecia
Switzerland	Suiza
Ukraine	Ucrania
United Kingdom	Reino Unido
Vatican City	Ciudad del Vaticano

North America/Norteamérica

Antigua and Barbuda	Antigua y Barbuda
Bahamas	Bahamas
Barbados	Barbados
Belize	Belice
Canada	Canadá
Costa Rica	Costa Rica
Cuba	Cuba
Dominica	Dominica
Dominican Republic	República Dominicana
El Salvador	El Salvador
Grenada	Granada
Guatemala	Guatemala
Haiti	Haití
Honduras	Honduras
Jamaica	Jamaica
Mexico	México, Méjico
Nicaragua	Nicaragua
Panama	Panamá
Saint Kitts and Nevis	San Cristóbal y Nieves, Saint Kitts y Nevis
Saint Lucia	Santa Lucía
Saint Vincent and the Grenadines	San Vicente y las Granadinas
Trinidad and Tobago	Trinidad y Tobago
United States of America	Estados Unidos de América

Oceania/Oceanía

Australia	Australia
Fiji	Fiji, Fiyi
Kiribati	Kiribati

Marshall Islands	Islas Marshall
Micronesia, Federated States of	Estados Federados de Micronesia
Nauru	Nauru
New Zealand	Nueva Zelanda, Nueva Zelandia
Palau	Palaos
Papua New Guinea	Papúa Nueva Guinea, Papua Nueva Guinea
Samoa	Samoa
Solomon Islands	Islas Salomón
Tonga	Tonga
Tuvalu	Tuvalu
Vanuatu	Vanuatu

South America/Sudamérica

Argentina	Argentina
Bolivia	Bolivia
Brazil	Brasil
Chile	Chile
Colombia	Colombia
Ecuador	Ecuador
Guyana	Guyana
Paraguay	Paraguay
Peru	Perú
Suriname	Surinam
Uruguay	Uruguay
Venezuela	Venezuela

Metric System : Conversions
(Sistema métrico : conversiones)

Length

unit	number of meters	approximate U.S. equivalents	
millimeter	0.001	0.039	inch
centimeter	0.01	0.39	inch
meter	1	39.37	inches
kilometer	1,000	0.62	mile

Longitud

unidad	número de metros	equivalentes aproximados de los EEUU	
milímetro	0.001	0.039	pulgada
centímetro	0.01	0.39	pulgada
metro	1	39.37	pulgadas
kilómetro	1000	0.62	milla

Area

unit	number of square meters	approximate U.S. equivalents	
square centimeter	0.0001	0.155	square inch
square meter	1	10.764	square feet
hectare	10,000	2.47	acres
square kilometer	1,000,000	0.3861	square mile

Superficie

unidad	número de metros cuadrados	equivalentes aproximados de los EEUU	
centímetro cuadrado	0.0001	0.155	pulgada cuadrada
metro cuadrado	1	10.764	pies cuadrados
hectárea	10,000	2.47	acres
kilómetro cuadrado	1,000,000	0.3861	milla cuadrada

Volume

unit	number of cubic meters	approximate U.S. equivalents	
cubic centimeter	0.000001	0.061	cubic inch
cubic meter	1	1.307	cubic yards

Volumen

unidad	número de metros cúbicos	equivalentes aproximados de los EEUU	
centímetro cúbico	0.000001	0.061	pulgada cúbica
metro cúbico	1	1.307	yardas cúbicas

Capacity

unit	number of liters	approximate U.S. equivalents		
		CUBIC	DRY	LIQUID
liter	1	61.02 cubic inches	0.908 quart	1.057 quarts

Capacidad

unidad	número de litros	equivalentes aproximados de los EEUU		
		CÚBICO	SECO	LÍQUIDO
litro	1	61.02 pulgadas cúbicas	0.908 cuarto de galón	1.057 cuartos de galón

Mass and Weight

unit	number of grams	approximate U.S. equivalents	
milligram	0.001	0.015	grain
centigram	0.01	0.154	grain
gram	1	0.035	ounce
kilogram	1,000	2.2046	pounds
metric ton	1,000,000	1.102	short tons

Masa y peso

unidad	número de gramos	equivalentes aproximados de los EEUU	
miligramo	0.001	0.015	grano
centigramo	0.01	0.154	grano
gramo	1	0.035	onza
kilogramo	1000	2.2046	libras
tonelada métrica	1,000,000	1.102	toneladas cortas